Intergalactic treachery, terror and hordes of monstrous mutants!!

You are Eizel Cloud, ace intergalactic investigator, and Wibarm is your most versatile weapon – you can transform it into a huge armored robot, land cruiser or star jet. You'll need all the help you can get as you battle the most loathsome monsters the galaxy has ever seen! *Wibarm* gives you the best of both worlds – blazing arcade action and intricate role-playing challenge.

Available for IBM PC/Tandy.

To buy: Visit your software dealer or for credit card purchases and ordering by mail, call (800) 521-6263, 8 am - 5 pm PT. For more information, write to Brøderbund Software-Direct, P.O. Box 12947, San Rafael, CA 94913-2947.

Brøderbund

THE NEW AMERICAN

DESK ENCYCLOPEDIA

A SIGNET BOOK

SIGNET
Published by the Penguin Group
Penguin Books USA Inc., 375 Hudson Street,
New York, New York 10014, U.S.A.
Penguin Books Ltd, 27 Wrights Lane,
London W8 5TZ, England
Penguin Books Australia Ltd, Ringwood,
Victoria, Australia
Penguin Books Canada Ltd, 2801 John Street,
Markham, Ontario, Canada L3R 1B4
Penguin Books (N.Z.) Ltd, 182–190 Wairau Road,
Auckland 10, New Zealand

Penguin Books Ltd, Registered Offices:
Harmondsworth, Middlesex, England

Published by arrangement with Concord Reference Books, Inc.

This book is a derivation and adaptation of the *University Desk Encyclopedia*.

First Printing, March, 1984
First Printing, Revised and Updated Edition, February, 1989
14 13 12 11 10 9 8 7 6

 REGISTERED TRADEMARK—MARCA REGISTRADA

Printed in the United States of America

HOW TO USE
THE NEW AMERICAN DESK ENCYCLOPEDIA

Articles in this encyclopedia are arranged in alphabetical order. The system of alphabetization is letter by letter—that is, spaces, hyphens, or apostrophes in the article title do not affect the alphabetization. For example, **DE FOREST** is alphabetized as though it were spelled **DEFOREST**; it follows **DEFOLIANTS** and precedes **DEGAS**.

Article titles are printed in bold letters. The key word (or words) in the title is printed in capitals; subordinate words are printed in capital and lower-case letters after a comma. In the article title **WASHINGTON, George**, the key word is **WASHINGTON**, the subordinate word is **George**. The key word is also **WASHINGTON** in the article title **WASHINGTON, Treaty of**. When looking for an article on a particular subject, try to think of the key word for that subject.

When article titles have the same key word (or words), they are arranged in this order: *people, places, things*. Thus **WASHINGTON, Booker Taliaferro**, **WASHINGTON, George**, and **WASHINGTON, Martha Custis** precede **WASHINGTON** (state) and **WASHINGTON** (city), which in turn precede **WASHINGTON, Treaty of**.

When people have the same name, their articles are arranged in this order: *saints, popes, emperors, kings, noblemen*, and *ordinary people*. Thus **JOHN, Saint** precedes **JOHN** (pope), which precedes **JOHN** (king), which precedes **JOHN, Augustus Edwin** (the painter). Kings with the same name are arranged alphabetically by country. When ordinary people have the same last name, they are alphabetized on the basis of their first names: **TAYLOR, Telford** precedes **TAYLOR, Zachary**. When ordinary people have the same first as well as last name, they are arranged in chronological order: **BACON, Francis** (1561-1626) precedes **BACON, Francis** (1909-   ).

Places with the same name are arranged in order of size: *country, state* or *province*, and *city*. Thus **WASHINGTON** (state) precedes **WASHINGTON** (city). When two states or provinces, or two cities, have the same name, they are arranged alphabetically by country.

Some articles are cross references. For example, the article "**DISSENTERS. See NONCONFORMISTS.**" tells you that the information you want about Dissenters will be found in the article titled **NONCONFORMISTS**.

Other cross references appear *within* articles. When you see words in the text set in SMALL CAPITALS, that means there is an article elsewhere in the encyclopedia with that title. Still other cross references appear within parentheses in the text or at the ends of articles. For example, the article about the 18th-century Scottish geologist James Hutton contains in its text a parenthetical cross reference—"(see UNIFORMITARIANISM)"—and it concludes with another cross reference—"(See also CATASTROPHISM.)." You will learn more about James Hutton by looking up and reading those related articles.

Abbreviations

A – ampere
A – mass number
Å – angstrom unit
AC – alternating current
AD – *anno domini* (in the year of our Lord)
AF – audio frequency
AFL-CIO – American Federation of Labor–Congress of Industrial Organizations
Ala. – Alabama
AM – amplitude modulation
ANZAC – Australian and New Zealand Army Corps
AP – Associated Press
ARC – American Red Cross
Ariz. – Arizona
Ark. – Arkansas
atm – atmosphere
AU – astronomical unit
AW – atomic weight

b. – born
BC – before Christ
Btu – British thermal unit

C – coulomb
c – circa, centi-
C° – centigrade degree
°C – degrees Celsius
Cal. – California
cal – calorie
CENTO – Central Treaty Organization
CIA – Central Intelligence Agency
Col. – Colorado
Conn. – Connecticut
cos – cosine
cot – cotangent
CSA – Confederate States of America
csc – cosecant
cu ft – cubic foot
cwt – hundredweight

d. – died
dB – decibel
DC – direct current
Del. – Delaware
DST – Daylight Saving Time

e – electron charge, base of natural logarithms

EEC – European Economic Community
EEG – electro-encephalogram
EHF – extremely high frequency

°F – degrees Fahrenheit
FAO – Food and Agriculture Organization
FBI – Federal Bureau of Investigation
Fla. – Florida
FM – frequency modulation
ft – foot

G – universal constant of gravitation, giga-
g – gram
g – acceleration due to gravity
Ga. – Georgia
gal – gallon
GATT – General Agreement on Tariffs and Trade
GNP – gross national product
gr – grain
Gs – gauss

H – henry
h – Planck constant
HF – high frequency
HMS – His/Her Majesty's Ship
hp – horse power
Hz – hertz

Ia. – Iowa
Ida. – Idaho
i.e. – *id est* (that is)
Ill. – Illinois
IMF – International Monetary Fund
in – inch
Ind. – Indiana
IQ – intelligence quotient
IRA – Irish Republican Army

J – joule

K – kelvin
k – kilo-
Kan. – Kansas
kg – kilogram
KGB – *Komitet Gosudarstvennoye Bezopastnosti* (Committee for State Security)
kn – knot
Ky. – Kentucky

l – litre
La. – Louisiana
lb – pound
LF – low frequency
log – common logarithm

M – mega-
m – metre, milli-
Mass. – Massachusetts
mbar – millibar
Md. – Maryland
Me. – Maine
MF – medium frequency
mi – mile
Mich. – Michigan
min – minute (time)
Minn. – Minnesota
MIT – Massachusetts Institute of Technology

Mo. – Missouri
Mont. – Montana
mph – miles per hour
Mx – maxwell

N – newton
N – Avogadro number, neutron number
NAACP – National Association for the Advancement of Colored People
NASA – National Aeronautics and Space Administration
NATO – North Atlantic Treaty Organization
N.C. – North Carolina
N.D. – North Dakota
Neb. – Nebraska
Nev. – Nevada
N.H. – New Hampshire
N.J. – New Jersey
N.M. – New Mexico
N.Y. – New York

OECD – Organization for Economic Cooperation and Development
Okla. – Oklahoma
Ore. – Oregon

Pa. – Pennsylvania
pH – hydrogen ion concentration
pop – population
ppm – parts per million

R – röntgen
RAF – Royal Air Force
RCAF – Royal Canadian Air Force
R.I. – Rhode Island
rpm – revolutions per minute
RSFSR – Russian Soviet Federated Socialist Republic
RSV – Revised Standard Version (Bible)

s – second
sb – stilb

S.C. – South Carolina
S.D. – South Dakota
SEATO – Southeast Asia Treaty Organization
sec – secant
SHF – superhigh frequency
sin – sine
sq mi – square mile
SSR – Soviet Socialist Republic
St. – Saint

tan – tangent
Tenn. – Tennessee
Tex. – Texas

U. – University
UHF – ultrahigh frequency
UK – United Kingdom
UN – United Nations
UNESCO – United Nations Educational, Scientific and Cultural Organization
UNICEF – United Nations Children's Fund
US – United States
USAF – United States Air Force
USCG – United States Coast Guard
USN – United States Navy
USS – United States Ship
USSR – Union of Soviet Socialist Republics
Ut. – Utah

V – volt
v. – *versus* (against)
Va. – Virginia
VHF – very high frequency
Vt. – Vermont

W – watt
Wash. – Washington
Wb – weber
WHO – World Health Organization
Wis. – Wisconsin
W.Va. – West Virginia
WWI – World War I
WWII – World War II
Wyo. – Wyoming

STAFF FOR THE 1982, 1984, AND 1989 EDITIONS

Editor in Chief: Robert A. Rosenbaum; *Executive Editors:* Eleanor M. Gates, Wesley F. Strombeck; *Managing Editor:* John Berseth; *Assistant Managing Editor:* Randy Blunk; *Senior Editors:* Francis Bloch, William B. Cummings, Walter Fox, Robert J. Quinlan, Patricia A. Rodriguez, Jo Ann White; *Contributing Editors:* Diane Barnard, Arthur Biderman, Eugene Brown, Mariana A. Fitzpatrick, Richard Foerster, Sarah I. Fusfeld, Murray Greene, A. Tom Grunfeld, Ernest Hildebrande, Joyce Kovalesk, Henry I. Kurtz, Frank B. Latham, Alan Lazar, Cynthia Lechan, Carol Mankin, Margaret Miner, Steven Moll, Kelly Monaghan, Barbara H. Nelson, Thomas D. O'Sullivan, Hugh Rawson, Edwin E. Rosenblum, Irina Rybacek, Diane Tasca, Heidi Thaens, Carol Ueland, Edward J. Vernoff, Kenneth D. Whitehead, Gerald M. Williams, Dan Woog, Donald Young.

Publisher: John Prescott
Assistant to the Publisher: Ronni Berger

1st letter of the English and of many other alphabets, derived from the Latin, Etruscan and Greek alphabets. The capital letter "A" is from the Greek *alpha*, which in turn came from an ancient North Semitic symbol. The small letter "a" came from the Roman. (See also ALPHABET.)

AACHEN (French: Aix-la-Chapelle), important West German industrial city in a coal region near the Belgian and Dutch borders. A spa since Roman times, it was the capital of the Frankish Emperor CHARLEMAGNE, who was founder of its famous cathedral which holds his tomb. Aachen was the coronation seat of the German Emperors until 1531, and site of two major European peace conferences (see AIX-LA-CHAPELLE, TREATIES OF). Pop 238,587.

AALTO, Alvar (1898–1976), Finnish architect and designer. His early buildings were functionalist (e.g., Toppila Mill at Oulu, 1930), as was his famous plywood furniture. But his later work, such as the dormitory at Massachusetts Institute of Technology (MIT), Cambridge, Mass., 1947, emphasized natural materials and free forms.

AARDVARK (Afrikaans: earth pig), southern African burrowing mammal (*Orycteropus afer*) of the family Orycteropidae. A nocturnal animal, up to 6ft in length and weighing up to 150lb, the aardvark has a stout body with a plump, ratlike tail, elongated piglike snout, large ears and powerful limbs. It feeds on TERMITES, picking them out of their nests with its long, sticky tongue.

AARON, in the Bible, brother of Moses and first high priest of the Hebrews. Later high priests and priests traced their descent from him.

AARON, Henry "Hank" (1934–   ), US baseball player who broke Babe Ruth's record in 1974 with his 715th career home run. He retired in 1976 with 755 homers. Aaron, an outfielder with the Milwaukee and Atlanta Braves, also set a National League record with 2,297 runs batted in.

ABACUS, or counting frame, a simple calculating instrument still widely used in Asia. It comprises a wooden frame containing a series of parallel rods divided into upper and lower portions. The rods represent the powers of 10, with each of the five beads on their lower portion counting 1 and the two on their upper portion each counting 5. In the hands of a skilled operator it allows addition, subtraction, multiplication and division problems to be solved with great rapidity.

ABBASIDS, dynasty of Arab caliphs descended from Abbas, uncle of the Prophet MOHAMMED. They ruled the Islamic Arab empire, following the Omayyads, from 750 until overthrown by the Mongol Hulagu Khan (grandson of Genghis Khan) in 1258. The Abbasids founded Baghdad (c762) as their capital and made it a center for the arts and sciences. The dynasty was at its most magnificent during the reigns of HARUN AL-RASHID (786–809) and his son al-Ma'mun (813–833).

ABBEY THEATRE, Irish repertory theater founded by W. B. YEATS and Lady GREGORY in 1904, during the Irish literary revival. It fostered playwrights and actors such as J. M. SYNGE, Sean O'CASEY, Barry Fitzgerald and Siobhan McKenna. In 1924 it became the first state-subsidized, English-speaking theater.

ABBOTT, Berenice (1898–   ), US photographer who served an apprenticeship under Man Ray in Paris, 1921–29. There she collected the photographs of Eugène Atget. Her subject became New York City after her return to the US. Her books include *Changing New York* (1939) and *Greenwich Village Today and Yesterday* (1949).

ABBOTT, Grace (1878–1939), US social worker who administered the first federal Child Labor Act (1917) and US Children's Bureau (1921–34).

A.B.C. POWERS, a loose entente between Argentina, Brazil and Chile, initiated in 1906 and taking its name from the countries' initials. The entente's mediation averted a US–Mexican war in 1915. Its aims were cooperation and mutual nonaggression, though a treaty signed by the three countries in May 1915 had little real effect.

ABD EL-KRIM (1882–1963), leader of the Rif tribes who fought (1920–26) against Spanish and French rule in Morocco. Captured in 1926, he spent 20 years as a prisoner on the island of Réunion before escaping to Egypt.

ABDOMEN, in VERTEBRATES, the part of the body between the chest and the pelvis. In man, it contains most of the

GASTROINTESTINAL TRACT (from the stomach to the colon) together with the LIVER, GALL BLADDER and SPLEEN in a potential cavity lined by peritoneum, while the KIDNEYS, ADRENAL GLANDS and PANCREAS lie behind this cavity, with the abdominal AORTA and the vein called the inferior vena cava. It is surrounded and protected by a muscular abdominal wall attached to the spine, ribs and pelvic bones and is separated from the chest by the diaphragm. In ARTHROPODS, the abdomen is the rear division of the body.

ABDUL HAMID, name of two Turkish sultans. **Abdul Hamid I** (1725–1789), succeeded in 1774. Turkey was weakened by the Treaty of Kuchuk Kainarji (1774) with Russia, by the forced cession of Bukovina to Austria (1775), and by continued foreign wars and internal revolt. **Abdul Hamid II** (1842–1918), succeeded in 1876. His war with Russia in 1877 resulted in Turkey's loss of many of her European territories. He was notorious for the bloody massacres of Armenians in 1894–96. In 1908, the Young Turks forced him to restore a parliamentary constitution, and he was deposed in 1909.

ABDULLAH IBN HUSSEIN (1882–1951), emir of Transjordan from 1921; king of Jordan from its independence in 1946. After the creation of Israel in 1948, he annexed most of the remainder of Palestine. He was assassinated by Arab extremists in 1951.

ABELARD, Peter (1079–1142), leading French Scholastic philosopher and teacher noted for his discussion of UNIVERSALS. His career was marked by controversy and by a famous love affair with Héloïse, one of his pupils. Following the birth of a child, Héloïse and Abelard married secretly, and in revenge Héloïse's uncle had Abelard castrated. After separating to take up monastic life, the couple exchanged a series of moving love letters. The church condemned Abelard's original teachings as heretical.

ABERDEEN, George Hamilton Gordon, 4th Earl of (1784–1860), British statesman. As British foreign secretary (1828–30; 1841–46), he negotiated the WEBSTER-ASHBURTON TREATY (1842) and the Oregon Treaty (1846) with the US. In 1852–55 he was prime minister of a coalition government that fell due to mishandling of the CRIMEAN WAR.

ABERNATHY, Ralph David (1926–   ), US Baptist minister and civil rights leader, successor to Martin Luther KING, Jr., as president (1968–77) of the Southern Christian Leadership Conference.

ABERRATION, Optical, the failure of a lens to form a perfect image of an object. The commonest types are chromatic aberration, where dispersion causes colored fringes to appear around the image; and spherical aberration, where blurring occurs because light from the outer parts of the lens is brought to a focus at a shorter distance from the lens than that passing through the center. Chromatic aberration can be reduced by using an achromatic lens and spherical aberration by separating the elements of a compound lens.

ABERRATION OF LIGHT, in astronomy, a displacement between a star's observed and true position caused by the earth's motion about the sun and the finite nature of the velocity of light. The effect is similar to that observed by a man walking in the rain: though the rain is in fact falling vertically, because of his motion it appears to be falling at an angle. The maximum aberrational displacement is 20.5″ of arc; stars on the ecliptic appear to move to and fro along a line of 41″; stars 90° from the ecliptic appear to trace out a circle of radius 20.5″; and stars in intermediate positions, ellipses of major axis 41″.

ABM TREATY. See ARMS CONTROL.

ABOLITIONISM, movement in the US and other countries which aimed at the abolition of slavery. The *Liberator*, an antislavery paper edited by William Lloyd GARRISON, began publication in 1831, and in 1833 the American Anti-Slavery Society was founded in Philadelphia. Some abolitionists used their homes as "stations" for fugitive slaves on the UNDERGROUND RAILROAD, and the movement produced much literature, such as Harriet Beecher STOWE's novel *Uncle Tom's Cabin*. In 1840 the abolitionists split over the formation of a political party, and John BROWN's single-handed effort to free the slaves in 1859 was a failure. Increasingly a crucial political issue, abolitionism was a major factor in the outbreak of the Civil War. Lincoln's Emancipation Proclamation (1863) and the 13th Amendment (1865) completed the abolition of slavery in the US. William Wilberforce and others led the movement in Britain to abolish the slave trade (1807) and slavery (1833).

ABOMINABLE SNOWMAN, See YETI.

ABORTION, ending of PREGNANCY before the fetus is able to survive outside the womb. It can occur spontaneously (in which case it is often termed **miscarriage**) or it can be artificially induced. Spontaneous abortion may occur as a result of maternal or fetal disease and faulty implantation in the WOMB. Induction may be mechanical, chemical or using HORMONES, the maternal risk varying with fetal age, the method used and the skill of the physician. In most countries, and until recently throughout the US, the practice was considered criminal unless the mother's life was at risk. In recent years, despite continuing moral controversy, abortion has become widely regarded as a means of BIRTH CONTROL.

ABORTION CONTROVERSY. Abortions were made illegal in the US during the second half of the 19th century. By 1900, every state had enacted statutes prohibiting or severely restricting abortion. Between 1966 and 1972, 14 states reformed their laws to permit abortion when pregnancy posed a serious danger to the woman's physical or mental health, when the child would be born with a grave physical or mental defect, or when the pregnancy resulted from rape or incest. In 1970, four other states repealed their antiabortion statutes, permitting abortion without restrictions.

Abortion was legalized nationwide in 1973 by the 7-2 decision of the US Supreme Court in *Roe v. Wade*, which struck down most state antiabortion laws, thereby permitting abortion with certain careful qualifications: in the first trimester (three months) of pregnancy, a constitutional right of privacy made abortion a decision entirely between the woman and her physician; in the second trimester, the state might regulate abortion to protect the health of the mother; in the third trimester, the state could prohibit abortion, except when necessary to preserve the life or health of the mother, in the interest of the fetus, which by then was considered viable — that is, capable of surviving outside the womb.

Though legal, abortions proved difficult and costly for many women seeking them. Many hospitals and physicians refused to perform abortions, either for religious or personal reasons or in deference to conservative opinion in their areas. The great majority of abortions have been performed in nonhospital facilities (abortion clinics) in metropolitan areas of the West Coast and of the northeast and mid-Atlantic states.

At first, Medicaid paid for abortions for poor women. But in 1977 the Supreme Court ruled that states and localities were not required to provide public funds for nontherapeutic abortions, and Congress withheld federal funds. A number of states, however, continued to fund medically necessary abortions under Medicaid even without the federal contribution.

Although polls find that a majority of the public supports a right to abortion, the opponents of abortion, led by the National Right to Life Committee, have the advantage of an absolutist viewpoint, fierce dedication, and focus on a single issue. Against them the National Abortion Rights Action League heads a coalition that includes the PLANNED PARENTHOOD FEDERATION, the NATIONAL ORGANIZATION FOR WOMEN, the AMERICAN CIVIL LIBERTIES UNION, and various church groups. The abortion-rights forces support the 1973 Supreme Court opinion that a constitutional right to privacy protects each woman's decision whether to bear a child. They oppose government regulation in the area of family life. And they especially oppose the attempt to incorporate into US law a particular theological dogma about the beginning of human life.

Since 1973, the opponents of abortion have tried to shut down abortion clinics by demonstrations and, in some cases, by arson and bombings. They have won lower-court decisions and state legislation making abortions more difficult to obtain. They failed to agree on a constitutional amendment that would have overturned *Roe v. Wade*, but in the late 1980s they were hopeful that the Supreme Court would itself reconsider and reverse its 1973 decision. In 1988, only four of the nine justices were known to favor abortion rights.

ABORTION RIGHTS ACTION LEAGUE, National. See ABORTION CONTROVERSY.

ABRAHAM, biblical father of the Hebrew people, first of the patriarchs and regarded as the founder of JUDAISM. The Book of Genesis describes him as a descendant of Shem, and son of Terah, being born in UR of the Chaldees. He vowed to worship God and was promised that his people should inherit Canaan through his son ISAAC. However, as a test of faith and obedience, God commanded Abraham to slay Isaac. Abraham unquestioningly obeyed, and Isaac was spared. Through Abraham's faith a covenant of plenty and fecundity was established between God and the Israelites.

ABRAHAM, Karl (1877–1925), German psychoanalyst whose most important work concerned the development of the libido, particularly in infancy. He suggested that various PSYCHOSES should be interpreted in terms of the interruption of this development.

ABRAHAM, Plains of, site of the decisive battle in the Canadian theater during the FRENCH AND INDIAN WARS when WOLFE defeated the French at Quebec (1759).

ABRAMOVITZ, Max (1908–), US architect who designed the interfaith chapel group (1955) at Brandeis U., the law school

(1962) at Columbia U. and is best known as the architect of New York City's Philharmonic Hall at Lincoln Center (1962).

ABRAMS, Creighton Williams (1914–1974), commander of US troops in Vietnam (1968–72) and US Army chief of staff (1972–74).

ABRASIVE, any material used to cut, grind or polish a softer material by abrasion. Mild abrasives such as chalk are incorporated in toothpaste, and others, silica, pumice or aluminum oxide, are used in household cleansers; but various industrial applications demand even harder abrasives (see HARDNESS) such as carborundum, borazon or diamond. Some abrasives are used in solid blocks (as with knife-grinding stones), but **coated abrasives** such as sandpaper, in which abrasive granules are stuck onto a carrier, make more economic use of the material. **Sandblasting** exemplifies a third technique in which abrasive particles are thrown against the workpiece in a stream of compressed air or steam. Sandblasting is used for cleaning buildings and engraving glass.

ABSCESS, a localized accumulation of PUS, usually representing one response of the body to bacterial infection. Abscesses, which may occur in any tissue or organ of the body, often show themselves in pain, redness and swelling. They may drain spontaneously, otherwise they should be incised.

ABSINTHE, a bitter, green, distilled liqueur principally flavored with an aromatic oil (also used in vermouth) obtained from the **wormwood** *Artemisia absinthium*, itself also known as absinthe. Allegations that absinthe is poisonous led to the drink's prohibition in many countries, including the US and Canada.

ABSOLUTE, in philosophy, refers to what is unconditional, noncontingent, self-existent or even arbitrary. In 19th-century IDEALISM, the Absolute (Idea) came to refer to the ultimate cosmic totality.

ABSOLUTE ZERO, the TEMPERATURE at which all substances have zero thermal ENERGY and thus, it is believed, the lowest possible temperature. Although many substances retain some nonthermal zero-point energy at absolute zero, this cannot be eliminated and so the temperature cannot be reduced further. Originally conceived as the temperature at which an ideal GAS at constant pressure would contract to zero volume, absolute zero is of great significance in THERMODYNAMICS, and is used as the fixed point for the absolute or KELVIN (k) temperature scale. In practice

the absolute zero temperature is unattainable, although temperatures within a few millionths of a Kelvin of it have been achieved in CRYOGENICS laboratories.

$$0°K = -273.16°C = -459.69°F$$

ABSOLUTISM, form of government in which all power is held by an unchecked ruler. Monarchies in the ancient world were usually absolute, but with the rise of FEUDALISM, the nobility often limited royal power. With the destruction of feudal rights opportunities for absolutism reappeared. In England the STUART attempt to rule by divine right failed, but in Europe, and especially France, absolutism flourished until the early 19th century. More sophisticated 20th-century forms such as NAZISM and COMMUNISM are better termed TOTALITARIANISM.

ABSTRACT ART, term applied to 20th-century paintings and sculptures which have no representational function. The precursors were CÉZANNE, SEURAT and GAUGUIN, who believed that the formal elements of painting—color, line and composition—could be used expressively. FAUVISM and CUBISM developed these ideas. The first completely abstract works were painted by KANDINSKY and MONDRIAN in 1912. By 1914 Kandinsky's pictures were composed of regular non-representational forms, and color was used freely. In Paris, DELAUNAY, Kupka, and Morgan Russell developed the Orphist movement which influenced the German painter MARC Mondrian and Van DOESBURG launched DE STIJL in Holland in 1917, which applied abstract theories to architecture and design. In Russia MALEVICH led the movement of SUPREMATISM and El Lissitzky and Tatlin were involved in CONSTRUCTIVISM. Many abstract artists went to the US before WWII, where they developed the tradition.

ABSTRACT EXPRESSIONISM, American movement of ABSTRACT ART which explored the emotional, expressive power of non-figurative painting. The "action painter" Jackson POLLOCK stressed the creative act and dripped and spattered paint on the canvas. KLINE and DE KOONING are also considered abstract expressionists.

ABU BAKR (c573–634), the first Muslim caliph of Arabia in 632, following MOHAMMED'S death. He ordered incursions into Syria and Iraq, thus beginning the Muslim conquests. He was Mohammed's closest companion and adviser.

ABU DHABI, largest (25,000sq mi) sheikhdom of the UNITED ARAB EMIRATES, located on the southern side of the Persian Gulf; mostly desert, it has extensive oil deposits. Pop 300,000.

ABUSE, a phenomenon of uncertain but undoubtedly large dimensions that began to attract public notice only in recent years. The term covers **child abuse**, the physical or sexual abuse of children, or their neglect, by parents, other family members, or nonfamily caretakers; **spouse abuse**, usually the physical abuse of women by their husbands or boyfriends; and **elder abuse**, the physical or psychological abuse, including neglect, of aged persons by their adult children or other caretakers.

ABU SIMBEL, archaeological site of two temples commissioned by RAMSES II (13th century BC) on the west bank of the Nile 762mi south of Cairo. The Aswan High Dam construction threatened to submerge the site, but a UNESCO project, supported internationally, saved the temples by removing them and reconstructing them above the future waterline.

ABYDOS, Greek name for a religious center in Middle Egypt inhabited since the early dynastic period (3100–2686 BC) and connected with the god Osiris. It is noted for its tombs of early dynastic kings and its 19th-dynasty temple (c1300 BC).

ABYSSINIA. See ETHIOPIA.

ACADÉMIE FRANÇAISE (French Academy), a literary, linguistic society officially recognized in 1635. Membership is limited to 40, the so-called "Immortals," and includes prominent public men as well as literary figures. It has been criticized for electing individuals with personal influence, while often ignoring those with real merit. MOLIÈRE and ZOLA were never elected. Over the centuries, the Academy has produced the *Dictionnaire*, considered the official arbiter of the French language.

ACADEMY AWARDS, the annual awards ("Oscars") given by the Academy of Motion Picture Arts and Sciences for outstanding achievement in various branches of film-making. The major awards are for best leading and supporting actor and actress, best direction, best screenplay and best film.

ACADIA, the name given to Nova Scotia and neighboring regions of New Brunswick, Prince Edward Island and parts of Quebec and Maine, by the French colonists who settled there starting in 1604. All but Prince Edward Island and Cape Breton passed under British control by the Treaty of Utrecht (1713). The French colonists, dispersed by the British in 1755, are the subject of LONGFELLOW's poem *Evangeline*. Those who went to Louisiana are the ancestors of the present-day CAJUNS.

ACADIA NATIONAL PARK covers 65.1sq mi in Me., centered on the Mount Desert Island area. Its mountains, forests and lakes make it an important wildlife reserve.

ACCELERATION, the rate at which the velocity of a moving body changes. Since velocity, a vector quantity, is speed in a given direction, a body can accelerate both by changing its speed and by changing its direction. The units of acceleration, itself a vector quantity, are those of velocity per unit of time—e.g., meters per second (m/s^2). In calculus notation, acceleration **a** is the first differential of velocity **v** with respect to time t:

$$a = \frac{dv}{dt}$$

According to NEWTON'S second law of motion, acceleration is always the result of a force acting on a body; the acceleration **a** produced in a body of mass m by a force **F** is given by $a = F/m$. The **acceleration due to gravity** (g) of a body falling freely near the earth's surface is about $9.81 m/s^2$. In the aerospace industry the accelerations experienced by men and machines are often expressed as multiples of g. Headward (vertical) accelerations of as little as $3g$ can cause pilots to black out.

ACCELERATORS, Particle, research tools used to accelerate electrically charged SUBATOMIC PARTICLES to high velocities. The resulting particle beams can be focused to interact with other particles or break up atomic nuclei in order to learn more about the fundamental nature of matter. Accelerators use electromagnetic fields to accelerate the particles in a straight line or in a circular or spiral path. The devices are rated according to the kinetic ENERGY they impart, which is measured in electron volts (eV).

The first accelerator was designed by J. D. Cockcroft and E. T. S. Walton in 1932. It used a transformer, a hydrogen-gas discharge ion source and a simple evacuated tube to accelerate PROTONS to energies of 700 keV. At about the same time, R. J. Van de Graaff designed an advanced electrostatic generator that could achieve voltages as high as 3 MeV. The first **linear accelerator**, or linac, was built in 1928 by R. Wideröe. The largest linear accelerator yet in operation is a device 2mi long at Stanford University, which can accelerate ELECTRONS to energies of 20 GeV. In linear accelerators, the particles pass through a series of electrodes that impart greater and greater velocities.

The first circular accelerator, the cyclotron, was built by E. O. Lawrence in 1931. The particles—mainly protons or deuterons—were accelerated twice in each revolution, spiraling outward and eventually shot out toward a target. The relativistic (see RELATIVITY) gain in mass of the particles tended to throw them out of phase with the acceleration pulses, however; the solution was the **synchrocyclotron**, or frequency-modulated cyclotron, which varies the acceleration frequencies to keep them in phase with the particles. The device was first suggested separately in 1945 by E. M. McMillan and V. I. Veksler; the largest synchrocyclotron today achieves energies of more than 700 MeV.

As still higher energies continued to be sought, the massive magnets needed to cover the whole spiral path of the particles became impractical. This problem was solved by the **synchrotron**, which guides the particles around a ring of magnets through a thin evacuated tube. As the particles continue to accelerate, the strengths of the magnetic fields are slowly increased in such a way that the size of the orbits remains constant. The first such devices used electrons, but most large synchrotrons today are proton accelerators. The first to pass the 1-GeV mark was the so-called Cosmotron of Brookhaven National Laboratory, which began operating in 1952; the largest now operating is at the Fermi National Accelerator Laboratory in Batavia, Ill., which achieves energies in excess of 500 GeV. The latest accelerators are **colliding-beam** machines, in which positive and negative particles circle in opposite directions. The resulting head-on collisions yield much higher effective energies than collisions with stationary targets. (See also SUPERCOLLIDER.)

ACCORDION, small portable reed organ, used for jazz as well as folk music. Tuned metal reeds are set in vibration by air directed at them from the central bellows through valves operated by pianotype keys on the instrument's right. Buttons on the left produce chords. Although they were known in ancient China, the first modern accordions were built in the 1820s.

ACCOUNTING, the recording and analysis of financial transactions in order to reveal the financial position of an individual or firm. While the bookkeeper merely records transactions and makes no attempt at analysis, it is the accountant who analyses the data thus collected and produces balance sheets and income (or profit-and-loss) statements. On a balance sheet assets must balance liabilities. An income statement balances income against expenditure over a given period, recording any difference between them as a profit or loss, and is used to assess the performance of a firm. All such financial statements are audited, that is, checked for accuracy and fairness by independent accountants. The US professional body for accountants is the American Institute of Accountants, founded in 1916.

ACHAEAN LEAGUE, ancient confederation of Greek cities of which Corinth was a leading member. In the 3rd century BC the league resisted Macedon, then allied with Macedon against Sparta and later Rome. Rome's destruction of Corinth in 146 BC ended Greek independence.

ACHAEANS, one of the four main ethnic groups of ancient Greece and traditionally victors in the TROJAN WAR (in HOMER synonymous with all Greeks). They may have entered northern Greece about 2000 BC and, moving south, created the Bronze Age civilization of MYCENAE. Other authorities believe they came to Greece only shortly before the DORIANS in the 12th century BC, dominating Mycenae only briefly before being displaced by the Dorians.

ACHAEMENIANS, Persian dynasty dominating much of W Asia (6th-4th centuries BC). The outstanding rulers were CYRUS THE GREAT (founder, reigned 559-529), DARIUS I and XERXES I. It ended when ALEXANDER THE GREAT defeated DARIUS III in 330.

ACHEBE, Chinua (1930–   ), Nigerian novelist, chronicler of the impact of Western culture on Africans, beginning with *Things Fall Apart* (1958) and including *Anthills of the Savannah* (1987).

ACHESON, Dean Gooderham (1893-1971), US statesman who helped rebuild Europe's economic and military strength after WWII. He served Roosevelt and Truman in the State Department (1941-53), becoming secretary of state in 1949. After the war he promoted the recovery of Europe and worked to curb Soviet expansion by helping to formulate the TRUMAN DOCTRINE, MARSHALL PLAN and the NORTH ATLANTIC TREATY ORGANIZATION.

ACHILLES, legendary Greek warrior of the TROJAN WAR, celebrated by HOMER. He was dipped in the River Styx by his mother Thetis and made invulnerable except at the point on his heel by which she had held him. Joining in the Greek attack on Troy, he killed many men including the Trojan hero Hector (in revenge for the death of Achilles' friend Patroclus). Achilles was himself killed when the god APOLLO guided an arrow from the Trojan prince Paris into his heel.

ACID, a substance capable of providing HYDROGEN ions (H+) for chemical reaction. In an important class of chemical reactions (acid-base reactions) a hydrogen ION (identical to the physicist's PROTON) is transferred from an acid to a BASE, this being defined as any substance which can accept hydrogen ions. The strength of an acid is a function of the availability of its acid protons (see pH). Free hydrogen ions are available only in SOLUTION where the minute proton is stabilized by association with a solvent molecule. In aqueous solution it exists as the hydronium ion (H_3O+).

Chemists use several different definitions of acids and bases simultaneously. In the Lewis theory, an alternative to the Brönsted-Lowry theory outlined above, species which can accept ELECTRON pairs from bases are defined as acids.

Many chemical reactions are speeded up in acid solution, giving rise to important industrial applications (acid-base CATALYSIS). Mineral acids including sulfuric acid, nitric acid and hydrochloric acid find widespread use in industry. Organic acids, which occur widely in nature, tend to be weaker. Carboxylic acids (including acetic acid and oxalic acid) contain the acidic group –COOH; aromatic systems with attached hydroxyl group (phenols) are often also acidic. AMINO ACIDS, constitutive of proteins, are essential components of all living systems.

ACIDOSIS, medical condition in which the acid-base balance in the blood PLASMA is disturbed in the direction of excess acidity, the pH falling below 7.35. It may cause deep-sighing breathing and drowsiness or coma. Respiratory acidosis, associated with lung disease, heart failure and central respiratory depression, results from under-breathing and a consequent buildup of plasma carbon dioxide. Alternative metabolic causes include the ingestion of excess acids (as in aspirin overdose), ketosis (resulting from malnutrition or diabetes), heavy alkali loss (as from a fistula) and the inability to excrete acid which occurs in some kidney disorders.

ACID RAIN, the popular name for the acidity from the atmosphere that is poisoning lakes, estuaries, forests, and farmlands in NE US and SE Canada. The acid comes from oxides of sulfur and nitrogen created by coal-burning power plants in the Ohio Valley. A great deal of acid pollution crosses the US–Canadian border, and the failure of the Reagan administration to take action on the problem was a source of friction between the two countries.

ACNE, a common pustular SKIN disease of the face and upper trunk, most prominent in ADOLESCENCE. Blackheads become

secondarily inflamed due either to local production of irritant fatty acids by BACTERIA or to bacterial infection itself. In severe cases, with secondary infection and picking of spots, scarring may occur. Acne may be aggravated by diet (chocolate and nuts being worst offenders), by HORMONE imbalance, by greasy skin or by poor hygiene. Methods of treatment include degreasing the skin, removing the blackheads, controlling diet or hormones, and exposure to ultraviolet radiation. Tetracyclines may be used to decrease fatty acid formation.

ACONCAGUA, snowcapped peak in the ANDES (22,834ft), the highest in the W Hemisphere. The summit is in NW Argentina, the W slopes in Chile. It was first climbed by E. A. Fitzgerald's expedition in 1897.

ACOUSTICS, the science of SOUND, dealing with its production, transmission and effects. Engineering acoustics deals with the design of sound-systems and their components, such as microphones, headphones and loudspeakers; musical acoustics is concerned with the construction of musical instruments, and ULTRASONICS studies sounds having frequencies too high for men to hear them. Architectural acoustics gives design principles of rooms and buildings having optimum acoustic properties. This is particularly important for auditoriums, where the whole audience must be able to hear the speaker or performers clearly and without ECHOES. Also, the reverberation time (the time taken for the sound to decay to one millionth of its original intensity) must be matched to the intended uses of the hall; for speech it should be less than 1 sec; for chamber music, 1-2 sec; for larger-scale works, 2-3 sec. All this is achieved by attending to the geometry and furnishings of the hall and incorporating the appropriate sound-absorbing, diffusing and reflecting surfaces. **Anechoic chambers,** used for testing acoustic equipment, are completely surfaced with diffusing and absorbing materials so that reverberation is eliminated. **Noise insulation engineering** is an increasingly important branch of acoustics.
ACQUIRED CHARACTERISTICS, modifications in an organism resulting from interaction with its environment. In 1801 LAMARCK proposed an evolutionary theory in which the assumption that acquired characteristics could be inherited provided the mechanism for species divergence. In later editions of *The Origin of Species*, DARWIN moved towards accepting this explanation in parallel to that of NATURAL

SELECTION, but eventually the Lamarckian mechanism was entirely discounted. It is now thought, however, that organisms which reproduce asexually (see REPRODUCTION) can pass on acquired characteristics. (See also ADAPTATION; EVOLUTION.)

ACQUIRED IMMUNE DEFICIENCY SYNDROME. See AIDS.

ACROPOLIS (Greek: high city), the fortified hilltop site of an ancient Greek city. Such places eventually became sanctuaries for city gods and centers of religious ceremonies. Remains of their defenses and temples are known from the sites of many ancient Greek cities. The most famous is the Acropolis of ATHENS, with its Parthenon.

ACROSTIC, written composition where the initial or final letters (sometimes both) in successive lines spell a word or phrase. A popular verse form among the rhetoricians of antiquity, it appears now in literary puzzles.

ACTH (adrenocorticotrophic hormone), or corticotropin, a HORMONE secreted by the PITUITARY GLAND which stimulates the secretion of various STEROID hormones from the cortex of the ADRENAL GLANDS. ACTH has been used in the treatment of a number of diseases including MULTIPLE SCLEROSIS.

ACTION, independent federal agency established in 1971 to administer volunteer service programs. ACTION includes VOLUNTEERS IN SERVICE TO AMERICA (VISTA), the FOSTER GRANDPARENT PROGRAM (FGP), the RETIRED SENIOR VOLUNTEER PROGRAM (RSVP), the Senior Companion Program (SCP), and the Volunteer Management Support Program (VMSP).

ACTION FRANÇAISE, French nationalist and anti-republican movement, formed in 1898 and led by Charles MAURRAS. Its newspaper *Action Française* (1908–44) advocated extreme rightwing monarchism. Although banned in 1936, the movement revived to make a pro-VICHY stand in WWII.

ACTION PAINTING. See ABSTRACT EXPRESSIONISM.

ACTIUM (now Akra Nikolaos), promontory on the W coast of Greece. A great sea battle was fought near it in 31 BC when Octavian's naval forces crushed those of Mark ANTONY and CLEOPATRA. Victory gave mastery of the Roman world to Octavian, later the first Roman emperor AUGUSTUS.

ACT OF SETTLEMENT, British parliamentary act of 1701 securing the succession of the Hanoverian line. It increased parliamentary control over the monarch, who was also required to belong to the Protestant CHURCH OF ENGLAND.

ACT OF UNION, four acts of the British parliament uniting England with Wales (1536), Scotland (1707) and Ireland (1801), and uniting Upper and Lower Canada (1840).

ACTON, John Emerich Edward Dalberg-Acton, 1st Baron (1834–1902), English Catholic historian and moralist, proponent of the Christian liberal ethic. He attacked nationalism, racism and authoritarianism and made the famous remark: "All power tends to corrupt, and absolute power corrupts absolutely." Lord Acton introduced German research methods into English history and launched the monumental *Cambridge Modern History.*

ACTORS STUDIO, the professional workshop for actors, established in New York City in 1947; Lee Strasberg became director in 1948. The school's training, often called "the Method," is based on the teachings of Constantin STANISLAVSKI and stresses an actor's psychological interpretation of his role and emotional identification with the personality of the character he plays.

ACTS OF THE APOSTLES, fifth book of the New Testament, a unique history of the early Christian Church. Probably written between 60 and 90 AD by the Evangelist Luke, it is a continuation of St. Luke's Gospel and deals mainly with the deeds of the apostles, Peter and Paul. Events described include the descent of the Holy Spirit at PENTECOST, St. Stephen's martyrdom, and St. Paul's conversion, journeys and missionary work.

ACUPUNCTURE, an ancient Chinese medical practice in which fine needles are inserted into the body at specified points, used for relieving pain and in treating a variety of conditions including MALARIA and RHEUMATISM. It was formerly believed that this would correct the imbalance between the opposing forces of YIN and YANG in the body which lay behind the symptoms of sickness. Although it is not yet understood how acupuncture works, it is still widely practiced in China and increasingly in the West, mainly as a form of ANESTHESIA.

ADAM, first man and father of the human race, according to the Old Testament Book of Genesis. This tells how God made Adam (Hebrew for "man") from *adamah* (Hebrew for "dust") and Adam's wife Eve from one of his ribs. The tale of their temptation, fall and expulsion from Paradise is the basis of such Judaic and Christian concepts as grace, sin and divine retribution.

ADAM, Adolphe-Charles (1803–1856),

French composer, best remembered for his ballet *Giselle* (1841). He also wrote operatic, religious and choral works.

ADAM, Robert (1728–1792) and **James** (1730–1794), Scottish architect brothers who developed the neoclassical "Adam style" in England. Robert's studies of ancient Roman architecture in Italy helped to inspire their joint designs of graceful and sumptuous buildings, interiors and furnishings which brought a new elegance to many town and country houses in Britain, the Continent and America.

ADAMS, Abigail (1744–1818), wife of President John ADAMS and mother of President John Quincy ADAMS. Largely self-educated but highly intelligent, she wrote letters giving a lively account of contemporary American life.

ADAMS, Ansel (1902–1984), US photographer. One of the foremost nature photographers of the 20th century, Adams is known for his dramatic black and white photos celebrating the natural beauty of California's Sierra Nevada range and the American Southwest. He pioneered in folio reproduction and wrote several instructional books.

ADAMS, Brooks (1848–1927), US historian, son of Charles Francis ADAMS, who saw economic history as a series of growth cycles. In 1900 he predicted that the US and Russia would be the only world powers in 1950, but that America's wealth would decline and her democratic tradition would be destroyed by uncontrolled private business.

ADAMS, Charles Francis (1807–1886), US diplomat and son of John Quincy ADAMS. He supported the new Republican Party after 1856 and, as minister to Britain (1861–68), helped to keep Britain neutral during the American Civil War. In 1871–72 he represented the US in the ALABAMA CLAIMS settlement.

ADAMS, Henry (Brooks) (1838–1918), major US historian, brother of Brooks ADAMS, whose history of the Jefferson and Madison administrations is a classic work. His other works include *Mont-Saint-Michel and Chartres* (1913), on the social and religious background of medieval culture, and his autobiography, *The Education of Henry Adams*, in which he attempted to show how ill-prepared his generation was for the technological society of the 20th century.

ADAMS, John (1735–1826), one of the leaders in America's struggle for independence and second president of the US (1797–1801).

Born at Braintree (now Quincy), Mass.,

he gained political prominence as one of the chief protesters against the STAMP ACT (1765). At the First Continental Congress called to protest against the INTOLERABLE ACTS of 1774 he helped draft a declaration of rights and a petition to the king. By then a major figure in colonial politics, at the Second Continental Congress he urged the creation of a Continental Army headed by George Washington, and later helped draft the DECLARATION OF INDEPENDENCE. In and after the REVOLUTIONARY WAR he served abroad as a diplomat (1777–88), gaining American support from France and Holland and helping to negotiate a peace treaty with Britain, to which he became the first American minister (1785–88).

Adams then began an active political career at home. As runner-up to Washington in the first two presidential elections he automatically became the nation's first vice-president (1789–96). When Washington retired, Adams was elected president in 1796, heading the new FEDERALIST PARTY favoring strong central government in opposition to the Republicans (later renamed Democrats) under Thomas Jefferson, who defeated his bid for re-election in 1800.

Adams soon faced major problems. His moderate federalism antagonized extreme Federalists including Alexander HAMILTON, who intrigued against him, especially when Adams refused to fight France over French seizures of American shipping in the Anglo-French conflict following the French Revolution. Instead, Adams sought peace with France, and (after the fiasco of the XYZ AFFAIR) secured a Franco-US treaty (1800)—but alienated Federalist supporters by not consulting Congress. He had already angered the pro-French Republicans by a seemingly autocratic distrust of popular democracy, and his (reluctant) involvement in the ALIEN AND SEDITION ACTS (1798) curbing criticism of Congress's military preparations against France.

Unpopularity lost Adams the election of 1800, but his policy of non-involvement had saved the country from what could have been a costly war. Adams was the first president to live in the White House in Washington.

ADAMS, John (Coolidge) (1947–   ), US composer and conductor whose works include the string septet *Shaker Loops* (1978), the opera *Nixon in China* (1987), and the orchestral work *Fearful Symmetries* (1988).

ADAMS, John Couch (1819–1892), English astronomer who first calculated the position of the then undiscovered planet

NEPTUNE. The French astronomer U. J. J. Leverrier, who independently made the same calculation, initially received sole credit for the discovery.

ADAMS, John Quincy (1767–1848), sixth president of the US (1825–29) and sole example of a son following his father (John ADAMS) to the presidency. However, his main achievement, promoting national expansion, came while he was secretary of state.

Trained in law and educated in international affairs by his father, he held diplomatic posts abroad under George Washington, John Adams and James Monroe, becoming the first American ambassador to Russia (1809–14) and helped to negotiate the Treaty of GHENT (1814).

As Monroe's secretary of state (1817–25), he helped formulate the MONROE DOCTRINE, declaring US opposition to European involvement in the Americas (a cornerstone of future US foreign policy), and urged recognition of the emergent Latin American states. He negotiated the ADAMS-ONÍS TREATY with Spain (1819) for the purchase of Florida and fixed a border with Mexico to the Pacific Ocean, prerequisites for national expansion. He also helped to restrict British influence to N of the 49th parallel as far W as the Rockies.

Elected president in 1824, Adams had been an unpopular compromise choice and faced a hostile congressional coalition headed by Andrew JACKSON. Congressional opposition largely blocked Adams' ambitious schemes for national improvements including a national bank and university, new roads and canals, and protective tariffs. His main presidential achievement, completion of the ERIE CANAL, was offset by the passing of the unpopular "Tariff of Abominations" (1828).

Adams lost the 1828 election but went on (1831–48) to be the only ex-president to sit in the House of Representatives.

ADAMS, Maude (1872–1953), US actress famous around the turn of the century. She is best remembered for her leading roles in plays by James BARRIE, Edmond ROSTAND and SHAKESPEARE.

ADAMS, Samuel (1722–1803), American revolutionary leader and signer of the Declaration of Independence. His forceful oratory and inflammatory writings increased colonial discontent with British rule. Adams opposed the Sugar and Stamp acts, helped organize the BOSTON TEA PARTY, pioneered the Committees of Correspondence and urged independence at the First Continental Congress (1774). He served as governor of Mass. (1794–97).

ADAMS-ONÍS TREATY, also called the **Transcontinental Treaty,** US–Spanish agreement (1819) defining the western boundary of the US, negotiated by J. Q. ADAMS and the Spanish minister Onís. Spain ceded Florida to the US in return for the abandonment of US claims to Texas.

ADAPTATION, the process of modification of the form or functions of a part of an organism, to fit it for its environment and so to achieve efficiency in life and reproduction. Adaptation of individual organisms is called acclimatization, and is temporary since it involves acquired characteristics; the permanent adaptation of species arises from transmitted genetic variations preserved by NATURAL SELECTION (see also EVOLUTION). Successful and versatile adaptation in an organism usually leads to widespread distribution and long-term survival. Examples include the development of lungs in amphibians and of wings in birds and insects. The term is sometimes also used for the modified forms of the organism.

ADAPTIVE RADIATION, a sequence of EVOLUTION in which an unspecialized group of organisms gives rise to various differentiated types adapted to specific modes of life. Early placental mammals, for example, gave rise to modern burrowing, climbing, flying, running and swimming forms.

ADDAMS, Jane (1860–1935), American social reformer who pioneered the settlement house movement in the US. (See SOCIAL SETTLEMENTS.) With Ellen Gates Starr she founded Chicago's Hull House (1889) which provided social and cultural activities for poor European immigrants. She was its resident head until her death. An ardent pacifist, she became first president of the Women's International League for Peace and Freedom, and was co-winner, with Nicholas Murray BUTLER, of the 1931 Nobel Peace Prize.

ADDICTION. See DRUG ADDICTION.

ADDING MACHINE. See CALCULATING MACHINE.

ADDIS ABABA, capital of Ethiopia (since 1889) and of Shoa province, stands on an 8,000ft central plateau. It has the former imperial palace and government buildings; new hospitals, theaters and factories have been built since the 1950s. The city is the headquarters of the Organization of African Unity. Pop 1,464,901.

ADDISON, Joseph (1672–1719), English man of letters and public servant, whose witty, elegant style had a lasting effect on English prose. He wrote plays, poems, and, above all, essays dealing with the literature, life and manners of the day in *The Tatler* and *The Spectator* (which he founded with Sir Richard STEELE). He was secretary of state 1717–18.

ADDISON'S DISEASE, failure of STEROID production by the ADRENAL GLAND cortex, first described by English physician **Thomas Addison** (1793–1860). Its features include brownish skin pigmentation, loss of appetite, nausea and vomiting, weakness, and malaise and faintness on standing. The stress associated with an infection or an operation can lead to sudden collapse. Autoimmune disease, tuberculosis and disseminated cancer may damage the adrenals, and long-term steroid therapy may suppress normal production. Treatment is normally by steroid replacement.

ADE, George (1866–1944), American newspaper humorist and playwright whose *Fables in Slang* (1899) used colloquialisms and down-to-earth characters to poke fun at society.

ADEN, seaport of the People's Democratic Republic of Yemen (Southern Yemen), on the Gulf of Aden. Under British rule (1839–1967) it became a coaling station for ships sailing between Europe and India via the Suez Canal. Although the city's importance as a port has declined, it is the country's industrial center, with an oil refinery. Pop 271,600.

ADENAUER, Konrad (1876–1967), first chancellor of West Germany (1949–63), who headed its spectacular postwar economic and financial recovery. A politician since before WWI, he was twice imprisoned by the Nazis. He became leader of the Christian Democratic Union party in 1947, and as chancellor made West Germany an integral part of W Europe, taking it into NATO and the European Common Market.

ADENOIDS, lymphoid tissue (see LYMPH) draining the nose, situated at the back of the throat. They are normally largest in the first five years and by adult life have undergone atrophy. Excessive size resulting from repeated nasal infection may lead to mouthbreathing, middle-ear diseases, sinusitis and chest infection. If these are prominent or persistent complications, surgical removal of the adenoids may be needed.

ADHESION, the force of attraction between contacting surfaces of unlike substances, such as glue and wood or water and glass. Adhesion is due to intermolecular forces of the same kind as those causing COHESION. Thus the force depends on the nature of the materials, temperature and the pressure between the surfaces. A liquid in contact with a solid surface will "wet" it if the adhesive force is greater than the cohesive force within the liquid.

ADHESIVES, substances that bond surfaces to each other by mechanical ADHESION (the adhesive filling the pores of the substrate) and in some cases by chemical reaction. Thermoplastic adhesives (including most animal and vegetable glues) set on cooling or evaporation of the solvent. Thermosetting adhesives (including the epoxy resins) set on heating or when mixed with a catalyst. There are now many strong, long-lasting adhesives designed for use in such varied fields as electronics, medicine, house-building and bookbinding, and for bonding plastics, wood and rubber.

ADIABATIC   PROCESS,   in THERMODYNAMICS, a change in a system without transfer of HEAT to or from the environment. An example of an adiabatic process is the vertical flow of air in the atmosphere; air expands and cools as it rises, contracts and grows warmer as it descends. The generation of heat when a gas is rapidly compressed, as in a piston engine or SOUND WAVES, is approximately adiabatic.

ADIPOSE TISSUE, specialized fat-containing connective TISSUE, mainly lying under the skin and within the abdomen, whose functions include fat storage, energy release and insulation. In individuals its distribution varies with age, sex and obesity.

ADIRONDACK MOUNTAINS, range in NE N.Y., in Hamilton, Essex, Franklin and Clinton Counties, source of the Hudson R. Although often taken as part of the Appalachians, they are in fact structurally related to the Laurentian (Canadian) Shield. Mt Marcy (5,344ft) is the highest peak. Many scenic lakes and millions of acres of woodland (largely included in the Adirondack Forest Preserve) make the region a tourist and sportsman's paradise. Important resources include lumber, iron ore and graphite.

ADLER, Alfred (1870–1937), Austrian psychiatrist who broke away from FREUD to found his own psychoanalytic school, "individual psychology," which saw AGGRESSION as the basic drive. Adler emphasized the importance of feelings of inferiority in individual maladjustments to society.

ADLER, Cyrus (1863–1940), US educator and Semitics scholar who founded the American Jewish Historical Society and wrote and edited several books on Jewish history and comparative religion. He was a founder of the American Jewish Committee

(1906) and president of Dropsie College (1908–40) and of the Jewish Theological Seminary (1924–40) in New York City.

ADLER, Dankmar (1844–1900), German-born US architect and engineer, whose partnership with Louis SULLIVAN from 1881 helped to create the famous Chicago School of architecture. His first important work was the Chicago Central Music Hall (1879).

ADLER, Felix (1851–1933), German-born American educator and social reformer, founder of the ETHICAL CULTURE movement. He held professorships in Semitic literature and in social and political ethics, and championed educational, housing and child-labor reforms.

ADOLESCENCE, in humans, the transitional period between childhood and adulthood. The term has no precise biological meaning, but adolescence is generally considered to start with the onset of PUBERTY and to end at the age of about 20. In primitive societies the period is marked by RITES OF PASSAGE such as those at puberty and at MARRIAGE. These rites are less specifically defined in more sophisticated cultures. Adolescence is both a biological and social concept. In industrialized societies, where the economic dependence of youth is prolonged, it lasts longer and is generally characterized by behavioral patterns and stresses unknown or rare elsewhere.

ADRENAL GLANDS, or **suprarenal glands,** TWO ENDOCRINE GLANDS, one above each kidney. The inner portion (medulla) produces the hormones ADRENALINE and noradrenaline and is part of the autonomic NERVOUS SYSTEM. The outer portion (cortex), which is regulated by ACTH, produces a number of . STEROID hormones which control sexual development and function, glucose metabolism and electrolyte balance. Adrenal cortex damage causes ADDISON'S DISEASE.

ADRENALINE, or **epinephrine,** a HORMONE secreted by the ADRENAL GLANDS, together with smaller quantities of **noradrenaline.** The nerve endings of the sympathetic NERVOUS SYSTEM also secrete both hormones, noradrenaline in greater quantities. They are similar chemically and in their pharmacological effects. These constitute the "fight or flight" response to stress situations: blood pressure is raised, smaller blood-vessels are constricted, heart rate is increased, METABOLISM is accelerated, and levels of blood glucose and fatty acids are raised. Adrenaline is used as a heart stimulant, and to treat serious acute ALLERGIES.

ADRIAN, name of six popes. **Adrian I** (d.795) was pope 772–95. He enlisted Charlemagne's help in crushing the Lombards and enlarging papal territories, condemned adoptionism and, through his legates at the second Council of NICAEA (787), joined in the condemnation of Iconoclasm. **Adrian IV** (c1100–1159), born Nicholas Breakspear, was the only English pope (1154–59). He died while preparing to lead a coalition of Italian forces against the Holy Roman Emperor Frederick I. **Adrian VI** (1459–1523) was the only Dutch pope. After his election in 1522 he attempted to correct abuses within the Church, but during his 20-month reign failed to check the advance of the Reformation.

ADRIAN, Edgar Douglas, 1st Baron Adrian of Cambridge (1889–1977), English physiologist who shared the 1932 Nobel Prize for Physiology or Medicine with Charles SHERRINGTON for work elucidating the functioning of the neurons of the NERVOUS SYSTEM.

ADRIANOPLE, Battle of, decisive victory of the VISIGOTHS and their allies, led by Fritigern, over the Romans in 378 AD. The Emperor Valens and two-thirds of his army perished. Theodosius I had to allow the Visigoth army to settle within the empire, opening the way for future barbarian inroads.

ADRIANOPLE, Treaty of, concluded the Russo-Turkish War of 1828-29. It gave Russia control of the Danube estuary and part of the Black Sea.

ADRIATIC SEA, arm of the Mediterranean, between Italy, and Yugoslavia and Albania. Along the Italian coast, which is straight and flat with shallow lagoons and marshes in the N, the chief ports include Venice, Ancona and Brindisi. At the head of the Adriatic on the Italian-Yugoslav border lies the port of Trieste. The indented Yugoslav coast is lined by the steep limestone cliffs and numerous islands of Dalmatia. Among the major ports are Rijeka, Split and Dubrovnik. On the marshy Albanian coast the main port is Durrës. The Adriatic coast extends for about 500mi with an average width of 110mi. The Straits of Otranto link it to the Ionian Sea to the S.

ADULT EDUCATION, learning undertaken by adults. It was at first an attempt to give people opportunities missed in youth. While this remains a major aim, adult education is now seen more as part of a continuing process. With improvements in formal education, the demand for adult education has increased. In America it started with the LYCEUM MOVEMENT, early in the 19th century. After the Civil War important advances were made by the CHAUTAUQUA MOVEMENT and in various federal agricultural education acts. During the Depression the Works Projects Administration provided education programs for 2,000,000 adults, and after WWII came the G.I. Bill of Rights. In the 1960s federal funds provided for basic literacy programs under the Economic Opportunity Act.

ADVENT (from Latin *adventus*, coming or arrival), in the church year, the season before Christmas. It includes four Sundays, starting from the Sunday nearest St. Andrew's Day (Nov. 30), and marks the beginning of the church year. Advent has been observed since the 6th century as a season of meditative preparation for Christmas and Christ's birth and second coming.

ADVENTISTS, Christian sects, mainly in the US, who believe in the imminent advent (SECOND COMING) of Christ. Adventism grew from the teachings of William MILLER, who announced the end of the world would come in 1843. After the failure of Miller's predictions new Adventist churches arose. The largest is the Seventh-day Adventists, formally organized in 1863. Its members observe Saturday as the Sabbath and support an extensive missionary program.

ADVERTISING, paid publicity designed to persuade people to buy a product or service or to adopt a viewpoint. Advertising started with storekeepers' signs, but modern advertisers include manufacturers, as well as political candidates and governments—using media ranging from billboards to magazines, newspapers, radio and television. In the US advertising provides these media with most of their income and is very big business, accounting for no less than $60 billion a year, involving some 5,000 advertising offices and employing over 100,000 specialists backed by as many clerical and administrative personnel.

Most advertising material comes from advertising agencies which formulate advertising campaigns, buy the necessary time or space in the media chosen, and produce the actual advertisements. Large agencies also offer specialized market research and other facilities. Most agency earnings come from commissions deducted from the payments that clients make for the space or time bought.

Key agency staff include: the agency chief in overall charge; account executives providing liaison between the agency and its clients; copywriters writing the texts of advertisements and working with artists and layout people handling illustrations and typography; the space-buyer; the research department assessing market potential; and the traffic department supervising work flow.

AEGEAN CIVILIZATION, a collective term for the BRONZE AGE civilizations surrounding the Aegean Sea, usually extended to include the preceding STONE AGE cultures there. Early archaeological work in the area was performed in the 1870s–80s by Heinrich SCHLIEMANN, whose successes included the location of Troy, and early in this century by Sir Arthur EVANS. The Bronze Age cultures of the Aegean have been identified as follows: **Helladic,** the cultures of the Greek mainland, including subdivisions such as Macedonian; **Cycladic,** the cultures not only of the Cyclades but of all the Aegean Islands except Crete; and **Minoan,** the cultures of Crete, so named by Evans for Minos, in legend the most powerful of Cretan kings. The Late Helladic cultures are often termed **Mycenaean.**

Around 3000 BC the region was invaded by Chalcolithic (i.e. bronze- and stone-using) peoples, displacing the previous Neolithic inhabitants. This population appears to have remained static until around 2000 BC, when the Greek tribes arrived on the mainland, overpowering and submerging the previous cultures. Around the same time Crete established a powerful seafaring empire, and throughout the area there were rapid and substantial advances in the arts, technology and social organization. Around 1550 BC it would appear that the Mycenaeans occupied Crete, and certainly by this time the Greeks were established as the dominant culture in the area. The Cretan civilization seems to have been eclipsed about 1400 BC. During the 17th century BC there emerged on the mainland a wealthy and powerful aristocracy, whose riches have been discovered in many of their tombs. It would appear that for several hundred years there was a period of stability, since fortifications were not added to the aristocrats' palaces until the 13th century BC. The artistry of this era is exquisite, as evidenced by archaeological discoveries in the tombs: gold cups superbly wrought, small sculptures, and delicate frescoes. During the 13th century BC there probably was a war with Troy, leading to a general decline of the civilizations as a whole.

AEGEAN SEA, arm of the Mediterranean Sea between mainland Greece and Turkey. It is about 400mi long and 200mi wide and has numerous islands: among them the N and S Sporades (including the Dodecanese) and Cyclades groups; Euboea, Lesbos and Samothrace. Many of the islands are the peaks of submerged mountains. Almost all are Greek. Islanders live by farming, fishing and tourism. The Aegean civilization was the first in Europe, and the area became the heart of the classical Greek world.

AEHRENTHAL, Count Alois Lexa von (1854–1912), Austro-Hungarian foreign minister (1906–12) who formally annexed BOSNIA AND HERZEGOVINA in 1908. This inflamed Slav opinion, eventually leading to WWI.

AENEAS, in Greek and Roman myth, a Trojan hero, son of Aphrodite and Anchises. He escaped from the fall of Troy to Carthage, where he lived with Dido. At the gods' command he deserted her and went to Italy, where he founded Lavinium, legendary parent city of Rome. VERGIL'S *Aeneid* tells Aeneas' story to glorify the Emperor Augustus, reputedly his descendant.

AERODYNAMICS, the branch of physics dealing with the flow of air or other gas around a body in motion relative to it. Aerodynamic forces depend on the body's size, shape and velocity; and on the density, compressibility, viscosity, temperature and pressure of the gas. At low velocities, flow around the body is streamlined or laminar, and causes low drag; at higher velocities turbulence occurs, with fluctuating eddies, and drag is much greater. "Streamlined" objects, such as airfoils, are designed to maintain laminar flow even at relatively high velocities. Pressure impulses radiate at the speed of sound ahead of the moving body; at supersonic velocities these impulses pile up, producing a shock wave—the "sonic boom" (see DOPPLER EFFECT). In AIRPLANE design all of these factors must be considered. In normal cruising flight all the forces acting on an airplane must balance. The lift provided by the wings must equal the aircraft's weight; the forward thrust of the engine must balance the forces of drag. Lift occurs because the wing's upper surface is more convex, and therefore longer, than the lower surface. Air must therefore travel faster past the upper surface than past the lower, which leads to reduced pressure above the wing. (See also WIND TUNNEL.)

AEROEMBOLISM, presence of air in the blood circulation. Direct entry of air into veins may occur through trauma, cannulation or surgery, and a large air embolus reaching the HEART may cause death. In acute decompression (as with flying to high altitude or sudden surfacing after deep diving) bubbles of air come out of solution.

These may block small blood vessels, causing severe muscle pains ("bends"), tingling and choking sensations and occasionally paralysis or coma. Recompression and slow decompression is the correct treatment.

AERONAUTICS, the technology of aircraft design, manufacture and performance. See AERODYNAMICS; AIRPLANE; AIRSHIP; BALLOON; FLIGHT, HISTORY OF; GLIDER; HELICOPTER.

AEROSOL, a suspension of small liquid or solid particles (0.1–100μm diameter) in a gas. Examples include smoke (solid particles in air), fog and clouds. Aerosol particles can remain in suspension for hours, or even indefinitely. Commercial aerosol sprays are widely used for insecticides, air fresheners, paints, cosmetics, etc.

AEROSPACE PLANE, National, hybrid airplane and spacecraft being developed by the US for flight in 1994. It will use hydrogen-fueled air-breathing jet engines in atmospheric flight and pure rocket engines in space. (See also HYDROGEN-POWERED AIRCRAFT.)

AERTSEN, Pieter (c1508–1575), Dutch painter of finely-detailed still lifes and domestic interiors. He is regarded as one of the founders of GENRE painting in the Netherlands.

AESCHINES (389–c314 BC), Athenian orator and rival of Demosthenes who argued against resistance to Macedonia.

AESCHYLUS (c525–456 BC), earliest of the three great dramatists of ancient Greece, regarded as the "father of tragedy." Only 7 of at least 80 plays survive, including *The Persians, Prometheus Bound* and the *Oresteia.* The latter is a trilogy based on the murder of Agamemnon by his wife Clytemnestra, and the subsequent revenge by their son Orestes. Aeschylus elaborated Greek dramatic form by adding a second actor and exploiting the dramatic possibilities of dialogue. His tragedies develop a belief that worldly success may lead to pride, incurring the punishment of providence. His style is marked by a unique grandeur and richness.

AESOP, traditional Greek author of animal fables, said to have been a slave on 6th-century BC Samos. He may be a wholly legendary figure. Rooted in folklore, Aesop's fables acquired literary additions and influenced writers such as LA FONTAINE.

AESTHETICS, the study of the nature of art and beauty. The term, from the Greek *aisthesis* ("sense perception"), was coined in the 18th century, though philosophers have discussed art and beauty since PLATO and ARISTOTLE. Modern aesthetics, however, recognizes that not all art is necessarily beautiful in the classic sense.

Philosophers have differed as to whether there are objective formal criteria of artistic value, or whether these criteria are entirely subjective. KANT tried to reconcile the two approaches by arguing that subjective aesthetic judgments involve universal attributes of imagination and understanding. Particularly influential in modern times, have been CROCE, who saw aesthetics as a matter of intuitive knowledge, and SANTAYANA, who argued that beauty lay in the pleasure experienced by the observer.

AFFIRMATIVE ACTION, any program or policy designed to increase the numbers of minority group members or of women in jobs or schools from which they were previously wholly or partly excluded. Affirmative action flourished in the 1960s under the leadership of Presidents Johnson and Kennedy, but under subsequent Republican administrations the program waned rapidly. Affirmative action was dealt a sharp blow in 1978, when the Supreme Court, in the BAKKE CASE, ruled against the use of strict racial quotas in affirmative-action programs.

AFGHANISTAN, republic in Central Asia. It is a mountainous and rugged country, bisected by the mountains of the Hindu Kush, which form a major watershed. The main rivers are the Amu Darya (Oxus), Hari Rud, Kabul, Farah Rud and Helmand. Temperatures can range from 0°F in winter to 113°F in summer.

Official name: Democratic Republic of Afghanistan
Capital: Kabul
Area: 251,825 sq mi
Population: 14,184,000
Languages: Pushtu: Dari Persian
Religions: Muslim (Sunni)
Monetary unit(s): 1 afghani = 100 puls
Economy and People. The economy is mainly pastoral and agricultural, and the chief exports are agricultural products. Though industrialization may be facilitated by further exploitation of natural gas

deposits, the emphasis is still on craft industries. Manufactured goods, including machinery and petroleum products, are imported. There are no railways and few good roads. Strategically placed between the USSR, China, Kashmir, Pakistan and Iran, Afghanistan has received substantial development aid from the US and USSR.

The main cities are Kabul (the capital), Kandahar, Jalalabad and Herat. Most Afghans live a traditional, rural life; about 2.5 million are nomadic. Though elementary education is compulsory, 90% of the people are illiterate.

History. Conquered by Alexander the Great in 330 BC, Afghanistan retained elements of Greek culture as the kingdom of Bactria (c250–150 BC). After a brief period of Buddhist culture, the country fell to the Arabs in the 7th century AD, and Islam became the dominant culture. Afghanistan was subsequently overwhelmed by Genghis Khan and Tamerlane, and from his base in Kabul, Babur (1483–1530) established the MOGUL EMPIRE in India.

Afghanistan became a united state in 1747 under AHMED SHAH, founder of the Durani dynasty. During the 19th century Britain and Russia contested influence over the country, but later Amanullah (ruled 1919–29) succeeded in wresting control of foreign policy from the British. He began modernizing Afghanistan, and proclaimed a monarchy in 1926. The last king, Mohammed Zahir Shah, ruled from 1933 to 1973, when he was overthrown in a coup led by Lt. Gen. Sardar Mohammed Daud Khan. The latter became president and prime minister of the new republic. Daud was overthrown in 1978 and a pro-Russian government installed, precipitating guerrilla warfare by right-wing groups. In Dec. 1979 the Soviet Union invaded Afghanistan to support the Marxist regime. Eight years of warfare followed between Soviet and Afghan government troops on the one hand and US- and Pakistani-supported Afghan guerrillas, or *mujahidin,* on the other. The former controlled the cities and highways, the latter the countryside. In 1988 Soviet troops began to withdraw from Afghanistan, leaving government forces exposed to increased attacks by the *mujahidin.*

AFRICA, the world's second-largest continent 11,677,239 sq mi in area, including offshore islands, or about 10% of the world's land area—a land of tropical forests, grasslands and deserts, famous for big game. It was perhaps man's first home, and was the cradle of the black peoples. Since the 1950s the new nations of Africa have seen great social and political change and have formed a new force in world politics while struggling to develop their often rich resources.

Land. Africa is a vast landmass straddling the equator and extending almost 5,000mi from N to S and 4,600mi from E to W. Only at the Suez isthmus does it touch another landmass (Asia). Except for the Atlas Mts, which are structurally related to the mountains of Europe, most of Africa is an ancient plateau that has been tilted and warped to form a number of basins (e.g. Congo Basin) in the N and W and highlands in the S and E. Africa's highest peak, Mt Kilimanjaro (19,340ft) is in Tanzania and the lowest point (436ft below sea level) is in Egypt. E Africa's GREAT RIFT VALLEY contains the world's second largest area of lakes. The Nile, Niger, Congo and Zambezi are major rivers. Coasts are smooth, lacking natural harbors.

Climate and Vegetation. W equatorial Africa is generally hot and rainy and supports dense rainforests, the home of gorillas, chimpanzees, monkeys and okapis. N, S and E of these forests are tropical areas with alternating dry and rainy seasons. Their savanna grasslands are roamed by lions, giraffes, antelopes and zebras. N of the northern savannas and SW of the southern savannas lie great deserts including the SAHARA and KALAHARI. Extreme N and S Africa have Mediterranean-type climates with mild wet winters and warm dry summers. Tough-leaved olives, cork oaks, etc. survive the summer drought, and animals include porcupines in the N and the Cape buffalo in the S. Grasslands cover Africa's high mountain slopes, scoured by birds of prey. Crocodiles and hippopotamuses live in lakes and rivers, where water birds include storks and flamingoes.

People. Some 70% of Africa's 623 million people are black, but whites predominate N of the Sahara and include Berbers and Arabs. Whites and blacks intermingle in Ethiopia and the Sahara. S of the Sahara live various black groups, Congo Forest pygmies, and (in the SW) the dwindling HOTTENTOTS and BUSHMEN. The S and SE also have large populations of European (mainly of Dutch and British) and Asian origins. Africa has around 50 major languages each (spoken by more than 1 million) and well over 1,000 lesser languages, excluding those established by Europeans. Islam, Christianity and animism are major religious forces. The population is fragmented by more than 50 national and numerous regional divisions. It is also changing rapidly as urbanization and modern ways disrupt traditional tribal life.

Economy. Outside the economically developed S and parts of the N, most African nations are part of the technologically developing Third World. Their agriculture mainly involves subsistence raising of millet, sorghum, maize (corn), cassava, etc., or nomadic cattle herding, and there are commercial tea, coffee, cocoa and citrus plantations geared to world markets. Africa provides one-twentieth of the world's minerals. These include gold and diamonds from South Africa, chrome and copper from Zimbabwe, uranium and copper from Zaire, oil from Nigeria, Libya and Algeria. Except in South Africa and the Mediterranean states, industrialization lags—mainly through insufficient capital, skilled labor and home markets, lack of a comprehensive rail or surfaced road network and other transportation problems. The continent mainly exports tropical crops and minerals, importing machinery and manufactured goods.

History. Fossil finds suggest that early man may have evolved in E Africa. By 3000 BC Egypt had one of the world's first civilizations and from the 9th century BC Phoenicians founded coastal colonies, later seized by Rome. In the 7th century AD Arabs overran N Africa and established trading contacts in the E. Powerful states developed S of the Sahara in the 8–15th centuries, but southern Africa remained unknown to Europe until the 1400s when Portugal explored and colonized its coasts. European trading posts and colonies were subsequently established along the coast, and in the 19th century European explorers probed interior Africa. By 1900 almost all Africa lay divided among colonial European powers (Great Britain, France, Belgium, Portugal, Spain, Italy, and Germany). By the 1960s most former colonies had become independent. Portugal withdrew from its colonies in the mid-1970s, and Rhodesia gained independence as Zimbabwe under black majority rule in 1980. By 1988 tentative agreement had been reached on independence for Namibia, which had been illegally ruled by South Africa since the end of WWII. Efforts to end white dominance in South Africa itself, however, remained unsuccessful.

AFRICAN LANGUAGES. More than 1,000 languages are spoken in Africa, many of them as different from one another as English is from Japanese. Systems of classifying these languages vary, however. In N Africa is the Hamito-Semitic, or Afroasiatic, family of languages; in the S are the Khoisan languages (which are click languages); and between them are at least two other language families: Nilo-Saharan and Congo-Kordofanian (including the Niger-Congo and Kordofanian groups). In the latter family is the important subfamily of Bantu languages. SWAHILI is a lingua franca.

AFRICAN METHODIST EPISCOPAL CHURCH, black Protestant denomination akin to but separate from white Methodist denominations. Founded in Philadelphia (1816) by the Rev. Richard Allen, it is the largest black Methodist body, with about 6,000 churches and 2,000,000 members.

AFRICAN METHODIST EPISCOPAL ZION CHURCH (The AME Zion Church), independent Methodist denomination founded in New York City by blacks disaffected by white prejudices. They built a church in 1800 and formed the denomination in 1821. It has over 1,000,000 members.

AFRICAN NATIONAL CONGRESS (ANC), organization opposing APARTHEID in South Africa. Founded in 1912, it was outlawed in 1960 in the aftermath of the SHARPEVILLE massacre and has since been based in Zambia and Angola. It embraces moderates and radicals, including Marxists, and pursues both political and terrorist tactics. Its titular leader, Nelson MANDELA, has been imprisoned in South Africa since 1964.

AFRICAN VIOLET, any of the genus *Saintpaulia* of hairy PERENNIAL herbs with velvety heart-shaped leaves and purple, pink or white violet-like flowers. The African violet is native to tropical E Africa, but the species *S. ionantha* is widely cultivated as a houseplant. Indoors, they should be placed in a sunny east or south window in winter, but moved to avoid direct sunlight in the summer. They grow well between 60°F and 80°F and should be regularly watered to keep the soil evenly moist. Propagation is by seeds, leaf cuttings and dividing the plants. Family: Gesneriaceae.

AFRIKAANS, an official language of South Africa. It evolved from the South Holland form of Dutch spoken by 17th-century BOER settlers, but incorporated Bantu, Hottentot, Malayo-Portuguese and English words.

AGA KHAN, spiritual leader of the Ismaili sect of SHI'ITE Muslims, an hereditary title. His millions of followers are dispersed through the Near East, India, Pakistan and parts of Africa, and are descended from 14th-century Hindus converted by Persian Ismailis. **Aga Khan I** (1800–1881), a Persian provincial governor who emigrated to India in 1840, was invested as leader of the sect in 1866. **Aga Khan II,** Ali Shah, held the title from 1881 until his death in 1885. **Aga Khan III,** Sultan Sir Mohammed Shah (1877–1957), spent much time in Europe and took an active part in international affairs. He represented British India at numerous conferences and as first president of the All-Indian Muslim League worked for Indian independence. **Aga Khan IV,** Prince Karim (1936–   ), inherited the title in 1957.

AGAMEMNON, in Greek legend, a son of Atreus and king of Mycenae who organized the expedition against Troy recounted in Homer's ILIAD. Before setting sail he was forced to sacrifice his daughter Iphigenia, and was murdered on his return by his wife Clytemnestra and her lover, his cousin Aegisthus. His death was avenged by his son Orestes and his daughter Electra. These events are the subject of AESCHYLUS' trilogy, the *Oresteia*.

AGAPE, Greek word for "love" that occurs frequently in the New Testament, where it signifies both God's love for men and Christian love and charity, as distinct from *philia* (love between friends) and *eros* (sexual love). In its charitable sense *agape* was used to describe a meal held by early Christians to promote fellowship and benefit the poor; it was a prototype of the Eucharist.

AGASSIZ, Jean Louis Rodolphe (1807–1873), Swiss-American naturalist, geologist and educator, who first proposed (1840) that large areas of the northern continents had been covered by ice sheets (see ICE AGES) in the geologically recent past. He is also noted for his studies of fishes. Becoming natural history professor at Harvard in 1848, he founded the Museum of Comparative Zoology there in 1859. On his death he was succeeded as its curator by his son, **Alexander Agassiz** (1835–1910).

AGASSIZ, Lake, a large prehistoric lake which covered parts of N.D., Minn., Manitoba, Ontario and Saskatchewan in the PLEISTOCENE epoch, named for Louis AGASSIZ. It was formed by the melting ice sheet as it retreated (see ICE AGES). When all the ice had melted, the lake drained northward, leaving fertile silt.

AGAVE, a genus of economically important, fleshy rosette plants of the family Agavaceae. There are about 300 species, growing mostly in arid regions of America. Some species, notably *A. americana*, are given the name century plant because they take as long as 50 or 60 years to produce the massive panicles of flowers. Useful fibers such as sisal are obtained from the leaves of certain agaves, and the sap of several species is fermented to make the popular Mexican drink pulque. Several small species are grown as house plants, where they should be placed in a sunny south window, avoiding temperatures below 45° F. They should be watered weekly in the spring and summer, but in other seasons they should only be watered when the soil becomes dry. Agaves are easily propagated by removing offsets.

AGEE, James (1909–1955), US writer remarkable for his sensitive character studies and polished prose style. *Let Us Now Praise Famous Men* (1941) portrayed the life of the Alabama sharecropper. From 1943 to 1948 Agee was film critic of *The Nation*, after which he wrote several screenplays, including *The Quiet One* (1949) and *The African Queen* (1951). His partly autobiographical novel, *A Death in the Family* (1957), won a Pulitzer Prize in 1958.

AGENCY FOR INTERNATIONAL DEVELOPMENT (AID), US government agency formed in 1962 to administer foreign economic aid. It administers two kinds of foreign assistance, normally on a bilateral basis: development assistance and economic support funds. Development assistance concentrates in the areas of: agriculture, rural development, and nutrition; health; population planning; education and human resource development; and private enterprise. Economic support funds are used flexibly to provide grants or loans in support of US economic, political, and security interests. AID also conducts humanitarian relief activities in the wake of such natural calamities as earthquakes, famines, floods, and droughts.

AGENT ORANGE, herbicide used by the US in the Vietnam War to defoliate the jungle. Agent Orange was contaminated with DIOXIN, a lethal poison, and its use had to be abandoned after Vietnamese women reported an extraordinary rise in birth defects. In postwar years, 60,000 veterans complained to the Veterans Administration that they had suffered lasting damage from Agent Orange poisoning, but they were refused compensation.

AGE OF REASON. See ENLIGHTENMENT, THE.

AGGLUTININS, ANTIBODIES found in BLOOD plasma which cause the agglutination (sticking together) of antigens such as foreign red blood cells and bacteria. Each agglutinin acts on a specific antigen, removing it from the blood. An agglutinin is produced in large quantities after immunization with its particular antigen. Agglutinins which agglutinate red blood cells are called isohemagglutinins, and the blood group of an individual is determined by which of these are present in his blood. Group O blood contains isohemagglutinins anti-A and anti-B; group A contains anti-B; group B contains anti-A, and group AB contains neither.

AGGRESSION, behavior adopted by animals, especially vertebrates, in the defense of their territories and in the establishment of social hierarchies. An animal's aggressive behavior is usually directed towards members of its own species, but it is possible that the behavior of predators, although not generally regarded as aggression, may be controlled by the same mechanism. Aggressive behavior is commonly ritualized, the combatants rarely inflicting serious wounds upon one another. Ritual fighting has become established by the evolution of a language of signs, such as the threat posture, by which animals make known their intentions. Equally as important are submission or appeasement postures, which signal that one combatant acknowledges defeat.

It has been claimed in recent years that such signs are particularly well developed in man, and that he is unique in having aggressive tendencies which have led to the extermination of large numbers of his own species. Critics of such claims point out that comparisons between social and political situations and those occurring in animal populations are invalid or, at best, misleading.

AGINCOURT, village in NW France, scene of a decisive battle in the HUNDRED YEARS' WAR. On Oct. 25, 1415, English forces under HENRY V routed the French under Claude d'Albret, demonstrating the power of the English longbow over a heavily armored enemy. The French lost over 7,000 men, the English only a few hundred.

AGING, Human, normal physiological and neurological deterioration over time, accelerating from around age 30. The process is probably genetically determined but may be influenced by diet and activity. Some hallmarks of aging: failing memory due to loss of brain cells; lower effectiveness of the immune system; decline in muscle mass; reduced efficiency of heart and lungs; bone loss; skin wrinkling and coarsening.

The US population is growing dramatically older. The median age, which was 16.7 years in 1820, reached 30.2 in 1950. It declined to 28.0 in 1970, reflecting the post-WWII "baby boom," but it again reached 30.0 in 1980 and 32.1 in 1987. The long-term aging of the population is a consequence of declining mortality due to improved living conditions and advances in medical science. During the first half of the 20th century mortality declines were concentrated among younger ages as medical science conquered the diseases of infancy and childhood. But since midcentury mortality declines have been significant in the older population. Average life expectancy at birth has increased from 47.3 years in 1900 to 74.7 in 1985. Increased longevity, coupled with low national fertility rates, is making aged persons both absolutely and relatively more numerous. Persons 65 and over constituted only 4% of the population in 1900 but 11.9% in 1985. By 2030, when the "baby boom" will have become a "senior boom," 18% of the population — 55 million Americans — will be 65 and over.

The aged population is not homogeneous. Most of the disabilities and dependencies of old age are concentrated among the "old old," persons aged 75 and over (as distinct from the "young old," those 65-74). Prevalent among the elderly are such chronic diseases as arthritis, vision and hearing impairment, heart conditions, and hypertension. The leading causes of death for both men and women 65 and over are heart disease, cancer, stroke, pneumonia, and influenza. The elderly account for nearly a third of all health-care expenditures.

The aging of the US population in the next decade is expected to affect every aspect of American life. A shortage of younger workers will increase the value of older workers and necessitate the redesign of jobs, work schedules, and workplaces. The tastes of older citizens will be reflected in the mix of consumer goods and services offered in the marketplace. Their health and security needs will impact with special force on government. In 1980, 23.8% of the federal budget was spent on programs for the elderly; it is estimated that by 2030 such programs will consume more than 40%. The claims of the elderly will inevitably be contested by younger citizens, on whom the financial burden of those programs will fall. The elderly are already politically powerful. (See also AMERICAN ASSOCIATION OF RETIRED PERSONS (AARP); OLD AGE.)

AGNEW, Spiro Theodore (1918–   ), US politician, Republican governor of Maryland 1967–69 and US vice president 1969–73 in the Nixon administration. He resigned in 1973 and pleaded no contest to a charge that he had failed to report income from payoffs by Maryland businessmen. He was fined $10,000.

AGNON, Shmuel Yosef (1888–1970), Galician-born Israeli author who shared the 1966 Nobel Prize for Literature.

AGNOSTICISM, doctrine that man cannot know about things beyond the realm of his experience, in particular about God. It is a skeptical reservation of judgment in the absence of proof rather than an explicit rejection of any divine order.

AGORA, the public square and marketplace of ancient Greek towns where civic and commercial meetings were held. Surrounded by colonnades and public buildings, it sometimes contained temples and statues of heroes. The famed Agora of Athens has been extensively excavated and reconstructed.

AGOSTINO DI DUCCIO (1418–1481?), Florentine sculptor famed for his subtle and delicate handling of marble. His finest works are the reliefs in ALBERTI's Tempio Malatestiano in Rimini and on the façade of S. Bernardino in Perugia.

AGRARIAN REVOLUTION, advances in farming methods in 18th-century England and Western Europe in which three English agriculturists played an important part. Robert Bakewell sponsored scientific breeding of animals. Jethro Tull invented new agricultural machinery and imported root crops and clover from Europe. Charles, Viscount Townshend used these crops and another new arrival, artificial grasses, in his new "four-course" system of crop rotation. This eliminated the fallow year and supplied more fodder for the animals, which no longer had to be slaughtered in quantity before winter, leaving more meat and more manure for cereal crops. Higher profits motivated renewed enclosure of land, thus encouraging the urban drift of peasant farmers.

AGRICOLA, Georgius (Georg Bauer; 1494–1555), German physician and scholar, "the father of mineralogy." His pioneering studies in geology, metallurgy and mining feature in his *De natura fossilium* (1546) and *De re metallica* (1556).

AGRICOLA, Gnaeus Julius (40–93 AD), Roman general. As proconsul of Britain (77-84) he defeated the Caledonians and extended Roman rule into Scotland. His son-in-law, the historian TACITUS, wrote the famous biography of Agricola.

AGRICULTURE, the science and practice of farming in the widest sense, including the production of crops of all types, the rearing of livestock and the care of the soil. Man's settled agricultural activities probably date back about 10,000 years. But the essential characteristic of true agriculture, the storing and sowing of seeds, did not develop until the Neolithic period (see STONE AGE). The practice probably originated in the highlands of the Near East and spread to the river valleys of Mesopotamia, Egypt and China. By the 4th or 5th millennium BC men were growing grain and keeping livestock, and using stone tools for chopping and digging the ground. Much of the agriculture was practiced by nomadic tribes, who moved from one place to another as soon as they had exhausted the fertility of the soil. As the density of population grew, and nomadic life became more difficult, more clearly defined agricultural systems arose. On these were based the great civilizations of antiquity.

Ancient Egypt possessed a highly productive agriculture owing to the fertility of the Nile valley, whose soil was perpetually replenished by the annual flooding of the river. The Egyptians were familiar with the principles of irrigation, crop rotation and livestock breeding. The Romans too were good farmers, and several of their agricultural treatises make interesting reading. The medieval European farm economy rested on the manorial system. The usual method adopted was a three-field crop rotation, one field being sown with wheat or rye, the second with a combination of barley, oats, beans and peas, and the third being left fallow to recover its fertility. With the coming of the industrial revolution, farming underwent radical changes. The AGRARIAN REVOLUTION of the 18th and 19th centuries replaced the old village communities with individual farms and estates. Farming therefore became concentrated in fewer hands, and its output was geared to supplying food for the urban population and raw materials for the manufacturers.

The Indians of North America were agriculturalists long before the Europeans arrived. The first colonists inherited methods already established for growing corn, beans, pumpkins, tobacco and many other crops. The great expansion of farming to the west of the Appalachians began after the Revolution. A new type of agriculture developed, combining large tracts of land with relatively small amounts of labor and capital. During the 19th century America led the world in agricultural development. Many factors played a part in this: the transportation revolution, the invention of such new machines as MCCORMICK's reaper, which opened up the prairies to wheat farmers, the introduction of artificial FERTILIZERS and the increase of specializa-

tion were all instrumental in raising the productivity of the farms.

Agriculture in most advanced countries is today marked by increasing specialization, with farmers tending to concentrate more and more on a particular line of production. This factor, together with the fall in the number of farm laborers, has led to a high degree of mechanization and produced great sophistication in agricultural techniques. Milking machinery, automated poultry farms, harvesting by combines, grain drying, and automatic potato planting and manure spreading are almost universal. Artificial insemination is commonly used as a means of improving cattle stock. Crops are selectively bred to improve yields and increase resistance to disease. Livestock are fattened in feedlots, weeds and pests are controlled by chemicals, and antibiotics are fed to farm animals to speed their growth.

AGRICULTURE, US Department of, executive department of the US government concerned with the promotion and regulation of agriculture. Established in 1862, the department today operates through research, credit extension, conservation, crop control, distribution and other programs.

AGRONOMY, the branch of agricultural science dealing with production of field crops and management of the SOIL. The agronomist studies crop diseases, selective breeding, crop rotation and climatic factors. He also tests and analyzes the soil, investigates soil erosion and designs land reclamation and irrigation schemes.

AGUINALDO, Emilio (1869–1964), leader of the Philippine independence movement against both Spain (1896–99) and the US (1899–1901). Used by the US to help capture the Philippines during the Spanish–American War (1898), he later led Filipino guerrilla warfare against US occupation and was finally captured in 1901. He withdrew from public life until WWII when, in 1942, he supported the Japanese occupation of the Philippines. Imprisoned by the US in 1945, he was granted an amnesty at the end of the war.

AGULHAS, Cape, southernmost point of Africa, about 100mi E of the Cape of Good Hope. The lighthouse at its tip marks the geographical divide between the Indian and Atlantic oceans. Seaward of the Cape lies the dangerous Agulhas Bank.

AHAD HA'AM (1856–1927), Hebrew pen name, meaning "one of the people," of Asher Ginzberg, Russian Hebrew writer and proponent of "spiritual Zionism." Opposed to political Zionism, he believed that a Jewish nation in Palestine was to be achieved through spiritual rebirth.

AHMED SHAH (c1723–1773), Afghan ruler who founded the Durani dynasty. Through several successful invasions of India he acquired a huge empire. Although unable to hold his empire together, he succeeded in strengthening and uniting Afghanistan, and is thus often thought of as founder of the modern nation.

AIDS, acronym for *a*cquired *i*mmune *d*eficiency *s*yndrome, a disorder that cripples the body's disease-fighting mechanisms. It is caused by a retrovirus (the HIV, or human immunodeficiency virus) that attacks certain white blood cells (the so-called helper T cells), the body's first line of defense. With the body's immune system weakened or destroyed, the carrier is subject to opportunistic infections of all kinds, characteristically pneumocystis carinii (a form of pneumonia) and Kaposi's sarcoma (a form of cancer). Years may elapse between infection with HIV and the appearance of disease, but AIDS invariably proves fatal.

AIDS was first observed in the late 1970s among male homosexuals and identified in 1981. Research worldwide has been intensive, especially since the isolation of the HIV in 1983. It is believed that the disease is transmitted only by inoculation—that is, the virus must be injected into the bloodstream for a person to become infected. This may happen, for example, through transfusions with contaminated blood (as with hemophiliacs), through use of contaminated hypodermic needles (as with intravenous drug users who share needles), or through anal intercourse, since the tissues of the rectum are unusually permeable to the virus contained in semen (as with homosexuals). Carriers of the HIV may be identified by antibodies in their blood, but not if infection was recent and not if MACROPHAGES rather than T cells are involved.

No preventive vaccine or cure for AIDS was available in 1988. In 1987 the US Food and Drug Administration approved the use of AZT (azidothymidine) for the treatment of AIDS. AZT inhibits the replication of the HIV in T cells (but perhaps not in macrophages) and so may prolong the lives of some patients. However, it is also toxic, and some patients cannot tolerate it. A variety of other drugs and foods, not officially approved as safe or effective, are used by desperate HIV carriers and AIDS patients.

In 1988 the US Centers for Disease Control in Atlanta reported 68,200 cases of AIDS nationwide and estimated that as many as 1.4 million people were infected with the HIV. The World Health Organization reported 100,000 AIDS cases worldwide and estimated that 5-10 million people were infected.

AID TO FAMILIES WITH DEPENDENT CHILDREN (AFDC), federal-state WELFARE program providing cash assistance to low-income, female-headed families with dependent children or to families where the male head is incapacitated. Half the states also provide AFDC benefits to two-parent families where the father is unemployed. Eligibility requirements, benefit levels, and participation rates vary from state to state. The federal contribution ranges from 50% in high-income states like Massachusetts and New York to 65% in low-income states like Louisiana and Mississippi. A 1988 welfare reform act required that single parents with children over 3 receiving AFDC get regular jobs and work their way off the dole. If they cannot get jobs immediately, they are required to enroll in educational or job-training courses, paid for by state and federal governments, that will prepare them for jobs. To smooth the transition, they will receive one year of day-care assistance for their children and one year of continued eligibility for Medicaid health coverage for the family.

AIKEN, Conrad Potter (1889–1973), US writer, whose *Selected Poems* (1929) won a Pulitzer Prize. His often incisive critiques and essays on poetry were published in *A Reviewer's ABC* (1958). Other prose works include the novel *Great Circle* (1933) and his sensitive autobiography *Ushant* (1952).

AILANTHUS, a genus of tropical-looking deciduous trees native to Asia and Australia but now widely cultivated in Europe and N America. The best-known species, *A. altissima*, grows rapidly to heights of up to 50ft and produces greenish, malodorous flowers. It thrives in polluted urban conditions in almost any kind of substrate. Family Simaroubaceae.

AILEY, Alvin (1931–   ), US dancer and choreographer, pupil of Lester Horton, with whom he made his debut in 1950. He began choreographing in 1953 and in 1958 formed his own company. *Blues Suite* (1958) and *Revelations* (1960) are among his most noted works.

AINU, the primitive hunting and fishing Australoid Japanese aborigines. They are distinguished by stockiness, pale skins and profuse body hair, hence their frequent description as "the Hairy Ainu." Ainu speech, little used now, bears no relation to any other language. They are now few in number, many having been absorbed into ordinary Japanese society.

AIR. See ATMOSPHERE.

AIR CONDITIONING, the regulation of the temperature, humidity, circulation and composition of the air in a building, room or vehicle. In warm weather an air-conditioning plant, working like a refrigerator (see REFRIGERATION), cools, dehumidifies and filters the air. In colder weather it may be reversed to run as a heat pump.

The first commercial air-conditioning installation dates from 1902, when W. H. CARRIER designed a cooling and humidifying system for a New York printing plant. During the 1920s, motion-picture theaters and then office buildings, department stores and hospitals began to install air-conditioning equipment. After WWII, home units became available, resulting in the rapid growth of the industry manufacturing the equipment. Room air conditioners (window units) are the most widely used domestic equipment, though the installation of the more versatile central air-conditioning equipment (unitary equipment) is becoming more widespread.

AIRCRAFT CARRIER, the largest type of warship in the world. While early carriers had straight flight decks, modern vessels use angled decks for simultaneous takeoffs and landings. Planes are launched by steam catapults, and arresting cables are used to bring landing aircraft to a halt. Each carrier is equipped with anti-aircraft guns and missiles, and is protected by its own planes and sister ships. The US Navy's Forrestal class carriers are over 1,000ft long, weigh 75,000 tons when loaded, and can carry approximately 70 airplanes. The largest built so far is the US nuclear-powered carrier *Enterprise* (1,102ft), displacing almost 90,000 tons full load and able to run five years without refueling.

The first successful takeoff from a ship's deck was made in 1910, and aircraft carriers played a limited role in WWI. They emerged fully in WWII as a decisive factor in the Pacific campaign. Despite the development of long-range aircraft and vulnerability to nuclear attack, they remain a vital part of the US fleet.

AIR FORCE, US, is headed by the chief of staff, who is responsible to the civilian secretary of the air force in the US Department of Defense. He is also the Air Force member of the JOINT CHIEFS OF STAFF. Major Air Force commands include the Logistics Command; the Training Command; the Airlift Command; the Strategic Air Command; the Tactical Air Command; the Europe, Pacific, and Alaskan air commands; and the Space Command. In 1986, 606,000 men and women served in the US Air Force.

AIR FORCE ACADEMY, US, center which trains students to become officers in the US Air Force. Established in 1954, it is located at Colorado Springs, Col. Studies include basic and military sciences, aeronautic theory and airmanship, in addition to liberal arts. Graduates are awarded a BS degree and are commissioned as second lieutenants in the Air Force.

AIR GUN, a weapon using compressed air to fire a dart or pellet with a maximum range of about 300ft. The charge of air released on pressing the trigger is produced either by prior compression or instantaneously by releasing a spring-loaded piston. In the similar **gas gun,** a replaceable carbon dioxide reservoir provides several hundred charges.

AIR LAW, the law governing the use and status of air space. A body of international rules was first formulated at the Paris Convention of 1919, which established that all nations have the right to control their air space. The Chicago Convention of 1944 (Convention on International Civil Aviation) recognized the right of civil aircraft of the signatory states to fly across or land in each other's territories for non-commercial purposes (subject to certain limitations). Commercial scheduled air services are arranged bilaterally. The Convention established the International Civil Aviation Organization (ICAO), which formulates technical standards and codifies the law with respect to liability, property rights and criminal acts, including hijacking.

AIR NATIONAL GUARD, reserve force of the US Air Force including men in all the states and territories. Enlistment is voluntary, and the men are given short periods of paid training throughout the year, under the supervision of the Continental Air Command. Normally under state command, the guard may be activated by the federal government.

AIRPLANE, a powered heavier-than-air craft which obtains lift from the aerodynamic effect of the air rushing over its wings (see AERODYNAMICS). The typical airplane has a cigar-shaped fuselage which carries the pilot and payload; wings to provide lift; a power unit to provide forward thrust; stabilizers and a tail fin for controlling the plane in flight, and landing gear for supporting it on the ground. The plane is piloted using the throttle and the three basic control surfaces: the elevators on the stabilizers which determine "pitch" (whether the plane is climbing, diving or flying horizontally); the rudder on the tail fin which governs "yaw" (the rotation of the plane about a vertical axis), and the ailerons on the wings which control "roll" (the rotation of the plane about the long axis through the fuselage). In turning the plane, both the rudder and the ailerons must be used to "bank" the plane into the turn. The airplane's control surfaces are operated by moving a control stick or steering column (elevators and ailerons) in conjunction with a pair of footpedals (rudder).

The pilot has many instruments to guide him. Chief among these are the air-speed indicator, altimeter, compass, fuel gauge and engine-monitoring instruments. Large modern aircraft also have flight directors, artificial horizons, course indicators, slip and turn indicators, instruments which interact with ground-based navigation systems and radar. In case any individual instrument fails, most are duplicated. (See also FLIGHT, HISTORY OF.)

AIR POLLUTION, the contamination of the atmosphere by harmful vapors, aerosols and dust particles, resulting principally from the activities of man but to a lesser extent from natural processes. Natural pollutants include pollen particles, salt-water spray, wind-blown dust and fine debris from volcanic eruptions. Most man-made pollution involves the products of COMBUSTION—smoke (from burning wood, coal, and oil in municipal, industrial and domestic furnaces; carbon monoxide and lead (from automobiles), and oxides of nitrogen and sulfur dioxide (mainly from burning coal)—though other industrial processes, crop-spraying and atmospheric nuclear explosions also contribute. Most air pollution arises in the urban environment, with a large portion of that coming from the AUTOMOBILE. Pollution control involves identifying the sources of contamination, developing improved or alternative technologies and sources of raw materials, and persuading industries and individuals to adopt these, if need be under the sanction of legislation. Automobile emission control is a key area for current research, exploring avenues such as the recycling and thorough oxidation of exhaust gases, the production of lead-free gasoline, and the development of alternatives to the conventional internal combustion engine. On the industrial front, flue-gas cleansing using catalytic conversion (see CATALYSIS) or centrifugal, water-spray or electrostatic precipitators is becoming increasingly widespread. The matching of smokestack design to local meteorological and topographic conditions is important for the efficient dispersal of remaining pollutants. Domestic pollution can be reduced by restricting the use of high-pollution fuels as in the UK's "smokeless zones." In the short term, the community must be prepared to pay the often high prices of such pollution-control measures, but bearing in mind the continuing economic rewards ensuing and the vital necessity of preserving the purity of the air we breathe, the sacrifice must be worthwhile. (See also ACID RAIN; POLLUTION).

AIR PRESSURE. See ATMOSPHERE.

AIR RIGHTS, rights to use of building space, especially over railroad tracks, highways, bridge and tunnel approaches and so on. Air rights were used in New York City over the New York Central track as early as 1910. As urban land grew scarcer in all big cities, such rights became increasingly valuable for housing developments and office construction.

AIRSHIP, or dirigible, a lighter-than-air, self-propelled aircraft whose buoyancy is provided by gasbags containing hydrogen or helium. The first successful airship was designed by Henri Giffard, a French engineer, and flew over Paris in 1852, though it was only with the development of the INTERNAL COMBUSTION ENGINE that the airship became truly practical. From 1900 Germany led the world in airship design, as Count Ferdinand von ZEPPELIN began to construct his famous "Zeppelins." Most of the large airships built during the next 40 years were of the "rigid" type, with a metal-lattice frame, and used hydrogen as the lifting gas. Their vulnerability in storms and a series of spectacular fire disasters brought an abrupt end to their use in about 1937. During WWII much use was made of small "nonrigid" patrol airships ("blimps") in which the gasbag formed the outer skin and altitude was controlled by inflating and venting air "ballonets" inside the main gas-bag. Most existing craft are of this type, with engines slung beneath the gasbag either on the cabin or in separate "nacelles." "Semi-rigid" airships are similar to blimps but, being larger, usually have a longitudinal metal keel. Airship enthusiasts envisage a great future for airships filled with nonflammable helium, noiselessly transporting freight right into the heart of large cities.

AIRSICKNESS. See MOTION SICKNESS.

AIX-LA-CHAPELLE, Treaties of, name of two agreements. The first treaty (1668) ended the War of DEVOLUTION between France and the TRIPLE ALLIANCE of England, Holland and Sweden over France's claim to the Spanish Netherlands. It allowed France to retain most of the Flanders towns captured the previous year. The second treaty (1748) concluded the War of the AUSTRIAN SUCCESSION, in which several nations, led by France and Prussia, had tried to annex the vast territories held by the Empress Maria Theresa of Austria. By the terms of the treaty the empress's right to the Hapsburg throne was recognized, and Prussia gained the important region of Silesia.

AKBAR (1542–1605), greatest of the MOGUL emperors, who extended Mogul power over most of Afghanistan and India. An excellent administrator, he pursued a policy of religious toleration and took an active interest in the study of religious sects. He also improved social laws, commerce and transportation.

AKELEY, Carl Ethan (1864–1926), American naturalist and sculptor of animals who pioneered large-scale museum displays of stuffed animals, especially African big game, in their natural habitats.

AKHENATON, or Ikhnaton, title taken by Amenhotep IV, king of Egypt c1379–1362 BC. Married to NEFERTITI, he started the cult of the sungod Aton, despite the opposition of the priesthood of Amon-Ra. Changing his name to Akhenaton ("he who serves Aton"), he moved the capital from Thebes, city of Amon, to Akhetaton (now Tell el-Amarna), where he fostered a naturalistic school of art and literature. After his death the old religion was reestablished and Akhenaton's name was erased from his monuments.

AKHMATOVA, Anna, pseudonym of Anna Andreyevna Gorenko (1888–1966), Russian poet who joined the reaction against Symbolist vagueness and obscurity. Her own poems, often confessional lyrics, are notable for clarity and formal precision.

AKIBA BEN JOSEPH (c40–135), famous Jewish rabbi, one of the greatest compilers of Hebrew law, whose work later formed the basis of the Mishnah. After supporting a revolt against the Romans, he was executed as a rebel.

AKKAD, Semitic kingdom in Lower Mesopotamia, N of Sumer, founded by Sargon c2360 BC. Its center was the strongly fortified city of Akkad (Agade), N of Nippur. The Akkadian dynasty overthrew the Sumerian Kish and ruled Mesopotamia from c2360 to 2180 BC.

AKSAKOV, Sergei Timofeyevich (1791–1859), Russian writer, whose *Family Chronicle* (1846–56) and *Years of Childhood* (1858) combine the novel and memoir forms. He was a prominent member of the Slavophile movement, as were his writer sons Konstantin (1817–1860) and Ivan (1823–1886).

AKSUM or AXUM, town in Tigre province, N Ethiopia, capital of the Aksumite Empire, which included much of present-day Ethiopia and Sudan, from about the 1st to the 7th centuries AD. Aksum is the most sacred city of Ethiopia's Coptic Christians: the biblical Ark of the Covenant is said to be kept in the Church of St. Mary Zion. Gigantic carved stelae, as large as the obelisks of Egypt, stand as the most impressive achievements of Aksumite art. The city is now an agricultural market center.

AKUTAGAWA RYUNOSUKE (1892–1927), Japanese writer of short stories, poetry and plays. From medieval themes he turned to autobiographical subjects. His work's fantastic and morbid nature reveals susceptibilities which led to his suicide. His most famous story is *Rashomon* (1915).

ALABAMA, state, SE US, bounded to the E by Ga., to the S by Fla. and the Gulf of Mexico, to the W by Miss. and to the N by Tenn.

Name of state: Alabama
Capital: Montgomery
Statehood: Dec. 14, 1819 (22nd state)
Familiar names: Cotton State, Yellowhammer State, the Heart of Dixie
Area: 51,609sq mi
Population: 4,052,000
Elevation: Highest—2,407ft, Cheaha Mountain. Lowest—sea level, Gulf of Mexico
Motto: *Audemus jura nostra defendere* ("We dare defend our rights")
State flower: Camellia
State bird: Yellowhammer
State tree: Southern pine
State song: "Alabama"
Land. NE Alabama runs into the SW end of the Appalachians. It includes the Cumberland Plateau, a series of forested mineral-rich ridges, and a section of the Piedmont region. The Black Belt, a narrow strip of prairie land, crosses the East Gulf Coastal Plain (drained by the Alabama, Tombigbee and other rivers), which

occupies most of the S two-thirds of the state. Climate is mild and moist.

People. About half the people now live in six urban areas, including the steel center of Birmingham in the N central part of the state, and Alabama's only Gulf port, Mobile.

Economy. Alabama's traditional agricultural economy, once based on cotton, has greatly changed since the 1930s. Economic diversification, aided by the exploitation of hydroelectricity, has led to marked industrial growth, particularly in iron and steel production. Coal, iron ore, limestone, bauxite, timber, petroleum and natural gas provide raw materials for the state's industries, which are now the chief source of income. Major manufactures include clothes, textiles, metal and wood products, processed foods and chemicals. In the N, TENNESSEE VALLEY AUTHORITY (TVA) dams provide low-cost hydroelectricity.

History. Choctaws, Creeks and other members of the FIVE CIVILIZED TRIBES originally peopled Alabama (the state is named for a Choctaw tribe). Spain's Hernando DE SOTO explored the region in 1540, and France's Sieur de BIENVILLE founded the first permanent European settlement in the Mobile area in 1702. France ceded the region to Britain (1763), which lost it to the US (1783), but Spain held the Mobile area until 1813. The defeat of the Creeks at the Battle of Horseshoe Bend (1814) opened S Alabama to settlers, who developed a slave-based plantation economy. At the outbreak of the Civil War Montgomery became the first Confederate capital. The state suffered greatly during the war and then afterward during Reconstruction. Industry began to develop towards the end of the century, but one-crop farming and the sharecropping system brought widespread agricultural depression and poverty, accentuated from 1915 by the infestation of the boll weevil. TVA projects and WWII boosted industry, and despite racial tension in the 1950s and 1960s, Alabama became a leader in the S in basing its economy firmly on manufacturing. Still, with a population increase of only 17.7% from 1970 to 1986, Alabama grew more slowly than neighboring states and its per capita income remained in the lowest 20% of the states. For more than 20 years, Alabama politics was dominated by Democrat George C. WALLACE, originally a segregationist but later a moderate who won black support. Wallace was governor 1963–67, 1971–79, 1983–87. His wife, Lurleen, was governor 1967–71. In 1986 Alabama elected its first Republican governor in a century although the state's legislature remained Democratic. In presidential elections 1968–88, Alabama voted Republican in 1972 and 1980–88.

ALABAMA CLAIMS, compensation claimed by the US from Britain for property seized and destroyed by the *Alabama* and other Confederate vessels during the Civil War. Britain was charged with violating its neutrality by allowing the Confederate warships to be built or equipped in its shipyards. In 1871 the dispute was submitted to an international tribunal, which found Britain liable and awarded the US $15,500,000 in gold.

ALAIN-FOURNIER, pseudonym of Henri Alban Fournier (1886–1914), French writer whose one novel, *Le Grand Meaulnes* (1913), is the haunting tale of a boy's attempt to rediscover the dreamlike setting of his meeting with a beautiful girl.

ALAMEIN, El. See EL ALAMEIN.

ALAMO, Spanish mission-fortress in San Antonio, Texas, the site of a heroic defense in 1836 by less than 200 Texans in the struggle for independence from Mexico. All the defenders, including such heroes as Davy CROCKETT and Jim BOWIE, died in a lengthy siege by 4,000 Mexicans under General SANTA ANNA.

ALAMOGORDO, town in S central N.M., seat of Otero Co. and the center of an agricultural, timber and recreation area which includes White Sands National Monument. The first atomic bomb was exploded near Alamogordo in a test on July 16, 1945. Pop 23,035.

ALANBROOKE, Alan Francis Brooke, 1st Viscount (1883–1963), British field marshal, one of the leading military strategists of WWII. Chief of the Imperial General Staff 1941–46, he participated in important wartime conferences of the Allies.

ALARCÓN, Pedro Antonio de (1833–1891), Spanish regional writer best known for his novel *The Three-Cornered Hat* (1874). His work is distinguished by sharp realistic observation and picturesque effects.

ALARCÓN Y MENDOZA, Juan Ruiz de (c1580–1639), Spanish playwright of the Golden Age who wrote brilliant moralizing comedies. The best-known, *The Suspicious Truth,* influenced the great French dramatist, CORNEILLE.

ALARIC, name of two Visigoth kings. **Alaric I** (c370–410) was commander of the Visigoth auxiliaries under the Roman Emperor Theodosius until the latter's death, when Alaric was proclaimed king by his countrymen. After invading Greece and N Italy, he captured and sacked Rome in

410. Alaric II (d. 507), ruled Spain and S Gaul from 484, and issued the Breviary of Alaric, a Visigoth code of Roman law, in 506. His army was defeated and he was slain by Clovis I, king of the Franks.

ALASKA, largest of the 50 states, and potentially one of the richest, America's "Last Frontier." It occupies the extreme NW corner of North America, bounded N by the Arctic Ocean, W by the Bering Sea, S by the Pacific Ocean, and E by the Yukon and British Columbia. Alaska lies only 51mi E of the Siberian mainland across the Bering Strait.

Name of state: Alaska
Capital: Juneau
Statehood: Jan. 3, 1959 (49th state)
Familiar names: Last Frontier; Land of the Midnight Sun; Great Fun Land
Area: 586,400sq mi
Population: 534,000
Elevation: Highest—20,320ft, Mt. McKinley. Lowest—sea level, Pacific coast
Motto: "North to the future"
State flower: Forget-me-not
State bird: Willow ptarmigan
State tree: Sitka spruce
State song: "Alaska's Flag"

Land. Including the coasts of thousands of offshore islands (notably the 1,200mi long Aleutian Islands, the Alexander Archipelago and the Pribilof Islands), Alaska's coastline exceeds those of all the other states combined. Major mountain chains are the Brooks Range in the N and the Alaska Range in the S (with Mt McKinley reaching 20,320ft), separated by the Central Plateau through which the Yukon R flows. In the far N, the lowland North Slope faces the Arctic Ocean. The climate is cold in the N and the interior, but during the long daylight hours of the brief interior summer temperatures can be extremely high. Warm ocean currents and sheltering mountains make the climate of the S relatively mild and moist.

People. Alaska is still the least populated of the 50 states, though its population grew by a third in the 1980s. Most people live in Anchorage (the largest city), Fairbanks and smaller centers in the Panhandle.

Economy. Minerals (especially oil from Prudhoe Bay and the Kenai Peninsula; also gravel, coal and copper) are the state's chief source of income. Hunting fur seals is also important, and Alaska has the largest commercial fisheries of any state. Processing of the fish catch and production of pulp and lumber are the largest industries. Tourism is a relatively new and fast-growing industry. Farms are few, and most food must be imported, which adds to the high cost of living. Transportation is difficult in this remote, rugged state where long winters hamper road construction and maintenance. The ALASKA HIGHWAY links Fairbanks with Canada and the US, and roads and a railroad join some S centers, but much travel is by sea or air.

History. Russia claimed Alaska after Vitus Bering and Alexander Chirikov sighted it (1741). Grigori Shelekhov founded the first permanent settlement, on Kodiak Island (1784). Secretary of State William H. Seward bought Alaska for the US in 1867 for $7.2 million (about 2 cents an acre), which some referred to as "Seward's Folly." Economic growth remained slow until the 1896 Klondike gold rush in the Yukon and after subsequent deposits were discovered in Nome (1899) and Fairbanks (1902). Crude oil began flowing along the Trans-Alaska pipeline to the port of Valdez in 1977, with more than 1¼ billion barrels being transmitted in the first three years of operation. Construction of a gas line from Prudhoe Bay also began. Alaska's revenues from oil and gas have been so large that the state income tax was repealed in 1980. A commission also was appointed that year to review Alaska's role within the federal union. Perceived by some as a cover for secessionist sentiments, the commission is mandated to study the statehood act and propose such lawful changes as may seem warranted. Debate continues on environmental issues, too. In a major compromise Congress in 1980 set aside more than 104 million acres for wilderness areas, wildlife refuges and national parks and preserves, while allocating other lands for mining and logging. Low oil prices in the 1980s reduced state revenues and depressed the economy. After 13 years as the leader among the states in per capita income, Alaska fell to third place in 1986. In presidential elections 1968–88, Alaska voted consistently Republican.

ALASKA BOUNDARY DISPUTE, disagreement concerning the demarcation of the border between the Alaska Panhandle and Canada, which arose in

1898 during the Klondike gold rush. Skagway and the head of the Lynn Canal, through which supplies reached the Yukon, were claimed to be in Canadian territory. The question was settled in favor of the US by a joint US–British commission in 1903.

ALASKA HIGHWAY, road extending 1,523mi from Fairbanks, Alaska, through Whitehorse, Yukon, to Dawson Creek, British Columbia. It was built by the US as a strategic all-weather military route in 1942, and in 1946 Canada took over control of the 1,221mi passing through its territory. Formerly known as the Alaskan International Highway and Alcan Highway, the road is kept open throughout the year.

ALASKA PIPELINE, oil pipeline with a flow potential of one million barrels daily, running 789mi from Alaska's North Slope to the port of Valdez. Constructed by a consortium of oil companies and finished in 1977, it was bitterly opposed by environmentalists for adversely affecting the ecology.

ALBA or **ALVA, Fernando Álvarez de Toledo, Duke of** (1507–1582), Spanish general who tyrannized the Netherlands. During his brutal campaign against rebellious Dutch Protestants (1567–73), he executed some 18,000 people, including the counts of Horn and Egmont. Hated for his atrocities and harsh taxes, and harassed by WILLIAM THE SILENT's liberating army, Alva was recalled to Spain in 1573. In 1580 he conquered Portugal for Spain.

ALBANIA, communist nation in SE Europe, the smallest Balkan State. Albania is bounded on the N and NE by Yugoslavia, S and SE by Greece, W by the Adriatic Sea. Barren mountains (reaching 9,026ft in the North Albanian Alps), with wooded lower slopes, dominate all inland Albania. They

Official name: The People's Socialist Republic of Albania
Capital: Tiranë
Area: 11,100sq mi
Population: 3,087,000
Languages: Albanian
Religions: No official religion
Monetary unit(s): 1 lek = 100 qintars

are pierced by the Drin, Vijosé and other rivers flowing W to the narrow fertile plain which flanks the N and central coast. Summers are hot and dry; winters mild and moist.

Albanians (mainly descendants of ancient Balkan hill tribes) are officially atheists; but traditionally Muslims outnumber Christians. Two Albanian dialects are spoken: Gheg in the N, Tosk in the S. Most people live on the coast or in the fertile mountain basins linked by poor roads. Agricultural products include corn, wheat, sugar beets, potatoes, fruit, tobacco and cotton. Industries are small but under rapid development. Copper, chromium, nickel, coal, naphtha and oil are being exploited, and Chinese aid helped hydroelectric schemes and farm mechanization. But agriculture remains the basis of the economy.

About 300 BC Albania was part of the region known as Illyria, which came under Greek, Roman and then Byzantine influence and control. Between 300 AD and 1100 AD it was successively invaded by Goths, Bulgars, Slavs and Normans. Later, the national hero Scanderbeg (d. 1468) delayed, but failed to stop, Ottoman Turkish conquest. Turkish rule Islamized Albania and suppressed nationalist aspirations until the First Balkan War (1912). Occupied in WWI, ruled by self-proclaimed King Zog I (1928–39), then annexed by Italy and occupied in WWII, Albania regained independence under Enver HOXHA's communist regime in 1945. Stalinist Albania broke with Russia in 1961 and allied with Communist China, but in the late 1970s it attacked the more moderate policies of China's post-Mao leadership. Albania remains probably Europe's poorest and most isolated country. After Hoxha's death in 1985, Albania slightly relaxed its isolationism by establishing diplomatic relations with several Western countries and permitting more tourists to enter.

ALBANY CONGRESS (1754), a meeting of 25 representatives from seven British colonies at Albany, N.Y., aimed at conciliating the Iroquois and improving the common defense of the colonies against the French. The congress adopted a plan, chiefly designed by Benjamin FRANKLIN, providing for greater colonial unity, one of the first significant attempts at colonial cooperation. The colonial governments later rejected the plan.

ALBATENIUS (c858–929), Arab mathematician and astronomer who improved on the results of Claudius PTOLEMY by applying

TRIGONOMETRY to astronomical computations. He had a powerful influence on medieval European ASTRONOMY

ALBATROSSES, the 14 species of large, long-winged, gliding, hook-billed seabirds forming the family Diomedeidae in the tubenose order, Procellariiformes. Two species form the genus *Phoebetria* (sooty albatrosses), the other 12 the *Diomedea*. Most albatrosses are white with darker markings on the back, wings and tail. The wandering albatross (*D. exulans*) has the broadest wingspan of any living bird—up to 12ft. Living mainly over the southern oceans, albatrosses have wings uniquely adapted for gliding flight.

ALBEE, Edward Franklin (1928–   ), US playwright who gained international fame with his play *Who's Afraid of Virginia Woolf?* (1962). He won Pulitzer Prizes for *A Delicate Balance* (1966) and *Seascape* (1975).

ALBENIZ, Isaac (1860–1909), Spanish composer and pianist. A child prodigy, he wrote operas and songs, but is best remembered for his later piano works, including the suite *Iberia* (1906–9), based on Spanish folk themes and popular music forms.

ALBERS, Josef (1888–1976), German-American painter, graphic artist and art teacher, whose style of geometrical abstraction and theories of art have influenced many modern artists. A teacher at the BAUHAUS in Germany (1923–33), he emigrated to the US (1933) and headed the department of design at Yale (1950–58).

ALBERT I (1875–1934), king of the Belgians (1909–34). Nephew and successor of LEOPOLD II, he did much to improve conditions in the Belgian Congo. In Belgium he strengthened national defense and the merchant fleet, and introduced various social reforms. During WWI he personally commanded the armed forces.

ALBERT, Prince (Francis Charles Augustus Albert Emmanuel; 1819–1861), prince consort of England, husband of Queen Victoria. German-born son of the Duke of Saxe-Coburg-Gotha, he married Victoria in 1840, and as her trusted adviser worked to establish the nonpartisan influence of the crown in government. He was active in promoting science and art. A man of irreproachable character, he was deeply mourned by Victoria after his early death.

ALBERT, Lake, 2,064sq mi lake between Uganda and Zaire, also known as Albert Nyanza or Lake Mobuto Sese Seko. The source of the Albert Nile, it is fed by the Semliki R, draining Lake Edward, and by the Victoria Nile. It was discovered 1864 by Sir Samuel Baker.

ALBERTA, Canada's westernmost prairie province, the country's leading petroleum producer and a rich agricultural region.
Name of province: Alberta
Joined Confederation: Sept. 1, 1905
Capital: Edmonton
Area: 255,285sq mi
Population: 2,348,021
Land. The S and E was originally covered by prairie grasslands, fertile but dry and rising towards the Rocky Mountains in the SW. The rugged Rockies (containing Banff, Jasper and other national parks) dominate the W; dense forests and swamp cover the N. The Peace, Athabasca and other rivers drain the province, and the Athabasca and Lesser Slave are the largest of many lakes. Long cold winters alternate with hot, sunny summers.
People. About 45% of all Albertans are of British origin; others are of German, Ukrainian, Scandinavian and French descent. Most of the 30,000 Indians live on reserves. Nearly half the rapidly growing population lives in the Edmonton and Calgary metropolitan areas, and the rural population has declined to less than a third of the total.
Economy. Since the 1950s Alberta's mineral wealth and manufacturing have become the chief source of income. The province produces 86% of Canada's crude oil and 80% of its natural gas, as well as coal from Canada's largest deposits. Two recovery plants are in operation N of Fort McMurray, but full exploitation of the immensely rich Athabasca oil sands still remains in the future. Oil refining and petrochemical production are major industries. Agriculture remains important with wheat and livestock the principal products.
History. In 1670 unexplored Alberta became part of RUPERT'S LAND, granted to the Hudson's Bay Company. Anthony Henday was its earliest European visitor (1754), and Fort Chipewyan (1788) was among the first of the settlements by fur traders and missionaries. But few white settlers arrived until after 1869, when the Canadian Government bought Rupert's Land. The arrival of the Mounties (1874), completion of the Canadian Pacific Railway (1885) and peace treaties handing most Indian lands to the Canadian government by 1899, encouraged immigrants. Alberta became a province in 1905. Depressed farm income during the 1920s and 1930s led to the victory of the SOCIAL CREDIT PARTY (1935), which stayed in power until 1971. Discovery of oil and natural gas at Leduc, near Edmonton, in 1947 opened a

new era in the province's history. Petroleum, natural gas, and coal have made Alberta one of Canada's richest provinces. The decline in oil prices in the 1980s slowed the province's economy, but an economic recovery began in 1987. In 1988 Calgary, the province's largest city, was the host of the 1988 winter Olympics.

ALBERTI, Domenico (c1710–1740), Venetian composer who gave his name to a style of accompaniment where the left hand plays broken chords, the "Alberti Bass."

ALBERTI, Leon Battista (1404–1472), Florentine Renaissance scholar, architect and art theorist whose contributions in the arts and sciences make him typical of the Renaissance "Universal Man." Architectural works include the Palazzo Rucellai in Florence and the Tempio Malatestiano (S. Francesco) in Rimini.

ALBERT NYANZA. See ALBERT, LAKE.

ALBERTUS MAGNUS, Saint (c1200–1280), German scholastic philosopher and scientist; the teacher of St. Thomas AQUINAS. Albert's main significance was in promoting the study of ARISTOTLE and in helping to establish Aristotelianism and the study of the natural sciences within Christian thought. In science he did important work in botany and was possibly the first to isolate ARSENIC.

ALBIGENSES, members of the heretical (actually non-Christian) CATHARI sect, active in the 12th and 13th centuries, who took their name from the city of Albi in S France. Believing that worldly things represented the forces of evil and that the human spirit alone was good, they attacked the Church. Pope Innocent III attempted to break the power of the sect in the Albigensian Crusade (1208–29), but it flourished for another century. See also DUALISM and MANICHAEISM.

ALBINO, an organism lacking the pigmentation normal to its kind. The skin and hair of albino animals (including man) is uncolored while the irises of their eyes appear pink. Albinism, which may be total or only partial, is generally inherited. Albino plants contain no CHLOROPHYLL and thus, being unable to perform PHOTOSYNTHESIS, rapidly die.

ALBINONI, Tomaso (1671–1750), Italian composer. A famous violinist, he also wrote over 50 operas. BACH, his contemporary, made use of several of Albinoni's themes in his own compositions.

ALBRIGHT, Ivan Le Lorraine (1897–1983), US painter of microscopically detailed canvases whose mood and symbolism focus on decay and human dissolution. His works include *That Which I Should Have Done I Did Not Do* (1941), which took ten years to complete, and a series of paintings for the film *The Picture of Dorian Gray* (1944).

ALBUMIN, group of PROTEINS soluble in water and in 50% saturated sulfate solution; present in animals and plants. Ovalbumin is the chief protein in egg white; serum albumin occurs in blood PLASMA, where it controls osmotic pressure.

ALBUQUERQUE, Afonso de (1453–1515), Portuguese admiral and second viceroy of Portuguese India, who extended Portuguese influence in the Far East (1503-15), and secured the Far Eastern trade routes from foreign intervention. He died at sea after having been deposed by rivals.

ALCAEUS, Greek lyric poet of c600 BC. Like his contemporary, Sappho, he came from the island of Lesbos and wrote in the Aeolic dialect. He is best remembered for poetry about his fondness for wine. The four-line Alcaic stanza, named for him, was widely used in Greek lyric poetry, and was adopted by the Latin poet Horace and by English poets such as Tennyson.

ALCAMENES (460–400 BC), Greek sculptor, somewhat younger than PHIDIAS. After Phidias' death he became the leading sculptor in Athens. Apart from a famous Roman copy of his statue of Hermes, few examples of his work survive.

ALCATRAZ, rocky island in San Francisco Bay, famous as the site (1933–63) of a federal prison for dangerous criminals, nicknamed "the Rock." In 1970 the island was occupied for a time by a group of American Indians. It is now part of the Golden Gate National Recreation Area.

ALCAZAR, name for the massive fortified palaces built in Spain under Muslim rule. The ALHAMBRA in Granada is a well-known and beautiful example. The Alcazar of Toledo withstood a famous siege in 1936 during the Spanish Civil War.

ALCHEMY, a blend of philosophy, mysticism and chemical technology, originating before the Christian era, seeking variously the conversion of base metals into gold, the prolongation of life and the secret of immortality. In the Classical world alchemy began in Hellenistic Egypt and passed through the writings of the great Arab alchemists such as Al-Razi (Rhazes) to the Latin West. The late medieval period saw the discovery of nitric, sulfuric and hydrochloric acids and ethanol (*aqua vitae,* the water of life) in the alchemists' pursuit of the "philosopher's stone" or *elixir* which would transmute base metals into gold.

In the early 16th century PARACELSUS set

alchemy on a new course, towards a chemical pharmacy (iatrochemistry), although other alchemists—including John Dee and even Isaac NEWTON—continued to work along mystical, quasireligious lines. Having strong ties with ASTROLOGY, alchemy, particularly in the hermetic writings, has never quite died out, though without any further benefit to medical or chemical science. (See also CHEMISTRY.)

ALCIBIADES (c450–404 BC), Athenian statesman and general, nephew of PERICLES and a favorite student of SOCRATES. Always a disturbing influence, during the Peloponnesian War he temporarily fell out of favor. Escaping to Sparta, he betrayed Athens, but later rejoined his fleet, which he led successfully against Sparta. Once more out of favor, he was assassinated in exile.

ALCOCK, Sir John William (1892–1919), British aviator who, with navigator Arthur Whitten Brown, made (1919) the first nonstop transatlantic flight, from Newfoundland to Ireland. A week later he died in an airplane accident.

ALCOHOLISM, compulsive drinking of alcohol in excess, one of the most serious problems in modern society. Many people drink for relaxation and can stop drinking without ill effects; the alcoholic cannot give up drinking without great discomfort: he is dependent on alcohol, physically and psychologically.

Alcohol is a depressant that acts initially by reducing activity in the higher centers of the BRAIN. The drinker loses judgment and inhibitions; he feels free of his responsibilities and anxieties. This is the basis for initial psychological dependence. With further alcohol intake, thought and body control are impaired (see also INTOXICATION). The alcoholic starts by drinking more and longer than his fellows. He then finds that the unpleasant symptoms of withdrawal—"hangover," tremor, weakness and hallucinations—are relieved by alcohol. In this way his drinking extends through the greater part of the day, and physical dependence is established. The alcoholic often has a reduced tolerance to the effects of alcohol and may suffer from AMNESIA after a few drinks. Social pressures soon lead to secretive drinking, work is neglected and financial difficulties add to the disintegration of personality; denial and pathological jealousy hasten social isolation. Alcohol depresses the appetite, and the alcoholic may stop or reduce eating. Many of the diseases associated with alcoholism are in part due to MALNUTRITION and VITAMIN deficiency: CIRRHOSIS, NEURITIS, dementia, and Korsakov's psychosis.

Prolonged alcohol withdrawal leads to DELIRIUM TREMENS. Treatment of alcoholism is very difficult. SEDATIVES and ANTABUSE may help to counteract dependence. Reconciliation of the patient to society is crucial; he must understand the reasons for his drinking and learn to approach his problems and fears realistically. Psychotherapy and Alcoholics Anonymous are valuable in this.

ALCOHOLS, class of aliphatic compounds, of general formula ROH, containing a hydroxyl group bonded to a carbon atom. They are classified as monohydric, dihydric, etc., according to the number of hydroxyl groups; and as primary, secondary or tertiary according to the number of hydrogen atoms adjacent to the hydroxyl group. Alcohols occur widely in nature, and are used as solvents and antifreezes and in chemical manufacture. They are obtained by fermentation, oxidation or hydration of alkenes from petroleum and natural gas, and by reduction of fats and oils.

Alcohols of lower molecular weight are colorless, flammable liquids, miscible with water. The simplest alcohols are METHANOL and ETHANOL (the intoxicating constituent of alcoholic beverages); others include benzyl alcohol, ethylene glycol and glycerol. (See also CARBOHYDRATES.)

ALCOTT, (Amos) Bronson (1799–1888), US educator, philosopher and author. As a teacher in several Conn. schools, his progressive methods were too advanced to be popular. In 1840 he retired to Concord, Mass., where he was closely associated with the TRANSCENDENTALISM of Emerson, Hawthorne, Thoreau and Channing. His writings include *Concord Days* (1872) and *Table Talk* (1877).

ALCOTT, Louisa May (1832–1888), US author of *Little Women* (1869) and other autobiographical books for children. Daughter of Amos Bronson ALCOTT, she began by publishing stories in magazines like the *Atlantic Monthly*. *Hospital Sketches* (1863) was based on her experiences as a Union nurse in the Civil War.

ALCUIN (735–804 AD), English prelate and scholar whose classical and humanist scholarship influenced medieval teaching of the liberal arts. In 781 he became master of the palace school of CHARLEMAGNE and supervised Charlemagne's program of ecclesiastical and educational reform among the Franks in the Carolingian empire.

ALDEGREVER, Heinrich (1502–c1555), German painter and engraver. One of the "little masters," he was influenced in his work by DÜRER'S assimilation of Italian Renaissance discoveries in classical art.

ALDEN, John (c1599–1687), a MAYFLOWER Pilgrim Father, an able assistant to the governor of Plymouth Colony. He is best known through LONGFELLOW'S poem *The Courtship of Miles Standish*, based on the legend that he courted Priscilla Mullens on behalf of Miles Standish, but married her himself.

ALDINGTON, Richard (1892–1962), English novelist, critic, biographer and pre-WWI IMAGIST poet, who wrote a controversial biography of T. E. LAWRENCE.

ALDRICH, Nelson Wilmarth (1841–1915), US politician, senator from Rhode Island (1881–1911). A spokesman for big business and leader of conservative opposition to President Theodore Roosevelt in the Republican Party, he advocated protective tariffs, the gold standard, and bank reform.

ALDRICH, Thomas Bailey (1836–1907). US editor and writer of poems, stories, novels and essays. He was editor of the *Atlantic Monthly* (1881–90). *The Story of a Bad Boy* (1870), his best-known book, tells of his youth in Portsmouth, N.H.

ALDRIDGE, Ira Frederick (1805–1867), first US black to achieve fame as an actor. Known in Britain and on the Continent for his bold interpretations of such Shakespearean roles as Lear, Othello and Macbeth, he eventually became a British citizen.

ALDUS MANUTIUS (1450–1515), Venetian founder of the *Aldine Press* whose scrupulous editions of Greek and Roman classics (including Aristotle) advanced Renaissance scholarship. He was the first man to use italic type (1501) especially cut in order to produce cheap, pocket-sized editions of the Latin classics.

ALE, in the US, a light-colored, top-fermented beer with an alcohol content of about 5%. It excludes bottom-fermented or continental-type beers. Malt liquors such as ale are generally called beer in England.

ALEATORY MUSIC (from Latin *alea*, dice), music dependent on chance applied to the post-1950 tendency of composers to leave some elements in their work to be settled by the performer's decision or by random chance. John CAGE'S work is perhaps the best-known example.

ALEICHEM, Sholem. See SHOLEM ALEICHEM.

ALEKSANDROV, Aleksandr Vassilievich (1883–1946), Russian composer who wrote operas, orchestral works and popular songs and choruses, including the Soviet national anthem. He also founded (1928) and directed the Red Army Chorus.

ALEMÁN, Mateo (1547–1614), Spanish writer of picaresque novels reflecting his own colorful life. *Guzman de Alfarache* (1599) was widely translated.

ALEMÁN VALDÉS, Miguel (1902–1983), president of Mexico (1946–1952), a successful lawyer, son of a revolutionary general. He initiated a vigorous program of economic development. After his presidency, he directed promotion of tourism, including development of Acapulco and bringing the 1968 Olympics to Mexico City.

ALEMBERT, Jean Le Rond d' (1717–1783), French philosopher, physicist and mathematician, a leading figure in the French ENLIGHTENMENT and coeditor with DIDEROT of the renowned *Encyclopédie*. His early fame rested on his formulation of d'Alembert's principle in mechanics (1743). His other works treat calculus, music, philosophy and astronomy.

ALEUTIAN ISLANDS, chain of some 150 Alaskan islands of volcanic origin, extending 1,200 mi SW and then NW from the Alaska Peninsula in a wide arc, and separating the Bering Sea from the Pacific. These treeless, rugged and foggy islands support a population of approximately 8,000; fishing is the chief occupation. In 1942 the Japanese occupied Agattu, Attu and Kiska, the westernmost islands of this strategic chain, and bombed the naval base at Dutch Harbor.

ALEXANDER, name of eight popes. **Alexander II** (Anselm of Lucca; d. 1073), pope 1061–73, laid the foundations of the reform movement that reached fruition under GREGORY VII. His deposition of the bishop of Milan for simony led to the investiture controversy. **Alexander III** (Orlando Bandinelli; d. 1181), pope 1159–81, continued the long battle against the Emperor FREDERICK I Barbarossa. Opposed by three antipopes, he was victor over Frederick at the Battle of Legano (1176). He convened the Third Lateran Council (1179) and forced King Henry II of England to recognize papal supremacy. He canonized Thomas à BECKET. **Alexander VI** (Rodrigo Borgia; 1431–1503), pope from 1492, was the most notorious of the Renaissance popes. Born in Valencia, Spain, he was deeply involved in the political turmoil of the Italy of his day. His efforts were directed at increasing the temporal power of the papacy and creating great hereditary domains for his children, among them Cesare and Lucrezia BORGIA. He was a keen patron of the great artists of his day. **Alexander VII** (Fabio Chigi; 1599–1667), pope from 1655, ruled at a time when the papacy was losing temporal power, and was worsted in controversy with Louis XIV of France.

ALEXANDER, name of three Russian tsars. Alexander I (1777–1825) succeeded his father, Paul I, in 1801, with a reform program which he later abandoned. In 1805 he joined England and Austria against Napoleon. After French victories at Austerlitz and Friedland, however, Napoleon proposed joint Franco-Russian domination of Europe. But mutual mistrust came to a head when Alexander encouraged British, not French, trade. Napoleon invaded Russia in 1812. Almost the whole French army was destroyed in the freezing Russian winter, and in 1814 Alexander entered Paris. In 1815 he formed a coalition with Austria and Prussia, the HOLY ALLIANCE. At his death, internal repression was abetted by a corrupt Church and enforced by the secret police, and the country itself faced economic ruin and rebellion. **Alexander II** (1818–1881) succeeded his father, Nicholas I, in 1855. Russian defeat in the CRIMEAN WAR and peasant unrest forced on him limited reforms, most importantly the emancipation of the serfs in 1861. But this did not satisfy revolutionary groups, and fear of their activities inspired him at first to more reactionary policies. He finally relented, but on the very day he signed a decree for moderate reform he was killed by nihilist bombs. In foreign policies he was a moderate, making peace in the Crimea and keeping out of the FRANCO-PRUSSIAN WAR (1870–71), though extending Russian power in the Far East as well as in Central Asia. **Alexander III** (1845–1894) succeeded his father Alexander II in 1881. He discarded the latter's proposals for moderate reform in favor of rigid repression and persecution of minorities. But industrial development prospered and construction of the TRANS-SIBERIAN RAILROAD began. In Europe his policies were peaceful.

ALEXANDER I (1888–1934), king of Yugoslavia from 1921 until his assassination by a Croatian terrorist at Marseille. He became prince-regent of Serbia in 1914 and commanded the Serbian forces in WWI. An autocratic ruler, he earned the enmity of separatist minorities.

ALEXANDER, Franz Gabriel (1891–1964), German-born US psychoanalyst who identified emotional factors based on human relationships as the cause of psychosomatic illness. He founded and directed (1932–56) the Chicago Institute for Psychoanalysis and wrote *Fundamentals of Psychoanalysis* (1948).

ALEXANDER, Grover Cleveland (1887–1950), one of the greatest right-handed pitchers of all times, playing with the Phillies, Cubs and Cardinals from 1911 to 1930. He gained the major league record for shutouts in a season (16) and the National League career record in complete games and shutouts.

ALEXANDER, Harold (Rupert Leofric George), 1st Earl Alexander of Tunis (1891–1969), British field marshal and statesman, in charge of the evacuation from DUNKERQUE (1940), later commander of British forces in the Middle East (under whom MONTGOMERY won the victory of EL ALAMEIN), and eventually Supreme Allied Commander in the Mediterranean and Italy. He was governor-general of Canada (1946–52) and British minister of defense (1952–54).

ALEXANDER NEVSKY (1220–1263), Russian national hero and saint. His victories over the Swedes at the Neva R (1240) and over the Teutonic Knights on the ice of Lake Peipus (1242) made him preeminent among Russian princes.

ALEXANDER THE GREAT (356–323 BC), king of Macedonia (336–323 BC) and conqueror of the Persian Empire. The son of PHILIP II of Macedonia, he was born in Pella and educated by ARISTOTLE, the great philosopher. In 338 Philip's defeat of the Thebans and Athenians at Chaeronea brought all the Greek city-states but Sparta under Macedonian rule. At the age of 20 Alexander succeeded his father and went on to execute Philip's plans for freeing the Greeks of Asia Minor from Persian rule. He invaded the Persian Empire with 30,000 infantry and 5,000 cavalry, but military victory was not his only concern; he also took with him a team of scholars, with the aim of bringing the blessings of Greek culture to Asia. After his defeat of the Persian King DARIUS III at Issus in 333, he pressed on to subdue Phoenicia and Egypt, founding Alexandria. As his dominions in the East spread, he thought of himself more and more as an Eastern prince, thus alienating much of his Macedonian army. In 331 Alexander again defeated Darius in the decisive battle of Gaugamela, after which the principal cities of the Persian Empire, Babylon, Susa and Persepolis, fell easily to his attack. He was proclaimed king of Asia, and then moved on eastward through Bactria and along the Indus Valley to the Indian Ocean. He had intended to go on to conquer India, but his men refused. On his return to Babylon he began planning further conquests, but did not have time to realize in detail his plans for consolidating the union he had achieved between the East and the West. With no legitimate succession, the empire was pulled apart after his death by rival generals, known collectively as the Diadochi. But though he lived to be only 33, he had conquered the greatest empire civilization had yet known, and he prepared the way for the HELLENISTIC AGE.

ALEXANDRIA, chief port and second-largest city of Egypt, at the NW corner of the Nile delta, 110mi NW of Cairo. Alexandria was founded by Alexander the Great c332 BC; it was the capital of Ptolemaic Egypt and a great center of trade and learning in the Hellenistic and Roman world. Among its ancient landmarks were the greatest library of antiquity, a renowned museum and school, and the famous lighthouse at Pharos. The city entered a long period of decline after the Arab conquest of 642, but since the time of MEHMET ALI it has grown into Egypt's principal channel for foreign trade, a cosmopolitan city with many of the country's industries. Pop (metro) 2,905,000.

ALEXANDRIAN LIBRARY, the greatest collection of books in antiquity, containing perhaps 400,000 manuscripts, in Alexandria, Egypt. Commenced under PTOLEMY Soter, it came to be housed mainly in the Museum (see ALEXANDRIAN SCHOOL). Portions were destroyed by fires between 47 BC and the final fall of the city to the Arabs in 646 AD.

ALEXANDRIAN SCHOOL, or *Museum* (place dedicated to the MUSES), founded c300 BC, the foremost center of learning in the ancient world during the HELLENISTIC AGE, and which housed the Alexandrian Library. The school was renowned from the first, its teachers including the mathematicians Apollonius of Perga, EUCLID and Hero; the physicians Erasistratus, Eudemus and Herophilus; the geographer Eratosthenes and the astronomer HIPPARCHUS. The last great Alexandrian scientist was Claudius PTOLEMY, who worked in the city between 127 and 151 AD. With the decline of Hellenistic culture, activity in the school turned away from original research towards compilation and criticism, the study of mystical philosophy and theology assuming an increasingly significant role.

ALEXIUS I COMNENUS (1048–1118), Byzantine emperor (1081–1118). He successfully defended the empire against Normans and Turks, restoring its power and prestige. Alarmed at the approach of the armies of the First Crusade, he provided them with money and transportation on condition that they return to him Byzantine territory recaptured from the Muslims. His daughter, ANNA COMNENA, wrote a valuable history of his reign.

ALFALFA, or **lucerne,** important forage plant, *Medicago sativa,* widely grown for pasture, hay and silage. The high protein content of this PERENNIAL makes it an excellent food for livestock, and the nitrogen-fixing BACTERIA in the nodules on its roots are important in enriching depleted soil. Alfalfa is of particular value in arid countries as its extremely long taproot enables it to survive severe drought. Alfalfa has trifoliate leaves and dense clusters of small purple, blue or yellow flowers. Family: Leguminosae.

ALFIERI, Count Vittorio (1749–1803), Italian dramatist and poet, founder of modern Italian tragic drama. Among his works are *Saul, Maria Stuarda* and *Oreste* (1787–89). Hatred of tyranny and a passionate republicanism marked his impetuous and stormy life.

ALFONSÍN, Raúl (1927–   ), Argentine political leader, elected president (1983) after the discrediting of the ruling military junta in the Falklands war. He brought top junta leaders to trial for human rights abuses committed during the "dirty war" against dissidents, but stopped short of pursuing lower-ranking officers. Under pressure from the International Monetary Fund, he imposed economic austerity measures to cope with Argentina's enormous foreign debt.

ALFONSO XIII (1886–1941), king of Spain, posthumous son of Alfonso XII, became king at birth and began personal rule in 1902. His intervention in politics brought instability and unpopularity and he associated himself with the dictatorship of PRIMO DE RIVERA. After a republican landslide in municipal elections he was forced to leave the country in 1931, though he refused to abdicate. His grandson JUAN CARLOS became king on General Franco's death.

ALFRED THE GREAT (c848–899), king of the West Saxons from 871. He halted the Danish invasions, making his kingdom of Wessex the nucleus of a unified England. Already a noted general, he came to the throne in the middle of a Danish invasion, which he had to buy off despite spirited resistance. He used the truce period to consolidate his army and navy, and won a conclusive victory at Edington (878). He occupied London in 886 and was recognized as overlord of all England not in the extensive DANELAW. A pious ruler, he had many writers, such as BOETHIUS and BEDE, translated for his subjects' benefit, and introduced educational and legal reforms.

ALGAE, a large and extremely diverse group of plants, including some of the simplest organisms known to man. They are mostly, aquatic, and range in size from microscopic single-celled organisms living on trees, in snow, ponds and the surface waters of oceans to strands of seaweed several yards long in the deep oceans. Some algae are free-floating, some are motile and some grow attached to a substrate.

Algae are separated into seven major divisions, primarily on the basis of pigmentation. Blue-green algae have also been grouped in the algae by some authorities but differ from other algae in that they are prokaryotic organisms. Green algae (division Chlorophyta) are found mainly in freshwater and may be single-celled, form long filaments (like *Spirogyra*) or a flat leaf-like mass of cells called a thallus (like the sea lettuce, *Ulva lactuca*). Golden-brown algae (division Chrysophyta) also include the diatoms. Brown algae (division Phaeophyta) include the familiar seaweeds found on rocky shores. The largest, the kelps, can grow to enormous lengths. Red algae (division Rhodophyta) are found mostly in warmer seas and include several species of economic importance. Desmids and dinoflagellates (both in division Pyrrophyta) are single-celled algae and are important constituents of marine plankton. Yellow-green algae and chloromonads (division Xanthophyta) are mainly freshwater forms, mostly unicellular and nonmotile. Motile unicellular algae such as *Euglena* (division Euglenophyta) are classified by some biologists as PROTOZOA, but most contain CHLOROPHYLL and can synthesize their own food.

Algae in both marine and freshwater plankton are important as the basis of food chains (see ECOLOGY). Many of the larger algae are important to man; for example, the red algae *Porphyra* and *Chondrus crispus* are used as foodstuffs. *Gelidium*, another red algae, is a source of agar, and the kelps (such as the giant kelp *Macrocystis*) produce alginates, one use of which is in the manufacture of ice cream. Other uses of algae are in medicine and as manure. (See also PLANT KINGDOM.)

ALGARDI, Alessandro (1595–1654), Italian baroque sculptor, pupil of Lodovico CARRACCI, contemporary and more conservative rival of BERNINI. His masterpieces include the tomb of Pope Leo XI (1642) and a great relief of St. Leo and Attila the Hun (1646–50), both in St. Peter's, Rome.

ALGEBRA, that part of mathematics dealing with the relationships and properties of numbers by use of general symbols (such as *a, b, x, y*) to represent mathematical quantities. These are combined by addition $(x+y)$, subtraction $(x-y)$, multiplication $(x \times y, x \cdot y$ or most usually $xy)$ and division $(x \div y,$ or most usually $x/y)$. The relationships between them are expressed by symbols such as $=$ ("is equal to"), $\neq$ ("is not equal to"), $\simeq$ ("is approximately equal to"), $>$ ("is greater than"), and $<$ ("is less than"). These symbols are also used in ARITHMETIC. Should a number be multiplied by itself one or more times it is said to be raised to a power:

$$x \cdot x = x^2,$$
$$x \cdot x \cdot x = x^3, \text{ etc.}$$

x^2 is termed "x to the power of two" or more usually "x squared"; x^3 is termed "x to the power of three" or more often "x cubed." From this emerges the concept of the ROOT: if $x^2 = y$ then x is the square root of y (or $\sqrt{y}$); if $x^3 = y$ then x is the cube root of y, written $^3\sqrt{y}$.

Expressions containing two or more terms, such as $x+y+z$, or x^2+2x+5, are called polynomials. A special case is an expression containing two terms, like $x+y$, which is termed a binomial. Algebraic operations obey the Associative, Commutative and Distributive Laws.

Addition and multiplication of numbers are said to be *commutative*:

$$a+b=b+a \text{ and } a \cdot b=b \cdot a$$

Addition and multiplication are also *associative*:

$$a+(b+c)=(a+b)+c$$
$$\text{and } a \cdot (b \cdot c)=(a \cdot b) \cdot c$$

Addition and multiplication are together *distributive*:

$$a \cdot (b+c)=a \cdot b+a \cdot c.$$

See also EQUATION.

ALGEBRA, Abstract, a branch of mathematics that deals with sets of abstract symbols on which certain formal operations are defined. The basic algebraic system is the group, in which there is one operation, which may be written as multiplication: $a \cdot b = c$, in which a, b and c all belong to the group. **Rings and fields** have both multiplication and addition and more closely resemble ordinary number systems; the real and complex number systems are fields. A **vector space** is an abstract system with formal properties similar to those used in ordinary vector algebra. Functions, or mappings, from one algebraic system to another that preserve the operations of the system play an essential role in abstract algebra. Mappings of vector spaces can be represented by matrices, the study of which has been an important part of abstract algebra.

ALGEBRAIC GEOMETRY, that branch of ALGEBRA concerned with the visual realization of algebraic FUNCTIONS, whether such realization is practically possible or not. An extension of ANALYTIC GEOMETRY, it is now used primarily as an intuitive aid in discovering or understanding THEOREMS.

ALGER, Horatio (1834–1899), US author of more than 100 boys' books, in which the heroes rise from rags to riches through virtue and hard work. Among his books were *Ragged Dick* (1867), *Luck and Pluck* (1869) and *Sink or Swim* (1870).

ALGERIA, socialist republic in North Africa extending from the Mediterranean deep into the Sahara Desert. The Atlas Mountains, running E-W, divide the country into three regions: the rugged coastal zone in the N, clothed with evergreen trees; the steepe, covered with scrub and grass, pocked by salt lakes and flanked by the Atlas ranges; and the stony and sandy Sahara Desert in the S, with the sharply fretted Ahaggar Mountains reaching 9,852ft in the SE. Apart from the Tafna and Chéliff (in the NW), most rivers are intermittent and useless for irrigation or hydroelectricity. The climate is marked by mild winters and warm, dry summers in the N, and by greater extremes on the steppe; the Sahara varies between roasting days and frosty nights.

Official name: Democratic and Popular Republic of Algeria
Capital: Algiers
Area: 919,595sq mi
Population: 23,116,000
Languages: Arabic, Berber, French
Religions: Muslim
Monetary unit(s): 1 Algerian dinar=100 centimes
People. Some 75% of Algerians (chiefly Muslim Arabs and Berbers, but still including some Christian Europeans) live in the fertile coastal area. The ports of Algiers, Oran and Annaga, and northern trading centers (Constantine, Sidi-bel-Abbes, Blida) provide urban employment, but most

Algerians still live on their land; their distribution reflects the mainly agricultural economy.

Economy. Northern farms produce citrus fruits, grapes, grain and vegetables. Nomads tend sheep, goats and cattle on the steppe; and desert oases yield dates. Algeria is one of the world's most important oil-producing countries and a primary exporter of liquefied natural gas. Oil and natural gas provide 95% of total export earnings. Industrial growth is assisted by extensive road and rail systems.

History. Phoenicians settled N Algeria c1200 BC. It became part of Carthage but after the victory of Rome in 201 BC became the Roman province of Numidia. Vandals (by 440 AD), Byzantines (in 534) and Arabs (in the 17th century) all conquered the area. Moors expelled from Spain became the Algerian-based Barbary pirates (from 1518 under nominal Ottoman Turkish control). They ravaged Mediterranean shipping until defeated by US warships. The French then absorbed all Algeria (1830–1909), and French colonists largely governed it until a nationalist revolt (1954–62) forced France to grant Algeria independence. An exodus of skilled French followed. Ahmed Ben Bella, Algeria's first president, was overthrown in 1965 by Houari Boumedienne, who died in 1979. Under his successor, Chadli Benjedid, Algeria took a leading role in North African affairs. In 1988, plunging oil prices and mismanagement of the country's highly centralized economy brought on the most serious social and economic crisis since independence.

ALGIERS, capital, major port and largest city of Algeria. Founded by Berbers in 935 on the site of the Roman settlement of Icosium, it was taken by the French in 1830. The modern city lies at the base of a hill overlooking the Bay of Algiers; higher up the slope is the old Moorish city, dominated by the Casbah, a citadel built by the Turks. Pop (city) 1,523,000; (metro) 2,700,000.

ALGONQUIN (or ALGONKIN) INDIANS, North American Indian tribe. Among the first with whom the French made an alliance, they were driven out of their territory along the St. Lawrence and Ottawa rivers by the Iroquois in the 17th and 18th centuries. Some united with the Ottawa Indians; a few remain in Ontario and Quebec. Originally the name "Algonquin" was applied only to the Weskarini of the Gatineau valley, but its application was widened to include other closely related tribes such as the Nipissing and Abitibi. The tribe gave its name to the Algonquian linguistic division.

ALGREN, Nelson (1909–1981), US naturalistic novelist, best known for his fiction describing Chicago slum life; author of *The Man with the Golden Arm* (1949) and *A Walk on the Wild Side* (1956).

ALHAMBRA, 13th-century citadel and palace dominating the city of Granada, the finest large-scale example of Moorish architecture in Spain. The name is Arabic for "the red castle." It is decorated in an elaborate but delicate style.

ALI (c600–661), cousin and son-in-law of the prophet Mohammed, 4th caliph (656–661) or ruler of ISLAM. He and his two sons were murdered, leading to the establishment of the Omayyad dynasty and a division of Islam between SUNNITES and SHI'ITES. The Shi'ites recognize Ali's descendants as the true successors to Mohammed.

ALI, Muhammad (1942–   ), US heavyweight boxer. Born Cassius Marcellus Clay in Louisville, Ky., he won the world heavyweight championship from Sonny Liston in 1964. Ali was stripped of his title in 1967 by the World Boxing Association while he was appealing against conviction for draft evasion, later overturned. He returned to the ring in 1971 only to be defeated by Joe Frazier, whom he beat in a return match in 1974. Ali defeated George Foreman for the title in 1974, lost it in 1978 to Leon Spinks, won it back the same year, then retired in 1979.

ALIEN AND SEDITION ACTS, four unpopular laws passed by the US Congress in 1798. Two empowered the president to expel or imprison aliens; one made naturalization more difficult; another, the Sedition Act, punished those who wrote or spoke "with intent to defame" the government. Enacted by the Federalists to prepare for a possible war with France (see XYZ AFFAIR), and to silence Jeffersonian criticism, the Alien Acts were not put into force. But several Jeffersonian newspaper editors were convicted under the Sedition Act. This led to the KENTUCKY AND VIRGINIA RESOLUTIONS.

ALIENATION, man's estrangement from society and from himself as an individual. The idea appears in ROUSSEAU, was first used as a term by HEGEL, and is now often connected with MARX. According to Marx, the sale of labor power as a commodity and the general conditions of production and exchange under capitalism deprive the individual of his essential humanity.

ALI KHAN, Liaquat (1895–1951), prime minister of Pakistan from independence in 1947 until his assassination by an Afghan fanatic. Chief aide of Muhammad Ali JINNAH, he became secretary of the MUSLIM LEAGUE in 1937.

ALIMENTARY CANAL. See GASTRO-INTESTINAL TRACT.

ALINSKY, Saul (1909–1972), US pioneer in community organization, known for his early community action work in the Chicago stockyards area (1939). Creator of the Woodlawn Organization on Chicago's South Side (1960), he founded a school for community organization there in 1969.

ALI PASHA (1741–1822), called "the Lion of Yannina," Ottoman pasha of Yannina (now Ioannina, NW Greece). After regaining his father's Albanian territories, in 1787 he crushed a rebellion at Scutari for the Turks, who appointed him pasha. With alternate British and French support he held Epirus, Albania and Thessaly until the Turks, fearing his power, had him murdered.

ALKALI, a water-soluble compound of the alkali metals (or ammonia) which acts as a strong BASE producing a high concentration of hydroxyl ions in aqueous solution. Alkalis neutralize acids to form salts and turn red litmus paper blue. Common alkalis are sodium hydroxide (NaOH), ammonia (NH_3), sodium carbonate (Na_2CO_3) and potassium carbonate (K_2CO_3). They have important industrial applications in the manufacture of glass, soap, paper and textiles. Caustic alkalis are corrosive and can cause severe burns.

ALKALOIDS, narcotic poisons found in certain plants and fungi. They have complex molecular structures and are usually heterocyclic nitrogen-containing BASES. Many, such as coniine (from hemlock) or atropine (deadly nightshade), are extremely poisonous. Others, such as morphine, nicotine and cocaine, can be highly addictive, and some, such as mescaline, are psychedelics. But in small doses alkaloids are often powerful medicines, and are used as analgesics, tranquilizers, and cardiac and respiratory stimulants. Other examples are quinine, reserpine and ephedrine. Caffeine (found in coffee and tea) is a stimulant. Although alkaloids may be found in any part of the plant, they are usually contained in the seeds, seed capsules, bark or roots. One plant, the opium poppy, contains about 30 alkaloids. Alkaloids are extracted from plants and separated by chromatography; synthetic alkaloids are seldom economically competitive.

ALLAH, Arabic name (*al-ilah*) for the supreme being, used by the prophet Mohammed to designate the God of ISLAM.

ALL-AMERICAN CANAL, completed 1940, brings water 80mi from the Imperial Reservoir on the Colorado R to irrigate 500,000 acres of the Imperial Valley, Cal., and also supplies water to San Diego. A branch delivering an equal amount of water to the Coachella Valley was opened in 1958.

ALLEGHENY MOUNTAINS, range of the central Appalachians extending from SW Va. through Md. into N central Pa. The Alleghenies run parallel to and W of the Blue Ridge Mountains, with average heights of 2,000ft in the N and more than 4,500ft in the S. The steep E slope is called the Allegheny Front. The upland region between the Cumberland Plateau and Mohawk Valley is known as the Allegheny Plateau.

ALLEGHENY RIVER rises in N central Pennsylvania and flows 325mi through Pennsylvania and New York before joining the Monongahela River at Pittsburgh to form the Ohio.

ALLEGORY, term applicable in any of the arts where the literal content of the work is subsidiary to its symbolic meaning. Concrete and material images are used to represent more abstract notions; thus death might be personified as a reaper. BUNYAN's *Pilgrim's Progress* is a classic example of allegory in literature; many modern writers also use allegory. It is common in the visual arts, perhaps most notably those of the Renaissance and Baroque periods, as for example in BOTTICELLI's *Primavera*.

ALLEN, Ethan (1738–1789), American revolutionary hero, leader of the GREEN MOUNTAIN BOYS of Vermont. In May 1775 he seized the British fort at TICONDEROGA, together with its valuable cannon, but in Sept. was captured in a reckless attack on Montreal. Released after almost three years, he was unsuccessful in petitioning Congress for Vt.'s statehood; he then attempted to negotiate the annexation of Vt. by British Canada.

ALLEN, Frederick Lewis (1890–1954), US journalist and social historian. After teaching at Harvard he entered journalism, becoming chief editor of *Harper's Magazine* (1941–54). His historical works, including *Only Yesterday* (1932), were readable and popular.

ALLEN, Hervey (1889–1949), US novelist and poet, co-founder of the Poetry Society of S.C. His best-known work is a long historical novel set in Napoleonic times, *Anthony Adverse* (1933), which was an international success.

ALLEN, Woody (1935–   ), US comedian, author and film director. An unprepossessing stature and self-effacing wit established him as one of the major comedic talents of the 1960s and 1970s. Following a nightclub career he broke into films (1965) and wrote, directed and starred in such successes as *Bananas* (1971), the Academy Award-winning *Annie Hall* (1977), *Manhattan* (1979), and *Hannah and Her Sisters* (1986).

ALLENBY, Edmund Henry Hynman, 1st Viscount Allenby (1861–1936), British field marshal who directed the brilliant campaign that won Palestine and Syria from the Turks in WWI. From 1919–25 he was British High Commissioner in Egypt.

ALLENDE, Salvador (1908–1973), Marxist founder of the Chilean Socialist Party, elected president of Chile in 1970, having won the largest minority vote. He subsequently failed to win a majority in the 1972 elections. His radical reform program disrupted the economy; strikes and widespread famine led to a military coup and to his death, reportedly by suicide.

ALLERGY, a state of abnormal sensitivity to foreign material (allergen) in susceptible individuals. It is essentially the inappropriate reaction of ANTIBODIES AND ANTIGENS defense responses to environmental substances. Susceptibility is often inherited but manifestations vary with age. Exposure to allergen induces the formation of antibodies; when, at a later date, the material is again encountered, it reacts with the antibodies causing release of HISTAMINE from mast cells in the tissues. INFLAMMATION follows, with local irritation, redness and swelling, which in skin appear as ECZEMA or urticaria (SEE HIVES). In the nose and eyes HAY FEVER results, and in the GASTROINTESTINAL TRACT diarrhea may occur. In the LUNGS a specific effect leads to spasm of bronchi, which gives rise to the wheeze and breathlessnness of ASTHMA. In most cases, the route of entry determines the site of the response; but skin rashes may occur regardless of route, and asthma may follow eating allergenic material. If the allergen is injected, anaphylaxis may occur. Localized allergic reactions in skin following chronic exposure to chemicals (e.g., nickel, poison ivy) are the basis of contact dermatitis. Common allergens include drugs (PENICILLIN, ASPIRIN), foods (shellfish), plant pollens, animal furs or feathers, insect stings and the house dust mite. Treatment includes ANTIHISTAMINES, cromoglycate, STEROIDS and desensitizing injections; ADRENALINE may be life-saving in severe allergic reactions.

ALLIES, two or more nations bound by treaty or alliance to act together against a common enemy in case of war. In WWI the "Allies" were the members of the TRIPLE ENTENTE, together with Serbia, Belgium, Japan, Italy and, as an "associated power," the US. In WWII "Allies" was the popular term for some 25 nations that opposed the Axis powers. The major nations among the Allies were the US, Britain, Russia, China and, later, the Free French. These five became the permanent members of the UN Security Council, established in 1945.

ALLIGATORS, two species of large, aquatic, carnivorous, lizard-like REPTILES comprising the genus *Alligator*. With the caimans, they form the family Alligatoridae of the order Crocodilia. The American alligator (*A. mississippiensis*), now largely restricted to Fla. and La., has been known to attain 20ft in length, but the rare Chinese alligator (*A. sinensis*), which inhabits the upper Yangtze valley, rarely exceeds 6ft. Alligators can live up to 75 years.

ALLITERATION, device in poetry of repeating a sound, usually a consonant, at the beginning of neighboring words; in the line from TENNYSON's *Lotos Eaters*, "Surely, surely, slumber is more sweet than toil," the "s" and "l" sounds are alliterative. Early Germanic, Old Norse and Old English verse is characterized by subtle accented alliterative measures, and it is often found in Gaelic and Welsh poetry. LANGLAND's *Piers Plowman* exemplifies a school of alliterative verse which survived in W England until the late 14th century.

ALLOTROPY, the occurrence of some elements in more than one form (known as allotropes) which differ in their crystalline or molecular structure. Allotropes may have strikingly different physical or chemical properties. Allotropy in which the various forms are stable under different conditions and are reversibly interconvertible at certain temperatures and pressures, is called enantiotropy. Notable examples of allotropy include DIAMOND and graphite, OXYGEN and OZONE.

ALLOY, a combination of metals with each other or with nonmetals such as carbon or phosphorus. They are useful because their properties can be adjusted as desired by varying the proportions of the constituents. Very few metals are used today in a pure state. Alloys are formed by mixing their molten components. The structures of alloys consisting mainly of one component may be substitutional or interstitial, depending on the relative sizes of the atoms. The study of alloy structures in general is complex.

The commonest alloys are the different forms of STEEL, which all contain a large proportion of iron and small amounts of

carbon and other elements. BRASS and BRONZE, two well-known and ancient metals, are alloys of copper, while PEWTER is an alloy of tin and lead. The very light but strong alloys used in aircraft construction are frequently alloys of aluminum with magnesium, copper or silicon. Solders contain tin with lead and bismuth. Among familiar alloys are those used in coins: modern "silver" coinage in most countries is an alloy of nickel and copper. Special alloys are used for such purposes as die-casting, dentistry, high-temperature use, and for making thermocouples, magnets and low-expansion materials.

ALLPORT, Gordon Willard (1897–1967), US psychologist, important figure in the study of personality, who stressed the "functional autonomy of motives." Among his many works, *The Nature of Prejudice* (1954) has become a classic in its field.

ALL SAINTS' DAY, religious feast day celebrating all Christian saints, observed by most Christian churches on Nov. 1. Its present form dates from the reign of Pope Gregory III (731–741).

ALLSTON, Washington (1779–1843), first major US landscape painter. He painted large dramatic canvases of biblical and Classical scenes, but this early Italianate style gave way to romanticism influenced by TURNER.

ALL-VOLUNTEER FORCE (AVF), descriptive name for the US armed forces since the end of the draft in 1973 (see DRAFT, MILITARY). The US is the only country to have attempted to maintain armed forces more than 2 million strong using volunteers alone. The AVF was a politically necessary response to national dissatisfaction with the draft as it operated in the Vietnam War. To attract volunteers, the AVF must offer pay, benefits, and living conditions competitive with those available to recruits in civilian life. Critics have questioned the AVF's cost, quality, and combat readiness. But its alternatives — a revived draft, UNIVERSAL MILITARY TRAINING, and some form of NATIONAL SERVICE that would include military service — also present serious problems, including the issue of fairness. In recent years pay raises and educational benefits have enabled the armed services to meet their recruitment goals handily. More than 90% of male and female enlistees have been high-school graduates, an important measure of the quality of recruits. However, the size of the male population aged 18-21 from which most recruits are drawn is declining, from 8.6 million in 1978 to a projected 6.6 million in 1995. Some experts believe that the shrinking pool of young men and the need to hold down costs may lead to a restoration of the draft.

ALMAGRO, Diego de (1475–1538), Spanish conquistador who helped to capture Peru. He joined Francisco PIZARRO in the conquest (1533), then fruitlessly sought gold in Chile. Returning to Peru, he claimed and seized Cuzco, then was defeated and executed by Pizarro's brother.

ALMANAC, originally a calendar giving the positions of the planets, the phases of the moon, etc., particularly as used by navigators (nautical almanacs), but now any yearbook of miscellaneous information, often containing abstracts of annual statistics.

ALMANACH DE GOTHA, handbook of the genealogies of Europe's royal and noble families, founded in Germany (1763) and later annually produced at Gotha. Publication stopped in 1944 but was resumed in 1959.

ALMEIDA, Francisco de (c1450–1510), first viceroy of Portuguese India (1505–09). His conquests, forts and trading posts strengthened Portuguese influence in coastal India and E Africa and spread it E to Sumatra.

ALMOHAD AND ALMORAVID, two medieval Muslim sects and dynasties originating among N African Berbers. First the Almoravids built an empire covering most of NW Africa and much of Spain (1063–1142). The Almohads conquered and enlarged the territory (1144–58), but their empire broke up after 1212 when the combined forces of the Christian kings of Aragon, Castile and Navarre defeated them at Las Navas de Tolosa in the south of Spain.

ALMQUIST, Carl Jonas Love (1793–1866), Swedish writer of romantic and increasingly realistic stories and plays, some unconventionally advocating free love. His best-known works appear in a massive collection, *The Book of the Briar Rose* (1832–50).

ALPACA, S American herbivore (*Lama pacos*) closely related to the LLAMA. It has a long body and neck, and is about 1m (3ft) high at the shoulder. Its long thick coat of black, brown or yellowish hair provides valuable wool. All alpacas are now domesticated, living mainly in the Andes above 13,000ft. Family: Camelidae.

ALPHABET (from Greek *alpha* and *beta*), a set of characters intended to represent the sounds of spoken language. Because of this intention (which in practice is never realized) written languages employing alphabets are quite distinct from those using characters which represent whole

words (see HIEROGLYPHICS). The word alphabet is, however, usually extended to describe syllabaries, languages in which characters represent syllables. The chief alphabets of the world are Roman (Latin), Greek, Hebrew, Cyrillic (Slavic), Arabic and Devanagari.

Alphabets probably originated around 2000 BC. Hebrew, Arabic and other written languages sprang from a linear alphabet which had appeared c1500 BC. From the Phoenician alphabet, which appeared around 1700 BC, was derived the Greek. Roman letters were derived from Greek and from the rather similar Etruscan, also a descendant of the Greek. Most of the letters we now use are from the Latin alphabet, U and W being distinguished from V, and J from I in the early Middle Ages. The Cyrillic alphabet, used with the Slavic languages, derives from the Greek. It is thought that Devanagari was possibly invented to represent Sanskrit.

Chinese and Japanese are the only major languages that function without alphabets, although Japanese has syllabary elements. (See also CUNEIFORM and WRITING, HISTORY OF; and, for the evolution of the letters of our alphabet, the headings to each alphabetical section.)

ALPHA CENTAURI, star in the constellation Centaurus, 3rd brightest in the sky.

ALPHONSUS LIGUORI, Saint (1696–1787), Italian priest who founded the Congregation of the Most Holy Redeemer (Redemptorist Order), a society of missionary preachers working with the rural poor. He was canonized in 1839.

ALPS, Europe's largest mountain system, 650mi long and 30–180mi wide. Its fold mountains result from earth movements in Tertiary times. The Western Alps, with the highest peak, Mont Blanc (15,771ft), run along the French-Italian border. The Central Alps run NE and E through Switzerland. The Eastern Alps extend through S Germany, Austria and NE Italy into Yugoslavia. Peaks are snowy and etched by ice action. The Alps are known for their magnificent mountain scenery, glacially deepened valleys and many glaciers.

ALSACE-LORRAINE, region in NE France occupying 5,608sq mi W of the Rhine. It produces grains and grapes; timber, coal, potash and salt (from the Vosges Mts); iron ore and textiles. Metz, Nancy, Strasbourg and Verdun are the chief cities.

The people are part French, part German in origin. France and Germany have long disputed control of the area. In medieval times it was in the Holy Roman Empire. France took Alsace after 1648 and Lorraine in 1766. Germany seized most of both in 1871, lost them to France after WWI, regained control in WWII, then lost it again.

ALTAIC LANGUAGES, group of languages comprising three subgroups: Mongol, Manchu-Tungus and principally the TURKIC LANGUAGES. The Altaic languages are spoken in the USSR, Turkey, Iran, Afghanistan, China and the Mongolian People's Republic.

ALTAMIRA, cave near Santander, N Spain, inhabited during the Aurignacian, upper Solutrean and Magdalenian periods. In 1879 the daughter of an amateur archaeologist discovered the striking cave paintings, believed to date from the Magdalenian period. They depict such animals as bison, boars, horses.

ALTDORFER, Albrecht (1480–1538), German painter and engraver. Most of his paintings had religious subjects, but because of the prominence of forest and mountain settings he is often held to be the first German landscape painter.

ALTGELD, John Peter (1847–1902), US political leader and jurist who sought to defend the individual against abuses of governmental power and vested interests. As a Cook Co., Ill. superior court judge he argued that legal practice was weighted against the poor. Elected Democratic governor of Illinois (1892), he backed labor and championed reform, arousing controversy by freeing three anarchists imprisoned for Chicago's HAYMARKET AFFAIR riot (1886) and by opposing President Cleveland's use of troops to crush the PULLMAN STRIKE of 1894.

ALTHUSSER, Louis (1918–   ), French philosopher, leading figure in the influential Marxist-structuralist school. He wrote *For Marx* (1965; tr. 1969) and *Reading Capital* (1965; tr. 1970).

ALTIMETER, an instrument used for estimating the height of an aircraft above sea level. Most are modified aneroid BAROMETERS and work on the principle that air pressure decreases with increased altitude, but these must be constantly recalibrated throughout the flight to take account of changing meteorological conditions (local ground temperature and air pressure reduced to sea level). **Radar altimeters,** which compute absolute altitudes (the height of the aircraft above the ground surface immediately below) from the time taken for RADAR waves to be reflected to the aircraft from the ground, are essential for blind landings.

ALTIPLANO, a high plateau region in S America between the W and E cordilleras of the Andes. Its bleak grasslands lie between 10,000 and 12,000ft and run S from Peru through Bolivia and into Argentina. It contains lakes Titicaca and Poopó.

ALTITUDE SICKNESS, a condition of OXYGEN lack in blood and tissues due to low atmospheric pressure. Night vision is impaired, followed by breathlessness, headache, and faintness. At 16,000ft mental changes include indifference, euphoria and faulty judgment, but complete acclimatization is possible up to those heights. At very high altitudes (20,000ft to 25,000ft), cyanosis, coma and death rapidly supervene. Treatment is by oxygen and descent. The use of pressurized cabins prevents the occurrence of the condition in air travel.

ALUMINUM (Al), silvery-white metal in Group IIIA of the PERIODIC TABLE, the most abundant metal, comprising 8% of the earth's crust. It occurs naturally as BAUXITE, cryolite, feldspar, clay and many other minerals, and is smelted by the Hall-Héroult process, chiefly in the US, USSR and Canada. It is a reactive metal, but in air is covered with a protective layer of the oxide. Aluminum is light and strong when alloyed, so that aluminum ALLOYS are used very widely in the construction of machinery and domestic appliances. It is also a good conductor of electricity and is often used in overhead transmission cables where lightness is crucial. AW 27.0, mp 660°C, bp 2467°C, sg 2.6989 (20°C).

Aluminum compounds are trivalent and mainly cationic, though with strong bases aluminates are formed. **Aluminum oxide** (Al_2O_3), or **alumina,** is a colorless or white solid occurring in several crystalline forms, and is found naturally as corundum, emery and bauxite. Solubility in acid and alkali increases with hydration. mp 2045°C, bp 2980°C. **Aluminum chloride** ($AlCl_3$) is a colorless crystalline solid, used as a catalyst. The hexahydrate is used in deodorants and as an astringent.

ALVARADO, Pedro de (c1485–1541), Spanish colonizer of Guatemala. He was CORTES's chief lieutenant in the conquest of Mexico (1519–21), then (1523–24) led the force that seized what are now Guatemala and El Salvador. As governor of Guatemala he instituted forced Indian labor and founded many cities.

ALVAREZ, Luis Walter (1911–1988), US physicist awarded the 1968 Nobel Prize for Physics for work on SUBATOMIC PARTICLES, including the discovery of the transient resonance particles. He helped develop much of the hardware of NUCLEAR PHYSICS. In the 1980s he and his son, Walter Alvarez, were leading proponents of the view that a collision of the earth and a comet some 65 million years ago caused the extinction of the dinosaurs.

ALZHEIMER'S DISEASE, progressive degeneration of the brain, with symptoms of memory loss, disorientation and other intellectual impairment. Although associated with the elderly and with "senile dementia," this disorder can also afflict the middle-aged. Both cause and cure of Alzheimer's disease are unknown.

AMADO, Jorge (1912–   ), Brazilian novelist, author of *The Violent Land* (1942) and *Gabriela, Clove and Cinnamon* (1958). His books are particularly concerned with the plight of the poor.

AMANA SOCIETY, religious community comprising Amana and associated villages, founded in Ia. in the mid-19th century. Originating in a German Pietist sect which stressed the divine inspiration of the Bible, the society farmed 25,000 acres of prairie and practiced self-sufficiency based on communal labor and property sharing. In 1932 it became a cooperative corporation.

AMATI, Italian family of violin makers in Cremona (16th–17th centuries). Noted members were **Andrea** (c1520–c1578), his sons Antonio and Girolamo, and Girolamo's son **Nicolò** (1596–1684), the most famous of all. His superb instruments became models for those of Andrea GUARNERI and Antonio STRADIVARI.

AMAZON RIVER, world's largest river in volume and drainage area, and second-longest, at 3,900mi. Its basin drains 40% of South America. The Amazon rises in Andean Peru near the Pacific Ocean and flows E through the world's largest equatorial forest to the Atlantic Ocean. It is a broad sluggish stream up to 30mi wide in flood, with hundreds of tributaries, 17 of which are more than 1,000mi long.

Fed by annual runoff from 70–120in of rain, the river pours an estimated one-fifth of all water falling on earth into the Atlantic Ocean, where its current extends 200mi out to sea. Tides are felt 600mi upstream, and oceangoing vessels can travel 2,300mi to Iquitos in Peru. Other ports are Belém and Manaus, handling river commerce in hardwoods and other forest products of sparsely peopled Amazonia. Spain's Vicente Pinzón discovered the river mouth in 1500; Francisco de Orellana was the first to travel downriver from the Andes to the Atlantic (1541).

AMAZONS, in Greek legend, a race of warrior women living in the Black Sea area. Their name derives from the Greek word for "breastless," due to their alleged practice of removing the right breast to aid archery. One myth relates how HERCULES, as his ninth labor, took the girdle of the Amazonian queen Hippolyta. Later tales associate Amazons with Brazil and with Dahomey in West Africa.

AMBEDKAR, Bhimrao Ramji (1893–1956), Indian politician who championed his fellow "untouchables," members of the lowest Hindu caste in India. He helped ensure that India's constitution of 1949 banned discrimination against them but failed to eliminate the untouchable castes from Hinduism.

AMBER, fossilized RESIN from prehistoric evergreens. Brownish-yellow and translucent, it is highly valued and can be easily cut and polished for ornamental purposes. Its chief importance is that FOSSIL insects up to 20 million years old have been found embedded in it.

AMBERGRIS, waxy solid formed in the intestines of sperm WHALES, perhaps to protect them from the bony parts of their squid diet. When obtained from dead whales, it is soft, black and evil-smelling, but on weathering (as when found as flotsam) it becomes hard, gray and fragrant, and is used as a perfume fixative and in the East as a spice.

AMBLER, Eric (1909–   ), English suspense writer, noted especially for stories in which ordinary, unheroic characters are caught up in international intrigue and danger. His numerous works include *Epitaph for a Spy* (1938) and *A Coffin for Dimitrios* (1939). *Here Lies* (1985) is his autobiography.

AMBROSE, Saint (c340–397), an important Father of the Latin Church. A Roman governor who became the influential bishop of Milan, he attacked imperial moral standards and strengthened the position of the Church amid the ruins of the Roman Empire by his preaching and writing. St. AUGUSTINE was one of his converts.

AMENHOTEP III (14th century BC), Egyptian king (1417–1379 BC) of the 18th dynasty. Ruling at the height of the ancient Egyptian empire, he built notable monuments at Thebes, Luxor, and Karnak. His son was AKHENATON.

AMERICA, the two major continents of the Western Hemisphere, North and South America, or only the United States. The term was coined in 1507 by the German geographer Martin Waldseemüller in honor of the Italian navigator Amerigo Vespucci, who supposedly discovered much of South

America—the area to which the term was originally confined.

AMERICA FIRST COMMITTEE, isolationist organization that opposed US involvement in WWII. It was founded by R. Douglas Stuart, Jr., in September 1940. Its supporters numbered 800,000 and included the HEARST newspapers and Charles LINDBERGH, but the Committee collapsed after Japan attacked Pearl Harbor.

AMERICAN ACADEMY OF ARTS AND LETTERS, organization to promote literature and the fine arts in the US, founded in 1904. Based in New York City, it originally had 50 members, outstanding in literature, art and music, chosen from the membership of its parent organization, the National Institute of Arts and Letters (1898). The groups subsequently combined in the American Academy and Institute of Arts and Letters, with 250 members. It makes awards to writers, artists and musicians and sponsors exhibitions.

AMERICAN ASSOCIATION FOR THE ADVANCEMENT OF SCIENCE (AAAS), the largest US organization for the promotion of scientific understanding. Founded in Boston in 1848 but now centered in Washington, it has 135,000 individual and 300 corporate members. Its publications include the weekly, *Science.*

AMERICAN ASSOCIATION OF RE-TIRED PERSONS (AARP), service and interest organization of people 50 and older, founded in 1958 and headquartered in Washington, D.C. In 1988 it had 24 million members.

AMERICAN BAR ASSOCIATION (ABA), organization of US lawyers, founded in 1878 and headquartered in Chicago, Ill. In 1988 it had 325,807 members.

AMERICAN CIVIL LIBERTIES UNION (ACLU), organization founded 1920 and dedicated to defending constitutional freedoms in the US. From its founding the ACLU has participated in the nation's most important civil liberties cases: the Scopes Trial (1925), which challenged a Tennessee law barring the right to teach Darwin's theory of evolution in schools; the federal court test (1933) that ended censorship of James Joyce's *Ulysses*; and the landmark *Brown v. Board of Education* (1954) case, which successfully challenged the constitutionality of racially segregated public schooling. In 1978 it upheld the American Nazi Party's right to march in Skokie, Ill., and to display swastika symbols. The organization became an issue in the 1988 presidential election when the Republican candidate attacked his Democratic opponent for being a "card-carrying member" of

the ACLU. Membership then was 250,000.

AMERICAN COLONIZATION SOCIETY, US organization formed in 1822 to found an overseas home for free Negroes. Some abolitionists thought it secretly pro-slavery. Its West African colony, established in 1816, became Africa's first black republic, LIBERIA, in 1847.

AMERICAN FEDERATION OF LABOR AND CONGRESS OF INDUSTRIAL ORGANIZATIONS (AFL-CIO), powerful US federation of labor unions created in 1955 by the merger of the AFL and CIO. Some 125 constituent unions represent about 15 million members. A national president, secretary-treasurer and 27 vice-presidents make up the executive council. This enforces policy decisions made at biennial conventions attended by several thousand delegates.

The organization's main objectives are more pay, fewer working hours and better working conditions for employees, obtained by union-management agreements that preserve industrial harmony and prosperity. Each affiliated union conducts its own collective bargaining and determines much of its own policy. The AFL-CIO takes influential stands on such issues as social welfare, conservation, education and international problems. It has recently backed Democratic presidential candidates.

The AFL originated in 1886 in the reorganized Federation of Organized Trade and Labor Unions. Initially led by Samuel GOMPERS, it comprised only craft unions, excluding unskilled and semiskilled workers, whose numbers multiplied as mass production increased in the early 1900s. To cater to these workers, AFL dissidents in 1935 formed the Committee for Industrial Organization, later the CIO, led by John L. LEWIS. In the 1950s laws hostile to organized labor encouraged union cooperation and in 1955 the AFL and CIO merged, with George MEANY (head of AFL) as president. Meany retired in 1979 and was replaced by his hand-picked successor, Lane KIRKLAND. Although nearly 40% of all union workers are women, it was not until 1980 that a woman labor leader was named to the AFL-CIO executive council: Joyce Miller, vice-president of the Amalgamated Clothing & Textile Workers.

AMERICAN FRIENDS SERVICE COMMITTEE, US Quaker philanthropic organization founded in Philadelphia, Pa., in 1917 to help in post-WWI relief and reconstruction abroad. With its British counterparts, it gained the 1947 Nobel Peace Prize for helping to build schools, orphanages and hospitals in war-ravaged parts of Europe. It has often helped in international relief operations after great disasters.

AMERICAN FUR COMPANY, the earliest US trading monopoly, founded 1808 by John Jacob Astor. With his Pacific Fur Co., it controlled the fur trade from the Great Lakes W to the Pacific and monopolized trade in the Mississippi valley.

AMERICAN INDEPENDENT PARTY, US political party with a strongly conservative position on social issues. Created 1968 as the vehicle for the presidential candidacy of George C. WALLACE, who polled 9,906,473 votes, or 13.5% of the total, it declined sharply after Wallace left the party.

AMERICAN LABOR PARTY, N.Y. State left-wing political party (1936–56). Founded by labor leaders, it helped elect its member Fiorello LA GUARDIA mayor of New York in 1937 and 1941 and Herbert LEHMAN governor in 1938. In WWII it split over attitudes to Russia: the right under David DUBINSKY accused Sidney Hillman's left of being communist-controlled. The party disbanded in 1956.

AMERICAN LEGION, organization of honorably discharged male and female wartime US veterans, founded in 1919 and headquartered in Indianapolis, Ind. In 1988 it had 2.7 million members.

AMERICAN LITERATURE began with accounts of the hopes, discoveries and disasters experienced by the explorers of the New World. The writings of established settlers followed in the 1600s, reflecting the Puritan and Colonial concerns of the time, and including Anne BRADSTREET's devotional poetry and Cotton MATHER's pious New England history, *Magnalia Christi Americana* (1702). The late 1700s heralded the eloquent prose of the American Revolutionaries, such as Thomas PAINE's *Common Sense* (1776) and Benjamin FRANKLIN's *Autobiography* (1790). After the Revolutionary War, the satirist Washington IRVING became the first American fiction writer to gain an international reputation with *Sketchbook* (1820), and James Fenimore COOPER became the first eminent American novelist with his rough-hewn historical romances such as *The Last of the Mohicans* (1826).

With the gradual development of the vast country during the 1800s, a distinctively American individualism began to assert itself in writings such as *Walden* (1854) by Henry David THOREAU and the essays of Ralph Waldo EMERSON, which championed independent thought and spiritual rejuvena-

tion. There also arose a cluster of major works that established a body of serious American fiction. Nathaniel HAWTHORNE's *The Scarlet Letter* (1850) and Herman MELVILLE's masterpiece *Moby Dick* (1851) displayed profound insight into the dilemmas of man's isolation, his place in nature and his capacity for evil. Edgar Allan POE, a pioneer of the short story and of the detective fiction genre, was also in the vanguard of the French Symbolist movement with such feverish works as the poem *The Raven* (1845) and the story *The Tell-Tale Heart* (1843). Walt WHITMAN's epic collection of poems, *Leaves of Grass* (1855–1892), celebrated the American experience with a vivid evocation of love and concern for the people and their democracy. With his innovative rhythms, Whitman influenced the free-verse poetry of the 20th century. Meanwhile, Emily DICKINSON wrote the compressed, idiosyncratic verse which has since established her as one of the most original of American poets. Henry Wadsworth LONGFELLOW, though his melodious narrative verse was not enduring, was the most popular poet of his day.

In the late 19th century, two men implanted a new realism in American literature: the expatriate Henry JAMES effected new psychological action in novels such as *Portrait of a Lady* (1881), and the humorist Mark TWAIN legitimatized the colloquial voice and the regional setting in his masterpiece *Huckleberry Finn* (1885). Meanwhile, the novelist and poet Stephen CRANE became the first American naturalist writer. These three influenced the work of such contemporaries as William Dean HOWELLS, Edith WHARTON and Theodore DREISER, and laid the foundations for a generation of early 20th century writers concerned with the effects of industrialized society on the individual, the focus of such works as Sinclair LEWIS's *Main Street* (1920), John DOS PASSOS' *U.S.A.* (1934) and John STEINBECK's *The Grapes of Wrath* (1939).

In the post WWI period, three important American writers emerged. F. Scott FITZGERALD precisely rendered the glamour and tragedy of the 1920s in novels such as *The Great Gatsby* (1925). William FAULKNER expanded the boundaries of the novel, taking it far beyond naturalism with works such as *The Sound and the Fury* (1929). And Ernest HEMINGWAY established a distinctively direct, spare and vivid prose style in short stories and his first novel, *The Sun Also Rises* (1926). Post WWII novelists of note include Saul BELLOW, Eudora WELTY, J.D. SALINGER, Norman

MAILER, John CHEEVER, and John UPDIKE.

Not until the 20th century did America produce a major dramatist—Eugene O'NEILL. In such powerful masterpieces as *Desire Under the Elms* (1924), *The Iceman Cometh* (1946) and *Long Day's Journey Into Night* (1957), O'Neill developed a realistic theatrical form that subsumed his own early experiments in expressionism and stream-of-consciousness. After WWII other major talents appeared, including Tennessee WILLIAMS, Arthur MILLER, Edward ALBEE, and Sam SHEPARD.

Early 20th-century heirs of the free-form poetry of Whitman and the verse of Dickinson included Amy LOWELL, Carl SANDBURG and Robert FROST. Between the world wars a New Poetry movement formed, influenced by Whitman, Dickinson, the French Symbolists and even the Chinese ideogram. It included such poets as Ezra POUND and Wallace STEVENS. T. S. ELIOT, whose poem *The Waste Land* (1922) was perhaps the most influential written in the 20th century, introduced the term "objective correlative" to describe the singular situation or image which a poet uses to convey a particular emotion. Wallace Stevens advanced a new "romantic" notion of the now-transcending imagination. After WWII, major names in US poetry have included Robert LOWELL and Sylvia PLATH.

AMERICAN MEDICAL ASSOCIATION (AMA), organization of US physicians, founded in 1847 and headquartered in Chicago, Ill. In 1988 it had 258,000 members.

AMERICAN MUSEUM OF NATURAL HISTORY, an institution in New York City founded in 1869 and dedicated to research and popular education in anthropology, astronomy, mineralogy and natural history. It is noted for its mounted specimens of birds and other animals from all over the world, fossil collections which include a 47-foot-long skeleton of a Tyrannosaurus rex, its gem collection with the Star of India sapphire, and the Hayden Planetarium.

AMERICAN PHILOSOPHICAL SOCIETY, the oldest US learned society, based in Philadelphia where it was founded by Benjamin FRANKLIN in 1743. The US counterpart of the ROYAL SOCIETY OF LONDON (1660), it currently has nearly 600 US and foreign members. It has an extensive library, much relating to early American science. Its publications commenced in 1769 with *Transactions*.

AMERICAN REVOLUTION. See REVOLUTIONARY WAR, AMERICAN.

AMERICAN STOCK EXCHANGE (AMEX), second largest securities market in the US (after the New York Stock Exchange). Located in the financial district of New York City, the Amex has 864 regular members and trades approximately 1,000 issues of stocks and bonds. Organized early in the 19th century, it received its present name in 1953.

AMERICA'S CUP, international yachting trophy awarded in a best-of-seven competition among 12-meter yachts in the waters of the previous winner. From 1851 to 1983 the cup was held by the New York Yacht Club, and races were conducted off Newport, R.I. The victory of *Australia II* over the US yacht *Liberty* in 1983 caused the cup's removal to Perth. The San Diego Yacht Club retrieved the cup in 1987 and retained it in 1988, when it pitted an unorthodox catamaran against a New Zealand monohull. The next America's Cup race is scheduled for 1991.

AMERICA THE BEAUTIFUL, popular patriotic song, with words written in 1893 by Katherine Lee Bates and music by Samuel A. Ward.

AMERINDS, term coined (1897–98) by John Wesley POWELL to denote the American INDIANS. It is believed that the Amerinds originated in NE Asia, having crossed the Bering Strait (perhaps by land bridge) before the 10th millennium BC. However, there are marked blood-type differences between them and the Asian Mongoloid peoples.

AMES, Fisher (1758–1808), US politician, a leading New England Federalist. As a US representative from Massachusetts (1789–97), he supported Alexander Hamilton against Thomas Jefferson and defended Jay's Treaty.

AMETHYST, transparent violet or purple variety of QUARTZ, colored by iron or manganese impurities. The color changes to yellow on heating. The best of these semiprecious gems come from Brazil, Uruguay, Ariz. and the USSR.

AMHARIC, official language of Ethiopia, spoken by some six million people. It is a Semitic tongue evolved mostly from ancient Ge'ez or Ethiopic. Its alphabet has 33 characters, each with seven forms that represent a consonant and different vowels.

AMHERST, Jeffrey Amherst, 1st Baron (1717–1797), British major-general who helped take Canada from the French. He captured Louisburg fortress on Cape Breton Island (1758), then Ticonderoga and Crown Point (1759) and lastly Montreal (1760). While governor-general of British North America (1760–63) he crushed a pro-French Indian rising led by PONTIAC.

AMIN DADA, Idi (c1925–   ), Ugandan soldier who became president in 1971, deposing Milton Obote. A flamboyant and dictatorial ruler, he expelled Uganda's Asian middle class in 1972 and purged many opponents. In 1975–76 he was president of the ORGANIZATION OF AFRICAN UNITY. Insurrectionists, aided by Tanzanian forces, drove Amin into exile in Saudi Arabia in 1979.

AMINO ACIDS, an important class of carboxylic acids containing one or more amino (-NH₂) groups. Twenty or so α-amino acids (RCH[NH₂]COOH) are the building blocks of the PROTEINS found in all living matter. They are also found and synthesized in cells. Amino acids are white, crystalline solids, soluble in water; they can act as ACIDS or BASES depending on the chemical environment (see pH). In neutral solution they exist as zwitterions. An amino acid mixture may be analyzed by CHROMATOGRAPHY. All α-amino acids (except glycine) contain at least one asymmetric carbon atom to which are attached the carboxyl group, the amino group, a hydrogen atom and a fourth group (R) that differs for each amino acid and determines its character. Thus amino acids can exist in two mirror-image forms. Generally only L-isomers occur in nature, but a few bacteria contain D-isomers. Humans synthesize most of the amino acids needed for NUTRITION, but depend on protein foods for eight "essential amino acids" which they cannot produce. Inside the body, amino acids derived from food are metabolized (see METABOLISM) in various ways. As each amino acid contains both an acid and an amino group, they can form a long chain of amino acids bridged by amide links and called peptides. Peptide synthesis from constituent amino acids is a stage in protein synthesis. Thus some are converted into HORMONES, ENZYMES and NUCLEIC ACIDS. Proteins may be broken down again by HYDROLYSIS into their constituent amino acids, as in digestion. When amino acids are deaminated (the amino group removed), the nitrogen passes out as urea. The remainder of the molecule enters the citric acid cycle, being broken down to provide energy.

Scientists have produced amino acids and simple peptide chains by combining carbon dioxide, ammonia and water vapor under the sort of conditions (including electric discharges) thought to exist on earth millions of years ago. This may provide a clue to the origin of LIFE.

AMIS, Kingsley (1922–   ), English novelist, poet and critic. He emerged as one of the ANGRY YOUNG MEN in *Lucky Jim*

(1954), an amusing attack on social and academic pretensions. Among his later works are *Take a Girl Like You* (1960) and *Jake's Thing* (1978).

AMISH, conservative group of the MENNONITE sect, founded by Jakob Ammann in Switzerland in the 1690s. In the 18th century members settled in what are now Ind., Ohio and Pa., and today they live in other states too. Literal interpretation of the Bible leads their farm communities to reject modern life (including electricity and cars). Amish wear old-style clothes, plow with horses and observe the Sabbath strictly. (See also PENNSYLVANIA DUTCH.)

AMISTAD CASE, US legal case of 1841, involving Negro slaves who mutinied aboard the Spanish slaveship *Amistad* and sought asylum as free men in the US. John Quincy ADAMS successfully defended them in the Supreme Court against the Van Buren administration's decision to return the Negroes to their Spanish masters.

AMMANN, Othmar Hermann (1897–1965), American engineer. He designed the George Washington Bridge in New York City (1931), the San Francisco Golden Gate Bridge (1935) and the Verrazano-Narrows Bridge in New York (1964).

AMMONIA (NH₃), colorless acrid gas; a covalent hydride. The pyramidal molecule turns inside out very rapidly, which is the basis of the ammonia clock (see ATOMIC CLOCK). Ammonia's properties have typical anomalies due to hydrogen bonding; liquid ammonia is a good solvent. Ammonia is a BASE; its aqueous solution contains ammonium hydroxide, and is used as a household cleaning fluid. Ammonia is used as a fertilizer, a refrigerant, and to make ammonium salts, urea, and many drugs, dyes and plastics. mp −78°C, bp −33°C.

On reaction with acids, ammonia gives ammonium salts, containing the NH₄+ ion, which resemble alkali metal salts. They are mainly used as fertilizers. **Ammonium chloride** (NH₄Cl), or **sal ammoniac,** a colorless crystalline solid used in dry cells and as a flux. **Ammonium nitrate** (NH₄NO₃), a colorless crystalline solid, used as a fertilizer and in explosives. mp 170°C.

AMNESIA, the total loss of MEMORY for a period of time or for events. In cases of CONCUSSION, **retrograde amnesia** is the permanent loss of memory for events just preceding a head injury while **posttraumatic** amnesia applies to a period after injury during which the patient may be conscious but incapable of recall, both at the time and later. Similar behavior to the latter, termed

fugue, occurs as a psychiatric phenomenon.

AMNESTY INTERNATIONAL, founded 1961 to aid political prisoners and others detained for reasons of conscience throughout the world. With thousands of members around the world, including the US, it has advisory status with the UN and other international organizations. Amnesty International received the Nobel Prize for Peace in 1977.

AMNIOCENTESIS, the procedure of obtaining a sample of the amniotic fluid surrounding a fetus by puncturing the abdomen of the pregnant woman with a very fine, hollow needle. Cells and other substances shed into the amniotic fluid by the fetus are used for diagnosing the presence of such disorders as DOWN'S SYNDROME, TAY-SACHS DISEASE and spinal malformations. Amniocentesis also can be used to determine the sex of an unborn child with 95% accuracy.

AMNION, a tough membrane surrounding the EMBRYO of reptiles, birds and mammals and containing the amniotic fluid, which provides a moist, aquatic environment for the EMBRYO. All land-laid EGGS contain amnions; those of fishes and amphibians do not, and thus they must be laid in moist surroundings or water.

AMOEBAS, a large order (Amoebida) of the class Sarcodina (Rhizopodea) of PROTOZOA. They are unicellular (see CELL), a relatively rigid outer layer of ectoplasm surrounding a more fluid mass of endoplasm, in which lie one or more nuclei. They move by extending pseudopodia, into which they flow; and feed by surrounding and absorbing organic particles. REPRODUCTION is almost always asexual, generally by binary FISSION, though sometimes by multiple fission of the nucleus; a tough wall of cytoplasm forms about each of these small nuclei to create cysts. These can survive considerable rigors, returning to normal amoeboid form when circumstances are more clement. (Some species of amoeba may form a single cyst to survive adversity.) Certain amoebas can reproduce sexually. Amoebas are found wherever there is moisture, some parasitic (see PARASITE) forms living within other animals: *Entamoeba histolytica,* for example, causes amoebic DYSENTERY in man. The type-species is *Amoeba proteus,* which has a single nucleus and can form only one pseudopodium at a time.

AMOS (8th century BC), Hebrew prophet, the first to proclaim clearly that there was one God for all peoples. A shepherd from Judah, he preached in neighboring Israel, denouncing its corruption until expelled by the king. The probably posthumous biblical Book of Amos is the earliest record of a prophet's sayings and life.

AMPÈRE, André Marie (1775–1836), French mathematician, physicist and philosopher best remembered for many discoveries in electrodynamics and electromagnetism. In the early 1820s he developed OERSTED'S experiments on the interaction between magnets and electric currents and investigated the forces set up between current-carrying conductors.

AMPHETAMINES, a group of stimulant drugs, including benzedrine and methedrine, now in medical disfavor following widespread abuse and addiction. They counteract fatigue, suppress appetite, speed up performance (hence "Speed") and give confidence, but pronounced DEPRESSION often follows; thus psychological and then physical addiction are encouraged. A paranoid PSYCHOSIS (resembling SCHIZOPHRENIA) may result from prolonged use, although it may be that amphetamine abuse is rather an early symptom of the psychosis. While no longer acceptable in treatment of OBESITY, they are useful in narcolepsy, a rare condition of abnormal sleepiness.

AMPHIBIA, a class of vertebrates, including frogs, toads, newts, salamanders and caecilians. Typically they spend part of their life in water, part on land. They are distinct from REPTILES in that their eggs lack amnions, and must hence be laid in moist conditions, and that their soft, moist skins have no scales. They are of the subphylum vertebrata, of the phylum Chordata. It is thought that amphibia were the first vertebrates to venture from the aquatic environment on to the land, and that they were the ancestors of all other vertebrates (see EVOLUTION). They are cold-blooded, and therefore many species hibernate (see HIBERNATION) during winter. Their development is in two stages: the egg develops into a larval form, which is usually solely aquatic, then the larva into an adult. All adult amphibia are carnivorous.

AMPLIFIER, any device which increases the strength of an input signal. Amplifiers play a vital role in most electronic devices: RADIO and TELEVISION receivers, PHONOGRAPHS, TAPE-RECORDERS and COMPUTERS: but nonelectronic devices such as the horn of a windup phonograph or the pantograph used for enlarging drawings are also amplifiers of a kind. Electronic amplifiers, usually based on TRANSISTORS or electron tubes, can be thought of as a sort of variable switch in which the output from a power source is controlled (modulated) by a weak input signal. An important factor is the fidelity (see HIGH-FIDELITY) with which the waveform of the output signal reproduces that of the input over the desired bandwidth.

AMPUTATION, the surgical or traumatic removal of a part or the whole of a limb or other structure. It is necessary for severe limb damage, infective GANGRENE, loss of BLOOD supply and certain types of CANCER. Healthy tissue is molded to form a stump as a base for artificial limb prosthesis. (See PROSTHETICS.)

AMSTERDAM, capital and largest city of the Netherlands, and one of Europe's great commercial, financial and cultural centers. It stands in N Holland at the S of man-made Lake IJssel. This "Venice of the North" is centered on a series of concentric semicircular canals. Other canals linked to the Rhine and North Sea make Amsterdam one of Europe's major transshipment ports. It is also a major rail center and has an international airport.

Amsterdam is world-famous for diamond cutting and polishing and produces chemicals, machinery, bicycles, beer and textiles. It has an important stock exchange, two universities and about 40 museums. Amsterdam grew from a medieval fishing village, and had become a major city by the 17th century. Pop (city) 677,360; (metro) 968,525.

AMTRAK, official nickname of the National Railroad Passenger Corp., established by Congress in an effort to halt the post-WWII deterioration of railroad passenger service. Amtrak began operations on May 1, 1971, and now operates an average of 210 intercity trains per day, serving over 500 station locations over a systems of approximately 24,000 route miles. Of this route system, Amtrak owns a right-of-way of 2,611 track miles in the northeast corridor (Washington-New York-Boston; New Haven-Springfield; Philadelphia-Harrisburg) and several small track segments in the east. Outside the northeast corridor, Amtrak contracts with 21 privately owned railroads for the right to operate over their tracks. In 1986, Amtrak transported over 200 million peoplefor more than 5 billion passenger miles. Costs have always exceeded revenues, however, and Congress provides an annual subsidy to make up the difference. In 1986, Amtrak's revenues covered 62% of its total costs.

AMU DARYA (ancient Oxus), the major river of Soviet Central Asia. Rising in the Pamir Mts, it flows 1,578mi, NW between the USSR and Afghanistan, then W and NW to enter the Aral Sea through a delta.

The lower 900mi are navigable, and this stretch also irrigates large arid areas.

AMUNDSEN, Roald (1872–1928), Norwegian polar explorer who was the first man to reach the S Pole (Dec 14, 1911). His party beat the ill-fated Robert F. SCOTT expedition by one month. In the Arctic he was the first to navigate the NORTHWEST PASSAGE (1903–06), later crossing the N Pole in the dirigible *Norge* (1926). He was lost over the Barents Sea in an air search for the Italian explorer Umberto Nobile.

AMUR RIVER, river in NE Asia. Rising in Mongolia, it flows 2,700mi NE through the USSR, then SE, dividing the USSR from China, then NE through the USSR into the Tatar Strait. Navigable for the six months it is not frozen, it carries oil, grain and lumber. The Amur has fisheries and hydroelectric installations.

ANABAPTISTS ("rebaptizers"), radical Protestant sects of the REFORMATION that sought a return to primitive Christianity. The first group was formed in 1523 at Zurich by dissatisfied followers of Ulrich ZWINGLI. Denying the validity of infant baptism, they rebaptized adult converts. Most stressed the dictates of individual conscience, and urged nonviolence and separation of church and state. Despite widespread persecution (notably at Münster) their doctrines spread, inspiring the MENNONITES in the Netherlands and the HUTTERITES in Moravia.

ANACONDAS, two species, subfamily Boidae, of South American BOA. *Eunectes notaeus* is found in Paraguay, and *E. murinus*, probably the largest SNAKE in the world with a length up to about 35ft, though more usually 10-20ft, throughout Brazil. Anacondas do not have a poisonous bite, killing prey by constriction. In general they shun human beings.

ANACREON (c582–c485BC), Greek lyric poet who celebrated wine and love in mellow, simple verses. These were later copied in the so-called Anacreontics; fashionable in 18th-century Europe. His main patrons were the "tyrants" of Samos and Athens.

ANALGESICS, drugs used for relief of pain. They mainly impair preception of, or emotional response to, pain by action on the higher BRAIN centers. ASPIRIN and paracetamol are mild but effective. Phenylbutazone, indomethacin and ibuprofen are, like aspirin, useful in treating rheumatoid arthritis by reducing INFLAMMATION as well as relieving pain. Narcotic analgesics derived from opium alkaloids range from the milder CODEINE and dextropropoxyphene, suitable for general use, to the highly effective euphoriants and addictive MORPHINE and HEROIN. These are reserved for severe acute pain and terminal disease, where addiction is either unlikely or unimportant. Pethidine (demerol) is an intermediate narcotic.

ANALYSIS, the branch of MATHEMATICS concerned particularly with the concepts of function and limit. Its important divisions are CALCULUS. ANALYTIC GEOMETRY and the study of differential equations.

ANALYSIS, chemical, determination of the compounds or elements comprising a chemical substance. Qualitative analysis deals with what a sample contains; quantitative analysis finds the amounts. The methods available depend on the size of the sample: macro ($>100mg$), semimicro ($1-100mg$), micro ($1\mu g-mg$), or submicro ($<1\mu g$). Chemical analysis is valuable in chemical research, industry, archaeology, medicine and many other fields. A representative sample must first be taken and prepared for analysis. Preliminary separation is often carried out by CHROMATOGRAPHY, ion-exchange, DISTILLATION or precipitation.

In qualitative analysis, classical methods involve characteristic reactions of substances. After preliminary tests—inspection, heating, and flame tests—systematic schemes are followed which separate the various IONS into groups according to their reactions with standard reagents, and which then identify them individually. Cations and anions are analyzed separately. For organic compounds, carbon and hydrogen are identified by heating with copper (II) oxide, carbon dioxide and water being formed; nitrogen, halogens and sulfur are identified by heating with molten sodium and testing the residue for cyanide, halides and sulfide respectively. Classical quantitative analysis is performed by gravimetric analysis (separation and weighing) and volumetric analysis (measurements of volume).

Modern chemical analysis employs instrumental methods to give faster, more accurate assessments than do classical methods. Many modern methods have the additional advantage of being nondestructive. They include colorimetry, spectrophotometry, polarography, mass spectroscopy, differential thermal analysis, potentiometric titration and methods for determining MOLECULAR WEIGHT. Neutron activation analysis subjects a sample to NEUTRON irradiation and measures the strength of induced radioactivity and its rate of decay. In X-ray analysis, a sample is irradiated with X RAYS and emits X rays of different, characteristic wavelengths.

ANALYTIC GEOMETRY, that branch of GEOMETRY based on the idea that a point may be defined relative to another point or to axes by a set of numbers. In plane geometry, there are usually two axes, commonly designated the x- and y-axes, at right angles. The position of a point in the plane of the axes may then be defined by a pair of numbers (x, y), its coordinates, which give its distance in units in the x- and y-direction from the **origin** (the point of intersection of the two axes). In three dimensions there are three axes, usually at mutual right angles, commonly designated the x-, y- and z-axes.

Equation of a curve. A curve may be defined as a set of points. A relationship may be established between the coordinates of every point of the set, and this relationship is known as the EQUATION of the curve. The simplest form of plane curve is the straight line, which in the system we have described has an equation of the form $y=ax+b$, where a and b are constants. All points whose coordinates satisfy the relationship $y=ax+b$ will lie on this line. Equations of curves may involve higher powers of x or y: a parabola may be expressed as $y=ax^2+b$. Since $x^2=(-x)^2$ for all values of x, the curve is symmetrical about the y-axis.

These principles may be applied to different coordinate systems, and to figures in more than two dimensions.

Analytic geometry was created by DESCARTES. Bringing algebra and geometry together in this way was a major advance in mathematics.

ANARCHISM, political belief that government should be abolished and the state replaced by the voluntary cooperation of individuals and groups. Like socialists, anarchists believe that existing governments tend to defend injustice, and they would do away with the institution of private property. But, unlike socialists, they believe that government is unnecessary and intrinsically harmful.

Pioneers of modern anarchism included England's William GODWIN (1756–1836), France's Pierre Joseph PROUDHON (1809–1865) and the Russian propagandist of violence, Mikhail BAKUNIN (1814–1876). Political leaders, such as President William McKinley (1901), have been assassinated by individual anarchists, and the SACCO-VANZETTI CASE strengthened the popular idea that anarchism was linked with crime. Outside SYNDICALISM, once strong in Spain, anarchism has had little political influence, but has recently become linked with student radicalism in Europe and America.

ANASTASIA (1901–1918?), Russian grand duchess. Daughter of the last czar, Nicholas II, she was probably murdered with her family during the Revolution. Several women later claimed to be Anastasia but none could prove her identity.

ANATOLIA, large mountainous plateau in Asian Turkey, now more or less identical with the peninsula of ASIA MINOR.

ANATOMY, the structure and form of biological organisms (see BIOLOGY) and their study. The subject has three main divisions: gross anatomy, dealing with components visible to the naked eye; microscopic anatomy, dealing with microstructures seen only with the aid of an optical MICROSCOPE; and submicroscopic anatomy, dealing with still smaller ultrastructures. Since structure is closely related to function, anatomy is related to PHYSIOLOGY

The study of anatomy is as old as that of MEDICINE, though for many centuries physicians' knowledge of anatomy left much to be desired. ANAXAGORAS had studied the anatomy of animals, and anatomical observations can be found in the Hippocratic writings (see HIPPOCRATES), but it was ARISTOTLE who was the true father of comparative anatomy. Human dissection (the basis of all systematic human anatomy) was rarely practiced before the era of the ALEXANDRIAN SCHOOL and the work of Herophilus and Erasistratus. The last great experimental anatomist of antiquity was GALEN. His theories, as transmitted through the writings of the Arab scholars Rhazes and AVICENNA, held sway throughout the medieval period. Further progress had to await the revival of the practice of human dissection by SERVETUS and VESALIUS in the 16th century. The latter founded the famous Paduan school of anatomy, which also included Fallopius and Fabricius, whose pupil William HARVEY reunited the studies of anatomy and physiology in postulating the circulation of the BLOOD in *De Motu Cordis* (1628). This theory was confirmed some years later when MALPIGHI discovered the capillaries linking the arteries with the veins. Since the 17th century many important anatomical schools have been founded and the study of anatomy has become an essential part of medical training. Important developments in the late 18th century included the foundation of HISTOLOGY by the Frenchman M. F. X. Bichat and that of modern comparative anatomy by CUVIER.

ANAXAGORAS (c500–c428 BC), Greek philosopher of the Ionian school, resident in Athens, who taught that the elements were infinite in number and that everything contained a portion of every other thing. He also discovered the true cause of ECLIPSES and thought of the sun as a blazing rock and showed that air has substance.

ANAXIMANDER (c610–c545 BC), Greek philosopher of the Ionian school who taught that the cosmos was derived from one "indeterminate" primordial substance by a process of the separating out of opposites. He was probably the first Greek to attempt a map of the whole known world and thought of the earth as a stubby cylinder situated at the center of all things.

ANAXIMENES OF MILETUS (6th century BC), Greek philosopher of the Ionian school who held that all things were derived from air; this becoming, for instance, fire on rarifaction, water, and finally earth on condensation.

ANCESTOR WORSHIP, ritual propitiation and veneration of dead kin in the belief that their spirits influence the fortunes of the living. It has figured strongly in Asian faiths, notably Confucianism in China, Shintoism in Japan and Hinduism in India, and also occurs in Africa and Melanesia.

ANDALUSIA, populous region of S Spain, extending to the Atlantic and Mediterranean and embracing eight provinces. It includes the Sierra Morena and Sierra Nevada Mts., and the warm fertile Guadalquivir River Valley—"the garden of Spain." There is metal mining, food processing and tourism along the Costa del Sol. Phoenicians first settled the area; later came Greeks, Romans and Vandals. Arabs and Berbers built a rich medieval culture. Today there is much rural poverty.

ANDERS, Wladislaw (1892–1970), Polish general whose Polish army-in-exile helped the Allies win Italy in WWII. In England after 1945 he was a leader of exiled anticommunist Poles.

ANDERSEN, Hans Christian (1805–1875), Danish writer, best remembered for his 168 fairy tales. Based on folklore and observation of people and events in Andersen's life, they have a deceptively simple, slyly humorous style and often carry a moral message for adults as well as children. Among his best known stories are *The Ugly Duckling, The Emperor's Clothes,* and *The Red Shoes.*

ANDERSON, Carl David (1905–   ), US physicist at Cal Tech who shared the 1936 Nobel Prize for Physics for his discovery of the positron (1932). Later he was codiscoverer of the first meson (see

SUBATOMIC PARTICLES).

ANDERSON, Elizabeth Garrett (1836–1917), one of the first Englishwomen to become a doctor (1865). She helped establish the place of women in the professions and founded a women's hospital and a medical school for women.

ANDERSON, (Franklin) Leroy (1908–1975), US composer and conductor. An orchestrator and arranger for the Boston Pops Orchestra (1936–50), he was also guest conductor of other US and Canadian symphony orchestras. His compositions include *The Syncopated Clock* and *Blue Tango*.

ANDERSON, John (1922–), US politician, a Republican member of the US House of Representatives from Illinois 1961–81. After losing a bid for the Republican presidential nomination in 1980, he ran for president as an independent and polled 5,719,722 votes, or 6.6% of the total.

ANDERSON, Dame Judith (1898–), Australian-born actress who worked in the US. She is best known for her tragic roles in the plays of Eugene O'NEILL and Shakespeare and in Robinson JEFFERS' version of *Medea* (1947). Her films included *Rebecca* (1940), *King's Row* (1941), and *Laura* (1944).

ANDERSON, Marian (1902–), US black contralto. Overcoming the handicaps of poverty and discrimination, she became an international singing star in the 1930s, and in 1955 was the first black to sing a leading role at the Metropolitan Opera—Ulrica in *A Masked Ball*.

ANDERSON, Maxwell (1888–1959), US playwright. After early realistic plays, he concentrated on the revival of verse drama, achieving some success with such plays as *Elizabeth the Queen* (1930), *Winterset* (1935) and *High Tor* (1936).

ANDERSON, Sherwood (1876–1941), US writer. His novels and short stories deal largely with men rebelling against contemporary industrial society. He is best remembered for *Winesburg, Ohio* (1919), stories of the frustrations of small-town Midwestern life, and such story collections as *The Triumph of the Egg* (1921) and *Horses and Men* (1923). His best novels are *Poor White* (1920) and *Dark Laughter* (1925).

ANDERSONVILLE, village in W Ga. where some 13,000 Union troops died of disease or wounds in a Confederate prison (1864–65). Its dreadful conditions provoked Union propaganda and reprisals. The site is now a federal park.

ANDES, South America's largest mountain system, 4,500mi long and averaging 200–250mi wide, running close to the entire W coast of the continent. Only the Himalayas exceed its average height of 12,500ft, and ACONCAGUA (22,835ft) is the highest peak in the W Hemisphere.

The Andes rose largely in the Cenozoic era (the last 70 million years), and volcanic eruptions and earthquakes suggest continuing uplift. There are three main sections. The S Andes form a single range (cordillera) dividing Chile and Argentina, with peaks ranging from 20,000ft in the N to 7,000ft in the S. The central Andes form two ranges flanking the high Bolivian plateau (the ALTIPLANO). The N Andes divide in Colombia and form four ranges ending in the Caribbean area. Many high Andean peaks are jagged and snowy, and glaciers fill some southern valleys.

ANDORRA, tiny semi-independent European state in the E Pyrenees between France and Spain. It is a land of mountains and mountain valleys, averaging over 6,000ft and ringed by peaks up to 10,000ft.

Official name: Andorra
Capital: Andorra la Vella
Area: 181sq mi
Population: 48,800
Languages: Catalan; French; Spanish
Religions: Roman Catholic
Monetary unit(s): French franc; Spanish peseta

The Andorrans are mainly Catalan-speaking Roman Catholics. Most live in six municipalities, Andorra la Vella being the largest. Tourism is the economic mainstay. But the people also grow tobacco, rye, barley, grapes and potatoes, raise sheep and cattle, and exploit local lead and iron. Smuggling is a common pursuit. Since 1278 Andorra has been a co-principality, now under the bishop of Urgel in Spain and the French head of state.

ANDRADA E SILVA, José Bonifácio de. See BONIFÁCIO, JOSÉ.

ANDRASSY, Count Gyula (1823–1890), first prime minister of Hungary within Austria Hungary (1867) and Austro-Hungarian foreign minister (1871–79). As foreign minister and supporter of Hungarian independence he forged close ties with Germany to counter Russian and Slav ambitions.

ANDRÉ, John (1750–1780), British army officer, hanged as a spy by the Americans during the Revolutionary War. He secretly met Benedict ARNOLD behind American lines to arrange Arnold's surrender of West Point, but was caught in civilian clothes, with incriminating papers.

ANDREA DEL SARTO (1486–1530), leading 16th-century Florentine painter, influenced by Michelangelo and Dürer and renowned for delicately-colored church frescoes. He rivalled Raphael's classicism but foreshadowed MANNERISM through his pupils Pontormo, ROSSO and VASARI.

ANDRÉE, Salomon August (1854–1897), Swedish Arctic explorer and balloonist. In 1897 he and two others tried to reach the N Pole from Spitsbergen by balloon, but were forced down after only 300mi. Their bodies were found in 1930.

ANDREW, Saint (1st century AD), one of Christ's 12 Apostles, formerly a fisherman and disciple of John the Baptist. He reputedly preached in what is now Russia and was martyred in Patras, Greece, on an X-shaped ("St. Andrew's") cross. He is the patron saint of Russia and of Scotland.

ANDREWES, Lancelot (1555–1626), English High Church bishop who developed the liturgy and molded ANGLICANISM by his copious writings. A royal chaplain, he helped produce the King James version of the Bible.

ANDREWS, Charles McLean (1863–1943), US historian. He stressed colonial America's dependence upon Britain in works like *The Colonial Period of American History* (1934–38), the first volume of which won him a Pulitzer Prize.

ANDREWS, Roy Chapman (1884–1960), US naturalist, explorer and author. From 1906 he worked for the AMERICAN MUSEUM OF NATURAL HISTORY (later becoming its director, 1935–41) and made important expeditions to Alaska, the Far East and Central Asia. Among many important discoveries he made in Mongolia were the first known fossil dinosaur eggs.

ANDREWS SISTERS (Patty, 1920– ; LaVerne, 1915–1967; Maxene, 1918–), US vocal group who achieved great popularity during WWII with "Beer Barrel Polka," "In Apple Blossom Time," and "Rum and Coca-Cola."

ANDREYEV, Leonid Nikolayevich (1871–1919), Russian novelist, short-story writer and playwright. Ranging from earlier realistic social protest to later symbolism, his work (e.g., *The Seven That Were Hanged*, 1908) reflects a basic pessimism and preoccupation with death.

ANDRIC, Ivo (1892–1975), Yugoslav novelist who won the Nobel Prize for Literature in 1961, largely for the epic quality of *The Bridge on the Drina*. His themes are man's insecurity and isolation in face of change and death.

ANDROGENS, STEROID hormones which produce secondary male characteristics such as facial and body hair and a deep voice. They also develop the male reproductive organs. The main androgen is TESTOSTERONE, produced in the testes; others are produced in small quantities in the cortex of the ADRENAL GLANDS. Small amounts occur in women in addition to the ESTROGENS and may produce some male characteristics. (See also ENDOCRINE GLANDS; PUBERTY.)

ANDROMEDA, constellation in the N Hemisphere. The Great Andromeda Nebula (M31), seen near the DOUBLE STAR Gamma Andromedae, is the most distant object visible to the naked eye in N skies. It is the nearest external GALAXY to our own, like it a spiral but larger (120,000 light-years in diameter), and about 2 million light-years from earth.

ANDROPOV, Yuri Vladimirovich (1914–1984), USSR political leader, who became general secretary of the Communist party in 1982 after the death of Leonid Brezhnev and also, in 1983, chief of state. Earlier he had served as ambassador to Hungary (1954–57) and as head of the KGB, the Soviet security service (1967–82).

ANDROS, Sir Edmund (1637–1714), British governor of the Dominion of New England, 1686–89. His attempt to curb the colonists' rights caused a rebellion. Imprisoned and sent to England for trial, he was acquitted and became governor of Virginia 1692–97.

ANEMIA, condition in which the amount of HEMOGLOBIN in the BLOOD is abnormally low, thus reducing the blood's oxygen-carrying capacity. Anemic people may feel weak, tired, faint and breathless, have a rapid pulse and appear pale.

Of the many types of anemia, five groups can be described. In **iron-deficiency anemia**, the red blood cells are smaller and paler than normal. Usual causes include inadequate diet (especially in PREGNANCY), failure of iron absorption, and chronic blood loss (as from heavy MENSTRUATION, HEMORRHAGE or disease of the GASTROINTESTINAL TRACT). Iron replacement is essential and in severe cases blood transfusion may be needed. In **megaloblastic anemia**, the red cells are larger than normal. This may be due to nutritional lack of VITAMIN B_{12} or folate, but the most important cause is **pernicious anemia**. B_{12} is needed for red-cell formation, but patients with pernicious anemia cannot absorb B_{12} because they lack a factor in the stomach essential for absorption. Regular B_{12} injections are needed for life. In **aplastic anemia**, inadequate numbers of red cells are produced by the bone MARROW owing to damage by certain poisons, drugs or irradiation. Treatment includes transfusions and androgens. In **hemolytic anemia**, the normal life span of red cells is reduced, either because of ANTIBODY reactions or because they are abnormally fragile. A form of the latter is **sickle-cell anemia**, a hereditary disease, common among NEGROIDS, in which abnormal hemoglobin is made. Finally, many chronic diseases including rheumatoid arthritis, chronic infection and uremia suppress red-cell formation and thus cause anemia.

ANEMOMETER, an instrument for measuring wind speed and often direction. The rotation type, which estimates wind speed from the rotation of cups mounted on a vertical shaft, is the most common of mechanical anemometers. The sonic or acoustic anemometer depends on the velocity of sound in the wind. For laboratory work a hot-wire instrument is used: here air flow is estimated from the change in resistance it causes by cooling an electrically heated wire.

ANEMONE, genus of mainly N temperate perennial herbs of the buttercup family (Ranunculaceae). Up to 3ft high, anemones have deeply cut, whorled leaves and white, pink, red, blue or, rarely, yellow flowers. Many are cultivated but some, such as the wood anemone and pasque flower, grow wild.

ANESTHESIA, or absence of sensation, may be of three types: general, local or pathological. **General anesthesia** is a reversible state of drug-induced unconsciousness with muscle relaxation and suppression of reflexes; this facilitates many surgical procedures and avoids distress. An anesthesiologist attends to ensure stable anesthesia and to protect vital functions. While ethanol and narcotics have been used for their anesthetic properties for centuries, modern anesthesia dates from the use of diethyl ether by William Morton in 1846, and of chloroform by Sir James Simpson in 1847. Nowadays injections of short-acting barbiturates, such as sodium pentothal, are frequently used to induce anesthesia rapidly; inhaled agents, including halothane, ether, nitrous oxide, trichlorethylene and cyclopropane, are used for induction and maintenance. **Local** and **regional anesthesia** are the reversible blocking of pain impulses by chemical action of cocaine derivatives (e.g., procaine, lignocaine). Nerve trunks are blocked for minor surgery and dentistry, and more widespread anesthesia may be achieved by blocking spinal nerve roots, useful in obstetrics and with patients unfit for general anesthesia. **Pathological anesthesia** describes loss of sensation following trauma or disease.

ANEURYSM, a pathological enlargement of, or defect in, a blood vessel. These may occur in the HEART after CORONARY THROMBOSIS, or in the AORTA and ARTERIES due to ARTERIOSCLEROSIS, high blood pressure, congenital defect, trauma or infection (specifically syphilis). They may rupture, causing HEMORRHAGE, which in the heart or aorta is rapidly fatal. Again, their enlargement may cause pain, swelling or pressure on nearby organs; these complications are most serious in the arteries of the BRAIN. SURGERY for aneurysm includes tying off and removal; larger vessels may be repaired by synthetic grafts.

ANGEL, supernatural messenger and servant of the deity. Angels figure in Christianity, Judaism, Islam and Zoroastrianism. In Christianity, angels traditionally serve and praise God, but guardian angels may protect the faithful against the evil of the Devil (the fallen angel Lucifer). The hierarchy of angels was said to have nine orders: Cherubim, Seraphim, Thrones; Dominions, Virtues, Powers; Principalities, Archangels, Angels.

ANGEL FALLS, world's highest known waterfall (3,212ft), on the Churún R in SE Venezuela. US aviator Jimmy Angel discovered it in 1935.

ANGELICO, Fra (c1400–1455), Italian painter and Dominican friar, a major figure in Renaissance art. His church frescoes and altarpieces, using religious figures, combined traditionally bright, clear colors with the new use of perspective settings. His Tuscan backgrounds are among the first great Renaissance landscapes.

ANGELL, Sir Norman (1874–1967), British economist and internationalist, awarded the Nobel Peace Prize in 1933. A journalist most of his life, he argued in his book *The Great Illusion* (1910) that war was futile and best prevented by the mutual economic interest of nations.

ANGELOU, Maya (1928–   ), black US author best known for her autobiographical books *I Know Why the Caged Bird Sings* (1970), *Gather Together in My Name* (1974), and *Now Sheba Sings the Song* (1987), which recount her struggles for identity in a hostile world.

ANGEVIN, name of two medieval royal dynasties originating in the Anjou region of W France. The earliest ruled in parts of France, Jerusalem, and in England after Henry II, son of Geoffrey of Anjou, became England's first Angevin (or Plantagenet) ruler in 1154. His descendants held power in England until 1485. The younger branch began in 1266 when Charles, brother of Louis IX of France, became king of Naples and Sicily. This dynasty ruled in Italy, Hungary and Poland until the end of the 15th century.

ANGINA PECTORIS, severe, short-lasting chest pain caused by inadequate blood supply to the myocardium (see HEART), often due to coronary artery disease such as ARTERIOSCLEROSIS. It is precipitated by exertion or other stresses which demand increased heart work. Pain may spread to nearby areas, often the arms; sweating and breathlessness may occur. It is rapidly relieved or prevented by sucking nitroglycerin tablets or inhaling amyl nitrite.

ANGIOSPERMS, or flowering plants, large and very important class of seed-bearing plants, characterized by having seeds that develop completely enclosed in the tissue of the parent plant, rather than unprotected as in the only other seedbearing group, the GYMNOSPERMS. Containing about 250,000 species distributed throughout the world, and ranging in size from tiny herbs to huge trees, angiosperms are the dominant land flora of the present day. They have sophisticated mechanisms to ensure that pollination and fertilization take place and that the resulting seeds are readily dispersed and able to germinate. There are two subclasses: monocotyledons (with one leaf) and dicotyledons (with two).

ANGKOR, extensive ruins in NW Cambodia the ancient KHMER EMPIRE, noted for the city Angkor Thom and the Angkor Wat temple complex. Covering 40sq mi and dating from the 9th–13th centuries, the remains were found in 1861. Angkor Thom with its temples and palace is intersected by a canal system and has a perimeter wall 8mi long. Angkor Wat is a massive complex of carved Hindu temples with a 2.5mi perimeter, and is the foremost example of Khmer art and architecture.

ANGLE, in plane GEOMETRY, the figure formed by the intersection of two straight lines. The point of intersection is known as the vertex.

Consider the two lines to be radii of a circle of unit radius. There is then a direct way of defining the magnitudes of angles in terms of the proportion of the circle's circumference cut off by their two sides: as the length of the circle's circumference is given by $2\pi r$, and $r=1$, the **radian** (rad) is defined as the magnitude of an angle whose two sides cut off $1/2\pi$ of the circumference. A **degree** (°) is defined as an angle whose two sides cut off $1/360$ of the circumference.

An angle of $\pi/2$ rad (90°), whose sides cut off one quarter of the circumference, is a **right angle,** the two lines being said to be perpendicular. Should the two sides cut off one half of the circumference (πrad or 180°), the angle is a straight angle or straight line. Angles less than $\pi/2$ rad are termed acute; those greater than $\pi/2$ but less than πrad, obtuse; and those greater than πrad but less than 2πrad, reflex. Pairs of angles that add up to $\pi/2$rad are termed complementary; those that add up to πrad, supplementary. Further properties of angles lie in the province of TRIGONOMETRY

In spherical geometry a **spherical angle** is that formed by intersecting arcs of two great circles: its magnitude is equal to that of the angle between the planes of the great circles.

A **solid angle** is formed by a conical surface (see CONE). Considering its vertex to lie at the center of a sphere, then a measure of its magnitude may be obtained from the ratio between the area (L^2) of the surface of the sphere cut off by the angle, and the square (R^2) of the sphere's radius. Solid angles are measured in steradians (sr), an angle of one steradian subtending an area of R^2 at distance R.

ANGLES, Germanic tribe from which England derives its name. Coming from the Schleswig-Holstein area of N Germany, the Angles, with the SAXONS and JUTES, invaded England from the 5th century and founded kingdoms including East Anglia, Mercia and Northumbria. (See also ANGLO-SAXONS.)

ANGLICANISM, the body of doctrines originally developed by the CHURCH OF ENGLAND and now broadly followed by the other members of the Anglican Communion. These include the Anglican Church of Canada, the EPISCOPAL CHURCH in the US, and other Episcopal churches in former British colonies and elsewhere.

ANGLO-SAXON CHRONICLE, historical record of England from early Christian times until after the Norman Conquest. Various versions were made between 890 and 1155, based on monastic annals, genealogies and episcopal records. They constitute the oldest W European history written in the vernacular, and the chief source for Anglo-Saxon history.

ANGLO-SAXONS, collective name for the Germanic peoples who dominated England from the 5th to the 11th centuries. They originated as tribes of ANGLES, SAXONS and JUTES who invaded England after Roman rule collapsed, creating kingdoms that eventually united to form the English nation. In modern usage, Anglo-Saxons are the English or their emigrant descendants in other parts of the world.

ANGOLA, independent state in SW Africa, formerly a Portuguese overseas province. Angola is bounded on the N and NE by Zaire; on the SE by Zambia; on the S by Namibia (SW Africa); and on the W by the Atlantic Ocean.

Official name: People's Republic of Angola
Capital: Luanda
Area: 481,350sq mi
Population: 9,105,000
Languages: Bantu; Portuguese
Religions: Roman Catholic; Protestant; Animist
Monetary unit(s): 1 kwanza = 100 lwei
Land. Beyond the coastal plain is a dominant central plateau 5,000ft high. Main rivers include the Congo, Zambezi, Cuanza and Cunene. The warm wet N has tropical rain forest; the cooler, seasonally dry plateau supports savanna. There is abundant savanna wildlife.
People. Over 90% of Angolans are Bantu with a few Bushmen. Bantu tongues and animist beliefs predominate among the largely illiterate majority. The capital, Luanda, and most towns lie in the W.
Economy. Angola has a prosperous oil industry and is expected to become a major oil-producing country. Crude oil is the principal export, followed by coffee, diamonds, iron ore, cotton and corn. There is some light industry.
History. The Bantu Bakongo kingdom held NW Angola when the Portuguese navigator Diogo Cam arrived in 1482. Portugal exerted control over Angola from 1576

onwards, and the export of Negro slaves to Brazil caused severe depopulation. Portuguese colonization and economic development grew in the early 20th century. Nationalist guerrillas were active in the fight for independence from 1961. Upon independence in 1975, conflict erupted among the three movements vying for power. With support from Cuba and the USSR, the Popular Liberation Movement of Angola gained control and established a Marxist government defended by Cuban troops. It was resisted by the National Union for the Total Independence of Angola (UNITA), led by Jonas Savimbi and supported by South Africa and the US. The presence of Cuban troops in Angola gave South Africa a pretext for its illegal occupation of Namibia (or South-West Africa), and South African troops were also involved in the Angolan civil war in support of UNITA. At the same time, the guerrilla forces of the South-West Africa People's Organization (SWAPO), the Namibian independence movement, were based in Angola in alliance with the Marxist government there. In 1988 a tentative agreement was reached among Angola, South Africa, and Cuba by which Cuba would pull its troops out of Angola and South Africa would end its occupation of Namibia.

ANGORA, term used for long-haired varieties of goats, cats and rabbits. Originally it referred to goats bred in the Angora (now Ankara) region of Turkey. The silky white hair of Angora goats has long been used for fine yarns and fabrics, especially for making mohair cloth.

ANGRY YOUNG MEN, post-WWII generation of British writers whose works reflected a mood scathingly critical of established social values, as in John OSBORNE's play *Look Back in Anger* (1956). Most had lower middle-class or working-class backgrounds and leftist political sympathies. They included Kingsley AMIS, Arnold WESKER, John Braine, John Wain, Alan Sillitoe and Doris Lessing.

ANGST, German word meaning dread or anxiety. It implies modern man's unease, frustration and sense of insignificance in face of an inexplicable universe, and reflects a loss of faith in God and of man's belief in himself. It appears in the literature of EXISTENTIALISM and in works by Franz KAFKA, T. S. ELIOT, W. H. AUDEN and others.

ANGSTROM, Anders Jonas (1814–1874), Swedish physicist who was one of the founders of SPECTROSCOPY and was the first to identify hydrogen in the solar spectrum (1862). The Angstrom unit is named in his honor.

ANIMAL, a living organism which displays most, if not all, of the following characteristics:

(1) it does not contain CHLOROPHYLL;

(2) it has the ability, at least at some time during its life-cycle, to move actively;

(3) its CELLS are limited by a cell membrane, rather than by a CELLULOSE or chitin wall;

(4) it is heterotrophic;

(5) it is limited in the extent of its growth (that is, it does not continue to grow larger and larger with increasing age, but reaches a maximum size at some point in its life-cycle);

(6) it produces male and female GAMETES, and its development includes the formation of an EMBRYO and often a larva.

In fact, many animals do not display all of these characteristics. For example, the PROTOZOA generally reproduce asexually by FISSION; and some contain chlorophyll. Slime molds show both plant and animal characteristics at different stages of their life cycles. Moreover, some PLANTS display some animal characteristics: FUNGI do not contain chlorophyll; BACTERIA are considered as plants although many types are motile.

Because of these borderline cases, the exact differentiation between plants and animals has long been a subject of dispute. Despite this, there is in general little confusion between the two kingdoms. (See also ANIMAL BEHAVIOR; ANIMAL KINGDOM; ECOLOGY; EVOLUTION; FOSSIL; TAXONOMY; ZOOLOGY.)

ANIMAL BEHAVIOR, the responses of animals to internal and external stimuli. Study of these responses can enable advances to be made in our understanding of human PSYCHOLOGY and behavior. Animal responses may be learned by the animal during its lifetime or may be instinctive or inherited (see HEREDITY; INSTINCT).

Even the simplest animals are capable of learning—to associate a particular stimulus with pain or pleasure, to negotiate mazes, etc. Moreover, there are critical periods in an animal's life when it is capable of learning a great deal in a very short time. Thus baby geese hatched in the absence of the mother will follow the first moving object they see, another animal or a human being. If, later, they must choose between this other animal and the mother, they prefer the other animal. This rapid early learning is called **imprinting.**

Among even the most intelligent animals much behavior is instinctive: the shape of a baby's head, for example, evokes an instinctive parental response in man. The complicated dance of the BEES, by which they inform the hive of the whereabouts of food, each species of bee having its own dance "dialect," is an example of more complex instinctive behavior. Instinctive ritual, too, plays its part. Instinct can determine the behavior of a single animal, or of a whole animal society (see HIBERNATION; MIGRATION).

ANIMAL HUSBANDRY, branch of agriculture dealing with the care and breeding of livestock, often making profitable use of land unsuitable for arable farming. Though scientific husbandry dates from only the 18th century, many special skills have been evolved to deal with various animals. Man, however, may have first domesticated an animal—the goat—about 8,000 years ago. (See also AGRICULTURE.)

ANIMAL KINGDOM, Animalia, one of the kingdoms into which all living organisms are classified. More than a million distinct species of animals have been identified, and these are divided into various groups, groups within groups, etc. (see TAXONOMY).

The animal kingdom is divided into phyla (singular, phylum). Within these phyla, animals are further divided into classes, based primarily on their bodily structure but also (though the two are usually equivalent) on their evolutionary history (see EVOLUTION); classes may be grouped into subphyla. Thus the phylum Chordata has, amongst others, the subphylum vertebrata, which includes classes such as AMPHIBIA, Pisces (FISHES), Reptilia (REPTILES), Aves (BIRDS) and Mammalia (MAMMALS). In the same way, classes contain (in descending order of magnitude) orders, families, genera, species and subspecies.

ANIMATION, cinematographic technique creating the illusion of movement by projecting a series of drawings or photographs showing successive views of an action. The first animated cartoons were made by Émile Cohl in France in 1907. Walt DISNEY pioneered sound and color in films such as the *Mickey Mouse* cartoons and the full-length *Fantasia,* which became world famous. In modern cartoon making, drawings on transparent celluloid ("cells") are superimposed to form each picture and only cells showing motion need changing from frame to frame.

ANIMISM, a term first used by E. B. TYLOR to designate a general belief in spiritual beings, which belief he held to be the origin of all religions. A common corruption of Tylor's sense is to interpret as animism the belief that all natural objects possess spirits. PIAGET has proposed that the growing child characteristically passes through an animistic phase.

ANJOU, former province of W France, now a wine-growing area in the department of Maine-et-Loire. Its name derives from the Celtic Andes tribe, which occupied the area before the Romans. Anjou was a county in the 9th century, later a powerful feudal state, and a duchy in 1360; it became part of the French monarchy in 1480.

ANKARA, capital of Turkey and of Ankara province in Asia Minor. It produces textiles, cement, flour and beer, and trades in local Angora wool and grain. Landmarks: the university, ATATURK's mausoleum and the old fortress. Ankara (formerly Ancyra or Angora) may be pre-Hittite in origin. It replaced ISTANBUL as Turkey's capital in 1923. Pop 2,235,035.

ANNA COMNENA (1083-d. after 1148), Byzantine princess and historian. Her *Alexiad* dealt mainly with the life of her father, Emperor Alexius I Comnenus, and gave a Byzantine viewpoint of the confrontation of East and West during the First Crusade.

ANNA IVANOVNA (1693–1740), empress of Russia from 1730, who stopped the decline of royal power. Elected "puppet" empress by the nobles' supreme privy council, she overthrew it and, with German advisers, waged costly wars against the Poles and Turks, and opened Russia's way to Central Asia.

ANNAM, ancient SE Asian Kingdom (now the republic of VIETNAM). Under Chinese domination from the 2nd century BC, Annam first became independent in 1428. It expanded S, was split in two in the 16th century, but was reunited with French help in 1802. By the later 1800s Annam was divided into French-dominated Tonkin, Annam and Cochin-China.

ANNAPOLIS, capital city of Md., seat of Anne Arundel Co. on the Severn R near Chesapeake Bay. A historic and beautiful city, it was settled in 1649 by Puritans from Va. and was given its present name in 1694. It was the site of the ANNAPOLIS CONVENTION of 1786. It has many historic buildings, including the statehouse (1772). It is the site of St. John's College (founded 1696) and the US Naval Academy (established 1845). There are a number of local industries, including the processing of seafood. Pop 31,740.

ANNAPOLIS CONVENTION (1786), meeting which foreshadowed the US Constitutional Convention. It was held at ANNAPOLIS, Md., to discuss problems of

interstate commerce. Alexander HAMILTON and James MADISON wanted its scope broadened to discuss revision of the ARTICLES OF CONFEDERATION. But only five of the 13 states were represented and thus a full-scale meeting was called for, which led to the Constitutional Convention at Philadelphia.

ANNAPURNA, Himalayan mountain in Nepal with the world's 11th-highest peak (26,391ft). Its conquest in 1950 by Maurice Herzog's team was the first such success involving any great Himalayan peak.

ANNE (1665–1714), Queen of Great Britain and Ireland 1702–14 and last of the Stuart monarchs. A devout Anglican Protestant of Whig persuasion, she was influenced in political and religious affairs by the Duke of MARLBOROUGH and his wife, Sarah. Her reign was dominated by the War of the SPANISH SUCCESSION (1701–14). It also saw the ACT OF UNION (1707) uniting England and Scotland to form the kingdom of Great Britain.

ANNEALING, the slow heating and cooling of metals and glass to remove stresses which have arisen in casting, cold working or machining. The annealed material is tougher and easier to process further. (See also METALLURGY.)

ANNENBERG, Walter (1908–   ), US publisher. He inherited a Philadelphia-based publishing empire which included the *Philadelphia Inquirer*, founded *Seventeen* magazine (1944) and *TV Guide* (1953) and bought the *Philadelphia Daily News* (1957). A heavy contributor to the Republican Party, he served (1969–75) as US ambassador to the UK.

ANNE OF CLEVES (1515–1557), queen consort and fourth wife of England's HENRY VIII. She was the daughter of a powerful German noble, and Henry married her (1540) on Thomas CROMWELL's advice to forge international bonds. But he disliked her and six months later had Parliament annul the marriage.

ANNUAL, plant that completes its life cycle in one growing season and then dies. Annuals propagate themselves only by seeds. They include such garden flowers and food plants as marigolds, cornflowers, cereals, peas and tomatoes. Preventing seeding may convert an annual, e.g. mignonette, to a biennial or a perennial.

ANNULMENT, decree to the effect that a marriage was invalid when contracted. Grounds for annulment include fraud, force and close blood links between the parties. The Roman Catholic Church recognizes annulment but not divorce.

ANNUNCIATION, in Christian belief, the

archangel Gabriel's announcement to the Virgin MARY that she would give birth to the Messiah. The Roman Catholic Church celebrates the annunciation as Lady Day, March 25. The annunciation appears in many Christian paintings.

ANOREXIA NERVOSA, pathological loss of appetite with secondary MALNUTRITION and HORMONE changes. It often affects young women with diet obsession and may reflect underlying psychiatric disease.

ANOUILH, Jean (1910–1987), French playwright of polished, highly theatrical dramas which emphasize the dilemma of modern man who must compromise in order to achieve happiness. His works include *Antigone* (1944), *The Lark* (1953) and *Beckett* (1959).

ANSCHLUSS, the union of Austria with Germany, effected (in violation of the VERSAILLES TREATY) when the Nazi army entered Austria on March 12, 1938. It had a logical basis in a common Austro-German language and culture, but was forced by Adolf Hitler for Nazi aggrandizement.

ANSELM, Saint (1033–1109), archbishop of Canterbury (from 1093) who upheld Church authority and became the first scholastic philosopher. He endured repeated exile for challenging the right of English kings to influence Church affairs. Anselm saw reason as the servant of faith and probably invented the ontological "proof" of God's existence: that our idea of a perfect being implies the existence of such a being.

ANSERMET, Ernest (1883–1969), Swiss conductor who directed many premieres of STRAVINSKY ballets. He founded the *Orchestre de la Suisse Romande* in 1918, conducting it until his death.

ANSKY, Shloime (pen name of Solomon Samuel Rapaport, 1863–1920), Russian Yiddish author and playwright, best known for *The Dybbik* (1916), an arresting tragedy of demonic possession. He was active in Russian Jewish socialism, but left Russia after the Revolution, and died in Poland.

ANSON, Adrian Constantine (known as "Cap" or "Pop" Anson; 1851–1922), great US baseball player. In 1939 he was elected to baseball's Hall of Fame as "the greatest hitter and greatest National League player-manager of the 19th century."

ANTABUSE, or disulfiram (tetraethylthiuram disulfide), drug used in treatment of ALCOHOLISM. Though nontoxic, it prevents the breakdown of acetaldehyde, a highly toxic product of ETHANOL metabolism. Thus if alcohol is drunk after Antabuse has been taken, unpleasant symptoms occur, including palpitations and vomiting.

ANTACIDS, mild ALKALIS or BASES taken by mouth to neutralize excess STOMACH acidity for relief of DYSPEPSIA, including peptic ULCER and HEARTBURN. Milk of magnesia, aluminum hydroxide and sodium bicarbonate are common antacids.

ANTARCTICA, a continental landmass of almost 6,000,000sq mi, covered by an icecap between 6,000 and 14,000ft thick, except where mountain peaks, such as the 16,900ft Vinson Massif, break through the ice. The general shape of the continent is circular, indented by the arc-shaped Weddell Sea (S of the Atlantic Ocean) and the rectangular Ross Sea (S of New Zealand). The Antarctic Peninsula and other areas facing Tierra del Fuego are structurally similar to the adjacent South American coast, while the rest of the continent resembles Australia and South Africa. Such facts provide evidence for the theory of CONTINENTAL DRIFT, also supported by recent fossil discoveries.

No warm ocean currents or winds reach the mainland, so the climate is intensely cold. All precipitation falls as snow, and in winter temperatures as low as $-80°F$ and winds up to 100mph occur frequently. Few animals other than mites, microscopic rotifers and tiny wingless insects can survive inland; but the coasts and offshore waters support seabirds, including penguins, skuas, petrels and fulmars, and marine mammals (whales and seals). Vegetation is limited to lichen, mosses and fungi S of the 62nd parallel, though it is richer in the N offshore islands.

Captain James CŌOK was the first to attempt a scientific exploration of the Antarctic region (1773), but he believed that the whole area was a frozen ocean. The mainland was probably first sighted in 1820 by the American sea captain, Nathaniel Palmer. Expeditions to the area were led by the Englishmen James Weddell (1823) and John Biscoe (1832) and the American Charles WILKES (1838–40). James Clark ROSS discovered the sea later named for him, and charted much of the Antarctic coast between 1840 and 1842, taking his English team as far as latitude 78°9'S. About the turn of the century a series of Belgian, Norwegian, German, British and French expeditions gathered much valuable data, and on Dec. 14, 1911, the Norwegian Roald AMUNDSEN reached the S Pole, a month before Captain Robert SCOTT. Sir Ernest SHACKLETON had come within 100mi of the Pole in 1909, and later led other expeditions (1914 and 1921). Admiral Richard Evelyn BYRD was responsible for many Antarctic expeditions, including "Operation High-jump" (1946–47).

Since the International Geophysical Year (1957–58), international cooperation in Antarctica has increased. On Dec. 1, 1959, 12 nations signed the 30-year Antarctic Treaty, temporarily setting aside various territorial claims and reserving the area S of 60°S for peaceful scientific investigation; 38 nations had signed the treaty by 1988. There are now over 40 permanent stations belonging to over 15 countries on the continent itself, the largest being McMurdo Station on the Ross Ice Shelf. In 1988 a new treaty was introduced. If ratified, it would permit controlled oil and mineral exploration on the continent. Some scientists contend that such activities could have serious local and even global environmental consequences.

ANTEATERS, four species of MAMMALS, family Myrmecophagidae, order Edentata, including the Giant Anteater (*Myrmecophaga tridactyla*) and the Tamandua, among others. They have long snouts, tubular mouths and long, sticky tongues with which they catch their food, chiefly ANTS and TERMITES. Other animals with the same adaptations and feeding habits, and thus also sometimes called anteaters, are the aardvark, echidna, numbat and pangolin.

ANTELOPES, swift-moving hollow-horned RUMINANTS of the family bovidae, order Artiodactyla. The term generally includes the American pronghorn, *Antilocapra americana*, the sole living member of the Antilocapridae family and not a true antelope. Common features include a hairy muzzle, narrow cheek teeth and permanent, backward-pointing horns. Distribution is throughout Africa and Asia (except for the pronghorn) in widely varying habitats. They range in size from the Royal Antelope, probably the smallest hoofed mammal, standing about 250mm (10in) high at the shoulders, to the giant eland, which may be as tall as 2m (6.6ft) at the shoulders.

ANTENNA, or **aerial**, a component in an electrical circuit which radiates or receives radio waves. In essence a transmitting antenna is a combination of conductors which converts AC electrical energy into ELECTROMAGNETIC RADIATION. The simple **dipole** consists of two straight conductors aligned end on and energized at the small gap which separates them. The length of the dipole determines the frequency for which this configuration is most efficient. It can be made directional by adding electrically isolated director and reflector conductors in front and behind. Other configurations include the folded dipole, the highly-directional loop antenna and the dish type used for MICROWAVE links. Receiving antennas can consist merely of a short dielectric rod or a length of wire for low-frequency signals. For VHF and microwave signals, complex antenna configurations similar to those used for transmission must be used.

ANTHEIL, George (1900–1959), US composer. He studied under Ernest BLOCH and brought popular motifs into serious music in works such as *Jazz Symphonietta* (1926) and the opera *Transatlantic* (1928–29). In later work he was more traditional, and after WWII he developed a neoclassical style influenced by STRAVINSKY.

ANTHONY, Saint (c250–355), Egyptian hermit. He lived alone in the desert for many years, resisting all the temptations of the devil. His organization of other hermits who gathered around him into a community established the model for Christian MONASTICISM.

ANTHONY, Susan Brownell (1820–1906), major US leader and organizing genius of the fight for women's rights. She was a N.Y. schoolteacher who backed the temperance and abolitionist movements, but devoted herself to female suffrage after befriending Elizabeth Cady STANTON. She co-founded the National Woman Suffrage Association (1869), and served as president of the National American Woman Suffrage Association (1892–1900). She also helped to write *The History of Woman Suffrage*.

ANTHONY OF PADUA, Saint (1195–1231), Franciscan friar, theologian and preacher. He was born near Lisbon, but taught and preached in France and Italy. Canonized a year after his death, he is the patron saint of the poor, and his feast day is June 13. He is invoked to aid the discovery of lost objects.

ANTHRAX, a rare BACTERIAL DISEASE causing characteristic SKIN pustules and LUNG disease; it may progress to SEPTICEMIA and death. Anthrax spores, which can survive for years, may be picked up from infected animals (such as sheep or cattle) or bone meal. Treatment is with PENICILLIN, and people at risk are VACCINATED; the isolation of animal cases and disinfection of spore-bearing material is essential. It was the first disease in which bacteria were shown (by KOCH) to be causative, and it had one of the earliest effective vaccines, developed by PASTEUR.

ANTHROPOID APES, the animals most closely resembling MAN (genus *Homo*) and probably sharing with him a common evolutionary ancestor (see EVOLUTION). Together the genera *Pan* and *Homo* form the family Hominidae in the suborder Anthropoidea (order PRIMATES). The apes concerned are the GORILLA, CHIMPANZEE, and the ORANG-UTAN (family Pongidae), the other members of the superfamily Hominoidea. (See also MONKEYS.)

ANTHROPOLOGY, the study of man from biological, cultural and social viewpoints. HERODOTUS may perhaps be called the father of anthropology, but it was not until the 14th and 15th centuries AD, with the mercantilist expansion of the Old World into new regions, that contact with unknown peoples kindled a scientific interest in the subject. In the modern age there are two main disciplines, physical anthropology and cultural anthropology, the latter embracing social anthropology. **Physical anthropology** is the study of man as a biological species, his past EVOLUTION and his contemporary physical characteristics. In its study of PREHISTORIC MAN it has many links with ARCHAEOLOGY, the difference being that anthropology is concerned with the remains or fossils of man himself while archaeology is concerned with the remains of his material culture. The physical anthropologist also studies the differences among RACES and groups, relying to a great extent on techniques of anthropometry and, more recently, genetic studies. **Cultural anthropology** is divided into several classes. Ethnography is the study of the culture of a single group, either primitive (see PRIMITIVE MAN) or civilized. Fieldwork is the key to ethnographical studies, which are themselves the key to cultural anthropology. ETHNOLOGY is the comparative study of the cultures of two or more groups. Cultural anthropology is also concerned with cultures of the past, and the borderline in this case between it and archaeology is vague. **Social anthropology** is concerned primarily with social relationships and their significance and consequences in primitive societies. In recent years its field has been extended to cover more civilized societies, though these are still more generally considered the domain of SOCIOLOGY.

ANTI-BALLISTIC-MISSILE (ABM) TREATY. See ARMS CONTROL.

ANTIBIOTICS, substances produced by microorganisms that kill or prevent growth of other microorganisms; their properties are made use of in the treatment of bacterial and fungal infection. PASTEUR noted the effect, and Alexander FLEMING in 1929 first showed that the mold *Penicillium notatum* produced PENICILLIN, a substance able to destroy certain bacteria. It was not until 1940 that FLOREY and CHAIN were able to manufacture sufficient penicillin for clinical use. The isolation of streptomycin by WAKSMAN, of gramicidin (from tyrothricin) by DUBOS, and of the cephalosporins were among early discoveries of antibiotics useful in fighting human infection. Numerous varieties of antibiotics now exist, and the search continues for new ones. Semi-synthetic antibiotics, in which the basic molecule is chemically modified, have increased the range of naturally occurring substances.

Each antibiotic is effective against a wider or narrower range of bacteria at a given dosage; their mode of action ranges from preventing cell-wall synthesis to interference with PROTEIN and NUCLEIC ACID metabolism. Bacteria resistant to antibiotics either inherently lack susceptibility to their mode of action or have acquired resistance by ADAPTATION (e.g., by learning to make substances which inactivate an antibiotic). Among the more important antibiotics are the penicillins, cephalosporins, tetracyclines, streptomycin, gentamicin and rifampicin. Each group has its own particular value and side effect, and antibiotics may induce ALLERGY. Many antibiotics are effective by mouth; injection or topical application can also be used.

ANTIBODIES AND ANTIGENS. As one of the body's defense mechanisms, PROTEINS called antibodies are made by specialized white cells to counter foreign proteins known as antigens. Common antigens are VIRUSES, bacterial products (including TOXINS) and allergens (see ALLERGY). A specific antibody is made for each antigen. Antibody reacts with antigen in the body, leading to a number of effects including enhanced phagocytosis by white cells, activation of complement (a substance capable of damaging cell membranes) and HISTAMINE release. Antibodies are produced faster and in greater numbers if the body has previously encountered the particular antigen. Immunity to second attacks of diseases such as MEASLES and CHICKENPOX, and VACCINATION against diseases not yet contracted are based on this principle. Antibody detection in blood samples may show agglutinins, precipitins or complement fixation, according to the technique used and the antibody involved.

ANTICOAGULANTS, drugs that interfere with blood CLOTTING, used to treat or prevent THROMBOSIS and clot EMBOLISM. The two main types are heparin, which is injected and has an immediate but short-lived effect, and the coumarins (including warfarin), which are taken by mouth and are longer-lasting. They affect different parts of the clotting mechanism, coumarins depleting factors made in the LIVER.

ANTI-COMINTERN PACT, an agreement between Germany and Japan (1936), ostensibly to counter the influence of a Russian-inspired anti-capitalist organization, the Comintern (Communist International). The pact was later joined by Italy, Spain, Bulgaria, Romania, Hungary, Denmark and Finland, countries that directly or indirectly aided the German war effort in WWII.

ANTIDEPRESSANTS, drugs used in the treatment of DEPRESSION; they are of two types: tricyclic compounds and monoamine oxidase inhibitors. Although their mode of action is obscure, they have revolutionized the treatment of depression.

ANTIETAM, Battle of, a bloody encounter which repulsed Confederate General Robert E. LEE's first northward thrust during the Civil War. It was fought in Sept. 1862 when 40,000 men under Lee met 70,000 Union troops under McCLELLAN at Antietam Creek, Md. McClellan used only two-thirds of his army and sustained 12,000 casualties, while Lee used his total force, losing almost a quarter of it. Halted before he could reach Washington, Lee was forced to retreat across the Potomac.

ANTIFEDERALISTS, name given in the US to those who opposed the ratification of the Federal Constitution of 1787. They feared that centralized power would become despotic. After the new government's inauguration, the Antifederalist group joined the Republicans to form the Democratic-Republican party under Jefferson.

ANTIFREEZE, a substance added to water, particularly that in AUTOMOBILE cooling systems, to prevent ice forming in cold weather. The additive most commonly used is ethylene glycol; METHANOL and ETHANOL, although cheaper alternatives, tend to need more frequent replacement, being much more volatile.

ANTIGENS. See ANTIBODIES AND ANTIGENS.

ANTIGONE, in Greek myth, the daughter of OEDIPUS, noted for her fidelity and courage. She followed her father into exile. Later she buried her brother Polynices against the orders of King Creon. Creon imprisoned Antigone, who killed herself, provoking the suicide of Creon's son Heamon, to whom she was bethrothed. Antigone is the heroine of plays by SOPHOCLES, EURIPIDES and ANOUILH.

ANTIGUA AND BARBUDA, independent nation in the West Indies, largest and most developed of the Leeward Islands.

Official name: Antigua and Barbuda
Capital: St. John's
Area: Antigua (108sq mi); Barbuda (62sq mi)
Population: 82,400
Language: English
Religion: Protestant
Monetary Unit: 1 East Caribbean dollar = 100 cents

Land. It includes the islands of Antigua and Barbuda, both low-lying and of volcanic origin. White sandy beaches, the nation's principal resource, fringe the coasts; few places rise to more than 1,000ft above sea level. The climate is tropical with a dry season Jul.–Dec.

People and Economy. The population is predominantly of African and British origins. St. John's is the largest town and chief port. Tourism is the principal economic activity, especially in the winter months. Cotton replaced sugar as the chief crop in the 19th century, and some tropical fruits are also grown. The US maintains a large naval and army base near Parham.

History. Antigua was discovered and named by COLUMBUS in 1493. The island passed briefly to Spanish and French control in the 17th century and to the British in 1666. With Barbuda as a dependency it became a self-governing West Indies Associated State in 1967 and independent in 1981. Leaders on Barbuda fought unsuccessfully to remain a British colony and continue to claim neglect by the government on more prosperous Antigua.

ANTIHISTAMINES, drugs that counteract HISTAMINE action; they are useful in HAY FEVER and HIVES (in which ALLERGY causes histamine release) and in some insect bites. They also act as SEDATIVES and may relieve MOTION SICKNESS.

ANTIKNOCK ADDITIVES, substances added to GASOLINE to slow the burning of the fuel and thus prevent "knocking," the premature ignition of the combustion mixture in the cylinder head. Most widely used is LEAD tetraethyl [$Pb(C_2H_5)_4$]. This is usually mixed with 1,2-dibromo- and 1,2-dichloroethane, which prevent the formation of lead deposits in the engine.

ANTI-MASONIC PARTY, US political faction active from 1827 to 1836. It emerged after the disappearance in 1826 of William Morgan, author of a book revealing the secrets of MASONRY. The Masons were accused of murdering him, and public outrage was exploited politically against Masons in office, first by Thurlow Weed and William H. SEWARD in New York state against Martin VAN BUREN and the Albany Regency (the Democrats' political machine), then by a national campaign to defeat President Andrew Jackson, himself a Mason, which won a number of congressional seats.

ANTIMATTER, a variety of MATTER differing from the matter which predominates in our part of the universe in that it is composed of antiparticles rather than particles. Individual antiparticles, many of which have been found in COSMIC RAY showers or produced using particle ACCELERATORS, differ from their particle counterparts in that they are oppositely charged (as with the antiproton-PROTON pair) or in that their magnetic moment is orientated in the opposite sense with respect to their SPIN (as with the antineutrino and neutrino). In our part of the universe antiparticles are very short-lived, being rapidly annihilated in collisions with their corresponding particles, their mass-energy reappearing as a gamma-ray PHOTON. (The reverse is also true; a high-energy gamma ray sometimes spontaneously forms itself into a positron-ELECTRON pair.) However, it is by no means inconceivable that regions of the universe exist in which all the matter is antimatter, composed of what are to us antiparticles. The first antiparticle, the positron (i.e., the antielectron), was discovered by C. D. ANDERSON in 1932, only four years after DIRAC had theoretically predicted the existence of antiparticles. (See also SUBATOMIC PARTICLES.)

ANTINOMIANISM, heretical doctrine that Christians are set free by grace from the obligation to obey the moral law, especially the TEN COMMANDMENTS. In the patristic period it was held by many gnostics (see GNOSTICISM) and the followers of MARCION and MONTANUS. At the Reformation it was revived by Johann Agricola and the ANABAPTISTS, though opposed by the Reformers, and was later held by radical sects during Cromwell's rule In England, by Anne HUTCHINSON in New England and by many METHODISTS and dispensationalists. Antinomians have often been accused of

licentiousness, in some cases justly.

ANTIOCH (now Antakya), ancient city in Asia Minor on the Orontes R. Founded c300 BC by Seleucus Nicator, it became the capital of the Seleucid Empire and, in 64 BC, the Asian capital of the Roman Empire. Antioch was an important center of early Christianity. Antakya, the modern commercial city, became part of French-administered Syria after WWI and joined Turkey in 1939. Pop 78,000.

ANTIPARTICLES. See ANTIMATTER; SUBATOMIC PARTICLES.

ANTIPOPE, a pretender to the papal throne, elected by faction in the Roman Catholic Church or by a secular ruler. The first antipope was Hippolytus (3rd century); the last was Felix V (abdicated 1449). In the GREAT SCHISM (1378) Italy elected Urban VI while France set up court for Clement VII in Avignon. Their successors were deposed by the Council of Constance (1415).

ANTI-SALOON LEAGUE, temperance organization established in 1893 to curb the sale of liquor. It played an important part in the campaign to achieve national PROHIBITION.

ANTI-SEMITISM, hostility towards Jews, ranging from social prejudice to genocide. Common motives for anti-Semitism include religious opposition to Judaism, national resentment of a people who remain in some ways apart from the life of the country they live in and simple jealousy of the Jews' material success. Anti-Semites have often justified their standing by claiming that the Jews' exile and persecution were punishment for their part in Christ's crucifixion. Segregation, expulsion and massacres have dogged Europe's Jewish communities, notably in the Middle Ages, and later in Tsarist Russia and in Nazi Germany before and during WWII, when some 6,000,000 Jews were put to death in concentration camps at AUSCHWITZ, BELSEN, BUCHENWALD and elsewhere. Despite the decline of avowed anti-Semitism since WWII, anti-Jewish feeling has increased in Arab lands hostile to the young Jewish state of Israel. Jews are still persecuted in the USSR.

ANTISEPTICS, or **germicides,** substances that kill or prevent the growth of microorganisms (particularly BACTERIA and FUNGI); they are used to avoid sepsis from contamination of body surfaces and surgical instruments. Some antiseptics are used as disinfectants to make places or objects germ-free. Vinegar and cedar oil have been used from earliest times to treat wounds and for embalming. Modern antisepsis was pioneered by SEMMELWEIS, LISTER and KOCH, and dramatically reduced deaths from childbirth and surgery. Commonly used antiseptics and disinfectants include IODINE, CHLORINE, hypochlorous acid, ETHANOL, isopropanol (see ALCOHOLS), phenols (including hexachlorophene), quaternary ammonium salts (see AMMONIA), formaldehyde, hydrogen peroxide, potassium permanganate, and acriflavine (an acridine dye). HEAT, ULTRAVIOLET and ionizing radiations also have antiseptic effects. (See also STERILIZATION; ASEPSIS.)

ANTITOXINS, antibodies produced in the body against the TOXINS of some bacteria. They are also formed after INOCULATION of toxoid, chemically inactivated toxin that can still confer IMMUNITY.

ANTONELLO DA MESSINA (c1430–1479), allegedly the first Italian to paint in oils. He was influenced by Dutch and Flemish painters and excelled in spatial composition. The S. Cassiano altarpiece in Venice and a *St. Sebastian* in Dresden are among his major works.

ANTONESCU, Ion (1882–1946), Romanian general and pro-Nazi right-wing leader. Becoming prime minister in 1940, he persuaded King Carol to abdicate and established a military dictatorship favoring the AXIS POWERS. He was executed as a war criminal.

ANTONINUS PIUS (86–161 AD), Roman emperor (138–161), the last to achieve relative stability in the empire. Chosen consul in 120, he adopted MARCUS AURELIUS and Lucius Verus as successors. He was a prudent and economical ruler, tolerant of Christians.

ANTONIONI, Michelangelo (1912–   ), Italian film director of international renown. His motion pictures include *L'Avventura* (1959), *La Notte* (1961), *Eclipse* (1962), *The Red Desert* (1964), *Blow Up* (1966) and *Zabriskie Point* (1969).

ANTONY, Mark (Marcus Antonius; c82–30 BC), Roman general who became one of three joint rulers of the Roman state. He fought notably in Gaul and became a tribune in 50 BC and a consul in 44 BC. After Caesar's murder, Antony, his brother-in-law Octavian (see AUGUSTUS) and Lepidus formed a Triumvirate (43 BC), dividing the empire into three. Antony controlled the E from the Adriatic to the Euphrates, but alienated Octavian by falling in love with the Egyptian queen, CLEOPATRA, and combining forces with her. Attacked by Octavian, Antony committed suicide after his naval defeat at ACTIUM.

ANTONY OF THEBES, Saint (c251–356), Egyptian hermit, considered the founder of Christian MONASTICISM. He founded a desert community of ascetics near Fayum, then lived alone in a mountain cave near the Red Sea and died aged over 100. He supported St. ATHANASIUS in the Arian controversy.

ANTS, social INSECTS of the family Formicidae of the order Hymenoptera, recognizable through the petiole or "waist" between abdomen and thorax. There are some 3,500 species of ant, each species containing three distinct castes: male, female and worker. **Males** can be found only at certain times of year: winged, they are not readmitted to the nest after the mating flight. The **queen** is likewise winged, but she rubs her wings off after mating; she may survive for as long as 15 years, still laying eggs fertilized during the original mating flight. The **workers** are sterile females, sometimes falling into two distinct size categories, the larger ones (soldiers) defending the nest and assisting with heavier work. The most primitive ants (*Ponerinae*) may form nests with only a few individuals; nests of wood ants (*Formica rufa*), however, may contain more than 100,000 individuals. *Dorylinae*, the so-called army ants, do not build nests at all but are nomadic, traveling in "armies" up to 150,000 strong: like *Ponerinae* (but unlike the more sophisticated species, which are vegetarian) they are carnivorous. Nesting ants welcome some insects, mainly beetles, to their nests and often "farm" APHIDS for honeydew.

ANTWERP, Belgium's second-largest city and leading port, on the Scheldt R 60mi from the North Sea. It is the capital of Antwerp province, the commercial and cultural center of Flemish Belgium (with a large university) and an important manufacturing city, with oil, metal, automobile and diamond industries. Around 1560 it was the leading port of Europe, and the center of the great Flemish school of painting: artists like BRUEGEL, RUBENS and VAN DYCK worked there. Pop 194,000.

ANZA, Juan Bautista de (1735–1788), Spanish explorer who founded San Francisco in 1776. He made one of the longest journeys in the history of North American exploration, probing N from the deserts of S Cal. via San Gabriel (Los Angeles) and Monterey.

ANZIO, Italian fishing port and seaside resort about 30mi S of Rome. As the ancient Roman Antium, the town was the birthplace of the emperors CALIGULA and NERO. Anzio was badly damaged when the Allies landed there in Jan. 1944, and a force of 50,000 men was pinned down at the beachhead by German counteroffensives.

ANZUS PACT, treaty signed on Sept. 1, 1951, by Australia, New Zealand and the US for mutual defense in the Pacific. The name consists of the initials of the participating countries, which meet annually. In 1985 New Zealand declared itself a nuclear-free zone, making the status of the treaty uncertain.

AORTA, the chief systemic ARTERY, distributing oxygenated blood to the whole body except the LUNGS via its branches. (See also BLOOD CIRCULATION; HEART.)

APACHE INDIANS, North American Indians of the Athabaskan linguistic family. The major tribes were the Jicarilla, Lipan, Mescalero, Airavaipa, Coyotero, Pinaleno, Kiowa and Chiricahua. Apaches lived in SW North America, maintaining a nomadic hunting culture that depended on free movement over a large area. The arrival of white settlers thus threatened their survival, and many Apaches rejected repeated federal government attempts to confine the tribes to reservations. Bloody conflicts followed, and Apache numbers were greatly decimated by 1896, when the last great Apache chief, GERONIMO, was captured. Most present-day Apaches live on federal reservations in Okla., N.M. and Ariz.

APARTHEID, policy of strict racial segregation practiced in the Republic of South Africa in order to maintain the domination of the white minority. Segregation and discrimination against non-white peoples is observed in housing, employment, education and public services, and enforced by legislation punishing dissent or resistance with imprisonment, exile or house arrest. The policy also involves the "separate development" of eight Bantu homelands, where black people have a measure of self-government. Apartheid is almost universally condemned outside South Africa. (See also AFRICAN NATIONAL CONGRESS (ANC).)

APELLES (4th century BC), Greek artist reputed to be the greatest painter of the ancient world. He worked as court painter of Macedonia, and his portraits of Alexander the Great were particularly famous. None of Apelles' paintings have survived.

APENNINES, mountain chain forming the backbone of the Italian peninsula. It is about 800mi long and 25–80mi wide. The highest peak is Monte Corno (9,560ft). The predominant rocks are limestone and dolomite; sulfur and cinnabar (sulfide of mercury) are mined in the volcanic area near Vesuvius. Olives, grapes and grains are widely grown; lack of fertile topsoil prevents intensive agriculture.

APES. See ANTHROPOID APES.

APHASIA, a speech defect resulting from injury to certain areas of the brain and causing inability to use or comprehend words; it may be partial (dysphasia) or total. Common causes are cerebral THROMBOSIS, HEMORRHAGE and brain TUMORS. (See SPEECH AND SPEECH DISORDERS.)

APHIDS, or **greenflies** or **plant lice,** some 4,000 species of sap-feeding insects, comprising the family Aphididae of the order Homoptera. They have needle-like mouthparts with which they pierce the plant tissue, the pressure within this forcing the sap into the insect's gut. Because of the damage caused by their feeding and because many species carry harmful VIRUSES, aphids are one of the world's greatest crop pests. The life cycle is a complex one, so that within a species there may at any one time be a diversity of forms; winged and wingless, reproducing sexually or parthogenetically. Aphids excrete (see EXCRETION) a substance known as honeydew, an important food source for ANTS and other insects.

APHRODITE, the Greek goddess of love, fertility and beauty. She was supposedly the daughter of ZEUS and Dione, or alternatively rose from the sea near Cyprus. Her intensely sensual beauty aroused jealousy among other goddesses, particularly after Paris chose her as the most beautiful goddess over Hera and ATHENA. Aphrodite was the wife of Hephaestus (but took divine and mortal lovers). Aeneas and Eros were her sons. The Greeks honored her with major shrines at Athens, Corinth, Sparta, Cos, Cnidus and Cyprus, and the Romans identified her with Venus.

APOCALYPSE, a prophetic revelation, usually about the end of the world and the ensuing establishment of a heavenly kingdom. Jewish and Christian apocalyptic writings appeared in Palestine between 200 BC and 150 AD and offered hope of liberation to a people under alien rule. (See also MESSIAH; REVELATION, BOOK OF.)

APOCRYPHA, writings not accepted by Jews or all Christians as canonical (that is, as part of Holy Scripture). Protestants use the term mainly for books written in the two centuries before Christ and included in the SEPTUAGINT and the VULGATE, but not in the Hebrew Bible. These include Esdras I and II, Tobit, Judith, additions to Esther, the Wisdom of Solomon, Ecclesiasticus, Baruch, the Song of the Three Children,

Susanna and the Elders, Bel and the Dragon, the Prayer of Manasses and Maccabees I and II. (See also BIBLE: PSEUDEPIGRAPHA.)

APOLLINAIRE, Guillaume (real name: Wilhelm Apollinaris de Kostrowitzki; 1880–1918), influential French avant-garde poet and critic. The friend of DERAIN, DUFY and PICASSO, he helped to publicize Cubist and primitive art. His poetry, as in the collections *Alcools* (1913) and *Calligrammes* (1918), often anticipated SURREALISM with its use of startling associations and juxtapositions.

APOLLO, major deity in Greek and Roman mythology. In the Greek myths, Apollo was the son of ZEUS and Leto, and twin of Artemis. Second only to Zeus, he had the power of the sun as giver of light and life. He was the god of justice and masculine beauty, and the purifier of those stained by crime. He was the divine patron of the arts, leader of the MUSES, and god of music and poetry. Apollo was a healer, but could also send disease, and from his foreknowledge he spoke through the oracle at DELPHI. The Romans adopted Apollo, honoring him as healer and as god of the sun.

APOPLEXY, obsolete term for STROKE due to cerebral HEMORRHAGE.

APOSTLES, the 12 disciples closest to Jesus, whom he chose to proclaim his teaching. They were Andrew, John, Bartholomew, Judas, Jude, the two Jameses, Matthew, Peter, Philip, Simon and Thomas. When Judas died, Matthias replaced him. Paul and Barnabas became known as apostles for their work in spreading the Gospel.

APOSTLES' CREED, a CREED ascribed to Christ's apostles and maintained in its present form since the early Middle Ages. The Roman Catholic Church uses it in the sacraments of baptism and confirmation. It is also used by various Protestant denominations.

APOSTOLIC FATHERS, early Christian writers of the first two centuries after Christ, regarded by tradition as the disciples of the 12 apostles. They include Paul's assistant Barnabas; Hermas, a 2nd-century Roman; St. Clement of Rome, a disciple of Peter; Polycarp and Papias, followers of John; and Ignatius, bishop of Antioch.

APOSTOLIC SUCCESSION, a doctrine held by several Christian churches. They believe that Christ's apostles ordained the first bishops and other priests, that these ordained their successors, and so on, forging an unbroken chain of succession reaching to the present day which thereby guarantees

their authority. Many Protestants, excepting Episcopalians, reject the doctrine as unproven and unnecessary.

APPALACHIA, region of the SE US embracing the economically poor S part of the Appalachian Mts. It includes parts of 13 states, covers 355 counties and has 16 million inhabitants. In 1965 Congress voted $1.2 billion towards rebuilding the region's declining economy and improving social conditions.

APPALACHIAN MOUNTAINS, mountain system of E North America about 1,800mi long and 120–375mi wide, stretching south from Newfoundland to central Ala. The system's ancient sandstone, limestone, slate and other rocks have been folded, eroded, uplifted and again eroded. Major ranges of the N include the Notre Dame, Green, and White Mts. The central area has the Allegheny Mts and part of the Blue Ridge Mts. The S contains the S Blue Ridge, Cumberland, Black and Great Smoky Mts. The highest peak is Mt Mitchell (6,684ft) in N.C.

Appalachian forests yield much timber, and rich deposits of coal and iron have stimulated the growth of such industrial areas as Birmingham and Pittsburgh. The Connecticut, Hudson, Delaware, Susquehanna, Potomac, Kanawha, Tennessee and other rivers have cut deep gaps in the ranges. But in the early years of the US the Appalachians were a barrier to westward expansion.

APPALACHIAN TRAIL, the longest marked hiking trail in the world, stretching over 2,000mi along the crest of the Appalachian Mts from Mt Katahdin in N Me. to Springer Mountain in N Ga.

APPEL, Karel (1921–   ), Dutch abstract expressionist painter, a founder of the experimental art group, CoBrA. His work is marked by colorful, aggressive sensuality.

APPENDICITIS, inflammation of the appendix, often caused by obstruction to its narrow opening, followed by swelling and bacterial infection. Acute appendicitis may lead to rupture of the organ, formation of an ABSCESS or PERITONITIS. Symptoms include abdominal pain, usually in the right lower ABDOMEN, nausea, vomiting and FEVER. Early surgical removal of the appendix is essential; any abscess requires drainage of PUS and delayed excision.

APPIA, Adolphe (1862–1928), Swiss stage designer whose ideas revolutionized early 20th-century theater. He stressed the use of three-dimensional settings and of mobile lighting with controlled intensity and color.

APPIAN WAY, the oldest and most famous Roman road. Built by Appius Claudius

Caecus in 312 BC to link Rome and Capua, it was later extended to Brindisi, covering in all about 350mi. Sections near Rome are still largely intact.

APPLE, popular edible fruit of the apple tree, *Malus sylvestris* (family Rosaceae), widely cultivated in temperate climates. Over 7,000 varieties are known but only about 40 are commercially important, the most popular US variety being Delicious. Some 15%–20% of the world's crop is produced in the US, mostly in the states of Wash., N.Y., Cal., Mich., and Va. There are three main types of apples: cooking, dessert, and those used in making cider.

APPLESEED, Johnny (1774–1845), US folk hero, a mild eccentric whose real name was John Chapman. A pioneer in the Ohio river region, he wandered around for some 40 years, planting and tending apple orchards.

APPOMATTOX COURT HOUSE, US historical site in central Va., where the Civil War was ended with Lee's surrender to Grant on April 9, 1865. The McLean House (where the surrender took place) and other buildings have been reconstructed as part of the 972-acre Appomattox Court House National Historical Park.

APPORTIONMENT, Legislative, the distribution of voters' representation in the lawmaking bodies. Although each state, whatever its size, elects two senators only, members of the US House of Representatives are elected from districts with equal populations, and the federal census results in a reapportionment of seats each decade. Since the 1980 census, each congressman represents about 500,000 voters.

In the past, state legislature district boundaries were often erratically drawn to give voting advantage to one political party (see GERRYMANDER). Also, most counties had equal representation in state senates; thus, one vote in a rural county might be worth 30 times that in a city, due to lower population. But in 1962 the Supreme Court ruled that unfair districting may be brought before federal courts, and later rulings established that one man's vote should be "worth as much as another's," or, "one man, one vote." This principle is slowly shifting political power from rural to urban areas.

APRICOT, orange-colored fruit of the apricot tree, *Prunus armeniaca* (family Rosaceae), native to China but grown throughout temperate regions. Commercial production is mainly in central and SE Asia, Europe and the US; over 90% of the US crop comes from California. Apricots are eaten fresh, or preserved by drying or canning; the kernels are used to make a liqueur. Apricot trees are often grown as ornamentals.

APRIL, fourth month of the year in the Gregorian Calendar; first full spring month in the Northern Hemisphere. The Christian EASTER and Jewish PASSOVER usually fall in April. The month is probably named from *aperire* (Latin: to open), referring to the opening spring buds. Birthstone: diamond. Astrological signs: Aries and Taurus.

APRIL FOOLS' DAY, or **All Fools' Day,** April 1, the traditional day for practical jokes. The custom probably began in France in 1564, when New Year's Day was changed from April 1 to Jan. 1. Those continuing to observe April 1 were ridiculed.

APTITUDE TESTS, tests designed to measure a person's potential ability. Although satisfactory in dealing with well-defined skills such as problem-solving, they are less successful in evaluating artistic skills. Widely used in vocational guidance and college entry, they are also used for staff selection by some companies.

APULEIUS, Lucius (c125–185 AD), Roman author of *Metamorphoses* or *The Golden Ass*. The hero of this story is turned into an ass, whose humorous adventures provide a fascinating insight into contemporary Roman society.

APULIA (Italian: *Puglia*), SE region forming the "heel" of the "boot" of Italy. It is composed of the provinces of Bari, Brindisi, Foggia, Lecce and Taranto. Its principal town and main port is Bari; it also contains the important naval base and steel industry of Taranto.

AQABA, Gulf of, NE arm of the Red Sea, between the Sinai Peninsula and Saudi Arabia. Geologically part of the GREAT RIFT VALLEY of Africa and Asia, it is some 110mi long and 5–17mi wide. At the N end of the Gulf stand the ports of Aqaba (Jordan) and Elat (Israel). The Egyptian blockade of Elat sparked off the 1967 Arab-Israeli Six Days' War.

AQUALUNG, or **scuba** (*s*elf-*c*ontained *u*nderwater *b*reathing *a*pparatus), a device allowing divers to breathe and move about freely underwater. It comprises a mouthpiece, a connecting tube, a valve and at least one compressed-air cylinder. The key component is the "demand valve" which allows the diver to breathe air at the PRESSURE prevailing in the surrounding water however great the pressure in his supply cylinder. Used air is vented into the water.

AQUATINT, an ENGRAVING process used with particular success by GOYA, in which the plate is repeatedly etched through a porous (usually resin) ground. What are to produce the white areas of the finished print are stopped out with acid-resisting varnish before the first ETCHING, the other areas being stopped out in order of increasing darkness between subsequent etchings. The color-wash effect of aquatint is particularly striking when used in combination with drypoint.

AQUAVIT, or akvavit, colorless spirits distilled from grain or potatoes and flavored with caraway seeds. It is popular in Scandinavia.

AQUEDUCT, man-made conduit for water. The Babylonians and Egyptians built large-scale underground aqueducts, but the Romans preferred a row of arches supporting the channels along which water flowed downhill from mountains to cities. Rome itself was supplied by nine aqueducts, but the most famous Roman ones are at Segovia and Tarragona, Spain, and near Nîmes, France (the *Pont du Gard*).

AQUIFER, an underground rock body through which GROUNDWATER can easily percolate and possessing the porosity required to store sufficient quantities of water to supply wells. SANDSTONES, gravel beds and jointed LIMESTONES make good aquifers.

AQUINAS, Saint Thomas (c1225–1274 AD), known as the "angelic doctor," major Christian theologian and philosopher who attempted to reconcile faith with reason. In his *Summa Theologica* he uses Aristotelian logic to examine the existence of God: he finds God the logical uncaused cause, the prime reason for order in the universe. He sees man as a rational social animal gaining knowledge from sensory experience. His morality is based on the principle of man's harmony with himself, with other men and with God. Thomism, the philosophy of St. Thomas, has been very influential, and his teachings are basic to Roman Catholic theology.

AQUINO, Corazon (1933–   ), Philippine political leader. The widow of Benigno S. Aquino, Jr., a prominent opponent of President Ferdinand MARCOS assassinated in 1983, she became president in 1986 after an election "officially" won by Marcos. In the face of popular demonstrations, however, Marcos went into exile in the US and Aquino formed a government. She survived several coup attempts prompted by the army's dissatisfaction with her initial policy of seeking reconciliation with communist insurgents. She was also criticized for the slowness of land-reform efforts. Her personal popularity proved her strongest resource.

AQUITAINE, historic French region, between the rivers Garonne and Loire, extending to the Pyrenees. Henry II of England's marriage to Eleanor of Aquitaine in 1152 resulted in centuries of Anglo-French territorial conflicts. The French crown regained control of Aquitaine in 1453, at the end of the HUNDRED YEARS' WAR.

ARAB, one whose language is ARABIC and who identifies with Arab culture. Besides the countries of the Arabian Peninsula, the Arab world includes Algeria, Egypt, Iraq, Jordan, Lebanon, Libya, Morocco, Sudan, Syria and Tunisia. Arab culture spread after the coming of MOHAMMED (c570 AD). In the 7th century the Arabs extended their hegemony from NW Africa and Spain to Afghanistan and N India, where many non-Arabic peoples were converted to the religion of ISLAM, adopting Arabic language and culture. Although Arab political control crumbled in the 10th and 11th centuries, elements of the culture remained.

The precepts of Islam, as set out in the KORAN, still govern much of Arab life and social institutions. Non-Muslim peoples who are also Arabs include Palestinian, Lebanese and Syrian Christians. In the 20th century the discovery and exploitation of petroleum in Arab lands has resulted in sudden wealth and modernization for many Arab countries. Arab reaction to the creation of the state of Israel has strengthened Pan-Arab nationalism and led to the ARAB-ISRAELI WARS.

ARABESQUE, elaborate decorative style characterized by curved or intertwining shapes with grotesque, animal, human or symbolic forms and delicate foliage. Arab culture promoted the use of geometric rather than figurative forms.

ARABIA (Arabic: *Jazirat al-Arab,* the "island of the Arabs"), SW Asian peninsula bounded by the Red Sea, Indian Ocean and Persian Gulf. It comprises Saudi Arabia, the Republic of Yemen, the Southern Yemen People's Republic, the Sultanate of Oman and the Persian Gulf States, including Bahrain, Kuwait, Qatar and the United Arab Emirates. The world's richest reserves of petroleum were discovered in the peninsula in the 1930s and have since flooded wealth into an almost feudal seminomadic society, creating large income-differentials within it. In 1973, Saudi Arabia and other Arab countries cut back oil supplies to the West, thus adding an important new economic weapon to the continuing Arab-Israeli conflict.

Between the birth of Christ and the emergence of MOHAMMED (c570 AD), various foreign powers influenced or controlled the area. Mecca, on a busy caravan route, was a prosperous trading center; but other towns remained little more than small oasis farming settlements. When Mohammed first achieved prominence, Arabia was divided between continually warring tribes. His founding of ISLAM resulted in a partial unification of the Arab tribes and rapid political and territorial expansion. By 800 Muslims controlled almost half the civilized world. But this power crumbled by the 11th century, when Turkey began its domination of the area. In the 18th and 19th centuries the Islamic Wahabi movement weakened this power. In the 19th century Britain gained considerable footholds in Aden and on the Persian Gulf. After the Turks joined the Central Powers at the start of WWI, the British successfully encouraged the Arabs to revolt (1916) and by 1932 Saudi Arabia had extended political control over most of the region.

ARABIAN GULF. See PERSIAN GULF.

ARABIAN NIGHTS, or *The Thousand and One Nights,* a collection of 8th–16th century Arabic stories, probably of Indian origin with Persian and Arab additions. The stories, which include *Aladdin, Ali Baba* and *Sinbad,* are linked by Scheherazade who, sentenced to die at dawn, tells her husband the king one story per night, leaving the ending till the next day. She is reprieved after 1,001 nights.

ARABIAN SEA, NW Indian Ocean, between India and Arabia. Connected with the Persian Gulf by the Gulf of Oman, and with the Red Sea by the Gulf of Aden. Its ports include Bombay and Karachi.

ARABIC, one of the SEMITIC LANGUAGES. The Arabic ALPHABET comprises 28 letters, all consonants, vowels being expressed either by positioned points or, in some cases, by insertion of the letters *alif, waw* and *ya* in positions where they would not otherwise occur, thereby representing the long *a, u* and *i* respectively. Arabic is written from right to left. Classical Arabic, the language of the Koran, is today used occasionally in writing, rarely in speech; a standardized modern Arabic being used for newspapers, etc. Arabic played a large part in the dissemination of knowledge through medieval Europe as many ancient Greek and Roman texts were available solely in Arabic translation.

ARAB-ISRAELI WARS, the results of persistent conflicts between Israel and the Arabs since the BALFOUR DECLARATION (1917) pronounced British Palestine a Jewish national home. When Britain's mandate ended, the Jews declared an independent state of Israel (May 14, 1948). The next day, Egypt, Iraq, Transjordan (Jordan), Lebanon and Syria attacked, but within a month Israel had occupied the greater part of Palestine. By July 1949, separate ceasefires had been concluded with the Arab states, where hundreds of thousands of Palestinian Arabs now sought refuge.

On Oct. 29, 1956, with the Suez Canal and Gulf of Aqaba closed to her ships, Israel invaded Egypt, which had nationalized the canal in July. British and French supporting troops occupied the canal banks, but were replaced by a UN force after international furor. By March 1957 all Israeli forces had left Egypt in exchange for access to the Gulf of Aqaba.

In 1967 Egypt closed the gulf to Israel, and on June 5, at the start of the Six-Day War, Israeli air strikes destroyed Arab air forces on the ground. Israel won the west bank of the Jordan R, the Golan Heights, the Gaza Strip, the Sinai Peninsula and the Old City of Jerusalem. A ceasefire was accepted by June 10. In the following years, worldwide Arab anti-Jewish terrorism became common, reaching a climax in the 1972 Munich Olympic massacre of Israeli athletes.

On Oct. 6, 1973, Yom Kippur (the Jewish Day of Atonement), Egypt and Syria attacked Israel to regain the lost territories. A ceasefire was signed on Nov. 11, 1973. Although Israeli troops penetrated deep into Syria and crossed onto the W bank of the Suez Canal, initial Arab success restored confidence and encouraged Arab states to use economic measures, principally an oil boycott, against Israel's Western sympathizers.

Talks between Egypt and Israel led to a peace treaty (1979). But tension ran high elsewhere, especially in Lebanon, used as a guerrilla base by the Palestinians and a target for Israeli attacks. In June 1982 Israel invaded Lebanon in order to destroy strongholds of the PALESTINE LIBERATION ORGANIZATION (PLO) guerrillas. Subsequently, under a US-sponsored plan, the guerrillas left Beirut for other countries willing to accept them, and a multinational peacekeeping force, including US marines, landed in Lebanon. Israeli troops withdrew but retained a security zone in S Lebanon. Terrorist attacks on Israel from Lebanon were answered with ground and air retaliation.

The so-called peace process, begun by the CAMP DAVID AGREEMENT of 1978, went nowhere. Israelis debated the wisdom of offering land (the West Bank) for peace; in any case, the PLO refused to renounce its commitment to Israel's destruction, and no Arab state would negotiate on behalf of the Palestinians. Violent demonstrations by Palestinian youths in the West Bank and Gaza (the *intifada*) throughout 1988, Jordan's abdication of its claim to the West Bank, and Israeli elections in Nov. 1988 raised the possibility that the peace process might be revived.

ARAB LEAGUE, an organization to promote economic, cultural and political cooperation among Arab states, set up on March 22, 1945. Although quite successful in its first two aims, it achieved real political unity of action only in 1956 (Suez Crisis), 1961 (Franco-Tunisian conflict) and 1973 (cutback of oil to the West). Egypt was an original member of the league but was suspended in 1979 after it signed a peace treaty with Israel, and the league's headquarters were moved from Cairo to Tunis. In the 1980s much of the league's attention was focused on the Iran-Iraq war. The organization supported the Palestinian uprising in the West Bank and Gaza that began in Dec. 1987. Member states (excluding Egypt) are Algeria, Bahrain, Djibouti, Iraq, Jordan, Kuwait, Lebanon, Libya, Mauritania, Morocco, Oman, Qatar, Saudi Arabia, Somalia, Sudan, Syria, Tunisia, the United Arab Emirates, Yemen, Southern Yemen, and the government of the Palestine Liberation Organization.

ARAFAT, Yasir (1929–   ), Palestinian political leader. Born in Jerusalem and educated as an engineer in Cairo, Arafat became head of the anti-Israel Al Fatah guerrilla movement, the largest component of the coalition PALESTINE LIBERATION ORGANIZATION (PLO). In 1969 he became chairman of the PLO. He won recognition of the PLO as the "sole legitimate" representative of the Palestinian people from the Arab states and gained diplomatic recognition from the United Nations and more than 100 countries. Regarded as a moderate, he adhered to the rejectionist policy demanded by extremists, never repudiating the PLO's commitment to the destruction of Israel and continuing to wage guerrilla warfare against that country. His authority was challenged by radicals when the PLO was driven from Lebanon in 1982, but he remained the only leader acceptable to all PLO factions.

ARAGO, Dominique François Jean (1786–1853), French physicist and mathematician whose work helped establish the wave theory of LIGHT. He discovered the polarization of light in quartz crystals (1811) and was awarded the Royal Society's Copley Medal in 1825 for demonstrating the magnetic effect of a rotating copper disk.

ARAGON, Louis (1897–1982), French novelist, poet and journalist, a leading figure in the dadaist and surrealist movements of the 1920s and 1930s, as is reflected in his early poetry. He joined the Communist Party in the 1930s, and thereafter turned to social realism. After WWII he edited the left-wing weekly *Les Lettres Françaises*.

ARAGON, historic region of NE Spain, stretching from the central Pyrenées to S of the Ebro R. The medieval kingdom of Aragon comprised what are now Huesca, Teruel and Saragossa provinces though the influence of the kings of Aragon was more extensive. King Ferdinand II of Aragon's marriage to Isabella of Castile (1469) laid the foundations of a unified Spain. Aragon's sovereignty was ended 1707–09 by Philip V during the war of SPANISH SUCCESSION (1701–14).

ARAL SEA, inland sea or saltwater lake covering 24,904sq mi in the S USSR. It is the fourth-largest lake in the world and is fed by the Amu Darya and Syr Darya rivers. The sea is commercially important for its bass, carp, perch and sturgeon.

ARAMAEANS, nomadic Semites of the N Syrian desert in the 11th to 8th centuries BC. They assimilated features of earlier FERTILE CRESCENT civilizations. Most of the smaller Aramaean tribes were subjugated by the Assyrians 740–720 BC. But the Chaldean tribe, which settled near the Tigris and Euphrates estuary, extended its control over all Mesopotamia, succeeding the Assyrians. (See also BABYLONIA AND ASSYRIA.)

ARAMAIC, the Semitic language of the ARAMAEANS. Its use spread throughout Syria and Mesopotamia from the 8th century BC onwards and it became the official language of the Persian Empire. Aramaic was probably spoken by Jesus and the apostles, being by then the everyday language of Palestine. Parts of the Old Testament are in Aramaic. Aramaic survives only in isolated Lebanese villages and among some NESTORIANS of N Iraq and E Turkey.

ARAPAHO, North American Indian tribe of the Algonquian family. They lived as nomadic buffalo hunters on the Great Plains in two groups—the N and S Arapaho. Fierce enemies of white settlement, they were forced onto reservations at the end of the 19th century. By the 1970s, only 5,000 remained, mostly on reservations in Okla. and Wyo.

ARARAT, Mount, dormant volcanic mountain in E Turkey with two peaks (16,950ft and 13,000ft) 7mi apart. Genesis 8:4 says that Noah's Ark landed "upon the mountains of Ararat." The Armenians venerate the mountain as the Mother of the World. The last eruption was in 1840.

ARAUCANIAN INDIANS, South American tribes famous for their resistance to the 16th-century Spanish invasion of what is now central Chile. Many Araucanians crossed the Andes into Argentina. During the 19th century the Araucanians were settled on Chilean and Argentinian reservations where they have since maintained much of their traditional culture.

ARAWAK INDIANS, linguistic group of often culturally distinct South American tribes, now living mostly in Brazil, the Guianas and Peru. They also inhabited the Caribbean islands at the time Columbus landed there in 1492, but were later exterminated by the CARIB INDIANS.

ARBITRATION, process for settling disputes by submitting the issues involved to the judgment of an impartial third party or arbitrator. In the recent past, most US industrial collective bargaining agreements have allowed for an arbitrator to act in cases where problems of interpretation arise. An arbitration service, providing panels for commercial and industrial disputes, has been established by the American Arbitration Association. Several state and federal laws ensure the enforcement of agreements to submit disputes to arbitration. The Taft-Hartley Act (1947) provides for emergency fact-finding boards if serious strikes loom but, as their decisions are not binding, they lack the power of arbitrating bodies.

ARBOR DAY, annual tree-planting day in some US states. In northern areas it is normally held in the spring and in southern areas in winter. It was first held in Neb. on April 10, 1872.

ARBUS, Diane (1923–1971), US photographer who achieved prominence during the 1960s for her photographs of dwarfs, giants, transvestites and other grotesques.

ARBUTHNOT, John (1667–1735), Scotsborn mathematician, physician to Queen Anne and eminent satirist. Arbuthnot belonged to the famous Scriblerus Club, together with Alexander POPE, Jonathan SWIFT, and John GAY. He is noted for *The History of John Bull* (1712) and his contributions to *The Memoirs of Martinus Scriblerus* (1741).

ARCADIA, ancient Greek region in central PELOPONNESUS, enclosed by mountains. The simple life of its rustic inhabitants amid its idyllic pastures and fertile valleys was used by Classical pastoral poets and later writers, such as Sir Philip SIDNEY, as the ideal of innocent, virtuous living.

ARCARO, Eddie (George Edward Arcaro; 1916–   ), the only US jockey to have won the triple crown twice (1941 and 1948). Arcaro was also the world's third-greatest race-winner (4,779 wins), and the second-greatest money-winner (more than $30 million).

ARC DE TRIOMPHE, Napoleon I's triumphal arch in the Place Charles de Gaulle at the end of the Champs Elysées, Paris. It was built 1806–36 and is 162ft high and 147ft wide. Inspired by Roman triumphal arches, it bears reliefs celebrating Napoleon's victories. The arch is also the site of the tomb of France's Unknown Soldier.

ARCH, structural device to span openings and support loads. In ARCHITECTURE the simplest form of arch is the round (semicircular): here, as in most arches, wedge-shaped stones (**voussoirs**) are fitted together so that stresses in the arch exert outward forces on them; downward forces from the load combine with these to produce a diagonal resultant termed the thrust. The voussoirs at each end of the arch are termed **springers**; that at the center, usually the last to be inserted, is the **keystone**. Although the arch was known in ancient Egypt and Greece, it was not until Roman times that its use became popular.

ARCHAEOLOGY, the study of the past through identification and interpretation of the material remains of human cultures. A comparatively new social science, involving many academic and scientific disciplines such as ANTHROPOLOGY, history, paleography and PHILOLOGY, it makes use of numerous scientific techniques. Its keystone is fieldwork.

Archaeology was born in the early 18th century. There were some excavations of Roman and other sites, and the famous ROSETTA STONE, which provided the key to Egyptian HIEROGLYPHICS, was discovered in 1799 and deciphered in 1818. In 1832 archaeological time was classified into three divisions—STONE AGE, BRONZE AGE and IRON AGE—though this system is now more commonly used to describe cultures of PRIMITIVE MAN.

However, it was not until the 19th century that archaeology graduated from its amateur status to become a systematized science. SCHLIEMANN, Arthur EVANS, C. L.

Woolley, Howard CARTER and others adopted an increasingly scientific approach in their researches.

Excavation is a painstaking procedure, as great care must be taken not to damage any object or fragment of an object, and each of the different levels of excavation must be carefully documented and photographed. The location of suitable sites for excavation is assisted by historical accounts, topographical surveys and aerial photography. Any object or fragment of an object that was produced by man is of interest to the archaeologist. These include such obvious items as tools, weapons, utensils and clothing. The discovery of a midden, or refuse pile, is especially welcome. Natural objects, such as seeds of cultivated plants, are also revealing. Each item on discovery is recorded on a map that establishes its physical relationship with other artifacts found, and is numbered and photographed. Once in the laboratory, the archaeologist will examine it more closely, comparing it with similar finds.

Dating is accomplished in several ways. First, of course, is comparison of the relative depths of objects that are discovered. Analysis of the types of pollen in an object can provide an indication of its date. The most widespread dating technique is RADIOISOTOPE DATING, incorporating the corrections formulated through discoveries in DENDROCHRONOLOGY.

Archaeology contains many divisions and areas of specialty. Some embrace the study of great civilizations, like those of Greece, Rome, Egypt, China and Mexico. Other scholars concentrate on the cultures of peoples of humble achievements. In the US a major field of study is that of the American Indian. Another area concentrates on settlements of colonial America—an example of historic archaeology, which deals with peoples who flourished during a time when written documents were left.

ARCHBISHOP, a metropolitan BISHOP of the Roman Catholic, Anglican and Eastern churches, and the Lutheran churches of Finland and Sweden, having jurisdiction over the bishops of a church province, or archdiocese, within which he consecrates bishops and presides over synods. Archbishops do not form a separate order of MINISTRY. The term may be applied to bishops of distinguished sees, or PATRIARCHS.

ARCHERY, shooting with bow and arrow, used in warfare by primitive peoples in the Americas, Africa and Asia, and in ancient Greece and the Near East. It was vital in medieval European warfare. The English longbow's superiority over the French crossbow won the Battle of AGINCOURT (1415). Between the 14th and 15th centuries, the bow's use in W Europe declined with the development of firearms. But in late 18th-century England archery was revived as a sport. The US National Archery Association was formed in 1879 and, since 1900, archery has been part of the Olympic Games. The sport involves shooting at a standard circular target marked with colored concentric circles.

ARCHES NATIONAL PARK, 82,953 acres in E Utah containing natural rock arches formed by weathering and erosion. The park was established in 1929.

ARCHIMEDES (c287–212 BC), Greek mathematician and physicist who spent most of his life at his birthplace, Syracuse (Sicily). In mathematics he worked on the areas and volumes associated with conic sections, fixed the value of PI (π) between $3\frac{10}{71}$ and $3\frac{1}{7}$ and defined the **Archimedean spiral** ($r=a\theta$). He founded the science of hydrostatics with his enunciation of **Archimedes' principle**. This states that the force acting to buoy up a body partially or totally immersed in a fluid is equal to the weight of the fluid displaced. In MECHANICS he studied the properties of the LEVER and applied his experience in the construction of military catapults and grappling irons. He is also said to have invented the **Archimedes screw,** a machine for raising water still used to irrigate fields in Egypt. This consists of a helical tube or a cylindrical tube containing a close-fitting screw with the lower end dipping in the water. When the tube (or screw) is rotated, water is moved up the tube and is discharged from the top.

ARCHIPENKO, Alexander (1887–1964), Ukrainian-born US sculptor, famous for nude female torsos in which naturalistic forms are reduced to elegant geometric shapes.

ARCHITECTURE has usually been defined as the art of building. The architect today is both an artist and an engineer who must combine a knowledge of design and construction, and of the available resources in labor, techniques and materials, to produce a harmonious, durable and functional whole. His building must be fitted to its environment and must satisfy the social needs for which it is required—whether it is a church, dwelling, factory or office building. In the past all this was accomplished in a traditional manner by largely anonymous builders; today the architect plans both the aesthetics and the construction of his building in a highly conscious manner, often deliberately attempting to communicate artistic concepts and abstract ideas through the structure itself.

The architect designs buildings for human activities; and most such buildings spring directly out of the culture of their time. Hence architecture in any period is one of the most visible and significant expressions of the culture that produced it. The Egyptian pyramid, for instance, as a royal tomb, translated the pharaohs' hopes for an eternal afterlife into huge, long-lasting piles of masonry, while the awesome, columned halls of the royal palace at Persepolis were built to display the majesty of the ancient kings of Persia. The Islamic mosque and the Gothic cathedral, one open to sunny skies, the other closed and vaulted against northern weather, provided equally generous spaces for communal worship. Rome and the modern city both produced apartment houses for urban living; the Pueblo Indians built them for agricultural communities. The English stately home expressed the power and aspirations of a remarkable ruling class, while the modern glass skyscraper fulfills the needs of our industrial and business society.

Architecture has always been limited by the materials and techniques at its command; conversely, architectural advances and the development of new styles have been marked by the adoption of new materials or the discovery of new techniques. Traditionally the materials have been stone, earth, brick, wood, glass, concrete, iron and steel—with plastics and new metals added today. With its great compressive strength, stone has been the material of most major buildings in the past. It gave rise to the common post-and-lintel type of construction, and to the arch, the latter culminating in the soaring lightness of the Gothic cathedrals. The acme of the ancient post-and-lintel construction was reached in the classic simplicity of the Greek temple, notably in the PARTHENON. To these elements the Romans added daring experiments in vaulting, made possible by the use of concrete, as in the PANTHEON (2nd century AD), carried still further in Byzantine, Romanesque and Islamic architecture. But the tensile strength of stone is poor, while wood and steel have tensile as well compressive strength. This made frame construction possible, as in the wooden buildings of Japan or the steel-framed modern building. Geodesic and stressed-frame methods of construction, with reinforced concrete, have further extended the range of the modern architect.

Not only new materials and techniques, but also developments in social and institutional needs, the exigencies of climate and the need to express new aspirations and ideals in differing cultures have brought about changing styles in architecture. Often new architectures have repeated and elaborated older styles, as in the Renaissance and the Greek and Roman revivals. The use of ornamentation or decoration in architecture—as in the intricate surface decoration of Islamic buildings or the elaborations of the Rococo—has varied in response to changing tastes. Today we are emerging from a period of intense reaction against surface decoration embodied in the plain and functional International style of recent modern architecture. Styles change, but at all times and in all places the architect has attempted to manipulate space, mass, light and color to produce the optimum proportion and scale called for by the human mind. Thus the importance of architecture in civilization is three-fold; it is an art, it is made for people, and it is always a major expression of culture. See also articles on various styles and periods, for example GOTHIC ART AND ARCHITECTURE, ROMANESQUE ART AND ARCHITECTURE; articles on building forms, such as BASILICA and SKYSCRAPER; and articles on architectural elements, such as DOME.

ARCHIVES, documents of a public body preserved in an organized fashion. Systematic collection and supervision by a central government agency began in 1789 with the French *Archives Nationales.* The US National Archives and Records Service (originating in 1934) houses records in the National Archives Building, Washington, D.C. It has the originals of the DECLARATION OF INDEPENDENCE and the CONSTITUTION. Corporations, foundations, universities and cities also keep archives, which now include tape recordings and space-saving microfilms.

ARC LAMP, an intensely bright and comparatively efficient form of LIGHTING used for lighthouses, floodlights and spotlights, invented by DAVY in 1809. An arc discharge is set up when two carbon electrodes at a moderate potential difference (typically 40V) are "struck" (touched together, then drawn apart). The light is emitted from vaporized carbon IONS in the discharge. In modern lamps the arc is enclosed in an atmosphere of high-pressure xenon.

ARCTIC OCEAN, 5,400,000sq mi, is the smallest ocean. Entirely within the Arctic Circle, it is covered with ice throughout the year. It is bordered by Norway, the Soviet Union, Alaska, Canada, and Greenland. It is connected to the Pacific Ocean by the Bering Strait and to the Atlantic Ocean by the Greenland Sea.

ARCTIC REGIONS, regions N of the Arctic Circle (66°30′N); alternatively regions N of the tree line. The Arctic comprises the Arctic Ocean, Greenland, Spitsbergen and other islands, extreme N Europe, N Siberia, Alaska and N Canada. The central feature is the Arctic Ocean, opening S into the N Atlantic Ocean and joined with the N Pacific Ocean by the Bering Strait. The Arctic Ocean comprises two main basins and has a shallow rim floored by the continental shelves of Eurasia and North America. Much of the ocean surface is always covered by ice.

The Arctic climate is cold. In midwinter the sun never rises and the mean Jan. temperature is −33°F, far lower in interior Canada and Siberia. Snow and ice never melt in high altitudes and latitudes, but elsewhere the short mild summer with 24 hours' sunlight a day thaws the sea and the topsoil. In spring, melting icebergs floating south from the Arctic Ocean endanger N Atlantic shipping. Vegetation is varied but confined mainly to shrubs, flowering herbaceous plants, mosses and lichens. Wild mammals include polar bears, reindeer, musk oxen, moose, wolves, weasels, foxes and lemmings. Geese, ducks, gulls, cranes, falcons, auks and ptarmigan all nest in the Arctic, and its seas harbor whales, seals, cod, salmon and shrimp. Invits (Eskimos), Lapps, Russians and others make up a human population of several million. Eskimos have lived in the Arctic for at least 9,000 years, and total 60,000 or more. Once exclusively hunters and fishermen, Eskimos now work in towns and on oil fields. There are scattered agricultural, mining and fishing industries; and the US, Canada and USSR man air bases and meteorological stations. Oil production began at Prudhoe Bay (Alaska) in 1978, the oil moving S to Valdez through the Trans-Alaska pipeline.

Vikings were the first recorded Arctic explorers: Norwegians visited the Russian Arctic in the 9th century and the Icelander ERIC THE RED established a Greenland settlement c982 AD. In the 16th and 17th centuries search for a NORTHWEST PASSAGE and a NORTHEAST PASSAGE to the Orient encouraged exploration. In the 16th century Martin Frobisher reached Baffin Island and Willem Barents explored Novaya Zemlya and saw Spitsbergen. Henry HUDSON probed E Greenland and the Hudson Strait in the early 17th century. But the longed-for passages remained undiscovered, and interest in Arctic exploration declined until Canadian and Russian fur traders revived it late in the 18th century. Early in the 19th century the British naval officers John and James Ross, W. E. Perry, John Rae and Sir John Franklin traveled to unexplored areas, James Ross discovering the north magnetic pole. N. A. E. Nordenskjöld of Sweden navigated the Northeast Passage (1878–79) and R. AMUNDSEN the Northwest Passage (1906) and in 1909 Robert E. PEARY reached the North Pole. Richard E. BYRD and Floyd BENNETT overflew the Pole in 1926, pioneering polar air exploration and transpolar air travel. In 1958 the US nuclear submarine *Nautilus* reached the Pole under the icecap.

ARCTURUS, star in the constellation Bootes, 4th brightest in the sky.

ARDENNES, forested upland in SE Belgium, N Luxembourg and around the Meuse valley of N France. The area is a sparsely populated plateau with some agriculture and quarrying. It was a battleground in WWI and WWII (see BATTLE OF THE BULGE).

ARENDT, Hannah (1906–1975), German-born US political philosopher. In 1959 she became the first woman to be appointed a full professor at Princeton U, and she later taught at the U of Chicago and the New School for Social Research in New York. In *The Origins of Totalitarianism* (1951) she traced nazism and communism back to 19th-century anti-Semitism and imperialism. Her controversial *Eichmann in Jerusalem* (1963), with its theory of the "banality of evil," analyzed Nazi war crimes and the 1960 trial of Adolph EICHMANN by the Israeli government.

ARETINO, Pietro (1492–1556), Italian satirist and playwright who wrote coarse, sensual and lively political satires. His works include *I Ragionamenti* (1534–36), dialogues between prostitutes describing the escapades of contemporary notables.

ARGALL, Sir Samuel (d. 1626), daring English navigator and soldier in North America. He pioneered a N sea route to Va. (1609), captured POCAHONTAS (1612), crushed French colonies in Me. and Nova Scotia and became deputy governor of Va. (1617–19).

ARGENTINA, second largest country in Latin America, economically one of its most advanced nations.

Land. Argentina occupies most of South America E of the Andes and S of Brazil. There are four main areas: W, N, Central and S. The W comprises the Andes Mts, which exceed 20,000ft in parts of the N but

Official name: Republic of Argentina
Capital: Buenos Aires
Area: 1,073,399sq mi
Population: 31,497,000
Languages: Spanish
Religions: Roman Catholic
Monetary unit(s): 1 Argentine peso = 100 centavos

are low in the S. The N consists largely of the forests of the Gran Chaco and the swampy region in the NE Central Argentina comprises great grassy plains or *pampas*, a temperate region and economically the most important area, with two-thirds of the population. In the S lie the barren and cold plateaus of Patagonia.

People. About 90% of the people are descended from S European immigrants. There are only 20-30,000 native Indians. The national language is Spanish, and about 90% of the population is Roman Catholic. Over 70% live in urban areas. Argentina has a better educational system and a higher literacy rate (93%) than most Latin American states.

Economy. Grain growing and cattle raising dominate the pampas, and the S is a big sheep raising region. Sugarcane, grapes, citrus fruits, tobacco, rice and cotton grow in the subtropical N. Oil and other minerals come from the N and the S. About 30% of the labor force works in industry, notably in food processing, chemicals, plastics machine tools and automobiles. Much of this industry is located in and around the capital, Buenos Aires.

History. Argentina's first Spanish settlers arrived in the 16th century. After nearly 300 years of Spanish rule, independence followed the war of 1816. The 19th century was a period of increasing European immigration and economic progress. Argentina's development during the 20th century has suffered from political uncertainties and social unrest. The reformist but dictatorial government of Juan PERÓN (1946–55) ended with a military uprising and was followed by several military and civilian governments. Widespread violence broke out in the early

1970s, and in 1973 popular demand restored the aging Perón to power. He died in 1974, however, and was succeeded by his wife Isabel Perón. She was unable to solve Argentina's problems, and after a brief lull was overthrown in 1976. A military junta took over. Kidnapings and terrorist activities were widespread in the late 1970s, and the military introduced stern measures to cope with the increasing instability. Some 20-30,000 people allegedly disappeared. In 1982 Argentina occupied the Falkland Islands, a British colony long claimed by Argentina. The British battled successfully to regain the islands; following the defeat the Argentine military government was reshuffled. The election as president in 1983 of Raúl Alfonsín, leader of the Radical (middle-class and anti-Peronist) Party, restored civilian government. Alfonsín brought the members of the military junta and other high ranking officers to trial for crimes committed during the "dirty war" of 1976–83 against alleged subversives. The deterioration of the economy was not halted by government retrenchment, privatization of state-run enterprises, and deregulation. In 1987 the Peronist Justicialista Party made a strong showing in elections for provincial governorships and the national chamber of deputies (the lower house of the legislature). A presidential election was scheduled for 1989.

ARGON (Ar), the commonest of the NOBLE GASES, comprising 0.934% of the ATMOSPHERE. It is used as an inert shield for arc welding and for the production of silicon and germanium crystals, to fill electric light bulbs and fluorescent lamps, and in argon–ion LASERS. AW 39.9, mp — 189°C, bp — 186°C.

ARGONAUTS, heroes of Greek mythology who set sail under Jason to find the Golden Fleece. They reputedly included such illustrious figures as Orpheus, Hercules, Caster and Pollux and Theseus. The Argonauts set forth in the ship *Argo* for Colchis E of the Black Sea, where the fleece was guarded by a dragon. After many perils they obtained the fleece and returned to mainland Greece.

ARGONNE FOREST, a wooded hilly region south of the Ardennes, in NE France. In 1792 it was the site of the French victory over the Prussians at Valmy. The Meuse-Argonne offensive of late 1918 was one of the major US actions fought in WWI.

ARGONNE NATIONAL LABORATORY, a nuclear power research center 25mi S of Chicago. The University of Chicago operates it for the US Energy Research and

Development Administration.

ARIANISM, 4th-century Christian heresy founded in Alexandria by the priest Arius. He taught that Christ was not coequal and coeternal with God the Father, for the Father had created him. To curb Arianism, the Emperor Constantine called the first Council of NICAEA (325), and the first Nicene Creed declared that God the Father and Christ the Son were of the same substance. Arianism later almost triumphed, but most of the church returned to orthodoxy by the end of the century (see TRINITY).

ARIAS SÁNCHEZ, Oscar (1941–   ), Costa Rican politician, leader of the liberal National Liberation Party (PLN) and president of Costa Rica from 1986. He initiated a treaty, signed (Aug. 1987) by himself and the presidents of Guatemala, El Salvador, Honduras, and Nicaragua, in which all five agreed to take certain measures to advance peace and democracy in Central America. For this Arias Sánchez was awarded the 1987 Nobel Peace Prize.

ARIOSTO, Ludovico (1474–1533), Italian poet best remembered for the epic *Orlando Furioso*. This continued the Roland legend, depicting the hero as a love-torn knight. The work greatly influenced later poets, such as SPENSER and BYRON.

ARISTARCHUS OF SAMOS (c310–230 BC), Alexandrian Greek astronomer who realized that the sun is larger than the earth and who is reported by ARCHIMEDES to have taught that the earth orbited a motionless sun.

ARISTIDES (c530–468 BC), Athenian statesman and general, a founder of the DELIAN LEAGUE. He fought at the battle of MARATHON, and was elected archon for 489 BC. Ostracized in 482 BC, he was recalled in 480 BC and helped repulse the Persians. Later he fixed Greek cities' contributions to the Delian League.

ARISTOCRACY (from Greek *aristos*, the best, and *kratos*, rule), originally meaning the ruling of a state by its best citizens in the interest of all. It was used by both PLATO and ARISTOTLE in this sense. Gradually the term came to mean a form of government ruled by a small privileged class. Today, the term refers to members of a family which traditionally has hereditary privileges and rank.

ARISTOPHANES (c450–385 BC), comic dramatist of ancient Greece. Political, social and literary satire, witty dialogue, vigorous ribaldry, cleverly contrived comic situations and fine choral lyrics all feature in his works. Eleven of his 40 plays survive, notably *The Frogs* (satirizing Euripides),

The Clouds (satirizing Socrates), *Lysistrata* (a plea for pacifism) and *The Birds* (a fantasy about a sky city).

ARISTOTLE (384–322 BC), Greek philosopher, one of the most influential thinkers of the ancient world. He was the son of the Macedonian court physician, and studied at PLATO's academy in Athens. In 343 BC he became tutor to the young ALEXANDER THE GREAT. In 335 BC Aristotle set up his own school at the Lyceum in Athens (see PERIPATETIC SCHOOL). Many of Aristotle's teachings survive as lecture notes. His work covered a vast range, including *Physics, Metaphysics, On the Soul, On the Heavens,* and several works on LOGIC and BIOLOGY, in both of which subjects he was a pioneer.

In studying such diverse topics as nature, man or the soul, Aristotle considered how things became what they were and what function they performed. In doing this he introduced his fourfold analysis of causes (formal, material, efficient and final), and such important notions as form and matter, substance and accident, actual and potential—all of which became philosophical commonplaces. In logic he invented the SYLLOGISM. The *Nicomachean Ethics* argues that virtue is a "mean" between extremes. *Politics* considers civic participation an outgrowth of human nature and reason. *Poetics* argues that a tragic drama brings emotional catharsis through "pity and fear" evoked by the stage action. Aristotle's writings reached the West through Latin translations in the 11th and 13th centuries and had a prevailing influence on medieval and later thought.

ARITHMETIC (from Greek *arithmos*, number), the science of number. Until the 16th century arithmetic was viewed as the study of all the properties and relations of all numbers; in modern times, the term usually denotes the study of the positive real numbers and zero under the operations of addition, subtraction, multiplication and division. Arithmetic can therefore be viewed as merely a special case of ALGEBRA, although it is of importance in considerations of the history of MATHEMATICS.

ARIZONA, state, SW US, bounded to the E by N.M., to the S by Mexico, to the W by Cal. and Nev., and to the N by Utah. Once a largely worthless desert area, Arizona has developed rapidly and in population is now one of the fastest growing states in the Union.

Land. The Colorado Plateau to the N contains such spectacular features as the Grand Canyon, the Painted Desert, the Petrified Forest and Monument Valley, all of which have helped to make tourism an

Name of state: Arizona
Capital: Phoenix
Statehood: Feb. 14, 1912 (48th state)
Familiar name: Grand Canyon State
Area: 113,909sq mi
Population: 3,319,000
Elevation: Highest—12,633ft, Humphrey's Peak. Lowest—70ft, Colorado River at the Mexican border
Motto: *Didat deus* ("God enriches")
State flower: Saguaro (Giant Cactus)
State bird: Cactus wren
State tree: Paloverde
State song: "Arizona"

important part of the economy. A mountain chain, heavily forested and rich in minerals, extends NW to SE, while desert occupies the SW.

People. Arizona's population is predominantly urban, about half being concentrated in the Phoenix metropolitan area. More Indians live in Arizona than in any other state, the majority on the 19 reservations that cover almost 25% of the total land area. The Navaho, Hopi and Apache are the largest of the tribes.

Economy. With the aid of irrigation and of a long growing season, Arizona has developed a varied and intensive agricultural economy. About 60% of farm income is from livestock products. More than 1.1 million cattle and about 500,000 sheep are raised on ranches and grazing land. Cotton is the principal cash crop, while truck farming is so extensive it has earned the state a reputation as the "Salad Bowl of the Nation."

Arizona is also rich in minerals, supplying half the nation's copper as well as mining gold, silver, tungsten, molybdenum, zinc and vanadium. Manufacturing began with the smelting of copper and other ores and the establishment of sawmills.

Since WWII, industrial growth has been rapid and manufacturing now contributes more than agriculture or mining to the state's wealth. The electronics and electrical industry centered in Phoenix employs the largest number of workers engaged in manufacturing. Other industries

include food processing, publishing, aircraft construction, and the production of metal goods.

History. Arizona was under Spanish influence from 1539, when it was first explored by Friar Marcos de Niza, until 1821 when it was ceded to Mexico. The Treaty of GUADALUPE HIDALGO (1848) granted most of present-day Arizona to the US, and in 1853–54, the Gadsden Purchase was made, thereby extending the area to the Gila R. Movement for statehood began after the defeat of the Navahos—by Kit CARSON (1863)—and the Apache (1886). Recently, Arizona has suffered some of the pains of growing too quickly. While its population increased 53.1% in the 1970s, unemployment also rose, reaching 8.1% at the decade's end. A continuing influx of illegal aliens helped aggravate ethnic tensions and the crime rate is high, with Phoenix ranking third among the nation's metropolitan centers in this unenviable category in 1978. Excessive use of water for agriculture has lowered water tables in the southern part of the state; in an effort to halt this, a state code regulating ground-water use was adopted in 1980. In 1988 the Arizona senate removed Gov. Evan Mecham from office, the first impeachment conviction of a US governor since 1929. In presidential elections 1968–88, Arizona voted consistently Republican.

ARKANSAS, state, SE central US on the W bank of the Mississippi R. and bounded to the S by La., to the W by Tex. and Okla. and to the N by Mo. Arkansas has suffered in the past from over-dependence on the cotton crop and from low per capita income, but industrial growth has accelerated since the mid-1950s. Now income from manufacturing exceeds that from agriculture.

Land. In addition to the Mississippi, Arkansas has several major rivers, including the Arkansas, Red, Ouachita, White and St. Francis rivers. To the N and W are the rugged Ozark and Ouachita Mts, while the alluvial plain in the E is the chief agricultural region. More than half the state is forested. Three national forests—in the Ozarks, the Ouachitas and the Gulf Coastal Plain—have been established to protect valuable timberlands. Climate is mild and rainy.

People. Arkansas is one of the least urbanized states with only one out of every two inhabitants living in urban areas. Little Rock is the largest city, followed by Fort Smith and Pine Bluff. The General Assembly consists of a 35-member Senate and 100-member House of Representatives.

Economy. Arkansas is the leading US

Name of state: Arkansas
Capital: Little Rock
Statehood: June 15, 1836 (25th state)
Familiar name: Land of Opportunity
Area: 53,104sq mi
Population: 2,372,000
Elevation: Highest—2,753ft, Magazine Mountain. Lowest—55ft, Ouachita River at the Louisiana border
Motto: *Regnat populus* ("The people rule")
State flower: Apple blossom
State bird: Mockingbird
State tree: Pine
State song: "Arkansas"

producer of rice and broiler chickens. It also supplies about 10% of the national cotton total while Mississippi Co. is the country's leading soybean producer. In the W, raising and processing livestock and poultry are major sources of income.

Arkansas has important mineral deposits and produces a large proportion of the bauxite mined in the US. There are also oil and natural gas fields, as well as deposits of barite, manganese, bromine, vanadium and coal. The first diamond field in the US (no longer in industrial use) was established near Murfreesboro in SE Arkansas. Arkansas' forests provide timber and pulp for lumber, paper and other wood products, which account for a major share of the state's industry. Other major manufactures include metal goods, electrical parts, clothes, building materials and petroleum products.

History. First explored by Hernando DE SOTO (1541) Arkansas passed from Spanish to French hands, and then to the US as part of the LOUISIANA PURCHASE (1803). It first entered the Union as a slave state in 1836 and was readmitted after the Civil War in 1868 over President Andrew Johnson's veto. The Reconstruction period was marked by controversy and discontent. Racism brought Arkansas into the headlines in 1957 when federal troops were called to enforce integration at a Little Rock school. In the 1970s, Arkansas was troubled by rising unemployment and business failures.

Agriculture was also depressed, the number of farms declining over 15% in 1978–87. In presidential elections 1968–88, Arkansas voted Republican in 1972 and 1980–88.

ARKANSAS RIVER, longest tributary of the Mississippi–Missouri R system. It rises in the Rocky Mts of central Col. and flows 1,450mi through Kan., Okla., and Ark. to the Mississippi R. It is the main water source for Ark. state, and is controlled by dams and locks to curb flooding.

ARKHANGELSK (Archangel), city and major port in NW USSR, the administrative center for Arkhangelsk oblast. It stands on the Northern Dvina R and although icebound for six months is of considerable economic importance, specializing in furs, timber, paper-making, fishing, and ship-building. Arkhangelsk was Russia's leading port until the founding of St. Petersburg (1703). Pop 408,000.

ARK OF THE COVENANT, in the Old Testament, the chest containing the tablets bearing the Ten Commandments received by Moses. The most sacred object of ancient Israel, it was carried into battle before it was deposited in the Temple.

ARKWRIGHT, Sir Richard (1732–1792), English industrialist and inventor of cotton carding and SPINNING machinery. In 1769 he patented a spinning frame which was the first machine able to produce cotton thread strong enough to use in the warp. He was a pioneer of the factory system of production, building several water- and later steam-powered mills.

ARLEN, Harold (1905–1986), US popular composer of "Stormy Weather," "Blues in the Night," and "Over the Rainbow."

ARLEN, Michael (1895–1956), English novelist, born in Bulgaria of Armenian parents. His novels, notably *The Green Hat* (1924), mirrored fashionable 1920s London.

ARLINGTON NATIONAL CEMETERY, famous US national cemetery in N Va. It was established in 1864 on land once owned by George Washington Custis and Robert E. LEE. Over 160,000 American war dead and public figures are buried here. Monuments include the Custis-Lee Mansion, the mast of the battleship *Maine*, the Tomb of the Unknown Soldier and the grave of John F. Kennedy with its eternal flame.

ARMADA, fleet of armed ships, in particular Spain's "Invincible Armada," 130 ships carrying 27,000 men sent by PHILIP II in 1588 to seize control of the English Channel for an invasion of England. After a running fight with Howard, DRAKE, and HAWKINS, the Spaniards took refuge in

Calais Roads. Driven out by fire ships, the surviving vessels battled storms as they attempted to return to Cadiz via N Scotland and W Ireland. About half the ships returned.

ARMADILLOS, about 20 species of armored MAMMALS (family Dasypodidae) of the order Endentata, which also contains ANTEATERS and SLOTHS. They range in length from about 120mm (5in) to about 1.5m (5ft). They are usually nocturnal, sometimes diurnal, and live in burrows either excavated by themselves or deserted by other animals. Polyembryony (production of several identical offspring from a single fertilized egg) is general amongst armadillos.

ARMAGEDDON, biblical site of the world's last great battle, in which the powers of good will destroy the forces of evil (Revelation 16:16). The name may refer to biblical Megiddo.

ARMAGNAC, hilly farming area of SW France noted for its brandy. Count Bernard VII of Armagnac was virtual ruler of France in 1413–18. Armagnac passed to the French crown in 1607. The chief city, Auch, is a commercial center.

ARMENIA, historic country in SW Asia S of the Caucasus Mts, now mainly divided between the Armenian Soviet Socialist Republic and NE Turkey. Primarily a tableland, the entire region averages some 6,000–7,000ft above sea level. A range of mountains cuts across it from E to W; the highest point being Mt Ararat (16,945ft) in Turkey. The Tigris, Euphrates, Kyros and Araxes rivers all have their source in the highlands.

Armenia's landscape extends from subtropical lowland to snow-covered peaks. Small mountain pastures provide rich grazing for sheep and cattle, while the valleys are fertile when irrigated. The main crops are green vegetables, barley, potatoes, wheat, sugar beets and grapes. Pomegranates, figs, peaches and apricots are also grown.

Mining is the chief industry, the mountains yielding small but useful quantities of copper, iron, manganese, nepheline and molybdenum. Transportation facilities are limited, but industrialization is increasing. Hydroelectric schemes, particularly on Lake Sevan, have been a prime factor in Soviet Armenia's economic growth.

Armenia was conquered in 328 BC by Alexander the Great and in 66 BC by Rome. In 303 AD it became the first country to make Christianity its state religion. Later it was successively under Byzantine, Persian, Arab, Seljuk, Mongol and Ottoman Turkish control. Russian influence grew in the 19th century. A short-lived Armenian republic emerged after WWI but was swiftly absorbed by the USSR and Turkey.

ARMENIAN CHURCH, the national church of Armenia. It evolved as part of the EASTERN CHURCH and adopted a form of MONOPHYSITISM. It was the first Christian church to be established.

ARMINIANS, or Remonstrants, group of Protestant congregations inspired by the Dutch theologian Jacobus Arminius (1560–1609). Arminianism attempted to show that, contrary to John CALVIN'S doctrine of PREDESTINATION, man's free will and God's sovereignty were not incompatible. The Arminians, though persecuted initially, were legally tolerated in the Netherlands from 1630. Arminian theology greatly influenced John WESLEY, founder of Methodism.

ARMINIUS (18 BC?–19 AD), leader of German resistance to Rome. His destruction of a Roman army commanded by Publius Quintus Varus in the Teutoberg forest in 9 AD ended Roman efforts to occupy territory east of the Rhine. In recent centuries Arminius was made a German national hero.

ARMOR, protective clothing or covering used in armed combat. The earliest armor consisted of boiled and hardened animal skins but, with the coming of organized military campaigns, armor became more sophisticated. Roman soldiers wore standardized armor made of iron. Later, chain mail, a fabric of interlocking metal rings, was developed. By the end of the 11th century it was the standard form of armor. It provided poor protection against heavy blows, however, and the Middle Ages saw the development of full suits of metal plates with chain mail joints for flexibility. Later, as these suits were used more for tournaments and state occasions, certain cities, notably Milan and Augsburg, became renowned for their armorial artistry. Full armor was used in Europe only until the 16th century. Modern armor employs nylon, fiberglass and other synthetic materials. New advances in tank armor include the British Chobham, consisting of laminated steel, aluminum, fabric and ceramic materials, which is designed to dissipate kinetic energy more effectively than steel alone, and the French appliqué with removable plates.

ARMORY SHOW, officially the International Exhibition of Modern Art, the first show of its kind to be held in the US at the

69th Regiment Armory, New York City, Feb.–March 1913. Comprising over 1,300 works it included a large section of paintings by contemporary Americans, and works by such modern European artists as BRANCUSI, BRAQUE, CÉZANNE, DUCHAMP, MATISSE and PICASSO. The avant-garde paintings caused much controversy but also the acceptance of modern art in the US.

ARMOUR, Philip Danforth (1832–1901), US meatpacking pioneer and philanthropist. He made his fortune supplying pork to Union forces in the Civil War, and in 1870 established Armour & Co. which soon made Chicago the meatpacking center of the US. He founded the Armour Institute of Technology in 1892.

ARMS CONTROL, limitation of armaments as a means of preventing war or of mitigating its destructiveness. Throughout history, victorious powers often destroyed or restricted the capacity of their enemies to make war (see, e.g., VERSAILLES, TREATY OF). Agreements negotiated among states in times of peace to limit arms are modern phenomena and have not been notably successful. The HAGUE PEACE CONFERENCES of 1899 and 1907 failed to restrain the arms race in Europe that led to WWI. The WASHINGTON CONFERENCE of 1921-22 produced an agreement on the relative strengths of the navies of the great powers that was soon violated. The 1925 Geneva Protocol, ratified by over 50 countries, prohibited the use of chemical and biological weapons; it too has been frequently violated (see CHEMICAL AND BIOLOGICAL WARFARE).

Since WWII and the start of the nuclear age, the US and the USSR have pursued arms-control agreements to enhance their own security and the security of their respective alliances, the NORTH ATLANTIC TREATY ORGANIZATION (NATO) and the WARSAW PACT. The principal negotiations and agreements involving the two superpowers and others are as follows:

Limited Test Ban Treaty (1963), signed by the US, USSR, and Britain, prohibits all nuclear tests above ground, under water, and in space, plus underground explosions big enough to send radioactive debris across a nation's borders.

Nuclear Nonproliferation Treaty (1968), signed by the US, USSR, Britain, and 134 other countries, bans the transfer of weapons to nonnuclear powers and the diversion of nuclear materials to nonpeaceful purposes.

Strategic Arms Limitation Talks (SALT I), from 1969 to 1972 between the US and USSR, aimed at preventing the expansion of strategic weapons in both countries. The 1972 ABM Treaty (below) resulted.

Anti-Ballistic-Missile (ABM) Treaty (1972), signed by the US and USSR, restricts the development, testing, and deployment of land-mobile, sea-based, air-based, and space-based defense systems against strategic ballistic missiles.

Convention Prohibiting Production of Biological Weapons (1972), signed by the US, USSR, Britain, and numerous other countries, bans the production and stockpiling of biological and toxin weapons and calls for the destruction of existing stocks.

Threshold Test Ban Treaty (1974), signed by the US and USSR, limits the size of underground nuclear-weapons tests to 150 kilotons. The treaty was not ratified, but the two superpowers have observed its provisions.

Peaceful Nuclear Explosions Treaty (1976), signed by the US and USSR, limits nonweapons-test nuclear explosions to 150 kilotons. The treaty was not ratified.

Strategic Arms Limitation Talks (SALT II), between the US and USSR, begun in 1972, led to the SALT II Treaty of 1979, by which the two superpowers agreed to limits of 2,400 strategic missiles and bombers each, to be reduced to 2,250 in two years. The treaty contained sublimits on specific weapons categories. The US Senate shelved the treaty in 1980 when the USSR invaded Afghanistan.

Intermediate-Range Nuclear Forces (INF) Treaty (1987), signed by the US and USSR, bans ground-launched, nuclear-armed missiles with ranges from 300 to 3,300mi. Missiles and launchers are to be destroyed within three years. Compliance is to be verified by inspections at missile bases and support installations.

Strategic Arms Reduction Talks (START), begun in 1982 between the US and USSR, aimed at reducing long-range strategic weapons such as ICBMs, submarine-launched ballistic missiles, and heavy bombers. The Soviets viewed the US Strategic Defense Initiative (SDI), or STAR WARS project, as an obstacle to a START agreement.

ARMSTRONG, Edwin Howard (1890–1954), US electronics engineer who developed the FEEDBACK concept for AMPLIFIERS (1912), invented the superheterodyne circuit used in radio receivers (1918) and perfected FM RADIO (1925–39).

ARMSTRONG, Henry (1912–1988), US boxer. Nicknamed "Perpetual Motion" for his aggressive style, he was the only fighter to hold three world championships (featherweight, welterweight and light-weight) simultaneously (1938).

ARMSTRONG, Louis Daniel (1900–1971), US jazz musician renowned as a virtuoso trumpeter and singer. A master of improvisation, he is considered perhaps the most influential and important figure in the early history of jazz. "Satchmo" grew up in the back streets of New Orleans, moved to Chicago in 1922 and by the 1930s was internationally famous. In later life he played at concerts around the world as "goodwill ambassador" for the State Department.

ARMSTRONG, Neil Alden (1930–   ), first man to set foot on the moon. Born in Wapakoneta, Ohio, he studied aeronautical engineering at Purdue U. (1947–55) with time out on active service in the Korean War. He joined NASA in 1962, commanding Gemini 8 (1966), and landing the Apollo II module on the moon on July 20, 1969. In 1971–79 he was professor of aerospace engineering at Cincinnati U and then became a computer company executive.

ARMSTRONG, Samuel Chapman (1839–1893), US educator and philanthropist. He was colonel of a Negro regiment in the Civil War and agent of the FREEDMAN'S BUREAU (Va.). Armstrong founded the Hampton Institute (1868), an industrial school for blacks and Indians.

ARMY, traditionally the land fighting force of a nation. By a narrower definition an army is also a large unit of ground forces under a single commander (e.g. the US Fifth Army).

The 20th century has shown how far the modern army depends upon technology and industry. Germany was defeated in WWII not by superior military power but by superior machine power. However, the constant development of weapons and detection systems makes any land force extremely vulnerable. Modern armies must, therefore, be highly mobile, a need which has led to a blurring of the traditional distinctions between army, navy and air force. Cooperation among the services is essential for the successful application of advanced technology. Canada, for example, has combined all three branches of her armed forces.

Primitive armies perhaps consisted of raiding parties mainly engaged in individual combat, using rudimentary weapons such as stones and clubs. Later, skills in handling horses and chariots increased the complexity and mobility of armies, while the development of artillery, which had its origins in catapult machines

and the revolutionary invention of gunpowder in China, extended their range of effectiveness. Formation tactics evolved through the Macedonian *phalanx* and Roman *legion*.

It might be said that the modern army has brought all these developments to a very high level of sophistication. Rapid mobility, first made practicable by the construction of rail networks in the 19th century, has been increased in the 20th century by the development of air transportation. Nuclear weaponry has taken the effective range of firepower virtually to its limits and the value of tactical formations has largely been eliminated by radar detection equipment, making unconventional military units (e.g. guerrillas, paratroops) increasingly important in warfare.

ARMY, US, is headed by the chief of staff, who is responsible to the civilian secretary of the army in the US Department of Defense. He is also the Army member of the JOINT CHIEFS OF STAFF. The major Army commands include the Forces Command, which comprises the six armies based in the US; the Training and Doctrine Command; the Matériel Command; the Intelligence Command; the Criminal Investigation Command; and the Corps of Engineers. In 1986, 781,000 men and women served in the US Army.

ARNE, Thomas Augustine (1710–1778), English composer whose settings of Shakespeare's *Blow, Blow, Thou Winter Wind* and *Where The Bee Sucks* became perennial favorites. He also composed the air *Rule, Britannia*.

ARNIM, Ludwig Joachim von (1781–1831), German Romantic poet. With Clemens BRENTANO he edited a famous collection of German folk poetry, *Des Knaben Wunderhorn* (1806).

ARNOLD, Benedict (1741–1801), American general and traitor in the Revolutionary War. He fought outstandingly for the American cause at Ticonderoga (1775) and Saratoga (1777) and in 1778 received command of Philadelphia. In 1780 Arnold was reprimanded for abusing his authority. That year, however, he assumed the important command of West Point and with John ANDRÉ plotted its surrender to the British in revenge for past criticisms. André's capture forced Arnold to flee to the British side, and in 1781 he went into exile in London.

ARNOLD, Henry Harley (1886–1950), pioneer aviator and US Air Force general who helped build US air power and develop the air force as a unified separate service. "Hap" Arnold held several early flying records, became chief of the Air Corps (1938), headed the Army Air Forces in WWII and was made general of the Army (1944), being later retitled general of the Air Force.

ARNOLD, Matthew (1822–1888), English poet and literary critic. His poetry, perhaps best represented by the collections *Empedocles on Etna, and Other Poems* (1852) and *New Poems* (1867), is characteristically introspective, though Arnold could equally achieve a classical impersonality. Both in his poetry and his criticism (*Culture and Anarchy* 1869; *Literature and Dogma* 1873) Arnold showed a keen awareness of the changing cultural climate of his time. He worked as a schools inspector (1851–86) and was Professor of Poetry at Oxford (1857–67).

ARNOLD, Thomas (1795–1842), English headmaster of Rugby School whose approach to teaching, with its stress on character development, radically influenced English public school education. He was the father of Matthew ARNOLD.

ARON, Raymond (1905–1983), French sociologist, political scientist and journalist. A professor at the Sorbonne 1955–68, he was a critic of both the Gaullists and left-wing intellectuals. His books include *Opium of the Intellectuals* (1955), *Main Currents in Sociological Thought* (1961), and *In Defense of Decadent Europe* (1977).

AROOSTOOK WAR, boundary dispute of 1839 between settlers of Me. and New Brunswick, Canada. Both sides claimed lands along the Aroostook R. War between the US and Britain was averted by a truce and the appointment of a boundary commission. Its findings were incorporated into the WEBSTER-ASHBURTON TREATY of 1842.

ARP, Jean or **Hans** (1887–1966), Franco-Swiss sculptor, painter and poet. Briefly associated with the BLAUE REITER, he was a cofounder of DADA in Zurich (1916) and later a Surrealist. From the 1930s he created sculptures and reliefs remarkable for their elemental purity and strength.

ARROW, Kenneth (1921–   ), US economist, at Harvard (1968–79) and Stanford (from 1979). He received the 1972 Nobel Prize in Economics.

ARSENIC (As), metalloid in Group VA of the PERIODIC TABLE. Its chief ore is arsenopyrite, which is roasted to give arsenic (III) oxide, or white arsenic, used as a poison. Arsenic has two main allotropes (see ALLOTROPY): yellow arsenic, As_4, resembling white PHOSPHORUS; and gray (metallic) arsenic. It burns in air and reacts with most other elements, forming trivalent

and pentavalent compounds, all highly toxic. It is used as a doping agent in TRANSISTORS; gallium arsenide is used in LASERS. AW 74.9, subl 613°C, sg 1.97 (yellow), 5.73 (gray).

ART. See COMMERCIAL ART; PAINTING; SCULPTURE. Also entries under various styles and periods, for example ABSTRACT ART; BAROQUE; CUBISM; IMPRESSIONISM.

ARTAUD, Antonin (1896–1948), French author, actor and director. His theories of a "Theater of Cruelty," where the elemental forces of the psyche would be spectacularly exposed, have had a strong influence on modern theater.

ART DECO, a style of design popular in the US and Europe from the late 1920s through the 1930s. It emphasized geometrical or modified geometrical shapes and simplified lines, representing a radical reaction to the ornateness of Victorian design and expressing implied admiration of functionalism and machine technology. Receiving impetus at the 1925 Paris Exhibition for Decorative Arts, the style was applied in architecture, interior decoration, furniture-making and the design of a wide range of objects, from locomotives to salt-and-pepper shakers. Prime existing examples of art deco are the Chrysler Building and the interior of the Radio City Music Hall in New York City.

ARTERIOSCLEROSIS, disease of arteries in which the wall becomes thickened and rigid, and blood flow is hindered. **Artherosclerosis** is the formation of fatty deposits (containing CHOLESTEROL) in the inner lining of an ARTERY, followed by scarring and calcification. It is commoner in older age groups, but in DIABETES, disorders of fat METABOLISM and high-blood pressure, its appearance may be earlier. Excess saturated fats in the blood may play a role in its formation. A rarer form, **medial sclerosis,** is caused by degeneration and calcification of the middle muscular layer of the artery. Narrowing or obstruction of cerebral arteries may lead to STROKE, while that of coronary arteries causes ANGINA PECTORIS and CORONARY THROMBOSIS. Reduced blood flow to the limbs may cause CRAMP on exertion, ULCERS and GANGRENE. Established arteriosclerosis cannot be reversed, but a low fat diet, exercise and the avoidance of smoking help in prevention. Surgery by artery-replacement or removal of deposits is occasionally indicated.

ARTERY, blood vessel which carries BLOOD from the HEART to the TISSUES (see BLOOD CIRCULATION). The arteries are elastic and expand with each PULSE. In most vertebrates, the two main arteries leaving the heart are the pulmonary artery, which carries blood from the body to the LUNGS to be reoxygenated, and the AORTA which supplies the body with oxygenated blood. Major arteries supply each limb and organ and within each they divide repeatedly until arterioles and CAPILLARIES are reached. Fish have only one arterial system, which leads from the heart via the GILLS to the body. (See also ARTERIOSCLEROSIS.)

ARTESIAN WELL, a well in which water rises under hydrostatic pressure above the level of the AQUIFER in which it has been confined by overlying impervious strata. Often pumping is necessary to bring the water to the surface, but true artesian wells (named for the French province of Artois where they were first constructed) flow without assistance.

ARTHRITIS, INFLAMMATION, with pain and swelling, of joints. **Osteoarthritis** is most common, though there is no true inflammation; it is a wear-and-tear arthritis, causing pain and limitation of movement. OBESITY, previous trauma and inflammatory arthritis predispose. Bacterial infection (e.g., by STAPHYLOCOCCI or TUBERCULOSIS), with PUS in the joint, and GOUT, due to deposition of crystals in synovial fluid, may lead to serious joint destruction. **Rheumatoid arthritis** is a systemic disease manifested mainly in joints, with inflammation of synovial membranes and secondary destruction. In the hands, tendons may be disrupted, and extreme deformity can result. Arthritis also occurs in many other systemic diseases including rheumatic fever, lupus erythematosus, psoriasis and some venereal diseases. Treatment of arthritis includes anti-inflammatory ANALGESICS (e.g., ASPIRIN), rest, local heat and PHYSIOTHERAPY. STEROIDS are sometimes helpful, but their long-term use is now discouraged. Badly damaged joints may need surgical treatment or replacement.

ARTHROPODA, largest and most diverse phylum of the ANIMAL KINGDOM, containing, amongst others, INSECTS, millipedes, CENTIPEDES, CRUSTACEA, arachnida, and king crabs. They are characterized by a segmented EXOSKELETON with jointed limbs. This is shed at intervals, the arthropod emerging in a new, soft exoskeleton which has developed beneath: often this molting is followed by rapid growth. Molting may cease on attainment of adulthood, but many crustacea molt periodically throughout their lives. FOSSIL arthropods include the trilobites.

ARTHUR, Chester Alan (1830–1886), 21st president of the US. Arthur was vice-president under James A. Garfield and became president on the latter's assassination in 1881. Born in Fairfield, Vt., he was the son of a teacher from N Ireland. He entered a New York City law office in 1853 and soon after won a reputation as a progressive attorney in two important civil rights cases. During the Civil War he became quartermaster-general of the N.Y. Militia.

Returning to the law after the war, Arthur became active in city politics as a Republican, and President Grant appointed him customs collector for the port of New York in 1871. In this post, Arthur's name became linked with the "spoils system" and, although his personal integrity was not openly doubted, he was eventually removed from office in 1878 following an inquiry instigated by President Hayes. Arthur attended the Republican National Convention of 1880 and was chosen to make up the ticket under Garfield. On Garfield's death, he supported demands for the reform of the civil service, and the important PENDLETON ACT was passed in 1883. His attempts to cut taxes and tariff duties failed to gain the backing of Congress.

Arthur's stand against narrow party interests won the approval of many of his critics but alienated his own party, and cost him the renomination in 1884. He retired to his law practice.

ARTHURIAN LEGENDS, the literature relating the feats of King Arthur and his knights. Arthur himself is mentioned in a 9th-century chronicle, but the basis of the legends is found in Geoffrey of Monmouth (1137). From then until the 16th century a cycle of romances of chivalry developed, mainly written in French and in both prose and verse, drawing upon Celtic folklore (probably from Brittany) and incorporating the life and death of Arthur himself, the loves of Lancelot and Guinevere and of Tristan and Yseult, the story of Merlin and the quest for the Holy Grail. From them Sir Thomas MALORY distilled his *Morte d'Arthur* (1485), which inspired Lord TENNYSON's *Idylls of the King* (1859) and T. H. White's *The Once and Future King* (1958).

ARTICLES OF CONFEDERATION, the first written framework of government for the US. They were drafted in 1776–77 after the Declaration of Independence, but it was 1781 before all 13 states ratified them. The states were wary of a centralized and remote government because of their experience of the English Parliament, and the national government they set up had limited powers. It was to operate through

Congress, in which each state had one vote, and to control foreign affairs, war and peace, coinage, the post office and some other matters. But "sovereignty, freedom and independence" remained with the separate states. Congress had no way of enforcing its decrees, and there were no federal courts. The shortcomings of the Articles were evident, particularly with reference to interstate trade, and the Constitutional Convention of 1787 abandoned them in favor of the present UNITED STATES CONSTITUTION which took effect in 1789.

ARTIFICIAL INSEMINATION, introduction of sperm into the vagina by means other than copulation. The technique is widely used for breeding livestock as it produces many offspring from one selected male (see HEREDITY). It has a limited use in compensating for human impotence and sterility.

ARTIFICIAL INTELLIGENCE, the capacity of a computer to perform functions that are normally associated with human intelligence, such as reasoning, learning, and self-improvement. For example, computer scientists are trying to make computers understand English or other human languages so that operators do not have to use special computer commands. Another goal is to make computer vision systems that can recognize objects — for example, to enable a robot to find objects on a conveyor belt. A third goal is to enable computers to "reason," to make decisions based on data they have been fed and have processed.

ARTIFICIAL RESPIRATION, the means of inducing RESPIRATION when it has ceased, as after drowning, asphyxia, in coma or respiratory paralysis. It must be continued until natural breathing returns, and ensuring a clear airway via the mouth to the lungs is essential. The most common first aid methods are: "mouth-to-mouth," in which air is breathed via the mouth into the lungs and is then allowed to escape, and the less effective Holger Nielsen technique, where rhythmic movements of the chest force air out and encourage its entry alternately. If prolonged artificial respiration is needed, mechanical pumps are used, and these may support respiration for months or even years.

ARTILLERY, once the term for all military machinery, it now refers to guns too heavy to be carried by one or two men. The branch of the army involved is also known as the artillery. Modern artillery may be said to have its origins in the 14th century when weapons that used gunpowder were first developed. The importance of artillery in battle increased as equipment became more mobile, and scientific advances improved its accuracy and effectiveness. WWII saw the development of specialized antitank and antiaircraft guns, and the first really effective use of rockets. Since then the guided MISSILE has been produced, with its long ranges and high accuracy offering a formidable threat.

Many advances have been made in recent years to increase the mobility of US artillery units and to improve the accuracy of their fire. These include the use of lighter tougher alloys for towed pieces, improved ammunition and ultra-modern target acquisition systems drawing on laser and radar technology. Accuracy is further increased by the use of electronic data processing in fire control systems.

ART NOUVEAU, late 19th-century art movement which influenced decorative styles throughout the West. Its themes were exotic or decadent and its characteristic line sinuous and highly ornamental. The movement aimed to reunite art and life, and so to produce everyday objects of beauty. It was of importance in the applied arts, some notable architecture, furniture, jewelry and book designs being produced in this style. Graphic art too was much affected by Art Nouveau, as seen in the work of Aubrey BEARDSLEY. Other notable artists of the movement were the painter Gustav KLIMT and the architects Antonio GAUDI and Victor Horta, and in the applied arts TIFFANY, Lalique and Charpentier.

ARUBA, small island off the Venezuelan coast, 45mi W of Curaçao, part of the NETHERLANDS ANTILLES. It is about 19mi long and 4mi wide, and is inhabited by people of Indian and Negro descent who speak a hybrid language called *Papiamento.* The island won internal autonomy in 1986; full independence is scheduled for 1996. Pop. 65,800.

ARYAN (Sanskrit: noble), name once used for the family of languages now known as Indo-European. The word acquired political connotations in Nazi Germany, being interpreted as "Nordic" or non-Jewish in race, and has thus been discredited in modern usage.

ASBESTOS, name of various fibrous minerals, chiefly chrysotile and amphibole. Canada and the USSR are the chief producers. It is a valuable industrial material because it is refractory, alkali- and acid-resistant and an electrical insulator. It can be spun to make fireproof fabrics for protective clothing and safety curtains, or molded to make tiles, bricks and automobile brake linings. Asbestos particles may cause PNEUMOCONIOSIS and lung CANCER if inhaled.

ASBURY, Francis (1745–1816), first Methodist bishop in the US. Born in England, he came to the US in 1771 as a Methodist missionary. With his energetic guidance, and despite his ill-health, Methodism in the US became widely established. Asbury was elected bishop in 1784.

ASCENSION, The, the bodily ascent into heaven of Jesus Christ on the 40th day after his resurrection. The event, described in the New Testament, signifies Christ's entry into glory and thus promises believers a heavenly life. Ascension Day is a major Christian festival.

ASCH, Sholem (1880–1957), leading Yiddish novelist and playwright. Born in Poland, he spent most of his life in the US. His many books deal with Jewish life both in Europe and the US, and with the relationship between Judaism and Christianity, as in *The Nazarene* (1939).

ASCOT, English town near Windsor. It is the site of the famous June horse race meeting, Royal Ascot, traditionally attended by British royalty.

ASGARD, in Norse mythology, the realm of the gods. It contained many halls and palaces; chief of these was VALHALLA, where ODIN entertained warriors killed in battle. The only entry to Asgard was by the rainbow bridge called Bifrost.

ASHANTI, a region of S Ghana, and the name of the people who live there. From the 17th century to 1902, when Britain annexed the region, the powerful Ashanti Confederacy linked several small kingdoms under one chief. The symbol of their unity was the sacred Golden Stool which, in their religion of ancestor-worship, represents the departed spirits of the Ashanti. The present-day Ashanti are a thriving agrarian people numbering about one million.

ASHBERRY, John Lawrence (1927–   ), US poet, recipient of Pulitzer (1976) and Bollingen (1985) prizes.

ASHCAN SCHOOL, or **"The Eight,"** name given to a New York City group of painters, formed in 1908. They were so called because they chose to paint everyday aspects of city life. The Eight—Arthur DAVIES, William GLACKENS, Ernest LAWSON, George LUKS, Maurice PRENDERGAST, Everett SHINN, Robert HENRI and John SLOAN—differed in many ways but were united in their dislike of academicism. They were instrumental in bringing the ARMORY SHOW to New York in 1913.

ASHKENAZIM, those Jews whose medieval ancestors lived in Germany. Persecution drove them to spread throughout central and E Europe, and in the 19th and 20th centuries overseas, notably to the US. Their ritual and Hebrew pronunciation differ from those of the SEPHARDIM (Jews of Oriental countries). Up to the beginning of the 20th century most Ashkenazim spoke Yiddish. Most Jews in the US and the majority of the world's Jews are Ashkenazim. (See also JEWS.)

ASHLEY, William Henry (c1778–1838), US fur trader and politician. He explored the area W of Missouri as far as the Great Salt Lake and helped to make known the OREGON TRAIL.

ASHTON, Sir Frederick (1906–1988), British dancer and choreographer. His work, which included such new productions as *Façade* (1931) and *La Fille Mal Gardée* (1960), has had great influence on British ballet. He was director of the Royal Ballet 1963–70.

ASHURBANIPAL (7th century BC), king (668–627 BC) of ancient Assyria at the height of its power. He won victories over the Egyptians, Elamites, and Chaldeans. From his palace at Nineveh have come remarkable reliefs and a large library of clay tablets. A few years after his death his empire fell to the Medes, Persians, and Babylonians.

ASH WEDNESDAY, first of the 40 days of the Christian fast of Lent. The name derives from the early practice of sprinkling penitents with ashes. Today the ash of burnt palms is used to mark the sign of the cross on the foreheads of believers.

ASIA, the world's largest continent, covers more than 17,139,000sq mi (nearly one-third of the earth's land surface) and has about 2,995,000,000 people (excluding Soviet Asia), or nearly 60% of the total world population. It extends from the Arctic Ocean in the N to the Indian Ocean in the S, and from the Pacific Ocean in the E to the Mediterranean in the W. Its traditional border with Europe is formed by the Black Sea, the Caucasus Mts, the Caspian Sea, the Ural R and the Ural Mts, but the USSR located W of the Urals is often excluded in modern usage. In the SW, Asia is separated from Africa by the Red Sea and the Suez Canal. The combined land mass of Europe and Asia is sometimes treated as a single continent, Eurasia.

Land. Asia is a continent of infinite diversity, with extremes of every kind, the ultimate physical contrast being between Mt Everest (29,028ft), the world's highest mountain, and the Dead Sea (1,294ft below sea level). At its heart is the great system of mountain chains and high plateaus focused on the Pamir Knot. Among these huge mountain chains are the Karakoram Range, Himalayas, Kunlun Shan, Tien Shan, Altai Mountains, Hindu Kush and Sulaiman Range. Extensions include the lesser ranges of Asia Minor and, in the E, the Arakan Yoma range (Assam and Burma) which reappears in Indonesia. Another system of ranges stretches from E Siberia to Japan and the Philippines. The major plateaus include the plateau of Tibet, the Tarim basin and the great plateau of Mongolia. The triangular lowland region N of the mountains embraces the W Siberian lowlands and the low plateau of central Siberia. Weaknesses in the earth's crust are reflected in the active volcanoes bordering the Pacific Ocean in Indonesia, the Philippines, Japan and the Kamchatka peninsula and also in Turkey and Iran.

The major rivers include the Ob and its tributary, the Irtysh, the Yenisey and Lena, all flowing to the Arctic Ocean; the Indus (Pakistan), Ganges (India and Bangladesh) and Brahmaputra (China and India); and the Yellow and Yangtze rivers in China. Lake Baikal is the largest freshwater lake. Deserts include the Gobi Desert in Mongolia and the Great Sandy Desert of Arabia.

Climate and Vegetation. Asia has every known type of climate, from the polar to the tropical. The heart of the continent has extremes of temperature in winter and summer and low rainfall while much of E and SE Asia is monsoonal and annual rainfall may reach 400in. Vegetation ranges from the tundra of the far north to the taiga (coniferous forest) of Siberia, the treeless grasslands of the steppes and the tropical rain forests of India and SE Asia.

People. The product of thousands of years of migrations, invasions, conquests and intermingling, the people of Asia belong mainly to three ethnic groups: Mongoloid (including Chinese, Japanese and Koreans), Caucasoid (including Arabs, Afghans, Iranians, Pakistanis and most Indian people) and Negroid (in parts of the Philippines and SE Asia). Racial mixtures are frequent in SE Asia, where the Malays are the largest group. The population is unevenly distributed, almost uninhabited areas like "High Asia" (the heart of the continent) and the deserts contrasting with the densely populated Ganges valley and the great cities of Japan and China. About one in every three Asians is urban-dwelling. A multitude of languages and dialects is spoken, derived from Indo-European, Altaic, Semitic, Sino-Tibetan and other

language families. Asia was the birthplace of several religions. Hinduism claims the largest following, but there are also millions of Buddhists and Muslims. Only about 4% of Asians are Christians. Because of this cultural diversity, it is usual to divide the continent into homogeneous cultural regions such as East Asia (China, Korea, Japan), South Asia (India, Pakistan, Sri Lanka), Southeast Asia (Malaysia, Indonesia, etc.) and SW Asia or Middle East.

Economy. About 66% of the population depend on agriculture, vital to a continent whose population is increasing at a rate of about 100,000 every 24 hours. Oil is the chief mineral resource and industrialization has been rapid in Japan, India, China, and the USSR. South Korea, Singapore, and Taiwan also developed flourishing export-oriented economies.

History. Man has lived in Asia for about 500,000 years. The earliest-known civilizations—Sumerian, Babylonian and Assyrian—evolved in SW Asia. In S Asia the Indus valley civilization flowered in the 3rd millennium BC, while China's remarkable culture began in the Yellow R valley about 4,000—5,000 years ago. European colonial powers (Britain, France, Portugal, Spain, Netherlands) ruled much of S and SE Asia in the 18th and 19th centuries, but except for a few (e.g. Hong Kong, Macao) most former colonies became independent after WWII. Agreements to return Hong Kong and Macao to China were reached in 1984 and 1987.

ASIA MINOR, peninsula in SW Asia comprising most of modern Turkey. Mountainous and surrounded on three sides by sea, it is bounded on the E by the upper Euphrates R. Civilizations such as that of Troy flourished here from the Bronze Age onwards. After the destruction of the Hittite empire in 1200 BC, the land belonged successively to the Medes, Persians, Greeks and Romans. In the 5th century AD it passed to the Byzantine emperors and remained among their last possessions, constantly eroded as their power declined until in the 15th century it became part of the OTTOMAN EMPIRE and remained so until the Republic of Turkey was founded (1923).

ASIMOV, Isaac (1920–   ), prolific US author and educator, best known for his science fiction books such as the *Foundation* trilogy (1951–53; sequel, 1982) and for his many science books for laymen. He also taught biochemistry at Boston U.

ASOKA (d. 232 BC), third emperor of the Maurya dynasty of India, whose acceptance of BUDDHISM as the official religion of his vast empire had a major effect on that faith's predominance in Asia. He was said to have been so repelled by a particularly bloody victory of his troops over what is now Orissa that he turned to nonviolence and the Buddhist way of righteousness, and sent missionaries into Burma, Ceylon (Sri Lanka), Syria, Greece and Egypt.

ASP, the Egyptian COBRA *Naja haje* (family: Elapidae), an extremely poisonous snake up to 7ft in length. Sacred in ancient Egypt, it was legendarily the cause of Cleopatra's death. The name is also applied to the horned and asp VIPERS.

ASPHALT, a tough black material used in road paving, roofing and canal and reservoir lining. Now obtained mainly from PETROLEUM refinery residues (although natural deposits are still worked), it consists mainly of heavy HYDROCARBONS.

ASPIRIN, or **acetylsalicylic acid,** an effective analgesic, which also reduces FEVER and INFLAMMATION and also affects BLOOD platelets. It is useful in HEADACHE, minor feverish illness, MENSTRUATION pain, RHEUMATIC FEVER, inflammatory ARTHRITIS, and may also be used to prevent THROMBOSIS. Aspirin may cause gastrointestinal irritation and HEMORRHAGE, and should be avoided in cases of peptic ULCER.

ASQUITH, Herbert Henry, 1st Earl of Oxford and Asquith (1852–1928), British prime minister 1908–16. His term as head of the LIBERAL PARTY was one of great activity and political reform, but his leadership foundered in Dec. 1916 over his conduct of WWI, coupled with the chaos brought about by the EASTER RISING in Ireland. He resigned in favor of the rival Liberal leader David LLOYD GEORGE.

ASS. See DONKEY.

ASSAD, Hafiz al- (1928?–   ), president of Syria from 1971. Commander of the Syrian air force and defense minister, he led a coup in 1970 that made him premier, and a year later, under a new constitution, he was elected president. At home, he rigorously suppressed dissent. Abroad, he opposed the existence of Israel, supported Iran in its war with Iraq (the only Arab leader to do so), extended Syrian influence in Lebanon, and sheltered anti-Western terrorists.

ASSASSIN, perpetrator of a political murder. The term derives from the name given to members of a fanatical sect of Islam founded by Hasan ibn-al-Sabbah, who refused to recognize the Seljuk regime in Persia at the end of the 11th century. His followers hid in the mountains and made periodic murderous raids on their enemies after smoking HASHISH; hence "hashshasin," which became "assassin."

ASSAYING, a method of chemical ANALYSIS for determining NOBLE METALS in ores or alloys, used since the 2nd millennium BC. The sample is fused with a flux containing LEAD (II) oxide. This produces a lead button containing the noble metals, which is heated in oxygen to oxidize the lead and other impurities, leaving a bead of the noble metals which is weighed and separated chemically.

ASSEMBLIES OF GOD, largest of the Protestant Pentecostal denominations in the US. They were organized as a separate entity in 1914, and later established their headquarters in Springfield, Mo. They now have over 1 million members.

ASSINIBOIN INDIANS, Sioux tribe of the North American plains who left the Yanktonai Sioux to spread out from Canada across the NW US. A nomadic people, they lived primarily by hunting. Like other Sioux, they took quickly to the use of horses and guns. They were easily defeated by the white settlers, because of the extinction of the buffalo, and were placed on reservations in 1884.

ASSISI, town about 15mi SE of Perugia in Italy, situated on Mt Subasio above the plains of Umbria. The birthplace of St. FRANCIS and St. CLARE, it is also noted for its medieval buildings, particularly the Gothic Basilica of St. Francis and the Church of St. Clare. Pop 23,800.

ASSISI, Saint Francis of. See FRANCIS OF ASSISI, SAINT.

ASSOCIATED PRESS (AP), the oldest and largest US news agency, founded in 1848 by six New York City newspapers, now with offices sending and receiving throughout the world. It is a non-profit organization financed by subscriptions from member newspapers, periodicals and broadcasting stations.

ASSOCIATION, in PSYCHOLOGY, the mental linking of one item with others: e.g., black and white, Tom with Dick and Harry, etc. The connections are described by the principles of association involving similarity, contiguity, frequency, recency and vividness. In association tests, subjects are presented with one word and asked to respond either with a specifically related word, such as a rhyme or antonym, or merely with the first word that comes to mind.

ASSOCIATIONISM, a psychological school which held that the sole mechanism of human learning consisted in the permanent association in the intellect of impressions which had been repeatedly presented to the senses. Originating in the philosophy of John LOCKE and developed through the work of John Gay, David HARTLEY, James and John Stuart MILL and Alexander Bain, the "association of ideas" was the dominant thesis in British PSYCHOLOGY for 200 years.

ASSOCIATION OF SOUTHEAST ASIAN NATIONS (ASEAN), a framework for regional cooperation created by the five non-Communist governments of Malaysia, Thailand, Indonesia, Singapore and the Philippines in 1967. Since 1976 the members have elected a secretary general to preside over implementation of decisions on a wide range of issues from tourism and tariff preferences to foreign-policy matters. It has consistently called for a Zone of Peace in the troubled area of Southeast Asia.

ASSUMPTION OF THE VIRGIN, official dogma of the Roman Catholic Church (declared by Pope PIUS XII in 1950) that the Virgin Mary was "assumed into heaven body and soul" at the end of her life. The feast day of the Assumption is August 15.

ASSYRIA. See BABYLONIA AND ASSYRIA.

ASSYRIAN CHURCH. See NESTORIANS.

ASTAIRE, Fred (1899–1987), US dancer, choreographer and actor, born Frederick Austerlitz. First in partnership with his sister Adele on the stage and later with Ginger Rogers in such films as *Top Hat* (1935) and *Swingtime* (1938), he became one of the most popular US musical comedy stars as well a dancer whose drive for originality and perfection made him the idol of other dancers. Later films, with other partners, included *Holiday Inn* (1942), *The Band Wagon* (1953) and *Funny Face* (1957).

ASTEROIDS, the thousands of planetoids, or minor planets, ranging in diameter from a few feet to 470 miles (Ceres), most of whose orbits lie in the asteroid belt between the orbits of Mars and Jupiter. Vesta is the only asteroid visible to the naked eye, although Ceres was the first to be discovered (1801 by Giuseppe Piazzi). Their total mass is estimated to be 0.001 that of the earth. A few asteroids have highly elliptical, earth-approaching orbits, and the so-called Trojan group of asteroids shares the orbit of the planet Jupiter. (See also METEOR; SOLAR SYSTEM.)

ASTHENOSPHERE, the worldwide "soft layer" underlying the rigid LITHOSPHERE and located some 70 to 250km below the earth's surface. The zone is considered part of the upper MANTLE and is characterized by low seismic velocities, suggesting that it may be partially molten. In plate tectonic theory,

rigid slablike plates of the lithosphere move over the asthenosphere. (See also PLATE TECTONICS.)

ASTHMA, chronic respiratory disease marked by recurrent attacks of wheezing and acute breathlessness. It is due to abnormal bronchial sensitivity and is usually associated with ALLERGY to house dust, motes, pollen, FUNGI, furs and other substances which may precipitate an attack. Chest infection, exercise or emotional upset may also provoke an attack. The symptoms are caused by spasm of bronchioles and the accumulation of thick mucous. Cyanosis may occur in severe attacks. Desensitization injections, cromoglycate, STEROIDS and drugs that dilate bronchi are used in prevention; acute attacks may require OXYGEN, aminophylline or ADRENALINE, and steroids.

ASTIGMATISM, a defect of VISION in which the lens of the EYE exhibits different curvatures in different planes, corrected using cylindrical lenses. Also, an ABERRATION occurring with lenses having spherical surfaces.

ASTOR, John Jacob (1763–1848), German-born US merchant who built a large fortune in the China trade, New York City real estate, and the fur trade. He founded (1808) the American Fur Company, which monopolized the US fur trade for decades.

ASTOR, Nancy, Viscountess Astor (1879–1964), first woman to sit in the British Parliament. She was born in Greenwood, Va., in the US but lived in England after marriage (her second) to Waldorf Astor in 1906. When her husband was elevated to the House of Lords she won his seat in Commons as a Conservative (1919). Serving until 1945, she supported welfare measures to assist women and children, but opposed socialism. Colorful and witty, she could also be controversial, as when, as hostess of the "Cliveden Set," she was linked with an attitude of appeasement toward Germany before WWII.

ASTROLABE, an astronomical instrument dating from the Hellenic Period, used to measure the altitude of celestial bodies and, before the introduction of the SEXTANT, as a navigational aid. It consisted of a vertical disk with an engraved scale across which was mounted a sighting rule or "alidade" pivoted at its center.

ASTROLOGY, system of beliefs and methods of calculation where practitioners attempt to divine the future from the study of the heavens. Originating in ancient Mesopotamia as a means for predicting the fate of states and their rulers, the astrology which found its way into Hellenistic culture applied itself also to the destinies of individuals. Together with the desire to devise accurate CALENDARS, astrology provided a key incentive leading to the earliest systematic ASTRONOMY and was a continuing spur to the development of astronomical techniques until the 17th century. The majority of classical and medieval astronomers, PTOLEMY and KEPLER among them, practiced astrology, often earning their livelihoods thus. Astrology exercised its greatest influence in the Graeco-Roman world and again in renaissance Europe (despite the opposition of the Church) and, although generally abandoned after the 17th century, it has continued to excite a fluctuating interest down to the present. The key datum in Western astrology is the position of the stars and planets, described relative to the 12 divisions of the ZODIAC, at the moment of an individual's birth.

ASTRONAUT, name given to US test pilots and scientists chosen by the NATIONAL AERONAUTICS AND SPACE ADMINISTRATION to man US space flights. The first seven astronauts were chosen in 1959. The first manned flight was made by Commander Alan B. Shepard in 1961. Lt. Col. John GLENN, Jr., became the first American to orbit the earth in 1962, and astronauts Edwin Eugene Aldrin, Jr., and Neil Alden ARMSTRONG became the first men on the moon in 1969. (See also SPACE EXPLORATION.)

ASTRONOMY, the study of the heavens. Born at the crossroads of agriculture and religion, astronomy, the earliest of the sciences, was of great practical importance in ancient civilization. Before 2000 BC, Babylonians, Chinese and Egyptians all sowed their crops according to calendars computed from the regular motions of the sun and moon.

Although early Greek philosophers were more concerned with the physical nature of the heavens than with precise observation, later Greek scientists (see ARISTARCHUS; HIPPARCHUS) returned to the problems of positional astronomy. The vast achievement of Greek astronomy was epitomized in the writing of Claudius PTOLEMY. His *Almagest,* passing through Arabic translations, was eventually transmitted to medieval Europe and remained the chief authority among astronomers for over 1,400 years.

Throughout this period the main purpose of positional astronomy had been to assist in the casting of accurate horoscopes, the twin sciences of astronomy and ASTROLOGY

having not yet parted company. The structure of the universe meanwhile remained the preserve of (Aristotelian) physics. The work of COPERNICUS represented an early attempt to harmonize an improved positional astronomy with a true physical theory of planetary motion. Against the judgment of antiquity that sun, moon and planets circled the earth as lanterns set in a series of concentric transparent shells, in his *De Revolutionibus* (1543) Copernicus argued that the sun lay motionless at the center of the planetary system.

Although the Copernican (or heliocentric) hypothesis proved to be a sound basis for the computation of navigators' tables (the need for which was stimulating renewed interest in astronomy), it did not become unassailably established in astronomical theory until NEWTON published his mathematical derivation of KEPLER'S LAWS in 1687. In the meanwhile KEPLER, working on the superb observational data of Tycho BRAHE, had shown the orbit of Mars to be elliptical and not circular, and GALILEO had used the newly invented TELESCOPE to discover SUNSPOTS, the phases of Venus and four moons of Jupiter.

Since the 17th century the development of astronomy has followed on successive improvements in the design of telescopes. In 1781 William HERSCHEL discovered Uranus, the first discovery of a new PLANET to be made in historical times. Measurement of the PARALLAX of a few stars in 1838 first allowed the estimation of interstellar distances. Analysis of the FRAUNHOFER LINES in the spectrum of the sun gave scientists their first indication of the chemical composition of the STARS.

In the present century the scope of observational astronomy has extended as radio and X-ray telescopes (see RADIO ASTRONOMY; X-RAY ASTRONOMY) have come into use, leading to the discovery of QUASARS, PULSARS and neutron stars. In their turn these discoveries have enabled cosmologists to develop even more self-consistent models of the universe. (See also COSMOLOGY; OBSERVATORY.)

ASTROPHYSICS deals with the physical and chemical nature of celestial objects and events, using data produced by RADIO ASTRONOMY and SPECTROSCOPY. By investigating the laws of the universe as they currently operate, astronomers can formulate theories of stellar evolution and behavior.

ASTURIAS, Miguel Angel (1899–1974), Guatemalan writer and diplomat. He won the Lenin Peace Prize in 1966 and the

Nobel Prize for Literature in 1967. His books *The Cyclone* (1950) and *The Green Pope* (1954) attacked the exploitation of Guatemalan Indians.

ASTURIAS, historic region of Spain, now part of the modern province of Oviedo. Originally a Visigothic refuge from the Moorish invasions, it became a powerful and independent Christian kingdom from the 8th to the 10th centuries. From 1388 until 1931 the heir to the Spanish throne was called Prince of Asturias. Today this mountainous region is a major mining center for coal and other minerals.

ASWAN HIGH DAM, one of the world's largest dams built on the Nile 1960–70, located 4mi above the 1902 Aswan dam. Having created the vast Lake Nasser, stretching some 300mi along the course of the Nile, the dam's waters drive one of the world's largest hydroelectric generating stations and are used to irrigate over 1 million acres of farmland.

ASYLUM, Right of, a nation's right to grant protection to a refugee from another country. Asylum is granted by most countries only to political fugitives; ordinary criminals are not usually given asylum, though political crimes are loosely defined. The right to asylum is recognized by signatories to the UN Universal Declaration of Human Rights (1948).

ATACAMA DESERT, extremely arid plateau in N Chile, 600mi long with an average width of 90mi. Rich in borax and saline deposits, it is a major source of natural nitrates, copper and other minerals.

ATAHUALPA (c1500–1533), last Inca emperor of Peru. He was the eldest son of Huayna Capac, who died in 1525, leaving the kingdom to his younger son Huascar. Atahualpa inherited the Quito region and a large army. In 1530 he attacked Huascar, deposing him in 1532, just before the arrival of the CONQUISTADORS under PIZARRO. Atahualpa refused to accept Christianity and Spanish suzerainty; the Spaniards kidnapped him, extorted a vast ransom and murdered him after a show trial.

ATATURK, Kemal (originally: Mustafa Kemal; 1881–1938), first president (1923–38) of the modern Turkish state he helped to found. Born in Salonika, he received a military education and, as a member of the Young Turk movement, helped depose the Ottoman Sultan Abdul Hamid II in 1909. After distinguished service in the Second Balkan War (1913) and WWI, he led the Turkish war of independence as the head of a provisional government in Ankara (1919–23), repulsing a Greek invasion of ANATOLIA. Heading the new republic, Kemal reduced the power of Islam, abolishing the caliphate and the DERVISH sects, substituted Roman for Arabic lettering, rid TURKISH of Arabic words and modernized Turkey's economy. In 1934 he passed a law requiring all Turks to use surnames in the Western style and himself took the name Ataturk—"Father of the Turks."

ATAVISM, the inheritance (see HEREDITY) by an individual organism of characteristics not shown by its parental generation. Once thought to be throwbacks to an ancestral form, atavisms are now known to be primarily the result of the random reappearance of recessive traits (see GENETICS), though they may result also from aberrations in the development of the embryo or from disease.

ATAXIA, impaired coordination of body movements resulting in unsteady gait, difficulty in fine movements and speech disorder. Caused by disease of the cerebellum or spinal cord, ataxia occurs with MULTIPLE SCLEROSIS, certain hereditary conditions and in the late stages of syphilis (see VENEREAL DISEASES).

ATHABASCA, river and lake in N Alberta and Saskatchewan, Canada. The river rises in Jasper National Park and flows 765mi to the 3,120sq mi lake. The Athabascan tar sands between Fort McMurray and Fort Chipewyan are rich in crude oil. Uranium mining and fur trapping are the region's main industries.

ATHANASIAN CREED (sometimes called *Quicumque Vult,* from its opening words), Latin CREED expounding chiefly the doctrines of the Trinity and the Incarnation, regarded as authoritative by the Roman Catholic and Anglican churches, and also by some Protestant churches. Modern scholars believe it was composed in the 5th century.

ATHANASIUS, Saint (c293–373), Egyptian ecclesiastical statesman of the early Church. A devout adherent of the orthodox faith and opponent of ARIANISM, he took an active part in the religious and political controversies of his time, suffering many banishments as a result.

ATHENA (Pallas Athene), Greek goddess of wisdom and war who sprang fully-grown from ZEUS's head. The patroness of Athens, she protected legendary heroes such as ODYSSEUS. In peacetime she taught men agriculture, law, shipbuilding and all the crafts of civilization. The Romans identified her with Minerva.

ATHENS, capital of Greece, on the SW side of the Attica peninsula. Athens lies on a plain near the Saronic Gulf, with mountains to the W, N and E. The city was already important by c1500 BC, but reached its political peak after the PERSIAN WARS (490–479BC) when it led the DELIAN LEAGUE. In the 5th century PERICLES used the League's funds to rebuild the ACROPOLIS. Athens became a major center of art, architecture, philosophy and drama, the home of SOPHOCLES, EURIPIDES, SOCRATES and PLATO. Athens lost her supremacy to SPARTA in the PELOPONNESIAN WAR (431–404 BC), and later became a subject of Macedon and Rome.

Greater Athens is today the administrative, political, cultural and economic center of Greece. Tourism is a major source of income, but Athens is also an industrial center. Among its products are carpets, ships, petroleum, chemicals, textiles, electrical goods and canned foods. Exports handled at the city's port, Piraeus, include tobacco, oil, wine, aluminum and marble. Pop (city) 885,737; (metro) 3,027,331.

ATHLETE'S FOOT, a common form of RINGWORM, a contagious fungal infection of the feet, causing inflammation and scaling or maceration of the skin, especially between the toes. It may be contracted in swimming pools or from shared towels or footwear. Treatment consists in foot hygiene, dusting powder, certain carboxylic acid and antifungal ANTIBIOTICS.

ATHOS, Mount, mountain (6,670ft) in NE Greece, since the Middle Ages the site of the famous monastic community, now including 20 monasteries and 3,000 monks. The mountain and surrounding Athos peninsula constitute the semi-independent theocratic republic of Mount Athos, which proclaimed itself independent in 1913 and was granted autonomy by Greece in 1927. No women or female animals are allowed to enter the region.

ATLANTA, capital and largest city of Ga., seat of Fulton Co. Founded 1837 as the terminus of the Western and Atlantic Railroad, Atlanta was a major supply center during the Civil War and was burned to the ground by Union forces in 1864. It was rapidly rebuilt, and is today the major commercial and financial center of the S Atlantic states. The town has more than 20 colleges and universities. Pop (city) 426,000, (metro) 2,472,000.

ATLANTA CAMPAIGN, a Union offensive in the Civil War, against the Confederacy's major rail center, begun in May 1864 at Chattanooga, Tenn. Gen. Sherman's 100,000 Union troops forced the retreat of 60,000 Confederate troops and captured Atlanta in September. His army set the city ablaze before leaving (Nov. 16) on "its march to the sea," which ended in the capture of Savannah and the splitting of the Confederacy.

ATLANTIC CABLES, the telegraph and telephone cables on the bed of the North Atlantic Ocean linking North America with Europe. The first successful cable was laid by promoter Cyrus West Field (1819–1892) under the direction of William Thomson (later Lord KELVIN) at the third attempt, in 1858, but this soon failed and was replaced by a more permanent one in 1866. The first Atlantic telephone cable was not laid until 1956 and the method is at present suffering strong competition from COMMUNICATIONS SATELLITES.

ATLANTIC CHARTER, declaration of common objectives signed by F.D. Roosevelt and Churchill on Aug. 14, 1941, before the US entered WWII. It affirmed the determination of the American and British governments not to extend their territories and to promote every people's right to independence and self-determination.

ATLANTIC CITY, seaside resort and convention center in SE N.J., home of the Miss America Pageant. The first legal gambling casino opened in 1978, and other hotels with casinos have been operating since then. Its famous Boardwalk (1870) is lined by hotels and restaurants and has the Convention Hall, one of the world's largest auditoriums. Pop (city) 40,000, (metro) 293,000.

ATLANTIC INTRACOASTAL WATER-WAY, a shallow sheltered water route extending 1,134mi along the Atlantic seaboard from Norfolk, Va., to Key West, Fla., and serving pleasure craft and light shipping. The Atlantic route and the GULF INTRACOASTAL WATERWAY together make up the Intracoastal Waterway.

ATLANTIC OCEAN, ocean separating North and South America from Europe and Africa and creating by its currents the GULF STREAM which moderates the climate of NW Europe. It is the second largest of the world's oceans, the Pacific being the largest. Lying between highly industrialized continents, the N Atlantic carries the greatest proportion of the world's shipping. About half the world's fish comes from the area, 60% from the GRAND BANKS; some Atlantic fish species are verging on extinction due to the rapid development of modern fishing techniques and increasing pollution.

ATLANTIS, a mythical continent from which the Atlantic takes its name. Atlantis, as described by PLATO in the *Timaeus* and *Critias*, is situated just beyond the PILLARS OF HERCULES. He presents it as an advanced civilization that was destroyed by volcanic eruptions and earthquakes, sinking into the sea. The legend has fascinated men since antiquity, and many searches for the lost continent have been made.

ATLAS MOUNTAINS, an extension of the Alpine mountain system of Europe into NW Africa, the highest peak being Mt Toubkal (13,660ft) in SW Morocco. Olive and citrus crops are cultivated on some of the moister N slopes; sheep grazing predominates on the Saharan margins. The Atlas Mts are rich in coal, oil, iron ore and phosphates.

ATMOSPHERE, the roughly spheroidal envelope of gas, vapor and aerosol particles surrounding the EARTH, retained by gravity and forming a major constituent in the environment of most forms of terrestrial life, protecting it from the impact of meteors, cosmic ray particles and harmful solar radiation. The composition of the atmosphere and most of its physical properties vary with altitude, certain key properties being used to divide the whole into several zones, the upper and lower boundaries of which change with latitude, the time of day and the season of the year. About 75% of the total mass of atmosphere and 90% of its water vapor and aerosols are contained in the **troposphere,** the lowest zone. Excluding water vapor, the **air** of the troposphere contains 78% nitrogen, 20% oxygen, 0.9% argon, and 0.03% carbon dioxide, together with traces of the other noble gases, and methane, hydrogen and nitrous oxide. The water vapor content fluctuates within wide margins as water is evaporated from the oceans, carried in clouds and precipitated upon the continents. The air flows in meandering currents, transferring energy from the warm equatorial regions to the colder poles. The troposphere is thus the zone in which weather occurs (see METEOROLOGY), as well as that in which most air-dependent life exists. Apart from occasional inversions, the temperature falls with increasing altitude through the troposphere until at the tropopause (altitude 4.3mi at the poles; 10mi on the equator) it becomes constant (about 217K), and then slowly increases again into the **stratosphere** (up to about 30mi). The upper stratosphere contains the ozone layer which filters out the dangerous ultraviolet radiation incident from the sun. Above the stratosphere, the **mesosphere** merges into the **ionosphere,** a region containing various layers of charged particles (IONS) of immense importance in the propagation of radio waves, being used to reflect signals between distant ground stations. At greater altitudes still, the ionosphere passes into the **exosphere,** a region of rarefied helium and hydrogen gases, in turn merging into the interplanetary medium. In all, the atmosphere has a mass of about 5.2×10^{18}kg, its density being about 1.23kg/m^3 at sea level. Its weight results in its exerting an average **air pressure** of 101.3kPa (1013mbar) near the surface, this fluctuating greatly with the weather and falling off rapidly with height. The other planets of the solar system (with the possible exception of Pluto) all have distinctive atmospheres, though none of these contains as much life-supporting oxygen as does that of the earth.

ATOLL, a typically circular CORAL reef enclosing a lagoon. Many atolls, often supporting low arcuate islands, are found in the Pacific Ocean.

ATOM, classically, one of the minute, indivisible, homogeneous particles of which physical objects are composed (see ATOMISM); in 20th-century science, the name given to a relatively stable package of MATTER, that is itself made up of at least two SUBATOMIC PARTICLES. Every atom consists of a tiny nucleus (containing positively charged PROTONS and electrically neutral NEUTRONS) with which are associated a number of negatively charged ELECTRONS. These, although individually much smaller than the nucleus, occupy a hierarchy of orbitals that represent the atom's electronic energy levels and fill most of the space taken up by the atom. The number of protons in the nucleus of an atom (the atomic number, Z) defines the chemical ELEMENT of which the atom is an example. In an isolated neutral atom the number of electrons equals the atomic number, but an electrically charged ION of the same atom has either a surfeit or a deficit of electrons. The number of neutrons in the nucleus (the neutron number, N) can vary between different atoms of the same element, the resulting species being called the ISOTOPES of the element. Most stable isotopes have slightly more neutrons than protons. Although the nucleus is very small, it contains nearly all the MASS of the atom—protons and neutrons having very similar masses, and the mass of the electron (about 0.05% of the proton mass) being almost negligible. The mass of an atom is roughly equal to the total number of its protons and neutrons. This number, $Z + N$, is known as the mass number of the atom, A, the mass of a proton being counted as one. In equations representing nuclear reactions, the atomic number of an atom is often written as a subscript preceding the chemical symbol for the element, and the mass number as a superscript following it. Thus an atomic nucleus with mass number 16 and containing 8 protons belongs to an atom of "oxygen-16," written $_8O^{16}$. The average of the mass numbers of the various naturally occurring isotopes of an element, weighted according to their relative abundance, gives the chemical ATOMIC WEIGHT of the element. Subatomic particles fired into atomic nuclei can cause nuclear reactions that give rise either to new isotopes of the original element or to atoms of a different element, and that emit alpha particles, or beta rays, sometimes accompanied by gamma rays.

The earliest atomistic concept, regarding the atom as that which could not be subdivided, was implicit in the first modern, chemical atomic theory, that of John DALTON (1808). Although it survives in the once-common chemical definition of atom—the smallest fragment of a chemical element that retains the properties of the element and can take part in chemical reactions—chemists now recognize that the MOLECULE, not the atom, is the natural chemical unit of matter. The atomic nuclei form the basic structure of the molecules; but the interaction of the valence electrons associated with these nuclei, rather than the properties of the individual component atoms, is responsible for the chemical behavior of matter.

According to the model of atomic structure put forward by Niels BOHR and later refined by the application of QUANTUM MECHANICS, the electrons in an atom exist in certain orbits of fixed energy and angular momentum. Only one pair of electrons of opposite SPIN can occupy each orbit, and one may think of the orbits as being filled up to a certain level. It is the outer, or valence, electrons that are mainly responsible for the chemical properties of the atom (see PERIODIC TABLE). When an electron drops into a vacancy in an orbit of lower energy, the difference in energy is radiated in the form of a PHOTON of energy $h\nu$, where h is the Planck constant and ν is the frequency of the radiation.

ATOMIC BOMB, a weapon of mass destruction deriving its energy from nuclear FISSION. The first atomic bomb was exploded at Alamogordo, N.M., on July 16, 1945. As in the bomb dropped over Hiroshima, Japan, a few weeks later (August 6), the fissionable material was uranium-235, but when Nagasaki was destroyed by another bomb three days after that, plutonium-239 was used. Together the Hiroshima and Nagasaki bombs killed more than 100,000 people. Since the early

1950s, the power of the fission bomb (equivalent to some 20,000 tons of TNT in the case of the Hiroshima bomb) has been vastly exceeded by that of the HYDROGEN BOMB, which depends on nuclear FUSION.

ATOMIC CLOCK, a device which utilizes the exceptional constancy of the frequencies associated with certain electron spin reversals (as in the cesium clock) or the inversion of ammonia molecules (the ammonia clock) to define an accurately reproducible TIME scale.

ATOMIC ENERGY. See NUCLEAR ENERGY.

ATOMIC NUMBER. See ATOM.

ATOMIC WEIGHT, the mean MASS of the ATOMS of an ELEMENT weighted according to the relative abundance of its naturally occurring ISOTOPES and measured relative to some standard. Since 1961 this standard has been provided by the CARBON isotope C^{12}, whose atomic mass is defined to be exactly 12. On this scale atomic weights for the naturally occurring elements range from 1.008 (HYDROGEN) to 238.03 (URANIUM).

ATOMISM, the theory that all matter consists of atoms—minute indestructible particles, homogeneous in substance but varied in shape. Developed in the 5th century BC by Leucippus and DEMOCRITUS and adopted by EPICURUS, it was expounded in detail by the Roman poet LUCRETIUS.

ATOM SMASHER. See ACCELERATORS, PARTICLE; SUPERCOLLIDER.

ATONALITY, systematic departure in music from established tonal centers. The notion of tonality was increasingly blurred in the 19th century by the fluid chromaticism of WAGNER, Richard STRAUSS and MAHLER, foreshadowing DEBUSSY'S "whole-tone" scale. SCHÖNBERG and his disciples BERG and WEBERN went one stage further, abandoning tonal structure altogether and substituting the TWELVE-TONE system. Schönberg's *Moses and Aaron* and Berg's *Wozzeck* are leading examples of atonal composition.

ATONEMENT, Day of. See YOM KIPPUR.

ATTILA (c406–453), king of the Huns, who claimed dominion from the Alps and the Baltic to the Caspian. From 441–50 he ravaged the Eastern Roman Empire as far as Constantinople and invaded Gaul in 451, this expedition earning him the title of "Scourge of God." The following year he invaded Italy, but retired without attacking Rome. He died of overindulgence at his wedding feast.

ATTLEE, Clement Richard Attlee, 1st Earl (1883–1967), British statesman and prime minister (1945–51). Attlee led the Labour party from 1935 and served in Winston

100   ATTU

CHURCHILL'S wartime coalition cabinet. During his administration he instituted a broad program of social change and nationalization.

ATTU, westernmost island of the Aleutians, in the N Pacific. Mountainous and rugged, it covers 388sq mi and has no permanent population. The Japanese held Attu briefly during WWII.

ATTUCKS, Crispus (c1723–1770), black and Indian American who was the first of five men to die in the BOSTON MASSACRE.

ATWOOD, Margaret (1939–   ), Canadian poet and novelist. Her spare, terse poems in such collections as *Power Politics* (1971) and *You Are Happy* (1974) have been widely admired. Her novels include *Life before Man* (1979) and *The Handmaid's Tale* (1985).

AUBER, Daniel François Esprit (1782–1871), French composer whose operas, with librettos by dramatist Eugène SCRIBE, influenced 19th-century *opéra comique* and, later, the development of romantic opera.

AUBREY, John (1626–1697), English natural philosopher and antiquary, better known for his *Brief Lives,* vivid biographical sketches, mainly of his contemporaries, first published in 1813.

AUCHINCLOSS, Louis Stanton (1917–   ), US novelist whose work, noted for its character analysis, often deals with East Coast upper-class life. His best known books include *The Rector of Justin* (1964) and *Honorable Men* (1985).

AUCHINLECK, Sir Claude John Eyre (1884–1981), British field marshal. He served in the Indian army and in the Middle East during WWI. After the war he again served in India. As commander in chief of British armies in the Middle East early in WWII, he at first routed the Germans in North Africa but then had to abandon Tobruk and was dismissed by Churchill. Returning to his old post in India, he turned back the Japanese.

AUDEN, W(ystan) H(ugh) (1907–1973), English poet and a major influence on modern poetry, particularly during the 1930s when his highly energetic, often witty verse probed and laid bare Europe's ailing culture in the years that were to lead to WWII. Auden went to the US in 1939, becoming an American citizen in 1946. From this point his work reflects his growing religious concern (*The Double Man,* 1941). Some of Auden's best mature writing appeared in *Nones* (1951) and *The Shield of Achilles* (1955). He also collaborated on drama and opera librettos, and wrote literary criticism.

AUDUBON, John James (1785–1851), US artist and naturalist famous for his bird paintings, born in Santo Domingo (Haiti) of French parents and brought up in France. Some years after emigrating to the US in 1803, he embarked on what was to become his major achievement: the painting of all the then-known birds of North America. His *Birds of America* (London: 1827–38), was followed by a US edition (1840–44) and other illustrated works on American natural history.

AUER, Leopold (1845–1930), Hungarian-born violinist, a famous teacher of the instrument. He taught in Russia, Germany and England before emigrating in 1918 to the US, where he taught in New York and Philadelphia.

AUERBACH, Arnold "Red" (1917–   ), US basketball coach. The most successful coach in the history of professional basketball, he led the Boston Celtics to nine championships in ten years (1957; 1959–66). He retired in 1966 after having won 1,037 professional games.

AUGSBURG, Peace of (1555), agreement between Ferdinand—future Holy Roman Emperor, acting for his brother Emperor Charles V—and the German princes to end the religious wars of the REFORMATION. It legalized the coexistence of Lutheranism (as the sole recognized form of Protestantism) and Roman Catholicism in the empire. Each territory was to adhere to the denomination of its ruling prince.

AUGSBURG, War of the League of (1689–97), war between Louis XIV of France and the Grand Alliance, comprising the League of Augsburg (Emperor Leopold I and Saxony, Bavaria, the Palatinate, Savoy, Sweden and Spain), the Netherlands and England. The immediate cause was French devastation of the Palatinate in 1688. By the Treaty of Ryswick which ended the war, Louis returned Luxembourg and Lorraine, but kept Strasbourg, and recognized William III as king of England.

AUGSBURG CONFESSION, statement of Lutheran beliefs presented to the Diet of Augsburg on June 25, 1530. The Confession was largely the work of Philip MELANCHTHON, and was an attempt to reconcile LUTHER'S reforms with Roman Catholicism. Emperor Charles V rejected the document, sealing the break between the Lutherans and Rome.

AUGUST, eighth month of the Gregorian CALENDAR, named in honor of Emperor Augustus in 8 BC. It was previously called *Sextilis,* since (until 153 BC) it had been the sixth month. It was made the same length as July (named for Julius Caesar) by taking a day from February.

AUGUSTAN AGE, the high point of Roman culture, marked by the reign of Emperor Augustus (27 BC–14 AD) and the literary works of Livy, Horace, Ovid and Vergil. In the first half of the 18th century, English neoclassicists sought to emulate such writers and the term Augustan denoted all that was admirable in art and politics, though, in a manner typical of the period's liking for paradox and representative of its political divisions, it was often used ironically.

AUGUSTINE, Saint (354–430), Christian theologian and writer, the most prominent of the Latin Fathers of the Church. During his early years in Carthage, N Africa, he embraced MANICHAEISM, but in Rome (where he arrived in 383) he was much influenced by NEOPLATONISM. Moving to Milan, he met and was greatly impressed by St. Ambrose, bishop of Milan, and became a baptized Christian in 387.

Ordained a priest in 391, he became bishop of Hippo in N Africa in 396. There followed many famous books, including the autobiographical *Confessions* (397–401) and *De Civitate Dei* (413–26), the great Christian philosophy of history.

AUGUSTINE, Saint (d. c604–07), first archbishop of Canterbury (from 601). A Benedictine monk, he was sent to England by Pope Gregory the Great to convert the pagans and bring the Celtic Church under the control of Rome. Arriving in 597, he was given support by King Ethelbert of Kent.

AUGUSTINIAN FATHERS, common name for the Order of the Hermit Friars of St. Augustine, a Roman Catholic order dedicated to the advancement of learning and to missionary work. It was created in 1256 by Pope Alexander IV from a number of Italian hermit groups and adopted the Rule of St. Augustine of Hippo.

AUGUSTUS (63 BC–14 AD), the honorific title given in 27 BC to Gaius Julius Caesar Octavius, great-nephew and heir of Julius Caesar. With Marcus Aemilius Lepidus and Mark ANTONY he formed a triumvirate which avenged his great-uncle's murder by the defeat and death of the main conspirators at Philippi (42 BC). The deposition of Lepidus (36 BC) and the suicide of Antony after his defeat at ACTIUM (31 BC) left Augustus sole master of the Roman world. He proceeded to make good the ravages of 50 years of civil war, instituting religious, legal and administrative reforms and patronizing literature and the arts. While nominally restoring the Republic, his control of the state's finances and armed forces made him the sole ruler.

He is accounted first Roman e title deriving from the Latin commander-in-chief, *imperator*. He was succeeded by his stepson TIBERIUS. (See also ROME, ANCIENT.)

AUKS, 22 species (including the extinct Great Auk) of marine diving birds of the family Alcidae (order Charadriiformes), including razorbills, puffins, guillemots and murres. Lengths vary from 6-30in; the smallest is dovekie, or Little Auk (*Plautus alle*), which is about the size of a ROBIN. They usually breed in colonies, sometimes millions of individuals, and nest on high ledges or in burrows.

AULD LANG SYNE, Scottish song traditionally sung on Hogmanay (New Year's Eve). Written by Robert Burns c1788, its title means "old long since," or old times.

AURELIAN (c215–275), Roman emperor (270–275) who reversed the territorial decline of the empire. Although he gave up Dacia to the Goths, he reestablished Roman authority in Britain, Gaul, Spain, Egypt, Syria, and Mesopotamia. Around Rome he built the Aurelian wall, 12mi long and averaging 40ft in height.

AURIC, Georges (1899–   ), French composer, especially of ballet and film music. The youngest member of the group of composers known as *Les Six*, he was administrator of the two Paris opera houses 1962–68.

AURIOL, Vincent (1884–1966), first president of the Fourth Republic of France (1947–54). An active socialist, he was finance minister in Léon BLUM'S government. He opposed the Vichy regime in 1940 and in 1943 managed to escape to England, where he worked with General DE GAULLE.

AURORA, or **polar lights,** striking display of lights seen in night skies near the earth's geomagnetic poles. The *aurora borealis* (northern lights) is seen in Canada, Alaska and N Scandinavia; the *aurora australis* (southern lights) is seen in Antarctic regions. Auroras are caused by the collision of air molecules in the upper atmosphere with charged particles from the sun that have been accelerated and "funneled" by the earth's magnetic field. Particularly intense auroras are associated with high solar activity. Nighttime airglow is termed the permanent aurora.

AUSCHWITZ, present-day Oświęcim in Poland, site of a notorious Nazi concentration camp in WWII. Some 4 million inmates, mostly Jews, were murdered there. The town is now a transportation center with a chemical industry. Pop 39,600.

AUSTEN, Jane (1775–1817), English novelist. Daughter of a clergyman, in novels like *Sense and Sensibility* (1811), *Pride and Prejudice* (1813) and *Emma* (1815–16), she portrayed the provincial middle-class of her time with great subtlety and ironic insight. Her novels are admired as among the finest in the English language.

AUSTERLITZ, town in what is now S Czechoslovakia where, on Dec. 2, 1805, Napoleon's army defeated the combined forces of Emperor Francis I of Austria and Tsar Alexander I of Russia. This "Battle of the Three Emperors" was among the French emperor's most brilliant campaigns and marked the beginning of his rise to mastery in Europe.

AUSTIN, John Langshaw (1911–1960), British philosopher who was a leader in the field of linguistic analysis. His important papers appeared in *How to Do Things with Words* (1961) and *Sense and Sensibilia* (1962).

AUSTIN, Stephen Fuller (1793–1836), US pioneer statesman who helped create the state of Texas. In 1821 he brought 300 families to Tex. and was made the settlement's administrator. Between 1822 and 1830 he presented Texan demands for autonomy to the Mexican government; the negotiations proved difficult, and the Mexicans went so far as to imprison Austin. On his release in 1835, he joined the Texan rebellion against Mexico. In 1836, Sam HOUSTON appointed Austin secretary of state of the Republic of Tex.

AUSTRALASIA, term sometimes used to indicate an area of the S Pacific that includes Australia, New Zealand, Tasmania and adjacent islands. In a wider sense, it has been used to include OCEANIA. The term's lack of adequate definition has led to a decline in its use and importance.

AUSTRALIA, island continent entirely occupied by a single nation, the Commonwealth of Australia, a federation of six states (New South Wales, Victoria, Queensland, South Australia, Western Australia and Tasmania) and two territories (Northern Territory and Australian Capital Territory containing Canberra, the federal capital).

Australia led Papua New Guinea, self-governing from 1973, toward full independence (1975) and controls Norfolk Island, the Cocos (Keeling) Islands, Christmas Island (Indian Ocean) and about 5,000,000sq mi of Antarctica.

Land. The flat Western Plateau or Australian Shield extends from the NE

Official name: Commonwealth of Australia
Capital: Canberra
Area: 2,966,200sq mi
Population: 16,188,000
Languages: English
Religions: Protestant, Roman Catholic
Monetary unit(s): 1 Australian dollar = 100 cents

coast across nearly half of the continent, sloping eastward with Lake Eyre, 43ft below sea level, as its lowest point. In the desert-like "Red Heart" of the continent are the rugged Macdonnell and Musgrave ranges. Plains stretch from the Gulf of Carpentaria to the S coast. Parallel to the E coast is the Great Dividing Range, running from N Queensland to Tasmania (Mt Kosciusko, 7,310ft, is Australia's highest peak). Along the Queensland coast is the Great Barrier Reef, the world's largest coral reef. Major rivers include the Murray (1,600mi) and its tributaries the Darling and Murrumbidgee.

Climate. Australia enjoys a mainly warm, dry and sunny climate. Summer maximum shade temperatures are well above 100°F in most areas. Annual rainfall sometimes exceeds 117in in E Queensland, but only a small part of Australia has plentiful rainfall, and evaporation is high. Basically the N is a monsoon zone of dry winters and wet summers, separated by a transitional zone from the S, where summer drought and winter rains prevail.

Gum trees (eucalyptus) and wattles (acacia) are the continent's typical vegetation. The unique wildlife includes the platypus and spiny anteater, the most primitive surviving mammals; the koala bear, kangaroo, wallaby and wombat; the dingo, a wild dog; the emu, kookaburra and other colorful birds; and the deadly tiger-snake and other reptiles.

People and Economy. The people are mainly of British origin, but there are some 200,000 aborigines and part-aborigines, now mostly detribalized, and many immigrants from Italy, Yugoslavia, Greece, Germany, the Netherlands and the US. Most of the population is concentrated in the coastal cities, of which the largest is Sydney.

Australia provides about 25% of the world's wool and is a major producer of wheat and meat. The rich mineral resources include iron ore, gold, copper, silver, lead, zinc, bauxite, uranium and some oil and natural gas. Australia is highly industrialized, and products range from aircraft, ships and automobiles to textiles, chemicals, electrical equipment and metal goods.

History. Discovered by the Dutch in the early 1600s, Australia was claimed for Britain by Capt James COOK (1770). New South Wales, the first area settled, began as a penal colony (1788). But free settlement began in 1816, and no convicts were sent to Australia after 1840. The gold rushes (1851, 1892) brought more people to Australia, and in 1901 the six self-governing colonies formed the independent Commonwealth of Australia. Since WWII, Australia has come to play an increasingly active role in regional affairs. The nation celebrated its bicentennial in 1988.

AUSTRALIAN ABORIGINES, aboriginal population of AUSTRALIA. They have dark wavy hair (except in childhood), medium stance, broad noses and narrow heads—typical Australoid features. Before white encroachment in the 18th and 19th centuries they lived by well-organized nomadic food-gathering and hunting and numbered about 300,000. Since the enfranchisement of the remaining 40,000 full-blooded aborigines in 1962, varyingly successful attempts at integration have been made. Recent researches have suggested that they may be the result of interbreeding between an original population of *Homo erectus* and the earliest members of *Homo sapiens* (see PREHISTORIC MAN).

AUSTRALOIDS, an ethnic group including the AUSTRALIAN ABORIGINES, the AINU, the DRAVIDIANS, the population of the Vedda of SRI LANKA and, debatably, Melanesians, Negritos and Papuans.

AUSTRIA, a federal republic in central Europe divided into nine provinces: Vienna, Lower Austria, Burgenland, Upper Austria, Salzburg, Styria, Carinthia, Tyrol and Vorarlberg.

Land. There are four physical regions: the Austrian Alps to the W, including the highest mountain in Austria, Grossglockner (12,457ft); the N Alpine foreland, a plateau cut by fertile valleys between the Danube and the Alps; the Austrian granite plateau, N of the Danube; and the E lowlands, where the capital, Vienna stands. Most rivers drain north from the mountains into the Danube and its tributaries. Climate varies widely: in general, summers are warm,

Official name: The Republic of Austria
Capital: Vienna
Area: 32,376sq mi
Population: 7,554,000
Languages: German, Slovenian, Croatian
Religions: Roman Catholic
Monetary unit(s): 1 schilling=100 groschen

winters fairly severe, with moderate rainfall throughout the year.

Economy. Austrian farms are small, and the only crops the country is self-sufficient in are sugar beets and potatoes. Other important crops include grains, grapes, fruits, tobacco, flax and hemp; wines and beers are produced in quantity. Almost 40% of the country is forested: wood and paper are important products. Iron ore is the most important mineral resource, but there are also deposits of lead, magnesium, copper, salt, zinc, aluminum, silver and gypsum. There is oil near Zisterdorf, but production has decreased in favor of natural gas. The areas around Vienna, Graz and Linz are the chief industrial centers. Manufacturing industries provide one third of the GNP. Tourism has also helped to stimulate economic growth in recent years.

History. Inhabited from prehistoric times, settled by the CELTS, and subsequently part of the Roman Empire, from the 3rd century AD Austria was devastated by invading Vandals, Goths, Alamanni, Huns and Avars. Early in the 9th century CHARLEMAGNE made Austria the East March, which the Babenberg family inherited in 967 and retained as a duchy until their extinction in 1246. In 1247 the HAPSBURGS acquired these lands as archdukes of Austria. Until their fall in 1918, the history of Austria is the history of the Hapsburg lands. (See AUSTRIA-HUNGARY; AUSTRIAN SUCCESSION, WAR OF; AUSTRO-PRUSSIAN WAR; FRENCH REVOLUTIONARY WARS; HOLY ROMAN EMPIRE; NAPOLEONIC WARS; SEVEN YEARS' WAR, SPANISH SUCCESSION, WAR OF; THIRTY YEARS' WAR.) By the Treaty of VERSAILLES, independent states (Czechoslovakia, Hungary, Yugoslavia) were created from what had wholly or partially been within the old empire, while Austria herself, the Hapsburg patrimony, became a republic. Following the ANSCHLUSS in 1938, Austria became part of HITLER's Third Reich, regaining independence following the Allied victory in 1945, although the last Allied occupation forces did not leave the country until 1955.

From 1945 to 1966 Austria was governed by a coalition based on the People's and Socialist parties. Then one party or the other dominated until 1986, when the coalition was revived. In 1986 Kurt WALDHEIM was elected president despite allegations of involvement in Nazi war crimes. An international panel appointed by Waldheim later confirmed some of these charges, but Waldheim retained his office.

Austria's contributions to culture, especially in music, have been large: MOZART, HAYDN, SCHUBERT, BRUCKNER and MAHLER were all Austrians, while BEETHOVEN, Johann STRAUSS, and Franz LEHAR spent most of their lives in Vienna. Vienna is also considered the home of Freudian psychoanalysis.

AUSTRIA-HUNGARY, name given to the empire formed by the union of the Kingdom of Hungary and the Austrian Empire in 1867. It ceased to exist at the end of WWI, and its lands were divided among the East European nations.

AUSTRIAN SUCCESSION, War of the (1740–1748), war fought between the Austrian Empire and European powers disputing the right of MARIA THERESA to Austrian territories inherited from her father. It was called King George's War by Americans because of the involvement of Britain's George II. The treaty of AIX-LA-CHAPELLE, ending the war, guaranteed Maria Theresa's right to the throne on condition that she ceded Silesia to Prussia.

AUSTRO-PRUSSIAN WAR, or Seven Weeks War, war fought in 1866 by Austria against Prussia and Italy. Count Otto von BISMARCK, the Prussian premier, involved Austria in a dispute over the joint Austro-Prussian rule of Schleswig-Holstein which forced her to declare war on June 14. By keeping the French neutral, he left Austria politically isolated. Despite the collapse of his Italian allies, the Prussian General Möltke broke the Austrians at the battle of Königgrätz on July 3. The Peace of Prague (signed Aug. 23) excluded Austria from the new German confederation and ceded Venice to Italy, a major step towards Bismarck's dream of German unification under Prussia.

AUTISM, mental disorder variously characterized by lack of emotion; failure to speak or to respond to speech; repetitive motions such as rocking back and forth or repeated hand flapping; and bizarre memory disorders (photographic recall of some things, total forgetfulness of others). Many autistic people are mentally retarded but others have normal intelligence although they appear withdrawn and absorbed in daydreaming. Autism occurs in 2-5 of every 100,000 live births, more commonly among boys than girls. It usually becomes evident before a child is three. It was formerly attributed to unresponsive parenting or brain damage during labor and birth. A current view is that it is a result of abnormal BRAIN development, particularly in the cerebellum and the limbic system.

AUTOBIOGRAPHY, biography written by the subject himself. St. Augustine's *Confessions* (5th century AD) is generally regarded as the first, and the modern form of autobiography is believed to have grown out of the Christian tendency towards self-examination. Today the influence of psychoanalysis and the need to assert individuality may have a similar influence. Some notable autobiographies include those written by CELLINI, Samuel PEPYS, Jean Jacques ROUSSEAU, Benjamin FRANKLIN, George SAND, Cardinal NEWMAN and HITLER.

AUTOMATIC PILOT. See GYROPILOT.

AUTOMATION, the detailed control of a production process without recourse to human decision-making at every point, typically involving a negative-FEEDBACK system. (See MECHANIZATION AND AUTOMATION.)

AUTOMOBILE, or passenger car, a small self-propelled passenger-carrying vehicle designed to operate on ordinary highways and usually supported on four wheels. Power is provided in most modern automobiles by an INTERNAL COMBUSTION ENGINE which uses GASOLINE (vaporized and premixed with a suitable quantity of air in the carburetor) as fuel. This is ignited in the (usually 4, 6 or 8) cylinders of the engine by spark plugs, fired from the distributor in the appropriate sequence. The gas supply and thus the engine speed is controlled from the accelerator pedal. The driving power is communicated to the road wheels through the TRANSMISSION, which includes a clutch (enabling the driver to disengage the engine without stopping it), a gearbox (allowing the most efficient use to be made of the engine power), various drive-shafts (with universal joints), and a differential which allows the driving wheels to turn at marginally different rates in cornering. Steering is controlled from a hand wheel which moves a transverse tie rod mounted between the independently-pivoted front wheels. Service BRAKES of various types are mounted on all wheels, an additional parking-brake mechanism being used when stationary. In modern automobiles service brakes and steering may be power-assisted and the transmission automatic rather than manually controlled with a gearshift. Although the first propelled steam vehicles were built by the French army officer Nicholas-Joseph Cugnot in the 1760s, it was not until Karl BENZ and Gottlieb DAIMLER began to build gasoline-powered carriages in the mid-1880s that the day of the modern automobile dawned. The DURYEA brothers built the first US automobile in 1893 and within a few years several automobile manufacturers, including Henry FORD, had started into business. The Ford Motor Company itself was founded in 1903, pioneering the cheap mass-market auto with the Model T of 1908. The AUTOMOBILE INDUSTRY expanded fitfully until the 1960s, improving automobile performance, comfort and styling, but subsequently was forced by economic considerations and the activity of consumer groups (led by Ralph NADER) to pay more attention to safety and environmental factors. (See also AUTOMOBILE EMISSION CONTROL; AUTOMOBILE RACING.)

AUTOMOBILE EMISSION CONTROL, the reduction of the AIR POLLUTION caused by AUTOMOBILES by modification of the fuel and careful design. The principal pollutants are unburnt HYDROCARBONS, CARBON monoxide, oxides of NITROGEN and LEAD halide particles. The last can be eliminated if alternatives to lead-based ANTIKNOCK ADDITIVES in the GASOLINE are used, but the others require redesigned cylinder heads, recycling and afterburning of exhaust gases and better metering of the gasoline supply through fuel injection. Another approach investigates alternatives to the conventional INTERNAL COMBUSTION ENGINE—battery- and fuel-cell-powered vehicles, gas-turbine and even steam-powered units.

AUTOMOBILE INDUSTRY, US, comprising companies manufacturing cars, buses, trucks and motorcycles, the second largest industry in the US (oil is first). The earliest US firms hand-produced small numbers of electric-, steam-, and gas-powered cars; by the 1890s, pioneers such as the DURYEA brothers, Ransom OLDS, and Henry FORD were custom building gas-powered cars in small but growing numbers. In 1913, Ford successfully introduced new assembly-line techniques for mass-

producing his Model T, the first car designed to be made and sold in volume. General Motors was established in 1908 by William C. DURANT, and was soon producing a range of cars in a number of price categories—a marketing strategy Ford refused to adopt until long after his company had lost its leading position to GM. By 1929, annual output of US cars totaled five million, with Ford, GM, and Chrysler forming the Big Three of auto manufacturers. There also were a number of smaller firms including Nash and Hudson, which merged to become American Motors in 1954; and Packard and Studebaker, which ended production in 1964.

American automobiles dominated the world market until the 1960s, when manufacturers in Europe and Japan began to cut into US sales abroad and even penetrated the market at home. By the late 1970s, small foreign cars with their relatively low fuel consumption were bought by Americans in ever larger numbers. Imports were a major factor in the record losses of the auto industry in 1980—the largest in the history of the industry—and the near-bankruptcy of Chrysler, which was rescued by federal government loan guarantees that it was subsequently able to repay.

AUTOMOBILE RACING, a variety of forms of competition using specially designed or adapted motor vehicles. The drivers of Formula One cars compete under FIA (Fédération Internationale de l'Automobile) rules for the title of world champion, won by scoring the highest points in nine out of 11 Grand Prix events. Sports car competition tends to be as keen between manufacturers as between drivers. Major U.S. races include the Indianapolis 500 and the Daytona 500, a stock car race. European events of note are the Grand Prix de Monaco and the Le Mans 24-hour race. Attempts on the land speed record are carefully scrutinized by the FIA; following the approval of jet-powered cars the record soared to over 400 mph. Stock car racing is controlled in the US by the National Association for Stock Car Racing.

AUVERGNE, region of extinct volcanoes and former province of S central France in the Massif Central now divided between three departments. Its principal city is Clermont-Ferrand. It was once the home of the Arverni, whose chief, Vercingetorix, rebelled against Julius Caesar.

AVEDON, Richard (1923–), US photographer. World famous for his on-location fashion photography for *Vogue* and *Harper's Bazaar*, he also took revealing portraits of celebrities, collected in *Observations* (1959) and *Portraits* (1976).

AVERNUS, or **Averno,** lake in Italy 10mi W of Naples. About 2mi wide and 118ft deep, it has no natural outlet. The sinister sulfurous fumes that rise from the lake led the ancients to regard it as an entrance to the underworld.

AVERROËS, Latin name of abu-al-Walid Muhammad ibn-Ahmad ibn-Rushd (1126–1198), Spanish/N African Arab philosopher, a commentator on Aristotle and Plato who exerted a great influence on the development of the later Latin scholastic philosophy.

AVESTA. See ZEND AVESTA.

AVIATION. See AERODYNAMICS; FLIGHT, HISTORY OF.

AVICENNA, Latin name of abu-Ali al-Husayn ibn-Sina (980–1037), the greatest of the Arab scientists of the medieval period. His *Canon of Medicine* remained a standard medical text in Europe until the Renaissance.

AVIGNON, French city on the E bank of the Rhone, capital of the Vaucluse department; its industries include the production of metals and textiles and food processing. It was a Roman outpost, and the home of the popes during the BABYLONIAN CAPTIVITY (1309–1378). Pop 173,000.

AVILA CAMACHO, Manuel (1897–1955), Mexican soldier and statesman. As Mexico's president (1940–46) he supported the US and promoted Latin American opposition to the Axis powers.

AVOCADO, *Persea americana.* tree native to middle America, Mexico and the West Indies. The fruit, the avocado or **"alligator" pear,** is green or purple with pale yellow flesh rich in protein, vitamins, iron and oil and a large central seed. Advocados are also grown as foliage house plants requiring a few hours of sunlight each day, although direct summer sun should be avoided. They grow well at average house temperatures, but fail to thrive above 75°F and should be watered regularly to keep the soil evenly moist. They are propagated by means of the pits (hard seeds). Family: Agavaceae.

AVOGADRO, Count Amedeo (1776–1856), Italian physicist who first realized that gaseous ELEMENTS might exist as MOLECULES which contain more than one ATOM, thus distinguishing molecules from atoms. In 1811 he published **Avogadro's hypothesis**—that equal volumes of all GASES under the same conditions of TEMPERATURE and PRESSURE contain the same number of molecules—but his work in this area was ignored by chemists for over

50 years. The **Avogadro Number** (N), the number of molecules in one MOLE of substance, 6.02×10^{23}, is named for him.

AVON, Earl of. See EDEN, ANTHONY.

AVON, name of several British rivers. The longest, the Warwickshire or "Shakespeare" Avon flows 96mi from near Naseby, through Stratford-on-Avon, to join the Severn at Tewkesbury.

AXIS POWERS, countries that fought against the Allies in WWII. The Rome-Berlin Axis, a diplomatic agreement between Hitler and Mussolini, was reinforced by an Italian-German military pact in 1939. In 1940 Japan joined the pact, then Hungary, Bulgaria, Romania, Slovakia and Croatia.

AYACUCHO, Battle of, encounter that led to Peruvian independence. In 1824 South American revolutionaries under Antonio José de Sucre defeated Spanish forces under Viceroy José de la Serna on the plains of Ayacucho, Peru, bringing the end of Spanish rule in South America.

AYATOLLAH, honorific title meaning "reflection of God" given to the more important Muslim clergymen in Iran. Many of the ayatollahs joined the movement against the Shah in the 1970s. After the Iranian revolution they became the dominant political leaders of the new Islamic republic, occupying most important positions of authority. While many of the ayatollahs participated in the excesses of the regime, others, more moderate, remained quiet.

AYER, Sir Alfred Jules (1910–1989), English philosopher whose *Language, Truth and Logic* (1936) was influential in founding the "Oxford school" of philosophy, with its emphasis on the careful analysis of the use of words. The LOGICAL POSITIVISM of the Vienna Circle was an important formative influence in his philosophy.

AYMARA, Amerindian group numbering some 500,000, in the central Andes, Bolivia and Peru. Mainly herdsmen, they lead a meager existence under harsh climatic conditions.

AYMÉ, Marcel (1902–1967), French author noted for his humorous novels, *The Green Mare* (1933) and *The Conscience of Love* (1960). He also wrote children's stories and several plays, including *Clérambard* (1949).

AYUB KHAN, Mohammad (1907–1974), president of Pakistan 1958–69. He won office by a military coup, introduced land, education and local government reforms and created a new constitution.

AZALEA, a number of species of the genus

RHODODENDRON, cultivated principally for ornamental purposes. Best known in the US are the pinxter, *R. nudiflorum*; the flame azalea, *R. calendulaceum*; and the rhodora, *R. canadense*. Azaleas have funnel-shaped, usually fragrant flowers with 5–10 stamens. As house plants they will bloom for weeks if kept in a sunny position at temperatures between 15°C and 21°C (60°F and 70°F) and the soil kept moist. They are propagated by shoot cuttings taken in the spring. Family: Ericaceae.

AZERBAIJAN (Azerbaidjan), mountainous region E of the Caspian Sea divided between Iran and the USSR by the Araks R. Settled by MEDES as part of the Persian Empire, it was periodically dominated by Romans, Arabs, Mongols and Turks, returning to Persia in the 16th century. The Russian Tsar Alexander I annexed N Azerbaidzhan in 1813. An independent republic was formed there in 1918 but was conquered by the Soviets in 1920. Now a Transcaucasian socialist republic, its subtropical plain produces cotton, wheat and tobacco. It is rich in minerals, especially oil, and its capital Baku is an industrial and refining city. Iranian Azerbaidzhan was made an autonomous republic by a communist revolt in 1945 but Iran regained it in 1946. Its eastern province (capital Tabriz) grows grain, its western (capital Rezaiveh) tobacco and fruit.

AZIMUTH, in navigation and astronomy, the angular distance measured from 0–360° along the horizon eastward from an observer's north point to the point of intersection of the horizon and a great circle (see CELESTIAL SPHERE) passing through the observer's zenith and a star or planet.

AZORES, nine mountainous islands in the N Atlantic 800mi W of Portugal. São Miguel to the E is the largest and most populated. Their economy is agricultural, producing fruits and grain. Colonized and under Portuguese rule since the mid-15th century, the islands enjoy considerable autonomy. Pop 250,700.

AZTECS, pre-Columbian Indians of Central Mexico, traditionally thought to have migrated from Aztlán in the N to the Valley of Mexico. A warrior tribe, they took over the cities of the Toltecs, from whom they also derived part of their culture. The Aztec empire consisted of a confederation of three city states, Tenochtitlán (the capital, site of present-day Mexico City), Tlacopan and Texcoco. Religious belief contributed greatly to Aztec political and social structure. The two chief gods were Huitzilopochtli, god of war and the sun, and QUETZALCOATL, god of learning. Thousands of human victims were sacrificed to these and other gods. The Aztecs were superb artisans, working in gold, silver and copper, and creating fine pottery and mosaics. They are famed for their lavishly decorated temples, such as those at Tenochtitlán, Tula, Cuicuilco, Xochicalco and Cholula. The arrival of the conquistador Hernán CORTÉS (1519) heralded the collapse of the Aztec empire. (See also MONTEZUMA.)

AZUELA, Mariano (1873–1952), Mexican novelist who was the pioneer writer of the Mexican revolution. A social realist who was the first Latin American novelist to utilize the masses as protagonist, he is best known for *The Underdogs* (1916), *The Bosses* (1917) and *The Flies* (1918).

2nd letter of the alphabet. It can be traced back to an ancient Semitic character, the origin of both the Hebrew *beth* ("house") and Greek *beta* (β). The lower-case "b" developed in late Roman times.

BAAL, Semitic word meaning "lord" or "owner," name of an ancient Near East fertility deity. Canaanite tablets dating from c2500 BC represent him combating Mot, god of drought and sterility. There were many local variants: in Babylonia, Baal was known as Bel, and in Phoenicia, as Melkart.

BAAL-SHEM-TOV (c1700–1760), founder of HASIDISM, a Jewish sect devoted to intensely orthodox but joyous religious observance. Born in Russia as Israel ben Eliezer, he pursued a variety of secular occupations. His religious teachings, and a reputation as a miracle healer, won him the name Baal-Shem-Tov, or Master of the Good Name (i.e., God's name).

BABANGIDA, Ibrahim B. (1941–   ), president of Nigeria from 1985. A Western-oriented general, he dealt with severe economic problems caused by declining oil revenues by pursuing free-market policies and government austerity. He proved adept at defusing clashes between Muslims and Christians; a Muslim himself, he determined to keep the state secular. In 1987 he announced a five-year program to restore civilian rule in

1992, but he did not hesitate to use force against dissidents and food rioters.

BABBAGE, Charles (1792–1871), English mathematician and inventor who devoted much labor and expense to an unsuccessful attempt to devise mechanical calculating engines (see CALCULATING MACHINE). More significant was the part he played with J. HERSCHEL and G. Peacock in introducing the Leibnizian "d" notation for CALCULUS into British mathematical use in place of the less flexible "dot" notation devised by NEWTON.

BABBITT, Irving (1865–1933), US scholar and noted opponent of Romanticism. He led the New Humanism, a movement in literary criticism which stressed classical reason and restraint. His works include *The New Laokoön* (1910) and *On Being Creative* (1932).

BABBITT, Milton (1916–), US composer of complex 12-tone and electronic music whose pioneering work on the synthesizer (1959) led to the establishment of the Electronic Music Center of Columbia and Princeton universities.

BABEL, Isaac Emanuilovich (1894–1941?), Russian short-story writer. The famous collection of stories *Red Cavalry* (1926) is based on his service with the Red Cossacks. His other works are often about Jewish life in Russia before and after the Revolution. Arrested c1938, he died in a Siberian prison camp.

BABEL, Tower of, in the Old Testament, a tower begun by Noah's descendants to try to reach heaven. Jehovah frustrated the builders by making them speak many languages. The story may refer to the ZIGGURAT of Babylon.

BABEUF, François Émile (1760–1797), French revolutionary agitator, also known as Gracchus. His "Manifesto of Equals" advocated common ownership of property and the right of all to work. He was executed for plotting to overthrow the Directory, which ruled France 1795–99.

BABISM, religious sect that developed among Persian Muslims in the 19th century predicting the coming of a "Promised One." Persecuted, the movement seceded from Islam and its members scattered. Babism was a forerunner of BAHAISM.

BABI YAR, a ravine near Kiev, in the Ukraine. On Sept. 29 and 30, 1941, German SS troops executed by gunshot, and buried, more than 33,000 Soviet Jews. The victims had been assembled and brought to the ravine on a promise of "resettlement." In his poem "Babi Yar" (1962) the Russian poet Yevgeni Yevtushenko indicted the Soviet Union for indifference toward the massacre.

BABOONS, social MONKEYS of the African savannas, distinguished by their long muzzles (particularly in the males) and large size. They move in troops containing as few as 20 individuals or as many as 150 or more. They are highly aggressive and dangerous omnivores. There is generally a hierarchical structure within each troop, though the nature of this may change with differing circumstances: females are always subordinate to males, though females with infants are treated with great consideration. Appeasement is usually by "presentation," the adoption even by males of a subservient sexual posture. Their bodies are covered with unusually long hair except for parts of the face, and the buttocks, which may be brightly colored. They belong to the PRIMATE order and the family Cercopithedidae.

BABUR or **BABAR** (Zahir Muhammad; 1483–1530), founder of the MOGUL EMPIRE in India, a descendant of TAMERLANE and GENGHIS KHAN. Losing Fergana, which he had inherited, and failing in his ambition to win Samarkand, Babur made his reputation by conquests over Afghan rulers in N India 1522–29, providing territory that his grandson AKBAR was to build into a great empire.

BABY BOOM, steep increase in the US birthrate following WWII. During 1946–64, 76 million people were born, accounting for nearly one-third of the US population in 1980; in the 1970s, the birthrate then dropped. The resulting uneven age distribution has had a multitude of social effects on educational systems, job markets, urban and suburban economies and so on, including almost every aspect of contemporary life.

BABYLON, capital of the ancient kingdom of Babylonia, between the Tigris and Euphrates rivers 55mi S of modern Baghdad. Prosperous under HAMMURABI (reigned c1729–1686 BC) and his successors, it was later attacked by Hittites, Kassites and Assyrians. The reign (605—561 BC) of NEBUCHADNEZZAR II was marked by the building of its great walls, temples, ZIGGURAT and Hanging Gardens. Cyrus of Persia took Babylon in 539 BC. Alexander the Great died at Babylon in 323 BC, his plans to rebuild part of the city coming to nothing. (See also BABYLONIA AND ASSYRIA.)

BABYLONIA AND ASSYRIA, ancient kingdoms of the Near East. Both lay in MESOPOTAMIA, the fertile area between the rivers Tigris and Euphrates. Around 3200 BC the SUMERIANS migrated westward into S Babylonia and established what is generally considered to be the first major civilization, based on CITY STATES such as Ur. Clay tablets from Sumer, inscribed in CUNEIFORM script, have preserved king-lists, historical records and even some literature from this period, including the Epic of GILGAMESH.

Babylonia. In the 24th century BC N Babylonia was conquered by a Semitic people who established the kingdom of Akkad. Its founder, Sargon the Great (c2360–2305 BC), conquered Sumer, but after two centuries Akkadian culture was shattered in the north by an invasion of Gutians from Iran. In the south a Sumerian renaissance flowered in the creation of such monuments as the ZIGGURATS.

In the first centuries of the 2nd millennium BC invading Semitic Amorites established Babylon as the center of power in Mesopotamia. HAMMURABI (c1728–1686 BC), the sixth king of the Amorite dynasty, drew up a remarkable code of laws, but his S Babylonian Empire did not long survive his death. In about 1531 BC Babylon was sacked by a HITTITE army, leaving Babylonia wide open to an invasion of Kassites, who ruled there until about 1150 BC. Despite flourishing trade and a strong alliance with Egypt, the Kassites were weakened by a series of internal conflicts and sporadic war with neighboring nations.

Assyria. The Assyrians took their name from Ashur, their first capital, on the banks of the Tigris. Conquered by Sargon of Akkad, they later came under Sumerian rule, and around 1475 BC the Hurrian king of Mitanni made Assyria a vassal state. Assyria only became a great military power after the decline of the Hurrian kingdom. King Adadnirari I (1308–1276 BC) captured Carchemish, defeated the Hittites and the Kassites, and reached the Euphrates. Under King Tiglath-Pileser I (1116–1078 BC) this Middle Assyrian Empire spread across Syria and Phoenicia into Anatolia and overwhelmed Babylon.

After a period of decline, Assyria rose to new power under such warrior kings as Shalmaneser III (859–825 BC), Tiglath-Pileser III (745–727 BC) and Sargon II (722–705 BC). In addition to Babylonia, Syria, Israel, Carchemish and Tyre, even Egypt became subject to Assyrian rule. Sargon's son Sennacherib (705–681 BC) made his capital, NINEVEH, into one of the most magnificent cities of its time. It is to ASHURBANIPAL (c669–630 BC) that we owe much of our knowledge of the literature of ancient Mesopotamia: some 25,000 tablets from his library are now in the British Museum, London. The kingdom collapsed

after his death, in the face of an alliance of CHALDEA with the SCYTHIANS and MEDES.

Neo-Babylonian Empire. Under the Chaldean King Nabopolassar (626–605 BC) Babylonia recovered its independence. The new empire was consolidated by his son Nebuchadnezzar II (605–562 BC), who continued his father's war with Egypt and put down revolts in Tyre and Judah, destroying Jerusalem in 586 BC. He also built the famous Hanging Gardens of Babylon. The internal power struggle following his death was settled by the accession of the usurper Nabonidus to the throne in 555 BC. Nabonidus' son Belshazzar held power in Babylon when CYRUS THE GREAT, king of the Medes and Persians, captured the city in 539 BC. Babylonia then became a province of the Persian Empire.

BABYLONIAN CAPTIVITY, exile of the Jews to Babylon after the conquest of Jerusalem by Nebuchadnezzar II in 597 BC and 586 BC. In 538 BC CYRUS THE GREAT, who had taken Babylon, allowed them to return to Judea. The term is also used in European history for the period from 1309 to 1377 when, under French domination, the popes resided at Avignon in S France. Pope Gregory XI returned to Rome in 1377, but after his death the papacy was split by the GREAT SCHISM.

BACCHUS, Roman god of wine and fertility, counterpart of the Greek DIONYSUS. The *bacchanalia* held in his honor became increasingly licentious, and the Senate banned them in 186 BC.

BACH, name of a family of musicians originating in Thuringia, Germany. **Johann Sebastian Bach** (1685–1750) was one of the greatest composers of all time. His music is a culmination and enrichment of the polyphonic tradition of BAROQUE music, but also reflects the harmonic innovations which were supplanting polyphony. Bach held posts at the courts of the Duke of Weimar and Prince Leopold of Köthen, and was musical director of St. Thomas' School, Leipzig.

Bach first excelled as an organist, and his works include many organ compositions. Other keyboard works include *The Well-Tempered Clavier* and the *Goldberg Variations*. Among his instrumental masterpieces are the works for solo violin and cello and the six *Brandenburg Concertos*. The bulk of Bach's work is religious in inspiration, as seen particularly in his choral works. In addition to more than 200 cantatas, these include the famous *St. Matthew Passion, St. John Passion, B Minor Mass* and *Christmas Oratorio.*

Of Bach's 20 children, some became composers in their own right. **Wilhelm Friedemann Bach** (1710–1784) was organist at Dresden and Halle, and left some undistinguished compositions. **Carl Philipp Emanuel Bach** (1714–1788) was an outstanding composer and keyboard musician, whose development of symphonic, concerto and sonata forms influenced Haydn, Mozart and Beethoven. His *Essay on the True Art of Playing Keyboard Instruments* remains an essential manual of 18th-century techniques. He was court musician to Frederick the Great and musical director at Hamburg. **Johann Christoph Friedrich Bach** (1732–1794) was chamber musician and *Konzertmeister* to Count Wilhelm of Bückeburg and a prolific composer. **Johann Christian Bach** (1735–1782) wrote numerous graceful orchestral and chamber works and several operas. He was particularly successful in England, where he spent the last 20 years of his life.

BACHE, Benjamin Franklin (1769–1798), US journalist, publisher of the Philadelphia *Aurora*, a Jeffersonian newspaper that violently attacked the Federalist administration of President John Adams. He was arrested under the Sedition Act but pardoned.

BACK, Sir George (1796–1878), British Arctic explorer. He accompanied Sir John Franklin on three expeditions, then led two of his own to the Arctic coast of Canada.

BACKUS, Isaac (1724–1806), New England Baptist clergyman, for 50 years a prominent preacher and evangelist. He wrote a valuable history of New England Baptists.

BACON, Francis (1561–1626), English philosopher and statesman who rose to become lord chancellor (1618–21) to JAMES I but is chiefly remembered for the stimulus he gave to scientific research in England. Although his name is indelibly associated with the method of induction and the rejection of a priori reasoning in science, the painstaking collection of miscellaneous facts without any recourse to prior theory which he advocated in the *Novum Organum* (1620) has never been adopted as a practical method of research. The application of the Baconian method was, however, an important object in the foundation of the ROYAL SOCIETY OF LONDON some 40 years later.

BACON, Francis (1909–), British painter. A self-taught artist, he developed a unique style which expresses the isolation and horror of the human condition, concentrating on distorted figures which manage to convey both panic and menace.

BACON, Roger (c1214–1292?), English scholar renowned in his own day for his great knowledge of science and remembered today for allegedly prophesying many of the inventions of later centuries: aircraft; telescopes; steam engines; microscopes. In fact he was a wealthy lecturer in the schools of Oxford and Paris with a passion for alchemical and other experiments, whose later life was overshadowed by disputes with the Franciscan Order, of which he had become a member in 1257.

BACON'S REBELLION, a rising in colonial America led by planter Nathaniel Bacon (1647–1676) against the governor of Va., Sir William BERKELEY. When Berkeley failed to defend the frontier against Indians, Bacon claimed the right of frontiersmen to form their own militia and led unauthorized forces against the Indians in 1676. Proclaimed traitor, he marched on Jamestown and briefly controlled the colony, instituting legal reforms. The subsequent civil war against forces raised by Berkeley ended shortly after Bacon's death.

BACTERIA, unicellular microorganisms between 0.3 and 2 μm in diameter. They differ from plant and animal cells in that their nucleus is not a distinct organelle surrounded by a membrane: they are usually placed in a separate kingdom, the Protista.

The majority of bacteria are saprophytic: they exist independently of living hosts and are involved in processes of decomposition of dead animal and plant material. As such they are essential to the natural economy of living things.

Some bacteria are parasitic, and their survival depends on their presence in or on other living cells. They may be commensals, which coexist harmlessly with host cells, or pathogens, which damage the host organism by producing toxins that may cause tissue damage (see BACTERIAL DISEASES). This distinction is not absolute: *Escherichia coli* is a commensal in the human intestine, but may cause infection in the urinary tract.

Bacteria are like plant cells in that they are surrounded by a rigid cell wall. Most species are incapable of movement, but certain types can swim using hairlike flagella. Bacteria vary in their food requirements: autotrophs can obtain energy by oxidizing substances which they have built up from simple inorganic matter; heterotrophs need organic substances for nutrition. Aerobic bacteria need oxygen to survive, whereas anaerobic species do not. Included in the latter group are the putrefactive bacteria, which aid decomposition. Bacteria generally reproduce asexually by binary FISSION, but some species reproduce sexually. Some can survive adverse conditions by forming highly resistant spores.

Bacteria are important to man in many ways. Commensal bacteria in the human intestine aid digestion of food; industrially they are used in the manufacture of, for example, acetone, citric acid and butyl alcohol and in many dairy products. Some bacteria, especially the actinomycetes, produce ANTIBIOTICS, used in destroying pathogenic bacteria.

Classification. There is no standard way of classifying bacteria. The higher bacteria are filamentous and the cells may be interdependent—they include the family actinomycetes. The lower bacteria are subdivided according to shape: cocci (round), bacilli (cylindrical), vibrios (curved), and spirilla (spiral). Cocci live singly, in pairs (diplococci), in clusters (staphylococci) or in chains (streptococci)—as a group they are of great medical importance. Spirochetes form a separate group from the above: although spiral, they are able to move. Bacteria are also classified medically in terms of their response to Gram's stain: those absorbing it are termed Gram-positive, those not, Gram-negative. (See also BACTERIOLOGY; MICROBIOLOGY.)

BACTERIAL DISEASES, diseases caused by BACTERIA or their products. Many bacteria have no effect and some are beneficial, while only a small number lead to disease. This may be a result of bacterial growth, the INFLAMMATION in response to it or of TOXINS (e.g., TETANUS, BOTULISM and CHOLERA). Bacteria may be contracted from the environment, other animals or humans, or from other parts of a single individual. Infection of SKIN and soft tissues with STAPHYLOCOCCUS or STREPTOCOCCUS leads to boils, carbuncles, impetigo, cellulitis, scarlet fever and erysipelas. ABSCESS represents the localization of bacteria, while SEPTICEMIA is infection circulating in the BLOOD. Sometimes a specific bacteria causes a specific disease (e.g., ANTHRAX, DIPHTHERIA, TYPHOID FEVER), but any bacteria in some organs cause a similar disease: in LUNGS, PNEUMONIA occurs; in urinary tract, CYSTITIS or pyelonephritis, and in the BRAIN coverings, MENINGITIS. Many VENEREAL DISEASES are due to bacteria. In some diseases (e.g., TUBERCULOSIS, LEPROSY, RHEUMATIC FEVER), many manifestations are due to hypersensitivity (see IMMUNITY) to the bacteria. While ANTIBIOTICS have greatly reduced death and ill-health from bacteria and VACCINATION against specific diseases (e.g., WHOOPING COUGH) has limited the number of cases, bacteria remain an important factor in disease.

BACTERIOLOGICAL WARFARE. See CHEMICAL AND BIOLOGICAL WARFARE.

BACTERIOLOGY, the science that deals with BACTERIA, their characteristics and their activities as related to medicine, industry and agriculture. Bacteria were discovered in 1676 by Anton van LEEUWENHOEK. Modern techniques of study originate from about 1870 with the use of stains and the discovery of culture methods using plates of nutrient agar media. Much pioneering work was done by Louis PASTEUR and Robert KOCH. (See also BACTERIAL DISEASES; SPONTANEOUS GENERATION.)

BACTERIOPHAGE, or **phage,** a VIRUS which attacks BACTERIA. They have a thin PROTEIN coat surrounding a central core of DNA (or occasionally RNA), and a small protein tail. The phage attaches itself to the bacterium and injects the NUCLEIC ACID into the cell. This genetic material (see GENETICS) alters the metabolism of the bacterium, and several hundred phages develop inside it: eventually the cell bursts, releasing the new, mature phages. Study of phages has revealed much about protein synthesis and nucleic acids.

BACTRIA, ancient Greek kingdom in central Asia. Once a province of the Persian Empire, it was conquered by Alexander the Great in 328 BC and ruled and fought over by Greek generals until about 130 BC, when it succumbed to tribal invaders.

BADEN-POWELL, Robert, 1st Baron Baden-Powell of Gilwell (1857–1941), British army officer, founder in 1907 of the Boy Scouts and in 1910, with his sister Agnes Baden-Powell, of the Girl Guides.

BADGERS, medium-sized omnivorous burrowing MAMMALS of the WEASEL family Mustelidae. There are six genera (seven including the ratel) distributed throughout Eurasia, North America and parts of Indonesia. They have potent anal scent GLANDS especially effective in the Oriental stink badgers *Mydaus* and *Suillotaxus*. Three genera, *Meles, Taxidea* (which includes the American badger, *T. Taxus*) and *Melogale*, have distinctive black and white facial masks. Badgers are almost always nocturnal.

BADLANDS NATIONAL PARK, some 243,302 acres of badlands in SW S.D. It comprises barren ravines and ridges of multicolored shale; its sandstone layers are famous for fossils. Created as a national monument in 1929, the area was renamed a national park in 1978.

BADOGLIO, Pietro (1871–1956), Italian field marshal and statesman, instrumental in Italy's seizure of Ethiopia (1935) and in MUSSOLINI's overthrow (1943). He became prime minister and surrendered Italy to the Allies on Sept. 3, 1943.

BAECK, Leo (1873–1956), German rabbi, a leader of Reform Judaism. He braved Nazi persecution rather than emigrate and was one of the few to survive the Theresienstadt concentration camp. His major work, *Essence of Judaism* (1905), stresses the ethical importance of Judaism.

BAEDEKER, Karl (1801–1859), German publisher who developed the tourist guidebooks which bear his name. "Baedekers" now cover most European and many non-European countries.

BAEKELAND, Leo Hendrik (1863–1944), Belgian-born chemist who, after emigrating to the US in 1889, devised Velox photographic printing paper (selling the process to EASTMAN in 1899) and went on to discover Bakelite, the first modern synthetic PLASTIC.

BAER, Karl Ernst von (1792–1876), Estonian-born German embryologist who discovered the mammalian egg (see REPRODUCTION) and the NOTOCHORD of the vertebrate embryo. He is considered to have been one of the founders of comparative EMBRYOLOGY.

BAFFIN, William (c1584–1622), English navigator and Arctic explorer. As pilot on a vessel seeking the Northwest Passage, he discovered Baffin Bay (1616) and reached 77°45′N—setting a record that stood for more than 200 years.

BAFFIN ISLAND, world's fifth largest island, between Greenland and Canada, part of Canada's Northwest Territories. It is a rugged, glaciated tract of some 183,810sq mi with an impressive 7,000ft-high mountain range along its E coast. The largely Eskimo population lives by fishing, fur-trading and whaling. There is also some coal mining.

BAGEHOT, Walter (1826–1877), English social scientist, editor and literary critic, a man of great originality and influence. Among his most important works are *The English Constitution* (1867), *Physics and Politics* (1872) and *Lombard Street* (1873). Bagehot, who came from a banking family, edited *The Economist* from 1861 until his death.

BAGHDAD, capital of Iraq, situated on the Tigris R, some 330mi inland from the Persian Gulf. It is Iraq's main communications, trading and industrial center, and manufactures petroleum products and textiles. Founded in 762 AD, it was a center of Muslim culture until 1258 when it was sacked and largely destroyed by the Mongols. Baghdad was ruled by Turkey from 1638, captured by Britain in WWI and finally made capital of the new nation of Iraq in 1921. Pop (city) 1,198,142; (metro) 4,400,000.

BAGPIPE, wind instrument in which air is blown into a leather bag and forced out through musical pipes. The melody is played on one or two pipes (the chanters) while one or more drone pipes sound bass tones. The bagpipe originated in Asia, but is best known as Scotland's national instrument.

BAGRATION, Piotr Ivanovich, Prince (1765–1812), Russian general who fought Napoleon at Austerlitz, Eylau, Friedland, and Borodino, where he was fatally wounded.

BAHA'I FAITH, religion founded by the Persian Mirza Husain Ali, known as Baha'u'llah ("glory of god"), in the second half of the 19th century. It developed from the teaching of the prophet Bab (1820–1850) who preached in Persia until Islamic leaders had him executed. Mirza Husain Ali (1817–1892) succeeded him and founded Baha'i, proclaiming himself a manifestation of God. The Baha'i faith is based on belief in human brotherhood and promotes peace and racial justice. It has a world-wide following.

BAHAMAS, a nation of some 700 subtropical islands and more than 2,000 islets or *cays* extending about 760mi from the SE coast of Fla. to the N coast of Haiti. The most important island is New Providence, where the capital, Nassau, is situated. Among the largest islands in the

Official name: Commonwealth of the Bahamas
Capital: Nassau
Area: 5,382sq mi
Population: 245,000
Language: English
Religions: Protestant, Roman Catholic
Monetary units: 1 Bahamian dollar = 100 cents

chain are Andros, Great Abaco, Grand Bahama and Inagua.

About 85% of the population is black. Most people live in Nassau or elsewhere on New Providence. The economy is based on tourism and fishing and on the export of wood products, cement, salt and crayfish.

Columbus probably made his first New World landfall on Watling Island (San Salvador). English settlement began in the 1640s, and British rule was almost unbroken until internal self-government in 1964. Full independence came in 1973. In recent years, the nation's involvement in the drug trade has strained its relations with the US.

BAHRAIN, independent Arab emirate, an archipelago, consisting of Bahrain Island and a number of smaller islands, in the Persian Gulf between the Saudi Arabian coast and the Qatar peninsula. The country has a desert climate, and agriculture is limited. The economy is based on oil drilling and refining, pearl fishing being now relatively unimportant. The main. population centers are Manama and Muharraq. A trading center in ancient times, Bahrain has been ruled as an emirate since 1783. Bahrain was a British protectorate 1861–1971, when it regained full independence. A causeway linking Bahrain Island to Saudi Arabia was opened in 1987, enhancing Bahrain's role as a commercial and service center for the entire Persian Gulf region.

Official name: State of Bahrain
Capital: Manama
Area: 267sq mi
Population: 481,000
Languages: Arabic, English
Religions: Muslim
Monetary unit(s): 1 Bahrain dinar = 1000 fils

BAIKIE, William Balfour (1825–1864), British explorer in Africa who helped establish British control in Nigeria.

BAILEY, Gamaliel (1807–1859), US abolitionist editor. He edited the *Philanthropist* in Cincinnati and then the *National Era* in Washington, in which he first published Harriet Beecher Stowe's *Uncle Tom's Cabin.*

BAILEY, James Anthony (1847–1906), US circus owner. In 1881 his circus merged with that of Phineas T. BARNUM, to form the famous Barnum & Bailey Circus. Bailey owned it after Barnum died.

BAILEY, Pearl (1918–), US jazz singer and actress. She sang with Count BASIE and Cootie Williams and acted in stage and motion-picture musicals, including *Porgy and Bess* and *Hello Dolly.*

BAILLY, Jean Sylvain (1736–1793), French astronomer and revolutionary politician. A prominent scientist, he was elected (1789) to the Estates-General and became president of the National Assembly, simultaneously serving as mayor of Paris (1789–91). Opposed to radical elements in Paris, he was held responsible for the July 1791 massacre when the National Guard fired into a Parisian crowd. For this he was later guillotined.

BAILYN, Bernard (1922–), US historian, at Harvard U from 1953. He received Pulitzer Prizes for his *Ideological Origins of the American Revolution* (1967) and *Voyagers to the West* (1986).

BAILY'S BEADS, named for Francis Baily (1774–1844), the apparent fragmentation of the thin crescent of the sun just before totality in a solar ECLIPSE, caused by sunlight shining through mountains at the edge of the lunar disk.

BAJA CALIFORNIA (Lower California), peninsula in NW Mexico W of the Gulf of California. A dry mountainous area, it extends for 760mi and is 25–150mi wide. To the N the state of Baja California forms the boundary with the US, while in the S is the territory of Baja California Sur. The main border cities, Mexicali and Tijuana, benefit from nearby US markets, but the region is generally undeveloped with agriculture limited by poor water supply. The peninsula is of great archaeological interest, settlement there probably dating back to around 21000 BC. The Spanish landed here in 1533.

BAKER, George Pierce (1866–1935), influential US teacher of dramatic composition. He was professor at Harvard (1905–24), and at Yale (1935–33), where he founded the experimental Yale drama school. His students included Eugene O'NEILL.

BAKER, Howard Henry, Jr. (1925–), US Republican politician, senator from Tennessee 1967–85, majority leader 1981–85. He left the Senate to practice law in Washington, D.C., and was reportedly considering running for president in 1988.

But in Feb. 1987 he accepted the position of chief of staff in the Reagan White House, replacing Donald Regan in the midst of the Iran-contra controversy. He resigned in 1988.

BAKER, James Addison (1930–   ), US public official. He was White House chief of staff during President Ronald Reagan's first administration and US secretary of the treasury during the second. He resigned in 1988 to manage the successful presidential campaign of his friend George Bush, who immediately announced that he would name Baker secretary of state in the new administration.

BAKER, Josephine (1906–1975), US-born, naturalized-French singer and dancer of international fame. Film and stage artist, philanthropist and social campaigner, Miss Baker, a black woman, won a special place in the hearts of the French people.

BAKER, Newton Diehl (1871–1937), US secretary of war (1916–21) in the cabinet of President Woodrow Wilson. A pacifist, he nevertheless won praise for his conduct of the War Department during WWI.

BAKER, Ray Stannard (1870–1946), US journalist and author, awarded a Pulitzer prize for his *Woodrow Wilson—Life and Letters* (1927–39). At the request of President Wilson, Baker led the American Press Bureau at the Paris Peace Conference (1919). He also wrote homely philosophical essays under the pseudonym David Grayson.

BAKER, Sir Samuel White (1821–1893), English explorer who discovered the sources of the Nile (1861–64), an achievement shared by John Hanning SPEKE. Baker explored and named Lake ALBERT.

BAKKE CASE, a suit brought by Allan Bakke in 1974 against the University of California claiming that as a result of the institution's affirmative-action program he had been wrongfully denied admission to medical school solely because he was white. On June 28, 1978, the US Supreme Court ruled five to four in Bakke's favor, concluding that the use of strict racial quotas in determining university admissions is unconstitutional.

BAKST, Lèon Nikolaevich (Lev Samuilovich Rosenberg; 1866–1924), Russian painter and theater designer. He designed sets and costumes for DIAGHILEV's ballets.

BAKUNIN, Mikhail Alexandrovich (1814–1876), Russian revolutionary, a founder of political ANARCHISM. He was involved in uprisings in Paris (1848) and Dresden (1849). Exiled to Siberia (1857), he escaped to England (1861). Bakunin founded anarchist groups in W Europe and joined the First INTERNATIONAL, but clashed bitterly with MARX and was expelled from the movement with his followers.

BALAKIREV, Mili Alekseyevich (1837–1910), Russian nationalist composer, leader of "The Five." His works include two symphonies; the symphonic poem *Tamara* (1867–82); piano pieces, notably a sonata and *Islamey* (1869); and many songs.

BALAKLAVA, seaport village in the Crimean region, SW USSR, and site of a CRIMEAN WAR battle (Oct. 25, 1854) commemorated by Tennyson's *The Charge of the Light Brigade* (1854).

BALALAIKA, plucked, usually three-stringed instrument of ancient Slavic origin used in Russian and E European folk music. It has a triangular body and long fretted neck. Its six sizes may be combined in ensemble playing.

BALANCHINE, George (real name: Georgy Melitonovich Balanchivadze; 1904–1983), Russian-born choreographer, founder of an American ballet style. He worked for DIAGHILEV in France and in 1948, with Lincoln KIRSTEIN, established the New York City Ballet, for which he created many brilliant ballets.

BALBO, Italo (1896–1940), Italian aviator, Fascist leader and first air minister (1929–33), who built up Italian air power. Distrusted by Mussolini, he was made governor of Libya, dying there when Italian troops shot down his plane, allegedly in error.

BALBOA, Vasco Nùnez de (c1475–1519), Spanish conquistador who discovered the Pacific Ocean. In 1510 he cofounded and became leader of the first lasting European settlement on the American mainland, Antigua in Darien (Panama). Encouraged by Indian tales of a wealthy kingdom on "the other sea," in 1513 Balboa led an expedition across the isthmus, saw the Pacific, and claimed it and all its coasts for Spain. Pedrarias Dávila succeeded Balboa in Darien and jealously had him executed on a false charge of treason.

BALCH, Emily Greene (1867–1961), US sociologist, economist and humanitarian, joint winner of the 1946 Nobel Peace Prize. Secretary of the Women's International League for Peace and Freedom 1919–22 and 1934–35, she was its honorary president from 1936.

BALCHEN, Bernt (1899–1973), Norwegian-American aviator, chief pilot on Richard E. Byrd's 1928–30 Antarctic expedition. With Byrd, he made (1929) the first flight over the South Pole.

BALD EAGLE, *Haliaetus leucocephalus,*

only North American native EAGLE, the national bird of the US since 1782. About 3ft long with a wingspan around 7ft, it is black, with white feathers on neck, tail and head giving it a bald appearance. It preys on fish and is protected in all states. Family: Accipitridae.

BALDNESS, or **alopecia,** loss of hair, usually from the scalp, due to disease of hair follicles. **Male-pattern baldness** is an inherited tendency, often starting in the twenties. **Alopecia areata** is a disease of unknown cause producing patchy baldness, though it may be total. Prolonged FEVER, lupus erythematosus and ringworm may lead to temporary baldness, as may certain drugs and poisons.

BALDUNG GRIEN, Hans (c1484–1545), German painter and engraver. He was at first influenced by DÜRER. His masterpiece is the Freiburg cathedral altarpiece containing the *Coronation of the Virgin*(1516). His morbid allegorical paintings include a dramatic "Death and the Maiden" series.

BALDWIN, Abraham (1754–1807), American political leader. Born in Connecticut, he represented Georgia in the Continental Congress (1785–88), the Federal Constitutional Convention (1787), the US House of Representatives (1789–99), and the US Senate (1799–1807). In the Constitutional Convention, he served on the committee that resolved the crucial issue of how the states would be represented in the national legislature.

BALDWIN, James (1924–1987), black U.S. novelist, essayist and playwright, dealing with racial themes. *Go Tell It On The Mountain* (1953) reflects his Harlem adolescence; *Another Country* (1962) deals with sexual and racial identity. His nonfiction includes *The Fire Next Time* (1963), on racial oppression.

BALDWIN, Matthias William (1795–1866), US industrialist, an early builder of steam locomotives at the Baldwin Locomotive Works in Philadelphia.

BALDWIN, Robert (1804–1858), Canadian statesman, leader, with Louis LaFontaine, of the first responsible Canadian administration: the "Great Ministry" (1848–51). He later worked for improved relations between English and French Canadians.

BALDWIN, Roger Nash (1884–1981), US lawyer, founder and director (1920–50) of the AMERICAN CIVIL LIBERTIES UNION (ACLU).

BALDWIN, Stanley (1867–1947) British Conservative statesman, prime minister 1923–24, 1924–29, 1935–37. He maintained stable government, but provoked labor hostility (before and after the General Strike of 1926) and failed to curb unemployment or to rearm against Nazi Germany. He handled the crisis of EDWARD VIII's abdication. He became Earl Baldwin of Bewdley on his retirement.

BALEARIC ISLANDS, group of Mediterranean islands off E Spain, under Spanish rule since 1349. The largest are Majorca, Minorca and Ibiza. Products include grapes, olives and citrus fruit. Tourism is important.

BALEWA, Sir Abubakar Tafawa (1912–1966), first prime minister of Nigeria (1957–66), murdered in a military coup. He founded and led a major political party, the Northern People's Congress.

BALFOUR, Arthur James Balfour, 1st Earl of (1848–1930), English statesman best known for the BALFOUR DECLARATION. He was an influential Conservative member of parliament 1874–1911; prime minister 1902–05; and foreign secretary 1916–19.

BALFOUR DECLARATION, statement of British policy issued in 1917 by Foreign Secretary Arthur BALFOUR. It guaranteed a Jewish national home in Palestine without prejudice to the rights of non-Jews there, but did not mention a separate Jewish state. In 1922 the League of Nations approved a British mandate in Palestine based on the Balfour Declaration. (See also PALESTINE; WEIZMANN, CHAIM.)

BALI, volcanic island (2,171sq mi) of the Lesser Sunda group, Indonesia, E of Java. Freed from Japanese occupation after WWII, it became an Indonesian province in 1950. Rice is the main crop. The largely Hindu Balinese are famous for dancing, gamelan music and decorative arts.

BALKAN PENINSULA, SE Europe S of the Danube and Sava rivers and abutting the Adriatic, Ionian, Mediterranean, Aegean and Black seas. It comprises Bulgaria, Albania, Greece, European Turkey and most of Yugoslavia. The region is mountainous and limited in natural resources. Its SLAVS, Turks and Greeks live mainly in small communities, raising sheep, goats, vines and cereals. Little industry exists outside big cities like Belgrade, Athens and Istanbul.

The area was influenced by Greece; ruled by Rome (c148 BC-mid-5th century AD); then partly controlled by the Byzantine Empire. Invading Slavs and others founded ancient Bulgaria and Serbia, and crusaders seized the S early in the 13th century. But by 1500 the Ottoman Turks held almost all the Balkans. New nations emerged through 19th-century nationalist movements, which also sparked off the BALKAN WARS and

WORLD WAR I. After WWII Albania, Bulgaria and Yugoslavia became communist; Turkey and Greece joined NATO.

BALKAN WARS, two wars in which the Ottoman Empire lost almost all its European territory. In the First Balkan War (1912–13) Serbia, Bulgaria, Greece and Montenegro conquered all Turkey's European possessions except Constantinople. But Bulgaria, Serbia and Greece disputed control in Macedonia. In the Second Balkan War (1913) Bulgaria attacked Serbia, but was itself attacked by Romania, Greece and Turkey. In the ensuing Treaty of Bucharest (Aug. 1913) Bulgaria lost territory to each of her enemies.

BALL, John (d. 1381), English priest, a follower of John Wycliffe and an advocate of social equality who popularized the couplet "When Adam delved and Eve span/Who was then the gentleman?" For his part in the Peasants' Revolt of 1381 led by WAT TYLER, he was executed.

BALL, Lucille Desiree (1911–   ), US film and television comedienne and producer, best known for her television role as "Lucy" (from 1951).

BALLA, Giacomo (1871–1958), Italian painter, a leading exponent of FUTURISM. His works include attempts to show objects in motion and pioneer abstract paintings.

BALLAD, simple verse narrative, often meant to be sung, originally anonymous and orally transmitted. Many ballads comprise rhymed four-line stanzas each followed by a refrain. Traditionally, ballads celebrated folk heroes or related popular romances, and were developed by European minstrels of the Middle Ages. Romantic writers, such as Sir Walter SCOTT, WORDSWORTH and COLERIDGE, adapted the form. In popular music today, the term is used loosely as a synonym for any kind of sentimental song, but the US has produced many ballads of the traditional type, ranging from the anonymous *Frankie and Johnny* to the work of Bob DYLAN and Joan Baez.

BALLET, form of theatrical dance that tells a story or expresses a theme, mood or idea. It originated in Renaissance Italian court entertainments introduced into France in 1581 by Catherine de Médicis. Louis XIV in 1661 established the first ballet school, whose ballet master, Pierre Beauchamp, originated the five basic foot positions of ballet.

Early 18th-century ballet was part of opera, and dancers were hampered by heavy costumes; but by the mid-18th century pantomime ballet, in which all meaning was conveyed by movement, had evolved. The French choreographer Jean-Georges Noverre made ballet an independent art uniting plot, music, decor and movement. The 19th-century emphasized lightness and grace: dancing *sur les pointes* (on the tips of the toes) and the short tutu appeared. Russia became the world center with the appointment of Marius PETIPA to the Imperial Ballet in 1862. He inspired the originals of *Swan Lake, The Nutcracker* and *The Sleeping Beauty.*

Early in the 1900s, in Paris, the Russian Ballet of Sergei DIAGHILEV, with NIJINSKY, PAVLOVA, MASSINE and FOKINE, revitalized dance drama. In 1933 Ninette de Valois formed England's first permanent company, now the Royal Ballet, noted for ASHTON's choreography. BALANCHINE established American ballet in the 1930s, his New York City Ballet fusing classical tradition with modern dance as developed by Isadora DUNCAN, Ruth ST. DENIS, Martha GRAHAM and Jerome ROBBINS. (See also CHOREOGRAPHY; DANCE.)

BALLISTIC MISSILE. See MISSILE.

BALLISTICS, the science concerned with the behavior of projectiles, traditionally divided into three parts. **Interior ballistics** is concerned with the progress of the projectile before it is released from the launching device. In the case of a gun this involves determining the propellant charge, barrel design and firing mechanism needed to give the desired muzzle velocity and stabilizing spin to the projectile. **External ballistics** is concerned with the free flight of the projectile. At the beginning of the 17th century GALILEO determined that the trajectory (flight path) of a projectile should be parabolic (see CONIC SECTIONS), as indeed it would be if the effects of air resistance, the rotation and curvature of the earth, the variation of air density and gravity with height, and the rotational INERTIA of the projectile could be ignored. The shockwaves accompanying projectiles moving faster than the speed of sound are also the concern of this branch.

Terminal or **penetration ballistics** deals with the behavior of projectiles on impacting at the end of their trajectory. The velocity-to-mass ratio of the impact particle is an important factor, and results are of equal interest to the designers of ammunition and of armorplate. A relatively recent development in the science is **forensic ballistics,** which now plays an important role in the investigation of gun crimes.

BALLOON, a nonpowered, nonrigid lighter-than-air craft comprising a bulbous envelope containing the lifting medium and a payload-carrying basket or "gondola" suspended below. Balloons may be captive (secured to the ground by a cable, as in the barrage balloons used during WWII to protect key installations and cities from low-level air bombing) or free-flying (blown along and steered at the mercy of the WIND). Lift may be provided either by GAS (usually HYDROGEN or noninflammable HELIUM) or by heating the air in the envelope. A balloon rises or descends through the air until it reaches a level at which it is in equilibrium in accordance with ARCHIMEDES' principle. In this situation the total weight of the balloon and payload is equal to that of the volume of air which it is displacing.

If the pilot of a gas balloon wishes to ascend, he throws ballast (usually sand) over the side, thus reducing the overall DENSITY of the craft; to descend he releases some of the lifting gas through a small valve in the envelope. The altitude of a hot-air balloon is controlled using the propane burner which heats the air; increased heat causes the craft to rise; turning off the burner gives a period of level flight followed by a slow descent as the trapped air cools.

The MONTGOLFIER brothers' hot-air balloon became the first manned aircraft in 1783, and in the same year the first gas balloon was flown by Jacques CHARLES. In 1785 Jean BLANCHARD piloted a balloon across the English Channel. In due time the powered balloon, or AIRSHIP, was developed, though free balloons have remained popular for sporting, military and scientific purposes. The upper atmosphere is explored using unmanned gas balloons, and radiosonde balloons are in regular meteorological use. In 1931 Auguste PICCARD pioneered high-altitude manned flights. Many modern sporting balloons are built on the hot-air principle.

In 1978 three Americans, Ben Abruzzo, Maxie Anderson and Larry Newman, were the first to cross the Atlantic in a balloon.

BALLOT. See VOTING.

BALLOU, Hosea (1771–1852), US clergyman, a leading exponent of UNIVERSALISM. Ballou separated Universalist doctrine from Calvinist influence and introduced aspects of UNITARIANISM. He was pastor of the Second Universalist Church in Boston 1817–52, and founder-editor of *The Universalist Magazine* 1819–28.

BALLPOINT PEN, pen designed to minimize ink leakage. At one end of a narrow, cylindrical ink reservoir a freely-rotating metal ball is held in a socket. The viscous ink is drawn through internal ducts in the socket by capillary action (see CAPILLARITY). Ballpoint pens came into general use in the late 1940s.

BALMORAL CASTLE, private residence of the British monarch, near Braemar, in Grampian, Scotland. It was built 1853–56 by Prince ALBERT, who bequeathed it to Queen Victoria.

BALTIC LANGUAGES, group of INDO-EUROPEAN LANGUAGES, closely related to the Slavonic languages, spoken in the area SE of the Baltic Sea. They include Lithuanian, Lettish and the now extinct Old Prussian.

BALTIC SEA, an arm of the Atlantic Ocean, bounded by Sweden, Finland, the USSR, Poland, Germany and Denmark. It is linked to the North Sea by the Skagerrak, Kattegat and Øresund. Its 163,000sq mi of weakly saline water freeze over in winter. There is a limited fishing industry based on herring, cod and salmon. Baltic trade flourished in the 14th century through the HANSEATIC LEAGUE, but declined in competition with Atlantic ports. Copenhagen, Stockholm, Helsinki, and Leningad are the main ports.

BALTIC STATES, the former Baltic coast republics of Estonia, Latvia and Lithuania. They became independent in 1918 but were annexed by the USSR in 1940.

BALTIMORE, largest city in Md., on the Patapsco R near Chesapeake Bay. It is the seventh-largest city in the US, one of the nation's busiest ports and an important road, rail and air transportation hub. Since WWI it has become a leading manufacturing center with metallurgical, electronic and food-processing industries. Baltimore is the educational center of Md., with Johns Hopkins U. and many other institutions. Established in 1729 and named for Lord Baltimore, the city grew as a grain-exporting port. It suffered economic disruption as a Civil War "border city," and was largely rebuilt after the great fire of 1904. Pop (city) 764,000, (metro) 2,253,000.

BALTIMORE ORIOLE, *Icterus galbula,* North American songbird of the family Icteridae (not Oriolidae, as are true orioles). About 8in long, it has a wingspan of about 12in. Males are black and bright orange; females and young are olive, yellow and brownish.

BALZAC, Honoré de (1799–1850), French novelist noted for his acute social observation and sweeping vision. In the nearly 100 works forming *La Comédie Humaine,* he attempted to portray all levels of contemporary French society, their interdependence and the influence of the environment upon them. The most famous such novels of this series are *Eugénie Grandet* (1833), *Le Père Goriot* (1834) and *La Cousine Bette* (1846). Balzac had a great capacity for hard work, but was also known for his debts and love affairs.

BAMBOO, woody grasses with hollow stems found in Asia, Africa, Australia and the southern US. Some species grow to 120ft. In Asia the young shoots are a major foodstuff, while mature stems are used in building houses and furniture. Amorphous silica from stems is used as a catalyst in some chemical processes.

BANANA, edible fruit of a large (30ft) perennial stooling herb that reaches maturity within 15 months from planting. Cultivated clones evolved in SE Asia from two wild species, *Musa acuminata* and *M. balbisiana*, and spread across the Pacific, Africa and the New World. Main areas of commercial cultivation are in tropical and South America and the West Indies, a major part of the crop being exported to the US and Europe; but bananas are of great importance locally in many tropical diets.

BANCROFT, George (1800–1891), US historian and statesman whose 10-volume *History of the United States* (1834–74) was the first attempt fully to cover US history. As secretary of the navy (1845–46), he helped develop the US Naval Academy, Annapolis. His *History* became a standard work, though it was later criticized for its strong nationalistic bias.

BANCROFT, Hubert Howe (1832–1918), US historian and publisher. The 39-volume history of western North America, the *West American Historical Series*, which he edited and partly wrote, remains a useful source for the history of the West.

BAND, a musical ensemble generally of wind and percussion instruments, though sometimes devoted to a particular type of instrument. Bands accompany military and civil parades and other ceremonies, and play dance music. Famous US bands have included those founded by John Philip SOUSA and Glenn MILLER.

BANDA, Hastings Kamuzu (1906–   ), African nationalist leader, first prime minister (1964–66) and president of Malawi (from 1966). As leader of the Nyasaland nationalists, and head of the Malawi Congress party from 1960, he sought dissolution of the Federation of Rhodesia and Nyasaland. He later had a moderating influence on African affairs.

BANDARANAIKE, Sirimavo Ratwatte Dias (1916–   ), prime minister of Sri Lanka and the world's first woman premier. After the assassination of her husband, Prime Minister Solomon Bandaranaike, in 1959, she led his Sri Lanka Freedom party to victory in 1960, continuing his pro-Buddhist and pro-Sinhalese policies.

She lost office in 1965 but was returned in 1970 with a landslide victory for her left-oriented coalition. Conservatives defeated her in 1977.

BANDELLO, Matteo (1485–1561), Italian writer, diplomat and monk. His 214 stories or *novelle* greatly influenced European literature, and provided the bases of plots used by SHAKESPEARE (*Romeo and Juliet*) and John WEBSTER (*The Duchess of Malfi*).

BANDICOOTS, several genera of the family Peramelidae. They are roughly rabbit-sized MARSUPIALS, probably most closely related to the dasyures. They have tapering snouts, varying in length from species to species. There are considerable reproductive differences from other marsupials: though gestation is for only 12 days, the newborn young are comparatively large; while in the uterus, the embryos are nourished by a complex placenta quite unlike those of other marsupials. Their FOSSIL history is problematic, so that their relationship to other marsupials is not fully understood.

BANDUNG CONFERENCE, first major conference on world affairs by 29 independent African and Asian nations, held in Bandung, Indonesia, April 1955. It condemned colonialism and urged world peace and economic and cultural cooperation.

BANERJEA, Sir Surendranath (1848–1925), Indian nationalist leader who opposed GANDHI's methods of civil disobedience, preferring constitutional means of achieving self-government.

BANGKOK, capital of Thailand, on the Chao Phraya R near the Gulf of Siam. It is Thailand's chief port, manufacturing center and university city, with many picturesque Buddhist temples. Also SEATO headquarters and regional headquarters for the World Health Organization and UNESCO. Pop (metro) 4,697,071.

BANGLADESH, republic in the NE of the Indian subcontinent, on the Bay of Bengal; formerly East PAKISTAN.

Land and People. It is a low-lying land centered on the alluvial Ganges-Brahmaputra Delta. A tropical monsoon climate prevails, and because of the seasonal heavy rains and severe cyclones, most of the country is subject to flooding. Overpopulation accentuates periodic famines and epidemics among the mainly Muslim Bengalis who constitute the great majority of the population.

Economy. Bangladesh produces nearly 90% of the world's jute; tea is the other main cash crop, and sugarcane is also grown. Rice and wheat are the major subsistence crops.

Official name: People's Republic of Bangladesh
Capital: Dacca
Area: 55,598sq mi
Population: 105,307,000
Languages: Bengali, English
Religions: Muslim, Hindu, Buddhist
Monetary unit(s): 1 taka = 100 paisa

Natural gas is the only important mineral resource, and manufacturing is largely limited to the processing of raw materials.
History. The region was created as East Pakistan (Pakistan's eastern province) in 1947. The province sought greater independence under Sheikh Mujibur RAHMAN, whose Awami League won a majority in the 1970 Pakistan election. West Pakistan refused autonomy and troops crushed large-scale opposition in the ensuing civil war (March–Dec. 1971). But guerrilla fighting continued, Bengalis exiled in India proclaimed a Bengali republic, and Indian invasion forces overran the West Pakistani forces. A Bangladesh government was established in Dacca in Dec. 1971, and Mujibur Rahman became prime minister in Jan. 1972. But the war had left the country with severe economic and political problems, and in 1975 Mujibur Rahman established a presidential, one-party regime. In Aug. 1975 he and his family were assassinated in a coup; two military counter-coups and martial law followed in Nov. 1975. Martial law was ended in 1979, when in general elections Ziaur Rahman (Zia) was chosen president. President Zia was assassinated in 1981, and the vice president was sworn in as acting president. In 1982 martial law was instituted following another coup led by Lt. Gen. H. M. Ershad. Ershad, who won election to the presidency of a parliamentary government following the lifting of martial law in 1986, suspended parliament in 1987. New legislative elections in 1988 were boycotted by the opposition. Later that year, Bangladesh suffered the worst floods in 70 years when 75% of the country was inundated.
BANJO, stringed musical instrument with a circular skin soundboard and a long fretted neck. Its 4–9 strings are played by plucking. The banjo originated among Negro slaves in North America, and may have derived from W African instruments. It became popular in 19th-century minstrel shows and early jazz bands and for some folk music.
BANK FOR INTERNATIONAL SETTLEMENTS, a European bank founded in 1930 in Switzerland to handle the payments of German war reparations. A major international bank, it is a focal point for the central banks of W Europe—whose presidents sit on its board of governors—and the agent for the European Fund of the European Community.
BANKHEAD, William Brockman (1874–1940), American politician. A Democratic US representative from Alabama (1917–40) and Speaker of the House (1936–40), he was a leading New Deal legislator. His brother was **John Hollis Bankhead** (1872–1946), US senator from Alabama (1931–46). His daughter was **Tallulah Brockman Bankhead** (1903–1968), a stage and motion picture actress.
BANKING, the business dealing with money and credit transactions. It can be traced back beyond 2500 BC, but modern banking originated in medieval Italy (taking its name from *banca*, the money-lender's bench). Banking grew among traders needing to exchange one country's coins for those of another, to buy and sell without handling bulky gold or silver, and to borrow cash to bridge the period between buying goods and selling them. Thus major trading cities such as Venice, Antwerp, Hamburg and London also became great banking centers.
Banking in the US. The first Bank of the United States (1791–1811) was promoted by Alexander HAMILTON to finance industrial and commercial expansion. But politicians prejudiced against national banks closed the bank and its successor (1816–36). For 30 years, before the Civil War, wildcat banks incorporated in western border states profited from selling largely worthless notes in east coast cities. The 1863 National Bank Act forced banks to pledge US government bonds with the treasury to back their note issues, but bank insolvencies continued in times of depression.

In 1913 the FEDERAL RESERVE SYSTEM was set up to strengthen the US banking system. Bank failures in 1933 led to a bank holiday (after which only solvent banks were allowed to reopen) and to the setting up of the FEDERAL DEPOSIT INSURANCE CORPORATION. Today, some states do not allow banks to maintain branches. There are restrictions, too, on the number and type of subsidiary companies a bank may own.

Banking services. Banks offer four main services: safe storage facilities; interest payments on deposits, which are in effect loans from the customer to the bank; money transfers in the form of checking accounts; and loans for home mortgages, automobile financing, business expansion, etc. In recent years, regulations which narrowly controlled the kinds of loans and the amount of interest banks could offer have been relaxed. Many banks now provide credit cards to credit-worthy customers, and will advance specified credit amounts to cardholders. Interest-paying checking accounts (NOW, or Negotiable Order of Withdrawal) are available. Certificates of Deposit, which pay high interest rates on specified amounts for a specified time (usually six months or one year), can be bought at most banks. These and other services are intended to attract customer deposits, which form the basis of a bank's ability to maintain its own investments and to loan money at interest. Every bank account is federally insured for the amount of the deposit, up to $100,000.

Banks as creators of money. Banks "create" money by lending sums banked by depositors. For instance, a $5,000 bank deposit may engender a $4,000 bank loan, which raises the money supply from $5,000 to $9,000. (The $1,000 not lent forms "liquid" assets which the bank keeps to cover depositors' claims for immediate repayments.) The money supply deeply affects a nation's economy, for money is the means of measuring the relative value of all commodities.

BANK OF THE UNITED STATES, name of two central banks set up in the early years of the US. In 1791 Alexander HAMILTON created the First Bank of the US, chartered by Congress for 20 years, with a central office in Philadelphia. It held government deposits and was able to extend some control over the issue of paper currency and the extension of credit. However, its constitutionality was questioned, and it was so strongly opposed by agrarian interests and by the state banks that its charter was not renewed.

The nation's chaotic financial system after the War of 1812 led Congress to charter the Second Bank of the US in 1816 for another 20-year period. However, opposition continued, especially in the West, and in 1832 President JACKSON refused to extend the charter. In the "Bank War" which followed, Nicholas BIDDLE, the bank's president, restricted national credit, and Jackson retaliated by withdrawing government deposits from the bank. The bank's charter was allowed to expire in 1836 without renewal. Only with the creation of the FEDERAL RESERVE SYSTEM in 1913 were the first real steps taken towards a central US banking system.

BANKS, Sir Joseph (1743–1820), British botanist and president of the ROYAL SOCIETY OF LONDON (1778–1820), the foremost British man of science of his time. He accompanied COOK as naturalist on his first expedition (1768–71) and was a key figure in the establishment of the Botanic Gardens at Kew, London.

BANKS, Nathaniel Prentiss (1816–1894), US politician and Union general in the American Civil War. Elected (1855) to the US House of Representatives as a Democrat, he became a Republican and served (1858–60) as governor of Massachusetts. In the Civil War he saw action in Virginia and Louisiana. He was again in Congress 1865–73, 1875–79, 1889–91.

BANNEKER, Benjamin (1731–1806), American mathematician and astronomer, notable as the first American black to gain distinction in science and the author of celebrated ALMANACS (1791–1802).

BANNISTER, Roger Gilbert (1929–   ), British athlete. He was the first man to run a mile in under four minutes, on May 6, 1954, at Oxford. His time was 3 minutes 59.4 seconds.

BANNOCKBURN, battlefield named for a village in Stirlingshire, Scotland. Here, in 1314, Scottish forces under Robert Bruce routed the numerically superior English army of King EDWARD II, assuring the throne of Scotland for Bruce and securing Scottish independence until the 18th century.

BANTING, Sir Frederick Grant (1891–1941), Canadian physiologist who, with C. H. Best, first isolated the hormone INSULIN from the pancreases of dogs (1922). For this he shared the 1923 Nobel Prize for Physiology or Medicine with J.J.R. Macleod, who had provided the experimental facilities.

BANTU, outmoded collective term for a group of tribes in central, E and S Africa possessing a common group of languages. The term may also be used in South Africa to denote black Africans as distinct from Afrikaners.

BANTUSTANS. See HOMELANDS.

BAO DAI (1913–   ), Vietnamese emperor during the French colonial period. He was the last emperor of Annam (1932–45), until overthrown by the Viet Minh. He was later made head of state of a unified Vietnam (1949–55) created by the French in a final bid to retain Indochina, but was forced into exile.

BAPTISM, Christian sacrament which constitutes an initiation into the Church. The ceremony involves the application of water; by sprinkling, pouring or immersion according to the denomination. Baptism has its origins in pagan and Jewish ceremony, and was commanded by Christ (Matthew 28:19).(See also JOHN THE BAPTIST.)

BAPTISTS, members of the many independent branches of the Baptist Church, one of the most diverse of Protestant denominations. There are more than 31 million Baptists in the world, most of whom live in America. In general, Baptist churches are lay churches having no elaborate priesthood, and are known for their evangelistic and revivalist traditions. The strongest unifying principle among all Baptist churches is the method of baptism by total immersion in water when a person who has reached the age of reason professes faith in Christ.

The history of the Baptists can be traced to religious dissension in Europe in the early 17th century, particularly in the Puritan movement. Baptist churches were established in the English colonies after the Restoration (1660), but it was only with America's 18th-century religious revival, the GREAT AWAKENING, that the Baptist tradition spread, notably in the Midwest and the South, where it is still most influential. The Baptists have always had a great interest in higher education and have founded many colleges and universities throughout the US.

BARA, Theda (1890–1955), US film star, born Theodosia Goodman. The word "vamp" (short for vampire) was coined to describe the evil but enticing women she portrayed between 1915 and 1920.

BARANOV, Aleksander Andreyevich (1746–1819), Russian trader in Alaska. Employed (1799–1817) by the Russian American Company, he established a settlement at Sitka and organized a profitable fur trade that extended down the coast as far as California, but he failed in his efforts to develop a Russian colony.

BARBADOS, a densely populated small island in the Caribbean; a parliamentary state, part of the British Commonwealth.

Land. About 21mi long and 14mi wide, Barbados lies 250mi NE of Venezuela. It is surrounded by coral reefs. The climate is pleasant, with a hot and rainy season from June to December.

People and Economy. The majority of the people are of African descent; about 5% are

Official name: Barbados
Capital: Bridgetown
Area: 166sq mi
Population: 254,000
Languages: English
Religions: Anglican, Methodist, Moravian, Roman Catholic
Monetary unit(s): 1 Barbados dollar = 100 cents

white. Known as "Little England," Barbados is the most British of the West Indies islands. Literacy rate is 97%. The fertile land, intensively cultivated, produces sugarcane. Tourism is the second most important source of income, and there is some light industry (food processing, plastic products, electrical components) for local consumption.

History. Barbados was occupied by the British in 1627 and remained a colony for over 300 years. Internal autonomy was attained in 1961 and full independence in 1966. Earl Barrow, the first prime minister (1966–76), resumed that post from 1986 until his death in 1987.

BARBAROSSA, Frederick. See FREDERICK I (Holy Roman Emperor).

BARBARY APE, small tailless macaques of Algeria, Morocco and Gibraltar; the genus *Macaca sylvana* of the Cercopithecidae family. Legend has it that the British will lose the Rock of Gibraltar should its small colony of Barbary apes depart.

BARBARY STATES, countries along the Mediterranean coast of N Africa, the region of present-day ALGERIA, TUNISIA, LIBYA and MOROCCO. Named for the Berber tribes who lived there, the Barbary states were known from the 16th to the 19th centuries as centers of piracy. The area was ruled earlier by Carthage, Rome and Byzantium, then conquered by the Arabs in the 8th century. After centuries of relative autonomy, the states were taken over largely by France, in the 19th century.

BARBARY WARS, two wars waged by the US against the BARBARY STATES of N Africa. By the late 18th century brigandage by the Barbary states had become a highly organized and lucrative trade. The first

Barbary War, or Tripolitan War, broke out in May 1801. For 15 years the US had been forced to pay tribute to protect its shipping. The war was sparked by new, exorbitant demands by the pasha of Tripoli. The US blockaded Tripoli, and subjected it to naval bombardment. But the war was not won until 1805, when Capt. William Eaton marched his forces 500mi across the desert from Alexandria to take Derna and threaten Tripoli itself. The second Barbary War was fought in 1815 with Algiers. Commodore Stephen DECATUR was dispatched to suppress an upsurge of piracy. Forcing his way into the harbor of Algiers, he compelled the dey of Algiers to sign a treaty ending piracy and freeing all US captives. Decatur went on to exact similar treaties from Tunis and Tripoli.

BARBER, Samuel (1910–1981), US composer. His works include *Adagio for Strings* (1936); the ballet *Medea* (1946); *Knoxville: Summer of 1915* (1947), for soprano and orchestra; and the operas *Vanessa* (1958) and *Antony and Cleopatra* (1966). He was awarded Pulitzer prizes in 1958 and 1963.

BARBIROLLI, Sir John (1899–1970), English conductor, famous for his interpretations of SIBELIUS and other late classics. After conducting the New York Philharmonic Orchestra (1937–42), he began a lifelong association with the Hallé Orchestra in Manchester, and conducted the Houston Symphony Orchestra (1961–67).

BARBITURATES, a class of drugs acting on the central NERVOUS SYSTEM; they include SEDATIVES, anesthetics and anticonvulsants. Barbiturates depress nerve cell activity, the degree of depression and thus clinical effect varying in different members of the class. Although widely used in the past for insomnia, their use is now discouraged in view of high rates of addiction and their danger in over-dosage; safer alternatives are now available. Short-acting barbiturates are useful in ANESTHESIA; phenobarbitone is used in treatment of convulsions, often in combination with other drugs.

BARBIZON SCHOOL, group of French painters of natural and rural subjects, active 1830–70, who frequented the village of Barbizon, near Paris. It included Théodore ROUSSEAU, Diaz de la Peña, COROT, MILLET, Dupré, Troyon, Daubigny and Jacque.

BARBUSSE, Henri (1873–1935), French author best known for his bitter WWI novel, *Le Feu* (*Under Fire*, 1916). *Clarté* (*Light*, 1919), his next novel, expressed Barbusse's ideas for the achievement of world peace. It inspired a short-lived international movement.

BARCELONA, Spain's second-largest city and chief port, and its greatest industrial and commercial center. Located in NE Spain on the Mediterranean, it is the historic capital of Catalonia. Barcelona was reputedly founded by Hamilcar Barca c230 BC. The countship of Barcelona was united with Aragon in 1137, and during the Middle Ages Barcelona became one of the Mediterranean's great maritime and commercial cities. The center of Catalan nationalism in modern times, it was the stronghold of left-wing politics and Republican allegiance in the Spanish Civil War. Pop 1,756,905.

BARCLAY DE TOLLY, Mikhail Bogdanovich, Prince (1761–1818), Russian general of Scottish descent. As commander of the Russian forces opposing Napoleon's 1812 invasion, he practiced a scorched-earth policy while retreating. Defeated (Aug. 17-18) at Smolensk, he was replaced by KUTUSOV, who, himself defeated at Borodino, resumed the strategy of retreat. After Kutusov's death in 1813, Barclay de Tolly again commanded the Russian army, participating in the battle of Leipzig (Oct. 16-19, 1813) and the capture of Paris (Mar. 31, 1814).

BAR COCHBA, Simon (d. 135 AD), leader of the last Jewish revolt against Roman rule in Palestine (132–135 AD), during the reign of Hadrian. Hailed as the Messiah by Rabbi AKIBA, he was at first successful and captured Jerusalem, but the revolt was finally put down and Bar Cochba slain.

BARD, Celtic poet-musician of ancient and medieval times, most notably in Ireland and Wales. The bards were highly esteemed figures, and bardic poetry reached a high level of sophistication. In Wales the tradition has been revived in the festivals called eisteddfods.

BARDEEN, John (1908–   ), US physicist who shared the 1956 Nobel Prize for Physics with W. B. Shockley and W. H. Brattain for their development of the TRANSISTOR. In 1972 he became the first person to win the physics prize a second time, sharing the award with L. P. Cooper and J. R. Schrieffer for their development of a comprehensive theory of SUPERCONDUCTIVITY.

BAREA, Arturo (1897–1957), Spanish novelist best known for his autobiographical trilogy *The Forging of a Rebel* (*The Forge*, 1941; *The Track*, 1943; *The Clash*, 1946), which described the agony of the Spanish Civil War (1936–39).

BAREBONE, Praise-God (c1596–1679), English republican and religious enthusiast, one of the "godly men" who served (1653) in Oliver Cromwell's short-lived Nominated Parliament, derisively called "Barebone's Parliament."

BARENTS, Willem (c1550–1597), Dutch navigator, for whom the Barents Sea is named. He made three voyages to the Arctic in search of a NE passage to Asia. After discovering Spitsbergen on his third voyage and wintering in the Arctic, he died before reaching home.

BARENTS SEA, shallow arm of the Arctic Ocean N of Norway and European Russia, bounded by Svalbard (Spitsbergen) to the NW, Franz Josef Land to the N and Novaya Zemlya to the E. The SW portion is warmed by the North Atlantic Drift and remains ice-free in winter; on its coast lies the strategic port of Murmansk.

BARIUM (Ba), silvery-white ALKALINE-EARTH METAL resembling CALCIUM. Barium is used to remove traces of gases from vacuum tubes; its compounds are used in making flares, fireworks, paint pigments and poisons. AW 137.3, mp 725 C, bp 1640 C, sg 3.5 (20 C). Barium sulfate (BaSO₄), highly insoluble and opaque to X-rays, can be safely ingested for X-ray examination of the GASTROINTESTINAL TRACT.

BARKLEY, Alben William (1877–1956), 35th vice-president of the US (1949–53), under Truman. A Democrat from Ky., Barkley served in the US House of Representatives (1913–27) and the Senate (1927–49), including 10 years (beginning 1937) as majority leader. He returned to the Senate in 1954.

BARLACH, Ernst (1870–1938), German Expressionist sculptor, graphic artist and playwright, whose powerful figures in bronze or wood owe much to a very personal combination of Gothic and cubist influences. Barlach also produced many woodcuts and lithographs, some of them to illustrate his own dramas.

BARLEY, *Hordeum vulgare* and *H. distichon,* remarkably adaptable and hardy cereal, cultivated since ancient times. The USSR is the world's largest producer, with Canada and the US following. Over half of the world crop is used for animal feed and 10% (more in the US and W Europe) is turned into MALT. For human consumption barley is ground into a flour used to make porridge or flatbread, or, in the US and elsewhere, polished to produce "pearl barley" commonly used in soup. Six-rowed and two-rowed barleys are the commonest varieties.

BARLOW, Joel (1754–1812), American man of letters and diplomat, one of the HARTFORD WITS. Barlow was author of the mock-pastoral *The Hasty Pudding* (1796) and a long epic about the promise of the New World, *The Vision of Columbus* (1787), revised as *The Columbiad* (1807). A friend of liberals in France and Britain, he was US consul to Algiers (1795–96) and an envoy to France (1811–12).

BARMECIDES, Persian family whose members attained positions of great wealth and power under the early ABBASID caliphs of Baghdad. In 803 AD, however, Caliph HARUN AL-RASHID brutally eliminated the family. The term Barmecide Feast, referring to an illusory magnificence, comes from a tale in the ARABIAN NIGHTS.

BAR MITZVAH (Hebrew: son of the commandment), Jewish religious ceremony marking a boy's coming of age at his 13th birthday. The event is usually celebrated in the synagogue by calling on the boy to read the weekly portion of the Law (Torah) or the Prophets. Some congregations have a ceremony for girls, the "Bas Mitzvah." Reform Judaism often has a joint confirmation ceremony at 15 or 16.

BARNACLES, marine CRUSTACEA of the subclass Cirripedia, whose free-swimming larvae are an important part of the PLANKTON. Most adults are HERMAPHRODITE. Their shells consist primarily of calcium carbonate. Adults attach themselves to solid surfaces (even the bodies of other sea animals) and trap plankton by means of feathery organs known as cirri. There are some 1000 species.

BARNARD, Christiaan Neethling (1922–), South African surgeon who performed the first successful human heart TRANSPLANT operation in 1967.

BARNARD, Edward Emerson (1857–1923), US astronomer who discovered the fifth satellite of JUPITER (1892). In 1916 he discovered Barnard's star, a red dwarf STAR only six light-years from the earth and which has the largest known stellar PROPER MOTION.

BARNARD, Frederick Augustus Porter (1809–1889), president of Columbia College (1864–89), which he helped transform into a great university. He was an advocate of higher education for women; Barnard College (founded 1889) bears his name.

BARNARD, George Grey (1863–1938), US sculptor, creator of a controversial statue of Lincoln in 1917. His private collection of medieval French art became the nucleus of the Cloisters, a branch of the Metropolitan Museum of Art in New York City.

BARNARD, Henry (1811–1900), US educator, pioneer in the improvement and better supervision of public education in the US. He was instrumental in the creation of the US Office of Education and was the first US commissioner of education (1867–70).

BARNATO, Barnett (1852–1897), South African diamond magnate. Born Barney Isaacs in London, he went to South Africa in 1873 and made a fortune in Kimberley diamond mining. In 1888 he combined his interests with those of Cecil Rhodes to form De Beers Consolidated Mines. He served in the South African parliament.

BARNAVE, Antoine Pierre Joseph Marie (1761–1793), French revolutionary. Elected (1789) to the Estates-General, he became a leader of the Jacobins in the National Assembly. The return of the royal family from their attempted flight (1791) awoke royalist sympathies in him. He quit the Jacobins and became leader of the Feuillants, advocates of a constitutional monarchy. He was guillotined in the Terror.

BARNBURNERS, in US history, a radical faction of the Democratic Party in New York State in the 1840s. Opposed to slavery, they split the national Democratic Party in 1848, permitting the election of the Whig candidate, Zachary Taylor.

BARNES, Djuna (1892–1982), US poet, playwright and novelist. Her works include a collection of stories and poems entitled *A Book* (1923), and the novels *Ryder* (1928) and *Nightwood* (1936).

BARNES, Harry Elmer (1889–1968), US historian who advocated the integration of the social sciences in the "new HISTORY."

BARNEY, Joshua (1759–1818), US naval officer who, with a force of sailors, valiantly covered the retreat of American troops at the battle of Bladensburg (Aug. 24, 1814) during the War of 1812. He was wounded and captured.

BARNUM, Phineas Taylor (1810–1891), US impresario, showman and publicist. The hoaxes, freaks and curiosities exhibited in his American Museum (founded 1841) in New York included the original Siamese twins and General Tom Thumb. He toured Europe, and in 1850 engaged soprano Jenny LIND for a US tour. In 1871 he opened his famous traveling circus show, which merged in 1881 with James A. Bailey's show to become the Barnum and Bailey "Greatest Show on Earth."

BAROMETER, an instrument for measuring air pressure (see ATMOSPHERE), used in weather forecasting and for determining altitude. Most commonly encountered is the aneroid barometer, in which the effect of the air in compressing an evacuated thin cylindrical corrugated metal box is amplified mechanically and read off on a scale or, in the **barograph,** used to draw a trace on a slowly rotating drum, thus giving a continuous record of the barometric pressure. The aneroid instrument is that used for aircraft ALTIMETERS. The earliest barometers, as invented by TORRICELLI in 1643, consisted simply of a glass tube about 800mm long closed at one end and filled with MERCURY before being inverted over a pool of mercury. Air pressure acting on the surface of the pool held up a column of mercury about 760mm tall in the tube, a "Torricellian" vacuum appearing in the closed end of the tube. The height of the column was read as a measure of the pressure. In the **Fortin barometer,** devised by Jean Fortin (1750–1831) and still used for accurate scientific work, the lower mercury level can be finely adjusted and the column height is read off with the aid of a Vernier scale.

BARON, Salo Wittmayer (1895–   ), Austrian-born American historian, professor of Jewish history at Columbia U 1930–63. His chief work is *A Social and Religious History of the Jews* (18 vols., 1937–83).

BARONS' WAR (1263–67), English civil war between a baronial faction led by Simon de MONTFORT, Earl of Leicester, and the supporters of King HENRY III. The war was the result of Henry's refusal to abide by the reforms of the Provisions of Oxford (1258). Henry was defeated at the Battle of Lewes (1264) and taken prisoner; de Montfort consolidated his own power and summoned a parliament. In 1265 Henry's son, the future EDWARD I, killed de Montfort at the Battle of Evesham and restored the monarchy.

BAROQUE, dynamic and expressive style that dominated European art c1600–1750. The term has been used to describe not only the painting, sculpture and architecture of the period, but also, by analogy, its music. Baroque was born in a rejection of the balance of Renaissance Classicism and the uncertainty of Mannerism. Much Baroque art is characterized by its emotional appeal, and by the energy and fluidity of its forms. From the works of CARAVAGGIO and, above all, BERNINI in Rome, the dramatic and illusionistic style of the High Baroque spread throughout Europe, glorifying faith in the Counter-Reformation Church and the absolutist state. In N Europe as well as in Italy, through painters as diverse as RUBENS and REMBRANDT, the Baroque created a new vocabulary of artistic expression.

BAROQUE MUSIC, that period of music

c1600–1750 which began with the development of OPERA, cantata, oratorio and recitative, and ended with the death of its two greatest composers, HANDEL and J. S. BACH. Baroque music shared with the visual arts of its time dynamism, exuberance and forceful emotional expression. Musically, this was shown by ornamented melodies and by a striking use of harmonies and strong rhythms. The idea of stylistic contrast between instruments developed the CONCERTO form. In addition, both the SONATA and FUGUE forms developed, because of the increased attention paid to counterpoint.

BARR, Alfred Hamilton, Jr. (1902–1981), US art historian. Called the most influential museum man of the 20th century, Barr directed New York's Museum of Modern Art, 1929–43 (where he remained until 1967) and organized some of the most important shows in the history of modern art. He also wrote three contemporary classics: *Cubism and Abstract Art* (1936), *Picasso* (1946) and *Matisse* (1951).

BARRAS, Paul François Jean Nicolas, Vicomte de (1755–1829), French revolutionary. At first a JACOBIN, in favor of Louis XVI's execution, he turned against ROBESPIERRE and commanded the troops that arrested him (1794). Barras became the most powerful member of the Directory (the revolutionary government), and aided Napoleon's rise to power. But after Napoleon's coup d'etat of 18 Brumaire (1799), Barras was exiled.

BARRAULT, Jean-Louis (1910–   ), French actor, director, producer and mime. A member of the Comédie Française 1940–46, he directed the Théâtre de France 1959–68. His most famous film role was that of mime in *Les Enfants du Paradis* (1944).

BARRÈS, (Auguste) Maurice (1862–1923), French man of letters and political figure, best known for his intransigent nationalism and emphasis on regional ties. Among his many influential novels, *The Uprooted* (1897) stands preeminent.

BARRIE, Sir James Matthew (1860–1937), Scottish playwright and novelist. His plays— including *The Admirable Crichton* (1902), *Peter Pan* (1904), *What Every Woman Knows* (1908), and *Dear Brutus* (1917)—are marked by charm and ingenuity, and range in tone from whimsy and sentimentality to satire and pathos.

BARRIOS, Eduardo (1884–1963), Chilean novelist, known for the psychological insight of such powerful novels as *The Love-Crazed Boy* (1915) and *Brother Ass* (1922).

BARRON, James (1769–1851), US naval officer whose ship, the *Chesapeake*, was stopped (June 22, 1807) by the British warship *Leopard* and forced to surrender four crewmen. The incident almost led to war. Barron was court-martialed and suspended from duty. Believing that Stephen DECATUR, one of the judges in his court-martial, was blocking his reinstatement, he challenged Decatur to a duel (Mar. 22, 1820), fatally wounding him.

BARROW, Sir John (1764–1848), English traveler and government official, an important promoter and patron of Arctic exploration and chief founder of the Royal Geographical Society. As second secretary of the Admiralty (1804–06, 1807–48), he was responsible for the voyages of Sir John ROSS, W.E. Parry and others in search of the NORTHWEST PASSAGE.

BARROW, Point, northernmost point on the North American continent (71°23'N), at the tip of Point Barrow Peninsula on the Arctic coast of Alaska. Named for Sir John Barrow, 19th-century British geographer. The city of Barrow lies some 12mi S.

BARRY, Sir Charles (1795–1860), English architect who, with his assistant A.W.N. Pugin, designed the Houses of Parliament in London (1840–65), a masterpiece of the GOTHIC REVIVAL. Among his other buildings was the Reform Club in London (1837).

BARRY, John (1745–1803), Irish-born naval hero famed for many brilliant exploits in the Revolutionary War, often called the "Father of the American navy." As ranking captain of the navy (from 1794) he commanded the frigate *United States* and saw action in the undeclared naval war with France (1798–1800).

BARRY, Philip (1896–1949), US playwright, best known for popular drawing-room comedies such as *Holiday* (1928) and *The Philadelphia Story* (1939).

BARRYMORE, name of a noted American theatrical family. The father was the British actor Herbert Blythe (1847–1905), who adopted the stage name Maurice Barrymore. He came to the US in 1875 and married actress Georgina Drew. Lionel Barrymore (1878–1954), their eldest child, became an outstanding character actor on stage and radio and in many films— continuing to act even after arthritis had confined him to a wheelchair. Ethel Barrymore (1879–1959), famous for her beauty, style and wit, gave many distinctive performances on stage and screen. She won an Academy Award for her supporting role in *None But the Lonely Heart* (1944). John Barrymore (1882–1942) was a distinguished interpreter of Shakespearean roles, particularly *Richard III* (1920) and

Hamlet (1922). Later he became a popular and flamboyant film actor, nicknamed "the great profile." His children, **Diana Barrymore** (1921–1960) and **John Barrymore, Jr** (1932–   ), also became actors.

BARTH, Heinrich (1821–1865), German explorer in Africa. In British service, he traveled (1849–55) in the Sudan and Nigeria and reached Timbuktu. Back in England, he wrote the important *Travels and Discoveries in North and Central Africa* (1857–58).

BARTH, John (1930–   ), US novelist known for his ironic style and use of comic and elaborate allegory. His best-known works include *The Sot-Weed Factor* (1960) and *Giles Goat-Boy* (1966).

BARTH, Karl (1886–1968), Swiss theologian, one of the most influential voices of 20th-century Protestantism. He taught in Germany 1921–35, was expelled by the Nazis and spent the rest of his life in Basel. In his "crisis theology," Barth stressed revelation and grace and reemphasized the principles of the Reformation, initiating a movement away from theological "liberalism."

BARTHELME, Donald (1931–1989), US short-story writer and novelist noted for his innovative techniques and surrealistic style. His works include the novels *Snow White* (1967) and *The Dead Father* (1975); the children's book *The Slightly Irregular Fire Engine or the Hithering Thithering Djinn* (1971), for which he won a National Book Award; and *Forty Stories* (1987).

BARTHES, Roland (1915–1980), French philosopher and social critic. His works include *Writing Degree Zero* (1968), *Mythologies* (1972), *A Lover's Discourse* (1978) and his autobiography, *Roland Barthes* (1975).

BARTHOLDI, Frédéric Auguste (1834–1904), French sculptor, creator of the Statue of Liberty (see LIBERTY, STATUE OF). His other monumental works include the *Lion of Belfort* at Belfort, France.

BARTHOU, Louis (1862–1934), French foreign minister assassinated in Marseilles with King Alexander of Yugoslavia by a Croatian nationalist. He had been briefly premier in 1913 and was the author of several biographies.

BARTLETT, John (1820–1905), US editor and publisher, best known for his famous *Familiar Quotations*, which has gone through more than a dozen editions since its first appearance in 1855.

BARTLETT, Robert Abram (1875–1946), US Arctic explorer. A member of expeditions led by Robert E. Peary and Vilhjalmur Stefansson, he later spent many years exploring Greenland.

BARTOK, Béla (1881–1945), Hungarian composer, one of the major figures of 20th-century music. He was also a virtuoso concert pianist, and taught piano at the Budapest Academy of Music (1907–34). In 1940 he emigrated to the US. His work owes much to the rhythmic and melodic vitality of E European folk music, on which he was an authority. Bartók's works include such masterpieces as his six string quartets (1908–39), *Music for Strings, Percussion and Celesta* (1936) and *Concerto for Orchestra* (1943).

BARTOLOMMEO, Fra (c1472–1517), Florentine painter of the High Renaissance, born Baccio della Porta. A Dominican monk, he painted religious subjects (largely altarpieces) with telling grandeur and simplicity.

BARTON, Bruce (1886–1967), US advertising executive who, in *The Man Nobody Knows* (1925), described Jesus as "the greatest advertiser of his own day."

BARTON, Clara (1821–1912), founder of the American Red Cross (1881) and its first president. She began a lifetime of relief work by organizing care and supplies for the wounded in the Civil War. On a trip to Europe (1869–73) she became involved in the activities of the International Red Cross and was later influential in extending the range of its relief work.

BARTRAM, name of two American naturalists, father and son. **John Bartram** (1699–1777) began planting America's first botanical garden at Kingessing, Pa., in 1728. **William Bartram** (1739–1823), became famous for his book *Travels* (1791), based on his travels with his father in the SE US, said to have inspired Wordsworth and Coleridge.

BARUCH, Bernard Mannes (1870–1965), US financier and public official, who made a fortune on Wall Street and became an influential adviser to US presidents. He served Woodrow Wilson as chairman of the War Industries Board in WWI and at the Versailles peace talks; was adviser to F. D. Roosevelt in WWII; and under Truman was US delegate to the UN Atomic Energy Commission, where he proposed the "Baruch Plan" for the international control of atomic energy.

BARUCH, Book of, a biblical work attributed to Baruch, the prophet Jeremiah's secretary. Relegated to the APOCRYPHA by Protestants, it is included in the Old Testament by Roman Catholics. The book survives in a Greek version, and is probably the work of several authors of Hellenistic times.

BARYSHNIKOV, Mikhail (1948–   ), Soviet dancer and choreographer who defected to the West in 1974. He was a soloist with the Kirov Ballet, Leningrad, from 1966. In the West he joined the American Ballet Theatre, appearing there and with other companies in modern and classical ballets. He became director of the American Ballet Theatre in 1980.

BASAL METABOLIC RATE (BMR), a measure of the rate at which an animal at rest uses energy. Human BMR is a measure of the heat output per unit time from a given area of body surface, the subject being at rest under certain standard conditions. It is usually estimated from the amounts of oxygen and carbon dioxide exchanged in a certain time. (See METABOLISM.)

BASE, in chemistry, the complement of an acid. Bases used to be defined as substances which react with acids to form SALTS, or as substances which give rise to hydroxyl ions in aqueous solution. Some such inorganic strong bases are known as ALKALIS. In modern terms, bases are species which accept a HYDROGEN ion from an acid, or which can donate an electron-pair to a Lewis ACID.

BASEBALL, America's national sport, had its beginnings more than a century ago. Its true origins are obscure, and the supposed role of Abner DOUBLEDAY has been hotly disputed. It is generally thought that the sport is a hybrid, loosely developed from the English games of cricket and rounders. Many of its rules were first set down by Alexander Cartwright of the New York Knickerbocker Baseball Club, founded in 1845. The National Association of Baseball Players was organized in 1858; the game became popular among Union troops in the Civil War, and in 1865 a convention of 91 amateur clubs met in New York.
The major leagues. In 1869 the Cincinnati Red Stockings became the first fully professional baseball team. The National Association of Professional Baseball Players was formed in 1871; it was replaced by a new National League of Professional Baseball Clubs in 1876. Attempts at creating a rival league failed until the turn of the century, when the American League had become sufficiently established to match the National League.

The first World Series between the leading teams in each league was played in 1903. In 1933 the first "All-Star" exhibition game was played, followed in 1939 by the establishment of a Baseball Hall of Fame in Cooperstown, N.Y. In 1953 the major leagues started shifting franchises to new cities, and a great expansion began. By 1969, each league had grown from eight to 12 teams, and by the 1980s, the American League had 14. Each league was divided into two divisions, with the division winners meeting in three-out-of-five game playoffs to determine the league champions.

BASEL, Council of, general Church council opened in Basel, Switzerland, in 1431, concerned with the heresy of Jan HUS and the continuing struggle over papal supremacy. Pope Eugene IV tried to dissolve the council, but it denied his right to do so, claiming that as an ecumenical council it, rather than the pope, held ultimate authority. Eugene relented, but in 1437 ordered it to move to Ferrara, Italy, to consider reunion with the Eastern Church. Most bishops complied, but a small number remained in Basel, deposing Eugene and electing the antipope Felix V in 1439, and continuing to meet until 1449.

BASIC ENGLISH, selected vocabulary of 850 English words, meant for use as an auxiliary or international language. Developed by English scholar C. K. Ogden between 1926 and 1930, it was the first attempt to create a usable, simpler language system out of an existing one.

BASIE, William "Count" (1904–1984), US jazz pianist, composer and bandleader. Count Basie's big band, which included some of the outstanding jazz musicians of the time, brought the ragged rhythm and improvisational verve of jazz into the smooth swing era of the late 1930s and 1940s.

BASILICA, in its earliest usage, a type of large public building of ancient Rome. The term came to refer to a building of characteristic rectangular layout, with a central area (nave) separated by rows of columns from two flanking side aisles with high windows. At one or both ends was a semicircular or polygonal apse. This design was adopted as a basic pattern for Christian churches from the time of Constantine. The term "basilica" is also a canonical title for certain important Roman Catholic churches.

BASIL THE GREAT, Saint (c330–379), one of the great Fathers of the Eastern Church, a founder of Greek monasticism and author of the *Longer* and *Shorter Rules* for monastic life. As Bishop of Caesarea, he also played a role in subduing ARIANISM. His brother was St. Gregory of Nyssa.

BASKERVILLE, John (1706–1775), English printer and type designer, whose elegant Baskerville type was the ancestor and inspiration of the "modern" group of typefaces. He took great care in all aspects of his craft and produced many handsome editions.

BASKETBALL, the most popular indoor sport in the US. Its object is to score points by propelling a ball through a hoop and net construction, the "basket," 18in in diameter and 10ft from the floor. It is played on a court with maximum dimensions of 94×50ft by two teams, each consisting of 12 players and a coach, with five players from each team on the court at any one time. The ball may be moved by "passing" from one player to another, or by "dribbling," in which case the ball must not be kicked or held for more than one pace. Rules vary in detail between organizations.

Conceived by Dr. James A. Naismith in 1891, the game quickly became popular. In 1898, teams from New York, Brooklyn, Philadelphia and southern New Jersey formed the first professional league, but these early leagues lasted only a few seasons. International interest was fostered by an exhibition game played at the 1904 Olympics in St. Louis, Mo. and the game subsequently became an Olympic sport and a popular scholastic and collegiate sport. The first National Invitation Tournament, featuring the nation's best college teams, was held in Madison Square Garden in NYC in 1938. The union of the National Basketball League, the Basketball Association of America and the American Basketball Association created a strong professional league whose popular following was still growing in the 1980s.

BASKIN, Leonard (1922–   ), American graphic artist and sculptor. He studied art at New York and Yale universities, and in Paris and Florence. After winning a Guggenheim Fellowship for graphics in 1953, he taught at Smith College, Mass., where he founded the Gehenna Press.

BASQUES, a people of unknown origin living mainly in the vicinity of the Pyrenees Mts (about 100,000 in France and 600,000 in NE Spain). Ethnically they seem to belong to the Caucasoid group, but research into their blood groups indicates a long separation from other Europeans; their language is remarkably conservative and quite unlike the Indo–European tongues. Basques were living along the Ebro valley in N Spain in the 3rd century BC, and have preserved many features of their ancient culture despite incursions by Romans, Visigoths, Moors and Franks, and eventual Spanish rule. After the Spanish Civil War, in which many Basques fought against General Franco, an effort was made to subdue the region. A surge of Basque nationalism in recent years was marked by the assassination of Admiral Luis Blanco by the Basque resistance movement ETA in Dec. 1973 and the execution of five terrorists shortly before Franco's death in 1975. Basque terrorist attacks continued into the 1980s.

BASS, Sam (1851–1878), US outlaw. He rode the West, first with the Joel Collins gang and then with one of his own. Called the "Robin Hood of Texas," he died of gunshot wounds.

BASS, or double bass, largest instrument of the violin family. Usually it stands about 6ft high, and has four, or sometimes five, 42.5in strings of copper or steel. It is played with a bow, or the strings may be plucked.

BASSANO, Jacopo (Jacopo da Ponte; c1510–92),leading member of a family of Italian painters. Arriving in Venice c1534, he was at first influenced by TITIAN, TINTORETTO and others. With its use of everyday scenes in religious subjects, his work tended towards GENRE painting, a tradition continued by his three sons.

BASSOON, the bass of the woodwind family, an 8ft conical tube bent double, with a double reed mouthpiece, 8 holes, and 20–22 keys. It has a range of 3.5 octaves (B-flat bass to E-flat alto) but irrational key placing and an unstable pitch make it difficult to play. The contrabassoon is 6ft long and sounds an octave lower.

BASTIAT, Frédéric 1801–1850), French economist, a classic expounder of laissez-faire and free trade.

BASTILLE, fortress in Paris built in 1370, destroyed during the French Revolution. It was first used to house political prisoners by Cardinal Richelieu, in the 17th century, but was almost empty by the time of the Revolution. It remained a symbol of oppression, however, and its capture on July 14, 1789, was the first act of the Revolution. Today, July 14 is the French national holiday.

BASTOGNE, small town on the Ardennes plateau in SE Belgium. During the German counter-offensive of 1944, the BATTLE OF THE BULGE. an American division under Gen. Anthony McAuliffe was surrounded here for some weeks before the Germans were driven back.

BASUTOLAND. See LESOTHO.

BATAAN, 30mi-long peninsula of S Luzon Island, Philippines, on the W side of Manila Bay. In WWII US–Filipino troops under Gen. Jonathan Wainwright defended Bataan against the Japanese until forced to surrender on April 9, 1942. Out of 600,000 prisoners made to march 70mi to prison camps, over 100,000 died of starvation or maltreatment. Bataan was retaken by US forces in Feb. 1945.

BATES, Katharine Lee (1859–1929), US author, best known for writing the lyrics of AMERICA THE BEAUTIFUL. She was professor of English at Wellesley College and wrote much children's literature.

BATESON, Gregory (1904–1980), British-born US anthropologist, best known for his study of New Guinea, *Naven* (1936; rev. 1958), and *Ecology of Mind* (1972). He wrote *Balinese Character* (1943) with his wife, Margaret MEAD.

BATH, famous resort city in the county of Avon, England, on the Avon R about 12mi from Bristol. Noted for its mineral springs since Roman times, it is distinguished for its elegant Georgian architecture. Its industries include bookbinding, printing and weaving. Pop 84,760.

BATH, Order of the, British honor, established by George I in 1725 (supposedly based on an order founded in 1399). There are two divisions, military and civil, with three classes in each: knight grand cross (G.C.B.), knight commander (K.C.B.) and companion (C.B.).

BATHORY, Hungarian noble family, princes of Transylvania in the 16th century. Stephen Báthory (1533–1586) was king of Poland (1575–86). Elizabeth Báthory (d. 1614) was reputed a werewolf who bathed in the blood of virgins to renew her youth. She was imprisoned from 1610.

BATHS AND BATHING. In the past baths have served a primarily religious, social or pleasurable function far more often than a hygienic one. The Egyptians, Assyrians and Greeks all used baths, but the Romans developed bathing as a central social habit, constructing elaborate public buildings, often ornately decorated and of enormous size, with several rooms for disrobing, exercise, and entertainment, as well as bathing. Men and women bathed at separate times, except for one brief period in the 1st century AD. The baths were tended by slaves. After the fall of the Roman Empire bathing declined in popularity in Europe, though it did survive as a part of monastic routine and in Muslim countries. In Russia and Turkey the steam bath became popular. The crusaders brought steam bathing back with them from the Middle East, but an association with immorality caused it to fall into disrepute.

In the 18th century, it became fashionable to spend a season at a watering-place, such as BATH in England, but only 19th-century research into hygiene made a virtue of bathing, often with primitive and usually portable cold baths at schools and institutions. Only after WWI

did plumbing and bathtub production allow the bath to become a permanent installation in the home.

BATHYSCAPHE, submersible deep-sea research vessel, invented by Auguste PICCARD in the late 1940s, comprising a small, spherical, pressurized passenger cabin suspended beneath a cigar-shaped flotation hull. On the surface most of the flotation tanks in the hull are filled with GASOLINE, the rest, sufficient to float the vessel, with air. To dive the air is vented and seawater takes its place. During descent, sea water is allowed to enter the gasoline-filled tanks from the bottom, compressing the gasoline and thus increasing the DENSITY of the vessel. The rate of descent is checked by releasing iron ballast. To begin ascent, the remaining ballast is jettisoned. As the vessel rises, the gasoline expands, expelling water from the flotation tanks, thus lightening the vessel further and accelerating the ascent. Battery-powered motors provide the vessel with a degree of submarine mobility.

BATIK, a dyeing technique. Before the fabric is dipped into the dye the portions which are to remain uncolored are covered with wax. When the dye is dry, the wax is removed by boiling. The technique was introduced into Europe from Indonesia by Dutch traders.

BATISTA Y ZALDÍVAR, Fulgencio (1901–1973), Cuban military dictator. Becoming army chief of staff after the overthrow of the Machado government in 1933, he appointed and deposed presidents at will. He was himself president 1940–44, and took the title permanently in 1952. After his overthrow by CASTRO in 1959 he lived in exile in Spain.

BATS, the order Chiroptera, the flying MAMMALS. Since they are all nocturnal, and many tropical, it is not generally realized that bats account for about one-seventh of mammalian species. There are two suborders: the Megachiroptera ("big bats"), with weights from 25g (0.9oz) to 1kg (2.2lb) and wingspans of about 250–1500mm (10in–5ft); and the Microchiroptera ("little bats"), weights of about 3–200g (0.1–7oz) and wingspans of 150–900mm (6–35in). The former usually have large eyes adapted for night vision, but the latter navigate by use of echolocation (see SONAR). Most are insectivorous, but some are vegetarian and yet others carnivorous—the three species of the family Desmodontidae (the VAMPIRE BATS) are blood suckers, preying on birds and mammals.

BATTANI, abu-Abdullah Muhammad ibn-Jabir, al-, or Latin **Albategnius** or

Albatenius (c858–929), Arab mathematician and astronomer who improved on the results of Claudius PTOLEMY by applying TRIGONOMETRY to astronomical computations. He had a powerful influence on medieval European ASTRONOMY.

BATTENBERG, German princely family dating from the 19th century. **Prince Louis of Battenberg** (1854–1921), an admiral in the British navy, became first sea lord in 1912 but was forced to resign at the start of WWI because of press agitation over his German origin. In 1917 he renounced his German title, anglicized his name as Mountbatten, and was raised to the peerage as marquess of Milford Haven. His son, Louis MOUNTBATTEN (1900–1979), was the last British viceroy of India. A grandson, Prince PHILIP (1921–   ), married Queen ELIZABETH II.

BATTERY, a device for converting internally-stored chemical ENERGY into direct-current ELECTRICITY. The term is also applied to various other electricity sources, including the solar cell and the nuclear cell, but is usually taken to exclude the fuel cell, which requires the continuous input of a chemical fuel for its operation. Chemical batteries consist of one or more electrochemical (voltaic) cells (comprising two electrodes immersed in a conducting electrolyte) in which a chemical reaction occurs when an external circuit is completed between the electrodes. Most of the energy liberated in this reaction can be tapped if a suitable load is placed in the external circuit, impeding the flow of ELECTRONS from cathode to anode. (The conventional current, of course, flows in the opposite sense.) Batteries are classified in two main divisions. In **primary cells,** the chemical reaction is ordinarily irreversible and the battery can yield only a finite quantity of electricity. Single primary-cell batteries are used in flashlights, shavers, light meters, etc. The most common type is the dry **Leclanché cell,** which has a ZINC cathode, a CARBON anode, and uses a zinc chloride and ammonium chloride paste as electrolyte. Manganese dioxide "depolarizer" is distributed around the anode (mixed with powdered graphite) to prevent the accumulation of the HYDROGEN gas which would otherwise stop the operation of the cell. The dry Leclanché cell gives a nominal 1.54V. For the higher voltages necessary to power transistor radios, batteries containing several thin laminar cells are used. In **alkaline cells,** potassium hydroxide is used in place of ammonium chloride; this permits higher currents to be drawn. The **mercury cell,** with a mercury and graphite cathode, is smaller than other cells of the same power.

Secondary cells, known also as storage batteries or accumulators, can be recharged and reused at will, provided too much electricity has not been abstracted from them. The most common type, as used in AUTOMOBILES, is the lead-acid types in which both electrodes are made of LEAD (the positive covered with lead (IV) oxide when charged) and the electrolyte is dilute sulfuric acid. Its voltage is about 2V, depending on the state of charge. The robust yet light nickel-iron battery (having a POTASSIUM hydroxide solution electrolyte) is widely used in telephone exchanges and other heavy-duty situations. In spacecraft, however, where the batteries must be airtight, nickel-cadmium batteries are used instead. Nickel oxide serves as the cathode, and potassium hydroxide is the electrolyte. Such batteries provide about 1.3V and can last about 25 years.

The first battery was the voltaic pile invented c1800 by VOLTA. This comprised a stack of pairs of silver and zinc disks, each pair separated by a brine-soaked board. For many years from 1836 the standard form of battery was the **Daniell cell,** with a zinc cathode, a copper anode and a porous-pot barrier separating the anode electrolyte (copper(II) sulfate) from the cathode electrolyte (sulfuric acid). The lead-acid storage battery was invented by Gaston Planté in 1859 and the wet Leclanché cell, the prototype for the modern dry cell, by Georges Leclanché in 1865.

BATTLE HYMN OF THE REPUBLIC, American patriotic song, unofficial hymn of Union troops in the Civil War. Written in 1861 by Julia Ward Howe and sung to the tune of *John Brown's Body,* it later became a Protestant hymn and a protest marching song.

BATTLE OF BRITAIN, air battle in WWII from Aug. 8 to Oct. 31, 1940, between the British Royal Air Force (RAF) and the German Luftwaffe. The Germans intended to weaken British defenses and morale before invading the country. The Luftwaffe forces were much greater than those of the RAF, but the latter proved to be technically and tactically superior. The Germans first bombed shipping and ports, then airfields and Midland industries and, finally, in Sept., London. Daylight raids proving too costly, the Germans turned to night attacks. At the end the RAF had lost some 900 planes, the Germans over 2,300, and Hitler had postponed his projected invasion indefinitely, thus tacitly admitting failure.

BATTLE OF THE ATLANTIC, the WWII air and sea effort of the Axis powers to stop US supplies coming to Britain and the USSR. Allied convoys, guarded by British, Canadian and later US destroyers and escort carriers, ran the gauntlet of German U-boats and surface raiders. Through antisubmarine devices, air patrols and bombing of submarine pens and factories the Allies gradually overcame the Axis threat at sea.

BATTLE OF THE BULGE, last major western counteroffensive by the Germans in WWII. They planned to capture Liège and Antwerp, thus dividing the Allied armies. The German assault in the Ardennes began on Dec. 16, 1944, and created a huge "bulge" into the Allied lines. Although suffering about 77,000 casualties, the Allies stopped the German advance by Jan. 16, 1945.

BATTLESHIP, historically the largest of conventionally-armed warships. Though some battleships are still kept in reserve, aircraft carriers superseded them during WWII as the largest fighting ships afloat. The first US battleships were the *Indiana, Massachusetts* and *Oregon*, completed in 1895–96. Since 1946 no more have been built. (See also NAVY.)

BATU KHAN (d. 1255 AD), Mongol conqueror of Russia, grandson of GENGHIS KHAN. He ruled the westernmost part of the MONGOL EMPIRE and threatened eastern Europe from 1235 to 1242. He founded the khanate of the GOLDEN HORDE which ruled southern Russian for 200 years, isolating it from western European developments.

BAUDELAIRE, Charles Pierre (1821–1867), French poet and critic, forerunner of SYMBOLISM. The poems in *Les Fleurs du Mal* (1857), with their sensitive probing of even the most bizarre sensations, outraged public opinion and led to the poet's being tried for obscenity. His later prose poems were posthumously published in *Le Spleen de Paris* (1869). He was also a brilliant critic of music and fine art, and was renowned for his translations of Edgar Allan POE.

BAUHAUS, the most influential school of design and architecture in the 20th century. Walter GROPIUS founded it in 1919 at Weimar, Germany, and its teachers included some of the leading artists of the time. Gropius' ideal of uniting form with function is now a universal canon of design, and the dictum "less is more" has influenced much US design. The Bauhaus left Weimar in 1925 and was installed in new premises designed by Gropius in Dessau in 1927. The school was closed by the Nazis in 1933. Bauhaus teachers Gropius, FEININGER and MIES VAN DER ROHE later moved to the US.

BAUM, Lyman Frank (1856–1919), US childrens' writer, author of the famous *Wonderful Wizard of Oz* (1900), a tale of a girl carried by a cyclone to a land of adventure. The 1939 film adaptation became a motion-picture classic.

BAUMEISTER, Willi (1889–1955), German artist who was, in turn, a constructivist, abstract and ideographic painter. His important canvases of the 1950s utilized brightly colored geometric forms.

BAUR, Ferdinand Christian (1792–1860), German Protestant theologian, professor at Tübingen university, and a pioneer of bibilical criticism using literary criteria.

BAUXITE, the main ore of ALUMINUM, consisting of hydrated aluminum oxide, usually with iron oxide impurity. It is a claylike, amorphous material formed by the weathering of silicate rocks, especially under tropical conditions. High-grade bauxite, being highly refractory, is used as a lining for furnaces. Synthetic corundum is made from it, and it is an ingredient in some quick-setting cements. Leading bauxite-producing countries include Jamaica, Australia, the USSR, Suriname, Guyana, France, Guinea and the US (especially Ark.).

BAVARIA (German: Bayern), largest state in West Germany. Its area is 27,239sq mi and its population 10.9 million. MUNICH is the capital and administrative center. Bavaria manufactures machinery, precision instruments, textiles and toys. Brewing is also important and the annual Munich beer festival is a European occasion. Bavaria is also famous as a cultural center, with three universities, a technical institute, academies of arts and sciences, two leading museums and the BAYREUTH festival. The Christian Social Union (CSU), Bavaria's own distinctive political party, has played a vital part in national politics since WWII.

BAX, Sir Arnold Edward (1883–1953), British composer best known for his romantic and richly orchestrated symphonic poems and symphonies. He was appointed master of the king's music in 1941.

BAY, popular name for the laurel tree (*Laurus nobilis*), also known as the sweet bay or bay laurel, native to the Mediterranean countries. Dried leaves are used to season foods. Bay trees are planted as ornamentals, and their leaves were used in classical Greece to crown heroes.

BAYAR, Mahmud Cêlal (1884–1986), president of Turkey 1950–60. He was prominent in ATATURK'S nationalist movement after WWI, and later became economics minister (1932–37) and prime minister (1937–38) of the Turkish republic. He founded the opposition Democratic Party in 1946.

BAYARD, Pierre Terrail, Seigneur de (c1473–1524), French commander famous for his bravery, who became the epitome of French chivalry. He first distinguished himself in French campaigns in Italy. Later at Mézières in 1521, with only 1,000 men against 35,000, he held off an invasion of central France by the emperor Charles V.

BAYEUX TAPESTRY, embroidered linen wallhanging of the early Middle Ages, depicting the Norman Conquest of England in 1066. It is 231ft long and 19.5in wide, and contains over 70 scenes. It is believed to have been commissioned by Bishop Odo, half-brother of WILLIAM the Conqueror, for Bayeux Cathedral in NW France.

BAYKAL, Lake, in SE Siberia. It is the world's largest (12,160sq mi) freshwater lake and the world's deepest (5,714ft) lake. Famous for its clear water, it has become polluted as a result of industrial development in the area.

BAYLE, Pierre (1647–1706), French philosopher, whose great *Historical and Critical Dictionary* (1697) embodied his skeptical critique of Christian orthodoxy. His rationalistic approach to belief strongly influenced 18th-century thinkers.

BAY OF PIGS, English name for Bahia de Cochinos, SW Cuba, scene of an abortive invasion of Cuba on April 17, 1961. The invaders were Cubans who had fled to the US after Fidel CASTRO seized power. Although Americans were not directly involved, the CIA had helped plan the invasion.

BAY PSALM BOOK, name commonly given to the first book printed in Colonial America. *The Whole Booke of Psalmes Faithfully Translated into English Metre* was published in Cambridge, Mass., in 1640 as a hymnal for the Massachusetts Bay Colony. It was the work of Richard MATHER, John Eliot and Thomas Weld and was printed by Stephen Day.

BAYREUTH, industrial city in NE Bavaria, in W Germany. It is famous as the last home of Richard WAGNER and as the site of his opera house, the *Festspielhaus*, where the annual Wagnerian festival (begun in 1876) is now run by Wagner's grandson Wolfgang. Pop 63,530.

BAZAINE, Achille François (1811–1888), French general. Famous for his service in Algeria, the Crimea, Italy, and Mexico, he was given command of the French armies by Napoleon III in the Franco-Prussian War. Trapped in Metz by the Prussians, he surrendered on Oct. 27, 1870. For this he was convicted (1873) of treason, but he escaped and lived thereafter in Italy and Spain.

BAZIOTES, William (1912–1963), US painter, a leading member of the New York abstract-expressionist group after WWII.

BEACH, Amy (1867–1944), US composer whose *Gaelic Symphony* (1896) was the first symphony known to have been composed by an American woman. She wrote over 150 works, including a piano concerto (1900), string quartet (1929), and a one-act opera, *Cabildo* (1932).

BEACH, Moses Yale (1800–1868), US journalist, publisher (1838–48) of the New York *Sun*, chief rival of James Gordon Bennett's New York *Herald*.

BEACH, Sylvia (1887–1962), US bookstore owner whose shop, Shakespeare & Co., was the center of expatriate literary life in Paris during the interwar period. She also published James JOYCE's *Ulysses* (1922).

BEAN, Roy (c1825–1903), US justice of the peace who called himself "the only law west of the Pecos." After an adventurous early life which included arrest, jail break and proprietorship of tent saloons, he settled at what later became Langtry in W Tex. He built a combination store, saloon and pool hall, and held court as justice and coroner. His decisions were more notable for six-gun drama and humor than legal sagacity.

BEAN, common name given to a number of species of the family Leguminosae, cultivated for the food value of their seeds, immature pods and shoots. Important species include: the SOYBEAN (*Glycine max*), the fruit of which has a high protein content and is a dietary staple in Asia and is now grown in the US; the common garden bean or French bean (*Phaseolus vulgaris*), grown extensively in Europe and the US; the scarlet runner bean (*P. multiflorus*), which may be grown as an ornamental plant as well as for its pods; the lima bean (*P. lunatus*), originating from South America; the broad bean (*Vicia fabo*) grown mainly in Europe; and the mung bean, the source of bean sprouts popular in Chinese cuisine and staple in Asia. Bean plants in general are of great value in replenishing nitrogen-deficient soils, using, in association with BACTERIA, a process known as nitrogen fixation.

BEARD, Charles Austin (1874–1948), controversial American historian, author of *An Economic Interpretation of the Constitution* (1913), and co-author, with his wife **Mary Ritter Beard** (1876–1958), of *The Rise of American Civilization* (1927), a popular survey. Beard's iconoclastic analysis of the origins of the Constitution in terms of the economic self-interest of its authors was a landmark in US historiography. He later became a bitter critic of the ROOSEVELT administration and the circumstances of US entry into WWII.

BEARD, Daniel Carter (1850–1941), organizer of the Boy Scouts of America. As National Scout Commissioner (1910–41), he gave the movement its distinctly American character, based on Indian and pioneer lore.

BEARDSLEY, Aubrey Vincent (1872–1898), English illustrator and author. By 1894 Beardsley had become art editor of the *Yellow Book* magazine and a prolific artist. His graphic style was one of sharp black-and-white contrasts, with flowing lines and detailed patterning; his subject matter tended towards the decadent or erotic, for instance, Oscar WILDE'S *Salomé*, or ARISTOPHANES' *Lysistrata*.

BEAR FLAG REPUBLIC, republic declared in 1846 by a group of American settlers in Sacramento Valley, Cal., who rejected Mexican rule. Their flag, with a grizzly bear, a single star and the words "California Republic," was raised at Sonoma in June 1846. The explorer John C. FREMONT aided the insurgents, but the Republic collapsed after the outbreak of the MEXICAN WAR in May 1846; this ended in Feb. 1848 with Cal. ceded to the US. The Cal. state flag is modeled on the "Bear Flag."

BEARS, the world's largest extant terrestrial carnivores, characterized by their heavy build, thick limbs, diminutive tail and small ears and included in a single mammalian family, Ursidae. The differences among the seven species are small and are mainly limited to details of the skeleton. All have coarse thick hair which is, with the exception of the POLAR BEAR, dark in color. The varieties of the brown bear have the widest distribution. Other species are the North American black bear, the spectacled bear, the Asiatic black bear, the sun bear and the sloth bear.

BEAT GENERATION, literary movement of the 1950s, which burst onto the American scene in 1956 with Jack KEROUAC'S *On the Road* (the adventures of the original social dropout), Allen Ginsberg's *Howl and Other Poems* and work by such poets as Lawrence Ferlinghetti and Gregory Corso, and later by the novelist William S. Burroughs. The movement was a protest against complacent middle-class values and, though shortlived, influenced artistic experiments for the next 15 years.

BEATITUDES, eight blessings pronounced by Christ as a prologue to the Sermon on the Mount (Matthew 5:3–10). Jesus calls "Blessed" those who are poor in spirit, the meek, those who mourn, those who seek after holiness, the merciful, the pure in heart, the peacemakers and those who suffer persecution for righteousness' sake.

BEATLES, The, English rock-music group that dominated popular music in the 1960s. Guitarists and composers **Paul McCartney** (1942–   ), **John Lennon** (1940–1980), and **George Harrison** (1943–   ), and drummer **Ringo Starr** (1940–   ) won fame in Britain with their recording "Please Please Me" (1963). The 1964 song "I Want To Hold Your Hand" introduced them to the US, where their concerts became scenes of mass adulation. *Revolver* (1966) and *Sgt. Pepper's Lonely Hearts Club Band* (1967) are ranked among their finest albums, and their first film, *A Hard Day's Night* (1964) is highly regarded. The group disbanded in 1970. Paul McCartney later formed the successful group Wings. John Lennon's murder by a demented fan in New York City caused mourning around the world.

BEATON, Sir Cecil Walter Hardy (1904–1980), English photographer and designer, well known for his royal portraits, collections such as *Cecil Beaton's Scrapbook* (1937) and for set and costume designs for shows and films such as *My Fair Lady* (stage, 1956; motion picture, 1964). He was knighted in 1972.

BEATON, David (1494–1546), Scottish Roman Catholic cardinal, chancellor for the child Mary Queen of Scots and able opponent of English king Henry VIII. For his persecution of Scottish Protestants, he was murdered.

BEATTY, David, 1st Earl Beatty of the North Sea and of Brooksby (1871–1936), British admiral famous for his part in the Battle of JUTLAND (1916). He served in Egypt and Sudan and in China during the BOXER REBELLION. A rear admiral in 1910, he was made first sea lord and given an earldom in 1919.

BEAUHARNAIS, French military family. **Alexandre, vicomte de Beauharnais** (1760–1794), born in Martinique, fought in the American Revolution and the French Revolutionary Wars. He was guillotined in the Terror. His widow, JOSEPHINE (1763–1814), married (1796) Napoleon Bonaparte. Alexandre's son, **Eugène de Beauharnais** (1781–1824), was an able general and viceroy of Italy under Napoleon. Alexandre's daughter, **Hortense de Beauharnais** (1783–1837), married Napoleon's brother Louis Bonaparte and was the mother of NAPOLEON III.

BEAUJOLAIS, hilly region in E France, producing red wines, mainly from vineyards on the Saône R.

BEAUMARCHAIS, Pierre Augustin Caron de (1732–1799), French dramatist and variously an artist, litigant and political agent. His best-known plays, *The Barber of Seville* (1775) and *The Marriage of Figaro* (1784; the basis of MOZART'S opera) ridiculed the established order and the nobility. He was instrumental in furnishing the Americans with arms and money at the outbreak of the Revolution.

BEAUMONT, Francis (c1584–1616), and **FLETCHER, John** (1579–1625), English Jacobean playwrights. Their many plays, both as individuals and in collaboration, strongly influenced English drama. Their best-known collaborations are *Philaster* (c1608), *The Maid's Tragedy* (c1609) and *A King and No King* (1611).

BEAUMONT, William (1785–1853), US army physician noted for his researches into the human DIGESTIVE SYSTEM. While on assignment in northern Mich. in 1822 he treated a trapper with a serious stomach wound; when the wound healed, an opening (or fistula) into the victim's stomach remained, through which Beaumont was able to extract gastric juices for analysis.

BEAUREGARD, Pierre Gustave Toutant de (1818–1893), Confederate general during the American Civil War. In 1861 Beauregard commanded the attack on FORT SUMTER, S.C., which opened the war. He distinguished himself at the First Battle of BULL RUN, shared command at SHILOH and held off Union naval attacks on Charleston. Joining General Joseph E. Johnston, he fell back to the Carolinas in the face of Sherman's Georgia campaign, and remained there until the end of the war.

BEAUVOIR, Simone de (1908–1986), French writer, friend of Jean-Paul SARTRE and a leading exponent of EXISTENTIALISM and the role of women in politics and intellectual life. Her best-known works are *The Second Sex* (1953) and *The Mandarins* (1956). She has also written an autobiographical trilogy, and a moving account of her mother's death, *A Very Easy Death* (1966).

BEAVERBROOK, William Maxwell Aitken, 1st Baron (1879–1964), Canadian-born British newspaper owner and Conservative cabinet minister. His government posts included minister of aircraft production 1940–42, and lord privy seal 1943–45. Among his mass-circulation newspapers were the *Daily Express, Sunday Express* and *Evening Standard.*

BEAVERS, large RODENTS (family Castoridae), weighing up to 100lb or over, of northern lands. They have thick, furry waterproof coats, powerful, webfooted hindlegs and small forelimbs with dexterous, sensitive paws. They are lissencephalic (smooth-brained), but nevertheless by far the most intelligent rodents: their technical constructive skill, exemplified by their building, from logs and mud, dams and lodges (domes up to 23ft in diameter in which they live), is surpassed only by that of man. The dominant features of their SKULLS are the powerful incisors (see TEETH), with which they fell trees and gnaw logs into shape. Their large, heavy tails are used on land for balance and in the water as rudders. Their respiratory system (see RESPIRATION) enables them to remain underwater for up to 15 minutes.

BEBEL, August (1840–1913), leading German socialist and co-founder of the Social Democratic party (1869). A strong anti-militarist and fighter for women's rights, his *Women and Socialism* was published in 1879.

BECCARIA, Cesare Bonesana, Marchese di (1738–1794), Italian criminologist and economist, instrumental in many major reforms in the treatment of criminals. His *Essay on Crimes and Punishments* (1764) recommended the abolition of capital punishment and torture.

BECHET, Sidney (1897–1959), US soprano saxophonist, a master of New Orleans jazz. He settled in Paris in 1949.

BECHUANALAND PROTECTORATE. See BOTSWANA.

BECK, Ludwig (1880–1944), German general, head (1933–38) of the army general staff. Resigning in protest of Hitler's designs on Czechoslovakia, he thereafter conspired against the dictator. After the attempt to assassinate Hitler on July 20, 1944, Beck was executed.

BECKER, Carl Lotus (1873–1945), US historian of Cornell University, Ithaca, N.Y., who brought an elegant style and original insights to such subjects as *The Declaration of Independence* (1922) and *The Heavenly City of the Eighteenth-Century Philosophers* (1932).

BECKET, Saint Thomas à (1118–1170), martyr and archbishop of Canterbury. He first served as chancellor under Henry II, becoming a close friend, but in 1162 was appointed archbishop of Canterbury. Thereafter he supported the Church against the monarchy, and soon he and the king were at odds. The rift culminated in Becket's refusal to approve the royal "Constitutions of Clarendon," which sought to limit Church authority. A threatened papal interdict brought a temporary reconciliation, but in 1170 the intransigent Becket was murdered in the cathedral at Canterbury by four knights inspired by some rash words of the king's. Becket was canonized in 1173.

BECKETT, Samuel Barclay (1906–   ), Irish dramatist and novelist, resident in France since 1937. His work, much of it written in French, deals with habit, boredom and suffering, and is deeply pessimistic. His novels include *Murphy* (1938) and the trilogy, *Molloy, Malone Dies*, and *The Unnamable* (1951–53). Among his plays are *Waiting for Godot* (1952) and *Happy Days* (1961). Beckett won the 1969 Nobel Prize for Literature.

BECKMANN, Max (1884–1950), German painter and graphic artist. An expressionist until c1917, he then fell under the influence of George GROSZ, developing a more individual and strongly symbolic style. In 1933 his work was declared degenerate by the Nazis. He took refuge in Holland (1937–47) and later the US.

BECQUEREL, Antoine Henri (1852–1908), French physicist who, having discovered natural RADIOACTIVITY in a URANIUM salt in 1896, shared the 1903 Nobel physics prize with Pierre and Marie CURIE.

BEDBUGS, a number of BUGS of the family Cimicidae, order Hemiptera, bloodsuckers parasitic (see PARASITES) on man and other animals. The common bedbug, *Cimex lectularius*, found throughout most of the world, is about 5mm (0.2in) long and 3mm (0.12in) broad, and colored usually mahogany brown, though it may appear reddish if it has recently fed or purplish if an older meal is still in its gut. Adults may survive for up to a year without feeding. Very occasionally they may transmit dangerous diseases.

BEDE, Saint (c673–735), known as "The Venerable," an Anglo-Saxon monk and scholar whose work embraced most of contemporary learning. His *Ecclesiastical History of the English Nation* is indispensable for the early history of England.

BEDLAM, familiar name for London's oldest insane asylum. It is a corruption of the name St. Mary of Bethlehem, founded in 1247 as a priory and made a hospital for the insane (1547). The term is now used for a madhouse or any uproar or chaos.

BEDOUIN, nomadic herdsmen of the Syrian, Arabian and Sahara deserts. Although Muslim, Bedouin society retains pre-Islamic beliefs. It is comprised of rigidly hierarchical tribal groups, some of which still practice slavery. Such values as obedience, generosity, honor, cunning, vengefulness and forgiveness are emphasized. (See ARAB.)

BEE, superfamily (Apoidea) of insects which convert nectar into HONEY for use as food. There are about 20,000 species. Bees and flowering plants are largely interdependent; plants are pollinated as the bees gather their pollen. Many farmers keep bees specially for this purpose.

Most bees are solitary and each female builds her own nest, although many bees may occupy a single site. Eggs are laid in cells provided with enough pollen-nectar paste to feed the larva until it becomes a flying, adult bee. Social bees (honeybees and bumblebees) live in complex societies of 10,000–50,000 members. Headed by the queen, whose function is to lay eggs (up to 2,000 a day), the community comprises female workers which collect pollen and build cells, and male bees, or drones, which fertilize the few young queens that appear each fall. Parasitic bees, not equipped to build hives, develop in the cells of the host working bees.

BEEBE, Charles William (1877–1962), US naturalist remembered for the descents into the ocean depths he made with Otis Barton in their bathysphere. Diving off Bermuda in 1934 they reached a then-record depth of 3,028ft.

BEECHAM, Sir Thomas (1879–1961), English conductor. He introduced many operas to England, notably Richard STRAUSS' *Der Rosenkavalier*, and was an eloquent advocate of the music of his friend DELIUS. Beecham founded two orchestras, the London Philharmonic and the Royal Philharmonic.

BEECHER, Catharine Esther (1800–1878), US educator, advocate of education for women, founder of schools and colleges for women in Connecticut and the Midwest.

BEECHER, Henry Ward (1813–1887), US clergyman, lecturer and author. Preacher of Plymouth Congregational Church (1847–87) in Brooklyn, N.Y., he was the subject of a notorious and sensational lawsuit for adultery. Like his father, Lyman BEECHER, he was renowned as an orator. He was a staunch advocate of ABOLITIONISM.

BEECHER, Lyman (1775–1863), US clergyman and liberal theologian who helped found the American Bible Society (1816). Beecher's sermons against slavery and intemperance made him one of the most influential orators of his time. His daughter was Harriet Beecher STOWE.

BEER, an alcoholic beverage made by fermenting cereals. Known since ancient times, beer became common where the climate was unsuited to WINE production. Beer includes all the malt liquors variously called ale, stout, porter (drunk in the UK and Ireland) and lager. The alcohol content is 3-7%.

BEERSHEBA, city in S Israel (the Negev,) 45mi SW of Jerusalem. Home of the biblical patriarchs ISAAC and ABRAHAM and once the southernmost town of JUDAH, it is now an industrial and trading center.

BEERBOHM, Sir Max (1872-1956), English satirical writer and caricaturist, educated at Merton College, Oxford. He is best known for the caustic yet benign wit of his caricatures of eminent Victorian and Edwardian figures, and for his satirical novel about Oxford, *Zuleika Dobson* (1911).

BEET, *Beta vulgaris,* biennial plant with a fleshy taproot. The most extensively grown variety is SUGAR BEET, which provides 33% of the world's SUGAR. Also cultivated are the garden (or red) beet, eaten either boiled or pickled, the mangelwurzel, used as forage, and the leaf beet (Swiss chard), used as a potherb.

BEETHOVEN, Ludwig van (1770-1827), German composer, born in Bonn. His prodigious talent was soon recognized: HAYDN singled him out and offered to take the young musician on as a pupil in Vienna. There Beethoven's remarkable piano playing attracted attention, as did his eccentric behavior. Beethoven's deafness began when he was about 30 and was total by the time he was in his late 40s. This did not interfere with his creativity, but he never heard much of his mature work.

Beethoven's musical life is commonly divided into three periods. The *Pathétique* piano sonata and the First Symphony belong to the first period, ending about 1802, when he was still influenced by Haydn and MOZART. To the middle period, ending about 1816, belong works in his own individual style, such as the Third (*Eroica*) and Fifth Symphonies, Fifth Piano Concerto (*Emperor*), the *Kreutzer* Violin Sonata and the opera *Fidelio*. His later, more intense, highly individual works include the Ninth (Choral) Symphony, the *Missa Solemnis* (Mass in D) and the innovating late string quartets, including the *Grosse Fuge*.

BEETLES, common name for all insects of the order Coleoptera, the largest in the animal kingdom. Beetles occur in diverse forms, colors and habitats and range from 0.4mm to over 150mm in length. They are distinguished by hard protective wing cases which enclose a more fragile pair of wings. Some, however, such as the ground beetles and weevils, are flightless. All beetles develop from eggs into larvae and then pupate (see PUPA) before becoming adults. The life cycle can range from the usual three larval stages to as many as 12 or more and may last for as little as 2-3 weeks or as much as 5 years. Beetles and their larvae eat animal, vegetable and even inorganic matter; some eat carrion, others live off dung and a number prey on other beetles. Among the economically harmful beetles are the potato-destroying Colorado beetle, and the woodworm and deathwatch beetles, which attack and destroy furniture and woodwork.

BEGIN, Menachem (1913-   ), Israeli prime minister. From boyhood in Poland he was active in the movement to establish a Jewish state in Palestine. After Israel won independence, he entered the Knesset (1948) and was an opposition leader for most of the next 30 years. He became the leader of the new Likud Party (1973) and won the prime ministership in 1977. He pressed Israel's claim to the West Bank of the Jordan and refused to consider sovereignty for the Palestinians. He signed a peace treaty with Egypt (1979) and was reelected in 1981. In 1978 he shared the Nobel Peace Prize with Egyptian President Anwar Sadat. Begin resigned in 1983.

BEGONIA, a genus of perennial plants with about 900 species. Mostly succulent herbs, native to tropical regions, they are cultivated in house and garden for their colorful foliage, for example *Begonia diadema, B. rex* (silver leaf) and *B. masoniana* (iron cross), or for their attractive large flowers, for example *B.tuberhybrida* and the Reiger begonias. They have tuberous, rhizomatous or fibrous roots. Indoors, begonias grow best in a sunny east or west window during the winter, but the degree of direct summer sunlight that individual varieties can tolerate varies. They grow best within the temperature range 60°F to 70°F, and hot dry air must be avoided. The soil should be kept evenly moist, avoiding extreme dryness or wetness. They can be propagated from seed, tuber and rhizome cuttings, leaf cuttings or division of the tubers. Family: Begoniaceae.

BEGUINES, religious organizations of women in medieval Europe. The women were not bound by vows or discipline; they usually lived in cottages and devoted themselves to charitable work. Beginning in the 12th century in Belgium and the

Netherlands, the movement spread through France and Germany. In the 13th and 14th centuries, the Beguines were often accused of heresy and immorality, and their communities dispersed. Men involved in a similar movement were called Beghards.

BEHAIM, Martin (c1436–1507), German geographer whose terrestrial globe, made in 1492, is still exhibited in his native Munich.

BEHAN, Brendan (1923–1964), Irish playwright and author, noted for his vivid ribaldry and satire. His best-known works, *The Quare Fellow* (1956), *The Hostage* (1959) and the autobiographical *Borstal Boy* (1958), deal largely with his experiences in the Irish Republican Army and subsequent imprisonment.

BEHAVIORAL SCIENCES, those sciences dealing with human behavior, individually or socially. The term, which is sometimes considered synonymous with SOCIAL SCIENCES, embraces such fields as PSYCHOLOGY, SOCIOLOGY, ANTHROPOLOGY.

BEHAVIORISM, school of PSYCHOLOGY based on the proposal that behavior should be studied empirically by objective observations of reactions (see EMPIRICISM) rather than speculatively. It had its roots in ANIMAL BEHAVIOR studies, defining behavior as the actions and reactions of a living organism (and, by extension, man) in its environment; and more specifically in the work of PAVLOV in such fields as conditioned REFLEXES. Behaviorism developed as an effective factor in US psychology following the work of J. B. WATSON just before WWI; and since then it has influenced most schools of psychological thought.

BEHISTUN ROCK, a massive rock near the village of Behistun, Iran. On it are carved reliefs and cuneiform inscriptions in old Persian, Susian and Assyrian. In 1835 Sir Henry RAWLINSON scaled the rock and copied the inscriptions. Once deciphered, they provided a key to the interpretation of ancient Mesopotamian and all other cuneiform texts.

BEHN, Aphra (1640–1689), English dramatist, novelist and poet, the first professional English woman writer. Her many works, including the novel *Oroonoko* and the plays *The Forced Marriage* and *The Rover* show technical ingenuity, wit and vivacity.

BEHRENS, Peter (1868–1940), German architect who pioneered a mode of functional design suited to industrial technology. His most influential work was the AEG turbine factory in Berlin (1908–09). He influenced LE CORBUSIER and GROPIUS.

BEHRMAN, Samuel Nathaniel (1893–1973), US dramatist noted for his comedies of manners (*Biography*, 1932; *No Time for Comedy*, 1939). He also wrote film scripts and a biography of satirist Max BEERBOHM (1960).

BEIDERBECKE, Leon Bismarck "Bix" (1903–1931), US jazz musician. An accomplished pianist and brilliant trumpet player, he joined the renowned Paul Whiteman band in 1928. Despite his early death through alcoholism and general ill health, he greatly influenced the development of jazz.

BEIRUT, capital and chief port of Lebanon on the E Mediterranean coast. It stands on a triangular peninsula at the foot of the Lebanon Mts. The city was long a major Middle Eastern commercial and transportation center. After the Lebanese civil war between Muslims and Christians broke out in 1975, sporadic fighting in Beirut destroyed much of the city and reduced its economic role. In 1982 invading Israeli troops fought to oust PALESTINE LIBERATION ORGANIZATION guerrillas from Beirut and heavy destruction resulted. A multinational peacekeeping force was stationed in the city, but it was withdrawn in 1984 after it was subjected to terrorist attacks, including the bombing on Oct. 23, 1983, of the US Marine Corps headquarters at the Beirut airport in which 241 US servicemen died and the almost simultaneous bombing of a barracks used by French paratroopers in which 58 were killed. Fighting among Lebanese factions, Muslim and Christian, and Palestinians continued. Pop 1,500,000.

BEISSEL, Johann Conrad (1690–1768), German-born founder (1732) of the Seventh-Day Baptist community at Ephrata, Pa. He was also a prolific composer of hymns.

BEJART, Maurice (1927–   ), French dancer and choreographer. He danced with various companies in Europe and organized his own company in 1954. As director of the Ballet of the 20th Century in Brussels, Belgium, from 1959 he gave the company an international reputation.

BELASCO, David (1853–1931), US playwright and theatrical producer. In New York after 1880 he became famous for mounting spectacular productions, with lavishly detailed sets, to promote newly-discovered stars.

BELAU. See PALAU.

BELAUNDE TERRY, Fernando (1912–   ), Peruvian political leader who organized the reformist Popular Action Party (1956) and was elected president in 1963. He was overthrown in a military coup 1968 but was reelected when political democracy was restored 1980.

BEL CANTO, style of singing in 19th-century Italian opera, characterized by the singer's extravagant ornamentation of the music in order to heighten the emotional content and display versatility. Two great modern exponents are Maria CALLAS and Joan SUTHERLAND.

BELFAST, seaport and capital of N Ireland (Ulster). Despite major shipbuilding and other industries, the area remains the most depressed in Britain. Since 1969 Belfast has seen violent clashes between the dominant Protestants and the Catholic minority. Pop 318,600.

BELFORT, fortress city in Alsace, E France. Because of its heroic 108-day resistance to a German siege during the Franco-Prussian War, the city was permitted to remain French while the rest of Alsace passed to Germany.

BELGIAN CONGO. See ZAIRE.

BELGIUM, kingdom of NW Europe, bordered to the S by France, to the E by Luxemburg and West Germany and to the N by the Netherlands. It has a short North Sea coastline. Belgium is one of Europe's most densely populated countries. There are nine regions: Antwerp, Brabant, E Flanders, W Flanders, Hainault, Liège, Limburg, Namur and Luxembourg.

Official name: Kingdom of Belgium
Capital: Brussels
Area: 11,783sq mi
Population: 9,861,000
Languages: French, Flemish, German
Religions: Roman Catholic
Monetary unit(s): 1 Belgian franc = 100 centimes

Land. Flanders borders the sea and is mostly flat plain with sandy beaches; further inland, the region is intensively cultivated and drained by the Leie, Scheldt and Dender rivers. Central Belgium consists of a low plateau (300–600ft), which is also a rich agricultural area. The southern edge of this plateau is bounded by the Sambre-Meuse valley, the main industrial and coal-mining region of Belgium. About 25% of all Belgians live in this area of only 800sq

mi. In SE Belgium lies the ARDENNES plateau, a mainly uncultivated area of peat bogs and woodlands, about 1000–1,500ft high. The country has a generally temperate climate.

People. Belgium is politically and culturally divided because it has never been linguistically united. A line running East-West, just S of Brussels, divides the Flemish-speaking Flemings in the north and the French-speaking Walloons in the south. Both languages are in official use.

History. The kingdom emerged only in the 1830s, when it seceded from the Netherlands. A revolutionary government proclaimed independence in 1830, and in 1839 Belgium was recognized as a perpetually neutral sovereign state. The country was led to prosperity under Kings LEOPOLD I and II.

Belgian neutrality was violated by Germany in 1914 and 1940, and massive destruction was caused before its liberation by Allied and resistance forces in 1944. Belgium recovered rapidly, economically and industrially, under King Baudouin, and is now a prosperous member of the EUROPEAN ECONOMIC COMMUNITY, thanks to successful manufacturing industries and transportation systems. Flanders and the north generally are more prosperous than the French-speaking south, heightening linguistic and ethnic tensions. Government by shifting coalitions has been the rule. In 1988 Wilfred Martens of the Christian People's Party formed his eighth government since 1979, ending a record 150-day caretaker regime.

BELGRADE, capital of Yugoslavia, a busy port and industrial center at the junction of the Danube and Sava rivers. Important products include machine tools, tractors, furniture and foodstuffs. Pop 1,087,915.

BELGRANO, Manuel (1770–1820), Argentine revolutionary leader who won decisive battles against Spanish royalists at Tucumán (1812) and Salta (1813). Subsequent defeats led to his replacement by José de SAN MARTIN.

BELINSKY, Vissarion Grigoryevich (1811– 1848), Russian literary critic who founded the socially conscious school of criticism dominant in Russia until the end of the 19th century. He championed what he saw as the social realism of GOGOL, LERMONTOV and PUSHKIN.

BELISARIUS (c505–565 AD), famous Byzantine general under JUSTINIAN I. He crushed the VANDALS in N Africa (533) and the OSTROGOTHS in Italy, taking Rome in 536. His later Italian campaigns (544–48) were largely unsuccessful. In 559 Belisarius was called from retirement to repel the Huns and Slavs from the gates of Constantinople.

BELIZE, formerly (until 1973) **British Honduras,** an independent nation since 1981.

Official name: Belize
Capital: Belmopan
Area: 8,867sq mi
Population: 176,000
Languages: English, Spanish, Indian dialects
Religion: Roman Catholic, Protestant
Monetary unit(s): 1 Belizean dollar = 100 cents
Land. Situated on the subtropical Caribbean coast of Central America, Belize is bordered by Mexico on the N and by Guatemala on the SW. The country, which is densely forested, is about the size of New Hampshire.
People and Economy. The population consists of Creoles (of mixed African and European origin), descendants of Carib Indians, Maya Indians, and a small minority of Europeans. Most people live on the coast. Timber used to be the mainstay of the export-oriented economy, but it has been supplanted by citrus fruits, bananas and sugarcane. Fishing and livestock industries are being developed.
History. European settlement began in the 17th century and in the 18th century African slaves were brought in to cut mahogany. The country became a British colony in 1862 and achieved internal self-government in 1964. Disputes with Guatemala concerning the latter's claim that Belize is an inheritance from Spain delayed the proclamation of independence until 1981. The first direct talks between Guatemala and Belize on their territorial dispute were held in 1987.

BELKNAP, William Worth (1829–1890), US secretary of war (1869–70) in the cabinet of President Ulysses S. Grant. Accused of accepting bribes, he was impeached but resigned to avoid conviction. The scandal was one of several that sullied the Grant administration.

BELL, Alexander Graham (1847–1922), Scottish-born US scientist and educator who invented the TELEPHONE (1876), founded the Bell Telephone Company and devised the wax-cylinder PHONOGRAPH and various aids for teaching the deaf. In later life he helped perfect the aileron for airplanes.

BELL, Alexander Melville (1819–1905), Scottish-born educator of deaf-mutes in Washington, D.C. The inventor Alexander Graham Bell was his son.

BELL, Clive (1881–1964), English art and literary critic and member of the BLOOMSBURY GROUP. He married Virginia WOOLF'S sister, Vanessa Stephen (1907). Some of his best criticism is to be found in his books *Art* (1914) and *Since Cézanne* (1922).

BELL, Daniel (1919–), US sociologist, author of the controversial *The End of Ideology* (1960) and *The Coming of Post-Industrial Society* (1973). He co-founded, with Irving Kristol, the quarterly *Public Opinion* (1965), and taught at Columbia U (1952–69) and Harvard (from 1969).

BELL, Gertrude Margaret Lowthian (1868–1926), English traveler in the Middle East who served in British intelligence during WWI. She acted as liaison with the Arab Bureau of Iraq and was influential in the selection (1920) of Faisal I as king of Iraq, a British mandate. Founder of the Iraqi national museum in Baghdad, she published books of travel and poetry.

BELL, John (1797–1869), "Tennessee Bell," presidential candidate of the CONSTITUTIONAL UNION PARTY (1860) who lost to Lincoln on the eve of the American Civil War. As congressman 1827–41 and senator 1847–59, he was leader of a conservative group of anti-secessionist southerners. He held Tenn. in the Union until President Lincoln's call to arms, when he openly, but not actively, espoused the rebel cause.

BELLAMY, Edward (1850–1898), US author. His Utopian *Looking Backward: 2000–1877* (1888) pictured a benevolent state socialism with worker-ownership. Following its success, "Bellamy Clubs" and a "Nationalist" movement to promote his ideas attracted a nationwide following.

BELLARMINE, Saint Robert (1542–1621), Italian Jesuit theologian and cardinal, a leader of the Catholic REFORMATION by virtue of his polemical and devotional writings. He was canonized in 1930 and declared a Doctor of the Church in 1931.

BELLEAU WOOD, Battle of (June 6–25, 1918), part of the WWI second battle of the Marne in which a brigade of US Marines, with French support, halted five German divisions. In 1923 the battlefield was dedicated as a memorial to the American dead.

BELLINI, family of Early Renaissance Venetian artists. **Jacopo** (c1400–c1470) evolved a much-imitated compositional technique of depicting small figures in vast, precisely detailed architectural settings. Few of his paintings survive, but he influenced others directly and through his sons and son-in-law, Andrea MANTEGNA. **Gentile** (c1429–1507), his elder son, is noted for his strong, realistic portraits as well as for his use of perspective to give a sense of true spatial depth. **Giovanni** (c1430–1516), the younger son, was the greatest Early Renaissance Venetian painter. His early works were influenced by Mantegna, but he later developed the poetic use of light and color for which he is famous. His pupils, TITIAN and GIORGIONE, continued and developed his style.

BELLINI, Vincenzo (1801–1835), Italian opera composer of the bel canto school. His most popular works today are his last three: *La Sonnambula* (1831), *Norma* (1831) and *I Puritani* (1835).

BELLOC, (Joseph Pierre) Hilaire (1870–1953), French-born English poet, essayist and historian. An ardent Roman Catholic polemicist and close friend of G. K. CHESTERTON, his first well-known work was *The Bad Child's Book of Beasts* (1896).

BELLOW, Saul (1915–   ), Canadian-born American novelist noted for his narrative skill and for his studies of Jewish-American life. His best-known books are *Herzog* (1964) and *The Adventures of Augie March* (1953). Other novels include *Dangling Man* (1944), *Henderson the Rain King* (1959), *Mr. Sammler's Planet* (1970), *Humboldt's Gift* (1975), and *More Die of Heartbreak* (1986). He received the 1976 Nobel Prize for Literature.

BELLOWS, George Wesley (1882–1925), US painter and lithographer. One of the best and most interesting early 20th-century "realists," he often succeeded in capturing the raw human energy of his countrymen. Bellows, who remained aloof from modern European influences, was also influential in reviving US lithography.

BELSEN, German village in Lower Saxony, former site of the infamous Nazi concentration camp where over 115,000 people, mostly Jews, were killed.

BELY, Andrei (pseudonym of Boris Bugaev, 1880–1934), Russian poet and novelist, a leading theoretician of the Russian Symbolist movement. In addition to several collections of verse, Bely wrote modernist novels, including *The Silver Dove* (1909), *Kotik Letaev* (1916) and his masterpiece, *Petersburg*, a novel of the 1905 Revolution set in the tsarist capital.

BEMBO, Pietro (1470–1547), Italian humanist, scholar, writer and cardinal. He played an important part in the Renaissance language debate, writing one of the first Italian grammars and advocating a literary language modeled on the examples of BOCCACCIO and PETRARCH.

BEMELMANS, Ludwig (1898–1962), Austrian–American writer and illustrator of *Hansi* (1934), *Madeline* (1939), *My War with the United States* (1937) and other satiric and children's stories.

BEMIS, Samuel Flagg (1891–1973), US historian. A Yale professor (1935–60), he was an expert on US diplomatic history. His books included *A Diplomatic History of the United States* (1936) and two Pulitzer Prize winning works, *Pinckney's Treaty* (1926) and *John Quincy Adams and the Foundations of American Foreign Policy* (1950).

BEN ALI, Zine el-Abidine (1936–   ), president of Tunisia from 1987. Educated as an electronics engineer, he entered the army and rose to the rank of general. He was ambassador to Poland 1980-84. Appointed by President Bourguiba interior minister in 1986 and prime minister in 1987, in Nov. 1987 he deposed Bourguiba as too old and senile to govern and assumed the presidency himself.

BENAVENTE Y MARTÍNEZ, Jacinto (1866–1954), Spanish playwright who wrote and staged 172 comedies and helped establish the modern theater in Spain. He was awarded the 1922 Nobel Prize for Literature for such popular plays as *Bonds of Interest* (1907) and *La Malquerida* (1913).

BEN BELLA, Ahmed (1918–   ), Algerian revolutionary who helped plan the 1954 anti-French revolt. After the post-independence power struggle of 1963, Ben Bella became president but was ousted by Col. BOUMEDIENNE'S coup of June 19, 1965.

BENCHLEY, Robert Charles (1889–1945), US writer, drama critic of *Life*, 1920–29, and the *New Yorker*, 1929–40. He is best known for his short humorous pieces, published in several collections, and his satirical short films. His grandson, Peter Benchley (1928–   ) wrote the best-selling novel *Jaws* (1975).

BENDA, Julien (1867–1956), French

novelist and philosopher. A leading rationalist, he was best known for his influential work *The Treason of the Intellectuals* (1927), which decried the contemporary decline of reason and the growth of political and racial ideologies.

BENEDICT, Ruth (née Fulton; 1887–1948), US cultural anthropologist, whose extensive fieldwork helped illustrate the theory of cultural relativism— that what is deemed deviant in one culture may be normal in another. (See ANTHROPOLOGY.)

BENEDICTINE ORDERS, the "Black Monks," order of monks and nuns following the rule of St. Benedict of Nursia. Their motto is "Pray and work." Stress is laid on a combination of prayer, choral office, study and manual labor under an abbot's supervision. There has been a great revival of the Benedictine rule since 1830 in Europe and the US.

BENEDICT OF NURSIA, Saint (c480–547), father of Western monasticism, whose "rule" set the pattern of monastic life from the mid-7th century. For three years he lived as a hermit near Subiaco, Italy. His piety attracted many followers, some of whom he later grouped in 12 monasteries. Benedict also founded the monastery of MONTE CASSINO.

BENEDICT XV (1854–1922), pope from 1914. Strictly neutral during WWI, he advanced several peace proposals and did much to aid war victims and prisoners of war.

BENELUX, a customs union between Belgium, the Netherlands and Luxembourg, established in 1944 and revised by the Hague protocol of 1947. Benelux is often used collectively for the countries themselves.

BENES, Eduard (1884–1948), cofounder, with Tomáš MASARYK, of the Czechoslovak Republic. He was foreign minister 1918–35, prime minister 1921–22, president 1935–38 and 1946–48, and head of a government-in-exile 1940–45. His appeals to Britain and France in 1938 failed to prevent Hitler's occupation of the Sudetenland. He died after the 1948 communist coup.

BENÉT, Stephen Vincent (1898–1943), US poet, novelist and short story writer, whose works center on US history and tradition. His epic poems *John Brown's Body* (1928) and *Western Star* (1943) won Pulitzer prizes. Among his most famous short stories is *The Devil and Daniel Webster* (1937).

BENGAL, region including Bangladesh and NE India on the Bay of Bengal. Its chief city, Calcutta, was capital of British India 1833–1912, and it was an autonomous province from 1935 until the partition of India in 1947. The W became West Bengal State and the E was included in Pakistan until Bangladesh's 1971 declaration of independence. Most of the S is occupied by the Ganges-Brahmaputra delta.

BENGALI, Indo-Aryan language, related to Assamese, Bihari and Oriya. One of the principal languages of the Indian subcontinent, it has a rich literary heritage and is spoken by some 90 million people in Bangladesh and 50 million in West Bengal.

BEN-GURION, David (1886–1973), Polish-born founder and first prime minister of Israel. After WWI he cofounded the *Haganah* underground Jewish army and the *Histadrut*, the General Federation of Jewish Labor (1920). He became leader of the *Mapai* labor party (1930) and the World Zionist Organization (1935). As prime minister and defense minister, 1949–53 and 1955–63, he, more than any other leader, molded modern Israel.

BENIN, historic W African kingdom, on the Guinea Coast. It flourished between the 14th and 17th centuries, later enjoying a lively trade in pepper and ivory. Its culture was highly sophisticated: Benin bronze sculpture is now world-famous. By the 19th century the slave trade had decimated its male population. It became part of British Nigeria in 1897.

BENIN, a republic in W Africa, bounded by Togo, Burkina, Niger, Nigeria and the Atlantic, until 1975 known as Dahomey.

Official name: People's Republic of Benin
Capital: Porto Novo
Area: 43,450sq mi
Population: 4,307,000
Languages: French; Fon, Mina, Yoruba, Dendi
Religions: Animist; Muslim, Roman Catholic, Protestant
Monetary unit(s): 1 CFA franc = 100 centimes
Land. Benin is long and narrow, extending inland some 450mi from the Gulf of Guinea to the Niger R. Beyond the lagoons that lie behind the coastal strip, the country is flat and forested. In the N, streams flow to the

Volta and Niger rivers. In the NW are the Atacora Mts, Benin's highest elevation, about 2,000ft. S Benin has an equatorial climate, with two rainy and two dry seasons. There is only one rainy season in the N, where the climate is tropical.

People. The population is concentrated in the S coastal region, where Cotonou, a major port city and commerce city, and Porto Novo, the capital, are located. There are four major tribes: the Fon, Adja and Yoruba in the S and the Bariba in the NE and central regions. There is a small European community, mostly French. There are some technical schools and one university, but illiteracy is high.

Economy. Benin is one of the world's poorer countries. Its economy is based on agriculture; the major cash crop is the oil palm. Other exports include hides and skins, cotton, peanuts and coffee. Excessive dependence on one commodity and on foreign aid have hampered economic growth; however, Benin's position as a transit point for Nigeria and landlocked Niger has provided the impetus for an expanding transport sector. Industry, on the whole, is presently small-scale.

History. Benin or Dahomey came under French influence in 1851, after taking a profitable part in the slave trading which earned the region the title of the Slave Coast. It became part of French West Africa in 1904 but gained independence in 1960 and joined the UN. Since then it has suffered from political turmoil, including a series of coups in the 1960s. A three-man Presidential Council was established in 1970. The council was overthrown by the army in 1972. Power was transferred to an elected legislature in 1979–80, although there was only one legal party and coup leader Mathieu Kérékou remained president. He was subsequently reelected.

BENJAMIN, Judah Philip (1811–1884), West Indian-born US politician and lawyer, called the "brains of the Confederacy." As US senator from La. (1853–61), he proved an able advocate of the Southern cause. After secession, Jefferson DAVIS, his personal friend, appointed him successively attorney general, secretary of war, and finally secretary of state (1862–65) in the Confederate government. On the collapse of the Confederacy Benjamin fled to England, where he became a highly successful barrister.

BENNETT, (Enoch) Arnold (1867–1931), English novelist, journalist and playwright. He is famous for his novels set in the potteries of Staffordshire: *Anna of the Five Towns* (1902), *The Old Wives' Tale*

(1908), *Clayhanger* (1910), *Hilda Lessways* (1911) and *These Twain* (1916).

BENNETT, Floyd (1890–1928), US aviator who piloted Richard BYRD on the first flight over the N Pole (May 9, 1926). He was awarded the Congressional Medal of Honor.

BENNETT, James Gordon (1795–1872), Scottish-born US newspaper publisher and editor, pioneer of modern news reporting. In 1835 he launched the popular, sensationalist *New York Herald*, becoming the first to print stock market items and use the telegraph as a news source. His son, **James Gordon Bennett** (1841–1918), sent H. M. STANLEY to find David LIVINGSTONE (1869), and founded the *New York Evening Telegram* (1869) and the *Paris Herald* (1887).

BENNETT, Richard Rodney (1936–   ), English composer known primarily for the strong dramatic sense with which he imbued his works. His opera *Mines of Sulphur* displays this dramatic gift above all in the emotional intensity of its orchestration.

BENNINGTON, Battle of (Aug. 14-16, 1777), REVOLUTIONARY WAR engagement at Bennington, Vt., in which American troops under John Stark and Seth Warren repelled German mercenaries belonging to the British army of John Burgoyne.

BENNY, Jack (Benjamin Kubelsky; 1894–1974), US radio, television, and film comedian. His radio show ran from 1932 to 1955.

BENT, William (1809–1869), US fur trader and pioneer, the first permanent white resident in Col. He formed Bent, St. Vrain & Company in the upper Arkansas valley and ran Bent's Fort.

BENTHAM, Jeremy (1748–1832), English philosopher, economist and jurist. He propounded UTILITARIANISM, the aim of which was to achieve "the greatest happiness of the greatest number," and argued that legislation should be governed by that aim. These ideas were expressed in *An Introduction to the Principles of Morals and Legislation* (1789). He had a major influence on prison and law reform in the 19th century, and on the thinking of J. S. MILL and D. RICARDO. His head and skeleton, dressed in his own suit, sit in University College, London.

BENTLEY, Eric (1916–   ), British-born US drama critic and university teacher. Through his translations and theater work he was instrumental in introducing the plays and ideas of BRECHT to the English-speaking world.

BENTON, Thomas Hart (1782–1858), US

statesman. He represented Mo. in the US Senate for 30 years (1821–51), championing the development of the West and the interests of the common man. Benton was a leader in the fight against the Second Bank of the United States, earning the nickname "Old Bullion Benton" for his advocacy of hard money. His principles led him to oppose the Mexican War, and his opposition to the spread of slavery lost him his Senate seat and brought his brief career in the House (1853–55) to an end.

BENTON, Thomas Hart (1889–1975), US painter, grandnephew of Senator T. H. Benton. He was a leader of the influential 1930s regionalist school of painting, devoted to depicting the life of rural America. He was particularly known for his vivid murals of the midwestern scene.

BENT'S FORT, a trading post on the Arkansas River built by William BENT and his brothers in 1833. For 20 years it was a center of trade with the Indian tribes of the region and a way station on the SANTA FE TRAIL.

BEN YEHUDA, Eliezer (1858–1922), Lithuanian-born Jewish scholar who settled (1881) in Palestine, where he worked to revive Hebrew as a modern language, in part through a 16-volume *Dictionary of Ancient and Modern Hebrew*.

BENZ, Karl (1844–1929), German engineer who built the first commercially successful AUTOMOBILE (1885). His earliest autos were tricycle carriages powered by a small INTERNAL-COMBUSTION ENGINE.

BENZENE (C_6H_6), colorless toxic liquid HYDROCARBON produced from PETROLEUM by refining, and from COAL GAS and COAL TAR. It is the prototypical aromatic hydrocarbon compound; its molecular structure, first proposed by KEKULÉ, is based on a regular planar hexagon of carbon atoms. Stable and not very reactive, benzene forms many substitution products, and also reacts with the halogens to give addition products—including γ-benzene hexachloride, a powerful insecticide. It is used as a solvent, in motor fuel, and as the starting material for the manufacture of a vast variety of other aromatic compounds, especially phenol, styrene, aniline and maleic anhydride. mp $5°C$, bp $80°C$.

BEN-ZVI, Itzhak (1884–1963), Russian-born second president of Israel (1952–63). He was active in Jewish pioneer and self-defense groups in Palestine from 1907, and in 1929 was a founder of the Vaad Leumi (National Council of Palestine Jews).

BEOWULF, anonymous heroic epic poem, c8th century, the greatest extant poem in Old English. The poem uses elements of Germanic legend and is set in Scandinavia. It tells of the hero Beowulf's victories over the monster Grendel and Grendel's mother, his battle with a dragon, and his death and burial. The only manuscript (c1000) is in the British Museum.

BERBERS, several culturally separate N African tribes who speak the Hamitic Berber language or any of its many dialects. Almost all the tribes are Muslim. They live mainly in Algeria, Libya, Morocco and Tunisia. Most are farmers or nomadic herders, but some are oasis-dwellers. They include the Jerbans, Kabyles, Mzabites, Riffians, Beraber, Shluh, Shawia and TUAREGS.

BERCHTESGADEN, small SE Bavarian resort town in the Bavarian Alps, West Germany. Nearby, HITLER built the Berghof, his fortified chalet retreat, with its deep mountainside bunkers. Pop 8,500.

BERCHTOLD, Count Leopold von (1863–1942), Austro-Hungarian foreign minister 1912–15. His ultimatum to Serbia (July 23, 1914), following the assassination of Archduke FRANZ FERDINAND, was the spark that ignited WORLD WAR I.

BERDYAEV, Nikolai Aleksandrovich (1874–1948), Russian religious philosopher. A Marxist in his youth, he later turned to Christianity and created a highly individual Christian existentialism. Expelled from the USSR in 1922, he settled in Paris.

BERENSON, Bernard (1865–1959), Lithuanian-born US art historian. An expert on Italian Renaissance painting, he wrote the definitive study *Italian Painters of the Renaissance* (1894–1907). Berenson bequeathed his Italian villa, art collection and library to Harvard.

BERG, Alban (1885–1935), Austrian composer of expressive TWELVE-TONE MUSIC. A pupil of SCHOENBERG, he adopted his technique in such works as his violin concerto (1935) and two operas, *Wozzeck* (1925) and the unfinished *Lulu* (1935). (See also ATONALITY.)

BERGEN, Edgar (1903–1978), US ventriloquist, in radio, television, and films from the 1930s with his principal dummy, Charlie McCarthy. His daughter, **Candice Bergen** (1946–   ), was a film and television actress.

BERGER, Victor Louis (1860–1929), the first US Socialist congressman (1911–13, 1918, 1919, 1923–29). Born in Austria, Berger was a founder and leader of the American Socialist party. In WWI he was sentenced to 20 years' imprisonment for aiding the enemy, but was freed on appeal.

BERGMAN, (Ernst) Ingmar (1918–   ), Swedish film and stage director, producer and writer. He combines realism with imaginative symbolism to explore themes such as good and evil, love, old age and death. Famous motion pictures include *The Seventh Seal* (1956), *Wild Strawberries* (1957), *Persona* (1966), *Cries and Whispers* (1971) and *Fanny and Alexander* (1983).

BERGSON, Henri Louis (1859–1941), French philosopher, the first exponent of process philosophy. Reacting against the physicists' definition of TIME and substituting a notion of experienced duration; rejecting the psychophysical parallelism of the day and asserting the independence of mind, and viewing EVOLUTION not as a mechanistic but as a creative process energized by an *élan vital* (vital impulse), Bergson was perhaps the most original philosopher of the early 20th century. He was awarded the Nobel Prize for Literature in 1927.

BERIA, Lavrenti Pavlovich (1899–1953), head of the Soviet secret police (1938–53). As commissar for internal affairs he was responsible for thousands of political executions. Shortly after Stalin's death he was secretly executed for treason.

BERIBERI, deficiency disease caused by lack of VITAMIN B₁ (thiamine); it may occur in MALNUTRITION, ALCOHOLISM or as an isolated deficiency. NEURITIS leading to sensory changes, and foot or wrist drop, palpitations, EDEMA and HEART failure are features; there may be associated dementia. Onset may be insidious or acute. Treatment is thiamine replacement; thiamine enrichment of common foods prevents beriberi.

BERING, Vitus Jonassen (1681–1741), Danish explorer. Sailing in the service of Russia, he probed N through the Bering Sea and discovered BERING STRAIT (1728) and Alaska (1741). He died of scurvy on Bering Island.

BERING SEA, the extreme N arm of the N Pacific Ocean, 885,000sq mi in area, bounded by E Siberia, Alaska and the Aleutian Islands. It contains Nunivak Island, St. Lawrence Island, the Pribilof Islands (all US) and the Komandorskiye Islands (USSR). The international dateline crosses it diagonally.

BERING SEA CONTROVERSY, Anglo-American dispute in the late 19th century. When indiscriminate slaughter by various nations threatened the valuable seal herds of the US-owned Pribilof Islands in the Bering Sea, the US seized three Canadian ships (1886) and claimed dominion over the Bering Sea (1889).

Britain objected, and in 1893 an arbitration tribunal declared the Bering Sea international.

BERKELEY, Busby (1895–1976), US choreographer and film director who revolutionized the staging of musical-production numbers in Hollywood films. He introduced lavish settings, revolving platforms and giant staircases upon which hundreds of extras performed in such extravaganzas as *Forty-Second Street* (1933) and *Gold Diggers of 1933.*

BERKELEY, George (1685–1753), Irish philosopher and bishop who, rejecting the views of LOCKE as to the nature of material substance, substituted the *esse-percipi* principle: to be is to be perceived (or to be capable of perception). Thus for Berkeley there is no material reality but only ideas belonging to minds and deriving from God. Berkeley's acute analysis of experience and his cogent argumentation rendered his "subjective idealism" an important influence on subsequent views of knowledge.

BERKELEY, Sir William (1606–1677), royal governor of Virginia (1642–52 and 1660–77). His autocratic rule in his second term and an inability or unwillingness to deal with Indian frontier attacks caused BACON'S REBELLION (1676). Berkeley's harsh treatment of the rebels led to his recall to England.

BERKMAN, Alexander (1870–1936), Polish-born US anarchist. During a steel strike, he tried to assassinate the Carnegie Steel Co. head, Henry C. FRICK (1892). He served 14 years' imprisonment. In 1917 he was imprisoned for draft obstruction, then deported to Russia in 1919.

BERLE, Adolf Augustus, Jr. (1895–1971), US economist, member of President Franklin D. Roosevelt's "brain trust" and assistant secretary of state 1938–44. He cowrote *The Modern Corporation* (1932), a study of economic concentration in the US.

BERLIN, Irving (1888–1989), US song writer, born in Russia as Israel Baline. He wrote over 900 popular songs, including *Alexander's Ragtime Band* (1911) and *God Bless America* and *White Christmas* (1942); film scores, including *Top Hat* (1935); and musicals such as *Annie Get Your Gun* (1946) and *Call Me Madam* (1950). He won a Congressional gold medal (1954) for his patriotic songs.

BERLIN, Sir Isaiah (1909–   ), Latvian-born British philosopher and historian of ideas. He is best known for a biography of Karl Marx (1939), his study of Tolstoy *The Hedgehog and the Fox* (1953), and *Historical Inevitability* (1955). He also wrote *Russian Thinkers* (1978) and

Against the Current (1980). He was president of Wolfson College, Oxford, 1966–75, and the British Academy 1974–78.

BERLIN, major city located in the E central part of East Germany, with a corridor to West Germany. It covers 341sq mi and stands on a sandy plain at the center of a network of roads, railroads and waterways.

Berlin was the capital of Germany, 1871–1945. Since WWII it has been divided into East Berlin (formerly the Russian zone, now capital of communist East Germany) and West Berlin (a state of West Germany, though not constitutionally part of it). West Berlin contains 12 districts of the original city and is divided into British, French and US zones. East Berlin contains 8 districts of the old city. The BERLIN WALL separates both halves of the city; East Germany and the USSR have restricted movement between them and at times between West Berlin and West Germany (see BERLIN AIRLIFT). The Four Power Agreement of June 1972 guaranteed freer access to West Berlin and allowed its citizens to visit the East.

Berlin emerged in the Middle Ages, became the capital of Prussia in 1701 and grew into one of Europe's greatest political, commercial and cultural centers. The city was shattered in WWII, but has been rebuilt and revitalized. In 1987 Berlin's 750th anniversary was separately celebrated in the two halves of the city. Pop.: East Berlin 1,135,000; West Berlin 1,900,000.

BERLIN, Conference of, held in Berlin (1884–85) by 14 countries to discuss colonial rivalries in Africa. It established the principle that occupation of African territory had to be effective to be legal, recognized the Congo Free State set up by Leopold of Belgium and discussed the control of the Congo and Niger rivers.

BERLIN, Congress of, international meeting held in June–July 1878 to settle problems created by the 1877–78 Russo-Turkish war, notably Russian claims to Balkan territory. The resultant Treaty of Berlin was signed on Aug. 24. Romania, Bulgaria, Serbia and Montenegro became independent; Romania gained N Dobrudja and ceded Bessarabia to Russia; Russian possession of the Caucasus was confirmed; the UK gained Cyprus, and Austria-Hungary was to administer Bosnia-Herzegovina. The congress was chaired by BISMARCK, acting as "honest broker."

BERLIN AIRLIFT, operation by the UK and US to fly essential supplies into West Berlin during the Russian blockade of Allied land and water routes to the city (June 28, 1948–May 12, 1949). It continued until Sept. 30, 1949, involving 250,000 flights, 2 million tons of supplies and a cost of $224 million.

BERLIN WALL, 27mi-long wall built in Aug. 1961 by the East Germans to separate East and West Berlin. Made of concrete, steel and barbed wire, it is floodlit and constantly patrolled by armed guards. There are 12 official crossing points.

BERLIOZ, Louis Hector (1803–1869), French Romantic composer of dramatic, descriptive works, some for immense orchestras. Major works include his *Symphonie Fantastique* (1830), *Requiem* (1837), the choral symphony *Romeo and Juliet* (1838–39), the oratorio *The Childhood of Christ* (1850–54) and the operas *Benvenuto Cellini* (1838) and *The Trojans* (1856–59). Berlioz also wrote music criticism, a valuable treatise on instrumentation (1844), and his memoirs (1870).

BERMUDA, British colony comprising about 150 coral islands of which 20 are inhabited. It lies in the N Atlantic Ocean, 580mi E of N.C. The main island is Bermuda Island, with the capital, Hamilton. The climate is warm and the vegetation lush and tropical. Bermuda's first British colonists arrived in 1609. Some 60% of present inhabitants are descendants of Negro slaves, and the rest are mainly British. The economy depends on tourism and two US bases. Pop 55,000.

BERMUDA TRIANGLE, an area roughly bounded by Bermuda, Puerto Rico, and Miami, in which many ships and planes are said to have vanished. Natural and supernatural causes, ranging from storms to space-time warps, have been proposed to explain the allegedly mysterious disappearances.

BERN or **Berne,** capital city of Switzerland and of Bern canton. It lies on the Aare R in the German-speaking area. It is an important commercial, industrial and cultural center and the headquarters of some major international communications organizations. Bern was founded in 1191 and retains many old buildings. Pop 139,591.

BERNADETTE, Saint (1844–1879), born Marie-Bernarde Soubirous, French peasant girl who claimed to have had 18 visions of the Virgin Mary in a LOURDES grotto in 1858. The grotto became a shrine, and she was beatified (1925) and canonized (1933). Her feast day is Feb. 18 in France, April 16 elsewhere.

BERNADOTTE, Count Folke (1895–1948), Swedish UN mediator in the

1948 Arab–Israeli war. In spring 1945 he was the go-between for HIMMLER'S offer to the Allies of a conditional Nazi surrender. It was rejected. On Sept. 17, 1948, he was assassinated in Jerusalem by the Zionist Stern gang.

BERNADOTTE, Jean Baptiste Jules (1763–1844), French general who founded Sweden's present royal dynasty. He became one of Napoleon's marshals (1804), and was elected Swedish crown prince in 1810. He fought Napoleon at Leipzig (1813) and ruled Sweden and Norway as Charles XIV (1818–44).

BERNANOS, Georges (1888–1948), French novelist whose theme was the struggle of good and evil forces for man's soul. His masterpiece was *Journal d'un Curé de Campagne* (Diary of a Country Priest, 1936).

BERNARD, Claude (1813–1887), French physiologist regarded as the father of experimental medicine. Following the work of the American William Beaumont he opened artificial fistulas in animals to study their DIGESTIVE SYSTEMS. He demonstrated the role of the PANCREAS in digestion, discussed the presence and function of glycogen in the LIVER (1856) and in 1851 reported the existence of the vasomotor nerves.

BERNARD OF CLAIRVAUX, Saint (1090–1153), French theologian and mystic who reinvigorated the CISTERCIANS and inspired the Second Crusade. The founder abbot of Clairvaux Abbey (1115–53), he established 68 religious houses. He was adviser to popes, kings and bishops and was instrumental in ABELARD'S condemnation (1140). Bernard was canonized in 1174. His feast day is Aug. 20. (See also CRUSADES.)

BERN CONVENTION, international copyright protection agreement signed in 1886 by over 40 countries and periodically revised. It now has 59 members. It covers literary publications, drama, motion pictures, artwork, music, records and photographs. The US did not sign but subscribed to the similar Universal Copyright Convention (1952).

BERNHARDT, Sarah (1844–1923), French actress of great emotional power, born Henriette Rosine Bernard. She achieved great successes in classic French plays, created many roles for Victorien Sardou and ROSTAND, and made several triumphant worldwide tours.

BERNINI, Giovanni Lorenzo (1598–1680), Italian sculptor and architect who gave Rome many of its characteristic BAROQUE features. He designed the tomb of Urban VIII, the canopy over the high altar in St.

Peter's, the Piazza S. Pietro, the *Four Rivers* fountain in the Piazza Navona and the statue *St. Teresa in Ecstasy.*

BERNOULLI, family of Swiss mathematicians important in establishing CALCULUS as a mathematical tool of widespread application. **Jacques (Jakob) Bernoulli** (1654–1705), who applied calculus to many geometrical problems, is best remembered in the Bernoulli numbers and the Theorem of Bernoulli that appeared in a posthumous work on PROBABILITY. **Jean (Johann) Bernoulli** (1667–1748), brother of Jacques, also a propagandist on behalf of the Leibnizian calculus, assisted his brother in founding the calculus of variations. **Daniel Bernoulli** (1700–1782), son of Jean, anatomist, botanist and mathematician—perhaps the family's most famous member—published his *Hydrodynamics* in 1738, applying calculus to that science. In it he proposed **Bernoulli's principle,** which states that in any small volume of space through which a fluid is flowing steadily, the total ENERGY, comprising the pressure, potential and kinetic energies, is constant. This means that the PRESSURE is inversely related to the VELOCITY. This principle is applied in the design of the airfoil, the key component in making possible all heavier-than-air craft, where the faster flow of air over the longer upper surface results in reduction of pressure there and hence a lifting force acting on the airfoil (see also AERODYNAMICS).

BERNSTEIN, Eduard (1850–1932), German political theorist and historian. He lived and worked in London (1888–1901), formulating a non-violent program of social reform for the German Social Democratic Party. He was influenced by MARX, ENGELS and the FABIAN SOCIETY.

BERNSTEIN, Leonard (1918–   ), US conductor–composer, best known for his musical *West Side Story* (1957). He rose to fame as conductor of the New York Philharmonic Orchestra (1958–69). His varied works include the symphony *The Age of Anxiety* (1949), and musical *On the Town* (1944) and *Mass* (1971).

BERNSTORFF, Johann Heinrich, Graf von (1862–1939), German ambassador to the US (1908–17) who warned his government that unrestricted submarine warfare would bring the US into WWI. A member of the Reichstag (1921–28), he went into exile when Hitler came to power.

BERRA, Lawrence Peter "Yogi" (1925–   ), US baseball player for the New York Yankees, 1946–63. He gained the record for world series games played (75) and the greatest number of series hits

(71). He won the American League's "Most Valuable Player Award" in 1951, 1954 and 1955. He managed the Yankees in 1964, 1984–85, the New York Mets 1972–75, and the Houston Astros from 1986.

BERRYMAN, John (1914–1972), US poet, active from the 1930s. His reputation was confirmed by the long poem *Homage to Mistress Bradstreet* (1956). Berryman's later work, distinguished by its black ironies and linguistic innovation, includes *His Toy, His Dream, His Rest* (1968) and *Dream Songs* (1969). He committed suicide, throwing himself off a bridge in Minneapolis.

BERTILLON, Alphonse (1853–1914), French criminologist who devised a system (*Bertillonage*) for identifying criminals based on anthropometric measurements, adopted by the French police in 1888 and used until the adoption of FINGERPRINTS as a method of identification.

BERTOIA, Harry (1915–1978) Italian-born US sculptor. His large metallic screens show the geometric influence of industrial design. He also was well-known as a furniture designer.

BERZELIUS, Jöns Jakob, Baron (1779–1848), Swedish chemist who determined the ATOMIC WEIGHTS of nearly 40 elements before 1818, discovered cerium (1803), selenium (1818) and thorium (1829), introduced the terms PROTEIN, isomerism and CATALYSIS and devised the modern method of writing empirical formulas (1813).

BESANT, Annie (1847–1933), British theosophist and social reformer, born Annie Wood. Mrs. Besant joined the FABIAN SOCIETY and was an early advocate of birth control. Madame BLAVATSKY'S writings converted her to THEOSOPHY and she joined the Theosophical Society (1889) and became international president (1907–33). She also championed independence for India, becoming president of the Indian National Congress (1917).

BESSARABIA, historic region of SE Europe, NW of the Black Sea, between the Dniester and Danube rivers. After various Russo–Turkish conflicts it was ceded to Russia in 1812. After the CRIMEAN WAR it passed to Moldavia (1856) but was regained by Russia (1878). Romania controlled it almost continuously from 1918 to 1944, when it joined the USSR as part of the Moldavian and Ukrainian SSR.

BESSARION, John (c1410–1472), Byzantine humanist scholar and churchman. As a Byzantine archbishop at the councils of Ferrara and Florence he tried to reunite the divided Greek and Latin churches. He stayed in Italy, becoming a cardinal and helping to spread Greek classical learning.

BESSEMER, Sir Henry (1813–1898), British inventor of the Bessemer process for the manufacture of steel, patented in 1856.

BEST, Charles Herbert (1899–1978), US-born Canadian physiologist, codiscoverer (1921) of INSULIN with Frederick G. BANTING. He went on to do other important work on diabetes and thrombosis.

BETANCOURT, Römulo (1908–1981), Venezuelan politician and founder of the left-wing Acción Democràtica party (1941). Provisional president 1945–47 and president 1958–63, he spent 1948–58 in exile after a military coup, and survived an assassination attempt in 1960.

BETEL NUT, fruit of the betel palm (*Areca catechu*), native to tropical Asia. It is boiled, sliced, dried and chewed as a stimulant with betel pepper vine leaves (*Piper betle*) and coral lime. Chewing produces red saliva that may temporarily stain the mouth orange-brown.

BETHE, Hans Albrecht (1906–   ), German-born US theoretical physicist who proposed the nuclear carbon cycle to account for the sun's energy output (1938). During WWII he worked on the Manhattan Project. He was awarded the 1967 Nobel physics prize for his work on the source of stellar energy.

BETHLEHEM, town in Israeli-occupied WEST BANK, 6mi S of Jerusalem, and sacred to Jews, Christians, and Muslims. It was the biblical city of David where he was anointed by Samuel; the traditional tomb of Rachel is outside the town, which was the birthplace of Christ. A basilica built by the Emperor CONSTANTINE over the Grotto of the Nativity (326–33) and rebuilt by JUSTINIAN I now forms the Church of the Nativity, a major attraction for tourists and pilgrims. Long contested by Christians and Muslims, it was taken by Israel during the 1967 Six-Day War. Pop 25,000.

BETHMANN-HOLLWEG, Theobald von (1856–1921), German chancellor (1909–17) who was opposed to WWI but defended Germany's role during it. His calling the international guarantee of Belgian neutrality "a scrap of paper" was considered typical German cynicism.

BETHUNE, Mary McLeod (1875–1955), black American educator and civil rights activist. She founded the Daytona Normal and Industrial School for Negro Girls (1904), now Bethune–Cookman College, and was Director of Negro Affairs in the National Youth Administration (1936–44) and President F. D. ROOSEVELT'S adviser on minority problems.

BETJEMAN, Sir John (1906–1984), English poet laureate and architectural conservationist, often called a lyrical satirist. His books include *New Bats in Old Belfries* (1945), *Selected Poems* (1948), *Collected Poems* (1958), *Victorian and Edwardian Architecture in London* (1969).

BETTI, Ugo (1892–1953), Italian playwright and poet, once a judge. His plays, deeply concerned with guilt and evil, are often shaped as judicial enquiries. His works include *La Padrona* (1927) and *Il Giocatore* (1951).

BEVAN, Aneurin "Nye" (1897–1960), British trade unionist and member of Parliament (1929–60), leader of The Labour party's left wing. As Minister of Health (1945–50) under ATTLEE, he introduced and administered the 1946 National Health Act, which established a vast national health program.

BEVERIDGE, Albert Jeremiah (1862–1927), US politician and historian. A Republican senator from Indiana (1899–1911), he helped organize the Progressive Party and was defeated (1912) as its candidate for governor of Indiana. Thereafter he devoted himself to history, publishing notable biographies of John Marshall and Abraham Lincoln.

BEVERIDGE, William Henry (1879–1963), British economist and social planner whose report on social insurance (1942) revolutionized the British welfare system. It became law under the 1945–51 Labor government. Beveridge became a knight in 1919 and a baron in 1946.

BEVIN, Ernest (1881–1951), British labor leader and statesman. He formed the Transport and General Workers' Union (1922), the nation's largest union. He was minister of labor in WWII and as foreign minister in 1945–51 took a tough pro-European, anti-Soviet stand.

BEZA, Theodore (1519–1605), French Calvinist theologian, CALVIN's successor in Geneva (1564). His Latin translation of the New Testament was a source for the King James version.

BHAGAVAD-GĪTĀ (song of the Lord), anonymous SANSKRIT poem of about 200 BC, embedded in the Mahābhārata epic, a world-famous religious discourse. It consists of a dialogue (700 verses), covering many aspects of Hindu religious thought, between Prince Arjuna and the god KRISHNA on a field of battle.

BHOPAL, city, central India, capital of Madhya Pradesh state and site of history's worst industrial accident. On Dec. 3, 1984, toxic gas leaked from a storage tank at a pesticide plant there, killing more than 2,000 people and injuring as many as 150,000. The plant, jointly owned by a US corporation, Union Carbide, and Indian investors, was built and operated by Indians. Authorities closed the plant after the accident.

BHUTAN, kingdom in the E Himalayas between Tibet and India. It is a mountainous land with fertile subtropical valleys. Rice, tea and other farm products dominate its mainly subsistence economy. Poor communications have hampered development. Some 65% of the people are Bhutias of Tibetan–Himalayan origin. There are also many Nepalese. Dzongkha is the official language and LAMAISM the major faith

Official name: Kingdom of Bhutan
Capital: Thimbu
Area: 18,150sq mi
Population: 1,338,000
Languages: Dzongkha
Religions: Buddhist, Hindu
Monetary unit(s): 1 Indian rupee = 2 tikchung = 100 paise

Bhutan's early history is a mystery. The British East India Company made a treaty with the king in 1774, and in 1910 the British took over Bhutan's foreign relations, a responsibility India assumed in 1947. Bhutan is ruled by the hereditary king (Druk Gyalpo) Jigme Singye Wangchuck with a council of ministers and national assembly. China has claimed Bhutanese territory since the 1950s. In the late 1980s the two nations held a series of talks aimed at resolving the border conflict.

BHUTTO, Zulfikar Ali (1928–1979), president and prime minister of Pakistan. Educated in the US and in England, he returned to Pakistan and served in several cabinet positions. He became president (1971) and then prime minister (1973), gaining power after the secession of Bangladesh. Ousted by a military coup in 1977, Bhutto was convicted and executed on a charge of having ordered the murder of a political opponent. His daughter, **Benazir Bhutto** (1953-   ), educated at Harvard and Oxford, led the political opposition to her father's successor, Mohammed Zia ul-Haq. In Nov. 1988, after Zia's death, Benazir Bhutto's Pakistan People's Party won the largest number of seats in parliament. In Dec. she was named prime minister, becoming the first woman to lead a modern Muslim state.

BIAFRA, name assumed by Nigeria's Eastern Region during its attempted secession (1967–70). Under the leadership of Colonel Ojukwu, the IBO people of the Eastern Region declared their independence in May, 1967, and the civil war, for which both sides had been preparing for some time, broke out. Outnumbered and outgunned, the Biafrans suffered heavy losses, with large numbers dying from starvation, before their final surrender. The former breakaway region was divided to form the East-Central, River and South-Eastern states.

BIALIK, Haim Nahman (1873–1934), one of the greatest of modern Hebrew poets. Born in the Ukraine, he settled in Palestine in 1924. Firmly rooted in tradition, his poetry gave fiery expression to Jewish national aspirations, making Bialik his people's national poet.

BIBLE, collection of sacred books of JUDAISM and CHRISTIANITY, often called the Holy Scriptures. Being inspired (that is, given by God), they form the basis for belief and practice (see CANON). Modern theologians generally regard the Bible as the record and vehicle of divine revelation: equally the word of God and the word of man. Major biblical themes center in God, his creation and care of the world, his righteousness, love, and saving activity (see JESUS CHRIST; CHURCH). The Bible has had an incalculable influence on the thought, attitudes, beliefs, art, science and politics of Western society.

The Christian Bible comprises the OLD TESTAMENT and the NEW TESTAMENT. The Hebrew Bible is essentially the Old Testament. Its 39 books, plus the 27 of the New Testament, make up the Protestant Bible. Most of the books of disputed authority, known as the APOCRYPHA, are included in the Old Testament by the Eastern and Roman Catholic Churches, while in Protestant editions they are excluded or placed between the two Testaments.

There have been many versions and many translations of the Bible. The original Old Testament, written almost entirely in Hebrew, was translated into Aramaic (the Targums) and later into Greek (see SEPTUAGINT) and Latin. The VULGATE is still the standard Latin version in the Roman

Catholic Church. It was the basis of the first major English version, named for John WYCLIFFE, and completed in 1388. The REFORMATION aimed to give the Bible to the common people, and Martin LUTHER's German version pioneered much translation work. Several scholarly English translations, including those by William TYNDALE and Miles COVERDALE, appeared in the 16th century. A significant Roman Catholic translation by the English colleges in exile in Rheims and Douai appeared in 1582 and 1610. Still supreme among English versions is the King James or Authorized Version (1611), a major work of English literature. This remains perhaps the most popular translation, although outmoded by later, more accurate versions, notably the Revised Version (1881 and 1885) and the Revised Standard Version (1952). The Roman Catholic Church has produced the Jerusalem Bible (1966) and Ronald Knox's version (1945 and 1949). The New English Bible (1962 and 1970), produced by an interdenominational committee, is another major modern translation.

The Bible has now been translated into more than 1400 languages, and millions of copies are sold annually throughout the world.

BICHAT, Marie François Xavier (1771–1802), French anatomist and pathologist, the founder of HISTOLOGY. Although working without the MICROSCOPE, Bichat distinguished 21 types of elementary TISSUES from which the organs of the body are composed.

BIDAULT, Georges (1899–1983), French statesman who opposed France's decolonization policies. He was provisional president (1946), prime minister (1946; 1949–50) and foreign secretary (1944; 1947–48; 1953–54). In 1962 he was exiled by President de Gaulle for backing militant opposition to Algerian independence, and went to Brazil. He returned to France in 1968.

BIDDLE, Francis (1886–1968), US government official. He was US attorney general (1941–45) and a US judge at the Nuremberg war crimes trials (1945–46).

BIDDLE, Nicholas (1786–1844), president of the second Bank of the United States (1823–36). He made it the nation's first authoritative central bank. Renewal of the bank's charter was vetoed by President Jackson after Biddle had unwisely made rechartering a major presidential election issue.

BIEDERMEIER, utilitarian bourgeois style of furniture prevailing in Germany between about 1810 and 1850. The term derived from the caricature bourgeois figure "Papa Biedermeier" who featured in a popular magazine of the 1850s, and came to apply disparagingly to German bourgeois taste of the period.

BIENVILLE, Jean Baptiste le Moyne, Sieur de (1680–1768), French naval officer who founded New Orleans. Born in Canada, he helped to colonize French Louisiana, which he governed at various periods between 1701 and 1743.

BIERCE, Ambrose (Gwinett) (1842–1914?), US short-story writer and satirical journalist. His works include the gloomy tales of *Can Such Things Be?* (1893) and the cynical definitions of *The Devil's Dictionary* (1906). He disappeared without trace during the Mexican Revolution of 1913–14.

BIERSTADT, Albert (1830–1902), German-born American landscape painter. He is famous for his massive, realistic Western scenes.

BIG BEN, the clock in the tower of the Houses of Parliament, London. It is named for Sir Benjamin Hall, commissioner of works in 1856 when the bell was installed. The name originally referred only to the 13-ton bell.

BIG BEND NATIONAL PARK, vast tract of mountains and desert on the Texan border with Mexico, in the Big Bend of the Rio Grande. The park, which covers some 708,221 acres, was established in 1944 and is the last great expanse of truly wild land left in Tex.

BIGELOW, John (1817–1911), US journalist, author and diplomat. As US consul in Paris (1861–64), he prevented the Confederate states from gaining French-built warships. Bigelow also served as minister to France (1865–66). He was co-editor of the New York *Evening Post* (1848–61).

BIGGS, E(dward) Power (1906–1977), English-born US concert organist. He was a master of old and modern music, and edited various organ works.

BIKINI, an atoll in the Marshall Islands in the central Pacific Ocean. It was the site of US nuclear bomb tests in the 1940s and 1950s. Inhabitants evacuated during the tests began to return in the early 1970s, but the island was again declared uninhabitable because of dangerously high radiation levels in 1978.

BIKO, Steve (1946–1977), South African black activist who died while in police custody, a martyr of the antiapartheid movement.

BILE, a yellow-brown fluid secreted by the liver and containing salts derived from CHOLESTEROL. Stored and concentrated in the GALL BLADDER and released into the duodenum after a meal, the bile emulsifies fats and aids absorption of fat-soluble vitamins A, D, E and K. Other constituents of bile are in fact waste products. Yellow bile and black bile were two of the humors of Hippocratic medicine.

BILLIARDS, name for several indoor games in which balls set on a felt-covered rectangular table are struck by the end of a long tapering stick (the cue). Obscure in origin, billiards was popular in France and England as early as the 14th century. The name came from the French *billard* which meant "a cue." Until the 19th century billiard balls were made of ivory, but now compressed plastic composition balls are most common. The cue has a rubber cushion tip. The table usually has a slate bed in a wooden frame and must be plumb level. In most forms of the game, the table has six pockets: one in each corner and one midway along each of the longer sides. The object is to sink balls into the pockets by playing one ball off another or, in games played without pockets, to hit the balls against each other successively. **Carom billiards** and **English billiards** feature two white cue balls and one red ball. **Snooker** has one white cue ball, 15 red balls and six balls of other colors. **Pool,** as played in the US, or **pocket billiards,** has one white cue ball and 15 numbered colored balls and is the billiard game most popular in the US.

BILLINGS, Josh (Henry Wheeler Shaw; 1818–1885), US humorist, popular for sketches written in a rural dialect and first collected in *Josh Billings: His Sayings* (1869).

BILL OF RIGHTS, a constitutional document which defines the rights of a people, safeguarding them against undue governmental interference. In the US these rights and safeguards are embodied in the first 10 amendments to the constitution. After the Revolutionary War there was great popular demand for constitutionally defined rights to limit the power of the new government. Bills of rights were drafted in eight states between 1776 and 1781, but when the constitution was drawn up in 1787 no such bill was included, and ratification by the states lagged until promises were made that a bill of rights would be added to the Constitution. When the first Congress met in 1789, James Madison presented a bill of rights. Twelve amendments to the constitution were proposed in the debate on Madison's bill, 10 of which were accepted, and on Dec. 15, 1791, Secretary of State Thomas Jefferson proclaimed the Federal

Bill of Rights in full force. The bill guarantees freedom of speech, of the press and of religion. It protects against arbitrary searches and self-incrimination. It sets out proper procedures for trials, giving to all the right to trial by jury and to cross-examine witnesses. In addition to these rights, the 5th Amendment provides that no person shall "be deprived of life, liberty, or property, without due process of law."

The Bill of Rights sought to protect the people against arbitrary acts by the federal government, not the states. In 1868 the states ratified the 14th Amendment, which granted citizenship to the newly freed Negroes and directed the federal government to protect the citizens of a state against arbitrary state actions. Over the years the US Supreme Court increasingly has used the "due process" clause of the 14th Amendment to apply the Federal Bill of Rights against the states.

BILL OF RIGHTS, English, an act passed by the English parliament in 1689 to consolidate constitutional government after the GLORIOUS REVOLUTION. It abolished the royal power to suspend laws, established free parliamentary elections and defined citizens' rights.

BILLY THE KID (1859–1881), nickname of a US outlaw born William H. Bonney. Notorious in the Southwest as a cattle thief and murderer, he was eventually captured and sentenced to hang. He escaped from jail by killing two guards but was soon tracked down and killed by Sheriff Pat Garrett.

BINARY NUMBER SYSTEM, a number system which uses the powers of 2. Thus the number which in our everyday system, the DECIMAL SYSTEM, would be represented as 25 ($\doteq (2 \times 10^1) + (5 \times 10^0)$) is in binary notation 11001 ($\doteq (1 \times 2^4) + (1 \times 2^3) + (0 \times 2^2) + (0 \times 2^1) + (1 \times 2^0)$), which is equivalent to (1×16) + (1×8) + (1×1) or ($16 + 8 + 1$). The system is of particular note since digital COMPUTERS use binary numbers for calculation.

BINET, Alfred (1857–1911), French psychologist who pioneered methods of mental testing. He collaborated with Théodore Simon in devising the Binet-Simon tests, widely used to estimate INTELLIGENCE.

BINGHAM, George Caleb (1811–1879), US genre painter noted for his Midwestern river scenes, for example *The Jolly Flatboatmen* (1846). He also treated political subjects with warmth, humor and vigor, as in *Canvassing for a Vote* (1851), and was, in fact, a politician himself in his home state of Missouri.

BINGHAM, Hiram (1875–1956), US archaeologist who studied and wrote about Inca ruins in S America. Later he was governor of Connecticut (1925) and a US senator (1925–33).

BINGO, a lottery game which, in its present form, originated c1880, though it can be traced to a 17th-century Italian game called *tumbule.* Bingo is now conducted both by gambling professionals for profit and by churches and other groups as a means of raising money for charitable enterprises.

BINOMIAL THEOREM, the theorem that a binomial ($a + b$) may be raised to the power n by application of the formula

$$(a+b)^n = a^n + na^{(n-1)}b + \frac{(n-1)\,n}{2}$$
$$\ldots a^{(n-2)}b^2 + an.b^{(n-1)} + b^n$$

Thus, for example,

$$(a+b)^4 = a^4 + 4a^3b + 6a^2b^2 + 4ab^3 + b^4.$$

Expansion of $((a - b)^n$ is equivalent to expansion of $(a + (- b))^n$. Thus, for example,
$(a-b)^4 = a^4 + \quad 4a^3(-b) + \quad 6a^2(-b)^2 + 4a(-b)^3 + (-b)^4$
$= a^4 - 4a^3b + 6a^2b^2 - 4ab^3 + b^4.$
Note that the expansion of $(a+b)^n$ has ($n+1$) terms.

BIOCHEMISTRY, study of the substances occurring in living organisms and the reactions in which they are involved. It is a science on the border between BIOLOGY and ORGANIC CHEMISTRY. The main constituents of living matter are WATER, CARBOHYDRATES, LIPIDS and PROTEINS. The total chemical activity of the organism is known as its METABOLISM. Plants use sunlight as an energy source to produce carbohydrates from carbon dioxide and water (see PHOTOSYNTHESIS). The carbohydrates are then stored as starch; used for structural purposes, as in the CELLULOSE of plant cell walls; or oxidized through a series of reactions including the citric acid cycle, the energy released being stored as adenosine triphosphate (see NUCLEOTIDES). In animals energy is stored mainly as lipids, which as well as forming fat deposits are components of all cell membranes. Proteins have many functions, of which metabolic regulation is perhaps the most important. ENZYMES, which control almost all biochemical reactions, and some HORMONES are proteins. Plants synthesize proteins using simpler nitrogenous compounds from the soil. Animals obtain proteins from food and break them down by HYDROLYSIS to AMINO ACIDS. New proteins are made according to the pattern determined by the sequence of NUCLEIC ACIDS in the GENES. Many reactions occur in all CELLS and may be studied in simple systems. Methods used by biochemists and chemists are similar and include labelling with radioactive ISOTOPES and separation techniques such as CHROMATOGRAPHY, which analyzes very small amounts of substances, and use of the high-speed CENTRIFUGE. Molecular structures may be determined by X-ray diffraction. Landmarks in biochemistry include the synthesis of urea by Friedrich Wöhler (1828), the pioneering research of VON LIEBIG, PASTEUR and BERNARD, and more recently the elucidation of the structure of DNA by James WATSON and Francis CRICK in 1953.

BIOFEEDBACK, electronically-produced signals indicating the occurrence of a specific kind of biological event, such as a rise in blood pressure, especially as used to help a person control otherwise unconscious physiological processes. Biofeedback techniques have been used with some success in the treatment of hypertension, chronic headaches, epilepsy and other disorders.

BIOGENESIS, theory that all living organisms are derived from other living organisms. It is the opposite of the theory of SPONTANEOUS GENERATION. (See also LIFE.)

BIOLOGICAL CLOCKS, the mechanisms which control the rhythm of various activities of plants and animals. Some activities, such as mating, migration and hibernation, have a yearly cycle; others, chiefly reproductive functions (including human menstruation), follow the lunar month. The majority, however, have a period of roughly 24 hours, called a **circadian rhythm**. As well as obvious rhythms such as the patterns of leaf movement in plants and the activity/sleep cycle in animals, many other features such as body temperature and cell growth oscillate daily. Although related to the day/night cycle, circadian rhythms are not directly controlled by it. Organisms in unvarying environments will continue to show 24-hr rhythms, but the pattern can be changed—the clock reset. Scientists in the Arctic, with 6 months of daylight, used watches which kept a 21-hr day, and gradually their body rhythms changed to a 21-hr period. The delay in adjustment is important in modern travel. After moving from one time zone to another, it takes some time for the body to adjust to the newly imposed cycle. Biological clocks are important in animal navigation. Many animals, such as migrating birds or bees returning to the hive, navigate using the sun. They can only do this if they have some means of knowing what time of day it is.

(See also MIGRATION.) Biological clocks are apparently inborn, not learned, but need to be triggered. An animal kept in the light from birth shows no circadian rhythms, but if placed in the dark for an hour or so immediately starts rhythms based on a 24-hr cycle. Once started, the cycles are almost independent of external changes, indicating that they cannot be based on a simple rhythm of chemical reactions, which would be affected by temperature. The biological clock may be somehow linked to external rhythms in geophysical forces, or may be an independent and slightly adjustable biochemical oscillator. In either case the mechanism is unknown. Not all biological rhythms are controlled by a "clock": in many cases they are determined simply by the time taken to complete a certain sequence of actions. For example, the heart rate depends on the time taken for the heart muscles to contract and relax. Unlike those controlled by biological clocks, such rhythms are easily influenced by drugs and temperature.

BIOLOGY, the study of living things, i.e. the science of plants and animals, including humans. Broadly speaking there are two main branches of biology, the study of ANIMALS (ZOOLOGY) and the study of PLANTS (BOTANY). Within each of these main branches are a number of traditional divisions dealing with structure (ANATOMY, CYTOLOGY), development and function (PHYSIOLOGY, EMBRYOLOGY), inheritance (GENETICS, EVOLUTION), classification (TAXONOMY) and interrelations of organisms with each other and with their environment (ECOLOGY). These branches are also split into a number of specialist fields (MYCOLOGY, ENTOMOLOGY.)

However, the traditional division into zoology and botany no longer applies since groups of biosciences have developed which span their limits, e.g. MICROBIOLOGY, BACTERIOLOGY, OCEANOGRAPHY, MARINE BIOLOGY. There are also biosciences that bridge the gap between the physical sciences of CHEMISTRY, PHYSICS and GEOLOGY, e.g. BIOCHEMISTRY, BIOPHYSICS and PALEONTOLOGY. Similarly there are those that relate to areas of human behavior, e.g. PSYCHOLOGY and SOCIOLOGY.

Disciplines such as MEDICINE, VETERINARY MEDICINE, AGRONOMY and HORTICULTURE also have a strong basis in biology.

To a large extent the history of biology is the history of its constituent sciences. Since the impetus to investigate the living world generally arose in a desire to improve the techniques of medicine or of agriculture, most early biologists were in the first instance physicians or landowners. An exception is provided by ARISTOTLE, the earliest systematist of biological knowledge and himself an outstanding biologist—he founded the science of comparative anatomy—but most other classical authors, as GALEN and the members of the Hippocratic school, were primarily physicians. In the medieval period much biological knowledge became entangled in legend and allegory. The classical texts continued to be the principal sources of knowledge, although new compilations, such as AVICENNA'S *Canon* of medicine, were produced by Muslim philosophers. In 16th-century Europe interest revived in descriptive natural history, the work of Konrad von Gesner (1516–65) being notable; physicians such as PARACELSUS began to develop a chemical pharmacology, and experimental anatomy revived in the work of VESALIUS and others. The discoveries of SERVETUS, HARVEY and MALPIGHI followed. Quantitative plant physiology began with the work of van HELMONT and was taken to spectacular ends in the work of HALES. In the 17th century, microscopic investigations began with the work of HOOKE and van LEEUWENHOEK; GREW advanced the study of plant organs and RAY laid the foundation for LINNAEUS' classic 18th-century formulation of the classification of plants. This same era saw BUFFON devise a systematic classification of animals and von HALLER lay the groundwork for the modern study of physiology.

The 17th century had seen controversies over the role of mechanism in biological explanation—LA METTRIE had even developed the theories of DESCARTES to embrace the mind of man; the 19th century saw similar disputes, now couched in the form of the mechanist-vitalist controversy concerning the possible chemical nature of life (see Claude BERNARD). Development biology, foreshadowed by LAMARCK, was thoroughly established following the work of DARWIN; in anatomy, SCHWANN and others developed the cell concept; in histology BICHAT's pioneering work was continued; in physiology, organic and even physical chemists began to play a greater role, and medical theory was revolutionized by the advent of bacteriology (see PASTEUR; KOCH). The impact of MENDEL's discoveries in genetics was not felt until the early 1900s. Possibly the high point of 20th-century biology came with the proposal of the double-helix model for DNA (see NUCLEIC ACIDS), the chemical carrier of genetic information, by CRICK and WATSON in 1953.

BIOLUMINESCENCE, the production of nonthermal light by living organisms such as fireflies, many marine animals, bacteria and fungi. The effect is an example of chemiluminescence. In some cases its utility to the organism is not apparent, though in others its use is clear. Thus, in the firefly, the ABDOMEN of the female glows, enabling the male to find her. Similarly, LUMINESCENCE enables many deep-sea fish to locate each other or to attract their prey. The glow in a ship's wake at night is due to luminescent microorganisms.

BIOPHYSICS, a branch of BIOLOGY in which the methods and principles of PHYSICS are applied to the study of living things. It has grown up in the 20th century alongside the development of ELECTRONICS. Its tools include the ELECTROENCEPHALOGRAPH and the ELECTRON MICROSCOPE, its techniques those of SPECTROSCOPY and X-ray diffraction and its problems the study of nerve transmission, BIOLUMINESCENCE and materials transfer in RESPIRATION and secretion.

BIORHYTHMS, cyclical patterns of biological activity. (See BIOLOGICAL CLOCKS.)

BIOSPHERE, the region inhabited by living things. It forms a thin layer around the earth, including the surface of the LITHOSPHERE, the HYDROSPHERE and the lower ATMOSPHERE. The importance of the concept was first pointed out by LAMARCK.

BIRD, type of animal adapted for flight and unique in its body covering of feathers. Birds are the largest group of VERTEBRATES, with over 8,500 extant species. They are descended from the group of prehistoric reptiles which took to living in trees. Their most striking anatomical features are those associated with flight. The forelimbs are modified as wings and are associated with enormous breast muscles which make powered flight possible. Even in flightless birds such as the PENGUIN and OSTRICH it is clear that the forelimbs were once used as wings. The rest of the skeleton is constructed of thin, light bones. A further weight reduction resulted from the replacement of the teeth by a horny beak or bill early in the evolutionary history of birds. Feathers, developed from scales (still present on the legs), streamline the body, and provide flight surfaces.

Flightless birds are mainly adapted for running or swimming. Runners such as the ostrich have strong legs; swimmers may have their wings modified as flippers as in the penguin. Birds have been able to adapt to diverse ways of life, ranging from that of the emperor penguin of the Antarctic to Egyptian plovers of equatorial desert regions, because, being warm-blooded, they can function independently of the surrounding temperature. Different groups of birds have evolved a variety of shapes and sizes of bill to take advantage of different food sources. The majority of birds are active by day. Owls, the prominent nocturnal group, have highly developed night vision estimated to be up to 100 times more sensitive than that of man. All birds lay eggs, sometimes in quite elaborate nests. Incubation is by one or both parents, dependent on species.

BIRDSEYE, Clarence (1886–1956), US inventor and industrialist who, having observed during furtrading expeditions to Labrador (1912–16) that many foods keep indefinitely if frozen, developed a process for the rapid commercial freezing of foodstuffs. In 1924 he organized the company later known as General Foods to market frozen produce.

BIRDSONG, the pattern of notes, often musical and complex, with which birds attract a mate and proclaim their territory. Ornithologists call all such sounds songs, though those that are harsh and unmusical are often referred to simply as the "voice."

BIRKBECK, George (1776–1841), English educator, founder of "mechanics' institutions" in Glasgow and London to teach scientific and technical subjects to working people. He was a founder of University College of the University of London.

BIRNEY, James Gillespie (1792–1857), leading US abolitionist. Birney, who came from an old slave-owning family, freed his slaves in 1834. He launched the abolitionist newspaper the *Philanthropist* in 1836, became executive secretary of the American Anti-Slavery Society in 1837 and founded the LIBERTY PARTY, standing as its presidential candidate in 1840 and 1844.

BIRTH, emergence from the mother's WOMB, or, in the case of most lower animals, from the EGG, marking the beginning of an independent life. The birth process is triggered by HORMONE changes in the mother's bloodstream. Birth may be induced, if required, by oxytocin. Mild labor pains (contractions of the womb) are the first sign that a woman is about to give birth. Initially occurring about every 20 minutes, in a few hours they become stronger and occur every few minutes. This is the first stage of labor, usually lasting about 14 hours. The contractions push the baby downward, usually head first, which breaks the membranes surrounding the baby, and the amniotic fluid escapes.

In the second stage of labor, stronger contractions push the baby through the cervix and vagina. This is the most painful part and lasts less than 2 hours. Anesthetics (see ANESTHESIA) or ANALGESICS are usually given, and delivery aided by hand or obstetric forceps. A CESARIAN SECTION may be performed if great difficulty occurs. Some women choose "natural childbirth," in which no anesthetic is used, but pain is minimized by prior relaxation exercises.

As soon as the baby is born, its nose and mouth are cleared of fluid and breathing starts, whereupon the UMBILICAL CORD is cut and tied. In the third stage of labor the placenta is expelled from the womb and bleeding is stopped by further contractions. Birth normally occurs 38 weeks after conception. Premature births are those occurring after less than 35 weeks. Most premature babies develop normally with medical care, but if born before 28 weeks the chances of survival are poor. (See also EMBRYO; OBSTETRICS; PREGNANCY.)

BIRTH CONTROL, prevention of unwanted births, by means of CONTRACEPTION, ABORTION, STERILIZATION, and formerly infanticide. Many believe abortion to be medically advisable if the child is likely to be defective. By limiting the size of families, birth control can help prevent poverty, while globally it could help prevent mass starvation.

Certain forms of birth control have been used from ancient times, but modern methods have been available only since the late 19th century. Arising out of the early women's rights movement, the first birth control clinics were opened in 1916 in the US by Margaret SANGER, and in 1921 in Britain by Marie STOPES. The need for worldwide birth control intensified from the 1920s onwards as the world population "exploded," with modern medicine cutting the death rate while the birth rate stayed high. In 1952 international groups formed the International Planned Parenthood Federation. In the 1960s the UN urged the universal adoption of voluntary birth control. Organizations promoting ZERO POPULATION GROWTH have become active. Birth rates have fallen in many developed countries and in some developing countries such as India and China, whose governments have instituted public birth-control practices. The chief hindrances are apathy, ignorance and social pressure for large families. Ethical and religious objections to artificial forms of birth control derive from the view that procreation is the primary purpose of marriage and of coitus, and (in the case of abortion) from the sanctity of life. The most influential proponent of this view is the Roman Catholic Church.

BIRTHMARKS, skin blemishes, usually congenital. There are two main types: pigmented nevuses, or moles, which are usually brown or black and may be raised or flat; and vascular nevuses, local growths of small blood vessels, such as the "strawberry mark" and the "port-wine stain." Although harmless, they are sometimes removed for cosmetic reasons or if they show malignant tendencies. (See also TUMOR.)

BISCAY, Bay of, arm of the Atlantic Ocean between Brittany in NW France and Spain. The French ports of Brest, Saint-Nazaire, La Rochelle, and Bayonne, and the Spanish ports of San Sebastian, Bilboa, and Santander, adjoin the bay.

BISHOP, Elizabeth (1911–1979), US poet and translator of Brazilian poetry, widely acclaimed for her succinct and lyrical style. Her books include the Pulitzer prizewinning *North & South–A Cold Spring* (1955), *Questions of Travel* (1965) and *Geography III* (1977).

BISHOP, highest order in the ministry of the Roman Catholic, Anglican, Eastern and some Lutheran Churches. As head of his diocese, a bishop administers its affairs, supervises its clergy and administers CONFIRMATION and ORDINATION. Roman Catholic bishops are appointed by the pope, Anglican bishops by the sovereign. In the US, Protestant Episcopal bishops are elected by both clergy and laity. (See also APOSTOLIC SUCCESSION; ARCHBISHOP; MINISTRY.)

BISMARCK, Prince Otto von (1815–1898), the "Iron Chancellor," who was largely responsible for creating a unified Germany. Born of Prussian gentry, he entered politics in 1847. From the first he was intent on increasing German power. He served as ambassador to Russia and France, then as chancellor (prime minister). He defeated Austria in the AUSTRO-PRUSSIAN WAR and annexed or coerced neighboring states into the North German Federation. Following his defeat of Napoleon III in the FRANCO-PRUSSIAN WAR, the German Empire was created and Bismarck made imperial chancellor and prince in 1871. He was forced to resign in 1890 after the accession of Kaiser William II.

BISMARCK SEA, between New Guinea's NE coast and the Bismarck archipelago in the SW Pacific. It is about 500mi from E to W. Allied aircraft destroyed a Japanese convoy here in 1943.

BISMUTH (Bi), metal in Group VA of the PERIODIC TABLE, brittle and silvery-gray with a red tinge. It occurs naturally as the metal, and as the sulfide and oxide from which it is obtained by roasting and reduction with carbon. In the US it is obtained as a byproduct of the refining of copper and lead ores. Bismuth is rather unreactive; it forms trivalent and some pentavalent compounds. Physically and chemically it is similar to LEAD and antimony. Bismuth is used in low-melting-point alloys in fire-detection safety devices. Since bismuth expands on solidification, it is used in alloys for casting dies and type metal. Bismuth (III) oxide is used in GLASS and CERAMICS; various bismuth salts are used in medicine. AW 209.0, mp 271°C, bp 1560°C, sg 9.747 (20°C).

BISON, ox-like animals, of the family Bovidae, which may weigh half a ton and stand 1.8m (6ft) tall. Their forequarters are covered by a shaggy mane. The American bison, often miscalled the buffalo, once grazed the plains and valleys from Mexico to W Canada in herds of millions and was economically vital to the Plains Indians. Hunted ruthlessly by the white man, it was almost extinct by 1900. There are still a few herds in US and Canadian national parks.

BITHYNIA, ancient country of NW Asia Minor, part of the Persian Empire until the destruction of that empire by Alexander the Great. In the quarrels among Alexander's successors, Bithynia established its independence. The last king of Bithynia, a client of Rome, willed (74 BC) the country to Rome, precipitating the last war between Rome and MITHRADATES VI of Pontus.

BIVALVE, name for some 7,000 species of shellfish, including the OYSTER, CLAM and mussel, that have two shells (valves) joined together by a muscular hinge. Most live in the sea, though there are some freshwater species. They range in size from the giant clam (almost 1.2m (4ft) long) to the turton clam (only 1mm (0.01in) long). The valves, open except when the animal is disturbed, contain the fleshy body. This consists of a foot, by which the animal moves, and the viscera. There is no head, only a mouth towards which food is directed by moving hairs known as cilia. Most bivalves feed on PLANKTON, though the "boring" bivalve feeds on wood. Bivalves are prey to whelks, birds, fish and aquatic mammals. They are also commercially important. (See also MOLLUSK.)

BIZET, Georges (1838–1875), French composer. The works for which he is now famous—the piano suite *Jeux d'Enfants* (1871), the incidental music for DAUDET'S *L'Arlésienne* (1872), the *Symphony in C* and the operas *Les Pêcheurs de Perles* (1863) and *Carmen* (1875)—were mostly ignored or vilified when first performed. The failure of *Carmen*, now one of the most popular of all operas, affected Bizet's health and may have contributed to his death.

BJERKNES, Vilhelm (1862–1951), Norwegian meteorologist, a pioneer in predicting weather by applying hydrodynamic and thermodynamic theories to atmospheric conditions. He taught at Oslo, Leipzig, and Bergen universities.

BJÖRLING, Jussi (1911–1960), internationally famous Swedish operatic tenor. He specialized in Italian opera, especially works by VERDI and PUCCINI.

BJØRNSON, Bjørnstjerne Martinius (1832–1910), major Norwegian poet, critic, novelist, dramatist and politician; winner of the Nobel Prize for Literature (1903). Concerned at first with Norwegian history, he later wrote about modern social problems.

BLACK, Hugo Lafayette (1886–1971), US politician and jurist, Supreme Court associate justice 1937–71, senator from Ala. 1927–37. He backed NEW DEAL legislation and, although an ex-Ku Klux Klan member, was a noted campaigner for civil rights.

BLACK, Joseph (1728–1799), Scottish physician and chemist who investigated the properties of CARBON dioxide, discovered the phenomena of latent and specific heats, distinguished HEAT from TEMPERATURE and pioneered the techniques used in the quantitative study of CHEMISTRY.

BLACK AND TANS, name for recruits to the Royal Irish constabulary and also to the "Auxis" or Auxiliary Division, made up of demobilized British officers, introduced into Ireland in 1920 to maintain order during the struggle for Home Rule. They wore black berets and khaki or tan uniforms. Their repressive measures earned "the Tans" lasting hatred in Ireland and did much to discredit British rule there.

BLACKBEARD (d. 1718), nickname of Edward Teach, an English pirate proverbial for his extreme savagery. A privateer in the War of the Spanish Succession, he turned to piracy in the West Indies and along the Atlantic coast. Blackbeard was killed when his ship was taken by a British force.

BLACKBIRD, name for several dark-colored birds, including the red-winged blackbird, yellow-headed blackbird and the grackle. Their song is loud and monotonous; they eat fruit, insects and worms. The European blackbird is a member of the THRUSH family Turdidae; the New World blackbird a member of the oriole family Icteridae.

BLACKBODY, in theoretical physics, an object which absorbs all the ELECTROMAGNETIC RADIATION falling on it. In practice, no object acts as a perfect blackbody, though a closed box admitting radiation only through a small hole is a good approximation. Blackbodies are also ideal thermal radiators.

BLACK CODES, laws enacted by the Southern states after the Civil War. Allegedly intended to facilitate the transition from slavery to freedom, they were in fact a veiled device to deny real equality to newly-freed blacks. In 1866 the Civil Rights Act provided full rights to Negroes and further amendments were made during the next four years. However, some codes persisted into the 20th century.

BLACK DEATH, name for an epidemic of bubonic PLAGUE which swept through Asia and Europe in the mid-14th century, annihilating whole communities and perhaps halving the population of Europe. Originating in China, it was carried by flea-infested rats on vessels trading to the West. Its economic effects were far-reaching. It also fanned the flames of superstition and religious prejudice. European Jews, accused of poisoning wells, were massacred, and the idea that the plague was punishment for sin led to a wave of fanatical penance.

BLACKFOOT INDIANS, tribes of the Algonquian linguistic family, chiefly the Siksika, Piegan and Blood. Originally hunters and trappers, they adopted firearms and kept vast herds of horses, giving them power in Mont., Alberta and Saskatchewan. The disappearance of the bison, a smallpox epidemic and "incidents" with the white man led to a great reduction in their numbers. There are now under 8,000 Blackfoot on reservations in Mont. and Alberta.

BLACK FOREST, wooded mountain range in the province of Baden-Württemberg, SW West Germany An area of great scenic beauty, it is an important tourist attraction, with lumbering, clock and toy industries.

BLACK FRIDAY, term referring to disasters, particularly financial, occurring on Fridays. The most famous American Black Friday was Sept. 24, 1869, when the speculators Jay GOULD and James FISK tried to corner the gold market with the connivance of government officials. Government gold sales were stopped and prices rose rapidly until the plot was discovered and sales resumed. The market collapsed, and many were ruined.

BLACK HAWK WAR, revolt by Sauk and Fox Indians (1832), following their removal in 1831 from fertile lands owned by the Indians in the Illinois country. Refusing to recognize government claims to the lands, a group of Sauk and Fox Indians, led by Black Hawk, returned to plant corn the following spring but were once more driven out, pursued, and finally almost completely annihilated at the Massacre of Bad Axe River.

BLACK HILLS, mountain range in S.D. and Wyo., famous for the Mt Rushmore Memorial. Here, the heads of four past US presidents are carved out of the mountainside. The Black Hills are rich in minerals, including gold. Highest point is Harney Peak (7,242ft).

BLACK HOLE, according to current physical theory, the final stage of evolution for very massive stars following total gravitational collapse. At the center of a black hole are the densely packed remains of the star, perhaps only a few km across; the condition of matter under such circumstances is not yet understood. The gravitational field of a black hole is so intense that nothing, not even ELECTROMAGNETIC RADIATION (including light), can escape. Black holes, if they exist, can be detected through their gravitational effects on other bodies and through the emission of X- and gamma rays by matter falling into them. Also, according to QUANTUM MECHANICS small black holes would produce pairs (particle and antiparticle) of SUBATOMIC PARTICLES in their immediate vicinity; one of each pair would escape, and the black hole would thus in effect radiate matter. It has been suggested that the end of the universe will be its becoming a single black hole. Astronomers have identified a number of possible black holes, but none as yet has been fully confirmed.

BLACK HOLE OF CALCUTTA, prison cell where 146 British captives were incarcerated on the night of June 20, 1756, during which all but 23 were suffocated. They were held by the Nawab of Bengal, who opposed the monopoly of the EAST INDIA COMPANY.

BLACK LUNG DISEASE, a lay term for PNEUMOCONIOSIS, which affects coal miners.

BLACK MONDAY, financial panic on Oct. 19, 1987, when the DOW JONES INDUSTRIAL AVERAGE plunged a record 508 points and a record 604.3 million shares changed hands on the NEW YORK STOCK EXCHANGE. The decline in market value of 22.6% was the worst since WWI, far greater than the 12.82% drop on Oct. 28, 1929. Unlike the 1929 crash, the 1987 crash did not lead to a depression. A year later, the market had regained half its losses.

BLACKMORE, Richard Doddridge (1825–1900), English author of 14 novels, notably *Lorna Doone* (1869), a romance set in the English west country during the 17th century.

BLACKMUN, Harry (1908–), US jurist, associate jusstice on the US Supreme Court from 1970. He wrote the controversial decision in *Roe v. Wade* (1973) legalizing abortions.

BLACKMUR, Richard Palmer (1904–1965), US critic, editor and poet. His criticism, for which he is best known, is closely analytical. Among his books are *The Expense of Greatness* (1940) and *Language as Gesture* (1952). He taught at Princeton U. (1940–43; 1946–65).

BLACK MUSLIMS, the chief US black nationalist movement, founded in 1930 by Wali Farad. He rejected racial integration, taught thrift, hard work and cleanliness, and foretold an Armageddon where Black would crush White. Under Elijah MUHAMMAD, the Muslims proclaimed black supremacy and demanded a nation within the US. Elijah Muhammad's son and successor, Wallace Deen Muhammad (1934–), abandoned his father's racist views and brought his followers into line with true Islamic principles under the name American Muslim Mission. An offshoot of the original movement is the Lost-Found Nation of Islam, led by Louis J. Farrakhan (1934–), who adheres to the old views of black supremacy and separatism.

BLACKOUTS, incidents of widespread loss of electric power. In the most famous blackout, on Nov. 9, 1965, the power failure extended from Canada down the East Coast of the US into N.J. and Penn. A large part of France was struck by a blackout on Dec. 19, 1978. Blackouts are usually the result of a failure of one component of a power-supply network, or grid, which causes a "chain reaction" that spreads through the complex system.

BLACK PANTHER PARTY, US black revolutionary party, founded in 1966, advocating "armed self-defense" by black people. Though small in numbers, it enjoyed considerable influence until weakened by disputes in the early 1970s. Under the leadership of Eldridge Cleaver and Huey P. Newton, the party opened community centers and bookshops and fought legal battles with the authorities, frequently securing the release of members held on violence charges.

BLACKS, American, descendants of slaves brought from Africa to North America from the 16th to the 19th centuries. They belong to the Negroid race, although about one third of Afro-Americans possess some Caucasoid genes. In 1980 there were about

26.5 million blacks in the US, roughly the same number in South America and about 32,000 in Canada.

History. During the nearly 400 years of the slave trade, some 10–15 million slaves were brought to the Americas. The slaves were first brought over by the Spanish and Portuguese and then by the American colonists. The slave trade reached its height in the 18th century. After the Revolutionary War, however, it seemed for a time that slavery was dying out, with at least six states passing anti-slavery laws. This was all changed by Eli WHITNEY'S invention of the cotton gin in 1793, for this made cotton a viable cash crop. The admission into the Union of the state of Louisiana (1812), quickly followed by Mississippi (1817) and Alabama (1819), opened up new lands for cotton and sugarcane. Although Congress prohibited the further importation of slaves (1808), the slave trade continued to flourish illegally, and by 1860 about half the population of the South were slaves. When the Civil War broke out there were nearly 4 million slaves in the US, plus about half a million freed slaves. However, the freed slaves never had a place in American society, and attempts were made to repatriate them to LIBERIA, on the W coast of Africa. The slavery issue was one of the main causes of the Civil War. While the slave-based cotton industry of the South had been booming, the North had been rejecting slavery. Of note are the founding of the American Anti-Slavery Society in 1833 (see ABOLITIONISM), and the publication in 1852 of Harriet Beecher STOWE'S *Uncle Tom's Cabin*. The Civil War saw an end to slavery in the US, but it did little to improve the position of the freed black in American society. With the withdrawal of federal troops in 1877, the black in the South was soon reduced to a condition little better than slavery—it must be remembered that until the early 20th century, 90% of US blacks lived in the South. Some black leaders (e.g., Booker T. WASHINGTON) were willing to accept the position of the black as a second-class citizen, but others, including W. E. B. DU BOIS, a co-founder of the NATIONAL ASSOCIATION FOR THE ADVANCEMENT OF COLORED PEOPLE (1909), believed in fighting for black equality. Basic socioeconomic change was to prove the precursor to social and political change.

In the first half of the 20th century, some 5 million blacks left the South for the overcrowded cities of the North. There they could begin to have some political effect, and some individual blacks were able to distinguish themselves professionally. However, it was not until the historic Supreme Court decision of May 17, 1954, ordering the integration of all schools, that the position of the Negro in American society began to change fundamentally. Under the leadership of Martin Luther KING, the civil rights movement spread all over the South, leading eventually to the Voting Rights Act of 1960, and the Civil Rights Act of 1964 and 1968. In northern cities, however, unemployment and poverty loomed as the most pressing problems for blacks, and between 1965 and 1967 many of the "black ghettos" exploded into violence. The late 1960s saw the emergence of the Black Power movement, with groups like the BLACK MUSLIMS and the BLACK PANTHERS. These groups rejected civil rights activity and wished to organize blacks into separate social and economic communities within a white America. By the mid-1970s the more violent aspects of Black Power had dissipated themselves. American blacks nevertheless asserted their own social and cultural identity. An indication of this was the rejection of the old term "Negro" in favor of "black" or "Afro-American." In the 1980s black progress continued to be promoted by AFFIRMATIVE ACTION but otherwise slowed as a result of budget cuts in many of the 1960s' social and economic programs. As the growing black middle class moved out of the ghettos, the black underclass was engulfed in a destructive CRACK epidemic.

BLACK SEA, tideless inland sea between Europe and Asia, bordered by Turkey, Bulgaria, Romania and the USSR, and linked to the Sea of Azov and (via the Bosporus) to the Mediterranean. It covers 180,000sq mi and is up to 7,250ft deep. The Danube, Dniester, Bug, Don and Dnieper rivers all flow into the sea, which is vital to Soviet shipping. The chief ports are Odessa, Sevastopol, Batumi, Constanta and Varna. Russia's Black Sea coast is an important resort area.

BLACK SEPTEMBER, terrorist group affiliated with Al Fatah, the Palestinian guerrilla organization. Created in 1971, Black September was named for the crackdown in 1970 by Jordan's King Hussein on Arab terrorist groups operating out of Jordan. Black September, using Lebanon as its base, claimed responsibility for, or was implicated in, many assassinations, airline hijackings and other violent acts. Members of the group killed 11 Israeli athletes at the 1972 Olympic Games in Munich.

BLACK SHIRTS, popular name for the street fighters organized by Italian Fascist leader Benito Mussolini in 1919 to attack opponents of his movement. Their march on Rome in Oct. 1922 brought Mussolini to power. A black shirt was the distinctive element of the Fascist uniform.

BLACK SOX SCANDAL, ironic term for the scandal which shook the world of baseball 1919–20 and led to radical reorganization in the administration of the sport. It involved members of the Chicago White Sox and broke out when Edward Cicotte confessed to accepting a bribe to influence the outcome of the 1919 World Series. He named seven other players allegedly involved. All eight were suspended for a season but were cleared of fraud.

BLACKSTONE, Sir William (1723–1780), English jurist whose *Commentaries on the Laws of England* (1765–69) deeply influenced jurisprudence and the growth of COMMON LAW. He was the first professor of English Law at Oxford 1758–63, became a member of parliament 1761 and was a judge in the Court of Common Pleas 1770–80.

BLACKWELL, Elizabeth (1821–1910), English-born first woman doctor of medicine. Rebuffed at first by the authorities and later ostracized by her fellow students, she went on to gain her degree, with the highest grades for her year, at Geneva, N.Y., in 1849. After study in Europe, she returned to the US in 1857 and opened a hospital run by women (later also a medical school for women) in New York City.

BLACK WIDOW, *Latroclectas matans,* a common US name for a SPIDER whose bite is dangerous to man. The female has a rounded shiny abdomen and a scarlet hourglass-shaped mark on the underside; the male is smaller and harmless.

BLADDER, a hollow muscular sac; especially the urinary bladder (see also GALL BLADDER), found in most vertebrates except birds. In humans it lies in the front of the PELVIS. URINE trickles continually into the bladder from the KIDNEYS through two tubes called ureters, and the bladder stretches until it contains about 500ml, causing desire to urinate. The bladder empties through the urethra, a tube which issues from its base, being normally closed by the external sphincter muscle. The female urethra is about 30mm long: the male urethra, which runs through the PROSTATE GLAND and the penis, is about 200mm long. The bladder is liable to CYSTITIS and to the formation of calculi.

BLADENSBURG, Battle of, fought during the War of 1812 at Bladensburg, a town in S central Md., 7mi ENE of Washington. On

Aug. 21, 1814, outnumbered British troops defeated American forces and went on to sack and burn many public buildings in Washington.

BLAINE, James Gillespie (1830–1893), US statesman and post-Civil War Republican leader. His career was marked by an intense rivalry with fellow Republican Roscoe Conkling and also by allegations of corruption. Blaine served as congressman 1863–76 (speaker 1869–75) and US senator 1876–81; he was secretary of state 1881, 1889–92, and presidential candidate 1884. He backed RECONSTRUCTION and protective tariffs but fostered PAN AMERICANISM as an extension of the MONROE DOCTRINE.

BLAIR, US family influential in 19th-century politics. **Francis Preston Blair** (1791–1876), politician and journalist, a member of Andrew Jackson's "kitchen cabinet," played an important part in forming the new Republican party and also in organizing the unsuccessful Hampton Roads peace conference. He lived at the famous Blair House. His eldest son, **Montgomery Blair** (1813–1883), an eminent lawyer, defended Scott in the DRED SCOTT CASE, and served as postmaster general under Lincoln 1861–64. After the Civil War he backed Andrew Johnson's moderate policies and became a Democrat. His brother, **Francis Preston Blair, Jr.** (1821–1875), was a soldier and an ardent abolitionist. As a Republican congressman he helped keep Mo. in the Union during the Civil War. He was Democratic vice-presidential candidate in 1868.

BLAIR, Henry, 19th-century US slave and inventor who became the first black to hold a patent when he obtained patents for a corn harvester (1835) and a cotton planter (1836). In 1858, however, it was ruled that slaves could not hold federal patents; this situation prevailed until after the Civil War.

BLAIR, James (1656–1743), English clergyman, sent to colonial Virginia in 1685 to reform the Anglican church there. He founded the College of William and Mary and served as its first president.

BLAIR HOUSE, official guest house of the US government, on Pennsylvania Ave. in Washington, D.C. It was used as a temporary White House by President Truman 1948–52. The house, built in 1824, was named for its second owner, Francis Preston BLAIR, whose family sold it to the government in 1942.

BLAKE, Eubie (1883–1983), US ragtime pianist and composer best known for his Broadway musical *Shuffle Along* (1921) and his songs "I'm Just Wild About Harry" and "Memories of You." Associated with the RAGTIME revival of the 1970s, he was still performing publicly in his 90s.

BLAKE, Robert (1599–1657), English admiral who fought for the parliamentarians in the English Civil War. He made an important contribution to the organization of the Commonwealth navy, which he was to command decisively against the Dutch in 1652–53, ending for the time being their naval supremacy.

BLAKE, William (1757–1827), English poet, painter and prophet. He was apprenticed to an engraver 1772–79 and developed his own technique of engraving plates with both text and illustrations which were then colored by hand. In this manner he reproduced his *Songs of Innocence* (1789) and *Songs of Experience* (1794), collections of lyrics that contrast natural beauty and energy with the ugliness of man's material world. Blake was a revolutionary in both politics and religion and this is reflected in his art, particularly in the powerful though often opaque "Prophetic Books" which form the bulk of his work. Among perhaps the most impressive of these are *The Marriage of Heaven and Hell* (1793) and the epic *Jerusalem* (begun c1804). Blake's work was little understood by his contemporaries.

BLAKELOCK, Ralph Albert (1847–1919), US painter of western landscapes. He gave up medicine for painting, but failed to achieve commercial success and lived in conditions of great hardship. He was institutionalized 1899–1916.

BLANC, (Jean Joseph Charles) Louis (1811–1882), French politician whose egalitarian ideas influenced modern socialism. He was a member of the provisional government in the 1848 Revolution, after which he was driven into exile in England. On his return to France (1871) he reentered politics but followed a less radical line.

BLANC, Mont, highest peak (15,771ft) in the European Alps, in SE France on the border with Italy. One of the world's longest vehicular tunnels (7.5mi), exceeded in Europe only by the 10.2mi St. Gotthard (1980), was constructed through Mont Blanc's base in 1965.

BLANCHARD, Jean Pierre François, (1753–1809), French balloonist and inventor who made the first aeronautical crossing of the English Channel (1785) and the first BALLOON ascent in America (1793). He also invented the PARACHUTE (1785).

BLANK VERSE, unrhymed verse in iambic lines of five stresses. It is basically 10-syllabled but not rigidly so. The form originated in Italy. It was introduced into England by the Earl of SURREY, used to great effect by MARLOWE and by SHAKESPEARE, whose innovations made it a vehicle for natural speech rhythms. MILTON's *Paradise Lost* is written in highly distinctive and flexible blank verse.

BLANQUI, (Louis) Auguste (1805–1881), French revolutionary thinker and activist, an advocate of class struggle as a means to achieving COMMUNISM. He was involved in the revolutions of 1830, 1848 and 1870, and spent some 40 years in prison or exile. The Blanquist party became part of the French Socialist party in 1905.

BLASCO IBAÑEZ, Vincente (1867–1928), Spanish novelist and novelist. He is best known for *Blood and Sand* (1909) and *The Four Horsemen of the Apocalypse* (1916), but his true literary worth is to be found in his earlier naturalistic novels, such as *The Cabin* (1899) and *Reeds and Mud* (1902).

BLAST FURNACE, furnace in which a blast of hot, high-pressure air is used to force combustion; used mainly to reduce IRON ore to pig iron, and also for lead, tin and copper. It consists of a vertical, cylindrical stack surmounting the bosh (the combustion zone) and the hearth from which the molten iron and slag are tapped off. Modern blast furnaces are about 100ft high and 30ft in diameter, and can produce more than 1,800 tons per day. Layers of iron oxide ore, COKE and LIMESTONE are loaded alternately into the top of the stack. The burning coke heats the mass and produces CARBON monoxide, which reduces the ore to iron; the limestone decomposes and combines with ash and impurities to form a slag, which floats on the molten iron. The hot gases from the top of the stack are burned to preheat the air blast.

BLAUE REITER (Blue Rider), group of Expressionist painters formed by KANDINSKY and MARC in Germany 1911–14. They issued an almanac, *Der Blaue Reiter*, containing the artists' essays and pictures, and essays by SCHOENBERG, BERG and WEBERN. KLEE and ARP were invited to show at the exhibitions they organized in Germany. (See EXPRESSIONISM.)

BLAVATSKY, Helena Petrovna (1831–1891), Russian occultist, founder of the Theosophical Society (1875). She expounded her theory of human and religious evolution in *Isis Unveiled* (1877). (See also THEOSOPHY.)

BLEGEN, Carl William (1887–1971), US archaeologist, at the U of Cincinnati 1927–57. His excavations at TROY and PYLOS confirmed Homer's descriptions.

BLENHEIM, Battle of, battle in the War of the SPANISH SUCCESSION. On Aug. 13, 1704, an English army under the Duke of Marlborough, with Austrian troops under Eugene of Savoy, defeated a superior French–Bavarian force near Blenheim, Bavaria. The battle ended Louis XIV's hopes of mastering Europe.

BLÉRIOT, Louis (1872–1936), French pioneer aviator and airplane manufacturer. In 1909 he became the first person to fly a heavier-than-air machine across the English Channel.

BLEULER, Eugen (1857–1939), Swiss psychiatrist who introduced the term SCHIZOPHRENIA (1908) as a generic term for a group of mental illnesses which he had learned to differentiate in a classic research project. He was an early supporter of FREUD but later criticized his dogmatism.

BLIGH, William (1754–1817), English admiral, captain of HMS *Bounty* at the time of the famous mutiny (1789). Master of the *Resolution* on COOK's last voyage to the Pacific, he later fought at Camperdown and Copenhagen. In 1805 he became governor of New South Wales, where his overbearing behavior caused another revolt. (See BOUNTY MUTINY.)

BLINDNESS, severe loss or absence of VISION, caused by injury to the EYES, congenital defects, or diseases including CATARACT, DIABETES, GLAUCOMA, LEPROSY, TRACHOMA and VASCULAR disease. MALNUTRITION (especially VITAMIN A deficiency) may cause blindness in children. Infant blindness can result if the mother had GERMAN MEASLES early in PREGNANCY; it was also formerly caused by gonorrheal infection of eyes at birth, but routine use of silver nitrate reduced this risk. Transient blindness may occur if one is exposed to a vertical ACCELERATION of more than 5g. Cortical blindness is a disease of the higher perceptive centers in the BRAIN concerned with vision: the patient may even deny blindness despite severe disability. Blindness due to cataract may be relieved by removal of the eye lens and the use of GLASSES. Prevention or early recognition and treatment of predisposing conditions is essential to save sight, as established blindness is rarely recoverable.

Many special books (using BRAILLE), instruments, utensils and games have been designed for the blind. With the help of guide dogs or long canes, many blind persons can move about freely. They can detect obstacles around them by the change of pitch of high-frequency sound from the feet or a cane, a skill acquired by training, and by using other senses.

BLISS, Sir Arthur (1891–1975), English composer and Master of the Queen's Music. He is best known for his ballet *Checkmate* (1937), his *Colour Symphony* (1922), cinema scores such as *The Shape of Things to Come* (1935), and the less successful opera, *The Olympians* (1949).

BLISS, Tasker Howard (1853–1930), US soldier, army chief of staff during WWI. He served on the Allied Supreme War Council and was a delegate to the Paris Peace Conference.

BLITZKRIEG, a German word meaning "lightning war." Originally used to describe German tactics in WWII, it is now applied to any fast military advance, such as the 1944 sweep through France by the US 3rd Army under PATTON.

BLITZSTEIN, Marc (1905–1964), US composer and librettist. He wrote the texts and music for the operas *The Cradle Will Rock* (1937) and *Regina* (1949) and the American text for the 1954 production of *The Three-Penny Opera.*

BLIXEN, Karen. See DINESEN, ISAK.

BLOCH, Ernest (1880–1959), Swiss-American composer. He made great use of traditional Jewish music, particularly in his *Israel: Symphony* (1916) and *Sacred Service* (1930–33) and *Three Jewish Poems* (1913).

BLOCH, Marc (1886–1944), French medieval historian, a founder of the influential journal *Annales,* which has promoted economic and social history. A Jew, he joined the French Resistance in WWII and was executed by the Germans.

BLOCK, Adriaen (fl. 1610–24), Dutch navigator who discovered (1614) Long Island Sound, the Connecticut River, Block Island, and Narragansett Bay.

BLOCK, Herbert Lawrence (1909–   ), US political cartoonist. His dry and witty cartoons have been appearing under the signature Herblock in the *Washington Post* since 1943. He was awarded Pulitzer prizes in 1942, 1954, and 1979.

BLOK, Alexander Alexandrovich (1880–1921), Russian dramatist and poet. He rose to fame as a symbolist poet before the 1917 Revolution, which he used as the backdrop in his great long poem *The Twelve* (1918).

BLOOD, the body fluid pumped by the heart through the vessels of those animals (all vertebrates and many invertebrates) in which diffusion alone is not adequate for transport of materials, and which therefore require BLOOD CIRCULATION systems. Blood plays a part in every major bodily activity. As the body's main transport medium it carries a variety of materials: oxygen and nutrients (such as glucose) to the tissues for growth and repair (see METABOLISM); carbon dioxide and wastes from the tissues for excretion; HORMONES to various tissues and organs for chemical signaling; digested food from the gut to the LIVER; immune bodies for prevention of infection and clotting factors to help stop bleeding to all parts of the body. Blood also plays a major role in homeostasis, as it contains buffers which keep the acidity (pH) of the body fluids constant and, by carrying heat from one part of the body to another, it tends to equalize body temperature.

The adult human has about 6 quarts of blood, half PLASMA and half blood cells (erythrocytes, or red cells; leukocytes, or white cells; and thrombocytes, or platelets). The formation of blood cells (hemopoiesis) occurs in bone MARROW, lymphoid tissue and the reticuloendothelial system. Red cells (about 5 million per mm^3) are produced at a rate of over 100 million per minute and live only about 120 days. They have no nucleus, but contain a large amount of the red pigment HEMOGLOBIN, responsible for oxygen transfer from lungs to tissues and carbon dioxide transfer from tissues to lungs. (Some lower animals employ copper-based hemocyanins instead of hemoglobin. Others, e.g., cockroaches, have no respiratory pigments.) White cells (about 6,000 per mm^3) are concerned with defense against infection and poisons. There are three types of white cells: granulocytes (about 70%), which digest bacteria and greatly increase in number during acute infection; lymphocytes (20–25%), which participate in immune reactions (see IMMUNITY; ANTIBODIES); and monocytes (3–8%), which digest nonbacterial particles, usually during chronic infection. (See also HODGKIN'S DISEASE; LEUKEMIA.) Platelets, which live for about 8 days and which are much smaller than white cells and about 40 times as numerous, assist in the initial stages of blood CLOTTING together with at least 12 plasma clotting factors and fibrinogen. This occurs when blood vessels are damaged, causing THROMBOSIS, and when HEMORRHAGE occurs (see also HEMOPHILIA.)

Blood from different individuals may differ in the type of antigen on the surface of its red cells and the type of ANTIBODY in its plasma. Consequently, in a blood TRANSFUSION, if the blood groups of the donor and recipient are incompatible with respect to antigens and antibodies present, a dangerous reaction occurs, involving aggregation or clumping of the red cells of the donor in the recipient's circulation.

Many blood group systems have been discovered, the first and most important being the ABO system by Karl Landsteiner in 1900. In this system, blood is classified by whether the red cells have antigens A (blood group A), B (group B), A and B (group AB), or neither A nor B antigens (group O). Another important antigen is the Rhesus antigen (or Rh factor). People who have the Rh factor (84%) are designated Rh+, those who do not, Rh−. Rhesus antibodies do not occur naturally but may develop in unusual circumstances. In a few cases, where Rh− women are pregnant with Rh+ babies, blood leakage from baby to mother causes production of antibodies by the mother which may progressively destroy the blood of any subsequent baby. (See also EDEMA; SEPTICEMIA; SERUM).

BLOOD CIRCULATION, the movement of BLOOD from the HEART through the ARTERIES, CAPILLARIES and VEINS and back to the heart. The circulatory system has two distinct parts in animals with lungs: the pulmonary circulation, in which blood is pumped from the right ventricle to the left atrium via the blood vessels of the lungs (where the blood is oxygenated and carbon dioxide is eliminated); and the systemic circulation, in which the oxygenated blood is pumped from the left ventricle to the right atrium via the blood vessels of the body tissues (where—in the capillaries— the blood is deoxygenated and carbon dioxide is taken up). As it leaves the heart, the blood is under considerable pressure—about 120mmHg maximum (systolic pressure) and 80mmHg minimum (diastolic pressure). Sustained high blood pressure, or hypertension, occurs in kidney and hormone diseases and in old age, but generally its cause is unknown. It may lead to ARTERIOSCLEROSIS and heart, brain and kidney damage. Low blood pressure occurs in SHOCK, TRAUMA and ADDISON'S DISEASE.

BLOOD POISONING. See SEPTICEMIA.

BLOOMER, Amelia Jenks (1818–1894), US feminist reformer. A famous lecturer, she also edited *The Lily*, a journal which campaigned for temperance and women's rights. In a search for more practical clothes for women she unsuccessfully tried to introduce the baggy pantaloons which were derisively nicknamed "bloomers."

BLOOMFIELD, Leonard (1887–1949), US linguist whose *Language* (1933) inaugurated the modern science of linguistics. He taught at the University of Chicago (1927–40) and Yale (1940–49).

BLOOMSBURY GROUP, name applied to a coterie of writers and artists who met in Bloomsbury, London, in the early 20th century. Influenced by G. E. MOORE, they gathered about Virginia and Leonard woolf, and Virginia's sister, Vanessa Bell. The group included Clive bell, E. M. forster, Roger fry, Duncan grant, J. M. keynes and Lytton strachey.

BLOOR, Mother (Ella Reeve Bloor; 1862–1951), US radical activist. She participated in the temperance and women's suffrage movements and was a Socialist Party organizer (1902–19) before becoming a cofounder of the US Communist Party (1919). Called the "Matron Saint" of the party, she served on its national committee from 1932 to 1948.

BLOUNT, William (1749–1800), US political leader, a member of the Continental Congress and the Federal Constitutional Convention. Elected (1796) one of Tennessee's first US senators, he was expelled from the senate because of his involvement in a plot to help the British seize Spanish Florida.

BLOW, John (1649?–1708), English composer, organist, and choirmaster at Westminster Abbey. Henry purcell was a student.

BLOWFLY, also known as the bluebottle or greenbottle. It is a large fly of the family Calliphoridae, that lays eggs in carrion, excrement or open wounds. It attacks livestock and because of its breeding habits spreads dysentery and perhaps jaundice and anthrax.

BLOWGUN, weapon used by some Pacific and South American tribes. It consists of a long tube from which a small dart is blown; it may be accurate up to 40yd or more. The dart is most effective with a poison such as curare or the sap of the upas tree.

BLÜCHER, Gebhard Leberecht von (1742–1819), Prussian commander, a fierce opponent of Napoleon. After distinguished service at Jena (1806), he was made a field marshal for his part in the Battle of Leipzig (1813). He led Prussian troops into Paris a year later. In 1815 the timely intervention of the Prussian army under Blücher made conclusive victory at Waterloo possible.

BLÜCHER, Vasily Konstantinovich (1889–1938), Soviet general active in the Far East. He expelled (1922) the Japanese from Vladivostok and later served as a military adviser in China. Appointed to command Soviet forces in the Far East and promoted marshal, he nevertheless fell victim to Stalin's purge of military leaders. He was rehabilitated in 1956.

BLUE BABY, infant born with a heart defect (a hole between the right and left sides, or malformation of the arteries) that permits much of the blood to bypass the lungs. The resulting lack of oxygen causes the bluish skin discoloration known as cyanosis. These conditions used to be fatal but can now often be corrected by surgery.

BLUEBEARD, villain of a traditional tale in which a rich man, who has had several wives, marries a young girl. He forbids her to enter a particular room in his castle; she disobeys him, and finds there the bodies of former wives he has murdered. In some versions he threatens to kill her also, but she is saved by her brothers. Perrault based on a tale on the legend. Bartok's opera *Duke Bluebeard's Castle* (1911) is a more modern symbolic treatment of the story.

BLUEBIRD, songbird which visits the US as a summer bird of passage. A member of the family Turdidae, it often nests near human habitations. Its upper part is sky-blue in color and its breast is chestnut. Its song is mellow and sweet. The female lays four or five eggs.

BLUEBOTTLE. See blowfly.

BLUEFISH, warm-water food and game fish found in the Indian Ocean, the Mediterranean Sea, and the Atlantic Ocean. They average 30in in length and 10-12lb in weight.

BLUEGRASS, a traditional country-music instrumental style, streamlined by an intense hard-driving pace. The style was developed in the late 1930s by Bill Monroe and his Bluegrass Boys, and by the famous banjo player Earl Scruggs.

BLUEJAY. See jays.

BLUE NILE, a river in Sudan which joins the White Nile at Khartoum to form the nile. The Blue Nile has its headwaters in Ethiopia and is the source of Egypt's historically important seasonal floods.

BLUE RIDGE MOUNTAINS, a range lying E of the Appalachians and stretching through Md., W. Va., Va., N.C. and Ga. for 615mi. Shenandoah National Park is sited here and part of the Appalachian Trail follows the crest of the range.

BLUES, type of US Negro music, often sad and slow, characterized by the use of flattened "blue notes." It derived from the work songs, spirituals and "field hollers" of the Negroes of the South and became a principal basis of the jazz idiom. The characteristic pattern of the blues is a 12-bar structure with certain distinctive harmonies, but the form is flexible and has undergone many adaptations. At first a song, usually with guitar, harmonica or piano accompaniment, the blues have since also become an instrumental form, and their influence has pervaded many types of modern music. They were first popularized by W. C. handy's *Memphis Blues* and *St. Louis Blues.*

BLUE WHALES, the largest animal that has ever lived, as much as 100ft in length and 120 tons in weight. Slate blue in color, they migrate between polar and equatorial seas. Their population has been greatly reduced by whaling.

BLUM, Léon (1872–1950), creator of the modern French Socialist party, and the first socialist and the first Jew to become premier of France. As premier 1936–37 he led the Popular Front, a coalition of Socialists and Radicals opposed to fascism. He carried out major domestic reforms and was greatly concerned with defense against the Rome-Berlin axis.

BLUMENBACH, Johann Friedrich (1752–1840), German physiologist generally regarded as the father of physical ANTHROPOLOGY. As a result of careful measurement of a large collection of skulls, he divided mankind into five racial groups: Caucasian, Mongolian, Malayan, Ethiopian and American.

BLUNT, Sir Anthony (1907–1983), English art historian and Soviet spy. A brilliant scholar, he became curator of the royal art collection (1945–72) and director of the Courtland Institute of Art (1947–74). He was knighted in 1956. In 1979 it was revealed that he had been a Soviet spy from his student days at Cambridge and during service in British intelligence in WWII. His knighthood was annulled and he retired.

BLUNTSCHLI, Johann Kaspar (1808–1881), Swiss political scientist, expounder of the organic theory of the state, according to which the state passes through the same developmental stages as a human.

BLY, Nellie, pen name of Elizabeth Cochrane (1867–1922), US woman reporter. Her most famous exploit was her successful attempt in 1889 to beat the record of Jules Verne's Phileas Fogg (*Around the World in Eighty Days*): it took her 72 days, 6 hours, 11 minutes and 14 seconds.

BOADICEA (d. 61 AD), British queen who led a revolt against the Roman occupiers of Britain. After successes at Colchester, London, and St. Albans, her army was defeated and she took poison.

BOAR, the wild pig, *Sus scrofa*, smaller than the domestic pig, dark gray or brown in color with large upward-pointing tusks. It inhabits many parts of Europe, N Africa and Asia. Its favorite habitat is marshy ground and deciduous woods, where it feeds on roots and grain and sometimes small animals. Boars have long been hunted for sport. The male domestic pig is also called a boar.

BOAS, Franz (1858–1942), German-born US anthropologist who played a leading part in the establishment of the cultural-relativist school of ANTHROPOLOGY in the English-speaking world. The first professor of anthropology at Columbia U. (1899–1936), he wrote more than 30 books, including *The Mind of Primitive Man* (1911) and *Anthropology and Modern Life* (1928).

BOAS, nonpoisonous snakes that kill their prey by squeezing and suffocating it. Boas range from 8–30ft in length and feed on birds and mammals. They are found mostly in tropical America and the West Indies, and live on the ground or in trees. Boas give birth to live young and have vestigial hind limbs and a rudimentary pelvis. There are 35 species, including the anaconda.

BOAT PEOPLE, thousands of people from Indochina who attempted to flee Communist rule in the aftermath of the Vietnam War. Most of them left in small boats, bribing guards and officials to let them try the perilous journey on the high seas, where they were easy prey for bandits and bad weather. Those who reached other shores were often placed indefinitely in poorly supplied camps and denied permanent homes. The US admitted thousands of these boat people after 1975. Cuban and Haitian refugees have also tried to reach the US in small boats. (See CUBAN BOAT LIFT; REFUGEE.)

BOBCAT, a wild cat, *Lynx rufus*, closely related to the LYNX, named for its short (6in) tail. It grows to a length of about 3ft and has a brown and white coat with black spots and stripes. It is nocturnal, feeding on rodents and occasionally on livestock. The bobcat is found in most parts of North and Central America.

BOBOLINK, *Dolichonyx oryzivorus*, a North American migratory songbird named for its distinctive song. Also called ricebird or reedbird, it is 6-8in long with a dull plumage—except in spring, when the male is black and yellow. The bobolink breeds in the US and S Canada, migrating to South America for the winter.

BOBSLED, a heavy sled used on packed snow or ice runs, having four runners and carrying two or four people. The bobsled derived from the toboggan in Switzerland and became popular in the early 20th century. Bobsledding has been included in the winter Olympic Games since 1928, but with its steep runs and speeds up to 100mph it is very dangerous and is not widely practiced.

BOBWHITE, *Colinus virginiarus*, North American gamebird related to the QUAIL and PARTRIDGE. It is about 10in long and reddish-brown in color. Bobwhites feed on insects and seeds and keep within a group or covey.

BOCCACCIO, Giovanni (1313–1375), great Italian writer and humanist of the early Renaissance whose work had a lasting influence on European literature. A classical scholar and a friend and admirer of PETRARCH, he wrote *Filostrato, Teseida* and the famous DECAMERON tales—the first literary expression of Renaissance humanist realism.

BOCCHERINI, Luigi (1743–1805), Italian composer and cellist, noted for his chamber music. His numerous charming and elegant works have been compared to those of HAYDN, his contemporary.

BOCCIONI, Umberto (1882–1916), Italian painter and sculptor. A pioneer of Italian FUTURISM, he was a signer of the "Manifesto of Futurist Painters" (1910). He tried to capture movement and the speed and sensations of modern life by using dynamic forms.

BOCK, Fedor von (1880–1945), German field marshal in WWII who led armies in Poland, the Low Countries, and France. In Russia, he failed to take Moscow (1941) and Stalingrad (1942). He was apparently executed in the last days of the war.

BÖCKLIN, Arnold (1827–1901), major Swiss painter who lived mainly in Italy and drew inspiration from that country's classical heritage. Primarily a landscape painter, he often used mythological subjects and strongly influenced German Romantic painting.

BODE, Johann Elert (1747–1826), German astronomer, director of the Berlin observatory. He devised **Bode's law**, a formula that expresses the relationship between the mean distances from the sun of the first seven planets. Neptune and Pluto do not fit the scheme.

BODIN, Jean (c1530–1596), French political philosopher who argued that stable government lay in a moderate absolutism founded on divine right, but subject to divine and natural law. Tolerant in religion, he also tried to show that religious differences could be settled by adherence to the Ten Commandments.

BODLEIAN LIBRARY, the library of Oxford University. Originally established in the 14th century, it was restored 1598–1602 by the English diplomat Sir Thomas Bodley (1545–1613). Its collection has grown from 2,000 to 2.5 million books, including many oriental and other MSS.

BODONI, Giambattista (1740–1813), Italian printer and type-designer. The Bodoni typeface, with its sharp contrast between thick and thin strokes, has been widely used in modern printing.

BODYBUILDING, an activity that usually involves the development of musculature by weight-lifting. It is also a sport in which competitors display their muscular development in posing routines, being rated by judges on muscle size, definition (absence of fat), symmetry, shape and general appearance. Several international competitions are held annually.

BOEHM, Martin (1725–1812), American clergyman, an itinerant preacher among German settlements in Pennsylvania and Maryland. Expelled from the Mennonite church, he was a founder and first bishop of the Evangelical United Brethern Church.

BOEHME, Jakob (1575–1624), German religious mystic whose ideas about God and human striving influenced German idealist and romantic philosophers of the 19th century.

BOERHAAVE, Hermann (1668–1738), Dutch physician, famed as a chemist, pathologist, and teacher, who made Leiden a leading medical center.

BOERS (Dutch: farmers), in South Africa, term once used for people of Dutch, German and Huguenot descent who settled in the Cape of Good Hope from 1652. The British annexed the Cape in 1806, and in 1835–43 the Boers left on the Great Trek to found the new republics of the Transvaal and the Orange Free State. Now called Afrikaners, they speak their own language (AFRIKAANS) and belong to the Dutch Reformed Church. Their racial attitudes resulted in the APARTHEID policy.

BOER WAR, or **South African War,** fought between the British and the Boers from 1899 to 1902. The Boers resented British territorial expansion, while the British aimed at a united South Africa and complained of the harsh treatment the Boers, under Paul KRUGER, gave to immigrant gold prospectors. In 1895 tension was increased by the Jameson Raid, aimed at supporting an anti-Boer rebellion in the Transvaal. Well-equipped by Germany, the more numerous Boer forces took the offensive in 1899. In the early part of the war the Boers besieged Ladysmith and Mafeking, but the arrival of British reinforcements turned the tide and by late 1900 the Boers had to resort to guerrilla tactics. Their resistance steadily weakened and the war ended with the treaty of Vereeniging in 1902. The British victory did not, however, end the conflict between Boers and British, which moved into the political arena.

BOETHIUS, Anicius Manlius Severinus

(c480–525), Roman philosopher, statesman and Christian theologian whose works were a major source of Classical thought for medieval Scholastic philosophers. A high official under Theodoric the Great, he was accused of treason and executed. While in prison, he wrote his influential work *On the Consolation of Philosophy*.

BOGAN, Louise (1897–1970), US poet, poetry editor of the *New Yorker* magazine for 38 years whose own poetry received critical recognition only after her death.

BOGART, Humphrey DeForest (1899–1957), US film actor, famous for his screen image as the cool, tough anti-hero. Some of his most notable films were *The Maltese Falcon* (1942), *Casablanca* (1942) and *The African Queen* (1951)—for which he won an Academy Award.

BOGOMILS, religious sect founded in Bulgaria in the 10th century by the priest Bogomil. Its members held that all material things were created by the devil and that therefore all close contact with matter, even the Eucharist, must be rejected. The sect flourished in the Balkans until the 14th century. (See also CATHARI.)

BOGOTÁ, capital and largest city of Colombia. Founded by the Spanish in 1538 on the site of Chibcha settlement, commercial and cultural center with several universities (the oldest from 1573). Its climate is mild because of its altitude of over 8,500ft, at the edge of an Andean plateau. Pop 4,500,000.

BOHEMIA, historic region in central Europe. It was once part of the Austro-Hungarian Empire. In 1918, after a war-torn history, it became a province in the republic of Czechoslovakia, of which its chief city, Prague, became the capital. In 1949 it lost its separate provincial status. The area is rich in minerals and in fine agricultural land.

BOHLEN, Charles Eustis (1904–1974), US diplomat and adviser on Soviet affairs. He served as adviser and interpreter at Russian conferences for presidents Roosevelt and Truman, and was US ambassador to the USSR (1953–57), the Philippines (1957–59) and France (1962–68).

BÖHM-BAWERK, Eugen (1851–1914), Austrian economist who introduced psychological factors into classical economic theories of interest and capital.

BÖHME, Jakob (1575–1624), German mystic and religious philosopher. Claiming divine revelation, he argued that all opposites, including good and evil, are reconciled in God. His ideas influenced many late philosophers and theologians.

BOHR, Niels Henrik David (1885–1962), Danish physicist who proposed the Bohr model of the ATOM while working with RUTHERFORD in Manchester, England, in 1913. Bohr suggested that a HYDROGEN atom consisted of a single electron performing a circular orbit around a central PROTON (the nucleus), the energy of the ELECTRON being quantized (i.e., the electron could only carry certain well-defined quantities of energy—see QUANTUM THEORY). At one stroke this accounted both for the properties of the atom and for the nature of its characteristic radiation (a SPECTRUM comprising several series of discrete sharp lines). In 1927 Bohr proposed the complementarity principle to account for the apparent paradoxes which arose on comparing the wave and particle approaches to describing SUBATOMIC PARTICLES. After escaping from Copenhagen in 1943 he went to the UK and then to the USA, where he helped develop the ATOMIC BOMB, but he was always deeply concerned about the graver implications for humanity of this development. In 1922 he received the Nobel Prize for Physics in recognition of his contributions to atomic theory. His son, **Aage Niels Bohr** (1922–   ), shared the 1975 Nobel Prize for Physics with B. Mottelson and J. Rainwater for contributions made to the physics of the atomic nucleus. Niels Bohr's brother, **Harald August Bohr** (1887–1951), was a distinguished mathematician.

BOIARDO, Matteo (1441?–1494), Italian poet. His *Orlando Innamorato* retold the Roland epic, combining Carolingian, Arthurian, and classical materials. The work was continued by ARIOSTO in *Orlando Furioso*.

BOIL, an ABCESS in a hair follicle, usually caused by infection with staphylococcus. A sty is a boil on the eyelid; a carbuncle is a group of contiguous boils. Small boils may heal spontaneously, but most cannot until pus has escaped, by thinning and rupture of overlying skin. This is hastened by local application of heat. In severe cases lancing and antibiotics may be required.

BOILEAU (-DESPRÉAUX), Nicolas (1636–1711), French poet, satirist and literary critic. His insistence on classical standards, notably in the didactic poem *L'Art poétique* (1674), greatly influenced literary taste both in France and England in the 18th century.

BOILER, device used to convert water into steam by the action of heat, usually to drive a STEAM ENGINE. A boiler requires a heat source (i.e., a furnace), a surface whereby the heat may be conveyed to the water, and enough space for steam to form. The two main types of boiler are the fire-tube, where the hot gases are passed through tubes surrounded by water, and the water-tube, where the water is passed through tubes surrounded by hot gases. Fuels include coal, oil and fuel gas; nuclear energy is also used. HERO designed boilers but used them only in toys. Steam power proper was barely considered until the 17th century and little used before the 18th.

BOILING POINT, the temperature at which the vapor pressure of a liquid becomes equal to the external pressure, so that boiling occurs; the temperature at which a liquid and its vapor are at equilibrium. Measurement of boiling point is important in chemical analysis and the determination of molecular weights.

BOITO, Arrigo (1842–1918), Italian poet and composer. His own operas include *Mefistofele* (1868; revised 1875) and *Nerone* (1918), though he is best known as the librettist of VERDI's *Otello* and *Falstaff* and of PONCHIELLI's *La Gioconda.*

BOK, Edward William (1863–1930), Dutch-born US editor, writer and philanthropist. In 1889 he became editor of *The Ladies' Home Journal* and used the magazine to campaign for good causes. In his retirement he wrote the Pulitzer prize-winning *The Americanization of Edward Bok* (1920).

BOKASSA (1921–   ), deposed emperor of the Central African Republic. As army chief of staff he staged a coup in 1966 to become president of the country that was once part of French Equatorial Africa. In 1977 he had himself crowned the "world's first socialist emperor." His lavish spending and autocratic and bizarre behavior led to his overthrow and exile in Sept. 1979. He lived in France until Oct. 1986, when he returned to the Central African Republic and was tried for mass murder and other crimes and sentenced to death.

BOLEYN, Anne (c1507–1536), second wife of HENRY VIII and mother of Elizabeth I. When he met her, Henry was already tiring of his first queen, who had failed to produce a son, and he married Anne in 1533 as soon as he was divorced. Their daughter Elizabeth was born later that year, but Anne too bore no living son. She was beheaded, having been convicted, on dubious evidence, of adultery and incest.

BOLINGBROKE, Henry St. John, 1st Viscount (1678–1751), English statesman. A member of the Tory party, as secretary of state he successfully handled the negotiations for the treaty of UTRECHT (1713). He lost office on the death of Queen Anne, and in 1715 was forced to seek exile in France,

where he remained for the next 10 years. Out of the mainstream of affairs, Bolingbroke devoted his time to political journalism and the study of history.

BOLÍVAR, Simón (1783–1830), South American soldier, statesman and liberator. Born of a wealthy Venezuelan family, he studied in Europe, where he was influenced by the work of the 18th-century rationalists, particularly by ROUSSEAU. Bolívar returned to South America in 1807, convinced that the Spanish colonies were ready to fight for independence. After two abortive attempts, he successfully liberated Venezuela in 1821. His country united with New Granada and Quito to form the state of Gran Colombia, with Bolívar as president. He went on to liberate Peru (1824) and to form, from Upper Peru, the republic of Bolivia (1825). Bolívar envisaged a united South America, but Peru and Bolivia turned against him in 1826. Venezuela seceded from Gran Colombia in 1829, and in the following year Bolívar resigned as president. He died of tuberculosis.

BOLIVIA, landlocked South American republic, bordered by Brazil to the N and E, Paraguay to the SE, Argentina to the S, and in the W by Peru and Chile.

Official name: Republic of Bolivia
Capital: La Paz
Area: 424,164sq mi
Population: 6,799,000
Languages: Spanish
Religions: Roman Catholic
Monetary unit(s): 1 boliviano = 100 centavos

Land. There are three main regions: the Oriente lowlands in the E, consisting largely of tropical rainforest and swamps; the Montanas, a central zone of mountains and fertile valleys; and in the W, the Altiplano, a bleak Andean plain of coarse grassland, the home of most of the people. At its northern end, shared with Peru, is Lake Titicaca, South America's largest lake and at 12,500ft the world's highest navigable stretch of water.

People. About 75% of the population is concentrated within Andean Bolivia. The

Oriente, in contrast, averages less than 2 persons per sq mi. The population consists of about 30% Quechua Indians, 25% Aymará Indians, 30% mestizos and 15% whites. The illiteracy rate is about 40%.
Economy. Bolivia is one of the poorest countries in South America. Minerals, particularly tin, but also, increasingly, petroleum and natural gas, dominate the country's economy and form more than 75% of its exports. Antimony, lead, tungsten, bismuth and zinc are also important, while there are also large, but as yet unexploited, deposits of iron and manganese. Inadequate transportation has considerably hampered Bolivia's growth. Some two-thirds of the population still depend on the land for a livelihood. On the Altiplano the main crops are sugar, potatoes, barley and beans. Sheep, llamas and alpacas are the chief livestock. Corn, wheat, barley, tobacco, dairy cattle and a wide variety of fruits and vegetables are raised in the Montana region.
History. Before the Spanish conquest an advanced Aymará civilization around Lake Titicaca was subjugated by the INCAS. During colonial times the region was known as Upper Peru and was famous for its mineral wealth. Freed from Spanish rule by Simon BOLÍVAR in 1825, Bolivia later lost more than its present territory in armed conflicts with Brazil, Chile and Paraguay. In the 20th century the country has had an unhappy history of recurring military coups. Although the country returned to civilian rule in 1982 and elections were held successfully in 1985, economic difficulties continue to threaten the nation's political stability.
BÖLL, Heinrich (1917–1985), German author and winner of the Nobel Prize for Literature in 1972. His books are bitterly satiric, exploring themes of despair and love in post-WWII Europe. Important among his works are *Billiards at Half Past Nine* (1961) and *The Clown* (1965).
BOLLINGEN PRIZE, a prize of $5,000 awarded to US poets by the Yale University Library. The prize was originally given by the Library of Congress and was first awarded, amid great controversy, to Ezra POUND (1949) who, at the time, stood accused of treason during WWII. Other winners have been E. E. CUMMINGS and Robert FROST.
BOLL WEEVIL, *Anthonomus grandis,* the most damaging cotton pest in the US. The beetle, which is 6mm long, lays eggs in cotton buds and fruit and feeds on the bolls and blossoms, causing an estimated loss of $200 million every year. It first appeared in

the US in the 1890s from Central America. Modern methods of combating it include soil improvement, cleansing its hibernating places and the use of insecticides.
BOLOGNA, Giovanni da (1529–1608), French sculptor who worked in Italy, one of the greatest sculptors of the Italian Renaissance. *Flying Mercury*, in Florence, is considered his masterpiece.
BOLOGNA, Italian city 51 mi N of Florence at the foot of the Apennines. It is an ancient Etruscan and Roman city, with a university founded c1088, many medieval buildings and some fine Renaissance paintings and sculptures. Capital of the Emilia Romagna region, it is an agricultural and industrial center, producing farm machinery and chemicals. Pop 445,139.
BOLSHEVISM, name given to the policy of the majority group (Russian *bolsheviki*) at the 1903 congress of the Russian Social Democratic Workers' party, as opposed to the minority or *mensheviki*. The bolsheviks, under the leadership of LENIN, formed a radical left-wing group in 1917 and took over the leadership of the Russian Revolution. Their doctrines derived from the work of MARX and ENGELS and upheld a revolution led by workers and peasants. (See COMMUNISM.)
BOLSHOI THEATER, Russian theater, ballet and opera house. The Bolshoi, which possesses one of the largest stages in the world, is the home of the famous ballet school. Its classical ballet and opera productions have a worldwide reputation.
BOLT, Robert (Oxton) (1924–   ), English dramatist best known for the play and movie about Thomas More, *A Man for All Seasons* (1962). Bolt also wrote the screenplays for *Lawrence of Arabia* (1962) and *Doctor Zhivago* (1966).
BOLTS AND SCREWS, devices in which the principle of the screw thread, which may be traced back as far as ARCHIMEDES, is applied to the fastening together of objects. A screw is essentially conical, with a sharp point and widening toward the head—which is usually shaped to take a screwdriver—with a helical ridge. If the point is pressed into the material (usually wood) and the screw is longitudinally rotated by means of a screwdriver, the screw will be driven into the wood and will be held in place by friction. A bolt is essentially cylindrical, again with a helical ridge, and has a broad head usually shaped to take a wrench. It is used in conjunction with a nut, a member containing a prethreaded hole into which the bolt fits. The objects to be fastened are held together by the pressure of the bolthead on one side, the nut on the

other. The distance between consecutive turns of a screw thread is termed the pitch of the thread.

BOLTZMANN, Ludwig (1844–1906), Austrian physicist who made fundamental contributions to THERMODYNAMICS, classical STATISTICAL MECHANICS and KINETIC THEORY. The **Boltzmann constant** (k), the quotient of the universal gas constant R and the AVOGADRO number (N), is used in statistical mechanics.

BOMBAY, large seaport in W India, capital of Maharashtra State, on the Arabian Sea. Bombay was built on several small islands, now joined to each other and to the mainland, forming an area of 25sq mi. Its large harbor deals with the bulk of India's imports, notably wheat and machinery, and many exports such as cotton, rice and manganese. Local industries include textiles, leather goods and printing. Bombay is an important cultural center, with a university founded in 1857. The city is overcrowded, with a fast growing, mainly Hindu, population. The site was ceded to the Portuguese in 1534 and passed to Great Britain in 1661. The city was a headquarters of the British East India Company (1668–1858). Pop (metro) 10,100,000.

BONAPARTE, family name of French emperor NAPOLEON I (1769–1821). Napoleon's father, Carlo Buonaparte (1746–1785), was a lawyer in Ajaccio, Corsica; his mother, Letizia Ramolino Buonaparte (c.1750–1836), was honored at Napoleon's court as Madame Mére. Napoleon's oldest brother, Joseph Bonaparte (1768–1844), became king of Naples and then Spain, after 1815 living mostly in the US. Another brother, Lucien Bonaparte (1775–1840), played an important part in Napoleon's rise to power, but he married against Napoleon's wishes and lived in virtual exile in Italy. Another brother, Louis Bonaparte (1778–1846), was compelled to marry Hortense Beauharnais, sister of the empress JOSEPHINE, and made king of Holland until Napoleon forced him to abdicate. Napoleon's youngest brother, Jerome Bonaparte (1784–1860), married an American, Elizabeth Patterson of Baltimore. Napoleon did not recognize the marriage. Jerome was made king of Westphalia and fought in Russia and at Waterloo. Napoleon had three sisters — Elisa (1777–1820), Pauline (1780–1825), and Caroline (1782–1839) — who also played parts in his imperial arrangements.

Napoleon and his second wife, Marie Louise of Austria, had a short-lived son who, though he never reigned, became known as NAPOLEON II. Louis Bonaparte's son eventually became emperor of the French (1852–70) as NAPOLEON III. Other Bonapartes were prominent in French politics and society. A grandson of Jerome Bonaparte and Elizabeth Patterson was **Charles Joseph Bonaparte** (1851–1921), a US politician who served as secretary of the navy (1905–06) and attorney general (1906–09) in the cabinet of President Theodore Roosevelt.

BONAVENTURE, Saint (1221–1274), Italian medieval scholastic philosopher and theologian. He taught principally at Paris and later became Master General of the Franciscan order. Called the "Seraphic Doctor," he distinguished between PHILOSOPHY, based on man's natural knowledge, and THEOLOGY, which attempts to understand the Christian mysteries.

BOND, Chemical, the links which hold ATOMS together in compounds. In the 19th century it was found that many substances, known as **covalent compounds**, could be represented by structural FORMULAS in which lines represented bonds. By using double and triple bonds, most organic compounds could be formulated with constant valences of the constituent atoms. Stereoisomerism showed that the bonds must be localized in fixed directions in space. **Electrovalent compounds** (see ELECTROCHEMISTRY) consist of oppositely charged IONS arranged in a lattice; here the bonds are nondirectional electrostatic interactions. The theory that atoms consist of electrons orbiting in shells around the nucleus (see PERIODIC TABLE) led to a simple explanation of both kinds of bonding: atoms combine to achieve highly-stable filled outer shells containing 2, 8 or 18 electrons, either by transfer of electrons from one atom to the other (**ionic bond**), or by the sharing of one electron from each atom so that both electrons orbit around both nuclei (**covalent bond**). In the **coordinate bond,** a variant of the covalent bond, both shared electrons are provided by one atom. QUANTUM MECHANICS has now shown that electrons occupy orbitals having certain shapes and energies, and that, when atoms combine, the outer atomic orbitals are mixed to form molecular orbitals. The energy difference constitutes the bond energy—the energy required to break the bond by separating the atoms. Molecular orbitals are classified as σ if symmetric when rotated through 180° about the line joining the nuclei, or π if antisymmetric. The energy and length of chemical bonds, and the angles between them, may be investigated by SPECTROSCOPY and X-ray diffraction. (See also HYDROGEN BONDING.)

BONE, the hard tissue that forms the SKELETON of vertebrates. Bones support the body, protect its organs, act as anchors for MUSCLES and as levers for the movement of limbs, and are the main reserve of calcium and phosphate in the body. Bone consists of living cells (osteocytes) embedded in a matrix of collagen fibers with calcium salts similar in composition to hydroxyapatite deposited between them. Some carbonates are also present. All bones have a shell of compact bone in concentric layers (lamellae) around the blood vessels, which run in small channels (Haversian canals). Within this shell is porous or spongy bone, and in the case of "long" bones (see below) there is a hollow cavity containing MARROW. The bone is enveloped by a fibrous membrane, the periosteum, which is sensitive to pain, unlike the bone itself, and which has a network of nerves and blood vessels that penetrate the bone surface. After primary growth has ended, bone formation (ossification) occurs where the periosteum joins the bone, where there are many bone-forming cells (osteoblasts). Ossification begins in the embryo at the end of the second month, mostly by transformation of CARTILAGE: some cartilage cells become osteoblasts and secrete collagen and a hormone which causes calcium salts to be deposited. Vitamin D makes calcium available from the food to the blood, and its deficiency leads to RICKETS. The two ends of a "long" bone (the epiphyses) ossify separately from the shaft, and are attached to it by cartilaginous plates, at which lengthwise growth takes place. Radical growth is controlled by the periosteum, and at the same time the core of the bone is eroded by osteoclast cells to make it hollow. Primary growth is stimulated by the PITUITARY and SEX HORMONES; it is completed in adolescence, when the epiphyses fuse to the shaft. Bones are classified anatomically as "long," cylindrical and usually hollow, with a knob at each end; "short," spongy blocks with a thin shell; and "flat" two parallel layers of compact bone with a spongy layer in between. Some hand and foot bones are short; the ribs, sternum, skull and shoulder-blades are flat; and most other bones are long. The shape and structure of bones are quickly modified if the forces on them alter. Disorders of bone include OSTEOMYELITIS and various TUMORS and CANCER. Dead bone is not readily absorbed and can be a focus of infection. In old age thinning and weakening of the bones by loss of calcium (osteoporosis) is common.

BONE CHINA, fine PORCELAIN first introduced c1800 (see SPODE). Made of china clay mixed with bone-ash and china stone, it is similar to hard porcelain but more workable and less easily chipped.

BONHEUR, Rosa (1822–1899), French artist famous for her animal paintings. She made her reputation with *The Horse Fair* (1853), a scene full of vigor and grace, representative of her most accomplished work.

BONHOEFFER, Dietrich (1906–1945), German Lutheran pastor and theologian. He was the author of many radical books on ecumenism and Christianity in a secular world. A prominent anti-Nazi, he was arrested in 1943 and executed at Flossenbürg concentration camp two years later.

BONIFACE, Saint (c672–754), English missionary, the apostle of Germany. Backed by the Frankish rulers CHARLES MARTEL and Pepin the Short, he organized the German church, reformed the Frankish clergy and advanced the conversion of the Saxons. He was martyred by the Frisians.

BONIFACE VIII (c1235–1303), pope 1294–1303. He steadfastly asserted papal authority over the political leaders of Europe and involved the papacy in a series of conflicts with leading powers. His bull "Unam Sanctam," which called for the subjugation of temporal to spiritual authority, led to a clash with Philip IV of France. In 1303 the king's emissaries attacked Benedict in his palace at Anagni, where he was about to excommunicate Philip: the populace intervened, but Boniface collapsed and died three weeks later in Rome.

BONIFÁCIO, José (1763–1838), Brazilian statesman. A geologist of international reputation, he encouraged the Portuguese prince regent to declare (1822) Brazil independent of Portugal and become emperor as PEDRO I. Bonifácio served Pedro as minister, but was banished for his liberalism. Later he returned and was tutor to PEDRO II.

BONINGTON, Richard Parkes (1801–1828), English artist noted for his watercolor landscapes and GENRE subjects. He spent most of his brief career in France; among those he influenced there were DELACROIX and COROT.

BONIN ISLANDS, group of volcanic islands about 500mi SE of Japan. In all there are 27 islands with some 200 inhabitants. They were administered by the US 1945–68, when they were returned to Japan.

BONN, capital of West Germany since the

partition of the country after WWII (1949). This historic city is situated on the Rhine, in North Rhine-Westphalia. The birthplace of Beethoven, it has a museum and hall devoted to the composer. Much of the city has been rebuilt since WWII. It is now West Germany's administrative center and has attracted many modern industries. Pop 290,769.

BONNARD, Pierre (1867–1947), French artist whose almost impressionist style gives sparkling life and color to the sunny interiors he favored. These made him known as a leader of the intimist school. While at the Acadèmie Julian he met Maurice Denis and Jean VUILLARD, with whom he formed the group known as the Nabis.

BONNET, Georges (1889–1973), French politician, an advocate of appeasement toward Nazi Germany. Foreign minister (1938–39), he helped negotiate the Munich pact, opposed war with Germany, and after the French defeat advocated collaboration. He moved to Switzerland after the war to avoid prosecution, but returned and again served (1956–68) in the Chamber of Deputies.

BONNEVILLE, Benjamin Louis Eulalie de (1796–1878), French-American soldier and frontiersman. He explored the far west (1832–35) and distinguished himself in the MEXICAN WAR (1846–48). But he is remembered largely because of Washington IRVING's romanticized biography, *The Adventures of Captain Bonneville, U.S.A.* (1837).

BONNEVILLE DAM, large hydroelectric dam spanning the Columbia R in NW Ore., about 40mi E of Portland. It is 170ft high and 1,250ft wide and was built 1933–43 as part of the New Deal program.

BONSAI, the ancient oriental art of growing trees in dwarf form. The modern enthusiast may spend three years cultivating the "miniature" trees, mainly by root pruning and shoot trimming. Plants that can be "dwarfed" include the cedars, myrtles, junipers, oaks, cypresses, pyracanthas and pines. Bonsai has spread throughout the world, and is a fast-growing hobby in North America, where there are many "bonsai" clubs.

BONUS MARCH, a demonstration, in 1932, in Washington, D.C. by some 15,000 jobless veterans of WWI. They hoped to persuade Congress to enable them to cash bonus certificates issued in 1924 in recognition of their war service. President Hoover worsened his reputation by ordering the military to drive the "Bonus Army" from the city. In 1936 Congress finally

passed a law, against a presidential veto, allowing the exchange of the certificates.

BOOKKEEPING, the systematic recording of financial transactions. The single-entry system consists of a single account which shows the debts owed to and by the firm in question. The double-entry system is more detailed; the debit and credit items are entered in a journal; they are then classified in a ledger. From this information a comprehensive balance sheet can be drawn up. The monthly system was developed to meet the needs of a complex commercial society. There are a number of separate daybooks, and the monthly totals are posted to the ledger accounts. ACCOUNTING differs in that it also includes the analysis of financial data.

BOOK OF CHANGES. See I CHING.

BOOK OF COMMON PRAYER, the official liturgy of the CHURCH OF ENGLAND, including (among others) the services of Morning and Evening Prayer and Holy COMMUNION, and the Psalter, Gospels and Epistles. The first Prayer Book was written by CRANMER (1549); a more reformed version (see ANGLICANISM; REFORMATION) was published in 1552 and, with minor revisions, 1559 and 1662. The 1662 Prayer Book has been used ever since, and has been a major formative influence on the English language. Since 1966, various modern experimental services have also legally been in use.

BOOK OF HOURS, book of prayers to be said at the canonical hours, widely used by laymen during the late Middle Ages. They were often masterpieces of the miniaturist's art; among the most famous are the Rohan and the de Berry Hours.

BOOK OF KELLS, a copy of the Gospels from the late 8th century, completed by the monks of Kells in County Meath, Ireland. Its richly elaborate decoration makes it one of the finest examples of medieval illuminated manuscripts. It is now in the library of Trinity College, Dublin.

BOOK OF MORMON. See MORMONS.

BOOK OF THE DEAD, name applied to funerary writings found on ancient Egyptian tombs and papyri. They include instructions and magic charms for the use of the deceased.

BOOLE, George (1815–1864), British mathematician and logician, chiefly remembered for devising **Boolean algebra,** which allowed mathematical methods to be applied to non-quantifiable entities such as logical propositions.

BOOMERANG, a primitive weapon developed uniquely in Australia. Deceptively simple in shape, this angular throwing club is precisely bent and balanced. When thrown, it follows a curved path, spinning end for end, and can strike a vicious blow. It can be thrown in such a way that it comes back to the thrower.

BOONE, Daniel (1734–1820), American pioneer and hunter. Beginning in 1767 he made a series of trips into what is now Ky. and in 1775 built a fort there, called Boonesboro. In 1778 he was captured by the Shawnee, who were allied with the British against the American revolutionaries. Boone escaped to warn settlers at Boonesboro of a planned attack, which they successfully resisted. Traditionally, he is hailed as the founder of Ky., which he was not, and more justly as a great frontiersman.

BOORSTIN, Daniel Joseph (1914–   ), US historian. A professor at the University of Chicago (1944–69), Boorstin wrote several notable works in American history including *The Americans* (3 vols., 1958–73). He served as the Librarian of Congress 1974–87.

BOOTH, an English family, founders and leaders of the SALVATION ARMY. **William Booth** (1829–1912) started his career as a Methodist minister but left the church in 1861 to work among the poor in the slums of London. In 1878 he founded the Salvation Army, assisted by his wife **Catherine Booth** (1829–1890), a noted orator who did valuable work for women's rights. **William Bramwell Booth** (1856–1929), the eldest son of William Booth, served as second general of the Salvation Army. **Ballington Booth** (1859–1940), second son, brought the Salvation Army to the US in 1887. With his wife Maud, he instituted the VOLUNTEERS OF AMERICA, a similar organization. **Catherine Booth-Clibborn** (1859–1905), the eldest daughter of William Booth, founded the Salvation Army in France and Switzerland. **Emma Moss Booth-Tucker** (1860–1903) helped to establish the Salvation Army in India in 1881. **Herbert Henry Booth** (1862–1926), the youngest son of William Booth, founded the Salvation Army in Australia and New Zealand. **Evangeline Cory Booth** (1865–1950), daughter of William Booth, was the Salvation Army's first woman general, with international command of the organization (1934–39). She also commanded the US Salvation Army (1904–34) and wrote popular evangelical songs.

BOOTH, Charles (1840–1916), British merchant and sociologist, who applied statistical research methods to sociology. The 17-volume *Life and Labour of the People in London* (1891–1903) is his major work. A member of the royal commission on the poor law (1905–09), Booth also wrote *Poor Law Reform* (1910).

BOOTH, Edwin Thomas (1833–1892), US actor, famous on both the New York and London stages. His Shakespearean roles, particularly Hamlet, were considered theatrical landmarks. The son of Junius Brutus BOOTH, he was the brother of Lincoln's assassin, John Wilkes BOOTH.

BOOTH, John Wilkes (1838–1865), US actor who assassinated Abraham Lincoln, a son of the actor Junius Brutus BOOTH. He was a Confederate sympathizer; eager to avenge the South's defeat, he shot President Lincoln during a performance at Ford's Theater, Washington, D.C., on April 14th, 1865. Booth, breaking a leg, escaped but was finally trapped in a barn near Bowling Green, Va., where he was either shot or shot himself.

BOOTH, Junius Brutus (1796–1852), English-born actor, founder of a famous American family of actors. Emigrating to the US in 1821, he achieved great success, particularly in Shakespeare. He was the father of Edwin and John Wilkes BOOTH.

BOP, or **bebop,** seminal style of modern JAZZ, named for its basic rhythmic feature. Inspired by musicians like Dizzy Gillespie and Charlie Parker, Bop emerged in the 1940s to break with the Blues tradition and explore new harmonic and rhythmic fields. It added greater sophistication and complexity to jazz, deepening and reinvigorating it.

BORAH, William Edgar (1865–1940), Republican senator from Ida. 1907–40, a vigorous and independent champion of progressive reforms. He opposed US membership in the League of Nations and was a prominent isolationist on the eve of WWII, but was also an able chairman of the Senate Foreign Relations Committee (1924–33).

BORDEAUX, city in SW France and capital of Gironde department, on the Garonne R. It is France's third-largest port and chief center for the French wine trade. Bordeaux also has canning and shipbuilding industries. The city dates from Roman times. Pop (city) 205,960; (metro) 628,000.

BORDEN, Gail (1801–1874), US inventor of the first process for making condensed milk by evaporation. He also influenced the development of Tex.: he helped to write its first state constitution, prepared the first topographical map of Tex. and laid out the city of Houston.

BORDEN, Lizzie Andrew (1860–1927), US woman accused of murdering her father and stepmother with an ax on Aug. 4, 1892.

She was acquitted but remained popularly condemned. The murder became part of American folklore.

BORDEN, Sir Robert Laird (1854–1937), Canadian prime minister (1911–20) who gave his country a new and more independent voice in world affairs. Borden became Conservative leader in 1901. He was a vigorous WWI prime minister, forming a Union party government with pro-conscription Liberals in 1917, and securing separate representation for Canada at the peace conference and in the League of Nations.

BORG, Bjorn (1956–   ), Swedish tennis player, winner of five straight Wimbledon men's singles titles (1976–80).

BORGES, Jorge Luis (1899–1986), Argentinian poet and prose writer. At first influenced by the metaphorical style of Spanish *Ultraísmo*, he later developed a unique form between short story and essay, the "fiction." Some of the best examples are in his *Ficciones* (1944) and *El Aleph* (1949).

BORGHESE, aristocratic Roman family, originally from Siena. **Camillo Borghese** (1552–1621) became Pope PAUL V. The many Borghese cardinals included the noted art collector, **Scipione Borghese** (1576–1633), patron of Giovanni Lorenzo BERNINI. He commissioned the Borghese Palace and Villa Borghese, two of Rome's finest Baroque buildings. **Prince Camillo Filippo Ludovico Borghese** (1775–1832) married Napoleon's sister Marie Pauline and became duke of Guastalla. Borghese family power declined with falling land values in the 1890s.

BORGIA, powerful Italian family descended from the Borjas of Valencia in Spain. **Alfonso de Borja** (1378–1458) became Pope Calixtus III. By bribery, his nephew **Rodrigo Borgia** (1431–1503) became Pope ALEXANDER VI in 1492 and worked to enrich his family by crushing the Italian princes. His son, **Cesare Borgia** (c1476–1507), used war, duplicity and murder to seize much of central Italy. Alexander's notorious daughter, **Lucrezia Borgia** (1480–1519), was probably a pawn in her family's schemes. As duchess of Ferrara (from 1505), she generously patronized the arts and learning.

BORGLUM, Gutzon (1867–1941), US sculptor best remembered for Mt Rushmore S.D. National Memorial, with its enormous portrait heads of Washington, Jefferson, Lincoln and Theodore Roosevelt. After Borglum's death the project was completed by his son. (See RUSHMORE, MOUNT.)

BORIC ACID (H_3BO_3), or boracic acid,

colorless crystalline solid, a weak inorganic acid. It gives boric oxide (B_2O_3) when strongly heated; SODIUM borate typifies its salts. Boric acid is used as an external antiseptic, in the production of glass and as a welding flux. Powdered boric acid is an effective agent against cockroaches.

BORK, Robert Heron (1927–   ), US legal scholar and judge. He taught at Yale Law School 1962–73, 1975–81. As US solicitor general (1973–75), he carried out President Nixon's order to fire WATERGATE special prosecutor Archibald Cox after his superiors in the Justice Dept. resigned rather than do so. In 1982 President Reagan appointed him to the US Court of Appeals in Washington, D.C., and in 1987 nominated him to the US Supreme Court. The nomination was rejected by the US Senate in a bitter controversy in which the majority felt that Bork's views on "judicial restraint" and "original intent" were out of the judicial mainstream. Bork resigned (1988) his Appeals Court position.

BORLAUG, Norman Ernest (1914–   ), US agricultural scientist who was awarded the 1970 Nobel Peace Prize for his part in the development of improved varieties of CEREAL CROPS, important in the GREEN REVOLUTION.

BORMANN, Martin Ludwig (1900–1945), German Nazi politician who wielded brutal power as Hitler's deputy from 1941. Though he vanished in 1945, he was sentenced to death for war crimes at the NUREMBERG TRIALS in 1946. It is now thought he was probably killed as Berlin fell.

BORN, Max (1872–1970), German theoretical physicist active in the development of quantum physics, whose particular contribution was the probabilistic interpretation of the SCHRÖDINGER wave equation, thus providing a link between WAVE MECHANICS and the QUANTUM THEORY. Sharing the Nobel physics prize with W. Bothe in 1954, he devoted his later years to the philosophy of physics.

BORN-AGAIN CHRISTIANS, term applied predominantly to Fundamentalist Christians who feel themselves regenerated through the experience of being "born again" (John 3:3). Related to the Calvinist doctrine of election, the experience today assumes a revivalist character. President Jimmy Carter proudly claimed the experience. In the late 1970s, citing a decline in morality, Born-again Christians became active in US politics through such organizations as the MORAL MAJORITY and such evangelists as the Rev. Jerry Falwell. See FUNDAMENTALISM.

BORNEO, largest island of the Malay Archipelago and third largest in the world (280,100sq mi). It contains the Indonesian provinces of Central, E, W, and S Kalimantan, with the sultanate of BRUNEI and the Malaysian states of Sabah and SARAWAK to the N and NW. Borneo is a mountainous equatorial island largely clad in tropical rain forest, and drained by several major rivers. Its highest point is Mt Kinabalu (13,455ft). Its peoples include Dayak, Malays, Arabs and Chinese. Products include copra, rubber, rice, timber, oil, bauxite and coal. The Portuguese reached Borneo in the 1500s, followed by the Dutch and the British, who had most influence in the 19th century.

BORODIN, Alexander Porfirevich (1833–1887), Russian composer and chemist, one of the group known as the Five. Though music came second to his scientific work in St. Petersburg, he wrote some notable works, including the opera *Prince Igor*; completed after his death by GLAZUNOV and RIMSKY-KORSAKOV.

BORODIN, Michael (Mikhail Markovich Gruzenberg; 1884–1951?), Russian revolutionary, special envoy (1923–27) in China, where he helped negotiate an alliance between the Chinese communists and the Nationalists. When the Nationalist leader, Chiang Kai-shek, broke with the communists, Borodin was recalled to Moscow. He was arrested in 1949 and died in a Siberian labor camp.

BORODINO, Russian village 70mi WSW of Moscow, where Napoleon gained a Pyrrhic victory over General KUTUZOV's Russian forces on Sept. 7, 1812.

BORROMEO, Saint Charles (1538–1584), Italian Roman Catholic religious reformer. As secretary of state to Pope Pius IV he influenced the Council of TRENT. As archbishop of Milan he developed popular children's "Sunday Schools" and priests' seminaries, and set a high personal standard of clerical selflessness.

BORROMINI, Francesco (1599–1677), major Italian BAROQUE architect, renowned for his dramatic use of space and light. Among his best-known works are the Roman churches of Sant'Ivo della Sapienza and San Carlo alle Quattro Fontane.

BOSANQUET, Bernard (1848–1923), British idealist philosopher whose best-known works were *The Philosophical Theory of the State* (1899) and *The Value and Destiny of the Individual* (1913). A controversial public figure, he was a champion of social reform and progressive education.

BOSCH, Hieronymous (c1450–1516), Dutch painter, from Hertogenbosch in North Brabant, whose work is unique in its grotesque fantasy. In paintings like the *Haywain* (c1485) and *The Garden of Earthly Delights* (1500) he uses an array of part-human, part-animal, part-vegetable forms to express symbolically his obsessive vision of worldly sin and its eternal damnation.

BOSE, Subhas Chandra (1897–1945), Indian nationalist, briefly (1938–39) president of the Congress Party, who collaborated with Japan in WWII to end British rule in India.

BOSNIA AND HERZEGOVINA, a constituent republic of Yugoslavia. Most of its 19,741sq mi are mountainous, with barren limestone in the SW (the Dinaric Alps), forests in the E and arable land in the N. The population of over 4,000,000 consists of Serbs (Orthodox), Croats (Roman Catholics) and Muslims. The capital is Sarajevo. Once independent states, they were held by the Ottoman Empire from the late 15th century until occupied (1878) and annexed (1908) by Austria–Hungary. Serbian terrorists, hostile to Austrian rule, assassinated the Austrian Archduke Francis Ferdinand in Sarajevo in 1914, precipitating WWI. After the war, Bosnia and Herzegovina became part of the new state of Yugoslavia.

BOSPORUS, Turkish strait 19mi long and about 0.5mi to 2.25mi wide connecting the Black Sea and Sea of Marmara. Historically important as the sole sea link between the Black Sea and the Mediterranean, it was bridged in 1973.

BOSSUET, Jacques Bénigne (1627–1704), French prelate and historian who was renowned for his eloquence as an orator, especially in his funeral orations. He was bishop of Condom (1669–71) and of Meaux (from 1681). He wrote the famous *Discourse on Universal History* (1681).

BOSTON, capital and largest city of Mass., a seaport on Massachusetts Bay. It is the most populous state capital, New England's leading city and the nearest major US seaport to Europe. It is also a major commercial, financial, manufacturing, cultural and educational center. Boston's industries include shipbuilding, electronics, chemicals, plastics, rubber products and printing. The city's wool market is the nation's largest. Historic buildings include the Old State House, Paul Revere House, Christ Church and Faneuil Hall. Boston itself has many notable educational institutions, and nearby Cambridge has Harvard University and the Massachusetts Institute of Technology. Settled by English

Puritans in 1630, Boston became the capital of Massachusetts Bay Colony and—in the BOSTON MASSACRE and BOSTON TEA PARTY—led colonial unrest that erupted into the REVOLUTIONARY WAR. Modern Boston shares the acute urban problems of most large US cities. Pop (city) 571,000, (metro) 2,832,000.

BOSTON MARATHON, annual marathon race held since 1897 from Hopkinton, Mass. to Boston.

BOSTON MASSACRE, an incident which strengthened anti-British feeling in America preceding the REVOLUTIONARY WAR. On March 5, 1770, some 60 Bostonians, enraged by the presence of British soldiers in Boston, harassed a British sentry. Troops came to his aid and fired on the mob, killing three and wounding eight (two died later).

BOSTON POLICE STRIKE, stoppage called on Sept. 9, 1919, when Mass. authorities had failed to recognize a police labor union or to offer better working conditions. Gangs terrorized Boston for two nights until Gov. Calvin Coolidge called out the state militia and ended the strike. His action catapulted him to the vice-presidency in 1920.

BOSTON TEA PARTY, American revolutionary incident at Boston on Dec. 16, 1773. In protest against the tea tax and British import restrictions, a party of colonial patriots disguised in Indian dress boarded three British East India Company ships and dumped their cargo of tea into the harbor.

BOSWELL, James (1740–1795), Scottish writer and advocate, most famous for his *Life of Johnson* (1791), one of the greatest of English biographies. In his private journals he recorded his life and times with great zest. From them he culled the accounts of his travels in Corsica and elsewhere, and the brilliant conversations which distinguish the portrait of his friend Samuel JOHNSON.

BOSWORTH FIELD, site of a battle near Leicester, England. There, on Aug. 22, 1485, Yorkist Richard III was defeated and killed by Lancastrians under Henry Tudor (Henry VII)—who thus ended the Wars of the ROSES and founded the Tudor dynasty.

BOTANY, the study of plant life. Botany and ZOOLOGY are the major divisions of BIOLOGY. There are many specialized disciplines within botany, the classical ones being morphology, physiology, GENETICS, ECOLOGY and TAXONOMY. Although the present-day botanist often specializes in a single discipline, he frequently draws upon techniques and information obtained from others.

The plant morphologist studies the form and structure of plants, particularly the whole plant and its major components, while the plant anatomist concentrates upon the cellular and subcellular structure, perhaps using the ELECTRON MICROSCOPE. The behavior and functioning of plants is studied by the plant physiologist, though since he frequently uses biochemical techniques, he is often called a plant biochemist. A plant geneticist uses biochemical and biophysical techniques to study the mechanism of inheritance and may relate this to the EVOLUTION of an individual. An important practical branch of genetics is plant BREEDING. The plant ecologist relates the form (morphology and anatomy), function (physiology) and evolution of plants to their environment. The plant taxonomist or systematic botanist specializes in the science of classification, which involves cataloging, identifying and naming plants using their morphological, physiological and genetic characters. CYTOLOGY, the study of the individual cell, necessarily involves techniques used in morphology, physiology and genetics.

Within these broad divisions there are many specialist fields of research. The plant physiologist may, for instance, be particularly interested in PHOTOSYNTHESIS or RESPIRATION. Similarly, the systematic botanist may specialize in the study of ALGAE (algology), FUNGI (mycology) or MOSSES (bryology). Other specialists study the plant in relation to its uses (economic botany), PLANT DISEASES (plant pathology) or the agricultural importance of plants (agricultural botany). BACTERIOLOGY is often considered to be a division of botany since bacteria are often classified as plants. (See also AGRONOMY; BIOCHEMISTRY; BIOPHYSICS; HORTICULTURE; PLANT; PLANT KINGDOM.)

The forerunners of the botanists were men who collected herbs for medical use long before philosophers turned to the scientific study of nature. However, the title of "father of botany" goes to THEOPHRASTUS, a pupil of ARISTOTLE, whose *Inquiry into Plants* sought to classify the types, parts and uses of the members of the plant kingdom. Passing over the work of the elder Pliny and that of his contemporary, Dioscorides, scholars offered botany few further lasting contributions until the Renaissance, the intervening period making do with the more or less fabulous "herbals" of the medical herbalists. The most famous pre-Darwinian classification of the plant kingdom was that of LINNAEUS, in which modern binomial names first appeared (1753). While GREW and RAY had laid the foundations for plant anatomy and physiology in the 17th and 18th centuries, and HOOKE had even identified the cell (1665) with the aid of the MICROSCOPE, these subjects were not actively pursued until the 19th century, when Robert Brown identified the nucleus and SCHWANN proposed his comprehensive cell theory. The work of DARWIN revolutionized the theory of classification, while that of MENDEL pointed the way to a true science of plant breeding.

BOTANY BAY, site in New South Wales, Australia, visited (1770) by Capt. James Cook. Australia's first penal colony was called Botany Bay, but it was located at Sydney.

BOTERO, Fernando (1932–), Colombian-born painter known for his cartoonlike satirical renderings of Latin American cultural archetypes, including generals, politicians and religious and historical figures.

BOTHA, Louis (1862–1919), Boer politician and general, first prime minister of the Union of South Africa (1910–19). He led guerrilla fighting in the BOER WARS (1899–1902), but as premier worked to reconcile Boers and British.

BOTHA, Pieter (1916–), prime minister (1978–84) and president (from 1984) of South Africa. Although his Afrikaner government was beset by scandals concerning misuse of funds and foreign bribes, he remained in office, a staunch defender of his country's apartheid policies.

BOTHWELL, James Hepburn, 4th Earl of (c1536–1578), powerful Scottish noble who married MARY QUEEN OF SCOTS in May 1567, after helping to murder her husband, Lord Darnley. In June he fled Scotland, and later died in a Danish prison.

BOTSWANA, formerly **Bechuanaland Protectorate**, landlocked republic bounded by South Africa, NAMIBIA (SW Africa) and ZIMBABWE.

Land. It is mainly plateau (at 3,300ft), with the Okavango Swamp in the N, the Kalahari Desert in the S and SW, and mountains in the E. Rivers include the Limpopo and Zambezi. The climate is generally subtropical, with one rainy season (averaging 18in of rain), supporting savanna vegetation except in the Kalahari Desert.

People and Economy. A few Bushmen survive in the desert and elsewhere, but Bantu-speaking blacks form the majority. They live chiefly in the SE around Gaborone, the capital. Cattle raising and export dominate the economy. Products include corn, peanuts, sorghum, asbestos

Official name: Republic of Botswana
Capital: Gaborone
Area: 224,607sq mi
Population: 1,168,000
Languages: English, Tswana, Khoisan
Religions: Christian, Animist
Monetary unit(s): 1 pula = 100 thebe

and manganese. Diamonds, beef and copper have fueled Botswana's economic growth, although a prolonged drought in the 1980s increased migration from rural areas to cities and contributed to rising unemployment. South Africa is the principal trade partner and the primary market for Botswana's beef.

History. Immigrant Negro tribes largely ousted the aboriginal Bushmen after 1600. In 1885 the area was placed under British supervision and became known as the Bechuanaland Protectorate. As Botswana, it became an independent member of the Commonwealth of Nations in 1966. Sir Seretse M. Khama was president from 1965 until his death in 1980. He was succeeded by vice president Quett K. Masire, who was reelected in 1984.

BOTTICELLI, Sandro (c1444–1510), one of the greatest painters of the Italian Renaissance, born Alessandro di Mariano Filipepi in Florence. His work is noted for superb draftsmanship, a use of sharp yet graceful and rhythmic line, and exquisite coloring. Among his most famous works are the allegorical tableaux on mythological subjects, *Primavera* and *The Birth of Venus.*

BOTULISM, usually fatal type of FOOD POISONING caused by a toxin produced by the anaerobic bacteria *Clostridium botulinum* and *C. parabotulinum*, which normally live in soil but may infect badly canned food. The toxin paralyzes the nervous system. Thorough cooking destroys both bacteria and toxin.

BOUCHER, François (1703–1770), French painter whose work epitomizes the ROCOCO taste of 18th-century France. Influenced by TIEPOLO, he painted airy, delicately-colored portraits and mythological scenes. He also designed

Gobelin tapestries and decorated interiors.

BOUCICAULT, Dion (c1822–1890), Irish-born actor and playwright active in London and New York. The 150 plays that he wrote or adapted, such as *London Assurance* (1841) and *The Shaughraun* (1874), ranged from light social drama to melodrama.

BOUGAINVILLE, Louis Antoine de (1729–1811), French officer and navigator who led the first French voyage around the world (1766–69), discovering Bougainville and visiting Tahiti, Samoa and the New Hebrides.

BOULANGER, Georges Ernest Jean Marie (1837–1891), French general, leader of an antirepublican movement which threatened the government in the late 1880s. War minister 1886–87 and a member of the Chamber of Deputies 1888 and 1889, he was convicted of treason in 1889, but had by then fled to Brussels. He later committed suicide.

BOULANGER, Nadia (1887–1979), enormously influential French teacher of musical composition. Her pupils included US composers Aaron Copland, Roy Harris and Virgil Thomson, as well as Darius Milhaud. She is also renowned as an instrumentalist and conductor.

BOULDER DAM. See HOOVER DAM.

BOULEZ, Pierre (1925–   ), versatile French composer and conductor, noted for his extension of 12-tone techniques in *Le Marteau sans maître* (1951) and *Pli selon Pli* (1960). He has conducted many of the world's leading orchestras.

BOULLE, Pierre (1912–   ), French novelist, best known for *The Bridge on the River Kwai* (1952) and *Planet of the Apes* (1963).

BOULT, Sir Adrian Cedric (1889–1983), English conductor. He was founder and first director of the BBC Symphony Orchestra (1930–49) and became noted for his interpretations of English composers, especially ELGAR and VAUGHAN WILLIAMS.

BOUMEDIENNE, Houari (real name: Mohammed Boukharouba; 1927–1978), president of Algeria. A teacher, he became active in the rebellion against France. After independence (1962), he was defense minister and vice-premier. In 1965 he overthrew President BEN BELLA and assumed power. He promoted nationalization and industrialization and was a radical spokesman for the Third World. He was president from 1976 until his death.

BOUNTY MUTINY, uprising on HMS *Bounty* in the S Pacific Ocean in 1789. Mutineers under master's mate Fletcher Christian cast their overbearing commander, Lt. William BLIGH, and 18 others adrift in a longboat. Bligh brought his party 3,618mi to Timor. Some of the mutineers founded a colony on Pitcairn Island.

BOURASSA, Henri (1868–1952), French Canadian journalist and politician who championed French Canadians. He was several times a member of the Canadian House of Commons, and was founder and editor of the Montreal daily *Le Devoir* (1910–32).

BOURBON. See WHISKEY.

BOURBONS, powerful French family which for generations ruled France, Naples and Sicily (the Two Sicilies), Parma and Spain, named for the castle of Bourbon NW of Moulins. The family is popularly remembered for its love of luxury and its obdurate resistance to political progress.

Bourbons became part of the French ruling house when a Bourbon heiress married Duke Robert, Louis IX's sixth son, in 1272. In 1589 their descendant, Henry of Navarre, founded France's Bourbon dynasty (as HENRY IV). Bourbon rule in France was interrupted with Louis XVI's execution in 1793, was restored in 1814 under Louis XVIII, and finally ended with the deposition of Charles X in 1830.

Meanwhile, Louis XIV's grandson came to the Spanish throne in 1700 as Philip V. In Italy, cadet branches of his family ruled Parma 1748–1860 and Naples and Sicily (the TWO SICILIES) 1759–1861. Bourbons ruled Spain to 1931, when Alfonso XIII abdicated. In 1947 Spain was again declared a monarchy, and in 1975 Prince Juan Carlos of Bourbon succeeded the head of state, General Franco.

BOURGEOIS, Léon Victor Auguste (1851–1925), French politician and diplomat who received the 1920 Nobel Peace Prize for his part in the founding of the LEAGUE OF NATIONS.

BOURGEOISIE, originally medieval town dwellers — tradesmen, artisans, etc. — outside the feudal relationship of peasants and noble landowners. As an increasingly powerful middle class, the bourgeoisie supported national monarchs and opposed the social and economic privileges of the aristocracy. In the 19th century, the bourgeoisie consisted of the haute bourgeoisie, comprising financiers and industrialists; the middle bourgeoisie, comprising managers and professionals; and the petite bourgeoisie, comprising shopkeepers and artisans. Karl Marx described the bourgeoisie as having performed a revolutionary role in the modernization of society. Critics of the bourgeoisie have regarded their virtues (e.g., sobriety, industriousness) as stultifying, and their values (e.g., materialism, conformism) as destructive of the life of the spirit. In the US, where the European class structure never took root, all but the very poor consider themselves middle class, and bourgois virtues and values are the norm.

BOURGUIBA,   Habib   Ben   Ali (1903–   ), Tunisian nationalist politician who became Tunisia's first president in 1957. He led the campaign for independence from the 1930s onwards and was imprisoned by the French several times. A pro-Western moderate, he ruled authoritatively, declaring himself president for life in 1975. In 1965 he proposed that the Arabs recognize Israel, but Tunis later became the seat of the Arab League and headquarters of the Palestine Liberation Organization. In 1987 he suppressed Muslim fundamentalists accused of attempting to overthrow the government. In Nov. 1987 Zine el-Abidine Ben Ali, whom Bourguiba had appointed prime minister only the month before, deposed the president as too ill and senile to govern.

BOURKE-WHITE,   Margaret (1906–1971), US photographer and war correspondent who covered WWII and the Korean War for Time-Life Inc.

BOUTS, Dirk (also Dierick or Thierry; c1420– 1475), Netherlands painter whose sober work conveys intense emotion. His backgrounds (especially landscapes) are vivid and lifelike, his figures dignified. His masterpiece is the Louvain altarpiece, *The Last Supper*.

BOUVINES, Battle of (1214), decisive battle in which Philip II of France, defeating a coalition of enemies that included King John of England, established French military prestige and power.

BOW BELLS, bells of the church at St. Mary-le-Bow in London. It is said that a true Londoner, or cockney, is born within sound of them.

BOWDITCH, Nathaniel (1773–1838), self-taught US mathematician and astronomer remembered for his *New American Practical Navigator* (1802), "the seaman's bible," later made standard in the US navy. He was the first to describe the plane curves known as Bowditch curves, or Lissajous' figures.

BOWDLER, Thomas (1754–1825), Scottish editor and doctor, whose popular *Family Shakespeare* expunged all supposedly blasphemous or indecent passages from Shakespeare's plays. The term "bowdlerize" came to mean any such misguided attempt to "clean up" a text.

BOWDOIN, James (1726–1790), American revolutionary leader and scientist. Bowdoin served in the Mass. legislature (1753–76) and supported the patriots' cause. As governor of Mass. (1785–87), he suppressed SHAYS' REBELLION. He was first president of the American Academy of Arts and Sciences.

BOWEN, Elizabeth (1899–1973), English-Irish novelist, born in Dublin, whose works are distinguished by their meticulous style and fine emotional sensitivity. They include *The Death of the Heart* (1938), *The Heat of the Day* (1949) and *Eva Trout* (1969).

BOWERS, Claude Gernade (1878–1958), US journalist, historian and diplomat whose popular historical accounts of the Jeffersonian era praised the early leaders of the Democratic Party. An editorial writer for the New York *World* (1923–31), he was active in Democratic party politics and served as ambassador to Spain (1933–39) and Chile (1939–53).

BOWIE, James (c1796–1836), Texan frontier hero who reputedly invented the Bowie hunting knife. He grew rich by land speculation and slave trading, moving W from Ga. to Ala., Miss., La., and eventually Tex. Bowie joined the Texan fight for independence from Mexico and was one of the leaders at the ALAMO, where he died.

BOWLES, Chester (1901–1986), US advertising man, politician and diplomat. He cofounded 1929 the advertising firm of Benton and Bowles, served on the War Production Board during WWII and was Democratic governor of Connecticut 1948–50. An internationalist, he served as ambassador to India 1951–53 and 1963–69, under secretary of state 1961 and special adviser to President John F. Kennedy 1961–63.

BOWLES, Paul (1910–   ), US author and composer living in Morocco, known for his exotic novels and short stories of alienation, despair and psychological horror. His works include *The Sheltering Sky* (1949) and *Collected Stories: 1939–1976* (1979).

BOWLING, popular indoor sport which involves rolling a ball to knock down wooden pins. In tenpin bowling, the most popular form in the US, players aim a large heavy ball down a long wooden lane at 10 pins set in a triangle. The number of pins felled determines the score. Bowling became popular in 14th-century Europe, and was brought to America by the Dutch in the 17th century. Tenpin bowling was standardized by the American Bowling Congress, founded in 1895.

BOWMAN, Isaiah (1878–1950), Canadian-born US geographer who did fieldwork in South America and served (1915–35) as director of the American Geographical Society. He was an adviser to President Woodrow Wilson at the Paris Peace Conference. From 1935 to 1948 he was president of Johns Hopkins U.

BOXER REBELLION, violent uprising in China in 1900 directed against foreigners and instigated by the secret society "Harmonious Fists" (called Boxers by the Europeans). Encouraged by the Dowager Empress TZ'U HSI, the Boxers showed their dislike of growing European influence and commercial exploitation in China, attacking missionaries and Chinese converts to Christianity. When the European powers sent troops to protect their nationals at Peking they were repulsed (June 10–26, 1900). The German minister in Peking was murdered and foreign legations were besieged for nearly two months until relieved by an international force. Boxer violence was the pretext for Russian occupation of S Manchuria. On Sept 7, 1901, China was forced to sign the humiliating Boxer Protocol, in which it promised to pay a huge indemnity to the US and the European powers concerned.

BOXING, the sport of skilled fist-fighting. Two contestants wearing padded gloves attack each other by punching prescribed parts of the body, and defend themselves by avoiding or blocking their opponent's punches. Boxing contests are arranged between opponents in the same weight division or class: there are 10 classes ranging from flyweight to heavyweight. Fights take place in a square roped-off ring and consist of a number of two- or three-minute rounds separated by rests. Scoring is usually made by a referee and two judges.

If a contest goes its full length, the contestant awarded the most points or rounds wins by a *decision*. But a win can occur earlier by a *knockout*, if a boxer legitimately knocks down his opponent and the man cannot regain his feet in 10 seconds. A fight may also end in a *technical knockout* if the referee decides that a boxer is physically unfit to go on fighting. Boxing rules are slightly different for amateurs and professionals, and interstate and international practices vary in some respects.

Boxing can be traced back to the Olympic Games of ancient Greece, and to Roman gladiatorial contests where fighters' hands were encased in an iron-studded guard called a *cestus*. Modern boxing has its roots in 18th-century English fairground fights between bareknuckled pugilists, who battered each other for bets until one could

no longer continue. James Figg (1696–1734) opened one of the first boxing arenas in London in 1719, and champion fighter John Broughton (1704–1789) designed the first boxing gloves and in 1743 introduced some rules of fair play.

Modern rules date from those introduced for glove fighting by the Marquis of Queensberry in 1867. Glove fighting became firmly established after 1892, when James J. CORBETT beat John L. SULLIVAN in New Orleans in the first acknowledged gloved heavyweight world championship contest. The National Sporting Club in England laid down weight ratings that helped to internationalize boxing. World heavyweight contests promoted by men like Tex Rickard (who set up the first million-dollar gate) continue to dominate public interest. Since 1900, the US has often held the heavyweight title, through holders like Jack Dempsey, 1919–26, Gene Tunney, 1926–28, Joe Louis, 1937–49, Rocky Marciano, 1952–56, Cassius Clay (Muhammad ALI), 1964–67 and 1974–78, and Joe Frazier, 1970–73.

BOYCOTT, the refusal to deal with a person or organization as a sign of disapproval or as a means of forcing them to meet certain demands. The word comes from **Captain Charles Boycott** (1832–1897), an English estate manager in Ireland who refused demands to lower rents and was isolated by the tenants who worked for him.

BOYD, Belle (1843–1900), Confederate spy in the American Civil War. An actress, she lived in Va., and passed military information to the South. Caught in 1862, she was released for lack of evidence in 1863.

BOYD-ORR, John Boyd Orr, 1st Baron (1880–1971), Scottish nutritionist concerned with problems of world hunger and poverty. Founding director (1945–48) of the UN FOOD AND AGRICULTURE ORGANIZATION (FAO), he received the 1949 Nobel Peace Prize.

BOYLE, Robert (1627–1691), British natural philosopher often called the father of modern CHEMISTRY for his rejection of the theories of the alchemists and his espousal of ATOMISM. A founder member of the ROYAL SOCIETY OF LONDON, he was noted for his pneumatic experiments.

BOYNE, Battle of the, battle on the R Boyne in E Ireland on July 1, 1690, which ended JAMES II's attempt to regain the English throne. WILLIAM III's 35,000 troops decisively defeated the Catholic JACOBITES' 21,000. Northern Ireland's Protestants celebrate (July 12) the victory to this day.

BOY SCOUTS OF AMERICA, US youth organization comprising Tiger Cubs (age 6), Cub Scouts (ages 7-10), Boy Scouts (ages 11-18), Explorers (male and female, ages 15-20). It was founded in 1910 and has headquarters in Irving, Tex. In 1988 it had 4.7 million members.

BOYS TOWN, village in E Nebr., near Omaha. It was founded in 1917 as a community for homeless and abandoned boys by Father Edward J. Flanagan and is governed by the boys. Pop c9,000.

BOZEMAN, John M. (1835–1867), US explorer and gold prospector, who pioneered in 1862–63 a new direct route linking Mont. and Col. through what became known as the Bozeman Pass. He was later killed by Indians. Bozeman, Mont., was founded by him.

BRADBURY, Ray (1920–   ) US science-fiction writer. A master of the short-story form, his characteristic tales deal with moral dilemmas. Among his best-known science-fiction works are *The Martian Chronicles* (1950) and *Fahrenheit 451* (1953).

BRADDOCK, Edward (1695–1755), commander-in-chief of British forces in North America, who was disastrously defeated in the FRENCH AND INDIAN WARS. Unused to frontier conditions, in 1755 he led a cumbersome expedition against Fort Duquesne (on the site of present-day Pittsburgh), which ran into a French and Indian ambush. Braddock was fatally wounded and his men were routed. Among the survivors was a Virginian officer, George Washington.

BRADFORD, William (1590–1657), Pilgrim Father who helped to establish PLYMOUTH COLONY and governed it most of his life (reelected 30 times from 1621). He described the *Mayflower's* voyage and the colony's first years in his *History of Plymouth Plantation*.

BRADLAUGH, Charles (1833–1891), English radical who was the first professed atheist to enter parliament.

BRADLEY, Omar Nelson (1893–1981), US general. In 1944–45 he led the 12th Army Group (1,000,000 men in four armies) in Europe. He was chief of staff of the US Army (1948–49) and first chairman of the joint chiefs of staff (1949–53).

BRADSTREET, Anne Dudley (c1612–1672), English–American colonial poet. She began writing after her emigration to Mass. in 1630. Her poems deal with personal reflections on the Puritan ethic and her coming to spiritual terms with it. Her collection, *The Tenth Muse Lately Sprung Up in America*, was published in England in 1650.

BRADY, James Buchanan ("Diamond Jim"; 1856–1917), US railroad tycoon and philanthropist. He acquired his fortune through the selling of railroad equipment and the establishing of two steel railroad car manufacturing firms. He is noted as a legendary spender on both entertainments and charities.

BRADY, Mathew B. (c1823–1896), US photographer of eminent people and historic events. He photographed 18 US presidents and spent his fortune in hiring 20 teams of photographers to take over 3,500 shots covering almost every big battle of the Civil War. The project bankrupted him. His most famous photographs are those of Lincoln and of the battles at Bull Run and Gettysburg.

BRAGG, Braxton (1817–1876), Confederate general. He led the Army of Tennessee which defeated William S. Rosecrans at Chickamauga (1863) but soon lost to Ulysses S. GRANT at Chattanooga, after which he forfeited his command.

BRAGG, Sir William Henry (1862–1942), British physicist who shared the 1915 Nobel Prize for Physics with his son, **Sir William Lawrence Bragg** (1890–1971), for learning how to deduce the atomic structure of CRYSTALS from their x-ray diffraction patterns (1912).

BRAHE, Tycho (1546–1601), Danish astronomer, the greatest exponent of naked-eye positional ASTRONOMY. KEPLER became his assistant in 1601 and was driven to postulate an elliptical orbit for MARS only because of his absolute confidence in the accuracy of Tycho's data. Brahe is also remembered for the "Tychonic system," in which the planets circled the sun, which in turn orbited a stationary earth, this being the principal 17th-century rival of the Copernican hypothesis.

BRAHMA, in HINDUISM, together with VISHNU and SHIVA part of the Trimurti. Traditionally the creator of the universe and personification of the Absolute, he is represented in Hindu art as having four arms and four faces.

BRAHMANISM, Indian religion based on belief in Brahma. It developed c500 BC from old Dravidian and Aryan beliefs. Its ritual, symbolism and theosophy came from the *Brahmanas*, sacred writings of the priestly caste, and from the UPANISHADS. It developed the "divinely ordered" caste system and gave rise to modern HINDUISM.

BRAHMAPUTRA RIVER, rises in the Himalayas and flows about 1800mi through Tibet, NE India, Bangladesh and S to the Ganges, forming the Ganges-Brahmaputra delta on the Bay of Bengal. A holy river to the Indians, its name means "son of Brahma."

BRAHMS, Johannes (1833–1897), major German Romantic composer. Though strongly influenced by Beethoven and the Romantic movement, he developed his own rhythmic originality and emotional intensity, while using classical forms. He lived largely in Vienna from 1863. His major works include four symphonies, two piano concertos, a violin concerto, a double concerto for violin and cello, piano and chamber works, songs, part-songs and choral works—notably *A German Requiem* (1868) and the *Alto Rhapsody* (1869).

BRAILLE, Louis (1809–1852), French inventor of BRAILLE. Accidentally blinded at the age of three, he conceived his raised-dot system at 15, while at the National Institute for the Blind in Paris. In 1829 he published a book explaining how his system could be used, not only for reading but also for writing and musical notation.

BRAILLE, system of writing devised for the blind by Louis BRAILLE. It employs patterns of raised dots that can be read by touch. Braille typewriters and printing presses have been devised for the mass-production of books for the blind.

BRAIN, complex organ which, together with the SPINAL CORD, comprises the central NERVOUS SYSTEM and coordinates all nerve-cell activity. In invertebrates the brain is no more than a ganglion; in VERTEBRATES it is more developed—tubular in lower vertebrates and larger, more differentiated and more rounded in higher ones. In higher MAMMALS, including man, the brain is dominated by the highly developed cerebral cortex. The brain is composed of many billions of interconnecting nerve cells (see NEURONS) and supporting cells (neuroglia). The BLOOD CIRCULATION, in particular the regulation of blood pressure, is designed to ensure an adequate supply of oxygen to these cells: if this supply is cut off, neurons die in only a few minutes. The brain is well protected inside the skull and is surrounded, like the spinal cord, by three membranes, the meninges. Between the two inner meninges lies the CEREBROSPINAL FLUID (CSF), an aqueous solution of salts and glucose. CSF also fills the four ventricles (cavities) of the brain and the central canal of the spinal cord. If the circulation of CSF between ventricles and meninges becomes blocked, HYDROCEPHALUS results. Relief of this may involve draining CSF to the atrium of the heart.

The human brain may be divided structurally into three parts: (1) the **hindbrain**, consisting of the *medulla oblongata*, which contains vital centers to control heartbeat and breathing; the *pons*, which, like the *medulla oblongata*, contains certain cranial nerve nuclei and numerous fibers passing between the higher brain centers and the spinal cord; and the *cerebellum*, which regulates balance, posture and coordination. (2) The **midbrain**, a small but important center for REFLEXES in the brain stem, also containing nuclei of the cranial nerves and the *reticular formation*, a diffuse network of neurons involved in regulating arousal: SLEEP and alertness. (3) The **forebrain**, consisting of the *thalamus*, which relays sensory impulses to the cortex; the *hypothalamus*, which controls the autonomic nervous system, food and water intake and temperature regulation, and to which the PITUITARY GLAND is closely related; and the *cerebrum*. The cerebrum makes up two-thirds of the entire brain and has a deeply convoluted surface; it is divided into two interconnected halves, or hemispheres. The main functional zones of the cerebrum are the surface layers of gray matter, the cortex, below which is a broad white layer of nerve fiber connections, and the *basal ganglia*, concerned with muscle control. (Disease of the basal ganglia causes PARKINSON'S DISEASE.) Each hemisphere has a motor cortex, controlling voluntary movement, and a sensory cortex, receiving cutaneous sensation, both relating to the opposite side of the body. Other areas of cortex are concerned with language (see APHASIA, SPEECH AND SPEECH DISORDERS), memory, and perception of the special senses (sight, smell, sound); higher functions such as abstract thought may also be a cortical function (see also INTELLIGENCE, LEARNING). Diseases of the brain include infections—specifically MENINGITIS, ENCEPHALITIS, syphilis (see VENEREAL DISEASES) and ABSCESSES; also trauma, TUMORS, STROKES, MULTIPLE SCLEROSIS, and degenerative diseases with early atrophy, either generalized or localized. Investigation of brain diseases includes X RAYS, using various contrast methods, SPINAL TAP (lumbar puncture)—to study CSF abnormalities—and the use of the ELECTROENCEPHALOGRAM. Treatments range from a variety of drugs, including ANTIBIOTICS and STEROIDS, to SURGERY.

BRAINE, John (1922–1986), English novelist best known for his first novel *Room at the Top* (1957), about the rise of a young, ambitious working-class man. Braine's other works include *The Queen of a Distant Country* (1972) and *J.B. Priestley* (1979).

BRAIN TRUST, popular name for the intellectuals advising Franklin D. Roosevelt in his 1932 campaign and first years in office. Professor Raymond Moley headed the group, which included Adolph A. Berle, Jr., Rexford G. Tugwell, Samuel I. Rosenman and Basil O'Connor.

BRAKES, devices for slowing or halting motion, usually by conversion of kinetic ENERGY into HEAT energy via the medium of FRICTION. Perhaps most common are **drum brakes,** where a stationary member is brought into contact with the wheel or a drum that rotates with it. They may be either *band brakes,* where a band of suitable material encircling the drum is pulled tightly against its circumference, or *shoe brakes,* where one or more shoes (shaped blocks of suitable material) are applied to the inner or outer circumference of the drum. Similar in principle are **disk brakes,** where the frictional force is applied to the sides of the wheel or a disk that rotates with it. The simplest form is the *caliper brake,* as used on bicycles, in which rubber blocks are pressed against the rim of the wheel. Almost all AIRPLANE, AUTOMOBILE and RAILROAD brakes are of drum or disk type.

Mechanically operated brakes cannot always be used, as when a single control must operate on a number of wheels, thus involving problems in simultaneity and equality of braking action. In such cases, pressure is applied to a HYDRAULIC system (usually oil-filled), and hence equally to the brakes. Similar in principle are vacuum brakes, where creation of a partial VACUUM operates a piston which applies the braking action, and air brakes. **Fluid brakes,** used mainly in trucks to restrict speed in downhill travel, must be used in combination with mechanical brakes if it is desired to halt the vehicle. They consist of a rotating and a stationary element, between which a liquid (usually water) is introduced. Here it is FLUID rather than mechanical friction that converts the kinetic energy. (Cooling is usually performed by circulation through the radiator.) **Electric brakes,** similarly, may only restrict motion. The most common type, used on electric trains on downhill runs, consists merely of a GENERATOR driven by the axle (the electricity generated may be used by the train).

BRAMANTE, Donato (1444–1514), leading Italian architect who developed the classical principles of High Renaissance architecture. In 1499, he moved from Milan to Rome, where his major designs included the Tempietto of S. Pietro in Montorio (1502) and the Belvedere Court at the Vatican (c1505). His greatest project, the reconstruction of St. Peter's, was not realized.

BRANCUSI, Constantin (1876–1957), Romanian sculptor famous for his simple, elemental, polished forms. Living in Paris from 1904, he rejected Rodin's influence, turning to abstract forms and the example of primitive art. Among his best-known works are *The Kiss* (1908) and *Bird in Space* (1919).

BRANDEIS, Louis Dembitz (1856–1941), US jurist, influential in securing social, political and economic reforms, especially while an associate justice of the Supreme Court (1916–39). As a lawyer he crusaded for organized labor against big business interests.

BRANDENBERG, former German principality, ruled from 1417 by the house of HOHENZOLLERN. In the 17th century its rulers, who were electors of the Holy Roman Empire, acquired territories in W Germany and the duchy of PRUSSIA in the E. FREDERICK WILLIAM, "the Great Elector," made Brandenberg a military power. His son took (1701) the title king of Prussia as Frederick I.

BRANDES, Georg Morris Cohen (1842–1927), Danish literary critic who deeply influenced the course of Scandinavian literature in the late 19th and early 20th centuries. Particularly important was his series of lectures published as *Main Currents in 19th-Century Literature* (1871–87).

BRANDO, Marlon (1924–   ), US stage and film actor who won fame for his portrayal of Stanley Kowalski in *A Streetcar Named Desire* (play, 1947; film, 1951). He won Academy Awards for *On the Waterfront* (1954) and *The Godfather* (1972).

BRANDT, Willy (1913–   ), Social Democratic chancellor of West Germany 1969–74, whose *Ostpolitik* (Eastern policy) marked a major step towards East-West detente in Europe. Born Karl Herbert Frahm, he was mayor of West Berlin 1957–66. As chancellor, he secured friendship treaties with Poland and the USSR (1970), with East Germany (1972) and with Czechoslovakia (1974). Brandt's initiative won him the 1971·Nobel Peace Prize. He was forced to resign as chancellor in 1974 over a spy scandal in his own administration. In 1987 he resigned the chairmanship of the Social Democratic Party and retired from politics.

BRANDY, alcoholic drink of distilled grape or other wine, usually matured in wood. Brandies include cognac, from French wines of the Cognac area, kirsch (made from cherries) and slivovitz (made from plums).

BRANDYWINE, Battle of, a British victory in the REVOLUTIONARY WAR. On Sept. 11, 1777, at Brandywine Creek in SE Pa., Gen. William Howe's 15,000 British troops surprised the right flank of Washington's 11,000 men protecting Philadelphia. Washington retreated to Germantown, and Howe went on to take Philadelphia.

BRANT, Joseph (1742–1807), Mohawk Indian chief, Episcopal missionary and British army colonel. His tribal name was Thayendanegea. He served with the British forces in the FRENCH AND INDIAN WARS and in the REVOLUTIONARY WAR, participating in the Cherry Valley Massacre (1778).

BRANT, Sebastian (c1458–1521), German poet, renowned for his satirical allegory, *The Ship of Fools* (1494), telling of 111 fools led by other fools to a fools' paradise.

BRANTING, (Karl) Hjalmar (1860–1925), Swedish Social Democratic politician, premier 1920, 1921–23, 1924–25. For resolving a dispute with Finland over the Aaland Islands he shared the 1921 Nobel Peace Prize.

BRAQUE, Georges (1882–1963), French painter and sculptor, a seminal figure in modern art. From FAUVISM he went on, together with PICASSO, to evolve CUBISM and to be among the first to use COLLAGE. Among his many major works are *Woman with a Mandolin* (1937) and the *Birds* series (1955–63).

BRASÍLIA, federal capital of Brazil since 1960, located on the Paraná R, 600mi NW of the old coastal capital, Rio de Janeiro. It was built to help open up the immense Brazilian interior. Its cross-shaped plan was designed by Lúcio Costa, while such major buildings as the presidential palace and the cathedral are the work of Oscar NIEMEYER. Pop 1,576,657.

BRASS, an ALLOY of COPPER and ZINC, known since Roman times, and widely used in industry and for ornament and decoration. Up to 36% zinc forms α-brass, which can be worked cold; with more zinc a mixture of α- and β-brass is formed, which is less ductile but stronger. Brasses containing more than 45% zinc (white brasses) are unworkable and have few uses. Some brasses also contain other metals: lead to improve machinability, aluminum or tin for greater corrosion-resistance, and nickel, manganese or iron for higher strength.

BRAUDEL, Fernand (1902–1985), French historian whose studies of the Mediterranean world in early modern times are considered classics of social history.

BRAZIL, fifth-largest country in the world, covering nearly half of South America. It derives its name from its vast dyewood (*pau-brasil*) forests. Brazil shares borders with all the S American countries except Ecuador and Chile.

Official name: Federative Republic of Brazil
Capital: Brasília
Area: 3,286,488sq mi
Population: 141,302,000
Languages: Portuguese
Religions: Roman Catholic
Monetary unit(s): 1 cruzeiro = 100 centavos
Land. There are two major geographical regions: the lowlands of the Amazon R basin, mostly tropical rain forests (*selvas*); and the Brazilian highlands, an extensive mountainous tableland in the S and E making up two-thirds of the country's land area. Brazil has over 4,600mi of coastline.
People. Brazil differs from its Spanish-speaking neighbors in having a racially integrated population. This consists of a three-fold mixture: the Portuguese inter-married both with the native Indians and with the black slaves imported from W Africa. About 200,000 Indians of several tribes live in the Amazon basin. The majority of Brazilians belong to the Roman Catholic Church, which also runs most state schools. About two-thirds of the people live in cities. As a result of a literacy drive in the 1970s, the illiteracy rate declined to about 14%.
Economy. Although Brazil is rich in natural resources, few of these have been developed. Iron ore deposits may be the largest in the world; and there is also manganese, chromium, tin, gold, nickel, coal, tungsten and bauxite. No big reserves of oil have been discovered. But Brazil is best known as South America's biggest producer of cattle, coffee and cocoa. In 1977 the country was the world's largest exporter of agricultural products. Manufactures include textiles, chemicals, plastics, appliances, and machinery. An impressive economic growth in the 1970s made Brazil the leading industrial power in Latin America and led

to improvements in transport, energy, and social welfare.

History. Brazil was explored by the Spanish navigator Vicente Yáñez Pinzón early in 1500, and later in the same year, independently, by Portugal's Pedro Álvares Cabral, but colonization did not begin until after 1532. Slaves were used extensively by the plantation owners, until Jesuit missionaries intervened in the 17th century. The country gained independence in 1822 under its governor, Dom Pedro, who then ruled Brazil as emperor for the next nine years. Largely under military rule after 1889 when it became a republic, Brazil made rapid technological progress under President Juscelino Kubitschek, who replaced the previous capital, Rio de Janeiro, by BRASÍLIA in 1960. The left-wing civilian government of João Goulart was overthrown by the military in 1964. The successive military governments were often accused of torture and other human-rights violations. In 1985 the military voluntarily surrendered power to a conservative civilian government led by José Sarney. The civilians proved no more able than the military to deal with Brazil's urgent economic problems, at the center of which was a foreign debt of $113 billion, the largest in the third world. In 1987, Sarney suspended interest payments on $68 billion owed to foreign banks, but payments were resumed the following year. Inflation and unemployment soared, punctuated by labor stoppages and riots. Meanwhile, a special assembly worked on a new constitution. Early in 1988 the military vetoed a proposal to replace the presidential system of government with a parliamentary system, and it ordered presidential elections, scheduled for later that year, postponed for at least another year.

BREAD, one of humanity's earliest and most important foods, basically comprising baked "dough"—a mixture of FLOUR and water. In developed western societies, WHEAT flour is most commonly used and the dough is "leavened" (i.e., increased in volume by introducing small bubbles of CARBON dioxide throughout) using YEAST. In making bread, the chosen blend of flours is mixed with water, yeast, shortening and salt (and sometimes sugar and milk) to form the dough. This is then kneaded to distribute the GLUTEN throughout the mix, left to rise, kneaded again, molded into shape and left to rise a second time before baking. Bread is generally high in CARBOHYDRATES though low in PROTEIN. The vitamin and mineral content depends on the ingredients and additives used.

BREASTED, James Henry (1865–1935), US archaeologist and historian, who advanced archaeological research in Egypt and W Asia. He specialized in Egyptology, and in 1919 organized the Oriental Institute at the U. of Chicago, subsequently sponsoring expeditions at Megiddo and Persepolis.

BREASTS, or **mammary glands,** the milk-secreting glands in MAMMALS. The breasts develop alike in both sexes, about 20 ducts being formed leading to the nipples, till puberty when the female breasts develop in response to sex HORMONES. In PREGNANCY the breasts enlarge and milk-forming tissue grows around multiplied ducts; later milk secretion and release in response to suckling occur under the control of specific pituitary hormones. Disorders of the breast include mastitis, breast CANCER (see also MASTECTOMY) and adenosis. In humans, the breasts are erogenous zones in both males and females.

BREATHING. See RESPIRATION.

BRECHT, Bertolt (originally, Eugen Berthold Friedrich Brecht; 1898–1956), German Marxist playwright and poet, who revolutionized modern theater with his production techniques and concept of EPIC THEATER. He left Nazi Germany in 1933, returning to East Berlin in 1948 to found the Berliner Ensemble. His plays include *The Threepenny Opera* (1928), *The Life of Galileo* (1938), *Mother Courage* (1939) and *The Caucasian Chalk Circle* (1949).

BRECKINRIDGE, John Cabell (1821–1875), US politician, vice-president of the US 1857–61. He became a congressman from Ky. in 1851, and was elected to the Senate while still vice-president. He was Democratic presidential candidate in 1860, but lost to Lincoln. He joined the Confederate government in the Civil War, becoming a major general and, in 1865, secretary of war.

BREEDING, the development of new strains of plants and animals with more desirable characteristics, such as higher yields or greater resistance to disease and suitability to the climate. Breeding has been practiced since prehistoric times— producing our modern domestic animals—but without firm scientific basis until MENDEL's theory of GENETICS. The breeder first decides which traits he wishes to develop, and observes the range of PHENOTYPES in the breeding population. Discounting variants due to environmental differences, he selects those individuals of superior GENOTYPE. This genetic variation may occur naturally, or may be produced by hybridization or MUTATIONS induced by radiation or certain chemicals. The selected individuals are used as parent stock for INBREEDING to purify the strain. (See also ANIMAL HUSBANDRY.)

BRENDAN, Saint (c484–578 AD), Irish monk who, according to the 8th-century *Voyages of St. Brendan*, may have reached America 900 years before Columbus.

BRENNAN, William Joseph, Jr. (1906–   ), US jurist, associate justice on the US Supreme Court from 1956. He was regarded as the leading liberal on an increasingly conservative court.

BRENNER PASS, important pass across the Alps, in the Tyrol, linking Innsbruck in Austria with Bolzano in Italy. The first good road along this ancient route was completed in 1772, and the railroad was built 1864–67.

BRENTANO, Clemens (1778–1842), German Romantic poet, novelist and dramatist. Together with Ludwig Joachim von Arnim he edited the famous *Des Knaben Wunderhorn* (1805–08), a collection of folksongs which greatly influenced later German lyric poetry.

BRENTANO, Franz (1838–1917), German philosopher and psychologist, a Roman Catholic priest from 1864 to 1873, who founded the school of intentionalism and taught both FREUD and HUSSERL.

BREST-LITOVSK, Treaty of, the separate peace imposed on Soviet Russia by Germany and her allies during WWI, signed March 3, 1918, at Brest-Litovsk (now Brest) in Belorussia. By it Russia lost the Ukraine, Finland, and its Polish and Baltic possessions. The treaty was nullified on Nov. 11, 1918.

BRETON, André (1896–1966), French poet and critic, a founder of SURREALISM. Associated at first with DADA, he broke with it and in 1924 issued the first of three Surrealist manifestos, becoming the new movement's chief spokesman. Among his works is the poetic novel, *Nadja* (1928).

BRETTON WOODS CONFERENCE, international gathering at Bretton Woods, N.H., in July 1944, at which 44 members of the United Nations planned to stabilize the international economy and national currencies after WWII. They also established the INTERNATIONAL MONETARY FUND and the WORLD BANK.

BREUER, Josef (1842–1925), Austrian physician who pioneered the methods of PSYCHOANALYSIS and collaborated with FREUD in writing *Studies in Hysteria* (1895). He also discovered the role of the semicircular canals of the inner EAR in maintaining balance (1873).

BREUER, Marcel (Lajos) (1902–1981), Hungarian-born US architect. A student

and teacher at the BAUHAUS 1920–28, he moved in 1937 to Harvard and continued working with GROPIUS. A pioneer of the International Style, he collaborated in the design of the UNESCO headquarters, Paris (1953–58).

BREUGHEL. See BRUEGEL.

BREUIL, Henri Édouard Prosper (1877–1961), French archaeologist famous for his studies of the paleolithic cave paintings in S France, N Spain, and Africa.

BREWSTER, William (1567–1644), a leader of the Plymouth Colony, New England. He led the Puritan congregation formed in England in 1606, and sailed with the Pilgrims on the MAYFLOWER in 1620. He played a major part in regulating the civil and religious affairs of the Plymouth Colony.

BREZHNEV, Leonid Ilyich (1906–1982), USSR political leader, who became first secretary of the Communist party in 1964 and, as such, effective head of the Soviet government. He first became a member of the party central committee in 1952, and was chairman of the presidium of the supreme soviet 1960–64. Brezhnev, KOSYGIN and PODGORNY took control when KHRUSHCHEV was ousted in 1964. Brezhnev assumed the additional office of chief of state in 1977. He pursued a policy of détente with the West while overseeing a massive buildup of Soviet military might. He was only partially successful in overcoming shortcomings in industry and agriculture.

BRIAN BORU (941–1014), king of Ireland from 1002. His reign marked the end of Norse domination but unified rule died with him. He was murdered after his victory against the Danes at Clontarf.

BRIAND, Aristide (1862–1932), French statesman, lawyer and socialist leader who was 11 times premier of France. As foreign minister (1925–32), he was the author of the KELLOGG-BRIAND PACT. He was awarded the Nobel Peace Prize in 1926.

BRICE, Fanny (Fannie Borach; 1891–1951), US singer and comedienne who starred in Ziegfield *Follies* and later on radio. *Funny Girl* (play, 1964; film, 1968) was based on her life.

BRIDGE, a card game developed from WHIST. Contract bridge, the form now universally adopted, was perfected by Harold S. Vanderbilt in 1925–26. It is played by two pairs of partners, who before starting play must make bids according to how many tricks they calculate they can win. Demanding great skill, bridge has become immensely popular as a social and competitive game, with international championships controlled by the World Bridge Federation.

BRIDGE, any device that spans an obstacle and permits traffic of some kind (usually vehicular, bridges that carry canals being more generally termed aqueducts) across it. The most primitive form is the **beam** (or **girder**) **bridge,** consisting of a rigid beam resting at either end on piers. The span may be increased by use of intermediate piers, possibly bearing more than one beam. A development of this is the **truss bridge,** a truss being a metal framework specifically designed for greatest strength at those points where the load has greatest moment about the piers. Where piers are impracticable, **cantilever bridges** may be built: from each side extends a beam (cantilever), firmly anchored at its inshore end. The gap between the two outer ends may be closed by a third beam. Another form of bridge is the **arch bridge,** essentially an ARCH built across the gap: a succession of arches supported by intermediate piers may be used for wider gaps. A **suspension bridge** comprises two towers that carry one or more flexible cables that are firmly anchored at each end. From these is suspended the roadway by means of vertical cables. **Movable bridges** take many forms, the most common being the **swing bridge,** pivoted on a central pier; the **bascule** (a descendant of the medieval drawbridge), whose cantilevers are pivoted inshore so that they may be swung upward; the **vertical-lift bridge,** comprising a pair of towers between which runs a beam that may be winched vertically upward; and the less common **retractable bridge,** whose cantilevers may be run inshore on wheels. The most common temporary bridges include the **pontoon,** or floating bridge, comprising a number of floating members that support a continuous roadway.

BRIDGER, James (1804–1881), US trader, explorer and army scout. He traded in the unexplored American West and Southwest. He discovered Great Salt Lake (1824), and founded Fort Bridger, Wyo.

BRIDGES, Harry (Alfred Bryant Renton Bridges; 1901–   ), US labor leader, born in Australia. He helped form the International Longshoremen's and Warehousemen's Union (ILWU) in 1937, and as its president fought to improve dockworking conditions. Until 1955 there were many government attempts to deport him as a communist.

BRIDGES, Robert Seymour (1844–1930), English poet laureate, noted for the technical mastery of his verse and his editing of the poetry of Gerard Manley

HOPKINS (1916). His works include the philosophical poem, *The Testament of Beauty* (1929).

BRIGHT, John (1811–1889), British politician and orator, of Quaker descent. He entered parliament in 1843, and held office under Gladstone. A champion of free trade and of electoral reform, he was a cofounder of the Anti-Corn-Law League and opposed British participation in the Crimean War.

BRIGHT'S DISEASE, a form of acute NEPHRITIS that may follow infections with certain STREPTOCOCCUS types. Blood and protein are lost in the urine; there may be EDEMA and raised blood pressure. Recovery is usually complete but a few patients progress to chronic KIDNEY disease.

BRILL, Abraham Arden (1874–1948), Austrian-born US psychiatrist, the "father of American PSYCHOANALYSIS," who introduced the Freudian method to the US and translated many of FREUD'S works into English.

BRISBANE, Albert (1809–1890), US Utopian philosopher and socialist. A disciple of FOURIER, he wrote the influential *Social Destiny of Man* (1840).

BRITAIN, modern form of the ancient name for the island now comprising England, Scotland and Wales. The Romans referred to the 1st-century BC Celtic inhabitants as *Pritani,* hence their own name for the island, *Britannia.* (See GREAT BRITAIN.)

BRITISH COLUMBIA, province on the W coast of Canada, bounded on the W by the Pacific Ocean and S Alaska and on the E by the province of Alberta.
Name of province: British Columbia
Joined Confederation: July 20, 1871
Capital: Victoria
Area: 366,255 sq mi
Population: 2,859,261
Land. About 500mi from E to W and about 770mi from N to S, it is the most rugged of Canada's provinces. There are two main mountain chains, the Coast Mts in the W and the Canadian Rocky Mts in the E. In the remarkable Rocky Mountain Trench the upper courses of many rivers can be found, notably the Columbia, the Fraser and the Kootenay. The 700mi coastline is broken by fjords; among the offshore chains of islands Vancouver Island and the Queen Charlotte Islands are the most important. Temperatures and rainfall differ greatly in various parts of the province, with a mild climate near the coast, but temperatures vary between 100°F and −35°F in the interior.
People and Economy. About 75% of the population, predominantly of British origin,

live in the milder SW part of the province, where Vancouver is the largest city. There are also considerable Chinese, Japanese and East Indian minorities. Forestry now generates about 50 cents of every dollar earned in the province, and many of the world's major newspapers are printed on paper produced there. Copper, molybdenum, zinc and lead are major minerals; oil and natural gas are produced in the NE. Dairy farming and the production of livestock and related products dominate the agricultural sector of the economy. A 200mi fishing zone was adopted in 1977 and has boosted the fishing industry. Manufacturing, with transportation equipment, chemicals, machinery and fabricated metals the chief producers, has expanded in recent years and is concentrated in the Vancouver/New Westminster area.

History. The area was first visited by the Spanish explorer Juan Pérez in 1774, and in 1778 Captain Cook anchored in Nootka Sound. Britain commissioned George Vancouver to survey the coast in 1792. Other early explorers were Alexander MACKENZIE, David Thompson and Simon FRASER. For a time, the region was called New Caledonia, and its trade was controlled by the Hudson's Bay Company after 1821. Settlement increased following the discovery of gold in 1858, when the colony of British Columbia was established. It became a province of Canada in 1871. A new era began in 1885, when the railroad reached Vancouver, which grew to become the capital. The Social Credit Party was led into power by W. A. C. Bennett in 1952, and retained control for 20 years. He built extensive road and rail networks, two of the largest hydroelectric projects in North America, introduced hospital insurance and began operation of the province's power-distribution system, railway and ferry fleet. The New Democratic Party government, led by Dave Barrett, in power 1972–75, introduced social policies in the areas of health care, old age security, auto insurance and housing and instituted the Land Commission Act to encourage family farming and conservation. Social Credit leaders, returned to power in 1975, focused on a program of fiscal austerity that slowed economic growth and resulted in a 1985 unemployment rate of 15%. By 1988, however, industries, especially forest products, were thriving.

BRITISH HONDURAS. See BELIZE.

BRITISH MUSEUM, national museum of antiquities and ethnography in London. Founded in 1753, when the British government acquired the art collection and library of Sir Hans Sloane, it opened to the public in 1759. Its present neoclassical premises were built 1823–47 and its natural history section was separated 1881–83. The museum has one of the world's foremost collections, including the ELGIN MARBLES.

BRITISH NORTH AMERICA ACT, an act passed by the British parliament in 1867 to create the Dominion of Canada, uniting Canada (Quebec and Ontario), New Brunswick and Nova Scotia under a federal government. The act served as Canada's constitution until 1982; under it, the British Parliament had to grant formal approval to amendments. The CONSTITUTION ACT, 1982, superseded the earlier law (now also known as the Constitution Act, 1867), thus "patriating" the constitution.

BRITTANY (French: Bretagne), historic peninsular region of NW France. The Romans conquered the area in 56 BC and named it Armorica. It was settled c500 AD by Celtic Britons fleeing the Anglo-Saxon invasion. After struggles for independence from the Franks and from Normandy, Anjou, England and France in turn, it became a French province in 1532. The Bretons retain their own cultural traditions and language.

BRITTEN, Benjamin (1913–1976), outstanding British composer. His works include several important operas, among them *Peter Grimes* (1945), *Billy Budd* (1951), *The Turn of the Screw* (1954) and *Death in Venice* (1973). Among his many notable instrumental and choral works are the *Variations on a Theme by Frank Bridge* (1937) and *War Requiem* (1962).

BROADCASTING NETWORKS, US, American companies which produce programs for broadcasting to the public over a network or affiliated group of radio or television stations, interlinked by wire or radio relay. The four prime US networks (all commercial) are NBC (National Broadcasting Company), which organized the first radio network (1926), introduced regular TV service in 1939 and began coast-to-coast TV broadcasting in 1951; CBS (Columbia Broadcasting System, Inc.), organized in 1927, which broadcasts radio and TV programs, manufactures electronic equipment and operates hundreds of stations through the US; ABC (American Broadcasting Companies, Inc.), founded 1943; and the Mutual Broadcasting System (MBS), with close to 500 affiliated independently-owned radio outlets, which became a coast-to-coast network in 1936. The Public Broadcasting System (PBS) was established in 1969 for educational, noncommercial public TV; it is funded by the federal government and private foundations.

BROD, Max (1884–1968), Czech author, best known as editor of the works of his friend Franz KAFKA, which he saved from destruction. His own works include the novel, *The Redemption of Tycho Brahe* (1916) and a biography of Kafka (1937). He emigrated to Palestine in 1939.

BRODSKY, Joseph (1940–   ), Soviet-born US poet and essayist who received the 1987 Nobel Prize for Literature. *History of the Twentieth Century* (1986) is a collection of his poems, *Less Than One* (1986) a collection of his essays.

BROGLIE, Louis Victor Pierre Raymond, Prince de (1892–1987), French physicist who was awarded the 1929 Nobel Prize in Physics for his suggestion that subatomic particles should display wave properties under appropriate conditions in the same way that ELECTROMAGNETIC RADIATION sometimes behaved as if composed of particles.

BROMFIELD, Louis (1896–1956), US novelist, winner of a 1926 Pulitzer Prize for his novel, *Early Autumn.* His other works include *The Rains Came* (1937) and *Pleasant Valley* (1945).

BRONCHI, tubes through which air passes from the trachea to the lungs. The trachea divides into the two primary bronchi, one to each lung, which divide into smaller branches and finally into the narrow bronchioles connecting with the alveolar sacs. The bronchi are lined with a mucous membrane which has motile cilia to remove dust, etc.

BRONCHITIS, inflammation of bronchi, tubes through which air passes from the trachea to the lungs. **Acute bronchitis**, often due to VIRUS infection, is accompanied by COUGH and FEVER and is short-lived; ANTIBIOTICS are only needed if there is bacterial infection. **Chronic bronchitis** is a more serious, often disabling and finally fatal disease. The main cause is SMOKING, which irritates the LUNGS and causes overproduction of mucus. The cilia fail, and sputum has to be coughed up. Bronchi thus become liable to recurrent bacterial infection, sometimes progressing to PNEUMONIA. Areas of lung become non-functional, and ultimately cyanosis and HEART failure may result. Treatment includes PHYSIOTHERAPY, antibiotics and bronchial dilator drugs. Stopping smoking limits damage and may improve early cases.

BRONK, Detlev Wulf (1897–1975), US biologist who was a pioneer in the application of physics to biological processes. He influenced the growth of medical research in the US as president of Johns Hopkins University (1949–53) and Rockefeller Institute for Medical Research (1953–68).

BRONTË, name of three English novelists, daughters of an Irish-born Anglican clergyman. They lived chiefly in the isolated moorland town of Haworth, Yorkshire. Their lives, marred by the early death of their mother and the dissipations of their brother, Branwell, were closely bound together, and this domestic intensity informed much of their work. **Charlotte Brontë** (1816–1855) published the partly autobiographical *Jane Eyre* (1847) under the name Currer Bell, and met with immediate success. Together with *Shirley* (1849) and *Villette* (1853), it represents an important advance in the treatment of women in English fiction. **Emily Brontë** (1818–1848), using the name Ellis Bell, published a single novel, *Wuthering Heights* (1847), a masterpiece of visionary power. **Anne Brontë** (1820–1849) published two novels, *Agnes Grey* (1847) and *The Tenant of Wildfell Hall* (1848), under the name Acton Bell.

BRONZE, an ALLOY of COPPER and TIN, known since the 4th millennium BC (see BRONZE AGE), and used then for tools and weapons, now for machine parts and marine hardware. Statues are often cast in bronze. It is a hard, strong alloy with good corrosion-resistance (the patina formed in air is protective). Various other components are added to bronze to improve hardness or machinability, such as aluminum, iron, lead, zinc and phosphorus. Aluminum bronzes, and some others, contain no tin.

BRONZE AGE, the phase of man's material cultural development following the STONE AGE, and the first phase in which metal was used. The start of the bronze age varies from region to region, but certainly the use of copper was known as early as 6,500 BC in Asia Minor, and its use was widespread shortly thereafter. By about 3,000 BC BRONZE was widely used, to be replaced around 1000 BC by iron.

BRONZINO, Il (1503–1572), Florentine painter noted for his sophisticated portraits of aristocrats in the mannerist style. (See MANNERISM.)

BROOK, Peter (1925–   ), English theatrical director noted for his inventive, unconventional productions of such classics as Shakespeare's *King Lear* and *A Midsummer Night's Dream.* A proponent of the avant garde, Brook directed highly acclaimed English performances of DÜRRENMATT's *The Visit* (1958) and Peter

WEISS' *Marat/Sade* (1964).

BROOKE, Sir James (1803–1868), English adventurer who became the ruler of Sarawak, Borneo. Appointed raja in 1841, he founded a dynasty which ruled Sarawak until 1946, when the region was ceded to Britain.

BROOKE, Rupert (1887–1915), English war poet whose patriotic sonnets were widely popular during the early days of WWI. His *Collected Poems* were published in 1918.

BROOK FARM, US Utopian community, founded at West Roxbury, Mass., by George RIPLEY in 1841. The aim was to create an egalitarian community of workers and thinkers. The community contained a noted progressive school and attracted many leading intellectuals, but lasted only until 1847.

BROOKHAVEN NATIONAL LABORATORY, center for nuclear research at Camp Upton, Long Island, N.Y. Under the aegis of the US Atomic Energy Commission, it has facilities for medical and agricultural research.

BROOKINGS INSTITUTION, nonprofit-making, public service corporation founded in 1927 in Washington, D.C., for research and information on government and economic problems. It was named for the St. Louis merchant, Robert S. Brookings.

BROOKLYN BRIDGE, famous suspension bridge in New York City between the borough of Brooklyn and Manhattan Island. It was built in 1869–83 by A. J. Roebling and his son, pioneers in the use of steel-wire support cables, which give the bridge its characteristic spider-web appearance. Its two huge masonry towers are supported by pneumatic caissons, another pioneering feat of the Roeblings.

BROOKS, Cleanth (1906–   ), US literary critic and editor, one of the New Critics. In such works as *The Well Wrought Urn* (1947), he argued that the essential core of poetry is metaphor and meter. With Robert Penn WARREN he wrote or edited several texts, including *Modern Rhetoric* (1949), *Understanding Poetry* (1938) and *Understanding Fiction* (1943).

BROOKS, Phillips (1835–1893), US Episcopal clergyman, the most famous preacher of his day, with a wide intellectual influence. Many of his sermons were published 1881–1902. He was minister at Trinity Church, Boston, 1869–91, and bishop of Mass. He is known for his hymn, *O Little Town of Bethlehem* (1868).

BROOKS, Preston Smith (1819–1857), US politician, congressman from S.C. from 1852. Enraged by Charles SUMNER'S denunciation of Brooks' uncle in an antislavery speech, he beat Sumner senseless with a cane in the Senate, rather than duel with a social inferior. Forced to resign, he was at once reelected. The incident revealed pre-Civil War tensions.

BROOKS, Van Wyck (1886–1963), US critic who examined American writers in the context of their contemporary society. In *America's Coming of Age* (1915), he saw the 19th-century US as torn between the idealistic and the materialistic. In biographies of Mark TWAIN, Henry JAMES, EMERSON and others he traced their development in this society.

BROUGHAM AND VAUX, Henry Peter Brougham, 1st Baron (1778–1868), influential Scottish lawyer, social reformer and politician. Cofounder of the *Edinburgh Review* (1802), he was a member of parliament 1810–12 and 1816–30. As lord chancellor 1830–34, he forced both legal reforms and the 1832 REFORM BILL through the House of Lords.

BROUWER, Adriaen (1605–1638), Flemish painter of humorous peasant scenes such as *The Smokers* (1626), *Drinkers at a Table, Peasant Interior* and *Tavern Brawl.* He was influenced by Pieter BRUEGEL and Frans HALS.

BROUWER, Luitzen Egbertus Jan (1881–1966), Dutch mathematician who developed the doctrine of intuitionism, which rejected the idea that formal logic was the foundation of mathematics. He was a pioneer in the study of TOPOLOGY and contributed to the theory of functions and the theory of sets.

BROWDER, Earl Russell (1891–1973), US Communist party secretary-general 1930–44, and president of the communist political association, 1944–45. Claiming "Communism is 20th-century Americanism" he won great support for the party. Although communist presidential candidate in 1936 and 1940, he was expelled as a deviationist in 1946.

BROWN, "Capability" (Lancelot Brown; 1715–1783), English garden and landscape designer. In his work for English estate owners, he made frequent references to the "capabilities" of a given landscape—thus his nickname.

BROWN, Charles Brockden (1771–1810), one of the first US professional writers. Influenced by William GODWIN, his *Alcuin: A Dialogue* (1798) and novel *Edgar Huntly* (1799) plead for social reform. *Wieland,* (1799) is an outstanding Gothic novel.

BROWN, Ford Madox (1821–1893), English literary, religious and historical painter, a precursor of the PRE-RAPHAELITE Brotherhood. He is famous for *Work* (1852–63) and *Pretty Baa-Lambs* (1851).

BROWN, George (1818–1880), Canadian politician and journalist, born in Scotland. In 1844 he founded the Toronto *Globe*, which had great political influence. He supported Canadian confederation.

BROWN, Jim (1936–   ), US football player, the all-time leading rusher in National Football League history, with 12,312yds gained, 1957–65. The Cleveland Browns star also set NFL records for most career touchdowns (126) and highest lifetime rushing average (5.2yds). After retiring from football, he became a film actor.

BROWN, John (1800–1859), US abolitionist whose exploits helped bring on the Civil War. He was involved in the slave UNDERGROUND RAILROAD in Pa. and then with his five sons moved to Kan. to help the antislavery settlers in 1855. After proslavery men burned down the town of Lawrence, Brown retaliated by murdering five proslavery men at Pottawatamie Creek. During 1857–58 Brown planned to establish a new state in the Va. mountains as a refuge for fugitive slaves and a base for antislavery activity. In October 1859 he seized the government arsenal at Harper's Ferry, Va., and awaited a massive slave insurrection. Instead, the arsenal was stormed; Brown was tried for treason and hanged.

BROWN, Norman O. (1913–   ), US social critic whose Freudian reappraisal of history, *Life Against Death* (1959), made him a hero in the emerging counterculture. His other books, *Love's Body* (1966) and *Closing Time* (1973), further enhanced his status.

BROWNE, Robert (c1550–1633), English Puritan clergyman, leader of a separatist group, the Brownists. He taught independence of the Church from secular government and duty to conscience rather than to outward regulation. His writings are considered the first expression of Congregationalism. (See CONGREGATIONAL CHURCHES.)

BROWNE, Sir Thomas (1605–1682), English physician and author. He is most famous for his book, *Religio Medici* (1643), a fine example of ornate English prose which displays religious toleration in an age of intolerance. His other major work is *Urne-Buriall* (1658), a meditation on death and immortality.

BROWNIAN MOTION, frequent, random fluctuation of the motion of particles suspended in a fluid; first described (1827) by Robert Brown (1773–1858) after observation of a SUSPENSION of pollen grains in water. It is a result of the bombardment of the particles by the MOLECULES of the fluid (see KINETIC THEORY): a chance greater number of impacts in one direction changes the direction of motion of a particle. The first theoretical analysis of Brownian motion was given by EINSTEIN in 1905 and helped to convince the scientific world of the reality of molecules.

BROWNING, Elizabeth Barrett (1806–1861), English poet. In her own day she was second in reputation only to Tennyson. She is now best known for *Sonnets from the Portuguese* (1850), inspired by her romance with Robert BROWNING, who "rescued" her from illness and family tyranny in 1846.

BROWNING, John Moses (1855–1926), US inventor of small arms, including the Browning automatic rifle (BAR) used by the US army in two world wars.

BROWNING, Robert (1812–1889), English poet. He perfected the dramatic monologue in such poems as "Andrea del Sarto" and "Bishop Blougram's Apology" (*Men and Women*; 1855). He also used it in what is considered his masterpiece, *The Ring and the Book* (1868–69), a 17th-century Roman murder story told from several different viewpoints. His psychological insight and use of colloquial language profoundly influenced 20th-century poets.

BROWNSON, Orestes Augustus (1830–1876), US transcendentalist writer on social and religious subjects. He was successively Presbyterian, Unitarian and Roman Catholic; and was interested in labor movements, social reform and emancipation.

BROWNSVILLE AFFAIR, an incident in 1906, in which Negro soldiers from Fort Brown, Tex. allegedly entered nearby Brownsville and fired on houses and townspeople. President Theodore Roosevelt ordered the dishonorable discharge of 167 soldiers, a decision reversed by the army in 1972.

BROWN v. BOARD OF EDUCATION OF TOPEKA, the historic case in which the US Supreme Court unanimously held on May 17, 1954, that "in the field of public education the doctrine of 'separate but equal' has no place." Thus the Court reversed *Plessy v. Ferguson*, an 1896 case in which a majority had held that "separate but equal accommodations" on railways did not necessarily stamp "the colored race with a badge of inferiority." That ruling had provided the constitutional umbrella for a host of state and local laws requiring segregation in practically every walk of life. Thus, *Brown v. Board of Education* was the first in a series of court decisions striking down those laws.

BRÜCKE, Die ("The Bridge"), name adopted by a group of German expressionists who worked together between 1905 and 1913. Leading members of Die Brücke were Ernst Ludwig KIRCHNER, Karl Schmidt-Rottluff, Erich Heckel, Emil NOLDE, Max Pechstein, and Otto Mueller. Like the FAUVES in France, these painters used bold colors and crude forms to convey violent emotion.

BRUCKNER, (Josef) Anton (1824–1896), Austrian composer, noted for his nine massive symphonies and his choral music. His deep Catholic piety permeated all his works. A major influence was Richard WAGNER, whom he greatly admired. Bruckner was a professor at the Vienna Conservatory from 1868. A simple and good-natured man, he ranks with MAHLER among the great late Romantic symphonists.

BRUEGEL, family of Flemish artists flourishing from the 16th to the 18th centuries. **Pieter Bruegel the Elder** (c1525–1569) was a great painter of landscapes and peasant scenes. Influenced at first by BOSCH, he was much impressed by the scenery of Italy, which he visited in 1552. His works, some on religious subjects, are often allegorical or satirical, profoundly affected by his view of the human condition. **Pieter Bruegel the Younger** (1564–1638), also called Hell Bruegel, worked in his father's manner, often with an emphasis on the grotesque. **Jan Bruegel** (1568–1625), also called Velvet Bruegel, the second son, painted landscapes and still lifes with great subtlety and delicacy. He often collaborated with RUBENS.

BRUGGE or **Bruges,** well-preserved medieval city in NW Belgium. Once a center for wool trade, and in the 15th century home of a school of painting led by the VAN EYCKS and Hans MEMLING, its commercial interest revived in the 19th century when the Zeebrugge Canal to the North Sea was opened. It manufactures lace and textiles. Pop 117,747.

BRUHN, Erik (1928–1986), Danish dancer. He made his debut with the Royal Danish Ballet in 1947, becoming its leading male dancer in 1949. He is considered one of the greatest classical dancers of his time.

BRUMMELL, George Bryan "Beau" (1778–1840), English man of fashion. He was a friend of the Prince of Wales (later George IV) and an arbiter of fashion in Regency society. He fled to France in 1816 to escape his creditors.

BRUNEI, independent sultanate on the N coast of the island of Borneo, on the South China Sea.

Official name: Negara Brunei Darussalam
Capital: Bandar Seri Begawan
Area: 2,226sq mi
Population: 300,000
Language: Malay; English, Chinese spoken
Religions: Muslim, Buddhist, Animist, Christian
Monetary unit(s): 1 Brunei dollar = 100 sen
Land. Brunei is surrounded by the Malaysian state of Sabah. It has a humid tropical climate that supports dense forests.
People and Economy. The population is 65% Malay and 20% Chinese, the latter running many small businesses. Malay is the chief language, Islam the official religion. Rubber and timber were superseded as main products after petroleum was found in 1929. Petroleum and natural gas, extracted both on and off shore, have given the tiny country one of the highest per capita incomes in the world; its citizens enjoy an impressive array of free social services.
History. A local sultanate was established here in the 15th century and during the 16th century controlled all of Borneo. It became a British protectorate in 1888 and a 1959 constitution gave it domestic autonomy. The country gained full independence on Jan. 1, 1984. The sultan rules by decree under a national state of emergency imposed following an attempted coup in 1962.

BRUNEL, Sir Marc Isambard (1769–1849), French-born British engineer and inventor who built the world's first underwater tunnel (under the River Thames) and devised machines for the mass production of pulley blocks and army boots. His son, **Isambard Kingdom Brunel** (1806–1859), pioneered many important construction techniques, designing the Clifton suspension bridge at Bristol, England, laying the Great Western Railway with a controversial 7ft (2.13m) gauge and building ironhulled steamships, including the giant *Great Eastern*.

BRUNELLESCHI, Filippo (1377–1446), first great Italian Renaissance architect. He was one of the first practitioners of linear perspective. Influenced by classical Roman and 11th-century Tuscan Romanesque architecture, his masterpiece is the dome of Florence cathedral (1420–36).

BRÜNING, Heinrich (1885–1970), German statesman. Chancellor of the Weimar Republic 1930–32, his measures to restore the German economy aroused opposition, and his dismissal from office by President von HINDENBURG led eventually to HITLER'S chancellorship.

BRUNO, Giordano (1548–1600), Italian pantheist philosopher, poet and cosmologist, an apostate Dominican, who taught the plurality of inhabited worlds, the infinity of the universe and the truth of the Copernican hypothesis. Burned at the stake for heresy, he became renowned as a martyr to science.

BRUSSELS, Belgian capital city, headquarters of the European Common Market, NATO and the Atomic Energy Commission. First commercially important in the 12th century, it was granted a ducal charter in 1312. From the 16th to the 19th centuries it was subject successively to Spain, Austria and France. It manufactures textiles, lace and furniture and is a transport center. Pop (metro) 980,196.

BRUTUS, name of an ancient Roman family. **Lucius Junius Brutus** (6th century BC) founded the Roman Republic by expelling King Lucius Tarquinius Superbus in 509 BC. **Decimus Junius Brutus** (d. 43 BC) served with Julius Caesar in Gaul and was one of his assassins. **Marcus Junius Brutus** (85–42 BC) was a highly respected statesman who helped lead the assassination plot against Caesar. He committed suicide after his defeat by Antony and Octavian at Philippi.

BRYAN, William Jennings (1860–1925), US political leader, orator and lawyer. Elected to Congress in 1890, he was an unsuccessful Democratic presidential candidate in 1896, 1900 and 1908 and secretary of state in 1913–15. His famous "cross-of-gold" speech at the 1896 Democratic convention led to his first nomination. A fundamentalist, he prosecuted at the SCOPES TRIAL in 1925, winning the case against teaching evolution in schools over defense attorney Clarence DARROW.

BRYANT, Paul "Bear" (1913–1983), US college football coach with the best winning average ever, more than eight victories per season. In over 35 seasons, his teams won or shared six national championships. In 1981 the Alabama U. coach broke Amos Alonzo STAGG's record of 314 career wins.

BRYANT, William Cullen (1794–1878), US poet and journalist. Editor of the New York *Evening Post* from 1829, he campaigned against slavery and for free speech. He wrote pastoral odes, the most famous being *Thanatopsis* (1817), and translated the *Iliad* and *Odyssey* (1870–72).

BRYCE, James Bryce, 1st Viscount (1838–1922), British statesman and historian. He wrote *The Holy Roman Empire* (1864) and *The American Commonwealth* (1888). He was British ambassador to the US 1907–13.

BRYCE CANYON NATIONAL PARK, an area of 36,010 acres in S Ut., created as a park in 1928. It contains extraordinary formations in colorful limestone and sandstone, the result of erosion.

BRZEZINSKI, Zbigniew (1928–   ), US political scientist and national security adviser (1977–81). Born in Poland, he became a professor and expert on Communist affairs at Harvard and Columbia universities. President Jimmy CARTER named him to the national security post, where he gained a reputation as an anti-Communist "hard-liner".

BUBBLE CHAMBER, device invented by Donald Glaser (1952) to observe the paths of SUBATOMIC PARTICLES with energies too high for a CLOUD CHAMBER to be used. A liquid (e.g., liquid HYDROGEN or OXYGEN) is held under PRESSURE just below its boiling point. Sudden reduction in pressure lowers this boiling point: boiling starts along the paths of energetic subatomic particles, whose passage creates local heating. At the instant of reduction, their paths may thus be photographed as a chain of bubbles.

BUBER, Martin (1878–1965), Jewish philosopher, born in Austria. Editor of a major German–Jewish journal, *Der Jude*, 1916–24, he was a leading educator and scholar of HASIDISM. An ardent Zionist, he moved to Palestine in 1938. His central philosophical concept is that of the direct "I-Thou" relationship between man and God and man and man.

BUBONIC PLAGUE. See BLACK DEATH; PLAGUE.

BUCER, Martin (1491–1551), German Protestant reformer noted for his efforts to reconcile the doctrines of Luther, Zwingli, and other reformers in order to achieve Protestant unity.

BUCHAN, John, 1st Baron Tweedsmuir (1875–1940), Scottish author and politician. He wrote historical works, biographies and such classic adventure stories as *The Thirty-Nine Steps* (1915). From 1935 he was governor-general of Canada.

BUCHANAN, James (1791–1868), 15th president of the US. A Pennsylvania lawyer, he was first a Federalist, later a Democrat. He was a US congressman 1821–31, minister to Russia 1831–33, and a US senator 1834–45. While he was secretary of state under President Polk (1845–49), the dispute with Britain over Oregon was settled and the Mexican War broke out, following the annexation of Tex. Under President Pierce he was minister to Britain 1853–56, and with J. Y. Mason and Pierre Soule worked out the controversial OSTEND MANIFESTO, stating that the US must protect its security by acquiring Cuba through purchase or force.

Though morally opposed to slavery, he believed the constitution gave individual states the right to decide the issue, and on this compromise platform won the presidency, serving 1857–61. He attempted to settle Kansas' admission to statehood by "popular sovereignty," allowing popular vote to decide the slavery issue in the territory. His proposal passed the Senate but failed in the House. His upholding of the DRED SCOTT DECISION aroused opposition in both houses. With the Democratic party divided, Abraham Lincoln won the 1860 election. When secession began, Buchanan tried desperately to maintain peace. He disapproved of secession but knew no constitutional authority to prevent it. Believing that federal troops should be used only to protect federal property, he eventually sent troops to Fort Sumter. After Lincoln took office, Buchanan supported the Union.

BUCHAREST, capital of Romania, on the Dâmbovita R. A medieval fortress, it became the residence of the princes of Walachia in 1459 and the capital when the new Romania was formed in 1861. It produces pharmaceutical and electrical goods, machinery and automobiles. Pop 1,961,189.

BUCHENWALD, Nazi concentration camp set up near Weimar in 1937 to hold political and "non–Aryan" prisoners. More than 100,000 (chiefly Jews) died there through starvation, extermination and medical experimentation.

BÜCHNER, Georg (1813–1837), German dramatist, forerunner of EXPRESSIONISM. His *Danton's Death* (1835) and *Woyzeck* (1837) use colloquial language and sometimes sordid settings. With psychological insight, they trace the powerlessness of isolated individuals, whether against historical forces or society. Woyzeck, for example, is a soldier pressured into murdering his unfaithful mistress. *Lenz*, unfinished, is about a dramatist on the verge of madness.

BUCK, Pearl Sydenstricker (1892–1973), US author. Most of her novels are set in China, where she lived up to 1934. She won the Pulitzer Prize in 1932 for *The Good Earth* (1931), and the 1938 Nobel Prize for Literature.

BUCKINGHAM, George Villiers, 1st Duke of (1592–1628), English nobleman whose influence over JAMES I and CHARLES I imflamed anti–monarchical feeling. He promoted costly and unsuccessful military ventures, notably the expedition to relieve the Huguenots of La Rochelle. Charles, however, shielded him from impeachment. He was eventually assassinated.

BUCKINGHAM PALACE, London residence of the British royal family, built in 1703 and bought by George III from the Duke of Buckingham in 1761. Queen Victoria, in 1837, was the first monarch to use it as an official residence.

BUCKLE, Henry Thomas (1821–1862), English historian. With the influential *History of Civilization in England* (1857–61), he broke from the tradition of treating only individuals, wars and politics and considered peoples, cultures and environments.

BUCKLEY, William Frank, Jr. (1925–   ), US author, editor and lecturer. He founded the weekly *National Review* (1955) to voice often controversially conservative views. A syndicated columnist and television host, he wrote popular adventure novels including *Saving the Queen* (1976) and *Mongoose, R.I.P.* (1988).

BUDAPEST, capital of Hungary, on the Danube R. Two settlements, Buda on the right bank and Pest on the left, date from Roman times but were destroyed by Mongol invaders in 1241. Buda became Hungary's capital in 1361. They declined under the Turks but revived under the Hapsburgs and were united in 1873. Textiles are the main industry. The city was virtually destroyed in WWII. It was the center of the Hungarian uprising in 1956. Pop 2,073,737.

BUDAPEST STRING QUARTET, musical group organized in Hungary in 1917. It soon became known for performances of Mozart and Bartok. Moving to the US in 1938, it was "quartet in residence" at the Library of Congress (1938–62). The group played all over the world and was famed for its Beethoven performances before it disbanded in 1968.

BUDDHA, Gautama (c563–483 BC),

founder of BUDDHISM. Son of the raja of Kapilavastu near Nepal, his name was Siddhartha Gautama. At the age of 29, confronting human misery for the first time, he at once set out to find the path to peace and serenity. For six years he studied under Brahman teachers, living as a hermit. Enlightenment came to him while seated under a *bodhi* or pipal tree; he remained there in contemplation of truth some six or seven weeks. Thereafter he preached and gathered disciples as Buddha ("the Enlightened One").

BUDDHISM, religion and philosophy developed from HINDUISM in the 6th century BC by Siddhartha Gautama, the BUDDHA. His monastic disciples shaved their heads, dressed in rags and devoted themselves to the philosophy of Enlightenment.

The Pali canon is the scriptural basis of Buddhism, transcribing from oral tradition Buddha's teaching and monastic rules. It was set down by the first Buddhist council at Rajagaha in the 5th century BC. The next council, at Vesali in the 4th century BC, saw Buddhism divided into two schools because of debate over the stringency of monastic regulations. The third, called by Emperor ASOKA in the 3rd century BC, sent missionaries throughout India and into Syria, N Africa and Ceylon. Spreading to Tibet in the 7th century AD, Buddhism combined with existing beliefs to form LAMAISM, and in China an Indian Buddhist, Bodhidharma, introduced spontaneous enlightenment, Ch'an (ZEN in Japanese). In the 6th century AD Buddhism reached Japan, where for the first time it became involved with politics.

Buddhist teaching advocates a middle course between mortification and the pursuit of ambition. Buddha's Four Noble Truths are: life involves suffering; the cause of suffering is desire; elimination of desire leads to cessation of suffering; the elimination of desire is the result of a method or path that must be followed. The Noble Eightfold Path (right mode of seeing things, right thought, right speech, right action, right way of living, right effort, right mindedness, right meditation) leads to the cessation of pain. Through these steps Nirvana is achieved, a state beyond thought which frees one from the perpetual cycle of birth, suffering, death and rebirth. Buddhism has no service, ritual or church. The stricter *Theravada* school is followed in Ceylon, Burma, Thailand and Cambodia (Kampuchea), the more lenient *Mahayana* school in Nepal, Korea, Indonesia, Japan and China. The religion numbers 300–500 million followers; many others in the East

and West practice Buddhist teaching to achieve self-awareness.

BUDGE, Donald (1915–   ), US tennis player, the first to win (1938) tennis's grand slam (British, French, Australian, and US championships in the same calendar year).

BUELL, Don Carlos (1818–1898), US Union general in the Civil War. Troops under his command contributed to victory in the Battle of Shiloh. At Perryville in 1862 he forced the Confederates to retreat from Ky., but was dismissed because he did not follow up the victory.

BUENA VISTA, a Mexican village 8mi from Saltillo. During the MEXICAN WAR, in Feb. 1847, US General Zachary TAYLOR with 5,000 troops here defeated a Mexican army of 20,000 under General SANTA ANNA.

BUENOS AIRES, capital of Argentina. On the Río de la Plata, it is a port for Argentine agricultural products, meat, hides, wool and cereals. It has several universities, an opera house (Teatro Colón) and is the world's leading Spanish language publishing center. Industries include food processing and textiles, automobiles and chemical manufactures. Founded in 1536, Buenos Aires became the capital of Río de la Plata viceroyalty in 1776. An impressive economic growth after 1850 has attracted many immigrants. Pop (city) 2,922,829; (metro) 10,728,000.

BUFFALO, name of several species of wild ox, incorrectly applied to the American BISON. They are members of the mammalian family Bovidae. The domesticated Indian water buffalo or carabao is a draft animal and gives milk. It weighs about a ton, is 1.5m (5ft) high and has large curved horns. Other types of Asiatic buffalo are the Philippine Tamarau and the small anoa of the Celebes. These are shy, but Cape buffaloes are dangerous big-game animals living in herds. Their populations have been reduced in the past by RINDERPEST, a cattle disease.

BUFFALO BILL, nickname of William Frederick Cody (1846–1917), US scout and showman. He claimed to have killed 4,280 buffalo to feed the builders of the Kansas Pacific Railway. He rode with the PONY EXPRESS in 1860 and during the Civil War was a scout in Tenn. and Mo. for the Union army. From 1872 he toured the US and Europe with his Wild West Show.

BUFFET, Bernard (1928–   ), French artist, book illustrator and stage designer. His austere, angular naturalistic style won him international fame in his youth, and his work has since been much sought after.

BUFFON, Georges Louis Leclerc, Comte de (1707–1788), French naturalist who was the first modern taxonomist of the ANIMAL KINGDOM and who led the team which produced the 44-volume *Histoire Naturelle* (1749–1804).

BUGLE. See WIND INSTRUMENT.

BUGS, common name for the insect order Hemiptera. They have beaks for piercing and sucking. Some, like the stinkbug, emit unpleasant odors, others secretions: aphids secrete honeydew; larvae of froghoppers (spittle bugs) secrete protective foam; scale insects secrete a waxy substance used in shellac. Most are plant-feeders and many are pests, attacking crops and transmitting diseases (e.g., squash bugs, lace bugs and whitefly). Some are blood-suckers (e.g., bedbugs and assassin bugs) which transmit disease. Others live on ponds (e.g., water skaters) or underwater (e.g., water scorpions). In America the word "bug" often colloquially refers to any insect.

BUKHARIN, Nikolai Ivanovich (1888–1938), an early Bolshevik theoretician and friend of Lenin, editor of *Pravda*. A party leader in the 1920s, he was ousted by Stalin in 1929, but was reinstated to edit *Izvestia* in 1934. He wrote several works on political science and economics. He was liquidated in the Great Purge in 1938. In 1988 a Communist Party commission reviewing the purge trials announced that Bukharin had been wrongly convicted.

BULB, a short, underground storage stem composed of many fleshy scale leaves that are swollen with stored food and an outer layer of protective scale leaves. Bulbs are a means of overwintering; in the spring, flowers and foliage leaves are rapidly produced when growing conditions are suitable. Examples of plants producing bulbs are daffodil, tulip, snowdrop and onion.

BULFINCH, Charles (1763–1844), US architect, designer of the Mass. statehouse, Boston (1800), University Hall, Harvard U. (1815) and the E portico of the Capitol, Washington, D.C. (1818). He emphasized the dignified neoclassical style in American civic architecture.

BULFINCH, Thomas (1796–1867), US mythologist. His classic, *The Age of Fable* (1855; "Bulfinch's Mythology"), popularized Greek, Roman, Nordic and oriental mythologies.

BULGAKOV, Mikhail Afanasievich (1891–1940), Russian author and playwright. His work, mostly suppressed until the 1960s, blends realism and fantasy with great humor, as in his most brilliant novel, *The Master and Margarita*, which describes the antics of the devil in modern Moscow.

BULGANIN, Nikolai Alexandrovich (1895–1975), Soviet leader. With the support of Nikita KHRUSHCHEV, he succeeded MALENKOV as premier in 1955. He was expelled from the central committee when Khrushchev became premier in 1958.

BULGARIA, republic located on the Balkan Peninsula, bordered by the Black Sea, the Danube and Yugoslavia. The country is traversed by the Balkan and Rhodope Mts; its climate is continental in the N and Mediterranean in the S. Until the 1940s most Bulgarians lived in peasant farming villages, but industrialization has greatly progressed since WWII. Industry produces machinery, textiles and chemicals; and lead, zinc, iron ore, copper and coal are mined. Wheat, corn, sugar beets and barley are the principal crops. Exports include tobacco, foodstuffs, minerals and machinery. The Black Sea resorts and the country's mineral springs are important tourist attractions.

Official name: The People's Republic of Bulgaria
Capital: Sofia
Area: 42,823sq mi
Population: 8,983,000
Languages: Bulgarian, Turkish
Religions: Bulgarian Orthodox
Monetary unit(s): 1 lev = 100 stotinki
History. Bulgars, Turkic people, conquered the Slavic population in the 7th century, adopting their language and customs. The Bulgar Empire was a major Balkan force until the 14th century, but from 1396 to 1878 Bulgaria was under rigid Ottoman rule. At the Congress of Berlin (1878), Turkish hegemony was restricted, and in 1908 Bulgaria proclaimed its independence under Ferdinand I. Bulgaria supported Germany in WWI and II, though not against the USSR. In 1944 the USSR occupied the country and the communist Fatherland Front seized power. In 1947 Bulgaria became a People's Republic. A new constitution was adopted in 1971, with Communist party chief Todor Zhivkov as president. Bulgaria has remained a faithful Soviet satellite. In 1987 Zhivkov announced major reforms in the party and government

on the model of the new Soviet policy of *perestroika*, but a year later caution prevailed and most reforms were postponed.

BULIMIA, eating disorder characterized by frequent binge eating followed by purging, often through self-induced vomiting, laxatives, strenuous exercise, or fasting. The results can be life-threatening biochemical imbalances. College women are considered most susceptible to the disorder, but recent studies have found only 1-3% of this population exhibit bulimic behavior.

BULLFIGHTING, Spanish national sport and spectacle, also popular in Latin America. Probably developed by the Moors, it was taken over by aristocratic professionals in the 18th century. The modern bullfight stresses the grace, skill and daring of the *matador*. (The most famous matadors have been Juan Belmonte, Joselito, Manolete and El Cordobes.) After a procession, the bull is released. Two mounted *picadors* jab the bull's neck with lances to lower its head for the matador's capework. Then three *banderilleros* thrust decorated wooden goads into the bull's back. The matador, after using his cape to make daring and graceful passes at the bull, kills it with a swordthrust between the shoulders.

BULLINGER, Heinrich (1504–1575), Swiss Protestant reformer. He played an important part in composing the First Helvetic Confession (1536), formulated the *Consensus Tigurinus* with CALVIN (1549) and composed the Second Helvetic Confession (1566), a popular CREED of the Reformation.

BULLITT, William Christian (1891–1967), US diplomat who, after a secret mission to Russia for President Woodrow Wilson in 1919, vainly recommended recognition of the Communist regime. When the US recognized (1933) the Soviet Union, Bullitt was appointed the first US ambassador (1933–36). He was ambassador to France 1936–40.

BULL RUN, Battles of, two clashes in the American Civil War around Manassas Junction near Bull Run Creek, 25mi SW of Washington, D.C. In the First Battle of Bull Run, July 1861, Union Gen. Irvin McDowell was sent against Confederates led by P.G.T. BEAUREGARD, but was repulsed by them. Gen. "Stonewall" JACKSON was so nicknamed for his tenacity in this battle. In the Second Battle of Bull Run, Aug. 1862, Jackson attacked Union Gen. John POPE and forced his retreat. (See also CIVIL WAR, AMERICAN.)

BULOW, Bernhard Heinrich Martin von
(1849–1929), German chancellor. He capped a distinguished diplomatic and political career by serving as chancellor 1900–09. Anxious to achieve imperial glory for Germany, he was responsible for causing Britain, France and Russia to draw closely together. His poor judgments on foreign policy helped bring on WWI.

BÜLOW, Hans Guido von (1830–1894), German pianist and noted virtuoso conductor. A pupil of LISZT and WAGNER, he championed their music and that of BRAHMS and Richard STRAUSS. He married Liszt's daughter, Cosima, who later left him for Wagner.

BULTMANN, Rudolf (1884–1976), German theologian who advocated "demythologizing" the New Testament and reinterpreting it in existentialist terms. He developed a critical approach to the Gospels, studying the oral tradition behind them. His books include *History of the Synoptic Tradition* (1921; tr. 1963) and the five-volume *Kerygma and Myth: A Theological Debate* (1948–55; tr. 1953–62).

BULWER-LYTTON, Edward George Earle Lytton, 1st Baron Lytton (1803–1873), English author and politician. His best-known works include the historical novels, *The Last Days of Pompeii* (1834) and *Rienzi* (1835), and the Utopian *The Coming Race* (1871).

BUNAU-VARILLA, Philippe Jean (1859–1940), French engineer who organized the Panama Canal Project. He was instrumental in arranging for the canal to go through Panama and then in planning the revolution which led to Panamanian independence from Colombia. As Panama's minister to the US, he negotiated the Hay-Bunau-Varilla Treaty (1903), giving the US control of the canal zone.

BUNCHE, Ralph Johnson (1904–1971), US diplomat. He entered the UN in 1946, and was undersecretary for political affairs in 1958. Having supervised the 1949 Arab-Israeli armistice, he became the first black to win the Nobel Peace Prize (1950).

BUNIN, Ivan Alekseyevich (1870–1953), Russian novelist, short-story writer and poet. He is best known for his short stories such as *The Gentleman from San Francisco* (1916). He emigrated to France in 1919, and won the Nobel Prize for Literature in 1933.

BUNKER HILL, Battle of, important early encounter of the American Revolutionary War, on June 17, 1775. As part of the encirclement of Boston, American militia under Col. William Prescott occupied Breed's Hill—although the original objective had been Bunker's Hill nearby. The first two British attempts to dislodge them, led by Maj. Gen. William Howe, resulted in heavy losses from close American fire. On the third assault the Americans ran out of ammunition and had to retreat. Though a British victory, the battle damaged British confidence and was a vital boost to American morale.

BUNSEN, Robert Wilhelm Eberhard (1811–1899), German chemist who, after important work on organo-arsenic compounds went on (with G. R. KIRCHHOFF) to pioneer chemical SPECTROSCOPY, discovering the elements cesium (1860) and rubidium (1861). He also helped to popularize the gas burner known by his name.

BUNUEL, Luis (1900–1983), Spanish-Mexican director of many outstanding films, often marked by their fierce realism, social criticism and wry humor. Surrealist fantasy has been another recurrent element in his work, ever since his first film, *Un Chien Andalou* (made with Salvador DALI in 1929).

BUNYAN, John (1628–1688), English author. A tinker by trade, he became a Baptist preacher in 1657. While imprisoned for unlicensed preaching (1660–72; 1675) he wrote his most famous work, *The Pilgrim's Progress* (1678), an allegory in simple prose describing Christian's journey to the Celestial City.

BUNYAN, Paul, in US frontier myth a lumberjack, a genial giant who worked with his huge blue ox Babe. By the time the first tall stories about this frontier hero were published in 1910, oral tradition had spread them across the country.

BUONARROTI, Michelangelo. See MICHELANGELO.

BURBAGE, Richard (c1567–1619), first great English actor. He played many of Shakespeare's leading roles, including Richard III, Hamlet, Othello and Lear. From his father, **James Burbage** (c1530–1597), builder of the first English theater (The Theatre, 1576), he and his brother Cuthbert inherited the Blackfriars Theatre in London. In 1599 they built the famous Globe Theatre.

BURBANK, Luther (1849–1926), US horticulturalist who developed more than 800 varieties of plants, including the Burbank potato.

BURCHFIELD, Charles Ephraim (1893–1967), US watercolorist known for his midwestern landscapes and small town scenes. A leader of the realistic movement in American painting, he liked to depict architectural relics of the late 1800s and was sensitive to lighting and atmospheric effects.

BURCKHARDT, Johann Ludwig (1784–1817), Swiss explorer employed by the English African Association. He traveled in Egypt, visited Petra and, disguised as a Muslim, went to Mecca and Medina. Several collections of his writings were published posthumously.

BURGER, Warren Earl (1907–   ), chief justice of the US 1969–87. Burger led the Supreme Court away from the judicial activism of his predecessor, Earl Warren, and toward a more conservative philosophy.

BURGESS, Anthony (1917–   ), English writer, mostly of satirical novels, best known for *A Clockwork Orange* (1962), about a violent gang leader in a corrupt, equally violent society of the near future. His other works include *Enderby* (1961), *Earthly Powers* (1980) and the critical study *Re Joyce* (1965).

BURGESS, Guy (1911–1963), British intelligence officer and Soviet spy associated with Kim PHILBY, Donald MACLEAN, and Anthony BLUNT. He fled (1951) with Maclean to Moscow, where he died.

BURGOYNE, John (1722–1792), Britis general in the American Revolutionary War. He fought in the Seven Years' War (1756–63), and became a fashionable playwright, socialite and politician. Posted to America, he attempted to put into effect his plan to split off the New England colonies but was eventually forced to surrender by Gen. Horatio GATES at Saratoga (1777).

BURGUNDY (French: Bourgogne), historic region of E France, occupying what are now the departments of Côte-d'Or, Saône-et-Lorie and Yonne. It was named for the Burgundians, a Germanic tribe. In 843 the area was divided into the E county of Franche-Comté and the W Duchy of Burgundy, which became virtually an independent state. From 1477 until the Revolution the duchy was a French province. A rich agricultural region, Burgundy is famous for its wines.

BURKE, Edmund (1729–1797), Irish-born British statesman, political philosopher and outstanding orator. He entered parliament in 1765, and advocated more just policies towards the American colonies, opposing the STAMP ACT and (in 1775) arguing for conciliation. Concerned for justice in India, he promoted the impeachment of Warren HASTINGS (1786–87). His famous *Reflections on the Revolution in France* (1790) presented his rational case against violent change.

BURKINA, formerly Upper Vola, a

landlocked West African republic, N of Ghana and S of Mali.

Official name: Burkina Faso
Capital: Ouagadougou
Area: 105,869sq mi
Population: 8,530,000
Languages: French; Mossi spoken
Religions: Animist; Muslim; Christian
Monetary unit(s): 1 CFA franc=100 centimes

Land. The country is a dry plateau drained by the upper streams of the Volta R. Rainfall averages 10–45in yearly, but is not retained by the thin soil, which supports little more than poor savanna; the N and NE is semidesert. Temperatures range between 68°F and 95°F. The wet season lasts from June to October.

People. The largest ethnic group is the Voltaic Mossi (48%); other Voltaic groups are the Bobo, Lobi and Gurunsi. There are also Mande and Senufo groups, and Fulani and Tuareg nomads. The population is 95% rural and concentrated in the S and E. The illiteracy rate is about 90%.

Economy. Burkina is among the poorest countries in the world, possessing few natural resources. Subsistence agriculture supports about 95% of the population. Principal exports are cotton, karite nuts and oil, live animals and peanuts. Landlocked, it relies on rail connections to the port of Abidjan in the Ivory Coast for imports and exports. As many as 1.5 million workers are employed outside the country, primarily in the Ivory Coast and Ghana. Their remittances home provide important revenues.

History. Part of the powerful Mossi empire since c1000 AD, the region of Upper Volta was annexed by the French in 1896 and became a French colony in 1919. It became independent in 1960. The military seized power in 1966 but permitted a civilian legislature from 1970 to 1974 and again from 1978 to 1980. Military rule returned in 1980, and there were coups in 1982 and 1983, when Capt. Thomas Sankara seized power. Sankara, who encouraged national pride and rural development and changed the name of the country to Burkina in 1984, was assassinated by his deputy, Blaise Campore, in 1987.

BURLESQUE, form of literary or stage humor characterized by exaggeration or distortion of its subject matter. Aristophanes' comedies are early examples. In mid-19th-century America the term was applied to a low-comedy, sometimes bawdy, entertainment, which developed into a form of variety show. After 1920 striptease acts became the main burlesque attraction, and the Minsky chain, with theaters in several US cities, became the leading provider of such entertainment.

BURLINGAME, Anson (1820–1870), US diplomat who helped China establish friendly relations with Western countries. The Burlingame Treaty (1868) between China and the US encouraged Chinese immigration.

BURMA, country in SE Asia on the Bay of Bengal, bounded by Bangladesh, India, China, Laos and Thailand. It comprises five federated states.

Official name: The Socialist Republic of the Union of Burma
Capital: Rangoon
Area: 261,228sq mi
Population: 39,218,000
Languages: Burmese
Religions: Buddhist
Monetary unit(s): 1 kyat = 100 pyas

Land. The country is fringed by high mountain ranges to the E, W and N, which enclose a fertile central plain watered chiefly by the Irrawaddy R and its great delta. Central and N Burma are thickly forested, and much of Burma has a tropical monsoon climate.

People. The Burmans, a Mongoloid people, form 75% of the population, the Karens and Shans being the other major groups; Indians and Chinese constitute significant minorities. Some 80% of the population lives in rural areas. Rangoon, the capital and chief port, is by far the largest city. Other centers include Mandalay and Moulmein.

Economy. Agriculture is the country's economic mainstay. Rice (grown particularly in the Irrawaddy basin and delta) is the main crop, followed by sugarcane and groundnuts. Forestry provides hardwoods for export. Industry is confined mainly to rice-milling, oil-refining and textiles. The country is rich in minerals, including oil, lead, tin and tungsten, but deposits are poorly exploited.

History. Burma was settled by the Burmans in the 9th century, establishing a kingdom which reached its height under Buddhist King Anawratha in the 11th century. In 1287 the kingdom fell to KUBLAI KHAN and was later divided among Shan and other rulers, though it was again unified in the 16th century. In the 1750s a new dynasty was established by King Alaungpaya, who made his capital at Rangoon. After a series of wars (1826–85), Britain annexed Burma as part of its Indian empire, and in 1937 granted the country separate dominion status. During World War II, Burma was occupied by the Japanese, who set up a puppet government. The independent Union of Burma was established in 1948. Its democratic constitution was suspended in 1962 by General Ne Win, and a new socialist constitution was announced in Dec. 1973. Under Ne Win's socialist dictatorship, the potentially rich country sank into poverty. In 1986 Burma applied to the United Nations for "least-developed nation" status that would enable it to receive more aid and credit. In 1988 Ne Win resigned as chairman of the nation's only political party in the midst of increasing antigovernment demonstrations.

BURNE-JONES, Sir Edward Coley (1833–1898), English artist, a member of the PRE-RAPHAELITE Brotherhood. His paintings (e.g. *King Cophetua and the Beggar Maid*) evince a romantic, dreamy medievalism. In 1858 he worked with ROSSETTI on the Oxford Union frescoes. He also designed many stained-glass windows for William MORRIS.

BURNET, Gilbert (1643–1715), British clergyman, an opponent of the Catholic James II and supporter of the Protestant William III, who made him bishop of Salisbury. He wrote a history of the Reformation in England and a notable *History of My Own Times.*

BURNETT, Frances (Eliza) Hodgson (1849–1924), English-born US author. She is particularly famous for her children's stories, *Little Lord Fauntleroy* (1885–86) and *The Secret Garden* (1910).

BURNEY, Frances "Fanny" (1752–1840), English novelist and diarist. Her first novel, *Evelina* (1778), won her the respect of Samuel JOHNSON. She spent five years from 1786 as a member of Queen Charlotte's household. Her *Early Diary: 1768–78* (1889) and *Diary and Letters: 1778–1840* (1842–46) provide interesting background to the period.

BURNHAM, Daniel Hudson (1846–1912), US architect, a pioneer of city planning. He built some of America's early skyscrapers, including the Masonic Temple Building, Chicago (1892), and the Flatiron Building, New York City (1902). He also designed the plan for the Columbian Exposition in Chicago (1893). Much of his improvement plan for Chicago (1907–09) was subsequently put into effect.

BURNHAM, James (1905–1987), US editor and author. A teacher of philosophy at New York U 1929–53, he was a follower of Leon TROTSKY in the 1930s but then rejected Marxism as both false and totalitarian. He helped found and edited (1955–77) the conservative magazine *National Review.* His books include the influential *The Managerial Revolution* (1941) and *The Coming Defeat of Communism* (1950).

BURNS, Arthur Frank (1904–1987), Austrian-born US economist. An expert on the BUSINESS CYCLE, he served as presidential adviser on economics 1953–56 and on labor management 1961–66. Among his many books, the most influential was *Measuring Business Cycles* (1946), written with Wesley Clair MITCHELL.

BURNS, George (Nathan Birnbaum; 1898–), and **Gracie Allen** (1906–1964), US entertainers, a team from 1922 in vaudeville, radio, television, and film, Burns playing straight man to illogical, birdbrained Allen. With Allen's death, Burns retired, but he returned to films at nearly 80 and won an Academy Award for *The Sunshine Boys* (1976).

BURNS, Robert (1759–1796), famous Scottish poet. The son of a poor farmer, he himself farmed for a living and later worked as a customs official. In 1786 he published *Poems, Chiefly in the Scottish Dialect* (enlarged 1787). His poetry, in Scots-English idiom, deals with rural human experience and feeling. He also wrote satires and radical poems, such as *The Twa Dogs* and *The Jolly Beggars.* Influenced by Scottish folk tradition, he was a master at writing songs to traditional airs—for example, *Auld Lang Syne.* At first taken up by fashionable society, he died neglected and in debt. Among his best-known poems are *Tam O'Shanter, To a Mouse* and *The Cotter's Saturday Night.*

BURNS AND SCALDS, injuries caused by heat, electricity, radiation or caustic substances, in which protein denaturation causes death of tissues. (Scalds are burns due to boiling water or steam.) Burns cause PLASMA to leak from blood vessels into the tissues and in severe burns substantial leakage leads to SHOCK. In **first-degree burns**, such as mild SUNBURN, damage is superficial. **Second-degree burns** destroy only the epidermis so that regeneration is possible. **Third-degree burns** destroy all layers of SKIN, which cannot then regenerate, so skin-grafting is required. Infection, ulceration, hemolysis, KIDNEY failure and severe scarring may complicate burns. Treatment includes ANALGESICS, dressings and ANTISEPTICS and fluids for shock. Immediate FIRST AID measures include cold water cooling to minimize continuing damage.

BURNSIDE, Ambrose Everett (1824–1881), Union general in the American Civil War. Succeeding McClellan as general of the Army of the Potomac, he resigned after the Union defeat at Fredericksburg in 1862. He was later governor of R.I. (1866–69) and US senator (1875–81). His whiskers gave rise to the term "sideburns."

BURR, Aaron (1756–1836), brilliant and controversial US vice-president, who killed Alexander HAMILTON in a duel (1804). Hamilton had blocked Burr's election as president in a tie vote with Jefferson in 1800, and (as Burr believed) his election as governor of N.Y. in 1804. Burr was admitted to the New York bar in 1782, was attorney general (1789–91) and US senator (1791–97) while helping to organize the new Republican party. After his term as vice-president (1800–05) he was involved in conspiracies to form an empire in the West, and was tried but acquitted of treason. After 1812 he returned to the law in N.Y.

BURROUGHS, Edgar Rice (1875–1950), US writer of adventure novels. He is most famous for *Tarzan of the Apes* (1914), whose characters have passed into comic strips, films and television.

BURROUGHS, John (1837–1921), US naturalist and author who made his reputation with philosophical nature essays. His *Notes on Walt Whitman* (1867) was the first biographical study of the poet, who was his friend.

BURSITIS, inflammation of a bursa (fibrous sac containing synovial fluid which reduces friction where tendons mover over bones), commonly caused by excessive wear and tear (as in housemaid's knee) or by rheumatoid ARTHRITIS, GOUT or various bacteria. It causes pain and stiffness of the affected part, and may require cortisone injections and, if infected, surgical drainage.

BURTON, Richard (1925–1984), British actor. Starting as a promising Shakespearean at the Old Vic, London, in the 1950s, he appeared on Broadway in *Camelot* (1960) and *Hamlet* (1964) and has made numerous films, including *Look Back in Anger* (1959), *Becket* (1964) and, with his then wife, Elizabeth Taylor, *Who's Afraid of Virginia Woolf?* (1966).

BURTON, Sir Richard Francis (1821–1890), English traveler and writer. An employee of the East India Company in India, he mastered Persian, Afghan, Hindustani, and Arabic, then used this knowledge to make (1853) a dangerous journey, in disguise, to the Muslim holy cities of Mecca and Medina. With John SPEKE, he explored in E and central Africa; later he explored in W Africa. He also visited the US and Brazil. He ended his life as British consul at Trieste. Burton wrote extensively about his travels, but his greatest work is his famous translation of the *Arabian Nights*.

BURTON, Robert (1577–1640), English clergyman, author of the *Anatomy of Melancholy* (1621), a compendious study of the causes and symptoms of melancholy, which, from the frankness and perception of its section "On Love Melancholy," has led to his being regarded as a precursor of FREUD.

BURUNDI, a small African state on the NE shore of Lake Tanganyika, originally part of Ruanda-Urundi.

Official name: Republic of Burundi
Capital: Bujumbura
Area: 10,747sq mi
Population: 4,989,000
Languages: Kirundi, French, Swahili
Religions: Roman Catholic, Animist, Muslim
Monetary unit(s)s: 1 Burundi franc = 100 centimes
Land. It consists mostly of high plateau, and is bordered to the N by Rwanda, to the E and S by Tanzania and to the W by Zaire. Burundi has a tropical climate with equable

temperatures and irregular rainfall.

People. Although exceptionally small in area, Burundi is Africa's second most-densely populated state, after Rwanda, its neighbor. The population is about 84% Hutu (Bahutu), 15% Tutsi (Watutsi or Watusi) and 1% pygmy Twa. The Hutu are mainly farmers; the Tutsi, cattle raisers; the Twa, hunters. Although a small minority, the Tutsi dominate politically and socially.

Economy. A poor country, Burundi depends almost exclusively upon coffee for its income. Reliance upon this one commodity and the poor transport infrastructure of this land-locked country are major obstacles to development.

History. The earliest inhabitants, the Twa hunters, were conquered by the Hutu, who in turn were reduced to serfdom by the Tutsi. In 1899, Germany claimed the Ruanda–Urundi territory; after WWI it was administered by Belgium as a trust territory under the League of Nations and, after WWII, under the UN. The two states separated in 1962; Burundi was granted independence that same year. In 1966 long-standing rivalry between the Hutu and Tutsi peoples erupted, and the monarchy was replaced by a military government. Civilian rule was restored in 1979, but there was another coup in 1987. In 1988, violence again broke out between the majority Hutu and the ruling Tutsi; thousands of Hutu fled to neighboring Rwanda.

BUSH, George Herbert Walker (1924–), 41st president of the US (1989–). Born in Milton, Mass., he was the son of Prescott Bush (1895–1972), an investment banker and US senator from Connecticut 1952–63. After graduating from Phillips Academy in Andover, Mass., Bush, at 18, became the youngest commissioned pilot in the US Navy during WWII, flying 58 combat missions in the Pacific. After the war, he graduated (1948) from Yale and moved to Texas, where he engaged in the oil business. In 1964 he ran for the US senate as a Republican and was narrowly defeated. He was a US representative from Texas in 1967–71. Defeated in a second race for the Senate in 1970, he was appointed ambassador to the UN by President Nixon in 1971. The next year he became Republican national chairman and in 1974 head of the US liaison office in China. He served President Ford as head of the CIA in 1976. After unsuccessfully seeking the Republican presidential nomination in 1980, he was chosen as Ronald Reagan's running mate and served as vice president in both Reagan administrations. As the Republican can-

didate for president in 1988, he won 54% of the popular vote and carried 40 states.

BUSH, Vannevar (1890–1974), US electrical engineer, director of the Office of Scientific Research and Development in WWII. In the 1930s he developed a "differential analyzer"—in effect the first analog COMPUTER.

BUSHIDO, code of honor among the SAMURAI (warrior) class of Japan, influenced by ZEN and CONFUCIANISM, which stressed military virtues, feudal loyalty and filial piety. It was formulated in the 12th–14th centuries, but the term itself was first used in the 16th century. After the abolition of the samurai class in 1868, it formed a basis for emperor-worship and nationalism.

BUSHMEN, a people of South Africa related to the pygmies, living around the Kalahari Desert. They average about 5ft in height and have yellowish-brown skin, broad noses and closely curled hair. They are nomadic hunters, living in bands of 25–60. Their language, related to Hottentot and belonging to the Khoisan group, employs a series of "clicks." Bushmen are a musical people, and are also noted for their vivid painting.

BUSINESS CYCLE, periodic fluctuation in the economy of an industrialized nation, between prosperity and recession or depression, with marked variations in growth rate and employment levels. Recession may be caused by overproduction, declining demand, changes in money supply and generally by a loss of confidence. Government interventions to strengthen the economy have become common in recent years.

BUSING, School, the most common means of desegregating US public schools on an area or citywide basis. In 1971, in *Swann v. Charlotte-Mecklenburg*, the US Supreme Court upheld the constitutionality of busing students to achieve racial balance. This decision applied to cases of *de jure* segregation (where segregation is due to official actions) but not to *de facto* segregation (the result of residential patterns). The issue continues to be extremely controversial in both the N and S. Many parents, blacks as well as whites, who otherwise agree with the principle of desegregation as enunciated by the Supreme Court in BROWN V. BOARD OF EDUCATION OF TOPEKA, nevertheless have grave reservations about busing their children away from neighborhood schools—particularly when the distant schools are perceived as being inferior.

BUSONI,   Ferruccio   Benvenuto

(1866–1924), Italian pianist and composer. His works include a lengthy piano concerto with chorus (1904) and the opera, *Doctor Faust* (1916–24). He also made many piano transcriptions of works by J. S. Bach and others.

BUSSOTTI, Sylvano (1931–   ), Italian avant-garde composer who devoted himself to applying the principles of abstract expressionism to music. He abandoned traditional notation and used instead drawings that the performer was required to duplicate in sound, as in his *Five Pieces for David Tudor* and *Frammento*.

BUTE, John Stuart, 3rd Earl of (1713–1792), favorite of King GEORGE III. Though unpopular, he dominated the king until 1765. As prime minister 1762–63, he ended the SEVEN YEARS' WAR.

BUTLER, Benjamin Franklin (1818–1893), US politician and Union general in the Civil War. Because of his harsh autocratic rule as military governor of New Orleans (1862), he was known as "Beast," and he was recalled by President Lincoln. As congressman (1867–75, 1877–79), he supported RECONSTRUCTION and the impeachment of President JOHNSON. A Populist party candidate, he was governor of Mass. (1882) and ran for president (1884).

BUTLER, John (1920–   ), US dancer and choreographer, a member of the Martha GRAHAM company 1945–55.

BUTLER, Nicholas Murray (1862–1947), US educator. He was president of Columbia College (1902–45), and developed it into Columbia U. He was president of the Carnegie Endowment for International Peace (1925–45) and, in 1931, shared the Nobel Peace Prize. He was also active in Republican politics and was president of the American Academy of Arts and Letters (1928–41).

BUTLER, Richard Austen (1902–1982), British political leader. He held a number of important cabinet posts in Conservative governments, including chancellor of the exchequer 1951–55, home secretary 1957–62 and foreign secretary 1963–64. Twice a favorite to be named prime minister, he was passed over twice.

BUTLER, Samuel (1612–1680), English poet, author of *Hudibras* (1663–78), a mock-heroic, anti-Puritan satire. He attacked the hypocrisy and pedantry of the Puritans of the Commonwealth.

BUTLER, Samuel (1835–1902), English novelist. He considered Darwinism too mechanistic and satirized it in *Erewhon* (1872), his version of Utopia. His major work is *The Way of All Flesh* (1903), an autobiographical novel satirizing Victorian morality.

BUTTER, a dairy product made by churning MILK or cream, containing fat, protein and water. Made in some countries from the milk of goats, sheep or yaks, it is made in the US from cows' milk only. Continuous mechanized production has been general since the 1940s. After skimming, the cream is ripened with a bacterial culture, pasteurized (see PASTEURIZATION), cooled to 40°F. and then churned causing the butterfat to separate from the liquid residue, buttermilk. The butter is then washed, worked, colored and salted.

BUTTERFLIES, a large group of INSECTS characterized by wide, brightly colored wings. With MOTHS, they comprise the order LEPIDOPTERA. The life history of the butterfly is composed of several stages, each divided by a METAMORPHOSIS. The egg grows into a larva called a CATERPILLAR, which feeds on vegetation. The next stage, the PUPA, does not feed and eventually produces the adult butterfly.

BUXTEHUDE, Dietrich (c1637–1707), Danish-born German composer and organist. His cantatas and organ toccatas and chorale preludes influenced J. S. Bach. The evening music concerts he held at Lübeck were famous.

BUZZARDS, a group of medium-sized hawks of the family Accipitridae, easily identifiable by their soaring flight, widespread wings and broad tail. They prey on small mammals by swooping from the air or from a perch. In North America they are called hawks, "buzzard" being applied to VULTURES.

BYNG, Julian Hedworth George Byng, 1st Viscount (1862–1935), British field marshal and distinguished WWI commander. In 1917 he took Vimy Ridge with the Canadian Corps in France, and later commanded the first-ever large-scale tank offensive. He was governor-general of Canada 1921–26.

BYRD, Harry Flood (1887–1966), US legislator and Democratic governor of Va. 1926–30. During his 32 years in the Senate (1933–65), he advocated stricter government economy and opposed most NEW DEAL programs, foreign aid and integration policies.

BYRD, Richard Evelyn (1888–1957), US aviator, explorer and pioneer of US exploration and research in Antarctica. He led the air unit with D. B. MacMillan's 1925 Arctic expedition and, with Floyd BENNETT, overflew the North Pole (1926); in 1929 he flew over the South Pole. He made five important expeditions to Antarctica (1928–56), established the base camp Little America there, and worked the whole winter of 1933–34 alone at an advance camp. He headed the US Antarctic program from 1955.

BYRD, Robert Carlyle (1917–   ), US politician, a US representative (1953–59) and senator (from 1959) from West Virginia. He was Democratic leader in the Senate 1977–88.

BYRD, William (1543–1623), English composer, one of Europe's greatest masters of POLYPHONY. His choral music includes the "Great Service" for the Anglican Church, three fine Roman Catholic mass settings, some superb motets, *Cantiones Sacrae* (1589; 1591) and many anthems. He also wrote important keyboard music and madrigals. He was closely associated with TALLIS, and in 1575 they were granted a joint monopoly for the printing and sale of music.

BYRD, William (1674–1744), colonial American planter at Westover, Va., active in political and cultural life. He laid out the city of Richmond on part of his family's vast estates. His delightful books and diaries are important records of his times.

BYRNES, James Francis (1879–1972), US statesman. He was director of WWII mobilization 1943–45, and as secretary of state 1945–47 he worked to lessen tensions with the USSR. He was Democratic governor of S.C. 1951–55.

BYRON, George Gordon Byron, 6th Baron (1788–1824), English poet, a leading figure of European ROMANTICISM. Lameness and an unhappy childhood bred morbidity, a scorn for authority and hatred of oppression. A disastrous marriage and the strictures of English society drove him to exile in Italy (1816). He later joined the Greek revolt against the Turks, dying of fever at Missolonghi, Greece. *English Bards and Scotch Reviewers* (1809), a savage riposte to his critics, brought overnight fame, and the first two cantos of *Childe Harold's Pilgrimage* (1812), a European reputation. The moody, defiant "Byronic" hero of the poetic drama, *Manfred* (1817), became a great Romantic theme. Major works include the incomplete satiric epic, *Don Juan* (1819–24), and *The Vision of Judgement* (1822), satirizing the poet laureate SOUTHEY and King George III.

BYZANTINE EMPIRE, historical term for the successor state to the Roman Empire in the East. Its capital was Constantinople (see ISTANBUL), founded by CONSTANTINE I in 330 AD at the ancient Greek Byzantium. Its heartlands were Asia Minor and the Balkans; at its height it ruled S Spain, Italy, Sicily, N Africa, Egypt, Syria, Palestine, the Crimean coast, Cyprus and the Aegean islands. Its religion was Eastern Orthodox Christianity; Byzantine missionaries took Christianity to Russia and Byzantine theologians are among the chief Church Fathers. Its literature was based on the ancient Greek classic. Byzantine art and architecutre influenced W Europe and Turkey, and Byzantine scholars contributed to Western Humanism.

The Roman Empire was divided after the death of Theodosius I in 395. By c500 the Western Empire had fallen, and Germanic invaders occupied Italy, Spain and N Africa. In the East, Roman institutions continued; JUSTINIAN I (527–565) reconquered Italy, S Spain and N Africa and made a great codification of Roman law. However, after c600 fundamental changes displaced Roman with typically Byzantine (Greek) institutions. By 700, S Spain, N Africa, Egypt and Syria were lost to the VISIGOTHS and ARABS, and the LOMBARDS were conquering Italy. Later, Bulgars occupied much of the Balkans and, after the disastrous Byzantine defeat at the Battle of Manzikert in 1071, the Seljuks pushed deep into Asia Minor. A 12th-century recovery ended when, in 1204, Venice and the Fourth Crusade sacked Constantinople. In 1261 Michael VIII regained the city, but the Turkish threat grew. Western Europe, considering the Eastern Church in schism since a break (1054) between the patriarch of Constantinople and the pope, refused to help. In 1453, the once great Eastern Christian empire fell when the Turks captured Constantinople.

On the rich trade routes from Asia and N Africa to Europe and Russia, Constantinople was the greatest city of the Christian world; its empire rested on a money economy, while feudalism and the Church dominated Western society and government. Byzantine emperors ruled through paid professional administrators, commanded paid professional armies and were supreme in religion as in politics, though affairs were often marked by court intrigues. They controlled early Church Councils and, during the 8th-century iconoclastic controversy, ordered images to be destroyed as idolatrous. Theological debate was a passion with all classes. Military success was expected of emperors, and military coups were frequent. Foreign diplomacy was subtle and usually successful. The Byzantines considered themselves to be the heirs to Rome; their high and ancient civilization justified their claim.

C 3rd letter of the English alphabet, a rounded form of the Greek *gamma*, used by the Romans instead of *k*. In some languages *c* retains both the *k* and *c* sounds (cat, certain, cycle, etc.). C is the chemical symbol for carbon and in Roman numerals equals 100.

CABAL, clandestine group or organization engaged in intrigues; also applied to the intrigues themselves. The term was already used in the 17th century for any secret council of the king. The conduct of English King Charles II's ministers Clifford, Arlington, Buckingham, Ashley and Lauderdale, whose initials spelled "cabal," gave it a sinister sense.

CABALA, or **Kabbalah** (Hebrew: tradition), a body of esoteric Jewish mystical doctrines dealing with the manifestations of God and his revelation. The Cabala attaches mystical significance to every detail in the TORAH. Its chief books are the *Sefer Yezirah* (Book of Creation; 3rd–6th centuries) and the *Sefer HaZohar* (Book of Splendor; 13th century). The Cabala arose in S France and Spain in the Middle Ages and was later a major influence on HASIDISM.

CABBAGE, *Brassica olearacea*, a biennial vegetable from which other brassicas, such as kale, cauliflower and broccoli have been developed. The cabbage originated many centuries ago from the European wild cabbage. It has a characteristic tight "head" of leaves. Cabbages can be boiled or pickled, or fermented in salt to give sauerkraut. They are also used as an animal feed.

CABELL, James Branch (1879–1958), US novelist, who combined an ironic, often anti-romantic style with a strong element of fantasy in plots and settings. His best-known novel is *Jurgen* (1919).

CABET, Étienne (1788–1856), French Utopian socialist, whose novel of an ideal communistic society, *Voyage en Icarie* (1840), gained wide readership. An unsuccessful attempt in 1848 to found an "Icarian" community in Texas was followed by other short-lived colonies, notably one led by Cabet himself (1849–56) at Nauvoo, Ill.

CABEZA DE VACA, Álvar Núñez (c1490–1557), Spanish explorer. Shipwrecked in 1528 on an expedition to Florida, he reached Mexico City after several years among the Indians. His account of the present-day SW US, including descriptions of "Seven Cities of Cíbola" supposedly laden with riches, stirred Spanish interest in the area. He was made governor of the Río de la Plata region in 1540, but after a rebellion against him was recalled to Spain. He was tried and exiled to Africa, but in 1552 he was pardoned by the king.

CABEZÓN, Antonio de (c1510–1566), Spanish composer of keyboard music. Blind from infancy, he served at the Spanish court, writing for the organ, harpsichord and vihuela. His theme–and–variations compositions were notable early examples of the form.

CABINET, in the US, top-level advisory council to the president, composed of the heads of the major executive departments. Though not mentioned in the US constitution, the cabinet has been accepted as a consultative body to the executive since George Washington. Normally the cabinet meets weekly with the president, though procedure varies.

Members of the cabinet are appointed by the president and are responsible as individuals to him: they are not members of either house of Congress and may not address them, though they are often called to testify before committees. In Great Britain and most of the Commonwealth the cabinet is a policy-making body of ministers chosen by the prime minister from the political party in power, and is collectively responsible to parliament. (See also US Departments of AGRICULTURE; COMMERCE; DEFENSE; EDUCATION; ENERGY; HEALTH AND HUMAN SERVICES; HOUSING AND URBAN DEVELOPMENT; INTERIOR; JUSTICE; LABOR; STATE; TRANSPORTATION; TREASURY; VETERANS AFFAIRS.)

CABLE, George Washington (1844–1925), US author noted for his depiction of New Orleans and Creole life in works such as *Old Creole Days* (1879) and *The Grandissimes* (1880).

CABLE TELEVISION, or **CATV** (*community antenna television*), system used originally in areas where mountains or tall buildings made TELEVISION reception poor or impossible, but now expanding throughout the US because of the multiplicity of channels and programs it makes available. Normally, subscribers' sets are connected by coaxial CABLE to a single ANTENNA erected in a suitably exposed position. Many signals are now fed to cable systems via satellite.

CABOT, John (Giovanni Caboto; c1450–1499), Italian navigator and explorer, probably the first European to reach the North American mainland. In 1497, after receiving letters patent from Henry VII of England authorizing his voyage, Cabot sailed in search of a western route to Asia and reached the coasts of Nova Scotia and Newfoundland. He made a landing and set up the English and Venetian flags. On a second voyage (1498) Cabot may have reached America again, but it is not clear what happened to the expedition. Cabot himself was not mentioned again, though he drew his English annuity for 1499.

CABOT, Sebastian (c1476–1557), explorer and navigator, son of John CABOT. Appointed pilot-major of Spain in 1518, he led an expedition to the Rio de la Plata region of South America in 1526. Its failure led to his banishment from Spain. Though eventually reinstated, he went to England in 1548, and later became governor of the Merchant Adventurers Company.

CABRAL, Pedro Álvares (c1467–1520), Portuguese navigator credited with the discovery of Brazil, where he landed in 1500 on a voyage from Lisbon to India. The expedition succeeded in establishing trading posts in India, but after his return in 1501 Cabral was given no other position of authority.

CABRILLO, Juan Rodríguez (d. c1543), Portuguese explorer in the service of Spain, best known for his discovery of California. In 1542 he explored the coastline from Lower California northwards to San Diego Bay, and may have succeeded in landing on some of the islands.

CABRINI, Saint Frances Xavier (1850–1917), Italian–American nun, first US citizen to be canonized (1946). She founded the Missionary Sisters of the Sacred Heart in 1880, and established 67 houses of the order throughout the world. In 1889 she immigrated to New York from Italy.

CACAO, Theobroma cacao, the tree that produces cacao or cocoa beans. The raw material for CHOCOLATE is prepared by roasting, grinding and pressing the dried seeds (or beans) from the woody cacao fruits. Pressing squeezes out cocoa butter and leaves a solid mass that is reground to make cocoa powder. Eating chocolate is made from a blend of ground beans, sugar and cocoa butter, with milk added for milk chocolate. The cacao tree grows in Africa and Middle America and has been cultivated since the time of the Aztecs, who used it for beverages and currency. Christopher Columbus introduced cocoa beans into Europe in 1502 and by the 1700s the hot chocolate drink was popular.

CACTI, family of prickly plants (Cactaceae) comprising over 1,500 species, almost all of which are native to America. The succulent cactus is a xerophyte and well adapted to life in the driest desert conditions. It has no leaves, the main source of water loss in other plants, and PHOTOSYNTHESIS takes place in the stem or trunk, which also stores a great deal of water. A network of roots radiating from the stem makes maximum use of brief desert showers. The characteristic spines have two functions: they prevent the stem from being eaten by animals; and where the spines form a dense covering, they help to retain water without obstructing light. Cacti bear beautiful flowers which are shortlived and often open only at night. Cacti are prized as ornamental plants. They are also the source of the drug MESCALINE, and some species are edible. As house plants they should be kept in sunny south-facing windows. They tolerate normal house temperatures, although some species require a cold period in winter to set buds. They should be well watered whenever the surface of the soil dries out. They can be propagated by means of seeds, cuttings or by dividing the plants. (See also PEYOTE.)

CADBURY, George (1839–1922), English chocolate manufacturer and social reformer who provided model housing for his workers at rural Bournville. He worked to ameliorate working conditions and to establish old-age pensions. His wife was **Dame Elizabeth Cadbury** (1858–1935), who was active in education, housing, and church affairs.

CADE, Jack (d. 1450), leader of the Kentish rebellion against Henry VI of England in 1450. His army occupied London for three days, but disbanded after the promise of concessions and pardons. Cade was captured and mortally wounded, and the concessions were revoked.

CADILLAC, Antoine Laumet de la Mothe (c1658–1730), French colonial governor and founder of Detroit (1701). Governor of Mackinac in 1694, he felt the site of Detroit would be a better strategic position. In 1710 he was appointed governor of Louisiana, but was recalled in 1717.

CADIZ, ancient city and port in SW Spain, on the Atlantic coast NW of Gibraltar. Founded by the Phoenicians in c1100 BC as Gadir, the city became prosperous under Roman rule. After the discovery of America it became important as the headquarters of the Spanish fleets. It is now a commercial port noted for sherry exports. Pop 167,014.

CAEDMON (7th century), early English Christian poet. After a dream commanding him to "sing the beginning of created things," he spent the rest of his life rendering biblical stories into verse. Only nine lines of his hymn to God survive.

CAESAR, family name of the Julian clan of Rome. The success of Julius CAESAR made it charismatic, and it was retained as a family name by the first five Roman emperors. The title was kept by later emperors for their heirs designate, and the German *kaiser* and Russian *tsar* were derived from it.

CAESAR, Gaius Julius (100–44 BC), Roman general, politician and writer, one of the most famous of the ancient Romans. Although a member of the ancient patrician Julian clan, he supported the antisenatorial party. His early career through various public offices won him popularity, and in 60 BC he formed the First Triumvirate with POMPEY, who supplied the army, and Crassus, who provided the money. With Caesar as consul in 59 BC they succeeded in controlling Roman politics, and in 58 BC he chose Gaul as his proconsular command.

Caesar's successful GALLIC WARS (58–51 BC) gained him great esteem and a loyal and well-trained army. Pompey was given extraordinary powers in Rome and tried to force Caesar to lay down his command, but in 49 BC Caesar crossed the Rubicon R (the boundary between his province and Rome), and civil war began. Pompey was finally defeated at Pharsalus in 48 BC, and by 45 BC Caesar had secured the defeat of all the Pompeian forces. In 44 BC he was made dictator for life, but on the Ides of March he was murdered by a group of senators. An outstanding writer (*Commentaries*) and orator, he introduced the Julian calendar.

CAESARIAN SECTION. See CESARIAN SECTION.

CAFFEINE, or trimethylxanthine ($C_8H_{10}N_4O_2$), an ALKALOID extracted from coffee, and also found in tea, cocoa and cola. Caffeine stimulates the central NERVOUS SYSTEM and HEART, and is a DIURETIC. It increases alertness, in excess causing insomnia (see SLEEP), and is mildly addictive. mp 238°C.

CAGE, John (1912–   ), US experimental composer and musical theoretician. He composed for "prepared piano," attaching objects to the strings to alter tone and pitch and get percussive effects. Later work included prolonged silences, improvisation, ALEATORY MUSIC and ELECTRONIC MUSIC.

CAGLIOSTRO, Alessandro, Conte (1743–1795), Italian adventurer who posed as a physician, hypnotist, and magician. He enjoyed a great reputation at the court of King Louis XVI of France. Returning to Italy at the start of the French Revolution, he was condemned by the Inquisition for sorcery and died in prison.

CAGNEY, James (1904–1986), US film actor who played cocky, aggressive tough guys in such classic gangster movies as *The Public Enemy* (1931) and *The Roaring Twenties* (1939). He won an Academy Award for his portrayal of George M. COHAN in *Yankee Doodle Dandy* (1942).

CAHAN, Abraham (1860–1951), Russian-born US journalist and novelist, cofounder in 1897 of the Social Democratic narty and the influential newspaper, the *Jewish Daily Forward.*

CAHOKIA MOUNDS, a group of prehistoric MOUNDS, mostly in the form of truncated pyramids, near East St. Louis, Ill. The largest of these, Monks Mound, is about 350m by 200m at base and some 30m high, and is the largest mound in the US. More than 300 of the mounds have in recent years been bulldozed to make way for agricultural and municipal expansion, but the 18 largest remain.

CAILLIE, René (1799–1838), French explorer in Africa, the first European to visit Timbuktu.

CAIN, James M(allahan) (1892–1977), US writer of crime novels admired for their accuracy of dialogue and characterization. His best-known works are *The Postman Always Rings Twice* (1934), *Serenade* (1937), *Mildred Pierce* (1941) and *Double Indemnity* (1943), all of which were made into films.

CAIRO, or **Al-Qāhirah,** capital of Egypt. It lies at the head of the Nile delta and is the largest African city. Founded in 969 by the Fatimids, it became and has remained the intellectual center of the Islamic world with the foundation of al-Azhar University (970–78). An Allied base during WWII and site of the CAIRO CONFERENCE, it became capital of republican Egypt (1952), and remains a major Arab political, economic and nationalist center. The nearby pyramids, sphinx and Memphis ruins make it a tourist center. Pop (city) 5,875,000; (metro) 7,700,000.

CAIRO CONFERENCE, WWII meeting of CHURCHILL, F. D. ROOSEVELT and CHIANG KAI-SHEK in Cairo, Egypt, Nov. 22–26, 1943. The Cairo Declaration (Dec. 1, 1943) asserted that on Japan's defeat her boundaries would revert to what they were before the late-19th–century conquests of Chinese territory.

CAJETAN, Saint (1480–1547), Italian

CALCULUS 207

churchman and reformer, founder of the congregation of the Theatines and a prominent figure in the COUNTER-REFORMATION.

CAJUNS, descendants of expatriate French–Canadians, living in S La. They were deported from Acadia (Nova Scotia) by the British in 1755. They have a distinctive patois: a combination of archaic French forms with English, Spanish, German, Indian and Negro idioms.

CALABRIA, autonomous Italian region; the "toe" of Italy's "boot." Its capital is Catanzaro and other chief cities are Cosenza and Reggio Calabria. It suffered disastrous earthquakes 1783–87, 1905 and 1908. Area: 5,822sq mi.

CALAIS, city in N France on the Strait of Dover. Held by the English from 1347 to 1558, it has always been a principal terminus of cross-channel travel.

CALAMITY JANE, nickname of Martha Jane Burke (c1852–1903), frontier-town prostitute and campfollower who roamed the West in male garb. Famous in Deadwood, S.D., during the 1870s gold boom, she claimed she had been an army scout, pony express rider, Custer's aide and Wild Bill Hickok's mistress.

CALCIUM (Ca), a fairly soft, silvery-white alkaline-earth metal, the fifth most abundant element. It occurs naturally as calcite, gypsum and fluorite. The metal is prepared by ELECTROLYSIS of fused calcium chloride. Calcium is very reactive, reacting with water to give a surface layer of calcium hydroxide, and burning in air to give the nitride and oxide. Calcium metal is used as a reducing agent to prepare other metals, as a getter in vacuum tubes, and in alloys. AW 40.1, mp 839°C, bp 1484°C, sg 1.55 (20°C).

Calcium compounds are important constituents of animal skeletons: calcium phosphate forms the bones and teeth of vertebrates, and many seashells are made of the carbonate. **Calcium carbonate** ($CaCO_3$), colorless crystalline solid, occurring naturally as calcite and aragonite, which loses carbon dioxide on heating above 900°C. It is an insoluble BASE. **Calcium chloride** ($CaCl_2$), colorless crystalline solid, a by-product of the Solvay process. Being very deliquescent, it is used as an industrial drying agent. mp 782°C. **Calcium fluoride** (CaF_2), or fluorite, colorless phosphorescent crystalline solid, used as windows in ultraviolet and infrared SPECTROSCOPY. mp 1423°C, bp c2500°C. **Calcium hydroxide** ($Ca(OH)_2$), or **slaked lime,** colorless crystalline solid, slightly soluble in water, prepared by hydrating calcium oxide and

used in industry and agriculture as an ALKALI, in mortar and in glass manufacture. **Calcium oxide** (CaO), or **quicklime,** white crystalline powder, made by calcination of calcium carbonate minerals, which reacts violently with water to give calcium hydroxide and is used in arc lights and as an industrial dehydrating agent. mp 2580°C, bp 2850°C. **Calcium sulfate** ($CaSO_4$), colorless crystalline. When the dihydrate is heated to 128°C, it loses water, forming the hemihydrate, **plaster of paris.** This re-forms the dihydrate as a hard mass when mixed with water, and is used for casts.

CALCULATING MACHINE, device that performs simple ARITHMETIC operations (see also ALGEBRA). There are two main classes: **adding machines,** for addition and subtraction only; and **calculators,** able also to perform multiplication and division. They may be mechanical, or electronic.

The forerunner of the calculating machine was perhaps the ABACUS. The first adding machine, invented by PASCAL (1642), was able to add and carry. A few decades later (1671), LEIBNIZ designed a device that multiplied by repeated addition (the device was built in 1694). The Englishman Charles Babbage built a small adding machine (1822); in 1833 he conceived his Difference Engine, a predecessor of the digital COMPUTER, but his device was never completed. (See also SLIDE RULE.)

CALCULUS, the branch of MATHEMATICS dealing with continuously varying quantities. It can be seen as an extension of ANALYTIC GEOMETRY, much of whose terminology it shares. It was invented by NEWTON and independently by LEIBNIZ.

Differential Calculus. Suppose a continuous FUNCTION $f(t)$ represents the position, x, along a road of a moving vehicle at any time t. In the interval between two times t and $t+\Delta t$, the vehicle travels a distance $\Delta x = f(t+\Delta t) - f(t)$ and its average velocity, which is defined as the distance traveled divided by the time taken to travel it, is

$$\frac{\Delta x}{\Delta t} = \frac{f(t+\Delta t)}{\Delta t}$$

Suppose we wish (as Newton did) to define the velocity of an instant t, i.e. the rate of change of x at the time t. We can approximate it as closely as we wish by taking a sufficiently short time interval Δt at t; the LIMIT of the average velocity $\Delta x/\Delta t$ as Δt approaches 0 is the instantaneous velocity, written

$$\frac{dx}{dt} \quad \text{or} \quad f'(t)$$

and called the **derivative** of x (or of the function $f(t)$) with respect to t. If x is plotted as a GRAPH against t, the derivative gives the slope of the tangent to the curve at t. One can take the derivative of the derivative of $f(t)$ and obtain the second derivative

$$\frac{d^2x}{dt^2} \text{ or } f''(x).$$

This is the rate of change of velocity, or acceleration.

There are simple rules for determining the derivatives of the elementary functions. For example (now calling the independent variable x instead of t), if $f(x)=x^2$, then $f'(x)=2x$; and in general, if $f(x)=x^n$, then $f'(x)=nx^{n-1}$. Equations that include derivatives are called differential equations and are widely used in science.

Integral calculus. In order to find the area under the curve representing a function $f(x)$, another limiting process is used. The area is divided into narrow vertical strips, and their areas are added; the limit of the sum as the width of the strips approaches 0 is the area under the curve, called the integral of $f(x)$ and written $\int f(x)dx$. This is a function of x, called the indefinite integral, because we have not specified which part of the curve we want the area under; the value of the area from $x=a$ to $x=b$ (a definite integral) is the value of the indefinite integral or $x=b$ minus its value for $x=a$.

CALCUTTA, capital of W Bengal and largest city of India, near the E border with Bangladesh. It lies in the Ganges delta on the Hooghly R. The principal port and industrial center of E India, it has manufactures that include jute products, chemicals, textiles and glass. It was founded by the British East India Company (1690), and Fort William was built on the site (1696). It was captured by Siruj-ud-Daula, Nawab of Bengal, in 1756; he imprisoned the British in what is known as the BLACK HOLE OF CALCUTTA. Calcutta was retaken by CLIVE (1757) and was capital of British India 1774–1912. In the 1947 Indian partition, it lost its valuable jute-producing hinterland and received thousands of religious refugees, causing severe overcrowding. MOTHER TERESA worked among its impoverished homeless. Pop 9,100,000.

CALDECOTT, Randolph (1846–1886), British painter and illustrator, particularly of children's books. Among his best-known illustrations are those for Irving's *Old Christmas* (1876) and Cowper's *John Gilpin* (1878). In 1938 the Caldecott Medal was established as an annual award for the best US children's picture book.

CALDER, Alexander (1898–1976), US abstract sculptor and creator of the "mobile." His mobiles consist of flat metal shapes connected by rods, wire or string, which are hung or balanced and moved by motors or by air currents.

CALDERÓN DE LA BARCA, Pedro (1600–1681), Spanish playwright and poet. He and LOPE DE VEGA were the leading dramatists of Spain's Golden Age. He wrote over 200 plays, distinguished by their heightened style and poetic symbolism, many on religious themes. Among his most famous works are *The Constant Prince* (1629), *Life Is a Dream* (1635) and *The Surgeon of His Honor* (1635).

CALDWELL, Erskine Preston (1903–1987), US author noted for his portrayal of poor Southern whites in short stories and novels such as *Tobacco Road* (1932), *God's Little Acre* (1933) and *Trouble in July* (1940).

CALENDAR, a system for reckoning the passing of time. The principal problem in drawing up calendars arises from the fact that the solar DAY, the lunar MONTH and the tropical YEAR—the most immediate natural time units—are not simple multiples of each other. In practice a solution is found in basing the system either on the phases of the moon (lunar calendar) or on the changing of the seasons (solar calendar). The difficulty that the days eventually get out of step with the moon or the seasons is got over by adding in (intercalating) one or more extra days or months at regular intervals in an extended cycle of months or years. The earliest Egyptian calendar had a year of 12 months with 30 days each, though later 5 extra days were added at the end of each year so that it approximated the tropical year of 365¼ days. In classical times, the Greeks came to use a lunar calendar in which three extra months were intercalated every eight years (the octennial cycle), though, about 432 BC, the astronomer Meton discovered that 235 lunar months fitted exactly into 19 years (the Metonic cycle), this becoming the basis of the modern Jewish and ecclesiastical calendars. The Roman calendar was reformed under Julius CAESAR in 46 BC, fixing the year at 365 days but intercalating an additional day every fourth year (thus giving an average 365¼-day year). The 366-day year is known as a leap year. This Julian calendar continued in use until the 16th century when it had become about 10 days out of step with the seasons, the tropical year in fact being a little less than 365¼ days. In 1582, therefore, Pope GREGORY XIII ordered that 10 days be omitted from that year.

Furthermore, century years would no longer be leap years unless divisible by 400, so that there would be no recurrence of any discrepancy. This Gregorian calendar was only slowly adopted, particularly in non-Catholic countries—the reform waiting until 1752 in England and its American colonies, by which time 11 days had to be dropped. But today it is in civil use throughout the world. Various proposals for further reform have come to nothing.

Years are commonly numbered in Western societies from the birth of Christ—as computed by a 6th-century monk. Years since that epoch are labeled AD, years before, BC. There is no year 0, 1 AD following directly from 1 BC. Astronomers, on the other hand, figure years BC as negative numbers one less than the date BC and include a year 0 (=1 BC). The astronomers' year − 10 is thus the same as 11 BC. (See also CHRONOLOGY.)

CALHOUN, John Caldwell (1782–1850), prominent US statesman and lifelong defender of Southern interests. He was a member of the House of Representatives 1811–17; secretary of war to Monroe 1817–25 and a member of the 1812 War Hawks. He was twice vice-president, under Adams (1825–29) and under Jackson (1829–32). Following Congress' 1828 "Tariff of Abominations," seen as an attack on the South, he wrote his *South Carolina Exposition* (1828), expounding the "doctrine of nullification": when a federal law violates the Constitution, a state can consider the law void. In 1832 he resigned the vice-presidency and became a senator for S.C. (1833–43; 1845–50) and secretary of state under Tyler (1844-45). He was fiercely proslavery, calling slavery the "perfect good." He argued against the 1846 WILMOT PROVISO, saying that slaves were property and could be moved at will. The last 20 years of his life were spent in fighting ABOLITIONISM.

CALIFORNIA, state SW US, on the Pacific, bounded to the N by Ore., to the W by Nev. and Ariz., and to the S by Mexico. It has the largest state population, and is third largest in area. Its capital is Sacramento, but the most important cities are LOS ANGELES and SAN FRANCISCO. Well over 50% of California's population lives in the Los Angeles-Long Beach and San Francisco-Oakland metropolitan areas. This high percentage of urban population, its sheer size and one of the highest per capita incomes in the US make California an increasingly influential power in national politics.

Land. California's land features are varied,

Name of state: California
Capital: Sacramento
Statehood: Sept. 9, 1850 (31st state)
Familiar name: Golden State
Area: 158,693sq mi
Population: 26,981,000
Elevation: Highest—14,494ft, Mt. Whitney, Lowest—282ft below sea level, Death Valley
Motto: *Eureka* ("I have found it")
State flower: Golden poppy
State bird: California valley quail
State tree: California redwood
State song: "I Love You, California"

including the Sierra Nevada Mts to the W, the coastal ranges to the E, and the Mojave Desert to the SW. There are occasional earth tremors in California, some caused by the San Andreas fault, which runs two-thirds of the state's length.

People. California has a diverse ethnic population. Before 1849 it was comprised of Indians, Mexicans and Spaniards. The Gold Rush brought an influx of US citizens of European descent, and by 1850 they were the vast majority. Extensive railway and road construction in the 1870s and 1880s brought a large number of Chinese immigrants. By 1900 the Japanese also began to emigrate to California as a labor force. After WWII California's population grew rapidly (almost 50% in 1950–60). Growth has continued but at a more moderate rate (14% in 1980–86). By 1990 Hispanics and Asians are each expected to constitute 20% of the population.

The state's system of higher education is constantly expanding. The University of California, founded 1868, moved from Oakland to Berkeley in 1873. Its campuses are located at Berkeley, Los Angeles, Davis, Santa Cruz, Irvine, Riverside, San Diego, Santa Barbara and San Francisco. California has a large number of state and private colleges and universities and a comprehensive system of community and junior colleges.

Economy. Although under 5% of California's population lives on farms, and under 9% of the area is cultivated, intensive irrigation gives California one of the highest state farm incomes. It produces every major US crop except tobacco, has the largest fishing industry, and produces nearly 85% of US wine and 15% of US petroleum. Major manufactures include processed foods, metal goods, machinery, electric and electronic equipment and chemicals. Los Angeles is the world capital of the TV and motion picture industry. Tourism is also a large industry.

History. The Spanish explorer CABRILLO is usually credited with California's discovery. In 1542 he named the present state's area Alta (Upper) California. In 1579 DRAKE ineffectively claimed the area for England, calling it New Albion. The first European settlement was the Spanish San Diego Franciscan mission and fort (1769). In 1822 the Californians changed their allegiance from Spain to the new Mexican Congress; and later US presidents Jackson (1835) and Polk (1845) unsuccessfully attempted to buy the area. On June 14, 1846, a group of Californian settlers declared the independent Republic of California in the "Bear Flag" revolt against Mexico. A few weeks later, the Mexican-US War broke out, and California was occupied by US forces. In 1848, the postwar Treaty of GUADALUPE HIDALGO ceded the area to the US. It was admitted to the Union as a free state under the COMPROMISE OF 1850 on Sept. 9, 1850. Before that, on Jan. 24, 1848, gold had been discovered on the American R. This caused the 1849 GOLD RUSH and within seven years the state's population leaped from 15,000 to 300,000. The present constitution was adopted in 1879. There have been over 420 amendments: since 1911 these can be proposed by petition and approved by popular vote. Voters can also propose measures through the power of initiative and challenge a new law by calling a referendum.

In recent years, the strong growth of the state's economy and population has continued. Supplying water to the densely populated S part of the state has been a problem for decades, and in 1980 a major and controversial extension of the monumental California Water Project (dating from 1960) was initiated at an estimated cost of $5.1 billion. In the 1980s, the state, although basically wealthy, faced a series of fiscal crises brought on in large part by the reduction of local property taxes required by Proposition 13, passed in 1978. In presidential elections 1968–88, California voted consistently Republican.

CALIFORNIA TRAIL, trade and travel routes to the early 1850s Cal. goldfield. In particular, the 800mi route from the Oregon Trail near Fort Bridger to Sutter's Fort near Sacramento. Now part of highways 26, 30, 40 and 50.

CALIGULA (12–41 AD), nickname (meaning "little boots") of Roman Emperor Gaius Caesar, 37–41 AD. He was insanely cruel and despotic and believed he was a god. He reputedly planned to make his horse a consul. His demands that his statue be erected in Jerusalem's temple almost precipitated a revolt in Palestine. He was assassinated by a tribune of his guard.

CALIPHATE (Arabic: *khalifa*, successor), highest office in ISLAM. Early caliphs were the successors of MOHAMMED. They were the rulers of the Muslim community throughout the world and guardians of Islamic law. In 632 AD the Muslims of Medina elected Abu Bakr as first caliph. He was succeeded by Omar (634–44), the first caliph to adopt the title "commander of the faithful." Omar was murdered, as were Othman (644–56) and Ali (656–61). The Omayyad dynasty of caliphs then ruled from Damascus until 750, when the Shiite Muslims, descendants of Ali, who had always claimed their right to the caliphate, massacred the Omayyad family. However, Abd-al-Rahman escaped, fled to Spain, and established an independent emirate at Cordoba which lasted from 750 to 1031. Meanwhile, the Shiite Muslims established the ABBASID family in the caliphate. They ruled from Baghdad until it was sacked by the Mongols in 1258. A puppet Abbasid caliphate also continued in Egypt from 909 until 1520. Until the fall of the Ottoman Empire the Turkish sultans used the title. The caliphate was abolished in 1924 by ATATURK.

CALLAGHAN, Sir (Leonard) James (1912–   ), prime minister of the UK 1976–79. He was elected Labour party leader on the resignation of Harold WILSON and became prime minister immediately. Labour lost the 1979 general election to Margaret Thatcher's Conservatives.

CALLAS, Maria (1923–1977), leading Greek–American operatic soprano, born Maria Kalogeropoulos. She was famous for her expressive phrasing and acting ability in a wide variety of roles in over 40 operas.

CALLES, Plutarco Elías (1877–1945), Mexican general and politician, ablest organizer of the Mexican Revolution which ousted President DIAZ in 1911. President 1924–28, he fought for land reform, educational improvements and greater social welfare. After his presidency he was a power behind the scenes until forced into exile in the US for a time (1936–41).

CALLIGRAPHY, the art of penmanship. Combining beauty with legibility, it evolved in the Far East, where it was a recognized art form as early as 250 BC. In early medieval Europe calligraphy was practiced in monastic communities, which developed the Carolingian and Insular scripts. A high point was reached with the BOOK OF KELLS and the Lindisfarne gospels. The superb Italian Renaissance manuscripts provided models for the first printed books and roman and italic types. The Englishman Edward Johnston (1872–1944) and his pupil Graily Hewitt (1864–1952) began the remarkable modern revival of calligraphy in the early 1900s.

CALLIMACHUS (c310–240 BC), Greek poet, grammarian and critic, leading member of the Alexandrian school. Only six hymns and 64 epigrams of his poetry survive. He also produced the *Pinakes*, the earliest work of systematic bibliography, now lost.

CALLIOPE, keyboard instrument dating from 1855 and much used in circuses and amusement parks. The original version was operated by steam forced through whistles controlled by a keyboard, but later models used compressed air.

CALLISTHENES (c360–328 BC), Greek historian, nephew of Aristotle. The official chronicler of ALEXANDER THE GREAT's Asian expedition, he criticized Alexander's adoption of Oriental customs and was thrown into prison, where he died. None of his works have survived.

CALLOT, Jacques (c1592–1635), French graphic artist, whose 1,500 etchings and engravings are among the greatest of their kind. The two series called *Miseries of War* (1633) are considered his greatest achievement; they were inspired by the Thirty Years' War and seek to depict its horrors. He also produced numerous light, playful works during his residence at the Florentine Medici court. REMBRANDT and WATTEAU, among others, benefited from Callot's example, and his technical innovations greatly refined engraving techniques.

CALLUS, or **callosity.** See CORNS AND CALLUSES.

CALORIC THEORY OF HEAT, the view, formalized by LAVOISIER toward the end of the 18th century, that heat consists of particles of a weightless, invisible fluid, caloric, which resides between the atoms of material substances. The theory fell from favor as physicists began to appreciate the equivalence of work and HEAT.

CALORIE, the name of various units of HEAT. The calorie or gram calorie (c or cal), originally defined as the quantity of heat required to raise 1g of water through 1°C at 1 atm pressure, is still widely used in chemical THERMODYNAMICS. The large calorie, kilogram calorie or kilocalorie (Cal or kcal), 1000 times as large, is the "calorie" of dietitians. The 15° calorie (defined in terms of the 1°C difference between 14.5°C and 15.5°C) is 4.184 joules; the International Steam Table calorie (cal$_{IT}$) of 1929, originally defined as 1/860 watt-hour, is now set equal to 1.1868J in SI UNITS.

CALVARY, or **Golgotha,** Jerusalem hill site of the crucifixion of Jesus. Although archaeologists are not agreed, it is traditionally accepted to be the hill on which Constantine founded the Church of the Holy Sepulcher in the 4th century.

CALVERT, English Roman Catholic family which founded and owned colonial Maryland. **George, 1st Baron Baltimore** (c1580–1632), occupied various public offices until 1625. He founded Ferryland, Newfoundland, in 1621, and lived there 1627–29. Seeking a warmer climate, he petitioned for a grant in N Virginia (present-day Md.), for which King Charles I granted a charter to his son Cecil in 1632. **Cecil (or Cecilius), 2nd Baron Baltimore** (c1605–1675), never visited Md., and left its administration to his younger brother **Leonard Calvert** (1606–1647). In 1649, the colony's Act of Toleration was the first practical expression of the principle of freedom of conscience in the New World. **Charles, 3rd Baron Baltimore** (1637–1715), son of Cecil, was governor of Md. from 1661, governed the colony in person 1679–84 and then returned to England. In 1689 his Md. administration was overthrown by a Protestant rebellion, and in 1691 the Crown withdrew his authority to govern.

CALVIN, John (1509–1564), French theologian and reformer. He studied in Paris, and was converted to Reformation doctrines c1533, becoming prominent in the reforming party. He was forced to flee to Basel, where he published his *Institutes of the Christian Religion* (1536). Guillaume FAREL persuaded him to help establish the Reformation in Geneva. They enforced subscription to a confession of faith, but were expelled from the city in 1538. Calvin joined Martin Bucer at Strasbourg. Geneva recalled him in 1541, and, despite controversy, he set up a church polity which became the paradigm for PRESBYTERIANISM and the REFORMED CHURCHES. Despite fragile health, Calvin worked unceasingly in preaching, lecturing and advising in the city councils, and aided foreign Protestant refugees. On his death, his work was continued by Theodore BEZA. (See also CALVINISM; REFORMATION.)

CALVINISM, the theological system of John CALVIN. Its key principle is that God, not man, is central and supreme. Hence scripture is the source of doctrine. Calvin's *Institutes of the Christian Religion* is a systematic account of biblical teaching, with much in common with early LUTHERANISM, including JUSTIFICATION BY FAITH, PREDESTINATION, assurance of SALVATION, and denial of FREE WILL since the Fall. One distinguishing feature is the view that in Holy COMMUNION the believer participates in Christ in heaven by faith. Calvinism became the doctrine of the REFORMED CHURCHES, which developed Calvin's theology in a scholastic fashion, elevating PRESBYTERIANISM to a major principle, and emphasizing the divine decrees and covenants. Calvinism has been influential in the CHURCH OF ENGLAND (see THIRTY-NINE ARTICLES), among the PURITANS and nonconformists, and in the Evangelical Revival. Recently Karl BARTH has popularized a modified Calvinism. (See also HUGUENOTS; REFORMATION.)

CALVINO, Italo (1923–1985), Italian writer notable for his use of fantasy. Calvino has written in several genres, including science fiction and historical allegory, but received his greatest acclaim for *Italian Folktales* (1956; repr. 1980) and the experimental *If on a Winter's Night a Traveler* (1979; trans. 1981).

CALYPSO, a West Indies musical style notable for its lyrics, which are usually improvised and often humorous or ironic. The music is typically played on steel drums.

CAMBACÉRÈS, Jean Jacques Régis de (1753–1824), French revolutionary and loyal associate of Napoleon I. He was a principal author of the CODE NAPOLÉON.

CAMBODIA. See KAMPUCHEA.

CAMBODIAN "INCURSION." On April 30, 1970, President NIXON announced that 70,000 US and South Vietnamese troops had begun an attack on North Vietnamese "sanctuaries" in Cambodia; he said that this was "not an invasion" since the areas were already under North Vietnamese control. This widening of a war that the president had previously said he was ending inspired many demonstrations in the US, and led to the tragic shooting by National Guardsmen that killed four students at Kent State University in Ohio on May 4. In the Senate, on June 30, the same day that the return of the troops was announced, an amendment was passed barring the use of funds to support future military action in Cambodia without the express approval of Congress.

CAMBRAI, Battle of, first major British WWI tank offensive (Nov. 20, 1917) and successful German counterattack (Nov. 30) at Cambrai, N France. The battle emphasized the tank's striking power, but also the necessity to consolidate territorial gains.

CAMBRIAN, the earliest period of the PALEOZOIC Era (see GEOLOGY), dated roughly 570–500 million years ago, and immediately preceding the ORDOVICIAN. Cambrian rocks contain the oldest FOSSILS that can be used for dating (see PRECAMBRIAN).

CAMBRIDGE, University of, one of the world's leading universities, at Cambridge, England. Its history dates from c1209, and its first college, Peterhouse, was established in 1284. Today, the university is coeducational, and has about 9,000 students. It has a total of 29 colleges and approved societies, and is a self-governing body, with authority vested in its senior members.

CAMBRIDGE PLATONISTS, an influential group of philosophers centered on the U. of Cambridge in the mid-17th century, founded by Benjamin Whichcote and including Henry More and Ralph Cudworth. Their philosophy was Platonist, their outlook was tolerant and one of their chief aims was the reconciliation of faith with scientific knowledge and rational philosophy.

CAMDEN, Battle of, August 16, 1780, during the American Revolution, near Camden, S.C. The Americans, under Gen. Horatio GATES, were badly defeated by the British under Lord CORNWALLIS.

CAMELOT, court of King Arthur and the Knights of the Round Table in ARTHURIAN LEGENDS. It has been identified variously with Caerleon (Wales), Camelford (Cornwall) and South Cadbury (Somerset), where excavations have taken place.

CAMELS, two species of haired, cud-chewing animals with humped backs, long necks and callosities on knee joints. The one-humped or Arabian camel, or dromedary, *Camelus dromedarius*, of N Africa and the Near East is a widely-kept domestic animal which has even been introduced into desert regions of Australia. The two-humped or Bactrian camel, *C. bactrianus* is found from Asia Minor to Manchuria, and there are still a few living wild in the Gobi Desert. Recorded as being domesticated in Babylonia from about 1100

BC, the animals are invaluable in the desert since they can carry enormous loads and are able to withstand the loss of about one-third of their body fluid without danger (not, however, exclusively from their humps, which are fatty tissue, not water storage vessels).

CAMERA, device for forming an optical image of a subject and recording it on a photographic film or plate or (in TELEVISION cameras) on a photoelectric mosaic. The design of modern cameras derives from the ancient camera obscura, represented in recent times by the pinhole camera. This consists of a light-tight box with a small hole in one side and a ground-glass screen for the opposite wall. A faint image of the objects facing the hole is formed on the screen, and this can be exposed on a photographic plate substituted for the screen.

Although the image produced in the pinhole camera is distortion-free and perfectly focused for objects at any distance, the sensitive materials used when photography was born in the 1830s required such long exposure times that the earliest experimentalists turned to the already available technology of the LENS as a means of allowing more light to strike the plate. From the start cameras were built with compound lenses to overcome the effects of chromatic aberration (see ABERRATION, OPTICAL) and the subsequent history of camera design has seen constant improvement in lens performance.

Today's simple camera consists of a light-tight box, a fixed achromatic lens, a simple shutter, a view finder and a film support and winding mechanism. The lens will focus all subjects more than a few feet distant and the shutter (usually giving an exposure of 1/30 or 1/50) admits sufficient light to expose negative materials on a sunny day. If exposures are to be made for reversal processing (see PHOTOGRAPHY) or of close-by or rapidly moving subjects, or in poor light, a more complex camera is required. This may include a movable lens perhaps coupled to a range finder (allowing the precise focusing of objects at different distances), a variable diaphragm (aperture) and shutter-speed mechanism (allowing adjustment to meet a wide range of light conditions) perhaps coupled to an exposure meter (light meter), a flash synchronization unit (allowing use of a flash gun) or a facility for interchangeable lenses (allowing the photographer to alter the width of the camera's field of view). With the advent of the MICROPROCESSOR, some cameras for amateurs have come to include refinements that leave little adjusting for the user to do.

Special types of camera include those that produce a finished print within seconds; the earliest of these was the Polaroid Land camera, first marketed by its inventor, E. H. LAND, in 1948. Another special camera is the stereo camera, which takes two pictures from slightly different points to create an illusion of depth when one picture is seen with each eye. Motion picture cameras take 24 successive photographs per second on a long reel of film (see MOTION PICTURES).

CAMERON, Julia Margaret (1815–1879), English photographer noted for her photographic portraits of prominent Victorians.

CAMERON, Simon (1799–1889), US politician. He built a powerful political machine in Pa., was a US senator (1845–49; 1857–61; 1867–77) and served as secretary of war under Lincoln (1861–62). His career was marked by considerable scandal and corruption.

CAMEROON, republic adjoining Nigeria and five other countries, stretching from the Gulf of Guinea to Lake Chad in W Africa.

Official name: Republic of Cameroon
Capital: Yaoundé
Area: 183,569sq mi
Population: 10,759,000
Languages: English, French, Bantu, Sudanic
Religions: Animist, Christian, Muslim
Monetary units(s): 1 CFA franc = 100 centimes
Land. The coastal plain is from 10–50mi wide, dominated by Cameroon Mountain. The S region is a densely forested 1,000ft plateau. Fertile grasslands lie in the central region, which rises to the N, where the vegetation changes from forest to savanna. The arid far north slopes down to Lake Chad. The entire country is tropical. In the S region, average annual temperatures are 70°F–82°F. The S has two rainy seasons; rainfall in some parts of the coastal plains can be excessive, while in the N, scant.
People. The population is ethnically diverse. In the S are aboriginal pygmies and Bantu farmers, settled in villages; in the N are

various Bantu, Sudanese, Hamite and Arab nomads. Some 34% of the population is urban, the main towns being Douala and Yaoundé. Expanded educational facilities have reduced the illiteracy rate to 35%. The Federal University at Yaoundé has 2,400 students.

Economy. The economy is based mainly on agriculture and forestry. Manioc, millet, sorghum and rice are grown for home consumption, and cattle and sheep are raised. Coffee, cocoa and timber are the main exports. Industry has been developed since independence, and includes textiles, food processing and aluminum smelting. Trade is mainly with France. Cameroon's road network is growing but not yet well-developed. Douala is the major seaport.

History. The Sao people, who produced a distinctive kind of art and cast objects in bronze, settled near Lake Chad about 900 AD. The Portuguese came in the 1400s. In 1884 Germany established a protectorate in the Cameroon area. British and French troops occupied the area during WWI, after which the League of Nations mandated the larger part to France (Cameroun) and the remainder to Britain (Southern and Northern Cameroons). In 1946 the territories became UN trust territories. In 1960 Cameroun became an independent republic. After plebiscites in 1961 N Cameroons joined Nigeria, and S Cameroons joined Cameroun to form the Federal Republic of Cameroon. In 1972 the federal system was abandoned in favor of a unitary republic. Amadou Ahidjo, who had served as president since independence, resigned in 1982. Paul Biya, his successor, was reelected in 1984 and 1988.

CAMOES or **CAMOENS, Luís Vaz de** (1524–1580), Portugal's greatest poet. His epic poem, *The Lusiads* (1572), is a celebration of Portuguese historical glory. Inspired by the AENEID, it centers around the voyages of Vasco da GAMA. Much of the rest of his poetry was published posthumously, in 1595.

CAMORRA, Italian secret society started in the Kingdom of Naples c1830. Although it specialized in extortion, smuggling, robbery and assassination, it was often used by the authorities, and it became very powerful. After unification with Italy in 1861 attempts were made to suppress it, but it survived until 1911.

CAMP, Walter Chauncey (1859–1925), the father of American FOOTBALL. As a player and coach at Yale U. (1876–92) and Stanford U. (1894–95), Camp helped initiate, implement and develop many of the changes that turned European rugby into American football.

CAMPAIGN FINANCING, how candidates meet the high cost of running for elective office. Campaign financing has long been a scandal of US political life. The costs of running for even a minor office are generally greater than most candidates can personally afford. Few have managed to finance their campaigns with their own money or with the aid of friends and neighbors. Invariably, they have had to turn to other sources.

Most candidates have found it more practicable to seek relatively few large contributions from wealthy individuals and special interests rather than many small contributions from average citizens. The successful candidate, therefore, is inevitably indebted to the major contributors to his campaign. Members of city councils, state legislatures, and the national Congress have sometimes been notorious as representatives of particular special interests rather than of their nominal constituents. The problem has become greater in recent years as spiraling campaign costs—due to reliance on television, direct mail, and other advertising to reach large constituencies—have made candidates increasingly dependent on wealthy supporters.

The Federal Elections Campaign Act of 1972, significantly amended in 1974 and 1976, required that candidates for federal office disclose the sources of their financing and placed ceilings on contributions and expenditures. It also provided for public financing of presidential election campaigns.

The 1972 act required candidates for federal office to disclose all campaign contributions over $100 and all campaign expenditures over $1,000. The 1974 amendments to the act required annual financial disclosure by members of Congress and by candidates. Further, for each election (primary, runoff, general) they placed a ceiling of $1,000 on individual contributions to candidates and of $5,000 on contributions by POLITICAL ACTION COMMITTEES (PACs). (While the law limits PAC contributions to candidates, the courts have ruled that it does not limit independent PAC spending on *behalf* of candidates). They also placed ceilings on candidates' total and personal expenditures in primary and general elections. Oversight of federal elections was entrusted to a Federal Election Commission (FEC) composed of three Democrats and three Republicans.

The 1974 act was immediately challenged in the courts. In 1976 the US

Supreme Court ruled that campaign spending was a form of political expression protected by the free-speech clause of the First Amendment; consequently, the act's limits on campaign spending were declared unconstitutional. The Court also rejected ceilings on the amount a candidate or a candidate's family could spend on a campaign. On the other hand, the Court upheld the constitutionality of limits on contributions to the candidate's campaign from other sources, and it upheld the act's disclosure requirements. The Court did, however, make a significant exception to its rejection of limits on campaign spending: such limits were permissible, the Court declared, if the candidate voluntarily accepted them as a condition of receiving public campaign subsidies.

The 1974 amendments to the Federal Elections Campaign Act authorized public financing of national political-party conventions and of presidential primary- and general-election campaigns. At the same time, Congress rejected public financing of congressional (House and Senate) campaigns. Since 1976, Democratic and Republican presidential candidates have accepted public financing of their campaigns. In 1976, each of the two major candidates in the general election received $21.8 million; in 1980, $29.4 million; in 1984, $40.4 million; in 1988, $46.1 million. Although spending by the candidates and party committees was strictly limited, PACs and other organizations were free to raise and funnel money to local party accounts for "party-building" and "get-out-the-vote" drives on behalf of favored candidates.

CAMPANIA, region of central Italy whose principal city is Naples. It is largely devoted to agriculture.

CAMPBELL, Alexander (1788–1866), US clergyman, founder of the DISCIPLES OF CHRIST (Campbellites). The Disciples were formed after a split between Campbell's congregation and the Baptist Church in 1830. He also founded Bethany College in Bethany, W. Va., in 1840.

CAMPBELL, Joseph (1904–1987), US scholar of mythology, at Sarah Lawrence College 1934–72. His many books include *The Masks of God* (4 vols., 1959–67).

CAMPBELL, Sir Malcolm (1885–1949), British racing driver, the first racer to average more than 300mph (Bonneville Salt Flats, Ut. 1935). He set three successive water-speed records, finally attaining 141.74mph in 1939. His son, **Donald Malcolm Campbell** (1921–1967), set a water-speed record of 276.33mph in 1964,

but was killed trying to establish a new record. All the vehicles of both father and son were called *Bluebird*.

CAMPBELL, Mrs. Patrick (1865–1940), English actress. Popular on stage for over 40 years, she created many classic roles, including Eliza Doolittle in Shaw's *Pygmalion* (1914), a part written for her. She is also remembered for her famous correspondence with Shaw.

CAMPBELL-BANNERMAN, Sir Henry (1836–1908), British prime minister 1905–08 and leader of the LIBERAL party from 1899. A member of the House of Commons from 1868 until his death, he held offices under Gladstone. He pursued a progressive policy: established old-age pensions, granted self-government to the Transvaal and the Orange Free State and attempted to end the veto power of the House of Lords.

CAMP DAVID, the woodland camp in the Catoctin mountains in Maryland near Washington, D.C., that has been used by presidents ever since F. D. ROOSEVELT as a retreat, workplace and environment to receive foreign dignitaries. It was called Shangri-La until EISENHOWER renamed it after his grandson, David. Composed of a number of log cabin-like structures snuggled in the mountain scenery, it nevertheless has all the communications and transportation facilities necessary for the work of the president.

CAMP DAVID AGREEMENT, a peace treaty worked out at CAMP DAVID by Egyptian President Anwar SADAT and Israeli Prime Minister Menachem BEGIN with the assistance of President Jimmy CARTER and signed in 1979. Some of the treaty's provisions were: a timetable for a phased withdrawal from the Egyptian Sinai by Israel to be concluded by 1982, mutual diplomatic recognition and setting up a framework for attempting to solve the Palestinian question. The peace process began with Sadat's historic trip to Jerusalem in 1977.

CAMPIN, Robert (1378–1444), Flemish painter best known for his religious paintings. His art reflects the influence of manuscript illumination, though with a keener sense of plasticity in rendering the forms. One of his major works is the triptych of the Annunciation (c1428) known as the *Mérode Altarpiece*. Eager to depict in realistic detail the daily life of the rising bourgeoisie, Campin became a founder of the Netherlandish school, influencing Jan VAN EYCK and Roger Van der WEYDEN, among others.

CAMPION, Saint Edmund (c1540–1581),

martyred English JESUIT. After a conversion to Roman Catholicism he entered the Society of Jesus in 1573. In 1580 he joined the first mission of Jesuits to England. He was arrested as a spy in 1581, tortured and executed. He was canonized in 1970.

CAMPION, Thomas (1567–1620), English poet, composer and physician. He is best known for his four books of *Ayres*, his lyric poetry and the controversial "attack" on rhyme, *Observations in the Art of English Poesie* (1602).

CAMUS, Albert (1913–1960), French novelist, essayist, dramatist and philosopher. Through fiction and reflective essays he communicated his vision of man in an absurd universe. He felt that the only true possibility for freedom and dignity lay in the awareness of this absurdity. His major works include the essay *The Myth of Sisyphus* (1942), which elucidated the philosophical basis of his novel *The Stranger* (1942). Other important works are the novels *The Plague* (1947) and *The Fall* (1956), the essay *The Rebel* (1951) and the play *Caligula* (1944). He won the Nobel Prize for Literature in 1957.

CANAAN, early name for PALESTINE, probably meaning Land of the Purple—from the purple dye made in the area. The region was inhabited from the second millennium by Semitic peoples, mainly AMORITES, whose script provides the earliest known alphabet. Their culture was a mixture of Egyptian, Mesopotamian and many other influences. During the 13th century BC Canaan was occupied by the Israelites (see JEWS), though in the next century its coasts were taken by the PHILISTINES. The latter were subdued by King David (1000–961 BC), who extended Israelite rule over all Canaan.

CANADA, country in North America, largest in the W hemisphere and second-largest in the world after the USSR. Ironically it derives its name from *Kanata*, a Huron-Iroquois word meaning a small village. It is bounded on the E by the Atlantic Ocean, on the N by the Arctic Ocean, on the W by the Pacific Ocean and Alaska, and on the S by its 3,987mi border with the US.

Canada comprises 10 provinces (Newfoundland, Prince Edward Island, Nova Scotia, New Brunswick, Quebec, Ontario, Manitoba, Saskatchewan, Alberta and British Columbia) and the Yukon and Northwest Territories. It is a Commonwealth country in which the British Crown is represented by a governor-general. The federal capital is Ottawa.

Land. Canada is basically a vast, stepped

Official name: Canada
Capital: Ottawa
Area: 3,849,675sq mi
Population: 25,853,000
Languages: English, French
Religions: Roman Catholic, United Church of Canada, Anglican
Monetary unit(s): 1 Canadian dollar = 100 cents

plain bordered on the W by the Rocky Mts, on the SE by the Appalachians and on the NE by the U-shaped Canadian shield formation of old and worn rocks, covering about half of Canada. In the S, bordering the Great Lakes, is the Ontario Peninsula, and farther E are the fertile St. Lawrence lowlands and the rolling valleys and uplands of Appalachian Canada. Around the center of the Shield are the lakes and muskegs of the Hudson Bay lowlands.

The Canadian Rockies have at least 30 peaks above 10,000ft, but Canada's highest mountain, Mt Logan (19,850ft) is in the St. Elias Mts in the Yukon. There are three major drainage systems, the Great Lakes-St. Lawrence, the Saskatchewan-Red-Nelson rivers system and the Mackenzie, Canada's longest river (2,635mi). Climate is mainly influenced by distance from the sea and distance north; it runs to extremes. Winters are usually long and cold, though milder on the W and SW coasts. Southern summers are usually warm. Rainfall is heaviest in the W and snowfall heaviest in the E. Vegetation ranges from the tundra of the N to mainly coniferous forest, mixed woodlands and prairie grasslands.

People. Canada's population is predominantly of British or French stock, though it includes many of German, Italian, Ukrainian, Dutch and other origins. Indians number about 320,000 and Inuit (Eskimos) about 23,000. Of the total population, 67% speak only English, 18% speak only French, 13.5% are bilingual and 1.5% speak neither. Both French and English are official languages, but the majority of new immigrants prefer to learn English. Population is concentrated in the S part of the country, the most populous provinces being Ontario, Quebec and British Columbia. About 76% of Canadians are urban, with Ontario the most urbanized of the provinces and Prince Edward Island the least. The largest urban areas are Toronto, Montreal, Vancouver, Ottawa, Edmonton, Calgary, Winnipeg, Quebec and Hamilton

Government. Canada has a parliamentary system of government, with executive power vested in a prime minister and cabinet. The federal legislature comprises a Senate of 104 appointed members and a House of Commons whose 282 members are elected for a 5-year term. Each of the 10 provinces has its own premier and elected legislature. The Yukon and Northwest Territories are governed by federally appointed commissioners and elected councils, and each sends one representative to the federal parliament.

Economy. During the present century Canada has emerged as a major manufacturing country and in the early 1980s was far more urban and industrial than rural and agricultural. Two-thirds of all manufacturing plants are located in Ontario and Quebec. Agriculture, however, remains important, ranking first in terms of employment and providing about 11% of Canada's total exports. Canada is one of the world's chief wheat producers, but also grows other grains, oilseeds, fruit (especially apples), vegetables and tobacco. Beef and dairy cattle, hogs, sheep and poultry are reared. Forestry and fisheries are major industries, and Canada remains a leading source of furs, both farmed and trapped. Mineral resources are rich and include petroleum and natural gas, molybdenum, platinum, copper, nickel, iron ore, zinc, lead, silver, gold, asbestos, elemental sulfur and coal. Oil and natural gas are produced mainly in Alberta and Saskatchewan, and are actively being sought in the MacKenzie delta. Abundant energy is provided by hydroelectric and thermal power plants, and several nuclear power plants are operating. Major hydroelectric installations are located on Niagara, St. Lawrence, Ottawa, St. Maurice, Saguenay, Bersimis, Manicouagan, Churchill, Peace and Columbia Rs; and there is great potential for further development in the N as the technology for long-distance transmission is improved.

Manufacturing accounts for about 20% of all employment. In terms of manufacturers' shipments the leading products were automobiles. Other important products include nonferrous metals, machinery, chemicals, plastics, electrical equipment and textiles. Among Canada's chief trading partners are the US, Britain, Japan, West Germany, Netherlands, China, Venezuela and the USSR.

History. Visited by 11th-century Vikings, Canada was later penetrated by explorers such as John CABOT, Jacques CARTIER and Samuel de CHAMPLAIN. The French founded Quebec in 1608 and made Canada the royal colony of New France (1663). Anglo-French rivalry culminated in the cession of New France to Britain (Treaty of PARIS, 1763). French rights were guaranteed by the QUEBEC ACT (1774). Only one serious revolt against British rule took place (1837–38), consisting of separate uprisings led by W. L. Mackenzie in Upper (English-speaking) Canada and Louis Papineau in Lower (French-speaking) Canada. The British North America Act (1867) established Canada as a dominion, the four founding provinces being Quebec, Ontario, Nova Scotia, and New Brunswick. The others entered later: Manitoba (1870), British Columbia (1871), Prince Edward Island (1873), Saskatchewan (1905), Alberta (1905) and Newfoundland (1949). The Northwest Territories, formerly administered by the Hudson's Bay Company, became a federal territory in 1870, and the Yukon was made a separate territory in 1898. Separatist tensions, particularly in French-speaking Quebec, developed during the 1960s and continued into the 1980s. Efforts begun in 1978 to amend the British North America Act in order to "patriate" the Canadian constitution resulted in the CONSTITUTION ACT, 1982. Quebec demanded special concessions under the new constitution, and these were granted in 1987, including recognition of Quebec as a "distinct society," unanimity instead of a seven-province majority for future major amendments, and a provincial voice in future senate and supreme court appointments. The 16-year government of Liberal prime minister Elliott TRUDEAU ended in 1984 with the election of a Conservative, Brian MULRONEY, whose ideology was compatible with that of US president Ronald Reagan. Hopes for improved relations with the US were advanced by the conclusion in 1987 of a bilateral trade agreement between the two leaders providing for elimination of tariffs by both countries over a 10-year period, the end of all restrictions on the import and export of energy, Canadian abandonment of all controls on US investment in Canada, and binding arbitration to resolve future bilateral disputes. The free-trade agreement was the central issue in general elections held in Nov. 1988. The Liberal and New Democratic parties denounced it as leading to further economic and cultural domination of Canada by the US. But Mulroney's Progressive Conservatives won 169 of the 295 seats in the House of Commons, and the prime minister recalled parliament to ratify the agreement.

CANADA GOOSE, *Branta canadensis,* a large migratory bird common to North America, Greenland and parts of Asia. It is recognizable by its long black head and neck and distinctive white cheek bars and is known for its habit of flying in group formations.

CANADIAN FOOTBALL, game resembling US FOOTBALL, but differing in the following ways: There are 12 men on a team, not 11; the extra player is a flanker on offense, a halfback on defense. Each team has three, rather than four, downs to gain 10 yds. There is no fair catch when receiving a kick. One point is scored by the punting team if the receivers are unable to move the ball out of the end zone, which is 25 yds deep, as against 10 in US football. The field size is 110 by 65 yds. as against 100 by 53 1/3 in the US game. All backs may be in motion, and no time-outs are allowed.

CANADIAN SHIELD, or **Laurentian Plateau,** that area of North America (including the E half of Canada and small portions of the US) which has remained more or less stable since PRECAMBRIAN times. Its surface rocks, which are igneous and metamorphic (see IGNEOUS ROCK; METAMORPHIC ROCK), are amongst the oldest in the world, younger structures having disappeared through EROSION, in some areas by GLACIERS of the PLEISTOCENE Epoch.

CANALETTO (1697–1768), born Antonio Canal, 18th-century Venetian painter preeminent in the depiction of architectural vistas. His best-known works, such as *View of the Grand Canal,* are scenes of Venice notable for their sense of spaciousness and light combined with very fine detail. He lived in London 1746–56, and painted many English views of similar quality. His very numerous drawings and etchings are also highly esteemed.

CANALS, man-made waterways used for transportation, drainage and IRRIGATION. They represent one of mankind's earliest attempts to change the environment to suit his convenience. As early as 521 BC a precursor of the Suez Canal joined the Nile to the Red Sea. In China, the Ling Ch'u canal was completed during the 3rd century BC and the Grand Canal, joining the Paiho, Yellow and Yangtze rivers, had sections in use by the 7th century AD. The Romans built many canals to supply their cities with water and canalized a number of European rivers to create an empire-wide transportation system. AQUEDUCTS were widely used long before Roman times to carry water across roads and valleys, but it was the development of the lock which allowed canals to cross other terrain. By the 15th century this simple device for raising boats from one land level to another was already in use, and one of its inventors, LEONARDO DA VINCI, built several canals with locks near the city of Milan.

Although one of the great engineering projects of the 19th century, the SUEZ CANAL to the Red Sea was built entirely without locks, the other great international waterway, the PANAMA CANAL, would not have been possible without them. Locks allowed a canal transport system to be built across England and Europe from the 16th century onwards. In North America, the canal system included the ERIE CANAL, completed in 1825 to link the Hudson R to Lake Erie and, more significantly, to provide an opening to the Middle West. The Welland Canal, opened in 1828 between Lake Erie and Lake Ontario, was the next step in an inland waterway transportation network completed by the opening of the ST. LAWRENCE SEAWAY, of which it is now a part, in 1959.

CANARIS, Wilhelm (1887–1945), German admiral, chief of military intelligence 1935–44. Involved in the opposition to Hitler, he was arrested after the attempt on Hitler's life in July 1944 and later executed by the Gestapo.

CANARY, name of several small song birds, particularly a finch native to the Canary Islands. The wild canary is usually gray or green in color, but tame birds have been bred to produce the characteristic "canary yellow." The birds have been kept and bred in Europe since the 16th century and are valued for their lovely song.

CANARY ISLANDS, group of volcanic islands in the Atlantic, about 65mi off the NW coast of Africa. Comprising two Spanish provinces, the main islands are Tenerife, Palma, Gomera, Hierro, Grand Canary, Fuerteventura and Lanzarote; their land area is nearly 3,000sq mi. Main industries are fishing, farming and tourism; Las Palmas and Santa Cruz are the principal ports. They were called "insulae canariae," or "islands of the dogs," by the Romans. The name passed on to the native wild finch, or CANARY.

CANAVERAL, Cape, promontory on the E coast of Fla., site of the John F. Kennedy Space Center, named Cape Kennedy

1963–73. It became famous with the launching of the first US satellite, Explorer I, in 1958; and first manned lunar exploration in 1969. The cape was established as a national seashore in 1975.

CANBERRA, federal capital city of the Commonwealth of Australia, built from 1913 onwards in the Australian Capital Territory. Australia's largest inland city, it is located on a plain about 1,900ft above sea level. There are various light industries, but the economy rests mainly on the public service and governmental departments. Pop 245,000.

CANCER, a group of diseases in which some body cells change their nature, start to divide uncontrollably and may revert to an undifferentiated type. They form a malignant TUMOR which enlarges and may spread to adjacent tissues; in many cases cancer cells enter the BLOOD or LYMPH systems and are carried to distant parts of the body. There they form secondary "colonies" called **metastases.** Such advanced cancer is often rapidly fatal, causing gross emaciation. Cancer may present in very many ways—as a lump, some change in body function, bleeding, ANEMIA or weight loss—occasionally the first symptoms being from a metastasis. Less often tumors produce substances mimicking the action of HORMONES or producing remote effects such as NEURITIS.

Cancers are classified according to the type of tissue in which they originate. The commonest type, **carcinoma,** occurs in glandular tissue, SKIN, or visceral linings. **Sarcoma** occurs in connective tissue, MUSCLE, BONE and CARTILAGE. **Glioma** is a sarcoma of BRAIN neuroglia, unusual in that it does not spread elsewhere. **Lymphoma,** including HODGKIN'S DISEASE, is a tumor of the lymphatic system (see LYMPH); LEUKEMIA can be regarded as a cancer of white blood cells or their precursors. The cause of cancer remains unknown, but substantial evidence points to damage to or alteration in the DNA of CHROMOSOMES. Certain agents are known to predispose to cancer including RADIOACTIVITY, high doses of X RAYS and ULTRAVIOLET RADIATION and certain chemicals, known as **carcinogens.** These include tars, oils, dyes, ASBESTOS and tobacco smoke (see SMOKING). A number of cancers are suspected of being caused by a VIRUS and there appear to be hereditary factors in some cases.

Prevention of cancer is mainly by avoiding known causes, including smoking, excess radiation and industrial carcinogens. People suffering from conditions known to predispose to cancer need regular surveil-lance. Treatments include surgical excision, RADIATION THERAPY, CHEMOTHERAPY, or some combination of these. The latter two methods destroy cancer cells or slow their growth; the difficulty is to do so without also damaging normal tissue. They have greatly improved the outlook in lymphoma and certain types of leukemia. Treatment can be curative if carried out in the early stages, but if the cancer has metastasized, therapy is less likely to succeed; all that may be possible is the relief of symptoms. Thus, if cure is sought, early recognition is essential.

CANETTI, Elias (1905–   ), Bulgarian-born author of prose and plays in the German language. Major works include the novel *Auto da Fé* (1935) and the political study *Crowds and Power* (1960). He received the 1981 Nobel Prize for Literature.

CANIFF, Milton Arthur (1907–1988), US cartoonist, originator (1934) of the comic strips *Terry and the Pirates* and (1947) *Steve Canyon.*

CANNABIS. See HEMP; MARIJUANA.

CANNAE, ancient town in S Italy, site of HANNIBAL's decisive defeat of the Romans in 216 BC. The encircling technique he perfected, which is regarded as a masterpiece of tactics, won him the battle and 10,000 prisoners.

CANNES, French resort and seaport on the Mediterranean coast, in the Alpes Maritime department. Its superb climate makes it a center for tourism and festivals, notably the annual International Film Festival. Pop (city) 71,100; (metro) 296,000.

CANNIBALISM, or **anthropophagy,** consumption by humans of human flesh, common throughout the world at various times in the past and still occasionally practiced, though now generally taboo. Among PRIMITIVE MAN the motive appears to be belief that eating an enemy or a respected elder transfers to the eater the strength, courage or wisdom of the dead.

CANNING, Charles John Canning, Earl (1812–1862), British statesman. He was governor general of India during the SEPOY REBELLION (1857–58). When the British government assumed (1858) control of India from the British East India Company, Canning became the first British viceroy.

CANNING, George (1770–1827), British statesman. As foreign secretary 1822–27 (following an earlier tenure, 1807–09), he opposed the HOLY ALLIANCE, pledged support for the independence of the Spanish American colonies (thus making possible the MONROE DOCTRINE) and secured Greek independence. He became prime minister in

1827, but died shortly afterwards.

CANNING, the process of preserving foods in sealed metal containers, developed by the French chef Nicolas Appert in 1809 and first patented in the US by Ezra Daggett in 1815. The fragile glass jars originally used were replaced by tin-coated iron cans after 1810. Today, a production line process is used. The food may reach the cannery a few hours after picking; it is first cleaned, and then prepared by removing inedible matter. After it has been peeled, sliced or diced as necessary, the food is blanched: hot water and steam are used to deactivate enzymes that might later spoil the flavor and color, and to shrink the product to the desired size and weight. The cans are then filled and heated to drive out dissolved gases in the food and to expand the contents, thus creating a partial vacuum when they are cooled after sealing. Finally, the cans are sterilized, usually by steam under pressure. (See also FOOD PRESERVATION.)

CANNON, Joseph Gurney (1836–1926), US legislator and speaker of the US House of Representatives 1903–11. Elected to the House by Ill. in 1872, he served for 46 years. As speaker, his arbitrary partisan rules became known as "Cannonism," and he had a dictatorial control of the House which was only finally curtailed when he was excluded from the rules committee in 1910.

CANO, Juan Sebastiàn del (1476–1526), Basque seaman who commanded the first ship to circumnavigate the globe (1521), after MAGELLAN's death.

CANON, Biblical, books accepted as part of the Bible and usually considered to have divine authority. The Jewish Old Testament canon was completed by the 1st century AD, and St. ATHANASIUS compiled the oldest canonical list of the New Testament in the 4th century.

CANONIZATION, the process by which a Christian church declares a deceased person to be a saint. In the Roman Catholic Church the process involves a long and careful investigation of the individual's life and reputation for sanctity, heroic virtue and orthodoxy. There is also a scrutiny of miracles reputedly effected by the candidate when alive or after death.

CANON LAW, the body of ecclesiastical laws (canons) governing the organization, administration and discipline of a church, most fully developed in the Roman Catholic Church. In the 12th century Gratian, a Benedictine monk, compiled the first systematic collection of canon law, based on papal decrees and the proclamations of synods. It was reinforced by further compilations under Pope PIUS X in 1904 and completed under Pope BENEDICT XV in 1917. Another revision was initiated in 1959.

CANOPUS, star in the constellation Carina, 2nd brightest in the sky.

CANOSSA, village in N Italy, site of a castle outside whose walls Holy Roman Emperor Henry IV reportedly stood barefoot in the snow for three days in 1077 as penance before Pope Gregory VII withdrew his excommunication. The incident dramatized the subordination of secular to ecclesiastical authority in the Middle Ages.

CANOVA, Antonio (1757–1822), Italian sculptor, a leading exponent of Neoclassicism. His works include *Cupid and Psyche* (1787–92), several statues of his patron Napoleon, and a famous statue of Pauline Bonaparte Borghese as the reclining *Venus Victrix* (1808).

CANTERBURY, city and county borough of Kent, on the Stour R 55mi SE of London. It was England's ecclesiastical capital from 597AD and the archbishop of Canterbury is primate of all England. Canterbury has many notable buildings, including the cathedral (where Thomas à BECKET was murdered in 1170), a Norman castle and Kent U. Pop 127,400.

CANTERBURY TALES, the best-known work of the English poet Geoffrey CHAUCER, written between 1387 and his death in 1400. In 17,000 lines (mostly heroic couplets) it describes a party of 30 pilgrims going to the shrine of St. Thomas à Becket, and their plan to tell four tales each on the journey. Only 24 tales were written, 4 of them unfinished, but the work presents a vivid cross-section of medieval society and the tales cover most medieval literary genres.

CANTINFLAS (Mario Moreno Reyes; 1911–), Mexican actor, popular in Spanish-language films for his Chaplinesque character.

CANTON, largest city in S China, capital of Kuang-tung (Guangdong) province, on the Pearl R about 75mi from Hong Kong. It is the chief seaport and the commercial and industrial center of the area, producing newsprint, textiles, machinery, chemicals, rubber and matches, and also processing many agricultural products. It has been a trading center since the 2nd century AD and was the first to trade with Europeans in the 16th century. Pop (city) 3,181,510; (metro) 5,669,640.

CANTOR, Eddie (Edward Israel Iskowitz; 1892–1964), US entertainer, an energetic song-and-dance vaudevillian who attained stardom in Florenz Ziegfeld's *Follies*. Thereafter he appeared on Broadway, in films, and (1931–39) in a weekly radio show.

CANTOR, Georg Ferdinand Ludwig Philip (1845–1918), German mathematician who pioneered the theory of infinite SETS.

CANUTE II THE GREAT (Cnut or Knut; c995–1035), king of England, Denmark and Norway, son of King Sweyn of Denmark. His victory at Ashingdon (1016) won him all England N of the Thames R. Edmund II Ironside's death gave him the south. He succeeded his brother Harold in Denmark (1019), seized the throne of Norway (1028) and was recognized as Scotland's overlord. His attempt to hold back the sea is apocryphal.

CANVASBACK, *Aythya vallisneria,* a diving duck found in coastal and inland waters of North America, about 600mm (2ft) long and 1.4kg (3.1lb) in weight. It feeds on aquatic plants, shrimps and small fish.

CANYONLANDS NATIONAL PARK, in E Ut., established in 1964. It covers an area of 337,258 acres and contains much remarkable scenery, including red rock canyons, stone needles, arches and rapids, and also rock carvings.

CAPA, Robert (born Andrei Friedmann, 1913–1954). Hungarian-born US photographer, a pioneer of journalistic photography, notably in the Spanish Civil War and the WWII Normandy landings.

CAPACITOR, or **condenser,** an electrical component used to store electric charge (see ELECTRICITY) and to provide reactance in alternating-current circuits. In essence, a capacitor consists of two conducting plates separated by a thin layer of insulator. When the plates are connected to the terminals of a BATTERY, a current flows until the capacitor is "charged," having one plate positive and the other negative. The ability of a capacitor to hold charge, its capacitance C, is the ratio of quantity of electricity on its plates, Q, to the potential difference between the plates, V. The electric energy stored in a capacitor is given by $\frac{1}{2}CV^2$. The capacitance of a capacitor depends on the area of its plates, their separation and the dielectric constant of the insulator. Small fixed capacitors are commonly made with metal-foil plates and paraffin-paper insulation; to save space the plates and paper are rolled up into a tight cylinder. Some small capacitors have a mica dielectric. Variable capacitors used in RADIO tuners consist of movable intermeshing metal vanes separated by an air gap. In electrolytic capacitors, the dielectric is an oxide film formed on the plates by the action of a solid electrolyte. They must be connected with the correct polarity.

CAPE BRETON ISLAND, in NE Nova Scotia, 110mi long, up to 75mi wide, separated from the Canadian mainland by the Strait of Canso (since 1955 joined by a causeway). Local industries include tourism, lumbering, fishing and the mining of coal and gypsum.

CAPE COD, peninsula in Barnstable Co., SE Mass., 65mi long, up to 20mi in width, site of the first Pilgrim landing in 1620. Shipping, whaling, fishing and salt production were early industries; today the cape is famous for its cranberries, and its summer resorts such as Provincetown and Hyannis.

CAPE HATTERAS, a promontory lying 30mi off the N.C. coast and long known as "the graveyard of the Atlantic" because of its rocky shoals.

CAPE HORN, lower tip of South America, known for its cold, stormy climate. Part of Chile, the cape's bare headland lies well S of the Strait of Magellan on Horn Island.

CAPEK, Karel (1890–1938), Czech writer whose works, known for their humor and anti-authoritarian stand, include the plays *R.U.R.* (*Rossum's Universal Robots,* 1920) and *The Insect Play* (1921) and the novel *War with the Newts* (1936).

CAPE OF GOOD HOPE, rocky promontory near the S tip of Africa, 30mi S of CAPE TOWN, chief navigational hazard in rounding Africa. It was discovered by Bartholomew DIAZ in 1488, who named it Cape of Storms. Vasco da GAMA first sailed around it in 1497 into the Indian Ocean.

CAPE PROVINCE, province of South Africa, 278,465sq mi in area. The capital and chief city is Cape Town. A Dutch colony since 1652, the Cape became British in 1806. Many Dutch settlers (BOERS) migrated N and W to found independent states (see GREAT TREK). Self-governing after 1872, Cape Colony joined the Union of South Africa in 1910.

CAPETIANS, ruling house of France (987–1328) which, by consolidating and extending its power, laid the basis for the French state. Hugh Capet, founder of the dynasty, was elected king in 987. Though his rule and territory were limited, his successors gradually increased their land and control. Under the Capetian dynasty many basic administration characteristics of the French monarchy were established, including the parlements (courts) and the States-General (national assembly).

CAPE TOWN (Kaapstad), legislative capital of South Africa and capital of Cape of Good Hope province. Founded by the Dutch East India Company in 1652, it has a pleasant climate, excellent beaches and attractive scenery, and the country's largest harbor. Among its major exports are gold, diamonds, fruits, wines, skins, wool, mohair and corn. Pop (city) 697,513; (metro) 1,107,763.

CAPE VERDE, independent nation in Africa, lies in the Atlantic Ocean some 400mi W of Senegal.

Official name: Republic of Cape Verde
Capital: Praia, on the island of São Tiago
Area: 1,557sq mi
Population: 350,000
Languages: Portuguese, Creole
Religion: Roman Catholic
Monetary unit(s): 1 escudo = 100 centavos
Land. Cape Verde consists of 10 islands and 5 islets, forming a 1500sq mi horseshoe. The islands are volcanic—only about 20% of the land is cultivable. The climate is tropical, with a rainy season, although recently there has been severe cyclical drought.

People and Economy. Over half of the population is of Portuguese and African extraction. Living standards and the rate of literacy are low. Despite a paucity of fertile land, the country is primarily agricultural. However, most food must be imported. The fishing industry provides the major source of exports. Canned fish, salt, bananas and frozen fish are the primary exports, most going to Portugal.

History. The Portuguese discovered the islands in the 15th century. Cape Verde became a supply station for ships and a transit point during the Atlantic slave trade. Blacks from Guinea were taken to the islands to work on Portuguese plantations. Portugal ruled the islands until 1975, when the islands became independent. Cape Verde and GUINEA-BISSAU are politically and culturally close, although they severed diplomatic relations from 1980 to 1982. In 1988 the two countries signed a cooperation agreement.

CAPILLARIES, minute BLOOD vessels concerned with supplying OXYGEN and nutrients to and removing waste products from the tissues. In the LUNGS capillaries pick up oxygen from the alveoli and release carbon dioxide. These processes occur by DIFFUSION. The capillaries are supplied with blood by ARTERIES and drained by VEINS.

CAPILLARITY, the name given to various SURFACE-TENSION phenomena in which the surface of a liquid confined in a narrow-bore tube rises above or is depressed below the level it would have if it were unconfined. When the attraction between the molecules of the liquid and those of the tube exceeds the combined effects of gravity and the attractive forces within the liquid, the liquid rises in the tube until equilibrium is restored. Capillarity is of immense importance in nature, particularly in the transport of fluids in plants and through the soil.

CAPITAL, in economics, those goods which are used in production—such as plant and equipment (*fixed capital*) and raw materials, components and semifinished goods (*circulating capital*)—as opposed to goods intended for immediate consumption. To classical economists, capital was one of three main factors of production, the others being labor and land. Modern economists include "management skill" and "human capital," i.e. education and training. The problem being to find the most profitable combination of resources in the manufacture of goods, the decision to invest in capital is determined by the cost and availability of labor and natural resources, and the cost of capital (e.g. interest on the money used to buy equipment). Other factors, such as the state of the market, are also important. Modern industrial countries are highly capitalized, but, among the less developed countries, the lack of capital is often acute.

CAPITALISM, economic system in which the means of production — land, machinery, labor — are privately owned (or hired) and managed for profit, as contrasted with SOCIALISM, where the means of production are publicly owned and managed for the welfare of society as a whole. Karl MARX believed that capitalism generated profits exclusively from its exploitation of labor, with the result that the working class was reduced to abject poverty while other social groups enjoyed luxuries. Historically, however, capitalism has proved more efficient and more productive of widespread material benefits than socialism, although it has also created economic inequality and insecurity. Modern capitalism developed in the later 18th and early 19th centuries in England and the US. It is commonly associated with the free-market or laissez-faire philosophy of Adam SMITH, but in fact capitalism existed only briefly free of government restraints. Modern industrial societies in the West have mixed economies, in which government regulates market competition, protects the interests of different groups, and pursues basic social objectives.

CAPITAL PUNISHMENT, in the US, was meted out by local state, and federal governments in the 18th and 19th centuries for a wide variety of crimes. Movements to reform or abolish it persisted through the 19th and 20th centuries. Reformers succeeded in ending public executions, in transferring executions from local to state authorities, in instituting more efficient and humane methods of execution, in limiting the death penalty to murder in the first degree (i.e., premeditated murder or murder committed during the perpetration of a felony), and in substituting discretionary for mandatory death sentences. Pennsylvania was the first state to abolish (1794) capital punishment for all crimes except first-degree murder. In 1972, 11 states had abolished the death penalty entirely; 5 others retained it for a few special crimes, such as the murder of a police officer or a prison employee.

Advocates of the death penalty argued that it was an essential weapon in the war on crime. Opponents argued, in part, that it had no measurable deterrent effect on criminals but that it brutalized the society that inflicted it. In the 1960s, the Legal Defense and Educational Fund of the NATIONAL ASSOCIATION FOR THE ADVANCEMENT OF COLORED PEOPLE (NAACP) undertook a systematic attack on capital punishment on the grounds that it was applied in a racially and economically discriminatory manner. Executions had been declining since the 1930s, but the NAACP's class-action suits based on the "due process" and "equal protection" clauses of the 14th Amendment brought them to a halt in 1968. In 1972 the US Supreme Court ruled that capital punishment was not in itself unconstitutional (i.e., it was not "cruel and unusual punishment") but that the arbitrary, capricious, and discriminatory fashion in which it was imposed made it so. All state and federal capital-punishment laws were thereby struck down. Those states that had had capital-punishment laws before 1972 quickly enacted new ones to satisfy the Court's requirement that capital punishment be administered in a regular and equitable manner. The Court rejected some of those laws but approved others, and executions were resumed in the US in 1977. From 1977 through 1987 there were 93 executions in the US. In 1988, 2,100 persons were under sentence of death. At that time, 37 states had capital punishment statutes. Thirteen states and the District of Columbia did not. Of those states, 18 authorized execution by lethal injection, 14 by electrocution, 7 by lethal gas, 2 by hanging, and 1 by firing squad.

CAPITOL, The, federal government building in Washington, D.C. which houses the US Congress. The Capitol, in classical style, was built on 3½ acres of high ground known as Capitol Hill in Washington's center. Designed by William Thornton in 1792, it was begun the next year when President Washington laid the cornerstone. The Senate occupies the N wing (completed 1800), and the House of Representatives the S wing (completed 1807). The building was severely damaged by the British in 1814. After its reconstruction (completed 1863) no significant alterations were made until 1958–62, when the E facade was extended 32½ feet.

CAPONE, Al (1899–1947), US gangster, born in Naples, became head of a lucrative Chicago crime syndicate, and was involved in many gang murders, including the St. Valentine's Day Massacre. Because of the difficulty in securing evidence against him he was eventually convicted only of income tax evasion.

CAPORETTO, Battle of (Oct.–Dec. 1917), major defeat of Italian military forces during WWI in NW Yugoslavia. The 600,000 Italian troops, weary after a 2½ year stalemate, either deserted or surrendered to the Austrian-German forces. The defeat caused Italy's allies to send reinforcements and eventually establish a unified Allied command.

CAPOTE, Truman (1924–1984), US writer known especially for *Breakfast at Tiffany's* (1958) and the "non-fiction" crime novel *In Cold Blood* (1965). His earlier works include *Other Voices, Other Rooms* (1948) and *The Grass Harp* (1951).

CAPP, Al (Alfred Gerald Caplin; 1909–1979), US cartoonist, author of the hugely successful comic strip *Li'l Abner* (1934–77).

CAPRA, Frank (1897–   ), US film director and three-time Academy Award winner. With a gift for gentle satire and comic improvisation, he directed, among other films, *Mr. Deeds Goes To Town* (1936), *You Can't Take It With You* (1938) and *Mr. Smith Goes to Washington* (1939).

CAPRI, Italian island resort in the Bay of Naples, site of the Villa Iovis of Roman Emperor TIBERIUS. Capri produces olive oil and wine, but its main industry is tourism.

Anacapri, at the island's W end, is approachable from the sea by hundreds of steps, called the "Phoenician Stairs."

CAPUCHINS, Roman Catholic order of friars and an independent branch of the Franciscans. Founded (1525) by Matteo di Basico, a Franciscan who sought a return to the simplicity of St. Francis' life, the order is distinguished by the pointed hood, or *capuccino.*

CARACALLA (Marcus Aurelius Antoninus; 188–217 AD), son of Septimius Severus, tyrannical Roman emperor (211–217) notable for his edict (212) granting Roman citizenship to all freemen of the Empire. He left the magnificent baths in Rome that bear his name.

CARACAS, Venezuelan capital, near the Caribbean Sea at an altitude of 3,020ft, founded in 1567 by Diego de Losada, and the birthplace of Simón BOLÍVAR in 1783. Independence from Spain was achieved in 1821, as part of the Republic of Gran Colombia. In 1829 Caracas became the capital of independent Venezuela.

After WWII and the discovery of oil in Maracaibo, Caracas greatly expanded. Industries include textiles, cement, steel products, paper, leatherwork and furniture. Pop (city) 1,232,254; (metro) 3,184,958.

CARAVAGGIO, Michelangelo Merisi da (1573–1610), Italian Baroque painter who achieved startling and dramatic effects with an interesting technique of shadow and light, called chiaroscuro. Among his finest works are the *Death of the Virgin* and *Supper at Emmaus.*

CARBOHYDRATES, a large and important class of aliphatic compounds, widespread and abundant in nature, where they serve as an immediate energy source; cellulose is the chief structural material for plants. Most carbohydrates have chemical formulas $(CH_2O)_n$, and so were named as hydrates of carbon—which, however, they are not. Systematic names of carbohydrates end in –ose. They are generally divided into four groups, the simplest being the **monosaccharides** or simple SUGARS and the **disaccharides** or double sugars. The **oligosaccharides** (uncommon in nature) consist of three to six monosaccharide molecules linked together. The **polysaccharides** are POLYMERS, usually homogeneous, of monosaccharide units, into which they are broken down again when used for energy, The main plant polysaccharides are CELLULOSE and STARCH; in animals a compound resembling starch, glycogen, is formed in the muscles and liver. Other polysaccharides include agar, algin, chitin, dextrin, gum acacia, insulin and pectin. Carbohydrates play an important role in food chains (see ECOLOGY): they are formed in plants by PHOTOSYNTHESIS, and are converted by ruminant animals into PROTEIN. They also form one of the major classes of human food (see NUTRITION). In Europe and the US they provide a third to a half of the calories in the diet, of which starch and the various sugars supply about half each. In less developed countries carbohydrates, especially starch, are even more important.

CARBON (C), nonmetal in Group IVA of the PERIODIC TABLE. It is unique among elements in that a whole branch of chemistry (ORGANIC CHEMISTRY) is devoted to it, because of the vast number of compounds in its forms. The simple carbon compounds described below are usually regarded as inorganic.

Carbon occurs in nature both uncombined (COAL) and as carbonates, carbon dioxide in the atmosphere, and PETROLEUM. It exhibits ALLOTROPY, occurring in three contrasting forms: DIAMOND, graphite and "white" carbon, a transparent allotrope discovered in 1969 by subliming graphite. So-called amorphous carbon is actually microcrystalline graphite; it occurs naturally, and is found as COKE, CHARCOAL and **carbon black** (obtained from the incomplete burning of petroleum, and used in pigments and printer's ink, and to reinforce rubber). Amorphous carbon is widely used for adsorption, because of its large surface area. A new synthetic form is carbon fiber, which is very strong and is used to reinforce plastics to make electrically-conducting fabrics.

Carbon has several ISOTOPES: C^{12} (used as a standard for ATOMIC WEIGHTS) is much the most common, but C^{13} makes up 1.11% of natural carbon. C^{10}, C^{11}, C^{14}, C^{15} and C^{16} are all radioactive. C^{14} has the relatively long half-life of 5730yr, and is continuously formed in the atmosphere by COSMIC RAY bombardment; it is used in radiocarbon dating.

The element (especially as diamond) is rather inert, but all forms will burn in air at a high temperature to give carbon monoxide in a poor supply of oxygen, and carbon dioxide in excess oxygen. Fluorine will attack carbon at room temperature to give carbon tetrafluoride, and strong oxidizing agents will attack graphite. Carbon will combine with many metals at high temperatures, forming carbides. Carbon shows a covalency of four, the bonds pointing toward the vertices of a tetrahedron, unless multiple bonding occurs. AW 12.011.

Carbides, binary compounds of carbon with a metal, prepared by heating the metal or its oxide with carbon. Ionic carbides are mainly acetylides (C_2^{2-}) which react with water to give acetylene, or methanides (C^{4-}) which give METHANE. There are also metallic interstitial carbides, and the covalent boron carbide (B_4C) and silicon carbide. **Carbon dioxide** (CO_2), colorless, odorless gas. It is nontoxic, but can cause suffocation. The air contains 0.03% carbon dioxide, which is exhaled by animals and absorbed by plants (see RESPIRATION; PHOTOSYNTHESIS). Carbon dioxide is prepared in the laboratory by reacting a carbonate with acid; industrially it is obtained by calcining LIMESTONE, burning coke in excess air, or from FERMENTATION. At atmospheric pressure, it solidifies at $-78.5°C$ to form "dry ice" (used for refrigeration and CLOUD seeding) which sublimes above that temperature; liquid carbon dioxide, formed under pressure, is used in fire extinguishers. Carbon dioxide is also used to make carbonated drinks. When dissolved in water an equilibrium is set up, with carbonate, bicarbonate and HYDROGEN ions formed, and a low concentration of **carbonic acid** (H_2CO_3). **Carbon disulfide** (CS_2), colorless liquid, of nauseous odor due to impurities; highly toxic and flammable. Used as a solvent and in the manufacture of rayon and CELLOPHANE. mp$-111°C$, bp 46°C, sg 1.261 (22°C). **Carbon monoxide** (CO), colorless, odorless gas. It is produced by burning carbon or organic compounds in a restricted supply of oxygen, for example, in poorly ventilated stoves, or the incomplete combustion of gasoline in an AUTOMOBILE engines. It is manufactured as a component of water gas. It reacts with the halogens and sulfur, and with many metals, to give carbonyls. Carbon monoxide is an excellent reducing agent at high temperatures, and is used for smelting metal ores (see BLAST FURNACE; IRON). It is also used for the manufacture of methanol and other organic compounds. It is a component of manufactured gas, but not of natural gas. Carbon monoxide is toxic because it combines with hemoglobin, the red BLOOD pigment, to form pink carboxyhemoglobin, which is stable, and will not perform the function of transporting oxygen to the tissues. mp$-199°C$. **Carbon tetrachloride** (CCl_4), colorless liquid, nonflammable but toxic, made by chlorinating carbon disulfide. Used as a fire extinguisher, a solvent (especially for dry-cleaning) and in the manufacture of freon. mp$-23°C$. bp 77°C. (See also CYANIDES.)

CARBONARI (Italian: charcoal burners), members of a revolutionary secret society in 19th-century Italy. Although originally formed to restore the Bourbons to Naples, the Carbonari later instigated many revolts against conservative regimes in Italy. The name was also used by French, Spanish and Portuguese revolutionaries.

CARBON CYCLE, in biology, a very important cycle by which carbon, obtained from the atmosphere as carbon dioxide, is absorbed by green plants, synthesized into organic compounds and then returned to the atmosphere as carbon dioxide. The organic compounds, particularly CARBOHYDRATES, are synthesized in plants from carbon dioxide and water in the presence of CHLOROPHYLL and light by a process known as PHOTOSYNTHESIS. The carbohydrates are then broken down to carbon dioxide and water either by the plant during RESPIRATION or after death by putrefying BACTERIA and FUNGI. (See also PLANT.)

CARBONIFEROUS, collective term used mainly in Europe for the combined MISSISSIPPIAN and PENNSYLVANIAN periods of the geologic time scale.

CARDANO, Girolamo (1501–1576), Italian physician and astrologer, chiefly remembered for his contributions to mathematics. He was responsible for the first systematic theory of possibilities.

CÁRDENAS, Lázaro (1895–1970), Mexican soldier and politician. He joined the Mexican revolutionary forces in 1913, rising to the rank of general. President 1934–40, he initiated many radical reforms, including the expropriation of land and nationalization of foreign-owned oil companies.

CARDIGAN, James Thomas Brudenell, 7th Earl of (1797–1868), British general in the CRIMEAN WAR, who led the charge against the Russians at Balaklava in which the Light Brigade was destroyed. A vain and quarrelsome man, he is remembered as an incompetent commanding officer.

CARDINAL, hierarchically high-ranking official of the Roman Catholic Church, whose principal duties include the election of the pope, counseling the papacy and administrating Church government. Cardinals are chosen by the pope, and have the title of Eminence. Their insignia consists of scarlet cassock, sash, biretta (skullcap) and hat, and a ring.

There are three orders: *cardinal bishops* of the sees near Rome; *cardinal priests* (cardinal archbishops) with responsibilities outside the district of Rome; and *cardinal deacons,* who have been titular bishops since 1962. Cardinal bishops and cardinal deacons are members of the Curia, the central administrative body of the Church. They head the *tribunals*, the courts of the Church. Together, the cardinals form the Sacred College, which elects the pope. The cardinalate originated in early 6th-century Rome. The term cardinal is derived from Latin *cardo*, meaning hinge, reflecting the essential working relationship between this institution and the papacy.

CARDOZO, Benjamin Nathan (1870–1938), US jurist and Supreme Court justice (1932–38) after an impressive career at the bar and in the N.Y. courts. He believed that the courts should not merely interpret the law but help create it, particularly in adapting it to changing social conditions. His many significant decisions reflect this view.

CARDS. See PLAYING CARDS.

CARDUCCI, Giosuè (1835–1907), Italian scholar and patriotic poet. His *Hymn to Satan* (1863) is an anticlerical, political satire; the *Barbarian Odes* (1877–89) are perhaps his best work. He won the 1906 Nobel Prize for Literature.

CARE (Cooperative for American Relief to Everywhere, Inc.), a charity founded in 1945, initially for aid to Europe but now operating worldwide. MEDICO (Medical International Cooperation Organization), a medical relief agency, became part of CARE in 1962.

CAREW, Thomas (c1594–1640), English poet and lyricist, in later life a courtier of CHARLES I. His verse, influenced by DONNE, combines a light "cavalier" style with metaphysical elements. He remains best known for his long amatory poem *The Rapture*.

CARGO CULTS, religious movements common among the natives of New Guinea and Melanesia, who believe that, by aping in ritual the European society they do not understand, they can persuade supernatural powers to give them European material wealth—"cargo." Often worshiping John Frum, a messianic figure, the cults have even involved building airstrips to receive the "cargo."

CARIBBEAN SEA, a warm oceanic basin bordered by Central America to the E, South America to the S, and the West Indies to the N and E. The GULF STREAM originates here. The construction of the Panama Canal from 1881 increased trade and traffic in the area.

CARIB INDIANS, inhabitants of the Caribbean before the Spanish conquest, living in the Lesser Antilles and parts of South America. They were farmers and formed villages presided over by headmen. Persistent raiders of other tribes, they ate their captives. The Caribs were practically exterminated after the Spanish settlement, apart from a few on the island of Aruba. Some descendants survive among the area's population today.

CARIBOU, *Rangifer tarandess*, the only member of the DEER family (Cervidae) in which both sexes bear antlers. They were at one time essential food animals for the Canadian Indians. They live wild in Canada and Siberia, while the semi-domesticated reindeer of the same family live in Greenland and Scandinavia. They can travel over boggy or snow-covered ground and they live on lichen, dry grass and twigs.

CARICATURE AND CARTOON. A **caricature** is a sketch exaggerating or distorting characteristics of its subject for satirical purposes; generally used of pictures, the term may also describe literary works. Caricature became an established form by the 18th century, in the hands of GOYA in Spain and HOGARTH in England, followed by ROWLANDSON, CRUIKSHANK and TENNIEL, and the savagely witty DAUMIER in France. It occasionally proved a powerful means of communication. NAST's political caricatures helped topple the Tweed Ring and TAMMANY HALL in New York after the Civil War. Today, artists such as David Levine and Albert Hirschfeld continue the tradition in the US.

Cartoons are related to, and often contain, caricature. Originally meaning a preparatory sketch, the term derives from a series of architectural "cartoons" parodied by *Punch* magazine in 1843. Today it also includes the COMIC STRIP, the political cartoon and cartoon ANIMATION. The cartoon has been increasingly adopted as an art form by POP ART. Prominent US cartoonists have included Charles Addams, Al Capp, Charles Schulz, Walt Kelly, Garry Trudeau and Herblock.

CARLETON, Sir Guy (1724–1808), British soldier and governor-general of Quebec. He was responsible for the QUEBEC ACT of 1774 which guaranteed the French the right to speak French and to practice their religion. During the American Revolution, he led the defense of Quebec against Benedict ARNOLD and later captured Crown Point, N.Y. In 1782 he was appointed commander-in-chief of the British army in North America; he was several times governor–general of Canada.

CARLISTS, Spanish supporters of the claim of Don Carlos (1788–1855) and his successors to the Spanish throne. They were part of the Falange during the Spanish Civil War. The present pretender is Prince Carlos Hugo de Bourbon-Parma.

CARLOTA (1840–1927), empress of Mexico, wife of Archduke MAXIMILIAN of Austria. When NAPOLEON III stopped supporting Maximilian as emperor, she returned to Europe to seek other assistance, but failed. Not long before Maximilian's execution she went mad and spent the rest of her life in seclusion in Belgium.

CARLSBAD CAVERNS, a series of underground caves in SE N.M. The caverns consist of a three-level chain of limestone chambers studded with magnificent stalactites and stalagmites. They were discovered in 1901 and are millions of years old. The main chamber is 4,000ft long and in places 300ft high; there are over 40mi of explored passages.

CARLSON, Chester Floyd (1906–1968), US inventor of XEROGRAPHY, first patented in 1940.

CARLSTADT (c1480–1541), German Protestant reformer. He supported Martin LUTHER, but Luther rejected his extreme emphasis on salvation by grace alone. He became a professor of theology at Basel.

CARLYLE, Thomas (1795–1881), Scottish historian and philosopher. His famous *French Revolution* (1837) is a vivid but idiosyncratic presentation of the event rather than a factual account. Believing that man's progress was due to individual "heroes," he scorned egalitarianism, always extolling the right of the stronger. Many of his books, such as *Sartor Resartus* (1833–39), *On Heroes* (1841) and *Past and Present* (1843), are still read, but as literature rather than history.

CARMAN, (William) Bliss (1861–1929), Canadian poet and essayist. He is now best remembered for *Low Tide on Grand Pré* (1893) and *Songs from Vagabondia* (1894, 1896, 1901), volumes of love and nature poems.

CARMELITES, Friars of Our Lady of Mount Carmel, a religious order of the Roman Catholic Church. It is named for Mount Carmel, in Israel, where it originated about 1150. The Carmelites' strict rule was based on silence and solitude but it was slightly relaxed by the English prior, Saint Simon Stock (d. 1265). The order of Carmelite Sisters was established in 1452. Saint TERESA OF ÁVILA and Saint JOHN OF THE CROSS were members. In 1593 a separate branch, the Discalced (Barefoot) Carmelites, was founded. The order's typical clothing consists of a brown habit and scapular, with a white mantle and black hood.

CARMICHAEL, Hoagland Howard "Hoagie" (1899–1981), US composer of popular songs, including "Stardust," "Rockin' Chair," "Georgia on My Mind," and "Lazybones."

CARMONA, António Óscar de Fragoso (1869–1951), Portuguese general and politician who took power in 1926. He outlawed the party system and remained president until his death. He was virtually a dictator but established internal stability.

CARNAP, Rudolf (1891–1970), German-US logician and philosopher of science, a leading figure in the Vienna Circle (see LOGICAL POSITIVISM), who later turned to studying problems of linguistic philosophy and the role of probability in inductive reasoning.

CARNARVON, George Edward Stanhope Molyneux Herbert, 5th Earl of (1866–1923), English Egyptologist. His excavations with Howard Carter in the Valley of Kings area revealed tombs of the 12th and 18th dynasties and, in Nov. 1922, the tomb of TUTANKHAMEN.

CARNEGIE, Andrew (1835–1919), US steel magnate and philanthropist. Born in Dunfermline, Scotland, he emigrated with his family and acquired his fortune entirely through his own efforts, rising from bobbin-boy in a cotton factory to railroad manager and then steel producer at a time of great demand. In an essay, *The Gospel of Wealth* (1889), he formulated his belief that the duty of the rich is to distribute their surplus wealth, and in 1900 he began to set up the vast number of charitable and educational institutions for which he is remembered, including libraries, pension funds, educational trusts, grants to universities in Scotland and the US, patriotic funds, a Temple of Peace at The Hague and the CARNEGIE FOUNDATIONS.

CARNEGIE, Dale (1888–1955) US author and lecturer whose book *How to Win Friends and Influence People* (1936) became the best-selling nonfiction work of modern times, second only to the Bible. He offered courses in effective speaking and human relations in more than 750 US cities and 15 foreign countries.

CARNEGIE FOUNDATIONS, philanthropic organizations established by Andrew CARNEGIE to advance education, research and world peace. The Carnegie Institution of Washington, D.C., supports research in physical and biological sciences. The Carnegie Foundation for the Advancement of Teaching works to improve higher education, and the Carnegie Corporation of New York endows projects in preschool education and education for the disadvantaged. The Carnegie Endowment for International Peace promotes peace through studies of international law and diplomacy. These and other organizations set a pattern for other major institutions such as the Ford and Rockefeller foundations.

CARNIVORA, order of flesh-eating MAMMALS. Daggerlike canine teeth, cutting cheek teeth (*carnassials*) and sharp claws are distinctive features.

CARNIVOROUS PLANTS. See INSECTIVOROUS PLANTS.

CARNOT, Lazare Nicolas Marguerite (1753–1823), French soldier and politician; "Organizer of Victory" for the Revolutionary armies. Disapproving of Napoleon he resigned as minister for war in 1800 and was exiled as a regicide by Louis XVIII in 1816.

CARNOT, Nicolas Léonard Sadi (1796–1832), French physicist who, seeking to improve the EFFICIENCY of the STEAM ENGINE, devised the **Carnot cycle** (1824) on the basis of which Lord KELVIN and R. J. E. CLAUSIUS formulated the second law of THERMODYNAMICS. The Carnot cycle, which postulates a heat engine working at maximum thermal efficiency, demonstrates that the efficiency of such an engine does not depend on its mode of operation but only the TEMPERATURES at which it accepts and discards heat ENERGY.

CARO, Anthony (1924–   ), British sculptor who created large and brightly painted abstractions out of steel plates, beams, and rods.

CARO, Joseph ben Ephraim (1488–1575), Jewish Talmudist and philosopher whose codification of Jewish law, the *Shulhan 'Arukh* (1565), became the standard authority. Caro's family were Spanish Jews who settled in Constantinople; in later life he became a leader of the Jewish community in Palestine.

CAROL, two kings of Romania. **Carol I** (1839–1914), elected prince 1866, became Romania's first king in 1881 when it became independent of the Ottoman Empire. His reign brought economic development but no solution to pressing rural and political problems. **Carol II** (1893–1953) became king in 1930. He established a royal dictatorship to counter the growing Fascist movement, but after losing territory to the Axis powers in WWII, he abdicated in 1940 and went into exile.

CAROLINE AFFAIR, incident in 1837 in which the US ship *Caroline* was sunk by loyal Canadians, killing a US sailor. The *Caroline* was running supplies to the Canadian rebel leader W. L. Mackenzie. The affair strained relations between Britain and the US, but the affair was settled in 1842 after the Webster-

Ashburton treaty.

CAROLINE ISLANDS, archipelago in the W Pacific, with over 900 islands, the largest being Ponape, Babelthuap, Yap and Truk, now part of the federated states of MICRONESIA. In WWII they were the scene of bitter fighting between US and Japanese forces and were part of the US Trust Territory of the Pacific Islands until 1986, when they became a sovereign state in free association with the US.

CAROLINGIANS, Frankish dynasty named for the Emperor CHARLEMAGNE. Its first members ruled under puppet MEROVINGIAN kings as mayors of the palace, but in 751 Pepin III the Short deposed Childeric III and ruled as king with the blessing of Pope Stephen III. Pepin III's son, Charlemagne, was crowned emperor of the West in 800. His reign was the golden age when the empire had its frontiers on the Elbe, the Danube and the Ebro, and included north and central Italy. However in 843 it was partitioned among his three grandsons, the first of many divisions. The reigns of Charlemagne and his successors are sometimes called "the Carolingian Renaissance" because of their artistic achievements. The superb palatine chapel at Aachen reflects the Carolingian merging of ancient Roman and Byzantine influences; Carolingian manuscripts are among the masterpieces of manuscript illumination, and from the Carolingian minuscule the present small letters are derived. The Carolingians encouraged close church-state relations and fostered feudal ideas which reached their full development in the Middle Ages.

CAROTHERS, Wallace Hume (1896–1937), US chemist who developed NYLON, the first synthetic fiber, and neoprene, a synthetic rubber, while serving as director of research at the Du Pont Company (1928–37).

CARPACCIO, Vittore (c1460–1526), Venetian Renaissance narrative painter. A major work is the cycle of paintings of the *Legend of St. Ursula* (1490–95), typical of his work in atmospheric use of color and meticulous detail to create fantasy settings. He was an accurate observer and delighted in presenting pageantry.

CARPATHIANS, European mountain range, about 900mi long, running from Czechoslovakia through Poland, the USSR and Romania. Though an extension of the Alps, they are much lower. The N Carpathians are densely forested, with isolated valleys inhabited by Slav and Magyar peoples. The S Carpathians (or Transylvanian Alps) are more accessible and have important oil fields.

CARPENTER, John Alden (1876–1951), US composer. A businessman until 1936, he composed in his spare time. His ballets *Krazy Kat* (19219 and *Skyscrapers* (1926) and orchestral suite *Adventures in a Perambulator* (1915) were particularly popular.

CARPENTERS' HALL, historic meeting place in Philadelphia, Pa., now within Independence National Historical Park. Seat of the CONTINENTAL CONGRESS in 1774, it served as a hospital in the REVOLUTIONARY WAR and in the 1790s was occupied by the First Bank of the United States. It has been restored and run by the Carpenters' Company since 1857.

CARPENTIER, Alejo (1904–1980), Cuban novelist and music historian best known for his novels *The Lost Steps* (1953) and *Explosion in a Cathedral* (1962) and for his encouragement of the Afro-Cuban movement in literature and the arts.

CARPET. See RUGS AND CARPETS.

CARPETBAGGERS, name give to Northern opportunists who moved into the South after the Civil War to make their fortunes out of postwar chaos and political spoils grabbed from disenfranchised Southerners. They secured many local and state political posts, mobilizing a politically unsophisticated Negro vote, and earned a reputation for graft, wasteful spending and influence-peddling.

CARR, Edward Hallett (1892–1982), British political scientist and historian best known for his 10-vol. *History of Soviet Russia* (1950–78). A specialist in international relations, he also wrote *The Twenty Years' Crisis* (1939) and the controversial *What Is History?* (1961).

CARRACCI, family of Bolognese painters. **Lodovico Carracci** (1555–1619), a painter of the Mannerist school, founded an academy of art in Bologna. **Agostino Carracci** (1557–1602) is famous primarily for his prints and *Communion of St. Jerome* (c1590). **Annibale Carracci** (1560–1609) is considered the greatest painter of the family. Much influenced by CORREGGIO, his work, particularly the vast decorations for the Farnese palace (1597–1604), introduced a strong classical element into a basically Mannerist style.

CARRANZA, Venustiano (1859–1920), Mexican political leader. He became governor of Coahuila state in 1910, and Mexican president in 1917, the first to be elected under Mexico's new consititution, which he had supported. It established basic reforms in land ownership and national control of natural resources. His restrictions on foreign acquisitions of Mexican property made for uneasy foreign relations. He fled an uprising led by General OBREGÓN, but was assassinated.

CARREL, Alexis (1873–1944), French surgeon who won the 1912 Nobel Prize for Medicine or Physiology for developing a technique for suturing (sewing together) blood vessels, thus paving the way for organ TRANSPLANTS and blood TRANSFUSION.

CARRIER, Willis Haviland (1876–1950), US industrialist and mechanical engineer, pioneer designer of AIR-CONDITIONING equipment. He invented an automatic humidity-control device first used in a New York printing plant in 1902—arguably the first commercial air-conditioning installation.

CARRIER PIGEON, breed of show pigeon derived from the rock pigeon, not used for message-bearing despite its name. (See also PIGEON.)

CARROLL, Charles (1737–1832), American Revolutionary leader. Owner of a large estate (Carrollton) in Maryland but barred from colonial politics as a Catholic, he nevertheless took an active part in Revolutionary affairs. He served in the Continental Congress and (1789–92) in the US Senate. He was the last surviving signer of the Declaration of Independence.

CARROLL, John (1735–1815), first US Roman Catholic bishop. A strong patriot, he helped establish the Catholic hierarchy in the US. In 1790 he was consecrated bishop of Baltimore, and was made archbishop in 1808. He founded a seminary which became Georgetown U.

CARROLL, Lewis (pseudonym of Charles Lutwidge Dodgson; 1832–1898), English mathematician best known for his children's books *Alice in Wonderland* (1865) and *Alice Through the Looking Glass* (1872). Lecturer in mathematics at Christ Church, Oxford, from 1854, he was ordained a deacon in 1861 but did not take further orders. The *Alice* books and poems such as *The Hunting of the Snark* (1876) are built on mathematical illogic and paradox. He was also a noted portrait photographer.

CARSON, Christopher "Kit" (1809–1868), US frontiersman, Indian agent, army officer and folk hero. He worked as a hunter and guide in the 1840s and explored Ore. and Cal. with FRÉMONT. He served in the Mexican War, and fought for the Union in the Southwest during the Civil War, finally becoming a brevet brigadier general.

CARSON, Rachel Louise (1907–1964), US marine biologist and science writer whose *Silent Spring* (1962) first alerted the US public to the dangers of environmental POLLUTION.

CARTE, Richard d'Oyly. See D'OYLY CARTE, RICHARD.

CARTEL, an association, often illegal, of individuals or firms who agree not to compete with each other in the open, domestic or international markets. The price and volume of goods can therefore be fixed and cartel members' profits increased.

CARTER, Elliott Cook (1908–   ), a major 20th-century US composer. Marked by unusual instrumentation and structure, his work is often complex and experimental. Among his best-known works are a ballet, *The Minotaur* (1947), the *Double Concerto* (1961) and *Concerto for Piano and Orchestra* (1965). Carter was awarded Pulitzer prizes in 1960 and 1973 and the Edward MacDowell Medal for lifetime achievement in 1983.

CARTER, Howard (1873–1939), English Egyptologist, famous for the Valley of the Kings' excavations with Lord CARNARVON that led to the discovery of the tomb of TUTANKHAMEN in 1922. Carter spent ten years in careful excavation and exploration of the tomb.

CARTER, James Earl ("Jimmy"), Jr. (1924–   ), 39th US president 1977–81. A Baptist, Carter grew up on a Georgia farm and graduated from the US Naval Academy in 1946. While in the navy he studied nuclear physics and worked under Admiral Rickover on the atomic submarine program. He then ran his family's farm and entered politics. Elected as a Democrat to the state senate (1962), he built up a reputation as a liberal on race relations. As governor of Georgia 1971–75 he simplified the complex system of government of the state and instigated electoral and social reforms. He won the Democratic presidential nomination in 1976 and defeated Republican incumbent Gerald FORD. The US Senate refused to ratify Carter's arms-limitation agreement with the USSR but it did approve treaties yielding US control over the Panama Canal. Carter gave full recognition to Communist China and was effective in securing a peace treaty between Egypt and Israel. His last year as president was plagued by Iran's seizure of more than 50 US hostages, who were released on Carter's last day in office. At home, he struggled with record interest and inflation rates and the threat of an energy shortage. He was defeated for reelection in 1980 by Republican Ronald Reagan.

CARTERET, Sir George (c1610–1680), English politician, admiral and lieutenant-governor of Jersey from 1643. A staunch Royalist, he was rewarded after the RESTORATION with proprietorships in New Jersey and Carolina.

CARTESIAN PHILOSOPHY. See DESCARTES, RENÉ.

CARTHAGE, ancient N African city which once stood on the Mediterranean coast near the site of modern Tunis. Established around 800 BC by Phoenician traders as an anchorage, by the 5th century BC it had become the capital of a sizeable empire, comprising African colonies, Corsica, Sardinia and much of Sicily and Spain. Greek opposition checked Carthaginian expansion from 480 BC until the 3rd century BC, when the famous rivalry with Rome began. (See PUNIC WARS.)

Although the fortunes of Carthage reached their zenith at this time under Hamilcar Barca and his son, HANNIBAL, in 201 BC the city forfeited all but its African possessions, and in 146 BC a Roman army razed it to the ground. Archaeologists have found very few traces of Phoenician Carthage. Julius CEASAR removed the 1st century BC colony to a different site. Roman Carthage had a checkered history, passing, after the decline of Rome, through Vandal and Byzantine hands before its final destruction in 698 AD by the forces of Islam.

CARTHUSIANS, contemplative and austere Roman Catholic monastic order founded in France in 1084 by St. Bruno. Each monk spends most of his life in solitude in his private cell and garden. Lay brothers prepare the Chartreuse liqueur which has made the order famous.

CARTIER, Sir George Étienne (1814–1873), Canadian statesman and leading French-Canadian advocate of confederation. Elected to the Canadian parliament in 1848, he was from 1857 to 1862 joint prime minister with Sir John MACDONALD, under whom he later served as minister of defense in the first dominion government.

CARTIER, Jacques (1491–1557), French explorer who, in search of a NORTHWEST PASSAGE, made two important voyages to Canada. In 1534 he explored the Gulf of St. Lawrence and claimed the Gaspé Peninsula for France. In 1535 he explored the St. Lawrence R as far as Mont Royal, which he named. His pessimistic reports on North America deterred many potential colonists.

CARTIER-BRESSON, Henri (1908–   ), internationally famous French documentary photographer who rose to fame with his coverage of the Spanish Civil War. He published many books and also made films, some with Jean RENOIR.

CARTILAGE, tough, flexible connective tissue found in all vertebrates, consisting of cartilage cells (chondrocytes) in a matrix of collagen fibers and a firm protein gel. The skeleton of the vertebrate embryo is formed wholly of cartilage, but in most species much of this is replaced by BONE during growth. There are three main types of cartilage: hyaline, translucent and glossy, found in the joints, nose, trachea and bronchi; elastic, found in the external ear, Eustachian tube and larynx; and fibrocartilage, which attaches tendons to bone and forms the disks between the vertebrae.

CARTLAND, Barbara (1901–   ), British writer of more than 300 titillating but virtuous "romance" novels, a pioneer in a publishing genre that found huge audiences among women in the 1960s and 1970s.

CARTOON. See ANIMATION; CARICATURE AND CARTOON.

CARTWRIGHT, Edmund (1743–1823), British inventor of a mechanical loom (c1787) that was the ancestor of the modern power loom. He also invented a wool-combing machine (c1790). (See also WEAVING.)

CARTWRIGHT, Peter (1785–1872), US Methodist preacher, frontier circuit rider—the "Kentucky Boy"—and Ill. politician. The life of circuit riders is vividly described in his *Autobiography* (1856).

CARUSO, Enrico (1873–1921), Italian operatic tenor famous both for his voice and his artistry. He was the first leading singer to recognize the possibilities of the phonograph, and his recordings brought him worldwide fame.

CARVER, George Washington (c1860–1943), US chemurgist, botanist and educator, born of slave parents in Mo. As director of agricultural research at TUSKEGEE INSTITUTE, Ala., from 1896, he fostered soil improvement by crop rotation, urging an end to the dependence of Southern agriculture on cotton alone. With this in mind he developed hundreds of industrial uses for peanuts and sweet potatoes.

CARVER, John (c1576–1621), leader of the Pilgrim Fathers and first governor of Plymouth Colony (1620–21). He was largely responsible (1617–20) for getting a charter and financial aid, and for chartering the *Mayflower*. He died during the colonists' disastrous first winter.

CARVER, Jonathan (1710–1780), US explorer and writer. He accompanied an early expedition into the Great Lakes area, commissioned by Major Robert Rogers, which he afterwards described in his popular *Travels Through the Interior Parts of North America in the Years 1766, 1767 and 1768* (1778).

CARY, (Arthur) Joyce (Lunel) (1888–1957), British novelist whose primary theme is the individual's struggle against society. His best-known works are *The Horse's Mouth* (1944) and *Prisoner of Grace* (1952), both parts of trilogies, and *Mister Johnson* (1939), a novel set in Africa.

CASABLANCA CONFERENCE, WWII meeting of Winston CHURCHILL and F. D. ROOSEVELT (Jan. 1943) in Casablanca, Morocco. It determined Allied strategy in Europe, and established that only unconditional surrender by Germany and Japan would be acceptable.

CASADESUS, Robert (1899–1972), distinguished French pianist and composer, noted for his interpretations of Mozart and Debussy, and also for the two- and three-piano concertos he composed and performed with his wife and eldest son.

CASALS, Pablo (1876–1973), virtuoso Spanish cellist and conductor. In 1919 he founded an orchestra in Barcelona to bring music to the working classes, but left Spain after the Civil War and never returned. He settled in Prades, SW France, and then (1956) in Puerto Rico, organizing annual music festivals in both places. A great interpreter of Bach, he was a model to a whole generation of cellists.

CASANOVA (DE SEINGALT), Giovanni Giacomo (1725–1798), Venetian author and adventurer whose name became a synonym for seducer. His memoirs, both sensual and sensitive, show him as a freethinking libertine; they also give an excellent picture of his times.

CASAS, Bartolomé de Las. See LAS CASAS, BARTOLOMÉ DE.

CASCADE RANGE, mountain range extending from N Cal. to British Columbia in Canada. Its highest peak is Mt Rainier (14,410ft). There are 14 dormant volcanoes and the recently active (1980) MOUNT SAINT HELENS. The range is named for the ferocious rapids in the Columbia R where it crosses the mountains.

CASEMENT, Sir Roger David (1864–1918), Irish politician, knighted for his humanitarian work in the Congo and South America. In WWI he was hanged for an attempt to arrange German support for the 1916 Irish EASTER RISING.

CASH, Johnny (1932–   ), US country-music singer and composer, often of songs about prisoners, outlaws, and other luckless people.

CASHMERE, very fine natural fiber, the soft underhair of the Kashmir goat, bred in India, Iran, China and Mongolia. Cashmere is finer than the best wools, although the name may be applied to some soft wool fabrics.

CASLON, William (1692–1766), English typefounder, inventor of Caslon type, for many years the basic typeface. Although superseded by the "newstyle" faces of John BASKERVILLE and others, versions of it are much in use today.

CASPIAN SEA, the world's largest inland sea (143,000sq mi), in the SW USSR and Iran. Tideless, it is 92ft below sea level. Although fed by several rivers, including the Volga, the level fluctuates because evaporation losses often exceed inflow. Astrakhan and Baku are the main ports. The northern part of the sea is a major sturgeon-fishing area.

CASS, Lewis (1782–1866), US soldier and political leader. Born in Exeter, N.H., he rose to the rank of brigadier general in the War of 1812, was governor of Michigan Territory (1813–31), and then became secretary of war under Andrew Jackson. Minister to France 1836–42, he was elected a senator for Mich. in 1844 and ran as Democratic presidential candidate in 1848. He lost to Zachary TAYLOR, due largely to the defection of the Barnburners (radical N.Y. state Democrats) to the FREE SOIL PARTY. Later he returned to the Senate 1849–57 and served as secretary of state.

CASSANDRA, in Greek legend, a Trojan princess given the power of prophecy by Apollo but with the condition that no one would believe her.

CASSATT, Mary (1845–1926), American Impressionist painter, strongly influenced by her friend DEGAS. She studied, exhibited and lived mainly in Paris. Most of her paintings are of domestic scenes, especially mother-and-child studies.

CASSETTE. See TAPE RECORDER.

CASSIN, René (1887–1976), French authority on international law, a principal author (1948) of the UNIVERSAL DECLARATION OF HUMAN RIGHTS and president (1965–68) of the European Court of HUMAN RIGHTS. He received the 1968 Nobel Peace Prize.

CASSIRER, Ernst (1874–1945), German–born philosopher. Based on the ideas of KANT, his work examines the ways in which man's symbols and concepts structure his world. He fled Nazi Germany in 1933, and taught at Oxford, in Sweden and from 1941 in the US.

CASSIUS LONGINUS, Gaius (d. 42 BC), Roman general and politician, one of the conspirators against Julius Caesar in 44 BC. After the assassination, he fled to Syria and with his army joined Brutus to fight Octavian and Mark Antony at Philippi in 42 BC. Despairing of victory, he killed himself during the battle.

CASTAGNO Andrea del (c1423–1457), outstanding Florentine painter of church frescoes, portraits and murals. Best known for his *Last Supper* (1445–50) and *Crucifixion* (1449–50), he stressed perspective and a stark, dramatic illumination. He is notable for the vigor and strength of his figure rendering.

CASTANEDA, Carlos (1931–   ), Brazilian-born US anthropologist whose accounts of the wisdom and culture of the Yaqui Indians, including *The Teachings of Don Juan* (1968) and *Journey to Ixtlan* (1972), established him as a cult figure.

CASTELNUOVO-TEDESCO, Mario (1895–1968), Jewish–Italian composer. Forced to leave Italy in 1939, he emigrated to the US. Besides his operas *All's Well That Ends Well* (1957) and *The Merchant of Venice* (1956), he wrote many Shakespeare settings, and also concertos and film music.

CASTE SYSTEM, the division of society into closed groups, primarily by birth, but usually also involving religion and occupation. The most caste-bound society today is probably that of Hindu India; caste divisions are mentioned in the Rig VEDA, dating from 3000 BC, and have not been discouraged until recently. The hierarchy consists of four Varnas (graded classes) with various subdivisions: Brahman (priestly), Kshatriyas (warrior), Vaisyas (merchants and farmers) and Sudras (menials and laborers). There was also a classless element, the outvarnas or untouchables, who performed the lowest tasks. The system solidified social structures by fixing from birth social contacts, thought, diet, ritual, occupation and marriage. Western influences weakened the Indian system in the 19th century; reform was hastened by GANDHI in the 1930s. In India today caste has been drastically modified but not destroyed, despite corrective legislation in the 1950s.

CASTIGLIONE, Baldassare (1478–1529), Italian courtier, diplomat and author famed for his *Libro del cortegiano* (1528), a portrait of the ideal courtier and his relationship with the prince he serves. The book greatly influenced Renaissance mores and inspired such writers as Spenser, Sidney and Cervantes.

CASTILE, traditional name for the central region of Spain, formerly the kingdom of Castile. First united in the 10th century, by the 12th century the kingdom was the dominant power in Spain. A royal union between Castile and Aragon (1479) created the core of modern Spain. Madrid, the capital, is in Castile, and the official language is Castilian. A wide plain bounded by mountains, its 54,463sq mi area is largely arid, but some areas support sheep. Wheat is also grown in some parts.

CASTING, the production of objects of a desired form by pouring the raw material (e.g., ALLOYS, FIBERGLASS, PLASTICS, STEEL) in liquid form into a suitably shaped mold. Both the mold and the pattern from which it is made may be either permanent or expendable. Permanent-mold techniques include **die casting,** where the molten material is forced under pressure into a die; **centrifugal casting,** used primarily for pipes, the molten material being poured into a rapidly rotating mold (see CENTRIFUGE); and **continuous casting,** for bars and slabs, where the material is poured into water-cooled, open-ended molds. Most important part of the expendable-mold process is **sand casting (founding);** here fine sand is packed tightly around each half of a permanent pattern, which is removed and the two halves of the mold placed together. The material is poured in through a channel (**sprue**); after setting, the sand is dispersed. In some processes, the mold is baked before use to remove excess water. (See also METALLURGY.)

CASTLE, Vernon (1887–1918) and **Irene** (1893–1969), couple who revolutionized ballroom dancing. They introduced the one-step and the Castle walk and popularized the hesitation waltz and tango during a meteoric career that began in 1912 and ended with Vernon's death in an air crash, 1918.

CASTLE, fortified dwelling, built to dominate and guard a region. The term derives from the Roman *castellum,* meaning fort or frontier stronghold. In Western Europe, most of the extant castles were built between 1000–1500, often on an artificial mound, with a palisaded courtyard. Later, the stockade was replaced by masonry keeps, defensive outer walls, and frequently a moat and drawbridge. With the decline of feudalism the castle evolved into the Renaissance CHÂTEAU, with its emphasis on splendor rather than on fortification.

CASTLEREAGH, Robert Stewart, Viscount (1769–1822), British statesman, creator of the Grand Alliance which defeated Napoleon. As secretary for Ireland, he suppressed the 1788 rebellion and forced the Act of Union through the Irish Parliament (1800). He was war minister 1805–06 and 1807–09 and then, as foreign secretary 1812–22, played a major role in the organization of Europe at the Congress of Vienna (1814). Much maligned in his time, he committed suicide.

CASTRATO, a male singer who was castrated to retain his high-pitched prepubescent vocal range. Such male sopranos flourished in Europe in the 17th and 18th centuries. Many major operatic roles were written for them.

CASTRO, Fidel (1926–   ), Cuban premier and revolutionary leader. After his law studies he led an abortive revolution in 1953 against the Cuban dictator Fulgencio BATISTA, and was imprisoned and exiled. On Dec. 2, 1956, he landed again in Cuba, with 81 men, and, after a guerrilla struggle against overwhelming odds, overthrew the regime and established himself as premier (1959–76) and head of state (from 1976). He brought about many far-reaching social and economic changes, becoming increasingly dependent on the USSR for financial support. His efforts to become a leader of developing "third world" nations were undercut by his reliance on the USSR.

CATACOMBS, the name given to underground cemeteries, particularly those of the early Christians. The best known and most extensive are at Rome. The oldest of the catacombs, those of Saint Sebastian and Saint Priscilla, date from the 1st century AD. They also served as a refuge from the religious persecutions of the Roman emperors. Construction was freely permitted provided they were situated outside the city walls. The catacombs extend through rocky soil at depths between 20ft and 65ft, sometimes at several levels, the oldest catacombs usually being uppermost. They form a labyrinthine network of narrow passages, the sides of which are lined with tiers of recesses (*loculi*) and frequently decorated with pictorial and written symbols. After a body had been placed in its recess, the opening was sealed with an inscribed slab of marble or terracotta.

CATALONIA, autonomous region in NE Spain, comprising the provinces of Lérida, Gerona, Barcelona and Tarragona. Densely populated, it was occupied by the Romans and Goths, who called it *Gothalonia.* It maintained its own customs and language even after its union with Aragon in 1137. It is now the chief industrial area of Spain, and is dependent on the interior for grain and protected markets. In 1980 the Spanish government handed over certain limited functions to a Catalan regional government with its own parliament and premier.

CATALYSIS, the changing of the rate of a chemical reaction by the addition of a small amount of a substance which is unchanged at the end of the reaction. Such a substance is called a catalyst, though this term is usually reserved for those which speed up reactions; additives which slow down reactions are called inhibitors. Catalysts are specific for particular reactions. In a reversible reaction, the forward and back reactions are catalyzed equally, and the equilibrium position is not altered. Catalysis is either homogeneous (the catalyst and reactants being in the same phase, usually gas or liquid), in which case the catalyst usually forms a reactive intermediate which then breaks down; or heterogeneous, in which adsorption of the reactants occurs on the catalytic surface. Heterogeneous catalysis is often blocked by impurities called poisons. Catalysts are widely used in industry, as in the contact process, the hydrogenation of oils, and the cracking of PETROLEUM. All living organisms are dependent on the complex catalysts called enzymes which regulate biochemical reactions.

CATAPULT, ancient military weapon used for hurling missiles. Some catapults were large crossbows, with a lethal range of over 400yd, while others (*ballistas*) used giant levers to hurl boulders. In the Middle Ages, catapults were an important part of siege artillery, but were made obsolete by the cannon. A modern steam-powered version of the catapult launches jets from aircraft carriers.

CATARACT, disease of the EYE lens, regardless of cause: the normally clear lens becomes opaque and light transmission and perception are reduced. Congenital cataracts occur especially in children born to mothers who have had GERMAN MEASLES in early PREGNANCY, and in a number of inherited disorders. Certain disturbances of METABOLISM or HORMONE production can cause cataracts, especially DIABETES. Eye trauma and INFLAMMATION are other causes in adults. Some degree of cataract formation is common in old age. Once a cataract is formed, vision cannot be improved until the lens is removed surgically. After this, glasses are required to correct loss of focusing power. It is among the commonest causes of BLINDNESS in developed countries.

CATASTROPHISM, in geology, the early 19th century theory that major changes in the geological structure of the earth occurred only during short periods of violent upheaval (catastrophes) which were separated by long periods of comparative stability. The theory fell from prominence after LYELL'S enunciation of the rival

doctrine of UNIFORMITARIANISM.

CATBIRDS, garden songbirds related to the MOCKING BIRD, named for the mewing notes in their song. They live in the US and in S Canada, migrating in winter to Middle America or to the West Indies.

CATEGORICAL IMPERATIVE, in the ethics of KANT, an absolute moral law, one which is not dependent on ulterior considerations. It was formulated thus: "So act that you could will the maxim of your action to be a universal law."

CATERPILLAR, the larva of a moth or a butterfly, with 13 segments, 3 pairs of true legs and up to 5 pairs of soft false legs. (See also INSECTS, LEPIDOPTERA.)

CATGUT, a strong, thin cord used to string musical instruments and rackets, and to sew up wounds in surgery, made from the intestines of herbivorous animals. In surgery, it has the advantage of being eventually absorbed by the body.

CATHARI, a heretical (actually non-Christian) sect widespread in Europe in the 12th and 13th centuries; called ALBIGENSES in S France. Their philosophy, akin to that of the BOGOMILS, was derived from GNOSTICISM and MANICHAEISM. They saw two principles in the world: good (the spirit) and evil (matter and the body). There were two classes of Cathari, the Believers and the Perfect, the latter practicing extreme asceticism.

CATHEDRAL, the principal church of a diocese, in which the bishop has his *cathedra*, his official seat or throne. A cathedral need not be particularly large or imposing, though its importance as a major center led to the magnificent structures of the Gothic and Renaissance periods. By its prominent position and size, a cathedral often dominated a city and served as the focus of its life. In Europe, most of the older cathedral cities were already important centers in Roman and early Christian times.

CATHER, Willa Sibert (1873–1947), US novelist noted for her psychologically astute portrayals of the people of Nebraska and the southwest. Her works include *O Pioneers!* (1913), *My Ántonia* (1918) and *Death Comes for the Archbishop* (1927). She was also a brilliant writer of short stories, the most famous being *Paul's Case.*

CATHERINE, name of two Russian empresses. **Catherine I** (1684–1727), of Lithuanian peasant origin, became the mistress and later the wife of Peter I. On his death in 1725 she succeeded him to the throne. **Catherine II, the Great** (1729–1796), daughter of a minor German prince, became the wife of the heir to the Russian throne, the future Peter III, in 1745. After his deposition and murder in 1762, she became empress and proposed sweeping reforms, but her apparent liberalism was quenched by E. I. Pugachev's peasant uprising (1773–74) and the French Revolution. She greatly extended Russian territory, annexing the Crimea (1783) and partitioning Poland (1772–95). She was also a great patron of the arts.

CATHERINE DE MÉDICIS. See MEDICI.

CATHERINE OF ARAGON (1485–1536), first wife of HENRY VIII of England. The daughter of Ferdinand and Isabella of Spain, she first married Prince Arthur (1501) and then, after his death, his brother, Henry VIII (1509). Henry's annulment of the marriage in 1533 without papal consent led to the English Reformation. She was the mother of Mary I of England.

CATHERINE OF BRAGANZA (1638–1705), Portuguese wife of King CHARLES II of England. The marriage (1662) was intended to promote the Anglo-Portuguese alliance; but she produced no heir. After Charles' death, she returned to Portugal in 1692, serving as regent (1704–05).

CATHERINE OF SIENA, Saint (1347–1380), Italian religious and mystic renowned for her visions, charity and diplomatic skills. Her influence over Pope Gregory XI (1331–1378) led him to leave Avignon in 1377 and return the papacy to Rome, thus ending the BABYLONIAN CAPTIVITY. Although formally unlettered, she was declared a Doctor of the Church by Paul VI in 1970 for her amazing knowledge. Her feast day is April 30.

CATHETER, hollow tube passed into body organs for investigation or treatment. **Urinary catheters** are used for relief of BLADDER outflow obstruction and sometimes for loss of nervous control of bladder; they also allow measurement of bladder function and special X-RAY techniques. **Cardiac catheters** are passed through ARTERIES or VEINS into chambers of the HEART to study its functioning and ANATOMY.

CATHODE RAY TUBE, the principal component of OSCILLOSCOPES and TELEVISION sets. It consists of an evacuated glass tube containing at one end a heated cathode and an anode, and widened at the other end to form a flat screen, the inside of which is coated with a fluorescent material. ELECTRONS emitted from the cathode are accelerated toward the anode, and pass through a hole in its center to form a fine beam which causes a bright spot where it strikes the screen. Because of the electric charge carried by the electrons, the beam can be deflected by transverse electric or magnetic fields produced by electrodes or coils between the anode and screen: one set allows horizontal deflection, another set, vertical. The number of electrons reaching the screen can be controlled by the voltage applied to a third electrode, placed near the cathode, which varies the electric field of the cathode. It is thus possible to move the spot about the screen and vary its brightness by the application of appropriately timed electrical signals, and sustained images may be produced by causing the spot to traverse the same pattern many times a second. In the oscilloscope, the form of a given electrical signal, or any physical effect capable of conversion into one, is investigated by allowing it to control the vertical deflection while the horizontal deflection is scanned steadily from left to right, while in television sets pictures can be built up by varying the spot brightness while the spot scans out the entire screen in a series of close horizontal lines.

CATHOLIC EMANCIPATION ACT, British law enacted on April 13, 1829, removing most of the civil disabilities imposed on British Roman Catholics. A controversial measure, it was introduced by Sir Robert PEEL, after considerable pressure from Irish campaigners headed by Daniel O'CONNELL.

CATHOLIC REFORMATION. See COUNTER-REFORMATION.

CATILINE (c108–62 BC), Roman aristocrat, who tried to seize power in 63 BC. He was trapped and killed in battle at Pistoia. CICERO attacked him in a series of four celebrated orations.

CATLIN, George (1796–1872), US artist, noted for his paintings of American Indian life. His books include *Notes on the Manners, Customs, and Conditions of the North American Indians* (1841).

CATO, name of two Roman statesmen. **Marcus Porcius Cato** (234–149 BC), called the Elder, was an orator and prose writer. He became consul in 195 BC and censor in 184 BC. His only surviving work is a treatise on agriculture. **Marcus Porcius Cato** (95–46 BC), called the Younger (great-grandson of Cato the Elder), was a model Stoic and defender of Roman republicanism. He supported POMPEY against Gaius Julius CAESAR in the Civil War, but after the final defeat of the republican army at Thapsus (46 BC), he killed himself at Utica.

CATS, members of the family Felidae, all of which are hunting carnivores. They vary in size from the small domestic cat to the large

LION and TIGER.

CATS, Domestic, popular household pets, thought to be descended from the African kaffir (or bush) cat, mixed with strains from the European wildcat. They were fully domesticated by the time of the ancient Egyptians, who venerated them. Mummies of cats have been found in Egyptian tombs.

The most common type of cat is the tabby (both striped and blotched). Though seemingly derogatory, the term alley or gutter cat (meaning mixed breed) applies to about 90% of cats in the world. Pedigree cats are divided primarily into two groups: shorthaired (including Siamese, Burmese, Russian blue, Manx and Abyssinian) and long-haired (including Persian and Angora).

CAT SCANNER, or CT scanner, advanced X-RAY instrument for medical diagnosis, the letters CAT standing for **computerized axial tomography.** A tomograph is an X-ray image that reveals a thin layer of the body, as opposed to the ordinary radiograph, which superimposes shadows of tissues at various depths. Tomography was developed in the 1930s to obtain more precise images of selected cross sections of the body by rotating the X-ray beam around the body in the plane of the desired section, with the receiving detector rotating in synchronization on the opposite side of the body. The CAT scanner further improved on this by linking the detector to a computer that reconstitutes a two-dimensional image of the cross section and displays it on a television screen. The computer can add false color for a vivid depiction of different tissue densities, and can build up a three-dimensional image with a series of cross sections. The CAT scanner first entered operation in 1973 and is now in widespread use in many medical centers. The same principle is now also being applied to scanning by means of nuclear magnetic resonance and positron emission.

CATSKILL MOUNTAINS, group of low mountains W of the Hudson R in SE N.Y., part of the Appalachian system. Geologically unique, with flat-topped plateaus divided by narrow valleys, they are a popular recreation area. The highest point is Slide Mountain (4,180ft).

CATT, Carrie Lane Chapman (1859–1947), US feminist, suffragette and founder of the LEAGUE OF WOMEN VOTERS. She was also an active advocate of international disarmament. (See also WOMEN'S LIBERATION MOVEMENT.)

CATTLE, large ruminant mammals of the family Bovidae, most of which have been domesticated, including BISON, BUFFALO, YAK, zebu or Brahman cattle and European cattle. The last two are fully domesticated. Western cattle are derived from the now extinct aurochs. By 2500 BC the Egyptians had several breeds of cattle, which may have been used as draft animals, still an important function in many places, and for leather. Their dung served as fuel and manure.

Today, beef cattle (like Aberdeen Angus or Hereford) are square, heavily built animals commonly kept on poor grazing land, whereas dairy breeds (like Holstein or Guernsey) are kept on good grazing. Recent breeds are mixed beef and dairy animals. A dairy cow can give as much as 14 tons of milk in one year.

CATTON, Bruce (1899–1978), US journalist and Civil War historian. He is best known for his trilogy on the Army of the Potomac: *Mr. Lincoln's Army* (1951), *Glory Road* (1952) and *A Stillness at Appomattox* (1953). He won the Pulitzer Prize in 1954.

CATULLUS, Gaius Valerius (c84–54 BC), Roman lyric poet, born in Verona, Italy. Influenced by Hellenistic Greek poetry, he wrote passionate lyrics, epigrams, elegies, idylls and vicious satires, of which only 116 survive. He influenced the later Roman poets HORACE and MARTIAL.

CAUCASIAN LANGUAGES, group of 40 Indo-European languages spoken by some 5 million people in the region of the Caucasus Mountains, of which Georgian is the only important modern language.

CAUCASOID, a racial division of man. Caucasoids have straight or curly fine hair, generally mesocephalic heads, thin lips, straight faces and well-developed chins. The RACE may have originated in W Asia.

CAUCASUS, mountain range in the USSR between the Caspian and Black seas, 700mi long and up to 120mi wide, including the highest mountain in Europe, Mt Elbrus (18,481ft). Its northern parts belong to Europe, but its southern regions (Transcaucasia), bordering on Turkey and Iran, are part of Asia.

CAVAIGNAC, Louis Eugène (1802–1857), French republican general who crushed working class unrest in Paris during the JUNE DAYS (1848). Cavaignac was defeated in the presidential election of Dec. 1848 by Louis Napoleon (see NAPOLEON III).

CAVALCANTI, Guido (c1255–1300), Florentine poet, a friend of DANTE. He was a leading exponent of the "sweet new style" and is remembered as the author of some 50 ballads and sonnets, generally dramatic poems about love.

CAVALIER POETS, group of English

poets of the 17th century at the court of Charles I. They include Thomas CAREW, Robert HERRICK, Richard LOVELACE and Sir John Suckling.

CAVALRY, military force that fights on horseback. It played a key role in warfare from about the 6th century BC to the end of the 19th century when the development of rapid fire rifles began to reduce its effectiveness. The advent of the tank during WWI and subsequent improvements in military hardware have rendered traditional cavalry redundant. The term is retained in the names of some modern armored units.

CAVE, any chamber formed naturally in rock and, usually, open to the surface via a passage. Caves are found most often in LIMESTONE, where rainwater, rendered slightly ACID by dissolved CARBON dioxide from the ATMOSPHERE, drains through joints in the stone, slowly dissolving it. Enlargement is caused by further passage of water and by bits of rock that fall from the roof and are dragged along by the water. Such caves form often in connected series; they may display STALACTITES AND STALAGMITES and their collapse may form a sinkhole. Caves are also formed by selective EROSION by the sea of cliff bases. Very occasionally they occur in LAVA, either where lava has solidified over a mass of ice that later melted, or where the surface of a mass of lava has solidified, molten lava beneath bursting through and flowing on.

CAVELL, Edith Louisa (1865–1915), British nurse who became a WWI heroine. As matron of the Berkendael hospital in Brussels, she was executed by the Germans for helping some 200 Allied soldiers to escape.

CAVEMEN, a term commonly applied to all STONE AGE men, although many of them did not live in caves. (See PREHISTORIC MAN.)

CAVENDISH, Henry (1731–1810), English chemist and physicist who showed HYDROGEN (inflammable air) to be a distinct GAS, water to be a compound and not an elementary substance and the composition of the ATMOSPHERE to be constant. He also used a torsion balance to measure the DENSITY of the earth (1798).

CAVIAR, the salted roe of certain STURGEON, a delicacy because of its scarcity. The best caviar comes from the Beluga sturgeon of the Caspian Sea.

CAVOUR, Count Camillo Benso di (1810–1861), Italian statesman largely responsible for the creation of a united Italy. Cavour, a native of Turin, founded the liberal newspaper *Il Risorgimento* in 1847

and, under Victor Emmanuel II, became premier of Piedmont in 1852. Cavour sought to unite the country by making piecemeal additions to Piedmont. A subtle diplomat, he exploited NAPOLEON III'S ambitions to engineer the defeat of Austria in 1859, through which he secured the central Italian states. He then invaded the Papal States and entered Neapolitan territory. GARIBALDI, who had taken Sicily and Naples, was left with little option but to cede these gains to Cavour. The unification was completed, except for Venice and the Province of Rome, in 1861, only a few months before Cavour's death.

CAXTON, William (c1422–1491), English printer, trained in Cologne. He produced *The Recuyell of the Histories of Troye* (Bruges, c1475), the first book printed in English, and *The Dictes and Sayenges of the Phylosophers* (1477), the first book printed in England.

CAYLEY, Sir George (1773–1857), British inventor who pioneered the science of AERODYNAMICS. He built the first man-carrying GLIDER (1853) and formulated the design principles later used in AIRPLANE construction, although he recognized that in his day there was no propulsion unit which was sufficiently powerful and yet light enough to power an airplane.

CAYUGA INDIANS, tribe of IROQUOIAN-speaking Indians, members of the Iroquois League. They inhabited the area of Cayuga Lake, N.Y., until the American Revolution. Favoring the British, many then moved to Canada and the others dispersed.

CECIL, Edgar Algernon Robert, 1st Viscount Cecil of Chelwood (1864–1958), British statesman, awarded the Nobel Peace Prize in 1937 for his part in the formation of the League of Nations.

CECIL, William, 1st Baron Burghley (1520–1598), English statesman who rose to power late in Henry VIII's reign. He was appointed chief secretary of state on the accession of Elizabeth I and remained her chief adviser for 40 years, becoming Lord High Treasurer in 1572. He was responsible for the execution of Mary Queen of Scots and for the defensive measures against the Spanish Armada.

CELESTIAL SPHERE, in ancient times, the sphere to which it was believed all the stars were attached. In modern times, an imaginary sphere of indefinite but very large radius upon which, for purposes of angular computation, celestial bodies are considered to be situated. The celestial poles are defined as those points on the sphere vertically above the terrestrial poles, and the **celestial equator** by the projection of the terrestrial EQUATOR onto the sphere. Astronomical coordinate systems are based on these great circles (circles whose centers are also the center of the sphere) and, in some cases, on the observer's celestial horizon. In the most frequently used, the equatorial system, terrestrial latitude corresponds to declination—a star directly overhead in New York City will have a declination of +41° (S Hemisphere declinations are preceded by a minus sign), New York City having a latitude of 41°N—and terrestrial longitude to right ascension, which is measured eastward from the first point of Aries. Right ascension is measured in hours, one hour corresponding to 15° of longitude.

CELIAC DISEASE, a disease of the small intestine (see GASTROINTESTINAL TRACT), among the commonest causes of food malabsorption. In celiac disease, ALLERGY to part of gluten, a component of wheat, causes severe loss of absorptive surface. In children, failure to thrive and DIARRHEA are common signs, while in adults weight loss, ANEMIA, diarrhea, tetany and VITAMIN deficiency may bring it to attention. Complete exclusion of dietary gluten leads to full recovery.

CELIBACY, voluntary abstinence from marriage and sexual intercourse. Celibacy of the clergy in the Roman Catholic Church was instituted by Pope Siricius (386), but abandoned by Protestants during the Reformation. In the Eastern Church, married men can be ordained as priests, though bishops must be celibates or widowers. Recently there has been opposition to celibacy among some Catholics.

CÉLINE, Louis-Ferdinand (1894–1961), pseudonym of Louis-Ferdinand Destouches, French novelist. His first novels, *Journey to the End of Night* (1932) and *Death on the Installment Plan* (1936), made his vivid, hallucinatory style famous.

CELL, the basic unit of living matter from which all plants and animals are built. A living cell can carry out all the functions necessary for life. BACTERIA, AMOEBAS and paramecia are examples of single-celled organisms. In multicellular organisms cells become differentiated to perform specific functions. All cells have certain basic similarities.

Nearly all cells can be divided into three parts: an outer membrane or wall, a nucleus and a clear fluid called cytoplasm.

Animal cells are surrounded by a plasma membrane. This is living, thin and flexible. It allows substances to diffuse in and out

and is also able to select some substances and exclude others. The membrane plays a vital role in deciding what enters a cell. Plant cells are surrounded by a thick, rigid, non-living CELLULOSE cell wall.

Other types of membrane are found in a cell. Around the nucleus is the nuclear membrane, which has in it tiny pores to allow molecules to pass between the cytoplasm and the nucleus. Another type of membrane is the much-folded endoplasmic reticulum, which seems to be a continuation of the cell or nuclear membrane. The endoplasmic reticulum is always associated with the RIBOSOMES where PROTEIN synthesis takes place, controlled by the CHROMOSOMES which are sited in the nucleus and are mainly made of DNA (see NUCLEIC ACIDS).

The cytoplasm contains many organelles. Among the most important are the rod-shaped mitochondria, containing the enzymes necessary for the release of energy from food by the process of RESPIRATION Other organelles whose function is still uncertain are the Golgi bodies, which may be involved in the synthesis of cell wall material, and the lysosomes, which may contain enzymes involved in autolysis and controlled destruction of tissues. The cytoplasm of green plants also contains chloroplasts, where PHOTOSYNTHESIS occurs.

New cells are formed by a process of division called MITOSIS. Each chromosome duplicates; mitosis involves the transfer of this new set of chromosomes to the new daughter cell. Gamete (reproductive) cells are formed by meiosis, which is a division that halves the number of chromosomes; thus a human cell that contains 46 chromosomes will produce gamete cells with 23.

Cells differentiate in a multi-cellular organism to produce cells as different as a nerve cell and a muscle cell. Cells of similar types are grouped together into TISSUES.

There are two broad types of cells. Firstly, **prokaryotic cells,** which have the genetic material in the form of loose filaments of DNA not separated from the cytoplasm by a membrane. Secondly, **eukaryotic cells,** which have the genetic material borne on chromosomes made up of DNA and protein that are separated from the cytoplasm by a nuclear membrane. Eukaryotic cells are the unit of basic structure in all organisms except bacteria and blue-green algae, which comprise single prokaryotic cells.

CELLINI, Benvenuto (1500–1571), Italian goldsmith and sculptor. Of his work in precious metals little survives except the gold saltcellar made for Francis I of France in 1543. His most famous work of sculpture is *Perseus with the Head of Medusa* (1545–54). His celebrated *Autobiography* (1558–62) is colorful and vigorous, though somewhat exaggerated.

CELLO, or **violoncello**, the second-largest instrument of the violin family, with four strings and a range of three octaves starting two octaves below middle C. It is the deepest-toned instrument in the string quartet (see CHAMBER MUSIC). It dates from the 16th century, but did not become a popular solo instrument until the 17th and 18th centuries. Among the finest music for solo cello are J. S. Bach's six cello suites. Many composers, including Elgar, Dvořák and Shostakovich, have written cello concertos.

CELLOPHANE, transparent, impermeable film of CELLULOSE used in packaging, first developed by J. E. Brandenburger (1911). Wood pulp is soaked in sodium hydroxide, shredded, aged and reacted with CARBON disulfide to form a solution of viscose (sodium cellulose xanthate). This is extruded through a slit into an acid bath, where the cellulose is regenerated as a film. It is dried and given a waterproof coating. If the viscose is extruded through a minute hole, rayon is produced (see SYNTHETIC FIBERS).

CELLULOID, the first commercial synthetic PLASTIC, developed by J. W. Hyatt (1869). It is a colloidal dispersion of nitrocellulose and camphor. It is tough, strong—resistant to water, oils and dilute acids—and thermoplastic. Used in dental plates, combs, billiard balls, lacquers, spectacle frames and (formerly) photographic films and toys, celluloid is highly inflammable, and has been largely replaced by other plastics.

CELLULOSE, the main constituent of the CELL walls of higher plants, many algae and some fungi; cotton is 90% cellulose. Cellulose is a CARBOHYDRATE with a similar structure to starch. In its pure form it is a white solid which absorbs water until completely saturated, but dissolves only in a few solvents, notably strong alkalis and some acids. It can be broken down by heat and by the digestive tracts of some animals, but it passes through the human digestive tract unchanged and is helpful only in stimulating movement of the intestines. Industrially, it is used in manufacturing textile fibers, CELLOPHANE, CELLULOID, and the cellulose PLASTICS, notably nitrocellulose (used also in explosives), cellulose acetate for toys and plastic boxes and cellulose acetate butyrate for typewriter keys.

CELSIUS, Anders (1701–1744), Swedish astronomer, chiefly remembered for his proposal (1742) of a centigrade TEMPERATURE scale which had 0° for the freezing point and 100° for the boiling point of water. The modern centigrade temperature scale is known as the **Celsius scale** in his honor, temperatures being quoted in "degrees Celsius" (°C).

CELSUS, Aulus Cornelius, 1st-century Roman medical writer, renowned in the Renaissance as the "Cicero of medicine" for the fine Latin style of his *De medicina*.

CELTIC CHURCH, churches organized along monastic lines in areas of Celtic settlement (Scotland, Ireland, Wales and Brittany) between about the 5th century and the Norman Conquest. They differed from Rome only in superficial matters, and were responsible for converting large areas of Europe.

CELTIC LANGUAGES, a major division of the INDO-EUROPEAN LANGUAGES, spoken widely over Europe from pre-Roman times though now confined chiefly to the UK and Brittany. There are two main branches: the now extinct Gaulish, about which little is known, and Insular, to which belong all the modern Celtic tongues. The latter branch is itself split into two: Gaelic, or Goidelic (Irish Gaelic, Scottish Gaelic and Manx), and Brythonic (Breton, Welsh and Cornish). Recent years have seen a revival in certain of these.

CELTIC RENAISSANCE, literary revival of the Gaelic tongues, particularly in Ireland and Wales, in the 19th and 20th centuries. Linked to the rise of nationalism, it resulted in a large and still growing body of literature and scholarship.

CELTS, a prehistoric people whose numerous tribes occupied much of Europe between c2000 and c100 BC, the peak of their power being around 500–100 BC. No European Celtic literature survives, but the later Irish and Welsh sources tell much about Celtic society and way of life. Primarily an agricultural people, though in local areas crafts and iron smelting developed, they grouped together in small settlements. Their social unit, based on kinship, was divided into a warrior nobility and a farming class, from the former being recruited the priests or DRUIDS, who ranked highest of all. Celtic art mixes stylized heads with abstract designs of scrolls and spirals. Remnants of CELTIC LANGUAGES are to be found in the forms of Gaelic, Erse, Manx and Welsh. The Celtic sphere of influence declined during the 1st century BC owing to the simultaneous expansion of the Roman Empire and the incursions of the Germanic races.

CEMENT, common name for Portland cement, the most important modern construction material, notably as a constituent of CONCRETE. In the manufacturing process, limestone is ground into small pieces (about 2cm). To provide the silica (25%) and alumina (10%) content required, various clays and crushed rocks are added, including iron ore (about 1%). This material is ground and finally burned in a rotary kiln at up to 1500°C, thus converting the mixture into clinker pellets. About 5% gypsum is then added to slow the hardening process, and the ground mixture is added to sand (for mortar) or to sand, gravel and crushed rock (for concrete). When water is added it solidifies gradually, undergoing many complex chemical reactions. The name "Portland" cement arises from a resemblance to stone quarried at Portland, England.

CENOBITES, monks who founded the first monastic communities in the 4th century. They differed from their hermit predecessors in that they formed communities rather than living in solitude. Western cenobitic monasticism was introduced by St. Benedict, and was the basis of the Benedictine Order.

CENOZOIC, the period of geological time containing the TERTIARY and QUATERNARY.

CENSORSHIP, supervision or control exercised by anybody in authority over public communication, conduct or morals. The official responsible is known as the censor. Early censorship in the Greek city-states curbed conduct insulting to the gods or dangerous to public order. In Rome the censor dictated public morality.

Censorship of books was not widespread (although some books were publicly burned) until the invention of printing in the 15th century. The first *Index of Prohibited Books* was drawn up by the Catholic Church in 1559 in an effort to stop the spread of subversive literature. Similar tactics were employed by Protestants and secular authorities. Milton's *Areopagitica* (1644) presented a strong case for freedom of the press, which was won in W Europe during the 18th and 19th centuries. In the US, freedom of the press is protected from federal interference by the First Amendment to the Constitution, but it was not applied to the states through the 14th Amendment until 1931. In 1957 the US Supreme Court extended First Amendment protection to material "having even the slightest redeeming social importance" and defined obscenity as "material which deals with sex in a manner appealing to prurient interest." But in 1973 the Court changed the requirement to one of "serious" social purpose. It has upheld film censorship as being within the police power of the states, but has struck down several censorship statutes for being too vague. (See also PORNOGRAPHY AND OBSCENITY LAWS.)

CENSUS, enumeration of persons, property or other items at a given time. Today most countries conduct a regular count of population but these vary greatly in reliability, especially in underdeveloped countries. India, for example, conducts only sample censuses; this is cheaper and allows more detailed examination of the chosen sample. Early censuses, such as those mentioned in the Old Testament, were primarily military inventories. Babylonia, China, Egypt and Rome all conducted a census for fiscal purposes. The modern concept dates from the 17th and 18th centuries when regular censuses were taken in some New World colonies. Among the first national censuses was that in the newly founded US in 1790, to determine each state's representation in Congress; since then, as required by the Constitution, a census has been conducted every 10 years. The British census began in 1801. Beyond merely determining the size and content of a country's population, the modern census may seek information on economic development and social issues, and is therefore an essential tool in government planning.

CENSUS, Bureau of the, in the US Department of Commerce, collects and publishes a wide variety of statistical data about the people and economy of the US. Its principal function is the decennial population census required by the US Constitution, but it conducts as well surveys of agriculture, manufacturing, mining, construction, transportation, retail and wholesale trade, imports and exports, and state and local government finances.

CENTENNIAL EXPOSITION, International, world's fair held in Philadelphia, Pa., from May to Nov. 1876, celebrating the 100th anniversary of the Declaration of Independence. Exhibits from the arts and sciences were displayed by 49 nations. Mass production techniques, then being pioneered in the US, were also put on show. The fair attracted almost 10 million visitors.

CENTER OF GRAVITY, the point about which gravitational FORCES on an object exert no net turning effect, and at which the mass of the object can for many purposes be regarded as concentrated. A freely suspended object hangs with its center of gravity vertically below the point of suspension, and an object will balance, though it may be unstable, if supported at a point vertically below the center of gravity. In free flight, an object spins about its center of gravity, which moves steadily in a straight line; the application of forces causes the center of gravity to accelerate in the direction of the net force, and the rate of spin to change according to the resultant turning effect.

CENTIPEDES, long-bodied members of the phylum Arthropoda with two legs to each of their 15–100 segments. They are usually 25–50mm (1–2in) long, though in the tropics some reach 0.3m (1ft). Normally insectivorous, they paralyze their food by injecting poison through a pair of pincers located near the head. Centipedes live in moist places under stones or in soil.

CENTRAL AFRICAN REPUBLIC, land-locked independent republic in Africa. It lies just N of the equator, bounded by Chad to the N and Sudan to the S, on a well-watered plateau 2,500ft above sea level. The country is mostly savanna, with dense tropical rain forest to the S. The chief river, the Ubangi, is the main link with the outside world. There are no railroads and only 50mi of paved road.

Official name: Central African Republic
Capital: Bangui
Area: 240,324sq mi
Population: 2,774,000
Languages: French, Sangho
Religions: Christian, Animist, Muslim
Monetary unit(s): 1 CFA franc = 100 centimes

People and Economy. The population is composed of various ethnic groups, with mainly Bantu and Nilotic cultures. The *lingua franca* is Sangho. There are various religious groups, but about 70% of the population are tribal animists. There are few towns, and education and living standards are poor.

History. Various tribes migrated into the area, most fleeing the slave trade in the 19th century. The French established outposts 1886–87, and the area was incorporated into French Equatorial Africa in 1910. It achieved independence on Aug. 13, 1960, under President David Dacko; he was overthrown in 1966 by Colonel Jean-Bedel Bokassa, who in 1972 was appointed president for life. In 1979 Dacko regained control with support from the French but was ousted in a military coup led by Gen. André Kolingba in 1981. Legislative elections were held in 1987 under a constitution approved in 1986; Kolingba remained president. Bokassa voluntarily returned to the Central African Republic in 1986 and was tried on several counts of murder and sentenced to death; in 1988 his sentence was commuted to life imprisonment.

CENTRAL AMERICA, narrow land bridge between Mexico and South America that includes seven independent republics: Belize, Costa Rica, El Salvador, Guatemala, Honduras, Nicaragua, and Panama.

People. Originally the land of MAYA Indians, Central America is now inhabited by Indians, Europeans, Africans, and people of mixed ancestry. There are great differences between countries: in Costa Rica most of the people are white, while in Guatemala almost half the population are pure Indians. Spanish is the most widely spoken language, except in Belize where English is the official language. Tribal dialects are used by many Indians. Although elementary education is free, Central America—with the exception of Costa Rica—has high illiteracy rates. Ancient customs still prevail in many Indian villages.

Economy. Much of the population still works in agriculture, either on plantations or on small farms, although the region is becoming increasingly urbanized. Export crops include bananas, coffee, cotton, and sugar, and the main subsistence crops are corn and beans. Civil strife has hampered efforts to spur regional trade and industrial growth and has contributed to a decline in tourism and foreign investment. Development is also hindered by transportation problems, caused partly by the rugged terrain.

History. The Maya civilization, one of the earliest in the Western Hemisphere, flourished in Central America AD 300-800. Following the Spanish conquest in the early 16th century, the region north of Panama became the Spanish colony of Guatemala. Panama belonged to the viceroyalty of New Granada (Colombia). After the independence proclamation in 1821, the former colony of Guatemala was for a short time the Central American Federation, but in 1838 independent republics were established. In the early 20th century, Central

America came under US influence: the Panama Canal was opened in 1914, US marines intervened in Honduras (1903 and 1923) and Nicaragua (1912 and 1924), and US companies became the chief foreign investors. Costa Rica is politically the most stable country; the others have suffered from external conflicts, dictatorships, revolutions, and guerrilla insurgencies. Violence and strife continued in the late 1980s despite the signing of a regional peace plan in 1987 by Costa Rica, El Salvador, Guatemala, and Nicaragua.

CENTRALIA MINE DISASTER, an explosion on Mar. 25, 1947, that killed 115 miners at the Centralia (Ill.) Coal Company's Mine Number 5. The operator had a long record of safety violations, but the disaster, the worst such in 19 years, came when the nation's coal mines were under government control and John L. Lewis, head of the United Mine Workers, defied the Supreme Court when he called his men out on a memorial strike. Four years later an even worse disaster occurred at another Illinois coal mine, in West Frankfort, where 119 died. The two tragedies spurred Congress to pass the Mine Safety Act of 1952.

CENTRAL INTELLIGENCE AGENCY (CIA), established in 1947 by the National Security Act to coordinate, evaluate and disseminate intelligence from other US agencies and to advise the president and the National Security Council on security matters. Though its field of operations widened considerably under Allen DULLES (director 1953–61), its estimated 15,000 employees spend most of their time in research and analysis at CIA headquarters in Langley, Va. The agency has no police, subpoena, or law-enforcement powers or internal-security functions.

CENTRAL POWERS, coalition of Germany, Austria–Hungary, Ottoman Turkey and Bulgaria in WWI. (See also ALLIES; TRIPLE ALLIANCE.)

CENTRAL TREATY ORGANIZATION (CENTO), mutual security alliance among Pakistan, Iran, Turkey, Iraq and Britain, with the US an associate member. It was established by the Baghdad Pact (1955). Iraq withdrew in 1959. After Iran and Pakistan withdrew (1979), CENTO became virtually defunct.

CENTRIFUGAL FORCE. See CENTRIPETAL FORCE.

CENTRIFUGE, a machine for separating mixtures of solid particles and immiscible liquids of different DENSITIES and for extracting liquids from wet solids by rotating them in a container at high speed.

The separation occurs because the centrifugal force experienced in a rotating frame increases with particle density. Centrifuges are used in drying clothes and slurries, in chemical ANALYSIS, in separating cream and in atomic ISOTOPE separation. Giant ones are used to accustom pilots and astronauts to large accelerations. The **ultracentrifuge,** invented by Theodor Svedberg (1884-1971), uses very high speeds to measure (optically) sedimentation rates of macromolecular solutes and so determine molecular weights.

CENTRIPETAL FORCE, the FORCE applied to a body to maintain it moving in a circular path. To maintain a body of MASS m, traveling with instantaneous VELOCITY v, in a circular path of radius r, a centripetal force F, acting toward the center of the circle, given by $F=mv^2/r$ must be applied to it. The equal and opposite force of reaction of the mass on its constraint is the **centrifugal force.**

CENTURY OF PROGRESS EXPOSITION, international exhibition celebrating Chicago's centenary, held on the shores of Lake Michigan 1933–34. Primarily concerned with science and technology, it also stimulated design and architecture.

CEPHALOPODA, class of predatory MOLLUSKS including the cuttlefish, OCTOPUS and SQUID. They swim by forcing a jet of water through a narrow funnel near the mouth. Cephalopods have sucker-bearing arms and a horny beak. The shell, typical of most mollusks, is absent or reduced.

CEPHEID VARIABLES, stars whose brightness varies regularly with a period of 1–50 days, possibly, but improbably, due to a fluctuation in size. The length of their cycle is directly proportional to their absolute magnitude, making them useful "mileposts" for computing large astronomical distances. (See VARIABLE STARS.)

CERAMICS, materials produced by treating nonmetallic inorganic materials (originally clay) at high temperatures. Modern ceramics include such diverse products as porcelain and china, furnace bricks, electric insulators, ferrite magnets, rocket nosecones and abrasives. In general, ceramics are hard, chemically inert under most conditions, and can withstand high temperatures in industrial applications. Many are refractory metal OXIDES. Primitive ceramics in the form of pottery date from the 5th millennium BC, and improved steadily in quality and design. By the 10th century AD porcelain had been developed in China. (See also CERMETS; CONCRETE; GLASS; POTTERY AND PORCELAIN.)

CEREAL CROPS, annual plants of the

grass family, including WHEAT, RICE, CORN, BARLEY, SORGHUM, millet, oats and RYE. Their grain forms the staple diet for most of the world. Though lacking in calcium and vitamin A, they have more CARBOHYDRATES than any other food, as well as PROTEIN and other VITAMINS. Cereal crops are relatively easy to cultivate and can cope with a wide range of climates. About 1,757 million acres of the world's arable land are sown with cereal crops each year. The US leads in production of corn, oats and sorghum.

CEREBELLUM. See BRAIN.

CEREBRAL PALSY, a diverse group of conditions caused by BRAIN damage around the time of BIRTH and resulting in a variable degree of nonprogressive physical and mental handicap. While abnormalities of MUSCLE control are the most obvious, loss of sensation and some degree of DEAFNESS are common accompaniments. Speech and intellectual development can also be impaired but may be entirely normal. SPASTIC PARALYSIS of both legs with mild arm weakness (diplegia), or of one half of the body (hemiplegia), are common forms. A number of cases have abnormal movements (athetosis) or ATAXIA. Common causes include birth trauma, anoxia, prematurity, Rhesus incompatibility and cerebral HEMORRHAGE. PHYSIOTHERAPY and training allow the child to overcome many deficits; deformity must be avoided by ensuring full range of movements at all joints, but surgical correction may be necessary. Sometimes transposition of TENDONS improves the balance of strength around important joints. It is crucial that the child is not deprived of normal sensory and emotional experiences. Improved antenatal care, OBSTETRIC skill and care of premature infants have reduced the incidence.

CEREBROSPINAL FLUID, watery fluid circulating in the chambers (ventricles) of the BRAIN and between layers of the meninges covering the brain and SPINAL CORD. It is a filtrate of BLOOD and is normally clear, containing salts, glucose and some PROTEIN. It may be sampled and analyzed by SPINAL TAP.

CEREBRUM. See BRAIN.

CERENKOV RADIATION, ELECTROMAGNETIC RADIATION emitted when a high-energy particle passes through a dense medium at a velocity greater than the velocity of light in that medium. It was first detected in 1934 by P. A. Cherenkov.

CERMETS, or ceramels, composite materials made from mixed METALS and CERAMICS. The TRANSITION ELEMENTS are most often used. Powdered and compacted with an oxide, carbide or boride, etc., they are heated to just below their melting point, when bonding occurs. Cermets combine the hardness and strength of metals with a high resistance to corrosion, wear and heat. This makes them invaluable in jet engines, cutting tools, brake linings and nuclear reactors.

CERN. See EUROPEAN ORGANIZATION FOR NUCLEAR RESEARCH (CERN).

CERRO GORDO, Battle of, major battle on April 17–18, 1847, in the MEXICAN WAR (1846–48). Winfield SCOTT's 8,500 US troops defeated 12,000 Mexicans led by General SANTA ANNA, 60mi NW of Veracruz. This opened the way to Puebla and ultimately to Mexico City.

CERVANTES SAAVEDRA, Miguel de (1547–1616), Spanish novelist and playwright, a major figure of Spanish literature. He left his studies in 1570 to join the army; his left hand was crippled at the sea battle of Lepanto (1571). Captured by pirates in 1575, he was enslaved in Algiers until ransomed in 1580. In 1585 he wrote *La Galatea,* a pastoral novel in verse and prose; after this he entered government service. In 1605 he published the first part of *Don Quixote de la Mancha,* his masterpiece. Not only a masterly debunking of pseudo-chivalric romance but a rich tragi-comic novel, it was an immediate success. He also wrote about 30 plays, of which 16 survive, a volume of short stories and the second part of *Don Quixote* (1615). His last work was *Persilas and Sigismunda* (1617).

CERVERA Y TOPETE, Pascual (1839–1909), Spanish admiral. Minister of marine in 1892, he commanded the Atlantic fleet during the SPANISH-AMERICAN WAR (1898). It was blockaded and sunk at Santiago de Cuba; Cervera was honorably acquitted at his court-martial.

CESARIAN SECTION, BIRTH of a child from the WOMB by abdominal operation. The mother is given an anesthetic, and an incision is made in the ABDOMEN and lower part of the uterus; the child is delivered and attended to; the placenta is removed, incisions are sewn up. Cesarian section may be necessary if the baby is too large to pass through the pelvis, if it shows delay or signs of anoxia during labor, or in cases where maternal disease does not allow normal labor. It may be performed effectively before labor has started. With modern ANESTHESIA and blood transfusion, the risks of Cesarian section are not substantially greater than those of normal delivery. It is believed that Julius Caesar was born in this way.

CETEWAYO, or **Cetshwayo** (c1826–1884), fourth and last Zulu king (1873–79). In 1879 he declared war on British and Boer settlers in the Transvaal, but was finally captured and deposed.

CEYLON. See SRI LANKA.

CÉZANNE, Paul (1839–1906), French painter, among the most influential of modern times. During his studies in Paris he met and was influenced by Pissarro and other Impressionists. His early work is Impressionist in style, but he later abandoned this to develop an approach of his own, lyrical and vibrantly colorful, as in the *Grandes Baigneuses* (1905). He sought to suggest depth through the use of color and to give his paintings a new structural strength and formal integrity. In his efforts "to treat nature in terms of the cylinder, sphere and cone . . . ," and to make his paintings autonomous objects, he became the prime innovator of modern art, anticipating Cubism and other movements.

CGS UNITS, a metric system of units based on the centimeter (length), gram (mass) and second (time), generally used among scientists until superseded by SI UNITS. Several variants are used for electrical and magnetic problems, including electrostatic units (esu or stat-units), electromagnetic units (emu or ab-units) and the Gaussian system. In this last, ab-units are used for quantities arising primarily in an electromagnetic context, stat-units for electrostatic quantities and both the permeability and the permittivity of free space are set equal to unity. As a result, the speed of light (c) tends to occur in equations in which electrostatic and magnetic quantities are mixed.

CHABRIER, Alexis Emmanuel (1841–1894), French composer best remembered for orchestral works such as *España* (1883) and various piano pieces. His work influenced DEBUSSY, RAVEL and SATIE.

CHACO WAR, war fought between Paraguay and Bolivia during 1932–35 over possession of part of the Chaco region. It caused significant damage to both countries, with over 200,000 casualties. It was settled by arbitration, largely in favor of Paraguay, the military victor.

CHAD, landlocked state in N central Africa bordered by six states, including Libya to the N and the Central African Republic to the S.

Land. Its N part extends into the Sahara desert, where the Tibesti highlands rise to 11,000ft. The S part consists largely of semiarid steppe with wooded grasslands (savannas) near Lake CHAD, watered by the Shari and Logone rivers. In the S rainfall

Official name: Republic of Chad
Capital: N'djamena
Area: 495,755sq mi
Population: 5,265,000
Languages: French, Arabic, Bantu
Religions: Muslim, Animist, Christian
Monetary unit(s): 1 CFA franc = 100 centimes

reaches 47in during the rainy season.

People. The N part of the country is inhabited by nomadic Muslim tribes such as the Fulani, the Wadai and the Toubou. In the more densely populated S, Negroid tribes predominate, the largest being the Sara. Most live in rural areas, are animists, and speak tribal languages. The rate of illiteracy is high. There are less than 5,000 Europeans, mainly French; French is the official language.

Economy.. Agriculture and cattle support the economy. Manufacturing is limited mostly to the processing of cotton, the chief export. Cattle, meat, fish, hides, cotton and groundnut oils and gum arabic are also exported. Trade is primarily with Europe, chiefly France, which has been a major investor and provider of aid.

History. The French had conquered Chad by 1900, and it became the northernmost of the four territories of Ubanga-Shari-Chad when French Equatorial Africa was formed in 1910. It became an independent republic in Aug. 1960, with François (Ngarta) Tombalbaye as president. He was killed during a military takeover in 1975 and various factions began to struggle for control of the government. The civil war was complicated by Libyan involvement. Hissène Habré, who became head of government in 1982, gradually consolidated his power with aid from France and the US. Libyan troops were finally driven from their bases in N Chad in 1987; in 1988, Libyan leader Muammar al-Qaddafi recognized the Habré government.

CHAD, Lake, in W central Africa, is bounded by Cameroon, Chad, Niger and Nigeria and fed by the Shari and Logone rivers. The area of the shallow lake varies from 4,000 to 10,000sq mi at low and high water respectively.

CHADWICK, Sir Edwin (1800–1890), English government official responsible in the 1830s and 1840s for major poor law and public health reforms.

CHADWICK, Florence (1918–   ), US distance swimmer who was the first woman to swim the English Channel in both directions (1950–51), and the first woman to swim the 21-mi Catalina Channel, off Long Beach, Calif. (1952). She also swam the Strait of Gibraltar and the Bosporus.

CHADWICK, Henry (1824–1908), English-born US sports journalist, a leader in organizing professional baseball and formulating its rules.

CHADWICK, Sir James (1891–1974), English physicist who was awarded the 1935 Nobel physics prize for his discovery of the NEUTRON (1932).

CHAGALL, Marc (1887–1985), Russian-Jewish painter. Influenced at first by his teacher BAKST, his work developed further in Paris 1910–14. His style is characterized by dreamlike, lyrical fantasy and bright but never harsh colors. His subjects are often derived from the traditions of folklore and pre-WWI Jewish life in Russia. Chagall, who left Russia in 1922 and later settled in France, also illustrated a number of books and created memorable works in stained glass.

CHAGAS' DISEASE, PARASITIC DISEASE found only on the American continent, caused by a trypanosome and carried by insects. In the acute form there is swelling around the eye, fever, malaise, enlargement of lymph nodes, liver and spleen, and edema. Most cases recover fully. The chronic form causes disease of the HEART and GASTROINTESTINAL TRACT.

CHAIN, Sir Ernst Boris (1906–1979), German-born UK biochemist who helped develop PENICILLIN for clinical use. For this he shared with H. W. Florey and A. Fleming the 1945 Nobel Prize for Physiology or Medicine.

CHAIN REACTION. See NUCLEAR ENERGY.

CHALDEA, name for S Babylonia, after its occupation by the Chaldeans in the 10th century BC. The Chaldeans were accomplished astronomers and astrologers, and ancient writers often used their name as a synonym for "magician." In 626 BC Nabopalassar founded the Chaldean Neo-Babylonian Empire, which held sway over the area until the death of Nebuchadnezzar in 561 BC. (See also BABYLONIA and ASSYRIA.)

CHALIAPIN, Fyodor Ivanovich (1873–1938), Russian operatic bass. Famous for his acting as well as for his voice, he settled in France after the Russian Revolution. His main successes were as MUSSORGSKY's *Boris Godunov* and Boito's *Mefistofele.*

CHALK, soft, white rock composed of calcium carbonate, $CaCO_3$; a type of fine-grained, porous LIMESTONE containing calcareous remains of minute marine animals. There are large deposits in Tex., Kan. and Ark. Chalk is widely used in lime and cement manufacture and as a fertilizer. It is also used in cosmetics, plastics, crayons and oil paints; school chalk is today usually made from chemically-produced calcium carbonate.

CHALLENGER, US SPACE SHUTTLE that exploded 74secs after lift-off from Cape Canaveral, Fla., on Jan. 28, 1986. Seven crew members, including schoolteacher Christa McAuliffe, died. Investigators identified the immediate cause of the disaster as the failure of seals (O-rings) in the solid-rocket boosters on either side of the shuttle. More fundamental, however, was the determination of the NATIONAL AERONAUTICS AND SPACE ADMINISTRATION to meet a schedule of 24 shuttle flights a year, with consequent disregard of known engineering problems and safety considerations.

CHALLENGER EXPEDITION, a round-the-world oceanographic-survey cruise made by the steam corvette HMS *Challenger* between 1872 and 1876 under the scientific direction of **Sir Charles Wyville Thomson** (1830–1882), the first and most comprehensive voyage of its type. Its results were published as the 50-volume *Challenger Report* (1881–95).

CHAMBERLAIN, family name of three prominent British statesmen. **Joseph Chamberlain** (1836–1914) entered Parliament in 1876 as a Liberal. He held office under Gladstone, but split with him, opposing home rule for Ireland (1886). As colonial secretary 1895–1903, he failed to prevent the Boer War. Until his paralysis by a stroke in 1906, he fought for integration of the Empire through preferential tariffs for Empire trade. His son, **Sir Joseph Austen Chamberlain** (1863–1937), entered parliament as a Conservative in 1892, and held various government offices from 1902. As foreign secretary 1924–29 under Baldwin, he helped secure the LOCARNO TREATIES, and shared the 1925 Nobel Peace Prize. Austen's half-brother, **Arthur Neville Chamberlain** (1869–1940), was a Conservative member of parliament from 1918. He held office under Baldwin, and succeeded him as prime minister in 1937. In his efforts to avert war with Germany, he followed a policy of appeasement and signed the MUNICH AGREEMENT, finally abandoning the policy when Hitler seized the rest of Czechoslovakia in March 1939. He resigned on May 10, 1940, during WWII, after the failure of an expedition to help Norway.

CHAMBERLAIN, Houston Stewart (1855–1927), Anglo-German writer. His *Foundations of the Nineteenth Century* (1899) was a racialist glorification of Germanic history from which Hitler and the Nazis drew many ideas. He was a son-in-law of Richard Wagner.

CHAMBERLAIN, Wilt (1936–   ), US basketball player. A center, he was professional basketball's all-time leading scorer. Combining great height (7ft, 1 1/8in) with great strength, he holds records for most points scored in a career (31,419), in a season (4,029) and in a game (100), and most rebounds per season (2,149).

CHAMBER MUSIC, term applied to a musical composition intended for a small ensemble. Originally it meant domestic music, that is music written by a house composer for his patron. It became established as a special genre during the 17th and 18th centuries. The instrumental combinations are varied, though they do not often exceed a total of 15 instruments. Chamber music is characterized by an intimacy of communication between the performers. The principal form of composition is the string quartet (2 violins, viola and cello), which was developed by HAYDN and MOZART, and expanded to new dimensions by BEETHOVEN.

CHAMBER OF COMMERCE, an association of businessmen set up to improve business conditions and practices, and to protect business interests. The first in the US was the New York Chamber of Commerce (1768) and now most sizeable US cities have one. Activities are coordinated through the US Chamber of Commerce, founded 1912. The International Chamber of Commerce, based in Paris, is mainly concerned with trade problems.

CHAMBERS, Whittaker (1901–1961), US journalist. A Communist, he engaged in espionage for the USSR during the 1930s but left the party in 1939 and became an editor of *Time* magazine. In 1948, in testimony before the House Committee on Un-American Activities, he identified Alger HISS, a former state Department official and then president of the Carnegie Endowment for International Peace, as also a former Communist and spy. The sensational confrontation of the two former friends ended eventually in Hiss's convic-

tion for perjury. Chambers wrote an autobiography, *Witness* (1952).

CHAMBERS, William (1800–1883), Scottish publisher who, with his brother, **Robert Chambers** (1802–1871), formed the firm of W. and R. Chambers, which published *Chambers's Edinburgh Journal* and *Chambers's Encyclopedia.*

CHAMELEONS, LIZARDS of the family Chamaeleonidae living in Africa and Madagascar with extraordinary adaptability to arboreal life. Their five toes are webbed into two groups of two and three between which they are able to grip branches. Their tails are prehensile, and their eyes can turn independently in all directions. They feed on insects which they catch with their long, sticky tongues, and the color of their skin undergoes swift alteration in response to changes of emotion or temperature. There are over 80 species, some viviparous, ranging in length from 50mm (2in) to 0.6m(2ft).

CHAMOIS, *Rupicapra rupicapra,* a goat-like mammal of the family Bovidae found in the mountain forests of Europe and Asia Minor. Chamois are famous for their agility, being capable of leaps of over 6m (20ft). They have thick brown coats and stand about 0.75m (2.5ft) at the shoulder. Their hides were once used for making "chammy" leather.

CHAMPAGNE, historic province in NE France, famous for the effervescent champagne wines from vineyards between Reims and Épernay. The ruling counts of Champagne were especially powerful during the 12th and 13th centuries, and the region had a central role in French history.

CHAMPLAIN, Samuel de (1567–1635), French explorer, first governor of French Canada. After voyages to the Canary Isles and Central America, he explored the St. Lawrence area in 1603 as far as the Lachine Rapids. In 1604–07 he explored much of what is now Nova Scotia. He founded Quebec in 1608 and discovered Lake Champlain in 1609. Virtual governor, when Quebec surrendered to the English in 1629, Champlain was imprisoned in England; on his release in 1633 he returned to Canada as governor.

CHAMPLAIN, Lake, narrow lake forming the border between Vt. and N.Y. and jutting partly into Canada. Its area is 435sq mi, excluding 55sq mi of islands. Lake Champlain is drained N by the Richelieu R, a tributary of the St. Lawrence R; though icebound for four months of the year, it is deep enough for commercial navigation. It is a leisure center and a site for many refining industries and was in the past the scene of several battles between American and British forces.

CHAMPOLLION, Jean François (1790–1832), French linguist and historian, the "father of Egyptology." Professor of history at Grenoble U. 1809–16, he was the first to effectively decipher Egyptian HIEROGLYPHICS, a result of his research on the ROSETTA STONE. A chair of Egyptian antiquities was created especially for him at the Collège of France in 1831.

CHANCELLOR, Richard (d.1556), English navigator who, in search of a Northeast Passage to Asia, reached Russia via the Arctic in 1553 and laid the foundations for trade with England. He died on his return from a second voyage to Russia.

CHANCELLORSVILLE, Battle of, fought during the US Civil War, May 1–5, 1863. Gen. Joseph Hooker's Union forces crossed the Rappahannock R to Chancellorsville, W of Fredericksburg, Va., in a bid to encircle Gen. Robert E. Lee's Confederate forces protecting Fredericksburg. The ploy failed; Lee's counteroffensive led to an indecisive battle claiming 30,000 lives, including that of Gen. "Stonewall" Jackson.

CHANDLER, Albert Benjamin "Happy" (1898–   ), US politician, governor of Kentucky (1935–39, 1955–59) and US senator (1939–45). From 1945 to 1951 he was a reforming commissioner of professional baseball.

CHANDLER, Charles Frederick (1836–1925), US chemist on the faculty of Columbia U 1864–1910. President (1873–84) of the New York City Board of Health, he accomplished important public-health reforms. He invented but did not patent the flush toilet.

CHANDLER, Raymond Thornton (1888–1959), US detective novelist whose seven novels have received critical acclaim. They combine wit and pace with strong characterization, particularly of their hero Philip Marlowe, a tough but honest private detective. Among his best-known works are *The Big Sleep* (1939) and *The Long Goodbye* (1954).

CHANDRAGUPTA (4th century BC), Indian emperor c321–297 BC, founder of the Maurya dynasty. He rose to power after Alexander the Great's withdrawal from India, winning territory from the Seleucids and extending his realm into Afghanistan. His grandson was the famous Emperor ASOKA.

CHANDRASEKHAR, Subrahmanyan (1910–   ), Indian-born US astrophysicist, a major figure in the theoretical study of stellar evolution, particularly that of dwarf stars. For his work on the structures of white dwarfs he was co-winner of the 1983 Nobel Prize for Physics.

CHANEY, Lon (1883–1930), US film actor who specialized in playing misshapen individuals and monsters. His skill in characterization and makeup won him the title of "Man with a Thousand Faces." His best-known films were *The Hunchback of Notre Dame* (1923) and *The Phantom of the Opera* (1925). His son, **Lon Chaney, Jr.** (1907–1973), also became famous as an actor, portraying the "Wolfman" in a series of horror movies.

CHANNEL ISLANDS, archipelago totalling 75sq mi in area, in the English Channel off NW France. Dependencies of the British crown since 1066, they are administered according to their own local constitutions. The two main bailiwicks are Jersey, including Les Minquiers and Ecrehou Rocks, and Guernsey, including Sark, Alderney, Herm, Jethou, Lihou and Brechou. The two main towns are St. Helier on Jersey and St. Peter Port on Guernsey. Pop 128,560.

CHANNEL ISLANDS NATIONAL PARK, consisting of eight islands off S Cal., extends over 150mi over the Pacific Ocean. The park was established in 1980 and includes Santa Barbara and Anacapa Islands, formerly part of the Channel Islands National Monument, and the islands of San Miguel, Santa Rosa, and Santa Cruz. The islands are known for sea mammals, including the California sea lion, and have rich fossil beds.

CHANNEL TUNNEL, 52-kilometer tunnel running from a terminal near Folkestone, England, to another near Calais, France, begun in 1987 and expected to be completed in the early 1990s at a cost of nearly $10 billion. It will consist of three parallel tubes — two for trains, one for service (ventilation, maintenance, and escape). A tunnel beneath the ENGLISH CHANNEL was conceived as early as the 18th century. Tunnel projects were organized several times during the 19th and 20th centuries but abandoned because of defense considerations and financing difficulties.

CHANNING, William Ellery (1780–1842), US theologian, writer and philanthropist, leader of the Unitarian movement in New England. He led the Unitarian withdrawal from Congregationalism in 1820–25. Active in antislavery, temperance and pacifist causes, he believed that moral improvement was man's prime concern.

CHANSON DE ROLAND (Song of Roland), most famous and probably the earliest of the CHANSONS DE GESTE. Written in the 11th century, probably by the Norman poet Turold, it tells of the death of Roland at the battle of Roncevaux (Roncesvalles) in 778. It was a formative influence on Spanish, Italian and even Icelandic epic poetry.

CHANSONS DE GESTE, medieval French epic poems. Around 80 have survived, and the form and style have given rise to hundreds of other poems in various languages. Most of them deal with the legendary exploits of the Emperor CHARLEMAGNE and his knights, the Paladins.

CHANUTE, Octave (1832–1910), US engineer and pioneer aviator. He designed the Union Stockyards in Chicago and the first bridge over the Missouri R. From 1889 on he made many types of glider; these influenced the WRIGHT brothers.

CHAOS, in MATHEMATICS, the recurrent yet unpredictable behavior exhibited by deterministic (causal, not random) natural systems, such as the atmosphere interacting with earth, oceans, and solar radiation; the ecology of fish and plankton; rain forests; crystals growing in solution; and the heart in patterns of arrhythmia. Chaotic systems are highly sensitive to initial conditions. Two states of a system that differ by extremely small amounts at one time can differ greatly at a later time. Thus uncertainties in temperature data over the earth at one time make it difficult to forecast weather beyond a few days.

CHAPLIN, Sir Charles Spencer (1889–1977), British film actor and director, great comedian of the silent cinema. A vaudeville player, he rose to fame in Hollywood 1913–19 in a series of short comedies, in which he established his "little tramp" character. After 1918 he produced his own feature-length films such as *The Gold Rush* (1925) and, with sound, *Modern Times* (1936) and *The Great Dictator* (1940). Accused of communist sympathies, he left America in 1952 to settle in Switzerland. He was awarded a special Academy Award in 1973 and knighted in 1975.

CHAPMAN, George (c1559–1634), English poet and dramatist. His translations of Homer (1598–1616), although imprecise and full of his own interjections, long remained standard, and they are still recognized as masterpieces. His plays include *Bussy d'Ambois* (1607).

CHAPULTEPEC, historic hill near Mexico City. Site of an Aztec royal residence and religious center in the 14th century, it is 200ft high. In 1847 the fort on the hill, built by the Spanish in 1783, was stormed by American forces in the MEXICAN WAR, two days before the occupation of Mexico City. It is now a museum and state residence.

CHARCOAL, form of amorphous CARBON produced when wood, peat, bones, cellulose or other carbonaceous substances are heated with little or no air present. A highly porous residue of microcrystalline graphite remains. Charcoal is a fuel and was used in BLAST FURNACES until the advent of COKE. A highly porous form, activated charcoal, is made by heating charcoal in steam; it is used for adsorption in refining processes and in gas masks. Charcoal is also used as a thermal insulator and by artists for drawing.

CHARCOT, Jean Martin (1825–1893), French physician and founder of modern neurology, whose many researches advanced knowledge of HYSTERIA, MULTIPLE SCLEROSIS, locomotor ATAXIA, ASTHMA and aging. FREUD was one of his many pupils.

CHARDIN, Jean-Baptiste-Siméon (1699–1779), French painter best known for his still lifes and for his middle-period genre paintings, affectionate depictions of the everyday life of the bourgeosie. All his work is characterized by a straightforward realism, with atmospheric use of light and color.

CHARIOT, light, open, horse-drawn vehicle, usually two-wheeled, used as a weapon of war by many primitive peoples because of its speed. Mesopotamia used chariots c3000 BC, and by c1500 BC Egypt and China made extensive use of them. Chariot racing was a popular sport in ancient Rome.

CHARISMA, New Testament term from the Greek for the gifts of the Holy Spirit, imparted to apostles, prophets and healers to promote God's kingdom. The term has come to mean those magnetic qualities in certain individuals, especially political leaders such as Napoleon, Lenin or John F. Kennedy, that enable them to win mass support or enthusiastic response from their followers.

CHARLEMAGNE (Charles the Great; c742–814), king of the FRANKS, founder of the HOLY ROMAN EMPIRE and, in legend, hero of the CHANSONS DE GESTE. In 771, on the death of his co-ruler, his brother Carloman, Charlemagne became sole ruler of the Franks and began to extend the kingdom. In response to an appeal by Pope Adrian I, he waged a successful campaign against Lombardy in 773–74. Bavaria was annexed in 788, and the Saxons and Avars (on the Danube) were subjugated and Christianized after some 30 years of war. In 800 Charlemagne was crowned emperor by Pope Leo III. From his court at AACHEN he not only controlled an efficient administrative system, but also fostered the Carolingian cultural renaissance, which spread through much of present-day France, Germany, Austria, Switzerland, Holland and Belgium.

CHARLES, name of seven Holy Roman Emperors. **Charles I** (see CHARLEMAGNE). **Charles II the Bald** (see CHARLES, kings of France). **Charles III the Fat** (839–888) was emperor 881–87. After his overthrow Charlemagne's empire disintegrated. **Charles IV** (1316–1378) was emperor from 1355. He was also king of Bohemia, in whose welfare he was most interested. Making Prague his capital, he founded the Charles University there and promulgated the Golden Bull of 1356, which determined the form of elections for the Holy Roman Emperor. **Charles V** (1500–1558) was emperor 1519–56, and ruler of more territory than any of his predecessors (Spain, with its American colonies, the Netherlands, Naples, Sicily and Austria). His reign was marked by struggles with Pope Clement VII and Francis I of France, by attempts to check the Turks and by the REFORMATION. Exhausted and disillusioned, he abdicated in 1556 and retired to Spain. **Charles VI** (1685–1740) was emperor from 1711. With no male heir, he arranged for the succession of his daughter MARIA THERESA by the PRAGMATIC SANCTION. (See AUSTRIAN SUCCESSION.) **Charles VII,** or Charles Albert (1697–1745), also known as Charles of Bavaria, was emperor from 1742. He disputed Maria Theresa's succession.

CHARLES, name of two Stuart kings of England, Scotland, and Ireland. **Charles I** (1600–1649) came to the throne in 1625. His absolutist beliefs and Roman Catholic sympathies alienated the Puritan-dominated parliaments. Forced to dissolve parliaments in 1625, 1626 and 1629, he ruled without one until 1640, when increasing fiscal problems made him call the LONG PARLIAMENT, which sought to curtail his powers. This precipitated the Civil War in 1642. Charles was defeated, and captured in 1647. His continual duplicity in dealing with his captors led to his trial and execution. (See CIVIL WAR, ENGLISH.) **Charles II** (1630–1685) returned from exile to succeed his father in 1660 after the death of Cromwell. His pro-Roman Catholic foreign policy, reflecting his own sympathies, made him distrusted, but he was much more tolerant in religious matters than his parliaments. A shrewder man than Charles I, he exhibited political expertise and cynicism that kept

him much of his power. In the end he retained the country's affection, if only for his flamboyant private life.

CHARLES, name of 10 kings of France. **Charles I** (see CHARLEMAGNE). **Charles II the Bald** (823–877) reigned as king of the Franks from 843 and as Holy Roman Emperor from 875. Numerous revolts and invasions troubled his reign. It was the last great reign of his dynasty and culturally the last flowering of the Carolingian renaissance. **Charles III the Simple** (879–929), grandson of Charles II, reigned 893–923. **Charles IV the Fair** (1294–1328) reigned from 1322. **Charles V the Wise** (1337–1380) reigned as regent 1356–64 and as king from 1364. Frail and poor in health, he nevertheless put down the Jacquerie (peasant) uprising and various plots by his nobles. He regularized taxation and used the increased revenues to build up his armies. He declared war upon England in 1369, and before his death his armies, under the great commander du Guesclin, had regained most French territory occupied by the English. **Charles VI the Mad** (1368–1422) reigned from 1380. Subject to frequent and severe fits of madness, he allowed corrupt advisers to reign in his stead. England overran most of N France once more, and Charles was forced to name Henry V of England his heir (1420). **Charles VII** (1403–1461) reigned from 1422. The early part of his reign was marked by his unwillingness to challenge the English occupation of France, even to the extent of allowing Joan of Arc to be burned as a heretic. With the influence of new advisers and the end of the Burgundian alliance with England, Charles introduced tax reforms, rebuilt his army and regained all occupied territory except Calais. **Charles VIII** (1470–1498) reigned from 1483. **Charles IX** (1550–1574), who reigned 1560–74, was dominated by his mother, Catherine de Médicis, who instigated the SAINT BARTHOLOMEW'S DAY MASSACRE. **Charles X** (1757–1836) reigned 1824–30. He returned to France from exile after the restoration of the monarchy, becoming king on the death of his brother Louis XVIII. He was exiled again after the 1830 revolution, largely provoked by his autocratic rule.

CHARLES, name of four kings of Spain. **Charles I** (see CHARLES V, Holy Roman Emperor). **Charles II** (1661–1700), last of the Spanish Hapsburgs, reigned from 1665. Feeble and degenerate, he could not produce an heir, and named Philip of Anjou, grandson of Louis XIV, his successor, causing the War of the SPANISH SUCCESSION. **Charles III** (1716–1788) reigned from

1759. A strongly absolutist monarch, his attempts to expand Spanish interests in South America met with defeat at British hands. His enlightened domestic policy, reducing the power of the Church and Inquisition and introducing administrative reforms, was considerably more successful. **Charles IV** (1748–1819) reigned 1788–1808. Spain was largely ruled by his wife, Maria Luisa of Parma, and her lover, Chief Minister Manuel de Godoy. Defeated by France in 1795, Charles allowed Spain to become a satellite of Napoleonic France, and was forced to abdicate in 1808.

CHARLES, Jacques Alexandre César (1746–1823), French physicist who with Nicholas Robert made the first ascent in a hydrogen BALLOON (1783). About 1787 he discovered **Charles' Law** which, stated in modern terms, records that for an ideal gas at constant pressure, its volume is directly proportional to its absolute temperature.

CHARLES, Ray (1932–   ), black US singer and pianist, blind since age 6, who performed gospel, soul, country and standard songs.

CHARLES ALBERT (1798–1849), liberal king of Sardinia (1831–49), a hero of the Italian RISORGIMENTO. He twice waged war on Austria but, defeated at Custozza (1848) and Novara (1849), abdicated in favor of his son, VICTOR EMMANUEL II, who became the first king of united Italy.

CHARLES BORROMEO, Saint (1538–1584), Italian churchman, major figure of the COUNTER-REFORMATION. Influential in the final stage of the Council of TRENT, he was appointed (1563) bishop of Milan, where he proved a strict disciplinarian and vigorous reformer of clerical education.

CHARLES MARTEL (c688–741), Frankish ruler, who as mayor of the palace (chief minister) from 714, ruled in place of the weak MEROVINGIAN kings. The son of Pepin II, he received his surname Martel (the hammer) after his famous victory at Tours against the Muslim invaders in 732. His policies assured the Frankish preeminence in N Europe which culminated in his grandson CHARLEMAGNE'S coronation as emperor (800).

CHARLES PHILIP ARTHUR GEORGE (1948–   ), PRINCE OF WALES and Duke of Cornwall, heir apparent to the British throne. The first child of Queen Elizabeth II and Prince Philip, he was educated at Cheam, Gordonstoun and Cambridge. In 1981 he married Lady Diana Spencer; their sons are Prince William (b. 1982) and Prince Henry (b. 1984).

CHARLES THE BOLD (1433–1477), last duke of Burgundy (from 1467). Having failed to defeat him in open war, LOUIS XI of France trapped him in conflicts with other powers, leading ultimately to his death in battle at Nancy.

CHARLESTON, city in S.C., seat of Charleston Co., on a peninsula between the Cooper and Ashley rivers, 3mi from the Atlantic Ocean. A major seaport, it produces fertilizer, cigars, asbestos, pulp, chemicals, paper, textiles and steel. Among Charleston's many attractions are colonial buildings, gardens and annual azalea and performing-arts festivals. Pop (city) 67,000, (metro) 482,000.

CHARLEVOIX, Pierre François Xavier de (1682–1761), French Jesuit traveler in North America. From Quebec he passed up the St. Lawrence, through the Great Lakes, and down the Mississippi to New Orleans. Back in France he published *Histoire de la Nouvelle France* (1744), which contains an account of his trip.

CHARLOTTETOWN CONFERENCE, convened Sept. 1, 1864, at Charlottetown, Prince Edward Island, Canada, first of a series of meetings which led to the formation of the Dominion of Canada.

CHARPENTIER, Gustave (1860–1956), French composer, noted for his opera *Louise* (1900), a lyrical work evoking the spirit of Paris.

CHARTER OAK, celebrated oak tree, formerly in Hartford, Conn., in which the Conn. colonial charter was hidden in 1687, to prevent its surrender to the royal governor of New England. In 1856 the Charter Oak was uprooted in a storm. Its age was estimated at 1000 years, and its trunk size was nearly 7ft in diameter.

CHARTISM, a radical and unsuccessful attempt by voteless British laborers to gain economic and social equality. It was one of the first working-class political movements in Britain. The Chartists took their name from the "People's Charter," drafted in 1838 by William Lovett of the London Workingmen's Association. The demands made were universal male suffrage, equal district representation, vote by ballot, abolition of property qualifications for officeholders, parliamentary salaries and an annual parliament.

CHARTRES, historic city in NW France, capital of the Eure-et-Loire department and commercial center of the Beauce region. It is famous for its Gothic cathedral of Notre Dame. Pop 41,000.

CHASE, Mary Ellen (1887–1973), US author of children's literature, novels, and books about the Bible. Among her more than 40 books are *The Silver Shell* (1930),

The Lovely Ambition (1960) and *The Psalms for the Common Reader* (1962).

CHASE, Philander (1775–1852), US clergyman. As Episcopal bishop of Ohio (1819–31) he founded the town of Gambier and Kenyon College there. He was bishop of Illinois from 1835.

CHASE, Salmon Portland (1808–1873), US senator 1849–55, 1860–61, governor of Ohio 1855–59, secretary of the treasury 1861–64 and chief justice of the US Supreme Court 1864–73. Active in the antislavery movement, he helped to form the FREE SOIL PARTY. As Lincoln's secretary of the treasury, he instituted a national banking system and issued paper money. Though occasionally a political antagonist of Lincoln, as chief justice he supported the moderate Republican view towards RECONSTRUCTION.

CHASE, Samuel (1741–1811), US Supreme Court justice 1796–1811. A signer of the Declaration of Independence, he was a member of the Maryland legislature and the Continental Congress. In 1804 an unsuccessful attempt to impeach him was made by President Jefferson, who believed Chase conducted his circuit court in a partisan pro-Federalist manner.

CHASE, Stuart (1888–1985), US economist and author, a prominent advocate of CONSUMER PROTECTION.

CHATEAU, the French term for castle, often applied to any stately mansion; originally a well-fortified medieval castle with moat (a *château fort*), used for defense rather than residence. By the 17th century the château became a refined and elegant home for royalty and nobility, often distinguished by intricate gardens.

CHATEAUBRIAND, François René, Vicomte de (1768–1848), French writer and diplomat, sometimes considered a founder of the Romantic movement in 19th-century French literature. His works include the North American romance *Atala* (1801), *René* (1802), and *Mémoires d'outre-tombe* (*Memoirs from Beyond the Tomb*; 1849–50).

CHATEAU-THIERRY, town in NE France on the Marne R, scene of the second Battle of the Marne in WWI. Its products include musical instruments.

CHATHAM, Earl of. See PITT, WILLIAM.

CHATTANOOGA, Battle of (Nov. 24–25, 1863), engagement in the American Civil War in which Union forces under U.S. GRANT drove Confederate forces under Braxton BRAGG from their positions on Lookout Mountain and Missionary Ridge, securing Union possession of Chattanooga, Tenn., for the remainder of the war.

CHATTERJEE, Bankim Chandra (1838–1894), Indian author whose novels heightened Indian nationalist sentiment.

CHATTERTON, Thomas (1752–1770), English poet who wrote poems in pseudo-medieval English which he presented as the work of a 15th-century monk, Thomas Rowley. His ruse was exposed in 1777–78. Despite the success of a burlesque opera, *The Revenge* (1770), he remained destitute and poisoned himself at age 17.

CHAUCER, Geoffrey (c1340–1400), one of the first great English poets, who established English as a literary language. His early writing, including an incomplete translation of *Le Roman de la Rose*, shows strong French influence. However, c1370 a new force, due to growing familiarity with BOCCACCIO and DANTE, began to exert itself. This is shown in *The Parliament of Fowls*. His two major works are *Troilus and Criseyde* and the CANTERBURY TALES.

CHAUNCY, Charles (1705–1787), influential American Congregationalist minister, a critic of the Great Awakening religious revival.

CHAUSSON, Ernest Amédée (1855–1899), French composer, a major figure in the post–Romantic movement, strongly influenced by FRANCK. Among his best-known works is the *Symphony in B Flat Major* (c1890).

CHAUTAUQUA MOVEMENT, US adult education movement which began at Lake Chautauqua, N.Y., in 1874, as a course for Sunday school teachers. The founders, John H. Vincent, a Methodist minister, and Lewis Miller, a businessman, organized lectures, concerts and recreation activities. (See ADULT EDUCATION; LYCEUM MOVEMENT.)

CHAUVINISM, excessive and blind patriotism, a term derived from Nicholas Chauvin, a soldier blindly devoted to Napoleon who came to represent the militaristic cult of his time. Gradually the term was applied to extreme nationalism of any kind.

CHÁVEZ, Carlos (1899–1978), Mexican composer who founded the Orquesta Sinfónica de México (1928). His compositions are strongly influenced by the rhythms and patterns of Mexican-Indian folk music.

CHÁVEZ, Cesar Estrada (1927–   ), revolutionary Mexican–American labor leader who, as head of the United Farmworkers of America AFL-CIO, was instrumental in organizing Cal.'s CHICANO migrant workers. The early history of his union was filled with strikes, picketing and violent clashes with both farmers and the International Brotherhood of TEAMSTERS.

CHECKERS, called **draughts** in Great Britain, a popular game of skill played on a board of 64 alternating light and dark squares. Each of the two players begins with 12 pieces (red or black checkers) placed on the 12 dark squares nearest him, that is, in the first three rows.

Black moves first, and the players then alternate moves. A player moves by advancing one piece diagonally forward to a vacant square. If that square is occupied by the opponent and the square beyond in the same diagonal direction is vacant, the player must capture the opponent's checker by jumping over it to the vacant square and removing the opponent's piece. If completion of the jump finds the player in the same situation, he must continue jumping until he no longer can. Hence part of the strategy of the game consists in forcing the opponent into jumps that leave him open to strong counterattack. When a player can jump in more than one way, he may take his choice.

When a checker reaches the farthest row, it becomes a king, and another checker is placed on top of it to indicate its new dignity. Since kings can move and capture either forwards or backwards (though always diagonally), they add greatly to a player's forces. The goal of the game is to capture or immobilize all the opponent's pieces.

Checkers is an ancient game, dating from the time of the pharaohs in Egypt, and was probably the precursor of the related game of chess. The game is mentioned in the writings of Homer and Plato, and is believed to have been learned by the Romans from the Greeks.

CHECKS AND BALANCES, term used to describe the separation and balance of three branches of government: the legislature which makes the law, the executive which enforces it and the judiciary which interprets it. The idea is based on the theory of SEPARATION OF POWERS advocated by MONTESQUIEU in 1748, which greatly influenced the men who drew up the US Constitution. The SENATE and the HOUSE OF REPRESENTATIVES, as separate organs of the legislature, were to act as checks upon each other in the national Congress.

In practice, however, the powers are not absolutely separated in the working of today's government. Tensions between the branches of government, usually between the president and Congress, often hold up the passage of essential legislation. Some modern critics have pointed out that delay and inefficiency are all too frequently the price that must be paid for a system of checks and balances. In recent years, however, much more criticism has been raised against abuses of power committed by individual branches of government against the spirit of the checks and balances system. (See also WATERGATE.)

CHEESE, nutritious food made from the milk of various animals, with a high protein, calcium and vitamin content. Cheesemaking was already common by 2000 BC. It involves first the curdling of milk by adding an acid or rennet, so that the fat and protein (mostly casein) coagulate to form the solid curds. After excess liquid whey has been drained off, the curds are compressed and enough moisture is removed to give the cheese the desired degree of hardness. Most cheeses (but not cottage cheese) are then subjected to a period of FERMENTATION, from two weeks to two years, called ripening or curing, during which they are salted and perhaps flavored. The consistency and flavor of the cheese depend on the time, temperature and humidity of storage and on the microorganisms present. Camembert, for instance, is ripened with two molds, *Penicillium candidum* and *P. camemberti*, which make it soft. Process cheese is a blend of several types of cheese melted together.

CHEETAH, *Acinonyx jubatus*, a member of the cat family Felidae. It is the fastest land animal, with a speed of up to 70 mph. The tawny coat covered with closely set spots makes the cheetah easily recognizable. Once common in Africa and SW Asia the cheetah is fast disappearing through hunting and the reduction in numbers of small deer and antelope, its main prey.

CHEEVER, John (1912–1982), US author. His witty novels about the conflicts of suburban life won major prizes: the National Book Award for *The Wapshot Chronicle* (1957) and the Howells Medal for *The Wapshot Scandal* (1964). His collected short stories, *The Stories of John Cheever* (1978), were awarded a Pulitzer prize.

CHEKA, Russian abbreviation of "Extraordinary Commission," the secret police set up by the Bolsheviks in 1917 to eliminate their opponents. Reorganized by STALIN in 1922 and renamed the GPU, it was the ancestor of the modern KGB.

CHEKHOV, Anton Pavlovich (1860–1904), Russian dramatist and short story writer. Between 1898 and 1904 his four major plays were produced by the Moscow Art Theater: *The Seagull, Uncle Vanya, The Three Sisters* and *The Cherry Orchard.* These plays realistically explore the frustrations and unhappiness of life, particularly among the Russian rural upper and middle classes of the time. His work (both plays and short stories) has exerted an immense influence on modern literature.

CHEMICAL AND BIOLOGICAL WAR-FARE, the use of poisons and diseases against an enemy, either to kill or disable personnel or to diminish food supply, natural ground cover, etc. According to legend, SOLON defeated a Megaran army c600 BC by poisoning their drinking water. THUCYDIDES records that the Spartans in the 5th century BC used in attack the fumes produced by burning wood, sulfur and pitch. Julius CAESAR mentions with disapproval the use of poisons in warfare. Greek fire (a kind of incendiary bomb) was in use from about the middle of the 7th century AD. In the US during the FRENCH AND INDIAN WAR, infected blankets were given to the Indians to spread SMALLPOX among them. During the CIVIL WAR, John Doughty proposed the use of an artillery shell containing the choking, corrosive gas CHLORINE. Chemical warfare on a large scale was first waged by the Germans in WWI at Ypres (1915), using chlorine against the Allies. Gas warfare on both sides escalated throughout the remainder of WWI; despite the use of the gas mask, around 100,000 may have died as a result of chlorine, PHOSGENE and mustard gas attacks. During WWII the Germans developed nerve gases, which attack the NERVOUS SYSTEM, but these (Sarin, Soman and Tabun) were not used. More deadly nerve gases have since been developed in the US: some may linger for months and kill in seconds. Binary nerve gas, which consists of two non-lethal substances packed separately which do not mingle into a toxic whole until airborne, is considered of special interest. The binaries, which would be packaged in artillery shells and bombs, are perceived as avoiding problems due to lethal leakage and death through improper handling. In the VIETNAM WAR, TEAR GASES were used in combat as distinct from their more normal role in riot control. Also in Vietnam, defoliants known as Agent Orange were sprayed from aircraft on enemy crops and on vegetation to deprive guerrillas of cover (see also NAPALM). As the 1980's began, the Soviets were accused of using chemicals including "yellow rain" against the people of Laos, Cambodia and Afghanistan.

Waging of biological warfare has been rare, mainly because its effects are hard to control. Nevertheless, most developed countries have encouraged military research in this field. Available preparations could, if used, unleash pneumonic PLAGUE, pulmonary ANTHRAX, and BOTULISM, among other fatal diseases; it has been estimated that 1oz of these would, if well distributed, be sufficient to kill the entire population of North America. Less fatal diseases, such as TULAREMIA, and certain HALLUCINOGENIC DRUGS are also available for such use. In 1979 the death of hundreds of Soviets from anthrax in the Russian town of Sverdlovsk led to suspicion that an explosion in a germ warfare station had caused a lethal cloud of anthrax spores to mix with the town's air. The incident at Sverdlovsk has never been convincingly resolved.

Of the international agreements outlawing the use of chemical and biological warfare, the oldest is the 1925 Geneva Protocol; the UK accepted its strictures only in part, reserving the right to retaliate; and the US, although signing the agreement in 1925, did not ratify until 1975. The Protocol was contravened by Italy against Ethiopia (1936), by Japan against China (1943), by Egypt against Yemen (1963), and by Iraq against Iran (1984-88). Most countries have signed the Biological Weapons Convention (1972), agreeing to cease production of biological weapons and destroy existing stockpiles. Bilateral negotiations between the US and the Soviets concerning chemical warfare began in Geneva in 1976.

CHEMISTRY, the science of the nature, composition and properties of material substances, and their transformations and interconversions. In modern terms, chemistry deals with ELEMENTS and compounds, with the ATOMS and MOLECULES of which they are composed, and with the reactions between them. It is thus basic to natural phenomena and modern technology alike. Chemistry may be divided into five major parts: ORGANIC CHEMISTRY, the study of carbon compounds (which form an idiosyncratic group); INORGANIC CHEMISTRY, dealing with all the elements, except carbon, and their compounds; chemical ANALYSIS, the determination of what a sample contains and how much of each constituent is present; BIOCHEMISTRY, the study of the complex organic compounds in biological systems; and PHYSICAL CHEMISTRY, which underlies all the other branches, encompassing the study of the physical properties of substances and the theoretical tools for investigating them. Related sciences include GEOCHEMISTRY and METALLURGY.

Practical chemistry originated with the art of the metallurgists and artisans of the ancient Middle East. Their products included not only refined and alloyed metals but also dyes and glasses, and their methods were and remain shrouded in professional secrecy. Their chemical theory, expressed in terms of the prevailing theology, involved notions such as the opposition of contraries and the mediation of a mediating third. Classical Greek science generally expressed itself in the theoretical rather than the practical, as the conflicting physical theories of THALES and ANAXAGORAS, ANAXIMENES and ARISTOTLE bear witness. An important concept, that matter exists as atoms—tiny individual material particles—emerged about this time (see ATOMISM) though it did not become dominant for another 2,000 years. During the HELLENISTIC AGE a new practical chemistry arose in the study of ALCHEMY. These early alchemists sought to apply Aristotelian physical theory to their practical experiments. Alchemy was the dominant guise of chemical science throughout the medieval period. Like the other sciences, it passed through Arab hands after the collapse of the Roman world, though, unlike the case with some other sciences, great practical advances were made during this time with the discovery of alcohol DISTILLATION and methods for preparing nitric and sulfuric acids. Chemical theory, however, remained primitive, and practitioners sought to guard their secret recipes by employing obscure and even mystical phraseology. The 16th century saw new clarity brought to the description of metallurgical processes in the writings of Georgius AGRICOLA and the foundation by PARACELSUS of the new practical science of iatrochemistry with its emphasis on chemical medicines. Jan Baptist van HELMONT, the greatest of his successors, began to use quantitative experiments. In the 17th century mechanist atomism enjoyed a revival, with Robert BOYLE leading a campaign to banish obscurantism from chemical description. The 18th century saw the rise and fall of the PHLOGISTON theory of combustion, promoted by G. E. Stahl (1660–1734) and adopted by all the great chemists of the age: BLACK, SCHEELE and PRIESTLEY (all of whom found their greatest successes in the study of GASES). The phlogiston theory fell before the oxygen theory of LAVOISIER and his associated binomial nomenclature, and the new century (the 19th) saw the proposal of DALTON's atomic theory, AVOGADRO's hypothesis—neglected for 50 years until revived by Stanislao Cannizzaro (1826–1910)—and the foundation of ELECTROCHEMISTRY which, in the hands of DAVY, rapidly yielded two new elements, SODIUM and POTASSIUM. During the 19th century chemistry gradually assumed its present form, the most notable innovations being the periodic table of MENDELEYEV, the BENZENE ring-structure of KEKULÉ, the systematic chemical THERMODYNAMICS of GIBBS and Robert Bunsen's chemical SPECTROSCOPY. In the opening years of the present century the new atomic theory revolutionized chemical theory and the interrelation of the elements was deciphered. Since then successive improvements in experimental techniques (e.g., CHROMATOGRAPHY; isotopic labeling; MICROCHEMISTRY) and the introduction of new instruments (infrared, nuclear-magnetic-resonance and mass spectroscopes) have led to continuing advances in chemical theory. These developments have also had a considerable impact on industrial chemistry and biochemistry. Perhaps the most significant recent change in the chemist's outlook has been that his interest has moved away from the nature of chemical substance itself towards questions of molecular structure, the energetics of chemical processes and reaction mechanisms.

CHEMOTHERAPY, the use of chemical substances to treat disease. More specifically, the term refers to the use of nonantibiotic antimicrobials and agents for treating CANCER. The drug must interfere with the growth of bacterial, parasitic or TUMOR cells, without significantly affecting host cells. In antimicrobial chemotherapy, the work of P. EHRLICH on aniline dyes and arsenicals (salvarsan) and of Gerhard Domagk (1895–1964) on Prontosil led to the development of sulfonamides (see SULFA DRUGS). Many useful synthetic compounds are now available for BACTERIAL and parasitic disease, although ANTIBIOTICS are often preferred for bacteria. Cancer chemotherapy is especially successful in LEUKEMIA and lymphoma; in carcinoma it is usually reserved for disseminated tumor. Nitrogen mustard, ALKALOIDS derived from the periwinkle, certain antibiotics and agents interfering with DNA metabolism are used, often in combinations and usually with STEROIDS.

CHÉNIER, André Marie de (1762–1794), French poet who renewed the classical tradition in French poetry. His work forms a bridge between CLASSICISM and ROMANTICISM, with many of the best characteristics of both. He was guillotined during the French Revolution.

CHENNAULT, Claire Lee (1890–1958), US pilot, founder of the WWII "Flying Tigers." In 1937 he went to China to organize CHIANG KAI-SHEK's air force in the war against Japan. He reentered US service in 1942 as commander of the US air forces in China.

CHERNENKO, Konstantin Ustinovich (1911–1985), Soviet political leader. A protégé of Leonid BREZHNEV, he was named to the Communist Party's Central Committee (1971) and Politburo (1974) and was chosen general secretary of the party on the death of Yuri ANDROPOV (1984). Already in poor health, he died 13 months later.

CHERNOBYL, nuclear power plant, near Kiev, USSR, one of whose reactors exploded on April 26 (Moscow time), 1986, igniting the graphite moderator. Radioactive debris was scattered over a wide area of the USSR and Europe. At least 31 plant workers died, and some 135,000 people living near the plant were evacuated. The burning reactor was ultimately entombed in concrete. The Chernobyl accident has been the worst in nuclear-power history, followed by that at THREE MILE ISLAND in the US.

CHERNYSHEVSKY, Nikolai Gavrilovich (1828–1889), Russian revolutionist and author. He advocated emancipation of the serfs and saw the village commune as the first step toward socialism. In prison, he wrote the influential novel *What Is to Be Done?* (1863).

CHEROKEE INDIANS, North American tribe of the IROQUOIS linguistic group. Once numerous in Ga., N.C., S.C. and Tenn., they were decimated by smallpox and conflicts with settlers in the 18th century. Deprived of their land, thousands died on a march west in 1838. Today about 40,000 Cherokee live in the West and another 3,000 in the East.

CHEROKEE STRIP, strip of land along the S border of Kan. which was guaranteed by treaty to the CHEROKEE INDIANS. In 1891 the US bought the land and added it to Okla.

CHERRY, a tree best known for its luscious, fleshy fruits with hard pits. Varieties of the European sweet cherry are grown in many states, from New York to California. Cherry trees are also grown as ornaments, their blossom being extremely attractive in the spring, and for their fine-grained timber, which is used for cabinet work. Native cherries include the chokecherry with sour fruits and the wild black cherry, which grows to 100ft.

CHERUBINI, Maria Luigi (1760–1842), Italian composer who spent most of his life in France. Now remembered mainly for his opera *Medea* (1797), and the *Requiem in D major* (1836).

CHERWELL, Frederick Alexander Lindemann, Viscount (1886–1957), British physicist, at Oxford U 1919–56. He was scientific adviser to Prime Minister Winston Churchill during WWII and played a major role in the development of atomic energy in Britain.

CHESAPEAKE AND OHIO CANAL, waterway running along the Potomac R between Washington, D.C., and Cumberland, Md. It was planned as a route to the Midwest, but went bankrupt because of competition with the railroads. The canal was taken over by the government in 1938 and established as a historical park in 1961.

CHESAPEAKE BAY, large inlet on the E coast of the US in both S Md. and N Va., an important trade route for oceangoing vessels. Baltimore, Norfolk and Newport, important shipping and industrial towns, are on its shores. The bay, formed by the submergence of the lower Susquehanna R, separates the Md.–Del. peninsula from mainland Md. and Va. The area is famous for its waterfowl and seafood.

CHESAPEAKE BAY BRIDGE-TUNNEL, complex of highways, bridges and tunnels stretching 17.65 mi across Chesapeake Bay. The world's largest bridge–tunnel system, it links the E shore of Va. with mainland Va. without obstructing shipping. The project cost $200 million, was built in 42 months, and opened to traffic in 1964.

CHESS, game for two players, each with 16 pieces, played on a board of 64 squares, colored light and dark alternately. Each chessman moves in a certain way. Chess is thought to have originated in India c500 AD, and to have spread to Europe by 1300, perhaps through Byzantium and the Moors; many piece names are of Eastern origin. Chroniclers in N Europe often used the name chess for any board game. Chess as we know it dates from 15th-century Italy and Spain. In the 18th century France was the game's chief center. The USSR gained ascendency in chess after the 1920s. Chess today has been given popularity by publicized international contests including world championship competitions such as those between FISCHER and SPASSKY in 1972 and KARPOV and Viktor Korchnoi in 1981.

CHESTERFIELD, Philip Dormer Stanhope, 4th Earl of (1694–1773), English statesman and wit. He is chiefly remembered for his *Letters to His Son,* which give a vivid and often amusing insight into the morality of the age.

CHESTERTON, Gilbert Keith (1874–1936), English author and critic, noted for his lyrical style and delight in paradox. He wrote many poems, short stories and novels; his essays condemn the moral and political evils of his day. He is best known for his Father Brown detective stories.

CHESTNUTS, trees of America and the Old World with edible nuts. The American chestnut was once an important tree of the eastern woodlands but it has been almost wiped out by a fungus, "chestnut blight," which was introduced from Asia in 1904 and is spread by woodpeckers. The related chinquapin of the southeastern states appears to be immune. Chestnuts were highly valued for their timber, which was used for decorative and heavy-duty work, for their nuts, which were roasted or ground into a meal for storage, and for their bark, from which tannin was extracted for tanning leather. Chestnuts for roasting are now imported from Europe, whose native chestnut still flourishes.

CHEVALIER, Maurice (1888–1972), popular French singer and film star. He gained international fame in the 1920s and 1930s as the embodiment of French charm and light–heartedness. His films include *The Love Parade* (1930), *Gigi* (1958) and *Can-Can* (1959).

CHEVERUS, Jean Louis Lefebvre de (1768–1836), French churchman, first Roman Catholic bishop of Boston (1810–23). Returning to France, he became archbishop of Bordeaux and cardinal.

CHEVROLET, Louis (1879–1941), Swiss-born US automobile racer and designer; in 1911 he designed and built (with William C. DURANT) the first "Chevrolet," a 6-cylinder car produced to compete with the Ford. He later designed the racers that won the 1920 and 1921 Indianapolis 500-mile race.

CHEWING GUM, confection made from sweetened and flavored sap. For centuries Indian tribes chewed chicle (gum from the juice of the sapodilla tree) or spruce resin. Early settlers adopted the habit, and chewing gum has been made commercially in the US since the 1860s. Modern gum contains chicle, other resins and waxes, sugar and corn syrup. US annual consumption is now about 200 sticks per person.

CHEYENNE INDIANS, North American tribe of the Algonquian linguistic group. By the mid-19th century they had become nomadic hunters on the Great Plains and fierce fighters against neighboring tribes and, after 1860, the encroaching whites. A history of Cheyenne raids and punitive actions by the government, of broken promises and starvation culminated in the defeat of General CUSTER in 1876 by the Sioux and Northern Cheyenne. Eventually all the Cheyenne were resettled in Okla. and Mont.

CHIANG CHING-KUO (1911?–1988), president of Taiwan from 1978. Son of Nationalist Chinese leader Chiang Kai-shek, who with some 2 million supporters fled to Taiwan when the communists took over mainland China, he promoted rapid economic development on the island and brought native Taiwanese into the government and the ruling party, the Kuomintang. In 1987 he ended 40 years of martial law.

CHIANG KAI-SHEK (1887–1975), Chinese soldier and political leader. He fought in support of SUN YAT-SEN during the Revolution of 1911. After the success of the revolution, Chiang joined the Kuomintang, the governing party, organized the nationalist army and rose rapidly in power. After Sun's death (1925), Chiang consolidated his position, in part through an association with the communists. By the time he had become president (1928) he had turned on them, but he then forged a new alliance when Japan invaded China in 1937. As generalissimo, Chiang commanded Chinese and later (1942) Allied forces in the China war theater against Japan. After WWII, conflict between Chiang and the communists resumed. US mediation failed, the civil war went badly and Chiang fled the mainland for Taiwan 1949, where he continued as president until he died. With US support he built Taiwan into an economic and military power in its own right.

CHIANTI, a mountainous district in central Italy, part of the Appenines. Its slopes produce the famous red and white Chianti wines.

CHIBCHA INDIANS, the inhabitants of the plateau of Bogota in central Colombia. Their society was based on farming and the worship of the Sun God. The Spaniards destroyed their culture in the 16th century. Over a million of their descendants survive in the area today.

CHICAGO, city situated on Lake Michigan in Ill. Two branches of the Chicago R divide it into three parts, known as the North, South and West sides. Chicago is the hub of the US road, rail and air systems; the city's wholesale outlets handle more goods than any city except New York. Industry is diverse and immense, including the famous meatpacking plants, grain elevators and chemical, metal and printing industries. Chicago has large public libraries and many museums and art galleries. It is the home of the U. of Chicago, the Chicago Symphony Orchestra and was the major center of "Urban Blues" music.

Chicago grew as a French trading post in the 1700s, but it was not until after the

BLACK HAWK WAR (1832) that the Indian threat was ended and a city developed. The arrival of the railroads in the mid-19th century placed Chicago in the path of the nation's economic expansion as the commercial hub of the vast northern plains. Even the Great Fire of 1871, which destroyed 2,000 acres of property, could not end the vitality of Chicago's growth. With sudden economic growth came a tradition of violence, culminating in the 1920s and 1930s in open gang warfare. A large influx of blacks during WWI and WWII created serious problems. Chicago's West and South sides have some of the worst slums in the US. Pop (city) 2,992,000, (metro) 6,177,000.

CHICAGO SCHOOL refers to the conservative, monetarist approach to economic policy strongly advocated at the University of Chicago after WWII by Milton FRIEDMAN and other economists (see ECONOMICS; MONETARISM).

CHICAGO STYLE, in jazz, referred originally to the music recorded by black New Orleans artists in Chicago during the early 1920s. The jazz played by white Chicago musicians in the 1920s was called "Dixieland." More recently, the two terms have been used interchangeably to connote a style closely related to, but smoother and more sophisticated than, that of the New Orleans jazz pioneers.

CHICANO, originally a pejorative nickname for an American of Mexican descent, derived from the common name "Chico." Like the word "black," it has now been accepted as a proud acknowledgement of racial identity. In the 19th century persons of Mexican descent were a majority in the US states bordering on Mexico, and they still constitute significant minorities in the W. In addition, according to 1980 census estimates, another 3-6 million illegal migrants from Mexico live in the US. These "undocumented" persons pose a variety of legal and economic issues; for example, should their children be allowed to attend public schools? Many Mexicans are expected to continue to emigrate as long as greater work opportunities exist north of the border. With their increasing numbers, Chicanos have begun to exercise more political power in some border states. A Chicano labor leader, Cesar CHAVEZ, organized the National Farm Workers Association, and achieved bargaining power for Chicano field workers after years of bitter struggle.

CHICHÉN-ITZÁ, important archaeological remains of a Maya city, in Yucatan state, Mexico. The ruins indicate two periods of prosperity. The first was around 1000 AD when Chichén-Itzá was a modest Maya city and a member of the League of Mayapan. A second period (with strong Toltec-Mexican influences) saw the construction of an astronomical observatory and the huge pyramid temples for the worship of the god QUETZALCOATL.

CHICHERIN, Georgi Vasilievich (1872–1936), Russian diplomat, foreign minister 1918–30. He served under the tsars but left Russia in 1904 to help revolutionary activity in Europe. He returned in 1918 and joined the Bolsheviks.

CHICHESTER, Sir Francis (1901–1972), British yachtsman who made three solo transatlantic crossings (1960, 1962, 1964) and a solo voyage around the world (1967).

CHICKADEES, common garden birds, of the family Paridae, with dark caps and bibs and white faces, noted for their tameness and agility. Their simple song can be heard throughout most of the year. They nest in tree cavities or nest boxes.

CHICKAMAUGA, Battle of, Confederate victory in the American Civil War, fought in N Ga. in Sept. 1863. After the victories of GETTYSBURG and Vicksburg in July, Union troops under General Rosecrans drove on Chattanooga, Tenn., a key railway hub. The Confederates under General Braxton BRAGG retreated south of the city, regrouped, and in the ensuing battle along Chickamauga Creek routed the Federals, despite the firm stand of Union General G. H. Thomas. Both sides lost heavily.

CHICKASAW INDIANS, one of the FIVE CIVILIZED TRIBES of North American Indians of the Muskogean linguistic group. They were moved from N Miss. to Okla. with the Choctaws. Both tribes fought for the Confederacy in the Civil War and lost one third of their territory as a punishment.

CHICKENPOX, or **varicella**, a VIRUS disease due to *Varicella zoster*, affecting mainly children, usually in EPIDEMICS. It is contracted from other cases or from cases of SHINGLES and is contagious. It causes malaise, FEVER and a characteristic vesicular rash—mainly on trunk and face. Infrequently it becomes hemorrhagic or LUNG involvement occurs. Chickenpox is rarely serious in the absence of underlying disease but it is important to distinguish it from SMALLPOX.

CHICKENS, domestic birds derived from the red jungle fowl, *Gallus gallus*, raised for their flesh and eggs. They were first domesticated in India by 2,000 BC. Champion layers like the white Leghorn produce over 300 eggs a year. Chickens raised for meat are sold as broilers and fryers at under three months old and as roasters at 4–8 months.

CHIFLEY, Joseph Benedict (1885–1951), Australian Labour politician, prime minister 1945–49.

CHILBLAIN, itchy or painful red swelling of extremities, particularly toes and fingers, in predisposed subjects. A tendency to cold feet and exposure to extremes of temperature appear to be factors in causation. Treatment is symptomatic.

CHILD LABOR, the employment of children in industrial or agricultural work often detrimental to their health, education and general well-being. The practice was rampant in the US in the 19th century. Despite public outrage, commercial interests opposed legislation until the Fair Labor Standards Act was passed in 1938. This act, with the 1961 amendment, forbids the employment of children under 16 in heavy industry, transport or commerce, and under 18 in occupations detrimental to health.

CHILDREN'S CRUSADE (1212), a sad attempt by 30,000 children to conquer the Holy Land after their elders had failed. Defying king, priests and parents, they set out from France and Germany, led by the youths Stephen of Vendôme and Nicholas of Cologne. Those who survived disease, starvation and the grueling journey over the Alps were mostly sold into slavery by unscrupulous sea captains when they reached the Mediterranean ports.

CHILE, South American republic on the Pacific coast.

Official name: Republic of Chile
Capital: Santiago
Area: 292,135sq mi
Population: 12,536,000
Languages: Spanish
Religions: Roman Catholic
Monetary unit(s): 1 Chilean peso = 100 centavos
Land. Chile is a long narrow country, which measures over 2,500mi from N to S, but only 250mi at its widest point. The Andes Mts run the whole length of the country. The N, Central and S parts form three distinct natural regions: the N is dominated by desert and has rich mineral deposits in its dry saline basins. Central Chile is made up of well-watered valleys and has a Mediterranean climate. The S is wetter and cooler, containing dense forests and rolling grasslands in the Southeast.

People. Nine out of ten Chileans live in the Central area, many in Santiago, the capital, and Valparaiso, the chief port. 70% of the population is of mixed Spanish-Indian blood, the other 30% being mainly of Spanish or other European origin. Spanish is spoken by the great majority.

Economy. Chile is one of the world's leading exporters of copper; other minerals include iron ore, nitrates, lead, zinc, iodine, gold, silver and manganese. In the late 1970s the government encouraged diversification of exports in order to lessen the country's vulnerability to fluctuations of world copper prices. After copper, timber is the second most important export. The main crops are grain, rice, beans and potatoes, but Chile is not agriculturally self-supporting. Manufacturing includes textiles, steel, cement and chemicals. After a severe overall crisis (with inflation of 506% in 1974) a gradual economic recovery took place in the late 1970s.

History. The original inhabitants of the region were the Araucanian Indians. Settled by the Spanish, Chile was dominated by Spain until 1818 when Bernardo O'HIGGINS and José de SAN MARTÍN led a successful war of independence. The addition of the valuable northern area to Chile after the WAR OF THE PACIFIC (1879–83) heralded a period of industrial expansion. Following a revolution in 1891, Chile embarked on a long period of parliamentary rule. In the 20th century it was one of the most democratic and politically stable countries in Latin America, but the 1970 election of Salvador Allende, a Marxist, to the presidency led to political polarization and economic collapse. A military take-over in 1973, one of the bloodiest coups in Latin American history, initiated a right-wing dictatorship intent on eradicating Marxism. Allende allegedly committed suicide during the coup. The military junta headed by Augusto Pinochet remained in control. Pinochet's authoritarian rule and free-market economics, together with a revival of copper prices, contributed to rapid economic growth in the late 1980s and prosperity for the middle class. In 1987 non-Marxist political parties were legalized, but Pinochet was the sole candidate for an eight-year term as president in a national yes-or-no referendum held in 1988.

Chileans voted "no." Pinochet accepted the result but determined to complete his current term, which ran to 1990. The opposition parties had difficulty in agreeing upon a successor.

CHIMPANZEE, *Pan troglodytes*, an intelligent African ape. Chimpanzees inhabit woodland or grassy savanna, and feed mainly on vegetable matter. They live in large societies of as many as 60 or 80 individuals.

CH'IN, Chinese dynasty (221–207 BC) whose first emperor, SHIH-HUANG-TI, unified China, and also completed the GREAT WALL OF CHINA and built new canals and roads. The Ch'in standardized Chinese script, abolished feudalism and initiated local government.

CHINA, republic in E Asia, the world's most populous country.

Official name: The People's Republic of China
Capital: Peking
Area: 3,696,100sq mi
Population: 1,072,330,000
Languages: Mandarin, local dialects
Religions: No official religion
Monetary unit(s): 1 yuan = 100 cents
Land. China is surrounded by natural barriers; sea to the E, and mountains and deserts to the SW and N. Within this framework are three natural regions: the W, an area of high plateaus and desert, the N, fertile plains, and the S, mostly hills and valleys. The two main rivers, the Yangtze R and the Yellow R, flow from the Tibetan plateau, and are of great economic importance. The climate and vegetation are varied, with monsoons and subtropical rain forest in the SE, areas of grassland and desert in the NW, and the Himalayan Plateau in the SW.
People. The Chinese belong to the Mongoloid race, and 95% are Chinese-speaking, though there are sizeable minorities of Mongols and Tibetans, who speak their own languages. The principal dialect is now MANDARIN, taught in all schools. (See also CHINESE.)

The traditional religions are Taoism, based on the teachings of LAO-TSE (6th century BC), BUDDHISM, introduced in the 3rd century AD, and CONFUCIANISM, based on the teachings of CONFUCIUS (551–479 BC); of these, Confucianism was most responsible for building the very strong family ties, based on patriarchal dominance, that characterized Chinese society. These ties have been replaced under communism by loyalty to the commune and state; and the status of women in society has greatly improved.

Although China is still an agriculturally-based nation, with only one in five living in cities, there are many large cities; in the N, Peking, the capital (pop 8,490,000), and Tientsin (pop 7,000,000); and in the S, Shanghai (pop 13,000,000) and Canton (pop 5,200,000).
Economy. The communist government is trying to raise the economy from subsistence to prosperity by a combination of industrialization and improved agriculture, despite the problems of the vast population, which is increasing by 20 million a year.

Although China is the third-largest food producer in the world, raising sheep and growing rice, corn, wheat, vegetables, tea and cotton, it has barely enough to feed the population; but increasing production is difficult as all available land is under cultivation.

Fishing, sea and fresh water, is an important food source. Timber resources have fallen, though reforestation is under way.

Surveys have shown that mineral resources are very rich, and production of coal and iron ore has dramatically increased. More heavy machinery is being built, giving China a sound basis for industrial expansion. Power sources are largely coal and hydroelectricity. While China has become an oil exporter much heavy work is still done by hand. In the late 1970s China embarked on an ambitious program to develop agricultural mechanization and light industry ("Four Modernizations") rapidly.

Transport is largely by canal and river and rail, as the road network is poor. Nearly all trade is by sea, main exports being raw materials and textiles, and imports being machinery and wheat.
History. Peking man and Lan-t'ien man lived in China well over 500,000 years ago, but the earliest farming settlements date from c4000 BC.

The Shang dynasty (c1523–1028 BC), ruling near the Yellow R, marks the beginning of the historical period and the

Bronze Age; it was succeeded by the Chou dynasty (1027–256 BC), who were powerful war lords. A period of local wars followed, which only ended when the powerful Ch'in dynasty (221–207 BC) united China. Under the subsequent Han dynasty (202 BC–220 AD), China expanded S to Vietnam and W to central Asia.

The arts and sciences flourished for two centuries, but army revolts and barbarian invasions brought chaos, and not until the Tang dynasty (618–906 AD) reinstated strong government did trade and civilization thrive again. Prosperity continued through the Sung dynasty (960–1279), but an invasion by mounted Mongol archers made China part of the great MONGOL EMPIRE. Soon, however, the Mongol Empire broke up and a Chinese ruling house, the Ming dynasty (1368–1644), drove the Mongols deep into Asia, and China resumed power in her own right.

The rich empire was again invaded by northern barbarians, this time the MANCHUS, who set up the Ch'ing dynasty (1644–1911), the last in Chinese history. Prosperity continued until the mid-19th century, when European expansion led to unfavorable competition. China lost wars against Britain, Russia and Japan, and nationalist revolts against the Manchus caused the fall of the empire.

A new republic was declared in 1912, led first by SUN YAT-SEN and then by YUAN SHIH-KAI. However it was not until 1927 that the nationalists under CHIANG KAI-SHEK, with the help of the communists led by MAO TSE-TUNG, gained control from the Chinese war lords. Though Chiang turned on the communists in 1927, they rejoined forces to fight the Japanese invasion in 1937, and fought together during WWII.

After WWII the communists gained control and drove the nationalists off the mainland to TAIWAN (then Formosa) in 1949. They then consolidated their position under the strong leadership of Chairman Mao, Vice Chairman LIU SHAO-CHI, and Premier CHOU EN-LAI. Agriculture was collectivized, industry was nationalized, and centralized economic planning and direction on the Soviet model was instituted with the objective of rapid industrialization. In 1958, the Great Leap Forward attempted to force the progress of industrialization at the expense of agriculture, with the result that 25-30 million people starved. The need for economic development caused a rift in the Communist Party between pragmatic moderates and doctrinaire Communists led

by Mao. In 1966 Mao launched the Cultural Revolution, in which fanatical Red Guards turned society upside down in an attempt to revitalize egalitarian revolutionary zeal. Again the result was economic disaster. After Mao's death in 1976, power shifted to the moderates. TENG HSIAO-PENG, who had been dismissed from power during the Cultural Revolution, became party vice chairman, dominating the government from that position. Teng rejected both Moscow's policy of centralized planning and Mao's insistence on national self-reliance. Rural communes were abolished in favor of private family farming, resulting in a 30% increase in grain production 1978–84 (production thereafter leveled off). Factory managers were given greater freedom together with responsibility for the profitability of their plants, but here the results were disappointing because of continued price controls and fears of unemployment. Finally, China was opened to foreign trade and investment, particularly in the eastern coastal provinces, which the Chinese hoped would develop rapidly in the same way that Japan, South Korea, and Taiwan had. Teng retired from the Central Committee in 1987, compelling many of his elderly conservative opponents also to retire and thereby strengthening the position of reformers in the party leadership. Student demonstrations for political reforms alarmed conservatives, and the election of LI PENG as premier in 1988 was interpreted as a setback for the reformers.

CHINA, Republic of, also **Taiwan** or **Formosa,** an island off SE mainland China, the Formosa Strait (about 120mi wide) intervening. It is the only province of China controlled by the (Nationalist) Republic of China and includes the Pescadores, Quemoy and Lan Hsü islands.

Land. Forested and mountainous (Yü Shan, 13,113ft), Taiwan has extensive plains in the W, a monsoon climate, tropical in the S, subtropical in the N, which permits two rice harvests.

People. Most people are of Chinese, largely Fukien province, origin. Taiwan is densely populated. In the late 1940s 1,000,000 mainland Chinese fled to Taiwan, increasing density even more. Most Taiwanese are Buddhists or Taoists. The 200,000 Malay-Polynesian aborigines live mainly in the E.

Economy. Taiwan's well-developed economy is no longer largely agricultural but highly industrialized into chiefly an export economy. Irrigation is vital in growing rice, sweet potatoes, soybeans, sugar, 'oolong' tea, fruits and cotton. There are rich

Official name: Republic of China
Capital: Taipei
Area: 13,900sq mi
Population: 19,630,000
Languages: Mandarin Chinese; Amoy, Hakka dialects
Religions: Buddhist, Taoist, Christian, Muslim
Monetary unit(s): 1 New Taiwan dollar = 100 cents

fisheries and abundant timber. Minerals include coal, natural gas and some oil, gold, copper and silver. Industry includes steel, aluminum, textiles, petrochemicals, wood and food-processing, and a wide range of manufactured goods. Exports include textiles, metals, machinery, chemicals, sugar and tea.

History. Named Formosa ('beautiful') by the Portuguese, and from 1624 under Dutch control, Taiwan fell to a Ming general in 1662 and then to the Manchus (1683). Ceded to Japan in 1895, it was taken over by CHIANG KAI-SHEK in 1949 when MAO TSE-TUNG ousted the Nationalists from mainland China. From 1951 to 1965 the US gave $1.5 billion economic aid and $2.5 billion military aid. Though Taiwan (Republic of China) was expelled from the UN in 1971, it continued to enjoy US protection under the Mutual Defense Treaty of 1954 until 1979, when the US recognized the People's Republic of China, severed diplomatic relations with Taiwan, and terminated the treaty. Since then, the export-oriented economy has flourished despite diplomatic isolation. In 1987 Chiang Kai-shek's son, Chiang Ching-kuo, who had become president in 1978, lifted the state of martial law that had been in effect since 1949. Political reform continued under Lee Teng-hui, the first native-born Taiwanese president, who assumed office following the death of Chiang Ching-kuo in 1988.

CHINA SEA, W part of the Pacific Ocean, along the E coast of Asia. Taiwan divides it into the E China Sea, 485,300sq mi in area, whose maximum depth is 9,126ft; and the S China Sea, whose area is 895,400sq mi, and

maximum depth is 15,000ft. Major seaports are CANTON and HONG KONG.

CHINAWARE. See POTTERY AND PORCELAIN.

CHINESE, a group of languages of the Sino-Tibetan family. MANDARIN, China's official language, is the most commonly used in the world, being spoken by nearly 700 million people. Other dialects include Cantonese, Hakka and Wu. Except for borrowing European technical terms, Chinese is self-sufficient; Japanese and Korean use a version of its writing system. There is evidence of its existence from c2000 BC. The earliest examples date from c1400 BC. The written Chinese of CONFUCIUS' time is still used in literature and scholarship, but the spoken word has developed differently, and is the basis for the new literary form, introduced in 1911. The writing system developed from pictorial representation into conventionalized designs, one character being composed of between one and 32 strokes. In the 20th century attempts have been made to simplify the script. Chinese literature spans 3,000 years, and is written in two styles: the classical and, since 1911, the vernacular.

CHINESE EXCLUSION ACTS, name of two acts to limit immigration of Orientals to the US. The first, passed in 1879, stemmed from anti-Chinese agitation on the W coast of the US. President HAYES vetoed the act on the grounds that it abrogated the Burlingame Treaty (1868), which allowed unlimited Chinese immigration. But in 1882 the second act suspended immigration for 10 years, and in 1902 the suspension was made indefinite.

CH'ING, MANCHU dynasty that ruled CHINA after seizing Peking in 1644. It was overthrown by Chinese nationalists in 1911.

CHINOISERIE, European art style using Chinese designs in architecture, ceramics, furniture and decorating, usually in conjunction with BAROQUE and ROCOCO styles. It reached its peak in the mid-18th century, and thereafter waned except for a brief revival in the 1930s.

CHINOOK, language group of several 18th-century settlements of Northwestern American Indians. Indians speaking Chinook lived in the area around the Columbia River and included the Clatsop, Wasco, Wishram and Clackama. They were primarily a fishing culture but also carried on a number of skilled crafts. What most impressed early European observers was their practice of flattening children's foreheads to indicate social class and the *potlatch* gift-giving ceremony common to many Northwestern Indians. Chinook jargon, a pidgin version of their highly developed language, was widely used ·by traders and other Indian tribes. The Chinook and their language became almost extinct as a cultural entity after a disastrous epidemic of smallpox in 1829, in which approximately 80% of their people died.

CHIPMUNKS, small striped ground-living SQUIRRELS. There are 16 species in North America, and one in Asia. They feed on fruits and nuts which they carry to a store in their cheek pouches; they may also eat small animals. Without hibernating, they sleep for long periods in winter.

CHIPPENDALE, Thomas (c1718–1779), famous English cabinetmaker whose elegant, individual style blended aspects of GOTHIC, ROCOCO and CHINOISERIE. He also worked from designs by Robert ADAM.

CHIPPEWA, common name for the OJIBWA Indians.

CHIRAC, Jacques René (1932–   ), French politician, leader of the neo-Gaullist Rally for the Republic (RPR). Premier (1974–76) under President Valery Giscard d'Estaing, he was again appointed (1986) premier by socialist president François Mitterrand when conservatives won a parliamentary majority. In 1988 he ran for president against Mitterrand, was defeated, and resigned as premier.

CHIRICO, Giorgio de (1888–1978), Greek-born Italian painter who as a founder of the *scuola metafisica,* was a forerunner of SURREALISM. His most characteristic works depict desolate, harshly hued cityscapes that might have been seen in a nightmare.

CHIROPODY. See PODIATRY.

CHIROPRACTIC, a health discipline based on a theory that disease results from misalignment of vertebrae. Manipulation, massage, dietary and general advice are the principal methods used. It was founded by Daniel D. Palmer in Davenport, Ia., in 1895 and has a substantial following in the US.

CHISHOLM TRAIL, 19th-century route for cattle drives between Tex. and Kan., named after the scout and trader Jesse Chisholm. It was superseded by the spread of the railroads.

CHIVALRY, knightly code of conduct in medieval Europe combining Christian and military ideals of bravery, piety, honor, loyalty and sacrifice. These virtues were particularly valued by the Crusaders, who founded the earliest chivalric orders. Chivalry was also associated with ideals of courtly love, and it was this, together with changing methods of warfare, that led to its degeneration and decline during the late Middle Ages.

CHLORINE (Cl), greenish-yellow gas with a pungent odor, a typical member of the halogens, occurring naturally as chlorides (see HALIDES) in seawater and minerals. It is made by electrolysis of SALT solution, and is used in large quantities as a bleach, as a disinfectant for drinking water and swimming pools, and in the manufacture of plastics, solvents and other compounds. Being toxic and corrosive, chlorine and its compound PHOSGENE have been used as poison gases (see CHEMICAL AND BIOLOGICAL WARFARE). Chlorine reacts with most organic compounds, replacing hydrogen atoms and adding to double and triple bonds. AW 35.5, mp −101°C, bp −35°C. **Chlorides,** the commonest chlorine compounds, are typical halides except for carbon tetrachloride (see CARBON), which is inert (see STEREOCHEMISTRY). Other chlorine compounds include a series of oxides, unstable and highly oxidizing, and a series of oxyanions—hypochlorite, chlorite, chlorate and perchlorate—with the corresponding oxy-acids, all powerful oxidizing agents. Calcium hypochlorite and sodium chlorite are used as bleaches; chlorates are used as weedkillers and to make matches and fireworks; perchlorates are used as explosives and rocket fuels.

CHLOROFORM, or trichloromethane (CHCl₃), dense, colorless volatile liquid made by chlorination of ETHANOL or acetone. One of the first anesthetics (see ANESTHESIA) in modern use (by Sir James Simpson, 1847), it is now seldom used except in tropical countries, despite its potency, since it has a narrow safety margin and is highly toxic in excess. It is also used in cough medicines and as an organic solvent; it is nonflammable. MW 119.4, mp −64°C, bp61°C.

CHLOROPHYLL, various green pigments found in plant chloroplasts. They absorb light and convert it into chemical energy, thus playing a basic role in PHOTOSYNTHESIS. Chlorophylls are chelate compounds in which a magnesium ion is surrounded by a porphyrin system.

CHMIELNICKI, Bohdan (c1595–1657), Ukrainian cossack *hetman* who led a successful rebellion against Polish rule but then placed the independent Ukraine under the protection of Russia, which shortly absorbed it.

CHOCOLATE, popular confectionary made from CACAO beans. Fermented beans are roasted and the outer husks removed by a process that breaks the kernels into fragments called nibs. Chocolate is made from ground nibs, cocoa butter (the fat released when the nibs are subjected to hydraulic pressure), sugar and sometimes milk. It is a high energy food that contains a small amount of the stimulant CAFFEINE. Chocolate may be molded into bars or used as a beverage and in some liqueurs.

CHOCTAW, North American Indian tribe which originated in what is now SE Miss. They remained at peace with the US government but, following the Removal Act of 1830, were forced, as members of the FIVE CIVILIZED TRIBES, to sell their lands and move to what is now Okla.

CHOLERA, a BACTERIAL DISEASE causing profuse watery DIARRHEA, due to *Vibrio cholerae*. It is endemic in many parts of the East, and EPIDEMICS occur elsewhere. A water-borne infection, it was the subject of a classic epidemiological study by John Snow in 1854. Abdominal pain and diarrhea, which rapidly becomes severe and watery, are main features, with rapidly developing dehydration and SHOCK. Without rapid and adequate fluid replacement, death ensues quickly; ANTIBIOTICS may shorten the diarrheal phase. It is a disease due to a specific TOXIN. VACCINATION gives limited protection for six months.

CHOLESTEROL ($C_{27}H_{46}O$), sterol found in nearly all animal tissue, especially in the NERVOUS SYSTEM, where it is a component of myelin. Cholesterol is a precursor of BILE salts and of adrenal and sex HORMONES. Large amounts are synthesized in the liver, intestines and skin. Cholesterol in the diet supplements this. Since abnormal deposition of cholesterol in the arteries is associated with ARTERIOSCLEROSIS, some doctors advise avoiding high-cholesterol foods and substituting unsaturated for saturated FATS (the latter increase production and deposition of cholesterol). It is a major constituent of gallstones.

CHOMSKY, Noam (1928–   ), US linguist. A professor at MIT from 1955, he revolutionized the study of language structure with his theory of generative grammar, first outlined in *Syntactic Structures* (1957). He was also an influential critic of US foreign policy both during and after the Vietnam War.

CHOPIN, Frédéric François (1810–1849), Polish composer and pianist who wrote chiefly for the solo piano. His music is Romantic, inspired by introspection and concern for the fate of his native Poland. Chopin gave his first public performance at the age of eight, in Warsaw. In 1831 he moved to Paris (his father was French) where he began serious composition. His chief works include two piano concertos, 24 preludes, 19 nocturnes, three impromptus, four scherzos, four ballades and many waltzes, mazurkas and polonaises. They

display an often startling technical virtuosity. In 1837 he began his famous friendship with the novelist George SAND. Their relationship ended unhappily in 1847 and Chopin, already ill with tuberculosis, died in Paris two years later.

CHOPIN, Kate O'Flaherty (1851–1904), US author noted for her realistic descriptions of Louisiana life.

CHORAL MUSIC, music sung by a choir or chorus. The unaccompanied choral music sung in monasteries and abbeys during the early Christian era is known as PLAINSONG. Choral music continued to be performed without accompaniment through the 16th century. Some of the finest works of this period were written by the Italian PALESTRINA. The development of instrumental accompaniment in the 17th and 18th centuries culminated in J. S. BACH'S orchestrated cantatas and passions and the ORATORIOS of HANDEL. Choral music lost some popularity with the development of secular and orchestral music but choral works continued to be written. BEETHOVEN'S innovative inclusion of a choir in the finale of his *Ninth Symphony* (1817–23) marks a turning point in the history of music. Notable among 20th-century choral works are ELGAR's *Dream of Gerontius* (1900) and STRAVINSKY's *Symphony of Psalms* (1930).

CHORDATES, group of animals comprising the phylum Chordata. They include all VERTEBRATES and little-known animals such as amphioxus, the hemichordates and the tunicates. At some stage in their development, all possess a primitive backbone-like structure called the NOTOCHORD.

CHOREA, abnormal, nonrepetitive involuntary movements of the limbs, body and face. It may start with clumsiness, but later uncontrollable and bizarre movements occur. It is a disease of basal ganglia (see BRAIN). **Sydenham's chorea,** or **Saint Vitus' dance,** is a childhood illness associated with STREPTOCOCCUS infection and RHEUMATIC FEVER; recovery is usually full. **Huntington's chorea** is a rare hereditary disease, usually coming on in middle age and associated with progressive dementia.

CHOREOGRAPHY, composition of steps and movements for dancing, especially BALLET. The most influential choreographers of the early decades of the 20th century created ballets for DIAGHILEV and include Michel FOKINE, NIJINSKY and George BALANCHINE. Pioneers in modern dance, such as Martha GRAHAM and Jerome ROBBINS, helped to free the dance theater from the restrictions of classical steps. Teaching is traditionally by demonstration, and written records of early dance steps are scant. A notation system was published 1699 by Raoul Feuillet (c1670–c1730) and, in the 20th century, Rudolf von Laban developed his *Labanotation*.

CHOU, Chinese dynasty that ruled from Hao, near present-day Sian, (c1122–770 BC) and then from Lo-yang (770–256 BC). The two periods, known respectively as the Western and Eastern Chou, were, despite political turmoil, a time of fundamental cultural growth. Irrigation projects were established, great advances were made in iron-casting techniques, and a money economy was evolved. Literature and philosophy flourished, particularly during the Eastern Chou which became the classical age of Chinese philosophy. (See CONFUCIUS; LAO-TSE; MENCIUS.)

CHOU EN-LAI (Zhou Enlai; 1898–1976), first prime minister of the People's Republic of China. Born into the gentry, he became a Marxist after studying in China, Japan and Paris. In 1924 he became political director of the Whampoa Military Academy while CHIANG KAI-SHEK was commandant. In 1926 he organized the Shanghai Strike for Chiang and escaped when Chiang betrayed the communists. He became a Comintern liaison man organizing the proletariat and eventually director of military affairs for MAO TSE-TUNG'S guerrilla forces. After commanding the first stages of the LONG MARCH (1934–35), he became Mao's champion and thereafter always deferred to his authority. As foreign minister (as well as prime minister) until 1958, he won support for China in the Third World. He was a moderating influence during Mao's Cultural Revolution in the 1960s and a major force in taking China into the UN (1971). Seeking to balance worsening Sino-Soviet relations, he was responsible for the rapprochement with the US, symbolized by President Nixon's visit to China in 1972.

CHOUTEAU, family of fur traders who helped to open up the Middle West. (René) **Auguste Chouteau** (1749–1829), co-founded with Pierre Laclède the trading post which was to become St. Louis (1764). Auguste's brother, (**Jean) Pierre Chouteau** (1758–1849), an Indian agent for all tribes W of the Mississippi R, co-founded the St. Louis Missouri Fur Company (1809). His son, **Auguste Pierre Chouteau** (1786–1838), was an Indian treaty commissioner and made many expeditions into the West. Auguste Pierre's brother, **Pierre Chouteau** (1789–1865), headed the AMERICAN FUR COMPANY from 1834. By pioneering the use of steamboats he monopolized trade on the Missouri R.

CHRÉTIEN DE TROYES (c1135–1183), French poet who wrote romances rooted in ARTHURIAN LEGEND. His five romances, *Erec, Cligès, Lancelot, Yvain* and the unfinished *Perceval*, were seminal, greatly influencing French and English literature through the next two centuries.

CHRIST (Greek *Christos*, anointed one), translation from the Hebrew *Mashiah* or Messiah. (See JESUS CHRIST; MESSIAH.)

CHRISTIAN BROTHERS, Roman Catholic teaching order founded in 1802 by Edmund Ignatius Rice at Waterford, Ireland, to care for poor Catholic boys. The order now has schools and colleges in many countries.

CHRISTIANITY, a major world religion; arising out of JUDAISM, and founded on the life, death and resurrection of JESUS CHRIST. Christians total some 28% of the world's population. Half of all Christians are in Europe, most of the rest in North and South America. The central Christian proclamation is that by the grace of God men are saved (see SALVATION) through faith in Christ, their sins are forgiven, and they receive new and eternal life in the fellowship of the CHURCH. Arising out of this are the various aspects of Christian life and teaching, broadly divided into worship, THEOLOGY, MISSION and personal and social obedience to God's will—that is, the practice of righteousness, love and mercy. The whole Church regards the BIBLE as authoritative, but the place given to tradition and reason varies.

After Jesus' resurrection and ascension (c30 AD), his APOSTLES and other followers traveled widely, spreading and developing Christian beliefs and worship. Christian communities emerged throughout the Roman Empire, meeting weekly for prayer and Holy COMMUNION. Soon an ecclesiastical structure began to evolve. Meetings were led by bishops, assisted by elders (see PRESBYTERS). Later the elders presided over local congregations and bishops had wider authority (see MINISTRY). Regions were organized into dioceses and provinces.

Christians suffered persecution until the Emperor CONSTANTINE proclaimed freedom of worship throughout the Roman Empire (313 AD). He made Christianity Rome's official religion in 324 AD, and in 325 called the first Ecumenical Council at Nicaea to settle major doctrinal disputes. In the 4th century MONASTICISM spread from Egypt to the West.

Almost from the beginning the Church had been divided into the Greek-speaking East and the Latin-speaking West, with divergent traditions. The Western church came to recognize the preeminence of the pope, the bishop of Rome, as the direct successor of St. Peter. But the EASTERN CHURCH looked to the patriarch of Constantinople as its head. This division finally led to the GREAT SCHISM of 1054. The MONOPHYSITE CHURCHES had previously separated from the Eastern ORTHODOX CHURCHES in the 6th century. The advance of ISLAM was an increasing threat to all the Eastern Churches.

In medieval Western Europe the increasing secular power and corruption of the Roman Church helped to spark off the 16th-century REFORMATION, from which PROTESTANTISM emerged as various national churches separated from the ROMAN CATHOLIC CHURCH, which responded by its own COUNTER-REFORMATION. The LUTHERAN and REFORMED CHURCHES came to dominate northern Europe. The Roman Catholic Church and (two centuries later) Protestant churches embarked on a vigorous missionary program to the Americas, Africa and Asia, often closely connected with colonial expansion.

Today, Christian churches, though still divided by differences of doctrine and practice, work together and share a concern for worldwide social justice, and the ECUMENICAL MOVEMENT offers hope of eventual reunion.

CHRISTIAN REFORMED CHURCH, Protestant denomination founded in 1857 by Dutch immigrants in the US who separated from the Protestant Dutch Church (now the Reformed Church in America). Originally known as the True Holland Reformed Church, the present name was adopted in 1890.

CHRISTIAN SCIENCE, a religious movement which believes in the power of Christian faith to heal sickness. It was founded by Mary Baker EDDY, who organized the first Church of Christ, Scientist at Boston, Mass., in 1879. There are now many affiliated churches throughout the world. The *Christian Science Monitor* is a widely respected international daily newspaper.

CHRISTIAN SOCIALISM, 19th-century movement of social reform based on Christian ideals rather than on secular socialist theories such as class struggle. (See also SOCIAL GOSPEL.)

CHRISTIE, Agatha (1891–1976), British writer of popular detective novels and plays. Her two central characters are the egotistical Hercule Poirot and the elderly Miss Jane Marple. Her play *The Mousetrap* opened in London in 1952 and was still being performed in the early 1980s,

the world's longest continuous run.

CHRISTINA (1626–1689), queen of Sweden 1632–54, successor to Gustavus Adolphus. She was a lavish patron of the arts and attracted many scholars to her court, among them Descartes. Christina refused to marry and in 1654 she abdicated, leaving the country in male disguise. She was received into the Roman Catholic Church at Innsbruck in the following year and settled in Rome. She failed in two attempts to regain her throne (1660 and 1667).

CHRISTMAS (Christ's Mass), annual Christian festival observed on Dec. 25 in the Western Churches to commemorate the birth of Jesus Christ. It is a public holiday in Christian countries, usually marked by the exchange of gifts—tokens of the gifts of the three wise men to the infant Jesus. Christmastide lasts from Dec. 25 to Jan. 6 (EPIPHANY).

CHRISTOPHE, Henri (1767–1820), king of N Haiti. He became president of Haiti in 1806, after the murder of DESSALINES. Opposed by Alexandre Pétion, after 1811 he ruled only N Haiti, as King Henri I, building the mountain fortress of La Ferrière. Faced with a revolt, he shot himself.

CHRISTOPHER, Saint (c3rd century AD), by tradition a Christian martyr and patron of travelers because, according to a popular legend, he once carried the Christ child across a river. The ROMAN CATHOLIC CHURCH has removed Christopher from its calendar of saints for lack of historical evidence as to his existence.

CHRISTUS, Petrus (d. 1473?), leading Flemish painter, early Netherlandish school. His work, strongly influenced by Jan VAN EYCK, was important in the 15th-century development of realistic perspective.

CHRISTY, Edwin P. (1815–1862), US actor who organized the highly successful Christy Minstrels troupe at Buffalo, N.Y., in 1842. He established the basic format of the MINSTREL SHOW, popular in the 19th century.

CHROMATIC SCALE, musical scale consisting of all 12 semitones within an octave. It contains every tone commonly used in Western music. (See also SCHOENBERG, ARNOLD; TWELVE TONE MUSIC.)

CHROMATOGRAPHY, a versatile technique of chemical separation and ANALYSIS, capable of dealing with many-component mixtures, and large or small amounts. The sample is injected into the moving phase, a gas or liquid stream which flows over the stationary phase, a porous solid or a solid support coated with a liquid. The various components of the sample are adsorbed by the stationary phase at different rates, and separation occurs. Each component has a characteristic velocity relative to that of the solvent, and so can be identified. In liquid-solid chromatography the solid is packed into a tube, the sample is added at the top, and a liquid eluant is allowed to flow through; the different fractions of effluent are collected. A variation of this method is ion-exchange chromatography, in which the solid is an ion-exchange resin from which the ions in the sample are displaced at various rates by the acid eluant. Other related techniques are paper chromatography (with an adsorbent paper stationary phase) and thin-layer chromatography (using a layer of solid adsorbent on a glass plate). The other main type of chromatography—the most sensitive and reliable—is **gas-liquid chromatography** (glc), in which a small vaporized sample is injected into a stream of inert eluant gas (usually nitrogen) flowing through a column containing nonvolatile liquid adsorbed on a powdered solid. The components are detected by such means as measuring the change in thermal conductivity of the effluent gas.

CHROMIUM (Cr), silvery-white, hard metal in Group VIB of the PERIODIC TABLE; a TRANSITION ELEMENT. It is widespread, the most important ore being chromite. This is reduced to a ferrochromium alloy by carbon or silicon; pure chromium is produced by reducing chromium (III) oxide with aluminum. It is used to make hard and corrosion-resistant ALLOYS and for chromium electroplating. Chromium is unreactive. It forms compounds in oxidation states $+2$ and $+3$ (basic) and $+6$ (acidic). Chromium (III) oxide is used as a green pigment, and lead chromate (VI) as a yellow pigment. Other compounds are used for tanning leather and as mordants in dyeing. AW 52.0, mp 1890°C, bp 2482°C, sg 7.20 (20°C).

CHROMOSOMES, threadlike bodies in cell nuclei, composed of GENES, linearly arranged, which carry genetic information responsible for the inherited characteristics of the organism (see HEREDITY). Chromosomes consist of the NUCLEIC ACID DNA (and sometimes RNA) attached to a protein core. All normal cells contain a certain number of chromosomes characteristic of the species (46 in man), in homologous pairs (diploid). GAMETES, however, are haploid, having only half this number, one of each pair, so that they unite to form a ZYGOTE with the correct number of chromosomes. In

man there is one pair of sex chromosomes, females having two X chromosomes, males an X and a Y; thus each egg cell must have an X chromosome, but each spermatozoon has either an X or a Y, and determines the sex of the offspring. In cell division, the chromosomes replicate and separate (see MITOSIS). Defective or supernumerary chromosomes cause various abnormalities, including DOWN'S SYNDROME. (See also MUTATION.)

CHRONICLES, two Old Testament books summarizing Jewish history from Adam through the Babylonian Captivity. The first consists mainly of genealogies up to Saul, and the second is largely a history of the Kingdom of Judah.

CHRONOLOGY, the science of dating involving the accurate placing of events in time and the definition of suitable time scales. In Christian societies, events are dated in years before (BC) or after (AD—*Anno Domini*) the traditional birth date of Christ. In scientific use, dates are often given BP (Before Present). In ARCHAEOLOGY, dating techniques include DENDROCHRONOLOGY and RADIOISOTOPE DATING. In GEOLOGY, rock strata are related to the geological time scale by examination of the FOSSILS they contain (see also POTASSIUM).

CHRONOMETER, an extremely accurate clock, especially one used in connection with celestial NAVIGATION at sea (see also CELESTIAL SPHERE). It differs from the normal clock in that it has a fusee, by means of which the power transmission of the mainspring is regulated so that it remains approximately uniform at all times; and a balance made of metals of different coefficients of expansion to minimize the effects of temperature changes. The device is maintained in gimbals to reduce the effects of rolling and pitching. A chronometer's accuracy is checked daily and its error noted; the daily change in error is termed the **daily rate**. Chronometers are always set to Greenwich mean time. The first chronometer was invented by John Harrison (1735). (See also ATOMIC CLOCK; CLOCKS AND WATCHES.)

CHRYSANTHEMUM, genus of popular flowering herbaceous plants of the daisy family (Compositae). The large, showy flowers are usually white, yellow, pink or red. Each flower consists of a number of florets. Chrysanthemums are native to temperate and subtropical areas. Many cultivated varieties have been developed.

CHRYSLER, Walter Percy (1875–1940), US industrialist who produced the first Chrysler car (1924) and established the

Chrysler Corporation (1925), which eventually became the third-largest auto producer in the US.

CHRYSOSTOM, Saint John (c347–407 AD), one of the CHURCH DOCTORS, called Chrysostom ("golden mouthed") for his powers of oratory. He was patriarch of Constantinople (398–404) and became its patron saint.

CHURCH, Frederick Edwin (1826–1900), US romantic landscape painter. He was a student of Thomas COLE and the most famous member of the HUDSON RIVER SCHOOL.

CHURCH, the community of Christian believers, a society founded as such by Jesus Christ (though springing from the Jewish community). The term is used both for the universal Church and for its national and local expressions. Governed and served by its MINISTRY, the Church is established by the Holy Spirit through the Scriptures and the SACRAMENTS. Its life, ideally characterized by holiness, is expressed in worship, teaching, MISSION and good works. The Church consists not only of its present members (the "Church Militant") but also of those departed, the "Church Triumphant" in heaven and (disputedly) the "Church Expectant" in purgatory. The traditional marks of the Church, as in the Nicene Creed, are that it is one, holy, Catholic and apostolic; the first is challenged by schism and the last by heresy. Protestant churches, while generally accepting the visible organization of the Church, have stressed more its spiritual nature, attempting to distinguish true Christians from nominal. (See also CHRISTIANITY.)

CHURCH DOCTORS, saints whose writings on Christian doctrine have special authority. The four great doctors of the E Church are saints ATHANASIUS of Alexandria, Basil the Great of Caesarea, Gregory of Nazianzus, and John CHRYSOSTOM. The four great doctors of the W Church are saints AMBROSE, AUGUSTINE, Gregory the Great (Pope GREGORY) and JEROME. The W has 20 other doctors, including saints Thomas AQUINAS, BONAVENTURE, CATHERINE OF SIENA and TERESA OF AVILA. The last two were declared doctors in 1970 by papal decree.

CHURCHES OF CHRIST, US religious denomination based on the primitive Church. It holds that the Church of Christ was founded at PENTECOST and refounded by Thomas Campbell (1763–1854). There are over 17,000 independent churches and 2,500,000 members.

CHURCH FATHERS, eminent early Christian bishops and teachers whose writings deeply influenced Church doctrine. They include the eight great CHURCH DOCTORS and the Apostolic Fathers.

CHURCHILL, Lord Randolph Henry Spencer (1849–1895), British politician, father of Sir Winston Churchill, famous in the 1880s for advocating a more democratic and reformist Conservative party. Entering the House of Commons in 1874, he led a group called the Fourth Party (1880–85) and was creator of Tory democracy. A brilliant orator, he became chancellor of the exchequer in 1886, but resigned the same year and never again held office.

CHURCHILL, Sir Winston Spencer Leonard (1874–1965), greatest modern British statesman, as a war leader the architect of victory in WWII. He was the son of Lord Randolph Churchill. After an early career as an army officer and war correspondent he became a Conservative member of Parliament, in 1901, changing to the Liberals in 1905. He was home secretary 1910–11, a dynamic first lord of the admiralty 1911–15 and held various government posts 1917–22. He was Conservative chancellor of the exchequer 1924–29 but in the 1930s his unpopular demands for war preparedness kept him from power. In WWII he was first lord of the admiralty 1939–40 and prime minister 1940–45. As such he became one of the greatest-ever war leaders; his oratory maintained Britain's morale, and he was one of the main shapers of Allied strategy working closely with President ROOSEVELT. A postwar reaction cost his party the 1945 election, but he was again prime minister 1951–55, remaining a nationally loved and revered figure for the rest of his life.

CHURCH OF CHRIST, SCIENTIST. See CHRISTIAN SCIENCE.

CHURCH OF ENGLAND, the English national church. Its doctrine is basically Protestant and its hierarchy and ceremony are rooted in Catholic tradition. The Church broke with Rome in 1534 (see REFORMATION) when HENRY VIII assumed the title of head of the Church. In the 16th and 17th centuries the Church was troubled by PURITAN agitation and later by nonconformity. But it remains the established state church with a nominal membership of 25–30 million (active members perhaps total only 10% of this figure). The 26 senior bishops (lords spiritual) sit in the House of Lords, and are led by the archbishop of Canterbury. (See also ANGLICANISM; MINISTRY.)

CHURCH OF SCOTLAND, the Scottish national church, based on PRESBYTERIANISM.

It is governed by the General Assembly, which is elected from the presbyteries. Parishes are presided over by kirk sessions elected by the congregation. Membership totals some 1,300,000. (See also KNOX, JOHN; COVENANTERS.)

CHURCH OF THE NAZARENE, Protestant evangelical denomination created in its present form in Tex. in 1908 when three groups merged. Its headquarters is in Kansas City, Mo.

CHURRIGUERA, José Benito (1665–1725), Spanish architect who gave his name to the Spanish Baroque style, better known as Churrigueresque (1650–1740). Churriguera designed grandiosely theatrical altars and the entire urban complex of Nuevo Baztán, in Madrid.

CHURUBUSCO, Battle of, a conflict in the MEXICAN WAR. On Aug. 20, 1847 Winfield SCOTT's US forces crushed SANTA ANNA's Mexican troops at Churubusco, a suburb of Mexico City.

CHU TEH (1886–1976), Chinese Communist leader. He studied in Germany, became a Communist, helped form the Chinese Red Army, and joined Mao Tse-tung. As commander in chief, he led the Long March (1934–35) and defeated the Nationalists (1949). He held various high posts in the Communist government.

CIANO, Count Galeazzo (1903–44), Italian Fascist statesman. He married Mussolini's daughter (1930) and became propaganda minister (1933). As foreign minister (1936–43), he was overshadowed by Mussolini. Dismissed, he voted against Mussolini at the 1943 Fascist Grand Council. He was caught by the Nazis, handed over to the Fascists in N Italy and shot.

CIARDI, John (1916–1986), US poet, translator and teacher. He made notable translations of Dante's *Inferno* (1954), *Purgatorio* (1961) and *Paradiso* (1970).

CIBBER, Colley (1671–1757), English actor-manager and dramatist who introduced sentimental comedy to the theater in *Love's Last Shift* (1696). His moral comedies were a reaction against Restoration drama. Cibber was made poet laureate in 1730.

CIBOLA, Seven Cities of, golden cities reported in the Southwest of North America in the 16th century. The legend attracted Spanish exploration, notably by Coronado with 300 Spanish cavalry and 1000 Indian allies (1540). In fact the cities were five or six Zuñi pueblos.

CICERO, Marcus Tullius (106–43 BC), Roman orator, statesman and philosopher. As consul (63 BC) he championed POMPEY

and saved Rome from civil war by crushing the CATILINE conspiracy. His refusal to submit to the First Triumvirate ruined his political career in 58 BC. Cicero's tacit approval of Caesar's murder and his defense of the Republic in his *First and Second Philippics* led Mark ANTONY to have him killed.

CID, El ("the Lord"), title given to Rodrigo Días de Vivar (c1043–1099), a Castilian Spanish national hero. He led the forces of Sancho II of Castile and Alfonso VI of León. Banished by Alfonso in 1081, he fought for the Moorish king of Saragossa and captured Valencia (1094), which he ruled until his death. His romanticized exploits appear in much literature, notably in *The Song of the Cid* (c1140) and CORNEILLE's *Le Cid* (1637).

CIMABUE, Giovanni (d1302?), Italian fresco painter of the 13th-century Florentine school. His work links Italian Byzantine and early Renaissance art. He possibly taught GIOTTO. He supervised the construction of mosaics in Pisa cathedral, whose *St. John* is said to be his.

CIMAROSA, Domenico (1749–1801), prolific Italian composer famous for his comic operas, notably *Il Matrimonio Segreto* ("The Secret Marriage") of 1792. He was court composer to Catherine the Great of Russia, 1787–91.

CINCHONA or **CHINCHONA,** genus of tropical evergreen trees and shrubs that are native to the Amazonian slopes of the Andes from Colombia to Bolivia. The main importance of these trees lies in the bark, which yields medicinal ALKALOIDS, notably QUININE, used as a cure for malaria. Cinchona seeds from Bolivia formed the basis of major plantations established in Java by the Dutch. Java is the chief source of cinchona bark today.

CINCINNATUS, Lucius Quinctius (c519–439? BC), early Roman hero renowned for selfless patriotism. He was twice appointed dictator (458 and 439 BC) to save Rome from disaster. Both times he reputedly defeated Rome's enemies and then resigned, rejected all rewards and returned to his farm.

CINDERELLA, heroine of a famous fairy tale in which her fairy godmother helps her escape from drudgery at home. She attends the prince's ball, and he falls in love with her, eventually finding her by means of a glass slipper which she dropped, and which she alone can wear. The tale is known the world over, and probably originated in 9th-century China. The English version comes from Perrault's *Cendrillon* (1697), *pantoufle en vair* (sable slipper) being mistranslated as glass slipper (*pantoufle en verre*).

CINEMA. See MOTION PICTURES.

CINÉMA VÉRITÉ, style of documentary filmmaking, characterized by the use of hand-held sound cameras to record scenes and events, ideally with maximum spontaneity and objectivity and minimal staging and direction. The approach dates back to the work of Dziga Vertov, and the term (literally "cinema truth") is a translation of his *Kino-Pravda*, a series of newsreels made in the USSR in the 1920s. Modern cinéma-vérité techniques have been especially popular in France and the US, a pioneer film being Jean Rouch's and Edgar Morin's *Chronique d'un Été* (1961).

CINQUE PORTS, originally five but ultimately thirty-two towns along the S coast of England which from the 11th-17th centuries enjoyed certain privileges in return for providing the crown with ships and men. England had no royal navy at this time.

CIPHERS. See CODES AND CIPHERS.

CIRCASSIANS, a pastoral and fruit-growing mountain people living in the NW Caucasus E of the Black Sea. Today they number over 350,000: 80% live in the Soviet Union, the rest live in Turkey and are descended from Muslims who fled there when Russia annexed Circassia in 1829.

CIRCE, in Greek mythology, the enchantress who lived on the island of Aeaea. Daughter of Helios (the Sun) and Perseus, she transformed the companions of ODYSSEUS into swine, but Odysseus himself escaped her spell. Later legends say that she had three sons by Odysseus, including Telegonus, doomed to slay his father.

CIRCUIT, Electric, assemblage of electrical CONDUCTORS (usually wires) and components through which current from a power source such as a BATTERY or GENERATOR flows (see ELECTRICITY). Components may be connected one after another (in series) or side by side (in parallel). If current may flow between two points, their connection is a closed circuit; if not, an open circuit; and if RESISTANCE between them is virtually zero, a short circuit. Short circuits between the terminals of the power source are dangerous (see CIRCUIT BREAKER; FUSE). (See also ELECTRONICS; KIRCHHOFF'S LAWS.)

CIRCUIT BREAKER, device now often used in place of a FUSE to protect electrical equipment from damage when the current exceeds a desired value, as in short-circuiting. The circuit breaker opens the circuit automatically, usually by means of a coil that separates contacts when the current reaches a certain value (see ELECTROMAGNETISM). One advantage of the circuit breaker is that the contacts may be reset (by hand or automatically) whereas a fuse has to be replaced. Small circuit breakers are used in the home (as in many TELEVISION sets), larger ones in industry.

CIRCULATION OF THE BLOOD. See BLOOD CIRCULATION.

CIRCUS, in the modern sense, an entertainment involving equestrian, acrobatic, animal, trapeze and clown acts. The modern circus first appeared in London in 1768, when Philip Astley launched an equestrian show to which other acts were added. The first US circus was opened by an Englishman, J. W. Ricketts, in Philadelphia in 1793. Its imitators often formed traveling shows, performing under an enormous tent, the "Big Top." The most famous American circuses, later combined, were those of BARNUM and BAILEY and the RINGLING BROTHERS, which became "three-ring" circuses as they expanded and added additional staging areas for their numerous acts.

CIRRHOSIS, chronic disease of the LIVER, with disorganization of normal structure and replacement by fibrous scars and regenerating nodules. It is the end result of many liver diseases, all of which cause liver-cell death; most common are those associated with ALCOHOLISM and following some cases of hepatitis, while certain poisons and hereditary diseases are rare causes. All liver functions are impaired, but symptoms often do not occur until early liver failure develops with EDEMA, ascites, JAUNDICE, COMA, emaciation, or gastrointestinal-tract HEMORRHAGE; BLOOD clotting is often abnormal and PLASMA proteins are low. The liver damage is not reversible, but if recognized early in the alcoholic, abstention can minimize progression. Treatment consists of measures to protect the liver from excess protein, DIURETICS and the prevention and treatment of hemorrhage.

CISTERCIANS, or White Monks, Roman Catholic religious order founded at Cîteaux, France, in 1098 by St. Robert of Molesme and at its height in the 12th and 13th centuries. Cistercians eat and work in silence and abstain from meat, fish and eggs.

CITIZENSHIP, a legal relationship between an individual and the country of his nationality, usually acquired by birth or naturalization. The terms for acquiring citizenship vary in different countries, but usually depend on a person's place of birth and the nationalities of the parents. In the

US, anyone born on American soil is an American citizen, unless born of foreign parents having diplomatic status. If born outside the US, the child can acquire US citizenship through either parent, by birth if at least one parent maintains residence in the US, or by residing in the US for at least five years between ages 13 and 21 if only one parent is an American citizen. A person may become a naturalized citizen of the US by residing there for five years under permanent status. The citizen is given a passport, government protection and constitutional rights, and must pay taxes and be ready to serve in the armed forces.

CITIZENS' PARTY, US political party, founded in 1979. It favors public control of energy industries, an end to nuclear power, institution of price controls and a cut in defense spending. The environmentalist and author Barry Commoner, its 1980 presidential candidate, polled 234,279 votes, or 0.3% of the total.

CITROEN, André Gustave (1878–1935), French engineer and industrialist who earned the name "the French Henry Ford" for mass producing the Citroën automobile (from 1919).

CITY, any large center of population, often distinguished from a town or village by the diversity of economic and cultural activities within it; or a center officially designated as a city for purposes of local government. Cities first developed in the Middle East, notably in Mesopotamia. One of the earliest true cities was UR in Sumer, dating back to at least 3500 BC. Thereafter cities proliferated throughout the Middle East and in any parts of the world where civilization developed, either as religious or governmental centers, or as centers of trade, transportation, markets and manufacturing. Few early cities had more than 20,000 inhabitants and even Rome, the largest in the Empire, had no more than 800,000. Urban life decayed in Western Europe during the Dark Ages, but proliferated elsewhere. Around the 6th to 8th centuries AD Ch'ang-an, the T'ang capital in China, was the largest and most cosmopolitan city in the world; Teotihuacan in Mexioo had possibly 200,000 inhabitants, and somewhat later Chan-Chan in Peru had possibly 250,000. In Europe the RENAISSANCE was ushered in by the revival of the cities as centers of trade and culture, but the giant cities of today were strictly a product of the INDUSTRIAL REVOLUTION.

US Cities. As long as water was the most economical means for the transportation of heavy freight, American cities were built on major bodies of water or on navigable rivers.

America's first important cities (Boston, Newport, New York, Philadelphia, Charleston) were seaports. As the line of settlement advanced westward, new cities were built on the inland rivers (Pittsburgh, Cincinnati, Louisville, St. Louis) and on the Great Lakes (Cleveland, Detroit, Chicago). All of these cities provided markets where the farmers of the hinterlands exchanged their products for imported manufactures.

The harnessing of steam power in the 19th century brought about an industrial revolution in America that profoundly affected urban life. Steamboats brought new prosperity to river towns, while the railroad made possible the growth of cities remote from major waterways but close to the natural resources—coal, iron, oil—demanded by industry. In the past, manufacturing had been limited to small shops or to scattered mills operated by water power. The steam engine made factories independent of mill streams. Now they concentrated in cities where transportation facilities and labor were available.

During the 19th century, American cities expanded in number and in size. Of the 50 largest cities in the US today, only 7 were incorporated before 1816; 39 were incorporated between 1816 and 1876. Most of these were in the northeastern and north central regions; until after the Civil War the south preserved its predominantly agricultural economy. In the northern cities, industrial and residential rings grew up around old commercial centers. Because workers had to live within walking distance of their jobs, developers erected three- and four-story tenements or tightly-packed rows of houses close to the factories. Only the wealthy could afford to live in outlying towns and commute to their offices or factories by railroad.

The invention of the passenger elevator in the 1850s encouraged even denser concentrations of people by permitting the vertical stacking of offices, factories, and apartments. In 1860, only 9 cities—all of them seaports—had populations of 100,000 or more; by the end of the century, there were 50 cities of that size.

The transformation of the US from a rural to an urban country was accomplished by massive migrations of population from rural areas to the cities. On each new rural generation the cities acted like magnets, offering economic opportunities and cultural amenities far more appealing than the hardship and isolation of farm life or the narrow constraints of life in small towns. Another source of urban growth was successive waves of foreign immigrants—

English, Irish, Germans, Italians, Poles, Greeks, Russians. Often poor and unskilled, the immigrants settled mostly in the large cities of the northeast and midwest where, like native migrants, they occupied the least desirable housing and filled the least desirable jobs.

The concentration of dense urban masses induced by steam power began to be reversed with the coming of electricity and then the internal-combustion engine. The electric trolley, which first appeared in the 1880s, provided relatively fast transportation at prices working people could afford. As electric street railways radiated from crowded downtowns, new housing developments sprang up along them. Those city dwellers who could afford to do so abandoned densely packed old neighborhoods for one- and two-family houses in the new suburbs, which were quickly annexed to the city.

What the electric trolley began, the automobile was to complete. Auto registrations grew from 2.5 million in 1915 to 26 million in 1930. Mass-produced automobiles, priced within reach of the middle class and of many blue-collar workers, speeded the exodus from old neighborhoods to the city's periphery and even to suburbs altogether outside the city's jurisdiction.

Beginning in the 1920s, while the movement of population into the cities continued and even accelerated, the distribution of population within cities began to change. Increasingly, people moved out of the aging inner cities to the urban fringes and beyond. This double population movement—into urban areas but away from urban cores—reached flood proportions after World War II. Low-cost mortgages guaranteed by the federal government, income-tax benefits for home buyers, the phenomenal multiplication of automobiles, and the construction in the 1950s and 1960s of the interstate highway system—all encouraged vast expansion of suburbs.

Industry soon followed population. Manufacturers left crowded quarters in the old industrial sections of the cities for the cheaper land and lower taxes of suburban industrial parks. Service industries followed their customers and work force into the burgeoning suburbs. The number of jobs in the suburbs grew faster than the number in the cities; indeed, in recent decades, many large cities have experienced net losses of jobs to their suburbs. Once merely residential communities dependent on a nearby city, suburbs have developed into economically diversified towns that compete with the dominant metropolis.

In 1920, the US Census found for the first time that more than half of the US population was urban—that is, lived in places with populations of 2,500 or more. In the first census (1790), only 5% of the total population of 4 million was urban. Increasingly, the Census Bureau's definition of an urban place came to have little relevance to the reality of US urban civilization. Since 1950, the unit of analysis used by the Census Bureau has been the metropolitan area, consisting of a large population nucleus together with adjacent communities that have a high degree of social and economic integration with that nucleus. In 1985, 332 metropolitan areas, occupying 16.2% of the US land area, contained 76.5% of the US population.

CITY PLANNING, planning for the growth of a city or town to take into consideration the physical, social and economic aspects of its environment. Most Roman cities, and many earlier ones in the ancient world, were built on a gridiron pattern, with the public buildings centrally and strategically placed. The cities of the Middle Ages, however, were rarely planned unless powerful monied interests made this possible. The Renaissance, especially in Italy, saw a revival of grandiose city planning, usually intended to glorify a ruler or to strengthen his military position. The Industrial Revolution and the enormous population movements it generated caused rapid piecemeal development, and the situation had become critical before any attempt was made to deal with it.

In the US various civic reform movements were already active before the Civil War, leading to legislation to enforce slum clearance and provide better educational and recreational facilities, while designers such as Frederick L. OLMSTED and Daniel BURNHAM (planner of Chicago's Columbian Exposition of 1893) stimulated their fellows to more imaginative efforts. Unfortunately the teams responsible for such work tended to impose their own class and moral values on other social classes. More recently efforts have been made to avoid such mistakes; large federal subsidies have been made available, notably for low-cost housing and city center renewal projects, and planning has begun to take human as well as physical factors into account. Local government has become increasingly professional in planning ahead, and over 30 US universities now offer courses in city planning.

CITY-STATES, politically independent communities controlling the lives of their own citizens and dominating the surrounding countryside. They flourished in three major areas of Western culture: among the ancient civilizations of the Middle East, notably in Sumeria (ancient Babylonia) and Phoenicia; in the classical period of Greece (emerging about 700 BC); and in Europe from the 11th to the 16th centuries, notably in Italy and Germany.

CIVETS, weasel-like carnivorous mammals of the family Viverridae, found in Africa and S Asia. The African civet, *Civettictis civetta,* is reared for the musky-smelling oily substance used as a base for perfumes that is produced by glands under the tail.

CIVIL DISOBEDIENCE, a form of political action involving intentional violation of the law in order to draw attention to alleged injustices. The aim is to enlist public sympathy, and the idea probably dates back to the essay *On Civil Disobedience* by the 19th-century American writer Henry David THOREAU. It was successfully used by the Indian leader GANDHI to help gain independence for India, and has been employed by movements as diverse as the Suffragettes and the Vietnam-War protesters, not always accompanied by Gandhi's technique of "passive resistance." In the US the civil rights movement has made the most widespread and striking use of civil disobedience.

CIVIL LAW, law dealing with private rights of individual citizens in contrast to branches of law, such as CRIMINAL LAW, which regulate relationships between individuals and the state. Thus civil law includes mortgages, marriage, inheritance, citizenship and property (COMMERCIAL LAW is often separate). The term civil law is also used for codified legal systems derived from Roman Law, not from the COMMON LAW.

The Romans distinguished civil law (*jus civile*) from international or public law (*jus gentium*). Codified by JUSTINIAN but replaced by customary laws in the Dark Ages, Roman law was rediscovered in the 12th century. It influenced France's CODE NAPOLÉON (1804), soon copied by other West European nations. Today, Western countries comprise civil law nations (most of Europe and Latin America) and common law countries (notably Great Britain, Canada and the US). In civil law countries, courts base judgments on codified principles rather than on precedents, and they do not feature trial by jury or the law of evidence.

CIVIL LIBERTIES, in the US, freedoms guaranteed by the 1st and 4th amendments to the US CONSTITUTION. Freedom of religion, speech, press, and assembly, and security of person, house, papers, and effects are not rights granted by these amendments. The amendments assume that Americans already possess them as NATURAL RIGHTS. The 1st and 4th amendments simply prohibit the government from infringing them.

Civil liberties are distinguished from two other classes of rights protected by the BILL OF RIGHTS and later amendments to the Constitution. CIVIL RIGHTS — particularly those embodied in the 13th, 14th, 15th, and 19th amendments — are concerned with equality of citizenship. Procedural rights — such as those contained in the 5th, 6th, and 14th amendments — provide such protections as fair trial and DUE PROCESS OF LAW. (See also AMERICAN CIVIL LIBERTIES UNION.)

CIVIL RIGHTS, in the US, rights granted by the US CONSTITUTION to ensure equality of citizenship of all Americans. The framers of the Constitution envisioned a republic of political equals, free of the hereditary privileges and disabilities of the Old World. Nevertheless, they excluded Indians and Negro slaves from citizenship and severely restricted the citizenship of women. The realization of the ideal of civil equality has been a principal theme of US history.

Blacks. Slavery was abolished in the US by the 13th Amendment. The 14th and 15th amendments, and a series of civil rights acts, sought to secure the rights of citizenship to the former slaves. Not until the 20th century, however, did Congress and the US Supreme Court not only effectively assure the voting rights of blacks but extend the concept of equal citizenship to the social and economic realms, outlawing segregation in schools and housing and discrimination in employment, public accommodations, and the criminal justice system. (See AFFIRMATIVE ACTION; BROWN V. BOARD OF EDUCATION OF TOPEKA.)

Women. The special but inferior status assigned women under English common law was largely preserved in the US until the 20th century. The 19th Amendment to the Constitution gave women the vote nationwide, and women have used the antidiscrimination laws originally enacted on behalf of blacks to achieve equal citizenship as currently understood despite the failure of the EQUAL RIGHTS AMENDMENT to win ratification in the early 1980s. (See WOMEN'S MOVEMENT.)

In general. The civil rights of all citizens have been enhanced by legislation and court decisions affecting elections, such as the judicial promulgation of the one-man-one-vote principle and regulation of CAMPAIGN FINANCING to minimize the disproportionate influence of wealth on elections. (See also CIVIL LIBERTIES.)

CIVIL RIGHTS COMMISSION, US government agency established by the Civil Rights Act of 1957 to oversee enforcement of federal civil rights laws. The eight commissioners and staff make findings of fact, which they submit to the president and Congress; they have no enforcement authority.

CIVIL SERVICE, the permanent body of civilian employees of a government, usually excluding elected officials, judges and military personnel. Appointment and promotion are generally based on merit, to secure efficiency and freedom from political influence. Civil services date from ancient China and Rome, and a civil service bureaucracy has become increasingly important as the functions of national governments have increased in scope and complexity.

In the US the civil service's integrity and continuity suffered from the SPOILS SYSTEM (gifts of government jobs as political rewards), firmly established from 1828 under President Andrew Jackson. Attempts to establish a merit system failed until the PENDLETON ACT (1883) set up the Civil Service Commission to administer a merit system of federal employment. The Hatch Acts of 1939 and 1940 forbade federal employees to play any active part in politics beyond voting. Since the 1880s many states, cities and countries have set up civil service systems for public employees.

CIVIL WAR, American (1861–1865), conflict between 11 Southern states, known as the CONFEDERATE STATES OF AMERICA, and the US Federal government. Because the 11 states had attempted to secede from the Union, the conflict was officially called the "War of Rebellion" in the North. Since it was a sectional struggle, it is also known, particularly in the South, as the "War between the States."

Significance. The Civil War was one of the most crucial events in American history. It was fought for total aims: restoration of the Union or independence for the South. The conflict destroyed slavery and the agrarian society of the South which depended on it, stimulated northern industry and ensured the supremacy of the Federal government over the states. Military historians often see the struggle as the first modern, or "total" war. The American Civil War was probably the greatest sustained combat in history before WWI.

Origins. The immediate cause of the war was the North's refusal to recognize the right of states to secede from the Union. The war's underlying cause lay in the socio-economic division between North and South. The economy of the South, based on the plantation system of agriculture, depended on slave labor, which became increasingly distasteful to the more industrialized non-slave-owning North. Political differences between the two sides came to a head over the question of westward expansion—whether slavery should be permitted in the new states and territories or remain confined to the South. Attempts to settle this question produced the MISSOURI COMPROMISE (1820) and the COMPROMISE OF 1850 which was nullified by the KANSAS-NEBRASKA ACT (1854). The DRED SCOTT DECISION (1857) and Lincoln's election as president (1860) inflamed the situation. Fearing that a Republican president would enforce abolition, S.C. seceded from the Union on Dec. 20, 1860 and was soon followed by six other states. The CONFEDERATE STATES elected Jefferson Davis provisional president, and after Lincoln ordered supplies to Federal-held Fort Sumter, in Charleston (S.C.) Harbor, Confederate guns opened fire on the fort on April 12. The fort surrendered, and four more states (N.C., Va., Ark. and Tenn.) joined the Confederacy. So began what Senator James M. Mason of Va. aptly called "a war of sentiment and opinion by one form of society against another form of society."

The war. The determination of both sides led to over 2,400 named battles. The war involved 1,600,000 Federal troops and nearly 1,000,000 Confederates. There were over 600,000 dead, Union armies suffering more than 600,000 casualties, the Confederates nearly half as many. The North outnumbered the South by 22,000,000 to 9,000,000 and was constantly reinforced by immigration from Europe. The North also had superior manufacturing, transportation and other facilities. The South had a poor railroad system, few good harbors and little industry. The North set out to crush the South by naval blockade and offensive war—waged both in the East and the West.

Congress gave Lincoln authority to recruit 500,000 men. When volunteers failed to come forward in sufficient numbers, the first national conscription act in American history was passed in March 1863. The South, too, enacted conscription. As the world's major cotton exporter, the South expected financial and diplomatic support from abroad, and what it lacked in numbers and equipment it largely made up for in the quality of its soldiers and their leaders.

The campaigns. The war, which opened in the East with the Federal disaster at BULL RUN, was won by the superior numbers and hard fighting of the Federals against the brilliant tactics of the South, and by the crippling naval blockade (see MONITOR AND MERRIMACK). Britain and France stayed neutral (though British aid to the South provoked the TRENT AFFAIR and ALABAMA CLAIMS). The war really began with the PENINSULA CAMPAIGN (1862) of G. B. MCCLELLAN which bogged down close to Richmond. The great southern commander, Robert E. LEE, harassed McClellan in the SEVEN DAYS' BATTLES, then blunted a Federal thrust, again at BULL RUN; but his own northward drive was stopped at ANTIETAM. (The victory gave LINCOLN the occasion to issue the preliminary EMANCIPATION PROCLAMATION.) Undaunted, Lee defeated Federal troops at Fredericksburg and CHANCELLORSVILLE (where he lost his brilliant commander, "Stonewall" JACKSON) and moved north again. In the war's climactic battle, Lee was turned back at GETTYSBURG, Pa. (July 1863). Meanwhile in the West Ulysses S. GRANT moved down into W. Tenn. to win the battle of SHILOH (1862), and W. S. ROSECRANS pushed Braxton BRAGG through Tenn. E. into Ga. at Murfreesboro and CHICKAMAUGA. New Orleans fell to David FARRAGUT. Grant's objective was VICKSBURG on the Mississippi R. When it fell, a day after Gettysburg, Grant became Supreme Commander and began relentlessly pounding at Lee in the East. From the West W. T. SHERMAN moved on Atlanta, marched to the sea, laying waste the countryside, then turned to join Grant. Caught in a pincers, Lee surrendered at APPOMATTOX COURT HOUSE, April 9, 1865.

The South was devasted, its economy in ruins, but the North emerged stronger than before. Slavery was abolished, but the balance of power between the states and the Federal government remained a problem. (See also CIVIL RIGHTS AND LIBERTIES; RECONSTRUCTION.)

CIVIL WAR, English (1642–51), the conflict between Royalists and Parliamentarians that led to the defeat and execution of CHARLES I, and the establishment of the Commonwealth under Oliver CROMWELL. It is also called the Puritan Revolution, because the king's opponents were mainly Puritan, and his supporters chiefly Episcopalian and Catholic. But the constitutional issue at stake was whether England should be effectively ruled by parliament or by a monarch claiming supreme authority by virtue of the divine right of kings. War between parliament's Roundheads and Charles' Cavaliers began after Charles opposed the LONG PARLIAMENT's efforts to curb his powers. No clear-cut social or geographical boundaries divided the forces.

In the first major battle, Charles' army held back Parliamentarian troops under Robert Devereux, Earl of Essex, at Edgehill near Warwick (1642). This enabled Charles to establish headquarters at Oxford. But Prince RUPERT lost to Cromwell's "Ironsides" at Marston Moor (1644). On June 14, 1645, Fairfax and Cromwell destroyed the Royalist army at Naseby, and by autumn 1646 parliament held most of England. Fighting flared up again after Charles' capture (1646), but Cromwell routed Scottish invaders at Preston. After Charles' execution (1649) fighting recurred. Cromwell brutally subdued Ireland (1649–50), crushed Scottish troops at Dunbar (1650) and defeated CHARLES II's Scottish forces at Worcester (1651). This was the last battle of the war.

CLAIBORNE, William (c1587–1677?), English-born fur trader from Virginia, who seized and briefly held Maryland (1644–46). His insurrection ousted the Catholic governor, Leonard Calvert, and in the 1650s he was one of four commissioners of England's Puritan government governing the colony.

CLAIR, René (René Chomette; 1898–1981), French film director, producer and writer, especially of screen comedies. Born in Paris, he worked on both silent and "talkie" films, including *Sous les toits de Paris* (1930).

CLAM, the general name given to many two-shelled BIVALVE mollusks. Giant clams on coral reefs may reach a diameter of 1.2m (4ft) and weigh 0.25 ton.

CLAPHAM SECT, evangelical Christian group, active 1790–1830, responsible for abolishing slavery and pioneering other social reforms. Founded in Clapham, London, by the banker H. Thornton, and led by William WILBERFORCE, the group included many members of parliament.

CLARE, Saint (or Clara; 1194–1253), Italian founder of the POOR CLARES. She was born at Assisi, and was influenced by St. FRANCIS OF ASSISI. Canonized 1255.

CLARENDON, Edward Hyde, 1st Earl of (1609–1674), English statesman and historian, author of the *History of the Rebellion*, a personal account of the English Civil War. As lord chancellor 1660–67, he was a chief adviser and minister of Charles II, but lost favor and fled to France.

CLARENDON CODE, penal laws against nonconformists, enacted in England 1661–65 during the RESTORATION to strengthen the Anglican Church. The code was named for Charles II's lord chancellor, the 1st Earl of CLARENDON (who opposed much of it).

CLARINET, woodwind instrument comprising a tube (usually wooden) with a flared bell and tapered mouthpiece with a single reed. Different tones are produced by the fingers opening and closing holes (some covered by keys) in the tube. Clarinets feature in dance bands, military bands, woodwind groups, symphony orchestras and as solo instruments. The clarinet was invented in Germany by Johann Christoph Denner early in the 18th century.

CLARK, George Rogers (1752–1818), US frontiersman and Revolutionary War officer who led the campaign against the British in the Northwest Territory. With about 175 volunteers, he succeeded in capturing key British forts north of the Ohio R, principally Kaskaskia (1778) and Vincennes (1779).

CLARK, James Beauchamp (1850–1921), US Congressman, Democratic Party leader and speaker of the House of Representatives. Born in Ky. but representing Mo. (1893–95, 1897–1921), "Champ" Clark helped to oust dictatorial House Speaker J. G. CANNON, whom he succeeded (1911–19).

CLARK, John Bates (1847–1938), US economist, professor at Columbia U 1895–1923 and author of the influential *Distribution of Wealth* (1899).

CLARK, Kenneth Bancroft (1914–   ), US psychologist whose 1950 report on school segregation was cited in the Supreme Court's 1954 ruling against segregation. A professor at CCNY 1942–1975, he was active in many civil rights and educational organizations and was the first black member of the New York State Board of Regents (1966–86).

CLARK, Kenneth MacKenzie, Baron Clark of Saltwood (1903–1983), British art critic, director of the National Gallery 1934–45 and chairman of the Arts Council 1953–60. He held many other important posts, but became most widely known through his television series *Civilisation*, first broadcast in Britain in 1969 and in the US in the late 1970s.

CLARK, Mark Wayne (1896–1984), US general, commander of Allied ground forces in Italy in WWII and commander of UN operations in the Korean War (1952–53). He led the invasion of Italy in 1943.

CLARK, Tom Campbell (1899–1977), US lawyer from Dallas, Tex., who was attorney general 1945–49 and an associate justice of the US Supreme Court (1949–67).

CLARK, William (1770–1838), US explorer, a leader of the LEWIS AND CLARK EXPEDITION 1804–06, and brother of George Rogers CLARK. Previously a frontier soldier (1791–96), he was subsequently superintendant of Indian affairs and governor of Missouri Territory (1813–21).

CLARK, William Andrews (1839–1925), US copper magnate, rival of Marcus DALY for control of copper deposits and political power in Montana. He was a US senator 1901–07.

CLARKE, Arthur Charles (1917–   ), British science fiction and science writer, best known as the author of the film *2001: A Space Odyssey* (1968) and for his detailed design for communications satellites in 1945. His best-known novel is *Childhood's End* (1953).

CLARKE, John (1609–1676), English Baptist clergyman, one of the founders of Rhode Island (1638) and a co-founder of Newport. With Roger WILLIAMS he helped to keep Rhode Island's government basically democratic and liberal, securing its royal charter in 1663.

CLASS ACTION SUIT, a lawsuit brought by one or more members of a large group on behalf of all members who share a common interest in the issues of law and fact, and have suffered a similar wrong for which they seek relief from the court. If the trial court agrees to hear the suit, all members of the group must be informed and be given the opportunity, if they so desire, to exclude themselves from the group. If a member does not exclude himself, he must accept the judgment of the court. One or more stockholders, for instance, may bring a class action suit on behalf of other stockholders who object to the policies of the corporation. Class action suits have been successfully brought against companies which, over a period of years, systematically discriminated against women or minorities in their pay and promotion policies.

CLASSICAL ORDERS, in architecture, the names given to various styles of COLUMN and adjoining parts, notably the entablature. They are: **Doric** (the oldest, without base, used in the PARTHENON), **Ionic** (developed in Asia Minor around the 6th century BC, then taken to Greece), **Corinthian** (the most ornate, appearing in Greece in the 4th century BC, but fully developed by the Romans and revived in the RENAISSANCE), **Tuscan** (the simplest, supposedly derived from the Etruscans) and **Composite** (a late-Roman blend of Ionic and Corinthian). As outlined by VITRUVIUS

(1st century BC) and described by Sebastiano Serlio (16th century AD), the classical orders deeply influenced architectural design in and after the Renaissance.

CLASSICISM, art forms and cultural periods characterized by the conscious emulation of classical antiquity, particularly the art and literature of ancient Greece and Rome. Emphasizing order, clarity, restraint and harmony of form, classicism was most notably exemplified by the Renaissance, the "rebirth" of classical civilization. After the Mannerist and Baroque periods, classicism reappeared in the 18th–19th-century movement known as NEOCLASSICISM. Influenced by Johann WINCKELMANN, principal exponents of the movement included Antonio CANOVA, J. L. DAVID and Robert ADAM.

CLASSIFICATION OF LIVING THINGS. See TAXONOMY.

CLAUDEL, Paul (1868–1955), French Roman Catholic dramatist, poet and diplomat. Influenced by RIMBAUD and intensely religious, he drew inspiration for his sensuous, lyrical verse from nature and Oriental thought.

CLAUDE LORRAIN (real name, Claude Gelée or Gellée; 1600–1682), a founder of French romantic landscape painting, lived and worked mostly in Rome. His canvases usually show a biblical or classical scene dominated by an idyllically lit landscape. His later works are almost visionary in their intensity and inspired such painters as TURNER.

CLAUDIUS, name of two Roman emperors. **Claudius I** (Tiberius Claudius Nero Germanicus; 10 BC–54 AD) reigned 41–54 AD. A sickly nephew of TIBERIUS, he was a scholar and writer. He invaded Britain (43 AD), annexed Mauretania, Lycia and Thrace (41–46 AD), improved Rome's legal system and encouraged colonization. He was poisoned by his second wife, Agrippina. **Claudius II, Gothicus** (Marcus Aurelius Claudius; 214–270 AD) reigned 268–70. An army officer, he succeeded Gallienus.

CLAUSEWITZ, Karl von (1780–1831), Prussian general, strategist and military historian, known mainly as the author of *On War* (1833), which revolutionized military thinking after his death. He defined war as an extension of diplomacy and urged the destruction of enemy forces, morale and resources. He has thus been called the prophet of total war (although he favored defensive fighting).

CLAUSIUS, Rudolf Julius Emanuel (1822–1888), German theoretical physicist who first stated the second law of THERMODYNAMICS (1850) and proposed the term ENTROPY (1865). He also contributed to KINETIC THEORY and the theory of ELECTROLYSIS.

CLAVICHORD, a stringed keyboard instrument used primarily between the 15th and 18th centuries. Its sound is produced by brass blades (tangents) hitting against pairs of strings. Although small-toned, it is especially sensitive and responsive. It was the usual household musical instrument in 16th–18th-century Germany.

CLAY, Cassius. See ALI, MUHAMMAD.

CLAY, Cassius Marcellus (1810–1903), US abolitionist, politician and statesman, founder of the antislavery journal *True American*, in Lexington, Ky., 1845. He was a founder of the Republican Party, 1854, and US ambassador to Russia (1861–62 and 1863–69).

CLAY, Henry (1777–1852), US statesman, famous for his attempts to reconcile North and South in the pre-Civil War period. Born near Richmond, Va., Clay served as both US representative and senator from Ky. 1806–1852, and secretary of state 1825–29. He helped produce the MISSOURI COMPROMISE on slavery (1820). In 1844 he was Whig presidential candidate but lost the election by alienating New York abolitionists on the issue of the annexation of Tex. as a slave state. His career culminated in the COMPROMISE of 1850, a complex package of "slave" and "free" provisions. Known as "the great compromiser," Clay lost support as the nation became more bitterly divided. He is also remembered as one of the WAR HAWKS of 1812 and for his controversial American System, a series of radical economic proposals.

CLAY, Lucius Dubignon (1897–1978), US general assigned to govern the American zone of West Germany 1947–49. He supervised the BERLIN AIRLIFT.

CLAY, an extremely important type of earth. Most clays consist of very small particles of hydrated aluminum silicates (kaolinites), although other minerals are often present. They are usually produced by the weathering of rocks. Clay is found in layers under the earth's crust and often at river mouths. When wet, clay is easily malleable and retains its shape when dried. If it is fired (baked) in a high-temperature oven or kiln it becomes extremely hard and, if first coated with a glaze, nonporous. For centuries clay has served man in the form of water jugs, pots, bricks and many other sorts of earthenware and it still has a multitude of practical uses. Electrical insulators, sewage pipes, cement, kitchen tiles, chinaware, bricks and paper manufacture all require clay. It is often used as an impermeable core of dams. Clay, moreover, is essential to the soil if crops are to be grown. It holds moisture and prevents organic material from being washed away.

Pure clay—kaolin or china clay—is white and finds extensive application in the manufacture of porcelain materials.

CLAYTON, John Middleton (1796–1856), US secretary of state (1849–50) who negotiated with British minister Sir Henry Bulwer the CLAYTON-BULWER TREATY.

CLAYTON ANTITRUST ACT, a law passed by Congress in 1914 to supplement the SHERMAN ANTITRUST ACT of 1890. The Clayton act specified illegal monopolistic practices, among them certain forms of interlocking directorates and holding companies. It also legalized peaceful strikes, picketing and boycotting. In 1921, however, the Supreme Court interpreted the act as doing no more than legalize labor unions and not their practices. (See MONOPOLY.)

CLAYTON-BULWER TREATY, an Anglo-American agreement of 1850 concerning a proposed canal across the Isthmus of Panama. Both sides agreed to control, finance and maintain the canal jointly, and "not to occupy, or fortify, or colonize . . . any part of Central America." But differing interpretations of the treaty produced friction and, after the second Hay-Pauncefote Treaty (1901), the US built the PANAMA CANAL alone.

CLEAN AIR ACT, first passed in 1963 and updated in subsequent years, empowered the federal government to give grants, conduct studies, and create and enforce regulations designed to combat air pollution. In particular, under this act, standards were set for limiting pollutants in auto emissions and restricting industrial air pollution in regions in which the atmosphere had become foul.

CLEAVAGE, physical property of a MINERAL, the tendency to split along certain preferred planes parallel to an actual or possible CRYSTAL face: e.g., galena, whose crystals are cubic, cleaves along three mutually perpendicular planes (parallel to 100, 010, 001). Such cleavage is useful in identifying minerals. Rock cleavage generally takes place along certain planes defined by the preferred orientation of minerals, or may represent numerous closely spaced cracks (joints) in the rock. Rock cleavage is usually inclined to the bedding of sedimentary rocks.

CLEFT PALATE, a common developmental deformity of the palate in which the two halves do not meet in the midline; it is often associated with HARELIP. It can be familial or follow disease in early PREGNANCY, but may appear spontaneously. It causes a characteristic nasal quality in the cry and voice. Plastic SURGERY can close the defect and allow more normal development of the voice and TEETH.

CLEISTHENES, two ancient Greek statesmen. **Cleisthenes of Sicyon,** tyrant of the house of Orthagoras, ruled c600–570 BC. He vigorously opposed and ridiculed the Argive Dorian ascendancy. During his rule DELPHI became a center of the Delphic Amphictyony, an association of neighboring states. His grandson **Cleisthenes of Athens** (late 6th century BC) is generally held to be the founder of Athenian democracy. He built upon SOLON'S reforms and broadened the base of government, which nevertheless may be seen as somewhat aristocratic when compared with that of his grandson PERICLES.

CLEMENCEAU, Georges (1841–1929), French statesman and journalist, a founder of the Third Republic and twice French premier, 1906–09 and 1917–20. Clemenceau was a committed republican. He worked with Léon Gambetta (1870) for the overthrow of the Second Empire and supported ZOLA in the DREYFUS AFFAIR. During his second premiership he made a major contribution to the Allied victory in WWI and to the drafting of the Treaty of VERSAILLES.

CLEMENS, Samuel Langhorne. See TWAIN, MARK.

CLEMENT, name of 14 popes. **Saint Clement I** (d.101?) became pope around 92. He is noted for a letter to the church at Corinth reflecting his sense of his authority as bishop of Rome. He died a martyr. **Clement V** (c1260–1314), pope from 1305, was a Frenchman. Crowned at Lyons, he settled at Avignon, beginning the BABYLONIAN CAPTIVITY of the papacy (1309–77), when it was subject to the influence of the kings of France. **Clement VII** (1478–1534), elected 1523, was a younger brother of Lorenzo de' MEDICI and a cousin of Pope LEO X. Because of his alliance with FRANCIS I of France against Holy Roman Emperor CHARLES V, Rome was sacked by imperial troops in 1527. He refused to invalidate the marriage of HENRY VIII of England to CATHERINE OF ARAGON, thereby causing the breach between England and Rome. Although a reformer himself, he did not appreciate the seriousness of the rise of LUTHERANISM in Germany. He was a patron of RAPHAEL and

MICHELANGELO.

CLEMENTE, Roberto (1934–1972), Puerto Rican-born US baseball player. A star outfielder for the Pittsburgh Pirates (1954–72), he amassed 3,000 hits, compiled a .317 lifetime batting average and was a five-time National League batting champion. He was elected to the Baseball Hall of Fame in 1973, soon after his death in an airplane crash.

CLEMENTI, Muzio (1752–1832), Italian composer and pianist, known as "the father of the piano." He enjoyed a successful concert career throughout Europe. The Irish virtuoso John Field was among his pupils. In 1799, in London, he became a partner in one of the first firms ever to manufacture pianos.

CLEMENT OF ALEXANDRIA (c150–c215 AD), theologian of the early Christian Church. His most important work is the trilogy *Exhortation to the Greeks*, the *Tutor* and *Miscellanies*. Born in Athens, Clement spent most of his life as a teacher in Alexandria.

CLEOPATRA, name of several queens of the Ptolemaic dynasty, the most famous being the Egyptian Queen Cleopatra VII (69–30 BC) who, as mistress of Julius CAESAR and later wife to Mark ANTONY, had a profound influence on Roman politics. Her marriage to Mark Antony contributed to Egypt's defeat by Rome, which in turn led to the couple's tragic suicide. A celebrated *femme fatale*, she is the subject of dramatic works by Shakespeare and G. B. Shaw.

CLEOPATRA'S NEEDLES, two large stone obelisks erected by Thutmose III at Heliopolis in Egypt, c1500 BC. One now stands on the Thames Embankment in London; the other is in Central Park, New York City.

CLEVELAND, (Stephen) Grover (1837–1908), twice Democratic president of the US, remembered for his unswerving honesty in government. Grover Cleveland was born in Caldwell, N.J. In 1855 he moved to Buffalo and entered the legal profession. In 1881 he was elected mayor of Buffalo, and little more than a year later was catapulted into the job of governor of N.Y. state. There his opposition to graft and opportunism earned him a countrywide following and, in 1884, despite the efforts of TAMMANY HALL, the Democratic presidential nomination.

First Term (1885–89). Cleveland's adherence to principle often cost him political support. He implemented the Pendleton Civil Service Act (1883), cutting by almost 12,000 the number of posts previously controlled by political patronage, and this cost him much of his own party's backing. Cleveland also angered Western timber companies, cattle ranchers and railroaders by exposing illicit land deals. And by trying to reduce tariffs, he antagonized Eastern bankers and industrialists. After losing the presidential election of 1888, Cleveland was renominated by the Democratic Party, once more in spite of Tammany Hall, in 1892.

Second Term (1893–97). Cleveland took office just as the US was beginning to experience severe economic depression. He saw the Sherman Silver Purchase Act (1890) as a major factor in causing the depression and forced its repeal in 1893, but this measure had little impact. Cleveland then attempted to replenish the treasury by buying gold from private financiers. Again, this proved to be no remedy. The situation deteriorated for Cleveland with the outbreak of labor troubles. He lost support by turning away Jacob COXEY and his "army" of unemployed citizens, and by using troops to break the PULLMAN STRIKE (1894). In 1896, with the president's popularity at its lowest ebb, FREE SILVER supporters gained control of the Democratic Party, nominating William Jennings Bryan for the presidency. Cleveland retired to Princeton, where he died.

CLIFF DWELLERS, prehistoric Indians who built multi-roomed houses, sheltered beneath overhanging cliffs, in the American Southwest. Most of the dwellings date from about 1000 AD. The Cliff Dwellers were a peaceful agricultural community whose settlements, built high above the canyon floors, were inaccessible to roving tribes. When the Spanish arrived in the Southwest in the 16th century, they found the settlements abandoned. The Cliff Dwellers are considered to be members of the PUEBLO culture. Cliff Dwellers ruins are found in Mesa Verde National Park, Col., and in national monuments in Ariz., N.M. and Ut.

CLIMATE, the sum of the weather conditions prevalent in an area over a period of time. Weather conditions include temperature, rainfall, sunshine, wind, humidity and cloudiness. Climates may be classified into groups. The system most used today is that of Vladimir Köppen, with five categories (A, B, C, D, E), broadly defined as follows:

A Equatorial and tropical rainy climates;

B Arid climates;

C Warmer forested (temperate) climates;

D Colder forested (temperate) climates; and

E   Treeless polar climates.

These categories correspond to a great extent to zoning by LATITUDE; this is because the closer to the EQUATOR an area is, the more direct the sunlight it receives and the less the amount of ATMOSPHERE through which that sunlight must pass. Other factors are the rotation of the earth on its axis (diurnal differences) and the revolution of the earth about the sun (seasonal differences).

Paleoclimatology, the study of climates of the past, has shown that there have been considerable long-term climatic changes in many areas: this is seen as strong evidence for CONTINENTAL DRIFT (see also PLATE TECTONICS). Other theories include variation in the solar radiation (see SUN) and change in the EARTH's axial tilt. Man's influence has caused localized, short-term climatic changes. (See CLOUDS; METEOROLOGY; TROPIC; WIND.)

CLINTON, De Witt (1769–1828), US politician who promoted the building of the ERIE CANAL and the Champlain–Hudson Canal. As mayor of New York for most of 1803–15 and N.Y. governor, 1817–23 and 1825–28, he set up important civic and political reforms and social relief for the Roman Catholics, slaves and the poor. He had Federalist and Republican support for his presidential candidacy in 1812, but lost to James Madison.

CLINTON, George (1739–1812), US vice president, statesman and revolutionary soldier, often called the "father of New York state." He built up N.Y.'s economy during seven terms as governor (1777–95; 1801–04). He was a leading opponent of the Federal Constitution. He was vice president for 1804–12 and a presidential candidate in 1804.

CLINTON, Sir Henry (c1738–1795), English general appointed (in 1778) commander-in-chief of British forces during the American Revolution after distinguishing himself at BUNKER HILL. He captured Charleston in 1780 but resigned in 1781. He was blamed for the British surrender at YORKTOWN in that year.

CLIPPER SHIPS, 19th-century sailing ships, the fastest ever built. They evolved from the Baltimore clippers and were built in the US and later in Britain. They had a very large area of sail, relied on a good crew, and traded with China and Australia where speed paid off. Two famous ships were Donald McKay's *Lightning* and the British *Cutty Sark* (now at Greenwich, England).

CLIVE OF PLASSEY, Robert Clive, 1st Baron (1725–1774), British soldier and administrator, twice governor of Bengal, who established British power in India. He defeated both the French at Arcot (1751) and the Bengal nawab, Siraj-ud-Daula, at Plassey, thus securing all Bengal for the EAST INDIA COMPANY. He reformed administrative corruption in Bengal. Although acquitted by parliament in a long and notorious trial of the charge of dishonesty when in office, he afterwards committed suicide.

CLOCKS AND WATCHES, devices to indicate or record the passage of time; essential features of modern life. In prehistory, time could be gauged solely from the positions of celestial bodies; a natural development was the sundial, initially no more than a vertical post whose shadow was cast by the sun directly onto the ground. Other devices depended on the flow of water from a pierced container; the rates at which marked candles, knotted ropes and oil in calibrated vessels burned down; and the flow of sand through a constriction from one bulb of an hourglass to the other. Mechanical clocks were probably known in ancient China, but first appeared in Europe in the 13th century AD. Power was supplied by a weight suspended from a rope, later by a coiled spring; in both cases an escapement was employed to control the energy release. Around 1657–58 HUYGENS applied the PENDULUM principle to clocks; later, around 1675, his hairspring and balance-wheel mechanism made possible the first portable clocks—resulting eventually in watches. Jeweled bearings, which reduced wear at critical points in the mechanism, were introduced during the 18th century, and the first CHRONOMETER was also devised in this century. Electric clocks with synchronous motors are now commonly found in the home and office, while the ATOMIC CLOCK, which can be accurate to within one second in 3 million years, is of great importance in science.

CLOISONNÉ, artistic process by which metal objects, such as jewel boxes and bases, are decorated by fusing colored enamel onto their surface. The design is created by the arrangement of metal strips soldered edgewise onto the surface of the object. The compartments (*cloisons*) created by these strips are filled with colored enamel and the object is then heated, thus fusing the enamel with the surface. After it is cooled, the surface is then highly polished. Originally a Persian technique, cloisonné spread throughout the Middle East and was highly developed during the Byzantine period. It was perfected by the Chinese, Japanese, and French.

CLONE, a cell or organism that is genetically identical to the cell or organism from which it was derived. **Cloning,** the creation of clones, is asexual, so there is no mixing of parental GENES. Clones may be produced by such reproductive methods as cell division in BACTERIA, cell budding in yeasts, or vegetative duplication (plant cuttings). The experimental cloning of mice has been achieved by replacing the nucleus of a fertilized mouse egg cell with the nucleus of a cell from a mouse embryo. The egg cell then develops into a mouse that is genetically identical to the donor embryo.

CLOSED SHOP, an establishment where the employer accepts only members of a specified union as his employees, and continues to employ them only if they remain union members. The TAFT-HARTLEY ACT of 1947 forbids closed shops in industries involved in or affecting interstate commerce.

CLOTHING. See FASHION.

CLOTTING, the formation of semisolid deposits in a liquid by coagulation, often by the denaturing of previously soluble ALBUMIN. Thus clotted cream is made by slowly heating milk so that the thick cream rises; the curdling of skim milk to make CHEESE is also an example of clotting. Clotting of BLOOD is a complex process set in motion when it comes into contact with tissues outside its ruptured vessel. These tissues contain a factor, **thromboplastin,** which activates a sequence of changes in the PLASMA clotting factors (12 enzymes). Alternatively, many surfaces, such as glass and fabrics, activate a similar sequence of changes. In either case, factor II (prothrombin, formed in the liver), with calcium ions and a platelet factor, is converted to **thrombin.** This converts factor I (fibrinogen) to **fibrin,** a tough, insoluble polymerized protein which forms a network of fibers around the platelets (see BLOOD) that have stuck to the edge of the wound and to each other. The network entangles the blood cells, then contracts, squeezing out the serum and leaving a solid clot. (See also ANTICOAGULANTS; EMBOLISM; HEMOPHILIA; HEMORRHAGE; THROMBOSIS.)

CLOUD CHAMBER, device, invented by C. T. R. Wilson (1911), used to observe the paths of subatomic particles. In simplest form, it comprises a chamber containing saturated vapor (see SATURATION) and some liquid, one wall of the chamber (the window) being transparent, another re-tractable. Sudden retraction of this wall lowers the temperature, and the gas becomes supersaturated. Passage of SUBATOMIC PARTICLES through the gas leaves charged IONS that serve as seeds for CONDENSATION of the gas into droplets. These fog trails (condensation trails) may be photographed through the window. (See also BUBBLE CHAMBER.)

CLOUDS, visible collections of water droplets or ice particles suspended in the ATMOSPHERE. Clouds whose lower surfaces touch the ground are usually called fog. The water droplets are very small, indeed of colloidal size (see AEROSOL); they must coagulate or grow before falling as rain or snow. This process may be assisted by **cloud seeding;** supercooled clouds are seeded with particles of (usually) dry ice (i.e., solid CARBON dioxide) to encourage condensation of the droplets, ideally causing rain or snow. **Types of Clouds.** There are three main cloud types: **Cumulus** (heap) clouds, formed by convection, and often mountain- or cauliflower-shaped, are found from about 2,000ft up as far as the tropopause, even temporarily into the stratosphere (see ATMOSPHERE). **Cirrus** (hair) clouds are composed almost entirely of icy crystals. They appear feathery, and are found at altitudes above about 20,000ft. **Stratus** (layer) clouds are low-lying, found between ground level and about 5,000ft. Other types of cloud include cirrostratus, cirrocumulus, altocumulus, altostratus, cumulonimbus, stratocumulus and nimbostratus.

CLOUET, Jean (c1485–1540), Flemish artist who was chief portrait painter at the court of Francis I of France. However, only one unsigned painting and about 130 drawings can be assigned to him.

CLOVES, the dried, unopened flowers of the evergreen clove tree. Originally grown in the Moluccas or Spice Islands, the Philippines and islands nearby, they were first appreciated by the Chinese for perfuming the breath. They were later imported to Europe and are now grown in the West Indies and Mauritius. Their main use nowadays is as flavoring and in medicine. Oil of cloves is used for digestive upsets, as a painkiller for toothache and as an antiseptic.

CLOVIS I (c466–511 AD), Frankish king, founder of the Frankish monarchy. He amassed a huge kingdom from the Rhine R to the Mediterranean, defeating the Romans at Soissons (486) and the Visigoths under Alaric II of Spain at Vouillé (507). He became a Christian in c498. Clovis compiled the code of Salic law, followed by his successors the MEROVINGIANS.

CLOWN, a comedy figure of the pantomime and circus. Modern clowns possibly derived from the vice figures of medieval miracle plays, but clowns were also known in ancient Greece and Rome, and as jesters or fools in medieval courts. They later figured as harlequins in the COMMEDIA DELL' ARTE; but their grotesque makeup, baggy clothes and slapstick and tumbling (see Joseph GRIMALDI) developed fully only in the 1800s. The best-known 20th-century circus clown was Emmett KELLY.

CLUBFOOT, deformity of the foot, with an abnormal relationship of the foot to the ankle; most commonly the foot is turned in and down. Abnormalities of fetal posture and ligamentous or muscle development, including CEREBRAL PALSY and spina bifida, may be causative. Correction includes gentle manipulation, PHYSIOTHERAPY, plaster splints and sometimes SURGERY.

CLUNIAC REFORM, movement in the medieval Catholic Church led by the Benedictine abbey at CLUNY, France, founded in 910. Independent of secular and diocesan authority, and enjoying the protection of the papacy, the monks of Cluny founded hundreds of religious houses, churches, and schools, revised the liturgy, and elevated standards of piety and learning. The movement was at its height in the 10th-12th centuries.

CLUNY, small town in E central France, 12mi NW of Mâcon. Its Benedictine abbey (910–1790) was the parent house of the Cluniac order. Only a part of its great basilica, once the largest church in W Europe, remains. Pop 4,300.

CLYDE, the most important river in Scotland and one of Britain's major commercial waterways, rising on the Lanarkshire-Dumfriesshire border in southwest Scotland and flowing some 106mi to its estuary, the Firth of Clyde. Its upper valley, Clydesdale, is noted for its fruit and market garden crops. Near Lanark, at the Falls of Clyde, the river is harnessed for hydroelectricity. From Lanark on, its valley is occupied by heavy industry. At the head of navigation is the city-seaport of Glasgow, Scotland's chief commercial center. To the west, on the northern bank, is Clydebank, with large engineering interests and the shipyards that built the *Queen Elizabeth II* and other large ships.

COAL, hard, black mineral burned as a FUEL. With its by-products COKE and COAL TAR it is vital to many modern industries.

Coal is the compressed remains of tropical and subtropical plants, especially those of the CARBONIFEROUS and PERMIAN periods. Changes in the world climatic pattern explain why coal occurs in all continents, even Antarctica. Coal formation

began when plant debris accumulated in swamps, partially decomposing and forming PEAT layers. A rise in sea level or land subsidence buried these layers below marine sediments, whose weight compressed the peat, transforming it under high-temperature conditions to coal; the greater the pressure, the harder the coal.

Coals are analyzed in two main ways: the "ultimate analysis" determines the total percentages of the elements present (carbon, hydrogen, oxygen, sulfur and nitrogen); and the "proximate analysis" gives an empirical estimate of the amounts of moisture, ash, volatile materials and fixed carbon. Coals are classified, or ranked, according to their fixed-carbon content, which increases progressively as they are formed. In ascending rank, the main types are: **lignite,** or brown coal, which weathers quickly, may ignite spontaneously, and has a low calorific value (SEE FUEL), but is used in Germany and Australia; **subbituminous coal,** mainly used in generating stations; **bituminous coal,** the commonest type, used in generating stations and the home, and often converted into COKE; and **anthracite,** a lustrous coal which burns slowly and well, and is the preferred domestic fuel.

Coal was burned in Glamorgan, Wales, in the 2nd millennium BC, and was known in China and the Roman Empire around the time of Christ. Coal mining was practiced throughout Europe and known to the American Indians by the 13th century AD. The first commercial coal mine in the US was at Richmond, Va., (opened 1745) and anthracite was mined in Pa. by 1790. The INDUSTRIAL REVOLUTION created a huge and increasing demand for coal. This slackened in the 20th century as coal faced competition from abundant oil and gas, but production is now again increasing. Annual world output is about 3 billion tons, 500 million tons from the US. World coal reserves are estimated conservatively at about 7 trillion tons, enough to meet demand for centuries at present consumption rates. (See also MINING.)

COAL GAS, a mixture of gases produced by the destructive distillation of COAL, consisting chiefly of hydrogen, methane and carbon monoxide. Other products are COKE and COAL TAR. Coal gas is used as a domestic fuel, but has been largely superseded by NATURAL GAS.

COAL TAR, a dense black viscous liquid produced by the destructive distillation of COAL; COKE and COAL GAS are other products. Fractional distillation of coal tar produces a wide variety of industrially important substances. These include ASPHALT (pitch), creosote (a wood preservative), and various oils used as fuels, solvents, preservatives, lubricants and disinfectants. Specific chemicals that can be isolated include benzene, toluene, xylene, phenol, pyridine, naphthalene and anthracene—the main source for the pharmaceutical and other chemical industries.

COAST GUARD, US, branch of the armed forces, is a service within the US Department of Transportation except when operating as part of the Navy in time of war. Its functions include search and rescue; maritime law enforcement; marine inspection and licensing; port safety and security; and waterways management. In 1985, 38,600 men and women served in the US Coast Guard.

COAST GUARD ACADEMY, US, an institution of higher education training career officers for the US COAST GUARD, located in New London, Conn. Students take a four-year course leading to a Bachelor of Science degree and an ensign's commission in the US coast guard.

COAST RANGES, a series of mountain ranges along the Pacific coast of North America from Kodiak Island, S Alaska, to S Cal. The mountains are of widely varied geological composition. The highest peak in the entire series is Canada's Mt Logan (19,850ft).

COBALT (Co), silvery-white, hard, ferromagnetic (see MAGNETISM) metal in Group VIII of the PERIODIC TABLE; a TRANSITION ELEMENT. It occurs in nature largely as sulfides and arsenides, and in nickel and copper ores; major producers are Canada, Zaire and Zambia. An ALLOY of cobalt, aluminum, nickel and iron ("Alnico") is used for magnets; other cobalt alloys, being very hard, are used for cutting tools. Cobalt is used as the matrix for tungsten carbide in drill bits. Chemically it resembles IRON and NICKEL: its characteristic oxidation states are +2 and +3. Cobalt compounds are useful colorants (notably the artists' pigment cobalt blue). Cobalt CATALYSTS facilitate hydrogenation and other industrial processes. The RADIOISOTOPE cobalt-60 is used in RADIATION THERAPY. Cobalt is a constituent of the vital VITAMIN B12. AW 58.9, mp 1495°C, bp 2870°C, sg 8.9 (20°C).

COBB, Tyrus Raymond (1886–1961), the "Georgia Peach," one of baseball's greatest players. In 24 years with the Detroit Tigers and the old Philadelphia Athletics he appeared in more games, batted more times and made more hits than any other major leaguer; his lifetime average was a record .367.

COBBETT, William (1763–1835), British radical writer and reformer, best known for his *Rural Rides* (1830), which portrayed the misery of rural workers. His radical views forced him to live in the US 1793–1800 and 1817–19. His *Weekly Political Register* (founded 1802) was the major radical newspaper of its day. He was elected to parliament after the 1832 Reform Act.

COBDEN, Richard (1804–1865), British politician and reformer. A textile merchant, he was known as "the Apostle of Free Trade". He was a founder member of the Anti-Corn Law League 1838–39, and its chief spokesman in parliament 1841–46. In two pamphlets, *England, Ireland and America* (1835) and *Russia* (1836), he surveyed international relations and argued against British interventionist policies.

COBRAS, poisonous snakes of the family Elapidae that spread the ribs of the neck to form a hood when alarmed. The king cobra, the longest poisonous snake, is about 5.5m (18ft) long. The Egyptian and Indian cobras are the traditional snake-charmer's snakes. They respond to movement, not to music, as they are deaf.

COCAINE, an ALKALOID from the coca leaf, the first local anesthetic agent and model for those currently used; it is occasionally used for surface ANESTHESIA. It is a drug of abuse, taken for its euphoriant effect by chewing the leaf, as snuff or by intravenous injection. Its abuse may lead to acute psychosis. It also mimics the actions of the sympathetic NERVOUS SYSTEM.

COCHIN CHINA, historic region of SE Asia comprising what is now S VIETNAM.

COCHISE (c1815–1874), Chiricahua Apache chief. Wrongly antagonized by soldiers, he began a savage campaign against whites in Ariz. in 1861 and effforcively drove them from the area. In 1862 he was driven back by troops to the Dragon Mts., which he held until his capture by Gen. CROOK in 1871. He escaped, but gave himself up when the Chiricahua Reservation was formed in 1872.

COCHRAN, Jacqueline (1912?–1980), US pilot. She obtained her pilot's license in 1932, after only three weeks' flying. First woman to fly in a Bendix transcontinental race (1934), she won it in 1938. She organized and headed the Women's Airforce Service Pilots (WASP) in WWII, and was the first woman to fly faster than sound.

COCKCROFT, Sir John Douglas (1897–1967), English physicist who first "split the atom." With E. T. S. Walton, he built a particle ACCELERATOR and in 1932 initiated the first man-made nuclear reaction by bombarding lithium atoms with PROTONS, producing alpha particles. For this work Cockcroft and Walton received the 1951 Nobel Prize for Physics. In 1946 Cockcroft became the first director of the UK's atomic research laboratory at Harwell, and in 1959, the first Master of Churchill College, Cambridge.

COCKNEY, nickname for a Londoner, especially one born within the sound of the bells of St. Mary-le-Bow church. It derives from a derogatory term used c1500 of anyone city-bred.

COCKROACHES, running, flat-bodied insects of the family Blattidae with long antennae and hardened forewings that protect the hindwings, as in BEETLES. They feed on fungi and on plant and animal remains, but also come indoors to eat exposed food, book bindings or even wood. There are about 70 species in the US.

COCONUT PALM, *Cocus nucifera*, an economically valuable tree found on many tropical coasts. It has a long trunk crowned by a cluster of large fronds. The fruits, coconuts, take one year to develop and a single palm normally produces up to 100 nuts in one year. Each nut is surrounded by a thick fibrous husk and contains a white kernel surrounding the "coconut milk." The kernel is dried to produce copra, which is the source of coconut oil, a vegetable oil much used in the US and Europe in detergents, edible oils, margarine, brake fluid etc. The fibers of the husk are used for mats and ropes.

COCTEAU, Jean (1889–1963), French author, artist and film director. He first rose to fame with poetry, ballets such as *Parade* (1917), and the novel *Thomas l'Imposteur* (1923). After overcoming opium addiction, he produced some of his most brilliant work, such as the play *Orphée* (1926) and the novels *Les Enfants Terribles* (1929) and *La Machine Infernale* (1934). A prolific writer in many fields, he also made several films, of which *Le Sang d'un Poète* (1932) is the most adventurous.

COD, members of the family Gadidae, important food fish of the N Atlantic and the Pacific, weighing up to 90kg (200lb). Cod form dense shoals, feeding on other fish and bottom-living animals. Females lay up to 6 million eggs at a time. The "cod banks" off New England and Newfoundland stimulated colonization of North America. The cod were salted, their livers yielded vitamin-rich cod liver oil and the swimbladder produced isinglass, a pure form of gelatin.

CODE, systematic and usually comprehensive set of legal rules. Many early bodies of law, such as that of HAMMURABI (c1800 BC), took this form. Roman law was codified in the Twelve Tables and again by the Emperor JUSTINIAN in the 6th century AD. The law reform movement in modern CIVIL LAW countries chose the code as the most accessible form of law; first of these was the CODE NAPOLÉON of 1804–10. Britain, the US and other COMMON LAW countries have made only limited use of codes.

CODEINE, a mild narcotic, ANALGESIC and COUGH suppressant related to MORPHINE. It reduces bowel activity causing CONSTIPATION and is used to cure DIARRHEA.

CODE NAPOLÉON, French legal CODE, officially the *Code Civil*. Napoleon I, as first consul, appointed a commission to devise a replacement for the confused and corrupt local systems formerly in force. The code, made up of 2,281 articles arranged in three books, was enacted in 1804 and, although much altered, is still in force today. Revision commissions were appointed in 1904 and 1945. The code has been the model for nearly all codes in CIVIL LAW countries. The La. civil code (1825) is closely based on it.

CODES AND CIPHERS, devices for conveying information secretly, mostly used in wartime and for espionage. In ciphers, individual letters or numerals that make up a message are transposed or replaced by other letters or numerals. But ciphers can often be "broken" because each letter of the alphabet tends to occur with a particular frequency.

Codes are based on units that may vary in length from letters to sentences. These units are given arbitrary code equivalents known to sender and receiver, who use identical code books listing code words and symbols. Machines have often been used to create complex codes and ciphers; today computers dominate the field. It is not clear how often cryptoanalysts break cryptographers' ciphers and codes, since successes are seldom made public, but a dramatic example of the importance of cryptoanalysis in wartime was the solving of Germany's so-called unbreakable Enigma system in the early years of WWII by British mathematicians and cryptoanalysts. This allowed Allied leaders to know virtually all of Germany's intentions during the hostilities before they were carried out. US breaking of Japanese codes was another major contribution to Allied victory.

The US National Security Agency, NSA, is America's top cipher maker and breaker today. It is presently attempting to monitor breakthroughs in the commercial and academic sectors to prevent foreign governments from picking up information through scientific and trade journals.

A recent breakthrough in cryptography, public key cryptography, allows the key to the code to be transmitted in the clear since in this unique system the sender can encode but not decode a message and the receiver can decode but not encode it.

COELACANTHS, fish, common as 70-million-year-old fossils, thought to be extinct until rediscovered by scientists in 1938 off the E African coast, where fishermen knew one species, *Latimeria chalumnae*, well.

COEUR D'ALENE INDIANS, Indian tribe who lived around Coeur d'Alene Lake in Ida. A peaceful people, they belonged to the Plateau cultures and spoke a Salish language. Their descendants live on a reservation in the area.

COFFEE, drink produced from the roasted fruit (beans) of the coffee plant. The coffee tree (or bush) belongs to the genus *Coffea*, the most extensively cultivated species being *Coffea arabica*. The coffee tree probably originated in Abyssinia. Its use as a drink rapidly spread through Arabia in the 13th century and it became popular in Europe during the 16th and 17th centuries. The US is now the largest market for coffee. Coffee is grown in many tropical countries. Brazil produces more coffee than any other country, but its share is becoming less. For many Latin American, African and Asian countries it is a very important export commodity. After picking, the ripe red berries are either naturally dried and the hulls, pulp and parchment removed (dry process), or are squeezed out of their skin and soaked when slight fermentation takes place, washed and then dried (wash process). The processed berries are roasted, which induces the coffee color and aroma, partly through the formation of CAFFEINE.

The coffee bush can also be grown as a house plant, requiring several hours sunlight in the winter, although young plants thrive under fluorescent light. Indoors, the temperature should not drop below 13°C (53°F) and the soil should be kept evenly moist. Propagation is by seeds and shoot tip cuttings.

COFFIN, Levi (1798–1877), US abolitionist, called "president of the Underground Railroad" for his help to fugitive slaves at "depots" in Newport, Ind., and Cincinnati, Ohio.

COGNAC, historic town in Charente department, W France. It gives its name to the famous brandy distilled in the area.

COHAN, George Michael (1878–1942), US popular songwriter, actor, playwright and producer. A celebrated Broadway song and dance man, he is best remembered for composing such hits as 'Give My Regards to Broadway,' 'You're a Grand Old Flag,' 'Yankee Doodle Dandy' and the popular WWI song 'Over There', for which Congress awarded him a special medal in 1940.

COHESION, the tendency of different parts of a substance to hold together. This is due to forces acting between its MOLECULES: a molecule will repel one close to it but attract one that is farther away; somewhere between these there is a position where WORK must be done either to separate the molecules or to push them together. This situation results both in cohesion and in ADHESION. Cohesion is strongest in a SOLID, less strong in a LIQUID, and least strong in a GAS.

COHN, Ferdinand Julius (1828–1898), German botanist renowned as one of the founders of BACTERIOLOGY. He showed that BACTERIA could be classified in fixed species and discovered that some of these formed endospores that could survive adverse physical conditions. He was also the first to recognize the value of KOCH'S work on the ANTHRAX bacillus.

COIN, piece of stamped metal, of fixed value and weight, issued to serve as money. Coins were probably invented in Lydia, Asia Minor, in the 8th century BC. Their use spread through the civilized world, and coins remained the main medium of exchange until the introduction of bank notes. Coins are made in licensed government mints. They carry a design on both sides, traditionally including inscriptions giving their value and the name of the issuing ruler or state. Gold, silver and copper are the traditional metals, often alloyed with harder metals to reduce wear. Unscrupulous debt-laden rulers also practiced debasement—reducing a coin's precious metal content without changing its face value. The Massachusetts Bay Colony produced the first US coins in 1652. The first US mint was established in Philadelphia in 1792. (See also MONEY.)

COKE, Sir Edward (1552–1634), English lawyer and parliamentarian who defended the supremacy of the common law and the rights of parliament and the judiciary against the attempts of JAMES I and CHARLES I to govern by royal prerogative. He drafted the PETITION OF RIGHT in 1628 setting out the rights of a citizen. First lord chief justice of England, he is best known for his four Institutes (1628–44).

COKE, form of amorphous CARBON (also containing ash, volatile residues and sulfur) remaining when bituminous COAL is heated in special furnaces to distill off the volatile constituents. Before the exploitation of NATURAL GAS, much COAL GAS was thus produced. In the US 95% of coke is used in METALLURGY, mostly in BLAST FURNACES. Such coke must be strong (to support the weight of the charge), porous and relatively pure. Some coke is used as a smokeless fuel, and to make water gas.

COLBERT, Jean Baptiste (1619–1683), French statesman, finance minister and comptroller general under LOUIS XIV. He transformed the finances of the state by reforming taxation, correcting abuses in the administration and encouraging industry and trade. He introduced protective tariffs, developed roads and canals, created the French navy and merchant marine, and was a patron of culture.

COLD, Common, a mild illness of the NOSE and throat caused by various types of VIRUS. General malaise and RHINITIS, initially watery but later thick and tenacious, are characteristic; sneezing, COUGH, sore throat and headache are also common, but significant FEVER is unusual. Secondary bacterial infection of EARS, SINUSES, pharynx or LUNGS may occur, especially in predisposed people. Spread is from person to person. Mild symptomatic relief only is required.

COLD-BLOODED ANIMALS, or **poikilotherms,** animals, in particular fish, amphibians and reptiles, that cannot maintain a constant body TEMPERATURE and which are therefore greatly affected by climatic changes.

COLDEN, Cadwallader (1688–1776), colonial American physician, administrator and naturalist. As lieutenant governor of N.Y. colony, he became unpopular for defending the British position during the STAMP ACT riots of 1765. He produced a botanical classification of American plants which was published by LINNEAUS in Sweden, and wrote a study of the IROQUOIS Indians, *History of the Five Indian Nations of Canada* (1727).

COLD HARBOR, locality in E central Va., 10mi ENE of Richmond. It was the scene of two Civil War battles; GAINES' MILL (1862) and Cold Harbor (1864), in which Robert E. LEE forced General GRANT'S troops to withdraw with massive losses.

COLD SORE, vesicular SKIN lesion of lips or nose caused by *Herpes simplex* VIRUS. Often associated with periods of general ill-health or infections such as the common COLD or PNEUMONIA. The virus, which is often picked up in early life, persists in the skin between attacks. Recurrences may be reduced by special antivirus drugs, applied during an attack.

COLD WAR, state of tension between countries, featuring mutually antagonistic policies but stopping short of actual fighting. The term is usually used to describe post-WWII relations between the Western powers led by the US and the communist bloc led by the USSR. Both sides built powerful alliances. The US established the NORTH ATLANTIC TREATY ORGANIZATION and the USSR organized the WARSAW PACT. Meanwhile a nuclear arms race gained momentum. Famous incidents in the Cold War included the BERLIN AIRLIFT (1948–49), the Cuban missile crisis (1962), in which the US forced Russia to dismantle its missile bases in Cuba, and the Russian invasion of Hungary (1956). The rise of a communist, but independent China and a growing assertiveness by nonaligned nations tended to weaken the leadership of the superpowers. By seeking détente and by negotiating arms-limitation treaties, the US and USSR sought to relax Cold War tensions.

COLE, George Douglas Howard (1889–1959), British economist and labor historian, a leading advocate of guild socialism and chairman of the Fabian Society 1939–46. A teacher at Oxford U 1925–57, he wrote several important books, including *A Short History of the British Working Class Movement* (3 vol., 1927; rev. 1948) and *A History of Socialist Thought* (5 vol., 1953–60).

COLE, Nat "King" (Nathaniel Adams Cole; 1919–1965), US singer and jazz pianist. He first became known as a pianist in the "Chicago Blues" manner, but it was his uniquely phrased, throaty singing style that brought him his greatest fame.

COLE, Thomas (1801–1848), British-born painter who founded the HUDSON RIVER SCHOOL. His best known works are views of the Catskills and the White Mountains. Cole's grandiose, Italianate paintings of the wilderness introduced landscape as a serious subject for US painting.

COLERIDGE, Samuel Taylor (1772–1834), leading English poet, essayist and critic. With WORDSWORTH he published *Lyrical Ballads* (1798), a landmark in early ROMANTICISM, in which Coleridge's major contribution was "The Rime of the Ancient Mariner," a tale in verse of the sea and fate. He is also remembered for an unfinished dream poem, "Kubla Khan," published in 1816. He gave notable lectures on Shakespeare and his *Biographia Literaria*

(1817) criticizes the philosophy of KANT, FICHTE and SCHELLING and the poetry of Wordsworth. Opium addiction blighted his early life.

COLES, Robert (1929–   ), US psychiatrist who studied migrant families, Southern black children involved in the civil rights struggle, and other people involved in the turmoil of social crisis. He is best known for *Children of Crisis* (5 vols., 1967–77) and *Women of Crisis* (2 vols., 1978–80).

COLET, John (c1466–1519), English theologian, dean of St. Paul's and founder of St. Paul's School, London. He was a friend of Thomas MORE and ERASMUS and a proponent of the new Renaissance HUMANISM.

COLETTE, Sidonie-Gabrielle (1873–1954), French writer and music-hall actress known for her sensuous and subtle characterizations of people, especially of slightly disreputable women in the demimonde which she knew so well. Her brilliant style was admired by PROUST. Her best-known heroine is Claudine, a thinly veiled self-portrayal.

COLFAX, Schuyler (1823–1885), US editor and politician, Speaker of the US House of Representatives (1863–69) and vice president (1869–73) under President Ulysses S. Grant. His political career was ruined by his involvement in the CRÉDIT MOBILIER and other scandals.

COLGATE, William (1783–1857), US soap manufacturer and philanthropist. Colgate University was renamed for him.

COLIC, intermittent pain; generally experienced as bouts of severe pain with pain-free intervals. It is due to irritation or obstruction of hollow viscera, in particular the GASTROINTESTINAL TRACT, ureter (see KIDNEY) and GALL BLADDER or bile ducts (see LIVER). Treatment of the cause is supplemented by ANALGESICS and drugs to reduce smooth muscle spasm.

COLIGNY, Gaspard de (1519–1572), admiral of France and French Protestant leader. As Huguenot commander in the second of the French Wars of RELIGION, he concluded the Treaty of St. Germain (1570) which favored the Protestants. But CHARLES IX turned against him and he was a victim in the massacre of St. Bartholomew's Day. (See SAINT BARTHOLOMEW'S DAY MASSACRE.)

COLITIS, INFLAMMATION of the colon (see GASTROINTESTINAL TRACT). Infection with VIRUSES, BACTERIA or PARASITES may cause it, often with ENTERITIS. Inflammatory colitis can occur without bacterial infection in the chronic diseases, ulcerative colitis and Crohn's disease. Impaired blood supply may also cause colitis. Symptoms include colic and DIARRHEA (with slime or blood). Severe colitis can cause serious dehydration or SHOCK. Treatments include ANTIBIOTICS and, for inflammatory colitis, STEROIDS, ASPIRIN derivatives or occasionally SURGERY.

COLLAGE, modern art form in which various objects and materials are glued onto a canvas or board and sometimes painted. Pablo PICASSO and Georges BRAQUE extended it to CUBISM in 1912–13, and DADAISM and SURREALISM developed it further. Collage gave rise to "assemblage," a modern art form using scrap-metal objects and wood.

COLLECTIVE UNCONSCIOUS, term used, especially by Carl JUNG, for those parts of the UNCONSCIOUS derived from racial, rather than individual, experience.

COLLECTIVISM, political doctrine which places control of economic activity in the hands of the community or the government, as opposed to CAPITALISM, which emphasizes private ownership. Collectivists, beginning with ROUSSEAU, hold that it is only through submission to the community that the individual can fulfill himself and that economic power is too important to be left to the self-interest of individuals.

COLLIER, John (1884–1968), US commissioner of Indian affairs (1933–45), initiator of the Indian Reorganization Act (1934), which reversed US Indian policy of individual land allotments by restoring tribal ownership of Indian lands.

COLLINS, Michael (1890–1922), Irish revolutionary leader. Imprisoned for opposing the British in the EASTER RISING of 1916, he later became a SINN FEIN leader and intelligence chief of the guerrilla IRISH REPUBLICAN ARMY. Collins helped to negotiate the treaty with Britain which set up the Irish Free State in 1921, and briefly headed the Irish army and finance ministry, but was ambushed and shot by Irish opponents.

COLLINS, (William) Wilkie (1824–1889), English novelist. A friend of DICKENS, he established his reputation in 1860 with the publication of *The Woman in White*, one of the first English detective stories.

COLLOID, or colloidal solution, a system in which two (or more) substances are uniformly mixed so that one is extremely finely dispersed throughout the other. A colloid may be viewed intuitively as a halfway stage between a SUSPENSION and a SOLUTION, the size of the dispersed particles being larger than simple MOLECULES, smaller than can be viewed through an optical MICROSCOPE (more precisely, they have at least one diameter in the range 1μ–1mm). Typical examples of colloids include FOG and BUTTER. Colloids may be classified in two ways: one by the natures of the particles (dispersed phase) and medium (continuous phase); the other by, as it were, the degree of permanency of the colloid. In the latter case, one may define a **lyophilic colloid** as one that forms spontaneously when the two phases are placed in contact; and a **lyophobic colloid** as one that can be formed only with some difficulty and maintained for a moderate elapse of time only under special conditions. Colloids have interesting properties, perhaps the most notable of which is light DISPERSION: it is due to colloidal particles in the atmosphere that the sky is blue in the daytime and the sunset red. Moreover, the property of ADSORPTION of molecules and IONS at the interface between particles and continuous phase plays a major part in water purification. (See also AEROSOL; BROWNIAN MOTION; DIALYSIS; ELECTROPHORESIS; OSMOSIS; TYNDALL.)

COLLOTYPE, PRINTING process, akin to LITHOGRAPHY, whereby photographs may be reproduced without a HALFTONE screen. A glass or ALUMINUM plate is coated in a light-sensitive GELATIN and POTASSIUM bichromate (dichromate, $K_2Cr_2O_7$) solution. On exposure, the gelatin hardens most in areas of brightest light. The plate is soaked in GLYCEROL which is absorbed most in the softest areas; during printing, the plate is kept moist by a glycerol-water mixture, the glycerol-soaked areas absorbing the moisture and repelling the INK. Collotype printing is slow and the plate lacks durability (print run at most about 5,000).

COLOGNE (Köln), river port and leading industrial city in West Germany, on the Rhine R in the W of the country. Its products range from heavy machinery to toilet water (eau de cologne). Cologne's prosperity dates from its membership of the HANSEATIC LEAGUE. The cathedral of St. Peter (built 1248–1880) is its most renowned landmark. Pop 916,153.

COLOMBIA, republic in NW South America. It is the only South American country with both Pacific and Caribbean coastlines.

Land. Colombia has four major regions: the Andes; the Caribbean coastal lowlands; the Pacific coastal lowlands; and the E plains. Some 80% of the people live in the Andean region. Three *cordilleras* (mountain ranges) branch out northwards from the Pasto knot in the S, some peaks exceeding 16,000ft. The Caribbean lowlands are drained by sluggish rivers that frequently flood, but in the dry season big herds of

Official name: Republic of Colombia
Capital: Bogotá
Area: 440,831sq mi
Population: 28,655,000
Languages: Spanish
Religions: Roman Catholic
Monetary unit(s): 1 Colombian peso=100 centavos

cattle find good grazing there. The Pacific lowlands are wet and scantily populated. The N section of the E region forms part of the South American *llanos* or tropical grasslands; the S section is equatorial rain forest containing Leticia, Colombia's only port on the Amazon R. The country's climate varies from extreme cold to humid heat according to altitude and proximity to the coast.

People. More than half of Colombians are mestizos (of mixed European and Amerindian ancestry); there are about 20% whites and minorities of mulattoes, blacks and Indians. The literacy rate is about 80%.

Economy. Colombia is a major world coffee producer. It also grows cotton, bananas, sugar, tobacco, cocoa, rice, sorghum, corn, wheat and barley. Rich in minerals, the country has the largest coal reserves in Latin America and substantial reserves of uranium. Other resources include oil, gas and precious metals. Transportation is hindered by mountain ranges, but cities are joined by road, rail or river and an advanced air network. Tourism is becoming an important source of foreign exchange.

History. CHIBCHA INDIANS of the E Cordilleras had a highly developed culture before the Spanish arrived in the early 16th century. Spain ruled the area until independence, which followed Simón BOLÍVAR's victory over the Spanish at Boyacá (1819). Greater Colombia then comprised what are now Colombia, Venezuela, Ecuador, and Panama. Venezuela and Ecuador became separate countries in 1850; Panama became independent in 1903. Throughout the 19th century and most of the 20th Colombia was deeply divided between centralizing and Catholic conservatives and federalist, anticlerical liberals. Their differences led to frequent civil wars and military dictatorships. Under Alberto Lleras Camargo (1906–   ), president 1945–46, 1958–62, relative stability was achieved. In the 1980s leftist guerrilla forces challenged government authority in the countryside. Government was also undermined by the growth of the cocaine trade, centered in the city of Medellín. Through violence and corruption, the drug lords of the "Medellín cartel" overpowered Colombia's courts and law-enforcement agencies.

COLOMBO PLAN, cooperative program for economic development in S and SE Asia, inaugurated in 1951 at Colombo, Ceylon (now Sri Lanka). The first participants were members of the Commonwealth, who were joined by the US, Japan and some SE Asian countries. A consultative committee meets annually to discuss national accomplishments and plans. Capital aid consists of grants and loans from the industrial members to the developing countries.

COLOR, the way the brain interprets the wavelength distribution of the LIGHT entering the eye. The phenomenon of color has two aspects: the physical or optical—concerned with the nature of the light—and the physiological or visual—dealing with how the eye sees color.

The light entering the eye is either emitted by or reflected from the objects we see. Hot solid objects emit light with wavelengths occupying a broad continuous band of the electromagnetic SPECTRUM, the position of the most intense radiation depending on the temperature of the object—the hotter the object, the shorter the wavelengths emitted. We see the shortest visible wavelengths as blue, the longest as red. Hot or electrically excited gases, consisting of nearly isolated atoms, emit light only at specific wavelengths characteristic of the atoms (see SPECTROSCOPY).

The EYE can only see colors when the light is relatively bright; the rods used in poor light see only in black and white. The cones used in color VISION are of three kinds, responding to light from the red, green or blue portions of the visible spectrum. The brain adds together the responses of the different sets of cones and produces the sensation of color. The three colors to which the cones of the eye respond are known as the three primary colors of light. By mixing different proportions of these three colors, any other color can be simulated, equal intensities of all three producing white light. This is known as the production of color by

addition, the effect being used in color TELEVISION tubes where PHOSPHORS glowing red, green and blue are employed. Color pigments, working by transmission or reflection, produce colors by subtraction, abstracting light from white and displaying only the remainder. Again a suitable combination of a set of three pigments—cyan (blue–green), magenta (blue–red) and yellow (the "complementary" colors of the three primaries)—can simulate most other colors, a dense mixture of all three producing black. This effect is used in color photography but in color printing an additional black pigment is commonly used.

Most colors are not found in the spectrum. These nonspectral colors can be regarded as intermediates between the spectral colors and black and white. Many schemes have been proposed for the classification and standardization of colors. The most widely used is that of Albert Henry Munsell, which describes colors in terms of their hue (basic color), saturation (intensity or density), and lightness and brightness (the degree of whiteness or blackness).

COLORADO, a W central state of the US bounded on the N by Wyo. and Neb., on the E by Kan., on the S by Okla. and N.M. and on the W by Ut. It is the highest state in the US.

Name of state: Colorado
Capital: Denver
Statehood: Aug. 1, 1876 (38th state)
Familiar name: Centennial State
Area: 104,247sq mi
Population: 3,267,000
Elevation: Highest—14,431ft, Mount Elbert, Lowest—3,350ft, Arkansas River
Motto: *Nil sine numine* ("Nothing without Providence")
State flower: Rocky Mountain columbine
State bird: Lark bunting
State tree: Colorado blue spruce
State song: 'Where the Columbines Grow"
Land. Colorado has three main areas: To the E, plateaus rise to meet the Rocky Mts. forming a narrow Piedmont (foothills) zone between the plateaus and the mountains.

Ranges of the Rocky Mts crisscross central Colorado from N to S, and include the state's highest point, Mt Elbert (14,431ft). To the W, along the Ut. border, lies a region of lower mountains and plateaus crossed by rivers flowing in deep canyons. The Colorado, South Platte, Arkansas and upper Rio Grande are the state's main rivers. The climate is largely dry and sunny; average annual rainfall is only 17in and water is scarce, restricting agriculture. Three million acres are irrigated for the cultivation of sugar beets, vegetables and fruit; another 40,000 acres provide grazing for cattle and sheep and land for dry crops such as wheat and hay.

People. Colorado's population increased by nearly one-third 1970–80 but only 13% in 1980–86. Denver is the largest city, followed by Colorado Springs, Aurora, Lakewood and Pueblo. All five cities are located in the Piedmont zone.

Economy. Mining has always been important to Colorado's economy; discoveries of gold and silver were followed by zinc, oil, natural gas, molybdenum, vanadium and uranium. Manufacturing includes processed foods, metal goods, electronic equipment, machinery and aerospace products. Agriculture ranks after manufacturing in value of output. Tourism is also important, with spectacular mountain scenery and skiing the major attractions.

History. Traces of an ancient Indian culture in Colorado are evident in the MESA VERDE and other cliff dwellings. In the 1500s Spanish explorers entered the territory to be followed by the French. US trappers hunting beaver and buffalo came in the early 1800s, and after the LOUISIANA PURCHASE (1803), explorers like Zebulon Pike and traders like William Bent began to open up the territory. In the MEXICAN WAR (1848) the US conquered further Colorado territory. The discovery of gold near Denver in 1858–59 brought a rush of prospectors. In 1876 Colorado became the Union's 38th state.

Colorado was one of the early states to benefit from the shift of business and population to the Sun Belt. But the boom of the 1970s became the bust of the 1980s when oil prices dropped, exploration slowed, unemployment increased, and mortgage defaults soared. Environmentalism gave way to boosterism as the state moved to broaden its economic base. In presidential elections 1968–88, Colorado voted consistently Republican.

COLORADO RIVER, a major US river, rising in the Rocky Mts of N Col. and flowing 1,450mi SW to enter the Gulf of Cal. Features include the GRAND CANYON and the HOOVER DAM, one of a series of dams that provide irrigation for seven states.

COLOR BLINDNESS, inability to discriminate between certain COLORS, an inherited trait. It is a disorder of the retina cones in the EYE. The commonest form is red-green color blindness (Daltonism), usually found in men (about 8%), the other types being rare.

COLOR-FIELD   PAINTING, contemporary school of painting that stresses the creation of large areas of color, often closely related in value or tone. Mark ROTHKO was a leading color-field painter. See MINIMALISM.

COLOSSEUM, huge oval amphitheater in Rome which held 45,000 spectators on several tiers of seats supported by arches. Built by the Flavian Emperor Vespasian and completed by his son, the emperor Titus, 80 AD, it was used for gladiatorial, wild beast and other displays up to the 5th century. It has been damaged by earthquakes and its marble was quarried as building stone in the Middle Ages.

COLOSSIANS, Epistle to the, book of the New Testament written by St. Paul to the Christians of Colossae in SW Asia Minor. It resembles EPHESIANS.

COLOSSUS OF RHODES, gigantic statue of Helios, the sun god, one of the SEVEN WONDERS OF THE WORLD. Erected about 290–280 BC by the sculptor Chares of Lindos, it stood at the harbor of Rhodes in commemoration of the island's successful defense against an invasion in 304 BC. It was made of bronze from the war machines left behind by the invaders, and stood 105ft high. The 16th-century story that it straddled the harbor entrance has no basis in fact. The Colossus collapsed in an earthquake (224 BC) and lay in ruins until 672 AD, when the Saracens sold the bronze to an Edessa merchant.

COLT, Samuel (1814–1862), US inventor and industrialist who devised the revolver, a single-barreled pistol with a revolving multiple breech (bullet chamber), in the early 1830s. His factories pioneered mass-production techniques and the use of interchangeable parts.

COLTER, John (c1775–1813), US trapper and guide, the first white man to cross the Wind River Mts and Teton Range (1807), now in Yellowstone National Park. He guided the 1803 LEWIS AND CLARK EXPEDITION and other expeditions up the Missouri R.

COLTRANE, John William (1926–1967), US saxophonist, a leader in changing jazz styles in association with Miles Davis,

Theolonius Monk, and others.

COLUMBA, Saint (c521–597 AD), Irish missionary to Scotland. After founding Irish monasteries at Derry and Kells, he made the island of Iona a base for the conversion of N Scotland.

COLUMBIA, District of. See WASHINGTON, D.C.

COLUMBIA RIVER, rises in the Rocky Mts of SE British Columbia, Canada. It flows 460mi to the US border and thence 745mi to the Pacific Ocean, forming the Wash.-Ore. border. The river's vast hydroelectric potential is partially harnessed by numerous dams, including Grand Coulee Dam.

COLUMBIA UNIVERSITY, New York City, one of the nation's major private universities. Founded as King's College in 1754, it was renamed Columbia College in 1784 and became a university in 1896. Its schools and faculties include important research institutes for international relations and schools of journalism, business and social work. Its libraries hold valuable rare books and MS collections. It has some 20,000 students.

COLUMBUS, Christopher (1451–1506), Genoese explorer generally credited with the discovery of America. An experienced navigator, he hoped to sail W across the Atlantic to pioneer a new short route to the spice-rich East Indies (formerly reached by sailing E). Columbus failed to win Portuguese backing but Queen Isabella and King Ferdinand of Spain eventually agreed to finance the voyage.

On Aug. 3, 1492, Columbus, commanding the *Santa María* and accompanied by the *Niña* and *Pinta*, sailed from SW Spain for the Canary Islands. On Sept. 6 he set out due W and on Oct. 12 landed on San Salvador Island (perhaps Samana Cay) in the Bahamas. After discovering Cuba and Hispaniola, he returned to Spain where he was created an admiral and governor of the new lands discovered and to be discovered.

Columbus made three further voyages to the New World. In Oct. 1493 he left Spain with 17 ships, planning to set up trading posts and colonies and carrying hundreds of colonists. He colonized Hispaniola, discovered Puerto Rico, Jamaica, the Virgin Islands and some of the Lesser Antilles and explored the S coast of Cuba. On his third voyage, 1498, he sighted South America and discovered Trinidad. But the Hispaniola colonists' discontent with living conditions threatened to break into revolt. Complaints against Columbus reached Spain, disorders continued, and Francisco de Bobadilla was sent out to replace him as

governor. Columbus was sent back to Spain in disgrace. His fourth and last voyage (1502–04) was again intended to find the elusive route to the East Indies. Instead he came upon the Central American coast at Honduras and followed it E and S to Panama. Columbus died two years after his last journey, poverty-stricken and almost forgotten.

COLUMN, in architecture, slim vertical structural support, usually cylindrical, consisting of a base, shaft and a capital. Columns support the entablature on which the roof rests. A row of columns forms a colonnade. Widely used in early architecture, columns were characteristic of Egyptian temples and of classical Greek architecture. The three main Greek forms were the Doric, Ionic and Corinthian orders (see CLASSICAL ORDERS).

COMA, state of unconsciousness in which a person cannot be roused by sensory stimulation and is unaware of his surroundings. Body functions continue but may be impaired, depending on the cause. These include POISONING, head injury, DIABETES, and BRAIN diseases, including STROKES and convulsions. Severe malfunction of LUNGS, LIVER or KIDNEYS may lead to coma.

COMANCHE, North American Indians, closely related to the SHOSHONE INDIANS. Brilliant horsemen and fierce warriors, they were dominant among the S Great Plains peoples, warring as far afield as Mexico. They stubbornly defended the buffalo hunting grounds against white incursions until the 1870s. Some 3,000 Comanche still live in W Okla.

COMBUSTION, or burning, the rapid oxidation of FUEL in which heat and usually light are produced. In slow combustion (e.g., a glowing charcoal fire) the reaction may be heterogeneous, the solid fuel reacting directly with gaseous oxygen; more commonly, the fuel is first volatilized, and combustion occurs in the gas phase (a flame is such a combustion zone, its luminance being due to excited particles, molecules and ions). In the 17th and 18th centuries combustion was explained by the PHLOGISTON theory, until LAVOISIER showed it to be due to combination with oxygen in the air. In fact the oxidizing agent need not be oxygen: it may be another oxidizing gas such as nitric oxide or fluorine, or oxygen-containing solids or liquids such as nitric acid (used in rocket fuels). If the fuel and oxidant are premixed, as in a Bunsen burner, the combustion is more efficient, and little or no soot is produced. Very rapid combustion occurs in an explosion (see

EXPLOSIVES), when more heat is liberated than can be dissipated, or when a branched chain reaction occurs. Each combustion reaction has its own ignition temperature below which it cannot take place, e.g. c400°C for coal. Spontaneous combustion occurs if slow oxidation in large piles of such materials as coal or oily rags raises the temperature to the ignition point. (See also INTERNAL-COMBUSTION ENGINE.)

COMEDY, literary work which aims primarily to amuse, often using ridicule, exaggeration or criticism of human nature and institutions, and usually ending happily. One of the two main traditional categories of drama (see also TRAGEDY), comedy also describes nondramatic art forms.

Comedy evolved in ancient Greece from the festivals of DIONYSUS and from the satyr plays, and developed in the satiric plays of ARISTOPHANES. It then became more consciously literary, employing stock characters and situations, as in the works of MENANDER, who was later imitated by the Roman poets PLAUTUS and TERENCE. Classical comedy elements survived the Middle Ages in folk plays and festivals. Roman comedies were revived in the Renaissance and influenced Italian COMMEDIA DELL'ARTE and the comedies of Spain's LOPE DE VEGA and the Elizabethans Ben JONSON and SHAKESPEARE. In 17th-century France MOLIÈRE wrote comic and satiric drama; the comedy of manners stemmed from his work and influenced CONGREVE and other writers of RESTORATION COMEDY. In the 18th century SHERIDAN and GOLDSMITH and Italy's Carlo GOLDONI wrote satiric, witty and more realistic comedies. From the 19th century onwards, outstanding writers of comedy in English included Oscar WILDE, who wrote drawing-room comedies; G. B. SHAW, who wrote unique comedies of ideas; James BARRIE, who wrote romantic comedies; J. M. SYNGE and Sean O'CASEY, who wrote native Irish comedy; Noel COWARD, who wrote witty farces; and George S. KAUFMAN, Thornton WILDER, and Neil Simon, in whose works humor is often mixed with serious social commentary. (See also BURLESQUE; FARCE; SATIRE.)

COMENIUS (Jan Amos Komenský; 1592–1670), Czech educational reformer and theologian; last bishop of the old MORAVIAN CHURCH. He advocated universal education, teaching in the vernacular and Latin as a common language. His most famous books are *The Great Didactic* (1628–32) and *The Visible World* (1658–59).

COMET, a nebulous body which orbits the sun. In general, comets can be seen only when they are comparatively close to the sun, though the time between their first appearance and their final disappearance may be as much as years. As they approach the sun, a few comets develop tails (some comets develop more than one tail) as long as 100 million mi. The tails of comets are always pointed away from the sun, so that, as the comet recedes into space, its tail precedes it. For this reason it is generally accepted that comets' tails are caused by the SOLAR WIND.

The head of the comet is known as the nucleus. Nuclei may be as little as 350ft or as much as 60mi in radius, and are thought to be composed primarily of frozen gases and ice mixed with smaller quantities of meteoritic material. Most of the mass of a comet is contained within the nucleus, though this may be less than 0.000,001 that of the earth. Surrounding the nucleus is the bright coma, a vast area that is composed of gas and possibly small particles erupting from the nucleus.

Cometary orbits are usually very eccentric ellipses, with some perihelions (see ORBIT) closer to the sun than that of MERCURY, aphelions as much as 100,000 AU from the sun. The orbits of some comets take the form of hyperbolas, and it is thought that these have their origins altogether outside the SOLAR SYSTEM, that they are interstellar travelers.

In Greco-Roman times it was generally believed that comets were phenomena restricted to the upper atmosphere of the earth. In the late 15th and 16th centuries it was shown by M. Mästlin and BRAHE that comets were far more distant than the moon. NEWTON interpreted the orbits of the comets as parabolas, deducing that each comet was appearing for the first time. It was not until the late 17th century that HALLEY showed that at least some comets returned periodically.

COMICS, cartoon drawings in a panel or series of panels (strips) with consistent characters involved in brief incidents or continuous stories. Captions or dialogue are often set in "balloons." The concept originated with satirical cartoons (18th–19th centuries), but developed in 20th-century America as a device to increase newspaper circulation. Early successes were *The Yellow Kid* (1895) and *The Katzenjammer Kids* (1897), while today's most popular comic strip is probably Charles Schulz's *Peanuts*. Comics range from humor or farce to adventure, crime and horror stories, science fiction, classics and satire and social criticism. See also

CARICATURE AND CARTOON.

COMINES, Philippe de (c.1447–1511), French chronicler and diplomat who served CHARLES THE BOLD of Burgundy and kings LOUIS XI and CHARLES VIII of France. His memoirs are highly regarded.

COMINFORM (Communist Information Bureau), an organization set up in 1947 to create unity among and assert Soviet influence over communist countries. Membership was limited to representatives of the communist parties of the USSR, its E European satellites, and France and Italy. Khrushchev disbanded the Cominform in 1956.

COMINTERN. See INTERNATIONAL, THE.

COMMEDIA DELL'ARTE, form of Italian COMEDY which originated in the Middle Ages and flourished in the 16th–18th centuries. Traveling professional actors (often wearing masks) improvised action and dialogue around outline plots with stock characters. The *commedia* spread through Europe and had a lasting influence on the theater.

COMMERCE, Chambers of. See CHAMBER OF COMMERCE.

COMMERCE, US Department of, the executive department of the government responsible for fostering and regulating domestic and foreign commerce. Its present name dates from 1913. The secretary of commerce, a member of the cabinet appointed by the president as chief adviser on federal policies affecting trade and industry, is aided by an under secretary and five assistant secretaries. The department operates the Maritime Administration, Office of Business Economics, Economic Development Administration, Bureau of International Commerce, National Oceanic and Atmospheric Administration, Office of Telecommunications, Bureau of the Census, National Bureau of Standards, Patent Office, and Office of Equal Opportunity, among others.

COMMERCIAL ART, art which helps sell a product, service or point of view; also "advertising art." It involves design, drawing and type matter in advertisements and illustrations for books, magazines and newspapers, posters and packages, display and exhibition material, television and films. Commercial artists need a wide knowledge of art techniques and reproduction methods. (See also ADVERTISING.)

COMMERCIAL LAW, body of law governing commercial transactions and commercial organizations. Transactions are governed largely by the law of CONTRACTS dealing with the negotiation, breach and performance of legally enforceable business agreements. The laws governing commercial organizations lay down the legal forms in which business bodies may be constituted, such as the incorporation of companies. The law of agency, making it possible for a person or corporation to transact business through employees, is important in this area.

Commercial law is as old as large-scale trade, but it expanded and consolidated after the Middle Ages. English mercantile law was gradually incorporated into the COMMON LAW and so inherited by the US, where it grew with the expansion of interstate trade in the 19th century, necessitating uniform legislation. Many states have adopted the Uniform Commercial Code of 1952 in an attempt to systematize national practice.

COMMERCIAL REVOLUTION, in European history, the shift of the greatest commercial activity from the Mediterranean to the Atlantic in the 16th century due to the establishment of national monarchies in W Europe, improvements in ships and instruments, and the discovery of America and sea routes to Asia.

COMMODITY MARKET, a formal market for dealings in raw materials and foods. Such exchanges trade simultaneously in present and future supplies, thus tending to minimize short-term price variations caused by supply fluctuation and allowing traders to hedge their purchasing. Coffee, oil, cotton, grain, livestock and metals are some of the commodities sold in this way. The largest commodity markets are in Chicago, New York City, and London. Their prices largely determine world prices.

COMMON CAUSE, a national nonpartisan citizens' lobby, organized in 1970 by John W. Gardner, former secretary of Health, Education, and Welfare. It has sought to reform campaign financing and end political corruption, to improve the internal workings of the federal and state governments and to protect the environment. With some 280,000 members, it monitors the work of Congress, recommends legislative reforms to its members, files lawsuits and engages in lobbying at the federal, state and local levels.

COMMONER, Barry (1917–   ), US biologist, ecologist and environmentalist who warned against the threats of technology and nuclear energy to the environment in such books as *The Closing Circle* (1971), *The Poverty of Power* (1976) and *The Politics of Energy* (1979).

COMMON LAW, body of law based upon custom and the established precedent of court decisions. Developed in England since early medieval times, it is the basis of the law of many other countries today, including the US. In late Anglo-Saxon and early Norman England, the growth of centralized government created a law common to all areas, administered by royal justices. Henry II and Edward I (12th–13th centuries) strengthened the law, laying the foundations of many modern practices and principles. Common law gradually absorbed much of English mercantile, sea and CANON LAW. By the 15th century, however, adherence to outdated, narrow and unsuitable legal formalities created many injustices. The lord chancellor, therefore, on behalf of the king, set up a court to "restore the equity" between parties involved in such situations. This created the modern body of EQUITY law, on which such concepts as TRUST and MORTGAGE are based.

At the same time, the custom of relying on precedents—preceding decisions—was becoming a firm principle, to be modified only by statute or a higher court. This contrasted with the CIVIL LAW system, derived from Roman law, which was popular in Europe. In this, the main legal rules are embodied in a central code such as the CODE NAPOLÉON, which courts theoretically apply without references to previous decisions. However, civil law often relies on precedent, just as many common law rules are codified by statute for convenience. Common law spread throughout the British colonies. It was generally adopted in the US, although La. state law is based upon the Code Napoléon and other states have partially codified systems.

COMMON MARKET. See EUROPEAN ECONOMIC COMMUNITY (EEC).

COMMONS, John Rogers (1862–1945), US labor economist and historian. He founded the U. of Wisconsin School of History and helped draft the exemplary reform legislation of the state of Wis.

COMMONS, House of. See HOUSE OF COMMONS.

COMMON SENSE SCHOOL, in philosophy, a group of Scottish thinkers, including Thomas REID and Dugald STEWART, who, reacting against the idealism of BERKELEY and the skepticism of HUME, affirmed that the truths apparent to the common man—the existence of material objects, the reality of causality, and so on—were genuine, reliable and not to be questioned.

COMMONWEALTH, form of government based on the consent of the people ("common weal" means common wellbeing). In the US, the states of Mass., Pa., Va. and Ky. are known as commonwealths. Various nations are associated with Britain in the COMMONWEALTH OF NATIONS; and the federated states of Australia form the Commonwealth of Australia. In English history, the Commonwealth was a period of republican rule (1649–60).

COMMONWEALTH OF NATIONS, free association of Britain and over 40 former colonies, now independent states, and their dependencies. It is not governed by a constitution or specific treaty; member countries are linked by a common heritage and economic and cultural interests and recognize the British sovereign as symbolic head of the Commonwealth. Commonwealth prime ministers and other officials meet at periodic conferences and exchange views on international, economic and political affairs of mutual interest. Member nations range in size from Canada, Australia and India to tiny Tonga. Membership increased as more British colonies gained independence and opted to join. Burma chose to remain outside the Commonwealth; Ireland, South Africa and Pakistan withdrew; and Fiji's membership lapsed when it declared itself a republic in 1987.

COMMUNE, cooperative community formed for ideological, political or religious reasons. The self-governing towns of medieval Europe were known as communes; the term is also used of the period's religious communities, and of those in 17th-century America. In the 19th century, with the growth of Utopian socialism, a number of experimental communes were established, notably NEW HARMONY and BROOK FARM in the US. The farm collective of China is a form of commune, as is the Israeli KIBBUTZ.

COMMUNICATIONS SATELLITE, artificial earth-orbiting satellite used to relay radio signals between points on earth. The orbits of most such satellites are above the equator at a height of 22,300mi; at that altitude a satellite orbits the earth at the same rate as the earth turns and thus remains over a fixed point on the surface. The satellite carries a number of **transponders** that receive radio beams from earth and retransmit them back to earth. The power for the electronic equipment comes from SOLAR CELLS. Communications satellites carry television programs, telephone calls and a variety of business data. The great bulk of data communications between continents is carried by satellites and handled by COMPUTERS at each end. (See also COMSAT.)

COMMUNICATIONS SATELLITE CORPORATION. See COMSAT.

COMMUNION, Holy, or **Lord's Supper** or **Eucharist,** a Christian SACRAMENT involving the consumption of the body and blood of Jesus Christ, which are received by eating and drinking consecrated bread and wine, as at the Last Supper. Whether this receiving is actual or only symbolic has been much disputed (see TRANSUBSTANTIATION). Nonconformists, following ZWINGLI, see Holy Communion as merely a symbolic commemoration. The manner in which communion is a SACRIFICE, if at all, is equally controversial. In Holy Communion, the central act of all Christian worship, the Church celebrates the atonement made by Christ as the basis of its common life and faith. (See also CONFIRMATION; MASS.)

COMMUNISM, political doctrine based on the writings of Karl MARX and Friedrich ENGELS, developed along a number of different lines during the course of the 20th century by various communist states and parties throughout the world. The term communism was originally used of communities, generally small and short-lived, whose members enjoyed common ownership of all property and material provision for all according to need. All communist parties share the general belief that a state-run economy is superior to private enterprise and that land should be organized for communal cultivation.

Marx and Engels saw communism as an advanced stage of SOCIALISM, and the term first acquired its modern associations with the appearance of their *Communist Manifesto* in 1848 (see MARXISM).

Communism differs from what in the West is generally called socialism in its adherence to the doctrine of revolution. The RUSSIAN REVOLUTION (1917) was the world's first successful communist revolution. It was led by LENIN, who had built upon 19th-century revolutionary POPULISM to create a disciplined Marxist movement (see BOLSHEVISM). Russia became the center of world communism.

The Comintern or Third INTERNATIONAL was founded in Moscow in 1919. It was to have been the spearhead of the world revolution which many saw as imminent. However, by March 1921 discontent at home and opposition to communism by European socialist parties forced Lenin to draw in his horns. He introduced the New Economic Policy, a compromise policy which meant a "temporary" abandoning of the world revolution and in time proved the seed of schism between right and left. On Lenin's death (1924), this schism broke out in the form of a power struggle between STALIN, whose priority was to strengthen socialism within Russia, and the internationalist TROTSKY. It was the first great rift in the world communist movement.

Stalin's repressive policies produced further rifts, such as that between Yugoslavia and the USSR (1948), throughout the European communist bloc as well as among communist parties in non-communist countries. The 1968 Soviet invasion of Czechoslovakia had much the same result.

The second great schism in world communism came after the success in 1949 of the Chinese Revolution, under the leadership of MAO TSE-TUNG. Within 15 years the reappearance of traditional tensions between the two giant neighbors, China and Russia, plus differences about the role each should play on the world stage, came to outweigh their nominal unity under the flag of Marxism-Leninism.

By the 1970s, there were communist movements in most countries throughout the world where not outlawed by the government. In Chile, under Salvador ALLENDE, the communists actually won power through free elections, but that regime was overthrown by a military coup. Attempts to build broad-based parties in the W, as in France and Italy, had mixed results. Widespread and outspoken hostility to the regime in POLAND, beginning in 1980, called attention to the failures of applied communist economic doctrine. At the same time, Soviet inability to put down resistance to the communist puppet regime in AFGHANISTAN underscored the limits to Soviet military power.

COMMUNIST PARTY, US, American political organization devoted to the ideals of COMMUNISM. Two parties, the Communist Labor Party and the Communist Party of America, emerged in 1919. They were united in 1921 and by 1925 were known as the Workers Party. In 1929 the party was renamed the Communist Party of the US, under the leadership of William Z. FOSTER. It became the leading revolutionary organization in the US, though post-depression economic recovery and the Nazi-Soviet pact of 1939 greatly reduced its appeal (see also Earl BROWDER). With the end of WWII and the onset of the COLD WAR, anti-communist legislation, for example the TAFT-HARTLEY ACT (1947), increased (see also MC CARTHY, JOSEPH). The party was virtually outlawed in 1954 but in 1966 it resumed open activity.

COMMUNITY CHEST, organization coordinating fund-raising by different groups to help voluntary and welfare agencies. This method of financing charities originated in Liverpool, England, in 1873.

COMOROS, independent nation occupying

most of the Comoro Islands, an archipelago in the Indian Ocean, off the E coast of Mozambique.

Official name: Federal and Islamic Republic of the Comoros
Capital: Moroni, on Grande-Comore
Area: 719sq mi
Population: 422,000
Languages: French, Comoran
Religions: Muslim and Christian
Monetary unit(s): 1 CFA franc = 100 centimes
Land. The Comoros consist of several small islands and three main islands—Grande-Comore, Anjouan and Moheli. The island of Mahore, previously Mayotte, remains under French administration. Climate, rainfall and vegetation vary from island to island, but all are volcanic in origin.
People. The majority of the population have mixed Arab, Malagasy and African ancestry and are Muslims.
Economy. The islands are poor in resources, and rank among the world's lowest income countries. Most of the population is engaged in farming, but soils are poor and most food must be imported. Coconuts, cassava and bananas are produced for local consumption. Ylang-ylang, a stabilizer used in French perfumes, vanilla, sisal, copra and cloves are the main exports. France is the principal trade partner.
History. Arabs landed on the islands during the 1400s and ruled each island as a separate sultanate, until ceding them to the French in 1841. In 1975 the Comoros declared independence, with France retaining responsibility for the island of Mayotte, where it has a naval base. Ahmed Abdalla, the nation's first president, was overthrown weeks after independence but returned to power in 1978 and was reelected in 1984. Comoros continues to claim Mayotte, and the issue has strained relations with France in recent years.

COMPARABLE WORTH, popular name for the concept of equal pay for work of equal value, which is intended to end the depreciation of female-dominated occupa-tions. Equal pay for equal work is guaranteed by the Equal Pay Act of 1963; complaints under this act need only show differences in pay between men and women in the same job. The principle of equal pay for work of equal value, or comparable worth, maintains that work of comparable difficulty, responsibility, and value to an organization should receive comparable pay. Thus, for example, a female nurse might argue that her work was of comparable worth to that of a male accountant employed by the same hospital.

COMPASS, device for determining direction parallel to the earth's surface. Most compasses make use of the EARTH'S magnetic field; if a bar magnet (see MAGNETISM) is pivoted at its center so that it is free to rotate horizontally, it will seek to align itself with the horizontal component in its locality of the earth's magnetic field. A simple compass consists of a magnet so arranged and a compass card marked with the four cardinal points and graduated in degrees (see ANGLE). In ship compasses, to compensate for rolling, the card is attached to the magnet and floated or suspended in a liquid, usually alcohol. Aircraft compasses often incorporate a GYROSCOPE to keep the compass horizontal. The two main errors in all magnetic compasses are **variation** (the angle between lines of geographic longitude and the local horizontal component of the earth's magnetic field) and **deviation** (local, artificial magnetic effects, such as nearby electrical equipment). Both vary with the siting of the compass, and may be with more or less difficulty compensated for. (See also GYROCOMPASS; NAVIGATION.) A **radio compass,** used widely in aircraft, is an automatic radio direction finder, calibrated with respect to the station to which it is tuned.

COMPIÈGNE, tourist center and man-ufacturing town in N France, 47mi NNE of Paris. It is famous for its château and forest where the WWI armistice was signed in Marshal FOCH's rail coach. Hitler accepted France's surrender in the same coach on June 22, 1940. Pop 28,381.

COMPLEX NUMBERS, pairs of real numbers that can be added, subtracted, multiplied and divided according to certain rules. The rule for addition is simply $(a, b) + (c, d) = (a+c, b+d)$, and similarly for subtraction. Complex numbers can be multiplied by writing them as $a+ib$ and using the rule $i^2 = -1$. Thus, $(a+ib)(c+id) = (ac-bd) + i(ad+bc)$. i is called the imaginary unit and numbers of the form $a+ib$ are called imaginary numbers (or pure imaginary numbers, the term imaginary number sometimes being applied to all complex numbers). This name arose because there is actually no number ("real" number) whose square root is -1. They were introduced into algebra so that every polynomial equation of degree n with real coefficients would have n roots. The equation $x^2 = -1$, for example, has no real roots; its roots are $+i$ and $-i$.

COMPOSITION, Chemical, the proportion by weight of each ELEMENT present in a chemical compound. The **law of definite proportions**, discovered by J. L. PROUST, states that pure compounds have a fixed and invariable composition. A few compounds, termed non-stoichiometric, disobey this law: they have latticed vacancies or extra atoms, and the composition varies within a certain range depending on the formation conditions. The **law of multiple proportions**, discovered by DALTON, states that, if two elements A and B form more than one compound, the various weights of B which combine with a given weight of A are in small whole-number ratios. (See also BOND, CHEMICAL.)

COMPROMISE OF 1850, attempt by the US Congress to reconcile North and South in the pre–CIVIL WAR period on the question of extending slavery to new territories. Approved by Congress in Sept. 1850, Senator Henry CLAY'S compromise Omnibus Bill admitted Cal. as a free state; prohibited slave trade in the District of Columbia; proposed a stricter FUGITIVE SLAVE LAW; deferred a decision on slavery in Ut. and N.M. until they applied for statehood; and paid the slave state of Tex. $10 million to relinquish much of its western territory to the federal government. The Compromise temporarily saved the Union; the factions were too entrenched for it to do any more.

COMPTON, Arthur Holly (1892–1962), US physicist who discovered the Compton effect (1923), thus providing evidence that X RAYS could act as particles as predicted in QUANTUM THEORY. Compton found that when monochromatic X rays were scattered by light elements, some of the scattered radiation was of longer wavelength, i.e., of lower ENERGY than the incident. Compton showed that this could be explained in terms of the collision between an X-ray PHOTON and an ELECTRON in the target. For this work he shared the 1927 Nobel physics prize with C. T. R. Wilson.

COMPTON-BURNETT, Dame Ivy (1892–1969), English novelist who portrayed late-Victorian upper middle class life. Her novels dealt with familial corruption, property and greed and proceed almost entirely through mannered yet dramatically flexible dialogue. Among her best-known works are *Men and Wives* (1931) and *Mother and Son* (1955).

COMPUTER, any device which performs calculations. In this light, the ABACUS, CALCULATING MACHINE and SLIDE RULE may all be described as computers; however, the term is usually limited to those electronic devices that are given a program to follow, data to store or to calculate with, and means with which to present results or other (stored) information.

Programming. A computer program consists essentially of a set of instructions which tells the computer which operations to perform, in what order to perform them, and the order in which subsequent data will be presented to it; for ease of use, the computer may already have subprograms built into its memory, so that, on receiving an instruction such as LOG X, it will automatically go through the program necessary to find the LOGARITHM of that piece of data supplied to it as X. Every model of computer has a different machine language or code; that is, the way in which it should ideally be programmed; however, this language is usually difficult and cumbersome for an operator to use. Thus a special program known as a **compiler** is retained by the computer, enabling it to translate computer languages such as ALGOL, COBOL and FORTRAN, which are easily learned and used by operators and programmers, into its own machine code. Programmers also make extensive use of ALGORITHMS to save programming and operating time.

Input. Programs and data are fed into computers using either the medium of punched tape or, more commonly in recent years, that of punched cards. In both cases it is the positions of holes punched in the medium which carry the information. These are read by a card or tape reader which usually consists of a light shining through the holes and activating PHOTOELECTRIC CELLS on the far side. The computer "reads" the resulting electrical pulses.

Storage. Machine languages generally take the form of a binary code (see BINARY NUMBERS), so that the two characters 0 and 1 may be easily represented by $+$ and $-$. Thus the ideal medium for data storage is magnetic, and may take the form of tapes, disks or drums. Magnetic tapes are used much as they are in a TAPE RECORDER; a magnetic head "writes" on the tape by creating a suitable magnetic flux, and can "read" the spots so created at a later date, retransmitting them in the form of electric pulses. Magnetic disks and drums work on a similar principle; the former are flat disks mounted in groups of up to twenty on a shared shaft, looking rather like a stack of phonograph records; drums are, as the name suggests, cylindrical, and are coated with a magnetic medium. Both drums and stacks of disks rotate constantly while the computer is in use, so that the maximum time taken for the read/write head to locate any specific area is that for one revolution. In all cases, each datum must be identified and given a specific "address" in the storage system, so that instructions for its retrieval may be given to the computer and so that the operator may take precautions against erasing it. (See INFORMATION RETRIEVAL.)

The computer's internal "memory" for programs and data that have been fed into it from these storage media usually consists of large-scale integrated circuit (LSI) chips that can store thousands of bits of information in a very small space.

Data processing. All the operations performed by the computer on the information it receives are collectively described as data processing. The main element of data processing is, of course, computation. This is almost exclusively done by addition, and performed using binary arithmetic. More complicated procedures, such as integration (see CALCULUS) or finding roots, are performed algorithmically, suitable subprograms being built into the computer. Again the characters 0 and 1 are represented by + and −, where this may refer to a closed or open switch, a direction of magnetic flux (see MAGNETISM), etc. Moreover, the computer contains logic circuits so that it may evaluate information while performing a calculation. If, for example, it were performing an algorithm to find √2 to a specified number of decimal places, it has to have a system whereby it can check at the end of each cycle of the algorithm whether or not its result is correct to the accuracy required. These circuits are designed using an application of Boolean algebra (see BOOLE, GEORGE) and are composed of simpler logic circuits that are electrical representations of the truth tables for the three operations *and*, *or* and *not*. Combinations of these three operations are capable of handling any logical operation required.

Output. Before being fed out, the information must be converted from machine code back into the programmer's computer language, numerical data being translated from the binary into the DECIMAL SYSTEM. The information is then fed out in the form of paper tape, punched cards or, using an adapted teleprinter, as a printout.

Types of computer. We have been talking almost exclusively about the **digital computer**, since this is the most widely-encountered and certainly the most versatile type. As we have seen, it requires information to be fed into it in "bits." Contrarily, the other main type of computer, the **analog computer**, is designed to deal with continuously varying quantities, such as lengths or voltages; the most everyday example of an analog computer is the slide rule. Electronic analog computers are usually designed for a specific task; as their accuracy is not high, their greatest use is in providing models of situations as bases for experiment. (See also CYBERNETICS.)

COMPUTER VIRUS, instructional code introduced into a computer program with the capacity to replicate itself in other computers with which the host computer has contact, causing anything from a mere nuisance to the destruction of stored data. Ingenious computer "hackers" regard the security measures by which such large computer users as government, banks, businesses, and universities try to prevent unauthorized access as irresistible challenges.

COMSAT (Communications Satellite Corporation), a private corporation established by act of Congress on Aug. 31, 1962, to develop satellite systems for relaying telephone, telegraph and television transmissions. Comsat is the US member and general manager of the International Telecommunications Satellite Consortium (Intelsat), formed in 1964 under the auspices of the United Nations. Comsat's first satellite, Early Bird, also known as Intelsat I, was launched Apr. 6, 1965.

COMSTOCK, Anthony (1844–1915), US moral crusader and a founder of the New York Society for the Suppression of Vice (1873). He successfully campaigned for stricter legislation against gambling and prostitution in N.Y. and the mailing of obscene matter.

COMSTOCK LODE, rich vein of silver discovered in the 1850s in W Nev. and named for Henry T. P. Comstock, one of the lode's first claimants. For some 30 years after its discovery it produced about half the US's silver output.

COMTE, Auguste (1798–1857), French philosopher, the founder of POSITIVISM and a pioneer of scientific sociology. His thinking was essentially evolutionary; he recognized a progression in the development of the sciences: starting from mathematics and progressing through astronomy, physics, chemistry and biology towards the ultimate goal of sociology. He saw this progression reflected in man's mental development. This had proceeded from a theological stage to a metaphysical one. Comte then sought to help inaugurate the final scientific or positivistic era. His social thinking reflected that of Henri de Saint-Simon and in turn his own works, particularly the *Philosophie positive* (1830–42), became widely influential in both France and England.

CONANT, James Bryant (1893–1978), US educator and diplomat who was president of Harvard (1933–53) and US high commissioner (1953–55) for and ambassador (1955–57) to West Germany. He wrote several influential works on education, including *Modern Science and Modern Man* (1952) and *Slums and Suburbs* (1961).

CONCENTRATION CAMP, term now most commonly associated with the forced-labor and extermination camps of Nazi Germany and the USSR. Prisoners in a concentration camp usually belong to a particular category and are often rounded up and interred without a legal trial. The modern concentration camp dates from the Boer War (1899–1902), when the British interred families of guerrillas. In the US during WWII, more than 100,000 persons of Japanese ancestry were removed from the West Coast and placed in 10 relocation centers. Although the camps had basic amenities, even schools, and although the inmates were not abused, the camps were universally condemned in later years as a gross injustice.

In Russia, before and after the 1917 revolution, political prisoners were routinely sent to remote, cold areas for forced labor. In the 1930s this punishment was meted out to others, including peasants, residents of newly annexed areas regarded as untrustworthy and suspected collaborators with the Germans—as well as German prisoners.

In 1933 the new Nazi regime in Germany established camps. Camp populations remained small until WWII when millions, mostly Jews, were interred in Germany and in occupied countries. Many were worked to death in forced-labor camps, and others were sent to camps whose purpose was extermination, usually by gassing or shooting. Estimates of the number of victims begin at 4,000,000 and range upward. The infamous camp names include Auschwitz, Treblinka, Dachau and Buchenwald.

CONCEPTUALISM, a modern term describing a position in scholastic philosophy with respect to the status of universals that was intermediate between the extremes of both NOMINALISM and REALISM. To a conceptualist, UNIVERSALS (general concepts such as chair-ness) indeed exist, but only as concepts common to all men's minds and not as things in the world of particular objects (such as chairs).

CONCERTO, composition opposing unequal musical forces, usually one solo instrument against a large orchestra. The three-movement orchestral form was elaborated by J. S. BACH out of the *concerto da camera*, a type of CHAMBER MUSIC. HANDEL added the cadenza as a regular feature. MOZART set the style for the modern concerto: the orchestra announces an opening subject with a *tutti,* a passage for full orchestra, then takes a subordinate position when the solo instrument enters, thus establishing the pattern of interchanges. BEETHOVEN added many novel touches to Mozart's basic form; others, including MENDELSSOHN, SCHUMANN, CHOPIN, BRAHMS and ELGAR have developed the concerto, using a wide range of solo instruments. The form remains popular with more recent composers such as BARTOK, PROKOFIEV, STRAVINSKY and SHOSTAKOVITCH.

CONCERT OF EUROPE, philosophy of cooperation shared by the major 19th-century European powers, aimed at maintaining the balance of power and settling disputes through negotiation. It originated in the Treaty of Chaumont 1814 (see also QUADRUPLE ALLIANCE) and remained intact until the CRIMEAN WAR 1854–56. The spirit of the Concert of Europe, however, may be said to have lasted through to the outbreak of WWI.

CONCORD, Battle of, second engagement in the American Revolutionary War, after Lexington (see LEXINGTON, BATTLE OF). Both were fought on April 19, 1775. The British, 700 strong, marched on Concord, Mass. to destroy military stores. The Americans retreated, but returned on seeing smoke from burning supplies. Under Major John Buttrick, they met the British at North Bridge and routed them, raising American morale. Casualties for both battles totaled 273 British, 95 Americans.

CONCORDAT, agreement between a pope and a secular government regulating religious affairs within that state, for instance the appointment of bishops and the status of church property. The first concordat was the Concordat of Worms, in 1122. The LATERAN TREATY (1929) recognized Vatican City as a sovereign state and established Roman Catholicism as Italy's only state religion.

CONCORDE, supersonic commercial passenger plane, developed by France and Britain. It began operation on Jan. 21, 1976 from Paris and London to South America and the Middle East, and on Nov. 22, 1977, from those cities to New York.

CONCRETE, versatile structural building material, made by mixing CEMENT, aggregate and water. Initially moldable, the cement hardens by hydration, forming a matrix which binds the aggregate. Various other ingredients—admixtures—may be added to improve the properties of the concrete; air-entraining agents increase durability. Since concrete is much more able to resist compressive than tensile stress, it is often reinforced with a steel bar embedded in it which is able to bear the tension. Prestressed concrete is reinforced concrete in which the steel is under tension and the concrete is compressed; it can withstand very much greater stresses. Concrete is used for all building elements and for bridges, dams, canals, highways etc., often as precast units.

CONCRETE MUSIC. See ELECTRONIC MUSIC.

CONCUSSION, a state of disturbed consciousness following head injury, characterized by AMNESIA for events preceding and following the trauma. Permanent BRAIN damage is only found in cases of repeated concussion, as in boxers who develop the punch-drunk syndrome.

CONDÉ, Louis II de Bourbon, Prince de (1621–1686), "the Great Condé," outstanding French general of the THIRTY YEARS' WAR, related to the royal family. He turned against MAZARIN, led troops in the FRONDE rebellion, and served with Spain; but was pardoned and fought for Louis XIV in the DUTCH WARS.

CONDENSATION, passage of substance from gaseous to liquid or solid state; CLOUDS are a result of condensation of water vapor in the ATMOSPHERE. Warm air can hold more water vapor than cool air; if a body of air is cooled it will reach a temperature (the dew point) where the water vapor it holds is at SATURATION level. Further decrease in temperature without change in pressure will initiate water condensation. Such condensation is greatly facilitated by the presence of condensation nuclei ('seeds'), small particles (e.g., of smoke) about which condensation may begin. Condensation trails behind high-flying jet aircraft result primarily from water vapor produced by the engines increasing the local concentration (see also CLOUD CHAMBER; GAS). Condensation is important in all processes using steam and in DISTILLATION, where the liquid

is collected, and condensed by removal of its latent heat of vaporization, in an apparatus called a condenser. In chemistry a condensation reaction is one in which two or more MOLECULES link together with elimination of a relatively small molecule, such as water.

CONDILLAC, Étienne Bonnot de (1715–1780), French philosopher, who broke with the teaching of LOCKE to found the doctrine of SENSATIONALISM, holding that all knowledge is derived from the senses.

CONDITIONING, term used to describe two quite different LEARNING processes. In the first, a human or animal response is generated by a stimulus which does not normally generate such a response (see REFLEX; PAVLOV). In the second, animals (and by extension humans) are trained to perform certain actions to gain rewards or escape punishment.

CONDOMINIUM, in real estate, individual ownership in property, such as an apartment, which is part of a larger complex owned in common. In the 1960s and 1970s, a sharp increase in condominiums occurred in the US. In many cases landlords sought to convert existing rental properties into condominiums for economic reasons. A cooperative building differs from a condominium in that tenants do not actually own their apartments; they hold shares in a corporation entitling them to a long-term "proprietary" lease.

CONDORCET, Marie Jean Antoine Nicholas de Caritat, Marquis de (1743–1794), French philosopher, mathematician and revolutionary politician chiefly remembered for his theory that the human race, having risen from barbarism, would continue to progress toward moral, intellectual and physical perfection. His principal mathematical work was in the theory of probability. He played a prominent role in the Revolution, though his moderate opinions led to his outlawry and suicide.

CONDORS, two species of New World vultures, the California condor *Gymnogypes californianus* and the Andean condor *Vultur gryphus*. The California condor is extremely rare, facing extinction.

CONDOTTIERE, mercenary soldier of 14th- and 15th-century Italy. Powerful condottieri raised armies and sold their services to the highest bidder among warring states. Famous leaders were Francesco Sforza, Bartolomeo Colleoni and an Englishman, Sir John Hawkwood.

CONDUCTING, the art of directing a group of musicians. Conducting evolved with the increasing complexity of music.

Choirs had leaders by the 15th century, while by HANDEL'S day CONTINUO players guided orchestral works; but the idea of a conductor whose sole task was training and directing an orchestra emerged in the time of BEETHOVEN (who conducted his own works). Conducting became a virtuoso skill in the 19th century.

CONDUCTION, Heat, passage of heat through a body without large-scale movements of matter within the body (see CONVECTION). Mechanisms involved include the transfer of vibrational ENERGY from one MOLECULE to the next through the substance (dominant in poor conductors), and energy transfer by ELECTRONS (in good electrical conductors) and phonons (in crystalline solids). In general, solids, especially metals, are good conductors, liquids and gases poor.

CONDUCTORS, Electric, substances (usually metals) whose high conductivity makes them useful for carrying electric current (see ELECTRICITY). They are most often used in the form of wires or cables. The best conductor is SILVER, but, for reasons of economy, COPPER is most often used. (See also SEMICONDUCTORS; SUPERCONDUCTIVITY.)

CONE, a solid geometrical figure traced by the rotation of a straight line A (the generator) about a fixed straight line B which it intersects, such that each point on A traces out a closed curve. A cone has therefore two parts (nappes) which touch each other at the point of intersection, termed the vertex of the cone, of lines A and B; the two parts being skew-symmetrical (see SYMMETRY) about the vertex and of infinite extent. Usually one considers only one of these parts, limited by a plane which cuts it. The tracing of the closed curve of rotation on this plane is the directrix, and the part of the plane bounded by the directrix is the base of the cone. The lines joining the vertex to each point of the directrix are the cone's elements. The perpendicular line from the vertex to this plane is the altitude or height of the cone; the line joining the vertex to the center of the base (if it has a center) is the axis, and in most cases coincides with line B. Should axis and altitude coincide, the cone is a right cone; otherwise it is oblique. A cone whose directrix is a circle is a circular cone, its volume being given by $\pi r^2 h/3$ where r is the radius of the directrix and h is the altitude. (See also CONIC SECTIONS.)

CONESTOGA WAGON, large covered wagon used by American pioneers. Originating about 1725 in the Conestoga region of Pennsylvania, it became the chief means of transporting settlers and freight across the Alleghenies until about 1850. It had big, broadrimmed wheels and a canvas roof supported by wooden hoops, and was pulled by four to six horses.

CONFEDERATE STATES OF AMERICA, government formed by the Southern states which seceded from the United States of America, Dec. 1860–May 1861. S.C. was the first state to leave the Union after the election of President LINCOLN and was followed by Miss., Fla., Ala., Ga., La., Tex., Va., Ark., Tenn. and N.C. Rebels from Mo. and Ky. (both of which remained in the Union) set up their own governments-in-exile under the Southern banner and brought the number of Confederate states hypothetically to 13.

A constitutional convention was called for Feb. 4, 1861, in Montgomery, Ala., which became the Confederate capital. Jefferson DAVIS (Miss.) and Alexander STEPHENS (Ga.) were elected president and vice-president. A constitution much like that of the US—but with strong "states' rights" provisions—was produced on March 11.

War with the North began on April 13 with the bombardment of Union-held Fort Sumter. Davis was reelected in Nov. and inaugurated on Feb. 22, 1862, in the new capital, Richmond, Va. He led some 9,000,000 people—of whom about 3,500,000 were slaves—at war with the nearly 23,000,000 citizens of the Union. By April he had been forced to initiate the draft and his need for wide wartime powers brought clashes with his "states' rights" Congress.

As the war continued, the government's problems deepened. Reluctant to impose taxes, it issued vast amounts of currency and war bonds which caused ruinous inflation. The essentially agricultural South suffered an increasingly desperate shortage of munitions, heavy industrial goods, domestic supplies and even of food, worsened by a successful Union naval blockade which hampered export of cotton, the country's one major crop. The South's chief cotton consumer, Britain, sent ships and munitions but refused to enter the war.

Superb military leadership provided the South's early victories and kept the conflict alive into 1865. After several desperate peace initiatives, the Confederacy had to acknowledge total military surrender. By then much of its land was devastated and the economy was in ruins. (See also CIVIL WAR, AMERICAN.)

CONFEDERATION, Articles of. See ARTICLES OF CONFEDERATION.

CONFESSION, admission of sin, an aspect

of repentance and thus required for absolution. General confession may be made in a congregation; private confession may be made to God, or also to a priest. The latter is a SACRAMENT of the Roman Catholic and Eastern churches, also observed in some Lutheran and Episcopalian churches.

CONFIRMATION, a rite of certain Christian churches, usually administered in adolescence. The candidates confirm the promises made at their BAPTISM and the bishop lays his hands on them, invoking the HOLY SPIRIT upon them. In the Roman Catholic and Eastern churches confirmation is a SACRAMENT.

CONFUCIANISM, philosophical system based on the teachings of CONFUCIUS and practiced throughout China for nearly 2,000 years. Confucianism teaches a moral and social philosophy and code of behavior based on peace, order, humanity, wisdom, courage and fidelity. Confucius refused to consider the question of God but Confucianists hold there is a state of heavenly harmony which man can attain by cultivating virtues, especially knowledge, patience, sincerity, obedience and the fulfillment of obligations between children and parents, subjects and ruler. Confucianism's encouragement of the acceptance of the *status quo* is at odds with the ideology of continuing revolution of the Communist Chinese government.

CONFUCIUS (K'ung Fu-tzu; c551–479 BC), founder of the Chinese ethical and moral system CONFUCIANISM. Born in the feudal state of Lu, he was poor and self-educated but began teaching and gathering disciples when aged about 20. Distressed by political disunity and oppressive rule, over the next 30 years he evolved a system of "right living," a guide for wise government preserved by his disciples in a collection of his sayings, the Confucian *Analects.* Confucius became a magistrate of the city of Chang-tu but resigned from what proved to be a position of impotence. Little else is reliably known of his life.

CONGO, a socialist republic in W central Africa, formerly part of French Equatorial Africa. It is about the size of Mont. and lies on the equator E of Gabon and the Atlantic and W of Zaire.

Land. A low, treeless plain along the coast gives way inland to the Myombé Escarpment, a mountainous rain forest. There is a savanna plateau in the N, and the Ubangi and Congo (Zaire) rivers and their hot, humid forests border the E and S.

People. Some 60% of the population is rural,

Official name: People's Republic of the Congo
Capital: Brazzaville
Area: 132,047sq mi
Population: 2,180,000
Languages: French, Bantu
Religions: Animist, Roman Catholic
Monetary unit(s): 1 CFA franc=100 centimes

but there has been a major drift to the towns, of which the largest are the capital Brazzaville and Pointe-Noire, the Atlantic port. Most people are Bantu speakers, notably the Bakongo whose roughly 15 tribes make up nearly half the population. Other main Bantu-speaking tribal groups are the Batcke and M'Bochi. French is the official language. The government has placed an emphasis on education, but the rate of illiteracy is still high. A national university catering to over 4,500 students was created in Brazzaville in 1972.

Economy. Although the Congo has rich oil resources, a varied manufacturing sector and ports providing it and its neighbors with vital outlets to the world market, it has had serious economic setbacks—due mainly to political instability and poor economic planning and management. The agricultural sector is undeveloped; the country has had to rely increasingly on food imports. Cocoa, coffee, sugar and palm oil are the main crops. Crude oil is the sole major cash earner, followed by timber and potash. The Congo R is a key waterway, and Brazzaville, the capital, is a major port city.

History. The Congo was originally part of the Kingdom of the Kongo, a region discovered by the Portuguese in the 15th century and later broken up into smaller states and exploited by European slave traders. It became a French colony in 1891, an overseas territory of France in 1946 and an independent republic in 1960. Periodic civil strife from 1963 onward led to an army takeover in 1968. Following a presidential assassination in 1977 and subsequent martial law, Col. Sassou Nguesso seized power and was declared president under a new constitution; he was subsequently reelected to successive terms by the Congolese Labor Party, the only legal party. In the late 1980s, an economic crisis caused by falling petroleum revenues forced the government to institute austerity measures.

CONGO (Kinshasha). See ZAIRE.

CONGO RIVER, also Zaire R, second-longest river in Africa. It exceeds 2,700mi from its source in the Chambezi R, Zambia, to the Atlantic Ocean in W Zaire. It drains 1,425,000sq mi, and in volume of water is second only to the Amazon. The Congo proper and its longest navigable portion (1000mi) begins below Boyoma (Stanley) Falls near Kisangani (Stanleyville) and runs to Pool Malebo (Stanley Pool), linked by channels to Brazzaville and Kinshasha. Below Livingstone Falls the Congo is navigable for 95mi from Matadi to the Atlantic. The river mouth was discovered by Diogo Cam in 1482, and David LIVINGSTONE explored its upper reaches first 1866–71. Henry Morton STANLEY first traced its course in 1874–77. It was renamed the Zaire by President Mobutu in 1971.

CONGREGATIONAL CHURCHES, Protestant churches which hold that each local church (congregation) should have complete autonomy, though they may form loose associations. In the 16th century Robert BROWNE first stated Congregational doctrine. In the 17th century Congregationalists established churches in the New England colonies and founded Harvard and Yale universities. Most US Congregationalists merged (1931) with the Christian Church (see DISCIPLES OF CHRIST) and then with the EVANGELICAL AND REFORMED CHURCH (1957) to form the UNITED CHURCH OF CHRIST. (See also MATHER; SEPARATISTS.)

CONGRESS OF RACIAL EQUALITY (CORE), US organization founded in 1942 by James FARMER to promote black CIVIL RIGHTS through nonviolent direct action projects. Its voter registration drives and "freedom rides" in the South led to civil rights legislation in the 1960s. In the 1970s CORE became more militant.

CONGRESS OF THE UNITED STATES, legislative branch of the US federal government. It consists of two houses, the Senate and the House of Representatives. Under the UNITED STATES CONSTITUTION, the powers vested in Congress are to introduce legislation, to assess and collect taxes, to regulate interstate and foreign commerce, to coin money, to establish post offices, to maintain armed forces and to declare war. Congress convenes on Jan. 3 and is in session until adjournment, usually in the

fall. A single Congress is two sessions; the first Congress met in 1789–90.

House of Representatives. Membership was 65 in 1789 and is now fixed at 435. Each state has at least one representative; the total number per state is proportional to state population as determined by official census; state legislatures set the boundaries for congressional districts. A representative must be over 25, a US citizen for at least seven years and resident in the state (and usually the district) which elects him. Elections for representatives are held every two years on the Tuesday after the first Monday in Nov. The House has special powers to impeach federal officials (who are then tried by the Senate), originate revenue bills and elect the president if no candidate gains a majority in the ELECTORAL COLLEGE.

The Senate. There are 100 senators, two from each state. Direct popular elections were introduced in 1913. Until then senators had been elected by state legislatures. Senators serve overlapping six-year terms, one-third being elected every two years. They must be over 30, citizens for at least nine years and resident in the state which elects them. The Senate's special powers are to advise and consent on the appointments of important government officials, including ambassadors and federal judges, and to approve treaties. Through its foreign relations committee, the Senate wields large influence on the conduct of foreign affairs. Officially the vice-president presides over the Senate, but often delegates the task.

The Work of Congress. For a bill to become law it must be approved by both the House and Senate and signed by the president. If he vetoes the bill, Congress may pass it by a two-thirds majority in each house. When the House and Senate disagree on a bill, a joint committee may resolve the differences in a compromise bill, or the bill may die. Each house has committees for drafting and studying bills. They are then debated by the house which originated them, and votes are taken to pass, reject or defer them. Debate is freer in the Senate than in the House because of the Senate's smaller numbers; a bill may be killed by FILIBUSTER unless a two-thirds majority can be reached to close the debate.

CONGREVE, William (1670–1729), English Restoration dramatist, master of the comedy of manners. Among his comedies are *The Old Bachelor* (1693), *Love for Love* (1695) and his masterpiece *The Way of the World* (1700), which is often performed today.

CONIC SECTIONS, plane curves formed

by the intersection of a PLANE with a right circular or right elliptical CONE: the three curves are the ellipse, the parabola and the hyperbola. An ellipse occurs when the ANGLE between the axis of the cone and the plane is greater than the angle between the axis and the generator (in special cases a circle may be produced). It may be defined as the locus of intersection of a plane with a right circular cone about two fixed foci F and F', such that $PF + PF' = c$, where c is a constant greater than the distance FF'. The major axis of an ellipse is its axis of SYMMETRY concurrent with FF'; its minor axis is the axis of symmetry perpendicular to this, their point of intersection being defined as the center of the ellipse. If the length of the minor axis is 2b, b being a constant, then $c^2 = (FF')^2 + b^2$. The eccentricity of an ellipse is given by the distance FF' divided by the length of the major axis. A parabola occurs when the angle between the axis and the plane equals the angle between the axis and generator (in special cases a straight line may be produced). It may be defined as the locus of a point P such that its distance from a fixed focus F is constantly equal to its perpendicular distance from a fixed straight line XY. The curve, which has only one axis of symmetry, perpendicular to XY and passing through F, is of infinite extent. The hyperbola occurs when the angle between axis and plane is less than that between axis and generator (in special cases a pair of intersecting straight lines may be produced). It may be defined as the loci of two points, P' and P', about two foci, F and F', such that $PF' - PF = c = P'F - PF'$, where c is a constant less than the distance FF'. The curve, which is of infinite extent, has a real axis of symmetry passing through F and F', and an imaginary axis of symmetry passing perpendicularly through the midpoint of FF'. The hyperbola, though of infinite extent in the direction of its real axis, is bounded in the direction perpendicular to this.

CONIFERS, cone-bearing trees and shrubs that include the yews, pines, redwood, cypress, and araucarias. They are found in the drier parts of the world, particularly in cold regions, and usually have needle- or scale-like leaves which reduce the loss of water from the plant. Except for the larches and bald cypress, conifers are evergreen, retaining their leaves all the year round.

The reproductive organs are cones, which are modified branches with scaly leaves. Each cone is a single sex and cones of each sex may be borne on separate trees. Male cones usually grow in clusters while female cones are solitary, a seed being borne on each cone scale.

CONJUNCTIVITIS, INFLAMMATION of the conjunctiva, or fine skin covering the EYE and inner eyelids. It is a common but usually harmless condition caused by ALLERGY (as part of HAY FEVER), foreign bodies, or infection with VIRUSES or BACTERIA. It causes irritation, watering and sticky discharge, but does not affect VISION. Eye drops may help, as can ANTIBIOTICS if bacteria are present.

CONNECTICUT, state, NE US, bounded to the E by R.I., to the S by Long Island Sound (an arm of the Atlantic Ocean), to the W by N.Y., and to the N by Mass.; one of the original 13 states.

Name of state: Connecticut
Capital: Hartford
Statehood: Jan. 9, 1788 (5th state)
Familiar names: Constitution State, Nutmeg State
Area: 5,009sq mi
Population: 3,189,000
Elevation: Highest—2,380ft, Mt. Frissell. Lowest—sea level, at Long Island Sound
Motto: *Qui transtulit sustinet* ("He who transplanted still sustains")
State flower: Mountain laurel
State bird: Robin
State tree: White oak
State song: "Yankee Doodle."

Land. Connecticut can be divided into three topographical areas: the Taconic Mts and Berkshires to the NW; a central lowland; and a hilly E upland. Major rivers include the Connecticut, Housatonic, and Thames. The climate is temperate and changeable.

People. Although about two-thirds of the state is forested, it is generally a highly urbanized area. Many residents in the SW commute to work in New York City. Population growth is minimal, less than 3% in 1976–86.

Economy. Most of the state's prosperity comes from industry: Connecticut produces transportation equipment, fabricated metal goods and machine tools. Hartford, the state capital, is an important insurance center in the US. Yale, founded in 1701, was the nation's third university. Bridgeport and Hartford are the largest cities, followed by New Haven, Waterbury and Stamford.

History. The Connecticut R was first explored in 1614 by the Dutchman Adriaen Block, and in 1633 a Dutch fur-trading post was established at Hartford. In the 1630s, Puritans from Massachusetts Bay Colony settled Wethersfield, Hartford, Windsor and Saybrook, while Congregationalists from the Plymouth Bay Colony founded New Haven Colony, restricting voting rights there to members of the Congregational Church. In 1639, the river towns joined to form the Connecticut Colony to which New Haven also belonged after 1665. Colonial agriculture prospered in the Connecticut Valley, and in the 18th century manufacturing developed with production of iron and tin products as well as textiles and clothing.

In 1788 Connecticut became the fifth state of the new union. It opposed Jefferson's Embargo Act of 1807 and the WAR OF 1812. The Hartford Convention, set up to protect New England interests during the War of 1812, was dissolved when the war ended; in 1818 the new state constitution was introduced. In the Civil War, Connecticut supported the Union. The war increased industry, immigration and urbanization. WWI aided industrial expansion and WWII revived the economy after the depression of the 1930s. Connecticut thereafter grew steadily in prosperity. Defense contracts remained important, Hartford maintained its leading position in the insurance industry, and Stamford became a center for corporate headquarters. Increased suburbanization brought problems of air and water pollution, but the state—with the highest per capita income in the nation—had the resources to deal with them. In presidential elections 1968–88, Connecticut voted Republican in 1972–88.

CONNECTICUT RIVER, the longest river in New England. Rising in northern New Hampshire, the Connecticut flows south 407mi through Massachusetts and Connecticut before emptying into Long Island Sound. Discovered by Dutch explorers in 1614, the river is of great historical, agricultural and industrial significance to the northeastern states. Many of its falls and rapids are harnessed for hydroelectric power.

CONNECTICUT WITS. See HARTFORD WITS.

CONNELLY, Marc (Marcus Cook Connelly; 1890–1980), US playwright, best known for his Pulitzer Prize-winning play, *The Green Pastures* (1930). He collaborated with George S. KAUFMAN on several plays, including *Beggar on Horseback* (1924).

CONNOLLY, Maureen Catharine (1934–1969), US tennis player, three-time Wimbledon champion (1952–54). In 1953 she also won the Australian, French, and US championships.

CONNORS, Jimmy (1952–   ), US tennis player. He was the top-ranked player in the world through most of the 1970s. He won the US Open (1974, 1976, 1978, 1982, 1983) and Wimbledon (1974, 1982), popularizing the left-handed, two-fisted backhand.

CONQUISTADORS, 16th-century military adventurers who founded Spain's empire in the Americas. Most famous among them were Hernán CORTÉS and Francisco PIZARRO.

CONRAD, Joseph (Jozef Teodor Konrad Korzeniowski; 1857–1924), Polish-born English novelist. He went to sea from 1874 to about 1894 and became a British citizen (1886). Conrad is best known for his studies of individuals and also of small groups or communities (such as those on board ship or in isolated jungle settlements) at moments of extreme moral crisis. His works include *The Nigger of the "Narcissus"* (1897), *Lord Jim* (1900), *Heart of Darkness* (1902), *Typhoon* (1903), *Nostromo* (1904) and *The Secret Agent* (1907).

CONRAIL, the official nickname for Consolidated Rail Corp., a quasi-governmental US organization created to take over seven bankrupt railroads in the NE and MW, including the Penn Central, Erie & Lackawanna, Lehigh Valley and Reading. Conrail began operations on Apr. 1, 1976. It carries c500,000 passengers daily and one-quarter of the nation's rail freight traffic.

CONSCIENTIOUS OBJECTOR, person who refuses to bear arms and opposes military training or service. The position of objectors is based on conscience, according to their religious, political or philosophical beliefs. Groups refusing to bear arms have been persecuted at various periods in history. Most countries now have legal provisions for objectors, who are generally drafted into alternative noncombatant military duty or socially useful civilian work. (See also DRAFT, MILITARY; PACIFISM.)

CONSCRIPTION. See DRAFT, MILITARY.

CONSERVATION, the preservation of the ENVIRONMENT, whether to ensure the long-term future availability of natural resources such as FUEL or to retain such intangibles as scenic beauty for future generations.

History. The conservation movement was born in the 19th century as a result of two developments: acceptance of the theory of EVOLUTION and the concept (later proved erroneous) of the BALANCE OF NATURE. It was estimated in that century that over 100 million acres of land in the US had been totally destroyed through SOIL EROSION caused by the reckless destruction of forests; Congress passed the Forest Reserve Act (1891) and the Carey Land Act (1894) but both were rendered ineffectual by commercial interests. The first genuinely conservationist president was Theodore ROOSEVELT, whose Newlands Reclamation Act of 1902 began the struggle for American conservation in earnest. More recently, where officialdom has been dilatory, conservation has been brought to the people by groups such as Friends of the Earth, earning through their efforts a powerful international membership.

The Role of Science. ECOLOGY, the study of the interrelationships of elements of an environment, has enabled many scientific disciplines to play a part in conservation. In AGRICULTURE, where protection of the soil from erosion is clearly of paramount importance, crop rotation, strip-cropping and other improvements in land use have been made. Important in all fields of human existence and endeavor is the conservation of WATER for IRRIGATION, industrial, drinking and other purposes. Careful use, plus the prevention or amelioration of POLLUTION, especially by industry, are essential. Conservation of raw materials is more complicated, since they cannot be replaced; however, much has been done in the way of good management, and science has developed new processes, artificial substitutes and techniques of RECYCLING. Conservation of wildlife, however, is probably the most dramatically successful of all conservation in this century. Many species, such as the koala and American bison, that were in danger of extinction are now reviving; and most governments are vigilant in areas such as hunting and industrial pollution. Important to all these efforts is the retention of the human population within reasonable limits. In this, CONTRACEPTION has a large part to play, and many governments are now active in their encouragement of it.

CONSERVATISM, term for social and political philosophies or attitudes, stressing traditional values and continuity of social institutions and rejecting sudden radical change, while at the same time maintaining ideals of progress. It was first used in the early 19th century of the policies of the British TORY party. Modern conservative political parties include the British Conservative and Unionist Party, the Canadian PROGRESSIVE-CONSERVATIVE PARTY and the American REPUBLICAN PARTY.

CONSIDÉRANT, Victor Prosper (1808–1893), French socialist. He promoted the doctrines of Charles FOURIER, edited *La Phalange*, the journal of Fourierism, and published *Destinée sociale* (1834–38) and *Principes du socialisme* (1847). He tried to establish a communistic community near Dallas, Tex. (1855–57).

CONSTABLE, John (1776–1837), English painter. He and J. M. W. TURNER were England's two greatest landscapists. Believing that painting should be pursued scientifically, he explored techniques of rendering landscape from direct observation of nature under different effects of light and weather. His naturalist approach had some influence on the French BARBIZON SCHOOL.

CONSTANCE, Council of (1414–18), council of the Roman Catholic Church that ended the GREAT SCHISM and asserted the supremacy of councils over popes. In its effort to extirpate heresy, the council ordered the arrest, trial, and execution of the Bohemian reformer Jan HUS.

CONSTANT, Benjamin (1767–1830), French writer and politician. He advocated constitutional monarchy in opposition to both NAPOLEON I and CHARLES X. His novel *Adolphe* (1816) and journals are highly regarded. He is also noted for his liaison with Madame de STAËL.

CONSTANTINE I (c280–337 AD), Roman emperor, known as the Great. He promoted and accepted Christianity, and transferred the empire's capital from Rome to Byzantium. He was proclaimed Caesar in the W by his father Constantius (306), who was Augustus in the W. After his father's death, he defeated one claimant for the throne, Maximilian (310), and then his son Maxentius at the battle of the Milvian Bridge (312), where he is said to have had a vision of a cross against the sun, which he adopted as his standard. In the Edict of Milan, Constantine, now Augustus in the W, and Licinius, Augustus in the E, agreed to tolerate Christianity in the empire. In 324 Constantine defeated Licinius and became sole emperor. His council at Arles (314) condemned Donatism (a schismatic Christian sect in North Africa), and the first general council of the Church at NICAEA (325) dealt with ARIANISM. He rebuilt Byzantium, inaugurating it as his eastern capital in 330 and renaming it Constantinople. He instituted a centralized bureaucracy, separated military from civil government and introduced many legal reforms.

CONSTANTINOPLE. See ISTANBUL.

CONSTANTINOPLE, Latin Empire of (1204–61), feudal empire set up by leaders of the Fourth Crusade, the Venetians and Latins. Throughout this disastrous period of Byzantine history, the city suffered massacres and pillages until its recapture by Greek Emperor Michael VIII. (See CRUSADES.)

CONSTELLATION, a group of stars forming a pattern in the sky, though otherwise unconnected. In ancient times the patterns were interpreted as pictures, usually of mythic characters. The ecliptic passes through 12 constellations, known as the zodiacal constellations (see ZODIAC).

CONSTIPATION, a decrease in the frequency of bowel actions from the norm for an individual; also increased hardness of stool. Often precipitated by inactivity, changed diet or environment, it is sometimes due to GASTROINTESTINAL TRACT disease. Increased dietary fiber, and taking of fecal softeners or intestinal irritants are usual remedies; enema may be required in severe cases.

CONSTITUTION, fundamental rules, written or unwritten, for the government of an organized body such as a nation. The US constitution defines the rights of citizens and of states, and the structure and powers of the federal government. It exists in documentary form, but those of many other nations do not. The British constitution is embodied in tradition and the law of the land. Some constitutions, such as that of the US, may only be altered by special procedures, while others, such as that of Britain, may be altered by a simple act of the legislature.

CONSTITUTION, USS, American frigate carrying 44 guns, known as "Old Ironsides." Launched in Boston in 1797, she served in the war with Tripoli and the War of 1812. In 1828 a plan to dismantle the warship provoked Oliver Wendell Holmes' poem "Old Ironsides." She was rebuilt, berthed in Boston, and opened to the public in 1934.

CONSTITUTION ACT (1982), Canadian law that superseded the BRITISH NORTH AMERICA ACT (1867) and effectively "patriated" Canada's constitution—eliminating the necessity of formal approval from the British Parliament for constitutional amendments. The basic constitution of Canada, proclaimed by Queen Elizabeth II in Ottawa on April 17, 1982, this document includes a Charter of Rights guaranteeing fundamental rights and freedoms.

CONSTITUTIONAL LAW, US, body of law which interprets the US Constitution. The original constitution did not precisely define the roles or the limits of power of governmental institutions. Constitutional law studies their historical development in relation to contemporary issues. **Judicial review** deals with the power of the courts, ultimately the Supreme Court, to determine the constitutionality of laws or acts of government. Although the Constitution did not provide for this activity, the Supreme Court has claimed it since Chief Justice John MARSHALL's decision in MARBURY V MADISON (1803). He asserted that since the Constitution is the supreme law, and it is the courts' duty to uphold the law, the courts must invalidate any law or action they consider in conflict with the Constitution.

Separation of powers (formulated by MONTESQUIEU) combats despotism by dividing governmental power into branches which check and balance each other. Thus legislative power is granted to Congress, judicial power to the courts and executive power to the president. Each is supreme in its own sphere, but the 20th century has seen growth in executive power, which now initiates legislation.

The federal system divides governmental powers between the federal and state governments. The Constitution designated the federal government's powers and reserved all others to the states. Recently the use by Congress of its right to make all laws necessary and proper to carry out its constitutional function and to regulate interstate commerce has enormously increased federal power. The conflict between centralized and state power is reflected in US political parties: Democrats tend to favor centralized power and financial control, while Republicans favor STATES' RIGHTS and decentralized financial administration.

CONSTITUTIONAL UNION PARTY, US political party (the Do-Nothing Party), formed from remnants of the Whig and American (Know-Nothing) parties, active 1859–60. Its platform upheld the Constitution and the Union, while ignoring the slavery issue. As a result, the vote in 1860 was split and LINCOLN was elected by the ELECTORAL COLLEGE, the first president without a popular majority.

CONSTRUCTIVISM, artistic movement which was developed in Russia 1913–20 by TATLIN, LISSITZKY, PEVSNER and GABO. Partly influenced by CUBISM and FUTURISM, it was related to technology and industrial materials. The geometric abstract work of Russian constructivists was influential in Germany (in the BAUHAUS), France, England and the US.

CONSUBSTANTIATION, doctrine that in the Eucharist the blood and body of Christ coexist substantially with the bread and wine of the sacrament. This was introduced by LUTHER in opposition to belief in TRANSUBSTANTIATION, the changing of the wafer and wine into the body and blood of Christ.

CONSUL, Roman, the two chief magistrates of the Roman Republic, elected annually by the legislative assembly. Consuls were the heads of state from the fall of the kings, c509 BC, until 27 BC; under the empire consulship became an honorary office.

CONSULATE, government of France (1799–1804) that replaced the DIRECTORY. It consisted of three consuls but was dominated by First Consul Napoleon Bonaparte, who was made first consul for life in 1802 and emperor in 1804. (See NAPOLEON I.)

CONSUMER PRODUCT SAFETY COMMISSION, independent US government agency established in 1972 to set mandatory product-safety standards to reduce the unreasonable risk of injury to consumers from consumer products.

CONSUMER PROTECTION, the body of laws and voluntary codes setting standards for goods and services sold and the agencies enforcing them, as well as the efforts of consumer groups. In recent years widespread recognition was given to the fact that the common law maxim "let the buyer beware" (*caveat emptor*) was no longer valid in superindustrial societies; today's buyer cannot necessarily protect his own best interests by judicious purchasing. The need for consumer protection arose because of the dangers of price-fixing by monopolies, of fraud and of the increasing difficulty in judging the quality or suitability of goods as technological production, packaging and sales techniques grow more sophisticated.

There are over 1000 consumer protection programs in the US under federal, state and local agencies. The federal government sets standards for weights and measures, product safety, packaging, food and drug composition and advertising descriptions. The FOOD AND DRUG ADMINISTRATION is the best known of the federal agencies. The departments of Justice, Transportation, Commerce, Housing and Urban Development, and the Federal Power, Trade, Communications and Interstate Commerce commissions are among those involved in consumer protection.

Consumer movements. The National Consumers' League was formed in 1899 to encourage purchase of articles made under good working conditions and of good standard. Its work inspired such books as *The Great American Fraud* by Samuel Hopkins Adams, which contributed to the passage of the Food and Drug Act in 1906 and the founding of the American Home Economics Association (1908). Upton SINCLAIR's *The Jungle* (1906) exposed the unsafe and unsanitary conditions in the meat-packing industry. F. J. Schlink, coauthor with Stuart Chase of *Your Money's Worth* (1924), helped to found a consumers' club that evolved into Consumers' Research Inc. (1929), which tested products and published its findings. An offshoot of this group formed the Consumers' Union in 1936 and began to publish *Consumer Reports,* which evaluates the cost and quality of products in an effort to protect consumers' interests. The Food, Drug and Cosmetic Act was passed in 1938.

Ralph NADER exposed defects in automobile design that affected motorists' safety in *Unsafe at Any Speed* (1965) and financed investigation of other products. With "Nader's Raiders," his volunteer assistants, he aroused consumer awareness, which was consolidated in boycotts and group lawsuits. Such action was at first bitterly opposed, but later won positive response from government, industry and the public. Congress approved the Auto safety Act (1965), Truth in Landing Act (1968), Consumer Protection Act (1969) and Consumer Products Safety Act (1972). Some companies have begun to manufacture products less harmful to consumers and the environment such as biodegradable detergents, lead-free gasoline, returnable bottles and foods free from chemical additives. The many governmental restrictions on production of consumer goods because of safety factors during the 1970s caused a backlash, however, and President Ronald Reagan's conservative administration began to relax some stringent controls on production of consumer goods in the early 1980s.

CONTINENT, one of the seven major divisions of land on earth: Africa, Antarctica, Asia, Australia, Europe, North America, South America. These continents have evolved during the earth's history from a single landmass, Pangaea (see also CONTINENTAL DRIFT; PLATE TECTONICS; CONTINENTAL SHELF).

CONTINENTAL ARMY, American force

in the REVOLUTIONARY WAR, organized (1775) and commanded by George WASHINGTON. It consisted of about 5,000 volunteers, joined at irregular intervals by state militia, sometimes raising the number to around 20,000. It was financed by individual states and foreign loans, and was always short of money, food, clothing and ammunition.

CONTINENTAL CONGRESS (1774–89), body of delegates representing the colonies which was summoned before and during the American REVOLUTIONARY WAR. The First Continental Congress met in Philadelphia, Sept. 5, 1774, to seek relief from England's commercial and political oppression. There were 56 delegates, from all colonies except Georgia. The congress drafted a declaration of rights setting forth the colonists' demands as British subjects, formulated a "plan of association," denounced "taxation without representation" and agreed to boycott trade with England until their demands were met. When the Second Continental Congress met on May 10, 1775, battles had already been fought at Lexington and Concord, Mass. It appointed George Washington commander-in-chief of the army. It approved the Declaration of Independence on July 4, 1776, and drafted the ARTICLES OF CONFEDERATION, which served as a US constitution from 1781 until the present constitution was drawn up (1787). In the meantime, the Continental Congress acted as a federal government in maintaining an army, issuing currency and dealing with foreign policy.

CONTINENTAL DIVIDE, imaginary line which divides a continent at the point where its rivers start flowing in opposite directions and empty into different oceans. In North America it follows the Rocky Mts, in South America the Andes.

CONTINENTAL DRIFT, theory first rigorously formulated by WEGENER to explain a number of geological and paleontological phenomena. It suggests that originally the land on earth composed a single, vast CONTINENT, Pangaea, which broke up.

CONTINENTAL SHELF, the gently sloping portion of a continent that is submerged in the OCEAN to a depth of less than 200m (650ft), resulting in a rim of shallow water surrounding the landmass. The outer edge of the shelf slopes towards the ocean bottom, and is called the continental slope.

CONTINENTAL SYSTEM, an attempted economic blockade of England by NAPOLEON I. Instituted in 1807, it would have brought privation and probable defeat to England if

it had been successful. However, a counter-blockade of the continent by England's superior seapower nullified it. The British blockade, because it interfered with American trade with the continent, was a major cause of the WAR OF 1812.

CONTRACEPTION, the avoidance of conception, and thus of PREGNANCY. Many different methods exist, none of which are absolutely effective. In the **rhythm method**, sexual intercourse is restricted to the days immediately before and after MENSTRUATION, when fertilization is unlikely. **Withdrawal** (*coitus interruptus*) is removal of the penis prior to ejaculation, which reduces the number of sperm released into the vagina. The **condom** is a rubber sheath, fitting over the penis, into which ejaculation occurs; the diaphragm is a complementary device which is inserted into the vagina before intercourse. Both are more effective with **spermicide creams**. **Intrauterine devices** (IUDs) are plastic or copper devices which are inserted into the WOMB and interfere with implantation. They are convenient but may lead to infection, or increased blood loss or pain at menstruation. **Oral contraceptives** ("the Pill") are sex HORMONES of the ESTROGEN and PROGESTERONE type which, if taken regularly through the menstrual cycle, inhibit the release of eggs from the ovary. While they are the most reliable form of contraception, they carry a small risk of venous THROMBOSIS, raised blood pressure and possibly other diseases. When the Pill is stopped, periods and ovulation may not return for some time, and this can cause difficulty in assessing fetal maturity if pregnancy follows without an intervening period. While the more effective forms of contraception carry a slightly greater risk, this must be set against the risks of pregnancy and induced ABORTION in the general context of FAMILY PLANNING.

CONTRACTS, legally enforceable promises or agreements. Most are written, but verbal contracts may be equally binding in law. A contract is a bargain in which one party agrees to the terms offered by another party. To be binding there must be consideration: one party promises to do something in return for something of value promised by the other. Contracts are usually enforced under civil rather than criminal law. A party failing to fulfill a contracted promise is in breach of contract, and the court may award financial damages to the other party.

CONTRERAS, Battle of, engagement in the MEXICAN WAR, near Contreras, 8mi SW of Mexico City. Finding his advance on

Mexico City blocked by generals SANTA ANNA and Valencia, US Maj. Gen. Winfield SCOTT outflanked and attacked Valencia, scattering his troops. Scott thus gained control of roads to Mexico City.

CONVECTION, passage of heat through a fluid by means of large-scale movements of material within the body of the fluid (see CONDUCTION). If, for example, a liquid is heated from below, parts close to the heat source expand and, because their DENSITY is thus reduced, rise through the liquid; near the top, they cool and begin to sink. This process continues until heat is uniformly distributed throughout the liquid. Convection in the ATMOSPHERE is responsible for many climatic effects (see METEOROLOGY).

CONWAY CABAL, plot to oust George Washington as commander-in-chief of the Continental Army in 1777, during the American Revolution. Washington had lost at Brandywine and Germantown, but General Horatio Gates had won at Saratoga. Washington intercepted a letter from Gen. Thomas Conway to Gates criticizing Washington and revealing plans by an army and Congressional cabal to replace Washington by Gates. Washington published the letter and rallied Congressional support. Conway was forced to resign his command.

COOK, Frederick Albert (1865–1940), US explorer who claimed to have climbed Mt McKinley in 1906 and to have discovered the North Pole in 1908, before Peary. Neither claim was widely believed.

COOK, James (1728–1779), English navigator and explorer who led three celebrated expeditions to the Pacific Ocean (1768–71; 1772–75; 1776–80), during which he charted the coast of New Zealand (1770), showed that if there were a great southern continent it could not be so large as was commonly supposed, and discovered the Sandwich Islands (1778). He died in an attack by Hawaiian natives.

COOK, Thomas (1808–1892), English travel agent, founder of Thomas Cook & Son and pioneer of packaged travel. He started tours in England (1841) and on the Continent (1855). In 1884 his firm transported a military expedition up the Nile.

COOKE, Jay (1821–1905), US financier who helped the federal government finance the Civil War. He formed the banking firm Jay Cooke & Co. in 1861, and sold over $1 billion in war bonds. His firm later underwrote the construction of the Northern Pacific Railway but failed in the financial crisis of 1873. Cooke made a second fortune in silver mining, 1878–79.

COOKERY. The transformation from raw to cooked food is based on several methods. **Boiling** involves cooking food in liquid at the boiling or bubbling point. The aim is either to retain the flavor of the meat or vegetable (and therefore the cook does not prolong the process) or to flavor the liquid (as in making soup). **Frying** means cooking in fat at high temperature; generally the food should be quite dry or coated in batter or crumbs. Deep-fat frying requires much fat; sautéing uses little fat, as does the Chinese technique of stir-frying. **Broiling** and **roasting** expose the food to direct, dry heat. The aim is to brown the food's surface but keep the inside juicy. **Steaming** is accomplished either by keeping food in a rack and tightly covered above boiling liquid or by using a little hot liquid or melted fat to steam the food gently. **Braising** and **stewing** impart tenderness to meat and a special flavor to all ingredients through a combination of methods: the food is first browned in fat, a small amount of liquid is added, and cooking proceeds at low temperature with the pot tightly covered.

Thickening and **sauce-mixing** can also be considered among basic cookery techniques. Thickening depends on using flour (or another starch) or egg yolk to thicken liquids. Other sauces (Hollandaise, mayonnaise, Béarnaise) are based on emulsions—combinations of egg yolks with butter or oil.

COOLEY, Charles Horton (1864–1929), pioneer US sociologist, on the faculty of the U of Michigan from 1891. He developed a comprehensive sociological theory in *Human Nature and the Social Order* (1902), *Social Organization* (1909), and *Social Process* (1918).

COOLIDGE, (John) Calvin (1872–1933), 30th president of the US (1923–29), a moderately conservative Republican who continued Warren G. Harding's policies but replaced corruption with honesty. Born at Plymouth, Vt., he became a lawyer in Mass. and rose in local political office. He was mayor of Northampton 1910–11, state senator 1912–15, lieutenant governor of Mass. 1916–18 and governor 1919–20. His firm handling of the BOSTON POLICE STRIKE gave him national prominence, and in 1920 he was chosen US vice president, succeeding to the presidency on the death of Harding. He was elected president in 1924 over Democrat John W. Davis and Progressive Robert M. La Follette. His administration was characterized by caution, governmental efficiency and delegation of responsibility to such able men as Secretary of Commerce Herbert Hoover, Secretary of the Treasury Andrew Mellon, and Secretary of State Frank B. Kellogg.

Disapproving of government interference in economic affairs and believing in government frugality, Coolidge vetoed the McNary-Haugen Bill for relief to agriculture. He lowered taxes, reduced the national budget and the national debt and protected industry with high tariffs, creating a short-lived prosperity. He handled with restraint and integrity the oil-lease scandals of the Harding administration. In foreign affairs the country's policy was isolationist. The US kept out of the League of Nations but took part in League-sponsored conferences. Coolidge's wish for US participation in the World Court was blocked by Senate opposition. He sponsored the KELLOGG-BRIAND PACT (1927) outlawing war. His administration passed the DAWES PLAN to lend Germany money to rebuild its economy.

COOLIDGE, William David (1873–1975), US chemist who developed (1911) the pliable TUNGSTEN filaments used in lightbulbs and (1913) a high-vacuum X-RAY tube (the Coolidge tube) which was a major breakthrough in RADIOLOGY.

COOPER, Gary (1901–1961), US film actor who portrayed laconic, romantic heroes in such films as *A Farewell to Arms* (1933) and *For Whom the Bell Tolls* (1943). He won Academy Awards for roles in *Sergeant York* (1941) and *High Noon* (1952).

COOPER, James Fenimore (1789–1851), first major US novelist, best known for narratives about the American frontier. The series of *Leatherstocking Tales* (1823–41), with their hero, the scout Natty Bumppo, includes *The Pioneers, The Last of the Mohicans, The Prairie, The Pathfinder* and *The Deerslayer*. His attitude is romantic, his characterization shallow, his dialogue stilted; yet his work is readable. He also invented the sea romance and wrote works of social criticism.

COOPER, Peter (1791–1883), US industrial innovator and philanthropist. His Baltimore iron works built the first US steam locomotive, *Tom Thumb* (1830). He introduced structural iron beams and popularized the BESSEMER process. In 1854 he founded Cooper Union in New York City for free instruction in arts and sciences. In 1876 he was GREENBACK PARTY presidential candidate.

COOPER, Thomas (1759–1839), British-born American educator, natural scientist, and political philosopher. Cooper was a professor of natural science who was sent to prison and fined $400 for writing pamphlets attacking the ALIEN AND SEDITION ACTS of 1798. He also campaigned against the slave trade and religious intolerance, but late in his career often sided with the South because of his strong belief in states' rights.

COOPERATIVE, in real estate. See CONDOMINIUM.

COOPERATIVE, an association of producers or manufacturers and consumers to share profits which would otherwise go to middlemen. The pioneer Rochdale Society of Equitable Pioneers, founded in England 1844, set precedents of unrestricted membership, democratic organization, educational facilities and service at cost. That same year John Kaulbach, a Boston tailor, formed the first US consumers' cooperative among members of his trade union. The National Grange, founded in the US 1867, promoted Rochdale principles (see GRANGE, THE). Current US cooperative activity consists of farmers' purchasing and marketing, credit and banking, mutual insurance, wholesaling, group medical programs and consumer cooperatives. There are over 800,000 cooperative societies in the world.

COPENHAGEN, seaport capital of Denmark, on Sjaelland and Amager islands. It handles most of Denmark's trade, exporting ham, bacon, porcelain, silverware and furniture. Its main industries are shipping, shipbuilding, brewing and light manufacturing. The Royal Copenhagen porcelain factory and Georg Jensen handmade silverworks are famous. Landmarks include Christianborg Palace, Rosenborg Palace, Tivoli amusement park, the National Museum and several art museums. The university, founded 1478, is a major center for research in theoretical physics. A small fishing port until the 11th century, Copenhagen grew as a center on the Baltic trade route. In 1443 it became the royal residence and expanded under Christian IV (1577–1648). It was occupied by the Germans 1940-45. Pop (city) 478,615; (metro) 1,358,540.

COPENHAGEN, Battle of (Apr. 2, 1801), naval battle in the FRENCH REVOLUTIONARY WARS occasioned by Denmark's joining other N European states in refusing to comply with England's rules for neutral navigation. It is famous for the incident in which English admiral Horatio NELSON put his telescope to his blind eye to avoid seeing his superior's command to withdraw and then proceeded to destroy the Danish fleet.

COPERNICUS, Nicolaus (Niklas Koppernigk; 1473–1543), Polish astronomer who displaced the earth from the center of man's conceptual universe and made it orbit a stationary sun. Belonging to a wealthy German family, he spent several years in

Italy mastering all that was known of mathematics, medicine, theology and astronomy before returning to Poland where he eventually settled into the life of lay canon at Frauenburg. His dissatisfaction with the earth-centered (geocentric) cosmology of PTOLEMY was made known to a few friends in the manuscript *Commentariolus* (1514), but it was only on the insistence of Pope Clement VII that he expanded this into the *De revolutionibus orbium coelestium* (*On the revolutions of the heavenly spheres*) which, when published in 1543, announced the sun-centered (heliocentric) theory to the world. Always the theoretician rather than a practical observer, Copernicus' main dissatisfaction with Ptolemy was philosophical. He sought to replace the equant, epicycle and deferent of Ptolemaic theory with pure circular motions, but in adopting a moving-earth theory he was forced to reject the whole of the scholastic physics (without providing an alternative—this had to await the work of GALILEO) and postulate a much greater scale for the universe. Although the heliocentric hypothesis was not immediately accepted by the majority of scientists, its proposal did begin the period of scientific reawakening known as the Copernican Revolution.

COPLAND, Aaron (1900–), US composer using a distinctively American idiom. His lyrical and exuberant music incorporates jazz and folk tunes. His works include the ballet scores *Billy the Kid* (1938) and *Appalachian Spring* (1944), the song cycle *Twelve Poems of Emily Dickinson* (1950), the opera *The Tender Land* (1954), symphonies, piano and chamber works and film scores. His many awards include the 1945 Pulitzer prize.

COPLEY, John Singleton (1738–1815), American portrait painter who brilliantly depicted colonial personalities. In 1774 he left America and settled in London. He became a member of the Royal Academy and painted large canvases with historical themes, including *The Death of Chatham* (1779–80).

COPPER (Cu), soft, red metal in Group IB of the PERIODIC TABLE; a TRANSITION ELEMENT. Copper has been used since c6500 BC (see BRONZE AGE). It occurs naturally as the metal in the US, especially Mich., and as the ores cuprite, chalcopyrite, antlerite, chalcocite, bornite, azurite and malachite in the US, Zambia, Zaire and Chile. The metal is produced by roasting the concentrated ores and smelting, and is then refined by electrolysis. Copper is strong, tough, and highly malleable and ductile. It is an excellent conductor of heat and electricity, and most copper produced is used in the electrical industry. It is also a major component of many ALLOYS, including BRASS, BRONZE, German silver, cupronickel (see NICKEL) and beryllium copper (very strong and fatigue-resistant). Many copper alloys are called bronzes, though they need not contain tin: copper + tin + phosphorus is phosphor bronze, and copper + aluminum is aluminum bronze. Copper is a vital trace element: in man it catalyzes the formation of HEMOGLOBIN; in mollusks and crustaceans it is the basic constituent of hemocyanin. Chemically, copper is unreactive, dissolving only in oxidizing acids. It forms cuprous compounds (oxidation state +1), and the more common cupric salts (oxidation state +2), used as fungicides and insecticides, in pigments, as mordants for dyeing, as catalysts, for copper plating, and in electric cells. **Copper (II) sulfate** ($CuSO_4.5H_2O$), or **blue vitriol**, blue crystalline solid occurring naturally as chalcanthite; used as above. AW 63.5, mp 1083°C, bp 2567°C, sg 8.96 (20°C).

COPPERHEADS, Northern Democrats who opposed the Lincoln administration's Civil War policy and advocated peace with the Confederates. The term originated in a newspaper article depicting them as poisonous copperhead snakes. Most urged peace through negotiation, but some secret societies (KNIGHTS OF THE GOLDEN CIRCLE, Order of American Knights, Sons of Liberty) harassed Northern sympathizers, helped deserters and sabotaged Union supplies.

COPRA. See COCONUT PALM.

COPTIC CHURCH, chief Christian Church in Egypt, led by a patriarch in Cairo and 12 diocesan bishops. Services are held in Greek, Arabic and the otherwise dead language Coptic, based on ancient Egyptian. The Copts broke from the Roman Church when the Council of Chalcedon in 451 rejected their doctrine of MONOPHYSITISM. After the 7th-century Arab conquest many Copts became Muslims. The Ethiopian Church derives from the Coptic.

COPYRIGHT, exclusive right of an author, artist or publisher to publish or sell a work. Anyone reproducing a copyrighted work without permission of the copyright holder is liable to be sued for damages and ordered to stop publication or distribution. Books, plays, musical compositions, periodicals, motion pictures, photographs, designs and other works of art, maps and charts, speeches and lectures may be copyrighted in the US. This involves publishing the work with the statutory copyright notice (usually followed by the year and copyright owner's name). Copies and a registration fee must be lodged with the US Copyright Office.

The first US Copyright Act of 1790 protected only books, maps and charts, but later legislation included other works. Current US copyright law grants exclusive rights for the creator's life plus 50 years, after which the work becomes public domain. International agreements protect rights of authors in the markets of other countries. The Buenos Aires Convention protects copyright among 17 Western countries including the US. The Universal Copyright Convention covers over 50 nations including the US. (See also BERN CONVENTION.)

CORALS, small marine invertebrates of the class Anthozoa (phylum Cnidaria) whose limestone skeletons form coral reefs and islands in warm seas. Most corals join together in colonies and secrete external LIMESTONE skeletons. Branches and successive layers are formed by budding and by the addition of new members, produced sexually, which swim freely before attaching themselves and secreting their skeletons. Older members of the colony gradually die, leaving their skeletons behind. Vegetation, such as coraline algae, cements the discarded skeletons, forming coral reefs, of which there are three types: *fringing reefs* along the shore, *barrier reefs* offshore and *atolls*, circular reefs enclosing a lagoon.

CORAL SEA, Battle of the, battle between US and Japanese naval forces in the Coral Sea May 4–8, 1942. Fought by aircraft launched from carriers, it was the first naval engagement in which opposing vessels never saw each other. US losses were the heavier, but the battle checked the Japanese advance towards New Guinea.

CORAL SNAKES, poisonous SNAKES with black, yellow or white and red rings. They feed on small reptiles and insects. Two species inhabit the southern US (*Micrurus julvius* and *M. euryxanthus*).

CORBETT, James John (1866–1933), US world heavyweight boxing champion, known as "Gentleman Jim." In 1892 he knocked out John L. Sullivan, to become the first man to win the world heavyweight championship under Marquess of Queensberry Rules. He lost his title to Bob Fitzsimmons in 1897. Later he took up a stage and film career.

CORCORAN, William Wilson (1798–1888), US banker, founder of the Corcoran Gallery of Art in Washington, D.C.

CORDAY, Charlotte (1768–1793), French assassin of the French revolutionary Jean Paul MARAT. Objecting to Marat's persecution of the GIRONDINS, she stabbed him to death in his bath on July 13, 1793. She was guillotined by order of the revolutionary tribunal.

CORDELIERS, political club of the French Revolution, active 1790–94, led by DANTON and MARAT, and later by Jacques Hébert. It espoused extremist policies, helping to overthrow the GIRONDINS in 1793 and disintegrating in 1794 after its leaders were executed for trying to seize power by force.

CORE. See CONGRESS OF RACIAL EQUALITY.

CORELLI, Arcangelo (1653–1713), Italian composer and violinist, pioneer of the concerto grosso form which led to the CONCERTO. He wrote largely for violin, viola and cello—instruments then replacing the older VIOL family.

CORINTH, ancient Greek city on the Isthmus of Corinth. Established under Dorian rule (9th century BC), it founded Syracuse and other colonies in the 7th century BC and was the chief Greek merchant city until outstripped by Athens. Destroyed by Rome in 146 BC, it was rebuilt by Julius Caesar in 44 BC. Modern Corinth (Kòrinthos) was founded in 1858 after an earthquake destroyed the old city. Pop 11,000.

CORINTH, Battle of, Civil War battle at the rail junction of Corinth, Miss., on Oct. 3–4, 1862. Union forces under Rosecrans repulsed Confederates under generals Van Dorn and Price.

CORINTHIANS, Epistles to the, two letters, the 7th and 8th books of the New Testament, written by St. Paul c52–55 AD to the Christian church of Corinth, Greece. The first discusses the discipline and organization of the divided church and ways of restoring unity. The second largely defends Paul's work and authority as an apostle.

CORIOLANUS, Gaius Marcius (5th century BC), legendary Roman patrician, hero of Shakespeare's *Coriolanus*. He was named for Corioli, a town he allegedly won for Rome from the Volscians in 493 BC. Exiled for his anti-plebeian attitude, he led a Volscian attack on Rome until his mother and wife persuaded him to relent.

CORIOLIS EFFECT, a FORCE which, like a centrifugal force (see CENTRIPETAL FORCE), apparently acts on moving objects when observed in a frame of reference which is itself rotating. Because of the rotation of the observer, a freely moving object does not appear to move steadily in a straight line as usual, but rather as if, besides an outward centrifugal force, a "Coriolis force" acts on it, perpendicular to its motion, with a strength proportional to its MASS, its VELOCITY and the rate of rotation of the frame of reference. The effect, first described in 1835 by **Gaspard de Coriolis** (1792–1843), accounts for the familiar circulation of air flow around CYCLONES, and numerous other phenomena in METEOROLOGY, oceanography and BALLISTICS.

CORK, protective, waterproof layer of dead cells that have thick walls impregnated with suberin, a waxy material. Cork is found as the outer layer of stems and roots of older woody plants. The cork oak (*Quercus suber*) of S Europe and North Africa produces a profuse amount of cork, which is harvested commercially every 3 to 4 years.

CORMORANTS, or shags, birds of the family Phalocrocoracidae related to PELICANS. Cormorants have long necks and bills, are usually black, and dive for fish food in coastal regions and in the larger lakes and rivers of the world.

CORN, or **maize,** *Zea mays,* a grain crop native to the New World, but now cultivated throughout the world and second among the world's crop plants to WHEAT in terms of acreage planted. The major area of cultivation is in the Midwest cornbelt of the US. Five main types of corn have been developed. Most of the US yield is dent corn (so-called from the indentation in the crown of each kernel) used for animal feed. Flint corn grows in colder climates, such as Canada. It has a hard kernel and is used for animal feed. Sweet corn, containing sugar, is a familiar vegetable. Popcorn kernels have hard outer coatings to prevent moisture escape. When heated the internal steam pressure causes them to burst. Flour corn, grown in Peru, Bolivia and Ecuador, has soft kernels and is used for flour and corn meal. The plants grow 3–15ft high and require a frost-free growing season of at least 100 days. Each plant develops 1–3 ears. The male flowers are in tassels on top of the stem. The female inflorescences consist of a number of rows of ovaries; each ovary is crowned by a silk that projects from the top of the "cob." Pollination is by the wind, the pollen falling on the silks. Corn is subject to numerous diseases. Fungi attack young plants, and improperly stored ears and bacterial leaf blights cause wilting. RUST, smut and VIRUS diseases also attack the crop. The corn borer is the worst insect pest. Corn is ground for feeding to animals and for human consumption. It is rolled and flattened for breakfast cereals. Cornbread,

hominy, mash, griddle cakes and confections are made from corn. Industrially corn is processed to make alcohol, syrup and oil and is used in manufacturing plastics. The stalk is sometimes used in paper and wall board manufacture. The term "corn" is also used locally to indicate the CEREAL CROPS most important in the district, e.g., in England corn refers to wheat and in some parts of Scotland to oats. (See also AGRICULTURE; PLANT DISEASES.)

CORNEILLE, Pierre (1606–1684), French dramatist, creator of French classical verse tragedy. His masterpiece, *Le Cid* (1637), though controversial in its time, was a great popular success. His many other plays included *Horace* (1640), *Cinna* (1641) and *Polyeucte* (1643). His popularity faded with the rise of his younger rival, RACINE.

CORNELL, Ezra (1807–1874), US businessman, a pioneer in telegraphy. He created America's first (Baltimore–Washington) telegraph line (1844) with Samuel MORSE, and was founder and director of the Western Union Telegraph Company (1855). His gifts helped create Cornell U., Ithaca, N.Y. (1868).

CORNELL, Katharine (1898–1974), US actress, noted for her major roles in serious dramas, often directed by her husband Guthrie McClintic. Her most famous part was Elizabeth Barrett Browning in *The Barretts of Wimpole Street* (1931).

CORNET, valved brass wind instrument somewhat like a trumpet. It has a mellow tone controlled by lip vibration at the cupped mouthpiece, a two-and-a-half octave range and is usually tuned to B flat. Cornets have traditionally been used in brass bands but rarely in symphony orchestras. They have however, formed an important place in JAZZ.

CORNISH. See CELTIC LANGUAGES.

CORN LAWS, various laws regulating English import and export of grain from the 14th century to 1849. After the Napoleonic Wars the corn price was raised to offset agricultural depression. But protests from the poor and from manufacturers objecting to agricultural subsidy helped COBDEN and BRIGHT, leaders of the Anti-Corn Law League (1839–46), to persuade Prime Minister Sir Robert PEEL to repeal the Corn Laws (1846 and 1849).

CORNS AND CALLUSES, localized thickenings of the horny layer of the SKIN, produced by continual pressure or friction. **Calluses** project above the skin and are rarely troublesome; **corns** are smaller, and are forced into the deep, sensitive layers of skin, causing pain or discomfort.

CORNWALLIS, Charles Cornwallis, 1st

Marquis of (1738–1805), British general, whose surrender to Washington at Yorktown (Oct. 19, 1781) ended the Revolutionary War. Earlier, he had defeated Nathanael Greene in the Carolinas. He later gave important service as governor-general of India 1786–93 and 1805, and as viceroy of Ireland 1798–1801.

CORONA, outer atmosphere of the SUN or other STAR. The term is used also for the halo seen around a celestial body due to DIFFRACTION of its light by water droplets in thin CLOUDS of the earth's ATMOSPHERE; and for a part appended to and within the corolla of some FLOWERS. Around high-voltage terminals there appears a faint glow due to the ionization (see ION) of the local air. The result of this ionization is an electrical discharge known as **corona discharge**, the glow being called a corona.

CORONADO, Francisco Vázquez de (1510–1554), Spanish explorer of SW North America. While governor of Nuevo Galicia (in Mexico) in 1540 he subdued the so-called Seven Cities of CIBOLA. Fruitlessly seeking gold, his expedition probed what is now N.M., Ariz., Tex. and Kan., and discovered the Grand Canyon.

CORONARY THROMBOSIS, myocardial infarction, or heart attack, one of the commonest causes of serious illness and death in Western countries. The coronary ARTERIES, which supply the HEART with OXYGEN and nutrients, may become diseased with ARTERIOSCLEROSIS which reduces BLOOD flow. Significant narrowing may lead to superimposed THROMBOSIS, which causes sudden complete obstruction and results in death or damage to a substantial area of heart tissue. This may cause sudden death, usually due to abnormal heart rhythm which prevents effective pumping. Severe persistent pain in the center of the chest is common, and it may lead to SHOCK or LUNG congestion. Characteristic changes may be seen in the ELECTROCARDIOGRAPH following myocardial damage, and ENZYMES appear in blood from the damaged heart muscle. Treatment consists of rest, ANALGESICS and drugs to correct disordered rhythm or inadequate pumping; certain cases must be carefully observed for development of rhythm disturbance. Recovery may be complete and normal activities resumed. Predisposing factors, including OBESITY, SMOKING, high blood pressure, excess blood FATS (including CHOLESTEROL) and DIABETES must be recognized and treated. Recent studies have found that aspirin helps prevent heart attacks. The clot-dissolving drug streptokinase, taken upon the onset of chest pains, has reduced deaths from heart attack.

COROT, Jean-Baptiste Camille (1796–1875), French landscape painter who broke with classical tradition to achieve subtle lighting effects by painting directly from nature. Although his more austere early works are highly regarded, he won fame with his misty, poetic, gray-green landscapes, influencing both the BARBIZON SCHOOL and the practitioners of IMPRESSIONISM.

CORPORATE STATE, in political theory, a society regarded as being composed of various functional or economic groups rather than individuals. The theory was particularly important in the ideology of Fascist Italy, but it also played a role in Portugal and Spain, and in Germany and Austria in the 1930s.

In theory, the various functional groups with a given society—labor unions, business firms and so on—name representatives to the central governing body, which is therefore able to take into account all points of view and make democratic decisions. In practice, however, the corporate ideology usually proved to be a mere slogan aimed at giving dictatorship a veneer of respectability.

CORPORATION, group of persons forming a legal entity independent of the individuals owning or managing it. As a legal "person" it may hold property, sue and be sued. Corporations may be public or private. Municipal corporations such as school districts and cities perform some governmental functions. National public corporations carry out large-scale enterprises. Private corporations carry on a vast range of business and other activities. Advantages of a corporation are that it can deal in its own name without risking the personal finances of its officers or stockholders; it has a permanence lacking in a partnership or individually owned business; and it may raise large amounts of capital by sale of stocks.

Corporations are chartered by state governments and usually managed by officers named by a board of directors elected by the votes of a stockholders' majority. Thus anyone owning 51% of the stock controls a corporation. Business corporations grew out of the great trading companies of 16th- and 17th-century England. In the US, N.Y. passed the first general corporation law in 1811. Today US corporations have assets valued at more than $1 trillion and employ over half the nation's work force.

CORREGGIO (real name: Antonio Allegri; c1494–1534), Italian Renaissance painter who influenced the BAROQUE style. His works (including most of his Parma frescoes) are primarily devotional, and are noted for softness and use of chiaroscuro.

CORREGIDOR, fortified rocky island (2sq mi) in the Philippines, at the entrance to Manila Bay. Under US control from 1898, it fell to the Japanese in May 1942 when Gen. Jonathan WAINWRIGHT surrendered after four months of fierce fighting. Recaptured in 1945, it is now a WWII memorial.

CORROSION, the insidious destruction of metals and alloys by chemical reaction (mainly OXIDATION) with the environment. The annual cost of corrosion was estimated in the 1970s as more than $5 billion in the US alone. In moist air most metals form a surface layer of oxide, which, if it is coherent, may slow down or prevent further corrosion. Tarnishing is the formation of such a discolored layer, mainly on copper or silver. (Rust—hydrated iron (III) oxide, $FeO(OH)$—offers little protection, so that iron corrodes rapidly.) Industrial AIR POLLUTION greatly speeds up corrosion, oxidizing and acidic gases (especially sulfur dioxide) being the worst culprits. Corrosion is usually an electrochemical process (see ELECTROCHEMISTRY): small cells are set up in the corroding metal, the potential difference being due to the different metals present or to different concentrations of oxygen or electrolyte; corrosion takes place at the anode. It also occurs preferentially at grain boundaries and where the metal is stressed. Prevention methods include bonderizing; a protective layer of paint, varnish or electroplate; or the use of a "sacrificial anode" of zinc or aluminum in electrical contract with the metal, that is preferentially corroded. Galvanizing—coating iron objects with zinc—works on the same principle.

CORSICA, Mediterranean island and French department N of Sardinia, off W Italy, occupying 3,352sq mi. It is largely mountainous, with much Mediterranean scrub and forest. Its products include olive oil, wine and citrus fruits. The capital is Ajaccio. Its rulers have included Carthaginians, Romans, Vandals, Goths, Saracens and (1347–1768) the Genoese, who sold it to France. There is strong nationalist feeling on the island. Napoleon Bonaparte was born here.

CORTÉS, Hernán (1485–1547), Spanish explorer, conqueror of Mexico. In 1504 he settled in Hispaniola (Santa Domingo) and in 1511 joined the conquest of Cuba, becoming mayor of Santiago. Sent to explore Yucatán, in 1519 he marched on the AZTECS' capital Tenochtitlán, where MONTEZUMA greeted him as the white god QUETZALCOATL. Cortés took Montezuma prisoner, but the latter was killed in an uprising against the Spaniards. Cortés retreated, but returned in 1521 and conquered the capital, ending the Aztec Empire. He later explored Honduras and Lower California.

CORTISONE, one of the group of hormones secreted by the cortex of the ADRENAL GLANDS. Cortisone was first isolated in 1935 and synthesized in 1944. It proved to be of immense value in treating diseases caused by malfunctioning of the adrenal cortex, such as ADDISON'S DISEASE, and in the treatment of arthritis, some forms of allergy, leukemia and many other diseases. However, cortisone, and the closely related hydrocortisone, have undesirable side effects. Among other things they cause the patient to become "moon-faced." As a result the drug is used with caution or replaced by a synthetic substitute. The secretion of cortisone is controlled by ACTH (adrenocorticotropic hormone), which is itself secreted by the anterior lobe of the pituitary gland.

COSGRAVE, William Thomas (1880–1965), Irish statesman, president of the Irish Free State 1922–32. He was in the 1916 EASTER RISING, served in the first republican ministry 1919–21 and, as president, brought stability to the Irish nation.

COSMIC RAYS, ELECTRONS and the nuclei of HYDROGEN and other ATOMS which isotropically bombard the earth's upper ATMOSPHERE at VELOCITIES close to that of light. These primary cosmic rays interact with molecules of the upper atmosphere to produce what are termed secondary cosmic rays, which are considerably less energetic and extremely shortlived: they are SUBATOMIC PARTICLES that change rapidly into other types of particles. Initially, secondary cosmic rays, which pass frequently and harmlessly through our bodies, were detected by use of the GEIGER COUNTER, though now it is more common to employ a spark chamber. It is thought that cosmic rays are produced by SUPERNOVAS, though some may be of extragalactic origin.

COSMOGONY, the science of the origins of the universe or of the SOLAR SYSTEM.

COSMOLOGY, the study of the structure and evolution of the universe. Ancient and medieval cosmologies were many, varied and imaginative, usually oriented around a stationary, flat earth at the center of the universe, surrounded by crystal spheres carrying the moon, sun, planets and stars, although ARISTARCHUS understood that the earth was spherical and circled the sun. With increasing sophistication of observational techniques and equipment, more realistic views of the universe emerged (see COPERNICUS; BRAHE; KEPLER; GALILEO; NEWTON). Modern cosmological theories, which take into account EINSTEIN'S Theory of RELATIVITY and the recession of galaxies shown by the RED SHIFT in their spectra (see SPECTRUM), divide into two main types.

Evolutionary Theories. The most important of these is the **big bang theory** resulting from HUBBLE'S observations of the galaxies. This theory proposes that initially the universe existed as a single compact ball of matter, the **cosmic egg**, that exploded to form a mass of gaseous debris which eventually began to condense to form stars. An alternative theory is of an **oscillating universe** that periodically reaches a maximum size, then begins to shrink until it is once more in the form of a cosmic egg, which in turn explodes to create a new universe.

Continuous Creation. The **steady state theory** of Bondi Gold and HOYLE, first put forward in 1948, proposes that the universe has existed and will exist forever in its current form, the expansion being caused by the continuous creation of new matter so that the average density and appearance of the universe remain the same at all times. This would necessitate a reexamination of the Law of Conservation of ENERGY.

In 1965 A. Penzias and R. Wilson discovered that the universe possesses an inherent radio "background noise," and it was suggested by R. Dicke that this was the relic of the radiation produced by the big bang. Further researchers have indicated the probability that space is filled with uniform BLACKBODY thermal radiation corresponding to a temperature of around 3K. This would support an evolutionary theory and, though it still has adherents, the steady state theory has now largely been abandoned. (See also ASTRONOMY; BLACK HOLE; PULSAR; QUASAR.)

COSSACKS, Slavic warrior peasants living on the Ukrainian steppe and famed for horsemanship. Self-governing under leaders like Bohdan CHMIELNICKI (c1595–1657), they resisted outside authority, but served the tsars as irregular cavalry, pioneered in Siberia and fought the Bolsheviks 1918–21. Collectivization broke up their communities in the 1930s, but Cossack cavalry served in WWII.

COSTA RICA, small republic in S Central America, bordered by Nicaragua on the N and Panama on the S.

Official name: Republic of Costa Rica
Capital: San José
Area: 19,730sq mi
Population: 2,613,000
Languages: Spanish
Religions: Roman Catholic
Monetary unit(s): 1 Costa Rican colon = 100 céntimos
Land. The country's topography varies from wet tropical plains on the coast to the temperate central plateau at about 3000ft, which is surrounded by two chains of volcanic mountains rising to over 12,000ft. A rainy season lasts from May to November.

People. The population is largely of Spanish descent; there are fewer mestizos in Costa Rica than in other Latin American countries. A small minority of blacks lives on the Caribbean coast. About 60% of the people live in rural areas, largely on small farms.

Economy. Coffee is Costa Rica's most important cash crop, monopolizing 95% of the arable land in the central plateau; bananas are grown in coastal areas. Agricultural exports bring in most of the country's foreign exchange. A lack of mineral resources has created an emphasis on light industry, producing for the home market, (food processing, textiles, fertilizers, plastic goods, chemicals, pharmaceuticals), but large sulfur deposits are now being exploited.

History. Columbus discovered Costa Rica in 1502, but because of its lack of resources the region escaped the ravages of the Conquistadors. Since few Indians survived, the white farmers worked their own land, establishing a significant middle class and avoiding the semifeudal peonage system so destructive in other Latin American countries. In 1821 Costa Rica declared independence from Spain, joining first the Mexican Empire and then the Central American Federation, which dissolved into anarchy in 1838. A power struggle followed, complicated by the invasion of the American adventurer William WALKER, defeated in 1857. Despite internal strife in

1919 and 1948, the country's history has been peaceful and its politics democratic. Oscar Arias Sánchez, who was elected president in 1986, was awarded the Nobel Peace Prize in 1987 for his efforts to bring peace to war-torn Central America.

COTOPAXI, the highest active volcano in the world, 19,347ft high. It is situated in the Andes in Ecuador, and last erupted in 1942.

COTTON, John (1584–1652), powerful Puritan minister of Boston, Mass., noted for his didactic writings. Born in England, Cotton fled to the colonies in 1632 to avoid religious persecution. He was later to become involved in the banishment of Anne HUTCHINSON and Roger WILLIAMS for their heretical views.

COTTON, a subtropical plant of the genus *Gossypium,* grown for the soft white fibers attached to its seed, which can be woven into cloth. The seeds are planted in the early spring and the plants bloom after four months. The white flowers redden and fall in a few days, leaving the seed pods, which are fully grown in another month or so. These pods then burst, showing the white lint, which is picked either by hand or mechanically. Each fiber is a single cell, with numerous twists along its length, which give it excellent spinning characteristics.

A number of species and their varieties are grown. Cultivated varieties of *Gossypium barbodeon* produce fibers 1.4–2.5in long, *G. hirsutum* (the American upland cotton) fibers 0.8–1.3in and the Asiatic species *G. herbaceum* and *G. arboreum* fibers 0.4–0.8in. Cotton is produced in more than 60 countries; total world production exceeds 55 million bales annually, each bale weighing 490lb.

Cotton is prone to many pests and diseases, which cause enormous damage to the crop (averaging nearly $300 million in the US every year). The main insect pests are the BOLL WEEVIL in the US and the pink boll worm in India and Egypt. Destructive fungus diseases that attack the plant include fusarium and verticillium wilt and Texas root rot. Boll rots can cause severe damage to the crop. Mechanization of the cotton processing industry was one of the first stages of the Industrial Revolution. It is still an important industry, although consumption of cotton has not risen since the development of man-made textiles. However, 80% of the yarn from spinning mills is still made into cloth, the remainder being used in industry. The seed is now used for oils and cattle food, while small fibers are made into cellulose. (See also COTTON GIN; PLANT DISEASES.)

COTTON GIN, device for separating cotton fibers from the seeds, invented by Eli WHITNEY (1793), which revolutionized the cotton industry in the US South. Whitney's original gin comprised a rotating drum on which were mounted wire spikes that projected through narrow slits in a wire grid. The spikes drew the fibers through these slits, leaving behind the seeds, which are broader. A revolving brush removed the fibers from the drum. In 1794, Hodgen Holmes replaced the wire spikes by a circular saw; modern cotton gins still work on this principle.

COUGAR. See PUMA.

COUGH, sudden explosive release of air from the LUNGS, which clears respiratory passages of obstruction and excess mucus or pus; it occurs both as a REFLEX and on volition. Air flow may reach high velocity and potentially infectious particles spread a great distance if the mouth is uncovered. Persistent cough always implies disease.

COUGHLIN, Charles Edward (1891–1979), Roman Catholic priest who became a national figure in the US in the 1930s with his radio broadcasts, attacking first the financial leaders he believed to be responsible for the Depression, and later F. D. ROOSEVELT. He formed the Union Party in 1936 in opposition to Roosevelt; its presidential candidate received 2% of the popular vote. In 1942 his activities were curbed by the Church, worried by his apparent Nazi sympathies.

COULOMB, Charles Augustin de (1736–1806), French physicist noted for his researches into friction, torsion, electricity and magnetism. Using a torsion balance, he established Coulomb's Law of electrostatic forces (1785). This states that the force between two charges is proportional to their magnitudes and inversely proportional to the square of their separation. He also showed that the charge on a charged conductor lies solely on its surface.

COUNCIL OF ECONOMIC ADVISERS, three-member commission established in the US in 1946 to help prevent postwar depressions. It advises the president on economic and monetary problems.

COUNCIL OF EUROPE. See EUROPE, COUNCIL OF.

COUNTERCULTURE, term that gained currency in the 1960s to refer to anti-establishment and antiwar movements and to those who were part of them. The counterculture disdained bourgeois, capitalist values, war (but not necessarily revolution), energy-wasteful technology and competitiveness. Participants favored "doing your own thing," civil disobedience in New Left causes, marijuana, rock music and natural foods and materials. The counterculture was celebrated in the best-selling *The Greening of America* (1970) by Charles Reich.

COUNTERFEITING, the forging of money in an attempt to pass it off as genuine. Since this threatens the monetary basis of any economy it is a serious offense, punishable by death in the USSR and China. As it requires a high degree of technical skill it is seldom successful as organized crime; successful counterfeiters are more often eccentric individuals rather than habitual criminals.

COUNTERPOINT, in music, a term for the art of combining two or more different melodic lines simultaneously in a composition. The term derives from latin *punctus contra punctum,* meaning "note against note." Originating in the *organum* style of the 10th century, it reached its zenith in BAROQUE music, especially that of J. S. BACH. It remains a widely used form; a mastery of counterpoint is considered essential for a composer.

COUNTER-REFORMATION, reform movement in the Roman Catholic Church during the 16th and 17th centuries, springing as much from internal demands for reform as from reaction to the Protestant REFORMATION. Many organizations, such as the Oratory of Divine Love, the CAPUCHINS and the Ursulines, were founded in an attempt to infuse more spiritual life into the Church. Most notable among these were the JESUITS, founded in 1534, whose emphasis on action and education did much to slow the spread of Protestantism. The reform movement within the Church culminated in the Council of TRENT, convened by Pope Paul III in 1545. Its reaffirmation of doctrine and its disciplinary reforms did much to improve the standing of the Church. The establishment of the congregation of the INQUISITION in Rome by Paul III helped check Protestant influence; there was also a revival of missionary work. A revival in the arts, which fostered BERNINI and PALESTRINA among others, accompanied the movement.

COUNTRY AND WESTERN MUSIC, a broad category of pop music that includes, at one end of its spectrum, country music derived from the traditional BLUEGRASS folk music of the SE US and, at the other, Western music (i.e., cowboy songs updated with swing and rock influences). The popularity of Country and Western rose rapidly in the 1960s and 1970s. Among its stars have been Loretta Lynn and Johnny Cash. The national center of Country and Western is the Grand Ole Opry theater in Nashville, Tenn.

COUPERIN, François (1668–1733), French composer, most celebrated member of an illustrious musical family. He wrote supremely for the harpsichord, which he taught to the French royal family. His authoritative treatise, *The Art of Harpsichord Playing* (1716), influenced J. S. BACH.

COURBET, Gustave (1819–1877), French painter noted for his development of the "Realist" style in paintings such as *The Burial at Ornans* (1849) and *The Studio* (1855). Influenced by the Dutch genre painters of the 17th century, he emphasized everyday life and landscape in his work, as a reaction to the Classical and Romantic schools.

COUREURS DE BOIS, illicit traders in 17th- and 18th-century French Canada, largely responsible for the corruption of the Indian population. In defiance of government regulations they ruthlessly exploited the fur trade, selling the Indians cheap alcohol at exorbitant rates.

COURT, Margaret (1942–   ), Australian tennis player, the fourth person (second woman) to win (1970) tennis's "grand slam" (British, French, Australian, and US championships in the same year).

COURTS, official assemblies for the administration of justice. A typical US court will consist of a judge, jury (when required), attorneys representing both parties to the dispute, a bailiff or marshal to carry out court orders and keep order, and a clerk to record the proceedings.

Though many nations have developed various types of judicial assembly, the court in Western countries is descended from the king's court, in which he dispensed justice. Since his justices were theoretically deputizing for him, their assemblies were still *curiae regis*—the king's courts. Unlike their European counterparts, the English courts did not base themselves upon Roman law but developed the system of legal interpretation known as the COMMON LAW, and this, with its accompanying judicial system, became one of Britain's most important and lasting exports to her colonies, including the US and Canada.

The US has two related court systems: federal and state. The federal court system covers cases involving the Constitution, the nation, foreign nationals, federal laws, interstate disputes and ships at sea. Federal courts comprise a SUPREME COURT, intermediate courts of appeals, and many district courts, as well as special courts such as the Tax Court, Court of Claims and the Court of Customs and Patent Appeals. In an individual state, the state court system deals with that state's affairs in both civil and criminal matters. Inferior (lower) state courts include magistrates' courts in urban areas, courts run by justices of the peace in rural areas, and juvenile and family courts, traffic courts, probate courts, rent courts and small-claims courts. Above these stand the county and municipal courts and other superior courts, and above these there are often appellate courts reviewing lower court decisions. The highest court in most states is called the state supreme court.

The US court system is a carefully designed judicial apparatus, but by the 1970s it was so overstrained that some defendants were waiting years for a trial. Expansion and procedural streamlining may improve the position.

Like the US, Canada has two related court systems: federal and provincial. The federal system features the Supreme Court (the highest court of appeal) and Exchequer Court (dealing largely with cases involving the national government). The provincial courts handle cases of federal and provincial law.

The INTERNATIONAL COURT OF JUSTICE meets at the Hague, in the Netherlands, to deal with cases under INTERNATIONAL LAW. Its 15 judges, each from a different country, are elected for nine-year terms by the UN Security Council.

COUSTEAU, Jacques-Yves (1910–), French naval officer and oceanologist who pioneered underwater exploration, coinventor of the aqualung and an underwater television system. His popular cinema and television films have made him world-famous.

COUSY, Robert Joseph (1928–), US basketball player, a star of the Boston Celtics (1951–63) and later a coach of college and professional teams.

COVENANTERS, 16th- and 17th-century Scottish Presbyterians pledged by covenants to defend their religion against Anglican influences. They were suppressed, both by Cromwell and the Stuart kings. Their savage persecution after the Restoration was known as the "killing time".

COVENTRY, industrial city in central England, noted for its association with Lady GODIVA and for a German air raid in November 1940 that destroyed the center of the town, including a 14th-century cathedral.

COVERDALE, Miles (1488–1569), English Protestant reformer, royal chaplain to Edward VI and later bishop of Exeter.

While studying in Europe, he produced in 1535 the first complete printed English translation of the Bible, revising large portions of it for inclusion in the Great Bible he prepared for Thomas Cromwell in 1539–40.

COWARD, Sir Noel (Pierce) (1899–1973), English actor, playwright and composer. He is famous for his witty comedies of manners, such as *Private Lives* (1930) and *Blithe Spirit* (1941), revues, musicals and serious plays such as *The Vortex* (1924). Their prevailing cynicism is offset by patriotic works such as the film *In Which We Serve* (1942).

COWBIRDS, birds of the family Icteridae, relatives of the grackles, so named because they follow cattle and feed on the insects they stir up. Two species live in the US but most are South American. Most lay eggs in the nests of other birds, which hatch and raise the cowbird young.

COWBOY, a person who herds cattle on horseback. The American cowboy, who was a product of the opening up of the vast central plains of the US after the Civil War, has become a legendary folk hero, celebrated in innumerable films and novels. The sometimes mournful cowboy songs are also very popular in the United States.

In areas such as Texas in the early 1800s (then part of Mexico) the American settlers took over the Spanish practice of using the plains for grazing cattle. At the same time they borrowed from the Spanish the typical equipment and methods of the cattle herder, including the broad-brimmed sombrero hat, the bandanna worn around the neck, the high-heeled boots which went with the heavy "western" saddle and covered stirrups, the leather chaps to protect the legs, and the lariat with which to rope cattle. Most of this came from the Mexican *vaquero*, and to it was added the "sixshooter" revolver. Thus equipped, the lean, bowlegged, swaggering cowboy rode into American mythology.

The cowboy was really created by the "long drive." As the frontier moved westward after the Civil War and the Plains Indians were driven off the open lands into reservations, large herds of cattle, tended by cowboys, began to be driven every year from the southern plains to the new railheads in the north central plains, grazing and fattening as they moved northward. By the 1880s and 1890s the settlement of the central plains and their enclosure with barbed wire put an end to the long drive, but the cowboy continued to be employed in ranch work and even today is still known for his riding and roping skills in that favorite

American carnival, the rodeo.

The modern cowboy is more likely to be equipped with a walkie-talkie and a jeep, but the romantic, legendary figure of the cowboy–tough, taciturn, independent, a hardworking man who leads a lonely life battling with the elements–has also persisted, thanks to the "western" films and to popular novels such as those of Zane GREY.

COWELL, Henry Dixon (1897–1965), US experimental composer. Like John CAGE. he sought to explore new sonorities in his music, as with "tone clusters," produced on the piano by striking groups of keys with the forearm.

COWLES, Gardner (1903–1985), US publisher whose *Des Moines Register and Tribune* became the nucleus of a newspaper, magazine, and broadcasting empire. He published *Look*, a weekly picture magazine, from 1937 to 1971.

COWPENS, Battle of, tactical victory in the Revolutionary War, fought on Jan. 17, 1781 in S.C. American troops under Gen. Daniel Morgan attacked Col. Banastre Tarleton's British troops in the Cowpens area. The Americans then withdrew, but met the British counterattack with bayonets and a flank attack, surrounding them. The British surrendered with 200 casualties to the Americans' 72.

COWPER, William (1731–1800), English poet. His work anticipates Romanticism in its lyrical delight in nature, expressed directly and simply. His best-known serious poem is *The Task* (1785). He also wrote many hymns, but is remembered for his comic ballad *John Gilpin* (1783).

COWPOX, a disease of cattle, caused by a VIRUS related to the smallpox virus. It was by noting the IMMUNITY to SMALLPOX conferred on humans who contracted cowpox by milking infected cattle that JENNER popularized VACCINATION against smallpox.

COX, James Middleton (1870–1957), US politician and journalist who championed liberal reform. He became nationally known as a newspaper publisher, Democratic congressman (1909–13) and governor of Ohio (1913–15; 1917–21). In 1920 he ran for president on the Democratic ticket but lost heavily to Warren G. Harding.

COXEY, Jacob Sechler (1854–1951), US self-made businessman who, with revivalist Carl Browne, led a "living petition" of 500 unemployed to Washington from Massillon, Ohio, in 1894, in support of his plan for national reconstruction. The march of "Coxey's Army," or the "Commonweal of Christ," ended when Coxey was jailed for

demonstrating on the Capitol lawn.

COXSACKIE VIRUSES, viruses named after the New York State village in which they were first identified. There are more than 30 of them, responsible for, among other things, herpangina, Bornholm disease and forms of meningitis.

COYOTE, *Canis latrans*, a wild dog that looks like a small wolf and has a characteristic howl. It has spread from the plains of NW America to the Atlantic coast. Coyotes hunt small mammals or live as urban scavengers, some interbreeding with dogs.

COZZENS, James Gould (1903–1978), US novelist. His books, such as *By Love Possessed* (1957) and *Ask Me Tomorrow* (1940), deal with moral conflicts of the professional classes, seen by Cozzens as the custodians of social stability. *Guard of Honor* (1948) won him a Pulitzer Prize.

CRABBE, George (1754–1832), English poet. His long narrative poems, such as *The Village* (1783) and *The Borough* (1810), seek to convey the harsh realities of village life as opposed to the conventional "poetic" view then popular.

CRABS, crustaceans with 10 pairs of legs, the first pair usually modified as pincers. They are closely related to LOBSTERS and SHRIMPS and start life as small, swimming, lobster-like larvae that repeatedly molt before settling on the bottom and becoming adult crabs. The adults have rounded protective shells covering head and thorax, the abdomen curling under the body to form a series of plates. Most of the 4,500 species live in the sea or brackish water, eating small animals and carrion. They range in size from the tiny pea crabs that live in oyster shells to the giant crab of the Pacific, a spider crab with a leg span of up to 3.8m (12.5ft).

CRACK, powerful form of COCAINE. It consists of light brown pellets of cocaine packaged in small vials and is used in freebasing, a practice where the drug is heated and inhaled. Free-basing cocaine causes rapid addiction and severe changes in the brain's chemistry.

CRAIG, Edward Gordon (1872–1966), English stage director and designer who helped to revolutionize theater production. He stressed the director's unifying role and abandoned realism in favor of a stark abstract style relying for its effects on lighting and mass.

CRAMP, the painful contraction of muscle—often in the legs. The cause is usually unknown. It may be brought on by exercise or lack of SALT; it also occurs in muscles with inadequate BLOOD supply.

Relief is by forcibly stretching the muscle or by massage.

CRANACH, Lucas the Elder (1472–1553), major German Renaissance painter and engraver. His early paintings are mainly on biblical themes and set in romantic landscapes; later mythological treatments introduced his characteristic sinuous female nudes. A great portraitist, especially for the Saxon court, he produced many propagandist woodcuts for his friend Martin Luther. **Lucas Cranach the Younger** (1515–1586), who took over his father's workshop, also enjoyed great popularity.

CRANBERRY, several low, berry-bearing shrubs related to the blueberry, native to N Eurasia and North America. The American cranberry (*Vaccinium macrocarpon*) is cultivated in Mass., N.J. and Wis., the berries being used in sauces and as a relish for meats, particularly turkey.

CRANE, (Harold) Hart (1899–1932), a major US poet, influenced by Edgar Allen POE and Walt WHITMAN. His masterpiece was *The Bridge* (1930), an attempted epic of the modern American experience using the Brooklyn Bridge as its central image. Beset by personal problems, he drowned himself on a return voyage from Mexico.

CRANE, Stephen (1871–1900), US novelist, short story writer and poet, best known for *The Red Badge of Courage* (1895), a sensitive study of a young man's development towards manhood during the Civil War. *Maggie: A Girl of the Streets* (1893) frighteningly describes a girl's poverty, seduction and suicide in New York's slums. Crane died of tuberculosis at 28.

CRANES, large birds of the family Gruidae, with long necks and legs, both of which project in flight. Most are mainly white or gray and some have partly naked heads. Their coiled windpipe helps to produce a trumpeting call. Cranes eat small animals and grasses in marshes and on plains, and perform graceful leaping courtship dances. Most of the 14 species spread around the world are now rare. The sandhill crane and the nearly extinct whooping crane are found in North America.

CRANMER, Thomas (1489–1556), first Protestant archbishop of Canterbury and leader of the English Reformation. He favored the ascendancy of state over church and obtained royal favor by helping Henry VIII to divorce his second, third, fourth and fifth wives. As counselor to Edward VI, Cranmer compiled the first BOOK OF COMMON PRAYER (1549), his most enduring monument. Under the Roman Catholic regime of Mary Tudor he was stripped of office and burned at the stake as a heretic.

CRASHAW, Richard (c1613–1649), English poet, whose poetry combined religious fervor with sensuous imagery. At first a High Church Anglican, he later became a Roman Catholic convert, and died as canon of Santa Casa Cathedral at Loreto. His *Carmen Deo Nostra* (1652) contains many of his best poems.

CRASSUS, Marcus Licinius (115?–53 BC), Roman politician. Because of his great wealth, CAESAR made him a member of the First TRIUMVIRATE together with his arch rival POMPEY. Crassus served as consul with Pompey in 70 and again in 55 BC, after which he became governor of Syria and campaigned against the Parthians. He was defeated and murdered.

CRATER LAKE NATIONAL PARK, a 250sq mi area centered on Crater Lake in the Cascade Mts in SW Ore., established as a park in 1902. The crater, which is volcanic, measures 6mi across and the lake within it, noted for its vivid blue color, reaches a depth of 1,932ft.

CRAWFORD, Joan (1908–1977), US film actress noted for her roles as self-made, tough-minded women. Her best-known movies were *Rain* (1932), *The Women*, (1939), *A Woman's Face* (1941) and *Mildred Pierce* (1945), for which she won an Academy Award.

CRAWFORD, Thomas (1813–1857), US neoclassical sculptor who worked mainly in Rome. His monumental figure *Armed Freedom*, cast posthumously, surmounts the dome of the capitol in Washington, D.C.

CRAWFORD, William Harris (1772–1834), US lawyer and senator, one of four candidates in the indecisive 1824 presidential election after which the House of Representatives chose John Quincy Adams for the presidency. Crawford was secretary of war 1815–16 and secretary of the treasury 1816–25.

CRAXI, Bettino (Benedetto Craxi; 1934–   ), Italian Socialist politician, leader of his party from 1976, first Socialist premier in Italian history (1983–88). Head of a five-party coalition, he pursued moderate policies.

CRAZY HORSE (c1840–1877), chief of the Oglala Sioux Indians and the inspiration behind Indian resistance to the white man's invasion of the N Great Plains. He led the SIOUX and CHEYENNE victory over Gen. George CROOK at Rosebud R (June 17, 1876) and eight days later led the Sioux massacre of Gen. CUSTER's forces at Little Bighorn. Arrested on his surrender in 1877, he was killed some months later while attempting to escape.

CREATIONISM, theory held by fundamentalist Christians that the Earth and living beings were created as described in Genesis rather than through a process of evolution, such as is accepted in modern geology and biology. Creationists have survived numerous setbacks, including the Scopes trial in 1925, the push in the 1960s to improve science education, and a Supreme Court ruling in 1975 striking down a Tenn. law requiring discussion of Genesis in schools. Espousing supposedly nonreligious "scientific creationism," creationists of the 1970s pressured textbook publishers and science teachers nationwide into equivocating with regard to the validity of scientific knowledge. In the 1980s court decisions overturned as unconstitutional laws in Ark. and La. that required the teaching of creationism.

CREATION MYTHS, accounts of the creation of the earth, or of man's known world, and of man himself. They often form a basis for religious doctrine and as such have determined the structure of particular societies. Supreme deity myths are typified by the biblical account in GENESIS. Emergence myths, such as that of the Navajo Indians, are analogous to gestation and birth, seeing creation as a gradual unfolding of forces within the earth. Hindu and other Asian cultures represent the moment of creation in terms of the breaking of an egg. World-parent myths generally deal in personifications of the earth (mother) and the sky (father) and include the Babylonian *Enuma Elish* myth. Diving myths posit a watery chaos with mud as the stuff of creation. In accounts by the Crow Indians a duck dives for the mud; a Romanian version has the devil in the role of diver. Antagonism between newly-emergent life forms is a common mythological feature and serves to account for life's subsequent imperfections.

CRÉCY, Battle of (Aug. 26, 1346), battle in the HUNDRED YEARS' WAR near Crécy-en-Ponthieu in N France. Edward III of England's smaller army, with its high percentage of longbowmen, devastated Philip VI's French forces (mainly mounted knights) after some of them launched a premature attack.

CREDIT, in business and economics, the ability of a borrower to raise funds, or the funds themselves. The person making the funds available is a creditor, and he generally makes a charge (interest) for his services; the borrower is the debtor. Only in the case of small-scale retail trade (the corner foodstore, for example) there is often no added charge for credit extended for a few days or weeks. Usually, creditors extend credit only if they are convinced of the ability of the debtor to repay within a reasonable time, or if the debtor pledges goods, stocks, or other property (called collateral) as a sign of his good faith.

The use of credit is an integral part of modern economies, extending from the large-scale operations of government and big corporations to the individual's purchases of appliances or a car. Credit, used on an individual basis, has been known throughout history, but it became important in business only in the late medieval and early modern period when trade developed on a large scale and credits were needed to finance shipments of goods. The need for credit increased during the Industrial Revolution. In today's highly industrialized economies, a high level of development depends upon the existence of an effective credit market to create purchasing power.

Commercial banks and similar banking institutions are the main means of channeling credit to potential users, though insurance and finance companies also contribute a share. Credit created by banks is a part of the money supply and is therefore linked with general economic activity. This means that central banks must pay close attention to the amount of credit available and take measures, where required, to tighten or increase it in order to check inflation or stimulate economic activity in case of recession.

CRÉDIT MOBILIER OF AMERICA, company involved in the construction of the Union Pacific railroad (1865–69). The subject of a financial scandal involving Congressman Oakes Ames, Crédit Mobilier came to symbolize corruption in US business during and after the RECONSTRUCTION period.

CREDIT UNION, a cooperative bank formed under government charter generally by groups of employees or members of a particular association or community. Members buy shares in the bank in return for which they can borrow at interest rates lower than those of commercial banks.

CREED, formal, authorized statement of religious belief, found in all major world religions, used in worship and to define and maintain doctrine. The Christian creeds grew out of early formulas of belief used in BAPTISM, and became standards of orthodoxy. The three "ecumenical creeds," accepted by virtually all WESTERN CHURCHES, the APOSTLES', NICENE and

ATHANASIAN CREEDS, all express belief in God the Father, Son and Holy Spirit, the first two creeds having thus three sections. The Protestant Confessions of the 16th and 17th centuries, including the AUGSBURG CONFESSION, the THIRTY-NINE ARTICLES and the WESTMINSTER CONFESSION, are longer creeds defining controverted points, as is the Roman Catholic *Decrees and Canons* of the Council of TRENT.

CREE INDIANS, North American Indian tribe of the Algonquian group. Originally they were all woodland Indians, hunting and trapping in the forest of S Manitoba, Canada, but in time part of the tribe moved onto the plains of Alberta, Canada, and into the N US, where they hunted buffalo.

CREEK INDIANS, confederacy of North American Indian tribes of the MUSKOGEAN linguistic family. An agricultural people, they lived in the SE US, occupying a large area including most of present day Ala. and Ga. Under chief TECUMSEH they resisted white domination in the Creek War (1813–14), but were routed at the Battle of Horseshoe Bend and as a result lost most of their lands. By 1840 they had been moved to the Indian Territory as one of the FIVE CIVILIZED TRIBES.

CREEL, George Edward (1876–1953), US journalist. Appointed (1917) by President Woodrow Wilson to head the Committee on Public Information, he directed the government's propaganda and information activities during WWI.

CREMONA, Italian city, capital of Cremona province, Lombardy, on the Po R, an agricultural market center. It was the home of the violin-making families of AMATI, STRADIVARI and GUARNIERI.

CREOLE, term first used in the 16th century to describe people of Spanish parentage born in the West Indies. It is now far less specific, serving to describe the descendants of Spanish, Portuguese and French settlers in the West Indies, Latin America and parts of the US—where in La., for example, the term applies to French-speaking people of either French or Spanish descent. French- and Spanish-based patois are known as Creole languages. (See PIDGIN.)

CRETACEOUS, final period of the Mesozoic Era, about 135 to 65 million years ago. It follows the JURASSIC period and is in turn followed by the Cenozoic Era. (See GEOLOGY.)

CRETE, mountainous but fertile Greek island in the E Mediterranean at the southern end of the Aegean. The largest of the Greek islands, it covers some 3,189sq mi. Agriculture is the mainstay, with grapes, oranges and olives the only significant cash crops. The island is of great historical interest, being the home of the ancient Minoan civilization, which had KNOSSOS, with its famous palace, as its leading city. The present-day capital is Canea.

CRETINISM, congenital disease caused by lack of THYROID hormone in late fetal life and early infancy, which interferes with normal development, including that of the BRAIN. It may be due to congenital inability to secrete the hormone or, in certain areas of the world, to lack of dietary IODINE (which is needed for hormone formation). The typical appearance, with coarse SKIN, puffy face, large tongue and slow responses, usually enables early diagnosis. It is crucial that replacement therapy with thyroid hormone should be started as early as possible to minimize or prevent the mental retardation that occurs if diagnosis is delayed.

CRÈVECOEUR, Michel-Guillaume Jean de (1735–1813), French-born writer and settler in America—where he was known as J. Hector St. John. His popular *Letters from an American Farmer* (1782) is an important documentary source on the period. He was French consul in New York 1783–90.

CRIBBAGE, card game essentially for two people, played with the standard deck and a special board with pegs for marking the score. Picture cards are valued at 10 points and all others at their face value. Each player discards two of his six cards, to create a spare hand, or crib, which goes to the dealer. The object is to make the pool of cards in play add up to no more than 31.

CRICK, Francis Harry Compton (1916–   ), English biochemist who, with J. D. WATSON, proposed the double-helix model of DNA. For this, one of the most spectacular advances in 20th-century science, they shared the 1962 Nobel Prize for Physiology or Medicine with M. H. F. WILKINS, who had provided them with the X-ray data on which they had based their proposal. Crick's subsequent work has been concerned with deciphering the functions of the individual codons or "vocabulary" in the genetic code.

CRICKET, field game that originated in England before 1700 and is now most popular in Commonwealth countries. Basically it is played between two teams of eleven. A pair of batsmen from one side defend two wickets, one at each end of a 22yd pitch. The other team act as fielders. A hard ball is "bowled" (thrown overhand with a straight arm) at the defended wicket from the other; the batsman tries to hit out into the field to give himself time to score by running between wickets. If the ball strikes his wicket either directly or while he is running, or if it is caught off his bat, he is out. When all the batsmen are out the teams exchange functions and the "innings" ends; a game consists of not more than two innings per team. The side with most runs wins and the game is drawn if the innings cannot be completed.

CRICKETS, a large group of orthopterous INSECTS. Male ground-dwelling crickets make a chirping sound (stridulation) by rapidly rubbing together the front edge of their wing covers. Crickets have long antennae. Most species have wings, and most have hind legs developed for jumping. An exception is the mole cricket, whose hind legs are undeveloped, but whose fore legs are adapted for burrowing.

CRIME, a voluntary, intentional violation of the criminal law. Criminal law defines a wide variety of offenses. The FEDERAL BUREAU OF INVESTIGATION (FBI) compiles crime statistics under 29 categories. It maintains a crime index of eight major offenses: the violent crimes of murder and nonnegligent manslaughter, forcible rape, robbery, and aggravated assault; and the property crimes of burglary, larceny, motor vehicle theft, and arson. These are the crimes that the average citizen perceives as serious and threatening and that the FBI uses to determine a "crime rate." Treating the eight index crimes apart from all other crimes removes most so-called white-collar crimes — by far the most costly — from consideration and thereby introduces socioeconomic and racial bias into discussion of crime.

The FBI counts only crimes known to the police. In 1985, it recorded 12.4 million index crimes for a crime rate of 5,207 crimes per 100,000 inhabitants. In the period 1981–85, the number of index crimes declined 7.4% and the crime rate declined 11.1%. The Justice Department's Bureau of Criminal Statistics, through its National Crime Survey (NCS), counts crimes by means of victimization surveys based on interviews with a national population sample. NCS data indicate that the number of crimes is actually several times that reported by the FBI, and they do not always confirm trends reported by the FBI. Both FBI and NCS agree, however, on the relative frequency of different types of crime, and they agree also in locating crime both geographically and socially. Crime rates are highest in cities, and the perpetrators are disproportionately male, poor, young, and black. The victims are also disproportionately male, poor, young, and black.

There are both psychological and sociological theories of the causes of crime, and neither type offers much guidance to policymakers compelled to deal with crime in the short run. The psychological theories, in fact, suggest that the causes of crime are so individual as to be beyond the influence of the state. The sociological theories can offer only vague, long-run prescriptions. Most criminologists agree that as the proportion of young people in the population declines, crime rates will also decline.

CRIMEA, peninsula 10,425sq mi in area on the N side of the Black Sea, an *oblast* (province) of the Ukrainian Republic, USSR; it is connected to the Ukrainian mainland by the Perekop Isthmus. Its population today is about 70% Russian and 20% Ukrainian, the indigenous Tatars having been absorbed or exiled.

Around 60% of the population lives in the major urban areas, which include the capital, Simferopol, Kerch, Sevastopol, Balaklava and Yalta. The Crimea is largely agricultural, but has important fisheries and mines, and the S is a popular resort area. The area belonged to the Ottoman Empire until 1783, when Catherine the Great annexed it to Russia. It was the scene of major battles in the CRIMEAN WAR, Russian Revolution and WWII.

CRIMEAN WAR (1853–56), war between Russia and an alliance of Britain, France, Turkey and later Sardinia. A chief cause was Russia's desire to expand to Constantinople and gain access to Mediterranean ports, justified by a claim to be protector of Christians in the Ottoman Empire. In July 1853, the Russians occupied the Turkish provinces of Moldavia and Walachia. In Oct., Turkey declared war on Russia. In March 1854, Britain and France allied with Turkey, out of concern at the general Russian threat to their interests elsewhere. On Oct. 17, the Allies began the siege and bombardment of Sevastopol. Major battles, chaotic and with heavy losses on both sides, followed at Balaklava (Oct. 25) and Inkerman (Nov. 5). The siege of Sevastopol ended in Sept. 1855 with Allied victory. After continued fighting, an armistice was concluded in Feb. 1856 and the Treaty of PARIS signed in March. It was the first conflict reported by war correspondents and photographers.

CRIMINAL LAW, defines those acts considered to be offenses against the state as distinct from civil wrongs committed against an individual. It also regulates legal procedures for the apprehension and trial of suspected offenders and limits the penalties of those convicted.

Modern US criminal law derives from the English common law system, with which it concurs on the broad definition of crime. An act cannot be a crime unless it contravenes a rule of law, customary or statutory, in two elements. The *actus reus* is the act (or failure to act) itself; it must be voluntary, but it is worth noting that self-induced incapacity (as through drugs or alcohol) is held to be reckless of consequences and therefore voluntary. The *mens rea* requires intention to commit the act, rather than mere mistake. Recklessness or carelessness is usually held to be sufficient *mens rea*, however.

The US system relies less on judicial precedent than its British ancestor. In several states, for example, no person may be tried for an offense not specified by statute in that state, although in other states offenses founded only on precedent, such as breach of the peace and conspiracy, still exist. In general, the flexible common law is not well adapted to the federal system of the US because it leads to inconsistencies between states. Since the 1800s La., Wis., Ill., Minn., N.M., N.Y. and Mich. have adopted penal codes on the lines of the CODE NAPOLÉON and other European codes, and many other states are studying them, especially the drafts produced by the American Law Institute in 1962 and the National Commission on Reform of Federal Criminal Laws in 1970.

CRITICISM, in general the act of analyzing and making judgments about any object or activity. In particular the term is applied most often to the examination and evaluation of works of art and of literature. Critical writings may take the form of prose, verse, essays, reviews or long books.

The criticism of a novel, a play, or a piece of music may be subjective and impressionistic—an attack on or a glorification of the work, often in personal terms. Or it may be a wide-ranging examination of a work of literature in which the critic, in order to evaluate the writer and his works, explores aspects of his language and style, his social and historical environment, his private life, and how his work compares with that of other writers.

Objective standards of evaluation have often been sought, but without much success except during certain periods, such as the 18th century, when almost all writers recognized certain conventions of style and content. Today we tend to recognize that most criticism has to reflect the personal taste of the critic, and the weight which we give to it depends upon our evaluation of his experience and judgment.

In periods of great literary and artistic productivity, an extremely fruitful relationship may develop between the writer and the critic, each stimulating the other, through their activities remain essentially different. Writers may be critics too (though critics are not so often creative writers). John DRYDEN, Alexander POPE, Dr. Samuel JOHNSON, Samuel COLERIDGE, Matthew ARNOLD and T. S. ELIOT are examples of excellent writer-critics.

In philsophy, criticism may be defined as an approach to problems in which the thinker weighs the evidence in the manner of a judge. More especially, the term *critical philosophy* is used to describe the theories of Immanuel KANT, whose *critiques* are actually critical examinations of various ideas.

CRITTENDEN COMPROMISE, measure sponsored by Senator John J. Crittenden in Dec. 1860 in an attempt to avert the Civil War. It proposed the abolition of slavery N of 36°30′, and the protection of slavery S of that line. The domestic slave trade was to be free of all restriction; there was also to be a constitutional amendment preventing Congress from interfering with slave states. The compromise failed in committee and Crittenden won no support for a national referendum.

CRIVELLI, Carlo (c1430–1495), Italian painter. A Venetian, he worked in exile in the March of Ancona. In his intensely religious paintings, outlines are sharp and ornamentation rich and varied, though his figures are somewhat flat and stylized.

CROATIA, a constituent republic of Yugoslavia, 21,829sq mi in area. Long a province of Austria-Hungary, Croatia became part of Yugoslavia after WWI. Political and religious differences led to friction between the Croats and Serbs, and Croatia became autonomous as an Axis satellite during WWII. In 1946, when Yugoslavia adopted a federal constitution, Croatia became one of the constituent republics. Croatian agitation for greater autonomy led to political crises and terrorist activity.

CROCE, Benedetto (1866–1952), major Italian philosopher, historian and literary critic. Influenced by HEGEL and VICO, he was a leading exponent of Neo-Idealist philosophy and founder of the review *La Critica* in 1903. He was an active critic of fascism before and during WWII, and in 1943 refounded the Italian Liberal Party, becoming its president; he held various government posts after 1944.

CROCHET, method of making fabrics, garments, lace-like dress trimmings and rugs from yarn or, more rarely, straw, by a series of looped chain stitches made with a special hook. Silk, cotton, wool, or artificial-fiber yarn may be used. Many primitive cultures, including the American Indians, used some form of crochet work; it became popular in the modern US when reintroduced by Irish immigrants.

CROCKER, Charles (1822–1888), US railroad builder. A founder (1861) with Collis P. HUNTINGTON, Mark HOPKINS, and Leland STANFORD of the Central Pacific Railway Company, he personally supervised construction of the railroad to Promontory Point, Utah, employing great numbers of Chinese immigrants. Later he organized the Southern Pacific Railroad, directed its construction, and in 1884 merged it with the Central Pacific.

CROCKETT, Davy (David) (1786–1836), US frontiersman, politician and folk hero. A farmer and Tenn. politician, he was elected to Congress as a Democrat 1827–31, but in 1833 was returned as a Whig. The Whigs built him up as a "backwoods" alternative to Andrew Jackson, and he became famous for his shrewd and humorous speeches, and his memoirs of frontier life. He lost his seat in 1835, and led a Tenn. volunteer force to the ALAMO, where he was killed.

CROCODILE, a family (Crocodylidae) of aquatic reptiles closely related to the ALLIGATOR and the gavial. There are over a dozen species, which are distinguished from alligators by their narrower snout. True crocodiles are members of the genera *Crocodylus, Osteoblepharon* and *Osteolaemus.* They are found in the warmer areas of the world. Young crocodiles feed on small creatures such as frogs or insects, then graduate to fish and, finally, to mammals and birds. Large prey is knocked down and drowned; man-eating has been known to occur.

CROESUS, last king of Lydia c560-546 BC, and last of the Mermnad dynasty, proverbial for his wealth and generosity. At his height he ruled a large part of Asia Minor, but he was overthrown by Cyrus the Great c546 BC. He apparently became an honored courtier of Cyrus.

CROGHAN, George (c1720–1782), Irish-born American frontiersman. An Indian trader, he was employed by the British to counter French influence among the Indians during the FRENCH AND INDIAN WARS. He negotiated (1766) the treaty that ended PONTIAC's Rebellion.

CROLY, Herbert David (1869–1930), US author and editor. His *The Promise of American Life* (1909) had great influence on Progressives in both the Republican and Democratic parties. He founded (1914) the magazine *The New Republic,* which he edited until his death.

CRO-MAGNON MAN, a race of primitive man named for Cro-Magnon, France, dating from the Upper Paleolithic (see STONE AGE) and usually regarded as Aurignacian, though possibly more recent. Coming later than Neanderthal man (see PREHISTORIC MAN), Cro-Magnon man was dolichocephalic with a high forehead and a large brain capacity, his face rather short and wide. He was probably around 5½ft tall, powerfully muscled and robust.

CROME, John (1768–1821), English landscape painter, also called Old Crome, founder of the Norwich school. He was almost entirely self-taught. His best works, such as *Mousehold Heath* (1815) and *Poringland Oak* (1817–21), were done in later life. His main influences were HOBBEMA and other Dutch painters.

CROMER, Evelyn Baring, 1st Earl of (1841–1917), British colonial administrator, who ruled Egypt as consul general 1883-1907. His progressive policies brought the economic and social advances he believed were essential for political progress, but he was distrusted by nationalists. He retired in 1907, becoming leader of the free-trade group in the Unionist party.

CROMWELL, Oliver (1599–1658), lord protector - of the Commonwealth of England, Scotland and Ireland 1653–58. A minor landowner, he became prominent in the early days of the English Civil War as a member of parliament and as commander of the "Ironsides" cavalry regiment he had created. Largely responsible for victory at Marston Moor (1644), he became lieutenant general of the New Model Army, leading his men to victory at Naseby and Langport in 1645. At first inclined to negotiate with Charles I, the king's untrustworthiness so infuriated him that he lent all his weight to the latter's trial and execution. As lord lieutenant of Ireland he led a campaign there (1649) marked by appalling massacres, and as captain general and commander-in-chief of the army he defeated the Scots at Dunbar in 1650. He summarily dissolved the oligarchic and bigoted RUMP PARLIAMENT in 1653. Its beleaguered successor handed power over to him as lord protector; he refused the crown in 1657. Essentially a dictator, he saw his wish to rule through parliament continually thwarted by the intransigence of the Puritan politicians. His regime, though benevolent, suppressed rather than solved the nation's problems and they broke out anew at his death.

CROMWELL, Richard (1626–1712), son of Oliver Cromwell, on whose death he became lord protector of England (1658). He was deposed by military coup in 1659, and went into exile for 20 years.

CROMWELL, Thomas, Earl of Essex (c1485–1540), English statesman under Henry VIII. A ruthless administrator and the main agent for destroying papal power in England, he supervised the king's break with Rome under the Act of Supremacy (1534) and the dissolution of the monasteries (1536–39). He arranged the king's marriage with Anne of Cleves, and on its failure he was executed without trial on charges of heresy and treason trumped up by his many enemies.

CRONIN, A(rchibald) J(oseph) (1896–1981), Scottish doctor who devoted himself to writing after the success of his first novel, *Hatter's Castle* (1931). His other novels include *The Citadel* (1937) and *The Keys of the Kingdom* (1942).

CROOK, George (1829–1890), US cavalry officer. After service in the Civil War, he led campaigns against the Apache Indians in Ariz. (1871–74) and the Sioux and Cheyenne forces led by Sitting Bull and Crazy Horse (1875–77). From 1883 Crook led a temporarily successful campaign to subdue Geronimo.

CROOKES, Sir William (1832–1919), English physicist who discovered the element thallium (1861), invented the radiometer (1875) and pioneered the study of cathode rays. By 1876 he had devised the Crookes tube, a glass tube containing two electrodes and pumped out to a very low gas pressure. By applying a high voltage across the electrodes and varying the pressure, he was able to produce and study cathode rays and various glow discharges.

CROQUET, lawn game of French origin that became popular in 19th-century England. Competitors have to drive colored balls with a longhandled mallet in strict sequence against each other and through a series of iron hoops stuck into the ground.

CROSBY, Bing (Harry Lillis Crosby; 1904–1977), US popular singer and actor. He became known as a big-band singer with Paul Whiteman's "Rhythm Boys" and as a "crooner" and a witty, affable host on one of network radio's most durable variety programs (1931–49). His many films include the famous *Road* series with Bob Hope and Dorothy Lamour, and he won an Oscar for his performance in *Going My Way* (1943). His recording of "White Christmas" was one of the all-time bestsellers.

CROSS, a structure consisting essentially of an upright and a crosspiece, used in ancient times for executions by crucifixion. It is now the principal symbol of the Christian religion. There are four basic forms of the cross: the Latin cross, in which the upright is longer than the transverse beam that crosses it near the top; the Greek cross, an upright crossed at right angles at its center by a beam of the same length; the tau, or St. Anthony's cross in the form of a T; and St. Andrews's cross in the form of an X. The other forms of the cross are mainly inventions for ecclesiastical or hierarchical purposes, such as the papal cross, an upright crossed by three bars.

CROSSBOW, medieval weapon consisting of a small but very powerful box fixed transversely on a stock, grooved to take the missile. Its bowstring latched onto a trigger mechanism, often by a lever or winch. It fired a shaft called a bolt or quarrel, about 10in long; some varieties also fired stones. It had less range and accuracy than the longbow and was slower to load.

CROSS-EYE. See STRABISMUS.

CROUP, a condition common in infancy due to VIRUS infection of LARYNX and TRACHEA and causing characteristic stridor, or spasm of larynx when the child breathes in. Often a mild and short illness, it occasionally causes so much difficulty in breathing that OXYGEN is needed.

CROW INDIANS, North American Indian tribe of the Siouan linguistic group, first encountered in Mont. and Wyo. A nomadic plains tribe living mainly by hunting bison and buffalo, they originally broke away from the Hidatsa tribe, and had two main divisions: the Mountain and River Crow. They now occupy a reservation in S Mont.

CROWS, a large group of black songbirds which are found worldwide. The true crows are members of the family Corvidae, related to ravens and jays. They are omniverous and are regarded as pests in agricultural areas. Crows are highly intelligent. They can imitate sounds and, with training, the human voice. The clough, jackdaw and rook are common forms of Eurasian crow.

CRUCIFIXION, execution by being nailed or tied to a cross by the limbs or, more specifically, the execution in this manner of Jesus Christ. Many countries of the ancient world used it as their most painful method of execution. The victim often suffered for days; death resulted from shock, exhaustion or exposure. The Romans inflicted crucifixion only on lower-class non-Roman criminals and on political agitators.

CRUIKSHANK, George (1792–1878), English artist and satirical caricaturist. He first won fame with his numerous political cartoons (1811–25), then turned to book illustration. His superb illustrations included those for Dickens' *Sketches by Boz* (1836–37) and *Oliver Twist* (1838).

CRUISER, warship designed for speed and long-range attack, in size between the destroyer and aircraft carrier. Used as a small battleship in WWII, its function has been to maintain lines of sea communication and to defend carriers against air attack. The three traditional types of cruiser, heavy, light and antiaircraft, with 8in, 6in and 5in guns respectively, are being converted to or replaced by guided-missile cruisers, and the first such cruiser with nuclear power, USS *Long Beach,* was launched in 1959.

CRUSADES, a series of religious wars from the end of the 11th to the 13th centuries, organized by European powers to recover Christian holy places in Palestine from the Muslims. Crusades arose from religious reform and revival, and because the SELJUKS of Asia Minor, who had taken Jerusalem (1071), were now threatening the Byzantine Empire, ruled by Alexius I. There was an enthusiastic response to Pope Urban II's appeal at the Council of Clermont to recover Jerusalem, but political and commercial interests on the part of European rulers confused the issues of religious zeal and wars of conquest.

The **First Crusade** (1095–99) was fought initially by French and German peasants, but they were massacred in Asia Minor. A second force of four large European armies routed the Turks at Dorylaeum (1097) and, led by Godfrey of Bouillon, captured Jerusalem in 1099, slaughtering thousands of Muslims and Jews. The crusaders set up the Latin kingdom of Jerusalem, with fiefs at Tripoli, Antioch and Edessa. The Turkish recapture of Edessa in 1144 caused the **Second Crusade** (1147–48), led by Louis VII of France and Conrad III of Germany. Their attack on Damascus failed because of mutual jealousy. The Muslims under SALADIN captured Jerusalem in 1187, thus provoking the **Third Crusade** (1189–92), led by the Holy Roman Emperor Frederick I, Philip II of France and RICHARD I of England. Disunited by rivalry, they were unable to take Jerusalem. However, Richard won Acre, gained a few coastal towns and made a truce with Saladin giving pilgrims access to Jerusalem.

The **Fourth Crusade** (1201–04) was diverted to Constantinople by Venetians and claimants to the Byzantine throne from Egypt. The Crusaders pillaged the city, and set up the Latin Empire of Constantinople (1204). The **Children's Crusade** (1212) was a fiasco: some children died on the way, others were sold into slavery. The **Fifth Crusade** (1218–21), against Egypt, the center of Muslim power, was the last launched by a papal legate. The invasion failed when the crusaders had to be evacuated from floodwaters near Cairo. On the peaceful **Sixth Crusade** (1228–29), the Holy Roman Emperor Frederick II claimed his title to Jerusalem and secured the city for the Christians; but it again fell to the Muslims in 1244. LOUIS IX, leading the **Seventh Crusade** (1248–54) to Egypt, was captured at Mansura; he undertook the **Eighth Crusade** in 1270 but died at Tunis. The last Christian city, Acre, fell to the Muslims in 1291 and there were no further large-scale Crusades. Although the Crusades were a military failure, Western Europe was profoundly affected by the prolonged contact with the East, and both culture and trade were stimulated. (See also KNIGHTS OF SAINT JOHN; KNIGHTS TEMPLAR; TEUTONIC KNIGHTS.)

CRUSTACEA, class of animals in the phylum Arthropoda, with jointed legs, including CRABS, SHRIMPS, waterfleas, BARNACLES and woodlice. A few live on land or are parasitic, but most are aquatic, breathing by gills or through the skin and bearing paired series of antennae and limbs down the body. They are vital to the economy of the sea, forming the food of many marine animals.

CRYOGENICS (from Greek *kruos,* frost), the branch of physics dealing with the behavior of matter at very low temperatures, and with the production of those temperatures. Early cryogenics relied heavily on the Joule–Thomson effect (named for James JOULE and William Thomson, later Lord KELVIN) by which temperature falls when a gas is permitted to expand without an external energy source. Using this, James Dewar liquefied HYDROGEN in 1895 (though not in quantity until 1898), and H. K. Onnes liquefied HELIUM in 1908 at 4.2K (see also ABSOLUTE ZERO). Several cooling processes are used today. Down to about 4K the substance is placed in contact with liquefied gases which are permitted to evaporate, so removing HEAT energy. The lowest temperature that can be reached thus is around 0.3K. Further temperature decrease may be obtained by para-magnetic cooling (adiabatic demagnetization). Here a paramagnetic material is placed in contact with the substance and with liquid helium, and subjected to a strong magnetic field (see MAGNETISM), the heat so generated being removed by the helium. Then, away from the helium, the magnetic field is reduced to zero. By this means temperatures of the order of 10^{-2}–10^{-3}K have been achieved (though, because of heat leak, such temperatures are always unstable). A more complicated process, nuclear adiabatic demagnetization, has been used to attain temperatures as low as 2×10^{-7}K.

Near absolute zero, substances can display strange properties. Liquid helium II has no viscosity and can flow up the sides of its container. Some elements display SUPERCONDUCTIVITY: an electric current started in them will continue indefinitely.

CRYPTOGRAPHY. See CODES AND CIPHERS.

CRYPTOZOIC, in GEOLOGY, the eon in which life first appeared (see EVOLUTION) and PRECAMBRIAN rocks were formed. The rocks do not contain FOSSILS that can be used for dating (see CAMBRIAN; CHRONOLOGY); hence the name Cryptozoic (hidden life). By contrast the eon of visible life, from the end of the Cryptozoic to the present, is called the PHANEROZOIC.

CRYSTAL PALACE, vast glass exhibition hall designed by Sir Joseph PAXTON for the Great London Exhibition of 1851. An innovative work, it was both the first cast-iron frame building and the first for which structural units were prefabricated and then assembled on site. It was destroyed by fire in 1936.

CRYSTALS, homogeneous solid objects having naturally-formed plane faces. The order in their external appearance reflects the regularity of their internal structure—i.e., the arrangement of their atoms or molecules—this internal regularity being the keynote of the **crystalline state**. Although external regularity is most obvious in natural crystals and those grown in the laboratory, most other inorganic solid substances (with the notable exceptions of PLASTICS and GLASS) also exist in the crystalline state, although the crystals of which they are composed are often microscopic in size. True crystals must be distinguished from cut gemstones, which, although often internally crystalline, exhibit faces chosen according to the whim of the lapidary rather than developed in the course of any natural growth process. The study of crystals and the crystalline state is the province of **crystallography**. Crystals are classified according to the SYMMETRY that they display. This gives the 32 crystal

classes, which can be grouped into the seven traditional crystal systems (six if trigonal and hexagonal are counted together). Crystals are allotted to their proper class by considering their external appearance, the symmetry of any etch marks made on their surfaces, and their optical and electrical properties. Although such observations enable the crystallographer to determine the type of "unit cell" which, when repeated in space, gives the overall lattice structure of a given crystal, they do not enable the actual dispositions of the constituent ATOMS or IONS to be determined. This can be done only by using X-RAY diffraction techniques. When a crystal is composed solely of particles of a single species and the attractive forces between molecules are not directionally localized, as in the crystals of many pure metals, the atoms tend to take up one of two structures that allow a maximum degree of close-packing. These are known as hexagonal close-packed (hcp) and face-centered cubic (fcc) and can both be looked upon as different ways of stacking planes of particles in which each is surrounded by six neighbors. Although much crystallography assumes that crystals perfectly exhibit their supposed structure, real crystals, of course, contain minor defects such as grain boundaries and dislocations. Many of the most important properties and uses of crystals depend on these defects.

CUBA, republic and largest island in the Caribbean Sea, at the entry to the Gulf of Mexico and 90mi S of the Florida Keys.

Official name: Republic of Cuba
Capital: Havana
Area: 42,804sq mi
Population: 10,302,000
Languages: Spanish
Religions: Roman Catholic
Monetary unit(s): 1 Cuban peso = 100 centavos
Land. Cuba has three mountain ranges, the Sierra de los Organos in the W, the Sierra de Trinidad in the center and the Sierra Maestra in the SE—where Turquino, Cuba's highest peak, rises to 6,560ft. Only a few of the country's many rivers are major

navigable waters. There are deep bays and natural harbors. The warm climate (temperatures between 72°F and 82°F), the usually plentiful rainfall, and the rich soil give Cuba a very wide variety of plant life (over 8,000 species) and great mountain forests. Hurricanes occur quite frequently.

People. The population is over 70% white, of Spanish origin; the rest are mulattoes and blacks. More than half of all Cubans live in cities or towns. Most of the rural population lives near sugar factories. The literacy rate is over 90%.

Economy. Cuba is dependent upon one crop, sugar; tobacco is the second most important export. The island's agriculture has been further diversified by the production of coffee, citrus fruit and rice crops. The fisheries are a growing industry. The largest mineral resource is iron ore, and there are also deposits of nickel, cobalt, copper and manganese. Before 1959 industrialization was limited; after a period of rapid development (1959–63) it has progressed slowly. Neglected for almost 20 years, tourism began to grow in the late 1970s. All trade, commerce and industrial production is nationalized, and most of the cultivated land has been reorganized as state cooperatives. Cuba benefits from an extensive transport network.

History. COLUMBUS discovered Cuba in 1492 and it became important as the base for Spanish exploration of America and as a harbor for Spanish treasure ships. The native Indians, decimated by ill-treatment and disease, were replaced as a work force by West African Negro slaves, particularly in the 18th century when the sugar plantations developed rapidly. In the 19th century Spain's colonial policy led to a series of nationalist uprisings, and after the SPANISH–AMERICAN WAR (1898) Cuba became an independent republic, though it was under US military occupation 1899–1902 and 1906–09. In return for rights of intervention, the US organized public services and invested heavily in Cuba's economy.

Between 1924 and 1959 Cuba was under virtually continuous dictatorship. Fulgencio BATISTA, who had come to power in 1940, was overthrown by Fidel CASTRO in 1959. Castro, as premier, established a socialist state and instituted sweeping land, industrial and educational reforms. After US firms had been nationalized, the US supported the abortive BAY OF PIGS invasion and enforced an economic blockade. Thereafter, the USSR and the communist bloc replaced US trade and provided great economic support. The USSR accounted for 80% of Cuba's international trade, becoming its principal supplier of oil, food, machinery, spare parts, chemicals, and other vital materials. It subsidized the Cuban economy through its supply of low-cost oil and its purchase of Cuban sugar at inflated prices. In 1962 Cuba permitted the installation of Russian nuclear missiles, which led to a major confrontation between the US and USSR until the missiles were withdrawn (see CUBAN MISSILE CRISIS). The Organization of American States (OAS) expelled Cuba in 1962 but lifted its sanctions in 1975. In the late 1970s a brief rapprochement between Cuba and the US seemed to promise reestablishment of diplomatic ties. Cuba permitted thousands of refugees to depart to the US (see CUBAN BOAT LIFT). Cuba's involvement in Africa, however, ended the prospect of reconciliation. In recent years the Cuban economy has deteriorated and the USSR has reduced its economic support. In 1988 Cuba's foreign debt per capita was one of the largest in the world.

CUBAN BOAT LIFT, a flotilla of hundreds of private vessels that carried refugees from Mariel, Cuba, to Key West, Fla., in the spring of 1980. Between Apr. and June some 125,000 new Cuban refugees entered the US, straining the capacity of Fla. and the nation generally to absorb them.

CUBAN MISSILE CRISIS, perhaps the world's closest approach to nuclear war. The crisis began officially on Oct. 16, 1962, when President John F. KENNEDY received photographs, taken by a U-2 reconnaissance plane, of launch sites being constructed for Soviet long-range missiles near San Cristóbal, Cuba. The president and his advisers leaned initially toward making a surprise air attack on the sites but decided instead on a naval blockade to prevent shipment of additional offensive weapons to Cuba. The idea was to apply sufficient pressure to force the Russians to remove their missiles but not so much pressure as to trigger an all-out nuclear war. Kennedy told the American nation about the missiles in Cuba and the imposition of the blockade in a televised address on Oct. 22. Emergency meetings of the ORGANIZATION OF AMERICAN STATES and the UN Security Council were called. Russian vessels en route to Cuba began turning back on Oct. 24, but work on the missile sites continued and contradictory messages were received from Soviet Chairman KHRUSHCHEV on Oct. 26. The first message offered to withdraw the missiles in return for assurances that the US would not invade Cuba while the second proposed a trade:

The Russian missiles would be removed if American missiles were pulled out of Turkey. It was decided to ignore the second message and accept the terms of the first. The crisis was settled on this basis on Oct. 28, with Khrushchev's agreement to dismantle the launch sites and return the missiles to Russia.

CUBISM, influential modern art style created by PICASSO and BRAQUE in Paris between 1907 and 1914. Until 1912, in the "analytic" period, Cubist paintings represented subject matter in the pictorial form of an elaborately-faceted surface. After 1912, in the "synthetic" period, Cubists also stuck objects to their canvases, instead of representing them, and stressed color, texture and construction in COLLAGE. Cubism had a wide effect on all the arts. (See also ABSTRACT ART.)

CUCKOO, family of birds (Cuculidae), including the anis, coucals, guiras and roadrunners. The common cuckoo of Europe, Asia and Africa lays its eggs in other species' nests where they are reared by their foster parents. The North American species raise their own broods.

CUKOR, George (1899–1983), US film director who was known for his polished social comedies and romances. His films featured many of Hollywood's leading actresses, including Katharine Hepburn (*Little Women,* 1933; *Philadelphia Story,* 1940), Greta Garbo (*Camille,* 1936), and Judy Garland (*A Star Is Born,* 1954). He won an Academy Award for *My Fair Lady* (1964).

CULLEN, Countee (1903–1946), black US poet and member of the HARLEM RENAISSANCE. He wrote about the "New Negro" who has proud roots in an African past. Among his works are *Color* (1925) and a novel, *One Way to Heaven* (1932).

CULLODEN MOOR, site of the battle near Inverness, N Scotland, where Charles Edward STUART, the Young Pretender, and the JACOBITES were finally defeated in 1746 by the Duke of Cumberland. About 1,000 of the 5,000 Scots were slaughtered.

CUMBERLAND GAP, a natural pass, 1,640ft high, through the Cumberland Mts near where Ky., Tenn. and Va. meet. Daniel Boone's WILDERNESS ROAD ran through the Gap, and it was one of the three early major routes to the West through the Appalachian Mts. In the Civil War it was a strategic point.

CUMMINGS, Edward Estlin (1894–1962), U.S. poet known as e. e. cummings, famous for his innovations in language, punctuation and typography. The content of his poems is often traditional and romantic, though colored by wit and satire. His best work is in the collection *Poems 1923–1954.*

CUMMINS, Albert Baird (1850–1926), US Republican politician, Progressive governor of Iowa (1901–08) and US senator (1909–27).

CUNARD, Sir Samuel (1787–1865), Canadian ship-owner, founder of the Cunard line. He pioneered regular transatlantic steamship lines from 1840 after he had won a contract to carry British and North American mail.

CUNEIFORM (from Latin *cuneus,* wedge, and *forma,* shape), one of the earliest known fully developed writing systems. Each character is formed by a combination of wedge- or nail-shaped strokes. Invented probably by the Sumerians before 3,000 BC, it was soon adopted by the Akkadians and then by other peoples, such as the Hittites and the Persians. The characters are stylizations of earlier pictographs, and were impressed in clay. Cuneiform was first deciphered in detail by Sir Henry Rawlinson (1810–95) in 1846.

CUNNINGHAM, Merce (1919–   ), U.S. dancer and choreographer whose avant-garde style emphasizes experimental music and abstract movement. Much of his work is set to the music of John CAGE.

CUPID, or **Amor,** in Roman mythology, the god of love, identified with the Greek Eros and the son and companion of Venus. He is usually depicted as a small boy, winged, naked and armed with bow and arrow. Those wounded by him fall in love.

CURAÇAO, largest island (182sq mi) of the Netherlands Antilles, West Indies, 60mi N of NW Venezuela. It is flat and barren. The chief industries are oil-refining and phosphate mining. The liqueur Curaçao originated here. The capital is Willemstad.

CURARE, arrow-poison used by South American Indian hunters, extracted from various plants, chiefly of the genera *Strychnos* and *Chondodendron,* killing by respiratory paralysis. Curare is a mixture of ALKALOIDS, the chief being *d*-tubocurarine. By competing with acetylcholine it blocks nerve impulse transmission to muscles, producing relaxation and paralysis. It has revolutionized modern surgery by producing complete relaxation without a dangerous degree of ANESTHESIA being required. (See also TETANUS.)

CURIE, Marie (1867–1934), born Marja Sklodowska, Polish-born French physicist who, with her French-born husband Pierre Curie (1859–1906), was an early investigator of RADIOACTIVITY, discovering the radioactive elements polonium and RADIUM in the mineral PITCHBLENDE (1898). For this the Curies shared the 1903 Nobel physics prize with A. H. BECQUEREL. After the death of Pierre, Marie went on to investigate the chemistry and medical applications of radium and was awarded the 1911 Nobel Prize for Chemistry in recognition of her isolation of the pure metal. She died of LEUKEMIA, no doubt contracted in the course of her work with radioactive materials. Pierre Curie is also noted for the discovery, with his brother Jacques, of piezoelectricity (1880) and for his investigation of the effect of TEMPERATURE on magnetic properties. In particular he discovered the **Curie point**, the temperature above which ferromagnetic materials display only paramagnetism (1895). The Curies' elder daughter, Irène JOLIOT-CURIE, was also a noted physicist.

CURLEY, James Michael (1874–1958), Democratic "boss" and mayor of Boston, Mass. for many years; also US congressman and governor of Mass. In 1947 he was convicted for fraudulent use of the mails, but his sentence was later commuted by President Truman. He was fully pardoned in 1950.

CURLING, a game introduced from Scotland and played in the US and Canada for over 150 years. In curling, granite stones of up to 3ft in circumference are propelled along "rinks" of ice 138ft long, with the object of hitting, or getting nearest to a *tee*—or target stone—at the other end. Canada and the US won all but one of the first eleven world championships, introduced in 1959, and as many as 25,000 spectators have watched a Canadian national championship final. Curling is also popular in Scandinavia, Switzerland (which has several curling "schools") and, of course, Scotland, where a curling stone dated 1551 is preserved.

CURRIER AND IVES, firm of American lithographers which produced over 7,000 different prints showing lively scenes from 19th-century American life. **Nathaniel Currier** (1813–1888) became known in 1835 by producing a lithograph of a major New York City fire only four days after the event. **James Merritt Ives** (1824–1895) became Currier's bookkeeper in 1852, his partner in 1857.

CURTIN, John Joseph (1885–1945), Australian Labour politician, prime minister (1941–45) during WWII.

CURTIS, Benjamin Robbins (1809–1874), US lawyer, a justice on the US Supreme Court 1851–57. He dissented in the DRED SCOTT CASE and resigned. In 1868 he was chief defense counsel in the impeachment trial of President Andrew JOHNSON.

CURTIS, Cyrus Hermann Kotzschmar (1850–1933), US founder of a publishing empire. From the age of 12, he started or bought magazines and newspapers including *The Saturday Evening Post*, *The Ladies' Home Journal* and the *New York Evening Post*.

CURTISS, Glenn Hammond (1878–1930), US aviation pioneer. He won trophies for the first public flight of more than a kilometer, for a 25mi flight, and for a flight from Albany to New York City. He developed the first practical seaplane. During WWI Curtiss's company manufactured "Jenny" biplanes for the army and navy.

CURZON OF KEDLESTON, George Nathaniel Curzon, 1st Marquess (1859–1925), British statesman, viceroy of India 1898–1905 and foreign secretary 1919–24. His reforms while viceroy included reorganizing government finance.

CUSH, Kingdom of, Egyptian-influenced Sudanese state flourishing c1000 BC—350 AD. Cushite kings, reigning from the capital, Napata, conquered Egypt, ruling as its 25th dynasty (8th–7th centuries BC). The later capital, MEROE, was Black Africa's first major iron-making center until its destruction in the 4th century AD.

CUSHING, Caleb (1800–1879), US lawyer and diplomat. As minister to China, he negotiated commerical treaties and established the principle of extraterritoriality. He served (1853–57) as US attorney general under President Franklin Pierce. A prominent Democrat and sympathetic to the South, he nevertheless supported the Union in the Civil War, and becoming a Republican, campaigned for Lincoln's reelection. He was (1871–72) chief US counsel at the arbitration of the ALABAMA CLAIMS and served (1874–77) as US minister to Spain.

CUSHING, Harvey Williams (1869–1939), US surgeon who pioneered many modern neurosurgical techniques and investigated the functions of the PITUITARY GLAND. In 1932 he described **Cushing's syndrome**, a rare disease caused by STEROID imbalance and showing itself in obesity, high blood pressure and other symptoms.

CUSTER, George Armstrong (1839–1876), controversial American cavalry officer, killed in a famous battle with Indians. He proved himself an outstanding Union cavalry leader during the Civil War. Made a lieutenant colonel in 1866, he joined General Hancock's successful expedition against the Cheyenne Indians in Kan. and subsequently saw western patrol duty. In 1876 Custer and the 7th US Cavalry Regiment moved to herd Sioux Indians in

Mont. into government reservations. Underestimating the size of an Indian village, Custer refused to await expected reinforcements and attacked, recklessly dividing his force into three columns. His own column was entirely wiped out. (See also CRAZY HORSE.)

CUVIER, Georges Léopold Chrétien Frédéric Dagobert, Baron (1769–1832), French comparative anatomist and the founder of PALEONTOLOGY. By applying his theory of the "correlation of parts" he was able to reconstruct the forms of many fossil creatures, explaining their creation and subsequent extinction according to the doctrine of CATASTROPHISM. A tireless laborer in the service of French Protestant education, Cuvier was perhaps the most renowned and respected French scientist in the early 19th century.

CUYP, Aelbert (1620–1691), outstanding member of a family of Dutch painters. His glowing river scenes with cattle are particularly fine, but he also painted portraits, still lifes and seascapes. He influenced later English landscape artists, and many of his best works are in Britain.

CYANIDES, compounds containing the CN group. Organic cyanides are called nitriles. Inorganic cyanides are salts of **hydrocyanic acid** (HCN), a volatile weak ACID; both are highly toxic. Sodium cyanide is made by the Castner process: ammonia is passed through a mixture of carbon and fused sodium. The cyanide ion (CN^-) is a pseudohalogen, and forms many complexes. Cyanides are used in the extraction of GOLD and SILVER.

CYBERNETICS, a field of science which compares the communication and control systems built into mechanical and other man-made devices with those present in biological organisms. For example, fruitful comparisons may be made between data processing in COMPUTERS and various functions of the BRAIN; and the fundamental theories of cybernetics may be applied with equal validity to both.

CYCLADES, a group of about 220 mountainous islands in the Aegean Sea belonging to Greece, the chief islands being Andros, Ceos (Kea), Delos, Melos, Naxos, Paros, Santorin, Syros (Siros), and Tenos (Tinos). Syros (Hermoupolis), on Syros, is the capital. Wine, wheat, fruit, olive oil and tobacco are produced; and iron, manganese, and sulfur mined. Their possession was contested in classical times. In the 13th century they passed to Venice, in 1566 to the Ottoman Empire. They became Greek in 1829.

CYCLONE, a low-pressure atmospheric disturbance (see ATMOSPHERE; METEOROLOGY) of a roughly circular form, a center towards which ground WINDS move, and at which there is an upward air movement, usually spiraling. Above the center, in the upper troposphere, there is a general outward movement. The direction of spiraling is counterclockwise in the N Hemisphere, clockwise in the S Hemisphere, owing to the CORIOLIS EFFECT. **Anticyclones,** by contrast, are high-pressure atmospheric disturbances characterized by out-blowing winds and a clockwise circulation in the N Hemisphere (counterclockwise in the S Hemisphere). (See also HURRICANE; TORNADO.)

CYCLOPS, in Greek mythology, a shaggy giant with a single large eye in the center of his forehead. HOMER's Cyclopes were lawless Sicilian herdsmen, one of whom (Polyphemus) was met by ODYSSEUS. But there were other mythological Cyclopes: the three blacksmith sons who were imprisoned in Tarturus by their father, Uranus, and who, in return for their freedom, helped Hephaestus make Zeus's thunderbolts in his forge under Mt. Etna; and the Cyclopes who built the great walls of Tiryns and Mycenae.

CYNICS, members of an ascetic Greek philosophical sect following DIOGENES (4th century BC), and influenced by SOCRATES. They ignored conventional standards, preached self-control, condemned immorality and renounced worldly comfort, living as simply as animals (hence, probably, their name: *kynikos* means "doglike"). Their movement influenced STOICISM but vanished in imperial Roman times.

CYPRIAN, Saint (Thascius Caecilianus Cyprianus; c200–258 AD), bishop of Carthage (248–258) and martyr, one of the CHURCH FATHERS. Converted to Christianity c246, Cyprian wrote and spoke influentially on order and conduct in the Church, stressing Church unity and episcopal authority. Feast day: Sept. 16.

CYPRUS, island republic in the NE Mediterranean, about 40mi from the S Turkish coast. It is the third-largest island in the Mediterranean after Sicily and Sardinia.

Land. The island consists of fertile central lowlands with rugged mountains to the N and S. The N range comprises the Kyrenia and Karpas mountains (Akromandra, 3,357ft). In the SW, the Troodos massif has Mt Olympus (6,403ft), the island's highest peak. On the Mesaoria lowland between the mountain systems is Nicosia, the capital. The mountains are partly forested (pine, cypress, and juniper) and have much poor

Official name: The Republic of Cyprus
Capital: Nicosia
Area: 3,572sq mi
Population: 719,000
Languages: Greek, Turkish
Religions: Greek Orthodox, Turkish Muslim
Monetary unit(s): 1 Cyprus pound = 1,000 mils

pasture. The climate is typically E Mediterranean.

People. The population is about 80% Greek and 20% Turkish. Both Greek and Turkish are official languages and English is widely spoken.

Economy. The economy normally depends heavily upon irrigated agriculture (citrus fruits, vines, tobacco, cereals and vegetables). Mineral resources include cupreous and iron pyrites, asbestos, chromite and gypsum. Tourism was formerly important.

History. Ruled successively by the Ottoman Turks (1570–1878) and Great Britain, Cyprus became an independent republic, with Archbishop Makarios III as president, in 1960. But strife between Greek and Turkish Cypriots continued, and in 1974 a military coup organized by Greek army officers favoring *enosis* (union with Greece) temporarily ousted Makarios, whereupon Turkey occupied the NE third of the island. In 1983 this split was formalized with the establishment of the Turkish Republic of Northern Cyprus. UN-sponsored talks on reunification collapsed in 1986. Archbishop Makarios's political heir, Spyros Kyprianou, was president from 1977 to 1988, when he was defeated by George Vassilou, thought to be less intransigent on the Turkish issue.

CYRANO DE BERGERAC, Savinien de (1619–1655), French author. He gave up a military career to write plays and prose. A freethinker, influenced by Pierre Gassendi (1592–1655), he satirized contemporary society in ingenious fantasies about voyages to the sun and moon. Edmond ROSTAND, in his play *Cyrano de Bergerac*, made him into a flamboyant Romantic hero, handicapped in love because of an unusually large nose.

CYRENAICS, members of a Greek school of philosophy centered in Cyrene in the 3rd and 4th centuries BC. Its founder, Aristippus (c435–356 BC), advocated seeking pleasure and avoiding pain. Pleasure was the only absolute good, but wisdom was a vital path to its attainment. Cyrenaic philosophy gave rise to EPICUREANISM.

CYRIL AND METHODIUS, Saints (c827–869 and c825–884), Greek missionaries, apostles to the Slavs, who deeply influenced Slavic culture. Invited to Moravia, from 863 the brothers rivaled Latin-speaking German missionaries in the Danube region, preaching in the local Slavic tongue, pioneering the Glagolitic script (precursor of Cyrillic) and translating biblical texts into Old Church Slavonic. Their feast day is July 7.

CYRUS, name of three rulers of ancient Persia. **Cyrus I** was king of Anshan in the late 7th century BC. **Cyrus II the Great** (c590/580–529 BC) was the son of Cambyses I and founder of the empire of the Achaemenians. Ruler of Anshan from c559 BC, he conquered Media, Lydia (c547 BC) and Babylonia (539 BC), building an empire from the Black and Caspian seas to the Arabian Desert and Persian Gulf (see also PERSIA, ANCIENT). He allowed the Jews to return to Palestine from their BABYLONIAN CAPTIVITY. **Cyrus the Younger** (d. 401 BC) was the second son of DARIUS II. Pardoned after unsuccessfully trying to oust his elder brother, Artaxerxes II, he rebelled and was killed by Artaxerxes at the Battle of Cunaxa—which led to the famous retreat of 10,000 Greeks under XENOPHON.

CYST, a fluid-filled sac, lined by fibrous connective tissue or surface EPITHELIUM. It may form in an enlarged normal cavity (e.g., sebaceous cyst), it may arise in an embryonic remnant (e.g., branchial cyst), or it may occur as part of a disease process. They may be present as swellings or may cause pain (e.g., some ovarian cysts). Multiple cysts in KIDNEY and LIVER occur in inherited polycystic diseases; here kidney failure may develop.

CYSTIC FIBROSIS, an inherited disease presenting in infancy or childhood causing abnormal GLAND secretions; chronic LUNG disease with thick sputum and liability to infection is typical, as is malabsorption with pale bulky feces and MALNUTRITION. Sweat contains excessive salt (the basis for a diagnostic test) and heat exhaustion may result. Significant disease of LIVER, SINUSES and salivary glands occurs. Prompt treatment of chest infection with PHYSIOTHERAPY and appropriate ANTIBIOTICS is crucial to minimize lung damage;

concentrated PANCREAS extract and special diets encourage normal digestion and growth, and extra salt should be given in hot weather. Although long-term outlook in this disease has recently improved, there is still a substantial mortality before adult life.

CYSTITIS, INFLAMMATION of the BLADDER, usually due to infection. A common condition in women, sometimes precipitated by intercourse. It occasionally leads to pyelonephritis, or upper urinary tract infection. Burning pain and increased frequency of urination are usual symptoms. ANTIBIOTICS are often needed. Recurrent cystitis may suggest an underlying disorder of bladder or its nervous control.

CYTOLOGY, the branch of BIOLOGY dealing with the study of CELLS, their structure, function, biochemistry, etc. Techniques used include tissue culture and ELECTRON MICROSCOPY. (See also HISTOLOGY.)

CZECHOSLOVAKIA, central European communist republic between Poland on the N and Hungary and Austria on the S. The USSR lies to the E, West Germany to the W and East Germany to the NW.

Official name: The Czechoslovak Socialist Republic
Capital: Prague
Area: 49,384sq mi
Population: 15,591,000
Languages: Czech, Slovak
Religions: Roman Catholic, Protestant
Monetary unit(s): 1 koruna = 100 haléřů
Land. It comprises four distinct geographical regions: Bohemia, Moravia, the Carpathians and Slovakia. Bohemia is the W plateau fringed by mountains—the Böhmer Wald (Bohemian Forest), Erzgebirge (Ore Mountains), the Sudetic Mountains (Sněžka, 5,256ft) and the Bohemian–Moravian Heights. Cutting through the uplands in the S is the Vltava R, which flows through Prague, the Czech capital, on its way to the Elbe. Moravia, E of Bohemia, has rolling hills and fertile soils and is drained by the Morava R and its tributaries and, in the N, by the Oder R. The forested arc of the Carpathians

dominates N Slovakia, the ridges separated by the Váh, Nitra and Hron rivers, all flowing to the Danube. In the High Tatra is Gerlachovka (8,711ft), the republic's highest peak. Slovakia's plains in the SW and SE are extensions of the Danube–Tisa (Pannonian) plain. The climate is central European, with hot, thundery summers and long, cold winters.

People. More than 60% of the population are Czech and about 30% Slovak, with Hungarians, Germans, Poles and Ukrainians accounting for the remainder. Prague is the only city with more than 1 million inhabitants. Other large cities are Brno, Bratislava, Ostrava, Plzeň and Košice.

Economy. Industry is the dominant sector of the economy. Heavy industry, especially engineering and chemicals, has been greatly expanded since WWII. Steel, armaments, machinery, precision instruments, electrical goods, glass, textiles and footwear are among Czechoslovakia's many products. Limited mineral resources (coal, oil, natural gas, iron ore, copper and lead-zinc ores) are supplemented by imports of bituminous coal, iron ore, oil and natural gas, mainly from the USSR. There are valuable forests (mainly spruce and beech). Agriculture has been collectivized and provides cereals, sugar beets, potatoes, hops, grapes, fruit and beef and dairy cattle.

History. With the disintegration of Austria–Hungary at the end of WWI, the Czechs and Slovaks proclaimed the independent republic of Czechoslovakia (1918), which developed as a Western-style democracy. Seized by Nazi Germany (1938–39), Czechoslovakia came under Russian domination after WWII, and a communist regime took power. In 1968–69 an attempt by the Communist Party leader, Alexander Dubček, to liberalize the country, the so-called Prague spring, was crushed by invading Russian and other Warsaw Pact troops. Dubček and other moderates were purged and the staunchly pro-Soviet Gustav Husák was put in control. An oppressive Stalinist regime settled on the country, buying cultural conformity and political silence from the population with food and consumer goods. But rigid planning and inept management undermined the economy, which stagnated during the 1980s. In 1987 Husák retired as party leader (but remained in the ceremonial office of president) and was succeeded by the equally conservative Milos Jakes. Except for a small dissident movement, Charter 77, the population remained apathetic. In 1988 the entire Council of Ministers resigned, enabling

Jakes to consolidate his power and bring Czechoslovakia cautiously into step with policies of change advocated by the Soviet Union.

4th letter of the English alphabet, originally derived from the triangular Semitic symbol *daleth* (meaning door). The present form comes from the Latin alphabet. In chemistry D stands for deuterium; it is the second note of the musical scale of C, and the Roman numeral for 500.

DACHAU, town in Bavaria, West Germany, 10mi NW of Munich. Many thousands were murdered at the Nazi concentration camp set up nearby in 1933, some in brutal medical experiments. Pop 33,000.

DACIA, ancient region corresponding to modern Romania and Transylvania. The emperor TRAJAN made it a Roman province and settled Roman colonists there whose Latin influenced modern Romanian.

DADA, artistic movement which arose in Zurich and New York in 1915–16, spreading to Berlin and Paris. The name was first used in Zurich by the poet Tristan TZARA, the artists Jean ARP and Marcel Janco, and the writers Hugo Ball and Richard Huelsenbeck. Dada was deliberately provocative, aiming at the destruction of aesthetic preconceptions. The Dadaists experimented with "ready-mades," phonetic or nonsense poetry, collage, anarchic typography and outrageous theater events. Dada was a prelude to SURREALISM and, though it effectively ended in 1923, it influenced many later artistic developments.

DAFFODIL, bulbous, perennial plants of the genus *Narcissus*, family Amaryllidaceae, producing yellow trumpet-shaped flowers. They are native to Europe and North Africa, but are now an important ornamental crop grown throughout the world.

DAGUERREOTYPE, the first practical photographic process, invented (1837) by Louis Daguerre (1789–1851) and widely used in portraiture until the mid-1850s. A brass plate coated with silver was sensitized by exposure to iodine vapor and exposed to light in a CAMERA for several minutes. A weak positive image produced by mercury vapor was fixed with a solution of salt. Hyposulfite soon replaced salt as the fixing agent, and after 1840 gold (III) chloride was used to intensify the image. (See also PHOTOGRAPHY.)

DAHL, Roald (1916–   ), English writer famous for his macabre short stories. He also wrote novels and children's books, including *Chitty Chitty Bang Bang* (1968).

DAHOMEY. See BENIN.

DAIMLER, Gottlieb Wilhelm (1834–1900), German engineer who devised an INTERNAL-COMBUSTION ENGINE (1883) and used it in building one of the first AUTOMOBILES about 1886.

DAIMYO, Japanese feudal barons. The SAMURAI were their armed retainers. Some daimyo became more powerful than the emperor and made themselves SHOGUNS, or military dictators, of the country. The daimyo IEYASU TOKUGAWA united the country under the TOKUGAWA shogunate in 1600. In the 19th century some daimyo, feeling that the decayed shogunate was too weak to resist Western intrusion, gave their support to the emperor Meiji. This led to the end of the Tokugawa shogunate, the restoration of imperial authority, and the abolition of feudal domains and privileges.

DAISY, common name given to several plants of the family Compositae. The common daisy (*Bellis perennis*) is native to Europe, and ornamental varieties are popular in North America and Europe. Similarly, the ox-eye daisy (*Chrysanthemum leucanthemum*) is native to Europe and naturalized in North America. Many varieties are in cultivation.

DALADIER, Édouard (1884–1970), French premier who, with Neville CHAMBERLAIN, signed the MUNICH AGREEMENT abandoning Czechoslovakia to Hitler. Premier in 1933, 1934 and 1938–40, he resigned in 1940 after failing to aid Finland against Russia. He was imprisoned by the Germans 1943–45, and later became leader of the Radical Party.

DALAI LAMA, title of the head of the dominant order of Tibetan Buddhists and, until 1959, Tibet's spiritual and temporal ruler. When a Dalai Lama dies, the next one is chosen from among young boys born within two years of his death. The 13th Dalai Lama (1875–1933) expelled occupying Chinese troops and declared Tibet independent in 1913. Independence was lost under the 14th Dalai Lama (1935–   ) when the Chinese communists invaded Tibet. The Dalai Lama went into exile in

India in 1959.

D'ALEMBERT, Jean Le Rond. See ALEMBERT, JEAN LE ROND D'.

DALEY, Richard Joseph (1902–1976), US Democratic politician, mayor of Chicago from 1955 until his death. Born in Chicago, he was a state senator 1939–43, director of revenue 1948–50 and clerk of Cook Co. 1950–55. As mayor he improved Chicago in many ways, but was criticized for his failure to curb racial segregation and for his rough handling of demonstrators at the 1968 Democratic Convention. He was an adviser to presidents Kennedy and Johnson.

DALHOUSIE, James Andrew Broun Ramsay, 1st marquess of (1812–1860), British governor general of India (1847–56). He annexed the Punjab, lower Burma, and a number of princely states, reformed Hindu practices, and encouraged Western education. He planned the Indian railway system, beginning heavy British investment in Indian economic development.

DALI, Salvador (1904–   ), Spanish surrealist painter whose works mix images as in dreams and hallucinations. Strongly influenced by Sigmund FREUD, Dali sought to portray the elements of the UNCONSCIOUS by using unusual methods and rich fantasy, combined with a refined draftsmanship.

DALLAPICCOLA, Luigi (1904–1975), Italian composer who adapted the 12-tone technique to his own emotionally expressive and melodic style. His works include vocal compositions and operas.

DALLAS, Alexander James (1759–1817), US secretary of the treasury (1814–16) who restored the country's finances after the War of 1812 by levying heavy new taxes and reestablishing (1816) the BANK OF THE UNITED STATES. His son, **George Mifflin Dallas** (1792–1864), was vice president (1845–49) under President James K. Polk and US minister to Great Britain (1856–61).

DALLAS, second-largest city in Tex., founded by John Neely Bryan in 1841 on the Trinity R and named for George Mifflin Dallas (1792–1864), vice-president under James Polk. In the 1870s the railroads brought Dallas growth and lasting importance as a cotton processing and shipping center. When oil was discovered in E Tex. in the 1930s, Dallas became a major oil center. The banking and insurance capital for the Southwest, it also has many thriving industries (textiles, paper, machinery), and cultural and educational institutions. Pop (city) 974,000, (metro) 2,312,000.

DALMATIA, region in W Yugoslavia consisting of a mountainous strip bordering the Adriatic, and including about 300 islands. The area has been dominated by the Romans (1st century BC–5th century AD), Venetians (1420–1797), Austrians (1815–1918) and many other foreign powers. The present, largely Croatian population lives on tourism, fishing and farming. They produce wine, olive oil, cotton, ships, bauxite and limestone.

DALTON, John (1766–1844), English Quaker scientist renowned as the originator of the modern chemical atomic theory. First attracted to the problems of GAS chemistry through an interest in meteorology, Dalton discovered his **Law of Partial Pressures** in 1801. This states that the PRESSURE exerted by a mixture of gases equals the sum of the partial pressures of the components and holds only for ideal gases. (The partial pressure of a gas is the pressure it would exert if it alone filled the volume.) Dalton believed that the particles or ATOMS of different ELEMENTS were distinguished from one another by their weights, and, taking his cue from the laws of definite and multiple proportions (see COMPOSITION, CHEMICAL), he compiled and published in 1803 the first table of comparative ATOMIC WEIGHTS. This inaugurated the new quantitative atomic theory. Dalton also gave the first scientific description of COLOR BLINDNESS. The red-green type from which he suffered is still known as **Daltonism**.

DALTON, Robert (1867–1892), US outlaw who, with his brothers Grattan and Emmet and others, became notorious for train robberies in California and Oklahoma Territory. Robert and Grattan were killed, and Emmet was wounded and captured, in an attempted bank robbery in Coffeyville, Kans.

DALY, Augustin (1838–1899), US playwright and theatrical producer. His many productions in New York, London, and Europe featured such outstanding performers as Otis Skinner, John Drew, Maurice BARRYMORE, and Joseph JEFFERSON.

DALY, Marcus (1841–1900), Irish-born US mining magnate. Prospecting for silver near Butte, Mont., he discovered copper and in 1891 organized the Anaconda Mining Company, which made him a multimillionaire.

DAM, a structure confining and checking the flow of a river, stream or estuary to divert its flow, improve navigation, store water for irrigation or city supplies or raise its level for use in power generation. Often a recreation area is made as a by-product. Dams are one of the earliest known man-made structures, records existing from c2900 BC of a 15m-high dam on the Nile. Construction methods were largely empirical until 1866, when the first scientifically designed dam was built in France. Dams are classified by profile and building material, these being determined by availability and site. They must be strong enough to hold back water; withstand ice, silt and uplift pressures, and stresses from temperature changes and EARTHQUAKES. The site must have stable earth or rock that will not unduly compress, squeeze out or let water seep under the dam. Borings, seismic tests, structural models and computer simulations are all design aids. **Masonry** or **concrete dams** are typically used for blocking streams in narrow gorges. The highest are around 300m high. A **gravity dam** holds back water by its own weight and may be solid, sloping downstream with a thick base, or buttressed, sloping upstream and strengthened by buttresses which transfer the dead weight sideways; these require less concrete. **Arch dams**, with one or more ARCHES pointing upstream, are often built across a canyon and transfer some water pressure to its walls. Hoover Dam, built in 1936, is a combination of arch and gravity types. **Embankment** or **earthfill dams** are large barriers of rock, sand, silt or clay for controlling broad streams. As in a gravity dam, their weight deflects the horizontal water thrust downward toward the broad base. The materials may be uniformly mixed or there may be zones of waterproof material such as CONCRETE either on the upstream face or inside the dam. During construction, temporary **cofferdams** are built to keep water away from the site. Automatic **spillways** for disposing of excess water from the dam, intakes, gates and bypasses for fish or ships are all important parts of a dam complex.

DAMASCUS, capital city of Syria, founded c2000 BC and reputed to be the oldest continuously inhabited city in the world. An oasis by the Anti-Lebanon Mts, it has been a halt for desert caravans since c1000 BC; it is still a market center, dealing in both produce and industrial products. The city's northern section is modern, the southern ancient, with the famous Great Mosque and a medieval citadel. The city has been controlled by Greeks, Macedonians, Romans, Arabs, Mongols, Turks, British and French until it became the capital of independent Syria in 1946. Pop 1,219,448.

DAMIEN, Father (Joseph de Veuster; 1840–1889), Belgian Roman Catholic missionary who spent his life in the leper colony of Molokai Island, Hawaii, which he turned from a mere refuge into a thriving community. He died of leprosy himself, having refused to be cured because he would have had to leave Molokai.

DAMPIER, William (1652–1715), English adventurer, explorer and author. For 11 years he sailed the Atlantic and Pacific as a buccaneer, then was commissioned by the British Admiralty to explore the SW Pacific. He was the first Englishman to reach Australia. He described his voyages in *A New Voyage Round the World* (1697) and other books.

DAMROSCH, Walter Johannes (1862–1950), German-born US conductor of the New York Symphony Orchestra (founded by his father, **Leopold Damrosch**, 1832–1885) and the Metropolitan Opera, where he introduced modern European composers to American audiences. He pioneered music broadcasting on the radio.

DANA, Charles Anderson (1819–1897), American journalist who developed the "human interest" story. From 1841–46 he lived in the Utopian BROOK FARM; he then joined the *New York Tribune*, and in 1849 became its managing editor. From 1864–65 he was assistant to the secretary of war. As editor of the *New York Sun* in 1868, he became a national figure.

DANA, Richard Henry, Jr. (1815–1882), American lawyer, social reformer and author of *Two Years Before the Mast* (1840). Written after he had sailed to Cal. round Cape Horn, it exposed in realistic and readable detail the harsh treatment of sailors and started a reform campaign. He was a founder of the FREE SOIL PARTY.

DANBURY HATTERS' CASE, a Supreme Court decision of 1908, that dealt labor unions a severe blow by upholding a suit by a non-union Danbury, Conn., hat manufacturer against the hatters' union for boycotting his product. The court held that the boycott was in violation of the Sherman Anti-Trust Act (1890) outlawing "every combination in restraint of trade."

DANCE, the art of moving the body rhythmically, usually to music. The movements may be enjoyed for their own sake, they may express an idea or emotion or tell a story, or they may be employed to induce a frenzied or trancelike state in the dancer. These possibilities of dance have made it a central feature of the religious, social and artistic life of most cultures. From earliest times dance has played an important part in courtship rituals—the root of most popular dances in the West today—and in the celebration of notable public and private occasions. Among primitive peoples a belief in the magical potency of dance found expression in fertility and rain dances, in dances of exorcism and resurrection, and in dances preparatory to hunting or fighting. Religious dance, associated with paganism, has been played down by the Christian Church since the 12th century. In contrast, in the East traditional dancing is wholly religious in origin and there is little tradition of social dancing. Communal dance as a powerful symbol of group cooperation and mutual regard underlies enduring traditions in FOLK DANCING. Classical BALLET had its origins in the court dances in 15th and 16th-century Italy and France, which were increasingly elaborated into complete entertainments. The 19th century saw the development of the waltz, in which social dancing reached the height of popularity. 20th-century dance styles, promoted by the syncopated rhythms of popular music, have become increasingly free and uninhibited, often resembling primitive dances. One conspicuous innovation has been the conscious invention and commercial promotion of dance styles.

DANDELION, *Taraxacum officinale* and related species of the family Compositae, with worldwide distribution. They are common weeds producing a sessile rosette of spreading leaves and an inflorescence of yellow flowers and fluffy heads of seeds. The name is derived from the French *dent-de-lion* (lion's tooth), referring to the points on each leaf. The roots and leaves are sometimes eaten and wine is made from the flowers.

DANDOLO, Enrico (c1108–1205), doge of Venice from 1192. He diverted the Fourth Crusade (see CRUSADES) to serve Venetian purposes. The crusaders reconquered Zara (1202), captured Constantinople (1204), and gave to Venice strategic Byzantine possessions in the E Mediterranean, including Cyprus.

DANDRUFF, scaling of the SKIN of the scalp, part of the chronic skin condition of seborrheic DERMATITIS; scalp involvement is usually diffuse and itching may occur. The condition is lifelong but usually little more than an inconvenience. Numerous remedies are advertised but few are effective.

DANELAW, Anglo–Saxon name for areas of England colonized by Danish Viking forces in the 9th century, during the reign of Alfred the Great. The W Saxon king Edgar (959–975) granted autonomy to the Danelaw in return for fealty, and a Danish customary law developed in the area.

DANIEL, Book of, Old Testament book, placed among the Prophets in the Christian BIBLE; in the Hebrew Bible it is placed in the Writings. Parts of it are in Aramaic. It is the story of Daniel, thought to have been a Judaean noble brought to Nebuchadnezzar's court during the BABYLONIAN CAPTIVITY, and of his exploits and his apocalyptic visions.

DANIELS, Josephus (1862–1948), US public official and newspaperman. Editor of the Raleigh, N.C., *News and Observer,* he was active in the campaigns of William Jennings Bryan and Woodrow Wilson, who made him secretary of the navy, 1913–21. He was ambassador to Mexico, 1933–42.

DANISH. See SCANDINAVIAN LANGUAGES.

D'ANNUNZIO, Gabriele (1863–1938), Italian writer and adventurer. His poetry first made him famous, its sensuous imagery reflecting his life-style. His novel *The Flame of Life* (1900) is an account of his long liaison with Eleonora DUSE. As a politician he helped bring Italy into WWI on the Allies' side, himself serving in the air force, and in 1919 he occupied the Dalmatian port of Fiume, ruling it as dictator until 1920.

DANTE (Dante Alighieri; 1265–1321), Italy's greatest poet, author of the *Divine Comedy.* Scion of an old Florentine family, he mastered the art of lyric poetry at an early age. He probably attended Bologna University during 1287. His first major work is *The New Life* (c1292) which describes his early life and great love for Beatrice—probably Beatrice Portinari, whom he had known since he was nine; she died in 1290, but remained his lifelong inspiration. He married Gemma Donati c1285. Politically, he was active in Florentine affairs, and was exiled from Florence in 1302. He finally settled in Ravenna in 1318 and died there. *The Divine Comedy* (probably written between 1308 and 1320) is an account of the poet's travels through Hell and Purgatory, and his final glimpse of Heaven. A poetic masterpiece in itself, it is also a diatribe against the corruption Dante saw in the world around him.

DANTON, Georges Jacques (1759–1794), one of the leaders of the FRENCH REVOLUTION. A lawyer, a powerful orator and, in the end, a moderate, Danton strove to reconcile the GIRONDINS and JACOBINS. He dominated the first Committee of Public Safety, but by 1793 began to lose power to the militant Robespierre. Believing the revolution won, he was unable to stop the Reign of Terror, was accused of treason and executed by the Jacobins.

DANUBE RIVER, major European river, 1,776mi long, second only to the Volga in length. From its official source near

Donaueschingen in West Germany, it flows through Austria, Czechoslovakia, Hungary, Yugoslavia, Romania, Bulgaria and along parts of the USSR border before emptying into the Black Sea. With over 300 tributaries, it drains almost one-tenth of Europe and provides a major transport system. It served as a major natural boundary for the Roman Empire and a useful highway for invaders from the east. The river becomes navigable at Ulm in Bavaria and flows through three capitals—Vienna, Budapest and Belgrade. Since 1856, international agreements have regulated its use, but seasonal obstructions and Europe's East–West political split have limited its traffic. In W Germany, the Main-Danube Canal links the Danube at Regensburg with the Main-Rhine river system at Bamberg, thus greatly stimulating development of a river formerly isolated from W Europe and exiting through Soviet-controlled E Europe.

DANZIG. See GDÁNSK.

DARDANELLES, narrow strait 44mi in length in NW Turkey, separating Asia Minor from Europe, formerly called the Hellespont; it is bordered on the W by the GALLIPOLI PENINSULA. It links the Sea of Marmora with the Aegean and is part of the waterway from the Black Sea to the Mediterranean. Together with the BOSPORUS, the Dardanelles are of great strategic importance for their control of access by Soviet vessels to the Mediterranean and the Suez Canal sea lanes.

DARÍO, Rubén, pen name of Felix Rubén García Sarmiento (1867–1916), Nicaraguan poet. He introduced the movement which revolutionized Spanish and Spanish-American literature, *modernismo*. His best-known works are *Profane Hymns* (1896) and *Songs of Life and Hope* (1905).

DARIUS, three Persian kings of the Achaemenid dynasty. **Darius I, the Great,** reigned from 522–486 BC. An able ruler, he reorganized his empire into 20 satrapies under officials responsible to him who were supervised by ministers and secret police; he introduced efficient transport, a postal system, taxation, coinage and legal systems. He attacked the SCYTHIANS, overran Thrace and Macedonia, then attempted to subdue Greece but was finally defeated at MARATHON in 490. **Darius II** reigned from 423 BC until his death in 404 BC; his reign was corrupt, but he achieved much influence in Greece in an alliance with Sparta against Athens. **Darius III** (reigned 336-330 BC) was the last ruler of an independent Persia. Defeated by ALEXANDER THE GREAT, he was murdered by one of his own satraps.

DARK AGES, general term for the centuries of decline in Europe, c500–1000 AD, after the fall of the Roman Empire. Documentation for the period is sparse because, in the general instability, classical culture was stifled, though remnants of Greek and Roman tradition were preserved by Christian monks in Ireland, Italy, France and Britain. Charlemagne's rule (800–814) briefly reunited Europe but the true flowering of the MIDDLE AGES came after 1000.

DARLAN, Jean François (1881–1942), French admiral who held various cabinet posts in the Vichy government, becoming vice premier, foreign minister and heir-designate to Pétain in Feb 1941. In Nov. 1942 he surrendered French North Africa to the Allies, but was soon afterward assassinated.

DARNLEY, Henry Stuart, Lord (1545–1567), second husband of MARY QUEEN OF SCOTS (1565); their son became James VI of Scotland and JAMES I of England. His intrigues for the Scottish crown led to his death by violence.

DARROW, Clarence Seward (1857–1938), US lawyer, a renowned defense attorney. After 20 years defending the interests of organized labor, he changed his practice to criminal cases. None of his clients on murder charges received the death penalty. His eloquence saved Leopold and Loeb in 1924 from the electric chair; and he won acclaim in 1925 for upholding the right of academic enquiry in his defense of John Scopes for teaching Darwin's theory of evolution.

DART, Raymond Arthur (1893–1988), Australian-born South African physical anthropologist, at the U of Witwatersrand from 1923. His discovery of fossil remains of *Australopithecus africanus*, an early human ancestor, at Taung, South Africa, lent support to the view that mankind originated in Africa.

DARTMOUTH COLLEGE CASE, US Supreme Court decision of 1819 which denied the N.H. legislature the right to revise Dartmouth's charter, originally granted during the reign of King George III. Such action was voided as impairing the the obligation of contracts, forbidden by the US Constitution. The decision encouraged the growth of corporations, chartered by the states, since it gave them a measure of freedom from state interference.

DARWIN, Charles Robert (1809–1882), English naturalist, who first formulated the theory of EVOLUTION by NATURAL SELECTION. Between 1831 and 1836 the young Darwin sailed round the world as the naturalist on board HMS *Beagle*. In the course of this he made many geological observations favorable to LYELL's uniformitarian geology, devised a theory to account for the structure of coral islands and was impressed by the facts of the geographical distribution of plants and animals. He became convinced that species were not fixed categories as was commonly supposed but were capable of variation, though it was not until he read MALTHUS' *Essay on the Principle of Population* that he discovered a mechanism whereby ecologically favored varieties might form the basis for new distinct species. Darwin published nothing for 20 years until, on learning of A. R. WALLACE's independent discovery of the same theory, he prepared a short paper for the Linnean Society to accompany Wallace's. The next year (1859) the theory was set before a wider public in his *Origin of Species*. The rest of his life was spent in further research in defense of his theory, though he always avoided entering the popular controversies surrounding his work and left it to others to debate the supposed consequences of "Darwinism."

DATA PROCESSING. See COMPUTER.

DATE LINE, International, an imaginary line on the earth's surface, with local deviations, along longitude 180° from Greenwich. As the earth rotates, each day first begins and ends on the line. A traveler going east over the line sets his calendar back one day, and one going west adds one day.

DAUDET, Alphonse (1840–1897), French writer noted for his stories of his native Provence. He wrote with humor and compassion about the poor, and is best remembered for *Lettres de Mon Moulin* (1866) and *Tartarin de Tarascon* (1872).

DAUGHERTY, Harry Micajah (1860–1941), US lawyer and politician who managed the career of Warren G. HARDING from lieutenant governor of Ohio to US senator and finally president. Harding appointed him attorney general. Lax in his administration of the Justice Department and suspected of corruption, Daugherty was dismissed by President Calvin Coolidge.

DAUMIER, Honoré (1808–1879), French caricaturist, painter and sculptor. In some 4,000 technically masterful lithographs, he satirized the bourgeoisie and contemporary politicians. In 1832, his cartoon of King Louis-Philippe earned him six months in jail. He was one of the first to paint scenes from modern life, and his acidly ironic vision has rarely been approached by others.

DAUPHIN, title given to the heir to the French throne after Philip VI purchased Dauphiné from the Count of Viennois in 1349. The title was renounced in 1830 following the abdication of Charles X.

DAUPHINÉ, historical region of SE France, now covering the departments of Drôme, Isére and Hautes Alpes. The Rhone valley is the main wine center; Grenoble the capital, manufacturing and cultural center.

D'AVENANT, Sir William (1606–1668), English poet, playwright, and theatrical producer, appointed poet laureate in 1638. He wrote the text of the first English opera, *The Seige of Rhodes* (1656–69).

DAVID (d. c961 BC), king of Israel. A Judaean from Bethlehem, he became arms bearer to King Saul of Israel, and an intimate friend to Saul's son Jonathan. David killed the Philistine giant Goliath, and his subsequent popularity aroused Saul's envy and wrath. After years as an outlaw, he was chosen king of Judah on Saul's death, soon extending his authority over the northern tribes. David then seized Jerusalem, making it the religious and political capital of Israel and of a large empire. His highly prosperous reign lasted 40 years. David was the prototype of the MESSIAH through whom God mediated his blessing to Israel, and an ancestor of Jesus Christ. He is the reputed author of many of the psalms.

DAVID, Gerard (c1460–1523), last great master of the 15th-century Bruges school of painting. He is noted for his emotional power and depth, and accomplished technique, as in the altarpieces *Rest on Flight into Egypt* and *Madonna with Angels and Saints.*

DAVID, Jacques Louis (1748–1825), French painter and leader of the French neoclassical movement. His style, which combines formal perfection with romantic feeling and didactic purpose, is exemplified in his *Oath of the Horatii* and *Death of Marat*. He appealed to the French Revolutionary spirit and was appointed painter to Napoleon. Exiled by Louis XVIII, he died in Brussels.

DAVIDSON, Jo (1883–1952), US sculptor, born N.Y. city, but lived in Paris. Among famous sitters for his portrait busts were Gertrude STEIN, Will ROGERS and Franklin ROOSEVELT.

DAVIES, Arthur Bowen (1862–1928), US painter in the romantic-idealist tradition. Davies was a leader of the American modern movement and a member of the ASHCAN SCHOOL as well as chief organizer of the 1913 ARMORY SHOW. Noted for the lyrical and abstract *Unicorns* and *Dreams*

(1908).

DAVIES, Joseph Edward (1876–1958), US diplomat. He was US ambassador to the Soviet Union (1937–38) and Belgium (1938–40). During WWII he chaired the President's War Relief Control Board (1942–46). His *Mission to Moscow* (1941) reported favorably on the USSR.

DA VINCI, Leonardo. See LEONARDO DA VINCI.

DAVIS, Alexander Jackson (1803–1892), US architect, practitioner of the Greek revival style in the design of several state capitols and other public buildings.

DAVIS, Benjamin Oliver (1877–1970), the first black general in the US Army. After service as a lieutenant of volunteers in the Spanish-American War, Davis enlisted in the regular army as a private and rose through the ranks to brigadier general (1940). During WWII he served in the European theater as an adviser on race relations in the army. His son, **Benjamin Oliver Davis, Jr.** (1912-   ), became the first black general in the US Air Force.

DAVIS, Bette (1908–1989), US movie actress. She won Academy Awards for *Dangerous* (1935) and *Jezebel* (1938), and in the 1960s won new fame in psychological thrillers. Her other films include *Dark Victory* (1939), *The Little Foxes* (1941) and *All About Eve* (1950).

DAVIS, Elmer (1890–1958), US writer and broadcaster. A political commentator for the *New York Times* (1914–24), he achieved fame as a CBS radio news analyst (1939–42) during the early years of WWII. He headed the Office of War Information (1942–45) before resuming his radio career with ABC. His bestselling *But We Were Born Free* (1954) was an attack on political witch-hunters.

DAVIS, Henry Winter (1817–1865), US Congressman and leader of the pre-Civil War Know Nothing party. A staunch Unionist who served in the House of Representatives from 1855–61 and 1863–65, he criticized Lincoln's lenient Reconstruction program for the South. With Benjamin Wade, he succeeded in getting his own Reconstruction bill through Congress, but Lincoln refused to sign it.

DAVIS, Jefferson (1808–1889), president of the Confederate States of America during the Civil War, born in Fairview, Ky. He represented Miss. in the US Senate (1847–51 and 1857–61) and was a leading defender of slavery and states' rights. He was a nationalist secretary of war, 1853–57, but when the Southern states began their secession Davis resigned from the Senate in Jan. 1861, when Miss. withdrew from the Union. His peace delegation to Lincoln was rebuffed and he ordered the attack on Fort Sumter, S.C., which opened the war. On Feb. 18, 1861, he became provisional president of the Confederacy and was elected for a six-year term. Although his leadership was criticized, he made the best of inferior numbers and poor industrial resources. In 1865 Davis was captured, and after two years in prison was released on bail.

DAVIS, John (d.1605), English navigator and one of the greatest early Arctic explorers. He discovered the Davis Strait between Greenland and Baffin Island as well as the Falkland Islands. He was also the author of valuable aids to navigation.

DAVIS, John William (1873–1955), US lawyer and diplomat. A W.Va. Democrat, he served (1911–13) in the US House of Representatives and (1913–18) as US solicitor general. In 1918 he was appointed ambassador to Great Britain, and he advised President Woodrow Wilson at the Paris Peace Conference. In 1924, after receiving the Democratic party's presidential nomination on the 103rd ballot, he was defeated by Calvin Coolidge. As a lawyer, he argued many important cases before the US Supreme Court.

DAVIS, Miles (1926–   ), US trumpeter, a pioneer of cool jazz in the 1940s. He led many small groups, blending contemporary musical trends with jazz.

DAVIS, Richard Harding (1864–1916), US journalist, famous as a traveler and war correspondent. He also wrote novels and plays.

DAVIS, Stuart (1894–1964), US abstract painter, illustrator and lithographer, studied in New York. A forerunner of the pop art movement, his style is characterized by brilliant colors, the use of printed words and interlocking shapes.

DAVIS CUP, international men's tennis trophy. In 1900 Dwight F. Davis, a US statesman, donated a silver bowl to promote international tennis competition between the United States and Europe. Since 1902 all countries in the world, divided into zones, have been allowed to compete for the annual award, but the major contenders have been the US, Australia, England, Sweden, Germany and France. After eliminating rounds between the countries from the losing zone of the previous year's tournament, the challenging country's teams play against the cup's defenders in a meet of four singles and one doubles match.

DAVITT, Michael (1846–1906), Irish nationalist, who in 1879 organized the Irish Land League, which sought to better the lot of the Irish tenant farmers. He was elected to parliament in 1892 and 1895 but resigned in 1899 over the South African War.

DAVY, Sir Humphry (1778–1829), English chemist who pioneered the study of ELECTROCHEMISTRY. Electrolytic methods yielded him the elements SODIUM, POTASSIUM, magnesium, CALCIUM, STRONTIUM and BARIUM (1807–08). He also recognized the elemental nature of and named CHLORINE (1810). His early work on nitrous oxide (see NITROGEN) was done at Bristol under T. Beddoes, but most of the rest of his career centered on the Royal Institution where he was assisted by his protégé, M. FARADAY, from 1813. A major practical achievement was the invention of a miner's safety lamp, known as the **Davy Lamp**, in 1815–16. From his Bristol days, Davy was a friend of S. T. Coleridge.

DAWES, Charles Gates (1865–1951), US statesman who shared the 1925 Nobel Peace Prize for his DAWES PLAN. Vice-president under Calvin Coolidge 1925–29, he was ambassador to Great Britain 1929–1932, when he became chairman of the Reconstruction Finance Corporation. He resigned the same year and returned to banking.

DAWES ACT (1887), or **General Allotment Act**, law sponsored by US senator Henry Laurens Dawes (1816–1903) intended to end the status of Indian tribes as "domestic nations" and to absorb the Indians into American life by allotting tribal lands as individual holdings. Disastrous for the Indians, the policy was reversed by the Indian Reorganization Act (1934), initiated by Indian affairs commissioner John COLLIER.

DAWES PLAN, plan developed by Charles Gates DAWES in 1924, to enable Germany to pay off WWI reparations by means of an international loan and mortgages on German industry and railways.

DAY, Dorothy (1897–1980), US social activist. A reporter for left-wing papers, she was active in the Socialist and Communist parties before joining the Roman Catholic Church (1927). Dorothy Day publicized the Catholic Church's social programs in the *Catholic Worker*, opened a house in New York for the hungry and homeless, and supported numerous liberal causes.

DAY or **DAYE, Stephen** (c1594–1668), American printer who set up in Cambridge, Mass., the first printing press in the American colonies. Forerunner of Harvard University Press, it printed the *Freeman's Oath* (1639) and the BAY PSALM BOOK (1640).

DAY, William Rufus (1849–1923), US statesman. Secretary of state (1898) during the Spanish-American War, he ensured the neutrality of France and Germany. As chairman of the US peace commission, he insisted that the US purchase the Philippines rather than claim them by right of conquest. He was (1903–22) an associate justice of the US Supreme Court.

DAY, term referring either to a full period of 24 hours (the civil day) or to the (usually shorter and varying) period between sunrise and sunset when a given point on the earth's surface is bathed in light rather than darkness (the natural day). Astronomers distinguish the sidereal day from the solar day and the lunar day depending on whether the reference location on the earth's surface is taken to return to the same position relative to the stars, to the sun or to the moon respectively. The civil day is the mean solar day, some 168 seconds longer than the sidereal day. In most modern states the day is deemed to run from midnight to midnight, though in Jewish tradition the day is taken to begin at sunset.

DAYAN, Moshe (1915–1981), Israeli military and political leader. Active in Israel's War of Independence (1948), he commanded the Israeli army in the 1956 Sinai Campaign. He was minister of defense during the Six-Day War of 1967 and from 1969 to 1974, when he resigned over the Yom Kippur War. He was foreign minister 1977–79.

DAY CARE, care of children while parents work. The need has grown in recent decades with the increasing entry of mothers into the LABOR FORCE. In 1986, 68.4% of married women with children aged 6-17, and 53.8% of those with children under 6, were in the labor force, compared to 39.0% and 18.6%, respectively, in 1960. Many mothers who want to work cannot because they cannot find or afford day care. The problem is particularly acute for poor and welfare mothers who can neither work nor receive job training because of their child-care responsibilities. The economic pressures that often compel mothers to work tend to blunt the consideration that, ideally, children might be better off with their mothers than in day-care facilities.

Currently, day care is provided by day-care facilities, licensed and unlicensed, of widely varying sponsorship and quality, and by relatives, housekeepers, and neighbors. Some employers provide day-care facilities for their employees. School-age children left without after-school supervision are called latch-key children. In 1971 President Richard Nixon vetoed a bill to establish a national system of publicly funded day care. In the late 1980s, similar bills were again before Congress.

DAY LEWIS, C. See LEWIS, CECIL DAY.

DAYLIGHT SAVING TIME, system that adjusts the clock to make maximum use of seasonal daylight; it was first adopted as a WWI fuel conservation measure.

D-DAY, in WWII, June 6, 1944, the day fixed for the Allied landing in Normandy beginning the invasion of Europe, under the command of General EISENHOWER. Over 5,000 ships were used, from which 90,000 British, American and Canadian troops landed; around 20,000 more were delivered by parachute and glider. After some initial difficulties, the forces had linked up in a solid front by June 11. The invasion, code-named *Overlord*, was one of the most complex feats of organization and supply in history.

DDT, dichlorodiphenyltrichloroethane, a synthetic contact INSECTICIDE which kills a wide variety of insects, including mosquitoes, lice and flies, by interfering with their nervous systems. Its use, in quantities as great as 100,000 tons yearly, has almost eliminated many insect-borne diseases, including MALARIA, TYPHUS, YELLOW FEVER and PLAGUE. Being chemically stable and physically inert, it persists in the environment for many years. Its concentration in the course of natural food chains (see ECOLOGY) has led to the buildup of dangerous accumulations in some fish and birds. This prompted the US to restrict the use of DDT in 1972. In any case the development of insect strains resistant to DDT was already reducing its effectiveness as an insecticide. Although DDT was first made in 1874, its insecticidal properties were only discovered in 1939 (by P. H. Müller).

DEACON, lowest rank in the threefold MINISTRY in episcopally-organized Christian churches, an elected lay official in some Protestant churches. Traditionally deacons have administered alms. Since the Second Vatican Council, a permanent office of deacon in the Roman Catholic Church has become open both to celibate and married men, where formerly it was a transitional rank as a step towards priesthood. In some Lutheran churches an assistant minister is called a deacon although fully ordained.

DEAD SEA, salt lake on the Israel–Jordan border. It extends around 50mi S from the mouth of the Jordan R (its main affluent) and is up to 11mi wide. Much of it is more than 1000ft deep, and with a surface 1,302ft below sea level it is the lowest point on earth. Its biblical name of Salt Sea derives from its extremely high salt content (over

20%), resulting from the rapid evaporation in the area's hot climate. Some minerals are extracted from it commercially.

DEAD SEA SCROLLS, manuscripts on papyrus and leather (and even one on copper) discovered in five sites in what is now Israel and Israeli-occupied territory. The first discovery was made by shepherds at Khirbat Qumran on the NW shore of the Dead Sea. These scrolls were possibly part of the library of a Jewish sect, the Essenes, that flourished from c200 BC to 68 AD. The area's 11 caves contained hundreds of manuscripts, including large portions of the Hebrew Old Testament. This has proved that the modern Hebrew Bible has hardly changed in 2,000 years. Another site at Wadi al-Murabba'ah, a few miles away, contained both religious and secular documents dating from the anti-Roman rebellion led by Bar Cochba in 132–135 AD. They were probably left by fugitives from his army, as were those at a third site near Ein Gedi.

A cave near Jericho and an excavation at Masada produced further documents that, together with the other finds, clarify much of the complex history of the area and throw new light on the beginnings of Christianity. The manuscripts are not well preserved, and their transcription and interpretation is made more difficult by the necessity of carefully unrolling the ancient scrolls, and of salvaging and putting together pieces often smaller than postage stamps.

DEADWOOD, city in the Black Hills of South Dakota; the seat of Lawrence County. A gold rush in 1876 brought a huge influx of prospectors to the area, many of whom settled in Deadwood Gulch, the site of present-day Deadwood. Colorful figures from the town's early days include Wild Bill HICKOK, CALAMITY JANE and Deadwood Dick. Deadwood has a flourishing tourist industry.

DEAF MUTE. See DUMBNESS.

DEAFNESS, or failure of hearing, may have many causes. Conductive deafness is due to disease of outer or middle EAR, while perceptive deafness is due to disease of inner ear or nerves of hearing. Common physical causes of **conductive deafness** are obstruction with wax or foreign bodies and injury to the tympanic membrane. Middle ear disease is an important cause: in *acute otitis*, common in children, the ears are painful, with deafness, FEVER and discharge; in *secretory otitis* or glue ear, also in children, deafness and discomfort result from poor Eustachian tube drainage; *chronic otitis*, in any age group, leads to a deaf discharging ear, with drum perforation. ANTIBIOTICS in adequate courses are crucial in acute otitis, while glue ear is relieved by tubes or "grommets" passed through the drum to drain the middle ear. In both, the ADENOIDS may need removal to relieve Eustachian obstruction. In chronic otitis, keeping the ears clean and dry is important, and antibiotics are used for secondary infection, while SURGERY, including reconstitution of the drum, may be needed to restore hearing. *Otosclerosis* is a common familial disease of middle age in which fusion or ankylosis of the small bones of the ear causes deafness. Early operation can prevent irreversible changes and improve hearing. **Perceptive deafness** may follow infections in PREGNANCY (e.g., GERMAN MEASLES) or be hereditary. Acute VIRUS infection and trauma to the inner ear (e.g., blast injuries or chronic occupational noise exposure) are important causes. Damage to the ear blood supply or the auditory nerves by drugs, TUMORS or MULTIPLE SCLEROSIS may lead to perceptive deafness, as may the later stages of MÉNIÈRE'S DISEASE. Deafness of old age, or *presbycusis*, is of gradual onset, mainly due to the loss of nerve cells. Early recognition of deafness in children is particularly important as it may otherwise impair learning and speech development. Hearing aids are valuable in most cases of conductive and some of perceptive deafness. Lipreading, in which the deaf person understands speech by the interpretation of lip movements, and sign language are useful in severe cases.

DEÁK, Ferenc (1803–1876), Hungarian statesman who negotiated the 1867 Compromise with the Austrian emperor, giving Hungary internal autonomy within the dual monarchy of AUSTRIA–HUNGARY. A lawyer, he entered the Diet in 1833. In the 1848 revolution he became minister of justice, but resigned in disagreement with the revolutionary KOSSUTH the same year. He returned to the Diet in 1861, becoming the country's acknowledged leader.

DEAKIN, Alfred (1856–1919), Australian Liberal politician, drafter (1897–98) of the constitution bill that created (1901) the Australian confederation. He served as prime minister 1903–04, 1905–08, 1909–10.

DEAN, Dizzy (Jay Hanna—erroneously Jerome Herman—Dean; 1911–1974), American baseball pitcher who played for the St. Louis Cardinals and Chicago Cubs 1932–41, winning 30 games in 1934, when the Cardinals won the World Series. He retired in 1941, and became a popular sports commentator.

DEANE, Silas (1737–1789), American diplomat, first envoy to Europe. Sent to France in 1776, he was successful in recruiting officers and obtaining arms. He was recalled on profiteering charges; these were never proved. Unpopular in America for urging reconciliation with England (1781), he went into exile in England.

DEARBORN, Henry (1751–1829), US soldier and politician. A captain of militia during the Revolution, he was secretary of war under President Thomas Jefferson (1801–09). During the War of 1812, as a general, he commanded the northern frontier, but incurred such heavy losses that he was relieved of his command in 1813. He also served as US representative (1793–97) and minister to Portugal (1822–24). Chicago's Fort Dearborn was named for him.

DEATH, the complete and irreversible cessation of LIFE in an organism or part of an organism. Death is conventionally accepted as the time when the HEART ceases to beat, there is no breathing and when the BRAIN shows no evidence of function. Ophthalmoscopic examination of the EYE shows that columns of BLOOD in small vessels are interrupted and static. Since it is now possible to resuscitate and maintain heart function and to take over breathing mechanically, it is not uncommon for the brain to have suffered irreversible death but for "life" to be maintained artificially. The concept of "brain death" has been introduced, in which reversible causes have been eliminated, when no spontaneous breathing, no movement and no specific REFLEXES are seen on two occasions. When this state is reached, artificial life support systems can be reasonably discontinued as brain death has already occurred. The ELECTROENCEPHALOGRAPH has been used to diagnose brain death but is now considered unreliable.

After death, ENZYMES are released which begin the process of autolysis or decomposition, which later involves BACTERIA. In the hours following death, changes occur in muscle which cause rigidity or rigor mortis. Following death, anatomical examination of the body (autopsy) may be performed. Burial, embalming or cremation are usual practices for disposal of the body in Western society.

Death of part of an organism, or necrosis, such as occurs following loss of blood supply, consists of loss of cell organization, autolysis and GANGRENE. The part may separate or be absorbed, but if it becomes infected, this is liable to spread to living tissue. Cells may also die as part of the normal turnover of a structure (e.g., SKIN or blood cells), after POISONING or infection (e.g., in the LIVER), from compression (e.g., by TUMOR), or as part of a degenerative disease. They then undergo characteristic involutionary changes.

DEATH PENALTY. See CAPITAL PUNISHMENT.

DEATH VALLEY, arid valley in Inyo Co., Cal. The highest recorded US temperature—134°F—was recorded here in 1913. Located near the Nevada border, it is 140mi long, and up to 15mi wide. The lowest point in the W Hemisphere, Badwater (282ft below sea level) is at the heart of the valley. Since rainfall is only 2in per year, it supports little vegetation. Large deposits of borax were discovered there in the late 19th century. In 1933 it was made part of the Death Valley National Monument.

DEBS, Eugene Victor (1855–1926), American labor organizer and socialist political leader. He was a national leader of the Brotherhood of Locomotive Firemen and in 1893 founded the American Railway Union. Debs was jailed in 1895 for defying a federal court injunction against strike action which interfered with the mails. Five times a socialist candidate for the presidency, he fought his last and most successful campaign in 1920 while still imprisoned under the WWI Espionage Act (1917) for his opposition to the war. He was released in 1921.

DEBUSSY, Claude (1862–1918), born Achille-Claude. French composer whose impact on the history of music was revolutionary. He involved music in the Impressionist movement (see IMPRESSIONISM) which was affecting painting and poetry at this time. His ideas on harmony and his innovations in orchestration and the use of the piano were highly influential in the development of 20th-century music. His works include songs, some outstanding piano music including *Clair de lune*, an opera, *Pelléas et Mélisande* (1902), and the orchestral pieces *Prélude à l'après-midi d'un faune* (1892–94) and *La Mer* (1905).

DECAMERON, The, collection of 100 stories by the 14th-century Italian writer, Giovanni BOCCACCIO, one of the outstanding works in Italian literature. Amusing and often bawdy, the tales provide a shrewd commentary on 14th-century Italian life.

DECATHLON, ten-event contest in modern Olympic games. It consists of the 100-meter dash; the 400-meter and 1,500-meter flat races; the 110-meter hurdle race; pole vaulting; discus throwing;

shot putting; javelin throwing; and the long and high jumps. Outstanding US Olympic decathlon champions have included Jim THORPE (1912), Bob Mathias (1948, 1952) and Bruce Jenner (1976).

DECATUR, Stephen (1779–1820), American naval hero. He was responsible for many victories in the BARBARY WARS, and later in the WAR OF 1812 until forced to surrender to the British in 1815. After the war he was sent to subdue Algiers, and then served as a US navy commissioner until his death in a duel. He is famous for his reply to a toast: "Our country, right or wrong."

DECCAN, name loosely applied to the entire peninsula of India, S of the Narmada R, more strictly the lava-covered plateau between the Narmada and Krishna rivers.

DECEMBER, 12th month of the year in the Gregorian calendar, taking its name from the 10th month in the Roman calendar. The winter solstice occurs about Dec. 21, and traditionally it is the month for celebrations, including CHRISTMAS.

DECEMBRIST REVOLT, unsuccessful uprising against the tsar of Russia (Dec. 1825). In the unrest following the French Revolution and the Napoleonic Wars, groups of officers and aristocrats formed secret revolutionary societies. On this occasion they attempted to take advantage of the confusion accompanying the accession of Nicholas I. They lacked effective organization and were quickly suppressed, but the uprising served as an inspiration to later Russian revolutionaries.

DECIBEL, a unit of measure used to express the intensity of sound. A sound that is just perceptible to the human ear exerts a pressure of 0.0002 dynes per sq cm on the membrane of the ear, and has an arbitrary value of 0 decibels (db). The scale increases logarithmically. A busy street may be rated 70 to 80 db and the sound near a jet engine may reach 130 db. A decibel is equal to one tenth of a *bel*, which was named for Alexander Graham Bell.

DECIDUOUS TREES, those that shed their leaves each year, usually in the fall. This is an adaptation to survive bad weather. Food material is reabsorbed from the leaves before they fall, and their loss greatly reduces the amount of water that evaporates from the tree. Trees that retain their leaves all the year round are called evergreens.

DECIMAL SYSTEM, a number system using the POWERS of ten; our everyday system of numeration. The digits used are 0, 1, 2, 3, 4, 5, 6, 7, 8, 9; the powers of 10 being written $10^0 = 1$, $10^1 = 10$, $10^2 = 100$, $10^3 = 1000$, etc. To each of these powers is assigned a place value in a particular number; thus (4×10^3) $+ (0 \times 10^2)$ $+ (9 \times 10^1)$ $+ (2 \times 10^0)$ is written 4092. Similarly, fractions may be expressed by setting their denominators equal to powers of 10—

$$\frac{3}{4} = \frac{75}{100} = \frac{7}{10} + \frac{5}{100} \quad \frac{(7 \times 10^{-1})+}{(5 \times 10^{-2})},$$

which is written as 0.75. Not all numbers can be expressed in terms of the decimal system: one example is the fraction ⅓ which is written 0.333 3..., the row of dots indicating that the 3 is to be repeated an infinite number of times. Fractions like 0.333 3... are termed **repeating decimals**. Approximation is often useful when dealing with decimal fractions.

DECLARATION OF INDEPENDENCE, manifesto in which the representatives of the 13 American colonies asserted their independence and explained the reasons for their break with Britain. It was adopted on July 4, 1776, in what is now known as Independence Hall, in Philadelphia. The date has since been celebrated annually as Independence Day.

American discontent with British attempts at taxation began in the 1760s, but in these disputes colonists demanded only their "rights" as Englishmen. Even after the military confrontations at Lexington and Concord (1775), the Second Continental Congress convened at Philadelphia in May disavowed any desire for independence. However, after continued British provocations in 1775, opinion began to shift. Thomas Paine's pamphlet *Common Sense* (1776), which attacked the monarchy and called for independence, was extremely influential. During 1776 definite moves towards independence were taken.

On June 7 Richard Henry Lee of Virginia resolved before the Congress that "These United Colonies are, and of right ought to be, free and independent States." A committee consisting of Thomas Jefferson, Benjamin Franklin, John Adams, Robert Livingston and Roger Sherman was selected to draft a formal declaration of independence. The draft, almost wholly Jefferson's work, passed on July 2, with 12 colonies voting in favor and New York temporarily abstaining. The ensuing debate made the most significant changes in omitting the clauses condemning the British people as well as their government, and, in deference to the Southern delegates, an article denouncing the slave trade.

In Europe, including Britain, the Declaration was greeted as inaugurating a new age of freedom and self-government.

As a manifesto for revolution it yielded to the French DECLARATION OF THE RIGHTS OF MAN AND THE CITIZEN, although its importance increased in the US. After the federal union was organized in 1789 it came to be considered as a statement of basic political principles, not just of independence.

The Declaration is on display for the public in the National Archives Building in Washington, D.C.

DECLARATION OF THE RIGHTS OF MAN AND THE CITIZEN, key philosophical document of the French Revolution, adopted by the National Assembly on Aug. 26, 1789. It reflects the French Enlightenment's rejection of the rule of absolute monarchy in favor of natural rights. These included fair taxation, self-determination in government and personal liberty under the rule of law. It was made the preamble to the 1791 Constitution.

DECONSTRUCTION, philosophy of literary criticism that maintains that all texts are inherently ambiguous and subject to conflicting interpretations, no matter what their authors may intend. Corollaries of this view are that language cannot be used to communicate objectively and that all claims to absolute knowledge are false. Deconstruction is associated with the French philosopher Jacques DERRIDA.

DECORATION DAY. See MEMORIAL DAY.

DECORATIONS AND MEDALS, awards for exceptional bravery in civil or military service. The highest US civil decoration is the Presidential Medal of Freedom; the Medal for Merit is also for outstanding services. The highest US military award, "for conspicuous gallantry at the risk of life" is the Congressional Medal of Honor. Soldiers wounded in action receive the Purple Heart. Important foreign decorations include the Victoria Cross and the George Cross (Britain and the Commonwealth), the Croix de Guerre and Legion of Honor (France), the Order of Merit for civilians (the German Federal Republic), the Order of Lenin (USSR), the Order of the Chrysanthemum (Japan) and the Order of the People's Liberation Army (China).

DEER, cloven-hoofed mammals of the family Cervidae, found in Europe, Asia and the Americas. The most remarkable characteristic of the deer family, which contains about 40 species, is the antlers of the males. Only the musk deer and the Chinese water deer lack antlers, while both sexes of the CARIBOU and the REINDEER are antlered. The smallest deer is the Chilean pudu, 13in at the shoulder, and the largest the North American MOOSE, up to 7ft, and over 1000lb in weight. Though many species are abundant, some, such as the axis deer of India and Ceylon, are fast becoming rare and the Chinese Pere David's deer survives only in zoos.

DEERE, John (1804–1886), US inventor who developed and marketed the first steel plows.

DEFENSE, US Department of, executive department responsible for national security. Defense is the largest of the federal departments and receives the major part of the federal budget. It was created by the National Security Act of 1947 as a National Military Establishment, bringing together the three previously separate departments of the Army, Navy and Air Force. It was established in its present form in 1949 with the aim of achieving a more unified defense structure. It is headed by a civilian secretary of defense, appointed by the President, who is a member of his cabinet.

DEFOE, Daniel (1660–1731), English author, one of the founders of the English novel. Originally a merchant, he took to writing essays and pamphlets, including a satire against the Anglican High Church for which he was fined and pilloried. He was nearly 60 when he began writing the realistic novels for which he is best known, including *Robinson Crusoe* (1719), *Moll Flanders* (1722) and *A Journal of the Plague Year* (1722).

DEFOLIANTS, chemicals that cause plants to lose their leaves. They are used in agriculture to remove excess foliage and in war to deprive the enemy of the cover of vegetation (see AGENT ORANGE; VIETNAM WAR).

DE FOREST, Lee (1873–1961), US inventor of the triode (1906), an electron tube with three ELECTRODES (cathode, anode and grid) which could operate as a signal AMPLIFIER as well as a rectifier. The triode was crucial to the development of RADIO.

DEGAS, Edgar (Hilaire-Germain Edgar de Gas; 1834–1917), French painter and sculptor associated with IMPRESSIONISM. The paintings of INGRES were the source of Degas' linear style, but his asymmetrical compositions were influenced by Japanese prints. His favorite subjects were ballet dancers, women dressing and horse racing. From the 1880s, Degas worked regularly in pastel, and produced small bronze sculptures of dancers and horses. Among his best-known paintings are *The Rehearsal* (1872) and *The Millinery Shop* (c1885).

DE GASPERI, Alcide (1881–1954), Italian statesman, premier 1945–53. Active in political life from 1911, he was twice imprisoned for his opposition to the fascist regime. He clandestinely organized the Christian Democratic Party during WWII and as its leader became the first premier of the new Italian Republic in 1945.

DE GAULLE, Charles André Joseph Marie (1890–1970), French soldier and statesman, president 1945–46 and 1958–69, noted for his sense of personal destiny and unswerving devotion to France. De Gaulle was trained at Saint-Cyr military academy, and served under PÉTAIN as a captain in WWI. He then taught military history at Saint-Cyr, developing his advanced tactical theories. When France fell in 1940, he started the Free French movement in England. In 1944, his provisional government took over liberated France and did much to restore national morale. After resigning in 1946 he returned the following year with a new party, but met with little success and retired in 1953. On June 1, 1958, he was named premier at the height of the Algerian crisis; he assumed new and wider powers and passed many reforms which strengthened the economy. The Algerian crisis worsened, but De Gaulle was largely responsible for its resolution in 1962. He failed in his aim to make France the leader of a European political community, and during the 1960s pursued a policy of national independence. He resigned in 1969 on the defeat of a referendum designed to give him further powers for constitutional reforms.

DE HAVILLAND, Sir Geoffrey (1882–1965), British aircraft designer and manufacturer. He designed fighter planes in WWI. His company built the famous Mosquito fighter-bomber of WWII as well as the world's first jet airliner (1948).

DEINSTITUTIONALIZATION, the movement of mental patients out of state hospitals and into local communities. Until the 1950s, huge state mental hospitals, lacking the resources for effective therapy, warehoused large numbers of patients at great cost and little benefit. The situation changed with the development of drugs that relieved some patients' most conspicuous symptoms; with the growing belief among psychiatrists that institutional life actually contributed to the patients' illness and that most would benefit from treatment in their communities or in short-term facilities; with the conviction of civil libertarians, influenced by the civil rights movement, that involuntary commitment of persons who were not dangerous to themselves or others was unconstitutional. In 1963, Congress passed the Community Mental Health Center Act, providing federal funds to encourage the development of 2,000 outpatient clinics throughout the country. The population of state mental hospitals fell from a peak of 558,000 in 1955 to 137,000 in 1980.

The hopes of all the proponents of deinstitutionalization have been disappointed. Fewer than half of the projected community mental health centers were ever established, and those did not reach the most seriously ill. Most of the chronically mentally ill now live in nursing homes or group residences rather than independently. Many live on the streets, constituting perhaps a third of the homeless population. Meanwhile, the state hospitals remain open, in part to care for the most dangerous patients and in part in response to the political pressures of the communities in which they are located.

DEISM, religious system developed in the 17th and 18th centuries, expounded by VOLTAIRE and Jean Jacques ROUSSEAU. Deists believed in a Creator God, but rejected PROVIDENCE, REVELATION and the supernatural, holding that religious truth is known by reason and the light of nature. (See also THEISM).

DEKKER, Thomas (c1570–c1632), English dramatist and pamphleteer. On many plays he collaborated with Philip MASSINGER, Thomas MIDDLETON, John FORD and John WEBSTER. His best-known work is the comedy *The Shoemaker's Holiday* (1600). He was a vigorous pamphleteer and witty observer of London life.

DE KOONING, Willem (1904–   ), Dutch-born US painter, a founder of ABSTRACT EXPRESSIONISM. Influenced by GORKY, MIRO and PICASSO, he painted abstract and figurative pictures with thickly applied pigment. One famous work is *Woman I* (1952).

DELACROIX, Ferdinand-Victor-Eugène (1798–1863), French painter whose literary and historical themes are typical of ROMANTICISM. Such early works as *The Massacre of Chios* (1824) were influenced by GÉRICAULT, but his mastery of rich color schemes and handling of paint were largely learned from RUBENS, as shown by *Death of Sardanapalus* (1827), *The Justice of Trajan* (1840) and the many official decorative schemes he undertook. His frescoes for Saint-Sulpice, Paris, influenced IMPRESSIONISM.

DE LA MADRID HURTADO, Miguel (1934–   ), president of Mexico (1982–88). His administration faced grave economic problems, including a huge foreign debt, despite Mexico's oil wealth. He was a leader in Latin American efforts to end the strife in neighboring Central American countries.

DE LA MARE, Walter John (1873–1956), English poet and novelist. His work, much of which was intended for children, is characterized by its power to evoke the atmosphere of dreams and the supernatural. His best-known works are the novel *Memoirs of a Midget* (1921) and the children's poetry collection *Peacock Pie* (1913).

DE LANCEY, James (1703–1760), political figure in colonial America. Of an influential New York family, he became chief justice of the New York Supreme Court in 1733. While a judge he also served as lieutenant-governor and acting governor of New York. He is remembered primarily as the presiding judge at the trial of John Peter ZENGER, and for his part in establishing Kings College (now Columbia U).

DELANY, Martin Robinson (1812–1885), US Negro leader. A newspaper publisher until 1849, he received a medical degree from Harvard in 1852, one of the first blacks to do so. He wrote and worked for abolitionist causes such as the UNDERGROUND RAILROAD and Negro emigration. In the Civil War he became an army surgeon, the first Negro to reach the rank of major. He later joined the FREEDMEN'S BUREAU and became a trial judge in Charleston, S.C.

DELAUNAY, Robert (1885–1941), French abstract painter who with his wife Sonia founded the Orphist movement in 1910. His pictures comprise forms of brilliantly contrasting color. His *Windows* (1912) developed the Cubist style.

DELAWARE, state, in E US, bounded by the Atlantic Ocean and the Delaware R to the E, Md. to the S and W, and Pa. to the N; it was the first state to ratify the US Constitution.

Land. Most of the state is part of the Atlantic coastal plain, long and narrow in shape. The greater part consists of lowland, but the Piedmont area in the NW has rolling hills. The main river is the Delaware, running down the E boundary of the state. It has many other rivers and lakes. The climate is temperate but humid with quite mild winters and hot summers.

People. The state has become mainly urban. Its population, swelled by interstate migration, is chiefly concentrated in the Wilmington metropolitan area. The state legislature, the General Assembly, consists of a Senate of 21 members, elected for four-year terms, and a House of Representatives with 41 members who serve

Name of state: Delaware
Capital: Dover
Statehood: Dec. 7, 1787 (1st state)
Familiar name: First State; Diamond State
Area: 2,057sq mi
Population: 633,000
Elevation: Highest—442ft, New Castle County. Lowest—sea level, Atlantic coast
Motto: "Liberty and independence"
State flower: Peach blossom
State bird: Blue hen chicken
State tree: American holly
State song: "Our Delaware"

for two years.

Economy. Until 1920 the economy was mostly rural, but now agriculture (led by broiler chickens, soybeans, vegetables, and dairy products) accounts for only a fraction of the state's production, while the chemical industry is the state's largest producer of goods. The manufacture of processed foods, transportation equipment, clothing and metal goods is also important. Corporation taxes are unusually low, attracting many companies whose main business is often not in Del.

History. The English explorer Samuel Argall sailed into the Delaware R in 1610 and named it for Baron De la Warr, then governor of Virginia. The area was occupied by the Dutch and the Swedes until seized by the English in 1664; it was ruled as part of Pennsylvania until acquiring its own assembly in 1704. After the Revolution Delaware prospered; flour-milling was then the leading industry. Gunpowder mills were built by DU PONT in 1802, becoming the basis of the state's chemical industry. Quaker influence around Wilmington meant that many slaves were freed by 1860. From WWI on, the industrialization and urbanization of the N part of the state proceeded steadily, led by the Wilmington-based Du Pont company. In the 1970s and 1980s the population became increasingly suburban. In presidential elections 1968–88, Delaware voted Republican in 1968–72 and 1980–88.

DELAWARE INDIANS, tribe of the Algonquian linguistic group who lived in the Delaware R basin area until driven out into Ohio in the 18th century by the incursions of colonists and the FRENCH AND INDIAN WARS. An agricultural tribe, they had a sophisticated culture and were respected by other tribes. Today their descendants are scattered through reservations in Okla. and Ontario, Canada.

DELAWARE RIVER, a major waterway, in the eastern US. Originating in the Catskill Mountains of New York, the river flows southeast, forming the Pennsylvania–New York border, and then southward through the Delaware Water Gap, forming the boundary between New Jersey and Pennsylvania, and empties into Delaware Bay. The river is about 410mi long. Draining an area of approximately 12,000 sq mi, it is an important source of hydroelectric power and serves as a navigable waterway for ships traveling as far up river as Trenton. It is connected to Chesapeake Bay on the west by the Chesapeake and Delaware Canal. The Delaware was first explored by Henry HUDSON in 1609.

DELBRÜCK, Max (1906–1981), German-born US biologist whose discovery of a method for detecting and measuring the rate of mutations in BACTERIA opened up the study of bacterial GENETICS.

DELCASSÉ, Théophile (1852–1923), French statesman. As foreign minister (1898–1905) he settled colonial differences with Great Britain, strengthened ties with Russia, and negotiated a secret nonaggression treaty with Italy, thereby determining the alignment of the European powers in WWI.

DELEDDA, Grazia (1875–1936), Italian novelist who received the 1926 Nobel Prize for Literature.

DE LEON, Daniel (1852–1914), US Marxist leader. An emigrant from Curaçao, he edited the Socialist Labor Party organ, *The People,* for some years. A cofounder of the INDUSTRIAL WORKERS OF THE WORLD in 1905, he was expelled from it in 1908, after which his influence declined.

DELFTWARE, earthenware covered with an opaque white glaze made from tin oxide. First produced in the Netherlands and particularly at Delft in the 16th century, it was designed to imitate Chinese porcelain. The style spread to England and remained popular until the 18th century, when porcelain was manufactured in the West.

DELHI, city in N India, its capital 1912–31. Adjacent to NEW DELHI, Delhi dates from the 17th century and has many historic buildings, such as the Red Fort, dating from that time. There are several light industries, and the city's craftwork in ivory, jewelry and pottery is famous. Most new building is now confined to New Delhi, and much of the old city, which has a much larger population, has become a slum. Pop 4,884,234.

DELIAN LEAGUE, confederacy of Greek states formed by Athens 478–477 BC to follow up the Hellenic League's victories against Persia. It was nominally governed by a council in which each member state had one vote, but was in fact entirely dominated by Athens. After considerable success against Persia, Athens began to turn the league into an empire, using its fleet to subjugate reluctant states such as Naxos. The so-called league endured until Athens was defeated by Sparta in the PELOPONNESIAN WAR. An attempt to revive it in 377 BC was crushed by Philip II of Macedon in 338 BC.

DELIBES, (Clément Philibert) Léo (1836–1891), French composer. Best known at first for his lighter works and operettas, some written in collaboration with OFFENBACH, he set a new high standard for ballet music with *Coppélia* (1870) and *Sylvia* (1876) and wrote the grand opera *Lakmé* (1883).

DELINQUENCY. See JUVENILE DELINQUENCY.

DELIRIUM, altered state of consciousness in which a person is restless, excitable, hallucinating and is only partly aware of his surroundings. It is seen in high FEVER, POISONING, drug withdrawal, disorders of METABOLISM and organ failure. SEDATIVES and reassurance are basic measures.

DELIRIUM TREMENS, specific delirium due to acute alcohol withdrawal in ALCOHOLISM. It occurs within days of abstinence and is often precipitated by injury, surgery or imprisonment. The sufferer becomes restless, disorientated, extremely anxious and tremulous; FEVER and profuse sweating are usual. Characteristically, hallucinations of insects or animals cause abject terror. Constant reassurance, SEDATIVES, well-lit and quiet surroundings are appropriate measures until the episode is over. Treatment of dehydration and reduction of high fever may be necessary, though fatalities do occur.

DELIUS, Frederick (1862–1934), English composer. An orange-grower in Fla. 1884–86, he studied in Leipzig, where he met and was influenced by Edward GRIEG. He is best known for orchestral pieces such as *Florida* (1886–87) and *Brigg Fair* (1907), and for tone poems such as *Summer Night on the River* (1911) and *Sea Drift* (1903). His best-known opera is *A Village*

Romeo and Juliet (1900–01). In old age he became blind and paralyzed, but continued to compose by dictation.

DELLA FRANCESCA, Piero. See PIERO DELLA FRANCESCA.

DELLA ROBBIA. See ROBBIA, DELLA.

DE LONG, George Washington (1844–1881), US Arctic explorer. In 1879 he sailed the *Jeannette* through the Bering Strait, hoping to be borne by currents to within reach of the North Pole. Instead, the ship was trapped in the ice for two years and then crushed. De Long and some of his men reached Siberia, but he died before they could be rescued. The expedition produced important information about Arctic geography and polar drift.

DELORME, Philibert (c1515–1570), French architect who introduced into Renaissance France a classical style he learned in Italy. He was court architect to Francis I, Henry II, and Catherine de Médicis.

DELPHI, classical Greek site located on the lower slopes of Mt PARNASSUS. Delphi was considered by the Greeks to be the center of the world, and was the seat of the most important oracle in ancient Greece. The oracular messages often had a strong influence on state policy. Excavations begun in 1892 revealed the magnificent temple of Apollo, now partially reconstructed, treasuries, a theater and a stadium.

DEL SARTO, Andrea. See ANDREA DEL SARTO.

DELVAUX, Paul (1897–), Belgian painter who often evoked a surrealistic atmosphere by creating disquieting images, such as those in which nude women and clothed men were posed together on otherwise deserted city streets. His paintings were influenced by DALI and MAGRITTE.

DEMAND. See SUPPLY AND DEMAND.

DE MILLE, Agnes George (1909–), US dancer and choreographer. She pioneered the combination of ballet and American folk music. Her ballets include *Rodeo* (1942) and *Fall River Legend* (1948). Her choreography for the Rodgers and Hammerstein musical *Oklahoma!* (1943) revolutionized dance in musical comedy by using ballet as an integral part of the plot acting.

DE MILLE, Cecil B(lount) (1881–1959), US motion picture producer and director, noted for his use of spectacle. He directed such epics as *The Ten Commandments* (1923 and 1956), *The Sign of the Cross* (1932), *Samson and Delilah* (1949) and *The Greatest Show on Earth* (1952).

DEMOCRACY, system of government

which recognizes the right of all members of society to influence political decisions, either directly or indirectly. Direct democracy, in which political decisions are made by the whole citizen body meeting together, is only possible where the population is small. (See GREECE, ANCIENT.) The direct democracy of some ancient Greek city-states has had little influence on the development of modern representative democracies, in which political decisions are made by elected representatives responsible to their electors.

Representative democracy began to evolve during the 18th and 19th centuries, in Britain, Europe and the US. Its central institution is the representative parliament, in which decisions are effected by majority vote. Institutions intrinsic to representative democracy are: regular elections with a free choice of candidates, universal adult suffrage, freedom to organize rival political parties and independence of the judiciary. Freedom of speech and the press, and the preservation of civil liberties and minority rights are also implicit in the idea of liberal representative democracy. The American and French revolutions, and the growth of the classes following the INDUSTRIAL REVOLUTION, were important influences in the formation of modern democracies. The concepts of natural rights and political equality expressed by such philosophers as John LOCKE in the 17th century, VOLTAIRE and Jean Jacques ROUSSEAU in the 18th century, and BENTHAM and J. S. MILL in the 19th century, are vital to the theory of representative democracy. (See also CONSTITUTION; PARLIAMENT; REPUBLIC; TOTALITARIANISM; UNITED STATES CONSTITUTION.)

DEMOCRATIC PARTY, one of the two major political parties in the US. Democrats trace their history back to the Democratic Republican Party (1792) of Thomas JEFFERSON, who favored popular control of the government. Following the inauguration of Andrew JACKSON in 1828, the party's base was broadened, with representation from the new West as well as the East. Jackson was a man of the people, and his administration marked the beginning of a period of dominance for the Democrats that only ended with the election in 1860 of Abraham Lincoln, the first successful candidate of the new REPUBLICAN PARTY. The slavery controversy and the Civil War split the party into northern and southern sections and, apart from the success of Woodrow WILSON just before WWI, it was not until the election of Franklin D. ROOSEVELT in 1932 that the

party reemerged with its old vigor. Roosevelt's NEW DEAL transformed the party's traditional policies, introducing broad governmental intervention in the economy and social welfare. This approach was continued on Roosevelt's death in 1945 by Harry S. TRUMAN, whose FAIR DEAL measures were, however, largely thwarted by a coalition of Republicans and Southern Democrats. In the 1950s, under Eisenhower's Republican administration, the party was led by Adlai E. STEVENSON. It controlled both houses of Congress from 1954, but the solidity of the South's adherence to the party began to fracture with the drive for black civil rights. The election of John F. KENNEDY in 1960 led to important legislation in this sphere, but also contributed further to the breakup of the traditional alliance between the urbanized North, with its many ethnic minorities, and the rural, disadvantaged South which had benefited from New Deal policies. On Kennedy's assassination in 1963, Vice-president Lyndon B. JOHNSON came to power. By 1968 the party was riven by dissent, particularly over policy in Vietnam. In 1968 Hubert H. HUMPHREY lost the presidential election to Richard M. NIXON, and in 1972 he was replaced as leader of the party by George S. MCGOVERN. The Democrats retained control of Congress. In 1976 Jimmy CARTER became party leader, but he lost his bid for a second term to Ronald Reagan in 1980. Democratic candidates Walter MONDALE in 1984 and Michael DUKAKIS in 1988 were also defeated, bringing the party's record to five defeats in the last six elections. Nevertheless, Democrats constituted majorities in both houses of the 101st Congress that convened in Jan. 1989.

DEMOCRATIC REPUBLICAN PARTY, one of the two political parties founded during the first decades of the United States. The party emerged in the 1790s in opposition to the dominant FEDERALIST PARTY. It was initially called the Republican Party, later the Democratic Republican Party, and since about 1830 the Democratic Party.

The Democratic Republican Party emerged following the resignation of Thomas Jefferson, secretary of state in President George Washington's cabinet, in 1793. Jefferson, a firm believer in an agrarian society, opposed the Federalist policies (framed primarily by Alexander HAMILTON) favoring the commerce and industry of New England and the Middle Atlantic area. The party came to power in 1800 with the election of Jefferson as president, and held the presidency through the administrations of Jefferson, James MADISON and James MONROE. With the emergence of Andrew JACKSON, new party alignments came into being.

DEMOCRITUS OF ABDERA (c460–370 BC), Greek materialist philosopher. One of the earliest exponents of ATOMISM, he maintained that all phenomena were explicable in terms of the nomic motion of atoms in the void.

DEMOGRAPHY, a branch of sociology, the study of the distribution, composition and internal structure of human populations. It draws on many disciplines (e.g., genetics, psychology, economics, geography), its tools being essentially those of STATISTICS: the sample and the CENSUS whose results are statistically analyzed. Its prime concerns are birth rate, emigration and immigration. (See also POPULATION.)

DEMOSTHENES (384–322 BC), famous Athenian orator and statesman. Demosthenes was the author of the *Philippics* (351–341 BC) and the *Olynthiacs* (349–348 BC)—speeches designed to awaken the Athenians to the danger of conquest by Philip II of Macedon. Demosthenes' most famous speech was *On the Crown* (330 BC), in which he vindicated himself against charges of financial corruption, cowardice in battle and indecisiveness in policy.

DEMPSEY, Jack (1895–1983), US boxer, one of the great heavyweights. He won the world championship from Jess WILLARD in 1919 at Toledo, Ohio, and held the title until defeated by Gene TUNNEY in 1926. Again defeated by Tunney in 1927, he retired from the ring in 1928.

DEMUTH, Charles (1883–1935), US watercolorist, painter and illustrator. Demuth, who was influenced by both CUBISM and EXPRESSIONISM and worked in a number of styles, is best known for his precise and delicate studies of flowers. He liked to paint the stark, simple shapes generated by the machine age and is also noted for his illustrations of works by Poe, Zola and Henry James.

DENDROCHRONOLOGY, the dating of past events by the study of tree-rings. A hollow tube is inserted into the tree trunk and a core from bark to center removed. The annual rings are counted, examined and compared with rings from dead trees so that the chronology may be extended further back in time. Through such studies important corrections have been made to the system of RADIOISOTOPE DATING.

DENGUE FEVER, or **breakbone fever,** a VIRUS infection carried by mosquitoes, with FEVER, headache, malaise, prostration and characteristically severe muscle and joint pains. There is also a variable skin rash through the roughly week-long illness. It is a disease of warm climates, and may occur in EPIDEMICS. Symptomatic treatment only is required.

DENG XIAOPING. See TENG HSIAO-PING.

DENIKIN, Anton Ivanovich (1872–1947), Russian leader of the anti-Bolshevik "White" forces in the civil war following the RUSSIAN REVOLUTION of 1917. In 1918 he succeeded KORNILOV as commander of the Whites in S Russia, but was convincingly defeated at Orel, 250mi from Moscow, in 1919. Denikin resigned his command the following year and fled to France. He emigrated to the US in 1945.

DENMARK, constitutional monarchy consisting of the Jutland peninsula, between the North and Baltic seas in NW Europe, and 482 islands off the peninsula, the two largest of which are Zealand (where Copenhagen is situated) and Fyn, and also the Faeroe Islands and GREENLAND. Denmark's 42mi S land boundary is with West Germany. Her E and N neighbors are respectively Sweden and Norway. Denmark is the smallest of the Scandinavian countries.

Official name: The Kingdom of Denmark
Capital: Copenhagen
Area: 16,638sq mi
Population: 5,127,000
Languages: Danish
Religions: Lutheran
Monetary unit(s): 1 krone=100 ore

Land. The W half of the country is fairly flat and consists of coastal dunes and lagoons and relatively infertile plains with sandy soil and peat bogs. The E has hilly moraines, cut by deep inlets and valleys, a pattern continued in the islands. The soils in this region are loamy and fertile. Climate is moist, with cool summers and, for the latitude, relatively warm winters.

The People. Denmark's population is almost entirely Scandinavian. A German minority of about 30,000 lives in SW Jutland, while some 40,000 Danes live in German

Schleswig. The majority of people live in the towns, with Greater Copenhagen the most densely populated district. Hinterlands are restricted and the Danes have become increasingly aware of the extent to which fertile farmland is being swallowed up by urban development. Denmark has a highly developed state education system and advanced social security schemes.

The Economy. Agriculture was the chief support of the economy until recently, and although some 60% of the country is given over to intensive farming, manufacturing now supplies more than 60% of Denmark's total exports. About 30% of the Gross National Product is provided by industry, 7% by agriculture and 16% by commerce. Industry employs about 30% of the work force, agriculture about 9%.

Among the major products are foodstuffs (particularly dairy products), furniture, glass, silverware, leather goods and clothing. There are important shipbuilding and agricultural engineering industries, while fishing and tourism also make an important contribution to the economy. Denmark depends heavily on imported raw materials, particularly iron, coal and oil. From 1958–72 it was a member of the EUROPEAN FREE TRADE ASSOCIATION; in 1973 it joined the COMMON MARKET.

History. Denmark has a rich early history as the center of VIKING expansion. She maintained her influence through to the 16th century, as a dominant partner in the Kalmar Union of Denmark, Norway and Sweden (1397–1523). From about 1600 Danish power waned under Swedish pressure. Norway remained under Danish rule until it was taken by Sweden in 1814. Prussia and Austria wrested Schleswig-Holstein from the Danes (1864), who eventually recovered N Schleswig after a plebiscite (1920). During WWII Denmark was occupied by Germany (1940–45). Denmark recovered rapidly after the war. A charter member of the United Nations in 1945, it broke a long tradition of neutrality by joining the NORTH ATLANTIC TREATY ORGANIZATION in 1949 and the EUROPEAN ECONOMIC COMMUNITY in 1972. In the late 1980s Denmark allowed its military forces to decline below NATO requirements.

DENSITY, the ratio of MASS to volume for a given material or object. Substances that are light for their size have a low density. Objects whose density is less than that of water will float in water, while a hot air BALLOON will rise when its average density becomes less than that of air. The term is also applied to properties other than mass: e.g., charge density refers to the ratio of electric charge (see ELECTRICITY) to volume.

DENTISTRY, the branch of MEDICINE concerned with the care of TEETH and related structures. Dental caries is responsible for most dental discomfort. Here the bacterial dissolution of dentine and enamel leads to cavities, especially in molars and premolars, and these allow accumulation of debris which encourages further bacterial growth; destruction of the tooth will gradually ensue unless treatment restores a protective surface. Each tooth contains sensitive nerve fibers extending into the dentine; exposure of these causes toothache, but the fibers then retract so that the pain often recedes despite continuing caries. The dentist removes all unhealthy tissue, often using ANESTHESIA, and fills the cavity with metal amalgam which hardens and protects the tooth; a severely damaged tooth may require extraction. Traumatic injury to teeth is repaired by a similar process. In some instances a tooth may be reconstructed on a "peg" of the original by using an artificial "crown." Maldeveloped or displaced teeth may need extraction or, during childhood, braces or plates to encourage realignment with growth. Wisdom teeth (rearmost molars), in particular, may need extraction if they erupt out of alignment or if they interfere with the normal bite. Infection of tooth pulp with ABSCESS formation destroys the tooth; pus can only be drained by extraction. False teeth or dentures, either fitted individually or as a group on a denture plate that sits on the gums, are made to replace lost teeth, to allow effective bite and for cosmetic purposes. Dentistry is also concerned with the prevention of carious decay and periodontal disease by encouragement of oral hygiene, including regular adequate brushing of teeth. Fluoride and protective films are important recent developments in preventive dentistry.

DEOXYRIBONUCLEIC ACID (DNA). See NUCLEIC ACIDS.

DEPRESSION, a common psychiatric condition marked by severe dejection, pathologically depressed mood, and characteristic somatic and sleep disturbance. Many authorities divide depressions into those due to external factors, and those where depression arises without obvious cause, including manic-depressive illness. SHOCK THERAPY, ANTIDEPRESSANTS and psychotherapy are the major methods of treatment.

DEPRESSION, in economics, a major decline in business activity, involving sharp reductions in industrial production, bankruptcies, massive unemployment and a general loss of business confidence. Although minor recessions occur regularly in industrial nations, the most serious and widespread depression was the GREAT DEPRESSION commencing in 1929 and lasting world wide through most of the 1930s.

DE QUINCEY, Thomas (1785–1859), English essayist and critic, author of *Confessions of an English Opium Eater* (1821), in which he recounted his experiences under opium. His output, affected by lifelong opium addiction, was erratic, but included some penetrating essays and powerful descriptions of drug-inspired dreams.

DERAIN, André (1880–1954), French painter, one of the original fauves (see FAUVISM). He was also attracted for a time to CUBISM. Later, rejecting nonrepresentational extremes, he returned to a more traditional style.

DERBY, Edward George Geoffrey Smith Stanley, 14th Earl of (1799–1869), British statesman and Conservative prime minister 1852, 1858 and 1866–68. His third and last administration saw the passing of the REFORM BILL of 1867, which increased the franchise.

DERBY, classic annual horse race at Epsom, England, instituted in 1780 by the 12th Earl of Derby. (See also KENTUCKY DERBY.)

DEREGULATION, reversal in the 1970s and 1980s of a century-long expansion of federal regulation of business. Federal regulation began in response to consumers' demands for protection. Thus the first regulatory agency, the INTERSTATE COMMERCE COMMISSION, was established in 1887 to prevent rate discrimination and other abuses by the railroads. The FEDERAL TRADE COMMISSION was established in 1914 to prevent unfair competition. The FOOD AND DRUG ADMINISTRATION was established in 1931, but some of its consumer-protection functions had been exercised by other agencies since 1906.

During the GREAT DEPRESSION, regulation was intended to protect not only consumers but businesses as well. Regulatory agencies established under the NEW DEAL included the NATIONAL RECOVERY ADMINISTRATION (1933), the SECURITIES AND EXCHANGE COMMISSION (1934), the FEDERAL COMMUNICATIONS COMMISSION (1934), and the NATIONAL LABOR RELATIONS BOARD (1935).

In succeeding decades, the flood of regulations issued by these and newer regulatory agencies — for example, the ENVIRONMENTAL PROTECTION AGENCY (1970), the OCCUPATIONAL SAFETY AND HEALTH ADMINISTRATION (1970), the CONSUMER PRODUCT SAFETY COMMISSION (1972) — were experienced by business people as excessively restrictive, burdensome, and costly. The process of deregulation began in the administration of President Jimmy CARTER, when Congress enacted laws deregulating the airlines, trucks, railroads, and banks. The REAGAN administration slowed the issuing of new regulations and relaxed enforcement of existing ones.

Deregulation has had mixed results. Increased competition has often produced lower prices for consumers, but sometimes at the cost of service and safety. It has also resulted in increased domination of some industries by a few large firms.

DERMATITIS, SKIN conditions in which INFLAMMATION occurs. These include ECZEMA, contact dermatitis (see ALLERGY) and seborrheic dermatitis (see DANDRUFF). Acute dermatitis leads to redness, swelling, blistering and crusting, while chronic forms usually show scaling or thickening of skin. Cool lotions and dressings, and ointments are used in acute cases, whereas tars are often useful in more chronic conditions. Avoidance of allergens in contact or allergic dermatitis is essential.

DERMATOLOGY, subspecialty of MEDICINE concerned with the diagnosis and treatment of SKIN diseases: a largely visual speciality, but aided by skin biopsy in certain instances. Judicious use of lotions, ointments, creams (including STEROID creams) and tars is the essence of treatment, while the recognition of ALLERGY, infection and skin manifestations of systemic disease are tasks for the dermatologist.

DERRIDA, Jacques (1930–   ), French philosopher and critic, the inventor of "deconstruction," the analysis of the language of literary and philosophical texts to identify their underlying metaphysical assumptions.

DERVISH, a Muslim mystic, member of one of the Sufi brotherhoods that emerged in about the 12th century. Members served a period of initiation under a teacher and each order had its own ritual for inducing a mystic state which stressed their dependence on the unseen world. The best known are the "whirling" and "howling" dervishes, who used forms of dancing and singing. (See also SUFISM.)

DESAI, Moraji (1896–   ), Indian political leader. A disciple of Mahatma Gandhi and a devout Hindu, he held cabinet posts under Nehru and was deputy prime minister for Indira Gandhi (1967–69) before breaking with her. She imprisoned him 18 months during a "state of emergency" but following her defeat he served as prime minister (1977–79).

DESALINATION, or **desalting,** the conversion of salt or brackish water into usable fresh water. DISTILLATION is the most common commercial method; heat from the sun or conventional fuels vaporizes brine, the vapor condensing into fresh water on cooling. Reverse OSMOSIS and electrodialysis (see DIALYSIS) both remove salt from water by the use of semipermeable membranes; these processes are more suitable for brackish water. Pure water crystals may also be separated from brine by freezing. The biggest problem holding back the wider adoption of desalination techniques is that of how to meet the high ENERGY costs of all such processes. Only where energy is relatively cheap and water particularly scarce is desalination economic, and even then complex energy conservation procedures must be built into the plant.

DESCARTES, René, or **Renatus Cartesius** (1596–1650), mathematician, physicist and the foremost of French philosophers, who founded a rationalist, a priorist school of philosophy known as **Cartesianism.** After being educated in his native France and spending time in military service (1618–19) and traveling, Descartes spent most of his creative life in Holland (1625–49) before entering the service of Queen Christiana of Sweden shortly before his death. In mathematics Descartes founded the study of ANALYTIC GEOMETRY, introducing the use of Cartesian coordinates. He found in the deductive logic of mathematical reasoning a paradigm for a new methodology of science, first publishing his conclusions in his *Discourse on Method* (1637). The occult qualities of late scholastic science were to be done away with; only ideas which were clear and distinct were to be employed. To discover what ideas could be used to form a certain basis for a unified a priori science, he introduced the method of universal doubt; he questioned everything. The first certitude he discovered was his famous *cogito ergo sum* (I think, therefore I am) and on the basis of this, the existence of other bodies, and of God, he worked out his philosophy. In science, Descartes, denying the possibility of a VACUUM, explained everything in terms of motion in a plenum of particles whose sole property was extension. This yielded his celebrated but ultimately unsuccessful vortex theory of the solar system and statements of the principle of INERTIA and the laws of ordinary REFRACTION. In psychology Descartes upheld a strict DUALISM: there were no causal relationships between physical and mental substances. In biology, his views were mechanistic; he regarded animals as but complex machines.

DESERTS, areas where life has extreme difficulty in surviving. Deserts cover about one third of the earth's land area. There are two types.

Cold Deserts. In cold deserts, water is unavailable during most of the year as it is trapped in the form of ice. Cold deserts include the Antarctic polar icecap, the barren wastes of Greenland, and much of the TUNDRA. (See also GLACIER.) Eskimos, Lapps and Samoyeds are among the ethnic groups inhabiting such areas in the N Hemisphere. Their animal neighbors include seals and the polar bear.

Hot Deserts. These typically lie between latitudes 20° and 30° N and S, though they exist also farther from the equator in the centers of continental landmasses. They can be described as areas where water precipitation from the ATMOSPHERE is greatly exceeded by surface EVAPORATION and plant TRANSPIRATION. The best known, and largest, is the Sahara. GROUNDWATER exists but is normally far below the surface; here and there it is accessible as SPRINGS or wells (see ARTESIAN WELL). In recent years, IRRIGATION has enabled reclamation of much desert land. Landscapes generally result from the surface's extreme vulnerability to EROSION. Features include arroyos, buttes, dunes, mesas and wadis. The influence of man may assist peripheral areas to become susceptible to erosion, and thus temporarily advance the desert's boundaries. (See also DUST BOWL.)

Plants may survive by being able to store water, like the CACTI; by having tiny leaves to reduce evaporation loss, like the paloverde; or by having extensive ROOT systems to capture maximum moisture, like the mesquite. Animals may be nomadic, or spend the daylight hours underground. Best adapted of all are the CAMELS.

DE SEVERSKY, Alexander Procofieff (1894–1974), Russian-born US aviator and aeronautical engineer whose Seversky (later Republic) Aircraft Corporation made important contributions to US military aviation. He wrote the influential *Victory Through Air Power* (1942).

DE SICA, Vittorio (1901–1974), Italian film director. His earlier films, such as *The Bicycle Thief* (1948), are outstanding for their compassionate treatment of social problems in the Neorealist style. The later films are not thought to be of the same standard, though many, like the *Garden of the Finzi Continis* (1971), have won international acclaim.

DE SMET, Pierre Jean (1801–1870), Belgian-born Jesuit missionary to the North American Indians. His work among several tribes won their friendship, and he often acted as a peacemaker for the government, as when he started negotiations with SITTING BULL and the SIOUX INDIANS.

DESMOULINS, Camille (1760–1794), journalist and leader in the FRENCH REVOLUTION. His oratory helped incite the mob to storm the BASTILLE in 1789, and his writings helped to radicalize public opinion. He and DANTON led the moderate faction in 1793–94, and were eventually arrested by Robespierre and guillotined.

DE SOTO, Hernando (1500–1542), Spanish explorer, discoverer of the Mississippi R. He served as second in command in PIZARRO's conquests in Peru (1531–35), and supported the Inca emperor ATAHUALPA. He returned to Spain with a fortune and set out again to explore the Florida region. He landed in 1539 at Charlotte Harbor and spent two years exploring what is now the SE US. He reached the Mississippi R in May 1541. Turning back in 1542, he died and his body was sunk in the Mississippi.

DESSALINES, Jean-Jacques (1758–1806), first black emperor of Haiti. Brought to Haiti as a slave, he took part in the rebellion against the French in the 1790s. After the final expulsion of the French in 1803 he became governor-general. In 1804 he proclaimed an independent country and took the title of Emperor Jacques I. His rule, characterized by extreme hostility to whites, ended when he was killed in a mulatto revolt.

DE STIJL, modern art movement in the Netherlands taking its name from the magazine *De Stijl* (*The Style*). Founded in 1917 by a group of artists including MONDRIAN and Van DOESBURG, it stressed purity of line and the use of primary colors. Its theories were also applied to interior decoration, furniture and architecture, of which the Schröder House in Utrecht (1924) is a good example.

DESTROYER, small, fast naval vessel which evolved in the 1890s out of earlier torpedo boats. In the two world wars destroyers were used principally as escorts for convoys and for attacking submarines. Some of the modern destroyers are nuclear-powered and many carry guided missiles. Some embark one or two helicopters. A new class of destroyer, the *Spruance* class, displacing 7,800 tons, is replacing some of the WWII destroyers still in service with the US Navy.

DÉTENTE (French for "relaxation"), the name given to the policy of easing tensions between the US and USSR that occurred in the late 1960s and 1970s. It was particularly associated with President NIXON (and his adviser Henry KISSINGER) during whose presidency the first STRATEGIC ARMS LIMITATION TALKS (SALT) agreement was signed (1972). It was continued by President FORD, who signed the HELSINKI ACCORDS in 1975. In the last years of the 1970s, however, tensions between the US and USSR rose again, and then détente was finally eclipsed by the Russian invasion of Afghanistan in 1980.

DETERGENTS, synthetic chemicals that have the same cleaning action as soaps, but unlike soaps do not form a scum when used in hard water. Most stains are caused by oily films holding dirt particles. The detergent molecules surround a particle of dirt and carry it into suspension in the water. Detergents are made with chemicals obtained from petroleum. Household detergents contain several ingredients. These include the basic detergent substances, which are also *surfactants*, or compounds that lower the surface tension of the water and make the cleaning action more effective; organic "builders," which enhance the emulsifying, foaming and dirt-suspending action of the detergent; germicides; bleaches; optical brighteners, which convert invisible ultraviolet rays striking the detergent into visible light, so that it looks brighter; stabilizers; colors and perfumes. These ingredients may be present in different amounts so that one detergent has a slightly different action from another. But apart from the "biological" or "enzyme" detergents, they are all basically the same. Biological detergents contain ENZYMES that digest organic matter and are very good at removing marks such as coffee stains, but they have been known to cause skin troubles.

Detergents are mostly used in water, but they may also be dissolved in other liquids. Hydrocarbons containing detergents are used in dry cleaning, and automobile engine lubricants use detergents to reduce buildup of carbon deposits.

DETERMINISM, the philosophical theory that all events are determined (inescapably caused) by preexisting events which, when considered in the context of inviolable physical laws, completely account for the subsequent events. The case for determinism has been variously argued from the inviolability of the laws of nature and from the omniscience and omnipotence of God. Determinism is often taken to be opposed to the principles of FREE WILL and indeterminacy.

DETROIT, city in SE Mich., situated on the W bank of the Detroit R., directly opposite the city of Windsor, Canada. The sixth-largest city in the US and one of the world's largest automobile manufacturing centers: over a quarter of all American-made cars are built there. It is also a major Great Lakes port and shipping center. A major steel center, Detroit produces a wide variety of metal goods and machine tools; pharmaceuticals, paints and chemicals are other important industries. One of the largest salt mines in the US lies beneath the city. Detroit is also a prominent educational and cultural center: Wayne State U. and the U. of Detroit, the city's symphony orchestra and the Detroit Institute of Arts are nationally known.

The city's history began in 1701 with the founding by Antoine CADILLAC, at "la place détroit," of a French trading post. It rapidly gained in importance and was a British possession 1706–96. Rebuilt after a fire in 1805, it was capital of Mich. until 1847; it achieved city status in 1815. Auto building had already begun by 1896, and within 10 years such famous firms as Cadillac, Ford, Oldsmobile and Packard were well established. Pop (city) 1,089,000, (metro) 4,319,000.

DEUTERONOMY, fifth book of the Old Testament and last book of the PENTATEUCH. Supposedly a testament left by Moses to the Israelites about to enter Canaan, it is primarily a recapitulation of moral laws and laws relating to the settlement of Canaan. Much of it was written long after Moses, parts being added during the reforms under King Josiah (621 BC). It may have been the "Book of the Law" discovered by Hilkiah in the Temple at that time.

DEUTSCH, Babette (1895–1982), US poet, writer of juvenile books and translator of Russian and German poetry. Her *Collected Poems, 1919–1962* was published in 1963. She also wrote several novels and an award-winning biography of Walt Whitman for children.

DE VALERA, Eamon (1882–1975), Irish statesman, prime minister 1937–48; 1951–54; 1957–59; and president of Ireland 1959–73. Born in New York City, he was raised in Ireland, and became an ardent republican. Only his US citizenship saved him from execution after the 1916 EASTER RISING. He was imprisoned by the Irish Free State for refusing to recognize the Anglo-Irish treaty of 1922; in 1924 he organized the Fianna Fáil party, which won power in 1932. In 1937 he declared Ireland independent of Britain, and during WWII preserved Irish neutrality.

DEVIL (from Greek *diabolos*, slanderer or accuser), in Western religions and sects, the chief spirit of evil and commander of lesser evil spirits or demons. Dualistic systems (see DUALISM)—notably ZOROASTRIANISM, GNOSTICISM and MANICHAEISM—have regarded the devil as the uncreated equal of God, engaged in an eternal war for evil against good. Such beliefs, often leading to devil worship, have appeared sporadically in connection with the occult. In Judaism, Christianity and Islam, the devil, Satan, is a fallen angel, powerful but subordinate to God, who opposes God and tempts mankind, but is to be utterly defeated and bound at the LAST JUDGMENT. (See also EXORCISM; MAGIC.)

DEVIL'S ISLAND, small island off the coast of French Guiana, formerly the site of a notorious French penal colony for political prisoners, among whom was Alfred Dreyfus (see DREYFUS AFFAIR). The penal colony was abolished in 1938.

DEVOLUTION, War of (1667–68), conflict between Spain and France over the right of succession to the Spanish Netherlands. LOUIS XIV claimed that by an old law of devolution the territory should have reverted to his wife MARIE THÉRÈSE upon the death of her father, Philip IV. Although his military campaign was successful, Louis was forced to withdraw in the face of the Triple Alliance of England, the United Provinces and Sweden; and the matter was settled in 1668 (see AIX-LA-CHAPELLE, TREATIES OF), Spain ceding to France 12 small fortified towns along the French border.

DEVONIAN, the fourth period of the PALEOZOIC, which lasted from about 400 to 345 million years ago. (See GEOLOGY.)

DE VOTO, Bernard Augustine (1897–1955), US journalist and author. He won national fame as a contributor to *Harper's Magazine.* His books include *Mark Twain's America* (1932), the Pulitzer prizewinning *Across the Wide Missouri* (1947) and the novel *The Crooked Mile* (1924).

DEW, the layer of water droplets that often forms at night on or near the ground. Dew may form in two ways: first water vapor may rise out of the ground by capillary action and form droplets on reaching cooler surfaces (leaves, rocks) near ground level. The second and principal way is the CONDENSATION of moisture from the air in contact with relatively cool objects. In arid and semi-arid areas, dew is an important source of moisture for plants.

DEWEY, George (1837–1917), US naval

hero promoted admiral of the navy—the highest possible rank—for his victory at the Battle of Manila Bay and the capture of the Philippines from Spain. On May 1, 1898, during the SPANISH-AMERICAN WAR, Dewey led the Asiatic squadron into Manila Bay and, without losing a man, destroyed the Spanish eastern fleet. In August, aided by Filipino rebels and US army forces, he received the surrender of Manila; the Philippines then fell to the US. Dewey later served as president of the general board of the Navy Department.

DEWEY, John (1859–1952), US philosopher and educator, the founder of the philosophical school known as instrumentalism (or experimentalism) and the leading promoter of educational reform in the early years of the 20th century. Profoundly influenced by the PRAGMATISM of William JAMES, Dewey developed a philosophy in which ideas and concepts were validated by their practicality. He taught that "learning by doing" should form the basis of educational practice, though in later life he came to criticize the "progressive" movement in education, which, in abandoning formal tuition altogether, he felt had misused his educational theory.

DEWEY, Thomas Edmund (1902–1971), US lawyer and Republican presidential candidate defeated in 1944 by Franklin D. Roosevelt and in 1948 by Harry S. Truman, although his election had been thought a foregone conclusion. In the 1930s, as US attorney for the southern district of N.Y. state and then as special prosecutor in New York City, Dewey gained a national reputation for successful campaigning against organized crime. He was governor of N.Y. 1943–55. He declined the post of chief justice under Richard M. Nixon (1968).

DEWEY DECIMAL SYSTEM, a system devised by Melvil Dewey (1851–1931) for use in the classification of books in libraries, and based on the DECIMAL SYSTEM of numbers. Dewey divided knowledge into ten main areas, each of these into ten subdivisions, and so on. Thus a book could fall into one of a thousand categories, from 000 to 999. Extensions of this system added further classificatory numbers after the decimal point.

DE WITT, Jan (1625–1672), Dutch statesman, grand pensionary (ruler) of Holland 1653–72, and republican opponent of the House of Orange. In 1667 he made peace with England and, in 1668, negotiated the Triple Alliance with England and Sweden against Louis XIV, to end the War of DEVOLUTION. When Louis XIV invaded Holland and the Dutch people called William III to power, he and his brother **Cornelius De Witt** (1623–1672) were brutally murdered by a mob.

DHARMA, important concept in HINDUISM, BUDDHISM and JAINISM. To Hindus, it denotes the universal law ordaining religious and social institutions, the rights and duties of individuals or, simply, virtuous conduct. Buddhists consider it the universal truth proclaimed to all men by Buddha. In Jainism, it also represents an eternal substance.

DIABETES, a common systemic disease, affecting between 0.5 and 1% of the population, and characterized by the absence or inadequate secretion of INSULIN, the principal hormone controlling BLOOD sugar. There are many causes, including heredity, VIRUS infection, primary disease of the PANCREAS and OBESITY. Though it may start at any time, two main groups are recognized: juvenile (beginning in childhood, adolescence or early adult life)—due to inability to secrete insulin; and late onset (late middle life or old age)—associated with obesity and with a relative lack of insulin. High blood sugar may lead to coma, often with keto-ACIDOSIS, excessive thirst and high urine output, weight loss, ill-health and liability to infections. The disease may be detected by urine or blood tests and confirmed by a glucose tolerance test. It causes disease of small blood vessels, as well as premature ARTERIOSCLEROSIS, retina disease, CATARACTS, KIDNEY disease and NEURITIS. Poor blood supply, neuritis and infection may lead to chronic leg ULCERS. Once recognized, diabetes needs treatment to stabilize the blood sugar level and keep it within strict limits. Regular medical surveillance and education is essential to minimize complications. Dietary carbohydrate must be controlled and for late onset cases this may be all that is needed; in this group, drugs that increase the body's insulin production are valuable. In juvenile and some late onset cases, insulin itself is needed, given by subcutaneous injection by the patient. Regular dosage, adjusted to usual diet and activity, is used, but surgery, PREGNANCY and infection increase insulin requirement. Control can be assessed by a simple urine test. Insulin overdose can occur, with sweating, confusion and COMA, and prompt treatment with sugar is crucial. EYE complications should be recognized early, especially in juvenile onset cases, as early intervention may prevent or delay BLINDNESS.

DIADOCHI, the generals of ALEXANDER THE

GREAT who, after his death in 323 BC, divided his empire among themselves. They included Antigonus, Antipater, PTOLEMY and Seleucus.

DIAGHILEV, Sergei Pavlovich (1872–1929), Russian impresario and founder (Paris, 1909) of the Ballets Russes which inaugurated modern BALLET. His magazine *World of Art* (1899–1904) led a movement for Russian involvement in Western European arts. He moved to Paris in 1906. The Ballets Russes broke with the formalism of classical choreography and aimed to unify music, dance and stage design. Its productions included the dancers and choreographers FOKINE, PAVLOVA, NIJINSKY and MASSINE, the composers STRAVINSKY and PROKOFIEV and the designers Aleksandr Benois and BAKST. MATISSE, PICASSO, DEBUSSY, RAVEL and many others also worked for Diaghilev.

DIALECTIC, in philosophy, variously: a method of forcing a respondent to alter his opinion by leading him into self-contradiction (SOCRATES); the process of getting to know the world of ideal forms (PLATO); sound reasoning from generally accepted opinions rather than from self-evident truths (ARISTOTLE); argument exposing the folly of reasoning that employs the categories of understanding outside the world of experience (KANT), or a dynamic logic, common to true philosophy and the historical process, in which apparent contradictories—theses and antitheses—are reconciled in syntheses (HEGEL).

DIALYSIS, process of selective DIFFUSION of ions and molecules through a semipermeable membrane which retains colloid particles and macromolecules. It is accelerated by applying an electric field. Dialysis is used for DESALINATION and in artificial kidneys. (See also OSMOSIS.)

DIAMOND, allotrope of CARBON (see ALLOTROPY), forming colorless cubic crystals. Diamond is the hardest known substance, with a Mohs hardness of 10, which varies slightly with the orientation of the crystal. Thus diamonds can be cut only by other diamonds. They do not conduct electricity, but conduct heat extremely well. Diamond burns when heated in air to 900°C; in an inert atmosphere it reverts to graphite slowly at 1000°C, rapidly at 1700°C. Diamonds occur naturally in dikes and pipes of kimberlite, notably in South Africa (Orange Free State and Transvaal), Tanzania, and in the US at Murfreesboro, Ark. They are also mined from secondary (alluvial) deposits, especially in Brazil, Zaire, Sierra Leone and India. The diamonds are separated by mechanical panning, and those of GEM quality are cleaved (or sawn), cut and polished. Inferior, or industrial, diamonds are used for cutting, drilling and grinding. Synthetic industrial diamonds are made by subjecting graphite to very high temperatures and pressures, sometimes with fused metals as solvent. sg 3.51.

DIARRHEA, loose and/or frequent bowel motions. A common effect of FOOD POISONING, GASTROINTESTINAL TRACT infection (e.g., DYSENTERY, CHOLERA) or INFLAMMATION (e.g., COLITIS, ENTERITIS, ABSCESS), drugs and systemic diseases. Benign or malignant TUMORS of the colon and rectum may also cause diarrhea. Slime or blood indicate severe inflammation or tumor.

DIAS or **DIAZ, Bartholomeu** (d. 1500), Portuguese navigator and explorer who, in 1488, discovered the sea route around Africa past the Cape of Good Hope to India. He explored much of the W coast of Africa. In 1500 he took part in Pedro CABRAL'S expedition, which discovered Brazil. He died at sea.

DIASPORA, the term used to describe Jewish settlements outside of Palestine. The name first referred to the Jewish community exiled to Babylonia in the 8th century BC and later included all Jews living outside the Holy Land. The largest Diaspora center in early Jewish history was Alexandria in the 1st century BC. Many modern thinkers have stressed the positive aspects of dispersion. They point out that the synagogue as an institution developed in Babylonia and that Judaism was broadened as a result of confrontation with other cultures. Others maintain that life in the Diaspora has been primarily a continuous history of persecution.

DÍAZ, Porfirio (1830–1915), Mexican general and president. Renowned for his part in the war against the French (1861–67), he came to oppose Benito JUÁREZ and gained power in 1877. President until 1880 and again from 1884, he was politically ruthless. However, his policies and foreign investment brought stability and prosperity, although peasant conditions were wretched. He was overthrown in 1911 and died in exile in Paris.

DIAZ DEL CASTILLO, Bernal (c1492–1581),· Spanish conquistador who accompanied Hernán CORTÉS in the conquest of Mexico, of which he wrote a valuable account.

DICE, two six-sided cubes with sides numbered from one to six. They are used in gambling games and in many board games. Dice in games of chance go back at least

5,000 years, the earliest such cubes having been found in the Sumerian royal tombs of Ur, dating to the third millennium BC.

DICKENS, Charles (1812–1870), one of the great English novelists. His brief childhood experience of a debtor's prison and work in a blacking factory shaped his future imagery and sympathies. Trained as a stenographer and lawyer's clerk, he began his literary career in London as a magazine contributor, under the pseudonym "Boz," publishing *Sketches by "Boz"* in 1836. His comic work *The Pickwick Papers* (1837) made him famous. Most of his novels were published first in monthly installments, for popular consumption, and this affected their structure and style. His chief concern was the effect of moral evil, crime and corruption on society. He created some memorable comic characters, as in *David Copperfield* (1850), which was based on his own experiences. His works include *Oliver Twist* (1838), *Bleak House* (1853), *Little Dorrit* (1857), *Great Expectations* (1861) and *Our Mutual Friend* (1865). Dicken's novels were dramatized, and he made successful reading tours of England and the US. His works influenced the Russian writer DOSTOYEVSKY.

DICKEY, James (Lafayette) (1923–), US poet, novelist and critic, best known for his novel *Deliverance* (1970), which was made into a movie in 1972. His collection of poems *Buckdancer's Choice* (1965), which like his novel explores themes of violence, won a National Book Award in 1966.

DICKINSON, Emily Elizabeth (1830–1886), important American poet. She spent most of her life secluded in her father's home in Amherst, Mass. Her concise lyrics, witty and aphoristic in style, simple, even sentimental, in expression and remarkable for metrical variations, are chiefly concerned with immortality and nature. Of 1,775 poems, only seven were published during her lifetime.

DICKINSON, John (1732–1808), American colonial statesman and political writer, who opposed British colonial policy but was against separation from Britain. He wrote *Letters from a Farmer in Pennsylvania* (1767 and 1768) and, while a member of the CONTINENTAL CONGRESS 1774–76, probably drew up the *Declaration of the Causes of taking up Arms*. He also wrote the first draft of the ARTICLES OF CONFEDERATION, in 1776. Dickinson refused to sign the DECLARATION OF INDEPENDENCE but supported the Constitution.

DICTATORSHIP, form of government in which one person holds absolute power and is not subject to the consent of the governed. The term derives from the Roman *dictator* who was a magistrate appointed to govern for a six-month period, following a state emergency. Both SULLA and Julius CAESAR, however, abolished the constitutional limits to their dictatorial power. In the 20th century, HITLER and STALIN assumed dictatorial powers and committed hideous atrocities; there have also been dictatorships in Portugal, Spain and Greece and in many South American and African countries. (See also TOTALITARIANISM.)

DICTIONARY, alphabetically arranged book giving the orthography, syllabication, pronunciation, meanings and uses, and etymology of words. Until the 18th century, dictionaries amounted to little more than lists, furnishing simple glossaries. The first large-scale compilation was *A New English Dictionary* (1702), containing 38,000 entries. Nathan Bailey's *Universal Etymological English Dictionary* (1721), besides containing etymologies, marked word stress and syllabication and established a methodology of word collection. In 1755 Samuel JOHNSON published the famous *Dictionary of the English Language*, in two volumes, the first English language dictionary to give literary examples of usage. Johnson's work was expanded by Noah WEBSTER in the US, who produced *An American Dictionary of the English Language* (1828). In 1857 Richard Chenevix Trench proposed *A New English Dictionary on Historical Principles* known, since 1894, as the *Oxford English Dictionary*. Its 12 volumes were published between 1884 and 1928; a 16-volume edition was published in 1986. Bilingual and special subject dictionaries are also made.

DIDEROT, Denis (1713–1784), French encyclopedist, philosopher and man of letters. His versatility as a novelist, playwright and art critic made him prominent in the ENLIGHTENMENT. His fame rests on the *Encyclopédie*, which he edited with d'ALEMBERT and published between 1751 and 1771. The *Encyclopédie*, comprising 17 volumes of text and 11 of engravings, contained essays on the sciences, arts and crafts by such eminent contributors as BUFFON, CONDORCET, Jean Jacques ROUSSEAU and VOLTAIRE, as well as by d'Alembert and Diderot themselves. It presented the scientific discoveries and more advanced thought of the time. As a result the French government tried to suppress it in 1759. Diderot's works included the play *Le Père de Famille* (1761) and the novel *Jacques le Fataliste* (1796).

DIDION, Joan (1934–), US essayist

and novelist concerned with the "atomization" of post-WWII society. Her works include the collections of essays *Slouching Towards Bethlehem* (1968) and *The White Album* (1979) and the novels *Play It As It Lays* (1970) and *A Book of Common Prayer* (1977).

DIEFENBAKER, John George (1895–1979), Canadian prime minister 1957–63. After repeated attempts he succeeded in being elected to parliament from Saskatchewan, in 1940. Becoming leader of the PROGRESSIVE CONSERVATIVE PARTY in 1956, he headed a minority government in 1957, after 22 years of Liberal rule. The 1958 election produced a record government majority. He instituted agricultural reforms but the economic recession, the Cuban missile crisis, and the nuclear arms debate, which aggravated relations with the US under Kennedy, brought on his defeat in 1963 by Lester PEARSON and the Liberals. He served in the Commons until his death.

DIEM, Ngo Dinh (1901–1963), American-backed president of the South Vietnam republic 1954–63. His Roman Catholic regime's harsh oppression of the Buddhist majority (leading to cases of self-immolation), his corrupt politics and failure to effect land reform, led to a withdrawal of US support. He was assassinated in a coup led by his own generals.

DIEN BIEN PHU, military outpost, in North Vietnam, where in 1954 France was finally defeated in the Indochina war. During a 55-day siege, the French army lost 15,000 men in their bid to resist the onslaught of Gen. Vo Nguyen Giap's Vietminh forces. France formally withdrew from Indochina at the Geneva Conference (1954).

DIES, Martin (1900–1972), Democratic US representative from Texas (1931–45, 1955–59) who established (1938) and presided over the HOUSE COMMITTEE ON UN-AMERICAN ACTIVITIES (HUAC). The "Dies committee" became extremely controversial for its uncovering of alleged Communist influence in organized labor, motion pictures, and government agencies.

DIESEL ENGINE, oil-burning INTERNAL-COMBUSTION ENGINE patented by **Rudolf Diesel** (1858–1913), a German engineer, in 1892 after several years of development work. Air enters a cylinder and is compressed by a piston to a high enough TEMPERATURE and PRESSURE for spontaneous combustion to occur when fuel is sprayed in. This method of operation differs from that of a gasoline engine in which air and fuel are mixed before entering the cylinder, there is less compression and a spark is needed to initiate combustion. In the first (intake) stroke of the cycle of a 4-stroke diesel engine, the piston moves down, drawing in air through a valve. In the second (compression) stroke, the piston returns up, compressing the air and heating it to over 300°C. (The exact value depends on the compression ratio, which may be between 12:1 and 22:1.) Near the end of the stroke, fuel is sprayed into the cylinder at high pressure through a nozzle and ignites in the hot air. In the third (power) stroke, the burning fuel–air mixture increases the pressure in the cylinder, pushing the piston down and driving the crankshaft. Then, in the fourth (exhaust) stroke, the piston moves up again and drives the burnt gases out of the cylinder. There are also 2-stroke diesel engines. These have only compression and power strokes, the exhaust gases being scavenged and new air introduced by a blower while the piston is at the bottom of its stroke. Diesel engines are less smooth-running, heavier and initially more expensive than gasoline engines but make more efficient use of cheaper fuel. They are widely used in ships, heavy vehicles and power installations, and increasingly in passenger cars.

DIETRICH, Marlene (1904–), German-born US film actress and cabaret artist. Her classic role was that of the "femme fatale" nightclub singer in the German film *The Blue Angel* (1930). She became famous for her sultry glamor and sophistication.

DIFFERENTIAL EQUATIONS, EQUATIONS involving derivatives (see CALCULUS).

DIFFERENTIAL GEOMETRY, the branch of GEOMETRY dealing with the basic properties of curves and surfaces, using the techniques of CALCULUS and ANALYTIC GEOMETRY.

DIFFERENTIATION. See CALCULUS.

DIFFRACTION, the property by which a WAVE MOTION (such as ELECTROMAGNETIC RADIATION, SOUND or water waves) deviates from the straight line expected geometrically and thus gives rise to INTERFERENCE effects at the edges of the shadows cast by opaque objects, where the wave-trains that have reached each point by different routes interfere with each other. Opaque objects thus never cast completely sharp shadows, though such effects only become apparent when the dimensions of the obstruction are of the same order as the wavelength of the wave motion concerned. It is diffraction effects which place the ultimate limit on the resolving power of optical instruments, RADIO TELESCOPES and the like. Diffraction is set to work in the diffraction grating. Here, light passed through a series of very accurately ruled slits or reflected from a series of narrow parallel mirrors produces a series of spectrums by the interference of the light from the different slits or mirrors. Gratings are ruled with from 70 lines/mm (for infrared work) to 1,800 lines/mm (for ultraviolet work).

DIFFUSION, the gradual mixing of different substances placed in mutual contact due to the random thermal motion of their constituent particles. Most rapid with gases and liquids, it also occurs with solids. Diffusion rates increase with increasing TEMPERATURE; the rates at which gases diffuse through a porous membrane vary as the inverse of the square root of their MOLECULAR WEIGHT. Gaseous diffusion is used to separate fissile URANIUM-235 from nonfissile uranium-238, the gas used being uranium hexafluoride (UF_6).

DIGESTIVE SYSTEM, the mechanism for breaking down or modifying dietary intake into a form that is absorbable and usable by an organism. In unicellular organisms this is by phagocytosis and enzyme breakdown of large molecules; in larger animals it occurs outside cells after liberation of ENZYMES. In higher animals, the digestive system consists structurally of the GASTROINTESTINAL TRACT, the principal absorbing surface which also secretes enzymes, and the related organs: the LIVER and PANCREAS, which secrete into the tract via ducts. Different enzymes act best at different pH, and **gastric juice** and BILE respectively regulate the acidity of the STOMACH and alkalinity of the small intestine. PROTEINS are broken down by pepsin in the stomach and by trypsin, chymotrypsin and peptidases in the small intestine. CARBOHYDRATES are broken down by specialized enzymes, mainly in the small intestine. FATS are physically broken down by stomach movement, enzymatically by lipases and emulsified by bile salts. Food is mixed and propelled by PERISTALSIS, while nerves and locally regulated HORMONES, including gastrin and secretin, control both secretion and motility. Absorption of most substances occurs in the small intestine through a specialized, high-surface area mucous membrane; some molecules pass through unchanged but most in altered form. Absorption may be either by an active transport system involving chemical or physical interaction in the gut wall, or simply by a passive DIFFUSION process. Some VITAMINS and trace metals have specialized transport systems. Most absorbed food passes via the portal system to the liver,

where much of it is metabolized and toxic substances removed. Some absorbed fat is passed into the LYMPH. BACTERIA colonize most of the small intestine and are important in certain digestive processes. **Malabsorption** occurs when any part of the digestive system becomes defective. Pancreas and liver disease, obstruction to bile ducts, alteration of bacteria and inflammatory disease of the small intestine are common causes.

DIGGERS, or **True Levellers,** 17th-century English radical cooperative movement, followers of Gerrard Winstanley. In April 1649, following the execution of King Charles I after the Civil War, they occupied the common land on St. George's Hill, Surrey, and began to cultivate it. They claimed land should be given to the poor and held in common. They were dispersed in 1650.

DIGITALIS, drug derived from the FOXGLOVE and acting on the muscle and systems of the HEART. In 1785 William Withering described its efficacy in heart failure or dropsy; it increases the force of cardiac contraction. It is also valuable in treatment of some abnormal rhythms; however, overdosage may itself cause abnormal rhythm, nausea or vomiting.

DILLINGER, John (1903–1934), notorious US gangster, who terrorized the Midwest in 1933 after escaping from jail. He was responsible for 16 killings and was shot in Chicago in 1934.

DILLON, Clarence Douglas (1909–), US financier and public official, chairman of the investment banking firm of Dillon, Read 1946–53. He was US ambassador to France (1953–57) and undersecretary of state (1958–61) in the Eisenhower administration and secretary of the treasury (1961–65) in the Kennedy and Johnson administrations.

DILTHEY, Wilhelm (1833–1911), German philosopher who sought to achieve for "historical reason" in the human sciences (law; religion; history; psychology and the arts), what KANT had achieved for the natural sciences in the *Critique of Pure Reason.*

DIMAGGIO, Joseph Paul "Joe" (1914–), US baseball outfielder. He played for the New York Yankees from 1936 until his retirement in 1951, set a new record with consistent safe-hitting in 56 consecutive games (1941), hit 361 home runs and had a career batting average of .325.

DIME NOVEL, fast-moving melodramatic tale of adventure. Dime novels were first popular from the 1860s to the 1890s. Selling for 10 cents, they usually told stories about the American Revolution, the frontier period or the Civil War. They became popular again from the 1920s to the 1940s, when they sold for 10 or 15 cents and were printed on pulp stock with soft covers. Their subjects, typically, were romance, horror, crime or science fiction.

DIMITROV, Georgi (1882–1949), Bulgarian Communist leader. He was accused of complicity in the Reichstag fire in Berlin in 1933 but brilliantly defended himself. Rewarded with Soviet citizenship, he headed the Comintern 1934–43. From 1944 he led the Communist Party in Bulgaria, becoming premier in 1946.

D'INDY, (Paul Marie Théodore) Vincent (1851–1931), French composer and teacher, a pupil of César FRANCK and cofounder of the Schola Cantorum academy, Paris (1894). He thought French 19th-century music superficial, admiring the German classics and Renaissance polyphony. He urged a renovated French style derived from folk idioms. His works include *Symphony on a French Mountain Air* (1886).

DINE, Jim (1935–   ), US artist. His work made use of "found" objects, such as old shoes or tools, which he often attached to his canvases to create a vivid imagery.

DINESEN, Isak, pseudonym of Karen Christence Dinesen, Baroness Blixen-Finecke (1885–1962), Danish author of romantic tales of mystery, such as *Seven Gothic Tales* (1934). The autobiographical *Out of Africa* (1937) was based on her 20 years in E Africa as a planter.

DINOSAURS, extinct REPTILES that flourished for 125 million years from the TRIASSIC to the Cretaceous periods. They ranged in size from small forms no larger than a domestic chicken to giants such as *Diplodocus* which was 90ft long and weighed about 30 tons. Early in their history two distinct dinosaur groups evolved: the Saurischia and the Ornithischia.

The **saurischians** (or lizard-hipped dinosaurs) had pelvic girdles typical of lizards, with three prongs to each side. They included the two-legged carnivorous theropods, such as *Tyrannosaurus* and *Allosaurus*, with enormous skulls and large teeth; and the four-legged herbivorous sauropods, such as *Brontosaurus* and *Diplodocus*, with very small heads and long necks and tails.

The **ornithischians** (or bird-hipped dinosaurs) had bird-like pelvic girdles, with four prongs to each side. All were herbivorous. Four-legged types include the

stegosaurs, with triangular bony plates along the back, and the armadillo-like ankylosaurs. The two-legged duck-billed dinosaurs were well equipped for swimming.

At the end of the Cretaceous period, about 65 million years ago, dinosaurs disappeared. The reasons for this sudden extinction are not known and are the subject of much debate and controversy among paleontologists.

DINWIDDIE, Robert (1693–1770), governor of colonial Virginia (1751–58) in the last of the FRENCH AND INDIAN WARS. In 1753 he sent George WASHINGTON to warn the French to leave the Ohio Valley, then attempted to build a fort on the present site of Pittsburgh. The French captured the fort (which they named Fort Duquesne) and then defeated Washington's militia at nearby Fort Necessity. Dinwiddie labored in support of the campaign of Gen. Edward BRADDOCK, which ended in disaster (1755).

DIOCLETIAN (Gaius Aurelius Valerius Diocletianus; c245–316), Roman emperor from 284 to 305, when he abdicated. He reformed the army and administration, dividing the empire into four regions (293), ruled by two emperors and two caesars. Much of his great palace at Split, Yugoslavia, survives. In 303 he initiated the last universal persecution of the Christians.

DIOGENES (c412–323 BC), Greek philosopher, living in Athens. He rejected tradition and social conventions. Contemptuous of his contemporaries and their values, he was nicknamed "the Dog" and his followers the CYNICS (*kynikos*, "doglike"). He abandoned all his possessions, begged his living and reputedly lived in a barrel. Supposedly, when Alexander the Great asked what he could do for him, Diogenes answered, "Just step out of my light."

DIONYSUS, Greek god of wine and fertility, also called Bacchus, a son of Zeus. He founded the art of vine culture. In early times his devotees, notably the Maenads, practiced an orgiastic cult of divine possession.

DIOXIN, a toxic chemical produced in some chemical-manufacturing processes; it contaminates various herbicides. The effects on human health of long-term exposure to dioxin are disputed, although it is generally accepted that dioxin causes chloracne, a skin ailment. US chemical workers have filed suits against employers for serious health problems, and Vietnam veterans also claimed damages for exposure to Agent Orange, a defoliant contaminated by dioxin. Cleanups in the 1980s of dioxin deposits on sites in Missouri and New Jersey cost millions of dollars.

DIPHTHERIA, BACTERIAL DISEASE, now uncommon, causing FEVER, malaise and sore throat, with a characteristic "pseudomembrane" on throat or pharynx; also, the LYMPH nodes may enlarge. The LARYNX, if involved, leads to a hoarse voice, breathlessness and stridor; this may progress to respiratory obstruction requiring tracheotomy. The bacteria produce TOXINS which can damage nerves and HEART muscle; cardiac failure and abnormal rhythm, or PARALYSIS of palate, eye movement and peripheral NEURITIS may follow. Early treatment with ANTITOXIN and use of ANTIBIOTICS are important. Protection is given by VACCINATION.

DIPLOMACY, conduct of negotiations and maintenance of relations in time of peace between sovereign states. A diplomatic mission is generally headed by an ambassador, supported by attachés, chargés d'affaires and other officials specializing in economic, political, cultural, administrative and military matters. An embassy building is considered to have "extraterritoriality," that is, to be outside the jurisdiction of the receiving state. Accredited diplomats are immune from prosecution and customs regulations. Abuse of this privileged diplomatic immunity can lead to a diplomat being asked to quit the host country as *persona non grata*. The most common abuse is espionage. The whole body of diplomats in a capital is known as the diplomatic corps and its spokesman is the longest serving ambassador.

International contacts have been handled by diplomats since ancient times. In medieval Europe they were generally appointed for the duration of specific missions. The first permanent residential missions were established by the Italian city states c1400. Diplomatic protocol and the forms of accreditation owed much to the practice of papal missions from the Vatican. Latin was the official language of diplomacy until the 17th century, when it was superseded by French, later joined by English. The Congress of Vienna (1815) further clarified diplomatic procedure. The traditional formulas of diplomatic exchange allow sharp expressions of protest without ruptures in international dealing. Improved communications have strengthened direct links between governments and diplomacy is now often conducted at "summit conferences" between heads of state. (See also INTERNATIONAL RELATIONS.)

DIRAC, Paul Adrien Maurice (1902–1984), English theoretical physicist who shared the 1933 Nobel physics prize with E. SCHRÖDINGER for their contributions to WAVE MECHANICS. Dirac's theory (1928) took account of RELATIVITY and implied the existence of the positive ELECTRON or positron, later discovered by C. D. ANDERSON. Dirac was also the codiscoverer of Fermi-Dirac statistics.

DIRECTORY, government of France 1795–99. It consisted of a group of five directors chosen by the Council of Ancients and the Council of Five Hundred. Corrupt and discredited by military reverses, it was replaced by the CONSULATE of Napoleon Bonaparte in the coup of 18 Brumaire (Nov. 9, 1799).

DIRIGIBLE. See AIRSHIP.

DISARMAMENT. See ARMS CONTROL.

DISCIPLES OF CHRIST, now the International Convention of Christian Churches, US religious body founded (1832) by followers of Alexander CAMPBELL. It has no formal ministry or creed, teaching simple, personal faith in the Bible and the primitive gospel of Christ. This, it holds, should be the basis for union of Christian churches. It has missions all over the world. Its membership in North America is about 1,600,000.

DISEASE, disturbance of normal bodily function in an organism. MEDICINE and SURGERY are concerned with the recognition or diagnosis of disease and the institution of treatment aimed at its cure. Disease is usually brought to attention by symptoms, in which a person becomes aware of some abnormality of, or change in, bodily function. Pain, HEADACHE, FEVER, COUGH, shortness of breath, DYSPEPSIA, CONSTIPATION, DIARRHEA, loss of BLOOD, lumps, PARALYSIS, numbness and loss of consciousness are common examples. Diagnosis is made on the basis of symptoms, signs on physical examination and laboratory and X-RAY investigations; the functional disorder is analyzed and possible causes are examined. Causes of physical disease in man are legion, but certain categories are recognized: trauma, congenital, infectious, inflammatory, vascular, tumor, degenerative, deficiency, poison, metabolic, occupational and iatrogenic diseases.

Trauma to body may cause SKIN lacerations and BONE fractures as well as disorders specific to the organ involved (e.g., CONCUSSION). Congenital diseases include hereditary conditions (i.e., those passed on genetically) and diseases beginning in the FETUS, such as those due to drugs or maternal infection in PREGNANCY. Infectious diseases include viral disease, BACTERIAL

DISEASE and parasitic disease, which may be acute or chronic and are usually communicable. Insects, animals and human carriers may be important in their spread, and EPIDEMICS may occur. INFLAMMATION is often the result of infection, but **inflammatory disease** can also result from disordered IMMUNITY and other causes. In **vascular diseases**, organs become diseased secondary to disease in their blood supply, such as ARTERIOSCLEROSIS, ANEURYSM, THROMBOSIS and EMBOLISM.

Tumors, including benign growths, CANCER and LYMPHOMA are diseases in which abnormal growth of a structure occurs and leads to a lump, pressure on or spread to other organs and distant effects such as emaciation, HORMONE production and NEURITIS. In **degenerative disease**, DEATH or premature aging in parts of an organ or system lead to a gradual impairment of function. **Deficiency diseases** result from inadequate intake of nutrients, VITAMINS, minerals, calcium, iron and trace substances; disorders of their fine control and that of hormones leads to **metabolic disease**. **Poisoning** is the toxic action of chemicals on body systems, some of which may be particularly sensitive to a given poison. An increasingly recognized side-effect of industrialization is the occurrence of **occupational diseases**, in which chemicals, dusts or molds encountered at work cause disease—especially PNEUMOCONIOSIS and other LUNG disease, and certain cancers. **Iatrogenic disease** is disease produced by the intervention of doctors, in an attempt to treat or prevent some other disease. The altered ANATOMY of diseased structures is described as **pathological**. **Psychiatric disease**, including psychoses (schizophrenia and depression) and neuroses, are functional disturbances of the BRAIN, in which structural abnormalities are not recognizable; they may represent subtle disturbances of brain metabolism. **Treatment** of disease by SURGERY or DRUGS is usual, but success is variable; a number of conditions are so benign that symptoms may be suppressed until they have run their natural course.

DISINFECTANTS. See ANTISEPTICS.

DISMAL SWAMP, coastal region of some 750sq mi in SE Va. and NE N.C. It has a rich and varied tree cover, though most of the swamp is now drained and used for lumbering and agriculture. In the center of the swamp is Lake Drummond.

DISNEY, Walt (Walter Elias Disney; 1901–1966), US pioneer of animated film cartoons. Starting in the 1920s, the Disney studios in Hollywood created the famous cartoon characters Mickey Mouse, Pluto, Donald Duck and Goofy. Disney's first full-length cartoon feature, *Snow White and the Seven Dwarfs* (1938), was followed by *Pinocchio* (1940), *Fantasia* (1940) and *Bambi* (1942) among others. He also produced many popular nature and live-action films.

DISNEYLAND, popular amusement center at Anaheim, Calif., built by animation impresario Walt DISNEY and opened in 1955. The park now includes over 160 acres of elaborately mechanized amusements and recreations of Disney cartoon characters. Built on a permanent World's Fair scale, the park is one of the major tourist attractions in the US. A similar and far larger park opened in 1971 on a 27,400-acre site near Orlando, Fla.

DISRAELI, Benjamin, 1st Earl of Beaconsfield (1804–1881), British Conservative statesman of Jewish descent, prime minister 1868 and 1874–80. A member of Parliament from 1837, he was chancellor of the exchequer 1852, 1858–59 and 1866–68. His influence was crucial in the passing of the 1867 Reform Bill, which enfranchised some 2 million working-class voters. His brief first ministry ended when the Liberals under GLADSTONE won the 1868 elections. His second period of office included domestic reforms: slum clearance, public-health reform and improvement of working conditions. Abroad, Disraeli fought imperial wars, bought control of the Suez Canal (1875), had Queen Victoria proclaimed Empress of India (1876) and annexed the Transvaal (1877). In the confrontation between Russia and Turkey (1877–78), he forced concessions on Russia (see BERLIN, CONGRESS OF). A prolific writer, he published many books, notably the novels *Coningsby* (1844) and *Sybil* (1845)—both on social and political themes.

DISSENTERS. See NONCONFORMISTS.

DISTEMPER, term applied to several animal diseases, but particularly referring to a specific viral disease of dogs. It commonly occurs in puppies, with FEVER, poor appetite and discharge from mucous membranes; bronchopneumonia and ENCEPHALITIS may be complications. VACCINATION is protective.

DISTILLATION, process in which substances are vaporized and then condensed by cooling, probably first invented by the ALEXANDRIAN SCHOOL and used in ALCHEMY, the still and the ALEMBIC being employed. It may be used to separate a volatile liquid from nonvolatile solids, as in the production of pure WATER from seawater, or from less volatile liquids, as in the distillation of liquid air to give oxygen, nitrogen and the noble gases. If the boiling points of the components differ greatly, **simple distillation** can be used: on gentle heating, the components distill over in order (the most volatile first) and the pure fractions are collected in different flasks. Mixtures of liquids of similar boiling points require **fractionation** for efficient separation. This technique employs multiple still heads and fractionating columns in which some of the vapor is condensed and returned to the still, equilibrating as it does so with the rising vapor. In effect, the mixture is redistilled several times; the number of theoretical simple distillations, or theoretical plates, represents the separating efficiency of the column. The theory of distillation is an aspect of phase equilibria studies. For ideal solutions, obeying Raoult's law, the vapor always contains a higher proportion than the liquid of the more volatile component; if this is not the case, an azeotropic mixture may be formed. When two immiscible liquids are distilled, they come over in the proportion of their vapor pressures at a temperature below the boiling point of either. This is utilized in **steam distillation**, in which superheated steam is passed into the still and comes over together with the volatile liquid. It is useful when normal distillation would require a temperature high enough to cause decomposition, as in **vacuum distillation**, in which the pressure reduction lowers the boiling points. A further refinement is **molecular distillation**, in which unstable molecules travel directly in high vacuum to the condenser.

DISTRICT OF COLUMBIA. See WASHINGTON, D.C.

DITTERSDORF, Karl Ditters von (1739–1799), Austrian composer and violinist. He composed light operas, establishing the singspiel form, and various other works. Among his works are the operas *Doktor und Apotheker* (1786), *Hieronymus Knicker* (1789) and *Das Rote Kappchen* (1790).

DIURETICS, drugs that increase urine production by the KIDNEY. Alcohol and CAFFEINE are mild diuretics. Thiazides and other diuretics are commonly used in treatment of HEART failure, EDEMA, high blood pressure, LIVER and KIDNEY disease.

DIVINATION, the term applied to various methods of foretelling the future, by means of oracles, omens or signs. These methods include dream interpretation, astrology, investigation of parts of the body, (e.g., palmistry, phrenology), the study of animal entrails, and the interpretation of the cries of birds and animals (augury). Divination is

one of the most ancient of practices, and has been found in almost all societies. (See ASTROLOGY.)

DIVINE, Father. See FATHER DIVINE.

DIVINE COMEDY. See DANTE.

DIVINE RIGHT, claim of early modern kings that their authority derived from God, not from the church or from the governed. English kings JAMES I and CHARLES I and LOUIS XIV of France made explicit claims to divine right.

DIVING. See SWIMMING AND DIVING.

DIVING, Deep Sea, the descent by divers to the sea bed, usually for protracted periods, for purposes of exploration, salvage, etc. Skin diving is almost as old as man—the Romans had primitive diving suits connected by an air pipe to the surface. This principle was also known in the early 16th century. A breakthrough came when John Lethbridge devised the forerunner of the armored suits used today in deepest waters (1715): it looked much like a barrel with sleeves and a viewport, and was useless for depths of more than a few yards. In 1802 William Forder devised a suit where air was pumped to the diver by bellows. And in 1837 (improving his earlier design of 1819) Augustus Siebe (1788–1872) invented the modern diving suit, a continuous airtight suit to which air is supplied by a pump. The diving suit today has a metal or fiberglass helmet with viewports and inhalation and exhalation valves, joined by an airtight seal to a metal chestpiece, itself joined to a flexible watertight covering of rubber and canvas; and weights, especially weighted boots, for stability and to prevent the diver shooting toward the surface. Air or, more often, an oxygen/helium mixture is conveyed to him via a thick rubber tube. In addition, he has either a telephone wire, or simply a cord which he can tug, for communication with the surface. Nowadays SCUBA diving, where the diver has no suit but carries gas cylinders and an AQUALUNG, is preferred in most cases since it permits greater mobility. In all diving great care must be taken to avoid the bends through too-rapid ascent to the surface. (See also BATHYSCAPHE.)

DIVORCE, legal dissolution of a valid marriage, as distinct from SEPARATION, in which the partners remain married but live apart, and ANNULMENT, in which the marriage is deemed to be invalid. In most cases, divorce leaves the partners free to remarry, sometimes after a set period. Divorce has existed in most cultures, but its availability and the grounds for it have varied widely. Christianity regards marriage as a sacrament which may not lightly be set aside, and this view has affected the Western concept of divorce. The Roman Catholic Church still does not allow it, but most other churches now allow divorce. In the US each state makes its own divorce laws and there is great divergence. The trend has been towards a liberal view, but it has created the migratory or "quickie" divorce, for which Nevada is renowned. Adultery is the most widely accepted ground for divorce; others include cruelty, alcoholism, insanity, desertion and conviction of a serious crime. A modern trend is to make irreparable breakdown of the marriage another ground, without involving the misconduct of either party; the first states to introduce this were California and Iowa. Divorce is a major social problem in the US; it has been estimated that it ends one in every four marriages. The possible effect of such marital instability upon the children involved and upon society is giving rise to serious concern.

DIX, Dorothea Lynde (1802–1887), US social reformer and crusader for the humane and scientific treatment of mental illness. In 1841 she was shocked to see mentally sick people in jail and launched a successful campaign to establish mental hospitals.

DIX, Otto (1891–1969), German painter and leader of the "new objectivity" school of social realism. His most famous work is the cycle of 50 etchings entitled *Der Krieg* (The War; 1924) depicting WWI horrors. He was jailed (1939–45) by the Nazi government. In later years he turned to a form of religious mysticism in his work.

DIXIECRATS, Southern faction of the US Democratic Party which opposed the 1948 party platform on civil rights. They ran their own candidates, Governor Strom Thurmond of S.C. for president and Governor Fielding Wright of Miss. for vice-president, against the incumbent President Truman, and received 1,169,000 national and 39 electoral votes.

DIXIELAND, name given to one of the earliest jazz styles. It originated in New Orleans as an attempt by white musicians to copy early Negro jazzmen. It has since come to be applied to a strictly standardized brand of jazz that stresses improvisation and is somewhat smoother and more sophisticated than early New Orleans jazz.

DJAKARTA. See JAKARTA.

DJIBOUTI, a republic in NE Africa, situated where the coast of Africa approaches the Arabian peninsula, bounded by Ethiopia and Somalia.

Land and Economy. Most of the country is stony desert. The climate is hot. Rainfall is

Official name: Republic of Djibouti
Capital: Djibouti
Area: 8,950sq mi
Population: 470,000
Languages: Arabic, French
Religion: Muslim
Monetary unit (s): 1 Djibouti franc = 100 centimes

usually scant, but in some years torrential rainfall causes flooding. Because of the character of the terrain, agricultural activity is limited. There are no known mineral resources, and industry is negligible. Livestock are important; hides and skins and live animals are the main exports.

People. The population is almost evenly divided into two main ethnic groups: the Afars (from Ethiopia) and the Issas (from Somalia), the latter having a slight predominance. Both groups are traditionally nomadic and depend on livestock; however, the Issas are more urbanized than the Afars. The nation's government is carefully balanced between the two groups, but historical rivalries persist. The capital, also called Djibouti, is the economic and political hub of the country, with a port and a railway terminus.

History. In 1896 France signed treaties with Britain, Italy and Ethiopia to define the boundaries of French Somaliland. In 1967 the colony voted to remain a French possession and became the French Territory of the Afars and the Issas. It became independent in 1977. Djibouti has remained neutral during strife between its neighbors, Somalia and Ethiopia, despite close ethnic ties, and has received considerable foreign assistance because of its strategic location. The country is a one-party state. Hassan Gouled Aptidon, the first president, was reelected in 1981 and 1987.

DJILAS, Milovan (1911–   ), Yugoslav communist leader and writer. He was a leading WWII partisan alongside TITO, and became a vice-president after the war. But because of his outspoken criticisms of the regime and his general indictment of communism as a form of government he was imprisoned 1956–66. Among his works are

The New Class (1957) and *Conversations with Stalin* (1962).

DNA, deoxyribonucleic acid, a NUCLEIC ACID comprising two strands of nucleotide wound around each other in a double helix, found in all living things and VIRUSES.

DNIEPER RIVER, second-longest river in the European USSR, about 1,400mi long. Rising in the Valdai Hills, it flows SW to empty into the Black Sea E of Odessa. Leading tributaries are the Desna, Pripyat, Berezina and Sozh. It is a major water transport route, and also has many hydroelectric plants.

DOBIE, James Frank (1888–1964), US folklorist, at Texas U 1925–47, who recorded the legends of Texas and the southwest in many books.

DOBZHANSKY, Theodosius (1900–1975), Russian-born US biologist, famed for his study of the fruit fly, *Drosophila*, which demonstrated that a wide genetic range could exist in even a comparatively well-defined species. Indeed the greater the "genetic load" of unusual genes in a species, the better equipped it is to survive in changed circumstances. (See EVOLUTION; HEREDITY.)

DOCTOROW, E(dgar) L(aurence) (1931–   ), US novelist. His critically acclaimed books include *The Book of Daniel* (1971), an historical novel about Julius and Ethel Rosenberg and their children; *Ragtime* (1975), which interweaves fictional portraits of Freud, Jung, Harry Houdini, and Henry Ford, among others; and *Loon Lake* (1980), a complex and haunting novel set during the Great Depression.

DODD, William Edward (1869–1940), US historian at the U of Chicago (1908–33) who served as US ambassador to Germany (1933–37). At first hopeful of improving German-American relations, he became a firm opponent of the Nazi regime.

DODECANESE, group of Greek islands in the SE Aegean Sea off Turkey. There are 12 main islands, and, except for Rhodes and Cos, they are largely rocky and infertile. Italy seized the group in 1912 from the Turks, but after WWII they were ceded to Greece.

DODECAPHONIC MUSIC. See TWELVE-TONE MUSIC.

DODGE, family name of two early developers of the automobile. Both **John Francis Dodge** (1864–1920) and **Horace Elgin Dodge** (1868–1920) were born in Michigan and began working with cars in Detroit in 1901. At first they built car parts in their machine shop for the Ford and Olds motor companies, but later began developing their own automobile. In 1914 they produced a car with an all-steel body. They founded the Dodge Company, which merged with the Chrysler Corporation in 1928.

DODGE, Mary Elizabeth Mapes (1831–1905), US children's author, who founded and edited the magazine *St. Nicholas* (1873). She is best known for her book *Hans Brinker, or The Silver Skates* (1865), a classic of children's literature.

DODGE CITY, city in SW Kan. on the Arkansas R, seat of Ford Co. In the late 1800s its was a cattle center on the Santa Fe Trail, at the head of the Santa Fe Railroad, and it became notorious for its wild frontier life. It now has railroad shops and makes agricultural implements. Pop 18,001.

DODGSON, Charles Lutwidge. See CARROLL, LEWIS.

DODO, a turkey-sized flightless bird with strong legs and a big bill, now extinct. Its home was the island of Mauritius until it succumbed to the depredations of settlers. The last dodo died around 1681, but a few museum specimens and skeletons survive.

DOENITZ, Karl (1891–1980), German admiral, head of the WWII U-boat service and later commander in chief of the German navy (1943–45). On Hitler's death in 1945 he became head-of-state, and subsequently surrendered to the Allies. He was tried for war crimes at Nuremberg and served 10 years in prison.

DOESBURG, Theo van (1883–1931), Dutch painter and author, a leader of the DE STIJL group. He turned to abstract art in 1916, influenced at first by MONDRIAN, and taught at the BAUHAUS 1921–23.

DOG, carnivorous mammal of the family Canidae, usually with long legs, long muzzle and bushy tail, that lives by chasing its prey. Many live in packs. Wild dogs include the raccoon dog of Asia and several South American forms like the bush dog and the maned wolf. Domestic dogs are members of the species *Canis familiaris.*

DOHNÁNYI, Ernst von (1877–1960), Hungarian composer and pianist, conductor of the Budapest Philharmonic Orchestra (1919–44). His music, influenced by Brahms, includes the light-hearted *Variations on a Nursery Song* (1913) and *Ruralia Hungarica* (1924), both for piano and orchestra.

DOLCI, Danilo (1924–   ), Italian writer and social reformer. Since 1952 he has worked to improve the lot of the Sicilians, despite opposition from both the authorities and the Mafia. He won the 1957 Lenin Peace Prize. His books include *To Feed the Hungry* (1959) and *"Where There's*

Smoke" (1971).

DOLE, James Drummond (1877–1958), US businessman who went (1899) to Hawaii and there founded and developed the Hawaiian pineapple industry.

DOLE, Robert J. (1923–   ), US politician, unsuccessful Republican vice-presidential candidate in 1976 as running mate of Gerald FORD. Twice decorated in WWII, he was Republican national chairman 1971–73 and senator from Kan. from 1974. He unsuccessfully sought the Republican presidential nomination in 1988.

DOLE, Sanford Ballard (1844–1926), US judge and leader of the Republic of Hawaii. In 1893, he led the movement which overthrew Queen Liliuokalani and resulted in the establishment of the Hawaiian republic, of which Dole was proclaimed president (1894–1900). After US annexation in 1898, he served as territorial governor 1900–03.

DOLL, a miniature representation of the human form, used as a toy or, in some societies, a sacred object. The practice of making dolls is an ancient one. Some of the earliest examples, made from a wide range of substances including wood, bone, ivory and clay, have been found in Pakistan at MOHENJO-DARO (c3000 BC) and on Babylonian, Egyptian and Aztec sites. In ancient societies dolls were often entombed with the dead. In America, they are still used in Hopi and Zuni Indian rites.

The modern doll has its origin in medieval doll nativity scenes and in the 14th-century fashion dolls of France and England. During the 16th century, Nuremberg in Germany became a major center of doll making, noted particularly for its figures carved from wood. Papier-mâché and wax were used in the 19th century as ideal materials for fashioning dolls' heads. Present-day dolls are made from a variety of synthetic materials, their designs incorporating such sales gimmicks as "voices," working limbs and moving eyelids.

DOLLFUSS, Englebert (1892–1934), Austrian chancellor and fascist dictator (1933–34). He allied with Mussolini to keep Austria independent of Hitler and banned the Austrian Nazi party. In Feb. 1934, his Fatherland Party decimated the Social Democrats in street fighting. Dollfuss was assassinated in an unsuccessful Nazi *putsch* the following July.

DÖLLINGER, Johann Joseph Ignaz von (1799–1890), German Roman Catholic historian and theologian, excommunicated (1871) for rejecting the doctrine of papal infallibility. He was professor of ecclesias-tical history and law at Munich Univ. (1826–71). His books include *The Pope and the Council* (1869), a collection of letters and articles criticizing papal authoritarianism. (See OLD CATHOLICS.)

DOLOMITES, Alpine mountain range in NE Italy mainly composed of vividly-colored dolomitic limestone. The highest peak is Marmolada (10,965ft). A popular tourist and climbing resort, its main center is Cortina d'Ampezzo.

DOLPHINS, a group of aquatic mammals. Dolphins are small-toothed WHALES living in schools and feeding mainly on fish. The largest, the KILLER WHALE, also feeds on seals. The pilot whale is another large dolphin, but the most well-known member of the family (Delphinidae) is the bottlenosed dolphin, a highly intelligent mammal with an amazingly developed system of echolocation (see ECHO) for finding food and avoiding obstacles. A second family of dolphins (Platanistidae) lives in fresh water, and includes the Chinese lake dolphin and the blind susu or Ganges dolphin. (See also PORPOISE.) The Pacific spout fish of the family Corphaenidae is also known as the dolphin. It has a blunt head and forked tail, and can swim at great speed. It is a popular Hawaiian food fish, called mahimahi. In the E Pacific dolphins often travel with schools of yellowfin tuna and are accidentally caught and killed in great numbers by tuna fishermen.

DOMAGK, Gerhard (1895–1964), German pharmacologist who discovered the antibacterial action of the dye prontosil red. This led to the discovery of other SULFA DRUGS. In recognition of this Domagk was offered the 1939 Nobel Prize for Physiology or Medicine, though the Nazi government did not allow him to accept it at the time.

DOME, in architecture, an oval or hemispherical vault, used to roof a large space without interior supports. The first domes were built around 1000 BC by the Persians and Assyrians, but these were small and the dome did not become architecturally significant until Roman times. The PANTHEON, in which the dome rests on a drum-shaped building, is an outstanding example of the large-scale dome. The Byzantine architects of HAGIA SOPHIA in Constantinople evolved the pendentive, a device enabling the construction of a great dome over a square central area. Brunelleschi's dome on the cathedral in Florence has an inner and an outer shell; Sir Christopher Wren's dome for St. Paul's, London, has three shells. Modern techniques and lightweight materials permit the spanning of vast areas, as at the Houston Astrodome. (See also GEODESIC DOME.)

DOMENICHINO (born Domenico Zampieri; 1581–1641), Italian Baroque painter from Bologna, noted for the landscape settings of his pictures. Trained by the CARRACCI brothers, he painted large fresco schemes, notably *The Life of St. Cecilia* (1613–14), in palaces and churches in Rome.

DOMESDAY BOOK, a survey of most of England compiled for William I the Conqueror in 1085–86. It describes "ploughland and habitations ... men ... both bond and free," housing conditions, services and rents owned by gentry and peasants, land values and every detail of rural economy in the years 1066–1085. It was compiled largely by itinerant commissioners with the aid of juries of inquiry. A statistical record unique in medieval Europe, it is an invaluable source for English national and local history.

DOMINGO, Placido (1941–), Spanish-born Mexican tenor. In 1961 he made his debut in Mexico as Alfredo in *La Traviata* and his US debut with the Dallas Civic Opera. He sang in Israel (1963–65), with the NY City Opera (1965–67) and joined the Metropolitan Opera in 1968.

DOMINIC, Saint (c1170–1221), Spanish churchman, founder of the DOMINICAN ORDER. From 1207 he was leader of a mission to the ALBIGENSIAN heretics of S France. In 1216 the pope approved Dominic's plans for a new preaching order based on ideals of poverty and scholarship. The order grew rapidly and Dominic spent the rest of his life supervising it. He was canonized in 1234. His feast day is Aug. 4.

DOMINICA, an independent state, is the largest island in the Windward Islands of the Lesser Antilles group, between Guadeloupe and Martinique.

Land. Dominica is crossed from N to S by a mountain range, which contains Morne Diablotin (4,747ft), the highest point in the Lesser Antilles. The climate is tropical, without great seasonal variations. Average temperature reaches 80°F and rainfall is heavy.

People and economy. Most people are Negroes or mulattoes. The rich volcanic soil produces bananas, coconuts, citrus fruits and cinnamon. Dominica also exports pumice. Tourism is not yet fully developed, but is actively encouraged by the government. Dominica's economy was badly hurt in 1979 when hurricane David destroyed almost all banana and citrus plantations.

History. Discovered by COLUMBUS in 1493

Official name: Commonwealth of Dominica
Capital: Roseau
Area: 290sq mi
Population: 87,700
Languages: English, French patois
Religions: Roman Catholic
Monetary unit(s): 1 East Caribbean dollar = 100 cents

and colonized by France in the early 17th century, Dominica was acquired by Britain in 1805 and became internally self-governing in 1967. In 1978 the island achieved full independence. In 1983 Dominica was among the Caribbean nations requesting US intervention in Grenada and sent a token force there. A 1987 proposal to join the six other members of the Organization of Eastern Caribbean States in a single nation was to be voted upon in a referendum.

DOMINICAN ORDER, officially the Order of Preachers (O.P.), Roman Catholic order of FRIARS. It was founded (1216) by St. DOMINIC, with approval from Pope Honorius III, as a band of highly trained priests, pledged to poverty, study and itinerant preaching. The first friaries were intended as hostels, not permanent residences. The "Black Friars," as they were popularly named for the black cloak they wore over their white habit while preaching, played a major role in the medieval INQUISITION and produced many great missionaries and theologians, notably AQUINAS. There were associated orders of nuns (see CATHERINE OF SIENA) and of lay men and women. The religious reformer SAVONAROLA was a Dominican.

DOMINICAN REPUBLIC, state in the eastern two-thirds of the island Hispaniola, which it shares with Haiti.

Land. Parallel mountain chains run from NW to SE. The biggest of these, the Cordillera Central, contains Pico Duarte, which at 10,490ft is the highest point in the West Indies. The main rivers (Yaque del Norte, Yaque del Sur and Yuna) rise there. To the N of the range lie the Cibao and Vega Real lowlands, the main agricultural area. The climate is subtropical, with an

Official name: Dominican Republic
Capital: Santo Domingo
Area: 18,704sq mi
Population: 6,708,000
Languages: Spanish
Religions: Roman Catholic
Monetary unit(s): 1 D.R. peso=100 centavos

annual rainfall averaging 50in. Hurricanes tend to occur between Aug. and Nov. In 1979 hurricane David devastated the island.

People. About 11% of Dominicans are black, 16% are Caucasians and 73% are of mixed blood. Slightly less than half of the people live in rural areas. About 30% of the population is illiterate.

Economy. Sugar, coffee, cocoa, tobacco and bananas are the principal crops. 75% of exports are agricultural. Industry is concentrated around the capital, and apart from agricultural processing includes cement, textile and plastic manufacture. There is also some mining of bauxite and nickel, and tourism is increasingly important.

History. Hispaniola was discovered by COLUMBUS in 1492. The E part remained Spanish, while the W part was ceded to France in 1697. After centuries of turmoil the independent Dominican Republic emerged in 1844, but continued to be torn by internal troubles under a succession of dictators and revolutions. It was occupied by the US Marines (1916–1924). In 1930 an army revolt put General TRUJILLO in power. His dictatorship ended with his assassination in 1961. Free elections followed, but the new left wing government of Juan Bosch was overthrown by a military coup in 1963. An attempt to reinstate Bosch prompted US intervention in the form of armed occupation of Santo Domingo (1965). Joaquín Balaguer served as president 1966–78 and was returned to office again in 1986.

DOMINION DAY, July 1, Canadian national holiday commemorating the creation of the independent Dominion of Canada under the BRITISH NORTH AMERICA ACT (1867).

DOMINOES, a game for two to four people, played with flat rectangular blocks usually made from wood, ivory, or bone. The game was introduced to Europe, probably from China, in the middle of the 18th century. Dominoes is normally played with a set of 28 pieces. The face of each piece is divided into two sections, each of which is either blank or has up to six dots or pips. The set of dominoes contains every possible combination of numbers from 0–0 (double blank) to 6–6 (double six). During play, each player in turn must attempt to match a number on one of the dominoes or bones in his hand with one of the two exposed ends on the table. If he fails, he must draw a further piece from the central pool, or *boneyard.* Play stops when a person has disposed of all his dominoes. A number of variations on the game have been devloped, and the number of pieces may also vary. Some Eskimo tribes gamble furiously at a game involving over 100 pieces.

DOMITIAN (51–96 AD), Roman emperor, 81–96, son of Vespasian and brother of TITUS, whom he succeeded. He governed efficiently but harshly, his last years amounting to a reign of terror. He was assassinated at the instigation of his wife.

DONATELLO (c1386–1466), Florentine sculptor, a major figure of the Italian Renaissance. He trained as a metal worker with GHIBERTI, and as a marble sculptor. His many commissions for the cathedral of Florence include the famous *putti* for the singing gallery. Other major works are *St. George Slaying the Dragon* (1415–17), the graceful bronze *David* (c1432) in the Bargello, Florence, and the equestrian statue known as the Gattamelata Monument (1447–53), in Padua.

DONATION OF CONSTANTINE, document purporting to be addressed to Pope Sylvester I by Emperor Constantine I (d. 337), but forged, probably in the 8th century. According to it, Constantine, the first Christian emperor, renounced imperial political authority over Italy and spiritual authority over the Church in favor of the pope. The forgery was exposed by the scholar Lorenzo Valla c1440, though the document's authenticity was contested on into the 18th century.

DONATISM, schism in the Christian church of North Africa during the 4th century. The event which triggered the schism occurred in 311 when Caecilian, who had renounced the church during the persecution of the Roman emperor Diocletian, was named bishop of Carthage. Donatus, who took over the leadership of the schism in 315, held that anyone who had once publicly denied the faith could not be readmitted to it, that sacraments administered by an unworthy minister were invalid, and that "sinners" could not belong to the church. Condemned by St. Augustine and later by both the synods of Aries (314) and Milan (316), the Donatists seceded to form their own church, which died out about 450.

DONG, Pham Van (1906–   ), Vietnamese political leader. A colleague of Ho Chi Minh from 1930, he was premier of North Vietnam (1955–76) and of united Vietnam (1976–81), when Vietnam became a close ally of the USSR and invaded neighboring Kampuchea.

DONIPHAN, Alexander William (1808–1887), US soldier and lawyer. In 1838, commanding the Mo. state militia, he refused orders to execute Joseph SMITH and other Mormon leaders. In 1846–47, during the Mexican War, he led his men on a celebrated long march of 3,600mi from Santa Fe, N.M., to Chihuahua, Mexico (which he captured) and then back to Mo.

DONIZETTI, Gaetano (1797–1848), Italian opera composer. Influenced by ROSSINI, he developed the traditions of serious and comic opera. His operas include *L'Elisir d'Amore* (1832) *Lucia di Lammermoor* (1835) and *Don Pasquale* (1843). He influenced VERDI.

DON JUAN, legendary libertine, often the subject of dramatic works in which, after a dissolute life, he was led off to hell. The earliest-known dramatization is TIRSO DE MOLINA's *The Rake of Seville* (1630). Other versions are by MOLIÈRE, MOZART (*Don Giovanni*), BYRON and G. B. SHAW (*Man and Superman*).

DONKEY, the domesticated form of the wild ass, it is descended from the African wild ass of Ethiopia. The donkey is related to the horse, but has long ears, a large head and a short mane, a tuft of hair on the end of the tail and no callosities on the hind legs. A dark band usually runs along the back and another over the shoulders. Crossbreeding with the horse produces the MULE or the hinny, which is sterile. It is surefooted and intelligent and much used as a pack animal.

DONNE, John (1572–1631), English METAPHYSICAL POET and divine. His love poems and religious verse and prose are characterized by sophisticated argument, complex metaphors and a passionate and direct tone. His imagery relies upon both Scholastic philosophy and 17th-century scientific thought. After a long period of exclusion from court life he took orders in 1615 and became dean of St. Paul's, London, where he gave many fine sermons.

His most famous writings are the love-lyrics *Songs and Sonnets*, and the religious works *Holy Sonnets, Sermons* and *Devotions*.

DONNELLY, Ignatius (1831–1901), US politician and writer. A Republican Congressman for Minn. 1863–69, he later led the GREENBACK PARTY and in the 1890s the Populist Party. He wrote the party platform and was the Populist nominee for vice-president in 1900. He wrote several speculative works, including the Utopian novel *Caesar's Column* (1891).

DONNER PARTY, group of 87 settlers from Ill., led by George Donner, who were trapped by snow in the Sierra Nevada, N Cal., in the winter of 1846–47. When food ran out, the surviving members resorted to cannibalism. Only about half the group were rescued.

DONOVAN, William Joseph (1881–1959), US soldier, attorney and government official. Nicknamed "Wild Bill," he won a Congressional Medal of Honor for his service in WWI. During WWII he created and headed the Office of Strategic Services (OSS), which was the forerunner of the CENTRAL INTELLIGENCE AGENCY.

DON QUIXOTE. See CERVANTES SAAVEDRA, MIGUEL DE.

DON RIVER, river in the USSR, about 1,224mi long. Rising SE of Tula (about 100mi S of Moscow) it flows SE to within 48mi of the VOLGA, to which it is linked by the Volga-Don Canal, and then SW to the Sea of Azov. It is mostly navigable and carries coal, timber and grain. The Don is rich in fish and has many fishing villages on its banks.

DOOLEY, Mr. See DUNNE, FINLEY PETER.

DOOLITTLE, Hilda (1886–1961), US poet, known as **H.D.** She lived in Europe after 1911. H.D. was one of the first IMAGISTS in America, and she continued to develop the Imagist style in her later poetry. Her works include *Sea Garden* (1916), *The Walls Do Not Fall* (1944) and the novel *Bid Me to Live* (1960).

DOOLITTLE, James Harold (1896–   ), US pilot and WWII air hero. Famous as a racing pilot in the 1920s and early 1930s, he led the first air raid on Tokyo on April 18, 1942. After the war he was an executive in the aerospace industry.

DOPPLER EFFECT, the change observed in the wavelength of a sonic, electromagnetic or other wave (see WAVE MOTION) because of relative motion between the wave source and an observer. As a wave source approaches an observer, each pulse of the wave is closer behind the previous one than it would be were the source at rest relative to the observer. This is perceived as an increase in frequency, the pitch of a sound source seeming higher, the color of a light source bluer. When a sound source achieves the speed of sound, a SONIC BOOM results. As a wave source recedes from an observer, each pulse is emitted farther away from him than it would otherwise be. There is hence a drop in pitch or a reddening in COLOR (see LIGHT; SPECTRUM). The Doppler Effect, named for **Christian Johann Doppler** (1803–1853) who first described it in 1842, is of paramount importance in astronomy. Observations of stellar spectra can determine the rates at which stars are moving towards or away from us, while observed red shifts in the spectra of distant galaxies are generally interpreted as an indication that the universe as a whole is expanding.

DORÉ, Gustave (1832–1883), French engraver, illustrator and painter. He created dreamlike, grandiose scenes in a fantastic, bizarre style and is known especially for line engravings of unusual power provided for editions of Balzac's *Contes Drolatiques* (1855), Dante's *Inferno* (1861), Cervantes' *Don Quixote* (1863) and the Bible (1866).

DORIA, Andrea (1466–1560), Italian statesman. In the ITALIAN WARS of the 16th century he fought for both FRANCIS I of France and then Emperor CHARLES V, preserving the independence of his native Genoa. He gave Genoa a new republican constitution, but ruled as a dictator to suppress factional strife.

DORIANS, people of ancient Greece. Originating from the lower Balkans, they probably defeated the ACHAEANS and conquered the Peloponnese between 1100 and 950 BC, subsequently extending their influence to the Aegean Islands, Crete, Sicily and parts of Asia Minor, Africa and Italy.

DORR, Thomas Wilson (1805–1854), US constitutional reformer and leader of Dorr's Rebellion. Elected to the R.I. state legislature in 1834, he became head of a popular party agitating for the extension of voting rights. In 1842 the R.I. state legislature and Dorr's party formed separate administrations, but Dorr's administration collapsed after an armed confrontation. He was jailed for treason 1844–45.

DORSEY, Jimmy (1904–1957) and **Tommy** (1905–1956), US swing musicians and band leaders. Jimmy, a clarinetist, and Tommy, a trombonist, together and separately led some of the most popular dance bands of the 1930s and 1940s, the "big band" era.

DOS PASSOS, John (Roderigo) (1896–1970), US novelist and writer of American social history. His trilogy, *U.S.A.* (1937), depicts 20th-century American life up to 1929, making use of innovative, collage-like reportage techniques. Other works are *Manhattan Transfer* (1925), *District of Columbia* (a trilogy; 1952) and *Midcentury* (1961).

DOSTOYEVSKY, Fyodor Mikhailovich (1821–1881), major Russian novelist. He spent several years in the army but resigned his commission in 1844 to devote himself to writing. Arrested in 1849 as a member of a socialist circle, Dostoyevsky was condemned to be shot; however, the sentence was commuted in the execution yard to four years' hard labor in Siberia. During the 1860s he founded two journals and traveled in Europe after his consumptive wife and his brother had died, and after he had incurred large gambling debts. He did not finally return to Russia until 1871. In 1876 he edited his own monthly *The Writer's Diary*. Suffering from epilepsy for most of his life, he died after an epileptic attack. Dostoyevsky's major novels, *Crime and Punishment* (1866), *The Idiot* (1868), *The Devils* (1871–72) and *The Brothers Karamazov* (1879–80), reveal his deep understanding of the complex psychology of human character and the problems of sin and suffering.

DOU, Gerard (1613–1675), Dutch painter. His father, a glass painter, first apprenticed him to an engraver, and he later (1628–1631) became a pupil of REMBRANDT. Dou developed the tradition of small, minutely finished pictures, with enamel-like surfaces, painting GENRE scenes, portraits, still lifes and landscapes.

DOUAY BIBLE, first official Roman Catholic English version of the Bible. It was translated from St. JEROME'S Latin VULGATE Bible by English Catholics exiled in Douai, N France. The New Testament was published in 1582, the Old Testament in 1609–10. The translation was revised by Bishop Challoner 1749–72.

DOUBLE-BASS, stringed musical instrument, contrabass of the violin family. About 6ft high, it has four strings tuned in fourths; a fifth string or an extension at the neck is sometimes added. The double-bass is usually bowed, but jazz basses are plucked.

DOUBLEDAY, Abner (1819–1893), US Union general, credited with the invention of baseball in 1839 at Cooperstown, N.Y. He fired the first Union gun in defense of Fort Sumter and was a hero of the Battle of Gettysburg.

DOUBLE JEOPARDY, principle embodied in the 5th Amendment of the US

Constitution, protecting a person against being tried twice on the same charge. The US Supreme Court, in *Benton v. Maryland* (1969), held that this principle was applicable to the states through the "due process" clause of the 14th Amendment. Neither federal nor state officers can appeal a verdict of acquittal, but the accused may appeal a verdict of guilty.

DOUBLE STAR or **binary star**, a pair of stars revolving around a common center of gravity. Less frequently the term "double star" is applied to two stars that merely appear close together in the sky, though in reality at quite different distances from the earth (optical pairs), or to two stars whose motions are linked but which do not orbit each other (physical pair). About 50% of all stars are members of either binary or multiple star systems, in which there are more than two components. It is thought that the components of binary and multiple star systems are formed simultaneously. **Visual binaries** are those which can be seen telescopically to be double. There are comparatively few visual binaries, since the distances between components are small relative to interstellar distances, but examples are Capella, Procyon, SIRIUS and Alpha Centauri. **Spectroscopic binaries**, while unable to be seen telescopically as doubles, can be detected by RED SHIFTS in their spectra, their orbit making each component alternately approach and recede from us. **Eclipsing binaries** are those whose components, due to the orientation of their orbit, periodically mutually eclipse each other as seen from the earth.

DOUGHTY, Charles Montagu (1843–1926), English writer, traveler and poet. *Travels in Arabia Deserta* (1888), written in Elizabethan style, describes his experiences living and traveling in Arabia in the mid-1870s.

DOUGHTY, Thomas (1793–1856), US landscape painter, a founder of the HUDSON RIVER SCHOOL. His pictures of woodlands, river valleys and lakes have a silvery light. Among his works are *On the Hudson* and *A River Glimpse*.

DOUGLAS, Donald Wills (1892–1981), US aircraft designer and manufacturer. Douglas Aircraft's twin-engine DC-3 (1936) was the most successful transport plane of the piston era. The company merged (1967) with McDonnell Aircraft.

DOUGLAS, Lloyd Cassel (1877–1951), US clergyman and author. His first novel, *Magnificent Obsession* (1929), was followed by other extremely popular works. *The Robe* (1942) was on bestseller lists for three years.

DOUGLAS, Stephen Arnold (1813–1861), US politician, affectionately known as the "Little Giant." He is remembered for his debates with Abraham Lincoln in the Ill. Senate elections (1858) which brought Lincoln to national attention. He was a Democratic congressman from Ill. 1843–47, and senator 1847–61. Involved in the issue of slavery in the new states, he helped draft the COMPROMISE OF 1850, based on SQUATTER SOVEREIGNTY, and the KANSAS-NEBRASKA ACT (1854). In 1860 he was the unsuccessful Democratic presidential candidate, but later supported Lincoln and the Union.

DOUGLAS, William Orville (1898–1980), justice of the US Supreme Court 1939–1975, longer than any other justice. An expert on business law, he had been chairman of the SECURITIES AND EXCHANGE COMMISSION. As a justice, he favored a broad exercise of court powers and was an ardent defender of civil rights and free speech. He wrote some 30 books, many defending nature and wilderness.

DOUGLAS-HOME, Alec (1903–   ), British Conservative prime minister 1963–64. After being foreign secretary 1960–63, he renounced six peerages in order to sit in the House of Commons while serving as prime minister. He followed a moderate anticommunist policy and achieved some compromise on Commonwealth racial issues. After serving again as foreign secretary 1970–74 he received a life peerage.

DOUGLASS, Frederick (1817–1895), US escaped slave (born Frederick Augustus Washington Bailey) who became a leading abolitionist and orator. He lectured for an antislavery society in Mass. and published *The Narrative of the Life of Frederick Douglass* (1845). He campaigned in England, purchased his freedom and returned to establish his own newspaper, *North Star*, in Rochester, N.Y. In the Civil War he recruited Negroes for the North, and during Reconstruction pressed for Negro civil rights. He held various federal posts and was US minister to Haiti 1889–91.

DOUKHOBORS, Russian pacifist religious sect, now settled in Canada. Founded in the 18th century, the sect rejected all forms of religious, ecclesiastical and secular authority in favor of individual direct revelation. The Doukhobors were often exiled and persecuted by the tsars. In 1898, assisted by their leader Peter Verigin and by Leo TOLSTOY, over 7,000 emigrated to Saskatchewan, some moving later to British Columbia. Their communities have developed economically, but there has been continuous trouble with the Canadian government, particularly from the extremist splinter group, Sons of Freedom, over issues of technology and compulsory education.

DOVE, Arthur Garfield (1880–1946), US painter, a precursor of the abstract expressionists.

DOVER, Strait of, narrow passage separating SE England from N France, connecting the English Channel with the North Sea. It is around 19mi across at its narrowest point. The chief ports are Dover, Folkestone, Calais and Boulogne. Of great strategic importance, the strait was the scene of the first repulse of the Spanish ARMADA (1588), the Dover (antisubmarine) Patrol of WWI and the evacuation from DUNKERQUE (1940). The strait is frequently crossed by long-distance swimmers.

DOW, Charles Henry (1851–1902), US journalist who, with Edward D. Jones, founded (1882) a financial news service, Dow Jones & Company. From 1889 the company published the *Wall Street Journal*, of which Dow was the editor. Dow also developed the index of stock prices known as the DOW-JONES INDUSTRIAL AVERAGE.

DOW, Herbert Henry (1866–1930), US chemist and industrialist. Successful at extracting chemicals and metals from brine, he founded (1897) the Dow Chemical Company, which became a giant in the industry.

DOW JONES INDUSTRIAL AVERAGE, the most frequently cited gauge of US stock market performance. Compiled since 1884, the Dow Jones Industrial Average is a composite of the prices of 30 leading industrial stocks. In addition, Dow Jones compiles a Transportation Average (20 stocks), a Utility Average (15 stocks) and a Combined Average (all 65). Other key market indicators are Standard and Poor's Stock Prices (500 issues) and the New York Stock Exchange Price Index (all stocks traded on the exchange).

DOWLAND, John (c1563–1626), English composer and lutenist, best known for his songs and the collection of lute pieces *Lachrimae* (1604). He traveled to France, Italy, Germany and Denmark in the service of various kings and princes. From 1612, he served in the court of James I.

DOWNING STREET, in Westminster, London, location of the British Foreign Office and of the prime minister's residence (No. 10) since the 18th century.

DOWN'S SYNDROME, congenital mental and physical retardation caused by an extra chromosome. The condition, also called Mongolism, is characterized by a flat face and epicanthic folds. Women over 35 are at greater risk than younger ones of giving birth to Down's syndrome children. Amniocentesis permits detection of the condition in the fetus.

DOWSON, Ernest Christopher (1867–1900), English poet, one of the so-called decadents of the 1890s. From a life of misery and squalor he produced a delicate, mellifluous poetry on themes of love and lost childhood. He influenced the early work of W. B. YEATS.

DOYLE, Sir Arthur Conan (1859–1930), British writer, creator of the detective Sherlock Holmes, in many short stories and four novels. A doctor, soldier and campaigner for law reform, he also wrote historical novels such as *Micah Clarke* (1889) and science fiction, as in *The Lost World* (1912). In later life he became an adherent of spiritualism.

D'OYLY CARTE, Richard (1844–1901), English impresario who produced GILBERT and SULLIVAN's first operetta *Trial by Jury*, in 1875. In 1878 he founded the D'Oyly Carte Opera Company, and in 1881 built the Savoy Theatre, London, as a stage for works by Gilbert and Sullivan.

DRACO (7th century BC), lawgiver in Athens. His code (c621 BC) made both serious and trivial crimes punishable by death—hence the term "Draconian" to describe any harsh legal measure. SOLON later repealed all the laws except those dealing with homicide.

DRACULA, in the book of that name by Bram STOKER, a Transylvanian VAMPIRE count, subject of many horror films. The name, meaning "demon," was applied to Vlad IV the Impaler, a 15th-century Walachian prince upon whom Stoker based the character.

DRAFT, Military, or conscription, system of raising armed forces by compulsory recruitment. The modern practice is more aptly described as selective service. Obligatory military service dates back to ancient times, but conscription as we know it began to evolve only in the late 18th century when, in France, Napoleon I imposed universal conscription of able-bodied males. Conscription in Prussia 1807–13 was used to build up large reserves of trained men. Peacetime conscription became standard practice in the 19th century, except in Britain where it was not imposed until prior to WWII (wartime conscription was practiced in both Britain and the US during WWI). During the American Civil War both North and South used conscription, but mainly to encourage volunteering. In the US peacetime conscription was first introduced in 1940 and, though dropped briefly in 1947, continued through to 1973 to meet the demands of the Korean and then the Vietnamese commitment. Conscription has frequently given rise to civil protest. During Johnson's presidency (1963–69), anti-draft demonstrations, with mass burning of draft cards, became a popular form of protest against involvement in Vietnam. In June 1980, President Carter reinstated the Selective Service System, which had been in a "standby" position since the start of the ALL VOLUNTEER FORCE in 1973. U.S. males born in 1960 or later and at least 18, including citizens, resident aliens and conditional entrants to the US, were required to register with the Service through the post office. In 1981 the US Supreme Court ruled that Congress could constitutionally exclude women from the draft. (See also CONSCIENTIOUS OBJECTOR; IMPRESSMENT.)

DRAFT RIOTS, in the American Civil War, violent protests against the Union Conscription Act (1863), which permitted a drafted man to avoid service by providing a substitute or paying $300. Mobs ruled New York City July 13–16, during which time blacks and abolitionists were murdered and arson and looting were widespread. Order was eventually restored by army, navy, militia, and police forces, and the draft was peacefully resumed in August.

DRAGON (from Greek *drakōn*, serpent), legendary monster, usually represented as a fire-breathing, winged serpent or lizard, with crested head and large claws. Apart from the wingless Chinese and Japanese dragons, which were beneficent, dragons were usually regarded as symbols of evil, and dragon-slayers, for example Saint GEORGE, as saints and heroes.

DRAGONFLIES, beautiful and predatory flying insects, readily identifiable by the long, slender abdomen, two pairs of transparent wings, each covered in a network of veins, and large compound eyes which may contain 30,000 separate facets. Dragonflies are superb fliers, some being credited with speeds of 60 mph, and can dart forward, hover, then shoot forward again with the greatest of ease. Each dragonfly patrols an area, usually near water, where it feeds on insects. The eggs are laid in water and the nymphs live under water for a year or more. They have gills inside the intestine and can shoot water out of the rectum in a form of jet propulsion. The food of the nymphs is small animals

which are caught in an extensible hooked "mask." They are sometimes pests of fish hatcheries.

The largest dragonfly, which lives in Borneo, has a 7in wingspan, but fossilized remains have been found of a crow-sized dragonfly with a 27in wingspan.

DRAKE, Sir Francis (c1543–1596), English admiral and explorer, the first Englishman to sail around the world (1577–80). During his circumnavigation aboard the *Golden Hind*, Drake seized a fortune in booty from Spanish settlements along the South American Pacific coast. He was knighted on his return by Queen Elizabeth I. In 1587 he destroyed a large part of the Spanish fleet at anchor in Cadiz harbor. The following year he was joint commander of the English fleet which, with the help of a storm, dispersed and destroyed the Spanish ARMADA.

DRAMA. See THEATER.

DRAVIDIANS, subgroup of the Hindu race, some 100,000,000 people of (mainly) S India. They are fairly dark-skinned, stocky, have rather more NEGROID features than other Indics, and are commonly dolichocephalic. (See also RACE.) The **Dravidian languages** are a family of some 22 languages, perhaps the most important from a philological point of view being Tamil, texts in which date back to at least the 1st century BC (see also PHILOLOGY).

DRAWING, the art of delineating figures, objects or patterns on a surface, usually paper. Two general types of medium are used: dry mediums such as graphite, metalpoint, charcoal, chalks and crayons, and wet mediums, inks and washes, applied by pen or brush. Drawings have traditionally served as preparatory studies for paintings, sculptures or works of architecture. Artists like the 13th-century architect Villiard d'Honnecourt or the Renaissance painter PISANELLO drew and collected together many detailed studies for use in other works. LEONARDO DA VINCI drew to create and elaborate his artistic ideas, and like RAPHAEL, DÜRER, MICHELANGELO and REMBRANDT made drawing an art form in its own right. During the 17th century, drawing evolved into an important artistic discipline. In the 19th century, INGRES was a major exponent of this discipline. Modern masters of drawing include PICASSO, KLEE and MATISSE.

DREADNOUGHT, British battleship (1906) of revolutionary design. Weighing 18,000 tons and capable of traveling at 21 knots, the *Dreadnought* carried ten 12in guns. At the time of her completion there was nothing afloat to match her for speed and firepower. By the outbreak of WWI nine *Dreadnought*-class ships and 12 other big-gun battleships were in service in the British navy.

DREAMS, fantasies, usually visual, experienced during sleep and in certain other situations. About 25% of an adult's sleeping time is characterized by rapid eye movements (REM) and brain waves that, registered on the ELECTROENCEPHALOGRAPH, resemble those of a person awake (EEG). This REM-EEG state occurs in a number of short periods during sleep, each lasting a number of minutes, the first coming some 90min after sleep starts and the remainder occurring at intervals of roughly 90min. It would appear that it is during these periods that dreams take place, since people woken during a REM-EEG period will report and recall visual dreams in some 80% of cases; people woken at other times report dreams only about 40% of the time, and of far less visual vividness. Observation of similar states in animals suggests that at least all mammals experience dreams. Dreams can also occur, though in a limited way, while falling asleep; the origin and nature of these is not known. **Dream interpretation** seems as old as recorded history. Until the mid-19th century dreams were regarded as supernatural, often prophetic; their possible prophetic nature has been examined in this century by, among others, J. W. Dunne. According to FREUD, dreams have a *latent content* (the fulfilment of an individual's particular UNCONSCIOUS wish) which is converted by *dreamwork* into *manifest content* (the dream as experienced). In these terms, interpretation reverses the dreamwork process.

DRED SCOTT CASE, suit brought by Scott, a slave from Mo., on the grounds that temporary residence in a territory in which slavery was banned under the MISSOURI COMPROMISE had made him free. The majority opinion of the US Supreme Court in 1857, read by Chief Justice TANEY, held that Scott, as an African Negro, could never be a citizen of any state, and therefore could not sue his owner in federal court. Taney should have ended his opinion here but, instead, plunged on to declare that even if Scott could sue, his sojurn in free territory did not make him free because Congress' ban on slavery in the Missouri Compromise was unconstitutional; furthermore, said Taney, Congress had no power to keep slavery out of any US territory. This decision inflamed and divided the nation, making the Civil War all but inevitable.

DREISER, Theodore (1871–1945), US novelist whose naturalistic fiction, concerned with the dispossessed and criminal, dealt with the grimmer realities of American life. Dreiser's work, often artistically raw, has at its best a massive energy and power. His novels include *Sister Carrie* (1900) and *An American Tragedy* (1925).

DRESDEN CHINA, also known as Meissen ware, after the town near Dresden where china has been made since 1710. Europe's first true porcelain, the process of its manufacture was discovered by Johann Friedrich Böttger c1707. (See POTTERY AND PORCELAIN.)

DRESS. See FASHION.

DREW, Charles Richard (1904–1950), black US physician, surgeon and medical researcher who founded the American Red Cross blood bank.

DREW, Daniel (1797–1879), US financier, notorious for his speculative dealing in connection with the Erie railroad, of which he became a director (1857). With Jay GOULD and James FISK, Drew conspired to thwart the ambitions of Cornelius VANDERBILT.

DREYFUS AFFAIR, notorious French political scandal of the Third Republic. In 1894, Alfred Dreyfus (1859–1935), a Jewish army captain, was convicted of betraying French secrets to the Germans. Further evidence pointed to a Major Esterhazy as the traitor; but when tried (Jan. 1898), he was acquitted on further secret, and forged, evidence. Dreyfus' conviction had aroused ANTI-SEMITISM; and although evidence against him had been forged, the army was reluctant to admit error. As public interest in the case was aroused, it became known that the Roman Catholic Church supported the conviction. After Esterhazy's acquittal, Émile ZOLA published an attack on the army's integrity, *J'accuse*, which roused intellectual and liberal opinion to a furor. With the suicide of an army officer who acknowledged the forgeries and Esterhazy's flight from France, a new trial began, but Dreyfus was found "guilty with extenuating circumstances" (Aug. 1899). Public opinion was outraged, and in Sept. the government gave him a pardon. He served in WWI and retired a lieutenant-colonel. The scandal had thrown the government, army and Church into disrepute. Legislation followed which led to separation of Church and State (1905). The original verdict against Dreyfus was quashed in 1906.

DRILLS, tools for cutting or enlarging holes in hard materials. There are two classes: those that have a rotary action, with a cutting edge or edges at the point and, usually, helical fluting along the shank; and those that work by percussive action, where repeated blows drive the drill into the material. **Rotary drills** are commonly used in the home for wood, plastic, masonry and sometimes metal. They are usually hand-turned, though electric motors are increasingly used to power drills in home workshops. In metallurgy the mechanical drilling machine or *drill press* is one of the most important machine tools, operating one or several drills at a time. As great heat is generated, LUBRICATION is very important. Most metallurgical drills are of high-speed STEEL. Dentists' drills rotate at extremely high speeds, their tips (of TUNGSTEN carbide or DIAMOND) being water-cooled: they are powered by an electric motor or by compressed air. Rotary drills are used for deeper oil-well drilling: a cutting bit is rotated at the end of a long, hollow drill pipe, new sections of pipe being added as drilling proceeds. **Percussive drills** are used for rock-boring, for concrete and masonry, and for shallower oil-well drilling. Rock drills are generally powered by compressed air, the tool rotating after each blow to increase cutting speed. The pneumatic drill familiar in city streets is also operated by compressed air. *Ultrasonic drills* are used for brittle materials; a rod, attached to a transducer, is placed against the surface, and to it are fed ABRASIVE particles suspended in a cooling fluid. It is these particles that actually perform the cutting. (See also ULTRASONICS.)

DROMEDARY. See CAMEL.

DROPSY. See EDEMA.

DROWNING, immersion in water causing DEATH by asphyxia, metabolic or blood disturbance, following inhalation of water. On immersion, reflex breath-holding occurs but is eventually overcome; if immersion continues, water is taken into the lungs. Spasm of the larynx leads to further asphyxia and abnormal heart rhythm. If death does not follow, water absorbed from the lungs alters the mineral concentration of blood, and red blood cells may be damaged. Acidosis, lung edema and distension of stomach may occur. Prompt resuscitation at an early stage by clearing the airway, ARTIFICIAL RESPIRATION and, if necessary, cardiac massage and correction of blood abnormalities, may be successful.

DRUG ADDICTION, an uncontrollable craving for a particular DRUG, usually a narcotic, which develops into a physiological or sometimes merely psychological dependence on it. Generally the individual acquires greater tolerance for the drug, and therefore requires larger and larger doses,

to the point where he may take doses that would be fatal to the nonaddict. Should his supply be cut off he will suffer **withdrawal symptoms** ("cold turkey") which are psychologically grueling and often physically debilitating to the point where death may result. Many drugs, such as ALCOHOL and TOBACCO, are not addictive in the strictest sense but more correctly habit forming (but see ALCOHOLISM). Others, such as the OPIUM derivatives, particularly HEROIN and MORPHINE, are extremely addictive. With others, such as LSD (and most other HALLUCINOGENIC DRUGS), COCAINE, HEMP and the AMPHETAMINES, the situation is unclear: dependence may be purely psychological, but it may be that these drugs interfere with the chemistry of the BRAIN; for example, the hallucinogen MESCALINE is closely related to ADRENALINE. The situation is even less clear with such drugs as MARIJUANA which appear to be neither addictive nor habit forming but nevertheless constitute a health problem. An inability to abstain from regular self-dosage with a drug is described as a **drug habit.** In the 1980s an inexpensive, highly addictive cocaine derivative, CRACK, threatened to overwhelm the nation's public-health and law-enforcement agencies. (See also WAR ON DRUGS.)

DRUG ENFORCEMENT ADMINISTRATION (DEA), federal agency created in 1973 to enforce narcotics laws. It concentrates on high-level narcotics smuggling and distribution in the US and abroad, working closely with such agencies as the Customs Service, the Internal Revenue Service, and the Coast Guard. In 1982 the US attorney general gave the FEDERAL BUREAU OF INVESTIGATION (FBI) concurrent jurisdiction with DEA over drug offenses. The DEA's administrator reports to the director of the FBI, and DEA agents work side by side with FBI agents in major drug cases.

DRUGS, chemical agents that affect biological systems. In general they are taken to treat or prevent disease, but certain drugs, such as the OPIUM narcotics, AMPHETAMINES, BARBITURATES and cannabis, are taken for their psychological effects and are drugs of addiction or abuse (see DRUG ADDICTION). Many drugs are the same as or similar to chemicals occurring naturally in the body and are used either to replace the natural substance (e.g., THYROID hormone) when deficient, or to induce effects that occur with abnormal concentrations as with STEROIDS or oral contraceptives. Other agents are known to interfere with a specific mechanism or antagonize a normal process (e.g., atropine, CURARE). Many other drugs are obtained from other biological systems; FUNGI or BACTERIA (ANTIBIOTICS) or plants (DIGITALIS), and several others are chemical modifications of natural products. In addition, there are a number of entirely synthetic drugs (e.g., barbiturates), some of which are based on active parts of naturally occurring drugs (as with some antimalarials based on QUININE).

In devising drugs for treating common conditions, an especially desirable factor is that the drug should be capable of being taken by mouth; that is, that it should be able to pass into the body unchanged in spite of being exposed to STOMACH acidity and the ENZYMES of the DIGESTIVE SYSTEM. In many cases this is possible, but there are some important exceptions, as with INSULIN, which has to be given by injection. This method may also be necessary if vomiting or GASTROINTESTINAL-TRACT disease prevent normal absorption. In most cases, the level of the drug in the BLOOD or tissues determines its effectiveness. Factors affecting this include: the route of administration; the rate of distribution in the body; the degree of binding to PLASMA PROTEINS or FAT; the rates of breakdown (e.g., by the LIVER) and excretion (e.g., by the KIDNEYS); the effect of disease on the organs concerned with excretion, and interactions with other drugs taken at the same time. There is also an individual variation in drug responsiveness which is also apparent with undesired **side-effects**. These arise because drugs acting on one system commonly act on others. Side effects may be nonspecific (nausea, DIARRHEA, malaise or SKIN rashes); allergic (HIVES, anaphylaxis), or specific to a drug (abnormal HEART rhythm with digitalis). Mild side effects may be suppressed, but others must be watched for and the drug stopped at the first sign of any adverse effect. Drugs may cross the placenta to reach the FETUS during PREGNANCY, interfering with its development and perhaps causing deformity as happens with THALIDOMIDE.

Drugs may be used for symptomatic relief (ANALGESICS, antiemetics) or to control a disease. This can be accomplished by killing the infecting agents; by preventing specific infections; by restoring normal control over MUSCLE (anti-Parkinsonian agents) or mind (ANTIDEPRESSANTS); by replacing a lost function or supplying a deficiency (e.g., VITAMIN B_{12} in pernicious ANEMIA); by suppressing inflammatory responses (steroids, ASPIRIN); by improving the functioning of an organ (digitalis); by protecting a diseased organ by altering the function of a normal one (e.g., DIURETICS for heart failure), or by toxic actions on CANCER cells (cancer CHEMOTHERAPY). The scientific study of drugs is the province of PHARMACOLOGY.

DRUGS, War on. See WAR ON DRUGS.

DRUIDS, ancient Celtic priestly order in Gaul (France), Britain and Ireland, respected for their learning in astronomy, law and medicine, for their gift of prophecy and as lawgivers and leaders. Little is known of their religious rites, though human sacrifice may have been involved. Because of their power, they were banned by the Romans.

DRUM, musical instrument of the percussion family, common to most cultures. It consists of a shell, usually cylindrical, with a membrane, or skin, stretched over one or both ends. The skin is struck with the hand or with sticks. The principal drum in the symphony orchestra is the kettledrum, or tympanum (see TIMPANI). Other types include the tenor, snare and bass drums. The last two also figure in jazz, where they are important in the rhythm section.

DRUNKENNESS. See INTOXICATION.

DRUZES or **DRUSES**, Islamic sect of about 300,000 living in Lebanon, Syria, Israel and the US. They form a closed community, and most of their doctrines are jealously guarded secrets. They have their own scriptures, and profess MONOTHEISM and the divinity of al-Hakim, 6th caliph (996–1021) of the Egyptian Fatimid dynasty.

DRYDEN, John (1631–1700), English poet and dramatist, also considered the father of English literary criticism. Dryden's career began around the time of the RESTORATION (1660). He became Poet Laureate in 1668 and Historiographer Royal in 1670. One of his best-known plays is *All for Love* (1677); his famous critical *Essay of Dramatick Poesie* appeared in 1668. *Absalom and Achitophel* (1681) and *Mac Flecknoe* (1682) are brilliant satirical poems. After the accession of William of Orange, Dryden worked largely on translations, notably of Vergil (1697).

DUALISM, any religious or philosophical system characterized by a fundamental opposition of two independent or complementary principles. Among religious dualisms are the unending conflict of good and evil spirits envisaged in ZOROASTRIANISM and the opposition of light and darkness in Jewish apocalyptic, GNOSTICISM and MANICHAEISM. The Chinese complementary principles of *yin* and *yang* exemplify a cosmological dualism while the mind–body dualism of DESCARTES is the best-known philosophical type. Dualism is often opposed to MONISM and pluralism.

DUARTE, José Napoléon (1926–   ), Salvadoran politician. Leader of the reformist Christian Democratic Party, he was elected president in 1972 but forced into exile by the army. After a coup in 1979, Duarte returned, headed the civilian-military government, and in 1984 was elected president. He received US economic and military air but was paralyzed by a guerrilla insurgency on the left and uncompromising anticommunists on the right whose death squads committed numberless atrocities. In 1988 he developed terminal cancer.

DUBAI, one of the sheikhdoms of the UNITED ARAB EMIRATES which extends about 45mi along the Persian Gulf, bordered on the S and W by Abu Dhabi. Over 90% of the population live in the capital, Dubai, a port with an international airport and a commercial center. Oil, shipbuilding, and aluminum production are mainstays of the economy. Pop 265,702.

DU BARRY, Marie Jeanne Bécu, Countess (1743–1793), the last mistress of LOUIS XV of France. Her years as mistress (1769–74) were marked by her generosity and good nature but little political influence. She was executed in Paris for coming out of retirement to aid royalist émigrés during the French Revolution.

DUBČEK, Alexander (1921–   ), Czechoslovak statesman. As first secretary of the Communist Party in 1968, he led popular measures to liberalize and "de-Stalinize" communism in Czechoslovakia. But USSR and Warsaw Pact forces invaded and put an end to hopes for "socialism with a human face." In 1975 Dubček was expelled from the Communist Party.

DUBINSKY, David (1892–1982), Russian-born US labor leader; president of the International Ladies Garment Workers Union (1932–66). Known for combating Communist and underworld infiltration of the union, he negotiated increased benefits for its members. He was also a founder of New York's Liberal Party (1944) and a vice-president of the AFL-CIO (1955–66).

DUBLIN, capital of the Irish Republic (Eire) and of County Dublin. Located at the mouth of the Liffey R and Dublin Bay on the Irish Sea, Dublin is the political and cultural center of Ireland. Its fine buildings include the Four Courts, the Custom House, Trinity College, the National Library, Museum and Gallery and the Royal Irish Academy, in addition to many Georgian streets and squares. There is also a famous medical center and zoological gardens dating from 1830, as well as the Abbey Theatre and University College. English rule, which severely restricted Dublin's commercial development, was finally removed after the EASTER RISING (1916) and the establishment of the Irish Free State (1921). Dublin is an industrial seaport and the city manufactures stout, whiskey and textiles. There is a direct rail and steamer link to London. Pop (city) 525,360; (metro) 915,115.

DU BOIS, William Edward Burghardt (1868–1963), US black educator and author, who helped transform the Negro view of the black man's role in America. Professor of economics and history at Atlanta U., 1897–1910, and head of its sociology department, 1934–44, he wrote *The Philadelphia Negro* (1899), *The Souls of Black Folk* (1903) and *Black Reconstruction* (1935). A hero of black intellectuals, he became increasingly alienated from the US and died in Ghana in self-imposed exile.

DUBOS, René Jules (1901–1982), French-born US microbiologist who discovered tyrothricin (1939), the first ANTIBIOTIC to be used clinically. He wrote more than 30 books, including *So Human an Animal* (Pulitzer Prize; 1969), and founded the René Dubos Center for Human Environments.

DUBUFFET, Jean (1901–1985), French artist influenced by spontaneous, primitive amateur art, known as *art brut* ("raw art"). He used gravel, tar etc. to produce fantastic impasto paintings that constitute fierce protests against conventional esthetic criteria.

DUCCIO DI BUONINSEGNA (c1255–c1319), Italian painter, first great master of the Sienese school. Combining Byzantine austerity with French Gothic grace, Duccio's work strongly influenced the development of Renaissance painting. The altarpiece *Maestà* is regarded as his masterpiece.

DUCHAMP, Marcel (1887–1968), French artist, a pioneer of DADA, CUBISM and FUTURISM, initially influenced by CÉZANNE. His *Nude Descending a Staircase* shocked the American public in 1913. Having settled in New York in 1915, he abandoned art for chess in 1923 and became an American citizen in 1955.

DUCHAMP-VILLON, Raymond (1876–1918), French sculptor whose concern with the fluidity of motion and the dissection of a dynamic figure into its component parts can be seen in his bust of Baudelaire and his studies of human and animal forms. His work influenced the later cubist sculptors.

DUCKS, aquatic birds comprising most of the smaller members of the family Anatidae, which also contains the GEESE and SWANS. The word "duck" also is used to describe the females of many members of the Anatidae, the males being called drakes. Ducks are, broadly, of two types: surface-feeding or dabbling, and diving ducks. The most familiar ducks are dabblers and include the mallard which is found throughout the N Hemisphere and is the ancestor of the domestic duck. Many ducks are killed for sport and food. Their down, particularly that of the eider, is of commercial importance.

DUEL, a prearranged armed combat between two persons, usually in the presence of witnesses, for the purpose of deciding a quarrel, avenging an insult (real or imagined), or vindicating the honor of one of the combatants or of a third party. While the purpose in modern times was seldom to kill the opponent, deaths did occur; and public outrage has resulted in the banning of duels in most modern nations. Swords or pistols were the customary weapons, and the person challenged had the choice of weapons.

The earliest form of duel was trial by battle, which probably originated among the Germanic tribes and became established in Europe in the early Middle Ages. If a man alleged in the presence of a judge that another had committed a crime, and the other denied it, the judge ordered them to meet in a duel. The accuser threw down a quantlet, which the opponent picked up as a sign of acceptance of the duel. Since God supposedly defended the right cause, the loser of the duel (if still alive) was executed in criminal cases or otherwise penalized in civil claims. In the 9th century, Pope Nicholas I proclaimed trial by battle to be legitimate. Judicial duels died out in France in the 16th century, but one took place in England as late as 1818.

Private duels or duels of honor were particularly common in France; and participants were often killed. Henry IV's edict of 1602 declared persons fighting unauthorized duels guilty of treason. But dueling remained popular, and duels for political reasons were frequent during the 19th century.

The most famous duels in the United States took place in 1804, when Aaron BURR killed Alexander HAMILTON, and in 1820, when James BARRON killed Stephen DECATUR. By the time of the Civil War the practice had ended.

DUE PROCESS, constitutional guarantee of fairness in the administration of justice. This concept can be traced back to MAGNA CARTA, and is embodied in the 5th Amendment to the US Constitution: "No person shall be . . . deprived of life, liberty or property without due process of law." The 14th Amendment extended this limitation on the federal government to include the states. Due process has two aspects. *Procedural* due process guarantees fair trial in the courts, and *substantive* due process places limitations on the content of law. It is under this latter heading that the Supreme Court has struck down many state laws restricting civil liberties as infringements of the Bill of Rights. (See also UNITED STATES CONSTITUTION.)

DUFAY, Guillaume (c1400–1474), Flemish composer, the greatest of his period. Attached to Cambrai Cathedral from 1445, he wrote church music and songs, developing the mass in a graceful, expressive style, much influenced by John DUNSTABLE.

DUFY, Raoul (1877–1953), French painter influenced by FAUVISM, CUBISM and the works of CÉZANNE. He is best known for lively sporting scenes in brilliant colors executed with great dash.

DUHAMEL, Georges (1884–1966), French writer who stressed human values and distrusted material progress. Works include war stories and two cycles of novels: *Salavin* (1920–32) and *The Pasquier Chronicle* (1933–45).

DUKAKIS, Michael Stanley (1933–   ), US politician, Democratic governor of Massachusetts (1975–79, 1983–   ). In 1979–82 he taught at the Kennedy School of Government at Harvard U. He was the unsuccessful Democratic candidate for president in 1988.

DUKAS, Paul Abraham (1865–1935), French composer of the colorful orchestral piece, *The Sorcerer's Apprentice.* He also wrote a symphony, a ballet, an opera and piano works.

DUKE, James Buchanan (1856–1925), US industrialist and philanthropist, member of a family with expanding tobacco interests. In 1890 he became president of the powerful merger-built American Tobacco Company. He helped found Duke U. in N.C. and endowed colleges, churches and hospitals.

DULCIMER, musical instrument with a set of strings stretched across a thin, flat soundbox and struck with mallets. Of ancient origin, it is still used in the folk music of Central Europe, where it is called the cimbalom.The Kentucky dulcimer, a

US folk instrument, is plucked.

DULLES, name of two prominent American brothers. **John Foster Dulles** (1888–1959), lawyer, US secretary of state under Eisenhower (1953–59), employed a strong foreign policy to block communist "cold war" expansion. He was legal counsel at the WWI peace conference, worked on the UN charter during WWII and negotiated the Japanese peace treaty, 1951. **Allen Welsh Dulles** (1893–1969), American lawyer and intelligence official, negotiated the Nazi surrender in Italy in WWII. He directed the CENTRAL INTELLIGENCE AGENCY 1953–61, considerably influencing foreign policy, as in the American-backed BAY OF PIGS invasion of Cuba.

DULUTH, Daniel Greysolon, Sieur (1636–1710), French explorer around Lake Superior from 1679. He befriended and influenced the OJIBWA and SIOUX Indians, and claimed the Great Lakes area for France. Duluth, Minn., was named for him.

DUMA, elected assembly in tsarist Russia, instituted by Nicholas II in 1906. The first two dumas were radical, and were swiftly dissolved. The third and fourth (1907–12 and 1912–17), though restricted, introduced some reforms. Revolution in 1917 did away with the institution.

DUMAS, name of two 19th-century French authors, a father and his illegitimate son. **Alexandre Dumas** (1802–1870), "Dumas père," wrote the famous historical novels *The Three Musketeers* (1844) and *The Count of Monte Cristo* (1845). Historically inaccurate and lacking in depth, these adventures nevertheless remain popular. **Alexandre Dumas** (1824–1895), "Dumas fils," won fame with his tragic play *La Dame aux Camélias* (known in English as *Camille*, 1852) which formed the basis of Verdi's opera *La Traviata*. He also wrote moralizing plays aimed at the reform of such social evils as prostitution and illegitimacy.

DU MAURIER, name of two English novelists. **George Louis Palmella Busson du Maurier** (1834–1896), caricaturist, illustrator and novelist, is best known for *Peter Ibbetson* (1891) and *Trilby* (1894). **Daphne du Maurier** (1907–), George's granddaughter, wrote romantic novels. Her most famous work is *Rebecca* (1938).

DUMBARTON OAKS CONFERENCE, meeting of diplomats of the "Big Four" (China, the US, USSR and UK), held Aug. 24–Oct. 7, 1944, at the Dumbarton Oaks estate in Washington, D.C. Its discussions were the first major step towards establishing a postwar international security system (see UNITED NATIONS).

DUMBNESS, inability to speak. Failure of speech development, usually associated with congenital DEAFNESS (deaf-mute) is the most common cause in childhood. APHASIA and hysterical mutism are the usual adult causes. If comprehension is intact, writing and sign language are alternative forms of communication, but in aphasia language is usually globally impaired. (See SPEECH AND SPEECH DISORDERS.)

DUNANT, Jean Henri (1828–1910), Swiss philanthropist, founder of the RED CROSS. Horrified by unrelieved suffering at the Battle of Solferino (1859) he publicized the need for effective aid for injured in war and peace. His efforts led to the Geneva Convention of 1864 (see GENEVA CONVENTIONS) and to the formation of the Red Cross. He shared in the first Nobel Peace Prize in 1901.

DUNBAR, Paul Laurence (1872–1906), black US poet and novelist. His poems about black rural life were influenced by the sentimental dialect poems of James Whitcomb RILEY. His works include *Lyrics of Lowly Life* (1896) and the novel *The Sport of the Gods* (1902).

DUNBAR, William (c1460–1520), greatest of the old Scottish poets. He became a priest, employed by James IV on court business. His mainly short poems show great satiric power, originality, versatility and wit.

DUNCAN, David Douglas (1916–), US photographer who covered WWII as a Marine photographer and the Palestine conflict and the Korean War for *Life* magazine. His publications include *This Is War* (1951) on Korea, and two books on Picasso (1958, 1961).

DUNCAN, Isadora (1878–1927), US dancer, a pioneer of modern dance, encouraging a spontaneous personal style. She danced in a loose tunic, barefoot, to symphonic music. After European concert successes, she founded schools of dancing in Germany, the USSR and the US. She was strangled by a scarf caught in a car wheel.

DUNHAM, Katherine (1910–), US dancer and choreographer, greatly influenced by her study of the dances and rituals of black people in the Caribbean and Brazil. She led her own dance troupes but also choreographed for Broadway and films.

DUNKERQUE or **Dunkirk,** seaport in Northern France, on the English Channel, 10mi from Belgium, a shipbuilding, oil-refining and food processing center, and railway terminus. In WWII (May 27–June 4, 1940) some 1,000 vessels evacuated 337,000 trapped British and Allied troops from here.

DUNKERS or **Dunkards**, any of several bodies of Brethren, or German Baptists. They are theologically rooted in 17th-century Lutheran PIETISM and named for their practice of triple baptismal immersion. The movement began in 18th-century Germany but most members went to America where they now number over 230,000, most in the Church of the Brethren.

DUNMORE, John Murray, 4th Earl of (1732–1809), English governor of New York (1770–71), Virginia (1771–75) and the Bahamas (1787–96). He launched "Lord Dunmore's War" (1774) against the Indians. Opposing the rebels, he three times dissolved the Virginia assembly (1772–74) but in 1776 an uprising forced him out of Virginia.

DUNNE, Finley Peter (1867–1936), US journalist and humorist. He created "Mr. Dooley," an Irish-American saloonkeeper, whose amusing and satirical comments on current events Dunne first published in the press, then in books such as *Mr. Dooley in Peace and War* (1898).

DUNS SCOTUS, John (c1265–1308), Scottish philosopher and theologian. He joined the Franciscans (1280), was ordained in 1291 and taught at Cambridge, Oxford, Paris and Cologne. His system of thought, embodied chiefly in his commentary on Lombard's *Sentences*, was adopted by the Franciscans and was highly influential. Typical of SCHOLASTICISM, it differs from AQUINAS in asserting the primacy of love and the will over reason. He was the first in the West to defend the IMMACULATE CONCEPTION.

DUNSTABLE, John (c1385–1453), English composer whose flowing, harmonious works influenced European music. He wrote some 60 works, including motets and secular part-songs.

DUODECIMAL SYSTEM, a number system using the powers of twelve, which are allotted place values as in the DECIMAL SYSTEM. The number written in decimals 4092 can be expressed as $(2 \times 12^3) + (4 \times 12^2) + (5 \times 12^1) + (0 \times 12^0)$ or, in duodecimals, 2450. Fractions are expressed similarly. Two extra symbols are needed for this system to represent the numbers 10 and 11; these are generally accepted as X (dek) and Σ (el) respectively. The advantage of this system can be realized by consideration of the integral factors of 10 and 12: 10 has two (2,5) while 12 has four (2,3,4,6). The most common examples of everyday use of this system are the setting of 12 inches to the foot and 12 months to the year.

DUPLEIX, Joseph François (1696–1763), governor-general of French possessions in India, 1742–54. He tried to extend French influence in central and S India by supporting Indian rulers against their British-backed rivals. Defeated by CLIVE, Dupleix was discredited and returned to France to die in poverty.

DU PONT, US industrial family of French origin. **Pierre Samuel du Pont de Nemours** (1739–1817), French economist and statesman, publicized the PHYSIOCRATS' doctrines. He was a reformist member of the Estates General (1789) and secretary general of the provisional government (1814). He fled to the US in 1799 and, having returned in 1802, fled again in 1815. His son **Éleuthère Irénée du Pont** (1771–1834) established a gunpowder factory near Wilmington, Del., in 1802. The company expanded enormously during the Mexican, Crimean and Civil wars under Éleuthère's son **Henry du Pont** (1812–1889), who in 1872 organized the "Gunpowder Trust" which soon controlled 90% of explosives output. **Alfred Irénée du Pont** (1864–1935), **Thomas Coleman du Pont** (1863–1930) and **Pierre Samuel du Pont** (1870–1954) reorganized the firm in 1902, and after WWI it exploited the valuable dye-trust patents confiscated from Germany. Under Pierre's brothers **Irénée du Pont** (1876–1963) and **Lammont du Pont** (1880–1952) the firm built up an immensely powerful synthetic chemicals industry, developing rayon, cellophane, neoprene, nylon and other materials.

DUPRÉ, Marcel (1886–1971), French organist and composer, director of the Paris Conservatoire 1954–56. His compositions include symphonies and many organ works.

DURAND, Asher Brown (1796–1886), US painter and engraver, a founder of the HUDSON RIVER SCHOOL. He made his name by engraving John Trumbull's painting *The Signing of the Declaration of Independence* (1820). He painted realistic landscapes and portraits, and also designed banknotes.

DURANT, Thomas Clark (1820–1885), US railroad pioneer, chief founder of the Union Pacific Railroad (1862). Founder president of the CRÉDIT MOBILIER OF AMERICA (1863–67), he was ousted by rivals, but remained a Union Pacific director till 1869.

DURANT, William Crapo (1861–1947), US automobile executive who founded the General Motors Corporation in 1916 with the aid of Louis Chevrolet (1879–1941). He lost control in 1920.

DURANT, William James (1885–1981), US educator and popular historian. He wrote the stylishly lively bestseller *The*

Story of Philosophy (1926) and, with his wife, **Ariel** (1898–1981), the 11-volume *The Story of Civilization* (1935–75).

DURAS, Marguerite (1914–   ), French novelist, playwright and scriptwriter, associated with the New Wave French writers of the 1950s and 1960s. Her works include the novels *The Sea Wall* (1950) and *The Lover* (1985) and the film script *Hiroshima, Mon Amour* (1960).

DÜRER, Albrecht (1471–1528), German artist who introduced Italian Renaissance outlook and style to Germany, though tempered by Gothic tradition. Bellini, Mantegna and Leonardo da Vinci all influenced Dürer after his visits to Venice (1494–95 and 1505–07). He became court painter to the emperors Maximilian (1512) and Charles V (1520), and produced a huge output of masterly, vividly detailed drawings, engravings, woodcuts and paintings. His themes included religious subjects, plant and animal studies and evocative landscapes in watercolor.

DURHAM, John George Lambton, 1st Earl of (1792–1840), English statesman, author of Durham's Report, which laid down the basic principles of British colonial administration. A radical Whig, he was lord privy seal 1830–33 and helped draft the Reform Bill of 1832. Governor general of Canada 1838, he was criticized for his leniency towards rebels, and resigned.

DURKHEIM, Émile (1858–1917), pioneer French sociologist who advocated the synthesis of empirical research and abstract theory in the social sciences and developed the concepts of "collective consciousness" and the "division of labor."

DURRELL, Lawrence (George) (1912–   ), English novelist and poet, known for the sensuous lyricism and rhythmic vitality of his style. His works include *The Alexandria Quartet*, four novels—*Justine* (1957), *Balthazar* (1958), *Mountolive* (1958) and *Cleo* (1960)— exploring one story from different viewpoints; and several volumes of poetry and travel literature.

DÜRRENMATT, Friedrich (1921–   ), Swiss playwright and novelist. His often bizarre tragicomedies employ biting satire, and include *The Visit* (1956) and *The Physicists* (1962). He has also written crime novels.

DURYEA, Charles Edgar (1861–1938), US inventor and manufacturer who, with **J. Frank** (1870–1967), built what was probably the first commercially viable gasoline-powered automobile in the US (1893). They manufactured cars independently from 1898 to 1914.

DUSE, Eleonora (1859–1924), Italian dramatic actress, rivaling Sarah Bernhardt as the greatest actress of her period, notably in plays by Ibsen and by Duse's lover Gabriele D'Annunzio.

DUST BOWL, area of some 150,000sq mi in the S Great Plains region of the US which, during the 1930s, the Depression years, suffered violent dust storms owing to accelerated SOIL EROSION. Grassland was plowed up in the 1920s and 1930s to plant wheat: a severe drought bared the fields, and high winds blew the topsoil into huge dunes. Despite rehabilitation programs, farmers plowed up grassland again in the 1940s and 1950s, and a repetition of the tragedy was averted only by the action of Congress.

DUTCH, West Germanic language spoken in the Netherlands and (as FLEMISH) in N Belgium, also in Suriname and the Dutch Antilles. AFRIKAANS, spoken in South Africa, is derived from Dutch. Dutch evolved largely from the speech of the Franks, who settled in the Low Countries in the 4th–5th centuries. About 20 million people speak Dutch.

DUTCH EAST INDIES, former Dutch overseas territory, now INDONESIA. Colonized by the Dutch East India Company in the 17th century, the area came under Dutch government in 1798, was occupied by Japan in WWII and gained independence in 1949 after a nationalist struggle.

DUTCH GUIANA. See SURINAME.

DUTCH REFORMED CHURCH, largest and oldest Protestant church of the Netherlands and dominant church in South Africa. It was the first reformed church from mainland Europe to be established in North America.

DUTCH WARS, three 17th-century wars fought by the Dutch and English for maritime supremacy. The *First Dutch War* (1652–54) began after England's First Navigation Act (1651) excluded the Dutch from trade with English possessions. The English temporarily lost control of the English channel and failed to sustain a blockade. War ended with the Treaty of Westminster (1654). British attacks on Dutch colonies provoked the *Second Dutch War* (1665–67), in which the French aided the Dutch. Impoverished by plague and the Great Fire of London, England signed the Treaty of Breda (1667). This gave the Dutch Surinam and relaxed the navigation laws, but gave England New Netherland (New York). In the *Third Dutch War* (1672–74), the English and French attacked the Dutch but failed to subdue the Dutch fleet. France invaded the Dutch Republic until halted by deliberate flooding and a powerful alliance including Austria, Spain and Brandenburg. Disheartened by lack of success, England made peace with the Dutch in 1674. But Franco-Dutch fighting continued until 1678.

DUTCH WEST INDIA COMPANY, association of Dutch merchants incorporated in 1621 to monopolize Dutch trade with Africa and the Americas and to found colonies there. It colonized Caribbean islands (1634–48) and Surinam (1667). Harassed by Spain, Portugal and England, it lost other New World possessions and was dissolved in 1674. Reorganized in 1675, it was absorbed by the Dutch state in 1791 and finally dissolved in 1794.

DUTCH WEST INDIES. See NETHERLANDS ANTILLES.

DUVALIER, François "Papa Doc" (1907–1971), president of Haiti from 1957. A physician, he was elected president with army backing, was reelected in 1961, and declared himself president for life in 1964. He ruled by terror, abetted by his merciless police, the Tonton Macoutes, and enriched himself while the country's economy deteriorated. He was succeeded as president for life by his son, **Jean Claude "Baby Doc" Duvalier** (1951–   ), whose regime was also corrupt and ineffective. After months of antigovernment demonstrations, he fled to France in 1982.

DUVEEN OF MILLBANK, Joseph Duveen, 1st Baron (1869–1939), English art dealer who advised wealthy American collectors such as MELLON and John D. ROCKEFELLER. He largely created and satisfied the American taste for fine old masters, now represented in many American art museums.

DVORAK, Antonín (1841–1904), major Czech composer, who developed the national style founded by SMETANA. A viola player, he composed richly lyrical music that began to win him acclaim in the 1870s. He spent 1892–95 in the US, as director of the National Conservatory of Music, New York City. His works include 9 symphonies, 10 operas, concertos, the Slavonic dances and other orchestral compositions, choral works and chamber music.

DWARFISM, or small stature. This may be a family characteristic or associated with congenital disease of CARTILAGE or BONE development (e.g., achondroplasia). Failure of growth-HORMONE (see PITUITARY GLAND) or THYROID-hormone production during growth, and excess STEROID, ANDROGEN or ESTROGEN can cause small stature by altering control of bone development. The condition can also arise from spine or limb deformity (e.g., scoliosis), MALNUTRITION,

RICKETS, chronic infection or visceral disease.

DWARF STAR, a star with a relatively small diameter. Because of their small size, dwarf stars do not appear very bright. The sun is an average-size star, and dwarf stars have diameters less than that of the sun.

There are two types of dwarf star, distinguished by their color. *Red dwarfs* are cooler than the sun. They are the most common type of star in the sky, and seem to be scaled-down versions of ordinary stars like the sun.

White dwarfs are much hotter—white hot, in fact. They may be twice the temperature of the sun. Although a white dwarf star contains as much matter as the sun, this mass is condensed into a sphere the size of a planet. Therefore white dwarf stars are very dense, and a thimbleful of white dwarf material would weigh many tons. White dwarfs are thought to represent the final stages of a star's life, when it has collapsed and is fading away. After several hundred million years a white dwarf will have cooled off so that it ceases to shine. In this invisible state it is called a *black dwarf*.

DWARF TREE. See BONSAI.

DWIGGINS, William Addison (1880–1956), US designer and calligrapher whose new typefaces and layouts revolutionized book and magazine design. He created Alfred A. Knopf's house style and wrote the influential *Layout in Advertising* (1928) and *MSS by WAD* (1949).

DWIGHT, Theodore (1764–1846), American author, one of the HARTFORD WITS. He served in Congress 1806–07 and was secretary of the Hartford Convention (1814–15), which sought federal redress of New England grievances. His journal on the convention was published in 1833.

DWIGHT, Timothy (1752–1817), US clergyman, educator, and author. A grandson of Jonathan EDWARDS, he became in turn the leading intellectual figure in New England. He was president of YALE from 1795.

DYER, Mary (d. 1660), Quaker martyr in Massachusetts. A supporter of Anne HUTCHINSON, she visited imprisoned Quakers and preached in Boston, despite orders banishing her from the settlement. She was reprieved in 1659, but was rearrested the following year and sentenced to be hanged.

DYER-BENNET, Richard (1913–   ), British singer, guitarist, lutenist and composer. His repertoire of Elizabethan, classic, and folk songs, which he presented annually in New York (from 1944), helped reawaken public interest in the art of minstrelsy.

DYES AND DYEING. Dyes are colored substances which impart their color to textiles to which they are applied and for which they have a chemical affinity. They differ from PIGMENTS in being used in solution in an aqueous medium. Dyeing was practiced in the FERTILE CRESCENT and China by 3000 BC, using natural dyes obtained from plants and shellfish. These were virtually superseded by synthetic dyes—more varied in color and applicability—after the accidental synthesis of mauve by Sir William Perkin (1856). The raw materials are aromatic hydrocarbons obtained from COAL TAR and PETROLEUM. These are modified by introducing chemical groups called chromophores which cause absorption of visible LIGHT (see also COLOR). Other groups, auxochromes, such as amino or hydroxyl, are necessary for substantivity—i.e., affinity for the material to be dyed. This fixing to the fabric fibers is by hydrogen bonding, adsorption, ionic bonding or covalent bonding in the case of "reactive dyes" (see BOND, CHEMICAL). If there is no natural affinity, the dye may be fixed by using a mordant before or with dyeing. Vat dyes are made soluble by reduction in the presence of alkali, and after dyeing the original color is re-formed by acidification and oxidation; indigo and anthraquinone dyes are examples. Dyes are also used as biological stains (see MICROSCOPE), indicators and in PHOTOGRAPHY.

DYLAN, Bob (born Robert Zimmerman; 1941-   ) US folk singer and composer. His distinctive blues style had a strong influence on popular music in the 1960s. He later turned to country and ballad music.

DYNAMITE, high EXPLOSIVE invented by Alfred NOBEL, consisting of NITROGLYCERIN absorbed in an inert material such as kieselguhr or wood pulp. Unlike nitroglycerin itself, it can be handled safely, not exploding without a detonator. In modern dynamite SODIUM nitrate replaces about half the nitroglycerin. Gelatin dynamite, or **gelignite,** also contains some nitrocellulose.

DYSENTERY, a BACTERIAL or PARASITIC disease causing abdominal pain, DIARRHEA and FEVER. In children, **bacillary dysentery** due to *Shigella* species is a common endemic or EPIDEMIC disease, and is associated with poor hygiene. It is a short-lived illness but may cause dehydration in severe cases. The organism may be carried in feces in the absence of symptoms. ANTIBIOTICS may be used to shorten the attack and reduce carrier rates. **Amebic dysentery** is a chronic disease, usually seen in warm climates, with episodes of diarrhea and CONSTIPATION, accompanied by mucus and occasionally BLOOD; constitutional symptoms occur and the disease may resemble noninfective COLITIS. Treatment with emetine, while effective, is accompanied by a high risk of toxicity; metronidazole is a less toxic antiamebic agent introduced recently.

DYSLEXIA, difficulty with reading, often a developmental problem possibly associated with suppressed left-HANDEDNESS, and spatial difficulty; it requires special training. It may be acquired by BIRTH injury, failure of learning, visual disorders or as part of APHASIA.

DYSPEPSIA, or indigestion, a vague term usually describing abnormal visceral sensation in upper abdomen or lower chest, often of a burning quality. Relationship to meals and posture is important in defining its origin; relief by ANTACIDS or milk is usual. HEARTBURN from esophagitis and pain of peptic (gastric or duodenal) ULCERS are usual causes.

DYSPHASIA. See APHASIA; SPEECH AND SPEECH DISORDERS.

DZERZHINSKI, Felix Edmundovich (1877–1926), Polish-born revolutionary, one of the founders of the USSR. From 1917 until his death he organized and headed the Cheka, the Soviet secret police, known after 1922 as the OGPU. He also became commissar of transport 1921 and was head of the supreme economic council 1924.

5th letter of the English alphabet, derived from an ancient Semitic letter and the Greek *epsilon*. It is a vowel and can be long as in *feet*, or short as in *met*, or it can lengthen the preceding vowel as in *bite*. In music, *E* is the note *mi* in the scale of *C*.

EADS, James Buchanan (1820–1887), US engineer, best known for the system of jetties he built in the delta of the Mississippi to keep the river channel open for oceangoing vessels. It was this that turned New Orleans into a seaport. Eads also designed the great steel-arched bridge across the Mississippi at St. Louis that bears his name, and built a number of ironclad riverboats for use on the Mississippi during the Civil War.

EAGLES, powerful birds of prey found in many highland regions such as North America, Scotland and Asia. Their nests (eyries) are found at elevations between 900–2,000ft. The eagles comprise four groups: sea and fish eagles; snake eagles; crested eagles; and "true" or aquiline eagles. All have characteristic soaring flights made possible by broad wings with spans of up to 2m (6.5ft). Being carnivores, eagles have hooked beaks and clawed feet. They are diurnal. Eagles have frequently figured in mythology, especially of North American Indians.

EAKINS, Thomas (1844–1916), important US realist painter, considered a major American portraitist. Among his most famous paintings is *The Gross Clinic* (1875). His insistence on paintings from nature—and especially from the nude—was controversial in his time, but his work became a powerful influence on younger US artists. Eakins was also an early action photographer.

EAMES, Charles (1907–1978), US designer, who influenced contemporary furniture design. He created plywood and fiberglass form-fitting chairs, and the upholstered "Eames chair."

EAR, a special sense organ in higher animals, concerned with hearing and balance. It may be divided into the outer ear, extending from the tympanic membrane or ear drum to the pinna, the inner ear embedded in the skull bones, consisting of cochlea and labyrinth, and between them the middle ear, containing small bones or ossicles. The cartilaginous pinna varies greatly in shape and mobility in different animals; a canal lined by skin leads from it and ends with the thin tympanic membrane stretched across it. The middle ear is an air-filled space which communicates with the pharynx via the eustachian tube. This allows the middle ear to be at the same pressure as the outer and also secretions to drain away. The middle ear is also connected with the MASTOID antrum. Three ossicles (malleus, incus, stapes) form a bony chain articulating between the ear drum and part of the cochlea; tiny muscles are attached to the drum and ossicles and can affect the intensity of SOUND transmission. The inner ear contains both the cochlea, a spiral structure containing fluid and specialized membranes on which hearing receptors are situated, and the labyrinth, which consists of three semicircular canals, the utricle and the saccule, all of which contain fluid and receptor cells. Nerve fibers pass from the cochlea and labyrinth to form the eighth cranial nerve.

In hearing, sound waves travel into the outer ear, funneled by the pinna, and cause vibration of the ear drum. The drum and ossicular chain, which transmits vibration to the cochlea, effect some amplification. The vibration set up in the cochlear fluid is differentially distributed along the central membrane according to pitch. By a complex mechanism, this membrane movement causes certain groups of receptor cells to be preferentially stimulated, giving rise to auditory nerve impulses, which are conducted via several coding sites to higher centers for perception. These centers can in turn affect the sensitivity of receptors by means of centrifugal fibers. In balance, rotation of the head in any of three perpendicular planes causes stimulation of specialized cells in the semicircular canals as fluid moves past them. The utricle and saccule contain small stones which respond to gravitational changes and affect receptor cells in their walls. All these balance receptor cells cause impulses in the vestibular nerve, which connects to higher centers.

Disease of the ear usually causes DEAFNESS or ringing in the ears. Peripheral disorders of balance include vertigo and ATAXIA, which may be accompanied by nausea or vomiting. MÉNIÈRE'S DISEASE is an episodic disease affecting both systems.

EARHART, Amelia (1898–1937), US pioneer aviator. She was the first transatlantic woman passenger (1928), first solo transatlantic woman pilot (1932) and made the first ever solo flight from Hawaii to the US mainland (1935). She disappeared over the Pacific Ocean on an attempted around-the-world flight in 1937.

EARLE, Ralph (1751–1801), American portrait painter. His distinctively rugged portraits were influenced by John Singleton COPLEY. He is noted for his Revolutionary War battle scenes.

EARLY, Jubal Anderson (1816–1894), Confederate general, famous for his advance on Washington (1864), in which he cleared the Shenandoah Valley of Union forces. His army was subsequently forced to retreat and defeated by Union troops under Philip SHERIDAN.

EARP, Wyatt Berry Stapp (1848–1929), US frontier lawman and folk hero. He was deputy sheriff and US marshal in several Kan. and Ariz. "cow towns." He is most famous for the gunfight at O.K. Corral in Tombstone, Ariz. (1881).

EARTH, the largest of the inner planets of

the solar system, the third planet from the sun and, so far as is known, the sole home of life in the solar system. To an astronomer on Mars, several things would be striking about our planet. Most of all, he would notice the relative size of our MOON: there are larger moons in the SOLAR SYSTEM, but none so large compared with its planet—indeed, some astronomers regard the earth as one component of a "double planet," the other being the moon. Our Martian astronomer would also notice that the earth shows phases, just as the moon and Venus do when viewed from earth. And, if he were a radio astronomer, he would detect a barrage of radio "noise" from our planet—clear evidence of the presence of intelligent life.

The earth is a bit larger than VENUS. It is slightly oblate (flattened at the poles), the equatorial diameter being about 7,926mi, the polar diameter about 7,900mi. It rotates on its axis in 23h 56min 4.09s (one sidereal day)—though this is increasing by roughly 0.00001s annually due to tidal effects (see TIDES)—and revolves about the sun in 365d 6h 9min 9.5s (one sidereal year: see SIDEREAL TIME). Two other types of year are defined: the tropical year, the interval between alternate EQUINOXES (365d 5h 48min 46s); and the anomalistic year, the interval between moments of perihelion (see ORBIT), 365d 6h 13min 53s. The earth's equator is angled about 23.5° to the ecliptic, the plane of its orbit. The direction of the earth's axis is slowly changing owing to PRECESSION. The planet has a mass of about 5.98×10^{21} tons, a volume of about 1.08×10^{21}cu m, and a mean DENSITY of about 5.52 tons/cu m.

Like other planetary bodies, the earth has a magnetic field (see MAGNETISM). The magnetic poles do not coincide with the axial poles (see NORTH POLE; SOUTH POLE), and moreover they "wander." At or near the earth's surface, magnetic declination (or variation) is the angle between true N and compass N (lines joining points of equal variation are isogonic lines); and magnetic dip (or inclination) the vertical angle between the magnetic field and the horizontal at a particular point. Isomagnetic lines can be drawn between points of equal intensity of the field. There is also evidence to suggest that the direction of the field reverses from time to time. These changes are of primary interest to the paleomagnetist (see PALEOMAGNETISM). The earth is surrounded by radiation belts, probably the result of charged particles from the sun being trapped by the earth's magnetic field (see VAN ALLEN RADIATION BELTS; AURORA).

There are three main zones of the earth: the ATMOSPHERE; the hydrosphere (the world's waters); and the LITHOSPHERE, the solid body of the world. The atmosphere shields us from much of the harmful radiation of the SUN, and protects us from excesses of heat and cold. Water covers much of the earth's surface (over 70%) in both liquid and solid (ice) forms (see GLACIER; OCEANS). There are permanent polar icecaps. The earth's solid body can be divided into three regions: The core (diameter about 4,350mi), at a temperature of about 3,000K, is at least partly liquid, though the central region (the inner core) is probably solid. Probably mainly of NICKEL and IRON, the core's density ranges between about 9.5 and perhaps over 15 tons/cu m. The mantle (outer diameter about 7,883mi), probably mainly of olivine, has a density around 5.7 tons/cu m toward the core, 3.3 tons/cu m toward the crust, the outermost layer of the earth and the one to which all human activity is confined. The crust is some 21.75mi thick (much less beneath the oceans) and composed of three classes of ROCKS: IGNEOUS ROCKS, SEDIMENTARY ROCKS and METAMORPHIC ROCKS. FOSSILS in the strata of sedimentary rocks give us a geological time scale (see GEOLOGY). The earth formed about 4.5 billion years ago; life appeared probably about 3.2 billion years ago, and man around 4 million years ago. Man has thus been present for about 0.1% of the earth's history, and civilization for less than 0.0001%.

It is now known that the earth's configuration of continents and oceans has changed radically through geological time—as it were, the map has changed. Originally, this was attributed to continents drifting, and the process was called CONTINENTAL DRIFT (see also Alfred WEGENER). However, although this term is still used descriptively, the changes are now realized to be a manifestation of the theory of PLATE TECTONICS, and so a result of the processes responsible also for EARTHQUAKES, MOUNTAIN building and many other phenomena.

EARTHQUAKE, a fracture or implosion beneath the surface of the earth, and the shock waves that travel away from the point where the fracture has occurred. The immediate area where the fracture takes place is the focus or hypocenter, the point immediately above it on the earth's surface is the epicenter, and the shock waves emanating from the fracture are called seismic waves.

Earthquakes occur to relieve a stress that has built up within the crust or mantle of the EARTH; fracture results when the stress exceeds the strength of the rock. The reasons for the stress build-up are to be found in the theory of PLATE TECTONICS. If a map is drawn of the world's earthquake activity, it can be immediately seen that earthquakes are confined to discrete belts. These belts signify the borders of contiguous plates; shallow earthquakes being generally associated with mid-ocean ridges where creation of new material occurs, deep ones with regions where one plate is being forced under another.

Seismic waves are of two main types. Body waves travel from the hypocenter, and again are of two types: P (compressional) waves, where the motion of particles of the earth is in the direction of propagation of the wave; and S (shear) waves, where the particle motion is at right angles to this direction. Surface waves travel from the epicenter and are largely confined to the earth's surface; Love waves are at right angles to the direction of propagation; Rayleigh waves have a more complicated, backward elliptical movement in the direction of propagation.

The experienced intensity · of an earthquake depends mainly on the distance from the source. Local intensities are gauged in terms of the Mercalli Intensity Scale, which runs from I (detectable only by SEISMOGRAPH) through to XII ("catastrophic"). Comparison of intensities in different areas enables the source of an earthquake to be located. The actual magnitude of the event is gauged according to the RICHTER SCALE.

The study of seismic phenomena is known as seismology. (See also FAULT; TSUNAMI.)

EAST ANGLIA, kingdom of Anglo-Saxon England, first settled by ANGLES in the 5th century. The Danes conquered it in 869 and it became part of the DANELAW in 886. EDWARD THE ELDER, king of Wessex, defeated the Danes in 917, after which East Anglia became an English earldom.

EASTER, chief festival of the Christian church year, celebrating the RESURRECTION of Jesus Christ, and subsuming the Jewish PASSOVER. Easter has been observed by the Western Church since the Council of NICAEA, on the Sunday after the first full moon following the vernal EQUINOX. It traditionally included a night vigil and the BAPTISM of catechumens. Easter is celebrated at a later date by the Eastern churches.

EASTER ISLAND, easternmost island of Polynesia in the S Pacific Ocean about

2,000mi W of Chile, which annexed the island in 1888. This small, grassy, volcanic island features hundreds of colossal stone statues up to 40ft high, carved and raised on burial platforms by a pre-Columbian culture, which have been the subject of much speculation by Thor Heyerdahl and others. Easter Island was discovered on Easter Sunday, 1722, by the Dutch admiral Jakob Roggeveen.

EASTERN CHURCH, one of the two great branches of the Christian Church. From the apostolic age itself a natural distinction arose between the Greek-speaking church of the eastern Roman empire and the Latin-speaking church of the west. The Eastern Church developed its own liturgical traditions, patriarchal government, outlook and ethos, and resisted the increasing claims of the papacy. It became a family of ORTHODOX CHURCHES, finally breaking with Rome in the Great Schism of 1054. The non-orthodox Monophysite Churches separated in the 5th and 6th centuries but share the common eastern tradition. (See also CHRISTIANITY.)

EASTERN QUESTION, the international political problems raised in the 19th century by the decline of the OTTOMAN EMPIRE. The rival ambitions of Russia, Austria-Hungary, Britain and France in the E Mediterranean led to the CRIMEAN WAR (1854–56) and BALKAN WARS (1912–13) and were partly responsible for the outbreak of WWI.

EASTER RISING, Irish rebellion against British rule, begun on Easter Monday, 1916. Although itself abortive, it proved a turning point in the Irish struggle for Home Rule. Sir Roger CASEMENT tried in vain to obtain arms from Germany, but the rising went ahead at the insistence of the nationalist leaders James Connolly and P. H. Pearse, and some 1,500 volunteers seized public buildings, notably the Post Office, in Dublin. The British suppressed the rebellion after fierce street fighting and executed its leaders, an act which further fueled the nationalist cause.

EAST INDIA COMPANY, name of several private trading companies chartered by 17th-century European governments to develop trade in the E Hemisphere, after the discovery of a sea route to India. They competed for commercial supremacy and eventually aided European colonial expansion. **The Dutch East India Company** (1602–1798) dominated trade with the East Indies but failed to survive the French invasion of Holland in 1795. **The British East India Company** (1600–1858) monopolized trade with India and, in the 18th century, gained administrative control of most of India. Its power was curbed by William PITT in 1784 and successive British governments took complete control of the Company and made India an imperial possession.

EAST INDIES, the former Dutch East Indies, now Indonesia. Modern usage confines the term to the Malay Archipelago. It is the largest island group in the world.

EASTMAN, George (1854–1932), US inventor and manufacturer who invented the Kodak CAMERA, first marketed in 1888. Earlier he perfected processes for manufacturing dry photographic plates (1880) and flexible, transparent film (1884). He took his own life in 1932. (See also PHOTOGRAPHY.)

EASTMAN, Max (1883–1969), US author and editor. He edited two influential socialist magazines and was a Communist Party member until 1923. He became a critic of Stalinism in such works as *Marxism, Is It Science?* (1940) and *Stalin's Russia* (1940). He was also a literary critic (*Enjoyment of Poetry*, 1913) and poet (*Poems of Five Decades*, 1954).

EAST PRUSSIA, historic region of Europe, bounded, (between WWI and WWII), by the Baltic Sea, Poland, Lithuania and Danzig. It was a stronghold of the Teutonic Knights in the Middle Ages, and later belonged variously to Poland, Prussia and Germany. East Prussia was separated from the rest of Germany from 1918 to 1939 by the "Polish Corridor," and after WWII it was partitioned between the USSR and Poland.

EAST RIVER, tidal strait connecting New York Bay with Long Island Sound and separating Manhattan and the Bronx from the other New York City boroughs of Brooklyn and Queens.

EBAN, Abba Solomon (1915–   ), Israeli political leader and diplomat. Born in South Africa and educated in England, he became Israel's first UN delegate (1949–59) and ambassador to the US (1950–59). He was then minister of education 1960, deputy prime minister 1963–65 and foreign minister 1966–74.

EBBINGHAUS, Hermann (1850–1909), German psychologist who developed experimental techniques for the study of rote LEARNING and memory. In later life he devised means of intelligence testing and researched into color VISION.

EBERT, Friedrich (1871–1925), first president (1919–25) of the German WEIMAR REPUBLIC. A lifelong Social Democrat and moderate Marxist, he initiated many social reforms and helped to reconstruct Germany after WWI.

ECCLESIASTES, Old Testament "wisdom" book, pessimistic and skeptical in tone. It was traditionally attributed to King Solomon, but modern experts favor a much later author, possibly of the 3rd century BC.

ECCLESIASTICUS, Old Testament book included in the APOCRYPHA by Jews and Protestants. It was written c180 BC by Jesus son of Sirach, and is a collection of instructive observations, influenced by the Book of PROVERBS.

ECHEGARAY, José (1832–1916), Spanish engineer, economist, and politician. He was also a leading dramatist, sharing the 1904 Nobel Prize in Literature with French poet Frédéric MISTRAL.

ECHINODERMS, members of a phylum of marine invertebrates, Echinodermata. They include STARFISH, crinoids, sea cucumbers and SEA URCHINS. Their body form is generally radially symmetrical; they move slowly by means of tube feet and the majority possess a calcite skeleton. The sexes are generally separate; most are suspension feeders, but some prey on mollusks.

ECHO, a wave signal reflected back to its point of origin from a distant object, or, in the case of RADIO signals, a signal coming to a receiver from the transmitter by an indirect route. Echoes of the first type can be used to detect and find the position of reflecting objects (echolocation). High-frequency SOUND echolocation is used both by boats for navigation and to detect prey and by man in marine SONAR. RADAR, too, is similar in principle, though this uses UHF radio and MICROWAVE radiation rather than sound energy. The range of a reflecting object can easily be estimated for ordinary sound echoes: since sound travels about 1,100ft/sec through the air at sea level, an object will be distant about 550ft for each second that passes before an echo returns from it.

ECK, Johann (1486–1543), German scholar and theologian. Though advocating church reform, he was a bitter opponent of LUTHER and the REFORMATION. He influenced the 1520 papal bull against Luther, and presented the Roman Catholic case at the Diet of Augsburg (1530).

ECKENER, Hugo (1868–1954), German aeronautical engineer and pioneer airship pilot who commanded the *Graf Zeppelin* on its historic 12-day round-the-world flight (1929). He later piloted the *Hindenburg*.

ECKERMANN, Johann Peter (1792–1854), German writer and literary assistant of GOETHE, notable for his *Conversations with Goethe* (3 volumes, 1836–48).

ECKHART, Johann (c1260–1327), also called Meister Eckhart, German Dominican theologian, regarded as the founder of German mysticism. He was influenced by neoplatonism and by the works of Saint AUGUSTINE and Thomas AQUINAS.

ECLIPSE, the partial or total obscurement of one celestial body by another; also the passage of the moon through the earth's shadow. The components of a binary star (see DOUBLE STAR) may eclipse each other as seen from the earth, in which case the star is termed an eclipsing binary. The moon frequently eclipses stars or planets, and this is known as OCCULTATION.

A **lunar eclipse** occurs when the moon passes through the umbra of the earth's SHADOW. This happens usually not more than twice a year, since the moon's orbit around the earth is tilted with respect to the ecliptic. The eclipsed moon is blood-red in color due to some of the sun's light being refracted by the earth's atmosphere into the umbra. A partial lunar eclipse occurs when only part of the umbra falls on the moon.

In a **solar eclipse**, the moon passes between the sun and the earth. A total eclipse occurs when the observer is within the umbra of the moon's shadow: the disk of the sun is covered by that of the moon, and the solar corona (see SUN) becomes clearly visible. Total eclipses are particularly important since only during them can astronomers study the solar corona and prominences. The maximum possible duration of a total eclipse is about 7½min. Should the observer be outside the umbra but within the penumbra, or should the earth pass through only the penumbra, a partial eclipse will occur.

An **annular eclipse** is seen when the moon is at its farthest from the earth, its disk being not large enough to totally obscure that of the sun. The moon's disk is seen surrounded by a brilliant ring of light.

ECOLOGY, the study of plants and animals in relation to their ENVIRONMENT. The whole earth can be considered as a large ecological unit: the term biosphere is used to describe the atmosphere, earth's surface, oceans and ocean floors within which living organisms exist. However, it is usual to divide the biosphere into a large number of ecological subunits or ecosystems, within each of which the organisms making up the living community in balance with the environment. Typical examples of ecosystems are a pond, a deciduous forest or a desert. The overall climate and topography within an area are major factors determining the type of ecosystem that develops, but within any ecosystem minor variations give rise to smaller communities within which animals and plants occupy their own particular niches. Within any ecosystem each organism, however large or small, plays a vital role in maintaining the stability of the community.

The most important factor for any organism is its source of energy or food. Thus, within any ecosystem, complex patterns of feeding relationships or **food chains** are built up. Plants are the primary source of food and energy; they derive it through PHOTOSYNTHESIS, utilizing environmental factors such as light, water, carbon dioxide and minerals. Herbivores then obtain their food by eating plants. In their turn, herbivores are preyed upon by carnivores, who may also be the source of food for other carnivores. Animal and plant waste is decomposed by microorganisms (BACTERIA, FUNGI) within the habitat, and this returns the raw materials to the environment. The number of links within a food chain is normally three or four, with five, six and seven less frequently. The main reason for the limited length of food chains is that the major part of the energy stored within a plant or animal is wasted at each stage in the chain. Thus if it were possible for a carnivore to occupy, say, position 20 within a food chain, the area of vegetation required to supply the energy needed for the complete chain would be the size of a continent.

The plants within an ecosystem, as well as the major environmental features, help create habitats suitable for other organisms. Thus, in a forest ecosystem, the humid, dimly illuminated environment covered by a thick canopy is suitable for mosses, lichens and ferns and their associated fauna. Within any ecosystem the raw materials nitrogen, carbon, oxygen and hydrogen (in water) are continually being recycled via a number of processes including the nitrogen cycle, CARBON CYCLE and photosynthesis.

Most natural ecosystems are in a state of equilibrium or balance so that few changes occur in the natural flora and fauna. However, when changes occur in the environment, either major climatic changes or minor alterations in the inhabitants, an imbalance results and the ecosystem changes to adapt to the new situation. The sequence of change that leads to a new period of equilibrium is called a succession and may take any length of time from a few years, for the establishment of a new species, to several centuries, for the change from grassland to forest.

Over millions of years, nature has moved toward the overall creation of stable ecosystems. Natural changes, such as adaptations to the slow change of climate, tend to be gradual. However, man often causes much more sudden changes—the introduction of a disease to a hitherto uninfected area, the cutting down of a forest or the polluting of a river. The effects of this type of change upon an ecosystem can be rapid and irreversible. Up to now these changes have not been too serious on a worldwide scale, but there is an increasing awareness of what could happen if a major disturbance in the biosphere occurred. The forms of life as they are known today depend entirely upon the sensitive balance within the environment, and any change with worldwide effects could have devastating consequences for man and for life in general.

ECONOMIC ADVISERS, Council of. See COUNCIL OF ECONOMIC ADVISERS.

ECONOMICS is basically concerned with the most efficient use of scarce resources (factors of production such as land, labor, capital) in producing various types of goods and services to satisfy numerous different and competing demands. The American economist Paul SAMUELSON has called economics the study of how, what and for whom to produce. The difficulty of defining economics precisely stems from the various concerns that have characterized the evolution of economic thought. Analytical economics began with XENOPHON, who coined the word *oikonomikos*, a combination of two Greek words, one meaning home or household, and the other to manage or rule. While theologians in the Middle Ages wrote about economic matters, serious and organized economic studies date only from the 17th century. Since then there have been seven major schools of economic thought: MERCANTILISM (17th and 18th centuries); PHYSIOCRATS (mid-18th century); classicists (18th and 19th centuries); Marxists (19th and 20th centuries); neoclassicists (19th and 20th centuries); Keynesians, and post-Keynesians (both of them 20th century).

Mercantilists were concerned with trade, especially foreign trade, and argued for a surplus of exports over imports. They also advocated development of local industries protected by tariffs from foreign competition as a means of reducing unemployment and minimizing the reliance on imports in times of national emergency. In contrast, the physiocratic school is best known for the *Tableau Économique*, a work by its founder François Quesnay (1694–1774). In this school the economy is visualized in terms of circular flows of outputs and income among its members, thus displaying the general interdependence of industries in the economy. The physiocrats were eventually eclipsed by the work of the three most eminent classicists: Adam SMITH, who favored free trade and competition (laissez-faire); Thomas MALTHUS and David RICARDO, whose treatises on rent and the labor theory of value have influenced all subsequent discussions on problems of distribution and value.

A separate school of thought, MARXISM, developed during this period. However, the work of its two founders, Karl MARX and Friedrich ENGELS, was preoccupied with describing and analyzing how the capitalist economy behaves. They used philosophical and sociological principles to postulate "inexorable laws of development," and concluded that capitalism was doomed and that socialism was inevitable.

The neoclassicists, of which the most famous were William Stanley JEVONS in England, Karl Menger in Austria and Léon Walras in Switzerland, were concerned with diverse theoretical aspects of the problems of value and distribution, and for the first time applied mathematics to the study of economics in systematic fashion. In the 20th century, two new schools of thought came into being. The Keynesians applied basic principles of supply and demand to analyze problems of national income, unemployment and inflation. The post-Keynesians concern themselves with issues of post-WWII economic development. Among these are growth economics (at what rate should the economy grow and what is the rate of investment needed?); economic planning (guidance and control of the economy to achieve certain objectives); and development economics (how best can developing countries industrialize?).

Under the influence of KEYNESIAN ECONOMICS, US government policies from the 1950s emphasized increasing demand by both manipulating tax rates and increasing the money supply. However, starting in the 1970s, inflation and a stagnating or decreasing gross national product brought these fiscal policies under question, strengthening the influence of non-Keynesian economists. The SUPPLY-SIDE ECONOMICS favored by President Reagan's administration advocated increasing the growth of input (capital, raw materials) by government policies that are intended to encourage investment, such as tax incentives to invest in new plants and machinery, increased depreciation write-offs and lowered tax rates on capital gains and high incomes. Monetarists (see MONETARISM) view inflation as today's prime economic problem and urge the FEDERAL RESERVE SYSTEM to keep a tight rein on the money supply, which by increasing lifts the rate of inflation.

ECUADOR, republic in NW South America, lying S of Colombia and N and W of Peru, on the Pacific coast. Its territory includes the GALAPAGOS ISLANDS in the Pacific.

Official name: Republic of Ecuador
Capital: Quito
Area: 103,930sq mi
Population: 9,923,000
Languages: Spanish
Religions: Roman Catholic
Monetary unit(s): 1 sucre = 100 centavos
Land. Ecuador is divided by two Andes ranges running N to S, between which lie about 10 plateaus around 8,000ft high. This is the most densely populated region of the country, and the capital, Quito, is situated in its N part. Between the Andes and the Pacific lie the coastal lowlands, also well populated, while to the E of the Andes there are almost uninhabited equatorial forests. The central Andean area has a mild climate all the year around, but the lowlands are hot and wet.
People. Of the population, roughly 10% are white, 10% black, 25% Indian and 55% mestizo—people of mixed Indian and white ancestry. The official language is Spanish but Quechua is widely spoken. Most Ecuadorians live near subsistence level either by working their own small landholdings or more commonly as laborers on large estates and plantations. Adult-education programs have helped reduce illiteracy to 15%.
Economy. Although only 5% of the land is cultivated, agriculture was the basis of Ecuador's economy until 1972, when exploitation of petroleum began. Ecuador became a leading producer of oil in Latin America, and oil revenues contributed to rapid economic growth in the 1970s. In the 1980s, a slump in world oil prices and a

devastating earthquake that totally halted exports for four months in 1987 caused a serious economic crisis. Other exports include bananas, coffee, cocoa, and fish products. Many foodstuffs, transportation equipment, chemicals and consumer goods must be imported. Manufacturing (textiles, food processing, cement and pharmaceuticals) grew substantially in the 1970s but contracted in the 1980s.
History. Following the conquest of the Incas by PIZARRO in 1533, Ecuador became part of the Spanish Empire. It has been an independent republic since 1830, but has always suffered from political instability, marked by conflict between the landed bourgeoisie of the Andean region, the mercantile interests centered in the leading port of Guayaquil and, more recently, the urban working classes. Military coups have been common—the most recent successful one in January 1976. A civilian government was installed in 1979; successive elections were held without incident.

ECUMENICAL COUNCIL, a general council of the leaders of the entire Christian Church. The first was at Nicaea (325) and there have been 20 since. The Orthodox Churches recognize only those that were truly ecumenical—the first seven, with the Trullan Synod (692), and give them supreme authority; the Roman Catholic Church also recognizes the 14 later Western councils, the last being the Second Vatican Council (1962–65), but denies their authority unless confirmed by the pope. Protestants generally honor the first four.

ECUMENICAL MOVEMENT, modern movement among the Christian churches to encourage greater cooperation and eventual unity. Various organizations such as the International Missionary Council, and the Life and Work and the Faith and Order conferences (after WWI) studied the churches' doctrinal differences. But substantial progress was not made until 1948, when representatives of 147 world churches agreed to form the WORLD COUNCIL OF CHURCHES. Most Protestant and Orthodox churches have since joined the council, and the Roman Catholic Church, though not a member, participates in some joint studies.

ECZEMA, form of DERMATITIS, usually with redness and scaling. It is often familial, being worst in childhood, and is associated with HAY FEVER and ASTHMA.

EDDA, name of two works of Old Icelandic literature known as the *Prose (Younger) Edda* and the *Poetic (Elder) Edda*. The *Prose Edda* was written c1200 by SNORRI STURLUSON for aspiring court poets as a guide to the subject matter and techniques of SKALDIC POETRY. The *Poetic Edda*, compiled later in the 13th century, contains 34 mainly alliterative poems written between c800 and 1200. It represents the finest extant body of ICELANDIC literature.

EDDINGTON, Sir Arthur Stanley (1882–1944), English astronomer and astrophysicist who pioneered the theoretical study of the interior of STARS and who, through his *Mathematical Theory of Relativity* (1923), did much to introduce the English-speaking world to the theories of EINSTEIN.

EDDY, Mary Baker (1821–1910), US founder of CHRISTIAN SCIENCE. After a period of study under Phineas QUIMBY she began to formulate her own ideas on spiritual healing and published these in *Science and Health* (1875). She founded the *Christian Science Monitor* newspaper in 1908.

EDDY, Nelson (1901–1967), US baritone who appeared in a number of romantic musical films in the 1930s with soprano **Jeannette MacDonald** (1907–1965).

EDEMA, the accumulation of excessive watery fluid outside the cells of the body, causing swelling of a part. Some edema is seen locally in INFLAMMATION. The commonest type is gravitational edema (**dropsy**), where fluid swelling is in the most dependent parts, typically the feet. HEART or LIVER failure, MALNUTRITION and nephrotic syndrome of the KIDNEY are common causes, while disease of VEINS or LYMPH vessels in the legs also leads to edema. Serious edema may form in the LUNGS in heart failure and in the BRAIN in some disorders of METABOLISM, trauma, TUMORS and infections. DIURETICS may be needed in treatment.

EDEN, Robert Anthony, Earl of Avon (1897–1977), British diplomat and prime minister (1955–57), famous for his antiappeasement stand in the 1930s and for his part in the SUEZ CANAL crisis of 1956. Eden became foreign secretary in 1935 but resigned in 1938 in protest against Chamberlain's negotiations with Hitler and Mussolini. He served again at the foreign office 1940–45 and 1951–55. As prime minister he promoted an ill-advised invasion of Egypt (1956) to restore Anglo-French control of the Suez Canal after the Egyptians had nationalized it. He resigned the next year because of ill health.

EDEN, Garden of, in biblical tradition, the garden paradise created by God for ADAM and EVE. In the Old Testament book of Genesis it is described as being watered by four streams, including the Tigris and the Euphrates, which suggests that it was set somewhere in ancient Mesopotamia.

EDERLE, Gertrude Caroline (1906–   ), US swimmer, the first woman to swim the English Channel. She broke all previous records, crossing the 35mi from France to England on Aug. 6, 1926, in 14hr 31min.

EDGEWORTH, Maria (1767–1849), Anglo-Irish novelist. Her gifts for social observation and colorful, realistic portrayal of Irish domestic life and young people influenced many later novelists including Sir Walter SCOTT. Among her works are *Tales of Fashionable Life* (1809–12).

EDINBURGH, capital of Scotland, the seat of Midlothian Co., and the second largest Scottish city, located on the S shore of the Firth of Forth. The Old Town, dominated by Edinburgh Castle, dates from the 11th century, but has remains of fortifications from c617. The city became Scotland's capital in 1437. It has always been Scotland's cultural center. Holyrood House, a royal residence, is situated here; Edinburgh U. was founded in 1583. The city has many public and private buildings which are beautiful examples of Neoclassical architecture. Since 1947 Edinburgh has been world-famous for its annual summer arts festival. Today the city is a thriving commercial center for banking, insurance and finance; its industries include brewing, distilling, engineering, printing and publishing. Pop 439,672.

EDISON, Thomas Alva (1847–1931), US inventor, probably the greatest of all time with over 1,000 patents issued to his name. His first successful invention, an improved stock-ticker (1869), earned him the capital to set up as a manufacturer of telegraphic apparatus. He then devised the diplex method of telegraphy which allowed one wire to carry four messages at once. Moving to a new "invention factory" (the first large-scale industrial-research laboratory) at Menlo Park, N.J., in 1876, he devised the carbon transmitter and a new receiver which made A. G. BELL's TELEPHONE commercially practical. His tin-foil phonograph followed in 1877, and in the next year he started to work toward devising a practical incandescent lightbulb. By 1879 he had produced the carbon-filament bulb and electric LIGHTING became a reality, though it was not until 1882 that his first public generating station was supplying power to 85 customers in New York.

Moving his laboratories to West Orange, N.J., in 1887 he set about devising a motion-picture system (ready by 1889) though he failed to exploit its entertainment potential. In all his career he made only one important scientific discovery, the Edison effect—the ability of electricity to flow from a hot filament in a vacuum lamp to another enclosed wire but not the reverse (1883)—and, because he saw no use for it, he failed to pursue the matter. His success was probably more due to perseverance than any special insight; as he himself said: "Genius is one percent inspiration and ninety-nine percent perspiration."

EDUCATION, Public. The idea of public education in America was born in colonial New England and spread, gradually and unevenly, through the rest of the country. The founders of the republic believed that an educated citizenry was essential for the success of their design. Their interest in education was shared by the rising class of businessmen, who required a literate and disciplined work force. During the 19th century, tax-supported elementary schools in every state largely supplanted various private, charity, and denominational schools. In the fall of 1980, 99.3% of all children aged 7-13 (grades 1-8) were enrolled in school, 88.4% of them in public schools.

Public secondary schools developed in the 19th century to serve middle-class young people destined for college, business, and the professions. Early in the 20th century the classical college-preparatory high-school curriculum was modified to accommodate the increasing numbers of students for whom high school was the final stage of education. In 1900, only 11.4% of persons aged 14-17 attended high school, and as late as 1950 only 76.7%. In 1985, 94.9% of young people aged 14-17 (grades 9-12) were enrolled in high school, and about three-quarters of them graduated. The median number of school years completed by all persons 25 years old and over was 9.3 in 1950 and 12.6 in 1985.

Although almost all young Americans go to school and three-fourths graduate from high school, there is persuasive evidence that Americans are poorly educated. More than 10% of US adults are functionally illiterate, unable to read an employment advertisement or complete a job application. Employers are appalled at the lack of basic reading, writing, and arithmetic skills among job applicants with high-school diplomas. American students compare poorly with foreign students on math and science exams. The academic achievement even of college-bound high-school juniors and seniors, as measured by the Scholastic Aptitude Test (SAT), declined precipitously from an average combined verbal and math score of 980 out of a possible 1600 in 1963 to 890 in 1980 before gradually recovering to 906 in 1986.

For this calamitous failure, the schools are universally blamed—perhaps unfairly, since locally controlled public schools probably reflect the values and desires of their communities more accurately than most institutions. The causes of the failure are probably very complex and inextricably involved with little-understood cultural and societal forces. Symptomatic of the confusion is the perennial debate between educational conservatives and educational liberals, each group blaming the schools' failure on the educational philosophy espoused by the other.

Liberals advocate educating "the whole child," developing his emotional as well as his intellectual capacities. They believe the elementary school should encourage the young child's natural eagerness to learn by providing an environment of freedom, discovery, and creativity. Because older children are most interested in the things that affect them directly, liberals advocate a high-school curriculum emphasizing "relevance" and offering a wide choice of electives. In view of the uncertain future, some liberals believe that the goal of education should not be knowledge itself but the skills needed to acquire knowledge.

Conservatives believe that there is a body of traditional knowledge that society has a duty to transmit to its youth and that youth has a right to receive. In the elementary grades, this means solid mastery of the "three R's." In the secondary grades, it means firm grounding in English, history, mathematics, science, and foreign languages. Conservatives do not believe that children are the best judges of what is educationally important. A curriculum so narrowly vocational or trivially "relevant" as to deny the high-school student a comprehensive basic education does him a disservice by foreclosing future occupational or educational options.

Neither of these views has ever prevailed to the exclusion of the other. But fashions in education continually swing, pendulumlike, between them. Conservatives point out that the periods of liberal dominance coincide with declining levels of academic achievement. Liberals claim that the schools have failed because they are authoritarian, stifling, and irrelevant.

While the battle over educational philosophies continues, educators and politicians are compelled to come up with proposals for better schools. It was long self-evident to believers in "quality education" that high educational expenditures (inputs) would produce superior educational results (outputs). Researchers have found that the connection between inputs and outputs is not as direct and important as was once believed.

Some educators have argued for innovative methodologies, like open class-rooms, team teaching, etc. Researchers have found that innovative methodologies produce little effect. In fact, the only methodology that has been found effective is one that emphasizes academic standards, denial of automatic promotion, and frequent evaluation of teacher performance.

A popular proposal in the early 1980s was competency testing—that is, requiring high-school seniors to pass examinations in the basics of reading, writing and mathematics and denying diplomas to those who fail. Critics argued that any standards low enough to be politically acceptable to parents would be educationally meaningless and that denial of a diploma—often essential for employment—would stigma-tize students for failures that are arguably the fault of the schools. There is less objection to tests if they are administered early enough in each student's high-school career to identify learning deficiencies that can be remedied before graduation.

A currently popular proposal is teacher accountability—holding teachers and administrators responsible for the success or failure of their schools. Increasingly, states are trying to raise teaching standards by requiring examinations and even intern-ships before certifying new teachers. Advocates of teacher accountability would like to see ineffective teachers weeded out and effective teachers rewarded. Teacher organizations, however, adamantly oppose all schemes of teacher accountability since, they argue, students' achievement is affected by many factors outside of the classroom.

EDUCATION, US Department of, established as a cabinet-level department Sept. 27, 1979, as part of President Jimmy Carter's plan to reorganize the federal government. With an initial budget of $14.1 billion and some 17,400 employees, the new department was split out of the Department of Health, Education, and Welfare, whose name was changed as a result to the Department of HEALTH AND HUMAN SERVICES.

EDWARD, eight kings of England. (See also EDWARD THE CONFESSOR.) **Edward I** (1239–1307), reigned 1272–1307. He subjugated Wales and, inconclusively, Scotland, centralized the national admini-stration and reduced baronial and clerical power. He summoned the Model Parli-ament (1295). **Edward II** (Edward of Caernarvon, 1284–1327), first heir appar-ent to be created Prince of Wales (1301), reigned 1307–27. He spent his reign trying to resist the barons. His poorly directed Scottish campaigns were highlighted by his defeat at Bannockburn (1314) by Robert Bruce. In 1326 he was unseated in a revolt led by his wife, Queen Isabella, and her paramour Roger de Mortimer. Edward was imprisoned, and forced to abdicate in favor of his son, and was probably murdered. **Edward III** (1312–1377) reigned 1327–77. Edward's claim to part of Guienne in France was one of the causes of the HUNDRED YEARS WAR. Despite decisive victories at Crécy (1346) and Poitiers (1356), he had lost most French territory by the end of his reign. In 1348–49, the BLACK DEATH decimated the population, resulting in major economic and social upheavals. **Edward IV** (1442–1483), reigned 1461–70 and 1471–83, during the Wars of the ROSES. A Yorkist, Edward deposed the Lancastrian Henry VI in 1461 and again in 1471 after the latter had been restored in 1470 by the Earl of WARWICK. Edward reestablished the power of the monarchy, improved admini-stration and law enforcement and increased England's trade and prosperity. **Edward V** (1470–1483?), reigned April–June, 1483, one of the "princes in the tower." He is believed to have been murdered at the order of his uncle and protector, Richard Duke of Gloucester, who became Richard III. Edward acceded to the throne as a minor and was immediately a victim of a ruthless power struggle between his uncles Gloucester and Earl Rivers. **Edward VI** (1537–1553), Henry VIII's only son, reigned 1547–53. A sickly child who was to die of consumption, he succeeded to the throne as a minor. Struggles over the succession, and between Protestants and Roman Catholics soon engulfed him. His reign saw the introduction, under Arch-bishop CRANMER, of the first *Book of Common Prayer* (1549). **Edward VII** (1841–1910), king of Great Britain and Ireland, 1901–10. A popular king, with a reputation as a *bon vivant*, he was particularly concerned with Britain's role in Europe and he helped to promote ENTENTES with France and Russia and to defuse the rivalry with Germany. **Edward VIII** (1894–1972), king of Great Britain and Ireland, Jan. 20–Dec. 11, 1936. Edward enjoyed great popularity as Prince of Wales and heir, but his association with the American divorcée, Wallis Warfield

Simpson, was treated as a scandal by the press and met stern opposition from government and Church. Edward acceded to the throne but to avoid a constitutional crisis abdicated, becoming Duke of Windsor. He married Mrs. Simpson in 1937 and thereafter lived mainly in France.

EDWARDS, Jonathan (1703–58), American theologian and philosopher of wide-ranging interests (see also ENLIGHTENMENT). A Calvinist in the Puritan tradition, he furthered the GREAT AWAKENING by his preaching, but was dismissed by his church in 1749 for his opposition to the HALF-WAY COVENANT. In 1757 he became president of the College of New Jersey (Princeton U.). Influenced by LOCKE, he wrote many works of philosophical theology, most notably *The Freedom of the Will* (1754) and *Religious Affections* (1746).

EDWARD THE BLACK PRINCE (1330–1376), prince of Wales, son and heir of Edward III. His nickname may derive from the color of his armor; he is remembered mainly as a brilliant soldier. Given his first independent command in France in 1355, he won the battle of POITIERS in 1356, capturing the French king. Made Prince of Aquitaine in 1362, he alienated his subjects, who revolted. Mortally ill, he returned to England in 1371 and died there a year before his father.

EDWARD THE CONFESSOR, Saint (c1003– 1066), king of England from 1042. Brought up in Normandy, he was respected for his piety. During most of his reign the government was dominated by the powerful Earl Godwin. Edward alienated the country by attempting to exile Godwin and introduce Normans into the government. He had named William of Normandy as his heir, but on his deathbed chose HAROLD, Godwin's son, precipitating the NORMAN CONQUEST.

EDWARD THE ELDER (d. 924), king of WESSEX (899–924), son and successor of ALFRED THE GREAT. He continued his father's warfare against the Danes and by 918 ruled all of England S of the Humber.

EELS, long slender fish of the order Anguilliformes, without pelvic fins and with dorsal and ventral fins joining the tail fin. They include the conger, moray, snake, snipe and freshwater eel families. Some eels are covered in slime, and some have tiny scales on the skin. Moray eels live in warm water and are a danger to divers. American and European freshwater eels spawn in the Sargasso Sea. The leaf-like larvae cross the ocean, and enter rivers as young eels or elvers. When adult they swim back to the

Sargasso Sea to spawn and die.

EFFICIENCY, in THERMODYNAMICS and the theory of MACHINES, the ratio of the useful work derived from a machine to the ENERGY put into it. The mechanical efficiency of a machine is always less than 100%, some energy being lost as HEAT in FRICTION. When the machine is a heat engine, its theoretical thermal efficiency can be found from the second law of thermodynamics, but actual values are often rather lower. A typical gasoline engine may have a thermal efficiency of only 25%, a STEAM ENGINE 10%.

EGALITARIANISM, the doctrine that all men, in spite of differences of character or intelligence, are of equal dignity and worth, and therefore are entitled to equal rights and privileges in society. Interpretation of this doctrine has varied from the notion of equal access to opportunity to that of equal satisfaction of basic needs or to the leveling of social, political and economic inequalities. Thus it has been claimed as a guiding principle by such diverse political philosophies as democratic capitalism, socialism and communism.

EGG, the female GAMETE, germ cell or ovum found in all animals and in most plants. Popularly, the term is used to describe those animal eggs that are deposited by the female either before or after fertilization and develop outside the body, such as the eggs of reptiles and birds. The egg is a single cell which develops into the EMBRYO after FERTILIZATION by a single sperm cell or male gamete. In animals, it is formed in a primary sex organ or gonad called the ovary. In fishes, reptiles and birds there is a food store of yolk enclosed within its outer membrane. In ANGIOSPERMS, the female reproductive organs form part of the FLOWER. The egg cell is found within the ovules, which upon fertilization develop into the embryo and SEED. (See also POLLINATION, REPRODUCTION.)

EGLEVSKY, André (1917–1977), Russian-born US virtuoso ballet dancer and teacher. A member of the Ballet Russe de Monte Carlo 1939–42 and the New York City Ballet 1951–58, he appeared with many of the world's greatest companies.

EGMONT, Lamoral, Count of (1522–68), popular Flemish nobleman, a Catholic, who attempted to take a moderate stand in the Dutch independence movement. He favored loyalty to Philip II of Spain but made a personal protest to him about the persecution of Protestants. When this was ignored he withdrew from the Council of State in 1565, but put down uprisings against the Spanish in Flanders. In 1568 the Duke of Alba, attempting to suppress the independence movement, had him beheaded.

EGRETS, a group of small herons with lacy, usually white, plumage. They are found around the world and the *great* or *common egret* ranges from Europe to New Zealand and throughout the Americas. Other American species include the *snowy egret* and *reddish egret*. The *cattle egret* feeds on insects, often following cattle to catch insects which they flush from the grass. At one time the plumes of the egret were highly valued as items of ceremonial or fashionable dress, and the birds were nearly hunted to extinction. They are now protected by law and are increasing once again.

EGYPT, Arab republic in NE Africa, bordered on the N by the Mediterranean, on the NE by Israel and the Red Sea, on the S by the Sudan and on the W by Libya. The Suez Canal and Gulf of Suez separate the Sinai Peninsula from the rest of Egypt.

Official name: Arab Republic of Egypt
Capital: Cairo
Area: 385,229sq mi
Population: 49,143,000
Languages: Arabic, French, English, Berber
Religions: Muslim, Coptic Christian
Monetary unit(s): 1 Egyptian pound = 100 piastres
Land is 96% desert, only some 13,800sq mi being habitable. The chief physical feature, the fertile Nile R valley, runs narrowly for about 930mi from the Sudanese frontier to the Mediterranean, developing, N of Cairo, into a large alluvial delta where most of the population lives. The Nile separates the Western Desert (260,000sq mi) from the Eastern Desert where the Red Sea Mts (Gebel Sha'ib, 7,175ft) parallel the coast. Egypt's highest peak, Gebel Katherina (8,652ft), is in the thinly populated Sinai Peninsula. The climate everywhere is arid and hot. Rainfall is low, being 3in annually or even less in most of the S.
People are mainly of Hamitic origin. There are small Greek and Armenian communities. The largest cities are Cairo, the capital, and Alexandria. Other important towns are

Giza, Port Said, Suez and Ismailia. Arabic is the official language, but most educated Egyptians also speak French or English. Almost 50% of the adult population is literate. Most Egyptians are Sunni Muslims, but Coptic Christians are numerous.
Economy. Agriculture (especially cotton, wheat, corn, millet and rice) depends mostly on irrigation from the Nile and provides about 30% of the GNP. Mineral resources include iron ore, salt, natural gas and petroleum, and phosphates. The production of textiles and processed foods dominates the industrial sector, although there is some oil refining, and manufacturing of iron and steel, cement, and rubber products. Tourism is highly developed. The ARAB-ISRAELI WARS severely strained the economy. Following the reopening of the Suez Canal (1975), Egypt sought foreign investment to redevelop the canal area.
History (see also EGYPT, ANCIENT). After the Arab invasion (641 AD), Egypt had a variety of rulers including the Mamluks and Ottomans. Financially insolvent after the opening of the Suez Canal (1869), Egypt was a British protectorate 1914–36. From 1948 it played a major role in the Arab-Israeli conflict. In 1952 an army coup deposed King Farouk; the republic was proclaimed in 1953. Col. Gamal Abdel NASSER became president in 1956. He used aid from the USSR to modernize the army and to a lesser extent industry, building the Aswan High Dam. Much Egyptian territory was lost in the Six-Day War with Israel. On Nasser's death (1970) Anwar al-SADAT became president; he joined Syria and Iraq in attacking Israel during the Yom Kippur War (1973). He expelled the Russians from Egypt and sought closer links with the US. In 1978 Sadat and Israeli Prime Minister Menachim Begin signed a peace accord. Israeli forces were withdrawn from the Sinai by 1982, although little progress was made in negotiations on the larger issue of Palestinian autonomy. After Sadat's "separate peace" with Israel, Egypt was severely isolated by the other Arab countries, leaving the country heavily dependent on the US for both economic and military aid. In 1981 Sadat was assassinated by Muslim fundamentalists; he was succeeded by Vice-President Lt. Gen. Muhammed Hosni Mubarak, who was reelected in 1987. Under Mubarak, Egypt was readmitted (1984) to the Islamic Conference Organization and subsequently resumed diplomatic ties with many Arab states.
EGYPT, Ancient, one of the cradles of

world civilization. Egyptian civilization began more than 5,000 years ago in the fertile Nile Valley. Actual dates are much disputed, but Upper and Lower Egypt seem to have been united c3110 BC under Menes, a southern ruler; he made his capital at Memphis, on the boundary between the two. In this period HIEROGLYPHICS developed.

The Old Kingdom (3rd–6th dynasties). The 4th dynasty of pharaohs developed the pyramid as a royal tomb. Under them Egypt became a massive and powerful state. Official worship centered on the sun god RA. The 94-year reign of Pepi II seems to have led to civil war, foreign infiltration and the breakup of the kingdom. After a century of anarchy a stable kingdom was set up in Middle Egypt.

The Middle Kingdom (11th–13th dynasties). The restoration of stability was completed by the 11th dynasty. Under the 12th dynasty the country flourished. Irrigation became more systematic, resulting in increased food production and raised standards of living. Trade extended to Crete and cultural activity reached a new peak. But the 13th dynasty evidently lost power to foreign nomadic rulers, the HYKSOS, who were overthrown by the 17th and 18th dynasties.

The New Kingdom (18th–21st dynasties). The 18th dynasty completed the reconquest, and under Thutmose III Egypt ruled from the Sudan east to the Euphrates. AKHENATON, rejecting traditional polytheism, introduced the sun worship of Aton and founded a new capital at Akhetaton (now Tell el-Amarna). Traditional religion revived under his son-in-law TUTANKHAMEN. Incursions by Hittites, Libyans and other foreign tribes were now weakening Egypt, despite revivals under RAMSES II and III.

The Late Period (21st dynasty–641 AD). Egypt now came increasingly under foreign control, divided between Libyan rulers and the Kingdom of Cush. Invaded by Assyria (668 BC), Egypt was later annexed by Persia (525 BC), then taken by Alexander the Great (332 BC). Alexander founded Alexandria and made his general PTOLEMY governor of Egypt. He fathered the Ptolemaic dynasty of Macedonian rulers which persisted until the death of Cleopatra in 30 BC. Egypt then became a Roman province. In the 4th century AD the country became Christian and c395 it passed under the control of the Byzantine Empire. Byzantine misrule made Arab conquest easy in 641. Egypt became a province of the Arab empire, from which it takes its present character. (For recent history see EGYPT.)

EHRENBURG, Ilya Grigoryevich (1891–1967), Russian author. He emigrated to Paris in 1911 and did not return to Russia until 1924; he then lived in Europe as a journalist until 1941. He received the Stalin Prize for the panoramic novel *The Fall of Paris* (1942). The novel *The Thaw* (1954) was a major work of the post-Stalin liberalization.

EHRLICH, Paul (1854–1915), German bacteriologist and immunologist, the founder of CHEMOTHERAPY and an early pioneer of hematology. His discoveries include: a method of staining (1882), and hence identifying, the TUBERCULOSIS bacillus (see also Robert KOCH); the reasons for immunity in terms of the chemistry of ANTIBODIES AND ANTIGENS, for which he was awarded (with Élie Metchnikoff) the 1908 Nobel Prize for Physiology or Medicine; and the use of the drug salvarsan to cure syphilis (see VENEREAL DISEASES), the first DRUG to be used in treating the root cause of a disease (1911).

EICHMANN, Adolf (1906–1962), lieutenant–colonel in the GESTAPO, head of the Jewish Division from 1939. He was responsible for the deportation, maltreatment and murder of European Jews in WWII. He escaped to Argentina, but was abducted, tried and executed in Israel.

EIFFEL, Alexandre Gustave (1832–1923), French engineer best known for his design and construction of the Eiffel Tower, Paris (1887–89), from which he carried out experiments in AERODYNAMICS. In 1912 he founded the first aerodynamics laboratory.

EIGHT, The. See ASHCAN SCHOOL.

EINHARD (c770–840), Frankish historian who wrote a valuable biography of CHARLEMAGNE.

EINSTEIN, Albert (1879–1955), German-born Swiss-American theoretical physicist, the author of the theory of RELATIVITY. In 1905 Einstein published several papers of major significance. In one he applied PLANCK'S QUANTUM THEORY to the explanation of photoelectric emission. For this he was awarded the 1921 Nobel Prize for Physics. In a second he demonstrated that it was indeed molecular action which was responsible for BROWNIAN MOTION. In a third he published the special theory of relativity with its postulate of a constant VELOCITY for LIGHT (c) and its consequence, the equivalence of MASS (m) and ENERGY (E), summed up in the famous equation $E=mc^2$. In 1915 he went on to publish the general theory of relativity. This came with various testable predictions, all of which were spectacularly confirmed within a few years. Einstein was on a visit to the US when

Hitler came to power in Germany and, being a Jew, decided not to return to his native land. The rest of his life was spent in a fruitless search for a "unified field theory" which could combine ELECTROMAGNETISM with GRAVITATION theory. After 1945 he also worked hard against the proliferation of nuclear weapons, although he had himself, in 1939, signed a letter to President F. D. Roosevelt alerting him to the danger that Germany might develop an ATOMIC BOMB, and had thus perhaps contributed to the setting up of the Manhattan Project.

EIRE. See IRELAND, REPUBLIC OF.

EISELEY, Loren Corey (1907–1977), US anthropologist, professor of anthropology and the history of science at the U of Pennsylvania from 1947. His books, beginning with *The Immense Journey* (1957), were meditations on man's place in nature.

EISENHOWER, Dwight David (1890–1969), supreme commander of Allied troops in Europe during WWII and 34th president of the United States (1953–61).

Born in Denison, Tex., the third of seven sons, he spent most of his childhood in Abilene, Kan. He left Abilene in 1909 to attend West Point. The year after his graduation he married Mary (Mamie) Geneva Doud, by whom he had two sons, Doud David (1917–1921) and John Sheldon Doud (1922–). In 1926 he graduated first out of 275 from the Fort Leavenworth Staff School. By 1941 he had become a brigadier-general, and in the summer of 1943 he was sent to London as commanding general of US forces in the European theater of operations. He directed victorious Allied operations in North Africa and Sicily. As supreme commander of the Allied Expeditionary Force he directed the D-Day assault in 1944 and the campaign which led to the German surrender at Rheims in 1945. He headed the occupation force until 1948, when he became president of Columbia University, taking leave of absence to serve as supreme commander of NATO in 1950.

He became the Republican presidential candidate in 1952, was elected by a large majority, and reelected in 1956. Domestically he sought "moderation," appealing, often fruitlessly, for bipartisan support from a Democratic Congress which consistently rejected such Republican programs as the repeal of the TAFT–HARTLEY ACT and a reduction in tariffs.

The CIVIL RIGHTS legislation of 1957 and 1960 was among the most significant measures of his presidency. Although he sent troops to Little Rock, Ark., to enforce an antisegregation court order, he personally doubted the ability of such legislation to effect social change. One of his first foreign-policy moves was to arrange a truce in the KOREAN WAR. He supported the COLD WAR strategy of his secretary of state, John Foster DULLES, which resulted in some of the highest peacetime military budgets ever proposed. Eisenhower himself warned of the massive potential for "misplaced power" such military expenditures entailed, in his famous "military-industrial complex" speech, given when he retired at the age of 70.

EISENSTAEDT, Alfred (1898–), pioneering American photojournalist who worked for *Life* magazine for over 30 years. From the early 1930s he helped to develop news and candid photography from mere reportage into an art form.

EISENSTEIN, Sergei Mikhailovich (1898–1948), Soviet film director who was a major influence on the development of the cinema. He extended editing techniques, especially the use of montage. His films, notably *The Battleship Potemkin* (1925), *Ten Days that Shook the World* (1927), *Alexander Nevsky* (1938) and *Ivan the Terrible* (1944–46), are undisputed classics.

EISNER, Kurt (1867–1919), German revolutionary who established a socialist republic in Bavaria at the end of WWI and became its premier. Opposed to Prussian leadership of Germany, he published Bavarian documents purporting to show German responsibility for the war. He was assassinated.

EL-ALAMEIN, Battle of, decisive British victory in the N African campaign in WWII. The 8th Army under General MONTGOMERY forced the Axis troops under Field-Marshal ROMMEL to withdraw from Egypt and Libya into E Tunisia, thus paving the way for their total defeat soon after.

ELAM, biblical name of a large and historically important country east of Babylonia and comprising the plain in southwestern Persia roughly corresponding to the modern Iranian province of Khuzistan. Its capital was Susa (Shushan). Elamite history and civilization are chiefly known as a result of the French excavations at Susa, which began in 1897. Throughout its history Elam was closely tied culturally to Mesopotamia. From numerous inscriptions the Elamite language is known up to the time of Darius I (550–486 BC), and, together with Persian and Babylonian, was one of the three official languages of the Persian Empire. Elam and the Elamites are mentioned in the Old Testament both as allies and enemies of various empires that threatened the nation of Israel.

ELAND, the largest antelope, heavily built with spiral horns and a short mane. Eland are found in central and southern Africa where they live in herds of up to 100. In recent years attempts have been made to domesticate eland, as they can survive in very dry conditions and give excellent milk and meat.

ELASTICITY, the ability of a body to resist tension, torsion, shearing or compression and to recover its original shape and size when the stress is removed. All substances are elastic to some extent, but if the stress exceeds a certain value (the elastic limit), which is soon reached for brittle and plastic materials, permanent deformation occurs.

ELBA, Italian island in the Mediterranean, 6mi SW of Tuscany, famous as the place to which NAPOLEON I was exiled. The island is about 20mi long and less than 10mi wide, and is very mountainous. Industries include iron mining, marble quarrying, fishing and agriculture.

ELBE RIVER, major river in central Europe. It rises in the Riesengebirge in NW Czechoslovakia and flows 725mi N through East and West Germany into the North Sea beyond Hamburg. The river is navigable for some 525mi and is connected by a canal system to the Oder. Important cities on the Elbe include Hamburg, Dresden and Magdeburg.

EL DORADO (Spanish: the gilded one), South American Indian chief who was reputed to cover himself with gold dust at festivals and then, as a sacrifice, wash it off in a lake into which his subjects also threw gold. Much of the Spanish exploration and conquest of South America was fired by the quest for the legendary city of El Dorado. (See also CIBOLA, SEVEN CITIES OF.)

ELEANOR OF AQUITAINE (c1122–1204), daughter and heiress of William, Duke of Aquitaine; queen consort first to Louis VII of France (marriage annulled 1152) and then to Henry II of England. Her marriage to Henry in 1152 brought almost all of W France under English domination. In 1173 she supported her sons (later kings Richard I and John) in rebellion against their father and was afterwards kept in captivity until Henry's death in 1185. She was subsequently active in politics in support of her sons.

ELEATICS, pre-Socratic school of Greek philosophy mentioned by PLATO and ARISTOTLE. Founded by PARMENIDES, it also included ZENO OF ELEA and Melissus, taking its name from Elea, their native city. The central Eleatic doctrine, in contrast to the theory of HERACLITUS, is that the world is one uniform whole, an abstract "being" remaining unchangeable and absolute, and change is a mere illusion of the senses. Because the Eleatics were the first to develop purely formal arguments they are often regarded as the founders of LOGIC.

ELECTION, method of choice by poll, often used by democratic bodies, including states, to select officeholders. Some public officials in ancient Greece and Rome were elected, but the modern system of government by elected representatives derives largely from the British parliamentary system and the American system based on it.

When the American states adapted the British system, however, they wished to avoid having a hereditary head of state and upper house, but did not wish to "degrade" these offices by putting them up for straightforward competitive election. President and Senate were therefore to be chosen by indirect election. The Senate is no longer elected by the state legislatures, but the president is technically still elected by the ELECTORAL COLLEGE.

Primary elections, a reform adopted by a number of states in the late 19th century, might also be considered a form of indirect election, since voters actually elect a delegate of a particular party, who is usually then pledged to vote in convention for those voters' candidate for the party's nomination. The general tendency in American government has been to extend the franchise, by giving all citizens, regardless of color, sex, etc., the right to vote, and individual representation has been channeled to the various people for whom each citizen votes—local officials, county officials, some judges, state governors and legislators, US Representatives and Senators and so on.

A system of proportional representation, as opposed to the plurality system, operates by awarding parties seats in a national legislature, for example, on the basis of the proportion of the total popular vote each party has received. Although operated widely in Europe, proportional representation has only been used experimentally in the US, except in the special case of some primary elections.

ELECTORAL COLLEGE, body created to elect the president and vice president of the US. The college was conceived as a compromise between direct popular elections for the nation's highest office and rule by appointment or inheritance. It was originally intended in the Constitution that the electors would be chosen by the state legislatures. But this has been modified so that the electors are chosen by the voters of each state—often without their names appearing on the ballot—by the indirect method of allowing voters to indicate their choice for president and vice president and then allowing the winning party's electors to cast the states' votes for the candidates chosen. Each state has as many votes in the college as the total number of its senators and representatives. If no candidate receives a majority of electoral votes, the House of Representatives elects the president from among the top three candidates. This happened twice in the 19th century—in 1800, when Thomas Jefferson was chosen by the House, and in 1824, when John Quincy Adams was chosen. Since the winning candidate in each state receives all that state's electoral votes, it is mathematically possible for the losing presidential candidate to receive more popular votes than the man elected by the college. This happened in 1824 with Jackson and Adams, in 1876 with Tilden and Hayes and in 1888 when Benjamin Harrison defeated Grover Cleveland. There has been constant dissatisfaction with the electoral college, but the institution still survives. (See also UNITED STATES CONSTITUTION.)

ELECTRIC CAR, an automobile driven by electric MOTORS and (usually) using storage BATTERIES as the ENERGY source. Although an electrically-powered carriage was built as long ago as 1837, it was only in the 1890s that electric cars became common. After WWI they lost ground to AUTOMOBILES with INTERNAL-COMBUSTION ENGINES although, particularly in Europe, electric traction has remained popular for urban delivery vehicles. With increasing concern being felt at the energy- and pollution-costs of the gasoline automobile, renewed interest is being shown in the electric car in spite of its relatively short range between charges. It is pollution-free, robust and simple to drive and maintain. The only difficulty is its low power-to-weight ratio, largely due to the weight of the lead-acid storage batteries commonly used. Much research is being put into finding alternative, lighter battery systems or powerful-enough fuel cells to make electric cars once again an attractive proposition for urban transportation.

ELECTRIC FISHES, several groups of unrelated fishes that have the ability to generate electric currents for stunning prey or enemies or for locating nearby objects. The electric currents are generated in specialized muscles. Fishes that stun their prey or their adversaries include the Mediterranean *electric ray* which delivers a charge of 200 volts, the *marine stargazers*,

the *electric catfish* of Africa and the *electric eel* of the Amazon, which is not a true eel. Its body organs are squeezed into the head end and most of the eel-like body is given over to an electric organ that discharges 500 volts. The electric eel also discharges a very weak current in the form of continuous pulses. These form an electromagnetic field around the fish and it can detect disturbances to this field caused by prey animals or other objects. The *elephant-snout fishes* and the *knifefish* of Africa also have this faculty.

ELECTRICITY, the phenomenon of charged particles at rest or in motion. Electricity provides a highly versatile form of ENERGY, electrical devices being used in heating, LIGHTING, machinery, TELEPHONES, and ELECTRONICS. **Electric charge** is an inherent property of matter; ELECTRONS carry a negative charge of 1.602×10^{-19} coulomb each, and atomic nuclei normally carry a similar positive charge for each electron in the ATOM. When this balance is disturbed, a net charge is left on an object; the study of such isolated charges is called **electrostatics.** Like charges repel and unlike charges attract each other with a force proportional to the two charges and inversely proportional to the square of the distance between them (the inverse-square law). This force is normally interpreted in terms of an electric field produced by one charge, with which the other interacts. A field is represented graphically by field lines beginning at the positive and ending at the negative charge. The lines show by their direction that of the field, and by their density its strength. Pairs of equal but opposite charges separated by a small distance are called dipoles, the product of charge and separation being called the dipole moment. Dipoles experience a torque in an electric field that tends to align them with the field, but they experience no net force unless the field is nonuniform. The amount of work done in moving a unit charge from one point to another against the electric field is called the electric **potential difference,** or voltage, between the points; it is measured in VOLTS (V = joules/coulomb). The ratio of a charge added to a body to the voltage produced is called the capacitance of the body.

Materials known as electric CONDUCTORS contain charges that are free to move about—for example, valence electrons in metals, and ions in salt solutions. The presence of an electric field in conductors produces a steady flow of charge in the direction of the field; such a flow constitutes an **electric current,** measured in amperes (A

= coulombs/second). The field implies a voltage between the ends of the conductor, which is normally proportional to the current (OHM'S LAW). This ratio, called the resistance of the conductor, is measured in ohms (ohms [Ω] = volts/amps); it normally rises with temperature. Materials with high resistance to currents are classed as insulators. (See also SEMICONDUCTOR.) The energy acquired by the charges in falling through the field is dissipated as heat—and light, if a sufficient temperature is reached—the total POWER output being the product of current and voltage. Thus, for example, a 1-kW heater supplied at 110 V draws a current of about 9 A, and the hot element has a resistance of about 12Ω.

Electric sources such as BATTERIES or GENERATORS convert chemical, mechanical, or other energy into electrical energy (see ELECTROMOTIVE FORCE), and will pump charge through conductors much as a water pump circulates water in a radiator heating system. Batteries create a constant voltage, producing a steady, or direct current (DC); many generators, on the other hand, provide a voltage that changes in sign many times a second, and so produce an alternating current (AC), in which the charges move to and fro instead of continuously in one direction. This system has advantages in generation, transmission, and application and is now used almost universally for domestic and industrial purposes.

An electric current is found to produce a magnetic field circulating around it, to experience a force in an externally generated magnetic field, and to be itself generated by a changing magnetic field. For more details of these properties, on which most electrical machinery depends, see ELECTROMAGNETISM.

Static electricity was known to the ancient Greeks; the inverse square law was hinted at by J. PRIESTLEY in 1767 and later confirmed by H. CAVENDISH and C. A. Coulomb. G. S. Ohm formulated his law of conduction in 1826, although its essentials were known before then. The common nature of all the "types" of electricity then known was demonstrated in 1826 by M. FARADAY, who also originated the concept of electric field lines.

ELECTRIC MOTOR. See MOTOR, ELECTRIC.

ELECTROCARDIOGRAPH, instrument for recording the electrical activity of the HEART, producing its results in the form of multiple tracing called an electrocardiogram (ECG or EKG). These are conventionally recorded with twelve combinations of electrodes on the limbs and chest wall. The electrical impulses in the conducting tissue and muscle of the heart pass through the body fluids, while the position of the electrodes determines the way in which the heart is "looked at" in electrical terms. ECGs allow detection of CORONARY THROMBOSIS, abnormal heart rhythm, disorders of the heart muscle and PERICARDIUM, as well as diseases of the METABOLISM that affect the heart.

ELECTROCHEMISTRY, branch of PHYSICAL CHEMISTRY dealing with the interconversion of electrical and chemical energy. Many chemical species are electrically-charged IONS (see BOND, CHEMICAL), and a large class of reactions—oxidation and reduction— consists of electron-transfer reactions between ions and other species. If the two half-reactions (oxidation, reduction) are made to occur at different electrodes, the electron-transfer occurs by the passing of a current through an external circuit between them (see BATTERY). The ELECTROMOTIVE FORCE driving the current is the sum of the electrode potentials (in volts) of the half-reactions, which represents the free energy (see THERMODYNAMICS) produced by them. Conversely, if an emf is applied across the electrodes of a cell, it causes a chemical reaction if it is greater than the sum of the potentials of the half-reactions (see ELECTROLYSIS). Such potentials depend both on the nature of the reaction and on the concentrations of the reactants. Cells arising through concentration differences are one cause of corrosion.

ELECTROENCEPHALOGRAPH, instrument for recording the BRAIN's electrical activity using several small electrodes on the scalp. Its results are produced in the form of a multiple tracing called an electroencephalogram (EEG). The "brain waves" recorded have certain normal patterns in the alert and sleeping individual. Localized brain diseases and metabolic disturbances cause abnormal wave forms either in particular areas or as a generalized disturbance. The abnormal brain activity in EPILEPSY, both during convulsions and when the patient appears normal, usually allows diagnosis. The interpretation of electroencephalographs requires skill and experience.

ELECTROLYSIS, production of a chemical reaction by passing a direct current through an electrolyte— i.e., a compound which contains IONS when molten or in solution. (See ELECTROCHEMISTRY.) The cations move toward the cathode and the anions toward the anode, thus carrying the current. At each electrode the ions are discharged according to FARADAY's laws: (1) the quantity of a substance produced is proportional to the amount of electricity passed; (2) the relative quantities of different substances produced are proportional to their equivalent weights. Hence one gram-equivalent of any substance is produced by the same amount of electricity, known as a **faraday** (96,500 coulombs). Electrolysis is used to extract electropositive metals from their ores, and to refine less electropositive metals; to produce sodium hydroxide, chlorine, hydrogen, oxygen and many other substances; and in electrometallurgy.

ELECTROMAGNET, a magnet produced (and thus easily controlled) by the electric current in a coil of wire which is usually wound on a frame of highly permeable material so as to reinforce and direct the magnetic field appropriately.

ELECTROMAGNETIC RADIATION, or radiant energy, the form in which ENERGY is transmitted through space or matter using a varying electromagnetic field. Classically, radiant energy is regarded as a WAVE MOTION. In the mid-19th century MAXWELL showed that an oscillating (vibrating) electric charge would be surrounded by varying electric and magnetic fields. Energy would be lost from the oscillating charge in the form of transverse waves in these fields, the waves in the electric field being at right-angles both to those in the magnetic field and to the direction in which the waves are traveling (propagated). Moreover, the velocity of the waves would depend only on the properties of the medium through which they passed; for propagation in a vacuum its value is a fundamental constant of physics—the **electromagnetic constant**, $c = 299{,}792.5$km/s. At the beginning of the 20th century PLANCK proposed that certain properties of radiant energy were best explained by regarding it as being emitted in discrete amounts called quanta. Einstein later proposed that the quanta should be regarded as particles, called PHOTONS, and that the energy travels through space in that form. The energy of each photon is proportional to the frequency of the associated radiation (see QUANTUM THEORY).

The different kinds of electromagnetic radiation are classified according to the energy of the photons involved, the range of energies being known as the electromagnetic SPECTRUM. (Equivalently, this spectrum arranges the radiations according to wavelength or frequency.) In order of decreasing energy the principal kinds are gamma rays, X-RAYS, ULTRAVIOLET RADIATION, LIGHT, INFRARED RADIATION, MICROWAVES and RADIO waves. In general, the higher the energies involved, the better the properties of the radiation are described in terms of particles (photons) rather than waves. Radiant energy is emitted from objects when they are heated (see BLACKBODY) or otherwise energetically excited (see LUMINESCENCE; SPECTROSCOPY); man uses it to channel and distribute both energy and information (see INFORMATION THEORY).

ELECTROMAGNETISM, the study of ELECTRIC and magnetic fields, and their interaction with electric charges and currents. The two fields are in fact different manifestations of the same physical field, the electromagnetic field, and are interconverted according to the speed of the observer. Apart from the effects noted under ELECTRICITY and MAGNETISM, the following are found:

1. Moving charges (and hence currents) in magnetic fields experience a FORCE, perpendicular to the field and the current, and proportional to their product. This is the basis of all electric MOTORS, and was first applied for the purpose by M. FARADAY in 1821.

2. A change in the number of magnetic field lines passing through a circuit "induces" an electric field in the circuit, proportional to the rate of the change. This is the basis of most GENERATORS, and was also established by M. Faraday, in 1831.

3. An effect analogous to the above, but with magnetic and electric fields interchanged, and usually much smaller. This was hypothesized by J. C. MAXWELL, who in 1862 deduced from it the possibility of self-sustaining electromagnetic waves traveling at a speed which coincided with that of LIGHT, thereby identifying the nature of visible light, and predicting other waves such as the RADIO waves found experimentally by H. HERTZ shortly afterwards.

ELECTRON, a stable SUBATOMIC PARTICLE, with rest MASS $9.109 \, 1 \times 10^{-31}$kg (roughly 1/183,6 the mass of a HYDROGEN atom) and a negative charge of 1.6021×10^{-19}C, the charges of other particles being positive or negative integral multiples of this. Electrons are one of the basic constituents of ordinary MATTER, commonly occupying the orbitals surrounding positively charged atomic nuclei. The chemical properties of ATOMS and MOLECULES are largely determined by the behavior of the electrons in their highest-energy orbitals. Both cathode rays and beta rays are streams of free electrons passing through a gas or vacuum. The unidirectional motion of electrons in a solid conductor constitutes an electric current. Solid conductors differ from nonconductors in that in the former some electrons are free to move about, while in the latter all are permanently associated with particular nuclei. Free electrons in a gas or vacuum can usually be treated as classical particles, though their wave properties become important when they interact with or are associated with atomic nuclei. The anti-electron, with identical mass but an equivalent positive charge, is known as a positron (see ANTIMATTER).

ELECTRONIC MUSIC, compositions in which musicians use sounds created solely on electronic equipment. **Concrete music** uses recordings of natural sounds as the basis for composition; and works mixing both approaches are called "tape music." Experiments with electronic composition began as early as the 1890s but widespread production began only after WWII, as universities and broadcasting authorities in many countries began setting up studios to encourage this use of modern technology. John CAGE, Karlheinz STOCKHAUSEN and Edgar VARÈSE have produced important works in this field.

ELECTRONICS, an applied science dealing with the development and behavior of electron tubes, SEMICONDUCTORS and other devices in which the motion of electrons is controlled; it covers the behavior of electrons in gases, vacuums, conductors and semiconductors. Its theoretical basis lies in the principles of ELECTROMAGNETISM and solid-state physics discovered in the late 19th and early 20th centuries. Electronics began to grow in the 1920s with the development of RADIO. During WWII, the US and UK concentrated resources on the invention of RADAR and pulse transmission methods and by 1945 they had enormous industrial capacity for producing electronic equipment. The invention of TRANSISTOR in 1948 as a small, cheap replacement for vacuum tubes led to the rapid development of COMPUTERS, transistor radios, etc. Now, with the widespread use of integrated circuits, electronics plays a vital role in communications (TELEPHONE networks, information storage, etc.) and industry. All electronic circuits contain both active and passive components and transducers (e.g., MICROPHONES) which change ENERGY from one form to another. Sensors of light, temperature, etc., may also be present. **Passive components** are normally conductors and are characterized by their properties of resistance (R), capacitance (C) and inductance (L). One of these usually predominates, depending on the function required. **Active components**

are electron tubes or semiconductors; they contain a source of power and control electron flow. The former may be general-purpose tubes (diodes, triodes, etc., the name depending on the number of electrodes) which rectify, amplify or switch electric signals. Image tubes (in TELEVISION receivers) convert an electric input into a light signal; photoelectric tubes (in television cameras) do the reverse. Semiconductor diodes and transistors, which are basically sandwiches made of two different types of semiconductor, now usually perform the general functions once done by tubes, being smaller, more robust and generating less heat. These few basic components can build up an enormous range of circuits with different functions. Common types include: power supply (converting AC to pulsing DC and then smoothing out the pulsations); switching and timing (the logic circuits in computers are in this category); AMPLIFIERS, which increase the amplitude or power of a signal, and oscillators, used in radio and television transmitters and which generate AC signals. Demands for increased cheapness and reliability of circuits have led to the development of microelectronics. In **printed circuits**, printed connections replace individual wiring on a flat board to which about two components per cu cm are soldered. Integrated circuits assemble tens of thousands of components in a single structure, formed directly by evaporation or other techniques as films about 0.03mm thick on a substrate. In monolithic circuits, components are produced in a tiny chip of semiconductor by selective diffusion.

ELECTRON MICROSCOPE, a microscope using a beam of ELECTRONS rather than light to study objects too small for conventional MICROSCOPES. First constructed by Max Knoll and Ernst Ruska around 1930, the instrument now consists typically of an evacuated column of magnetic lenses with a 50–1500 kV electron gun at the top and a fluorescent screen or photographic plate at the bottom. The various lenses allow the operator to see details almost at the atomic level (0.1 nm) at up to a million times magnification, although many specimens deteriorate under the electron bombardment at these limits. The greater magnification results from the shorter wavelengths of electrons compared to the light waves of optical microscopes.

Standard instruments are called *transmission* electron microscopes because the beam is transmitted through the thin-sliced specimen. In the *scanning* electron microscope, which resembles a

TELEVISION system, a beam of 1-20 kV intensity is instead focused to a point and scanned over the specimen area. A synchronized television screen displays the intensity of the secondary electrons reflected back, or scattered, from the surface. Resolution is limited to about 3 nm, but the surface topography is seen as an image. Scanning electron microscopes can also be used in a *transmission* mode.

In the *field emission* electron microscope, invented by Erwin Müller in 1936, the object itself—the sharp tip of a metal or semiconductor specimen—is the source of the electrons, when it is subjected to a strong electric field. An image of the tip's surface appears on a fluorescent screen without the use of a focusing system. Very high resolutions can be obtained by using charged atoms instead of electrons; images of individual atoms in the tip have been obtained in this way.

Electron microscopes are used for structural, defect and composition studies in a wide range of biological and inorganic materials.

ELEGY, in classical poetry, refers to a lyric poem of alternate two-line stanzas written in a distinctive meter on a variety of themes. However, the term has been used since the Renaissance to describe any poem expressing sorrow, particularly about death, such as Milton's *Lycidas* (1637) or Thomas Gray's *Elegy Written in a Country Churchyard* (1750).

ELEMENT, Chemical, simple substance composed of ATOMS of the same atomic number, and so incapable of chemical degradation or resolution. Elements are generally mixtures of different ISOTOPES. Of the 106 known elements, 88 occur in nature, and the rest have been synthesized (see TRANSURANIUM ELEMENTS). The elements are classified by physical properties as METALS, metalloids and nonmetals, and by chemical properties and atomic structure according to the PERIODIC TABLE. Most elements exhibit ALLOTROPY, and many are molecular (e.g., oxygen, O_2). The elements have all been built up in STARS from HYDROGEN by complex sequences of nuclear reactions, e.g., the CARBON CYCLE.

ELEMENTARY PARTICLES. See SUBATOMIC PARTICLES.

ELEPHANTIASIS, disease in which there is massive swelling and hypertrophy of the SKIN and subcutaneous tissue of the legs or scrotum, due to the obstructed flow of LYMPH. This may be a congenital DISEASE, due to trauma, cancer or infection with filariasis, tuberculosis and some venereal diseases. Recurrent secondary bacterial infections are common, and chronic skin ULCERS may form. Elevation, elastic stockings, DIURETICS and treatment of infection are basic to relief, while some cases are helped by SURGERY.

ELEPHANTS, the largest living land mammals, comprising two species, the African *Loxodonta africana* and the Indian *Elephas maximus.* The African elephant is up to 12ft tall and may weigh 6.6 tons; the Indian species is slightly smaller. Both species are characterized by their trunks, elongated extensions of the nose and upper lip, and by huge incisor teeth in the males prized as the source of ivory. The African elephant has large ears that distinguish it from the Indian species. Both live in herds feeding on grass and foliage. In spite of, and because of, its size the Indian elephant has long been tamed as a beast of burden.

ELEUSINIAN MYSTERIES, secret religious rites of the seasons in ancient Greece. They were originally performed in honor of Demeter, goddess of agriculture, at Eleusis near Athens and dramatized the descent of her daughter Persephone into the underworld. Later the rites were performed in Athens.

ELGAR, Sir Edward William (1857–1934), English composer. In general Elgar followed the German orchestral and choral traditions of the 19th century, but his *Enigma Variations* (1899) and *Pomp and Circumstance* marches reflected a style which was clearly English in character. His other works include the oratorio *The Dream of Gerontius* (1900); two symphonies, violin and cello concertos, and the concert overture *Cockaigne (1901).*

ELGIN MARBLES, ancient sculptures (mostly from the Athenian ACROPOLIS) brought to Britain by Thomas Bruce, 7th Earl of Elgin and British envoy at Constantinople (1799–1802). Now in the British Museum, they include a frieze from the Parthenon and parts of the Erechtheum temple.

EL GRECO. See GRECO, EL.

ELIJAH, Hebrew prophet of the late 9th century BC, mentioned in the Koran and the Old Testament Book of Kings. He fought against the worship of BAAL introduced from Phoenicia during the reign of King Ahab of Israel by his Queen, Jezebel. In the New Testament Elijah appears with Christ at the Transfiguration.

ELIJAH MUHAMMAD. See MUHAMMAD, ELIJAH.

ELIOT, Charles William (1834–1926), US educator, president of Harvard University from 1869–1909 and editor of the original *Harvard Classics* series. Eliot had a

profound influence on American education.
ELIOT, George (1819–1880), pseudonym
of the famous English novelist, Mary Ann
Evans. Her work, notably *Adam Bede*
(1859), *The Mill on the Floss* (1860), *Silas
Marner* (1861), *Middlemarch* (1871–72)
and *Daniel Deronda* (1876) brought a new
breadth of intellect, technical sophistication
and moral scope to the English novel and
greatly influenced later novelists. Her
creative work was encouraged by writer and
editor George Henry Lewes, with whom she
lived for 24 years, defying convention. She
was a friend of Herbert SPENCER. was
subeditor of the *Westminster Review*
(1851–53) and a notable translator of
German works.
ELIOT, John (1604–1690), Puritan clergyman known as the "apostle to the Indians."
Born in England, he emigrated to Mass. in
1631 and devoted himself to the conversion
of local Indians. He established over a dozen
missions in New England, most of which
were destroyed in KING PHILIP'S WAR.
ELIOT, T(homas) S(tearns) (1888–1965),
major 20th-century poet and critic. Born in
St. Louis, Mo., he settled permanently in
England. He was a leading modernist who
found his own poetic voice as early as
Prufrock and Other Observations (1917).
His most famous poem, *The Waste Land*,
appeared in 1922, and was noted for its
portrayal of the chaos and squalor of
modern life. His criticism (*The Sacred
Wood*, 1920) expressed belief in tradition
and the life of the spirit, however.
Increasingly meditative and philosophical
poetry followed (e.g. *Ash Wednesday*, 1930,
and his masterpiece, the *Four Quartets*,
1944). He wrote successful poetic dramas
such as *Murder in the Cathedral* (1935)
and *The Cocktail Party* (1950). He was
awarded the Nobel Prize for Literature in
1948.
ELISHA, Hebrew prophet, a disciple of and
successor to ELIJAH. Greatly gifted as a
soothsayer and healer, he was successful in
driving out BAAL worship from the northern
state of Israel.
ELIZABETH (1709–1762), empress of
Russia from 1741, daughter of PETER the
Great. In 1741 she staged a coup against her
cousin, the regent, and reasserted her
father's principle of government. She rid the
court of German influence, founded
Moscow University, and pursued the SEVEN
YEARS' WAR against Prussia.
ELIZABETH I (1533–1603), queen of
England and Ireland 1558–1603, and the
last TUDOR monarch. A daughter of HENRY
VIII, who had broken with the Catholic
Church to marry Anne BOLEYN, her mother,

her initial task as queen was to reestablish
her supremacy over the English Church
after the reign of her Catholic sister, MARY I.
The defeat by her navy of the Spanish
ARMADA (1588) established England as a
major European power. At home, industry,
agriculture and the arts (especially
literature) throve under conditions of
relative peace and financial stability, while
colonization of the New World was
encouraged. The settlement of the
Protestant succession became the *bête noire*
of the reign as Elizabeth was unmarried and
childless. After the execution of her
Catholic cousin, MARY QUEEN OF SCOTS, a
possible heir, Elizabeth finally acknowledged the succession of JAMES VI of Scotland,
Mary's son, thus securing the peaceful
union of England and Scotland.
ELIZABETH II (1926–   ), queen of the
United Kingdom of Great Britain and
Northern Ireland (from 1952) and head of
the COMMONWEALTH OF NATIONS. One of the
world's few remaining monarchs, she is
extremely popular at home and abroad and
has traveled extensively as her country's
representative. She is married to Philip
Mountbatten, Duke of Edinburgh, and has
four children.
ELK, large member of the DEER family
Cervidae. It inhabits some of the forest
areas of N Europe and Asia and is closely
related to the larger American MOOSE. The
American elk is also called the WAPITI.
**ELKS, Benevolent and Protective Order of
(BPOE),** US fraternal organization, founded 1868, with headquarters in Chicago, Ill.
In 1988 it had 1.5 million members.
ELLESMERE ISLAND, Canadian Arctic
island off northwest Greenland. It occupies
about 80,000 sq mi and broadly consists of
ice-capped plateaus and mountains flanked
by a coastline pierced by deep fjords. Cape
Columbia (83°07') is North America's
northernmost point. The island supports
musk oxen and caribou but its only human
inhabitants are a few Eskimos and
technicians. Natural gas was found there in
1969. Ellesmere Island was discovered in
1616 by William BAFFIN.
ELLICE ISLANDS. See TUVALU.
ELLINGTON, Edward Kennedy "Duke"
(1899–1974), US composer, pianist and
orchestra leader, one of the giants of JAZZ
music. After a formal musical education,
Ellington formed his first band in 1918 and
by the 1930s enjoyed an international
following. His superbly disciplined orchestra remained the envy of the jazz world for
several decades, playing music composed by
its leader for its well-known instrumental
soloists. Ellington wrote such hit songs as

"Mood Indigo," "Sophisticated Lady" and "Satin Doll," suites such as *Black, Brown and Beige* (1943) and, late in life, considerable sacred music. He was awarded the Presidential Medal of Freedom in 1969.

ELLIS, (Henry) Havelock (1859–1939), British writer chiefly remembered for his studies of human sexual behavior and psychology. His major work was *Studies in the Psychology of Sex* (1897–1928).

ELLIS ISLAND, island of about 27 acres in upper New York Bay, within the boundaries of New York City. Bought by the government in 1808, it was the site of a fort and later an arsenal. From 1891 to 1954, it was an immigration station through which some 20 million immigrants entered the US.

ELLISON, Ralph Waldo (1914–   ), black US writer. He is best known for his novel *Invisible Man* (1952), a story of black alienation in a hostile white society, which won a National Book Award.

ELLSWORTH, Lincoln (1880–1951), US polar explorer and the first man to cross both the Arctic and Antarctic by air. He flew from Spitsbergen to Alaska with AMUNDSEN and the Italian Umberto Nobile in the dirigible *Norge* (1926), and in 1935 he made a 2,300mi flight over the Antarctic in a single-engine airplane.

ELLSWORTH, Oliver (1745–1807), American statesman and jurist reputedly responsible for the use of the term "United States" in the American Constitution. He represented Conn. at the Constitutional Convention (1787), where he helped promote the "Connecticut compromise," providing equal state representation in the Senate. He was Senator from Conn. 1789–96, and chief justice of the US 1796–1800.

ELM, a deciduous tree growing to 160ft. It has toothed leaves and the seeds are carried on the wind by a "wing." Elms have tough wood, used in furniture and barrels, and are often grown along streets. The American elm is rapidly being killed off by a fungus disease called *Dutch elm disease*, which is carried by the elm bark beetle. The disease was first identified in the Netherlands and appeared in the US in the 1930s. It has spread rapidly from New England. Other, less valuable elms, are immune to the disease.

ELMAN, Mischa (1891–1967), Russian-born US violinist. He made his international debut in Berlin (1904), and first performed in the US in 1908. He became an American citizen in 1923.

EL SALVADOR, the smallest Central American republic, bordered by Guatemala and Honduras, and having a Pacific coastline.

Official name: Republic of El Salvador
Capital: San Salvador
Area: 8,124sq mi
Population: 4,974,000
Languages: Spanish
Religions: Roman Catholic
Monetary unit(s): 1 Salvadoran colón = 100 centavos

Land. Two parallel volcanic mountain ranges cross the country from SE to NW enclosing high fertile plateaus and valleys irrigated in the W by the Lempa R. To the E of the narrow coastal plain the Gulf of Fonseca forms a natural harbor for the chief port, La Unión.

People. About 89% of the population are mestizos, 10% Indians and 1% white. Some Indians still speak Nahuatl. The country has one of the highest illiteracy rates in Latin America (almost 40%).

Economy. El Salvador depends on agriculture, which supports most of its population at subsistence level. Corn, rice, sugar, cotton and beans are grown, and coffee, from the rich volcanic areas of the highlands, is the chief export. The developing industries include food processing and the production of textiles, cement and asbestos. The country trades mainly with the US, importing machinery, foodstuffs and chemical products, and since 1961 has been a member of the Central American Common Market.

History. El Salvador was discovered in 1524 by a Spanish expedition led by ALVARADO. Unrest during the early 19th century led to independence from Spain in 1821. After brief involvement in the Mexican Empire, El Salvador joined the first Central American Federation 1823–38. It became an established independent republic in 1841. From the beginning the nation was beset by ideological disputes, political rivalries and military coups. A long-standing hostility between El Salvador and Honduras erupted into an armed conflict in 1969. The 1970s and 1980s were marked by armed violence between government forces, backed by the US, and leftist guerrillas. By 1988 the civil war had killed 70,000 Salvadorans, and more than 1 million had fled abroad. The army and right-wing elements represented by the Nationalist Republic Alliance (ARENA), led by Roberto d'Aubuisson, murdered thousands of suspected leftists. Despite substantial US economic and military assistance, the government of Christian Democrat José Napoleón Duarte suffered from corruption, economic mismanagement, and failure to end the civil war. In 1988 ARENA won control of the national legislature and seemed likely to win the presidential election scheduled for 1989.

ELY, Richard Theodore (1854–1943), US political economist. He advanced the study of economics and helped found the American Economic Association (1885). As a leader of the Society of Christian Socialists, he supported the growth of the labor unions.

EMANCIPATION PROCLAMATION, decree issued by Abraham Lincoln on Jan. 1, 1863, during the Civil War. It abolished slavery in the rebel states, although Lincoln was not an abolitionist and pledged in 1860 not to interfere with slavery. It was a shrewd military and political maneuver designed to deprive the Confederacy of its economic base, namely slavery. Nevertheless, the proclamation boosted the abolitionist cause and three years later the 13th Amendment brought all slavery in America to an end. (See also CIVIL WAR, AMERICAN.)

EMBARGO ACT (1807), legislation requested by President Thomas JEFFERSON in response to restrictions imposed on neutral shipping by both Britain and France, who were at war. The act forbade all international trade to and from US ports, the object being to persuade Britain and France of the value of neutral commerce. Enforcement of the act provoked serious resistance in New England without affecting Britain or France. The policy was abandoned in 1810.

EMBOLISM, the presence of substances other than liquid BLOOD in the BLOOD CIRCULATION, causing obstruction to ARTERIES or interfering with the pumping of the HEART. The commonest embolism is from atheromatous plaques (see ARTERIOSCLEROSIS) or THROMBOSIS on a blood vessel or the HEART walls. FAT globules may form emboli from bone MARROW after major bone FRACTURES, and amniotic fluid may cause embolism during childbirth. Stroke or transient cerebral episodes, pulmonary embolism, CORONARY THROMBOSIS and obstruction of limb or organ blood supply with consequent cell DEATH are common results, some of them fatal. Some may be removed surgically, but prevention is preferable.

EMBROIDERY. See NEEDLEWORK.

EMBRYO, the earliest stage of the life of a FETUS, the development from a fertilized egg through the differentiation of the major organs. In man, the fertilized egg divides repeatedly, forming a small ball of cells which fixes by IMPLANTATION to the wall of the womb; differentiation into placenta and three primitive layers (endoderm, mesoderm and ectoderm) follows. These layers then undergo further division into distinct organ precursors, and each of these develops by a process of migration, differentiation and differential growth. The processes roughly correspond to the phylogeny or evolutionary sequence leading to the species. Much of development depends on formation of cavities, either by splitting of layers or by enfolding. The HEART develops early at the front, probably splitting into a simple tube, before being divided into separate chambers; the gut is folded into the body, although for a long time the bulk of it remains outside. The NERVOUS SYSTEM develops as an infolding of ectoderm, which then becomes separated from the surface. Facial development consists of mesodermal migration and modification of the bronchial arches, remnants of the gills in phylogeny; primitive limb buds grow out of the developing trunk. The overall control of these processes is not yet understood; however, infection (especially GERMAN MEASLES) in the mother, or the taking of certain DRUGS (e.g., THALIDOMIDE) during PREGNANCY may lead to abnormal development and so to congenital defects, including heart defects (e.g., BLUE BABY), limb deformity, HARELIP and CLEFT PALATE. By convention, the embryo becomes a fetus at three months' gestation.

EMBRYOLOGY, the study of the development of EMBRYOS of animals and humans, based on anatomical specimens of embryos at different periods of gestation, obtained from animals or from human ABORTION. The development of organ systems may be deduced and the origins of congenital defects recognized, so that events liable to interfere with development may be avoided. It may reveal the basis for the separate development of identical cells and for control of growth. The ANATOMY of an organism may be better understood and learnt by study of embryology. The principal embryologists of past ages have included ARISTOTLE; William HARVEY and Marcello MALPIGHI in the 17th century, and

Karl Ernst von Baer in the 19th century.

EMERALD, valuable green GEMSTONE, a variety of beryl. The best emeralds are mined in Colombia, Brazil and the USSR. Since 1935 it has been possible to make synthetic emeralds.

EMERSON, Ralph Waldo (1803–1882), US philosophical essayist, poet and lecturer. He resigned a Unitarian pastorate (1831) and, after traveling in Europe, settled in Concord, Mass. His *Nature* (1836) was the strongest motivating statement of American TRANSCENDENTALISM. After 1837 he became renowned as a public speaker and after 1842 as editor of the Transcendentalist journal, *The Dial.* He later adjusted his idealistic view of the individual to accommodate the American experience of man's historical and political limitations, especially over the issue of slavery.

ÉMIGRÉ, one who leaves a country, usually for political reasons. During the FRENCH REVOLUTION, many members of the nobility and clergy left France. When they returned after 1815 they formed a reactionary, ultraroyalist element. After the 1917 Bolshevik revolution, Russian émigrés were familiar figures in W Europe.

EMILIA-ROMAGNA, fertile, low-lying historic region in N Italy, bounded by the Po R, the Adriatic and the Apennines. Named for the ancient Roman road, the Via Aemilia, whose route is now followed by a railroad, it was once part of the Papal States, and contains the noted art centers of Bologna, Ferrara, Ravenna and Parma.

EMMET, Robert (1778–1803), Irish patriot. After a poorly planned uprising against the British in 1803, Emmet was tried and hanged for treason, which assured his fame as a martyr and romantic hero.

EMMETT, Daniel Decatur (1815–1904), US entertainer who organized one of the first black-faced minstrel troupes. His song "Dixie's Land" attached the name Dixie to the south and became the unofficial anthem of the Confederacy.

EMOTION, in psychology, a term that is only loosely defined. Generally, an emotion is a sensation which causes physiological changes (as in pulse rate, breathing) as well as psychological changes (as disturbance) which result in attempts at adaptations in the individual's behavior. Some psychologists differentiate types of emotion: one such classification is into primary (e.g., fear), complex (e.g., envy) and sentiment (e.g., love, hate); but such schemata are controversial. The causes of emotion are not fully understood, but they may be associated with biochemical changes in various parts of the body. (See also INSTINCT.) Modern psychoanalysts generally prefer the term affect for emotion.

EMPEDOCLES (c490–430 BC), Sicilian Pythagorean philosopher who developed the notion that there were four fundamental elements in matter—earth, air, fire and water. In medicine he taught that blood ebbed and flowed from the heart and that health consisted in a balance of the four HUMORS in the body.

EMPEROR, ruler of an empire. The word comes from the Latin *imperator,* supreme military commander. The successors of Julius CAESAR adopted the title, and it continued in use in the Western Roman Empire until 476 and in the Eastern Roman (Byzantine) Empire until 1453. The title was revived in the West with the crowning of CHARLEMAGNE in 800; it designated the ruler of the Holy Roman Empire from 936 to 1806. In 1545 IVAN IV THE TERRIBLE assumd the title emperor (tsar) of Russia, which he considered the heir to the Byzantine Empire. NAPOLEON I took the title in 1804; he was followed by the rulers of Austria, Germany, Great Britain (for India), Mexico, and Brazil. The rulers of China, Japan, and Ethiopia have also used the title.

EMPHYSEMA, condition in which the air spaces of the LUNGS become enlarged, due to destruction of their walls. Often associated with chronic BRONCHITIS, it is usually a result of SMOKING but may be a congenital or occupational disease. Subcutaneous emphysema refers to air in the subcutaneous tissues.

EMPIRE STATE BUILDING, office building in New York City. Rising 1,250ft, it is one of the highest buildings in the world. It is one of the most popular tourist attractions in New York and on a clear day there is a 50-mile view from the top of its 102 stories. It was built in 1930–31.

EMPIRE STYLE, Neoclassical style in architecture, interior decoration and furniture design which reached its peak during the Napoleonic empire (1804–14). In architecture, Roman grandeur was imitated; mahogany and gilt were favored materials for furniture; and costume design was inspired by Classical drapery. The style evolved into the German BIEDERMEIER and the English Regency styles. (See also NEOCLASSICISM.)

EMPIRICISM, in philosophy, the view that knowledge can be derived only from sense experience. Modern empiricism, fundamentally opposed to the RATIONALISM that derives knowledge by deduction from principles known a priori, was developed in the philosophies of LOCKE, BERKELEY and HUME. Other thinkers in the "British empiricist tradition" include J. S. MILL and the Americans J. DEWEY and W. JAMES.

EMS DISPATCH, report of an encounter at Ems between Prussian king WILLIAM I and French ambassador Vincent Benedetti telegraphed on July 13, 1870, to Prussian premier Otto von BISMARCK in Berlin. The king had already acceded to French demands by ordering a relative to withdraw as a candidate for the Spanish throne. When Benedetti demanded that the king promise never to allow such a candidacy in the future, the king refused. Bismarck edited and published the telegram in such a way as to exaggerate the king's rebuff of Benedetti, thereby provoking France to declare war. The result was the FRANCO-PRUSSIAN WAR, desired by Bismarck, in which France appeared to be the aggressor.

ENAMEL, vitreous glaze (see CERAMICS; GLASS) fused on metal for decoration and protection. Silica, potassium carbonate, borax and trilead tetroxide (see LEAD) are fused to form a glass (called flux) which is colored by metal oxides; tin (IV) oxide makes it opaque. The enamel is powdered and spread over the cleaned metal object, which is then fired in a furnace until the enamel melts.

ENCEPHALITIS, infection affecting the substance of the BRAIN, usually caused by a VIRUS. It is a rare complication of certain common diseases (e.g., mumps, herpes simplex) and a specific manifestation of less common viruses, often carried by insects. Typically an acute illness with HEADACHE and FEVER, it may lead to evidence of patchy INFLAMMATION of brain tissue, such as personality change, EPILEPSY, localized weakness or rigidity. It may progress to impairment of consciousness and COMA. A particular type, *Encephalitis lethargica*, occurred as an EPIDEMIC early this century leading to a chronic disease resembling PARKINSON'S DISEASE but often with permanent mental changes.

ENCLOSURE, in Britain especially, the practice of fencing off land formerly open to common grazing or cultivation. It began in the 12th century and increased from the 15th century onwards as land values rose, often causing social dislocation and hardship in the countryside.

ENCOMIENDA, system of tributary labor imposed by the Spanish in South America in the 16th century. Spanish settlers, *encomenderos*, were assigned groups of Indians, from whom they exacted tribute and labor. The Spaniards were ostensibly supposed to pay the Indians, protect them and Christianize them. The system died out in the 18th century.

ENCYCLICAL, in modern times a circular letter addressed by the pope to the bishops of the Roman Catholic Church. Papal encyclicals are statements concerned with the general welfare of the faithful and usually set out guidelines for the application of the theological and social teachings of the church. Catholics are bound to accept any doctrinal teachings they may contain. Encyclicals are known by their opening words. Among the best-known encyclicals of recent times are *Rerum Novarum* (1891), on the condition of the working classes, by Leo XIII; *Quadragesimo anno* (1931), in which Pius X wrote on social questions; *Mater et Magistra* (1961) by John XXIII, on social question, and *Pacem in Terris* (1963) on relationships between the church and state; and the controversial *Humanae Vitae* (1968) by Paul VI, on birth control.

ENCYCLOPEDIA, reference work comprising alphabetically or thematically arranged articles selectively covering the whole range or a part of human knowledge. The earliest extant encyclopedia is the *Natural History* of PLINY the Elder (1st century AD) in 37 volumes. The most famous medieval encyclopedia was the *Speculum Majus* of Vincent de Beauvais (13th century), and in 1481 William CAXTON issued one of the earliest encyclopedias in English, the *Mirror of the World*. Ephraim Chambers' *Cyclopaedia* (1728) used specialist writers and formed the basis of the most ambitious and influential work of its kind, the French *Encyclopédie* (1751–72; see DIDEROT, DENIS). The *Encyclopaedia Britannica*, which first appeared 1768–71, and the *Great Soviet Encyclopedia*, whose production began in the 1920s, are the most compendious of the world's general encyclopedias.

ENDANGERED SPECIES. See WILDLIFE CONSERVATION.

ENDECOTT, John (1588–1665), Puritan founder of Salem, Mass., a deputy governor and governor of the Massachusetts Bay colony. He persecuted religious dissenters, especially Quakers.

ENDOCRINE GLANDS, ductless glands in the body which secrete HORMONES directly into the BLOOD stream. They include the PITUITARY GLAND, THYROID and parathyroid glands, ADRENAL GLANDS and part of the PANCREAS, testes and OVARIES. Each secretes a number of hormones which affect body function, development, mineral balance and

METABOLISM. They are under complex control mechanisms including FEEDBACK from their metabolic function and from other hormones. The pituitary gland, which is itself regulated by the HYPOTHALAMUS, has a regulator effect on the thyroid, adrenals and gonads.

ENDORPHINS, substances produced in the brain that inhibit certain brain cells from transmitting impulses and thereby block or reduce the sensation of pain. Morphine and similar drugs are thought to owe their effectiveness to their chemical similarity to endorphins. Synthetic endorphins may prove to be effective and non-addictive painkillers.

ENERGY, to the economist, a synonym for fuel; to the scientist, one of the fundamental modes of existence, equivalent to and interconvertible with MATTER. The MASS-energy equivalence is expressed in the Einstein equation, $E=mc^2$, where E is the energy equivalent to the mass m, c being the speed of LIGHT. Since c is so large, a tiny mass is equivalent to a vast amount of energy. However, this energy can only be realized in nuclear reactions and so, although the conversion of mass may provide energy for the STARS, this process does not figure much in physical processes on earth (except in nuclear power installations). The law of the conservation of mass-energy states that the total amount of mass-energy in the universe or in an isolated system forming part of the universe cannot change. In an isolated system in which there are no nuclear reactions, this means that the total quantities both of mass and of energy are constant. Energy then is generally conserved.

Energy exists in a number of equivalent forms. The commonest of these is HEAT—the motion of the MOLECULES of matter. Ultimately all other forms of energy tend to convert into thermal motion. Another form of energy is the motion of ELECTRONS. ELECTRICITY. Moving electrons give rise to electromagnetic fields, and these too contain energy. A pure form of electromagnetic energy is ELECTROMAGNETIC RADIATION **(radiant energy)** such as light. According to the QUANTUM THEORY, the energy of electromagnetic radiation is "quantized," referable to discrete units called PHOTONS, the energy E carried by a photon of radiation of frequency v being given by $E=hv$, where h is the PLANCK constant. When macroscopic bodies move, they too have energy in virtue of their motion; this is their kinetic energy and is given by $\frac{1}{2}mv^2$ where m is the mass and v the velocity of motion. To change the

velocity of a moving body, or to set it in motion, a FORCE must be applied to it and work must be done. This work is equivalent to the change in the kinetic energy of the body and gave physicists one of their earliest definitions of energy: the ability to do work. When work is done against a restraining force, **potential energy** is stored in the system, ready to be released again. The restraining force may be electromagnetic, torsional, electrostatic, tensional or of any other type. On earth when an object of mass m is raised up to height h, its gravitational potential energy is given by mgh, where g is the acceleration due to gravity. If the object is let go, it falls and it will strike the ground with a velocity v, its potential energy having been converted into kinetic energy $\frac{1}{2}mv^2$. SOUND energy is kinetic energy of the vibration of air. Chemical energy is the energy released from a chemical system in the course of a reaction. Although all forms of energy are equivalent, not all interconversion processes go with 100% EFFICIENCY (the energy deficit always appears as heat—see THERMODYNAMICS). The SI UNIT of energy is the joule.

ENERGY, US Department of, created Aug. 4, 1977, to centralize national energy planning at the cabinet level. The new department consolidated activities previously conducted within the Department of the Interior and by the Energy Research and Development Administration, the Federal Energy Administration, and the Federal Power Commission.

ENESCO or **ENESCU, Georges** (1881–1955), Romanian composer and violinist. Strongly influenced by folk music, he is best known for his two Romanian Rhapsodies.

ENEWETAK, Pacific atoll at the NW end of the Ralik Chain of the NW Marshall Islands. It served as a US test site for atomic weapons in the 1940s and 1950s and was declared (1978) uninhabitable for at least 30-50 more years because of radiation levels.

ENGELS, Friedrich (1820–1895), German socialist, philosopher and close associate of Karl MARX. Born into a wealthy German family, he went to England in 1842 as the manager of a family factory and there became interested in SOCIALISM. In 1844 he met Marx, whom he supported both financially and politically. Four years later he and Marx published the influential *Communist Manifesto.* Engels edited the 2nd and 3rd volumes of Marx's *Capital,* and among other works wrote *Anti-Duehring: Socialism, Utopian and Scientific* (1878) and *The Origin of the Family, Private Property and the State* (1884).

ENGINE, a device for converting stored ENERGY into useful WORK. Most engines in use today are heat engines which convert HEAT into work, though the EFFICIENCY of this process, being governed according to the second law of THERMODYNAMICS, is often very low. Heat engines are commonly classified according to the fuel they use (as in gasoline engine); by whether they burn their fuel internally or externally (see INTERNAL-COMBUSTION ENGINE), or by their mode of action (whether they are reciprocating, rotary or reactive). (See DIESEL ENGINE; JET PROPULSION; STEAM ENGINE; STIRLING ENGINE; TURBINE.)

ENGINEERS, Army Corps of, technical and combatant corps of the US army. It performs civil as well as military construction and maintenance operations on projects such as harbors, waterways, airfields and missile bases. In war it provides combat and supply support.

ENGLAND, largest and most populous part of the UK, covers 50,333sq mi and has a multiracial population of over 46 million. It is bounded on the S by the English Channel, on the N by Scotland, on the W by the Atlantic Ocean, Wales and the Irish Sea, and on the E by the North Sea. It includes the Isle of Wight and the Scilly Isles, and its coast is much indented. Physical features include the Pennine Chain (Cross Fell 2,930ft) running N from Derbyshire; the Cumbrian Mts containing the country's highest point (Scafell Pike 3,210ft); and numerous lowlands and low hills such as the London basin between the Chiltern Hills and North Downs, the Fens bordering on the Wash and, in the SW, the Cotswold Hills, Exmoor, Dartmoor and Bodmin Moor. Among the largest cities are London, capital of both England and the UK, Birmingham, Manchester, Liverpool, Newcastle, Sheffield, Leeds and Bradford, all centers of industry. Leading industries, some now state-controlled or nationalized, include mining (especially coal), iron and steel, chemicals and manufacturing of all kinds (including automobiles, ships and aircraft). Agriculture is important, but much food—and industrial raw materials, too—has to be imported. See also UNITED KINGDOM.

ENGLAND, Church of. See CHURCH OF ENGLAND.

ENGLAND, John (1786–1842), Irish-born Roman Catholic bishop of Charleston, S.C., from 1820, where he founded schools and charitable organizations and fought discrimination against Catholics.

ENGLISH, language native to the British Isles, spoken there and in North America and Australasia, also in parts of Africa, in India and throughout many other former British colonies. English is taught as the first foreign language in numerous countries over six continents. It is the foremost international language. Several centuries of British colonial expansion facilitated its dispersal while, given the stability this expansion ultimately afforded, the language's qualities of relative simplicity and flexibility enhanced its chances of taking root and surviving in foreign lands.

English is of the INDO-EUROPEAN LANGUAGE family, its parent tongue being referred to as Proto-Indo-European, and it evolved from West Germanic (as did Dutch, Flemish and Frisian). The first steps in its development may be traced back to the Jute, Saxon and Angle settlement in Britain during the 5th and 6th centuries, a settlement gradually given cohesion by the spread of Christianity, and hence of Latinate influences, which followed St. Augustine's landing in Kent in 597. The language that evolved from this settlement is known as Anglo-Saxon or Old English, of which there were four dialects: Northumbrian, Mercian, West Saxon and Kentish. Of these, West Saxon, the dialect of Wessex in which the period's literature has survived, is referred to as standard Old English. It is the language of such works as BEOWULF and the ANGLO-SAXON CHRONICLE. Incursions by VIKING invaders in the 9th century left their mark on the language in the form of numerous Scandinavian loan words.

The Middle English period begins with the Norman Conquest of 1066 and extends to the 15th century, the death of CHAUCER in 1400 being chosen as a convenient closing point. The language absorbed many French (and thereby also many Latin) influences during the period. Two factors are of key importance: the requirement through the Statute of Pleading (1362) that all court proceedings should be in English, and the fact that Chaucer chose to write his major works not in Latin or French, nor even Italian, but in the East Midlands English dialect then spoken in London.

After 1400, there followed a century of transition in which London speech became established, the language undergoing a process of standardization which was to be aided by the introduction of printing by CAXTON in 1476.

With the RENAISSANCE, a host of Greek and Latinate words were introduced and, amid considerable controversy, the English vocabulary expanded. By Shakespeare's time the language was only a little more inflected than it is today. The King James Bible appeared in 1611 and just under a century and a half later Dr. Johnson's *Dictionary* (1755) was published. (See also DICTIONARY.)

American English dates from the 17th century. It diverges to a degree in spelling, being often more accurate phonetically, and is also idiomatically different. Its influence on the language has been considerable, especially in the sphere of new coinages, among which scientific words predominate.

ENGLISH CHANNEL, an arm of the Atlantic Ocean separating England and France, called *La Manche* by the French. About 300mi long, it varies in width from about 112mi to about 21mi at the Strait of Dover. Plans to construct a tunnel under the channel (proposed in 1874) began in 1974 but were later abandoned. There are frequent crossings by ferries and Hovercraft. A CHANNEL TUNNEL, projected for more than a century, was begun in 1987.

ENGLISH CIVIL WAR. See CIVIL WAR, ENGLISH.

ENGLISH HORN, an alto oboe, somewhat larger than a standard oboe. Its "bell" is a pear-shaped bulb that helps to give the instrument a dark, melancholy tone.

ENGLISH LITERATURE. Early English literature divides into two periods. ANGLO-SAXON literature ends roughly with the Norman Conquest (1066). Poems which survive, such as the epic BEOWULF (8th century), the religious and quasi-mystical *Dream of the Rood,* and the historical narrative *The Battle of Maldon,* remind us both of the rich culture that produced them and of the pre-literary oral traditions that influenced them. The prose ANGLO-SAXON CHRONICLE is a major chronicle of the age of King Alfred. After the Conquest, as the language developed, the literature widened in range and subject manner. *Sir Gawain and the Green Knight* is perhaps the finest Arthurian poem in the 14th century, and such poets as John Gower and LANGLAND were notable, but Geoffrey CHAUCER (c1340–1400) is the indisputable genius of the era. He is accessible to modern readers because he wrote in the Midlands dialect upon which modern English is based (see ENGLISH) and because his style and temperament have the timeless quality of all great writers. Modern literature can be said to begin with his work, which was the first in English to synthesize successfully a number of widespread European influences. The Middle English period ends by 1476 when CAXTON's press became a decisive

factor in completing the standardization of the language. Poetry in the 15th century is dominated by the name of John SKELTON (c1460–1529) although there was a steady production of anonymous lyrics and ballads. Memorable prose of this period includes MALLORY's *Morte d'Arthur* (c1470) and the Paston letters; while the MYSTERY and MORALITY PLAYS presaged the drama.

The continuing political stability after the Wars of the ROSES permitted a belated appearance of RENAISSANCE humanism under the TUDORS. In this period PROTESTANTISM was established; the language, like the country, grew prosperous, confident and eclectic; in every genre a rich flair for linguistic experimentation and development of new forms reflected the spirit of adventure of a country that was exploring the globe. Sir Thomas WYATT (1503–1542) and Henry Howard, Earl of Surrey (c1517–1547) introduced Italian literary influences into England, particularly adapting the SONNET, and Surrey's early experiments with blank verse were of major importance to dramatists. As important to the linguistic termperament of the era were Sir Philip SIDNEY's *Arcadia* (1590) and *Defence of Poesie* (1595), both widely known in manuscript before publication. The quintessential Renaissance allegory, uniting moral vision with aesthetic virtues, is Edmund SPENSER's *The Faerie Queene* (1590–96). The specific voice of Puritanism appeared, among other places, in Roger Ascham's *The Schoolmaster* (1570). Prose works like LYLY's *Euphues* (1578–80) and Robert Greene's fiction seemed to presage development of the novel, but it was in the field of drama that the glory of the age was expressed. In the theater, human insight and poetic development united to entertain and stir an insatiable audience. In one generation the theater progressed from tentative efforts such as Sackville and Norton's blank verse tragedy *Gorboduc* (1562) and the anonymous farce *Gammer Gurton's Needle* (1575) to the plays of KYD, MARLOWE, DEKKER, Ben JONSON, MARSTON, and, of course, the consummate artistry of SHAKESPEARE. The impetus given to drama after the building of theaters in the 1570s carried through to the Civil War and the closing of the theaters in 1642, adding such names as BEAUMONT AND FLETCHER, WEBSTER, MIDDLETON, MASSINGER and FORD to the list of major dramatists. It was also the period of such offshoots of theater as the MASQUE. A flowering of Elizabethan and Jacobean prose was reached within the Authorized Version of the BIBLE (1611), but the English genius for discursive prose continued to develop in Robert BURTON's *Anatomy of Melancholy* (1621), the work of Sir Thomas BROWNE (1605–1682), and Thomas HOBBES's *Leviathan* (1651).

The dual trauma of the English Civil War and the Puritan Commonwealth produced a profound shift in sensibility. The diaries of Samuel PEPYS (1644–1703) reflect the social flavor of the Restoration period. In the theater a brief flourish of sophisticated, artificial RESTORATION COMEDY gave way by c1800 to a taste for sentiment and prudery that constrained the English drama until the 20th century, except for the brief resurgence of wit in the plays of SHERIDAN and GOLDSMITH in the late 18th century. The great poet of the Puritan movement was John MILTON (1608–1674), who, in retirement after the Restoration, wrote the incomparable Christian epic *Paradise Lost* (1667), a study of the origin of evil which is Homeric in scope. John DRYDEN (1631–1700) was another pivotal writer of the times. Inheritor and supreme exponent of the ideals of the Renaissance, he produced prose, poetry and drama which looked forward to the tone and ambitions of the succeeding era of Neoclassicism. BUNYAN's *The Pilgrim's Progress* (1678) is perhaps the major achievement of Puritan prose literature.

The first years of the prosperous 18th century were the years of ADDISON and STEELE's suave prose and fashionable periodicals. Alexander POPE (1688–1744) was the most famous and admired poet of his era, subtle in his experimentation, wide-ranging in his wit, irony and compassion, while his friend Jonathan SWIFT (1667–1745), also a considerable poet, was a master prose-satirist. His *Gulliver's Travels* (1726) can be seen along with fictitious narratives by Daniel DEFOE (1660–1731)—such as *Robinson Crusoe* (1719) and *Moll Flanders* (1722)—as prime stimulators of the growth of the novel. Coincidental with the increase in economic and political dominance of the middle classes, the new genre was established with the epistolary novels of RICHARDSON (*Pamela*, 1740) and the satirical novels of FIELDING (*Joseph Andrews*, 1742). Tobias SMOLLETT (1721–1771) and Laurence STERNE (1713–1768) were also among the first professional novelists. Increasingly in the 18th century, prose literature in all forms dominated the taste and outlook of the age, the labors and personality of Samuel JOHNSON (1709–1784) being of major importance along with BOSWELL's *Life of Dr. Johnson* (1791–99), and GIBBON's mon-

umental *History of the Decline and Fall of the Roman Empire* (1776–88). Following upon the Gothic mysteries of Horace WALPOLE (1717–1797) and Mrs. RADCLIFFE (1764–1823), precursors of ROMANTICISM, the novels of Jane AUSTEN (1775–1817) are rooted in the 18th-century standards of moderation and elegance, while they established new complexities of irony, psychology and social observation. Later novelists were to develop the territory which she mapped out and to take as models her achievement in formal and technical skills.

The 19th century began with the impact of the Romantic era in poetry: WORDSWORTH, COLERIDGE, BYRON, SHELLEY and KEATS reflected both German literary and French Revolutionary movements. The novels of Sir Walter SCOTT (1771–1826) are as much in keeping with Romantic restlessness, gusto and individuality of utterance as are the criticism of HAZLITT, LAMB and COLERIDGE and the confessional writings of Thomas DE QUINCEY (1785–1859). The Victorian Age which followed, seemingly more staid, was troubled by the early results of the industrial revolution and the political consequences of expanding imperialism in the post-Napoleonic era. Despite adherence to certain conventions, the mid-century poetry of TENNYSON, BROWNING and ARNOLD is innovative in content as well as style. Thomas MACAULAY and Thomas CARLYLE satisfied the Victorian taste for heavy and moralizing nonfiction. The controversies instigated by Cardinal John Henry NEWMAN (1801–1890) and Charles DARWIN (1809–1882) raged with much publicity and rebuttal and reached wide audiences. It was also an age of popular and literary magazines, in which many of the most famous novels first appeared as serials. The great novels of DICKENS, THACKERAY, Emily and Charlotte BRONTË and George ELIOT dominated the period 1830–75 and reflected the major social, political, psychological and historical debates of the country.

Transitional novels by TROLLOPE (1815–1882), MEREDITH (1828–1909) and GISSING (1857–1903) led to the novels of Thomas HARDY (1840–1928) and American-born Henry JAMES (1843–1916) who in their different ways usher in the modern era. Joseph CONRAD (1857–1924), a Pole who chose to write in English, and E. M. FORSTER (1879–1970) were among those who even before WWI introduced foreign influences into English literature. It was about this time, however, that a split began to occur between "serious" and "popular" literature: the more journalistic fiction of Arnold BENNETT (1867–1931), John GALSWORTHY (1867–1933) and H. G. WELLS (1866–1946), along with imperialistic and conservative prose and poetry by Rudyard KIPLING (1865–1936), Hilaire BELLOC (1870–1953) and G. K. CHESTERTON (1874–1936), were also more widely read. This division has been exacerbated since WWI by the increasing complexity of various schools of "modernism." Symbolism, Expressionism and Vorticism were but three experiments in literature (and the visual arts) of the first decades of the 20th century. James JOYCE (1882–1941), Virginia WOOLF (1882–1941) and D. H. LAWRENCE (1885–1930) came to dominate fiction in the interwar period (1918–1939) while YEATS (1865–1939) and T S. ELIOT (1888–1965) established the new voice of modern poetry. For the first time in 200 years there was a major revival in drama (coinciding with the European revival led by IBSEN, STRINDBERG and CHEKHOV), headed by the Irishmen Oscar WILDE (1854–1900) and George Bernard SHAW (1856–1950) in London and J. M. SYNGE (1871–1909), Sean O'CASEY (1884–1964), and Yeats in association with the ABBEY THEATRE in Dublin.

By WWII a new generation of writers had begun to appear. Concern about the tortured politics of Europe was reflected by poets such as W. H. AUDEN (1907–1973) and C. Day LEWIS (1904–1972) and the journalist-novelists Arthur KOESTLER (1905–1983) and George ORWELL (1903–1950). Graham GREENE (b. 1904), Christopher ISHERWOOD (b. 1904) and Evelyn WAUGH (1903–1966) were among the most interesting novelists of the same generation.

Since the war, the most consistently lively activity in England has been in the theater: John OSBORNE (b. 1929), Harold PINTER (b. 1930), Athol Fugard (b. 1932) and Tom STOPPARD (b. 1937) have produced striking work. Individual works in other genres have attracted attention. William GOLDING (b. 1911) and Doris Lessing (b. 1919) among novelists, and Philip Larkin (b. 1922) and Seamus Heaney (b. 1937) among poets have been of particular interest. It has also become evident that the critical writings of T. S. ELIOT, William Empson (b. 1906) and F. R. LEAVIS (b. 1895) among others, have established a new age of the prose essay in English literature.

For the literature of the US, see AMERICAN LITERATURE.

ENGRAVING, various craft and technological techniques for producing blocks or plates from which to print illustrations, banknotes etc.; also, an individual print made by one of these processes. Line engraving refers to preparing a plate by scratching its smooth surface with a highly-tempered steel tool called a burin or graver. If the desired design is left standing high as is common with woodcuts and linocuts, this is known as a relief process. If the ink is transferred to the paper from lines incised into the plate, the surface of the inked plate having been wiped clean, this is known as intaglio. Drypoint and mezzotint are mechanical engraving processes developed from line engraving; other techniques, including AQUATINT, involve chemical ETCHING processes. (See also PRINTING.)

ENIWETOK. See ENEWETAK.

ENLIGHTENMENT, The, also known as the Age of Reason or *Aufklärung,* a term applied to the period of European intellectual history centering on the mid-18th century. The empiricist philosophy of LOCKE and scientific optimism following the success of NEWTON'S *Principia* provided men with the confidence to deem reason supreme in all the departments of intellectual enquiry.

ENNIUS, Quintus (239–169 BC), classical Roman poet. His most important work was the *Annales,* a history of Rome beginning with the fall of Troy and ending with his own times, of which only about 600 lines have survived. It was the national poem of Rome until the *Aeneid* of VERGIL.

ENOCH, Books of, three books describing experiences and visions of the Old Testament patriarch Enoch. The first, complete only in an Ethiopic version, is one of the Jewish PSEUDEPIGRAPHA. It is an important aid to New Testament study. The second is written in Slavonic and the third, which is sometimes anti-Christian in tone, is in Hebrew.

ENSOR, James Sydney, Baron (1860–1949), Belgian painter whose bizarre, sometimes macabre canvases were influenced by BOSCH and BRUEGEL and anticipated SURREALISM. Among his best-known works are *Entry of Christ into Brussels* and *The Temptation of St. Anthony,* both painted in the late 1880s.

ENTEBBE, town in S Uganda near Kampala, at whose international airport on July 4, 1976, airborne Israeli commandos carried out a daring hostage rescue. On June 27 Arab terrorists hijacked an Air France plane en route from Tel Aviv to Paris and took it to Entebbe, where they were protected by Ugandan president Idi AMIN DADA. The hijackers released more than half of the plane's passengers but kept 102, mostly Israelis, plus the plane's crew as hostages, demanding the release of Palestinian terrorists imprisoned in several countries, including Israel. On July 4, an Israeli force flown 2,500mi nonstop from Israel landed at Entebbe, stormed the building where the hostages were kept, and returned with the hostages to Israel. Three hostages died; a fourth, left behind in a Kampala hospital, was later murdered. The Israelis suffered only one casualty, the commander of the strike force.

ENTENTE (French: understanding), political term for a friendly relation between countries, based on diplomatic agreement rather than formal treaty. The term originated in the 17th century and has been applied particularly to the relationship between Britain and France, the Entente Cordiale (1904), which in 1907, when it included Russia, became the TRIPLE ENTENTE.

ENTERITIS, INFLAMMATION of the small intestine (SEE GASTROINTESTINAL TRACT) causing abdominal colic and DIARRHEA. It may result from VIRUS infection, certain BACTERIAL DISEASES or FOOD POISONING, which are in general self-limited and mild. The noninfective inflammatory condition known as Crohn's disease causes a chronic relapsing regional enteritis, which may result in weight loss, ANEMIA, abdominal mass or VITAMIN deficiency, as well as colic and diarrhea. In bacterial enteritis, ANTIBIOTICS may help, while Crohn's disease is sometimes helped by anti-inflammatory drugs or STEROIDS; SURGERY may also be required, but is often hazardous and may lead to fistula formation.

ENTITLEMENTS, government benefits to which eligible citizens have a legally enforceable right. Some major entitlement programs are Social Security (including Medicare), public assistance (including Medicaid), veterans' benefits, and public-employee retirement payments. Federal expenditures on entitlement programs have risen dramatically in recent years, rising from about a quarter of the federal budget in 1960 to more than half in the late 1980s. Most benefits do not go to the needy: total federal expenditures on public assistance in the mid-1980s were less than a fourth of spending on Social Security (including Medicare) alone. In 1980, 40% of all US households received income from one or more entitlement programs.

ENTOMOLOGY, the study of INSECTS. In a broader sense the term is sometimes erroneously used to describe studies on other arthropod groups. Entomology is important, not only as an academic discipline, but because insects are among the most important pests and transmitters of disease.

ENTROPY, the name of a quantity in STATISTICAL MECHANICS, THERMODYNAMICS, and INFORMATION THEORY representing, respectively, the degree of disorder in a physical system, the extent to which the ENERGY in a system is available for doing work, the distribution of the energy of a system between different modes, or the uncertainty in a given item of knowledge. In thermodynamics the infinitesimal entropy change δS when a quantity of HEAT δQ is transferred at absolute TEMPERATURE T is defined as $\delta S = \delta Q / T$. One way of stating the second law of thermodynamics is to say that in any change in an isolated system, the entropy (S) increases: $\Delta S \geq 0$. This increase in entropy represents the energy that is no longer available for doing work in that system.

ENVER PASHA (1881–1922), also known as Enver Bey, Ottoman leader who organized the Young Turk revolution of 1908 and one of the triumvirate that ruled Turkey from 1913–18. As minister of war he took Turkey into WWI on Germany's side (1914). Edged from power by Mustafa Kemal (SEE ATATURK), he died leading Turkish Uzbek factions against Russia.

ENVIRONMENT, the surroundings in which animals and plants live. The study of organisms in relation to their environment is called ECOLOGY. Organisms are affected by many different physical factors in their environment, such as temperature, water, gases, light, pressure and also biotic factors such as food resources, competition with other species, predators and disease.

ENVIRONMENTAL PROTECTION AGENCY (EPA), US agency established in 1970 to coordinate government action on environmental issues. It absorbed several existing agencies as well as serving as the public's advocate in pollution cases; it also coordinates research by state, local government and other groups.

ENZYMES, PROTEINS that act as catalysts (see CATALYSIS) for the chemical reactions upon which LIFE depends. They are generally specific for either one or a group of related reactions. Enzymes are responsible for the production of all the organic materials present in living CELLS, for providing the mechanisms for energy production and utilization in MUSCLES and in the NERVOUS SYSTEM, and for maintaining the intracellular environment within fine limits. They are frequently organized into subcellular particles which catalyze a whole sequence of chemical events in a manner analogous to a production line. Enzymes are themselves synthesized by other enzymes on templates derived from NUCLEIC ACIDS. An average cell contains about 3,000 different enzymes. In order to function correctly, many enzymes require the assistance of metal IONS or accessory substances known as coenzymes which are produced from VITAMINS in the diet. The action of vitamins as coenzymes explains some of the harmful effects of a lack of vitamins in the diet. A majority of enzymes function in a neutral aqueous environment although some require different conditions. For instance, those which digest food in the stomach require an ACID environment. Cells also contain special activators and inhibitors which switch particular enzymes on and off as required. In some cases a substance closely related to the substrate (the substance on which the enzyme acts) will compete for the enzyme and prevent the normal action on the substrate; this is termed competitive inhibition. Again, the product of a reaction may inhibit the action of the enzyme so that no more product is produced until its level has dropped to a particular threshold, this being known as FEEDBACK control. Enzymes either synthesize or break down chemical compounds or transform them from one type to another. These differing actions form the basis of the classification of enzymes into oxidoreductases, transferases, hydrolases, lyases, isomerases and synthetases. Enzymes normally work inside living cells but some (e.g., digestive enzymes) are capable of working outside the cell. Enzymes are becoming important items of commerce and are used in "biological" washing powders, food processing and brewing.

EOCENE, the second epoch of the TERTIARY period, lasting from about 55 million to about 37–38 million years ago. (See also GEOLOGY.)

EPHESIANS, Epistle to the, New Testament book attributed to the apostle Paul, closely resembling COLOSSIANS. Probably written during Paul's first imprisonment in Rome c60 AD, its main theme is the universality and unity of the church, Jewish and Gentile Christians alike being saved in Christ.

EPHESUS, ancient Greek city of Asia Minor, a seaport famous for its wealth. Its temple of Artemis was one of the SEVEN WONDERS OF THE WORLD. Conquered by Lydians, Persians, and Alexander the Great, it was the leading city of the Roman province of Asia and an early center of Christianity. The city was abandoned after

the 5th century because of malaria and the silting up of its port.

EPIC, long narrative poem concerned with heroism, either of individuals or of a people. GILGAMESH, the earliest known epic, dates from c2000 BC, but epics were considered the highest literary form until at least the 14th century. Many, such as the ODYSSEY and ILIAD, and BEOWULF, must have existed as oral tradition before being written down; the *Kalevala,* Finland's national epic, was collated only in the 19th century. Others, such as VERGIL's *Aeneid,* SPENSER's *Faerie Queene* and MILTON's *Paradise Lost,* draw on traditional material but are very much individual works. Many epics, such as the NIBELUNGENLIED, are nationalistic in flavor, blending actual history with myth and fable. (See also, for example, ARTHURIAN LEGENDS; CHANSONS DE GESTE; CHANSON DE ROLAND; SAGA.)

EPICTETUS (c55–135 AD) , Greek Stoic philosopher. An educated Roman slave, after he was freed he taught philosophy, but was expelled with other philosophers by Emperor Domitian in 90 AD, moving to Nicopolis in Greece. His teachings, recorded by his pupil Arrian, indicate that the key to conduct is self-control and acceptance of the natural order—itself the will of God. (See also STOICISM.)

EPIC THEATER, form of theater developed in the 1920s and 1930s by Erwin Piscator and BRECHT, emphasizing the narrative and political aspect of staged events. Brecht's theories stressed the arousal of a critical response by alienating the spectator from the staged action.

EPICUREANISM, philosophy propounded by EPICURUS in the 4th century BC. It regarded the purpose of human life as the attainment of pleasure, by which was meant contentment and peace of mind in a frugal life. The school was viciously attacked, particularly by Christians; and this has debased the name into merely signifying sensual hedonism.

EPICURUS (c341–270 BC), Athenian philosopher, the author of epicureanism. Reviving the ATOMISM of DEMOCRITUS, he preached a materialist, sensationalist philosophy which emphasized the positive things in life and remained popular for more than 600 years.

EPIDEMIC, the occurrence of a disease in a geographically localized population over a limited period of time; it usually refers to infectious disease which spreads from case to case or by carriers. Epidemics arise from importation of infection, after environmental changes favoring infectious organisms or due to altered host susceptibility. A

pandemic is an epidemic of very large or world-wide proportions. Infectious disease is said to be **endemic** in an area if cases are continually occurring there. Travel through endemic areas may lead to epidemics in nonendemic areas.

EPIDEMIOLOGY, the study of the factors contributing to the occurrence and distribution of a disease, injury or other physiologic debilitation prevalent within a human population. Epidemiology uses statistical and other methods to discover causative agents, determine the elements affecting rate of incidence and degree of severity, and establish the means of control.

EPIGRAM, terse and pointed saying in either prose or verse, often in couplet form. It is named for Greek monumental inscriptions, but the modern form was established by the Romans, particularly CATULLUS and MARTIAL. COLERIDGE defined it thus:

What is an epigram? A dwarfish whole.
Its body brevity, and wit its soul.

EPILEPSY, the "sacred disease" of HIPPOCRATES, a chronic disease of the BRAIN, characterized by susceptibility to convulsions or other transient disorders of NERVOUS-SYSTEM function and due to abnormal electrical activity within the cerebral cortex. There are many types, of which four are common. **Grand mal** convulsions involve rhythmic jerking and rigidity of the limbs, associated with loss of consciousness, urinary incontinence, transient cessation of breathing and sometimes cyanosis, foaming at the mouth and tongue biting. **Petit mal** is largely a disorder of children in which very brief episodes of absence or vacancy occur, when the child is unaware of the surroundings, and is associated with a characteristic ELECTROENCEPHALOGRAPH disturbance. In **focal or Jacksonian epilepsy,** rhythmic movements start in one limb, progress to involve others and may lead to a grand mal convulsion. **Temporal lobe or psychomotor epilepsy** is often characterized by abnormal visceral sensations, unusual smells, visual distortion or memory disorder, and may or may not be followed by unconsciousness. **Status epilepticus** is when attacks of any sort occur repetitively without consciousness being regained in between; it requires emergency treatment.

Epilepsy may be either primary, due to an inborn tendency, often appearing in early life, or it may be symptomatic of brain disorders such as those following trauma or brain SURGERY, ENCEPHALITIS, cerebral ABSCESS, TUMOR, or vascular disease. The electroencephalograph is the cornerstone of diagnosis in epilepsy, helping to confirm its presence and localize its origin, and suggesting whether there is a structural cause. If epilepsy is secondary, the cause may respond to treatment such as surgery, but all cases require anticonvulsant medication in the long term. Phenytoin (Dilantin), phenobarital (see BARBITURATES), ethosuccimide, carbamazepine, diazepam and related compounds are important anticonvulsants, suitable for different types. Dietary food (ketogenic diet) may be effective in some cases.

EPIPHANY (from Greek *epiphania,* manifestation), feast of the church year held on Jan. 6. Originating in the 3rd century in the Eastern Church, where it commemorates Christ's baptism, it came into the Western Church in the 4th century and there celebrates the manifestation of Christ to the gentiles, represented by the MAGI.

EPIPHYTE, or airplant, a plant that grows on another but which obtains no nourishment from it. Various lichens, MOSSES, FERNS and ORCHIDS are epiphytes, particularly on trees. Epiphytes thrive in warm, wet climates.

EPISCOPAL CHURCH, Protestant, US denomination that formed itself from the remnants of the Church of England in the colonies after the Revolutionary War, and was finally given a constitution at a convention in Philadelphia in 1789. It now has 100 dioceses and a membership of around 3,000,000. Its administrative body is the Executive Council in New York, and it is governed by the triennial General Convention, composed of a House of Bishops and a House of Clerical and Lay Deputies. It is part of the Anglican Communion, and in recent years has been prominent in the ecumenical movement and in social action among minority groups.

EPISTEMOLOGY, from the Greek *episteme* (knowledge), the branch of philosophy that inquires about the sources of human knowledge, its possible limits, and to what extent it can be certain or only probable. Epistemology is connected with other branches of philosophy, such as psychology and logic.

EPITHELIUM, surface tissue covering an organ or structure. Examples include skin and the mucous membranes of the LUNGS, gut and urinary tract. A protective layer specialized for water resistance or absorption, depending on site, it usually shows a high cell-turnover rate.

E PLURIBUS UNUM ("out of many, one"), Latin motto referring to the unification of the original 13 American colonies. Chosen for the Continental Congress by John Adams, Franklin and Jefferson, it is now inscribed on the great seal of the US and on many US coins.

EPSTEIN, Sir Jacob (1880–1959), American-born sculptor, living in London, whose work often caused controversy. His early sculptures were influenced by African sculpture, Constantin BRANCUSI and vorticism, but after 1915 he turned, in more conventional style, to religious subjects and portraiture. His works include *Rock Drill* (1913) and *Ecce Homo* (1935).

EQUAL EMPLOYMENT OPPORTUNITY COMMISSION (EEOC), federal agency created by the Civil Rights Act of 1964 to eliminate employment discrimination based on race, color, religion, sex, national origin, or age. It investigates charges of discrimination, tries to remedy unlawful practices through informal conciliation, and, failing that, brings suit in an appropriate federal district court.

EQUALITY, in mathematics, the relation between two or more expressions which represent the same thing, represented by the symbol "=". Thus $3 + 4 = 7$ is an equality. The expressions need not represent numbers but may denote SETS, GROUPS or any other kind of mathematical object.

EQUAL RIGHTS AMENDMENT (ERA), a proposed Constitutional amendment prohibiting the denial or abridgment of a person's Constitutional rights because of sex. First introduced in Congress in 1923, it finally passed in 1972. Ratification by the states proceeded expeditiously at first but then faltered; the deadline for ratification was extended in 1978 to 1982. But the June 30, 1982, deadline passed without the necessary 38-state ratification.

EQUATION, a statement of equality. Should this statement involve a variable it will, unless it is an invalid equation, be true for one or more values of that variable, though those values need not be expressible in terms of real numbers: $x^2 + 2 = 0$ has two imaginary (see COMPLEX NUMBERS) roots, $+\sqrt{-2}$ and $-\sqrt{-2}$.

Linear equations are those in which no variable term is raised to a POWER higher than 1. Solution of linear equations in one variable is simple. Consider the equation $x + 3 = 7$. The equation will still be true if we add or subtract equal numbers from each side:

$$x + 3 = 7,$$
$$x + 3 - 3 = 7 - 3$$
$$\text{and } x = 4.$$

Linear equations are so called because, if considered as the equation of a curve (see

ANALYTIC GEOMETRY), they can be plotted as a straight line (see also FUNCTION).

Quadratic equations are those in a single variable which appears to the power 2, but not higher. A quadratic equation always has two roots, though these roots may be equal.

Cubic equations are those in a single variable which appears to the power 3, but not higher. Cubic equations always have three roots, though two or all three of these may be equal.

Degree of an equation. Linear, quadratic and cubic equations are said to be of the 1st, 2nd and 3rd degrees respectively. More generally, the degree of an equation is defined as the sum of the EXPONENTS of the variables in the highest-power term of the equation. In $ax^5 + bx^3y^3 + cx^2y^5 = 0$, the sums of the exponents of each term are, respectively, 5, 6 and 7; hence cx^2y^5 is the highest-power term, and the equation is of the 7th degree.

Radical equations are those in which roots of the variables appear: e.g., $a\sqrt{x} + b\sqrt{x} + c = 0$. Radical equations can always be simply converted into equations of the nth order, where $n = 1,2,3 \ldots$, by raising both sides of the equation to a power, repeating the process where necessary.

Simultaneous equations. A single equation in two or more variables is generally insoluble. However, if there are as many equations as there are variables, it is possible to solve for each variable. Consider

$$2x + xy + 3 = 0 \qquad (1)$$
$$\text{and} \qquad x + 2xy = 0 \qquad (2)$$

Multiplying equation 1 by 2 we have

$$4x + 2xy + 6 = 0 \qquad (3)$$

and, subtracting equation 2 from this,

$$3x + 6 = 0.$$

Hence $x = -2$.

Substituting this value into equation (1) we find the value $y = -\frac{1}{2}$. More complicated simultaneous equations can be solved in the same way.

EQUATOR, an imaginary line equal to the circumference of the earth drawn about the earth such that all points on it are equidistant from the N and S poles (see NORTH POLE; SOUTH POLE). All points on it have a latitude of $0°$, and it is the longest of the parallels of latitude. (See also CELESTIAL SPHERE; LATITUDE AND LONGITUDE.)

EQUATORIAL GUINEA, the least populated and only Spanish-speaking black African country, is a tiny republic on the W coast of Africa. It consists of two provinces: the mainland territory of Rio Muni (bordered by Cameroon and Gabon and the Gulf of Guinea); and the island of Bioko, which lies in the Gulf of Guinea about 100mi from Rio Muni.

Official name: Republic of Equatorial Guinea
Capital Malabo
Area: 10,831sq mi
Population: 328,000
Languages: Spanish, African languages
Religions: Roman Catholicism, animism
Monetary unit(s): 1 CFA franc = 100 centimos

People. Main ethnic groups are the Fang, in Rio Muni, and the Bubi, in Bioko. Spanish is the official language, but tribal languages and a form of pidgin English are widely spoken.

Economy. Agriculture, including forestry, is the mainstay of the economy, engaging most of the labor force. Cocoa is the main export, followed by coffee, wood, and bananas. Despite the richness of its soil and its potential natural resources, the country is exceedingly poor.

History. In 1778 Portugal gave Spain the island now called Bioko. In 1885 Spain formally obtained Rio Muni. Independence was granted in 1968; Macías Nguema (president 1968–79) proclaimed himself life president in 1975. His erratic leadership and internal unrest brought the country close to economic ruin. In 1979 the military seized power, and Macías Nguema was subsequently executed. Under a constitution adopted in 1982, legislative elections were held in 1983; new parliamentary and direct presidential elections are scheduled for 1989.

EQUINOXES, (1) the two times each year when day and night are of equal length. The spring or **vernal equinox** occurs in March, the **autumnal equinox** in September. (2) The two intersections of the ecliptic and equator (see CELESTIAL SPHERE). The vernal equinox is in Pisces, the autumnal between Virgo and Leo.

EQUITY, legal term for the application of certain principles by the judiciary to prevent injustice that would result from strict application of the law. In fact, however, in English and US COMMON LAW these principles have hardened into rules of law and have been incorporated into the system. They originated in the judicial remedies of the English Court of Chancery, which introduced and shaped such essential legal forms as the TRUST, easement and MORTGAGE.

ERA. See EQUAL RIGHTS AMENDMENT.

ERA OF GOOD FEELING, a newspaper's term for the two administrations of President James Monroe, 1817–25. Coined after Monroe's friendly reception by Boston Federalists and the virtual disappearance of the Federalist party nationally, it was belied by the ill feeling and discord in the Republican administration among Monroe's potential successors.

ERASISTRATUS (3rd century BC), Greek physician who is credited with the foundation of PHYSIOLOGY as a separate discipline.

ERASMUS, Desiderius (c1466–1536), Dutch Roman Catholic humanist and advocate of church and social reform. The illegitimate son of a priest, he was forced by his guardians to enter a monastery and was ordained in 1492. Studies in Paris imbued him with a deep dislike of Scholastic theology, and on a visit to England in 1499 he met and was influenced by the humanists John Colet and Thomas MORE. He published *The Christian Soldier's Handbook* (1503), with an emphasis on spiritual simplicity. *In Praise of Folly* (1509) is a light, witty satire on Church corruption, paving the way for the REFORMATION. The foremost scholar of his time, Erasmus produced the first critical edition of the Greek New Testament (1516) and edited the works of the CHURCH FATHERS. Although a moderate reformer, he called for religious peace, and opposed LUTHER in his *Diatribe on Free Will* (1524), which drew a crushing reply from Luther. Erasmus died embittered by the Reformation controversies, accepted by neither side.

ERASTIANISM, doctrine that the state should have complete control over the affairs of the Church. It is named for ERASTUS who, in fact, believed that only a Christian state could administer church discipline.

ERASTUS, Thomas (1524–1583), Swiss physician for whom ERASTIANISM was named. An adherent of ZWINGLI, he clashed with the Calvinists, particularly over the practice of excommunication, which he opposed in his *Explicatio gravissimae quaestionis* (1589).

ERATOSTHENES (c275–c195 BC), Greek scholar, head of the library at Alexandria. A man of many accomplishments, he is especially noted for having determined the circumference of the earth, the sizes of the sun and moon, and their distances from the earth.

ERECHTHEUM, marble temple on the ACROPOLIS at Athens, built in the 5th century BC to replace a temple destroyed by the Persians.

ERGOT, disease of GRASSES and sedges caused by fungal species of the genus *Claviceps*. Also, the masses of dormant mycelia (sclerotia) formed in the flower heads of the host plant. Ergots contain toxic ALKALOIDS which, if eaten by animals or man, can cause serious poisoning (ergotism or St. Anthony's fire).

ERHARD, Ludwig (1897–1977), West German economist and political leader. Forced out of academic life by the Nazis in 1942, he was appointed to various posts by the occupying powers in 1945–49. In 1949 he became economics minister under Konrad ADENAUER, and in this post he was the prime architect of West Germany's post-WWII revival. He succeeded Adenauer as chancellor in 1963, but was removed from the chancellorship and party leadership in 1966 after the economy began to decline.

ERICSON, Leif (flourished 999–1002 AD), Norse explorer, son of ERIC THE RED. On a voyage from Greenland in 1000 AD, he discovered some part of the North American coast (called VINLAND in old Norse sagas). Modern scholars do not agree on the location of Vinland, but excavation at a Norse site in Newfoundland in the 1960s lends credence to the story.

ERICSSON, John (1803–1889), Swedish-born US engineer and inventor. He developed the screw propeller to replace the paddlewheel on steamships. In 1861–62 he designed and built the ironclad *Monitor*, which sank the Confederate ironclad *Virginia* at Hampton Roads. The *Monitor* introduced a new era of steam-powered, propeller-driven, iron warships with heavy guns mounted in revolving turrets.

ERIC THE RED (10th century AD), Norse chieftain and discoverer of Greenland. He settled in Iceland with his exiled father, but was banished for manslaughter about 980. Eric sailed W and discovered Greenland, then returned to Iceland where he organized a voyage about 985 to colonize Greenland. He founded settlements near present-day Julianehaab and Osterbygd, which may have survived for as long as 500 years.

ERIE, Battle of Lake, major naval engagement in the WAR OF 1812. The US forces, led by Commodore Oliver Hazard PERRY, defeated the British at Put-in-Bay, Ohio, Sept. 10, 1813. The victory gave the US control of Lake Erie and the NE.

ERIE, Lake, one of the five GREAT LAKES of North America, bordered by N.Y., Pa., Ohio, Mich. and Ontario, Canada. Named for the Erie Indians, it is the shallowest and fourth-largest (9,910sq mi) of the Great Lakes. Erie is icebound part of the year and is heavily polluted by waste from industry and large cities. Some of its chief ports are Buffalo, N.Y., Erie, Pa., Cleveland and Toledo, Ohio. The US–Canadian boundary passes through the center of the lake. (See also SAINT LAWRENCE SEAWAY.)

ERIE CANAL, historic artificial waterway in the US, which once connected Buffalo, N.Y., on Lake Erie with Albany, N.Y., on the Hudson R. The New York State Barge Canal now follows part of the old Erie Canal route, which was completed in 1825 as a result of the political support of N.Y. Governor DeWitt CLINTON. The canal, originally 365mi long, stimulated the growth and financial development of New York and many Midwestern cities.

ERIGENA, John Scotus (c810–877), Irish theologian and philosopher, who taught at Paris, probably the most advanced thinker of his time. He attempted to combine Christian theology and NEOPLATONISM.

ERIKSON, Erik Homburger (1902–   ), German-born US psychoanalyst who defined eight stages, each characterized by a specific psychological conflict, in the development of the ego from infancy to old age. He also studied the identity, introducing the concept of the identity crisis.

ERITREA, province of N Ethiopia, on the W coast of the Red Sea. Eritrea is populated by many ethnic groups, with diverse socio-cultural systems. Less than 5% of this hot, dry, mountainous region is cultivated. The capital, Asmara, produces some food products, textiles and hide. Roads, a railroad and air service link the province with the Sudan and the rest of Ethiopia. Eritrea became an Italian colony in 1890 and an Ethiopian province in 1952. From 1961 a guerrilla movement—led from 1981 by the Marxist Eritrean People's Liberation Front—fought to establish the independence of Eritrea, first against Emperor Heile Selassie and after 1974 against the Marxist government of Mengistu Haile Mariam.

ERMINE, term for any WEASEL which turns white in winter. In the Middle Ages ermine fur was used only by royalty; it was later associated with high-court judges. Ermine fur is obtained from the Russian stoat and several species of North American weasel.

ERNST, Max (1891–1976), German-born artist, leader of the DADA and SURREALISM movements in Paris. Foremost among the expressive techniques that Ernst developed were COLLAGE and *frottage* (rubbing on paper placed over textured surfaces). He also painted in oil and produced graphics and sculpture, revealing in all genres an exceptionally adventurous imagination.

EROSION, the wearing away of the earth's surface by natural agents. Running water constitutes the most effective eroding agent, the process being accelerated by the transportation of particles eroded or weathered farther upstream: it is these that are primarily responsible for further erosion. GROUNDWATER may cause erosion by dissolving certain minerals in the rock. Ocean waves and especially the debris that they carry may substantially erode coastlines. GLACIERS are extremely important eroding agents, eroded material becoming embedded in the ice and acting as further abrasives. Many common landscape features are the results of glacial erosion (e.g., drumlins, fjords). Rocks exposed to the atmosphere undergo **weathering**: mechanical weathering usually results from temperature changes (e.g., in **exfoliation**, the cracking off of thin sheets of rock due to effects of "unloading"; chemical weathering results from chemical changes brought about by, for example, substances dissolved in RAIN water. Wind erosion may be important in dry, sandy areas. (See also SOIL EROSION.)

ERVIN, Samuel James, Jr. (1896–1985), US lawyer and public official. After serving in the US House and on the superior and supreme courts of North Carolina, Ervin was a US Senator 1954–75. The Senate's leading authority on the Constitution, he headed the committee investigating the WATERGATE affair. He fought President Nixon's use of executive privilege to withhold evidence and testimony, and enlivened the hearings with humor and quotations from the Bible.

ERVING, Julius Winfield (1950–   ), US basketball player with the Virginia Squires (1972), the New York Nets (1973–76), and the Philadelphia 76ers (1976–88).

ERYSIPELAS, or **St. Anthony's fire**, a SKIN infection, usually affecting the face, caused by certain types of STREPTOCOCCUS. It is common in infancy and middle age. Erythema (redness of the skin) and swelling spread with a clear margin and cause blistering. It is a short illness with FEVER; if it affects the trunk it may however cause prostration and can prove fatal. PENICILLIN is the ANTIBIOTIC of choice.

ERZBERGER, Matthias (1875–1921), German politician, a member of the Catholic Center Party. An imperialist at the start of WWI, he sponsored a 1917 peace resolution, signed the 1918 armistice, and advocated acceptance of the Treaty of Versailles. As finance minister in the republican government, he attempted major reforms opposed by conservatives. Forced to resign, he was later assassinated.

ESCAPE VELOCITY, the speed an object must reach in order to break free from the gravitational pull of a massive body, such as a star or planet. The escape velocity depends upon the mass of the body and the distance of the moving object from it. Once an object has attained escape velocity it needs no further power to carry it beyond the gravitational pull. The escape velocity near the surface of the earth is about 7 mi per second (25,000 mph). The escape velocity for the moon is about 1.5 mi per second.

ESCHATOLOGY, the study of the "last things." A universal theme in religion, especially Christianity and Judaism, eschatology deals with the meaning of history and the final destiny of the world, mankind and the individual. Old Testament eschatology centers on the expected MESSIAH. Christian eschatology includes the doctrines of death, RESURRECTION, HEAVEN, HELL, the SECOND COMING of Christ and the LAST JUDGMENT (see also MILLENNIUM). The benefits of the "age to come" are in part realized now in the Church.

ESCOBEDO v. ILLINOIS (1960), US Supreme Court case that nullified the confession of a criminal suspect made without legal counsel.

ESCOFFIER, Georges-Auguste (1846–1935), world-famous French chef, director of the Carlton and Savoy Hotel kitchens (London), and author of many cookbooks, including *Ma Cuisine* (1924). He was awarded the *Légion d'Honneur* (1920) for his culinary achievements.

ESCORIAL, monastery and palace in central Spain, 26mi NW of Madrid. One of the most magnificent buildings in Europe, it was built (1563–84) by PHILIP II and houses a church, palace, college, library and a mausoleum in which many Spanish kings are buried. Its famous art collection contains works by VELÁSQUEZ, El GRECO and TINTORETTO, among others.

ESDRAS, the Latin form of EZRA, a Jewish priest often called the "second Moses." Esdras is the name given to four Old Testament books, two in the Jewish canon (Ezra and Nehemiah) and two in the Protestant APOCRYPHA (1 and 2 Esdras, called 3 and 4 Esdras in the Vulgate). (See also PSEUDEPIGRAPHA.)

ESENIN, Sergei (1895–1925), Russian poet. Born to a peasant family, he celebrated village life in lyric verse infused with religious and folk themes. He welcomed the Russian revolution, but became disillusioned and went abroad. Married briefly to Isadora DUNCAN, he committed suicide in 1925.

ESHKOL, Levi (1895–1969), Israeli political leader and prime minister, 1963–69. He emigrated from Russia to Palestine (1914), helped found one of the first *kibbutzim* (1920) and *Histadrut* (the labor federation). He succeeded BEN-GURION as prime minister, unified the labor parties in Israel to gain a majority in the Knesset and led the country in the Six-Day War (1967).

ESKIMO, a Mongoloid race native to the Arctic coasts of Greenland, North America and NE Asia, believed to have crossed the Bering Strait from Asia in about 2000 BC. Considering their widespread distribution, the Eskimos, who speak dialects of the Eskimo-Aleut language family and today number some 70,000, have preserved their cultural identity to a remarkable degree. Although the white man's influence has been important in education and medical welfare and in the establishment of cooperatives, the Eskimos have only intermarried with white settlers, to any significant extent, on Greenland. Many still live by hunting and fishing, using traditional skills to exploit the unyielding Arctic environment. Seals, fish, walrus and whales are hunted for food, fuel and clothing. Travel on land is by dog-sled and on the water by kayak or *umiak*, a skin boat. During hunting expeditions, temporary igloo shelters are sometimes built, but the basic home, in which the Eskimos live in small communal groups, is made of sod, driftwood and stone. Tents of hide or sealskin are used in the summer. The traditional Eskimo religion draws heavily on a rich folklore. On Greenland, many Eskimos are Christian. SHAMANISM is also practiced.

ESOPHAGUS, the thin tube leading from the pharynx to the STOMACH. Food passes down it as a bolus by gravity and PERISTALSIS. Its diseases include reflux esophagitis (HEARTBURN), ULCER, stricture and CANCER.

ESP, or **extrasensory perception,** perception other than by the recognized senses of an event or object; and, by extension, those powers of the mind (such as **telekinesis,** the moving of distant objects by the exercise of willpower) that cannot be scientifically evaluated. The best known and most researched area of ESP is **telepathy,** the ability of two or more individuals to communicate without sensory contact: though laboratory tests (see PARAPSYCHOLOGY) have been inconclusive, it seems probable that telepathic communication between individuals can exist. Another important area of ESP is **precognition,** the prior knowledge of an event: again, despite a mass of circumstantial evidence, laboratory tests have been inconclusive. The term **clairvoyance** is sometimes used for ESP.

ESPERANTO, artificial language created by Dr. L. L. Zamenhof (1859–1917) of Poland to enable people of different linguistic backgrounds to communicate more easily and with less misunderstanding. Consisting of "root words" derived from Latin, Greek and the Romance and Germanic languages, Esperanto is easy to learn and has enjoyed more popularity since its introduction in 1887 than other artificial "universal" languages such as Volpük and Interlingua. (See also BASIC ENGLISH.)

ESPIONAGE, clandestine attempt to gather confidential information, usually of a political, military or industrial nature. Espionage is an ancient practice; it is mentioned in the Bible and in the *Iliad*. Espionage activities are primarily carried on by individual nations to gain data on other nations, although industrial espionage is becoming widespread. Undercover espionage may be severely penalized; although espionage is not illegal under international law, every country has laws against it. (See also CENTRAL INTELLIGENCE AGENCY; NATIONAL SECURITY COUNCIL; OFFICE OF STRATEGIC SERVICES.)

ESPOSITO, Phil (1942–   ), Canadian hockey player with the Boston Bruins 1967–74, when he won five scoring championships and was named the National Hockey League's most valuable player in 1969 and 1974. He played for the New York Rangers 1975–81.

ESSENCE, in philosophy, a term referring to the permanent actuality of a thing, the that-by-which it can be recognized, whatever its outward appearance. Different philosophers have used the term with various detailed significations; LOCKE, for instance, distinguished a thing's real essence, the what-it-is-in-itself, from its nominal essence, the what-it-appears-to-be, the name men give it.

ESSENES, ascetic sect which flourished in Palestine from about 200 BC to about 100 AD. Gathered in small monastic communities, the Essenes held property in common and observed the law of Moses strictly. The DEAD SEA SCROLLS may have been written by a community of Essenes.

ESSEX, Robert Devereux, 2nd Earl of

(1567–1601), a favorite of Queen ELIZABETH I. He acquired some fame in European military campaigns and was knighted in 1589 and made lord lieutenant of Ireland in 1599, a post he lost by failing to crush the Earl of Tyrone's rebellion. Unfailingly ambitious for power, he later attempted a coup to establish his own party at court, was defeated and then executed.

ESSEX, kingdom of Anglo-Saxon England, first settled by SAXONS in the 6th century. Dominated by Mercia and then Wessex, it became part of the DANELAW in 886. It was recaptured by EDWARD THE ELDER in 917 and restored as an earldom.

ESSEX JUNTO, name of a group of US New England Federalist property owners who supported Alexander HAMILTON and earlier had opposed Mass. radicals in the American Revolution. They were regarded as traitors by many Americans.

ESTAING, Jean Baptiste Charles Henri Hector, Compte d' (1729–1794), French admiral, commander of a French fleet which assisted the Americans in the REVOLUTIONARY WAR. In 1779 he took part with General Benjamin Lincoln in the abortive attack on Savannah.

ESTE, Italian noble family, rulers of Ferrara (1240–1597) and Modena (1288–1796). Prominent since the 11th century, they were particularly notable as patrons of Renaissance writers and artists.

ESTERHÁZY, Hungarian noble family. **Paul Esterházy** (1635–1713) became regent of Hungary in 1681 and distinguished himself in war against the Turks. He was made a prince of the Holy Roman Empire in 1687. **Prince Nikolaus Joseph Esterházy** (1714–1790) was the generous patron of Joseph HAYDN. He rebuilt the lavish Esterhazy palace in Eisenstaedt, Austria.

ESTERS, organic compounds formed by CONDENSATION, of an ACID (organic or inorganic) with an ALCOHOL, water being eliminated. This reaction, esterification, is the reverse of HYDROLYSIS. Many esters occur naturally: those of low molecular weight have fruity odors and are used in flavorings, perfumes and as solvents; those of higher molecular weight are FATS and WAXES.

ESTHER, Old Testament book. It tells of Esther, formerly named Hadassah, a Jewess, queen of the Persian King Ahasuerus (probably XERXES I) who prevented the king's favorite, Haman, from massacring all Persian Jews. Instead the Jews' enemies were slain. The story is the origin of the feast of PURIM.

ESTONIA, or **Estonian Soviet Socialist Republic,** constituent republic of the USSR, S of the Gulf of Finland and E of the Baltic Sea. The largest cities are Tallin, the capital, Tartu and Pärnu. A third of the land, which consists of plains and low plateaus, is forested. The climate is temperate. Estonians are ethnically and linguistically related to the Finns. More than half the population is urban, although agriculture, especially dairy farming, is the chief industry. Other important industries are shipbuilding, electrical engineering, cement, fertilizers and textiles. Ruled at various times by the Danes, the TEUTONIC KNIGHTS, the Swedes and the Russians, Estonia became independent in 1918. Its annexation by the USSR in 1940 along with that of LATVIA and LITHUANIA is not recognized by the US. In the mid-1980s Estonia and the other Baltic republics responded eagerly to Soviet leader Gorbachev's encouragement of local economic initiatives, and there was speculation that Gorbachev regarded the Baltic republics as a kind of economic laboratory. Nevertheless, demonstrations in Tallinn in Aug. 1988 marked the anniversary of the 1939 Hitler-Stalin nonaggression pact that divided Eastern Europe into German and Soviet spheres of influence and permitted Stalin to annex the Baltic states in 1940. In Nov. the Estonian Supreme Soviet (the republic's legislature) unanimously declared that it had the right to reject Soviet legislation that infringed on Estonian autonomy. (See also UNION OF SOVIET SOCIALIST REPUBLICS.)

ESTRADA PALMA, Tomás (1835–1908), Cuban revolutionist against Spanish rule, first president (1902–06) of independent Cuba. His reelection in 1906 was challenged by his rival, José Manuel GOMEZ, who led a revolt that brought US intervention. Estrada Palma resigned rather than accept US terms for a settlement.

ESTROGENS, female sex HORMONES concerned with the development of secondary sexual characteristics and maturation of reproductive organs. They are under the control of pituitary-gland gonadotrophins, and their amount varies before and after MENSTRUATION and in PREGNANCY. After the menopause, their production decreases. Many pills used for CONTRACEPTION contain estrogen, as do some preparations given to menopausal women. Their administration may lead to venous THROMBOSIS and some other diseases.

ETCHING, an ENGRAVING technique in which acid is used to "bite" lines into a metal plate which is then printed, usually intaglio. The plate, usually copper or zinc, is first coated with a resin "ground" through which the design is drawn with a needle. Only the exposed metal is etched away. Different line thicknesses can be obtained by selective stopping out and repeated exposure to the acid. (See also AQUATINT.)

ETHANOL (C_2H_5OH), or **ethyl alcohol**, also known as grain alcohol; the best-known ALCOHOL; a colorless, inflammable, volatile, toxic liquid, the active constituent of alcoholic beverages. Of immense industrial importance, ethanol is used as a solvent, in ANTIFREEZE, as an ANTISEPTIC and in much chemical synthesis. Its production is controlled by law, and it is heavily taxed unless made unfit for drinking by adulteration (denatured alcohol). Most industrial ethanol is the azeotropic mixture containing 5% water. It is made by FERMENTATION of sugars or by catalytic hydration of ethylene. MW 46.1 mp −112°C, bp 78°C.

ETHELBERT (d. 616), king of Kent, 560-616. Converted to Christianity by Saint AUGUSTINE of Canterbury, he was the first Christian king to rule in Anglo-Saxon England. He promulgated the first extant code of Anglo-Saxon laws which established the legal rights of clergy.

ETHELRED THE UNREADY (968?-1016), king of England, 978-1016. His name refers to his lack of sound counsel. He succeeded his brother Edward the Martyr, whom he possibly murdered. Danish power spread in England during his reign and he paid Danegeld (tribute) to the Danes. Ethelred fled when the Danes ruled England, 1013-14, and then negotiated his restoration in a pact with his subjects.

ETHER, a hypothetical medium postulated by late 19th-century physicists in order to explain how LIGHT could be propagated as a wave motion through otherwise empty space. Light was thus thought of as a mechanical WAVE MOTION in the ether. The whole theory was discredited following the failure of the MICHELSON-MORLEY EXPERIMENT to detect any motion of the earth relative to the supposed stationary ether.

ETHEREGE, Sir George (1634?-1691), English dramatist, an important writer of RESTORATION COMEDY, who influenced both CONGREVE and WYCHERLEY. His three plays are *The Comical Revenge* (1664), *She Wou'd if She Cou'd* (1668) and *The Man of Mode* (1676).

ETHICAL CULTURE, movement based on the belief that ethical tenets are not necessarily dependent on philosophical or religious dogma. Ethical Culture has undertaken programs of social welfare, education and race relations. The movement was founded by Felix Adler in 1876 in New York City and has now spread throughout the world.

ETHICS, principles or moral values of a person or a group of people which guide their actions and behavior. The term comes from the Greek word *ethos* which in the plural means character.

Ethical actions may be approved of in that they are "good," "desirable," "right" or "obligatory," or disapproved of because they are "bad," "wrong," "undesirable" or "evil." In philosophy ethics is the study of moral principles. A traditional philosophical question is whether right and wrong are inherent in the nature of things and therefore "absolute," or mere conventions and thus "relative" to time and place. Some recent thinkers claim that an ethical judgment, such as "Lying is bad," can be neither true nor false but only an expression of the speaker's feelings. See PLATO; ARISTOTLE; SPINOZA; KANT; MILL; MOORE; and other main philosophers, and doctrines such as UTILITARIANISM.

ETHIOPIA, East African state lying between Sudan and the Red Sea, with Kenya and Somalia to the S and E, formerly known as Abyssinia.

Official name: Ethiopian Socialist Democratic Republic
Capital: Addis Ababa
Area: 472,400sq mi
Population: 45,997,000
Languages: Amharic, many tribal languages and dialects
Religions: Christian (Ethiopian Orthodox Church), Muslim
Monetary unit(s): 1 birr=100 cents
Land. It consists basically of mountainous W and E highlands divided by the GREAT RIFT VALLEY. In the center of the W highlands, or Abyssian Plateau, is the capital Addis Ababa, 8,000ft above sea level. Spectacular river gorges, including that of the Abbai R (or Blue Nile), which runs from Lake Tana, cut through the

Plateau. Ras Dashan in the N is Ethiopia's highest peak (15,158ft). In the SE is the great plain of the Ogaden and the Haud. Average highland rainfall is 40in, but overall rainfall varies from 80in in the S and W to 4in on the Red Sea Coast. The lowlands are tropical.

People. The Ethiopians comprise many linguistic, cultural and racial groups. The Galla are the largest single group (40% of the population) but the Amhara and the Tigre (together 40%) have been historically and politically the most important peoples. Other significant groups are the Walamo, the Somali and the Gurage. Although education is expanding, only a small minority is literate. The majority of the population is concentrated in the fertile high-rainfall area of the highlands. About a fifth of the population is town-dwelling, and the chief towns are Addis Ababa, Asmara, Dire Dawa and Harar.

Economy. In the late 1970s and 1980s renewed drought, complicated by civil war, severely affected the Ethiopian economy, which is largely dependent on agriculture and livestock. Coffee is the most important export, followed by skins and hides. Imports exceed exports, and manufacturing activity is limited. A deposit of natural gas has been found, but a general lack of natural resources has hampered industrialization. There is some gold and platinum, and iron, potash and copper, but large mineral deposits have not been discovered. All agricultural land was nationalized in 1975. Smallholdings by individuals are allowed, and state farms are being encouraged.

History. Ethiopia is one of the most ancient kingdoms of the world. Former kings claimed descent from the son of King Solomon and the Queen of Sheba. The kingdom of Aksum, prominent from the 1st to the 8th century, was converted to Coptic Christianity in the 4th century. In medieval times Ethiopia was isolated and was thought to be the realm of PRESTER JOHN. Frequent Muslim invasions and internal feuds for long undermined Ethiopian power, but MENELIK II reconsolidated the empire and defeated the Italians in 1896 at Adowa. The Italians remained in ERITREA and in 1935–36 invaded Ethiopia, which was liberated in 1941 when Emperor HAILE SELASSIE was restored to the throne. Ethiopia made considerable economic and technical advances, but after unrest the army mutinied in 1974 and Haile Selassie was deposed. In 1975 a socialist one-party state replaced the military government. The Workers' Party of Ethiopia became the sole legal party in 1984 and the country was declared a people's democratic republic in 1987. Mengistu Haile Mariam, who has headed the government since 1977, ruthlessly stamped out opposition to his Marxist regime. An insurgency in the Ogaden backed by Somalia was largely put down by 1978 with Soviet and Cuban aid, although an Ethiopian attempt to topple the Somali government in 1982 failed. Secessionist movements in drought-stricken Eritrea and Tigré provinces continued into the late 1980s.

ETHNIC GROUP, individuals united by ties of culture and/or heredity who are conscious of forming a subgroup within society. Racial minorities may constitute ethnic groups, but this is not always the case. Major US ethnic groups include Irish, Italian, Polish, Jewish, Chinese, Japanese and Hispanic Americans. At times they have clashed with each other or with blacks. Similar tensions due to a diversity of ethnic groups also mark British and Canadian society.

ETHNOLOGY, the science dealing with the differing races of man, where they originated, their distribution about the world, their characteristics and the relationships between them. More generally, the term is used to mean cultural ANTHROPOLOGY.

ETHOLOGY, meaning literally the "study of behavior," is applied particularly to the European school of behavioral scientists. Their concern is the behavior of the animal in the wild, paying special attention to patterns of behavior, or "instinctive" behavior. This contrasts with the interests of most American behaviorists, whose work stems largely from comparative psychology and is concentrated on the study of the learning process, studies which are mainly if not entirely laboratory based. The founders of ethology were Konrad LORENZ and Nikolaas TINBERGEN, whose ideas on instinctive behavior supplied the stimulus for renewed study of animals in the wild.

ETNA, frequently active volcano in NE Sicily, highest volcano in the Mediterranean region. Its height (about 10,900ft) varies with eruptions. The peak is snow-covered through much of the year. The fertile lower slopes are intensely cultivated.

ETON, town in Berkshire, England, on the Thames R, near Windsor, most famous for Eton College. Founded in 1440–41 by Henry VI, the college is possibly the most prestigious private school for boys in Britain.

ETRUSCANS, ancient race of Etruria, located in what is now modern Tuscany,

Italy. Their civilization lasted from the 8th to the 1st century BC but had begun to decline from the beginning of the 5th century BC. It is generally accepted that the Etruscans migrated from the Aegeo-Asian region to Italy in the 8th century BC, although some may have settled there as early as the 13th century BC. The Etruscans called themselves the "Rasenna" but the Romans named them the "Tusci" or "Etrusci."

No Etruscan literary works are extant and, even though some documents and funerary inscriptions remain, so far it has only been possible to understand a few words. Etruria comprised 12 "populi" or city-states, including Arretium, Caere, Perusia, Tarquinii, Veii, Volci, Volsinii and Volterrae. The cities were associated in a league but each was politically independent. The early governments were monarchical and changed subsequently to republican states which were controlled by oligarchies. The Etruscans were extremely powerful. They enjoyed extensive maritime trade with the Greeks and Phoenicians, and had colonies in Sicily, Corsica, Sardinia, the Balearic Islands and Spain. Another source of wealth were the rich mineral deposits, especially those of copper, lead and iron. The Etruscans are famous for their gold and bronze craftsmanship and for their black *bucchero* ceramic ware. They decorated their tombs with large mural paintings. After the 5th century BC the Etruscan cities were absorbed by the expanding Roman state.

ETYMOLOGY (from Greek *etymos*, true meaning, and *logos*, word), the history of a word or other linguistic element; and the science, born in the 19th century, concerned with tracing that history, by examining the word's development since its earliest appearance in the language; by locating its transmission into the language from elsewhere; by identifying its cognates in other languages; and by tracing it and its cognates back to a (often hypothetical) common ancestor. Cognates (from Latin *co*, together, and *nasci*, to be born) of English words appear in many languages: our "father" is cognate with the German "*Vater*" and French "*père*" all three deriving from the Latin "*pater*." An *etymon* is the earliest known form of a word, though the term is sometimes applied to any early form. (See also LINGUISTICS; PHILOLOGY.)

EUBOEA, second largest island in the Greek archipelago. In the Aegean Sea close to the E coast of Greece, it is dominated by three mountain ranges with fertile and well-wooded valleys and plains. Its ancient cities of Chalcis and Eretria led the Greek colonization of southern Italy, and the fine white marble of Euboea was used in the building of imperial Rome.

EUCHARIST. See COMMUNION, HOLY.

EUCLID (c300 BC), Alexandrian mathematician whose major work, the *Elements*, is still the basis of much of geometry (see EUCLIDEAN GEOMETRY): its fifth postulate (the Euclidean axiom) cannot be proved, and this lack of proof gave rise to the non-Euclidean geometries. Other ascribed works include *Phaenomena*, on spherical geometry, and *Optics*, treating vision and perspective.

EUCLIDEAN GEOMETRY, the branch of GEOMETRY dealing with the properties of three-dimensional space. It is commonly split up into plane geometry, which is concerned with figures and constructions in two or less dimensions, and solid or three-dimensional geometry, which deals with three-dimensional figures and the relative spatial positions of figures of three dimensions or less. It takes its name from EUCLID, whose *Elements*, written c300 BC, summarized all the mathematical knowledge of contemporary ancient Greece into 13 books; those on geometry were taken as the final, authoritative word on the subject for well over a millennium and still form the basis for many school geometry textbooks. (See also PYTHAGORAS' THEOREM.)

EUDOXUS OF CNIDUS (c400–c350 BC), Greek mathematician and astronomer who proposed a system of homocentric crystal spheres to explain planetary motions; this system was adopted in ARISTOTLE's cosmology (see ASTRONOMY). He was probably responsible for much of the content of Book V of EUCLID's *Elements*.

EUGENE OF SAVOY, Prince (1663–1736), Austrian general, one of Europe's greatest commanders. He served the emperors Leopold I, Joseph I and Charles VI, and won many victories, most notably over the Turks at Zenta (1697), Peterwardein (1716) and Belgrade (1717). He was also a patron of the arts.

EUGENICS, the study and application of scientifically directed selection in order to improve the genetic endowment of human populations. Eugenic control was first suggested by Sir Francis GALTON in the 1880s. People supporting eugenics suggest that those with "good" traits should be encouraged to have children while those with "bad" traits should be discouraged or forbidden from having families.

EUGÉNIE (1826–1920), empress of the French 1853–70 as wife of NAPOLEON III. The daughter of a Spanish noble, she was a major influence on her husband and was three times regent in his absence. After his downfall she escaped to England.

EULENSPIEGEL, Till, trickster hero of a group of German tales originally published c1515. The historic Till may have been a 14th-century Brunswick peasant. His pranks demonstrated peasant cunning triumphing over establishment figures of his day. He was the subject of the Richard STRAUSS tone poem that bears his name.

EULER, Leonhard (1707–1783), Swiss-born mathematician and physicist, the father of modern ANALYTIC GEOMETRY and important in almost every area of mathematics. He introduced the use of analysis (especially CALCULUS, a field which he also profoundly affected) into the study of MECHANICS; and made major contributions to modern ALGEBRA. **Euler's Relation** links the logarithmic and trigonometric functions: $e^{ix} = \cos x + i \sin x$ (see COMPLEX NUMBERS; TRIGONOMETRY). He worked also on a theory to explain the motions of the MOON and pioneered the science of HYDRODYNAMICS.

EUPHRATES RIVER, 2,235mi long, is the major river in SW Asia. It rises in NE Turkey and crosses the plains of Iraq where it finally joins the TIGRIS R to form the Shatt-al-Arab. It fostered the great civilizations of MESOPOTAMIA.

EURASIA, landmass composed of Asia and Europe, politically and culturally separate continents. In fact there is hardly any physical division, although the Ural and Caucasus Mts may be taken as a border.

EURATOM. See EUROPEAN ATOMIC ENERGY COMMUNITY (EURATOM).

EURIPIDES (c480 BC–406 BC), one of the greatest Greek playwrights. He appears to have been unpopular in Athens in his lifetime, possibly because of his agnostic and cynical views. He is thought to have written 92 plays, of which 19 have survived. The best-known are *Medea, The Trojan Women, Electra, Orestes* and *The Bacchae.*

EUROPE, the world's second smallest continent after Australia, is bounded on the N by the Arctic Ocean, on the W by the Atlantic and on the S by the Caucasus Mts and Black and Mediterranean seas. Because its E boundary, conventionally the Ural Mts and Ural R, is not generally agreed, and because Europe has thousands of offshore islands (including the British Isles and Iceland), estimates of its area range from 3,800,000sq mi to over 4,000,000sq mi. With Asia it forms a vast, single landmass (Eurasia).

The Land is dominated by great mountain systems including the Kjolen Mts and other peaks in Scandinavia, and the Hercynian system—the mosaic of plateaus, uplands and mountains extending E from Brittany and the Iberian peninsula and embracing the Massif Central of France, the Bohemian plateau and the Urals. Alpine Europe, including the Pyrenees, Alps, Carpathians and Caucasus, has many high peaks such as Mont Blanc (15,777ft) in the Alps and Elbrus (18,481ft) in the Caucasus, Europe's highest peak. Peninsular Italy has the Apennines, and the Dinaric fold mountains swing through Yugoslavia and into Greece. Volcanoes occur in Iceland and in Mediterranean Europe (especially Italy), and earthquakes and tremors are common in the Balkans. The most prominent lowland is the North European Plain, which broadens eastward from Belgium and The Netherlands reaching across N Poland and into Russia. Other lowlands are associated with major rivers like the Rhine and Danube. Europe's longest river is the Volga. Other important rivers include the Rhône, Elbe, Oder, Vistula and Don.

Climate and Vegetation. Most of Europe has a relatively mild climate, though winters in the N and E are long and severe. Rainfall is mostly plentiful. Mediterranean lands are known for their hot, dry summers and mild, wet winters. Vegetation ranges from the tundra plants and coniferous forests of the N to the alpine plants and varied forests of the high mountains, and the olives, cypress and scrub of the Mediterranean lands. The W has much natural grassland.

The People. Some 690,000,000 people, about 14% of the world's population, live in Europe. It is the most densely-populated continent. Its peoples are of many different ethnic and linguistic groups. It has 34 countries and more than 60 languages. Some areas, due to their harsh environments, are thinly populated. Rural densities of population are highest in the lowlands, while the highest concentrations are centered on coal fields and industrial centers. In most areas people are tending to move from the countryside and into the towns. The pattern has also been changed by the influx of millions of migrant workers from the Mediterranean lands into highly-industrialized W countries like France and West Germany. Though it has more than 4,000,000 Jews and about 13,000,000 Muslims, Europe is mainly a Christian continent, Roman Catholics being by far the most numerous.

EUROPE, Council of, organization of European countries founded in 1949 and headquartered in Strasbourg, France, to work for greater European unity, human rights, and the principles of parliamentary democracy. Its principal organs are the Committee of Ministers, composed of the foreign ministers of all member states, and the Parliamentary Assembly, whose members are drawn from the parliaments of member countries and apportioned according to population. In 1988 the 21 members of the Council of Europe were Austria, Belgium, Cyprus, Denmark, France, West Germany, Greece, Iceland, Ireland, Italy, Liechtenstein, Luxembourg, Malta, the Netherlands, Norway, Portugal, Spain, Sweden, Switzerland, Turkey, and the United Kingdom.

EUROPEAN ATOMIC ENERGY COMMUNITY (Euratom), one of the three EUROPEAN COMMUNITIES, established in 1957 by France, West Germany, Italy, Belgium, the Netherlands, and Luxembourg to combine their efforts in the development of nuclear power.

EUROPEAN COAL AND STEEL COMMUNITY (ECSC), the first of the three EUROPEAN COMMUNITIES, established in 1952 at the initiative of French foreign minister Robert Schuman to create a common market for coal and steel as a means of guaranteeing European peace. The original members were France, West Germany, Italy, Belgium, the Netherlands, and Luxembourg.

EUROPEAN COMMUNITIES (EC), or **European Community**, collective name for the EUROPEAN COAL AND STEEL COMMUNITY (ECSC), the EUROPEAN ECONOMIC COMMUNITY (EEC, or Common Market), and the EUROPEAN ATOMIC ENERGY COMMUNITY (EURATOM). The 12 members of the EC are Belgium, Denmark, France, the Federal Republic of Germany, Greece, Ireland, Italy, Luxembourg, the Netherlands, Portugal, Spain, and the United Kingdom. The EC's common institutions are: a Council of Ministers, representing the member governments, which provides overall policy direction; a 17-member Commission, which exercises executive authority; a 518-member European Parliament, elected directly by the peoples of the member countries, which has budgeting authority and may dismiss the executive Commission; and a Court of Justice, which decides whether acts of the common institutions or member governments are compatible with the governing treaties.

EUROPEAN ECONOMIC COMMUNITY (EEC), one of the three EUROPEAN COMMUNITIES, established in 1957 with the object of creating a common market among its members. The original members were France, West Germany, Italy, Belgium, the

Netherlands, and Luxembourg. The United Kingdom, Ireland, and Denmark joined in 1973, Greece in 1981, Spain and Portugal in 1986. Despite difficulties arising from different levels of economic development and agricultural and industrial competition, the EEC aims to complete the elimination of all intra-EEC trade barriers by 1992.

EUROPEAN FREE TRADE ASSOCIATION (EFTA), trading group organized in 1960 by Austria, Britain, Denmark, Norway, Portugal, Sweden, and Switzerland, none of them members of the original six-member EUROPEAN ECONOMIC COMMUNITY (EEC), to enable these so-called "outer seven" to bargain with the "inner six" as well as to liberalize trade among themselves, chiefly by eliminating trade barriers on nonagricultural goods. This last was accomplished in 1967. Finland became an associate member in 1961 and a full member in 1985. Iceland joined in 1970. Britain, Denmark, and Portugal later withdrew to join the EEC, leaving the EFTA currently with six members.

EUROPEAN ORGANIZATION FOR NUCLEAR RESEARCH (CERN), organization, founded in 1954 and headquartered in Geneva, through which 14 European countries — Austria, Belgium, Denmark, France, West Germany, Greece, Italy, the Netherlands, Norway, Portugal, Spain, Sweden, Switzerland, the United Kingdom — collaborate on fundamental nuclear research of a nonmilitary character. It replaced the Conseil Européen pour la Recherche Nucléaire (CERN), founded in 1952, but retained its acronym.

EUROPEAN SPACE AGENCY (ESA), organization established in 1980 and headquartered in Paris through which 13 member states — Austria, Belgium, Denmark, France, West Germany, Ireland, Italy, the Netherlands, Norway, Spain, Sweden, Switzerland, the United Kingdom — cooperate in space research and technology for peaceful purposes.

EURYTHMICS, art of expressing musical rhythms through body movement. It was developed by the Swiss professor of music Emile Jaques-Dalcroze in an attempt to increase his students' awareness of rhythm, and has been a major influence on modern dance and, most recently, physical fitness programs.

EUSEBIUS OF CAESAREA, bishop, 4th-century scholar, remembered for his *Ecclesiastical History*, a primary source for the early history of the Church. Originally an Arian sympathizer, he was exonerated of heresy by the Council of NICAEA (325).

EUTHANASIA, the practice of hastening

or causing the DEATH of a person suffering from incurable DISEASE. While frequently advocated by various groups, its practical and legal implications are so controversial that it remains illegal in most countries.

EUTROPHICATION, the increasing concentration of plant nutrients and FERTILIZERS in lakes and estuaries, partly by natural drainage and partly by POLLUTION. It leads to excessive growth of algae and aquatic plants, with oxygen depletion of the deep water, causing various undesirable effects.

EVANGELICAL AND REFORMED CHURCH, Protestant church formed by the union of the Reformed Church of America and the Evangelical Synod of North America (1934); since 1957 part of the UNITED CHURCH OF CHRIST.

EVANGELICALISM, meaning "pertaining to the Gospel," the name of a theological movement, found in most Protestant denominations, that emphasizes the primary authority of the Bible. It stresses Christ's atoning death, human sinfulness, JUSTIFICATION BY FAITH, the necessity of personal conversion and expository preaching, and opposes Roman and Anglo-Catholicism.

EVANGELICAL UNITED BRETHREN (EUB), Protestant church, essentially Methodist, formed by the merger (1946) of the Evangelical Church and the Church of the United Brethren in Christ. In 1968 they became part of the United Methodist Church.

EVANS, Sir Arthur John (1851–1941), English archaeologist famous for his discovery of the MINOAN CIVILIZATION from excavations at KNOSSOS in Crete. He was curator of the Ashmolean Museum, Oxford 1884–1908 and professor of prehistoric archaeology at Oxford from 1909.

EVANS, Mary Ann. See ELIOT, GEORGE.

EVANS, Walker (1903–1975), US photographer who documented the Depression in the southern US. He published his work in *Let Us Now Praise Famous Men* (1941) and in *Fortune* magazine, of which he was an editor.

EVAPORATION, the escape of molecules from the surface of a liquid into the vapor state. Only those molecules with sufficient kinetic ENERGY are able to overcome the cohesive forces holding the liquid together and escape from the surface. This leaves the remaining molecules with a lower average kinetic energy, and hence a lower TEMPERATURE. In an enclosed space, the pressure of the vapor above the surface eventually reaches a maximum, the saturated vapor pressure (SVP). This varies according to the substance concerned and, together with the rate of evaporation, increases with temperature, equalling atmospheric pressure at the liquid's boiling point.

EVE, the first woman, according to the Bible, wife of ADAM, from whose rib God created her. She is the subject of Jewish, Christian and Muslim legend.

EVELYN, John (1620–1706), English writer and humanist whose *Diary*, published in 1818, is one of the most important sources for English life in the 17th century.

EVEREST, Mount, highest mountain in the world (29,028ft), situated in the Himalayas on the Nepalese-Tibetan border. It is named for Sir George Everest, British surveyor general of India 1830–43. After several unsuccessful attempts, it was first climbed on May 29, 1953 by Edmund HILLARY and Tenzing Norkay.

EVERETT, Edward (1794–1865), US statesman and orator. A Unitarian clergyman, he received from the University of Göttingen the first Ph.D. given to an American (1817). He became professor of Greek at Harvard in 1815, was a congressman 1825–35, governor of Mass. 1836–39, minister to England 1841–45, president of Harvard 1846–49, secretary of state 1852–53 and in 1860 the Constitutional Union Party's vice-presidential candidate.

EVERGLADES, swampy region in S Fla. Covering an area of about 5,000sq mi, the Everglades extend from Lake Okeechobee in the N to the S end of the Florida peninsula. The flooded sawgrass swamps support abundant wild animals and plants, many peculiar to the area. Indians inhabited the Everglades before the 1500s. In the 1830s the US tried to drive the SEMINOLE Indians out. Part of the Everglades was drained in the late 19th century, producing rich agricultural land, but drainage now conflicts with conservation plans. In 1947 the Everglades National Park was established in the S.

EVERGOOD, Philip (Philip Blashki; 1901–73), US artist. An advocate of social realism, he was best known for murals painted while he was participating in the Federal Works Project during the 1930s. His later work emphasized biblical and mythological symbolism.

EVERT, Chris (1954–   ), US tennis player, six-time US Open champion (1975–78, 1980, 1982), three-time Wimbledon champion (1974, 1976, 1981).

EVERYMAN, late 15th-century morality play about a man (Everyman) who, when summoned by Death, finds that of all his friends only Good Deeds aided by Knowledge accompanies him. The allegory has been often used by dramatists.

EVIDENCE, in law, that which is advanced by parties to a legal dispute as proving, or contributing to the proof, of their case. To be admissible in court evidence must conform to various rules in order to ensure a clear and fair presentation of it to the trier of fact, a jury or a judge. Such evidence may consist of the oral testimony of witnesses summoned by either side, of documentary evidence of physical objects, as for example an alleged murder weapon. The evidence may be direct, supporting the facts of the case, or it may be circumstantial, evidence from which those facts may reasonably be deduced. An eyewitness account of an auto accident is direct evidence; unaccountable damage to the defendant's auto may be circumstantial evidence. Evidence may be excluded for three main reasons—if it is not sufficiently relevant, if it arises out of privileged circumstances, and if it is hearsay—"second-hand" evidence arising out of a statement made outside court by a person not called as a witness, who cannot therefore be cross-examined. In a 1970 case the US Supreme Court held that a state's rules on hearsay evidence do not necessarily have to be as strict as those in federal courts. Business and public records likely to be accurate are exempted from the hearsay rule, as in some circumstances is a statement made by a dying person. Privileges protect certain interests, such as the right not to incriminate oneself, and certain relationships considered essential to society, such as that between a husband and wife, who are therefore not required to give evidence against each other.

EVOLUTION, the process by which living organisms have changed since the origin of life. The formulation of the theory of evolution by NATURAL SELECTION is credited to Charles DARWIN, whose observations while sailing around the world on the *Beagle*, when taken together with elements from MALTHUS' population theory and viewed in the context of LYELL's doctrine of UNIFORMITARIANISM, led him to the concept of natural selection, but the theory also later occurred independently to A. R. WALLACE. Other theories of evolution by the inheritance of acquired characteristics had earlier been proposed by Erasmus Darwin (1731–1802) and LAMARCK. Darwin defended the mechanism of natural selection on the basis of three observations: that animals and plants produced far more offspring than were required to maintain the size of their population; that the size of any natural population remained more or less stable over long periods; and that the members of any one generation exhibited variation. From the first two he argued that in any generation there was a high mortality rate, and from the third that, under certain circumstances, some of the variants had a greater chance of survival than did others. The surviving variants were, by definition, those most suited to the prevailing environmental conditions. Any change in the environment led to adjustment in the population such that certain new variants were favored and gradually became predominant.

The missing link in Darwin's theory was the mechanism by which heritable variation occurs. Unknown to him, a contemporary, G. MENDEL, had demonstrated the principle of GENETICS and had deduced that the heritable characters were controlled by discrete particles. We now know these particles to be GENES which are carried on the CHROMOSOMES. Mendel's variants were caused by recombination and MUTATION of the genes. Natural selection acts to eradicate unfit variants either by mortality of the individual or by ensuring that such individuals do not breed. How then can natural selection lead to the evolution of a new character? The key is that a character that is advantageous to an individual in the normal environment may become disadvantageous if the environment changes. This means that individuals that happen through variation to be well adapted to the new set of circumstances will tend to survive and thus become the norm.

An example of natural selection at work is provided by studies carried out recently on North American sparrows. Large numbers of sparrows were trapped and their various characteristics recorded. In this way the "normal" sparrow was identified. A further collection was made of dead sparrows which had succumbed to the adverse conditions of a particularly severe winter. It was found that the individuals in the second sample were all different in some important respect from the "normal" sparrow. Natural selection could thus be seen to be maintaining a population that was ideally suited to the North American environment.

Today, the evidence for evolution is overwhelming and comes from many branches of biology. For instance, the comparative anatomy of the arm of a man, the foreleg of a horse, the wing of a bat and the flipper of a seal reveals that these superficially different organs have a very similar internal structure, this being taken to indicate a common ancestor. Then, the study of the embryos of mammals and birds reveals that at some stages they are virtually indistinguishable and thus have common ancestors. Again, vestigial organs such as the appendix of man and the wing of the ostrich have no use to these mammals, but in related species such as herbivores and flying birds they clearly are of vital importance. Evidently these individuals have progressively evolved in different ways from a common ancestor. The hierarchical classification of plants and animals into species, genus, family etc. (see TAXONOMY) is a direct reflection of the natural pattern that would be expected if evolution from common ancestors occurred. Again, the geographical distribution of animals and plants presents many facts of evolutionary significance. For example, the tapir is today centered in two widely separated areas, the E Indies and South America. However, it probably evolved in a single center, migrated across the world and then became extinct in many areas as habitats changed. Indeed FOSSILS of tapirs have been found in Asia, Europe and North America. Fossils in general provide convincing evidence of evolution. Thus, the theory of the evolution of birds indicates descent from now extinct reptiles. The fossil archaeopteryx, a flying reptile with some bird-like features, was believed to represent the missing link in this development.

LIFE probably first evolved from the primeval soup some 3-4 billion years ago, when the first organic chemicals were synthesized due to the effects of lightning. Primitive ALGAE capable of synthesizing their own food material have been found in geological formations some 2 billion years old. Simple forms of animals and fungi then evolved. From that time there has been a slow evolution of multicellular organisms.

EWING, William Maurice (1906–1974), US oceanographer, at Columbia 1944–72. He was the first recipient (1960) of the Vetlesen Prize honoring leaders in earth sciences.

EXCLUSIONARY RULE, law derived from the Supreme Court ruling in *Mapp v. Ohio* (1961), which held that in a criminal case, evidence seized illegally cannot be used in a trial of the case. This law had already been established by federal courts and some state courts. The High Court pointed out that blanket exclusion appears to be the only way to prevent police abuses, but the rule has never been popular with law-enforcement officers. In 1981 the Court delivered rulings which peripherally weakened the rule.

EXCLUSION PRINCIPLE, a law, proposed by W. PAULI, accounting for the different chemical properties of the ELEMENTS and numerous other phenomena. Applying to those particles called fermions, particularly ELECTRONS, it is a consequence of the fact that particles of the same kind are indistinguishable, and states that only one such particle can occupy a given quantum state (see QUANTUM MECHANICS) at a time. In atoms, the energy levels fill up as the number of electrons increases; it is the electrons in the outer unfilled "shells" that are responsible for the chemical properties of an atom.

EXCOMMUNICATION, ecclesiastical censure, common to all Christian denominations, usually denoting formal exclusion of an offender from sharing in the communion of the church. In the Roman Catholic Church an excommunicate may not attend mass or receive the sacraments and is denied a Christian burial. Excommunication was important in the Middle Ages as a punishment meted out by ecclesiastical courts. It was sometimes used to force temporal rulers to submit to papal authority.

EXCRETION, the removal of the waste products of METABOLISM either by storing them in insoluble forms or by removing them from the body. Excretory organs are also responsible for maintaining the correct balance of body fluids. In VERTEBRATES the excretory organs are the KIDNEYS: blood flows through these and water and waste products are removed as URINE. Other forms of excretory organs include the Malpighian tubes of insects, arachnids and myriapods, the contractile vacuoles of Protozoa and the nephridia of annelids. In plants, excretion usually takes the form of producing insoluble salts of waste products within the cells.

EXECUTIVE, that part of government which carries out the business of governing. In the US it shares power with the legislature and the judiciary. Under the Constitution it is charged with taking care "that the laws be faithfully executed." It is headed by the president, who appoints all executive officers, usually subject to Senate approval. His cabinet, federal departments such as the defense department, foreign ambassadors and hundreds of boards and commissions come under the jurisdiction of the executive. The term is also used of that part of a private organization or company that manages and controls its business. (See also SEPARATION OF POWERS.)

EXERCISE, or physical exertion, the active

use of skeletal muscle in recreation or under environmental stress. In exercise, MUSCLES contract actively, consuming OXYGEN at a high rate, and so require increased BLOOD CIRCULATION; this is effected by increasing the HEART output by raising the PULSE and increasing the blood expelled with each beat. Meanwhile, the CAPILLARIES in active muscles dilate. The raised demand for oxygen and, more especially, the increased production of carbon dioxide in the muscles increase the rate of RESPIRATION. Some energy requirements can be supplied rapidly without oxygen but, if so, the "oxygen debt" must be made good afterward. GASTROINTESTINAL TRACT activity is reduced during exercise. Changes in the autonomic and central NERVOUS SYSTEMS, HORMONES and local regulators are responsible for adaptive changes in exercise. In athletes, exercise increases muscle efficiency and cardiac compensation.

EXILE, The. See BABYLONIAN CAPTIVITY.

EXISTENTIALISM, the 20th-century branch of philosophy which stresses that since "existence precedes essence," man is what he makes himself and is also responsible for what he makes of himself. It is a rejection of traditional metaphysical thought, which views truth as timeless and unchanging and sees man as subject to external verities termed "essences." The important precursor of Existentialism was Søren KIERKEGAARD, who held that man's sense of dread and despair arose from his responsibility for his own decisions and for his relationship with God. Theologians influenced by Kierkegaard are Karl BARTH, Martin BUBER, Karl JASPERS, Reinhold NIEBUHR and Paul TILLICH. Edmund HUSSERL's philosophy of PHENOMENOLOGY influenced his two students Martin HEIDEGGER and Jean-Paul SARTRE to consider the nature of human experience and of responsibility and freedom. Sartre, who eventually became a Marxist, influenced Albert CAMUS and Simone de BEAUVOIR.

EXOBIOLOGY, or xenobiology, the study of life beyond the earth's atmosphere. Drawing on many other sciences (e.g., biochemistry, physics), it is for obvious reasons a discipline dealing primarily in hypotheses (though FOSSIL organic matter has been found in certain meteorites—see METEOR). An important branch deals with the effects on man of nonterrestrial environments.

EXODUS, second book of the Old Testament, and of the TORAH. The book describes the escape of the Israelites from slavery in Egypt, the covenant made at Mt

Sinai between Moses and Yahweh and includes the Ten Commandments.

EXORCISM, the expulsion of demons from places or persons, common in pagan religions, and found also in Judaism and Christianity. In the New Testament, Jesus cast out demons from the possessed by a word, and the apostles did likewise in his name. In the early Church anyone so gifted could exorcise; in the 3rd century exorcism was restricted to ordained clergy, in particular a minor order called exorcists, finally suppressed in 1972. Now somewhat controversial, exorcism is practiced as a last resort and with medical advice. Regulated by canon law and requiring episcopal permission, it is a ceremonial rite with set prayers. An exorcism to ward off evil (not presupposing possession) forms part of the Roman Catholic service of baptism.

EXOSKELETON, any skeletal material that lies on the surface of the animal's body. In this position it not only performs the mechanical functions common to any other SKELETON but, in addition, affords protection. Exoskeletons are particularly well developed in arthropods such as crabs, lobsters and insects.

EX PARTE MILLIGAN. See MILLIGAN, EX PARTE.

EXPLOSIVES, substances capable of very rapid COMBUSTION (or other exothermic reaction) to produce hot gases whose rapid expansion is accompanied by a high-velocity shock wave, shattering nearby objects. The detonation travels 1000 times faster than a flame. The earliest known explosive was GUNPOWDER, invented in China in the 10th century AD, and in the West by Roger BACON (1242). Explosives are classified as primary explosives, which explode at once on ignition and are used as detonators, and high explosives, which if ignited at first merely burn, but explode if detonated by a primary explosion. The division is not rigid. Military high explosives are usually mixtures of organic nitrates, TNT, RDX, and picric acid, which are self-oxidizing. Commercial blasting explosives are less-powerful mixtures of combustible and explosive substances; they include DYNAMITE (containing NITROGLYCERIN, ammonium nitrate and sometimes nitrocellulose), ammonals (ammonium nitrate+aluminum) and Sprengel explosives (an oxidizing agent mixed with a liquid fuel such as nitrobenzene just before use). Obsolete explosives include the dangerous chlorates and perchlorates, and the uneconomical liquid oxygen explosives (LOX). Explosives which do not ignite firedamp are termed "permissible," and may be used in coal mines. Propellants for guns and rockets are like explosives, but burn fast rather than detonating.

EXPONENT, a number such as x in the expression a^x, a being a number to be used as a FACTOR x times: e.g., $a \cdot a \cdot a$. In the expression, a is termed the base.

EXPORT–IMPORT BANK OF THE UNITED STATES (Eximbank), US government agency set up in 1934 to assist foreign exports. It makes loans to foreign borrowers who wish to buy US goods and services. After developing world trade and particularly that of Latin America and the Allied countries after WWII, Eximbank now supports US exports especially to developing countries.

EX POST FACTO LAW, law acting retrospectively, most commonly to make illegal actions which were legal when committed. The US Constitution prohibits *ex post facto* criminal laws; in English law they are permitted but are rare. The NUREMBURG TRIALS were based on *ex post facto* legislation.

EXPRESSIONISM, early 20th-century movement in art and literature which held that art should be the expression of subjective feelings and emotions. Expressionist painters preferred intense coloring and primitive simplified forms, in that these seemed to convey emotions directly. VAN GOGH, ENSOR and MUNCH influenced the movement which developed in both France and Germany after 1905. In France the style was represented by the Fauvists (see FAUVISM), MATISSE and ROUAULT, and in Germany by Die Brücke and the BLAUE REITER artists like KANDINSKY, KIRCHNER, KOKOSCHKA, NOLDE, GROSZ, and MARC. Expressionist writers include STRINDBERG, WEDEKIND and KAFKA.

EXTERNAL-COMBUSTION ENGINE, an engine that burns its fuel in a separate container outside the engine itself, as in the STEAM ENGINE, steam or gas TURBINE and also the STIRLING ENGINE. Unlike an INTERNAL-COMBUSTION ENGINE (gasoline or DIESEL ENGINE), an external-combustion engine requires only a source of heat and thus is not dependent on refined petroleum fuels designed to burn inside its cylinders.

EXTORTION, seeking to obtain money from a person by non-physical intimidation, often by the threat of a criminal charge or the exposure of some secret. Physical intimidation is usually considered robbery. Some specific kinds of extortion are usually known as blackmail.

EXTRASENSORY PERCEPTION. See ESP.

EXTRATERRITORIALITY, privilege granted by a country to resident foreign nationals, allowing them to remain under the jurisdiction of the laws of their own country only. It is generally extended only to diplomatic agents.

EXTREMELY LOW FREQUENCY (ELF), a system aimed at improved linkage of submarines to communication networks. Water being notoriously opaque to electromagnetic signals, submarines have been forced to rise to the surface to receive or send signals on conventional radio frequencies. ELF radiowaves, however, have good penetrating power. For over a decade the US Navy has been trying to develop an ELF radio wave system using a giant broadcast antenna. The first plan, involving the sinking of 5,000 miles of antenna wire through Wisconsin and Michigan was stalled by environmentalists and others fearing possible low radiation effects. In late 1981, President Reagan gave the go-ahead for a Michigan and Wisconsin-based system using a total of 84 miles of cable. By 1985, 20 US submarines are scheduled to be fitted with receivers and the ELF system is slated to become operational.

EXTREME UNCTION, or anointing of the sick, a SACRAMENT of the Roman Catholic and Eastern Orthodox churches; a rite including anointing with oil, laying on of hands and prayer for healing. From the Middle Ages until recently in the Roman Catholic Church it was administered chiefly to the dying as preparation for death, but its healing use is now emphasized.

EYE, the specialized sense organ concerned with VISION. In all species it consists of a lens system linked to a LIGHT-receptor system connected to the central NERVOUS SYSTEM. In man and mammals, the eye is roughly spherical in shape, has a tough fibrous capsule with the transparent cornea in front, and is moved by specialized eye muscles. The exposed surface is kept moist with tears from lacrymal glands. Most of the eye contains vitreous humor—a substance with the consistency of jelly—which fills the space between the lens and the retina, while in front of the lens there is watery or aqueous humor. The colored iris or aperture surrounds a hole known as the pupil. The focal length of the lens can be varied by specialized ciliary muscles. The retina is a layer containing the nerve cells (rods and cones) which receive light, together with the next two sets of cells in the relay pathway for vision. The optic nerve leads back from the retina to the BRAIN.

Rods and cones receive light reflected from a pigment layer and contain pigments (e.g., rhodopsin) which are bleached by light and thus set off the nerve-cell reaction.

EYE BANK, a department in a hospital or some other organization where eyes or corneas are stored (for up to three weeks) for use in corneal grafts by ophthalmic surgeons. Sometimes removed in a necessary operation on someone living, the eyes usually come from the dead (within 10 hours of decease) by permission either of a will or of surviving relatives.

EZEKIEL, early 6th-century BC Hebrew priest and prophet. He lived in Jerusalem but in 597 BC was taken by Babylon. The Old Testament book which bears his name foretells the destruction of Jerusalem, pronounces judgment on foreign nations and predicts the restoration of Israel.

EZRA, 5th-century BC Babylonian Jewish priest and religious leader, whose teachings are recorded in the Old Testament Book of Ezra. He advocated an exclusive and legalistic doctrine, prohibiting marriages between Jews and gentiles.

6th letter of the English alphabet, and also of the Roman and early Greek alphabets. In science, F is the symbol for farad, the SI UNIT of capacitance, and °F for degrees Fahrenheit.

FABER, John Eberhard (1822–1879), German-born US manufacturer who in 1861 established the first pencil factory in the US. He introduced the rubber eraser on the pencil's end.

FABERGE, Peter Carl (1846–1920), Russian goldsmith famous for the jewelry he made for the Russian tsars and other royalty, especially the bejeweled "Easter eggs." He went into exile in 1917.

FABIAN SOCIETY, English society for the propagation of socialism, established 1883–84, taking its name from the delaying tactics of the Roman general Fabius Cunctator. Fabians rejected violent revolution, seeking to change society gradually. They helped form the Labour Representation Committee which became the Labour Party in 1906. Leading Fabians were Sidney and Beatrice WEBB and George Bernard SHAW.

FABIUS CUNCTATOR (Quintus Fabius Maximus Verrucosus; d. 203 BC), Roman general, famous for his delaying tactics in the war against HANNIBAL. He harassed the Carthaginian army but avoided pitched battle, giving Rome time to recover its strength.

FABLE, a fictional story, generally one illustrating a moral. The characters are often animals whose behavior caricatures human folly. Famous collections of fables are those by AESOP and Jean de LA FONTAINE.

FABRE, Jean Henri (1823–1915), French entomologist who used direct observations of insects in their natural environments in his pioneering researches into insect instinct and behavior.

FACTOR, an INTEGER which may be divided into another integer without remainder. Thus the factors of 12 are 1, 2, 3, 4 and 6, since each of these may be divided exactly into 12. In general it is of use to consider only the factors of a number which are NATURAL NUMBERS. The prime factors of a number are those PRIME NUMBERS which are its factors. The prime factors of 12 are 1, 2 (twice), and 3.

In ALGEBRA the factors of a POLYNOMIAL are found by a mixture of guesswork and rules of thumb. This is helped by certain standard rules:

$$x^2 - y^2 = (x+y)(x-y)$$
$$x^3 - y^3 = (x-y)(x^2 + xy + y^2)$$
$$x^3 + y^3 = (x+y)(x^2 - xy + y^2)$$
$$x^2 + 2xy + y^2 = (x+y)^2.$$

FACTORY, establishment for the manufacture of goods in quantity. In the US most goods are factory-made and almost 25% of the population is employed in factories. Factories as we know them originated in the INDUSTRIAL REVOLUTION and were soon focal points for overcrowding and slums caused by the massive influx of workers into urban areas. Working conditions were often bad and had to be improved by legislation. The factory today is attacked because of the POLLUTION it can cause, and because a town may become economically dependent on a few factories and so suffer disproportionately in a recession.

FADEYEV, Aleksander Alexandrovich (1901–1956), Russian novelist. In 1918 he fought for the Bolsheviks in Siberia, the setting of his best-known novel, *The Nineteen* (1927).

FAHD IBN ABDUL AZIZ (1922–   ), king of Saudi Arabia from 1982. Fahd, a son of IBN SAUD, was interior minister from 1962 to 1975, when his half-brother King Khalid named him crown prince. He succeeded upon the death of Khalid, whose cautious policies he generally followed.

FAHRENHEIT, Gabriel Daniel (1686–1736), German-born Dutch instrument maker who introduced the mercury-in-glass thermometer and discovered the variation of boiling points with atmospheric PRESSURE, but who is best remembered for his **Fahrenheit temperature scale**. This has 179 divisions (degrees) between the freezing point of water (32°F) and the boiling point (212°F). Although still commonly used in the US, elsewhere the Fahrenheit scale has been superseded by the Celsius scale.

FAINTING, or **syncope,** transient loss or diminution of consciousness associated with an abrupt fall in blood pressure. In the upright position, head and BRAIN are dependent on a certain blood pressure to maintain BLOOD CIRCULATION through them; if the pressure falls for any reason, inadequate flow causes consciousness to recede, often with the sense of things becoming more distant. The body goes limp and falls, so that, unless artificially supported, the effect of gravity on brain flow is lost and consciousness is rapidly regained. Fainting may result from sudden emotional shock, HEMORRHAGE, ANEMIA or occur with transient rhythm disorders of the HEART.

FAIRBANKS, Douglas Sr. (1883–1939), US film actor famous for his romantic and swashbuckling roles in films such as *Robin Hood* (1922) and *The Black Pirate* (1926). In 1919 he founded United Artists Studio with his wife Mary PICKFORD, Charlie CHAPLIN, and D. W. GRIFFITH.

FAIR DEAL, domestic program put before Congress by President Truman 1945–48, covering civil rights, education, health services, agriculture and employment. Congress rejected many of the proposals as being too expensive, but the 1946 Employment Act and some other measures resulted.

FAIR EMPLOYMENT PRACTICES COMMITTEE (FEPC), wartime federal agency (1941–46) created by executive order to promote the fullest use of manpower by eliminating discrimination in employment. (See also EQUAL EMPLOYMENT OPPORTUNITY COMMISSION (EEOC).)

FAIRFAX OF CAMERON, Thomas Fairfax, 6th Baron (1693–1781), English landowner in colonial Virginia. Inheriting the proprietorship of the Northern Neck, more than 5 million acres between the Rappahannock and Potomac rivers, he moved to Virginia in 1747, eventually settling (1750) in the Shenandoah Valley near Winchester. After the Revolution, the state of Virginia ended the proprietorship. His cousin, William Fairfax, was a friend and neighbor of the young George Washington.

FAIR LABOR STANDARDS ACT, passed in 1938 by the Roosevelt administration to ensure for most workers a minimum wage and a 44hr maximum working week. The act was subsequently extended and improved.

FAIRY TALE, general term for a tale involving fantastic events and characters, not necessarily fairies. Many of these originate in myth and folklore, but an equal number have been written or collected to provide sophisticated adult entertainment, among them those by Charles PERRAULT, the brothers GRIMM, GOETHE, E. T. A. HOFFMANN and some by Hans Christian ANDERSEN. Many modern writers, such as J. R. R. TOLKIEN and C. S. LEWIS, invented and incorporated fairy-tale elements in their works.

FAISAL or **Feisal,** two kings of Iraq. **Faisal I** (1885–1933) took part in the Arab revolt against the Ottoman Turks in 1915 and was king 1921–33. **Faisal II** (1935–58) reigned from 1939. His uncle, Abdul Ilah, ruled Iraq as regent till 1953. In 1958 they were both murdered in a revolution.

FAISAL or **Feisal** (1905–1975), king of Saudi Arabia from 1964, when his brother King Saud was forced to abdicate. A pious, moderate and able ruler, Faisal instituted a far-ranging program of social reform. Friendly to the West, he nevertheless joined the campaign against Israel and supported the Arab oil cartel. He was assassinated by a nephew in March 1975.

FAITH HEALING, the treatment of DISEASE by the evocation of faith, usually induced during a public ceremony or meeting; chanting and laying on of hands are common accompaniments. Greatest success is often with disease that tends to remit spontaneously and in HYSTERIA; in some instances, patients are helped to come to terms with disease. Substantiation of cures is rare.

FALANGE, Spanish political party founded in 1933 in emulation of Italian FASCISM but differing from other varieties of fascism by its support of the Catholic church. The Falange supported Francisco FRANCO in the Spanish civil war and after.

FALASHAS, Ethiopian Jews, probably descendants of converts made by Jewish merchants or soldiers from Arabia or Egypt. Isolated from other Jews for two millennia, until recently they practiced a form of pre-Talmudic Judaism, with priests but not rabbis, based on the Old Testament. The word "falasha" is an Ethiopian slave name meaning "stranger" or "exile," and the Falashas were persecuted by Christian Ethiopians. In recent years they endured with other Ethiopians famine and civil war. In 1984–85 the Israelis airlifted about 6,000 Falasha refugees from the Sudan to Israel in "Operation Moses." An equal number or more remain in Ethiopia.

FALCONS, name generally applied to about 60 species of hawk, though the true falcons of the family Falconidae number about 35 species. They are birds of prey, feeding mainly on other birds which they kill in the air. They inhabit most parts of the world, making their nests on rocky ledges or tree forks. Falcons in the US include the prairie falcon and the sparrow hawk.

FALKLAND ISLANDS, self-governing British colony, a group of islands totalling 4,700sq mi in the S Atlantic about 480mi NE of Cape Horn. Possession is disputed with Argentina (which calls them Islas Malvinas); in 1982 Argentina seized them but Britain fought successfully to regain the islands. They number about 200, the largest of which are E Falkland and W Falkland. The inhabitants are mostly of British descent; the economy rests largely on sheep raising. Capital: Stanley. Pop 1,800.

FALLA, Manuel de (1876–1946), major Spanish composer. He studied in Madrid and Paris. His work was heavily influenced by RAVEL and native Andalusian folk music, evident in the famous ballets *El Amor Brujo* (1915) and *The Three-Cornered Hat* (1919). Other famous works are the opera *La Vida Breve* (1905) and *Nights in the Gardens of Spain* (1911–15), for piano and orchestra.

FALLEN TIMBERS, Battle of (Aug. 20, 1794), in which a large force of regulars and militia led by US general Anthony WAYNE decisively defeated the Indians. It was fought at the Maumee River rapids southwest of modern Toledo, Ohio, and was so named because the Indians concealed themselves behind trees brought down by a storm. The Indians had risen to oppose settlement beyond the Ohio River, and had previously surprised and routed General Arthur St. Clair near the Miami villages (1791). Wayne's victory at Fallen Timbers opened up the Old Northwest to settlement. He concluded the Treaty of Greenville (Aug. 3, 1795) with the Indians, who ceded nearly all of what soon became Ohio (1803).

FALL LINE, a line in the E US along which a number of rivers have waterfalls, marking the progress of the rivers from hard rock underlying the Piedmont to softer rock forming the Atlantic Coastal Plain. Since this marks the farthest inland point navigable from the sea, and because the falls can supply hydroelectric power, many important industrial centers have sprung up along fall lines, including Philadelphia and Baltimore.

FALLOPIAN TUBE, narrow tube leading from the surface of each ovary within the female pelvis to the womb. Its abdominal end has fimbria which waft peritoneal fluid and eggs into the tube after ovulation. Fertilization may occur in the tube, and if followed by implantation there, the PREGNANCY is ectopic, and ABORTION, which may be life-threatening, is inevitable. In STERILIZATION, the tubes are divided.

FALLOUT, Radioactive, deposition of radioactive particles from the ATMOSPHERE on the earth's surface. Three types of fallout follow the atmospheric explosion of a nuclear weapon. Large particles are deposited as intense but short-lived local fallout within about 150mi of the explosion; this dust causes radiation burns. Within a week, smaller particles from the troposphere are found around the latitude of the explosion. Long-lived RADIOISOTOPES such as strontium-90, carried to the stratosphere by the explosion, are eventually deposited worldwide.

FALSE DECRETALS, collection of papal letters and decrees and other documents, many of them forgeries, published in the 9th century to support the claims of bishops to greater independence. Influential during the Middle Ages, the forgeries were suspected from the start and fully exposed in the 16th century.

FALWELL, Jerry (1933–   ), US Baptist radio and television evangelist who preaches a politically oriented pro-family, pro-morality and pro-American gospel to millions of faithful followers. In 1979 he founded Moral Majority, Inc., which played an important role in electing conservatives, including Ronald Reagan, to office in the 1980 elections. In 1987 he resigned the presidency of Moral Majority and renounced political activism.

FAMILY, a social unit comprising a number of persons in most cases linked by birth or MARRIAGE. There are four main types of families: the conjugal or nuclear family, a single set of parents and their children; the extended or consanguine family, which includes also siblings and other relations and generations (e.g., brothers, grandparents, grandchildren, uncles and aunts); the corporate family, a group organized around an important activity such as hunting, sharing of shelter, religion or customs; and the experimental family, a group whose members are generally unrelated to each other genetically, but who choose to live together and perform the traditional roles of the nuclear or consanguine family. The *kibbutzim* of Israel and the commune are examples of experimental families.

The descent within a family is usually either patrilineal, through its male members, or matrilineal, through its female members. Occasionally descent is bilineal, through either male or female lines, or bilateral, through both males and females.

By far the most common forms of families are the **nuclear** and **consanguine.** There are sound reasons for this: psychological security through membership of a close, intimate group; ready sexual and emotional satisfaction between husband and wife; and physical security based on a family's sense of duty and willingness to protect its members. Moreover, it would seem that these types of families are the most efficient insofar as childrearing is concerned, with older generations or siblings acting as mentors during the child's formative years. In the West, the nuclear family has in recent years become generally more democratic, the male's absolute authority being tempered to permit wives and children greater freedom and responsibility.

FAMILY PLANNING, the practice of regulation of family size by judicious use of CONTRACEPTION. STERILIZATION and, occasionally, induced ABORTION; increased survival of children and increasing world population have created the need for such an approach. Planning of numbers and timing to accord with economic and social factors are greatly aided by modern methods of contraception, so unwanted PREGNANCY should be a rarity. However, ignorance and neglect have prevented the realization of this ideal. Adoption, ARTIFICIAL INSEMINATION and treatment of infertility are used for parents unable to conceive.

FAMILY VIOLENCE. See ABUSE.

FAMINE, acute food shortage resulting in widespread starvation. It is usually caused by natural disasters such as drought, floods or plant diseases, causing crop failure. Famines have often dramatically influenced the course of history. One such was the Irish famine (1846–47) caused by potato blight. Millions died and around a million and a half emigrated, mostly to the US. Recently there have been crippling famines in Bangladesh and Ethiopia.

FANEUIL HALL, historic marketplace and meeting hall in Boston, Mass. Built by Peter Faneuil in 1742, it was burned in 1761, and rebuilt by the town in 1763. It was a meeting place for American patriots during the Revolutionary period and received the name "Cradle of Liberty." It is still in use as a marketplace and meeting hall, and contains a historical museum.

FANNIN, James Walker (c1804–1836), US soldier. A colonel in the Texan army, he was active in the revolutionary movement against Mexico. He was captured on March 19, 1836 and by order of SANTA ANNA he and most of his men were shot.

FANON, Frantz Omar (1925–1961), French black psychoanalyst and social philosopher. He condemned racism in his book *Black Skin, White Masks* (1952). In *The Wretched of the Earth* (1961) he advocated extreme violence against whites as a cathartic expression for black peoples.

FANTIN-LATOUR, Ignace Henri Jean Théodore (1836–1904), French painter known for his flower-paintings, his illustrations of the work of WAGNER and BERLIOZ, and his portraits of artistic celebrities as in the grouping in *A Studio at Batignolles* (1870).

FARADAY, Michael (1791–1867), English chemist and physicist, the pupil and successor of H. DAVY at the Royal Institution, who discovered BENZENE (1824), first demonstrated electromagnetic INDUCTION (see also HENRY, Joseph) and invented the dynamo (1831—see GENERATOR. ELECTRIC), and who, with his concept of magnetic lines of force, laid the foundations of classical field theory later built upon by J. Clerk MAXWELL. In the course of many years of researches, he also discovered the laws of ELECTROLYSIS which bear his name and, in showing that the plane of polarization of plane POLARIZED LIGHT was rotated in a strong magnetic field, demonstrated a connection to exist between LIGHT and MAGNETISM.

FARCE, comedy based on exaggeration and broad visual humor. Its traditional ingredients are improbable situations and characters developed to their limits. Farcical elements are present in the plays of ARISTOPHANES. PLAUTUS. SHAKESPEARE. MOLIÈRE and many others, but only through such 19th-century writers as Georges Feydeau and W. S. GILBERT did farce become a respectable theatrical form.

FAREL, Guillaume (1489–1565), French reformer, converted to REFORMATION doctrines c1520. A powerful preacher, he was a leader in the REFORMED CHURCHES of French-speaking Switzerland, and brought

John CALVIN to Geneva. From 1538 he worked at Neuchâtel.

FARGO, William George (1818–1881), cofounder of Wells and Company (later Wells-Fargo), the pioneer express service, in 1844. In 1850 it merged with other companies to become the American Express Company, of which he was president until his death.

FARINELLI, Carlo Broschi (1705–1782), famed Italian CASTRATO who gave up his public career to sing exclusively for Philip V of Spain.

FARLEY, James Aloysius (1888–1976), US politician. A businessman active in New York State Democratic politics, he played a major role in the election of Franklin D. ROOSEVELT as governor and president. He served (1933–40) as postmaster general, but opposed Roosevelt's renomination for third and fourth terms.

FARM CREDIT ADMINISTRATION, US federal agency formed in 1933 by President Franklin D. ROOSEVELT out of other agencies to provide adequate finance facilities to revive farming. Part of the Department of Agriculture 1939–53, it then became independent again.

FARMER, Fannie Merritt (1857–1915), US cookery instructor, author of the *Boston Cooking School Cook Book* (1896) which introduced standard level measurements. She served as the director of the Boston Cooking School 1891–1902, when she opened a school of her own.

FARMER, James Leonard (1920–   ), US civil rights leader who founded the Congress of Racial Equality and headed it 1942–66, utilizing nonviolent techniques of protest. He was assistant secretary of health, education, and welfare 1969–70.

FARMER, Moses Gerrish (1820–1893), US inventor whose many electrical inventions included an incandescent lamp 20 years before Thomas A. EDISON developed a more practical one.

FARMER-LABOR PARTY, minor US political party founded 1919 to promote the interests of small farmers and city workers. The party soon foundered nationally, but the separate Minn. Farmer-Labor Party elected its candidate, F. B. Olsen, governor in 1930, 1932 and 1934. The party merged with the Minn. Democratic Party in 1944.

FARNESE, Italian noble family, dukes of Parma and Piacenza from 1545 to 1731. The family produced a pope (PAUL III), a great general (Alessandro FARNESE), and patrons of Renaissance writers and artists. The Farnese Palace in Rome is one of the city's most magnificent.

FARNESE, Alessandro (1545–1592),

Italian nobleman, general and diplomat in the service of his uncle, Philip II of Spain, for whom he reconquered the southern provinces of the Netherlands from the Protestants. Later he led a Spanish army in France in support of the Catholic League against the Protestant Henry IV.

FARNSWORTH, Philo Taylor (1906–1971), US inventor who demonstrated a television system as early as 1927.

FAROUK (1920–1965), king of Egypt 1936–52. He was weak and incompetent, and his rule was marked by corruption, alienation of the military and many internal rivalries. This led to a military coup headed by Gamar Abdel NASSER, which forced Farouk's abdication.

FARQUHAR, George (1678–1707), English comic dramatist. His most successful plays, *The Recruiting Officer* (1706) and *The Beaux' Stratagem* (1707), are characterized by vigorous language and pungent satire, and more realism than was then fashionable.

FARRAGUT, David Glasgow (1801–1870), US admiral, a Civil War hero. In 1862 he captured New Orleans, a Confederate supply center, by a bold maneuver. In 1863 he gained control of the Mississippi R. In a daring attack on Mobile Bay, Ala., in 1864 he gave the now proverbial command "Damn the torpedoes! Full speed ahead!"

FARRAR, Geraldine (1882–1967), US soprano. She made her debut in 1901 as Marguerite in *Faust* in Berlin. Her famous roles included Mimi in *La Bohème*, Carmen and Cio-Cio-San in *Madame Butterfly*, and in 1921 she introduced Charpentier's *Louise* at the Metropolitan.

FARRELL, Eileen (1920–   ), US soprano who won fame on the radio and concert stage before singing (1960–66) with New York's Metropolitan Opera.

FARRELL, James Thomas (1904–1979), US writer. He is known for his social novels, particularly the *Studs Lonigan* trilogy (1932–35), which depicts the often harsh life of the Irish on the Chicago South Side.

FARSIGHTEDNESS. See HYPEROPIA.

FASCISM, strictly, the political social system of Italy under MUSSOLINI 1922–45; (the name is derived from the ancient Roman symbol of the fasces); more generally, an authoritarian and anti-democratic political philosophy placing the corporate society, as embodied in the party and the state, above the individual, and stressing absolute obedience to a glorified leader. It is a reaction against the achievements of the ENLIGHTENMENT, the FRENCH REVOLUTION and LIBERALISM. It rejects both the 19th-century neutral state based on economic laissez-faire and also socialism, because fascism denies to separate social groups any independent political and economic activity. Instead it promotes an organic social order whereby the individual will find his own place in family, profession and society according to his character and ability. Nationalism and militarism are its logical products and thus it has close ties with NAZISM. "Fascist" has become a term of abuse for many because of the ugly aspects of fascism, and is often used of anyone whose views are right wing.

The roots of fascism in Italy lie in the stagnant political situation with its chronic poverty, social unrest and manifold dissensions, worsened by the fact that the country had "won the war (WWI) but lost the peace." In 1919 Mussolini founded the *Fasci Italiani di Combattimento*, mainly ex-soldiers in black shirts who strove to overthrow the government by means of street fighting units. Regular fights ensued during 1921 between them and the communists. On Oct. 28, 1922, Mussolini, with four companions and followed by thousands of supporters, marched on Rome from Naples, where the king refused the prime minister's request for extraordinary powers, thus making way for Mussolini's first cabinet three days later.

Fascist movements spread to most western countries between WWI and WWII following in the wake of the economic crisis. Dollfuss and Schuschnigg headed a fascist government in Austria from 1933 until its incorporation into Germany in 1938, Horthy led one in Hungary, Pilsudski in Poland, Metaxas in Greece and Perón in Argentina. The longest surviving fascist regimes were in Portugal under Salazar and in Spain under Franco and the Falange.

FASHION, the prevailing style of dress, particularly new designs representing changes from previous seasons. Fashion in both dress and interior design is believed to have originated in 14th-century Europe and was set by monarchs and other prominent persons, with descriptions conveyed by travelers or in letters. The fashion doll was a popular means of transmitting the latest costume designs until the emergence of the first fashion magazine, thought to have originated in late 16th-century Germany. In the US, *Godey's Ladies' Book*, a precursor of *Vogue, Harper's Bazaar* and *Mademoiselle*, was established in 1830. For many decades it was the leading US source of fashion news, bringing to American women the latest creations from Paris, the

leading arbiter of fashion since the Renaissance. By the mid-19th century, designer-dressmakers became prominent in the fashion world for the first time, and this coincided with a certain decline in the influence of celebrities. Fashion houses became the trend setters in female styles, Paris taking its place as the undisputed capital of *haute couture*, a distinction it continues to hold despite inroads by Italian, English, and, most recently, American designers. London led the way in men's fashions in the early 1800s, when such Regency dandies as Beau BRUMMELL were widely emulated, and briefly became a women's fashion leader in the mid-1960s with the Carnaby Street look, characterized by the popular mini-skirt. By the late 1970s, US designers had begun to compete successfully with Paris fashion greats, and such names as Halston, Blass and Galanos were rivaling those of Dior and Saint-Laurent in lustre.

FASHODA INCIDENT, confrontation between the French and British (Sept. 18, 1898), at the small town of Fashoda in the Sudan, over the desire of both nations to consolidate their African territories. The British under KITCHENER forced the French to relinquish claims to the region.

FAST, Howard Melvin (1914–), US writer of historical fiction, known for his strong stand on social issues. His works include *Citizen Tom Paine* (1943), *Spartacus* (1952), and *The Pledge* (1988). A one-time communist, he was imprisoned in 1947 for refusing to cooperate with the House Un-American Activities Committee and then blacklisted. In *The Naked God* (1957) he recounted his disillusion with communism.

FASTING, abstention, wholly or in part, from food or drink, a practice common to many religions, usually linked with prayer and penance. YOM KIPPUR is a major Jewish fasting period, and RAMADAN the main Muslim fast. Many Christians fast at various times, such as during LENT and before Holy COMMUNION, to aid spirituality and self-discipline. Fasting is also used as a form of peaceful political protest.

FATHER DIVINE, pseudonym of George Baker (c1877–1965), black US religious leader whose Peace Mission sect, popular on the East Coast in the 1930s, demanded worship of him as God incarnate and communal celibate living.

FATHER'S DAY, so named in honor of fathers, first celebrated in the US in 1910. It is observed on the third Sunday in June. Although not a national holiday, it has been officially recognized by several presidents.

FATIMA, village and sanctuary in central Portugal, famous for its shrine of the Virgin Mary. The shrine was created after several apparitions of the Virgin were reported here in 1917.

FATIMIDS, Muslim dynasty which ruled a N African empire from its conquest of Egypt in 969 AD until 1171. The first rulers claimed descent from Fatimah, Mohammed's youngest daughter. In 969 al-Mu'izz established his capital at Cairo, bringing a religious and cultural renaissance to the city. At one time all of N Africa, Sicily and Syria was under Fatimid rule, but the dynasty was overthrown in 1171 by SALADIN.

FATS, ESTERS of carboxylic acids with glycerol which are produced by animals and plants and form natural storage material. Fats are insoluble in water and occur naturally as either liquids or solids; those liquid at 68°F are normally termed oils and are generally found in plants and fishes. Oils generally contain esters of oleic acid which can be converted to esters of the solid stearic acid by hydrogenation in the presence of finely divided nickel. This process is basic to the manufacture of MARGARINE. Fats are the most concentrated sources of energy in the human diet, giving over twice the energy of STARCHES. Diets containing high levels of animal fats have been implicated as causative factors in heart disease, and substitution of animal fat by plant oils (e.g., peanut oil, sunflower oil) has been suggested. Fats particularly of fish and plant origin represent important items of commerce. Of major importance are soybean oil, sunflower, palm, peanut, cottonseed, rapeseed and coconut oil and olive and fish oil. Major producers include the US (soybean oil), the USSR (sunflower oil and cottonseed oil) and India (peanut oil).

FAULKNER, William (1897–1962), major US writer, known for his vivid characterization and complex, convoluted style in novels and short stories set in the fictional Yoknapatawpha Co., Miss. His best works are the novels *The Sound and the Fury* (1929), an experimental work influenced by James JOYCE, and *Light in August* (1932) and the haunting short story "A Rose for Emily." He painted a vivid picture of the decadent and dying South, seeing in it a microcosm of human destiny. In 1949 he was awarded the Nobel Prize for Literature. He also won two Pulitzer prizes (1955 and 1963).

FAULT, a fracture in the earth's crust along which there has been relative movement and displacement. *Dip-slip faults* involve movement up or down an inclined fault plane. Thus, *normal faults* result from tensional stress and involve a downward relative displacement of overlying rocks with respect to rocks underlying the fault plane. A *reverse* or *thrust fault* involves relative displacement upward of the overlying rocks and results from compressive stress. *Strike-slip faults* involve horizontal displacement and result from shearing stress. In PLATE TECTONICS, an important type of strike-slip fault that trends at right angles to and offsets plate boundaries along an oceanic ridge is called a *transform fault. Oblique-slip faults* are also known. The sudden release of accumulated long-term stresses through sudden rupturing of rock either creates a new fault or involves renewed displacement along an existing fault, a process responsible for most EARTHQUAKES.

FAURÉ, Gabriel Urbain (1845–1924), influential French composer, director of the Paris Conservatory 1905–20, where his pupils included RAVEL and ENESCO. He is famous for his songs, chamber music and large-scale works such as the *Requiem* (1887).

FAUST, legendary German enchanter, based on a 16th-century charlatan, who sold his soul to the devil Mephistopheles for knowledge and pleasure. Faust has been a favorite literary subject. MARLOWE, in *Dr. Faustus* (c1590), made the tale a tragedy of human presumption while GOETHE, in *Faust* (1808 and 1832), made Faust a Romantic idealist whose sins are forgiven because of his continual striving after good.

FAUST, Frederick Schiller (1892–1944), US author, fertile producer of "westerns" under various pseudonyms, most notably Max Brand. He also wrote film scripts for the *Dr. Kildare* series.

FAUVISM, art movement that developed in early 20th-century France, characterized by its bold use of brilliant color and rhythmic line. Hostile critics dubbed the group of artists painting in the style *"fauves,"* wild beasts. Its main members were MATISSE, DERAIN, BRAQUE, ROUALT, VLAMINCK and DUFY. The movement, lasting c1898–c1908, was largely transitional; some Fauvists moved on to CUBISM.

FAWKES, Guy (1570–1606), Roman Catholic Englishman, hired by the GUNPOWDER PLOT conspirators as an explosives expert while he was serving in the Spanish army. Arrested while setting explosives beneath the House of Lords, he was tortured and hanged. In England he is burnt in effigy on Guy Fawkes Day, Nov. 5.

FEATHERS, the covering of a bird's body,

equivalent to the hair of a mammal and made of the same material, *keratin*. The layer of feathers which make up a bird's plumage is an effective insulating device to keep the bird warm. The coloring of the feathers may play an important part in courtship. The long feathers of the wings and tail provide light, but strong, flight surfaces. A feather is made up of a central *shaft*, with the hollow *quill* at the tip, and the vane or web on each side. The vane consists of rows of fine threads called *barbs* which are held together by hooked *barbules*.

FEBRUARY, the second month of the year. Before Julius Caesar decreed that the year should begin in January, February was the last month of the year. The name is from the Latin *febrarius*, purification; the month was then a time of religious purification for the new year.

FEDERAL AVIATION ADMINISTRA-TION (FAA), an agency of the US Department of Transportation created in 1958 to regulate air commerce; control the use of navigable airspace of the US; promote and develop civil aeronautics; consolidate research and development with respect to air navigation facilities; develop and operate a common system of air traffic control and navigation for both civil and military aircraft; and develop programs to control aircraft noise, sonic boom, and other environmental effects of civil aviation.

FEDERAL BUREAU OF INVESTIGA-TION (FBI), investigative branch of the US Department of Justice. Established in 1908, it is headed by a director appointed by the president, subject to Senate confirmation. Its headquarters are in Washington, D.C. In general, the FBI is responsible for the investigation of possible violations of all federal laws except those for which enforcement is specifically assigned to another agency; the Bureau is also concerned with internal security, counter-espionage, organized crime and corruption. FBI history was dominated by J. Edgar HOOVER, director 1924–72, a conservative figure who held the post until his death.

FEDERAL COMMUNICATIONS COM-MISSION (FCC), an independent agency of the federal government, directly responsible to the US Congress, which regulates communication by radio, television, wire, cable, and satellite. Created in 1934, it has five members appointed by the president. Its most important functions are the licensing of commercial radio and television stations, the assignment of broadcasting frequencies, the supervision of other radio services and regulation of interstate communications services.

FEDERAL CONSTITUTIONAL CON-VENTION. See UNITED STATES CONSTITUTION.

FEDERAL DEPOSIT INSURANCE CORPORATION (FDIC), federal agency which insures almost all bank deposits in the US, created by the 1933 Banking Act. All FEDERAL RESERVE SYSTEM banks must insure with FDIC. In the case of failure of an insured bank, the FDIC reimburses each depositor up to $100,000. It also acts as a watchdog over banking practices.

FEDERAL ELECTION COMMISSION (FEC), independent US government agency established to administer the Federal Election Campaign Act of 1971, which provides for the public funding of presidential elections, public disclosure of financial activities of political committees involved in federal elections, and limitations and prohibitions on contributions and expenditures made to influence federal elections.

FEDERAL ENERGY REGULATORY COMMISSION (FERC), an independent, five-member commission within the US Department of Energy, sets rates and charges for the transportation and sale of natural gas and for the transmission and sale of electricity and the licensing of hydroelectric power projects. It also establishes rates and charges for the transportation of oil by pipeline. The FERC replaced the Federal Power Commission.

FEDERALISM, system of government in which two or more independent states form a union by granting a central government supreme power in common or national affairs, while retaining their independent existence and control over local affairs. A federal system is opposed to a confedera-tion, under which independent states form a loose union for a common purpose, but retain complete autonomy; and to a unitary system, under which all power is centralized in the national government, with no subdivisions (such as states or provinces) exercising independent powers. In theory, a federal form of government presents a balance under which the national govern-ment is strong enough to provide peace and security, while the states or provinces retain sufficient powers to regulate local matters of which they have better knowledge.

The US and Canada both have federal forms of government, but with a key difference. Although the US Constitution states that all powers not specifically delegated to the federal government are reserved to the states or the people, Supreme Court decisions and the actual course of events have concentrated ever more power in the hands of the central government. State and local governments now possess relatively little power compared to the influence of the government in Washington. In Canada, on the other hand, all powers not specifically allotted to the constituent provinces are reserved to the national government; but court decisions have tended to enlarge the powers of the provinces at the expense of the central government in Ottawa. In recent years, however, the central government has gradually extended its power.

In the US, the federal government is supreme in defense, foreign affairs, the postal and monetary systems, patents and copyrights, and interstate and foreign commerce. The federal judiciary, headed by the Supreme Court, has the final word in all matters presenting a substantial federal question, but state tribunals have exclusive jurisdiction in strictly state and local questions if no constitutional issues arise. All levels of government may levy taxes and spend money; but the federal government accounts for the vast majority of public spending.

In a federal government the citizen owes his allegiance directly to the central (national) government. He may also owe loyalty to the state, but not in a way that runs counter to the national government. The 10th Amendment clearly reserves to the states all powers not delegated to the national government.

FEDERALIST PAPERS, collection of American political essays written in support of the proposed US Constitution, published serially 1787–88. Written anonymously by Alexander HAMILTON. James MADISON and John JAY. the papers were later collected in book form and published under the title *The Federalist*. They provide a classic exposition of the US federal system.

FEDERALIST PARTY, first true US political party. Founded by Alexander HAMILTON c1789, it was in general supported by prosperous citizens who wanted a strong central government. It dominated the government 1794–1800 but lost support among the lower middle class to Thomas JEFFERSON's Democratic Republican Party. After Jefferson won the election of 1800, the Federalist Party endured until 1816 only, remaining as a New England party until the 1820s.

FEDERAL NATIONAL MORTGAGE ASSOCIATION (FNMA, or "Fanny Mae"), government-sponsored corporation which acts as a secondary mortgage market for banks. Created by Congress in 1938,

Fanny Mae helped make mortgage funds widely available in the post-WWII housing surge.

FEDERAL RESERVE SYSTEM, central US banking authority, created by the Federal Reserve Act of 1913. It consists of a board of governors, 12 Federal Reserve banks, the Federal Open Market Committee; the Federal Advisory Council; the Thrift Institutions Advisory Council; and the nation's financial institutions, including commercial banks, savings and loan associations, mutual savings banks, and credit unions. All national banks must belong to the System; state banks may also join. The System is the basic arm of the monetary side of national economic management. By buying securities it expands bank reserves, enabling banks to expand loans and stimulate economic activity. When it sells, it contracts bank reserves, reducing lending and slowing the economy (these are called open-market operations). The System may also affect the volume of banks' lending by changing the statutory amount of reserves they must hold and by changing the rate at which member banks may borrow from the System.

FEDERAL STYLE, in architecture and the decorative arts, the dominant style in the US from c1790 to c1830. Like the colonial style but more developed and often more monumental, it is based on French and Italian Renaissance designs as well as English Palladian precedents. Graceful in proportions and delicate in design, the federal style is typified by slender, fluted columns; large, freestanding porticoes; brick walls trimly accented with white at the openings; entrances topped by fanlights and, in general, curvilinear decorative forms. Major exponents were Charles BULFINCH in Boston and Samuel McIntire in Salem, Mass. The style is seen in many state capitols.

FEDERAL TRADE COMMISSION (FTC), a federal agency established in 1914 to prevent unfair business practices, particularly monopolies, and to maintain a competitive economy. Its five commissioners are appointed by the president subject to Senate confirmation. The FTC studies the effects of business mergers and price agreements, issuing cease and desist orders if their effects prove undesirable. It also attempts to prevent misleading advertising and protect public health.

FEEDBACK, the use of the output of a system to control its performance. Many examples of feedback systems can be found in the life sciences, particularly in ecology, biochemistry and physiology. Thus the population of a species will grow until it overexploits its food supply. Malnutrition then leads to a reduction in population. In the design of machines, SERVOMECHANISMS and governors also exemplify feedback systems. The most important application of the feedback concept in modern technology comes in ELECTRONICS, where it is common practice to feed some of the output of an AMPLIFIER back to the input to help reduce NOISE, distortion or instability. Most often used is "negative feedback" in which the effect of the feedback is to reduce the amplifier's output while stabilizing its performance. The howling that can occur when too much sound from a loudspeaker enters the MICROPHONE of a public address system is an example of positive feedback. Feedback plays an essential role in CYBERNETICS. (See also MECHANIZATION AND AUTOMATION.)

FEIFFER, Jules (1929–   ), US cartoonist whose satiric examinations of contemporary mores first appeared in New York City's *Village Voice* in 1956 and have been syndicated since 1959. His other works include the play *Little Murders* (1967) and the screenplay *Carnal Knowledge* (1971). He received a Pulitzer Prize in 1986.

FEININGER, Lyonel (1871–1956), US artist. Influenced by CUBISM, his style is based on interpenetrating prismatic planes of color that create geometric designs. He lived in Germany 1887–1936, teaching at the BAUHAUS 1919–32. Also a caricaturist, he produced a memorable weekly comics page for the Chicago *Tribune* in 1906–07.

FELDSTEIN, Martin (1939–   ), US economist. A professor of economics at Harvard (from 1967), he was chairman of the Council of Economic Advisers 1982–84.

FELLER, Robert William Andrew "Bob" (1919–   ), US baseball star, a pitcher with the Cleveland Indians 1936–42 and 1944–56. In 1946 he set a season record of 348 strike-outs.

FELLINI, Federico (1920–   ), Italian film director. His early films, such as *La Strada* (1954) and *La Dolce Vita* (1960), portray human disillusionment in a corrupt society. Later films such as *8½* (1963), *Juliet of the Spirits* (1964), *Satyricon* (1970) and *Amarcord* (1974), have a more personal style, often dream-like and fantastic.

FELONY, a criminal offense more serious than a misdemeanor. In US law the distinction between the two categories is generally the severity of the prescribed penalty for the offense. Homicide, robbery, burglary, theft and rape are the main felonies.

FENCING, sport of combat with swords. It is descended from the duel, but in fencing the object is only to touch, not to wound, one's opponent. Fencers wear protective clothing and masks. Three weapons are used; the light, rectangular foil, the stiffer, triangular épée and the triangular two-edged saber. Only the tip of the foil and épée may be used to score hits; saber scores may be made with the point or by a cut. In foil and saber fencing hits may only be made on certain parts of the body. Matches take place on a measured strip or *piste*. In men's bouts the first to be hit five times loses, in women's four times.

FÉNELON, François de Salignac de la Mothe (1651–1715), French theologian, archbishop of Cambrai from 1695. His reform writings were far in advance of their day. He opposed JANSENISM. He tutored the duke of Burgundy, heir of Louis XIV of France, and wrote for him *Fables: Dialogues of the Dead* (1690) and *Telemachus* (1699).

FENIAN   BROTHERHOOD, Irish-American revolutionary society, founded in 1858 by Irish exile John O'Mahony. The movement achieved little in Ireland but made sporadic terrorist attacks in Canada 1866–71. It collapsed with O'Mahony's death in 1877.

FERBER, Edna (1887–1968), US author famous for her epic popular novels set in the 19th- and 20th-century US, such as *So Big* (1924), for which she won a 1925 Pulitzer Prize, *Show Boat* (1926), *Cimarron* (1930), *Saratoga Trunk* (1941) and *Giant* (1952).

FERDINAND, name of three Holy Roman Emperors. **Ferdinand I** (1503–1564), emperor 1558–64, was king of Bohemia and Hungary from 1526. His agreement to the Peace of AUGSBURG ended the crippling religious conflict in Germany. Elected emperor after his brother Charles V abdicated, he stabilized the unwieldy empire by capable administration. **Ferdinand II** (1578–1637) was elected emperor in 1619. An advocate of the COUNTER-REFORMATION, his attempts to enforce Catholicism in Protestant Bohemia led to a revolt in 1619, which began the THIRTY YEARS' WAR. In the Peace of Prague (1635) he was forced to make concessions to the Protestants. **Ferdinand III** (1608–1657) succeeded his father Ferdinand II as emperor in 1637. A capable ruler, he compromised with the Protestant powers in the Peace of WESTPHALIA (1648).

FERDINAND, name of several kings of Spain. **Ferdinand II of Aragon** (1452–1516) married Isabella of Castile in 1469, becoming her consort in Castile in 1474. In

1492 he conquered the Moorish kingdom of Granada, becoming effective king of Spain. A supporter of the Spanish Inquisition, he expelled the Jews from Spain. Isabella, rather than he, was COLUMBUS' sponsor. **Ferdinand VI** (1713–1759) came to the throne in 1746. A capable ruler and patron of the arts, he carried out many administrative reforms and managed to keep Spain neutral during the SEVEN YEARS' WAR. **Ferdinand VII** 1784–1833) acceded in 1808 when his father Charles IV was deposed by a revolt; he was himself deposed by Napoleon two months later and imprisoned until his restoration in 1814. A cruel and repressive absolutist, he was deposed 1820–23 and only restored by a French army. Of limited ability, he was unable to prevent the complete loss of Spain's American possessions.

FERENCZI, Sándor (1873–1933), Hungarian psychoanalyst, and an early colleague of FREUD, best known for his experiments in PSYCHOTHERAPY, in course of which he broke away from Freud's classic psychoanalytic theory. (See PSYCHOANALYSIS.)

FERMAT, Pierre de (1601–1665), French mathematician best remembered for **Fermat's Principle**, that the path of light traveling between two points by reflection is that taking the least time; and **Fermat's Last Theorem**, that $x^n + y^n - z^n = 0$, where x, y, $z \neq 0$ and $n > 2$, is impossible for integral x, y, z and n.

FERMENTATION, the decomposition of CARBOHYDRATES by microorganisms in the absence of air. Louis PASTEUR first demonstrated that fermentation is a biochemical process, each type being caused by one species. It is an aspect of bacterial and fungal METABOLISM, in which glucose and other sugars are oxidized by ENZYME catalysis to pyruvic acid. Pyruvic acid is then reduced to lactic acid or degraded to carbon dioxide and ETHANOL. Considerable energy is released in this process: some is stored as the high-energy compound ATP, and the rest is given off as heat. Fermentation by YEAST has been used for centuries in brewing and making bread and wine; fermentation by lactic acid bacteria is used to make cheese. Special fermentations are used industrially for the manufacture of acetone, butanol (see ALCOHOLS), GLYCEROL, CITRIC ACID, glutamic acid and many other compounds. (See also RESPIRATION.)

FERMI, Enrico (1901–1954), Italian atomic physicist who was awarded the 1938 Nobel Prize for Physics. His first important contribution was his examination of the properties of a hypothetical gas whose particles obeyed Pauli's EXCLUSION PRINCIPLE; the laws he derived can be applied to the ELECTRONS in a metal, and explain many of the properties of metals. Later he showed that NEUTRON bombardment of most elements produced their RADIOISOTOPES. He built the world's first NUCLEAR REACTOR (1942).

FERNS, nonflowering plants of the class Filicineae having creeping or erect rhizomes (rootstocks) or an erect aerial stem and large conspicuous leaves. Spores are produced on the underside of the leaf within sporangia and germinate to form the gametophyte or sexual stage of the life cycle. Ferns are widely distributed throughout the world, but the majority grow in the tropics. Many ferns are popular house plants, e.g. *Nephrolepis* (Boston ferns), *Pteris* (maidenhair ferns), *Platycerium* (staghorn ferns) and *Asplenium* (bird's nest ferns). Indoors they require a reasonably bright position but avoiding direct sunlight; they flourish under fluorescent lighting. They grow best at temperatures between 60°F and 70°F and will tolerate temperatures as high as 75°F so long as the air is fresh and humid. They should be watered often enough to keep the soil evenly moist, benefiting most from daily misting. They can be propagated from spores, but normally by division of the plant or by rhizome cuttings.

FERRARI, Enzo (1898–1988), Italian auto racer and manufacturer, after WWII, of racing and sport cars.

FERRARO, Geraldine (1935–), US Democratic politician, a representative from Queens, N.Y., 1979–84. She was the Democratic candidate for vice president on the ill-fated ticket headed by Walter Mondale in 1984.

FERRIS, George Washington Gale (1859–1896), US engineer whose "Ferris wheel," 250ft high, was a sensation at the 1893 Columbian Exposition in Chicago.

FERRY, Jules François Camille (1832–1893), French statesman. A republican opponent of the Second Empire, he held many offices in the Third Republic, becoming premier 1880–81 and 1883–85. He sought to exclude the clergy from education, and directed the acquisition of many colonies.

FERTILE CRESCENT, area in the Middle East, extending in an arc or crescent from the N coast of the Persian Gulf to the E coast of the Mediterranean. Natural irrigation made this semi-arid land fertile; it gave birth to the Sumerian, Phoenician and Hebrew civilizations. (See also MESOPOTAMIA.)

FERTILIZATION, the union of two GAMETES. or male and female sex cells, to produce a CELL from which a new individual, animal or plant, develops. The sex cells contain half the normal number of CHROMOSOMES. and fertilization therefore produces a cell with the normal number of chromosomes for any particular species. Fertilization may take place outside the organism's body (external fertilization), or inside the female (internal fertilization) as a result of copulation.

FERTILIZERS, materials added to the SOIL to provide elements needed for plant NUTRITION, and so to enable healthy growth of crops with high yield. The elements needed in large quantities are NITROGEN. PHOSPHORUS. POTASSIUM. SULFUR. CALCIUM and magnesium; the last three are usually adequately supplied in the soil or incidentally in other fertilizers. Small amounts of trace elements are also needed, and usually supplied in fertilizers. The choice of compounds or materials containing nitrogen, phosphorus and potassium depends mainly on cost. The traditional natural fertilizers—bone meal, guano and manure—are now too expensive to be much used outside HORTICULTURE. Potassium is supplied as potassium chloride, widely available as sylvite. Phosphorus fertilizers are obtained from mineral PHOSPHATES. especially apatite; some is used as such, but most is converted to ammonium phosphate or superphosphate. Nitrogen is supplied as AMMONIA (injected under pressure), ammonium salts, nitrates (ammonium nitrate being most useful) and urea. Fertilizers in excess may harm crops and cause EUTROPHICATION.

FESSENDEN, Reginald Aubrey (1866–1932), US inventor who, from Brant Rock, Mass., made (1906) the first radio broadcast of voice and music.

FESSENDEN, William Pitt (1806–1869), US politician. An early organizer of the Republican Party, he was US senator from Maine (1855–64, 1865–69) and briefly secretary of the treasury (1864–65). As chairman of the Joint Congressional Committee on Reconstruction, he supported the Radical Republican position but opposed the impeachment of President Andrew JOHNSON.

FETTERMAN MASSACRE, destruction (Nov. 1966) by Indians under RED CLOUD of a party of 80 US soldiers from Fort Phil Kearny, Wyoming, imprudently led by William Judd Fetterman. As a result the BOZEMAN TRAIL was partially abandoned.

FETUS, the developing intrauterine form of an animal, loosely used to describe it from the development of the fertilized egg (EMBRYO), but strictly referring in man to the period from three months gestation to BIRTH. During fetal life, organ development is consolidated and specialization extended so that function may be sufficiently mature at birth; some organs start to function before birth in preparation for independent existence. During the fetal period most increase in size occurs, both in the fetus and in the placenta and womb. The fetus lies in a sac of amniotic fluid which protects it and allows it to move about. BLOOD CIRCULATION in the fetus is adapted to the placenta as the source of OXYGEN and nutrients and site for waste excretion, but alternative channels are developed so that within moments of birth they may take over. Should the fetus be delivered prematurely, immaturity of the LUNGS may cause respiratory distress, that of the LIVER, resulting in JAUNDICE.

FEUDALISM, system of social, economic and political relationships that shaped society in medieval Europe. It originated in the 8th century and flourished from the 10th to the 13th centuries. Thereafter it declined, although in Europe and Russia many feudal institutions persisted into the 19th century. The system rested on the obedience and service of a vassal to his lord in return for protection, maintenance and, most particularly, a tenancy of land (a *fief*). The duty owed by a vassal included military service, counsel and attendance at court, and contribution towards the lord's extraordinary expenditures such as ransoms or dowries. At the apex of the social pyramid was the king, vassal only to God. His vassals were his great nobles, holding land or some other source of income in fief from him. They in turn invested, or *enfeoffed* (so, "feodal" or "feudal") their own vassals, the lords of the manor. At the base of the pyramid were the serfs, or villeins, permanently tied to the land. They worked both for the lord and for themselves, unpaid; serfdom offered a degree of security in that if a serf could not leave the land, neither could it be taken from him.

In effect feudalism tended to allow vassal lords unrestricted freedom, at least in their own holdings. With the tendency towards centralized government this liberty was curbed. The system assumed a subsistence economy; the growth of trade and of economically powerful towns attacked it, and by the 15th century it was dying out.

FEUERBACH, Ludwig Andreas (1804–1872), German materialist philosopher, a major influence on MARX. He rejected HEGEL's Idealism, and in such works as *The Essence of Christianity*

(1841) he analyzed the Christian concept of God as an illusory fulfillment of human psychological needs. His father, **Paul Johann Anselm von Feuerbach** (1775-1833), was a legal philosopher who prepared for Bavaria a liberal and widely influential criminal code.

FEUILLANTS, political club during the FRENCH REVOLUTION that split off from the JACOBINS in 1791 to support a constitutional monarchy. The Jacobins eliminated them during the TERROR.

FEVER, raising of body TEMPERATURE above normal (37°C or 98.6°F in man), usually caused by DISEASE. Infection, INFLAMMATION, heat stroke and some TUMORS are important causes. Fever is produced by pyrogens, which are derived from cell products, and alter the set level of temperature-regulating centers in the HYPOTHALAMUS. Fever may be continuous, intermittent or remittent, the distinction helping to determine the cause. Anti-inflammatory drugs (e.g., ASPIRIN) reduce fever; STEROIDS mask it.

FEYNMAN, Richard Phillips (1918–1988), US physicist awarded with SCHWINGER and TOMONAGA the 1965 Nobel Prize for Physics for their independent work on quantum electrodynamics (see QUANTUM MECHANICS). With Murray GELL-MANN he developed an important theory of weak interactions such as the emission of electrons from radioactive nuclei.

FIBER, a thin thread of natural or artificial material. **Animal fibers** include wool, from the fluffy coat of the sheep, and silk, the fiber secreted by the silkworm larva to form its cocoon. **Vegetable fibers** include COTTON, flax, hemp, jute and sisal: they are mostly composed of lignin, though CELLULOSE is also important. **Mineral fibers** are generally loosely termed ASBESTOS. These fibrous mineral silicates are mined in South Africa, Canada and elsewhere. **Man-made fibers** are of two types: regenerated fibers, extracted from natural substances (e.g., rayon is cellulose extracted from wood pulp); and SYNTHETIC FIBERS. Most PAPER is made from wood fiber. (See also COTTON GIN; SPINNING; WEAVING.)

FIBERGLASS, GLASS drawn or blown into extremely fine fibers that retain the tensile strength of glass while yet being flexible. The most used form is fused QUARTZ, which when molten can be easily drawn and which is resistant to chemical attack. Most often, the molten glass is forced through tiny orifices in a platinum plate, on the far side of which the fine fibers are united (though not twisted) and wound onto a suitable spindle. Fiberglass mats (**glass wool**) are

formed from shorter fibers at random directions bonded together with a thermo-setting RESIN; they may be pressed into predetermined shapes. Known in ancient Egypt, fiberglass is now used in insulation, automobile bodies, etc.

FIBER OPTICS. See OPTICAL FIBER.

FIBONACCI, Leonardo, or **Leonardo of Pisa** (c1180–c1240), Italian mathematician whose *Liber Abaci* (1202) was probably the first European account of the mathematics of India and Arabia, including some material on ALGEBRA.

FICHTE, Johann Gottlieb (1762–1814), German philosopher, an early exponent of ethical idealism, for whom the ego was the primary metaphysical and epistemological principle. His work influenced HEGEL and SCHOPENHAUER, among others. Some of his theories prefigured socialism; his concept of the nation as a manifestation of divine order, combined with his fanatical patriotism, stimulated German nationalism.

FICINO, Marsilio (1433–1499), Italian philosopher who headed the Renaissance revival of Platonism. He translated all of PLATO into Latin, and under the aegis of Cosimo de MEDICI taught a form of Platonism reconciled with Christianity.

FIEDLER, Arthur (1894–1987), US conductor of the Boston Pops Orchestra from 1930.

FIELD, US family prominent in law and industry in the 19th century. **Cyrus West Field** (1819–1892), an industrialist, financed the laying of the first permanently operational transatlantic telegraph cable in 1866. His elder brother **David Dudley Field** (1805–1894), a jurist, was appointed by N.Y. in 1857 to draw up civil, political and penal codes, the last of which was subsequently adopted. Other states adopted all three. In 1873, he became the first president of the International Law Association. A third brother, **Stephen Johnson Field** (1816–1899) was also a distinguished jurist. He rose to become chief justice of Cal. and in 1863 was appointed to the US Supreme Court.

FIELD, influential US mercantile and publishing family. **Marshall Field I** (1834–1906) established one of the world's first and largest department stores. His donations established the U. of Chicago and the city's Art Institute and Field Museum of Natural History. **Marshall Field III** (1893–1956), publisher and philanthropist, began the *Chicago Sun* (later Sun-Times) in 1941, and published the *World Book Encyclopedia*, and various magazines. **Marshal Field IV** (1916–1965), expanded and increased the Field publishing concerns.

FIELD HOCKEY, a team sport played with a stick curved at the end. Usually played by women and girls in the US, it is played by both men and women in 70 other countries. **History.** Hockey is believed to have originated in ancient Persia, although the first record of it is a drawing on a tomb at Beni-Hassan in the Nile Valley, and something similar was known to the ancient Greeks. The modern world's first national hockey organization was formed in England in 1886, but the game there was probably introduced from France. The word hockey comes from Old French, *hoquet*, meaning shepherd's crook. It was introduced into the US in 1902 at a match played at Vassar College, Poughkeepsie, N.Y., promoted by an English woman, Constance Applebee. By 1922 the U.S. Field Hockey Association was formed and in 1927 the International Federation of Women's Hockey Associations. **Rules.** Hockey is played between teams of eleven on each side on a field measuring 90–100 yds long by 50–60 yds wide. There are two playing periods of 35 minutes each, and the object is to score as many goals as possible, the goals at each end measuring 4 yds wide and 7 ft high. The goalkeeper is the only player allowed to kick the ball, which is made of leather with a circumference of 8–9 in. A hockey eleven comprises five forwards; a right and left wing, a right and left inner, and a center forward. The other players are a right, center, and left halfback; a right and left fullback; and a goalkeeper.

FIELDING, Henry (1707–1754), English novelist, dramatist and essayist. His satirical comedies angered the Whig premier Sir Robert WALPOLE, and Fielding had to abandon the stage and turn to the law. He then wrote two novels, *Joseph Andrews* (1742) and *Tom Jones* (1749). Boisterous, picaresque works, they burlesque the stilted sentimentality then fashionable. He became a magistrate in 1748; he helped organize the Bow Street Runners, an early police force.

FIELD-ION MICROSCOPE, an instrument producing very beautiful pictures of the arrangement of individual ATOMS in materials drawn out into, or evaporated on to, a fine tip, typically 40nm in radius. Invented by Erwin Wilhelm Müller (1911–   ) in 1936, the microscope is lensless, the image being produced on a fluorescent screen by IONS created in a low pressure gas by the intense electric field at the tip when it is positively charged to a few kilovolts.

FIELDS, W. C. (William Claude Dukenfield; 1880–1946), US comedian and actor, characterized both on and off stage as a cantankerous but witty misogynist and child-hater. He began in VAUDEVILLE as a juggler but rose to fame in movies, many of which, such as the classic farce *The Bank Dick* (1940), he wrote himself. He was acclaimed for his portrayal of Mr. Micawber in *David Copperfield* (1935).

FIGS, shrubs and trees belonging to the genus *Ficus,* family Moraceae, particularly *Ficus carica,* the common fig, which is widely cultivated in SW Asia and the Mediterranean. The edible fruits are in fact a mass of male and female flowers enclosed in a fleshy receptacle. Dried figs are used medicinally as laxatives and poultices and are a staple food in Mediterranean regions. *F. elastica* (rubber tree) and *F. benjamina* (weeping fig) are popular house plants, the former producing large dark green leaves, and the latter small leaves on a much more compact bush. They grow best at average house temperatures in sunny east or west windows or a short distance from south-facing windows. They should be well watered whenever the soil surface dries out and are propagated by air layering or taking shoot tip cuttings.

Official name: Republic of Fiji
Capital: Suva
Area: 7,056sq mi
Population: 726,000
Languages: Fijian; Hindustani; English
Religions: Christian, Hindu
Monetary unit(s): 1 Fiji dollar=100 cents
FIJI, since 1970 an independent state within the British Commonwealth, an island group in the SW Pacific. It contains around 100 inhabited islands, of which the largest are Viti Levu, with the capital city Suva, and Vanua Levu. The larger islands are volcanic in origin, the rest are coral atolls or reefs. The climate is tropical, rainfall averaging over 100in a year and temperatures 65°–95°F. The original Melanesian and Polynesian inhabitants are now only 44% of the population, outnumbered by Indian immigrants.

Sugarcane, coconuts, and ginger are the leading commercial crops. Tourism, fishing, and food processing are also important to the economy.

Settled by about 500 BC and visited by Abel TASMAN in 1643 and by James COOK in 1744, the islands were offered to Britain by a chieftain in 1874 and remained a British colony until 1970. Growing tensions between indigenous Fijians and the Indian majority, complicated by the election of an Indian-backed government, led the Fijian army to stage the first military coup in the Pacific in May 1987. The British governor-general then briefly took control of the government, followed by a second coup in September. In October, Fiji's military leader declared the nation a republic. He returned power to a civilian government on Dec. 5 but insisted that there would be a new constitution guaranteeing the political dominance of the indigenous Fijians.

FILENE, Edward Albert (1860–1937), US merchant who, as president of William Filene's Sons, Boston, pioneered such new methods of retailing as the "bargain basement." He was also a founder of the US Chamber of Commerce.

FILIBUSTER, in a legislative body, the practice of prolonging debate to prevent the adoption of a measure or procedure. It is usually used by a member of the minority as an obstacle to the passage of a measure favored by the majority. In modern times, this tactic has been used mostly in the US Senate. Since the Senate permits almost unlimited debate, opponents of a measure can organize a continuous succession of long speeches. However, two-thirds of the senators present can vote to close the debate, known as imposing *cloture*, and end the filibuster. One of the longest Senate filibusters in recent years came over a debate on a civil rights bill when Strom Thurmond managed to keep the floor for 24 hours and 18 minutes.

FILLMORE, Millard (1800–1874), 13th US president. Fillmore stepped into office on the death of President Zachary Taylor in 1850. He served only 2½ years and assumed the role of moderator in the fierce national and congressional debates of the pre-Civil War period.

Born in Summerhill, N.Y., and trained as a lawyer, Fillmore was first elected to the US House of Representatives in 1832, serving from 1833–35 and again from 1837–43. In 1848 he was elected to the vice-presidency on the Whig ticket under Taylor. His principal achievement as president 1850–53 was a trade agreement

with Japan. He supported the COMPROMISE OF 1850 as avoiding a North–South clash, although himself against slavery. This damaged his reelection chances, and on March 4, 1853, Fillmore left office after failing to win renomination with the Whig party. He finally retired from public life in 1856 after an unsuccessful candidacy for the KNOW-NOTHING Party.

FILM. See MOTION PICTURES.

FILMER, Sir Robert (c1588–1653), English royalist political writer. His *Patriarcha; or The Natural Power of Kings* (1680), although much criticized by LOCKE and others, is a valid picture of the development of society up to his time.

FILSON, John (c1753–1788), American pioneer. His *Discovery, Settlement and Present State of Kentucky* (1784) included a pseudo-autobiographical account of the adventures of Daniel BOONE and established the frontiersman in American legend.

FINCHES, small seed-eating birds of the family Fringillidae—canaries, grosbeaks, sparrows, cardinals, crossbills and buntings. Finches are characterized by their conical bills, used for opening seeds. Many members of the family number among the familiar song-birds of town and country.

FINGER LAKES, 11 narrow, glacially formed lakes in N.Y. The largest are Seneca, Cayuga and Canandaigua. The lakes are situated in rolling, wooded countryside, with many resorts.

FINGERPRINTS, impressions of the loops and whorls of the papillary ridges of the fingertips, a valuable tool for identification by police and other authorities because the ridge patterns are considered individually unique. The first police system was developed (1888) by Jean Vucetich in Argentina. The fingerprinting system most in use today was developed by Sir Edward Richard Henry from the work of Sir Francis GALTON. Replacing the anthropometric techniques of BERTILLON, it was adopted in the UK in 1901, the US in 1903. In **dactyloscopy** (fingerprinting) the tips of the fingers are well cleaned, rolled on printer's ink spread on a glass sheet and then impressed onto coated cards.

FINK, Mike (1770?–1823), US frontiersman and folk hero. A Mississippi keelboatman and famous sharp-shooter, he was renowned for his drinking, brawling and bragging. He was murdered by a friend of a man he had killed in a drunken game.

FINLAND, independent republic in N Europe, bordered by arms of the Baltic Sea in the SW and W, by the USSR in the E and by Norway and Sweden in the N and NW. An independent country only since 1917, it has made great contributions to European culture, among them the music of Jan SIBELIUS and the work of architects Alvar AALTO and Eliel and Eero SAARINEN.

Official name: Republic of Finland
Capital: Helsinki
Area: 130,559sq mi
Population: 4,942,000
Languages: Finnish, Swedish, Lappish
Religions: Evangelical Lutheran Church
Monetary unit(s): 1 markka = 100 penni
Land. The central plateau, glacial relatively recently, is low-lying. Lakes, which cover about 9% of the whole country, extend over about 20%–50% of the central lakeland, creating a labyrinth of waterways. The N uplands, about 40% of the country, pass from forest into swamplands, and then into barren Arctic tundra; 30% of the country lies above the Arctic circle. The coastal lowlands are fertile, with a mild climate. The major cities, Turku and Helsinki, are situated here, as is most of the country's farmland. The coastal archipelago is largely barren.
People. The Lapps, nomadic reindeer herders, live in the N, numbering only about 1,500. There is a Swedish-speaking minority along the coasts, but the remaining 92% of the people are Finns. Around 60% of the population is now urban, compared with 9% in 1880. Educational standards have long been high, and illiteracy is minimal; there are five universities. Government is by elected president and single-chamber parliament.
Economy. Before WWII Finland remained predominantly agricultural, but manufacturing has now expanded until agriculture and forestry account for around only 8% of the national output. The economy is largely managed by private enterprise, but the government has often intervened because of capital shortages. Forests remain the most important national resource, covering 70% of the total land area. Trade with the USSR has become increasingly important.
History. Finland was colonized from the S, and by the 9th century formed three tribal states, Karelia, Tavastenland and Suomi.

Sweden progressively colonized the area, and after the 14th century Finland became a Swedish grand duchy. In 1809 Sweden was forced to cede it to Russia. Tsar Alexander I maintained the country as a grand duchy but allowed it considerable autonomy under a governor-general. This period saw the rise of nationalism: the Swedish language was replaced by Finnish, particularly after the publication of the national folk-epic, the *Kalevala*. In 1863 the legislative Diet was revived and political parties developed. Under Alexander III a policy of "Russification" was adopted and generally bitterly resisted until WWI. In 1917 the parliament declared independence from the new regime in Russia, and Bolshevik forces were defeated in a brief civil war. In 1919 a republic was declared. In 1939, in breach of a non-aggression pact, the USSR invaded Finland, but was stalled by fierce resistance. For the German aid Finland then received it was made to pay massive postwar reparations to the USSR and lost S Karelia. During the postwar period, the Finnish government, dominated by the Social Democratic Party and the Center (formerly Agrarian) Party under U. K. Kekkonen, has sought a peaceful rapprochement with the USSR, despite much Soviet interference in Finnish affairs. Kekkonen's successor as president, Manno Koivisto, was elected to a second 6-year term in 1988.

FINLAY, Carlos Juan (1833–1915), Cuban physician who first proposed (1881) that YELLOW FEVER is transmitted by the MOSQUITO. Despite his considerable research, this was unproved until 1900.

FINNEY, Charles Grandison (1792–1875), US evangelist and educator. His emotional revival meetings throughout New England and the Middle Atlantic states in the 1820s dismayed more conventional clergymen. He was professor of theology at Oberlin College in Ohio from 1835 and served as the college's president 1851–66; all the while continuing his evangelistic work.

FINNISH, the most important of the UGRO-FINNIC LANGUAGES, spoken by around 5 million people in Finland. It has a written tradition dating from the 16th century but only achieved official status in the 19th century.

FIRBANK, (Arthur Annesley) Ronald (1886–1926), English novelist known for his eccentric and often innovative style and his fluent verbal wit. Among his best-known works are *Vainglory* (1915), *Inclinations* (1916) and *Valmouth* (1919).

FIRDAUSI, pen name of the great Persian poet Abul Qasim Mansur (c940–1020), author of the *Shah-Nameh* (Book of Kings), Persia's national epic and first great literary work. The poem, 60,000 verses long, took him 35 years to complete.

FIRE. See COMBUSTION.

FIRE ANTS, mainly tropical ants with extremely painful stings. Two species, one introduced from Argentina, are found in the southern US, and are a pest in fruit plantations.

FIREARMS, weapons in which missiles are projected by firing explosive charges. They are classified as either ARTILLERY or small arms. The latter seem to have originated in 14th-century Europe in the form of metal tubes, closed at one end, into which GUNPOWDER and the missile were packed, the charge being ignited via a touch hole. The heavy harquebus was one of these. The 15th century saw the introduction of the matchlock in which a spring-loaded lever mechanism was used to introduce a smoldering match (a hemp cord soaked in saltpeter) to the powder. This was superseded in the next century by the wheel lock. In this a serrated wheel rotated against a flint and ignited the powder with a spark. In the 17th century the flintlock was introduced. Here a flint held in a spring-loaded arm, or cock, struck a metal hammer, or frizzen, to produce the spark. The perfecting of the gas-tight breechblock and the modern percussion lock in the early 19th century led to the development of the breech-loading rifle and the repeating pistol. By the end of the century, machine guns were in an advanced state of development. Shotguns, used mainly for sport, fire a cartridge containing numerous small pellets. (See also AIR GUN; AMMUNITION; PISTOL.)

FIRE EXTINGUISHER, a portable appliance for putting out small fires. Extinguishers work either by cooling or by depriving the fire of OXYGEN (as typified by the simplest, a bucket of water or bucket of sand), and most do both. The soda-acid extinguisher contains a SODIUM bicarbonate solution and a small, stoppered bottle of SULFURIC ACID: depression of a plunger shatters the bottle, mixing the chemicals so that CARBON dioxide (CO_2) gas is generated, forcing the water out of a nozzle. Foam extinguishers employ a foaming agent (usually animal PROTEIN or certain detergents) and an aerating agent: they are effective against oil fires, as they float on the surface. Carbon dioxide extinguishers provide a smothering blanket of CO_2; and dry chemical extinguishers provide a powder of mainly sodium bicarbonate, from which the fire's heat generates CO_2.

FIREFLIES, mainly tropical soft-bodied BEETLES which produce an intermittent greenish light in their abdominal organs. The light is created by the oxidation of luciferin under the influence of an ENZYME, luciferase. In some species females are without wings and are known as glowworms. The lights serve to attract mates.

FIRE PROTECTION, the prevention and control of fires, one of the most essential community services. Volunteer firefighting organizations are known to have existed in ancient Egypt, Rome and many other countries, but the first attempts to cope with fires in the modern fashion began after the Great Fire of London in 1666. After this the first regulations controlling building materials and techniques to avoid fire risks were passed. Also at this time the flourishing fire insurance companies set up brigades with pumps mounted on hand-carts, to attend to their customers only. In the early 19th century fast horsecarts were used to carry the pumps, and soon after steam-driven pumps were introduced. The extensible ladder was developed c1800, and the wheeled escape ladder in 1837. In 1865 the communal fire department of the insurance companies was taken over and expanded into the London Metropolitan Fire Brigade, ancestor of modern brigades. In the US the trend was similar. The first volunteer fire organization in America was founded by Benjamin Franklin in Philadelphia in 1736. In the US also it was the insurance companies which established fire brigades, and these were eventually taken over by the municipalities. Small towns, however, often still have a wholly or partly volunteer service.

FIRESTONE, Harvey Samuel (1868–1938), US industrialist, founder of one of the largest rubber companies in the world, the Firestone Tire & Rubber Company. His million acre rubber plantation in Liberia played a large role in the country's economic development from 1926.

FIREWORKS, combustible or explosive preparations used for entertainment, probably first devised in ancient China to frighten off devils. Their initial European use was as weaponry and not until after about 1500 were they employed for entertainment. Compounds of CARBON, POTASSIUM and SULFUR are the prime constituents in fireworks, colors being produced by metallic salts (e.g., blue, COPPER; yellow, SODIUM; red, lithium or STRONTIUM; green, barium), sparks and crackles by powdered IRON, CARBON or ALUMINUM, or by certain LEAD salts. (See also EXPLOSIVES; GUNPOWDER.)

FIRS, evergreen trees of the pine family. They are pyramidal in shape with two rows of large flattened needles running along the twigs. The large cones stand erect. Firs are grown mainly for wood pulp and as Christmas trees. The *Douglas fir* provides twice as much timber as any other tree in the US. (See also CONIFERS.)

FIRST AID, treatment that can be given by minimally-trained people for accident, injury and sudden illness, until more skilled persons arrive or the patient is transferred to a hospital. Recognition of the injury or the nature of the illness and its gravity are crucial first measures, along with prevention of further injury to the patient or helpers. Clues such as medical bracelets or cards, tablets, lumps of sugar, alcohol and evidence of external injury should be sought and appropriate action taken. Arrest of breathing should be treated as a priority by clearing the airway of dentures, gum, vomit and other foreign material and the use of ARTIFICIAL RESPIRATION; likewise cardiac massage may be needed to restore BLOOD CIRCULATION if major PULSE cannot be felt. In traumatic injury, FRACTURES must be recognized and splinted to reduce pain; the possibility of injury to the spine must be considered before moving the patient, to avoid unnecessary damage to the SPINAL CORD. External HEMORRHAGE should be arrested, usually by direct pressure on the bleeding point; tourniquets are rarely needed and may be dangerous. Internal hemorrhage may be suspected if SHOCK develops soon after collapse or trauma without obvious bleeding. BURNS AND SCALDS should be treated by immediately cooling the burnt surface to reduce the continuing injury to SKIN due to retained heat. The use and, if necessary, improvisation of simple dressings, bandages, splints and stretchers should be known; simple methods of moving the injured, should this be necessary, must also be understood. Accessory functions such as contacting ambulances or medical help, direction of traffic and different aspects of resuscitation should be delegated by the most experienced person present. The inquisitive should be kept away and a calm atmosphere maintained.

Prevention as a part of first aid includes due care in the home: avoiding highly polished floors and unfixed carpets, obstacles on or near stairs, loose cords, overhanging saucepan handles, unlabeled bottles of poison and DRUG cupboards accessible to children. Attention to fireguards, adequate lighting and suitable education of children are also important.

Effective first aid depends on prevention, recognition, organization and, in any positive action, adherence to the principle of "do no harm."

FISCHER, Bobby (Robert James Fischer; 1943–   ), US chess player. In 1958, he became the youngest player (age 15) to attain the rank of international grand master. In 1972 in Iceland, he became the first American to win the world championship, defeating the Russian Boris Spassky in a widely-publicized tournament. He subsequently refused to defend his title, which was awarded to Anatoly KARPOV in 1975.

FISCHER-DIESKAU, Dietrich (1925–   ), German baritone. He achieved international fame in the 1950s as an opera singer and an interpreter of German lieder (see SONG), notably those of SCHUBERT and WOLF.

FISCHER VON ERLACH, Johann Bernhard (1656–1723), Austrian architect, who served the Hapsburgs and was a leading exponent of the Austrian BAROQUE style. Among his works are the original Schönbrunn Palace (Vienna) and the Kollegienkirche (Salzburg). He wrote *A Plan of Civil and Historical Architecture* (1721).

FISH, Hamilton (1808–1893), US statesman. A governor and US senator for New York, Fish was a Whig who joined the Republicans (1856) as an antislavery moderate. He served as a capable secretary of state under President U. S. Grant and helped bring about the 1871 Treaty of Washington which settled the ALABAMA CLAIMS with Britain.

FISH AND WILDLIFE SERVICE, US federal agency within the Department of the Interior, created in 1956, concerned with conservation and development of fish and wildlife resources, wilderness areas and river basins. It maintains waterfowl refuges and fish hatcheries, prepares federal hunting regulations, performs research for the fishing industry, protects threatened wildlife, manages the fur seal herds of Alaska and administers international agreements.

FISHER, Geoffrey Francis (1887–971), English clergyman, archbishop of Canterbury (1945–61) and president of the World Council of Churches (1946–54). His visit to the pope in 1960 was the first by an archbishop of Canterbury since the Reformation.

FISHER, Harry Conway "Bud" (1884–1954), US cartoonist, creator (1908) of *Mutt and Jeff,* the first comic strip featuring the same characters to be widely syndicated.

FISHER, John (c1469–1535), English cardinal, saint and martyr. As bishop of Rochester (1504–34), he refused to recognize Henry VIII's claim to royal ecclesiastical supremacy, was imprisoned in the Tower and later beheaded.

FISHER, John Arbuthnot Fisher, 1st Baron (1841–1920), British admiral, who as second (1892–97) and then first sea lord (1902–10), introduced wide-ranging naval reforms, including the encouragement of submarine development. His measures helped ensure British naval superiority in WWI.

FISHERIES, the commercial harvesting of marine and freshwater animals (and some plants) to provide food for men and animals. The main catch is of FISHES, but shellfish and marine mammals including seals and whales are also important. About 75% of the world harvest is caught in the cold and temperate zones of the Northern Hemisphere. The chief fishing nations are Peru, China, the USSR, Norway, Japan and the US; in the next rank are Canada, India, Spain, Great Britain and Iceland. Inland fisheries—in lakes, rivers and ricefields—account for less than 10% of recorded catches. The most important groups of fish caught are herring and its relatives, and cod and its relatives. Modern fishing vessels are equipped with radar, depth sounders and echo sounders to locate fish shoals; increasingly used are factory ships which process the fish and freeze or can them. Modern nets are very strong, being made from synthetic fibers. Trawlers draw a bag-shaped net behind them; drift nets are fastened to a buoy; lining involves trailing many-hooked lines in deep water; and in seining a large net encircles the fish and is gradually closed as it is drawn in. The supply of fish can no longer be regarded as practically inexhaustible: it is depleted by the vast catches of efficient modern fishing and also by POLLUTION. Conservation is therefore important, and there are international agreements against overfishing and to regulate the meshes of nets so that young fish can escape. Fish farming is also being developed. International disputes have often arisen over fishing rights in coastal waters.

FISHES, a large group of cold-blooded aquatic vertebrates that breathe by means of GILLS, and whose bodies bear a vertical tail fin. Most fishes fall within this definition, but a few breathe atmospheric air by means of a lung or lung-like organ; some species have a body temperature slightly above that of the surrounding water; and in certain fishes the tail may be missing or reduced to a filament. There are four classes of fish-like vertebrates: the jawless fishes (Agnatha); the placoderms (Placodermi); the cartilaginous fishes (Chondrichthyes), and the bony fishes (Pisces).

The Agnatha are now represented solely by the lampreys and hagfishes. When they first appeared, during the Ordovician period 530 million years ago, they were fish-like in shape, but had poorly formed fins and lacked jaws.

The placoderms are now entirely extinct. They are known only as fossils, mainly from rocks of Devonian age (about 400 million years old). They had jaws and paired fins, with ossified skeletons.

The Chondrichthyes include the SHARKS, rays and chimaeras as well as certain fossil forms. They are characterized by skeletons that are composed of cartilage, gills that are located in pouches and tooth-like scales.

The most widespread class comprises the Pisces or bony fish, which include the COELACANTH, lungfishes and ray-finned fishes. Ray-finned fishes contain the chondrosteans (bichirs, sturgeons and one entirely fossil order); the holosteans (bowfins and five fossil orders), and finally the teleosteans. The overwhelming majority of present-day fishes are teleosts. There are at least 20,000 different species of teleosts and countless millions of individuals inhabiting the seas, lakes and rivers of the world. They show an amazing diversity of form, from eels to the sea horse, but have a number of characteristics in common. They range in size from a total length of over 20ft in the oarfish and a weight of over 2 tons in the ocean sunfish, to an adult length of only 0.5in in a Philippine goby (*Paudaka pygmaea*), the latter qualifying as the smallest of all vertebrates. Typically, the body is streamlined, rising smoothly from the head and tapering gently to the tail, but in particular cases the body shape reflects the mode of life of the fish. In most fishes swimming is achieved by throwing the body into a series of lateral undulations which travel along the length of the body, growing in amplitude toward the tail. The tail provides the final thrust and evens out the oscillations of the body. One characteristic (but not invariable) feature of fishes is the presence of scales on the body.

FISHING, the catching of fish for consumption or for sport. It is one of the world's most popular participant sports. There are millions of fishermen (almost 30 million in the US alone), or anglers, who fish for recreation or in competition. World records by weight, length and girth exist for every type of fish. The first fishing club in America was the Schuylkill Fishing Company of Philadelphia (established 1732). There are three main types of sports fishing: game, coarse and sea angling, or deep-sea fishing. Game anglers fish trout, salmon and other fish in fast-moving streams which require accurate casting of the right lure. Coarse anglers fish in slow, deep rivers. Sea anglers generally fish for shark, tuna, tarpon or barracuda.

FISK, James (1834–1872), US financial speculator, notorious for stock manipulation. With Jay GOULD he engaged in a brutal stock market struggle for control of the Erie Railroad and together their attempt to corner the gold market in 1869 led to the BLACK FRIDAY scandal. He was shot by a business associate and rival for the affections of an actress.

FISKE, Minnie Madden (1865–1932), US actress and director, a major figure on the New York stage from 1893. She was noted for her portrayals of Ibsen and Shakespeare heroines.

FISSION, the division of CELLS, or sometimes multicellular organisms, to produce identical offspring. Binary fission results in the production of two equal parts and multiple fission in the production of more than two equal parts. The term is normally applied to the reproduction of multicellular organisms such as members of the phylum PROTOZOA.

FISSION, Nuclear, the splitting of the nucleus of a heavy ATOM into two or more lighter nuclei with the release of a large amount of ENERGY. Fission power is used in NUCLEAR REACTORS and the ATOMIC BOMB.

FITCH, John (1743–1798), US inventor and engineer who built the first practical steamboat (1787), larger vessels being launched in 1788 and 1790. All were paddle-powered; his later attempt to introduce the screw propeller was a commercial failure.

FITZGERALD, Edward (1809–1883), English poet and scholar. FitzGerald is famous for his "translation" of OMAR KHAYYAM's *Rubaiyat* (1859) in which he managed to capture the spirit of the original while at the same time creating a new masterpiece using his own images and structure.

FITZGERALD, F. Scott (Francis Scott Key Fitzgerald; 1896–1940), US novelist and short story writer. The "spokesman" of the Jazz Age in the 1920s, his works deal with the frenetic life style of the post-WWI generation and the spiritual bankruptcy of the so-called American Dream. His celebrated novel *The Great Gatsby* (1925) explores the ruthless society of the 1920s. *Tender Is the Night* (1934) draws upon his experience of American expatriates in Paris and upon the schizophrenic gaiety and breakdown of his wife, Zelda. He spent his last years as a Hollywood scriptwriter.

FITZGERALD, Garret (1926–   ), Irish politician, a member of the business-oriented Fine Gael Party, prime minister in coalition governments with the Labour Party 1981–87. In Nov. 1985 he signed an agreement with the British government giving Ireland a consultative role in the governing of Northern Ireland.

FITZPATRICK, Thomas (c1799–1854), US fur trader and guide, one of the MOUNTAIN MEN. A fur trader for William ASHLEY and William SUBLETTE, he later guided the first emigrant trains to California and Oregon. He also served as guide for John C. FREMONT and Stephen W. KEARNY.

FITZSIMMONS, Robert Prometheus (called "Bob" or "Ruby Robert"; 1863–1918), English world boxing champion. Middleweight (1891–97), heavyweight (1897–99) and light-heavyweight (1903–05) champion of the world, he fought in New Zealand and Australia and in the US from 1890.

FIVE CIVILIZED TRIBES, term for the CHEROKEE, CHICKASAW, CHOCKTAW, CREEK and SEMINOLE Indian tribes of North America. Between about 1830–50 they were forced to settle in Indian Territory but were recognized as domestic, dependent nations with constitutions and laws based on those of the US. After the Civil War they were restricted to areas in E Okla. and the US followed a detribalization policy which left the five with little autonomy.

FLAG, a piece of cloth or other material, usually rectangular, bearing a distinctive design and displayed as a symbol or signal. Regimental flags date back to ancient battle standards—symbolic objects borne on poles. Personal standards of heads of state derive from the heraldic banners of medieval knights. Early national flags often used royal insignia, like the fleur-de-lis of France, or religious devices. The United Kingdom's *Union Jack* combines the crosses of St. George (England), St. Andrew (Scotland) and St. Patrick (Ireland). The *Stars and Stripes* of the US, officially adopted by Congress on June 14, 1777, now consists of 13 alternate red and white stripes for the original colonies, and 50 stars for the present states. Betsy ROSS supposedly made the first *Stars and Stripes*. International organizations, including the Red Cross and UN, have their own flags. Other internationally used flags include the white flag of surrender and the yellow flag for infectious disease (representing Q in the international code of signals used at sea).

FLAG DAY, June 14, anniversary of the adoption in 1777 of the Stars and Stripes as the US flag.

FLAGG, James Montgomery (1877–1960), US painter and illustrator famous for a WWI recruiting poster showing a beckoning Uncle Sam who says "I want YOU." Flagg also drew homely scenes of American life in a vigorous pen-and-ink technique for several popular magazines.

FLAGLER, Henry Morrison (1830–1913), US financier who helped develop Fla. In partnership with John D. Rockefeller, he helped form the Standard Oil Company in 1870, then built hotels and railways that made Fla. a vacation center.

FLAGSTAD, Kirsten (1895–1962), Norwegian singer, one of the greatest Wagnerian sopranos. She made her New York debut as Sieglinde in *Die Walküre* in 1935 and retired from public singing in 1953, though she continued making records.

FLAHERTY, Robert Joseph (1884–1951), US pioneer documentary filmmaker. He is chiefly famous for *Nanook of the North* (1922), a study of Eskimo life, and *Man of Aran* (1934), about life on the Aran Islands of Ireland.

FLAMENCO, name given to the folk music of Andalusia in southern Spain. Like most folk music traditions, flamenco combines singing and dancing, and the influence of Moorish music has helped to create one of the most distinctive, colorful, and exciting of all folk music styles. True flamenco singing and dancing requires a considerable amount of training and skill, and professional flamenco groups are admired throughout the world.

FLAMINGO, several species of colorful water birds, of the family Phoenicopteridae, related to HERONS. They have long spindly legs and necks, and large bills with bristles which they use to sift their food from the water. Their plumage is white, pink and black. They live in large flocks on alkaline lakes in America, Africa and S Eurasia.

FLAMINIAN ROAD, ancient Roman road connecting Rome with Cisalpine Gaul. Begun in 220 BC, it originally extended some 200mi to modern Rimini.

FLANAGAN, Edward Joseph (1886–1948), Irish-born US Roman Catholic priest who founded BOYS TOWN, a self-governing community of homeless boys,

near Omaha, Neb., in 1917. After WWII he helped organize youth facilities abroad for the US government.

FLANDERS, medieval county on the coast of NW Europe, largely corresponding to N Belgium, with smaller portions in the Netherlands and France. In the 14th and 15th centuries, wealth from trade and textile manufacture enriched the chief towns (Antwerp, Ypres, Bruges and Ghent) and made Flanders a major cultural center. Its famous artists included Bruegel, Rubens and Van Dyck.

FLATFOOT, deformity of the foot in which the longitudinal or transverse arches of the feet are flattened or lost; this results in loss of spring and the inefficient use of the feet in walking or running. It may result from muscle weakness or be congenital. Corrective exercises and shoe wedges may relieve the condition.

FLATHEAD INDIANS, North American tribe of the Salish linguistic family inhabiting W Mont. The name derives from the head-flattening practiced by tribes from whom the Flatheads took slaves. The Flatheads were early converts to Christianity, and most now live at Flathead Lake, Mont.

FLAUBERT, Gustave (1821–1880), French novelist; a scrupulous observer and stylist, whose work influenced much subsequent French writing. His first work, *Madame Bovary* (1856–57), brought him immediate fame. The vividly naturalistic tragedy of a provincial wife who attempts to live out her fantasies, it was unsuccessfully prosecuted as an offense against public morality in 1857. The exotic Carthaginian setting of *Salammbô* (1862) showed an equal mastery of Romantic style. His *Three Tales* (1877), set in modern, medieval and ancient times, combined both Romanticism and realism.

FLAX, an important plant of temperate and subtropical areas grown for its fiber and for linseed oil. Flax was first cultivated in the Mediterranean basin, and has been an important crop for thousands of years.

The native flax of Eurasia is a straw-like annual, about 2 or 3 ft high, bearing blue or whitish flowers. The flowers ripen into seed capsules or bolls. The plants germinate quickly and flower within about two months. Crops are usually harvested after about 14 weeks. After the fibers have been separated from the seed, they are freed from the woody portion of the stem by soaking (*retting*) and scraping (*scutching*). The longer fibers are separated by a combing process called *hackling*, and are spun into yarn.

FLEAS, wingless INSECTS with legs developed for jumping, and a laterally compressed body. They suck the blood of host animals, and can carry such diseases as the bubonic PLAGUE. The flea survives its early stages in insanitary conditions; when newly emerged, adults leap onto passing hosts.

FLEMING, Sir Alexander (1881–1955), British bacteriologist, discoverer of lysozome (1922) and penicillin (1928). Lysozome is an ENZYME present in many body tissues and lethal to certain bacteria; its discovery prepared the way for that of ANTIBIOTICS. His discovery of PENICILLIN was largely accidental; and it was developed as a therapeutic later, by Harold FLOREY and Ernst CHAIN. All three received the 1945 Nobel Prize for Physiology or Medicine for their work.

FLEMING, Ian (1908–1964), British novelist, creator of secret agent James Bond, known also as 007.

FLEMING, Peggy (1948–   ), US ice skater, winner of US, Olympic, and world figure skating titles 1963–68.

FLEMISH, the form of DUTCH traditionally spoken in N Belgium. Given official equality with French in 1898, it became the official language of N Belgium in 1934.

FLETCHER, John. See BEAUMONT, FRANCIS, AND FLETCHER, JOHN.

FLEURY, André Hercule de (1653–1743), French cardinal and statesman. As tutor and adviser to Louis XV from 1726, he was the effective ruler of France.

FLEXNER, Abraham (1866–1959), US educator who profoundly changed medical teaching in the US. His survey of medical schools (1910) led to drastic reorganization. He was founder and first director (1930–39) of the Institute for Advanced Study, Princeton, N.J. His brother, **Simon Flexner** (1863–1946), made major contributions to viral-disease research as director of laboratories (1903-35) and director (1920-35) of the Rockefeller Institute (now Rockefeller University).

FLIES, members of the INSECT order Diptera which number about 85,000 species, and whose second pair of wings has been reduced to a pair of halteres, or balancing organs, which act as GYROSCOPES. These give flies great agility. They have two compound eyes; the antennae act as tactile, and possibly also smelling and hearing, organs. Their mouths are adapted either for sucking (as in the house fly), or piercing (as in mosquitoes). Their larvae, called maggots, live on plants or decaying flesh. Adults feed on NECTAR, other insects, decaying matter or animal blood. The MOSQUITO and TSETSE FLY carry MALARIA and SLEEPING SICKNESS respectively.

FLIGHT, History of. LEONARDO DA VINCI was the first man to attempt the scientific design of flying machines. But in his time no motor was available which was powerful enough to lift a man into the air. Man's first ascents from the ground had to await the late 18th century and the invention of the MONTGOLFIER brothers' hot-air BALLOON and J. Charles' hydrogen balloon (1783). The addition of steam engines to the balloon gave the first maneuverable AIRSHIP (1852). Meanwhile G. CAYLEY designed and built flying GLIDERS (1810–1853) and William Henson designed a steam-powered model airplane with twin propellers (1842). It was not until the advent of the gasoline INTERNAL-COMBUSTION ENGINE, though, that the powered heavier-than-air machine became a practical possibility. The first successful controlled airplane flight was made by the WRIGHT brothers near Kitty Hawk, N.C., on December 17, 1903, and within a few years there were many competing manufacturers and fliers of airplanes. Airplane technology was greatly stimulated by WWI, and after 1919 commercial aviation developed rapidly. Meanwhile, the AUTOGIRO was invented by J. de la Cierva (1923), to be followed by SIKORSKY'S HELICOPTER in 1939. JET PROPULSION was developed in several countries during WWII and by the mid-1950s had come to be used in the majority of military and commercial airplanes. RADAR navigation systems came into general use in this period. The early 1970s saw the introduction of widebodied jet airliners (jumbo jets) with vastly increased carrying capacity and the development of the first supersonic jet airliners.

FLINT, or **chert**, sedimentary rock composed of microcrystalline QUARTZ and chalcedony. It is found as nodules in LIMESTONE and CHALK, and as layered beds, and was mainly formed by alteration of marine sediments of siliceous organisms, and by replacement, preserving many FOSSIL outlines. A hard rock, flint may be chipped to form a sharp cutting edge, and was used by STONE AGE men for their characteristic tools.

FLINTLOCK, firearm developed in the 17th century and named for its use of flint ignition. It had a' cock or hammer containing a piece of flint. When the trigger was pulled the flint struck a steel hammer or frizzen and the resulting spark ignited the charge. It was superseded by the percussion system which was introduced in the 19th century.

FLODDEN FIELD, Battle of, English victory in which James IV of Scotland and at least 10,000 of his troops were killed near Branxton in NE England, on Sept. 9, 1513. They had invaded England to support their ancient ally, France.

FLOODS AND FLOOD CONTROL. River floods are one of mankind's worst enemies. In 1887, when the Hwang Ho overflowed, around 900,000 lost their lives; and, as recently as 1970, 200,000 died in E Pakistan when a cyclone struck the Ganges delta. Clearly the development of ways to control and contain floods must be a preoccupation of man.

Often floods are caused by unusually rapid thawing of the winter snows: the river, unable to hold the increased volume of water, bursts its banks. Heavy rainfall may have a similar effect. Coastal flooding may result from an exceptionally high TIDE combined with onshore winds, or, of course, from a TSUNAMI.

River floods can be forestalled by artificially deepening and broadening river channels or by the construction of suitably positioned DAMS. Artificial levees may also be built (in nature, levees occur as a result of sediment deposited while the river is in flood; they take the form of built-up banks). Vegetation planted on uplands helps to reduce surface runoff.

Flood control can create new problems to replace the old. In Egypt the Aswan Dam has halted the once regular flooding of the Nile, thus robbing farmlands of a rich annual deposit of silt. But flood control made possible the civilization of ancient Mesopotamia and plays a vital role in modern water conservation. (See also RIVERS AND LAKES.)

FLORENCE or **Firenze,** historic city in central Italy, capital of Firenze province, on the Arno R at the foot of the Apennines. A town on the Cassian Way during Roman times, it grew to become a powerful medieval republic, dominating Tuscany. Florence was a major commercial and artistic center during the Renaissance. It retains many architectural and other art treasures which, together with the proximity of the Apennines, serve to make the city an important tourist center. The great art museums of Florence include the Uffizi Gallery, the Pitti Palace and the Accademia. Famous figures associated with Florence include BRUNELLESCHI, DANTE, GIOTTO, MACHIAVELLI, MASACCIO, MICHELANGELO and SAVONAROLA. Glass and leatherware, pottery, furniture and precision instruments are among its products. In 1966 floods seriously damaged many of Florence's art treasures. Pop 438,304.

FLOREY, Howard Walter, Baron Florey of Adelaide (1898–1968), Australian-born British pathologist who worked with E. B. CHAIN and others to extract PENICILLIN from *Penicillium notatum* mold for use as a therapeutic drug (1934–44). He shared with Chain and Alexander FLEMING the 1945 Nobel Prize for Physiology or Medicine.

FLORIDA, state, SE US, bounded to the E by the Atlantic Ocean, to the W by the Gulf of Mexico, and to the N and NW by Ga. and Ala. It is a major resort area and one of the fastest growing states in the US.

Name of state: Florida
Capital: Tallahassee
Statehood: Mar. 3, 1845 (27th state)
Familiar name: Sunshine State
Area: 58,560sq mi
Population: 11,675,000
Elevation: Highest—345ft, in Walton Co. Lowest—sea level, Atlantic Ocean
Motto: "In God we trust"
State flower: Orange blossom
State bird: Mockingbird
State tree: Sabal palm
State song: "Swanee River"

Land. The greater part of the state consists of a low 400mi-long peninsula between the Gulf of Mexico and the Atlantic, with the Straits of Florida skirting its S coast. Sandbars and islands flank the smooth E coast. The string of islands known as the Florida Keys and the Dry Tortugas Islands extend SW from Biscayne Bay on the S coast. The W coast is indented and swampy. The central plains run from the NW to central Florida. Big Cypress Swamp and the EVERGLADES are situated in the marshlands of the S. There are some 30,000 lakes, including the 700sq mi Okeechobee, and numerous rivers. Florida enjoys a subtropical climate.

People. More than 80% of the people live in rapidly expanding urban areas, such as Jacksonville, Miami, Orlando, St. Petersburg and Fort Lauderdale. Florida's population grew fivefold between 1940 and

1980; by 1986 it was the fifth largest state. The state is administered by a governor elected for 4 years, a 40-member Senate and a 120-member House of Representatives. The state's numerous institutions of higher learning include the U. of Florida and Miami U.

Economy. Tourism, manufacturing (processed foods, paper, chemicals, electrical products) and agriculture, which produces a large proportion of the nation's citrus fruit, are the three leading industries. Mining and fishing are also important economically. Florida's transportation system includes international airports, interstate bus, rail and road systems and a number of deepwater harbors. Lake Okeechobee links the ATLANTIC INTRACOASTAL WATERWAY to the Gulf of Mexico, via the Caloosahatchee and St. Lucie canals and rivers.

History. Juan PONCE DE LEÓN discovered and named Florida in 1513 and claimed the territory for Spain. Early European settlements met with failure, but in 1565 Spain founded Saint Augustine, which survives as the oldest permanent white settlement in the US. Spain soon controlled all Florida. Britain held it from 1763 until 1783, when it was returned to Spain. American colonists began moving in, and in 1819 Spain ceded Florida to the US. Resistance to white settlement by Seminole Indians culminated in the brutal Seminole War (1835–42). Admitted to the Union in 1845, Florida seceded in 1861. It was readmitted in 1868. Major economic growth began only late in the 19th century when an expanding railroad system encouraged the development of tourism and of the citrus fruit industry. Economic expansion has been phenomenal since WWII, putting increasing strains upon the fragile environment, public servies, transportation and the dwindling tracts of subtropical wilderness. In the 1970s, Florida was the leading point of entry for Caribbean refugees. More than half the population of Miami is of Cuban origin. Trade with Latin America became increasingly important in the 1980s. At the same time, southern Florida became a major drug trafficking area, with an attendant rise in crime and other social problems. In presidential elections 1968–88, Florida voted Republican in 1968–72 and 1980–88.

FLORIDA KEYS, chain of about 20 small coral islands off S Fla. Their arc curves SW from Biscayne Bay S of Miami to Key West. Causeways bearing some 160mi of highway link most of the islands, which support fishing and farming and attract vacationers.

FLOTSAM, JETSAM AND LAGAN are all terms in maritime law relating to goods lost at sea as distinct from goods washed ashore from a wreck. Goods found floating on the surface are *flotsam*. Goods thrown overboard (to lighten a ship) and that sink are *jetsam*; but if they sink and are marked by a buoy or flag, to indicate ownership, they are *lagan* (or *ligan*). All lagan must be returned to the owner. But flotsam and jetsam need not be returned unless the owner claims them. Flotsam, jetsam and lagan are all subject to the law of salvage whereby the finder or rescuer of the goods is entitled to reward, provided it was not his legal duty to recover goods so lost.

FLOUR, fine powder ground from the grains or starchy portions of WHEAT, RYE, CORN, RICE, POTATOES, BANANAS or BEANS. Plain white flour is produced from wheat; soft wheat produces flour used for cakes and hard wheat, with a higher GLUTEN content, makes flour used for bread. Flour is made from the endosperm, which constitutes about 84% of the grain; the remainder comprises the bran, which is the outer layers of the grain, and the germ, which is the embryo. Grain used to be milled by hand between two stones, until the development of wind, water or animal driven mills. In modern mills, the grain is thoroughly cleaned and then tempered by bringing the water content to 15%, which makes the separation of the bran and germ from the endosperm easier. The endosperm is broken up by rollers, and the flour is graded and bleached. It may then be enriched with VITAMINS. Byproducts are used mainly for cattle food, although wheat germ is an important source of vitamin E.

FLOWER, the part of an ANGIOSPERM that is concerned with REPRODUCTION. There is a great variety of floral structure, but the basic organs and structure are similar. Each flower is borne on a stalk or pedicel, the tip of which is expanded to form a receptacle that bears the floral organs. The **sepals** are the first of these organs and are normally green and leaflike. Above the sepals there is a ring of **petals**, which are normally colored and vary greatly in shape. The ring of sepals is termed the **calyx**, and the ring of petals, the **corolla**. Collectively the calyx and corolla are called the **perianth**. Above the perianth are the reproductive organs comprising the male organs, the **stamens** (collectively known as the **androecium**) and female organs, the **carpels** (the **gynoecium**). Each stamen consists of a slender stalk, or filament, which is capped by the pollen-producing **anther**. Each carpel has a swollen base, the **ovary**, which contains the **ovules** that later form the **seed**. Each carpel is connected by a **style** to an expanded structure called the **stigma**. Together, the style and stigma are sometimes termed the **pistil**.

There are three main variations of flower structure. In hypogynous flowers (e.g. buttercup) the perianth segments and stamens are attached below a superior ovary, while in perigynous flowers (e.g. rose) the receptacle is cuplike, enclosing a superior ovary, with the perianth segments and stamens attached to a rim around the receptacle. In epigynous flowers (e.g. dandelion) the inferior ovary is enclosed by the receptacle and the other floral parts are attached to the ovary. In many plants, the flowers are grouped together to form an inflorescence (flower cluster).

Pollen produced by the stamens is transferred either by insects or the wind to the stigma, where POLLINATION takes place. Many of the immense number of variations of flower form are adaptations that aid either insect or wind pollination. (See also PLANT KINGDOM.)

FLU. See INFLUENZA.

FLUID, a substance which flows (undergoes a continuous change of shape) when subjected to a tangential or shearing FORCE. Liquids and GASES are fluids, both taking the shape of their container. But while liquids are virtually incompressible and have a fixed volume, gases expand to fill whatever space is available to them.

FLUIDICS, application of fluid flow to perform such functions as sensing, control, actuation, amplification and information processing. Many of these functions can also be accomplished by electronic circuitry, but fluidic devices are preferable in certain hostile environments where electronic components would fail, such as under conditions of excessive heat, humidity or vibrations. A fluidic device is especially efficient for systems in which the flow of fluid plays an integral part, such as certain chemical-engineering processes and automotive fuel systems.

FLUID MECHANICS, the study of moving and static FLUIDS, dealing with the FORCES exerted on a fluid to hold it at rest and the relationships with its boundaries that cause it to move. The scope of the subject is wide, ranging from HYDRAULICS, concerning the applications of fluid flow in pipes and channels, to aeronautics, the study of airflow relating to the design of AIRPLANES and ROCKETS. Any fluid process, such as flow around an obstacle or in a pipe, can be described mathematically by a specific equation that relates the forces acting, the dimensions of the system and its properties such as TEMPERATURE, PRESSURE and DENSITY. Newton's laws of motion and viscosity, the first and second laws of THERMODYNAMICS and the laws of conservation of MASS, ENERGY and momentum are applied as appropriate. Much use is also made of experimental evidence from models, wind tunnels, etc., to determine the process equation. Many types of flow occur: in laminar flow in a closed pipe, distinct layers of fluid slide over each other, their velocity decreasing to zero at the pipe wall; in turbulent flow the fluid is mixed by eddies and vertices, and a statistical treatment is needed. (See also ARCHIMEDES; BERNOULLI; PASCAL'S LAW.)

FLUKES, parasitic flatworms, some of which are important disease carriers. The sheep liver fluke lives in the bile duct of mammals. Its eggs pass out of the intestine into water, where the larvae infect water snails, then wait on vegetation to be eaten by mammals. The blood fluke bilharzia is responsible for the disease SCHISTOSOMIASIS, which is thought to affect 250 million people throughout the world.

FLUORIDATION, addition of small quantities of fluorides (see FLUORINE) to public water supplies, bringing the concentration to 1 ppm, as in some natural water. It greatly reduces the incidence of tooth decay by strengthening the teeth. Despite some opposition, many authorities now fluoridate water. Toothpaste containing fluoride is also valuable.

FLUORINE (F), the lightest of the halogens, occurring naturally as fluorite, cryolite and fluorapatite. A pale-yellow toxic gas, fluorine is made by electrolysis of potassium fluoride in liquid hydrogen fluoride. It is the most reactive, electronegative and oxidizing of all elements, reacting with almost all other elements to give fluorides (see HALIDES) of the highest possible oxidation state. It displaces other nonmetals from their compounds. Most nonmetal fluorides are highly reactive, but sulfur hexafluoride (used as an electrical insulator) and carbon tetrafluoride are inert (see STEREOCHEMISTRY). Fluorine is used in rocket propulsion, in URANIUM production, and to make FLUOROCARBONS. (See also FLUORIDATION.) AW 19.0, mp—220°C, bp—188°C.

FLUOROCARBONS, HYDROCARBONS in which hydrogen atoms are replaced (wholly or in part) by fluorine. Because of the stability of the carbon-fluorine bond, they are inert and heat-resistant. Thus they can be used in artificial joints in the body, and where hydrocarbons would be decomposed by heat, such as in spacecraft heatshields, the coating of nonstick pans or as lubricants. Liquid fluorocarbons are used as refrigerants.

FLUOROSCOPE, device used in medical diagnosis and engineering quality control which allows the direct observation of an X-RAY beam which is being passed through an object under examination. It contains a fluorescent screen which converts the X-ray image into visible light (see LUMINESCENCE) and, often, an image intensifier.

FLUTE, reedless woodwind instrument of ancient origin. The modern concert flute is a transverse or side-blown instrument, the earlier form being, like the RECORDER, end-blown. It was in widespread use by the end of the 18th century. The C flute with a three octave range is the standard instrument. Other types include the bass flute and the piccolo, about half the size of the flute and the highest pitched instrument in the orchestra. The piccolo is widely used in military bands.

FLYING FISHES, members of the family Exocoetidae, tropical fish which propel themselves out of the sea by an elongated lobe of the tail. They can glide on their fins for over 0.4km (0.25mi) but the flights are usually 55m (180ft) or less. The reason for flying is to escape predatory fish.

FLYING SAUCER, popular term for Unidentified Flying Object (UFO). UFOs have been reported for many years, but only caught the public imagination in the 1950s' "saucer scare." Most sightings are obviously erroneous, but a number of reliable observations remain unexplained.

FLYING SQUIRRELS, members of the family Sciuridae, a family of SQUIRRELS which glide on a web of skin between their legs. They use their tails to balance and as a rudder. Flying squirrels are found throughout the world but are most common in SE Asia. Their habits are similar to those of other squirrels.

FOCH, Ferdinand (1851–1929), outstanding French army marshal. His courageous stand against the Germans at the Marne in 1914 led to further commands and (1917) becoming chief of the French general staff. He commanded the Allied armies in France, April–Nov., 1918, launching the Aisne-Marne offensive which ended WWI.

FOG, in essence, a cloud touching or near to the earth's surface. A fog is suspension of tiny water (sometimes ice) particles in the air. Fogs are a result of the air's HUMIDITY being high enough that CONDENSATION occurs around suitable nuclei; they are found most often near coasts and large inland bodies of water. In industrial areas, fog and smoke may mix to give **smog**. Persistent **advection fogs** occur when warm, moist air moves over cold land or water. (See also CLOUDS.)

FOKINE, Michel (1880–1942), Russian-born US dancer and choreographer, a founder of modern ballet. Influenced by the work of Isadora DUNCAN, he stressed the total effect of expressive dancing, costume, music and scenery. He worked in Paris as chief choreographer of DIAGHILEV's Ballets Russes 1909–14, and from 1925 directed his own company in the US.

FOKKER, Anthony Herman Gerard (1890–1939), Dutch-American pioneer in aircraft design. In WWI he designed pursuit planes for Germany, developing a synchronizer mechanism by which guns could be fired from directly behind a plane's propeller blades. In 1922 Fokker emigrated to the US where he designed for the Army Air Corps and built transport planes, such as the Fokker T-2, which in 1923 made the first nonstop flight across the US.

FOLD, a buckling in rock strata. Folds convex upward are called **anticlines**; those convex downward, **synclines**. They may be tiny or up to hundreds of miles across. Folds result from horizontal pressures in the EARTH's crust and result in crustal shortening. The upper portions of anticlines have often been eroded away.

FOLGER SHAKESPEARE LIBRARY, Washington, D.C., institution possessing the world's largest collection of Shakespeariana, including 79 First Folios, and a host of material on the Tudor and Stuart periods. Opened in 1932, the collection was assembled initially by American philanthropist Henry Clay Folger (1857–1930) and his wife.

FOLK DANCING, traditional popular dancing, often stylistically peculiar to a nation or region. Folk dances derive variously from ancient magic and religious rituals and also from the sequences of movement involved in certain forms of communal labor. Famous national dances include the Irish jig, Italian tarantella and Hungarian czardas. The American Folk Dancing Society popularizes American folk dances, notably the SQUARE DANCE where an expert "caller" gives rhyming instructions. Many US dances have European origins, but their barn dance setting is authentically American. (See also DANCE.)

FOLKLORE, a culture's traditional beliefs, customs and superstitions handed down informally in fables, myths, legends, proverbs, riddles, songs and ballads. Folklore studies were developed in the

1800s, largely through collection and collation of material by the GRIMM brothers, and folklore societies were set up in Europe and the US. The American Folklore Society was founded in 1888. The extent to which folktale themes are echoed and paralleled among distinct and isolated cultures is truly remarkable. One of the major studies of this phenomenon is Sir James FRAZER's *Golden Bough* (1890). (See also FABLE; MYTHOLOGY.)

FOLK MUSIC, traditional popular music stylistically belonging to a regional or ethnic group. Compositions are usually anonymous and, being in the main orally transmitted, often occur in several different versions. Folk music of the US includes the English ballads of Kentucky, Mexican music of the Southwest, and black music of the South. Among classical composers influenced by folk music are Béla Bartók, Zoltán Kodaly, Aaron Copland and Ralph Vaughan Williams.

FOLSOM, prehistoric American Indian culture. The existence of Folsom man has been deduced from the evidence of spearheads, stone tools and animal bones first discovered in 1928 at Folsom, New Mexico. The Folsom points, or flint spearheads, are leaf-shaped and have a lengthwise groove. Folsom culture is thought to have been nomadic, based mainly on hunting now extinct species of bison, camel, and mastodon. Archaeologists estimate the age of the Folsom implements as more than 10,000 years. Important Folsom remains have been found in northeastern Colorado and as far afield as Alberta, Canada, and southern Texas.

FONDA, family of US stage and screen actors. Henry Fonda (1905–1982) played earnest, idealistic heroes in *Young Mr. Lincoln* (1939), *The Grapes of Wrath* (1940), and *The Ox-Bow Incident* (1943). He repeated his stage success in *Mr. Roberts* in the 1955 film. His daughter, Jane Fonda (1937–   ), developed from sex-kitten roles to powerful dramatic achievements in *They Shoot Horses Don't They* (1969) and *Klute* (1971). She was active in the anti-Vietnam War movement. Her brother, Peter Fonda (1939–   ), produced and starred in *Easy Rider* (1969), a film that reflected the mood of 1960s youth.

FONTAINEBLEAU, town in the department Seine-et-Marne, France. Situated 37mi SE of Paris, the town did not develop until the 19th century. Fontainebleau is primarily a recreation and tourist town. The magnificent palace of the French kings, built in the 16th century on the site of a royal hunting lodge, stands just outside of the town. It was the scene of Napoleon's farewell to his army after his abdication in 1814. Fontainebleau forest, once a royal hunting ground, was a favorite subject for the 19th-century landscape painters known as the Barbizon school.

FONTANA, Domenico (1543–1607), Italian architect and civil engineer. As chief architect to Pope Sixtus V he completed the dome of St. Peter's (1585–90) and designed the Lateran Palace and the Vatican Library (1588).

FONTANE, Theodor (1819–1898), German writer whose realistic novels portray Berlin society.

FONTENELLE, Bernard le Bovier de (1657–1757), French writer best known as a popularizer of new scientific ideas. As secretary of the Royal Academy of Sciences (1699–1741) and through such works as *Conversations on the Plurality of Inhabited Worlds* (1686) he paved the way for the skeptical philosophers of the French ENLIGHTENMENT.

FONTEYN, Dame Margot (Dame Margot Fonteyn de Arias; 1919–   ), English prima ballerina of the Royal Ballet. Before WWII she had danced leads in *Giselle*, *Swan Lake* and *The Sleeping Beauty*, and ASHTON had begun choreographing works for her. She retired from the Royal Ballet in 1959, but continued to appear as a guest star and in 1962 formed a dance partnership with NUREYEV that won new international fame for both of them.

FOOD AND AGRICULTURE ORGANIZATION (FAO), agency of the UN, established in 1945, with headquarters in Rome. It provides member nations with information on food and agricultural problems and with technical and financial aid.

FOOD AND DRUG ADMINISTRATION, US (FDA), Federal agency in the Department of Health and Human Services, set up in 1940 to enforce the laws maintaining standards in the sale of food and drugs. Originally concerned largely with preventing adulteration and poor food hygiene, the FDA is now also involved in testing the safety, reliability and usefulness of drugs and chemicals, and assessing the effects on health of "accidental additives" such as PESTICIDES.

FOOD POISONING, disease resulting from ingestion of unwholesome food, usually resulting in colic, vomiting, DIARRHEA and general malaise. While a number of VIRUS, contaminant, irritant and allergic factors may play a part in some cases, three specific types are common:

those due to STAPHYLOCOCCUS, clostridium and SALMONELLA bacteria. Inadequate cooking, allowing cooked food to stand for long periods in warm conditions and contamination of cooked food with bacteria from humans or uncooked food are usual causes. **Staphylococci** may be introduced from a boil or from the nose of a food handler; they produce a TOXIN if allowed to grow in cooked food. Sudden vomiting and abdominal pain occur 2–6 hours after eating. *Clostridium* poisoning causes colic and diarrhea, 10–12 hours after ingestion of contaminated meat. *Salmonella* enteritis causes colic, diarrhea, vomiting and often fever, starting 12–24 hours after eating; poultry and human carriers are the usual sources. BOTULISM is an often fatal form of food poisoning. In general, food poisoning is mild and self-limited, and symptomatic measures only are needed; ANTIBIOTICS rarely help.

FOOD PRESERVATION, a number of techniques used to delay the spoilage of food. There are two main causes of spoilage: one is the PUTREFACTION that follows the death of any plant or animal; the other is over-ripening, the result of the action of certain plant ENZYMES. Heating destroys these enzymes and the BACTERIA responsible for putrefaction but, before it cools, the food must be sealed in sterile cans or bottles, isolated from air-borne bacteria. Freezing slows the enzyme action and the REPRODUCTION of the bacteria and preserves flavor better. Dehydration, irradiation and preservatives are also used. Traditional means of preservation include smoking, salting and pickling. (See also FOOD POISONING; REFRIGERATION.)

FOOD STAMPS, federal WELFARE program, administered by the states, that provides needy households with monthly allotments of stamps or coupons exchangeable like money for food in most food stores. Most households receiving welfare benefits are automatically eligible for food stamps. Other households, including single persons and childless couples, may qualify on the basis of need. The value of the monthly stamp allotment is inversely proportional to household income.

FOOTBALL, popular US sport, played with a leather-covered oval-shaped ball, by two teams of 11 players. The football gridiron or field is 120 yd long by 53 yd 1 ft wide, with two end zones 10 yd deep, each with an H-shaped goal post having a crossbar 10 ft high. Playing time for men is 60 min, divided into two halfs of two quarters each. To score, a team must run or pass the football over the opponent's goal line, or kick it through the uprights of the goal post. A touchdown (running or passing the ball over the goal line) scores six points, a field goal (kicking the ball over the goal post) three points, and after a touchdown an extra point or conversion (usually by kicking the ball over the crossbar) one point. Possession of the ball is the key to scoring; the offensive team has four plays, or downs, to advance 10 yd and keep possession of the ball by gaining a new first down. The defense obtains the ball by stopping the offense from gaining 10 yd within four downs, by intercepting a pass or by recovering a fumble (dropped ball).

Early US football was similar to SOCCER, but today's game evolved from rugby, which permits handling of the ball. In the 1880s the main rules and tactics of American football were devised by Yale U's Walter CAMP, the "father" of the game. The new college sport soon became popular, but public criticism of its physical violence brought about a meeting of President Theodore Roosevelt and college team representatives in 1906 that resulted in banning mass formations and other dangerous practices. Forward passing of the ball was legalized, opening up the strategy and tactics of the game.

Organized professional football began in 1921 with formation of the National Football League, although the Depression of the 1930s and WWII retarded the NFL's development. After the war the televising of the pros' faster, more skillful and hard-hitting style of play contributed to making the sport extremely popular. The two major pro leagues merged in 1966 into the NFL's American and National conferences, each having 14 teams in the early 1980s; a Super Bowl championship game between the conference winners has been played every January since 1967. Canadian football more closely resembles the US game than it does either soccer or rugby.

FORAMINIFERA, single-celled sea animals. Each species has a limy shell which sinks when the foraminifer dies. These shells form deposits of foraminiferan ooze which cover one third of the ocean floor.

FORBES, John (1710–1759), British general in the FRENCH AND INDIAN WARS. In 1758 he commanded an expedition, which included a detachment led by George Washington, from Halifax, Nova Scotia, against Fort Duquesne, on the Ohio R. Despite great hardship Forbes' troops took the fort, renaming it Fort Pitt (now Pittsburgh, Pa.). Emaciated and exhausted, Forbes was taken to Philadelphia where he died.

FORBIDDEN CITY, walled enclosure in Peking, China, containing the imperial palace, its grounds, reception halls and state offices. In imperial times, the Forbidden City was closed to the public.

FORCE, in mechanics, the physical quantity which, when it acts on a body, either causes it to change its state of motion (i.e., imparts to it an ACCELERATION), or tends to deform it (i.e., induces in it an elastic strain. Dynamical forces are governed by NEWTON's laws of motion, from the second of which it follows that a given force acting on a body produces in it an acceleration proportional to the force, inversely proportional to the body's MASS and occurring in the direction of the force. Forces are thus VECTOR quantities with direction as well as magnitude. They may be manipulated graphically like other vectors, the sum of two forces being known as their resultant. The SI UNIT of force is the newton, a force of one newton being that which will produce an acceleration of 1cm/sec^2 in a mass of 1 gram.

FORCES, Fundamental, natural forces posited by scientists to account for all the phenomena of the universe. Until recently, there were four fundamental forces: gravity, the attraction one body exerts on another; electromagnetism, the source of light, radio waves, and other forms of radiation; the "strong force," which binds particles in the nucleus of the atom; and the "weak force," which makes atoms break down in radioactive decay. Albert EINSTEIN and other theoreticians sought to develop a UNIFIED FIELD THEORY in which three and perhaps all four forces would be found to be manifestations of a single force. In recent years, scientists have found evidence of a fifth force, believed to counteract gravity, and a sixth force that seems to enhance gravity.

FORD, Ford Madox (1873–1939), influential English man of letters, born Ford Madox Hueffer. His novels *The Good Soldier* (1915) and *Parade's End* (1924–28), a tetralogy, described the decline of the English upper classes before WWI. As first editor of *The English Review* (1908–11), he encouraged such writers as Conrad (with whom he also collaborated), Pound, Frost and D. H. Lawrence.

FORD, Gerald Rudolph, Jr. (1913–   ), 38th president of the US. Born Leslie King, Jr., in Omaha, Neb., Ford was adopted and renamed before he was two by his mother's second husband. Ford grew up in Grand Rapids, Mich., graduated from the U. of Michigan, where he had been a star football

player, worked his way through Yale U. Law School as a coach, and returned home to practice law in 1941. He served four years in the Navy during WWII, becoming a lieutenant-commander.

Ford ran for Congress in 1948 and won. He became a hard-working Congressman and remained in the House of Representatives for 25 years. He obtained a seat on the powerful House Appropriations Committee and was known as a conservative and an internationalist. In 1964 Ford became Republican Minority Leader of the House.

Several times Ford was considered as a possible vice-presidential nominee, but he remained in the House. On Oct. 12, 1973, President Nixon nominated Ford to succeed Spiro Agnew as vice-president. On Aug. 9, 1974, Nixon resigned the presidency over the WATERGATE crisis and Ford took the oath of office, declaring, "Our long national nightmare is over . . . Our Constitution works." Ford lost popularity because of his pardon of Nixon and because of inflation and economic recession. The US-supported regime in Vietnam was overthrown by the communists in 1975. Ford narrowly lost the 1976 presidential election to Jimmy CARTER.

FORD, Henry (1863–1947), American automobile production pioneer. He produced his first automobile in 1896 and established the Ford Motor Company, Dearborn, Mich., in 1903. By adopting mass-assembly methods, and introducing the moving assembly line in 1913, Ford revolutionized automobile production. Ford saw that mass-produced cars could sell at a price within reach of the average American family. His Model T sold 15 million (1908–26). Ford was a paradoxical and often controversial character. Although a proud anti-intellectual, he set up several museums and the famous FORD FOUNDATION. A violent anti-unionist, he reduced the average working week, introduced profit-sharing and the highest minimum daily wage of his time. In 1938 he accepted a Nazi decoration and became a leading isolationist. At the outbreak of war, however, he built the world's largest assembly plant, to produce B-24 bombers.

FORD, Henry II (1917–1987), US automotive executive, the grandson of Henry Ford. He revivified the ailing Ford Motor Co. during the 1940s and 1950s and served as its chief executive officer from 1960 to 1979.

FORD, John (1586–1640?), English dramatist. Three tragedies, *'Tis Pity She's a Whore* (c.1627), *The Broken Heart* (c.1629) and *Love's Sacrifice* (1630), are his best-known works. Considered decadent by earlier critics because of his lack of moral comment, Ford's insight into human passion has been admired in the 20th century.

FORD, John (1895–1973), US motion picture director. One of the great masters of his craft, he began directing the first of his more than 125 films in 1917. He won Academy Awards for *The Informer* (1935), *The Grapes of Wrath* (1941), *How Green Was My Valley* (1942), and *The Quiet Man* (1953). In later years, his principal output was Westerns, a form he had pioneered with such early films as *The Iron Horse* (1924) and *Stagecoach* (1939).

FORD FOUNDATION, philanthropic corporation founded by Henry Ford in 1936. With assets of over $3 billion, it is the world's largest philanthropic trust. The foundation uses its funds for educational, cultural, scientific and charitable purposes in the US and abroad.

FOREIGN LEGION, elite mercenary army created in 1831 by the French to save manpower in Algeria. The legion fought mainly outside France until Algerian independence (1962): in Morocco, Madagascar, Spain, Mexico, the Crimea and Indochina.

FOREIGN SERVICE, diplomatic and consular employees of the US Department of State. They staff embassies and consulates, promote friendly relations between the US and countries where they serve, advise on political and economic matters, protect and aid US citizens abroad and deal with aliens seeking entry to the US. (See also STATE, US DEPARTMENT OF.)

FORENSIC MEDICINE, the branch of MEDICINE concerned with legal aspects of DEATH, DISEASE or injury. Forensic medical experts are commonly required to examine corpses found in possibly criminal circumstances. They may be asked to elucidate probable cause and approximate time of death, to investigate the possibility of POISONING, trauma or suicide, to analyze links with possible murder weapons and to help to identify decayed or mutilated bodies.

FORESTER, C(ecil) **S**(cott) (1899–1966), English novelist, best known for his popular Captain Hornblower novels set in the Napoleonic period. An earlier novel, *The African Queen* (1935), was made into an Academy Award-winning film in 1951.

FORESTRY, management of forests for productive purposes. In the US, a forestry program emerged in the 1890s because of fears of a "timber famine" and following exploitation of the Great Lakes pine forests.

Congress authorized the first forest reserves in 1891; creation of the FOREST SERVICE in 1905 put forestry on a scientific basis.

The most important aspect of forestry is the production of lumber. Because of worldwide depletion of timber stocks, it has become necessary to view forests as renewable productive resources, and because of the time scale and area involved in the growth of a forest, trees need more careful planning than any other crop. Forestry work plans for a continuity of timber production by balancing planting and felling. Other important functions are disease, pest, fire and flood control. The forester must control the density and proportions of the various trees in a forest and ensure that man does not radically disturb a forest's ecological balance.

The science of forestry is well advanced in the US, which is the world's largest timber producer and has more than 25 forestry schools across the country. However, only 20% of the world's forests are being renewed, and timber resources are declining.

FOREST SERVICE, US, Department of Agriculture agency, created in 1905 to manage and protect the national forests. Nearly 190 million acres of national forests and grasslands, as well as 480 million acres of forests and watersheds belonging to state and local governments and private owners, benefit from the service's conservation, research, development and advisory programs.

FORGERY, in law, the making or altering of a written instrument with intent to defraud. As a general term it is used of anything, such as a work of art or literature, made or altered with intent to deceive whether fraudulently or not. This is usually not criminal unless done for some kind of gain. Art forgeries are common, but are easier to detect than is commonly supposed; literary forgeries, such as Thomas Chatterton's pseudo-medieval "Rowley" poems, have seldom survived for long. Forgeries are usually detected through errors in either content or material. It is almost impossible, for example, to age paper or canvas artificially. The most successful modern art forger, however, the Dutchman Hans van Meegeren, was detected only when he confessed to forgery to escape a charge of selling art treasures to the Nazis. The term for forgery of money is COUNTERFEITING.

FORGING, the shaping of metal by hammering or pressing, usually when the workpiece is red hot (about 400–700°C) but sometimes when it is cold. Unlike

CASTING, forging does not alter the granular structure of the metal, and hence greater strength is possible in forged than in cast metals. The most basic method of forging is that of the blacksmith, who heats the metal in an open fire (forge) and hammers it into shape against an anvil. Today, metals are forged between two dies, usually impressed with the desired shape. Techniques include: **drop forging**, where the workpiece is held on the lower, stationary die, the other being held by a massive ram which is allowed to fall; **press forging**, where the dies are pressed together; and **impact forging**, where the dies are rammed horizontally together, the workpiece between. (See also METALLURGY.)

FORMOSA. See CHINA, REPUBLIC OF.

FORMULA, Chemical, a symbolic representation of the composition of a MOLECULE. The **empirical formula** shows merely the proportions of the atoms in the molecule, as found by chemical ANALYSIS. e.g., water H_2O, acetic acid CH_2O. (The subscripts indicate the number of each atom if more than one.) The **molecular formula** shows the actual number of atoms in the molecule, e.g., water H_2O, acetic acid $C_2H_4O_2$. The atomic symbols are sometimes grouped to give some idea of the molecular structure, e.g., acetic acid CH_3COOH. This is done unambiguously by the **structural formula**, which shows the chemical BONDS and so distinguishes between isomers. The **space formula** shows the arrangement of the atoms and bonds in three-dimensional space, and so distinguishes between stereoisomers; it may be drawn in perspective or represented conventionally.

FORREST, Edwin (1806–1872), prominent American tragedian; the first US actor actively to encourage native playwrights. His feud with English actor William Macready led to a notorious riot at New York's Astor Place Opera House on May 8, 1849.

FORREST, Nathan Bedford (1821–1877), Confederate cavalry general, esteemed for bravery and brilliant leadership. His several victories over Union forces included capturing Fort Pillow, Tenn., during which many Negro defenders were killed. Later that year (1864) he commanded all cavalry under J. B. HOOD in the Tenn. campaign.

FORRESTAL, James Vincent (1892–1949), US public official. An investment banker, he was appointed undersecretary of the navy (1940), secretary of the navy (1944), and the first secretary of defense (1947).

FORSTER, E(dward) M(organ) (1879–1970), a major English novelist of the early 20th century. His novels are *Where Angels Fear to Tread* (1905), *The Longest Journey* (1907), *A Room with a View* (1908), *Howard's End* (1910), *A Passage to India* (1924) and *Maurice* (1971). Forster's major themes concern conflict in human relations—between truth and falsehood, "culture" and instinct or emotion, and the inner and outer life. His *Aspects of the Novel* (1927) was an influential critical work.

FORTAS, Abe (1910–1982), US lawyer and Supreme Court justice. Although he held several governmental offices, he achieved greatest success as a lawyer. He was named to the court in 1965, but in 1968 the Senate rebuffed President Johnson's attempt to promote him to chief justice. He resigned (1969) after allegations of conflict of interest in financial dealings.

FORT DEARBORN, military post built on the site of Chicago (1803) and named for Secretary of War Henry DEARBORN, who ordered its construction. On the outbreak of the War of 1812, it suffered an Indian attack and many of the garrison were killed and others made captive. The fort was later rebuilt (1816–17), and was one of the centers around which Chicago developed. It was finally abandoned in 1837, the year in which Chicago received its city charter.

FORT DUQUESNE, French fortification in the FRENCH AND INDIAN WARS built in 1754 on the present site of Pittsburgh, Pa. Target of English general Edward BRADDOCK's unsuccessful expedition in 1755, it was taken by Gen. John FORBES in 1758 and renamed Fort Pitt.

FORT HALL, historic fur-trading port on the Snake R, SE Idaho, an important landmark and garrison post on the OREGON TRAIL. It was built in 1834 and operated until 1855.

FORTIFICATION, military construction for defense or protection. Two main types are permanent fortification (forts, castles, defense zones), usually built in peacetime, and field works, temporary defense systems in combat zones. Permanent structures such as walls, forts or castles have been important in most countries thoughout world history. Artillery revolutionized fortification: walls and towers became lower and thicker; bastions and gun platforms were set at calculated angles in walls; and concrete came into use. Field works can be hasty (fox or shell hole, shallow trench) or deliberate (rampart, trench, bunker, obstacles such as mines or wire), and have been used in war since ancient times.

FORT KNOX, a US military reservation in N Hardin Co., N central Ky., 33,000 acres in size and established in 1917 as a training camp. It has been a permanent military post since 1932, and the site of the US Gold Bullion Depository since 1936. Godman Air Force Base is also there.

FORT McHENRY, fort in Baltimore harbor, Md. During the War of 1812, it withstood overnight bombardment by a British fleet. This inspired Francis Scott Key, a spectator, to write the words to *The Star-Spangled Banner*, which became the US national anthem.

FORT NECESSITY, entrenchment built by George WASHINGTON in SW Pa. in July 1754, at Great Meadows. The clash with French troops which led to Washington's surrender on July 4 was one of the early battles in the last of the FRENCH AND INDIAN WARS.

FORT NIAGARA, National Monument in NW N.Y., a stone fortress built (1726) by the French at the mouth of the Niagara R. Captured in 1759 by the British, it was ceded to the US in 1796. During the WAR OF 1812 it was briefly recaptured by the British.

FORTS HENRY AND DONELSON, Confederate fortifications protecting Nashville, Tenn. In the first major Union victories of the Civil War, Gen. U.S. GRANT took Fort Henry, on the Tennessee R, on Feb. 6, 1862, and Fort Donelson, on the Cumberland R, on Feb. 16, after which the Confederates abandoned Nashville.

FORT SUMTER, fort in Charleston harbor, S.C., where the first shots in the Civil War were fired on April 12, 1861. When S.C. seceded from the Union (1860), US Maj. Robert Anderson received a rebel summons to surrender his garrison. He refused, Sumter was fired upon, and the war had begun. The fort was retaken when Confederates evacuated Charleston in Feb. 1865.

FOSDICK, Harry Emerson (1878–1969), US Protestant clergyman, founder (1931) with John D. Rockefeller, Jr., of New York's nonsectarian Riverside Church.

FOSS, Lukas (Lukas Fuchs; 1922–   ), German-born US composer who developed a method of simultaneous improvisation, and experimented with electronic effects, the use of prerecorded tape, and aleatory composition, as in *Echoi* (1961–63) and *Cello Concerto* (1966). He championed contemporary music as conductor of the Buffalo, Brooklyn, and Milwaukee symphony orchestras.

FOSSE, Robert Louis (1927–1987), US dancer, choreographer, and stage and film director. His Broadway successes included *Pajama Game* (1954) and *Damn Yankees* (1955). He choreographed and directed the films *Sweet Charity* (1966), *Cabaret* (1972), and *All That Jazz* (1979).

FOSSIL FUELS, fuels — namely oil, gas, and coal — that are residues of fossil plants. Currently they supply over 90% of US energy needs. Because their supply is finite and nonrenewable, the fossil-fuel era in world history, which began with the industrial use of coal in the 19th century, will be relatively short. Nevertheless, world supplies of fossil fuels remain considerable. Present reserves of oil and natural gas may be enlarged by exploration of hitherto neglected areas of Africa, South America, and Asia. There are vast quantities of petroleum trapped in tar sands and oil shale. Coal reserves are sufficient for several centuries. The development of these resources, however, will be accomplished only at significantly higher costs and with important consequences for the environment. Eventually, fossil fuels will have to be superseded by other, renewable energy sources such as GEOTHERMAL ENERGY, HYDROELECTRICITY, NUCLEAR ENERGY, and SOLAR ENERGY.

FOSSILS, evidences of ancient life preserved in sediment or rock. The preservation of most body fossils usually requires the possession of hard skeletal parts and rapid burial of the organism so as to prevent its decay and/or destruction. Common skeletal materials include bone, calcium carbonate, opaline silica, chitin and tricalcium phosphate. Preservation of an organism in its entirety (i.e., unaltered hard and soft parts together) is exceptional, e.g. MAMMOTHS in Siberian PERMAFROST. Unaltered hard parts are common in post-Mesozoic sediments but become increasingly scarcer further back in geologic time.

Petrification describes two ways in which the shape of hard parts of the organism may be preserved. In permineralization, the pore spaces of the hard parts are infilled by certain minerals (e.g., silica, PYRITE, calcite) that infiltrate from the local GROUNDWATER. The resulting fossil is thus a mixture of mineral and organic matter. In many other cases, substitution (or replacement) occurs, where the hard parts are dissolved away but the form is retained by newly deposited minerals. Where this has happened very gradually, even microscopic detail may be preserved; but generally only the outward form remains.

Often the skeletal materials are dissolved entirely, leaving either internal or external molds. The filling of a complete mold may also occur, forming a cast. The complete filling of a hollow shell interior may form a core or **steinkern** such as the corkscrewlike filling of a coiled snail shell.

In the process of **carbonization** the tissues decompose, leaving only a thin residual CARBON film that shows the outline of the organism's flattened form. In addition to interest in body fossils, there is also much interest in trace fossils, which include more indirect evidences of the former presence of an organism.

FOSTER, Stephen Collins (1826–1864), US composer of over 200 songs and instrumental pieces. His *Oh! Susannah, My Old Kentucky Home* and *Old Black Joe* and other Southern dialect songs are essentially so simple that they are often considered folk music.

FOSTER, William Zebulon (1881–1961), US communist leader, organizer of the 1919 steel strike. He joined the Communist Party (c1921) and was its candidate for president (1924; 1928; 1932) and for governor of N.Y. (1930).

FOSTER GRANDPARENT PROGRAM (FGP), volunteer program instituted in 1965 and administered by ACTION. It offers men and women over 60 opportunities to help children with special needs in schools and hospitals for the mentally retarded or handicapped; in care centers, hospital wards, and corrections institutions; and in homes for disadvantaged, dependent, or neglected children.

FOUCAULT, Jean Bernard Léon (1819–1868), French physicist best known for showing the rotation of the earth with the FOUCAULT PENDULUM, for inventing the GYROSCOPE and for the first reasonably accurate determination of the velocity of LIGHT.

FOUCAULT, Michel (1926–1984), French philosopher best known for his social history and epistomology. His works include *Madness and Civilization* (1965), *The Order of Things* (1971), *The Archeology of Knowledge* (1972) and *The History of Sexuality* (1978).

FOUCAULT PENDULUM, a long pendulum used to demonstrate the rotation of the earth. In 1851, Jean FOUCAULT, a French physicist, suspended a large iron ball by 200ft of wire from the center of the dome of the Pantheon in Paris. He laid a thin layer of sand on the floor and set the pendulum swinging. With each swing, the ball traced a fine groove in the sand. It soon became evident that the line of the swing was turning slowly clockwise, and that the pendulum was moving independently of the earth's rotation. The swing of a Foucault pendulum is clockwise in the Northern

Hemisphere and anticlockwise in the Southern Hemisphere. At the equator there is no swing, and the greatest swing (15° per hour) occurs at the poles. Foucault's demonstration was conclusive proof that the earth rotates.

FOUCHÉ, Joseph (1759–1820), French revolutionary. A Jacobin who played a leading part in the Terror, he later served Napoleon as police minister.

FOUNTAIN OF YOUTH, a rejuvenating spring located according to legend on the Bimini Islands off the coast of Fla. The Spaniard PONCE DE LEON discovered Florida in 1513, probably on an expedition to find the fountain.

FOUQUET, Jean (c1420–1480), French painter who helped bring the Italian Renaissance style to France. His miniatures, panels, portraits and manuscript illuminations are realistic and precisely detailed. One of his finest works is the *Melun Diptych* (c1450).

FOUR FREEDOMS, freedom of speech, freedom of worship, freedom from want, freedom from fear. These principles were first presented by President Roosevelt in 1941 as a basis for world peace. After WWII the freedoms became enshrined in the UN Charter. (See DECLARATION OF HUMAN RIGHTS.)

FOUR HORSEMEN OF THE APOCALYPSE, allegorical biblical figures in the book of Revelation (often called the Apocalypse) 6:1-8. The red horse's rider represents war, the black's famine, the pale horse's rider death, while the rider on the white horse is usually taken to represent Christ.

FOUR HUNDRED, The, term used to describe elite society in New York City, or generally. The phrase is derived from Ward MCALLISTER'S controversial comment (1892) that there were only about 400 important members of N.Y. society.

FOURIER, François Marie Charles (1772–1837), French Utopian socialist. Rejecting CAPITALISM, he devised a social system based on cooperative, primarily farming COMMUNES of about 400 families. Fourierism gained considerable following in France and the US, but attempts to put his theories into practice, as at BROOK FARM, were short-lived. (See also UTOPIA.)

FOURIER, Jean Baptiste Joseph, Baron (1768–1830), French mathematician best known for his equations of HEAT propagation and for showing that all periodic oscillations can be reduced to a series of simple, regular WAVE MOTIONS.

FOURTEEN POINTS, war objectives for the US, proposed by President Wilson in

Jan. 1918, incorporated in the armistice of Nov. 1918. The points were that there should be: open covenants of peace; freedom of the seas; abolition of trade barriers; general disarmament; settlement of colonial claims; evacuation of conquered Russian territories; evacuation and restoration of Belgium; return of Alsace-Lorraine to France; readjustment of Italian frontiers; autonomy for the subject peoples of Austria and Hungary; guarantees for the integrity of Serbia, Montenegro and Romania; autonomy for the subject peoples of the Ottoman Empire; an independent Poland; and a general association of nations. These points formed the basis of the Treaty of VERSAILLES and the LEAGUE OF NATIONS.

FOURTH DIMENSION. See SPACE-TIME.

FOWLER, Henry Watson (1858–1933), distinguished English lexicographer, best-known for his masterly *A Dictionary of Modern English Usage* (1926). Fowler collaborated with his brother on several books, including *The Concise Oxford Dictionary of Current English* (1911).

FOWLES, John (1926–   ), English novelist. Often attempting to reconcile the Victorian novel form with more philosophical concerns, he has written such passionate, sometimes difficult works as *The Magus* (1966; rev. version, 1978), *The French Lieutenant's Woman* (1969) and *A Maggot* (1985).

FOX, Charles James (1749–1806), English statesman and orator, champion of political and religious freedom and fierce opponent of George III and the power of the crown. He served in Parliament from 1768 as a Tory and as a Whig, both in and out of government. He championed the colonists in the REVOLUTIONARY WAR (1775–83) and in the 1790s supported the French Revolution.

FOX, Fontaine Talbot Jr. (1884–1964), US cartoonist, creator of *Toonerville Folks* (1915–55).

FOX, George (1624–1691), English religious leader, founder of the Society of Friends or QUAKERS (1652). Although frequently harassed and imprisoned by the authorities, Fox traveled widely in Europe and North America preaching his doctrine—derived from his conversion experience (1646)—that truth comes through the inner light of Christ in the soul. (See also MYSTICISM.)

FOX, William (1879–1952), Hungarian-born US film producer, founder (1915) of the Fox Film Corp., which became (1935) 20th Century-Fox. He introduced (1927) *Movietone News*.

FOXES, small members of the dog family

Canidae, noted for their cunning and solitary habits; foxes feed mainly on small mammals. The common red fox of the N Hemisphere is the quarry of British fox-hunts; American foxes include the gray fox, the desert kit fox and the now rare swift fox. The Arctic fox lives in northern tundras and has a white winter coat. Africa offers the insect-eating Bat-eared fox and South America the crab-eating fox.

FOX TALBOT, William Henry. See TALBOT, WILLIAM HENRY FOX.

FOXX, James Emory (1907–1967), US baseball player. In a 21-season career with the Philadelphia Athletics (1925–35), the Boston Red Sox (1936–42), the Chicago Cubs (1942–44) and the Philadelphia Phillies (1945), he hit 534 home runs. His usual position was first base.

FRA ANGELICO. See ANGELICO, FRA.

FRACTURES, mechanical defects in BONE caused by trauma or underlying DISEASE. Most follow sudden bending, twisting or shearing forces, but prolonged stress (e.g., long marches) may lead to small fractures. Fractures may be *open*, in which bone damage is associated with SKIN damage, with consequent liability to infection; or *closed*, in which the overlying skin is intact. Comminuted fractures are those in which bone is broken into many fragments. *Greenstick* fractures are partial fractures where bone is bent, not broken, and occur in children. Severe pain, deformity, loss of function, abnormal mobility of a bone and HEMORRHAGE, causing swelling and possibly SHOCK, are important features; damage to nerves, ARTERIES and underlying viscera (e.g., LUNG, SPLEEN, LIVER and BRAIN) are serious complications. Principles of treatment are: reduction, or restoring the bone to satisfactory alignment, by manipulation or operation; immobilization with plaster, splints or internal fixation with metal or bone prostheses, until bony healing has occurred, and rehabilitation, which enables full recovery of function in most cases. Early recognition and appropriate treatment of associated soft tissue injury is crucial. **Pathological fractures** occur when congenital defect, lack of mineral content, TUMORS etc. weaken the structure of bone, allowing fracture with trivial or no apparent injury.

FRAGONARD, Jean-Honoré (1732–1806), French ROCOCO painter and noted portraitist. His work is characterized by a lightness of touch and a use of radiant color. Among his masterpieces are *The Swing* (1766) and *Fête at St. Cloud* (1775), which convey the atmosphere of erotic playfulness and gaiety cultivated at the court of Louis

XV.

FRANCE, Anatole (Jacques Anatole François Thibault; 1844–1924), French novelist and critic, a renowned stylist. Though he believed in and worked for social justice, his work is deeply pessimistic. Among his best-known books are *Penguin Island* (1908) and *The Revolt of the Angels* (1914). He won the 1921 Nobel literature prize.

FRANCE, officially the French Republic, the largest country in W Europe, covering some 211,000sq mi. It is bordered on the N by the English Channel; on the NE by Belgium and Luxembourg; on the E by West Germany, Switzerland and Italy; on the S (where Monaco forms a small enclave) by the Mediterranean, Spain and Andorra; and on the W by the Atlantic Ocean; and it includes the island of Corsica. The whole area is known as metropolitan France, and is divided administratively into 95 departments grouped into 22 regions. In addition, the former colonies of Guadeloupe, French Guiana, Martinique, Réunion, and Saint Pierre and Miquelon rank as overseas departments.

Official name: The French Republic
Capital: Paris
Area: 210,026sq mi
Population: 55,623,000
Languages: French
Religions: Catholic, Protestant, Jewish
Monetary unit(s): 1 French franc=100 centimes

Land. More than 50% of metropolitan France is lowlying and less than 25% is highland. The main mountain ranges form natural frontiers: the Pyrenees in the SW, the French Alps (with Mont Blanc, 15,781ft, the highest peak in W Europe) in the SE, and the Jura and Vosges (separated by the Belfort Gap, an important routeway) in the E. A major physical feature is the Massif Central (central plateau) W of the Saône and Rhône rivers and terminated in the S by the Cévennes Mts. Its features include lava plateaus and *puys* (ash and lava cones). In the NW is the small and much lower Armorican Massif. The

lowlands are mainly in the N and W and include the Paris Basin (about 29,000sq mi) between the English Channel and the Massif Central, the Ile-de-France, a fertile plateau and the triangular Aquitaine lowland in the SW.

Draining the country are five major river systems: the Seine (historically and commercially France's most important river), Loire, Garonne-Gironde, Rhône-Saône, and Rhine. Most have important canal links, and some provide hydroelectric power, notably the Rhône. Coastal features include the *rias* (long inlets) of the Armorican Massif, the sand dunes and lagoons of the Landes in the SW, and the marshy lagoons of the Rhône delta.

The climate is mainly mild but has many regional variations. More than half of France has less than 80 days with frost annually, and most areas average 20-50in of rain yearly. The Riviera and Corsica have a typically Mediterranean climate. Vegetation ranges from the beech and oak of N and central France to the drought-resistant scrub and wild olives of Mediterranean areas.

People. Due to invasions by Romans, Celts, Franks and Mediterranean peoples, the French are of mingled racial types. Distinctive groups include the Celtic Bretons of Brittany and the Basques living along the Spanish frontier. The population also includes more than 750,000 Algerians and some 3,500,000 migrant workers, including many Spaniards and Italians. More than 70% of the people live in the cities and towns; the largest is Paris, the capital. The Paris megalopolis has more than 15% of the total population. Other large conurbations are Lyons, Marseilles and Lille-Roubaix-Tourcoing. People are increasingly moving from the rural areas into the towns.

Most French people are baptized Roman Catholic, but many are not practicing Catholics. Minority groups include Protestants, Jews and Muslims. The French are proud of their education system; illiteracy is negligible. French culture has had worldwide influence on social intercourse, diplomacy, arts, crafts and architecture since the Middle Ages.

Economy. France is a major agricultural and industrial country, leading W Europe in food production. Leading crops include wheat (especially in the Paris Basin and Flanders), oats, rye and corn, sugar beets (Brittany and Flanders), rice (the Camargue) and all kinds of fruits. Millions of beef and dairy cattle, sheep and hogs are reared. The NW is known for its dairy products. France is the world's third-largest silk-producer and leads in the production of high-quality wines from such areas as Champagne, Bordeaux and lower Burgundy. About 20% of the land is forested, and fisheries, centered on such ports as Boulogne and Lorient, are important. France has coal (Nord, Pas de Calais, Lorraine), oil (Parentis), natural gas (Lacq), abundant iron ore (mainly Lorraine but also in Normandy), bauxite and other minerals. Industry includes iron and steel production, mainly in the N and E (especially Dunkerque) but also in the S (Fos-sur-Mer), oil refining (mainly of imported oil) and petrochemicals, aircraft, automobiles and textiles (Lyons, Roubaix, Lille, Tourcoing, Castres). Paris is the chief manufacturing center. Tourism is important, and so is the production of high fashion clothing, gloves, perfume, jewelry and watches.

History. Among early inhabitants were the Stone Age hunter-painters of such caves as Lascaux (Dordogne) and the megalith builders in Brittany. Greeks founded Marseilles about 600 BC. The country was progressively settled and unified under the Gauls, Romans and Franks. On Charlemagne's death (814 AD) the Frankish Empire disintegrated and feudal rulers became powerful. Their territories were increasingly welded together under the CAPETIANS (987–1328), and the HUNDRED YEARS' WAR (1338–1453) saw the eviction of the English. Under Louis XI (1461–83) and later monarchs, royal power was strengthened, reaching its zenith with Louis XIV (1643–1715). Continuing royal extravagance culminated in the FRENCH REVOLUTION (1789), the execution of Louis XVI and the establishment of the First Republic. The Bourbon restoration following on the downfall of NAPOLEON (1815) was short-lived, and Louis Philippe was put on the throne (July Revolution, 1830). After his deposition, Louis Napoleon Bonaparte headed the Second Republic (1848), then made himself Emperor NAPOLEON III (1852). Defeat in the Franco-Prussian War (1870) led to his downfall and to the Third Republic. WWI left France victorious but devastated, and in WWII the country was occupied by Germany (1940). The Fourth Republic (1946) proved unstable and Gen. Charles DE GAULLE was recalled to head the Fifth Republic (1958). He established a strong presidential government, gave independence to most French possessions (notably Algeria, 1962) but pursued conservative policies at home, and stressed greater independence from the United

States in foreign policy. After De Gaulle resigned over a constitutional issue (1969), his conservative policies were maintained by his successors Georges POMPIDOU and Valéry GISCARD D'ESTAING. In 1981 François MITTERRAND, a socialist, was elected president and instituted substantial changes in French domestic policy. The socialists lost their parliamentary majority in 1986, and Mitterrand was compelled to appoint Jacques CHIRAC, a Gaullist, as premier. In this government of "cohabitation," Mitterrand controlled foreign policy, Chirac domestic policy. In the latter area, Chirac pursued a privatization program, selling off state-owned enterprises to private investors. The economy grew slowly, and unemployment was high. Chirac sought the presidency himself in 1988 but was defeated by Mitterrand and resigned. The socialists were again a majority in parliament, and Mitterrand appointed as premier a popular moderate socialist, Michel Rocard.

FRANCIS, name of two Holy Roman Emperors. **Francis I** (1708–1765), Holy Roman Emperor from 1745, was consort of Maria Theresa of Austria from 1736. **Francis II** (1768–1835), last Holy Roman Emperor (1792–1806) and first emperor of Austria (from 1804), was defeated by Napoleon in 1796, 1805 (AUSTERLITZ) and 1809. He then sided with Napoleon until 1813, when he joined the anti-Napoleonic side. At the Congress of VIENNA, through the diplomacy of METTERNICH, he regained most of the Austrian territories.

FRANCIS, two kings of France. **Francis I** (1494–1547), king from 1515, strengthened royal power at the expense of the nobility. He conducted costly wars against the Hapsburgs, including abortive Italian campaigns. He suppressed Protestantism but fostered Renaissance ideals; he was a great patron of art and letters, and a great builder of palaces. **Francis II** (1544–1560), king from 1559, first husband of MARY QUEEN OF SCOTS. A weak-willed man, he was dominated by the House of Guise and his mother, Catherine de MEDICIS.

FRANCISCANS, largest order in the Roman Catholic Church. Three orders were founded by St. FRANCIS OF ASSISI between 1209 and 1224. They were called Grey Friars for the color of their habits; modern habits are dark brown. Dissension within the First Order divided it into three main branches, the Observants, Conventuals and CAPUCHINS. The Second Order are nuns, known as Poor Clares for their foundress St. Clare. The Third Order is mainly a lay fraternity, though some members live in community under vows.

FRANCIS OF ASSISI, Saint (c1181–1226), Italian Roman Catholic mystic, founder of the FRANCISCANS. In 1205 he turned away from his extravagant life and wealthy merchant family to a wandering religious life of utter poverty. With his many followers he preached and ministered to the poor in Italy and abroad, stressing piety, simplicity and joy in creation, and the love of all living things. Given oral sanction by Pope Innocent III, his order expanded beyond the control of its founder; he relinquished the leadership in 1221. His feast day is Oct. 4.

FRANCIS OF SALES, Saint (1567–1622), Roman Catholic bishop of Geneva-Annecy from 1603. Author of popular works such as *Introduction to the Devout Life* (1608), he was respected even by the Calvinists for his good nature and humility. He helped found the Order of the Visitation (1610). His feast day is Jan. 24.

FRANCIS XAVIER, Saint (1506–1552), Spanish missionary. A friend of St. IGNATIUS OF LOYOLA, he was a founder member of the JESUITS. In 1541 he set out as a missionary, reaching the East Indies, Goa, India, Malacca and Ceylon. In 1549 he established a Jesuit mission in Japan and in 1552 sought to extend his work to China, but died before he reached there. His feast day is Dec. 3.

FRANCK, César Auguste (1822–1890), Belgian French composer. Organist of St. Clothilde, Paris, from 1858, he became a professor at the Paris Conservatory in 1872. Though at first little appreciated, his compositions greatly influenced French Romantic music. Among his famous works are the tone poem *The Accursed Hunter* (1882) and the *Symphony in D minor* (1888).

FRANCO, Francisco (1892–1975), Spanish general, *caudillo* (Spanish: leader, head of state) of Spain from 1939. Kept in foreign commands by leftwing governments, he joined the 1936 military revolt in Spain from Morocco and in 1937 became leader of the Falange party and head of the anti-republican army. After the fall of Madrid he became head of state. Although he had been aided against the Soviet-backed Loyalists by Germany and Italy he remained neutral in WWII. In the postwar period his rule became less totalitarian but he retained all his power. In the late 1960s increasing unrest caused him to harden the regime once more; he remained in control until shortly before his death, when he was succeeded by Prince JUAN CARLOS as king.

FRANCO-PRUSSIAN WAR (July 1870–May 1871), arose from BISMARCK's desire to unify the German states against a common enemy and NAPOLEON III's fear of an alliance against him if a Prussian prince succeeded to the Spanish throne. Provoked by the Ems Dispatch (Bismarck's version of French demands concerning the Spanish question), France declared war; the more efficient Prussians trapped a large French army at Metz, and in Sept. 1870 captured the main French army and Napoleon himself at Sedan. The Second Empire fell and Paris was besieged; despite vigorous resistance led by Leon Gambetta, the city capitulated in Jan. 1871. William I of Prussia was declared German emperor at Versailles. The PARIS COMMUNE revolt followed. In the treaty, France lost Alsace-Lorraine and incurred crushing indemnities.

FRANK, Anne (1929–1945), German Jewish girl who with her family lived in hiding from the Nazis in Amsterdam 1942–44; betrayed and sent to a concentration camp, she died there of typhus. Her diary, published in 1947, provided the material for a popular play and film.

FRANKENSTEIN, novel by Mary SHELLEY. In an attempt to recreate life, its title character makes a hideous, suffering creature who wavers between good and evil and finally kills his creator. The name has become attached to the creature, particularly as portrayed on film by Boris Karloff.

FRANKENTHALER, Helen (1928–), US painter whose work is considered transitional between abstract expressionism and color-field painting. She often used stains and diluted paints to achieve her effects.

FRANKFURT AM MAIN, historic city on the Main R in West Germany, since medieval times a world center of commerce, industry and finance. Its prosperity was founded on the textile trade, and on the great medieval trade fairs; the city remained independent until taken by Prussia in 1866. It was largely devastated in WWII but some old buildings, including its Gothic cathedral, still survive. A major river port, it is a rail and road junction with Germany's busiest airport. It has a wide range of industries. Pop 595,348.

FRANKFURTER, Felix (1882–1965), US Supreme Court Justice 1939–62, legal adviser to presidents Wilson and F. D. Roosevelt. Known for his liberal views, he advocated the doctrine of judicial restraint, minimizing the judiciary's role in the process of government; he was equally opposed to attempts to obstruct "progressive" legislation and to attempts to further it by undue interpretation.

FRANKLIN, Benjamin (1706–1790), American writer, printer, philosopher, scientist and statesman of the American revolution. Tolerant, urbane and intellectual, he combined the spirit of the ENLIGHTENMENT with his puritan upbringing. Born of a poor family in Boston, Mass., he moved to Philadelphia (1723) and married Deborah Read, by whom he had two children. By his own efforts he made enough money as a publisher and printer to retire at the age of 42 and devote himself entirely to writing, science and public life. His writings include letters, journals, satires, economic and social essays, a revealing *Autobiography* and the aphoristic *Poor Richard's Almanack* (1732). A founder of the American Philosophical Society (1743), he was an enthusiastic researcher and inventor. Experiments in electrostatics (1750–51) led to his famous kite experiment, which proved that lightning was a form of electricity; from this he invented the lightning conductor. He also invented bifocal spectacles, the glass harmonica and the efficient Franklin stove, and developed theories of electricity, heat absorption, meteorology and ocean currents.

In Philadelphia's civic affairs he helped found an insurance company, a hospital, a public library, a night watch and in 1747 the first militia. He served as deputy postmaster general of the colonies 1753–1754 and in 1754 organized defenses in the FRENCH AND INDIAN WARS. As Pennsylvania's delegate to the Albany Congress, he was largely responsible for a plan to unite the colonies under the British crown. He was an important influence for conciliation in pre-Revolutionary years when he acted as Pennsylvania's agent in London.

When he returned home, he helped draft the Declaration of Independence. He was the rebel colonies' commissioner in the French court from 1776 and his diplomatic skill gained them vital French support in the war. He led the independence negotiations and returned home in 1785 to serve as president of the Pennsylvania Executive Council. Franklin supported the abolition of slavery and at 81 became a member of the Constitutional Convention, where despite ill-health he helped formulate the compromise that made the US Constitution possible.

FRANKLIN, Sir John (1786–1847), British rear admiral and explorer who in expeditions during 1819–22 and 1825–27 charted much territory from Hudson Bay N to the Arctic. He set out in 1845 with two ships to find the NORTHWEST PASSAGE; trapped in the ice, the entire expedition perished and was not traced until 1859.

FRANKLIN, John Hope (1915–   ), black US historian, educator and author of books on Negro history, including *From Slavery to Freedom* (6th ed. 1987).

FRANKS, Germanic tribes, living originally E of the Rhine. In the 3rd–5th centuries AD they repeatedly invaded Gaul and finally overran it. CLOVIS I united the disparate tribes under his rule, founding the Christian MEROVINGIAN dynasty; this was weakened by internal conflict, and finally deposed by the CAROLINGIANS in the 8th century. Under the rule of CHARLEMAGNE the Franks reached the height of their power. France and Franconia in Germany are named for them.

FRANZ FERDINAND (1863–1914), archduke of Austria and heir to the Austro-Hungarian Empire. His children's right of succession was forfeited by his morganatic marriage to Sophie Chotek of the lesser nobility. Their assassination at Sarajevo triggered off WWI.

FRANZ JOSEF (1830–1916), emperor of Austria from 1848 and king of Hungary from 1867. He came to the throne in a year of revolutions and was at first highly absolutist. He suppressed a Hungarian revolt in 1849, but in 1867 further unrest forced him to create the Dual Monarchy, giving Hungary internal autonomy. Alliance with Germany (1879) and Italy (1882) created the TRIPLE ALLIANCE. His harsh policies against Serbia were among the causes of WWI. A conservative autocrat but a patron of arts and learning, he was generally liked and respected by his subjects.

FRASER, James Earle (1876–1953), US sculptor, best known for his bronze *The End of the Trail*, one of many works influenced by his youthful friendship with the Dakota Indians. Many of his busts, statues, and bronzes are in Washington, D.C. and New York City. He also designed medals and the Indian head and buffalo on the US 5-cent piece.

FRASER, Malcolm (1930–   ), Australian Liberal prime minister (1975–83). He pursued a policy of cutbacks in public expenditures in order to halve the inflation rate; however, unemployment continued high.

FRASER, Simon (1776–1862), Canadian fur-trader who in establishing a chain of trading posts explored the interior of British Columbia. In 1808 he sailed down most of the British Columbia R (now the Fraser River). In 1816 he was acquitted of the massacre of the Red River Settlement.

FRAUNHOFER'S LINES. When sunlight is examined through a spectroscope it is found that the spectrum is traversed by an enormous number of dark lines parallel to the length of the slit. These dark lines are known as Fraunhofer's lines. KIRCHHOFF conceived the idea that the sun is surrounded by layers of vapors which act as filters of the white light arising from incandescent solids within and which abstract those rays which correspond in their periods of vibration to those of the components of the vapors. Thus reversed or dark lines are obtained due to the absorption by the vapor envelop, in place of the bright lines found in the emission spectrum.

FRAZER, Sir James George (1854–1941), British social anthropologist. In *The Golden Bough: A Study in Magic and Religion* (1890; enlarged 1907–15) he proposed a parallel evolution of thought in all peoples: from magic through religion to science, each with its distinct notion of cause and effect. Despite the apparent error of his conclusions, his work in surveying primitive customs and beliefs was of great value to cultural anthropology.

FRAZIER, Joe (1944–   ), US boxer declared world champion in 1970 after Muhammad Ali's deposition. His title was disputed, but he defeated Ali in the ring in 1971. In 1973 he lost the title to George Foreman.

FREDERICK, name of three Holy Roman Emperors. **Frederick I Barbarossa** (c1123–1190) was elected king of Germany in 1152. Having pacified Germany, where he promoted learning and economic growth, he occupied Lombardy and was crowned king of Italy in 1154 and Holy Roman Emperor in 1155. He was drowned while leading the Third Crusade, and passed into legend as Germany's savior. **Frederick II** (1194–1250) became king of Sicily in 1198 and of Germany in 1211. He was crowned Holy Roman Emperor in 1220. Made titular king of Jerusalem in 1227, he acquired territory in the Holy Land and was crowned in 1229. He was continually at odds with the papacy and was excommunicated three times. A capable administrator, scholar and patron of the arts, he went into a decline after a serious defeat at Parma in 1248. **Frederick III** (1415–1493) was chosen king of Germany in 1440 and obtained election as Holy Roman Emperor in 1452 by making concessions to the papacy, weakening the empire.

FREDERICK, name of three kings of Prussia. **Frederick I** (1657–1713), elector of Brandenburg from 1688, sought the title of

king from the Emperor Leopold I. In 1700 he obtained it in exchange for military aid and crowned himself king of Prussia, the major part of his domain, in 1701. **Frederick II the Great** (1712–1786) was one of the greatest 18th-century monarchs. As a boy his inclinations were artistic rather than military. His father, Frederick William II, resented this and so maltreated the prince that he attempted to escape. He was captured, imprisoned and forced to watch the execution of a friend. Eventually he was readmitted to court and succeeded his father in 1740. He almost immediately used his father's strong army to win Silesia from Austria, thus precipitating the War of the AUSTRIAN SUCCESSION. There followed a period of peace, which he used to strengthen Prussia, encouraging both arts and commerce. Fearing attack by an alliance of Austria, Russia and France, he made a preemptive attack on Saxony in 1756, beginning the SEVEN YEARS' WAR, from which Prussia emerged unscathed but exhausted. Frederick rebuilt the economy at considerable personal expense. Through the partition of Poland and the War of the Bavarian Succession he made further territorial gains for Prussia. By the end of his reign he had doubled the country's area and left it rich, powerful, more humanely governed and dominant in Germany. **Frederick III** (1831–1888), son of Emperor William I, was a cultivated and liberal man. A distinguished army commander, he was a determined opponent of BISMARCK'S imperial policies. Much was expected of his reign, but he died of cancer only three months after his coronation.

FREDERICKSBURG, Battle of (Dec. 13, 1862), in the American Civil War, costly Union defeat in which the Army of the Potomac under Ambrose BURNSIDE failed to dislodge Confederate defenders of Fredericksburg, Va., under Robert E. LEE.

FREDERICK WILLIAM, name of four kings of Prussia. **Frederick William I** (1688–1740), king from 1713, centralized and radically reformed his administration. He spent freely on building up a powerful army but was otherwise frugal to the point of miserliness. **Frederick William II** (1744–1797) reigned from 1786. Nephew of Frederick the Great, he lacked his uncle's military and administrative skill, being most noted as a patron of the arts. Prussia made large territorial gains in his reign, however, by inheritance and through the partition of Poland. **Frederick William III** (1770–1840) reigned from 1797. He resisted demands for internal reforms until the collapse of Prussia in the Napoleonic

Wars. **Frederick William IV** (1795–1861) reigned from 1840, a time of unrest and the growth of the movement for German unity. He resisted most demands for reform until forced by the 1848 revolution to make drastic changes.

FREDERICK WILLIAM (1620–1688), elector of Brandenburg from 1640, known as the Great Elector. By skillful shifting of alliances in an attempt to establish a balance of power he was able to shield his country from the worst of the THIRTY YEARS' WAR and add Prussia to Brandenburg. This and the modern army he created laid the foundations for the country's future predominance in Germany.

FREEDMEN'S BUREAU, the US Bureau of Refugees, Freedmen and Abandoned Lands (1865–72), established during RECONSTRUCTION to act as a welfare agency for freed slaves in the South. It was headed by Major O. O. Howard. Handicapped by inadequate funding and personnel, the bureau nevertheless built Negro hospitals, schools and colleges. It had little success in improving civil rights, due to judicial and congressional hostility; its influence had declined by the time it was dissolved.

FREEDOM OF INFORMATION ACT (FOIA) gives the public right of access to governmental records. Enacted in 1966 and strengthened in 1974, FOIA provides that agencies must respond to requests for information within 10 working days; appeals are supposed to be settled in another 20. FOIA has helped reporters gather material for such important stories as those on the MY LAI massacre and the FBI's illegal harassment of domestic political groups. Most requests under the act come from businesses seeking information in governmental files about their competitors. Some records are exempted from the act, including confidential files of law enforcement and intelligence agencies and information gained by the Federal Trade Commission through subpoenas.

FREEDOM OF RELIGION, right to believe and worship freely, without legal restraint. Religious practices considered contrary to public interest, however, e.g. polygamy, snake handling, and withholding medical treatment from minors, are usually forbidden in the US.

FREEDOM OF SPEECH, right to express facts and opinions without legal restraint. In practice this is usually limited by the laws of libel, and, in extreme cases, sedition. (See also BILL OF RIGHTS; FOUR FREEDOMS.)

FREEDOM OF THE PRESS, right of private individuals to print and distribute information and opinions without interfer-

ence, subject only to laws against indecency, libel and in extreme cases sedition. (See also BILL OF RIGHTS.)

FREEDOM OF THE SEAS, concept in international law to describe the legal status of the high seas as free from the sovereignty of any nation. The high seas are held to be those areas outside the territorial waters of all nations. The concept has never been generally accepted and is increasingly called into question in the matter of sea and seabed resources, such as fish and minerals.

FREEDOM RIDES, bus trips from the North to the South organized in 1961, originally by the CONGRESS OF RACIAL EQUALITY (CORE), for the purpose of protesting and breaking racial-segregation practices in Southern interstate bus terminals. After the first black and white Freedom Riders encountered violence in Ala., other civil rights groups joined the movement, and ugly confrontations between Freedom Riders and racist crowds and local officials continued for some months. In Nov. 1961, the Interstate Commerce Commission banned such segregation.

FREEMASONRY. See MASONRY.

FREE SILVER, 19th-century US political issue started by Western silver interests in an attempt to boost the price of silver, which had been hit by world prices and demonetization in 1873. The idea of "free silver" as an economic panacea was nonsensical but had great appeal among the economically ignorant and those whose debts would be lessened by a cheaper dollar. After the 1893 depression (which it in fact helped precipitate) it became the major issue of the 1896 presidential campaign, with William Jennings BRYAN as its most fervent advocate.

FREE SOIL PARTY, a short-lived US coalition party formed in N.Y. in 1848 to oppose the extension of slavery into the territories. It attracted many famous men, including President Martin VAN BUREN, but polled few votes in the 1848 and 1852 elections, and most members merged with the Republican Party in 1854.

FREE TRADE, international commerce, free from tariffs, quotas or other legal restriction, except nonrestrictive tariffs levied for revenue only. The opposite of free trade is PROTECTIONISM. Among early advocates of free trade were the PHYSIOCRATS, Adam SMITH, David RICARDO and J. S. MILL. Modern economists generally accept free trade but advocate varying degrees of protection to safeguard employment and developing industries, as in the theories of J. M. KEYNES. The US has traditionally been protectionist but since WWII has become committed to freer trade.

FREE VERSE (from French *vers libre*), verse without conventional rhythm or meter, relying instead upon the cadences of the spoken language. It was first developed in 19th-century France as a reaction to the extreme formality of accepted styles. Among its many exponents in English are Walt WHITMAN, D. H. LAWRENCE, Ezra POUND and T. S. ELIOT.

FREE WILL, in philosophy, a faculty of originating an action or decision man is alleged to require if he is to be able to make moral choices. Philosophical theories in which man is assumed to have free will formally conflict with those in which his actions are considered to be determined by causes beyond his control. However, the choice between theories of free will and DETERMINISM may admit of other, intermediate alternatives.

FREEZING POINT, the TEMPERATURE at which a liquid begins to solidify—not always well-defined or equal to the melting point. It usually rises with PRESSURE, solids being slightly denser than liquids, though water is a notable exception; it is lowered by solutes in the liquid, the amount providing an accurate means of determining MOLECULAR WEIGHTS. The solid separating from a solution usually has a different composition from the liquid, and repeated freezing can be used to separate substances. Pure substances can often be "supercooled" below their freezing point for limited periods, as the formation of the solid CRYSTAL requires enucleation by rough surfaces in contact with or particles suspended in the liquid. The freezing point of water is 32°F or 0°C.

FREGE, Gottlob (1848–1925), German logician, father of mathematical LOGIC. Inspired by the earlier work of LEIBNIZ, he tried to show that all mathematical truths could be derived logically from a few simple axioms. After RUSSELL's criticism that his system allowed at least one paradox, he wrote little more; but his work influenced later thinkers such as PEANO, RUSSELL and WHITEHEAD. (See also LOGICAL POSITIVISM.)

FREMONT, John Charles (1813–1890), US explorer, general, politician and popular hero. He mapped much of the territory between the Mississippi valley and the Pacific during the early 1840s. He was caught up in the struggle with Mexico over California, being at one time appointed military governor and the next convicted of mutiny (1847–48), a sentence later commuted by President Polk. Frémont

stood as the Republican Party's first presidential candidate (1856) but was defeated by James BUCHANAN. He had to resign as commander of the Department of the West during the Civil War for exceeding his office by declaring martial law. He was governor of Arizona territory 1878–83.

FRENCH, Daniel Chester (1850–1931), US sculptor best known for his monumental statuary, such as his first work, *The Minute Man* (1875) in Concord, Mass., and the seated *Lincoln* (1922) in the Lincoln Memorial, Washington, D.C.

FRENCH, John Denton Pinkstone, 1st Earl of Ypres (1852–1925), British field marshal, commander of the British Expeditionary Force at the beginning of WWI. He was relieved of his command after the costly retreat from Mons and the battles of Ypres and Loos 1914–15.

FRENCH, Romance language spoken in France and parts of Belgium, Switzerland, Canada and former French and Belgian colonies; it is the official language of 21 countries. It developed from Latin during and after the Roman occupation of Gaul and also from Celtic and Germanic elements. By the 11th century two dialects had developed: in the south the *langue d'oc*, in the north the *langue d'öil*. From the latter came *francien*, the Paris dialect which became modern French as spoken and written since the 17th century.

FRENCH ACADEMY. See ACADÉMIE FRANÇAISE.

FRENCH AND INDIAN WARS, 1689–1763, struggle for supremacy in North America between the British and French and their respective Indian allies. Both countries sought to expand from their initial settlements; their clashes reflected European wars but in general arose from local problems. The first three wars were named for the British monarch of the day. **King William's War** (1689–97) was the American phase of the War of the League of AUGSBURG. It consisted of bloody but disorganized raids on both sides, and was inconclusively ended by the Treaty of RYSWICK. **Queen Anne's War** (1702–13) reflected the War of the SPANISH SUCCESSION. French raids on British territory in the N were beaten off and Acadia (Nova Scotia) was taken. In the S French and Spanish forces unsuccessfully attacked Charleston, S.C. In the Peace of UTRECHT much territory was theoretically ceded to Britain. **King George's War** (1744–1748) was the American phase of the War of the AUSTRIAN SUCCESSION. After much disorganized raiding, New England troops captured Louisbourg in 1745; it was returned in the Treaty of AIX-LA-CHAPELLE, which restored the status quo. **The French and Indian War** (1754–63) was the American arena of the SEVEN YEARS' WAR, and the final British-French clash. It centered on the upper Ohio valley, territory claimed by both sides. The French sought to encircle the British colonies by linking their territory along the St. Lawrence R and the Great Lakes with their Mississippi territory, confining the British E of the Appalachian Mts. In 1753 the French began constructing a line of forts to do this, some on territory claimed by Va. An expedition to build a competing fort there, led by George Washington, was forced back in 1754. In 1755 Gen. Edward BRADDOCK'S expedition to attack Fort Duquesne was ambushed and he was killed; the few successes before 1757 were by colonial troops. In 1758 William PITT came to power in Britain and developed a new strategy; in 1758 Forts Frontenac, Duquesne and Louisbourg were taken, cutting the French lines of communication. In 1759 Gen. James WOLFE captured Quebec. Montreal fell in 1760, and in 1763 the Treaty of PARIS ceded all Canada and a large part of La. to Britain. By thus freeing the colonists from the French threat and giving their troops war experience, the French and Indian War paved the way for the REVOLUTIONARY WAR.

FRENCH GUIANA, French overseas department on the NE coast of South America. The chief town is Cayenne. It is bounded by Suriname on the W and Brazil on the E and S, and consists of a strip of lowland along the 200mi Atlantic coastline and a hilly interior stretching c225mi inland. Its economy rests on forestry and shrimp fishing. The French government, which continues to provide many jobs, opened a space center there in the 1960s. Pop 88,000.

FRENCH HORN. See HORN.

FRENCH REVOLUTION, the first major revolution of modern times. It overthrew the most famous monarchy in Europe, executed the royal family, ended the privileged position of the nobility and replaced the traditional institutions of France with new ones based upon popular sovereignty and democratic rights. Subsequently, through its wars, the Revolution spread the explosive ideas of the sovereignty of the people, liberty of the individual and equality before the law throughout Europe. Although the immediate sequel to the Revolution was the establishment of the Napoleonic empire, its impact survived the Napoleonic interlude, and inaugurated the liberal and democratic movements of the 19th century.

By 1788, in a time of rapid economic growth and the consequent rise of the middle classes, the country was still ruled by the privileged nobility and clergy, the two upper Estates of the STATES-GENERAL. The tax burden fell on the Third Estate, made up of the middle classes and the landowning peasantry; this was further increased by the corruption of the fiscal system. Into this situation the philosophy of the ENLIGHTENMENT introduced the ideal of progress, scientific materialism and the concepts of constitutional monarchy and republicanism on the British and American models. When the nobility thwarted attempts by the royal ministers to reform government finance the king was forced to summon the Estates-General for the first time since 1614. The Third Estate, which outnumbered the other two chambers, demanded that votes be counted individually and not by chamber, giving them a majority; when this was not immediately granted the Third Estate, with sympathetic members of the other two, declared itself the National Assembly on June 20, 1789. Louis XVI agreed to this, but brought troops to Versailles; mobs stormed the BASTILLE prison on July 14, and pillaged the nobility's country estates. On Aug. 4 the Assembly abolished the feudal system and approved the DECLARATION OF THE RIGHTS OF MAN; the royal family was threatened by mobs, the Church disestablished and largely suppressed. The royal family fled in June, hoping to join their sympathizers who had fled abroad, but were arrested at Varennes and returned to Paris. In Oct. 1791 the Legislative Assembly convened under a new constitution, and became increasingly radical in form. Threat of attack from abroad precipitated the FRENCH REVOLUTIONARY WARS. In the face of this crisis the mob again threatened the king, forcing him to replace the Assembly with a radical Convention elected in Sept. 1792, during mob massacres of jailed royalists. The king was tried for treason and executed in Jan. 1793. In the face of royalist insurrection and foreign hostility the JACOBINS now seized power from the more moderate GIRONDINS, transferring power from the Convention to arbitrary bodies such as the Committees for Public Safety and General Security. Dominated by DANTON and ROBESPIERRE, these brought about the REIGN OF TERROR. This ended with Robespierre himself being executed by the Convention in July 1794. The Convention then introduced a new constitution, setting up the DIRECTORY, which proved ineffectual and corrupt. In 1799 it was overthrown by the army, led by the popular general NAPOLEON. He established the Consulate, effectively ending the revolutionary period.

FRENCH REVOLUTIONARY WARS, waged by revolutionary France before the accession of NAPOLEON I. In 1789 France preemptively declared war on and defeated Austria. The First Coalition (Austria, Britain, Prussia, Russia, Spain, and the Netherlands) was defeated 1793–95, France showing surprising if costly military strength. The Second Coalition of Britain, Austria and Russia was defeated 1799–1800, although Napoleon's strike at British-held Egypt failed in 1801.

FRENCH SOMALILAND. See DJIBOUTI.

FRENCH WEST AFRICA, federation of eight French overseas territories, 1895–1958. Its members were Dahomey (now Benin), Guinea, Ivory Coast, Mauritania, Niger, Senegal, Sudan (now Mali) and Upper Volta (now Burkina).

FRENCH WEST INDIES, comprises two islands: MARTINIQUE and GUADELOUPE. They were French colonies until 1946.

FRENEAU, Philip (1752–1832), US poet and journalist, an influential supporter of Thomas Jefferson as editor of the *National Gazette* and other papers.

FREQUENCY MODULATION (FM). See RADIO.

FRESCO, type and technique of wall painting common in ancient Crete and China, and in Europe from the 13th to the 17th centuries. In true fresco, dry earth pigments mixed with water were painted on fresh wet lime-plaster, setting with it. Preparatory drawings (*sinopia*) were often done in red paint on an underlying layer. In *fresco secco* (dry fresco) varnishes are painted on a smooth, non-absorbent surface. Among famous fresco painters are GIOTTO and MICHELANGELO.

FRESCOBALDI, Girolamo (1583–1643), Italian organist, an early master of organ and instrumental composition. His style is bold but logical. He was organist of St. Peter's, Rome, 1608–28 and from 1634.

FRESNEL, Augustin Jean (1788–1827), French physicist who evolved the transverse-wave theory of LIGHT through his work on optical INTERFERENCE. He worked also on reflection, REFRACTION, DIFFRACTION and polarization, and developed a compound LENS system still used for many lighthouses.

FREUD, Anna (1895–1982), Austrian-born British pioneer of child psychoanalysis. Her book *The Ego and Mechanisms of Defense* (1936) is a major contribution to the field. After escaping with her father

Sigmund FREUD from Nazi-occupied Austria (1938), she established an influential child-therapy clinic in London.

FREUD, Sigmund (1856–1939), Austrian neurologist and psychiatrist, founder and author of almost all the basic concepts of PSYCHOANALYSIS. He graduated as a medical student from the University of Vienna in 1881; and for some months in 1885 he studied under J. M. CHARCOT. Charcot's interest in HYSTERIA converted Freud to the cause of psychiatry. Dissatisfied with HYPNOSIS and electrotherapy as treatment techniques, he evolved the psychoanalytic method, founded on DREAM analysis and FREE ASSOCIATION. Because of his belief that sexual impulses lay at the heart of NEUROSES. he was for a decade reviled professionally, but by 1905 disciples such as Alfred ADLER and Carl Gustav JUNG were gathering around him; both were later to break away. For some thirty years he worked to establish the truth of his theories, and these years were especially fruitful. Fleeing Nazi anti-Semitism, he left Vienna for London in 1938, and there spent the last year of his life before dying of cancer.

FREYRE, Gilberto de Mello (1900–1987), Brazilian anthropologist, historian, man of letters, and statesman. His most famous work is *The Masters and the Slaves* (1933), the first part of a tetralogy on the history of Brazil.

FRIAR, member of any of the medieval Roman Catholic mendicant orders. Friars were forbidden to hold property in common, not bound to one convent, and enjoyed various controversial ecclesiastical privileges. Some were distinguished by the color of their habits as Black Friars (DOMINICANS), Grey Friars (FRANCISCANS) and White Friars (CARMELITES); Augustinians or Austin Friars were the other main order.

FRICK, Henry Clay (1849–1919), US industrialist and art collector. He started a coke business in 1868, and in 1882 he became an associate of Andrew CARNEGIE and managed his steel company 1889–99. He bequeathed his extensive art collection, housed in his New York mansion, for public exhibition.

FRICTION, resistance to motion arising at the boundary between two touching surfaces when it is attempted to slide one over the other. As the FORCE applied to start motion increases from zero, the equal force of "static friction" opposes it, reaching a maximum "limiting friction," just before sliding begins. Once motion has started, the "sliding friction" is less than the limiting. Friction increases with the load pressing the surfaces together, but is nearly independent of the area in contact. For a given pair of surfaces, limiting friction divided by load is a dimensionless constant known as the coefficient of friction. LUBRICATION is used to overcome friction in the bearings of machines.

FRIEDAN, Betty (1921–   ), US feminist leader. Her book *The Feminine Mystique* (1963) challenged attitudes which had led women to become housewives and mothers at the expense of more ambitious careers. She was founding president of the NATIONAL ORGANIZATION FOR WOMEN (1966–70) and helped organize the National Women's Political Caucus (1971). *It Changed My Life* (1976) concerns her participation in the women's movement; *The Second Stage* (1981) charts the movement's course.

FRIEDMAN, Milton (1912–   ), US economist, at Chicago U from 1946. A famed monetarist, he was awarded the 1976 Nobel Prize in Economic Science.

FRIEDRICH, Caspar David (1774–1840), German Romantic painter, known for the land and seascape compositions he imbued with rich light effects and deep religious symbolism, such as *Cross in the Mountains* (1807) and *Man and Woman Gazing at the Moon* (1809).

FRIENDLY ISLANDS. See TONGA.

FRIENDS, Society of. See QUAKERS.

FRIML, (Charles) Rudolf (1879–1972), Czech-born US composer of widely popular operettas and film scores. His best-known works include *The Firefly* (1912), *Rose Marie* (1924) and *The Vagabond King* (1925).

FRISCH, Karl von (1886–1982), Austrian zoologist best known for his studies of bee behavior, perception and communication, discovering the "dance of the bees." With TINBERGEN and LORENZ he was awarded the 1973 Nobel Prize for Physiology or Medicine for his work.

FRISCH, Max (1911–   ), Swiss architect, journalist and playwright best known for his play *The Firebugs* (1958) and the novels *Stiller* (1954), *Homo Faber* (1957), and *Man in the Holocene* (1980). His dominant theme is the destructive effect of modern society upon individuals.

FROBISHER, Sir Martin (c1539–1594), English navigator and explorer. In search of a NORTHWEST PASSAGE to the Pacific, he led three expeditions to N Canada 1576–78, landing at Labrador and Frobisher Bay and at Greenland.

FROEBEL, Friedrich Wilhelm August (1782–1852), German educator noted as the founder of the kindergarten system. He

believed in play as a basic form of self-expression, and in the innate nature of mystical understanding. Though much criticized, he has profoundly influenced later educators.

FROGS, jumping, tailless AMPHIBIA. Strictly, the name applies only to true frogs, members of the family Ranidae, but other members of the order Anura (which also includes the TOADS) are sometimes called frogs. True frogs are characterized by shoulder-girdles that are fused down the midline. They are found throughout the world except in the southern parts of South America and Australia.

FROHMAN, Charles (1860–1915), US theatrical producer who developed such stars as John Drew, Maude Adams, Ethel Barrymore, Julia Marlowe, Billie Burke, William Gillette, and Elsie de Wolfe. He went down on the *Lusitania*.

FROISSART, Jean (c1338–1410?), French poet and chronicler who traveled widely in search of material for his *Chronicles of France, England, Scotland and Spain*, which present a colorful picture of events between 1325 and 1400. His poetry ranges from light verse to the romance *Meliador*.

FROMM, Erich (1900–1980), German-born US psychoanalyst who combined many of the ideas of Freud and Marx in his analysis of human relationships and development in the context of social structures and in his suggested solutions to problems such as alienation. His books include *Escape from Freedom* (1941), *The Art of Loving* (1956) and *The Anatomy of Human Destructiveness* (1973).

FRONDE, a series of uprisings against the French crown 1648–53. At first largely popular uprisings against heavy taxation, they were later fomented by the *parlements* and discontented members of the aristocracy, such as Prince Louis II de Condé, against the autocratic chief minister, Cardinal MAZARIN, whose decisive intervention in 1653 finally crushed the Fronde.

FRONTENAC, Louis de Buade, Comte de Palluau et de (1622–1698), French soldier who became governor of New France in 1672. He badly mismanaged Indian relations and damaged the fur trade. Recalled to France in 1682, he returned in 1689 and in King William's War successfully held Quebec against the English. He maintained the French position in New France up to the Treaty of Ryswick (1697).

FRONTIER, in American history, the boundary between the settled and unsettled areas of the country. It was constantly changing as the descendants of the original settlers of the 13 colonies spread out N, S and especially W. In the early days expansion was slow, consisting largely of migrations into the Appalachian area and into what is now Pa. By the time of Independence, Ky. had been settled and the frontier was in Tenn. The new government provided for surveying, settlement and administration of new areas. The frontier moved steadily W, and new states were formed in quick succession until by 1848 Mexico had been forced to cede the SW, and settlement had begun on the W coast. The Indians suffered badly under the government's policy of moving them to make way for settlers, and struggled to resist it. After the Civil War, Indian wars broke out again, but by the 1870s and 1880s the growth of cities and the enclosure of much of the land meant that the settlers were firmly established. In 1890 the Bureau of the Census officially declared the frontier closed; its way of life and the peculiar mythology it created have had a great influence on American culture.

FROST, Robert (1874–1963), eminent US poet. For most of his life he supported himself by farming and part-time academic work. His first two volumes of poetry *A Boy's Will* (1913) and *North of Boston* (1914) were published during a stay in England. His reputation grew in America, and he won many honors, including four Pulitzer prizes. His style is individual, clearly influenced by rural life, religion and much personal tragedy. Frost's complete poems were published in 1967.

FROST, frozen atmospheric moisture formed on objects when the temperature is below 0°C, the freezing point of water (see FREEZING POINT). **Hoarfrost** forms in roughly the same way as dew but, owing to the low temperature, the water vapor sublimes from gaseous to solid state to form ice crystals on the surface. The delicate patterns often seen on windows are hoarfrost. **Glazed frost** usually forms when rain falls on an object below freezing: it can be seen, for example, on telegraph wires. **Rime** occurs when supercooled water droplets contact a surface that is also below 0°C; it may result from FOG or drizzle. The first frost of the year signifies the end of the growing season. (See also ICE.)

FROSTBITE, damage occurring in SKIN and adjacent tissues caused by freezing. (The numbness caused by cold allows considerable damage without pain.) DEATH of tissues follows and they separate off. Judicious rewarming, pain relief and measures to maximize skin blood flow may reduce tissue loss.

FRUIT, botanically, the structure that develops from the ovary and accessory parts of a FLOWER after FERTILIZATION. True fruits are formed from the carpels, while in false fruits other parts of the flower are involved; for example, in apple the fleshy pulp is derived from the receptacle. Fruits may be simple (derived from the ovary of one pistil), aggregate (formed by a single flower with several separate pistils, e.g. raspberry) or multiple (formed from the flowers of an inflorescence e.g. FIG). Simple fruits may be fleshy or dry. Fleshy fruits include the berry and the drupe. Dry fruit may split open to disperse the seeds (dehiscent), the main types being the legume (or pod), follicle capsule and silique. Some dry fruits do not break open (indehiscent), the main types here being the achene, grain, samara and nut.

The main function of the fruit is to protect the seeds and disperse them when ripe.

FRUIT FLIES, small flies of the genus *Drosophila*, which feed on decaying vegetation and ripe fruit, sometimes causing great damage to crops. Some species are used for genetics experiments because they breed rapidly. As a result, the fruit fly is one of the most studied animals in the world today.

FRY, Christopher (1907–   ), British verse dramatist, whose plays, although often in ancient or medieval settings, deal with contemporary themes. His best-known play, *The Lady's Not for Burning* (1948), is a dry comedy centering on witchcraft hysteria. *A Sleep of Prisoners* (1951) and *The Dark Is Light Enough* (1955) are essentially religious plays.

FRY, Elizabeth Gurney (1780–1845), British Quaker philanthropist whose inspections of prisons throughout Britain and Europe led to great advances in the treatment of the imprisoned and the insane. Her proposed reforms of London's notorious Newgate prison, including segregation of the sexes and the provision of employment and religious instruction, were largely accepted.

FRY, Roger Eliot (1866–1934), British art critic and painter. A member of the London group, he was among the first to champion CÉZANNE and POSTIMPRESSIONISM. In 1933 he was appointed Slade Professor of Fine Art at Cambridge.

FUAD (1868–1936), modern Egypt's first monarch, son of the khedive Ismail Pasha. He became sultan on his brother's death in 1917 and assumed the title of king when the British protectorate ended in 1922.

FUCHS, Klaus (1911–1988), German-born

physicist and convicted spy. During WWII, Fuchs—by then a British citizen and active Soviet agent—worked on the top-secret, atomic-bomb project in the US (1943–45). He supplied the Russians with designs for both the uranium and plutonium bombs. Released from a British prison in 1959, he returned to East Germany.

FUCHS, Sir Vivian Ernest (1908–   ), British geologist and explorer, who led the British Commonwealth Trans-Antarctic expedition that made the first overland crossing of Antarctica 1957–58.

FUEL, a substance that may be burned (see COMBUSTION) to produce heat, light or power. Traditional fuels include dried dung, animal and vegetable oil, wood, PEAT and COAL, supplemented by the manufactured fuels CHARCOAL, COAL GAS, COKE and WATER gas. In this century PETROLEUM and NATURAL GAS have come into widespread use. The term "fuel" has also been extended to include chemical nuclear fuels (see NUCLEAR ENERGY), although these are not burned. Specialized high-energy fuels such as hydrazine are used in rocket engines. The chief property of a fuel is its calorific value—the amount of heat produced by complete combustion of a unit mass or volume of fuel. Also of major importance is the proportion of incombustibles—ash and moisture—and of sulfur and other compounds liable to cause AIR POLLUTION.

FUGITIVE SLAVE ACTS, laws passed by Congress in 1793 and 1850 to deter slaves from fleeing to abolitionist states. The 1793 act denied runaway slaves the benefit of jury trial. The 1850 measure was a reaction to the growing opposition this provoked. It imposed severe fines and imprisonment on US marshals and citizens who helped or failed to apprehend runaway slaves. The acts only hardened opposition and were another divisive factor between North and South.

FUGUE, a musical form in which two or more parts (voices) combine in introducing and developing a theme. The principal idea behind fugal composition is that of developing contrasts which produce a specific texture and density. The fugue's history dates from the 16th-century canon and round. The greatest achievements in this form are by J. S. BACH, whose unfinished *The Art of Fugue* (1748–50) is a major study of fugal form.

FUJI, Mount, or **Fujiyama,** highest mountain in Japan (12,388ft), long considered sacred by the Japanese and a source of inspiration to artists and poets. A dormant volcano crowned by a wide crater, it last erupted in 1707.

FULANI, an ancient people of W Africa found over a wide area from Senegambia to W Sudan. They include nomadic pastoralists as well as settled communities. The Fulani have a deep-rooted culture based on Islam and have strong ties with the HAUSA. They number some 7 million.

FULBRIGHT, James William (1905–   ), US political leader and lawyer, initiator of the Fulbright Act (1946), providing for international exchange of students and teachers. After teaching law at Arkansas U. Fulbright was elected to the House of Representatives in 1942, and served in the Senate 1944–75. He was chairman of the Senate Foreign Relations Committee 1959–74, becoming an outspoken critic of US policy in Vietnam.

FULBRIGHT SCHOLARSHIP PROGRAM, educational exchange program conceived by US Senator J. William Fulbright in 1946 under which, initially, foreign credits held in the US from the sale of surplus war property overseas would be used to send US students to study in those countries. In 1988 the program had 156,000 alumni, with 4,500 new exchanges each year of students, teachers, and scholars in 120 participating countries.

FULLER, Margaret (1810–1850), influential American critic and advocate of female emancipation. A friend of EMERSON, she edited the Transcendentalist magazine *The Dial* 1840–42. She became literary critic for the New York *Tribune* in 1844 and in the following year published *Woman in the Nineteenth Century*. She was drowned with her husband and child in a shipwreck off Fire Island, N.Y.

FULLER, R(ichard) Buckminster (1895–1983), US inventor, philosopher, author and mathematician. He was a prolific source of original ideas, many of which have had important consequences. He is best known for his concept "Spaceship Earth" and for inventing the GEODESIC DOME.

FULTON, Robert (1765–1815), US inventor who improved both the submarine and the steamboat. His submarine *Nautilus* was launched at Rouen, France (1800), with the aim of using it against British warships: in fact, these repeatedly escaped and the French lost interest. His first steamship was launched on the Seine (1803), and after this success he returned to the US, launching the first commercially successful steamboat (see FITCH, John), the *Clermont*, from New York (1807). He built several other steamboats and the *Demologus*, the first steam warship (launched 1815).

FUNCTION, a rule by which each element of one set, for example the real NUMBERS, is assigned an element of another set. (The two sets may share some or all elements.) The same element of the second set may be assigned to more than one element of the first set. In Cartesian coordinates a function of one real variable may be plotted by setting x along one axis and $f(x)$ (read "function of x") along the other. (See also ANALYTIC GEOMETRY; GRAPH.) If the rule defining the function is square the number, add twice the number and subtract three; this is expressed as $f(x)=x^2+2x-3$.

If a function of one variable is plotted as a graph or curve as above, it is said to be **continuous** if the curve has no breaks. More precisely, it is continuous if any two points $f(x)$ and $f(x')$ can be brought as close together as desired by bringing x and x^1 sufficiently close together. This definition can be extended to sets of any kind (not necessarily numbers), provided a meaning can be given to "close" (see TOPOLOGY).

FUNCTIONALISM, the principle that all design should be dictated by the function of what is being designed, all unnecessary elements being discarded. This was derived from a dictum of the architect Louis SULLIVAN, "form follows function," and was a moving principle of the BAUHAUS school. Functionalism influenced many modern architects, notably Frank Lloyd WRIGHT, and LE CORBUSIER.

FUNDAMENTALISM, US conservative Protestant movement, upholding EVANGELICALISM against MODERNISM, which has flourished, particularly in the South, since the early 20th century. Its chief doctrines, set out in a series of pamphlets, *The Fundamentals* (1910–1912), are Christ's virgin birth, physical resurrection and second coming, the substitutionary theory of the atonement, and the absolute infallibility of the Bible. The last led to a denial of biblical criticism and the theory of evolution. Leading advocates of the movement included W. J. BRYAN and the theologian John Gresham Machen. Modern fundamentalism is mostly anti-intellectual, dispensationalist, pietist and revivalist.

FUNDY, Bay of, an arm of the Atlantic Ocean between New Brunswick and Nova Scotia about 94mi long and about 50mi at its widest. It is remarkable for a massive fluctuation in tidal level, which has reached 70ft. Its chief harbor is St. John, in New Brunswick.

FUNGAL DISEASES, DISEASES caused by FUNGI which, apart from common SKIN and nail ailments such as ATHLETE'S FOOT, tinea cruris and RINGWORM, develop especially in people with disorders of IMMUNITY or DIABETES and those on certain DRUGS (STEROIDS, immunosuppressives, ANTIBIOTICS). Thrush is common in the mouth and vagina but rarely causes systemic disease. Specific fungal diseases occur in some areas (e.g., histoplasmosis, blastomycosis) while aspergillosis often complicates chronic LUNG disease. In addition, numerous fungi in the environment lead to forms of ALLERGY and lung disease.

FUNGI, a subdivision (Eumycotina) of the PLANT KINGDOM which comprises simple plants that reproduce mostly by means of SPORES and which lack CHLOROPHYLL, hence are either saprophytes or PARASITES.

The closely related slime MOLDS produce naked (no cell walls) amoeboid states, and the YEASTS are single-celled, but the majority of true fungi produce microscopic filaments (hyphae) that group together in an interwoven weft, the mycelium or spawn. REPRODUCTION is sometimes by budding (yeasts) but more normally by the production of asexual and sexual spores. Some fungi produce large fruit bodies, which are the structures commonly associated with fungi. The classification of fungi is complicated and several systems have evolved, mostly based on the types of spore produced. Fungi belong to the division mycota, which also includes the Myxomycetes or slime molds. The true fungi are divided into a number of classes, the main ones being: the Chytridomycetes, which produce motile gametes or zoospores that have a single flagellum; the Oomycetes, which have biflagellate zoospores and produce dissimilar male and female reproductive organs and gametes; Zygomycetes, which do not produce motile zoospores and reproduce sexually by fusion of identical gametes; the Ascomycetes, including yeasts, which reproduce asexually by budding or by the production of spores (conidia) and sexually by the formation of ascospores within sac-like structures (asci) that are often enclosed in a fruiting body or ascocarp; the Basidiomycetes, including bracket fungi and agarics in which the sexual spores are produced, or enlarged cells called basidia, that often occur on large fruiting bodies; and the Deuteromycetes, or imperfect fungi, which are only known to reproduce asexually, although sexual forms are often classified in the Ascomycetes and Basidiomycetes. (See also FUNGAL DISEASES; PLANT DISEASES; RUST.)

FUNGICIDE, substance used to kill FUNGI and so to control FUNGAL DISEASES in man and plants. In medicine some ANTIBIOTICS,

SULFUR, carboxylic acids and potassium iodide are used. In agriculture a wide variety of fungicides is used, both inorganic—Bordeaux mixture and sulfur—and organic—many different compounds, generally containing sulfur or nitrogen. They are applied to the soil before planting or around seedlings, or are sprayed or dusted onto foliage. (See also PESTICIDE.)

FUR, the soft, dense, hairy undercoat of certain mammals. Fur is an excellent heat insulator and protects against the cold of the northern regions where most furbearing animals are found. It is generally interspersed with guard HAIRS, longer and stiffer, that form a protective outer coat and prevent matting. Skins or pelts are cleaned, softened and converted to a leatherlike state by "dressing," a process resembling TANNING. In some cases the guard hairs are sheared or plucked. The pelt is then dyed or bleached and then glazed, chemically or by heat, to give it a lustrous sheen. To make the furs into a garment, they are matched for color and texture, cut to shape, sewn together, and finally dampened and nailed to the pattern to dry smooth and the exact shape wanted. Fur clothing has long been valued for its beauty and warmth, and was an aristocratic luxury until the discovery of America, in whose exploration and economic development trapping and fur trading played a major role. Demand is still high, threatening some furbearing species with extinction; this has led to fur-farming of suitable animals such as mink and to the development of artificial furs made of synthetic fibers.

FURTWANGLER, Wilhelm (1886–1954), German conductor whose free, passionate style made him one of the great interpreters, particularly of Beethoven and Wagner.

FUSE, safety device placed in an electric circuit to prevent overloading. It usually comprises a wire of low-melting-point metal mounted in or on an insulated frame. Current passing through the wire heats it, and excessive current heats it to the point where it melts, so breaking the circuit. In most domestic plugs, the fuse consists of a cylinder of glass, capped at each end by metal, with a wire running between the metal caps. Similar, but larger, cartridge fuses are used in industry.

FUSELI, Henry (1741–1825), Anglo-Swiss painter and writer, appointed professor of painting at the Royal Academy in 1799. His paintings, of which the most famous is probably *The Nightmare* (1782), are highly stylized and have an often sinister sensuality.

FUSION, Nuclear, a nuclear reaction in which the nuclei of light ATOMS combine to produce heavier, more stable nuclei, releasing a large quantity of ENERGY. Fusion reactions are the energy source of the SUN and the HYDROGEN BOMB. If they could be controlled and made self-sustaining man would have a safe and inexhaustible energy source using deuterium or tritium extracted from seawater. Only small amounts of fuel would be needed, and none of the by-products would be radioactive. But if they are to fuse, the light, positively charged nuclei must collide with sufficient energy to overcome their electrostatic repulsion. This can be done by using a particle ACCELERATOR, but to get a net energy release the material must be heated to very high temperatures (around 10^9K) when it becomes a PLASMA. However, plasmas are difficult to contain and, as yet, no apparatus has been designed which allows more energy to be extracted than is used in heating and containing the plasma. (See also NUCLEAR ENERGY.)

FUTURISM, 20th-century Italian art movement based on two manifestos of Futurist poetry and painting, issued in 1909 and 1910 by the poet Filippo MARINETTI and an allied group of artists. It sought to express the speed, violence and dynamism of a mechanical age.

7th letter of the English alphabet, developed from the Semitic *ghimel* and a differentiated form of the Greek *gamma*. English has a hard "g" sound as in "go" and a soft "g" sound, mostly before e, i, and y, as in "gentle." In music G is the fifth note in the scale of C.

GABIN, Jean (1904–1976), French film actor who often played tough but decent heroes. The most popular French star of the 1930s, he made such memorable films as *Pépé le Moko* (1936) and *La Grande Illusion* (1937).

GABLE, Clark (1901–1960), US film star, winner of a 1934 Academy Award for a comedy role in *It Happened One Night*. His most famous role was Rhett Butler in *Gone with the Wind* (1939). Called "the King," he was a leading box-office "draw" for more than two decades.

GABO, Naum (Naum Pevsner; 1890–1977), Russian sculptor, a pioneer of CONSTRUCTIVISM. With his brother Anton PEVSNER, he issued the *Realist Manifesto* (1920). He left Russia and taught at the BAUHAUS (1922–32). In 1946 he emigrated to the US. He is noted for his kinetic sculptures and geometrical constructions in metal, plastic and nylon.

GABON, small republic on the Atlantic coast of W Africa.

Official name: Gabonese Republic
Capital: Libreville
Area: 103,347sq mi
Population: 1,195,000
Languages: French, Fang, Bantu
Religions: Roman Catholic, Animist, Muslim
Monetary unit(s): 1 CFA franc=100 centimes

Land. Most of the country, lying across the Equator, is rain forest; a mountain range separates the narrow coastal area from the heartland plateaus. The climate is hot and humid, with heavy rainfall.

People. Gabon's relatively small population has a wide range of ethnic groups: the largest, the Fang, constitutes about 30% of the population and dominates politics and industry; the Omyene are a small but important coastal group. Most of the people are village dwellers, but about 30% live in the main towns of Libreville, Port-Gentil and Lambarene, site of Albert SCHWEITZER'S famous hospital. There is a strong emphasis on education and a large number of children attend school.

Economy. Gabon is the richest country in sub-Saharan Africa in terms of per capita income, and the second richest in all of Africa, after Libya. Oil dominates Gabon's export earnings; manganese and uranium are also exported. Agricultural output is low and much food is imported from France, a main trading partner. Despite national wealth, living standards are generally low.

History. Gabon became an important slave-trade center after discovery by the Portuguese in the 15th century. The Omyene peoples dominated Gabon until gradually displaced by the Fang in the 19th century. France maintained a naval base on the coast from 1843, but occupied the country only when its economic possibilities became apparent. A French colony from 1886, in 1946 it became an overseas territory of France. It achieved self-government in 1958, independence in 1960, and became a one-party state in 1968. Omar Bongo, who became president in 1967, has since been reelected unopposed.

GABRIEL, Jacques Ange (1698–1782), French architect employed by Louis XV, a master of the ROCOCO style.

GABRIELI, family of Italian composers. **Andrea** (c1520–1586), organist at St. Mark's, Venice, composed sacred motets and psalms, madrigals and organ works. **Giovanni** (c1556–1612), Andrea's nephew and successor at St. Mark's, composed vocal and instrumental music noted for its dramatic style and use of counterpoint.

GADDI, Taddeo (c1300–1366), Florentine painter, a pupil of GIOTTO, whom he succeeded as decorator of S. Croce in Florence. His frescoes of the lives of Christ, St. Francis and St. Bonaventure are perhaps his greatest works.

GADSDEN, James (1788–1858), US soldier and diplomat who, as minister to Mexico, negotiated the GADSDEN PURCHASE. In the WAR OF 1812 he served against the Seminole Indians and was in charge of their removal to S Fla. in 1825 and to the W in 1832.

GADSDEN PURCHASE, Mexican territory bought by the US in 1853, to add to lands acquired in the war of 1848. The extra land, some 45,000 sq mi, cost $10 million. It provided a rail route through the conquered land to the Pacific. The purchase was negotiated by James Gadsden, US minister to Mexico.

GAELIC, group of CELTIC LANGUAGES, native to Ireland (Irish Gaelic), the Isle of Man (Manx) and the Scottish Highlands (Scottish Gaelic).

GAELIC LITERATURE, writings in the Gaelic language. There are two main traditions. Irish Gaelic is divided into three periods, Old Irish (up to c10th century), Middle Irish (up to mid-15th century) and Modern Irish. The early literature consists chiefly of lyric verse and sagas, of which the *Ulster Cycle* is a famous example. Scottish Gaelic diverged from the Irish tradition in c1300 and developed an impressive body of poetry, with some prose work.

GAELS, or **Goidels,** the Gaelic-speaking Celtic peoples of Ireland, Scotland and the Isle of Man, as opposed to the Celtic people of Wales, Cornwall or Brittany, who speak Brythonic.

GAGARIN, Yuri Alekseyevich (1934–1968), Soviet astronaut, first man in space. His capsule was launched on April 12, 1961, and orbited the earth once. A deputy to the Supreme Soviet from 1962, he died in a plane crash.

GAGE, Thomas (1721–1787), British general, from 1763 commander-in-chief of British forces in North America and military governor of Mass. from 1774. In April 1775 his attempt to take an arms depot at Concord resulted in the first battles (at Lexington and Concord) of the REVOLUTIONARY WAR. He resigned after the debacle at BUNKER HILL.

GAG RULES, resolutions passed in the US House of Representatives 1836–40 to prevent discussion in the House of petitions regarding slavery. The rules infringed the right of petition; they were repealed in 1844 as the result of a campaign led by John Quincy ADAMS and Joshua Giddings.

GAINES'S MILL, Battle of, in the American Civil War, part of the Confederate counteroffensive to end the PENINSULAR CAMPAIGN, near Richmond, Va. On June 27, 1862, forces led by Generals Jackson and Longstreet attacked and routed Union forces under Gen. Fitz-John Porter.

GAINSBOROUGH, Thomas (1727–1788), English portraitist and landscape painter. He painted numerous society portraits; in 1780 he was commissioned to portray George III and Queen Charlotte. Many of his portraits are actually set in landscapes, which were his primary interest. His work influenced CONSTABLE and English landscape painting in the 19th century.

GAITSKELL, Hugh (Todd Naylor) 1906–1963), British politician, Labour Party leader 1955–63. He entered Parliament in 1945 and was chancellor of the exchequer in 1950. In opposition he was a leading critic of Conservative policies and managed to reunite the party after a split in 1960.

GALACTIC CLUSTERS, clusters of stars lying in or near the galactic plane, each of which contains a few hundred stars. Due to their irregular shape they are also termed **open clusters.** The best known galactic cluster in N skies is the Pleiades.

GALÁPAGOS ISLANDS, group of volcanic islands in the Pacific, on the equator W of Ecuador. They were named for the giant tortoises found there in 1535 by the Spaniard Thomas de Berlanga. They have unique vegetation and wildlife, the study of which confirmed Charles DARWIN in his theory of evolution. There are large marine and land iguanas, scarlet crabs, penguins, a flightless cormorant, unique finches and the giant tortoises, now rare. The main islands are Isabella, Santa Cruz, Fernandina, San Salvador and San Cristobal; they are now a national park and wildlife sanctuary.

GALATIA, an ancient territory of central Asia Minor overrun by Gauls in the 3rd century BC. Subjugated by Rome in 189 BC, it became part of the Roman province of Galatia (which extended south) in 25 BC, and by 200 AD had merged with Anatolia.

GALATIANS, Epistle to the, ninth book of the NEW TESTAMENT, a letter written by St. Paul to the Christians in N or S Galatia to counter the influence of Judaizers who taught that Christians must keep all the law of Moses. It sets forth the basis of Christian freedom, man's union with Christ through faith.

GALAXY, the largest individual conglomeration of matter, containing stars, gas, dust and planets. Galaxies start life as immense clouds of gas, out of which stars condense. Initially a galaxy is **irregular** in form; that is, it has neither a specific shape nor any apparent internal structure. It contains large amounts of gas and dust in which new stars are constantly forming. It rotates and over millions of years evolves into a **spiral** form, looking rather like a flying saucer, with a roughly spherical nucleus surrounded by a flattish disk and orbited by GLOBULAR CLUSTERS. In the nucleus there is little gas and dust and a high proportion of older stars; in the spiral arms, a great deal of gas and dust and a high proportion of younger stars (our SUN lies in a spiral arm of the MILKY WAY). Over further millions of years the spiral arms "fold" toward the nucleus, the end result being an **elliptical** galaxy containing a large number of older stars and little or no gas and dust. The ultimate form of any galaxy is a sphere, after which it possibly evolves into a BLACK HOLE. The nearest external galaxy to our own is the Andromeda Galaxy. Similarly spiral, though rather larger, it has two satellite galaxies which are elliptical in form. Originally it was thought to be a NEBULA within our own galaxy, but in 1924 HUBBLE showed that it was a galaxy in its own right. Study of the Andromeda Galaxy is important as it enables us better to understand our own, most of which is obscured from us by clouds of gas and dust. Galaxies emit radio waves, and the strongest sources are known as **radio galaxies.** One group of these, spiral with active nuclei, are named **Seyfert galaxies** for the US astronomer Carl Seyfert. (See also PULSAR; QUASAR.) Galaxies tend to form in clusters. The Milky Way and the Andromeda Galaxy are members of a cluster of around 20 galaxies.

GALBRAITH, John Kenneth (1908–   ), US economist, at Harvard 1948–75. He served as US ambassador to India 1961–63. His books include *The Affluent Society* (1958) and *The New Industrial State* (1967). *A Life in Our Times* (1981) is his autobiography.

GALEN (c130–c200 AD), Greek physician at the court of the Roman Emperor Marcus Aurelius. His writings drew together the best of classical medicine and provided the form in which the science was transmitted through the medieval period to the Renaissance. He himself contributed many original and careful observations in anatomy and physiology.

GALICIA, historic region in E central Europe N of the Carpathian Mts, now part of Poland and of Russia's Ukrainian SSR. It is both rich in minerals and a productive agricultural area. Part of Poland since the 14th century, it was annexed by Austria in the 18th century. Galicia was again Polish after WWI. After WWII its eastern portion passed to the USSR.

GALICIA, mountainous region of NW Spain, one of the ancient kingdoms of Castile. A distinctive school of lyric poetry in the Galician-Portuguese language flourished in the 13th century. Santiago de Compostella has been a pilgrimage center since the 9th century. Agriculture and fishing are the chief occupations.

GALILEE, hilly region of N ancient Palestine between the Sea of Galilee and the Jordan R. It was the homeland of Jesus, who was sometimes referred to as the Galilean.

GALILEE, Sea of (Lake Tiberias), lake in N Israel 696ft below sea level and 104sq mi in area, fed by the Jordan R. The only body of fresh water in Israel, it has been a fishing center since biblical times. Many sites on its shores are associated with Jesus' ministry.

GALILEO GALILEI (1564–1642), Italian mathematical physicist who discovered the laws of falling bodies and the parabolic motion of projectiles. The first to turn the newly invented TELESCOPE to the heavens, he was among the earliest observers of SUNSPOTS and the phases of Venus. A talented publicist, he helped to popularize the pursuit of science. However, his quarrelsome nature led him into an unfortunate controversy with the Church. His most significant contribution to science was his provision of an alternative to the Aristotelian dynamics. The motion of the

earth thus became a conceptual possibility and scientists at last had a genuine criterion for choosing between the Copernican and Tychonic hypotheses in ASTRONOMY.

GALL, Saint, 7th-century Irish monk, companion of St. Columban on a mission to France. He then lived as a hermit with the Alamanni tribe in N Switzerland. His feast day is Oct. 16.

GALL, Franz Joseph (1758–1828), German-born Viennese physician who was one of the earliest proponents of the theory of cerebral localization (that different areas of the BRAIN control different functions) and who founded the pseudoscience of PHRENOLOGY.

GALLATIN, (Abraham Alfonse) Albert (1761–1849), Swiss-born American statesman and diplomat. As congressman 1795–1801 he defended US relations with France during the XYZ AFFAIR. Secretary of the treasury 1801–13, he objected to the drain on national economy caused by the War of 1812 and helped negotiate the Treaty of GHENT, 1814. He was minister to France 1816–23 and Britain 1826–27.

GALLAUDET, Thomas Hopkins (1787–1851), US educator of the deaf. After study at the Royal Institute for Deaf-Mutes in Paris, he founded the first free school for the deaf in the US at Hartford, Conn. (1817).

GALL BLADDER, small sac containing BILE, arising from the bile duct which leads from the LIVER to the duodenum. It lies beneath the liver and serves to concentrate bile. When food, especially fatty food, reaches the STOMACH, local HORMONES cause gall bladder contraction and bile enters the GASTROINTESTINAL TRACT. In some people the concentration of bile favors the formation of gallstones, usually containing CHOLESTEROL. These stones may cause no symptoms; they may obstruct the gall bladder causing biliary colic or INFLAMMATION (cholecystitis), or they may pass into the bile duct and cause biliary obstruction with JAUNDICE or, less often, pancreatitis. Acute episodes are treated with ANALGESICS, antispasmodics and ANTIBIOTICS, but SURGERY is frequently necessary later. Recent advances suggest that in some instances stones may be dissolved by DRUG therapy.

GALLEGOS, Rómulo 1884–1968), Venezuelan novelist and statesman. Elected president of Venezuela in 1948, he was almost immediately overthrown by a military coup. His short stories and novels, of which the best known is *Dona Barbara* (1929), are primarily didactic and ideological works concerned with social reform.

GALLEY, early seagoing warship, propelled by oars, sometimes with auxiliary sails. The ancient Greek and Roman navies were comprised of galleys, which were classified according to the number of banks of oars on each side: *uniremes* (one bank), *biremes* (two banks), and *triremes* (three banks). There were usually about 25 oars per bank. The oars were 40 to 50 ft long and as many as seven slaves were required to man each oar. These ships were long and narrow. Though fast, they were difficult to handle in rough seas. They were equipped with catapults, and carried archers and soldiers who would board an enemy ship after ramming it. Galleys continued to be used in the Mediterranean and other seas until late in the 17th century.

GALLICANISM, in the French Roman Catholic church, tradition of resistance to papal authority, in opposition to ULTRAMONTANISM.

GALLIC WARS, a series of campaigns by Julius CAESAR, 58–51 BC. The name is derived from Caesar's *Commentaries on the Gallic War* (c50 BC). As governor of Transalpine Gaul, Caesar carried out a combined strategy of driving out invading German tribes and in the process occupying more territory in Gaul, until almost the whole country was in Roman hands (55 BC). In 53–52 BC he put down revolts by the chieftains Ambiorix and VERCINGETORIX. The latter's defeat at Alesia (52 BC) effectively ended the wars, with the Romans in control.

GALLIENI, Joseph Simon (1849–1916), French general, governor of French Sudan and then Madagascar (1896–1905). Military governor of Paris 1914–15, his strategy precipitated the Battle of the Marne, which saved the city. He became famous for rushing reserves to the front by Paris taxicabs. He was minister of war 1915–16.

GALLIENUS, Publius Licinius Egnatius (c218–268 AD), Roman emperor 253–268. Under pressure from German, Persian and Gothic invasions and provincial revolutions, he reorganized the army and reduced the power of the Senate. He ended official persecution of the Christians. Gallienus was assassinated in Milan while quelling a revolt.

GALLIPOLI PENINSULA, a 50mi long strip of land in European Turkey between the Aegean Sea and the Dardanelles. A strategic point of defense for Istanbul, it was fought over during the Crimean War and WWI. In 1915 an Allied expedition of British, Australian, French and New Zealand forces failed to dislodge Turkish troops in an effort to gain control of the Dardanelles.

GALLOWAY, Joseph (1731–1803), American loyalist statesman. A member and speaker of the Pennsylvania Assembly 1756–76, he proposed at the First CONTINENTAL CONGRESS a plan for legal settlement of differences between Britain and the colonies, but was forced by the war to join the Loyalists. See GALL BLADDER.

GALLSTONES. See GALL BLADDER.

GALLUP, George Horace (1901–1984), American pollster. In 1935 he established the American Institute of Public Opinion which undertakes the Gallup polls, periodic samplings of public opinion on current issues. His several books include *The Pulse of Democracy* (1940) and *The Gallup Poll: Public Opinion, 1935–71* (1972).

GALSWORTHY, John (1867–1933), English novelist and playwright. His works, especially the famous cycle of novels *The Forsyte Saga* are concerned with the life and attitudes of the wealthier English middle classes, typified by the "man of property" Soames Forsyte. He was awarded the Nobel Prize for Literature in 1932.

GALT, Sir Alexander Tilloch (1817–1893), Canadian statesman, influential proponent of confederation. He served (1880–83) as the first Canadian high commissioner in London.

GALTON, Sir Francis (1822–1911), British scientist, the founder of EUGENICS and biostatistics (the application of statistical methods to animal populations); the coiner of the term "anticyclone" and one of the first to realize their meteorological significance; and the developer of one of the first FINGERPRINT systems for identification.

GALVANI, Luigi (1737–1798), Italian anatomist who discovered "animal electricity" (about 1786). The many varying accounts of this discovery at least agree that it resulted from the chance observation of the twitching of frog legs under electrical influence. A controversy with VOLTA over the nature of animal electricity was cut short by Galvani's death.

GAMA, Vasco da (c1469–1524), Portuguese navigator whose discovery of a new sea-route around the Cape of Good Hope and destruction of the Muslim trade monopoly made possible large-scale European trade with the East. In his first voyage (1497–99) his trade negotiations in India were thwarted by Muslim merchants. On his second voyage (1502–03) his fleet established Portuguese supremacy in the area by a ruthless destruction of the Malabar Muslim fleet. Later appointed viceroy to India, he died soon after his arrival there.

GAMBETTA, Léon Michel (1838–1882), French republican statesman who assumed virtually dictatorial power after Napoleon III's defeat at Sedan, but was unable to prevent capitulation to Prussia. Premier in 1881, he was distrusted as an opportunist and lasted only three months in office.

GAMBIA, republic in W Africa, smallest state on the continent.

Official name: Republic of the Gambia
Capital: Banjul
Area: 4,127sq mi
Population: 787,000
Languages: English, French, Mandinka, Wolof
Religions: Muslim, Animist
Monetary unit(s): 1 dalasi = 100 butut
Land. It extends for around 200mi from the W coast narrowly along the Gambia R, almost bisecting Senegal. A low-lying country, it ranges from coastal mangrove areas to interior scrublands.
People and Economy. The Mandingo peoples constitute around 40% of the population; others are the Fulani, Wolof, Jola and Sarahule. Most are small farmers, producing millet, corn and rice for local consumption. Goats and sheep are raised, and the Fulani breed cattle. Peanuts and peanut oil are the main exports. Britain is the principal trade partner. There is little industry.
History. In ancient times Gambia was part of the Mali Empire. During the 1400s Portuguese began trading for slaves along the coast. Gambia was born of the struggle between Britain and France for supremacy in W Africa. The French territory became Senegal and the British territory became Gambia. The first legislative assembly was elected in 1960; independence came in 1965. The country became a republic within the Commonwealth in 1970, with Sir Dawda Jawara as its first head of state. Following an attempted coup in 1981, Senegal and Gambia formed a confederation in 1982. Although each country retains its sovereignty, their armed forces have been integrated.

GAMETE, or **germ cell,** a sexual reproductive CELL capable of uniting with a gamete of the opposite sex to form a new individual or ZYGOTE; this process is termed FERTILIZATION. Each gamete contains one set of dissimilar chromosomes and is said to be haploid. Thus when gametes unite, the resultant cell contains a diploid or paired set of CHROMOSOMES. The gametes of some primitive organisms are identical cells capable of swimming in water, but in most species only the male gamete (sperm) is mobile while the female gamete (ovary or egg) is a larger static cell. In higher PLANTS the male gametes or pollen are produced by the anthers and the female gametes (ovules) by the ovary. In animals gametes are produced by the gonads, namely the testes in the male and ovaries in the female.

GAME THEORY, an application of mathematics to decision-making in games and, by extension, in commerce, politics and warfare. In singular games (e.g., solitaire) the player's strategy is determined solely by the rules. In dual games (e.g., chess, football) one side's strategy must take into account the possible strategies of the other. Dual games are usually zero-sum: one side's gain exactly equals the other's loss. In practical situations, however, they may be non-zero-sum, as where two conflicting nations negotiate a truce that benefits both. A player in a zero-sum dual game, knowing that whatever he does his opponent will maximize his own gain, should play in such a way as to maximize his minimum gain. VON NEUMANN showed in his **minimax theorem** that if both players follow this principle, then, if they use "mixed strategies" in which their moves are chosen at random but with certain probabilities in each situation, the game has a determinate result (as a long-run average, because of the chance element) in which each player achieves his optimum result in the sense defined above. Games with more than two players are more difficult to analyze.

GAMMA GLOBULIN, the fraction of blood protein containing antibodies (see ANTIBODIES AND ANTIGENS). Several types are recognized. Although they share basic structural features they differ in size, site, behavior and response to different antigens. Absence of all or some gamma globulins causes disorders of IMMUNITY, increasing susceptibility to infection, while the excessive formation of one type is the basis for **myeloma,** a disease characterized by BONE pain, pathological FRACTURES and liability to infection. Gamma globulin is available for replacement therapy, and a type from highly immune subjects is sometimes used to protect against certain diseases (e.g., serum hepatitis, TETANUS).

GANDHI, Indira Priyadarshini (1917–1984), first woman prime minister of India. Daughter of Jawaharlal NEHRU, she became president of the Congress Party in 1959. As prime minister (1966–77) she became more friendly with the USSR and less so with the US, and defeated Pakistan in a war. In 1975, she was found guilty of electoral malpractice. During the ensuing constitutional crisis she declared a state of emergency and jailed nearly 700 political opponents. The Indian Supreme Court overruled the verdict against her and upheld her electoral and constitutional changes. Briefly turned out of office, she regained the premiership in 1980. Her suppression of violent political agitation for an autonomous Sikh state in the Punjab led to her assassination by Sikh members of her bodyguard.

GANDHI, Mohandas Karamchand "Mahatma" (1869–1948), Indian nationalist leader. After studying law in London, he went to South Africa, where he lived until 1914, becoming a driving force in the Indian community's fight for civil rights. During this campaign he developed the principle of satyagraha, nonviolent civil disobedience, and held to it despite persecution and imprisonment. When he returned to India he had achieved substantial improvements in civil rights and labor laws. In India he became leader of the Congress Party, initiating the campaign which led to the independence of India after WWII. He was assassinated by a Hindu fanatic who disapproved of his tolerance of Muslims.

GANDHI, Rajiv (1944–   ), Indian politician, son of Indira GANDHI and grandson of Jawaharlal NEHRU. When his younger brother, Sanjay, who was being groomed as his mother's successor, was killed (1980) in an airplane crash, Rajiv gave up his position as a pilot with Indian Airlines to enter politics. He was elected (1981) to parliament and helped his mother run the government and reorganize the Congress Party. In 1983 he became general secretary of the party. When his mother was assassinated in 1984, Rajiv became prime minister. Early popularity based on his personal charm and anticorruption stance gave way to rising criticism of his autocratic style, charges of corruption in his administration, and his inability to stem communal violence, particularly by the Sikhs in Punjab.

GANGES RIVER, in India the most sacred Hindu river, believed to be the reincarnation of the goddess Ganga. It rises in the Himalayas and flows through N and NE India, following a SE course across the plain of India. It joins the Brahmaputra R in Bangladesh, then continues through the vast Ganges delta to empty through several mouths (Meghna, Tetulia, Hooghly) into the Bay of Bengal. The river waters irrigate a populous agricultural area. Many cities line the river's banks, including the holy Indian cities of Váranasi (Benares), Allahábád, and Calcutta, and Dacca (Bangladesh) on the delta.

GANGLION, a small collection of nerve cells, sometimes with SYNAPSE formation, common in autonomic or peripheral NERVOUS SYSTEMS.

GANGRENE, DEATH of tissue following loss of blood supply, often after obstruction of ARTERIES by trauma, THROMBOSIS or EMBOLISM. Dry gangrene is seen when arterial block is followed by slow drying, blackening and finally separation of dead tissue from healthy. Its treatment includes improvement of the blood flow to the healthy tissue and prevention of infection and further obstruction. Wet gangrene occurs when the dead tissue is infected with BACTERIA. Gas gangrene involves infection with gas-forming organisms (*Clostridium*) and its spread is particularly rapid. ANTIBIOTICS, HYPERBARIC CHAMBERS and early AMPUTATION are often required.

GANNETT, Frank (1876–1957), US newspaper publisher who founded (1906) a communications empire that eventually included radio and television stations and twenty-two urban newspapers. An anti-New Deal conservative, he ran unsuccessfully for the 1940 Republican presidential nomination.

GAPON, Georgi Apollonovich (1870–1906), Russian priest, prominent in the 1905 revolution. He helped set up a workers' association to deal with grievances. On Jan. 22, 1905 (known as "Bloody Sunday"), he led workers to the Winter Palace in St. Petersburg to petition the tsar for better conditions, but troops shot over 100 people. He was murdered in Finland by socialist revolutionaries.

GARAMOND, Claude (c1480–1561), French type designer and publisher. He created typefaces which helped establish roman in place of Gothic or black letter as standard type. His royal Greek and italic types were also highly influential. (See also TYPOGRAPHY.)

GARBO, Greta (1905–   ), Swedish-American film actress, born Greta Lovisa Gustafsson. She was a talented actress known for her aura of glamour and mystery; her 24 films included *Anna Christie* (1930),

Camille (1937) and *Ninotchka* (1939). She retired in 1941, and was given an Academy Award in 1954.

GARCIA LORCA, Federico. See LORCA, FEDERICO GARCIA.

GARCÍA   MÁRQUEZ,   Gabriel (1928–   ), Colombian writer whose novels include *One Hundred Years of Solitude* (1967). He received the 1982 Nobel Prize for Literature.

GARCÍA Y IÑIGUEZ, Calixto (1839–1898), Cuban revolutionary. He commanded Cuban forces in the Ten Years War (1868–78) against Spain. After being imprisoned in Spain, he helped lead the Cuban revolt in 1895–98 which led to the SPANISH-AMERICAN WAR. His name became a famous byword in the US after publication of a magazine article, *A Message to Garcia* (1899), dealing with an incident in the war.

GARDEN, Mary (1877–1967), Scottish-US soprano. She made her debut in 1900 at the Opéra-Comique in Paris in Charpentier's *Louise* and later became famous as Mélisande in Debussy's *Pelléas et Mélisande* and in Massenet's *Thaïs*. She was a member (1910–31) of the Chicago Opera Company.

GARDENS, land cultivated for flowers, herbs, trees, shrubs and vegetables. Early man made the first gardens when he discovered he could plant and then harvest edible roots, greens and fruits. The Hanging Gardens of Babylon (about 600 BC) were considered one of the seven wonders of the ancient world. Ancient Greek, Roman and medieval monastic gardens cultivated herbs for medicinal uses. The Greeks had the first potted plant gardens and the Romans planted roof gardens. The elaborate gardens of Renaissance Italy were copied in Tudor England. The formal gardens of Versailles were the most impressive of 17th-century French landscape architecture. In 18th- and 19th-century England, idealized natural landscapes were created by landscape gardeners such as Lancelot "Capability" Brown (1715–1783). The US tended to imitate English and European garden design, but after WWI emphasis was on private suburban gardens. "Garden apartments" with shared parklike facilities became increasingly common after WWII. (See also HORTICULTURE.)

GARDINER, Stephen (c1490–1555), English bishop of Winchester. By the end of HENRY VIII's reign he was regarded as the chief opponent of the REFORMATION in England. Secretary to Cardinal WOLSEY and then to Henry, he aided negotiations for the king's annulment from Queeen Catherine and accepted royal supremacy over the English church; but he opposed many of CRANMER's reforms, was jailed under Edward VI and became Lord High Chancellor under MARY I.

GARDNER, Erle Stanley (1889–1970), US mystery writer, creator of lawyer-detective Perry Mason. Gardner wrote over 140 novels under his own name and the pseudonym A. A. Fair.

GARFIELD, James Abram (1831–1881), 20th president of the US, the second to be assassinated in office. He was born in a log cabin near Orange in Cuyahoga Co., Ohio, the son of pioneer farmers. In his youth he worked as a farmer and on canal boats. He graduated from Williams College in 1856 and then became a teacher and principal of Hiram College (Ohio), and was admitted to the bar. A distinguished officer of Ohio volunteers in the Civil War, he was commissioned major general in the Union army (1863). He resigned to take a seat in the House of Representatives (1863–80). During his years in Congress he was chairman of the House appropriations committee (1871–75) and Republican House leader, helped establish an Office of Education (1867), served as a Smithsonian Institution regent and helped create the US Geological Survey. He favored a conservative policy on money, fought inflation and supported RECONSTRUCTION measures against the South. In 1880 he was elected to the Senate, but the same year was chosen as compromise Republican presidential candidate and defeated W. S. Hancock in the election. Garfield's brief term of office was notable for the start of friendlier US–Latin American relations under Secretary of State James G. BLAINE and for exposure of the "star route" mail frauds in the W. He gained prestige by asserting presidential power in a patronage struggle with New York state Republican Party boss Roscoe Conkling. When the president was shot, the nation was outraged, and the postal and civil service reforms he had advocated were hastened (supported by his successor, Chester A. ARTHUR). (See also SPOILS SYSTEM.)

GARIBALDI, Giuseppe (1807–1882), Italian patriot and general, one of the creators of modern Italy. As a young man he joined the republican Young Italy society set up by MAZZINI. In 1834 he first fought in a republican uprising in Genoa and then fled to South America. There he became famous as a guerrilla leader in revolutions in Brazil and Uruguay. In 1848, the "year of revolutions," he returned to Italy to fight against Austrian, French and Neapolitan armies in support of Mazzini's short-lived

Roman Republic. On its collapse, Garibaldi fled to the US until 1854. Again returning to Italy, from 1859–62 he led brilliant guerrilla campaigns against Austria and captured Sicily and Naples with a volunteer army, his famous "Red Shirts," in the most decisive campaign of the RISORGIMENTO. He surrendered the territories to King Victor Emmanuel, effectively unifying Italy. Twice (in 1862 and 1867) Garibaldi unsuccessfully tried to capture Rome from the pope. Subsequently he fought for the French against Prussia (1870). In 1874 he was elected to the Italian parliament, but retired in 1876.

GARLAND, (Hannibal) Hamlin (1860–1940), US writer. His fiction portrays pioneering Middle Western farm life with bitterness and realism. Among his best work is the story collection *Main Travelled Roads* (1891) and his autobiographical "Middle Border" stories (4 vols., 1917–1928).

GARLAND, Judy (1922–1969), US singer and movie actress, born Frances Gumm. Famous for her performances of popular songs such as "You Made Me Love You," she starred in *The Wizard of Oz* (1939) and *A Star is Born* (1954).

GARNER, Erroll (1921–   ), US jazz musician who developed a most distinctive piano style, based on an emphatic left hand accompaniment and certain chord groupings, which won him great popularity. He composed the popular ballad *Misty*.

GARNER, John Nance (1868–1967), US vice-president, 1933–40 under Franklin ROOSEVELT. A Democratic member of the US House of Representatives (1903–33) and its speaker 1931–33, he was a skillful behind-the-scenes politician. He ran unsuccessfully for the Democratic presidential nomination in 1940.

GARRETT, Patrick Floyd "Pat" (1850–1908), US frontier sheriff. He arrested BILLY THE KID in 1880, and after "the Kid's" escape from jail in N.M. pursued and shot him in 1881.

GARRICK, David (1717–1779), English actor-manager and dramatist. He introduced a more natural acting style to the English stage in roles such as Hamlet and partially restored the original versions of Shakespeare's plays. From 1747–1776 he was manager of the Drury Lane Theatre.

GARRISON, William Lloyd (1805–1879), US leader of the abolitionist movement. From 1831–65 he published *The Liberator*, an influential crusading journal which opposed slavery, war and capital punishment and supported temperance and women's rights. (See ABOLITIONISM.)

GARTER, Order of the, the highest order of British knighthood, established in the mid-14th century by King Edward III. It consists of the sovereign, the Prince of Wales, 25 knights companions and such foreign rulers and others as the monarch may name. Its patron is St. George and its famous motto is *Honi soit qui mal y pense* ("Shame to him who thinks ill of it").

GARTER SNAKES, harmless snakes of the genus *Thamnophis*. They are the most common snakes of North America, growing usually to a length of 500–750mm (20–30in) and feeding on frogs or salamanders. Some are aquatic or semiaquatic and kept as pets.

GARVEY, Marcus Moziah (1887–1940), US Negro leader, born in the British West Indies. In 1914 he founded the Universal Negro Improvement Association in Jamaica and in 1916 introduced it to the US where it gained a widespread following. It emphasized the kinship of all Negroes and a "back to Africa" movement. He promoted the Black Star Line, a shipping company for trade with Africa but in 1925 was convicted of mail fraud in connection with its funds. His sentence commuted by President Coolidge (1927), he was deported to Jamaica.

GARY, Elbert Henry (1846–1927), US lawyer and industrialist. He organized the US Steel Corporation and was its chairman, 1901–27. He founded the city of Gary, Ind., named for him, and promoted good working conditions, but opposed unions.

GARY, Romain (1914–1980), French novelist of Russian origin, born Romain Kacev. He fought in WWII and was a diplomat. His works include *The Roots of Heaven* (1956) and *Promise at Dawn* (1960).

GAS, one of the three states (solid, liquid, gas) into which nearly all matter above the atomic level can be classified. Gases are characterized by a low DENSITY and viscosity; a high compressibility; optical transparency; a complete lack of rigidity, and a readiness to fill whatever volume is available to them and to form molecularly homogeneous mixtures with other gases. Air and steam are familiar examples. At sufficiently high temperatures, all materials vaporize, though many undergo chemical changes first. Gases, particularly steam and CARBON dioxide, are common products of COMBUSTION, while several available naturally or from PETROLEUM or COAL (e.g., HYDROGEN, METHANE) are used as fuels themselves. The great bulk of the universe is gaseous, in the form of interstellar hydrogen. Gases will often dissolve in liquids, the solubility rising with PRESSURE and falling with TEMPERATURE; a little dissolved carbon dioxide is responsible for the bubbles in soda.

In contrast to solids and liquids, the MOLECULES of a gas are far apart compared with their own size, and move freely and randomly at a wide range of speeds of the order of 325ft/sec. For a given temperature and pressure, equal volumes of gas contain the same number of molecules ($2.7 \times 10^{25} m^{-3}$ at room temperature and atmospheric pressure). The impacts of the molecules on the walls of the container are responsible for the pressure exerted by gases.

GASCONY, historic region of SW France. Once occupied by the Romans and settled by the Basques, it was semi-independent of France until the 17th-century.

GASKELL, Elizabeth Cleghorn (Stevenson) (1810–1865), English novelist. Her most famous works are *Cranford* (1853), about middle-class village life, *North and South* (1855), a social portrayal of industrial towns, and *The Life of Charlotte Brontë* (1857).

GASOHOL, a nine-to-one mixture of gasoline with ethanol (ethyl or grain alcohol) or with methanol (methyl or wood alcohol), each of which can be produced from certain agricultural waste products. The alcohol increases the octane rating of the gasoline, reduces gasoline-produced pollutants and is considered promising in augmenting gasoline supplies.

GASOLINE, or petrol, a mixture of volatile HYDROCARBONS having 4 to 12 carbon atoms per molecule, used as a FUEL for INTERNAL-COMBUSTION ENGINES and as a solvent. Although gasoline can be derived from oil, coal and tar or synthesized from carbon monoxide and hydrogen, almost all is produced from PETROLEUM by refining, cracking and alkylation, the fractions being blended to produce fuels with desired characteristics. Motor gasoline boils between 30°C and 200°C, with more of the low-boiling components in cold weather for easy starting. If, however, the fuel is too volatile, vapor lock can occur—i.e., vapor bubbles form and hinder the flow of fuel. Aviation gasoline contains less of both low- and high-boiling components. The structure of gasoline components is also carefully controlled for maximum power and efficiency, as reflected in the octane rating; this may be further improved by ANTIKNOCK ADDITIVES. Other additives include lead scavengers (ethylene dibromide and dichloride), antioxidants, metal deactivators (which remove metal ions that catalyze oxidation), anti-icing agents and detergents.

GASPÉ PENINSULA, peninsula, c170mi long, in SE Quebec, Canada, projecting into the Gulf of St. Lawrence. Scenic and popular with tourists, it has a forested interior with lakes and rivers, providing excellent hunting and fishing.

GASSENDI, Pierre (1592–1655), French philosopher important for his role in tipping the balance away from the old and toward the new science. A friend and ally of KEPLER and GALILEO, he attacked the prevalent Aristotelianism and supported ATOMISM. He also made a number of important astronomical observations and named the *aurora borealis* (see AURORA).

GASTROENTERITIS, group of conditions, usually due to viral or bacterial infection of the upper GASTROINTESTINAL TRACT, causing DIARRHEA, vomiting and abdominal colic. While these are mostly mild illnesses, in young infants and debilitated or elderly adults, dehydration may develop rapidly and fatalities may result. (See also ENTERITIS; FOOD POISONING.)

GASTROINTESTINAL SERIES, X-RAY examination of the GASTROINTESTINAL TRACT using radio-opaque substances, usually barium salts. In barium swallow and meal, an emulsion is taken and the ESOPHAGUS, STOMACH and duodenum are X-rayed. A follow-through may be performed later to outline the small intestine. For barium enema, a suspension is passed into the rectum and large intestine. CANCER, ULCERS, diverticulae and forms of ENTERITIS and COLITIS may be revealed.

GASTROINTESTINAL TRACT, or gut, or alimentary canal, the anatomical pathway involved in the DIGESTIVE SYSTEM of animals. In man it starts at the pharynx, passing into ESOPHAGUS and STOMACH. From this arises the small intestine, consisting of the duodenum and the great length of the jejunum and ileum. This leads into the large bowel, consisting of the cecum (from which the vermiform appendix arises), colon and rectum. The parts from the stomach to the latter part of the colon lie suspended on a mesentery, through which they receive their blood supply, and lie in loops within the peritoneal cavity of the ABDOMEN. In each part, the shape, muscle layers and epithelium are specialized for their particular functions of secretion and absorption. Movement of food in the tract occurs largely by PERISTALSIS, but is controlled at key points by sphincters. There are many gastrointestinal tract diseases. In GASTROENTERITIS, ENTERITIS and COLITIS, gut segments become inflamed. Peptic ULCER affects both the duodenum and stomach, while CANCERS of the esophagus, stomach, colon and rectum are relatively common. Disease of the small intestine tends to cause malabsorption. Methods of investigating the tract include GASTROINTESTINAL SERIES, and endoscopy, in which viewing tubes are passed in via the mouth or anus to examine the gut epithelium.

GATES, Horatio (c1727–1806), American Revolutionary War general. As a commander of the Army of the North he gained credit for the defeat of General Burgoyne at the battle of SARATOGA in 1777, after which the CONWAY CABAL plotted unsuccessfully to replace Washington by Gates as commander-in-chief. Gates took command in the South in 1780 and was badly defeated at CAMDEN, by General Cornwallis.

GATES, Sir Thomas (d. c1621), English colonial governor of the Virginia colony 1611–14. In 1606 he was one of the first petitioners granted a charter for the London Company to settle Virginia. After Virginia was almost abandoned in 1610, Gates helped to reestablish the colony in 1611.

GATLING, Richard Jordan (1818–1903), US inventor who developed a practical MACHINE GUN. Adopted by the US army in 1866, it had 10 barrels that revolved on a central shaft and could fire 350 rounds per minute.

GAUCHO, cowboy of the South American pampas who flourished in the 18th and 19th centuries. Gauchos were skilled riders, and were usually employed to herd cattle. Their function ceased with the fencing of the pampas and reorganization of the cattle industry, but like the US cowboy they survived as local folk heroes.

GAUDÍ, Antonio (1852–1926), Spanish architect, born Antonio Gaudí y Cornet. The fluidity, intricacy and bizarre aspect of his designs are an expression of ART NOUVEAU. He used glazed tiles to color his architecture. He worked mostly in Barcelona where he created the Milá House, the Güel Park and the Church of the Holy Family.

GAUDIER-BRZESKA, Henri (1891–1915), French sculptor, born Henri Gaudier, who worked in England. His abstract animal sculptures attracted the interest of Ezra POUND and Wyndham LEWIS. He was killed in WWI.

GAUGAMELA, Battle of, battle in 331 BC near modern Mosul, Iraq, where ALEXANDER THE GREAT defeated the larger army of DARIUS III of Persia. This battle, sometimes called the Battle of Arbela, marked the final overthrow of the Persian Empire.

GAUGUIN, Paul Eugéne Henri (1848–1903), French post-impressionist painter noted for his pictures of Polynesian life. After painting in a symbolist style at Pont-Aven, Brittany and working with VAN GOGH, he went to Tahiti and the Marquesas in 1891 where he lived for the rest of his life. He painted scenes in brilliant colors and flattened, simplified forms. His concept of primitivism in art influenced EXPRESSIONISM.

GAUL, ancient designation for a region in W Europe comprising present-day France, Belgium, western Germany and northern Italy. The region was named for the invaders the "Galli" (Celts) who conquered it. Northern Italy, *Cisalpine Gaul* (Gaul this side of the Alps), was conquered in the 5th century BC by Celts who were subjected by Rome in 222 BC. The inhabitants were given Roman citizenship in 49 BC. *Transalpine Gaul* (Gaul the other side of the Alps), now France and parts of Germany, Belgium, Holland and Switzerland, was gradually conquered by the Celts from the 8th to the 5th century BC. However, by 121 BC Rome had occupied the S portion. In his GALLIC WARS, 58–51 BC, Julius Caesar defeated incursions of Germanic tribes and conquered all the Gallic tribes. Under Roman dominion Gaul prospered; roads were built and cities founded. In the 5th century AD it was overrun by Germanic tribes.

GAUSS, Johann Karl Friedrich (1777–1855), German mathematician who discovered the method of least-squares (for reducing experimental errors), made many contributions to the theory of numbers (including the proof that all algebraic equations have at least one root of the form $(a+ib)$ where i is the imaginary operator and a and b are real numbers), and discovered a NON-EUCLIDEAN GEOMETRY. He won fame when he showed how to rediscover the lost ASTEROID Ceres (1801), then later (1831) turned to the study of MAGNETISM, particularly terrestrial magnetism. He is also remembered for his contributions to STATISTICS and CALCULUS.

GAUTIER, Theophile (1811–1872), French poet, novelist and critic. He was a supporter of the aesthetic movement, "art for art's sake," which he explained in the preface to his novel *Mademoiselle de Maupin* (1835–36). He wrote outstanding art, drama and ballet criticism. His volumes of verse include *Enamels and Cameos* (1852).

GAY, John (1685–1732), English poet and dramatist, author of *The Beggar's Opera* (1728). Using English ballads for the music, he satirized Italian operatic forms and contemporary politics in this comedy of highwaymen, thieves and prostitutes. BRECHT based his *Threepenny Opera* on *The Beggar's Opera*.

GAY-LUSSAC, Joseph Louis (1778–1850), French chemist and physicist best known for Gay-Lussac's Law (1808), which states that, when gases combine to give a gaseous product, the ratio of the volumes of the reacting gases to that of the product is a simple, integral one. AVOGADRO's hypothesis is based on this and on DALTON's law of multiple proportions (see COMPOSITION, CHEMICAL). He also showed that all gases increase in volume by the same fraction for the same increase in temperature 1/273.2 for 1C°; and made two balloon ascents to investigate atmospheric composition and the intensity of the EARTH's magnetic field at altitude. His many important contributions to inorganic chemistry include the identification of cyanogen.

GAZA STRIP, narrow piece of land in the former SW Palestine, about 26 mi long, 4–5 mi wide. After the Arab–Israeli war in 1948, it was granted to Egypt and many Arab refugees fled there. Israel occupied the area in 1967. Some of the Arab population has been resettled. Although the Israeli-Egyptian peace treaty (1979) provided for negotiations on self-rule in Gaza, little progress was made, and in Dec. 1987 the inhabitants launched an uprising aimed at ending Israeli occupation.

GAZELLE, a slender, graceful ANTELOPE of Asia and Africa. Males are horned; females may have short spikes. They are usually 2–3ft high at the shoulder, swift and light-footed. They inhabit dry open country. Thompson's and Grant's gazelles live in Africa; the goitered gazelle, so called from a swelling in the throat, in Asian deserts; Speke's gazelle, with an inflatable nose, in Somali deserts. The gerenuk or giraffe-necked gazelle has a long neck and legs.

GDÁNSK (formerly Danzig), large Polish industrial city and port on the Baltic Sea with some of the world's largest shipyards. Its economy rests on mechanical engineering and chemical industries. Once a major city in the Hanseatic League, since 1772 Gdánsk has alternated several times between being a free city and under German or Polish control. Pop 457,000.

GEAR, a toothed wheel forming part of a system by which motion is transmitted between rotating shafts.

One of the simplest gears is the spur gear, which connects parallel shafts. The teeth are cut in the edge of the gear wheel parallel to the axis of rotation. When the wheels

mesh, the driven shaft turns in the opposite direction to the driving shaft. The two shafts can be made to rotate in the same direction by means of an intermediate "idling" gear, the three gears then comprising a gear train. Where smoother transmission is necessary, helical gears are used. They resemble spur gears, but the teeth are cut at a slight angle, forming part of a helix. For carrying high loads, double helical gears are usually employed. Bevel gears transmit motion between the ends of two shafts at right angles to each other; the teeth are cut at angles to the axis of rotation. Worm gears have one gear similar to a spur gear and one gear, the worm, in the form of a spiral along the axis of the shaft, like a screw thread. This combination can be used to transmit power between shafts at right angles, but whose axes do not intersect.

By selecting gear wheels with different numbers of teeth, the shafts can be made to rotate at different speeds from each other, giving reducing or multiplying gears. The ratio between the numbers of teeth is the gear ratio. In an automobile gearbox, sets of gear wheels are meshed together in different "gears" to give a wide range of road speeds while allowing the engine to run near its most efficient speed. Automatic gearboxes have sets of epicyclic or planetary gears, which automatically select the appropriate gear combination.

GECKOES, small lizards living in warm climates all over the world. They appear in the US in Fla. and Cal. They are about 6in long, eat insects and are able to climb vertical surfaces by means of suction pads and minute hairs on the feet. Some can change color to match their background. Most live in trees, but some are found in the desert.

GEDDES, Sir Patrick (1854–1932), Scottish biologist and sociologist who played a formative role in early sociological and urban-planning studies.

GEERTGEN TOT SINT JANS (c1465–c1495), Netherlandish painter. His dramatic style, brilliant coloring, the individuality of his figures and lyrical landscapes prefigure later developments in Dutch art.

GEERTZ, Clifford James (1926–   ), US anthropologist, at the Institute for Advanced Study, Princeton, N.J., from 1970. Fieldwork in Java (1952–54), Bali (1957–58), and Morocco (1965–66) provided the foundation for his theories of interpreting societies.

GEESE, water birds of 14 species closely related to DUCKS and SWANS. There are two natural groups of true geese: gray geese of the genus *Anser*, and black geese (genus *Branta*). They are all confined to the N Hemisphere, breeding in arctic or subarctic regions. They are gregarious, feeding and migrating in large flocks. In flight a flock usually adopts a characteristic V-formation. Geese feed by grazing on the banks of rivers and lakes, or may fly quite a distance from water to feed on grain or in stubble. Domestic geese are derived from the graylag goose, *A. anser*.

GEHRIG, "Lou" (Henry Louis Gehrig; 1903–1941), US baseball player, known as the "Iron Man." As first baseman for the New York Yankees he set a record by playing 2,130 consecutive games. He had a .361 batting average in seven world series, a lifetime average of .341 and 493 home runs. He died of a rare muscle-wasting disease, amyotrophic lateral sclerosis, which now bears his name.

GEIGER COUNTER, or **Geiger-Müller tube,** an instrument for detecting the presence of and measuring radiation such as alpha particles, beta-, gamma- and x-rays. It can count individual particles at rates up to about 10,000/s and is used widely in medicine and in prospecting for radioactive ores. A fine wire anode runs along the axis of a metal cylinder which has sealed insulating ends, contains a mixture of ARGON or neon and METHANE at low pressure, and acts as the cathode, the potential between them being about 1kV. Particles entering through a thin window cause ionization in the gas; ELECTRONS build up around the anode, and a momentary drop in the inter-electrode potential occurs which appears as a voltage pulse in an associated counting circuit. The methane quenches the ionization, leaving the counter ready to detect further incoming particles.

GEISEL, Theodor. See SEUSS, DR.

GEISHA, Japanese professional female entertainer, especially for businessmen's parties in restaurants. The name means "art person" and a Geisha's accomplishments include singing, dancing, playing instruments and conversation, ranging in subject from a knowledge of history to contemporary gossip. Geishas are not prostitutes. Training for the profession, which has existed since the 18th century, begins early with a highly-organized apprenticeship.

GELL-MANN, Murray (1929–   ), US physicist awarded the 1969 Nobel Prize for Physics for his work on the classification of SUBATOMIC PARTICLES (notably K-mesons and hyperons) and their interactions. He (and independently G. Zweig) proposed the quark as a basic component of most subatomic particles.

GEMARA. See TALMUD.

GEMINI, the twins, a constellation in the Northern Hemisphere of the sky. It is also a sign of the Zodiac. Gemini lies near the Milky Way. Its brightest stars are called Castor and Pollux after two twins in Greek mythology. The constellation gives its name to the Geminid meteor shower, seen in December.

GEMS, stones prized for their beauty, and durable enough to be used in jewelry and for ornament. A few—AMBER, CORALS, PEARLS, and jet—have organic origin, but most are well-crystallized MINERALS. Gems are usually found in IGNEOUS ROCKS (mainly pegmatite dikes) and in contact METAMORPHIC ZONES. The chief gems have HARDNESS of 8 or more on the Mohs scale, and are relatively resistant to CLEAVAGE and fracture, though some are fragile. They are identified and characterized by their specific gravity (which also determines the size of a stone with a given weight in carats and optical properties, especially refractive index (see REFRACTION). Gems of high refractive index show great brilliancy (also dependent on transparency and polish) and prismatic dispersion ("fire"). Other attractive optical effects include chatoyancy, dichroism, opalescence and asterism—a star-shaped gleam caused by regular intrusions in the crystal lattice. Since earliest times gems have been engraved in intaglio and cameo. Somewhat later cutting and polishing were developed, the cabochon (rounded) cut being used. Not until the late Middle Ages was faceting developed, now the commonest cutting style, its chief forms being the brilliant cut and the step cut. Some gems are dyed, impregnated, heated or irradiated to improve their color. Synthetic gems are made by flame-fusion or by crystallization from a melt or aqueous solution.

GENERAL ACCOUNTING OFFICE (GAO), an independent agency of the US Congress, created in 1921 for auditing government spending. Headed by the US Comptroller General, it sets up accounting and management standards, settles claims for or against the government, collects debts and assesses the practicability and legality of public expenditures of most government agencies.

GENERAL AGREEMENT ON TARIFFS AND TRADE (GATT), a set of agreements which aim to abolish quotas and reduce tariffs and other restrictions on world trade, originally agreed to by 23 countries in 1947. By 1988 there were 85 nations participating in GATT.

GENERAL SERVICES ADMINISTRA-TION (GSA), an independent US federal agency, established 1949, to maintain government property and records. Its five branches deal with quality-controlled supplies for government use, emergency stockpiles of strategic materials, erection and management of public buildings, transportation and telecommunications and the preserving of historical records and archives.

GENERATOR, Electric, or **dynamo,** a device converting mechanical ENERGY into electrical energy. Traditional forms are based on inducing electric fields by changing the magnetic field lines through a circuit (see ELECTROMAGNETISM). All generators can be, and sometimes are, run in reverse as electric MOTORS.

The simplest generator consists of a permanent magnet (the **rotor**) spun inside a coil of wire (the **stator**); the magnetic field is thus reversed twice each revolution, and an AC voltage is generated at the frequency of rotation. In practical designs, the rotor is usually an ELECTROMAGNET driven by a direct current obtained by rectification of a part of the voltage generated, and passed to the rotor through a pair of CARBON **brush/slip** ring contacts. The use of three sets of stator coils 120° apart allows generation of a three-phase supply.

Simple DC generators consist of a coil rotating in the field of a permanent magnet: the voltage induced in the coil alternates at the frequency of rotation, but it is collected through a **commutator**—a slip ring broken into two semicircular parts, to each of which one end of the coil is connected, so that the connection between the coil and the brushes is reversed twice each revolution—resulting in a rapidly pulsating direct voltage. A steadier voltage can be achieved through the use of multiple coil/commutator arrangements and except in very small generators, the permanent magnet is again replaced by an electromagnet driven by part of the generated voltage.

For large-scale generation, the mechanical power is usually derived from fossil-fuel-fired steam TURBINES, or from dam-fed water turbines, and the process is only moderately efficient. The magneto-hydrodynamic generator, currently under development, avoids this step, and has no moving parts either. A hot conducting fluid (treated coal gas, or reactor-heated liquid metal) passes through the field of an electromagnet, so that the charges are forced in opposite directions, producing a DC voltage. In another device, the electrogasdynamic generator, the voltage is

produced by using a high speed gas stream to pump charge from an electric discharge, against the electric field, to a collector.

Generators originated with the discovery of induction by M. FARADAY in 1831; the considerable advantages of electromagnets over permanent magnets were first exploited by E. W. von SIEMENS in 1866.

GENES, the carriers of the genetic information which is passed on from generation to generation by the combination of GAMETES. Genes consist of chain-like molecules of NUCLEIC ACIDS, DNA in most organisms and RNA in some VIRUSES. The genes are normally located on the CHROMOSOMES found in the nucleus of the CELL. The genetic information is coded by the sequences of the four bases present in nucleic acids, with a differing 3-base code for each AMINO ACID so that each gene contains the information for the synthesis of one PROTEIN chain.

GENESIS (Greek: origin or generation), the first book of the OLD TESTAMENT and of the PENTATEUCH. It tells of the Creation, the Fall (see ORIGINAL SIN), the Flood, the origins of the Hebrews, and the early PATRIARCHS with whom God made his Covenant. The book accounts for the Israelites' presence in Egypt, and so leads into EXODUS.

GENET, Edmond Charles Édouard (1763–1834), French diplomat. He tried to bring the US into the war against Britain during the FRENCH REVOLUTION, thus creating the first international crisis for America. "Citizen Genêt" was sent as minister to the US (1792–94). His demands were opposed by President Washington, and Genêt was replaced.

GENET, Jean (1910–1986), French playwright and novelist. He spent much of his life in prisons. His writing concerns the homosexual underworld of France and the borderline between acceptable and unacceptable social behavior. His works include the novel *Our Lady of the Flowers* (1944), *The Thief's Journal* (1948) and the plays *The Balcony* (1956) and *The Blacks* (1958).

GENETIC ENGINEERING, manipulation of genetic material, or DNA, to effect a particular result. Gene splicing, which creates RECOMBINANT DNA, has been the most prominent technique of genetic engineering since 1973; it promises to revolutionize any number of enterprises from pharmaceuticals to agriculture; for example, by implanting an insulin-producing gene into a DNA ring of the common bacterium *E. coli*, one can create (given the rapid reproduction of these bacteria) a virtual insulin factory. Similarly, with such gene transference, one should be able to develop new characteristics in plants selectively and immediately, as opposed to the time-consuming, imprecise method of cross-breeding. The scientists who developed the basic techniques of gene splicing are the 1980 Nobel Prize winner Paul Berg of Stanford University, first to make recombinant DNA, and Stanley N. Cohen of Stanford University and Herbert W. Boyer of the University of California at San Francisco.

GENETICS, the branch of biology dealing with HEREDITY, which studies the way in which GENES operate and the way in which they are transmitted from parent to offspring. Genetics can be subdivided into a number of more specialized subjects including classical genetics (which deals with the inheritance of parental features in higher animals and plants), cytogenetics (which deals with the cellular basis of genetics), microbial genetics (which deals with inheritance in microorganisms), molecular genetics (which deals with the biochemical basis of inheritance) and human genetics (which deals with inheritance of features of social and medical importance in man). Genetic counseling is a branch of human genetics of growing importance. Here couples, particularly those with some form of inherited defect, are advised on the chances that their children will have similar defects.

GENEVA, city and capital of Geneva canton, SW Switzerland, on Lake Geneva at the Rhône R outlet. It is the headquarters of the WORLD HEALTH ORGANIZATION, the INTERNATIONAL LABOR ORGANIZATION and the International RED CROSS. It is an important cultural, scientific, theological, industrial and banking city and the center of the Swiss watchmaking industry. The Collège de Genève was founded (1559) by John CALVIN. Pop (city) 159,710; (metro) 377,313.

GENEVA, Lake, crescent-shaped lake between Switzerland and France, extending about 45mi from east to west, and varying from 1 to 10mi in width. The Rhône River enters the lake at its eastern end, and emerges at Geneva. The lake, lying between the Alps and the Jura Mountains, at a height of 1,220 ft is much celebrated for the grandeur of the surrounding scenery and the beauty of its shores.

GENEVA CONFERENCE, name of several international conferences held in Geneva, Switzerland. Among the most significant is that of April-July 1954, between the US, Britain, the USSR, France, Communist China, SE Asian countries and other interested parties to discuss settlement of the French-Indochinese and the Korean wars. Cease-fires were agreed for Cambodia, Laos and Vietnam, which was divided into North and South. (See VIETNAM WAR.)

GENEVA CONVENTIONS, four international agreements for the protection of soldiers and civilians from the effects of war, signed by 58 nations and the Holy See in Aug. 1949, at Geneva, Switzerland. Convention I derived from a conference in 1864 in which the work of Jean DUNANT, founder of the RED CROSS, led to an agreement to improve conditions for sick and wounded soldiers in the field. Convention II deals with armed forces at sea, Convention III with treatment of prisoners of war and Convention IV with protection of civilians.

GENGHIS KHAN (1167?–1227), Mongol ruler of one of the greatest empires in world history, born Temujin. After 20 years of tribal warfare, he was acknowledged Genghis Khan (Universal Ruler) in 1206. He campaigned against the Ch'in empire in N China (1213–15) and in 1218–25 he conquered Turkestan, Iran, Afghanistan and S Russia. His empire stretched from the Caucasus Mts to the Indus R and from the Caspian Sea to Peking. Genghis Khan was not only a fearsome warrior but also a skilled political leader. (See MONGOL EMPIRE.)

GENOA, capital of Genoa province and of the region of Liguria, NW Italy, 71mi SSW of Milan. It is Italy's largest port and is second only to Marseilles on the Mediterranean. In ancient times it was the headquarters of the Roman fleet. In the 12th and 13th centuries it was an independent republic with its own fleet and possessions in the LEVANT. The city's principal industries include shipbuilding, iron and steel making and oil and sugar refining. Pop 742,442.

GENOCIDE (from Greek *genos*, race), the deliberate extermination of a racial, ethnic, political or religious group of people. The term is widely credited to the Polish-American scholar Raphael Lemkin. He believed that Nazi persecution of the Jews and other groups called for an international code on the subject. This was achieved when the UN General Assembly in 1948 approved the Convention on the Prevention and Punishment of the Crime of Genocide. By 1988, 97 countries had ratified the Genocide Convention. The US Senate approved the treaty in 1986, and Congress passed implementing legislation in 1988.

GENOTYPE, the total genetic makeup of a particular organism consisting of all the GENES received from both parents. For any individual the genotype determines their strengths and weaknesses during their whole life and is unique and constant for each individual. Duplication of the genotype except in identical twins is statistically impossible except in the simplest organisms. (See also PHENOTYPE.)

GENRE, form of painting which takes its subjects from everyday life. The term derives from the French *de tout genre* (of every kind). Dutch, Flemish and Italian genre schools flourished in the 16th and 17th centuries. Among the great artists of the genre are Pieter BRUEGEL, VERMEER, WATTEAU, LONGHI and CHARDIN. The 19th and 20th centuries saw their own genre movements, such as the American ASHCAN SCHOOL.

GENSERIC, or Gaiseric (c390–477 AD), king of the VANDALS and the Alani from 428. He led his people from S Spain to N Africa, took Carthage in 439, gained control of the Mediterranean and in 455 sacked Rome. By the time of his death he controlled Sardinia, Corsica, Sicily, Roman Africa and the Balearic Islands.

GENTILE, Giovanni (1875–1944), Italian educator and philosopher. He wrote for Benedetto CROCE's *La Critica* and became known as the philosopher of FASCISM. As Fascist education minister (1922–24), he reformed the public educational system; in the period 1925–43 he edited the *Enciclopedia italiana*.

GENTILE DA FABRIANO (c1370–1427), Italian painter, a major exponent of the international Gothic style. His rich, exotic manner with its profusion of color and gilt is seen in his masterpiece, the *Adoration of the Magi* (1423), an altarpiece now in the Uffizi in Florence.

GENTLEMEN'S AGREEMENT, an informal agreement between Japan and the US in 1907. The US promised to discourage any laws restricting Japanese immigration, and the Japanese agreed to stop unrestricted emigration to America. It lapsed in 1924 when the US Congress restricted Japanese immigration. The term also applies to any informal agreement not legally binding.

GENUS. See TAXONOMY.

GEOCHEMISTRY, the study of the CHEMISTRY of the EARTH (and other planets). Chemical characterization of the earth as a whole relates to theories of planetary formation. Classical geochemistry analyzes rocks and MINERALS. The study of phase equilibria has thrown much light on the postulated processes of ROCK formation.

(See also GEOLOGY.)

GEODESIC DOME, architectural dome-like structure composed of polygonal (usually triangular) faces of lightweight material. It was developed by Buckminster FULLER. A geodesic dome housed the US exhibit at Expo '67 (Montreal).

GEODESY, an area of study concerned with the determination and explanation of the precise shape and size of the EARTH. The first recorded measurement of the earth's circumference that approximates to the correct value was that of Eratosthenes in the 3rd century BC. Modern geodesists use not only the techniques of SURVEYING but also information received from the observations of artificial SATELLITES.

GEOFFREY OF MONMOUTH (c1100–1155), British bishop and chronicler whose *History of the Kings of Britain* (c1135) is a romantic and fictional account of early Britain. Highly popular in medieval Europe, it introduced the ARTHURIAN LEGENDS to the continent.

GEOFFREY PLANTAGENET (1113–1151), duke of Normandy from 1135 and count of Anjou, Maine and Touraine from 1131. In 1128 he married Matilda, daughter of Henry I of England; their son Henry thus became Henry II of England, founding the line of PLANTAGENETS.

GEOGRAPHY, the group of sciences concerned with the surface of the earth, including the distribution of life upon it, its physical structures, etc. Geography relies on surveying and mapping, and modern cartography (mapmaking) has rapidly adapted to the new needs of geography as it advances and develops. (See MAP; SURVEYING.) Biogeography is concerned with the distribution of life, both plant and animal (including man), about our world. It is thus intimately related to BIOLOGY and ECOLOGY. Economic geography describes and seeks to explain the patterns of the world's commerce in terms of production, trade and transportation, and consumption. It relates closely to ECONOMICS. Mathematical geography deals with the size, shape and motions of the EARTH, and is thus linked with ASTRONOMY (see also GEODESY). Physical geography deals with the physical structures of the earth, also including climatology and oceanography, and is akin to physical GEOLOGY. Political geography is concerned with the world as nationally divided; regional geography with the world in terms of regions separated by physical rather than national boundaries. Historical geography deals with the geography of the past: paleogeography at one level, exploration or past political change or settlement at another. Applied geography embraces the applications of all these branches to the solution of socioeconomic problems. Its subdivisions include urban geography and social geography; and it contributes to the science of SOCIOLOGY. (See also ETHNOLOGY; HYDROLOGY; METEREOLOGY.)

Development of Geography. Geography had its origins in the Greek attempts to understand the world in which they found themselves. Once it was realized that the earth was round, the next step was to estimate its size. This was achieved in the 3rd century BC by Eratosthenes. The classical achievement in geography, like that in astronomy, was summed up by Claudius PTOLEMY. His world MAP was used for centuries. Geographical knowledge next leapt forward in the age of exploration that opened with the voyages of DIAS and COLUMBUS. The 17th century saw continuing discovery and greatly improved methods of survey. The earliest modern geographical treatises, including that of Varenius, also appeared in this era. The 19th century brought with it the works of F. H. A. von HUMBOLDT and Karl RITTER, the former stressing physical and systematic geography, the latter the human and historical aspects of the science. Encompassing so many different studies, geography since the mid-19th century has become a battleground for the strife between different schools of geographers. While some have encouraged a regional approach, others have preferred to develop a landscape-concept. Others have stressed the study of the physical environment or have concentrated on political and economic factors. Perhaps the most recent group to come to the fore favors the collection of precise numerical data to use in building mathematical models of geographic phenomena.

GEOLOGICAL SURVEY, US government bureau, within the Dept. of the Interior, established in 1879, responsible for the location and control of water and mineral resources on federal land, and for the chartering of water resources and the location of potential problem areas. It carries out and supervises research in the earth sciences.

GEOLOGY, the group of sciences concerned with the study of the earth, including its structure, long-term history, composition and origins.

Physical Geology deals with the structure and composition of the EARTH and the forces of change affecting them. The sciences that make up physical geology thus include structural geology, petrology, mineralogy, geomorphology, geophysics, geochemistry and environmental geology. Much of modern physical geology is based on the theory of PLATE TECTONICS.

Historical Geology deals with the physical history of the earth in past ages and with the EVOLUTION of life upon it. It embraces such sciences as paleoclimatology, geography, paleontology and stratigraphy, and attempts to integrate these with the accumulated data of physical geology in a plate tectonics-oriented reconstruction of earth history embracing some 4.5-5 billion years of geologic time.

Economic Geology lies between these two and borrows from both. Concerned with the location and exploitation of the earth's natural resources (see ORE), it includes such disciplines as petroleum geology, mining geology, and groundwater geology, and utilizes modern geochemical and geophysical methods of exploration.

Geology of Other Planets. Except for the MOON, it is not yet possible to examine the rocks of other planets, but telescopic and spectroscopic examinations and unmanned probes have revealed much. Volcanism is known on the moon and MARS (one volcano is some 375mi across), and "moonquakes" have been detected.

Development of Geology. Most early geological knowledge came from the experience of mining engineers, some of the earliest geological treatises coming from the pen of Georgius AGRICOLA. The interest of the 16th century in FOSSILS was also reflected in the writings of K. von Gesner. In the 17th century the biblical timescale of about 6,000 years from the Creation to the present largely constrained the many speculative "Theories of the Earth" that were issued. The century's most notable geological observations were made by N. STENO. The late 18th century saw the celebrated controversy between A. G. Werner's "Neptunists" and J. HUTTON's "Plutonists" as to the origin of rocks. The first decades of the 19th century witnessed the decline of speculative geology as field observations became ever more detailed. William SMITH, the "father of stratigraphy," showed how the succession of fossils could be used to index the stratigraphic column, and he and others produced impressive geological maps. C. LYELL's classic *Principles of Geology* (1830-33) restated the Huttonian principle of UNIFORMITARIANISM and provided the groundwork for much of the later development of the science. L. AGASSIZ pointed to the importance of glacial action in the recent history of the earth (1840), while mining engineering continued to contribute to the pool of geologic data. The most significant recent development in the earth sciences has been the acceptance of the theory of PLATE TECTONICS, foreshadowed by A. WEGENER'S 1912 theory of CONTINENTAL DRIFT.

GEOMAGNETISM, the magnetic field of the EARTH; and the study of it, both as it is in the present and as it was in the past (see PALEOMAGNETISM). (See also GEOPHYSICS; MAGNETISM.)

GEOMETRY, the branch of MATHEMATICS which studies the properties both of space and of the mathematical constructs—lines, curves, surfaces and the like—which can occupy space. Today it divides into algebraic geometry; ANALYTIC GEOMETRY; descriptive geometry; differential geometry; EUCLIDEAN GEOMETRY; and projective geometry, but many of these divisions have grown up only in the last few hundred years. The name geometry reminds us of its earliest use—for the measurement of land and materials. The Babylonian and Egyptian civilizations thus gained great empirical knowledge of elementary geometric figures, including how to construct a right-angled triangle. The Greek philosophers transformed this practical art into an intellectual pastime through which they sought access to the secrets of nature. About 300 BC EUCLID collected and added to the Greek rationalization of geometry in his *Elements.* Later Alexandrian geometers began to develop TRIGONOMETRY. The revival of interest in life-like painting in the Renaissance led to the development of projective geometry, though it is to the philosopher–scientist DESCARTES that we owe the invention of the algebraic (coordinate) geometry which allows algebraic FUNCTIONS to be represented geometrically. The next new branch of geometry to be developed followed fast upon the invention of CALCULUS: differential geometry. The greatest upset in the history of geometry came in the 19th century. Men such as J. K. F. GAUSS, N. I. LOBACHEVSKI and János Bolyai began to question the Euclidean parallel-lines axiom and discovered hyperbolic geometry, the first non-Euclidean geometry. The elliptic non-Euclidean geometry of G. F. B. RIEMANN aided EINSTEIN in the development of the theory of general RELATIVITY.

GEOPHYSICS, the physics of the EARTH, as such including studies of the LITHOSPHERE, e.g. SEISMOLOGY, GEOMAGNETISM, GRAVITATION, RADIOACTIVITY, electric properties, heat flow. Also included are studies of the ATMOSPHERE and HYDROSPHERE. Geophysical techniques are used extensively in the search for mineral deposits, an area known as exploration geophysics or geophysical PROSPECTING. (See also HYDROLOGY; OCEANOGRAPHY; METEOROLOGY.)

GEOPOLITICS, the study of politics in relation to geography and demography. The term was originally applied to the theories of the biologist and geographer Friedrich Ratzel (1844–1904), who sought to apply evolutionary theory to the rise and fall of nations. In the 1900s the British geographer Sir Halford Mackinder extended these, seeing the international struggle for survival as hanging on control of the heartlands, or interior lands, of the world's great landmasses, particularly the "World Island" of Eurasia. The German Karl HAUSHOFER combined these theories to preach the eventual regeneration of Germany through her inevitable demand for *Lebensraum* (German: living space, space to expand), which would have to be sacrificed by the seaboard countries to the more dynamic countries of the heartland. This was seized upon by Adolf Hitler and became a cornerstone of Nazi doctrine, thus entirely discrediting the theory.

GEORGE, Saint, the patron saint of England. He is an obscure figure, possibly a Christian convert martyred in 303. Many medieval legends became connected with his name, including his rescue of a maiden from a dragon. His feast day was April 23, but since 1969 the Roman Catholic Church has merely commemorated him on Jan. 1.

GEORGE, name of six kings of Britain. **George I** (1660–1727), Elector of Hanover from 1698, came to the throne in 1714. Shrewd and not very popular, he never learned English; this left much power in the hands of his chief minister Sir Robert WALPOLE. **George II** (1683–1760), born in Hanover, succeeded his father, George I, in 1727. He was considerably more popular. Strongly in favor of peace, he allowed the country to be drawn into the War of Austrian Succession (1740–48), losing influence and prestige. After 1750 he took little interest in politics, becoming a great patron of musicians such as HANDEL; Parliament was dominated by the Whigs WALPOLE and PITT the elder. **George III** (1738–1820) was king from 1760. Much of his reign was spent in conflict with the Whig oligarchy in Parliament, which had become entrenched under his father's rule. Ironically, he became the American colonists' principal symbol of English oppression although Whig policy was really responsible. Before the onset of insanity in his later years, George III was a well-meaning ruler in a time of great stress abroad and at home. **George IV** (1762–1830) was regent from 1811 and king from 1820. A loose-living dandy, he cared little about government. The scandal surrounding his divorce from Caroline of Brunswick lowered public esteem for the monarchy. **George V** (1865–1936) ascended the throne in 1910. He was immediately thrown into a constitutional crisis over the power of the House of Lords, in which he played a moderating role. He proved a popular monarch in WWI, seeking to unify the country; he later played an important part in the formation of a coalition government in the economic crisis of 1931. **George VI** (1895–1952) ascended the throne after the abdication crisis of 1936. He and his consort did much to restore confidence in the monarchy; during WWII they were an example of tireless devotion to duty. In 1939 George VI became the first reigning monarch to visit the US.

GEORGE, Henry (1839–1897), US journalist whose *Progress and Poverty* (1879) saw the prime cause of inequality as the possession of land. His proposed SINGLE-TAX on land was never endorsed by economists but won him popular support.

GEORGE, Stefan (1868–1933), German lyric poet. Associated with the PRE-RAPHAELITES and symbolists, he based his poetry on classical Greek humanism, free of naturalistic influences.

GEORGE WASHINGTON BRIDGE, suspension bridge across the Hudson R linking New York City and Fort Lee, N.J. Designed by Othmar AMMANN, it was completed in 1931. It has a main span 3,500ft in length.

GEORGIA, or Georgian Soviet Socialist Republic, constituent republic of the USSR since 1936. The Caucasus Mts run across the N of the republic. Georgia has a subtropical climate, and the lowland areas near the Black Sea produce tea, fruit, wine, tobacco and cereals. Georgia provides the Soviet Union with petroleum and many essential minerals. There is much heavy industry, with steel and other metals, textiles and chemicals the main products. Around two-thirds of the population still work on the land. The Georgian people have a long cultural history. The ancient kingdom of Georgia, ravaged by Turkey and Persia, was annexed to Russia in 1801; an attempt to regain independence after the Revolution was crushed in 1921. Georgia was the home of STALIN. (See UNION OF SOVIET SOCIALIST REPUBLICS.)

GEORGIA, state in SE US, bordered to the E by the Atlantic Ocean and S.C., to the S by Fla., to the W by Ala., and to the N by Tenn. and N.C.; one of the 13 original states.

Name of state: Georgia
Capital: Atlanta
Statehood: Jan. 2, 1788 (4th state)
Familiar name: Peach State, Empire State of the South
Area: 58,876sq mi
Population: 6,104,000
Elevation: Highest—4,784ft, Brasstown Bald Mountain. Lowest—sea level, Atlantic Ocean
Motto: "Wisdom, justice and moderation"
State flower: Cherokee rose
State bird: Brown thrasher
State tree: Live oak
State song: "Georgia on My Mind"
Land. More than half the state consists of plains which extend from the Atlantic coast to the Piedmont region. The rest consists of rolling hill country. On the coastal plains, average temperatures range from a winter low of 54°F to a summer high of 82°F; the Piedmont is a little cooler in winter.
People. The majority of Georgians live in urban areas—over one million live within the urban area of Atlanta, the capital. Until the late 1950s Georgia was primarily rural in character, but today fewer than 10% of Georgians live on farms, and most of the rural population commute to work in the towns.
Economy. The structure of Georgia's economy has changed radically in the last 40 years; manufactures include textiles, transportation equipment, processed foods, clothing, paper and wood products, chemicals and cigarettes. In the 1980s jobs in the service sector increased over 30%. Agriculture still accounts for about a quarter of the state's income. No longer totally dependent on cotton, however, it produces peanuts, peaches, tobacco and chickens; cattle and hog raising are also of importance.
History. The first permanent settlement in

Georgia was made by the English in 1733. In 1749 a ban on the importation of slaves was removed and Georgia quickly prospered. Before the Civil War Georgia was one of the world's leading cotton producers, and by 1860 a large proportion of the state's inhabitants were black slaves. Georgia seceded from the Union on Jan. 19, 1861, and suffered greatly in the Civil War. After the war, resentment aroused by harsh RECONSTRUCTION measures ensured Democratic control over the state's politics for a century. Little changed fundamentally until the combined effects of crop destruction by the boll weevil and low cotton prices in the 1920s and 1930s drove thousands of smaller farmers from the land. After WWII Georgia experienced rapid industrialization. Atlanta became a major commercial and financial center and led the way in accepting racial integration. In 1976 former governor Jimmy Carter became the first native Georgian to be elected pesident of the US. In the 1980s, the state's economy continued to grow, although the farm sector was depressed by low prices and the 1988 drought. In presidential elections 1968–88, Georgia voted Republican in 1972 and 1984–88.

GEOTHERMAL ENERGY, energy contained in underground reservoirs of steam, hot water, hot saline fluids, and hot dry rock. The basic technology for using high-temperature hydrothermal resources is well established. Power plants that exploit such resources are less costly to build and operate than fossil-fuel or nuclear plants because they do not require boilers or fuel. Exploitation of hydrothermal energy, however, poses environmental problems: land subsidence, noise, noxious gases, waste heat, and waste water of high alkalinity that must be reinjected into the earth rather than drained off. The technology is not yet available for economic exploitation of other geothermal energy sources.

GERANIUM, genus of cosmopolitan hardy perennial herbs, some of which are cultivated in gardens and as house plants. Geranium is also the name given to popular pot and bedding plants of the genus *Pelargonium*. Common or zonal geraniums (hybrid races derived from *Pelargonium zonale*) have white, salmon pink or red, flowers single or semidouble, some with bronze or maroon zones on the leaves. A range of dwarf or miniature varieties are available in this group. Another decorative-leaved variety is the ivy-leaved geranium (*P. peltatum*). Indoors, geraniums grow well in sunny south-facing windows, and the miniature varieties are particularly suited to fluorescent-light gardens. Ideally, geraniums should grow at temperatures between 16°C and 21°C (60°F and 70°F) and they should be well watered whenever the soil surface becomes nearly dry, making sure that the soil never completely dries out. Propagation is by seeds and taking shoot tip cuttings. Family: Geraniaceae.

GERBILS, small RODENTS found in arid areas of Africa and Asia. Known as sand rats, they have fine, dense fur, long tails and can move fast by hopping.

GERIATRICS, the branch of MEDICINE specializing in the care of the elderly. Although concerned with the same DISEASES as the rest of medicine, the different susceptibility of the aged and a tendency for multiple pathology make its scope different. In particular the psychological problems of old age differ markedly from those encountered in the rest of the population and require special management. The social and medical aspects of long-term care involve the coordination of family, voluntary and hospital services; the geriatrician must nevertheless seek to maximize the individuality and freedom available to the geriatric patient.

GÉRICAULT, (Jean Louis André) Théodore (1791–1824), French painter whose style combined a massive, dynamic romanticism with a minutely detailed realism. As seen in such well-known works as his studies of lunatics, his horse paintings and the *Raft of the Medusa* (1818–19), Géricault's daringly revolutionary approach helped eclipse the classical school in French painting.

GERM, microorganism capable of causing disease. Germs may be VIRUSES, BACTERIA, PARASITES and PROTOZOA.

GERMAN, official language of Germany and Austria and an official language of Switzerland and Luxembourg, native tongue of more than 100 million people. Modern German is descended from two main forms. Low German, spoken mainly in the N, is the ancestor of both Dutch and Flemish. High German, spoken in central and S Germany is, historically, the classical German. A large part of medieval German literature, such as the 12th and 13th century epics, is in Middle High German. Today the written language is standardized but there are still great differences between spoken N and S German. Modern German is a highly inflected language with three genders and four cases, and requires agreement in number, gender and case, as in Latin. Many words are formed by compounding.

GERMAN **CONFEDERATION,**

organization of 39 German states established by the Congress of Vienna in 1815 in place of the defunct HOLY ROMAN EMPIRE. The Confederation was dominated by Austria. In the AUSTRO-PRUSSIAN WAR (1866), Prussia expelled Austria and organized a North German Confederation under its own leadership.

GERMAN DEMOCRATIC REPUBLIC. See GERMANY, EAST.

GERMAN FEDERAL REPUBLIC. See GERMANY, WEST.

GERMAN MEASLES, or **rubella,** mild VIRUS infection, usually contracted in childhood and causing FEVER, SKIN rash, malaise and LYMPH node enlargement. Its importance lies in the fact that infection of a mother during the first three months of PREGNANCY leads to infection of the EMBRYO via the placenta and is associated with a high incidence of congenital DISEASES including CATARACT, DEAFNESS and defects of the HEART and ESOPHAGUS. VACCINATION of intending mothers who have not had rubella is advisable. If rubella occurs in early pregnancy, ABORTION may be induced to avoid the BIRTH of malformed children.

GERMANTOWN, Battle of, fought on Oct. 4, 1777, during the REVOLUTIONARY WAR. American troops under Washington sought to regain the Philadelphia area from the English under Burgoyne and Cornwallis, but they were routed and driven off.

GERMANY, nation in western Europe now divided into two effectively independent states, East and West Germany. It occupies the heartland of Europe and is composed of the North German Plain in the N, and highlands in the center and S. West Germany has a maritime climate with average temperatures in July 64°F and in January 32°F. In East Germany the temperature varies more widely. About 28% of Germany is still forest and about 39% is farmland; the soil, however, is fairly poor in most areas.

The People. The German people are of two distinct strains: the tall, fair-skinned, blue-eyed Nordic people of the N, and the darker, stockier Alpine types of the S; the two types are well-mingled throughout the country. About three-quarters of the population now lives in urban areas. Germans are known for their liking of outdoor sports and also for their folk traditions. German culture has made major contributions to European art, thought, science, and especially music, through such composers as BEETHOVEN and WAGNER.

Economy. Germany's greatest natural asset has been her coal. The soft coal mines of the Ruhr supply much of the fuel needed for the whole W European steel industry. Other important minerals are salt, potash, silver, copper, lead, zinc and nickel. The Ruhr is still one of the centers of heavy industry in W Europe. More traditional industries include the making of fine clocks, toys and cameras.

History. Although Rome conquered the left bank of the Rhine, the Teutonic tribes of central Germany were never brought into the empire. CHARLEMAGNE united most of the territory of modern France and Germany into the Frankish empire, which was eventually divided among his three grandsons; the area E of the Rhine went to Louis the German. From the 10th to the 13th centuries attempts to retain a united Germany were unsuccessful, and until the 19th century Germany was composed of independent states, loosely united in name only as the Holy Roman Empire. The Protestant Reformation, launched by Luther in the 16th century, influenced much of Europe, but German disunity was intensified by strife between Catholic and Protestant states, culminating in the devastating Thirty Years' War (1618–48). The foundation of modern Germany was largely the work of Otto von BISMARCK, prime minister of Prussia from 1862. After defeating Austria in 1866 and France in 1871, he unified Germany in a Prussian-dominated empire. In the last decades of the 19th century there was massive industrial development in Germany; she began to compete with Britain and France, a competition that culminated in WWI. Germany was defeated and the WEIMAR REPUBLIC was declared on Nov 9, 1918. However, resentment aroused by the harsh Treaty of VERSAILLES (1919), economic chaos in the 1920s and 1930s and lack of democratic traditions all served to undermine support for the Republic.

HITLER became chancellor in 1933 and quickly established a dictatorial, one-party regime. His aggressive expansionist policies led to WWII in Sept. 1939 and although German armies overran most of Europe in 1939 and 1940, the war in Europe ended with Germany's unconditional surrender, May 7–8, 1945. The US, France, Britain and the USSR divided the defeated country into four zones of occupation, the first three of which became West Germany, the fourth, Russian zone becoming East Germany. The former capital, Berlin, although situated in East Germany, was divided between the Western powers and East Germany. (See also GERMANY, EAST and GERMANY, WEST.)

GERMANY, East, customary name for the

Official name: German Democratic Republic
Capital: East Berlin
Area: 41,827sq mi
Population: 16,598,000
Language: German
Religions: Protestant; Roman Catholic
Monetary unit(s): 1 mark (M)=100 pfennige

German Democratic Republic (GDR). The population has dropped by around two million since 1948 due to emigration to West Germany before the erection of the Berlin Wall in 1961. The standard of living is the highest in the Eastern bloc, including the USSR itself. East Germany's free educational system stresses science, mathematics, sports and public service.

Economy. The East German economy is socialized, though there are private firms in the retail trade and in handicrafts. Over 90% of industrial output comes from state-owned establishments. East Germany is now a major industrial nation. Important industries include chemicals, electronics, textiles and metallurgy. Trade is oriented towards the USSR, which accounts for more than one third of the country's imports and exports. Agriculture is now highly mechanized; main products are rye, wheat, barley, potatoes and sugar beet. Livestock is also important.

History. The German Democratic Republic came into being in 1949. It lacked popular support and a revolt in 1953 by students and workers was violently suppressed with the help of Soviet troops. East Germany was not recognized by many Western countries in the 1950s and 1960s and there were continual crises, particularly over the status of West Berlin. The 1970s saw important steps towards improvements of relations between East Germany and the rest of the world, and in Sept. 1973, East Germany was admitted to the UN. Always the most orthodox communists in Eastern Europe, the leaders of the GDR were unenthusiastic about the political and economic reforms initiated by Mikhail Gorbachev in the USSR. Nevertheless, in 1987 the GDR

Official name: Federal Republic of Germany
Capital: Bonn
Area: 96,026sq mi
Population: 60,924,000
Languages: German
Religions: Protestant; Roman Catholic
Monetary unit(s): 1 deutsch mark (DM) = 100 pfennige

amnestied thousands of political prisoners and abolished the death penalty, the first communist state to do so. State and party leader Erich Honecker visited West Germany that year, the first East German leader ever to do so. He used the occasion, however, to declare that the division of Germany between capitalist and communist states was irreversible.

GERMANY, West, customary name for the **Federal Republic of Germany (FRG).** The country has a federal constitution: power is shared between the central government in Bonn and the 10 state governments. West Germany has a well-developed state educational system; there are very few private schools.

Economy. The country's economic progress since WWII has been so striking that it has become known as the *Wirtschaftswunder* (economic miracle). West Germany now has one of the highest living standards in the world. This is the result of the German capacity for hard work, injections of American capital in the COLD WAR period, and a good supply of immigrant labor. West Germany's vast and diverse industries include automobiles, electronics, oil refining, textiles, chemicals and shipbuilding. Industrial products, especially machinery and transport equipment, play a central part in West Germany's highly successful export trade. The country has to import many of her foodstuffs.

History. The Federal Republic of Germany came into being in 1949. The Christian Democratic Party leader, Konrad ADENAUER, became chancellor, and held office for 14 years. In the early years West Germans hoped above all for the reunification of their country, and to this end refused to recognize East Germany. In recent years, however, the existence of two German states has come to be seen as an inescapable reality at least for the time being. The government of Willy BRANDT in 1969 took the first steps towards improving relations with East Germany. This resulted in a nonaggression pact with the USSR (1970) and a treaty recognizing East Germany (1972). West Germany was committed to eventual reunification but, in a first-time visit to Bonn in 1987, East German leader Erich Honecker emphasized that the division of the country was irreversible. West Germany joined the EUROPEAN ECONOMIC COMMUNITY in 1951, the NORTH ATLANTIC TREATY ORGANIZATION in 1955, and the UNITED NATIONS in 1973. Domestically, the West German economy flourished under Social Democratic chancellor Helmut SCHMIDT (1974–82), but in the late 1980s, under conservative Christian Democrat Helmut KOHL (1982–   ), it turned sluggish, due in some part to labor inflexibility, overregulation, and high government subsidies. Corporate taxes were high, investment was low, and economic growth was slow. In anticipation of the ending of internal trade barriers by the European Community in 1992, large German companies shifted plants and investments to lower-cost countries.

GERM CELL. See GAMETE.

GERMICIDES. See ANTISEPTICS.

GERMINATION, the resumption of growth of a plant embryo contained in the SEED after a period of reduced metabolic activity or dormancy. Conditions required for germination include an adequate water supply, sufficient oxygen and a favorable temperature. Rapid uptake of water followed by increased rate of respiration are often the first signs of germination. During germination, stored food reserves are rapidly used up to provide the energy and raw materials required for the new growth. The embryonic root and shoot which break through the seed coat are termed the radicle and plumule, respectively. There are two general forms of germination: hypogeal and epigeal. In the former, the seed leaves, or cotyledons, remain below the ground, as in the broad bean, while in the latter they are taken above the ground and become the first photosynthetic organs, as in the castor oil seed.

GERM PLASM, a special type of PROTOPLASM present in the reproductive cells or gametes of plants and animals, which A. WEISMANN suggested passed on unchanged from generation to generation. Although it gave rise to the body cells, it

remained distinct and unaffected by the offspring.

GERONIMO (1829–1909), greatest war leader of the APACHE INDIANS of Ariz. When his tribe was forcibly removed to a barren reservation he led an increasingly large band of hit-and-run raiders 1876–86. Twice induced to surrender by Lt.-Col. George CROOK, he was driven to escape again by maltreatment. Persuaded to surrender a third time by Gen. Nelson Miles, he was summarily exiled to Fla. and resettled in Okla., where he became a farmer.

GERRY, Elbridge (1744–1814), US politician for whom the GERRYMANDER was named. He signed the Declaration of Independence and attended the Constitutional Convention (1787), was a member of Congress 1789–93, governor of Mass. 1810–12 and vice-president under Madison 1813–14.

GERRYMANDER, an unfair practice usually employed by a party in power, involving a redivision of electoral boundaries in its favor. The term originated during Elbridge Gerry's governorship of Mass. in 1812, when the state senatorial districts were reapportioned to produce a majority in his party's favor.

GERSHWIN, George (1898–1937), US composer. From a Jewish immigrant family, he rose to fame first as a songwriter and then with musical shows such as *Lady Be Good!* (1924), his first Broadway success, and the satirical *Of Thee I Sing* (1931), among many others. He also wrote highly regarded orchestral pieces, *Rhapsody in Blue* (1924), *Piano Concerto* (1925), *An American in Paris* (1928), and and an opera *Porgy and Bess* (1935), noted for its unusual lyricism and emotional power. These works show the influence of RAVEL, STRAVINSKY and, especially, American jazz.

GERSHWIN, Ira (1896–1983), US lyricist known primarily for his collaborations with his brother George in the 1920s and 1930s on many shows, songs and the opera *Porgy and Bess* (1935). After George's death he collaborated with Kurt WEILL and others.

GESNER, Konrad von (1516–1565), Swiss naturalist whose major work, *Historia Animalium* (4 vols., 1551–58), an encyclopedic study of many varieties of animals, is considered the foundation stone of modern zoology.

GESTALT PSYCHOLOGY, a school of psychology concerned with the tendency of the human (or PRIMATE) mind to organize PERCEPTIONS into "wholes"; for example, to hear a symphony rather than a large number of separate notes of different tones.

Gestalt psychology, whose main proponents were WERTHEIMER, KOFFKA and KÖHLER, maintained that this was due to the mind's ability to complete patterns from the available stimuli.

GESTAPO, abbreviated form of *Geheime Staatspolizei* (Secret State Police), the executive arm of the Nazi police force 1936–45, with almost unlimited power. Under the overall control of Heinrich HIMMLER, it shared responsibility for internal security and administered the concentration camps. It was declared a criminal organization at the NUREMBERG TRIALS.

GESTATION, the development of young mammals in the mother's uterus from FERTILIZATION to BIRTH. With some exceptions, the gestation period is proportional to the adult size of the animal; thus, for the human young the gestation period is about 270 days, but for the elephant it is closer to two years. (See EMBRYO; FETUS; PREGNANCY.)

GESUALDO, Carlo (1560–1613), Italian composer, a master of the madrigal form. Of his five collections (1594–1611) the last two are noted for their revolutionary use of harmony and their handling of chromaticism and dissonance.

GETHSEMANE (from Hebrew *gat semanim*, oil press), the garden across the Kidron valley, on the Mount of Olives, E of the old city of Jerusalem, where Jesus prayed on the eve of his crucifixion, and was betrayed. Gethsemane was probably an olive grove; its precise location is disputed.

GETTYSBURG, Battle of, the major conflict of the US Civil War, fought July 1–3, 1863. In a daring maneuver Confederate General Robert E. LEE struck deep into Union territory, reaching Pa. in June 1863. He and the Union Army of the Potomac, under Gen. George S. MEADE, converged upon Gettysburg, Pa. On July 1 and 2 there were many inconclusive attacks and counterattacks; Union reinforcements arrived on July 2. On July 3 suicidal Confederate attacks broke the Union line on Cemetery Ridge, but were driven back in disorder. On July 4, after a day of stalemate, Lee retreated under cover of night and rain. Union losses were over 23,000, around 25%; Confederate losses were around 20,000, a similar percentage. The costly battle marked a reversal in the fortunes of the Confederacy which paved the way for the eventual Union victory.

GETTYSBURG ADDRESS, speech delivered by President LINCOLN at the dedication of the national cemetery at Gettysburg, Pa., on Nov. 19, 1863. A brief masterpiece of oratory, it combined the themes of grief for the dead with the maintenance of the principles they had died to uphold.

GETZ, Stanley (1927–   ), US jazz musician. He played the saxophone under Stan Kenton, Benny Goodman and Woody Herman before forming smaller groups to develop his own style of "cool" jazz.

GEYSER, a hot spring, found in currently or recently volcanic regions, that intermittently jets steam and superheated water into the air. It consists essentially of a system of underground fractures analogous to an irregular tube leading down to a heat source. GROUNDWATER accumulates in the tube, that near the bottom being kept from boiling by the PRESSURE of the cooler layers above. When the critical temperature is reached, bubbles rise, heating the upper layers which expand and well out of the orifice. This reduces the pressure enough for substantial steam formation below, with subsequent eruption. The process then recommences. The famous Old Faithful in Yellowstone National Park used to erupt every 66½min, but has recently become less reliable.

GHANA, republic in West Africa, on the Gulf of Guinea, formerly the British colony of the Gold Coast.

Official name: Republic of Ghana
Capital: Accra
Area: 92,098sq mi
Population: 13,482,000
Languages: English; Twi; Fanti; Ga; Hausa and others
Religions: Christian; Animist; Muslim
Monetary unit(s): 1 new cedi=100 pesewas
Land. Generally a low-lying country, it is characterized by tropical rain forests in the S, a central inland plateau that forms a divide between the White Volta and the Black Volta rivers, and rolling savanna in the N. Lake Volta, in central Ghana, is one of the world's largest man-made lakes. Ghana has a hot climate with, generally, one rainy season in the N and two in the S.
People. The population is made up of various tribal groups. Compared with other

African states, Ghana has a high level of education with 10 years of free and compulsory basic schooling and subsidized further education. Most Ghanaians still live on the land, but large numbers have moved to the cities.

Economy. Once one of the most prosperous countries in Africa, Ghana underwent serious economic decline in the 1970s and 1980s. At independence, Ghana was the world's leading producer of cocoa; production subsequently declined more than 50%, although cocoa still accounts for more than half of export earnings. Minerals and forest products are other important exports. Principal mineral exports are gold, industrial diamonds, manganese and bauxite. The manufacturing sector is well developed but has declined because of its heavy reliance upon imported oil and spare parts.

History. In 1482 the Portuguese began trading at Elmina in gold, ivory and then slaves. The Gold Coast was then controlled by the French, Dutch and finally the British, under whom the economy expanded, bringing prosperity. Ghana was the first West African country to become independent, on March 6, 1957, with Kwame NKRUMAH as premier. In 1960 he declared the country a republic, with himself as life president. While he made reforms in education, transportation and other social services, during his rule political opponents were jailed and government became increasingly inefficient and corrupt. In 1966 Nkrumah was deposed by a coup that had popular support. In 1969 Kofi Busia was elected premier; he was deposed in 1972. Following a series of coups, civilian rule was restored in 1979. Economic conditions did not improve subsequently; at the end of 1981 the military, under Jerry Rawlings, again took control. Under Rawlings, government involvement in the economy was reduced. The nation celebrated the 30th anniversary of its independence in 1987.

GHATS, Eastern and Western, two mountain ranges forming the E and W boundaries of the Deccan Plateau of peninsular India. The Western Ghats receive between 200in and 400in of rain a year from the monsoons and are the source of several rivers. Both ranges are between 3,000 and 5,000ft high and about 1,000mi long.

GHAZZALI, AL- (1058–1111), important medieval Muslim philosopher and mystic who taught at Baghdad. His system evidences his mistrust of purely intellectual inquiry in theology; for a time he gave up philosophy to seek certainty as a Sufi mystic, an experience he attempted to reconcile with orthodox Islamic teachings.

GHENT, historic city in Belgium, at the junction of the Lys and Scheldt rivers. Former capital of Flanders, it was the textile center of medieval Europe; the textile industry is still important, along with paper, chemical and metal production. It also has a major port. In the 16th and 17th centuries it was a center of Flemish art. Pop 234,653.

GHENT, Treaty of, concluded on Dec. 24, 1814, in Ghent, Belgium, formally ending the WAR OF 1812 between Britain and the US. Because the war had developed into a military stalemate, the treaty was essentially a return to prewar status. No concession was made over the impressment of former British citizens from US ships, a major US grievance, but the resulting British withdrawal from interference in the affairs of the American Northwest opened the frontier to westward expansion.

GHETTO, in European history, the street or section of a city once set aside for the compulsory residence of Jews. Today the term is often used to refer to the slum areas of inner cities where blacks and other minority groups are compelled to live, not by law, but by the forces of discrimination and poverty. The word itself is probably derived from the name of the area of Venice to which the Jews of that city were confined in 1516. Ghettos spread throughout Italy during the Counter-Reformation (the late 16th century) but had already been in existence in northern Europe for hundreds of years. The ghetto was surrounded by walls and it was illegal for a Jew to remain outside its gates after curfew. The French Revolution and reform movements of the 19th century removed legal discrimination against Jews in Western Europe and the ghettos were abolished.

GHIBERTI, Lorenzo (c1378–1455), Italian sculptor, goldsmith, painter, writer and architect. A Florentine, he was one of the leading figures of the early Renaissance. His most famous work is probably his second pair of bronze doors for the Florence baptistery, known as the *Gates of Paradise* (1425–52).

GHIRLANDAIO, Domenico (1449–1494), Florentine Renaissance painter said to have taught MICHELANGELO. Probably his most famous frescoes are those of *Saint Jerome* (1480) and the *Last Supper* (1480), both in the Church of Ognissanti, Florence. He is also noted for his portraits, among them *Grandfather and Grandson*.

GHOSE, Aurobindo (1872–1950), Indian

nationalist leader and mystic philosopher. Arrested by the British as the head of a secret terrorist organization opposed to the 1905 partition of Bengal, he underwent a religious transformation in jail. Upon his release (1910), he renounced politics, established a religious retreat in India, and gained a large following. He devoted his life to the study of Hindu philosophy and became known as Sri Aurobindo. His writings include *The Synthesis of Yoga* (1948) and *The Divine Life* (1949).

GHOST DANCE, millenarian cult originating among the PAIUTE INDIANS in W Nev. in 1870, named for its ceremonial dance. It was led by the religious mystic Wovoka who prophesied the rebirth of the dead and the restoration of the Indians to their lands. The massacre of Ghost Dance believers at WOUNDED KNEE in 1890 did much to suppress the cult.

GHOSTS, disembodied spirits of the dead. Ghosts and apparitions figure in the literature and folklore of all countries, from Homer's *Odyssey* to Shakespeare's *Hamlet* to the stories of Edgar Allan Poe. Ghosts are usually said to appear in the places they inhabited when alive. The spirits of the dead may be condemned to haunt the earth as punishment for their sins; they may return to seek vengeance; or they may even appear to warn people of impending disaster. The word "ghost" originally referred to the essential part of a man's soul that was immortal: the phrase "giving up the ghost" is derived from this meaning. Superstitious belief in ghosts has declined over the centuries, but in recent years ghosts and similar apparitions have become subjects of serious study in parapsychology, the division of psychology concerned with apparently inexplicable phenomena.

GHOST TOWNS, abandoned communities, usually mining towns vacated when the mineral deposits ran out. Found in Canada and Australia, they are most common in the W US, where many are now tourist attractions.

GIACOMETTI, Alberto (1901–1966), Swiss-born sculptor and painter who spent most of his life in Paris. He is best known for his elongated and skeletal human figures which convey a sense of extreme spiritual isolation. His early work was influenced by primitive art and SURREALISM.

GIANTS, semi-human creatures of great size and strength; they figure in the myth and folklore of almost every culture, usually as survivors of races that lived before mankind. The Greek Titans were to some extent personifications of elements and natural forces. Other giants, such as the

biblical Goliath, are probably exaggerated memories of very large and fierce men.

GIANT'S CAUSEWAY, spectacular rock structure near Portrush, Northern Ireland, formed by cooling LAVA. Initially, generally hexagonal cracks appeared on the surface, formed by localized contractions toward discrete centers: these developed downward, forming 38,000 basalt columns. According to folk legends, it was formed by giants as part of a roadway to Staffa, the site of a similar structure.

GIAP, Vo Nguyen (1912–   ), Vietnamese general. As commander of the Viet Minh, he defeated the French at Dien Bien Phu (1954). In the Vietnam War he directed N Vietnamese and Viet Cong strategy against S Vietnam.

GIBBON, Edward (1737–1794), English historian, author of the *History of the Decline and Fall of the Roman Empire* (1776–88), the greatest historical work of the 18th century and a literary masterpiece. The *Decline and Fall* is particularly well known for its skeptical treatment of Christianity. Gibbon served somewhat unsuccessfully as a member of Parliament (1774–82).

GIBBON, the smallest of the apes, distinguishable by its very long arms. It is the only ape to walk upright with ease. There are six species living in SE Asia from Borneo to Assam. They can leap over 9m (30ft) and swing along the branches of trees in which they live without pausing between bounds. (See also ANTHROPOID APES.)

GIBBONS, Grinling (1648–1721), English carver and sculptor. While still a young man he was engaged by WREN to work on St. Paul's Cathedral. His wood carvings decorate many of England's country houses, among the most notable being at Petworth, Sussex.

GIBBONS, James (1834–1921), US Roman Catholic cardinal and archbishop, author of *The Faith of Our Fathers* (1876), a popular work of Catholic apologetics. In 1886 Pope Leo XII made him cardinal; he was only the second American to hold this office.

GIBBONS, Orlando (1583–1625), English composer, one of the last of the polyphonic school. A talented keyboard player, he was made organist of the Chapel Royal when only 21. In 1623 he became organist of Westminster Abbey. He composed madrigals, motets and music for viol and virginal.

GIBBONS v. OGDEN, US Supreme Court decision of March 2, 1824, important in defining the power of Congress. Ogden, a steamship operator, held a license from a company given a monopoly of steamship traffic by the N.Y. legislature. He sought to prevent Gibbons, who held a license from the federal government, from competing with him. Chief Justice Marshall's decision upholding Gibbons was widely praised because it affirmed Congress's power over interstate commerce and broke up a powerful and hated monopoly of steamboat travel.

GIBBS, James (1682–1754), Scottish architect, designer of the present church of St. Martin's-in-the-Fields, London, and the Radcliffe Camera, Oxford. Trained in Rome, he developed a simple but striking style unlike the then fashionable Palladian architecture. His *Book of Architecture* (1728) was a major influence in the 18th century.

GIBBS, Josiah Willard (1839–1903), US physicist best known for his pioneering work in chemical THERMODYNAMICS, and his contributions to STATISTICAL MECHANICS. In *On the Equilibrium of Heterogeneous Substances* (2 vols., 1876 and 1878) he states Gibbs' Phase Rule for chemical systems. In the course of his research on the electromagnetic theory of LIGHT, he made fundamental contributions to the art of vector analysis.

G.I. BILL OF RIGHTS, the Serviceman's Readjustment Act of 1944, which provided government aid for demobilized servicemen after WWII. It was designed to prevent a repetition of the social problems that had resulted after WWI. It provided financial aid for the purchase of houses, farms and businesses, and for veterans' hospitals; unemployment benefits; and vocational training. Most significnt, however, was the educational aid, which in effect paid for four years of college education, including basic living expenses. Veterans of the Korean and Vietnam wars also received benefits.

GIBRALTAR, self-governing British colony, 2.3sq mi in area, on the Rock of Gibraltar at the S tip of the Iberian peninsula. The population is mixed; natives are of English, Genoese, Portuguese and Maltese descent. The economy rests on light industry, shipping and tourism, and on the important British naval and airbases. Gibraltar was captured from Spain in 1704. A 1967 referendum showed overwhelming opposition to a return to Spanish rule. Pop 29,000.

GIBRAN, Kahlil (1883–1931), Lebanese-American essayist, philosopher–poet and painter who blended elements of Eastern and Western mysticism. He was influenced by BLAKE and NIETZSCHE. His best-known

work is *The Prophet* (1923).

GIBSON, Althea (1927–   ), US tennis player, the first black to win all the world's women's singles titles, including consecutive British and US titles (1957–58).

GIBSON, Charles Dana (1867–1944), US artist, a fashion illustrator who created the "Gibson Girl." Based on his wife, she was an elegant and high-spirited figure who came to typify the ideal of American womanhood in the early 20th century.

GIBSON, Josh (1911–1947), black US baseball player, a catcher for Pittsburgh teams in the Negro League from 1930. Although no official records were kept, he is estimated to have hit more than 950 home runs, including more than 70 in 1931 and 1933. He had a lifetime batting average of .423.

GIDE, André Paul Guillaume (1869–1951), French writer and moralist, whose relentless examination of his own standards and assumptions, and the resulting inner conflicts, made him one of the foremost figures in French literature in the first half of the 20th century. In 1947 he was awarded the Nobel Prize for Literature. Among his best-known works are the novels *The Immoralist* (1902) and *The Counterfeiters* (1925) and four volumes of *Journals* (1889–1949).

GIDEON v. WAINWRIGHT, case involving the right of a defendant in a criminal case to legal counsel. In 1963 the US Supreme Court ruled that Clarence Gideon, an indigent convicted of burglary by a Fla. court, had been wrongfully imprisoned because, not being able to afford a lawyer, he had defended himself. The Supreme Court held that all defendants in criminal cases are entitled to counsel, and that attorneys must be provided for defendants who are indigent.

GIELGUD, Sir (Arthur) John (1904–   ), British actor, producer and director, famous early in his career for his Shakespearean roles, especially Hamlet and Richard III. Famous for his versatility, he created many modern roles in his maturity in numerous stage, film and television appearances.

GIEREK, Edward (1913–   ), first secretary of the Polish Communist Party (1970–80). He was appointed to improve the standard of living following food riots in late 1970. A failing economy and massive national labor unrest led to his fall from power in 1980.

GIESEKING, Walter (1895–1956), German pianist who was best known for his refined interpretations of the works of DEBUSSY and RAVEL.

GIGANTISM, or abnormally large stature

starting in childhood, may be caused by a constitutional trait or by HORMONE disorders during growth. The latter are usually excessive secretion of growth hormone or thyroid hormone before the epiphyses have fused.

GIGLI, Beniamino (1890–1957), Italian tenor, who made his debut in 1914. After bowing at the Metropolitan Opera in 1920 as Faust in Arrigo Boito's *Mefistofele* he was a principal tenor of the company until 1932, assuming many of the roles formerly sung by Enrico CARUSO.

GILA MONSTER, stout-bodied lizard, up to 2ft long. It and the related beaded lizard are the only poisonous lizards. Both live in the deserts of the SW states and in Mexico. The gila monster is so rare that it is protected by law.

GILBERT, Cass (1859–1934), US architect most famous for the Woolworth Building in New York (1913). His characteristic neoclassical style appears also in his other designs, such as the Supreme Court Building in Washington, D.C.

GILBERT, Sir Humphrey (c1537–1583), English soldier and explorer who founded England's first North American colony, at St. John's, Newfoundland (1583). He was granted a royal charter to colonize unclaimed lands in North America (1578). His first expedition had to turn back after being attacked by the Spanish. He went down with his ship while returning from his second, otherwise successful voyage.

GILBERT, William (1544–1603), English scientist, the father of the science of MAGNETISM. Regarding the earth as a giant magnet, he investigated its field in terms of dip and variation (see EARTH), and explored many other magnetic and electrostatic phenomena.

GILBERT, Sir William Schwenck (1836–1911), English author and humorist who collaborated with Sir Arthur SULLIVAN on the cycle of comic operettas named for them. He combined facetiousness with a mordant wit in satires more vigorous in their day than they appear to modern audiences.

GILBERT AND ELLICE ISLANDS. See TUVALU.

GILBERT AND SULLIVAN. See GILBERT, SIR WILLIAM SCHWENCK; SULLIVAN, SIR ARTHUR SEYMOUR; D'OYLY CARTE, RICHARD.

GILDED AGE, sardonic name for the post-Civil War period up to around 1880 in the US, a time of rampant corruption in politics and commerce. The term derives from the title of a novel by Mark TWAIN and C. D. Warner.

GILELS, Emil Grigorevich (1916–1985), Russian pianist, winner of the Stalin Prize in 1946 and the Lenin Prize in 1962. Noted for his crystalline technique, he was one of the first Soviet artists to tour the US (1955) after WWII.

GILGAMESH, Epic of, the earliest known epic poem, written in the Akkadian language and originating in Mesopotamia in the 3rd millennium BC. The fullest surviving text, carved on tablets, was found in a 7th-century BC library at Nineveh in 1872. The poem tells of the semi-divine hero Gilgamesh (a historical 3rd-millennium king of Uruk), and of his friend Enkidu. They clash with the gods, who cause Enkidu's death. Gilgamesh then goes on a quest to find the secret of eternal life, which in the end eludes him. The epic contains a flood story with close parallels to that in Genesis.

GILLESPIE, John Birks "Dizzy" (1917–), US jazz musician. A trumpet player, he pioneered with saxophonist Charlie Parker the style known as bebop.

GILLRAY, James (1757–1815), English caricaturist whose violent and often scurrilous cartoons both expressed and influenced public opinion in his time. He reduced all the major political figures of his day, including George II and the royal family, to ridiculous grotesques.

GILLS, the respiratory organs of many aquatic animals. They take in OXYGEN from the water and give off CARBON dioxide waste. They are thin-walled so that gases pass easily through and usually take the form of thin flat plates or finely divided feathery filaments. The higher invertebrates, crabs and lobsters for instance, have gills protected by an EXOSKELETON and maintain an adequate oxygen supply by pumping water over them. The gills of most fish are protected by a bony operculum and movements of the throat provide a water current over them. (See RESPIRATION.)

GILMAN, Daniel Coit (1831–1908), US educator. He taught physical and political geography at Yale and in 1872 became president of the U. of California at Berkeley. He was first president of Johns Hopkins U. 1875–1901 and then first president of the Carnegie Institute until 1904.

GILSON, Étienne Henri (1884–1978), French historian and philosopher. A neo-Thomist, most of his writings are either studies of medieval Christain philosophy or applications of Thomist principles to modern problems. He became a member of the French Academy in 1947.

GIN, liquor distilled from grain flavored with juniper berries. Sometimes coriander, orange or lemon peel, cardamom and orris roots are added as flavoring agents. It contains 40–47% alcohol (80–94 US proof). It originated in the Netherlands, apparently from a juniper-berry medicine.

GINASTERA, Alberto (1916–1983), leading Argentinian composer. Despite his advanced techniques he is an essentially nationalistic composer, making much use of local idioms. His best-known work is his opera *Don Rodrigo* (1964).

GINGIVITIS, or gum INFLAMMATION, due to bacterial infection or disease of the TEETH and poor mouth hygiene.

GINSBERG, Allen (1926–   ), US poet of the 1950s BEAT GENERATION and spokesman for the COUNTERCULTURE of the 1960s. *Howl* (1956) and *Kaddish* (1961) are principal works.

GIOLITTI, Giovanni (1842–1928), Italian politician who served as premier five times between 1892 and 1921; the period 1901–14 is called the Age of Giolitti. Responsible for major liberal reforms, including universal male suffrage (1912), he maintained power through a form of political corruption called *giolittismo.*

GIORGIONE (c1478–1510), Renaissance painter and student of Giovanni BELLINI who is regarded as the founder of the Venetian school in Italian art of the 1500s. Painting with a soft subordination of line to light and color, he achieved a unity of human figures with landscape which greatly influenced TITIAN and several other painters of note. Among the works attributed to him are *The Tempest* (c1505), *Madonna and Child Enthroned* (1504) and *The Three Philosophers* (1510).

GIOTTO (Giotto di Bondone; c1266–1337), Italian painter and architect of the Florentine school. He had a profound influence on his own time and on future generations of artists throughout Europe. Breaking away from the Byzantine style of graceful but static representation, he painted monumental figures dramatically and emotionally, giving his vast FRESCO scenes a sense of movement and spatial depth. Among his famous works are frescoes in Padua, Florence and the Church of St. Francis at Assisi.

GIOVANNI DI PAOLO (c1403–1483), Italian painter of the Sienese school whose work, in the style of the preceding century, is rich in fantasy and imagination.

GIRAFFE, *Giraffa camelopardalis,* the tallest living mammal, reaching 5.5m (18ft) in the male, some 2m (6.6ft) of which are taken up by the head and extremely long neck. Its coat is a neutral buff color spotted with red-brown patches. A short, rather bristly mane runs along its spine from head to tail. Giraffes live by grazing, often on trees, aided by their long necks and tongues. They are speedy runners. Giraffes are related to deer as is evidenced by their short horns.

GIRAUDOUX, (Hippolyte) Jean (1882–1944), French playwright. Known for his imaginative, satirical dramas, his major works include *Tiger at the Gates* (1935) and *Electra* (1937), both based on Greek mythology, and *The Mad Woman of Chaillot* (1945).

GIRL SCOUTS OF THE USA, US girls organization comprising Daisy Girl Scouts (ages 5-6), Brownie Girl Scouts (ages 6-8), Junior Girl Scouts (ages 8-11), Cadette Girl Scouts (ages 11-14), Senior Girl Scouts (ages 14-17). It was founded in 1912 and has headquarters in New York City. In 1988 it had 2.2 million members.

GIRONDINS, or **Girondists,** French political group of republicans, representing the middle classes and favoring a federal republic, prominent in the FRENCH REVOLUTION. The group's original members came from the Gironde department in SW France. They came into power under the 1791 Constitution but lost ground to the JACOBINS. In June 1793, a Jacobin-led mob forced the expulsion of 29 Girondins from the National Convention; many Girondins were guillotined in the TERROR.

GIRTY, Simon (1741–1818), American frontiersman called the "Great Renegade." He was captured by the Seneca Indians at age 15. During the REVOLUTIONARY WAR, he deserted the Colonists to serve the British as a scout and interpreter and led numerous, often brutally savage Indian raiding parties.

GISCARD D'ESTAING, Valéry (1926–   ), president of France 1974–81. In 1962–66 he was minister of finance, a post he resumed (1969) under Georges POMPIDOU, supporting the Common Market and closer ties with the US. He ran for president as an independent Republican with Gaullist support. His austerity program failed to solve problems related to inflation, unemployment, and the balance of payments. He was defeated for reelection by the Socialist candidate, François Mitterrand.

GISH, Lillian Diana (1896–   ) and **Dorothy** (1898–1968), American sisters, famous stage and screen actresses who appeared in the pioneering epics of D. W. GRIFFITH. In *The Birth of a Nation* (1915), Lillian won world fame; later she appeared in many notable plays, including *All the Way Home* (1960) and *Uncle Vanya*

(1973).

GISSING, George Robert (1857–1903), English novelist. He is noted for his starkly realistic studies of late Victorian lower and middle class life. His most famous novel, *New Grub Street* (1891), depicts much of the drudgery and hardship he himself experienced as an aspiring writer.

GIST, Christopher (c1706–1759), American frontiersman, who explored parts of Ky. 18 years before Daniel BOONE and was the first to explore and map the Ohio R valley in western Va. He served in the FRENCH AND INDIAN WARS, during which he is said to have twice saved George WASHINGTON's life.

GIULIO ROMANO (born Giulio Pippi; c1492–1546), Italian painter and architect in the style of MANNERISM. RAPHAEL's pupil, his masterpiece is the Palazzo del Té, Mantua, where his architecture is highly fanciful and the frescoes exciting examples of illusionism.

GJELLERUP, Karl Adolph (1857–1919), Danish poet and novelist, who shared the 1917 Nobel literature prize. His novels, radical and idealist in tone, include *An Idealist* (1878), *Minna* (1889) and *The Pilgrim Kamanita* (1906).

GLACIER, a large mass of ice formed from the burial, compaction and recrystallization of snow, which is flowing or has flowed in the past under the influence of gravity. There are three recognized types of glacier: ice sheets and caps; mountain or valley glaciers; and piedmont glaciers. Glaciers form wherever conditions are such that annual precipitation of snow, sleet and hail is greater than the amount that can be lost through evaporation, melting, or otherwise. The occurrence of a glacier also depends much on the position of the lower limit of perennial snow (*snowline*), which generally varies with latitude (see LATITUDE AND LONGITUDE) and also on local topography: there are several glaciers at high elevations on the Equator. The world's largest glacier is the ice sheet which covers over 90% of the Antarctic continent and has ice thicknesses exceeding 10,000ft. Mountain glaciers are more numerous and are found in the Alps, Himalayas, Andes and other high ranges of the world, including about 50 in the NW US (excluding Alaska). **Mountain glaciers** usually result from snow accumulated in snowfields which grow to form glaciers and occupy mountain valleys originally formed through stream erosion; **piedmont glaciers** occur when such a glacier spreads out of its valley into a contiguous lowland area. (See also EROSION; ICE; ICE AGES; ICEBERG.)

GLACIER NATIONAL PARK, wilderness area of over 1 million acres in the Rocky Mts, NW Mont. Part of the Waterton-Glacier International Peace Park, it is noted for its spectacular peaks and glacier-fed lakes. It was established in 1910.

GLACKENS, William James (1870–1938), US illustrator and painter. A member of the ASHCAN SCHOOL in New York City, he painted GENRE subjects and landscapes. Among his works are *Hammerstein's Roof Garden* (1901) and *Chez Mouqin* (1905).

GLADDEN, Washington (1836–1918), US Congregational minister and social reformer. His many books and public lectures popularized the idea of a Christian solution to modern social problems.

GLADIATORS, warrior-entertainers of ancient Rome. They fought in public arenas against each other and against wild beasts with a variety of weapons including swords (Latin *gladius*, a short sword), three-pronged tridents and nets, for the favor of the crowds. They were recruited from prisoners of war, slaves, criminals and sometimes freemen. The tradition survived into the 5th century AD.

GLADSTONE, William Ewart (1809–1898), British statesman; four times prime minister (1868–74; · 1880–85; 1886; 1892–94). Originally a TORY, he later dominated the LIBERAL PARTY, 1868–94. He was a powerful and popular orator, a dedicated social reformer and a deeply religious man. Among his many accomplishments from the time he entered Parliament (1832) were the introduction of the secret ballot, the extension of the franchise, the abolition of sales of army concessions, the first Education Act, the Irish Land Act and the disestablishment of the Anglican Church in Ireland. (See also REFORM BILLS.)

GLANDS, structures in animals and plants specialized to secrete essential substances. In plants they may discharge their secretions to the outside of the plant (via glandular hairs), or into special secretory canals. External secretions include NECTAR and insect attractants; internal secretions, pine resin and RUBBER latex. In animals they are divided into ENDOCRINE GLANDS, which secrete HORMONES into the BLOOD stream, and **exocrine glands**, which are the remainder, usually secreting materials via ducts into internal organs or onto body surfaces. LYMPH nodes are sometimes termed glands. In man, SKIN contains two types of gland: *sweat glands*, which secrete watery fluid (PERSPIRATION), and *sebaceous glands*, which secrete sebum. *Lacrimal glands* secrete TEARS. The cells of mucous membranes or the EPITHELIUM of internal organs secrete mucus, which serves to lubricate and protect the surface. *Salivary glands* (parotid, submandibular and sublingual) secrete SALIVA to facilitate swallowing. In the GASTROINTESTINAL TRACT, mucus-secreting glands are numerous, particularly in the STOMACH and colon, where solid food or feces need lubrication. Other stomach glands secrete hydrochloric acid and pepsin as part of the DIGESTIVE SYSTEM. Small-intestinal juices containing ENZYMES are similarly secreted by minute glandular specializations of the epithelium. The part of the PANCREAS secreting enzyme-rich juice into the duodenum may be regarded as an exocrine gland. Analysis of gland secretion may be helpful in diseases of digestion, of the EYES and salivary glands and in CYSTIC FIBROSIS.

GLASGOW, Ellen (1873–1945), US novelist, winner of the Pulitzer Prize in 1941 for *In This Our Life*. Her realistic novels about the American South satirized the code of Southern chivalry. They include *The Descendants* (1897) and *Barren Ground* (1925).

GLASGOW, Scotland's largest city and principal port, on the Clyde R. It is a major commercial and industrial center for shipbuilding, metal working and manufacturing of locomotives, machinery, chemicals, paper, leather, whisky and textiles. Glasgow U. was founded in 1451. Pop 733,794.

GLASS, Carter (1858–1946), US Democratic politician from Virginia, a US representative (1902–18), secretary of the treasury (1918–20), and US senator (1920–46). As chairman of the House Committee on Banking and Currency, he was a principal author of the FEDERAL RESERVE SYSTEM. In the Senate, he was a conservative opponent of the NEW DEAL.

GLASS, Philip (1937–   ), US composer whose work was influenced by Asian and African rhythms as well as by contemporary rock and progressive jazz. His best-known work is the opera *Einstein on the Beach* (1975).

GLASS, material formed by the rapid cooling of certain molten liquids so that they fail to crystallize (see CRYSTAL) but retain an amorphous structure. Glasses are in fact supercooled liquids which, however, have such high viscosity that they behave like solids for all practical purposes. Some glasses may spontaneously crystallize or devitrify. Few materials form glasses, and almost all that are found naturally or used commercially are based on silica and the silicates. Natural glass is formed by rapid cooling of MAGMA, producing chiefly

OBSIDIAN, or rarely by complete thermal metamorphism. The earliest known manufactured glass was made in Mesopotamia in the 3rd millennium BC. Glass was shaped by molding or core-dipping, until the invention of glassblowing by Syrian craftsmen in the 1st century BC. Essentially still used, the process involved gathering molten glass on the end of a pipe, blowing to form a bubble, and shaping the vessel by further blowing, swinging, or rolling it on a surface. They also blew glass inside a shaped mold; this is now the chief process used in mechanized automatic glassblowing. Modern glass products are very diverse, including windows, bottles and other vessels, optical devices, building materials, fiberglass products, etc. Most are made of soda-lime glass. Although silica itself can form a glass, it is too viscous and its melting point is too high for most purposes. Adding soda lowers the melting point, but the resultant sodium silicate is water-soluble, so lime is added as a stabilizer, together with other metal oxides as needed for decolorizing, etc. The usual proportions are 70% SiO_2, 15% Na_2O, 10% CaO. Crown glass, used in optical systems for its low dispersion, is of this type, with barium oxide (BaO) often replacing the lime. Flint glass, or crystal, is a brilliant clear glass with high optical dispersion, used in high-quality glassware and to make lenses and prisms. It was originally made from crushed flints to give pure, colorless silica; later, sand was used, with an increasing amount of lead (II) oxide. Pyrex is a borosilicate glass, used where high thermal stresses must be withstood. The manufacture of the various kinds of glass begins by mixing the raw materials—sand, limestone, sodium nitrate or carbonate, etc.—and melting them in large crucibles in a furnace. The molten glass, having been refined (free from bubbles) by standing, is formed to the shape required and then annealed (see ANNEALING). Some SAFETY GLASS is not annealed but is rapidly cooled to induce superficial compressive stresses which yield greater strength. Plate glass is made by passing a continuous sheet of soft glass between rollers, grinding and polishing it on both sides, and cutting it up so as to eliminate flaws. A newer method (the float glass process) involves pouring the molten glass onto molten metal, such as tin, and allowing it to cool slowly: the surface touching the metal is perfectly flat and needs no polishing. Special glass products include foam glass, made by sintering a mixture of glass and an agent that gives off a gas on heating, used for insulation;

photosensitive glass, which darkens reversibly in bright light; and FIBERGLASS. (See also ENAMEL.)

GLASSES, or **spectacles,** LENSES worn in front of the EYES to correct defects of VISION or for protection. Converging lenses have been worn to correct farsightedness (HYPEROPIA) since the late 13th century and diverging lenses for shortsightedness (MYOPIA) since the 16th. Glasses with cylindrical lenses are used to correct ASTIGMATISM, and those having bifocal lenses (i.e., having two different powers in the upper and lower areas of each lens) or even trifocals (three powers) may be worn for PRESBYOPIA. Most spectacle lenses are worn in a metal or plastic frame which rests on the nose and ears, though in some cases contact lenses fitting directly onto the eyeball may be suitable. Protective glasses include sunglasses and safety glasses.

GLASTONBURY, historic town in Somerset, SW England, famous for its abbey. It stands on a peninsula which is alleged to be the Isle of Avalon of ARTHURIAN LEGEND. Tradition and legend also suggest that Joseph of Arimathea founded England's first Christian church here. Pop 6,571.

GLAUCOMA, raised fluid pressure in the EYE, leading in chronic cases to a progressive deterioration of VISION. It arises from a variety of causes, often involving block to aqueous humor drainage. Glaucoma is relieved using drugs or surgically.

GLAZUNOV, Aleksandr Konstantinovich (1865–1936), Russian composer. A pupil of RIMSKY–KORSAKOV, with whom he worked on the completion of Borodin's *Prince Igor,* he was director 1906–17 of the St. Petersburg Conservatory. He wrote eight symphonies and numerous other works including the ballet *The Seasons* (1889).

GLEASON, Jackie (1916–1987), US comedian, immensely popular on television in the 1950s. He also played dramatic roles in films such as *The Hustler* (1961) and *Nothing in Common* (1987).

GLENDOWER, Owen (c1354–c1416), the last independent prince of Wales, a Welsh national hero. He led one of the last Welsh rebellions against English rule (1400–13), exploiting baronial unrest in England against Henry IV. His gains were finally recovered by Henry V.

GLENN, John Herschel, Jr. (1921–   ), first US astronaut to orbit the earth. He served as a pilot in WWII and in the Korean War. On Feb. 20, 1962, in the space capsule *Friendship 7,* he orbited the earth three times. Active in Ohio politics after retiring from the US Marines as a colonel, he served in the US Senate from 1975.

GLIDER, or **sailplane,** nonpowered airplane which, once launched by air or ground towing, or by using a winch, is kept aloft by its light, aerodynamic design and the skill of the pilot in exploiting "thermals" and other rising air currents. Sir George CAYLEY built his first model glider in 1804 and in 1853 he persuaded his coachman to undertake a short glide—the first manned heavier-than-air flight. Otto LILIENTHAL made many successful flights in his hang gliders (planes in which the pilot hangs underneath and controls the flight by altering his body position, hence moving the craft's CENTER OF GRAVITY) from 1891 until his death in a gliding accident in 1896. Later, the WRIGHT brothers developed gliders in which control was achieved using moving control surfaces, as a prelude to their experiments with powered flight. Gliding as a sport was born in Germany after WWI and is now popular throughout the world. Recent years have seen a particular resurgence of interest in hang gliding.

GLIÈRE, Reinhold Moritzovich (1875–1956), Russian composer whose pupils included PROKOFIEV. Among his works are the ballet *The Red Poppy* (1927) and *Symphony No. 3* (1911).

GLINKA, Mikhail Ivanovich (1804–1857), Russian composer. His two operas, *A Life for the Tsar* (1836) and *Russlan and Ludmilla* (1842), marked the start of a nationalistic Russian school of music.

GLOBE THEATRE, the principal public theater of the Elizabethan acting company, the Lord Chamberlain's Men, where most of SHAKESPEARE's plays were first performed. It was an open-air theater with three galleries and a platform stage and stood on the S bank of the Thames. Built in 1598, it was destroyed by fire in 1613, rebuilt in 1614 and finally destroyed in 1644 by the Puritans.

GLOBULAR CLUSTERS, apparently ellipsoidal, densely packed clusters of up to a million stars orbiting a GALAXY. The MILKY WAY and the Andromeda Galaxy each have around 200 such clusters. They contain high proportions of cool red stars and RR Lyrae VARIABLE STARS. Study of the latter enables the distances of the clusters to be calculated.

GLORIOUS REVOLUTION, events of 1688–89 which drove King James II from England and brought William III of Orange and his wife Mary to the throne. Distrusting Parliament, the Catholic James had kept a large standing army. The birth of his son threatened to turn England into a permanently Catholic monarchy. This finally caused the Whigs and Tories to unite and invite the Dutch prince and his wife to become joint rulers. James fled to France after his army deserted him. In 1689, Parliament redefined and restricted royal powers in the BILL OF RIGHTS.

GLOSSOLALIA, speech in an unknown or fabricated language uttered by individuals under HYPNOSIS, suffering from certain MENTAL ILLNESSES or in trance, or by groups undergoing religious ecstasy. In the Christian Church, glossolalia has sometimes accompanied revivals, and characterizes the PENTECOSTAL CHURCHES. A spiritual gift (see CHARISMA) common in the early Church, its use was regulated by St. Paul.

GLOUCESTER, Humphrey, Duke of (1390–1447), youngest son of Henry IV of England. He fought with his brother King Henry V at AGINCOURT in 1415, and in the absence of his brother the duke of Bedford, was protector of the realm 1422–29. He was called "good Duke Humphrey" because of his support of scholars and scholarship.

GLUBB, Sir John Bagot (1897–1986), British army officer who commanded (1939–56) Jordan's Arab Legion. Successful against the Israelis in the 1948–49 ARAB-ISRAELI WAR, he was forced to resign during the 1956 war because of anti-English sentiment in the Arab world. He was also known as Glubb Pasha..

GLUCK, Christoph Willibald von (1714–1787), German operatic composer. His first 10 operas were produced in Italy, and he traveled extensively in Europe before he settled in Vienna. In *Orfeo ed Euridice* (1762) he discarded many of the static operatic conventions of the previous hundred years and made the opera a dramatic musical work. In the preface to *Alceste* (1767) he set out his ideas for operatic reform which considerably influenced later operatic composers such as MOZART.

GLUCOSE ($C_6H_{12}O_6$), also **dextrose,** a naturally occurring simple SUGAR (monosaccharide) found in honey and sweet fruits. It circulates in the BLOOD of mammals, providing their cells with energy. Other sugars and CARBOHYDRATES are converted to glucose by digestion before they can be utilized.

GLUES, widely used adhesive substances of animal or vegetable origin. Animal glues are made from bones, hides, fish bones, fish oil or the milk protein casein; vegetable glues from natural gums, STARCH (e.g., flour and water) or soybeans. Though in use for millennia, it is not yet fully understood how glues work. Nowadays, synthetic RESINS are replacing glues for many purposes. (See also ADHESIVES.)

GLUTEN, a mixture of two proteins (gliadin and glutenin) found in wheat and other cereal flours. In the rising of BREAD gluten forms an elastic network which traps the carbon dioxide, giving a desirable crumb structure on baking. The proportion of gluten in wheat flour varies from 8% to 15%. The level determines the suitability of the flour for different uses. The high gluten content of hard wheat is right for bread and pasta, while soft wheat (low gluten) is used for biscuits.

GNOME, a dwarf-like creature in mythology and folklore. Gnomes dwell within the earth, mine precious minerals and fashion intricate metal ornaments and weapons, hence their reputation as guardians of hidden treasure. They are generally depicted as misshapen.

GNOSTICISM, syncretic religious system of numerous pre-Christian and early heretical Christian sects. A form of DUALISM, Gnosticism held that matter (created by the Demiurge) is evil and spirit good, and that salvation comes from secret knowledge (gnosis) granted to initiates. A large Gnostic library was found in Egypt in 1945. The sources of Gnostic beliefs range from Babylonian, Egyptian and Greek mythology to the CABALA and ZOROASTRIANISM. Gnosticism threatened early Christianity, but declined after the 2nd century AD. (See also MANICHAEISM.)

GNU. See WILDEBEEST.

GOA, former Portuguese colony on the W coast of India. Since Dec. 1961 it has been part of the Union Territory of Goa, Daman and Diu in the Republic of India.

GOATS, members of the Bovidae closely related to SHEEP. Goats are widely kept as domestic stock and, as browsers (feeding on the twigs and leaves of bushes), they can be kept in areas not suitable for other domestic stock. They will eat anything, and the barrenness of many Mediterranean countries is largely due to overgrazing by goats. Probably the earliest-domesticated ruminant, the domestic goat is derived from the wild goat (*Capra aegagrus*) of Western Asia.

GOBELIN, French family of clothmakers and dyers. Their workshops, established in the mid-15th century, were bought by Louis XIV (1662) whose finance minister COLBERT created from them a factory to make fine TAPESTRY and furniture. The Gobelin factory is still state-controlled.

GOBI, vast desert in central Asia, which lies mainly in Mongolia, but extends to N China. It covers about 500,000sq mi in the Mongolian plateau and has an average altitude of between 3,000ft and 5,000ft.

Parts of the desert's steppeland fringes are inhabited by Mongol herdsmen.

GOBINEAU, Joseph Arthur, Comte de (1816–1882), French diplomat and author. His essay *The Inequality of the Human Races* (1853–55) propounded a pseudo-scientific theory of Nordic superiority which, as *gobinisme*, enjoyed some popularity in Germany. He is today more admired for his novel *The Pleiads* (1874).

GOBLIN, or **hobgoblin**, a dwarf-like sprite in folklore and legend, grotesque in appearance. A household mischief-maker, the goblin is sometimes evil.

GOD, a supernatural being worthy of worship; especially, the supreme being who is the creator of the universe and on whom all else depends. Many religions are based on POLYTHEISM, having a pantheon of many gods which are generally local, tribal or which have particular functions. Behind some such pantheons lies a more or less explicit belief in a supreme being, an idea that comes to fruition in the MONOTHEISM of Judaism, Christianity and Islam; and, in a different form, in the Good Power of DUALISM, who is not merely one of many gods, yet not wholly supreme. Many scholars have supposed that religions evolve from ANIMISM through polytheism to monotheism. In monotheistic religions and philosophies the knowledge of God (absent from AGNOSTICISM—and impossible in atheism) has been approached via reason (in particular, the classical arguments for the existence of God), via God's self-disclosure, or via an existential encounter in which the knowledge is personal rather than intellectual. The attributes of God as held by traditional monotheism—though now often questioned—are derived partly from revealed scripture, partly from the results of controversy with pagans, and partly from Greek philosophy. God is described as one, eternal, all-powerful, all-knowing, omnipresent, self-existent, unchangeable, and perfectly good, just, holy and true. Being infinite, his nature is ineffable, and the human mind is incapable of fully grasping it. The relation of God to the world is differently held in DEISM, PANTHEISM and THEISM; theism, as in orthodox Christianity, balances God's immanence and transcendence. Christianity also teaches that God is a TRINITY—that the one God exists as three Persons—a doctrine which in early and modern Christianity has been controversial, and which is rejected by Jews, Muslims and Unitarians as being inconsistent with the absolute unity of God. (See also RELIGION; THEOLOGY.)

GODARD, Jean Luc (1930–   ), French film director who became famous in the early 1960s as a pioneer of the French "new wave" school with his film *Breathless*. Godard was a remarkable technician whose impressive imagery and innovative camera techniques influenced a generation of filmmakers. His later films became increasingly formless and simplistic.

GODDARD, Robert Hutchings (1882–1945), US pioneer of rocketry. In 1926 he launched the first liquid-fuel rocket. Some years later, with a Guggenheim Foundation grant, he set up a station in N.M., there developing many of the basic ideas of modern rocketry: among over 200 patents was that for a multistage rocket. He died before his work received US Government recognition.

GODDEN, (Margaret) Rumer (1907–   ). British author whose novels, poems, and children's books are distinguished by their warm characterization and lyric style. Her novels of life in India include *Black Narcissus* (1939) and *The River* (1946).

GÖDEL'S THEOREM, showing the futility of attempting to set up a complete axiomatic formalization of mathematics. Kurt Gödel (1906–1978) proved (1931) that any consistent mathematical system must be incomplete; i.e., that in any system formulae must be constructed that can be neither proved nor disproved within that system. Moreover, no mathematical system can be proved consistent without recourse to axioms beyond that system. Gödel's Theorem has had profound effects on attitudes toward the foundations of MATHEMATICS. (See also LOGIC.)

GODEY, Louis Antoine (1804–1878), US magazine publisher. *Godey's Lady's Book*, founded in Philadelphia in 1830, contained notable fiction and fashion pictures in color, and was the first successful US periodical for women.

GODFREY OF BOUILLON (c1058–1100), a leader of the First CRUSADE. On the capture of Jerusalem from the Muslims in 1099, he was elected Protector of the Holy Sepulcher. He became a legendary figure and the hero of several CHANSONS DE GESTE.

GODIVA, Lady (c1040–80), noted for her legendary ride through Coventry, England. Her husband Leofric, Earl of Mercia, promised to reduce the people of Coventry's heavy taxes if she rode naked through the city streets on a white horse. "Peeping Tom" alone essayed to gaze upon the spectacle.

GODKIN, Edwin Lawrence (1831–1902), US newspaper editor. He founded the influential weekly review the *Nation* (1865). He was chief editor of the *New York Evening Post* by 1883 and became famous as an independent, incorruptible social and political critic.

GODOLPHIN, Sidney Godolphin, 1st Earl of (1645–1712), English statesman. A powerful court politician from 1679 to 1710, he maintained the treasury with great financial expertise during a constitutionally unstable period, and supported the Duke of MARLBOROUGH'S campaigns. The unpopular War of the SPANISH SUCCESSION eventually led to his downfall.

GODUNOV, Boris Fedorovich (c1551–1605), tsar of Russia (1598–1605). A close adviser to IVAN IV ("the Terrible") and regent for Feodor I, Ivan's son and heir, Boris was virtual ruler of Russia. On Feodor's death (1598), Boris was elected tsar and continued Ivan IV's policies of subjugating the boyars (upper nobility) and expanding Russian boundaries. His life is the subject of a drama by PUSHKIN upon which MUSSORGSKY based his famous opera.

GODWIN (d. 1053), earl of Wessex. The chief adviser to CANUTE II THE GREAT, on the king's death (1035) Godwin became the most powerful earl in England. He challenged the power of EDWARD THE CONFESSOR and was exiled (1051); in 1052, he led an armed invasion of England and regained his former power. He was succeeded by his son Harold, who became king of England in 1066 (see HAROLD II).

GODWIN, William (1756–1836), English political theorist and novelist. In his *Enquiry Concerning Political Justice* (1793) and in his novels such as *The Adventures of Caleb Williams* (1794), Godwin rejected all government as corrupting and expressed his belief that humans are rational beings able to live without laws and institutions. He was the father of Mary SHELLEY.

GOEBBELS, Paul Joseph (1897–1945), German Nazi propaganda chief. He had a brilliant academic career before joining the Nazi party. Appointed minister of propaganda by Hitler in 1933, Goebbels skillfully organized political campaigns and used the mass media to promote NAZISM throughout Germany until the end of WWII. He committed suicide with his family in Berlin in 1945.

GOERING, Hermann Wilhelm (1893–1946), German political leader and Hitler's deputy, 1939–45. He organized the STORM TROOPERS and the GESTAPO and, as commander of the German Air Force, prepared for the aerial *blitzkrieg* campaigns of WWII. By 1936 Goering was

economic dictator of Germany, but his power dwindled when he failed to stop Allied air attacks. Convicted of WAR CRIMES at the NUREMBERG TRIALS in 1946, he poisoned himself in his prison cell.

GOES, Hugo van der. See VAN DER GOES, HUGO.

GOETHALS, George Washington (1858–1928), US army engineer who completed construction of the PANAMA CANAL, 1907–14. Apart from solving the complicated technical problems of the project, Goethals successfully overcame unexpected difficulties caused by the climate, disease and the labor force. He served as governor of the Canal Zone from 1914–16.

GOETHE, Johann Wolfgang von (1749–1832), German poet, novelist and playwright, one of the giants of world literature, and perhaps the last European to embody the ideal of the Renaissance man. His monumental work ranges from poems, novels, plays, and a famous correspondence with SCHILLER to 14 volumes of scientific studies and is crowned by *Faust* (part I, 1808; part II, 1833), written in stages during 60 years, in which he synthesized his life and art in a poetic and philosophical statement of man's search for complete experience and knowledge.

Born in Frankfurt-am-Main, Goethe achieved national recognition with his STURM UND DRANG play *Götz von Berlichingen* (1773) and the romantic novel *The Sorrows of Young Werther* (1774). From 1775 until his death, he lived at the ducal court of Saxe-Weimar, where he published, among many other works, *The Apprenticeship of Wilhelm Meister* (1795–96), a novel of the maturing artist to which he later wrote a sequel. A visit to Italy in 1786–88 gave Goethe inspiration for the plays *Iphigenie auf Tauris* (1787) and *Egmont* (1788). Thomas CARLYLE is among his notable English translators; the Weimar edition of Goethe's complete works was published in 133 volumes, 1887–1919.

GOFFMAN, Erving (1922–1982), Canadian-born US sociologist, known for his description of life in a "total institution," *Asylum* (1961), and for his analyses of everyday social transactions in *Relations in Public* (1972).

GOGARTY, Oliver St. John (1878–1957), Irish physician and writer associated with the Irish Renaissance. An acquaintance of Yeats, Joyce and Russel (AE), Gogarty recalled his youthful days in Dublin in his memoirs *As I Was Going Down Sackville Street* (1937) and *Tumbling in the Hay* (1939). The character of Buck Mulligan in

Joyce's *Ulysses* is based on him.

GOGH, Vincent van. See VAN GOGH, VINCENT.

GOGOL, Nikolai Vasilievich (1809–1852), Russian short story writer, novelist and dramatist. Considered the father of Russian realism, his comic stories of Ukrainian peasant life and later more bizarre and intense tales set in St. Petersburg, such as *The Overcoat* (1872), put him among the most original of Russian authors. Adverse reaction in Russia to his satirical drama *The Inspector-General* (1836) drove Gogol into a self-imposed exile abroad, where he wrote more macabre stories and also his masterpiece, the picaresque novel *Dead Souls* (1834–52), of which only the first part survives.

GOITER, enlargement of the THYROID GLAND in the neck, causing swelling below the LARYNX. It may represent the smooth swelling of an overactive gland in thyrotoxicosis or more often the enlargement caused by multiple CYSTS and nodules without functional change. Endemic goiter is enlargement associated with IODINE deficiency, occurring in certain areas where the element is lacking in the soil and water. Rarely, goiter is due to CANCER of the thyroid. If there is excessive secretion or pressure on vital structures SURGERY may be needed, although DRUG'S or RADIATION THERAPY for excess secretion are often adequate.

GOLD (Au), yellow NOBLE METAL in Group IB of the PERIODIC TABLE; a transition element. Gold has been known and valued from earliest times and used for jewelry, ornaments and coinage. It occurs as the metal and as tellurides, usually in veins of QUARTZ and PYRITE; the chief producing countries are South Africa, the USSR, Canada and the US. The metal is extracted with CYANIDE or by forming an AMALGAM, and is refined by electrolysis. The main use of gold is as a currency reserve (see GOLD STANDARD). Like SILVER, it is used for its high electrical conductivity in printed circuits and electrical contacts, and also for filling or repairing teeth. It is very malleable and ductile, and may be beaten into gold leaf or welded in a thin layer to another metal (rolled gold). For most uses pure gold is too soft, and is alloyed with other noble metals, the proportion of gold being measured in carats. Gold is not oxidized in air, nor dissolved by alkalis or pure acids, though it dissolves in aqua regia or cyanide solution because of ligand complex formation, and reacts with the halogens. It forms trivalent and monovalent salts. Gold (III) chloride is used as a toner in

photography. AW 197.0, mp 1063°C, bp 2966°C, sg 19.32 (20°C).

GOLDBERG, Arthur Joseph (1908–   ), US labor lawyer and public servant. He served as secretary of labor (1961–62), associate justice of the Supreme Court (1962–65) and US representative to the United Nations (1965–68).

GOLDBERG, "Rube" (Reuben Lucius Goldberg; 1883–1970), US cartoonist and sculptor, known for his bizarre "inventions" of ridiculously complicated machinery to perform everyday tasks. In 1948 he won the Pulitzer Prize for political cartoons.

GOLD COAST. See GHANA.

GOLDEN BULL, name applied to any medieval document bearing a gold seal (*bulla*). The most famous bull was issued by the Holy Roman Emperor Charles IV in 1356. It formulated the procedures by which the emperor would be selected by the Electors (the heads of the chief German principalities); guaranteed the Electors considerable territorial sovereignty; and excluded papal influence from elections of the German ruler. (See also HOLY ROMAN EMPIRE.)

GOLDEN GATE BRIDGE, bridge spanning the entrance to San Francisco Bay, Cal., built in 1933–37. Its 4,200ft central span, between two 746ft towers, is the second longest in the world and carries six traffic lanes 220ft above the water.

GOLDEN HORDE, name for the Mongol rulers of much of Russia from the 13th to the 15th century, and their khanate or empire. Led by Batu Khan, the horde swept across Russia in 1237–40. The khanate slowly came under Turkish influence, but at the end of the 14th century was reconquered by TAMERLANE. (See also MONGOL EMPIRE; TATARS.)

GOLDEN RULE, the precept stated by Jesus in the SERMON ON THE MOUNT: "Always treat others as you would like them to treat you." The name, implying that this is the chief ethical principle, has been used since the 16th century. The golden rule is not peculiarly Christian, and is also found (in a negative form) in Jewish writers, Confucius, Aristotle, Plato, Isocrates and Seneca.

GOLDFISH, *Carassius auratus*, a common pet fish related to the carp. In the wild state, the goldfish—native to the rivers and streams of China—is dull brown in color. Chance MUTATION produces a form in which all pigments are missing except red (a form of albinism [see ALBINO] well-known in carp-like species). Such mutants breed true, and goldfish have now been kept as pets for over 2,000 years.

GOLDING, William (Gerald) (1911–   ), English novelist. His powerful allegorical works explore the nature of mankind, and include *Lord of the Flies* (1954), *The Inheritors* (1955), *The Spire* (1964) and *Darkness Visible* (1979). He received Britain's prestigious Booker McConnell Prize in 1980 and the Nobel Prize for Literature in 1983.

GOLDMAN,   Emma   (1869–1940), Russian-born anarchist who worked in the US c1890–1917. She was imprisoned (1893, 1916, 1917) for inciting riots, advocating birth control and obstructing the draft. She was temporarily deported (1919) and later lived in England and Canada and was active in the Spanish civil war, 1936.

GOLDMARK, Peter Carl (1906–1977), Hungarian-born US engineer and inventor who, at CBS Laboratories, developed the first practical color TELEVISION (1940) and the first long-playing PHONOGRAPH record. He was also a pioneer in the field of educational television and in the development of electronic video recording.

GOLDONI, Carlo (1707–1793), Italian dramatist. His type of character comedy led to the decline in popularity of the rival COMMEDIA DELL' ARTE. Goldoni directed the Comédie Italienne in Paris, 1762–64. Among his 150 comic plays are *The Mistress of the Inn* (1753) and *The Fan* (1763).

GOLD RUSH, general term for an influx of gold prospectors following the discovery of a new gold field. From 1848–1915, in the Americas, Australia and South Africa, there were numerous gold rushes. Three main North American gold strikes attracted thousands of prospectors: in California (1849), Colorado (1858–59) and the Klondike (1897).

GOLDSMITH,   Oliver   (c1730–1774), Anglo-Irish man of letters. His best-known works are the novel *The Vicar of Wakefield* (1766), the comedy *She Stoops to Conquer* (1773) and the pastoral poem *The Deserted Village* (1770). An unsuccessful physician, he achieved both a considerable literary reputation and widespread popularity in his day. His works attacked pedantry and sentimentalism and stressed the simple virtues of humility, courage and humor.

GOLD STANDARD, a monetary system in which a standard currency unit equals a fixed weight of gold and central banks must be prepared to exchange currency for gold and vice versa. In an *internal* gold standard system, gold coins circulate in a country as legal tender. In an *international* system, gold (or gold-based currency) is used for making international payments. Since WWII most countries no longer have an internal gold standard, but do use a limited international standard in which they convert their currencies into gold or US dollars for international payments. The US went on the gold standard in 1900, but the Gold Reserve Act of 1934 prohibited the redemption of dollars into gold. And in 1970 the US Treasury ended its requirement that Federal Reserve notes be backed 25% by gold deposits, in effect taking the US completely off the gold standard.

GOLDWATER, Barry Morris (1909–   ), leading US conservative senator from Ariz. 1953–65, 1969–87. As Republican presidential candidate in 1964, Goldwater won only six states running against Lyndon B. JOHNSON. Goldwater's writings include *The Conscience of a Conservative* (1960) and *Why Not Victory?* (1962). An Air Force officer in WWII, he became an authority on defense issues in the Senate.

GOLDWYN, Samuel (1882–1974), Polish-born US motion picture pioneer. He produced over 70 films and in 1916 founded a unit in the future Metro-Goldwyn-Mayer film company, though he worked as an independent producer after 1924. He won an Academy Award (1947) for *The Best Years of Our Lives.*

GOLEM, in Jewish medieval legend, an effigy (often of clay) magically endowed with life. The golem was a faithful mechanical servant, protecting its owner in times of danger. The most famous golem, supposedly created by Rabbi Löw in 16th-century Prague, was a forerunner of the creature FRANKENSTEIN.

GOLF, the most popular outdoor sport in the US, a game in which individual competitors drive a small hard ball with variously-shaped clubs towards and into a hole. A game consists of playing into either 9 or 18 consecutive holes spread over an extensive ground known as a golf course or links. The winner of individual stroke (or medal) play is the player who holes his ball in the fewest strokes over the course; in match play the winner is the player who wins the most individual holes. Playing a hole involves driving the ball from a raised peg or *tee* across the fairway towards the distant closely-mown *putting green* around the hole (which may be 100 to 600yd from the tee). The player seeks to keep the ball on the intervening mown fairway, avoiding the flanking "rough"—water and sand trap hazards. A player's score is based on *par*, the number of strokes an expert golfer would need to hit the ball from the tee into the hole in a given distance and course difficulty. Par varies from three to six strokes per hole. An expert golfer would average a score of 72 strokes for 18 holes—or an average of four per hole.

Written records of golf date from the 15th century in Scotland, where the traditional international rulemaking body, the Royal and Ancient Club of St. Andrews, was founded (1754). Early Scottish colonists probably introduced golf to the US in the 17th century. The game slowly gained popularity, and the Professional Golfers' Association (PGA) championship began in 1916. American golfers have tended to dominate the world game, from Bobby Jones to Ben Hogan, Arnold Palmer and Jack Nicklaus. More than 10 million Americans play golf, which is a multimillion-dollar leisure business.

GOLIAD, city in Tex., seat of Goliad Co., 22mi W of Victoria. It is an historic site of the Mexican revolt against Spain (1812–13). In the Texas revolt against Mexico in 1836, James FANNIN's troops were massacred at Goliad on SANTA ANNA's orders. Pop 1,709.

GÓMEZ, Juan Vincente (1864–1935), dictator of Venezuela (1908–35). A ruthless tyrant, he attracted foreign investors and used oil revenues to modernize the country and enrich himself.

GOMPERS, Samuel (1850–1924), pioneer American labor leader. A leader in the cigar makers' union, he helped found and became first president, 1886–94, 1896–1924, of the AMERICAN FEDERATION OF LABOR (AFL). Gompers led the labor fight for higher wages, shorter working hours and more freedom. He opposed militant political unionism and as head of the War Committee on Labor (WWI), he greatly helped organized labor gain respectability in the US.

GOMULKA, Wladyslaw (1905–1982), Polish communist leader. He helped organize communist underground resistance in WWII, became Poland's deputy premier, 1945–49, and cochairman of the COMINFORM (from 1947). A Polish nationalist, he opposed Russian domination and was imprisoned, 1951–54. After the Poznan uprising (1956) he became first secretary of the Polish Communist Party (1956–70), encouraging some social and economic freedoms for Poles while maintaining close ties with the USSR. He resigned following food price riots.

GONCHAROV, Ivan Aleksandrovich (1812–1891), Russian novelist. His novel, *Oblomov* (1859), satirized realistically the indolence of Russian landed gentry in the 1860s. As a result, the Russian word *oblomovism* was coined to describe the hero's typical aristocratic laziness.

GONCOURT, two French brothers, known as "les deux Goncourt," art historians and pioneer authors of the naturalist school of fiction. **Edmond Louis Antoine Huot de Goncourt** (1822–1896) and **Jules Alfred Huot de Goncourt** (1830–1870) wrote novels exploring aspects of French society, notably *Germinie Lacerteux* (1864), a study of working-class life. They also wrote perceptively on art and social history and published a famous journal depicting Parisian society, 1851–95. Edmond provided money in his will for the Goncourt Academy which annually awards the prestigious literary Goncourt Prize.

GÓNGORA Y ARGOTE, Luis de (1561–1627), Spanish poet. Often called the greatest poet of Spain's cultural Golden Age, he created an ornate, difficult poetic style called Gongorism. His greatest work, *Las Soledades* (1613), led to long controversy over his grandiose and abstruse, yet technically skilled and never dull style.

GONORRHEA. See VENEREAL DISEASES.

GONZAGA, Italian princely family, rulers of Mantua (1328–1708) where their court was a brilliant center of Renaissance arts and letters.

GONZÁLEZ MÁRQUEZ, Felipe (1942–), Spanish socialist politician, premier from 1982. He led (1986) Spain into the European Common Market.

GOOD FRIDAY, the Friday in HOLY WEEK before Easter, observed in most Christian churches as a day of fasting and repentance in commemoration of the CRUCIFIXION of Jesus Christ, of which it is the anniversary. Its observance dates from the 2nd century.

GOOD HOPE, Cape of. See CAPE OF GOOD HOPE.

GOODMAN, Benny (Benjamin D. Goodman; 1909–1986), American clarinetist and band leader, one of the most famous jazz soloists and dandeband leaders of the 1930s and 1940s "swing" era. His virtuoso playing inspired classical compositions for the clarinet, notably *Contrasts* (1938) by Bela BARTÓK and concertos by COPLAND and HINDEMITH.

GOOD NEIGHBOR POLICY, pact signed at the 1933 Pan-American conference by the US and Latin American countries, as outlined by President Franklin D. ROOSEVELT. Ending the "gun-boat diplomacy" long practiced by the US to protect its interests in Latin America, the policy stated that no nation would interfere in another's affairs. Exchange programs were set up for teachers and technical experts and the US agreed to help develop

Latin American agriculture, business, education and health facilities.

GOODYEAR, Charles (1800–1860), US inventor of the process of vulcanization of rubber (patented 1844). In 1839 he bought the patents of Nathaniel Manley Hayward (1808–1865), who had had some success by treating RUBBER with SULFUR. Working on this, Goodyear accidentally dropped a rubber/sulfur mixture onto a hot stove, so discovering vulcanization.

GOPHERS, the name applied in North America to any burrowing rodent, but properly referring to the pocket gophers, a group confined to arid areas of North America. Gophers are solitary animals feeding on bulbs and roots collected in their underground tunnels. They possess fur-lined cheek pouches for storing food, which open on the outside of each cheek.

GORBACHEV, Mikhail Sergeyevich (1931–), general secretary of the USSR Communist Party from 1985, succeeding Konstantin Chernenko. A native of the Stavropol region of S Russia, he became party first secretary there in 1970. He was called to Moscow in 1978 as agricultural minister; in 1980 he became the youngest member of the Politburo. His selection as party leader after a succession of elderly, conservative men signaled a dramatic change in political direction. Concerned at the economic backwardness and stagnation of the USSR compared to capitalist and even some socialist economies, Gorbachev determined upon policies of economic decentralization and party democratization. The words *glasnost* ("openness") and *perestroika* ("restructuring") reflected the new direction. In international relations, he adopted unusually flexible positions on arms control. He was elected chairman of the presidium of the Supreme Soviet in 1988.

GORDIAN KNOT, in Greek mythology, an intricate knot by which King Gordius of Phrygia joined the yoke and pole of an oxcart. A prophecy held that anyone undoing the knot would rule all Asia. The knot defied all comers until the conqueror ALEXANDER THE GREAT severed it with his sword. Hence, "cutting the Gordian knot" describes any problem solved by bold, unorthodox action.

GORDIMER, Nadine (1923–), South African writer whose novels, such as *July's People* (1981) and *A Sport of Nature* (1987), depict the subtle effects of apartheid.

GORDON, Charles George (1833–1885), British soldier, popularly known as "Chinese Gordon." He helped suppress the TAIPING REBELLION (1863–64) in China, was governor of the Sudan (1877–80), where he established law, improved communications and attempted to suppress the slave trade. In 1885 he defended Khartoum against the MAHDI's forces for 10 months, but was killed on Jan. 26 before relief arrived on Jan. 28. British indignation over his abandonment led to the collapse of GLADSTONE's government.

GORDON, Lord George (1751–1793), English Protestant agitator. In June 1780 he precipitated the violent Gordon riots in London, which destroyed Roman Catholic homes, chapels and other buildings and caused over 450 deaths.

GORGAS, William Crawford (1854–1920), US Army sanitarian. After Walter REED's commission had proved (1900) Carlos FINLAY's theory that YELLOW FEVER is transmitted by the MOSQUITO, Gorgas conducted in Havana a massive control program; he repeated this in Panama (1904–1913), facilitating the digging of the Panama Canal.

GORGES, Sir Ferdinando (c1566–1647), English colonizer. He helped found the PLYMOUTH COMPANY (1606) and the Council of New England (1620) for colonizing eastern North America between lat. 40°N–48°N, and supported numerous colonizing and trading ventures in North America. In 1639 he received a royal charter for the province of Me. After his death, his grandson sold all rights in Me. to Mass. (1677).

GORGIAS (c483–376 BC), Greek sophist and teacher of rhetoric. He believed that objective truth or knowledge was impossible, and hence that the ability to argue on either side of a question was of prime value to an educated man. He is a central figure of Plato's *Gorgias* dialogue. (See SOPHISTS; SKEPTICISM.)

GORILLA, *Gorilla gorilla*, the largest of the PRIMATES, with a scattered distribution throughout central Africa. They live in groups with a single dominant "silverback" male, feeding on vast quantities of vegetable material as they wander over their range of 10–15sq mi. Gorillas are quadrupedal, rising to two legs only when displaying. They spend most of their time on the ground, but may make nests on the ground or in trees to sleep in at night. Though huge apes (a male weighs 350–440lb), they are peaceable and will not attack unprovoked. The well-known chest-beating display is not a threat, but an intraspecific social signal.

GORKI, Maxim (1868–1936), pen name of Aleksey Maksimovich Peshkov, Russian author recognized as the father of SOCIALIST

REALISM. His works, noted for their stark naturalism, include the play *The Lower Depths* (1902), the novel *Mother* (1906) and the autobiographical trilogy *Childhood* (1914), *In the World* (1915) and *My Universities* (1923). After the Revolution, Gorki headed state publishing up to 1921 and later served as propagandist for the Stalin regime.

GORKY, Arshile (1904–1948), Armenian-born US painter, a pioneer of ABSTRACT EXPRESSIONISM. His seemingly spontaneous, organic abstracts influenced the work of Jackson POLLOCK and Willem DE KOONING.

GOSPEL MUSIC, folk music in which a religious text is sung in a blues style, created originally by blacks in the S US. Mahalia JACKSON was the best known singer of gospel.

GOSPELS, The, first four books of the NEW TESTAMENT, named for their reputed authors: Matthew, Mark, Luke and John. Each is a collection of the acts and words of Jesus. Didactic in intention rather than biographical, they were written to help spread the gospel ("good news") of Christian salvation. All broadly cover the key events of Jesus' life, death and resurrection, but narrative styles and details, and intended readership, differ. The Gospel— an excerpt from the Gospels—is one of the readings at Holy COMMUNION. (See also SYNOPTIC GOSPELS.)

GOSSE, Sir Edmund William (1849–1929), English writer of literary criticism and biographies, remembered for his moving autobiographical *Father and Son* (1907).

GOTHIC ART AND ARCHITECTURE. The Gothic style of art and architecture flourished in Europe, particularly in France, from the mid-12th century to the end of the 15th century. The style was first referred to as "gothic" in the Renaissance by artists and writers who sought to condemn it as barbaric.

Gothic architecture in fact developed from the Romanesque, combining the latter's barrel vault and the stone rib to produce its most characteristic feature, the rib vault. This was first perfected at the Abbey Church of St. Denis near Paris, in 1140. It made possible a lighter, almost skeletal building. The flying buttress, also characteristic, was first used at Notre Dame in Paris. During the 13th century, High Gothic was perfected and cathedrals with higher vaults and more slender columns and walls were constructed, as at Chartres and Reims in France, Salisbury in England and Cologne in Germany. In the 14th and 15th centuries Gothic became more elaborate and ornate. (See PERPENDICULAR STYLE.)

Sculptural decoration was an essential part of Gothic architecture, as were stained glass windows, the most notable examples of which are at Chartres. The period is also noted for its manuscript illumination in missals, books of hours, Bibles and psalters.

GOTHIC NOVEL, genre of fiction whose terror-laden stories are usually set against a menacing, medieval background. Famous early examples of the genre are Horace WALPOLE'S *Castle of Otranto* (1765) and Ann RADCLIFFE'S *The Mysteries of Udolpho* (1794). The term now embraces a wide range of popular fiction, including formulaic historical romances.

GOTHIC REVIVAL, 18th- and 19th-century revival of interest in medieval culture, chiefly in England and the US. It involved a somewhat dilettante liking for such phenomena as the GOTHIC NOVEL and pseudomedieval country houses, but there was also a more serious appeal to the standards of the Middle Ages, as by the architect Pugin and by John RUSKIN.

GOTHS, ancient Germanic peoples, reputed to have originated in S Scandinavia, who invaded and settled in Roman Spain and Italy in the 5th century AD. In the 2nd century AD, they settled on the N and NW Black Sea coast and during the next century occupied the Roman province of Dacia. The Goths in Dacia became known as VISIGOTHS and those around the Black Sea as OSTROGOTHS.

GOTTFRIED VON STRASSBURG, 13th century German poet famous for his masterpiece *Tristan* (c1210), an epic based on Celtic legend, and stressing the ennobling ideals of courtly love. Richard WAGNER used the work as the basis of his opera *Tristan und Isolde* (1859).

GOTTLIEB, Adolph (1903–1974), US artist. His oversized abstract-expressionist landscapes, featuring bursts of color, gained him much popularity in the 1950s. He derived his early style from "pictographs," arranging abstract symbols in grids.

GOTTSCHALK, Louis Moreau (1829–1869), US composer and pianist, internationally celebrated as a virtuoso. He studied in Europe, toured there and in North and South America, and wrote operas, orchestral works and piano pieces.

GOTTWALD, Klement (1896–1953), Czech communist politician. Premier (1946–48), he organized the communist coup of 1948 and replaced Eduard Beneš as president. He created a Stalinist state, purging dissident communists as well as noncommunists. A purge trial in 1952 sentenced 11 communist leaders to death.

GOUJON, Jean (c1510–1568?), French sculptor and architect. He is famous for his elongated and elegant statues. His finest work, part of which is in the Louvre in Paris, is generally agreed to be the *Fontaine des Innocents* (1547–49).

GOULART, João (1918–1976), Brazilian politician. A protégé of Getúlio VARGAS, he led Brazil's Labor Party (PTB) and became president in 1961. His program of agrarian reform and industrial development was frustrated by inflation and a hostile congress. He was overthrown (1964) by a military coup and went into exile.

GOULD, Chester (1900–1985), US cartoonist, creator (1931) of the comic strip *Dick Tracy.*

GOULD, Glenn (1932–1982), Canadian virtuoso pianist, famous for his performances of BACH, BEETHOVEN and BRAHMS. From the late 1960s he abandoned live performances, making records and documentary films.

GOULD, Jay (1836–1892), US railroad speculator. He denied Cornelius VANDERBILT control of the Erie Railroad by selling stock illegally. With James FISK he tried cornering the gold market (1869) and triggered the BLACK FRIDAY panic. From 1872 he built up the Gould railroad system in the SW, which included the Union Pacific. He also gained a controlling interest in the Western Union Telegraph Company.

GOULD, Morton (1913–   ), US composer, conductor and pianist who began his wide-ranging career as a teenage pianist and later composed works blending popular American themes and classical forms, such as *Cowboy Rhapsody* (1942). He also composed music for films, musical comedies and ballet.

GOUNOD, Charles François (1818–1893), French composer, best known for the operas *Faust* (1859) and *Romeo and Juliet* (1867). He wrote 10 other operas, as well as oratorios, masses, songs and piano pieces in a melodic and often sentimental style.

GOUT, a DISEASE of purine metabolism characterized by elevation of uric acid in the BLOOD and episodes of ARTHRITIS due to uric acid crystal deposition in synovial fluid and the resulting INFLAMMATION. Deposition of urate in CARTILAGE and subcutaneous tissue (as *tophi*) and in the KIDNEYS and urinary tract (causing stones and renal failure) are other important effects. The arthritis is typically of sudden onset with severe pain, often affecting the great toe first and large joints in general. Treatment with allopurinol prevents recurrences.

GOVERNMENT PRINTING OFFICE (GPO), US government agency in Washington D.C., one of the world's largest printing establishments. Created in 1860, it prints and publishes official documents and supplies writing materials to other government agencies.

GOWER, John (c1330–1408), English poet, a friend of CHAUCER. He is best known for his narrative poem in English, *Confessio amantis* (c1390), but he also wrote in French and Latin. His work, characterized by its moral tone, was widely influential.

GOWON, Yakubu (1934–   ), Nigerian general, head of state (1966–75). He crushed secessionist BIAFRA in a bloody civil war (1967–70), then announced an amnesty and launched a reconciliation program. He was deposed in a bloodless coup and took up residence in England.

GOYA Y LUCIENTES, Francisco José de (1746–1828), Spanish painter and etcher, famous as much for his delightful paintings and portraits for the Spanish court as for his grim depictions of the French invasion of Spain in 1808–14. During the 1790s he painted some of his most delicately and brilliantly colored portraits, including *La Tirana* (1794) and, after he became first court painter in 1799, the *Family of Charles IV* (1800). The etchings *Caprices* (1793–98) and *Disasters of War* (1810–14) are scenes of absurd and savage human behavior.

GOYEN, Jan Josephszoon van (1596–1656), Dutch landscape painter. Exploiting a narrow range of colors, he depicted Dutch rural, city, coast and winter scenes, using low horizons surmounted by delicately atmospheric skyscapes.

GOZZOLI, Benozzo (Benozzo di Lese; 1420–1497), Italian painter and goldsmith. He assisted Fra ANGELICO and is best known for the frescoes in which he treated contemporary Florentine life. His finest work is in the Medici Palace chapel, Florence.

GRACCHUS, family name of two Roman brothers, reformers and statesmen, known as the Gracchi. **Tiberius Sempronius** (163–133 BC) was elected a tribune of Rome in 133 and proposed a law redistributing public land (largely farmed by rich senators) to landless citizens to restore the middle class of small independent farmers. To push his law through he illegally renominated himself. He was killed in an election riot. **Gaius Sempronius** (154–121 BC) was elected a tribune in 123 and 122. He, too, tried to restrict the powers of the Senate and to help the poor and the underprivileged middle class—for instance by issuing cheap grain, establishing overseas colonies and proposing Roman citizenship for all free Italians and Latins. The Senate moved to revoke his bills, fighting Brute out, and Sempronius was killed in a riot.

GRACE, in Christian theology, the undeserved favor shown by God towards needy and sinful men through Jesus Christ. In biblical thought, especially in St. Paul, grace is at the heart of SALVATION, and is necessary for faith and good works; the relation between them has been controversial (see AUGUSTINE; CALVINISM; PELAGIANISM). The "means of grace" include holy scripture, the sacraments, prayer and Christian fellowship. The term is also applied to a formal thanksgiving for food.

GRACES, Greek goddesses of fertility, personifying charm, beauty and grace, also known as the Charites. They usually number three: Aglaia (radiance), Euphrosyne (joyfulness) and Thalia (bloom) —daughters of Zeus and Hera. The Graces sometimes attended Aphrodite, goddess of love, and sang with the Muses and Apollo, and hence were linked with the arts.

GRADY, Henry Woodfin (1850–1889), US journalist and orator who encouraged reconciliation between North and South after the Civil War. He delivered a famous speech, *The New South*, in New York City in 1886.

GRAF, Stefanie Maria (1969–), West German tennis player, the fifth person (third woman) to win (1988) tennis's grand slam (British, French, Australian, and US championships in the same year).

GRAFFITI (sing.: graffito), from Italian, "scratchings," a term generally used to mean a casual writing on an interior or exterior wall. Graffiti are found in great numbers on ancient Egyptian monuments, the walls of Pompeii, etc., and are of special interest in paleography as they show the corruptions and transmutations of alphabetical characters. Ancient graffiti, like their modern counterparts, are mainly of a political or obscene nature. In some US urban centers in the 1970s, the use of spray-paint cans added a new dimension to the practice. In the fine arts, **graffito** designates a technique in which a second covering of color is partially scraped away to reveal a primary covering of color below.

GRAFTING, the technique of propagating plants by attaching the stem or bud of one plant (called the scion) to the stem or roots of another (the stock or rootstock). Only closely related varieties can be grafted. Roses and fruit trees are often grafted so that good flowering or fruiting varieties have the benefit of strong roots.

GRAHAM, Billy (William Franklin Graham; 1918–), US evangelist. Ordained a Southern Baptist minister, 1939, he gained national prominence on the revivalist circuit about 1949 and went on to establish an international reputation as a leader of mass religious rallies. He was friendly with Presidents Eisenhower and Nixon.

GRAHAM, Katherine Meyer (1917–), US publisher. One of the most influential women in the US, she was publisher of the *Washington Post* (1968–78) and head of its parent company, which also controlled *Newsweek* magazine and several television stations.

GRAHAM, Martha (1895–), US dancer and choreographer, a major pioneer of modern dance. Influenced by Isadora DUNCAN, Ruth SAINT DENIS and Ted SHAWN, she made her solo concert debut in 1926. She choreographed over 100 works, most notably *Appalachian Spring* (1944) and *Clytemnestra* (1958). In 1976 she was awarded the US Medal of Freedom.

GRAHAM, Sylvester (1794–1851), US temperance advocate who recommended the use of coarsely ground, unsifted flour, which came to be called graham flour.

GRAHAME, Kenneth (1859–1932), British writer, author of the famous children's story *The Wind in the Willows* (1908), featuring animals with appealingly human characteristics.

GRAIL, Holy. See HOLY GRAIL.

GRAIN, a dry one-seeded FRUIT, usually containing a high percentage of starch, produced by, for example, CORN, oats, BARLEY, RYE and other CEREAL CROPS. Grain crops have a high food value, store well and are a primary food stuff, contributing over half the world's calorie intake. (See also FLOUR.)

GRAINGER, Percy Aldridge (1882–1961), Australian-born composer and pianist, a naturalized American from 1919. Influenced by his friend GRIEG, he collected and edited English folk music, basing short orchestral pieces upon it.

GRAMMAR, the structures of language and of its constituents; and the science concerned with the study of those structures. The grammarian concentrates on three main aspects of language: syntax, the ways that words are put together to form sentences; accidence, or morphology, the ways that words alter to convey different senses, such as past and present or singular and plural; and phonology, the ways that sounds are used to convey meaning.

Syntax. In English, the simplest sentence

has a noun followed by a verb: "Philip thinks." More complicated is "Philip thinks little," where the verb is qualified by an adverb. In both of these, order is important: in "Little Philip thinks" the change in order has brought about a change in meaning. In contrast, sentences of widely different outward form may have the same meaning (for example, using active and passive forms of the verb), and this suggests to many grammarians that superficial structure is not ultimately important, that there is a deep-lying structure of language which can be resolved into a few basic elements whose combinations can be used to produce an infinite number of sentences. Here grammatical studies are probing at the very roots of the human psyche; and ethnographical studies of the syntaxes of different languages, primitive and civilized, have been of primary importance in cultural ANTHROPOLOGY. (See also CHOMSKY, NOAM.)

Accidence. Most English nouns have different endings for singular and plural: "knight" and "knights." Again, there is a change of ending for the genitive (possessive) case: "knight's" (the obsolete full form is "knightes") and "knights'." Most other cases are dealt with by prepositions: "to the knight" (dative); "from the knight" (ablative). Similarly, verb-endings are changed for two tenses only, past and present, the remainder being dealt with by use of the "auxiliary" verbs "to be" and "to have." Most other languages have a profusion of noun and verb endings to deal with different cases and tenses, and so have less flexibility than English.

Phonology. Much of our speech depends for meaning on our tone of voice: "Philip is thinking" may have several meanings, depending on the stress placed on each of the words. These stresses are thus an important part of grammar, less so in English than in many other tongues: in the Sino-Tibetan languages, for example, a word may have two utterly different meanings depending upon the tone of voice in which it is said. (See also ETYMOLOGY; LANGUAGE;   LINGUISTICS;   PHILOLOGY; PHONETICS; SEMANTICS.)

GRAMM-RUDMAN ACT (1985), congressional legislation intended to reduce the federal budget deficit to zero in 1991 by setting five successive and diminishing deficit limits. If the budgets negotiated by Congress and the president failed to meet the   Gramm-Rudman   "ceilings,"   the congressional General Accounting Office was authorized to make across-the-board cuts in all government programs to meet the act's targets. The US Supreme Court found that the assignment of such responsibility to a congressional agency was unconstitutional, and the act was amended to give the executive branch's Office of Management and Budget the budget-cutting authority. By 1988, the target date of 1991 for zero deficit had slipped to 1993.

GRAMSCI, Antonio (1891–1937), Italian left-wing intellectual, cofounder (with TOGLIATTI) of the Italian Communist Party, 1921. He edited the left-wing journal *L'Ordine Nuovo* and led communists in the Chamber of Deputies (1924–26). He was arrested under Fascism and imprisoned for 11 years.

GRAM'S STAIN, a stain for BACTERIA which divides them into Gram-positive and Gram-negative groups. Since the cell walls determine not only the staining difference but also behavior and ANTIBIOTIC sensitivity of bacteria, the stain has considerable medical value.

GRANADA, Kingdom of, medieval Moorish kingdom in S Spain. Founded 1238 by the Nasrid dynasty, who made Granada its capital, the state pursued an independent Moorish policy and was a center of Moorish culture. In the 15th century internal dissensions furthered Castile's slow conquest, completed when Boabdil surrendered to Ferdinand and Isabella in 1492.

GRANADOS, Enrique (1867–1916), Spanish composer and pianist who helped create a distinctively Spanish musical style. He is best known for his songs and the *Goyescas* piano pieces (1912–14), inspired by Goya's paintings, and used in one of Granados' seven operas.

GRAN CHACO, lowland region in central S America, occupying 300,000sq mi between the Amazon forests and Argentinian pampa. Prone to droughts and flooding, it is mostly scrub with areas of swamp, grassland and desert.

GRAND ALLIANCE, War of the. See AUGSBURG, WAR OF THE LEAGUE OF.

GRAND ARMY OF THE REPUBLIC (GAR), organization of Union Civil War veterans founded in 1866 and numbering 400,000 at its peak in 1890. A powerful political force in support of the Republican Party, the GAR's principal activity was lobbying for veterans' pensions. Its last annual "encampment" was in 1949; its last member died in 1956.

GRAND BANKS, underwater plateau in the N Atlantic Ocean, extending 350mi off Newfoundland, where the Labrador Current and Gulf Stream meet. Averaging 240ft in depth, the shallow waters abound in plankton that directly and indirectly support millions of food fish, notably cod. This is one of the world's richest fishing grounds.

GRAND CANAL, in China, connects Peking (Beijing) and Hangchow, a distance of 1,000mi. Begun in the 6th century BC, it is still an important north-south waterway. Another Grand Canal is the chief traffic artery of Venice, Italy.

GRAND CANYON, spectacular gorge cut by the Colorado R in NW Ariz. It is about 217mi long, 4–18mi wide, up to 1mi deep, and flanked by a plateau 5,000–9,000ft above sea level. The main canyon contains smaller canyons, peaks and mesas, and is walled by colorful, horizontal rock strata dating back to the PRECAMBRIAN era. It is an important geological site, contains a wealth of animal and plant life, and attracts 1,500,000 visitors a year. The most impressive part forms the 673,575-acre Grand Canyon National Park.

GRAND COULEE DAM, concrete dam on the Columbia R, Wash., 85mi WNW of Spokane. Built 1934–42, it is one of the world's largest hydroelectric generating plants with an ultimate capacity of 10,080 megawatts resulting from expansion work during the 1980s.

GRANDFATHER CLAUSE, legal device used in Southern states to deny blacks the vote, by giving it to males with high literacy and property qualifications or to those whose fathers and grandfathers had been qualified to vote on Jan. 1, 1867 (before the 15th Amendment had enfranchised Southern blacks). First used in S.C. in 1895, it was declared unconstitutional in 1915.

GRAND GUIGNOL, a theater in Paris that presented plays with horror themes. Ingenious devices were invented to simulate the flow of blood and to give verisimilitude to depictions of murder, torture, and other kinds of violence in order to shock and amuse the audience. Founded in 1897, the theater closed in 1962, but has given its name to any play that makes use of its distinctive themes.

GRAND NATIONAL, most famous steeplechase in horse-racing, held annually since 1834 at the Aintree race course in England. The difficult and dangerous 4½mi course includes 30 jumps, and many participants fail to finish.

GRAND TETON NATIONAL PARK, spectacular area of the Rocky Mts in NW Wyo., just S of Yellowstone National Park. It comprises major peaks of the Teton Range and the valley of Jackson Hole from which the peaks rise abruptly. Created in 1929, the park occupies c500sq mi. It is a major tourist area and wildlife preserve.

GRANGE, Harold Edward George "Red" (1903–   ), US football player known as the "Galloping Ghost" as an All-American at the U of Illinois. He played professionally for the New York Yankees (1926–27) and the Chicago Bears (1929–35).

GRANGE, The, American farmers' organization, officially the National Grange of the Patrons of Husbandry. Founded as a fraternal order in 1867, in the 1870s it led the Granger Movement to protect farmers against the railroad monopolies, which fixed high prices on freight and storage. Soon individual states pioneered laws to curb these charges. Upheld in the Granger Cases, such laws led to government regulation of transportation and utilities. The Grange united farmers throughout the country as a political force, encouraged technical and educational exchanges and laid a basis for farm cooperatives. It is now a social and educational organization, still representing farmers' interests when necessary.

GRANGER CASES, six Supreme Court cases in 1876 which established a state's right to regulate privately owned services affecting the public interest. The cases arose from the Granger Movement, which aimed at curbing high prices imposed on farmers by railroads and grain processors. The first and most important Granger case was *Munn v. Illinois,* a landmark in US law. (See also GRANGE, THE.)

GRANITE, coarse- to medium-grained plutonic IGNEOUS ROCK, composed of feldspar (orthoclase and microcline predominating over plagioclase) and QUARTZ, often containing biotite and/or amphibole. It is the type of the family of granitic rocks, plutonic rocks rich in feldspar and quartz, of which the CONTINENTS are principally made. Most granite was formed by crystallization of MAGMA, though some may be METAMORPHIC, formed by "granitization" of previously existing sedimentary rock. It occurs typically as large plutonic masses called batholiths. A hard, weather-resistant rock, usually pink or gray, granite is used for building, paving and road curbs.

GRANT, Cary (1904–1986), English-born US actor, a dapper leading man for more than five decades. His films include *She Done Him Wrong* (1933), *Bringing Up Baby* (1938), *The Philadelphia Story* (1940), *To Catch a Thief* (1955) and *North By Northwest* (1959).

GRANT, Duncan James Corrowr (1885–1978), Scottish painter and designer, whose pictures are characterized by bright colors and bold brushwork. He was influenced by POSTIMPRESSIONISM and his friendship with the BLOOMSBURY GROUP.

GRANT, Ulysses Simpson (1822–1885), 18th president of the US 1869–77, and military leader who secured Union victory in the Civil War. A man of great personal integrity, he led an administration infiltrated by corruption.

Army career. Son of an Ohio farmer and tanner, he entered West Point in 1839, graduated four years later and first saw action in 1846 as a second lieutenant in the MEXICAN WAR. He then returned to St. Louis, and married his fiancée, Julia Dent. Though made a captain in 1853, he resigned from the army in 1854, disheartened by an uncongenial posting. For the next seven years he wandered from job to job, but on the outbreak of the Civil War became colonel of the 21st Illinois Regiment. Promoted to brigadier general, he fought at Paducah, Ky. (1861), then won victories at Forts Henry and Donelson (1862)—the first major Union successes. His subsequent victories at Shiloh, Vicksburg and Chattanooga eventually cut the Confederacy in two. Lincoln made Grant a lieutenant-general in 1864, with command of the entire Union Army and control of the Virginia campaign that eventually ended the war.

The politician. Created a full general in 1866, Grant was now a national hero. He impressed Republicans by opposing President Johnson's unpopular attempt to oust Edwin M. Stanton as secretary of war and to put Grant in his place. Becoming the Republican presidential candidate, Grant defeated Democrat Horatio Seymour in the 1868 election by a small popular majority. He was reelected in 1872, defeating Horace Greeley. As president, Grant pursued a lenient RECONSTRUCTION policy, reduced the national debt and worked to prevent a currency crisis. His administration improved relations with Britain. But Grant's scheme to annex Santo Domingo foundered, and his Force Acts (to enforce Negro civil and voting rights) failed to help Southern Negroes. Above all, corruption affected the government—partly because the inexperienced Grant chose personal friends rather than the most able Republicans to fill government offices. Grant's brother-in-law was involved in an attempt to corner the gold market that led to the 1869 business panic (see BLACK FRIDAY). W. W. Belknap resigned as secretary of war to avoid impeachment for taking bribes. The CRÉDIT MOBILIER OF AMERICA frauds and the WHISKEY RING were among other scandals, though none of these touched Grant

personally. After leaving the presidency, Grant undertook a world tour, then lost all his capital in an investment swindle. Virtually penniless and suffering from throat cancer, he wrote two volumes of Civil War memoirs that helped to ensure his family's financial security.

GRANVILLE-BARKER, Harley (1877–1946), English actor, director, playwright and seminal Shakespeare critic. He produced several of G. B. SHAW's plays for the first time. His best-known plays include *The Voysey Inheritance* (1905), *Waste* (1907) and *The Madras House* (1910).

GRAPE, *Vitis vinifera* and other species of the genus *Vitis*, family Vitaceae. The grapevine is a hardy deciduous climber cultivated for its edible golden-green or red-purple fruits that are used as table fruit, dried as raisins and used for making WINE. The grapevine is native to temperate regions of W Asia, N Africa and S Europe, and many varieties are cultivated throughout the temperate regions of the world, France, Italy and Spain having the greatest areas planted. Grapes grow best in sandy, fertile, well-drained soils in open, sunny areas. They are propagated from cuttings or by GRAFTING. A number of insect pests and diseases can cause serious losses, notably grape phylloxera, an insect pest.

GRAPEFRUIT, large citrus fruit so-named because it grows in bunches likes grapes. Originating in Asia, it is now grown in Florida, Texas, and California as well as in Mediterranean countries.

GRAPHS, plottings of sets of points whose coordinates are of the form $(x, f(x))$, where $f(x)$ is a FUNCTION of x (see ANALYTIC GEOMETRY). These points may define a curve or straight line. Graphs are a powerful tool of STATISTICS, since it is often profitable to plot one variable (such as age) along one axis against another (such as height) plotted along the other; the points on statistical graphs need not define a continuous curve. The axes on a graph are not always marked off regularly: in some cases it is useful to mark off one or both on a nonlinear scale—e.g., using logarithmic (see LOGARITHM) or exponential (see EXPONENT) scales.

GRASS, Günter Wilhelm (1927–   ), German novelist and playwright. His works, deeply affected by the post-WWII sense of national guilt, are usually centered around grotesque motifs and have a strong moral content. His best-known works include the novels *The Tin Drum* (1959), *Local Anaesthetic* (1969) and *The Flounder* (1977) and the controversial play *The Plebeians Rehearse the Uprising*

(1965).

GRASSE, François Joseph Paul, Comte de (1722–1788), French naval commander whose fleet made possible Washington's decisive victory over the British at the siege of YORKTOWN (1781). Grasse landed 3,000 troops to aid the siege, and remained off Chesapeake Bay to keep the British fleet from aiding the British force under Cornwallis.

GRASSES, large group of ANGIOSPERMS that are of great importance to man. Strictly speaking, grasses only include those species belonging to the family Graminae, but the name applies to any plant with a similar growth habit. Grasses are wind- or self-pollinated and have hollow or pithy, jointed stems, bearing lanceolate leaves. The fruit is a GRAIN. Grasses include CEREAL CROPS, such as WHEAT, RICE and CORN, SUGARCANE, SORGHUM, millet and BAMBOO.

GRASSHOPPERS, active jumping INSECTS related to the CRICKETS. The hindlegs are greatly enlarged for jumping. Adults usually have two pairs of fully developed wings; these are lacking in immature stages. Many grasshoppers can produce sounds by rubbing the hind legs against the folded wings. Grasshoppers feed entirely on grasses and other plants. A few species form large migratory swarms; certain of these species are known as LOCUSTS.

GRASSLAND, the areas of the earth whose predominant type of vegetation consists of GRASSES, rainfall being generally insufficient to support higher plant forms. There are three main types: savanna, or tropical grassland, has coarse grasses growing 3-12ft high, occasional clumps of trees and some shrubs; it is found in parts of Africa and South America. Prairie has tall, deep-rooted grasses and is found in Middle and North America, Argentina, the Ukraine, South Africa and N Australia. Steppes have short grasses and are found mainly in Central Asia. Grasslands are of great economic importance as they provide food for domestic animals and often excellent cropland for cultivation.

GRATIAN, early 12th-century Italian monk who founded CANON LAW with his *Concordia discordantium canonum* (c1140), the first attempt to resolve over 3,000 conflicting texts on ecclesiastical discipline.

GRATTAN, Henry (1746–1820), Irish nationalist politician. An eloquent champion of economic reform and Roman Catholic emancipation, he served in both the Irish and British parliaments.

GRAVES, Morris Cole (1910–   ), US painter whose interest in Eastern art and American Indian mythology is seen in his delicate images of, for example, blind birds, pine trees and waves. His best-known work is probably the *Little Known Bird of the Inner Eye* (1941).

GRAVES, Robert Ranke (1895–1985), English poet and novelist, best known for his novels set in imperial Rome, *I, Claudius* (1934) and *Claudius the God* (1934). Less popular but equally successful were *Goodbye to All That* (1929), describing his experiences in WWI, and *The Long Week-End*, on the interwar period. He was professor of poetry at Oxford from 1961-66.

GRAVITATION, one of the fundamental forces of nature, the force of attraction existing between all MATTER. It is much weaker than the nuclear or electromagnetic forces and plays no part in the internal structure of matter. Its importance lies in its long range and in its involving all masses. It plays a vital role in the behavior of the universe: the gravitational attraction of the SUN keeps the planets in their orbits, and gravitation holds the matter in a STAR together. NEWTON'S **law of universal gravitation** states that the attractive FORCE F between two bodies of MASSES M_1 and M_2 separated by distance d is $F = GM_1 M_2/d^2$ where G is the **Universal Gravitational Constant** (6.670×10^{-11} Nm^2 kg^{-2}). The force of gravity on the earth is a special case of all attraction between masses and causes bodies to fall toward the center of the earth with a uniform acceleration $g =. GM/R^2$ where R and M are the radius and mass of the earth. Assuming, with Newton, that the inertial mass of a body (that which is operative in the laws of motion) is identical with its gravitational mass, application of the second law of motion gives the WEIGHT of a body of mass m, the force with which the earth attracts that body, as mg. Bodies on the earth and moon thus may have the same mass but different weights. Again, the gravitational force on a body is proportional to its mass but is independent of the type of material it is. Newton's theory explains most of the observed motions of the planets and the TIDES and is still sufficiently accurate for most applications. The Newtonian analysis of gravitation remained unchallenged until, in the early 20th century, EINSTEIN introduced radically new concepts in his theory of general RELATIVITY. According to this, mass deforms the geometrical properties of the space around it. Einstein reaffirmed Newton's assumption regarding the equivalence of gravitational and inertial mass, proposing that it was impossible to distinguish experimentally between an accelerated coordinate system and a local gravitational field. From this he predicted that LIGHT would be found to be deflected a certain amount toward massive bodies by their gravitational fields and this effect indeed was observed for starlight passing close to the sun. It was also predicted that accelerated matter should emit gravitational waves with the velocity of light, but the existence of these has not as yet been demonstrated.

GRAVURE. See PRINTING.

GRAY, Asa (1810–1888), the foremost of 19th-century US botanists. Being a prominent Protestant layman, his advocacy of the Darwinian thesis carried special force. However, he never accepted the materialist interpretation of the evolutionary mechanism and taught that NATURAL SELECTION was indeed consistent with a divine TELEOLOGY.

GRAY, Elisha (1835–1901), US inventor whose claim to have invented the device used by BELL in his telephone led to a famous legal battle. The invention appears to have been almost simultaneous; Gray's device was in fact the more practical of the two, but the legal battle was won by Bell.

GRAY, Harold Lincoln (1894–1968), US cartoonist, creator (1924) of the comic strip *Little Orphan Annie*.

GRAY, Robert (1755–1806), sea captain, first American to circumnavigate the world. Between 1787–90 Gray sailed westward around the world, starting from Boston. In 1792 he penetrated the mouth of the Columbia R and established the American claim to the Oregon territory.

GRAY, Thomas (1716–1771), English poet. His *Elegy Written in a Country Churchyard* (1750) is one of the most popular English poems; among his other main works are the odes *The Progress of Poesy* and *The Bard* (both 1757).

GREAT AMERICAN DESERT, a term applied to the desert areas of SW US and N Mexico. Beginning in S Cal., it stretches N along the E side of the Sierra Nevada into Ida. and Ore. It continues E to the Rockies and S into Mexico where the Lower California peninsula and the E shore of the Gulf of California are desert.

GREAT AWAKENING, an intense and widespread religious revival in 18th-century America, forming part of the international evangelical revival. Starting in N.J. (c1726), the movement quickly spread across New England. In reaction to the prevailing rationalism and formalism, its leaders—notably Jonathan EDWARDS and George WHITEFIELD—preached evangelical CALVINISM and discouraged excessive emo-

tionalism. The 1740s saw the zenith of the Awakening, which led to the rapid growth of the Presbyterian, Baptist and Methodist churches, continuing to the end of the century. A similar revival beginning in the 1790s is known as the Second Great Awakening.

GREAT BARRIER REEF, series of massive coral reefs off the NE coast of Australia, extending for about 1,250mi. The reef, which is the world's largest coral formation, can only be safely crossed at certain passages, the chief of which is Raines Inlet.

GREAT BASIN, desert region in the W US between the Wasatch and Sierra Nevada Mts and parts of adjacent states. A subdivision of the Basin and Range physiographic province, the Great Basin of Nev. contains Death Valley, Reno, Las Vegas, and Salt Lake City. Mineral mining and agriculture are the main industries.

GREAT BEAR, or Ursa Major, a constellation of the northern sky. The seven brightest stars form the group known as the Big Dipper.

GREAT BRITAIN, name of the main island of the British Isles comprising England, Scotland and Wales. (See UNITED KINGDOM.)

GREAT DEPRESSION, a period of US and world economic depression during the 1930s which was immediately precipitated by the disastrous stockmarket collapse in Wall Street on BLACK FRIDAY, Oct. 29, 1929. This heralded a period of high unemployment, failing businesses and banks and falling agricultural prices. Millions of workers were unemployed during the period (some 16 million in the US alone in 1933). There were many causes of the depression: easy credit had led to widespread stock speculation; the world had not completely recovered from WWI; US economic policies under President HOOVER had created domestic overproduction and less foreign trade. Franklin ROOSEVELT, elected president in 1932, brought in the NEW DEAL measures, but full recovery of the economy only occurred with the beginnings of defense spending immediately prior to WWII.

GREAT DIVIDE. See CONTINENTAL DIVIDE.

GREAT LAKES, chain of five large freshwater lakes in North America, forming the largest lake group in the world and covering an area of 95,170sq mi. From E to W the lakes are: Ontario, Erie, Huron, Michigan and Superior. They are connected by several channels, including the St. Lawrence R, Niagara R, and Lake St. Clair and the Welland Canal, Sault Sainte Marie (Soo) Canals and St. Lawrence Seaway and are now navigable by ocean-going vessels from Duluth, Minn., on Lake Superior to the Atlantic. The lake system is used for the transportation of iron ore, steel, petroleum, coal, grain and heavy manufactured goods. Trading ports on the waterways include Duluth, Chicago, Detroit, Cleveland, Buffalo, Port Arthur, Toronto and Montreal. In recent years, the lakes, particularly Lake Erie, have suffered from serious pollution.

GREAT PLAINS, large plateau in W central North America, extending for over 1,500mi from the Saskatchewan R in NW Canada to the Rio Grande in Mexico and the Gulf coastal plain in the S US. The plateau slopes gently downwards from the Rockies in the W, extending about 400mi E. The natural vegetation is buffalo grass, and the area generally has hot summers and cold winters with an average annual rainfall of 20in. The plains are known as the "granary of the world" owing to their vast wheat production; livestock is also important.

GREAT RIFT VALLEY, a large down-faulted depression extending more than 3,000mi from SE Africa to N Syria. In Africa, its W course is partly occupied by lakes Malawi (Nyasa), Tanganyika, Kivu, Edward and Albert (Mobutu Sese Seko); its E course by Lake Turkana. In Asia, the Sea of Galilee, the Jordan R, the Gulf of Aqaba, the Red Sea and the Gulf of Aden are in the Great Rift Valley. Volcanic and seismic activity are common throughout the length of the rift, tending to support the hypothesis that the rift represents an early stage in the development of an ocean that will in the geologic future separate E Africa from the rest of the continent. (See also PLATE TECTONICS.)

GREAT SALT LAKE, a shallow saline inland sea in NW Ut., about 5mi NW of Salt Lake City. Its size and depth vary yearly, but on average the lake is 72mi long and 30mi across at its widest point, with a maximum depth of 27ft. It is the largest brine lake in North America. Industrial plants along the shore extract some 300,000 tons of salt from the lake every year, and plans are under way for tapping other mineral resources. In 1987 a $60 million flood-control program was begun to lower the level of the lake, which had risen 12ft to a historic high.

GREAT SCHISM, two divisions in the Christian Church. The first was the breach between the EASTERN CHURCH and the Western church. Long-standing divergences in tradition, combined with political and theological disputes, came to a head in 1054 when Pope Leo IX sent legates to refuse the title of Ecumenical Patriarch to the Patriarch of Constantinople and to demand acceptance of the *filioque* ("and from the Son") clause in the Nicene Creed (see HOLY SPIRIT). The Patriarch refused and rejected the claim of papal supremacy. Reciprocal excommunications and anathemas followed. Later Councils were unsuccessful in healing the breach.

The second Great Schism was the division within the ROMAN CATHOLIC CHURCH from 1378 to 1417, when there were two or three rival popes and antipopes (see PAPACY), each with his nationalistic following. The Council of Constance ended the schism by electing Martin V sole pope.

GREAT SMOKY MOUNTAINS, range of the Appalachian Mts, forming the border between N.C. and Tenn. The "Great Smokies" are almost entirely within the 800sq mi Great Smoky Mountains National Park, established 1934. The mountain valleys are often filled with a smoky-blue haze, from which the name of the range derives.

GREAT SOCIETY, collective name for the domestic programs of President Lyndon B. JOHNSON. It derives from his aim (first stated in a speech in 1964) to build a great society in the US. Such a society, as Johnson envisioned it, would offer "abundance and liberty for all" and an "end to poverty and racial injustice."

GREAT STONE FACE, a stone profile formed by erosion on Profile Mt in the Franconia range of the White Mts., N N.H. Also known as the "Old Man of the Mountain," the Great Stone Face is a tourist attraction.

GREAT TREK, a migration between 1835 and 1845, of about 14,000 Afrikaners out of Cape Colony, South Africa, to escape British domination. They settled Natal, but when in 1843 it was taken by Britain, they trekked on across the Drakensberg Mts to form the Orange Free State and the Transvaal.

GREAT WALL OF CHINA, the world's longest wall fortification, N China. It extends over 1,500mi, roughly following the S border of the Mongolian plain. Construction was begun in the Ch'in dynasty (3rd cent. BC) to defend China against invasion from the N and mostly completed during the Ming dynasty (1368–1644). Its average height is 25ft; it is wide enough (about 12ft) for horsemen to ride along it.

GREBES, a group of highly specialized aquatic birds all closely related; family: Podicipedidae. They are diving birds of lakes or coastal waters; the feet are not webbed but "lobed" with flaps along the toes. Many of the grebes are highly ornamental birds, brightly colored and bearing tufts or crests. Courtship displays are often complex and extremely spectacular. All grebes eat quantities of their own feathers which collect around fishbones in the gut allowing these indigestible remains to be formed into a pellet and cast.

GRECO, El (1541–1614), one of the greatest and most individual Spanish painters, born Domenikos Theotokopoulos in Greece. First in Venice, where he was influenced by TINTORETTO, and later in Toledo, Spain, he developed his distinctive style of painting characterized by dramatically elongated figures and contrasting colors. Among his most famous works are *The Burial of the Count of Orgaz* (1586), the *Portrait of Cardinal Niño de Guevara* (c1600), and *View of Toledo* (1608).

GREECE, a European republic which occupies the S part of the Balkan peninsula and the surrounding islands in the Ionian, Mediterranean and Aegean seas.

Official name: Hellenic Republic
Capital: Athens
Area: 50,949sq mi
Population: 10,010,000
Language: Greek
Religions: Greek Orthodox; Muslim
Monetary unit(s): 1 drachma=100 leptae
Land. Of the country's total land area, almost 20% is accounted for by islands, among them Corfu, the Ionian Isles, Crete, the Cyclades, Sporades and Dodecanese. Over 75% of the land is mountainous; the Pindus range runs SE down the length of the country and then continues S into the Peloponnesus. The S and coastal areas of Greece have hot summers and mild winters, but Macedonia and the mountainous northern interior have cold winters. Much of Greece receives only about 15in of rain a year, but W Greece can receive as much as 50in.
People and Economy. The Greek people, who call themselves Hellenes, are a racial mixture of the many peoples who invaded the Balkans before and after classical times.

Language and culture, rather than race, define the Greeks. Half of Greece's population live in rural communities of fewer than 2,000 inhabitants, and about 30% are engaged in agriculture. In the last two decades there has been a trend towards urbanization. The capital, Athens, with its port Piraeus, is the largest city. The official language is modern Greek. Religious life is dominated by the Greek Orthodox Church. Elementary and secondary education are free, but private secondary schools are widespread. The country's biggest universities are at Athens, Thessaloniki, Patras and Ioannina.

The leading farm products are fruit and vegetables, wheat, cotton, tobacco, wine and olive oil. Both sheep and goats are raised in large numbers. The country is rich in mineral resources which have not been fully exploited. The bulk of the country's manufacturing is located in or near Athens, but efforts are being made to develop industrialization and thus provide a wider economic base for future growth. Greece has traditionally had a prosperous shipping industry; in 1987 its merchant fleet ranked third in the world. Despite problems with terrorism, tourism has become increasingly important to Greece's economy. In 1981 Greece joined the EUROPEAN ECONOMIC COMMUNITY.

History. Conquered by the Turks in the 15th century, Greece fought a successful War of Independence (1821–29) and established a constitutional monarchy. Thereafter Greece was characterized by political instability and conflict between monarchists and republicans. In WWI the country fought against Germany and Turkey. During WWII Greece was invaded by Italy in 1940, then by Germany, which occupied the country until Oct. 1944. A civil war was fought between 1944 and 1949, and US intervention was a major factor in ensuring the victory of the monarchists over communist and other left-wing groups. Political instability continued during the 1950s and 1960s, leading to a military coup and eventual dictatorship in April 1967. The monarchy was abolished in July 1973, and another military coup in Nov. of that year overthrew the dictatorship. In 1974 the Greek people voted for a constitutional republic rather than a restoration of the monarchy, and a new constitution was adopted in June 1975. Andreas PAPANDREOU's victory in the 1981 elections resulted in Greece's first socialist government. In 1986 the president's role was weakened and full executive powers were given to the prime minister. The

Papandreou government lost popularity as problems developed in the economy, church-state relations, corruption in government, and the prime minister's domestic life.

GREECE, Ancient, the independent cities and states of classical times occupying the Balkan peninsula and the surrounding islands. The name Greece comes from the Greek *graikoi*—the original inhabitants of the area around Dodona, the most ancient shrine of ZEUS. The Greeks called their land Hellas and themselves Hellenes. Ancient Greek culture is recognized as profoundly significant for Western man, for it provided the foundation of civilization in the West.

Greece was settled by about 3500 BC, and the Greek people probably moved into the area around 2000 BC. These settlers were strongly influenced by the Minoan civilization on the island of Crete. In the next few centuries the Mycenaean civilization (named after the city of Mycenae on the mainland; see AEGEAN CIVILIZATION) flourished (1600–1200 BC). The writings of HOMER provide a vivid picture of Mycenaean times. In the period between 1200–750 BC (known as the "Dark Ages" of Greek history), Dorian invaders overwhelmed the culture of Mycenae, bringing with them the knowledge of working with iron. In the 8th and 7th centuries BC the first Greek CITY-STATES emerged, generally consisting of a fortified hilltop such as the Athenian ACROPOLIS and the surrounding market town and countryside. Trade with Egypt, Syria and Phoenicia grew, and the city-states formed colonies throughout the Mediterranean area. From the 6th century ATHENS and SPARTA became the two most powerful city-states, embodying, respectively, a liberal and an authoritarian approach to government and society. Athens became a DEMOCRACY; Sparta became a military state. The 5th century BC began with attempted invasions of Greece by the Persians. The Persians were defeated on land at the Battles of Marathon (490 BC) and Plataea (479 BC) and at sea near Salamis. Athens emerged as the undisputed leader of Greece and led a number of Ionian cities in the formation of the DELIAN LEAGUE, whose purpose was to protect commerce and resist any further Persian invasions. From this league the Athenian empire emerged. The latter half of the 5th century, especially during PERICLES' leadership, was the Golden Age of Athens—a period of unparalleled cultural activity ranging from the building of the PARTHENON (see also PHIDIAS) to the ideas of SOCRATES. However, growing resentment against Athenian power led eventually to Athens' defeat by Sparta in the PELOPONNESIAN WAR (431–404 BC).

In the 4th century BC Athens' artistic and intellectual achievements continued to flourish under PLATO, ARISTOTLE, the sculptor PRAXITELES and others. However, in 338 BC Philip of Macedon became ruler of Greece, depriving the people of political liberty they were not to regain for more than 2,000 years. Philip's son Alexander the Great (356–323 BC) carried out a plan of conquest which would have far-reaching effects on the world. In the period that followed his death, the HELLENISTIC AGE, Greek culture and civilization spread over all the known world. Macedonia controlled Greece for more than a hundred years, although some city-states tried to restore a measure of their lost power by forming two confederations: the Aetolian League and the Achaean League.

Rome first became involved in Greek affairs in 220 BC in support of the Aetolian League against Macedonia, and in 197 BC the leagues helped the Romans defeat Macedonia. The Romans were hailed as liberators, but after the revolt of the Achaean League against Rome (146 BC), Greece was dominated by Rome and in 27 BC became the Roman province of Achaea. Greece still remained the cultural and intellectual center of the Mediterranean world, but economically and politically was unable to regain her former power. From 395 AD when the Roman Empire was divided into W and E, Greece was incorporated into the BYZANTINE EMPIRE (395–1453 AD). In the DARK AGES (from the 4th to the 9th centuries), Greece suffered from barbarian incursions, and after the fall of Constantinople in 1453 it became part of the Turkish OTTOMAN EMPIRE.

GREEK, the language of ancient and modern Greece, one of the oldest INDO-EUROPEAN LANGUAGES. The ancient and modern tongues use the same alphabet (which the Greeks adopted from the Phoenicians in the 8th century BC), but differ greatly in grammar, vocabulary and pronunciation. The earliest known records of ancient Greek date from around 1400 BC and use a form of writing known as MINOAN LINEAR SCRIPT. Classical Greek is based on Athenian dialects spoken from the 6th to the 4th centuries BC. During Hellenistic times a simplified Greek known as Koine became the common language of the civilized world. There are two forms of modern Greek: Koine for everyday use and an official state language which incorporates classical forms and words.

GREEK ART AND ARCHITECTURE.
The art of ancient Greece was the tangible expression of its religion and philosophy. Greek culture is essentially humanist, and the expressive possibilities of the human figure played a preeminent part in Greek art. Gods took human forms and abstract qualities were personified.

Sculpture. The Greeks first began to carve large scale marble sculptures around 650 BC. Their finest achievements date from the Classical Age beginning about 480 BC—idealized majestic figures of great harmony and fluidity. Notable examples are MYRON'S *Discus Thrower,* POLYCLITUS' *Spearbearer* and PHIDIAS' PARTHENON sculptures and his *Zeus,* a 40ft statue of gold and ivory at Olympus, one of the seven wonders of the ancient world. From the 4th century, Greek sculpture embodied emotional appeal, as in PRAXITELES' *Aphrodite of Cnidus,* the Hellenistic *Venus de Milo* and *Winged Victory of Samothrace.*

Vase Painting. The history of Greek painting in which portraiture and perspective were skilfully developed is illustrated primarily from painted pottery which has survived from about 900 BC. The earliest Dipylon vases, decorated with human figures in funeral and battle scenes, were grave markers. In the 7th century BC black-figure ware appeared, with carefully incised silhouette forms. In the mid-6th century BC Athenian red-figure ware appeared with carefully painted-on details and scenes which conformed to the shape of the pottery.

Architecture. Classical Greek architecture, which flourished in the 5th century BC, had its origins in the 6th century when stone and then marble replaced wood in civic buildings and temples. Greek architecture is characterized by harmony and symmetry. There are three specific styles of decoration: the earliest Doric style has great columns with wide flutes as in the Parthenon of Athens; the later Ionic and Corinthian styles have slenderer columns with more elaborate capitals (see CLASSICAL ORDERS).

GREEK FIRE, liquid mixture of unknown composition that took fire when wet, invented by a Syrian refugee in Constantinople in the 7th century AD and used by the Byzantine Empire and others for the next 800 years. Thrown in grenades or discharged from syringes, it wrought havoc in naval warfare until superseded by gunpowder. It appears to have been a petroleum-based mixture.

GREEK REVIVAL, a movement in art and architecture, in Europe and America, during the late 18th and 19th centuries, characterized by renewed interest in classical antiquity. Private and public buildings were modeled on Classical designs. Notable examples include the U. of Va. by Thomas JEFFERSON and the WASHINGTON MONUMENT. (See also NEOCLASSICISM.)

GREELEY, Horace (1811–1872), US journalist and reformer, founder and editor of the popular New York *Tribune* (1841). One of the most influential figures of the pre-Civil War period, he endorsed abolitionism, helped found the Republican Party and was instrumental in the candidature and election of Lincoln. However, his popularity was diminished during and after the Civil War by his confused attitude towards the South, and by his pleas for total amnesty for the Confederacy. He was defeated for the presidency in 1872.

GREELY, Adolphus Washington (1844–1935), US army officer and explorer. In 1881–89 he was one of only six survivors from an expedition to establish observation stations near the N pole. Chief signals officer from 1887, he introduced radio telegraphy to the Signal Corps.

GREEN, Thomas Hill (1836–1882), English idealist philosopher at Oxford who was the leading critic of the empiricist philosophies of J. S. MILL and H. SPENCER in mid-Victorian England. His influence long survived his death, declining only with the resurgence of the empirical approach in the 20th century.

GREEN, William (1873–1952), American labor leader. A union official from an early age, he served as president of the AMERICAN FEDERATION OF LABOR (1924–52).

GREENBACK, the first paper currency not backed by specie, issued by the US Treasury. Greenbacks were introduced in 1862 to help finance the Civil War. Because they were not backed by gold or silver, their issue was controversial and their value fell during the war.

GREENBACK PARTY, US political group active between 1876 and 1884. Founded largely by farmers, its main aim was to expand the circulation of greenback currency to bring about inflation, and thus end the depressed agricultural prices and make debts easier to pay. In 1878 the party sent 14 congressmen to Washington, but it rapidly declined in the 1880s. Many of the party's supporters and leaders turned to POPULISM in the 1890s.

GREENBERG, Hank (Henry Benjamin Greenberg; 1911–1986), US baseball player, first baseman for the Detroit Tigers (1933–42, 1944–46). He had a career total of 331 home runs, including 58 in 1938, and was voted the American League's most valuable player in 1935 and 1940.

GREENE, Graham (1904–   ), British novelist, best known for the works he defined as "entertainments," such as *The Third Man* (1950) and *Our Man in Havana* (1958). His more serious work is influenced by Roman Catholicism, expressing the need for faith and the possibility of personal salvation, as in *Brighton Rock* (1938), *The Power and the Glory* (1940), *The Heart of the Matter* (1948) and *The End of the Affair* (1951). Greene has also written short stories, several plays and the autobiographical volumes *A Sort of Life* (1971) and *Ways of Escape* (1980).

GREENE, Nathanael (1742–1786), American military commander in the REVOLUTIONARY WAR. Washington's second-in-command, he became general of the Southern army in 1780. His strategy at the battles of Guilford Court House, Hobkirks Hill and Eutaw Springs in 1781 did not bring outright victory, but wore out the British forces.

GREENHOUSE EFFECT, increase of average global temperature due to the trapping of heat in the ATMOSPHERE by carbon dioxide and other industrial gases. Sunlight radiated at visible and near-ultraviolet wavelengths provides most of the earth's incoming energy. After absorption it is reradiated, but at longer, infrared wavelengths, the earth being much cooler than the sun (see BLACKBODY). Although the atmosphere is transparent to the incoming solar radiation, that reradiated from the earth's surface is strongly absorbed by atmospheric water vapor and carbon dioxide. That absorbed is again reradiated, the majority back toward the surface. The amount of carbon dioxide in the atmosphere has risen from 280 to 340 parts per million in the last century, probably because of the burning of FOSSIL FUELS and the destruction of forests whose trees absorb carbon dioxide. Scientists believe that this increase has contributed to a more or less steady rise of the earth's temperature during this period. Their mathematical models predict that the average global temperature will rise from 59°F in 1950-80 by 3-9°F by 2030. Warming of the earth will cause major changes in climatic patterns and a gradual rise in sea level as polar ice melts.

GREENLAND, the world's largest true island, part of the kingdom of DENMARK. It is located mainly N of the Arctic Circle, to the NE of Canada. An ice cap which may reach a depth of over 1mi covers four-fifths of the island; the only habitable areas are two small coastal strips. Vegetation is sparse, but there is a variety of Arctic fauna such as musk ox and caribou. About 90% of the population live on the SW coast, near the capital Nuuk (formerly Godthaab). Greenlanders have in general a blend of ESKIMO and Danish blood, but enjoy a distinct racial identity and have their own language. Health services and education are free. Known mineral resources are now largely exhausted, and the economy rests on fishing and agriculture.

It is uncertain when Eskimo tribes first arrived from N Canada. VIKINGS, led by ERIC THE RED, established a colony in Greenland around 982, but the settlers appear to have died out in the 14th century. Greenland was rediscovered in the 16th century; it became a Danish colony in 1815, and a Danish settlement was established in 1894. The island was made an integral part of Denmark in 1953, with representatives in parliament. In 1979 it achieved home rule.

GREEN MOUNTAIN BOYS, organization formed in the Green Mountains of what is now Vt. in the 1760s. Led by Ethan ALLEN, its original purpose was to assault and rob N.Y. state officials and settlers in areas disputed between N.Y. and N.H. In the REVOLUTIONARY WAR the Green Mountain Boys directed their activities against the British, and helped take Crown Point and Fort Ticonderoga.

GREENOUGH, Horatio (1805–1852), US neoclassical sculptor and art critic who spent most of his working life in Italy. His best-known work is the grandiose statue of George Washington in the Smithsonian Institution (1841).

GREENPEACE, international organization of environmental activists, particularly protesting against nuclear and atomic testing and waste.

GREEN POLITICS, political movements in West Germany (*die Grüne*), Belgium, the Netherlands, Switzerland, and France, to promote parliamentary measures to protect the environment from pollution and similar political issues.

GREEN REVOLUTION, an agricultural trend of recent years which has greatly increased crop production in India, Pakistan and Turkey. It is based on the introduction of new varieties of crops and is dependent on the use of large quantities of PESTICIDES and FERTILIZERS. It was once hoped that the Green Revolution could solve the problem of feeding the world's increasing population, but these hopes have faded in the face of high prices and of secondary ecological effects. (See POLLUTION.)

GREENSPAN, Alan (1926–), US economist and public official, chairman of the Council of Economic Advisers (1974–77) under President Gerald Ford, appointed (1987) chairman of the Federal Reserve Board by President Ronald Reagan to replace Paul A. Volcker.

GREENWICH OBSERVATORY, Royal, observatory established in 1675 at Greenwich, England, by Charles II to correct the astronomical tables used by sailors and otherwise to advance the art of NAVIGATION. Its many famous directors, the "astronomers royal," have included J. Flamsteed (the first), E. HALLEY and Sir George Airy. The original Greenwich building, now known as Flamsteed House and run as an astronomical museum, was designed by Sir Christopher WREN. The observatory is presently sited at Herstmonceux, Sussex, where it moved in the late 1940s. The observatory itself is thus no longer sited on the Greenwich meridian, the international zero of longitude.

GREENWICH VILLAGE, area between Spring and West 14th Streets in New York City, famous since the 19th century as an "artists' colony." The area's Bohemian atmosphere has made it a popular tourist attraction.

GREGG, John Robert (1867–1948), inventor of the Gregg system of shorthand, using the phonetic principle and the forms of ordinary handwriting. Easy to learn, it is now taught in most US schools, and is adopted for use in 20 languages.

GREGG, Josiah (1806–1850), Santa Fe trader, author of *Commerce of the Prairies* (1844), a classic of the frontier. He led various exploratory expeditions in N Cal., and during one of these was killed falling from his horse.

GREGORIAN CHANT. See PLAINSONG.

GREGORY, name of 16 popes. **Saint Gregory I** (c540–604), called Gregory the Great, was pope 590–604. His papacy laid the foundation for the political and moral authority of the medieval papacy. He reorganized the vast papal estates scattered all over Italy, providing an economic foundation for the Church's power. In 596 he sent St. AUGUSTINE to Britain, beginning its conversion to Christianity. His feast day is March 12. **Saint Gregory II** (c669–731), pope 715–731, held office at a time of increasing conflict between Rome and Byzantium, and eventually excommunicated Patriarch Anastasius of Byzantium. His feast day is Feb. 11. **Saint Gregory III** (d. 741), pope 731–41, continued to be involved in conflicts with Byzantium, excommunicating Byzantine Emperor Leo III. His

feast day is Nov. 28. **Saint Gregory VII** (c1025–1085), called Hildebrand, was pope 1073–85. One of the great medieval reform popes, he attacked corruption in the Church, insisted on the celibacy of the clergy and on the sole right of the Church to appoint bishops and abbots. These reforms threatened the power of the German monarchy, leading to disputes and war with Henry IV of Germany. In 1084 Henry seized Rome, forcing Gregory to flee. His feast day is May 25. **Gregory IX** (c1170–1241) was pope 1227–41. His papacy was marked by conflict with Holy Roman Emperor Frederick II, leading eventually to war in Italy between Imperial and papal factions. **Gregory XI** (1329–1378) was pope 1370–78. Elected pope in Avignon, he managed to return the papal court to Rome in 1377. **Gregory XIII** (1502–1585), pope from 1572–85, promoted the COUNTER-REFORMATION through his pledge to execute the decrees of the Council of Trent. A patron of the Jesuits, he is remembered for the calendar reform he sponsored and for his lavish building program, which emptied the papal treasury. He celebrated the massacre of the Huguenots on St. Bartholomew's Day, 1572, with a *Te Deum*. **Gregory XVI** (1765–1846), pope 1831–46, strengthened the papacy, aligning it with Austria under METTERNICH, with whose help he suppressed a revolt in the Papal States. He opposed the introduction of gas lighting and railways.

GREGORY, Lady Isabella Augusta (1852–1932), Irish dramatist and director, largely responsible for the production of YEAT'S and SYNGE's plays at the famous ABBEY THEATRE in Dublin. Their works have tended to overshadow her own plays, such as *The Rising of the Moon* and *The White Cockade* (1904–08).

GRENADA, one of the smallest independent countries in the Western Hemisphere.

Land. Grenada is the southernmost of the Windward Islands in the West Indies, 90mi N of Trinidad. The state consists of the main island, which is mountainous, and of the S group of the GRENADINES. The climate is semitropical.

People and Economy. Over half of the population are blacks, about 45% mulattoes, and 1% whites. Exports include nutmeg, cocoa, mace, sugar, cotton, coffee, lime oil and bananas. Tourism is becoming an important source of income, but Grenada is still a very poor country.

History. Discovered by COLUMBUS in 1498, Grenada was first colonized by the French but became British in 1762. It achieved internal self-government in 1967 and

Official name: State of Grenada
Capital: St. George's
Area: 133sq mi
Population: 104,000
Languages: English, French-African patois
Religions: Roman Catholic, Anglican
Monetary unit(s): 1 East Caribbean dollar = 100 cents

became fully independent within the Commonwealth in 1974. After a bloodless coup in 1979 a left-wing government was installed. In the course of an army-supported coup in 1983, Prime Minister Maurice Bishop and several other leaders were slain. The US then sent troops, aided by units from other Caribbean nations, to protect about 1,000 Americans on the island and to restore constitutional government. Elections were held in 1984, and the last foreign forces were withdrawn in 1985. Since then, substantial foreign aid and the opening (1987) of a new international airport have helped improve the economy.

GRENADINES, a group of c600 small islands, part of the WINDWARD ISLANDS in the West Indies, between Grenada and St. Vincent. The N group, and the N part of Carriacou (the largest island) belong to St. Vincent. The S Group belongs to Grenada.

GRENFELL, Sir Wilfred Thomason (1865–1940), English physician, missionary and author who devoted himself to establishing hospitals, nursing stations and schools in Labrador and Newfoundland. He founded the International Grenfell Association. His books include *Forty Years for Labrador* (1932).

GRENVILLE, George (1712–1770), English statesman who tried to impose internal taxation on the American colonies by means of the STAMP ACT, which was a precipitant of the American Revolution. He was prime minister 1763–65.

GRENVILLE, Sir Richard (1542–1591), Elizabethan "sea dog." He commanded RALEIGH'S first expedition (1585) to colonize Roanoke Island, N.C. When his ship the *Revenge* became isolated from the rest of the fleet in a British attempt (1591) to intercept Spanish treasure ships off the Azores, Grenville held an entire Spanish fleet in combat for 15 hours before he was mortally wounded and captured. The story is told in Tennyson's "The Revenge."

GRESHAM, Sir Thomas (c1519–1579), English financier, merchant and government official under Elizabeth I. He restored the coinage (devalued under Henry VIII) and proposed stabilization of the pound. He was founder of the Royal Exchange and of Gresham College, London.

GRESHAM'S LAW, the economic principle (attributed to Sir Thomas Gresham) that "bad money drives out good." This means that when coins of the same face-value but of different market-value circulate together, the coins of higher market-value will disappear from circulation to be hoarded or used as an open-market commodity.

GRETZKY, Wayne (1961–   ), Canadian hockey player, with the Edmonton Oilers 1978–88 and the Los Angeles Kings from 1988. He was elected the National Hockey League's most valuable player 1980–87.

GREUZE, Jean-Baptiste (1725–1805), French painter who started a vogue with his sentimental and moralistic GENRE painting, e.g. *The Village Bride* (1761). He is also known for his popular erotic studies of young girls, such as *The Broken Pitcher* (c1773).

GREVILLE, Charles Cavendish Fulke (1794–1865), British diarist whose writings are a main source of information on British politics of his time. He was clerk of the privy council under George IV, William IV and Victoria.

GREY, Charles, 2nd Earl Grey (1764–1845), English prime minister responsible for the passage of the REFORM BILL (1832), which extended the franchise to the middle classes. A long-time leader of the liberal Whig party in opposition, he was in office from 1830 to 1834.

GREY, Lady Jane (1537–1554), queen of England for nine days in 1553. The Duke of Northumberland, her father-in-law and powerful adviser to the dying Edward VI, persuaded the king to name Jane heir to the throne. She reluctantly accepted the crown, but Mary Tudor, Edward's half-sister, had the country's support, and was proclaimed queen by the Lord Mayor of London. Lady Jane and her husband were beheaded for treason.

GREY, Zane (1875–1939), US author of sagas about the American West. His 54 novels, of which *Riders of the Purple Sage* (1912) is the most popular, have sold over

15 million copies.

GREY OF FALLODEN, Edward Grey, Viscount (1862–1933), British foreign secretary 1905–16 who brought about a conference of the Great Powers to negotiate a settlement of the BALKAN WARS, and attempted similarly to avert WWI after the assassination of Archduke Ferdinand. He was responsible for the Treaty of London that brought Italy into WWI in 1915.

GRIEG, Edvard Hagerup (1843–1907), Norwegian composer who based his work on traditional national folk music. He wrote many songs and piano pieces. His best known orchestral works are: the *Piano Concerto* (1869), the *Peer Gynt* suites (1876) and the *Holberg Suite* (1885).

GRIFFITH, Arthur (1872–1922), Irish nationalist who founded SINN FEIN, a major force in Ireland's struggle for independence from England. He led the Irish delegation in negotiating the treaty (1921) that established the Irish Free State. He was the first vice-president of the Dáil Éireann and, in 1922, briefly succeeded De Valera as its president.

GRIFFITH, D(avid) W(ark) (1880–1948), US silent film director and producer, often considered the father of modern cinema. His immensely popular *Birth of a Nation* (1915) introduced major principles of film technique. Griffith also pioneered the film "spectacular." Among his other films are *Intolerance* (1916), *Way Down East* (1920) and *Orphans of the Storm* (1922).

GRILLPARZER, Franz (1791–1872), Austria's foremost dramatist. His poetic tragedies introduced a new realism to the romantic tradition out of which they grew. His major works include *Hero and Leander* (1831) and *A Dream Is Life* (1834).

GRIMALDI, Joseph (1779–1837), English clown. Born of a family of pantomimists, he first appeared on stage at age two. His legendary success (1806) in *Mother Goose* established him as one of the comic masters of all time.

GRIMKÉ, Angelina Emily (1805–1879) and **Sarah Moore** (1792–1873), US abolitionists and women's rights crusaders. Angelina's *An Appeal to the Christian Women of the South* and Emily's *An Epistle to the Clergy of the Southern States* (both 1836) urged opposition to slavery.

GRIMM, Jakob (1785–1863) and **Wilhelm** (1786–1859), German philologists, most famous for their collections of folk tales, notably *Grimm's Fairy Tales* (1812–1815). Jakob's *German Grammar* (1819–37) formulated a linguistic law (Grimm's Law) explaining the systematic sound-changes of consonants in the Germanic languages from their Indo-European roots. In 1838 the brothers began work on the great *German Dictionary*, completed only in 1960.

GRIMMELSHAUSEN, Hans Jakob Christoffel von (1625–1676), German novelist whose picaresque romance *Simplicissimus* (1669), set in the Thirty Years' War, ranks as the great 17th-century German novel.

GRIS, Juan (1887–1927), Spanish cubist painter, born José Victoriano González. A follower of PICASSO, he developed the style known as Synthetic CUBISM, which he applied to still lifes in increasingly free compositions.

GRIZZLY BEAR, *Ursus arctos horribilis*, one of the largest of the North American brown bears. The name refers to the grizzled coat rather than to the beast's temper, but despite this the grizzly has more or less been exterminated in the US. Though classed with the CARNIVORA, the grizzly is largely vegetarian and rarely eats flesh. An imposing, even terrifying, animal, the grizzly plays a big role in the legends of the North American pioneers.

GROFÉ, Ferde (1892–1972), US composer and pianist. His best-known works are the *Mississippi Suite* (1924) and the *Grand Canyon Suite* (1931) and the orchestration of George GERSHWIN's *Rhapsody in Blue* (1924).

GROMYKO, Andrei Andreyevich (1909–   ), Soviet diplomat. In a rapid rise after Stalin's purges, he became ambassador to the US in WWII and UN representative of the USSR after the war. Named foreign minister in 1957, he held that post for over a quarter century during periods of cold war, disarmament talks, détente, and incidents of Soviet military interventions in several countries. From 1985 to 1988 he was chairman of the presidium of the Supreme Soviet, a largely honorific post sometimes called the presidency of the USSR. He was succeeded as foreign minister by Eduard Shevardnadze.

GROOTE, Gerhard (1340–1384), Dutch monastic reformer and founder of the Brethren of the Common Life. A mystic, he stressed simple piety.

GROPIUS, Walter (1883–1969), German–American architect and teacher who originated the profoundly influential BAUHAUS style, characterized by a marriage of form and function, and the use of modern materials (especially glass). His designs include the Bauhaus in Dessau (1926) and (in collaboration) the Pan Am Building in New York.

GROPPER, William (1897–1977), US satirical cartoonist and painter whose theme was social and economic injustice. In the 1930s his expressionist paintings won widespread recognition. He also painted murals in important public buildings.

GROS, Antoine-Jean, Baron (1771–1835), French painter, most notably of Napoleon's military campaigns.

GROSSETESTE, Robert (c1168–1253), English scholar and prelate whose teaching and writings turned Oxford into a major institution of learning and helped lay the basis for medieval SCHOLASTICISM. Grosseteste translated and commented on Aristotle and wrote scientific works on mathematics, physics, and astronomy. Bishop of Lincoln from 1235, he vigorously defended the rights of the Church against the monarchy and chastised his superiors in Rome for corruption.

GROSS NATIONAL PRODUCT (GNP), the total value of goods and services produced by a national economy before any deduction has been made for depreciation (the *net national product*). The annual growth of the GNP is often taken as an indicator of the state of a country's economy, but its significance is limited because it does not take inflation into account. Its chief purpose is to indicate a nation's comparative national wealth.

GROSVENOR, Gilbert Hovey (1875–1966), US editor who transformed the *National Geographic Magazine* from a technical bulletin of the National Geographic Society in Washington to a hugely popular illustrated magazine whose subscribers were also members of the society. He was editor of the magazine 1903–54 and president of the society 1920–54.

GROSZ, George (1893–1959), German–American satirical artist. He was an early member of the DADA movement. His caricatures, especially those attacking corruption and militarism in post-WWI Germany, are among the most persuasive expressions of misanthropy in the 20th century. He moved to the US in 1933.

GRÓSZ, Károly (1930–), prime minister of Hungary from 1987, general secretary of the Hungarian Communist Party from 1988, succeeding János Kádár. An orthodox party bureaucrat, he accepted the policy of economic reform prevailing in Moscow though in the context of strict political control.

GROTIUS, Hugo (1583–1645), Dutch jurist, considered the father of international law. In 1619 he was condemned to life imprisonment for his political activity, but he escaped to Paris. There he wrote *On the Law of War and Peace* (1625). This was a study of all the laws of mankind with an emphasis on rules of conduct applying to states, nations and individuals.

GROUNDHOG, a familiar North American member of the ground squirrels popularly referred to as the WOODCHUCK.

GROUNDWATER, water accumulated beneath the earth's surface in the pores of rocks, spaces, cracks, etc. Most underground water is *meteoric* and originates as precipitation that sinks into soil and rocks. Permeable, water-bearing rocks are AQUIFERS; rocks with pores small enough to inhibit the flow of water through them are aquicludes. Build-up of groundwater pressure beneath an aquiclude makes possible construction of an ARTESIAN WELL. The uppermost level of groundwater saturation is the water table. (See also PERMAFROST; SPRING.)

GROUP, a set of algebraic elements in which there is an operation * such that: (1) for all elements a, b, in the set, * is associative (see ALGEBRA) and $a*b$ is a member of the set; (2) there is an identity element e defined by $a*e=a$ for every element a of the set; (3) every element a has an inverse a^{-1}, also a member of the set, where $a*a 03^{WI}=e$. If $a*b=b*a$ for every a and b, the group is said to be commutative, or abelian. Groups are important in pure and applied mathematics partly because many sorts of operations, for example all the rotations of space or all the ways of rearranging a set of objects, form groups. See SYMMETRY; ALGEBRA, ABSTRACT.

GROUSE, a family (Tetraonidae) of game birds usually brown, gray or black in plumage. They are ground birds living on open moorland or heath, and are well-camouflaged. Three species moult into a white or parti-colored winter plumage for camouflage in snow. Grouse feed largely on plant material—shoots, buds and fruits—but will also eat insects. In many species males perform elaborate courtship displays at established display grounds, or "leks." These lek species, and many others, are polygamous.

GROVE, Lefty (Robert Moses Grove; 1900–1975), US baseball player, left-handed pitcher for the Philadelphia Athletics (1925–33) and the Boston Red Sox (1934–41). He won 20 or more games in seven consecutive years (1925–31), including a 31-4 record in 1931.

GROVES, Leslie Richard (1896–1970), US army officer who headed the MANHATTAN PROJECT to develop the atomic bomb, and was responsible for the vast construction program involved. Before the war he supervised all US military construction, including the building of the PENTAGON.

GROWTH, the increase in the size of an organism, reflecting either an increase in the number of its CELLS, or one in its protoplasmic material, or both. Cell number and protoplasmic content do not always increase together; cell division can occur without any increase in PROTOPLASM giving a larger number of smaller cells. Alternatively, protoplasm can be synthesized with no cell division so that the cells become larger. Any increase in protoplasm requires the synthesis of cell components such as nuclei, mitochondria, thousands of enzymes, and cell membrane. These require the synthesis of macromolecules such as PROTEINS, NUCLEIC ACIDS and polysaccharides from AMINO ACIDS, SUGARS and fatty acids. These subunits must be synthesized from still simpler substances or obtained from the environment. **Growth curves,** which plot time against growth (such as the number of cells in a bacterial culture, the number of human beings on earth, the size or weight of a plant seedling, an animal or an organ of an animal) all have a characteristic S-shape. This curve is divided into three parts: the lag phase, during which cells prepare for growth; the exponential phase when actual growth occurs, and the stationary phase when growth ceases. The time any particular cell or group of cells remains in any phase depends on their type and the particular condition prevailing. The *lag phase* represents a period of rapid growth of protoplasm so that the cells become larger without any increase in their number. The duration of the lag phase depends on the resynthesis of the enzyme systems required for growth and the availability of the necessary raw materials. Basically each original cell must obtain sufficient components to form two new cells. During the *exponential phase*, each cell gives rise to two cells, the two to four and so on, so that the number of cells after n generations is 2^n. The generation or doubling time for any particular cell is constant throughout the exponential phase. The time for organisms to double their mass ranges from 20 min for some bacteria to 180 days for a human being at birth. If exponential growth were unlimited, one bacterial cell in 24 hours would give rise to some 4,000 tons of bacteria. However, the exponential growth usually ceases (giving the *stationary phase*) either because of lack of an essential nutrient or because waste products produced by the cells pollute the environment. Again, in higher animals population growth is often slowed by parasite-carried epidemics.

The S-type growth pattern can be readily seen in unicellular organisms. Although growth in organisms containing different types of cells obeys the same basic rules, the relationships of the different types of cells complicate the pattern. But although all parts of a multicellular organism do not grow at the same rate or stop growing at the same time, the overall growth curve is still S-shaped.

GRÜNEWALD, Mathias (c1475–1528), German painter who, with his contemporary DÜRER, is considered one of the two great masters of the German Renaissance. His most characteristic theme is the crucifixion, a subject in which he combined beauty and delicacy of style with a savage and harrowing realism. His masterpiece is the altarpiece for St. Anthony's monastery at Isenheim, with subjects such as the *Resurrection* and the *Temptation of St. Anthony* (1513–15).

GUADALCANAL, largest of the SOLOMON ISLANDS in the S Pacific. Volcanic in nature, it supports extensive coconut plantations which are the economic mainstay; copra and timber are the main exports. The island was the scene of a decisive battle of WWII in 1943, when it was recaptured by Allied troops from the Japanese.

GUADALUPE HIDALGO, Treaty of, was signed by the US and Mexico at this Mexican town in 1848 to end the Mexican War. Mexico agreed to cede what are now Tex., Cal., Utah., Nev., and parts of N.M., Ariz., Col., and Wyo. to the US in return for $15 million and other benefits. The treaty guaranteed Mexicans' land rights, but these were not respected.

GUADALUPE MOUNTAINS NATIONAL PARK covers 128.6sq mi of Tex. E of El Paso. An area of geological interest, particularly for its limestone formations, it contains prehistoric Indian ruins and a wide variety of wildlife; established 1966.

GUADELOUPE, overseas department of France composed of two islands in the E Caribbean Sea, Grande-Terre and Basse-Terre. With some smaller islands they cover a total area of 687sq mi. A French settlement since 1635, it was captured by the British in the Seven Years' War and confirmed as French in 1815; the largely black population speaks a French patois. Bananas, coffee, cacao and vanilla are produced, and tourism is important. Pop 335,000.

GUAM, largest and southernmost of the MARIANA ISLANDS, in the Pacific Ocean 6,000mi W of San Francisco. A US territory since 1898 and an important US naval and air base, Guam was captured by the Japanese in 1941, and was recaptured by the US in 1944.

GUANTÁNAMO BAY, large natural harbor in Cuba, site of a US naval base strategically placed with access to the Caribbean and Panama. It has been leased to the US since 1903 but since 1960 has been isolated and harassed by the hostile Castro regime.

GUARANI INDIANS, group of primitive South American tribes, linked by language, who once lived in an area now covered by parts of Paraguay, Brazil and Argentina. Conquered by Spain in the 16th century, their numbers have been reduced by disease. Their language, however, is now the second language of Paraguay.

GUARDI, Francesco (1712–1793), Venetian landscape, architectural and figure painter, noted for his romantic, visionary views of Venice executed with a high degree of individualism and ellipticism in a style inspired by CANALETTO. His characteristic work, typified by his *Feast of the Ascension at Venice* (c1763), was done in later life.

GUARINI, Guarino (1624–1683), influential Italian architect, one of the masters of the Baroque. Most of his major works were churches and palaces in Turin, such as San Lorenzo, the Capella della Sacra Sindone, and the Palazzo Carignano.

GUARNERI, family of violin makers of Cremona in Italy. **Andrea** (c1626–1698), with STRADIVARI an apprentice of AMATI, founded the dynasty. His sons **Giuseppe** (1666–1739?) and **Pietro Giovanni** (1655–c1740), and **Pietro** (1695–c1765), a grandson, continued the trade, but the most renowned member of the family was the eccentric and experimental **Giuseppe "del Gesù"** (c1687–1745).

GUATEMALA, northernmost republic in Central America.

Land. Guatemala is a mountainous country

Official name: Republic of Guatemala
Capital: Guatemala City
Area: 42,042sq mi
Population: 8,434,000
Languages: Spanish; Maya-Quiché dialects
Religions: Roman Catholic
Monetary unit(s): 1 quetzal=100 centavos

composed largely of volcanic highland at altitudes of 2,000–6,000ft, although mountain peaks such as Mount Tajumulco (13,845ft) rise much higher. The E and W highlands are not very fertile, lacking the rich volcanic soils of the coast or the cooler climate and high rainfall of the N central area. To the N is the Petén, a rain forest plateau with areas of savanna covering a third of the country. The climate varies from the tropical Petén and coastal areas to the subtropical and temperate highlands.

People. The native Indians moved into the highland areas as Spanish colonizers occupied the valleys, and many of them still live there. Today they account for over 54% of the population, only 4% being white; the remainder are mestizos (*Ladinos*). The Indians maintain a traditional family-oriented village culture, speaking mainly their own dialects.

Economy. Coffee plantations account for almost half the nation's revenues. Cotton is also an important product, having superseded banana cultivation since the 1930s. Other exports are tobacco, vegetables, fruit and beef. Guatemala has only limited mineral resources; nickel, chromate, silver, lead and zinc are produced. Manufacturing industries are mainly devoted to the processing of local produce, but they are steadily expanding. Although Guatemala joined the Central American Common Market in 1961, the US remains its principal trading partner, taking over 30% of its exports and providing about 40% of its imports.

History. The Indian MAYAS ruled the area from about 300 AD, but their civilization declined and they were unable to offer much resistance to the invading Spaniards under ALVARADO in 1524. With the breakup of the Spanish New World, Guatemala became independent in 1821, and subsequently was a member of the Central American Federation (1824–39). The post-WWII governments, especially under Jacobo Arbenz Guzmán, had socialist tendencies. After a military coup in 1954 Guatemala has been plagued by left- and right-wing terrorism, political assassinations and further coups. Left-wing guerrilla attacks and right-wing human-rights abuses continued into the late 1980s despite the restoration of civilian government in 1986 and the signing of a preliminary Central American peace agreement in 1987.

GUDERIAN, Heinz (1888–1954), German army officer whose tank warfare and *blitzkrieg* techniques were successful in the German invasion of Poland (1939) and of France (1940).

GUELPHS AND GHIBELLINES, two opposing political factions in 13th- and 14th-century Italy. The Guelphs supported the pope, while the Ghibellines backed imperial Germany. Both originated in 12th century Germany, in opposition over territories of the Holy Roman Empire. After 1268, the rivalries became purely political between cities and families. In Florence the ruling Guelphs split into rival groups of Whites and Blacks.

GUERICKE, Otto von (1602–1686), German physicist credited with inventing the vacuum pump. His best-known experiment was with the Magdeburg hemispheres (1654): he evacuated a hollow sphere composed of two halves placed together, and showed that two 8-horse teams were insufficient to separate the halves. (See PUMPS.) He is also credited with inventing the first electric GENERATOR.

GUERNICA, town in N Spain in the Basque province, destroyed by bombing in 1937 by German planes fighting for FRANCO in the Spanish Civil War. PICASSO's picture commemorating the event is in the Prado in Madrid. Pop 15,000.

GUERRILLA WARFARE is waged by irregular forces in generally small-scale operations, often in enemy-held territory. The term (Spanish: little war) originally applied / to the tactics of Spanish–Portuguese irregulars in the Napoleonic Wars. Traditional guerrilla warfare is generally waged against larger and better-equipped conventional forces; it is usually part of a wider strategy, as for example the activities of the resistance movements in Nazi-occupied Europe, which were part of overall Allied strategy. Guerrilla fighters must avoid open battle as much as possible, exploiting the mobility gained from lack of equipment and supply lines. To compensate for these they must have a wide degree of popular support. They must rely on hit-and-run tactics, ambush, sabotage and the psychological effects of unpredictable attack.

Recent years have seen the development of the "urban guerrilla," whose desire is not to expel an invader by a general insurrection but to so disorganize the fabric of society that a faction can seize power without relying on popular support. To this end ambush, hijacking and bombing, directed both at specific targets and simply at the populace at large, have become increasingly common. Such revolutionary guerrilla warfare tends to be offensive rather than defensive. It is ideological rather than patriotic in nature. More centralized than conventional guerrilla fighting, it is easier to suppress in the earlier stages.

With the advent of the nuclear age, guerrilla warfare is perceived to have distinct advantages. No longer relegated to the underdog, it avoids large-scale confrontations which might lead to escalation, is less expensive for aggressors than all-out war and can be easier to disclaim.

GUEVARA, Che (Ernesto Guevara de la Serna; 1928–1967), Argentinian-born Cuban communist revolutionary and guerrilla leader, who helped organize CASTRO's coup in 1959. After serving as president of the Cuban national bank and minister of industry, he went to Bolivia in 1966 to direct the guerrilla movement there. He was captured by the Bolivian army and executed.

GUGGENHEIM, name of a family of US industrialists and philanthropists. **Meyer** (1828–1905) emigrated to Philadelphia from Switzerland in 1847 and set up a business importing Swiss lace. Aided by his seven sons he later established large smelting and refining plants. One son, **Daniel** (1856–1930), extended the concern internationally and set up an aeronautics research foundation. Another son, **Simon** (1867–1941), was a US senator from Col. and established a memorial foundation awarding fellowships to artists and scholars. The sixth son, **Solomon Robert** (1861–1949), founded the Guggenheim Museum in New York.

GUIANA, British. See GUYANA.

GUIANA, Dutch. See SURINAME.

GUIANA, French. See FRENCH GUIANA.

GUICCIARDINI, Francesco (1483–1540), Italian statesman and historian. He held various offices in his native Florence and in the service of Pope Leo X. His history of Italy during the ITALIAN WARS is considered a Renaissance masterpiece.

GUIDE DOG. See SEEING-EYE DOGS.

GUIDO D'AREZZO (c990–1050), Italian musical theorist and monk whose great work *Micrologus* (c1025) reformed musical notation. He introduced a four-line staff so that certainty of pitch in notation was established.

GUILD, association of merchants or craftsmen in the same trade or craft to protect the interests of its members. Guilds had both economic and social purposes and flourished in Europe in the Middle Ages. Merchant guilds were often very powerful, controlling trade in one area, or in the case of the HANSEATIC LEAGUE much of N Europe. The guilds of individual craftsmen such as goldsmiths, weavers or shoemakers, regulated wages, quality of production and working conditions for apprentices. Wealthy guilds built extensive head-quarters for themselves, some of which still stand. The guild system declined from the 16th century because of changing trade and work conditions.

GUILD SOCIALISM, the English version of SYNDICALISM, calling for the organization of industry in independent worker-controlled guilds. In the early 20th century, guild socialists, led by S. G. Hobson and G. D. H. Cole, rejected the violent general strike in favor of parliamentary methods and, although the guilds themselves disappeared, strongly influenced the growth of the modern British Labour Party.

GUILFORD COURTHOUSE, Battle of, battle in the REVOLUTIONARY WAR in North Carolina on March 15, 1781, between the Southern Army under Nathanael GREENE and the British under CORNWALLIS. Greene was defeated, but the British suffered great losses and withdrew, abandoning the drive to capture the center of the state.

GUILLOTINE, device for beheading; an oblique blade between two upright posts falls, when a supporting cord is released, onto the victim's neck below. It came into use during the French Revolution in response to J. I. Guillotin's call for a "humane" form of execution. Used for the last time in France in 1971, it was abolished with the elimination of the nation's death penalty in 1981.

GUIMARD, Hector (1867–1942), French ART NOUVEAU architect and designer. He is famous for the Castel Béranger (1894–98), an apartment building in Paris, and the Paris métro station's decorative cast-iron gates (c1900).

GUINEA, West African republic, between Guinea-Bissau and Sierra Leone, sharing frontiers with Senegal, Mali, Ivory Coast and Liberia.

Land. It is a tropical country. The Atlantic coastline has many estuaries and mangrove swamps, which have been reclaimed for the cultivation of rice and bananas. Behind the narrow coastal plain is the high and extensive Fouta Djallon plateau, the slopes of which are densely forested. Mt Nimba in the SE is the highest peak (5,800ft). The annual rainfall is especially heavy in the coastal region, the average being 169in. The climate and vegetation support a richly varied wildlife.

People and Economy. The population is made up of about 16 ethnic groups, notably the Fulani, Malinke, Soussou and Kissi. The majority of Guineans are Muslims, but many are animist. Most of the people live in villages. Although most Guineans are

Official name: Republic of Guinea
Capital: Conakry
Area: 94,926sq mi
Population: 6,380,000
Languages: French; Soussou; Manika
Religions: Muslim; Animist; Christian
Monetary unit(s): 1 sily = 100 corilles

illiterate, free education is having a strong impact. Besides the capital Conakry, the principal towns are Kankan and Kindia. Agriculture is central to the country's economy, engaging some 85% of the work force and accounting for about 30% of the gross national product. Traditional export crops, including palm kernels, coffee, pineapple and bananas, have been declining in recent years, and aluminum, bauxite, iron ore and diamonds play an increasingly important role in the economy. Manufacturing is negligible. Large herds of small Ndama cattle are bred on the plateau.

History. Portuguese exploration began in the 15th century and by the 17th there was extensive trade with Europe. A French colony, Guinea became independent in 1958, whereupon France stopped supplying aid, which was subsequently accepted from both communist and non-communist countries. After independence politics were dominated by Sékou TOURÉ, who served as president from 1958 until his death in 1984. The army then seized power, freeing many political prisoners and reversing Touré's socialist policies in an effort to halt the nation's economic decline.

GUINEA-BISSAU, formerly **Portuguese Guinea,** a republic in W Africa, is wedged between Senegal to the N and the Republic of Guinea to the E and S, with various coastal islands and an offshore archipelago in the Atlantic.

Land. Low-lying and crossed by many rivers, the mainland consists of coastal swamps, a heavily forested central plain and savanna grazing land to the E. The climate is hot and humid, with heavy rains May–Oct.

People and Economy. Africans form 98% of the population; most are engaged in agriculture, on which the economy is based.

Official name: Republic of Guinea-Bissau
Capital: Bissau
Area: 13,948sq mi
Population: 912,000
Languages: Cape Verde-Guinean Crioulo; Portuguese
Religions: Animist, Muslim, Roman Catholic
Monetary unit(s): 1 Guinea-Bissau peso=100 centavos

The chief export is peanuts; the main food crop, rice. Seafood is an increasingly important export. Industry is limited but expanding. The largest town and main port is Bissau, the capital.

History. First visited by the Portuguese in 1446–47, the country became a Portuguese colony and a center of the slave trade. It became an overseas province of Portugal in 1951, and in 1963 nationalists started a war of independence which continued for 10 years. The independence of Guinea-Bissau was proclaimed in 1973 and recognized by Portugal in 1974. The same political party worked for independence in both Guinea-Bissau and Cape Verde. The close relations between the two countries were strained by the military overthrow of Guinea-Bissau's president in 1980, although diplomatic relations have since been restored.

GUINEA PIG, *Cavia porcellus,* a domestic pet related to the cavies of South America. The plump body, absence of tail and extremely short legs are quite distinctive.

GUINNESS, Sir Alec (1914–   ), English stage and screen actor, remarkable for his versatility in both comic and serious roles. His films include *Kind Hearts and Coronets* (1950) and *The Bridge on the River Kwai* (1957), for which he won an Academy Award.

GUISE, powerful French noble family in the 16th and 17th centuries. They were leaders of the Catholic cause in the French Wars of Religion (see RELIGION, WARS OF) and the opposition to the Protestant Henry IV.

GUITAR, stringed musical instrument, related to the lute, played by plucking. Its curved sides form a waisted shape. The Moors introduced the guitar into Spain about the 13th century, and the Spanish guitar with five strings evolved in the 1500s, becoming the Spanish national musical instrument. The modern guitar has six, sometimes metal, strings.

GUITRY, Sacha (1885–1957), Russian-born French actor, playwright and film producer. His prolific output included 130 comedies. His best-known films are *The Comedian* (1921) and *The Cheat* (1935).

GUIZOT, François Pierre Guillaume (1787–1874), French statesman and historian. Under LOUIS PHILIPPE he held various offices, notably the education and foreign ministries. He became premier in 1847 but resigned when the monarchy was overthrown in 1848. Thereafter he wrote history, most notably a history of the 17th-century English revolution.

GUJARATI, INDO-ARYAN LANGUAGE of the Indian states of Gujarat and Maharashtra. Spoken by around 20,000,000 people, it is written in a form of Devanāgāi script.

GULF INTRACOASTAL WATERWAY, system of navigable waterways, both natural and man-made, running about 1,100mi along the Gulf of Mexico from Apalachee Bay, Fla., to Brownsville, Tex.

GULF OF CALIFORNIA, 700mi arm of the Pacific Ocean separating Baja (Lower) California, Mexico, from the Mexican states of Sonora and Sinaloa to the E.

GULF OF MEXICO, off the SE coast of North America between the US and Mexico, and bounded to the E by Cuba. It is linked to the Atlantic by the Strait of Florida and to the Caribbean by the Strait of Yucatan. Extensive petroleum deposits are worked offshore.

GULF OF TONKIN RESOLUTION, put before the US Congress on Aug. 4, 1964 by President Lyndon B. JOHNSON, following attacks by North Vietnamese vessels on US destroyers in the Gulf. The resolution gave the president power to take measures necessary to repel other attacks and prevent aggression. The resolution was later seen as the beginning of full-scale US involvement in the VIETNAM WAR and was attacked for giving excessive power to the president. In July 1970 the Senate voted to revoke its authorizations.

GULF STREAM, warm ocean current flowing N, then NE, off the E coast of the US. Its weaker, more diffuse continuation is the E flowing **North Atlantic Drift**, which is responsible for warming the climates of W Europe. The current, often taken to include also the Caribbean Current, is fed by the N Equatorial Current, and can be viewed as the western part of the great clockwise water circulation pattern of the N Atlantic. (See also OCEAN CURRENTS.)

GULLAH, descendants of freed slaves who settled in the coastal districts of S.C. and Ga. The name is also used for their Creole dialect, a blend of various African languages and English; it resembles neither very closely.

GULLS, strong-flying and swimming seabirds forming the subfamily Larinae. The plumage is basically white with darker wings and back. Some species develop a dark hood in the breeding plumage. There are altogether some 40 species of gulls and the group is widespread. Gulls are a very successful and adaptable group and many species have now become common inland as scavengers on refuse, or on plowed land.

GUNPOWDER, or **black powder,** a low EXPLOSIVE, the only one known from its discovery in the West in the 13th century until the mid-19th century. It consists of about 75% POTASSIUM (or SODIUM) nitrate, 10% SULFUR and 15% CHARCOAL; it is readily ignited and burns very rapidly. Gunpowder was used in fireworks in 10th-century China, as a propellant for firearms from the 14th century in Europe and for blasting since the late 17th century. It is now used mainly as an igniter, in fuses and in fireworks.

GUNPOWDER PLOT, conspiracy of a group of English Roman Catholics led by Robert Catesby to blow up King James I, his family and government in the Houses of Parliament on Nov. 5, 1605. Guy FAWKES was arrested while setting charges under the Houses of Parliament and under torture disclosed the names of the conspirators, who were executed. In England Nov. 5 is celebrated with bonfires, fireworks and the burning of effigies.

GUNTHER, John (1901–1970), US journalist and author. His background as a foreign correspondent enabled him to write the highly successful "Inside" books, the first being *Inside Europe* (1936); in describing various countries these blended personal observation with historical and economic analysis to provide a vivid picture.

GUPTA DYNASTY, N Indian dynasty which ruled c320–550 AD, a period which produced some of the finest Indian art and literature. From a small area in the Ganges valley their power spread out to most of India, and under Chandragupta II (385–414) scholarship, law and art reached new heights. The White Hun invasion c450 reduced the Gupta empire to a portion of Bengal.

GURKHAS, dominant Hindu race in Nepal, and its ruling dynasty. The name has

become attached to the Nepalese soldiers serving in the British army. Gurkha regiments are famous for their great courage, endurance, discipline and loyalty. The Gurkhas carry the famous *kukhri,* a long knife with a hooked blade.

GUSTAVUS, name of six kings of Sweden. **Gustavus I Vasa** (1496?–1560) was founder of the modern Swedish nation. A Swedish noble, he led the successful revolt against the Danes 1520–23 and was elected king. Instrumental in the establishment of Lutheranism and the growth of the economy, he took firm control of the country and established an hereditary monarchy. **Gustavus II Adolphus** (1594–1632) reigned from 1611. One of the great generals of modern times, he made Sweden a European power. When he came to the throne, Sweden was at war with Denmark, Russia and Poland. In 1613 he ended victoriously the Danish war and in 1617 the Russian. With his chancellor Count Oxenstierna he introduced wide internal reforms. He joined the THIRTY YEARS' WAR in 1631, scoring the first Protestant victory at Breitenfeld (1631). He was killed in his victory at Lützen in 1632. **Gustavus III** (1746–1792) became king in 1771, at a time of factionalism and unrest. He regained much of the monarchy's lost power in 1772, and ruled well, introducing many liberal reforms. He was assassinated by a conspiracy of discontented nobles. **Gustavus IV** (1778–1837) reigned 1792–1809. In 1805 he joined a coalition against Napoleon and lost Swedish Pomerania and territory in Germany; despite English help he lost Finland to Russia in 1808. He was then deposed and exiled. **Gustavus V** (1858–1950), a popular sovereign, reigned from 1907. **Gustavus VI Adolphus** (1882–1973) reigned from 1950. He was an able and popular monarch; in 1971 the monarchy was stripped of its powers, but this was deferred during his reign. He was also a noted archaeologist.

GUSTON, Philip (c1913–1980), Canadian-born US painter, a follower of ABSTRACT EXPRESSIONISM; his *White Painting* series is often reminiscent of MONET.

GUTENBERG, Johann (c1400–1468), German printer, usually considered the inventor of PRINTING from separately cast metal types. By 1450 he had a press in Mainz, financed by **Johann Fust** (c1400–c1466) but in 1455 he handed over the press (and his invention) to Fust in repayment of debts. By now the Gutenberg (or Mazarin) Bible was at least well under way: each page has two columns of 42 lines. Gutenberg possibly founded another press some time later.

GUTHRIE, Sir (William) Tyrone (1900–1971), influential British stage director, famous for his experimental approach to traditional works. His Shakespeare productions and his vigorous and realistic opera productions, such as *Peter Grimes* (1946) and *Carmen* (1949 and 1952), set new standards in their time. The establishment in 1963 of the Tyrone Guthrie Theater at Minneapolis, Minn., under his direction, spurred the development of regional theater in the US.

GUTHRIE, Woody (Woodrow Wilson Guthrie; 1912–1967), US folksinger whose compositions and guitar style have had enormous influence on modern folk music. He developed the characteristic themes of his "protest" songs as a migrant worker in the 1930s.

GUTIÉRREZ, Gustavo (1928–   ), Peruvian Roman Catholic priest, professor of theology at the Catholic U in Lima. Influenced by the poverty and violence around him, he developed in the 1960s LIBERATION THEOLOGY, a blend of Marxist and Christian doctrine, to deal with the concerns of the poor. He wrote *A Theology of Liberation* (1971).

GUYANA, independent republic on the NE coast of South America, largest of the three countries in the Guiana region.

Official name: Co-operative Republic of Guyana
Capital: Georgetown
Area: 83,000sq mi
Population: 802,000
Languages: English, Hindi, Chinese; Portuguese also spoken
Religions: Christian, Hindu, Muslim
Monetary: unit(s): 1 Guyana dollar=100 cents

Land. The sparsely settled interior is largely massive sandstone plateaus, up to 500ft in height, sloping up to the Guiana Highlands in the S. Much of the more densely populated coastal strip, 10–40mi in width, lies below sea level; some of it is reclaimed land. About 85% of the country is tropical rain forest. Heat is constantly around 80°F with average humidity of about 75%; rainfall at the coast is around 90in a year.

People. More than 90% of the population lives along the coast. The main ethnic groups are East Indians (descendants of imported labor), 55%, and blacks, 36%; there are also about 30,000 Amerindians. Many of the professional classes are European or Chinese. Education is compulsory between 6 and 14, and literacy is around 85%.

Economy rests on agriculture, especially sugarcane grown on plantations near the coast. Rice is the other major crop. Important mineral reserves include bauxite (Guyana's chief export), diamonds and manganese. Hardwood from the enormous forests is also becoming an important resource.

History. Guyana's original inhabitants were CARIB and ARAWAK Indians. The Dutch were the first to colonize the area, setting up POLDERS to reclaim land and importing Negro slaves to cultivate sugar and tobacco. The region became British in 1815 and was subsequently known as British Guiana. East Indian labor was imported in the 19th century. Amid political, economic and racial unrest Guyana achieved internal self-rule in 1961 and full independence in 1966. The country has long-standing border disputes with Venezuela and Suriname. In 1979, a mass suicide-execution of 911 members of Rev. Jim Jones's People's Temple cult took place in the Guyana jungle. Forbes Burnham, who led the country to independence, served as president until his death in 1985

GWYN, Nell (1650–1687), English actress, favorite mistress of Charles II from 1669. Daughter of a brothel-keeper, she became an orange-seller in the King's theater, and 1666–69 its most popular actress. She bore Charles two sons.

GYMNASTICS, a system of exercise designed not only to maintain and improve the physique, but also as a sport. In ancient Greece gymnastics were important in education, including track and field athletics and training for boxing and wrestling. Competitive gymnastics are a series of exercises on set pieces of apparatus: parallel bars, horizontal bar, side and vaulting horses, beam and asymmetric bars. The US system, derived from the German, is designed to assist physical growth; the Swedish system aims at rectifying posture and weak muscles; and the Danish system seeks general fitness and endurance.

GYMNOSPERMS, the smaller of the two main classes of seed-bearing plants, the other being the ANGIOSPERMS. Gymnosperms are characterized by having naked seeds usually formed on open scales produced in cones. All are perennial plants and most are evergreen. There are several orders, the main ones being the Cycadales, the cycads or sago palms; the Coniferales, including pine, larch, fir and redwood; the Ginkgoales, the ginkgo; and the Gnetales, tropical shrubs and woody vines.

GYNECOLOGY, branch of MEDICINE and SURGERY, specializing in diseases of women, specifically disorders of the female reproductive tract; often linked with OBSTETRICS. CONTRACEPTION, ABORTION, STERILIZATION, infertility and abnormalities of MENSTRUATION are the commonest problems. The early recognition and treatment of CANCER of the WOMB cervix after Pap smear tests have become important. Other TUMORS of womb or ovaries, benign or malignant, and disorders of genital tract or closely related BLADDER following PREGNANCY, commonly require gynecological surgery. Dilatation of the cervix and curettage of womb endometrium (D and C) is used frequently for diagnosis and sometimes for treatment of menstrual disorders or postmenopausal bleeding. HYSTERECTOMY, or removal of the womb, is the commonest major operation of gynecologists.

GYPSIES, nomadic people of Europe, Asia and North America. They are believed to have originated in India; their language, ROMANY, is related to Sanskrit and Prakrit. The gypsies probably began their westward migration about 1000 AD. By the 15th century they had penetrated the Balkans, Egypt and North Africa. In the 16th century they were to be found throughout Europe. Often known as thieves and tricksters, they have met with little toleration. In WWII many European gypsies were executed by the Nazis. There is a strong gypsy tradition of folklore, legend and song, and this, combined with the independence of their lives, has inspired the romantic imagination of many musicians, artists and writers.

GYPSUM, mineral composed of calcium sulfate and water, used to make wallboard and for casts and molds.

GYPSY MOTH, *Porthetria dispar,* a pretty moth originating in Europe and later introduced to North America. Here, in the absence of natural enemies, it has become a serious pest: the caterpillars feed on the leaves of deciduous trees, particularly fruit trees, and their occasional mass outbreaks can lead to complete defoliation.

GYROCOMPASS, a continuously-driven GYROSCOPE which acts as a COMPASS. It is unaffected by magnetic variations and is used for steering large ships. As the earth rotates the gyroscope experiences a torque if it is out of the meridian. The resulting tilting is sensed by a gravity sensing system which itself applies a torque to the gyroscope which returns it to the N–S meridian. The sensitivity of such instruments decreases with latitude away from the equator.

GYROPILOT, an automatic device for keeping a ship or airplane on a given course using signals from a gyroscopic reference. The marine version operates a ship's rudder by displacement signals from the GYROCOMPASS. In an airplane, the device is usually known as an **automatic pilot** and consists of sensors to detect deviations in direction, pitch and roll, and pass signals via a computer to alter the controls as necessary.

GYROSCOPE, a heavy spinning disk mounted so that its axis is free to adopt any orientation. Its special properties depend on the principle of the conservation of angular MOMENTUM. Although the scientific gyroscope was only devised by J. B. L. Foucault in the mid-19th century, the child's traditional spinning top demonstrates the gyroscope principle. The fact that it will stay upright as long as it is spinning fast enough demonstrates the property of **gyroscopic inertia:** the direction of the spin axis resists change. This means that a gyroscope mounted universally, in double gimbals, will maintain the same orientation in space however its support is turned, a property applied in many navigational devices. If a FORCE tends to alter the direction of the spin axis (e.g., the weight of a top tilting sideways), a gyroscope will turn about an axis at right-angles to the force for as long as it is applied; this movement is known as **precession.** Instrument gyroscopes usually consist of a wheel having most of its mass concentrated at its rim to ensure a large moment of inertia. The wheel is kept spinning in frictionless bearings by an electric motor. Once the wheel is set spinning its response to applied torques can be monitored or used in control servomechanisms.

GYROSTABILIZER, a gyroscopic device for stabilizing a ship, airplane or instrument mounting. Originally giant gyroscopes (up to 4m in diameter) were used to counteract roll in ships, but they were found to be too cumbersome. Now fins protruding from the ship's hull are moved hydraulically to oppose roll under the control of signals from small GYROSCOPES that sense roll angle and velocity.

8th letter of the English alphabet, derived from the Semitic letter *cheth*. Usually a glottal spirant, it is silent in many Romance languages. In thermodynamics it is the symbol for enthalpy.

HAAKON VII (1872–1957), king of Norway from 1905. A Danish prince, he was elected constitutional monarch when Norway became independent of Sweden. He spent WWII in England, the symbol of his country's resistance to Germany.

HABAKKUK, Book of, the eighth of the Old Testament Minor Prophets, dated probably late 7th century BC. Nothing is known of Habakkuk himself. The first part explores the problem of God's using the evil Chaldeans to punish Judah, and includes the influential statement, "The righteous shall live by his faith." The final chapter is a psalm.

HABEAS CORPUS (Latin: you have the body), in COMMON LAW a writ issued by the judiciary to compel a person held in custody to be brought before a court, so that it may determine whether or not the detention is lawful. Habeas corpus originated in medieval England, becoming a major civil right through the 1679 Habeas Corpus Act. Embodied in the US Constitution, it may not be suspended except in cases of rebellion or invasion. President Lincoln suspended it in 1861, at the onset of the Civil War. The writ may also be used in some non-judicial cases, as by an inmate in a mental hospital.

HABERMAS, Jürgen (1929–   ), German philosopher at Frankfurt U who expanded the scope of "critical theory" first propounded by Marxist scholars at the Frankfurt Institute for Social Research in the 1920s. He was best known for his work on epistemology, communication theory, the legitimation function of science and the theory of capitalist crisis.

HADRIAN (Publius Aelius Hadrianus; 76–138), Roman emperor from 117, successor of TRAJAN. He traveled the empire for 12 years, reforming and restoring imperial rule. An able administrator, builder and soldier, he was a talented poet and an admirer of Greek civilization. He was responsible for construction (120–123) of Hadrian's Wall to defend Britain against the Picts. His plan to build a new city at Jerusalem, however, sparked off a Jewish revolt 132–135, which he savagely repressed. His later years were saddened by the death of his favorite, Antinoüs.

HADRIAN'S WALL, Roman fortification built by Emperor HADRIAN, running 74mi across the N of England. Intended to exclude the dangerous northern tribes, it had a series of forts along its length. Twice breached, it was abandoned after 383.

HAECKEL, Ernst Heinrich (1834–1919), German biologist best remembered for his vociferous support of DARWIN's theory of EVOLUTION, and for his own theory that ontogeny (the development of an individual organism) recapitulates phylogeny (its evolutionary stages), a theory now discarded.

HAFIZ, Shams ud-Din Mohammed (c1325–c1390), great Persian lyric poet, a courtier at Shiraz. He adopted the hitherto frivolous verse form *ghazal,* using it to express a sensuality and gaiety heightened by the philosophical mysticism of SUFISM.

HAGANAH (Hebrew: defense), Jewish volunteer militia in Palestine, formed after WWI to protect the Jewish community there. Although outlawed by the British, it was moderate and well-disciplined. It fought alongside the Allies in WWII and against the Arabs in 1947; in 1948 it was made into the Israeli national army.

HAGGAI, Book of, the tenth of the Old Testament Minor Prophets, dated 520–519 BC. It consists of four oracles urging the Jews to rebuild the Temple at Jerusalem and prophesying the glories of the Messianic Age.

HAGGARD, Sir Henry Rider (1856–1925), British novelist, best known for *King Solomon's Mines* (1885), *She* (1887) and other romantic adventure novels with an authentic African background. He was also a pioneering agriculturalist.

HAGGIS, traditional Scots pudding, made of the heart, liver and lungs of a sheep with oatmeal and suet, seasoned and cooked in the sheep's stomach (a plastic skin is sometimes used today). A cheap, tasty and long-lasting winter food, it should be eaten with vegetables and beer—*not* with neat whisky.

HAGIA SOPHIA, or Santa Sophia, massive cathedral raised at Constantinople (now Istanbul) by JUSTINIAN I: completed in 537, it became a mosque after the Turkish conquest (1453). Now a museum, the domed basilica, richly decorated, is the finest remaining example of Byzantine architecture.

HAGUE, Frank (1876–1956), US Democratic politician, mayor of Jersey City, N.J. 1917–47 and leader of one of the country's most powerful political machines.

HAGUE, The (Dutch: Gravenhage or Den Haag), historic city, seat of government of the Netherlands and capital of South Holland province. It has many ancient buildings and is one of the country's handsomest cities, with many parks and woodland areas. The Binnenhof palace houses the two chambers of the legislature. The economy rests more on administration than on industry. The city is also an educational and cultural center. Pop 456,900.

HAGUE PEACE CONFERENCES, two conferences held in 1899 and 1907 at The Hague, the Netherlands, at Russia's request. They achieved little beyond some clarification of belligerency rules and war conventions, but established the International Permanent Court of Arbitration (the HAGUE TRIBUNAL).

HAGUE TRIBUNAL, an international Permanent Court of Arbitration. Established by the first Hague Peace Conference (1899), it is now supported by 71 nations, each of which may appoint up to four jurists. The court will supply arbitrators to decide international disputes submitted to them by international agreement. After WWI it was supplemented by the World Court and later the INTERNATIONAL COURT OF JUSTICE.

HAHN, Otto (1879–1968), German chemist awarded the 1944 Nobel Prize for Chemistry for his work on nuclear FISSION. With Lise Meitner he discovered the new element protactinium (1918); later they bombarded URANIUM with NEUTRONS, treating the uranium with ordinary barium. Meitner showed that the residue was radioactive barium formed by the splitting (fission) of the uranium nucleus.

HAHNEMANN, Christian Friedrich Samuel (1755–1843), German physician, the father of HOMEOPATHY.

HAIG, Alexander (1924–   ), US general and secretary of state (1981–82). Deputy to Henry KISSINGER on the National Security Council in 1969, he became chief of staff in the NIXON White House. He then served as supreme commander of NORTH ATLANTIC TREATY ORGANIZATION forces in Europe until 1979. He was appointed secretary of state by President Reagan.

HAIG, Douglas Haig, 1st Earl (1861–1928), field-marshal, British commander in WWI. He has been unfairly blamed for the misconduct of the Somme and Ypres campaigns 1916–17. Hampered by the hostility of British premier LLOYD GEORGE, he was denied effective command until 1918, when he displayed far greater generalship.

HAIKU, traditional Japanese verse form, consisting of three lines of 5, 7 and 5 syllables each. Developed by MATSUO BASHO and others around the 17th century from an older 31-syllable form, it is now considered the major traditional form. Typically a *haiku* uses an image, often drawn from nature, to suggest or evoke a mood or feeling; a good *haiku* is compact and intense.

HAILE SELASSIE (1892–1975), reign-name of Ras Tafari, emperor of Ethiopia 1930–74. A benevolent despot, he won great popularity by his determined resistance to the Italian invasion of Ethiopia 1935–41, when British forces restored him to his throne. Efficient at first, his autocracy degenerated in later years. In the face of a nationwide famine he was deposed by his army in 1974 and died in captivity.

HAIR, nonliving filamentous structure made of keratin and pigment, formed in the skin hair follicles. Racial and genetic factors determine both coloring and shape (by heat-labile sulfur bridges). In man all skin surfaces except the palms and soles are covered with very fine hair. This assists in TOUCH reception. In the cold, these hairs are erected to create extra insulation. Scalp hair is prominent in man. Pubic and axillary hair develop at PUBERTY in response to sex HORMONES. Their patterns differ in the sexes; facial hair is ANDROGEN-dependent. Hair growth is more rapid in the summer. Hormone abnormalities alter hair distribution, while BALDNESS follows hair loss.

HAITI, independent republic in the Caribbean Sea, the W portion of the island of Hispaniola, which it shares with the Dominican Republic.

Land. Haiti is mainly mountainous; the coastline has beaches, coral reefs, mangrove swamps and cliffs. The climate is tropical, with two rainy seasons. There are extensive forests in the interior and many coffee and fruit plantations on the coast.

People. The people are mostly of African descent, with a powerful mulatto minority. The official language is French, the main tongue is CREOLE. The official religion is Roman Catholicism, but VOODOO dominates the life of the people. Only about 20% of the population is literate and education, although theoretically compulsory, is scant. The standard of living is low; government, army and professions are in the hands of the mulattoes.

Official name: Republic of Haiti
Capital: Port-au-Prince
Area: 10,579sq mi
Population: 5,532,000
Languages: French; Creole spoken by majority
Religions: Roman Catholic, Voodoo
Monetary unit(s): 1 gourde = 100 centimes
Economy. The economy is poor, based on subsistence agriculture. Coffee is the major cash crop, and some sisal, sugarcane, cotton and cocoa is processed and exported, as are wood and, on a small scale, minerals. The tourist trade is the second-largest source of foreign exchange.
History. COLUMBUS claimed Haiti for Spain in 1492. Spanish exploitation wiped out the aboriginal ARAWAK INDIANS. The island was ceded to France in 1697, and became a plantation center to which African slaves were imported. In 1804 a slave revolt led by TOUSSAINT L'OUVERTURE and Jacques DESSALINES finally won independence. Political chaos then continued until the US occupation 1915–47. In 1957 François DUVALIER became dictator, and with the brutal backing of his *tontons macoutes* (secret police) held power until his death in 1971; he was succeeded by his son, Jean-Claude, under whom the regime became slightly less repressive. That in turn led to better foreign relations, increased foreign investment and more tourism. However, Haiti continued to be the most densely populated and the poorest nation in the Western Hemisphere. In 1986, "Baby Doc" Duvalier was ousted in a popular revolt. A provisional government headed by Gen. Henri Namphy promised elections for Nov. 1987, but these were aborted by bloody violence by soldiers, police, and former members of the Tontons Macoute. Another election in Jan. 1988, in which only 10% of voters took part, was won by Leslie Manigat, but in June he was driven from the country in another military coup led by Namphy, who was shortly overthrown in turn.

HAKLUYT, Richard (c1552–1616), pioneering British geographer. He published many early accounts of the Americas and a major account of English voyaging and discoveries. He lectured on geography at Oxford.

HALDANE, John Burdon Sanderson (1892–1964), British geneticist whose work, with that of Sir Ronald Aylmer Fisher and Sewall Wright, provided a basis for the mathematical study of population GENETICS.

HALDANE, Richard Burdon Haldane, 1st Viscount (1856–1928), British statesman and lawyer, a Liberal member of Parliament 1885–1911. As secretary of state for war 1905–12 he introduced sweeping army reforms, founding the Territorial Army and national and imperial general staffs. He was Lord Chancellor 1912–15 and in 1924. A founder of the London School of Economics (1895), he wrote several philosophical works.

HALDIMAND, Sir Frederick (1718–1791), Swiss-born British general, governor of Quebec 1778–86. A former mercenary, he commanded the British North American Army 1773–74. In Quebec he managed to prevent any revolutionary outbreaks at the time of the REVOLUTIONARY WAR.

HALE, George Ellery (1868–1938), US astronomer who discovered the magnetic fields of SUNSPOTS, and who invented at the same time as Henri Alexandre Deslandres (1853–1948) the spectroheliograph (c1892). His name is commemorated by the Hale Observatories in Cal.

HALE, Nathan (1755–1776), American revolutionary. A former schoolteacher, he was caught in disguise behind the British lines on Long Island, and hanged as a spy on Sept. 22, 1776. His last words are said to have been that he regretted having but one life to lose for his country; the quotation actually comes from Joseph ADDISON's play *Cato*.

HALE, Sarah Josepha (1788–1879), US feminist journalist, Editor of *Ladies' Magazine* (1828–37) and *Godey's Lady's Book* (from 1837), she championed higher education for women.

HALE OBSERVATORIES, formerly the Mt Wilson and Palomar Observatories, renamed (1970) for G. E. HALE and since 1948 operated jointly by the Carnegie Institution and the California Institute of Technology. At Mt Wilson (Cal.) are two reflecting TELESCOPES and two solar towers; at Palomar Mountain (Cal.) a 200-in reflector, until 1973 the largest in the world, and two Schmidt telescopes.

HALEVI, Jehuda. See JUDAH HA-LEVI.

HALF-LIFE, the time taken for the activity

of a radioactive sample to decrease to half its original value, half the nuclei originally present having changed spontaneously into a different nuclear type by emission of particles and energy. After two half-lives, the radioactivity will be a quarter of its original value and so on. Depending on the type of nucleus and mode of decay, half-lives range from less than a second to over 10^{10} years. The half-life concept can also be applied to other systems undergoing random decay, e.g. certain biological populations.

HALFTONE, reproduction of a photograph or other picture containing a range of continuous tones, by using dots of various sizes but uniform tone. The dots are small enough to blend in the observer's vision to give the effect of the original. The picture is photographed through a screen on which a fine rectangular grid has been scribed (2 to 6 lines/mm); the dots arise by DIFFRACTION. From the screened negative is made a halftone plate used for PRINTING by all processes.

HALF-WAY COVENANT, a religious-political compromise adopted by the New England Congregationalists (Puritans) in 1662, which allowed baptized persons not publicly professing conversion to be regarded as church members in a sense, though not admitted in Holy Communion. This gave them political rights, and entitled their children to baptism and membership. In the 18th century the churches reverted to the stricter policy of requiring for membership a statement of personal conversion.

HALICARNASSUS, ancient Greek city, capital of Caria, Asia Minor; its site is now Bodrum, Turkey. HERODOTUS was born here. The monumental tomb of the Carian king Mausolus, the original MAUSOLEUM, was built here c355 BC.

HALIFAX, Edward Frederick Lindley Wood, 1st Earl of (1881–1959), British statesman, a Conservative member of Parliament 1910–25. As viceroy of India 1925–31 he was sympathetic to the independence movement. Foreign secretary 1938–40, he advocated appeasement of Hitler, helping to negotiate the MUNICH AGREEMENT. He was ambassador to the US 1941–46.

HALL, Granville Stanley (1844–1924), US psychologist and educator best known for founding the *American Journal of Psychology* (1887), the first US psychological journal. He was first president of the American Psychological Institute (1894), a body whose foundation he had assisted.

HALLECK, Henry Wager (1815–1872), US Civil War general and military theorist, whose *Elements of Military Art and Science* (1846) was an influential training manual in the Civil War. After service in the Mexican War he left the army in 1853 to practice law. At the onset of the Civil War he was appointed major-general in command of the Western theater and in 1862 general in chief. In 1864 he was relieved, and served as chief of staff until 1865.

HALLER, Albrecht von (1708–1777), Swiss biologist, best known for his work on human anatomy and physiology, and also a poet. A pupil of Hermann Boerhaave and much influenced by him, he is credited with being the founder of experimental ANATOMY. In physiology he investigated RESPIRATION, the BLOOD CIRCULATION, the NERVOUS SYSTEM and the irritability and sensibility of different types of body tissue—in all cases relying on experiment.

HALLEY, Edmund (1656–1742), English astronomer. In 1677 he made the first full observation of a transit of Mercury; and in 1676–79 prepared a major catalog of the S-hemisphere stars. He persuaded NEWTON to publish the *Principia*, which he financed. In 1720 he succeeded John Flamsteed as astronomer royal. He is best known for his prediction that the comet of 1680 would return in 1758 (see HALLEY'S COMET), based on his conviction that COMETS follow elliptical paths about the sun.

HALLEY'S COMET, the first periodic comet to be identified (by HALLEY, late 17th century) and the brightest of all recurring comets. It has a period of about 76 years. Records of every appearance of the comet since 240 BC, except that of 163 BC, are extant; and it is featured on the BAYEUX TAPESTRY. The comet was intensively studied from earth and space when it returned in 1986. It will next appear in 2061.

HALLMARK, stamped symbol on silver and gold objects guaranteeing that the metal conforms to certain legal standards. Various distinguishing marks indicate the maker, date and assaying authority. The term hallmark derives from the Goldsmith's Hall, London, which was responsible for the marking, beginning in 1300. In America only the maker's mark and sometimes the date is used, but neither is mandatory.

HALLOWEEN, festival on Oct. 31, eve of All Saints' Day or Hallowmas, originally a Celtic festival to mark the new year, welcoming the spirits of the dead and assuaging supernatural powers. It was introduced to the US by Scots and Irish immigrants, and is now a children's festival famous for "trick-or-treat."

HALLSTATT, term referring to the late BRONZE AGE and early IRON AGE in W and Central Europe, from Hallstatt, Austria, where there is a prehistoric cemetery and salt mines which have been in constant operation since 2500 BC. It was characterized by extremely fine, decorated pottery, though the quality deteriorated toward the end of the period.

HALLUCINATION, an experience similar to a normal PERCEPTION but with the difference that sensory stimulus is either absent or too minor to explain the experience satisfactorily. Certain abnormal mental conditions (see MENTAL ILLNESS) produce hallucinations, as does the taking of HALLUCINOGENIC DRUGS. Hallucinations may also result from exhaustion or FEVER; or may be experienced while falling asleep (hypnogogic) or waking (hypnopompic), and also by individuals under HYPNOSIS.

HALLUCINOGENIC DRUGS, DRUGS which cause hallucinations or illusions, usually visual, together with personality and behavior changes. The last may arise as a result of therapy, but more usually follow deliberate exposure to certain drugs for their psychological effects ("trip"). Lysergic acid diethylamide (LSD), HEROIN, MORPHINE and other OPIUM NARCOTICS, MESCALINE and psilocybin are commonly hallucinogenic and cannabis sometimes so. The type of hallucination is not predictable and many are unpleasant ("bad trip"). Recurrent hallucinations may follow use of these drugs; another danger is that altered behavior may inadvertently cause death or injury. Although psychosis may be a result of their use, it may be that recourse to drugs represents rather an early symptom of SCHIZOPHRENIA.

HALS, Frans (c1580–1666), Dutch painter, one of the great portraitists. In his time he was not especially famous and known mainly in his native Haarlem. Many of his greatest works, such as the *Lady Governors of the Old Men's Home* (1664), are civic portraits. His later works have a somber serenity, but many portraits and genre scenes, such as *Banquet of the Officers of St. George* (1616) and the so-called *Laughing Cavalier* (1624), are infused with a rich joviality. Working freely and rapidly without wasting a brush stroke, he was able to capture the reality of his subjects on canvases that sparkle with color and light.

HALSEY, William Frederick "Bull," Jr. (1882–1959), US admiral, WWII. After commanding a Pacific carrier division with great distinction 1940–42, he took command of the Pacific theater. As commander of the 3rd Fleet he helped destroy the Japanese fleet at LEYTE GULF in 1944. He resigned as fleet admiral in 1947 and entered business.

HAMBLETONIAN STAKE, premier harness racing event in the US. Limited to three-year-old trotters, it has been held annually since 1926 and, since 1978, has been contested at New Jersey's Meadowlands. The victor must win two one-mile heats. The race is named for a trotting horse called *Rydyk's Hambletonian* (1849–76), the ancestor of most modern trotters.

HAMBURG, historic seaport, now the largest city in West Germany, near the mouth of the Elbe R. Probably founded by CHARLEMAGNE, it was a dominant member of the HANSEATIC LEAGUE, and always a flourishing commercial center. Devastated in WWII, it has been rebuilt and now has shipyards and a wide range of industries. A transport hub, it is the center of the country's fishing industry. Pop 1,579,884.

HAMILCAR BARCA (d. c228 BC), Carthaginian general, father of HANNIBAL. He became commander of Sicily in 247 BC, in the First PUNIC WAR, and from there harassed the mainland. In 241 he returned to Carthage; he quelled a mercenary revolt and became a political leader. In 238 he led a successful occupation of Spain, but was later killed there.

HAMILTON, Alexander (c1755–1804), a founding father of the US. Successively a revolutionary, first secretary of the treasury, founder of the first American political party, adviser to Washington and a powerful statesman, he was one of the most important figures in the new nation. His hauteur and elitist political outlook antagonized many people, but his integrity was beyond doubt. The young republic would have had less chance of surviving without his determination to make it fiscally sound with a strong central government.

A pamphleteer for the Revolution, he joined the army and became Washington's aide-de-camp in 1777. After the war he campaigned for central government and served in the Continental Congress and the New York legislature, becoming its delegate to the ANNAPOLIS CONVENTION and the Constitutional Convention of 1787. With John JAY and MADISON he wrote the *Federalist Papers* (1787–88), still considered classics of political theory. Not a democrat, he advocated an intellectual aristocracy maintained by the "enlightened self-interest" of the wealthy. This brought him into conflict with JEFFERSON, who supported the French Revolution and sought to abolish privilege. As first secretary of the treasury from 1789, Hamilton created the Bank of the United States (1791) and became leader of the Federalist Party; Jefferson and Madison led the Republicans, the Hamiltonians becoming the Federalists. Hamilton left the cabinet in 1795 but he continued to influence the executive from behind the scenes until John ADAMS became president. When the latter lost his bid for reelection, an electoral tie occurred between Aaron BURR and Jefferson. The Federalists in Congress wanted Burr, but Hamilton intervened in favor of his old opponent and Burr lost. Burr challenged him to a duel, in which Hamilton was killed.

HAMILTON, Alice (1869–1970), US physician and social reformer. The first woman on the faculty of the Harvard Medical School (1919–35), she was the first researcher to study industrial diseases and industrial hygiene in the US. Her work was instrumental in the passage of WORKMEN'S COMPENSATION laws.

HAMILTON, Andrew (1676–1741), Philadelphia lawyer whose successful defense of the publisher John Peter ZENGER on a libel charge in 1735 established a precedent that contributed towards freedom of the press in America.

HAMILTON, Edith (1867–1963), US educator and classical scholar. Founder and headmistress of Bryn Mawr school for girls in Baltimore, she interpreted classical civilizations in such influential books as *The Greek Way* (1930), *The Roman Way* (1932) and *The Echo of Greece* (1957).

HAMILTON, Emma, Lady (1765–1815), celebrated beauty who became the mistress of Lord NELSON. A blacksmith's daughter, she was the wife of Sir William Hamilton, British envoy in Naples. She exercised great influence over Nelson. After his death she died in poverty.

HAMITIC LANGUAGES, a group within the **Hamito-Semitic** language family, including Berber, Cushite and Ancient Egyptian (the former two still being spoken today). Other Hamito-Semitic languages include SEMITIC and Chadic.

HAMLET, Danish prince in SHAKESPEARE'S tragedy of that name. The story is that of Amleth, whose vengeance on his usurping uncle is recounted in Saxo Grammaticus' *History of Denmark* (12th century). The legend of the prince who feigns madness to outwit a tyrant, however, has origins in Roman and Eastern legend. Shakespeare probably found the story in François de Belleforest's *Histoires Tragiques* (1570) or

in Thomas KYD's play, now lost, drawn from it.

HAMLIN, Hannibal (1809–1891), US vice-president under Lincoln 1861–65. A Democrat at first, he joined the Republicans in 1856 because of his antislavery views. He was a senator from Me. 1848–56 and 1869–81, and an ardent Reconstructionist.

HAMMARSKJÖLD, Dag (Hjalmar Agne Carl) (1905–1961), Swedish statesman and economist, UN secretary general 1953–61. He greatly increased UN power and prestige. He was instrumental in negotiations over the Korean War truce and the Suez crisis of 1956. In 1960 he directed UN attempts to end the fighting in the Congo, and his actions were condemned by the USSR. He refused to resign, but was killed in an aircrash in the Congo. He was posthumously awarded the 1961 Nobel Peace Prize.

HAMMER, Armand (1898–   ), US business executive. A newly graduated physician, he went (1921) to the Soviet Union to help fight epidemics but was encouraged by Lenin to develop US-USSR economic ties. Back in the US, he made fortunes in a variety of business ventures, notably with the Occidental Petroleum Corp. He remained an influential economic and cultural intermediary between the US and the Soviet Union.

HAMMERSTEIN, name of two US theatrical producers. **Oscar Hammerstein I** (1846–1919) was a German-born tobacco magnate who became an opera impresario, opening theaters in New York, London and Philadelphia. **Oscar Hammerstein II** (1895–1960), his grandson, became famous as a writer and producer of musical comedies in partnership with Richard RODGERS and others. Among his successes with Rodgers were *Oklahoma!* (1943), *Carousel* (1945), *South Pacific* (1949), *The King and I* (1951) and *The Sound of Music* (1959).

HAMMETT, (Samuel) Dashiell (1894–1961), US detective-story writer and left-wing political activist. His novels are "hard-boiled" and realistic. His main character, Sam Spade, became the prototype of the fictional American detective, especially as portrayed by Humphrey Bogart in the film of Hammett's best-known work, *The Maltese Falcon* (1930). *The Thin Man* (1932) featured more amiable detectives, Nick and Nora Charles.

HAMMURABI, more correctly Hammurapi (d. 1750 BC or 1686 BC), 6th king of the 1st dynasty of Babylon, from 1792 BC or

1728 BC. Over many years of wars and alliances he conquered and united Mesopotamia, though his empire did not long survive him. An able administrator, he was responsible for the Code of Hammurabi, a compilation and expansion of earlier laws which is the fullest extant collection of Babylonian laws. The best source of the code is a black diorite stela found at Susa, Iran, in 1901.

HAMPDEN, John (1594–1643), English Parliamentary leader. He provoked a test case by refusing to pay ship money, a royal tax not approved by Parliament, in 1636. King Charles I's attempted seizure of him and other Parliamentary leaders in 1642 was one of the incidents which provoked the English Civil War, in which Hampden was killed.

HAMPTON, Wade (1818–1902), US politician and soldier. Although opposed to secession, he joined the Confederate army, becoming famous as General LEE's cavalry commander. He was governor of S.C. (1877–79) and U.S. senator (1879–91).

HAMPTON COURT CONFERENCE, meeting held at Hampton Court Palace in 1604 to consider Puritan demands for reform in the Church of England, especially of the episcopal system of Church government and the *Book of Common Prayer*. James I rejected most of these but agreed to sponsor a new translation of the Bible, which became the Authorized Version now also named for him.

HAMPTON ROADS PEACE CONFERENCE, informal peace talks held on board a ship in the Hampton Roads in Feb. 1865, in an attempt to reconcile the Union and the Confederacy. Abraham LINCOLN and William H. SEWARD represented the Union, and Alexander H. STEPHENS led the Confederate delegates. The talks broke down over the question of reunion, upon which Lincoln insisted.

HAMSTERS, short-tailed RODENTS of Europe and Asia. Living in dry areas—steppe country or the edge of deserts—hamsters feed chiefly on cereals, but also on fruits, roots and leaves. Large cheek pouches are used for carrying food back to their nests—where it may be stored against the winter. The most familiar species, the golden hamster, *Mesocricetus auratus*, makes an attractive pet, though both it and the related common hamster, *Cricetus cricetus*, are nocturnal.

HAMSUN, Knut (1859–1952), Norwegian novelist. In his youth he led a wandering life, which became the theme of many of his novels, such as *Hunger* (1890). His masterpiece, *Growth of the Soil* (1917),

brought him the Nobel Prize for Literature in 1920.

HAN, powerful Chinese dynasty lasting from 206 BC to 220 AD. Usually divided into Western Han and the later Eastern Han, it was founded by Liu Pang after a period of oppressive centralized rule under the Chi'in dynasty. At the height of its expansion, the dynasty extended from Korea and Vietnam to Uzbekistan, and presided over a period of great cultural growth.

HANCOCK, John (1737–1793), American Revolutionary leader. President of the Continental Congress (1775–77) and first signer of the Declaration of Independence, he used much of his inherited wealth to support the American cause. First governor of Mass. 1780–93, he presided over the convention that ratified the US Constitution in 1788.

HANCOCK, Winfield Scott (1824–1886), US general and politician. He distinguished himself in the Civil War and, as commander of the 2nd Corps, played a major role at Gettysburg. Democratic nominee for the presidency in 1880, he was narrowly defeated by James A. GARFIELD.

HAND, (Billings) Learned (1872–1961), prominent US jurist noted for his profoundly reasoned rulings in almost 3,000 cases. He served 52 years as a New York federal district judge and, from 1924, member and later chief of the federal Court of Appeals. Although never a Supreme Court justice, he was greatly influential.

HANDEDNESS refers to the side of the body, and in particular to the hand, that is most used in motor tasks. Most people are right-handed and few are truly ambidextrous (either-handed). In the BRAIN, the paths for sensory and motor information are crossed, so the right side of the body is controlled by the left cerebral hemisphere and vice versa. The left hemisphere is usually dominant and also contains centers for speech and calculation. The nondominant side deals with aspects of visual and spatial relationships, while other functions are represented on both sides. In some left-handed people, the right hemisphere is dominant. Suppression of left-handedness may lead to speech disorder.

HANDEL, George Frederick (1685–1759), German-born composer who settled in England in 1712. He is considered one of the greatest composers of the baroque period; he enjoyed both public favor and royal patronage in his lifetime. Established as an opera composer in Germany and Italy, he turned to oratorio to suit British taste. His most famous such works are *Saul* (1739),

Israel in Egypt (1739), *The Messiah* (1742) and *Belshazzar* (1745). Among the rest of his vast output, the *Water Music* (1717) and the *Music for the Royal Fireworks* (1749) are best known. His career was ended by blindness in 1751–52.

HANDY, **W(illiam)** **C(hristopher)** (1873–1958), US songwriter, band leader and jazz composer. He conducted his own band 1903–21. In 1912 he published one of the first popular blues songs, *Memphis Blues*, and in 1914 wrote the famous *St. Louis Blues*. He became a music publisher in the 1920s.

HANGING GARDENS OF BABYLON, terraced roof gardens traditionally built by Nebuchadnezzar II of Babylon for his queen in the 6th century BC. Considered one of the SEVEN WONDERS OF THE WORLD in Classical times, no certain remains of them have yet been discovered.

HANNA, **Marcus Alonzo "Mark"** (1837–1904), US Republican politician and industrialist whose financial backing of William MCKINLEY helped bring about the latter's victory over William Jennings BRYAN in the 1896 presidential elections. Hanna was appointed and subsequently elected US Senator from Ohio 1897–1904 and remained a close presidential adviser.

HANNIBAL (247–183 BC), brilliant Carthaginian general who almost defeated Rome in the Second PUNIC WAR. Son of the great general Hamilcar Barca, he commanded Carthaginian forces in Spain against a city allied to Rome. When Rome declared war in 218 BC, he set off across the Pyrenees with around 40,000 seasoned troops and a force of elephants. In an extraordinary feat of organization, he took his forces across the Alps in wintry conditions and defeated Roman forces under SCIPIO at the Trebia R, then won great victories at Lake Trasimene (217 BC) and at Cannae (216 BC). Rome then detained him by harassing tactics while Roman armies reduced Carthaginian possessions in Spain and began to strike at Carthage itself. Hannibal was recalled, only to be defeated at Zama in 202 BC. Driven into exile c195 BC, he joined Syrian operations against Rome. When the defeated Syrians had to promise to surrender him to Rome, he poisoned himself.

HANOI, capital of North Vietnam 1954–76 and of Vietnam from 1976. Dating from the 7th century, it is an important shipping, industrial and transport center on the Red R., part European and part Annamese in style. The city suffered from US bombings during the VIETNAM WAR. Pop (metro) 2,000,000.

HANOVER, House of, reigning family of Hanover, in Germany, and of Great Britain (1714–1901). In 1658 the 1st Elector of Hanover married Sophia, granddaughter of James I, named heir to the British throne by the ACT OF SETTLEMENT, 1701. Her son became GEORGE I of Britain. By Salic law, Victoria could not become queen of Hanover, and from 1837 the thrones separated. On Edward VII's accession the family name became Saxe-Coburg (after Prince Albert) and in 1917 was changed to WINDSOR.

HANSARD, official report of the British Parliament's debates, named for the Hansard family, who began printing Parliamentary papers in 1774. From 1909, *Hansard* became an official verbatim government report, published daily for sale to the public.

HANSEATIC LEAGUE, a medieval confederation (c1157–1669) organized by N German towns and merchants to protect their trading interests in the Baltic Sea and throughout Europe. The town of Lübeck on Germany's N coast was the League's administrative center. Diets were held there to decide on monopolies, trading rights and other policy matters. From the late 13th to 14th centuries, the *hanse* (or guild) had over 100 members and exercised wide commercial powers, backed by monopoly and boycott, and strong political influence. Members of the *hanse* established commercial centers in numerous foreign towns such as Bergen (Norway), London and Novgorod (Russia). The League's strength declined with the rise of nationalism in Europe.

HANSON, Howard (1896–1981), US conductor, teacher and composer in the Romantic tradition. He won a Prix de Rome (1921) and was director of the Eastman School of Music, Rochester, N.Y., 1924–64. Hanson's Fourth Symphony won a Pulitzer Prize in 1944.

HANUKKAH, Jewish Feast of Dedication in Nov.–Dec., which marks the rededication (164 BC) of the Temple in Jerusalem after Judas Maccabaeus' victory over Antiochus IV (see MACCABEES, BOOK OF). This "Festival of Lights" is celebrated by lighting candles, one on the first night, two on the second and so forth, for eight days.

HAPPENING, in art, a performance combining prepared and random effects, aural as well as visual, frequently including some degree of audience participation. The happening may make use of any materials and take place in any environment, from an art gallery or theater to a gym or city street. John CAGE's pieces in the 1950s, combining music with other media, provided the inspiration for the art form, but the term itself comes from painter Allan Kaprow's *18 Happenings in 6 Parts*, first performed in 1959 at New York City's Reuben Gallery.

HAPSBURG, House of, European dynasty from which came rulers of Austria (1278–1918), the HOLY ROMAN EMPIRE (1436–1806), Spain (1516–1700), Germany, Hungary, Bohemia and other countries. Count Rudolf, elected king of Germany in 1273, founded the imperial line. Thereafter Hapsburg power and hereditary lands grew until under CHARLES V they included most of Europe (excepting France, Scandinavia, Portugal and England). After Charles, the Hapsburgs were divided into Spanish and imperial lines. When the Spanish line died out, Charles V's granddaughter, MARIA THERESA, gained the Austrian title. Her husband, Francis I (Duke of Lorraine), became Holy Roman Emperor (1745); the Hapsburg-Lorraine line ruled the Holy Roman Empire until its demise. The last Hapsburg ruler, Charles I, emperor of Austria and king of Hungary, abdicated in 1918.

HARA-KIRI, or *seppuku,* ancient Japanese act of ceremonial suicide, in which a short sword was used to slash the abdomen from left to right, then upwards; used by warriors to escape capture by the enemy, and also by the Samurai (warrior) class to avoid dishonorable execution after breaking the law. The Japanese favored hara-kiri to avoid capture even during WWII.

HARDECANUTE (c1019–1042), king of Denmark (from 1035) and last Danish king in England, the son of Canute II and Emma of Normandy. On his father's death (1035) Hardecanute, in Denmark, laid claim to the English throne, but his half brother, Harold I, succeeded. On Harold's death (1040), Hardecanute reigned with the support of GODWIN of Wessex.

HARD-EDGE PAINTING, a modern school of painting that stresses the optical relationships between flat areas of color arranged with geometrical precision. Josef ALBERS' works, such as *Homage to the Square,* are well-known examples. See MINIMALISM.

HARDENBERG, Karl August, Fürst von (1750–1822), Prussian statesman who continued the modernizing reforms begun by STEIN, thereby preparing PRUSSIA to resume the war against NAPOLEON I.

HARDENING OF THE ARTERIES. See ARTERIOSCLEROSIS.

HARDIE, James Keir (1856–1915), pioneer British socialist and first leader of the Labour Party. A mine worker from age 10, he was elected the first independent labor member of Parliament (1892) and helped form the Labour Party in 1906.

HARDIN, John Wesley (1853–1895), US western outlaw, born in Bonham, Tex. He killed over 30 men, served a prison term and was pardoned in 1894.

HARDING, Warren Gamaliel (1865–1923), 29th president of the US. He died after only 30 months in office, during which his administration was marred by high-level corruption, culminating in the TEAPOT DOME oil reserve scandal, which involved Secretary of the Interior Albert B. Fall accepting large bribes.

Born in Ohio and educated at a backwater college, Harding became part owner of the Marion, Ohio, *Star* (1884), which he turned into a successful small-town daily. In 1891 he married Mrs. Florence Kling DeWolfe; their domestic life was unhappy and led to Harding's involvement in liaisons which hurt his personal reputation. A genial man with a flair for vague rhetoric, Harding entered politics, becoming a Republican state senator and Ohio's lieutenant-governor. Defeated in the 1910 gubernatorial race, but elected US Senator in 1914, he was a conservative and popular member of Congress though he did little of consequence.

In 1920 he was adopted as a presidential candidate when the Republican convention became deadlocked over the leading contenders. He won a sweeping victory on a "return to normalcy" platform, appealing to a nation weary of wartime restraints. Many of Harding's political appointments were disastrous; he rewarded political cronies with office, and their corruption and dishonesty seriously damaged both his administration and the reputation of the Republican Party. Harding's cabinet did include some distinguished political figures: Charles Evans Hughes (State), Herbert Hoover (Commerce), Andrew Mellon (Treasury) and Henry C. Wallace (Agriculture). He also appointed former President Taft as chief justice and created the Bureau of the Budget, introducing modern budgetary systems into government. Determined that America should join the League of Nations' World Court, despite Congressional disapproval, Harding set out on a cross-country tour to take the issue to the people. Already suffering from a serious heart condition, Harding died in San Francisco on Aug. 2, 1923, during the tour. After his death, the scandals of his administration and personal life that came to light destroyed his reputation. Harding is now recognized as a well-intentioned, ingenuous man who did not have the leadership capabilities to fulfill the office of president.

HARDNESS, the resistance of a substance to scratching, or to indentation under a blow or steady load. Resistance to scratching is measured on the **Mohs' scale,** named for Friedrich Mohs (1773–1839), who chose 10 MINERALS as reference points, from talc (hardness 1) to DIAMOND (10). The **modified Mohs' scale** is now usually used, with 5 further mineral reference points. Resistance to indentation is measured by, among others, the Brinell, Rockwell and Vickers scales.

HARD WATER, water containing CALCIUM and magnesium ions and hence forming scum with soap and depositing scale in boilers, pipes and kettles. **Temporary hardness** is due to calcium and magnesium bicarbonates; it is removed by boiling, which precipitates the carbonates. **Permanent hardness** (unaffected by boiling) is due to the sulfates. Hard water may be softened by precipitation of the metal ions using CALCIUM hydroxide and SODIUM carbonate, followed by sodium PHOSPHATE; or by a zeolite or ion-exchange column, which exchanges the calcium and magnesium ions for sodium ions.

HARDY, Thomas (1840–1928), English novelist and poet. Born in Dorset (Wessex in his novels), he practiced architecture until the popular success of his novel *Far From the Madding Crowd* (1874). Nine novels, including *The Return of the Native* (1878) and *Tess of the d'Urbervilles* (1891), appeared in the next 20 years. *Jude the Obscure* (1894), partially autobiographical, so offended Victorian morality that Hardy abandoned writing novels but continued writing poetry. His heroic verse drama *The Dynasts* (1903–08) and later lyric poetry are as highly regarded as his novels. The "last of the great Victorians," Hardy directly influenced 20th-century English literature. His view of life was essentially tragic; his characters often seem victims of malignant fate, especially if they rebel against "nature." Hardy is almost unsurpassed in his skill at describing rustic life and the English countryside.

HARE KRISHNAS, popular name for members of a strict monastic order (the International Society for Krishna Consciousness), famous for their orange robes, shaved heads, public chanting of "Hare Krishna" (in praise of the Hindu god Krishna), and aggressive begging. The movement was founded in 1965 in New York City by A. C. Bhaktivedanta Swami Prabhupada. Among the group's international string of residences and temples is the Palace of Gold, on 2,000 acres in W. Va., opened in 1980.

HARELIP, a congenital DISEASE with a cleft defect in the upper lip due to impaired facial development in the EMBRYO, and often associated with CLEFT PALATE. It may be corrected by plastic SURGERY.

HAREM, from the Arabic *harim* (meaning forbidden), the secluded part of a Muslim dwelling reserved for the women of the household. An ancient Semitic practice, the harem was fostered by Muslims, who practiced polygamy and concubinage. Today, harems are dying out as Muslim women move out of their seclusion and attain more social freedom.

HARES, the genus *Lepus*, animals resembling RABBITS and including the JACKRABBITS, adapted for swift running and characterized by long ears, long, powerful hindlegs and feet and short tails. Hares are herbivorous, living entirely above ground in grasslands in Eurasia, Africa and North America and, by introduction, in South America, Australia and New Zealand. Various species molt into a white pelage over winter. Male European hares indulge in wild boxing matches during the rut—the origin of the expression "mad as a March hare." Young hares, leverets, are born well-developed, alert and capable of independent movement.

HARGREAVES or **HARGRAVES, James** (c1720–1778), British inventor of the spinning jenny (c1764), a machine for SPINNING several threads at once. Public uproar forced him to flee his native Blackburn for Nottingham (1768), where he patented the jenny (1770). In 1777 he adopted ARKWRIGHT'S more sophisticated machinery.

HARLAN, two associate justices of the US Supreme Court, grandfather and grandson. **John Marshall Harlan** (1833–1911), appointed in 1877, served 34 years. A court independent, he is best known for his 1896 dissenting opinion that Jim Crow laws, which established the principle of "separate but equal" racial segregation, in fact deprived black citizens of equal protection of the law. **John Marshall Harlan** (1899–1971) was appointed to the court by President Eisenhower in 1955. He had been an assistant US attorney, chief counsel to the N.Y. State Crime Commission and member of the US Court of Appeals.

HARLEM, primarily Negro and Hispanic community, in the N part of Manhattan borough, New York City. A Dutch settlement from 1658 (Nieuw Haarlem), it was a rural and then a fashionable residential area. From the 1920s it became chiefly black; overcrowding helped turn Harlem into a notorious slum. Government-funded programs since the 1960s have attempted to improve conditions there.

HARLEM HEIGHTS, Battle of, Sept. 16, 1776, skirmish in the struggle for Manhattan Island during the American Revolutionary War. The repulse of the British momentarily revived American spirits and William HOWE, the British commander, gave up the idea of frontal attack.

HARLEM RENAISSANCE, period of cultural development among US blacks, centered on Harlem, New York City, in the 1920s. In this period black American literature changed from works in dialect and imitations of white writers to penetrating analyses of black culture and to novels of protest, displaying racial pride. Notable writers included Countee CULLEN, Langston HUGHES and Jean Toomer.

HARLEQUIN, comic character who usually performed in PANTOMIME, often wearing a standard costume of multicolored diamond-shaped patches. He is derived from Arlecchino, a character of the COMMEDIA DELL'ARTE in the 16th–17th centuries.

HARLOW, Jean (1911–1937), US film actress who was the voluptuous Hollywood sex symbol of the 1930s. Her films included *Hell's Angels* (1930), *Platinum Blonde* (1932) and *China Seas* (1935).

HARMONICS, vibrations at frequencies which are integer multiples of that of a fundamental vibration: the ascending notes C, C, G, C', E', G' comprise a fundamental with its first five harmonics. Apart from their musical consonance, they are important because any periodically repeated signal—a vowel sound, for example—can be produced by superimposing the harmonics of the fundamental frequency, each with the appropriate intensity and time lag.

HARMONY, in music, the simultaneous sounding of two or more tones or parts; also the structure, relation and progression of chords and the rule governing their relationship. Traditional harmony is based upon a triad, a three-tone musical structure, with notes named for their position on the musical SCALE: the lowest tone is called the root, the middle tone is called the third (located a third scale tone above the root), the next is called the fifth (a fifth scale tone above the root). The triad becomes a chord in four-part writing when one tone is doubled. Chords can be erected on any note of the traditional eight-note scale. In the 20th century, harmonic rules and standards, developed over the preceding 400 years, were largely discarded. (See also ATONALITY; HARMONICS.)

HARMONY SOCIETY, or **Rappites**, religious group of 600 German immigrants to the US, led by George RAPP, which established Utopian communities in Pa. and Ind. (1804–1906). They held property in common and believed in Christ's imminent coming. The celibate society prospered until Rapp's death (1847), but thereafter attracted few converts.

HARNACK, Adolf von (1851–1930), influential German church historian, professor at Leipzig, Gressen, Marburg and Berlin. His masterpiece was the *History of Dogma* (1885–89). He advocated a return to the simplicity of the Gospels.

HARNESS, working gear of any draft animal, which hitches an animal to machinery or wagons; used mainly with horses. The main parts are the *collar* and *hames*, resting on the horse's shoulders or chest; the *traces* or *shafts*, which extend from the collar along the horse's sides to the vehicle; the *saddle pad* or *back band*, held by the girth and crupper, which retains the traces or shafts; and the *headgear*, the bit, bridle, blinkers and reins or lines.

HARNESS RACING. See HORSE RACING.

HAROLD II (c1020–1066), last Anglo-Saxon king of the English, son of Godwin and earl of East Anglia, Wessex and Kent. Harold accepted the crown on the death of Edward the Confessor. Nine months later, he was killed at the Battle of HASTINGS when William, duke of Normandy, began his conquest of England.

HARP, stringed instrument, usually triangular in shape, with a resonating chamber nearly perpendicular to the plane of the strings. The harp is of ancient origin, although the Greeks and Romans favored the LYRE. The modern "double-action" harp, developed in 1800, is chromatic throughout its range. To alter their pitch, strings are shortened by means of seven pedals.

HARPERS FERRY, town in NE W.Va., scene of John BROWN's raid in Oct. 1859. Its location at the confluence of the Potomac and Shenandoah rivers made it an important Civil War strongpoint. It changed hands many times; its spirited resistance in 1862 seriously delayed Robert E. LEE's march N. The Civil War sites are preserved in the Harpers Ferry National Historical Park.

HARPIES, in Greek mythology, bird-like

monsters with the heads of women. Originally they may have been tomb demons, but in the myths they are agents of divine punishment.

HARPSICHORD, keyboard instrument in which the strings are plucked, rather than hit as in a piano. The range is small, but tonal effects are achieved by stops or "registers." Larger harpsichords have two keyboards. The harpsichord was very popular from c1550 until the advent of the piano in the early 1800s, and much great music was written for it, most notably by Bach, Couperin and Scarlatti. It is now enjoying renewed popularity.

HARRIMAN, father and son prominent in US commerce and government. **Edward Henry Harriman** (1848–1909) formed syndicates to buy the Union Pacific railroad in 1898 and the Southern Pacific in 1901, and created a Wall Street panic in his fight for the Northern Pacific in 1901. His son, **William Averell Harriman** (1891–1986), board chairman of Union Pacific 1933–46, served under Franklin D. Roosevelt in the National Recovery Administration, and carried on lend-lease negotiations in Britain 1941–42. Named US ambassador to Moscow in 1943, he took part in all the major wartime conferences. Ambassador to London in 1946, he became secretary of commerce 1946–48 and governor of N.Y. 1955–59. As ambassador-at-large he was instrumental in the Laos peace talks 1961–62 and in achieving the limited test ban treaty in 1963. In 1968–69 he took part in the Vietnam peace talks.

HARRINGTON, James (1611–1677), English philosopher, best known for his *Commonwealth of Oceana* (1656), a treatise on the ideal state and ideal ruler. In 1661 he was arrested on a charge of plotting Charles II's overthrow, but this was never proved.

HARRINGTON, Michael (1928–1989), US socialist leader and writer; his book *The Other America* (1962) described the "invisible poor" in the contemporary US and was credited with inspiring the federal antipoverty programs of the 1960s. He was chairman of the Socialist Party (1968–72) and the Democratic Socialist Organizing Committee (from 1973).

HARRIS, Frank (1856–1931), British writer, editor of three London newspapers 1892–98. A prolific writer, he is best remembered for his biographies of Shakespeare, Oscar Wilde and G. B. Shaw, and for his humorous, erotic and unreliable autobiography *My Life and Loves* (1925–29).

HARRIS, Joel Chandler (1848–1908), US journalist and author. His tales of plantation life, many featuring the old slave and folk philosopher Uncle Remus, are noted for their charming narrative style rendered in authentic dialect.

HARRIS, Julie (1925–), US stage and film actress whose first great success was as 12-year-old Frankie Adams in *The Member of the Wedding* (play, 1950; film, 1953). Her other stage credits include *I Am a Camera* (1951), *The Lark* (1955), and *The Belle of Amherst* (1976).

HARRIS, Louis (1921–), US pollster who founded Louis Harris and Associates (1956), one of the most influential public opinion polling organizations in the US.

HARRIS, Roy Ellsworth (1898–1979), US composer who studied in Paris with Nadia BOULANGER. Well known as a teacher, he was twice awarded the Guggenheim Fellowship (1927–28). The *Third Symphony* (1937) is perhaps his best-known work.

HARRIS, Townsend (1804–1878), US diplomat. A New York merchant, he settled in the Far East in 1847, becoming the first US consul-general in Japan 1855. He negotiated a preferential commercial treaty with the shogunate in 1858.

HARRISON, Benjamin (1833–1901), 23rd president of the US (1889–93). Grandson of William Henry Harrison, 9th president, he studied law in Cincinnati, and in 1854 began practice in Indianapolis. There he became active in the new Republican Party, was elected city attorney in 1857, and became reporter of the Ind. Supreme Court in 1860. During the Civil War, he served heroically in Sherman's Atlanta campaign of 1864. He returned to his law practice and politics, supporting Garfield in 1880 and entering the US Senate in 1881. There he backed high tariffs, helped to create the Interstate Commerce Commission and worked to expand the national park system. In 1888 he won the Republican presidential nomination, to oppose the then president, Grover Cleveland. The ensuing election was fought largely on the tariff issue; Harrison defeated Cleveland in the electoral vote, although trailing in the popular vote. As president, Harrison pursued a vigorous foreign policy. US claims to Samoa were established; the first and highly successful Pan American conference was held in Washington. A dispute with the UK over Bering Sea fur-seal exploitation went to arbitration. He had less influence over domestic legislation, although he signed the SHERMAN ANTITRUST ACT and the McKinley Tariff Act, convinced that the nation wanted high import duties. In 1890, the

Democrats captured Congress, due to low farm prices, the rise of the Populist party and the rising cost of living. This made Harrison's last years in office unfruitful and lost him personal popularity; he was reluctantly renominated in 1892. His wife died two weeks before the election. Growing agrarian unrest and bitter labor disputes helped to give Cleveland an easy victory; Harrison returned to Indianapolis to pursue a distinguished legal career.

HARRISON, Peter (1716–1775), foremost American architect of his time. He introduced a strong Palladian influence, as may be seen in such buildings as Christ Church, Cambridge, Mass., and King's Chapel in Boston.

HARRISON, Rex (Reginald Carey Harrison; 1908–   ), British stage and film actor, notably as Professor Higgins in the musical *My Fair Lady* (play, 1956; film, 1964).

HARRISON, Wallace Kirkman (1895–1981), US architect who coordinated work on the UN building and Lincoln Center, both in New York City. His First Presbyterian Church in Stamford, Conn., is noted for its clever use of colored light.

HARRISON, William Henry (1773–1841), 9th president of the US (March 4–April 4, 1841). Born on a Va. plantation and son of a former state governor, Harrison entered the army on his father's death in 1791 and fought in Indian campaigns in the Northwest Territory. He finally settled in North Bend, Ohio, and in 1800 became governor of the new Indiana Territory. In treaties with the Indians, Harrison opened up 133,650sq mi of Ohio and Ind. to white settlement. During the 1811 Indian uprising, led by TECUMSEH, Harrison's troops repulsed an Indian attack at the Battle of TIPPECANOE; he became a national hero, "Old Tippecanoe." When the War of 1812 began, he was made brigadier-general in charge of the Northwestern army, and major-general in 1813. At the war's end in 1814, he entered politics, serving in the Ohio Senate 1819–21 and in Congress 1816–19 and 1825–28. First minister to Colombia 1828–29, he retired to North Bend when Jackson took office.

In 1839 Harrison won the Whig presidential nomination at its first national convention on the strength of his military record and broad political views. He and his running mate, John Tyler, were launched by a campaign more colorful than any yet seen in the US. With the famous slogan, "Tippecanoe and Tyler, too," Harrison was put forward as a war hero and a son of the people with simple tastes. This image

appealed to a country caught in a serious economic depression and he won by an overwhelming electoral vote. He appointed an able cabinet, headed by Daniel WEBSTER, and called a special session of Congress to act on the nation's financial difficulties. He delivered his inaugural address in pouring rain, however, and caught a cold which quickly turned to pneumonia. He died one month to the day after taking office.

HART, Lorenz Milton (1895–1943), US lyricist who collaborated with Richard RODGERS on 29 musical comedies. The most famous are *A Connecticut Yankee* (1927), *The Boys from Syracuse* (1938) and *Pal Joey* (1940).

HART, Moss (1904–1961), US dramatist and director. With George S. KAUFMAN, he wrote *You Can't Take It With You* (1936) and *The Man Who Came to Dinner* (1939). He directed the Broadway hits *My Fair Lady* (1956) and *Camelot* (1960).

HART, William S. (1870–1946), US stage and film actor. An authentic cowboy, he became the first cowboy film star (1910–25), writing and directing many of his pictures.

HARTE, Bret (1836–1902), influential US writer. His short stories of frontier life helped create the mythology of the West. Among the stories that brought him worldwide fame are *The Luck of Roaring Camp* (1868) and *The Outcasts of Poker Flat* (1869). When his popularity in America declined, he settled in Britain.

HARTFORD CONVENTION, assembly of Federalist delegates from Mass., Conn., R.I. and Vt. It met secretly from Dec. 15, 1814, to Jan. 5, 1815, and put forward seven constitutional amendments to redress New England's grievances, resulting largely from federal neglect during the WAR OF 1812. With the arrival of peace, however, opponents were able effectively to ruin the Federalist party by accusing it of attempted secession.

HARTFORD WITS, a literary circle who met in Hartford, Conn., during the last quarter of the 18th century. Mostly Yale men, they were all Federalists; their main product was political satire, typified by the *Anarchiad*, a jointly-written mock verse epic. A collection of their work, *Echo*, was published in 1807.

HARTLEY, David (1705–1757), English physician and a founder of the school of psychology known as ASSOCIATIONISM. In his *Observations on Man* (1749), he taught that sensations were communicated to the brain via vibrations in nerve particles and that the repetition of sensations gave rise to the association of ideas in the mind.

HARTLEY, Marsden (1877–1943), US artist who abandoned an early interest in abstraction to produce impressionistic depictions of natural scenes. He was best known for paintings of his native Maine.

HARTMANN, Heinz (1894–1970), Austrian-born US psychologist who was a leader of the second generation of Freudians and was best known for the expansion of the basic theory of the ego. He wrote *Essays in Ego Psychology* (1964) and collaborated on the annual *Psychoanalytic Study of the Child*.

HARUN-AL-RASHID (c766–809), fifth ABBASID caliph of Baghdad, from 786, whose rule extended from N Africa to the Indus R in India; he exacted tribute from the Byzantine Empire. His reign marked both the height and decline of the caliphate, and is remembered in the ARABIAN NIGHTS as a golden age.

HARVARD, John (1607–1638), American clergyman, first benefactor of Harvard College. Born in London, he emigrated to Mass. in 1637 to become Charlestown's minister. In 1638 he bequeathed half his estate and his library to the college, which was named for him in 1639.

HARVARD UNIVERSITY, founded by the General Court of Mass. in 1636, is the oldest university in the US. It has long been influenced by European patterns of education, but under the 40-year presidency of C. W. ELIOT developed a distinctive character of its own, especially in the growth of graduate schools. It now has nearly 200 allied institutions such as libraries, laboratories, museums and observatories.

HARVEY, William (1578–1657), British physician who discovered the circulation of the blood. He showed that the HEART acts as a pump and that the blood circulates endlessly about the body; that there are valves in the heart and VEINS so that blood can flow in one direction only; and that the necessary pressure comes only from the lower left-hand side of the heart. His discoveries demolished the theories of GALEN that blood was consumed at the body's periphery and that the left and right sides of the heart were connected by pores. He also made important studies of the development of the EMBRYO.

HARZ MOUNTAINS, range in N Germany on the border between lower Saxony and East Germany. In medieval times it was a major mining center for various metals, but the area's economy now rests on tourism, especially for winter sports. The range's highest point is Brocken peak.

HASDRUBAL (d. 207 BC), Carthaginian general in the second PUNIC WAR. He marched from Spain in 207 BC to reinforce his brother HANNIBAL in Italy. The Romans defeated him and so deprived Hannibal of forces that might have brought him victory.

HASEK, Jaroslav (1883–1923), Czech novelist whose *The Good Soldier Schweik* (1920–23) satirizes the WWI Austrian military machine. Schweik became the archetypical "little man," who outwits authority despite apparent stupidity.

HASHEMITE DYNASTY, Arab royal family claiming descent from the grandfather of the prophet MOHAMMED, hereditary sherifs of MECCA from the 11th century until 1919. After WWI the Hashemites FAISAL I and ABDULLAH IBN HUSSEIN became kings of IRAQ and JORDAN respectively; Abdullah's grandson HUSSEIN is the present king of Jordan.

HASHISH, or **cannabis,** a drug produced from a resin obtained from the HEMP plant (*Cannabis sativa*), particularly from its flowers and fruits. It is a non-addictive drug whose effects range from a feeling of euphoria to fear. Hashish is mainly produced in the Middle East and India, and has been in use for many centuries, although it is still illegal in many countries. (See MARIJUANA.)

HASIDISM, Jewish pietistic movement established in 18th-century Poland by Israel ben Eliezer. Reacting against emphasis on rabbinical learning and strict observance of the law, he stressed the ecstatic, joyous element in religion. The movement became grouped around *tzadikkim,* holy men or saints. Hasidism still flourishes in Israel and New York. In Hebrew, *hasidim* means "the pious ones." It is also applied to fiercely orthodox sectarians who fought in the 2nd-century BC Maccabaean wars.

HASMONEAN, Jewish dynasty which ruled Judea c164–63 BC. It descended from Mattathias who, with his son JUDAS MACCABAEUS, rebelled against Syria in 168 BC (see MACCABEES, BOOKS OF). From Jonathan (d. 142 BC) onwards the Hasmoneans were also high priests. The family's power, at its height under John Hyrcanus (d. 104 BC) and Alexander Jannaeus (d. 76 BC), ended with the Roman conquest of Jerusalem in 63 BC.

HASSAM, Childe (1859–1935), US painter and graphic artist. He studied in Paris, and was one of the first US artists to adopt IMPRESSIONISM, painting many New York and New England landscapes.

HASSAN II (1929–   ), king and spiritual head of Morocco since 1961. He initiated partial democratization in 1962, but has retained effective absolute power despite an abortive coup in 1971–72.

HASTINGS, Battle of, the prelude to the Norman conquest of England, fought between King HAROLD II and Duke William of Normandy on Oct. 14, 1066. Delayed all summer by unfavorable winds, William was finally able to cross the English Channel just when Harold was in N England defeating a Norwegian invasion. Forced marches brought Harold south with an exhausted and depleted force to meet William at Senlac (renamed Battle), near Hastings. Harold's axmen were only swept from a strong hilltop position, and Harold killed, when William, after a day's fighting, successfully managed a feigned retreat.

HASTINGS, Warren (1732–1818), first governor-general of British India (1772–85). Starting as a clerk in 1750, he rose high in the British East India Company and as governor fought corruption and banditry, but also amassed a large personal fortune. Criticized in England as an aggressive and occasionally arbitrary governor, he resigned and was impeached. Despite fierce prosecution speeches, notably by Edmund BURKE, during the celebrated trial (1788–95), Hastings was honorably acquitted.

HATCH ACTS, two unrelated acts passed by the US Congress. In 1887 William Henry Hatch successfully sponsored an act promoting scientific research in agriculture. In 1939 Senator Carl Hatch of N.M. sponsored an act to regulate political expenditure and corruption in national elections, by barring federal employees from political activity and setting limits on campaign-fund contributions and expenditures.

HATFIELD-McCOY FEUD, bloody clan vendetta in the 1880s between the Hatfields of Logan Co., W. Va., and the McCoys of Pike Co., Ky. Originating during the Civil War, it erupted in 1882 over the attempted elopement of Johnse Hatfield and Rosanna McCoy.

HATHAWAY, Anne (c1556–1623), wife of William Shakespeare. Eight years his senior, she married him in 1582, bearing him three children. Her family home, "Anne Hathaway's Cottage," is at Shottery, near Stratford-upon-Avon.

HATSHEPSUT, queen of Egypt, 18th dynasty (15th century BC). She ruled with her husband and half-brother Thutmose II, becoming regent to his son and then assuming the powers and titles of a pharaoh. She presided over a period of prosperity, and built the great temple of Deir el-Bahri near Thebes.

HAUGHEY, Charles James (1925–   ), Irish politician, prime minister 1979–81, 1982, 1987–   . To make Ireland competitive with other EUROPEAN ECONOMIC COMMUNITY members when trade barriers are removed in 1992, he cut government borrowing and spending and encouraged private enterprise.

HAUPTMANN, Gerhart (1862–1946), German author and playwright who pioneered naturalism in the German theater. His first play, *Before Dawn* (1889), dealing with social problems, won him overnight fame, and was followed—among others—by *The Weavers* (1892), a drama of working-class life. He won the Nobel Prize for Literature, 1912.

HAUSA, a people of NW Nigeria and neighboring Niger, numbering about 9 million and Muslim since the 14th century. Early in the 19th century they were mostly conquered by the FULANI. Their language is much used in W African trade.

HAUSHOFER, Karl Ernst (1869–1946), German theoretician of geopolitics. His development of earlier theories of *Lebensraum* or "living space" influenced Hitler's ideas. Under investigation as a war criminal, he committed suicide.

HAUSSMANN, Georges-Eugène, Baron (1809–1891), French civic official (1853–70) responsible for planning and rebuilding central Paris under Napoleon III. Besides the famous boulevards, he laid out improved water and sewage systems.

HAVANA, capital of Cuba, on the Gulf of Mexico. One of the largest cities in the West Indies, it was founded by the Spanish in c1515. It has an excellent harbor. The U. of Havana was opened in 1728. Tobacco from the neighboring Vuelta Abajo is used for the famous Havana cigars. Until Fidel CASTRO's revolution (1959), the city's economy rested on gambling and tourism controlled from the US. Since then Havana has been subordinated to the general economy of Cuba. Pop 2,014,806.

HAWAII, 50th state of the US in the North Pacific Ocean, a chain of some 130 islands, over 1,500mi long.

Land. The main islands, at the SE end of the chain and about 2,400mi from the mainland, are Hawaii, Maui, Kahoolawe, Lanai, Molokai, Oahu, Kauai and Niihau. Oahu is the most developed, and contains the naval base at Pearl Harbor, the capital Honolulu, and more than three-fourths of the state's population.

MAUNA LOA, Mauna Kea and KILAUEA, active volcanoes on Hawaii Island, still cause frequent damage. Prevailing trade

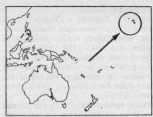

Name of state: Hawaii
Capital: Honolulu
Statehood: Aug. 21, 1959 (50th state)
Familiar name: Aloha State
Area: 6,450sq mi
Population: 1,062,000
Elevation: Highest—13,796ft., Mauna Kea.
Lowest—sea level, Pacific Ocean
Motto: *Ua mau ke ea o ka aina i ka pono*
("The life of the land is perpetuated in righteousness")
State flower: Hibiscus
State bird: Né-né (Hawaiian goose)
State tree: Kukui (Candlenut)
State song: "Hawaii Ponoi" (Hawaii's Own)

winds give an equable climate with daytime temperatures of 75°–80°F.

People. Settled by Polynesians c400–800 AD, it now has a population of mixed descent, more than half E Asian. Remnants of the old culture, such as the *lei* (flower-necklace), the *hula* dance and the *luau* or Hawaiian feast, survive as tourist attractions.

Economy. The more than 1 million tourists annually, agriculture based on pineapple and sugarcane and military spending are mainstays of the economy. Industry is largely devoted to food processing and the manufacture of clothing. In the 1980s, Japanese businesses made large investments in Hawaii, buying hotels, office buildings, and other real estate.

History. In 1778 Captain James COOK discovered the islands, and the arrival of US missionaries from 1820 began the process of westernization. They introduced writing and new political concepts and opened the way to trade. Treaties (1875, 1887) freed Hawaiian sugar of duty but also gave the US Pearl Harbor as a way station. Agitation by US residents brought the fall of the monarchy in 1893, and in 1898 the US annexed the new republic. In 1908 Pearl Harbor became a US naval base; the Japanese attack on it (Dec. 7, 1941) brought the US into WWII. An expanding postwar economy and resentment at taxation by the US without representation

fueled agitation for admission to the Union. Statehood was granted on Aug. 21, 1959 under a constitution amended in 1958. Since then, Hawaii has continued to grow (with a population increase of about 70% in 1960–87) and to remain prosperous. Growth has brought problems characteristic of many other states (a rise in crime, a debasement of the environment), and has led to concerns about the quality of life in Hawaii. In presidential elections 1968–88, Hawaii voted Democratic in 1968, 1976–80, and 1988.

HAWAII VOLCANOES NATIONAL PARK, on Hawaii Island, established 1916, has among the largest and most active volcanoes in the world. MAUNA LOA (13,680ft) has the Mokuaweoweo crater on its summit, and KILAUEA crater on its E slope which is 4,090ft high and over 4sq mi in area with a fiery floor called Halemaumau. Area of park: 317sq mi.

HAWKE, Bob (Robert James Lee Hawke; 1929–), Australian Labour Party politician, prime minister from 1983. Criticized by the left wing of his party, he sponsored tax reforms and free-market policies that reduced inflation and resulted in economic growth.

HAWKING, Stephen (1942–), British theoretical physicist and cosmologist who has applied general RELATIVITY and QUANTUM MECHANICS to the theory of BLACK HOLES in novel ways and produced results of great originality. He wrote a popular *Brief History of Time* (1988).

HAWKINS, Coleman (1904–1969), US jazz musician whose virtuosity on the saxophone made it a major instrument of jazz performance.

HAWKINS, Sir John (1532–1595). Elizabethan sea captain and, as treasurer of the navy, sponsor of reforms in ship design and gunnery which contributed to victory over the Spanish ARMADA (1588). He commanded one of the English squadrons. In 1562–63 he had captained the first English slaving voyage, breaking the Spanish West Indies trade monopoly.

HAWKS, fast-flying, diurnal birds of prey. The name is properly restricted to the genus *Accipiter*, though, especially in North America, it is taken as a general name for any bird of prey. True hawks are broad-winged birds of woodland or forest, the shape of the wings and the long tail enabling them to maneuver rapidly among trees. They prey mostly on small birds, approaching behind cover and making a swift dash to kill.

HAWKSMOOR, Nicholas (1661–1736), English baroque architect. He achieved dramatic and massive designs, notably the Castle Howard Mausoleum.

HAWTHORNE, Nathaniel (1804–1864), major US novelist and short story writer, born in Salem, Mass. At first unable to earn a living by writing, he worked at the Boston custom house. Later he was US consul in Liverpool (1853–57). His great novels, *The Scarlet Letter* (1850) and *The House of the Seven Gables* (1851), set in Puritan New England, are masterpieces of psychological portraiture and dark atmosphere. His short stories collected in *Twice-Told Tales* (1842) and *Mosses from an Old Manse* (1846) mark him as a master of that genre.

HAY, John (Milton) (1838–1905), US statesman and author, and when young, President Lincoln's secretary (1860–65). Secretary of State under McKinley and Roosevelt (1898–1905), he established US sovereignty over Hawaii and the Philippines, negotiated the Hay-Pauncefote Treaties (1899, 1901) and the Hay-Bunau-Varilla Treaty (1903) which together ensured US control of the Panama Canal, and evolved the OPEN DOOR POLICY in China. His writings include *Pike County Ballads* (1871) and (with J. G. Nicolay) *Abraham Lincoln: A History* (10 vols., 1890).

HAY-BUNAU-VARILLA TREATY, pact signed on Nov. 18, 1903, between the US and the 15-day-old state of Panama, giving the US sovereignty over a 10mi-wide corridor across the isthmus of Panama, in return for a guarantee of the independence of Panama. Drawn up by John Hay and Philippe Bunau-Varilla, promoter of the New Panama Canal Company, the treaty allowed the US to build a canal on payment of $10 million and a $250,000 annuity to begin nine years later. (See also PANAMA CANAL.)

HAYDN, Franz Joseph (1732–1809), Austrian composer who established the accepted classical forms of the symphony, string quartet and piano sonata. The architect of classicism, Haydn nevertheless drew inspiration from folk music in many of his works. His greatest music combines vigor, lyricism and poignancy with frequent flashes of wit. For 48 years court musician to the Esterhazy family, his huge output includes 107 symphonies, hundreds of chamber works as well as violin and piano concertos, some 25 operatic works, a number of great masses, notably the *Nelson* mass, and other great religious works, such as the oratorio *The Creation*. In the 1790s he visited England, where he won great acclaim for his 12 "London" or "Salomon" symphonies, which were commissioned by the impresario Salomon.

HAYEK, Friedrich August von (1899–), Vienna-born British economist (naturalized 1938), professor at London U. 1931–1950, Chicago U. 1950–62, and Freiburg U. 1962–69. He wrote prolifically on monetary theory and the history of capitalism. He shared the Nobel Prize for Economics with Gunnar MYRDAL in 1974.

HAYES, Helen (1900–), US actress, born Helen Hayes Brown. Beginning her career at age five, she became one of America's most versatile and admired performers, winner of numerous awards for stage, screen, radio and television. She married playwright Charles MacArthur. A New York theater was named for her.

HAYES, Rutherford Birchard (1822–1893), 19th president of the US who won office in the most bitterly contested of all presidential elections. Born in Delaware, Ohio, he graduated from Harvard Law School in 1845 to begin a successful legal career. In the Civil War he was four times wounded in action and rose to become a major general of volunteers. Elected to Congress while on active service (1865) he later won three terms as governor of Ohio (1867–75). At the Republican Convention of 1876 he won the nomination from the better known James G. BLAINE. In the election, the Democrat reform governor of New York, Samuel J. TILDEN, revived his party's fortunes to win a popular majority. But disputed results in S.C., Fla., La. and Ore. led to the formation of a special electoral commission with a Republican majority, which awarded all the disputed votes to Hayes.

President. Hayes' contribution as president has undoubtedly been underrated. Following pre-inaugural pledges to Southern Democrats for their acquiescence in the commission's decision, he recalled Federal troops from the South, thus ending 11 years of Republican military RECONSTRUCTION. Despite opposition in his own party, he appointed ex-Confederates to administration posts and began a much-needed reform of the civil service by insisting upon recruitment by competitive examination rather than political patronage. In economic affairs, although his hard money policies were modified, even overridden by Congress, he has been credited with restoring business confidence. Hayes, whose personal integrity was never impugned, refused to stand for a second term. Yet he had slowly mollified opposition resentment over the "stolen" election and he had helped to repair Republican credibility after the corruption and scandals of Grant's presidential terms.

HAY FEVER, common allergic disease causing RHINITIS and CONJUNCTIVITIS on exposure to allergen. The prototype is ALLERGY to grasses, but pollens of many trees, weeds and grasses (e.g., ragweed, Timothy grass) may provoke seasonal hay fever in sensitized individuals. Allergy to FUNGI or to the house-dust mite may lead to perennial rhinitis; animal fur or feathers may also provoke attacks. Susceptibility is often associated with ASTHMA, ECZEMA and ASPIRIN sensitivity in the individual or his family. Treatment consists of allergen avoidance, desensitizing injections and cromoglycate, ANTIHISTAMINES or STEROID sprays in difficult cases.

HAY-HERRAN TREATY, agreement between the US and Colombia, signed in 1903, but refused ratification by the Colombian congress, which would have given the US rights to the Panama Canal Zone. After the refusal, US president Theodore ROOSEVELT gave aid to a revolutionary force which declared Panama independent. (see also HAY-BUNAU-VARILLA TREATY.)

HAYMARKET AFFAIR, violent confrontation between labor organizers and police in Chicago's Haymarket Square on May 4, 1886. After several workers had been killed or injured on May 3, a protest meeting was held. During the meeting a bomb was thrown at the police who intervened, and rioting started; four workers and seven policemen died. Of the eight anarchists later sentenced to death for murder, four were hanged, one committed suicide and three, in 1893, were pardoned.

HAYNE, Robert Young (1791–1839), US lawyer, politician and spokesman for the South. In a famous two-week debate in 1830 with Daniel WEBSTER, he championed states' rights and supported state NULLIFICATION of federal laws.

HAY-PAUNCEFOTE TREATY, agreement between the US and Great Britain, signed in 1901, giving the US the sole right to control and fortify the proposed Panama Canal Zone, and abrogating the CLAYTON-BULWER TREATY. Effectively the US acquired naval supremacy in the Caribbean and policing powers on the major searoute between the Atlantic and Pacific Oceans. It also brought about the American construction of the PANAMA CANAL.

HAYS, Arthur Garfield (1881–1954), US lawyer, famous for his powerful defense in the SCOPES TRIAL in Tenn. (1925) and for the SACCO-VANZETTI CASE of 1927. From 1923, Hays was associated with the AMERICAN CIVIL LIBERTIES UNION.

HAYS, Will (William Harrison Hays; 1879–1954), US politician, president (1922–43) of the Motion Pictures Producers and Distributors of America, in which role he imposed a code of morality (the "Hays code") on the movies that assured their wide acceptance.

HAYWOOD, William Dudley (1869–1928), US labor leader and principal organizer of the INDUSTRIAL WORKERS OF THE WORLD (1905). His membership in the Socialist party ended with expulsion because of his advocacy of sabotage and violence. In WWI he was convicted of sedition but escaped to Russia in 1921.

HAZLITT, William (1778–1830), one of England's greatest literary critics and essayists. His perceptive and sympathetic observations of culture, politics and English manners appeared in *Characters of Shakespeare's Plays* (1817) and *Lectures on the English Comic Writers* (1819). His wit and versatility are reflected in the miscellaneous essays of *Table Talk* (1821–22) and *The Spirit of The Age* (1825).

H.D. See DOOLITTLE, HILDA.

HEADACHE, the common symptom of an ache or pain affecting the head or neck, with many possible causes including FEVER, emotional tension (with spasm of neck MUSCLES) or nasal SINUS infection. **Migraine,** due to abnormal reactivity of blood vessels, is typified by zig-zag or flashing visual sensations or tingling in part of the body, followed by an often one-sided severe throbbing headache. This may be accompanied by nausea, vomiting and sensitivity to light. There is often a family history. **Meningeal inflammation,** as in MENINGITIS and subarachnoid HEMORRHAGE, may also cause severe headache. The headache of raised intracranial pressure is often worse on waking and on coughing and may be a symptom of brain TUMOR, ABSCESS or HYDROCEPHALUS. Headaches are often controlled by simple ANALGESICS, while migraine may need drugs that act on blood vessels (e.g., ERGOT derivatives).

HEAD START, US government program, set up in 1964 by the Economic Opportunity Act, to prepare "culturally deprived" children of preschool age for school, and to involve parents and local communities in the effort. The "Head Start" program was so popular that "Follow Through" programs for children in kindergarten were added in 1967.

HEALTH AND HUMAN SERVICES, US Department of (HHS), executive department established 1939 as the Federal

Security Agency and reestablished 1953 as the Department of Health, Education and Welfare. It was designated the Department of Health and Human Services in 1979, when the Office of Education became a new department. As the second-largest federal department (after the Department of Defense), HHS is responsible for over 300 federal health and human service programs, including the Offices of Human Developmental Services, Public Health Service, Social Security Administration and Child Support Enforcement.

HEALTH MAINTENANCE ORGANIZATION (HMO), prepaid group medical practice, devised as a strategy to control the rising cost of medical care. Private medical insurance, as well as MEDICARE and MEDICAID, adhere to the fee-for-service model in which the insurer pays the physician and hospital for whatever medical services they provide, thereby encouraging overutilization of medical resources. Although HMOs differ widely, their common feature is that, for an annual premium, the subscriber and his family receive as much medical care as they need. The cost advantage of HMOs lies in their emphasis on preventive care and the absence of any financial incentive to prescribe unnecessary procedures or hospitalization. Although HMOs' costs have risen more slowly than those of insurance companies, HMOs have not been dramatically successful in curbing medical-cost inflation.

HEARN, Lafcadio (1850–1904), US writer of Irish-Greek origin. His move to Japan in 1890 and naturalization as a Japanese citizen brought about his best work: *In Ghostly Japan* (1899), *Shadowings* (1900), *Kwaidan* (1904) and *Japan: An Attempt at Interpretation* (1904).

HEARNE, Samuel (1745–1792), English explorer and fur trader. In 1770 he led an expedition which traced the Coppermine R to the Arctic Ocean. Subsequently he discovered that a short NORTHWEST PASSAGE did not exist.

HEARST, William Randolph (1863–1951), US publisher, head of a vast newspaper empire. His early success as a newspaper publisher in "yellow journalism" was largely due to his papers' sensationalism, low prices, the introduction of color cartoons, banner headlines and Sunday supplements. In 1895 he bought the New York *Journal* and engaged in an epic circulation war with Joseph PULITZER's *World*. Both were accused of having helped to bring on the 1898 war with Spain to increase circulation. He also pursued a largely unsuccessful political career.

HEART, vital organ in the chest of animals, concerned with pumping the BLOOD, thus maintaining the BLOOD CIRCULATION. The evolution of the vertebrates shows a development from the simple heart found in fish to the four-chambered heart of mammals. In man, the circulation may be regarded as a figure-eight, with the heart at the cross-over point, but keeping the two systems separate by having two parallel sets of chambers. The pumping in the two sets, right and left, is coordinated, ensuring a balance of flow. Each set consists of an atrium, which receives blood from the LUNGS (left) or body (right), and a ventricle. The atria pump blood into the ventricles, which pump it into the lungs (right) or systemic circulation (left). The bulk of the heart consists of specialized MUSCLE fibers which contract in response to stimulation from a pacemaker region relayed via special conducting tissue. Between each atrium and ventricle are valves, the mitral (left) and tricuspid (right). Similarly, between the ventricles and their outflow tracts are aortic and pulmonary valves. The heart is lined by pericardium and receives its blood supply from the AORTA via the coronary ARTERIES. The cells in the right atrium have an inbuilt tendency to depolarize and thus to set up an electrical impulse in the conducting tissue. In **heart action** this passes to both atria, which have already filled with blood from the systemic or pulmonary veins. Blood is then pumped by atrial contraction into the ventricles, though much of it passes into the latter before the atria contract. The same electrical impulse is conducted to both ventricles and there sets up a coordinated contraction (*systole*), which leads to the forceful expulsion of blood into the aorta or pulmonary artery and to the closure of the mitral and tricuspid valves. When the contraction ceases (*diastole*), the pressure in the ventricle falls, and the aortic and pulmonary valves close. The force generated by systole is propagated into the major arteries, providing the driving force for the circulation. Heart output may be increased (e.g., in EXERCISE) through several agencies including increased rate (*tachycardia*) and force of contraction (mediated by the sympathetic NERVOUS SYSTEM and ADRENALINE), and the increased return of venous blood (effected by a muscle pumping action on the valved, collapsible VEINS). **Disorders of the heart** include: *Congenital disorders* of the structure of the chambers or valves (e.g., BLUE BABY), and disease following RHEUMATIC FEVER, leading to stenosis or incompetence of the valves, especially the mitral and aortic. These disorders may be improved by DRUG treatment, but they frequently require cardiac SURGERY to correct or repair defects or to insert PROSTHETICS (e.g., artificial heart valves). Coronary thrombosis causes DEATH or injury to areas of heart muscle. This may lead to defects in pumping and heart failure, rhythm disorder, ANEURYSM or, rarely, cardiac rupture. *Rhythm disturbance* may follow damage to conducting tissue (where abnormal conducting or pacemaker tissue exists), in certain metabolic disorders (thyrotoxicosis—see THYROID GLAND), and in valve disease. *Bradycardia* is very slow heart rate. This may be due to disease but can be normal in fit athletes in whom it indicates increased heart efficiency. Rhythm disorders are often treated with drugs including DIGITALIS, sympathetic-nervous-system stimulants or blockers, atropine, and certain agents used in local ANESTHESIA. *Heart failure*, in which inadequate pumping leads to imbalance between the two parts of the circulation or the failure of both, may be due to coronary thrombosis, cardiac muscle disease or fluid overload. It causes pulmonary EDEMA with shortness of breath on exercise or on lying flat, or peripheral edema. DIURETICS and digitalis are the cornerstones of treatment, relieving edema and increasing pump efficacy. *Infection of abnormal valves* with BACTERIA or FUNGI is a serious disease causing FEVER and other systemic manifestations including EMBOLISM, heart failure and valve destruction. Its prevention, in high-risk patients, and treatment involve careful use of selected ANTIBIOTICS. Valve replacement may also be needed. Investigation of the heart can involve the use of the ELECTROCARDIOGRAPH, chest X-RAY or cardiac CATHETER (to study ANATOMY and flow) and the study of serum ENZYME levels.

HEART, Artificial, mechanical device used to replace or temporarily sustain a diseased human heart. The first artificial heart to replace a human heart was the Jarvik-7, invented by Dr. Robert Jarvik of the U of Utah Medical Center. A plastic and metal pump implanted in the patient's chest, it was operated by compressed air supplied through tubes in the patient's abdomen from an external pump and monitoring console about the size of a small refrigerator. Between 1982 and 1985 the Jarvik-7 was implanted in four patients; the longest survival was 620 days. The patients experienced infections, kidney failure, excessive bleeding, clots, fever, and strokes. Many experts concluded that the Jarvik-7 should be used only as a "bridge" to sustain

the patient until a donor heart was available for transplantation. Meanwhile, smaller, permanently implanted pumps are being developed to boost the action of a failing heart rather than replace it altogether. These are currently powered by external energy sources.

HEART ATTACK. See CORONARY THROMBOSIS.

HEARTBURN, or esophagitis, burning sensation of "indigestion" localized centrally in the upper ABDOMEN or lower chest. It is frequently worse after large meals or on lying flat, especially with hiatus HERNIA. Acid STOMACH contents irritate the esophageal EPITHELIUM and may lead to ULCER; relief is with ANTACIDS. Heartburn is also losely applied to other pains in the same situation.

HEART MURMUR, abnormal sound heard on listening to the chest over the HEART with a STETHOSCOPE. Normally there are two major heart sounds due to valve closure, separated by silence. Murmurs arise in the disease of heart valves, with narrowing (stenosis) or leakage (incompetence). Holes between chambers, valve roughening and high flow also cause murmurs.

HEAT, the form of ENERGY that passes from one body to another owing to a TEMPERATURE difference between them; one of the basic functions in THERMODYNAMICS. The energy residing in a hot body is also loosely called heat, but is better termed internal energy, since it takes several different forms. Despite an earlier view by some philosophers that heat was a form of agitation, in the 18th century the CALORIC THEORY OF HEAT predominated, until disproved by the experiments of Sir Humphry DAVY and Count RUMFORD (1798) showing that mechanical work could be converted to heat. James JOULE confirmed this by many ingenious experiments and found a consistent value for the **mechanical equivalent of heat** (the ratio of work done to heat produced). In the mid-18th century Joseph BLACK first clearly distinguished heat from temperature, a conceptual advance which allowed heat to be measured in terms of the temperature rise of a known mass of water, the unit being the CALORIE (or the British Thermal Unit). In SI UNITS heat is measured, as a form of energy, in joules. A given mass m of any substance shows a characteristic temperature rise θ when an amount of heat Q is supplied: $Q=ms\theta$ where s is the specific heat of the substance. If the substance changes its state, however, by melting, freezing, boiling or condensing, latent heat is absorbed or produced without any temperature change, the internal energy being changed by altering the molecular interrelations, not merely their degree of motion. Heat is commonly produced as required for space heating or to power ENGINES, by conversion of chemical energy (burning fuel—see COMBUSTION), electrical energy or nuclear energy. There are three processes by which heat flows from a hotter to a cooler body: CONDUCTION and CONVECTION, in which molecular motion is transferred, and radiation, in which INFRARED RADIATION is emitted and propagates through space. Heat transfer may be hindered by means of thermal insulation. NEWTON's law of cooling states that the rate of loss of heat by a body in a draft (forced convection) is proportional to its temperature difference from its surroundings.

HEATH, Edward Richard George (1916–   ), British prime minister 1970–74. He was elected to parliament in 1950, and became Conservative Party leader in 1965. As prime minister, he brought Britain into the Common Market. He employed austerity measures to fight inflation and resorted to a 3-day work week to save fuel during a miners' strike. In 1975, a year after being turned out of office, he resigned as party leader.

HEAVEN, the celestial regions in which the heavenly bodies—sun, moon, stars and planets—exist; the abode of God, angels and the righteous after death. These two concepts have been progressively differentiated, especially since the 16th-century scientific revolution made the three-decker universe archaic. In the Old Testament, God, who dwells in heaven, also transcends it. Not until late Judaism was heaven generally regarded as the abode of the righteous; the dead were previously believed to have a shadowy existence in *sheol*. In Christian thought, heaven is the eternal home of true believers, or the state of living in full union with Christ, which the perfected soul enters after death—or, in Roman Catholic doctrine, after PURGATORY—there "to glorify God, and to enjoy him for ever," an experience sometimes known as the beatific vision. In Islam likewise heaven is the joyful dwelling-place of faithful Muslims after death. Similar concepts are found in some other religions. (See also ASCENSION; ESCHATOLOGY; HELL; RESURRECTION.)

HEAVISIDE, Oliver (1850–1925), British physicist and electrical engineer best known for his work in telegraphy, in course of which he developed operational calculus, a new mathematical system for dealing with changing wave-shapes. In 1902, shortly after A. E. Kennelly, he proposed that a layer of the atmosphere was responsible for reflecting RADIO waves back to earth. This, the E layer of the IONOSPHERE, was found by E. V. Appleton and others (1924), and is often called the **Kennelly-Heaviside Layer,** or **Heaviside Layer.**

HEAVY WATER, or deuterium oxide (D_2O), occurs as 0.014% of ordinary WATER, which it closely resembles. It is used as a moderator in nuclear reactors and as a source of deuterium and its compounds. It is toxic in high concentrations. Water containing tritium or heavy isotopes of oxygen (O^{17} and O^{18}) is also called heavy water; mp 3.8°C, bp 101.4°C.

HÉBERT, Jacques René (1757–1794), French political journalist in the French Revolution. Through his newspaper *Le Père Duchesne* he roused the extremist sansculottes and was prominent in the REIGN OF TERROR. He was executed in March 1794.

HEBREW, the Semitic language in which the Old Testament was written and which is now the official language of Israel. The earliest extant Hebrew writings date from at least the 11th century BC, since when there has been a continuous Hebrew literature. Hebrew is now a sacred tongue and a common written language for religious Jews of all nationalities. Hebrew died out as a spoken language by the 3rd century BC. It was revived as the language of the modern Jewish nation, largely owing to Eliezer Ben Jehudah, who compiled a Hebrew dictionary in the 19th century. Hebrew script, written from right to left, was influenced by ARAMAIC, and adopted the square letters still used in writing Hebrew.

HEBREWS, Epistle to the, a NEW TESTAMENT book of unknown authorship, though traditionally ascribed to Paul. Addressed to Jewish converts to Christianity who were in danger of apostasy, it explains the fulfillment in Christ of the Old Testament.

HEBRIDES, or Western Islands, a group of about 500 islands off the NW coast of Scotland, fewer than 100 of them inhabited. The Outer Hebrides include Harris, Lewis, North and South Uist, Benbecula and Barra, while Skye, Mull and Iona lie among the Inner Hebrides. Apart from tourism, industries include fishing, farming, sheep-raising, distilling, quarrying and tweed-making.

HECHT, Ben (1894–1964), US dramatist, short story writer and novelist. After working as a journalist he collaborated with Charles MacArthur on the highly successful plays *The Front Page* (1928), and

Twentieth Century (1932). He also worked on the filmscripts of *Gunga Din* (1938), *Wuthering Heights* (1939) and *Notorious* (1946). His autobiography is *A Child of the Century* (1954).

HECKER, Isaac Thomas (1819–1888), US Roman Catholic priest, founder in 1858 of the PAULIST FATHERS, an order dedicated to the conversion of American non-Catholics. To this end Hecker lectured widely, and established the *Catholic World* and the Catholic Publication Society for the distribution of Catholic literature.

HEDGEHOGS, small, spine-covered insectivores of Asia, Africa and Europe. The Eurasian species is the common hedgehog, *Erinaceus europaeus*. Nocturnal mammals, they wander about searching the ground for worms, beetles and slugs. Each spine is a modified hair about 25mm (1in) long. Hedgehogs are able to roll up for protection against predators, and become entirely enclosed by the spiny part of the skin.

HEDONISM, a philosophical theory which regards pleasure as the ultimate good for man. The view of the CYRENAICS and Aristippus was that the sentient pleasure of the moment was the only good. EPICURUS thought man's aim should be a life of lasting pleasure best attained by the guidance of reason. The 19th-century theory of UTILITARIANISM, for "the greatest good of the greatest number," was a revival of hedonism. Hedonism has often been attacked, for instance by Joseph Butler who saw pleasure as a bonus when a desire is fulfilled, not as an end in itself.

HEGEL, Georg Wilhelm Friedrich (1770–1831), German philosopher of IDEALISM who had an immense influence on 19th and 20th-century thought and history. During his life he was famous for his professorial lectures at the University of Berlin and he wrote on logic, ethics, history, religion and aesthetics. The main feature of Hegel's philosophy was the dialectical method by which an idea (*thesis*) was challenged by its opposite (*antithesis*) and the two ultimately reconciled in a third idea (*synthesis*) which subsumed both. Hegel found this method both in the workings of the mind, as a logical procedure, and in the workings of the history of the world, which to Hegel was the process of the development and realization of the World Spirit (*Weltgeist*). Hegel's chief works were *Phenomenology of the Mind* (1807) and *Philosophy of Right* (1821). His most important follower was MARX.

HEGIRA, the flight of MOHAMMED from Mecca to Medina in 622 AD, which is the year from which Muslims date their calendar.

HEIDEGGER, Martin (1889–1976), German philosopher. Influenced by KIERKEGAARD and HUSSERL, he was concerned with the problem of how man's awareness of himself is dependent on a sense of time and his impending death. Heidegger rejects traditional metaphysics and criticizes many aspects of modern technological and mass culture as a "forgetfulness of being." His major work *Being and Time* (1927) has been fundamental in the development of existentialism, although Heidegger denied he was an existentialist. (See also EXISTENTIALISM; PHENOMENOLOGY.)

HEIDELBERG, historic city in West Germany, in Baden-Württemberg on the Neckar R. Overlooking the city is the ruined castle of the former Electors of the Palatinate. Heidelberg has the oldest German university (1386). The city is European headquarters of the US army. Pop 134,724.

HEIFETZ, Jascha (1901–1987), Russian-born US violinist. He was a child prodigy, giving concerts by 1911, and his virtuosity and technique have been compared to those of PAGANINI. He has transcribed many works for the violin and made many recordings.

HEINE, Heinrich (1797–1856), German romantic lyric poet and essayist. His best-known work, *Book of Songs* (1827), was influenced by German folk songs. His prose writings such as *Travel Pictures* (1827–31), although poignant, were often very satirical. His poems have been set to music by such composers as SCHUMANN, SCHUBERT and MENDELSSOHN.

HEINKEL, Ernst Heinrich (1888–1958), German aircraft designer of the first jet airplane (He 178) to fly, in 1939, and of rocket-propelled airplanes. After WWII he designed mass-produced motor scooters.

HEINLEIN, Robert Anson (1907–1988), prolific US writer of science fiction, including *A Stranger in a Strange Land* (1961).

HEISENBERG, Werner Karl (1901–1976), German mathematical physicist generally regarded as the father of QUANTUM MECHANICS, born out of his rejection of any kind of model of the ATOM and use of mathematical matrices to elucidate its properties. His famous UNCERTAINTY PRINCIPLE (1927) overturned traditional physics.

HEISMAN TROPHY, the John W. Heisman Memorial Trophy, awarded annually since 1935 to the best college football player. It is most often bestowed on a running back.

HEJAZ, NW province in Saudi Arabia, on the E coast of the Red Sea, the holy land of Islam. The cities of MECCA and MEDINA are the most important Muslim pilgrimage sites. Saudi Arabia annexed Hejaz in 1924.

HELD, John Jr. (1889–1958), US cartoonist and illustrator who captured the mood of the 1920s with his famous line drawings of bobbed-haired flappers and their raccoon-coated escorts. His work appeared frequently in such sophisticated magazines as *The New Yorker, Smart Set* and *Vanity Fair.*

HELEN OF TROY, the most beautiful of all women, according to Greek mythology. Daughter of ZEUS and Leda, she was wife of Menelaus, king of Sparta, from whom Paris abducted her to Troy, thus provoking the TROJAN WAR. After the war she returned to Greece with Menelaus.

HELICOPTER, exceptionally maneuverable aircraft able to take off and land vertically, hover, and fly in any horizontal direction without necessarily changing the alignment of the aircraft. Lift is provided by one or more rotors mounted above the craft and rotating horizontally about a vertical axis. Change in the speed of rotation or in the pitch (angle of attack) of all the blades at once alters the amount of lift; cyclic change in the pitch of each blade during its rotation alters the direction of thrust. Most helicopters have only a single lift rotor, and thus have also a tail-mounted vertical rotor to prevent the craft from spinning around; change in the speed of this rotor is used to change the craft's heading.

Helicopter toys were known to the Chinese and in medieval Europe, but, because of problems with stability, it was not until 1939, following the success of the autogiro (1923), that the first fully successful helicopter flight was achieved by SIKORSKY. Used in combat in Vietnam, the helicopter has become increasingly important in military use. It has given ground forces entree to areas hitherto inaccessible. Its firepower and maneuverability permit close air support of ground forces. Its extreme mobility allows evasive action and the potential to surprise the enemy. Its capacity to hover makes it a relatively stable weapons platform.

In civilian use, helicopters have proved valuable for city-to-airport and city-to-suburb transportation and for such uses as monitoring traffic, spotting forest fires, patrolling pipelines, and rescue work. (See also AERODYNAMICS.)

HELIOGABALUS, or **Elagabalus** (c205–222 AD), Roman emperor with the imperial name Marcus Aurelius Antoninus (reigned 218–222). He outraged Rome by his corrupt homosexual favoritism and by the indecent rites offered to Elagabalus, a Syrian sun-god.

HÉLION, Jean (1904–1987), French painter, an influential abstractionist in the 1930s who turned to representational painting after WWII.

HELIOPOLIS (city of the sun), one of the most important cities of ancient Egypt. Sited at the apex of the Nile Delta, it was the center of worship of the sun god RA, pharaohs being known as the "sons of Ra."

HELIUM (He), one of the NOBLE GASES, lighter than all other elements except hydrogen. It is a major constituent of the SUN and other STARS. The main source of helium is natural gas in Tex., Okla. and Kan. Alpha particles are helium nuclei. Helium is lighter than air and nonflammable, so is used in balloons and airships. It is also used in breathing mixtures for deep-sea divers, as a pressurizer for the fuel tanks of liquid-fueled rockets, in helium-neon LASERS, and to form an inert atmosphere for welding. Liquid helium He^4 has two forms. Helium I, stable from 2.19K to 4.22K, is a normal liquid, used as a refrigerant (see CRYOGENICS; SUPERCONDUCTIVITY). Below 2.18K it becomes helium II, which is a superfluid with no viscosity (the ability to flow as a film over the side of a vessel in which it is placed) and with other strange properties explained by QUANTUM THEORY. He^3 does not form a superfluid. Solid helium can be produced only at pressures above 25atm. AW 4.0, mp 1.1K (25atm), bp 4.22K.

HELL, the abode of evil spirits (see DEVIL) and of the wicked after death, usually thought of as an underworld or abyss. In many ancient religions hell is merely the dark, shadowy abode of the dead—Hades or its equivalent—and the word is so used when Christ is said to have descended into hell. Zoroastrianism and many Eastern religions saw it as a place of chastisement and purification, resembling the Roman Catholic PURGATORY. In later Judaism, Christianity and Islam, hell is the place of eternal punishment of unrepentant sinners condemned at the LAST JUDGMENT. The New Testament describes hell (or Gehenna) as a place of corruption and unquenchable fire and brimstone—images which have often been taken literally. Modern theology usually regards hell as ultimate separation from God, the confirmation of the sinner's own choice. Many Christians deny the eternity or the existence of hell (see UNIVERSALISM).

HELLENISTIC AGE, the period in which

Greco-Macedonian culture spread through the lands conquered by Alexander the Great. It is generally accepted to run from Alexander's death (323 BC) to the annexation of the last Hellenistic state, Egypt, by Rome (31 BC) and the death of Cleopatra VII, last of the Ptolemies (30 BC). After Alexander's death, and despite the temporary restraint imposed by Antipater, his empire was split by constant warring between rival generals eager for a share of the territory. Even after the accomplishment of the final divisions (Egypt, Syria and Mesopotamia, Macedonia, the Aetolian and Achaean Leagues in Greece, Rhodes and Pergamum), Greek remained the international language throughout most of the known world and a commercial and cultural unity held sway. The age was marked by cosmopolitanism, sharply contrasting with the parochialism of the earlier Greek era, and by advances in the sciences (see ARCHIMEDES; ARISTARCHUS; EUCLID; THEOPHRASTUS). The art was powerfully naturalistic if occasionally bathetic. Traditional religious cults weakened and were superseded by others either imported from the east or increasing in influence; such as the cults of Isis, Sarapis, Cybele and Mithras. The Hellenistic age saw the emergence of Stoicism (see ZENO) and Epicureanism (see EPICURUS).

HELLER, Joseph (1923–   ), US novelist and playwright best known for *Catch-22* (1961), a grotesquely humorous novel about an American bombadier's "deep-seated survival anxieties" during WWII. Other satiric works include the play *We Bombed in New Haven* (1967) and the novel *God Knows* (1984).

HELLESPONT, ancient name for the DARDANELLES, the strait separating Asia Minor from Europe, named for the legendary Helle, who was drowned here fleeing to Colchis with her brother Phrixus.

HELLMAN, Lillian (1905–1984), US playwright, screenwriter, and autobiographer. A mordant social critic, she wrote plays, such as *The Children's Hour* (1934), *The Little Foxes* (1939) and *Watch on the Rhine* (1941), that studied the evil effects of ruthless ambition and exploitation in personal, social and political situations. Her books of reminiscences, such as *An Unfinished Woman* (1969, National Book Award 1970) and *Scoundrel Time* (1976), are fascinating for their portraits of famous people and events.

HELLS CANYON, also **Grand Canyon of the Snake**, gorge of the Snake R on the Ida.–Ore. boundary. At a depth of 7,900ft it is the deepest in North America. An area of great natural beauty, it extends for 40 mi.

HELMHOLTZ, Hermann Ludwig Ferdinand von (1821–1894), German physiologist and physicist. In the course of his physiological studies he formulated the law of conservation of ENERGY (1847), one of the first to do so. He was the first to measure the speed of nerve impulses (see NERVOUS SYSTEM), and invented the ophthalmoscope (both 1850). He also made important contributions to the study of ELECTRICITY and NON-EUCLIDEAN GEOMETRY.

HELMONT, Jan Baptista van (1580–1644), Flemish chemist and physician, regarded as the father of biochemistry. He was the first to discover that there were airlike substances distinct from air, and first used the name "gas" for them.

HÉLOÏSE. See ABÉLARD, PETER.

HELPER, Hinton Rowan (1829–1909), US racialist author from the South. In his *The Impending Crisis in the South and How to Meet It* (1857), he attacked slavery on economic rather than moral grounds; the resulting furor in the heated atmosphere of the pre-Civil War South forced him to move to the North. He eventually committed suicide.

HELSINKI, capital of Finland, situated on a rocky peninsula. Called "white city of the north" because much of it is built of local white granite, it is Finland's chief industrial center and seaport. Its main industries are shipbuilding, foundries, textiles and paper and machinery manufacture. Chief exports are timber, pulp and metal goods. Founded by Swedish king Gustavus Vasa in 1550, its Swedish name is Helsingfors. Pop (city) 485,029; (metro) 948,361.

HELSINKI ACCORDS. On Aug. 1, 1975, the US, Canada, the USSR and 35 European countries signed this document as the final act of the Conference on Security and Cooperation in Europe that began in 1972. Though nonbinding, it outlines a broad basis for peaceful relations in Europe. It includes the promise to give 21 days notice of military maneuvers by more than 25,000 men by either the East or West bloc, respect for human rights and recognition of existing European frontiers. Each side later accused the other of violating these accords. In Sept. 1983, nonetheless, 35 foreign ministers met in Madrid to mark the end of three years of negotiations on a document to augment the 1975 accords.

HELVETIUS, Claude Adrien (1715–1771), French philosopher and Encyclopedist whose *The Mind* (1758), considered godless, caused a furor in France. He was attacked by his fellow

Encyclopedists, VOLTAIRE and ROUSSEAU, but his work later influenced UTILITARIANISM.

HEMINGWAY, Ernest (1899–1961), influential US novelist and short story writer whose terse prose style was widely emulated. His first major novel, *The Sun Also Rises* (1926), chronicled the postwar experiences of what his friend Gertrude STEIN called the "lost generation" of WWI. *A Farewell to Arms* (1929) and *For Whom the Bell Tolls* (1940) were based on his own experiences in WWI and the Spanish Civil War respectively and added greatly to his reputation as a writer. *The Old Man and the Sea* (1952) won a 1953 Pulitzer Prize and he won the Nobel Prize for Literature the next year. Increasingly depressed and ill in later years, he committed suicide.

HEMLOCK, various herbs of the parsley family, Umbelliferae. They produce poisonous ALKALOIDS, used in ancient Greece to put condemned prisoners to death.

HEMLOCK, popular name for evergreen conifers of the genus *Tsuga* from the pine family, Pinaceae. They are native to North America, the Himalayas and E Asia. The western hemlock (*Tsuga heterophylla*) is an important source of lumber in the US, primarily in Ore. and Wash.

HEMOGLOBIN, respiratory pigment found in the BLOOD of many animals including man. It contains heme, an iron-containing molecule, and globin, a large protein, and occurs in red blood cells. The whole molecule has a high affinity for oxygen, being converted to oxyhemoglobin. In the LUNG capillaries, hemoglobin is exposed to a high oxygen concentration and oxygen is taken up. The redder blood then passes via the HEART into the systemic circulation. In the tissues the oxygen concentration is low, so oxygen is released from the erythrocytes and reduced hemoglobin returns to the lungs. Carbon monoxide has an even higher affinity for hemoglobin than oxygen and thus acts as a poison by displacing oxygen from hemoglobin, causing anoxia. Abnormal hemoglobin structures occur in certain races and may cause red-cell destruction and anemia. Lack of hemoglobin, regardless of cause, produces ANEMIA.

HEMOPHILIA, inherited disorder of CLOTTING in males, carried by females who do not suffer from the disease. It consists of inability to form adequate amounts of a clotting factor (VIII) essential for the conversion of soluble fibrinogen in blood to form fibrin. Prolonged bleeding from wounds or tooth extractions, HEMORRHAGE into joints and MUSCLES with severe pain are important symptoms. Bleeding can be stopped by giving PLASMA concentrates rich in factor VIII and, if necessary, BLOOD TRANSFUSION. Similar diseases of both sexes are **Christmas disease** (due to lack of factor IX) and **von Willebrand's disease** (factor VIII deficiency with additional CAPILLARY defect).

HEMORRHAGE, acute loss of BLOOD from any site. Trauma to major ARTERIES, VEINS or the HEART may lead to massive hemorrhage. GASTROINTESTINAL TRACT hemorrhage is usually accompanied by loss of altered blood in vomit or feces and may lead to SHOCK; ULCERS and CANCER of the bowel are important causes. **Antepartum hemorrhage** is blood loss from the WOMB in late PREGNANCY and may rapidly threaten life of both mother and FETUS; **postpartum hemorrhage** is excessive blood loss after BIRTH due to inadequate womb contraction or retained placenta. STROKE due to BRAIN hemorrhage may damage vital structures and cause COMA, while *subarachnoid bleeding* around the brain from ANEURYSM or malformation causes severe HEADACHE. FRACTURES may cause sizeable hemorrhage into soft tissues. Blood loss may be replaced by TRANSFUSION, and any blood clots may need to be removed.

HEMORRHOIDS, or **piles**, enlarged VEINS at the junction of the rectum and anus, which may bleed or come down through the anal canal, usually on defecation, and which are made worse by CONSTIPATION and straining. Sentinal pile is a SKIN tag at the anus. Bleeding from the rectum may be a sign of bowel CANCER and this may need to be ruled out before bleeding is attributed to piles.

HEMP, *Cannabis sativa*, tall herbaceous plant native to Asia, but now widely cultivated for fiber, oil and a narcotic drug called **cannabis**, HASHISH or MARIJUANA. The fibers are used in the manufacture of rope. They are separated from the rest of the plant by a process called retting (soaking), during which BACTERIA and FUNGI rot away all but the fibers, which are then combed out. Hemp oil obtained from the seed is used in the manufacture of paints, varnishes and SOAPS. (See also DRUGS.)

HENDERSON, Arthur (1863–1935), British Labour Party politician and trade unionist who held various cabinet posts 1916–17 and 1924–31. He was awarded the Nobel Peace Prize in 1934 for his work for collective security and disarmament.

HENDERSON, (James) Fletcher (1898–1952), US jazz pianist, leader of jazz orchestras in New York City in the 1920s and 1930s. Considered the creator of "swing," he wrote arrangements for the

Dorsey brothers and Benny Goodman.

HENGIST AND HORSA, two brothers who apparently led a group of Saxon mercenaries invited to settle in Kent by the British king Vortigern c446 AD. Six years later they turned on him and captured Kent. Horsa was killed and Hengist became the first Anglo-Saxon king of Kent.

HENIE, Sonja (1912–1969), Norwegian-US figure skater, winner of ten consecutive world amateur titles (1927–36) and three Olympic gold medals (1928, 1932, 1936). Thereafter she appeared in films and ice revues.

HENLEY ROYAL REGATTA, the oldest major event in rowing. It was begun in 1839 at Henley-on-Thames, England, and is now held annually over four days in early July. The eight oars and single scullers cups are the most coveted awards in rowing.

HENNEPIN, Louis (1640–1701?), Belgian Franciscan missionary and explorer. He went to Quebec (c1675) as chaplain to LA SALLE and joined his 1679 expedition. Captured but well treated by Sioux Indians, he was rescued in 1680. His exaggerated accounts of his travels were very popular.

HENRI, Robert (1865–1929), US painter and art teacher, founder of the ASHCAN SCHOOL of realistic painters. He studied and traveled in Europe 1888–1900, then taught in New York, where he organized the 1908 exhibition of the Eight and the 1910 Independent Artists Exhibition.

HENRY, name of seven kings of Germany, six of whom were also Holy Roman emperors. **Henry I** (c876–936), reigned 919–36, known as Henry the Fowler. He established Germany as a new kingdom. **Henry II** (973–1024), reigned 1002–24, emperor from 1014. By political astuteness he ensured secular and clerical support. Canonized in 1146, his feast day is July 15th. **Henry III** (1017–1056), reigned 1039–56, emperor 1046–56. During his reign the Holy Roman Empire was probably at its greatest power and unity. He carried out important papal reforms. **Henry IV** (1050–1106), reigned 1056–1105 and emperor 1084–1105. He deposed Pope Gregory VII, but Gregory excommunicated him and Henry yielded to papal authority at Canossa in Italy in 1077. Gregory then supported a rival king of Germany, and Henry replaced him with the antipope Clement III. He captured Rome in 1084 and was crowned emperor. After two sons rebelled against him he was forced to abdicate in favor of his son, Henry V. **Henry V** (1081–1125), reigned 1105–25, emperor 1111–25. He unified Germany and continued Henry IV's struggle against the

papacy. **Henry VI** (1165–1197), reigned 1190–97 and was emperor from 1191. He was made king of Sicily in 1194; he died before being able to implement plans to invade the Holy Land. **Henry VII** (c1275–1313), reigned 1308–13, emperor from 1312. He invaded Italy in 1310 in an abortive attempt to make it the base of imperial power.

HENRY, name of eight kings of England. **Henry I** (1068–1135), reigned 1100–35. Son of William I, he seized the English throne on the death of his brother William II and became Duke of Normandy in 1106. **Henry II** (1133–1189), reigned 1154–89, the first of the ANGEVIN kings. By marrying Eleanor, Duchess of Aquitaine in 1152, he acquired vast lands in France. His policy of establishing royal authority in England led to Thomas à BECKET's murder. Henry made many legal and judicial reforms. **Henry III** (1207–1272), reigned 1216–72. His unpopular rule was marked by administrative and diplomatic incompetence and by the revolts of nobles who forced him to yield power to them. **Henry IV** (1366–1413), reigned 1399–1413, known as Henry of Bolingbroke, the first ruler of the House of LANCASTER. He usurped the throne after forcing Richard II to abdicate. His reign was marked by struggles with Owen GLENDOWER and Sir Henry Percy. **Henry V** (1387–1422), reigned from 1413, son of Henry IV. He defeated the French at AGINCOURT in 1415, married Catherine of Valois and became successor to the French throne. He established civil order in England and was a great popular hero. **Henry VI** (1421–1471), reigned 1422–61 and 1470–71. A weak, unstable ruler, he was frequently dominated by factions, and this led to the dynastic Wars of the ROSES. He was deposed for nine years, and finally murdered. **Henry VII** (1457–1509), reigned 1485–1509, the first of the TUDOR rulers. He killed Richard III in the last battle of the Wars of the ROSES and united the houses of LANCASTER and YORK by marrying Elizabeth of York. He restored order to England and Wales, and promoted efficient administration. **Henry VIII** (1491–1547), son of Henry VII, reigned 1509–47, one of the most powerful and formative rulers in British history. His religious policies led to the Act of Supremacy (1534) in which Parliament renounced papal authority and established the Church of England with the king as supreme head. He replaced feudal authority with a central system of government, albeit despotic at times, and he created a navy which was to become the basis of British power for centuries to come. His matrimonial problems arose originally from his search for a male heir; he was married successively to CATHERINE OF ARAGON, whom he divorced for Anne BOLEYN (mother of ELIZABETH I) whom he beheaded, Jane SEYMOUR (mother of Edward VI), ANNE OF CLEVES (divorced within a year), Catherine HOWARD (beheaded) and Catherine PARR, who survived him.

HENRY, name of four kings of France. **Henry I** (c1008–1060), reigned 1031–60. His rule was disturbed by feudal conflicts organized by his mother and brother. One of his chief enemies was the future William I of England. **Henry II** (1519–1559), reigned 1547–59. In 1533 he married Catherine de Médici, but he was dominated by his mistress Diane de Poitiers and his military commander, the Duc de Montmorency. A fanatic Catholic, he persecuted the HUGUENOTS and continued the war against the Holy Roman Emperor and Spain. **Henry III** (1551–1589), reigned 1574–89. He collaborated with his mother Catherine de Médici in the SAINT BARTHOLOMEW'S DAY MASSACRE (1572). He was dominated by the Guise family, and his reign was unstable. He was assassinated by a Jacobin friar. **Henry IV** (1553–1610), reigned 1589–1610, king of Navarre 1572–1610, the first French BOURBON king. A Protestant leader of the Huguenots, he converted to Roman Catholicism in 1593, granting religious freedom with the Edict of NANTES (1598). He brought unity and economic stability to France, but was assassinated by a Catholic extremist.

HENRY, Joseph (1797–1878), US physicist best known for his electromagnetic studies. His discoveries include INDUCTION and self-induction, though in both cases FARADAY published first. He also devised a much improved ELECTROMAGNET by insulating the wire rather than the core; invented one of the first ELECTRIC MOTORS; helped MORSE and Wheatstone devise their telegraphs; and found SUNSPOTS to be cooler than the surrounding photosphere.

HENRY, O. (1862–1910), pseudonym of William Sidney Porter, US short story writer noted for the "surprise ending." He began writing stories while imprisoned in Ohio for embezzlement, and was already popular when released. He moved to New York City in 1902, and wrote over 300 stories, collected in *The Four Million* (1906), *The Voice of the City* (1908) and many other books. His last years were marred by an unhappy second marriage, financial difficulties and alcoholism.

HENRY, Patrick (1736–1799), statesman, orator and prominent figure of the American Revolution. A lawyer, he came to public notice with his defense of the Va. legislature over a law repealed by King George II as unjust. Elected to the legislature himself in 1765, he persuaded it to reject the Stamp Act, then joined the first CONTINENTAL CONGRESS in 1774. In a speech at Va.'s second revolutionary convention in 1775, advocating war rather than negotiations, he coined the famous phrase "Give me liberty, or give me death!" He served as governor of Va. 1776–79 and 1784–86, but furiously opposed the ratification of the US CONSTITUTION in 1788.

HENRY THE NAVIGATOR (1394–1460), Portuguese prince, third son of King John of Portugal, whose active interest inaugurated Portuguese maritime exploration and expansion overseas. He sponsored the exploration and mapping of the W coast of Africa, and his expeditions discovered the Madeiras and the Azores and rounded Cape Verde.

HENSON, Josiah (1789–1881), US slave, thought to have been the model for Uncle Tom in Harriet STOWE's book *Uncle Tom's Cabin*. He became a Methodist Episcopal preacher, and escaped to Canada in 1830, where he aided fugitive slaves and established the British-American Institute for the "colored inhabitants of Canada."

HENSON, Matthew Alexander (1866–1955), US Negro Arctic explorer, who with Robert PEARY discovered the North Pole in 1909. He had already accompanied Peary to the Arctic seven times.

HENZE, Hans Werner (1926–   ), German composer known for his symphonies, concertos and operas, which include *Elegy for Young Lovers* (1961), for which W. H. AUDEN and Chester Kallman wrote the libretto.

HEPATITIS, INFLAMMATION of the LIVER, usually due to VIRUS infection, causing nausea, loss of appetite, FEVER, malaise, JAUNDICE and abdominal pain; liver failure may result. It can occur as part of a systemic disease (e.g. YELLOW FEVER, MONONUCLEOSIS). In two forms infection is restricted to the liver: **infectious hepatitis** is an EPIDEMIC form, transmitted by feces and is of short INCUBATION; it is rarely serious or prolonged. **Serum hepatitis** is transmitted by BLOOD (e.g., used needles and syringes, TRANSFUSION), it develops more slowly but may be more severe, causing death. It is common among drug addicts; carriers may be detected by blood tests and immunization of those at risk may be helpful. Amebiasis and certain DRUGS can also cause hepatitis.

HEPBURN, Katharine (1909–   ), US stage and film actress. She is famous for many performances during a long career, which includes several films with Spencer Tracy, and has won four Academy awards. Her films include *Alice Adams* (1935), *The Philadelphia Story* (1940), *The African Queen* (1951), *Long Day's Journey Into Night* (1962) and *On Golden Pond* (1981).

HEPPLEWHITE, George (d. 1786), famous English furniture-maker and designer, influenced by Robert ADAM. In the *Cabinet-maker and Upholsterer's Guide* (1788), his furniture is characterized by elegant, fine carved forms and painted or inlaid wood.

HEPTARCHY, name for the seven kingdoms of Anglo-Saxon Britain before the 9th-century Danish conquests, comprising Kent, Sussex, Wessex, Essex, Northumbria. East Anglia and Mercia.

HEPWORTH, Dame Barbara (1903–1975), British sculptor, and one of the most famous woman artists of the 20th century. Her abstract work, in stone and bronze, like that of Henry MOORE, is concerned with surface textures and the contrast of space and mass.

HERACLITUS (c540–c480 BC), Greek philosopher from Ephesus, called "the Obscure" for his cryptic style. He is known to us through some 125 fragments of his own work and by comments of later authors. Believing in universal impermanence ("everything is in flux") and that all things (notably opposites) were interrelated, he considered fire the fundamental element of the universe. His view of the transience of all things exerted a strong influence on PLATO.

HERALDRY, the system of devising and granting armorial designs or insignia, and of establishing family genealogies. The designs are displayed on shields or coats of arms and identify individuals or families (in which case they are hereditary), towns, universities, military regiments and nations. The term derives from the work of the heralds of the Middle Ages who announced tournaments and became expert in identifying the armorial bearings of the participants. The practice of bearing coats of arms was adopted by the crusaders and spread through Europe in the 12th century. The arrangement of the devices on the shields was subject to strict conventions. Coats of arms became so general in England that Richard III established the Herald's College (1483) to regulate their adoption.

HERB, in botany, any plant with soft aerial stems and leaves that die back at the end of the growing season to leave no persistent parts above ground. In everyday terms, herbs are plants used medicinally and to flavor food. (See COOKERY; MEDICINE.)

HERBART, Johann Friedrich (1776–1841), German philosopher and educator best remembered for his pedagogical system, now called **Herbartianism**, in which he stressed the importance of ethics (to give social direction) and psychology (to understand the mind of the pupil) acting together.

HERBERT, George (1593–1633), English poet and clergyman. His poetry, generally termed Metaphysical, deals for the most part with his own intense religious experiences, expressed in a complex but elegant, sometimes witty style. His work was first published posthumously in a collection entitled *The Temple* (1633).

HERBERT, Victor (1859–1924), Irish-American operetta composer and conductor, famous for *Babes in Toyland* (1903) and *Naughty Marietta* (1910). He also wrote two grand operas and a cello concerto.

HERBICIDES, chemical compounds used to kill plants. Originally, general herbicides were used in agriculture to kill weeds, but these dangerous substances have been largely superseded since WWII by a host of selective weedkillers, complex organic compounds which at suitable dosage are much more toxic to the prevailing weeds than to the crop. These chemicals have also proved to be dangerous to human and animal life and must be used with great care. (See also DEFOLIANTS; DIOXIN.)

HERBIVORES, a dietary classification of the Animal Kingdom—including all animals which feed exclusively on plant materials. Preyed on by many carnivorous animals, they form the lower links of food chains.

HERCULANEUM, ancient Roman city at the foot of Mt Vesuvius in Italy. Like nearby POMPEII, it was destroyed in 79 AD, by the eruption of Vesuvius which engulfed it in volcanic mud that hardened and preserved even wood and textiles. Rediscovered in 1709, it is still being excavated.

HERCULES or **Heracles**, Greek mythological hero famed for his strength and courage. The son of ZEUS, he performed 12 seemingly impossible labors. He killed the Nemean lion and the Hydra; captured the wild boar of Mt Erymanthus and the hind of Arcadia, a deer with golden antlers; killed the man-eating birds of the Stymphalian marshes; cleaned, in one day, the Augean stables; captured the savage bull of King Minos of Crete and the man-eating mares of King Diomedes of

Thrace; obtained the girdle of the Amazon queen Hippolyta; seized the cattle of the monster Geryon; fetched the golden apples of the Hesperides and brought Cerberus from the underworld.

HERDER, Johann Gottfried von (1744–1803), German philosopher and literary critic in the STURM UND DRANG movement. He initiated the study of comparative folk literatures and in his *Outlines of the Philosophy of Man* (1784–91) he developed the influential concept of the evolution of human culture and the singularity of each historical epoch.

HEREDITY, the process whereby progeny resemble their parents in many features but are not, except in some microorganisms, an exact duplicate of their parents. Patterns of heredity for a long time puzzled biologists and it was not until the researches of Gregor MENDEL, an Austrian monk, that any numeric laws of heredity were discovered. Although Mendel's work was published in the mid-1860s, it went ignored by the majority of biologists until the opening of the 20th century.

Mendel showed that hereditary characteristics are passed on in units called GENES. When GAMETES (reproductive cells) are formed by meiosis, the genes controlling any given characteristic "segregate" and become associated with different gametes. Thus, if the height of a pea plant is controlled by the genes T (for tallness) and t (for shortness) and pollen from a pure-breeding dwarf strain (of genotype tt) is used to fertilize ovules of a pure-breeding tall strain (of genotype TT), the resulting plants (of the "first filial"—F_1—generation), are of genotype Tt. Now the gametes of the F_1 generation contain equal numbers of genes T and t, both in the pollen and the ovules. The second filial (F_2) generation thus contains 50% of the "heterozygote" Tt, together with 25% each of the "homozygotes" TT and tt. In many cases, the heterozygote is indistinguishable from one of the homozygotes. In this case the gene that is expressed in the heterozygous condition is called a *dominant* gene; that which only manifests itself when homozygous is termed *recessive*. In the case of Mendel's peas, since T was dominant and t recessive, in the F_1 generation (100% Tt) all the plants were tall, while in the F_2 generation 75% were of the tall phenotype (i.e., the 25% TT and the 50% Tt) and 25% (the tt) of the short one.

Mendel also showed that when two or more pairs of genes segregate simultaneously the distribution of any one is independent of the distribution of the others. This work was done by crossing peas pure-breeding for round yellow seeds ($RRYY$) with peas pure-breeding for wrinkled green seeds ($rryy$). All the first-cross seeds were round yellow, showing that round is dominant over wrinkled and yellow over green. The possible number of genotypes is 16 but only 4 phenotypes appeared: in the ratio of 9 round yellow seeds to every 3 round green, 3 wrinkled yellow and 1 wrinkled green. This "independent segregation" applies only to genes on different CHROMOSOMES; genes on the same chromosome are "linked" and do not segregate independently.

It is now known that the genes are normally located on the chromosomes in the nucleus of the CELL. Each chromosome carries many genes which may be transmitted together and are said to be in *coupling*. However, genes are exchanged between chromosome pairs so that recombination occurs. Because of the occurrence of recombination the linkage of genes is not complete.

In the vast majority of animals and higher plants sex is determined by a special sex chromosome which in humans is the XY chromosome. Men are XY and women XX, so that all ova are X while a sperm is either X or Y. Therefore there should be an equal number of males and females in a population. In practice Y-bearing sperm are more successful in fertilizing ova than X, so that more boys are born than girls.

Genes not only replicate themselves to pass on genetic information and direct the synthesis of PROTEINS within individual cells, they also interact with each other both directly at the chromosomal level and indirectly through gene products. Although a particular characteristic of an organism is probably under the control of a single gene, the characteristic may be modified by a large number of other genes. For example, mice have a gene which can either slightly shorten the tail or result in early death through kidney failure, depending on the presence of other genes. Other genes exist for the sole function of suppressing the effects of another gene. The translocation of genes on chromosomes probably plays an important role in gene interaction.

In most organisms the majority of abnormal or mutant genes are recessive. But in man mutant genes tend either to be dominant or show no dominance. As humans generally avoid marrying close relatives, different combinations of genes are always being formed, giving rise to the great variation seen among human beings. A reduction of variability occurs in thoroughbred animals where matings are controlled so as to select for desired constant features.

It has been estimated that throughout EVOLUTION there have been over 500 million different species of plants and animals; therefore there must have been at least 500 million different genes. Genes are composed of DNA (see NUCLEIC ACIDS) which is capable of an enormous number of variations. A sequence of 15 nucleotides composed of four different bases is capable of over 500 million alternatives. It is possible using the four different nucleotides in DNA to construct a code of 64 three-nucleotide sequences capable of indicating all the differing AMINO ACIDS.

HERMAN, Woodrow Charles "Woody" (1913–1987), US jazz clarinetist and leader from 1936 of a succession of popular bands, each called "The Thundering Herd."

HERMAPHRODITE, any organism in which the functions of both sexes are combined. Usually, an individual functions in only one sexual role at a time, but in a few species, e.g., earthworms, each of a pair of partners fertilizes the other during copulation. Hermaphrodite plants are usually referred to as being bisexual.

HERMITAGE, Soviet art museum in Leningrad, one of the world's most outstanding art collections. The huge collection was begun by Empress Catherine II in the 18th century. It has art treasures from all over the world and masterpieces by Rembrandt, Picasso and Matisse.

HERMIT CRABS, a group of crustaceans with soft bodies which occupy the empty shells of sea snails. Most members of the group occupy spiral whelk shells, and in all of them the appendages on the right side of the abdomen are not developed. Detritus feeders, hermit crabs have well-developed pincers and two pairs of walking legs, and can withdraw into their borrowed shells if attacked. Not infrequently the shell is shared by one or more sea-anemones, commensal with the hermit crab.

HERNDON, William Henry (1818–1891), US lawyer and biographer (1889) of Abraham Lincoln. Lincoln's friend and law partner from 1843, he was faulted for his somewhat uncritical portrayal of Lincoln. Nevertheless his book is an invaluable record of the president's life.

HERNIA, protrusion of abdominal contents through the abdominal wall in the inguinal or femoral part of the groin, or through the diaphragm (**hiatus hernia**). Hernia may occur through a congenital defect or through an area of MUSCLE weakness. Bowel and omentum are commonly found in hernial sacs, and if there is a tight constriction at the neck of the sac (the hernia is "strangulated"), the bowel may be obstructed or suffer GANGRENE. In hiatus hernia, part of the STOMACH lies in the chest. Hernia may need SURGERY to reposition the bowel and close the defect, but this is rare in hiatus hernia.

HEROD, family name of a dynasty in Palestine which ruled for nearly 150 years around the time of Christ. They were clients of Rome. **Herod the Great** (c73–4 BC), first important ruler of the dynasty, king of Judaea from 37 BC. He strengthened his position by keeping on good terms with the Romans, including Mark ANTONY and Augustus. Although an able ruler and generous builder (especially the Temple at Jerusalem) he was hated for his ruthlessness. He was responsible for the deaths of many of his family and, according to the New Testament, ordered the massacre of the Innocents. **Herod Antipas** (c21 BC–39 AD), son of Herod the Great, ruler of Galilee at the time of Christ's crucifixion. He was tricked by his wife and her daughter Salome into having John the Baptist executed. **Herod Agrippa I** (c10 BC–44 AD), grandson of Herod the Great, king of Judaea 41–44 AD. Helped in his career by his friendship with the Roman emperors Caligula and Claudius, he earned the support of the Jews by his adherence to Jewish tradition. **Herod Agrippa II** (c27–93 AD), son of Herod Agrippa I, king of Chalcis, last important ruler of the Herodian dynasty. Lacking his father's tact in the treatment of the Jews, he contributed to their discontent, and sided with the Romans in the Jewish revolt 66–70 AD.

HERODOTUS (c484–425 BC), Greek historian, renowned as "the Father of History" for his work seeking to describe and explain the causes of the Greco-Persian wars of 499–479 BC. This involved him in a monumental survey of the whole of mankind's previous history, collected from the stories he had heard during his extensive travels. He is also famed as a geographer and ethnologist.

HEROIN, OPIUM alkaloid with narcotic ANALGESIC and euphoriant properties, a valuable DRUG in severe pain of short duration (e.g., CORONARY THROMBOSIS) and in terminal malignant disease. It is abused in DRUG ADDICTION, taken intravenously for its psychological effects and later because of physical addiction. SEPTICEMIA and hepatitis may follow unsterile injections, and early death is common.

HERONS, long-billed and long-legged wading birds of the subfamily Ardeinae, and including the egrets. Herons are the only birds that fly with the neck tucked back and the head between the shoulders. Gregarious at nesting time, most species disperse after breeding. Waterside or marsh birds, they feed on frogs, fish, eels and watervoles, stabbing with their heavy bills.

HERO OF ALEXANDRIA (c62 AD), or **Heron**, Greek scientist best known for inventing the aeolipile, a steam-powered engine that used the principle of jet propulsion, and many other complex steam- and water-powered toys. Other works ascribed to him deal with mensuration, optics (containing an early version of FERMAT's Principle) and MECHANICS.

HEROPHILUS (c300 BC), Alexandrian physician regarded as the father of scientific ANATOMY, and one of the first dissectors. He distinguished nerves from tendons and partially recognized their role. His work survives only through GALEN's writings.

HERPES, in general, any of several viral diseases of the skin. Herpes simplex is characterized by vesicles or blisters on skin or mucous membranes (see COLD SORE; VENEREAL DISEASES). Herpes zoster or SHINGLES is distinguished by pain from inflamed nerves as well as by vesicular eruptions.

HERRICK, Robert (1591–1674), English lyric poet. Writing in the classical tradition of the Latin lyricists, he was also greatly influenced by the dramatist Ben JONSON. Most of his poems are concerned with the pleasures of nature, wine and love, and he is probably best known for the line "Gather ye rosebuds while ye may."

HERRIMAN, George Joseph (1880–1944), US cartoonist, creator (1911) of the comic strip *Krazy Kat*.

HERRINGS, or clupeid fishes, a large family of important food fishes of worldwide distribution, characterized by a forward extension of the swimbladder into the skull forming two small capsules associated with the ears, and a short, deep lower jaw. Some species of shoaling fishes are found in enormous numbers: shoals of herring may be 9mi across. The herring family includes the round herring, shad and menhaden.

HERRIOT, Édouard (1872–1957), French statesman and scholar, leader of the Radical Socialists from 1919. Mayor of Lyon from 1905, he became a senator in 1912. He was a minister, premier of France three times and president of the Chamber of Deputies. In 1942 he was imprisoned by the Germans for opposition to the Vichy government. After WWII he became president of the National Assembly, 1947–54.

HERSCHEL, family of British astronomers of German origin. Sir **Frederick William Herschel** (1738–1822) pioneered the building and use of reflecting TELESCOPES, discovered URANUS (1781), showed the sun's motion in space (1783), found that some DOUBLE STARS were in relative orbital motion (1793), and studied NEBULAE. His sister **Caroline Lucretia** (1750–1848) assisted him and herself discovered eight COMETS. His son Sir **John Frederick William Herschel** (1792–1871), with BABBAGE and Peacock, helped establish Leibnizian CALCULUS notation in Britain, was the first to use SODIUM thiosulfate (hypo) as a photographic fixer, studied POLARIZED LIGHT and made many contributions to ASTRONOMY, especially that of the S Hemisphere.

HERSEY, John Richard (1914–), US author who won a Pulitzer Prize with his first novel, *A Bell for Adano* (1944). His experiences as a war correspondent provided him with material for his books, which include *Hiroshima* (1946), *The Wall* (1950), and *The Call* (1987).

HERSKOVITS, Melville Jean (1895–1963), US anthropologist. He was particularly interested in culture change and African ethnology, and in 1927 he founded the first US university course in African studies at Northwestern University.

HERTZ, Heinrich Rudolph (1857–1894), German physicist who first broadcast and received RADIO waves (c1886). He showed also that they could be reflected and refracted (see REFRACTION) much as light, and that they traveled at the same velocity, though their wavelength was much longer (see ELECTROMAGNETIC RADIATION). In doing so he showed that light (and radiant heat) are, like radio waves, of electromagnetic nature.

HERTZOG, James Barry Munnik (1866–1942), South African prime minister 1924–39. Founder of the Nationalist Party (1914), he worked for separate development of Afrikaner culture and an independent republic of South Africa.

HERTZSPRUNG, Ejnar (1873–1967), Danish astronomer who showed there was a relation between a STAR's brightness and color: the resulting Hertzsprung–Russell Diagram (named also for Henry RUSSELL) is important throughout astronomy and cosmology. He also conceived and defined absolute MAGNITUDE; and his work on CEPHEID VARIABLES has provided a way to measure intergalactic distances.

HERZEN, Aleksander Ivanovich (1812–1870), Russian writer and early advocate of socialism. He was banished in 1834 for subversive activities and left Russia permanently in 1847. His writings were smuggled into Russia and did much to shape the revolutionary movement there.

HERZL, Theodor (1860–1904), Austrian writer and founder of the political Zionist movement. Convinced by the anti-Semitism surrounding the DREYFUS AFFAIR that Jewish assimilation was impossible, he proposed the establishment of a Jewish state and in 1897 organized the first World Zionist Congress (see ZIONISM). After the establishment of Israel, his body was removed from Vienna to Jerusalem.

HESCHEL, Abraham Joshua (1907–1972), US Jewish philosopher, at New York's Jewish Theological Seminary from 1945. Active in the civil rights movement, he wrote *Man Is Not Alone: A Philosophy of Religion* (1951) and *God in Search of Man: A Philosophy of Judaism* (1955).

HESIOD (8th century BC), Greek epic poet. His major works are the didactic *Theogeny*, describing the gods and heroes of Greek mythology, and *Works and Days*, which departed from the heroic tradition of Homer in dealing with the everyday life of a farmer.

HESS, Dame Myra (1890–1965), British pianist noted for her interpretations of Bach, Mozart and Scarlatti. She is especially remembered for her morale-boosting lunch-time concerts in London's National Gallery during WWII.

HESS, Rudolf (1894–1987), German Nazi leader and Hitler's deputy, 1933–39. Depressed by his loss of influence, in 1941 he flew to Scotland to try personally to arrange a settlement between Germany and Britain. Arrested and interned in Britain during the war, he was condemned to life imprisonment for war crimes at the NUREMBERG TRIALS in 1946. He eventually became the only inmate in Berlin's Spandau Prison. The USSR rejected appeals for his release.

HESSE, Hermann (1877–1962), German-born Swiss poet and novelist. The duality of man's nature, particularly with regard to the artist, is a recurrent theme in his work, with a later emphasis on symbolism and psychoanalytic insights. His novels include *Demian* (1919), *Siddhartha* (1922), *Steppenwolf* (1927) and *The Glass Bead Game* (1943). In 1946 he won the Nobel Prize for Literature.

HESSIANS, German mercenaries, mostly from Hesse-Kassel, who fought with distinction on the British side during the American REVOLUTIONARY WAR. They suffered a serious defeat at Trenton, N.J., in Dec. 1776. After the war many settled in the US and Canada.

HEURISTICS, an approach to problem-solving in which a formally unjustifiable solution is assumed as an aid in exploring the implications of the problem. In science, even theories that ultimately prove misconceived can be of great heuristic value in research.

HEYDRICH, Reinhard (1904–1942), notoriously cruel German Nazi leader, deputy head of the Gestapo 1934–39, then put in charge of all security. He became known as "the Hangman," and was assassinated while acting as "protector" in Czechoslovakia (see LIDICE).

HEYERDAHL, Thor (1914–), Norwegian ethnologist famous for his expeditions to prove the feasibility of his theories of cultural diffusion, and for his books. On the *Kon-Tiki*, a primitive balsawood raft, he and his crew sailed from the W coast of South America to Polynesia, demonstrating the possibility that the Polynesians originated in South America (1947). On *Ra*, a facsimile of an ancient Egyptian papyrus reed boat, he and his cosmopolitan crew succeeded at the second attempt in sailing from Morocco to Barbados, showing the possibility that the pre-Columbian cultures of South America were influenced by Egyptian civilization (*Ra* I, 1969, *Ra* II, 1970). On *Tigris*, another primitive reed vessel, he demonstrated that the ancient Sumerians of Mesopotamia could have reached the Indus Valley and Africa by sea (1977–78).

HEYSE, Paul Johann Ludwig von 1830–1914), German writer. Center of the traditionalist Munich circle, he was noted for his romantic short stories. He won the Nobel Prize for Literature in 1910.

HEYWARD, DuBose (1885–1940), US author, best known for his novel *Porgy* (1925), on which GERSHWIN based his opera *Porgy and Bess*. Much of his work deals with the plight of Southern blacks.

HEYWOOD, Thomas (c1574–1651), English dramatist and actor. He was a prolific writer, claiming over 200 dramas, but only about 20 have survived. Excelling at themes based on everyday life, often set in London, his best known play is *A Woman Kilde with Kindnesse* (1607).

HIAWATHA, semi-legendary American Indian chief. He founded the Iroquois League (c1450) to end intertribal warfare, and has been immortalized in LONGFELLOW's *Song of Hiawatha*.

HIBERNATION, a protective mechanism whereby certain animals reduce their activity and apparently sleep throughout winter. At its most developed it is a characteristic of warm-blooded animals but a comparable phenomenon, diapause, is found in cold-blooded forms. Diapause is a direct physiological response to cold temperatures: metabolic activity in cold-blooded animals is entirely dictated by external temperature. In hibernating animals, internal preparations, such as laying down a store of fat, begin several weeks before the onset of hibernation. Then, when temperatures drop, the animal goes to sleep. Pulse rate and breathing drop to a minimum. With metabolism reduced, the animal can live on food stored in its body till spring. Winter food supplies would not be sufficient to maintain the animal in a fully-active state. When an animal remains torpid throughout the summer, this is known as **aestivation**.

HICCUP, brief involuntary contraction of the diaphragm that may follow dietary or alcoholic excess and rapid eating. It may also be a symptom of UREMIA, mineral disorders and brain-stem disease. Rebreathing into a paper bag or repeated swallowing are effective remedies; chlorpromazine also suppresses hiccups.

HICKOK, Wild Bill (1837–1876), American scout and frontier law officer. During the Civil War he was a Union scout and spy. As US marshal at Hays City and Abilene, Kan. (1869–71), both lawless frontier towns, he won a reputation for marksmanship and daring which he demonstrated in 1872–73 on tour with BUFFALO BILL.

HICKS, Edward (1780–1849), US primitive painter. A Quaker preacher, he is best known for his illustrations of biblical passages, including over 50 versions of *The Peaceable Kingdom*, based on Isaiah's prophecy of peace among all creatures.

HICKS, Elias (1748–1830), US Quaker preacher, one of the first advocates of the abolition of slavery in the US. His idea that beliefs could be continually revised caused a split among the Friends, and his liberal followers became known as Hicksites.

HIDALGO Y COSTILLA, Miguel (1753–1811), Mexican revolutionary, known as "the father of Mexican independence." A village priest, when Napoleon annexed Spain he plotted independence from Spain. The plot discovered (1810), he rang his church bells and shouted the famous *grito* (cry) *de Dolores*, demanding revolution against Spain. He led a peasant revolt which after initial success was suppressed in 1811. Hidalgo was executed, but the anniversary of his *grito* (Sept. 16) is celebrated as Mexico's Independence Day.

HIDATSA INDIANS (sometimes known as the Gros Ventre), North American tribe of the Siouan language family, originating in the upper Missouri area. In the 19th century they formed one group with the neighboring MANDAN and Arikara, and now live on the Fort Berthold Reservation, N.D.

HIEROGLYPHICS, system of writing using pictorial characters (hieroglyphs), especially that found on Egyptian monuments. Egyptian hieroglyphics are first found from c3000 BC, their use declining during the 3rd century AD. Initially there were a fairly limited number of hieroglyphs. This was followed by a rapid expansion of the number of characters in order to reduce ambiguity, and by a further expansion around 500 BC. There were two derived cursive scripts, hieratic and demotic. **Hieratic script**, initially used only for sacred texts, coexisted with true hieroglyphics from early on until c100 AD. The less legible, more cursive **demotic script** appeared around 660 BC and disappeared around 450 AD. The writings of other ancient peoples, e.g., the Hittites and Mayas, are also termed hieroglyphics. (See also ROSETTA STONE.)

HIGGINSON, Thomas Wentworth (1823–1911), US pastor and abolitionist. His liberal ideas lost him his first post, and after the Fugitive Slave Act (1850) he helped runaway slaves, including Anthony Burns. In the Civil War he was colonel of the first Negro regiment. After 1864 he turned to writing.

HIGH BLOOD PRESSURE. See BLOOD CIRCULATION.

HIGH-FIDELITY, an adjective applicable to systems carrying a signal with very little distortion, such as a sound CAMERA or RADIO transmitter, but also a generic noun ("Hi-Fi") for a wide range of domestic equipment for sound reproduction. The input signal may arise from a phonograph disc, in which case a high-compliance (flexibility) stylus following a groove produces a piezoelectric or induced (see ELECTROMAGNETISM) voltage; from magnetic tape, on which the signal is recorded in the variations of magnetization of a ferromagnetic (see MAGNETISM) coating, produced by a finely focused ELECTROMAGNET (the recording head) and inducing a voltage in the small playback head coil; or from a radio receiver which detects the slight variations in intensity (AM) or frequency (FM) of a broadcast electromagnetic wave. The resulting voltage is amplified electronically and passed to a loudspeaker, consisting typically of a paper cone, vibrated by an electromagnet, in an enclosure which attempts to compensate for the uneven response of the cone for different directions and frequencies. The most important measures of the overall faithfulness are the frequency response (the range of frequencies passed with intensities unchanged within a quoted tolerance), the harmonic distortion (the change in the balance of the HARMONICS of a signal—particularly a boost in the high harmonics), the hum and NOISE levels (in the absence of a signal), and the flutter and wow (fluctuations in speed of record or tape decks).

HIGH SEAS, in maritime law, the sea beyond territorial waters. Since the 19th century freedom of the seas has been recognized as a rule of international law, but recently the discovery of minerals under the sea and the importance of the airspace above it have made the concept crucial. Attempts by any state to extend its jurisdiction, for example, to protect fishing rights, should be ratified by international agreement. The Law of the Sea Treaty (1982) received majority approval in the UN, largely because of Third World support, but the US voted against it.

HIGHWAY, major road, often with controlled access. The term goes back to the Roman roads which were on a mound (hence "high way"), made by earth from the side ditches thrown into the center. The first roads were probably Mesopotamian, but the earliest recorded long-distance road was the Persian Royal Road stretching c1,775mi from Susa to Smyrna. The Romans were the best of the ancient road-builders, and their greatest road, the APPIAN WAY, begun 312 BC, set the standard for road-building for 2,000 years.

Until the 18th century European roads were neglected and hard to travel, but Pierre Marie Jérôme Trésaguet (1716–93) in France and John Metcalf (1777–1810) in England pioneered modern road-building. The Scots, Thomas Telford and John Loudon McAdam, developed lightweight road construction, and the MACADAM road relied on a compacted subgrade with a thin surface of broken stone to support the load, as opposed to the heavy Roman system.

The composition was improved in the 20th century by the addition of tar or bitumen as a binder. The coming of the automobile and increasing loads meant that totally new requirements were introduced. It became necessary for highway systems to be integrated, so although local roads are usually still the responsibility of cities, major highways are administered on a national basis to ensure continuity and uniformity. In the US this is seen to by the Federal Highway Administration. Finances are supplied by the user, with motor-fuel taxes as the main single source of revenue. Vehicles are usually licensed on the basis of weight, and toll roads are popular in areas of high demand. In road construction the major operation is earth moving, and the soil then has to be suitably prepared to make the roadbed. The pavement, or road surface laid on the roadbed, will depend on the traffic anticipated and the nature of the ground.

First-class highways, especially designed for fast-moving traffic, are variously described as expressways, superhighways, throughways or freeways, and parkways are built in park-like country and are often landscaped. The growing numbers of automobiles and the increase in road usage demands a constant rethinking of highway policy. Compromise is often necessary to avoid conflicts with community or environmental amenities. (See also INTERSTATE SYSTEM.)

HILBERT, David (1862–1943), German mathematician whose most important contributions were in the field of mathematical LOGIC. With the advent of the NON-EUCLIDEAN GEOMETRIES it had become clear that the axiomatic basis of EUCLID's work needed further examination. This Hilbert did, establishing a logical axiomatic system for geometry.

HILL, Ambrose Powell (1825–1865), US Confederate general, one of the outstanding leaders in the Civil War. He joined the Confederates in 1861 and his force, called the "Light Division" because of its speed in marching, came to be one of the best in the South and played a decisive role in the Battle of ANTIETAM (1862). He was killed in action at Petersburg.

HILL, James Jerome (1838–1916), US railroad magnate who established a continental rail system in the NW. Purchasing the St. Paul and Pacific Railroad, he extended it to the Canadian border and to the Pacific at Seattle (1893). Later, working with J. P. MORGAN, he consolidated his holdings in the Great Northern Railway Company.

HILL, Joe (born Joseph Hillstrom; 1879–1915), Swedish-American labor organizer for the INDUSTRIAL WORKERS OF THE WORLD in California. He wrote many labor songs. Tried and executed on a murder charge, his funeral was attended by about 30,000 people.

HILL, Sir Rowland (1795–1879), English postal reformer and the founder of "penny postage" (1837). He worked for the government, 1838–64, establishing an efficient postal service.

HILLARY, Sir Edmund Percival (1919–   ), New Zealand explorer and mountaineer. In 1953 he and Tenzing Norkay, a Sherpa from Nepal, became the first men to reach the summit of Mount EVEREST, the world's highest mountain.

HILLEL (d. 10 AD), Jewish scholar, who was one of the great founders of rabbinic Judaism, and ethical leader of his generation. He was opposed by Shammai, another teacher. His "Seven Rules" of exegesis laid the groundwork for a liberal rather than literal interpretation of scriptural law.

HILLIARD, Nicholas (c1537–1619), English miniature painter and portraitist. As court miniaturist and goldsmith to Elizabeth I, his style of "limning" was characterized by exquisite jewel-like, detailing and fine drawing.

HILLMAN, Sidney (1887–1946), US labor leader. A Lithuanian immigrant, Hillman became the first president of the Amalgamated Clothing Workers of America (1914). He was a powerful supporter of industrial unions, a founder of the Congress of Industrial Organizations (CIO), and government adviser on labor relations.

HILLQUIT, Morris (1869–1933), US lawyer and Socialist leader, born in Riga, Russia. He was a leader of the SOCIAL DEMOCRATIC PARTY and the SOCIALIST PARTY and defended lawyers against espionage charges. He was involved in the PROGRESSIVE PARTY.

HILTON, James (1900–1954), English popular novelist. His books include *Lost Horizon* (1933), and *Random Harvest* (1941), which were made into films.

HIMALAYAS, the highest mountain system in the world, over 1,500mi long, extending from NW Pakistan and across Kashmir, N India, S Tibet, Nepal, Sikkim, Bhutan to the bend of the Tsangpo-Brahmaputra R. The Himalayas consist of a series of parallel ranges that are thought to have originated when the Indian subcontinent moved N and collided with Eurasia (see PLATE TECTONICS). The Great Himalayas lie in the N, then the Lesser Himalayas, and the Outer Himalayas in the S. The average elevation is 20,000ft in the Great Himalayas, where Mt Everest rises to 29,028ft and there are 11 other mountains of over 26,000ft. The Himalayas protect S and W China from the moisture-laden monsoons which strike Bhutan, Sikkim and Nepal, but this results in semiarid and desert conditions in those parts of China. The Indus, Sutlej, Brahmaputra and Ganges rivers all rise in the mountains.

HIMMLER, Heinrich (1900–1945), Nazi leader, police chief and politician. Head of the SS from 1929 and the GESTAPO from 1936, he was largely responsible for the CONCENTRATION CAMPS and the murder of millions of Jews and others considered undesirable to the Nazi regime in the 1930s and 1940s. He became interior minister in 1943, but fell from Hitler's favor in 1945. After the German defeat in 1945 he committed suicide.

HINDEMITH, Paul (1895–1963), influential German composer and teacher. Considered a modernist because of his dissonant harmonies and counterpoint, he nevertheless embraced the classical musical forms of Bach and Mozart in a modern idiom. He viewed the composer as a craftsman who ought to write music for specific uses (*Gebrauchsmusik*). Among his many major works are the opera and symphony *Mathis der Maler* (1934) and *Symphonic Metamorphoses on Themes of Carl Maria von Weber* (1943).

HINDENBURG, Paul von (Paul Ludwig Hans Anton von Hindenburg und Beneckendorff; 1847–1934), German general, military hero of WWI and president of Germany (1925–34). Together with LUDENDORFF he directed the German WWI effort and military strategies. As president he was chiefly a figurehead, becoming increasingly senile. During his presidency the Nazis gradually gained popular support until HITLER became chancellor in 1933.

HINDI, the official language of India, a written form of HINDUSTANI. It is written in Devanagari script (or SANSKRIT), reading from left to right.

HINDUISM, one of the major world religions: the civilization, in all its aspects, of the Hindus, the people of India and neighboring countries, with outposts elsewhere in SE Asia and Africa. A comprehensive culture embracing diverse beliefs and practices, it tolerates almost any belief, but regards none as essential. Even other religions are accepted, though not their exclusivism. Thus Hinduism has no dogma, and is almost indefinable. It had neither beginning nor founder, and has no hierarchy or source of authority. Abstract philosophies co-exist with magic, animism, pantheism, polytheism, mysticism, asceticism and cultic sexuality. Nevertheless there are some characteristics common to most Hindus. These include belief in Brahman, the One that is the All, the absolute and ultimate principle which is the Self of all living things. Brahman is sometimes personified as Brahma, a background figure who, with Shiva and Vishnu, forms the Trimurti, in some ways analogous to the Christian TRINITY. This element of monotheism plays almost no part in popular Hinduism, where countless gods are worshiped. Hindus have great respect for all life, many being vegetarian and revering and protecting the cow. The upper-caste class of Brahmins is respected as sacrosanct. The doctrine of TRANSMIGRATION OF SOULS in an endless cycle, under the law of KARMA, is universally believed. The three paths of escape from the cycle are duty, knowledge (sought by meditation and YOGA) and devotion to God. Hinduism has its roots in Vedism, the religion of the early Indo-Aryans who settled in India in the late 2nd millennium BC. The authority of the VEDA is still generally recognized, though in practice the Veda is hardly known. Vedism, a chiefly ritual system, developed into BRAHMANISM, in which, from about 700 BC, philosophy developed and was enshrined in the UPANISHADS. A period of great change followed, in which the sects (as they were at first) of BUDDHISM and JAINISM arose. True Hinduism began in the 2nd century BC, marked by the BHAGAVAD-GITA (found in the epic MAHABHARATA); the cults of Vishnu and Shiva developed, becoming major sects, and were followed by the cult of Shakti, often associated with TANTRA, esoteric practices both ritual and sensual. Modern Hinduism has seen the rise of innumerable reform movements and sects, some influenced by Islam or Christianity. Although in present-day India traditional Hindu social structures (see CASTE SYSTEM) are weakened, Hinduism is readily adapting to modern conditions. (See also KRISHNA; RAMAKRISHNA; RAMAYANA.)

HINDU KUSH, mountain range in Asia, stretching from NE Afghanistan to N Pakistan. High altitude passes cross the range. The range's highest peak is Tirich Mir (25,260ft).

HINDUSTANI, the most widespread language of N India, particularly of the Hindu-speaking areas. It is the spoken form of HINDI and URDU, and derives from the Prakrits (vernacular forms of classical Sanskrit). Hindustani grammar is less complex than Sanskrit in that it avoids noun inflections, gender agreement and irregular forms, and instead of prepositions it has postpositions, which explain the grammatical function of preceding words. GANDHI, at the time of India's independence in 1947, wanted Hindustani to be adopted as the national Indian language, because of its simple grammar and since it can be written in Devanagari or Urdu. However, Hindi was adopted as the official language.

HIPPARCHUS (c130 BC), Greek scientist, the father of systematic ASTRONOMY, who compiled the first star catalog and ascribed stars MAGNITUDES, made a good estimate of the distance and size of the moon, probably first discovered PRECESSION, invented many astronomical instruments, worked on plane and spherical trigonometry, and suggested ways of determining LATITUDE AND LONGITUDE.

HIPPIES, term first applied in the 1960s to a sizable group of people, principally under 25, who constituted an anti-establishment subculture in the US, rejecting conservative values and all forms of traditional authority. They were in the forefront of opposition to the Vietnam War. Many "straight" Americans despised them for their loose sexual conventions, their use of drugs and even their long hair. Centers of hippie culture in the US included NYC's East Village, San Francisco's Haight-Ashbury district and, later, Boulder, Colo. Their numbers peaked in the late 1960s and early 1970s.

HIPPOCRATES (c460–c377 BC), Greek physician generally called "the Father of Medicine" and the probable author of at least some of the Hippocratic Collection, some 60 or 70 books on all aspects of ancient MEDICINE. The authors probably formed a school centered around Hippocrates during his lifetime and continuing after his death. The Hippocratic Oath, traditionally regarded as the most valuable statement of medical ethics and good practice, probably represents the oath sworn by candidates for admission to an ancient medical guild.

HIPPOPOTAMUS, *Hippopotamus amphibius,* one of the largest living terrestrial mammals, distantly related to pigs. With a massive body set on short legs, each with four toes with hoof-like nails, the hippo spends the day submerged in water, coming to land at night to graze a strip extending up to 10km (6mi) inland. Highly adapted to its daytime life in water, the hippo has its sense organs, nose, eyes and ears, on top of its head, so that they are the last parts to submerge. Indeed it rarely submerges completely, and then only for short periods. The common hippopotamus is still widespread in the lakes and rivers in Africa.

HIROHITO (1901–1989), emperor of Japan from 1926 and a distinguished marine biologist. After WWII his status dramatically changed from a god-like position to being a "symbol of the state and unity of the people," without political or sovereign power. In 1971 he visited Alaska and Europe in the first trip abroad for a reigning emperor.

HIROSHIGE, Ando (1797–1858), Japanese painter and printmaker of the *ukiyo-e* (popular) school led by MANET and WHISTLER. He is famous for his sets of woodblock color prints depicting atmospheric landscapes of snow, rain, mist and moonlight. These inspired a number of his contemporaries in the West, including MANET and WHISTLER. Among his works is *53 Stages of the Tokaido Highway* (1833), a series of landscapes.

HIROSHIMA, industrial city on SW Honshu Island, Japan, located on a bay in the Inland Sea. As a thriving industrial and commercial center, it was chosen as the target for the US atomic bomb attack of Aug. 6, 1945, which caused enormous havoc and destruction; there were about 130,000 casualties. It has been largely rebuilt since 1950 and is again an important industrial and marketing center. Pop 1,052,500.

HIRSHHORN MUSEUM AND SCULPTURE GARDEN, museum of modern art in Washington, D.C., part of the Smithsonian Institution. It exhibits the collection of industrialist Joseph H. Hirshhorn (1899–1981), which he donated to the US in 1966.

HISPANIOLA, second largest island in the West Indies, located W of Puerto Rico and E of Cuba. The island is shared between the Republic of Haiti and the Dominican Republic.

HISS, Alger (1904–   ), US public official accused of spying for Russia. Hiss was an adviser to the US State Department on economic and political affairs. In 1948 he was brought before the House Committee on Un-American Activities, and in 1950 was convicted of perjury. He served four years in prison. Maintaining his innocence, Hiss devoted the rest of his life to clearing his name.

HISTAMINE, amine concerned with the production of INFLAMMATION, and particularly of HIVES and the allergic spasm of the bronchi in ASTHMA and anaphylaxis; it enhances STOMACH acid secretion and has several effects on BLOOD CIRCULATION. ANTIHISTAMINES and cromoglycate can interfere with its release; ADRENALINE counteracts its serious effects.

HISTOLOGY, the study of the microscopic ANATOMY of parts of organisms after DEATH (autopsy) or removal by SURGERY (biopsy). Tissue is fixed by agents that denature PROTEINS, preventing autolysis and bacterial degradation; they are stained by dyes that have particular affinity for different structures. Histology facilitates the study

both of normal tissue and of DISEASED organs, or pathological tissue.

HISTORY, man's study of his own past, the collective memory of mankind. Primitive peoples keep the past alive in songs and poems, but these hardly try to describe or explain and are not truly historical, although they might serve as sources for an historian. The ancient Egyptians and Chinese kept extensive records, but since these were never combined together into a connected narrative, they cannot be regarded as history either, though, again, the historian of today could find them extremely valuable for his own work.

True history begins in Greece in the 5th century BC, and HERODOTUS is usually considered the first man to have written a proper historical work. He described the wars between Greece and Persia, and attempted to explain them as a clash between different kinds of states, an oriental autocracy and a league of Greek cities, who misunderstood and distrusted each other. Herodotus, however, had not wholly emancipated himself from reliance on legend and hearsay, and the historical method remained to be fully developed by a Greek of the late 5th century BC, THUCYDIDES. He described the Peloponnesian War, and sought to explain its underlying causes by emphasizing the rivalry of democratic, cosmopolitan Athens and militaristic, isolated Sparta.

Roman Latin historians such as LIVY and TACITUS emulated their Greek predecessors, but few of the monks whose chronicles described the emergence and spread of the Christian religion had any regard for accuracy or analysis. Christianity did, however, introduce a new concept of time and change into man's view of his past. In the classical age history was seen as a cyclical process. Empires rose and declined, and events repeated themselves. Christianity saw time moving in a straight line. The Crucifixion was an actual historical event, and God's plan was gradually being unfolded as the world progressed to Judgment Day. With the help of printed books and newly discovered classical manuscripts, historians of the Renaissance began to rewrite history from a secular viewpoint. It was they who invented the words "Dark Ages," and they were convinced that human nature was uniform through time and that specific lessons could be drawn from the past.

The historians of the ENLIGHTENMENT, impressed by the methods and findings of science, attempted to apply a similar rational system to the writing of history, and they saw the future as one of gradual but steady progress, a secular version of Christianity's linear conception of the past.

In the early 19th century came what some scholars have called the "historical revolution." Instead of trying to apply universal laws to the past, judging it as though it were the present, historians and philosophers began to appreciate development and uniqueness in history. Spurred on by the new ideas of evolution, historians saw the past in terms of biological metaphors: "organic change," "growth," "stages of development."

In the 20th century historians have become increasingly skeptical of the idea that history accumulates more and more facts until, at last, the past can be perfectly known. In place of great speculative systems which tried to explain the "goals" and "direction" of history, philosophers of history now deal with technical questions: "What is a cause of an event?" or "What have historians done when they say they have explained something?" There is a new self-consciousness about the writing of history, and new questioning of the historian's proper task.

HITCHCOCK, Alfred Joseph (1899–1980), English film director known for his skillful suspense and macabre humor. He made over 50 films, among the best of which were *The Thirty-Nine Steps* (1935), *The Lady Vanishes* (1938) and, in Hollywood, *Rebecca* (1940), *Spellbound* (1945), *Notorious* (1946), *Rear Window* (1954) and *Psycho* (1960).

HITCHCOCK, Lambert (1795–1852), US cabinetmaker who in 1818 established a furniture factory in Barkhamsted, Conn. Here he manufactured "Hitchcock chairs," which combined simplicity with elegance. They are now collector's pieces.

HITLER, Adolf (1889–1945), Austrian-born dictator of Germany 1933–45. Hitler will for a long time remain a highly controversial figure. He was without doubt an evil man, coarse and unstable by nature, but he had political genius and was one of the phenomena of the 20th century. He hardly put a foot wrong politically between 1931 and 1941, and conquered an area of Europe larger than NAPOLEON did. He was the first man to understand and exploit the politics of the mass age and set up a radicalism of the right which won mass support and beat the radicals of the left on their own ground, something which earlier conservative and reactionary parties had failed to do. A powerful orator, he was one of the first to understand how to use political propaganda, including the propaganda value of violence and terror. He was indeed one of the inventors of the politics of violence from which recent decades have suffered.

The son of a customs official, he grew up near Linz, Austria. He left school at 16 and made a scanty living as a hack artist 1908–13. Drafted in WWI, he was twice awarded the Iron Cross. In 1919 he joined the small German Workers' Party, which he turned into the National Socialist Workers' Party (see NAZISM). In 1923, after an abortive coup against the Bavarian government, he served nine months in prison; there he wrote *Mein Kampf*, setting out his plans for restoring greatness to Germany. He then began to make the Nazis into a national party, and by 1932, aided by unemployment and economic chaos, he made it the largest party in the country. In 1933 he became chancellor, and in 1934 secured his position by liquidating potential opponents within the party. He took full credit for the economy's recovery and prepared it for war. He paid little further attention to domestic affairs, except to intensify persecution of the Jews. After 1935 he turned increasingly to foreign affairs.

In 1936 he reoccupied the Rhineland, in 1938 annexed Austria, and in 1939 seized parts of Czechoslovakia. On September 1 his invasion of Poland began WWII. At first his conduct of the war was effective, but his invasion of Russia in 1941 was precipitate and proved disastrous. Unable to maintain two fronts, German forces lost N Africa and were pushed back on both sides after D-DAY. Hitler maintained popular support despite an assassination attempt in 1944, but became increasingly ill and unbalanced. In 1945 he retreated to his Berlin bunker. After marrying his mistress, Eva Braun, he committed suicide with her on April 30, 1945.

HITTITES, important Indo-European people of the Middle East in the second millennium BC.

History. Of unknown origin, they appear to have first settled in southern Turkey c1900 BC; they conquered central Turkey and became a dominant power. By c1650 BC they had established a kingdom of city states (the Old Kingdom), with its capital at Hattusas (Boğazköy), just E of modern Ankara. Mursilis I overran Syria and even Babylon c1600 BC, but lost them almost at once.

The Hittite Empire proper starts with Tudhaliyas II (c1450 BC), who regained much lost territory. A period of decline followed but by the mid-14th century BC more lasting conquests were made by Suppiluliumas, who finally controlled Syria as far as the Euphrates and the Lebanon, and all Anatolia. At the battle of Kadesh c1285 BC the Hittites under Muwatallis drove off Egyptians under RAMSES II, but were seriously weakened. The final downfall of the Hittite empire came c1200 BC, when it was overrun and fragmented by a vast migration of uncertain origin, called by the Egyptians "peoples of the sea." Individual states continued to flourish, however, until Sargon II of Assyria captured Carchemish in 715 BC.

Culture. Much of what we know about the Hittites comes from clay tablets, some written in CUNEIFORM and some in Hittite HIEROGLYPHICS, which were part of the royal archives. The main Hittite language is Indo-European in origin, though other non-Indo-European tongues were apparently also current.

The Old Kingdom was a league of city states controlled by a royal governor. Each king nominated his successor. The society was essentially feudal, consisting of nobles (the land-owning warrior caste), artisans, peasants and also slaves, who had some rights, such as owning property and marriage with free persons.

During the Hittite empire the ruler became absolute and hereditary; regarded as the representative of the weather-god, the supreme god in the polytheistic Hittite religion, he was deified at his death. The Hittite legal system was in some ways more just and liberal than the Mesopotamian and Mosaic codes. Prices were regulated, and silver pieces were used as money. The economy was based on agriculture: the main crops were wheat and barley. As well as livestock, bees were kept and horses bred for the chariotry that was the basis of the Hittite army. Copper, lead and silver were mined; iron smelting was well developed, at first for religious objects and later for military purposes. Much of Hittite architecture and art is powerful and vigorous rather than beautiful. Their surviving literature, excluding political texts, is largely religious and folkloric in nature; many epics were translated and adapted from foreign sources.

HIVES, or urticaria, an itchy SKIN condition characterized by the formation of weals with surrounding erythema, and due to HISTAMINE release. It is usually provoked by ALLERGY to food (e.g., shellfish, nuts, fruits), pollens, FUNGI, DRUGS (e.g., PENICILLIN) or parasites (SCABIES, worms). But it may be symptomatic of infection, systemic disease or emotional disorder. **Dermographism** is a condition in which slight skin pressure may produce marked hives, as in the linear marks which appear after writing on the skin.

HOBAN, James (c1762–1831), Irish-American architect. He designed the WHITE HOUSE (1792–1801) and supervised construction of the Capitol and other buildings in Washington, D.C.

HOBBEMA, Meindert (1638–1709), Dutch landscape painter, taught by Jacob van RUISDAEL. His early atmospheric river landscapes and his later forest and road scenes, such as *The Avenue at Middelharnis* (1689), had little influence in their time but foreshadowed CONSTABLE and others.

HOBBES, Thomas (1588–1679), English political philosopher who sought to apply rational principles to the study of human nature. In both the physical and moral sciences reasoning was to proceed from cause to effect: certain knowledge could only flow from deductive reasoning based upon known principles. Hobbes' view of man was materialistic and pessimistic—men's actions were motivated solely by self-interest. This led Hobbes to consider that the existence of a sovereign authority in a state was the only way to guarantee its stability. *Leviathan* (1651), which gave voice to this opinion, was his most celebrated work. Hobbes saw matter in motion as the only reality: even consciousness and thought were but the outworkings of the motion of atoms in the brain. During and after his lifetime, Hobbes was well known as a materialist and suspected as an atheist, but in the 20th century his reputation as an able thinker has overshadowed his former notoriety.

HOBBY, Oveta Culp (1905–), US publisher and public servant. Director of the Women's Army Corps, 1942–45, she became the first secretary of health, education and welfare under EISENHOWER 1953–55 and was editor and president of the Houston *Post* 1938–42 and 1955–83.

HOBSON, John Atkinson (1858–1940), British economist, a forerunner of KEYNES. He believed that the root cause of depression was a predominance of savings at the expense of consumption, with a resultant drop in production. He wrote many books, most notably *The Physiology of Industry* (1889).

HOCHHUTH, Rolf (1931–), controversial German playwright whose first play, *The Deputy* (1963), attacked Pope Pius XII for his stand on the Jews in WWII and whose second, *Soldiers* (1967), portrayed Churchill as a murderer.

HO CHI MINH (1890–1969), president of

North Vietnam (1954–69). From 1911 to 1941 he lived in England, France, Russia, and China, where he founded the Vietnamese Communist party. In 1941 he returned to Vietnam and organized an independence movement, the Viet Minh, that fought against the Japanese in WWII and then against the restored French colonial government. After the decisive Viet Minh victory over the French at Dien Bien Phu in 1954, Vietnam was temporarily divided at the 17th parallel, and Ho became president of North Vietnam. South Vietnam's refusal to hold national elections led to the VIETNAM WAR, during which Ho and his military commander, Gen. Vo Nguyen GIAP, proved resolute and tenacious war leaders. In failing health, Ho lived to see the Tet offensive of 1968 and the start of peace negotiations that led ultimately to North Vietnamese victory.

HO CHI MINH CITY, formerly Saigon, city in Vietnam, 60mi from the South China Sea, on Saigon R. It is an industrial center and river port with a trade in rice and textiles. It was established as an Annamese settlement in the 17th century and was taken by the French in 1859. The city was capital of South Vietnam (1954–75) and suffered considerable damage during the VIETNAM WAR. Pop (metro) 2,600,000.

HOCKNEY, David (1937–   ), British artist whose emphasis on figurative work and brilliant color, often using acrylic paints, brought him immediate fame. One of his most characteristic paintings, *A Bigger Splash* (1967), was also the title of a semi-autobiographical documentary film made in 1974.

HODGKIN'S DISEASE, the most important type of LYMPHOMA or malignant proliferation of LYMPH tissue. Usually occurring in young adults, it may begin with lymph node enlargement, weight loss, FEVER or malaise; the SPLEEN, LIVER, LUNGS and BRAIN may be involved. Treatment has radically improved the outlook in a proportion of cases; it consists of local RADIATION THERAPY or systemic intermittent CHEMOTHERAPY with a combination of agents and STEROIDS.

HOE, Richard March (1812–1886), US inventor who developed many machines associated with PRINTING and invented the first successful rotary printing press (c1847).

HOFFA, James Riddle (1913–1975), US labor leader, president of the International Brotherhood of Teamsters from 1957. After an investigation, led by Robert F. KENNEDY, into his underworld links, Hoffa was convicted in 1964 of tampering with a jury over a bribery charge and jailed 1968–71. In 1975 he disappeared mysteriously and is thought to have been murdered.

HOFFER, Eric (1902–1983), self-educated US author and philosopher. A migratory worker and longshoreman until 1967, he won immediate acclaim with his first book, *The True Believer* (1951), a study of mass movements. *The Passionate State of Mind* (1955), a volume of maxims, followed.

HOFFMAN, Malvina (1887–1966), US sculptress. A student of RODIN'S, she is best known for the 100 portraits of ethnic types executed in bronze for the Museum of Natural History, Chicago, 1930–33.

HOFFMANN, Ernst Theodor Amadeus (1776–1822), German romantic author, composer, man of the theater and critic. He is best remembered today for his fantastic short stories, which inspired POE and others, and an opera, *Tales of Hoffmann*, by OFFENBACH.

HOFFMANN, Josef (1870–1956), Austrian architect who championed ART NOUVEAU in Austria and who was appointed city architect of Vienna in 1920. His masterpiece was the Stoclet House (1905–11) in Brussels.

HOFMAN, Josef (1876–1957), Polish-born US pianist who made a spectacular debut in New York City at the age of 11 and was noted for his authoritative interpretations of the works of CHOPIN and LISZT. He directed the Curtis Institute of Music in Philadelphia.

HOFMANN, Hans (1880–1966), German-American artist and teacher, prominent in the ABSTRACT EXPRESSIONISM movement. His vigorous and colorful style, inspired by KANDINSKY, is exemplified by *The Gate* (1959). In 1934 he opened his influential Eighth Street School in New York.

HOFMANNSTHAL, Hugo von (1874–1929), Austrian neo-romantic poet and dramatist. His early style was influenced by the German poet Stefan George (1868–1933) and the Pre-Raphaelites. An adaptation of Sophocles' *Elektra* (1903) was made into an opera by Richard STRAUSS in 1909, beginning a long collaboration on such operas as *Der Rosenkavalier* (1911), *Ariadne auf Naxos* (1912), *Die Frau ohne Schatten* (1919) and many others. Poems, plays such as *Jedermann* (1911), and his opera librettos make him a major figure of Austrian literature.

HOGAN, Ben (William Benjamin Hogan; 1912–   ), US golfer, four-time winner of the US Open (1948, 1950, 1951, 1953), two-time winner of the Masters (1951, 1953), and two-time PGA champion (1946, 1948).

HOGARTH, William (1697–1764), English painter and engraver, best known for his three series of moralistic and satirical engravings, *The Harlot's Progress* (1732), *The Rake's Progress* (1735) and *Marriage à la Mode* (1745). His first success was as a portraitist. Some of his finest work, such as *Captain Thomas Coram* (1740), is in this field. A master of the early ROCOCO style, he foreshadowed his later style in such works as *The Shrimp Girl* (c1760).

HOGS, or **pigs,** or **swine,** members of the hog family (Suidae), including the babirusa, wild BOAR, bushpig and warthog. They are usually sociable animals, but older boars tend to be solitary. The upper or lower canines are developed in all species to form slashing tusks. Hogs live in forests or thickets, though the warthog is more commonly found in more open country, feeding on a variety of vegetable foodstuffs—grass, roots and tubers, fallen fruits and nuts—and, in addition, insects, earthworms, eggs and other animal material. The many varieties of **domestic pig** are all descended from the European boar (*Sus scrofa*). Pigs are bred primarily either for their fat (lard) or for their meat (bacon and pork). China has the largest number of domestic swine in the world; in the US they are concentrated in the corn belt.

HOHENSTAUFEN, medieval German dynasty of Swabian origin, whose members ruled Germany and the HOLY ROMAN EMPIRE. The great Hohenstaufen emperors were Conrad III, Frederick I Barbarossa, Henry VI, Frederick II and Conrad IV. Their concept of a strongly centralized empire brought them into continual conflict with the papacy, and the two powerful opposing groups: GUELPHS AND GHIBELLINES.

HOHENZOLLERN, German ruling dynasty that first rose to prominence in the 12th century. In 1192 Frederick III of Zollern became the ruler of Nuremburg, and his descendants founded the Swabian and Franconian lines. From the latter were descended the electors of Brandenburg and the dukes and kings of Prussia, who ruled as emperors of Germany, 1871–1918.

HOHOKAM CULTURE, pre-Columbian North American Indian culture based along the Gila and Salt Rivers, Ariz., from c300 BC to c1400 AD. They built a complex network of irrigation canals, made various types of pottery, and built their houses over shallow pits.

HOKKAIDO, northernmost major island of Japan, second largest but least populated. Its aboriginal inhabitants are the AINU. Its economy rests on mining, crop agriculture and fisheries. Its main town is Sapporo.

HOKUSAI, Katsushika (1760–1849), Japanese painter, printmaker and book illustrator, greatest master of the Japanese *ukiyo-e* (popular) school. Interested in every aspect of life, Hokusai worked under a number of different names in a variety of styles, producing over 30,000 drawings of great imagination, compositional mastery and technical excellence. The most famous collections are *36 Views of Fuji* (1823–29) and *Mangwa,* or *Ten Thousand Sketches* (1814–18), many of which were admired in Paris and London as well as the Far East.

HOLBACH, Paul Henri Dietrich, Baron d' (1723–1789), French encyclopedist and materialist philosopher, best known for *The System of Nature* (1770), published as by "J. B. Mirabeau," which included a scathing attack on religion. He translated articles for DIDEROT's *Encyclopédie.*

HOLBEIN, name of two German painters. **Hans Holbein the Elder** (c1465–1524) was a German Gothic painter of great distinction, best known for his many altarpieces and other church decorations, such as the Kaisheim altar (1502). His middle and later work may have been influenced by GRÜNEWALD. **Hans Holbein the Younger** (c1497–1543), a religious painter and portraitist, is generally considered the greater of the two. He lived in many European countries and later entered the service of Henry VIII of England, whose most famous portraits are by him.

HÖLDERLIN, Johann Christian Friedrich (1770–1843), among the greatest of German lyric poets, notable for the grandeur of his images, usually deriving from classical Greek themes. Among his best-known poems are *Bread and Wine, The Rhine* and the *Empedocles* poems. *Hyperion* (1797–99) is a semi-autobiographical prose novel. Suffering from extreme emotional pressures, he finally went mad in 1806.

HOLIDAY, "Billie" (Eleanora Fagan; 1915–1959), US jazz singer. She started her career at 16, singing in Harlem cafés and night spots. Her highly individual style was soon recognized, and she sang with many famous bands and small groups in the 1930s and 1940s. In later years she suffered from heroin addiction.

HOLINESS CHURCHES, group of fundamentalist Protestant churches. Their central dogma is that a state of perfection—"holiness"—may be achieved in this life through "sanctification," a religious experience similar to but following conversion.

HOLINSHED'S   CHRONICLES,

purported histories of England, Scotland and Ireland, largely edited by Raphael Holinshed (c1525–c1580). Colorful, imaginative and inaccurate, they provided plots for many Elizabethan dramatists, including SHAKESPEARE.

HOLLAND, John Philip (1840–1914), Irish-born US inventor who built the first fully successful SUBMARINE, the *Holland*, launched in 1898 and bought by the US Navy in 1900.

HOLLAND, former countship in the W NETHERLANDS, roughly corresponding to the present provinces of North and South Holland. Outside the Netherlands the term is frequently applied to the whole country.

HOLLAND TUNNEL, second-largest underwater vehicular tunnel in the US. Its twin tubes, each 29½ft in diameter and 9,250ft long, pass beneath the Hudson R to link Jersey City, N.J., with downtown New York City. Begun in 1919, it was completed in 1927.

HOLLIDAY, John Henry "Doc" (1852–1887), US gunman and folk hero. A dentist who went to live in Tombstone, Ariz., to cure his tuberculosis, he soon became a gambler and gunfighter. He sided with Wyatt EARP at the O.K. Corral gunfight.

HOLLYWOOD, district of Los Angeles, Cal. Its name became synonymous with the US film industry in the 1920s. Few films are made there, but it now produces a very large percentage of US television material.

HOLMES, Oliver Wendell (1809–1894), US author and physician, best known for his light essays and poems which appeared in the *Atlantic Monthly* from 1857, and in book form as *The Autocrat of the Breakfast Table* (1858) and three sequels. He taught at Harvard, 1847–82; his paper *The Contagiousness of Puerperal Fever* (1843) is considered the first major contribution to medicine by an American.

HOLMES, Oliver Wendell, Jr. (1841–1935), US jurist, Supreme Court justice 1902–32. He is often called "the great dissenter," but this reflects the significance rather than the number of his dissenting judgments. In *Lochner v. New York* (1905) and *Hammer v. Dagenhart* (1918) he reinforced arguments for legislative checks on the economy. His dissent in *Abrams v. United States* (1919) was a powerful defense of free speech.

HOLMES, Sherlock. See DOYLE, SIR ARTHUR CONAN.

HOLOCAUST, term applied to the systematic execution of 6,000,000 European Jews by the German Nazi regime 1933–45. Hitler had exploited anti-Semitic

feelings on his rise to power and later called for a "final solution to the Jewish question." Most Jews in countries overrun by the Nazis who did not emigrate in time were victims of the Holocaust, which effectively obliterated the Jewish secular and religious life that had flourished in Europe for centuries.

HOLOCENE, also known as the Recent, the later epoch of the QUATERNARY Period, representing the time since the last ICE AGE (PLEISTOCENE Epoch) up to and including the present; i.e., about the last 10,000 years. (See also GEOLOGY.)

HOLOGRAPHY, a system of recording LIGHT or other waves on a photographic plate or other medium in such a way as to allow a three-dimensional reconstruction of the scene giving rise to the waves, in which the observer can actually see around objects by moving his head. The apparently unintelligible plate, or hologram, records the INTERFERENCE pattern between waves reflected by the scene and a direct reference wave at an angle to it; it is viewed by illuminating it from behind and looking through rather than at it. The high spatial coherence needed prevented exploitation of the technique, originated in 1948 by D. GABOR, until the advent of LASERS. Color holograms are possible, and three-dimensional TELEVISION may ultimately be feasible.

HOLST, Gustav Theodore (1874–1934), English composer. He is best known for *The Planets* (1918), a massive symphonic suite, each piece representing a planet characterized in myth and astrology. Its popularity has overshadowed his other work, such as the opera *Savitri* (1908).

HOLY ALLIANCE, collective security agreement created at the Congress of VIENNA in 1815 by Russia, Austria and Prussia and later joined by most other powers except Britain, Turkey and the Vatican. Its avowed aim was to conduct mutual relations according to Christian principles. It had little importance in itself, except as a symbol of reaction; revolts in Spain and Naples in the 1820s were suppressed in its name.

HOLY GHOST. See HOLY SPIRIT.

HOLY GRAIL, legendary talisman, given various forms in various versions of the tale. In his *Conte del Graal* (c1180) CHRÉTIEN DE TROYES made it the chalice from which Christ drank at the Last Supper and which was used to catch his blood on the Cross. The knight Perceval, who in the poem by WOLFRAM VON ESCHENBACH became *Parzival* (c1210), seeks the Grail to redeem himself and others. The *Queste del Saint Graal* (c1200) linked the Grail with the

ARTHURIAN LEGENDS, and was the source of MALORY's *Morte d'Arthur* (c1470). The Grail legends have inspired such modern writers as T. H. WHITE, T. S. ELIOT and TENNYSON. and also WAGNER's operas *Lohengrin* (1848) and *Parsifal* (1882).

HOLY ROMAN EMPIRE, European empire centered in Germany which endured from medieval times until 1806. First founded by Charlemagne, it was effectively established in 962 when the pope crowned OTTO I. king of Germany, emperor at Rome. At its height in the 10th and 11th centuries, it included all the German lands, Austria, and modern W Czechoslovakia, Switzerland, the Low Countries, E France and N and central Italy. The emperor was usually the dominant German sovereign, elected by the princes and, until Maximilian I, crowned by the pope. The empire was originally seen as a universal monarchy, modeled on the Roman Empire, the temporal equivalent and ally of the papacy. From the 11th to the 13th centuries, however, it clashed continually with the papacy for European supremacy. At the Reformation a further split developed between the Catholic emperor and Protestant princes, whose sovereignty was confirmed by the Treaty of Westphalia in 1648, leaving the Emperor no more than a figurehead. The empire endured in name until Napoleon, as Emperor of the French, ceased to recognize it in 1806; Francis II of Austria then abdicated the imperial title.

HOLY SEPULCHRE (officially, Church of the Resurrection), multidenominational church in the Old City of Jerusalem, on what is traditionally regarded as the site of the tomb of Jesus. The first church was built by CONSTANTINE I c336 AD, but it has been destroyed and rebuilt many times.

HOLY SPIRIT, or Holy Ghost, in Christian theology, the third Person of the TRINITY. proceeding from the Father and the Son (according to Western churches; Eastern churches reject the phrase "and the Son," Latin *filioque*). In the Old Testament the idea unfolds of the Spirit as God in action, both in creation and in man: the Spirit, bringing wisdom and holiness, was bestowed especially on the prophets, and was promised to dwell in the MESSIAH and to characterize the coming Messianic age. The New Testament shows the Holy Spirit as empowering Jesus Christ throughout his life, and at PENTECOST descending on the apostles, filling them with power and inaugurating the Christian Church as such. The Holy Spirit is basic to the Christian life, being the agent of new (spiritual) birth, given through BAPTISM and CONFIRMATION,

and producing in the Church Christian character and charismatic gifts (emphasized by PENTECOSTAL CHURCHES). By the title **Paraclete** (Greek *parakletos*) the Holy Spirit is described as a comforter or advocate.

HOLY WEEK, in the church year, the week preceding EASTER, observed in most churches as a time of solemn devotion to the passion of Christ. From the 4th century the events of the week of the crucifixion have been liturgically re-enacted, now especially on PALM SUNDAY, MAUNDY THURSDAY, GOOD FRIDAY, Holy Saturday and Easter Day.

HOME ECONOMICS, term used in education to embrace all the disciplines necessary to home maintenance: cookery, nutrition, sewing, the nature and use of textiles, household equipment and budgeting. Originally it was not considered to be a scholastic subject, but today it is a common high school elective, and colleges offer degree courses in it. In the UK it is called domestic science.

HOMELANDS, or "black states," areas set aside for black South Africans. **Bantustans** was the original name for these areas. In theory, the homelands, which are delineated on the basis of tribal language, were created to enable the "separate" economic and political development of blacks in areas outside "white" SOUTH AFRICA, where blacks are excluded from the general franchise. In practice, the homelands are poverty-stricken, generally poor in soil and in natural resources, depending to a large extent on South African aid and revenues generated by commuter workers, those who work in white areas but reside in homelands. According to plan, each of the homelands, of which there are ten, is to become an "independent" nation. Transkei, Bophuthatswana, Venda and Ciskei have become independent, although they are not recognized by any country other than South Africa. The other homelands are Gazankulu, KwaZulu, Lebowa, Qwaqwa, Ndebele and KaNgwane. Efforts to transfer KaNgwane and part of KwaZulu to Swaziland in the early 1980s were blocked by the South African courts. In 1987, KwaZulu established a joint executive council with Natal province to oversee matters of mutual concern.

Together, the homelands encompass only about 13% of the total land area of South Africa and are densely populated despite the fact that 55% of black South Africans live outside their borders. Critics of the homelands concept contend that it is a separatist structure enabling further entrenchment of white rule in South Africa.

HOMELESS, people without homes who live on the streets of US cities or in temporary shelters provided by public agencies and private charities. Their existence became conspicuous in the early 1980s, and their numbers have grown since then. Estimates vary between 250,000 nationwide at any one time to 3 million over the course of a year. The homeless population is not homogeneous. Many are conventional vagrants, particularly alcohol and drug abusers. A third or more are mentally ill people unable to manage organized lives. Perhaps a quarter are poor people — some employed — unable to afford current rents. The causes of homelessness most often cited are lack of low-income housing (due to the inability of the housing market to provide it and government cutbacks in public and subsidized housing programs) and the DEINSTITUTIONALIZATION of the mentally ill. The remedies involve major public commitments to housing, psychiatric care, and other human services.

HOMEOPATHY, system of treatment founded in the early 19th century by C. F. S. Hahnemann, based on a theory that DISEASE is cured by DRUGS whose effects mimic it and whose efficacy is increased by the use of extremely small doses, achieved by multiple dilutions.

HOMEOSTASIS, the self-regulating mechanisms whereby biological systems attempt to maintain a stable internal condition in the face of changes in the external environment. It was the 19th-century French physiologist Claude BERNARD who first realized that the internal environment of any free living organism was maintained constant within certain limits. Homeostasis is generally achieved through two types of regulating systems: on-off control and FEEDBACK control. HORMONES often play a vital role in maintaining homeostatic stability.

HOMER, Greek epic poet, probably of the 8th century BC, to whom are ascribed the ILIAD and ODYSSEY. Nothing is known of his life, nor even of the genesis of the poems. Since they were probably composed orally and based on traditional tales of real events in Bronze Age Greece, it is hard to say whether Homer actually was the author; most scholars now hold, though, that one man gave a final shape to each poem, and that it was the same man in both cases. Homer has come to represent, for many different ages and tastes, the epitome of poetry; this is still true in the 20th century, as witness his influence on POUND and JOYCE.

HOMER, Winslow (1836–1910), US painter who often worked in watercolor, best known for his landscapes and sea studies of New England and Florida, such as *Gulf Stream* (1899). Originally an illustrator, he recorded the Civil War for *Harper's Weekly*. His quasi-Impressionist paintings revolutionized the style of American painting in the 1880s and 1890s.

HOME RULE, Irish, movement to win Ireland control over its domestic affairs. The movement began in the early 1870s, and was initially peaceful despite the Phoenix Park murders, the assassination of two British officials in Dublin in 1882. As a result of the influence of Charles PARNELL. the Liberal Party under GLADSTONE adopted it as policy in 1886. Opposed by the Conservatives, nothing came of this; two Home Rule Bills in 1886 and 1893 foundered, and increasingly the Home Rule movement was dominated by violent radicals uninterested in constitutional solutions. A third bill was finally passed in 1914 but its implementation was postponed until after WWI. In 1916, however, extremists, fearful of losing influence, precipitated the EASTER RISING, which created lasting bitterness. LLOYD GEORGE, in 1922, finally overcame Ulster's objections by agreeing to partition. S Ireland then became completely independent as the Republic of IRELAND.

HOMESTEADING, the claiming and settling of federal lands under the Homestead Act (1862), which proved crucial in developing the US West. From independence, settlers in the West had complained at being charged for virgin lands which, they said, were valueless before being developed by their labor. The homestead movement, for the free distribution of such land, had won wide support by the 1830s and advocacy from such popular figures as Thomas Hart BENTON and Horace GREELEY. The 1862 act awarded land patents on 160-acre plots to individual settlers who paid a nominal registration fee, built a homestead and cultivated the land for five years. Despite much subsequent legislation there were flaws. The best lands were generally outside the provisions while loopholes left scope for bulk acquisition by railroads and speculators. Of the 250 million acres homesteaded by the 1950s, much was in large aggregates.

HOMESTEAD STRIKE, bitter labor dispute (1892) between steel workers and the Carnegie Steel Company, in Homestead, Pa., a landmark in the history of the US labor movement. A clash between strikers and the company's 300 PINKERTON guards left 10 dead. The national guard was sent in and the strike was broken, but at a high cost to the union movement and to the reputations of Carnegie and President Benjamin Harrison.

HOMICIDE, the killing of a human being by another. Criminal homicide is classified as either murder or manslaughter. But some homicides are excusable (occurring by accident) and others are justifiable (killing by a law officer in the line of duty or killing in self-defense or in the defense of property in certain cases).

HOMING PIGEON, a bird of the family Columbidae able to return to its loft from vast distances, and selectively crossbred to combine speed and ever greater stamina. Although the bird's navigational methods are still not fully understood, man has used the homing pigeon since ancient times, particularly to communicate over long distances. The racing of homing pigeons has been a popular sport since the 19th century. A well-trained bird may travel over 1000mi; the record flight is over 2,300mi.

HOMOGENIZATION, process to delay the separation of fat in milk. Milk, a rather unstable emulsion, contains fat globules that tend to coalesce. In homogenization the MILK is heated to about 140°F and passed at pressure through small openings. The fatty clusters are broken up by shearing as they pass through the holes, by the action of pressure and by impact with components of the homogenizer.

HOMOLOGUE, in biology, a structure or organ that has the same evolutionary origin as an apparently different structure in another species. For instance, there is little apparent similarity between a horse's leg and the flipper of a whale, but they have similar embryonic histories. (See EVOLUTION.)

HOMO SAPIENS. See PREHISTORIC MAN; RACE.

HOMOSEXUALITY, sexual activity or inclination involving members of the same sex; in women it is termed *lesbianism*. Freud believed that children pass through a homoerotic phase and that some persons retain and amplify their feelings from that period. While few specialists believe that anyone is "born homosexual," no one can fully explain why some persons and not others become disposed toward homosexuality. Some evidence suggests that a predisposition to homosexuality occurs when the child is quite young and that the tendency may be initiated or enforced if the child, for whatever reason, has low self-esteem or concern about his or her ability to fulfill the role society expects of a member of that sex. Homosexuality has been tolerated in certain societies, as in ancient Greece, but it has encountered hostility among fundamentalist Christians, who believe it to be proscribed by the Bible. In many countries, homosexual acts are not a crime, but the reverse is true in most states of the US.

HONDURAS, the second-largest and most mountainous Central American republic.

Official name: Republic of Honduras
Capital: Tegucigalpa
Area: 43,277sq mi
Population: 4,657,000
Language: Spanish
Religions: Roman Catholic
Monetary unit(s): 1 lempira = 100 centavos
Land. Mountain ranges, high open valleys and plateaus cover Honduras. The hot and humid low-lying areas are the lower reaches of the Ulúa and Chamelecón rivers, the swampy coastal plain in the NE and the narrow coastal plain on the Gulf of Fonseca. Rainfall varies from less than 40in to 120in. The terrain renders communications difficult.
People. Spanish-Indian *mestizos* compose 90% of the population; there are white, black and Indian minorities. Most people are concentrated in the rural areas of the central highlands. Illiteracy runs to 40%. Poverty is endemic: most Hondurans occupy poor subsistence farms.
Economy. US-owned banana plantations dominate the economy, and the bulk of the population works on the land. Coffee replaced bananas as the main export in 1975; other exports are timber, meat, cotton and tobacco. The mineral resources, which include silver and gold, are poorly exploited. There is little industry and poor transport facilities.
History. From the 4th to the 7th centuries AD the ancient city of Copán was a center of the civilization of the MAYAS, but when COLUMBUS touched the Honduran coast on his 1502 voyage the country was inhabited only by semi-nomadic Indian tribes. As a Spanish colony for almost 300 years, Honduras was mostly governed from Guatemala; in 1821 it won independence

from Spain to become part of the Mexican empire. Subsequently, Honduras joined the Central American Federation of which the Honduran patriot Francisco Morazán was president until its dissolution in 1838. As an independent republic since that time, its history has been generally marked by conflicts, revolutions and military rule. In 1969 El Salvador invaded Honduras in a dispute over Salvadoran laborers in Honduras and the fighting left tens of thousands homeless. In April 1975 General Oswaldo López Arellano (proclaimed as president in 1965) was ousted following charges of accepting bribes from a US fruit company to reduce export levies on bananas. A civilian constituent assembly met in 1980, and elected civilian presidents assumed office uneventfully in 1982 and 1986. The 1980s were marked by Honduras's growing involvement in conflicts elsewhere in Central America, particularly Nicaragua, despite the signing of a Central American peace plan in 1987.

HONDURAS, British. See BELIZE.

HONECKER, Erich (1912–   ), East German political leader, protégé and successor (1971) of Communist Party secretary general Walter Ulbricht. He continued Ulbricht's policies of close ties to the Soviet Union, domestic repression, and hostility to the West.

HONEGGER, Arthur (1892–1955), Swiss-French composer, member of the French Les SIX group, best known for his popular *Pacific 231* (1923) and his oratorio *King David* (1921–23).

HONEY, a sweet, sticky confection, formed of partially-digested SUGARS. Nectar, collected from flowers by foraging worker BEES, is returned to the hive, mixed with digestive "saliva" and often a little pollen, and stored in the cells of a wax honeycomb to act as a winter food supply for the hive. Combs, with their familiar hexagonal cells, are used for a variety of purposes in the hive, and honeycombs are not always distinct from combs of grubs. Where honey is taken from domestic hives for man's use, the beekeeper must replace the food supply by feeding sugar throughout the winter.

HONG KONG, British crown colony on the S China coast, consisting of mainland territories and numerous offshore islands. Hong Kong island was ceded to the British after the OPIUM WAR in 1842. Mainland Hong Kong includes Kowloon, acquired in 1860, and the New Territories (360sq mi of the colony's total area), leased to Britain for 99 years in 1898. China, while not recognizing British sovereignty, still accepts these arrangements as convenient to its

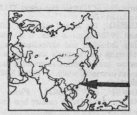

Official name: The Crown Colony of Hong Kong
Capital: Victoria
Area: 400sq mi
Population: 5,602,000
Languages: English, Cantonese, Mandarin
Religions: Buddhist, Taoist, Christian, Muslim, Hindu
Monetary unit(s): 1 Hong Kong dollar = 100 cents

international trade.

Of the rocky land surface, 75% is unsuitable for building and a mere 14% urbanized, accommodating 90% of the population. Since the early 1900s refugees from China's political upheavals have swelled the colony's population. During Japanese wartime occupation (1941–45) the trend was briefly reversed, but since then the population has increased rapidly and necessitated reclamation since 1945 of about 6sq mi of land along the harbor. Hong Kong is a free trade area and one of the world's principal ports. There is much light industry, particularly textiles and electrical goods. The colony depends on China for most of its food and water. In 1984 Britain agreed to turn its crown colony back to China when its lease expired in 1997, but it extracted from China written promises that Hong Kong would remain capitalist for 50 years and that it would enjoy a high degree of autonomy as a special administrative region of China. In 1988, the first draft of a Basic Law for Hong Kong, prepared by a committee appointed by China, indicated that China would interpret "autonomy" as it pleased. Anticipating the colony's reversion to China, thousands of entrepreneurs, business managers, and government officials began to emigrate to Australia, Canada, and the US.

HONOLULU, capital and chief seaport of Hawaii, seat of Honolulu Co. It is located on the SE coast of Oahu Island. Honolulu grew from a fishing village in 1820 to the capital of independent Hawaii, and then territorial capital when Hawaii was annexed to the US. It is important as a shipping center, for sugar and pineapple processing and as the tourist hub of Hawaii. Pop (city) 373,000, (metro) 815,000.

HONSHU, the largest island of Japan, about 89,000sq mi in area. It is Japan's prime industrial and agricultural region, containing the country's six major cities. Narrow coastal plains surround a mountainous interior of which Mt Fuji (12,388ft) is the highest peak.

HOOCH or **HOOGH, Pieter de** (c1629–c1684), Dutch painter best known for his portrayals of the domestic life of the wealthy burghers of Delft, similar in style to the works of his contemporary VERMEER.

HOOD, John Bell (1831–1879), Confederate general in the American Civil War, a daring commander in the second Battle of Bull Run, the battle of Gettysburg and in the resistance to General William Sherman's drive on Atlanta (1864). Disastrously defeated at the battle of Nashville (Dec. 1864), he was relieved of his command at his own request.

HOOD, Thomas (1789–1845), English comic poet, known to contemporaries for his *Comic Annuals* (1830–39, 1842). He is also remembered for his poems of protest against industrial conditions, especially "Song of the Shirt" (1843).

HOOD, Mount, extinct volcano in the Cascade Mts, about 50mi E of Portland, Ore. The peak (11,245ft) is the center of Mount Hood National Forest, an all-season recreation area of over a million acres.

HOOF AND MOUTH DISEASE, or foot and mouth disease, a VIRUS infection of cattle and pigs, rarely affecting domestic animals and man. Vesicles of the SKIN and mucous membranes, and FEVER are usual. It is highly contagious and EPIDEMICS require the strict limitation of stock movements and the slaughter of affected animals.

HOOK, Sidney (1902–   ), US philosopher, at New York U 1927–72, intellectual leader of the anticommunist left from the late 1930s.

HOOKE, Robert (1635–1703), English experimental scientist whose proposal of an inverse-square law of gravitational attraction (1679) prompted NEWTON into composing the *Principia*. From 1655 Hooke was assistant to R. BOYLE, but he entered into his most creative period in 1662 when he became the ROYAL SOCIETY OF LONDON's first curator of experiments. He invented the compound MICROSCOPE, the universal joint and many other useful devices. His microscopic researches were published in the beautifully illustrated *Micrographia* (1665), a work which also introduced the term "cell" to biology. He is best remembered for his enunciation in 1678 of

Hooke's Law. This states that the deformation occurring in an elastic body under stress is proportional to the applied stress.

HOOKER, Joseph (1814–1879), American Civil War general, called "Fighting Joe." Appointed commander of the Army of the Potomac (1863), he was defeated by General Robert E. Lee at CHANCELLORSVILLE and relieved as army commander.

HOOKER, Richard (c1554–1600), English theologian—a man of wide learning— whose eight-volume work, *Of the Laws of Ecclesiastical Polity*, in masterly English prose defended the Elizabethan religious settlement against both Roman Catholics and PURITANS. A landmark of Anglican theology, it acknowledged the authority of the Bible, but gave authority to the Church and reason when Scripture was silent or unclear. Hooker's political theories, modern in tendency, influenced John LOCKE.

HOOKER, Thomas (1586–1647), early American Puritan and founder of Hartford, Conn. A religious exile from England, he came to Massachusetts via Holland (1633), and became minister at the New Town (now Cambridge) settlement. But conflicts with the Massachusetts leaders drove him and his congregation to Connecticut (1635–36). He wrote the Fundamental Orders for the new settlements there (1639).

HOOKWORMS, intestinal PARASITES of man and his domestic animals, belonging to the nematodes. The life cycle involves a free-living larval stage and direct infection of the final host. No intermediate host is involved. The parasitic adults are blood feeders and attack vessels in the wall of the intestine. Each worm may cause the loss of up to 0.25ml of blood a day.

HOOTON, Earnest Albert (1887–1954), US physical anthropologist best remembered for his attempts to relate behavior to physical or racial type, and for books such as *Up From the Ape* (1931) and *The American Criminal* (1939).

HOOVER, Herbert Clark (1874–1964), 31st US president, 1929–33. Born in West Branch, Ia., he graduated as a mining engineer from Stanford U. in 1895, and managed mining operations in various parts of the world until 1914. Already a millionaire, he then became chairman of the voluntary Commission for Relief in Belgium and in 1917 was appointed US Food Administrator, responsible for increasing production and conservation of supplies. This he did with considerable success, providing large supplies for war-stricken Europe. He became secretary of commerce under Warren G. Harding in 1921. A national figure, he had already been considered as a Republican presidential nominee, but it was not until 1928 that he won the nomination. He ran on a conservative platform, proposing a program for "The New Day" to realize the country's full economic potential.

In Oct. 1929 the Wall Street crash began the Depression. In the belief that the root cause was psychological he tried to restore business confidence by cutting public expenditure and balancing the budget. He stressed the responsibility of states for relief programs and would allow the government to help only indirectly. The Reconstruction Finance Corporation was formed in 1932 and, in its first year, lent $1½ billion to help businesses survive. In the same year, Hoover lost a great deal of popularity over his harsh handling of the BONUS MARCH. Clearly unable to cope with the economic situation, he suffered a crushing defeat by F. D. Roosevelt in the 1932 election. His foreign policy had been more successful; he had done much to assure the Latin American states that the US would not intervene in their affairs. The London Naval Treaty (1930) had improved European relations. He retired from public life until he helped organize European relief after WWII. He also headed two "Hoover Commissions" on the organization of the executive branch of government in 1947–49 and 1953–55. These recommended many measures to improve efficiency and management, which Congress accepted.

HOOVER, John Edgar (1895–1972), first director of the FEDERAL BUREAU OF INVESTIGATION (FBI). A lawyer in the Department of Justice 1919–29, he became director of the then Bureau of Investigation in 1924, at a time when it enjoyed a bad reputation for political corruption. Effectively ridding it of political appointees, he instituted rigorous selection and training methods. He established the world's largest fingerprint file and introduced the most up-to-date scientific criminology and research programs. Hoover held the directorship until his death at the age of 77.

HOOVER DAM, formerly Boulder Dam, on the Colorado R in Ariz. It is 726ft high and 1,244ft in length; while providing flood control and irrigation it supplies electricity to S Cal., Ariz., and Nev. and water supplies to several cities. Built 1931–35, it began operating in 1936; it was named for President Herbert Hoover.

HOP, *Humulus lupulus* and related species; tall, perennial twining vine, the female inflorescence of which is used to flavor BEER. Hops are cultivated throughout the world, the US, Germany and England being the leading producers. Family: Cannabinaceae.

HOPE, Anthony (1863–1933), pseudonym of Sir Anthony Hope Hawkins, British author of adventure romances. The most famous were *The Prisoner of Zenda* (1894) and its sequel *Rupert of Hentzau* (1898).

HOPE, Bob (Leslie Townes Hope; 1903–   ), English-born US comedian, in radio, television, and films from the 1930s. Beginning with WWII, he performed frequently for US troops around the world.

HOPE, John (1868–1936), US educator and civil rights leader. Son of a black mother and white father, he could have lived as a white but threw in his lot with the black community, advocating advanced education at a time when Booker T. WASHINGTON was inclined to restrict Negro education to the purely technological. First Negro president of Morehouse College in Atlanta, Ga., in 1906, he became the first president of Atlanta U. in 1929.

HOPEWELL CULTURE, pre-Columbian culture of MOUND builders, flourishing c500 BC–c500 AD and centered in S Ohio. They appear to have had a fairly sophisticated social structure, made decorated pottery, carved stone and were skilled metallurgists.

HOPI, Pueblo Indian tribe of NE Ariz. An agricultural people, they have a complex society based on clans organized around matrilineal extended households. They are peaceful and deeply religious, the *kachina*, or beneficial spirit, being the center of their way of life. Around 6,000 Hopis survive today.

HOPKINS, Esek (1718–1802), American merchant sea-captain, commander of the Continental Navy 1775–78. In Feb. 1776, he captured New Providence, in the Bahamas, from the British.

HOPKINS, Gerard Manley (1844–1889), English poet and Jesuit priest. Largely misunderstood in his lifetime, Hopkins' work was experimental. It exploits natural speech rhythms, using what he called "sprung rhythm" rather than a syllable count, and is highly mimetic, as for example in the poem *The Windhover* and the more unconventional *Harry Ploughman*. His work was published posthumously in 1918. By the 1930s Hopkins had become a major influence on modern poetry.

HOPKINS, Harry Lloyd (1890–1946), US administrator under F. D. Roosevelt who did much to implement the NEW DEAL. He was successively administrator of the Federal Emergency Relief Administration (1933), director of the Works Project

Administration (1935), secretary of commerce (1938) and US Lend-Lease administrator (1941). He was Roosevelt's aide throughout WWII, and at its close carried out important negotiations with Russia for President Truman.

HOPKINS, Johns (1795–1873), US financier and philanthropist. A Quaker, he made his fortune as a wholesale grocer. He bequeathed $7 million to endow Johns Hopkins U. and Johns Hopkins Hospital in Baltimore.

HOPKINS, Mark (1802–1887), US educator. As a Congregational minister and president of Williams College, Williamstown, Mass., where he was professor of moral and intellectual philosophy 1830–87, he was widely influential in academic life.

HOPKINS, Mark (1813–1878), US railroad tycoon, who worked as a commission merchant until 1853, when he became a partner of Collis P. HUNTINGTON, with whom he founded the Central Pacific Railroad.

HOPKINSON, Francis (1737–91), American composer. He was a delegate to the Continental Congress and signer of the Declaration of Independence. His 1788 song collection, dedicated to George Washington, included "My Days Have Been So Wondrous Free," generally regarded as the first native American secular song. His son **Joseph Hopkinson** (1770–1842) wrote the words of "Hail, Columbia."

HOPPER, Edward (1882–1967), US painter and engraver. First recognized for his etchings, he returned to painting late in life, and became known for large, quiet urban studies that revealed a subtle sense of composition and often reflected his feeling of loneliness and alienation.

HOPPNER, John (1758–1810), British portraitist, much influenced by Sir Joshua REYNOLDS. Portrait painter to the Prince of Wales (1789), he was elected to the Royal Academy 1795. His portaits include studies of such eminent men as Nelson, Wellington, and Sir Walter Scott.

HORACE (Quintus Horatius Flaccus; 65–8 BC), Roman lyric poet and satirist. At first supported by the rich patron Maecenas, he later became the favored poet of AUGUSTUS. Horace's surviving work includes four books of *Odes*, two of *Satires*, two of *Epistles* and his *Epodes*. These and the *Art of Poetry* have been a profound and lasting influence on European literature.

HORATIUS (Publius Horatius Cocles), legendary Roman hero. In c508 he and two companions are said to have held the Sublician Bridge, the only remaining bridge across the Tiber, against the invading Etruscan army.

HORIZON, the apparent line where the sky meets the land or sea. At sea, its distance varies in proportion to the square root of the height of the observer's eyes above sea level: if this is, say, 2m the horizon will be about 5.57km distant. The **celestial horizon** is the great circle on the CELESTIAL SPHERE at 90° from the zenith (the point immediately above the observer).

HORMONES, substances produced in living organisms to affect GROWTH, differentiation, METABOLISM, digestive function, mineral and fluid balance, and usually acting at a distance from their site of origin. Plant hormones, auxins and gibberellins, are particularly important in growth regulation. In animals and man, hormones are secreted by ENDOCRINE GLANDS, or analogous structures, into the BLOOD stream, which carries them to their point of action. The rate of secretion, efficacy on target organs and rate of removal are all affected by numerous factors including FEEDBACK from their metabolic effects, mineral or sugar concentration in the blood, and the action of controlling hormones. The latter usually originate in the PITUITARY GLAND, and those controlling the pituitary in the HYPOTHALAMUS. Important hormones include INSULIN, THYROID hormone, ADRENALINE, STEROIDS, parathyroid gland hormone, glucagon, gonadotrophins, ESTROGEN, PROGESTERONE, ANDROGENS, pituitary growth hormone, vasopressin, thyroid stimulating hormone, adrenocorticotrophic hormone, gastrin and secretin.

HORMUZ, Strait of, strategically important waterway and only maritime exit from the Persian Gulf. Most tanker-borne Middle East oil exports pass through the strait, which is commanded by Qishm Island (Iran) and three other islands—Greater Tunb, Lesser Tunb and Abu Musa—currently held by Iran but claimed also by the United Arab Emirates.

HORN, in music, a brass wind instrument. It is derived from the primitive horns—actual animal horns—used by primitive societies. Metal was found to produce a better tone, and horns became increasingly sophisticated and complex. The principal modern horn, the French horn, which is derived from hunting horns, blends well in small brass or woodwind ensembles and is frequently combined with violin and piano. Horns were introduced into orchestral music in the early 18th century. Valved horns were developed in the 19th century.

HORNBOOK, children's primer used before printed books became cheap and widely available. They were printed sheets with the alphabet, numerals, and so on, pasted to a wooden, short-handled tablet and covered with a thin transparent layer of horn for protection.

HORNE, Marilyn (1934–), US mezzo-soprano. A pupil of Lotte LEHMANN, she appeared in 1960 with the San Francisco Opera and soon began thrilling audiences with her brilliance in difficult BELLINI and ROSSINI operas. She made her Metropolitan Opera debut in 1970 as Adalgisa in Bellini's *Norma*.

HORNETS, large WASPS which, unlike the commoner yellow jackets which nest underground, build their nests in trees or in human dwellings. The nest is enclosed in a paperlike shell and consists of a series of horizontal combs. The papery material used is manufactured by the hornets by chewing woody plant matter. Hornets can inflict an extremely painful sting. Family: Vespidae.

HORNEY, Karen (1885–1952), German-born US psychoanalyst who stressed the importance of environment in character development, thus rejecting many of the basic principles of FREUD's psychoanalytic theory, especially his stress on the libido as the root of personality and behavior (see PSYCHOANALYSIS).

HORNS, strictly, keratinous structures with a bony core, borne on the forehead of many ungulates. They show a variety of forms. Horns are usually permanent structures, though the antlers (which are all bone) of many DEER are cast and regrown annually. Horns appear occasionally to be purely ornamental, but usually they are used for defense or in intra-specific aggression. In such species horns are borne only by the males.

HORNSBY, Rogers (1896–1963), US baseball player-manager, one of the greatest right-handed batters in the game's history. His greatest successes were with the St. Louis Cardinals from 1915. He was elected to the Baseball Hall of Fame in 1942.

HOROLOGY, science of the measurement of time and of the construction of timepieces. See CLOCKS AND WATCHES.

HOROWITZ, Vladimir (1904–1989), Russian-born US virtuoso pianist. After a brilliant debut at Kiev (1922), he toured Russia and Europe (1924) and the US (1928). He became a US citizen in 1944.

HORSEFLIES, biting flies, so called because they bite horses as well as other mammals, including man. Only the females bite, piercing the skin with specialized mouthparts and sucking blood. Like MOSQUITOES female horseflies require a blood-meal before laying eggs. They transmit a few diseases, but their main significance as a pest is in the pain of their bite.

HORSE RACING, sometimes called the sport of kings, is among the most popular spectator sports. It is watched by millions of people in many countries, but chiefly in North America, Western Europe, Australasia and South America. Its interest as a spectator sport is considerably enlarged by the practice of on- and off-track betting.

The oldest stake race is the English St. Leger, first run in 1776. In America the most famous race is the KENTUCKY DERBY, first run in 1875. Today the three premier stake races in the US are the Derby, the Preakness Stakes and the Belmont Stakes, all for three-year-olds. Besides flat racing there are also STEEPLECHASING and harness racing. In the latter, special trotting horses known as trotters or pacers are used. They pull carts called sulkies and are trained not to break into a gallop. The major annual event in US harness racing is the Hambletonian.

HORSES, single-toed, ungulate, herbivorous mammals. Wild horses occurred in prehistoric times over most of Eurasia. True wild horses are represented now only by Przewalski's horse (*Equus przewalskii*) of Siberia, Mongolia and western China. These live in groups of 10–15 led and protected by a stallion. Many feral strains of the domestic breeds have however become established—the famous herds of the Camargue and of Sable Island off Nova Scotia. Domestic horses (*E. caballus*) are bred in many different races and can be grouped as ponies, heavy draft horses, lightweight draft and riding horses. Barbs and Arabs, the two most popular riding horses, originated from N African stock. Thoroughbreds are descended from Arabs and both are used widely in breeding light draught and riding horses. The ponies, especially the Icelands, are considered to be descendants of a Celtic stock of domestic horses, while heavy draft animals—Belgians, Percherons, Clydesdales, Shires and Suffolks—come from a breeding stock of central and west Europe. The fossil record of the horse family is so well documented that it provides a classic example of EVOLUTION in action. The earliest animal which can be placed in the family was *Hyracotherium*, or *Eohippus*, from the EOCENE of Europe and North America. This was a small animal the size of a fox terrier with three toes of equal size on each hindfoot and four toes on the forefeet. The development of the single-toed foot of modern horses—an adaptation to running on hard dry grassland (while the side toes represented by splint bones in the foot of the modern horse provided a flatter foot for the marshy habitat of *Hyracotherium*); the change in tooth pattern to allow the animal to eat grasses, a very abrasive food, and the increase in size, may be followed through a continuous series of intermediate stages through to the present day.

HORSESHOE BEND, Battle of, battle fought at Tohopeka, Ala., on March 27, 1814, in which Gen. Andrew JACKSON's forces defeated the Creek Indians led by William Weatherford.

HORTHY DE NAGYBÁNYA, Miklós (1868–1957), Hungarian admiral and politician. In 1919 he headed the counter-revolutionary army which overthrew the communist and socialist coalition under Béla KUN. From 1920–44 he acted as regent, preventing Emperor Charles I from regaining his throne. He joined the Axis powers in WWII, but in 1944, after trying to make peace with Russia, was imprisoned in Germany. He was freed by US forces and in 1949 settled in Portugal.

HORTICULTURE, branch of agriculture concerned with producing fruit, flowers and vegetables. It can be divided into pomology (growing fruit), olericulture (growing vegetables) and floriculture (growing shrubs and ornamental plants). About 3% of US cropland is devoted to horticulture. It was originally practiced on a small scale, but crops such as the POTATO and TOMATO are now often grown in vast fields.

HORUS, ancient Egyptian god. Originally a sky god, depicted as a falcon or as falcon-headed, he became thought of as the son of Isis and Osiris. He avenged his father's murder by defeating Set, the spirit of evil, and succeeded Osiris as king.

HOSEA, Book of, the first of the Old Testament Minor Prophets. Its material originated in the prophecies of Hosea, delivered in Israel in the 8th century BC. It compares God's abiding love for idolatrous Israel to Hosea's love for his prostitute wife, whom he divorced but remarried.

HOSPICE, facility for the care of terminally ill patients. Its professional staff seeks to provide alleviation of pain (rather than life-prolonging medical services), supportive psychological and spiritual counseling, and easy access for family and friends in a dignified and noninstitutional environment. The first hospice was opened in England in 1967 by Dr. Cecily Saunders. In the US, the cost of hospice care is now reimbursable under both Medicaid and Medicare.

HOSPITAL, institution for the care of the sick or injured. Early hospitals and medical schools were usually attached to the temples of certain gods, for example, Aesculapius and Hygeia in Greece, and the association with religion continued; many hospices and hostels were founded by Christian religious orders, such as the KNIGHTS OF ST. JOHN. As refuges for the sick poor, hospitals tended to spread disease rather than prevent or cure it. Only in the 19th century did they improve and then they did so dramatically, as a result of Louis PASTEUR's work on germ theory, LISTER's on infection and aseptic surgery and Florence NIGHTINGALE's organization of the nursing profession. Charitable, voluntary subscription and church hospitals increased greatly in number in Europe and North America from the 18th century, while the 19th saw new government hospitals for the old, sick poor and insane.

Modern hospitals are often large, complex institutions. In most countries the majority are government-owned, but in the US only a third (mostly long-stay hospitals for the mentally ill) are government-owned. Most general hospitals in the US and over half the total are "voluntary," run by religious and other non-profit bodies. Because most charge for treatment, many people take out medical insurance. One in seven hospitals is privately run and makes a profit from fees. There are about 7,000 hospitals in the US with well over a million beds. Every year they admit over 30 million sick people, who stay on average just over one week. General hospitals (over 80% of hospitals) may have equipment for diagnosis, a pharmacy, laboratory, maternity division, operating and recovery rooms, and departments for physical and occupational therapy, for outpatients and emergencies. While larger hospitals may cover sophisticated surgery and intensive care, training of medical staff, and research, there is increased emphasis everywhere on health checks, short stays and outpatient treatment.

HOSTAGE CRISIS. On Nov. 4, 1979, militants in Iran stormed the US embassy, taking as hostages 66 members of the diplomatic and military staff. The action was precipitated by the decision of President Jimmy CARTER, some two weeks earlier, to allow the former shah to enter the US for medical treatment. The militants, supported by the Ayatollah Ruhollah KHOMEINI, demanded extradition of the shah to stand trial for alleged crimes against the Iranian people. The US refused to comply. Toward the end of the year, with the help of the Algerian government, Deputy Secretary of State Warren M. Christopher worked out an agreement that called for the return to Iran of $12 billion in Iranian assets (frozen on Nov. 4) and the prohibition of retaliatory law suits against Iran in US courts in exchange for the hostages. Their release was effected on Jan. 20, 1981, a few minutes after Ronald REAGAN was inaugurated president.

HOT LINE, direct White House–Kremlin emergency communications link, established 1963. It aims to reduce the risk of war occurring by mistake or misunderstanding. Telegraphic and radio circuits run via London, Copenhagen, Stockholm and Helsinki.

HOT ROD, automobile with improved engine or body design, giving greater acceleration and speed. Following WWII, a cult of street racing developed in the US, consisting of acceleration races between traffic lights. In the 1950s, "drag racing" on special tracks was encouraged by police departments to try to prevent this. The term "hot rod" now includes recognized "stock" sedans and especially designed "dragsters."

HOT SPRINGS NATIONAL PARK, in the Ouachita Mts, central Ark. It is a popular tourist and health resort noted for its 47 thermal springs. The park, created in 1921, comprises 3,535 acres.

HOTSPUR. See PERCY, SIR HENRY.

HOTTENTOTS, people of South Africa similar to the Bushmen. Small in stature, they have brown skins, prominent cheekbones, broad noses, coarse hair and pointed chins, and are dolichocephalic and commonly steatopygic. Originally known to themselves as the Khoikhoin, they were nomadic herdsmen and farmers, but this way of life has largely disappeared.

HOUDINI, Harry (1874–1926), born Erich Weiss, US magician and escapologist. He was world famous for his escapes from seemingly impossible situations, as for example from a sealed chest underwater. He also pursued a campaign of exposing fake mediums and spiritualists.

HOUDON, Jean-Antoine (1741–1828), French sculptor famous for his portraits. His sitters included Catherine the Great (1773), Voltaire (1781) and Benjamin Franklin (1791). The best known of his mythological works is *Diana* (1777).

HOUPHOUËT-BOIGNY, Félix (1905–), president of the Ivory Coast since it gained independence (1960). In 1946 he helped found the Rassemblement Démocratique Africain (RDA), which paved the way for independence of the French West African colonies.

HOURGLASS, ancient instrument to measure the passage of time. A quantity of fine, dry sand is contained in a bulb constricted at its center to a narrow neck. The device is turned so that all the sand is in the upper chamber: the time taken for the sand to trickle into the lower chamber depends on the amount of sand and on the diameter of the neck. Small hourglasses are used in the home as eggtimers.

HOUSE, Edward Mandell (1858–1938), US diplomat and adviser to President Woodrow Wilson. He helped Wilson secure the 1912 Democratic nomination. In WWI, he acted for Wilson in Europe, and was responsible for arranging the peace conference and acceptance of Wilson's FOURTEEN POINTS. In 1919, his conciliatory approach during the Treaty of Versailles negotiations led to a rift with Wilson.

HOUSE COMMITTEE ON UN-AMERICAN ACTIVITIES (HUAC), a committee of the US House created in 1938 to investigate fascist, communist and other organizations deemed to be "un-American." Its chairmen, beginning with Martin Dies (Democrat, Texas), were conservatives, and they directed much of their attention to the bureaucracies created by the New Deal. Although the committee was criticized for abusing witnesses and for proceeding on the basis of flimsy or dubious evidence, its status was changed from temporary to permanent in 1945. When 10 prominent film-industry figures (the "Hollywood 10") refused to provide information on alleged communist infiltration, they were imprisoned for contempt. It was before this committee that Alger HISS gave the testimony for which he was subsequently convicted of perjury. A new name, the House Committee on Internal Security, was adopted in 1969, but a changing political climate led to the committee's abolition in 1975.

HOUSE OF COMMONS, lower house of the British parliament. It consists of 635 M.P.s elected by simple majority in single-member constituencies. It is the assembly to which the government is ultimately responsible; it legitimizes legislation, votes money and acts as a body in which complaints can be raised. Proceedings are regulated by the speaker, and a majority of members must assent before a bill becomes law. (See also PARLIAMENT.)

HOUSE OF LORDS, upper house of the British parliament. Members consist of the Lords Temporal: hereditary peers, life peers and ex-officio law lords, and Lords Spiritual: the 2 archbishops and 24 most senior bishops. Of over 1,100 members, only about 200 attend regularly. It is the highest court of appeal and can delay the passage of a Commons bill for up to a year. (See also PARLIAMENT.)

HOUSING AND URBAN DEVELOP-MENT, US Department of (HUD), executive department of the federal government, established 1965, to coordinate programs relating to housing problems. It took over the Housing and Home Finance Agency (HHFA). The department supervises the federal aid programs of both the Model Cities Program and the 1965 Housing and Urban Development Act. Its other programs include urban renewal and planning, mortgage insurance, housing for the elderly, low rent public housing and community facilities.

HOUSMAN, Alfred Edward (1859–1936), English poet and classical scholar. His poetry, narrow in range but at its best intensely felt and always craftsmanlike, is collected in *A Shropshire Lad* (1896), *Last Poems* (1922) and *More Poems* (1936).

HOUSTON, Sam (Samuel) (1793–1863), American frontiersman and politician, leader in the struggle against Mexico to create an independent Texas (1835–36). He commanded a force of fewer than 800 settlers in a decisive battle at San Jacinto (1836) and went on to become the first president of the Republic of Texas 1836–38. During a second term as president 1841–44 he worked to bring Tex. into the Union (1845). Houston served as US senator 1846–59 and was governor of Tex. 1859–61. He was deposed after refusing to support the Confederacy.

HOUSTON, city and seat of Harris Co. in SE Tex., a major US seaport. It is situated about 25mi SW of Galveston Bay on the Houston Ship Channel. Founded in 1836 and named for Sam HOUSTON, it remained relatively unimportant until 1901 when oil was discovered in the area. It is now an industrial, manufacturing and wholesale distribution center. Major industries include chemicals and petroleum refineries, and the NASA Manned Spacecraft Center (1961) has contributed to the growth of medical and technological research. Houston is a cultural center with museums, a symphony orchestra and several colleges and universities, including the U. of Houston. Pop (city) 1,706,000, (metro) 3,222,000.

HOVHANESS, Alan (1911–), US composer noted for his innovative use of Eastern musical materials. He is of Armenian descent, and this is evidenced in his works, among the best-known of which are *Mysterious Mountain* (1955) and

Magnificat (1957).

HOWARD, Catherine (c1521–1542), fifth wife of King Henry VIII of England, niece of the influential duke of Norfolk. Henry annulled his marriage to ANNE OF CLEVES (arranged by Thomas CROMWELL) and married Catherine on July 28, 1540, the day of Cromwell's execution. But when inquiries into premarital misconduct pointed to actual adultery, Catherine's fate was soon decided. She was beheaded at the Tower of London.

HOWARD, John (1726–1790), English public official and noted reformer. Serving as high sheriff of Bedfordshire, Howard had access to Bedford jail, where the conditions in which prisoners were kept appalled him. His subsequent efforts led to an act of Parliament (1774) to improve sanitation in prisons and abolish the system of discharge fees. He visited prisons throughout Britain and Europe and published *The State of Prisons in England and Wales* (1777), a study that inspired further reform.

HOWARD, Oliver Otis (1830–1909), Union general in the American Civil War and commissioner of the FREEDMEN'S BUREAU (1865–72). He helped provide ex-slaves with food, hospitals, labor contracts and schools and colleges. He was cofounder and president (1869–73) of Howard U., Washington, D.C.

HOWARD, Roy Wilson (1883–1964), US journalist and publisher. One of the most powerful newspapermen of the 20th century, Howard was board chairman (1921–36) and president (1936–52) of United Press and of the Scripps-McRae (later Scripps-Howard) newspaper chain. He edited the New York *World-Telegram* (later the *World-Telegram and Sun*) from 1927 to 1960.

HOWARD, Sidney (1891–1939), US playwright whose work is noted for its realism. He won the 1925 Pulitzer Prize with *They Knew What They Wanted* (1924). Other well-known plays include *Lucky Sam McCarver* (1925) and *The Silver Cord* (1926).

HOWE, name of two brothers who were British commanders in the American REVOLUTIONARY WAR. **Richard, Earl Howe** (1726–1799), commanded the British fleet in America 1776–78 but is best known for his victory over the French off Ushant (1794) as commander of the Channel Fleet. **William, 5th Viscount Howe** (1729–1814), was a commander in the British army 1775–78. He won two major victories in 1777 at Brandywine and Germantown.

HOWE, name of an American couple who were prominent social reformers. The physician and teacher **Samuel Gridley Howe** (1801–1876) ran a school for the blind in Boston (later the Perkins School for the Blind), where he achieved outstanding successes, most notably in teaching the deaf-blind child Laura Bridgman. He was also an active abolitionist and published the anti-slavery journal *Commonwealth*. His wife, the author **Julia Ward Howe** (1819–1910), is best known for her "Battle Hymn of the Republic" (1862). She was coeditor of *Commonwealth* and a campaigner for women's rights.

HOWE, Elias (1819–1867), US inventor of the first viable SEWING MACHINE (patented 1846). The early machines were sold in Britain, as in the US there was at first no interest. Later Howe fought a protracted legal battle (1849–54) to protect his patent rights from infringement in the US.

HOWE, Gordie (1928–   ), record-setting US ice hockey player. He played 26 seasons in the NHL and holds career records for most games, goals, assists and points. He was selected as an all-star 22 times and, as a 52-year-old grandfather, played on the same team as his sons.

HOWELLS, William Dean (1837–1920), US author, critic and chief editor of the *Atlantic Monthly* (1871–81). He was a pioneer of American social fiction; his finest and most famous novel is *The Rise of Silas Lapham* (1885). Among those influenced by his work were Stephen CRANE and Theodore DREISER.

HOXHA, Enver (1908–1985), Albanian leader. He helped found the Albanian Communist Party in 1941 and was the first premier of the new communist government (1944–54). Continuing as party secretary after 1954 he remained a Stalinist and fell out with the USSR during the latter's destalinization phase. Hoxha became allied with Communist China in the early 1960s. Later this friendship cooled when China moved toward closer ties with the West.

HOYLE, Edmond (1672–1769), English authority on card and board games, especially whist. He wrote *A Short Treatise on the Game of Whist* (1742), as well as treatises on other games, including chess and backgammon. The expression "according to Hoyle," meaning according to the rules, derives from his name.

HOYLE, Sir Fred (1915–   ), British cosmologist best known for formulating with T. Gold and H. Bondi the steady state theory (see COSMOLOGY); and for his important contributions to theories of stellar evolution, especially concerning the successive formation of the elements by nuclear FUSION in STARS. He is also well known as a science fiction writer and for his popular science books such as *Frontiers of Astronomy* (1955).

HRDLICKA, Aleš (1869–1943), Bohemian-born US physical anthropologist best known for expounding the theory that the Amerinds are of Asiatic origin, which is still generally accepted today.

HUAC. See HOUSE COMMITTEE ON UN-AMERICAN ACTIVITIES.

HUA KUO-FENG (Hua Guofeng; c1920–   ), Chinese political leader, Communist Party chairman from 1976. Achieving swift promotion during the Cultural Revolution, he was made premier following CHOU EN-LAI's death, and then succeeded MAO TSE-TUNG. As China turned toward more pragmatic policies, Hua's close identification with Mao proved a handicap, and he fell from power in 1981.

HUAYNA CAPAC (d. 1525), Inca emperor of Peru. He extended the empire to its farthest limits, but on his death left it to his two sons, and thus bequeathed the civil war which had only just ended when the Spanish arrived.

HUBBELL, Carl Owen (1903–1988), US baseball player, left-handed pitcher for the New York Giants (1928–43). He won 253 games, including 24 consecutive wins in 1936–37, but is best remembered for his performance in the 1934 All-Star game when he struck out Babe Ruth, Lou Gehrig, Jimmy Foxx, Al Simmons, and Joe Cronin in succession.

HUBBLE, Edwin Powell (1889–1953), US astronomer who first showed (1923) that certain NEBULAE are in fact GALAXIES outside the MILKY WAY. By examining the REDSHIFTS in their spectra, he showed that they are receding at rates proportional to their distances.

HUDSON, Henry (d. 1611), English navigator and explorer who gave his name to the Hudson R, Hudson Strait and Hudson Bay. After voyages for the English Muscovy Company to find a northeast passage to China (1607 and 1608), Hudson turned to the west where, with Dutch and then once more English backing (1609 and 1610), he made his most successful voyages. He reached the river known as the Hudson in 1609 and the following year entered Hudson Strait and Hudson Bay, establishing an English claim to the area. After the bitter winter, he was set adrift by a mutinous crew and left to die.

HUDSON, William Henry (1841–1922), English author and naturalist, born in Argentina. Of his early books, romances set in the South American pampas, the best-known is *Green Mansions* (1904). He also wrote studies of bird life and books on the English countryside, such as *A Shepherd's Life* (1910).

HUDSON BAY, shallow, epicontinental sea in N Canada, named for Henry HUDSON. Up to about 850mi long and 600mi wide, it is linked to the Atlantic by the Hudson Strait and to the Arctic Ocean by Foxe Channel. James Bay, the largest inlet, extends southwards between Ontario and Quebec provinces. Hudson Bay shipping is restricted since the bay freezes over in winter. (See also HUDSON'S BAY COMPANY.)

HUDSON RIVER, American river rising in the Adirondacks, flowing generally S for 315mi through N.Y., and emptying into the Atlantic at New York City. It was discovered in 1524, but only explored fully by Henry HUDSON in 1609. It is an important commercial waterway, being navigable by ocean ships as far upstream as Albany. A canal system links it to the Great Lakes. A major program was begun in 1975 to prevent further pollution and make the river safe for fishing and swimming.

HUDSON RIVER SCHOOL, group of 19th-century American landscape painters. The founders were Thomas COLE, Thomas DOUGHTY and Asher DURAND, who were especially interested in the Hudson River Valley and New England. The school later included artists who took their inspiration from other parts of the US.

HUDSON'S BAY COMPANY, mercantile corporation established by the British in 1670 for trading in the Hudson Bay region. The original intention was also to colonize the area and seek a northwest passage, but the company's major activity was fur-trading with the Indians. It played an important part during the next two centuries in opening up Canada. Although its vast lands were sold to the Dominion in 1870, it is still a major fur-trading company and one of Canada's chief business firms with holdings in metal ores, oil, gas and timber.

HUERTA, Victoriano (1854–1916), Mexican general and dictator (1913–14). After first supporting President Porifiro DÍAZ and then Francisco MADERO, he rebelled, proclaimed himself president in February 1913 and had Madero and his vice-president murdered. A combination of revolution at home and hostility from the US finally forced him into exile.

HUGH CAPET (c938–996), king of France 987–96, founder of the CAPETIAN dynasty. The son of Hugh the Great, the duke of the Franks, he was elected king in the place of the legitimate Carolingian heir, Charles of Lower Lorraine.

HUGHES, Charles Evans (1862–1948), US jurist and statesman. He was Republican governor of New York 1906–10 and narrowly missed becoming president in 1916 when Woodrow Wilson was elected. He served as secretary of state 1921–25 and as chief justice 1930–41 during the NEW DEAL.

HUGHES, Howard Robard (1905–1976), US industrialist, aviator and film producer. President of the Hughes Aircraft Company and of the Hughes Tool Company, he was a billionaire who in his later years became an eccentric recluse. Years of litigation over his will followed his death.

HUGHES, John Joseph (1797–1864), Irish-born American priest, the first Roman Catholic archbishop of New York. He held controversial views, being, for example, an opponent of abolitionism while deploring slavery.

HUGHES, Langston (1902–1967), black US poet and writer. He is best known for adapting the rhythms of Afro-American music to his poetry. His works include *The Weary Blues* (1926) and *Not Without Laughter* (1930).

HUGHES, Richard (1900–1976), English writer. His works include plays, poems, novels and short stories but he is best known for his novel *A High Wind in Jamaica* (1929), published in the US as *The Innocent Voyage*, and for *The Fox in the Attic* (1961), part of a projected long novel *The Human Predicament*.

HUGHES, Ted (1930–   ), English poet whose work is noted for its brutal, often violent animal imagery. Among his many collections are *The Hawk in the Rain* (1957), *Lupercal* (1960), *Crow* (1970), *Selected Poems: 1957–1967* (1972) and *Moortown* (1980). He was married to Sylvia PLATH.

HUGHES, Thomas (1822–1896), English jurist, reformer and novelist. He wrote *Tom Brown's School Days* (1857) which, through its emphasis on the Christian virtues and on athletic ability, did much to shape the popular image of the English public school.

HUGHES, William Morris (1864–1952), English-born Australian politician. As prime minister (1915–23) he vigorously led Australia's war effort, forming the Nationalist Party when his own Labour Party failed to support him. At the Paris Peace Conference he gained Australian control over German possessions in the S Pacific.

HUGH OF ST. VICTOR (1096–1141), German theologian in Paris, orthodox contemporary of Peter ABELARD and one of the principal formulators of SCHOLASTICISM.

HUGO, Victor Marie (1802–1885), major French novelist, playwright and poet, best known for his historical novel *The Hunchback of Notre Dame* (1831). Among his several important collections of verse are *Les Feuilles d'Automne* (1831) and *Les Châtiments* (1853). Hugo went into exile when Napoleon III became emperor (1851), and during this period produced his famous, socially committed novel *Les Misérables* (1862). He spent his last years in France, recognized as one of his country's greatest writers and republicans.

HUGUENOTS, French Protestants, followers of John CALVIN's teaching. The Huguenot movement originated in the 16th century as part of the REFORMATION and found support among all sections of French society, despite constant and severe persecution. (See SAINT BARTHOLOMEW'S DAY MASSACRE.) Some respite was provided by Henry IV's Edict of NANTES (1598), but this was revoked in 1685, and many thousands of Huguenots were forced into exile. Full civil and religious liberty was not granted to Huguenots until 1789.

HULA, traditional Hawaiian folk-dance. Its undulating, sensuous movements offended missionaries; despite their attempts to suppress it, it remains popular. The accompanying chants have now been influenced by Western music, but the subtle, graceful hand gestures that are part of the hula have remained basically unchanged.

HULAGU KHAN (c1217–1265), a grandson of GENGHIS KHAN, first of the Mongol Il-Khans of Iran. In 1256 he destroyed the ASSASSINS of N Iran; in the next year he defeated and executed the last ABBASID caliph. In 1258 he captured and sacked Baghdad. He captured Syria, but an Egyptian army drove him back to NW Iran.

HULL, Cordell (1871–1955), American statesman, secretary of state 1933–44 under ROOSEVELT. He developed the "Good Neighbor" policy in relations with South American states and helped maintain relations with the USSR in WWII. He was a Congressman 1907–21 and 1923–30 and senator 1931–33. After the war he was a major force behind US acceptance of the UN, for which he was awarded the 1945 Nobel Peace Prize.

HULL, Isaac (1773–1843), US naval officer, commander of the frigate *Constitution* ("Old Ironsides") in the War of 1812, defeating the British frigate *Guerrière*. He commanded the Pacific Squadron 1824–27 and the Mediterranean Squadron 1838–41.

HULL HOUSE, one of the first US social settlement houses. Founded in Chicago in 1889 by Jane ADDAMS and Ellen Gates Starr, it provided community services and recreational facilities to a poor community.

HUMAN BODY, the physical substrate of man, *Homo sapiens*. In terms of ANATOMY, it consists of the head and neck, a trunk divided into the chest, abdomen and pelvis, and four limbs: two arms and two legs. The head contains (within the bony structure of the skull) the BRAIN, which is connected by cranial nerves to the special sense organs for VISION (EYES), hearing and balance (EARS), SMELL (nose), and TASTE. On the front of the head is the face, specialized for communication (including the special senses, and through which the VOICE emanates). The head sits at the top of the spinal column of VERTABRAE, which continue through the neck, thorax and lumbar region to the sacrum and coccyx. The spinal column is the central structural pillar of the musculoskeletal system, and that onto which the ribs, chest and abdominal walls, and pelvic bones articulate. Within the bony spinal canal is the SPINAL CORD, the downward extension of the brain concerned with relaying information to and from the body and with segmental REFLEX behavior. It is linked with the various parts of the body by the peripheral and autonomic NERVOUS SYSTEMS. The chest, abdomen and pelvis contain many vital organs comprising the various functional systems.

The internal functions of the human body include: the BLOOD CIRCULATION, which supplies all organs with OXYGEN and nutrients and removes waste products from them (see AORTA; ARTERIES; CAPILLARIES; HEART; VEINS); RESPIRATION, which provides oxygen for the blood and removes carbon dioxide via the LUNGS, BRONCHI and TRACHEA; the DIGESTIVE SYSTEM, which starting at the mouth and pharynx, leads into the GASTROINTESTINAL TRACT; systems for EXCRETION and METABOLISM, including particularly the LIVER, KIDNEYS and BLADDER; BLOOD, formed in the bone MARROW and circulating throughout the body; the *lymphoreticular system*, which has a major role in IMMUNITY and blood degradation (see LYMPH; SPLEEN); sites of HORMONE secretion, or ENDOCRINE GLANDS; and the *reproduction system*, essential for the propagation of the species. The *limbs* are primarily concerned with locomotion and fine movement (see JOINTS; MUSCLES; TENDONS) and with tactile sensibility (see TOUCH).

The whole body surface is covered with

SKIN, which is a protective layer also concerned with temperature and fluid regulation, specialized for tactile sensation and bearing many HAIRS. The mucous membranes of the nose, mouth, respiratory tract and gastrointestinal tract and of exocrine GLANDS are made of surface EPITHELIUM. The thin layer of blood vessels (*endothelium*) is a surface which, when intact, prevents the CLOTTING of the contained blood. Other TISSUES found in the body include muscle, both striated (or skeletal) and smooth (or visceral); connective tissue; ADIPOSE TISSUE; BONE; CARTILAGE, and the specialized tissue of the organs discussed above.

The basic unit of the body is the CELL. In the early stages of the development of an individual, this is a multipotential structure containing all the genetic information (in GENES on the CHROMOSOMES of its nucleus) required for the development, differentiation, growth and function of any and all the parts of the body. Each cell divides repeatedly and forms a cell line which gradually specializes into a particular aspect of body structure and PHYSIOLOGY, while suppressing its other potentialities. In this way the highly complex and subspecialized body develops, the integration and control of development being perhaps genetically inbuilt or, alternatively, controlled by hormones and the nervous system. The early development of the EMBRYO and FETUS before BIRTH continue in childhood with subtler differentiation and increase of bulk, a further growth spurt and much sexual development occurring at PUBERTY. After early adult life, the optimal function of organs begins to become impaired with the degenerative processes of aging. Added to these are the DISEASES to which the human body is susceptible; these range from environmental influences such as trauma and infection to specific diseases such as CANCER. Disease and degeneration determine the finite quality of human life, leading to its termination in DEATH.

HUMANISM, originally, the RENAISSANCE revival of the study of classical (Latin, Greek and Hebrew) literature after the medieval absorption with SCHOLASTICISM. In a broader sense it has come to mean a philosophy centered on man and human values, exalting human free will and superiority to the rest of nature; man is made the measure of all things. Renaissance thinkers such as PETRARCH began a trend towards humanism which embraced such diverse figures as BOCCACCIO, MACHIAVELLI, Thomas MORE and ERASMUS and which became the ancestor of much subsequent

secular thought and literature, as well as—in another direction—of the REFORMATION. Modern humanism tends to be nontheistic (see AGNOSTICISM), emphasizing the need for man to work out his own solutions to life's problems, but has a strong ethic similar to that of Christianity. Both Roman Catholic and Protestant theologians (such as Karl BARTH) have sought to show that Christian beliefs embody true humanism.

HUMANITIES, branches of learning concerned with culture, excluding the sciences. Originally the term was limited to the study of ancient Greek and Roman literature, but has been extended to include all languages, literature, religion, philosophy, history and the arts.

HUMAN RIGHTS, 20th-century adaptation of the NATURAL RIGHTS philosophy classically embodied in the US DECLARATION OF INDEPENDENCE (1776) and the French DECLARATION OF THE RIGHTS OF MAN AND THE CITIZEN (1791). During the 19th century, the doctrine of individual rights antecedent and superior to the powers of the state was severely criticized, but the experience of Nazism and WWII revived it. The Charter of the UNITED NATIONS, signed in 1945, reaffirmed "faith in fundamental human rights," and the UNIVERSAL DECLARATION OF HUMAN RIGHTS, adopted by the UN General Assembly in 1948, enumerated them. Two additional UN covenants, the International Covenant on Civil and Political Rights (1976) and the International Covenant on Economic, Social, and Cultural Rights (1976), further elaborated the concept of human rights. In the HELSINKI ACCORDS (1975) the USSR subscribed to a restatement of these rights in exchange for recognition of its western frontiers. Human rights violations are regularly monitored by such international bodies as the Commission on Human Rights of the UN Economic and Social Council and the INTERNATIONAL LABOR ORGANIZATION (ILO), by independent human rights organizations like AMNESTY INTERNATIONAL, and by the world media.

HUMBOLDT, Friedrich Heinrich Alexander, Baron von (1769–1859), German naturalist. With the botanist **Aimé Jacques Alexandre Bonpland** (1773–1858) he traveled for five years through much of South America (1799–1804), collecting plant, animal and rock specimens and making geomagnetic and meteorologic observations. Humboldt published their data in 30 volumes over the next 23 years. In his most important work, *Kosmos* (1845–62), he sought to show a fundamental unity of all natural phenomena.

HUMBOLDT, Karl Wilhelm, Baron von (1767–1835), German philologist regarded as the father of comparative PHILOLOGY. He maintained both that the nature of language reflects the culture of which it is a product, and that man's perception of the world is governed by the language available to him.

HUMBOLDT CURRENT, or **Peru Current,** cold OCEAN CURRENT originating in the S Pacific, and flowing N along the coasts of N Chile and Peru, whose climates it moderates, before turning W to join the S Equatorial Current.

HUME, David (1711–1776), Scottish Enlightenment philosopher, economist and historian, whose *Treatise of Human Nature* (1739–40) is one of the key works in the tradition of British EMPIRICISM. But it was his shorter *Enquiry Concerning Human Understanding* (1748) which prompted KANT to his most radical labors. His influential *Dialogues Concerning Natural Religion* were published posthumously in 1779, long after their composition. In EPISTEMOLOGY Hume argued that men had no logical *reason* to associate distinct impressions as cause and effect; if they did so, it was only on the basis of custom or psychological habit. His SKEPTICISM in this respect has always been controversial. In his own day, Hume's most popular work was his *History of England* (1754–63).

HUMIDITY, the amount of water vapor in the air, measured as mass of water per unit volume or mass of air, and is also called the dew point. Saturation of the air occurs when the water vapor pressure reaches the vapor pressure of liquid water at the TEMPERATURE concerned; this rises rapidly with temperature. Relative humidity, expressed as a percentage, is the amount of water in the air at any given time compared with the amount the air could hold at that temperature before becoming saturated. The physiologically tolerable humidity level falls rapidly as temperature rises, since humidity inhibits body cooling by impeding the EVAPORATION of sweat.

HUMMEL, Johann Nepomuk (1778–1837), Hungarian composer and pianist. A child prodigy, he studied with MOZART. After some years of European travel and further study in Vienna under HAYDN, he became court conductor at Weimar in 1819, and remained there till his death. He wrote masses, ballets, operas and piano works; the latter influenced CHOPIN and SCHUMANN. His *Pianoforte School* (1828), a new fingering method, influenced subsequent keyboard techniques.

HUMMINGBIRDS, an enormous family (Trochilidae) of tiny nectar-feeding birds of the New World, which take their name from the noise of their rapid wingbeats—up to 70 a second in smaller species—as they hover at flowers to feed. Colorful birds, the body size in most species is 50mm (2in) or less. With their small size and fierce activity, hummingbirds must feed about once every 10–15 min. Highly adapted to flight, hummingbirds have short legs and little feet, used only for perching. They can hover in one place and are the only birds capable of flying backwards.

HUMORS, in ancient and medieval medicine, the four bodily fluids whose balance was required for the individual's health. They correspond to the four elements (see ARISTOTLE): *blood* to fire; *phlegm* to water; *choler* (or *yellow bile*) to air; and *melancholy* (or *black bile*) to earth. Excess of blood (hot and dry), for example, made one sanguine; phlegm (cold and wet), phlegmatic; etc. Cure was by enantiopathy, so that a fever would be treated with cold, and so forth. The idea may have originated with EMPEDOCLES in the 5th century BC, and we still retain something of it in modern words such as "choleric" and "phlegmatic."

HUMPERDINCK, Engelbert (1854–1921), German composer. He was much influenced by WAGNER, whom he assisted at the Bayreuth Festival. He wrote several operas; only one, *Hansel and Gretel* (1893) is widely performed today, although *The Royal Children* (1910) is revived from time to time.

HUMPHREY, Doris (1895–1958), US dancer and choreographer, a leader in modern dance. Influenced by Ruth SAINT DENIS and Ted SHAWN, under whom she studied before setting up her own school with Charles Weidman in 1928, she broke away to develop her own expressive style, based upon her theories of movement and her concept of dance as an expression of human dignity.

HUMPHREY, Hubert Horatio (1911–1978), US political leader, who was vice president 1965–1969. A Democrat, he was mayor of Minneapolis, then was elected Senator from Minnesota in 1948. Identified with many liberal causes, as vice president under Lyndon Johnson he vocally supported US Vietnam policy. Unsuccessful as the Democratic candidate for president (1968), he returned to the Senate (1970) until his death.

HUNCHBACK, or **kyphosis,** deformity of the spine causing bent posture with or without twisting (scoliosis) and abnormal bony prominences. TUBERCULOSIS of the spine may cause sharp angulation, while congenital diseases, ankylosing spondylitis, vertebral collapse and spinal TUMORS cause smooth kyphosis.

HUNDRED DAYS, March 20-June 28, 1815, the period between NAPOLEON's return to Paris from exile on Elba and the second Bourbon restoration. Napoleon attempted in this period to reinstate himself as ruler of France on a more liberal basis; this was unacceptable to the Allies, and he had to meet their challenge at the battle of WATERLOO.

HUNDRED YEARS' WAR, sporadic series of wars fought mainly between England and France 1337–1453. They originated in disputes over English possessions in France, and the claims of Edward III of England to the throne of France. In 1337 he invaded Gascony and won the battles of Sluis (1340), CRÉCY (1346) and POITIERS (1356) and seized Calais, gaining important concessions at the Treaty of Brétigny (1360). The French under Charles V regained much of their lost territory 1369–75 and attacked the English coast. Henry V of England destroyed the resulting uneasy truce when he invaded France in 1415, in pursuit of a vainglorious dream of establishing himself as monarch of Britain and France; he captured Harfleur and defeated a superior French force at AGINCOURT. At the Treaty of Troyes (1420) Henry V was recognized as heir to the French throne, and from 1422 his infant son, Henry VI, ruled the dual monarchy, with John, Duke of Bedford as French regent. His able rule won French support, and only the resurgence led by JOAN OF ARC in 1429 halted English gains. Although the Dauphin was crowned Charles VII at Reims in 1429, the English position was not assailed until 1435, when Philip the Good of Burgundy recognized Charles VII as king of France. After 1444 the English were driven back until they held only Calais (until 1558) and the Channel Islands.

HUNGARIAN, or **Magyar,** one of the UGRO-FINNIC LANGUAGES in the Uralic group. It is spoken mainly in Hungary, but also by groups in Czechoslovakia, Romania and Yugoslavia. It has many loan-words from the non-Uralic tongues within it, but retains its own distinct identity. Its six dialects do not differ widely. Standard Hungarian is the speech of the Budapest area.

HUNGARY, people's republic in central Europe, bordered by Czechoslovakia on the N, the USSR and Romania on the E, Yugoslavia on the S and Austria on the W.
Land is mainly low plain, the Kisalföld (Little Plain) in the NW and the Nagyalföld (Great Plain) in the center and

Official name: Hungarian People's Republic
Capital: Budapest
Area: 35,921sq mi
Population: 10,608,000
Languages: Hungarian
Religions: Roman Catholic; Protestant
Monetary unit(s): 1 forint = 100 fillér

E. Crossing the country are two major rivers, the Danube and Tisza, the area between the two (Cumania) being sandy plateau and reclaimed marsh. Other plains lie E of the Tisza including the Hortobagy with its dry steppes (*puszta*). In the W and SW is the more rolling Mezoföld (Middle Plain), and in the S the forested Mecsek massif. Lake Balaton (about 230sq mi) is Europe's largest natural lake. Highlands include the Bakony Forest, Vértes, Gerecse and Pilis hills, and the Carpathian foothills (Kékes, 3,330ft, Hungary's highest peak). Winters are cold and summers hot and dry. Rainfall is heavier in the W, and floods can occur in spring and early summer, though the E and S can have serious summer droughts.

People. Most of the people are Magyars (Hungarians) who speak an Ugro-Finnic language distantly related to Finnish. There are German, Slovak, Croat, Serb and Romanian minorities. About half of the population are urban-dwelling, the largest cities being Budapest, the capital (2,060,000), Miskolc, Debrecen and Szeged.

Economy. There has been expansion as a result of the "New Economic Mechanism" (inaugurated 1968). But mineral resources, including coal, oil, natural gas and iron ore are relatively poor, though bauxite is plentiful. Industrial centers include Budapest (engineering and transportation equipment) and Dunaújvaros (iron and steel). There are important electrical, chemical, food-processing and textile plants. Most of the farmland is owned by the state or by cooperatives. Leading crops include corn, wheat, oats, rye, potatoes, sunflowers and sugar beets. Apricots, grapes, paprika and tobacco are also grown, and hogs, sheep and cattle reared.

History. The area was conquered by the Magyars under Arpád about 896 AD and Christianized in the 900s. Resistance to Turkish invasion ended with the defeat of King Lewis II at Mohács (1526), and most of the country was divided between the Ottoman Empire and Austria, the W and N coming under Hapsburg rule in 1687. A bid for independence led by Lajos Kossuth (1848) failed, but led to the Dual Monarchy (1867), the Austrian Emperor Francis Joseph I being crowned King of Hungary. After WWI, ruled by regent Admiral Horthy, Hungary came under German influence and was Nazi Germany's ally in WWII. Occupied by Russia (1945), Hungary soon turned communist (1949). An uprising against the repressive regime was crushed by Russia (1956) and a puppet government under János Kádár set up. In 1968 Hungary helped other Warsaw Pact countries crush the Dubček regime in Czechoslovakia. In domestic matters, Kádar proved to be nondogmatic, expanding the possibilities for private enterprises. For a time, his "goulash communism" made Hungary the most prosperous state in the Eastern bloc, but in the 1980s the economy stagnated, inflation rose, real wages fell, and unemployment threatened. In 1988 Kádar was replaced as party chief by Károly Grósz, who promised continued market-oriented reforms combined with austerity and discipline. Perhaps to boost Grósz's popularity, the Soviets announced plans to withdraw all 65,000 Russian troops from Hungary.

HUNS, nomadic, probably Mongolian, race who invaded SE Europe during the 4th and 5th centuries. They crossed the Volga R in c372 and attacked the Germanic Goth tribes. By 432 they had invaded the Eastern Empire. Under their great leader ATTILA, they threatened the Roman Empire, unsuccessfully invading Gaul in 451. In 452 their Italian invasion was halted at Lake Garda. After Attila's death in 453, the Hun empire gradually disintegrated.

HUNT, Leigh (1784–1859), English critic, journalist and poet. Editor of the liberal *Examiner*, 1808–22, and later of other journals, Hunt was a friend of the leading literary figures of his day, notably Keats and Shelley whose poetic careers he furthered, Lamb, Hazlitt, Byron and eventually Carlyle. His most highly regarded works are *Lord Byron and Some of His Contemporaries* (1828), his *Autobiography* (1850) and the short lyric poems "Abou Ben Adhem" (1834) and "Jenny Kissed Me" (1844). His literary and dramatic criticism is considered first-rate.

HUNT, Richard Morris (1828–1895), US architect. He trained and worked in Europe 1843–54, and his style in America was historically eclectic. He built the Statue of Liberty base and the 1893 Chicago Exposition administrative building.

HUNT, William Holman (1827–1910), English painter who helped to found the PRE-RAPHAELITE movement. His work is noted for its brilliant coloring and accurate details. His best-known painting is *The Light of the World* (1853).

HUNTER, John (1728–1797), British anatomist and biologist who made many contributions to SURGERY, ANATOMY and PHYSIOLOGY. He is often regarded as the father of scientific surgery.

HUNTINGTON, name of two US railroad tycoons. **Collis Potter Huntington** (1821–1900) was chief promoter of the first railroad company in the West, the Central Pacific (1861). In 1884 he established the Southern Pacific. His nephew and heir, **Henry Edwards Huntington** (1850–1927), formed an outstanding art collection and library at San Marino, Cal. It specializes in English 18th-century art and literature and is now a research center.

HUNTINGTON'S DISEASE, rare, inherited, and incurable neurological disorder that typically strikes people aged 30-60. Early signs are memory problems, loss of balance, and lack of muscular coordination. Within several years involuntary jerking movements of the arms, legs, torso, and facial muscles appear. Mental and physical functions decline until the patient becomes incapacitated. Nearly all victims must eventually be institutionalized; most die within 10-20 years of the start of symptoms. About 25,000 Americans have the disease, and 125,000 more are at risk of developing it. The folksinger Woody GUTHRIE was a well-known victim.

HUNYADI, János (c1387–1456), Hungarian leader and general. Much of his career was spent in successfully preventing the Turkish invasion of Hungary, particularly in 1441–43. His victory against the Turks in 1456 ensured Hungarian independence for a further 70 years.

HURON, Lake, the second largest of the GREAT LAKES, covering some 23,010sq mi, with Canada to the N and E, and Mich. to the S and W. It belongs to the Great Lakes–St. Lawrence Seaway navigation passage. Its principal ports are Sarnia, Owen Sound and Midland in Canada; Alpena, Port Huron and Bay City in the US. Georgian Bay is the largest inlet.

HURON INDIANS, league of four North

American Indian tribes who lived in S Ontario and in c1615 numbered some 20,000. They belonged to the Iroquoian language group, and lived by agriculture. In 1650 the Iroquois virtually destroyed the league. Small numbers of Hurons remain in Quebec and in Okla.

HURRICANE, a tropical cyclone of great intensity. High-speed winds spiral in toward a low-pressure core of warm, calm air (the eye): winds of over 185mph have been measured. The direction of spiral is clockwise in the S Hemisphere, counterclockwise in the N (see CORIOLIS EFFECT). Hurricanes form over water (usually between latitudes 5° and 25°) when there is an existing convergence of air near sea level. The air ascends, losing moisture as precipitation as it does so. If this happens rapidly enough, the upper air is warmed by the water's latent heat of vaporization. This reduces the surface pressure and, thus, accelerates air convergence. Since they require large quantities of moist warm air, hurricanes rarely penetrate far inland. Hurricanes of the N Pacific are often called typhoons. (See also CYCLONE; WIND.)

HUS, Jan (c1370–1415), Bohemian religious reformer and Czech national hero. Influenced by John WYCLIFFE. Hus attacked Church and papal abuses. He defended his ideas at the Council of Constance in 1414, where he was arrested, tried and burned at the stake as a heretic. His followers, the Hussites, demanded many reforms in the Roman Catholic Church with which they were involved in a series of wars in Bohemia in the 15th century.

HUSEIN IBN ALI (c1854–1931), sharif of Mecca 1908–16, and king of Hejaz 1916–24. In 1916 he led the WWI Arab revolt against the Turks, and proclaimed himself king of all Arabia. Assisted by T. E. LAWRENCE, he drove the Turks from Syria, Northern Arabia and Transjordan. In 1924 IBN SAUD forced him to abdicate, and he died in exile.

HUSSEIN (1935–   ), king of Jordan since 1953. His policies are generally pro-Western, and he is a spokesman for moderation in the conflict between the Arab nations and Israel. Jordan's loss of the West Bank in the 1967 ARAB-ISRAELI WAR led to civil war in 1970, when King Hussein gained firmer control over the country. He declined to endorse the Camp David agreements between Israel and Egypt. His fourth wife, Elizabeth Halaby, an American, whom he married in 1978, became Queen Noor.

HUSSERL, Edmund (1859–1938), Czechborn German philosopher who founded PHENOMENOLOGY. Professor at Göttingen and Freiburg universities, he was concerned with what constitutes acts of consciousness and how they relate to experience. He held that consciousness is "intentional" in that it is always "consciousness of" an object. Husserl's investigations of consciousness strongly influenced HEIDEGGER, SARTRE, and other thinkers of twentieth-century EXISTENTIALISM.

HUSTON, the name of two film personalities. **Walter Huston** (1884–1950), Canadian-born American actor, is best known for his roles in the play *Dodsworth* (1936), the musical comedy *Knickerbocker Holiday* (1938) and the film *The Treasure of Sierra Madre* (1947) directed by his son **John Huston** (1906–1987), Hollywood writer, then director, whose films include: *The Maltese Falcon* (1941), *The Asphalt Jungle* (1950), *The African Queen* (1951), *Beat the Devil* (1954) and *Moby Dick* (1956).

HUTCHESON, Francis (1694–1746), Scottish philosopher who propounded the moral sense theory in ETHICS. He held that man has an innate faculty to distinguish between good and bad actions. His main work is *System of Moral Philosophy* (1755).

HUTCHINS, Robert Maynard (1899–1977), influential US educator, president of Chicago U. 1929–45, chancellor 1945–51. He advocated the integration and synthesis of academic disciplines. In 1959 he founded the Center for the Study of Democratic Institutions as an ideal "Community of Scholars." His books include *The Higher Learning in America* (1936) and *University of Utopia* (1953).

HUTCHINSON, Anne (c1600–1643), English Puritan religious leader, one of the founders of Rhode Island. She emigrated to Mass. in 1634, where she preached that faith alone could achieve salvation. She opposed obedience to the strict laws of the Puritan community. In 1638 she and her followers were banished, and they established a settlement on Aquidneck island (now Rhode Island). She was killed by Indians.

HUTCHINSON, Thomas (1711–1780), American colonial governor of Massachusetts, 1770–74. A political enemy of Samuel ADAMS, he opposed American independence, and enforced the STAMP ACT (1765) although considering the act unwise. In 1773 he insisted that duty be paid on tea cargoes at Boston, which led to the BOSTON TEA PARTY. In 1774 he went to England where he served George III as an adviser.

HUTTERITES, or **Hutterian Brethren,**

Protestant sect found primarily in S.D., and Canada. Like the MENNONITES, they believe in common ownership of goods and are pacifists. The sect originated in 1533 as a branch of the ANABAPTISTS and takes its name from Jacob Hutter, martyred in 1536.

HUTTON, James (1726–1797), Scottish geologist who proposed, in *Theory of the Earth* (1795), that the earth's natural features result from continual processes, occurring now at the same rate as they have in the past (see UNIFORMITARIANISM). These views were little regarded until LYELL'S work some decades later. (See also CATASTROPHISM).

HUXLEY, distinguished British family. **Thomas Henry Huxley** (1825–1895) is best known for his support of DARWIN'S theory of EVOLUTION, without which acceptance of the theory might have been long delayed. Most of his own contributions to paleontology and zoology (especially taxonomy), botany, geology and anthropology were related to this. He also coined the word "agnostic." His son **Leonard Huxley** (1860–1933), a distinguished man of literature, wrote *The Life and Letters of Thomas Henry Huxley* (1900). Of his children, three earned fame. **Sir Julian Sorell Huxley** (1887–1975) is best known as a biologist and ecologist. His early interests were in development and growth, genetics and embryology. Later he made important studies of bird behavior, studied evolution and wrote many popular scientific books. **Aldous Leonard Huxley** (1894–1963) was one of the 20th century's foremost novelists. Important works include *Crome Yellow* (1921), *Antic Hay* (1923) and *Point Counter Point* (1928), characterized by their wit and attitude toward lofty pretensions, and the famous *Brave New World* (1932) and *Eyeless in Gaza* (1936). After experimenting with hallucinogenic drugs he became interested in mysticism. Later works include *The Devils of Loudon* (1952), *The Doors of Perception* (1954) and *Island* (1962). **Andrew Fielding Huxley** (1917–   ) shared the 1963 Nobel Prize for Physiology or Medicine with A. L. Hodgkin and Sir J. Eccles for his work with Hodgkin on the chemical basis of nerve impulse transmission (see NERVOUS SYSTEM).

HU YAOBANG (1915–   ), Chinese Communist leader, general secretary of the Chinese Communist party 1980–87. A protégé of Teng Hsiao-ping, he was ousted in the wake of student unrest, being replaced by Zhao Ziyang, who had been premier. Hu retained his seat on the ruling Politburo.

HUYGENS, Christiaan (1629–1695), Dutch scientist who formulated a wave theory of LIGHT, first applied the PENDULUM to the regulation of CLOCKS, and discovered the surface markings of MARS and that SATURN has rings. In his optical studies he stated **Huygens' Principle**, that all points on a wave front may at any instant be considered as sources of secondary waves that, taken together, represent the wave front at any later instant.

HYBRIDIZATION, the crossing of individuals belonging to two distinct species. MULES, for example, are the result of hybridization between a horse and an ass. Hybrid offspring are often sterile, especially in animals.

HYDRAS, freshwater chidaria, perhaps the most familiar of the Hydrozoa. Occurring only as polyps, hydras have no medusoid, or jelly-fish, stage; they are found in ponds, lakes and streams throughout the world. The body is an elongated column with a mouth at one end surrounded by tentacles. Normally attached by the other end to the substrate, hydras can move by "looping" across a plane surface or by free-swimming. Hydras reproduce by asexual budding when food is abundant. When food is scarce, ovaries and testes develop on the column, and sexual REPRODUCTION gives rise to resistant, dormant embryos.

HYDRAULICS, application of the properties of liquids (particularly WATER), at rest and in motion, to engineering problems. Since any machine or structure that uses, controls or conserves a liquid makes use of the principles of hydraulics, the scope of this subject is very wide. It includes methods of water supply for consumption, IRRIGATION or navigation and the design of associated DAMS, canals and pipes; HYDROELECTRICITY, the conversion of water power to electric energy using hydraulic TURBINES; the design and construction of ditches, culverts and hydraulic jumps (a means of slowing down the flow of a stream by suddenly increasing its depth) for controlling and discharging FLOOD water, and the treatment and disposal of industrial and human waste. Hydraulics applies the principles of hydrostatics and HYDRODYNAMICS and is hence a branch of FLUID MECHANICS. Any hydraulic process, such as flow of liquid through a turbine, may be described mathematically in terms of four basic equations derived from the conservation of ENERGY, MASS, MOMENTUM and the relationship between the specific FORCES and internal mechanics of the problem. In hydraulic machines which transmit energy through liquids and convert it into mechanical power, three principles of liquid behavior that have been known for centuries are applied. Toricelli's law states that the speed of liquid flow from a hole in the side of a vessel increases with the depth of the hole below the surface of the liquid in it. PASCAL's law states that the PRESSURE (force per unit area) in an enclosed body of liquid is transmitted equally in all directions. (This law is applied directly in a **hydraulic press**, in which a force applied over a small area by a piston is transmitted through the liquid filling the system to another piston with a larger area on which a much larger force will be exerted.) BERNOULLI's law states that at any point in a tube through which liquid is flowing, if no work is done, the sum of energies due to the pressure, motion (kinetic energy) and elevation (potential energy) of the liquid is constant. Thus by increasing the cross-section of the tube and slowing the flow down, kinetic energy is converted to pressure energy. The development of pumps in the 19th century, which converted mechanical to hydraulic energy and produced greater fluid velocities and pressures than had previously been obtainable, meant that hydraulic principles could usefully be applied to operate a wide variety of machines. Self-contained hydraulic units consisting of an engine, a pump, control valves, a motor to convert hydraulic to mechanical energy, and a load were soon developed for use in industry and transportation. Hydraulics is now one of the main technologies for transmitting energy, comparing well with mechanical and electrical systems and having the advantages of being fast and accurate and good at multiplying forces. Hydraulic systems containing water, oil or special fire-resistant fluids are now used in AIRPLANE landing systems, AUTOMOBILE braking systems and many other industrial applications.

HYDRAXES, rabbit-sized animals of Africa and S Asia, remarkable in that their closest relatives are the ELEPHANTS. There are two species of tree hyrax and half a dozen species of rock hyrax, or dassies. They feed on plants and fruits and have rigid feeding times.

HYDROCARBONS, organic compounds (see ORGANIC CHEMISTRY) composed of CARBON and HYDROGEN only. Other organic compounds may be said to derive formally from the various hydrocarbon structures by the addition of functional groups and by the substitution of other groups or ELEMENTS. Hydrocarbons can be divided into aliphatic, alicyclic, and aromatic compounds. **Aliphatic** hydrocarbons, which are made of carbon atoms linked in straight or branched chains, can be further subdivided into **alkanes** (paraffins), which are *saturated* hydrocarbons, in which all possible sites for hydrogen atoms are filled; **alkenes** (olefins), *unsaturated* hydrocarbons in which one or more double bonds exist between the carbon atoms; and **alkynes** (acetylenes), also unsaturated, but with a triple bond between carbon atoms. Alicyclic hydrocarbons are made of carbon atoms that are linked to form one or more rings, and in general resemble analogous aliphatic structures. Aromatic compounds also contain one or more rings, but have a more stable structure than alicyclic compounds, and in many cases include a BENZENE ring. Some hydrocarbons occur in plant oils, but by far the largest sources of all kinds of hydrocarbons are PETROLEUM, NATURAL GAS, and COAL GAS. They are used as FUELS, for LUBRICATION, and as starting materials for a wide variety of industrial syntheses.

HYDROCEPHALUS, enlargement of the BRAIN ventricles with increased CEREBROSPINAL FLUID (CSF) within the skull. In children it causes a characteristic enlargement of the head. Brain tissue is attenuated and damaged by long-standing hydrocephalus. It may be caused by block to CSF drainage in the lower ventricles or brain stem aqueduct (e.g., by TUMOR and malformation, including those seen with spina bifida), or by prevention of its reabsorption over the brain surface (e.g., following MENINGITIS). Apart from attention to the cause, treatment may include draining CSF into the atrium of the HEART.

HYDRODYNAMICS, the branch of FLUID MECHANICS dealing with the FORCES, ENERGY and PRESSURE of FLUIDS in motion. A mathematical treatment of ideal frictionless and incompressible fluids flowing around given boundaries is coupled with an empirical approach in order to solve practical problems.

HYDROELECTRICITY, or **hydroelectric power,** the generation of ELECTRICITY using water power, is the source of about a third of the world's electricity. Although the power station must usually be sited in the mountains and the electricity transmitted over long distances, the power is still cheap since water, the fuel, is free. Moreover, running costs are low. An exciting modern development is the use in coastal regions of the ebb and flow of the tide as a source of electric power. Hydroelectric power uses a flow of water to turn a TURBINE, which itself drives a GENERATOR.

Convenient heads of water sometimes occur naturally, but more often must be created artificially by damming a river (see

DAM); an added advantage is that the reservoir that forms behind the dam may be tapped for drinking or irrigation water.

The powerhouse, which contains the turbines and generators, may be at the foot of the dam or some distance away, the water then being transported in tunnels and long pipelines called penstocks. The turbines are of two main types: impulse (e.g., the Pelton wheel) and reaction (e.g., the Francis and Kaplan wheels). The Pelton wheel has buckets about its edge, into which jets of water are aimed, so turning the wheel. The Francis wheel has spiral vanes: water enters from the side and is discharged along the axis. The Kaplan wheel is rather like a huge propeller immersed in the water.

HYDROFOIL, a structure which, when moved rapidly through water, generates lift in exactly the same way and for the same reasons as does the AIRFOIL (see also AERODYNAMICS). It is usually mounted beneath a vessel (also called a hydrofoil). Much of a conventional boat's power is spent in overcoming the drag (resistance) of the water; as a hydrofoil vessel builds up speed, it lifts out of the water until only a small portion of it (struts, hydrofoils and propeller) is in contact with the water. Thus drag is reduced to a minimum. Hydrofoils can exceed 75mph as compared with conventional craft, whose maximum speeds rarely approach 50mph.

HYDROGEN (H), the simplest and lightest element, a colorless, odorless gas. Hydrogen atoms make up about 90% of the universe, and it is believed that all other elements have been produced by fusion of hydrogen (see STAR; FUSION, NUCLEAR). On earth most hydrogen occurs combined with oxygen as WATER and mineral hydrates, or with carbon as HYDROCARBONS (see PETROLEUM). Hydrogen is produced in the laboratory by the action of a dilute ACID on zinc or other electropositive metals. Industrially it is made by the catalytic reaction of hydrocarbons with steam, or by the water gas process, or as a by-product of some ELECTROLYSIS reactions. Two-thirds of the hydrogen manufactured is used to make ammonia by the Haber process. It is also used in hydrogenation, PETROLEUM refining and metal smelting. Methanol and hydrogen chloride are produced from hydrogen. Being flammable, it has now been largely superseded by helium for filling BALLOONS and AIRSHIPS. Hydrogen is used in oxy-hydrogen WELDING; liquid hydrogen is used as fuel in rocket engines, in BUBBLE CHAMBERS, and as a refrigerant (see CRYOGENICS). Hydrogen is fairly reactive, giving hydrides with most other elements on

heating, and a moderate reducing agent. It belongs in no definite group of the PERIODIC TABLE, but has some resemblance to the halogens in forming the ion H^-, and to the alkali metals in forming the ion H^+ (see ACIDS); it is always monovalent. A hydrogen atom consists of one ELECTRON orbiting a nucleus of one PROTON. A hydrogen molecule is two atoms combined (H_2). In parahydrogen both the protons have the same spin: in orthohydrogen the protons have opposite spin. They have slightly different properties. At room temperature, hydrogen is 75% orthohydrogen, 25% parahydrogen. Deuterium (H^2) and tritium (H^3) are ISOTOPES of hydrogen. (See also HYDROGEN BOMB.) AW 1.008, mp $-259°C$, bp $-253°C$.

HYDROGEN BOMB, or thermonuclear bomb, very powerful bomb whose explosive energy is produced by nuclear FUSION of two deuterium atoms or of a deuterium and a tritium atom. The extremely high temperatures required to start the fusion reaction are produced by using an ATOMIC BOMB as a fuse. Lithium-6 deuteride (Li^6D) is the explosive; neutrons produced by deuterium fusion react with the Li^6 to produce tritium. The end products are the isotopes of HELIUM, He^3 and He^4. In warfare hydrogen bombs have the advantage of being far more powerful than atomic bombs, their power being measured in megatons (millions of tons) of TNT, capable of destroying a large city. In defensive and peaceful uses they can be modified so that the radioactivity produced is reduced. Hydrogen bombs were first developed in the US (1949–52) by Edward TELLER and others, and have been tested also by the USSR, Great Britain, China and France.

HYDROGEN-POWERED AIRCRAFT, aircraft powered by liquid hydrogen rather than petroleum-based jet fuel. Hydrogen power for airplanes was pioneered in the US by the National Aeronautics and Space Administration (NASA) in the 1950s and again proposed in the 1970s during the oil shortage. Since liquid hydrogen costs much more than jet fuel, the project was abandoned when oil prices fell. In April 1988 the USSR tested a hydrogen-powered commercial airliner capable of using liquified natural gas as well. Liquid hydrogen has the advantage of being much lighter than conventional jet fuel, and it leaves an exhaust of only steam rather than of toxic pollutants, including carbon dioxide. (See also AEROSPACE PLANE, NATIONAL.)

HYDROLOGIC CYCLE, the circulation of the waters of the earth between land, oceans and atmosphere. Water evaporates from the oceans into the ATMOSPHERE, where it may form CLOUDS (see also EVAPORATION). Much of this water is precipitated as rain (or snow, sleet, hail) back to the earth's surface. Of this, some is returned to the atmosphere by the TRANSPIRATION of plants, some joins rivers and is returned to the sea, some joins the GROUNDWATER and eventually reaches a sea, lake or river, and some evaporates back into the atmosphere from the surface of the land or from rivers, streams, lakes, etc. Over 97% of the earth's water is in the oceans. (See also HYDROLOGY.)

HYDROLOGY, the branch of geophysics concerned with the hydrosphere (all the waters of the EARTH), with particular reference to water on and within the land. The science was born in the 17th century with the work of Pierre Perrault and Edmé Mariotte. (See also HYDROLOGIC CYCLE.)

HYDROLYSIS, a double decomposition effected by WATER, according to the general equation

$$XY + H_2O \rightarrow XOH + YH.$$

If XY is a salt of a weak ACID or a weak BASE, the hydrolysis is reversible, and affects the pH of the solution. Reactive organic compounds such as acid chlorides and acid anhydrides are rapidly hydrolyzed by water alone, but others require acids, bases, or ENZYMES as catalysts (see also DIGESTIVE SYSTEM). Industrial hydrolysis processes include the alkaline saponification of oils and fats to glycerol and SOAP, and the acid hydrolysis of starch to glucose.

HYDROPHOBIA. See RABIES.

HYDROPONICS, the technique by which plants are grown without soil. It is also known as soil-less culture. All the minerals required for plant growth are provided by nutrient solutions in which the roots are immersed. The technique has been highly developed as a tool in botanical research, but commercial exploitation is limited primarily because of the difficulty of aerating the water and providing support for the plants. Gravel culture has overcome these problems to some extent and is used to grow some horticultural crops.

HYDROSPHERE, all the waters of the earth, in whatever form: solid, liquid, gaseous. It thus includes the water of the ATMOSPHERE, water on the EARTH'S surface (e.g., oceans, rivers, ice sheets) and GROUNDWATER. (See also HYDROLOGY; LITHOSPHERE.)

HYDROSTATICS. See FLUID MECHANICS.

HYENAS, three species of carnivorous mammals of essentially African distribution. They are distinctive in having the shoulders considerably higher than the hindquarters and have also an unusual gait, moving both limbs on one side of the body together. All three species have massive heads with powerful jaws. Though reviled as scavengers and carrion-feeders, hyenas are active and skilful predators in their own right, hunting in packs of up to 20. Family: Hyaenidae.

HYGROMETER, device to measure HUMIDITY (the amount of water vapor the air holds). Usually, hygrometers measure relative humidity, the amount of moisture as a percentage of the SATURATION level at that temperature. The hair hygrometer, though of limited accuracy, is common. The length of a hair increases with increase in relative humidity. This length change is amplified by a lever and registered by a needle on a dial. Human hair is most used. The wet and dry bulb hygrometer (psychrometer) has two thermometers mounted side by side, the bulb of one covered by a damp cloth. Air is moved across the apparatus (e.g., by a fan) and evaporation of water from the cloth draws latent heat from the bulb. Comparison of the two temperatures, and the use of tables, gives the relative humidity. The dewpoint hygrometer comprises a polished container cooled until the dew point is reached: this temperature gives a measure of relative humidity. The electric hygrometer measures changes in the electrical resistance of a hygroscopic (water-absorbing) strip.

HYKSOS, Asian invaders of Egypt who formed the 15th and 16th dynasties. They introduced the Asian light horse and chariot, bronze weapons and the compound bow. (See also EGYPT, ANCIENT.)

HYMN, a sacred song in praise of gods or heroes, found in almost all cultures. The Jewish PSALMS, sung in the Temple worship, were adopted by the early Christian Church and supplemented by distinctively Christian hymns such as the canticles. Greek and, later, Latin hymns became common, mostly in metrical verse. At the Reformation the REFORMED CHURCHES and the Church of England mainly used metrical psalms. But there is a continuous English hymn tradition from the 7th century, including the 16th-century carols. Modern hymns were developed by Isaac WATTS, John WESLEY and many others, fostered by both the evangelical revival and the OXFORD MOVEMENT. The Lutheran churches from the beginning had many fine hymns.

HYNDMAN, Henry Mayers (1842–1921), English Marxist socialist, founder (1881) of an organization that eventually became (1911) the British Socialist Party, of which he was chairman.

HYPATIA (d. 415 AD), probably the first and one of the most famous women philosophers and mathematicians. She probably occupied the chair of Neo-Platonic philosophy at Alexandria. She was murdered by a Christian mob in an Alexandrian riot.

HYPERBARIC CHAMBER, chamber built to withstand and be kept at pressures above atmospheric. The high OXYGEN pressures achieved in them may destroy the anaerobic bacteria (*Clostridia*) responsible for gas GANGRENE; SURGERY may be done in the chamber. It is also used for aeroembolism in decompression.

HYPEROPIA, or **hypermetropia** or **far-** or **longsightedness,** a defect of VISION in which light entering the EYE from nearby objects comes to a focus behind the retina. The condition may be corrected by use of a converging spectacle LENS.

HYPERTENSION. See BLOOD CIRCULATION.

HYPERTHYROIDISM. See THYROID GLAND.

HYPNOSIS, an artificially induced mental state characterized by an individual's loss of critical powers and his consequent openness to suggestion. It may be induced by an external agency or by the individual himself (**autohypnosis**). Hypnotism has been widely used in medicine and especially in PSYCHIATRY and PSYCHOTHERAPY. Here, the particular value of hypnosis is that, while in trance, the individual may be encouraged to recall deeply repressed memories (see MEMORY) that may be the cause, for example, of a complex; once such causes have been elucidated, therapy can proceed.

Hypnosis seems to be as old as man. However, the first definite information on it comes from the late 18th century with the work of MESMER. who held that disease was the result of imbalance in the patient's "animal magnetism," and hence attempted to cure by use of magnets. In fact, some of his patients *were* cured, presumably by suggestion; and the term **mesmerism** is still sometimes used for hypnotism. Early psychotherapeutic uses include that of CHARCOT and his pupil FREUD, though Freud later rejected hypnosis and instead used his own technique, free association. Little is known of the nature or root cause of hypnosis, and its amateur use is dangerous.

HYPOCHONDRIA, or **hypochondriasis,** involves undue anxiety about real or supposed ailments, usually in the belief that these are incurable. Hypochondriacs may unconsciously, or even consciously, use their symptoms to gain attention and sympathy.

HYPOTHALAMUS, central part of the base of the BRAIN. closely related to the PITUITARY GLAND. It contains vital centers for controlling the autonomic NERVOUS SYSTEM. body temperature and water and food intake. It also produces HORMONES for regulating pituitary secretion and two systemic hormones.

HYSTERECTOMY, or surgical removal of the WOMB. with or without the OVARIES and FALLOPIAN TUBES. It may be performed via either the ABDOMEN or the vagina and is most often used for fibroids, benign TUMORS of womb muscle, CANCER of the cervix or body of womb, or for diseases causing heavy MENSTRUATION. If the ovaries are preserved, HORMONE secretion remains intact, though periods cease and infertility is inevitable.

HYSTERIA, psychiatric disorder characterized by exaggerated responses, emotional lability with excess tears and laughter, over-activity and hyperventilation. It is often a manifestation of attention-seeking behavior. **Conversion systems** or mimicry of organic disease are often termed hysterical; the simulation of a particular disorder fulfills some psychological need in response to certain stresses and results in an unconscious gain or release from anxiety.

9th letter of the English alphabet. It derives from a Semitic form adopted into the Greek alphabet as *iota*. The dot above the lower-case *i* was introduced in the 11th century. With the advent of printing *j* was formally distinguished from *i*.

IACOCCA, Lee (Lido Anthony Iacocca; 1924–   ), US businessman. President (1970–78) of the Ford Motor Co., he left in a dispute with Henry Ford II and took over Ford's failing competitor, the Chrysler Corp. As president (1978–79) and chairman (from 1979) he restored it to profitability—with the aid of government loan guarantees and tax concessions.

IBERIAN PENINSULA, landmass in SW Europe, occupied by Spain and Portugal; cut off from the rest of Europe by the Pyrenees Mts and separated from North Africa by the Strait of Gibraltar.

IBERT, Jacques (1890–1962), French composer of piano pieces, orchestral works, symphonic poems and operas. Among his well-known works are a cantata, *Le Poète et la Fée* (Prix de Rome, 1919), a ballet based on Oscar Wilde's *Ballad of Reading Gaol* (1922), the orchestral suites *Escales* (1922) and *Divertissement* (1930) and the light opera for radio *Barbe-bleue* (1943).

IBERVILLE, Pierre le Moyne, Sieur d' (1661–1706), French-Canadian fur trader and explorer; founder of Louisiana. In 1699 he began exploring the mouths of the Mississippi R; he built a fort on Biloxi Bay and established a post at the site of Mobile, Ala.

IBEX, seven species of wild goats which differ from true GOATS in their flattened foreheads and usually broad-fronted horns. Always found in mountainous areas, ibex live for most of the year in separate-sexed herds, with the males only forming harems during the 7–10-day rut.

IBISES, stork-like birds of moderate size, characterized by long thin downward-curving bills. Ibises have a worldwide distribution in tropical, subtropical and temperate regions, and are usually found near fresh water, feeding on small aquatic animals. Ibises are gregarious and frequently raucous. The best known species are the sacred ibis (*Threskiornis aethiopica*), honored in ancient Egypt, and the scarlet ibis, *Eudocimus ruber*, a Caribbean species with scarlet plumage.

IBN BATTUTA (1304–1368?), greatest Arab traveler of the Middle Ages. Born in Tangier, Morocco, he spent about 25 years traveling in Africa, the Middle East, Persia, India and the Far East. His notes (the *Rihlah* or *Travels*) provide a priceless account of life in the oriental world before the rise of Europe.

IBN GABIROL, Solomon ben Judah (c1021–c1057), influential Spanish Jewish poet and neo-Platonic philosopher. His famous hymn *Keter Malkhut* (Royal Crown) concludes with a confession of sin which has been adapted for the Jewish Yom Kippur (Day of Atonement) service.

IBN KHALDUN (1332–1406), Arab historian and sociologist. The introduction to his great history of the Persians, Arabs and Berbers of North Africa contains the first attempt to interpret the pattern of history in purely secular terms of geography, sociology and allied subjects.

IBN SAUD (c1880–1953), creator of the kingdom of Saudi Arabia. Inheriting the leadership of the orthodox WAHABI movement, in 1900 he and a small band of followers captured the city of Ryadh, from which his family had been exiled, and by 1912 had conquered the Nejd from Turkey. During WWI the British favored his rival, King HUSEIN IBN ALI of Hejaz, in their campaign against the Turks, but in 1924–25 Ibn Saud defeated Husein, combining Hejaz and the Nejd to form the kingdom of Saudi Arabia. He imposed order and religious orthodoxy. In the 1930s he awarded oil concessions to US companies from which his family began to derive enormous wealth. Neutral in WWII, Ibn Saud took little part in the Arab-Israeli war of 1948.

IBO, African ethnic group of SE Nigeria numbering several million. After independence (1963) they came to dominate the civil service and commerce of Nigeria. Hostilities between Ibo and other tribal groups led to the secession of BIAFRA, the Ibo homeland, in 1967. In the civil war which followed, about 2 million Ibos died in battle or from starvation.

IBSEN, Henrik Johan (1828–1906), Norwegian playwright and poet. The pioneer of modern drama, his work developed from national Romanticism (*The Vikings at Helgoland*; 1858) to the realistic and effective presentation of contemporary social problems and moral dilemmas in such plays as *A Doll's House* (1879), *Ghosts* (1881), *The Wild Duck* (1884), and *Hedda Gabler* (1890). Very different, but as important to his philosophy, are his verse-dramas *Brand* (1866) and *Peer Gynt* (1867).

ICE, frozen WATER: a colorless crystalline solid in which the strong, directional hydrogen bonding produces a structure with much space between the molecules. Thus ice is less dense than water, and floats on it. The expansion of water on freezing may crack pipes and automobile radiators. Since dissolved substances lower the freezing point, ANTIFREEZE is used. For the same reason, seawater freezes at about −2°C. Ice has a very low coefficient of FRICTION, and some fast-moving sports (ice hockey, ice skating and iceboating) are played on it; slippery, icy roads are dangerous. Ice deposited on AIRPLANE wings reduces lift. Ice is used as a refrigerant and to cool some beverages. mp 0°C, sg 0.92 (0°C). (See also GLACIER; ICE AGES; ICEBERG.)

ICE AGES, periods when glacial ice covers large areas of the earth's surface that are not normally covered by ice. Ice ages are characterized by fluctuations of climatic conditions: a cycle of several glacial periods contains interglacial periods, perhaps of a few tens of thousands of years, when the climate may be as temperate as between ice ages. It is not known whether the earth is currently between ice ages or merely passing through an interglacial period.

There seem to have been several ice ages in the PRECAMBRIAN, and certainly a major one immediately prior to the start of the CAMBRIAN. There were a number in the PALEOZOIC, including a major ice age with a complicated cycle running through the MISSISSIPPIAN, PENNSYLVANIAN and early PERMIAN. The ice age that we know most about, however, is that of the QUATERNARY, continuing through most of the PLEISTOCENE and whose last glacial period ended about 10,000 years ago, denoting the start of the HOLOCENE. (See GEOLOGY.) At their greatest, the Pleistocene glaciers covered about a third of the earth's surface, or some 45 million km^2, and may have been up to 3km thick in places. They covered most of Canada, N Europe and N Russia, N parts of the US, Antarctica, parts of South America, and some other areas in the Southern Hemisphere.

Theories about the cause of ice ages include that the SUN's energy output varies, that the earth's axis varies in its inclination and in the shape and eccentricity of its orbit, that CONTINENTAL DRIFT and polar wandering may alter global climatic conditions, and that volcanic dust or dust produced by meteorite impact in the ATMOSPHERE could reduce the amount of solar heat received by the surface. (See EARTH; GLACIER; VOLCANO.)

ICEBERG, a large, floating mass of ice. In the S Hemisphere, the Antarctic ice sheet overflows its land support to form shelves of ice on the sea; huge pieces, as much as 200km across, break off to form icebergs. In the N Hemisphere, icebergs are generally not over 150m across. Most are "calved" from some 20 GLACIERS on Greenland's W coast. Small icebergs (growlers) may calve from larger ones. Some 75% of the height and over 85% of the mass of an iceberg lies below water. Northern icebergs usually float for some months to the Grand Banks, off Newfoundland, there melting in a few days. They endanger shipping, the most famous tragedy being the sinking of the *Titanic* (1912). The International Ice Patrol now keeps a constant watch on the area.

ICE CREAM, popular frozen dairy food whose main constituents are sugars, milk products, water, flavorings and air. Ice cream has a high caloric value, and a very high VITAMIN A content, as well as being protein and calcium-rich. It is also a source of, in smaller quantities, iron, phosphorus, riboflavin and THIAMIN. Water ices, which contain no milk products, have been known since ancient times in Europe and Asia. Ice cream probably reached the US in the 17th century, and was first commercially manufactured by Jacob Fussel (1851). Today, the US is the world's largest producer and consumer.

ICE HOCKEY, modern version of field hockey played on ice. Two teams of six skaters each attempt to score goals using wooden sticks to hit a hard rubber disk (the puck) into a small cage (the opponent's goal). Ice hockey is an exciting game which places a premium on speed, strength, mobility and stamina. The game originated in Canada, where it is a national sport. Canada and the US provide teams for the National Hockey League (NHL). The International Ice Hockey Federation governs amateur groups in North America and Europe. Television has made ice hockey popular.

ICELAND, island republic in the N Atlantic Ocean just touching on the Arctic Circle. Geologically young and volcanic in origin, the island is still being molded by volcanic activity. Surtsey, a new island off the S coast, first emerged from the sea in 1963, and Heimay had to be evacuated when the Helgafell volcano erupted in 1973.

Official name: Republic of Iceland
Capital: Reykjavik
Area: 39,769sq mi
Population: 245,000
Languages: Icelandic
Religions: Lutheran
Monetary unit(s): 1 króna=100 aurar
Land. Iceland is mainly a high inland plateau surrounded by mountains; Hvannadalshnjúkur is the highest peak (6,952ft) and Hekla (4,747ft) is the best-known volcano. Large surface areas are covered by cooled laval flows and there are many glaciers, eroded valleys and fjords. Numerous geysers and hot springs are used for central heating and irrigation. The climate is cool and temperate, and the weather very changeable. Temperatures at Reykjavik average 30°F in Jan. and 52°F

in July; rainfall averages 34in yearly at Reykjavik, but is heavier in the SE. Vegetation is mainly mosses, lichens and occasional small trees and shrubs, with some coastal grassland. Soils are thin.

People. The population of Iceland lives mainly in small towns along the coast, in N valleys and the SE lowlands. The largest town is Reykjavik, the capital, chief port and cultural center. Icelanders are a homogenous mixture of Nordic and Celtic racial stock. Their language, ICELANDIC, developed from Old Norse, and has changed little over the centuries. Iceland has a rich literary tradition of heroic medieval sagas and bardic poems which are still read by the people today. Education is free and compulsory from age 7 to 15; illiteracy is practically nonexistent.

Economy. Fishing (especially cod, haddock and herring) and fish-processing are the mainstay industries and provide almost three-quarters of Iceland's exports. A long dispute with Great Britain over fishing rights in the waters off Iceland led to a series of "cod wars." In 1975 Iceland extended its "economic" sea limits to 200mi, and the next year broke diplomatic relations with Britain temporarily. There is some small scale agriculture (cattle, sheep, potatoes, turnips) and manufacturing (fertilizer, appliances, food, clothing and books). Iceland has vast resources of natural energy in her rivers, hot streams and geysers as well as important volcanic mineral potential. In the 1980s Iceland experienced high inflation.

History. Discovered by Norsemen c870 AD, Iceland was under Norwegian rule from 1262, and under the Danes from 1380. The tradition of democratic government dates from 930 AD when the Althing, the world's oldest parliament, was established. Iceland was entirely self-governing from 1918, and became a fully independent republic in 1944. Postwar governments have been led by coalitions, generally center-left. In 1980 Vigdís Finnbogadóttir was elected Iceland's first woman president.

ICELANDIC, the official language of Iceland, developed from Old Norse, which was brought to Iceland from W Norway in the 9th and 10th centuries. Although pronunciation and spelling have changed, the old grammatical structure has remained. Icelanders are still able to read their medieval literature and the SAGAS.

I CHING, or **Book of Changes,** ancient Chinese literary classic dating to c12th century BC. It consists of a set of symbols and texts for DIVINATION. There has been a revival of interest in the *I Ching* in recent years.

ICHTHYOLOGY (from Greek *ichthys*, fish, and *logos*, knowledge), the study of fishes. The word was first used in 1646, respectively 60 and 120 years before the study of birds and insects achieved similar scientific recognition.

ICKES, Harold LeClair (1874–1952), US government official, secretary of the interior, 1933–46, and head of the Public Works Administration 1933–39. An able and responsible administrator, he was a central figure in Roosevelt's NEW DEAL.

ICON, from the Greek for image, a term used for religious images venerated in the Eastern and Russian Orthodox Churches. They also play an important part in liturgy. The Virgin Mary and Jesus were traditional icon figures; by the 7th century icon worship was an officially encouraged cult in the Byzantine Christian Church.

ICONOCLASTIC   CONTROVERSY, Christian dispute over the popular use of ICONS within the Eastern Orthodox (Byzantine) Church. With public support from Emperor Leo III, the iconoclasts (Greek for "image breakers") succeeded (726) in destroying works of art and in persecuting icon worshipers for idolatry and heresy. Under Empress Irene, icon veneration was officially restored (787), an event still celebrated in the Eastern Church as the Feast of Orthodoxy.

ICTINUS (5th century BC), one of the great Greek architects of the Age of PERICLES, famous for his work on the Parthenon in Athens, the Temple of the Mysteries at Eleusis (c430 BC) and the Temple of Apollo Epicurius at Bassae. (See GREEK ART AND ARCHITECTURE; PARTHENON.)

IDAHO, state, NW US, in the Rocky Mts, bounded by Mont. and Wyo. to the E, Utah and Nev. to the S, Wash. and Ore. to the W, and Canada to the N.

Land. Idaho contains about 81 mountain ranges, over 2,000 lakes and 10 major rivers, including the Clearwater, Salmon and Snake (a tributary of the Columbia R), which flows across the entire southern part of the state. The climate is widely varied with dry heat in the S, cold in the snow-laden Rockies and warm moist air from the Pacific in the N. Average July temperatures are 75°F–70°F; average Jan. temperatures are 30°F–16°F. Snowfall ranges from 14in (SW) to more than 200in (in the mountains). Rain varies from below 10in in the Snake R plains to 30in in the Panhandle. Evergreen forests cover two-fifths of Idaho. Wildlife is abundant, and includes elk, antelope, black bear, beaver, muskrat, game and other birds and fish.

Name of state: Idaho
Capital: Boise
Statehood: July 3, 1890 (43rd state)
Familiar name: Gem State
Area: 83,557sq mi
Population: 1,002,000
Elevation: Highest—12,662ft., Borah Peak. Lowest—710ft, Snake River at Lewiston
Motto: *Esto perpetua* ("It is forever")
State flower: Syringa (mock orange)
State bird: Mountain bluebird
State tree: Western white pine
State song: "Here We Have Idaho"

People. Population density is one of the lowest in the US; 70% of all Idahoans live within about 30mi of the Snake R in the fertile agricultural areas. The people are about 98% native-born Americans with about 1% non-Caucasian residents; about 6,000 descendants of French and Spanish Basques live in metropolitan Boise. Some 100 local school districts provide free public elementary and secondary education. The U. of Idaho (at Moscow), Idaho State U. (at Pocatello), and the College of Idaho (at Caldwell) are among the state's institutions of higher education.

Economy. Manufacturing (especially food processing), farming (Idaho potatoes are famous), tourism, mining (silver, lead, gold, zinc, copper and phosphates), livestock raising, manufacturing (especially food processing), lumbering and tourism are the state's chief sources of wealth. Sun Valley is a famous vacation resort. Other attractions include HELL'S CANYON, one of the deepest gorges in North America, Craters of the Moon National Monument, Mount Saint Helens volcano, fish and game reserves and designated "wilderness" areas. The state has vast water resources, and huge dams on the rivers provide hydroelectric power and water for irrigation.

History. The LEWIS AND CLARK EXPEDITION crossed the area in 1805. Fur traders and missionaries arrived in the next few decades. Discovery of gold (1860) brought a rush of prospectors followed by lumbermen, farmers and ranchers. Idaho became a territory (with Wyo. and Mont.) in 1863.

The territorial area was transformed to present-day boundaries, and in 1890 Idaho became the Union's 43rd state. In the 20th century, Idaho has been prosperous, and during the 1970s the population increased by 30%. Growth slowed in the 1980s, and there were problems of water pollution, natural resources management, and unemployment. In 1987 the state's jobless rate dropped below 5% for the first time since 1979. In presidential elections 1968–88, Idaho voted consistently Republican.

IDEA, in psychology, a loosely defined term describing any conscious (see CONSCIOUSNESS) mental event that is not stimulated by immediate PERCEPTION (e.g., a MEMORY). Some psychologists hold that idea-forming is present in perception also; e.g., when bread has just been baked, one smells an aroma and recognizes from experience that it is the aroma of new-baked bread, rather than sensing the bread directly. Others, particularly behaviorists (see BEHAVIORISM), hold that ideas do not exist but are merely reflections of other mental processes.

IDEALISM, name adopted by several schools of philosophy, all of which in some way assert the primacy of ideas, either as the sole authentic stuff of reality or as the only medium through which we can have knowledge or experience of the world. Idealisms are commonly contrasted both with the various types of REALISM and with philosophical MATERIALISM. They are often associated with methodological RATIONALISM because they usually seem to owe more to reasoning upon a priori principles than to any appeal to experience. The idealism of PLATO, in which ideas were held to have an external objectivity, is unrepresentative of modern varieties, of which that of BERKELEY is archetypal. KANT and HEGEL were foremost in the German idealist tradition, while T. H. Green, F. H. Bradley and J. Royce were representative of more recent English-speaking idealists. Idealism has, however, been in eclipse in the 20th century.

IDEOGRAM, a written symbol which directly conveys an idea or represents a thing, rather than representing a spoken word, phrase or letter. **Logograms,** symbols that each represent an entire word, are also often called ideograms. Egyptian HIEROGLYPHICS comprised a writing system partly ideogramic, partly logogrammatic and partly phonetic. (See also WRITING, HISTORY OF.)

IDES OF MARCH, 15th day of Mar. in the ancient Roman calendar, and the day on which Julius CAESAR was assassinated in the

Senate; thereafter known as an *ater dies*, black day, and hence unlucky. In the Roman calendar, the 15th of Mar., May, July or Oct. and the 13th of the other months were called the ides.

IDRIS (1890–1983), king of Libya, 1951–69; chief of the powerful Muslim brotherhood, Sanusi. From Egyptian exile (1923–49), he led the struggle against the Italian occupation, and became king when Libya gained independence. He was deposed when a military junta proclaimed the Libyan Arab Republic.

IEYASU TOKUGAWA (1542–1616), Japanese feudal baron (daimyo) who played a major part in the reunification of Japan during its turbulent 16th century. He founded the Tokugawa shogunate (military government) which lasted from 1603–1867 and established its center at Edo (Tokyo).

IGNATIUS OF ANTIOCH, Saint (d. c100 AD), Christian bishop of Antioch, condemned to death in TRAJAN's reign. Ignatius wrote seven letters (now precious early church documents) in which "catholic church" was first used to denote Christians everywhere and in which he tried to prove that Docetism, a doctrine which held that Christ's bodily sufferings were only "appearance," was heresy.

IGNATIUS OF LOYOLA, Saint (1491–1556), Spanish founder of the Society of Jesus (see JESUITS). Having spent his youth as a Basque nobleman and soldier, Loyola became converted to the religious life in 1521 while recovering from a serious wound. He wrote the famous *Spiritual Exercises* (begun 1522–23), and later went to Paris where, with St. FRANCIS XAVIER, he formed the Society of Jesus (1534). Loyola was its first general, and the author of its *Constitutions* (1547–50).

IGNEOUS ROCKS, one of the three main classes of rocks, those whose origin is the solidification of molten material, or detrital volcanic material. They crystallize from LAVA at the earth's surface (extrusion) or from MAGMA beneath (intrusion). There are two main classes: **Volcanic rocks** are extruded (see VOLCANISM), typical examples being LAVA and pyroclastic rocks. **Plutonic rocks** are intruded into the rocks of the EARTH's crust at depth, a typical example being GRANITE: those forming near to the surface are sometimes called **hypabyssal rocks**. Types of intrusions include batholiths, dikes, sills and laccoliths. As plutonic rocks cool more slowly than volcanic, they have a coarser texture, more time being allowed for crystal formation. (See also ROCKS.)

IGOR (1151–1202), Russian prince. He led a disastrous expedition into the Don steppes to try to keep the Polovtskys (Cumans) from marauding in S and W Russia; described in the famous Russian epic poem *Tale of the Host of Igor* (c1187) and BORODIN's opera.

IGUANAS, the largest and most elaborately marked lizards of the New World. The family (Iguanidae) includes insectivorous, carnivorous and herbivorous forms. Many species are territorial. Iguanas characteristically show ornamental scales and a dorsal fringe, and bear tubercles on the head and body. Some species have an erectile throat fan. There are two major groups: ground iguanas and green iguanas; there is also one species of marine iguana. All species are hunted for food, although this is greatly depleting their numbers.

ILE-DE-FRANCE, historic name for the limestone plains area of the Paris basin, N central France— between the Oise, Aisne, Marne and Seine rivers—the traditional political power center of France.

ILEITIS, INFLAMMATION of the ileum, part of small intestine (see ENTERITIS; GASTROINTESTINAL TRACT).

ILIAD, ancient Greek epic poem of 24 books in hexameter verse, attributed to HOMER; internal references suggest it was composed in the mid-8th century BC. It describes a quarrel during the siege of Troy between the Greek warrior-hero Achilles and King Agamemnon which results in Achilles' brutal slaying of Hector, the Trojan warrior-prince. A companion to the ODYSSEY, the *Iliad* is one of the world's greatest tragic works of literature.

ILLICH, Ivan (1926–   ), Austrian-born educator and social critic of modern Western industrial society. He founded (1961) and directed the Intercultural Center of Documentation (Cuernavaca, Mexico), a "think tank" for those seeking radical social, economic and political change in Latin America. His best known book is *De-Schooling Society* (1971).

ILLINOIS, state, in NE central US, at the heartland of US transportation with a vast network of railroads, highways, airways, lake and river routes. CHICAGO, its largest city, is the crossroads of America.

Land. Illinois is bounded in the N by Wis., in the E by its 60mi shoreline on Lake Michigan, Ind., and the Wabash R, in the SE by the Ohio R and Ken. and in the SW and W by Mo., Ia., and the Mississippi R. Flat prairies and fertile deep black soil plains cover the central and northern areas with rolling hills in the S. Some 4 million acres of forest exist in the S, mostly in Shawnee National Forest. The climate is temperate with summers averaging 70°F

Name of state: Illinois
Capital: Springfield
Statehood: Dec. 3, 1818 (21st state)
Familiar name: Land of Lincoln, Prairie State
Area: 56,400sq mi
Population: 11,552,000
Elevation: Highest—1,241ft, Charles Mound. Lowest—269ft, Mississippi River at Cairo
Motto: "State sovereignty, national union"
State flower: Native violet
State bird: Cardinal
State tree: Oak
State song: "Illinois"

(in the S) and 77°F (in the N); cold, snowy winters average 22°F (in the N) and 37°F (in the S). Rainfall averages 32–48in (N) and 48–64in (S). Plant life is varied, with N and S tree varieties ranging from oak, white pine and hickory to cypress and tupelo gum. The state has large numbers of waterfowl, game birds, small animals and fish.

People. The first wave of settlers moved into the Ohio R valley from the E and S. They pushed the local Indians (after whom the state is named) westward by the 1820s. Since the Civil War the state has had a steady influx of blacks, primarily from the South, and of European immigrants, among them Germans, Poles and Italians. Regionalism has always been a characteristic of Illinois; the people are divided in outlook and political attitudes between the metropolitan Chicago area and "downstate" (the smaller cities and rural areas towards the S). More than 80% of the state's people live in urban areas.

Economy. About one-third of the labor force is employed in manufacturing industries, based mainly in the Chicago area and in the East St. Louis area. A leading agricultural state, it produces corn, hogs, cattle and soybeans. Industry is exceptionally varied and includes the manufacture of machinery, electrical and electronic equipment, processsed foods, metal products and chemicals. Illinois is a leading coal producer and also has significant oil resources.

There is a large system of free public schools; over 100 institutions of higher learning include Northwestern U., the U. of Illinois, U. of Chicago and Illinois Institute of Technology. Unofficially named "the Land of Lincoln," the state has many tourist attractions, including Abraham Lincoln's home and tomb in Springfield and a reconstruction of his earlier home in New Salem.

History. The state was first explored by fur traders and then by JOLIET and MARQUETTE (1673) and by LASALLE (1680). The British took the area from the French after the French and Indian Wars (1763). Following the American Revolution, Illinois became part of the NORTHWEST TERRITORY (1787). In 1818 Illinois was admitted to the Union as a state. The people split over the question of states' rights and slavery at the time of the Civil War. After the war, construction of railroads aided industrial expansion. Through the later part of the 19th and early 20th centuries, Illinois was the scene of labor unrest and bitter strikes, but the result was that the state became a leader in social welfare legislation and progressive labor-employer relations. Following the 1930s depression, industrialization in "downstate" Illinois accelerated enormously. But the state suffered from the economic shift to the Sun Belt. From 1970 to 1986 the population grew only 4%; Chicago's declined 12%. In the late 1980s heavy industry, including steel, revived and out migration declined. In presidential elections 1968–88, Illinois voted consistently Republican.

ILLINOIS INDIANS, a tribal confederation of American Indians belonging to the Algonquian linguistic group and related to Ojibwas and Miamis. Their territory originally included Ill. and parts of Ia., Wis. and Mo. After tribal wars with the IROQUOIS and other northern Indians, the few survivors moved to Kan. (1832) and later to an Okla. reservation (1867).

ILLUMINATION, Manuscript, the decoration of a handwritten text with ornamental design, letters and paintings, often using silver and gold leaf. Illumination flourished between the 5th and 16th centuries AD. The art was highly developed in the Near East, the Orient and in Christian Europe where monks and others skilled in CALLIGRAPHY and painting often devoted their lifetimes to embellishing manuscripts of all kinds, particularly religious. Among the most celebrated manuscripts are the Irish BOOK OF KELLS, the Carolingian *Utrecht Psalter* and the *Très riches heures* commissioned by Jean duc de Berry from the LIMBOURG brothers.

ILLYRIA, an ancient country in the NW part of the Balkan peninsula. It was settled by the 10th century BC by Illyrians, an Indo-European people, who extended their influence from the Danube R to the Adriatic Sea in modern-day Yugoslavia and Albania. It became the Roman province of Illyricum (168 BC).

ILYUSHIN, Sergei Vladimirovich (1894–1977), leading Russian aircraft designer. He created the famous Stormovik dive-bomber (1939) used in WWII and civil aircraft like the IL-62 jet passenger transport (1962).

IMAGISTS, a group of poets writing in the early 20th century in the US and England who rebelled against the artificiality and sentimentality of much 19th-century poetry. Free, idiomatic verse, unusual rhythms and sharp, clear imagery were characteristics of their work which was influenced by French SYMBOLISM. The movement embraced Ezra POUND, Hilda DOOLITTLE (H.D.), Amy LOWELL, D. H. LAWRENCE and James JOYCE.

IMHOTEP, ancient Egyptian architect of the Step Pyramid at Saqqara. Chief minister, priest and scribe to Pharaoh Zoser (3rd millennium BC), Imhotep's fame spread and after his death he became a god of medicine. He is considered the first doctor known to history by name.

IMMACULATE CONCEPTION, Roman Catholic dogma, officially defined in 1854, that the Virgin MARY was conceived free from ORIGINAL SIN, owing to a special act of redemptive grace. It implies that Mary was always perfectly sinless.

IMMERSION FOOT, or trench foot, disease of the feet after prolonged immersion in water, due to a combination of vasoconstriction and waterlogging. It usually starts with red, cold and numb feet, which on warming develop through EDEMA and blistering to ulceration and sometimes skin GANGRENE.

IMMIGRATION. For nearly a century, the US made no effort to limit immigration. Between 1820 (when immigration records began to be kept) and 1890, the US received 15.4 million immigrants, chiefly from those countries of W and N Europe — England, Ireland, Germany, Scandinavia — to which most Americans at that time traced their ancestry. This "old immigration" was succeeded by the "new immigration," which between 1891 and 1920 brought 18.2 ‍‍‍‍on newcomers, the majority from S and ‍‍‍ope — chiefly Italy, Austria-‍‍‍ Romania, and Russia.

‍‍‍ Congress began to exclude certain classes of immigrants, beginning with convicts but eventually also paupers, the insane, the diseased, prostitutes, alcoholics, illiterates, anarchists, and communists. Chinese laborers were barred in 1882, Japanese in 1907. Immigration acts in 1921, 1924, and 1952 established a "national origins" quota system that set ceilings on the number of immigrants admissible each year and also favored those from W and N Europe. The national origins quota system was ended by the immigration act of 1965, which established new criteria for entry preference — occupation and family reunification — and a ceiling (from which immediate relatives of US citizens were exempt) of 290,000 immigrants a year, 170,000 from the E hemisphere, 120,000 from the W hemisphere. Under the 1965 act, immigrants from S and E Europe again replaced those from W and N Europe as the predominant European group. Asians, now competing with Europeans on an equal basis, quickly outnumbered them. But immigration from the W hemisphere exceeded that from Europe and Asia. Between 1980 and 1985, legal immigration to the US averaged 566,000 per year.

Meanwhile the nation became concerned at the tides of illegal immigration, particularly across the US-Mexican border. As many as 2.5 million persons were estimated to be entering the US illegally each year, of whom perhaps 500,000 sought to remain permanently. Hundreds of thousands of Mexicans crossed and recrossed the inadequately guarded US-Mexican border each year. To control illegal immigration, the immigration act of 1986 imposed sanctions on US employers who knowingly hired illegal aliens. At the same time, it permitted illegal aliens who could prove residence in the US since 1982 to apply for legal status leading to citizenship. (See also IMMIGRATION AND NATURALIZATION SERVICE; REFUGEE.)

IMMIGRATION AND NATURALIZA-TION SERVICE, substantially independent branch of the US Justice Department which controls entry of aliens and oversees their presence in the US. It is responsible for enforcing federal immigration, naturalization, exclusion and deportation laws.

IMMORTALITY, the life of the soul after death. This belief is found in both primitive and advanced cultures. It was important in Greek philosophy, notably that of PLATO. Immortality is a fundamental tenet of Christianity and of Islam and is generally accepted in Judaism. Their doctrines of eternal life include the RESURRECTION of the body. Hinduism, Buddhism and Jainism do not recognize individual immortality but believe souls can reach an immortal state or nirvana. (See also ESCHATOLOGY; HEAVEN; HELL; SPIRITUALISM.)

IMMUNITY, the system of defense in the body which gives protection against foreign materials, specifically, infectious microorganisms—BACTERIA, VIRUSES, PARASITES and their products. For many DISEASES, prior exposure to the causative organism in disease itself or by VACCINATION provides acquired resistance to that organism; further infection with it is unlikely or will be less severe. This type of immunity is usually mediated by ANTIBODY AND ANTIGEN reactions and is known as **humoral immunity.** The antigens of microorganisms provoke the formation of the antibody specific to that antigen. Once formed the antibody tends to neutralize (viruses) or to bind to antigens, encouraging phagocytosis and destruction of bacteria. In some diseases the development of antibodies is of value in the phase of recovery from the primary infection; once immunity has been thus primed, the easy and rapid availability of antibody protects against further infection. ALLERGY and anaphylaxis are also largely mediated by humoral immunity. A number of diseases are due to the systemic effects of **immune complexes** (antibody linked to antigen) which may arise in the appropriate response to an infection, or in serum sickness, and these especially affect the KIDNEYS, SKIN and JOINTS. In **autoimmunity** antibodies are produced to antigens of the body's own tissues for reasons that are not always clear; secondary tissue destruction may occur. The second major type of immunity is **cell-mediated immunity** (delayed type hypersensitivity); this system is mediated by lymphocytes and monocytes (including tissue macrophages). It is a reaction only occurring with certain types of infection (TUBERCULOSIS, histoplasmosis and FUNGAL DISEASES) and in certain probable auto-immune diseases; it is also important in the immunity of TRANSPLANTS. Lymphocytes are primed by infection with the appropriate organisms or by the autoimmune or graft reaction and produce substances which affect both lymphocytes and monocytes and result in a type of INFLAMMATION with much tissue damage. The understanding of the role of immunity and its disorders in the causation and manifestations of many diseases has seen a substantial advance in recent years. This has led to the development of DRUGS and other agents which are able to interfere with abnormal or destructive immune responses. **Immune deficiency diseases,** although rare, have provided models for the separate parts of the immune system, and have led to methods of replacement of absent components of immunity. (See also AIDS.) **Passive immunity** is the transfer of antibody-rich substances from an immune subject to a non-immune subject who is susceptible to disease. It is important in infancy, where maternal antibodies protect the child until its own immune responses have matured. In certain diseases such as TETANUS and RABIES, immune serum gives valuable immediate passive protection in non-immune subjects.

IMPALA, *Aepyceros melampus,* one of the most abundant African antelopes. They are about 1m (39in) high and red-brown in color; males have long, black, lyre-shaped horns. Animals of the woodland edge, impala live in big herds in the dry season, breaking up into single male harems in the wetter months for breeding. Impala herds often associate with BABOONS for protection against predators.

IMPEACHMENT, a formal accusation of a crime or other serious misconduct brought against a public official by a legislature. The term sometimes includes the trial by the legislature which follows. Impeachment began in England as a way of putting officials on trial who were derelict in their duties. The impeachment of Warren HASTINGS (1785–95) was a famous English case. Under US constitutional procedure the House of Representatives has the power to impeach; the Senate tries the impeached officials. Grounds for impeachment are: "Treason, Bribery or other high Crimes and Misdemeanors," generally interpreted as being limited to demonstrably criminal acts in the US. Conviction requires a two-thirds vote of all senators present and voting, providing there is a quorum, and entails automatic removal from office. The Chief Justice of the US presides. In US history Congress has impeached 11 officials and convicted four. President Andrew JOHNSON was impeached but acquitted in the Senate by one vote. In 1974, after the House Judiciary Committee recommended his impeachment, Richard M. NIXON resigned as president of the US.

IMPERIALISM, policy of one country or people, usually "developed," to extend its control or influence over other territories or peoples, usually "under-developed" ones. There are many different kinds of imperialism—political, financial, economic, military and cultural. The justification for imperialism has been that backward countries were advanced technologically, economically and culturally by the influence of more developed nations.

However, imperialist policies have also restricted individual and national freedoms and have often exploited undeveloped natural resources and native populations.

IMPERIAL VALLEY, important agricultural area in the low-lying SE Cal. desert, extending into Mexico, called the "Winter Garden" of America. Since the construction of the 80mi-long All-American irrigation canal and soil reclamation projects in the 1940s and 1950s, the valley has become a highly fertile farm region producing alfalfa, melons, tomatoes, lettuce and sugar beets. Even the January temperature averages 53°F.

IMPETIGO, superficial SKIN infection, usually of the FACE, caused by STREPTOCOCCUS or STAPHYLOCOCCUS. It starts with small vesicles which burst and leave a characteristic yellow crust. It is easily spread by fingers from a single vesicle to affect several large areas and may be transmitted to others. It is common in children and requires ANTIBIOTIC creams, and systemic PENICILLIN in some cases.

IMPRESSIONISM, dominant artistic movement in France from the mid-1860s to c1890. The Impressionist painters, who include MANET, MONET, PISSARRO, and others, painted landscapes and scenes of leisure in contemporary Paris. They usually worked out-of-doors, recording the scenes before them spontaneously and directly. Their pictures were executed in bright contrasting colors in order to convey the impression of light and they emphasized the individual brushstrokes. The term "impressionist" was first used as a criticism of Monet's *Impression: Soleil levant (Sunrise),* 1874. The artists organized eight independent exhibitions for their pictures. The American painters CASSATT and HASSAM were influenced by the Impressionists. Impressionism also describes other art forms, notably literature which uses symbolic imagery (see RILKE) and music which expresses mood and feeling (see DEBUSSY).

IMPRESSMENT, the seizure of persons or property for the purpose of placing them in public service. Common in many countries, impressment was used by the British to obtain seamen until the 19th century. Impressment of British deserters and US citizens from American ships aroused public indignation in the US and was one of the causes of the WAR OF 1812.

INBREEDING, the breeding of individual plants or animals that are closely related. Inbreeding tends to bring together recessive GENES with, usually, deleterious effects. This is because recessive genes are often harmless in the heterozygous condition but harmful in the homozygous condition (see GENETICS). For this reason, inbreeding has long been regarded as a practice to be discouraged; in human cultures, consanguinity is frequently forbidden by law or discouraged by custom.

INCA, title of the ruler of an empire in W South America which, at the time of the Spanish conquest, occupied what is now Peru, parts of Ecuador, Chile, Bolivia and Argentina. It extended some 3,000mi from N to S, stretching back between 150 and 250mi from the narrow Pacific coastal plain into the high Andes. Communications were maintained along brilliantly engineered and extensive roads, carried over the sheer Andean gorges by fiber cable suspension bridges. Trained relay runners carried messages 150mi a day and the army had quick access to trouble spots. Restive subject tribes were resettled near Cuzco, the capital. Detailed surveys of new conquests were recorded by *quipu,* a mnemonic device using knotted cords. Writing, like draft animals and wheeled transport, was unknown; so too was monetary currency. Taxation and tribute were levied in the form of labor services. In other respects the culture was highly advanced. At sites such as MACHU PICCHU Inca architects raised some of the world's finest stone structures; precious metals from government-controlled mines were worked by supremely-skilled goldsmiths; bronze was also used; ceramic and textile design was outstanding. Agriculture was based on elaborate irrigation and hillside terracing.

INCARNATION, embodiment of a deity as a human or animal. In Hindu belief, Vishnu has manifested himself in different incarnations or *avatara.* In Christianity the doctrine of the incarnation is that the Son of God (see TRINITY) took human nature and was born as JESUS CHRIST, who was thus fully God and fully man. This doctrine, much debated in the early Church, was finally defined at the Council of Chalcedon, 451. By the incarnation, redeemed mankind is in Christ united to God.

INCEST, sexual concourse between persons to whom marriage is forbidden on grounds of kinship. The grounds vary with culture and epoch. First cousin marriage, for example, once prohibited in Christian law, is now generally permissible. Almost universally forbidden are marriages between parents and children, or between siblings, but ancient Egypt and the Incas allowed brother-sister marriages in the ruling family.

INCOME TAX, the major source of

government revenue. As opposed to excise taxes levied on goods, it is a tax on the incomes of individuals, proportionate to their incomes, or on corporations. At first imposed only to meet extraordinary expenditures such as war financing, income tax became permanent in Britain in 1874. In the US it was levied during the Civil War, but an attempt to make it a permanent federal tax was ruled unconstitutional. The 16th Amendment (1913) authorized the federal government to levy the tax and since 1919 most states have also adopted this mode of revenue raising. It is assessed on net income after allowances have been deducted for family dependents, contributions to charities and certain other expenditures. In the most thorough tax reform since WWII, intended both to simplify and lower taxes, Congress in 1986 fixed two tax rates for individuals (15% and 28%) and one for corporations (34%). The new legislation also removed 6 million low-income households from the tax rolls.

INCUBATION, a method of keeping microorganisms such as BACTERIA or VIRUSES warm and in an appropriate medium to promote their growth (e.g., in identification of the organisms causing DISEASE); also, the period during which an organism is present in the body before causing disease. Infectious disease is contracted from a source of infective microorganisms. Once these have entered the body they divide and spread to different parts, and it is some time before they cause symptoms due to local or systemic effects. This incubation period may be helpful in diagnosis and in determining length of quarantine periods.

INCUNABULA (Latin: swaddling clothes), books printed before 1501 in the "infancy" years of typography. The 35,000 known editions include the works of such printers as GUTENBERG, CAXTON and ALDUS MANUTIUS. (See also PRINTING.)

INDENTURED SERVANT, person bound to labor for a stated period, usually five to seven years. In America he had often agreed to this in return for his passage to the colonies, but many were enticed or kidnapped, and convicts were sometimes sentenced and deported to indentured labor.

INDEPENDENCE DAY, US, the Fourth of July, the principal non-religious holiday which commemorates the signing of the DECLARATION OF INDEPENDENCE (July 4, 1776).

INDEPENDENCE HALL, the old state house of Philadelphia, Pa., where the DECLARATION OF INDEPENDENCE was proclaimed and the Constitutional Convention of 1787 met. It now houses the LIBERTY BELL and a small museum.

INDEPENDENT TREASURY SYSTEM, US banking structure in which the treasury was isolated from the nation's banking and finance system, originally to prevent the transfer of government funds to state banks. It functioned for brief periods from 1846 but could not meet the strains of financing the Civil War. The FEDERAL RESERVE Act (1913) marked its demise.

INDETERMINACY PRINCIPLE. See UNCERTAINTY PRINCIPLE.

INDEX OF FORBIDDEN BOOKS (*Index Librorum Prohibitorum*), official list of books banned by the Roman Catholic Church as being in doctrinal or moral error. A book could be removed from the Index by expurgation of offending passages, and permission could be given to read prohibited books. The index ceased publication in 1966.

INDIA, a federal republic of 22 states and nine union territories, in S Asia. It occupies a land mass ranging from the Himalayas southward to Cape Cormorin on the Indian Ocean, and shares the triangular-shaped Indian subcontinent with PAKISTAN, NEPAL, BHUTAN and BANGLADESH. The world's second most populous country, India has sought development aid wherever it is offered, and follows a policy of non-alignment.

Official name: Republic of India
Capital: New Delhi
Area: 1,222,559sq mi
Population: 783,044,000
Languages: Hindi, English; 14 other official national languages
Religions: Hindu, Muslim, Christian, Sikh, Buddhist, Jainism
Monetary unit(s): 1 rupee=100 paisa
Land. The chief geographical regions of N India are the Thar Desert along the Pakistan border; the mountain valleys of KASHMIR (disputed with Pakistan); the fertile plains of the GANGES and Brahmaputra rivers; and the Himalaya Mts, with Nanda Devi (25,645ft), India's highest peak. The mountains shield India from the

cold winter winds of central Asia. The Deccan plateau, bordered by the Western and Eastern Ghats mountain ranges, occupies most of S India. Here rivers flow sluggishly to the Eastern Ghats, then descend through broad valleys to the Bay of Bengal. The rich volcanic soil is used mainly for cotton-growing, though there are important mineral deposits. Most of the country has a tropical MONSOON climate, temperatures reaching 120°F in the hot season on the Northern Plains and, in the cool season, falling below freezing point in the mountains. The monsoon rains are especially heavy on the Western Ghats and in NE India; some places average more than 426in of rain a year. The rainy season lasts from May to September.

People. In 1983, India's population was over 730 million; despite birth control programs it is still rapidly expanding. The ethnic composition is complex, but there is a basic division between the light-skinned Indo-Aryans in the N and the darker DRAVIDIANS in the S. About 80% of the population live in small villages, though the towns are growing fast. The chief cities are the seaports of BOMBAY, CALCUTTA and MADRAS and the capital NEW DELHI. The dominant religion is HINDUISM which, through its CASTE system, profoundly affects the nation's social structures. Most Indians live on the poverty line in crowded slums or primitive villages, eating a mainly vegetarian diet.

Economy. India is an importer of food and industrial goods and an exporter of raw materials. Two-thirds of the labor force is engaged in agriculture. Rice, beans, peas, tea, sugarcane, jute, pepper and timber are the main agricultural products. Output, despite recent increases, is relatively low overall. Improvements are being sought by irrigation, land reclamation projects and the introduction of improved strains of crops and fertilizers. There are iron and steel mills, and electronic and engineering plants, but about 45% of the industrial manpower works in the jute, cotton and other textile mills. Mineral resources include oil, iron ore, coal, natural gas, copper, bauxite, manganese and mica, but are poorly exploited. Energy is supplied by hydroelectric plants and India's first atomic power station, at Tarapur, which came into operation in 1969.

History. The INDUS VALLEY CIVILIZATION, in modern Pakistan, was the first great culture on the subcontinent. It succumbed c1500 BC to Aryan peoples invading through the NW mountain passes; they brought the SANSKRIT language and Hinduism to India.

The Maurya Empire and Gupta dynasties represented high points of Buddhist and Hindu rule, but India was never united, and from the 10th century AD, Muslim invaders added to the conflicts. In the 14th century the Delhi Muslim sultanate and the Hindu kingdom of Vijayanagar in the S were dominant; in the 1520s the Muslim empire of the MOGULS was founded. Europeans also began to exert influence in the Indian subcontinent. In 1510 the Portuguese took Goa, and soon the Dutch, British and French were vying for Indian trade. In the 18th century English and French interests contested for control of the by then moribund empire. Victory went to the British EAST INDIA COMPANY, whose first governor-general of India was Warren HASTINGS (1774). After the Sepoy Rebellion (1857–58), the British government took over rule of much of the country, and the remaining independent princes, both Muslim and Hindu, recognized British primacy. The British did nothing to weaken religious rivalries but did give the subcontinent a unified code of law, a single administrative language and the world's greatest railroad network. In 1885, the Indian National Congress Party was set up; under Mahatma GANDHI and Jawaharlal NEHRU it led the movement for independence. JINNAH led the MUSLIM LEAGUE urging partition into India and Pakistan on religious grounds. Many thousands died in fierce communal riots following partition in 1947.

India achieved sovereign status in 1948. The constitution (1949) provided for a bicameral democratically-elected parliament and a cabinet government with prime minister and a president. The Congress Party has been the dominant party, first under Nehru and (since 1966) under his daughter Indira GANDHI. Domestic politics have been concerned with the vast problem of food supply, the drive towards large-scale industrialization, the mitigation of the worst injustices of the caste system and, since the late 1960s, tension between the central and provincial governments. Foreign policy was long overshadowed by the dispute with Pakistan over Kashmir, which flared into war in 1965. A frontier war in 1962 also emphasized the strained relations between India and China. SIKKIM became an Indian state in 1975, the same year Mrs. Gandhi was convicted of election irregularities. She declared a state of emergency, jailed her opponents and began to rule by decree. Mrs. Gandhi's party was defeated in the general elections in 1977 by the Janata Party, a coalition. The new government dismantled the state of emergency. The coalition, however, began to disintegrate, and in 1980 Mrs. Gandhi again became prime minister. In 1984 Mrs. Gandhi was assassinated by Sikh members of her bodyguard in retaliation for her suppression of Sikh extremists seeking autonomy for the state of Punjab. She was succeeded as prime minister by her son, Rajiv GANDHI, whose policies of reduced taxes, tariffs, and government regulation contributed to the greatest industrial expansion in India's history. But the new prosperity did not extend to the countryside, and Sikh extremists continued to terrorize Hindus. Rajiv Gandhi's initial popularity faded among charges of arbitrariness, corruption, and foreign influence.

INDIANA, Robert (Robert Clark; 1928–   ), US artist who adopted the name of his home state as his pseudonym. His use of verbs and numbers as artistic symbols won him fame in the 1960s. His poster design, "Love," appeared on 400 million US postage stamps.

INDIANA, state, in NE central US; it was created from the NORTHWEST TERRITORY and is bounded to the N by Mich. and Lake Michigan, on the E by Ohio, on the S by the Ohio R., which forms the border with Ky., and on the W by Ill.

Name of state: Indiana
Capital: Indianapolis
Statehood: Dec. 11, 1816 (19th state)
Familiar name: Hoosier State
Area: 36,291 sq mi
Population: 5,504,000
Elevation: Highest—1,257ft, Wayne County. Lowest—320ft, Ohio River in Posey County
Motto: "The crossroads of America"
State flower: Peony
State bird: Cardinal
State tree: Tulip tree (yellow poplar)
State song: "On the Banks of the Wabash"
Land. There are three main regions in Indiana. In the N are the Great Lakes Plains, in the center the Till Plains, and to the S the Southern Hills and Lowlands.

Glacial cover created many small lakes and left rich soil in the N and center. Main rivers are the Wabash, Kankakee and Maumee. The climate is humid, with summer temperatures from 65°F to 90°F typical; in winter the average is as low as 27°F, with heavy snow in the N.

People. Indiana's population swelled after statehood, driving out the Indians by about 1840. Since WWI it has become increasingly urbanized with the growth of industry, and in 1980 more than 65% of the population lived in urban areas. The 1816 constitution was the first to specifically provide free public education; the state now has state universities and many private institutions of higher education.

Economy. Before WWI the state's economy rested on agriculture, but it then expanded and is now among the top ten industrial states. Its largest industry is steel and other metal production, particularly in the Lake Michigan area, which also has major oil refineries. The cities, especially Indianapolis, are manufacturing centers, where transportation equipment, electrical and electronic products, machinery, chemicals and processed foods are produced. Indiana is among the top ten states in farm output; major crops are corn and soybeans, and the most plentiful livestock are hogs, cattle and poultry.

History. Algonkin, Iroquois and Delaware Indians occupied the area when French fur traders explored it in the 17th century. After the FRENCH AND INDIAN WARS, the area passed to the British (1763) and to the US after the Revolution. In 1800 it became a territory, with William Henry HARRISON as governor. Initial Indian resistance to white settlement ended after the battle of Fallen Timbers (1794), but revived under the Shawnee chief TECUMSEH until the battle of TIPPECANOE (1811). In 1816 Indiana became a state, although its settlements were too isolated to form a coherent political body until about 1850. In the Civil War it supported the Union, but despite this and the growth of industrialization it remained a rural and conservative state. In the 20th century, increased prosperity was accompanied by social and cultural advances. In the 1970s and early 1980s Indiana was hard hit by the general decline of heavy industry. There was an economic turnaround in the late 1980s as heavy industry revived and the state diversified economically. In presidential elections 1968–88, Indiana voted consistently Republican.

INDIAN AFFAIRS, Bureau of, US federal agency, part of the Department of the

Interior, set up in 1824 to safeguard the welfare of American Indians. It acts as trustee for tribal lands and funds, supervises the reservations and provides welfare and education facilities.

INDIANAPOLIS 500, the premier American automobile race. The 500-mile event has been held annually on Memorial Day at Indianapolis (Ind.) Speedway since 1911.

INDIAN OCEAN, at about 28,350,000sq mi the world's third largest ocean. It is bounded by Antarctica to the S, Africa to the W, and Australia and Indonesia to the E. The Indian subcontinent divides the N part of the ocean into two great arms, the Arabian Sea to the W and the Bay of Bengal to the E. Largest of its many islands are Madagascar and Sri Lanka; others include Zanzibar, Mauritius and the Seychelles. Major inflowing rivers include the Limpopo, Zambezi, Ganges and Indus. The deepest recorded point is in the Java or Sunda Trench (25,344ft).

INDIANS, American, name given by European explorers to the aboriginal inhabitants of the Western Hemisphere. It is generally believed that the ancestors of these first Americans migrated from Asia c26,000 years ago across a land bridge (now the Bering Strait) between Siberia and Alaska. A less popular theory suggests that the native Americans evolved on the American continent. It is certain that by 6000BC the Indians were distributed widely throughout North and South America.

Central and South American Indians are, like their counterparts in the N, believed to be of Asiatic origin. The major Indian groups in Central and N South America at the beginning of the European conquest (16th century) included the CARIBS, ARAWAKS, AZTECS, MAYAS and INCAS. The Maya civilization had reached its zenith some 700 years before, but the Inca and Aztec were at their peak. The three cultures had developed complex political and religious structures, built great temples, roads and bridges and achieved sophisticated astronomical and calendrical calculations, yet writing was rudimentary and wheeled transport unknown. The cultures were overthrown and millions of Indians killed by warfare and disease during the 16th-century Spanish conquest. The Spanish government proclaimed the Indians to be subjects and not slaves, but the settler community treated them as chattels and subjected them to forced labor. The situation was little better in Portuguese Brazil, though Jesuit-run plantations here and elsewhere treated their Indians humanely. Where they were able to, Indians

withdrew physically and psychologically from European culture. South American independence in the 19th century did little to improve their status. Atrocities committed against them by rubber barons in the early 20th century brought a degree of government protection. In Mexico Indian influence in the 1910–17 revolution, the restitution of certain Indian property rights and some integration between Indian and European cultures greatly improved the status of Indians. In South America progress is fitful, however, for cultural more than racial reasons. Indian tribal values lay more emphasis on the communal good and the sanctity of the soil; they cannot be easily integrated into a money economy. There is still a good deal of exploitation and maltreatment of remote tribes, often by government officials; they are still sometimes brutally driven off their lands, or simply massacred.

North American Indians. By the time of the European incursion, there appeared to have been about 900,000 Indians N of the Rio Grande. European weapons, diseases and destruction of natural resources took their toll, however, and the Indian population declined rapidly. The Indians had hundreds of peoples and nations, with as many languages. These may be divided into six broad culture areas: Eastern Woodlands, Plains, Southwest, Plateau, Northwest Coast and North or Sub-Arctic; the ESKIMOS are treated separately.

Early inhabitants of the Eastern Woodlands region in the E US were the Mound Builders of the Mississippi Valley. Later tribes in the area belonged to the great Algonquian and Iroquoian linguistic families; they included Cherokee, Chickasaw, Choctaw and Creek. In the SE the SEMINOLE were the dominant tribe. The IROQUOIS confederacy had effective political structures which were strengthened when the colonists appeared. Their main occupations were farming, tribal warfare and religious ceremonies.

The vast Plains area lay between the Mississippi R and the Rocky Mts. It was uninhabited until the 1600s, when the introduction of horses and guns by settlers made it possible for tribes to live as nomadic buffalo hunters. These included the Apache, Cheyenne, Sioux, Comanche, Blackfoot and Arapaho. The buffalo herds supplied food, fuel, bone utensils and skin for shelter and clothing. Status was achieved by success in warfare, often in defense of hunting grounds. The Plains Indians maintained a long resistance to white encroachment with skill and courage.

The original inhabitants of the Southwest, what is now Ariz., N.M., S Col. and S Ut., included a group called the Basket Makers (100–700 AD), who may have been the ancestors of the PUEBLO INDIANS. The peace-loving Pueblo peoples depended on agriculture for food, while their neighbors, tribes of the Apache and Navaho, relied on hunting and marauding. The Apaches were seminomadic, whereas the Navaho lived, and still live, in wooden hogans. Today there are about 200,000 sheep-farming Navaho on their reservation in Ariz., the largest existing Indian group.

The plateau region included most of what is now Cal. and the Great Basin between the Rocky Mts and the Sierra Nevada Ranges. Food was plentiful in the W part, and most tribes lived simply by gathering. Their culture was not sophisticated and there was little warfare. The dietary staple was acorn flour; rabbits, deer, elk and caribou were hunted, and there was fishing in the N.

The tribes of the Northwest Coast, notably the Haida, Kwakiutl and Nootka, lived along the Pacific coast from S Alaska to N Cal. The area was rich in food, principally fish, freeing the tribes to develop an elaborate and sophisticated culture. Art, particularly carving, was complex and developed; it still flourishes today, often commanding high prices. Social status was based on the surplus wealth available, mainly through the POTLATCH ceremony, in which office or status was gained by the distribution or destruction of wealth. The N tribes retain much of their culture today.

The peoples of the sparse North region from Newfoundland to Alaska belonged to the Athabascan language group in the W and the Algonquian group around Hudson Bay. Warfare played small part in their seminomadic life styles; too much energy went into the search for food.

Religion. Most Indian religion, even the fasts and self-mortification of the Plains Indian SUN DANCE, reveals a deep-felt communion with nature and a belief in a divine power. Individuals and kin groups of many tribes had spiritual ties with particular "totem" birds and animals. Shamans performed sacred rituals and treated the sick. The 1880s saw the tragic rise and fall of another Indian religion, the millenarian GHOST DANCE.

Indians and the Whites. The paternalistic attitudes of the first English colonists did not stop their encroachment on Indian lands (see INDIAN WARS). Indians were caught up in British and French rivalry in the FRENCH AND INDIAN WARS. Unscrupulous land speculators hardened mistrust. With the

NORTHWEST ORDINANCE (1787) the newly independent US, in need of Indian support, proclaimed a policy of peaceful coexistence, yet with new expansion hostilities increased. The Indian Removal Act of 1830 was followed from 1850 by campaigns against Plains Indians, which ended in the massacre of Indians at Wounded Knee, S.D., in 1890. In 1871 Congress ceased to recognize the Indian nations' independent rights; the Dawes Act (1887), by breaking up tribal land into individual grants, deprived the Indians of around 86 million acres, more than half their territory. A decline in the Indian population due to disease, war and starvation led to a belief that Indians were "naturally" dying out by natural selection; no long-term provision was therefore made for them. Reform began with the Indian Reorganization Act of 1934, aimed at increasing Indian autonomy and improving their economic position; it restored some lands. Other reforms followed, but poverty, poor education and unemployment are still a terrible problem on the reservations where the majority of about 800,000 US Indians still live. However, there is now a strong revival of Indian culture and an increasing awareness of their political and social identity. US courts have upheld Indian land claims and treaty rights.

INDIAN TERRITORY, region W of Ark., into which the FIVE CIVILIZED TRIBES were forcibly moved under the 1830 Indian Removal Act. In 1866 they were penalized for supporting the South in the Civil War by having other tribes resettled in the W part of this territory. Massive white settlement of other portions after 1889 led to disorder and the collapse of tribal government; by 1906 whites outnumbered Indians six to one, and the territory was incorporated into the state of Okla.

INDIAN WARS, the continuing struggle between the North American Indians and white colonizers from the earliest colonial times to the late 19th century. The first permanent English settlement was established at JAMESTOWN, Va., in 1607; despite peaceful trade with the Indians under POWHATAN, hostilities began in 1622 and by 1644 the Indians had been crushed. In New England, early relations between Puritan settlers and local Indians were good; but in 1636 war broke out with the PEQUOT tribe, resulting in their massacre. With the end of KING PHILIP'S WAR in 1678 Indian resistance in New England was broken.

The FRENCH AND INDIAN WARS (1689–1763) involved the NE tribes in constantly shifting alliances. In the long struggle for possession of North America both France and Britain offered guns and liquor to win Indian allies. In 1763 the tribal alliance headed by PONTIAC resulted in British recognition of Indian territorial and hunting rights. This was ignored and flouted by the colonists and corrupt officials.

With the Revolutionary War in 1775 the colonists needed Indian alliances, and trade regulations were introduced to protect the Indians from exploitation. Trade and land companies continued to cheat the Indians, however, provoking uprisings which government troops were sent in to crush. In 1811 an alliance of southern and western tribes under the Shawnee chieftain TECUMSEH was defeated at the Tippecanoe R by William Henry HARRISON; Tecumseh's death in 1813, after an abortive alliance with the British in the WAR OF 1812, virtually ended Indian resistance in this area. The SEMINOLE in Fla., however, continued hostilities until 1816. In 1830 the Indian Removal Act, passed by President JACKSON, authorized the transfer of SE tribes to land W of the Mississippi. Indian resistance was met by illegal force; Jackson even ignored a Supreme Court order upholding the land rights of the CHEROKEES.

In 1855, the defeated NEZ PERCÉ tribes were given land in the NW states, but when gold was found in the area they were again forced to move. Chief JOSEPH led an unsuccessful revolt against this in 1877. The Cal. GOLD RUSH also led to the overrunning of Indian lands and to the deaths of thousands of Indians 1848–58. The second half of the 19th century saw the final suppression of the Indians. The NAVAHO, holding the land between the Rio Grande and Cal., were defeated by Kit CARSON in 1863 and transferred to NW Ariz. After the Civil War attempts were made to restrict the Apaches, though COCHISE and others resisted; their last war chief, GERONIMO, surrendered in 1886. In 1871 the government ceased to recognize Indian tribes as independent nations.

The Great Plains, home of the SIOUX, APACHE and CHEYENNE, were subdued 1870–90 by a combination of military force and the depletion of buffalo herds. The Indian victory at the battle of Little Bighorn only hastened their defeat; it was marked by the surrender of CRAZY HORSE in 1877, and the suppression of the GHOST DANCE in 1890.
INDIGO, a blue dye obtained from LEGUMINOUS PLANTS of the genus *Indigofera.* The dye is produced by natural acidation of a solution containing pieces of the plants. Cultivation of indigo plants was once carried out on a large scale in India, but cheap synthetic indigo is now mainly used. Family: Leguminosae.

INDO-ARYAN LANGUAGES, group of languages of the family of INDO-EUROPEAN LANGUAGES, spoken on the Indian subcontinent. The oldest known is SANSKRIT, from which the others are directly or indirectly descended. Most widely spoken today are Hindi-Urdu, Bengali, Marathi, Punjabi, Gujarati, Oriya, Bihari and Rajasthani. Romany, the language of the Gypsies, is known to be descended from an Indo-Aryan original.

INDOCHINA, political term for peninsular SE Asia between China and India. It was formerly French Indochina, now divided into VIETNAM, LAOS and KAMPUCHEA. The area contains two densely-peopled, rice-rich deltas (Red R in the N, Mekong R in the S) separated by Annamite Mt. chain. Thais, Laos and Annamese (Vietnamese) settled Indochina from the N. From the second century AD, many states and cultures, affected by India and China, rose and fell there, including Funan, the KHMER EMPIRE, Champa and Annam. European penetration began in the 16th century; France concluded a treaty with Annam in 1787, annexed Cochin China in 1862 and by 1900 had welded separate states into the single political unit of French Indochina. WWII and militant nationalism destroyed France's authority and in 1949 Cambodia and Laos gained independence. The communist Vietminh drove the French out of Vietnam; the US continued France's anti-communist role in the long VIETNAM WAR, but by 1976 Indochina was effectively under communist control. Since then, hundreds of thousands of BOAT PEOPLE have fled Indochina. Vietnam, which invaded Kampuchea in 1979 and installed a Vietnamese-backed government there, remains the dominant country in the region, although the number of Vietnamese troops stationed in Laos and Kampuchea was greatly reduced in the late 1980s.

INDO-EUROPEAN LANGUAGES, one of the most important language families, spoken throughout most of Europe and much of Asia, and descended from a hypothetical common ancestor, Proto-Indo-European, extant more than 5,000 years ago. There are two main branches, Eastern, with six main groups, and Western, with four. The Eastern branch includes the extinct Anatolian and Tocharian groups, as well as Albanian, Armenian, Balto-Slavic and Indo-Iranian (with its important sub-group, the INDO-ARYAN LANGUAGES). The Western branch includes Celtic, Greek, Romance or

Italic (Latin and the languages derived from it) and Teutonic or Germanic (one of which is English). Until the beginning of the 20th century it was thought that SANSKRIT inscriptions represented the oldest written form of any of the family; however, both ancient Hittite and Linear B (see MINOAN LINEAR SCRIPTS), which have since been deciphered, are older. (See also LANGUAGE.)

INDO-IRANIAN LANGUAGES, easternmost branch of the INDO-EUROPEAN family of languages, and itself divided into two subgroups: 1) Indo-Iranian (Indic), sometimes called INDO-ARYAN, includes ancient Vedic-SANSKRIT, and the modern languages HINDI, BENGALI-Assamese, Punjabi, GUJARATI, SINHALESE (spoken in Sri Lanka), URDU (spoken in Pakistan), Nepali and others; this subgroup represents some 400 million speakers in India and neighboring countries; the Gypsy language, ROMANY, also belongs to this group. 2) Indo-Iranian (Iranian) includes Old Persian and modern PERSIAN (Fārsī), Pashto (spoken especially in Afghanistan), Kurdish and others spoken by some 50 million people in Iran and neighboring countries.

INDONESIA, republic in SE Asia, occupying most of the enormous Malay Archipelago.

Official name: Republic of Indonesia
Capital: Jakarta
Area: 741,101 sq mi
Population: 172,245,000
Languages: Bahasa Indonesia; many others
Religions: Muslim, Christian, Buddhist
Monetary unit(s): 1 rupiah = 100 sen
Land. Indonesia consists of more than 13,000 islands and islets strung out along the equator from Sumatra to New Guinea. There are three main island groups: the Greater Sunda Islands, including Java, SUMATRA, Indonesian Borneo (Kalimantan) and Sulawesi (Celebes); the Lesser Sunda Islands, including BALI, Flores, Lombok, Sumba, Sumbawa and Timor; and the MOLUCCAS (Maluku), including Ambon, Aru Island, Banda Islands, Buru, Ceram, Halmahera and the Tanimbar Islands. Indonesia also has Irian Jaya (W New

Guinea). The islands are mountainous and volcanic (many actively so), with tropical rain forests nourished by a hot, wet equatorial climate. There is abundant wild life, including many marsupials and the Komodo dragon.

People. Two-thirds of the population live on Java, site of the capital and chief port, Jakarta. The population can be broadly divided into Malays and Papuans, with Chinese, Arabs and others; Bahasa Indonesia is the official language but over 250 other languages are spoken. Education is compulsory and most Indonesians are literate. There are more than 50 universities and technological institutes.

Economy. Some 70% of the population are farmers, producing rice, coconuts, cassava, corn, peanuts, sweet potatoes, spices, and coffee and raising cattle, goats, hogs and chickens. Forest products include hardwoods, rubber, palm oil, quinine and kapok. The economy rests largely on agriculture, forestry and fisheries, but mineral resources are being increasingly exploited. Coal, bauxite, copper, manganese, nickel and precious metals are mined. Indonesia's most important products are oil, its chief export, and tin, of which it is one of the world's major producers. In general raw materials are exported and manufactured goods imported. There is some light manufacturing, mostly centered on Java. The multitude of islands, most of them rugged and mountainous, hinder transportation; air links are important.

History. Primitive man existed on Java c1 million years ago. Civilization grew under Indian influence after the 4th century AD; several kingdoms flourished from the 12th to 14th centuries. Islam spread swiftly in the 15th century. European impact began in 1511 when the Portuguese captured Malacca. But Portugal eventually kept only E Timor, losing control to the competing English and Dutch. The victorious Dutch EAST INDIA COMPANY founded Batavia (Jakarta) in 1619 and dominated the so-called Dutch East Indies until the Netherlands assumed control in 1798. Britain occupied the islands (1811–16) during the Napoleonic Wars, then returned them to the Dutch, who greatly expanded cash-crop exports during the 19th century. Nationalist movements emerged in the early 1900s, and after Indonesia's occupation by Japanese forces in WWII (1942–45), SUKARNO proclaimed Indonesia an independent republic; the Dutch were forced to grant independence in 1949. President Sukarno's dictatorial, anti-Western regime and extravagant spending damaged the economy; General SUHARTO deposed Sukarno in 1968. He suppressed left-wing groups; severed links with communist China and restored relations with the West. He sought to stabilize the economy, and in 1971 held the first free elections since 1955. In 1975, after Portugal withdrew from East Timor, Indonesian troops invaded, and in 1976 the region was proclaimed a province of Indonesia, a move not recognized by the UN. Domestically, Suharto welcomed foreign investors and turned national development over to a team of technocrats most of whom had been educated in the US. Internationally, Indonesia became a stabilizing influence in SE Asia. Suharto helped create the ASSOCIATION OF SOUTHEAST ASIAN NATIONS (ASEAN), and in 1987 he insisted that the group's third summit meeting be held in Manila as a gesture of support for Philippine president Corazon Aquino. He was also active in seeking Vietnam's withdrawal from Cambodia. Nevertheless, Suharto was increasingly criticized for his closed political system, his growing isolation and personality cult, and corruption among his friends and family.

INDUCTION, Electromagnetic, the phenomenon in which an electric field is generated in an electric circuit when the number of magnetic field lines passing through the circuit changes; independently discovered by M. FARADAY and J. HENRY. The voltage induced is proportional to the rate of change of the field, and large voltages can be produced by switching off quite small magnetic fields suddenly. Frequently, the magnetic field is itself generated by an electric current in a coil, in which case the voltage induced is proportional to the rate of change of the current. The principle finds numerous applications in electric GENERATORS and MOTORS, TRANSFORMERS, MICROPHONES, and engine ignition systems.

INDULGENCE, in the Roman Catholic Church, a remission of the temporal punishment (on earth or in PURGATORY) that remains due for sin even after confession, absolution and doing penance. In consideration of prayers and good works, the Church may grant plenary (full) or partial indulgences by administering the merits of Christ and the saints. Sale of indulgences was denounced by the Protestant reformers, and the abuse was abolished by the Council of TRENT.

INDUS RIVER, rising in the Himalayas of W Tibet and flowing 1,800mi through Kashmir and Pakistan to its 75mi-long delta on the N Arabian Sea. Cradle of the ancient INDUS VALLEY CIVILIZATION, it is now an important source of hydroelectric power and irrigation.

INDUSTRIAL RELATIONS, the conduct of relations between organized labor and management, and the relations between individual workers and their immediate supervisors. Wage rates, work conditions and productivity are among potential sources of conflict between the two sides. Unresolved conflicts can result in strikes and lockouts that cut output and profits and thus harm employees and employer alike. In the US the federal government helps to settle major industrial disputes, the National Labor Relations Board serving as adjudicator. US industrial relations are largely governed by the WAGNER ACT of 1935 and the TAFT-HARTLEY ACT of 1947. (See also ARBITRATION; LABOR; UNIONS.)

INDUSTRIAL REVOLUTION, in a country's history a period of rapid transition from an agrarian to an industrial society; specifically, the prototype of such periods, the late 18th and early 19th centuries in the UK. This period saw Britain transformed from a predominantly agricultural society into the world's first industrial nation. In the 18th century, British expansionism, inventiveness, economic sophistication and natural resources combined to provide unique opportunities for building business fortunes. The growth of capitalism developed the FACTORY system to harness new inventions that cheaply mass-produced textiles to exploit the expanding world market for British cloth. Key inventions in textile production included John Kay's flying shuttle (c1733), James Hargreaves' spinning jenny (c1764), Richard Arkwright's water frame (1769), and Edmund Cartwright's powered loom (1785). In 1709 Abraham Darby had learned to smelt iron with coke; in 1781, James WATT patented a steam engine producing rotary motion. Soon many factories were using steampowered iron machinery. Canals and, from the 1830s, railroads and steamships provided a transportation network linking new industrial cities with sources of supply and markets. The urban masses were supported by increasingly efficient agriculture, due to scientific advances and the stimulus to self-sufficiency of the NAPOLEONIC WARS. Largely through improvements in food supply, sanitation and medicine Britain's population rose from under 7 million in 1750 to over 20 million in 1850, creating both an increased labor force and escalating consumer demand. Factory workers endured appalling conditions before legislation brought improvements.

The wealth they had created, however, made possible a more general prosperity.

INDUSTRIAL WORKERS OF THE WORLD (IWW), American labor organization, founded 1905 by revolutionary socialists to radicalize the labor movement. It reached its greatest influence 1912–17, with a policy of confrontation, often violent; at its peak it had almost 100,000 members. Unlike the American Federation of Labor (AFL) it aimed not at improving labor conditions but at revolution. It lost support by attempting to exploit WWI; its strikes were considered treasonable. IWW leaders were imprisoned and the movement almost wholly suppressed.

INDUS VALLEY CIVILIZATION, centered around the Indus R in India and Pakistan, the earliest known urban culture of the Indian subcontinent. Superimposed on earlier stone- and bronze-using (see STONE AGE; BRONZE AGE) cultures dating from c4000 BC, the Indus Valley civilization, with its main cities Harappa and Mohenjo-Daro, lasted from c2500 to c1750 BC. About 100 of its towns and villages, some with fortified citadels, have been identified.

INERT GASES, former name for the NOBLE GASES.

INERTIA, property of all MATTER, representing its resistance to any alteration of its state of motion. The MASS of a body is a quantitative measure of its inertia; a heavy body has more inertia than a lighter one and needs a greater FORCE to set it in motion. NEWTON's laws of motion depend on the concept of inertia. In EINSTEIN's theory of RELATIVITY, inertia, or mass, is equivalent to ENERGY.

INFALLIBILITY, Papal. See PAPACY.

INFANTILE PARALYSIS. See POLIOMYELITIS.

INFANTRY, body of soldiers who fight on foot using light weaponry, such as rifles, machine guns, bazookas, mortars and grenades. Despite the mechanization of warfare, infantry units still form the largest combat branch of most armies. In the US army an infantry division consists of about 15,000 infantrymen and normally comprises eight infantry battalions and two supporting armored battalions equipped with tanks and heavy weapons.

INFECTIOUS DISEASES, DISEASES caused by any microorganism, but particularly viral and BACTERIAL DISEASES and parasitic diseases, in which the causative agent may be transferred from one person to another (directly or indirectly). Knowledge of the stages at which a particular disease is liable to infect others and of its route (via SKIN scales, COUGH particles, clothing, urine, feces, SALIVA, or by insects, particularly MOSQUITOS and TICKS) help physicians to limit the spread of diseases in EPIDEMICS.

INFINITY (∞), a quantity greater than any finite quantity. In modern mathematics infinity is viewed in two ways. In one, the word infinity has a definite meaning; and with transfinite cardinal numbers, for example, it may have a plurality of meanings. In the other, infinity is seen as a limit: to say that parallel lines intersect at infinity, for example, means merely that the point of intersection of two lines may be made to recede indefinitely by making the lines more and more nearly parallel. Similarly, in $f(x)=1/x$, it is meaningful to say that $f(x)$ tends to infinity as x tends to zero; again, the sequence $1,2,3,...,n$, tends to infinity since, however large n is chosen, there is an $(n+1)$ greater than it. In advanced set theory an infinite set is defined as one whose elements can be put in a one-to-one correspondence with those of a proper subset of the set (i.e., a subset that is not the whole set).

INFLAMMATION, the complex of reactions established in body TISSUES in response to injury and infection. It is typified by redness, heat, swelling and pain in the affected part. The first change is in the CAPILLARIES, which dilate, causing erythema, and become more permeable to cells and PLASMA (leading to EDEMA). White BLOOD cells accumulate on the capillary walls and pass into affected tissues; foreign bodies, dead tissue and bacteria are taken up and destroyed by phagocytosis and ENZYME action. Active substances produced by white cells encourage increased blood flow and white cell migration into the tissues. LYMPH drainage is important in removing edema fluid and tissue debris. ANTIBODY AND ANTIGEN reactions, ALLERGY and other types of IMMUNITY are concerned with the initiation and perpetuation of inflammation. Inflammatory DISEASES comprise viral and BACTERIAL DISEASE, parasitic disease and disorders in which the inflammatory response is activated inappropriately (e.g., by autoimmunity) causing tissue damage.

INFLATION, economic phenomenon characterized by rising prices of goods and services and resulting in the diminished purchasing power of a nation's money. It is the opposite of deflation, where prices and costs are falling. Inflation in the US is measured by the Consumer Price Index, which reflects price changes of a "market basket" of goods and services commonly purchased by householders and which indicates the cost of living. Inflation is generally considered unfavorable because (1) it may lead to undesirable redistribution of real income where people with fixed incomes or whose money income rises more slowly than the rate of inflation suffer a loss in their purchasing power; (2) unless interest rates rise, saving is discouraged as the sum saved falls in value over time; (3) higher prices and costs make a nation's exports less competitive in the international market, thus adversely affecting domestic production, employment and the balance of payments. The two principal theories on the causes of inflation are the Cost-Push theory, which explains inflation as stemming from higher costs of production leading to higher prices, and the Demand-Pull theory, which attributes inflation to excessive aggregate demand caused by an excess volume of money relative to the available supply of goods and services, driving up prices. Remedies for inflation depend on which of these two theories is accepted. Demand-Pull theorists advocate use of fiscal and monetary policies (control over money supply) to restrain aggregate demand. Cost-Push theorists, by contrast, would either allow unemployment to rise or would intervene in wage negotiations to curtail inflationary wage claims.

INFLORESCENCE, term applied to the conspicuous clusters of FLOWERS that are produced by many ANGIOSPERMS. There are several types of inflorescence, the forms of which vary according to the arrangement of individual flowers. In the type of inflorescence known as a raceme the flowers are attached to the main flower axis by short stalks, or pedicels, of equal length, for example the hyacinth, while in the spike there are no pedicels and the flowers are directly attached to the main axis, for example the gladiolus. Plants such as lilac and oats have an inflorescence similar to a raceme, but the pedicels bear more than one flower. This formation is called a panicle. In the corymb, the pedicels are of unequal length so that the inflorescence has a flat-topped appearance, for example hawthorn. In some plants, particularly those of the family Compositae, all the flowers are bunched on a flat disk, this arrangement being known as a head. In the simple umbel the pedicels appear to arise from a central point, while in the compound umbel several simple umbels are borne on a single stalk or ray and each inflorescence comprises a number a rays growing from the tip of the main axis. A simple umbel is produced by the milkweed and most members of the carrot family (Umbellifer-ae) produce compound umbels.

INFLUENZA, grippe, or **'flu,** a group of viral diseases causing mild respiratory symptoms, FEVER, malaise, muscle pains and HEADACHE, and often occurring in rapidly   spreading   EPIDEMICS. GASTROINTESTINAL TRACT symptoms may also occur. Rarely, it may cause a severe viral PNEUMONIA. A characteristic of influenza viruses is their property of changing their antigenic nature frequently, so that IMMUNITY following a previous attack ceases to be effective. This also limits the usefulness of influenza VACCINATION.

INFORMATION RETRIEVAL, a branch of technology of ever-increasing importance as man attempts to cope with the "information explosion." To store and have reference to the vast amount of printed matter produced annually is impossible for most libraries. The problem can be solved by microphotography. Pages are photographed at a reduction (typically to about $\frac{1}{20}$) and stored on 35mm or 16mm film (microfilm), on transparent cards measuring about $100 \times 150mm$ (microfiches) or as positive prints on slightly smaller cards (microcards). Videotape is also used. Reference may be manual or by machine, usually computer. The information must be classified so that the user may gain rapid access *either* to a particular book or paper *or* to all the relevant material on a particular subject.

In COMPUTERS, information retrieval involves a reverse of those operations used for data storage. The operator inserts a classification which the computer matches with the classification in its memory.

INFORMATION   THEORY,   or **communication theory,** a mathematical discipline that aims at maximizing the information that can be conveyed by communications systems, at the same time as minimizing the errors that arise in the course of transmission. The information content of a message is conventionally quantified in terms of "bits" (binary digits). Each bit represents a simple alternative—in terms of a message, a yes-or-no; in terms of the components in an electrical circuit, that a switch is opened or closed. Mathematically, the bit is usually represented as a 0-or-1. Complex messages can be represented as series of bit alternatives. Five bits of information only are needed to specify any letter of the alphabet, given an appropriate code. Thus able to quantify "information," information theory employs statistical methods to analyze practical communications problems. The errors that arise in the transmission of signals, often termed NOISE, can be minimized by the incorporation of **redundancy**. Here more bits of information than are strictly necessary to encode a message are transmitted, so that if some are altered in transmission, there is still enough information to allow the signal to be correctly interpreted. Clearly, the handling of redundant information costs something in reduced speed of or capacity for transmission, but the reduction in message errors compensates for this loss. Information theoreticians often point to an analogy between the thermodynamic concept of ENTROPY and the degree of misinformation in a signal.

INFRARED RADIATION, ELECTROMAGNETIC RADIATION of wavelength between 780nm and 1mm, strongly radiated by hot objects and also termed heat radiation. Detected using PHOTOELECTRIC CELLS, bolometers and photography, it finds many uses—in the home for heating and cooking and in medicine in the treatment of muscle and skin conditions. Infrared absorption SPECTROSCOPY is an important analytical tool in organic chemistry. Military applications (including missile-detection and guidance systems and night-vision apparatus) and infrared PHOTOGRAPHY exploit the **infrared window**, the spectral band between 7.5 and 11m in which the ATMOSPHERE is transparent. This and the high infrared reflectivity of foliage give infrared photographs their striking, often dramatic clarity, even when exposed under misty conditions.

INF TREATY. See ARMS CONTROL.

INGE, William (1913–1973), US playwright, noted for psychological studies of life in small Midwest towns, in such plays as *Come Back, Little Sheba* (1950), *Picnic* (1953) which won a Pulitzer Prize, *Bus Stop* (1955) and *A Loss of Roses* (1959).

INGERSOLL, Robert Green (1833–1899), US orator, an eloquent and provocative challenger of religious belief. He attracted large audiences and his lectures were widely read and denounced. At the 1876 Republican convention he placed James G. Blaine in nomination with a famous speech in which he called Blaine the "plumed knight."

INGRES, Jean Auguste Dominique (1780–1867), French neoclassical painter renowned for his mastery of line and superb draughtsmanship. *The Vow of Louis XIII* (1824) won him acclaim as the foremost classicist of his time, but today he is better known for portraits and nude studies such as the *Odalisque* (1814). A disciple of RAPHAEL, he was a determined opponent of

the romantic movement and an inspiration to many later artists, including DEGAS, RENOIR, and PICASSO.

INHERITANCE TAX, levy or assessment on property bequeathed by a deceased person to a specific legatee. It thus differs from an estate tax, levied on a deceased person's estate as a whole. In the US most states levy both estate and inheritance taxes; since 1916 the federal government has levied only an estate tax.

INITIATIVE, REFERENDUM AND RECALL, methods by which a country's citizens may directly intervene to influence government policy between elections. Initiative, provided for in most US states, is a procedure whereby a new law is proposed in a petition, then submitted to a vote by the legislature or electorate or both. Laws so passed are generally not subject to veto. Referendum allows citizens a direct vote on proposed laws and policies. A referendum may be demanded by petition, but in most US states it is mandatory for measures such as constitutional amendments and bond issues. Recall, adopted by many cities and some states, provides for the removal of an elected official by calling a special election. Such an election must usually be demanded in a petition whose signers number at least 25% of the votes originally received by the official. Recall has rarely succeeded at state level.

INKBLOT TEST. See RORSCHACH, HERMANN.

INNATE IDEAS, the theory that knowledge is inherent rather than acquired by means of sense experience to which reason is then applied. Derived from PLATO (c427–347 BC), the theory was vigorously denied by John LOCKE (1632–1704), who held the mind to be a *tabula rasa* or clean slate, and other ENLIGHTENMENT philosophers.

INNES, George (1825–1894), US landscape painter. His best-known work, such as *The Lackawanna Valley* (1855), shows the influence of COROT and the BARBIZON SCHOOL. His later work, such as *The Home of the Heron* (1893) is less realistic and more atmospheric.

INNOCENT, name of 13 popes. **Saint Innocent I** (d. 417), was pope from 401. He championed papal supremacy, but failed to prevent the sack of Rome by ALARIC in 410. **Innocent III** (c1161–1216), was pope from 1198. Under him the medieval papacy reached the summit of its power and influence. In an assertion of temporal power he forced King John of England to become his vassal and had Emperor Otto deposed in favor of Frederick II. He initiated the

Fourth Crusade (1202) and supported the crusade against the ALBIGENSES (1208). He presided over the Fourth Lateran Council (1215), culmination of the entire medieval papacy. **Innocent IV** (c1190–1254), pope from 1243, clashed with Emperor Frederick II over the temporal power of the papacy, and was forced to flee to Lyons, France, until Frederick's death. He worked for the unification of the Christian churches. **Innocent VIII** (1432–1492), pope from 1484, was worldly and unscrupulous. He fomented the witchcraft hysteria and meddled in Italian politics. For a fee he kept the brother and rival of Sultan Bayazid II imprisoned. **Innocent XI** (1611–1689), was pope from 1676. An opponent of QUIETISM, he favored toleration of Protestantism, and over this and the issue of papal power clashed with Louis XIV of France. **Innocent XII** (1615–1700), was pope from 1691. A stern reformer, he abolished nepotism and was renowned for his piety and charity. **Innocent XIII** (1655–1724), was pope from 1721. He bestowed Naples and Sicily on their de facto possessor, the Emperor Charles VI, and recognized the claims of James, the Old Pretender, to the British throne in the hope of a Catholic revival there.

INNS OF COURT, the four legal societies in London which, since the Middle Ages, have controlled admissions to the English bar. They are Lincoln's Inn, Gray's Inn, the Inner Temple and the Middle Temple.

INOCULATION, the INJECTION or introduction of microorganisms or their products into living TISSUES or culture mediums. It is used in man to establish antibody formation and IMMUNITY in VACCINATION.

INÖNÜ, Ismet (1884–1973), Turkish statesman, twice prime minister between 1923 and 1937, and second president of Turkey (1938–50). Militarily and politically second in command to ATATURK, he helped found the republic. In 1950 he held free elections, his own party being defeated. Following the military coup of 1960, he won further terms as premier (1961–65).

INORGANIC CHEMISTRY, major branch of CHEMISTRY comprising the study of all the elements and their compounds, except carbon compounds containing hydrogen (see ORGANIC CHEMISTRY). The elements are classified according to the PERIODIC TABLE. Classical inorganic chemistry is largely descriptive, synthetic and analytical; modern theoretical inorganic chemistry is hard to distinguish from PHYSICAL CHEMISTRY.

INQUISITION, a medieval agency of the Roman Catholic Church to combat heresy, first made official in 1231, when Pope Gregory IX appointed a commission of Dominicans to investigate heresy among the ALBIGENSIANS of S France. It aimed to save the heretic's soul, but a refusal to recant was punished by fines, penance or imprisonment, and often by confiscation of land by the secular authorities. Later the penalty was death by burning. Torture, condemned by former popes, was permitted in heresy trials by Innocent IV (d. 1254). The accused was not told the name of his accusers but could name his known enemies so that their hostile testimony might be discounted. Often the Inquisition was an object of political manipulation. In 1542 it was reconstituted to counter Protestantism in Italy; its modern descendant is the Congregation of the Doctrine of the Faith.

The Spanish Inquisition, founded in 1478 by Ferdinand V and Isabella, was a branch of government and was distinct from the papal institution. Its first commission was to investigate Jews who had publicly embraced Christianity but secretly held to Judaism. Under the grand inquisitor TORQUEMADA, it became an agency of official terror—even St. Ignatius Loyola was investigated. It was extended to Portugal and South America and not dissolved until 1820.

INSANITY, in psychology and psychoanalysis, a loose synonym for PSYCHOSIS. In criminal law, insanity is defined as an individual's inability to distinguish right from wrong and, therefore, to assume responsibility for his acts.

INSECTICIDE, any substance toxic to INSECTS and used to control them in situations where they cause economic damage or endanger the health of man and his domestic animals. There are three main types: **stomach insecticides,** which are ingested by the insects with their food; **contact insecticides,** which penetrate the cuticle; and **fumigant insecticides,** which are inhaled. Stomach insecticides are often used to control chewing insects like CATERPILLARS and sucking insects like APHIDS. They may be applied to the plant prior to attack and remain active in or on the plant for a considerable time. They must be used with considerable caution on food plants or animal forage. Examples include ARSENIC compounds, which remain on the leaf, and organic compounds, which are absorbed by the plant and transported to all its parts (systemic insecticides). Contact insecticides include the plant products NICOTINE, derris and pyrethrum, which are quickly broken down, and the synthetic compounds such as DDT (and other chlorinated HYDROCARBONS, organophosphates [malathion, parathion] and carbamates. Polychlorinated biphenyls (PCBs) are added to some insecticides to increase their effectiveness and persistence. Highly persistent insecticides may be concentrated in food chains and exert harmful effects on other animals such as birds and fish (see ECOLOGY).

INSECTIVORA, an order of small insectivorous MAMMALS, regarded as the most primitive group of placental mammals, having diverged little from the ancestral form. The skull is generally long and narrow, with a primitively large complement of unspecialized teeth in the jaw. Ears and eyes are small and often hidden in fur or skin. The group includes SHREWS, HEDGEHOGS and MOLES.

INSECTIVOROUS PLANTS, or **carnivorous plants,** specialized plants whose leaves are adapted to trap and digest insects. They normally live in boggy habitats or as EPIPHYTES. The insects may be caught in vase-like traps, by leaves that spring shut, by a trapdoor or on sticky leaves. The captured insects are broken down by ENZYMES secreted from the plants and the products absorbed.

INSECTS, animals having an external skeleton of chitin, characterized by having the body divided into three distinct sections: head, thorax and abdomen. The thorax typically bears two pairs of wings and three pairs of legs. This last is the most diagnostic feature and gives them their alternative name: Hexapoda. The insects are by far the most diverse class of invertebrates, and many are highly specialized. In terms of numbers they are undoubtedly the most successful group in the ANIMAL KINGDOM: the number of species alone exceeds that of all other groups of animals combined. The head bears the mouth, complex mouthparts, the antennae and eyes. The mouthparts above all reflect the diversity of the group. Although they are composed of the same six basic structures in all species, the mouthparts show incredible modifications to specialized modes of feeding. Primitively distinct, heavy, serrated structures for chewing and crushing in the cockroach, they form piercing stylets in MOSQUITOES and APHIDS, with animal or plant juices drawn up a central groove. The long, coiled proboscis of BUTTERFLIES and MOTHS, adapted for sucking nectar, is also a tube—but one formed from the modification of different mouthparts. In WASPS and BEES some of the mouthparts have formed a tube for drawing up nectar, while others

have retained their chewing form, for handling wax and pollen. The thorax also reflects the great diversity of the insects. Typically a thorax has three segments, each bearing a pair of legs, with the last two segments each having a pair of wings; wings are absent in some primitive forms (the Apterygota) and modified in others. In the BEETLES, and other groups, one pair of wings loses its flight function and forms a protective case for the other, flying wings. In the FLIES the second pair of wings is modified as a balancing organ. Insects have highly-developed sense organs: on the head are compound eyes and antennae, which are covered with little "hairs" sensitive to the chemical stimuli of smell and taste. Little hairs over the body are sensitive to touch and smell. The life history of insects usually involves a larval stage. As the larva grows, it passes through a series of molts before it reaches the adult stage, each time shedding the existing, rigid EXOSKELETON, after laying down another, larger one within. The new cuticle is at first soft and can be extended. It hardens on contact with air. Larvae are of two types: those which, with each succeeding molt, not only increase in size but also show a progressive development of adult features; and those which remain totally unlike the adult during growth, but pass through a resting stage, or PUPA, when the internal and external structures are completely reorganized to form the adult insect (see METAMORPHOSIS). Some insects, such as grasshoppers, instead of a larval stage, have a nymph stage in which they already resemble the adult insect.

INSTINCT, a phenomenon whose effects can be observed in animals and man. In general, one can say that instinctive behavior comprises those fixed reactions to external stimuli that have not been learned, such as the sucking instinct or fear of smothering in infants. In fact, such behavior seems to stem from a complex of hereditary and environmental factors characteristic of their species. Animals placed from birth in artificial environments display some, but not all, instinctive reactions characteristic of their species. Numbered among the instincts are the sex drive, aggression, TERRITORIALITY and the food urge; but much debate surrounds such classification. In psychoanalysis, "instinct" (sometimes called **drive**) has a similar meaning, with special emphasis on the response as a complex one (see REFLEX). Frustration of, or conflict between, instincts engenders NEUROSES. FREUD suggested the existence of two fundamental instincts: the life instinct and its opposite, the death instinct.

INSTITUTE FOR ADVANCED STUDY, research center in Princeton, N.J., founded for graduate study in various fields. It has long specialized in the physical sciences and social studies. It was opened in 1933 and one of its first members was Albert Einstein.

INSTRUMENTS, Scientific, devices used for measurement and hence for scientific investigation and control (see also MECHANIZATION AND AUTOMATION). They extend the observing faculties of the human senses, providing accuracy and a greater range. They can also direct and measure phenomena such as X rays which man cannot sense. Early instruments, used mainly in the fields of astronomy, navigation and surveying, measured the basic quantities of mass, length, time and direction (see ASTROLABE; CLOCKS AND WATCHES; COMPASS). With the rise of modern science came several instruments including the MICROSCOPE; TELESCOPE and THERMOMETER. During the Industrial Revolution and after were invented instruments too many to mention; and today in science, industry and even the home there are a host of instruments to measure every conceivable quantity. A few simple instruments, such as the ruler or balance, work by direct comparison, but most are transducers, representing the quantity measured by another sensible quantity (usually the position of a pointer on a scale). All instruments require initial calibration against a known or calculable standard. In general, an instrument interacts with the measured phenomenon, and the resultant change in its state is amplified if necessary, displayed by means of a pointer, pen, light beam, oscilloscope, etc., and recorded, usually on chart paper or by photography. Although precision instruments are designed for high accuracy, inevitably errors are introduced: amplification produces NOISE, the slowness of the instrument's response results in lag and damping, and the intrinsic nature of the response may be defective owing to hysteresis or drift; moreover, the observer may misread the scale because of parallax or interpolation errors. Most fundamental of all, the act of measuring a system may significantly alter the state of the system (see also UNCERTAINTY PRINCIPLE).

INSULAR CASES, decisions by the US Supreme Court in 1900–01 defining the legal status of Puerto Rico, under US sovereignty since 1899. The cases established that US sovereignty does not of itself confer full constitutional rights.

INSULATION, Electric, the containment of electric currents or voltage by materials (insulators) that offer a high resistance to current flow, will withstand high voltages without breaking down, and will not deteriorate with age. Resistance to sunlight, rain, flame or abrasion may also be important. The electrical resistance of insulators usually falls with temperature (paper and asbestos being exceptions) and if chemical impurities are present. The mechanical properties desired vary with the application: cables require flexible coatings, such as polyvinyl chloride, while glass or porcelain are used for rigid mountings, such as the insulators used to support power cables. In general, good thermal insulators are also good electrical ones.

INSULATION, Thermal, the reduction of transfer of heat from a hot area to a cold. Thermal insulation is used for three distinct purposes: to keep something hot; to keep something cold; and to maintain something at a roughly steady temperature. HEAT is transferred in three ways, CONDUCTION, CONVECTION and RADIATION. The vacuum bottle thus uses three different techniques to reduce heat transfer: a vacuum between the walls to combat conduction and convection; silvered walls to minimize the transmission of radiant heat from one wall and maximize its reflection from the other; and supports for the inner bottle made of CORK, a poor thermal conductor.

INSULIN, HORMONE important in METABOLISM, produced by the islets of Langerhans in the PANCREAS, which act as an ENDOCRINE GLAND. Insulin is the only hormone which reduces the level of SUGAR in the BLOOD and is secreted in response to a rise in blood sugar (e.g., after meals or in conditions of stress); the sugar is converted into glycogen in the cells of MUSCLE and the LIVER under the influence of insulin. Absence or a relative failure in secretion of insulin occurs in DIABETES, in which blood sugar levels are high and in which sugar overflows into the urine. The isolation of insulin as a pancreatic extract by F. G. Banting and C. H. Best in 1921 was a milestone in medical and scientific history. It is a PROTEIN made up of 50 AMINO ACIDS as two peptide chains linked by sulfur bridges. Because it is destroyed in the GASTROINTESTINAL TRACT, it has to be taken via subcutaneous injection by diabetics with severe insulin lack. Its use in diabetics has revolutionized treatment of this disease; the aim in its administration is to be as close to natural secretion patterns as possible. If insufficient insulin is taken, diabetic COMA may result, while in excess, hypoglycemia supervenes; both require prompt medical treatment.

INSULL, Samuel (1859–1938), English-born US financier. Secretary to Thomas Edison in the 1880s, he became head of the Chicago Edison Co and built a huge conglomerate supplying electricity throughout Ill. and other states. It collapsed in 1932. Later tried for fraud, he was acquitted.

INSURANCE, method of financial protection by which one party undertakes to indemnify another against certain forms of loss. An insurance company pools the payments for this service and invests them to earn further funds. Each insured person pays a relatively small amount, the *premium*, for a stated period of coverage. In return the company will, subject to an assessment of his claim, reimburse him for loss caused by an event covered in the policy. Forms of insurance have existed since the earliest civilizations. Modern insurance began with the medieval GUILDS, which sometimes insured members against trade losses. The specialized fields of fire and maritime insurance developed in the 17th and 18th centuries. The development of PROBABILITY theory allowed the statistical likelihood of damage to be calculated, making insurance as a business possible.

INTEGRATION. See CALCULUS.

INTEGRATION, Racial, the right to equal access for people of all races to such facilities as schools, churches, housing and public accommodations. It became an issue of public importance in the US after the Civil War and the passage of the 13th, 14th and 15th Amendments to the Constitution, 1864–70, which declared the Negro free and equal, and the Civil Rights Act of 1866. Although slavery was ended as a legal institution state laws were passed during the reaction against RECONSTRUCTION to enforce the physical segregation of blacks and whites. Tennessee adopted the first "Jim Crow" law in 1875, segregating public transportation. In 1896 the Supreme Court approved "separate but equal" accommodations for blacks, following which segregation laws proliferated. In the North segregation in housing created the black slum ghettos; while less common than in the South it still continued in factories, unions and restaurants. In 1910 the NATIONAL ASSOCIATION FOR THE ADVANCEMENT OF COLORED PEOPLE (NAACP) was founded in New York, followed by the National Urban League in 1911. Several activist groups were formed in the 1940s, including the CONGRESS OF RACIAL EQUALITY (CORE). The NAACP won its greatest legal victories in 1954 and 1955, when the Supreme Court outlawed segregation in the public schools and ordered that integration be implemented "with all deliberate speed." Among black leaders advocating passive resistance to discriminatory local laws was Martin Luther KING, Jr. His SOUTHERN CHRISTIAN Leadership Conference and the more radical Student Non-Violent Coordinating Committee exerted political pressure to enact the Civil Rights Act of 1964 and Voting Rights Act of 1965. Integration was more generally accepted during the 1970s, although serious unrest occurred over busing practices to end school segregation in many cities.

INTELLIGENCE, the general ability to solve problems. Since man is the animal of highest intelligence, most investigations of intelligence have been carried out in human beings. Intelligence tests are structured upon the following bases: numerical ability (the speed and accuracy with which the individual can solve problems of simple arithmetic); verbal fluency; verbal meaning (the ability to understand words); the ability to remember; the speed of perception; and, most importantly, the ability to reason. Such tests are of considerable use, though their limitations must be recognized. Disagreement about whether intelligence tests validly measure intelligence has led some psychologists to define human intelligence as "that which can be measured by intellgence tests."

Throughout the animal kingdom, there is a good correlation between the intelligence of an animal and the size of its brain relative to that of its body. There is an even better one when the surface area of the BRAIN is considered: the higher mammals have a more convoluted cortex (outer layer) than do the lower. After man, the most intelligent animal is the DOLPHIN. Perhaps surprisingly, ANTS show an ability to solve mazes that compares with that of some mammals.

The ways in which animals solve problems are a useful indication of their intelligence. The two important ways are trial-and-error, which is a LEARNING process dependent upon intelligence, and insight. This latter is displayed only by the higher animals.

The evolution of intelligence is unclear, though obviously it has had a profound effect on the emergence of man as earth's dominant animal. Equally obviously, intelligence is a considerable aid to species survival. Much effort has been expended in recent years to examine how much of an individual's intelligence is determined by hereditary factors, how much by environmental factors. Although results have not been conclusive, it would seem that about half the difference in intelligence between people is determined by inheritance, the remainder by early environmental conditions. (See also HEREDITY.)

INTELLIGENCE QUOTIENT. See IQ.

INTEREST, money paid for the use of money loaned. It is generally expressed as a percentage of the principal (sum loaned) per period (usually per year or per month). In "simple" interest, where the principal does not change, the interest can be calculated by the formula $I=prt$, where I is interest, p is principal (the amount borrowed), r the rate of interest and t the time. "Compound" interest is added periodically to the principal; interest is subsequently paid on the resulting compound total. The formula for this is $S=p(1+r/k)^n$ where S is the final amount, p and r are as before, k is the time interval between compounding and n is the number of times the interest is compounded.

Medieval Christian law forbade the taking of interest on moral grounds as "usury," but Jewish businessmen were freely used as bankers; in the face of this the Church was eventually forced to relax its attitude. Today, with credit playing a major economic role worldwide, interest rates affect the viability of every sort of economic venture, from buying a family home to the exploration of space. In the US, interest rates in recent years were driven upward by government deficits, inflation and the tight-money policy of the Federal Reserve Board.

INTERFERENCE, the interaction of two or more similar or related WAVE MOTIONS establishing a new pattern in the amplitude of the waves. It occurs in all wave phenomena including SOUND, LIGHT and water waves. In most cases the resulting amplitude at a point is found by adding together the amplitudes of the individual interfering waves at that point. Interference patterns can only result if the interfering waves are of related wavelength and exhibit a definite phase relationship.

Optical interference. Light from ordinary sources is "incoherent"—there is no definite relationship between the phases of the waves associated with different PHOTONS. Until recently the only way to demonstrate optical interference was to use light from a single source which had been divided and led to the interference zone along paths of differing length, thus ensuring that the interfering beams were coherent at least with each other. In this way Thomas YOUNG in 1801 first demonstrated optical interference, showing,

because interference effects cannot be explained on either ray or particle models, that light was indeed to be regarded as a wave phenomenon. Young passed light from a single pinhole source through two parallel pinholes in an opaque screen and found that interference fringes—alternate bands of light and dark—were formed on another screen placed beyond the slits. The bright bands resulted from the constructive interference of the two beams, the wave amplitude of each reinforcing the other; the dark bands, destructive interference, the amplitude of one wave canceling the effect of that of the other because the difference in path length was such that the "peaks" of one wave coincided with the "troughs" of the other. Newton's rings, colored fringes seen in thin transparent films, are a similar interference effect. In recent years LASERS (which produce coherent light—radiation having a uniform and controllable phase structure) have enabled physicists to produce optical interference effects much more easily, an important application being HOLOGRAPHY. (See also INTERFEROMETER.)

INTERFEROMETER, any instrument employing INTERFERENCE effects used: for measuring the wavelengths of LIGHT, RADIO, SOUND or other wave phenomena; for measuring the refractive index (see REFRACTION) of gases (Rayleigh interferometer); for measuring very small distances using radiation of known wavelength; or, in ACOUSTICS and RADIO ASTRONOMY, for determining the direction of an energy source. In most interferometers the beam of incoming radiation is divided in two, led along paths of different but accurately adjustable lengths and then recombined to give an interference pattern. Perhaps the best known optical instrument is the Michelson interferometer devised in 1881 for the MICHELSON-MORLEY EXPERIMENT. More accurate for wavelength measurements is the Fabry-Perot interferometer in which the radiation is recombined after multiple partial reflections between parallel, lightly-silvered glass plates.

INTERFERON, substance produced by living tissues following infection with VIRUSES, BACTERIA etc., which interferes with the growth of any organism. It is responsible for a transient and mild degree of nonspecific IMMUNITY following infection.

INTERIOR, US Department of the, executive branch of the federal government, headed by the secretary of the interior. Founded in 1849, its original task was to administer the census and Indian affairs, and to regulate the exploitation of natural resources. In recent years, however, it has been increasingly exercised by the need for conservation of resources and protection of the environment. Today it has five major areas of responsibility, each in the charge of an assistant secretary. These are Fish, Wildlife, Parks and Marine Resources; Mineral Resources; Water and Power Development; Water Quality and Research, and Public Land Management, which as well as agencies responsible for federally owned lands includes the Office of the Territories, which administers US territories and trust territories, and the Bureau of INDIAN AFFAIRS.

INTERIOR DECORATION, the design and arrangement of decorative elements in a home or public building. Until relatively recently, architectural and interior styles were almost inseparable and the names used to characterize each period applied both to the architecture of buildings and their interior decor.

In medieval Europe attention to interior display was confined largely to churches which, by late medieval times, exemplified the Gothic. It was only with the Renaissance that important styles of interior design began to emerge. Italian Renaissance design took classical architecture and ornament as its model, and Italian influences were soon seen throughout Europe, especially in the great French chateaus of the time and in the English Tudor, Elizabethan and Jacobean styles, which combined earlier Gothic with Italian forms. Baroque (c1600–1750) accented the grandiose and elaborate. Rococo (1700s, especially in France and Germany) was smaller-scale, with a generous use of curves. The Baroque-Rococo era also saw the development of the Louis period styles of interior decoration. Neoclassicism in France and Georgian in England (18th and early 19th centuries) both returned to the lighter forms reminiscent of classical design. Directoire and Empire were influential post-revolutionary French styles. In England, the Victorian period was undistinguished except for the attempt of artist William MORRIS and his Arts and Crafts Movement to return to the simpler hand-crafted forms of the past. In America, early utilitarian colonial designs were succeeded by the Georgian-influenced Federal style that characterizes the beginning 1800s. The early 1900s saw the curvilinear forms of ART NOUVEAU, and the later, more geometric work of the ART DECO movement. The BAUHAUS style of the 1920s, which emphasized simplicity and functional design, is still influential today. Through the years, the major furniture designers, such as CHIPPENDALE, HEPPLEWHITE, SHERATON, PHYFE and EAMES have also greatly influenced decorative styles.

INTERMEDIATE-RANGE NUCLEAR FORCES (INF) TREATY. See ARMS CONTROL.

INTERNAL-COMBUSTION ENGINE, type of ENGINE—the commonest now used—in which the fuel is burned inside the engine and the expansion of the combustion gases is used to provide the power. Because of their potential light weight, efficiency and convenience, internal-combustion engines largely superseded STEAM ENGINES in the early 20th century. They are used industrially and for all kinds of transport, notably to power AUTOMOBILES. There are three classes of internal-combustion engine: reciprocating engines, which include the gasoline engine, the DIESEL ENGINE and the free-piston engine; rotary engines, including the gas turbine, the turbojet (see JET PROPULSION) and the WANKEL ENGINE; and ROCKET engines and non-turbine jet engines, working by reaction. Although originally coal gas and even powdered coal were used as fuel, now almost all fuels used are PETROLEUM products: diesel oil, GASOLINE, bottled gas and NATURAL GAS. The first working (though not usable) internal-combustion engine was a piston engine made by HUYGENS (1680) that burned gunpowder. In 1794 Robert Street patented a practicable though inefficient engine into which the air had to be pumped by hand. In 1876 N. A. Otto built the first four-stroke engine, using the principles stated earlier by Alphonse Beau de Rochas. The cycle is (1) intake of fuel/air mixture; (2) compression of mixture; (3) ignition and expansion of burned gases; (4) expulsion of gases as exhaust. Only the third stroke is powered, but the engine is highly efficient, and modern gasoline engines are basically the same. Generally four, six or eight cylinders are linked to provide balanced power. The engine is cooled by water circulating through pipes or by air from a fan. The fuel/air mixture is produced in the carburetor; greater power is given by supercharging, by which the proportion of air and the initial pressure of the mixture are increased. The two-stroke engine, giving greater power for a given size, but less efficient in fuel use, does not usually have valves, but an inlet and an exhaust port in the cylinder, blocked and uncovered in turn by the piston. At the end of the powered stroke, the piston drives fresh fuel mixture from the crankcase into the cylinder, pushing out the exhaust gases. The

EFFICIENCY of an internal-combustion engine increases with the compression ratio; if this is too high, however, "knocking" occurs due to irregular burning and detonations. It is avoided by using fuel of high octane number, and by using ANTIKNOCK ADDITIVES. (See also AIR POLLUTION.)

INTERNAL REVENUE SERVICE (IRS), agency of the US Department of the Treasury. Created by Congress in 1789, it assesses and collects domestic or "internal" taxes. These include federal taxes on goods and services, income taxes and corporate taxes, as well as gift and estate taxes. The service is headed by a commissioner of internal revenue appointed by the president. Its headquarters are in Washington, D.C., and it has seven regional and 58 district offices.

IRS rules are based on the Internal Revenue Code, a huge compilation of tax laws passed by Congress and interpreted through regulations issued by the IRS. As administered by the agency, the tax system has been called inequitable and inefficient by some critics who claim that IRS regulations are intricate, confusing and frequently not fully understood even by the IRS itself. To gain the full benefit of the tax laws, taxpayers must frequently buy the services of expert tax accountants.

INTERNATIONAL, The, common name of a number of socialist-communist revolutionary organizations. Three of these have had historical significance. The First International, officially the International Working Men's Association, was formed under the leadership of Karl MARX in London in 1864 with the aim of uniting workers of all nations to realize the ideals of the *Communist Manifesto.* Divisions grew up between reformers and violent revolutionaries; these became increasingly bitter, culminating in the expulsion of the faction led by Mikhail BAKUNIN after a leadership struggle in 1872. The association broke up in 1876. The Second, commonly called the Socialist International, was founded in Paris in 1889 by a group of socialist parties that later made their headquarters in Brussels. The leading social democratic parties, including those of Germany and Russia, were represented. Among representatives were Jean JAURÉS, Ramsay MACDONALD, LENIN and TROTSKY. It influenced international labor affairs until WWI, when it broke up. The Third or Communist International, generally known as the Comintern, was founded by Lenin in 1919 in an attempt to win the leadership of world socialism; ZINOVIEV was its first

president. Soviet-dominated from the outset, it aimed, in the 1920s, to foment world revolution. In the 1930s, under STALIN, it sought contacts with less extreme left-wing groups abroad, to assuage foreign hostility. Stalin dissolved it in 1943 as a wartime conciliatory gesture to the Allies.

INTERNATIONAL ATOMIC ENERGY AGENCY (IAEA), intergovernmental agency closely related to the UN. Established in 1957, it promotes and conducts research into peaceful uses of atomic energy and seeks to ensure adequate safety standards. It is particularly concerned that agency assistance should not be used for military purposes.

INTERNATIONAL CIVIL AVIATION ORGANIZATION (ICAO), UN agency seeking to foster and coordinate cooperation among the world's airlines.

INTERNATIONAL COURT OF JUSTICE, highest judicial organ of the UN, founded in 1946 to provide a peaceful means of settling international disputes according to the principles of INTERNATIONAL LAW. Like its predecessor under the LEAGUE OF NATIONS, the World Court, it sits at the Hague. In practice its authority is limited by frequent refusals to accept its decisions.

INTERNATIONAL DEVELOPMENT ASSOCIATION (IDA), organization affiliated to the WORLD BANK. It was established in 1960 to make loans for development projects to member countries on less economically burdensome terms than World Bank loans; a service charge is substituted for interest.

INTERNATIONAL LABOR ORGANIZATION (ILO), UN agency with headquarters in Geneva, formed in 1919 to develop and improve working conditions worldwide. In 1934 the US joined; in 1946 the organization became affiliated to the UN.

INTERNATIONAL LADIES' GARMENT WORKERS' UNION, AFL-CIO union in the US women's and children's clothing industry. It was founded in 1900 by AMERICAN FEDERATION OF LABOR charter. Strikes in New York 1909–10 led to Louis BRANDEIS' Protocol of Peace, which set a pattern for labor-management cooperation. Under David DUBINSKY (president 1932–66) the ILGWU grew fast in the 1930s, was active in the AFL-CIO debate and pioneered union welfare schemes. Its membership totals 348,000 (1980).

INTERNATIONAL LAW, body of laws assumed to be binding among nations by virtue of their general acceptance. Although customary rules on maritime matters and on ambassadorial immunity had long existed, the real beginnings of international law lay in attempts to humanize the conduct of war. The seminal work of Hugo GROTIUS, *On the Law of War and Peace* (1625), was one such, but he also formulated several important principles, including a legal basis for the sovereignty of states. The works of Grotius and his successors were widely acclaimed but never officially accepted; however, legal principles were increasingly incorporated into international agreements such as the Congress of VIENNA as well as into the constitution of the UNITED NATIONS. International laws may arise through multilateral or bilateral agreements, as with the GENEVA CONVENTION, or simply by long-established custom, as with a large part of MARITIME LAW. In some cases, as with the war crimes rulings of the NUREMBERG TRIALS, they may be said to arise retrospectively. Because few nations are willing to relinquish any sovereignty, the law lacks a true legislative body and an effective executive to enforce it. The INTERNATIONAL COURT OF JUSTICE is the international judicial body; the UN in the process of compiling an international legal code, is the nearest thing to a legislature, but all these bodies are limited by the willingness of states to accept their decisions, as was the LEAGUE OF NATIONS in the 1930s. These difficulties have led some theorists to deny international law true legal status, but this is an extreme view; the need for international rules is widely recognized, as shown by the increasing tendency to anticipate problem areas such as space exploration and exploitation of seabed resources and to attempt to develop international rules to regulate them.

INTERNATIONAL MONETARY FUND (IMF), international organization, affiliated to the UN, existing to develop international monetary cooperation, in particular to stabilize exchange rates by providing international credit. Members cannot make changes greater than 10% in the exchange rate of their national currency without consulting the Fund. Established by the BRETTON WOODS CONFERENCE, it began operating in 1947. Operating funds are subscribed by member governments; the Group of Ten (US, UK, Belgium, Canada, France, West Germany, Italy, Japan, Netherlands and Sweden) are pledged to lend further funds if necessary. (See also WORLD BANK.)

INTERNATIONAL RELATIONS, relationships between nations, through politics, treaties, military confrontation or cooperation, economics or culture. Peacetime contact is generally maintained through DIPLOMACY; each nation maintains embassies in other countries it recognizes as nations. Even when states do not maintain mutual embassies, however, they may find it desirable to keep contacts open, often through the offices of a third nation. The other primary link is through membership in international organizations, either for global politics as with the UNITED NATIONS, defense as with NATO or the WARSAW PACT, or simply mutual convenience, as with the UNIVERSAL POSTAL UNION. From 1946 on international relations were dominated by the concept of the COLD WAR, in which the complications of world diplomacy were reduced to an oversimplified model of an ideological contest between two global antagonists, the communist and capitalist systems as personified by the USSR and US. In the 1960s the rise of the Third World countries negated this simple division, though many of these took one or the other side. In the 1970s relations between the US and USSR improved, largely through trade and nuclear limitation agreements and also because of the rise of China as a rival superpower. The endurance and value of the resulting detente, however, remained doubtful as the 1980s saw new—and continuing old—areas of conflict between the superpowers. (See also INTERNATIONAL LAW; INTERNATIONAL TRADE.)

INTERNATIONAL STYLE, architectural style, best defined in its widest sense as the dominant trend in large-scale buildings in industrialized countries since the 1920s. It emphasizes a clean functionalism, open space with large areas of glass, and reinforced concrete construction. Among pioneering exponents were Walter GROPIUS, MIES VAN DER ROHE, LE CORBUSIER, Pier Luigi NERVI and in the US Philip C. JOHNSON and R. I. NEUTRA.

INTERNATIONAL TRADE, or world trade, the exchange of goods and services between nations. Since the 18th century it has become a vital element in world prosperity. One reason for this is that it is generally thought more profitable for countries to specialize in making those things in which such factors as natural resources, climatic conditions, availability of raw materials, a skilled labor force or low labor costs give them a special advantage. This is known as the international division of labor. Some countries, such as Japan, rely largely on exports; US exports amount to 15% of the world total, but are less vital to its economy.

Even in prehistoric times the amber route carried trade between tribes thousands of miles apart. The ancient Greeks, Romans and Phoenicians were active traders. Chinese merchants penetrated most of Asia, and Arabs operated trade routes on the Indian Ocean and in Africa. Most explorers before the 20th century sought to open trade routes. Early trade was largely in goods yielding high prices on small amounts because of the difficulty of transportation. Only with modern transport did international trade become economically vital.

The financing of world trade relies on the foreign exchange market, where an importer can buy the necessary currency to pay his foreign supplier. Most countries keep a record of their balance of payments with foreign trading partners; a large surplus or deficit in this is often a good economic indicator.

After WWII efforts were made to promote free trade throughout the world. In 1948 the US and 23 other nations made an agreement within the framework of the UN known as the GENERAL AGREEMENT ON TARIFFS AND TRADE (GATT). In 1962 Congress passed the Trade Expansion Act, enabling President KENNEDY to lower or remove tariffs affecting the European COMMON MARKET countries. Subsequently, a series of tariff reductions have been negotiated under what is known as the "Kennedy Round." The Common Market had as its main aim free trade among its members, but it also created a system of common external tariffs in agriculture, a source of continual controversy.

One of the biggest unsolved problems of international trade is the balance between industrialized and developing countries of the Third World. Since they export mainly food and raw materials, which rise only slowly in price, and import manufactured goods, their expansion is much slower than that of rich countries.

INTERPOL, contraction of the International Criminal Police Organization, established in 1923. Its headquarters are now in Paris. It is a clearing house for police information and specializes in the detection of counterfeiting, smuggling and trafficking in narcotics.

INTERSTATE COMMERCE COMMISSION (ICC), independent US government agency, the first regulatory commission in US history. It was established in 1887 in response to western farmers' protests against the rate-setting practices of the railroads. Eventually its authority was extended over all surface transportation of passengers and freight across state lines. The deregulation movement of recent years has seen the curtailment of ICC power over railroads (1980), trucking (1980), and intercity buses (1982).

INTERSTATE SYSTEM, or National System of Interstate and Defense Highways, national intercity highway system totaling more than 43,000mi built since 1956. The cost was shared by the federal and state governments on a 90-10 matching basis. The federal share came from the Highway Trust Fund, which received the revenue from federal taxes on fuel, lubricants, vehicles, and parts. The state share derived from similar state taxes that are traditionally applied to highway construction and maintenance. Although the Interstate System accounts for only 1% of the nation's total road mileage, it carries 20% of its traffic. Even before its completion, the Interstate System, which was built to last 20 years, had fallen into serious disrepair.

INTERSTELLAR MATTER, thinly dispersed matter, in the form of gas and dust, between the stars, detectable through its light-absorbing effects. Thicker clouds are seen as NEBULAS. There is in the arms of the MILKY WAY almost as much interstellar as stellar matter. It is thought that STARS form out of interstellar matter.

INTESTINE. See GASTROINTESTINAL TRACT.

INTOLERABLE ACTS, also known as Coercive Acts, five acts of the British Parliament passed in 1774 to penalize dissidents in Mass. The Boston Port Act closed the harbor in default of compensation for the BOSTON TEA PARTY. The Massachusetts Bay Regulating Act suspended many of the colony's original rights. The Impartial Administration of Justice Act ordained that British officials accused of crimes within the colonies should be tried in other colonies or in England. The Quartering Act required colonists to shelter and feed British troops. The QUEBEC ACT extended Quebec's boundary S to the Ohio R. These strong measures were widely protested throughout the colonies and led to the calling of the First Continental Congress and hence the REVOLUTIONARY WAR.

INTOXICATION, state in which a person is overtly affected by excess of a DRUG or poison. It is often used to describe the psychological effects of drugs and particularly ALCOHOL, in which behavior may become disinhibited, facile, morose or aggressive and in which judgment is impaired. Late stages of intoxication affecting the BRAIN include stupor and COMA. Ingestion of very large amounts of water causes water intoxication and may lead to coma and death. POISONING with TOXINS and drugs may cause intoxication of other organs (e.g., HEART with DIGITALIS overdosage).

INVENTION, the act of devising an original process or device which facilitates or makes possible what was previously more difficult or impossible; also, such a process or device. Inventiveness is one of man's most valuable characteristics. Some of his earliest inventions—the stone ax, painting, wood and ivory carving—are shrouded in the mists of prehistory. But, although invention continued at a steady rate throughout the ancient and medieval periods, most of the inventions that have created the modern world date from 1500 AD at the earliest and the majority belong to the 20th century. If the 19th century was the age of the independent inventor, individually patenting (legally protecting) and marketing his invention, Thomas EDISON pointed the way to a later era in 1876 when he opened his first "invention factory." Today the majority of inventions flow from industrial research laboratories and the costly *development* of a new product is as important as the *research* which produces the basic idea for it: invention has become an industrial activity. The relations of science and invention have often been disputed; on balance it seems fair to admit that benefits have flowed in both directions.

INVERSION, Temperature, a relatively uncommon condition of the lower part of the atmosphere in which temperature increases with increase in height above the surface. Normally, temperature decreases upward through most of the lower ATMOSPHERE, but cold nights and certain atmospheric disturbances (e.g., a FRONT) can create inversions by creating cooler conditions at ground level and warmer conditions aloft. Inversions sometimes aggravate AIR POLLUTION, as the cooler air trapped near the surface cannot rise and so carry away the pollutants.

INVERTEBRATES, animals without backbones, a miscellaneous collection of groups from single-celled PROTOZOA to highly-specialized INSECTS and SPIDERS. Apart from the universal lack of an internal backbone of VERTEBRAE, many of these groups have little in common.

INVESTITURE CONTROVERSY, conflict between European rulers and the papacy in the 11th and 12th centuries. Originally a dispute about the appointment of bishops and abbots, it became a power struggle between church and state. In England a compromise was reached in

1107; in Germany the issue was resolved in 1122 by the Concordat of Worms.

INVESTMENT, the productive employment of resources (*capital*) or the transformation of savings into active wealth (*capital formation*), also the use of funds to obtain dividends, for example, from corporate stock or government bonds.

Investment is now one of the prime areas of concern for governments seeking to influence or control the progress of their economies. Planned investment in modern industry is achieved through an elaborate system of institutions and intermediaries including stock markets, investment banks, industrial finance corporations and commercial banks. This system enables individual investors to handle their assets easily and to choose the degree of risk they are willing to take.

Foreign investment can take two forms: *portfolio* investment, the purchase of the stock of foreign corporations, and *direct* investment, the establishment or expansion of an investor-controlled corporation in a foreign country. (See also BANKING; CAPITAL; ECONOMICS; STOCKS AND STOCK MARKET.)

INVESTMENT BANKING, system of banking that enables companies—and sometimes countries—to raise capital by selling new issues of stocks and bonds to investors. Investment bankers often join together to try and sell these substantially priced securities to insurance companies, pension funds, commercial banks and members of the investing public.

IODINE (I), the least reactive of the halogens, forming black lustrous crystals which readily sublime to pungent violet vapor. Most iodine is produced from calcium iodate ($Ca[IO_3]_2$), found in Chile saltpeter. In the US, much is recovered from oil-well brine, which contains sodium iodide (NaI). Chemically it resembles bromine closely, but has a greater tendency to covalency and positive oxidation states. It is large enough to form 6-coordinate oxy-anions. Most plants (especially seaweeds) contain traces of iodine; in the higher animals it is a constituent of the thyroxine hormone secreted by the THYROID GLAND. Iodine deficiency can cause GOITER. Iodine and its compounds are used as antiseptics, fungicides and in the production of dyes. The RADIOISOTOPE I^{131} is used as a tracer and to treat goiter. Silver iodide, being light-sensitive, is used in PHOTOGRAPHY. AW 126.9, mp 113.5°C, bp 184°C, sg 4.93 (20°C).

ION, an ATOM or group of atoms that has become electrically charged by gain or loss of negatively-charged ELECTRONS. In general, ions formed from metals are positive (cations), those from nonmetals negative (anions). CRYSTALS of ionic compounds consist of negative and positive ions arranged alternately in the lattice and held together by electrical attraction (see BOND, CHEMICAL). Many covalent compounds undergo ionic dissociation in solution. Ions may be formed in gases by radiation or electrical discharge, and occur in the IONOSPHERE (see also ATMOSPHERE). At very high temperatures gases form PLASMA, consisting of ions and free electrons. (See ELECTROLYSIS; ION PROPULSION.)

IONESCO, Eugène (1912–), Romanian-born French playwright, a leading figure in the so-called theater of the absurd. Among his best-known works are *The Bald Soprano* (1950), *Rhinoceros* (1959) and *Exit the King* (1962).

IONIAN ISLANDS, group of islands off the SW mainland of Greece, chief of which are Cephalonia, Cerigo, Corfu, Ithaca, Leukas, Paxos and Zante. A Byzantine province in the 10th century, the islands passed through periods of Venetian, French, Russian and British control before becoming part of Greece in 1864. Exports include wine, cotton, olives and fish.

IONIANS, ancient Greek people who colonized the W coast of Asia Minor that became known as Ionia. They are said to have been driven from the mainland by invading DORIANS. The Ionians made a major contribution to classical Greek poetry and philosophy.

IONIAN SEA, arm of the Mediterranean Sea, between SE Italy and W Greece. It is connected to the Adriatic by the Strait of Otranto and the Tyrrhenian Sea by the Strait of Messina.

IONOSPHERE, the zone of the earth's ATMOSPHERE extending outward from about 50mi above the surface in which most atoms and molecules exist as electrically charged IONS. The high degree of ionization is maintained through the continual absorption of high-energy solar radiation. Several distinct ionized layers, known as the D, E, F_1, F_2 and G layers, are distinguished. These are somewhat variable, the D layer disappearing and the F_1, F_2 layers merging at night. Since the free ELECTRONS in these layers strongly reflect radio waves, the ionosphere is of great importance for long-distance radio communications.

ION PROPULSION, or ion drive, drive proposed for spacecraft on interstellar or longer interplanetary trips. The vaporized propellant (liquid cesium or MERCURY) is passed through an ionizer, which strips each

atom of an ELECTRON. The positive IONS so formed are accelerated rearward by an electric field. The resultant thrust is low, but in the near-vacuum of space may be used to build up huge velocities by constant acceleration over a long period of time. The drive has been tested in orbit.

IOWA, state, in central US, bounded to the E by Wis. and Ill., to the S by Mo., to the W by Neb. and S.D. and to the N by Minn. It lies E-W between the Mississippi and Missouri rivers, which have contributed to its development, as routes first for exploration and then commerce.

Name of state: Iowa
Capital: Des Moines
Statehood: Dec. 28, 1846 (29th state)
Familiar name: Hawkeye State
Area: 56,290sq mi
Population: 2,851,000
Elevation: Highest—1,675ft, Ocheyedan Mound. Lowest—480ft, Mississippi River in Lee County
Motto: "Our liberties we prize and our rights we will maintain"
State flower: Wild Rose
State bird: Eastern Goldfinch
State tree: Oak
State song: "The Song of Iowa"
Land. Iowa consists of a gently rolling plain, sloping towards the SE, about two-thirds of which lies at 800–1,400ft. It is crossed by several large rivers, tributaries of the Mississippi and the Missouri. From 85% to 90% of the state's area is suitable for cultivation.
People. The first settlers came to Iowa from the states in the E and S, but from the 1840s many Europeans, particularly those with farming experience, joined them. Major ethnic groups include the Germans, Scandinavians, English and Dutch. More than 55% of the population lives in urban areas.
Economy. The state's income from agriculture is one of the nation's highest. Cattle and hogs are the most important livestock, and the major crops are corn and soybeans. After the sharp decline in farm prices in the 1930s, Iowa began a drive to

diversify its economy. Principal manufactures include farm implements, electronic goods, appliances, furniture, chemicals and automobile parts. Mineral production is relatively small, but the state is one of the nation's leading producers of gypsum. Good railroad and road systems have contributed to the growth of industry.

History. French explorers visited the region in 1673, and by 1682 France had claimed the area, naming it Louisiana for the French king. The territory W of the Mississippi was ceded to Spain (1762–1800), but in 1803 France sold the area to the US under the LOUISIANA PURCHASE. From 1804 to the early 1830s it was Indian land, not open to legal settlement, but by 1851 the entire area had been opened to settlers. The Territory of Iowa was created in 1838, and it became the 29th state of the US in 1846. In 1857 a second constitution was adopted and the state capital established at Des Moines. In the 20th century, Iowa has remained stable, prosperous, and still essentially agricultural. The state was hard hit by the farm crisis of the 1980s. In 1978–88 the number of farms fell 15%. In presidential elections 1968–88, Iowa voted Republican in 1968–84 but Democratic in 1988.

IOWA INDIANS, Siouan-speaking tribe of North American Indians. Farmers and buffalo-hunters, they lived in what is now Iowa. Today they are scattered through Neb., Kan, and Okla.

IPPOLITOV-IVANOV, Mikhail Mikhailovich (1859–1935), Russian composer and conductor. His work, which includes orchestral pieces, chamber music and operas, bridges Russian pre-revolutionary and post-revolutionary music.

IQ (*I*ntelligence *Q*uotient), a measure of an individual's INTELLIGENCE. IQ's are determined by an individual's performance on a variety of verbal, mathematical, perceptual and problem-solving tasks. Each individual's performance is considered in relation to average scores achieved by others of the same age group. IQ scores between 90 and 109 are considered average, the mean score being defined as 100; scores of 130 and above are considered very superior; while scores of 69 and below indicate mentally defective functioning. IQ scores of children vary moderately during childhood and adolescence as a result of environmental and emotional factors. (See also PSYCHOLOGICAL TESTS.)

IQBAL, Sir Muhammad (1873–1938), Indian Muslim poet, philosopher and politician. He was president of the Muslim League in 1930 and is considered one of the spiritual founders of Pakistan.

IRAN, formerly (until 1935) **Persia,** a republic in SW Asia, a major oil-exporting country. It is bordered by the USSR and the Caspian Sea in the N, Afghanistan and Pakistan in the E and Turkey and Iraq in the W. The Perisan Gulf and the Gulf of Oman lie to the S.

Official name: Islamic Republic of Iran
Capital: Teheran
Area: 636,372sq mi
Population: 49,930,000
Languages: Persian (Farsi) Kurdish; Luri; Turkish; Arabic; French
Religion: Muslim
Monetary unit(s): 1 Iranian rial=100 dinars

Land. Most of the country is a high mountainous plateau above 4,000ft, with an interior desert which contains a salt waste about 200mi long and half as wide. The climate ranges from subtropical to subpolar. About 11% of the land is forested.

People. Iran is multi-lingual and culturally diverse. The Kurds are an independent and nomadic people living in the W mountains, where about 350,000 Lurs, thought to be aboriginal Persians, also live. Other smaller nomadic tribal groups inhabit the mountainous fringes, and ethnic Arabs live in the SW. There are Armenians, who are primarily concerned with commerce and live in big cities, and groups of Turks and Jews. About 50% speak Persian, and although the Turkish groups are small, about 26% of Iranians speak Turkish— there was a long period of Turkish rule in the N. About 98% of the people are Shi'ite Muslims, although most of the tribal minorities are Sunnites.

Economy. In the early 1970s Iran's growth rate was one of the highest in the developing countries, because of profits from the oil industry. Agriculture remains important, employing about one-third the economically active population. Crops include cereals, cotton, tobacco and olives, and livestock is raised. In the late 1970s Iran was the world's fourth largest producer of oil. Natural gas was becoming important, though Iran's other mineral resources, including coal, chromium, lead and copper, were largely undeveloped. In 1954 the government instituted a major drive for self-sufficiency, and by the 1970s manufactures included machine tools, textiles, steel and automobiles.

History. Iran's history before 650 AD is treated under the entry on Ancient PERSIA. In 1055 Iran was invaded by the Turks, who in turn were overthrown by the Mongol leader GENGHIS KHAN in 1219. Between 1381 and 1404 there were frequent attacks by TAMERLANE, and it was not until 1501 that the Safavid dynasty, which ruled until 1736, was established, making Iran into a national state. There followed the rule of NADIR SHAH, and then, after 50 years of factional rivalry, the Kajar dynasty was established in 1795 and ruled until 1925. During this time Iran was dominated politically and economically by the European powers, especially Britain and Russia. After WWI Reza Khan, an army officer, overthrew the Shah and as REZA SHAH PAHLAVI founded the Pahlavi dynasty. In 1941 under pressure from the Western powers, he abdicated in favor of his son, Mohammed Reza Pahlavi. In 1951 Prime Minister Mohammed Mossadegh nationalized the oil industry, precipitating a crisis in which the US and European powers backed the Shah and Mossadegh was deposed. The Shah assumed complete control of the government in 1963. His regime—supported by the US—became increasingly repressive, and popular opposition, which grew in 1977–78, forced the Shah to leave the country in 1979. The exiled Islamic fundamentalist leader, Ayatollah Ruhollah Khomeini, returned, establishing an Islamic republican government under his effective control. Militants seized the US embassy in Nov. 1979, holding its staff hostage until Jan. 1981. The new regime, headed by Muslim clergy, succeeded in its primary goals: ending foreign domination and eradicating Western secularism. It sought but did not find a way to apply fundamentalist Islamic doctrine in economic affairs, legal matters, education, labor relations, and everyday life. It was disappointed by its inability to export its fundamentalist revolution to other Muslim countries; even Shi'ite Arabs did not support the Persian Shi'ites, identifying more strongly as Arabs than as Muslims. Most decisively, a war with Iraq that proved unwinnable cost innumerable lives and wrecked the Iranian economy (see IRAN-IRAQ WAR). Despairing of victory, Iran's clerical leaders turned increasingly to domestic problems even before the 1988 cease-fire. Conflicts sharpened among traditionalists, reformists, and radicals on how to devise an effective Islamic state. In 1987 Khomeini gave the government the power to overrule Islamic law whenever necessary. A new parliament elected in 1988 subordinated the war to economic reform, including widespread nationalizations and redistribution of agricultural land.

IRAN-CONTRA AFFAIR, Reagan administration scandal in which high officials of the NATIONAL SECURITY COUNCIL, with some degree of presidential authorization, sold US arms to Iran (ostensibly to establish contacts with "moderates" in that country but actually to obtain the release of US hostages held by pro-Iranian extremists in Lebanon) and then diverted profits from those sales to support the CONTRAS fighting the Sandinista regime in Nicaragua. The sale of arms to Iran violated national policy against such sales and against ransoming hostages; the diversion of funds to the contras violated congressional prohibition of such support by any US agency. The arms-for-hostages exchange secured the release of three hostages but did not prevent the taking of three more. Only a fraction of the profits from the scheme reached the contras. The operation, which began early in 1985, was exposed in the fall of 1986. Congressional and other investigations, including one by a special prosecutor, led to the indictment of a former national security adviser and NSC staff member and two business associates on charges of conspiracy, fraud, and theft. A former Central Intelligence Agency station chief in Costa Rica was indicted on charges of conspiracy and lying to federal investigators. Another former national security adviser pleaded guilty to charges of unlawfully withholding information from Congress.

IRAN-IRAQ WAR (1980-88), disastrous war precipitated by disputes over boundaries and access to the Persian Gulf but with deep roots in the ancient rivalry between Arabs and Persians and in the conflict between Iraq's socialist secularism and Iran's Islamic fundamentalism. Already identified as an enemy by Iran, which gave aid to Kurdish separatists in Iraq, Iraq's president Saddam Hussein sought to take advantage of the turmoil in Iran following the Islamic revolution of Ayatollah Ruhollah KHOMEINI to seize Iran's oil-producing Khuzistan region and to gain control of the disputed SHATT-AL-ARAB waterway, Iraq's crucial transit point to the PERSIAN GULF. The war that ensued was fought along the 730-mile border between the two countries. Iraqi troops invaded Iran in Sept. 1980. Iran counterattacked in 1981, driving the Iraqis back to their own borders and in 1982 invading Iraq, only to be driven back in turn. From 1984 through 1987 the Iranians launched a succession of costly but futile "final offenses" aimed especially at Basra in the S, Iraq's second-largest city and a major port. In these offenses Iran had the advantage in manower, Iraq in weapons, including aircraft, missiles, tanks, and poison gas. The military balance was moving in Iraq's favor when, in 1988, Khomeini reluctantly accepted a United Nations call for a truce. The eight-year war had cost an estimated 1 million dead and 1.7 million wounded.

IRAQ, independent Arab republic in SW Asia, a major oil-producing state. It is bounded by Turkey in the N, Iran in the E, and Syria and Jordan in the W. The S border is with Kuwait, the Persian Gulf and Saudi Arabia.

Official name: Republic of Iraq
Capital: Baghdad
Area: 169,235sq mi
Population: 16,476,000
Language: Arabic
Religions: Muslim; Christian
Monetary unit(s): 1 Iraqi dinar=1,000 fils

Land. Iraq consists of a largely level region between the Tigris and Euphrates rivers, whose waters are utilized for irrigation. In the south the rivers join to form the Shatt al-Arab, flowing through extensive marshlands. There are two climatic regions, a hot arid lowland in the W and SW desert and a damper area in the NE, where rain is sufficient for crops. In the N and E there is steppe vegetation with bushes and thorns, but the S and W support only salt-resistant shrubs.

People. Most Iraqis are Sunnite Muslim Arabs. The principal minority is the tribal Kurds, who comprise less than 15% of the population and live in the Zagros Mts of the N and adjacent portions of Turkey and Iran. They have long demanded independence. Other minorities include small groups of Iranians and Turkomans, other tribes and a Christian minority. The government has devoted considerable oil wealth to raising the standard of living, and primary education is now widely available.

Economy. Although agriculture employs nearly 40% of the labor force, oil production, begun in 1928, domintes the economy. Until 1961 the oil industry was monopolized by the largely British-owned Iraq Petroleum Co., but the government then took over much of IPC's holdings and the oil industry was nationalized in 1972. Oil revenues have been used to provide social services and to diversify the previously underdeveloped industrial sector. In the 1980s, despite the construction of pipelines to carry Iraqi oil to Turkish and Saudi Arabian ports, the economy was adversely affected by the long and costly IRAN-IRAQ WAR; Iraqi ports were forced to shut down and industrial centers such as Baghdad and Basrah came under repeated attack.

History. For the history of the region before the 7th century see under the entries BABYLONIA AND ASSYRIA and MESOPOTAMIA. When the Arabs settled in the area now known as Iraq in the 7th century AD, they brought about a cultural and scientific revival. Baghdad became the capital of the ABBASID caliphate. After the Mongol invasion in the 13th century the country was impoverished, and continuing political instability prevented its rebuilding. Ottoman control was solidified in 1638, although Iraq often maintained some autonomy. Iraq's modern history begins in 1914, with the British invasion during WWI. It was not until 1932, after years of violence and unrest, that the British granted independence to Iraq. Unrest continued, particularly over Kurdish demands for self-government. In 1945 Iraq joined the ARAB LEAGUE but then in 1955 joined the Baghdad Pact (see CENTRAL TREATY ORGANIZATION). The Arab socialist Baath Party took control of the government in 1968, nationalizing much of the economy. Violent conflict with the Kurds erupted in 1962. Kurdish rebels, who continued to demand autonomy despite a 1975 peace treaty, were supported by Iran during the long Iran-Iraq War that erupted in 1980. A UN-sponsored cease-fire went into effect in 1988 and negotiations aimed at a permanent peace settlement began. After the cease-fire, Iraq turned its attention to rebuilding the war-torn economy and ending the Kurdish rebellion. After government forces attacked Kurdish strongholds in the N, more than 60,000 Kurds sought refuge in Turkey.

IRELAND, Northern, comprises six counties of Ulster in NE Ireland. Since 1922 it has been a province of the UK. Covering 5,452sq mi, it has a predominantly Protestant population with a Roman Catholic minority swelled in recent years to around 30%. The largest towns are the capital, Belfast, and Londonderry. Major manufactures include machinery and shipbuilding, textiles (man-made fibers and linen) and electronics.

History. The Ulster counties chose to remain British after Ireland (Eire) became independent in 1922 and maintained this resolve despite occasional outbreaks of terrorism by the IRISH REPUBLICAN ARMY. Discrimination against the growing Catholic minority led them to form a civil rights movement (1968), which was used to justify renewed IRA terrorism. The resulting violence and civil unrest led the UK government to suspend the Northern Ireland Parliament at Stormont (1972) and assume direct rule of the province. Though a new Northern Ireland Assembly was elected in 1982 but dissolved in 1986, the violence continues. Pop 1,609,000.

IRELAND, Republic of, or **Eire,** independent country in the British Isles occupying all of the island of Ireland except the NE (see IRELAND, NORTHERN).

Official name: Irish Republic
Capital: Dublin
Area: 27,137sq mi
Population: 3,560,000
Languages: Irish, English
Religions: Roman Catholic, Protestant
Monetary unit(s): 1 pound (punt) = 100 pence

Land. The chief physical feature is the broad central limestone plain; seldom rising above 400ft, it is marked by numerous *loughs* (lakes) and large peat bogs. Rimming the plain are groups of hills and mountains, the most extensive being the Wicklow Mts in the E. The country's highest peak, Carrantuohill (3,414ft), rises in Macgillycuddy's Reeks in the SW near the beautiful Lakes of Killarney. The chief river is the Shannon (240mi), longest in the British Isles; like the Erne R it is harnessed for hydroelectric power. The long Shannon estuary is one of many inlets of the much-indented W coast, which is fringed by many islands. The climate is mild and damp, with annual rainfall ranging from 30–40in in the lowlands to over 60in in the W uplands. This has helped create the lush green pastures which have made Ireland "the Emerald Isle." Rainfall and high winds are more frequent in the W and N than in the sunnier E.

People. In 1845 about 8.5 million people lived in Ireland. A century later, the whole island had about half that many inhabitants. This unique demographic decline resulted from the POTATO FAMINE of 1845–48 and subsequent emigration especially from the rural W. Today the population of the republic is concentrated mainly in or near the cities, the largest of which are Dublin, the capital, Cork and Limerick. The Irish are a Celtic people; since 1922 the government has encouraged the revival of the Irish language (often known as Gaelic), although English remains the principal language. About 95% of the people are Roman Catholics; about 5% are Protestants, of whom the largest denomination is the Church of Ireland.

Economy. It is based mainly on small mixed farms rearing cattle or engaged in dairying (especially in the S) with barley, wheat, oats, potatoes, turnips and sugar beets as the chief arable crops. Ireland is relatively poor in minerals, but some coal is mined, along with recently-discovered deposits of lead, zinc, copper and silver. Peat from the bogs is a valuable fuel, used for home heating and electricity generation. Industries include food-processing, distilling, brewing, tobacco products, textiles, clothing and small-scale engineering. Foreign manufacturers, mainly W German and Japanese, have been encouraged to set up export-oriented plants, and tourism is important.

History. In the 4th century BC the Gaels evolved a Celtic civilization which in its full flowering, after St. PATRICK introduced Christianity in the 5th century, produced superb works of art (see BOOK OF KELLS) and sent religious and cultural missionaries to the rest of Europe. It was severely damaged by the VIKINGS in the 9th and 10th centuries, until their defeat by BRIAN BORU in 1041. In 1166 the Anglo-Normans invaded Ireland and thereafter the English tried constantly to assert their authority over the native Irish and the settlers, who quickly became assimilated with them. The Tudors and Stuarts promoted English and Scottish settlement (see ULSTER), and tried to anglicize the country, constantly embittered by religious differences, through wars until Oliver CROMWELL's pacification. Roman Catholic gentry fled when Protestant ascendency was confirmed by WILLIAM III's victory at the Boyne (1690). In the Rebellion of 1798 the Irish peasantry, roused by such patriots as Wolfe Tone, rebelled, but were ruthlessly suppressed. The Act of Union (1801) ended parliamentary independence from England; nevertheless, despite the potato famine and FENIAN violence, a measure of independence by constitutional means was slowly attained through agitation for Catholic Emancipation and the emergence of leaders like Daniel O'CONNELL and C. S. PARNELL. One result was the cultural CELTIC RENAISSANCE of the 1890s. The inability of British governments to implement HOME RULE led to the bitter EASTER RISING (1916). In 1920 Britain separated Northern Ireland, where Protestants were in the majority, from the rest of Ireland, which in 1922 was given dominion status as the Irish Free State. In 1937 Prime Minister Eamon DE VALERA declared Ireland (or Eire) a sovereign nation within the British Commonwealth. Ireland severed all ties with Britain in 1949, becoming the Republic of Ireland. It entered the United Nations in 1955 and the European Economic Community in 1973. Ireland has a relatively impoverished economy. Its wealth is less than two-thirds of the European average, unemployment is high, and many of its best-educated young people emigrate. In the late 1980s, Prime Minister Charles J. HAUGHEY instituted a program of government austerity and emphasis on private enterprise to make Ireland competitive with other EEC members when trade barriers come down in 1992.

IRIDESCENCE, production of colors of varied hue by INTERFERENCE of light reflected from front and back of thin films (as in soap bubbles) or from faults and boundaries within crystalline solids such as mica or opal. The colors of mother-of-pearl and some insects are due to iridescence.

IRISH REPUBLICAN ARMY (IRA), illegal revolutionary force operating in Ireland. The IRA evolved from militant remnants of the Irish Volunteers, who planned and fought the Easter Rising (1916). Refusing to accept the separation of Northern Ireland, it became a secret terrorist organization responsible for bombings and raids on both sides of the border. Loss of popular support because of its violence and pro-German activities in WWII, and strong repressive action by the government reduced its role until the 1960s.

In 1969 the IRA split into the anti-terrorist "officials" and the terrorist "Provisionals," who rely on Irish-American financial aid. The Provisionals then launched a campaign of indiscriminate bombings and assassinations in Northern Ireland and in England.

IRISH SEA, arm of the Atlantic, separating Ireland from England. Connected to the Atlantic by the North Channel to the NW and St. George's Channel to the S, it is about 130mi across.

IRON (Fe), silvery-gray, soft, ferromagnetic (see MAGNETISM) metal in Group VIII of the PERIODIC TABLE; a transition element. Metallic iron is the main constituent of the earth's core (see EARTH), but is rare in the crust; it is found in meteorites (see METEORS). Combined iron is found as hematite, magnetite, limonite, siderite, geothite, taconite, chromite and pyrite. It is extracted by smelting oxide ores in a BLAST FURNACE to produce pig iron, which may be refined to produce cast iron or wrought iron, or converted to STEEL in the open-hearth process or the Bessemer process. Many other iron ALLOYS are used for particular applications. Pure iron is very little used; it is chemically reactive and oxidizes to RUST in moist air. It has four allotropes (see ALLOTROPY). The stable oxidation states of iron are $+2$ (ferrous), and $+3$ (ferric), though $+4$ and $+6$ states are known. The ferrous ion (Fe^{2+}) is pale green in aqueous solution; it is a mild reducing agent and does not readily form ligand complexes. **Iron(II) sulfate** ($FeSO_4 7H_2O$), or green vitriol, or copperas, green crystalline solid, made by treating iron ore with sulfuric acid, used in tanning, in medicine to treat iron deficiency, and to make ink, fertilizers, pesticides and other iron compounds, mp $64°C$. The ferric ion (Fe^{3+}) is yellow in aqueous solution; it resembles the ALUMINUM ion, being acidic and forming stable ligand complexes, especially with cyanides. **Iron(III) oxide** (Fe_2O_3), red-brown powder used as a pigment and as jewelers' rouge (see ABRASIVES); occurs naturally as hematite; mp $1565°C$. In the human body, iron is a constituent of HEMOGLOBIN and the cytochromes. Iron deficiency causes ANEMIA. AW 55.8, mp $1535°C$, bp $2750°C$, sg 7.874 ($20°C$).

IRON AGE, the stage of man's material cultural development, following the STONE AGE and BRONZE AGE, during which iron is generally used for weapons and tools. Though used ornamentally as early as 4000 BC in Egypt and Mesopotamia, iron's difficulty of working precluded its general use until efficient techniques were developed in Armenia, c1500 BC. By c500 BC the use of iron was dominant throughout the known world, and by c300 BC the Chinese were using cast iron. Some cultures, as those in America and Australia, are said never to have had an iron age.

IRONCLADS, the first armored warships, wooden-hulled ships with iron plate armor, developed by the French and British in the CRIMEAN WAR. The first engagement between ironclads came in the US Civil War, involving the famous MONITOR. Iron-hulled ships superseded ironclads in the 1890s.

IRON CURTAIN, term for the self-imposed isolation of the communist countries, especially during the Stalinist era. The term was popularized by Sir Winston CHURCHILL in a speech at Fulton, Mo., on March 5, 1946.

IRON GATE, at 2,600ft the deepest gorge in Europe, 2mi long. It lies on the Danube R at the Romania-Yugoslavia border; the two countries run a joint hydroelectric project in the gorge.

IROQUOIAN, family of languages spoken by North American Indians chiefly in what is now N.N.Y. The languages of the first five confederated IROQUOIS tribes and Wyandot, the Huron language, are the most closely related. The two southern languages are Tuscarora and Cherokee.

IROQUOIS, North American Indian tribes of the IROQUOIAN linguistic family, members of the Iroquois League. This political union of the Mohawk, Oneida, Onondaga, Cayuga and Seneca tribes was founded in the 16th century by the Onondaga chief Hiawatha and Dekanawida, formerly a Huron. Villages and tribes were sometimes adopted into the League, as with the Tuscarora in 1722. Hunters and farmers, the Iroquois tribes lived in stockaded villages of *longhouses*; families were matrilineal, and belonged to an intertribal clan system. In the 1600s they were supplied with firearms and metal weapons by the Dutch, and became supreme in the NE. During the FRENCH AND INDIAN WARS the Iroquois supported the British, but the league split over the REVOLUTIONARY WAR.

IRRAWADDY RIVER, main waterway of Burma, formed by the confluence of the Mali and Nmai rivers. It flows S for about 1,350mi to empty into the Bay of Bengal. Its delta is one of the world's richest rice-growing areas.

IRREDENTISM (from *Italia irredenta*: unredeemed Italy), Italian nationalist movement begun after unification (1866) to acquire Italian-speaking lands still under foreign rule, an end achieved after WWI. The term is now used for any movement attempting to free territory from foreign control.

IRRIGATION, artificial application of water to soil to promote plant growth. Irrigation is vital for agricultural land with inadequate rainfall. The practice dates back at least to the canals and reservoirs of ancient Egypt. Today over 320 million acres of farmland throughout the world are irrigated, notably in the US, India, Pakistan, China, Australia, Egypt and the USSR. There are three main irrigation techniques: **surface irrigation,** in which the soil surface is moistened or flooded by water flowing through furrows or tubes; **sprinkler irrigation,** in which water is sprayed on the land from above; and **subirrigation,** in which underground pipes supply water to roots. The amount of water needed for a particular project is called the **duty of water,** expressed as the number of acres irrigated by 1cu ft of water per second.

IRVING, Sir Henry (1838–1905), stage name of John Henry Brodribb, greatest British actor and actor-manager of his day. At the Lyceum Theater, London, 1878–1902, he staged spectacular Shakespeare productions, often with Ellen TERRY as his leading lady.

IRVING, Washington (1783–1859), first US writer to achieve international acclaim. Born in N.Y., he became a casual writer and publisher; he went to Europe in 1815 on business and remained there until 1832. His most famous stories, *Rip Van Winkle* and *The Legend of Sleepy Hollow,* appeared in *The Sketch Book of Geoffrey Crayon* (1820). None of his later works approached the success of this collection. He served as minister to Spain 1842–46, but spent the rest of his life at Tarrytown, N.Y., near the setting of many of his tales.

ISAAC, in the Old Testament, second of the Hebrew patriarchs. Son of Abraham and Sarah, he was spared at the last moment from being sacrificed as proof of his father's faith. He married Rebecca and fathered Esau and JACOB, who cheated Esau out of Isaac's last blessing.

ISAAC, Heinrich (c1450–1517), major Flemish composer. He served Lorenzo de MEDICI and Emperor MAXIMILLIAN I. The bulk of his work was church music, particularly masses, but he also wrote many German and Italian secular songs.

ISABELLA, name of two queens of Spain. **Isabella I** (1451–1504), was queen of Castile from 1474 and of Aragon from 1481 by marriage to the future Ferdinand II of

Aragon (1469). The marriage unified Christian Spain; royal power was strengthened and the INQUISITION reestablished, Isabella supporting its call for the expulsion of Spanish Jews. She financed COLUMBUS' expedition in 1492. She helped direct the conquest of Moorish Granada. **Isabella II** (1830–1904), was queen of Spain 1833–68, under a regency until 1843. Her succession was disputed by the Carlists, provoking civil war 1833–39; after the regency was ended by a revolt her personal rule proved arbitrary and ineffectual. Promiscuous and irresponsible, she was ousted in 1868 and abdicated in 1870.

ISAIAH, great Hebrew prophet of the 8th century BC, for whom the Old Testament Book of Isaiah is named; probably only the first 36 chapters represent his teachings, the remainder (often known as Deutero—and Trito—Isaiah) being additions by his followers. Isaiah condemns the decadence of Judah, foretelling coming disaster; he warns against trusting in foreign alliances rather than in God and heralds the Messiah.

ISHERWOOD, Christopher William Bradshaw (1904–1986), English-born novelist and playwright who settled in the US in 1939. His best-known novels are *Mr. Norris Changes Trains* (1935) and *Goodbye to Berlin* (1939), set in the decaying Germany of the 1930s, later adapted by others into plays and films (*I Am a Camera* and *Cabaret*). He collaborated with W. H. AUDEN on three plays, the best-known being *The Ascent of F-6* (1936).

ISHII, Viscount Kikujiro (1866–1945), influential Japanese diplomat, ambassador to France 1912–15 and 1920–27. He negotiated the GENTLEMAN'S AGREEMENT and the LANSING-ISHII AGREEMENT with the US. He opposed Japan's alliance with the Axis powers in WWII, favoring the Allies, but was killed in a US air raid.

ISIS, in ancient Egyptian mythology the dominant mother goddess, protectress of living and dead. Sister and wife of Osiris, she temporarily restored him to life after his murder and dismembering by Set, and so conceived Horus. Her cult spread from Lower Egypt throughout the Roman world as one of the MYSTERIES.

ISLAM (Arabic: submission to God), major world religion, founded by Mohammed in the 7th century AD; a monotheistic faith, it incorporates elements of Judaic and Christian belief. Today there are about 600 million MUSLIMS ("ones who submit"), mainly in the Arab countries and SW Asia, and in N and E Africa, Turkey, Iran, Afghanistan, Pakistan, India, SE Asia and the USSR. The Prophet MOHAMMED was a merchant of Mecca in the early 7th century; on his journeys he came into contact with Jews and Christians. Inspired by a vision of the archangel Gabriel, he began to preach the worship of the one true God (Arabic: *Allah*), and to denounce idolatry. In his lifetime Mecca was converted to Islam. In the century after his death (632 AD) Muslim armies forged an Arab Empire extending from Spain to India.

Teachings. The KORAN, the holy book of Islam, sets forth the fundamental tenets of Islam as revealed by God to Mohammed. These include the five basic duties of Muslims and also rules for their social and moral behavior. Muslims also study the prophet's teachings, or *Sunna,* collected in the *Hadith* ("traditions"). A legal system, the *Shari'a,* based on the Koran and the Sunna, has been the law of many Muslim countries.

Worship. Public worship takes place in MOSQUES; these are often highly decorated in abstract patterns, because representational art is forbidden as idolatrous. Before entering a mosque, Muslims must ritually cleanse themselves. Special services are held at midday on Friday. Devout Muslims must pray five times daily, facing in the direction of Mecca. Islam has no priests as such; worship is led by a lay leader, the *imam.* A *muezzin* calls the faithful to prayer from a rooftop or minaret. Other leaders in Muslim communities include the *ulema,* experts on the *Shari'a,* who give guidance and may even decide legal disputes.

ISLE ROYALE NATIONAL PARK, wildlife reserve, established in 1940, comprising more than 100 islands in NW Lake Superior, N Mich. Isle Royale itself (229sq mi) is the site of pre-Columbian Indian copper mines; its wildlife includes moose, timber wolves and diverse bird life.

ISMAILIS, Muslim SHI'ITE sect sometimes known as Seveners because they venerated the religious leader Ismail (d. 760) as the seventh imam. Among branches of the Ismaili faith were the ASSASSIN sects of Iran and Syria. The Ismaili spiritual leader today is the Harvard-educated AGA KHAN IV.

ISMAIL PASHA (1830–1895), Ottoman viceroy of Egypt 1863–79. He extended Egyptian rule in the Sudan. In Egypt he improved administration, education and communications, opening the Suez Canal in 1869. Huge debts resulted from his schemes and he was dismissed by the Ottoman sultan in 1879.

ISOCRATES (436–338 BC), Athenian orator who founded a celebrated school of

RHETORIC there. His vision of a Greece united to invade Persia influenced ALEXANDER THE GREAT.

ISOLATIONISM, national policy of avoiding entanglement in foreign affairs, a recurrent phenomenon in US history. In 1823 the MONROE DOCTRINE tried to exclude European powers from the Americas. The US entered WWI reluctantly, stayed out of the League of Nations it helped create and entered WWII only when attacked. Thereafter it joined the UN and international defense pacts (NATO, SEATO) and played an active role in international affairs. British policy was essentially isolationist in the period between the wars.

ISOMERS, chemical compounds having identical chemical COMPOSITION and molecular FORMULA, but differing in the arrangement of atoms in their molecules, and having different properties. The two chief types are **stereoisomers,** which have the same structural formula, and **structural isomers,** which have different structural formulas. The latter may be subdivided into positional isomers, which have the same functional groups occupying different positions on the carbon skeleton; and functional isomers, which have different functional groups.

ISOMORPHISM, the formation by different compounds or MINERALS of CRYSTALS having closely similar external forms and lattice structure. Isomorphous compounds have similar chemical composition—ions of similar size, charge, and ionization potential being substituted for each other—and form mixed crystals. Cations are usually involved in the interchange, although anions may also replace each other. A mineral series showing a continuous isomorphous change between end members constitutes a *solid solution* as in the plagioclase feldspars where sodium and calcium are the cations involved.

ISOTOPES, ATOMS of a chemical ELEMENT which have the same number of PROTONS in the nucleus, but different numbers of NEUTRONS, i.e., having the same atomic number but different mass number. Isotopes of an element have identical chemical and physical properties (except those determined by atomic mass). Most elements have several stable isotopes, being found in nature as mixtures. The natural proportions of the isotopes are expressed in the form of an **abundance ratio.** Because some isotopes have particular properties (e.g., 0.015% of HYDROGEN atoms have two neutrons and combine with oxygen to form HEAVY WATER, used in NUCLEAR REACTORS),

mass-dependent methods of separating these out have been devised. These include MASS SPECTROSCOPY, DIFFUSION, DISTILLATION and ELECTROLYSIS. A few elements have natural radioactive isotopes (RADIOISOTOPES) and others of these can be made by exposing stable isotopes to RADIATION in a reactor. These are widely used therapeutically and industrially; their radiation may be employed directly, or the way in which it is scattered or absorbed by objects can be measured. They are useful as tracers of a process, since they may be detected in very small amounts and behave virtually identically to other atoms of the same element. They may also be used to "label" particular atoms in complex molecules, in attempts to work out chemical reaction mechanisms.

ISRAEL, Jewish republic on the E extremity of the Mediterranean. Founded in 1948, it is bounded by Lebanon on the N, Syria and Jordan on the E and Egypt on the S and W. Although small in itself, in various wars Israel captured large territories, including the Golan Heights, WEST BANK of the Jordan R., GAZA STRIP, and the Sinai Desert, from which Israel withdrew in 1979–82. The other territories are the subject of continual international controversy.

Official name: State of Israel
Capital: Jerusalem
Area: 7,992sq mi
Population: 4,449,000
Languages: Hebrew, Arabic
Religions: Judaism, Muslim, Christian
Monetary unit(s): 1 shekel = 100 new agorot
Land. Israel has a long straight Mediterranean coastline, and to the S access to the Red Sea from the port of Elath through the Gulf of Aqaba. There are three main regions: the mountainous but fertile Galilee area in the N, the more fertile coastal plain in the W and in the S the Negev Desert, barren but with important mineral resources. In the E a depression contains the Huleh Valley, Sea of Galilee, Jordan R and Dead Sea. Summers are hot and dry, winters mild; rainfall (mainly in winter, or Nov.–April)

varies from 40in in the N to almost nil in the S. Because much of Israel's potential farmland lacks water supplies a vast irrigation program has been put into operation; huge areas of formerly barren land are now productive. Available water resources, however, are already almost fully exploited.

People. About 83% of Israelis living within the country's 1949 boundaries are Jews. Nearly 60% of them were born in Israel; the remainer are immigrants, mostly from central and E Europe, the Middle East, N Africa and the USSR. Minorities include Christian and Muslim Arabs, DRUZES, CIRCASSIANS and SAMARITANS. Although thousands of Jews have settled in the West Bank, the great majority of the people in the occupied territories are Palestinian Arabs. The official language is HEBREW, but Arabic is also important and English, French, German and Yiddish are widely spoken. Elementary schooling is free and compulsory, and there are seven institutions of higher learning. Most of the population is urban, living mostly in Tel Aviv, Jaffa, Haifa and Jerusalem. Jews in rural areas generally live in *kibbutzim* (collective agricultural settlements) and *moshavim* (cooporative farming villages).

Economy. Heavy defense expenditure, immigration and limited natural resources have produced an unstable economy; assistance has come from American aid, German reparation and Jews abroad. Many immigrants bring technical and administrative skills. Land reclamation and irrigation have nearly trebled the cultivated area since 1955, so that the country produces most of its own food. Major crops include citrus fruit, grains, olives, melons, grapes. Mineral resources include gypsum, natural gas, oil and phosphates; potash, magnesium and bromine come from the Dead Sea. Light industry is developing, and manufactures include chemicals, textiles and paper. Citrus fruits, diamonds, chemicals and textiles are major exports. Tourism is a major industry. Because of heavy defense spending and reliance on imported oil, Israel suffers from severe payments deficits and a high rate of inflation.

History. (For the early history of the Jews in Palestine see JEWS; PALESTINE.) In 1947 the UN voted to divide Palestine (then under British mandate) into Jewish and Arab states. After the subsequent British withdrawal, Palestine Arabs and Arab troops from neighboring countries immediately tried to eradicate Israel by force, but the Israelis defeated them, capturing almost all Palestine (see ARAB-ISRAELI

WARS). Arab refugees, settled in S Lebanon, the West Bank and Gaza Strip in UN-administered camps, are a continuing social and political problem; also, refugee camps have proved a fruitful recruiting area and cover for Palestinian guerrilla groups. Egypt nationalized the SUEZ CANAL in 1956 and closed it to Israeli shipping; Israeli troops then overran Gaza and Sinai, winning the right of passage from Elath to the Red Sea. In the Six-Day War (1967) Israel acquired large tracts of its neighbors' territories including the West Bank and East Jerusalem; these it refused to return without a firm peace settlement. It lost some of these in the Yom Kippur War (1973). Relations with Egypt improved; in 1978 the two countries reached the so-called CAMP DAVID AGREEMENT and the Sinai was returned to Egypt by 1982. Subsequent negotiations between Egypt and Israel on the future of the Palestinian Arabs made little progress. In 1982 Israeli forces invaded Lebanon, from which Palestinian guerrillas had launched attacks on Israel. Palestinian guerrillas were forced to leave Beirut, and most Israeli forces were withdrawn by 1985. In Dec. 1987, frustrated by Israeli settlement of the West Bank and the lack of progress on Palestinian autonomy, Palestinian Arabs in the West Bank and Gaza Strip launched an uprising aimed at ending Israeli occupation. The Nov. 1988 Israeli elections offered voters a choice between the hard-line Likud Party and the Labor Party, which expressed a willingness to exchange land for peace. Likud won 40 seats, Labor 39 in the 120-member parliament. Likud's leader, Prime Minister Yitzhak Shamir, was asked to form a new government.

ISRAEL, Kingdom of, Hebrew kingdom, first as united under Saul, David and Solomon c1020 BC–922 BC, and then the breakaway state in the N founded by Jeroboam I in the territory of the 10 tribes. In 722 BC this was overrun by the Assyrians; the tribes were apparently killed, enslaved or scattered.

ISSUS, Battle of, important victory of ALEXANDER THE GREAT over DARIUS III of Persia near the Gulf of Issus (now Iskenderun in Turkey), 333 BC.

ISTANBUL, largest city in Turkey, divided by the Bosporus. Until 1930 its official name was Constantinople, of which Istanbul was originally a contraction. Built on the site of a former Greek town, Byzantium, in 330 AD by CONSTANTINE I, it became the capital of the BYZANTINE EMPIRE; it reached its cultural height under JUSTINIAN I in the 6th century. The city was taken and sacked by the Fourth Crusade in 1204; after years of decay it was taken by the Ottoman Turks in 1453, and was rebuilt as the Turkish capital, which it remained until 1923 when the capital was moved to Ankara. It is still the economic and cultural heart of Turkey, a port, transport hub and manufacturing center. Pop 5,475,982.

ISTRIA, mountainous peninsula in NW Yugoslavia, on the N Adriatic Sea. It became part of Yugoslavia in 1947. Its population's chief occupations are fruit growing, fishing and mining.

ITALIAN, one of the ROMANCE LANGUAGES, spoken in Italy and in parts of Switzerland, France and Yugoslavia. It derives from colloquial LATIN. The Tuscan dialect established as a literary language by Dante, Petrarch and Boccaccio became the foundation of modern Italian. Since the Renaissance, words from other Romance languages have been added. There are regional dialects.

ITALIAN WARS (1494–1559), series of wars in which France and Spain fought for control of Italy, begun by a French invasion in 1494. The Holy Roman Empire (Emperor CHARLES V was also king of Spain) and England also participated to frustrate French ambitions. The numerous small Italian states, including the papacy, tried to preserve their independence by alliances with each other and with the major powers. The wars ended with Spain dominant in the peninsula.

ITALO-ETHIOPIAN WAR (1935–36), Fascist Italy's conquest of Ethiopia, launched from Italian-held Eritrea and Somalia. Refusing to accept the League of Nations proposals for settling border disputes, Mussolini used planes, guns and poison gas to overwhelm the ill-equipped Ethiopians, and to forge a new empire. Too weak to halt aggression, the League merely voted economic sanctions against Italy, which simply left the League.

ITALY, republic in S Europe comprising a long, narrow peninsula and nearby Sicily, Sardinia and smaller Mediterranean islands. Italy is a land of great natural beauty, with an immensely rich historical and artistic heritage. It made a phenomenal economic recovery after the devastation suffered during WWII.

Land. Italy is predominantly mountainous. In the N is the great curve of the Alps, while the Apennine chain forms the peninsula's spine. Between the two lies the N plain containing the Po R—Italy's largest natural waterway, flowing E to the Adriatic Sea. The Arno and Tiber flow W from the Apennines, respectively to the Ligurian and

Official name: Italian Republic
Capital: Rome
Area: 116,324sq mi
Population: 57,256,000
Languages: Italian
Religions: Roman Catholic
Monetary unit(s): 1 lire=100 centesimi

Tyrrhenian seas. Except in the cooler, wetter mountains, summers are hot and dry, winters mild and rainy. Forest and scrub cover much of the mountains; the lowlands are largely cultivated.

People. People of short, dark, Mediterranean stock predominate in the S; in the N live taller, fair-haired peoples of Celtic and Alpine origin. Italy is densely populated, with the highest concentrations in the industrial cities of the N, the Po Valley, Rome and Naples. About half the population is urban. Rural poor from the underdeveloped S migrate to the N and abroad. Italian is the official language, but French and German are spoken respectively in the extreme NW and N. Over 90% of Italians are nominal Catholics. In 1985 a concordat with the Vatican ended Roman Catholicism's position as the state religion. Education is free and compulsory for ages 6-14, and more than 40 cities and towns have university centers.

Economy. Foreign aid and founder membership in the European Common Market vastly boosted Italy's postwar economy before the crises of the 1970s oil damaged it. Increased industrial output (steel, chemicals, automobiles, typewriters, machinery, textiles and shoes) enriched the N, but a faltering agriculture kept the S poor. The main farm products are grapes, citrus fruits, olives, grains, vegetables and cattle. Mineral resources are limited, but Italy has hydroelectric power, natural gas and oil. There are also a few nuclear power stations. Tourism helps the trade balance. Italy has an advanced system of roads and railroads

History. The Romans—a Latin people of central Italy—held most of the peninsula by 200 BC, absorbing the ETRUSCAN civilization in the N and Greek colonies (dating from the 8th century BC) in the S. (See ROME, ANCIENT.) In the 5th–6th centuries AD, barbarian tribes (VISIGOTHS, OSTROGOTHS and LOMBARDS) overran Italy, forming Germanic kingdoms. These kingdoms were disputed by the Byzantine Empire, whose lands in Italy became the core of the PAPAL STATES. Italy was to remain divided for over 1,000 years, although nominally part of Charlemagne's empire from 774 and part of the Holy Roman Empire from 962.

In the Middle Ages the S came under Norman rule (see NAPLES, KINGDOM OF). Powerful rival city-states (see GUELPHS AND GHIBELLINES) emerged in the center and N, from the late Middle Ages under the MEDICI and other dynasties. Italy pioneered the RENAISSANCE, but Spain (from the late 1400s) and Austria (from the early 1700s) controlled much of the land until the RISORGIMENTO culminated in unity and independence under Victor Emmanuel II (1861). Italy gained Eritrea, Italian Somaliland and Libya in Africa, and fought alongside the Allies in WWI. In 1922 the Fascist dictator Benito MUSSOLINI seized power, later conquering Ethiopia and siding with Nazi Germany in WWII. Defeated Italy emerged from the war as a republic shorn of its overseas colonies and firmly allied with the West.

Since a republican constitution went into effect in 1948, Italy has been governed by a long series of coalitions, generally dominated by the Christian Democrats. In the 1970s the country was plagued by domestic terrorism, culminating in the kidnap-murder of former premier Aldo Moro in 1978. Bettino Craxi formed Italy's first Socialist-led government in 1983; it held power for 3½ years, longer than any other postwar administration.

ITURBIDE, Agustin de (1783–1824), Mexican revolutionary, emperor of Mexico 1822–23. A royalist officer, he united the revolutionaries with his Plan of Iguala (1821), which proclaimed Mexican independence. Exploiting political divisions, he became emperor of independent Mexico. But opposition to his capricious rule brought abdication, exile and (on his return) execution.

IVAN, name of six Russian rulers. **Ivan I Kalita** (c1304–1340), was grand prince of Moscow 1328–40. **Ivan II Krasnyi** (1326–1359), was grand prince of Moscow 1353–59. **Ivan III the Great** (1440–1505), was grand prince of Moscow 1462–1505. He paved the way for a unified Russia by annexing land, repelling the Tatars, strengthening central authority over the

Church and nobility, and revising the law code. **Ivan IV the Terrible** (1530–1584), was grand prince from 1533 and the first tsar of Russia 1547–84. He annexed Siberia, consolidated control of the Volga R, and established diplomatic and trading relations with Europe. He strengthened the law and administration, but was notoriously cruel. **Ivan V** (1666–1696), was co-tsar (with Peter I) 1682–96. **Ivan VI** (1740–1764), was tsar 1740–41.

IVANOV, Vsevolod (1895–1963), Russian writer. Born in Siberia, he often used it as a setting for his stories. His most popular novels, *The Guerillas* (1921) and *Armored Train* (1922), treat the Russian Revolution and Civil War in epic fashion.

IVES, Charles Edward (1874–1954), US composer, a major 20th-century innovator. His music (mostly pre-1915) incorporated popular songs and hymn tunes, and exploits dissonance, polytonality and polymetric construction. Ignored by his contemporaries, he influenced later composers. His best-known works include *Three Places in New England* (1903–14) and the *Second (Concord) Piano Sonata* (1909–15). His *Third Symphony* (1904–11) won a 1947 Pulitzer Prize.

IVORY, hard white substance obtained from the tusks of ELEPHANTS, HIPPOPOTAMUSES, WALRUSES and NARWHALS. It is no more than a thickened form of dental enamel, yet carved ivory has been greatly prized—and priced—for centuries. Elephant ivory is the most sought-after, due to its greater length and finer grain; the poaching of elephants for their tusks threatens their existence in Africa. A vegetable ivory is also produced, from the nuts of the doum palm.

IVORY COAST, one of the most prosperous West African republics, located on the N coast of the Gulf of Guinea and bordering Liberia, Guinea, Mali, Burkina, and Ghana.

Land. One-third of the country is covered by dense rain forest, with a grassy and wooded plateau to the N and mountains to the NW. The climate is hot and rainy in the S, drier and cooler in the N. Wildlife includes African big game animals.

People. There are some 60 tribal groups and some 3 million foreigners, about two-thirds of whom are Africans from neighboring countries. Over 40% of the population is urban. Tribal languages and animist faiths predominate. Some two-fifths of the population is aged under 15, and spending on basic education is relatively high. There is a university at Abidjan.

Economy. Farming, forestry and fisheries

Official name: Côte d'Ivoire
Capital: Abidjan
Area: 123,847sq mi
Population: 11,154,000
Languages: French, African languages
Religions: Animist, Muslim, Roman Catholic
Monetary unit(s): 1 CFA franc=100 centimes

provide most of the gross national product. Major cash crops are cotton, coffee and cocoa. Palm-oil, pineapples and bananas are also exported, as are hardwoods including mahogany, iroko, satinwood and teak. Diamonds and manganese are mined. An expanding manufacturing industry produces palm-oil, instant coffee, fruit juices and textiles. Trade is chiefly with European COMMON MARKET countries and the US. Exports usually exceed imports in value.

History. In the 16th century the Portuguese traded in slaves and ivory along the coast. In the 18th century Ashanti peoples entered the region, while French trade and missionary activity increased in the E. France began systematic occupation in 1870, declaring a protectorate in 1893. A railroad built in 1903 made the Ivory Coast potentially the most prosperous colony in FRENCH WEST AFRICA. In 1946 Fèlix HOUPHOUET-BOIGNY founded an all-African political party. He became president of the Ivory Coast upon independence (1960). His government's policies encouraged foreign investment, exploited natural resources and raised living standards. By the late 1980s, however, the aging president's unwillingness to designate a successor had become a cause of increasing concern.

IVY, hardy, evergreen climbers of the genus *Hedera,* family Araliaceae. In the juvenile stage the plants have lobed leaves and numerous aerial roots, while in the adult or arborescent stage the leaves are entire, there are no aerial roots and flowers and fruits are produced. The English ivy (*H. helix*) is a popular house plant, coming in a number of dwarf, climbing and variegated varieties. Indoors, they should be grown in bright positions, although they survive for a long time under artifical light. They grow best at temperatures between (60°F and 70°F), and the soil should be kept evenly moist. Propagation is by shoot tip cuttings. Several other plants which have ivy-like leaves are also called ivy, for example ground ivy (*Glectoma hederacea*), Boston or grape ivy (Cissus) and German ivy (*Senecio milk-anoides*), the latter being a popular house plant requiring similar cultural practices to English ivy although it is less tolerant of low light intensities. The red ivy (*Hemigraphis*) is so-named because of its trailing habit, but apart from this is quite unlike and unrelated to English ivy. Red ivy is also a popular house plant grown mainly for its ornamental foliage that is maroon or burgundy colored. It should be grown in a bright window avoiding strong sunlight, at average house temperatures, and should be watered often enough to keep the soil evenly moist.

IWO JIMA, Japanese island in the NW Pacific, scene of a fierce battle in WWII. Largest of the Volcano Islands (about 8sq mi), it was annexed by Japan in 1891 and captured by US marines in Feb.–March 1945 at the cost of over 21,000 US casualties. US administration ended in 1968.

IWW. See INDUSTRIAL WORKERS OF THE WORLD.

10th letter of the English alphabet, a variant of the letter *i*, from which it became formally distinguished with the advent of printing. It has a *y* sound in most European languages but French influence has given it a *dzh* sound in modern English.

JACKALS, carnivorous mammals closely related to DOGS and wolves. The four species are distributed throughout Africa and S Asia. All are extreme opportunists— although often considered to be primarily scavengers, they will also hunt and kill birds, hares, mice and insects. Small packs may be formed temporarily, but they are usually solitary animals.

JACKRABBITS, true HARES of the genus *Lepus.* All seven species are found in

Central and W North America. Jackrabbits have enormously large ears functional in body temperature control. Found in open, comparatively arid plains they actually flourish in drought-stricken, overgrazed areas. Among the most abundant of American Lagomorpha, they constitute a considerable pest in agricultural areas.

JACKSON, Andrew (1767–1845), seventh president of the US. The first from W of the Appalachians, he was a self-made statesman championing the common man against monopoly and privilege.

Born in a log cabin in the Waxhaw settlement, S.C., Jackson had a minimal education; he joined the militia at 13 and was briefly captured by the British in 1781. He decided to study law, was admitted to the N.C. bar in 1787 and began his political career in 1796 as a member of the Tenn. constitutional convention. He became the first congressman from Tenn. 1796–97, senator from Tenn. 1797–98 and a superior court judge in Nashville 1798–1804. In the WAR OF 1812 he became a national hero as commander of the Tenn. militia; at the Battle of Horseshoe Bend he forced the Creek Indians to yield 23 million acres, opening much of the South for settlement. In 1815 he led a decisive victory over the British at the battle of NEW ORLEANS. Jackson's rough personality and leadership earned him the epithet "Old Hickory." As commander of the US army in the South he campaigned against the SEMINOLE Indians, entering and raiding Spanish-owned Florida; this accelerated the sale of Florida to the US (1819). Military governor of the Florida Territory in 1821, he was reelected to the US Senate from Tenn. in 1823. A presidential candidate in 1824, Jackson received the most electoral votes but no overall majority, and the House of Representatives chose runner-up John Quincy Adams. Jackson considered this a "corrupt bargain"; bitter personal attacks disfigured the campaign for the 1828 election, which Jackson resoundingly won.

Inaugurated in 1829, he attempted to root out corruption in the bureaucracy by dismissing over 2,000 government employees and appointing his political supporters in their place; he thus created the SPOILS SYSTEM. He also built up a KITCHEN CABINET of personal advisers. Opposition to his powerful executive control eventually produced the Whig Party, revitalizing the two-party system. In 1832 Jackson vetoed a bill to recharter the BANK OF THE UNITED STATES, denouncing the bank as an unconstitutional monopoly. Making the bank a presidential campaign issue, Jackson easily defeated Henry CLAY and won reelection in 1832. Later that year Jackson prepared to send troops to S.C. to prevent secession, after it had rejected federal tariff laws. The president paid off the national debt in 1835, and his Specie Circular (1836) requiring that public lands be sold only for silver or gold helped halt land speculation. In 1837 Jackson retired to the Hermitage, his estate near Nashville. He had helped found the modern Democratic Party, strengthened respect for democratic government, and established the role of the president as a popular leader.

JACKSON, Helen (Maria) Hunt (1831–1885), US author who publicized the mistreatment of Indians. *A Century of Dishonor* (1881) condemned governmental malpractice; the novel *Ramona* (1884) described the plight of California's mission Indians.

JACKSON, Henry Martin (1912–1983), US political leader, Democratic senator from Washington from 1953; he was a congressman 1941–53. Chairman of the Senate committee on energy and natural resources, as ranking Democrat on the armed forces committee he became a major spokesman on national defense issues. In foreign affairs, he was a leading advocate of the US interventionist policy in Vietnam and was an articulate ally of Israel. In 1972 and 1976 he sought but did not win the Democratic presidential nomination.

JACKSON, Jesse Louis (1941–   ), US clergyman and Chicago-based black activist who directed Operation Breadbasket (1968) and founded People United to Save Humanity (PUSH), organizations set up to improve the economic and educational standards of blacks in the US. In 1984 and again in 1988 he sought the Democratic presidential nomination, in the latter year winning 13 primaries and caucuses and entering the party's national convention with 1,200 delegates.

JACKSON, Mahalia (1911–1972), US black gospel singer with a powerful and expressive contralto voice; her concerts and recordings gained worldwide recognition for Negro religious music. In the 1960s she was active in the civil rights movement.

JACKSON, Robert Houghwout (1892–1954), US Supreme Court justice from 1941, chief US prosecutor in the NUREMBERG TRIALS. A supporter of the NEW DEAL, he served as solicitor general 1938–40 and attorney general 1940–41.

JACKSON, Shirley (1919–1965), US author. Her best-known works, such as *The Haunting of Hill House* (1959) and the short story *The Lottery* (1948), blend

Gothic horror with psychological insight. Autobiographical works such as *Raising Demons* (1957) are in a contrastingly humorous vein.

JACKSON, Thomas Jonathan "Stonewall" (1824–1863), brilliant Confederate general, one of America's greatest commanders. After service in the MEXICAN WAR he was given command of a regiment at the outbreak of the Civil War. As a brigadier-general at the First Battle of BULL RUN, 1861, he was nicknamed "Stonewall" for his stand against Union troops. After his bold tactics in the 1862 Shenandoah Valley campaign he fought brilliantly at the battles of Richmond, the Seven Days' Battles, Cedar Mt, the Second Battle of Bull Run, Antietam and Fredericksburg. At CHANCELLORSVILLE he was accidentally mortally wounded by his own troops.

JACKSON, William Henry (1843–1942), US photographer and painter, known for his post-Civil War documentation of the scenery and historic events of the Wild West. His photos of Yellowstone for the US Geological Survey led to its being named the first national park. He worked as a painter after 1924.

JACOB, in the Old Testament, son of ISAAC and Rebecca, progenitor of the Israelites. He fled after tricking his elder brother Esau out of his birthright; he settled in Mesopotamia, where he married, then returned to Canaan. In a vision he wrestled with and overcame an angel, and was honored with the name Israel. In a time of famine he migrated to Egypt, where he died, after a period of staying with his favorite son JOSEPH.

JACOBINS, powerful political clubs during the FRENCH REVOLUTION, named for the former Jacobin (Dominican) convent where the leaders met. Originally middle-class, they became increasingly radical advocates of terrorism. After they seized power in 1793 the extremists, led by ROBESPIERRE, instituted the reign of TERROR. In the THERMIDOR reaction the clubs were suppressed, to revive under the Directory and be finally put down by NAPOLEON.

JACOBITE CHURCH, or Syrian Orthodox Church, Christian church of Syria, India and Iraq. One of the MONOPHYSITE CHURCHES, it was founded in 6th century Syria by Jacobus Baradaeus. Its head is the patriarch of Antioch, who now resides at Damascus, and its ritual language is Syriac. An offshoot of the Jacobites is the Syrian Catholic Church, one of the UNIATE CHURCHES.

JACOBITES, supporters of that branch of the House of Stuart exiled by the GLORIOUS REVOLUTION of 1688; a large number were Highland Scots. Jacobites sought to regain the English throne for JAMES II and his descendants, notably James Edward Stuart (1699–1766), "The Old Pretender," and Charles Edward STUART, "Bonnie Prince Charlie." After rebellions in 1715, 1719 and 1745 they were effectively crushed at the battle of CULLODEN MOOR (1746).

JACOBSEN, Jens Peter (1847–1885), major Danish writer, known for his early Romantic poetry and his translation of DARWIN'S works. He later turned to NATURALISM in the novels *Marie Grubbe* (1876) and *Niels Lyhne* (1880), developing a rich style despite suffering from serious tuberculosis after 1873.

JACQUARD, Joseph Marie (1752–1834), French inventor of the **Jacquard loom** (completed 1801), which could weave complex patterns according to instructions coded on punched cards (a technique adopted by BABBAGE for his calculator and still used for COMPUTERS). Modern looms are still based on Jacquard's principles. (See also WEAVING.)

JACQUERIE, peasant revolt in NE France in 1358, named for "Jacques Bonhomme," the popular nickname for peasants. A reaction against the hardships of the HUNDRED YEARS' WAR, famine and oppression, it was savagely crushed by baronial armies.

JACQUES-DALCROZE, Émile (1865–1950), Swiss composer and educator, best known for his invention of eurhythmics as a teaching aid for musicians.

JADE, either of two tough, hard minerals with a compact interlocking grain structure, commonly green but also found as white, mauve, red-brown or yellow; used as a GEM stone to make carved jewelry and ornaments. Jade carving in China dates from the 1st millennium BC, but the finest examples are late 18th century AD. **Nephrite**, the commoner form of jade, is an amphibole, a combination of tremolite and actinolite, occurring in China, the USSR, New Zealand and the western US. **Jadeite**, rarer than nephrite and prized for its more intense color and translucence, is a sodium aluminum found chiefly in upper Burma.

JAGUAR, *Panthera onca*, the only true "big cat" of the American continent. The coat bears black spots arranged in rosettes on a background varying from almost white and buff, through black, where the rosettes appear only as a variation in texture. It lives in thick cover in forests or swamps and although an accomplished swimmer, hunts mostly on the ground or in trees.

JAHN, Friedrich Ludwig (1778–1852),

German educator and soldier, a pioneer of gymnastics. In 1811 he founded the *Turnvereinen* (German: gymnastics clubs) to promote physical fitness and a romantic German nationalism.

JAI ALAI, also known as **pelota**, a fast and demanding Spanish-Basque game similar to handball, from which it evolved in the 17th century. The ball, 2in in diameter, is made of hard rubber covered with goatskin. During a game it can attain speeds of more than 150mph. Each player is equipped with a *cesta*, a basket-shaped racket of wicker about 2ft long, which is strapped to his wrist. The jai alai court is enclosed by three walls, the fourth side consisting of a wire screen that protects spectators.

The American jai alai court is 176ft long, 55ft wide, and 40ft high. The game is played mostly in Florida. It is extremely popular in Cuba, Mexico, and Spain and is associated in most countries with betting.

JAINISM, philosophy and religion—an offshoot of HINDUISM—largely confined to India, with 2 million adherents. It was founded alongside BUDDHISM, which it resembles, in about the 6th century BC by Mahavira, an ascetic saint who taught the doctrine of *ahimsa* or non-injury to all living creatures. Jains do not believe in a creator God but see in the universe two independent eternal categories: "Life" and "Non-life" (see DUALISM), maintaining that man can reach perfection only through ascetic, charitable and monastic discipline.

JAKARTA (formerly Batavia), capital and largest city of Indonesia, in NW Java. It is the country's commercial, transport and industrial center, manufacturing automobiles, textiles, chemicals and iron products, and processing lumber and food. Much of Indonesia's external trade passes through the port. The city is also the administrative center and the home of the University of Indonesia. It grew out of the Dutch East India company settlement of Batavia (1614–19) and became British 1811–14. With independence in 1949 it was made national capital and renamed Djakarta, now officially spelled Jakarta. Pop 6,503,449.

JAKOBSON, Roman (1896–1982), Russian-born US linguist and philologist best known for his pioneering studies of the Slavic languages. He was a founder of the Prague School of Linguistics.

JAMAICA, island republic in the Caribbean.
Land. The body of the island is a limestone plateau with an E-W backbone of mountains and volcanic hills. The climate is tropical, with heavy rainfall.

Official name: Jamaica
Capital: Kingston
Area: 4,244sq mi
Population: 2,372,000
Language: English; Creole
Religions: Protestant, Roman Catholic
Monetary unit(s): 1 Jamaican dollar=100 cents

People. The majority of Jamaicans are of African descent, but there are East Indians, Chinese and Europeans also. Despite a massive literacy campaign in the 1970s, about 25% of the population remains illiterate.

Economy. The economy is largely agricultural, relying on sugar processing for its major industry. Bauxite and gypsum mining has become important, as has tourism.

History. Discovered by COLUMBUS in 1494, Jamaica was a Spanish settlement until captured by the British in 1655. The original ARAWAK INDIANS had been wiped out, and the British, under such governors as Sir Henry MORGAN, accelerated the importation of Negro slaves to man the sugar industry. After the full emancipation of former slaves in 1838 the sugar industry declined; poverty, unemployment and overpopulation led to serious unrest in the 19th and 20th centuries. Crop diversification and reforms improved conditions. Full internal self-government came in 1959, within the West Indies Federation, and full independence within the British Commonwealth in 1962. Under Prime Minister Michael Manley (1972–80), the government initiated a number of social reforms and took control of mining and the sugar industry. Manley's successor, Edward Seaga, steered a moderate course, but his hopes for improving the economy were shattered in 1988 when Hurricane Gilbert damaged or destroyed four-fifths of the nation's housing, devastated agriculture, and wiped out much of Jamaica's infrastructure.

JAMES, name of two saints, both Apostles. **St. James the Greater** (d. c43 AD), son of Zebedee and brother of St. John, was killed by Herod Agrippa I. There is a famous shrine to him at SANTIAGO DE COMPOSTELA. **St. James the Less** (1st century AD) was possibly the son of Alphaeus and Mary.

JAMES, name of two kings of England and Scotland. **James I and VI** (1566–1625), was king of Scotland from 1567, after his mother MARY QUEEN OF SCOTS was forced to abdicate, and king of England from 1603. James gained control over the nobles who sought to dominate him in 1583. Anxious to be Elizabeth I's heir, he condoned her execution of his mother. Early popularity in England, reinforced when he escaped the GUNPOWDER PLOT, waned as James sought autocratic control over Parliament, bolstered by his belief in the divine right of kings. His extravagance and dubious personal life alienated many, as did the execution of Sir Walter RALEIGH, part of a pro-Spanish policy. He was, however, scholarly and in some ways progressive. He established a large Presbyterian settlement in IRELAND and encouraged the first English colonies in America. He wrote the treatise on government *Basilikon Doron* and commissioned the Authorized Version of the Bible (1611). **James II** (1633–1701), reigned 1685–88. Although able, he sought to disregard Parliament and alienated many by his attempt to introduce toleration of Roman Catholicism. It was suspected—perhaps correctly—that he intended to make it the state religion. His Dutch son-in-law William of Orange was invited to invade Britain, deposing James in the GLORIOUS REVOLUTION. James' forces were driven out of Ireland also at the battle of the BOYNE.

JAMES, name of seven Stuart kings of Scotland. **James I** (1394–1437), technically reigned from 1406, but was a prisoner in England 1406–24. There he wrote his great poem, *The Kingis Quair* (1424), of his captivity and romance with Joan Beaufort, whom he married. A capable and energetic ruler, he suppressed a turbulent aristocracy; he was assassinated during an abortive aristocratic revolt. **James II** 1430–1460), reigned from 1449. **James III** (1451–1488), reigned from 1469. **James IV** (1473–1513), king from 1488, was the great Renaissance king of Scotland. He reformed law and administration, and extended royal authority; he built a powerful navy. A patron of arts and sciences, he married Margaret, daughter of Henry VII of England. He was killed at the battle of Flodden Field. **James V** (1512–1542), was king from 1513, but reigned 1528–42, during the beginnings of the REFORMATION. He supported Catholicism for financial and political reasons.

His daughter by his wife Mary of Guise was MARY QUEEN OF SCOTS. He died soon after his army was defeated by the English at Solway Moss. (For James VI and James VII of Scotland, see JAMES, two kings of England and Scotland.)

JAMES, Epistle of, 20th book of the NEW TESTAMENT, traditionally attributed to St. James, kinsman of Jesus and first bishop of Jerusalem. One of the Catholic (general) Epistles, it is primarily a homily on Christian ethics.

JAMES, Henry (1843–1916), American-born novelist and critic, brother of William JAMES. He settled in London (1876) and became a British citizen in 1915. A recurring theme in his work is the corruption of innocence, particularly as shown by the contrast between sophisticated and corrupt Europe and brash, innocent US society. His most famous works, distinguished by subtle characterization and a precise, complex prose style, include *The Americans* (1877), *Daisy Miller* (1878), *The Portrait of a Lady* (1881), *The Turn of the Screw* (1898) and *The Golden Bowl* (1909).

JAMES, Jesse Woodson (1847–1882), US outlaw. A member of William QUANTRILL'S raiders in the Civil War, he and his brother Frank led the "James Gang" 1866–79, robbing banks and trains from Ark. to Col. and Tex. Living as an ordinary citizen in St. Joseph, Mo., he was murdered for reward by gang member Robert Ford.

JAMES, William (1842–1910), US philosopher and psychologist, the originator of the doctrine of PRAGMATISM, brother of Henry JAMES. His first major contribution was *The Principles of Psychology* (1890). Turning his attention to questions of religion, he published in 1902 his Gifford Lectures, *The Varieties of Religious Experience*, which has remained his best-known work.

JAMESON, Sir Leander Starr (1853–1917), British colonial administrator in Southern Africa. In 1895, at the instigation of Cecil RHODES, he led the illegal and disastrous Jameson Raid into the Boer colony of Transvaal to support a rebellion intended to form a South African federation. He later served as prime minister of the Cape Colony (1904–08).

JAMESTOWN, former village in SE Va. on the James R, the first permanent English settlement in North America. Founded in 1607 by colonists from the London Company led by John SMITH, it was named for King James I. Lord De la Warr reinforced it in 1610 and John ROLFE introduced tobacco cultivation in 1612. In 1619 the House of Burgesses, the first representative government of the colonies, met here.

JANÁCEK, Leoš (1854–1928), major Czech composer and collector of Moravian folk music, best known for the *Sinfonietta* (1926) and the opera *Jenufa* (1904). Other operas include *Mr. Brouček* (1920), *Katya Kabanova* (1921), *The Cunning Little Vixen* (1924), *The Makropoulos Case* (1926), and *From the House of the Dead* (1928). First professor of composition at Prague Conservatory (1919), he wrote many songs, chamber and choral works, especially the *Glagolitic Mass* (1926).

JANET, Pierre Marie Félix (1859–1947), French psychologist and neurologist, best known for his studies of HYSTERIA and NEUROSIS. He played an important role in bringing the theories of psychology to bear on the clinical treatment of mental disease.

JANISSARIES, elite Turkish infantry of the 14th–19th centuries, conscripted from prisoners of war and Christian children abducted and reared as fanatical Muslims. From c1600 Turks gradually infiltrated the highly privileged corps, which became increasingly corrupt. Unruly and rebellious, it was massacred by order of Sultan Mahmud II in 1826.

JANSENISM, French and Flemish Roman Catholic reform movement, based on the ideas of the Flemish theologian Cornelius Jansen (1585–1638) and centering on the convent of Port-Royal, near Paris. Jansen stressed St. Augustine's teaching of redemption by divine grace and also accepted PREDESTINATION; opponents charged his followers with CALVINISM. Cultivated at first by French statesmen because it opposed the Catholic establishment, Jansenism and its prominent leaders, Antoine Arnauld and Blaise PASCAL, were condemned by Pope Innocent X. In the 18th century persecution in France, especially under Louis XIV, drove much of the movement into the Netherlands, where there are still Jansenist bishops (now OLD CATHOLICS). In France it survived mainly as a school of thought within the church.

JANUARY, first month of the year in the Julian calendar, named for the god Janus.

JAPAN (Nippon), an island country off the E Asian coast, now a leading industrial superpower.

Land. The Japanese archipelago, about 2,000mi long, comprises some 3,500 islands. The four major islands are HOKKAIDO, HONSHU, SHIKOKU and KYUSHU. Around 80% of the country is mountainous, and there are more than 190 active volcanoes; earth tremors and quakes are frequent. Many of the fast-flowing rivers are harnessed for

Official name: Japan
Capital: Tokyo
Area: 145,870sq mi
Population: 122,100,000
Language: Japanese
Religions: Shinto, Buddhism
Monetary unit(s): 1 yen = 100 sen

hydroelectric power. Lowland is scarce, consisting mainly of coastal plains, including the 5,000sq mi Kanto plain on Honshu. About 70% of the land is forested, only 16% cultivable. The monsoonal climate is moderated by latitude and the sea. Winters are very cold, summers hot and humid with frequent typhoons. Rainfall is high and winter snowfall heavy.

People. The Japanese are basically a Mongoloid race. Japan is the world's most densely populated country in terms of arable land per person. Most Japanese live in the non-mountainous areas and more than 66% in cities like Tokyo, the capital, Osaka and Yokohama. The population includes about 15,000 aboriginal AINUS and more than 737,000 foreigners, mostly Koreans. The literacy rate is the highest in Asia. Buddhism and Shintoism are the chief religions, but Japanese thought has also been greatly influenced by Confucianism.

Economy. Since 1945 Japan has become a leading industrial power. Products range from ships and automobiles to electronic equipment, cameras and textiles for world markets, notably the US. Imports include coal, petroleum and industrial raw materials; Japan has few mineral resources. Agriculture, once the mainstay, continues to decline; rice is still the chief crop. Because of inaccessibility, only 27% of Japan's forests are commercially exploited. The country has extensive fisheries.

History. Artifacts dating from at least 4000 BC have been found in Japan. Asiatic invaders drove the aboriginal Ainus into the extreme N. The first Japanese state was ruled by the Yamato clan, from whom the present imperial house supposedly descends.

Japan was subject to powerful cultural influences from China through Korea. Rice cultivation had been introduced from China c250 BC and Buddhism from Korea (c538 AD). Under the Taika Reforms (646–702 AD) the Chinese ideographic script (somewhat adapted to Japanese) and T'ang Dynasty administrative system was adopted. Clan chiefs became imperial officials, and land became the property of the emperor, who distributed it according to rank. The powerful Fujiwara family tried to maintain strong government centered on a figurehead emperor, and were dominant from the 9th to the 12th century; theirs was a classical age in art and literature.

In 1192 Yoritomo Minamoto seized power as SHOGUN (military dictator). Successive *shoguns* ruled absolutely, with the emperors relegated to purely ritual functions. Power was based on a vassal class of warrior knights, SAMURAI. Feudal warfare (1300–1573) brought the rise of powerful lords, often free of *shogun* rule. In 1543 the Portuguese visited Japan, and other European traders followed; Christianity, introduced by St. FRANCIS XAVIER (1549), became involved with politics and was banned in 1614, with savage persecution. A policy of isolation (*sakoku*) closed Japan to all foreigners except a few Dutch and Chinese traders until 1853–54, when US Commodore Matthew PERRY negotiated a trade treaty. Similar treaties with Britain, France, the Netherlands and Russia followed. The shogunate collapsed in 1867, and under Emperor Meiji (1867–1912) Tokyo became the capital; a program of westernization began. A new constitution (1889) established a parliamentary system under the divine emperor, and finance, industry and trade were developed by the *zaibatsu*, powerful family corporations.

Japan's spectacular victories over Russia and China (see RUSSO-JAPANESE WAR and SINO-JAPANESE WARS) won her recognition as a world power, as did her support of the Allies in WWI. In the 1930s a militarist regime took power after an economic crisis; Japan then built a large Asian colonial empire. The regime increasingly favored Nazi Germany, signing an Anti-Comintern Pact in 1936. Japan entered WWII with the surprise attack on PEARL HARBOR in 1941; war brought economic ruin and finally nuclear devastation at HIROSHIMA and NAGASAKI. Following the Japanese surrender (1945), Japan was occupied by US troops. A new democratic constitution was introduced (1947), and full sovereignty and independence were restored by the San Francisco Peace Treaty (1951). With US aid the economy was rebuilt, making Japan a vast industrial giant, with an economy second in size only to that of the US. By the late 1980s, however, the nation's economic success led to increasing demands that Japan open its markets to foreign imports and shoulder a larger share of the costs of Western strategic interests.

JAPAN CURRENT, or **Kuroshio,** warm strong ocean current running NE along the SE Japanese coast. In summer, some splits off eventually to reach the Sea of Japan: most, however, turns E past the Aleutians to form the North Pacific Current.

JAPANESE, language probably related to the ALTAIC group. Written Japanese originally used only adapted Chinese characters (*kanji*) despite their unsuitability; in the 8th century phonetic characters (*kana*) were added. Since 1945 both types have been simplified, their number reduced and romanized writing introduced.

JARRELL, Randall (1914–1965), US poet and influential critic. His poetry is emotional and often pervaded with a sense of tragedy and alienation; best-known collections are *Selected Poems* (1955), *The Woman at the Washington Zoo* (1960) and *The Lost World* (1965). *Poetry and the Age* (1953) is the first of three collections of his criticism.

JARRY, Alfred (1873–1907), eccentric French poet and dramatist whose *Ubu* plays (1896–1902) anticipated SURREALISM, DADA and the theater of the absurd. Brilliant but disordered, Jarry became an alcoholic while still young. The revoltingly gross, comic but sinister Ubu embodies his view of the bourgeoisie.

JARUZELSKI, Wojciech (1923–   ), Polish general and politician, appointed both premier and Communist party leader in 1981 to resolve the crisis occasioned by the rise of the independent trade union SOLIDARITY. He arrested the Solidarity leaders and imposed martial law until the government felt secure, but he was unable to remedy the country's economic difficulties.

JASPERS, Karl Theodor (1883–1969), German philosopher, noted for his steadfast opposition to National Socialism and his acute yet controversial analyses of the state of German society. Early work in psychopathology led him into the Heidelberg philosophical faculty in 1913. He there became one of Germany's foremost exponents of EXISTENTIALISM.

JAUNDICE, yellow color of the SKIN and sclera of the EYE caused by excess bilirubin pigment in the BLOOD. HEMOGLOBIN is broken down to form bilirubin which is excreted by the LIVER in the BILE. If blood is broken down more rapidly than normal (hemolysis), the liver may not be able to remove the abnormal amount of bilirubin fast enough. Jaundice occurs with liver damage (HEPATITIS, late CIRRHOSIS) and when the bile ducts leading from the liver to the duodenum are obstructed by stones from the GALL BLADDER or by CANCER of the PANCREAS or bile ducts.

JAURÈS, Jean (1859–1914), French pacifist politician, one of the founders of the French Socialist Party (1905). He was a member of the Chamber of Deputies 1885–88, 1893–98 and 1902–14; in 1904 he founded the socialist journal *Humanité*. Jaurès, who opposed war with Germany in 1914, was assassinated by a fanatic.

JAVA, island in southeastern Asia, part of the Republic of Indonesia, about 600mi by 120mi and bounded on the south and southwest by the Indian Ocean. Java accommodates nearly two-thirds of the population of Indonesia, together with the capital, Jakarta. Other important cities are Bandung, Surabaja, and Semarang.

Java is traversed from east to west by a chain of volcanic mountains, the highest of which is Mt. Semeru (12,060ft). The fertile tropical plain along the northern coast is drained by the Solo and Brantas rivers, and rainfall is heavy, for Java lies just south of the equator.

The Javanese are mainly farmers (many are smallholders), producing rubber, coffee, tea, sugar, cocoa, and cinchona bark (from which quinine is derived) for export. Small-scale manufacture of consumer goods was encouraged by the former Dutch administration and has been further developed by the present Indonesian government. For centuries handicrafts have been important to the economy, and Java is noted for its artistic silverwork and batik textiles. By far the most important of Java's mineral resources, oil is found in the northeastern part of the island and is well exploited. Other mineral deposits include gold, phosphate and manganese.

JAVA SEA, Battle of the, WWII naval engagement in Feb. 1942 in which the Allies were seriously defeated by the Japanese fleet. The defeat left Java open to Japanese occupation.

JAY, John (1745–1829), American statesman. An attorney, he drafted the N.Y. state constitution in 1777. In 1778 he was elected president of the Continental Congress and in 1779 first minister to Spain. In 1782, with Benjamin FRANKLIN and John ADAMS, he negotiated peace with Britain, resulting in the Treaty of PARIS (1783). As secretary for foreign affairs 1784–89 he supported the new Constitution, believing in the need for a strong central government. He was the first Chief Justice of the Supreme Court 1789–95. In 1794 he negotiated the unpopular JAY TREATY. A conservative member of the FEDERALIST PARTY, he served as governor of N.Y. 1795–1801.

JAYS, a diverse group of birds in the crow family, Corvidae, many of which are brightly-colored, with screeching, raucous voices. Adaptable and omnivorous, they have evolved to fill a variety of ecological roles and habitats. The original bearer of the name is the European jay, *Garrulus glandarius*, found in the woodlands of most of Europe and Asia, a striking bird with a pinkish body, black, white and blue wings and a white rump. There are in addition some 30 species of New World jays.

JAY TREATY, agreement between the US and Britain negotiated by John JAY, 1794. The British held forts in US territory and were inciting Indians against American settlers. Some American ships trading with the French were being seized and American seamen impressed. The Jay Treaty provided for British evacuation of NW forts, compensation for confiscated shipping, American repayment to Britain of prewar debts and limited trading concessions to the US. No mention was made of impressment, incitement of the Indians or compensation for abducted slaves. The treaty, considered a capitulation to the British, made Jay and the FEDERALIST PARTY unpopular. It led France to break its alliance with America and to pursue an undeclared naval war (1798–1800), but it averted a potentially crippling war with Britain.

JAZZ, form of music which grew out of Southern US black culture. Rhythmically complex, with a strong emphasis on syncopation, it is often highly improvisatory. Jazz may be said to have been born in the work songs, laments and spirituals of slaves and Southern black communities and to derive ultimately from African music. It was popularized by street bands that played for special occasions, particularly in New Orleans. By the 1900s such early forms as Stomp and RAGTIME had developed, and the BLUES had begun to evolve.

In the 1920s jazz moved north with the black populations to the cities, notably Chicago and New York. With increasing musical sophistication, new styles developed, and jazz found a wider audience through radio and phonograph. Big bands developed a commercialized jazz called Swing in the 1930s and 1940s. In the early 1940s black musicians pioneered a vivid new style, BOP. "West Coast" and "cool" styles appeared in the 1950s and 1960s, which saw the development of "free form" jazz.

Among early-jazz musicians were "King" Oliver, Sidney Bechet, "Jelly Roll" Morton, Louis ARMSTRONG, "Fats" Waller and "Bix" BEIDERBECKE. "Duke" ELLINGTON and "Count" BASIE led bands from the 1930s and Glenn MILLER, Benny GOODMAN and Woody Herman dominated the "swing era" (c1937–1947). Bessie SMITH and "Billie" HOLIDAY are considered two of the greatest jazz singers. Among more modern artists are Lester Young, Charlie PARKER, Dizzy Gillespie, Miles Davis, John Coltrane and the "free-form" pioneers Ornette Coleman and Cecil Taylor.

JEANS, Sir James Hopwood (1877–1946), British mathematician and astrophysicist who applied mathematical principles to his studies of physics and astronomy. He contributed to the KINETIC THEORY of gases, researched the origin of binary STARS and (after 1929) wrote several popular books explaining astronomy and the philosophy of science to the layman.

JEFFERS, (John) Robinson (1887–1962), American poet. His powerful poetry is violently disillusioned, seeing man as a mere doomed animal and glorifying nature. *Tamar and Other Poems* (1924) is his best-known collection, but his chief success was a searing adaptation of EURIPIDES' *Medea* (1946).

JEFFERSON, Joseph (1829–1905), US actor most famous in the role of Rip van Winkle. Already a successful actor, he created this role in London in 1865 and played it regularly for the rest of his life.

JEFFERSON, Thomas (1743–1826), third president of the US. The son of a Va. planter, he was admitted to the bar in 1767. He entered politics in 1769 as a member of the Va. House of Burgesses. In reply to the INTOLERABLE ACTS of 1774 he wrote *A Summary View of the Rights of British America*, in which he entirely denied Britain any right of government in the colonies. In 1775 he was a delegate to the second Continental Congress. In 1776, as leading member of a five-man committee, he wrote most of the DECLARATION OF INDEPENDENCE.

Jefferson was governor of Va. 1779–81 and after a short retirement was elected to Congress. In 1785 he succeeded Benjamin FRANKLIN as minister to France and secured trade concessions for the US there. From 1789 to 1793 he was secretary of state under Washington. Two parties, the Democratic-Republicans and the Federalists, formed respectively around Jefferson—who believed in agrarian egalitarianism based on the rationality of man—and Alexander HAMILTON, secretary of the treasury, who favored a strong central government led by a wealthy and able aristocracy.

In 1796 Jefferson ran as presidential candidate against the Federalist John ADAMS. Though he received the larger popular vote he lost by three electoral votes and became vice-president. During this time he wrote a *Manual of Parliamentary Practice*, and, with James MADISON, the KENTUCKY AND VIRGINIA RESOLUTIONS, protesting against the Federalists' ALIEN AND SEDITION ACTS which restricted freedom of speech and the press. From these resolutions there evolved the doctrines of STATES' RIGHTS and NULLIFICATION.

In 1800 Jefferson ran against Adams again and, gaining the same number of electoral votes as his opponent Aaron BURR, was chosen president by Congress. His administration was notable in foreign affairs and domestic expansion. He negotiated the LOUISIANA PURCHASE in 1803 and sent out the LEWIS AND CLARK EXPEDITION. He balanced the budget and reduced the national debt.

He was reelected in 1804 and during his second term tried to maintain US neutrality during the Napoleonic wars. He attempted to combat the seizure of ships and impressment of seamen with the Embargo Act of 1807, prohibiting American exports, but this damaged American agricultural and commercial interests and violated his principle of individual liberty. He repealed it in 1809, and in that year retired to his home, Monticello. A noted scholar, he founded the U. of Virginia (1819–25).

JEFFERSON MEMORIAL, monument in Washington, D.C., dedicated in 1943 to the memory of Thomas Jefferson. A white marble structure in classical style, it was designed by John Russell Pope and contains a statue of Jefferson by Rudulph Evans.

JEFFRIES, James J. (1875–1953), US heavyweight boxer who won the championship from Bob Fitzsimmons in 1899. He retired undefeated in 1905; returning to the ring in 1910 he was defeated by Jack Johnson.

JEHOVAH, variant of the Old Testament personal name for God. The sacred name YHWH, probably pronounced "Yahweh," was not used by the Jews after about 300 BC for fear of blaspheming. Hence in reading the Hebrew Bible *Adonai* (Lord) was substituted. Medieval translators combined the consonants of one name with the vowels of the other, arriving at

"Jehovah."

JEHOVAH'S WITNESSES, religious movement founded in 1872 by Charles Taze Russell in Pittsburgh, Pa. There is no formal church organization. Their central doctrine is that the Second Coming is at hand; they avoid participation in secular government which they see as diabolically inspired. Over a million members proselytize by house-to-house calls and through publications such as *The Watchtower* and *Awake*, issued by the Watchtower Bible and Tract Society.

JELLICOE, Sir John Rushworth, 1st Earl Jellicoe (1859–1935), British admiral, commander of the British fleet at the battle of Jutland in 1916. He was governor-general of New Zealand 1920–24.

JELLYFISH, familiar marine cnidarians with a pulsating "jelly" bell and trailing tentacles. Many cnidarian classes display alternation of generations, where a single species may be represented by a polyp form, usually asexual, and a medusoid, sexually reproductive stage. These medusoid forms are frequently referred to as jellyfish. The true jellyfish all belong to the class Scyphozoa, where the medusa is the dominant phase and the polyp or hydroid is reduced or absent. Jellyfish are radially symmetrical. Rings of muscle around the margin of the bell contract to expel water and propel the jellyfish forward.

JENKINS' EAR, War of, a conflict between England and Spain, 1739–41. The allegation by ship's master Robert Jenkins that a Spanish coast guard in the West Indies had cut off his ear while pillaging his ship was exploited to foment popular anger in England.

JENNER, Edward (1749–1823), British pioneer of VACCINATION. He examined in detail the country maxim that dairymaids who had had COWPOX would not contract SMALLPOX: in 1796 he inoculated a small boy with cowpox and found that this rendered the boy immune from smallpox.

JENSEN, Johannes Vilhelm (1873–1950), Danish winner of the 1944 Nobel Prize for Literature. His main works are a series of more than 100 tales entitled *Myths* (1907–44) and a six-volume novel cycle on the rise of man, *The Long Journey* (1908–22).

JEREMIAH (c650–c570 BC), prophet of Judah, and the primary author of the Old Testament Book of Jeremiah, a collection of his oracles. He prophesied the subjugation of Judah by Babylon and the destruction of Jerusalem and the Temple, and called for submission to the conquerors as God's agents in punishing idolatry. He was distressed by his message, but endured imprisonment for treason and threats to his life.

JERICHO, village in Jordan, 14mi ENE of Jerusalem, built 825ft below sea level. Dating possibly from 9000 BC, it was captured from the Canaanites by Joshua in 1400 BC. It has regularly been destroyed and rebuilt; HEROD the Great built a Jericho 1mi S of the Old Testament city. In 1967 it was occupied by Israel.

JEROME, Saint (Sophronius Eusebius Hieronymus; c347–c420), biblical scholar, one of the first theologians to be called a Doctor of the Christian Church. After being educated in classical studies he fled to the desert as a hermit in 375 to devote himself to prayer. He was subsequently papal secretary and translated the Old Testament into Latin (see VULGATE) and wrote New Testament commentaries.

JEROME, Jerome Klapka (1859–1927), English humorist and playwright, who wrote the classic comic novel *Three Men in a Boat* (1889), a work cherished for its broad humor and sentimentality.

JERSEY, largest and southernmost of the British CHANNEL ISLANDS. Its main industries are tourism and agriculture. It contains numerous remnants of prehistoric life, and was known to the Romans as Caesarea.

JERUSALEM, capital of Israel, and holy city for Jews, Christians and Muslims. The city stands on a ridge at an altitude of 2,500ft, W of the Dead Sea and 35mi from the Mediterranean. It retains many grandiose shrines and the cobbled streets of the Old City.

The city dates from possibly the 4th millennium BC. In c1000 BC King DAVID captured the city from the Jebusites and made it his capital. The great Temple was built by his son SOLOMON c970 BC. David's dynasty was ended in 586 BC by the invasion of King NEBUCHADNEZZAR, who sacked the Temple and deported most of the Jews to Babylon. The Jews were allowed to return by CYRUS II of Persia, and the Temple was rebuilt. Jerusalem subsequently bacame part of Syria, but in 165 BC JUDAS MACCABEUS freed the city, and it was ruled by the HASMONEAN dynasty. From 37 BC the HEROD family led the state under the aegis of the Roman Empire. The Jewish revolts, in 66 AD and 132 AD led to the destruction of the Temple and complete subjugation to the Romans until the 4th century, when Christianity became the religion of the Byzantine Roman Empire.

The city was captured by the Persian king Khosrau II in 614, from whom it passed to the religiously tolerant rule of the Muslim Omar. In 1099 the knights of the First Crusade took Jerusalem and set up the Latin Kingdom of Jerusalem. However, in 1187 the Muslims under SALADIN recaptured the city. The MAMELUKES and then the Ottoman emperor SULEIMAN I restored Jerusalem. The city declined as a religious and economic center from the 16th to the 19th centuries. It was conquered by the British in 1917 and became the capital of Palestine. The 1947 UN resolution made it an international city, but in the 1948 Arab–Israeli conflict it was divided, the Old City being under Jordanian administration, and the New City becoming the capital of Israel. In the 1967 ARAB-ISRAELI WAR, Israel took the Old City, and all Jerusalem was placed under unified administration.

There are traditional Armenian, Christian, Jewish and Muslim quarters in the Old City. Government, tourism and religious activity dominate life in Jerusalem. Pop 457,700.

JESUIT RELATIONS, reports sent by French Jesuit missionaries in North America between 1632 and 1673. They are valuable records of French exploration and accounts of Indian tribes before the arrival of settlers.

JESUITS, name given to members of the Society of Jesus, an order of Roman Catholic priests and brothers dedicated to foreign missions, education and studies in the humanities and sciences. Jesuit life is regulated by the constitutions written by the founder of the Society, St. IGNATIUS OF LOYOLA. Vows of poverty, chastity and obedience to the pope are taken, and training may last up to 15 years. After its foundation in 1540 the order undertook notable missions in the Far East, under St. FRANCIS XAVIER, and in Europe worked for Counter-Reformation. Their influence and power eventually led to their expulsion from many countries, and in 1773 Pope Clement XIV dissolved the Society, but it was restored in 1814.

JESUS CHRIST, or Jesus of Nazareth (c6 BC–c3 AD), the founder of CHRISTIANITY. The four GOSPELS, embodying early Christian tradition, are the primary sources for his life. Born in Bethlehem, Judaea, to MARY (see VIRGIN BIRTH), Jesus grew up with his parents in Nazareth in Galilee. Little is known of his life before he began his public ministry at the age of about 30; this was inaugurated when he was baptized in the Jordan R by JOHN THE BAPTIST. For the next three years he journeyed, mainly in Galilee, gathering a band of disciples, in particular the 12 APOSTLES, teaching and training

them, preaching to large crowds and healing the physically and mentally ill. His homely parables are memorable teaching aids; the miracles, few but significant, had the same function. The chief theme of Jesus' teaching was the imminent coming of the Kingdom of God and his own central role as the agent of God, bringing redemption and requiring commitment. He disavowed the popular wish for a pular MESSIAH, but made claims in which he transformed the traditional idea of the Messiah; toward the end of the three years, as he and his disciples traveled to Jerusalem, he introduced teaching about his coming humiliation, suffering and death. Appealing throughout to the Old Testament, he antagonized the Scribes and Pharisees by denouncing their legalism. In the last week of his life he entered Jerusalem and taught there; after the Last Supper he was betrayed by JUDAS ISCARIOT and arrested in the garden of GETHSEMANE. The Jewish authorities handed him over to the Roman governor, Pontius Pilate, who had him executed by CRUCIFIXION. Two days later his tomb was found to be empty, and many recognizable appearances of Jesus to his disciples convinced them of his RESURRECTION. According to the Acts of the Apostles, 40 days later he ascended to HEAVEN (see ASCENSION). The early Church soon crystallized its beliefs about Jesus, accepting him as Messiah, Lord and Son of God (see also INCARNATION; TRINITY) and as the Savior who by dying redeemed mankind. Muslims believe Jesus to have been the greatest prophet before Mohammed, but deny his deity.

JET PROPULSION, the propulsion of a vehicle by expelling a fluid jet backward, whose MOMENTUM produces a reaction that imparts an equal forward momentum to the vehicle, according to NEWTON's third law of motion. The squid uses a form of jet propulsion. Jet-propelled boats, using water for the jet, have been built, and air jets have been used to power cars, but by far the chief use is to power AIRPLANES and ROCKETS, since to attain high speeds, jet propulsion is essential. The first jet engine was designed and built by Sir Frank WHITTLE (1937), but the first jet-engine aircraft to fly was German (Aug. 1939). Jet engines are INTERNAL-COMBUSTION ENGINES. The turbojet is the commonest form. Air enters the inlet diffuser and is compressed in the air compressor, a multistage device having sets of rapidly rotating fan blades. It then enters the combustion chamber, where the fuel (a kerosene/gasoline mixture) is injected and ignited, and the hot, expanding exhaust gases pass through a TURBINE that drives the compressor and engine accessories. The gases, sometimes heated further in an afterburner, are expelled through the jet nozzle to provide the thrust. The nozzle converges for subsonic flight, but for supersonic flight one that converges and then diverges is needed. The fanjet or turbofan engine uses some of the turbine power to drive a propeller fan in a cowling, for more efficient subsonic propulsion; the **turboprop**, similar in principle, gains its thrust chiefly from the propeller. The **ramjet** is the simplest air-breathing jet engine, having neither compressor nor turbine. When accelerated to supersonic speeds by an auxiliary rocket or turbojet engine, the inlet diffuser "rams" the air and compresses it; after combustion the exhaust gases are expelled directly. Ramjets are used chiefly in guided missiles.

JET STREAM, a narrow band of very fast E-flowing winds, stronger in winter than in summer, found around the level of the tropopause (see TROPOSPHERE; ATMOSPHERE). Speeds average about 40mph in summer, about 80mph in winter, though over 200mph has been recorded.

JEVONS, William Stanley (1835–1882), English economist and logician. In 1862 he introduced the marginal utility theory of value, stating that value was determined by utility. His most famous work was *Theory of Political Economy* (1871).

JEWETT, Sarah Orne (1849–1909), US novelist and writer of realistic short stories based on small-town life in upper New England. Her best-known work is *The Country of the Pointed Firs* (1896).

JEWS, a people who share common racial origins, history and culture and who date from at least 1500 BC. It is nevertheless very difficult to define what constitutes Jewishness. In Israel there are Jews from many origins and races, but most Jews in Israel are not observant or practicing religious Jews.

According to the Old Testament the history of the Jewish people begins with ABRAHAM, who led his family from Mesopotamia to Canaan. The Egyptians reduced the Israelites to captivity, until MOSES led his people into the wilderness of Sinai. After 40 years of wandering the tribes reached and conquered Canaan. External threats forced the 12 tribes to unite under SAUL, whose successor, King DAVID, brought peace and prosperity to the country. Under the rule of David's grandson, Jeroboam, however, the northern 10 tribes seceded to form the kingdom of Israel. Israel was defeated in 721 BC by the

Assyrians, and these tribes lost their identity in captivity. The southern kingdom, Judah, was defeated by the Babylonians in 586 BC, and the people were sent into exile in Babylon, where they later introduced the SYNAGOGUE as a place of study and prayer. Babylon was conquered by the Persian CYRUS THE GREAT in 538 BC; he allowed the Jews to return to Judah. Their later conquest by ALEXANDER THE GREAT meant a gradual imposition of Greek culture, until a rebellion under JUDAS MACCABAEUS in 165 BC led to the foundation of the HASMONEAN dynasty. The religious strife and disagreement between the SADDUCEES, PHARISEES and such sects as the ESSENES brought about Roman intervention in 53 BC, when POMPEY's legions entered Jerusalem and Palestine became a Roman province. In c33 AD Jesus was executed because he was regarded as a threat to the security of the Roman rule. A Jewish revolt in 66 led to the destruction of Jerusalem by the Romans; after a further revolt in 131 led by BAR COCHBA the Jewish state was completely crushed by the Romans; Judah was renamed Syria Palestina, and Jews were forbidden to enter Jerusalem. Fearing the loss of their religion, Jewish scholars and rabbis codified the oral law into the Mishnah and the TALMUD.

Many Jews moved to Western Europe, and their culture flourished, particularly in Spain. However, the CRUSADES led to widespread suppression of the Jews and throughout Western Europe there were laws confining them to GHETTOS, excluding them from most trades and professions other than that of money-lending, and barring them from owning land. From the end of the 13th century they were in turn banished from England, France and from Spain, where they were persecuted by the INQUISITION. By the end of the Middle Ages only small parts of Germany and Italy still allowed Jews within their borders. Many of the exiles perished; some of the descendants of the Spanish Jews, the SEPHARDIM, settled in the Ottoman Empire, while others, the Marranos, reestablished Jewish communities in England, France and the Netherlands in the 17th century. In 1654, 23 Dutch Jews founded the first Jewish congregation at New Amsterdam (New York). The descendants of German Jews, the ASHKENAZIM, took refuge in E Europe, in Poland and Lithuania, but many found themselves trapped in ghettos and persecuted by the Russians. Some adopted HASIDISM, a form of religious mysticism.

In Western Europe tolerance for the Jews increased after the French Revolution, and

Jewish communities grew. Nevertheless there was considerable opposition to the Jewish race and religion, as manifested by the DREYFUS AFFAIR in France. Between 1880 and 1922 harsh conditions in E Europe and the Russian POGROMS brought about both a massive Jewish emigration from E Europe, especially to the US, and the modern movement of ZIONISM led by Theodor HERZL and Chaim WEIZMANN, who hoped to reestablish a state of Jewry in Palestine. In Palestine most new Jewish immigrants from Europe settled on the land. The 1917 BALFOUR DECLARATION guaranteed "a national home for the Jewish people" in Palestine, but increasing Jewish settlement aroused the hostility of the Arab inhabitants, whose own national aspirations were beginning to awaken.

From the 1930s NAZISM brought virulent ANTI-SEMITISM in Germany; before the outbreak of WWII the Nazis were systematically murdering European Jews, and by 1945 they had exterminated over 6 million. Many Jews moved to Palestine after the war, and world reaction to the WWII catastrophes led to the establishment of the state of ISRAEL in 1948. Its presence, however, has resulted in continuous hostility and warfare between Israel and Arab countries. (See ARAB-ISRAELI WARS.) The majority of Jews now live in Israel, in the US and in Russia, where their cultural and religious life is seriously restricted.

JIM CROW, name for a system of laws and customs in the Southern US to segregate Negroes from white society. The name comes from a minstrel song. The laws dated from the 1880s and applied to schools, transportation, theaters and parks. After the mid-1950s, Supreme Court rulings overturned the legislation. (See CIVIL RIGHTS AND LIBERTIES; INTEGRATION.)

JIMÉNEZ, Juan Ramón (1881–1958), major Spanish poet. At first influenced by SYMBOLISM, in *Diary of a Poet and the Sea* (1917) he developed a free, direct style of his own, *poesía desnuda* (Spanish: naked poetry). After the Spanish Civil War he moved to Puerto Rico. He received the Nobel Prize for Literature in 1956.

JIMENEZ DE QUESADA, Gonzalo (c1500–1579), Spanish conquistador who claimed the Colombia area for Spain as New Granada. He settled there, doing much to improve the colonists' lot. He led a disastrous expedition in search of EL DORADO 1569–71.

JINNAH, Mohammed Ali (1876–1948), Indian Muslim lawyer and statesman, founder of Pakistan. At first a member of the Indian Congress Party, he resigned in 1921 because of its Hindu bias. From 1934 head of the MUSLIM LEAGUE, he campaigned for Muslim rights in an independent state, and in 1947 became Pakistan's first head of state.

JOAN OF ARC, Saint (c1412–1431), French heroine of the HUNDRED YEARS' WAR, a peasant girl from Domrémy, Lorraine, who heard "voices" telling her to liberate France from the English. Given command of a small force by the Dauphin Charles, she inspired it to victory at Orléans and in the surrounding region in 1429. She stood beside the Dauphin when he was crowned Charles VII that year, but failed to relieve besieged Paris because he denied her adequate forces. Captured at Compiègne (1430), she was tried for heresy by French clerics who sympathized with the English, and burnt at the stake. The verdict was reversed in 1456 and she was canonized in 1920.

JOB, 18th book of the OLD TESTAMENT. It seeks to show that suffering need not be God's penalty for sin. God permits Satan to torment the virtuous Job with the loss of family, wealth and health. Finding small comfort in wife and friends, Job is bitterly questioning but remains faithful, and is restored to good fortune in old age.

JODL, Alfred (1890–1946), German soldier, chief of operations staff in WWII. He signed the surrender at Rheims, May 7, 1945. Convicted of war crimes at the NUREMBERG TRIALS, he was executed.

JOEL, second book of the Minor Prophets in the OLD TESTAMENT. Messianic in nature, it forecasts the Day of the Lord in apocalyptic terms. Its prophecy of the outpouring of the Spirit upon all flesh is regarded by the Christian Church as fulfilled at PENTECOST.

JOFFRE, Joseph-Jacques-Césaire (1852–1931), commander-in-chief of the French army 1914–16. He underestimated German power at the start of WWI, but shared with Gen. J. S. Gallieni credit for the victory on the Marne. After the mismanagement of VERDUN he resigned, but was immediately made a marshal of France.

JOFFREY, Robert (1930–1988), US dancer and choreographer. He founded his school, the American Ballet Center, in 1953 and his first company, the Robert Joffrey Theater Dancers, in 1956. By 1976, when it became the Joffrey Ballet, it was one of the most highly regarded of US companies. The touring Joffrey II Company was formed in 1970 to develop young dancers.

JOHANAN BEN ZAKKAI, Jewish

PHARISEE who, after the destruction of the Temple by Rome in 70 AD, founded the academy at Jamnia (Yibna), thus ensuring the survival of Judaism.

JOHANSON, Donald Carl (1943–   ), US physical anthropologist whose fossil discoveries in E Africa, including a nearly complete skeleton of a human ancestor he named Lucy, led him to posit the emergence of the human species as recently as 2 million years ago.

JOHN, Saint (called the Evangelist or the Divine), son of Zebedee and brother of James, is usually thought to be the author of three New Testament Epistles and possibly the fourth GOSPEL. The Gospel of John, written c100 AD and based on a series of long discourses by Jesus, has little in common with the SYNOPTIC GOSPELS; it emphasizes Jesus' deity, and is spiritual and theological in tone.

JOHN, name of 22 popes and 2 antipopes. **Saint John I** (d. 526), pope from 523, was sent to Constantinople by Theodoric, the Ostrogoth king, to win toleration for ARIANISM from the emperor; Theodoric imprisoned him when he failed. **John VIII** (d. 882), reigned from 872. He sought political power for the papacy, intervening, with mixed success, in the rivalries of the CAROLINGIAN imperial house and excommunicating his opponent Formosus. In 877 he had to bribe SARACEN raiders to spare Rome. He resolved a dispute with the Eastern Church by recognizing Photius as patriarch of Constantinople in 879. He was assassinated by a household conspiracy. **John XXII** (c1249–1334) reigned from 1316. The second pope at Avignon, he filled the college with French cardinals. A skillful administrator, he lost popularity for his persecution of the Spiritual FRANCISCANS, who sought to observe a strict rule of evangelical poverty. He contested the election of Emperor LOUIS IV; Louis attempted to have him declared a heretic, but John imprisoned the antipope Louis appointed, Nicholas V. **John XXIII** was first taken as a name by Baldassare Cossa (d. 1419), schismatic antipope 1410–15. He promoted the council of PISA (1408) to end the GREAT SCHISM. Elected pope by the Pisa cardinals, he defended Rome against his rival Gregory XII. Prompted by Emperor Sigismund, he convened the Council of Constance. There he agreed to abdicate if his two rivals did, but reneged; the Council deposed all three. Cossa was made a cardinal-bishop in 1419. The name **John XXIII** was therefore taken by Angelo Giuseppe Roncalli (1881–1963). Of peasant stock, he was an army chaplain in

WWI. He was made a titular archbishop in the Vatican diplomatic corps 1925–35 and nuncio 1925–53, serving in Turkey, the Balkans and France; in this post he won great popularity. Made cardinal in 1953, he was elected pope in 1958. He revolutionized the church, promoting cooperation with other Christian churches and other religions in the face of world problems; the encyclical *Mater et Magister* (1961) advocated social reform in underdeveloped areas of the world. In 1962 he called the influential Second VATICAN COUNCIL.

JOHN (1167–1216), king of England from 1199. Youngest son of HENRY II, he succeeded his brother Richard I. John refused to accept a papal nominee as archbishop of Canterbury, and so was excommunicated in 1209; he faced invasion by Philip II of France, to whom he had lost England's French possessions. Expensive military provisions had alienated the barons, already curbed by Henry II; in 1215 they rose in revolt and forced John to sign the MAGNA CARTA, confirming their feudal rights. John later repudiated it and waged a new war against the barons, who summoned French support. John died while the issue was still in doubt.

JOHN, Augustus Edwin (1878–1961), leading British painter, famous for his portraits of contemporary celebrities such as George Bernard SHAW, Dylan THOMAS and James JOYCE. He is noted for his vigorous use of rich color and his excellent draughtsmanship.

JOHN, Epistles of, three NEW TESTAMENT epistles ascribed to St. John the Apostle. The first and longest seeks to strengthen Christians by giving the signs of the faith; the second attacks gnostic denials of Christ's incarnation; the third urges an obstinate church leader to receive genuine missionaries.

JOHN, Gospel of, the fourth GOSPEL in the New Testament, written c100 AD and traditionally ascribed to St. John the Apostle. Based on a series of long discourses by Jesus, it has little in common with the SYNOPTIC GOSPELS; it emphasizes Jesus' deity and is spiritual and theological in tone.

JOHN BULL, personification, favorable or otherwise, of the typical Englishman, usually portrayed as a burly good-natured farmer or tradesman wearing a Union Jack waistcoat. The name derives from a satire by John ARBUTHNOT.

JOHN OF AUSTRIA (1547–1578), Spanish military commander, illegitimate son of Emperor Charles V. Noted for his skill and gallantry, he commanded the Christian fleet at LEPANTO (1571) and conquered Tunis (1573). Governor-general of the Spanish Netherlands (1576–78), he fought the rebellion of WILLIAM THE SILENT.

JOHN OF DAMASCUS, Saint (c675–749), Orthodox Syrian theological writer and antagonist of iconoclasm. He resigned an inherited post under the Saracen caliph to become a monk.

JOHN OF GAUNT (1340–1399), fourth son of Edward III, became duke of Lancaster in 1362. Born at Ghent (hence "Gaunt"), he was a commander in France 1367–74, during the HUNDRED YEARS' WAR. From 1371 he ruled England for his senile father and young nephew RICHARD II; his economic policies and alliance with John WYCLIF made him unpopular in many quarters, as did his unsuccessful campaigns to claim the Castilian throne 1369–73. His eldest son became HENRY IV.

JOHN OF LEIDEN (1509–1536), Dutch innkeeper who became leader of the ANABAPTISTS in Münster and in 1534 set up a brutally corrupt theocracy, the "Kingdom of Zion" with himself as king, in which private ownership was abolished. In 1535 the bishop of Münster crushed the revolt; John was tortured and executed.

JOHN OF SALISBURY (c1110–1180), English churchman and leading SCHOLASTIC philosopher. Friend and secretary to Archbishop Thomas à Becket, he shared his exile 1163–70. John, who studied under Peter ABELARD, was a principal theorist of REALISM.

JOHN OF THE CROSS, Saint (1542–1591), Spanish poet and mystic, founder of a reformed Carmelite order. Influenced by St. TERESA OF AVILA, he is remembered for poems such as *The Dark Night of the Soul*. Canonized in 1726, he was made a CHURCH DOCTOR in 1926.

JOHN PAUL I (Albino Luciani; 1912–1978), Italian-born pope. A moderate traditionalist of humble village background, he was cardinal and patriarch of Venice when elected pope in 1978. He died of a heart attack one month later, ending the shortest papal reign in nearly 400 years.

JOHN PAUL II (Karol Jozef Wojtyla; 1920–   ), Polish-born Roman Catholic pope who was the first non-Italian to be elected pontiff (1978) in 455 years. A personable world traveler, he has maintained a theologically conservative position on such controversial issues as birth control and abortion. He survived an assassination attempt in 1981.

JOHNS, Jasper (1930–   ), US painter, a leading exponent of POP ART in such works as *Flag* (1958), a copy of the US flag, and *Painted Bronze* (1960), two cast beer cans.

JOHNSON, Alvin Saunders (1874–1971), US economist, editor, and educator. He cofounded (1919) and directed (1923–45) the New School for Social Research in New York City. In 1933, he established the "University in Exile" as a refuge for European scholars fleeing Nazi Germany; this eventually became the New School's Graduate Faculty. With the aid of the Rockefeller Foundation, Johnson brought more than 200 refugee scholars to the US. He was also an editor of the *New Republic* and the *Encyclopedia of the Social Sciences*.

JOHNSON, Andrew (1808–1875), 17th president of the US. He was born in Raleigh, N.C., of a poor family and at 10 apprenticed to a tailor. In 1826 he moved to Greenville, Tenn., where in 1827 he married Eliza McCardle; she taught him writing and arithmetic. He took an active part in public life, and after becoming mayor was elected to the Tenn. house of representatives and then the state senate. A Democrat, he served 10 years as a US congressman. Governor of Tenn. 1853–57, he was then elected to the Senate. Though supporting some measures by the pro-slavery South he introduced a HOMESTEADING bill which was opposed by slave owners and most Southern congressmen. After Lincoln became president in 1860, Tenn. seceded; Johnson, the only Southern senator not to join the Confederate cause, was made military governor of Tenn., establishing a working basis for civilian rule. In 1865 he was elected vice-president, but six weeks later became president when Lincoln was assassinated. He inherited the problems of RECONSTRUCTION. On May 29, 1865, with Congress adjourned, he issued a proclamation of amnesty, allowing Southern states the right to adopt new constitutions and elect governments. His policy offended radical Republicans because it threatened their absolute control of Congress and robbed them of the chance of holding office in the South. In a mid-term election characterized by a vicious and emotive campaign by Johnson's opponents, they were returned with a two-thirds majority. On March 2, 1867 the first radical reconstruction act was passed. To further restrict Johnson Congress passed, over his veto, the Tenure of Office Act, forbidding the dismissal of certain federal officeholders. Despite this he dismissed the secretary of war, Edwin Stanton, and in March 1868 Johnson was impeached. The vindictiveness of the radical attack won him sympathy and he escaped conviction by one vote. He failed to capture the Democratic nomination, and attempts to reenter Congress failed until he was elected senator from Tenn. in 1874. He served a short session in 1875 and died of a stroke soon after.

JOHNSON, Charles Spurgeon (1893–1956), US educator, sociologist and first black president of Fisk University, Tenn. (1946–56). After research work for race relations organizations, he helped reorganize the Japanese educational system after WWII and was US delegate to UNESCO.

JOHNSON, Eyvind (1900–1976), Swedish novelist who shared the 1974 Nobel Prize for Literature.

JOHNSON, Hiram Warren (1866–1945), US statesman. As a prosecuting attorney in San Francisco he successfully prosecuted corrupt political bosses (1908); he became governor of Cal, 1911–17. A senator from 1917, he was a hard-line isolationist, opposing US membership in the League of Nations and any war preparations.

JOHNSON, Jack (1878–1946), US boxer. In 1908 he became the first black to win the world heavyweight championship. Unpopular with the white boxing world, he jumped bail on serious charges and fled abroad (1912). He lost the title to Jess Willard in Havana in 1915.

JOHNSON, James Weldon (1871–1938), black US author and statesman. He was US consul in Venezuela and Nicaragua (1906–12) and secretary of the NATIONAL ASSOCIATION FOR THE ADVANCEMENT OF COLORED PEOPLE 1916–30. He wrote *God's Trombones* (1927), a collection of verse sermons, and edited *The Book of American Negro Poetry* (1922).

JOHNSON, Lyndon Baines (1908–1973), 36th president of the US. He became chief executive on Nov. 22, 1963, after the assassination of John F. KENNEDY.

Johnson was born on a farm near Stonewall, SW Tex., of a prominent local family. He did not go to college until 1927, and taught after graduating in 1930. In 1931 he became secretary to the Republican congressman Richard Kleberg. In 1934 he married Claudia Alta Taylor, nicknamed "Lady Bird." He was Texan administrator of the NEW DEAL National Youth Administration 1935–37, and was elected to Congress as a Democratic New Deal supporter 1937–48, with a period of naval service 1941–42; he served on the House Naval and later Armed Services Committees. Elected to the Senate in 1948, he became the youngest majority leader in its history when the Democrats regained

control in 1954. He used his influence and mastery of procedure to secure a unanimous Democratic condemnation of Senator J. R. MCCARTHY and passage of important CIVIL RIGHTS bills. After losing the presidential nomination in 1960 Johnson became vice-president under John F. Kennedy, despite prior disagreements. He influenced committee decisions on space projects and civil rights and traveled abroad as a kind of roving ambassador, but remained in the background politically.

After Kennedy's assassination Johnson quickly and capably assumed his presidential responsibilities. With the same cabinet and presidential staff he implemented the faltering Kennedy tax reform and civil rights programs, as well as a massive anti-poverty program of his own. Winning a landslide victory in 1964, with Hubert HUMPHREY as vice-president, Johnson pushed through extensive liberal legislation to build the "Great Society," including the MEDICARE program and the Voting Rights Act. He equally vigorously extended Kennedy's policy of US involvement in the VIETNAM WAR, despite mounting hostility from sections of the public. Campus demonstrations and general civil unrest caused three years of turbulence rarely equalled in US history. On Mar. 31, 1968, Johnson announced that he would neither seek nor accept renomination, and retired to his home in Tex., where early in 1973 he suffered a fatal heart attack.

JOHNSON, Philip Cortelyou (1906–   ), US architect, a major exponent of the INTERNATIONAL STYLE. His "Glass House" (1949) at New Canaan, Conn., won him international recognition. In the 1950s he worked with MIES VAN DER ROHE on the Seagram Building, New York. His later work is less severely functional.

JOHNSON, Samuel (1709–84), English man of letters, poet, critic, essayist and lexicographer. After failing as a schoolmaster he supported himself in London by journalism and hack writing. He published the poems *London* (1738) and *The Vanity of Human Wishes* (1749). From 1746 to 1755 he prepared his pioneering *Dictionary of the English Language* (1755), an idiosyncratic but brilliant work which won him a wide reputation. The satirical *Rasselas* (1759) was produced as a quick moneymaker. In 1763 he met James BOSWELL, his biographer, who recorded much of Johnson's fiery but polished conversation. The critical works, particularly the edition of Shakespeare (1765) and *Lives of the Most Eminent English Poets* (1781) combine excellent writing and insight with, often, what many consider eccentric judgments.

JOHNSON, Thomas Loftin (1854–1911), US municipal reformer, an Indianapolis businessman who made a fortune from streetcar investments. Democratic congressman 1891–95, he advocated single tax and public ownership of public utilities. Mayor of Cleveland 1901–10, he introduced many reforms.

JOHNSON, Walter Perry, called "Big Train" (1887–1946), US baseball pitcher famous for his speed. With the Washington Senators 1907–27 he won 414 games and in 1913 pitched 56 consecutive scoreless innings. In 1936 he was one of the first five players elected to the Baseball Hall of Fame.

JOHNSON, Sir William (1715–1774), British superintendent of Indian affairs in North America. His just and honest conduct kept the IROQUOIS tribes, into which he was adopted, on the British side in the FRENCH AND INDIAN WAR. He commanded the victorious colonial forces at the battle of Lake George.

JOHNSTON, Albert Sydney (1803–1862), brilliant Confederate general, secretary of war for the Texas Republic 1838–40. Confederate second-in-command, he was driven back by superior forces on the Mississippi-Allegheny front. His daring strategy almost won the battle of SHILOH, but he was mortally wounded in the first day's fighting.

JOHNSTON, Joseph Eggleston (1807–1901), Confederate general, credited with the victory at BULL RUN in 1861. Wounded at Fair Oaks, he was replaced after a feud with Jefferson DAVIS in 1863; he returned to command in 1865 but had to surrender to SHERMAN after two months.

JOHN THE BAPTIST, Saint (d. c30 AD), preacher who proclaimed the coming of Christ and urged repentance, baptizing his followers in the Jordan R. He denounced HEROD Antipas for marrying Herodias, wife of Herod's brother, and was beheaded at her instigation.

JOINT, specialized surface between BONES allowing movement of one on the other. Major joints, especially of limbs, are **synovial joints**, which are lined by synovial membrane and CARTILAGE and surrounded by a fibrous capsule; they contain synovial fluid, which lubricates the joint surfaces. Parts of the capsule (e.g., in the ankle) or overlying tendons (e.g., in the knee) form ligaments important in joint stability, though at some joints (e.g., the shoulder) resting activity in MUSCLES ensures stability, while in others (e.g., the hip) it is due to the shape of the bony surfaces. **Fibrous and cartilaginous joints** between bones are relatively fixed except under special circumstances (e.g., the widening of the symphysis pubis in PREGNANCY). Joint disease causes ARTHRITIS, with pain, limitation of movement and sometimes increase in fluid.

JOINT CHIEFS OF STAFF, US committee of military advisers to the president, the NATIONAL SECURITY COUNCIL and the secretary of defense. Set up in 1942, its members are the Army, Navy and Air Force chiefs of staff, the Marine Corps commandant, and a chairman.

JOINVILLE, Jean, sire de (c1224–1317), French soldier whose *Histoire de saint-Louis* (c1309) is a moving account of the Seventh CRUSADE, its leader Louis IX and the frank and amiable author. He refused to join Louis' fatal crusade to Tunis (1270).

JOLIET, Louis (c1645–c1700), French-Canadian explorer who, with Father MARQUETTE, led the first expedition down the Mississippi R. In 1672–73 they reached its confluence with the Arkansas R, but turned back when they found it led not to the Pacific but into the Spanish-held Gulf of Mexico.

JOLIOT-CURIE, Irène (1897–1956), French physicist, the daughter of Pierre and Marie CURIE. She and her husband, **Jean Frédéric Joliot** (1900–1958), shared the 1935 Nobel Prize for Chemistry for their discovery of artificial RADIOACTIVITY. Both later played a major part in the formation of the French atomic energy commission but, because of their communism, were removed from positions of responsibility there (Frédéric 1950, Irène 1951). Like her mother, Irène died from LEUKEMIA as a result of prolonged exposure to radioactive materials.

JOLSON, Al (Asa Yoelson; 1886–1950), Lithuanian-born US entertainer, a Broadway star in the 1920s for such sentimental songs, sung in blackface, as "Swanee," "Mammy," "Sonny Boy," and "April Showers." He starred in *The Jazz Singer* (1927), the first part-sound feature film, in which he declared prophetically, "You ain't heard nothin' yet!"

JONAH, Book of, fifth book of the Minor Prophets, unique in its entirely narrative form. Jonah is portrayed as so intolerant of Gentiles that he disobeys God's command to convert the city of Nineveh. He sails away and in a storm is swallowed by a "great fish," now usually identified as "whale." Three days later he leaves the fish's body and returns to Nineveh to fulfill his mission.

JONES, (Alfred) Ernest (1879–1958), British psychoanalyst. A member of Freud's inner circle, he helped disseminate psychoanalysis in Britain, Canada, and the US, founded and edited (1920–39) the *International Journal of Psychoanalysis*, and wrote a three-volume biography of Freud (1953–57).

JONES, Bob (1883–1968), US evangelist who spent his life spreading an old-time, fundamentalist Protestant religion. He established his first Bob Jones College in Fla. (1927), trained ministers and missionaries, published books at the school's press and preached via radio broadcasts.

JONES, Bobby (Robert Tyre Jones, Jr.; 1902–1971), US amateur golfer, four-time winner of the US Open (1923, 1926, 1929, 1930), five-time US amateur champion.

JONES, Casey (John Luther Jones; 1863–1900), US railroad engineer and folk hero who drove the Cannon Ball express from Memphis, Tenn. to Canton, Miss. When it collided with a freight train on April 30, 1900, Jones stayed in the cab to apply the brakes. He was killed, but his actions saved the passengers and crew.

JONES, Inigo (1573–1652), English architect who introduced the classical style to England. While staying in Italy he had been influenced by the works of PALLADIO. Surveyor of the King's Works 1615–44, his masterpieces include the Queen's House at Greenwich, Whitehall Banqueting Hall and St. Paul's Church, Covent Garden. His sets and costumes for court MASQUES greatly influenced subsequent stage design.

JONES, James (1921–1977), US novelist. His first book, *From Here to Eternity* (1951), portrayed the degradation of army life on the eve of WWII. Other works include *Some Came Running* (1957), *The Pistol* (1959) and *The Thin Red Line* (1962).

JONES, John Paul (1747–1792), US naval hero, born John Paul in Kirkudbrightshire, Scotland. Serving at first in British ships, he killed one of his crew (1773) and deserted to America. In the Revolution he joined the Continental navy, taking command of the *Alfred* in 1775, in 1776 the *Providence*, and in 1777 the *Ranger*. His successes against British Atlantic shipping won him command of the French-donated *Bon Homme Richard* (1779). After petty raiding around the Scottish and Irish coasts he attacked a convoy escorted by the British ship *Serapis*. In a fierce battle the *Richard* was irreparably damaged, but Jones refused to surrender with the famous words "I have not yet begun to fight!" He managed to capture the *Serapis* as the *Richard* sank.

Service in the Russian navy 1788–89 left him physically and mentally broken, and he died in Paris.

JONES, Mother (Mary Harris Jones; 1830–1930), US labor activist, agitator and organizer among coal miners and other industrial workers from the 1870s through the 1920s. She helped found the INDUSTRIAL WORKERS OF THE WORLD (1905) and was the focal point of many of the most significant strikes of the early 20th century.

JONES, Robert Edmond (1887–1954), US stage designer whose "new stagecraft," featuring spare and abstract sets, lighting and costumes, revolutionized the American theater. He designed notable Shakespearean productions, many of Eugene O'Neill plays, and the popular *Lute Song* (1946) and *Green Pastures* (1951).

JONES, Samuel Milton "Golden Rule" (1846–1904), Welsh-born US businessman, an advocate of good management relations and a political reformer. Mayor of Toledo 1897–1904, he stood independently when political factions tried to remove him; he introduced many labor reforms for city employees.

JONESBORO, Battle of, fought at Jonesboro, W Ga., S of Atlanta. A tactical victory for Union forces under Gen. SHERMAN, it opened their way to Atlanta.

JONGKIND, Johann Barthold (1819–1891), Dutch painter, a precursor of IMPRESSIONISM. Resident in France from 1846, he met COROT there and painted in Normandy with Boudin. His landscapes and seascapes continued the Dutch tradition with a new exploration of light and atmospheric effects, a major influence on MONET.

JONGLEURS, itinerant entertainers in medieval France and England. They performed acrobatics, juggling, magic, and dancing, as well as singing and storytelling. (See MINSTRELS.)

JONSON, Ben (1572–1637), English dramatist and lyric poet. He served in the Dutch wars in the 1590s, returning to London to act and write for the stage. *Every Man in his Humour* (1598) established him as a playwright. His tragedies *Sejanus* (1603) and *Catiline* (1611) are still admired, but it is the comedies that are most often performed, especially *Volpone* (1606) and *The Alchemist* (1610); both of these are sardonic depictions of human gullibility before the lure of gold. Under James I Jonson and Inigo JONES collaborated on masques for the court, but he fell from favor under Charles I.

JOPLIN, Scott (1868–1917), US black composer who in lyrical and elegant pieces such as *Maple Leaf Rag* (1899) sought to establish RAGTIME as serious music. When ambitious ventures such as the opera *Treemonisha* (1911) failed, Joplin declined into mental illness. In the 1970s his works enjoyed a great revival.

JORDAENS, Jacob (1593–1678), Flemish baroque painter. Influenced by RUBENS, with whom he studied, he painted religious and allegorical scenes, genre works and portraits in a vigorous if occasionally crude style. Among his best-known works is *The King Drinks* (1638).

JORDAN, Arab HASHEMITE monarchy in the Middle East, bordered to the E by Saudi Arabia, the N by Syria and Iraq, and the W by Israel and the Israeli-occupied West Bank.

Official name: Hashemite Kingdom of Jordan
Area: 34,443sq mi
Population: 2,853,000
Languages: Arabic
Religions: Islam
Monetary unit(s): 1 Jordanian dinar=1,000 fils

Land. Jordan is bisected by the GREAT RIFT VALLEY through which flows the JORDAN R. The country is largely a desert plateau rising to greener highlands. In the SW is the capital, Amman, and the only port, Aqaba. The climate ranges from Mediterranean in the highlands to subtropical in the Jordan valley; the desert receives minimal rainfall.

People and Economy. The population is mainly Arab, but there is a wide cultural gulf between the traditionally nomadic BEDOUIN and the Palestinians, who number more than 100,000 and live in refugee camps or in the large urban centers—Amman, Irbid and Zarqa. Almost 95% of the people are Sunni Muslims, the remainder Christians. Jordan's economy is largely agricultural, with wheat, barley and fruits the principal crops; outside the irrigated Jordan valley yields are low due to reliance on sometimes insufficient rainfall. Most industry is limited to food processing and textiles, although there is some oil refining, and cement and fertilizer

manufacturing. Phosphate is mined. The economy was greatly disrupted by the loss of the West Bank (occupied by Israel in 1967), and Jordan relies heavily on foreign aid, mostly from Saudi Arabia and the US.

History. In biblical times the West Bank was settled by the Israelites, the E region by their enemies the Ammonites, Moab and Edom. This region later became the Nabatean empire, its capital at Petra. Later ruled by Rome and Byzantium, it was conquered by the Arabs in the 7th century. Jordan was part of the OTTOMAN EMPIRE from 1516 until the 20th century, but during WWI a Hashemite Arab revolt was backed by the British forces (see FAISAL I; LAWRENCE, T. E.). In 1923 it was made into the British-supervised state of Transjordan, ruled by the Emir ABDULLAH. Its army, the Arab Legion, was trained by British officers led by Sir John Glubb. In 1946 Transjordan won full self-government as Jordan, Abdullah becoming king; in 1948 the Arab Legion conquered the West Bank. In 1951 Abdullah, who had made a truce with Israel, was assassinated; his grandson HUSSEIN was enthroned in 1953. Jordan, which maintained strong ties with the United Kingdom and had troubled relations with the Palestinians, was often in conflict with its neighbors Egypt (until a 1967 mutual defense pact) and Syria. Jordan's subsequent involvement in the Six-Day War cost her the West Bank, occupied by Israel, and the PALESTINE LIBERATION ORGANIZATION (PLO) was expelled. In 1970 the growing power of the Palestian guerrillas in Jordan led to a short civil war in which they were defeated. In 1974 Hussein recognized the PLO as the sole legitimate representative of the Palestinian people, but the West Bank continued to be represented in the Jordanian parliament until 1988, when Jordan formally severed all legal and administrative links to the West Bank in favor of the PLO.

JORDAN RIVER starts at a confluence in the Hula basin in N Israel and flows about 200mi S through the Sea of Galilee and the Ghor valley to the Dead Sea. It occupies the Asian continuation of the GREAT RIFT VALLEY. Honored in the Christian, Moslem and Jewish religions, it is an important source of water in an arid region.

JOSEPH, Saint, husband of Mary, mother of Jesus. A carpenter, he was a descendant of David. Warned by God, he took Mary and the infant Jesus into Egypt to escape the wrath of Herod. He is honored as patron saint of the Roman Catholic Church.

JOSEPH, Jewish patriarch, favorite son of JACOB. His jealous brothers sold him into slavery in Egypt. There he won favor with Pharaoh by correctly interpreting premonitory dreams, and was eventually made chief minister. He forgave his brothers and rescued the family from famine.

JOSEPH, name of two Holy Roman Emperors. **Joseph I** (1678–1711), reigned from 1705, during the War of the SPANISH SUCCESSION and a Hungarian revolt led by Francis Rakoczy. **Joseph II** (1741–1790), reigned from 1765, but until 1780 with his mother, MARIA THERESA. When she died he began to institute a massive social reform program on ENLIGHTENMENT principles, abolishing serfdom and attacking feudal, class and property systems. His religious, administrative and language reforms made him unpopular in Austria and caused revolts abroad. His attempt at enlightened despotism was hindered by his tactless autocracy, and few of his reforms survived him.

JOSEPH, Chief (c1840–1904), Nez Percé Indian chief. In 1877, faced with forcible resettlement under a basically fraudulent treaty, he led his people in a mass flight from their Oregon lands to Canada. The Nez Percé were defeated only 30mi from the frontier; Joseph won popular sympathy for his heroic and brilliant resistance.

JOSEPHINE (1763–1814), empress of the French as wife of NAPOLEON I. The widow of Alexandre de BEAUHARNAIS, who was guillotined during the French Revolution, she married Napoleon Bonaparte in 1796. They had no children, and Napoleon had the marriage annulled in 1809 so he could marry Marie Louise, daughter of the emperor of Austria.

JOSEPHUS, Flavius (c37–100 AD), Jewish historian, governor of Galilee in the Roman-Jewish War of 66 AD. He later took Roman citizenship. His *History of the Jewish War* (c79 AD) and histories of the Jews are masterpieces of Jewish literature.

JOSHUA, sixth book of the OLD TESTAMENT. It describes the conquest of CANAAN by the Israelites under Joshua, associate of and successor to MOSES, and its division among the TWELVE TRIBES OF ISRAEL.

JOSQUIN DES PRÉS (c1450–1521), major Flemish composer. He traveled widely in Europe; much of his work was done in Italy. Technically brilliant, his music ranges from the almost mystical fervor in his 20 masses and 90 motets to the gaiety and elegance of his secular songs. His music has enjoyed a revival since the 1950s.

JOULE, James Prescott (1818–1889), British physicist who showed that HEAT energy and mechanical energy are equivalent and hinted at the law of conservation of ENERGY. From 1852 he and Thomson (later Lord KELVIN) performed a series of experiments in THERMODYNAMICS, especially on the Joule–Thomson effect (see CRYOGENICS). The joule (unit) is named for him.

JOWETT, Benjamin (1817–1893), English classical scholar, master of Balliol College, Oxford from 1870 and vice-chancellor of Oxford University, 1882–86. His translations of PLATO'S *Dialogues* (1871) and *Republic* (1844) are literary and scholastic masterpieces.

JOYCE, James Augustine Aloysius (1882–1941), Irish novelist and poet whose novel *Ulysses* (1922) is a seminal work of 20th-century literature. Within the framework of Homeric myth he dissects his characters' thoughts and actions in the course of a single day through STREAM OF CONSCIOUSNESS techniques and the creation of an allusive private language. This he developed in *Finnegans Wake* (1939), a complex cyclical exploration of dream consciousness. Dublin, where Joyce grew up, is central to his writing as in *Dubliners* (1914), and the autobiographical *A Portrait of the Artist as a Young Man* (1916), but from 1904 he lived abroad, in Paris, Trieste and Zurich, where he died.

JUANA INÉS DE LA CRUZ (1651–1695), Mexican-Spanish poet and scholar. As a girl she left court to become a nun. Criticized for her "unwomanly" studies, she defended women's education in a vigorous letter to her bishop (1691). Her lyric poems, especially the sonnets, are among the finest in Spanish. She died nursing epidemic victims in Mexico City.

JUAN CARLOS (1938–   ), king of Spain from Nov. 1975, after the death of Gen. FRANCO. Educated as Franco's successor, he was so named in 1969 in preference to his father Don Juan, son of ALFONSO XIII. In 1962 he married Princess Sophia of Greece, by whom he had three children. On becoming king, he proved to be an unexpectedly strong force for stability and democracy. Personally popular, he was instrumental in thwarting an attempted right-wing military coup in 1981.

JUAREZ, Benito Pablo (1806–1872), Mexican national hero, effective ruler from 1861. Of Indian descent, he was imprisoned and exiled as a liberal 1853–55, when he was made justice minister in the administration that ousted SANTA ANNA (1855). His reforms attacked privilege in the Church and the army, precipitating civil war 1855–61. In 1861 he was elected president. The French incursion under MAXIMILIAN 1864–67 forced him to conduct a guerrilla campaign, which he won with US backing. He continued to serve as president from 1867 until his death, but his last years in office saw insurrections.

JUDAH, Kingdom of, territory in S Palestine, held by the tribes of Judah and Benjamin, after the breakup of SOLOMON's kingdom under Rehoboam, c931 BC. The house of David ruled Judah until the destruction of Jerusalem in 587 BC.

JUDAH HA-LEVI (c1075–1141), Jewish rabbi, philosopher and poet who lived and worked in Muslim Spain. His *Sefer ha-Kuzari* remains his monument.

JUDAISM, the religion of the Jews, the most ancient of the world's surviving monotheistic religions and as such deeply influential on CHRISTIANITY and ISLAM. It sees the world as the creation of a living god and the Jews as his chosen people. Central is the idea of the Covenant made between God and Abraham, ancestor of the Jews. This was sealed and is commemorated by the ceremony of male circumcision; it was reaffirmed at the time of the EXODUS by the Pesach or Passover. Abraham bound himself and his descendants to carry the message of one God to the world in return for His protection. The relationship between God and His chosen people is the major theme of the Hebrew Bible.

Its first five books, the PENTATEUCH, constituted the TORAH, or law, which is the foundation of the religion. It contains a history of the Jews until the death of MOSES, the Ten Commandments and a corpus of ritual and ethical precepts. The Torah is supplemented by a body of oral traditions and interpretations and instructions, set down in the 1st century and known as the Mishnah. With a commentary on it, known as the Gemara, it is part of the TALMUD. Yet doctrinally Judaism is not a dogmatic religion. No analytical statement of the nature of God exists, the concept of the afterlife is undefined, and there is no formulaic creed of beliefs.

The faith was many times in danger of destruction by conquest or corruption from within. Its survival was, often, due to great kings, but principally to spiritual leaders (among whom Moses ranks almost as a second founder), PROPHETS and scholars. Until the conquest of Jerusalem by Babylon in 586 BC the Temple built by SOLOMON was the great religious center. Its destruction and the dispersion of Jewish communities through the ancient world made the SYNAGOGUE, or local meeting, increasingly important. Judaism survived the catastrophic destruction of the second Temple and depopulation of Jerusalem by Romans in 70 AD, thanks largely to Johanan ben Zakkai. His emphasis on the Torah, with the consolidation of the synagogue, provided Judaism with the intellectual and community strongholds to withstand the persecution of ensuing centuries. Also important was the ancient concept of the MESSIAH, a descendant of the house of David to be sent by God to restore and rule a triumphant Israel, and the strict observance of Judaic rituals and customs. An important holy day is the weekly SABBATH; others are ROSH HASHANAH, YOM KIPPUR, SHAVUOT, HANUKKAH, PASSOVER.

JUDAS ISCARIOT (d.c30 AD), the APOSTLE who betrayed Jesus. For 30 pieces of silver he identified Jesus to the soldiers at GETHSEMANE by a kiss of greeting. According to MATTHEW he later repented and hanged himself.

JUDAS MACCABEUS (d. 160 BC), Jewish leader of the HASMONEAN dynasty. He defeated Antiochus IV, a SELEUCID king seeking to force paganism on the Jews, and in 165 BC reconsecrated the Temple. This event is commemorated by the festival of HANUKKAH.

JUDE, Saint, one of the APOSTLES, possible author of the New Testament Epistle of Jude, which combats heresy. Jude is an anglicized form of Judas, to distinguish him from JUDAS ISCARIOT.

JUDGES, seventh book of the Old Testament. It recounts the exploits of military leaders, known as "judges," between the time of Joshua and the birth of Samuel. Israel's successive apostasies from God are punished by enemy oppression, until God sends a judge to deliver the people. The main judges are Barak, Deborah, Gideon, Abimelech, Jephthah and Samson.

JUDICIAL REVIEW. See SUPREME COURT; UNITED STATES CONSTITUTION.

JUDICIARY, body of public officials, usually called judges or magistrates, whose task it is to interpret the laws of a state made by its LEGISLATURE and executed by its EXECUTIVE (see SEPARATION OF POWERS). The US federal judicial system was established by the Judiciary Act, passed by Congress Sept. 24, 1789. It set up the federal COURTS and defined their powers, procedures and jurisdiction. Under COMMON LAW systems such as exist in the US and UK the rules of precedent give the judiciary such wide powers that they are often said to help make as well as interpret the law. (See also LEGAL PROFESSION.)

JUDITH, book of the Old Testament APOCRYPHA. During an Assyrian invasion a young Jewish widow, Judith, seduces the

Assyrian general Holofernes in order to murder him. She shows his head to the Jewish army, which routs its leaderless enemy.

JUDO, a form of unarmed combat, a sport developed by Jigoro Kano in 1882 as a less violent form of Japanese *jujitsu*. It uses grappling and throwing holds, combined with a skillful use of balance and timing, to turn an opponent's strength against him; judo can thus enable a weaker person to overcome a stronger. Colored belts, ranging from white for beginners to black for experts, denote proficiency grades. Introduced into the US in 1902, it has been regulated by the Amateur Athletic Union since 1952, and has been featured in the OLYMPIC GAMES since 1964.

JUGENDSTIL, German ART NOUVEAU style c1890–c1910. Centering particularly on Munich and Vienna, it was named for the magazine *Die Jugend* (Youth). Among major exponents was Henri van de VELDE.

JUGULAR VEINS, a pair of veins on each side of the neck which collect venous blood from the BRAIN (internal jugular vein) and the rest of the head (external jugular vein). Their proximity to the surface makes them liable to trauma with HEMORRHAGE and aeroembolism.

JUGURTHA (c156–104 BC), king of Numidia from 118 BC. He was not hostile to Rome but lost its support through irresponsible murders. He defeated Roman invasions in favor of his rival Adherbal, but was captured in 106 BC and murdered at Rome.

JUILLIARD STRING QUARTET, musical group founded in 1946 by William SCHUMAN, then president of the Juilliard School of Music, New York City. In 1962 it became "quartet in residence" at the Library of Congress. The group has given premieres of many American compositions.

JUJITSU. See JUDO.

JULIAN THE APOSTATE (c331–363 AD), Roman emperor from 361, proclaimed by the army he commanded. He greatly reduced taxes by cutting court expenditure and corruption. He attempted to restore paganism but did not persecute Christians. In 363 he was killed in battle with the Persians.

JULIUS II (1443–1513), pope who reigned from 1503. As Cardinal Giuliano della Rovere he dominated Innocent VIII but went into exile 1492–1503 when his bitter enemy Rodrigo Borgia became pope as ALEXANDER VI. As pope, Julius commanded the armies that reconquered the papal states, and led the Holy League against France (1510). The Fifth LATERAN Council, which he assembled, criticized the French Church and attacked Church corruption. Patron of RAPHAEL, MICHELANGELO and BRAMANTE, he laid the foundation stone of the new SAINT PETER'S BASILICA.

JULY, the seventh month of the year, named for Julius Caesar, who reorganized the CALENDAR. It has 31 days.

JULY REVOLUTION, popular rising in France, July 26–30, 1830, against the reactionary aims of King Charles X. Middle-class opposition was aroused when the king's ultraroyalist minister Polignac published the July Ordinances, which suspended freedom of the press, dissolved the chamber of deputies and reduced the small electorate by 75%. Rioting broke out on July 27, and by July 29 most of Paris was in insurgent hands; on July 30 Charles repealed the Ordinances, but was forced to abdicate. His cousin the duke of Orleans became king as LOUIS PHILIPPE.

JUMPING BEAN, the seeds of various Mexican shrubs, principally those of the genus *Sebastiania*, which contain the larvae of the moth *Carpocapsa saltitans*, movement of which cause the seeds to "jump."

JUNE, sixth month of the year, named for the Roman goddess Juno; it has 30 days.

JUNE DAYS, phase in the February Revolution in France, June 23–26, 1848. The unemployed of Paris rose in riot when the insensitive provisional government abolished the national workshops (a primitive dole system). Gen. Cavaignac suppressed the rioting with great savagery.

JUNG, Carl Gustav (1875–1961), Swiss psychiatrist who founded analytical psychology. He studied PSYCHIATRY at Basel University, his postgraduate studies being of PARAPSYCHOLOGY. After working with the Swiss Eugen Bleuler and JANET, he met FREUD (1907), whom he followed for some years. His disagreement with Freud's belief in the purely sexual nature of the libido, however, led to a complete break between the two in 1913. In *Psychological Types* (1921) he expounded his views on introversion and extroversion. Later he investigated anthropology and the occult, which led to his theory of archetypes, or universal symbols present in the collective unconscious. (See also PSYCHOANALYSIS; PSYCHOLOGY.)

JÜNGER, Ernst (1895–   ), German writer whose earlier works, such as *Storm of Steel* (1920), glorified war as a purifying factor in a corrupt society. He opposed Hitler and WWII, however, and later works such as *On the Marble Cliffs* (1939) call for a unifying peace.

JUNKER, Prussian landowner of the middle aristocracy. The junkers were powerful in the Prussian bureaucracy and army from the 17th century. In the 19th century the name was applied to German aristocratic conservatives generally.

JUNKERS, Hugo (1859–1935), German airplane engineer. He built the first internally braced cantilever monoplane in 1915. Junkers founded one of the early airlines and developed widely used passenger planes.

JUPITER, the largest and most massive planet in the solar system (diameter about 89,400mi, mass 317.8 times that of earth), fifth of the major planets from the sun. Jupiter is larger than all the other planets combined and, with a mean solar distance of 5.20AU and a "year" of 11.86 earth-years, is the greatest contributor to the solar system's angular MOMENTUM. Jupiter is believed to consist mainly of solid, liquid and gaseous HYDROGEN. Its disk, observed at close range by two US VOYAGER PROGRAM space probes in 1979, is marked by prominent cloud-belts paralleling its equator. These are occasionally interrupted by stormlike turbulences and particularly the Great Red Spot, an elliptical area about 30,000mi long and 10,000mi wide: unlike most other features of Jupiter's disk, which have a lifetime of a few days, it has been observed for about 150 years. Another long-term feature, the South Tropical Disturbance, was first observed in 1901 and disappeared in 1939. Jupiter's day is about 9.92h, and this high rotational velocity causes a visible flattening of the poles: the equatorial diameter is some 7% greater than the polar diameter. Jupiter has 16 known moons, the two largest of which, Callisto and Ganymede, are larger than MERCURY. Io exhibits volcanism, probably because of tidal action resulting from its close proximity to Jupiter. The planet also has a ring system, much fainter than that of Saturn and invisible from earth. Jupiter radiates energy, possibly because of nuclear reactions in its core or a gravitational contraction of the planet. Another US space mission to Jupiter, called Galileo, is scheduled for launching in 1989.

JURA MOUNTAINS, range in W Europe. It runs from the Rhône R to the R on the Swiss-German border, a series of heavily forested ridges crossed by gorges and with fertile valleys. The highest peak is Crêtede la Neige (5,652ft).

JURASSIC, the middle period of the Mesozoic era, lasting from about 190 to 135 million years ago. (See also GEOLOGY.)

JURISPRUDENCE. See LAW.

JURY, in COMMON LAW, body of people responsible for deciding points of fact in legal proceedings such as inquests and trials. The jury, probably a product of the Norman practice of calling character witnesses, was adopted from English law into the US system; the 6th and 7th Amendments to the Constitution provide for jury trial in most criminal and civil cases. A grand jury, usually of 23 persons, hears evidence and decides whether it should go for trial; a petit (small) jury of 12 persons sits at the trial proper and its verdict was until recently required to be unanimous. In 1970 and 1971, however, the Supreme Court held that six-person juries and less-than-unanimous verdicts were permissible in state (but not federal) criminal trials.

JUSTICE, US Department of, federal executive department created by Congress in 1870. Headed by the attorney general, its functions are to enforce federal laws, administer federal prisons and supervise district attorneys and marshals. It also represents the federal government in legal matters and legally advises the president.

JUSTIFICATION BY FAITH, Pauline doctrine that justification is given freely by God on the grounds of Christ's Atonement and by imputation of his righteousness. Justification is God's declaration that a person is righteous. The sinner is justified through believing in Jesus Christ, not by his own works. The Reformers, especially LUTHER, emphasized the doctrine in opposition to the popular medieval Roman Catholic belief in justification by works. It is no longer controversial.

JUSTINIAN I (483–565), Byzantine emperor 527–565, the last to rule in the West. His generals Belisarius and Narses reconquered Italy and North Africa 533–534. Justinian's attempts to impose heavy taxation and religious Orthodoxy on the diverse peoples and sects of the empire, especially the MONOPHYSITES, caused periodic unrest. In 532 political rivalries in the capital caused the Nika riots, quelled only by the decisiveness of the empress Theodora. Justinian commissioned the great *Digest* of Roman law and built such great churches as HAGIA SOPHIA and San Vitale.

JUSTIN MARTYR, Saint (c100–165), Christian theologian who conducted a school of Christian studies in Rome; he was martyred under Marcus Aurelius. His *Apology* defended Christianity against charges of impiety and sedition.

JUTES, Germanic people who originated in Scandinavia, probably in Jutland. With the

Angles and SAXONS they invaded Britain in the 5th century AD, settling in S and SE England. Their national identity was soon lost, although some cultural influence seems to have survived in Kent.

JUTLAND, peninsula in NW Europe, comprising continental Denmark and N Schleswig-Holstein state, West Germany.

JUTLAND, Battle of, only major naval battle in WWI, fought between the British and German fleets off the coast of Jutland on May 31, 1916, for domination of the North Sea. The British fleet under Admiral JELLICOE lost more ships but won a tactical victory.

JUVENAL (c60–130 AD), Roman poet whose 16 *Satires* (100–128 AD) are scathing attacks on the corruption of social and political life in Rome, which he contrasts with older standards. Many of his epigrammatic sayings—for example, "A sound mind in a sound body"—have passed into everyday use.

JUVENILE COURT, a court dealing with young offenders. Because children are not regarded as bearing legal responsibility for their actions, most juvenile courts seek to rehabilitate rather than punish. The first US juvenile court was established in Ill. in 1899; they are now found in every state. Their proceedings are less formal than those of adult courts, and they can deprive a minor of such civil rights as the right to remain silent, in order to achieve greater flexibility. The juvenile court has wide discretionary powers and may even remove children from their parents if the home environment seems harmful.

JUVENILE DELINQUENCY, term for crime committed by minors. The fact that youths, particularly males, are more active criminally than older persons is well known among criminologists. Sociologists suggest that in the US fully 90% of all adolescents commit at least one delinquent act. The majority of adolescents who engage in delinquent behavior are never caught and outgrow this proclivity. Chronic delinquents, however, may continue their criminal activity as adults but at diminishing rates. In 1985, 30.8% of all persons arrested for serious (crime index) crimes were under 18. Personal factors such as poor health, environmental factors such as cultural deprivation and the general emotional crises of adolescence are all seen as contributing to juvenile delinquency. Young offenders in the US are generally dealt with in juvenile courts. Often their sentences depend on reports from a social worker, psychiatrist or welfare worker, the policy being to "cure" rather than suppress criminal tendencies, but in extreme cases offenders may be sent to correctional institutions.

11th letter of the English alphabet, from the Semitic *kaph*, representing the palm of the hand, and the ancient Greek *kappa*. K stands for *King* in chess.

K2 (also, unofficially, Mt Godwin Austen or Dapsang), at 28,250ft the world's second highest peak after Mt Everest. Situated in the Karakoram Range in N Kashmir, it was first climbed in 1954.

KAABA, most sacred shrine of ISLAM, in the courtyard of the Great Mosque at Mecca, Saudi Arabia. Pilgrims must circle the flat-roofed Kaaba seven times and at its E corner kiss the Black Stone, which is said to have been given to Adam on his fall from paradise.

KABALEVSKY, Dmitri (1904–1987), Russian composer and critic. His work includes symphonies, ballet, chamber music and operas such as *Colas Breugnon* (1938) and *The Taras Family* (1949).

KABUKI, traditional Japanese popular theater which developed in the 17th century in contrast to the aristocratic NOH theater. A blending of dance, song and mime, the kabuki dramatized both traditional stories and contemporary events in a stylized but exuberant fashion. It remains popular today and has influenced much Western theatrical thought.

KABUL, capital and largest city of Afghanistan, lying in a mountain valley (elev. 5,900ft) on both banks of the Kabul R. The city is a commercial and manufacturing center with cement and textile industries. Founded in ancient times, Kabul fell to many conquerors because of its strategic location near important mountain passes. It was occupied by Russian troops in 1979. Pop 1,127,417.

KÁDÁR, János (1912–   ), Hungarian politician, premier in 1956–58 and 1961–65 and first secretary of the Socialist Workers' Party. As leader of the counter-revolutionaries during the 1956 anti-Soviet uprising, he had many rebel leaders executed. In power, while remaining close to the USSR, he allowed a slightly flexible "goulash communism" to evolve. In 1988 he was replaced as party leader by Károly Grósz.

KAFKA, Franz (1883–1924), German-language writer born in Prague of Jewish parents. Most of Kafka's stories confront his protagonists with nightmarish situations which they cannot resolve or escape from. They reflect his profound sense of alienation, and his inhibitions and shortcomings, particularly in relation to the powerful figure of his father. Kafka died of tuberculosis at age 40. His friend and executor Max BROD ignored his instructions to destroy all his work, and subsequently published Kafka's many short stories and his novels *The Trial* (1925), *The Castle* (1926) and *Amerika* (1927).

KAHN, Louis Isadore (1901–1974), US architect, noted for his work on housing projects and university buildings, particularly the Richards Medical Research Laboratories at the U. of Pennsylvania, where he was a professor.

KAHN, Otto Hermann (1867–1934), German-born US banker and patron of the arts. As a member of the New York Metropolitan Opera Company board he instituted many reforms, and appointed TOSCANINI as principal conductor.

KAISER, Henry John (1882–1967), US industrialist, founder of the Kaiser-Frazer Corporation. He contributed greatly to the Allied war effort in WWII by his development of faster production techniques for ships, aircraft and military vehicles, especially the famous "jeep."

KAISER, title, derived from Latin *Caesar*, sometimes used by rulers of the HOLY ROMAN EMPIRE (800–1806) and the German Empire (1871–1918).

KALAHARI DESERT, arid plain of some 100,000sq mi in S Africa. It lies mainly in Botswana but extends into Namibia and South Africa. The region has low annual rainfall and only seasonal pasture for sheep. It is inhabited only by Bushmen. There is a wide variety of game.

KALININ, Mikhail Ivanovich (1875–1946), Russian revolutionary leader. A loyal Stalinist, Kalinin was chairman of the central executive (now the presidium) from 1919 and a member of the Politburo from 1925.

KALMAR UNION, treaty whereby Denmark, Norway and Sweden were united under Margaret of Denmark and her heirs. It was signed at the Swedish port of Kalmar (1397), which became the Union's political center. The Union endured until 1523.

KALMUCK, or Kalmyk, a Mongoloid people who originally lived a wandering life in central Asia. Today Kalmucks live in parts of western China and in the Soviet Union, especially in the Kalmyk Autonomous Soviet Socialist Republic along the lower Volga River. The Kalmucks are short, sturdy people with flat Mongoloid faces. Most are Buddhists, but some are Muslims or Christians. The Kalmucks were traditionally fine horsemen and good soldiers. They originally raised horses and cattle and in more recent times have engaged in agriculture as well. Some Kalmucks emigrated to the US after World War II and settled in New Jersey.

KAMCHATKA PENINSULA, land area and oblast in the USSR which extends about 750mi S from NE Siberia to separate the Sea of Okhotsk from the Bering Sea. It is largely tundra and pine forest, and has Siberia's highest peak, Klyuchevskaya Sopka (15,584ft) and includes 22 active volcanoes, along with geysers and hot springs. Its main city is Petropavlovsk-Kamchatsky.

KAMEHAMEHA I (c1738–1819), Hawaiian monarch from 1790, a benevolent despot who united the islands (1810). He encouraged foreign contact and trade, but always sought to preserve the independence of his country and its people.

KAMENEV, Lev Borisovich (1883–1936), Russian politician, an associate of Lenin in exile. As president of the Moscow Soviet 1918–26, he sided with his brother-in-law TROTSKY and with ZINOVIEV against Stalin after Lenin's death (1924). Stalin used the murder of Sergei KIROV as a pretext for arresting Kamenev; he was executed after a "show-trial."

KAMIKAZE ("Divine Wind"), Japanese force of suicide pilots in WWII. Inspired by the ancient SAMURAI code of patriotic self-sacrifice, they deliberately crashed bomb-bearing planes onto Allied ships and installations. They inflicted particularly heavy damage at Okinawa.

KAMPUCHEA, formerly Cambodia, republic in SE Asia, known as the Khmer Republic, 1970–75. Laos lies to the N, Vietnam to the E and Thailand to the W and N.

Land. About half of Kampuchea is covered by tropical forest; at the center of the country the Mekong R flows from N to S, providing 900mi of navigable waterways. During the rainy season, May-Oct., the river backs up to the Tonle Sap Lake, vastly increasing its size and leaving rich fertile silt, excellent for rice production. There are two mountain ranges: the Dong Rek to the N and the Cardamom to the SW.

Official name: Democratic Kampuchea
Capital: Phnom Penh
Area: 69,898sq mi
Population: 7,688,000
Languages: Khmer; French
Religions: Hinayana Buddhist
Monetary unit(s): 1 riel = 100 sen

People. About 85% of the population are Khmers, with sizeable minorities of Chinese and Vietnamese, and smaller groups of Cham-Malays, Mayao-Polynesian and Austro-Asian hill tribes. The official language is Khmer but many people speak French. Kampuchea is one of the few countries in SE Asia which is sparsely populated and in which the majority of the people work in agriculture. The capital and largest city is Phnom Penh.

Economy. The economy was severely disrupted during most of the 1970s; famine was widespread in 1979 after warfare had prevented the planting of the rice crop. In normal times the principal product is rice. Other crops are corn, tobacco, sugar and pepper, and fishing is locally significant. Rubber cultivation was very important to the Cambodian economy and, like rice, was one of the largest exports. The rubber plantations were badly damaged in the fighting in the early 1970s and production has not recovered. Forests are extensive but underexploited. Mineral reserves, including phosphates and iron ore, are limited.

History. The Funan kingdom was established in Kampuchea for the first six centuries AD, but late in the 6th century the Funans were overcome by the Khmers from the neighboring Chenla state who founded the powerful KHMER EMPIRE. This empire, with its capital at ANGKOR, extended to modern Laos, Thailand and S Vietnam and lasted until the 15th century. From the 14th to the 19th centuries Cambodia's area was reduced by Thai conquests in the N and by the Annamese in the S. In 1863 Cambodia asked for, and was placed under, French protection. This lasted until 1954, when Cambodia became independent, largely owing to Prince Norodom SIHANOUK'S negotiations. Sihanouk, as head of state

from 1960, tried to keep Cambodia neutral in the VIETNAM WAR but this proved increasingly difficult. He broke off relations with the US, 1965–69, and allowed the Vietnamese communists to set up base camps in E Cambodia. In 1970 Gen. Lon Nol overthrew Sihanouk and, with US encouragement, attempted to drive out the Vietnamese. Meanwhile, a rebel insurgency developed controlled by the Khmer Rouge. The most extreme and violent faction of the Cambodian Communist Party, the Khmer Rouge was led by Saloth Sar, who adopted the pseudonym POL POT. In April 1975 the Khmer Rouge occupied the capital, Phnom Penh. They immediately ordered the evacuation of the cities, established a gigantic system of slave-labor camps in the countryside, and slaughtered hundreds of thousands of suspected opponents. Perhaps 1-3 million Cambodians were murdered or died of hunger, exhaustion, or disease. In 1979 Vietnam invaded Cambodia and established a pro-Vietnam government in Phnom Penh called the People's Republic of Kampuchea. It was resisted by three guerrilla forces combined under the title Coalition Government of Democratic Kampuchea, nominally headed by Sihanouk and recognized by the United Nations as the Cambodian government. The three forces were Sihanouk's own anticommunist National Front, the anticommunist Khmer People's National Liberation Front, and Pol Pot's Khmer Rouge. The US and other countries supported the two anticommunist groups; China supported the Khmer Rouge. In 1988 Vietnam began to withdraw its troops from Cambodia. The two anticommunist guerrilla forces continued to fight against the Vietnam-imposed government in Phnom Penh. The Khmer Rouge, however, the most powerful opposition group, made its own preparations for a rapid takeover once Vietnam troops were gone and the pro-Vietnam government collapsed.

KANDINSKY, Wassily (1866–1944), Russian painter, widely regarded as one of the fathers of ABSTRACT ART. A founder (1911) of the BLAUE REITER group of artists, he taught at the BAUHAUS design school 1922–33. His works, largely abstract, are characterized by their dynamic color and style.

KANE, Elisha Kent (1820–1857), US Arctic explorer and physician who led an expedition to find Sir John FRANKLIN and establish whether there was an open sea around the North Pole. He found neither but carried out much pioneering Arctic research.

KANGAROOS, MARSUPIAL mammals with large hind feet, strong hind limbs and a tail. Normally quadrupedal, they rise to a bipedal stance when moving quickly, progressing in huge leaps. The tail in true kangaroos is heavily built and serves to balance the body in bipedal locomotion. It may also be used as a prop during fighting when a kangaroo can kick with both hind feet together. Female kangaroos have a pouch containing the teats, in which the young, born singly and at a very "premature" stage, are raised. Kangaroos are herbivorous; the alimentary canal shows strong similarities to the stomach of placental, ruminant mammals. A diverse group, kangaroos include true kangaroos, WALLABIES, tree kangaroos and rat kangaroos.

KANSAS, state, central US, bounded to the E by Mo., to the S by Okla., to the W by Col. and to the N by Neb. The state's name was derived from the Kansas or Kansa Indians, earliest inhabitants of the area.

Name of state: Kansas
Capital: Topeka
Statehood: Jan. 29, 1861 (34th state)
Familiar name: Sunflower State
Area: 82,264sq mi
Population: 2,460,000
Elevation: Highest—4,039ft., Mt. Sunflower. Lowest—680ft., Verdigris River in Montgomery County
Motto: *Ad astra per aspera* ("To the stars through difficulties")
State flower: Sunflower
State bird: Western meadowlark
State tree: Cottonwood
State song: "Home on the Range"
Land. Kansas is not all prairie, as is sometimes thought. Its soils are generally dark, fertile loam, irrigated by a system of over 100 artificial lakes. The two major river systems are the Kansas and the Arkansas, with their tributaries. Kansas has cold winters and warm to hot summers. Rainfall averages about 40in in the SE and under 18in in the W.
People. The population is concentrated in the E of the state and, reflecting the change from a farm to a mixed farm-factory economy, nearly two-thirds live in urban areas. Kansas is still governed under its original constitution of 1859.
Economy. Since WWII manufacturing has developed rapidly and is now the state's chief money earner. Kansas is the nation's largest wheat producer, and livestock, dairy products and poultry account for a major proportion of agricultural income. Petroleum, natural gas and helium are important mineral resources. Principal manufactures include processed foods, aerospace equipment, farm machinery and petroleum products.
History. The Kansas area remained in European hands for some time, but in 1803 the US acquired most of Kansas under the LOUISIANA PURCHASE and used the region for Indian resettlement from the E. The cutting of the SANTA FE TRAIL (1821) and the OREGON TRAIL (1830) led to the first permanent white settlements. In 1854 the KANSAS-NEBRASKA ACT made the territory the focus of the growing slavery problem, a dispute which resulted in virtual civil war. Anti-slavery forces finally gained control and in 1861 Kansas achieved statehood. After the Civil War came rapid settlement and economic expansion, aided by railroad construction and cattle ranching in the W; mineral exploitation in WWI and growth in manufacturing industries after WWII gave Kansas a solid industrial, agricultural and mining economy. In the mid-1980s, manufacturing, especially aerospace, boomed, but lower prices for oil and farm products slowed economic growth. The state's farm economy was hard hit by the 1988 drought. In presidential elections 1968–88, Kansas voted consistently Republican.

KANSAS-NEBRASKA ACT, bill passed by Congress in 1854 which upset the balance of power between slave and free states and helped bring on the Civil War. It established Kansas and Nebraska with a provision that each territory, and subsequent ones, could decide for itself whether or not to introduce slavery. Settlers were poured in by both North and South in an attempt to establish control. The act upset the MISSOURI COMPROMISE (1820–21) and led to the formation of the REPUBLICAN PARTY.

KANT, Immanuel (1724–1804), German philosopher, one of the world's greatest thinkers. He was born and lived in Königsberg (Kaliningrad). The starting point for Kant's "critical" philosophy was the work of David HUME, who awakened Kant from his "dogmatic slumber" and led him to make his "Copernican revolution in philosophy." This consisted of the radical view found in *Critique of Pure Reason* (1781) that objective reality (the phenomenal world) can be known only because the mind imposes the forms of its own intuitions—time and space—upon it. Things that cannot be perceived in experience (noumena) cannot be known, but as Kant says in *Critique of Practical Reason* (1788) their existence must be presumed in order to provide for man's free will (see CATEGORICAL IMPERATIVE). In his third major work, *Critique of Judgment* (1790), his aesthetic and teleological judgments serve to mediate between the sensible and intelligible worlds which he divided sharply in the first two *Critiques*.

KAOLIN, or china clay, soft, white clay composed chiefly of kaolinite, mined in England, France, Saxony, Czechoslovakia, China and the S US. It is used for filling and coating paper, filling rubber and paints and for making POTTERY and PORCELAIN.

KAPITZA, Peter Leonidovich (1894–1984), Russian physicist best known for his work on low-temperature physics (see CRYOGENICS), especially his discovery of the superfluidity of HELIUM II. During the 1920s and early 1930s he worked at England's Cavendish Laboratory and directed the Institute for Physical Problems after he returned to the USSR (1934). He was an outspoken advocate of freedom of thought and scientific exchange and was awarded the 1978 Nobel Prize for Physics.

KARACHI, former capital (1947–59) and largest city of Pakistan. The country's major port and industrial center, it stands on the Arabian Sea near the Indus Delta in Sind province, of which it is the capital. Among its manufactures are automobiles, steel, petroleum products and textiles. Karachi began to develop as a trading center in the early 18th century. Pop 5,180,262.

KARAJAN, Herbert von (1908–1989), Austrian conductor. He directed the Berlin State Opera 1938–45; the Vienna State Opera 1954–64 and concurrently from 1954 the Berlin Philharmonic Orchestra.

KARAKORAM RANGE, mountain chain in N Kashmir, extending for some 300mi between India, China and Tibet. Among its 60 or so peaks it has the world's second highest mountain, K2 (28,250ft).

KARAKORUM, ancient capital of Genghis Khan's empire. Its ruins stand in what is now the Mongolian People's Republic, on the Orhon R. Established early in the 13th century, it had fallen into decay by the 16th century. Marco POLO visited here around

1275.

KARAMANLIS, Constantine (1907–), Greek statesman who in 1974 returned to national acclaim as prime minister and leader of the New Democratic Party after the overthrow of the Colonels' junta (1967–74). He served as prime minister (1974–80) and president (1980–85).

KARATE, unarmed combat and sport, originating in ancient China, popularized throughout the world by the Japanese. Calloused skin pads are developed on hands, knees, elbows and feet, which are all used to deliver blows against vulnerable pressure points on the body. (See also JUDO.)

KARLFELDT, Erik Axel (1864–1931), Swedish poet who received the 1931 Nobel Prize for Literature.

KARMA, Sanskrit term denoting the inevitable effect of man's actions on his destiny in successive lives, central to Buddhist and Hindu thought. (See also TRANSMIGRATION OF SOULS.)

KÁRMÁN, Theodore von (1881–1963), Hungarian-born US aeronautics engineer best known for his mathematical approach to problems in aeronautics (especially in jet engineering) and astronautics.

KARNAK, village E of LUXOR, on the Nile in Central Egypt, part of ancient THEBES. It is the site of the famous temple of Amon, perhaps the finest example of ancient Egyptian religious architecture.

KARPOV, Anatoly (1951–), Soviet chess player. He became (1975) world champion by default when Bobby Fischer refused to defend his title. He lost the title to Garri Kasparov in 1985 and failed to regain it in a 1987 match.

KARSH, Yousuf (1908–), Turkish-Armenian born Canadian portrait photographer, whose company used the professional name Karsh of Ottawa. In 1935 he was appointed the Canadian government's official photographer.

KASAVUBU, Joseph (c1915–1969), African politician, first president of the Republic of Congo (now Zaire) 1960–65. He ousted Premier Patrice LUMUMBA but was himself supplanted (1965) by Col. Joseph MOBUTU.

KASHMIR, territory administered since 1972 by India (Jammu and Kashmir) and Pakistan (Azad Kashmir), bordered by those countries and by Afghanistan and China. Ever since Indian partition in 1947 the territory, which was formerly one of India's largest princely states, has been a cause of conflict between India and Pakistan, with some interference from China 1959–63, cease-fire lines being drawn and redrawn repeatedly. An agreement in 1972 confirmed the positions held by both sides at the end of the 1971 war. The Jhelum R forms the rich and scenically beautiful Vale of Kashmir. The region is mainly agricultural but also produces timber, medicines, silk, carpets and perfume oil. The chief cities are Srinagar (Jammu) and Muzaffarabad (Azad).

KASKASKIA, historic settlement, now almost uninhabited, on Kaskaskia Island in the Mississippi R, SE Ill. It was Illinois Territory capital (1809–18) and state capital (1818–20). Persistent flooding restricted further development.

KASPAROV, Garri Kimovich (1963–   ), Soviet chess player who became the youngest world champion in history when he defeated Anatoly Karpov in 1985. He retained the title in a 1987 match with Karpov.

KATAYEV, Valentin Petrovich (1897–1986), Russian novelist and playwright. Among his best-known works are the novels *The Embezzlers* (1927), *Lonely White Sail* (1936), *The Small Farm in the Steppe* (1956) and the farce *Squaring the Circle* (1928).

KATHMANDU, capital of Nepal, in a high valley of the E Himalayas. It stands on an ancient route from India to Tibet and China and remains an important transportation center. Pop (metro) 235,160.

KATYN FOREST, site in the USSR of a massacre of some 4,250 Polish officers in WWII. The mass grave was reported in 1943 by the Germans, who accused the Russians, who in their turn accused the Germans. Stalin refused a Red Cross enquiry; the Polish government in exile in London took this as an admission of Russian guilt.

KAUFMAN, George Simon (1889–1961), US dramatist who collaborated on several successful plays noted for their dry satirical humor. Among his works are, with Marc Connelly, *Beggar on Horseback* (1924); and with Moss Hart *You Can't Take it With You* (1936). He won Pulitzer prizes in 1932 and 1937.

KAUNDA, Kenneth David (1924–   ), first president of Zambia, from 1964. From 1953 he worked ardently for African rule in the then British colony of N Rhodesia, suffering exile and imprisonment. Released in 1960, he headed the new United National Independence Party. Kaunda maintained a hard line against white regimes in southern Africa.

KAUTSKY, Karl Johann (1854–1938), German Marxist. Influenced by Eduard Bernstein, and a friend of ENGELS, he was a great popularizer of MARXISM. After the revolution in Russia (1917) he became a staunch opponent of BOLSHEVISM

KAVAFIS, Konstantinos Petrou, or **Constantine Cavafy** (1863–1933), Greek poet. He spent most of his life in his native Alexandria. His ironic poetry, of great breadth and dramatic power, has proved widely influential since his death.

KAWABATA, Yasunari (1899–1972), Japanese novelist. He is noted for his impressionistic, lyrical style and a preoccupation with loneliness and death; he finally committed suicide. One of his best-known works is *Snow Country* (1947). He was awarded the 1968 Nobel Prize for Literature.

KAY, John (1704–c1764), British inventor of the flying shuttle (patented 1733), which greatly increased the speed of WEAVING while reducing the number of workers required.

KAZAKHSTAN, one of the 15 main republics of the Soviet Union, covering 1,048,030 sq mi of central Asia, from the Caspian Sea in the west to the Chinese frontier in the east. Over 50% of the population is Russian and Ukrainian, the Kazakhs forming nearly 30%. The capital is Alma-Ata. An important producer of wheat, cotton, sheep and cattle, Kazakhstan is also one of the Soviet Union's leading industrial republics. Its rich mineral deposits include coal, tungsten, oil, copper, lead, zinc, nickel, chrome and manganese.

KAZAN, Elia (1909–   ), Turkish-born US film and stage director best known for realistic films on social issues, such as *On the Waterfront* (1954). Among his many other films are *A Streetcar Named Desire* (1951) and *Viva Zapata!* (1952). He wrote and directed *The Arrangement* (1967) and *The Assassins* (1972).

KAZANTZAKIS, Nikos (1883?–1957), prolific Greek writer and statesman, minister of public welfare 1919–27 and minister of state 1945–46. Among his best-known works are the novels *Zorba the Greek* (1946) and *The Greek Passion* (1951) and his epic poem *The Odyssey: A Modern Sequel* (1938).

KAZIN, Alfred (1915–   ), influential US critic. His book *On Native Grounds* (1942) was a major study of contemporary US prose literature. His autobiographical *Walker in the City* (1951) is an evocation of a Brooklyn Jewish childhood.

KEAN, Edmund (1787–1833), leading English actor of his time. His greatest roles were in Shakespearian tragedy, notably as Othello, to which he introduced a dynamic naturalistic style.

KEARNY, Stephen Watts (1794–1848), US general. During the MEXICAN WAR (1846–48) he conquered N.M. by diplomacy, persuading the more powerful Mexican force to withdraw peacefully. He subdued Cal. also, despite conflict with fellow-officers Robert Stockton and John FRÉMONT. Governor of Vera Cruz and Mexico City in 1848, he died there of yellow fever.

KEATON, (Joseph Frank) Buster (1895–1966), US silent-film comedian. In such films as *The Navigator* (1924) and *The General* (1926), now considered masterpieces of comic inventiveness, he created the character of an innocent in conflict with malevolent machinery. His apparently deadpan face was actually subject to a considerable range of subtle expressions.

KEATS, John (1795–1821), one of the greatest English Romantic poets. He gave up medicine in 1816 to devote himself to poetry. His earlier poems and the Spenserian epic *Endymion* (1817) attracted little attention except politically motivated abuse. In 1817 his brother Tom died of tuberculosis, and his own health suffered after a long walking tour. The epic *Hyperion*, the ballad *La Belle Dame sans Merci* and *The Eve of St. Agnes* were written at this time. A developing romance with Fanny Brawne was offset by serious financial troubles caused by his guardian. In May 1819 he wrote the four great odes—*To a Nightingale, On a Grecian Urn, On Melancholy,* and *On Indolence. Lamia* and *To Autumn,* effectively his last works, followed that summer. In Jan. 1820 he developed definite tuberculosis symptoms. Taken to winter in Italy, he died in Rome, where he is buried.

KEFAUVER, (Carey) Estes (1903–1963), US Democratic politician, senator from Tennessee from 1949. He sought the Democratic presidential nomination in 1952 and 1956 and ran unsuccessfully for vice president on the 1956 ticket headed by Adlai Stevenson. He chaired Senate investigations of crime, the pharmaceutical industry, and professional sports.

KEITEL, Wilhelm (1882–1946), German field-marshal, head of the armed forces high command during WWII. A man of little ability or experience, he was primarily Hitler's puppet. He was convicted at NUREMBERG of violations of international law and executed.

KEKULÉ VON STRADONITZ, Friedrich August (1829–1896), German chemist regarded as the father of modern ORGANIC CHEMISTRY. At the same time as **Archibald Scott Couper** (1831–1892) he recognized the quadrivalency of CARBON and its ability to form long chains. With his later inference of the structure of BENZENE (the "benzene ring"), structural organic chemistry was born.

KELLER, Helen Adams (1880–1968), US author and lecturer. Born blind, deaf and dumb, she became famous for her triumph over her disabilities. Taught by Anne SULLIVAN from 1887, she learned to read, write and speak, and graduated from Radcliffe College, Cambridge, Mass., with honors in 1904. Her books include *The Story of My Life* (1902) and *Helen Keller's Journal* (1938).

KELLEY, Florence (1859–1932), US social reformer and lawyer. A campaigner for labor legislation to protect women and children, she was director of the National Consumer's League from 1899.

KELLOGG, Frank Billings (1856–1937), US diplomat, senator 1917–23 and ambassador to Britain 1923–25. His most important achievement was the KELLOGG-BRIAND PACT of 1928. A judge of the Permanent Court of International Justice 1930–35, he was awarded the 1929 Nobel Peace Prize.

KELLOGG, Will Keith (1860–1951), US industrialist and philanthropist. He made his fortune through the breakfast cereal industry he established in 1906 at Battle Creek, Mich., originally to manufacture the cornflakes developed as a health food by his physician brother.

KELLOGG-BRIAND PACT, agreement signed on Aug. 27, 1928, by 15 nations (later observed by 64 others) renouncing "war as an instrument of national policy." Conceived by Aristide BRIAND of France and Secretary of State F. B. Kellogg of the US, it left many loopholes, and ultimately proved ineffectual.

KELLY, Edward Joseph (1876–1950), US Democratic politician, mayor of Chicago 1933–47 and one of the country's most powerful political bosses.

KELLY, Emmett (1898–1979), US circus clown. He created "Weary Willie," the mournful clown who chased elusive spotlights and "cleaned" the ring with a frayed old broom. He appeared with circuses throughout Britain and the US.

KELLY, Petra (Petra Karin Lehmann; 1947–), German politician. Raised and politically active in the US, she returned to Europe in 1970. Disillusioned with the German Social Democratic Party, she helped found (1979) the Green Party, a loose alliance of environmentalists, antinuclear activists, feminists, and independent Marxists. Campaigning (1983) against the deployment of US missiles in Germany, Kelly and 26 other Greens were elected to parliament.

KELLY, Walt (1913–1973), US cartoonist, creator (1948) of the comic strip *Pogo*.

KELSEN, Hans (1881–1972), Austrian-born US legal scholar, at Harvard Law School (1940–43) and the U of California at Berkeley (1943–73). He was one of the century's most important theorists of international law.

KELVIN, William Thomson, 1st Baron (1824–1907), British physicist who made important contributions to many branches of physics. In attempting to reconcile CARNOT's theory of heat engines and JOULE's mechanical theory of HEAT he both formulated (independently of CLAUSIUS) the 2nd Law of THERMODYNAMICS and introduced the absolute temperature scale, the unit of which is called Kelvin for him. His and FARADAY's work on ELECTROMAGNETISM gave rise to the theory of the the electromagnetic field, and his papers, with those of Faraday, strongly influenced J. Clerk MAXWELL's work on the electromagnetic theory of LIGHT (though Kelvin himself rejected Maxwell's over-abstract theory). His work on wire-telegraphic signaling played an essential part in the successful laying of the first ATLANTIC CABLE.

KENDALL, Edward Calvin (1886–1972), US biochemist awarded with P.S. Hench and Tadeus Reichstein the 1950 Nobel Prize for Physiology or Medicine for his work on the corticoids and isolation of cortisone (see STEROIDS), applied by Hench to the treatment of rheumatoid ARTHRITIS.

KENNAN, George Frost (1904–   ), US diplomat, one of the main authors of the US postwar policy of "containment" of Russian expansionism. Ambassador to the USSR 1952 and Yugoslavia in 1961–63, he wrote *Russia Leaves the War* (1956), for which he received the Pulitzer Prize, and *Memoirs, 1925–1950* (1968), which won another Pulitzer.

KENNEDY, Anthony M. (1936–   ), US jurist. An appeals court judge 1976–88, he was appointed an associate justice of the US Supreme Court in 1988.

KENNEDY, Edward Moore (1932–   ), US political leader. The brother of President John Kennedy, he was elected to the Senate from Massachusetts in 1962. With the deaths of his brothers John and Robert, he became a national leader of the Democratic party and an articulate advocate of liberal causes. His career suffered (1969) when a woman companion drowned after he drove his car off a bridge on Chappaquiddick Island. He challenged President Carter for the 1980 presidential nomination, but failed.

KENNEDY, John Fitzgerald (1917–1963), 35th president of the US, was the youngest man and the first Roman Catholic to be elected president; he was the fourth president to be assassinated. The second son of Joseph P. KENNEDY, he was brought up in Boston and New York. Popular but undistinguished at school, he was overshadowed by his older brother Joseph Jr., upon whom their father's ambitions focused. In his senior year at Harvard in 1939, however, his thesis on British policies leading to the MUNICH AGREEMENT was well-received and published as *Why England Slept* (1940). He joined the US Navy in 1941; when his torpedo boat was sunk by the Japanese in 1943 he led survivors to safety, himself towing an injured man three miles through rough seas. His already bad health was seriously weakened by a back injury and malaria, and he was discharged in 1945 with the Purple Heart and the Navy and Marine Corps medal. His brother Joseph had been killed in 1944 and the family ambition now rested on him. In 1952 he was elected senator (D-Mass.), taking a position on the moderate right. In 1953 he married Jacqueline Bouvier. While convalescing after operations on his injured back he wrote *Profiles in Courage* (1956); a study of US statesmen who put national interest before party, it won the Pulitzer Prize for biography in 1957. By 1957 he was becoming known for his liberal views on race, social and foreign issues.

Narrowly missing the 1956 vice-presidential nomination, in 1960 he was nominated as Democratic presidential candidate, running with Lyndon B. Johnson, and defeated Richard M. Nixon in the election. The abortive BAY OF PIGS invasion of Cuba in 1961 rocked the new administration, but the action was supported by both parties. More serious was the growing confrontation with the USSR under KHRUSHCHEV over West Berlin. Kennedy met the Russian challenge with equal obstinacy and the crisis was gradually defused, despite the construction of the BERLIN WALL. A more serious confrontation threatened in Oct., 1962, when aerial reconnaissance revealed Russian missile bases under construction in Cuba. Kennedy immediately imposed a quarantine on all weapons shipments to Cuba, threatening to search and turn back any such consignments. After a week of tense confrontation the USSR capitulated, a considerable victory for Kennedy, as was his part in persuading the USSR to sign a limited nuclear test-ban treaty, a significant check to COLD WAR policies. A massive foreign aid program for Latin America and his support of the European COMMON MARKET won him considerable support abroad. On Nov. 22, 1963, he was shot dead by Lee Harvey OSWALD in a motorcade through Dallas, Tex. Theories of a conspiracy are unsupported by evidence.

KENNEDY, Joseph Patrick (1888–1969), US businessman and diplomat. Having amassed a fortune in banking, the stock market and other areas in the 1920s, he was active in government and served as US ambassador to Britain 1937–40. His sons John Fitzgerald and Robert Francis were both assassinated in high office; his fourth son, Edward, continues to represent the family in politics.

KENNEDY, Robert Francis (1925–1968). Younger brother of John F. KENNEDY, he served as US attorney general 1961–64 and was senator for New York from 1965. After his brother's death, he became a popular leader of the liberal wing of the Democratic Party and ran as presidential candidate in 1968. On June 4, 1968, the evening of his victory in the Cal. primary, he was assassinated by Sirhan Sirhan.

KENNESAW MOUNTAIN, Battle of, fought in the Civil War near Atlanta, Ga., on June 27, 1864. Union troops under Gen. William SHERMAN made a frontal attack on Confederate positions but were repulsed with heavy losses. They forced a Confederate withdrawal by outflanking.

KENNY, Sister Elizabeth (1886–1952), Australian nurse best known for developing the treatment of infantile paralysis (see POLIOMYELITIS) by stimulating and reeducating the muscles affected.

KENSINGTON RUNE STONE, found in 1898 on a farm near Kensington, Minn. Inscribed in RUNES dated 1362 is an account of Norse exploration of the Great Lakes of North America. The stone is in a special museum in Alexandria, Minn., but most scholars now think it to be a forgery.

KENT, James (1763–1847), American jurist. He was the first professor of law at Columbia College 1794–98 and judge (from 1798) and chief judge (from 1804) of the N.Y. supreme court. As chancellor of the N.Y. court of chancery (1814–23) he revived EQUITY law in the US. He wrote the monumental *Commentaries on American Law* (1826–30).

KENT, Rockwell (1882–1971), US writer

and artist. He is best known for his illustrations of popular classics and his own works, which include *Wilderness* (1921) and *This is My Own* (1940).

KENTUCKY, state, E central US, bounded to the E by W.V. and Va., to the S by Tenn., to the W by Mo. and to the N by Ill., Ind., and Ohio.

Name of state: Kentucky
Capital: Frankfort
Statehood: June 1, 1792 (15th state)
Familiar name: Bluegrass State
Area: 40,395sq mi
Population: 3,729,000
Elevation: Highest—4,145ft, Black Mountain. Lowest—257ft, Mississippi River in Fulton County
Motto: "United we stand, divided we fall"
State flower: Goldenrod
State bird: Cardinal
State tree: Kentucky coffee tree
State song: "My Old Kentucky Home"
Land. The state is roughly triangular in shape and may be divided into three regions. In the W, the land slopes down to the Jackson Purchase Area, including swampland flanking the Mississippi R. The Interior Low Plateau consists of the W coalfield and the gently rolling Bluegrass Region, where there are rich soils and where the largest cities and major industries are also situated. The blue blossoms of the grasses around Lexington, in this region, have given Kentucky its nickname. The third land region, the Appalachian Plateau, is a mountainous area of narrow valleys, in which the CUMBERLAND GAP is one of the few natural passes to the West. The most important rivers are the Ohio and the Tennessee, dammed at Gilbertsville to create Kentucky Lake. Kentucky has a mild climate with warm summers and cool winters.
People. The majority of Kentuckians now live in urban areas, the drift to the cities having been considerable through the past 50 years. Louisville and Lexington are the chief cities.
Economy. Industry is concentrated along the Ohio R; the chief products are

foodstuffs, machinery, textiles, metal products and cigarettes. Kentucky is the second largest producer of tobacco in the US. Other important products are coal, gas, oil, livestock, grains and bourbon whiskey. Kentucky, home of the world-famous KENTUCKY DERBY, ranks first in the US in thoroughbred racehorse breeding.

History. The first permanent settlement was established by James Harrod in 1774 after Daniel BOONE's expeditions over the Appalachians 1769–71. After the Revolutionary War, new settlers flowed in. In 1792 a constitution for the Commonwealth of Kentucky was adopted and in the same year Kentucky became the 15th state in the Union. On the eve of the Civil War, Kentucky had vast tobacco plantations worked by slaves, but as much of the land was occupied by small farmers raising corn and hogs, the state was divided during the war. The legislature declared allegiance to the Union although a good number of Kentuckians enlisted in the Confederate armies.

After the war, burley tobacco became the mainstay of Kentucky's agriculture, though the new railroads opened up the coalfields of the Appalachians. Following the depression years of the 1930s, WWII brought economic recovery and since then industrial expansion has continued. Coal production increased during the energy crises of the 1970s, but poverty persisted in Appalachian mining towns. The state experienced an economic slump during most of the 1980s. In presidential elections 1968–88, Kentucky voted Republican in 1968–72 and 1980–88.

KENTUCKY AND VIRGINIA RESOLUTIONS, passed by the legislatures of Ky. and Va. in 1798 and 1799, after the Federalist-controlled Congress had passed the ALIEN AND SEDITION ACTS. The Kentucky Resolutions, drafted by Thomas JEFFERSON, claimed that the federal government was the result of a compact between the states. If it assumed powers not specifically delegated to it, the states could declare any acts under these powers unconstitutional. The Virginia resolutions, drafted by James MADISON, declared the same theory in milder form. The resolutions were concerned principally with individual civil liberties, but John CALHOUN and other Southern leaders used them as the basis for the doctrines of NULLIFICATION and SECESSION.

KENTUCKY DERBY, famous US horse-race. It is an annual classic for three-year-olds run over a course of 1¼mi at Churchill Downs, Louisville, Ky. It was founded in 1875 by Col. M. Lewis Clark. (See also HORSE RACING.)

KENYA, East African republic, bounded by the Sudan, Ethiopia, Somalia, Uganda and Tanzania, famous for its national parks and game reserves.

Official name: Republic of Kenya
Capital: Nairobi
Area: 224,961sq mi
Population: 22,020,000
Languages: English, Swahili, Kikuyu, Luo widely spoken
Religions: Animist, Christian, Muslim, Hindu
Monetary unit(s): 1 Kenya shilling=100 cents

Land. The country straddles the equator and has four main regions: the narrow fertile coastal strip, with rain forests and mango swamps; the vast dry scrubland pastures of the Niyika, crossed by Kenya's two chief rivers, the Tana and the Athi; the highlands, cut by the Great Rift Valley, where Mt Kenya (17,058ft) and Mt Elgon (14,178ft) stand and where the rich volcanic soil, moderate temperatures and ample rainfall provide most farm crops; the western (Nyanza) plateau, stretching to Lake Victoria, an area of farmlands, forests and grasslands.

People. Nearly 98% of the population is African, comprising more than 40 ethnic groups, chief among which are the Kikuyu. There are also Indian, Arab and European (primarily British) communities. More than eight million Kenyans live in the SW, mainly in the highlands where Nairobi, the capital and largest city, is situated.

Economy. Agriculture is the major occupation, with coffee, tea, timber, fruit and vegetables the main exports. Chief industries center around food processing, textiles, footwear and clothing. There is also a large livestock industry. Kenya has few natural resources, and its reliance upon imported oil places a strain on the economy. Hydroelectric power sources and a geothermal power project are being developed. Tourism is also important.

History. Until 1887 the coast was under

Arab control; the British then opened the interior with imported Indian labor and encouraged European settlement. In 1944 the first African nationalist party was set up, Jomo KENYATTA becoming its leader in 1947. Discontent led to the formation of the MAU MAU terrorist organization. Pacified by reforms, Kenya gained independence in 1963, becoming a republic in 1964 under Kenyatta's presidency. In 1978 Kenyatta died. His vice president and successor, Daniel arap Moi, transformed Kenya into a one-party state. In 1988 he began his third five-year term as president.

KENYATTA, Jomo (1893?–1978), Kenya's first president (1964–78). His early political career was concerned with rights of his Kikuyu people. In 1953 he was imprisoned on charges of leading the MAU MAU. His release came in 1961 following pressure from African nationalists. Kenyatta was one of the most influential of the early African nationalist leaders, and his policies preserved Kenya's stability and prosperity.

KEPLER, Johannes (1571–1630), German astronomer who, using BRAHE'S superbly accurate observations of the planets, advanced COPERNICUS' heliocentric model of the SOLAR SYSTEM in showing that the planets followed elliptical paths. His three laws (see KEPLER'S LAWS) were later the template about which NEWTON formulated his theory of GRAVITATION. Kepler also did important work in optics, discovering a fair approximation for the law of REFRACTION.

KEPLER'S LAWS, three laws formulated by Johannes KEPLER to describe the motions of the planets in the solar system. (1) Each planet orbits the sun in an ellipse of which the sun is at one focus. (2) The line between a planet and the sun sweeps out equal areas in equal times: hence the planet moves faster when closer to the sun than it does when farther away. (3) The square of the time taken by a planet to ORBIT the sun is proportional to the cube of its mean distance from the sun.

KERENSKY, Alexander Feodorovich (1881–1970), Russian moderate revolutionary leader and head of the provisional government July to Oct. 1917. Overthrown in the Bolshevik Revolution (October 1917), he emigrated to Western Europe and in 1940 went to the US. His books include *The Catastrophe* (1927) and *The Kerensky Memoirs* (1966).

KERN, Jerome David (1885–1945), US composer. His most famous work is the score of *Show Boat* (1927) which includes the song "Ol' Man River." Among his classic songs are "Smoke Gets in Your Eyes" and "The Song is You."

KERNER COMMISSION, appointed by President L. B. Johnson in 1967 to investigate the causes of the race riots of the mid-1960s. The commission, headed by Gov. Otto Kerner of Ill., put most of the blame on "white racism." It concluded that the US was moving towards two societies, one black and one white— "separate but unequal." It suggested improvements in schools and housing and better police protection for residents of black ghettoes:

KEROSENE, or paraffin oil, a mixture of volatile HYDROCARBONS having 10 to 16 carbon atoms per molecule, used as a FUEL for jet engines (see JET PROPULSION), for heating and lighting and as a solvent and paint thinner. Although it can be derived from oil, coal and tar, most is produced from PETROLEUM by refining and cracking—it was the major product until gasoline's ascendancy. Kerosene boils between 150°C and 300°C.

KEROUAC, Jack (1922–1969), US novelist. His best-known book is *On the Road* (1957), describing his life of freedom from conventional middle-class ties and values. He was a leading figure of the BEAT GENERATION.

KESSELRING, Albert (1885–1960), German field marshal of WWII. He became commander in chief in Italy (1943) and in the West (1945). He was convicted of war crimes (1947) and sentenced to life imprisonment, but was released in 1952.

KETTERING, Charles Franklin (1876–1958), US inventor of the first electric cash register and the electric self-starter, who made many significant contributions to AUTOMOBILE technology.

KETTLEDRUM. See TIMPANI.

KEY, Francis Scott (1779–1843), American lawyer who wrote the words to the STAR-SPANGLED BANNER. He wrote it after witnessing the night bombardment of Fort McHenry by the British in September 1814. It became the national anthem of the US by act of Congress (1931).

KEY, in music, the prescribed system of tones forming a major or minor scale, often used synonomously with TONALITY. It includes all the tones in the scale, and the chords built upon them, and receives its name from the lowest note of the scale to which it belongs. Thus the key of C Major has C as its principal note. In musical notation the key of a piece of music is shown at the beginning by the key signature, composed of the sharps and flats necessary for that particular key.

KEYBOARD INSTRUMENTS, musical instruments played by depressing a row of levers called keys. The organ has keyboards for both hands and feet but the term usually refers to instruments like the harpsichord and piano which have a keyboard consisting of long keys covered with ivory, and short keys covered with ebony, which when pressed by the fingers hit or pluck a string to produce a note. Since WWII, the name has also been applied to instruments with keyboards that produce piano-like or organ-like notes electrically.

KEYNES, John Maynard, 1st Baron Keynes of Tilton (1883–1946), British economist at Cambridge University, a major pioneer in the development of modern economics. He resigned in protest as treasury representative at the VERSAILLES Peace Conference, stating his objections to the possible outcome of the treaty in *The Economic Consequences of the Peace* (1919). His chief work, *The General Theory of Employment, Interest, and Money* (1936), formed the basis of the "new" or Keynesian economics. It argued against the traditional idea that the economy was best left to run itself and showed how government policies could maintain high levels of economic activity and employment. He attended the BRETTON WOODS CONFERENCE. Keynes was a prominent member of the BLOOMSBURY GROUP. (See also KEYNESIAN ECONOMICS.)

KEYNESIAN ECONOMICS, economic theories of John Maynard KEYNES and other theories derived from them. In analyzing the causes of the GREAT DEPRESSION, Keynes focused on the relationship among demand, production, and unemployment. He concluded that when national demand falls critically short of productive capacity, this leads to a state of economic depression—high unemployment, low prices, business stagnation—that may last indefinitely. In the Keynesian view, the cure is to create demand by government spending and low taxes; excessive demand, by contrast, leads to inflation and should be curbed by tight-budget policies.

KHACHATURIAN, Aram Ilich (1903–1978), Soviet-Armenian composer, greatly influenced by the folk music of Armenia and other Soviet nationalities. He is famous for the *Violin Concerto* (1940) and the "Saber Dance" in his ballet *Gayne* (1942).

KHAFRE, Egyptian pharaoh of the 4th dynasty who reigned late in the 26th century BC. He built the second pyramid at Giza, smaller only than that of his father KHUFU (Cheops).

KHALID IBN ABDUL-AZIZ (1913–1982), king of Saudi Arabia. Appointed crown prince in 1965, he acceded to the throne in 1975 on the death of his brother FAISAL. His regime showed some restraint on oil prices and otherwise took cautious positions on Middle East issues.

KHARTOUM, capital of Sudan, at the junction of the White and Blue Niles, a cotton trading center linked by rail and river to Egypt and Port Sudan. General GORDON was killed here in 1885 defending the city against the MAHDI. Pop 561,000.

KHAZARS, a Turkic people whose empire in S Russia and the Caucasus controlled trade between the N Slavs, Byzantium and the Far East from c550 until the Byzantines and Russians overwhelmed it (969–1030). The king and nobility adopted Judaism c740.

KHMER EMPIRE, ancient Cambodian empire dating from the 6th century, which at its acme under the Angkors occupied much of modern Laos, Thailand and South Vietnam. The capital, Angkor Thom, and the Hindu temple of Angkor Wat (12th century) were architectural masterpieces. After the empire fell to the Thais in 1434 the court moved to Phnom Penh. (See also ANGKOR.)

KHOMEINI, Ayatollah Ruhollah (1901–   ), spiritual and political leader of Iran. In 1962 he was recognized as one of the six grand ayatollahs (religious leaders) of Iranian Shi'ite Islam. The next year he was forced into exile because of his opposition to the rule of the shah, MOHAMMED REZA PAHLAVI. In exile in Turkey, Iraq and France he emerged as the leader of the anti-shah forces, which overthrew the Pahlavi regime. He returned to Iran in Jan. 1979 to become absolute leader of his new Islamic republic. His efforts to apply Islamic fundamentalism in the governance of Iran were complicated by an eight-year war with Iraq (see IRAN-IRAQ WAR), which he refused to end until the overthrow of Iraqi president Saddam Hussein. Only in 1988, when continuation of the war threatened the survival of his Islamic revolution, did he reluctantly consent to a United Nation's truce proposal.

KHRUSHCHEV, Nikita Sergeyevitch (1894–1971), Ukrainian-born Soviet statesman and premier of the USSR, 1958–64. He rose in the communist hierarchy to membership of the Presidium (1952). On STALIN's death he succeeded him as party secretary, but at the 20th Party Congress (1956) denounced Stalinism. He ousted the other members of the "collective leadership" to assume sole power (1958). His rule saw the launching of Sputnik satellite, the break with China and a rapprochement with the West, but the failure of his farm policy and loss of face in the Cuban missile crisis led to his fall.

KHUFU, or Cheops, Egyptian pharaoh of the 4th dynasty, early 26th century BC. He built the great pyramid at Giza, the largest single structure ever erected.

KHYBER PASS, mountain pass on the Pakistan border between Peshawar and KABUL, Afghanistan; historically crucial for the control of India, it is the site of a strategic military road and railroad. It is about 28mi long.

KIBBUTZ, type of cooperative farming settlement in Israel jointly owning or leasing land. All work, economic and municipal activities are done communally. Kibbutzim provide food, accommodation, nursery and elementary education. They began in Israel in the early 20th century.

KICKAPOO   INDIANS, Algonquian-speaking tribe living in SW Wisconsin in the 17th century and moving to central Illinois after 1769. They were formidable warriors, fighting against the US in the Revolutionary and 1812 wars. Ceding their Ill. land to the US in 1819, most went to Kan. or Mo., but later many to Mexico and Okla. Today only 800 Kickapoo remain.

KIDD, William (c1645–1701), famous British pirate. Settling in New York, he was employed in 1696 by the British governor there to privateer against French ships in King William's War. He later plundered the British in the Indian Ocean and was hanged in London for murder and piracy.

KIDNEYS, two organs concerned with the excretion of waste products in the urine and the balance of salt and water in the body. They lie behind the peritoneal cavity of the ABDOMEN and excrete urine via the ureters, thin tubes passing into the pelvis to enter the BLADDER. The basic functional unit of the kidney is the *nephron*, consisting of a glomerulus and a system of tubules; these feed into collecting ducts, which drain into the renal pelvis and ureter. BLOOD is filtered in the glomerulus so that low-molecular-weight substances, minerals and water pass into the tubules; here most of the water, sugar and minerals are reabsorbed, leaving behind wastes such as urea in a small volume of salt and water. Tubules and collecting ducts are concerned with the regulation of salt and water reabsorption, which is partly controlled by two HORMONES (vasopressin and aldosterone). Some substances are actively secreted into the urine by the tubules, and the kidney is the route of excretion of many DRUGS. Hormones concerned with erythrocyte

formation and regulation of aldosterone are formed in the kidneys, which also take part in protein METABOLISM. DISEASES affecting the kidney may result in acute NEPHRITIS, including BRIGHT'S DISEASE, the nephrotic syndrome (EDEMA, heavy protein loss in the urine and low plasma albumin) or acute or chronic renal failure. In acute renal failure, nephrons rapidly cease to function, often after prolonged SHOCK, SEPTICEMIA, etc. They may, however, recover. In chronic renal failure, the number of effective nephrons is gradually and irreversibly reduced so that they are unable to excrete all body wastes. Nephron failure causes UREMIA. Disease of the kidneys frequently causes hypertension (see BLOOD CIRCULATION). Advanced renal failure may need treatment with dietary foods, dialysis and renal TRANSPLANT.

KIEL CANAL, German canal 61mi long from the Elbe R mouth to Holtenau near Kiel. It opened in 1895 and as a major commercial-naval canal cut 300mi off the sea route between the North and Baltic Seas. After WWI it was internationalized until 1936.

KIERKEGAARD,   Sören   Aabye (1813–1855), Danish religious philosopher, precursor of EXISTENTIALISM. Opposing HEGEL, he emphasized that man has free will and can pass from the aesthetic (or material) to the ethical point of view and finally, through "a leap of faith," to the religious. His attack on systematic philosophy and rational religion was ignored in the 19th century but has influenced 20th-century Protestant theology and much modern literature and psychology. His main works are *Either/Or* (1843) and *Philosophical Fragments* (1844).

KIESINGER, Kurt Georg (1904–1988), West German Christian Democrat chancellor of the Federal Republic 1966–69. He governed in coalition with the Social Democrats, and generally pursued the West-oriented policies of his predecessors ADENAUER and ERHARD, with particular emphasis on Franco-German relations.

KIEV, third largest city in the USSR and capital of the Ukraine, on the Dnieper R. Known in Russia as "the mother of cities," it was founded before the 9th century and was the seat of the Russian Orthodox Church from 988. Much of Kiev (more than 40%) was destroyed in WWII, but after extensive reconstruction it is now a flourishing industrial, communications and cultural center. Pop 2,448,000.

KIKUYU, agricultural Bantu-speaking tribe, one of the largest groups in Kenya, living N of Nairobi. Racial and tribal tensions led to "Mau-Mau," a Kikuyu nationalist uprising against European colonists in the late 1940s and 1950s.

KILAUEA, world's largest active volcano, located on SE Hawaii island, Hawaii. Its elevation is 4,090ft, and it is 2mi wide, 3mi long and over 700ft deep. Kilauea erupts frequently.

KILIMANJARO, Africa's highest mountain, in NE Tanzania, near the Kenyan border. It is an extinct volcano and its highest peak, Kibo, reaches 19,340ft and is snow-capped.

KILLER WHALE, *Orcinus orca,* a true DOLPHIN, but lacking a beak. Fast and voracious predators, they eat dolphins, porpoises, seals and fish. They may hunt in small groups or form packs of 40 or more, driving their prey into shallow water where escape is impossible. Huge animals, average length about 20ft, killer whales are found throughout the world.

KILMER, Joyce (1886–1918), US poet remembered for his sentimental poem *Trees* (1913). He was killed in WWI.

KILOGRAM (kg), the base unit of MASS in SI UNITS, defined as the mass of a platinum-iridium prototype kept under carefully controlled conditions at the International Bureau of Weights and Measures, near Paris, France.

KILPATRICK, William Heard (1871–1965), US educator, called the father of progressive education in the US. A disciple of John DEWEY and professor at Columbia Teachers College 1909–38, he stressed a child-centered approach to education and rejected organized subjects.

KIM IL SUNG (1912–), North Korean political leader. A Communist, fought the Japanese, received training in Russia, and returned to Korea as head of a provisional government, supported by the Russians, in 1946. Invading South Korea, he precipitated the Korean War, and only Chinese intervention saved his regime. He then launched a vast industrial and military buildup. In 1972 he gave up the premiership and became president.

KINDERGARTEN, school for children aged 4–6, conceived by FROEBEL in 1837. The school aims to develop a child's self-expression and sociability through games, play and creative activities. One of the first American schools was opened in 1860 by Elizabeth PEABODY. Over 50% of children aged five in the US are enrolled in kindergartens.

KINETIC ART, style of art concerned with movement. There are several forms: OP ART involving dynamic optical effects; mobiles whose structure moves randomly and unaided; and works which are mechanically powered and use lights, water or electromagnets. The style first evolved about 1910.

KINETIC ENERGY. See ENERGY.

KINETIC THEORY, widely used statistical theory based on the idea that matter is made up of randomly moving ATOMS or MOLECULES whose kinetic ENERGY increases with TEMPERATURE. It is closely related to STATISTICAL MECHANICS, and predicts macroscopic properties of solids, liquids and gases from motions of individual particles using MECHANICS and PROBABILITY theory. Gases are particularly suited to treatment by kinetic theory, and the basic laws connecting their pressure, temperature, density, diffusion and other properties have been deduced with its aid. (See GAS; DIFFUSION.)

KING, Billie Jean Moffitt (1943–), US tennis player, six-time Wimbledon champion (1966–68, 1972–73, 1975), four-time US Open winner (1967, 1971–72, 1974).

KING, Ernest Joseph (1878–1956), US admiral, the only officer who was both commander of the US fleet and naval operations chief in WWII. His stress on the superiority of aircraft carriers to battleships led to Japan's naval defeat.

KING, Martin Luther, Jr. (1929–1968), black American clergyman and civil rights leader, recipient of the 1964 Nobel Peace Prize for his work for racial equality in the US. Born in Atlanta, Ga., King organized the boycott of the Montgomery, Ala. transit company in 1955 to force desegregation of the buses. Under his leadership in the late 1950s and 1960s civil disobedience and non-violent tactics, like the Washington March of 250,000 people in 1963, brought about the Civil Rights Act and Voting Rights Act in 1965. Black militants challenged his methods in 1965, but in 1966 he extended his campaign to slum conditions in the N cities of the US and set up the Poor People's Campaign in 1968. He was less successful in this area since the Vietnam War distracted national attention from the civil rights and urban issues. He was assassinated in Memphis, Tenn. In 1983 Congress designated the third Monday in January a national holiday to commemorate his birthday. (See also CIVIL RIGHTS AND LIBERTIES.)

KING, Stephen Edwin (1947–), US novelist and short-story writer. His best-selling occult thrillers about children and families threatened by malevolent supernatural forces include *Carrie* (1974), *The Shining* (1976), *Cujo* (1981), and *It*

(1986).

KING, William Lyon Mackenzie (1874–1950), Canadian statesman, three times Liberal prime minister. In his first term, 1921–26, he established Canada's right to act independently in international affairs; in his second, 1926–30, he introduced old age pensions—Canada's first national social security scheme; and in his third, 1935–48, he united Canada as the "arsenal of democracy" in WWII making the national economy a federal responsibility.

KINGFISHERS, a family, Alcedinidae, found worldwide, of brightly-colored fish-eating birds of rivers, lakes and streams. When hunting, the bird watches from a perch until prey is sighted, then dives arrowlike into the water to take the fish. Certain African species do not frequent water, and are insectivorous.

KING GEORGE'S WAR. See FRENCH AND INDIAN WARS.

KING PHILIP'S WAR (1675–76), last Indian resistance to the whites in S New England. In 1675, the Plymouth colony executed three Indians for an alleged murder. Metacom, a Wampanoag chief also called "King Philip," led an alliance of tribes in fierce guerrilla raids. The whites replied in kind, and Metacom was killed when his secret refuge was betrayed. The colonists then drove most of the Indians from S New England.

KINGS, Books of, two books of the OLD TESTAMENT (one book in Hebrew), numbered as 1 and 2 Kings by Protestants, but as 3 and 4 Kings by Roman Catholics (see SAMUEL). Related to DEUTERONOMY and religious in aim, they cover Israelite history from the reign of Solomon through the period of the two kingdoms of Israel and Judah to the destruction of Judah by the Babylonians.

KINGS CANYON NATIONAL PARK, area of about 460,330 acres in the Sierra Nevada, S central Cal., established as a national park in 1940. The canyon is formed by the Kings R and is noted for its surrounding snow-covered peaks and rich wildlife.

KINGSLEY, Charles (1819–1875), English writer and clergyman and an ardent advocate of social reform. His early novel, *Alton Locke* (1850) is a sympathetic study of working class life. He also wrote historical novels, notably *Westward Ho!* (1855) and the famous children's fantasy *The Water Babies* (1863).

KINGSLEY, Sidney (1906–), US playwright noted for his treatment of social problems. His first play, *Men in White*

(1933), won a Pulitzer Prize.

KING'S MOUNTAIN, Battle of, battle in the REVOLUTIONARY WAR in Oct. 1780 at King's Mt on the borders of N.C. and S.C. Some 900 American sharpshooters defeated a larger British force, checking CORNWALLIS in his Carolina campaign.

KING WILLIAM'S WAR. See FRENCH AND INDIAN WARS.

KINO, Eusebio Francisco (c1644–1711), Italian Jesuit missionary who explored Lower Cal. (1683–85) and into Ariz. from 1689. He established stock ranches at his missions. His map (1705) remained the basis of maps of the SW and of NW Mexico for a century.

KINSEY, Alfred Charles (1894–1956), US zoologist best known for his statistical studies of human sexual behavior, published as *Sexual Behavior in the Human Male* (1948) and *Sexual Behavior in the Human Female* (1953).

KIOWA INDIANS, tribe of the S Great Plains. A warlike nomadic people, they were settled in Okla. in 1868. A serious Kiowan uprising was put down in 1874. The Kiowas were followers of SUN DANCE and GHOST DANCE cults.

KIPLING, Rudyard (1865–1936), English writer, born in India. Kipling is perhaps now most admired for his short stories about Anglo-Indian life, as in the collection *Plain Tales from the Hills* (1888), and for his verse, including such pieces as *Mandalay* and *Gunga Din*, while his children's stories, among them *Kim* (1901) and the *Just So Stories* (1902), are perennial favorites. After an English education he worked as a journalist in India 1882–89. He lived in Vt. 1892–96 and in England from 1900. Kipling was enormously popular in his day. He was the first English winner of the Nobel Prize for Literature (1907).

KIRBY-SMITH, Edmund (1824–1893), Civil War general, the last Confederate commander to surrender, May 26, 1865. A major in the US army, he joined the Confederacy when Fla., his native state, entered the war. He was commander of the Trans-Mississippi Dept. 1863–65.

KIRCHHOFF, Gustav Robert (1824–1887), German physicist best known for his work on electrical conduction, showing that current passes through a conductor at the speed of light, and deriving KIRCHHOFF'S LAWS. With BUNSEN he pioneered spectrum analysis (see SPECTROSCOPY), which he applied to the solar spectrum, identifying several elements and explaining the Fraunhofer Lines in the spectrum of the sun.

KIRCHHOFF'S LAWS, two laws governing electric circuits involving Ohm's-law conductors and sources of electromotive force, stated by G. R. KIRCHHOFF. They assert that the sums of outgoing and incoming currents at any junction in the circuit must be equal, and that the sum of the current-resistance products around any closed path must equal the total electromotive force in it.

KIRCHNER, Ernst Ludwig (1880–1938), German expressionist graphic artist and painter, cofounder of the Brücke (Bridge) movement (1905–13). He is noted for his powerful, savagely expressive woodcuts and, in his painting, for his vigorous distorted use of color and form. His work condemned by the Nazis as degenerate, Kirchner committed suicide.

KIRIBATI, independent island republic in the central Pacific, consists of three groups of coral atolls astride the equator.

Official name: Republic of Kiribati
Capital: Tarawa
Area: 328sq mi
Population: 66,800
Languages: Kiribatian, English
Religion: Christian
Monetary unit(s): 1 Australian dollar = 100 cents

Land. The 33 atolls of Kiribati include the 16 Gilbert Islands, Banaba Island and eight each in the Phoenix and Line island groups. There are no rivers but most of the atolls enclose a lagoon. Because scanty soil covers the coral, little vegetation grows on the atolls. Temperatures are high and vary little during the year. Rainfall occurs between Oct. and Mar.

People. The administrative center is on Tarawa, the most populous and westernized island, where over 30% of the total population lives. Most of the inhabitants of Kiribati are Micronesian. English is the official language.

Economy. Fishing constitutes the mainstay of the subsistence economy, supplemented by the cultivation of taro and fruits. Coconuts are cultivated, and copra is virtually the only export since phosphate mining on Banaba ceased in 1979.

History. Most European exploration occurred between 1765 and 1826. In 1892 the British declared the islands a protectorate. During World War II some of the fiercest fighting between Japanese and US forces took place, and much of the native population died or was deported by the Japanese. Independence from the UK, achieved in 1979, had been slowed because Banaba had initially demanded separate status. In a quest for outside economic assistance, Kiribati signed a controversial one-year fishing agreement with the USSR that was allowed to expire in 1986.

KIRKLAND, (Joseph) Lane (1922–   ), US labor leader. Joining the AFL in 1948, he became executive assistant to President George Meany in 1960 and secretary-treasurer of the AFL-CIO in 1969. Succeeding Meany as president in 1979, he became known as a strong supporter of civil rights and national defense.

KIRKPATRICK, Jeane (1926–   ), US ambassador to the UN (1981–85). A professor of political science at Georgetown University, she was a charter member of the conservative Coalition for a Democratic Majority, a group that advocated a tougher American foreign policy.

KIROV, Sergei Mironovich (1886–1934), Russian revolutionary leader, one of Stalin's chief aides. He was assassinated, probably on the instruction of Stalin, who used his death as an excuse for a wave of purges.

KIRSTEIN, Lincoln (1907–   ), US ballet promoter who persuaded George BALANCHINE to come to the US and helped him organize the School of American Ballet in New York, 1934, and the New York City Ballet, 1948. Kirstein also wrote several books on ballet.

KISSINGER, Henry Alfred (1923–   ), German-born US adviser on foreign affairs and one of the most influential men in government. He was professor at Harvard when his book *Nuclear Weapons and Foreign Policy* (1957) brought him international recognition. Kissinger served as special assistant for national security affairs (1969–75) and secretary of state (1973–77) under presidents Nixon and (after 1974) Ford. He was instrumental in initiating the STRATEGIC ARMS LIMITATION TALKS on disarmament (1969), in ending US involvement in Vietnam and opening US policies toward China. In 1974–75 he made major peace initiatives in the Middle East and, in 1976, in southern Africa. His policy of détente toward the Soviet Union came under criticism from political conservatives. He received the Nobel Peace Prize in 1973.

KITASATO, Shibasaburo (1852–1931), Japanese bacteriologist who discovered, independently of A. E. J. Yersin, the PLAGUE bacillus; and with Emil von Behring discovered that graded injections of toxins could be used for immunization (see ANTITOXINS).

KITCHEN CABINET, popular name for an unofficial body of advisers to President Andrew Jackson (1829–31). It included politicians, editors and government officials.

KITCHENER, Horatio Herbert Kitchener, 1st Earl (1850–1916), British field marshal, secretary of state for war in WWI. In the Sudan in 1898, he defeated the Mahdis at Omdurman and retook Khartoum. He was commander in chief in the Boer War, 1900–02, and in India to 1909. At the outbreak of WWI he foresaw a long war, and his appeals raised thousands of patriotic volunteers. He died when a ship taking him to Russia hit a mine and sank.

KITCHEN MIDDEN, or shell mound, refuse heap of usually STONE AGE origin in which, among bones, shells, etc., archaeologists may find potsherds and implements of stone, horn and bone. They are 3-10ft high, 130-230ft wide and up to 1,300ft long.

KITE, recreational aircraft consisting of a light frame covered with thin fabric (e.g., paper) and tethered to a long line. Kites fly in the wind by AERODYNAMIC lift. Originating in the ancient Far East, kite flying has long been a popular sport, and has been used for meteorological observations.

KITES, a diverse assemblage of birds of prey, worldwide in distribution but especially developed in America and Australia. The name is properly restricted to Old World fork-tailed kites of the genus *Milvus*, but it is also used for 25 other species. Most kites are mainly or entirely insectivorous. A few species are scavengers: the black and red kites of Europe were formerly common scavengers of city streets.

KITTY HAWK, peninsula in N.C., scene of the first power-driven flight, Dec. 17, 1903. The flight, by the WRIGHT BROTHERS, lasted 12 seconds, and is commemorated by a monument on Kill Devil Hill.

KIWANIS INTERNATIONAL, worldwide service organization of business and professional men, founded 1915, with headquarters in Indianapolis, Ind. In 1988 it had 315,000 members.

KIWI, the genus *Apteryx*, three species of flightless New Zealand birds about 460mm (18in) high, lacking a tail and, unlike most flightless birds, even lacking visible wings. The feathers are gray-brown and hairlike in texture. The long slender bill is adapted for probing into soil as they feed at night on worms, insects and berries. Birds of damp forests, they are extremely shy and rarely seen.

KLAMATH INDIANS, North American Indians of SE Ore. and N Cal., neighbors of the MODOC INDIANS, with whom they share a reservation around Upper Klamath Lake, established in 1864.

KLAMATH MOUNTAINS, mountain range of the Pacific Coast Ranges in SW Ore. and NW Cal. It has peaks and ridges reaching 9,000ft.

KLEE, Paul (1879–1940), Swiss painter and graphic artist. In Munich, from 1906, he exhibited with the BLAUE REITER group, and developed a subtle color sense. In 1920–31 he taught at the BAUHAUS, publishing an important textbook on painting. Sensitive line, color and texture are combined in Klee's varied paintings with wit and fantasy.

KLEIN, Lawrence (1920–   ), US economist, known as "the father of econometric model-making." A professor at the Wharton School of the U. of Pa. from 1958, he was an adviser to President Jimmy Carter (1976–81) and winner of the 1980 Nobel Prize in Economic Science.

KLEIN, Melanie (1882–1960), Austrian-born psychoanalyst whose development of a psychoanalytic therapy for small children radically affected techniques of child psychiatry and theories of child psychology.

KLEIST, (Bernd) Heinrich (Wilhelm) von (1777–1811), German dramatist and writer of novellas, known for his power and psychological insight. His works include the plays *Penthesilea* (1808) and *Prince Friedrich of Homburg* (1821), and the novels *Michael Kohlhaas* and *The Marquise of O* (1810–11).

KLEMPERER, Otto (1885–1973), German conductor. As director of the Kroll opera house, Berlin (1927–33) he introduced many modern works and new interpretations of classics. After a period of crippling illness he revived his career from 1947, notably as an interpreter of BEETHOVEN and MAHLER.

KLIKITAT INDIANS, Shahaptian tribe noted for their sophisticated trading methods. They lived in Klikitat and Skamania counties, Wash., until resettled in 1855 on the Yakima reservation.

KLIMT, Gustav (1862–1918), Austrian painter and designer, a leader of the Vienna Secession (1897) who was noted for his lavishly ornamented, mosaic-patterned style. His interior designs, as for the Palais Stoclet, Brussels, and in Vienna, influenced

JUGENDSTIL.

KLINE, Franz Joseph (1910–1962), US abstract expressionist painter. His huge, stark, black-and-white compositions influenced the "calligraphic" style of the 1950s New York school. Later, Kline reintroduced color into his works.

KLONDIKE, subarctic region S of the Klondike R in the W central Yukon, site of the gold rush of 1896. By 1900 $22 million was being panned annually, but the creeks were quickly worked out.

KLOPSTOCK, Friedrich Gottlieb (1724–1803), German poet. His *Der Messias* (1749–73), on Christ's salvation of mankind, an epic modelled on Milton and Homer, freed German poetry from the conventions of French classicism.

KLUCKHOHN, Clyde (1905–1960), US anthropologist, best known for his studies of the Navaho Indians and work on the theory of culture and personality. A professor at Harvard (1935–60), he wrote several books including *Mirror for Man* (1949).

KNELLER, Sir Godfrey (1646–1723), German-born English portrait painter, a court painter from 1688. He founded the first English painting academy (1711); his finest works are the 42 portraits of members of the Kit-Cat Club, a London political and literary group.

KNIGHTS OF LABOR, early US labor group, precursor of the American Federation of Labor. Founded in 1869 to organize all workers in one union, it led successful strikes in 1884–86, but declined after the HAYMARKET AFFAIR.

KNIGHTS OF SAINT JOHN (officially, Order of the Hospital of St. John of Jerusalem; also known as Hospitalers, Knights of Rhodes, and Knights of Malta), religious order founded by papal charter (1113) to tend sick pilgrims in the Holy Land. It became a military order as well c1140, and after the fall of Jerusalem was based successively on Cyprus (1291), Rhodes (1309) and Malta (1530) to provide a defense against Muslim seapower. Expelled from Malta by Napoleon in 1798, the Knights have been established at Rome since 1834 in their original humanitarian role.

KNIGHTS OF THE GOLDEN CIRCLE, semimilitary US secret society organized in the Midwest states during the Civil War to set up proslavery colonies in Mexico, to help the South against the North. It merged with the Order of American Knights, later the Sons of Liberty, and disbanded in the 1860s.

KNIGHTS OF THE WHITE CAMELLIA, southern US secret society to sustain white supremacy after the Civil War. It was dissolved in the 1870s.

KNIGHTS TEMPLAR, Christian military order founded c1118, with its headquarters on the site of Solomon's Temple in Jerusalem, to protect pilgrims. It provided elite troops for the kingdom of Jerusalem. Its immense riches from endowments and banking excited the greed of Philip IV of France, who (1307–14) confiscated its property, forced the pope to suppress the order and executed the Grand Master and other knights. What remained of its possessions in France and elsewhere were transferred to the KNIGHTS OF ST. JOHN.

KNITTING, production of fabric by using needles to interlock yarn or thread in a series of connected loops. The basic handknitting stitches are plain (or jersey) and purl. It was practiced in North Africa in the 3rd century BC and was taken to Europe by Arab traders. In the Middle Ages there were knitting guilds. The first knitting machine was invented by William Lee in England in 1589.

KNOPF, Alfred Abraham (1892–1984), US publisher. He founded Alfred A. Knopf, Inc. (1915) which published many Nobel Prize-winning authors and became perhaps the most prestigious publishing house in the US. He also co-founded and edited (1924–34) the magazine *American Mercury.*

KNOSSOS, ancient city near Candia on the N coast of Crete, center of the Minoan civilization. Excavations by Sir Arthur Evans revealed settlements from the 3rd millennium and the great 2nd-millennium palace, now partly restored. Associated with the mythological King Minos, it comprises more than five acres of halls, ceremonial rooms and staircases. It has magnificent fresco decorations, advanced sanitation and every amenity of luxury. Fire destroyed it c1400 BC.

KNOW-NOTHING PARTY, US political party formed to restrict immigration and exclude naturalized citizens and Roman Catholics from politics. It won success in the 1854 election as the American Party, but split irremediably in 1856 over the slavery issue. Its name came from its members' habit of saying they "knew nothing" of the movement.

KNOX, Henry (1750–1806), US general and secretary of war under his friend Washington. He was artillery commander at Bunker Hill, Yorktown and other important battles of the Revolution. He proposed the establishment of the West Point military academy.

KNOX, John (c1514–1572), Scottish

Protestant Reformation leader, preacher and chronicler of the Scottish Reformation. A converted Roman Catholic priest, Knox was active in the English Reformation, but fled in 1554 from the Roman Catholic regime of Queen Mary I to Geneva, where he was a follower of CALVIN. He returned to Scotland in 1559 ardently preaching Protestantism. When it became the state religion (1560) Knox gained great political influence, opposing Mary Queen of Scots. His fiery prose includes a history of the Reformation in Scotland and the *First Blast of the Trumpet Against the Monstrous Regiment of Women* (1556–58). He also wrote the *Book of Common Order*, which regulated Scottish worship.

KOALA, *Phascolarctos cinereus,* a large, arboreal, superficially bear-like MARSUPIAL of eastern Australia. It feeds on the foliage of *Eucalyptus* and a few other trees. Alone among the marsupials but for the WOMBATS, koalas have a true allantoic placenta, though the young are brooded in a marsupial pouch. The koala has been considered an endangered species but is now increasing in numbers again.

KOCH, Edward I. (1924–), US Democratic congressman from New York 1969–77, controversial mayor of New York City from 1977. He failed to win the Democratic nomination for governor in 1982. He wrote *Mayor* (1984).

KOCH, Robert (1843–1910), German medical scientist regarded as a father of BACTERIOLOGY, awarded the 1905 Nobel Prize for Physiology or Medicine for his work. He isolated the ANTHRAX bacillus and showed it to be the sole cause of the disease; devised important new methods of obtaining pure cultures; and discovered the bacilli responsible for TUBERCULOSIS (1882) and CHOLERA (1883).

KÖCHEL, Ludwig von (1800–1877), Austrian musicologist (and also scientist), whose 1862 catalogue of Mozart's compositions, though revised, is still standard. The works are usually identified with a "K" number.

KODÁLY, Zoltán (1882–1967), Hungarian composer and, with BARTÓK, an ardent researcher of Hungarian folk music. Folk influences are evident in such works as the cantata *Psalmus Hungaricus* (1923), the opera *Háry János* (1925–26) and the orchestral *Peacock Variations* (1938–39).

KOESTLER, Arthur (1905–1983), Hungarian-born British writer. His novel *Darkness at Noon* (1940), based on his own experience in a Spanish death cell, analyzed the psychology of victims of Stalin's 1930s

purges. Many later works on philosophical and scientific subjects include *The Sleepwalkers* (1964), *The Case of the Midwife Toad* (1971) and *The Thirteenth Tribe* (1978).

KOFFKA, Kurt (1886–1941), German-born US psychologist who, with KÖHLER and WERTHEIMER, was responsible for the birth of GESTALT PSYCHOLOGY.

KOHL, Helmut (1930–), West German politician. Leader of the conservative Christian Democratic party, he succeeded Social Democrat Helmut Schmidt as chancellor in 1982. His free-market philosophy was frustrated by powerful interest groups, including employers and unions wedded to the status quo. His own party insisted on adding benefits to an already generous welfare system. The once dynamic German economy turned sluggish, with slow growth and high unemployment. In foreign affairs, Kohl stressed close ties to the US, cooperation with France, and improved ties with the East. In 1987 he welcomed East German leader Erich Honecker in Bonn, demonstrating his government's commitment to German reunification while pressing the East Germans for improvements in human rights.

KÖHLER, Wolfgang (1887–1967), German-born US psychologist, a founder of GESTALT PSYCHOLOGY. He devoted much of his career to studying problem-solving among chimpanzees.

KOKOSCHKA, Oskar (1886–1980), Austrian painter and writer who was a leader of German EXPRESSIONISM. He is known for such psychologically acute portraits as *The Tempest* (1914), a self-portrait with Alma Mahler, and for his lyric landscapes and townscapes. He became a naturalized British subject in 1947.

KOLCHAK, Alexander Vasilievich (1873–1920), Russian admiral, leader of the White Russian forces 1918–20. He took power in Omsk in 1918, proclaiming himself head of state. Defeated by the Red Army and overthrown after his move to Irkutsk in 1919, he was finally executed by the Bolsheviks.

KOLLEK, Theodore (1911–), Austrian-born Israeli politician, mayor of Jerusalem from 1965 who tried to reconcile Arabs and Jews in the city.

KOLLWITZ, Käthe (1867–1945), German artist admired particularly for her lithographs and woodcuts. Actively opposed to social injustice, she depicted human misery and tragedy in haunting fashion, often through the theme of mother and child.

KOLMOGOROV, Andrei Nikolayevich (1903–1987), Soviet mathematician. Considered to be the most influential Soviet mathematician of the 20th century, he made fundamental contributions to the theory of functions, TOPOLOGY, PROBABILITY theory, CYBERNETICS and INFORMATION THEORY.

KONEV, Ivan Stepanovich (1897–1973), USSR field marshal of WWII, who drove the Germans from the Ukraine, captured Prague and took part in the fall of Berlin. He headed the Warsaw Pact armies 1955–60.

KONOYE, Prince Fumimaro (1891–1945), Japanese premier 1937–39 and 1940–41. A moderate, he appeased the military extremists and so furthered expansionism. He killed himself when listed for trial as a war criminal.

KON-TIKI. See HEYERDAHL, THOR.

KORAN, sacred scripture of the religion of ISLAM, regarded by Muslims as God's actual words revealed to the prophet MOHAMMED in the 7th century AD. A canonical text was established in 651–52 AD, and Arabic itself was molded and preserved by its highly-charged, poetic language. Comprising laws, moral precepts and narrative, the Koran is divided into 114 *suras* or chapters, arranged according to length from the longest to the shortest except for the brief opening prayer. The Koran demands total surrender to the will of Allah (God), and stresses Allah's compassion and mercy. It contains much in common with the Judeo-Christian tradition, and indeed all Christians and Jews are regarded as believers since they accept the existence of one God. Today Islam places a greater emphasis on the spirit than on the letter of Koranic laws which govern, for instance, moral behavior and social life. The Koran remains, however, the inspiration and guide for millions of Muslims and is the supreme authority of the Islamic tradition.

KORDA, Sir Alexander (1893–1956), Hungarian-born British film producer and director. His historical extravaganzas, such as *The Private Life of Henry VIII* (1933), *The Scarlet Pimpernel* (1934), *Rembrandt* (1936) and *The Four Feathers* (1939), enhanced the international status of the British film industry. He was the first filmmaker to be knighted (1942).

KOREA, 600mi-long peninsula of E Asia, separating the Yellow Sea from the Sea of Japan. It is bounded N by China and the USSR, and S by Korea Strait. Korea is two countries: the communist Democratic People's Republic (North Korea) and the

Republic of Korea (South Korea). The division, which runs along 38°N, was made in 1945 and formalized in 1948. Korea is mostly mountainous, with coastal plains in the W. Most rivers flow W and S from the mountains to the Yellow Sea. The climate is varied with extremes of cold and humidity.

Official name: Democratic People's Republic of Korea
Capital: Pyongyang
Area: 42,250sq mi
Population: 21,390,000
Language: Korean
Religions: No official religion
Monetary unit(s): 1 won = 100 jun

Official name: Republic of Korea
Capital: Seoul
Area: 38,279sq mi
Population: 42,082,000
Language: Korean
Religions: Buddhist, Confucian, Christian
Monetary unit(s): 1 won = 100 jeon
People. South Korea, though smaller, has more than twice the population of North Korea. The Koreans are mostly agricultural workers, and less than a third of the people live in towns. In the North, as in other communist countries, religious belief is discouraged. In the South, Buddhism, Confucianism and Christianity coexist.
Economy. Agricultural crops are still of primary importance in Korea, but in the 1960s rapid industrial expansion, facilitated by foreign aid, profoundly altered the economy of both North and South. The North especially is now highly industrialized, and produces large quantities of iron and steel. Farming is cooperative and

mechanized. The North also has the dominant share of the country's mineral wealth and is one of the world's few totally self-sufficient nations. The South has one of the fastest growing economies in the world. Its widely mixed industry, including plywood, chemicals and textiles, is largely export-oriented.

History. After more than 1,000 years of Chinese settlements among the Korean tribes, the first of several native kingdoms arose, in the N, c100 AD. Korea was not united until the 7th century. Most of its early civilization was destroyed by the Mongol invasions of the 13th century; but with the establishment (1392) of the Yi dynasty, Korea entered an age of stability and outstanding cultural achievement which included the first known printing with movable metal type. In 1592 Japan invaded the peninsula, followed soon after by the Manchu. Korea became a Chinese vassal state, entirely cut off from the world. Commercial contact with Japan in the late 1800s foreshadowed Japan's annexation of Korea in 1910. After Japan's 1945 capitulation in WWII Korea was divided into a Russian zone of occupation in the N and a US zone in the S. Negotiations to unite the country failed, and in 1948 separate regimes were established. The North became a communist state under the former guerrilla leader, KIM IL SUNG. Elections in the South produced a republic under Syngman RHEE. On June 25, 1950, the communists of the North invaded South Korea, thus beginning the KOREAN WAR. The heavy fighting was eventually stopped (July 1953) by an armistice. In the South, Syngman Rhee's increasingly autocratic and corrupt regime was displaced (1960). A military coup in 1961 brought General PARK CHUNG HEE to power. President under a new constitution after 1963, he gained wider powers and the right to unlimited terms of office in 1972. In July 1979 he was assassinated and replaced by General Chun Doo Hwan, who established his own autocratic rule. In 1987, after widespread antigovernment demonstrations, Chun abandoned plans to name his own successor and agreed to a presidential election. Chun's candidate, Roh Tae Woo, was elected president but with only a third of the total vote despite government influence on his behalf and alleged vote fraud. The survival of the regime was due in large part to the country's astonishing economic growth during the preceding 20 years, when per capita gross national product quadrupled. In 1988 Seoul hosted the summer Olympics.

In North Korea, Kim Il Sung presided over a drab and disciplined state in which he was the object of a personality cult. He groomed his son, Kim Jong Il, to succeed him. In 1988 he demanded that North Korea cohost the Olympics. His demand was rejected by South Korea and unsupported by other communist countries. But negotiations were undertaken between north and south toward some accommodation, although the reunification of the peninsula was unlikely.

KOREAN, language spoken by the Korean people, numbering about 60 million. Of uncertain origin, Korean is considered by some to belong to the ALTAIC LANGUAGES. The official script has a simple phonetic alphabet called *hankul*, with 11 vowels and 14 consonants.

KOREAN WAR (1950–1953), a conflict between forces of the United Nations (primarily the US and South Korea) on one side and forces of North Korea and (later) communist China on the other. KOREA had been divided along latitude 38°N in 1945, Russia becoming the occupying force N of this line, and the US S of it. The war began when, having attempted to topple the government of the south by indirect means, North Korea launched a surprise invasion. UN forces were sent to assist South Korea under General Douglas MACARTHUR. By July the UN forces had been pushed SE to a small area around Pusan, but MacArthur's surprise landing at Inchon, near the captured capital Seoul, altered the complexion of the war. The UN forces destroyed the North Korean army in the south, retook Seoul, and advanced into North Korea. By November 1950 they were approaching the Yalu R on the Chinese border. At this point nearly 300,000 Chinese troops went into action and there was another major reversal as the UN forces were beaten back into South Korea. They recovered, and the fighting moved back and forth over the 38th parallel. MacArthur, urging a direct attack on China herself, was replaced in April 1951 by General RIDGWAY. Two years of negotiations, begun in July, achieved only an armistice (signed at Panmunjom on July 27, 1953). By then the communists had suffered about 2,000,000 casualties and the UN nearly 1,500,000. A peace treaty has never been signed and Korea remains divided as before.

KORNGOLD, Erich Wolfgang (1897–1957), Austrian-US composer. The Metropolitan Opera presented his *Die Tote Stadt* in 1921 and *Violanta* in 1927. In the 1930s he began composing scores for such films as *Anthony Adverse* and *The Adventures of Robin Hood*.

KORNILOV, Lavr Georgeyevich (1870–1918), Russian general placed in command of the armies after the February Revolution of 1917. His efforts to restore military discipline led KERENSKY to suspect him of planning an army takeover. Imprisoned, he escaped to lead the anti-Bolsheviks after the October Revolution and died in battle.

KORSAKOV'S PSYCHOSIS, or Korsakov syndrome, a condition involving organic brain damage observed particularly among alcoholics (see ALCOHOLISM). It is named for the Russian neurologist S.S. Korsakov (1854–1900).

KORZYBSKI, Alfred Habdank Skarbek (1879–1950), Polish-born US scientist who formulated the philosophical linguistic system, General SEMANTICS.

KOSCIUSKO, Thaddeus (1746–1817), Polish soldier and patriot who fought as a volunteer in the American Revolution. As colonel of engineers he helped build defense works at Saratoga and West Point. He was given US citizenship and made brigadier general. Returning to Poland in 1784, he instigated and led (1794) an unsuccessful fight for independence and unification. He died in exile in Switzerland.

KOSHER, Hebrew word meaning "proper" or "fit," used especially of food prepared according to Orthodox dietary and religious laws. Forbidden are pork, horseflesh, shellfish and parts of beef and lamb. All meat and poultry must be killed by a Jew trained in the prescribed ritual, then soaked or salted to remove all blood. Milk and its products must not be eaten with meat.

KOSINSKI, Jerzy (1933–   ), Polish-born US writer best known for his semi-autobiographical novel *The Painted Bird* (1965), which with vivid, often shockingly brutal imagery deals with "daily life among the violations of the spirit and body of human beings." Among his other works are *Steps* (1968), for which he won a National Book Award, and *Being There* (1971).

KOSSUTH, Lajos (1802–1894), Hungarian patriot and statesman who campaigned against Austrian rule and led the Hungarian revolution of 1848–49. A minister in the government which was set up in April 1848, he engineered Hungary's declaration of independence as a republic the following year, and became president. Austria, with the aid of Russian troops, forced a surrender, and Kossuth fled. Received as a hero in the US and England, where he lived many years, he died in Italy.

KOSYGIN, Aleksei Nikolaevich (1904–1980), Soviet premier, elected 1964. He joined the Communist Party in 1927, and by 1939, with much industrial–managerial experience behind him, was on the Central Committee. In 1948 he was made a full Politburo member and in 1960 became first deputy to Khrushchev, whom he succeeded. Sharing leadership with others from 1964, Kosygin concentrated on modernizing industry and agriculture. He resigned as premier in 1980, just before his death.

KOTZEBUE, Otto von (1787–1846), Russian explorer who circumnavigated the world 1803–06, 1815–18, and 1823–26. He discovered many Pacific islands and explored much of the Alaskan coast. Kotzebue Sound is named for him.

KOUFAX, Sandy (1935–   ), star Brooklyn (Los Angeles) Dodgers left-handed pitcher. He joined the Dodgers in 1958. He established several pitching records, including a record number of strikeouts in one season (382 in 1965), and was the first man to pitch four no-hit games in the major leagues.

KOUSSEVITSKY, Serge (1874–1951), Russian-US conductor. He left Russia in 1920 and settled in the US as conductor of the Boston Symphony Orchestra (1924–49). In 1940 he established the Berkshire Music Center at Stockbridge, Mass. He is remembered as a champion of contemporary composers.

KRAFFT-EBING, Richard, Baron von (1840–1902), German psychologist best known for his work on the psychology of SEX. He also showed there was a relation between syphilis and general PARALYSIS.

KRAKATOA, volcanic island in the Sunda Strait, Indonesia. The eruption of Aug. 1883, one of the most violent ever known, destroyed most of the island, caused a tidal wave killing 36,000 people in neighboring Java and Sumatra, and threw debris as far as Madagascar.

KRAKÓW, or Cracow, city in S Poland on the Vistula R, administrative center of Kraków province. Capital of Poland from 1320 to 1609, the city has much outstanding architecture, including that of Jagiellonian U. (founded 1364). Still today a center of culture and learning, modern Krákow is also a major industrial city. Notable products are iron, steel, machinery and chemicals. Pop 743,363.

KREISKY, Bruno (1911–   ), Austrian socialist politician, foreign minister (1959–66) and federal chancellor (1970–83).

KREISLER, Fritz (1875–1962), world-renowned Austrian-US violinist of great brilliance and elegance of style. His compositions included musical forgeries of various 17th- and 18th-century composers, which he later admitted were his own. He lived in the US from 1943.

KREMLIN, medieval fortified center of a Russian city, especially that of MOSCOW. The Moscow Kremlin's great wall, built in the 15th century, encloses magnificent palaces and churches from the time of the tsars. The Kremlin is the administrative and political center of the Soviet Union.

KRENEK, Ernst (1900–   ), Austrian-US composer of the jazz opera *Johnny Strikes Up* (1926), and of TWELVE TONE MUSIC such as the *Fourth Symphony* (1947). He moved to the US in 1938.

KRETSCHMER, Ernst (1888–1964), German psychiatrist and neurologist who developed a "constitutional theory of personality" which linked behavior and psychological disorders to physical stature.

KREUGER, Ivar (1880–1932), Swedish industrialist, financier and swindler. Known as the "Match King," he lent governments large sums of money in exchange for a monopoly over their match production, controlling about half the world's match production by 1928. After his suicide it was discovered that his empire was based on forgery and financial manipulation, and that ' he had perpetrated perhaps the greatest fraud in financial history.

KRISHNA, or **Govinda** or **Gopala,** major deity in later Hinduism, depicted as a blue-skinned, sportive youth generally playing the flute; he is worshiped as an incarnation of Vishnu. He is the hero of the MAHABHARATA; his teachings, related in the BHAGAVAD-GITA, advocate selfless action.

KRISHNAMURTI, Jiddu (1895–1986), Hindu religious thinker and teacher. His meeting (1909) with Annie BESANT led to claims that he was the reincarnation of Buddha, which he later denied. Since 1969 he has led the Krishnamurti Foundation in Cal.

KROEBER, Alfred Louis (1876–1960), US anthropologist who made contributions to many areas of cultural ANTHROPOLOGY and ARCHAEOLOGY, particularly with reference to the Amerinds. His books include *The Nature of Culture* (1952) and *Style and Civilization* (1957).

KRONSTADT, fortress and naval base in the USSR, on Kotlin Island in the Gulf of Finland. For most of the 18th and 19th centuries it was of primary importance, both as port and as garrison, to the then Russian capital of St. Petersburg (present-day Leningrad). The scene of several mutinies (the last, in 1921, against the Soviets) it also played a significant part in WWII.

KROPOTKIN, Peter Alexeyevich, Prince (1842–1921), Russian theorist of ANARCHISM whose writings, especially *Mutual Aid* (1902), won international respect. An established geographer, he abandoned (1871) career and social position to pursue revolutionary activities. Imprisoned (1874) in Russia, he escaped to Europe, where after a further spell of imprisonment in France (1883–86) he lived in England and devoted himself to studying, writing and lecturing. He returned to Russia in 1917, but denounced the October (Bolshevik) Revolution and lived in retirement until his death.

KRUGER, Paul (Stephanus Johannes Paulus Kruger; 1825–1904), South African Boer leader. He opposed the annexation (1877) of the Transvaal by the British and played a leading part in the Boer rebellion of 1880. Elected president of the new self-governing Transvaal Republic (1883), he attempted to extend the frontiers of Transvaal territory, and his pursuit of anti-British policies ultimately led to the second BOER WAR (1899–1902). In 1900 he went to Europe and sought vainly for support for the Boers. He died in Switzerland.

KRUPP, family of German industrialists famous as armaments makers and long associated with German militarism. The Essen firm was founded in 1811 by Friedrich Krupp (1787–1826) with a small steel casting factory, and under his son Alfred (1812–1887) became the largest cast steel enterprise in the world. It played a key role in the Franco-Prussian War, WWI and WWII. The Krupps clung to family ownership and opposed unionism. After WWII, Alfred Krupp von Bohlen und Halbach (1907–1967), head of the firm from 1943, was imprisoned (1948–51) for war crimes. The company, reorganized but retaining much of its holdings, now concentrates on heavy industrial equipment.

KRUPSKAYA, Nadezhda Konstantinovna (1869–1939), Soviet revolutionary and educationist. She married LENIN in 1898 while both were exiled in Europe, thereafter sharing his life in Europe and his return (1917) to Russia. An opponent of Stalin, she lost her considerable influence in the Communist Party after Lenin's death.

KRYLOV, Ivan Andreyevich (1769–1844), Russian author of nine books of fables (from 1809) which have become popular classics of satire. Influenced by or adapted from AESOP and LA FONTAINE, they are nonetheless typically Russian in spirit.

KUALA LUMPUR, capital and largest city of Malaysia, on the S Malay Peninsula. It is Malaysia's commercial, transportation, cultural and educational center. Founded as a mining camp in 1857, the city owed much of its subsequent rapid growth to the local abundance of tin and rubber. During WWII the city was occupied (1942–45) by the Japanese. Pop 919,610.

KUBELIK, Rafael (1914–   ), Czech conductor and composer. He was musical director of the Chicago Symphony Orchestra (1950–53), of the Covent Garden Opera (1955–58) and of the Metropolitan Opera (1973–74).

KUBITSCHEK, Juscelino (1902–1976), president of Brazil 1956–61. He encouraged scientific and industrial progress, but economic problems followed the building of the new capital BRASILIA. In 1964 he was accused of corruption and went into exile for some years.

KUBLAI KHAN (c1216–1294), Mongol emperor from 1259, founder of the Mongol Yüan dynasty of China and grandson of GENGHIS KHAN. By 1279, the last resistance of the Chinese SUNG dynasty crushed, his empire reached from the Pacific to the Volga R and into Poland. Under his skilled and tolerant rule China flourished both economically and culturally. His new capital Cambuluc, described by Marco POLO, became the nucleus of modern Peking.

KUBLER-ROSS, Elisabeth (1926–   ), US-Swiss psychiatrist who pioneered in the care of dying patients. Her books include *On Death and Dying* (1969).

KUHN, Walt (1877–1949), US painter and sculptor. As organizer of New York's 1913 Armory show, he brought leading post-impressionists and cubists, such as MATISSE, VAN GOGH and PICASSO, to the attention of the American public. His own painting career began in 1925, and his best-known canvases feature clowns and acrobats in posed situations.

KU K'AI-CHIH (c344–406 AD), reputedly the first great Chinese painter, noted especially for his portraits and also for landscapes. They are known only from ancient writings and from paintings thought to be copies. Of these last the most famous is *The Admonitions of the Instructress to the Palace Ladies* (7th century).

KU KLUX KLAN, secret organization originally begun (1866) to conduct a campaign of terror against newly enfranchised blacks. Founded by Confederate veterans, it spread from Tenn. throughout the South. Its members adopted an arcane hierarchy and dressed in hoods and white sheets to play on their victims' belief in vengeful ghosts. Its emblem was a fiery cross. It was officially disbanded in 1869, although many members remained active throughout RECONSTRUCTION and beyond. The second Klan, organized in 1915, extended its hostilities to Jews, Catholics, pacifists, the foreign born, radicals and labor unions. A membership of nearly 5,000,000 was claimed in the 1920s and its political power extended to some northern states. Officially disbanded once more in 1944, the Klan again revived in recent years as a response to desegregation and was involved in violent confrontations with anti-Klan and civil rights groups in the 1980s.

KULAKS, term for the historical class of prosperous peasants in Russia: those, e.g., who owned large farms and could employ labor. Stalin designated the kulaks an anachronism in a state-planned economy; they were dispossessed (1929–34) and deported en masse to labor camps.

KUN, Béla (1886–c1939), Hungarian politician and communist premier of Hungary for four months in 1919. Forced to flee by counterrevolutionists, Kun settled in Moscow, returning briefly to Hungary in 1928 to attempt another revolution. He was liquidated in Russia during the 1930s purges.

KÜNG, Hans (1928–   ), Swiss Roman Catholic theologian. A liberal professor and prominent advocate of ecumenism, he served as an official theologian at the Second Vatican Council. His rejection of papal infallibility in such books as *Infallible? An Inquiry* (tr. 1971) led to his censure by the Vatican (1979). Among his other books are *On Being a Christian* (tr. 1978) and *Does God Exist?* (tr. 1980).

KUNIYOSHI, Yasuo (1893–1953), Japanese-born US painter. Undertones of his Oriental heritage surface through somber tones and rich symbolism that pervade his still lifes. This style replaced the whimsy of his early work, which featured fantastic landscapes, mischievous boys and the like.

KUNLUN MOUNTAINS, great chain of mountain ranges in China, on the N extremity of the Tibetan plateau, extending E-W for over 1,800mi. Because they are the longest continuous mountain chain in Asia, they are called the "Backbone of Asia." The highest peak is Ulugh Mus Tagh (25,340ft).

KUOMINTANG (Chinese: National People's Party), political party of CHINA founded (1912) by SUN YAT-SEN to stand for an independent Chinese republic with a moderate socialist reform program. In 1924 Sun's "Three People's Principles" (nationalism, democracy and work for all) were accepted by a coalition that included the communists. After Sun's death (1925) CHIANG KAI-SHEK took over the leadership and in 1927 expelled the communists. Most of China was under Kuomintang rule until 1947, but corruption and galloping inflation hastened communist victory (1949). The Kuomintang survives in the Republic of CHINA.

KUPKA, Frank (Frantisek Kupka; 1871–1957), Czech-born French painter who was among the first "nonobjective" artists. He was noted for the use of bright colors and geometric shapes.

KURCHATOV, Igor Vasilevich (1903–1960), Russian nuclear physicist largely responsible for the development of Soviet nuclear armaments and for the first Soviet nuclear power station. The Soviets have named the transuranium element rutherfordium *kurchatovium* for him.

KURDISTAN, mountainous region in W Asia that includes parts of Turkey, Iran, Iraq, Syria, and Soviet Armenia. It is inhabited by about 8 million Kurds, formerly nomadic herdsmen but now mostly settled farmers. The majority are Sunnite Muslims. For generations the Kurds have sought autonomy from the countries in which they live. Revolts of Turkish Kurds after WWI were severely repressed. Turkey today suppresses any manifestation of Kurdish nationalism. Iraq has long resisted Kurdish demands for self-rule. The 1960s and 1970s saw heavy fighting between Iraqi troops and the Kurds. During the IRAN-IRAQ WAR, Iraqi Kurds sided with Iran. When the war ended, Iraq unleashed a devastating attack against its Kurds, using poison gas. Thousands of Kurds were killed; many survivors sought refuge in Turkey.

KURIL ISLANDS, USSR, chain of 56 volcanic islands, stretching from the Kamchatka Peninsula of Siberia to Hokkaido Island, Japan. Sparsely inhabited, the islands are the subject of a territorial dispute between Japan and the USSR following Russian occupation during WWII. They remain the only Japanese land still under foreign occupation and consequently the major obstacle to close Russo-Japanese economic and diplomatic ties.

KUROSAWA, Akira (1910–   ), Japanese movie director whose outstanding talent and originality have been internationally recognized. His films include *Rashomon* (1950), the widely-distributed epic *Seven Samurai* (1954), *Throne of Blood* (1957), a Japanese interpretation of *Macbeth,* and *Kagemusha* (1981).

KURUSU, Saburo (1886–1954), Japanese diplomat. He held a number of foreign posts (1910–45), including ambassador to Germany, in which position he signed (1940) the Axis pact between Japan, Germany and Italy. In the US in 1941 he and Ambassador Nomuru negotiated with Secretary of State Cordell Hull before the Pearl Harbor attack. After war was declared, he was interned in the US until exchanged for US diplomats in 1942.

KUTUZOV, Mikhail Illarionovich, Prince (1745–1813), Russian field marshal in charge of the forces opposing NAPOLEON I's invasion of Russia in 1812. After a heavy defeat at Borodino Kutuzov successfully adopted evasive tactics, then hounded Napoleon during the retreat from Moscow.

KUWAIT, independent Arab state on the NW coast of the Persian Gulf, bounded S by Saudi Arabia and N and W by Iraq. The country is nearly all desert and the bulk of the population lives in the cities, chief of which is Kuwait, the capital and major port.

Official name: State of Kuwait
Capital: Kuwait
Area: 6,880sq mi
Population: 1,873,000
Languages: Arabic, English
Religions: Muslim
Monetary unit(s): 1 Kuwait dinar=100 fils

Only about half the population is Kuwaiti; the rest are mostly Palestinian, Pakistani and Iranian. A major oil-producer since the 1940s, Kuwait is now a leading economic power with an estimated 20% of the world's oil reserves. Oil revenues finance free education and medical care for all, housing, power stations and water supplies, as well as providing Kuwait with the highest per capita income in the world. Since its foundation in the 18th century, Kuwait has been ruled by the al-Sabah dynasty. Even when a part of the Ottoman Empire, Kuwait retained independence, relying upon the port of Kuwait as its main source of income. A British protectorate from 1899 to 1961, Kuwait has successfully resisted territorial claims from both Saudi Arabia and Iraq; oil revenues from the so-called Partitioned Zone are now divided between Saudi Arabia and Kuwait. In 1975 the oil industry was completely nationalized. Threats to Kuwaiti shipping precipitated US naval involvement in the Persian Gulf during the IRAN-IRAQ WAR, which ended in a cease-fire in 1988.

KUZNETS, Simon Smith (1901–1985), Russian-born US economist. He pioneered development of a conceptual basis for national income accounts in the US, for which he won the Nobel Prize for Economics in 1971. He is noted for studies of structural changes in economic development and growth of nations.

KUZNETSOV, Anatoli (1929–1979), Soviet novelist best known for his documentation of the annihilation of Russian Jews by the Nazis in *Babi Yar* (1970). He defected to England in 1969.

KWAKIUTL INDIANS, North American Indians of Wakashan linguistic stock, native to Vancouver Island and coastal British Columbia, Canada. Skilled in fishing and crafts, they had a strictly hierarchical society in which the POTLATCH ceremony played a significant part. In 1970 the Kwakiutl numbered about 1,500.

KWASHIORKOR, PROTEIN malnutrition simultaneous with the maintenance of relatively adequate calorie intake. In affected children it causes EDEMA, SKIN and HAIR changes, loss of appetite, DIARRHEA, LIVER disturbance and apathy. Treatment involves rehydration, treatment of infection and a balanced diet with adequate protein.

KYD, Thomas (1558–1594), English dramatist, whose *The Spanish Tragedy* (c1586) was a prototype of the Elizabethan and Jacobean revenge tragedy. The work is partly modeled on Seneca but is both more lurid and more psychologically acute. Kyd may have written a version of the Hamlet story.

KYOTO, city in Japan, Honshu Island, about 25mi NE of Osaka. The national capital from its foundation in 794 AD until supplanted by Tokyo in 1868, Kyoto is rich in architectural relics and art treasures. Still today a cultural and religious center, it also has leading educational establishments and large-scale mixed industry with manufactures that include electrical equipment, cameras, chemicals, silk and porcelain. Pop 1,481,126.

KYUSHU, most southerly of the four major islands which make up JAPAN. Area 16,205sq mi.

12th letter of the English alphabet, derived from the Semitic *lamedh* and the Greek *lambda*. In Roman numerals, L represents 50. The symbol £, a form of L, is an abbreviation of the Latin *libra*, a pound in weight.

LABOR, the act of physical work or the social group that does it, namely the labor force; also an economic term applied to any kind of service that commands an economic return. The economic concept of labor was developed in the mid-18th century by Adam SMITH, and later by MALTHUS and above all by MARX in his labor theory of value.

In ancient civilizations manual laborers were generally slaves. In medieval Europe agriculture was carried on by serfs while other productive processes came to be controlled by master craftsmen, who formed GUILDS largely consisting of journeymen. Apprentices were used for simple preparatory operations. Such distribution of production tasks is found even in primitive economies, but it was the mechanization of the INDUSTRIAL REVOLUTION that made division of labor fundamental. This breaks down a given production process into as many simple, repetitive functions as possible, to minimize time-consuming skill and judgment. The immediate result was improved productivity, but also the degradation of work from a potentially creative act to a tedious chore. At the same time, regular hours were needed to get maximum output from machinery, and, because of the fluctuating demand patterns of a growth economy, labor had to be available or dismissible at will. The notion of "free labor" evolved. This replaced the master-servant relationship with a simple implied contract in which the wages, paid only for work done, became full quittance for the laborer's service. The day-laborer, the exception in early civilizations, became the norm. The labor contract released the employer from even notional responsibility for the laborer, but gave the laborer a highly limited freedom to contract where he would.

Labor UNIONS grew from employees'

determination to force employers to observe the labor contract, to acknowledge obligations of humanity in terms of pay and working conditions, and then to improve these terms and conditions. Working hours have diminished from about 70 hours per week (c1800) to about 40 hours in industrialized countries by the 1980s. In many countries organized labor has come to be represented by political parties.

LABOR, US Department of, federal department, independent since 1913, responsible for US workers' welfare. Headed by the secretary of labor, a cabinet member, it is concerned with the enforcement of federal laws regulating hours, wages and safety measures; it collects and issues industrial statistics; it administers job-training programs and provides information in labor disputes. It has several specialized divisions.

LABOR DAY, official holiday in the US and Canada since 1894, held on the first Monday in September. In socialist countries and most others, labor is honored on MAY DAY.

LABOR FORCE, Civilian, as defined by the BUREAU OF LABOR STATISTICS, consists of all employed, self-employed, and unemployed persons (that is, everyone who is working or looking for work) in the civilian, noninstitutional population 16 years of age and older. Military personnel are counted in the total labor force but not the civilian labor force. Inmates of prisons, mental hospitals, sanitariums, and homes for the aged, infirm, and needy are excluded from both the total and the civilian labor force.

LABOR STATISTICS, Bureau of (BLS), agency of the US Department of Labor that collects and analyzes data relating to employment, unemployment, and other characteristics of the labor force; prices and family expenditures; wages, other worker compensation, and industrial relations; productivity and technological change; and occupational safety and health. Most of the data are collected in surveys conducted by the BLS, the Bureau of the Census, or on a cooperative basis with state agencies. The BLS has no enforcement or regulatory functions.

LABOR THEORY OF VALUE, economic theory propounded by David RICARDO and others, which became a central thesis of Karl MARX'S analysis of capitalism. The value of a product is defined in terms of the amount of labor required to manufacture it. This concept has had influence on non-Marxian economics; its prime Marxian corollary is that the value of the products the laborer can buy with his wages is less than that of those he produces. The differential, or **surplus value,** makes the profit of the capitalist.

LABOR UNIONS. See UNIONS.

LABRADOR. See NEWFOUNDLAND.

LABRADOR CURRENT, cold ocean current originating in the Davis Strait. Bearing ICEBERGS, it flows S down the W side of the Labrador Sea to meet the GULF STREAM. (See also OCEAN CURRENTS.)

LA BREA TAR PITS, asphalt bog in Hancock Park, Los Angeles, containing skeletons of prehistoric (PLEISTOCENE) animals, including mammoths, saber-toothed cats and giant sloths, preserved by the tar.

LA BRUYÈRE, Jean de (1645–1696), French moralist. His *Les Caractères* (1688) is partly a translation of THEOPHRASTUS, but mostly his satirical impressions of contemporary society.

LACAN, Jacques (1901–1981), French psychiatrist, an unorthodox Freudian whose controversial theories influenced philosophy and literature.

LACHAISE, Gaston (1882–1935), French-born US sculptor who was best known for his heavy-set nudes, often sculpted larger than life size.

LACLOS, Pierre Ambroise François Choderlos de (1741–1803), French army officer and writer, best known for his novel *Les Liaisons Dangereuses* (1782), which cynically recounts the callous maneuvers of two seducers. He served as a general under Napoleon.

LACROSSE, team game derived by French settlers from the North American Indians' game of baggataway, and now the national game of Canada. It is played with a stick called a cross having a net at one end, and a hard rubber ball. The cross is used to catch, throw and carry the ball with the aim of sending it into the opposing goal. In men's lacrosse, played in Canada, the US and the UK, each team has 10 members. Women's lacrosse is usually played with 12 to a side.

LACTATION, the production of MILK by female mammals. Shortly before the birth of her young, hormonal changes in the mother result in increased development of the mammary glands and teats. Glandular cells in the body of the mammaries secrete milk which is released to the young when the teats are stimulated. Lactation and the feeding of young on milk are characteristic of the MAMMALS.

LACTOSE ($C_{12}H_{22}O_{11}$), a disaccharide SUGAR forming about 4.5% of MILK. It yields GLUCOSE and galactose with the ENZYME lactase.

LADD, William (1778–1841), US pacifist,

founder (1828) of the American Peace Society and author of *Essay on a Congress of Nations* (1840).

LADINO, or **Judeo-Spanish,** language of Jewish communities in the Balkans, Near East and N Africa brought by 15th-century Spanish refugees (see SEPHARDIM). It is an archaic form of Spanish, written in Hebrew characters.

LADYBUGS, or **ladybirds,** small brightly-colored beetles with 5,000 species of worldwide distribution. In length 2.5–7.5mm (0.1–0.3in), they are harlequin-patterned insects with, commonly, black spots on a red background or yellow spots on black. The colors are borne on the wingcases, modified forewings covering the true flying wings. Ladybugs and their larvae feed on plant aphids and have considerable economic value in controlling pest populations.

LA FARGE, Christopher Grant (1862–1938), US architect, best known as a designer of churches, particularly of the early plans of the Cathedral of St. John the Divine in New York City.

LA FARGE, John (1835–1910), influential US artist noted for his fine mural painting and stained glass, chiefly executed for churches such as the mural *Ascension* in the Church of the Ascension, New York. These works are held to be unequaled of their kind in the US. He also produced fine watercolors and drawings and was known for his writing and lectures.

LAFAYETTE, Marie Joseph Paul Yves Roch Gilbert du Motier, Marquis de (1757–1834), French soldier and statesman who fought in the American Revolution and worked for French–American alliance. He came to America 1777, joined Washington's staff as major general and fought in the campaigns of 1777–78 and at Yorktown (1781). On a visit to France (1779) he persuaded Louis XVI to send troops and a fleet to aid the colonists. In the French Revolution he supported the bourgeoisie, helped set up the National Assembly, drafted the Declaration of the Rights of Man, and commanded the National Guard, but fell from power after ordering his troops (July 1791) to fire on the populace. In 1824 he revisited the US, hailed as a hero. He was one of the leaders of the JULY REVOLUTION (1830).

LA FAYETTE, Marie Madeleine Pioche de la Vergne, Comtesse de (1634–1693), French writer and pioneer of the novel of character. She is especially noted for *The Princess of Clèves* (1678).

LAFAYETTE ESCADRILLE, in WWI a flight of US volunteer airmen with the French air service. In 1918 they became the US 103rd Pursuit Squadron.

LAFFITTE or **LAFITTE, Jean** (c1780–1825?), French pirate and smuggler who attacked Spanish ships S of New Orleans. He and his men received a pardon from President Madison in return for aiding Andrew Jackson against the British in 1815, but later went back to piracy. When he attacked US ships (1820) the navy sailed against him, and he set out in his favorite ship the *Pride*, never to be seen again.

LA FOLLETTE, Robert Marion, Sr. (1855–1925), US statesman and reform legislator. He served in the House of Representatives 1885–91. He became Wis. governor (1901–06), supported by progressive Republicans, and initiated the "Wisconsin idea" reform program, proposing direct primaries and a state civil service. He served as senator (1906–25), founded the PROGRESSIVE PARTY, opposed US entry to WWI and the League of Nations, and ran for president 1924.

His son **Robert Marion La Follette, Jr.** (1895–1953), was senator 1925–47, and another son, **Philip Fox La Follette** (1897–1965), was twice governor of Wis.

LA FONTAINE, Jean de (1621–1695), French writer, remembered especially for his *Fables* (1668–94), moral tales drawn from AESOP and oriental sources which he used to comment satirically on contemporary society; and for his humorous, bawdy *Tales* (1664–66).

LAFONTAINE, Sir Louis Hippolyte (1807–1864), Canadian statesman and judge. Leader of the French Canadians from 1837 and joint prime minister with Robert BALDWIN in 1842–43 and of the "great ministry" 1848–51 (its legislation included the Rebellion Losses Bill), he was chief justice of Lower Canada from 1853.

LAGERKVIST, Pär Fabian (1891–1974), Swedish poet, novelist and dramatist, winner of the 1951 Nobel Prize for Literature. He was much disturbed by WWI and later also protested against fascism. His works, which include *Barabbas* (1950), explore the problem of good and evil in man.

LAGERLÖF, Selma Ottiliana Lovisa (1858–1940), Swedish novelist, the first woman to win a Nobel Prize for Literature (1909). Her works, rooted in legend and the folklore of her native Värmland, include *Gösta Berlings Saga* (1891).

LAGRANGE, Joseph Louis (1736–1813), French mathematician who made important contributions to CALCULUS, DIFFERENTIAL EQUATIONS and especially the application of techniques of ANALYSIS to

MECHANICS. He worked also on celestial mechanics, in particular explaining the MOON's libration.

LA GUARDIA, Fiorello Henry (1882–1947), US statesman and reforming mayor of New York. A Republican member of Congress 1917–19 and 1923–33, he supported liberalizing and pro-labor measures, including the Norris–La Guardia Act forbidding the use of injunctions in labor disputes. As mayor 1933–45 he instituted major reforms in New York and fought corruption.

LAHR, Bert (Irving Lahrheim; 1895–1967), US comedian who graduated from burlesque and vaudeville to Broadway. He played the Cowardly Lion in the film *The Wizard of Oz* (1939) and scored a dramatic success in the play *Waiting for Godot* (1956).

LAING, Ronald David (1927–1989), Scottish psychiatrist who argued that mental illness was a response to an insane world. His books include *The Divided Self* (1960) and *The Politics of the Family* (1976).

LAISSEZ-FAIRE (French: let things alone), doctrine which opposes state intervention in economic affairs. First enunciated by the French PHYSIOCRATS in the 18th century as a reaction against MERCANTILISM, the idea was taken up by Adam SMITH and became a cornerstone of classical economics.

LAKE, Simon (1866–1945), US naval architect and engineer who was known as the "father of the modern SUBMARINE." He built the first experimental underwater boat (1894) and the first submarine to be operated successfully in open waters, the gasoline-powered *Argonaut* (1897).

LAKE DISTRICT, region in NW England, since 1951 a national park. It contains the highest mountain in England (Scafell Pike, 3,210ft) and 15 lakes including Windermere, Ullswater and Derwentwater. Its scenic beauty has made it a popular walking and tourist area. William and Dorothy Wordsworth, Samuel Coleridge, and Robert Southey all made their homes here in the early 19th century. (See also LAKE POETS.)

LAKE DWELLING, dwelling built on stilts or piles in the waters of a lake. In parts of Europe can be found STONE AGE and BRONZE AGE lake dwellings, and in some parts of the world they are still built. Crannogs, strongholds built on artificial islands, were built in Ireland, Scotland and England from the Late Stone Age until the Middle Ages.

LAKE POETS, name given to the English poets WORDSWORTH, COLERIDGE and SOUTHEY,

who lived in the LAKE DISTRICT for a time and were described by the critic Jeffrey as constituting the "Lake school of poetry." Although all three were friends, they do not really form a group, for Southey's style differed widely from the others'.

LALANDE, Michel Richard de (1657–1726), French composer. Organist to four Paris churches in his youth, he became director of all sacred music at the court of Louis XIV. He is remembered for his 42 motets for chorus and orchestra.

LALO, Édouard (1823–1892), French composer. A fine orchestrator, he is remembered for his *Symphonie espagnole* (1875) for violin and orchestra, the ballet *Nanouma* (1882) and the opera *Le roi d'Ys* (1888).

LAMAISM, popular term for Tibetan BUDDHISM (Mahayana), a distinctive form that evolved from the 7th century AD; it incorporated strict intellectual disciplines, YOGA and ritual, and large monastic orders as well as the shamanistic features of the old folk-religion. Spiritual and temporal power combined in the DALAI LAMA and PANCHEN LAMA, and the continuity provided by reincarnating lamas created an intensely religious society which remained unchanged until the Chinese invasion (1959). Like Hinduism, Lamaism has innumerable deities with consorts and families to represent symbolically the inner life. It survives in Bhutan, Sikkim, S Siberia, Nepal and Mongolia, and, since 1959, has been gaining new converts in the West.

LAMAR, Lucius Quintus Cincinnatus (1825–1893), US statesman, a prominent Confederate who devoted himself after the Civil War to reconciling north and south. He was US representative (1873–77) and senator (1877–85) from Mississippi, secretary of the interior (1885–88) in the Grover Cleveland administration, and associate justice of the US Supreme Court (1888–93).

LAMAR, Mirabeau Buonaparte (1798–1859), vice-president (1836–38) and president (1838–41) of the Republic of Texas. While in office he resisted union with the US, though he later supported it. He set up a system of public education in Texas.

LAMARCK, Jean Baptiste Pierre Antoine de Monet, Chevalier de (1744–1829), French biologist who did pioneering work on taxonomy (especially that of the invertebrates) which led him to formulate an early theory of EVOLUTION. Where DARWIN was to propose NATURAL SELECTION as a mechanism for evolutionary change, Lamarck felt that organisms could develop new organs in response to their need for them, and that these acquired characteristics could be inherited.

LAMARTINE, Alphonse Marie Louis de (1790–1869), French poet and statesman, briefly head of government after the 1848 revolution (see REVOLUTIONS OF 1848). His collection *Poetic Meditations* (1820) was a landmark of French Romantic literature; lyric evocations of love and nature are underlaid by gentle melancholy and religious feeling.

LAMB, Lady Caroline (1785–1828), wife of 2nd Viscount MELBOURNE, notorious for her passionate affair with Lord BYRON. She wrote several minor novels, including *Glenarvon* (1816), which contains a caricature of Byron. She was famed for her unconventionality and impetuosity.

LAMB, Charles (1775–1834), English essayist and critic. With his sister Mary he wrote *Tales from Shakespeare* (1807) for children. His famous *Essays of Elia* (1823, 1833) contain personal comments on many subjects written with humor and brilliance. He helped revive interest in Elizabethan drama with *Specimens of English Dramatic Poets* (1808).

LAME DUCK AMENDMENT, 20th amendment to the US Constitution, passed in 1933, providing for a new Congress to start work on Jan. 3 after an election, as opposed to the previous date of March 4. It abolished "lame duck" legislative sessions including congressmen who had not been re-elected.

LAMENNAIS, Félicité Robert de (1782–1854), French Roman Catholic cleric, an advocate of ULTRAMONTANISM as necessary for an independent and liberal church in France. He was excommunicated.

LAMENTATIONS, book of the OLD TESTAMENT, traditionally ascribed to Jeremiah, though this is disputed by modern scholars. It consists of a series of five poems in dirge meter (the first four are acrostics) lamenting the fall of Jerusalem at the hands of the Babylonians (586 BC).

LA METTRIE, Julien Offray de (1709–1751), French physician and philosopher who took the idea of "man as machine" to its extreme. He held that all mental phenomena resulted from organic changes in the NERVOUS SYSTEM.

L'AMOUR, Louis (1908–1988), prolific US author of westerns, beginning with *Hondo* (1953), the first novelist to be awarded a congressional gold medal. At his death, all 101 of his books were in print with about 200 million copies in circulation.

LAMPEDUSA, Giuseppe di (1896–1957), Italian novelist. A Sicilian prince, he won critical and popular acclaim with *The Leopard,* posthumously published in 1958.

LAMPREYS, one of the two remaining groups of jawless fishes, Agnatha, found both in freshwater and in the sea. The body is eel-like and there is a round, sucking mouth with horny teeth with which they rasp away at their prey. Many species are parasitic when adult, feeding on the flesh of living fishes. The blind, worm-like, filter-feeding larva, or ammocoete, is totally unlike the adult, and lives only in fresh water. Sea lampreys migrate into fresh waters to breed.

LAMY, Jean Baptiste (1814–1888), French-born Roman Catholic bishop (from 1853) and archbishop (from 1875) in the US southwest. He is the subject of Willa Cather's novel *Death Comes for the Archbishop* (1927).

LANCASTER, House of, English royal family which produced the kings HENRY IV, HENRY V and HENRY VI. Edmund Crouchback, second son of HENRY III, was first earl of Lancaster (1267); his son Thomas (d. 1322) led baronial opposition to EDWARD II. JOHN OF GAUNT became duke of Lancaster by marriage in 1362, and his son became HENRY IV in 1399. The Lancastrians were deposed by the house of YORK during the Wars of the ROSES, but the heir to their claims, Henry TUDOR, reestablished the line in 1485 as HENRY VII.

LAND, Edwin Herbert (1909–   ), US physicist and inventor of Polaroid, a cheap and adaptable means of polarizing light (1932), and the Polaroid Land Camera (1947). In 1937 he set up the Polaroid Corporation to manufacture scientific instruments and antiglare sunglasses incorporating Polaroid.

LANDAU, Lev Davidovich (1908–1968), Soviet physicist who made important contributions in many fields of modern physics. His work on CRYOGENICS was rewarded by the 1962 Nobel Prize for Physics for his development of the theory of liquid HELIUM and his predictions of the behavior of liquid He^3.

LANDER, Richard Lemon (1804–1834), English explorer in Africa who established (1830–31) the course of the Niger R.

LANDERS, Ann (Esther Pauline Friedman Lederer; 1918–   ), US columnist, widely syndicated adviser on life and love from 1955 when she joined the Chicago *Sun-Times.* Her chief rival was her twin sister, **Abigail Van Buren** (Pauline Esther Friedman Phillips; 1918–   ), whose "Dear Abby" column began in the San Francisco *Chronicle* in 1956.

LAND-GRANT COLLEGES, US colleges

set up with the proceeds of land sales. By the Morrill Act of 1862 Congress granted the states federal lands to be sold to establish agricultural and mechanical arts colleges. There are some 70 land-grant colleges in existence today, including many state universities.

LANDIS, Kenesaw Mountain (1866–1944), US judge and first baseball commissioner, appointed (1921) after the "Black Sox" scandal. He barred from organized baseball the eight Chicago White Sox players charged with bribery in the 1919 World Series and imposed strict discipline on players and managers thereafter.

LANDON, Alfred Mossman (1887–1987), governor of Kan. (1933–37) and Republican presidential candidate in 1936, when he lost to Franklin D. ROOSEVELT. His daughter, Nancy Kassebaum, was elected to the Senate in 1978.

LANDOR, Walter Savage (1775–1864), English poet and prose writer. He wrote epics, dramatic fragments, lyrics and epigrams, but is best known for his *Imaginary Conversations* (1824–53), a series of 150 stylish and amusing dialogues between notable characters from different ages.

LANDOWSKA, Wanda (1877–1959), Polish harpsichord virtuoso, largely responsible for the modern revival of the harpsichord. Living in Paris 1900–40, and then in the US, she was famous as a performer, teacher and authority on early music.

LANDSCAPE ARCHITECTURE, the art of modifying land areas to make them more attractive, useful and enjoyable. Highly developed in the ancient civilizations—in China and Japan it had symbolic significance—the art was neglected in Europe after the fall of Rome, but was revived in Renaissance Italy and spread through Europe. The French stress on geometric formality, as at VERSAILLES, was superseded in early-18th-century England by picturesque and dramatic, yet apparently natural hills and lakes and vistas, often over large areas; this style shaped the US tradition. Today landscaping is used in parks, highways and other public amenities. (See also BROWN, CAPABILITY; OLMSTEAD, FREDERICK LAW.)

LANDSEER, Sir Edwin Henry (1802–1873), English artist whose sentimental animal paintings, such as *The Monarch of the Glen* (1851), were enormously popular and frequently reproduced as engravings. He also modeled the lions around Nelson's Column in Trafalgar Square, London.

LANDSTEINER, Karl (1868–1943), Austrian-born US pathologist awarded the 1930 Nobel Prize for Physiology or Medicine for discovering the major BLOOD groups and developing the ABO system of blood typing.

LANE, James Henry (1814–1866), US politician. A US representative (1853–55) from Indiana, he voted for the KANSAS-NEBRASKA ACT, then moved to Kansas and took a leading part in the free-state movement. When Kansas became a state (1861), Lane was one of its first US senators.

LANFRANC (d. 1089), Italian churchman, chief advisor to WILLIAM the Conqueror and from 1070 archbishop of Canterbury. He appointed reforming Norman bishops, enforced clerical celibacy and strengthened the monasteries. As a scholar he helped shape the doctrine of TRANSUBSTANTIATION.

LANFRANCO, Giovanni (1582–1647), Italian painter in the high BAROQUE style who worked principally in Rome and Naples.

LANG, Andrew (1844–1912), Scottish writer and scholar. He pioneered the use of anthropology in folklore in *Custom and Myth* (1884) and *Myth, Literature and Religion* (1887), as well as publishing translations of Homer, popular fairy tale collections, poetry and historical and miscellaneous works.

LANG, Fritz (1890–1976), Austrian film director, one of the masters of EXPRESSIONISM in the silent film. *Metropolis* (1926) was a bleak futuristic drama; in the *Doctor Mabuse* films (1922, 1932, 1960) and above all *M* (1931), about a child murderer, Lang explored the psychology of evil. He left Germany in 1933, and his Hollywood films include the social drama *Fury* (1936), westerns, *Clash by Night* (1952) and *Beyond a Reasonable Doubt* (1956).

LANGE, Christian L. (1869–1938), Norwegian historian and statesman who shared the 1921 Nobel Peace Prize for his work (1909–33) with the Inter-Parliamentary Union.

LANGE, David Russell (1942–   ), New Zealand Labour Party politician, prime minister and foreign minister from 1984. He signed a pact with Australia and other countries of the region declaring the South Pacific a nuclear-free zone and banned nuclear-armed ships from New Zealand ports.

LANGE, Dorothea (1895–1965), US documentary photographer. Her powerful, stark pictures of Depression victims, migrant workers and the rural poor created a profound impression and greatly influenced subsequent photojournalistic technique. In 1939 she published *An American Exodus*.

LANGER, Susanne Knauth (1895–1985), US philosopher whose *Philosophy in a New Key* (1942) propounded for the nondiscursive symbolism of art a meaning and significance equal to that of the discursive symbolism of language and science. Other works include *Mind: An Essay on Human Feeling* (2 vols., 1967, 1972).

LANGLADE, Charles Michel de (1729–1800), Canadian soldier and pioneer settler. Half Indian, he fought against the British in the FRENCH AND INDIAN WAR (1755–59), but later supported them in the REVOLUTIONARY WAR. In retirement at Green Bay, Wis., he became known as the father of Wisconsin.

LANGLAND, William (c1332–c1400), presumed poet of *The Vision of Piers Plowman*, a religious allegory representing a dream-vision of the Christian life and one of the finest examples of Middle English alliterative verse.

LANGLEY, Samuel Pierpont (1834–1906), US astronomer, physicist, meteorologist and inventor of the bolometer to measure radiant energy (1878) and of an early heavier-than-air flying machine. His most important work was investigating the sun's role in bringing about meteorological phenomena.

LANGTON, Stephen (c1155–1228), English cardinal, whose appointment as archbishop of Canterbury (1207) led to a quarrel between Pope INNOCENT III and King JOHN. Despite a papal interdict, John kept him out of his see until 1213. Langton led baronial opposition to the king, and his is the first signature on the MAGNA CARTA. He was a distinguished theologian, noted for his Old Testament commentaries, and helped to develop English canon law and the autonomy of the English Church.

LANGTRY, Lillie (1853–1929), British actress, known as the "Jersey Lily." A famous beauty, she was a mistress of King EDWARD VII.

LANGUAGE, the spoken or written means by which man expresses himself and communicates with others. The word "language" comes from the Latin *lingua*, tongue, demonstrating that speech is the primary form of language and writing the secondary. Language comprises a set of sounds that symbolize the content of the message to be conveyed. It is peculiar to man, constituting as it does a formal system with rules whereby complex messages can be built up out of simple components (see GRAMMAR). Languages are the products of their cultures, arising from the cooperative effort required by societies. There are some 3,000 different languages spoken today, added to which are many more regional dialects. Languages may be classified into families, groups and subgroups. To us the most important language family is the Indo-European, to which many Asian and most European languages (including English) belong. Other important families are the Hamito-Semitic, Altaic, Sino-Tibetan, Austro-Asiatic, and Dravidian, among others. (See also ETYMOLOGY; LINGUISTICS; PHILOLOGY; SEMANTICS; SEMIOLOGY; SHORTHAND; WRITING, HISTORY OF.)

LANGUEDOC, historic region of S France, W of the Rhône R. Montpellier and Nîmes are the main cities, and the chief product wine. Its name comes from *langue d'oc*, the language of the PROVENÇAL culture. Languedoc was the center of the ALBIGENSIAN heresy, and later of French Protestantism.

LANIER, Sidney (1842–1881), US poet and musician. A Southerner who fought in the Civil War (recalled in his novel *Tiger-Lilies*, 1867), he practiced law, and became a professional flutist. After publication of his *Poems* (1877) he became a lecturer at Johns Hopkins U.

LANSBURY, George (1859–1940), British Labour Party politician who devoted himself to the cause of the poor and unemployed. In Parliament (1910–12, 1922–40), he advocated unilateral disarmament, resigned as party leader over the imposition of sanctions on Italy in 1935, and personally visited Hitler and Mussolini to plead for peace.

LANSING, Robert (1864–1928), US international lawyer and statesman. He founded the *American Journal of International Law* (1907), and as secretary of state (1915–20) he concluded the Lansing-Ishii agreement with Japan, 1917, reaffirming the Open Door policy towards China.

LANSING-ISHII AGREEMENT, signed by Robert LANSING for the US and Kikujiro ISHII for Japan, Nov. 1917. It reaffirmed the OPEN DOOR POLICY towards China, while recognizing Japan's imperial interests.

LAOS, landlocked country of SE Asia, bordered by China to the N, Vietnam to the E, Kampuchea (Cambodia) to the S and Thailand and Burma to the W.

Land. Laos is dominated by mountain chains and plateaus, which are cut by deep, narrow valleys. The terrain is covered by forests interspersed with grassland. In the S, limestone plateaus slope W to rice-growing

Official name: Lao People's Democratic Republic
Capital: Vientiane
Area: 91,400sq mi
Population: 3,757,000
Languages: Lao; French widely used
Religions: Buddhist, Animist
Monetary unit(s): 1 kip=100 at

plains along the Mekong R, which forms the border with Burma and most of the border with Thailand and is for 300mi the main transport route of Laos. The wet season of the monsoon climate is from May to Oct., while Nov. to April is a time of near drought. Average temperature in the valleys is above 70°F. Animal life includes elephants, used for lumbering, draft buffalo, and tigers.

People. The Lao, by far the largest ethnic group, are a Thai people; Hinayana (Theravada) Buddhism is the religion of their chiefly valley communities. Animist cults predominate among the mountain peoples, the Meo (Hmong) and Yao (in the N) and Kha (S). In the Mekong towns Chinese and Vietnamese traders are important minorities. Vientiane, the capital, is the only sizeable city.

Economy. Laos has few manufactures (some silk and silver products). Tin (found in central Laos) and timber (teak from the largely unexploited N forests) are the main exports. Opium poppies have traditionally been cultivated as a cash crop in the N. In the valleys in the center and S rice is the chief crop, though tobacco, cotton, tea and coffee are also grown. There are some hydroelectric and irrigation schemes and, in the NW, unexploited iron-ore deposits.

History. Part of the KHMER EMPIRE, the territory was settled from the 10th to 13th centuries by Thai Lao, forced out of Yünnan in S China. By the 17th century a powerful Lao kingdom, based on Khmer culture and Buddhism, had emerged; but in the early 1700s it split into the principalities of Luang Prabang in the N and Vientiane in the S. Civil wars invited foreign dominance, notably from Siam, but in 1893 France established hegemony. After WWII nation-al insurgency of various factions (including the Communist Pathet Lao with Vietnamese support) won the country independence within the French Union in 1949; it remained in the French Union until 1954. In 1959 renewed civil war between the neutralist premier Souvanna Phouma and right- and left-wing rivals brought intervention from the great powers. A coalition government was formed in 1973. In Dec. 1975 the king abdicated, and the country became a Communist republic under the Pathet Lao. The first nationwide elections under Communist rule were held in 1988. That same year, the number of Vietnamese troops stationed in Laos was reduced by half.

LAO-TSE or **LAO-TSU** ("Old Master"), Chinese philosopher of the 6th century BC, said to be the founder of TAOISM and the author of *Tao Te Ching*. His actual existence is uncertain, but he was allegedly a librarian at the Chou court. Tao, or the Way, emphasizes simplicity, naturalness and spontaneity in all the essentials of life.

LA PAZ, largest city and administrative capital of Bolivia (the legal capital is Sucre). Founded in 1548 by the CONQUISTADORS, it is located in La Paz river valley, some 12,000ft above sea level, the world's highest capital. Local products include cement, glass, textiles and consumer goods. Pop. 992,592.

LAPLACE, Pierre Simon, Marquis de (1749–1827), French scientist known for his work on celestial mechanics, especially for his nebular hypothesis, for his many fundamental contributions to mathematics, and for his PROBABILITY studies.

LAPLAND, region in the extreme N of Europe, the homeland of the LAPPS. Within the Arctic Circle, it embraces parts of Norway, Sweden, Finland and Russia, with an area of about 150,000sq mi. It has tundra vegetation.

LAPPS, a people of N Europe who speak an Ugro-Finnic language and may have come originally from central Asia. They number about 30,000 and live mostly in N Norway. Many are nomads who live off their wandering reindeer herds; others engage in fishing, hunting, forestry and agriculture, and live in settled communities.

LARDNER, "Ring" (Ringgold Wilmer Lardner; 1885–1933), US sports journalist and short-story writer. Stories in racy sports idiom, as in *You Know Me, Al* (1916), satirize vulgarity and greed in US life and the success cult. With G. S. Kaufman, he wrote the comedy *June Moon* (1929).

LARES AND PENATES, in ancient Rome, household guardian gods, originally spirits of fields and crossroads. The *lares* became, in the main, deified ancestor figures; the *penates* were seen as personified natural powers bringing prosperity. But the names were generally interchangeable.

LARIONOV, Mikhail (1881–1964), Russian painter and illustrator. He was the originator of the "rayonist" movement which attempted to combine elements of pointillism and cubism. In 1914 he moved permanently to Paris and designed for DIAGHILEV's Ballets Russes, 1914–29.

LARKS, small terrestrial songbirds of Europe, Asia, and Africa, forming the family, Alaudidae. Streaked brown birds, they feed on insects and seeds, walking or running at great speed along the ground. Larks are renowned for their beautiful songs, usually delivered on the wing.

LA ROCHEFOUCAULD, François, Duc de (1613–1680), French writer known for his *Memoirs* (1662) of the FRONDE, and his *Maxims* (1665), a collection of more than 500 moral reflections and epigrams, generally paradoxical, often pessimistic, usually acute.

LARYNGITIS, or INFLAMMATION of LARYNX, usually due to either viral or bacterial infection or chronic VOICE abuse, and leading to hoarseness or loss of voice.

LARYNX, specialized part of the respiratory tract used in VOICE production (see SPEECH AND SPEECH DISORDERS). It lies above the trachea in the neck, forming the Adam's apple, and consists of several CARTILAGE components linked by small MUSCLES. Two folds, or *vocal cords*, lie above the trachea and may be pulled across the airway so as to regulate and intermittently occlude air flow. It is the movement and vibration of these that produce voice.

LA SALLE, René Robert Cavelier, Sieur de (1643–1687), French explorer and fur trader in North America, who claimed the Louisiana territory for France. In Canada from 1666, he commanded Fort Frontenac, sailed across Lake Michigan (1679) and explored the Illinois R and followed the Mississippi R to its mouth on the Gulf of Mexico. In 1684, sailing to plant a colony there, his fleet was wrecked by storms and Spanish raiders. He was killed by a mutinous crew.

LAS CASAS, Bartolomé de (1474–1566), Spanish missionary in the West Indies, South and Central America. He exposed the oppression of the Indians, notably the forced labor of the ENCOMIENDA system, persuaded Madrid to enact the New Laws for Indian welfare (1542) and in his monumental *History of the Indies* recorded data valuable to modern anthropology.

LASCAUX CAVE, cave near Montignac, France, containing many outstanding examples of Aurignacian cave paintings. It was opened to the public in 1940, but deterioration of the paintings led to its being closed in 1963. (See also ALTAMIRA.)

LASCH, Christopher (1932–   ), US social historian, at Rochester U from 1970. His critique of contemporary society is reflected in *Haven in a Heartless World* (1977) and *The Culture of Narcissism* (1979).

LASER, a device producing an intense beam of parallel LIGHT with a precisely defined wavelength. The name is an acronym for "*l*ight *a*mplification by *s*timulated *e*mission of *r*adiation." It works on the same principle as the maser, but at visible rather than microwave frequencies.

The light produced by lasers is very different from that produced by conventional sources. In the latter, all the source atoms radiate independently in all directions, whereas in lasers they radiate in step with each other and in the same direction, producing **coherent light**. Such beams spread very little as they travel, and provide very high capacity communication links. They can be focused into small intense spots, and have been used for cutting and WELDING—notably for refixing detached retinas in the human EYE. Lasers also find application in distance measurement by INTERFERENCE methods, in SPECTROSCOPY and in HOLOGRAPHY.

The active material in laser operation is enclosed between a pair of parallel mirrors, one of them half-silvered; light traveling along the axis is reflected to and fro and builds up rapidly by the stimulated emission process, passing out eventually through the half-silvered mirror, while light in other directions is rapidly lost from the laser.

In pulsed operation, one of the end mirrors is concealed by a shutter, allowing a much higher level of pumping than usual; opening the shutter causes a very intense pulse of light to be produced—up to 100MW for 30ns—while other pulsing techniques can achieve 10^{13} W in picosecond pulses.

Among the common laser types are ruby lasers (optically pumped, with the polished crystal ends serving as mirrors), liquid lasers (with RARE EARTH ions or organic dyes in solution), gas lasers (an electric discharge providing the high proportion of excited states), and the very small SEMICONDUCTOR lasers (based on electron-hole recombination).

LASKI, Harold Joseph (1893–1950), English political theorist, economist and author, active in the FABIAN SOCIETY and the Labour Party. From 1920 he lectured at the London School of Economics and was a visiting lecturer in many countries. In the 1930s he moved from political pluralism to Marxism. His books include *Democracy in Crisis* (1933), *Liberty in the Modern State* (1948) and *The American Democracy* (1948).

LASKY, Jesse Louis (1880–1958), US film producer who, with Samuel Goldwyn and Cecil B. DeMille, produced the first feature-length film made in Hollywood, *The Squaw Man* (1914). Later their firm merged with others to form Paramount Pictures.

LASSALLE, Ferdinand (1825–1864), German socialist and lawyer, co-founder (1863) of the General German Workers' Association, later the Social Democratic Party, the first labor party in Germany. A Hegelian influenced by Marx's economic theories, he nevertheless favored state action, not revolution, as the way to socialism.

LASSUS, Roland de, or Orlando di Lasso (c1530–1594), Flemish Renaissance composer. He was choirmaster at St. John Lateran, Rome, and from 1556 director of music at the ducal court at Munich. His vast and varied output includes religious motets, secular chansons and the great *Penitential Psalms of David* (1584). His expressive integration of music and text anticipated the BAROQUE.

LASSWELL, Harold Dwight (1902–1978), US political scientist, at Chicago U (1924–38) and Yale (1945–75), who introduced psychoanalytic perspectives into the study of politics.

LAST JUDGMENT, in Christian theology, the judgment of all men by God at the end of the world. According to the New Testament, at Christ's SECOND COMING the dead will be raised (see RESURRECTION) and, with those then living, assembled before God to be judged by what they have done: the unrighteous thrown into HELL with Satan, the righteous admitted to HEAVEN. (See also ESCHATOLOGY; PURGATORY.)

LAST SUPPER, the final PASSOVER meal held by Jesus and his disciples in Jerusalem before his crucifixion. In it he distributed bread and wine to them, inaugurating the Christian sacrament of Holy COMMUNION. A popular subject in art, the best-known example is Leonardo da Vinci's fresco in Milan.

LAS VEGAS, city in SE Nev., seat of Clark Co.; world-renowned for "The Strip" with its casinos (state-legalized gambling), luxury hotels, bars and night clubs. The city is also a mining and cattle-farming center.

There are artesian springs nearby. Pop (city) 183,000, (metro) 557,000.

LA TÈNE, late IRON AGE culture of European CELTS, named for the site of the same name at the E end of Lake Neuchâtel, Switzerland. Originating c450 BC, when the Celts came into contact with Greco-Etruscan influences, it died out c50 AD as the Celts became subservient to Rome. La Tène ornaments are decorated with round, S-shaped and spiral patterns.

LATENT HEAT, the quantity of HEAT absorbed or released by a substance in an isothermal (constant-temperature) change of state, such as FUSION or vaporization. The temperature of a heated lump of ice will increase to 0°C and then remain at this temperature until all the ice has melted to water before again rising. The heat energy absorbed at 0°C overcomes the intermolecular forces in the ordered ice structure and increases the kinetic ENERGY of the water molecules.

LATERAN, district of SE Rome, given to the church by Emperor Constantine I in 311. The Lateran palace—the papal residence until 1309—was rebuilt in the 16th century. The basilica of St. John Lateran is the cathedral church of the pope as bishop of Rome.

LATERAN COUNCILS, five ecumenical councils of the Roman Catholic Church held in the Lateran Palace in Rome. The fourth, in 1215, convened by Pope INNOCENT III, was particularly important for its definition of TRANSUBSTANTIATION and its requirement of annual confession and communion at Easter as the minimum for church membership.

LATERAN TREATY, concordat between the papacy and the government of Italy, signed 1929 in the Lateran palace and confirmed by the 1948 Italian constitution. It established Roman Catholicism as Italy's state religion and VATICAN CITY as an independent sovereign state.

LATEX. See RUBBER.

LATHROP, Julia Clifford (1858–1932), US social worker, founder of the first US JUVENILE COURT (1899) and first head of the Children's Bureau of the Department of Labor (1912–21).

LATHROP, Rose Hawthorne (1851–1926), US philanthropist, daughter of Nathaniel Hawthorne. Converting (1891) to Catholicism, she worked among poor cancer patients in New York City. After her husband died (1898), she became a nun.

LATIMER, Hugh (c1490–1555), English Protestant martyr and REFORMATION leader. He defended Henry VIII's divorce from Catherine of Aragon, and was made bishop of Worcester 1535, but resigned 1539 in protest against the king's Six Articles. With Nicholas Ridley, he was burned at Oxford as a heretic, by order of the Roman Catholic Mary I.

LATIN, INDO-EUROPEAN LANGUAGE of the Italic group, the language of ancient Rome and the ancestor of the ROMANCE languages. Originating in Latium c8th century BC, Latin spread with Roman conquests throughout the Empire, differentiating into vulgar Latin and classical (literary) Latin. It is a logical and highly inflected language that has furnished scientific and legal terminology and is still used in the Roman Catholic Church. It was the international language of scholarship and diplomacy until the 18th century. About half of all English words are Latin in origin, many derived through Old French.

LATIN AMERICA, traditionally 20 independent republics in Middle and SOUTH AMERICA where Romance languages are spoken: Spanish in Mexico, Cuba, Dominican Republic, Costa Rica, El Salvador, Guatemala, Honduras, Nicaragua, Panama, Argentina, Bolivia, Chile, Colombia, Ecuador, Paraguay, Peru, Uruguay, and Venezuela; Portuguese in Brazil; and French in Haiti. Sometimes the term includes Guyana, Suriname, and French Guiana in South America, and, less often, also all the Caribbean Islands.

People. About 429 million people live in Latin America (including Central America and the Caribbean). They have Indian, black, and white ancestry. The population growth of some 2.2% a year is one of the highest in the world. Differences in educational levels and social structure are great—the predominantly white, literate, middle-class populations of Argentina, Uruguay and Costa Rica have little in common with traditional Indian communities of Mexico, Bolivia, Peru and Ecuador. Despite educational campaigns, illiteracy rates remain high, especially in remote highlands. The universities, which are seldom technologically oriented, suffer from lack of full-time teaching staffs. After World War II, large numbers of people moved from rural to urban areas in search of employment, and most large cities are now surrounded by extensive squatter colonies. Housing, social, and medical services are usually inadequate.

Economy. Historically, Latin American economies depended on one export commodity—oil, copper, tin, coffee, bananas, livestock, fish—to earn foreign currency. In several countries there have been efforts at diversification, but economic develop-ment is hampered by poor transport, political instability, and burdensome effects of foreign aid. Persistent unequal income distribution and urban unemployment (reaching up to 50%) are two great problems that still defy solution. Although about half of the people work on the land, agriculture is mostly primitive and inefficient. Important changes in recent decades include the emergence of Brazil as a leading industrial power, and use of oil revenues in Mexico and Venezuela to finance economic growth. Argentina, Brazil, Mexico and other nations borrowed huge sums from the INTERNATIONAL MONETARY FUND and from private banks, leading to a near-crisis in the 1980s when they were unable to repay their debts.

History. Before the arrival of COLUMBUS in 1492, several highly developed civilizations flourished in the region, most notably the MAYAS, AZTECS and INCAS. During the conquest the indigenous populations were decimated by war and European diseases. Spanish and Portuguese colonial rule lasted about three hundred years, and by 1825 most of the colonies, inspired by the leadership of BOLÍVAR and SAN MARTÍN, gained their independence. Power and wealth, however, remained in the hands of tiny minorities, and political life was marked by corruption and instability. In the 20th century, several countries (Mexico, Chile, Costa Rica, Uruguay) enjoyed long peaceful periods of constitutional rule. The 1960s and 1970s saw an upsurge of military dictatorships throughout the region and violent factional strife in Central America. Since 1979, many nations have returned to democratic rule, including Argentina, Brazil, Ecuador, Peru, Uruguay, Guatemala, Honduras, Bolivia, and El Salvador; the US intervened in Grenada to restore democracy there. Unrest in Central America continued, however, despite the 1987 signing of a regional peace accord.

LATIN KINGDOM OF JERUSALEM, feudal state in Palestine and Syria created (1099) by the Crusaders. GODFREY OF BOUILLON was elected its first king. The feudal lords fought constantly among themselves and against the Turks, Egyptians, and Byzantines. SALADIN recaptured Jerusalem in 1187, and the last Latin stronghold, Acre, fell in 1291.

LATITUDE AND LONGITUDE, the coordinate system used to locate points on the earth's surface. **Longitude** "lines" are circles passing through the poles whose centers are at the center of the earth; they divide the earth rather like an orange into segments. Longitudes are measured

0°–180°E and W from the line of the GREENWICH OBSERVATORY. Assuming the EARTH to be a sphere, we can think of the **latitude** of a point as the ANGLE between a line from the center of the earth to the point and a line from the center to the equator at the same longitude. Each pole, then, has a latitude of 90°, and so latitude is measured from 0° to 90° N and S of the EQUATOR. latitude "lines" being circles parallel to the equator that get progressively smaller towards the poles. (See CELESTIAL SPHERE.)

LATIUM, historic region of Italy, "the cradle of the Roman people," extending from the Tiber R to the Alban Hills; now part of the W coast region of Latium, or Lazio. This includes the provinces of Rome, Frosinone, Latina, Rieti and Viterbo.

LA TOUR, Georges de (1593–1652), French painter of religious and genre subjects. Renowned in his lifetime, he was virtually forgotten until 1915. Influenced indirectly by CARAVAGGIO, his work exploited indirect lighting sources and candle light and was characterized by simple forms and warm colors.

LATROBE, Benjamin Henry (1764–1820), English-born US architect and engineer. His work includes the S wing of the Capitol in Washington and Baltimore's Roman Catholic cathedral. A pioneer of the Classical revival, he was the first major professional architect in the US.

LATTER-DAY SAINTS, Church of Jesus Christ of. See MORMONS.

LATTER-DAY SAINTS, Reorganized Church of Jesus Christ of, sect which split from the main body of MORMONS when Brigham Young became leader at the death of Joseph Smith. They chose Smith's son as their leader, becoming formally organized in 1852. They follow the main Mormon beliefs but admit blacks as priests. The headquarters are at Independence, Mo.

LATTIMORE, Owen (1900–   ), US orientalist, an expert on China, who edited (1934–41) the magazine *Pacific Affairs* and taught (1939–53) at Johns Hopkins U. In 1950, US senator Joseph MCCARTHY accused him of being a Soviet spy. Finally cleared in 1955, he worked abroad in 1953, at Leeds U, England, 1963–70.

LATTIMORE, Richmond Alexander (1906–1984), US poet, noted for his poetic insights into the history, philosophy, and literature of Greece. His major works are *Sestina for a Far-Off Summer* (1962), *The Stride of Time* (1966), *Poems from Three Decades* (1972).

LATTRE DE TASSIGNY, Jean de (1889–1952), French general who led Free French forces in the invasion of S France

(1944) and Germany (1944–45) and represented France at the German surrender on May 8, 1945. He was French commander in chief in Indochina 1950–52.

LATVIA, a republic of the USSR, bordering on the Baltic Sea, between Estonia and Lithuania; its capital is RIGA. It is a lowland country, covering some 24,600sq mi, with a moderate continental climate. Nearly a third of the people are Russians, but the majority are Letts, an ancient Baltic people. Cattle and dairy farming, fishing and lumbering are still important, but there are highly developed industries, including steel, shipbuilding, engineering, textiles, cement and fertilizers. Christianized by the German Livonian Knights in the 13th century, Latvia was ruled by Poles, Swedes and, from the 18th century, Russians. From 1920 to 1940, when it was reabsorbed in Russia, it enjoyed a precarious independence. In the late 1980s, taking advantage of the relaxed political and economic climate initiated by Soviet leader Mikhail Gorbachev, Latvian demonstrators denounced Russia's 1940 annexation of the country and called for greater control of local economies, an end to russification of the culture, and the right to limit the immigration of Russians. (See also UNION OF SOVIET SOCIALIST REPUBLICS.)

LAUD, William (1573–1645), archbishop of Canterbury from 1633 and a chief advisor of CHARLES I. He enforced High Church beliefs and ritual, and his authoritarianism and persecution of English Puritans and Scottish Presbyterians provoked parliamentary impeachment (1640). He was executed for treason.

LAUGHTON, Charles (1899–1962), English-born actor, a US citizen from 1950. Films include the award-winning *The Private Life of Henry VIII* (1933) and *The Hunchback of Notre Dame* (1939). He directed *Night of the Hunter* (1955).

LAUREL AND HARDY, famous Hollywood comedy team. The English-born **Stan Laurel** (Arthur Stanley Jefferson; 1890–1965) and the American **Oliver Hardy** (1892–1957), thin man and fat man, simpleton and pompous heavy, made over 200 films between 1927 and 1945 in a style, shaped by Laurel, which ranged from slapstick to slow-paced comedy of situation and audience anticipation.

LAURIER, Sir Wilfrid (1841–1919), first French-Canadian prime minister of Canada 1896–1911. Leader of the federal Liberal party 1887–1919, he encouraged provincial autonomy while seeking to unite the country. Many of his attempts to better the rights of French-Canadians, particularly in education, met with little success. Defeated in the 1911 election, he was supported by Quebec and rejected by the rest of Canada in the 1917 election, a divisive result he worked against.

LAUSANNE, Treaty of (1923), peace treaty between the WWI Allies and Turkey replacing the earlier Treaty of SÈVRES, which Kemal ATATÜRK rejected. The Treaty of Lausanne recognized Turkish independence and sovereignty and exacted no reparations in return for Turkey's renouncing claims to prewar territory.

LAUTARO (c1533–1557), leader of the ARAUCANIAN INDIANS who almost reconquered Chile from the Spanish. He is a symbol of Chilean independence.

LAVA, both molten ROCK rising to the earth's surface through VOLCANOES and other fissures, and the same after solidification. Originating as MAGMA deep below the surface, most lavas (e.g., basalt) are basaltic (subsilicic) and flow freely for considerable distances. Lavas of intermediate silica content are called andesite. Silica-rich lavas such as rhyolite are much stiffer. Basaltic lavas solidify in a variety of forms, the commonest being *aa* (Hawaiian, rough) or block lava, forming irregular jagged blocks, and *pahoehoe* (Hawaiian, satiny) or ropy lava, solidifying in ropelike strands. Pillow lava, with rounded surfaces, has solidified under water, and slowly-cooled basalt may form hexagonal columns.

LAVAL, François de Montmorency (1623–1708), vicar-apostolic of New France (1659) and first bishop of Quebec, Canada, from 1674. He frequently clashed with the administrators of New France, bitterly opposing the profitable liquor trade with the Indians. He retired in 1684 to the Quebec Seminary (now Laval U.) founded by him in 1663.

LAVAL, Pierre (1883–1945), French politician who collaborated with the Germans in WWII. A socialist and pacifist, he served three unsuccessful terms as premier 1931–32, 1932 and 1935–36. Believing that Nazi victory was inevitable, he allowed himself to be installed as a Nazi puppet premier 1942–44. He fled abroad, returned for trial (1945) and was executed.

LAVER, Rod (Rodney George Laver; 1938–   ), Australian tennis player, the only player to win (1962, 1969) two grand slams (British, French, Australian, and US championships in the same year).

LA VERENDRYE, Pierre Gaultier de Varennes, Sieur de (1685–1749), French-Canadian explorer and fur trader. He founded a trail of important fur-trading posts as far as Mo. in his unsuccessful efforts to find an overland route to the Pacific.

LAVIGERIE, Charles Martial Allemand (1825–1892), French cardinal, archbishop of Algiers (from 1867). He worked against slavery and directed missionary activity among African Muslims. He is most famous for calling (1890) on Catholics to support the Third Republic.

LAVOISIER, Antoine Laurent (1743–1794), French scientist who was foremost in the establishment of modern CHEMISTRY. He applied gravimetric methods to the process of COMBUSTION, showing that when substances burned, they combined with a component in the air (1772). Learning from J. PRIESTLEY of his "dephlogisticated air" (1774), he recognized that it was with this that substances combined in burning. In 1779 he renamed the gas *oxygène*, because he believed it was a component in all acids. Then, having discovered the nature of the components in water, he commenced his attack on the PHLOGISTON theory, proposing a new chemical nomenclature (1787), and publishing his epoch-making *Elementary Treatise of Chemistry* (1789). In the years before his tragic death on the guillotine, he also investigated the chemistry of RESPIRATION, demonstrating its analogy with combustion.

LAW, Andrew Bonar (1858–1923), Canadian-born Scottish politician. He succeeded BALFOUR as leader of the Conservative Party in 1911. Colonial secretary in the 1915 war cabinet, he was chancellor of the exchequer under LLOYD GEORGE 1916–18 and prime minister 1922–23.

LAW, John (1671–1729), pioneering Scottish financier. After the success of a private bank he established in Paris in 1716 he founded his Mississippi Company, winning a monopoly of La. commerce; it later bought up the French East India Co. His bank became the state bank and he was made controller-general of France. Lacking experience of inflation, he created a boom by issuing unredeemable paper money. Ruined in the resulting collapse, he had to leave France and died in poverty.

LAW, body of rules governing the relationship between the members of a community and the individual and the state. In England, the British Commonwealth and the US the law is based upon statute law, laws enacted by legislative bodies such as Congress, and upon COMMON LAW, the body of law created by custom and adherence to rules derived from previous judgments. This also covers the body of law created by EQUITY. The other main system,

CIVIL LAW, derives from the laws of ancient Rome and relies not on precedent but on a code of rules established and modified only by statute. This is the dominant system in most of Europe and in many other countries of the world. In fact the division is not absolute. Many areas of the common law are codified by statute for convenience; there is often unofficial but very real reliance on previous decisions in civil law countries.

All major bodies of law break down into two divisions, public law and private law (often called civil law also). Public law governs matters which concern the state. CRIMINAL LAW is public because a crime is an offense against the state; other kinds of public law are administrative law, INTERNATIONAL LAW and CONSTITUTIONAL LAW. Private law governs the relationship between individuals (including corporate bodies such as companies) in such matters as CONTRACT,, and the law of TORT; this covers damaging acts done by one individual to another which are not necessarily crimes.

History of law. The first legal system of which we have any detailed knowledge is that of the Babylonian King HAMMURABI in c1700 BC, a complex code linking crime with punishment and regulating the conduct of everyday affairs. Like the Hebrew Mosaic Law, it treated law as a divine ordinance; the ancient Greeks were probably the first to regard law as made by man for his own benefit. Roman law was based on the Twelve Tables, compiled c451–450 BC; it developed a complex equity system when these became outdated. The emperor JUSTINIAN produced the last definitive code in an attempt to clear up resulting difficulties. Much medieval law was based on Church law, although an independent system arose quite early in England. This grew into the common law and spread outwards with the growth of the British Empire. Napoleon revised Roman law as the basis for his CODE NAPOLÉON, the model for most subsequent civil law codes. US law grew out of the common law, but has been much modified by the federal system.

LAW OF THE SEA CONFERENCE, an international assembly that first met in Geneva in 1958. Issues relating to control of the high seas include the extent of national off-shore territory and free passage of foreign ships through international straits. The most important and difficult matter is the access to valuable minerals on the ocean floor, especially manganese nodules, which also hold deposits of cobalt and copper. A draft accord was reached in 1980 by some 150 nations, and in 1982 the Law of the Sea Treaty received majority approval in the UN, largely because of Third World support, but the US voted against it.

LAWRENCE, D(avid) H(erbert) (1885–1930), major English author. He combined a vivid prose style with a solid background of ideas and intense human insight. Stressing the supremacy of instinct and emotion over reason in human relationships, he advocated absolute sexual candor; his novel *Lady Chatterley's Lover* (1928) is known for this to the exclusion of its other themes. Perhaps his best works are *The Rainbow* (1915) and *Women in Love* (1920). From a working-class background (reflected in *Sons and Lovers*, 1913), he was for some years a teacher. He died of pleurisy at Vence in France.

LAWRENCE, Ernest Orlando (1901–1958), US physicist awarded the 1939 Nobel Prize for Physics for his invention of the cyclotron (1929; the first successful model was built in 1931).

LAWRENCE, James (1781–1813), US naval officer, captain of the frigate *Chesapeake*, sunk by the British frigate *Shannon* off Boston in 1813. He was mortally wounded; his dying words "Don't give up the ship!" have become proverbial.

LAWRENCE, Sir Thomas (1769–1830), English painter, the most fashionable portraitist of his time. President of the Royal Academy from 1820, he never had the success he wished for as a history painter. His style is richly colorful, fluid and vigorous, but occasionally careless.

LAWRENCE, T(homas) E(dward), called "Lawrence of Arabia" (1888–1935), English scholar, writer and soldier, legendary guerrilla fighter with the Arabs against the Turks in WWI. As a British intelligence officer he carried out with Prince FAISAL a successful guerrilla campaign against Turkish rail supply lines, and was with the Arab forces that captured Damascus in 1918. In *The Seven Pillars of Wisdom* (1926) he described his wartime experiences and his personal philosophy. A neurotic, lonely man, he joined the Royal Air Force and Royal Tank Corps under assumed names 1923–25 and again 1925–35. He was killed in a motorcycle crash.

LAWSON, Ernest (1873–1939), US Impressionist painter. One of the eight members of the ASHCAN SCHOOL, he exhibited at their controversial ARMORY SHOW. Seeking a greater degree of naturalism, he specialized in serene landscapes, often rendered in glowing colors, such as *Winter* (1914) and *High Bridge* (1939).

LAXNESS, Halldór Kiljan (1902–   ), Iceland's greatest modern writer. He became famous with his novel *Salka Valka* (1934). This and later books such as *The Atom Station* (1945) are harsh but compassionate descriptions of Icelandic rural life and post-WWII problems. He was awarded the Nobel Prize in 1955.

LAYARD, Sir Austen Henry (1817–1894), British archaeologist known for his excavations of Assyrian and Babylonian remains, and especially for his confirmation of the site of Nineveh.

LAZARUS, Emma (1849–1887), US poet best known for the sonnet *The New Colossus* engraved at the base of the Statue of Liberty. Of a Sephardic Jewish family, she based much of her work on Jewish culture and supported Jewish nationalism.

LEACOCK, Stephen Butler (1869–1944), Canadian economist, at McGill U 1908–36. He is best remembered for his humorous essays.

LEAD (Pb), soft, bluish-gray metal in Group IVA of the PERIODIC TABLE, occurring as galena and also as cerussite and anglesite (lead sulfate). The sulfide ore is converted to the oxide by roasting, then smelted with coke. Lead dissolves in dilute nitric acid, but is otherwise resistant to corrosion because of a protective surface layer of the oxide, sulfate, etc. It is used in roofing, water pipes, coverings for electric cables, radiation shields, ammunition, storage BATTERIES, and alloys, including solder (see SOLDERING), PEWTER, babbitt metal and type metal. Lead and its compounds are toxic (see LEAD POISONING). AW 207.2, mp 327.5°C, bp 1740°C, sg 11.35 (20°C).

Lead forms two series of salts; the lead(II) compounds are more stable than the lead(IV) compounds. **Lead(II) oxide** (PbO), or **litharge**, yellow crystalline solid, made by oxidizing lead; used in lead-acid storage batteries, glass and glazes; mp 888°C. **Lead(IV) oxide** (PbO_2), brown crystalline solid, a powerful oxidizing agent used in matches, fireworks, and dyes; it decomposes at 290°C. **Trilead tetroxide** (Pb_3O_4), or **red lead**, orange-red powder, made by oxidizing litharge, used in paints, inks, glazes and magnets. **Lead tetraethyl** ($Pb[C_2H_5]_4$), colorless liquid, made by reacting a lead/sodium alloy with ethyl chloride. It is used as an ANTIKNOCK ADDITIVE to GASOLINE.

LEADBELLY. See LEDBETTER, HUDDIE.

LEAD POISONING, DISEASE caused by excessive LEAD levels in TISSUES and BLOOD. It may be taken in through the industrial use of lead, through AIR POLLUTION due to lead-containing fuels or, in children, through eating old paint. BRAIN disturbance with COMA or convulsions, peripheral NEURITIS, ANEMIA and abdominal colic are important effects. Chelating agents are used in treatment, but preventive measures are essential.

LEAF, green outgrowth from the stems of higher plants and the main site of PHOTOSYNTHESIS. The form of leaves varies from species to species but the basic features are similar. Each leaf consists of a flat blade, or lamina, attached to the main stem by a leaf stalk or petiole. Leaf-like stipules may be found at the base of the petiole. The green coloration is produced by CHLOROPHYLL which is sited in the chloroplasts. Most leaves are covered by a waterproof covering or cuticle. Gaseous exchange takes place through small openings called stomata, through which water vapor also passes (see TRANSPIRATION). The blade of the leaf is strengthened by veins which contain the vascular tissue that is responsible for conducting water around the plant and also the substances essential for METABOLISM.

In some plants the leaves are adapted to catch insects (see INSECTIVOROUS PLANTS), while in others they are modified to reduce water loss (see SUCCULENTS). Leaves produced immediately below the FLOWERS are called bracts, and in some species, e.g., poinsettia, they are more highly colored than the flowers.

LEAGUE OF NATIONS (1920–46), the first major international association of countries; a total of 63 states were members, although not all simultaneously. In WWI Allied leaders, particularly President WILSON, became convinced of the need for an international organization to resolve conflicts peacefully and avert another devastating war. The charter of the proposed League of Nations was incorporated in the Treaty of VERSAILLES. Ironically, however, Wilson was unable to persuade the US Senate to ratify the treaty and thus join the League; this may have been the League's greatest weakness. The Covenant embodied the principles of collective security against an aggressor, arbitration of international disputes, disarmament and open diplomacy.

Established at Geneva, Switzerland, the League grew during the 1920s, taking in many new members, but it never had much influence. It could do little to stop the Italian invasion of Corfu in 1923 or the CHACO WAR. It did no more than investigate and protest the Japanese invasion of

Manchuria in 1931. Its failure to take decisive action against Italy over the invasion of Ethiopia in 1934 was the final blow to its prestige; WWII proved it a failure. Its subsidiary organizations, however, such as the INTERNATIONAL LABOR ORGANIZATION and the INTERNATIONAL COURT OF JUSTICE, have endured, as have the public health bodies it created.

LEAGUE OF WOMEN VOTERS, nonpartisan organization with about 125,000 members in the US and Puerto Rico, founded in 1920 by members of the National American Women Suffrage Association. Apart from political education for its members, the league studies and campaigns on economic and social issues. It does not sponsor electoral candidates or political parties.

LEAHY, Frank William (1908–1973), US college football coach, most notably at Notre Dame (1941–53), where his record was 107-13-9.

LEAKEY, Louis Seymour Bazett (1903–1972), British archaeologist and anthropologist best known for his findings of human FOSSILS, especially in the region of Olduvai Gorge, Tanzania, and for his (sometimes controversial) views on their significance. His wife, **Mary Leakey** (1913–   ), collaborated with him. Their son **Richard Leakey** (1944–   ) continued their work.

LEANING TOWER OF PISA, white marble bell tower or *campanile* in Pisa, Italy. Building was started in 1174, reputedly by Bonanno Pisano, but the foundations were unsound and the 184.5ft tower had already begun to lean by the time of its completion in the 14th century. It now tilts more than 17ft from the perpendicular.

LEAP YEAR. See CALENDAR.

LEAR, Edward (1812–1888), English artist, traveler and versifier, best known for his limericks and nonsense rhymes. *The Owl and the Pussy-Cat* is a famous example. His landscapes and illustrated journals are highly regarded.

LEARNING, refers to the acquisition of new knowledge and new responses. If it were not for early learning you would be unable either to read these words or to understand them. The concepts of learning and MEMORY are closely related, though learning is usually considered to be the result of practice, which in itself is encouraged by a particular stimulus. The simplest learned response is the conditioned REFLEX. The most powerful learning stimulus is the satisfaction of instinctive drives (see INSTINCT). For example, a dog might learn that if he sits up and "begs" he will be fed by his owner. Here the stimulus is positive, in that the result of his response is a reward, rather than negative, where the correct response earns only escape from punishment: positive stimuli are more effective encouragements to learning than are negative. All animals display the ability to learn, and even some of the most primitive have the ability to become bored with the tests of experimenters (where the reward is not an adequate stimulus). In humans, learning ability depends to a great extent on INTELLIGENCE, though social and environmental factors clearly play a part. (See also CONDITIONING.)

LEASE, Mary Elizabeth (1853–1933), US agrarian protester and temperance advocate. An active supporter of POPULISM in the 1890s, she urged farmers to "raise less corn and more hell."

LEATHER, animal hide or skin that has been treated by tanning to preserve it from decay and to make it strong, supple, water-resistant and attractive in appearance. The skins are typically preserved temporarily by soaking in brine and kept in cold storage. They are washed and soaked in an alkaline solution, then scraped to remove the hair. Rapidly rotating blades remove residual fat and flesh. The hides are then neutralized and softened by soaking in pancreatic enzymes, and pickled in dilute acid to make them ready for tanning. The tanned leather is finished by being squeezed to remove excess liquid, lubricated with oil, slowly dried and impregnated with resins. It is commonly dyed, and a shiny surface is produced by compression. Most leather is made from the hide of sheep, cows, calves, goat, kids and pigs; for exotic products, from the skins of crocodiles, sharks and snakes. Leather is used to make shoes, gloves, coats and other garments, upholstery, bags and luggage, wallets, transmission belts, etc. and to bind books. Chamois leather, for cleaning, is now made from sheepskin.

LEAVEN, substance used to make dough rise during baking by producing gases which expand to make the food light and porous. YEAST produces CARBON dioxide by FERMENTATION; baking powder and SODIUM bicarbonate produce carbon dioxide by chemical reaction. Air may be introduced by vigorous whipping.

LEAVIS, F(rank) R(aymond) (1895–1978), influential English literary critic and lecturer. Leavis judged works by their moral standpoint and condemned low standards in modern culture. He edited the quarterly review *Scrutiny* (1932–53) and wrote *New Bearings in English Poetry*

(1932), *The Great Tradition* (1948) and *The Common Pursuit* (1952).

LEBANON, Mediterranean republic in SW Asia, a small Arab state bordered by Syria and Israel.

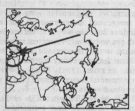

Official name: Republic of Lebanon
Capital: Beirut
Area: 3,950sq mi
Population: 2,762,000
Languages: Arabic; French and English widely used
Religions: Muslim, Christian
Monetary unit(s): 1 Lebanese pound=100 piastres

Land. The four main regions, paralleling the sea, are the flat, fertile, coastal strip; the Lebanon Mountains; the narrow, fertile Bekaa (Biqa) Valley and the Anti-Lebanon Mountains. Lebanon has more rain (15–50in per year) and a more moderate climate than its neighbors. Only a few groves of the famous "cedars of Lebanon" remain on the once-forested mountains.

People. Lebanon is an Arab state. The last official census, taken in 1932, showed Christians (mainly MARONITES) in the majority. Muslims include SUNNITES, SHI'ITES, and DRUZES (a small sect historically of great importance). The uneasy balance of power maintained by Muslims and Christians over the centuries has been upset by an influx of Palestinian refugees since 1948, many of whom subsequently settled in various refugee camps in the S.

The level of education is highest in the Middle East, with about 85% of the population literate. There are five universities, including the American University of Beirut (1866) which has an international reputation.

Economy. About half the labor force works in agriculture, producing grains, olives and citrus fruits. Until the 1975–76 civil war the country had a service-oriented economy, with Beirut the financial and banking capital of the Middle East. Remittances sent home by Lebanese working abroad are a major source of income.

History. The site of ancient PHOENICIA,

Lebanon is a land of great antiquity and resilience. Although engulfed by successive invaders—Greek, Roman, Arab and Turkish—it preserved some degree of autonomy. Lebanon's inaccessible mountains were an early refuge for persecuted religious groups, especially Christians, whose influence was entrenched during the CRUSADES. Freed from Turkish rule after WWI, the country passed into French hands, becoming effectively independent in 1943. During the early Arab-Israeli conflicts Lebanon was able to steer a course of noninvolvement. Civil war erupted in 1975 between the conservative Christian Phalangists and leftist Muslim and Palestinian militias, including the PALESTINE LIBERATION ORGANIZATION. Despite a 1976 ceasefire, sporadic fighting continued, mostly in Beirut. Beginning in the late 1970s S Lebanon was the scene of fighting between Palestinian guerrillas and Israeli troops. In 1982 Israel invaded Lebanon, occupying Beirut and eventually forcing many PLO guerrillas to leave the country. During the Israeli occupation Christian forces massacred 700–800 Palestinian refugees in two camps near Beirut. A multinational peace-keeping force, including US marines, arrived (1982) in Beirut but was withdrawn in 1984 after being subjected to terrorist attacks. Most Israeli troops were withdrawn from the country by mid-1985. Conflict continued despite efforts by Syria, which had had a military presence in Lebanon since 1976, to arrange a peace accord. In 1988, Lebanon's political leaders were unable to agree upon a successor to retiring president Amin Gemayel and established rival Christian and Muslim governments, posing an additional obstacle to Lebanese unity.

LE BRUN, Charles (1619–1690), French artist, "first painter" to Louis XIV and virtual dictator of the arts in France 1662–83. He directed the GOBELIN tapestry works and decorated the Palace of Versailles.

LE CARRÉ, John (David John Moore Cornwell; 1931–), English author of realistic novels of international espionage, including *The Spy Who Came In from the Cold* (1963), *Tinker, Tailor, Soldier, Spy* (1974), *Smiley's People* (1980) and *A Perfect Spy* (1987).

LECKY, William Edward Hartpole (1838–1903), British historian, noted for his *History of England in the Eighteenth Century* (8 vols., 1878–90).

LECLERC, Charles Victor Emmanuel (1772–1802), French general sent by Napoleon to reclaim Haiti from the native revolutionaries. He captured the black leader TOUSSAINT L'OUVERTURE by treachery, but the Haitians fought on and expelled the French, who were decimated by yellow fever. Leclerc died of the disease.

LECLERC, Jacques Philippe (1902–1947), name assumed by Jacques Philippe, Vicomte de Hauteclocque, WWII Free French commander. He led his forces from French Equatorial Africa 1,500mi across the Sahara to Tunisia 1942–43. In 1944 he received the surrender of Paris.

LECOMPTON CONSTITUTION, proslavery state constitution approved at Lecompton, Kan., 1857. Overwhelmingly rejected by referendum in 1858, and replaced by the antislavery Wyandotte Constitution, 1859, it helped to delay the admission of Kan. into the Union until 1861.

LECONTE DE LISLE, Charles Marie René (1818–1894), French poet and translator of classical verse. Established by his *Poésies barbares* (1862) as chief among the PARNASSIANS, he succeeded Victor HUGO at the Académie Française (1886).

LE CORBUSIER (1887–1965), professional name of Charles-Édouard Jeanneret: Swiss-born, French-trained architect, a founder of the INTERNATIONAL STYLE. His austere, rectangular designs made in the 1920s and 1930s reflected his view of a house as a "machine to live in." Later influential designs (featuring reinforced concrete) include apartments at Marseilles, a chapel at Ronchamp and Chandigarh, in India.

LEDBETTER, Huddie ("Leadbelly"; c1888–1949), US Negro blues and folk singer and guitarist, born in La. His repertoire and powerful singing style impressed the folk historian and archivist John Avery LOMAX, who became his patron. Leadbelly sang in New York nightclubs in the 1940s.

LEDERBERG, Joshua (1925–   ), US geneticist awarded with G. W. Beadle and E. L. Tatum the 1958 Nobel Prize for Physiology or Medicine for his work on bacterial genetics. With Tatum, he showed that the offspring of different mutants of *Escherichia coli* had genes recombined from those of the original generation, thus establishing the sexuality of *E. coli*. Later he showed that genetic information could be carried between *Salmonella* by certain bacterial viruses. (See also BACTERIA; GENETICS; VIRUS.)

LEDUC, Violette (1907–1972), French writer, best known for the autobiographical *La Bâtarde* (1964).

LEE, Ann (1736–1784), English-born religious mystic, founder of the SHAKERS in North America. Imprisoned in 1770 for street-preaching, in 1774 she emigrated to America, founding the first Shaker colony near Albany, N.Y., in 1776.

LEE, Arthur (1740–1792), American diplomat who sought aid in Europe 1776–79 as an agent of the CONTINENTAL CONGRESS. He made little headway in Spain and Berlin and quarreled with fellow commissioners Silas DEANE and Benjamin FRANKLIN. But in 1778 all three signed treaties with France.

LEE, Charles (1731–1782), American major general in the Revolutionary War. He refused orders from George Washington (1776), planned betrayal while in British captivity (1776–78), and retreated at the Battle of Monmouth (1778), robbing Washington of a victory. He was court-martialed, deprived of his command and later dismissed.

LEE, Fitzhugh (1835–1905), Confederate cavalry general in the American Civil War, a nephew of Robert E. Lee. He was governor of Virginia 1886–90.

LEE, Henry ("Light Horse Harry"; 1756–1818), dashing American cavalry officer in the Revolutionary War, highly praised by George Washington. He was governor of Va. 1791–94 and a representative in Congress 1799–1801. Civil War general Robert E. LEE was his son.

LEE, Richard Henry (1732–1794), American Revolutionary statesman from Va., member of the CONTINENTAL CONGRESS 1774–79, 1784–87, president 1784–85. On June 7, 1776, he introduced the motion that led to the DECLARATION OF INDEPENDENCE. He opposed ratification of the US Constitution, fearing its effects on states' rights. As a US senator from Va., 1789–92, he helped secure adoption of the BILL OF RIGHTS.

LEE, Robert Edward (1807–1870), commander of the Confederate armies in the American Civil War. Son of Henry LEE, he was born at Stratford, Va., graduated from WEST POINT (1829) and served brilliantly as a field engineer in the MEXICAN WAR 1846–48. He was superintendent of West Point 1852–55, and in 1859 arrested John BROWN at HARPERS FERRY. Lee opposed slavery and secession, but from loyalty to his native Va., declined Lincoln's offer of command of the Union armies in 1861 and reluctantly accepted a Confederate post. He became a full general in May 1861 and a year later gained command of the Army of Northern Virginia. His first great success was the defense of Richmond in the Seven Days' Battle (June 26–July 2, 1862). After the Confederate victory at the second Battle of BULL RUN, Lee invaded Maryland but was halted at ANTIETAM. Victory at CHANCELLORSVILLE encouraged a further offensive into Pa., but he was turned back at the Battle of GETTYSBURG. Lee finally surrendered to Ulysses S. GRANT at APPOMATTOX COURT HOUSE on April 9, 1865. Universally respected for his personal qualities and brilliant generalship, he ended his days as a college president.

LEECHES, annelid worms, segmented, with a prominent attachment sucker at the posterior end and another sucker around the mouth. Leeches are hermaphroditic. Freshwater or semiterrestrial animals, they feed by sucking the blood or other body fluids of mammals, small invertebrates, worms, insect larvae or snails. The crop is capable of great distention to enable large meals to be taken as occasion permits, for, with many species, meals are available only at intervals, and then only by chance. A fully-grown medicinal leech can survive for a whole year on a single blood meal.

LEE KUAN YEW (1923–   ), first prime minister of independent Singapore (from 1959). Originally a socialist, he became progressively more conservative, allowing no substantive opposition while presiding over an economic boom.

LEE TENG-HUI (1923–   ), first native Taiwanese to become (1988) president of Taiwan, succeeding Chiang Ching-kuo, who, with his father, Chiang Kai-shek, had ruled the island since fleeing mainland China in 1949.

LEEUWENHOEK, Anton van (1632–1723). Dutch microscopist who made important observations of CAPILLARIES, red BLOOD corpuscles and sperm cells, and who is best known for being the first to observe BACTERIA and PROTOZOA (1674–6), which he called "very little animalcules." (See also MICROSCOPE.)

LEEWARD ISLANDS, chain of about 15 islands and many islets in the West Indies, northernmost group of the Lesser Antilles. They include Antigua, Anguilla, Montserrat, and the British Virgin Islands (British colonies); St. Kitts-Nevis (a former British colony, independent since 1983); St. Eustatius, Saba and S St. Martin (Dutch); Guadeloupe and dependencies (French); and the Virgin Islands of the US.

LEFEBVRE,   Georges   (1874–1959), French historian, author of major works on the French Revolution and Napoleon.

LEFEBVRE   D'ETAPLES,   Jacques (c1450–1536), French theologian, a leading Christian humanist who advocated reform of the church. He translated the Bible into French.

LEFT-HANDEDNESS. See HANDEDNESS.

LE GALLIENNE, Eva (1899–   ), US actress, producer, and director, founder (1926) of the Civic Repertory Theater and cofounder (1946) of the American Repertory Theater, both in New York, where she produced and directed classic revivals.

LEGAL PROFESSION, body of people concerned with the interpretation and application of the law. The first law school in the US was started at Harvard U. in 1817. Students wishing to qualify as attorneys must usually complete at least two years of college, graduate from law school and pass a state bar examination. Since requirements vary from state to state, lawyers may usually practice only in the state in which they qualified. There are different types of legal careers. Lawyers may enter private practice, where they will advise individuals or firms on matters ranging from criminal defense to divorce, income tax, wills, contracts, trusts, mortgages and claims for injury. Then there are law firms that specialize in corporation law, advising clients on such matters as labor laws, antitrust laws, tax laws and corporate organization and finance. Large corporations often possess their own legal department. State and federal governments employ lawyers as city attorneys, judges, prosecutors and in legal aid organizations. Most lawyers belong to a professional legal association, the largest of which is the American Bar Association. Many states have their own bar association. The other main branch of the legal profession is the bench. A JUDGE is a member of the bench just as a lawyer is a member of the bar. Judges serve at all levels from district and municipal courts to the US SUPREME COURT. Federal judges are appointed by the president with the Senate's advice and consent and may only be removed by impeachment. State judges are elected and serve for a given number of years. The legal profession in England differs chiefly in retaining the official separation of barrister and solicitor. (See also JUDICIARY.)

LEGAL TENDER CASES, US Supreme Court cases which tested Congress's constitutional right to make US notes legal tender. The ruling in *Hepburn v. Griswold* (1870) declared that greenbacks were not legal tender. This ruling was reversed in *Knox v. Lee* (1871) and *Juillard v. Greenman* (1884).

LEGER, Fernand (1881–1955), French painter. A Cubist, he used strong colors and geometrical shapes and introduced such objects as cogwheels and pistons. His preoccupation with the machine age may be seen in such paintings as *The City* (1919). He designed huge murals for the UN in New York. (See also CUBISM.)

LEGIONNAIRE'S DISEASE, a mysterious pneumonia-like illness that broke out among people who attended an American Legion convention in July 1976 at Philadelphia's Bellevue Stratford Hotel. The disease got national attention as the number of deaths mounted, eventually reaching 29, and as doctors searched frantically for its cause and cure. Not until Jan. 18, 1977, was Dr. Joseph E. McDade, a scientist at the government's Center for Disease Control in Atlanta, Ga., able to report that he had traced the illness to a bacterium that, though probably widespread and the cause of other, earlier outbreaks of fatal pneumonia, had not previously been identified. The most effective treatment was found later to be erythromycin, an antibiotic.

LEGISLATURE, representative assembly empowered to enact, revise or repeal the laws or statutes of a community. The earliest modern legislatures were the British PARLIAMENT and the French STATES-GENERAL, which were forerunners of the contemporary bicameral system of upper and lower houses. In the US the two chambers are the Senate and the House of Representatives, which together are called CONGRESS. In most bicameral systems both chambers must usually approve a bill before it becomes law. Under a parliamentary system, such as Britain's or Canada's, a government can only remain in power if it retains a majority in the main legislative chamber. Under the US system, the president stays in office for his term even if he lacks a majority in the legislature.

LEGUMINOUS PLANTS, general name for plants of the pea family (Leguminosae), the fruit of which are called legumes (pods). In terms of number of species, this family is second in size only to the Compositae. There are many economically important species, including acacia, alfalfa, bean, lentil, pea and soybean. The roots of leguminous plants produce nodules containing nitrogen-fixing bacteria.

LEHAR, Franz (1870–1948), Hungarian composer famous for Viennese-style light opera. His most successful work was the melodious operetta *The Merry Widow* (1905).

LEHMAN, Herbert Henry (1878–1963), US Democratic politician. A banker, he was governor of New York (1933–43), the first director of the UNITED NATIONS RELIEF AND REHABILITATION ADMINISTRATION (1943–46), and US senator (1949–57).

LEHMANN, Lotte (1888–1976), German-US soprano. She sang with the Vienna State Opera (1914–38) and in the US at the Metropolitan (1934–45). Famous for her Marschallin in *Der Rosenkavalier*, she created roles in other Richard STRAUSS operas and was a skilled interpreter of lieder.

LEHMBRUCK, Wilhelm (1881–1919), German sculptor noted for his images of pathos and heroism of spirit. Influenced by Gothic sculpture and the modern works of PICASSO and MODIGLIANI, he depicted his human subjects as ascetic, angular figures.

LEIBNIZ, Gottfried Wilhelm von (1646–1716), German philosopher, historian, jurist, geologist and mathematician, codiscoverer of the CALCULUS and author of the theory of monads. His discovery of the calculus was independent of though later than that of NEWTON, yet it is the Leibnizian form which predominates today. He devised a calculating machine and a symbolic mathematical logic. His concept of the universe as a "pre-established harmony," his analysis of the problem of evil, his epistemology, logic, and philosophy of nature place him in the foremost rank of philosophers and helped mold the mind of the ENLIGHTENMENT.

LEICESTER, Robert Dudley, Earl of (c1532–1588), favorite and one-time suitor of Elizabeth I of England. Although his political and military performances were poor and his reputation was marred by suspicions of treason, wife-murder and bigamy, he wielded great power and was made a privy councillor and army commander.

LEIF ERICSON. See ERICSON, LEIF.

LEINSDORF, Erich (1912–   ), Austrian conductor who began his career as assistant to Bruno Walter and Arturo Toscanini at the Salzburg festival in 1934. By 1940 he had become a principal conductor at New York's Metropolitan Opera and was its director 1957–62. He directed the Boston Symphony Orchestra 1962–69.

LEIPZIG, city in S central East Germany, capital of Leipzig District. A major cultural, commercial and manufacturing center, it has fine medieval and renaissance architecture. Karl Marx U. (formerly Leipzig U.) is there. Pop 552,133.

LEISLER, Jacob (1640–1691), German-born leader of an insurrection in colonial New York. A Protestant, he welcomed the succession of William III in England and seized control of New York in the belief that the royal officials there were Catholics and that a French invasion was imminent. When a new royal governor arrived, Leisler was hanged as a traitor.

LELY, Sir Peter (1618–1680), Dutch-English portrait painter, born Pieter van der Faes. He moved to England about 1641 and became court painter to Charles I and Charles II. His works include portrait series of court beauties and English admirals.

LEMAÎTRE, Georges Édouard (1894–1966), Belgian physicist who first proposed the "big bang" model of the universe, explaining the RED SHIFTS of the galaxies as due to recession (see DOPPLER EFFECT), thereby inferring that the universe is expanding. The theory holds that the origins of the universe lie in the explosion of a primeval atom, the "cosmic egg."

LEMMINGS, small rodents, about 3–6in long, closely related to voles. They are the characteristic rodents of the Arctic tundra and are well adapted to severe conditions. Like many small mammals of simple ecological systems lemmings show periodic fluctuations in numbers with a periodicity of 3–4 years. These result in spectacular mass migrations whereby surplus animals in a high population area emigrate to find new ranges.

LEMON, *Citrus limon*, a small evergreen tree which produces the popular, sour, yellow fruits that are rich in VITAMIN C. The fruits also contain an oil that is used in cooking and the manufacture of perfume. The US and Italy are the chief producers of lemon fruit. Family: Rutaceae.

LEMURS, cat-sized primates found on Madagascar and small islands nearby, related to primitive ancestors of the whole primate group of monkeys and apes. They are nocturnal and strictly arboreal, feeding on insects, fruit, even small mammals. The family Lemuridae includes two subfamilies: the Cheirogaleinae, or mouse lemurs, and the Lemurinae, true lemurs.

LENDL, Ivan (1960–   ), Czech-born US tennis player, US Open winner 1985–87.

LEND-LEASE, program by which the US sent aid to the Allies in WWII, during and after neutrality. President Roosevelt initiated the program in 1941 to help countries "resisting aggression." Total aid exceeded 50 billion dollars and not only bolstered Allied defense but developed the US war industries and helped mobilize public opinion.

L'ENFANT, Pierre Charles (1754–1825), French-American engineer and architect who fought in the Revolutionary War and was commissioned (1791) to plan Washington, DC. Because of opposition his plans were shelved and L'Enfant was long dead when they were revived to become (1901) the basis for the development of the city. L'Enfant also designed Federal Hall in New York City.

LENIN, Vladimir Ilyich (1870–1924), Russian revolutionary, founder of the Bolshevik (later Communist) Party, leader of the Bolshevik Revolution of 1917 and founder of the Soviet state. Born Vladimir Ilyich Ulyanov, Lenin became a revolutionary after his elder brother was executed (1887) for participating in a plot to assassinate the tsar. By then a follower of Karl MARX, Lenin was exiled to Siberia (1887–90) for his activities; on his release he went to W Europe. In 1902 he published his famous pamphlet *What Is to Be Done?* arguing that only professional revolutionaries trained to lead a proletarian-peasant rising could bring Marxist socialism to Russia. Subsequent factional disputes between proponents of Lenin's BOLSHEVISM and the less radical MENSHEVIKS were interrupted only by the abortive Russian revolution of 1905, when Lenin and his fellow Marxists returned briefly to Russia. Lenin's confidence in the imminence of revolution was profoundly shaken by the rush of the socialist parties of Europe to support their own governments at the outbreak of WWI, and news of the 1917 RUSSIAN REVOLUTION, when it came, was sudden and unexpected. Lenin returned at once to Russia with German aid, and within six months the Bolsheviks controlled the state. Against overwhelming odds, and at the massive cost of the German-Russian treaty of BREST-LITOVSK, Lenin maintained and consolidated power. The history of his remaining years is that of the birth of Soviet Russia.

Lenin influenced COMMUNISM more than anyone else except Karl Marx. He adapted Marxist theory to the realities of Russia's backward economy but displayed his continuing hope of world-wide socialist revolution by founding the Comintern. Before his death from a series of strokes he warned against STALIN's growing ambition for power.

LENINGRAD, second largest city and chief port of the USSR, on the Gulf of Finland, capital of Leningrad oblast and former Russian capital (as St. Petersburg 1712–1914, Petrograd 1914–24). Founded (1703) by Peter the Great and linked by its port with W Europe, it rapidly became a cultural and commercial center. Industrial expansion during the 19th century was followed by a temporary decline during WWI and the RUSSIAN REVOLUTION. The city was renamed for Lenin in 1924. There was great destruction and loss of life in the German siege (1941–44) during WWII, since when Leningrad has been restored and enlarged. Today industries include heavy machinery manufacturing, shipbuilding, chemicals and textiles. The city has a university, outstanding libraries and art galleries, museums and palaces. Pop 4,867,000.

LE NÔTRE, André (1613–1700), French landscape architect who dominated European garden design for many years. His strictly geometrical creations, including the gardens of VERSAILLES, featured splendid vistas and radiating paths.

LENS, Optical, a piece of transparent material having at least one curved surface and which is used to focus light radiation in CAMERAS, glasses, MICROSCOPES, TELESCOPES and other optical instruments. The typical thin lens is formed from a glass disk, though crystalline minerals and moulded plastics are also used and, as with spectacle lenses, shapes other than circular are quite common.

The principal axis of a lens is the perpendicular to its surface at its center. Lenses which are thicker in the middle than at the edges focus a parallel beam of light traveling along the principal axis at the principal focus, a point on the axis on the far side of the lens from the light source. Such lenses are converging lenses. The distance between the principal focus and the center of the lens is known as the focal length of the lens; its focal power is the reciprocal of its focal length and is expressed in diopters (m^{-1}).

A lens thicker at its edges than in the middle spreads out a parallel beam of light passing through along its principal axis as if it were radiating from a virtual focus one focal length out from the lens center on the same side as the source. Such a lens is a diverging lens.

Lens surfaces may be either inward curving (concave), outward bulging (convex) or flat (plane). It is the combination of the properties of the two surfaces which determines the focal power of the lens. In general, images of objects produced using single thin lenses suffer from various defects including spherical and chromatic aberration (see ABERRATION, Optical), coma (in which peripheral images of points are distorted into pear-shaped spots) and astigmatism. The effects of these are minimized by designing compound lenses in which simple lenses of different shapes and refractive indexes (see REFRACTION) are combined. Achromatic lenses reduce chromatic aberration; aplanatic lenses

reduce this and coma, and anastigmatic lenses combat astigmatism. (See also LIGHT.)

LENT, period of 40 days dedicated by Christians to penitential prayer and fasting as a preparation for EASTER. In the West it begins on ASH WEDNESDAY.

LENYA, Lotte (1900–1981), Austrian-born US singer and actress. She performed on the stage in Berlin 1920–33, notably in *The Three-Penny Opera* (1928), composed by her husband, Kurt WEILL, in collaboration with BRECHT. In the US after 1933 she sang and acted in productions of several Weill works, including a 1954 revival of *The Three-Penny Opera*. She also appeared in motion pictures.

LEO, name of 13 popes. **Saint Leo I** (d. 461), called "the Great," reigned 440–461. He suppressed heresy and established his authority in both the West and the East. He persuaded the barbarian leaders ATTILA (in 452) and Genseric (in 455) not to destroy Rome. **Saint Leo III** (d. 816), reigned 795–816, crowned CHARLEMAGNE "Emperor of the Romans" in Rome on Christmas Day, 800, thus allying church and state. **Saint Leo IX** (1002–1054), reigned 1049–54, fought against simony and vigorously enjoined clerical celibacy. The GREAT SCHISM began in his reign. **Leo X** (1475–1521) reigned 1513–21. A MEDICI, he made Rome a center of the arts and literature, and raised money for rebuilding St. Peter's by the sale of indulgences—a practice attacked by Martin LUTHER at the start of the REFORMATION. **Leo XIII** (1810–1903), reigned 1878–1903, worked to reconcile Roman Catholicism with science and liberalism, and generally applied Christian principles to the religious and social questions of his time. His famous encyclical *Rerum Novarum* (1891), on the condition of the working classes, strengthened Roman Catholicism's links with the working-class movement and helped counter anticlericalism at home and abroad.

LEÓN, medieval kingdom of NW Spain, today a region which includes the provinces of León, Salamanca and Zamora. Forged in the 10th century by the rulers of ASTURIAS, the kingdom for a while spearheaded the Christian reconquest of Spain from the Moors. It was permanently joined to Castile in 1230.

LEONARDO DA VINCI (1452–1519), Italian RENAISSANCE painter, sculptor, architect, engineer and naturalist celebrated as history's outstanding "Renaissance man." Born in Vinci, Tuscany, the illegitimate son of a notary, he studied painting with VERROCCHIO in Florence. He worked at Ludovico Sforza's court in Milan as an architect, military engineer, inventor, theatrical designer, sculptor, musician, scientist, art theorist and painter. His fresco, *The Last Supper* (c1495), in Milan, is noted for its innovative composition and variety of gesture. He thought that painting should express the laws of light and space and of sciences like anatomy, botany and geology, and this he attempted in *Virgin of the Rocks* (c1506). He made thousands of sketches and notes in connection with his investigations into the laws of nature; his growing sense of awe of the world is reflected in the painting *Mona Lisa* (c1514), now in the Louvre, Paris. In Rome, 1513–16, he was preoccupied by the dynamic movement to be found in nature. He spent his last years at the French court of FRANCIS I, venerated as a genius.

LEONCAVALLO, Ruggiero (1858–1919), Italian opera composer. He wrote many operas, of which only the melodramatic *I Pagliacci* (The Clowns, 1892) is now widely known.

LEONIDAS (d. 480 BC), king of Sparta who, with 300 Spartans and about 1,000 other Greeks, died heroically defending the pass of THERMOPYLAE against the huge invading Persian army of XERXES.

LEONTIEF, Wassily (1906–   ), Russian-born US economist, who developed the techniques of input-output analysis. He came to New York in 1931 and subsequently worked at Harvard U. and New York U. In 1973 he won the Nobel Memorial Prize in Economics.

LEOPARD, *Panthera pardus*, a big cat similar to the JAGUAR, with a yellow coat marked with black rosettes. Found in a variety of habitats across Africa and Asia, they are agile cats which rely when hunting on their power to spring quickly. The leopard is well known for its habit of dragging its kill up into a tree out of the reach of jackals and hyenas. The kill may weigh more than the leopard itself.

LEOPARDI, Giacomo, Count (1798–1837), Italian poet and philosopher, one of the foremost writers of his time. Acutely unhappy almost all his life, he expressed himself most fully in his brilliant, supple, lyric poetry of which the major volume is *Songs* (1836). *Moral Essays* (1827) reveals his bleak philosophy.

LEOPOLD, three kings of the Belgians. Leopold I (1790–1865), a Saxe-Coburg, was elected king by the Belgians in June 1831. He did much to create national unity and carried out some reforms. He was the uncle of England's Queen Victoria. Leopold

II (1835–1909), his son, reigned from 1865. He promoted exploration in Africa and in 1885 established the Congo Free State (see ZAÏRE), which he exploited for personal gain until it was taken over by the Belgian government in 1908. There was great commercial and industrial growth in Belgium during his reign. Leopold III (1901–1983), reigned 1934–51. He lost popularity by ordering surrender to the Nazis in 1940, and was compelled to abdicate in favor of his son BAUDOUIN.

LEOPOLD, Nathan Jr. (1904–1971), and **Richard Loeb** (1905–1931), US murderers. Brilliant sons of wealthy Chicago families, they kidnapped and murdered (1924) 14-year-old Bobby Franks in a "perfect murder." Defended by Clarence DARROW, they were sentenced to life imprisonment. Loeb was murdered in prison. Leopold, released in 1958, worked as a medical technician in Puerto Rico.

LEPANTO, Battle of, Christian naval victory over the Muslim Turks, Oct. 7, 1571. John of Austria led combined Spanish, Venetian and papal fleets which crushed the Turkish fleet in the Gulf of Patras near Lepanto, Greece. The battle somewhat moderated the power of the OTTOMAN EMPIRE.

LEPIDOPTERA, the insect order that includes the BUTTERFLIES and MOTHS. Their bodies and wings are covered with minute scales of chitin often pigmented to produce the colors and patterns characteristic of these insects. The mouthparts of the adults are formed into a *proboscis*, a tube for sucking up liquid such as the nectar from flowers. The life history includes the egg, a larva or CATERPILLAR, a PUPA or chrysalis and the usually winged adult. The caterpillar is totally different in structure and habit from the adult, feeding with chewing mouthparts on a variety of vegetable materials, completely separated ecologically from the adult. Caterpillars feed voraciously and those of many species are agricultural pests. In the chrysalis, a resting stage, the structure of the adult insect is organized (see METAMORPHOSIS).

LEPRECHAUN, in Irish folklore, mischievous fairy usually depicted as a little old man. Traditionally each leprechaun has buried a crock (pot) of gold, the location of which it can be forced to reveal.

LEPROSY, or Hansen's disease, chronic disease caused by a mycobacterium and virtually restricted to tropical zones. It leads to SKIN nodules with loss of pigmentation, mucous membrane lesions in nose and pharynx, and NEURITIS with nerve thickening, loss of pain sensation and patchy weakness, often involving face and intrinsic hand muscles. Diagnosis is by demonstrating the organisms in stained scrapings or by skin or nerve biopsy. The type of disease caused depends on the number of bacteria encountered and basic resistance to the disease. Treatment is with sulfones (Dapsone).

LERMONTOV, Mikhail Yurevich (1814–1841), Russian poet and novelist. Initially influenced by BYRON, he wrote outstandingly fine lyric and narrative poetry. His prose masterpiece is the novel *A Hero of Our Time* (1840), an early example of psychological realism. He died in a duel.

LE SAGE, Alain René (1668–1747), French novelist and dramatist. His picaresque masterpiece *Gil Blas* (1715–35) greatly influenced the development of the realistic novel in France. It is a witty satirical account of all levels of French society.

LESOTHO, formerly **Basutoland,** landlocked kingdom surrounded by, and economically dependent on, the white-ruled Republic of South Africa.

Official name: Kingdom of Lesotho
Capital: Maseru
Area: 11,720sq mi
Population: 1,628,000
Languages: Sesotho, English
Religions: Christian, Animist
Monetary unit(s): 1 loti = 100 cents
Land. Part of the great plateau of S Africa, Lesotho lies mainly between 8,000ft and 11,000ft. In the E and N is the Drakensberg mountain range. The chief rivers are the Orange R and its tributaries. Annual rainfall averages under 30in and temperatures vary seasonally from 93°F to 30°F. Sparsely forested, Lesotho is mainly dry grassland.
People and Economy. The Basuto, who comprise all but 1% of the population, are chiefly rural. Education is mainly in the hands of missionaries; there is a literacy rate of about 50%, and about 70% of the people are Christian. An agricultural country, Lesotho is heavily dependent on livestock and food crops such as wheat and maize.

Poor farming techniques have resulted in a shortage of good land. Although Lesotho is opposed to apartheid, it depends heavily upon South Africa for trade and employment.
History. The nation was established c1829 by Chief Moshoeshoe I, who secured British protection from Boer encroachment. As Basutoland, it was under British rule from 1884, gaining independence in 1966. Chief Leabua Jonathan was prime minister from independence until 1986, when he was overthrown in a military coup. King Moshoeshoe II, whom Jonathan had stripped of all political authority under a state of emergency (1970–83), swore in the coup's leader as prime minister.

LESSEPS, Ferdinand Marie, Vicomte de (1805–1894), French diplomat whose idea for a canal to cross the isthmus of Suez resulted in the SUEZ CANAL. Lesseps supervised the building of it (1859–69) himself. His later plans for a Panama canal failed.

LESSING, Doris (1919–), British novelist, and short story writer, raised in Southern Rhodesia, who has dealt perceptively with the struggles of intellectual women for political, sexual, and artistic integrity. Her major works include *The Golden Notebook* (1962), *The Four-Gated City* (1969) (part of *The Children of Violence* series) and *The Good Terrorist* (1985).

LESSING, Gotthold Ephraim (1729–1781), German playwright, critic and philosopher, founder of a new national literature. He rejected French classicism and pioneered German bourgeois tragedy with *Miss Sara Sampson* (1755). He also wrote the influential comedy *Minna von Barnhelm* (1767), the prose tragedy *Emilia Galotti* (1772) and the dramatic poem *Nathan the Wise* (1779). The treatise *Laokoön* (1766) critically contrasted the natures of poetry and painting.

LEUCTRA, Battle of, battle in 371 BC that made Thebes supreme in Greece. The Thebans under Epaminondas crushed the numerically superior Spartans by using brilliant innovatory tactics.

LEUKEMIA, malignant proliferation of white blood cells in BLOOD or BONE marrow. It may be divided into acute and chronic forms for both granulocytes and lymphocytes. In acute forms, primitive cells predominate and progression is rapid with ANEMIA, bruising and infection. Acute lymphocytic leukemia is commonest in young children. Chronic forms are present in adult life with mild systemic symptoms, susceptibility to infection and enlarged

LYMPH nodes (lymphatic) or SPLEEN and LIVER (granulocytic). Cancer CHEMOTHERAPY and ANTIBIOTICS have greatly improved survival prospects.

LEUTZE, Emanuel (1816–1868), US historical painter. His large-scale, patriotic works include *Westward the Course of Empire Takes its Way* and *Washington Crossing the Delaware*.

LEVANT, the E Mediterranean countries, from Turkey to Egypt (inclusive), so named from the French *lever* (to rise), Levant implying lands of the sunrise, that is, of the east.

LE VAU, Louis (1612–1670), French architect employed by Louis XIV on the Louvre and the palace at Versailles.

LEVELLERS, radical reformers of the English Civil War and Commonwealth period. Their leader, John LILBURNE, advocated a republic, economic reforms and political and religious equality. Oliver Cromwell, to whom they were bitterly opposed, broke their power.

LEVER, the simplest MACHINE, a rigid beam pivoted at a *fulcrum* so that an *effort* acting at one point of the beam may be used to shift a *load* acting at another point on the beam. There are three classes of lever: those with the fulcrum between the effort and the load; those with the load between the fulcrum and the effort, and those with the effort between the fulcrum and the load. The part of the beam between the load and the fulcrum is the load arm; that between the effort and the fulcrum, the effort arm. The effort multiplied by the length of the effort arm equals the load multiplied by the length of the load arm: a load of 50kg, 5m from the fulcrum, may be moved by any effort 10m from the fulcrum greater than 25kg (the longer the effort arm, the less effort required). Load divided by effort gives the mechanical advantage; in this case 2. A first-class lever (e.g., a crowbar) has a mechanical advantage greater, less than or equal to 1; a second-class (e.g., a wheelbarrow), always more than 1; a third-class (e.g., the human arm), always less than 1. (See also ARCHIMEDES; MECHANICS.)

LEVERRIER, Urbain Jean Joseph (1811–1877), French astronomer whose calculations from the perturbations of Uranus led to the discovery of the planet NEPTUNE.

LÉVESQUE, René (1922–1987), Canadian politician, a founder and leader of the Parti Quebecois committed to independence for Quebec. He was elected (1976) premier of Quebec, but a referendum on separation was rejected (1980) and the party dropped (1985) that goal. Lévesque resigned as party leader and premier.

LEVI, Carlo (1902–1975), Italian painter and writer. His exile to S Italy for anti-Fascist activities led to his best-known book, *Christ Stopped at Eboli* (1945).

LEVIATHAN, in the Bible, the name of a primordial monster, or, as in the Book of Job, a sea monster, perhaps a whale. The name is commonly used for anything massive, particularly ships. It was used by HOBBES as an allegorical title for the state.

LEVINE, Jack (1915–   ), US satirical painter. Believing that art must have some social significance, he rejects abstract art in favor of a satirically distorted realism, seen in such works as *Feast of Pure Reason* (1937), *Welcome Home* (1946) and *Gangster Funeral* (1953).

LEVINE, James (1943–   ), US pianist, conductor and opera executive. In 1964–70 he was an apprentice conductor of the Cleveland Symphony Orchestra under George Szell and then assistant conductor. In 1972 he became principal conductor at the Metropolitan Opera, where he was appointed music director in 1975. He received the additional post of artistic director in 1983.

LEVINE, Philip (1900–1987), US medical scientist, a pioneering researcher in serums and antibodies who discovered the Rh factor in human BLOOD.

LÉVI-STRAUSS, Claude (1908–   ), Belgian–born French social anthropologist, best known for his advocacy of *structuralism*, an analytical method whereby different cultural patterns are related so that the universal logical substructure underlying them may be elicited. His writings include *Structural Anthropology* (1958) and *The Savage Mind* (1962).

LEVITES, in ancient Israel, the tribe descended from Levi, son of Jacob. As priestly auxiliaries the care of the Ark and the Sanctuary was their special responsibility, and in Jerusalem they had hereditary duties at the Temple and were later teachers of the Law.

LEVITICUS, in the Old Testament, third of the five books of the PENTATEUCH. It is essentially a collection of liturgical and ceremonial laws.

LEVITT, William Jaird (1907–   ), US builder who revolutionized the housing industry after WWII with moderately priced, mass-produced, one-family suburban houses in Levittowns in New York, New Jersey, and Pennsylvania.

LÉVY-BRUHL, Lucien (1857–1939), French anthropologist who studied the differences between primitive and civilized mentalities.

LEWES, George Henry (1817–1878), English author and critic. He wrote on philosophy, but his most successful work was his *Life of Goethe* (1855). He greatly influenced George ELLIOT, with whom he lived from 1854.

LEWIN, Kurt (1890–1947), German-born US psychologist, an early member of the GESTALT PSYCHOLOGY school, best known for his development of field theory and especially the concept of group dynamics.

LEWIS, Carl (1961–), US track star who won four gold medals in the 1984 Los Angeles Olympics, duplicating the 1936 feat of Jesse OWENS.

LEWIS, Cecil Day (1904–1972), English poet and critic, POET LAUREATE from 1968. *The Magnetic Mountain* (1933) is his best known work from the 1930s, but his style matured fully after 1945. He wrote novels under his own name and detective novels as "Nicholas Blake."

LEWIS, C(live) S(taples) (1898–1963), British author, literary scholar and Christian apologist. Of more than 40 books his best-known is *The Screwtape Letters* (1942), a diabolical view of humanity. *The Allegory of Love* (1936), his major critical work, is a study of love in medieval literature. He also wrote a well-known science-fiction trilogy and the *Narnia* fantasies for children.

LEWIS, Gilbert Newton (1875–1946), US chemist who suggested that covalent bonding consisted of the sharing of valence-electron pairs. His theory of ACIDS and bases involved seeing acids (Lewis acids) as substances which are able to accept electron pairs from bases which are electron-pair donating species (Lewis bases). In 1933, Lewis became the first to prepare HEAVY WATER (D_2O).

LEWIS, John Llewellyn (1880–1969), colorful American labor leader, president of the United Mine Workers of America 1920–60. He organized the Congress of Industrial Organizations in 1935 as a rival to the AMERICAN FEDERATION OF LABOR, beginning a bitter rivalry; he resigned as president of CIO in 1940.

LEWIS, Matthew Gregory "Monk" (1775–1818), English poet, dramatist and novelist, best known for the Gothic romance *Ambrosio, or The Monk* (1796), which blended natural and supernatural horror with perverse sexuality. A member of Parliament 1796–1802, he sought humanitarian reforms of slavery in the West Indies.

LEWIS, Meriwether (1774–1809), American explorer and commander of the LEWIS AND CLARK EXPEDITION, which penetrated to the NW Pacific coast 1804–06. In 1808 he became governor of the Louisiana Territory, but was badly affected by the pressures of the post. En route for Washington, he was found dead at a lonely inn in Tenn., either by murder or suicide.

LEWIS, Oscar (1914–1970), US anthropologist. He presented the controversial thesis of the "culture of poverty" in notable biographical accounts of impoverished Latin Americans such as *Five Families* (1959), *The Children of Sanchez* (1961) and *La Vida* (1966).

LEWIS, Sinclair (1885–1951), US novelist, best known for five novels satirizing small-town life in the Middle West, an environment in which he himself grew up and only escaped from at college. *Main Street* (1920) was his first major success. *Babbitt* (1922), a satire on the provincial small businessman, is perhaps his best-known book. He refused a Pulitzer Prize for *Arrowsmith* (1925); it was followed by *Elmer Gantry* (1927) and *Dodsworth* (1929). In 1930 he became the first American to win the Nobel Prize for Literature, but his work declined thereafter.

LEWIS, Wyndham (1882–1957), controversial English painter, critic and writer, the founder of the vorticism movement. He is best known for his savage satirical novel *The Apes of God* (1930).

LEWIS AND CLARK EXPEDITION, first overland American expedition to the NW Pacific coast under the command of Meriwether LEWIS and William CLARK, with Sacagawea, the Indian wife of an expedition member, acting as interpreter and guide. Setting out from St. Louis in May, 1804, the expedition pushed westwards through the Rockies, reaching the Pacific Ocean at the mouth of the Columbia R in Nov., 1805. They returned to St. Louis in Sept., 1806.

The expedition was dispatched by President Jefferson to explore the newly-purchased Louisiana Territory which expanded America's borders to the Continental Divide. It caught the popular imagination and played a major part in establishing the view that it was the "Manifest Destiny" of the US to expand to the Pacific Ocean.

LEXINGTON, Battle of, first engagement of the American REVOLUTIONARY WAR on April 19, 1775. A force of around 700 British troops marching to destroy illegal military stores at Concord, Mass., were met at Lexington by 70 MINUTEMEN. These obeyed an order to disperse, but one fired a shot which was returned by a volley, killing eight Americans and wounding ten. The British marched on unopposed, but were turned back at the battle of CONCORD.

LEYDEN JAR, the simplest and earliest form of CAPACITOR, a device for storing electric charge. It comprises a glass jar coated inside and outside with unconnected metal foils, and a conducting rod which passes through the jar's insulated stopper to connect with the inner foil. The jar is usually charged from an electrostatic generator. The device is now little used outside the classroom.

LEYTE, fertile mountainous island in the Philippines, scene of a major landing by US forces in the WWII Philippines campaign. The economy rests on rice and corn and various cash crops, although manganese deposits are also exploited.

LEYTE GULF, Battle of, a major air-sea battle off Leyte Island in the Philippines on Oct. 25–26, 1944, in which the Japanese were decisively defeated in an attempt to decoy the US 3rd Fleet N and attack the landing on Leyte it was protecting.

LHASA, former capital of Tibet, now capital of the Tibetan Autonomous Region of China. Western visitors were discouraged before the 20th century, and Lhasa became known as the "Forbidden City." Centered around a massive Buddhist temple, it is dominated by the Potala, former citadel of the DALAI LAMA, on a 400ft hillside above the city. It was a trading center before it was occupied by the communist Chinese in 1951. Most of the former inhabitants have been resettled, and the population is now substantially Chinese. Some light industry has also been developed. Pop 343,240.

LHEVINNE, Jozef (1874–1944), Russian-born US pianist noted for his brilliant performances of the music of CHOPIN and TCHAIKOVSKY. He and his wife, **Rosina** (1880–1976), also a concert pianist, emigrated in 1919 to the US, where both joined the faculty of the Juilliard School of Music in New York. Rosina Lhevinne became one of the century's most celebrated teachers of piano.

LIAQUAT ALI-KHAN (1895–1951), Pakistani political leader. A leader of the Muslim League and chief lieutenant to Mohammed Ali JINNAH in Indian politics, he became (1947) the first prime minister of Pakistan. He was assassinated.

LIBBY, Willard Frank (1908–1980), US chemist awarded the 1960 Nobel Prize for Chemistry for discovering the technique of radiocarbon dating (1947), the first method of RADIOISOTOPE DATING.

LIBBY PRISON, notorious Confederate prison for Union officers in Richmond, Va.,

1863–64. A converted warehouse, it lacked heat, ventilation and sufficient sanitation. Up to 1,200 prisoners were confined there, and when food supplies became inadequate many died in the bad conditions.

LIBEL, a false and malicious statement in writing or other durable form (such as on film), tending to injure the reputation of a living person, or blacken the memory of the dead. In US law the truth of the statement creates a valid defense in an action for libel. The 1st Amendment to the US Constitution shields the press against certain libel suits unless malice or reckless disregard for truth is proved.

LIBERAL ARTS, term now applied to college curriculums covering such subjects as languages, philosophy, history, literature and pure science, when these are studied as the basis of a general or liberal education, and not as professional or vocational skills.

LIBERALISM, a political philosophy that stresses individual liberty, freedom and equality of opportunity. Liberalism tends to place its faith in progress. Classical liberalism developed in Europe in the 18th century, characterized by a rational critique of traditional institutions and a distrust of state power over individuals and interference in the economy. Modern liberalism accepts state interference in the economy but is still very concerned with social issues such as civil rights and equality of opportunity. In the US, a degree of liberalism has been the dominant creed of both major political parties.

LIBERAL REPUBLICAN PARTY, a party formed during the administration of President U. S. GRANT, seeking reconciliation with the South and action against corruption in government and public service. In 1872 the Liberal Republicans nominated Horace GREELEY for president, but when he was soundly defeated the party effectively broke up.

LIBERATION THEOLOGY, Roman Catholic intellectual movement, particularly in Latin America, that combines biblical and Marxist themes in its critique of oppressive social and political structures. Its followers have sometimes been active in revolutionary movements. In 1984 the Vatican repudiated liberation theology for its adoption of the Marxist concept of class struggle in pursuit of social justice.

LIBERIA, oldest black republic in Africa. It is on the W coast of Africa, bordered by Sierra Leone, Guinea and the Ivory Coast.
Land. Liberia is only slightly larger than Ohio. Beyond a narrow coastal plain it consists of tropical rain forests, with mountainous plateaus in the interior. The

Official name: Republic of Liberia
Capital: Monrovia
Area: 38,250sq mi
Population: 2,356,000
Languages: English; tribal
Religions: Protestant, Roman Catholic; Muslim; Animist
Monetary unit(s): 1 Liberian dollar = 100 cents

climate is hot and humid, with an average temperature of 80°F, and up to 150in of rain a year.

People. Liberia was settled in the early 19th century as a haven for freed American slaves, whose descendants dominated the country's economy and politics until recently. Called Americo-Liberians, they are Christian, English-speaking and generally live in coastal urban areas. Literacy is high among this group, many of whom are professionals. Indigenous Africans, 90% of the population, generally speak tribal languages and live in rural areas, engaging in subsistence farming. There are 16 principal tribes. Most practice traditional African religions, although about 15% adhere to Islam and 10% to Christianity; most are illiterate.

Economy. The Liberian economy is still underdeveloped. Its main industries are rubber plantations, established in the 1920s, and the mining of iron ore, dating from the 1950s. Both of these have been run and maintained by US firms. Apart from iron ore and rubber, Liberia exports several crops including coffee, sugarcane, bananas and cocoa. Valuable foreign exchange is also earned by registering foreign ships under extremely lax rules; this practice has made the Liberian merchant navy appear to be one of the world's largest. By 1987, however, the economy was in shambles, and the US sent in a team of economists to help the government as a condition for further aid.

History. The first repatriated slaves arrived from the US in 1822 under the aegis of the American Colonization Society. The settlement was named Monrovia in honor of US President James Monroe. In 1847 the settlers declared their independence. Liberia gradually extended its territory by signing treaties with local chiefs, or by buying or claiming land. Inequities in wealth and political power have caused antagonisms between Americo-Liberians and indigenous Africans over the years. William V. S. Tubman was president from 1944 until his death in 1971. His successor, William R. Tolbert, Jr., was assassinated in 1980 by soldiers of indigenous origin who assumed control of the government. Coup leader Samuel K. Doe remained president following a return to civilian rule in 1985.

LIBERTARIAN PARTY, US political party which stresses individual rights. It favors the unfettered right of private property and a laissez-faire, free-market economy. Libertarians regard the state as the greatest threat to liberty and oppose government snooping in private lives and the use of taxes for war preparations.

LIBERTY, Statue of, or in full, *Liberty Enlightening the World,* a 152ft copper female figure on Liberty Island in New York Harbor. The statue, designed by Frédéric BARTHOLDI, was given to the US by France on the 100th anniversary of US independence. In July 1986, following a two-year $70 million restoration, the centennial of the statue was marked with four days of celebration in and around New York Harbor.

LIBERTY BELL, famous American bell housed in Independence Hall, Philadelphia. It was cast in London and arrived in America in 1752. It rang on many historic occasions, including the announcement of the Declaration of Independence on July 8, 1776; having been twice recast, it reputedly cracked while tolling for the funeral of Chief Justice John Marshall in 1835.

LIBERTY PARTY, antislavery political party founded in 1839 by J. G. BIRNEY and other abolitionists. In 1840 and 1844 it put up presidential candidates, but in 1848 the party united with other groups to form the FREE SOIL PARTY.

LIBRARY. The earliest libraries were kept by the ancient peoples of Mesopotamia; inscribed clay tablets have been found going back to about 3500 BC. The most famous library of the ancient world was begun at Alexandria by Ptolemy I Soter (305–283 BC) and destroyed in various fires. The Roman Empire had many libraries, but during the Dark Ages the Church alone kept the library tradition alive in Europe. The Renaissance saw the formation of many new libraries such as the Vatican Library (1447), and the growth of libraries was further stimulated by the invention of printing in the 15th century. The Bodleian Library, Oxford, dates from 1602, but it was the 18th century that saw the formation of many of the great national libraries: the British Museum Library (1753), Italy's National Central Library at Florence (1741), and Russia's Saltykov-Shchedrin Library in Leningrad.

The United States. The oldest library in the US originated in the 320 books bequeathed by John HARVARD (1638), Harvard U.'s chief benefactor. The present LIBRARY OF CONGRESS developed from a purchase (1814/15) of JEFFERSON's personal library by Congress. The first tax-supported public library was established in New Hampshire in 1833. The American Library Association was founded in 1876. An important figure in library history is Melvil Dewey, whose decimal classification system has now been adopted in many countries. In the late 19th century great industrialists such as Andrew CARNEGIE were often benefactors of libraries. In the 20th century the public library system has been extended and consolidated. There are many types of libraries, ranging from the great university research libraries to school libraries, business libraries and area public libraries. (See also INFORMATION RETRIEVAL.)

LIBRARY OF CONGRESS, national library of the US, located to the E of the Capitol in Washington, D.C. Originally established by Congress in 1800, it now contains more than 70 million items, including books and pamphlets. Since 1870 the library has been entitled to two free copies of all material copyrighted in the US. The library's catalog, the National Union Catalog, lists books in libraries all over the US and Canada.

LIBYA, independent republic in North Africa, a historic state once an important part of the Roman empire.

Land. Most of the country is in the Sahara Desert, although there is a fertile strip along the Mediterranean coast where 90% of the population lives, with an average rainfall of 10in and a warm Mediterranean climate.

People. The population is predominantly Arab, but there are many Berbers—the original inhabitants—of Hamitic stock, with a strong Negroid strain. They live by small-crop, primitive farming along the Mediterranean coast and in the desert to the S. There are also Bedouins and Tuaregs in the Sahara regions. Sunnite Muslims predominate, and Islam is the state religion. Only about 30% of the total population live in urban areas, the largest of which is Tripoli, located on the coast. Illiteracy has been reduced to about 25% as oil revenues

Official name: Socialist People's Libyan Arab Jamahiriya
Capital: No official capital; government offices dispersed
Area: 685,524sq mi
Population: 4,132,000
Languages: Arabic; Italian used
Religion: Muslim
Monetary unit(s): 1 Libyan dinar = 1,000 dirhams

have funded free and compulsory primary education.

Economy. In 1959 the discovery of vast petroleum reserves in the desert revolutionized the economy. New homes, power stations, roads, irrigation projects, schools and hospitals have been built, and from 1962 to 1975, GNP increased twentyfold. In the 1980s declining oil revenues due to a drop in world oil prices led to a cutback in development projects; nevertheless, work on a canal to transport water from under the Libyan desert to coastal cities began in 1984. Crude oil still accounts for more than 95% of export revenues, although agriculture employs a much larger share of the labor force. In the coastal area barley, wheat, millet, oranges, olives, almonds and groundnuts are grown. Dates are plentiful in the desert oases, and nomads raise livestock. Libya consumes much of its own agricultural produce, and is a net importer of foodstuffs. Petrochemicals have been added to the traditional textile and leather industries.

History. Because of Libya's strategic position on the Mediterranean coast, it has been occupied by many foreign powers throughout its history—the ancient Greeks, Egyptians, Romans, Arabs and Ottoman Turks controlled the country successively. In 1912 Italy annexed Libya, although it was not able to end Libyan armed opposition until 1932. In WWII Libya was an Axis military base and the scene of desert fighting between the Axis powers and the British. In 1951 the UN declared Libya an independent sovereign state under the rule of King Idris I. He was overthrown on Sept. 1, 1969, by a military coup led by Colonel

Muammar al-Qaddafi who proclaimed Libya a republic; it is in effect an Islamic military dictatorship. In 1973 he launched a "cultural revolution," running the country along socialist lines, including nationalization of key industries. A prominent follower of pan-Arabism, he has unsuccessfully attempted to unite Libya with Egypt, Syria, Sudan, Tunisia, Chad, Morocco, and Algeria. A fervent opponent of Israel, Qaddafi has supported various international terrorist groups; this support led to a US air attack on Libya in 1986. He has also been charged with intervening in the internal affairs of neighboring countries, particularly Chad, where Libyan troops suffered major defeats in 1987.

LICE, wingless parasitic insects of two orders: Mallophaga, bird lice or biting lice, and Anoplura, mammalian or sucking lice. Dorsoventrally flattened with a broad, clearly-segmented abdomen, lice are well-adapted to moving between hair or feathers, and are usually host-specific. Bird lice feed with chewing mouthparts on feather fragments or dead skin, occasionally biting through the skin for blood. Mammalian lice feed purely on blood obtained with needle-like sucking mouthparts. The human lice are instrumental in the spread of several diseases.

LICHEN, name given to plants that are in fact an association between FUNGI and ALGAE. The fungus prevents the alga from drying-out, while the alga probably provides assistance to the fungus in mineral absorption. This relationship is a form of SYMBIOSIS. Lichens occur on the bark of trees, rotting wood, rock and soil. They are particularly important because they are primary colonizers of bare rock.

LICHTENSTEIN, Roy (1923–   ), US painter prominent in the POP ART movement of the early 1960s. He depicted comic strip frames and used commercial art techniques, such as Benday dots, in his work.

LICK OBSERVATORY, astronomical observatory, opened in 1888, on Mt Hamilton, Cal. Financed by James Lick (1796–1876), it was turned over by him to the U. of California. Among its six major telescopes are the second largest refracting telescope in the world (36in) and a 120in reflecting telescope.

LIDDELL, Henry George (1811–1898), English scholar, dean (1855–91) of Christ Church, Oxford, coauthor with Robert Scott of a famous *Greek-English Lexicon* (1843). His daughter, Alice Liddell (d. 1934), was the child for whom Lewis CARROLL wrote *Alice in Wonderland* (1865).

LIDICE, Czech village, about 16mi NW of Prague, destroyed by the Gestapo in 1942 as a reprisal for the assassination of Reinhard HEYDRICH, the Nazi governor of Bohemia. A new village has been built near the site, which is now a national memorial.

LIE, Trygve Halvdan (1896–1968), Norwegian statesman, first secretary-general of the United Nations 1946–53. He believed in the UN as an effective peace agency, and incurred Russian hostility by his support for UN action in Korea. He resigned in 1953 to ease the tension over Korea. Returning to Norway, he served in ministerial and ambassadorial posts, and as governor of Oslo.

LIEBER, Francis (1798–1872), German-born US political philosopher, editor of the first edition of the *Encyclopedia Americana* (13 vols., 1829–31). He wrote significant books on law and government while teaching at South Carolina College (now U of South Carolina; 1835–56) and Columbia U (from 1856).

LIEBERMANN, Max (1847–1935), German painter of the Impressionist and Realist schools. Heavily influenced by Courbet and Millet, his GENRE paintings of peasant life, such as *Potato Harvest* (1875) and *Beach at Scheveningen* (1908), are nonetheless German in style.

LIEBIG, Baron Justus von (1803–1873), German chemist who with Friedrich Wöhler proposed the radical theory of organic structure. This suggested that groups of atoms such as the benzoyl radical (C_6H_5CO-), now known as the benzoyl group, remained unchanged in many chemical reactions. He also developed methods for organic quantitative analysis and was one of the first to propose the use of mineral fertilizers for feeding plants.

LIEBKNECHT, Karl (1871–1919), German socialist leader, one of the founders of the German Communist Party. He was mainly known as a campaigner against militarism. With Rosa LUXEMBURG he took part in the SPARTACUS LEAGUE's abortive uprising in 1919, after which he was arrested and shot.

LIECHTENSTEIN, tiny European principality in the mountains between Switzerland and Austria.

Industry has developed rapidly since WWII. Precision instruments are exported. Because of low taxes and bank secrecy, Liechtenstein is the nominal headquarters of thousands of international corporations. Foreign workers make up between a fourth and a third of the population. The mild climate and attractive scenery make Vaduz, the capital, a thriving tourist center.

Official name: Principality of Liechtenstein
Capital: Vaduz
Area: 62sq mi
Population: 27,500
Language: German
Religion: Roman Catholic
Monetary unit(s): 1 Swiss franc = 100 rappen

Independent since 1719, Liechtenstein was closely linked with Austria until 1919; since then it has been tied to Switzerland. In 1986 women were granted the right to vote.

LIEDER. See SONG.

LIE DETECTOR, or polygraph, device which gives an indication of whether or not an individual is lying. Though much used in criminal investigation, its results are only conditionally admissible as legal evidence. Its use is based on the assumption that lying produces emotional, and hence physiological (see EMOTION), reactions in the individual. It usually measures changes in BLOOD pressure, PULSE rate and RESPIRATION; sometimes also muscular movements and PERSPIRATION. Success varies with the individual.

LIFE, the property whereby things live. Despite the vast knowledge that has been gained about life and the forms of life, the term still lacks any generally accepted definition. Indeed, biologists tend to define it in terms that apply only to their own specialisms. Physiologists regard as living any system capable of eating, metabolizing, excreting, breathing, moving, growing, reproducing and able to respond to external stimuli. Metabolically, life is a property of any object which is surrounded by a definite boundary and capable of exchanging materials with its surroundings. Biochemically, life subsists in cellular systems containing both NUCLEIC ACIDS and PROTEINS. For the geneticist, life belongs to systems able to perform complex transformations of organic molecules and to construct from raw materials copies of themselves which are more or less identical, although in the long term capable of EVOLUTION by natural selection. In terms of THERMODYNAMICS, it has been said that life is exhibited by localized regions where net order is increasing (or net ENTROPY decreasing). But the scientist has no monopoly over the use of the term, and for poets, philosophers and artists, it carries another myriad significations.

Life on earth is manifest in an incredible variety of forms—over 1 million species of animals and 350,000 species of plants. Yet, despite superficial differences, all organisms are closely related. The form and matter of all life on earth is essentially identical, and this implies that all living organisms shared a common ancestor and that life on earth has originated only once.

LIGHT, ELECTROMAGNETIC RADIATION to which the human EYE is sensitive. Light radiations occupy the small portion of the electromagnetic SPECTRUM lying between wavelengths 400nm and 770nm. The eye recognizes light of different wavelengths as being of different COLORS, the shorter wavelengths forming the blue end of the (visible) spectrum, the longer the red. The term light is also applied to radiations of wavelengths just outside the visible spectrum, those of energies greater than that of visible light being called ultraviolet light, those of lower energies, infrared. (See ULTRAVIOLET RADIATION; INFRARED RADIATION.) White light is a mixture of radiations from all parts of the visible spectrum. Bodies which do not themselves emit light are seen by the light they reflect or transmit. In passing through a body or on reflection from its surface, particular wavelengths may be absorbed from white light, the body consequently displaying the colors which remain. Objects which reflect no visible light at all appear black.

For many years the nature of light aroused controversy among physicists. Although HUYGENS had demonstrated that REFLECTION and REFRACTION could be explained in terms of waves—a disturbance in the medium—NEWTON preferred to think of light as composed of material corpuscles (particles). YOUNG'S INTERFERENCE experiments reestablished the wave hypothesis and FRESNEL gave it a rigorous mathematical basis. At the beginning of the 20th century, the nature of light was again debated as PLANCK and EINSTEIN proposed explanations of blackbody radiation and the PHOTOELECTRIC EFFECT respectively, which assumed that light comes in discrete quanta of ENERGY (see PHOTON). Today physicists explain optical phenomena in terms either of waves (reflection, refraction, diffraction, interference) or quanta (blackbody radiation, photoelectric emission) as is required by each case (see QUANTUM MECHANICS).

Light from the sun is the principal source of energy on earth, being absorbed by plants in PHOTOSYNTHESIS. Many other chemical reactions involve light (see PHOTOCHEMISTRY; PHOTOGRAPHY) though few artificial light sources are chemical in nature. Most light sources employ radiation emitted from bodies which have become hot or have been otherwise energetically excited (see LASER; LUMINESCENCE). Light can be converted into electricity using the PHOTOELECTRIC CELL. Light used for illumination is the subject of the science of photometry. (See also OPTICS.)

LIGHTHOUSE, tower with a light at its head, erected on or near the coast, or on a rock in the sea, as a warning to ships. One of the earliest lighthouses was on the Pharos peninsula at Alexandria, built in the 3rd century BC, and one of the SEVEN WONDERS OF THE WORLD. In modern lighthouses, the lantern usually consists of a massive electric light with an elaborate optical system, producing intense beams which sweep the horizon. Radio signals may be transmitted, and foghorns are sometimes used. Where conditions make it difficult to build a lighthouse, an anchored lightship may be used. Most lighthouses are operated by small teams of men who may live isolated in the lighthouse for weeks at a time.

LIGHTING, Artificial, the illumination of sectors of man's physical environment in the absence of natural LIGHT. In the course of EVOLUTION, EYES sensitive to the solar radiation penetrating the earth's atmosphere to the surface developed in many of the planet's animals. Man's eyes are thus sensitive to light of these same wavelengths, so artificial light sources must be designed to produce radiations having an intensity SPECTRUM similar to that of natural sunlight.

Oil lamps, brushwood torches and candles formed man's earliest means of artificial lighting, developments leading towards the KEROSENE lamp of the late 19th century. Gas lighting dates from 1792, when the British engineer William Murdock used coal gas to light his Cornish home. The modern portable camping lamp burns butane gas to heat an incandescent mantle.

In the 20th century the industrialized nations have come to use ELECTRICITY for most lighting purposes because it offers an instant source of bright, clean, fume-free light. One of the earliest electrical lighting sources was the ARC LAMP, which utilizes the flame arcing between two pointed carbon electrodes maintained with a moderate voltage between them. Successful incandes-

cent filament lamps date from 1879, when Sir Joseph William Swan and EDISON demonstrated lamps in which a carbon filament enclosed in an evacuated glass bulb was heated electrically until it glowed. After 1913 these gave way to lamps having tungsten filaments, coiled to improve efficiency (from 1918) and filled with an unreactive gas such as nitrogen. In 1937 efficiency was further improved by coiling the coiled filament (coiled-coil lamp). A more recent development is the tungsten-halogen lamp (an early type of which was the quartziodine lamp) in which efficiency is improved and life extended by filling the bulb with a halogen with which tungsten evaporating from the filament can combine, preventing deposition of the metal on the envelope (which is sometimes made of quartz). Because discharge lamps (in which a glow discharge is set up in mercury or sodium vapor—glowing bluegreen and yellow respectively) do not produce light in all parts of the solar spectrum they find their greatest use in highway rather than domestic lighting. More recent high-pressure sodium lamps, however, offer a fuller light spectrum. Cold-discharge tubes containing neon (glowing red) or argon (glowing blue) are contorted into exotic shapes for use in advertising signs. Fluorescent lamps produce light similar to sunlight by using a PHOSPHOR coating on the inside of the tube to convert ultraviolet light produced in a mercury-vapor discharge. Although they require more complex circuitry than filament lamps, they are much more efficient and last longer. Other light sources such as light-emitting diodes (LEDs—see SEMICONDUCTORS) and electroluminescent panels find use in instrument display panels. (See also FIREWORKS; PHOTOMETRY.)

LIGHTNING, a discharge of atmospheric electricity resulting in a flash of light in the sky. Flashes range from a few mi to about 95mi in length, and typically have an energy of around 300kWh and an electromotive force around 100MV.

Cloud-to-ground lightning usually appears forked. A relatively faint light moves towards the ground at about 75mi/sec in steps, often branching or forking. As this first pulse (leader stroke) nears the ground, electrical discharges (streamers) arise from terrestrial objects; where a streamer meets the leader stroke, a brilliant, high-current flash (return stroke) travels up along the ionized (see ION) path created by the leader stroke at about 50,000mi/sec (nearly ⅓ the speed of light). Several exchanges along this same path may occur. If strong wind moves the ionized path, **ribbon lightning** results.

Sheet lightning occurs when a cloud either is illuminated from within or reflects a flash from outside, in the latter case often being called **heat lightning** (often seen on the horizon at the end of a hot day). **Ball lightning**, a small luminous ball near the ground, often vanishing with an explosion, and **bead lightning**, the appearance of luminous "beads" along the channel of a stroke, are rare.

Lightning results from a buildup of opposed electric charges in, usually, a cumulonimbus CLOUD, negative near the ground and positive on high (see ELECTRICITY). There are several theories which purport to explain this buildup. Understanding lightning might help us probe the very roots of life, for lightning was probably significant in the formation of those organic chemicals that were to be the building blocks of life.

LIGHT YEAR, in astronomy, a unit of distance equal to the distance traveled by light in a vacuum in one sidereal year, equal to 9,461Tm (about 6 million million miles). The unit has largely been replaced by the PARSEC (1 1y=0.3069pc).

LIGNITE, or brown coal. See COAL.

LI HUNG-CHANG (1823–1901), Chinese general and westernizing statesman. He helped crush the TAIPING REBELLION (1850–64). As governor general of the capital province, Chihli (1870–95), he tried to modernize the army and introduce western industries, and was virtually in charge of conducting China's relations with the West.

LILBURNE, John (c1614–1657), English pamphleteer and leader of the LEVELLERS. Imprisoned 1638–40, he became a commander in the CIVIL WAR (1640–45), but was then persecuted, spending much time in prison or exile. He remained popular, however, and was twice (1649, 1653) acquitted of treason by a London jury.

LILIENTHAL, David Eli (1899–1981), US lawyer and government official. He was a director (from 1933) and chairman (1941–46) of the TENNESSEE VALLEY AUTHORITY. As chairman (1946–50) of the Atomic Energy Commission, he championed civilian control of atomic energy.

LILIENTHAL, Otto (1848–1896), German pioneer of aeronautics, credited with being the first to use curved, rather than flat, wings, as well as first to discover several other principles of AERODYNAMICS. He made over 2,000 glider flights, dying from injuries received when one of his gliders crashed. (See also FLIGHT, HISTORY OF.)

LILIUOKALANI (1838–1917), queen of Hawaii, who reigned 1891–93. She succeeded her brother King Kalakaua. When she tried to assert her royal powers, Americans living in Hawaii fostered a revolt in which she lost her throne. She wrote the well-known farewell song "Aloha Oe."

LIMA, historic capital and largest city of Peru, about 8mi inland from the port of Callao. Founded 1535, Lima was the chief residence of the Spanish viceroys. Earthquakes in 1687 and 1746 destroyed most of the city, but it still retains its old character. The university dates from 1551. Rapidly expanding, Lima has many industries, including textiles, chemicals, oil refining and food processing. Pop (city) 5,008,400; (metro) 5,700,000.

LIMAN VON SANDERS, Otto (1855–1929), German general who commanded Turkish armies in WWI at GALLIPOLI and in Palestine.

LIMBOURG, Pol de (d. 1416?), Flemish manuscript illuminator, one of three brothers who after 1404 worked for the Burgundian duke of Berry. Their renowned devotional book of hours, the *Très riches heures du duc de Berry*, shows courtly life and landscape in brilliant detail and dazzling color. (See also ILLUMINATION, MANUSCRIPT.)

LIMESTONE, sedimentary rock consisting mainly of calcium carbonate (see CALCIUM), in the forms of CALCITE and aragonite. Some limestones, such as CHALK, are soft but others are hard enough for use in building. Limestone may be formed inorganically (oolites) by evaporation of seawater or freshwater containing calcium carbonate, or organically from the shells of mollusks or skeletons of coral piled up on sea beds and compressed. In such limestone fossils usually abound.

LIMOGES, city of S central France, on the Vienne R. Renowned from the 13th to the 17th century for its enamels, since the 18th century it has been an important porcelain manufacturing center. Other industries include shoes and textiles. Pop 139,320.

LIMÓN, José (1908–1972), Mexican-US dancer and choreographer. In the 1930s he danced with the Humphrey-Weidman company. With Doris HUMPHREY as artistic director, he formed his own company in 1946 and choreographed for it *Moor's Pavane* (1949), *The Visitation* (1952) and *A Choreographic Offering* (1963).

LIMPOPO RIVER, or Crocodile R, some 1,100mi long, rising in South Africa, and flowing in a great arc N, E and then SE through Mozambique to the Indian Ocean. It forms South Africa's NW frontier with

Botswana and its N frontier with Zimbabwe.

LINCOLN, Abraham (1809–1865), 16th president of the US who, while leading the North in the Civil War, preserved the Union, which he saw as a bastion of democratic government. By his EMANCIPATION PROCLAMATION in 1863, he abolished slavery in the CONFEDERATE STATES. He was not free from faults and vacillations, but his patience, fortitude and fierce devotion to the Union made him one of America's greatest presidents.

Lincoln was born in a log cabin in backwoods Ky., and raised in poverty. His father Thomas, and stepmother Sarah Bush Johnston Lincoln, were barely literate. In 1831 Abraham set up house in New Salem, Ill., and taught himself law in his spare time, eventually becoming one of the leading lawyers in the state. From 1834 to 1841 he served in the Ill. state legislature. He retained something of his rough frontier manner, even after a well-connected marriage, in 1842, to Mary Todd.

Lincoln entered the House of Representatives in 1847 as a Whig, but his opposition to the MEXICAN WAR lost him his seat in 1849. Returning to politics in 1854 he took his stand on slavery. Though not an abolitionist, he opposed the KANSAS-NEBRASKA ACT of Senator Stephen DOUGLAS, which by repealing part of the MISSOURI COMPROMISE seemed likely to introduce slavery into the new Western territories. Lincoln's speeches against slavery in 1854 aligned him with the new REPUBLICAN PARTY, which he joined in 1856. In 1858 he contested a senate seat with Douglas, challenging him in a series of historic debates in which, though he lost the election, Lincoln emerged as an orator of national stature. In 1860 he was nominated as a compromise presidential candidate, winning against a split Democratic vote.

Before he took office as president seven Southern states had already seceded from the Union. Determined to hold FORT SUMTER in S.C. for the Union, Lincoln ordered supplies to its beleaguered garrison. War broke out on April 12, 1861 (see CIVIL WAR, AMERICAN). At first the North suffered numerous reverses, but Lincoln built up the army, blockaded southern ports and personally directed strategy as commander in chief until, in March 1864, he gave Ulysses S. GRANT command of the armies in the field. Grant and gifted subordinates like William T. SHERMAN carried out Lincoln's grand strategy of multiple coordinated offensives against the numerically inferior South. In the continuing debate on slavery,

Lincoln put the Union before abolition, but in response to increasing demands made the Emancipation Proclamation on Jan. 1, 1863. It was to be followed by the 13th Amendment to the UNITED STATES CONSTITUTION, sponsored by Lincoln.

The tide turned with Grant's victory at Vicksburg and LEE's defeat at GETTYSBURG (1863), where Lincoln made his famous address. In 1864 came the victories of the Shenandoah Valley, ATLANTA and MOBILE BAY, and Lincoln, who had lost some political ground, was reelected. In his second inaugural address in March, 1865, he made plain his lenient intentions towards the South. Within four weeks Grant took Richmond, and on April 9 Lee surrendered. Five days later Lincoln was shot in his box at the theater by John Wilkes BOOTH, and died early on April 15.

LINCOLN, Benjamin (1733–1810), American officer in the REVOLUTIONARY WAR. Made commander of the South (1778), he was forced to surrender Charleston in 1780. He became secretary of war 1781–83 and, in 1787, suppressed SHAYS' REBELLION.

LINCOLN, Mary Todd (1818–1882), wife of US president Abraham LINCOLN. The daughter of a socially prominent Kentucky family, she married Lincoln in 1842. Of their four children—Robert (1843–1926), Edward (1846–1850), William (1850–1862), and Thomas (1853–1971)—only Robert outlived her. Her eccentric behavior caused her to be briefly institutionalized in 1875.

LINCOLN, Robert Todd (1843–1926), son of Abraham Lincoln. Having served on GRANT's staff in the Civil War, he became a corporation lawyer, and was US secretary of war (1881–85) and minister to Great Britain (1889–93).

LINCOLN CENTER FOR THE PERFORMING ARTS, in New York City, a complex of buildings, designed by leading modern architects, to accommodate such cultural organizations as the New York Philharmonic Orchestra, Metropolitan Opera, Juilliard School, theaters and a library of the performing arts.

LINCOLN MEMORIAL, marble memorial to Abraham Lincoln at the end of the Mall in Washington, D.C., dedicated in 1922. Its 36 Doric columns represent the states of the Union when Lincoln was president. The great hall contains a huge statue of Lincoln by Daniel Chester FRENCH.

LINCOLN TUNNEL, road tunnel, 8,216ft long, under the Hudson R from Manhattan Island, New York City, to Weehawken, N.J. The first tube was opened in 1937; the second and third in 1945 and 1957.

LIND, Jenny (1820–1887), Swedish soprano, the "Swedish nightingale." With a voice of exceptional flexibility and clarity, she had brilliant success in opera, and after 1849 in oratorio and concert recitals.

LINDBERGH, Anne Morrow (1906–   ), US author and wife of Charles A. LINDBERGH, noted for popular books about the environment, works of poetry, and writings that eloquently express her personal philosophy, gathered in two autobiographies and three volumes of diaries and letters (1972–1980).

LINDBERGH, Charles Augustus (1902–1974), US aviator who made the first solo nonstop flight across the Atlantic, in 33½ hours, on May 20, 1927, in "The Spirit of St. Louis." A hero overnight, he became an airline consultant and made many goodwill flights. The kidnapping and murder of his son in 1932 led to a federal law on kidnapping, popularly known as the Lindbergh Act. Criticized for his pro-German, isolationist stance 1938–41, he later flew 50 combat missions in WWII. His autobiography, *The Spirit of Saint Louis* (1953), won a Pulitzer Prize.

LINDISFARNE, or Holy Island, off the coast of NE England, the earliest center of Celtic Christianity in England. Settled by St. Aidan in 635 AD, it became a bishopric until the Danish invasions in 875. The *Lindisfarne Gospels,* a famous illuminated manuscript, was created here c700.

LINDSAY, (Nicholas) Vachel (1879–1931), US poet of rhythmic, ballad-like verse designed to be read out loud. Among the best known are "The Congo" (1914) and "Abraham Lincoln Walks at Midnight" (1914).

LINDSEY, Benjamin Barr (1869–1949), US jurist, judge (1900–27) of the first US JUVENILE COURT (Denver).

LINEN, yarn and fabric manufactured from the fibers of the flax plant. The stems of the flax plant must first be softened by soaking in water (retting). Next, the fibers are separated from the woody core in a "scutching" mill. The short fibers (tow) are combed out from the long fibers (line) in the "hackling" mills. The tow is finally spun into yarn.

LINGUA FRANCA, auxiliary, usually hybrid language used between people of different tongues. Examples are PIDGIN English, SWAHILI and the Chinoor language. The original lingua franca developed among medieval traders in the Mediterranean. A language used in diplomacy, such as French, may also be called a lingua franca.

LINGUISTICS, the scientific study of language. Interest in how language works and the differences among languages extends back to ancient times (witness the attention given to grammar in the classical curriculum). In the late Middle Ages and Renaissance, the study of biblical and other ancient texts marked the emergence of what is now called **historical, or diachronic, linguistics**. In the 19th century comparative language studies (comparative PHILOLOGY) and analyses of grammatical systems led the way to modern **synchronic linguistics** (i.e., the study of contemporary language use); the great 19th-century theorist Karl Wilhelm von HUMBOLDT anticipated structuralist and behaviorist concepts vital in the 20th-century linguistics. The first modern linguist was Ferdinand de SAUSSURE, whose major work (1916) introduced linguistic **structuralism**, i.e., the thesis that there exists a structure underlying a language distinct from the sounds or utterances made; elaboration of this view has dominated all later linguistics. In Europe, the influential Prague school of linguists has tried to combine study of structure with study of the many functions performed by language. American linguists (including Franz BOAS, Edward SAPIR, Benjamin Lee Whorf, and Leonard Bloomfield) emphasized descriptive methods of analyzing languages; American structuralism also became distinctly behavioristic, and thus deliberately excluded SEMANTICS (study of meaning) or theories about if or how the mind produced language. With Zellig S. Harris and his student Noam CHOMSKY (the most influential contemporary linguist), the tide turned. Chomsky's system of transformational-generative grammar, as he developed it in the 1960s, postulates a deep structure to language that corresponds to universal features of the human mind, and the rules of the system aim to demonstrate how sound is related to meaning. Technically, linguistics may be considered as having three aspects: the studies of sound (phonology), of word formation (morphology), and of syntax and vocabulary (which are called the "lexicon"). Many branches of linguistics reach into other fields of study, including **psycholinguistics** (concerned mainly with language acquisition), **anthropological** and **sociolinguistics** (which relate language to culture and to socialization), **applied linguistics** (which focuses on methods of teaching languages), **dialectology** and **geographical linguistics**, and so on.

LINNAEUS, Carolus (1707–1778), later **Carl von Linné**, Swedish botanist and physician, the father of TAXONOMY, who brought system to the naming of living things. His classification of plants was based on their sexual organs (he was the first to use the symbols ♂ and ♀ in their modern sense), an artificiality dropped by later workers; but many of his principles and taxonomic names are still used today.

LIN PIAO (1907–1971), Chinese communist general and statesman. He was a leader in the LONG MARCH (1934–35) and, by his capture of Manchuria in 1948, crucial in the final defeat of CHIANG KAI-SHEK. Minister of defense from 1959, he was a leader of the "Cultural Revolution" (1965–69). In 1969 he was designated the successor of MAO TSE-TUNG. He was killed in an air crash, and the Chinese press later reported that he had been escaping to Russia after an abortive coup.

LINTON, Ralph (1893–1953), US anthropologist best known for the eclecticism of his studies in cultural ANTHROPOLOGY, as expressed in *The Study of Man* (1936) and *The Tree of Culture* (1955).

LION, *Panthera leo,* one of the largest of the big cats, distributed through Africa and Asia. They live in family groups loosely associated into large social units or prides, which share a range. Lionesses usually kill for the pride, though the big-maned males are well able to kill for themselves, and frequently do so—particularly those in bachelor groups of immature males. Amazingly powerful animals, they are characteristic of bush or veld, killing zebra, wildebeest, even buffalo by dragging on the neck, bringing the prey to the ground and breaking its neck. The roar of a male lion is a territorial proclamation.

LIONS CLUBS INTERNATIONAL, worldwide service organization of business and professional men, founded 1917, with headquarters in Oak Brook, Ill. In 1988 it had 1.3 million members.

LIPCHITZ, Jacques (1891–1973), Russian-born sculptor whose early works in Paris were constructed in terms of spaces and volumes, as in CUBISM. From 1925 he produced a series he called "transparents," in which, as in the *Harpist* (1928), contour was emphasized. His later work was more romantic and metaphorical.

LI PENG (1928–   ), premier of China from 1987. The orphaned son of a Communist martyr, he was adopted by CHOU EN-LAI and brought up at MAO TSE-TUNG's Communist base in Yenan. He was trained (1948–55) in Moscow as an electrical engineer, worked in the Chinese power industry, and eventually held ministerial positions in electric power and

education. He was elected to the ruling Politburo in 1985. In Oct. 1987 he was named acting premier, and was confirmed in that post by China's parliament, the National People's Congress, in Apr. 1988. Well connected to the Communist Party's old guard, he was not counted among the disciples of reformer TENG HSIAO-PING.

LI PO (c700–762), Chinese poet of the T'ANG dynasty, a prolific writer on themes of romance, natural beauty, and the pleasures of wine.

LIPPI, name of two Italian early RENAISSANCE painters in Florence. **Fra Filippo Lippi** (c1406– 1469) was influenced by MASACCIO, DONATELLO and by Flemish painting. His frescoes in Prato cathedral have a prettiness derived from Fra ANGELICO. **Filippino Lippi** (c1457–1504), his son, influenced by BOTTICELLI, painted the brilliantly-detailed *Adoration of the Magi* (1496).

LIPPMANN, Walter (1889–1974), influential US political columnist and foreign affairs analyst. His column, "Today and Tomorrow," first appeared in the *New York Herald-Tribune* in 1931, and eventually won two Pulitzer prizes (1958, 1962). Books include *Public Opinion* (1922) and *The Good Society* (1937).

LIPTON, Sir Thomas Johnstone (1850–1931), British food merchant and yachting enthusiast who failed five times to win the AMERICA'S CUP.

LIQUID, one of matter's three states, the others being SOLID and GAS. Liquids take the shape of their container, but have a fixed volume at a particular temperature and are virtually incompressible (see COHESION). Nearly all substances adopt the liquid state under suitable conditions of temperature and pressure. (See also FLUID.)

LIQUID CRYSTAL, a state of matter, exhibited by certain chemical compounds, resembling both the liquid and the solid crystalline state. The molecules of liquid crystals are free to move around, as in liquids, but they tend to orient themselves spatially in a regular way, as in crystalline solids. The first known observation of this phenomenon was made by an Austrian botanist, Friedrich Reinitzer, in 1888, while working with cholesteryl benzoate. Compounds that have a liquid-crystal phase at ordinary environmental temperatures have been put to a variety of uses, since they are sensitive to minute changes in temperature, pressure or applied electrical or magnetic fields. Some, which can change from clear to opaque in response to changes in electric current, are widely used in image displays such as in calculators and digital watches.

Others change color in response to small changes in temperature and can be applied to surfaces to reveal patterns of temperature variation.

LISBON, capital and largest city of Portugal, on the Tagus R estuary. Its fine harbor handles the bulk of the country's foreign trade. Reconquered from the Moors in 1147, Lisbon became the capital c1260. Much of the city was rebuilt after the disastrous earthquake of 1755. Industries include steelmaking, petroleum refining, textiles, chemicals, paper and metal products. Pop 807,167.

LISSITSKY, Eliezer (El) Markovich, (1890–1941), Russian abstract painter, designer and architect, proponent of CONSTRUCTIVISM and SUPREMATISM. His series of paintings and drawings, *Proun*, applied geometric forms to art and architecture.

LIST, Friedrich (1789–1846), German-US economist and author of *The National System of Political Economy* (1841). Exiled in 1825 for his liberalism, in 1832 he returned to Germany as US consul at Leipzig. He argued for a German customs union, but advocated tariffs to protect developing industries.

LISTER, Joseph Lister, 1st Baron (1827–1912), British surgeon who pioneered antiseptic SURGERY, perhaps the greatest single advance in modern medicine. PASTEUR had shown that microscopic organisms are responsible for PUTREFACTION, but his STERILIZATION techniques were unsuitable for surgical use. Lister experimented and, by 1865, succeeded by using carbolic acid.

LISZT, Franz (1811–1886), Hungarian Romantic composer and virtuoso pianist who revolutionized keyboard technique and became a public idol. He was director of music at Weimar 1843–61, and then lived in Rome where he took minor holy orders in 1865. His highly programmatic music includes 13 symphonic poems, a form he invented; program symphonies such as *Faust* (1854); the great B minor piano sonata (1853); *Transcendental Studies* for piano (1852); and 20 *Hungarian Rhapsodies*. His daughter Cosima married WAGNER.

LITHOGRAPHY. See PRINTING.

LITHOSPHERE, the worldwide rigid outer shell of the EARTH extending to a depth of 70km and overlying the ASTHENOSPHERE; it includes the continental and oceanic crust and the uppermost part of the MANTLE. Seismically, the zone is one of high velocity and efficient wave propagation, suggesting solidity and strength. In plate tectonic theory, the lithosphere consists of a number of plates in motion over the soft asthenosphere. (See also PLATE TECTONICS.)

LITHUANIA, constituent republic of the USSR, bounded N by Latvia, E by Belorussia, S by Poland and W by the Baltic. The country is mainly flat with many lakes and forests, and is drained by the Neman R. The climate is generally mild and humid in summer, cold in winter. The population is 80% Lithuanian.

Although timber and agricultural produce remain important, Lithuania is now 60% urban, with machinery manufacture, shipbuilding, and building materials the most important industries. The chief cities and industrial centers are Vilnius, the capital, Kaunas and Klaipeda, the main port. Roman Catholicism is the traditional religion.

Fourteenth-century Lithuania, comprising Belorussia and parts of the Ukraine and Russia, was central Europe's most powerful state. In 1386 Lithuania and Poland were united under Grand Duke Jagiello. In 18th-century partitions of Poland, Lithuania became a Russian province. From 1918 to 1940, when it was reabsorbed by Russia, it had an independent regime. In the late 1980s, Soviet leader Mikhail Gorbachev's relaxation of economic and political controls resulted in increased expressions of Lithuanian national sentiment. In Aug. 1988 large crowds in Vilnius marked the anniversary of the Hitler-Stalin pact of 1939 that enabled Stalin to annex the Baltic states in 1940. Demonstrators denounced the Russian annexation and demanded greater local autonomy and protection of the Lithuanian language and culture. (See also UNION OF SOVIET SOCIALIST REPUBLICS.)

LITTLE AMERICA, US Antarctic base on the Ross Ice Shelf S of Whale Bay. It was set up by Richard E. BYRD in 1928 and used by him on his subsequent expeditions.

LITTLE BIGHORN, Battle of, in SE Mont. on June 25, 1876, known as "Custer's last stand." General George A. CUSTER was killed and his troops annihilated by Cheyenne and Sioux Indians led by chiefs SITTING BULL and CRAZY HORSE.

LITTLE ENTENTE, political, economic and military alliances formed in 1920–21 between Yugoslavia, Czechoslovakia and Romania, backed by France. The entente began to weaken in the 1930s, then finally collapsed in 1938 with the German annexation of Czechoslovakia.

LITVINOV, Maxim Maximovich (1876–1951), Russian revolutionary and commissar for foreign affairs from 1930–39. He maintained a policy of cooperation with the

West, negotiating US recognition of the USSR in 1933 and taking Russia into the League of Nations in 1934. From 1941–43 he was ambassador to the US.

LIU SHAO-CHI (Liu Shaoqui; 1898–1969), Chinese communist leader, who succeeded MAO TSE-TUNG as chairman of the Chinese People's Republic (1959) and came to be seen as his heir. But in 1968 he was publicly denounced for "taking the capitalist road" and dismissed. He died in mysterious circumstances. In 1980 he was rehabilitated and exonerated by China's new leaders.

LIVER, the large organ lying on the right of the ABDOMEN beneath the diaphragm and concerned with many aspects of METABOLISM. It consists of a homogeneous mass of cells arranged around blood vessels and bile ducts. Nutrients absorbed in the GASTROINTESTINAL TRACT pass via the portal VEINS to the liver, and many are taken up by it; they are converted into forms (e.g., glycogen) suitable for storage and release when required. PROTEINS, including ENZYMES, PLASMA proteins and CLOTTING factors, are synthesized from amino acids. The liver converts protein breakdown-products into urea and detoxifies or excretes other substances (including drugs) in the blood. Bilirubin, the HEMOGLOBIN breakdown product, is excreted in the BILE; this also contains bile salts, made in the liver from CHOLESTEROL and needed for the DIGESTIVE SYSTEM.

Diseases of the liver include CIRRHOSIS and HEPATITIS, while abnormal function is manifested as JAUNDICE, EDEMA, ascites (excessive peritoneal fluid) and a variety of BRAIN and NERVOUS SYSTEM disturbances including DELIRIUM and COMA. Chronic liver disease leads to SKIN abnormalities, a bleeding tendency and alterations in routes of BLOOD CIRCULATION, which may in turn lead to HEMORRHAGE. Hepatitis may be caused by VIRUSES (e.g., infectious and serum hepatitis); their high infectivity has made them a hazard in hospital dialysis units. Many drugs may damage the liver, causing disease similar to hepatitis, and both drugs and severe hepatitis can cause acute liver failure.

LIVERPOOL, industrial city and second largest port in Britain, on the Mersey R, 3mi from the Irish Sea. The borough was chartered in 1207; in the 18th century it was a major slave-trading port. Its extensive docks are now among Europe's finest. Pop 491,500.

LIVINGSTON, Robert R. (1746–1813), US statesman. He was a delegate at the CONTINENTAL CONGRESS and assisted in drafting the DECLARATION OF INDEPENDENCE. In 1777 he helped draft the N.Y. state constitution. As chancellor of N.Y. state 1777–1801, he administered the presidential oath of office to George Washington. In 1801–04 he negotiated the LOUISIANA PURCHASE. The Livingston family was prominent in N.Y. and national affairs 1680–1823.

LIVINGSTONE, David (1813–1873), Scottish missionary and explorer in Africa, from 1841. He discovered the Zambesi R in 1851 and explored it in three remarkable journeys (1852–56, 1858–63, 1866–73). In 1855 he reached the waterfall he was to name as Victoria Falls. His historic meeting with the New York journalist Henry Morton STANLEY took place in 1871. Livingstone was a sworn enemy of the slave trade. He died in central Africa; his body was carried to the coast by two African followers.

LIVY, or Titus Livius (c59 BC–17 AD), important Roman historian. Of his 142-book *History of Rome* 35 books survive, with fragments and an outline of the rest. This work, which set out to praise the ancient republican virtues, won the approval of AUGUSTUS.

LIZARDS, a diverse group of REPTILES, placed with SNAKES in the order Squamata. Lizards usually possess well-developed limbs, though these are reduced or absent in some species. In some families the tail vertebrae have a predetermined plane of fracture where the tail can be cast if seized by a predator. The missing portion of tail can usually be regenerated. The various groups are adapted to a wide variety of environments, and lizards are found even in dry or desert conditions. A number of African species of lacertid lizards live in tropical forest where they climb among trees. Some of these have flattened flaps of skin which can be stretched between hind and fore limbs, permitting the lizard to glide down from tree to tree. Lizards are typically insectivorous, though some will take eggs or small mammals. The group includes GECKOES, CHAMELEONS, skinks, true lacertid lizards and monitors.

LLAMA, domestic form of a *Lama* species, the generic name for humpless New World camellids including the llama and ALPACA, with the wild guanaco and VICUNA. It has thick fleece which may be used for wool, and is the principal beast of burden of Indians from Peru to Chile, thriving at altitudes of 7,500–13,000ft.

LLANOS (Spanish: plains), a vast area in the Orinoco R basin in E Colombia and Venezuela. It comprises about 200,000sq mi of grassland and is used for raising livestock.

LLOYD, Harold Clayton (1894–1971), US comedian of the silent screen. He is famous for his role as the naive young man in glasses and straw hat, forever teetering on the brink of disaster only to be saved at the last moment. Among his best-known films are *Safety Last* (1923), *The Kid Brother* (1927) and *Feet First* (1930).

LLOYD, Henry Demarest (1847–1903), US reforming journalist or MUCKRAKER. He exposed the sharp practices of big business, notably in *Wealth Against Commonwealth* (1894), a history of the Standard Oil Company.

LLOYD GEORGE, David, 1st Earl Lloyd-George of Dwyfor (1863–1945), Welsh statesman, British prime minister from 1916–22, one of Britain's greatest war leaders and a brilliant orator. He was elected a Liberal member of Parliament in 1890 and served the same Welsh constituency for 54 years. As chancellor of the exchequer he forced through the so-called "people's budget" 1910–11, virtually founding British welfare legislation. The budget was at first rejected by the House of Lords, an incident which led to effective curtailment of their power of veto. In WWI, Lloyd George became successively minister of munitions, minister of war, and in 1916 prime minister of a coalition government. He was one of "the Big Four" at the Paris Peace Conference, 1919. His later policies, particularly over Ireland, lost him support; he was forced to resign in 1922. In the 1930s he opposed policies of appeasement towards Nazi Germany.

LLOYD'S OF LONDON, the world's largest marine insurance association, also involved in other types of insurance. Risks are assured by individual "underwriters," grouped in some 300 "syndicates." The underwriters assume unlimited personal liability for their portion of any given claim.

LOBACHEVSKI, Nikolai Ivanovich (1792–1856), Russian mathematician who, independently of János Bolyai (1802–60), developed the first NON-EUCLIDEAN GEOMETRY, hyperbolic or LOBACHEVSKIAN GEOMETRY, publishing his developments from 1826 onward.

LOBACHEVSKIAN GEOMETRY, or **hyperbolic geometry,** the branch of NON-EUCLIDEAN GEOMETRY based on the hypothesis that for any point P not lying on a line L, there are at least two lines that can be drawn through P parallel to L.

LOBOTOMY, operation in which the frontal lobes are separated from the rest of the BRAIN, used in the past as treatment for extremely severe and chronic psychiatric conditions. It leads to a characteristically disinhibited type of behavior and is now rarely used.

LOBSTERS, large marine decapod crustaceans with the first pair of legs bearing enormous claws. True lobsters, genus *Homarus*, are animals of shallow water living among rocks in crannies feeding on carrion, small crabs and worms. The two large claws differ in both structure and function, one of them always adapted for crushing, the other adapted as a fine picking or scraping claw. The dark blue pigment of the living lobster is a complex compound broken down by heat to the familiar red.

LOCARNO TREATIES, a series of pacts drawn up in Locarno, Switzerland, in 1925, among seven European nations, guaranteeing existing borders in E and W Europe. They also established arbitration procedures to solve disputes, notably between France and Germany, the latter being treated as an equal among the European powers for the first time since WWI. The "spirit of Locarno" died in 1936 when Germany denounced the pacts and occupied the Rhineland.

LOCHNER, Stephan (c1400–1451), German painter of the Cologne school who brought a new feeling of naturalism and pure color to the Gothic traditions. His most famous work · is the triptych altarpiece (1440s) in Cologne Cathedral, in which the central panel depicts the Adoration of the Magi.

LOCHNER v. NEW YORK, landmark 1905 case in which the US SUPREME COURT invalidated the 10-hour limit that New York State had placed on the working day of bakers. Justices Oliver Wendell HOLMES and John M. HARLAN, dissenting, deplored the court's refusal to let a state protect the health of its workers.

LOCKE, John (1632–1704), English empiricist philosopher whose writings helped initiate the European Enlightenment. His *Essay Concerning Human Understanding* (1690) is one of the highlights of English philosophy. In it he opposed innate ideas, offered a critique of our ideas on the basis of how we get them, and stressed the limitation of human knowledge. His *Second Treatise of Civil Government* (1690) presents a classical statement of social contract theory. His *A Letter Concerning Toleration* (1689) and *The Reasonableness of Christianity* (1695) were seminal for British religious thought of the 18th century.

LOCKHART, John Gibson (1794–1854), Scottish editor and author whose biography of his father-in-law, *Memoirs of the Life of Sir Walter Scott* (7 vols., 1837–38), is ranked second only to Boswell's *Life of Johnson* among English biographies.

LOCKJAW. See TETANUS.

LOCKS AND KEYS. The earliest known mechanical lock is from ancient Egypt, c2000 BC. The bolt was hollow, with a number of holes bored in its top; one of the bolt staples held a number of wooden pegs which fell into the holes in the bolt, holding it in place. The key could be fitted into the bolt; it had spikes in the same pattern as the holes, and thus could lift the pegs clear. The ancient Greeks situated their locks on the inside of the door, access being achieved via a keyhole to whose shape the key conformed. The Romans improved the Egyptian design by having pegs of different shapes and using springs to drive the pegs home; they also invented the **warded lock**, whose key must be slotted to clear wards, obstacles projecting from the back of the lock. Early portable locks, and later padlocks, also used this principle. The modern *lever-tumbler lock* was invented by Robert Barron (1778): levers fit into a slot in the bolt patterned such that each lever must be raised a different distance by the key to free the bolt. Jeremiah Chubb added another lever to jam the lock if the wrong key were tried (1818). The *Bramah lock*, invented by Joseph Bramah (1784), has a cylindrical key slotted to push down sprung slides, each of which must be depressed a different distance to clear an obstacle. Most domestic locks are now *Yale locks*, invented by Linus Yale (1861). An inner cylindrical plug has holes into which sprung drivers press pins of different lengths. The key is patterned to raise each pin so that its top is flush with the cylinder, which can then turn. Modern safes have combination locks and time devices so that they can only be opened at certain times.

LOCOMOTION, the means by which animals move from point to point—crawling or running over hard surfaces; burrowing in sand or soil; flying and swimming. Animals that can move are termed *motile*, contrasted with those that cannot, which are *sessile*. There are two anatomical features that make locomotion possible for the vast majority of animals—a skeletal system and a muscle system. The skeletal system is frequently composed of chitin, CARTILAGE or BONE and provides mechanical levers which are operated by MUSCLES. Soft-bodied animals employ a hydrostatic skeleton composed of water-filled cavities that are distorted by muscular walls to produce movement (see AMOEBA).

Among VERTEBRATES there are many variations of the basic locomotor organ, the limb. In birds and bats it has been modified to form a wing, while in various groups, notably snakes, the limbs are lost and the animal moves by undulations of the body. In aquatic animals, the tail is the most important organ of locomotion, the main function of the fins being steering and stabilization.

LOCOMOTIVE, originally locomotive engine, power unit used to haul railroad trains. The earliest development of the railroad locomotive took place in the UK, where R. TREVITHICK built his first engine c1804. R. STEPHENSON's famous *Rocket* of 1829 proved that locomotive engines were far superior to stationary ones and provided a design that was archetypal for the remainder of the steam era. Locomotives were first built in the US c1830. These pioneered many new design features including the leading truck, a set of wheels preceding the main driving wheels, guiding the locomotives over the usually lightly-constructed American tracks. For most of the rest of the 19th century, locomotives of the "American" type (4-4-0) were standard on US passenger trains, though towards the end of the century, progressively larger types came to be built. Although electric locomotives have been in service in the US since 1895, the high capital cost of converting tracks to electric transmission has prevented their widespread adoption. Since the 1950s, most US locomotives have been built with DIESEL ENGINES. Usually the axles are driven by electric motors mounted on the trucks, the main diesel engine driving a generator which supplies power to the motors (diesel-electric transmission). Elsewhere in the world, particularly in Europe, much greater use is made of electric traction, the locomotives usually collecting power from overhead cables via a pantograph. Although some gas-turbine locomotives are in service in the US, this and other novel power sources have not made much headway.

LOCOWEED, poisonous LEGUMINOUS PLANTS of the genera *Astragalus* and *Oxytropis*, which are native to dry regions of the W and SW US. Poisoning causes livestock to become stuporous and to stagger, a disease commonly known as locoism.

LOCUST, a name restricted to about 50 species of tropical GRASSHOPPERS which have a swarming, gregarious stage in the life cycle. In the arid regions where they occur they have become opportunists, breeding in large numbers where conditions are suitable, then flying in huge swarms to wherever food may be abundant. Here they can rapidly effect an agricultural disaster. They lay their eggs in bare earth just after rain. The young hoppers which hatch thus have new vegetation on which to feed when they emerge. Then they form into bands which march across the country eating the leaves of grasses, herbs and bushes as they go. Once they fledge, a swarm of desert locusts can cover 30mi a day, devastating the vegetation as it proceeds.

LODGE, name of two US statesmen. **Henry Cabot Lodge** (1850–1924), senator from Mass. 1893–1924, known for his successful opposition to US membership of the LEAGUE OF NATIONS, which he felt threatened US sovereignty. Instructor in American history at Harvard 1876–79, he was a prominent historian even during his Senate career. His grandson, the diplomat **Henry Cabot Lodge** (1902–1985), was a Republican senator 1937–44 and 1947–52, when he lost his seat to John F. KENNEDY. In 1960 he was Richard Nixon's vice-presidential candidate. He served as ambassador to the UN 1953–60 and ambassador to South Vietnam 1963–64 and 1965–67. Ambassador to West Germany 1968–69, he was also chief negotiator at the Vietnam peace talks in Paris (1969).

LOESS, fine-grained, unstratified, unconsolidated, wind-deposited silt found worldwide in deposits up to 165ft thick. Its main components are QUARTZ, feldspar, calcite and clay minerals. Extremely porous, it forms highly fertile topsoil, often chernozem. It is able to stand intact in cliffs.

LOFTING, Hugh (1886–1947), English-born US author and illustrator of the famous *Dr. Dolittle* stories, begun in letters to his children. *The Voyages of Dr. Dolittle* (1922), the second in the series, won him the Newbery medal in 1923.

LOGAN, Joshua (1908–1988), US theatrical producer, director, and author, whose successes included *Annie Get Your Gun* (director; 1946), *Mr. Roberts* (coauthor, director; 1948), and *South Pacific* (coauthor, coproducer, director; 1949).

LOGARITHMS, a method of computation using EXPONENTS. A logarithm is the power (see ALGEBRA) to which one number, the base, must be raised in order to obtain another number. For example, since $10^2 = 100$, $\log_{10} 100 = 2$ (read as "log to the base 10 of 100 equals 2"). The most common bases for logarithms are 10 (common logarithms) and the exponential, e (natural logarithms).

Since $a^0 = 1$ for any a, $\log 1 = 0$ for all bases. In order to multiply two numbers together, one uses the fact that $a^x \cdot a^y = a^{x+y}$, and hence $\log (x.y) = \log x + \log y$. We therefore look up the values of $\log x$ and $\log y$ in logarithmic tables, add these values, and then use the tables again to find the number whose logarithm is equal to the result of the addition. Similarly, since

$$\left(\frac{a^x}{a^y} \right) = a^{x-y}, \log \left(\frac{x}{y} \right) = \log x - \log y; \text{ and}$$

and since $(a^x)^y = a^{xy}$, $\log x^y = y.\log x$. Log$_x$ $x = 1$ since $x^1 = x$. The antilogarithm of a number x is the number whose logarithm is x; that is, if $\log y = x$, then y is the antilogarithm of x. A *logarithmic curve* is the plotting of a FUNCTION of the form $f(x) = \log x$.

LOG CABIN, primitive dwelling erected by early settlers in North America. It was built from logs, stripped of their bark and branches, laid horizontally and notched at each end to overlap and interlock at the corners. No nails were necessary, and few tools. Gaps between the logs were filled with clay or mud. It was usually roofed with branches or bark; in later versions, with shingles or slate.

LOGIC, the branch of PHILOSOPHY concerned with analyzing the rules that govern correct and incorrect reasoning, or inference. It was created by ARISTOTLE, who analyzed terms and propositions and in his *Prior Analytics* set out systematically the various forms of the SYLLOGISM; this work has remained an important part of logic ever since. Aristotle's other great achievement was the use of symbols to expose the form of an argument independently of its content. Thus a typical Aristotelian syllogism might be: all A is B; all B is C; therefore all A is C. This formalization of arguments is fundamental to all logic.

From the 12th century onward Latin translations of Aristotle's logical works (collectively called the *Organon*) were intently studied, and a kind of program emerged, which was based on Aristotle and included much that would nowadays be regarded as GRAMMAR, EPISTEMOLOGY and linguistic analysis. Among the most important medieval logicians were William of Ockham, Albert of Saxony and Jean Buridan. After the Renaissance an anti-Aristotelian reaction set in, and logic was given a new turn by Petrus Ramus and by Francis BACON's prescription that induction (and not deduction) should be the method of the new science. In the work of George BOOLE and Gottlob FREGE the 19th century saw a vast extension in the scope and power of logic. In particular, logic became as bound up with mathematics as it was with philosophy. Logicians became interested in whether particular logical systems were either consistent or complete. (A consistent logic is one in which contradictory propositions cannot be validly derived.) The climax of 20th-century logic came in the early 1930s when Kurt Gödel demonstrated both the completeness of Frege's first-order logic and that no higher-order logic could be both consistent and complete.

LOGICAL POSITIVISM, the doctrines of the "Vienna Circle," a group of philosophers founded by M. SCHLICK. At the heart of logical positivism was the assertion that apparently factual statements that were not sanctioned by logical or mathematical convention were meaningful only if they could conceivably be empirically verified. In this sense only mathematics, logic and science were deemed meaningful; ethics, metaphysics and religion were meaningless. The influence of logical positivism tended to decline after WWII.

LOGOS (Greek; word, reason), term used in Greek philosophy to describe the divine reason and will that was seen to be implicit in the order of the universe. It was adopted in later Judaism (notably by PHILO) and used by Christian writers to define the role of Jesus Christ as the "Word of God" made flesh, the active will of God and an embodied revelation of it to mankind.

LOIRE RIVER, at 627mi the longest river of France. It rises in the Cévennes mountains and flows NW to Orléans, then SW to the ports of Nantes and Saint-Nazaire to empty into the Bay of Biscay. It drains an area of 44,000sq mi, more than a fifth of all France. Canals link the Loire with the Saône, Rhône and Seine rivers.

LOLLARDS ("idlers" or "babblers"), derisory name given to the 14th-century followers of the English religious reformer John WYCLIFFE. Wandering preachers, the Lollards sought to base their beliefs solely on the Bible and simple worship, rejecting the organized Church altogether. Although considered to have declined during the 15th century, Lollard beliefs were linked with radical social unrest and remained as underground influences on later movements.

LOMAX, John Avery (1867–1948), pioneering US folk musicologist. His collections of American folksongs include *Cowboy Songs and Other Frontier Ballads* (1910) and *Our Singing Country* (1938).

LOMBARD, Peter (c1100–1160), Italian theologian, archbishop of Paris from 1158. He is best known for his four *Books of Sentences,* written as source material for theological students and drawing on both biblical and patristic texts and on his contemporaries.

LOMBARDI, Vincent Thomas (1913–1970), US football coach, with the Green Bay Packers (1959–69), with whom he compiled a 141-39-4 record. His teams won five league championships and victories in Superbowls 1 and 2 (1967, 1968).

LOMBARDS, Germanic people who moved down from NW Germany in the 4th century AD towards Italy; in 568 they crossed the Alps and conquered most of N Italy, dividing it into dukedoms until 584, when they united into a kingdom against the threat of Frankish invasion. The kingdom reached its height under Liutprand in the 8th century, but was soon overrun by the Franks c770.

LOMBARDY, region of N Italy, once a kingdom of the Lombards, for whom it is named. The country's main industrial and commercial region, it also has efficient and prosperous agriculture. Its capital, Milan, is a major transport hub and commercial center. In area Lombardy is 9,202sq mi and has about 16% of Italy's total population.

LOMBROSO, Cesare (1836–1909), Italian physician who pioneered scientific criminology. His view that criminals were throwbacks to earlier evolutionary stages (see ATAVISM) has now been generally discarded. In retrospect his most valuable work is seen to have been his defense of the rehabilitation and more humane treatment of criminals.

LOMONOSOV, Mikhail Vasilievich (1711–1765), Russian scientist and man of letters, best known for his corpuscular theory of matter, in the course of developing which he made an early statement of the KINETIC THEORY.

LONDON, Jack (1876–1916), US writer of novels and short stories, many set during the Yukon GOLD RUSH, that treat the struggles of men and animals to survive as romantic conflicts with nature. The best examples are *The Call of the Wild* (1903), *White Fang* (1906) and *Burning Daylight* (1910), but perhaps his finest work is the autobiographical novel *Martin Eden* (1909).

LONDON, capital of the UK. Divided into 33 boroughs, Greater London covers over 650sq mi along both banks of the Thames R in SE England, all the historic city and county of London. The national center of government, trade, commerce, shipping, finance and industry, it is also one of the cultural centers of the world.

The Port of London handles over 33% of UK trade. London is also an important industrial region in its own right, with various manufacturing industries. Many of the most important financial and business institutions such as the Bank of England, the Stock Exchange and Lloyd's of London, as well as many banking and shipping concerns, are concentrated in the single square mile known as the City; the ancient nucleus of London, it has its own Lord Mayor and corporation. To the W of it are the Law Courts and the INNS OF COURT, and the governmental area in Westminster centered on the HOUSE OF COMMONS and HOUSE OF LORDS.

London is also a historic city with many beautiful buildings: the TOWER OF LONDON, WESTMINSTER ABBEY and BUCKINGHAM PALACE are major tourist attractions. Home of universities, colleges and some of the world's greatest museums and libraries, it also has a flourishing night life. London's art galleries, concert halls, theaters and opera houses are world-famous. Distant areas of London are linked by the complex and highly efficient subway system known as the Underground. Pop (city) 6,767,500; (metro) 10,400,000.

LONDON BRIDGE, actually a historical succession of bridges in London, for centuries the only bridge in the whole area. The first stone bridge, built c1176–1209, had many buildings along it, including a chapel and defensive towers. Rebuilt many times, it was demolished and replaced in the 1820s by New London Bridge. It was again replaced in the 1960s, when its facing was sold and shipped to Lake Havasu City, Ariz., where it was rebuilt as a tourist attraction.

LONDONDERRY, or **Derry,** seaport in Northern Ireland, on the Royle R. It has a traditional shirtmaking industry and some light manufacturing industries. Since 1968 it has been a center of violent conflict between Protestants and Roman Catholics (see IRELAND, NORTHERN). Pop 88,000.

LONG, Crawford Williamson (1815–1878), US physician who first discovered the surgical use of diethyl ETHER as an anesthetic (1842). His discovery followed an observation that students under the influence of ether at a party felt no pain when bruising or otherwise injuring themselves.

LONG, Huey Pierce (1893–1935), US political leader of La., called the "Kingfish." He entered the state administration in 1918. Governor after a landslide victory in 1928, he put through economic and social reforms, but virtually suspended the democratic process and ruthlessly used his powers of patronage to create what some saw as a semi-fascist system of state government. A US senator from 1931, he attacked NEW DEAL policies, advocating his own "share-the-wealth" program and openly proclaiming his presidential ambitions. He was assassinated at Baton Rouge by Dr. Karl Weiss. His brother, **Earl Long** (1895–1960), was governor 1939–40, 1948–52, 1956–60; his son, **Russell Long** (1918–   ), was US senator 1948–87.

LONG, Stephen Harriman (1784–1864), US explorer, army engineer and surveyor. He explored the Rocky Mts, where Long's Peak is named for him, the upper Mississippi R and the Minnesota R. He also surveyed for the Baltimore and Ohio railroad.

LONGFELLOW, Henry Wadsworth (1807–1882), the most popular US poet of his age. A contemporary of HAWTHORNE at Bowdoin College, he became a professor there and then at Harvard (1836–54). His principal works were *Ballads and Other Poems* (1841) and the narrative poems *Evangeline* (1847), *The Golden Legend* (1851), *The Courtship of Miles Standish* (1858) and above all *The Song of Hiawatha* (1855), which created romantic American legends. Famous individual poems are "The Wreck of the Hesperus" and "Excelsior."

LONGHI, Pietro (1702–1785), Venetian painter best known for his small-scale GENRE works of Venetian life, like *The Exhibition of a Rhinoceros* (1750) and *The Family Concert* (1741).

LONGHORN CATTLE, a Mexican breed of cattle. It became the basic stock of the US ranch herds during the 19th century. They are known as strong and hardy animals; however they have nearly been bred out of existence in favor of meatier types.

LONG ISLAND, island off the SE coast of N.Y., extending E from the mouth of the Hudson R. It is about 118mi long and 12–23mi wide, and covers an area of 1,723sq mi. Brooklyn and Queens Co. at the W end are part of New York City, and many residents of the island work there. Nassau Co. and Suffolk Co., formerly predominantly agricultural, now have much residential and light industrial development. Its beaches and bays make it a popular resort and fishing center.

LONG ISLAND, Battle of, Aug. 1776, an opening engagement of the American REVOLUTIONARY WAR. Five months after the British evacuated Boston, General Sir William HOWE landed troops on Long Island and drove WASHINGTON's defending army back to Brooklyn Heights. After a few days' siege, the American troops were successfully evacuated.

LONGITUDE. See LATITUDE AND LONGITUDE.

LONG MARCH, 1934–35, the epic march of the Chinese communists, from Kiangsi in the SE to Shensi in the extreme NW, which saved the movement from extermination by the Nationalist (Kuomintang) forces of CHIANG KAI-SHEK. The communists were surrounded by the Kuomintang. Led by MAO TSE-TUNG, CHOU EN-LAI and LIN-PIAO, the Red Army of some 100,000 broke the trap to begin a 6,000mi trek which took them over 18 mountain ranges and 24 rivers under constant air and land attack by Kuomintang troops and local warlords. Thousands were killed but the heroism and determination of the survivors made the Long March the founding legend of Revolutionary China.

LONG PARLIAMENT, English legislative assembly that met between 1640 and 1660. Convened by CHARLES I, it immediately tried to check his power. The conflict culminated in the attempted arrest of John PYM, and the CIVIL WAR (1642), during which the parliament remained in session. In 1648 it was "purged" (see RUMP PARLIAMENT), and in 1653 abolished altogether under the PROTECTORATE. It was briefly reconvened in 1660 prior to the RESTORATION.

LONGSTREET, James (1821–1904), Confederate general in the US CIVIL WAR, who fought many important battles in Va. His delay in attack at GETTYSBURG (1863), where he was second in command, is generally thought to have lost the battle. He fought in the Battle of the Wilderness (1864) and in the last defense of Richmond.

LOOKOUT MOUNTAIN, Battle of, 1863, also called the "Battle above the Clouds," a Union victory in the CIVIL WAR. The Confederates were swept from the ridge of Lookout Mt. near Chattanooga, by General HOOKER.

LOPE DE VEGA CARPIO, Félix (1562–1635), poet and Spain's first great dramatist. He created the *comedia,* a drama with comic, tragic, learned and popular elements. Vitality, wit and intricate plot typify *Peribáñez, Fuenteovejuna* and *The Knight of Olmedo.* Lope's 500 surviving works also include lyrical verse, the autobiographical *La Dorotea* (1632), religious and light "cloak-and-sword" plays.

LÓPEZ MATEOS, Adolfo (1910–1969), president of Mexico (1958–64) after being a successful minister of labor (1952–58). His presidency was characterized by

agrarian reform and a vast industrialization program.

LORAN (*long range navigation*) a NAVIGATION system in which an aircraft pilot may determine his position by comparing the arrival times of pulses from two pairs of RADIO transmitters. Each pair gives him enough information to draw a line of possible positions on a map, the intersection of the two lines marking his true position.

LORCA, Federico García (1898–1936), celebrated Spanish poet and dramatist inspired by his native Andalusia and by gypsy folklore. He made his reputation with *Gypsy Ballads* (1928) and surrealism influenced *Poet in New York* (published 1940), but he returned to folk themes in the plays *Blood Wedding* (1933), *Yerma* (1935) and *The House of Bernarda Alba* (1936). He was also a talented musician and theater director. He was murdered by the Nationalists in the Civil War.

LORD'S PRAYER, the chief Christian prayer, taught by Christ to his disciples and prominent in all Christian worship. Addressed to God the Father, it contains seven petitions, the first three for God's glory, the last four for man's bodily and spiritual needs. The closing doxology ("For thine is the kingdom" etc.) is a very clear addition.

LORELEI, rock on the Rhine R in Germany, between Koblenz and Bingen. It rises some 430ft above a point where the river narrows. The legend of its river maiden who lured boatmen to their death by her singing is the subject of HEINE's famous poem, "Die Lorelei."

LORENTZ, Hendrik Antoon (1853–1928), Dutch physicist awarded with P. Zeeman the 1902 Nobel Prize for Physics for his prediction of the Zeeman effect. Basing his work on J. Clerk MAXWELL'S equations, he explained the reflection and REFRACTION of light; and proposed his *electron theory,* explaining many electromagnetic phenomena by the effects of the electromagnetic field and electrons in atoms on each other, at a time when nothing was known of electrons. One such effect is the splitting of certain lines in the spectra of atoms by a magnetic field. This was experimentally shown by P. Zeeman (1896).

But the theory was inconsistent with the results of the MICHELSON-MORLEY EXPERIMENT, and so Lorentz introduced the idea of "local time," that the rate of time's passage differed from place to place; and, incorporating this with the proposal of George Francis Fitzgerald (1851–1901) that the length of a moving body decreases in the direction of motion (the Fitzgerald contraction), he derived the *Lorentz transformation*, a mathematical statement which describes the changes in length, time and mass of a moving body. His work, with Fitzgerald's, laid the foundations for EINSTEIN'S Special Theory of RELATIVITY.

LORENZ, Konrad (1903–   ), Austrian zoologist and writer, the father of ETHOLOGY, awarded for his work the 1973 Nobel Prize for Physiology or Medicine with Karl von Frisch and Nikolas Tinbergen. He is best known for his studies of bird behavior and of human and animal AGGRESSION. His best-known books are *King Solomon's Ring* (1952) and *On Aggression* (1966).

LORENZETTI, name of two Sienese painters influenced by GIOTTO. **Ambrogio** (c1290–1348) is best known for the fresco cycle *Good and Bad Government* (c1338–48) in Siena. His brother **Pietro** (c1280–1348) painted the *Passion* cycle in the Orsini Chapel, Assisi.

LOS ALAMOS, town in N.M., 25mi NW of Santa Fe. It grew up around the scientific laboratory (1943) where the world's first atomic and hydrogen bombs were developed. Pop 11,039.

LOS ANGELES, city in S Cal., second largest in the US. It is a sprawling city of some 464sq mi dominated by freeways and the automobile, and the center of a metropolitan area with a population of over 7 million. Situated between sea and mountains, it has no extremes of temperature, which average 55°F in January and 73°F in July. It is the third largest industrial center in the US, producing among other things aircraft, electrical equipment, automobiles, glass, furniture, rubber, canned fish and refined oils (but industrialization has made smog a serious problem). It is the world capital of the motion-picture and television industry (see HOLLYWOOD) and also a distribution and commercial center for the nearby mining regions, oilfields and rich farm areas. Its port, San Pedro, handles more tonnage than any other US Pacific port, and accommodates a large fishing fleet. Tourism is another source of wealth. The city is dominated by fine buildings, including a number by Frank Lloyd WRIGHT. It has several museums, many fine churches and libraries, and four universities. Taken from the Mexicans in 1846, it was incorporated in 1850. It was linked with the transcontinental railroad system in the 1870s and 1880s. Oil was discovered in the region in the 1890s. Los Angeles hosted summer Olympics in 1932 and 1984. Pop (city) 3,097,000, (metro) 8,109,000.

LOST COLONY, an English settlement (1587) on Roanoke Island off the coast of N.C., which disappeared without trace. It was founded by 117 settlers led by John White, sponsored by Sir Walter RALEIGH. Supplies ran out and White visited England for help. When he returned in 1590, the colony had disappeared, possibly having been wiped out by hostile Indians.

LOST GENERATION, a term for the US writers of the post-WWI generation, coined in a remark by Gertrude STEIN to Ernest HEMINGWAY. Besides them they included Scott FITZGERALD, John DOS PASSOS, E. E. CUMMINGS and others. Their ideals shattered by the war, they felt alienated from the materialism of America in the 1920s, and many lived bohemian expatriate lives in Paris.

LOTTO, Lorenzo (c1480–1556), Italian painter influenced by RAPHAEL and the Venetians, notably TITIAN. He painted portraits, landscapes and mystical and religious subjects which became, as in *St. Anthony Giving Alms* (1542), increasingly direct and moving in style.

LOTUS-EATERS, mentioned in Homer's *Odyssey*, the legendary inhabitants of the N coast of Africa. They lived on the fruit and flowers of the lotus tree, which drugged them into happy forgetfulness. TENNYSON wrote a famous poem with this title.

LOUIS, name of 18 kings of France. **Louis I** (778–840), Holy Roman Emperor 814–40, known as "the Pious." He was the third son of CHARLEMAGNE. He divided the empire among his sons, thereby contributing to its fragmentation, but laying the foundations of the state of France. **Louis II** (846–879), reigned 877–79. **Louis III** (c863–882), reigned 879–82. As king of N France he defeated Norman invaders. **Louis IV** (c921–954), reigned 936–54. He was called "Transmarinus" because of his childhood exile in England. **Louis V** (c966–987), reigned 986–87. The last Carolingian ruler of France, he was known as "the Sluggard." **Louis VI** (1081–1137), reigned 1108–37. He subdued the robber barons around Paris, granted privileges to the towns and aided the Church. He engaged in war against Henry I of England (1104–13 and 1116–20). **Louis VII** (c1120–1180), reigned 1137–80. He joined the second Crusade (1147–49) in defiance of a papal interdict. From 1157 onwards, Louis was at war with Henry II of England who had married Louis' former wife, Eleanor of Aquitaine. **Louis VIII** (1187–1226), reigned 1223–26. Nicknamed "the Lion," he was a great soldier and was at first successful in his attempts to aid the barons rebelling against King John of England. **Louis IX, Saint** (1214–1270), reigned 1226–70. He repelled an invasion by Henry III of England (1242), and led the sixth Crusade (1248), but was defeated and captured in Egypt and had to be ransomed. In 1270 he led another crusade, but died of plague after reaching N Africa. A just ruler, he was regarded as an ideal Christian king and was canonized in 1297. His feast day is Aug. 25. **Louis X** (1289–1316), reigned 1314–16, a period in which the nobility reasserted their strength. **Louis XI** (1423–1483), reigned 1461–83. A cruel and unscrupulous king, he had plotted against his father for the throne, but unified most of France. **Louis XII** (1462–1515), reigned 1498–1515. Nicknamed "Father of the People," he was a popular ruler who inaugurated reforms in finance and justice and was ambitious for territorial gains. **Louis XIII** (1601–1643), reigned 1610–43. A weak king, he was greatly influenced by his chief minister Cardinal RICHELIEU. **Louis XIV** (1638–1715), reigned 1643–1715, known as "Louis the Great" and "the Sun King." The archetypal absolute monarch, he built the great palace at VERSAILLES. "The state is myself," he is said to have declared. His able ministers, MAZARIN and COLBERT, strengthened France with their financial reforms. But Louis squandered money in such escapades as the War of DEVOLUTION (1667–68) and the War of the SPANISH SUCCESSION (1701–13), which broke the military power of France. **Louis XV** (1710–1774), reigned 1715–74, nicknamed "the Well-Beloved." He was influenced by Cardinal Fleury until the cardinal's death in 1743. A weak king dependent on mistresses (especially Madame de POMPADOUR), his involvement in foreign wars ran up enormous debts. **Louis XVI** (1754–1793), reigned 1774–92. Although he accepted the advice of his ministers TURGOT and Jacques Necker on the need for social and political reform, Louis was not strong enough to overcome the opposition of his court and his queen, MARIE ANTOINETTE. This led to the outbreak of the FRENCH REVOLUTION in 1789, with the formation of the National Assembly and the storming of the Bastille. In 1791 Louis attempted to escape but was brought back to Paris and guillotined on Jan. 21, 1793. **Louis XVII** (1785–1795), son of Louis XVI, king in name only. He was imprisoned in 1793 and was reported dead in 1795. **Louis XVIII** (1755–1824), brother of Louis XVI. He escaped from France in 1791. For more than 20 years he remained in exile, but after the final defeat of Napoleon in the Battle of WATERLOO (1815),

he became firmly established. He proclaimed a liberal constitution, but on his death the reactionary Ultraroyalists gained control under Charles X.

LOUIS, Joe (Joseph Louis Barrow; 1914–1981), known as the "Brown Bomber," heavyweight boxing champion of the world 1937–49. Louis, who defended his title 25 times, was beaten only three times, finally by Rocky MARCIANO.

LOUISBOURG, town in NE Nova Scotia, Canada, on the Atlantic. A French fortress founded in 1713, it was captured by the American colonials in 1745, restored to France in 1748, but taken by the English in 1758. The remains of the fortress are now part of a National Historic Park, and Louisbourg is a port for coal-shipping and fishing.

LOUISIANA, state, S central US, on the Gulf of Mexico, at the mouth of the Mississippi R, bounded to the E by Miss., to the W by Tex., and to the N by Ark.

Name of state: Louisiana
Capital: Baton Rouge
Statehood: April 30, 1812 (18th state)
Familiar name: Pelican State
Area: 48,523sq mi
Population: 4,501,000
Elevation: Highest— 535ft, Driskill Mountain. Lowest—5ft below sea level, at New Orleans
Motto: "Union, justice and confidence"
State flower: Magnolia
State bird: Brown pelican
State tree: Bald cypress
State song: "Give Me Louisiana"
Land. Louisiana can be divided into three geographical regions: the E and W Gulf coastal plains, and between them the Mississippi alluvial plain. The two coastal plains are mainly composed of rolling hills and prairie. The flat and fertile alluvial plain extends into the Mississippi delta which covers about a third of the state's land area. Louisiana has long, hot and humid summers, and brief cool winters.
People. About two-thirds of Louisiana's population live in urban areas, about one-third of the people are black. The port

of New Orleans is the largest city. The N of the state is a Protestant Anglo-Saxon area, but the people of the S are descended from French and Spanish settlers, and this has clearly influenced the area's culture.

Economy. Louisiana is among the nation's leading producers of sugarcane, rice and sweet potatoes. Livestock and dairy products are of importance, as are soybeans, cotton, corn and sugarcane. Louisiana is also one of the country's largest producers of petroleum; natural gas, sulfur and salt are also produced. The most important industries are chemicals, foodstuffs, paper and paper products and electronic and transportation equipment. Tourism and commercial fishing are also important.

History. In the 18th century, Louisiana was controlled alternately by the French and the Spanish, but in 1803 was sold to the US as part of the LOUISIANA PURCHASE. Louisiana was admitted to the Union in 1812 and quickly prospered. Her population increased almost tenfold between 1812 and the Civil War; but at the outbreak of the war, half the population was composed of slaves. The pre-Civil War period saw the heyday of the great Mississippi steamboats. Louisiana's prosperity, however, was checked by the Civil War and the harsh policies of RECONSTRUCTION. The discovery of oil and natural gas early in the 20th century brought new investment to Louisiana, but it remained basically a poor state, particularly during the 1930s depression. Governors Huey P. Long in the 1930s and Earl K. Long (elected 1948 and 1956) ran the state in a notoriously monarchistic manner but from populist platforms. Since WWII, industrialization has increased markedly, and in the 1970s the population grew by more than 15%. The state's economy was hard hit by the decline in oil prices in the 1980s. In presidential elections 1968–88, Louisiana voted Republican in 1972 and 1980–88.

LOUISIANA PURCHASE, the huge territory purchased by the US from France in 1803. It stretched from the Mississippi R to the Rockies, and from the Canadian border to the Gulf of Mexico, some 828,000sq mi. Its acquisition more than doubled the area of what was then the US.

From 1762 the old French province of Louisiana, roughly where Louisiana is today, had been held by Spain. In 1800 Napoleon persuaded the Spanish to return the province to France. President Jefferson received reports of this with alarm, realizing that Napoleon hoped to establish an empire in North America. Jefferson instructed Livingston and Monroe to purchase New Orleans and other strategic parts of the Louisiana province from France. Much to their surprise, Napoleon, who was expecting renewed war with England, in April 1803 offered to sell the huge Louisiana Territory to the US, and the envoys quickly accepted the offer for a total price of $15 million. The purchase had greatly exceeded Jefferson's instructions, and there was some opposition from US businessmen, but most Americans saw the doubling of their territory as a triumph.

LOUIS PHILIPPE (1773–1850), king of the French 1830–48. Exiled from France in 1793, he traveled in Europe and the US until 1815, when he was accepted as a compromise candidate for the crown. As king from 1830 he was unwilling to extend the voting franchise, and the revolution of Feb., 1848, led to his abdication.

LOURDES, center of Roman Catholic pilgrimage, in SW France where, in 1858, the Virgin is said to have appeared to a 14-year-old peasant girl, now St. BERNADETTE. Lourdes is visited by some three million pilgrims annually—including, in 1983, Pope John Paul II.

LOUSE. See LICE.

L'OUVERTURE, Toussaint. See TOUSSAINT L'OUVERTURE.

LOUVRE, historic palace in Paris, mostly built during the reign of LOUIS XIV. Now one of the world's largest and most famous art museums, its treasures include paintings by Rembrandt, Rubens, Titian and Leonardo da Vinci, whose *Mona Lisa* is there. Other masterpieces in its collection are the painting *Arrangement in Gray and Black,* called "Whistler's Mother," and the famous ancient Greek statues, the *Venus de Milo* and *Winged Victory of Samothrace.*

LOVEBIRDS, eight or nine species in a genus of African PARROTS, *Agapornis,* so-called because of their close pair-bond and the frequency with which paired birds preen each other.

LOVEJOY, surname of two American brothers, both dedicated advocates of ABOLITIONISM. **Elijah Parish Lovejoy** (1802–1837) published newspapers in St. Louis and in Alton, Ill., advocating abolitionism. He was killed while defending his press from a mob. **Owen Lovejoy** (1811–1864), pastor, and later abolitionist leader in Illinois. A supporter of Abraham Lincoln, he was elected to Congress in 1856 and constantly denounced slavery there.

LOVELACE, Richard (1618–1657?), English Royalist soldier and one of the CAVALIER POETS. His poems, in two volumes, entitled *Lucasta,* were published in 1649 and 1660. They are noted at their best for a fine melodic line.

LOVELL, Sir (Alfred) Bernard (1913–), British astronomer who was a pioneer in the field of RADIO ASTRONOMY. As director of the Jodrell Bank Experimental Station (now Nuffield Radio Astronomy Laboratories) he was instrumental in constructing one of the world's largest steerable radio telescopes (1957).

LOW, Sir David (1891–1963), New Zealand-born British editorial cartoonist for the London *Star* (1919–27) and *Evening Standard* (1927–50). His cartoons of the Hitler era and WWII were particularly memorable.

LOW, Juliette Gordon (1860–1927), founder of the Girl Scouts in the US. She organized the first troop in her home town, Savannah, Ga., in 1912. By the time of her death there were 140,000 Girl Scouts in the US.

LOW COUNTRIES. See BELGIUM; NETHERLANDS; LUXEMBOURG.

LOWELL, Amy (1874–1925), US critic and poet of the IMAGIST school. Her collections of verse include *Sword Blades and Poppy Seed* (1914), *Men, Women and Ghosts* (1916) and *What's O'Clock?* (1925), which was awarded the Pulitzer prize.

LOWELL, James Russell (1819–1891), US poet, editor, essayist and diplomat. His best poems, including the famous *Vision of Sir Launfal* (1848), were written before his wife's death in 1853. His reputation as a political satirist was made by the witty *Bigelow Papers* (1848 and 1867). In 1855 he became professor of modern languages at Harvard, and was minister to England 1877–85.

LOWELL, Percival (1855–1916), US astronomer and writer who predicted the existence of and initiated the search for PLUTO; but who is best known for his championing the theory (now discarded) that the "canals" of MARS were signs of an irrigation system built by an intelligent race.

LOWELL, Robert (1917–1977), US poet and playwright. For his collection *Lord Weary's Castle* (1946) he won the Pulitzer Prize. Later books, *The Mills of the Kavanaughs* (1951), the autobiographical *Life Studies* (1959) and *For the Union Dead* (1964), established his reputation as a major poet. His dramatic trilogy *The Old Glory* was published in 1965. His free adaptations of Greek tragedy and various European poets brought him acclaim as a translator.

LOWIE, Robert H. (1883–1957), Austrian-born US anthropologist who was best known for his studies of the North American Indian, *The Crow Indians* (1935) and *Indians of the Plains* (1954). His classic theoretical studies were *Primitive Society* (1920) and *Social Organization* (1948).

LOWRY, Malcolm (1909–1957), English novelist. While living on the coast of British Columbia (1940–54) he published his greatest work, *Under the Volcano* (1947), concerned in part with the problem of alcoholism, which eventually proved fatal to the author. Two volumes of short stories were published posthumously.

LOYOLA, Saint Ignatius of. See IGNATIUS OF LOYOLA, SAINT.

LSD, lysergic acid diethylamide, a HALLUCINOGENIC DRUG based on ERGOT alkaloids. It may lead to psychotic reaction and bizarre behavior.

LUBITSCH, Ernst (1892–1947), German film director, noted chiefly for the sophisticated comedies he made after his emigration to Hollywood in 1923. Among his films are *Forbidden Paradise* (1924), *Ninotchka* (1939), *The Merry Widow* (1939), *The Shop Around the Corner* (1940) and *Heaven Can Wait* (1943).

LUBRICATION, the introduction of a thin film of lubricant—usually a semiviscous fluid—between two surfaces moving relative to each other, in order to minimize FRICTION and abrasive wear. In particular, bearings are lubricated in engines and other machinery. Liquid lubricants are most common, usually PETROLEUM fractions, being cheap, easy to introduce, and good at cooling the parts. The viscosity is tailored to the load, being made high enough to maintain the film yet not so high that power is lost. Multigrade oils cover a range of viscosity. The viscosity index represents the constancy of the viscosity over the usual temperature range—a desirable feature. Synthetic oils, including SILICONES, are used for high-temperature and other special applications. Greases—normally oils thickened with soaps, fats or waxes—are preferred where the lubricant has to stay in place without being sealed in. Solid lubricants, usually applied with a binder, are soft, layered solids including graphite, molybdenite, talc and boron nitride. Teflon, with its uniquely low coefficient of friction, is used for self-lubricating bearings. Rarely air or another gaseous substance is used as a lubricant. Additives to liquid lubricants include antioxidants, detergents, pour-point depressants (increasing low-temperature fluidity), and polymers to improve the viscosity index.

LUCAN (Marcus Annaeus Lucanus;

39–65), Roman poet best known for his *Bellum Civile* (or, incorrectly, *Pharsalia*), an epic poem on the clash between Julius Caesar and Pompey. He was a protégé of Nero's but eventually aroused the latter's jealousy. Lucan joined the Pisonian conspiracy against Nero and when this failed, committed suicide.

LUCAS VAN LEYDEN (c1494–1533), foremost Dutch painter of his day. A noted engraver and printmaker, he was as highly regarded as his acquaintance DÜRER. He painted biblical themes, such as *Lot and His Daughters* (c1509); some of his work foreshadows that of the great GENRE painters.

LUCE, Henry Robinson (1898–1967), US editor and publisher of *Time*, which he founded with Briton Hadden in 1923. He also produced *Fortune* (1930), *Life* (1936) and *Sports Illustrated* (1954), as well as many books, radio series and newsreels. His wife, **Clare Booth Luce** (1903–1987), was a playwright (*The Women*, 1936), Republican US representative from Connecticut (1943-47), and US ambassador to Italy (1953-57).

LUCIAN (c125–c190 AD), Syrian-Greek satirist. Among his best-known works are *Dialogues of the Gods*, a parody of mythology; *Dialogues of the Dead*, a biting satire on human vanities; and the *True History*, a lampoon of fantastic travellers' tales, which influenced RABELAIS and Jonathan SWIFT.

LUCRETIUS (c95–55 BC), Roman poet, the author of *De rerum natura*, and the last and greatest classical exponent of ATOMISM. His description of atoms in the void and his vision of the progress of man suffered undeserved neglect on account of his antireligious reputation.

LUDDITES, bands of English textile workers who destroyed labor-saving textile machinery in the early 19th century. They were protesting against unemployment and low wages which resulted wherever the new machinery was introduced and also against the poor quality of goods produced on the machines. Repressive government measures and an improving economic climate combined to end the rioting by 1816.

LUDENDORFF, Erich (1865–1937), German general who with Hindenburg did much to defeat the invading Russian armies in WWI, particularly at TANNENBERG. He was responsible for much German policy 1917–18 and for the request of an armistice in 1918. After the war he led a nationalist movement; he took part in Hitler's abortive coup in Munich in 1923, but severed relations with him soon after.

LUDLOW, Roger (1590–c1664), English colonizer and Puritan politician. A director of the MASSACHUSETTS BAY COMPANY, he became colonial deputy governor in 1634. In 1635 he headed colonizing projects in the Conn. area and wrote the Fundamental Orders, its first legal code. He returned to England in 1654.

LUENING, Otto (1900–   ), US composer, conductor and flutist known primarily for his innovative use of taped and electronic music both alone and in combination with live performance, as in *Gargoyles* (1961) for violin and synthesizer.

LUFTWAFFE (German: air arm), title of the German air force. Formed in 1935 under Hitler, it was commanded by Herman GOERING during WWII.

LUKACS, Gyorgy (1885–1971), Hungarian-born leading Marxist literary critic. He was made professor of aesthetics at Budapest U. in 1945. After the 1956 Hungarian uprising, Lukacs fell from political favor. Among his major works are *Studies in European Realism* (1946) and *The Historical Novel* (1955).

LUKE, Saint, by tradition the author of the third GOSPEL and its sequel, the ACTS OF THE APOSTLES. Luke was a Gentile and worked as a physician, probably in Antioch. He was influenced by his friend, St. Paul, whom he accompanied on his missionary journeys. The Gospel, written for Gentiles, claims to be based on eyewitness accounts.

LUKS, George Benjamin (1867–1933), US realist painter, one of the ASHCAN SCHOOL. Primarily a painter of figures, his bold and vigorous style in such works as *The Wrestlers* (1905) may have owed something to his work as a cartoonist.

LULLY, Jean-Baptiste (1632–1687), Italian-born French composer who became Louis XIV's favorite musician. He wrote much stage music, for MOLIÈRE among others, and his operas, particularly *Alceste* (1674) and *Armide* (1686), founded a French operatic tradition.

LUMBAGO, popular term for low back pain or lumbar back ache. It may be of various origins including chronic ligamentous strain, SLIPPED DISK (sometimes with SCIATICA), certain types of ARTHRITIS affecting the spine and congenital disease of the spine. Diagnosis and treatment may be difficult.

LUMBER, cut wood, especially when prepared for use ("dressed"). Lumbering, the extraction of timber from the forest, is a major industry in the US, which still has vast natural forests. In world timber production, the USSR is first, followed by the US, Japan and Canada. The demand for lumber is vast; it takes as many as 20 trees to make a ton of paper. Annual US paper production exceeds 35 million tons. The forests would soon be depleted without modern conservation and reforestation programs.

Trees used for lumber are classed as either softwoods or hardwoods. Softwoods, which thrive in cold regions, are the evergreen conifers such as fir, pine, cedar and spruce. Hardwoods, which thrive in temperate regions, include the deciduous trees like oak, birch, aspen and beech. The softwoods, used in building, make up 75% of the US timber market.

In the vast softwood forests of the US lumbering has become a mechanized industry, using power saws to fell and cut to size the trees and tractors or tractor winches to drag logs to a central clearing by cable. Since forests are often located in inaccessible regions, roads and new railroads may have to be built to transport the logs. Logs are often floated down mountain streams to broader rivers and lakes on whose banks sawmills are often located. Great masses of logs can be towed by tug down river, inside huge floating collars or booms. Once at the mill they may be stored until needed in a huge log pond, or millpond, protected by the water from fire and disease. After sorting, the logs are fed onto a conveyor belt and into the mill. Each log is clamped to a carriage and fed back and forth against a vertical bandsaw. The boards then pass to an edger, which removes the bark, and a trimmer, which cuts them to standard lengths. Other logs are cut into sheets or veneer, for plywood. The newly-cut wood, still green with moisture, is then seasoned (dried) before it is used commercially. (See FORESTRY; PAPER; TREE.)

LUMIÈRE, Louis (1864–1948), French pioneer of motion PHOTOGRAPHY who, with his brother Auguste (1862–1954), invented an early motion-picture system (patented 1895), the *cinématographe*; and made what is regarded as the first movie (1895).

LUMINESCENCE, the nonthermal emission of ELECTROMAGNETIC RADIATION, particularly LIGHT, from a PHOSPHOR. Including both fluorescence and phosphorescence (distinguished according to how long emission persists after excitation has ceased, in fluorescence emission ceasing within 10ns but continuing much longer in phosphorescence), particular types of luminescence are named for the mode of excitation. Thus in photoluminescence, PHOTONS are absorbed by the phosphor and lower-energy radiations emitted; in

chemiluminescence the energy source is a chemical reaction; cathodoluminescence is energized by cathode rays (ELECTRONS), and BIOLUMINESCENCE occurs in certain biochemical reactions.

LUMUMBA, Patrice Emergy (1925–1961), first prime minister of the Republic of the Congo (Zaire). He negotiated independence from Belgium (1960). Soon after, the army mutinied and Katanga seceded. Following his dismissal by President Joseph Kasavubu in Sept. 1960, he was arrested by General Joseph Mobutu and killed in mysterious circumstances some time later.

LUNDY'S LANE, Battle of, fought during the WAR OF 1812 in Canada near Niagara Falls (July 25, 1814). It halted the US advance into Canada at Fort Erie, but it was otherwise inconclusive, despite heavy casualties.

LUNGS, in vertebrates, the (usually) two largely airfilled organs in the chest concerned with RESPIRATION, the absorption of OXYGEN from and release of carbon dioxide into atmospheric air. In man, the right lung has three lobes and the left, two. Their surfaces are separated from the chest wall by two layers of *pleura,* with a little fluid between them; this allows free movement of the lungs and enables the forces of expansion of the chest wall and diaphragm to fill them with air. Air is drawn into the trachea via mouth or nose; the trachea divides into the bronchi which divide repeatedly until the terminal air sacs or *alveoli* are reached. In the alveoli, air is brought into close contact with unoxygenated BLOOD in lung CAPILLARIES; the BLOOD CIRCULATION through these comes from the right ventricle and returns to the left atrium of the HEART. Disorders of ventilation or of perfusion with blood leads to abnormalities in blood levels of carbon dioxide and oxygen. Lung DISEASES include ASTHMA, BRONCHITIS, PNEUMONIA, PLEURISY, PNEUMOTHORAX, PNEUMOCONIOSIS, EMBOLISM, CANCER and TUBERCULOSIS; lungs may also be involved in several systemic diseases (e.g., sarcoidosis, lupus erythematosus). Symptoms of lung disease include COUGH, sputum, blood in the sputum, shortness of breath and wheeze. Sudden failure of breathing requires prompt ARTIFICIAL RESPIRATION. Chest X RAY and estimations of blood gas levels and of various lung volumes aid diagnosis.

LURIA, Aleksandr Romanovich (1902–1977), Soviet neuropsychologist. A world-renowned authority on the human brain, he made important advances in brain surgery and postsurgical restoration of brain function.

LUTE, fretted stringed instrument related to the guitar, played by plucking the strings with the fingers. It was perhaps the most popular single instrument between 1400 and 1700, both for solo playing and as accompaniment to songs and madrigals; the great 16th-century composer John Dowland wrote mostly for the lute.

LUTHER, Martin (1483–1546), German REFORMATION leader and founder of LUTHERANISM. Following a religious experience he became an Augustinian friar, was ordained 1507, and visited Rome (1510), where he was shocked by the worldliness of the papal court. While professor of Scripture at Wittenberg U. (from 1512) he wrestled with the problem of personal salvation, concluding that it comes from the unmerited grace of God, available through faith alone (see JUSTIFICATION BY FAITH). When Johann Tetzel toured Saxony 1517 selling papal INDULGENCES, Luther denounced the practice in his historic 95 Theses, for which he was fiercely attacked, especially by Johann ECK. In 1520 he published *To the Christian Nobility of the German Nation.* It denied the pope's final authority to determine the interpretation of Scripture, declaring instead the priesthood of all believers; and it rejected papal claims to political authority, arguing for national churches governed by secular rulers. Luther denied the special spiritual authority of priests, advocated clerical marriage and denied the doctrine of TRANSUBSTANTIATION, adhering to CONSUBSTANTIATION. In Dec. 1520 he publicly burned a papal bull of condemnation and a copy of the canon law; he was excommunicated 1521. Summoned by Emperor Charles V to renounce his heresies at the Diet of Worms (1521), he refused, traditionally with the words, "Here I stand: I can do no other." He was outlawed but, protected by Frederick III of Saxony, he retired to the Wartburg castle. There, in six months, he translated the New Testament into German and began work on the Old. His hymns have been translated into many languages, and he wrote two catechisms (1529), the basis of Lutheranism. Against ERASMUS he wrote *The Bondage of the Will* (1525). He directed the reform movement from Wittenberg, aiming to moderate more extreme elements (see ANABAPTISTS), and opposed the PEASANTS' WAR, condoning princely repression of the revolt. In 1525 he married a former nun; they had six children.

LUTHERAN CHURCHES, the churches adhering to LUTHERANISM and springing from the German REFORMATION. From the beginning they were state churches ruled by the local princes; national Lutheran churches also formed in the Scandinavian countries. (See also THIRTY YEARS' WAR.) In 1817 Frederick William III of Prussia enforced union between the Prussian Lutheran and Reformed Churches, provoking the first of several schisms to form free Lutheran churches. A united German Lutheran Church was formed in 1949. Lutheran migrants to the US and Canada formed numerous churches that merged into three major groups: the American Lutheran Church, the Lutheran Church in America and the Lutheran Church—Missouri Synod. In 1987 the ALC and the LCA merged into one church with the smaller Evangelic Lutheran Churches to form the fourth largest US Protestant denomination with 5.3 million members. The Lutheran World Federation has about 70 million members.

LUTHERANISM, Protestant doctrinal system based on the teachings of Martin LUTHER. It regards the Bible as the only source of doctrine; stresses JUSTIFICATION BY FAITH alone; and recognizes only two SACRAMENTS: baptism and Holy Communion (see also CONSUBSTANTIATION). Luther's two catechisms (1529) and the AUGSBURG CONFESSION (1530) were collected with other basic standards in the *Book of Concord* (1580), consolidating Lutheranism against both Roman Catholicism and CALVINISM. (See also PIETISM.)

LUTHULI, Albert John (1898–1967), Rhodesian-born Christian leader in South Africa, an unyielding opponent of APARTHEID. A Zulu chief, he was elected president of the African National Congress (1952). In 1959 he was confined to his village by the South African government. He won the 1960 Nobel Peace Prize.

LUTOSLAWSKI, Witold (1913–   ), Polish composer whose work allowed for improvisation on the part of the individual members of the orchestra (as in *Venetian Games*) or chorus (as in *Three Poems by Henri Michaux*). He is best known for his *Little Suite* (1951), *Mourning Music* (1958) and *Concerto for Orchestra* (1954).

LÜTZEN, Battle of (1632), engagement at Lützen, SW of Leipzig, Germany, in the THIRTY YEARS' WAR; a brilliant victory over the imperial army of WALLENSTEIN by King GUSTAVUS II of Sweden, who was, however, killed in the battle.

LUXEMBOURG or **Luxemburg**, constitutional monarchy of W Europe, bounded by West Germany, Belgium and France. It is about 55mi long and 35mi wide. Luxembourg extends into the rugged

Official name: Grand Duchy of Luxembourg
Capital: Luxembourg
Area: 999sq mi
Population: 367,000
Languages: French; German; Letzeburgesch
Religion: Roman Catholic
Monetary unit(s): 1 Luxembourg franc = 100 centimes

ARDENNES upland in the N; the agriculturally fertile "Good Country" is in the S lowlands; the SE region along the Moselle R produces wine and fruit. The industrial SW, rich in iron ore, provides much of the national income. Agriculture, banking, and tourism are other major industries. Formerly including the Luxembourg province of Belgium, the country was a duchy of the medieval empire; a Hapsburg possession 1482–1795; and a French possession 1795–1815. In 1815 it became a Grand Duchy under the King of the Netherlands. The present ruling house of Nassau came to the throne in 1890. Luxembourg formed an economic union with Belgium in 1922; it is a member of the NORTH ATLANTIC TREATY ORGANIZATION and since the 1950s a member of BENELUX and the EUROPEAN ECONOMIC COMMUNITY.

LUXEMBURG, Rosa (1871?–1919), Polish-born German Marxist revolutionary, cofounder with Karl LIEBKNECHT of the SPARTACUS LEAGUE, Germany's first communist party. In the 1918 Berlin revolution she edited their journal, *Red Flag*. She and Liebknecht were arrested and murdered in 1919.

LUXOR, city in Upper Egypt on the E bank of the Nile R on part of the site of the ancient city of THEBES. Its famous temple of Amon, built by Amenhotep III, is 623ft long and has a colonnade and hall of hypostyle columns. Pop 84,600.

LUTYENS, Sir Edwin Landseer (1869–1944), British architect and president of the Royal Academy. A designer of Edwardian country homes, he was commissioned as planning supervisor of New Delhi, the new Indian capital, where his design for the viceroy's residence (1915–30) combined classical and Mogul Indian features.

LUZON, the main island of the PHILIPPINES. It is mountainous with several active volcanoes, and produces gold, chromite, iron, coconuts, hemp, rice and lumber. The chief cities are Manila, the republic's seat of government, and Quezon City, the official capital.

LVOV, Prince Georgi Yevgenyevich (1861–1925), Russian liberal statesman, prime minister of the first provisional government 1917 (see RUSSIAN REVOLUTION). After the Bolshevik Revolution he fled to Paris.

LYCEUM MOVEMENT, US associations for popular ADULT EDUCATION, influential in the 19th century. The first was founded by Josiah Holbrook in 1826 in Millbury, Mass. (See also CHAUTAUQUA MOVEMENT.)

LYDIA, ancient kingdom of W Asia Minor, of legendary wealth. The Lydians invented metal coins in the 7th century BC. During the 6th century BC its magnificent capital, Sardis, was the cultural center of a growing empire. Its zenith came under CROESUS, but he was defeated c546 BC by Cyrus of Persia.

LYELL, Sir Charles (1797–1875), British geologist and writer whose most important work was the promotion of geological UNIFORMITARIANISM (originally developed by James HUTTON) as an alternative to the CATASTROPHISM of CUVIER and others. The prime expression of these views came in his *Principles of Geology* (1830–33).

LYLY, John (c1554–1606), English author best known for his *Euphues* (part I, 1578; II, 1580), a prose romance in a highly artificial and allusive style. Lyly also wrote elegant comedies on classical themes, and was influential on other Elizabethan playwrights.

LYME DISEASE, a tick-borne bacterial infection named for Lyme, Conn., where it was first described in 1974, but now found in 35 states. Aside from a characteristic rash, symptoms are common and variable, mimicking dozens of other illnesses, from flu to multiple sclerosis. They include headache, malaise, fever, nausea, fatigue, joint pain, and partial facial paralysis. Left untreated, the symptoms may come and go mysteriously over the years. The disease can cause crippling arthritic pain, heart problems, facial paralysis, difficulties in movement, and visual, emotional, and memory disturbances. If caught early, uncomplicated Lyme disease can usually be treated with a 3-6-week course of oral antibiotics. If it is not discovered early, treatment may be long and costly.

LYMPH, fluid which drains from extracellular fluid via lymph vessels and nodes (glands). Important node sites are the neck, axilla, groin, chest and abdomen. Fine ducts carry lymph to the nodes, which are filled with lymphocytes and reticulum cells. These act as a filter, particularly for infected debris or PUS and for CANCER cells, which often spread by lymph. The lymphocytes are also concerned with development of IMMUNITY. From nodes, lymph may drain to other nodes or directly into the major thoracic duct, which returns it to the BLOOD. Specialized lymph ducts or lacteals carry FAT absorbed in the GASTROINTESTINAL TRACT to the thoracic duct. In addition, there are several areas of lymphoid tissue at the portals of the body as a primary defense against infection (TONSILS, ADENOIDS, Peyer's patches in the gut). Lymph node enlargement may be due to INFLAMMATION following DISEASE in the territory drained (SKIN, pharynx), or to development of an ABSCESS in the node (STAPHYLOCOCCUS, TUBERCULOSIS) due to INFECTIOUS DISEASE, secondary spread of cancer and the development of LYMPHOMA or LEUKEMIA. BIOPSY is valuable in diagnosis.

LYMPHOMA, malignant proliferation of LYMPH tissue, usually in the lymph nodes, SPLEEN or GASTROINTESTINAL TRACT. The prototype is HODGKIN'S DISEASE, but a number of other forms occur with varying HISTOLOGY and behavior. Cancer CHEMOTHERAPY and RADIATION THERAPY have much to offer in these disorders.

LYNCHING, illegal "execution" conducted by a self-appointed body, or a killing by mob violence; probably named for Charles Lynch, a Va. magistrate who in 1780 dispensed summary justice to Tory conspirators. Vigilante bodies in pioneer communities sometimes authorized lynchings. Lynchings in this century have occurred mainly in the South, often instigated by the KU KLUX KLAN, where blacks were usually the victims; always rare, the practice seems to have died out.

LYND, Robert Staughton (1892–1970), and **Helen Merrell Lynd** (1896–1982), US sociologists who used anthropological methods in their pioneering studies of small town America. Their books, *Middletown* (1929) and *Middletown in Transition* (19379, later identified as studies of Muncie, Ind., are regarded as classics of American sociology.

LYNX, bobtailed members of the CAT family, of both Old and New Worlds. Tawny yellow cats, lynxes live in forests, especially of pine, leading solitary lives,

hunting by night for small deer, badgers, hares, rabbits and small rodents—as well as occasionally raiding domestic stock.

LYON, Mary (1797–1849), US pioneer of women's higher education. A teacher from the age of 17, she was founder and first president of Mount Holyoke Female Seminary (1837), South Hadley, Mass.

LYON or Lyons, major city in E central France at the confluence of the Rhône R and the Saône; capital of the Rhône department. Founded by the Romans and long famed for its silk, it now also produces rayon, nylon, pharmaceuticals, trucks and electrical appliances. Pop (city) 408,860; (metro) 1,170,000.

LYRE, STRINGED INSTRUMENT originating in ancient Greece and the FERTILE CRESCENT. The strings, usually plucked, stretch between the body and a crossbar joining two arms. (See also KITHARA.)

LYRIC POETRY, originally poetry sung to the accompaniment of the LYRE. It now denotes any poem, usually short, such as the SONNET, expressing strongly felt personal emotion.

LYSANDER (d. 395 BC), Spartan admiral and statesman. In the PELOPONNESIAN WAR he enlarged the Spartan fleet, crushed Athenian sea power and entered Athens in triumph, 404 BC. He set up the government of the Thirty Tyrants there.

LYSENKO, Trofim Denisovich (1898–1976), Soviet agronomist whose antipathy for GENETICS and position of power under the Stalin regime led to the stifling of any progress in Soviet biological studies for 25 years or more. Refusing on ideological grounds to believe in GENES, he adopted a peculiar form of Lamarckism (see LAMARCK), and forced other Soviet scientists to support his views. He was removed from power in 1964.

LYSIAS (c459–c380 BC), Athenian orator noted for clarity and elegance of style. Exiled under the Thirty Tyrants, he helped restore democracy and impeached the tyrant Eratosthenes. Some 35 of his speeches survive.

13th letter of the English ALPHABET. It

corresponds to the Semitic letter *mem* and the Greek *mu*. It represents a labial nasal sound.

MA, Yo-Yo (1955–), French-born US cellist of Chinese descent, considered the preeminent cellist of his generation.

MAAZEL, Lorin (1930–), US conductor. A child prodigy, Maazel led orchestras at the age of nine. He conducted the Cleveland Symphony (1972–82) and the Vienna State Opera (1982–84).

MABUSE, Jan de c1478–1532), Flemish painter, born Jan Gossaert. He visited Italy in 1508 (the first of many Netherlandish painters to do so) and his work developed an Italianate style. One of his best known paintings is *Danaë*.

MACADAM, road-building system devised by the Scots engineer **John Loudon McAdam** (1756–1836). The soil beneath the road, rather than foundations, takes the load, the road being waterproof and well-drained to keep this soil dry. For modern highways a first layer of larger rocks is laid, then smaller rocks and gravel, the whole being bound with, usually, ASPHALT or tar.

McADOO, William Gibbs (1863–1941), US lawyer and politician. He was secretary of the treasury (1913–18), US director general of railways (1917–19), first chairman of the Federal Reserve Board, which he helped institute (1913) and manager of the government financing of WWI. He served as a Democratic US senator from California 1933–39.

McALLISTER, (Samuel) Ward (1827–1895), US society leader. In 1892 he claimed that there were "only about 400 people in New York society," and his phrase the "Four Hundred" passed into American idiom. He wrote *Society as I Have Found It* (1890).

MACAO, Portuguese overseas territory in SE China, on the estuary of the Canton (Pearl) R, 6sq mi in area. It comprises the peninsula of Macao and adjacent islands of Taipa and Colôane. Macao is a popular resort and gambling center and important commercial port. Fishing is a major economic activity. The territory came into Portuguese possession in 1557. It was granted broad autonomy in 1976, and in 1987 Portugal and China negotiated an agreement for the return of Macao to China in 1999 under a plan similar to that approved for Hong Kong. Pop 400,000.

MACAPAGAL, Diosdado (1910–), Liberal president of the Philippines (1962–65). His attempts at reform were hampered by his party's minority position in the government, and he lost the 1965 election to Ferdinand MARCOS.

MacARTHUR, Douglas (1880–1964), US general and hero of WWII. He commanded the 42nd (Rainbow) Division in WWI, and was superintendent of West Point (1919–22). In 1930 he became chief of staff of the US army, the youngest man ever to hold the post, and was promoted to general. He retired from the army in 1937, but was recalled in 1941 as commander of US army forces in the Far East. In 1942 he became Allied supreme commander of the Southwest Pacific Area and in 1944 general of the army. Signatory of the Japanese surrender, he led the reconstruction of Japan as Allied supreme commander from 1945. When the KOREAN WAR broke out (1950) he was selected commander of the UN forces sent to aid South Korea. His unwillingness to obey President TRUMAN's orders to restrict the war to Korea led to his dismissal the following year.

MACAULAY, Dame Rose (1881–1958), English author who won recognition as a social satirist with such novels as *Told by an Idiot* (1923) and *Staying with Relatives* (1930). Her works include outstanding travel books, poems and literary criticism.

MACAULAY, Thomas Babington (1800–1859), English historian and essayist. He sacrificed a flourishing political career to undertake his *History of England* (5 vols, 1849–61), but he died before completing it. Its clarity and readability made it an immediate success. Like the *History*, his *Essays* display great range and brillance, together with supreme confidence of judgment.

MACBETH (d. 1057), king of Scotland, formerly chief of the province of Moray, who killed King Duncan in battle (1040) and took the throne. SHAKESPEARE's famous tragedy *Macbeth*, based on Holinshed's *Chronicles*, gives a historically inaccurate picture of him as a villainous usurper.

MacBRIDE, Sean (1904–1988), Irish politician, foreign minister 1948–51, active thereafter in European and United Nations affairs. He was a founder (1961) and chairman (1961–75) of AMNESTY INTERNATIONAL and secretary general (1963–70) of the International Commission of Jurists. For his work on behalf of HUMAN RIGHTS he shared the 1974 Nobel Peace Prize.

MACCABEES, Books of, two books of the Old Testament APOCRYPHA which tell the story of the Maccabees or HASMONEANS, Jewish rulers of the 2nd and 1st centuries BC who fought for the independence of Judea from Syria. 1 Maccabees, a prime historical source, was written c100 BC. 2

Maccabees is a devotional work of low historical value, written before 70 AD. Two other books, 3 and 4 Maccabees, are among the PSEUDEPIGRAPHA.

McCARRAN, Patrick Anthony (1876–1954), US Democratic senator from Nevada (1933–54). He sponsored two controversial measures, the McCarran-Wood Act (1950), requiring the registration of communists, and the McCarran-Walter Act (1952), which tightened controls over aliens and immigrants.

McCARTHY, Eugene Joseph (1916–   ), US Democratic senator from Minn. (1959–71). A consistent opponent of the VIETNAM WAR, he campaigned for the presidential nomination in 1968 and attracted considerable support. He lost the nomination to Hubert HUMPHREY, but his campaign helped to consolidate public opposition to the war.

McCARTHY, Joseph Raymond (1908–1957), US Republican senator from Wis. (1947–57) who created the "McCarthy era" in the mid-1950s through his sensational investigations into alleged communist subversion of American life. These investigations were first made (1950) into federal departments, then into the army and among prominent civilians. McCarthyism became a word for charges made without proof and accompanied by publicity. After the national publicity directed on his activities by the Army-McCarthy hearings (1954), McCarthy was formally censured by fellow senators, and his influence steadily diminished.

McCARTHY, Joseph Vincent (1887–1978), US baseball figure, manager (1931–46) of the New York Yankees. Under his leadership the Yankees won eight pennants and seven World Series, including four straight (1936–39).

McCARTHY, Mary ((1912–   ), US writer, best known for her satirical novel *The Group* (1963), about the lives of a generation of Vassar graduates. Her nonfiction works include *Memories of a Catholic Girlhood* (1957), *Vietnam* (1967) and a body of outstanding literary criticism. *Memories of a Catholic Girlhood* (1972) and *How I Grew* (1987) are autobiographical.

McCLELLAN, George Brinton (1826–1885), controversial Union general in the American Civil War. In July 1861 he was given command of the Army of the Potomac, and later that year the supreme command. His hesitation in taking the offensive, and his failure to take Richmond and to follow up his success at the Battle of ANTIETAM, brought his dismissal in 1862. In 1864 he ran unsuccessfully for the presidency against Abraham LINCOLN.

McCLOSKEY, John (1810–1885), US Roman Catholic prelate. He became archbishop of New York (1864) and was created the first US cardinal (1875). He was responsible for the completion of St. Patrick's Cathedral in New York City.

McCLURE, Sir Robert (1807–1873), British Arctic explorer and naval officer. On a search (1850–53) in the Arctic Archipelago for Sir John FRANKLIN, he discovered McClure Strait and became the first to prove the existence of the NORTHWEST PASSAGE.

McCLURE, Samuel Sidney (1857–1949), US editor and publisher who founded (1884) the first US newspaper syndicate. *McClure's Magazine*, of which he was founder (1893) and editor, presented many famous writers to the American public.

McCORMACK, John (1884–1945), Irish-American tenor. He began his operatic career in London, first appearing in the US in 1909. He gained his greatest popularity as a concert singer, especially of Irish songs.

McCORMICK, Cyrus Hall (1809–1884), US inventor and industrialist who invented an early mechanical reaper (patented 1834), the first models appearing under license from 1841 onward.

McCORMICK, Robert Rutherford (1880–1955), US newspaper publisher who became sole owner of the Chicago *Tribune* after WWI. Pursuing an extreme right-wing policy, it won the largest circulation of any paper in the Midwest.

McCOY, John Jay (1895–   ), US public official and banker. Assistant secretary of war (1941–45) during WWII, he played a leading role in the postwar reconstruction as president (1947–49) of the World Bank and high commissioner (1949–52) in occupied West Germany. He was president (1952–60) of the Chase Manhattan Bank.

McCOY, Joseph Geating (1837–1915), US cattleman who developed (1867) Abilene, Kansas, as the shipping point for Texas cattle driven north on the Chisholm Trail. As eastern Kansas became more settled, the terminus for the Long Drive shifted west to Dodge City.

McCRAE, John (1872–1918), Canadian physician and poet of WWI, famous for his poem "In Flanders Fields," which was written under fire. It was first published in *Punch* in December 1915.

McCULLERS, Carson (1917–1967), US novelist. Her novels, set in her native South, deal with the problems of human isolation. Her best known book is *The Member of the Wedding* (1946).

McCULLOCH v. MARYLAND, case before the US Supreme Court in 1819 in which it was ruled that Congress has implied powers other than those specifically granted by the Constitution. The case involved the Baltimore branch of the BANK OF THE UNITED STATES, which refused to pay a tax imposed by Maryland. The court ruled that the tax was unconstitutional as it interfered with an arm of the federal government.

MacDIARMID, Hugh (1892–1978), Scottish poet, born Christopher Murray Grieve. Founder of the Scottish Nationalist Party, he gave fresh impetus to Scottish literature. He is best known for the long rhapsodic poem *A Drunk Man Looks at the Thistle* (1926).

MACDONALD, Dwight (1906–1982), US political and cultural critic. He moved from the business magazine *Fortune* to the radical *Partisan Review*, where he became (1938–43) a leading figure in left intellectual circles. He left *Partisan Review* to protest its support of WWII. He was a staff writer for the *New Yorker* (1951–71) and film critic for *Esquire* (1960–66).

MacDONALD, James Ramsay (1866–1937), British statesman who was the chief founder of Britain's Labour Party (1900) and prime minister of the first and second labour governments (Jan.–Oct. 1924 and 1929–31). He lost most of his party's confidence when he headed a national coalition (1931–35) to deal with the Depression.

MACDONALD, Sir John Alexander (1815–1891), Canadian statesman, first premier of the Dominion of Canada. Elected to the Ontario legislature in 1844, he became premier in 1857 as head of a Conservative coalition which was joined (1864) by George Brown and others. He led subsequent negotiations which resulted (1867) in the confederation of Canada. The Pacific Scandal (1873), involving corruption charges, caused his government's resignation, but he was again premier from 1878 until his death.

MacDONALD, Ross (Kenneth Millar; 1915–1983), US mystery writer, creator of detective Lew Archer.

MACDONOUGH, Thomas (1783–1825), US naval officer who defeated the British at the decisive Battle of Plattsburgh (1814) during the WAR OF 1812. His victory saved New York and Vermont from invasion.

McDOUGALL, William (1871–1938), British psychologist best known for his fusion of the disciplines of PSYCHOLOGY and ANTHROPOLOGY in order to obtain a better understanding of the roots of social behavior. He also conducted important researches into PARAPSYCHOLOGY.

MacDOWELL, Edward Alexander (1861–1908), US composer and pianist. He is most remembered for his lyrical piano works and for the orchestral *Indian Suite* (1897). His wife founded the MacDowell Colony in Peterborough, N.H., a retreat for creative artists.

MACEDONIA, mountainous region of SE Europe, the ancient Macedon. It extends from the NW Aegean coast into the central Balkan peninsula. Divided among GREECE, YUGOSLAVIA and BULGARIA, it covers 25,636sq mi. Ethnically it is very mixed, but there are mainly Slavs in the N and Greeks in the S. The region is primarily agricultural, with tobacco, grains and cotton the chief crops. One of the great powers of the ancient world under ALEXANDER THE GREAT, Macedonia was later ruled by Romans, Byzantines, Bulgars and Serbs. From 1389 to 1912 it was part of the OTTOMAN EMPIRE. The present boundaries derive from the BALKAN WARS (1912–13).

McENROE, John (1959–   ), US tennis player, four-time US Open winner (1979–81, 1984), three-time Wimbledon champion (1981, 1983–84).

MacFADDEN, Bernarr (1868–1955), US publisher. An advocate of health foods, natural cures, and exercise, he founded (1899) *Physical Culture*, the first of his numerous popular magazines, including the "pulps" *True Story, True Romances, True Detective*, and *Photoplay*. He also published (1931–42) *Liberty* magazine as well as newspapers in ten cities.

McGILL, Ralph (1898–1969), US journalist and publisher who edited (from 1942) and published (from 1960) the Atlanta *Constitution*. Called "the conscience of the South," he was a champion of civil rights and supporter of school desegregation.

McGOVERN, George Stanley (1922–   ), US Senator from South Dakota and the 1972 Democratic presidential candidate. A leading advocate of an end to the Vietnam War, he campaigned for a broad program of social and political reforms. He attracted initially substantial support from liberals, but with serious party divisions his campaign went badly and Richard NIXON won with a record 61% of the popular vote. He sought his party's nomination again in 1984.

McGRAW, John Joseph (1873–1934), US professional baseball player and manager. A star third baseman for the Baltimore Orioles, he became manager of Baltimore's American League team (1901). He went to the New York Giants as manager in 1902 and by his retirement in 1932 his team had won ten league championships and three World Series.

McGUFFEY, William Holmes (1800–1873), US educator. His series of six *Eclectic Readers* (1836–57) sold an estimated 122 million copies. Almost universal readers for elementary schools in the Middle West and South, they had an immense influence on public education.

MACH, Ernst (1838–1916), Austrian physicist and philosopher whose name is commemorated in the Mach number, defined as speed (as of an airplane) expressed as a multiple of the speed of sound under the same conditions. His greatest influence was in philosophy, where he rejected from science all concepts which could not be validated by experience. This freed EINSTEIN from the absoluteness of Newtonian space-time (and thus helped him toward his theory of RELATIVITY) and helped inform the LOGICAL POSITIVISM of the Vienna Circle.

MACHADO Y MORALES, Gerardo (1871–1939), president of Cuba (1925–33). His rule began with a program of reforms but became increasingly despotic and repressive until he was forced into exile.

MACHAUT, Guillaume de (c1300–1377), French poet and composer. He was a leading figure in the 14th-century Ars Nova ("new art") school of music, which developed many new forms. His *Mass for Four Voices* was the first complete polyphonic setting by a single composer.

MACHEL, Samora Moises (1933–1986), Mozambican political leader, president of Mozambique from 1975 when the Portuguese withdrew. A Marxist, he tried to impose a socialist regime, but economic reverses and military pressure forced him to moderate his policies. In 1984 he signed a nonaggression pact with South Africa, which then withdrew its support from Mozambican guerrillas. He was killed in a plane crash.

MACHIAVELLI, Niccolò (1469–1527), Florentine statesman and political theorist. He served the Republic of Florence, and was its emissary on several occasions. When the MEDICI family returned to power in 1512 he was imprisoned; on his release he devoted himself principally to writing. Despite his belief in political morality and his undoubted love of liberty, as revealed in his *Discourses on Livy* (1531), his master work, *The Prince* (1532; written 1513), describes the amoral and unscrupulous political calculation by which an "ideal" prince maintains his power. It is often seen as a cynical guide to power politics, although Machiavelli's motives in writing it are much debated. He also wrote a brilliant *History of Florence* (1532).

MACHINE, a device that performs useful work by transmitting, modifying or transforming motion, forces and energy. There are three basic machines, the inclined plane, the lever, and the wheel and axle: from these, and adaptations of these, are built up all true machines, no matter how complex they may appear. There are two essential properties of all machines: *mechanical advantage*, which is the ratio load/effort, and *efficiency*, the ratio of actual performance to theoretical performance. Mechanical advantage can be less than, equal to or greater than 1; while efficiency, owing to such losses as FRICTION, is always less than 100% (otherwise a PERPETUAL MOTION machine would be possible). (See also EFFICIENCY; ENERGY; FORCE; LEVER.)

Simple machines derived from the three basic elements include: from the inclined plane, the *wedge* (effort at the top being translated to force at the sides) and the *screw* (an inclined plane in spiral form); from the lever, the wrench or spanner (the balance also uses the principle of the lever); and from the wheel and axle, the PULLEY, (which can also be viewed as a type of lever).

MACHINE GUN, a military small arm capable of rapid fire. The need for such a weapon was recognized soon after the development of firearms. Early inventors, including Leonardo da Vinci, concentrated on designs with numerous barrels which were fired either simultaneously or in sequence. These guns were cumbersome and took a long time to reload. They also suffered from the unreliability of the priming mechanism. After the invention of the percussion cap by Joshua Shaw, an American sea captain, the reliability of firing was greatly increased, and numerous machine guns were soon developed. In 1862, Richard Jordan Gatling invented a single-barreled machine gun with a rotary chamber, and, in 1862, the Confederates fired volleys from the Williams gun, making it the first machine gun to be used in warfare. The Union army was using Gatling's gun by the end of the war. Gatling later developed his famous handcranked multibarreled gun, incorporating automatic loading and ejection of cartridges, which had in the meanwhile been greatly improved. Gatling's multibarreled gun was capable of firing up to 3,000 rounds a minute.

The first fully automatic machine gun, a

single-barreled water-cooled weapon patented by Hiram Steven Maxim in 1885, was highly successful. The operation of the Maxim gun depended on the recoil force to push back the barrel and bolt. Then, in 1892, the American inventor John Moses Browning patented a machine gun operating on a new principle. This gun was the first successful "gas-operated" machine gun. The gases obtained from a hole in the side of the barrel moved a piston which was coupled to the automatic mechanism. In 1911, Isaac Lewis, an American colonel, patented the first lightweight automatic machine gun. It weighed 27 lb and was cooled by air. Browning's most famous machine gun, a belt-fed weapon, was developed in 1917 and manufactured in various calibers, in both water-cooled and air-cooled versions. Various guns designed by Lewis and Browning were used in World War I, and the devastating effectiveness of the machine gun against infantry forces is indicated by the fact that it was responsible for well over 80% of all casualties during the war.

In World War II, Browning machine guns were used effectively by Allied forces, while the Germans used MG34s and MG42s, which had firing rates well in excess of 1,000 rounds per minute. In 1957, the US Army replaced the Browning by the M60, a German-influenced lightweight gun. In the same year, the US Air Force introduced the Vulcan gun, smilar in design to the Gatling, and capable of firing up to 7,000 rounds per minute. High firing rates like this became necessary with the development of supersonic aircraft, although many modern airplanes carry rockets and guided missiles rather than machine guns.

MACHINE TOOLS, nonportable, power-driven tools used industrially for working metal components to tolerances far finer than those obtainable manually. The fundamental processes used are cutting and grinding, individual machines being designed for boring, broaching, drilling, milling, planing and sawing. Essentially a machine tool consists of a jig to hold both the cutting tool and the workpiece, and a mechanism to allow these to be moved relative to each other in a controlled fashion. A typical example is the lathe. Auxiliary functions facilitate the cooling and lubrication of the tool and workpiece while work is in progress using a cutting fluid. The rate which any piece can be worked depends on the material being worked and the composition of the cutting point. High-speed steel, tungsten carbide and corundum are favored materials for cutting edges. Where several operations have to be performed on a single workpiece, time can be saved by using multiple-function tools such as the turret lathe, particularly if numerically rather than manually controlled. Modern industry would be inconceivable without machine tools. It was only when these began to be developed in the late 18th century that it became possible to manufacture interchangeable parts and thus initiate MASS PRODUCTION.

MACH NUMBER, ratio of the speed of an object or fluid to the local speed of SOUND, which is temperature dependent. Speeds are subsonic or supersonic depending on whether the mach number is less than or greater than one.

MACHU PICCHU, ancient (15th-century?) INCA city in Peru, an impressive ruin dramatically situated on a high ridge of the Andes. It was discovered in 1911 by the American explorer Hiram Bingham.

MACK, Connie (1862–1956), famous US baseball player and manager. As owner and manager of the Philadelphia Athletics from 1901 to 1950, he led his team to victory in five world series.

McKAY, Claude (1890–1948), US black poet and novelist born in Jamaica. His was the first and most militant voice of the New York Negro movement in the 1920s. His works include *Harlem Shadows* (1922) and the novel *Home to Harlem* (1927).

McKAY, Donald (1810–1880), US naval architect, master builder of clipper ships. His *Great Republic* (1853) was at 4,555 tons the biggest clipper ever built. The use of steam brought a decline in business that forced him to close his Boston shipyards in 1855.

MACKENZIE, Sir Alexander (c1764–1820), Canadian fur trader and explorer, the first white man to cross the northern part of North America to the Pacific. Born in Scotland, he emigrated to Canada and in 1789 made an expedition down the Mackenzie River (named for him). In 1793 he crossed the Rockies to the Pacific coast.

MACKENZIE, Alexander (1822–1892), Canadian statesman. Born in Scotland, he went to Canada in 1842. He entered the legislative assembly in 1861, having worked his way up to the editorship of a Liberal paper. From 1873 until 1878 he was Canada's first Liberal prime minister.

MACKENZIE, William Lyon (1795–1861), Canadian journalist, radical politician and leader of the December revolution (1837), an unsuccessful attempt to achieve self-government in Canada. He fled to the US, then returned in 1849 and was reelected to Parliament in 1851.

MACKENZIE RIVER, in NW Canada, flowing from Great Slave Lake to the Arctic Ocean. The Mackenzie itself is 1,060mi in length, the total length of the system about 2,500mi, the second largest in North America. It is named for Sir Alexander MACKENZIE.

McKIM, Charles Follen (1847–1909), US architect, founder of his own firm (1878) and of the American Academy in Rome. His best-known projects, such as the University Club in New York City (1900), are in neoclassical style.

MACKINAC, Straits of, channel separating Upper and Lower Michigan. It connects lakes Huron and Michigan and is spanned by the MACKINAC BRIDGE from Mackinaw City to St. Ignace.

MACKINAC BRIDGE, 7,400ft long, connects Upper and Lower Michigan. It is one of the longest suspension bridges in the world, with a main span of 3,800ft.

MACKINDER, Sir Halford John (1861–1947), British geopolitician who argued that the Eurasian heartland was the "pivot" of history and advocated formation of an Atlantic community of Europe and North America to counter it. His ideas were taken up by the German geopolitician Karl Ernst HAUSHOFER.

McKINLEY, William (1843–1901), 25th president of the US. The son of a small ironfounder in Niles, Ohio, he enlisted as a private in the 23rd Ohio Volunteers at the outbreak of the CIVIL WAR, at the age of 18. By the end of the war he had reached the rank of brevet major. He then studied law in Albany, N.Y., and set up practice in Canton, Ohio, where, in 1871, he married Ida Saxton. Although she became a chronic invalid after the early deaths of their two daughters, the marriage was a happy one.

McKinley was elected to Congress as a Republican in 1876 and stayed there, except for one term, until 1891. He sponsored the Tariff Act of 1890, which set record-high protective duties. This unpopular measure contributed to his defeat in the 1890 congressional elections. He had, however, attracted the backing of the wealthy Cleveland irondealer, Marcus Alonzo HANNA, with whose help he was elected governor of Ohio in 1891, and again in 1893. Again with Hanna's backing, he was chosen Republican presidential candidate in 1896. His Democratic opponent, William Jennings BRYAN, had early successes with his chosen issue of FREE SILVER, but with the help of $3.5 million that Hanna collected, McKinley's "front porch"

campaign was effective enough to gain him a decisive victory.

Immediately after his inauguration he called a special session of Congress, which raised duties still higher, though without the reciprocal measures that McKinley wanted. The Gold Standard Act of 1899 killed Free Silver. With prosperity rising at home, he turned hs attention to foreign affairs. The SPANISH–AMERICAN WAR over Spanish outrages in Cuba was followed by a revolt against American rule in the Philippine Islands, and in 1899 the "Open Door" policy on trade with China was introduced. Reelected in 1900, McKinley was assassinated in 1901 by the anarchist Leon Czolgosz. He had presided over a period characterized by rapidly growing prosperity and the emergence of the US as a world power.

McKINLEY, Mount, highest peak (20,320ft) in North America. Part of Mount McKinley National Park in S central Alaska, much of it is covered by permanent snowfields and glaciers. It was first climbed in 1913.

MacLEAN, Donald (1913–1983), British public official and Soviet spy, member of a group at Cambridge including Guy BURGESS, Kim PHILBY, and Anthony BLUNT that was recruited by Soviet intelligence. He entered (1935) the British foreign office, serving (1944–48) as first secretary of the British embassy in Washington. In 1951 when his role as a Soviet agent was suspected he escaped to the Soviet Union.

MacLEISH, Archibald (1892–1982), US poet and playwright. *Conquistador* (1932), a narrative poem on the conquest of Mexico, *Collected Poems* (1952), containing his best lyrical verse, and *J.B.* (1958), a verse drama based on Job, all won Pulitzer prizes. Cultural adviser to President ROOSEVELT, he was Librarian of Congress 1939–44.

McLUHAN, (Herbert) Marshall (1911–1980), Canadian professor of humanities and mass communications specialist, best known for his book *Understanding Media* (1964), which contains the famous phrase "the medium is the message"; that is, the content of communication is determined by its means, with the implication that modern mass communications technology, particularly television, is transforming our way of thinking and perceiving.

MacMAHON, Marie Edmé Patrice de (1808–1893), French marshal, president of France 1873–79. Elected president by the monarchist majority in the national assembly, he was hostile to the Third Republic. When a new assembly with a republican majority was elected in 1876, he forced the resignation of the republican premier, Jules SIMON, appointed a royalist cabinet, and dissolved the assembly. Republicans again won a majority in the assembly, but MacMahon again appointed a royalist cabinet. He was finally forced to accept the principle of ministerial responsibility to the assembly rather than to the president. He resigned before the end of his term.

MacMILLAN, Donald Baxter (1874–1970), US explorer of the Arctic. His first expedition was with Commander Robert PEARY in 1908. In all he undertook 31 Arctic expeditions, and made many scientifically valuable contributions to knowledge of the region.

MACMILLAN, (Maurice) Harold (1894–1986), British statesman and Conservative prime minister from 1957 to 1963. He entered Parliament in 1924 and became an opponent of appeasement in the 1930s. Having served in ministerial posts in WWII and the 1950s, he became prime minister after the SUEZ CANAL intervention. He restored Anglo-US relations, tried to take Britain into the COMMON MARKET and presided over an economic boom, which, however, was already over when he resigned in ill health.

McNAMARA, Robert Strange (1916–   ), secretary of defense under presidents KENNEDY and JOHNSON (1961–68), who played an important part in the shaping of US defense policy, including Vietnam policy. Before this he had been president of the Ford Motor Company, and in 1968 he became president of the World Bank, serving until 1981.

MacNEICE, Louis (1907–1963), British poet, born in Northern Ireland. His low-keyed, socially committed poetry links him with the "Oxford Group" of the 1930s, which included W. H. AUDEN and Stephen SPENDER. His *Collected Poems* appeared in 1949.

McPHERSON, Aimee Semple (1890–1944), US evangelist, famed for her flamboyant preaching. She worked as a missionary in China, then returned to the US to become an itinerant preacher and faith-healer, eventually founding the Foursquare Gospel Church in Los Angeles. She was married three times, and involved in numerous legal actions.

MACPHERSON, James (1736–1796), Scottish poet and member of Parliament from 1780, famous for his purported translations of the Gaelic bard Ossian, published 1760–75. Disputed by Samuel JOHNSON and others, they appear to have been Macpherson's own work, loosely based on contemporary Gaelic verse.

MACREADY, William Charles (1793–1873), English actor and manager, with Edmund KEAN one of the outstanding tragedians of his day. He managed Covent Garden and Drury Lane. His rivalry with the American tragedian Edwin FORREST led to the Astor Place riot in New York in 1849.

McREYNOLDS, James Clark (1862–1946), US jurist, attorney general (1913–14) and associate justice of the US Supreme Court (1914–41). An archconservative opponent of the NEW DEAL, he was one of the targets of President F. D. Roosevelt's "court-packing" plan.

MACROECONOMICS, the study of aggregates in the national economy, as opposed to that part of economics concerned with the constituent elements, MICROECONOMICS. Macroeconomics studies key economic quantities (such as national income, savings, INVESTMENT and balance of payments), the factors determining them and the relationships between them.

MACROPHAGE, large scavenging cell (the name literally means "big eater") concerned with attacking and ingesting germs which is found wandering in the blood in areas where there is great activity against germ invasion. It is not a true white cell, but is produced in the reticuloendothelial system.

MADAGASCAR, formerly Malagasy Republic, republic in the Indian Ocean comprising the large island of Madagascar and several small islands.

Official name: Democratic Republic of Madagascar
Capital: Antananarivo
Area: 226,658sq mi
Population: 10,605,000
Languages: Malagasy, French. Hova spoken
Religions: Christian, Animist, Muslim
Monetary unit(s): 1 Malagasy franc (FMG) = 100 centimes
Land. It is separated from the SE African mainland by the Mozambique Channel.

The island has rugged central highlands and fertile low-lying coastal plains. The highlands have several extinct volcanoes and mountain groups which rise to over 9,000ft. They have a pleasantly cool, and occasionally cold, climate. The coastal plains tend to be hot and humid, with luxuriant tropical vegetation. Soil erosion is a serious problem, and destructive hurricanes may occur between December and April.

People. The island's population can be broadly divided into two groups: those of Indonesian-Polynesian descent (Merinas), living mainly in the highlands, and those of African Negro descent (*côtiers*), living mainly in the coastal regions. Traditional antagonisms exist between the two groups. French, Indian and Chinese nationals are prominent in commerce. About 75% of the people live in rural areas. The main cities are Antananarivo (Tananarive), the capital and largest city, Antairanana, Toamasina, Mahajanga, and Toliara.

Economy. The island is predominantly farming and stock-raising country. Coffee, cloves and vanilla are principal foreign-exchange earners. Meat and prawns are also exported. Chromite, graphite, mica and phosphates are important minerals. Oil and gas deposits have been discovered. Industries include food processing, oil refining, vehicle assembly and textile making.

History. Portuguese, French and English rivalry for control of Madagascar ended in French invasion and annexation (1885-1905). In 1947, a revolt against French rule was crushed, but in 1958 the island gained self-government within the French Community as the Malagasy Republic. It achieved full independence in 1960. In 1972 the civilian government handed over power to the military. Didier Ratsiraka, who became president in 1975 under a new constitution, was reelected to successive terms. Lt. Col. Désiré Rakotoar-ijaona served as prime minister from 1977 until his retirement in 1988.

MADEIRA, archipelago in the N Atlantic some 360mi W of Morocco, constituting the Funchal district of Portugal. Madeira, the largest island, is mountainous; settlement, including the capital Funchal, is largely on the coast. The islands produce sugarcane, bananas and the famous Madeira wine. Their scenic beauty and warm climate make them a year-round tourist resort.

MADERNO, Carlo (1556-1629), Italian architect of the early BAROQUE. Chief architect of St. Peter's, Rome, from 1603, he designed the nave and facade. He designed the church of Sta. Maria della Vittoria (1620) and began the Palazzo Barberini for Urban V in 1625.

MADERO, Francisco Indalecio (1873-1913), president of Mexico 1911-13. A democratic idealist, he opposed Porfirio DÍAZ in the 1910 election and was imprisoned. He escaped to Tex. and there declared a revolution; joined by Francisco VILLA and ZAPATA, he deposed Díaz in 1911 and was elected president. His administration was marred by his own ineptitude, and division and corruption among his followers. In the face of widespread revolt he was deposed and murdered by Gen. Victoriano HUERTA.

MADISON, Dolley Payne (1768-1849), wife of James MADISON from 1794. Of Quaker family, she was the widow of John Todd. She was known as a charming and lavish hostess when her husband was secretary of state and president.

MADISON, James (1751-1836), fourth president of the US 1809-17. Born at Port Conway, Va., he graduated from the College of New Jersey (Princeton U.) in 1771. In 1776 he helped draft Va.'s constitution and served in the CONTINENTAL CONGRESS 1780-83. He pressed the need for a stronger central government than was possible under the ARTICLES OF CONFEDERATION. In the Va. house of delegates 1784-86 he advocated federal unity; he promoted the ANNAPOLIS CONVENTION which led in turn to the Federal Constitutional Convention (1787). He submitted a series of proposals to it, the general framework of which is reflected in the UNITED STATES CONSTITUTION adopted by the Convention. This and his skillful conduct in the debates has earned him the title of "father of the Constitution." He was one of the authors of the FEDERALIST PAPERS. As a congressman 1789-97 he advocated the BILL OF RIGHTS.

An influential secretary of state under JEFFERSON 1801-08, he was chosen by Jefferson as his successor. As president himself from 1809 Madison took a firm grip on affairs, writing all major state papers in the first two years. In foreign affairs, he sought to free US shipping of the trade restraints imposed by Britain and France in the NAPOLEONIC WARS. Trusting dubious French assurances, Madison imposed an embargo on trade with Britain in 1810. This and a popular desire to conquer Canada provoked the WAR OF 1812 in which Madison's prestige suffered, especially after the burning of the White House by the British in 1814. After the war Madison presided over a period of new prosperity and expansion. He retired in 1817 to his Va. plantation Montpelier. Rector of the University of Virginia from 1826, he became interested in the abolition of slavery.

MADISON SQUARE GARDEN, world-famous indoor sports, entertainment and convention center in New York City. The first Garden was built on the site of a railroad terminal at Madison Square; the second Garden was at 49th Street and Eighth Avenue (1925). A new Madison Square Garden center was built 1964–69 on the site of the old Pennsylvania Station. It includes a 20,000-seat arena and a 5,200-seat forum.

MADONNA (Italian: my Lady), name given to the Virgin Mary, especially as depicted in works of art. The Madonna is often shown with the infant Jesus or, in the PIETA, mourning over his body taken down from the Cross.

MADRID, capital of Spain and of Madrid Province, on the Manzanares R in New Castile. A 10th-century Moorish fortress captured by Castile in 1083, it was made the capital by PHILIP II (1561). Now Spain's administrative and financial headquarters, it has a wide range of industries. A cultural center, its landmarks include the Prado art gallery, the royal palace and the university city. Pop 3,217,461.

MADRIGAL, part song for two or more voices. Originating in 14th-century Italy, it reached the height of its popularity in the 16th century, through the works of MONTEVERDI and GESUALDO. Thomas MORLEY and others developed a distinctive English form.

MAECENAS, Gaius (d. 8 BC), Roman statesman famous as the patron of HORACE, VERGIL and Propertius. Friend, adviser and agent of the emperor AUGUSTUS, he was criticized by SENECA for his extravagance. His name came to symbolize patronage.

MAENADS, in Greek mythology, female devotees of DIONYSUS. Also called *bacchantes* (for Bacchus, Dionysus' other name), they were known for their ecstatic frenzies.

MAETERLINCK, Maurice (1862–1949), Belgian poet and playwright. His early work was influenced by SYMBOLISM; he is best known for the tragedy *Pelléas and Mélisande* (1892), set as an opera by DEBUSSY, and the dramatic fable *The Blue Bird* (1908). He was awarded the Nobel Prize for Literature in 1911.

MAFEKING, town in N South Africa, in Cape Province, a cattle and dairy-farming center. In the BOER WAR a British garrison under Lord BADEN-POWELL was besieged there for 217 days. Pop 6,900.

MAFIA, Italian-American criminal organization. Its name derives from 19th-century Sicilian bandits who dominated the peasantry through terrorism and the tradition of the vendetta. Despite repression by successive governments, including MUSSOLINI, the Mafia remains very powerful in Italy. In 1987–88, 391 Mafia members were convicted in two mass trials and jailed. *Mafiosi* emigrated to the US and set up sophisticated criminal bodies there, organized in "families." These prospered during PROHIBITION, and diversified from bootlegging into gambling, narcotics, vice, labor unions and more recently into some legitimate business. In the 1950s and 1960s attention was drawn to the Mafia by the fruitless trial of 60 of its leaders, caught in conference at Apalachin, N.Y., in 1957, and the disclosures of former *mafioso* Joseph Valachi. In the 1980s increasing numbers of organized crime leaders were successfully prosecuted.

MAGDALENIAN, upper-Paleolithic culture named for La Madeleine cave, Dordogne, France, noted for the quality of its painting and bone engraving (see also ALTAMIRA; STONE AGE.)

MAGELLAN, Ferdinand (c1480–1521), Portuguese navigator who commanded the first expedition to sail around the world. Accused of embezzlement during his service in the Portuguese Indian army, he fell from favor at court and so sought Spanish backing for his proposed voyage in search of a western route to the Spice Islands or East Indies, then believed to be only a few hundred miles beyond America. Financed by Charles I, Magellan sailed from Sanlúca de Barrameda with five ships on Sept. 20, 1519. In Jan. 1520 he explored the Río de la Plata, then sailed S to Patagonia, where he put down a mutiny. In Oct. 1520 he discovered the strait now named for him. With three ships he entered the Pacific, proceeded N up the coast of South America, then sailed W across the Pacific. For two months no land was sighted and the expedition was near starvation; in March 1521 they reached Guam, and in April the Philippines. Magellan was killed in a skirmish with natives there on April 27. Only one ship, the *Victoria*, under Juan del CANO, returned to Spain, having sailed around the world. Although he did not survive the journey, Magellan was undoubtedly responsible for its success.

MAGELLAN, Strait of, separates mainland South America from Tierra del Fuego and islands to the S. Around 330mi long, and an important route before the building of the Panama Canal, it was first navigated by Ferdinand MAGELLAN in 1520.

MAGELLANIC CLOUDS, two irregular GALAXIES that orbit the MILKY WAY, visible in S skies. The Large Magellanic Cloud (Nubecula Major), about 15,000 light-years in diameter, has a well-marked axis suggesting that it may be an embryonic spiral galaxy. The Small Magellanic Cloud (Nubecula Minor) is about 10,000 light-years across. Both are rich in CEPHEID VARIABLES and about 150,000 light-years from the earth.

MAGI, Persian priestly caste or tribe. Little is known of them beyond their reputation for wisdom and supernatural powers. Zoroaster was probably a Magus; the Magi headed ZOROASTRIANISM, which may have been based upon their original religion. The Three Wise Men were reputedly Magi.

MAGIC, in entertainment, conjuring tricks or manipulated feats of illusion, such as making flowers appear, pulling rabbits out of hats, levitation, or sawing a person in half. Included are spectacular escapes—from strait jackets, handcuffs, locked trunks—of the kind that made Harry HOUDINI the best known of magician-entertainers.

MAGIC, Primitive, the prescientific belief that an individual, by use of a ritual or spoken formula, may achieve a result that would otherwise be beyond his, or human, powers. Should the magic fail to work, this is assumed to be due to deviations from the correct formula. FRAZER classified magic under two main heads, imitative and contagious. In **imitative magic** the magician acts upon or produces a likeness of his desired object: rainmakers may light fires, the smoke of which resembles rainclouds; voodoo practitioners stick pins in wax models of their intended victims. In **contagious magic** it is assumed that two objects once close together remain related even after separation: the magician may act upon hair clippings in an attempt to injure the person from whose body they came. Magic is crucial to many primitive societies, most tribes having at least an equivalent to a medicine man (see SHAMANISM) who is believed to be able to provide them with extra defense against hostile tribes or evil spirits.

MAGIC SQUARE, square array of numbers such that the sums along each row, column and diagonal are equal; e.g.:

6 7 2
1 5 9
8 3 4

MAGINOT LINE, massive French fortifications system, built 1930–34 between the Swiss and Belgian borders. Named for war minister André Maginot (1877–1932), it consisted of linked underground fortresses. Obsolete before it was completed, it was easily bypassed by the German mobile advance in WWII.

MAGLEV (*magnetic levitation*), phenomenon in which one object is suspended above another through the repulsion of like magnetic poles. A prototype passenger train employing this principle was operational in Japan in the mid-1980s. In a maglev system, the train's cars are suspended about 1 ft above an aluminum or copper track. An alternating current running through the track propels the cars by creating magnetic waves. The system eliminates friction and wear, the cars are relatively light and inexpensive, and the necessary electricity requires little fossil fuel. Recent advances in SUPERCONDUCTIVITY promise to make such a system even more efficient.

MAGMA, molten material formed in the upper mantle or crust of the EARTH, composed of a mixture of various complex silicates in which are dissolved various gaseous materials, including WATER. On cooling magma forms IGNEOUS ROCKS, though any gaseous constituents are usually lost during the solidification. Magma extruded to the surface forms LAVA. The term is loosely applied to other fluid substances (e.g., molten salt) in the earth's crust.

MAGNA CARTA (Latin: great charter), major British constitutional charter forced on King JOHN I by a baronial alliance at Runnymede in June 1215. The barons rebelled because of John's heavy taxation to finance wars and his exclusion of them from government. He sought to repudiate the charter but died soon after. It falls into 63 clauses, designed to prevent royal restriction of baronial privilege and feudal rights. It also safeguarded church and municipal rights and privileges. Altered forms of it were issued on John's death in 1216, in 1217 and 1225. In fact a reactionary measure, its vagueness allowed many later commentators to find in it the roots of whatever civil rights they wished to defend, such as HABEAS CORPUS and JURY trial. It did, however, pave the way for constitutional monarchy by implicitly recognizing that a king may be bound by laws enforceable by his subjects.

MAGNES, Judah Leon (1877–1948), US rabbi and Zionist who emigrated (1922) to Palestine, where he was a founder, chancellor (1925–35), and president (1935–48) of the Hebrew University. Magnes differed from other Zionists by advocating a binational Arab-Jewish rather than a Jewish state in Palestine.

MAGNETISM, the phenomena associated with "magnetic dipoles," commonly encountered in the properties of the familiar horseshoe (permanent) magnet and applied in a multitude of magnetic devices.

Man first learned of magnetism through the properties of the *lodestone*, a shaped piece of magnetite that had the property of aligning itself in a roughly north-south direction. Eventually he found how to use a lodestone to magnetize a steel bar, thus making an artificial **permanent magnet**. The power of a magnet was discovered to be concentrated in two "poles," one of which always sought the north, and was called a north-seeking pole, or north pole, the other being a south-seeking pole, or south pole. It was early learned that, given two permanent magnets, the unlike poles were attracted to each other and the like poles repelled each other according to an inverse-square law. Furthermore, dividing a magnet in two never resulted in the isolation of an individual pole, but only in the creation of two shorter two-poled magnets. The explanation of these properties in terms of magnetic "lines of force" was an early achievement of the science of magnetostatics.

Today, physicists explain magnetism in terms of *magnetic dipoles*. Magnetic dipole moment is an intrinsic property of fundamental particles. ELECTRONS, for example, have a moment of 0.928×10^{-23} A·m^2 parallel or antiparallel to the direction of observation. The forces between magnetic dipoles are identical to those between electric dipoles (see ELECTRICITY). This leads scientists often to regard the dipoles as consisting of two magnetic charges of opposite type, the poles of traditional theory. But unlike electric charges, magnetic poles are believed never to be found in isolation.

In **ferromagnetic materials** such as IRON and COBALT, spontaneous dipole alignment over relatively large regions known as *magnetic domains* occurs. Magnetization in such materials involves a change in the relative size of domains aligned in different directions, and can multiply the effect of the magnetizing field a thousand times. Other materials show much weaker, nonpermanent magnetic properties.

Magnetism is intimately associated with electricity (see ELECTROMAGNETISM). Electric currents generate magnetic fields circulating around themselves—the EARTH's magnetic field is maintained by large currents in its liquid core—and small current loops behave like magnetic dipoles

with a moment given by the product of the loop current and area.

MAGNITUDE, Stellar, a measure of a star's brightness. The foundations of the system were laid by HIPPARCHUS (c120 BC), who divided stars into six categories, from 1 to 6 in order of decreasing brightness. Later the system was extended to include fainter stars which could be seen only by telescope, and brighter stars, which were assigned negative magnitudes (e.g., Sirius, -1.5). Five magnitudes were defined as a 100-times increase in brightness. These *apparent magnitudes* depend greatly on the distances from us of the stars. *Absolute magnitude* is defined as the apparent magnitude a star would have were it at a distance of 10pc from us: Sirius then has magnitude $+1.4$. Absolute magnitudes clearly tell us far more than do apparent magnitudes. Stars are also assigned red, infrared, bolometric and photographic magnitude.

MAGRITTE, René (1898–1967), Belgian Surrealist painter. He was an adherent of SURREALISM from about 1925, developing a style which often juxtaposed realistically portrayed subjects in a deeply disconcerting manner.

MAGSAYSAY, Ramón (1907–1957), president of the Philippines 1953–57. In WWII he led anti-Japanese guerrillas on Luzon. As defense secretary 1950–53, he defeated the Hukbalahap (Huk) communist guerrillas.

MAGYARS, speakers of the Hungarian language. A nomadic warrior people, originally from the Urals, they entered central Europe in the 9th century and settled in the region which is now Hungary. The Magyar language belongs to the Ugro-Finnic linguistic group. (See also HUNGARY.)

MAHĀBHĀRATA, great Hindu epic poem, comprising some 110,000 32-syllable couplets, probably written before 500 BC, though with many later passages. It concerns the lengthy feud between two related tribes, the Pandavas and the Kauravas, and has as its central episode the BHAGAVAD-GĪTĀ, a later insertion. There are numerous editorial passages on mythology, religion, philosophy and morals.

MAHAN, Alfred Thayer (1840–1914), US naval officer and historian. His works on the historical significance of sea power are classics in their field. They include *The Influence of Sea Power upon History, 1660–1783* (1890) and *The Influence of Sea Power upon the French Revolution and Empire, 1793–1812* (1892). His work stimulated worldwide naval expansion.

MAHDĪ (Arabic: the guided one), the prophet or savior who Sunni Muslims believe will bring peace and justice to the world. A notable claimant was 'Ubayd Allah (reigned 909–34), founder of the Egyptian Fatimid dynasty. Another was Muhammad Ahmad (d. 1885), who raised a revolt against Egyptian rule in the Sudan and fought the British 1883–85.

MAHFOUZ, Naguib (1911–   ), Egyptian writer of plays, screenplays, short stories, and novels, most notably the "Cairo trilogy" (1956–57). In 1988 he became the first Arabic writer to receive the Nobel Prize for Literature.

MAHLER, Gustav (1860–1911), Austrian composer and conductor. He wrote nine symphonies (a tenth was unfinished) and a number of song cycles. The symphonies are a culmination of 19th-century Romanticism, but their startling harmonic and orchestral effects link them with early 20th-century works. Among other positions, Mahler was director of the Imperial Opera in Vienna 1897–1907.

MAHMUD OF GHAZNI (971–1030), Afghan conqueror who ruled Ghazni and Khorasan from 998. A devout Muslim, he invaded India many times, destroying Hindu temples and bringing the Punjab and Kashmir into his empire. He led a new era of Islamic dominance.

MAHRATTA or **MARATHA**, central Indian HINDU warrior people. Their empire was founded by Sivaji in 1674; it dominated India for about 150 years, following the MOGUL empire, but by the mid-19th century the British had broken its power.

MAIDU INDIANS, aboriginal Indians of N Cal. They lived mainly in the Sacramento Valley and the Sierra Nevada Mountains. The Maidus are part of the Penutian linguistic family. Today they number fewer than 200.

MAILER, Norman (1923–   ), US novelist and journalist. After the great success of his first novel, *The Naked and the Dead* (1948), he became a trenchant critic of the American way of life. He developed an amalgam of journalism, fiction and autobiography, first evident in his collection *Advertisements for Myself* (1959). He shared a 1969 Pulitzer Prize for *The Armies of the Night* (1968), an account of the 1967 Washington peace march. Later works include *Marilyn* (1973) and *The Executioner's Song* (1979).

MAILLOL, Aristide (1861–1944), French sculptor and painter. His chief subject was the female nude, which he sculpted in monumental, static forms that represent a revival of Classical ideals. In the early 1900s he was linked with the artists called Nabis, as a painter; but when he was nearly 40 years old he took up sculpture.

MAIMONIDES, Moses (Moses ben Maimon, or Rambam; 1135–1204), the foremost medieval Jewish philosopher. He was born in Muslim Spain, but persecution drove his family to leave the country. They eventually settled near Cairo in Egypt, where Maimonides became renowned as court physician to Saladin. Two of his major works were the *Mishneh Torah* (1180), a codification of Jewish doctrine, and *Guide to the Perplexed* (1190), in which he attempted to interpret Jewish tradition in Aristotelian terms. His work influenced many Jewish and Christian thinkers.

MAINE, Sir Henry James Sumner (1822–1888), English jurist and legal historian whose *Ancient Law* (1861) traced the development of societies from customary to positive law.

MAINE, the northeasternmost state of the US, bounded to the N and E by New Brunswick, to the S by the Atlantic Ocean, and to the W by NH and Quebec.

Name of state: Maine
Capital: Augusta
Statehood: March 15, 1820 (23rd state)
Familiar name: Pine Tree State
Area: 33,215sq mi
Population: 1,173,000
Elevation: Highest—5,268ft, Mount Katahdin. Lowest—sea level, Atlantic Ocean
Motto: *Dirigo* ("I direct")
State flower: White-pine cone and tassel
State bird: Chickadee
State tree: White pine
State song: "State of Maine Song"
Land. There are three distinct land regions in the state—the Seaboard (coastal) Lowlands, the New England Upland running SW–NE and the White Mountain region in the NW.
People. Maine is among the least urbanized of the states with about half of the population living in urban areas in 1986. Portland is the largest city, followed by Lewiston and Bangor. There are several Indian tribal reservations.

Economy. Some 80% of the state is forested, and much of its economy is based on wood and wood products. The scenic forests, lakes, hills, rivers and coastal regions make tourism an important industry. Acadia National Park is second only to Yellowstone in number of visitors. Manufacturing employs nearly 25% of the state's labor force. Major products in addition to paper and wood items include textiles, leather goods and processed foods. Maine is also famous for its lobsters and potatoes. Population growth in the increasingly urban SE has prompted laws to slow construction and control pollution.

History. In the early 1600s the Algonquin Indians who inhabited the region offered little resistance to the establishment of the first white settlements on the coast and along the navigable rivers. But Maine was the scene of many conflicts during the FRENCH AND INDIAN WARS and came under English control after the Treaty of Paris in 1763. Settlement began to increase, but remained low in comparison with other states until the 19th century.

Maine's soldiers played an active part in the Revolutionary War and the first naval engagement of the war took place off the state's coast, near Machias. In 1775 the British burned the town of Falmouth (now Portland). During the WAR OF 1812 the British easily captured and held the eastern portion of the state. In 1820, Maine, which had been a part of Mass. since 1691, became a separate state. The 12th largest state in 1820, by 1986 it ranked 38th. In 1980, the Penobscot Indians reached a settlement over their claim to half of Maine's territory. The worst floods in Maine's history caused over $100 billion damage in 1987. In presidential elections 1968–88, Maine voted Republican 1972–88.

MAINE, US battleship, sent to protect US citizens and property in Cuba; it mysteriously blew up in Havana harbor on Feb. 15, 1898, with a loss of 260 men. The incident helped spark the SPANISH-AMERICAN WAR.

MAINTENON, Françoise d'Aubigné, Marquise de (1635–1719), second wife of Louis XIV of France. After the death of her first husband (1660), she became governess to the sons of Louis and his mistress Mme de Montespan. She replaced the latter in Louis' affections and, on the death of the queen, married him.

MAISTRE, Joseph Marie, Comte de (1753 –1821), French philosopher, author and founder of the Ultramontanist movement. A staunch conservative, he believed papal and royal power should be absolute and was an inveterate opponent of the French Revolution.

MAITLAND, Frederic William (1850– 1906), English jurist and legal historian. He was particularly concerned with early English law and founded the Selden Society (1887). Notable among his works is *The History of English Law before the Time of Edward I* (1895), written with Sir Frederick Pollock.

MAIZE. See CORN.

MAJDANEK, Polish village near Lublin, site of a German concentration camp where 1.5 million Jews, Russians, and Poles were killed during WWII.

MAJORCA, or **Mallorca,** largest of the Balearic Islands of Baleares province, Spain. Majorca lies in the W Mediterranean, 115mi E of the Spanish coast. It is a major tourist center with many resorts, including its capital, Palma.

MAKARIOS III (Michael Christodoulos Mouskos; 1913–1977), the first president of independent Cyprus (from 1959), archbishop and primate of the Cypriot Orthodox Church from 1950. During British rule he led the movement for *enosis* (union with Greece). He had links with the EOKA terrorist group and was exiled by the British 1956–57. He fled temporarily during the political disturbances of 1974.

MAKAROVA, Natalia (1940–), Soviet-born US ballerina. A soloist with the Kirov Ballet from 1959, she defected (1970) to the West and joined the American Ballet Theater in New York.

MAKEMIE, Francis (c1658–1708), Irish-born missionary in America from c1682, founder of Presbyterianism in America. In 1706 he united parishes in Maryland, Pennsylvania, New Jersey, and Virginia into the first American presbytery.

MALABAR CHRISTIANS, or **St. Thomas Christians,** a group mostly found in Kerala state, SW India. Considered heretics by the Portuguese, though traditionally aligned with Rome since the 6th century, they broke with Rome in 1653. The majority reverted to Catholicism in 1661, but some joined the Syrian Orthodox Church.

MALABAR COAST, coastal region of SW India, from Goa to Cape Comorin peninsula. The principal industries are fishing and rice growing. In the 16th century it was an important Portuguese trading area.

MALACHI, Book of (Hebrew: my messenger), the 12th of the Old Testament Minor Prophets. Written anonymously about the 5th century BC, it prophesies judgment for insincerity and negligence in religion at the coming of the MESSIAH.

MALAGASY REPUBLIC. See MADA-GASCAR.

MALAMUD, Bernard (1914–1986), US novelist and short story writer. He won a National Book Award for his stories in *The Magic Barrel* (1958) and the Pulitzer Prize for his novel *The Fixer* (1966). Malamud's work deals mainly with Jewish life and traditions in the US. The heroes of his books are often humble, solitary individuals, though *Dubin's Lives* (1979) marked a departure in subject matter.

MALAN, Daniel François (1874–1959), South African politician. He founded the Purified Nationalist Party (1934) and was prime minister of South Africa (1948–54). He was a dedicated believer in APARTHEID.

MALAPARTE, Curzio (1898–1957), pen name of Kurt Suckert, Italian writer with a penchant for the grotesque. His war correspondent experiences with the German army in Russia formed the background of *Kaputt* (1944); those with the US army in Italy were transmitted into *The Skin* (1949).

MALARIA, tropical ·parasitic disease causing malaise and intermittent FEVER and sweating, either on alternate days or every third day; bouts often reoccur over many years. One form, cerebral malaria, develops rapidly with ENCEPHALITIS, COMA and SHOCK. Malaria is due to infection with *Plasmodium* carried by mosquitos of the genus *Anopheles* from the BLOOD of infected persons. The cyclic fever is due to the parasite's life cycle in the blood and LIVER; diagnosis is by examination of blood. QUININE and its derivatives, especially chloroquine and primaquine, are used both in prevention and treatment, but other chemotherapy (atabrine, pyrimethamine) may also be used. Mosquito control, primarily by destroying their breeding places (swamps and pools), provides the best method of combating the disease.

MALAWI, formerly Nyasaland, a republic in E central Africa. High plateaus, 2,500ft–4,500ft in elevation, comprise much of the country, and over 20% of the area is occupied by Lake Malawi (or Nyasa), lying in the GREAT RIFT VALLEY. The valley climate is hot; that of the Highlands, moderate. Most of the population are Bantu-speaking Africans, and 90% live in villages. The largest towns are Blantyre, Lilongwe, the capital, and Zomba. Malawi has no significant mineral deposits, and the economy is based on agriculture, particularly the growth of tea, tobacco and cotton, which are all exported. There is light industry at Blantyre and Lilongwe and bauxite deposits on Mt Mulanje. Roads and rails linking Malawi with Mozambique have been cut by war. Blantyre has an international airport.

Official name: Republic of Malawi
Capital: Lilongwe
Area: 45,747sq mi
Population: 7,499,000
Languages: English, Bantu languages, Swahili
Religions: Christian, Muslim, Animist
Monetary unit(s): 1 kwacha = 100 tambala
History. In 1859 the Scottish missionary David LIVINGSTONE visited the area. Missions were later set up and the Arab slave trade suppressed. In 1891 a British protectorate of Nyasaland was formed, becoming the British Central Africa Protectorate in 1893. In 1907 the name reverted to Nyasaland. From 1953–63 the country was part of the Federation of Rhodesia and Nyasaland. In 1964 it became the independent state of Malawi, remaining within the British Commonwealth, and Dr. Hastings Banda became premier. It was made a republic in 1966 with Banda as president for life. In the late 1980s, the nation suffered food shortages. The economy was further burdened by an influx of refugees from war-torn neighboring Mozambique.

MALAY, general term for a group of about 100 million people who live on the Malay Peninsula and on islands of the Philippines and Indonesia. They are a short, brown-skinned, Mongoloid people. They probably emigrated originally from central Asia. By the 2nd century AD, the powerful Malay kingdom of Srivijaya ruled in Sumatra, Indonesia.

MALAY ARCHIPELAGO, formerly the East Indies, the world's largest group of islands, off the coast of SE Asia, between the Indian and Pacific Oceans. They include the 3,000 islands of Indonesia, the 7,000 islands of the Philippines, and New Guinea.

MALAYO-POLYNESIAN LANGUAGES, or **Austronesian Languages**, family of some 500 languages found throughout the

Central and S Pacific (except New Guinea and Australia, but including New Zealand) and especially in Malaysia and the Indonesian islands. There are two main groups, Oceanic to the E and Indonesian to the W.

MALAY PENINSULA, the southernmost peninsula in Asia, comprising West Malaysia and SW Thailand. It is one of the world's richest producers of rubber and tin.

MALAYSIA, independent federation in Southeast Asia, comprising West Malaysia on the Malay Peninsula and, 400mi away across the South China Sea, East Malaysia, formed by Sabah and Sarawak on the island of Borneo.

Official name: Federation of Malaysia
Capital: Kuala Lumpur
Area: 127,581sq mi
Population: 16,538,000
Languages: Malay; English, Chinese, Tamil
Religions: Muslim, Buddhist, Hindu
Monetary units(s): 1 Malaysian dollar = 100 cents

Land. The landscape of Malaya (West Malaysia) is mainly mountainous (rising to over 7,000ft) with narrow coastal plains and lush equatorial forests. The climate is hot and very humid. Sarawak and Sabah also have mountainous interiors and large areas of rain forest. Many rivers flow from central Borneo to the coastal swamps. Malaysia's highest mountain, Mt. Kinabalu (13,455ft), is in Sabah.

People. The predominantly rural popula-tiion is more than 50% Malay, 32% Chinese, and 8% Indian. Another 8% are indigenous tribal peoples concentrated in Sarawak and Sabah. The largest cities are Kuala Lumpur, the capital, Penang (George Town) and Ipoh, in the W, Kota Kinabalu in Sabah, and Kuching in Sarawak. Government is by constitutional monarchy, a paramount ruler being elected from among the hereditary rulers of nine of the 14 states for five-year terms.

Economy. Malaysia has rich natural resources. It is one of the world's leading producers of natural rubber and tin. The forests also provide valuable timber, palm oil and coconuts. Rice is the chief food crop, and bananas, yams, cocoa, pepper, tea and tobacco are also grown. Malaysia produces petroleum, iron ore, bauxite, coal and gold. The principal exports are petroleum, rubber, tin, palm oil and timber.

History. In the 9th century Malaya was the seat of the Buddhist Srivijava empire. Beginning in the 14th century the population was converted to Islam. The Portuguese took Malacca in 1511 but were ousted by the Dutch in 1641. The British formed a trading base of the East India Company in Penang in 1786, and in 1826 united Penang, Singapore and Malacca into the Straits Settlement. Between 1888 and 1909 the British established many protectorates in Malaya and Borneo. After the WWII Japanese occupation (1941–45), Malaya was reorganized as the Federation of Malaya (1948), gaining independence within the British Commonwealth (1957). In 1963 the union of Malaya with Singapore, Sarawak and Sabah formed the Federation of Malaysia. Indonesia waged guerrilla warfare against the Federation during 1963–65. In 1965 Singapore seceded to become an independent republic. Parliament was suspended for 22 months in 1969 after racial riots broke out between Malays and Chinese in West Malaysia. Ethnic tensions resurfaced in 1978 and 1980. Premier Mahathir bin Mohammed came to power in 1981 and remained head of government following the 1982 and 1986 elections. In 1988, however, the courts declared his ruling United Malays National Organization illegal, intensifying a leader-ship struggle among Malay politicians.

MALCOLM X (Malcolm Little; 1925–1965), US black radical leader. While in prison 1946–52, he was converted to the BLACK MUSLIMS and became their leader in 1963. In 1964 he formed the rival Organization of Afro-American Unity, pleading for racial brotherhood instead of separation. He was assassinated at an OAAU meeting in New York City.

MALDIVES, Republic of, formerly the **Maldive Islands,** a group of 19 coral atolls in the Indian Ocean. They lie about 400mi SW of Ceylon and comprise some 2,000 islands, of which about 220 are inhabited. The people are Muslims, and their language, Divehi, is related to Old Sinhalese. The capital, Malé, lies on the island of the same name. The chief industry is fishing, although coconuts and some grains are grown on a limited scale. Since 1985, royalties from foreign fishing fleets operating offshore have provided additional

Official name: Republic of Maldives
Capital: Malé
Area: 115sq mi
Population: 195,000
Languages: Divehi (Maldivian)
Religions: Muslim
Monetary unit(s): 1 Maldivian rupee = 100 larees

revenues. The Maldives may have been settled in prehistoric times. From the 12th century the Maldive Islands were governed as a sultanate. The Islands were under British protection 1887–1965, becoming independent in 1965 and a republic in 1968. In 1988 Indian troops suppressed a coup by invading Tamil mercenaries from Sri Lanka.

MALEBRANCHE, Nicolas (1638–1715), French philosopher, scientist and Roman Catholic priest, noted for the doctrine of "occasionalism" as an explanation of causation and the mind-body relation. In both philosophy and science he was much influenced by the thought of DESCARTES, in the former field attempting to reconcile Cartesian philosophy with that of St. Augustine, in the latter field researching LIGHT, VISION and the CALCULUS.

MALENKOV, Georgy Maksimilianovich (1902–1988), Soviet premier 1953–55, after STALIN's death. Malenkov was replaced in 1955, then expelled from the PRESIDIUM (1957), accused of forming an "antiparty" group, and from the Party in 1961.

MALEVICH, Kasimir (1878–1935), Russian painter, a pioneer of ABSTRACT ART. In 1913 he began painting works based on geometric shapes and published a manifesto to propagate SUPREMATISM. Among his works is *White on White*, 1918.

MALHERBE, François de (1555–1628), French court poet to Henry IV and Louis XIII. A critic of the classical style of the PLÉIADE poets, he emphasized the importance of French classic language and of a precise form of writing.

MALI, landlocked republic in W Africa, lying to the S of Algeria.
Land. Mali is largely desert, but the great

Official name: Republic of Mali
Capital: Bamako
Area: 478,841sq mi
Population: 7,653,000
Languages: French; tribal languages
Religions: Muslim, Animist
Monetary unit(s): 1 CFA franc = 100 centimes

Niger R flows across S Mali, and its channels and marshy lakes form an "inland delta" suitable for rice and cotton growing. Without irrigation from the Niger and Senegal Rivers agriculture would be impossible. Middle Mali is arid, with shrub, thorn and acacia. The NE and SW regions are mountainous.

People. Mali has many ethnic groups, negroid farming peoples in the S like the Bambara and Malinké, the Dogon in central Mali, the Peuls (Fulani) in the Niger Valley and white nomadic pastoralists, the Tuareg, Moors and Arabs in the N. The capital and largest town is Bamako in the S on the Niger R.

Economy. Mali, whose economy depends on agriculture and livestock, has recently faced acute food shortages as a result of drought. Major cash crops are cotton and peanuts; industry is largely restricted to processing these and other agricultural products. Mineral resources are being developed on a limited basis, and dependence on imported oil has strained the economy.

History. In the 14th century the Mali Empire was at its height, and as late as 1507 TIMBUKTU was still a flourishing cultural center. By the mid-17th century Mali had crumbled under external attacks and internal rivalries. In 1896 the area came under French rule, and in 1904 it became the French Sudan. In 1958 the colony accepted autonomy within the French Community. During 1959–60, with Senegal, it composed the Sudanese Republic. In 1960 Mali became fully independent under President Keita, who was overthrown in 1968 in a military coup led by Col. Moussa Traoré. The country returned to civilian rule as a one-party state in 1979, with Traoré as president. He was reelected in

1985.

MALI EMPIRE, greatest of the Sudanese empires of Africa. Founded in the 13th century, it reached its height under Mansa Musa who reigned c1312–37. He and his successors were devout Muslims. The towns of Mali and TIMBUKTU became centers both of the caravan trade and of Islamic culture. The empire declined in the 15th century, mainly because of SONGHAI expansion.

MALINOWSKI, Bronislaw Kasper (1884–1942), Polish-born British anthropologist, generally accepted as the founder of social ANTHROPOLOGY. In his functional theory all the mores, customs or beliefs of a society perform a vital function in it. From 1927 to 1938 he was a professor at London University; from 1939 until his death, a professor at Yale.

MALIPIERO,   Gian   Francesco (1882–1973), Italian composer who, with Alfredo Casella, was a leader of the Italian school of modern classical music. He wrote many operas, eight major symphonies, seven quartets, and five oratorios, including the avant-garde *Impressioni dal Vero* (1910). He directed the Venice Conservatory, 1940–52.

MALLARMÉ, Stéphane (1842–1898), French Symbolist poet (see SYMBOLISM). He held that the subject of poetry should be the ideal world which language would suggest or evoke, but not describe. Although the syntactical and grammatical structure of his poems is difficult, he had considerable influence on French poetry. His works include *The Afternoon of a Faun* (1876), which inspired DEBUSSY, and *A Throw of the Dice Will Never Eliminate Chance* (1897).

MALLON, Mary (1870?–1938), US cook, a carrier of typhoid fever although immune to the disease herself. Reportedly responsible for 51 cases of typhoid and three deaths, she was confined (1907–10, 1914–38) in an isolated New York City hospital. She is popularly known as "Typhoid Mary."

MALLORY, George Herbert Leigh (1886–1924), English mountain climber who disappeared on a final and perhaps successful drive to the summit of Mt. Everest.

MALNUTRITION, inadequate nutrition, especially in children, which may involve all parts of diet (marasmus), or may be predominantly of PROTEINS (KWASHIORKOR) or VITAMINS (PELLAGRA, BERIBERI, SCURVY). In *marasmus*, essential factors for METABOLISM are derived from the breakdown of body TISSUES; extreme wasting and growth failure result. In adults, starvation is less rapid in onset, as the demands of growth are absent, but similar metabolic changes

occur.

MALONE, Dumas (1892–1986), US historian, at the U of Virginia (1923–29, 1959–86) and Columbia U (1945–59). He was also editor in chief of the *Dictionary of American Biography* (1931–36) and director of Harvard University Press (1936–43). His biography of Thomas Jefferson (6 vols., 1948–81) received a Pulitzer Prize in 1975.

MALORY, Sir Thomas (d. 1471), English writer and adventurer, author of *The Book of King Arthur and His Noble Knights of the Round Table*, which CAXTON published as *Morte d'Arthur*, 1485. Much of the work is based on French versions of the ARTHURIAN LEGENDS.

MALPIGHI,   Marcello   (1628–1694), Italian physician and biologist, the father of microscopic ANATOMY, discoverer of the CAPILLARIES (1661), and a pioneer in several fields of medicine and biology.

MALRAUX, André (1901–1976), French writer, critic and politician. He fought in China, in the SPANISH CIVIL WAR and in the resistance in WWII. He was minister of information 1945–46 and 1958, and of cultural affairs 1959–69. His novels *Man's Fate* (1933) and *Man's Hope* (1938) reflect his experiences in China and Spain; nonfiction works such as *The Voices of Silence* (1951) and *The Metamorphosis of the Gods* (1957) are concerned with art and civilization.

MALT, the product made from any cereal grain by steeping it in water, germinating and then drying it. This activates dormant ENZYMES such as diastase, which converts the kernel STARCH to maltose. Malt is used as a source of enzymes and flavoring.

MALTA, independent country strategically placed in the central Mediterranean. It comprises the islands of Malta, Gozo, Comino and two uninhabited islets.

Malta has almost no natural resources. The economy depends on light industry, tourism, agriculture, and shipbuilding and ship repair. The latter is the island's most important industry.

Inhabited since the 4th millennium BC, Malta was visited by Phoenicians, Greeks and Carthaginians before succumbing to Roman control in 218 BC. In c60 AD St. Paul was shipwrecked on Malta. In 1530, after occupation by the Arabs, Normans and Spaniards, the islands were granted to the KNIGHTS OF SAINT JOHN. The Knights defeated the Turks in the Great Siege of 1565 and built Valletta. In 1798 they were briefly ousted by the French, and in 1814 the British took over the islands. In 1942 Malta was awarded the British George

Official name: Malta
Capital: Valletta
Area: 122sq mi
Population: 345,000
Languages: Maltese, English; Italian widely spoken
Religion: Roman Catholic
Monetary unit(s): 1 pound (M) = 100 cents

Cross for the courage of its people under siege and bombardment in WWII. The country became an independent member of the British Commonwealth in 1964, a republic in 1974. The last British troops were withdrawn in 1979. In 1980–84 Malta had a defense and aid agreement with Italy, guaranteeing the island's neutrality. In 1985 Malta aligned itself with Libya.

MALTESE, Semitic language of the inhabitants of Malta. Punic-Arabic in origin, it contains elements of several other Mediterranean languages.

MALTHUS, Thomas Robert (1766–1834), English clergyman best known for his *Essay on the Principle of Population* (1798; second, larger edition, 1803). In this he argued that the population of a region would always grow until checked by famine, pestilence or war. Even if agricultural production were improved, the only result would be an increase in population and the lot of the people would be no better. Although this pessimistic view held down the provision of poor relief in England for many decades, it also provided both C. DARWIN and A. R. WALLACE with a vital clue in the formulation of their theory of EVOLUTION by natural selection.

MALVERN HILL, Battle of (July 1, 1862), last of the Seven Days' Battles in Union Gen. McCLELLAN's Peninsular Campaign. Nine Union brigades successfully repulsed a series of attacks by 16 Confederate brigades near Richmond, Va.

MAMELUKES, or **Mamluks,** originally non-Arab slaves forming the personal bodyguard of the Egyptian caliphs and sultans. In 1250 the Mamelukes overthrew the sultanate and ruled until defeated by the Ottomans (1517). They then became an important part of the Turkish army. But in 1811 the Egyptian pasha Muhammad Ali ordered a massacre of all Mamelukes. A very few escaped to Lower Nubia, but soon dispersed.

MAMMALS, a class of VERTEBRATES distinguished by the possession of mammary glands in the female for suckling the young, and of body hair. Living mammals are divided into monotremes, egg-laying mammals; MARSUPIALS, pouched mammals that bear their young in an undeveloped state, and PLACENTAL MAMMALS that nourish the young in the uterus with a placenta. Monotremes (echidnas and the duck-billed platypus) are a very divergent group with many reptilian characteristics. Placental mammals and marsupials show closer affinities. Mammals evolved from synapsid reptiles; these diverged early from the main reptilian stem and have no living representatives. Thus the actual origin of mammals is a matter for speculation. Certainly many groups of late synapsids independently developed mammal-like characteristics, and it is probable that more than one group crossed the "mammal line," i.e., that mammals are of polyphyletic origin.

MAMMOTH, a name that properly applies to only one species of large hairy elephant, the woolly mammoth, *Elephas primigenius,* which lived in the late Pliocene, but is now used for a whole group of large, extinct ELEPHANTS. These resembled modern forms but were covered with reddish hair and bore tusks far longer than any of today.

MAMMOTH CAVE, limestone cavern about 85mi SW of Louisville, Ky., containing a series of vast subterranean chambers. It includes lakes, rivers, stalactites, stalagmites and formations of gypsum crystals. The mummified body of a pre-Columbian man has been found there. It is part of Mammoth Cave National Park.

MAN, *Homo sapiens,* the most widespread, numerous, and reputedly the most intelligent (see INTELLIGENCE) of the PRIMATES. For man's evolutionary history see PREHISTORIC MAN; for the varieties of man see RACE, and for his earliest social development see PRIMITIVE MAN.

MAN, Isle of, island in the Irish Sea off the NW coast of England. It became the base for Irish missionaries after St. Patrick, and at one time was a Norwegian dependency sold to Scotland in 1266. It is now a British dependency with its own legislature (Court of Tynwald) and representative assembly (House of Keys). Tourism is the main industry. The Manx language is now virtually extinct.

MANAGEMENT AND BUDGET, Office of, US government office established in 1970 by executive order as part of the Executive Office of the President. It helps the president prepare the federal budget and formulate fiscal programs.

MANATEES, large and fully-aquatic herbivorous mammals of tropical and subtropical Atlantic coasts and large rivers. With the dugongs they are the only living sea-cows (order: Sirenia). Heavily-built and torpedo-shaped, they have powerful rounded tails which are flattened horizontally. The forelimbs are small and hindlimbs completely absent; the tail provides all propulsion.

MANCHESTER SCHOOL, a group of English businessmen and members of Parliament, c1820–1860, mostly from Manchester, who advocated worldwide free trade. They were led by John BRIGHT and Richard COBDEN. In 1839 Cobden formed the Anti-Corn-Law League, which brought about the repeal of the corn laws in 1846.

MANCHURIA, region of NE China comprising Heilungkiang (Heilongjiang), Kirin (Jilin) and Liaoning provinces. It is an important agricultural and industrial area.

Historically, Manchuria was the home of the MANCHUS. Chinese settlement in the area increased rather steadily, especially after 1900. It was a barren steppe until Western exploitation of its vast mineral resources began in the 19th century. In the 1890s Russia had declared an interest in the province; but Russia's defeat in the 1904–05 Russo-Japanese War brought Japanese domination, first of S Manchuria, then, in 1932, of the whole country. The puppet state of Manchukuo was created and rapidly industrialized. In 1945 Russian forces occupied the area, dismantling the industries upon their withdrawal. Bitterly contested in the Chinese civil war, Manchuria was captured in 1948 by the communists, who redrew the provincial boundaries. The name Manchuria is no longer used in China.

MANCHUS, a Manchurian people who conquered China and formed the Ta Ch'ing dynasty (1644–1912). They originated from the Jurchen tribe of the Tungus and were originally a nomadic, pastoral people. The Manchus have now been racially and culturally absorbed by the Chinese, and their language is virtually extinct.

MANCO CAPAC, name of two Inca rulers. **Manco Capac I** was the legendary 13th-century founder of the Inca dynasty. **Manco Capac II** (c1500–1544) was the last of the Inca rulers. He led a revolt against the Spanish and sacked Cuzco city (1536), but was later forced to withdraw.

MANDALAY, capital of the Mandalay division and district, N Burma on the Irrawaddy R. It is a Buddhist center with numerous pagodas and a trade point with air, railroad and river connections. Mandalay was founded in the mid-19th century and served (1860–65) as the last capital of the kingdom of Burma. Pop 532,895.

MANDAN INDIANS, Indian tribe of the upper Missouri valley. Of Siouan linguistic stock, they inhabited what is now N.D. The tribe was almost wiped out by smallpox in the early 19th century. A few hundred Mandans survive on the Fort Berthold Reservation, N.D.

MANDARIN, name of nine grades of important civil servants or military officials in imperial China. Mandarin Chinese, formerly an upper-class language, is now the official national language of China, though many dialects still exist.

MANDATE, the authority to administer a territory, granted under Article 22 of the Covenant of the LEAGUE OF NATIONS. This "caretaker" system was devised to administer former Turkish territories and German colonies after WWI. With the formation of the UN, the mandate system was replaced by the TRUST TERRITORY system.

MANDELA, Nelson (1922–   ), African National Congress leader, imprisoned since 1962 on a variety of charges, including conspiracy and sabotage. From his cell in Pollsmoor Prison near Cape Town, he has become an almost messianic figure, incarnating the aspiration of South Africa's 24 million blacks.

MANDELSTAM, Osip Emilievich (1891–1938?), Russian poet. At first a member of the neoclassicist Acmeist school, he was arrested in 1934 and exiled until 1937. Rearrested in 1938, he reportedly died soon afterwards in a Siberian prison. His works include *Stone* (1913) and *Tristia* (1922). After his death, his widow, **Nadezhda Mandelstam** (1899–1981) spent many years collecting his verse and smuggling it to the West. Her memoirs, *Hope Against Hope* (1970) and *Hope Abandoned* (1972) were powerful indictments of Stalinism.

MANDEVILLE, Bernard (c1670–1733), Dutch-born English philosopher and satirist. Best-known as the author of a work in verse, *The Fable of the Bees* (1714), he attempted to establish that every virtue is based on self-interest.

MANDEVILLE, Sir John (active 1350), putative author of *Mandeville's Travels*. Most of the book is drawn from previous works, including those of Vincent de Beauvais, William of Boldensele and Odoric of Pordenone. Mandeville's real identity is unknown.

MANDRAKE, *Mandragora officinarum,* perennial plant with purplish to white flowers, of the POTATO family, Solanaceae. In medieval Europe, the thin stalk and forked root were associated with the human form. The mandrake was said to scream when pulled from the soil. Its poisonous root has been used as an emetic, purgative and pain-killer. In North America, the May apple (*Podophyllum peltatum*) is called mandrake.

MANET, Édouard (1832–1883), French painter. Though partly influenced by GOYA and VELÁZQUEZ, his work introduced a new pictorial language, and was often severely criticized by the artistic establishment. His paintings *Olympia* and *Le Déjeuner sur l'Herbe* (both 1863) were thought scandalously bold. He strongly influenced the Impressionists, though he refused to exhibit with them.

MANGROVE, shrubs and small trees of the genera *Rhizophora* and *Avicennia,* which are native to tropical and subtropical coasts, estuaries and swamps. The seeds germinate in the fruit to produce a long root, which embeds in the mud when the fruit falls. Mangrove trees produce masses of aerial adventitious roots, which result in the mass of tangled vegetation typical of mangrove swamps. The mangrove's bark is rich in tannin.

MANHATTAN PROJECT, US project to develop an explosive device based on nuclear FISSION. It was established in Aug. 1942, and research was conducted at Chicago, California and Columbia universities, as well as at Los Alamos, N.M., and other centers. By Dec. 1942 a team headed by FERMI initiated the first self-sustaining nuclear chain reaction. On July 16, 1945 the first ATOMIC BOMB was detonated near Alamogordo, N.M., and similar bombs were dropped the following month on Hiroshima (Aug. 6) and Nagasaki (Aug. 9).

MANIC-DEPRESSIVE PSYCHOSIS, a PSYCHOSIS characterized by alternating periods of deep depression and mania. Periods of lucidity may intervene.

MANICHAEISM, religion founded by Mani (c216–c276 AD), a Persian sage who preached from c240 and claimed to be the Paraclete (intercessor) promised by Christ. Mani borrowed ideas from BUDDHISM, CHRISTIANITY, GNOSTICISM, Mithraism and ZOROASTRIANISM. A form of DUALISM, Manichaeism contained an elaborate cosmic mythology of salvation. Man was created by Satan, but had particles of divine light in him, which had to be released. St. AUGUSTINE was a Manichee in his youth. In the Middle Ages, Manichaean doctrines surfaced among the BOGOMILS and CATHARI.

MANIFEST DESTINY, a phrase coined in 1845. It implied divine sanction for the US "to overspread the continent allotted by Providence for the free development of our multiplying millions." The concept was used to justify most US territorial gains.

MANILA, city on the E shore of Manila Bay in SW Luzon, Philippines. It is the capital and commercial, industrial and cultural center and chief port of the islands. Manila was occupied by the Japanese 1942–45 and almost completely rebuilt after the war. Pop (city) 1,728,441; (metro) 6,720,050.

MANILA BAY, Battle of (May 1, 1898), an important naval battle early in the SPANISH-AMERICAN WAR. US Commodore George DEWEY's squadron completely destroyed a Spanish fleet, with almost no US losses. The victory made Dewey a national hero.

MANIN, Daniele (1804–1857), Italian revolutionary against Austrian rule in Venice. In the REVOLUTIONS OF 1848 he became head of a Venetian republic, which he defended against the Austrians until Aug. 1849. Thereafter he lived in Paris.

MANITOBA, easternmost of central Canada's "prairie" provinces.
Name of province: Manitoba
Joined Confederation: July 15, 1870
Capital: Winnipeg
Area: 251,000sq mi
Population: 1,054,909
Land. Manitoba comprises four regions. The Saskatchewan Plain is a rich farming area. The Manitoba Lowland is a region of forests, lakes and swamps. Both are part of the W Interior Plains. The Hudson Bay Lowland is a flat, thinly populated plain extending 50–100mi inland from the bay's S shore. The fourth region is an area of lakes, rivers, forests, muskeg (sphagnum bog) and mineral-rich rock; it covers 60% of Manitoba and is part of the vast Canadian Shield area. About 60% of the province is forested, and about 15% is covered by rivers and over 100,000 lakes.
People. Most people live in the S, and more than 75% are urban. Winnipeg is the largest city. About 43% of the population is of British origin; other ethnic groups include Germans, Ukrainians, Dutch, Scandinavians, Finns, French Canadians and Indians.
Economy. Manitoba is one of Canada's

more prosperous provinces with growing agricultural, mining and manufacturing sectors. Manufactures include processed food (especially meat packing), metals, machinery, transportation equipment and clothing. Agriculture focuses on wheat and livestock production, with Winnipeg being Canada's leading grain market. Important minerals include nickel, zinc and copper; there are oil deposits near the town of Virden.

History. Manitoba's first white settlers were fur traders of the HUDSON'S BAY COMPANY (1670) and the North West Company (1783). There was intermarriage with native Indian women, the offspring being called Métis. In 1812 Thomas Douglas founded the first farming settlement along the Red R. The Métis rebelled against this interference with the fur trade, but by 1821 peace was restored. When the Dominion of Canada gained Manitoba from the Hudson's Bay Company in 1869, the Métis again rebelled (under Louis RIEL). They were afraid of losing their lands to British-Canadian settlers. Their rights were respected in the 1870 Manitoba Act, but waves of immigrants did come from Britain, Scandinavia and Central Europe. Today over half Manitoba's total population lives in the Winnipeg metropolitan area. In 1987, to comply with a court ruling requiring a bilingual judicial system, many provincial laws were rewritten in English and French.

MANN, Horace (1796–1859), US educator, lawyer and politician. He served in the Mass. house of representatives (1827–33), and was state senator (1835–37), secretary of the state board of education (1837–48) and US congressman (1848–53). Mann, who published 12 annual reports (1837–48) promoting public education for all children, greatly raised educational standards in Mass.

MANN, Thomas (1875–1955), German novelist, essayist and winner of the 1929 Nobel Prize for Literature. He left Germany (1933), settled in the US (1938) and became a US citizen (1944). His works include *Buddenbrooks* (1901), *Death in Venice* (1912), *The Magic Mountain* (1924) and *Joseph and His Brothers* (4 novels; 1933–43). His literary themes are often concerned with the effects of a changing world on people's inner thoughts and lives; with death in the midst of life; and with the artist's isolation. His brother, **Heinrich Mann** (1871–1950), was also a novelist. An early work, *Professor Unrat* (1905), was made into the film *The Blue Angel* (1930). Heinrich Mann emigrated

(1933) to France and later to the US.

MANNERHEIM, Baron Carl Gustaf Emil von (1867–1951), Finnish soldier and statesman. He successfully led the Finnish nationalists against the Russo-Finnish communists in 1918. He also led the Finnish forces in the RUSSO-FINNISH WAR (1939–40), holding the "Mannerheim Line" defenses on the Karelian Isthmus. He was president of Finland 1944–46.

MANNERISM, the artistic and architectural style between the RENAISSANCE and the BAROQUE. It was developed in Bologna, Florence and Rome during the early 16th century and flourished until the century's end. Marked by strained (though apparently executed with great facility) human postures and crowded compositions, the style was a reaction against the Renaissance's classical principles. Mannerists included Parmigianino and Pontormo.

MANNHEIM, Karl (1893–1947), Hungarian-born sociologist. His *Man and Society in an Age of Reconstruction* (1940) stressed the importance of science in effecting sociological change. He taught in Britain at London U., from 1933.

MANNING, Henry Edward (1808–1892), English cardinal. He was an Anglican priest 1833–50 and a member of the OXFORD MOVEMENT. In 1851 he entered the Roman Catholic Church and in 1865 became archbishop of Westminster, being made a cardinal in 1875. He founded the League of the Cross temperance movement and mediated in the 1889 London dock strike.

MANOLETE (1917–1947), famous Spanish bullfighter. He was recognized as a true professional at Seville (1939) and remained the world's leading matador until fatally gored.

MAN O' WAR, legendary US racehorse. Known as "Big Red," he won 20 of 21 races, including the Belmont and Preakness stakes, in 1920 (he was not entered in the Kentucky Derby). His prize money amounted to a then-record $249,465.

MAN RAY (1890–1976), US abstract artist and photographer, a founder of the New York DADA movement. He recreated several "lost" photographic techniques and produced surrealist films.

MANSART, Nicolas François (1598–1666), French architect who popularized, but did not invent, the high-pitched mansard roof. He helped initiate the purity of the French classical style of architecture.

MANSFIELD, Katherine (Kathleen Mansfield Beauchamp; 1888–1923), New Zealand-born British short story writer, poet and essayist. The short stories collected in *The Garden Party* (1922) are among her finest mature work.

MANSFIELD, William Murray, 1st Earl of (1705–1793), English jurist, lord chief justice (1756–88) who worked to modernize the principles and procedures of English law.

MANSHIP, Paul (1885–1966), US sculptor. He is best known for his interpretations of classical mythological subjects, among which is his statue of *Prometheus* (1934) at Rockefeller Center, New York.

MANTEGNA, Andrea (c1431–1506), Italian painter and engraver. He was a member of the Paduan school, acclaimed for his mastery of anatomy and illusionistic perspective. Among his most famous works are the cartoons of the *Triumph of Caesar* (c1495). His frescoes in the Eremitani church, Padua (1448–57), were almost totally destroyed by bombing in 1944.

MANTISES, long, narrow, carnivorous insects usually found in the tropics. Most species are well-camouflaged as leaves or twigs. Mantids feed on other insects and sit motionless waiting for prey to approach within striking distance when the long front legs are shot out at great speed to catch it. Many sit "praying" with forelegs raised and clasped together when awaiting prey. The female usually devours the male after mating.

MANTLE, zone of the earth's interior underlying the crust and surrounding the core. The mantle is found from continental depths of about 40km (MOHOROVIČIĆ DISCONTINUITY) to 2900km (Gutenberg Discontinuity) and includes the ASTHENOSPHERE and lowermost LITHOSPHERE in its upper part. Forming 82.3% of the volume and 67.8% of the mass of the EARTH, the mantle is thought to be composed of dense iron- and magnesium-rich silicates.

MANTLE, Mickey (1931–   ), US baseball player, a switch-hitting center fielder for the New York Yankees (1951–68). He was voted the American League's most valuable player 1956, 1957, and 1962. In 1961 he hit 54 home runs.

MANTRA, in HINDUISM and BUDDHISM, sacred utterance believed to possess supernatural power. The constant repetition of *mantras* is used to concentrate the mind on an object of meditation, e.g. the syllable *om*, said to evoke the entire VEDA.

MANUEL I (1464–1521), king of Portugal (1495–1521). During his reign Vasco da GAMA pioneered the sea route to India, and Francisco de ALMEIDA and Afonso de ALBUQUERQUE built a Portuguese commercial empire in the East. In 1500 Pedro CABRAL discovered Brazil, establishing

Portuguese claim to that part of the New World. Wealth poured into Portugal, turning the attention of the Portuguese away from the economic development of their own country. Another setback to internal development was the expulsion of the Jews and Moors as a condition of Manuel's marriage to a daughter of FERDINAND and ISABELLA of Spain.

MANX, Celtic dialect of the Isle of MAN. See CELTIC LANGUAGES.

MANZIKERT, Battle of (1071), historic battle at Manzikert in E Turkey. Turkish leader Alp Arslan captured Emperor Romanus IV, defeated his largely mercenary army and effectively crushed the BYZANTINE EMPIRE's power in Asia Minor. The consequent blocking of pilgrim routes to the Holy Land by the Seljuk Turks was a direct cause of the CRUSADES.

MANZONI, Alessandro Francesco Tommaso Antonio (1785–1873), Italian novelist and poet. He was a leading figure in the Romantic movement and his novel *The Betrothed* (1825–27) influenced many later writers. Manzoni's death inspired VERDI's *Requiem* (1874).

MANZÙ, Giacomo (1908–   ), Italian sculptor, noted for his portraits. He also executed bronze doors for St. Peter's in Rome and Salzburg Cathedral in Austria.

MAORIS, the pre-European inhabitants of New Zealand. They are a Polynesian people who migrated to New Zealand c1200–1400 AD. When the first Europeans arrived, the Maoris were a well-organized Neolithic tribal society. Some of their tribes fought the British in the Maori Wars of the 1860s. The Maoris have full political rights, and intermarriage with whites is widespread.

MAO TSE-TUNG (Mao Zedong; 1893–1976), Chinese communist leader, a founder of the People's Republic of China. Son of an educated peasant in Shao-shan, Hunan province, he became interested in various political creeds, including anarchism; in 1921 he joined the newly-founded Shanghai Communist Party, and in 1927 led the Autumn Harvest uprising. This was crushed by the local KUOMINTANG militia, and Mao fled to the mountains. There he built up the Red Army, and in 1931 proclaimed a republic in Kiangsi. Surrounded by Kuomintang forces in 1934, the army was forced to embark on the famous LONG MARCH to Yenan, Shensi. The appalling rigors of the march united the communists behind Mao, and he was elected chairman. In 1937 an uneasy alliance was made with the Kuomintang under CHIANG KAI-SHEK against the Japanese; after WWII Mao's forces drove the

Kuomintang to Taiwan. Mao then became chairman of the new People's Republic. During the 1950s and 1960s he steered China ideologically further away from the USSR. In 1966 he launched the "Cultural Revolution" to clear the party of "revisionists." In the 1970s Mao appeared to favor a degree of détente with the West, especially Europe. In 1972, his meeting with President Nixon signaled better relations with the US. From 1974 age and ill-health forced him increasingly to withdraw from public life. It is uncertain how much influence his wife CHIANG CH'ING had on his rule. (See also CHINA.)

MAP, diagram representing the layout of features on the earth's surface or part of it. Maps have many uses, including routefinding; marine or aerial NAVIGATION (such maps are called *charts*); administrative, political and legal definition; and scientific study. **Cartography,** or mapmaking, is thus an important and exact art. The techniques of SURVEYING and GEODESY are used to obtain the positional data to be represented. Since the EARTH is roughly spheroidal— the geoid being taken as the reference level—and since the surface of a sphere cannot be flattened without distortion, no plane map can perfectly represent its original, the distortion becoming worse the larger the area. But spherical maps, or *globes*, are impractical for large-scale work. Thus plane maps use various projections, geometrical algorithms for transforming the spherical coordinates into plane ones. The choice of projection depends on the purpose of the map; one may aim for correct size or correct shape, but not both at once: a suitable compromise is generally reached. Projections fall into three main classes: *Cylindrical projections* are obtained by projection from the earth's axis onto a cylinder touching the equator. MERCATOR's projection from the center of the earth is a well-known example: its graticule (net of parallels and meridians) takes the form of a rectangular grid with the scale increasing toward the poles, which are infinitely distant; straight lines represent rhumb lines. *Conic projections,* best suited to middle latitudes, are obtained by projection onto a cone that caps the earth, touching a given parallel. *Azimuthal projections* are from a single point onto a plane. In this class the *gnomonic* projection, having the point at the center of the earth, represents great circle routes by straight lines. The *orthographic* projection has the point at infinity, the projective rays being parallel; distortion is great, but the map looks like the globe. These geometric projections are now seldom used as such, but are modified to give correct relative areas, distances or shapes. The *scale* of a map (assuming it to be constant) is the ratio of a distance on the map to the distance that it represents on the earth's surface. It may be expressed directly as the ratio or representative fraction (1:63,360), as a unit ratio (1in to 1mi) or by a graphic graduated scale. Maps use standard symbols and colors to show features, giving the maximum information clearly. Types of map include physical, political, economic, demographic, historical, geological and meteorological maps; there are also star maps (see CELESTIAL SPHERE).

Maps have been drawn from earliest times, but until the Middle Ages most were little more than sketch maps based on impressions and guesswork, except for those of the Greek geographers, notably PTOLEMY of Alexandria. In the 14th century, Mediterranean sea charts were in use which were remarkably accurate, owing to the introduction of the COMPASS and good estimates of distances sailed. The great voyages of discovery, the rediscovery of Ptolemy's map, and accurate surveying in the Low Countries revolutionized cartography in the 16th and 17th centuries, the work of Gerardus Mercator and Abraham Ortelius (who produced the first modern atlas) being well-known. Louis XIV promoted a national survey of France, the British Ordnance Survey (1791) followed suit, and in the 19th century most developed countries produced extensive maps. Remote sensing data are increasingly used in modern cartography.

MAPLE, common name for trees of the genus *Acer,* which are found throughout the N Hemisphere. The wood is hard and suitable for making furniture. The foliage of some species is noted for the red and orange colors produced in the fall. Maples are often grown as ornamental garden trees. The North American sugar maple (*Acer saccharum*) is tapped to produce MAPLE SYRUP. Family: Aceraceae. **Flowering maples** are not related to the true maples but belong to the genus *Abutilon,* family Malvaceae. They have maple-like leaves and produce funnel-shaped, droopy flowers. They are often grown as house plants, requiring a sunny position in winter, less so in summer; the temperature should drop from about 70°F in the daytime to about 63°F at night. The soil should be kept evenly moist, particularly avoiding extreme dryness, which causes leaf and flower-bud drop. Propagation is by shoot tip cuttings.

MAPLE SYRUP, crop produced solely in

North America and obtained from the sap (sweet water) of the sugar MAPLE (*Acer saccharum*). Up to 50qt of sap are required to produce 1qt of syrup; the flavor and coloring are imparted to the syrup as the sap is concentrated by evaporation.

MARAT, Jean Paul (1743–1793), French Revolutionary politician and demagogue. A doctor and journalist, he was elected to the National Convention in 1792, and came to lead the radical faction. Chief instigator of the September Massacre (1792) at which over 1,200 died, he was an active supporter of the REIGN OF TERROR. Marat was murdered in his bath by Charlotte CORDAY.

MARATHON, famous plain in Greece, about 25mi NE of Athens, where in 490 BC MILTIADES led an Athenian force of about 11,000 to victory over 20,000 Persians led by DARIUS I. Fearing Athens might surrender prematurely, to the Persian fleet, Miltiades sent the runner Pheidippides to report the victory. On reaching Athens, he delivered the message, collapsed and died. The modern OLYMPIC GAMES marathon race commemorates this incident.

MARBURY v. MADISON, historic US Supreme Court decision. In 1803, William Marbury sued James Madison, then secretary of state, for failure to deliver a commission given by the previous administration. Chief Justice John Marshall held the act upon which Marbury relied to be unconstitutional, thus establishing the judicial right to review the constitutionality of legislation.

MARC, Franz (1880–1916), German expressionist painter, with KANDINSKY a cofounder of the BLAUE REITER group. His work is characterized by vigorous lines and a vivid and symbolic use of color.

MARCEAU, Marcel (1923–   ), perhaps the greatest modern MIME. Born in France, he studied drama in Paris, rising to fame with a brief mime role in the film *Les Enfants du paradis* (1944). His most famous characterization is the white-faced clown, Bip. He became world famous with stage appearances in the 1950s.

MARCH, third month of the Gregorian CALENDAR. It corresponds to the Roman month Martius (after Mars, god of war), first month of the Roman calendar until 153 BC, when Jan. 1 was made New Year's Day. March has 31 days; the spring equinox occurs about March 21.

MARCH, Fredric (Frederick McIntyre Bickel; 1897–1975), US stage and film actor, winner of Academy Awards for his performances in the films *Dr. Jekyll and Mr. Hyde* (1932) and *The Best Years of Our Lives* (1946). His Broadway credits include *Long Day's Journey Into Night* (1956).

MARCIANO, Rocky (Rocco Marchegiane; 1923–1969), US boxer, world heavyweight champion 1952–56, when he retired. He is the only major prizefighter to have remained undefeated throughout his professional career. Marciano fought 49 bouts in 9 years, winning 43 by knockout. He was killed in an air crash.

MARCION (d. c160 AD), founder of a heretical Christian sect. He joined the church in Rome c140 but was excommunicated in 144. Influenced by GNOSTICISM, he taught that there were two rival Gods: one, the tyrannical creator and lawgiver of the Old Testament; the other, the unknown God of love and mercy who sent Jesus to purchase salvation from the creator God. Marcion rejected the Old Testament wholly, and of the New Testament he accepted only expurgated versions of Luke's Gospel and 10 of St. Paul's Letters. This forced the orthodox Church to fix its canon of Scripture. Marcionism spread widely but by the end of the 3rd century had mostly been absorbed by MANICHAEISM.

MARCONI, Guglielmo (1874–1937), Italian-born inventor and physicist, awarded (with K. F. Braun) the 1909 Nobel Prize for Physics for his achievements. On learning of Hertzian (RADIO) waves in 1894, he set to work to devise a wireless TELEGRAPH. By the following year he could transmit and receive signals at distances of about 2km. He went to the UK to make further developments and, in 1899, succeeded in sending a signal across the English Channel. On Dec. 12, 1901, in St. John's, Newfoundland, he successfully received a signal sent from Poldhu, Cornwall, thus heralding the dawn of transatlantic radio communication.

MARCOS, Ferdinand Edralin (1917–1989), president of the Philippines (1965–86). Confronting Muslim rebels and Communist and other resistance to his regime, Marcos imposed martial law in 1972 and the following year, under a new constitution, assumed near-dictatorial authority. Although he lifted martial law in 1981, he retained several martial-law powers. Marcos's wife, Imelda, shared a large measure of power, holding major government posts. Marcos was driven from power in 1986 by popular demonstrations after "officially" winning an election in which his opponent was Corazon Aquino, widow of an anti-Marcos leader who had been assassinated in Manila in 1983. The Marcoses took refuge in Hawaii. The Philippine government began efforts to recover vast sums it alleged that the Marcoses had stolen. In 1988, a federal grand jury in New York indicted Marcos, his wife, and several others on charges of participating in a scheme in which the Marcoses used more than $100 million in embezzled cash to buy real estate in New York City. The Marcoses were also charged with defrauding two American banks of more than $165 million.

MARCUS AURELIUS (121–180 AD), one of the greatest of Roman emperors. Adopted at 17 by his uncle Antoninus Pius, he succeeded him as emperor in 161 AD, after a distinguished career in public service. During this time he wrote his famous *Meditations*, his personal philosophy; he was one of the major exponents of STOICISM. His reign was marred by plague, rebellion, barbarian attacks along the Rhine and Danube, and his own savage persecution of Christians, to whom he had taken a dislike strange in so humane a man. His government was otherwise noted for social reform, justice and generosity.

MARCUSE, Herbert (1898–1979), German-born US political philosopher who combined Freudianism and Marxism in his social criticism. According to Marcuse modern society is automatically repressive and requires violent revolution as the first step towards a Utopian society. He became a cult figure of the New Left in the US in the 1960s.

MARCY, William Learned (1786–1857), US statesman, famous for coining the phrase, "spoils system." Marcy held high state offices under the patronage of Martin VAN BUREN and supported him as a US senator 1831–33. Governor of N.Y. 1833–38, he was secretary of war 1845–49, during the Mexican War. He was a particularly successful secretary of state 1853–57, concluding the GADSDEN PURCHASE and settling many other international problems.

MARDI GRAS (literally "fat Tuesday"), festivities on Shrove Tuesday, the last day of carnival before the start of Lent. Celebrated as a holiday in various Catholic countries, it was introduced into the US by French settlers and is now observed in many places, most particularly in New Orleans.

MARENGO, Battle of, major victory of NAPOLEON's second Italian campaign, against Austrian troops on the Marengo plain near Alessandria, Lombardy, on June 14, 1800. It gave Napoleon control of much of N Italy.

MARGARET OF ANJOU (1429–1482), French queen consort of HENRY VI of England from 1445. Her attempt at autocratic rule through the ineffectual king was one of the causes of the Wars of the ROSES. Margaret was imprisoned 1471–76 by EDWARD IV, who had Henry and her son murdered. Ransomed by LOUIS XI, she returned to France.

MARGARET OF PARMA (1522–1586), natural daughter of CHARLES V, regent of the Netherlands 1559–67. A benevolent ruler, she attempted to quell growing resistance to Spanish rule. Although a capable ruler, she resigned in protest against the brutal duke of ALBA in 1567, but returned to head the civil administration 1580–83.

MARGARET OF SCOTLAND, Saint (c1045–1093), queen consort of Malcolm III of Scotland. She did much to implement the Gregorian reform of the Church and improved relations with England. She died during a siege of Edinburgh castle, where her chapel still stands. Canonized in 1250, her feast day is on June 10.

MARGARINE, a spread high in food value, prepared from vegetable or animal fats together with milk products, preservatives, emulsifiers, butter and salt. It was first developed in the late 1860s by the French chemist Hippolyte Mège-Mouriès, inspired by a competition launched by Napoleon III to find a cheap BUTTER substitute. The fats used were, early on, primarily animal, with whale oil being particularly popular in Europe, but recently vegetable oils (especially soybean and corn) have been used almost exclusively.

MARIANA, Juan de (1536–1624), Spanish Jesuit historian and political philosopher who, in an era of developing absolutism, condoned tyrannicide.

MARIANA ISLANDS, group of islands in the W Pacific. Lying 1,500mi E of the Philippines, their total area is 184sq mi. Discovered by MAGELLAN in 1521, they were named the Ladrones (Thieves) Islands until renamed in 1668 by Jesuit missionaries. After WWI they were under a Japanese mandate until seized by the US in WWII. They became part of the UN Trust Territory of the Pacific Islands in 1947. In 1978 the NORTHERN MARIANA ISLANDS became internally self-governing; they became a US commonwealth on Nov. 3, 1986. The majority of the population lives on the largest and southernmost island, Guam, a US outlying territory. The group's economy rests on subsistence agriculture, copra export and government and military installations.

MARIANA TRENCH, world's deepest discovered submarine trench, in the W North Pacific E of the Mariana Islands. More than 1,500mi long, it averages over

40mi in width and has maximum known depths of 36,201ft.

MARIA THERESA (1717–1780), empress, archduchess of Austria, queen of Hungary and of Bohemia and wife of the Holy Roman Emperor Francis I, one of the most able of Hapsburg rulers. Despite the PRAGMATIC SANCTION, its signatories launched the War of the AUSTRIAN SUCCESSION against her as soon as she succeeded her father in 1740. This lost Silesia to Prussia; she allied with France in the SEVEN YEARS' WAR against Prussia, but was defeated. A capable ruler, she introduced administrative and fiscal reforms and maintained a strong army. Married to Francis of Lorraine in 1736, she arranged his election as emperor.

MARICOPA INDIANS, American Indian tribe of the Yuman linguistic group. Driven from the Lower Colorado R area by intertribal rivalry, they now live on the Gila and Salt R reservations in Ariz. with the Pima tribe. They united with the Pima to drive off the invading Yuma in a great battle in 1857.

MARIE ANTOINETTE (1755–1793), queen of France from 1774. Daughter of Maria Theresa and the Emperor Francis I, she married the Dauphin in 1770 and became queen on his accession as Louis XVI. Youthful extravagances made her many enemies, as did her unwitting involvement in a confidence trick perpetrated on the Cardinal de Rohan. When the French Revolution broke out she advised the attempted escape of the royal family which ended with its capture at Varennes. Imprisoned with Louis, she was guillotined nine months after him, in Oct. 1793.

MARIE LOUISE (1791–1847), empress of France. Eldest daughter of FRANCIS II of Austria, she married NAPOLEON after he divorced Josephine, and was the mother of Napoleon II. She was never popular in France. After Napoleon was exiled in 1814 she became duchess of Parma.

MARIGNANO, Battle of, victory of a French and Venetian army over Swiss mercenaries defending Milan on Sept. 13–14, 1515, during FRANCIS I of France's first Italian campaign; it won him the duchy of Milan.

MARIJUANA, term applied to any part of the HEMP plant (*Cannabis sativa*) or extract from it. The intoxicating drug obtained from the flowering tops is also called **cannabis** or HASHISH. This drug is usually smoked in cigarettes or pipes, but can also be sniffed or taken as food. It is mainly used for the mild euphoria it produces, although other symptoms include loss of muscular coordination, increased heart beat, drowsiness and hallucination. Its use, the subject of much medical and social debate, is widespread throughout the world.

MARIN, John (1870–1953), US painter and print maker best known for his expressionistic watercolors (influenced by CÉZANNE and the German Expressionists) of Manhattan and the Maine coast, such as *Singer Building* (1921) and *Maine Islands* (1922).

MARINE BIOLOGY, the study of the flora and fauna in the sea, from the smallest PLANKTON to massive WHALES. It includes the study of the complex interrelationships between marine organisms that make up the food chains (see ECOLOGY) of the sea. It has become apparent in recent years that if the sea is to remain a major and increasing source of food for man, CONSERVATION measures must be taken, particularly to retain adequate stocks of breeding fish. POLLUTION must also be controlled.

MARINE CORPS, US, a separate service within the Department of the Navy, is headed by a commandant who is a member of the JOINT CHIEFS OF STAFF. Major Marine operating forces are the Fleet Marine Force, Pacific, and the Fleet Marine Force, Atlantic. In 1986, 199,000 men and women served in the US Marine Corps.

MARINETTI, Filippo Tommaso (1876–1944), Italian writer, progenitor of FUTURISM. His *Manifesto* (1909), published in *Le Figaro* in Paris, called for the abandonment of art of the past and the creation of a new art based on continual revolution and change. He came to support Fascism as the best means of revolution.

MARION, Francis (c1732–1795), guerrilla leader in the REVOLUTIONARY WAR. Commander of S.C. troops, he fought at Charleston in 1776. In 1780 he and his men were forced to take refuge in the swamps, from which they waged a ceaseless guerrilla warfare on Loyalist farms and on British troops, who nicknamed Marion "the Swamp Fox." He served in the state senate 1782–90, and on the state constitutional convention.

MARIONETTE. See PUPPET.

MARIS, Roger (1934–1985), US baseball player. An outfielder with the New York Yankees (1960–66), he made sports history by hitting 61 homeruns in 1961, breaking Babe Ruth's single-season homerun mark of 60 set in 1927.

MARISOL (Marisol Escobar; 1930–   ), Venezuelan-born US sculptor, who satirized and caricatured human society by creating POP ART-type figures, usually from wood and clay. Reminiscent of South

American folk art, her sculptures are stark representations, with many of the details drawn on them.

MARITAIN, Jacques (1882–1973), leading French Neo-Thomist philosopher. He turned to the study of THOMISM after his conversion to Catholicism in 1906. Professor of modern philosophy at the Catholic Institute, Paris, 1914–39, he was French ambassador to the Vatican 1945–48 and a professor at Princeton U. 1948–60.

MARITIME LAW, body of law, based on custom, court decisions and statutes, seeking to regulate all aspects of shipping and ocean commerce such as insurance, salvage and contracts for carriage of goods by sea. It is international to the extent that firm general principles exist, but these have no legal force except as they are incorporated by individual countries into their own legal systems; they are often modified in the process. Many derive from decisions of medieval maritime courts. In the US maritime law is administered by the federal district courts.

MARIUS, Gaius (157–86 BC), Roman general and politician. After successes in the field he was elected consul seven times. In 88 BC he was defeated in a civil war by his rival SULLA. He returned from exile in 86 BC and massacred his opponents but died soon after.

MARIVAUX, Pierre Carlet de Chamblain de (1688–1763), French playwright and novelist, best known for his witty comedies. Sparkling dialogue is still termed *marivaudage*. His most famous works are the comedy *A Game of Love and Chance* (1730) and the novel *The Parvenu Peasant* (1735–36).

MARK, Saint (John Mark; flourished 1st century AD), Christian evangelist, traditional author of the second GOSPEL, which derived information from St. Peter in Rome. The Gospel is the earliest and simplest and was a source for the other SYNOPTIC GOSPELS. Mark accompanied Barnabas (his cousin) and Paul on their missionary journeys.

MARKHAM, Edwin (1852–1940), US poet and lecturer whose poem of social protest, *The Man with the Hoe* (1899), based on a painting by MILLET, brought him a fortune and worldwide acclaim.

MARK TWAIN. See TWAIN, MARK.

MARLBOROUGH, John Churchill, 1st Duke of (1650–1722), British soldier and statesman, one of the country's greatest generals. He helped suppress the Duke of Monmouth's rebellion (1685) for James II, but transferred his allegiance to William of Orange in 1688 and was made an earl and a member of the Privy Council. His wife was Sarah Jennings, a friend and attendant of Princess (later Queen) Anne; together they had great influence with the queen. After her accession in 1702 Marlborough commanded English, Dutch and German forces in the war of the SPANISH SUCCESSION. In 1704 he won a great victory over the French at BLENHEIM; a palace of that name was built for him at the queen's expense. Further victories followed at Ramillies (1706), Oudenarde (1708) and Malplaquet (1709). His wife fell from favor with the Queen in 1711, and Marlborough was dismissed; in 1714, however, he was restored to favor by George I.

MARLOWE, Christopher (1564–1593), English poet and dramatist, a major influence on Shakespeare. He developed the use of dramatic blank verse in a rhetorically rich and splendid language. In *Dr. Faustus* (c1589) he developed a new concept of tragedy, the struggle of a great personality doomed to inevitable failure by its own limitations. In *Tamburlaine* (c1581) he treated a heroic theme without the depth of characterization that appears in his most mature work, *Edward II* (c1592). Often accused of homosexuality, atheism and of being a government spy, he was stabbed to death in a tavern brawl.

MARNE, Battles of the, two WWI battles fought in the Marne R area of France. In the first, in Sept. 1914, the German advance on Paris was halted by an Allied offensive. The second, in July 1918, countered the last German offensive of the war.

MARONITES, a sect of eastern Christians who in the 7th century espoused MONOTHELISM. In the 12th century they became affiliated with the Roman Catholic Church (see UNIATE CHURCHES). Although some Maronites have settled in Cyprus, Syria and Egypt, their largest community is still in Lebanon, where their immediate spiritual head under the pope, the Maronite patriarch, also resides.

MARQUAND, J(ohn) P(hillips) (1893–1960), US novelist best known for his detective stories centered around the Japanese agent Mr. Moto, and for his gentle satires of New England society, such as *The Late George Apley* (1937), for which he won a 1938 Pulitzer Prize, and *Point of No Return* (1949).

MARQUESAS ISLANDS, two clusters of mountainous and volcanic islands in the S Pacific, 740mi NE of Tahiti. Their total area is about 492sq mi; the largest islands are Hiba Oa and Nuku Hiva. The S group was discovered by the Spanish in 1595; both were annexed by France in 1842. The islands are fertile, producing breadfruit, coffee, vanilla and copra for export.

MARQUETTE, Jacques (1637–1675), French Jesuit missionary and explorer. With Louis JOLIET he left St. Ignace mission, Mich., in 1673 on a search for the mouth of the Mississippi. They traced its course as far as the mouth of the Arkansas R and learned that it entered the Gulf of Mexico. In 1674 Marquette went back to Ill. to found a mission among Indians who had befriended him, but his health deteriorated. He died on the E shore of Lake Michigan while returning to St. Ignace.

MARQUIS, Don (Donald Robert Perry; 1878–1937), US literary journalist, poet and playwright, best known as the creator of "archy," a poet reincarnated as a cockroach, and his friend "mehitabel," a disreputable cat, who appeared in Marquis' columns in the *New York Sun* 1912–22 and *Tribune* 1922–25, and in subsequent books.

MARRANOS, derogatory term for Portuguese and Spanish Jews who were baptized to escape persecution in the 14th century; most continued to practice Judaism in secret. With the expulsion of the Jews and the establishment of the INQUISITION in the late 15th century, most fled abroad. The remainder died out, except in Portugal and the Balearic Islands.

MARRIAGE, durable union between man and woman for the purpose of cohabitation and usually also for raising children. In the broadest sense it is not an exclusively human institution; some animal pair-bonds may endure for life. Most human marriages are at least intended to last for life, but most societies have some provision for divorce, ranging from the easy to the almost impossible. The modern trend is towards monogamy, union between one man and one woman only. Many societies still permit POLYGAMY, but it is increasingly rare, even among Muslims. Forms of group and communal marriage have been tried from time to time, though with little success or social acceptance.

Marriage is in some senses a contract, often involving property and in some societies a dowry or a bride-price. In US law today marriage creates special ownership rights in marital property. It is, however, still also a religious matter in many countries; marriage is a minor sacrament of the Roman Catholic Church.

Most societies limit marriage in certain ways. It is forbidden in most countries between partners who have too close a blood relationship, or consanguinity, though the degree permissible varies widely among countries, religions and even among US states. In US COMMON LAW a purported marriage involving bigamy is void; other conditions, such as non-consummation, render marriage void or voidable, generally through the courts. A marriage is also void if not carried out in the prescribed legal form, although in some states common-law marriage may arise after long cohabitation without any formality. Marriages in the US are performed either by civil authority or by a religious ceremony with civil authorization; the ceremonies of most denominations are so authorized in most states. In general a marriage valid in one state is recognized in the others. Some states require a waiting period, and some religions require banns to be posted.

MARROW, Bone, the material in the center of BONES, in which erythrocytes, white blood cells and platelets are made. Mature cells only are released unless the marrow is diseased, as in LEUKEMIA, secondary CANCER or in serious infections. Bone marrow aspiration or biopsy is often valuable in diagnosis.

MARRYAT, Frederick (1792–1848), English author of sea adventures such as *Mr. Midshipman Easy* (1836) based on his 24 years of service in the British navy.

MARS, the fourth planet from the sun, with a mean solar distance of 228Gm (about 1.52AU) and a "year" of 687 days. During the Martian day of about 24.62h, the highest temperature at the equator is about 30°C; the lowest, just before dawn, is about −100°C. Mars has a mean diameter of 6,750km, with a small degree of polar flattening, and at its closest to earth is some 56Gm distant. Its tenuous atmosphere consists mainly of carbon dioxide, nitrogen and NOBLE GASES, and the distinctive Martian polar caps are composed of frozen carbon dioxide and water ice.

Telescopically, Mars appears as an ocher-red disk marked by extensive dark areas: these latter have in the past been erroneously termed *maria* (seas). Several observers in the past reported sighting networks of straight lines on the Martian surface—the famous canals— but observations with large telescopes and the photographs sent back by the US's Mariner and Viking space probes showed these to be an optical illusion. Mars actually has a cratered surface marked with canyons, ancient volcanoes, and jumbled terrains. No probe has yet found evidence that life ever existed on the planet. Mars has two moons, Phobos and Deimos.

Two US Viking spacecraft landed on Mars in 1976. In 1988, the USSR launched two spacecraft to Mars designed to study the smaller of its two moons, Phobos, and then to orbit the planet itself for two years, examining its surface and atmosphere. The only approved US mission in 1988 was Mars Observer, a reconnaissance craft scheduled to orbit the planet in 1992. US engineers were studying plans to land a roving vehicle on Mars and return a soil sample by 1998.

MARSALIS, Wynton (1961–   ), US trumpeter who won awards for both jazz and classical recordings.

MARSEILLAISE, French national anthem composed in 1792 by Claude Rouget de Lisle, a Revolutionary engineer captain. Named for its popularity with the Marseilles soldiers, it was banned by NAPOLEON I, LOUIS XVIII and NAPOLEON III until 1879.

MARSEILLES, city in SE France, the second largest city in the country, its chief Mediterranean seaport and a major industrial center. It was originally the Greek settlement of Massilia, annexed by Rome in 49 BC. The city's recent expansion began with the conquest of Algeria and the opening of the SUEZ CANAL in the 19th century. It has a wide range of industries; its port handles around 25% of French maritime trade. Pop (city) 867,260; (metro) 1,170,000.

MARSH, Dame (Edith) Ngaio (1899–1982), New Zealand actress and theater producer who turned mystery writer, creating the cultured detective Roderick Alleyn.

MARSH, Reginald (1898–1954), US painter. A newspaper illustrator, he later turned to the realistic depiction of New York City life in egg TEMPERA paintings such as *Twenty-Cent Movie* (1936).

MARSHALL, Alfred (1842–1924), British economist, professor of political economy at Cambridge 1885–1908. His *Principles of Economics* (1890) systematized economic thought up to that time, and was the standard text for many years. Through his work on cost and value Marshall developed a viable concept of marginal utility.

MARSHALL, George Catlett (1880–1959), US general and statesman. As chief of staff 1939–45 he influenced Allied strategy in WWII. Special ambassador to China in 1945, he was then made secretary of state (1947–49) by President TRUMAN. He introduced the European Recovery Program, or MARSHALL PLAN. He was active in the creation of the NORTH ATLANTIC TREATY ORGANIZATION, serving as US secretary of defense 1950–51. He was awarded the 1955 Nobel Peace Prize.

MARSHALL, James Wilson (1810–1885), US pioneer in California whose discovery of

gold on the property of John A. SUTTER launched the California GOLD RUSH in 1849. Both he and Sutter died poor.

MARSHALL, John (1755–1835), fourth chief justice of the US, known as the "Great Chief Justice." He established the modern status of the SUPREME COURT. Born in Va., he served in the REVOLUTIONARY WAR, studied law and was elected to the Va. legislature in 1782. A staunch Federalist, he supported acceptance of the Constitution. He declined ministerial posts but became one of the US negotiators who resolved the XYZ AFFAIR. Elected to Congress 1799, he was made secretary of state by President ADAMS 1800–01; in 1801 he became chief justice. He labored to increase the then scant power and prestige of the Supreme Court. In MARBURY V. MADISON he established its power to review a law and if necessary declare it unconstitutional. An opponent of STATES' RIGHTS, he established in McCULLOCH V. MARYLAND and GIBBONS V. OGDEN (and incidentally in the DARTMOUTH COLLEGE CASE) the superiority of federal authority under the Constitution. In 1807 he presided over the treason trial of Aaron BURR.

MARSHALL, Sir John Hubert (1876–1958), British archaeologist. As director of the Indian Archaeological Survey (1902–31), he directed the excavation of the buried cities of Harappa and Mohenjo-Daro in the Indus River delta.

MARSHALL, Thomas Riley (1854–1925), US Democratic politician, a reform governor of Indiana (1909–13) and vice president of the US (1913–21) in the administration of Woodrow Wilson. He is chiefly remembered for the observation, "What this country needs is a good five-cent cigar."

MARSHALL, Thurgood (1908–   ), US judge, first black member of the US SUPREME COURT. Chief counsel for the NATIONAL ASSOCIATION FOR THE ADVANCEMENT OF COLORED PEOPLE 1938–61 and solicitor general 1965–67, he was appointed to the Supreme Court by President JOHNSON in 1967.

MARSHALL ISLANDS, group of 34 islands in the W Pacific, formerly part of the Trust Territory of the Pacific Islands.

Land. The Marshall Islands consist of two parallel chains of low-lying coral islands with a total land area of 70sq mi. The climate is tropical with little seasonal variation in temperature. Rainfall averages 145-180in per year.

People and Economy. Many of the 39,000 Micronesian inhabitants are subsistence farmers growing coconuts and root crops, raising pigs and catching fish for their own use. Copra is the leading export. A US missile testing range on Kwajalein also provides employment. Manjuro is the capital.

History. The islands were sighted by Spanish navigators in 1526 and became a German protectorate in the 1880s. They were controlled by Japan from 1914 to the end of WWII and became part of the US-administered Trust Territory of the Pacific Islands in 1947. Several atolls, including BIKINI and ENEWETAK, were contaminated by US nuclear testing between 1946 and 1958. The Marshall Islands became internally self-governing in 1979 and gained sovereignty in 1986 in free association with the US, which remains responsible for their defense.

MARSHALL PLAN, the European Recovery Program 1947–52, named for its originator, US Secretary of State George C. MARSHALL. In general it succeeded in its design, which was to help Europe's economic recovery after WWII and so check Eastern bloc communist influence. Material and financial aid amounting to almost 13 billion dollars was sent to the 17 European countries who formed the Organization for European Economic Cooperation. The plan was administered by the US Economic Cooperation Administration, headed by Paul G. Hoffmann.

MARSH GAS. See METHANE.

MARSILIUS OF PADUA (c1275–1343), Italian political philosopher whose *Defensor pacis* (Latin: defender of peace; 1324) denied the Church's temporal power and proposed its subjugation to the sovereign, who ruled by popular mandate. He was protected from papal attacks by his patron, Emperor Louis IV.

MARSTON, John (1576–1634), English playwright best known for his tragicomedy *The Malcontent* (1604) and his rivalry with Ben JONSON. Both were imprisoned for offending JAMES I in their collaboration *Eastward Ho!* (1605). Marston was ordained 1609.

MARSUPIALS, MAMMALS with a double womb, giving birth to incompletely developed young which continue development attached to the mother's teats. Differences in the reproductive system are the only infallible way of separating marsupials from true mammals: in marsupials the urinary ducts from the kidneys separate the developing sex ducts, so that in the female both uterus and vagina are double structures. In the male, the urinary ducts lie between the sperm ducts; in PLACENTAL MAMMALS, they lie outside

them. The pouch, or marsupium, is not an exclusive or even universal feature of the group. Marsupials are at their most developed in Australia, where, in the absence of placental mammals, they achieved great diversity of form. In addition, there remain a number of groups in the Americas.

MARTHA'S VINEYARD, island off the coast of SE Mass. About 100sq mi in area, it is separated from Cape Cod by Vineyard Sound. Discovered and named by Bartholomew Gosnold (1602), it was settled c1632. A major whaling center in the 18th and 19th centuries, it is now a popular summer resort.

MARTÍ, José Julian (1853–1895), major Cuban poet and hero of the anti-Spanish independence movement. He founded the Cuban Revolutionary Party in the US 1881–95. His best known poems appear in *Ismaelillo* (1882), *Versos libres* (1913) and *Versos sencilles* (1891). A leader of the 1895 independence campaign, Martí was killed at the battle of Dos Rios.

MARTIAL (Marcus Valerius Martialis; c40–c104 AD), Spanish-born Latin epigrammatic poet. He lived in Rome 64–98 AD, and was favored by emperors TITUS and DOMITIAN and befriended by PLINY the Younger, JUVENAL and QUINTILIAN. Martial wrote 15 books of epigrams.

MARTIAL LAW, temporary superimposition of military on domestic civil government, usually in wartime or other national emergency. The army takes over executive and judicial functions, and civil rights such as HABEAS CORPUS may be suspended. When an invading army assumes control of a country it is said to act not under martial law but as a military government; law applying only to those in military service is not martial but military.

MARTIN, Glenn Luther (1886–1955), pioneering US aircraft designer and manufacturer. A former barnstorming flyer, he developed various military designs after WWI, one of which became the famous B-26 bomber. Many of his other planes and flying boats were used in WWII.

MARTIN, Joseph William, Jr. (1884–1968), US politician, speaker of the House of Representatives 1947–49 and 1953–55. A newspaper publisher, he was elected Republican congressman from Mass. 1925–67 after service in the state legislature. He chaired every Republican national convention 1940–56, and was minority leader in the House 1939–59, except when speaker.

MARTIN, Mary (1913–   ), US star of musical comedies beginning with *Leave It* *to Me* (1938). She created and for two years (1949–51) played the role of Nellie Forbush in *South Pacific*.

MARTIN, William McChesney Jr. (1906–   ), US economist and government official, chairman of the Federal Reserve Board (1951–70) during six presidential administrations.

MARTIN DU GARD, Roger (1881–1958), French novelist known for his objective but somber exploration of human relationships and the large backgrounds in which he sets them. In *Jean Barois* (1913) it is the DREYFUS AFFAIR; in *The Thibaults* (1922–40) it is WWI. In 1937 he won the Nobel Prize for Literature.

MARTINEAU, Harriet (1802–1876), English writer on economics and the philosophy of Auguste COMTE. A visit to the US in 1834 resulted in the unflattering *Society in America* (1837). Her brother, **James Martineau** (1805–1900), was a philosopher and Unitarian clergyman who defended theism against science.

MARTINELLI, Giovanni (1885–1969), Italian tenor, at New York's Metropolitan Opera 1913–46.

MARTINI, Simone (c1284–1344), Italian painter of the Sienese school. Influenced by DUCCIO and the French Gothic, he painted many altarpieces and chapel decorations. His portraits, such as one of Laura for his friend PETRARCH, introduced secular themes into Sienese art.

MARTINIQUE, island in the Windward group in the E Caribbean, an overseas department of France since 1946. Discovered by COLUMBUS c1493, it was colonized by France as a sugar-growing center after 1635; slave labor was used until 1848, and much of the present population is of African descent. The economy still rests on sugar, and also rum, fruit and tourism. The island is volcanic, and so is rugged and mountainous but very fertile. Its main town is Fort-de-France.

MARTIN OF TOURS, Saint (d. 397), bishop of Tours. Son of a pagan, he served in the Roman army but after a vision of Christ sought a religious life. Bishop of Tours from c372, he encouraged monasticism and opposed execution of heretics.

MARTINS, Peter (1946–   ), Danish dancer. From 1964–67 he danced with the Royal Danish Ballet, then joined the New York City Ballet, where he became a leading male dancer in such BALANCHINE works as *Violin Concerto* and *Duo Concertant* (both 1972). In 1983, following Balanchine's death, he became ballet master-in-chief (with Jerome ROBBINS).

MARTINSON, Harry Edmund (1904–1978), Swedish novelist and poet who shared with Egvind Johnson the 1974 Nobel Prize for Literature.

MARTINŮ, Bohuslav (1890–1959), Czech composer who lived in Paris 1923–40, and the US 1940–46. Although incorporating Czech folk themes, his highly individual work is usually neoclassical in style, as in the ballet *Istar* (1922) and the powerful *Double Concerto* (1940).

MARTIN V (1368–1431), pope (1417–31). His election by the Council of Constance ended the GREAT SCHISM of 1378–1417. He returned (1420) to Rome and attempted to restore papal prestige by denouncing the conciliar theory advanced at Constance that church councils were superior to popes. Nevertheless, he called the Council of Basle, where the issue was revived. Martin died before the council convened.

MARTIN v. HUNTER'S LESSEE, case decided by the US SUPREME COURT in 1816, in which Va.'s attempt to confiscate British-owned land was held to be overridden by treaties made by the federal government with Britain. The decision established the Supreme Court's power to review state court decisions.

MARTOV, L. or Julius (Iulii Osipovich Tsederbaum; 1873–1923), Russian revolutionary. Favoring a mass rather than an elite revolutionary party, he broke with Lenin in 1903 and thereafter led the anti-Leninist Mensheviks. He supported the Bolsheviks in the Russian civil war but opposed their dictatorial methods. When the Mensheviks were outlawed in 1920, Martov emigrated to Berlin.

MARVELL, Andrew (1621–1678), English METAPHYSICAL POET. Assistant to John MILTON from 1657, he was a member of Parliament from 1659. A Puritan, he was known as a wit and satirist, but is today best remembered for his lyric poetry such as "To His Coy Mistress" and "The Garden."

MARX, Karl Heinrich (1818–1883), German philosopher and social and economic theorist, the most important of socialist thinkers. Born at Trier of Jewish parents, Marx studied at Bonn and Berlin. When the Cologne newspaper he edited was suppressed (1843), he moved with his wife Jenny von Westphalen to Paris, Brussels and London, where he spent most of his life in great poverty.

With Friedrich ENGELS, his lifelong friend and collaborator, Marx published the *Communist Manifesto* (1848) on the eve of the REVOLUTIONS OF 1848. It summarizes Marx's social philosophy. In London Marx cofounded (1864) and led the International Workingmen's Association (First

INTERNATIONAL). But most of his energy went into his writing, of which *Capital* (3 volumes: 1867, 1885, 1894) is the most important.

In developing dialectical materialism, Marx adapted HEGEL's dialectic to his own economic interpretation of history. Ethics, politics and religion are the products of socioeconomic relations. Accepting the labor theory of value of RICARDO, Marx argued that the surplus value, or profit, extracted by the capitalist from his workforce would in time inevitably decline. CAPITALISM, the inevitable successor to FEUDALISM, would in turn inevitably be replaced by SOCIALISM and eventually COMMUNISM. The class war between the capitalist and the worker he exploits would end in the overthrow of capitalism. (See MARXISM.)

MARX BROTHERS, Groucho, Harpo and Chico, famous US film comedy team. The original team consisted of **Chico** (Leonard; 1887–1961), **Groucho** (Julius; 1890–1977), **Gummo** (Milton; c1892–1977), **Harpo** (Arthur; 1887–1964) and **Zeppo** (Herbert; 1901–1979). Gummo and Zeppo left the team by 1934. After appearing on Broadway, the Marx brothers made about a dozen movies (1933–46). Their anarchic humor is seen to best advantage in *Duck Soup* (1933) and *A Night at the Opera* (1935). Groucho also starred as a popular TV game show host in the 1950s and 1960s.

MARXISM, the foundation philosophy of modern COMMUNISM, originating in the work of Karl MARX and Friedrich ENGELS. Three basic concepts are: that productive labor is the fundamental attribute of human nature; that the structure of any society is determined by its economic means of production; and that societies evolve by a series of crises caused by internal contradictions, analyzable by dialectical materialism. Marx held that 19th-century industrial CAPITALISM, the latest stage of the historical process, had arisen from FEUDALISM by class struggle between the aristocracy and the rising bourgeois capitalist class. Dialectical materialism predicted conflict between these capitalists and the working class, or PROLETARIAT, on which the new industrialism depended. The triumphant dictatorship of the proletariat, an idea further developed by LENIN, would give way to a classless, stateless communist society where all would be equal, contributing according to their abilities and receiving according to their needs. A key concept of Marxist economics is the labor theory of value, that value is created by labor and profit is surplus value creamed off

by the capitalist. The fact that he owns the means of production makes this exploitation possible. It also means that the worker cannot own the product of his labor and thus suffers ALIENATION from part of his own humanity and the social system. Marx believed capitalism would be swept away by the last of a catastrophic series of crises. Among numerous later Marxist theorists are Karl KAUTSKY and Rosa LUXEMBURG. In *The Accumulation of Capital* (1913), Luxemburg argued that capitalism was able to adapt and survive by exploitation of its colonial empires. In Russia STALIN proclaimed Marxist-Leninism, an active philosophy of society in forced evolutionary conflict. In China MAO TSE-TUNG adapted Marxism to an agricultural peasant situation. Yugoslavia's TITO gave Marxism a nationalist bias, still more marked in the thinking of Fidel CASTRO of Cuba. Western economists, sociologists and historians have been widely influenced by Marxism.

MARY, the mother of JESUS CHRIST, also called the Blessed Virgin. The chief events of her life related in the Gospels are her betrothal to JOSEPH; the ANNUNCIATION of Christ's birth; her visit to her cousin Elizabeth, mother of John the Baptist; the birth of Christ; and her witnessing his crucifixion. In the Roman Catholic Church Mary is accorded a special degree of veneration, called hyperdulia, superior to that given to other saints, and is regarded as mediatrix of all graces and coredemptress. Roman Catholic doctrine holds she was born free from sin, remained always a virgin and was assumed bodily into heaven (see IMMACULATE CONCEPTION; ASSUMPTION OF THE VIRGIN).

MARY, name of two English queens. **Mary I** (1516–1558), daughter of HENRY VIII and Catherine of Aragon, succeeded EDWARD VI in 1553. She tried to restore Roman Catholicism in England. Some 300 Protestants were burnt as heretics—a persecution unparalleled in England, which earned her the name "Bloody Mary." Her unpopular alliance with and marriage to PHILIP II of Spain (1554) led to war with France and the loss of Calais (1558). **Mary II** (1662–1694), was the Protestant daughter of JAMES II and wife of her cousin WILLIAM III. She was proclaimed joint sovereign with him in 1689.

MARYKNOLL FATHERS, popular name for the Catholic Foreign Mission Society of America. It was founded in 1911 with headquarters at Maryknoll, N.Y. It has sent missions to Asia, Latin America and the Pacific islands.

MARYLAND, state, E US, on the Atlantic

Ocean, bounded to the N by Pa., to the NE by Del., to the S and SW by Va. and Washington, D.C., and to the W by W.V.; one of the 13 original states.

Name of state: Maryland
Capital: Annapolis
Statehood: April 28, 1788 (7th state)
Familiar name: Old Line State, Free State
Area: 10,577sq mi
Population: 4,463,000
Elevation: Highest—3,360ft., Backbone Mountain. Lowest—sea level, Atlantic Ocean
Motto: *Fatti maschii, parole femine* ("Manly deeds, womanly words")
State flower: Black-eyed susan
State bird: Baltimore oriole
State tree: White oak
State song: "Maryland, My Maryland"
Land. Maryland has three major regions: the Atlantic coastal plain in the E, the Piedmont-Blue Ridge region in the center and the Appalachian-Allegheny Mts in the W. The Potomac R, forming the state's W border, flows into CHESAPEAKE BAY, which divides Md. from N to S, separating the E Shore from the rest of the state. Much of the state is covered by forests, including 12 state forests. The average annual temperature is 53°F.
People. Maryland's population is heavily urban (over 75%). The principal urban areas are Baltimore and the suburbs of Washington, D.C.
Economy. A diversified economy is dominated by shipbuilding and the manufacture of metals, chemicals, electrical and electronic products and processed foods. There are also large livestock, horsebreeding and fishing industries.
History. Maryland was first explored by John Smith in 1608. In 1632 George CALVERT, Lord Baltimore, was granted the territory and founded a colony named for Henrietta Maria, wife of Charles I of England. The colony's initial religious freedom was eroded by the Puritans' ascendancy. The MASON-DIXON line set the boundary between Md. and Pa. Staunchly anti-loyalist during the War of Indepen-

dence, Md. was the seventh state to ratify the US Constitution (1788). In 1790–91 it ceded a tract of land along the Potomac R for the new national capital, Washington, D.C. In the 19th century an extensive transportation system was constructed, and Baltimore became a major US shipbuilding center. Although locally divided, Md. remained in the Union during the Civil War.

The opening in 1952 of the Chesapeake Bay Bridge led to the industrialization of the Eastern Shore. In recent years, Maryland has undergone economic changes, reflected in low population growth (less than 6% from 1970 to 1986) and a population shift from the cities to the suburbs. On the other hand, since the late 1970s Baltimore has been experiencing a much-publicized "Renaissance," emanating from the restored and redesigned inner harbor district. In the 1980s environmental concerns centered on the pollution of Chesapeake Bay, which has hurt the traditionally important fishing industry. In presidential elections 1968–88, Maryland voted Republican in 1972 and 1984–88.

MARY MAGDALENE, Saint, in the New Testament, the woman of Magdala from whom Jesus cast out seven demons (Luke 8:2). She became his devoted follower and was present at his death and burial. Mary was the first person to see the risen Jesus.

MARY OF BURGUNDY (1457–1482), daughter and heir of CHARLES THE BOLD of Burgundy, wife of Maximilian of Austria, later Holy Roman Emperor MAXIMILIAN I. Her marriage (1477) was critical in European history, eventually bringing the Netherlands, Artois and Franche-Comté to the imperial HAPSBURG house.

MARY QUEEN OF SCOTS (1542–1587), queen of Scotland (1542–67), daughter of James V (d. 1542) and Mary of Guise. Brought up in France, she married (1558) the Dauphin, king as FRANCIS II (d. 1560). Returning to Scotland (1561) she married (1565) Lord DARNLEY. In 1566 he murdered her favorite, David Rizzio, but was himself later murdered, supposedly by the Earl of BOTHWELL, whom Mary married. Public outrage and Presbyterian opposition forced her abdication, and in 1568 she fled to England. Mary, heir presumptive of ELIZABETH I and a Roman Catholic, soon became the natural focus of plots against the English throne. Parliament demanded her death, but it was only in 1587, after Anthony Babington's plot, that Elizabeth reluctantly agreed. Mary's trial and execution at Fotheringay castle inspired SCHILLER's tragedy *Maria Stuart*.

MASACCIO (Tommaso Guidi; 1401–1428), Florentine painter of the RENAISSANCE, one of the great innovators of western art. He was possibly a pupil of MASOLINO. By taut line, austere composition, and inspired use of light Masaccio created expressive monumental paintings, notably in the Brancacci chapel, S. Maria del Carmine, Florence.

MASADA, rock fortress near the SE coast of the Dead Sea, Israel, the historic scene of Jewish national heroism. The castle-palace complex, built largely by Herod the Great, was seized from Roman occupation by Jewish Zealots in 66 AD. A two-year siege, 72–73, was needed to recover it, but the garrison committed suicide rather than surrender. The site has been excavated and restored.

MASAI, a people of E Africa who speak the Masai language of the Sudanic group. The nomadic pastoral Masai of Kenya, the largest Masai tribe, practice polygyny and organize their society on a system of male age sets, graded from junior warrior up to tribal elder. They subsist almost entirely on livestock.

MASARYK, name of two Czechoslovakian statesmen. **Thomas Garrigue Masaryk** (1850–1937) was chief founder and first president of Czechoslovakia (1918–35). Professor of philosophy at Prague from 1882, he was a fervent nationalist. During WWI he lobbied western statesmen for Czech independence and helped delimit the frontiers of the new state. His son **Jan Garrigue Masaryk** (1886–1948) was foreign minister of the Czech government in exile in London in WWII, broadcasting to his German-occupied country. He continued as foreign minister in the restored government (1945). Soon after the communist coup (1948) he was said to have committed suicide.

MASCAGNI, Pietro (1863–1945), Italian opera composer of the *verismo* (realist) school, known for the one-act *Cavalleria Rusticana* (Rustic Chivalry, 1890). In 1929 he became musical director of La Scala, Milan.

MASEFIELD, John (1878–1967), English poet, novelist and playwright. As a youth he served on a windjammer ship, and love of the sea pervades his poems. He won fame with such long narrative poems as *The Everlasting Mercy* (1911), *Dauber* (1913) and *Reynard the Fox* (1919). In 1930 he became POET LAUREATE.

MASER, a device used as a MICROWAVE oscillator or amplifier, the name being an acronym for "microwave (or molecular) amplification by stimulated emission of radiation." As OSCILLATORS they form the basis of extremely accurate ATOMIC CLOCKS; as AMPLIFIERS they can detect feebler signals than any other kind, and are used to measure signals from outer space.

ATOMS and MOLECULES can exist in various states with different energies; changes from one energy level to another are accompanied by the emission or absorption of ELECTROMAGNETIC RADIATION of a particular frequency. Maser action is based on the fact that irradiation at the frequency concerned stimulates the process. If more atoms are in the higher energy (excited) state than in the lower state, incident waves cause more emission than absorption, resulting in amplification of the original wave.

The main difficulty is one of maintaining this arrangement of the states, as the equilibrium configuration involves more atoms being in the lower than in the excited state. In the AMMONIA gas maser, molecules in the lower state are removed physically through their different response to an electric field, while in solid-state masers, often operated at low temperatures, a higher frequency "pumping" wave raises atoms into the excited state from some state not involved in the maser action.

MASLOW, Abraham (1908–1970), US psychologist, the major figure in the humanistic school of psychology. Rejecting BEHAVIORISM and PSYCHOANALYSIS, he saw man as a creative being striving for self-actualization. His books included *Motivation and Personality* (1954) and *Toward a Psychology of Being* (1960).

MASOLINO DA PANICALE (1383–1447?), Florentine painter, born Tommaso di Cristoforo Fini. His decorative Gothic style was modified to greater realism under the influence of MASACCIO (possibly his pupil), with whom he executed notable frescoes in the Brancacci chapel, Florence.

MASON, George (1725–1792), American statesman who helped draft the US Constitution but refused to sign it because of its compromise on slavery and other issues. His Va. declaration of rights became the basis for the BILL OF RIGHTS. Much of the Va. Constitution was also his work.

MASON, James Murray (1798–1871), US senator from Virginia (1847–61) and Confederate commissioner to England who, with John Slidell, was involved in the TRENT AFFAIR. In England, Mason was never officially recognized.

MASON, Lowell (1792–1872), US composer and music educator whose system of music education, based on the theories of J. H. PESTALOZZI, was adopted by the Boston public schools. He composed more than 1,200 hymns, including "Nearer, My God, to Thee."

MASON-DIXON LINE, the S boundary of Pa., surveyed by two English astronomers, Charles Mason and Jeremiah Dixon, in the 1760s. It settled a dispute between the proprietary families of Pa. and Md. In 1779 it was extended westward to become the boundary between Va. and Pa. Up to the Civil War the line was popularly taken as the boundary between free and slave states.

MASONRY, or **Freemasonry,** common name for the practices of the order of Free and Accepted Masons, one of the world's largest and oldest fraternal organizations. Members participate in elaborate, secret rituals and are dedicated to the promotion of brotherhood and morality. Membership, of which there are several grades, is restricted to men and allegiance to some form of religious belief is required. Modern Masonry emerged with the Grand Lodge of England, founded in 1717, though masons trace their ancestry to the craft associations or "lodges" of medieval stone masons. The first US lodge was founded in Philadelphia, Pa. in 1730. The basic organization of Masonry is the blue lodge. In the US each state has a grand lodge and grand master, who presides over all the blue lodges in the state. There are associated organizations for women, boys and girls. The worldwide membership is more than six million, including one million in the US.

MASQUE, or **mask,** a dramatic entertainment popular at the early 17th-century English court. It concentrated on spectacle rather than plot. Members of the aristocracy often took part with the actors and masks were generally worn (hence the name). Ben JONSON was the most famous masque writer and Inigo JONES designed many of the lavish sets.

MASS, term for the celebration of Holy COMMUNION in the Roman Catholic Church and in Anglo-Catholic churches, derived from the final words of the Latin rite: *Ite, missa est* (Go, you are dismissed). Roman Catholics believe that the bread (host) and the wine became Christ's body and blood (see TRANSUBSTANTIATION), which are offered as a sacrifice to God. The text consists of the "ordinary," spoken or sung at every celebration, and the "proper," sections which change according to the day (Gospel, including Collect and Epistle) or occasion—for example, the requiem mass has its own proper. In high mass, celebrated with priest, deacon and choir, the text is sung to plainsong with choral responses. The ordinary comprises the Kyrie, Gloria, Creed, Sanctus, Benedictus, Agnus Dei and the Missa est. Medieval choral settings of the mass are the first great masterpieces of western music, remaining a major musical form into the 20th century. Low mass, said by a single priest, is the basic Roman Catholic service. In 1965 the Vatican sanctioned the use of vernacular languages in place of Latin.

MASS, a measure of the linear INERTIA of a body, i.e., of the extent to which it resists acceleration when a FORCE is applied to it. Alternatively, mass can be thought of as a measure of the amount of MATTER in a body. The validity of this view seems to receive corroboration when one remembers that bodies of equal inertial mass have identical WEIGHTS in a given gravitational field. But the exact equivalence of inertial mass and gravitational mass is only a theoretical assumption, albeit one strongly supported by experimental evidence. According to EINSTEIN's special theory of RELATIVITY, the mass of a body is increased if it gains ENERGY; according to the famous Einstein equation: $\Delta m = \Delta E/c^2$ where Δm is the change in mass due to the energy change ΔE,, and c is the electromagnetic constant. It is an important property of nature that in an isolated system mass–energy is conserved. The international standard of mass is the international prototype kilogram.

MASSACHUSETTS, state, NE US, on the Atlantic Ocean, bounded to the S by R.I. and Conn., to the W by N.Y. and to the N by Vt. and N.H.; one of the 13 original states.

Land. Massachusetts consists of a coastal plain and a central hilly region which is separated from the more rugged Berkshire Hills and Taconic Mts in the W by the Connecticut R valley. The climate is temperate, with the hillier regions in the W being colder than the eastern plains.

People. Massachusetts is small and densely populated, with a majority of its citizens and principal industries located along the E coastal plain. BOSTON is the seat of government; other large cities include Worcester, Springfield and Cambridge. Mass.'s public school system dating from the 1630s is the oldest in the nation, and its universities and colleges, including HARVARD UNIVERSITY and Massachusetts Institute of Technology, rank among the world's foremost.

Economy. Principal manufactures include electrical and nonelectrical machinery, fabricated metal products, foodstuffs, textiles, printed materials and leather products. Agriculture, fishing and mining,

Name of state: Massachusetts
Capital: Boston
Statehood: Feb. 6, 1788 (6th state)
Familiar name: Bay State
Area: 8,257sq mi
Population: 5,832,000
Elevation: Highest—3,491ft., Mount Grey-lock. Lowest—sea level, Atlantic Ocean.
Motto: *Ense petit placidam sub libertate quietem* ("By the sword we seek peace, but peace only under liberty")
State flower: Mayflower
State bird: Chickadee
State tree: American elm
State Song: "Hail Massachusetts"

once of prime importance to the state's economic base, are now minor branches of the economy. Electronics industries, serving communications and space research and development, and tourism have become increasingly important. In 1986, Massachusetts had the fourth highest per capita income in the US.

History. The first permanent colony in Mass. was founded by the PILGRIM FATHERS in 1620. (See also MAYFLOWER; MAYFLOWER COMPACT.) In 1629 a group of English Puritans was granted a charter (see MASSACHUSETTS BAY COMPANY), and the following year they established a settlement at Boston. The colony remained a Puritan theocracy until its original charter was revoked by the English crown in 1684.

The expansion of white settlement aroused Indian resistance, culminating in KING PHILIP'S WAR (1675–76). Mass. played a major role in the events leading up to the American Revolution (see BOSTON MASSACRE; BOSTON TEA PARTY). The depression which followed the revolution fell most heavily on the farmers and led to SHAYS' REBELLION in 1786, which influenced the state's leaders to ratify the Federal Constitution. As farmers moved W in the 19th century, shipbuilding and whaling became leading industries, but by the end of the century manufacturing was the basis of the state's economy. Mass. played a leading role in abolitionism, under such leaders as William Lloyd GARRISON and Wendell

Phillips. Between the Civil War and WWI, thousands of European immigrants, notably Irish, came to Mass., and gradually they wrested political power from the established families, creating a powerful Democratic machine. From 1947 to 1987, three US representatives from Massachusetts served as Speaker of the House of Representatives for a total of 23 years. A US senator from the state, John F. Kennedy, was elected president in 1960, and the state's governor, Michael Dukakis, was the Democratic candidate for president in 1988. In presidential elections 1968–88, Massachusetts voted Democratic in 1968–76 and 1988.

MASSACHUSETTS BAY COMPANY, joint stock company set up by royal charter in 1629 and styled the "Governor and Company of the Massachusetts Bay in New England." This gave the company self-government subject only to the king; the charter effectively became the constitution of the colony. In 1630 almost 1,000 immigrants landed in Mass., led by John WINTHROP, who became the first governor. The franchise was then restricted to Puritan "freemen," and the colony became an independent Calvinistic theocracy; it coined its own money and restricted freedom of worship. As a result the charter was revoked in 1684 and Massachusetts became a royal colony.

MASSASOIT, or **Ousamequin** (d. 1661), powerful Wampanoag Indian chief who signed a treaty with the PILGRIM FATHERS of Plymouth in 1621. He befriended the Plymouth colony, teaching the settlers much that they needed to know to survive. When he fell ill in 1623, the Pilgrims nursed him back to health, and he kept up friendly relations until his death.

MASSENET, Jules Émile Frédéric (1842–1912), French composer, best known for his operas *Manon* (1884), *Esclarmonde* (1889), *Werther* (1892) and *Thaïs* (1894). He also wrote oratorios, stage music and over 200 songs. He was a very influential teacher of composition at the Paris Conservatory from 1878.

MASSEY, Vincent (1887–1967), Canadian statesman, minister to the US (1926–36), high commissioner to Britain (1935–46), and governor general of Canada (1952–59). His brother, **Raymond Massey** (1896–1983), was a noted stage and film actor, remembered especially for *Abe Lincoln in Illinois* (play, 1938; film, 1940).

MASSINE, Léonide (1896–1979), Russian-born US dancer and choreographer. He made his early career with the DIAGHILEV company, and was choreographer, dancer and director of the Ballet Russe de Monte Carlo 1932–41.

MASSINGER, Philip (1583–1640), English dramatist best known for satirical comedies such as *A New Way to Pay Old Debts* (1626?) and romantic tragedies such as *The Duke of Milan* (1621–22). He wrote many works in collaboration with others such as DEKKER and John FLETCHER.

MASSON, André (1896–1987), French painter and graphic artist. Influenced by SURREALISM, he developed a style of drawing ("automatic drawing") intended to be spontaneous and without conscious intent to portray a specific subject.

MASS PRODUCTION, the production of large numbers of identical objects, usually by use of mechanization. The root of mass production is the assembly line, essentially a conveyer belt which transports the product so that each worker may perform a single function on it (e.g., add a component). The advantages of mass production are cheapness and speed; the disadvantages are the lack of job satisfaction for the workers and the resultant sociological problems.

MASS SPECTROSCOPY, spectroscopic technique in which electric and magnetic fields are used to deflect moving charged particles according to their mass, employed for chemical ANALYSIS, separation, ISOTOPE determination or finding impurities. The apparatus for obtaining a mass spectrum (i.e., a number of "lines" of distinct charge-to-mass ratio obtained from the beam of charged particles) is known as a mass spectrometer or mass spectrograph, depending on whether the lines are detected electrically or on a photographic plate. In essence, it consists of an ion source, a vacuum chamber, a deflecting field and a collector. By altering the accelerating voltage and deflecting field, particles of a given mass can be focused to pass together through the collecting slit.

MASS TRANSIT, system for conveying large numbers of people in and around cities. Transit includes buses, heavy-rail systems (subway and elevated), light-rail systems (streetcars), and paratransit (minibuses or vans providing special service for the elderly and handicapped). The amount and type of transit service varies with a city's age, size, and shape. It is most extensive in older cities that were built before the ascendancy of the automobile. Cities with populations over 2 million account for 75% of all transit activity. Between 1945 and 1972, transit ridership fell from 19 billion passengers a year to 6 billion. Most of the decline occurred in cities with populations under 500,000. With the rising cost of gasoline and efforts by transit authorities to make their systems more attractive, ridership began to increase. Transit currently accounts for perhaps 6% of all urban trips, although during the twice-daily rush hours 60-70% of all urban trips are made by transit. During nonrush hours and on weekends, transit is little used. Researchers have found that transit use is inversely related to personal income: as their incomes rise, people turn to private transportation.

MASTABA, ancient Egyptian rectangular stone tomb. Its sloping sides supported a flat roof. It usually had three chambers; in the third, entered by a vertical shaft, the mummy was sealed off.

MASTECTOMY, removal of a BREAST including the skin and nipple; LYMPH nodes from the armpit and some chest wall muscles may also be excised. Mastectomy, often with RADIATION THERAPY, is used for breast CANCER.

MASTERS, Edgar Lee (1869–1950), US poet, novelist, biographer and playwright whose best-known work is *Spoon River Anthology* (1915), which reveals the life of a small town as seen through the epitaphs of its inhabitants. He also wrote critical biographies of Lincoln and Mark Twain.

MASTERS, William H. (1915–   ), and **Virginia E. Johnson,** (1925–   ), US sex researchers whose book *Human Sexual Response* (1966) was the first complete study of the physiology and anatomy of sexual activity.

MASTERSINGER. See MEISTERSINGER.

MASTERSON, William Barclay "Bat" (1853–1921), US frontiersman. Son of a farmer, he was a professional gambler and law officer in early life; he is most famous as Wyatt EARP's assistant at Tombstone, Ariz. in 1880. In 1902 he became a sports journalist in New York.

MASTODONS, ELEPHANTS intermediate between the earliest elephant types and those of today. In North America, mastodons survived alongside the elephants into postglacial times. *Mastodon americanus* even outlived elephants in this part of the world.

MASTOID, air spaces lined by mucous membrane lying behind the middle EAR and connected with it; they are situated in the bony protuberance behind the ear. Mastoid infection may follow middle ear infection; block to its drainage by INFLAMMATION and pus may make eradication difficult. ANTIBIOTICS have reduced its incidence, and surgery to clear or remove the air spaces is now infrequent.

MATA HARI (1866–1917), pseudonym of

Margaretha Zelle, Dutch-born dancer, courtesan and spy. Having lived in Indonesia, she appeared as Mata Hari in Paris in 1905; her Oriental erotic dances soon made her world famous. She became the mistress of many French officials, and began to spy for Germany before and during WWI, for which she was tried and executed.

MATCH, short splint of wood or cardboard having a head that can be ignited by friction, used to kindle fire (see COMBUSTION). Early matches were complex, unreliable and somewhat dangerous (e.g., dipping a match treated with potassium chlorate and sugar into a bottle of concentrated sulfuric acid). Friction matches of the modern type were first produced in 1827, containing antimony (III) sulfide and potassium chlorate. Soon white PHOSPHORUS was introduced for strike-anywhere matches. This, however, caused the disease "phossy jaw" in match-factory workers, and was banned from about 1900, being replaced by phosphorus sesquisulfide (P_4S_3) and potassium chlorate, with iron (III) oxide, ground glass and glue. The head of a safety match is composed of potassium chlorate, manganese (IV) oxide, sulfur, iron oxide, ground glass and glue. These matches ignite only when struck on the mixture on the side of the box, which consists of red phosphorus, antimony (III) sulfide and an abrasive. The matchstick is coated with paraffin wax to give a better flame.

MATERIALISM, in philosophy, as opposed to IDEALISM, any view asserting the ontologic primacy of MATTER; in psychology, any theory denying the existence of mind, seeing mental phenomena as the mere outworking of purely physico-mechanical processes in the BRAIN; in the philosophy of religion, any synthesis denying the existence of an immortal soul in man. The earliest thoroughgoing materialists were the classical atomists (see ATOMISM), in particular DEMOCRITUS and LUCRETIUS. The growth of modern science brought a revival of materialism, which many have argued is a prerequisite for scientific thought, particularly in the field of psychology.

MATERIALS, Strength of, a branch of MECHANICS concerned with the behavior of materials when subjected to loads. When force is applied to an object, there is a tendency for it to deform: the internal forces resulting from the applied force are called stresses; the deformations are called strains. **Stress.** The four main types of stress are: shearing (e.g., the forces set up in a rivet joining two plates that are pulling in opposite directions); bending; tension and compression (which tend to elongate or shorten the member); and torsion (twisting). When we analyze a structure, we are concerned with the stresses that each component is called upon to resist, and with its ability to resist that stress without undue strain.
Strain. Materials deform in different ways under load. Basic properties include ELASTICITY, where a material regains its original dimensions when load is removed; plasticity, where the deformation is permanent; brittleness, where deformation is negligible before fracture; and creep, deformation under a constant load over a period of time. Within limits, elastic materials deform in proportion to the stress;

i.e., stress = a constant (HOOKE's Law). The strain

value of the constant depends on the material and on the type of stress. For tensile and compressive forces it is called Young's modulus, E (see YOUNG, THOMAS); for shearing forces, the shear modulus, S; and, for forces affecting the VOLUME of the object, the bulk modulus, B. There comes a point (the elastic limit), however, when further stress results in a permanent deformation of the material being used.

MATHEMATICS, the fundamental, interdisciplinary tool of all science. It can be divided into two main classes, pure and applied mathematics, though there are many cases of overlap between these. Pure mathematics has as its basis the abstract study of quantity, order and relation, and thus includes the sciences of NUMBER—ARITHMETIC and its broader realization, ALGEBRA—as well as the subjects described collectively as GEOMETRY (e.g., ANALYTIC GEOMETRY, EUCLIDEAN GEOMETRY, NON-EUCLIDEAN GEOMETRY, TRIGONOMETRY and sometimes TOPOLOGY) and the subjects described collectively as ANALYSIS (of which the most elementary part is CALCULUS). In modern mathematics, many of these subjects are treated in terms of SET theory. Abstract algebra (see ALBEGRA, ABSTRACT) deals with generalizations of number systems, such as GROUPS, and has important relationships to other parts of mathematics. Applied mathematics deals with the applications of this abstract science. It thus has particularly close associations with PHYSICS and ENGINEERING. Specific subjects that come under its aegis are GAME THEORY; INFORMATION THEORY; PROBABILITY, and STATISTICS.

MATHER, family of American colonial

divines. **Richard Mather** (1596–1669) emigrated to Mass. in 1635 and there became an influential preacher. A coauthor of the BAY PSALM BOOK, he wrote the *Platform of Church Discipline* (1649), the basic creed of Massachusetts Congregationalism. **Increase Mather** (1639–1723), son of Richard, was president of Harvard 1685–1701. A renowned preacher and scholar, he helped negotiate the colony's new charter with William III in 1692. In that year he also intervened to mitigate the witchcraft persecution. **Cotton Mather** (1663–1728), son of Increase, was also a famous preacher and scholar; his early work contributed to the witchcraft hysteria, which he always defended in part. His *Magnalia Christi Americana* (1702) is a brilliant religious history of the colonies. He helped found Yale U.; his wide scientific interests made him the first native American to be elected to the Royal Society of London.

MATHEWSON, Christopher "Christy" (1880–1925), US baseball player, one of the most successful of pitchers. During a 17-year career he won 373 games while losing 188 and set the National League strikeout record of 2,499. He pitched three shutouts in six days against the Philadelphia Athletics in 1905. Gassed in WWI, he died of tuberculosis.

MATILDA, or **Maud** (1102–1167), queen of England and Holy Roman Empress until the death of her husband Emperor Henry V in 1125. Her claim to the English throne was recognized in 1127, but countered successfully by Stephen of Blois in 1135. Her eldest son, however, became HENRY II in 1154.

MATISSE, Henri Émile Benôit (1869–1954), French painter, one of the most important artists of the 20th century. He studied under MOREAU and was much influenced by IMPRESSIONISM. The brilliance of color in such paintings as *Woman with a Hat* (1905) and *Joy of Life* (1906) caused the style of his circle to be dubbed FAUVISM. He visited and exhibited in the USSR and US, and in 1917 settled in Nice, France. A prolific painter, he also produced lithographs, etchings, designs, illustrations and much sculpture. He himself considered the decor of the Dominican Nunnery chapel at Vence, France, his masterpiece.

MATSUO BASHO, pseudonym of Matsuo Munefusa (1644–1694), the greatest Japanese exponent of *haiku* poetry. A follower of ZEN, he introduced this philosophy into the formerly trivial *haiku* form with compact and delicate imagery. He is also remembered for his *renga* verses and his accounts of travels.

MATSUOKA, Yosuke (1880–1946), Japanese businessman and statesman, educated in the US. He was an extreme nationalist; he headed the delegation to the LEAGUE OF NATIONS that walked out in 1932. Foreign minister 1940–41, he brought about the Tripartite Pact with the Axis powers in 1940. He died before his impending trial as a war criminal.

MATSYS, Quentin (c1466–1530), Flemish painter. Influenced by LEONARDO DA VINCI and the Italian Renaissance, he is best known for portraits, genre scenes and religious works, particularly the *Holy Kinship* and *Pietà* triptych altarpieces (1509 and 1511, respectively).

MATTEOTTI, Giacomo (1885–1924), Italian socialist politician who, after denouncing dictator Benito Mussolini in parliament, was abducted and murdered by Fascist thugs.

MATTER, material substance, that which has extension in space and time. All material bodies have inherent INERTIA, measured quantitatively by their MASS, and exert gravitational attraction on other such bodies. Matter may also be considered as a specialized form of ENERGY. There are three physical states of matter: solid, liquid and gas. An ideal solid tends to return to its original shape after forces applied to it are removed. Solids are either crystalline or amorphous; most melt and become liquids when heated. Liquids and gases are both FLUIDS: liquids are only slightly compressible, but gases are easily compressed. On the molecular scale, the state of matter is a balance between attractive intermolecular forces and the disordering thermal motion of the molecules. When the former predominate, MOLECULES vibrate about fixed positions in a solid crystal lattice. At higher temperatures, the random thermal motion of the molecules predominates, giving a featureless gas structure. The short-range intermolecular order of a liquid is an intermediate state between solid and gas.

MATTERHORN (French: Mont Cervin; Italian: Monte Cervino), 14,691ft high mountain in the Alps on the Swiss-Italian frontier. It was first climbed by Edward Whymper in 1865.

MATTHEW, Saint, one of the twelve APOSTLES, traditionally the author of the first GOSPEL. He was a tax-collector before Jesus called him; little more is known of him. The gospel, the fullest of the four, was written probably c80 AD for Jewish Christians. By many Old Testament quotes it shows Jesus as the promised MESSIAH.

(See also SYNOPTIC GOSPELS.)

MATTHIAS CORVINUS (c1443–1490), elected king of Hungary in 1458, son of the soldier Janos HUNYADI. In a successful reign he defended himself against the Turks and against the Emperor Frederick III, his rival. A patron of arts and learning, he made his capital at Buda famous throughout Europe.

MAUGHAM, W(illiam) Somerset (1874–1965), British author. After qualifying as a medical student he became a successful playwright and novelist; in WWI he served as a secret agent. His plays are no longer popular, and his fame rests on his many short stories and four of his novels, *Of Human Bondage* (1915); *The Moon and Sixpence* (1919), inspired by the life of GAUGUIN; *Cakes and Ale* (1930); and *The Razor's Edge* (1944). These reveal a cynical but sometimes compassionate view of humanity.

MAULDIN, William Henry (1921–   ), US cartoonist who became famous during WWII for his cartoons featuring G.I.'s Willie and Joe in the army newspaper *Stars and Stripes*. Later he was an editorial cartoonist for the St. Louis *Post-Dispatch* and the Chicago *Sun-Times*. He won Pulitzer Prizes in 1945 and 1959.

MAU MAU, Kenyan Kikuyu terrorist organization whose main aim was to expel the British. Organized on the lines of a cult or secret society, the Mau Mau ran a campaign of murder and sabotage 1952–60, although the movement was contained with the minimum of bloodshed after 1956. In all, however, 100 Europeans and 11,000 rebels had been killed; 20,000 were detained, among them Jomo KENYATTA. The Mau Mau also murdered at least 2,000 Africans who were from other tribes or were reluctant to join the organization.

MAUNA LOA (long mountain), highly active volcano in the HAWAII VOLCANOES NATIONAL PARK, which erupts about once every 3.5 years. It is 13,680ft in height and has several other large craters on its SW slope.

MAUNDY THURSDAY, the Thursday before EASTER (see HOLY WEEK), commemorating Christ's washing of his disciples' feet and institution of Holy COMMUNION at the Last Supper. The English monarch distributes special "Maundy money" to poor persons on this day.

MAUPASSANT, (Henri René Albert) Guy de (1850–1893), French short-story writer and novelist. A pupil of FLAUBERT, from 1880 to 1891 he produced some 300 short stories of outstanding quality, which excel in the unsentimental portrayal of the less attractive aspects of life and human nature.

His direct style, pessimism and NATURALISM are seen at their best in "Boule de suif" (1880) and "The House of Madame Tellier" (1881).

MAUPERTUIS, Pierre Louis Moreau de (1698–1759), French mathematician and astronomer who showed the EARTH to be flattened at the poles (1738), and who formulated the *principle of least action*, which assumes that, in nature, phenomena such as the motion of bodies occur with maximum economy.

MAURIAC, François (1885–1970), French writer whose novels of middle-class life concern man's vulnerability to sin and evil; they reflect his deeply-held Roman Catholic faith. In 1952 he won the Nobel Prize for literature. His works include *A Kiss for the Leper* (1922), *Génitrix* (1923), *The Desert of Love* (1925), *Thérèse Desqueyroux* (1927) and *Vipers' Tangle* (1932).

MAURICE, Frederick Denison (1805–1872), English clergyman and social reformer. A leading Christian socialist, he helped found Queen's College for women (1848) and the Working Men's College (1854), both in London.

MAURICE OF NASSAU (1567–1625), prince of Orange from 1618, Dutch statesman and military leader. A son of WILLIAM THE SILENT, he conducted a successful war against Spanish rule and was an architect of the emerging Dutch republic. He was virtually ruler of the Netherlands, executing his former ally OLDENBARNEVELDT in 1619, and establishing the supremacy of the house of ORANGE.

MAURITANIA, Islamic republic on the NW coast of Africa, bounded by Western Sahara on the NW, Algeria NE, Mali E and S and Senegal SW.

Official name: Islamic Republic of Mauritania
Capital: Nouakchott
Area: 398,000sq mi
Population: 1,844,000
Languages: Arabic, French
Religion: Muslim
Monetary unit(s): 1 ouguiya = 100 khoums

Land. The interior is largely desert and rocky plateau at an average height of 500ft. The climate is hot, with average rainfall less than 4in except in the fertile Senegal R valley in the S, where it rises to 24in.

People. Moors of Arab-Berber descent, traditionally nomadic herdsmen, form some 80% of the population; FULANI form about 13%, and Negro groups such as the Soninke, Bambara and Wolof, most of whom live in the S, make up the remainder. Following severe droughts in 1969–74 and again in the 1980s, the nation's nomadic population was reduced from nearly 85% of the total to 25% in 1986. More than a third of the population lives in Nouakchott, the capital and largest town. A new port opened nearby in 1986.

Economy. Basic crops, grown in the S, are millet, sorghum, rice and other cereals and vegetables; sheep, goats, cattle and camels are raised. There are large iron ore, gypsum and copper deposits, and oil exploration has been undertaken. Iron exports account for about 80% of the value of all exports.

History. In the 11th century the Ghanaian empire, to which most of Mauritania then belonged, was shattered by invading nomad Berbers of the Almoravid group. In the 13th century S Mauritania fell to the Mali Empire and Islam was firmly established. The Portuguese probed the coast in the 15th century; the French penetrated the interior in the 19th century. A French colony by 1921, Mauritania left the French Community at full independence in 1960. In 1968 military officers overthrew the government. During the 1970s a war against the Polisario Front guerrillas over claims to the Western Sahara brought political and economic instability. Mauritania relinquished its claims to the territory in 1979. Soon after, Mauritania's head of state was deposed and a new leader assumed power. Yet another coup occurred in 1984.

MAURITIUS, island republic of the British Commonwealth, 500mi E of the island of Madagascar in the Indian Ocean, comprising the islands of Mauritius and Rodrigues and associated archipelagos. Its warm and humid climate has average temperatures of 79° F from Nov. to April and 72°F in winter. The wet season, Dec. to March, is a time of dangerous cyclones.

People. Indians, descended from indentured laborers brought in to work the sugar plantations, form about 67% of the population, and Creoles about 30%. Europeans, French, Africans and Chinese constitute the remainder. Rapid population increase, coupled with unemployment and ethnic rivalries, has exacerbated political

Official name: Mauritius
Capital: Port Louis
Area: 788sq mi
Population: 1,040,000
Languages: English, French, Creole
Religions: Hindu, Christian, Muslim
Monetary unit(s): 1 Mauritian rupee = 100 cents

problems.

Economy. Sugar is the single most important export, and manufacturing centers around sugar processing, which makes the economy very sensitive to fluctuations in world market prices for sugar. Clothing is the second-largest export. Tea and tobacco are also cash crops. The capital, Port Louis, is the chief port.

History. Formerly uninhabited, Mauritius was settled by the Portuguese in the early 1500s but then abandoned. After a period of Dutch occupation in the 17th century, the French settled the island in 1715, founding the sugar industry. When slavery was abolished in the colonies in 1831, the planters turned to India for labor. The British took Mauritius during the Napoleonic wars (1810), initiated moves to representative government in the late 19th century and granted independence in 1968. Sir Seewoosagur Ramgoolam served as prime minister 1968–82 and as governor general from 1983 until his death in 1985.

MAURRAS, Charles (1868–1952), French poet, journalist and political theorist of "integral nationalism," a forerunner of fascism; he led the "romane" school of anti-SYMBOLIST poets (1891), and helped found *L'Action française* (1899), a promonarchist journal which became a vehicle for his ideas.

MAURY, Matthew Fontaine (1806–1873), US naval officer, head of the Depot of Charts and Instruments, 1842–61. His profile of the bed of the Atlantic and his *Physical Geography of the Sea* (1855) helped pioneer the science of oceanography.

MAURYA, Indian imperial dynasty ruling c325–c183 BC, founded by Chandragupta Maurya, with its capital near modern Patna. His grandson ASOKA (d. 232) ruled almost the whole subcontinent and made Buddhism the state religion. Mauryan art, influenced by Greek and Persian styles, marks a great flowering of Indian Buddhist culture.

MAUSOLEUM, large sepulchral monument, named for the tomb of Mausolus of Caria (built c352 BC) at Halicarnassus in Asia Minor, one of the SEVEN WONDERS OF THE WORLD. About 100ft square and 150ft high, it had superb sculptures, some preserved in the British Museum. Other mausoleums are the TAJ MAHAL and Lenin's tomb in Moscow.

MAWSON, Sir Douglas (1882–1958), Australian Antarctic explorer. A member of SHACKLETON's 1907–09 expedition, he led Australian expeditions in 1911–14 and 1929–30, claiming more than 2 million square miles of Antarctic territory for Australia.

MAXIM, Sir Hiram Stevens (1840–1916), US inventor, known chiefly for the fully automatic MACHINE GUN, which he developed and manufactured in England. He became a British subject in 1900 and was knighted in 1901.

MAXIMILIAN, name of two Hapsburg Holy Roman emperors. **Maximilian I** (1459–1519), reigned from 1493. He married first MARY OF BURGUNDY (1477) and then a Milanese princess, and arranged other family marriages that brought the Hapsburgs much of Burgundy, the Netherlands, Hungary, Bohemia and Spain. He reorganized imperial administration and set up a supreme court of justice, but had to recognize Switzerland's independence (1499), and failed to hold Milan. Loans from the Fugger bank supported his finances, which were severely strained by continual warfare in support of his dynastic ambitions. **Maximilian II** (1527–1576), emperor from 1564, was king of Bohemia from 1549 and of Hungary from 1563. A humanist, he adopted a policy of religious toleration which brought a respite from the struggles of the REFORMATION.

MAXIMILIAN (1832–1867), Austrian archduke and emperor of Mexico from 1864. Liberal and idealistic, he was offered the throne as a result of NAPOLEON III's imperial intrigues. He believed the Mexicans would welcome him, and attempted to rule liberally and benevolently, but found French troops essential against popular support for President JUAREZ. After US pressure had secured his recall he was defeated by Juarez's forces and executed.

MAXIMILIAN OF BADEN, Prince (1867–1929), last chancellor of imperial Germany. Appointed chancellor in Oct.

1918, he formed a coalition cabinet and negotiated with the Allies for an armistice. When the kaiser refused to abdicate, Prince Max announced (Nov. 9) the abdication anyway and turned over the government to Friedrich EBERT.

MAXWELL, James Clerk (1831–1879), British theoretical physicist whose contributions to science have been compared to those of Newton and Einstein. His most important work was in ELECTROMAGNETISM, THERMODYNAMICS, and STATISTICAL MECHANICS. **Maxwell's equations,** four linked differential equations, extend the work of FARADAY and others and completely define the classical theory of the electromagnetic field. The fact that they remain unchanged by LORENTZ transformations of space and time was the principal inspiration for EINSTEIN's theory of RELATIVITY.

MAY, Rollo (1909–   ), US psychologist. An existential psychotherapist, he was a leader of the humanistic movement in psychology and wrote several popular books including *The Meaning of Anxiety* (1950), *Love and Will* (1969) and *Power and Innocence* (1972).

MAY, fifth month of the year, with 31 days. The name is perhaps derived from Maia, the Roman goddess of growth. (See also MAY DAY.)

MAYAKOVSKY, Vladimir Vladimirovich (1893–1930), Soviet futurist poet and playwright whose powerful, declamatory verse, innovative in rhythm and diction, expresses his sense of being a new man in a revolutionary epoch. Notable works are the elegiac lament for *Lenin* (1924), *Very Good!* (1927) on a decade of Soviet successes and the play *The Bedbug* (1928), satirizing Soviet bureaucracy. He committed suicide.

MAYAS, American Indians whose brilliant civilization in central America was at its height c300–c900 AD. The Maya confederation covered the Yucatán peninsula, E Chiapas state in Mexico, most of Guatemala and the W parts of El Salvador and Honduras. They were a farming people of the rain forests and grew corn, cassava, cotton, beans and sweet potatoes and kept bees for wax and honey. The hierarchy of priest-nobles under a hereditary chief had an involved, hieroglyphic form of writing, still undeciphered, and a remarkable knowledge of mathematics, astronomy and chronology. The priests devised two calendars: a 365-day civil year astronomically more accurate than the western Gregorian CALENDAR and a sacred year of 260 days. Mayan art comprises fine sculpture in the round and relief, painted frescoes and manuscripts, ceramics and magnificent architecture. The chief feature of their great cities was the lofty stone pyramid, topped by a temple. By 900 AD their main centers, such as Palenque, Peidras and Copán, were abandoned to the jungle for reasons unknown. A "post-classical" tradition, under TOLTEC influence, sprang up in new centers, notably Chichén Itzá, but in the early 1500s the whole region came under Spanish rule.

MAY DAY, spring festival on May 1. Traces of its pagan origins survive in the decorated maypoles and May queens of England. Declared a socialist labor festival by the Second INTERNATIONAL in 1889, it is celebrated, particularly in communist countries, by parades and demonstrations.

MAYER, Julius Robert von (1814–1878), German physician and physicist who contributed to the formulation of the law of conservation of ENERGY.

MAYER, Louis Burt (1885–1957), Russian-born US motion picture producer and tycoon. As head of the Metro-Goldwyn-Mayer Corporation, MGM (1924–51), he "discovered" such stars as Greta Garbo, Joan Crawford and Clark Gable.

MAYFLOWER, the ship that carried the PILGRIM FATHERS to America in 1620, leaving Plymouth, England, on Sept. 21 and reaching Provincetown, Mass., on Nov. 21; the Pilgrims sailed on to settle what is now Plymouth, Mass., after signing the MAYFLOWER COMPACT. A two-decker, probably some 90ft long and weighing about 180 tons, the ship has not survived, but an English-built replica, *Mayflower II*, sailed the Atlantic in 1957 and is now at Plymouth, Mass.

MAYFLOWER COMPACT, agreement signed by 41 of the PILGRIM FATHERS on Nov. 21, 1620. Having landed outside any civil jurisdiction, and fearing that their group might split up, they undertook to form a "civil body politic" and to "frame just and equal laws." The compact became the basis of the government of the colony of Plymouth.

MAYHEW, Henry (1812–1887), British journalist, miscellaneous writer, social commentator, and a founder of the magazine *Punch* (1841). His 4-volume *London Labour and the London Poor* (1851–62), a sympathetic and penetrating study, is an invaluable source of social history.

MAYO, distinguished US family of surgeons. **William Worrall Mayo** (1819–1911) founded St. Mary's Hospital, Rochester, Minn. (1889), which was to become the famous Mayo Clinic. His sons, **William James Mayo** (1861–1939) and **Charles Horace Mayo** (1865–1939), traveled to many countries both to discover new surgical techniques and to attract foreign surgeons to the Clinic; in 1915 they set up the Mayo Foundation for Medical Education and Research. Charles' son, **Charles William Mayo** (1898–1968), was also a distinguished surgeon.

MAYO, George Elton (1880–1949), Australian pioneer of industrial sociology and psychology. Teaching at the Harvard Graduate School of Business Administration (1926–47), he organized a classic study of labor-management relations at the Western Electric Co. (1927).

MAYO CLINIC, one of the world's largest medical centers, founded in 1889 at Rochester, Minn., as a voluntary association of physicians. It developed from an emergency hospital set up by Dr. William W. Mayo to help cyclone victims. The Clinic treats about 175,000 patients a year and is financed by the Mayo Foundation.

MAYS, Willie Howard Jr. (1931–   ), baseball player who joined the New York Giants in 1951. A great hitter and spectacular outfield player, he won four National League home run titles and two Most Valuable Player awards before retiring in 1973.

MA YUAN (c1160–c1225), Chinese Sung period artist, one of China's greatest landscape painters. He was noted for his spare and dramatically asymmetrical compositions.

MAZARIN, Jules (1602–1661), Italian-born French statesman and cardinal who strengthened the French monarchy and by successful diplomacy increased France's influence abroad. After the deaths of RICHELIEU (1642) and LOUIS XIII (1643), he became the trusted chief minister of the regent, Anne of Austria, and educator of her son, the future LOUIS XIV. His policy of centralized power and his imposition of taxes provoked the revolts known as the FRONDE (1648–53), which he eventually crushed decisively. In foreign policy he gained favorable terms in the treaties that ended the THIRTY YEARS' WAR (1648) and the war with Spain (1659). He amassed a huge fortune and was a patron of the arts.

MAZEPA, **Ivan** **Stepanovich** (c1640–1709), Cossack *hetman* (chief) who vainly aided CHARLES XII of Sweden against PETER THE GREAT, hoping to win independence for his native Ukraine. BYRON's *Mazeppa* immortalizes a youthful incident in which he is said to have been tied to a wild horse by a jealous Polish nobleman.

MAZZINI, Giuseppe (1805–1872), Italian patriot and a leading propagandist of the RISORGIMENTO. A member of the CARBONARI, he was exiled in 1831, formed the "Young Italy" societies, and from France, Switzerland and England promoted his ideal of a united, democratic Italy. In 1849 he became a leader of the short-lived republic of Rome, but was soon in exile again, continuing his revolutionary propaganda and organizing abortive uprisings. His relations with the moderate CAVOUR were strained, and the actual unification of Italy, in which he took little part, fell short of his popular republican ideals.

MBOYA, Tom (1930–1969), Kenyan political leader. General secretary of the Kenya Federation of Labor (1953–63), and a member of the colonial legislative assembly (1957), he played a key role in securing Kenya's independence. Economics minister from 1964, he was established as a likely successor to KENYATTA, and his assassination led to rioting and political tension.

MEAD, George Herbert (1863–1931), US social psychologist and philosopher. Initially influenced by HEGEL, he then moved toward PRAGMATISM. He attempted to explain social psychology in terms of the evolution of the self, and through analyses of spoken language.

MEAD, Margaret (1901–1978), US cultural anthropologist best known for books such as *Coming of Age in Samoa* (1928), *Growing Up in New Guinea* (1930), *The Mountain Arapesh* (3 vols., 1938–49), and *Male and Female* (1949). A first autobiography, *Blackberry Winter*, appeared in 1972. She was associated with New York's American Museum of Natural History, from 1926 until her death.

MEADE, George Gordon (1815–1872), Union general in the US CIVIL WAR who, as commander of the Army of the Potomac, won the Battle of GETTYSBURG. Criticized for not following up his victory, he kept his command but served under Grant's direction.

MEANY, George (1894–1980), US labor leader, president (1955–79) of the AMERICAN FEDERATION OF LABOR AND CONGRESS OF INDUSTRIAL ORGANIZATIONS (AFL-CIO). He was president of the N.Y. State Federation of Labor (1934) and secretary-treasurer (1939) and president (1952) of the AFL.

MEASLES, common infectious disease, caused by a VIRUS. It involves a characteristic sequence of FEVER, HEADACHE and malaise followed by CONJUNCTIVITIS and RHINITIS, and then the development of a typical rash, with blotchy erythema affecting the SKIN of the face, trunk and limbs. COUGH may indicate infections in small bronchi, and this may progress to virus PNEUMONIA. Secondary bacterial infection may lead to middle EAR infection or pneumonia. ENCEPHALITIS is seen in a small but significant number of cases and is a major justification for VACCINATION against this common childhood disease. Recently, an abnormal and delayed IMMUNITY to measles virus has been associated with a number of BRAIN diseases, including MULTIPLE SCLEROSIS.

MEAT, the flesh of any animal, in common use generally restricted to the edible portions of cattle (beef and veal), sheep (lamb) and swine (pork), and less commonly applied to those of the rabbit, horse, goat and deer (venison). Meat consists of skeletal MUSCLE, connective TISSUE, FAT and BONE; the amount of connective tissue determines the toughness of the meat. Meat is an extremely important foodstuff. A daily intake of 100g (3½ oz) provides 45% of daily PROTEIN, 36% of daily iron and important amounts of B VITAMINS, but only 9% of daily energy. Meat protein is particularly valuable as it supplies eight of the AMINO ACIDS which human beings cannot make for themselves.

MECCA, Arabic Makka, chief city of the Hejaz region of Saudi Arabia, birthplace of MOHAMMED and the most holy city of ISLAM. Non-Muslims are not allowed in the city. The courtyard of the great Haram mosque encloses the sacred shrine, the KAABA; nearby is the holy Zem-Zem well. Pilgrimage to Mecca, the *hajj*, is a duty for all Muslims able to perform it, and each year over a million pilgrims arrive. The economy of Mecca depends on the pilgrims. The population includes Muslims of many nationalities. Pop 366,801.

MECHANICS, the branch of applied mathematics dealing with the actions of forces on bodies. There are three branches: kinematics, which deals with relationships among distance, time, velocity and acceleration; dynamics, dealing with the way forces produce motion; and statics, dealing with the forces acting on a motionless body.

Kinematics. In kinematics we deal with distance and time, which are scalar quantities (having no direction), and with velocity and acceleration, which are vector quantities. Velocity is the rate of change of position of a body in a particular direction with respect to time: it thus has both magnitude and direction. Its magnitude is the scalar quantity speed (S), related to distance (s) and time (t) by the equation $S=s/t$; similarly velocity (v) is related to distance and time by $v=ds/dt$ (see CALCULUS). Acceleration is rate of change of velocity with respect to time: $a = dv/dt = d^2s/dt^2$. Thus, if velocity is measured in km/s, acceleration is measured in km/s^2.

Dynamics is based on NEWTON's three laws of motion: that a body continues in its state of motion unless compelled by a force to act otherwise; that the rate of change of motion (acceleration) is proportional to the applied force and occurs in the direction of the force; and that every action is opposed by an equal and opposite reaction. The first gives an idea of INERTIA, which is proportional to the MASS and opposes the change of motion: combining the first with the second, we find that F is proportional to ma, where F is the force, m the mass of the body and a the acceleration produced by the FORCE. In practice we choose units such that $F=ma$. (See also MOMENTUM.)

Statics. We can combine forces much as we do velocities. If forces P_1 and P_2, with resultant R, act at a point, there must be a third force, P_3, equal and opposite to R, for equilibrium. We can combine forces similarly over more complex structures. For a bridge whose weight (w) acts as a downward force W at the center, the upward reactions R_1 and R_2 at the piers must be such that $R_1 + R_2 = -W$ for it to be in equilibrium. Similarly, we examine the members of the bridge to determine the stresses acting on each.

MECHANICSVILLE, Battle of, also called the Battle of Beaver Dam Creek, June 26, 1862, one of the Seven Days' battles in the US CIVIL WAR. The Confederate force of A. P. Hill was defeated some 7mi NE of Richmond, Va.

MECHANIZATION AND AUTOMA-TION, the use of machines wholly or partly to replace human labor. The two words are often used synonymously, but it is of value to distinguish mechanization as requiring human aid, automation as self-controlling.

The most familiar automated device is the domestic THERMOSTAT. This is set to switch off the heating circuit if room temperature exceeds a certain value, to switch it on if the temperature falls below a certain value. Once set, no further human attention is required: a machine is in full control of a machine.

The thermostat is a sensing element; the information it detects is fed back to the production mechanism (the heater), which adjusts accordingly. All automated processes work on this principle. In fact, fully automated processes are still rare: most often the role of sensing element will be taken over by a human being, who will check the accuracy of the machine and adjust it if needed.

The most versatile devices we have are COMPUTERS: very often, the complexity of their physical construction is more than matched by that of the network of subprograms which they contain. Data can be fed in automatically or by human operators, and the computer can be programmed to respond in many ways: to present information; to adjust and control other machines; or even to make decisions. Computerized automation plays an increasingly important role in our lives: airline and theater agents often book seat reservations with a computer, not a staffed box office; food manufacture is often automatically controlled from raw materials to packaged product; atomic energy is controlled automatically where radiation prohibits the presence of humans, possible leaks or even explosions being forestalled by machine; the justification of the columns of this book has been performed by a fully automated process. In addition, man would not have reached the moon had it not been for computerized automation.

Since mechanization and automation emerged in the "Second Industrial Revolution," they have been associated with all kinds of sociological problems and upheavals. Long-term benefits to the human race have to be balanced against such major problems as unemployment and depersonalization. (See also SERVOMECHANISM.)

MEDAWAR, Sir Peter Brian (1915–1987), British zoologist who shared with F. M. Burnet the 1960 Nobel Prize for Physiology or Medicine for their work on immunological tolerance. Inspired by Burnet's ideas, Medawar showed that if fetal mice were injected with cells from eventual donors, skin grafts made onto them later from those donors would "take," thus showing the possibility of acquired tolerance and hence, ultimately, organ TRANSPLANTS.

MEDELLIN, city in central Colombia, a manufacturing and mining center. In the 1980s it became notorious as the center of the Colombian drug trade, "Medellin cartel" referring to the group of drug lords whose wealth and violence menaced governments throughout the hemisphere.

MEDES, ancient Indo-European people of W Asia. Originally nomadic warrior herdsmen, they settled Media (in modern NW Iran) c900 BC. They controlled PERSIA by 700 BC, and in 612 BC, in alliance with Babylon, destroyed the Assyrian empire (see BABYLONIA AND ASSYRIA). c550 BC CYRUS THE GREAT captured Ecbatana, the Median capital, and made Media a Persian province.

MEDIATION. See ARBITRATION.

MEDICAID, federal-state WELFARE program that pays for medical services to needy persons under 65. It was enacted in 1965 at the same time that MEDICARE was added to the SOCIAL SECURITY system. Originally intended for recipients of AID TO FAMILIES WITH DEPENDENT CHILDREN and SUPPLEMENTAL SECURITY INCOME, Medicaid has been expanded in recent years to cover poor children, pregnant women, and elderly people who do not qualify for welfare.

MEDICARE, national social-insurance program partially covering the cost of medical care of the aged — not merely the aged poor — through the SOCIAL SECURITY system. It was established in 1965 at the same time as MEDICAID, the federal WELFARE program providing medical care for the needy.

Medicare consists of two parts: a mandatory hospital-insurance plan and an optional supplementary medical-insurance plan. Hospital insurance is financed by the Social Security taxes paid by employees, employers, and the self-employed. It covers all persons 65 and over who are entitled to receive Social Security or Railroad Retirement benefits; persons under 65 who are entitled to receive those benefits on the basis of disability; otherwise ineligible persons, 65 and over, who enroll voluntarily and pay the full cost of their coverage; and persons under 65 with chronic kidney disease. Supplementary medical insurance is available to all persons 65 and over who pay the monthly premium. In 1988 Congress added catastrophic insurance to Medicare, covering prolonged hospital stays, home health services, and hospice care for an additional premium. Medicare expenditures have vastly exceeded original expectations.

MEDICI, Italian family of bankers, princes and patrons of the arts who controlled Florence almost continually from the 1420s to 1737, and provided cardinals, popes Leo X, Clement VII and Leo XI and two queens of France. The French spelling of the name is Médicis.

The foundations of the family's power were laid by Giovanni di Bicci de' Medici (1360–1429). His son Cosimo de' Medici (1389–1464), was effectively ruler of Florence from 1434 and was voted "Father of the Country" after his death. He founded the great Laurentian Library and patronized such artists as DONATELLO and GHIBERTI. His grandson Lorenzo (1449–1492), called "the Magnificent," was Italy's most brilliant Renaissance prince. Himself a fine poet, he patronized BOTTICELLI, GHIRLANDAIO, the young MICHELANGELO and many other artists. His son Piero (1471–1503), was expelled from Florence (1494) by a popular rising led by SAVONAROLA. The family were restored in 1512; Lorenzo (1492–1519), ruled from 1513 under the guidance of his uncle Giovanni (1475–1521), who as Pope Leo X was a magnificent patron of the arts in Rome. The ruthless Cosimo I (1519–1574), doubled Florentine territory and power and was created grand duke of Tuscany in 1569. The later Medicis were less distinguished, and the line died out with Gian Gastone (1671–1737).

Catherine de Médicis (1519–1589), wife of HENRY II of France, was regent from 1560 for her second son CHARLES IX, and helped plan the SAINT BARTHOLOMEW'S DAY MASSACRE. Marie de Médicis (1573–1642), second wife of HENRY IV of France (1600), was powerful regent for her son LOUIS XIII (1610–17), but was forced into exile (1630) by Cardinal RICHELIEU.

MEDICINE, the art and science of healing. Within the last 150 years or so medicine has become dominated by scientific principles. Prior to this, healing was mainly a matter of tradition and magic. Many of these prescientific attitudes have persisted to the present day.

The earliest evidence of medical practice is seen in Neolithic (see STONE AGE) skulls in which holes have been bored, presumably to let evil spirits out, a practice called trepanning. Treatment in primitive cultures was either empirical or magical. Empirical treatment included bloodletting, dieting, primitive surgery and the administration of numerous potions, lotions and herbal remedies (some used in modern medicines). For serious ailments, magical treatment, involving propitiation of the gods, special rituals or the provision of charms, was performed by the medicine man or witch doctor, who was usually both doctor and priest (see SHAMANISM). Exorcism, the casting out of devils, and FAITH HEALING are still practiced in modern societies. ACUPUNCTURE and OSTEOPATHY, both being ancient and empirical, are also practiced today.

The growth of scientific medicine began with the Greek philosophy of nature. The great Greek physician HIPPOCRATES, with whose name is associated the Hippocratic oath which codifies the physician's ideals of humanity and service, has justly been called the father of medicine. GALEN OF PERGAMUM, the encyclopedist of classical medicine, clearly distinguished ANATOMY from PHYSIOLOGY. Medieval medicine was basically a corrupted Galenism. The 16th century saw the dawn of modern medicine. Men such as Fabricius, VESALIUS and William HARVEY revived the critical, observational approach to medical research. Perhaps the most far-reaching advances since then have been in preventive medicine, anesthesia and drug therapy. Preventive medicine was attempted in medieval times when ships arriving in Europe during the Black Death were "quarantined" for 40 days. More recent major milestones have been Edward JENNER'S work on VACCINATION and the "germ theory of disease" proposed by Louis PASTEUR and developed by Robert KOCH. ANESTHESIA and asepsis (see LISTER, JOSEPH) made possible great advances in SURGERY. Crawford LONG and James Simpson were both pioneers of their use. Drug therapy originated with herbal remedies, but perhaps the two most important discoveries in this field both came in the 20th century: that of INSULIN by Frederick BANTING and Charles Best, and that of PENICILLIN by Alexander FLEMING. (See also ANTIBIOTICS; CHEMOTHERAPY; DRUGS; SULFA DRUGS.)

Medical training to high set standards is used to protect society against charlatans and is usually undertaken in universities and hospitals. Since the progress of medical knowledge is very rapid, doctors today undergo continual retraining to keep them up to date. Socialized medicine, under the name MEDICARE, was set up in the US in 1965 and helps to pay the costs of medical care. However, several other countries have more comprehensive programs of socialized medicine.

The success of medicine in preventing disease is largely responsible for today's population explosion. This has stimulated an extensive re-examination of traditional attitudes to medical ethics, particularly in the areas of CONTRACEPTION, ABORTION and EUTHANASIA. (See also DISEASE.)

MEDILL, Joseph (1823–1899), Canadian-born US editor and publisher of the *Chicago Tribune*, and a founder of the REPUBLICAN PARTY. A strong emancipationist and admirer of Lincoln, he was elected mayor of Chicago in 1871.

MEDINA, holy Muslim city and place of pilgrimage in Hejaz, Saudi Arabia, 210mi N of MECCA. The prophet Mohammed came to Medina after his Hegira (flight) from Mecca (622 AD), and the chief mosque contains his tomb. A walled city, Medina stands in a fertile oasis noted for its dates, grains and vegetables. Pop 198,186.

MEDINA SIDONIA, Alonso Perez de Gusmán, duque de (1550–1615), Spanish nobleman appointed by Philip II to command the ARMADA sent against England in 1588. With no naval experience, and well aware of the deficiencies in the fleet, he did his duty loyally, leading the remnant of the defeated armada around Scotland and Ireland and back to Spain.

MEDITERRANEAN FRUIT FLY, *Ceratitis capitata*, a serious pest of fruit in Africa, Australia and South America, attacking, in particular, peaches, apricots and citrus fruits. The larvae completely destroy the fruits and whole harvests may be lost. The maggots are capable of prodigious leaps of about 100mm (4in) high and over distances of 200mm (8in).

MEDITERRANEAN SEA, intercontinental sea between Europe, Asia and Africa, connected to the Atlantic Ocean in the west by the Strait of Gibraltar and to the Black Sea by the Dardanelles and Bosporus. The man-made Suez Canal provides the link with the Indian Ocean via the Red Sea. Peninsular Italy, Sicily, Malta, Pantelleria and Tunisia's Cape Bon mark the dividing narrows between the eastern and western basins. The many islands of the western basin include Sicily, Sardinia, Elba, Corsica and the Balearics. Crete, Cyprus, Rhodes and the numerous Aegean islands are contained in the eastern basin. Geologically, the Mediterranean is a relic of Tethys, an ocean which separated Eurasia from Africa 200 million years ago and was partially uplifted to form the Alps, S Europe, and the Atlas Mts. Its name (from the Latin, "middle [of the] land"), given by the Romans, reflects its central position and importance in the ancient world. The limited access from the Atlantic and the confined entries to both the Black and Red seas have given it great strategic importance throughout history.

MEDVEDEV, Roy Aleksandrovich (1925–), Soviet historian, a communist who attacked Stalinism and advocated democratic reforms in the Soviet Union. For his dissident views, he was expelled from the Communist Party. His twin brother, **Zhores Aleksandrovich Medvedev** (1925–), a biologist, criticized the genetic theories of T. D. LYSENKO, for which he was temporarily confined in a psychiatric hospital. While he was working in London in 1973, his Soviet citizenship was revoked.

MEGALITHIC MONUMENTS, large,

usually undressed stone monuments found principally in Europe but also in many other parts of the world, believed to date usually from the late STONE AGE and early BRONZE AGE. They are of four main types: the menhir (from Breton *hir*, long, and *men*, stone) or single standing stone; the stone circle, or circles, as exemplified by STONEHENGE; the chamber or room, usually associated with a tomb, the most ancient of which is the dolmen; and the alignment, or row of stones, such as those at Carnac, France.

MEGIDDO, ancient fortified city 15mi S of Haifa, Israel, overlooking the plain of Esdraelon. Excavations have shown that it was inhabited c4000–450 BC. The city was the scene of many battles: the eschatological ARMAGEDDON was named for it.

MEHMET ALI (or Mohammed Ali; c1769–1849), an Albanian soldier who in 1806 became pasha (governor) of the Turkish province of Egypt and founder of the dynasty which ruled until 1952. He extended Egypt's borders and improved the economy. His power rivaled that of his overlord, the Sultan of Turkey.

MEHTA, Zubin (1936–), Indian-born conductor who studied at the Vienna Academy of Music and later acted as musical director of the Montreal Symphony (1961–67), Los Angeles Philharmonic (1962–78), and New York Philharmonic (from 1978).

MEIJI (1852–1912), emperor of Japan (1867–1912). At the start of his reign, the TOKUGAWA shogunate (see SHOGUN) came to an end, and power was nominally restored to the emperor (the so-called Meiji Restoration). In fact, the emperor was only a national symbol. Power was wielded by his advisers—the elder statesmen, or *genro*—who selected premiers responsible to the emperor rather than to the legislature (the diet). Under this narrow, authoritarian government, Japan was quickly transformed into a modern industrial state and, by the time of Meiji's death, was a world power.

MEINECKE, Friedrich (1862–1954), German historian, a nationalist and liberal. The experience of WWI and WWII caused him to reappraise his earlier approval of a powerful state as the embodiment of German cultural values.

MEIR, Golda (1898–1978), Israeli leader, prime minister of Israel 1969–74. Born Golda Mabovitch in Kiev, USSR, she was raised in the US and emigrated to Palestine in 1921. She was a prominent figure in the establishment of the State of Israel (1948). Elected to the Knesset (parliament) in 1949, she became foreign minister in 1956

and in 1966 was elected general secretary of the dominant Mapai party, later the Israel Labor Party (1968). In 1969 she succeeded Levi Eshkol as premier and formed a broad coalition government. During her time in office the Israelis fought off a Syrian-Egyptian surprise attack, called the Yom Kippur War (1973). In 1974 Mrs. Meir resigned.

MEISTERSINGER, a coveted title taken by poets and singers belonging to certain 15th-century German guilds who had perfected their art in accordance with an elaborate set of rules and traditions. WAGNER's opera *Die Meistersinger von Nürnberg* touches on the lives of these artists.

MEKONG RIVER, one of the chief rivers of SE Asia. Rising in the Tibetan highlands, it flows 2,600mi southward through the Yunnan province of China and Laos, along the Thailand border and through Kampuchea to its wide fertile delta in S Vietnam, on the South China Sea. The lower 340mi can accommodate medium-sized vessels and PHNOM-PENH is an important port.

MELANCHTHON, Philipp (1497–1560), German scholar and humanist, second to LUTHER in initiating and leading the Protestant REFORMATION in Germany. His *Loci communes* (1521), a systematic statement of Lutheran beliefs, was the first great Protestant work on religious doctrine; and his *Augsburg Confession* (1530) was one of the principal statements of faith in the Lutheran Church.

MELANESIA, one of three main ethnographic divisions of the Pacific islands, the other two being MICRONESIA and POLYNESIA. (See also OCEANIA.)

MELANIN, black pigment which lies in various SKIN layers and is responsible for skin color, including the racial variation. It is concentrated in MOLES and freckles. The distribution in the skin determines skin coloring and is altered by light and certain HORMONES.

MELBA, Dame Nellie (1861–1931), Australian soprano, born Helen Porter Mitchell. For almost 40 years (1887–1926) hers was one of the most celebrated coloratura voices on the operatic stage. She made her debut as Gilda in Verdi's *Rigoletto* in Brussels in 1887.

MELBOURNE, William Lamb, 2nd Viscount (1779–1848), British statesman. A member of the House of Commons from 1806, he served as chief secretary to Ireland 1827–1828, entered the House of Lords (1829) and as home secretary (1830–34) suppressed agrarian unrest. He became prime minister briefly in 1834 and again

1835–41, when he instructed the young Queen Victoria in her duties.

MELBOURNE, second largest city in Australia and state capital of Victoria, on the Yarra R. Founded by settlers in 1835, the city is now one of the nation's chief ports and ranks with Sydney as a major industrial center. Manufactures include textiles, leather goods and aircraft, and oil refineries have been built. Pop (metro) 2,864,600.

MELCHIOR, Lauritz (1890–1973), Danish opera singer, at New York's Metropolitan Opera 1926–50, the most prominent Wagnerian tenor of his time.

MELLON, Andrew William (1855–1937), US financier and industrialist who was an outstandingly able US treasury secretary (1921–31). He served under three presidents, and reduced the national debt by some $9 billion. He was US ambassador to Britain (1932–33). A multimillionaire himself, he founded the Mellon Institute of Industrial Research. His vast art collection formed the basis of the NATIONAL GALLERY OF ART.

MELVILLE, Herman (1819–1891), one of the greatest of US writers. His world reputation rests mainly on the masterpiece, *Moby Dick* (1851), and the short novel *Billy Budd*, published posthumously (1924). His whaling and other voyages provided material for several of his earlier, very popular books. *Typee* (1846), his first, was based on his adventures after jumping ship in the Marquesas Islands. *Moby Dick* is a deeply symbolic work, combining allegory with adventure. Too profound and complex for its audience, the novel was not successful and subsequent books did not recapture his former popularity. It was not until the 1930s that his talent was fully recognized.

MEMBRANES, layers that form part of the surface of CELLS and which enclose organelles within the cells of all animals and plants. The membranes of the cell wall function to allow some substances into the cell, to exclude others, and actively to transport others into the cell even though the direction of movement may be against existing concentration gradients. Membranes are composed of layers of lipid or FAT molecules which sandwich a layer of PROTEIN molecules. The protein layer is double but appears as a single layer when viewed under the ELECTRON MICROSCOPE. Thus most membranes appear to be triple-layered, although some appear to be composed of a single layer. Triple-layered membranes are normally 5–10mm thick.

MEMLING, Hans (c1430–1494), Flemish painter famous for his portraits and religious works, among which the paneled *Shrine of St. Ursula* (c1489) is one of the most famous. He worked in Bruges, Belgium, and was probably a pupil of Rogier van der WEYDEN.

MEMORIAL DAY, or Decoration Day, a US holiday, honoring the dead of all wars, observed on the last Monday in May. Traditionally, Memorial Day originated in the South after the Civil War when the graves of both Confederate and Union soldiers were decorated.

MEMORY, the sum of the mental processes that result in the modification of an individual's behavior in the light of previous experience. There are several different types of memory. In rote memory, one of the least efficient ways of storing information, data is learned by rote and repeated verbatim. Logical memory is far more efficient: only the salient data are stored, and each may be used in its original or in a different context. Mnemonics, which assist rote memory, superimpose what is in effect an artificial logical structure on not necessarily related data. Testing of the efficiency of memory may be by recall (e.g., remembering a string of unrelated syllables); recognition (as in a multiple-choice test, where the candidate recognizes the correct answer among alternatives); and relearning, in which comparison is made between the time taken by an individual to commit certain data to memory, and the time taken to recommit it to memory after a delay. Though recent studies of certain COMPUTER functions have thrown light on some of the workings of memory (see also CYBERNETICS), little is known of its exact physiological basis. It appears, however, that chemical changes in the brain, particularly in the composition of RNA (see NUCLEIC ACIDS), alter the electrical pathways there. Moreover, it seems that some form of initial learning takes place in the NERVOUS SYSTEM before data are stored permanently in the BRAIN. (See also ELECTROENCEPHALOGRAPH; INTELLIGENCE; LEARNING.)

MEMPHIS, capital of the Old Kingdom of ancient Egypt until c2200 BC. Probably founded by Menes, the first king of a united Upper and Lower Egypt, c3100 BC, the city stood on the W bank of the Nile some 15mi S of modern Cairo. Excavations have revealed the temple of Ptah, god of the city, and the two massive statues of RAMSES II.

MENANDER (c342–c291 BC), leading Greek writer of New Comedy. Out of over 100 plays, only *Dyscolos* (The Grouch) survives complete, though there are adaptations by PLAUTUS and TERENCE. His plots are based on love-affairs and he's noted for his elegant style and deft characterization.

MENCIUS (c370–c290 BC), Chinese philosopher, a follower of CONFUCIUS. He held that man is naturally good and that the principles of true moral conduct are inborn. He was a champion of the ordinary people and exhorted rulers to treat their subjects well.

MENCKEN, Henry Louis (1880–1956), US journalist and author, caustic critic of American society and literature. He wrote for the Baltimore *Sun* and founded and edited the *American Mercury* (1924). His collected essays appeared in *Prejudices* (1919–27), and he wrote an authoritative study, *The American Language* (1919).

MENDEL, Gregor Johann (1822–1884), Austrian botanist and Augustinian monk who laid the foundations of the science of GENETICS. He found that self-pollinated dwarf pea plants bred true, but that under the same circumstances only about a third of tall pea plants did so, the remainder producing tall or dwarf pea plants in a ratio about 3:1. Next he crossbred tall and dwarf plants and found this without exception resulted in a tall plant, but one that did not breed true. Thus, in this plant, both tall and dwarf characteristics were present. He had found a mechanism justifying DARWIN's theory of EVOLUTION by NATURAL SELECTION; but contemporary lack of interest and his later, unsuccessful experiments with the hawkweeds discouraged him from carrying this further. It was not until 1900, when H. de Vries and others found his published results, that the importance of his work was realized. (See also HEREDITY; POLLINATION.)

MENDELEYEV, Dmitri Ivanovich (1834–1907), Russian chemist who formulated the Periodic Law, that the properties of elements vary periodically with increasing atomic weight, and so drew up the PERIODIC TABLE (1869).

MENDELSOHN, Erich (1887–1953), German-born expressionist architect, who designed "sculptured" and functional buildings, notably the Einstein Tower, Potsdam (1921). He worked in England 1933–37, Palestine 1937–41 and the US, where he was naturalized.

MENDELSSOHN, Felix (1809–1847), German Romantic composer. He wrote his concert overture to *A Midsummer Night's Dream* when only 17. Other works include his *Hebrides Overture* (also known as "Fingal's Cave"), *Scottish* (1830–42) and *Italian* (1833) symphonies, a violin concerto, chamber music and the oratorio *Elijah*. He was also a celebrated conductor, notably of the Leipzig Gewandhaus orchestra, and revived interest in BACH's music.

MENDELSSOHN, Moses (1729–1786), Jewish philosopher, a leading figure of the Enlightenment in Prussia and a promoter of Jewish assimilation into German culture. He was the model for the hero of LESSING's play *Nathan the Wise*, and a grandfather of the famous composer.

MENDÈS-FRANCE, Pierre (1907–1982), French political leader. As center-left prime minister (1954–55), he ended France's war in Indochina and kept France out of a projected European Defense Community. He granted Tunisia internal self-government, but was defeated over his liberal Algerian policy.

MENDOZA, Antonio de (1490?–1552), Spanish colonial administrator, first viceroy of New Spain (Mexico) (1535–50) and viceroy of Peru (1551–52). He brought order and good government to Mexico after the Spanish conquest, encouraging religion, education, and economic development, and directing exploration northward.

MENELIK II (1844–1913), emperor of Ethiopia from 1889, founder of the modern Ethiopian nation. He unified Ethiopia and doubled its territory, crushed invading Italian forces at Adwa (1896) and instituted reforms and modernization.

MENÉNDEZ DE AVILÉS, Pedro (1519–1574), Spanish adventurer and conquistador who founded St. Augustine, Fla., oldest city in the US. Authorized by Philip II of Spain to start a Spanish colony in Florida and end French HUGUENOT influence there, in 1565 he built a fort on St. Augustine Bay and destroyed the rival French colony, Fort Caroline.

MENES (flourished c3100 BC), traditional name of the founder of the 1st dynasty in ancient Egypt. He is identified by some modern scholars with King Narmer, and is said to have united N and S Egypt and to have founded the city of Memphis.

MENGELE, Josef (1911–1979), German war criminal, chief physician (1943–44) at Auschwitz concentration camp, where he selected 400,000 persons for death and conducted grotesque experiments. After WWII he escaped to South America, living in Argentina and Paraguay. In 1985 an international team of forensic scientists identified the body of a man who had drowned at a Brazilian beach in 1979 as that of Mengele.

MENGISTU HAILE MARIAM (1937–), Ethiopian political leader. Head of the Marxist military junta that overthrew Emperor Haile Selassie in 1974, he imposed a one-party Soviet-model dictatorship on Ethiopia. With financial and military aid from the USSR, he continued military campaigns against Eritrean and Somali separatists, and was accused of obstructing famine relief to disaffected areas.

MÉNIÈRE'S DISEASE, disorder of the cochlea and labyrinth of the EAR, causing brief acute episodes of vertigo, with nausea or vomiting, ringing in the ears and DEAFNESS. Ultimately permanent deafness ensues and vertigo lessens. It is a disorder of inner-ear fluids and each episode causes some destruction of receptor cells. Drugs can reduce the vertigo.

MENINGITIS, INFLAMMATION of the meninges (see BRAIN) caused by BACTERIA (e.g., meningococcus, pneumococcus, hemophilus) or VIRUSES. **Bacterial meningitis** is of abrupt onset with HEADACHE, vomiting, FEVER. neck stiffness and avoidance of light. Early and appropriate ANTIBIOTIC treatment is essential as permanent damage may occur in some cases, especially in children. **Viral meningitis** is a milder illness with similar signs in a less ill person; symptomatic measures only are required. **Tuberculous meningitis** is an insidious chronic type which responds slowly to antituberculous drugs. Some FUNGI, unusual bacteria and syphilis (see VENEREAL DISEASES) may also cause varieties of meningitis.

MENNIN, Peter (1923–1983), US composer whose distinctive works are characterized by dissonant harmonies and lively rhythms. He served as president of Baltimore's Peabody Conservatory of Music and of New York City's Juilliard School of Music.

MENNINGER, Karl Augustus (1893–), US psychiatrist who, with his brother **William Claire Menninger** (1899–1966) and father **Charles Frederick Menninger** (1862–1953), set up the Menninger Foundation (1941), a nonprofit organization dedicated to the furtherance of psychiatric research in Topeka, Kan.

MENNONITES, Protestant sect originating among the ANABAPTISTS of Zurich, Switzerland. They became influential, particularly in the Netherlands, and are named for the Dutch reformer Menno SIMONS. They base their faith solely on the Bible, believe in separation of Church and State, pacifism, and baptism only for adults renouncing sin. Despite persecution, the sect spread and now totals about 550,000 with some 89,000 members in Canada and 20,000 in the US. They are known for the strict simplicity of their life and worship. (See also AMISH: HUTTERITES.)

MENOMINEE INDIANS, North American Indian tribe of the Algonquian linguistic group. Most lived in upper Mich. and Wis., along the W shore of Green Bay, gathering wild rice (*Menominee* means "wild rice people"). In 1854 they were settled on a reservation on the Wolf and Oconto rivers in Wis., now a county, where their descendants (about 4,000) still live.

MENON, (Vengalil Krishnan) Krishna (1897–1974), Indian diplomat and politician. As Indian ambassador to the United Nations (1953–62), he criticized the US and defended Indian neutrality between the superpowers. He was defense minister (1957–62) but was forced to resign after India's defeat in the 1962 war with China.

MENOPAUSE. See MENSTRUATION.

MENOTTI, Gian Carlo (1911–), Italian-born US composer of dramatically powerful operas with his own librettos, and founder (1958) of the Two Worlds festival at Spoleto, Italy. His works include *The Medium* (1946) and the television opera *Amahl and the Night Visitors* (1951). *The Consul* (1950) and *The Saint of Bleecker Street* (1954) won Pulitzer prizes.

MENSHEVIKS, minority group in the Russian Social Democratic Workers' Party, opposed to the Bolsheviks, the majority group led by LENIN (see BOLSHEVISM). Unlike Lenin, the Menshevik theoretician Georgi Plekhanov favored mass membership and thought a spell of bourgeois rule must precede communism. Led by L. Martov, the Mensheviks emerged in 1903, backed KERENSKY's government and opposed the Bolshevik seizure of power. By 1921 they had been eliminated.

MENSTRUATION, specifically the monthly loss of BLOOD (period), representing shedding of WOMB endometrium, in women of reproductive age; in general, the whole monthly cycle of hormonal, structural and functional changes in such women, punctuated by menstrual blood loss. After each period, the womb-lining endometrium starts to proliferate and thicken under the influence of gonadotrophins (follicle stimulating hormone) and ESTROGENS. In midcycle a burst of luteinizing hormone secretion, initiated by the HYPOTHALAMUS, causes release of an egg from an ovarian follicle (*ovulation*). More PROGESTERONE is then secreted, and the endometrium is prepared for implantation of a fertilized egg. If the egg is not fertilized, PREGNANCY does not ensue and blood-vessel changes occur leading to the shedding of the endometrium and some blood; these are lost through the vagina for several days, sometimes with pain or colic. The cycle then restarts. During the menstrual cycle, changes in the BREASTS, body temperature, fluid balance and mood occur, the manifestations varying from person to person. Cyclic patterns are established at PUBERTY (*menarche*) and end in middle life (age 45–50) at the *menopause*, the "change of life." Disorders of menstruation include heavy, irregular or missed periods; bleeding between periods or after the menopause, and excessively painful periods. They are studied in GYNECOLOGY.

MENSURATION, the branch of GEOMETRY dealing with the measurement of length, area and volume. The base of all such measurements is length, since the areas and volumes of geometric figures can be calculated from suitable length measurements. The area of a rectangle is bh, where b is the length of one side (the base) and h that of the other (the height). It is easy to show that this formula holds also for the parallelogram, if h stands for the altitude (the perpendicular distance from one side to that facing it) rather than for the height; from this can be found the formula for the area of a triangle (which can be thought of as half a parallelogram), $\frac{1}{2}bh$, and those for other polygons.

The area and circumference of a circle, which can be considered as a regular polygon with an infinite number of infinitely small sides, are πr^2 and $2\pi r$ respectively, where π is a constant (see PI) and r is the radius. The area of an ellipse is given by πab where a is the semi-major and b the semi-minor axis; the circumference of an ellipse cannot be expressed in algebraic terms.

From this information, it is fairly easy to determine formulas for the volumes of regular solids, such as the polyhedron, cone, cylinder, ellipsoid, pyramid and sphere. The areas of irregular plane shapes can be approximated by considering a large number of extremely small strips, each being almost trapezoidal, formed in them by the construction of a large number of parallel chords; the same principle can be applied to finding the approximate volumes of irregular solids: this process is akin to integral CALCULUS.

MENTAL ILLNESS, or **psychiatric disorders**, is characterized by abnormal functioning of the higher centers of the BRAIN responsible for thought, perception, mood and behavior. Although some mental disorders are organically based (e.g. Korsakov's psychosis), others, such as NEUROSES and most SCHIZOPHRENIAS, are considered to be functional or learned. The borderline between disease and the range of normal variability is indistinct and may be determined by cultural factors. Crime may result from mental disease, but modern Western society is careful to consider it as a possible cause before subjecting a criminal to justice. However, in certain repressive regimes, political or ideological nonconformity can be grounds for admission to a mental hospital. Mental disease has been recognized since ancient times, and both HIPPOCRATES and GALEN evolved theories as to its origins; but in many cultures, over the centuries, madness has been equated with possession by evil spirits, and sufferers were often treated as witches. In the 15th century, PARACELSUS proposed that the moon determined the behavior of mad people (hence "lunacy"), while in the 18th century MESMER favored the role of animal magnetism (from which HYPNOSIS is derived). The first humane *asylum* for the mentally ill was founded in Paris by Philippe Pinel (1795). Originally only socially intolerable cases were admitted to such hospitals, but today voluntary admission is more common. The *Viennese school* of psychology, in particular Sigmund FREUD and his pupils, emphasized the importance of past (especially childhood) experiences, sexual attitudes and other functional factors. PSYCHOANALYSIS and many modern psychotherapies derive from this school. On the other hand, the influence of subtle organic factors (e.g., brain biochemistry) was favored by others; this led to using LOBOTOMY, SHOCK THERAPY and DRUGS.

Mental illness may be classified into PSYCHOSIS, neurosis and personality disorder. **Schizophrenia** is a psychosis causing disturbance of thought and perception in which mood is characteristically flat and behavior withdrawn. Features include: auditory hallucinations; delusions of identity ("I'm the King of Spain"), of surroundings, and about other people (e.g., suspicion of conspiracy in PARANOIA); blocking, insertion and broadcasting of thought, and knight's-move thinking, or nonlogical sequence of ideas. Conversation lacks substance and may be in riddles and neologisms; speech or behavior may be imitative, stereotyped, repetitive or negative. Phenothiazine drugs, especially chlorpromazine and long-acting analogues, are particularly valuable in schizophrenia.

In **affective psychoses**, disturbance of mood is the primary disorder. Subjects usually exhibit DEPRESSION with loss of drive and inconsolably low mood, either in response to situation (exogenous) or for no apparent reason (endogenous). Loss of appetite, CONSTIPATION and characteristic sleep disturbance also commonly occur. ANTIDEPRESSANTS and shock therapy are valuable, but psychotherapy may also be needed. In hypnomania or mania, excitability, restlessness, euphoria, ceaseless talk, flight of ideas and loss of social inhibitions occur. Financial, sexual and alcohol excesses may result. Chlorpromazine, haloperidol and lithium are effective. Neuroses include anxiety, the pathological exaggeration of a physiological response, which may coexist with depression but responds to benzodiazepines (Valium) and psychotherapy; obsessional and compulsive neuroses, manifested by extreme habits, rituals and fixations (which may be recognized as irrational); PHOBIAS, excessive and inappropriate fears of objects or situations; and HYSTERIA, the last two of which are helped by behavior therapy. Psychopathy is a specific disorder of personality characterized by failure to learn from experience. Irresponsibility, inconsiderateness and lack of foresight result, and may lead to crime. Other personality disorders are exhibited by a variety of people, often with unstable backgrounds, who seem unable to cope with the realities of everyday adult life; attempted suicide is a common gesture. In sexual disorders with antisocial or perverse sexual fixations, behavior therapy may be of value. (See also ALCOHOLISM; ANOREXIA NERVOSA; DRUG ADDICTION.)

MENTALLY   ILL.   See DEINSTITUTIONALIZATION.

MENTAL RETARDATION, low intellectual capacity arising, not from MENTAL ILLNESS, but from impairment of the normal development of the BRAIN and NERVOUS SYSTEM. Causes include genetic defect (as in DOWN'S SYNDROME); infection of the EMBRYO or FETUS; HYDROCEPHALUS or inherited metabolic defects (e.g., CRETINISM), and injury at BIRTH including cerebral HEMORRHAGE and fetal anoxia. Disease in infancy such as ENCEPHALITIS may cause mental retardation in children with previous normal development. Retardation is initially recognized by slowness to develop normal patterns of social and learning behavior and is confirmed through intelligence measurements. It is most important that affected children should receive adequate social contact and education, for their development is retarded and not arrested. In particular, special schooling may help them to achieve a degree of learning and social competence.

MENUHIN, Sir Yehudi (1916–   ), US violinist and conductor. He made his concert debut at seven, played to Allied forces in WWII, and later to raise cash for war victims. He has revived forgotten masterpieces, aroused interest in Eastern music and directed festivals. In 1963 he opened a school for musically gifted children in England.

MENZIES, Sir Robert Gordon (1894–1978), Australian prime minister 1939–41, 1949– 66. He was attorney general 1935–39 and leader of the opposition 1943–48. As leader of the Liberal-Country Party coalition 1949–66, he pursued a conservative anti-communist policy and encouraged rapid industrial growth.

MEPHISTOPHELES, in medieval legend, the devil to whom Faust sold his soul. He is primarily a literary creation, and appears in the famous plays by MARLOWE and GOETHE.

MERCANTILISM, in economic history, theories prevailing in 16th- to 18th-century W Europe, reflecting the increased importance of the merchant. Mercantilists favored TARIFFS to secure a favorable INTERNATIONAL TRADE balance and maintain reserves of precious metals, considered essential to a nation's wealth. Their PROTECTIONISM was succeeded by the FREE TRADE arguments of the French PHYSIOCRATS.

MERCATOR, Gerardus (1512–1594), Flemish cartographer and calligrapher, best known for Mercator's Projection (see also MAP), which he first used in 1569 for a world map. The PROJECTION is from a point at the center of the earth through the surface of the globe onto a cylinder that touches the earth around the equator.

MERCER, Johnny (1909–1976), US songwriter who wrote the lyrics for many popular hits, including "Moon River," "That Old Black Magic," and "Blues in the Night." He was also a composer and wrote the entire score for the musical *Top Banana* (1951).

MERCHANT MARINE ACADEMY, US, at Kings Point, N.Y., established 1936 (opened 1942) to train officers for the US merchant marine, coeducational since 1974. Enrollment in 1988 was 957.

MERCIA, kingdom of Anglo-Saxon England, settled by Angles c500. In the 8th century it dominated S England but thereafter was overshadowed by Wessex.

MERCURY (Hg), or **quicksilver,** silvery-white liquid metal in Group IIB of the PERIODIC TABLE; an anomalous transition element. It occurs as cinnabar, calomel and rarely as the metal, which has been known from ancient times. It is extracted by roasting cinnabar in air and condensing the mercury vapor. Mercury is fairly inert, tarnishing only slowly in moist air, and soluble in oxidizing acids only; it is readily attacked by the halogens and sulfur. It forms Hg^{2+} and some Hg_2^{2+} compounds, and many important organometallic compounds. Mercury and its compounds are highly toxic. The metal is used to form amalgams, for electrodes, and in barometers, thermometers, diffusion PUMPS and mercury-vapor lamps (see LIGHTING, ARTIFICIAL). Various mercury compounds are used as pharmaceuticals. AW 200.6, mp −39°C, bp 357°C, sg 13.546 (20°C). **Mercury (II) cyanate** (Hg[ONC]$_2$), or **mercury fulminate**, is a white crystalline solid, sensitive to percussion, and used as a detonator. **Mercury (II) chloride** (HgCl$_2$), or **corrosive sublimate**, is a colorless crystalline solid prepared by direct synthesis. Although highly toxic, it is used in dilute solution as an antiseptic, and also as a fungicide and a polymerization catalyst. mp 276°C, bp 302°C. **Mercury (I) chloride** (Hg$_2$Cl$_2$), or **calomel**, is a white rhombic crystalline solid, found in nature. It is used in ointments and formerly found use as a laxative. A calomel/mercury cell with potassium chloride electrolyte (the Weston cell) is used to provide a standard ELECTROMOTIVE FORCE. mp 303°C, bp 384°C.

MERCURY, the planet closest to the sun with a mean solar distance of 36 million mi. Its highly eccentric ORBIT brings it within 28.5 million mi of the sun at perihelion and takes it 43.5 million mi from the sun at aphelion. Its diameter is about 3,031 mi its mass about 0.054 that of the earth. It goes around the sun in just under 88 days and rotates on its axis in about 59 days. The successful prediction by Albert EINSTEIN that Mercury's orbit would be found to advance by 43in per century is usually regarded as a confirmation of the General Theory of RELATIVITY. Night surface temperature is thought to be about 110K, midday equatorial temperature over 600K. The airless planet's average density (5.2 gr per cc) indicates a high proportion of heavy elements in its interior. In 1974 and 1975, the US Mariner space probe revealed that Mercury has a moonlike heavily cratered surface, and a slight magnetic field.

MEREDITH, George (1828–1909), English novelist and poet. His best-known novel is the tragicomic *Ordeal of Richard Feverel* (1859). The sonnet sequence *Modern Love* (1862) grew out of the breakdown of his marriage. Other well-known works are *The Egoist* (1879) and *Diana of the Crossways* (1885).

MEREZHKOVSKI, Dmitri Sergeyevich

(1865–1941), influential Russian author and critic. A mystic, he saw life and literature as divided between seers of the flesh and of the spirit. An opponent of both tsarism and bolshevism, he emigrated after the Revolution.

MERIDIAN, on the celestial sphere, the great circle passing through the celestial poles and the observer's zenith. It cuts his horizon N and S. (See also CELESTIAL SPHERE.) The term is used also for a line of terrestrial longitude.

MÉRIMÉE, Prosper (1803–1870), French author, historian, archaeologist and linguist. He is best known for short stories such as *Mateo Falcone* (1829) and the romance *Carmen* (1847), source of BIZET's opera.

MERLEAU-PONTY, Maurice (1908–1961), French philosopher. A leading phenomenologist, he wrote *Phenomenology of Perception* (1945; tr. 1962) and co-edited the journal *Les Temps Modernes* (with Jean-Paul Sartre). He also wrote several controversial Marxist works on political philosophy, including *Humanism and Terror* (1947; tr. 1969).

MERMAN, Ethel (Ethel Zimmerman; 1909–1984), US musical comedy star in such Broadway hits as *Girl Crazy* (1930), *Anything Goes* (1934), *Annie Get Your Gun* (1946), *Call Me Madam* (1950), and *Gypsy* (1959).

MEROVINGIANS, dynasty of Frankish kings 428–751. They were named for the 5th-century king Merovech; his grandson CLOVIS I first united much of France. The kingdom was later partitioned, but enlarged and reunited (613) under Clotaire II. The Merovingians governed through the remnants of the old Roman administration and established Catholic Christianity. After Dagobert I in the 7th century the kings became known as *rois-fainéants* (do-nothings), and power passed to the mayors of the palace, nominally high officials; the last of these, Pepin the Short, deposed the last Merovingian, Childeric III.

MERRILL, James Ingram (1926–   ), US poet who won a Pulitzer Prize for *Divine Comedies* (1977) and National Book Awards for *Nights and Days* (1967) and *Mirabell* (1979).

MERRILL, Robert (Robert Miller; 1917–   ), US baritone, at New York's Metropolitan Opera 1945–73.

MERTON, Robert King (1910–   ), US sociologist, at Columbia U 1941–84. He did important work on social deviance and anomie, bureaucracy, and sociological theory, and pioneered in the sociology of science.

MERTON, Thomas (1915–1968), US religious writer of poetry, meditative works and the autobiography *The Seven Storey Mountain* (1948). Converted to Roman Catholicism, he became a Trappist monk (1941) and later a priest.

MESABI RANGE, hills in NE Minn., NW of Lake Superior from Babbitt to Grand Rapids; highest point is 2,000ft. The range is famous for its iron ore deposits, lying near the surface. They have been mined since the 1890s.

MESA VERDE NATIONAL PARK, area of 52,074 acres in SW Col., established in 1906. It contains extensive pueblo ruins built by the cliff dwellers over 1,300 years ago, and much distinctive wildlife.

MESCALINE, HALLUCINOGENIC DRUG, derived from a Mexican cactus, whose use dates back to ancient times when "peyote buttons" were used in religious ceremonies among American Indians. The hallucinations experienced during its use were among the first to be described (by Aldous HUXLEY) and resemble those of LSD.

MESMER, Franz Anton (1734–1815), German physician, controversy over whose unusual techniques and theories sparked in CHARCOT and others an interest in the possibilities of using "animal magnetism" (or mesmerism, i.e., HYPNOSIS) for psychotherapy.

MESOLITHIC AGE. See STONE AGE.

MESOPOTAMIA (Greek: between the rivers), ancient region between the Tigris and Euphrates rivers in SW Asia, home of many early civilizations. (See also FERTILE CRESCENT.) Most of it lies in Iraq, between the Armenian and Kurdish Mts in the N and the Persian Gulf in the S; the N is mainly grassy, rolling plateau; the S is a sandy plain leading to marshes. Since ancient times the rivers have been used to irrigate the area, most notably under ABBASID rule (749–1258 AD), but the ancient systems degenerated under Mongol invasion and OTTOMAN rule, and were not replaced until the 20th century. Neolithic farming peoples were settling Mesopotamia by 6000 BC, followed by the Tell Halaf and al'Ubaid cultures after 4000 BC. By 3000 BC the SUMERIANS had created a civilization of independent city-states in the S. From c3000–625 BC Mesopotamia was successively dominated by Sumer, AKKAD, the SUMERIAN dynasty of UR, the empires of BABYLONIA AND ASSYRIA and CHALDEA. In 539 BC the Persian Empire absorbed Mesopotamia; in 331 BC it was conquered by Alexander the Great. It then came under Roman, Byzantine and Arab rule. The Abbasid caliphs made BAGHDAD their

capital in 762 AD, but prosperity collapsed with the Mongol invasion of 1289. Mesopotamia was under Ottoman rule 1638–1918, when it was largely incorporated into IRAQ.

MESOSPHERE, the layer of the ATMOSPHERE immediately above the stratosphere, marked by a temperature maximum (about 10°C) between altitudes of about 30mi and 50mi.

MESOZOIC, geologic era between the PALEOZOIC and the CENOZOIC, extending from about 225 million years ago to 65 million. It is divided into the TRIASSIC, JURASSIC, and CRETACEOUS periods. Reptiles, including dinosaurs, dominated animal life, conifers plant life.

MESSERSCHMITT, Wilhelm "Willy" (1898–1978), German pioneer aircraft designer famous for his fast monoplane fighters used in WWII. They included the Me-109 (1934) and the Me-262, the first jet plane used in war (1944).

MESSIAEN, Olivier Eugène Prosper Charles (1908–   ), influential French composer and organist. His music is extremely personal, such works as *The Ascension* (1955) being influenced by Roman Catholic mysticism. Others such as the *Turangalila* symphony (1949) are based on oriental music, or birdsong as in the *Catalog of Birds* (1959).

MESSIAH (Hebrew: anointed one), according to Israelite prophets, especially ISAIAH, the ruler whom God would send to restore Israel and begin a glorious age of peace and righteousness (see ESCHATOLOGY). He would be a descendant of King DAVID. Christians recognize Jesus of Nazareth as the Messiah (or CHRIST); his role as "suffering servant" was alien to Jewish hopes of a political deliverer. The concept of a forthcoming divine redeemer is common to many religions.

MESSINA, Strait of, 20mi long and 2–10mi wide, channel separating Sicily from Italy. It contains dangerous rocks and whirlpools which in classical times gave rise to myth of SCYLLA AND CHARYBDIS.

MESTIZO (Spanish: mixture), person of mixed racial ancestry, especially one of mixed Spanish and Amerind parentage. Mestizos form a large percentage of the population in many Latin American countries.

MESTROVIĆ, Ivan (1883–1962), Yugoslav-born US sculptor. He studied at Vienna and Rome, and was influenced by classical Greek styles and RODIN. Professor of fine arts at Notre Dame U. from 1955, he executed mainly religious subjects and portraits.

METABOLISM, the sum total of all chemical reactions that occur in a living organism. It can be subdivided into **anabolism,** which describes reactions that build up more complex substances from smaller ones, and **catabolism,** which describes reactions that break down complex substances into simpler ones. Anabolic reactions require ENERGY, while catabolic reactions liberate energy. Metabolic reactions are catalyzed by ENZYMES in a highly integrated and finely controlled manner so that there is no overproduction or underutilization of the energy required to maintain life. All energy required to maintain life is ultimately derived from sunlight by PHOTOSYNTHESIS, and most organisms use the products of photosynthesis either directly or indirectly. The energy is stored in most living organisms in a specific chemical compound, adenosine triphosphate (ATP). ATP can transfer its energy to other molecules by a loss of phosphate, later regaining phosphate from catabolic reactions. (See also BASAL METABOLIC RATE.)

METAL, an element with high specific gravity; high opacity and reflectivity to light (giving a characteristic luster when polished); that can be hammered into thin sheets and drawn into wires (i.e., is malleable and ductile), and is a good conductor of heat and electricity, its electrical conductivity decreasing with temperature. Roughly 75% of the chemical elements are metals, but not all of them possess all the typical metallic properties. Most are found as ores and in the pure state are crystalline solids (mercury, liquid at room temperature, being a notable exception), their atoms readily losing electrons to become positive IONS. ALLOYS are easily formed because of the nonspecific nondirectional nature of the metallic bond.

METALLURGY, the science and technology of METALS, concerned with their extraction from ores, the methods of refining, purifying and preparing them for use and the study of the structure and physical properties of metals and ALLOYS. A few unreactive metals such as silver and gold are found native (uncombined), but most metals occur naturally as MINERALS (i.e., in chemical combination with nonmetallic elements). Ores are mixtures of minerals from which metal extraction is commercially viable. Over 5,000 years man has developed techniques for working ores and forming alloys, but only in the last two centuries have these methods been based on scientific theory. The production of metals from ores is known as process or extraction metallurgy; fabrication metallurgy concerns the conversion of raw metals into alloys, sheets, wires etc., while physical metallurgy covers the structure and properties of metals and alloys, including their mechanical working, heat treatment and testing. Process metallurgy begins with ore dressing, using physical methods such as crushing, grinding and gravity separation to split up the different minerals in an ore. The next stage involves chemical action to separate the metallic component of the mineral from the unwanted nonmetallic part. The actual method used depends on the chemical nature of the mineral compound (e.g., if it is an oxide or sulfide, its solubility in acids etc.) and its physical properties. Hydrometallurgy uses chemical reactions in aqueous solutions to extract metal from ore. Electrometallurgy uses electricity for firing a furnace or electrolytically reducing a metallic compound to a metal. Pyrometallurgy covers roasting, SMELTING and other high-temperature chemical reactions. It has the advantage of involving fast reactions and giving a molten or gaseous product which can easily be separated out. The extracted metal may need further refining or purifying: electrometallurgy and pyrometallurgy are again used at this stage. Molten metal may then simply be cast by pouring into a mold, giving, e.g., pig iron, or it may be formed into ingots which are then hot or cold worked, as with, e.g., wrought iron. Mechanical working, in the form of rolling, pressing or FORGING, improves the final structure and properties of most metals; it tends to break down and redistribute the impurities formed when a large mass of molten metal solidifies. Simple heat treatment such as ANNEALING also tends to remove some of the inherent brittleness of cast metals. (See also BLAST FURNACE; STEEL.)

METAMORPHIC ROCKS, one of the three main classes of rocks of the earth's crust. They consist of rocks that have undergone change owing to heat, pressure or chemical action. In plate tectonic theory, the collision of lithospheric plates leads to widespread *regional metamorphism.* Igneous intrusion leads to changes in the rocks close to the borders or contacts of the cooling magma, and these changes, largely due to the application of heat, constitute *contact (thermal) metamorphism.* Common metamorphic rock types include marble, quartzite, slate, schist and gneiss. Some occurrences of granite are also thought to be of metamorphic origin.

METAMORPHOSIS, in animals (notably

FROGS, TOADS and INSECTS), a marked and relatively rapid change in body form. This alteration in appearance is associated with a change in habits. Perhaps the best known example is the change which occurs when a tadpole becomes a frog.

METAPHYSICAL POETS, early 17th-century English lyric poets characterized by an involved style relying on the metaphysical *conceit*, an elaborate metaphorical image. Most famous among them is John DONNE; others include Andrew MARVELL, George HERBERT, Richard CRASHAW, Henry VAUGHAN and Thomas CAREW. The Metaphysicals (a term first used by Samuel JOHNSON) extended the range of lyric poetry by writing about death, decay, immortality and faith. They declined in popularity after about 1660, but their complex intellectual content and rich exploration of feeling have made them a major influence on 20th century poetry.

METAPHYSICS, the branch of philosophy concerned with the fundamentals of existence or reality, such as the existence and nature of God, the immortality of the soul, the meaning of evil, the problem of freedom and determinism, and the relationship of mind and body. Metaphysical thinking was criticized by KANT, who claimed that traditional metaphysics sought to go beyond the limits of human knowledge.

METASTASIO, Pietro (born Pietro Antonio Domenico Bonaventura Trapassi; 1698–1782), Italian poet and dramatist. He is best known for his melodramas used as opera librettos, including *Artaxerxes* and *La Clemenza di Tito*.

METAXAS, Ioannis (1871–1941), Greek general and from 1936 ultra-royalist premier and dictator of Greece. He made important social and economic reforms. He tried to maintain Greek neutrality in WWII, but after successfully resisting the Italian invasion in 1940 joined the Allied powers.

METEOR, the visible passage of a meteoroid (a small particle of interplanetary matter) into the earth's atmosphere. Due to friction it burns up, showing a trail of fire in the night sky. The velocity on entry lies in the range 7-45mi/sec.

Meteoroids are believed to consist of asteroidal and cometary debris. Although stray meteoroids reach our atmosphere throughout the year, for short periods at certain times of year they arrive in profuse numbers, sharing a common direction and velocity. It was shown in 1866 by G. V. Schiaparelli that the annual Perseid meteor shower was caused by meteoroids orbiting the sun in the same orbit as a comet observed some years before; moreover, since their period of orbit is unrelated to that of the earth, the meteoroids must form a fairly uniform "ring" around the sun for the shower to be annual. Other comet-shower relationships have been shown, implying that these streams of meteoroids are cometary debris.

Meteors may be seen by a nighttime observer on average five times per hour: these are known as sporadic meteors or shooting stars. Around 20 times a year, however, a meteor shower occurs and between 20 and 35,000 meteors per hour may be observed. These annual showers are generally named for the constellations from which they appear to emanate: e.g., Perseids (Perseus), Leonids (Leo). Large meteors are called fireballs, and those that explode are known as bolides.

Meteorites are larger than meteoroids, and are of special interest in that, should they enter the atmosphere, they at least partially survive the passage to the ground. Many have been examined. They fall into two main categories: "stones," whose composition is not unlike that of the earth's crust; and "irons," which contain about 80%–95% iron, 2–5% nickel and traces of other elements. Intermediate types exist. Irons display a usually crystalline structure which implies that they were initially liquid, cooling over long periods of time. Sometimes large meteorites shatter on impact, producing large craters like those in Arizona and Siberia.

METEOROLOGY, the study of the ATMOSPHERE and its phenomena, weather and climate. Based on atmospheric physics, it is primarily an observational science, whose main application is weather forecasting and control. The rain gauge and WIND vane were known in ancient times, and the other basic instruments— ANEMOMETER, BAROMETER, HYGROMETER and thermometer— had all been invented by 1790. Thus accurate data could be collected; but simultaneous observations over a wide area were impracticable until the development of the telegraph. Since WWI observations of the upper atmosphere have been made, using airplanes, balloons, radiosonde, and since WWII (when meteorology began to flourish) ROCKETS and artificial SATELLITES. RADAR has been much used. Observed phenomena include CLOUDS, precipitation and HUMIDITY, WIND and air pressure, air temperature, storms, CYCLONES, air masses and fronts.

METER (m), the SI base unit of length, defined as the length equal to 1,650,763.73

times the wavelength of radiation corresponding to the transition between the energy levels $2p_{10}$ and $5d_5$ of the krypton-86 atom (see SI UNITS). It was originally intended that the meter represent one ten millionth of the distance from the N Pole to the equator on the MERIDIAN passing through Paris. But the surveyors got their sums wrong, and for 162 years (to 1960) the meter was defined as an arbitrary distance marked on a metal bar (from 1889–1960, the "international prototype meter," a bar of platinum-iridium which is still kept under controlled conditions near Paris).

METHANE (CH_4), colorless, odorless gas; the simplest alkane (see HYDROCARBONS). It is produced by decomposing organic matter in sewage and in marshes (hence the name *marsh gas*), and is the "firedamp" of coal mines. It is the chief constituent of NATURAL GAS, occurs in coal gas and water gas, and is produced in PETROLEUM refining. Methane is used as a FUEL, for making carbon-black, and for chemical synthesis. MW 16.0, mp $-183°C$, bp $-164°C$.

METHODISTS, members of Protestant churches that originated in the 18th-century evangelical revival led by John and Charles WESLEY. The name "Methodist" was used first in 1729 for members of the "Holy Club" of Oxford U., led by the Wesleys, who lived "by rule and method." Influenced by the MORAVIAN CHURCH, Methodism began as an evangelical movement in 1738 when the Wesleys and George WHITEFIELD began evangelistic preaching; banned from most Anglican pulpits, they preached in the open air and drew vast crowds. Converts were organized into class meetings and itinerant lay preachers appointed. Wesleyan Methodism was Arminian; Whitefield's followers were CALVINIST but predominated only in Wales. After Wesley's death in 1791 the societies formally separated from the Church of England and became the Wesleyan Methodist Church. The American Methodist movement was established after 1771 by Francis ASBURY and Thomas Coke. Methodist polity in Britain is in effect presbyterian; in the US it is episcopal. Methodism traditionally stresses conversion, holiness and social welfare. In both the US and England Methodist groups have often seceded from the main church, but most have since reunited. Worldwide there are more than 43 million Methodists. (See also AFRICAN METHODIST EPISCOPAL CHURCH; AFRICAN METHODIST EPISCOPAL ZION CHURCH.)

METRIC SYSTEM, a decimal system of WEIGHTS AND MEASURES devised in Revolutionary France in 1791 and based on the METER, a unit of length. The original unit of MASS was the gram, the mass of a cubic centimeter of water at $4°C$, the TEMPERATURE of its greatest DENSITY. Auxiliary units were to be formed by adding Greek prefixes to the names of the base units for their decimal multiples and Latin prefixes for their decimal subdivisions. The metric system forms the basis of the physical units systems known as CGS UNITS and MKSA units (or Giorgi system), the present International System of Units (SI UNITS) being a development of the latter. SI also provides the primary standards for the US Customary System of units. This means that exact interconversion can be easily accomplished.

METROPOLITAN MUSEUM OF ART, the world's largest and most comprehensive art museum. Founded in 1870 in New York City, its collections include art from ancient Egypt, Greece, Rome, Babylonia and Assyria and it has outstanding collections of musical instruments, prints, and of famous paintings and sculpture from all periods. Medieval art is housed in the Cloisters, constructed from actual medieval buildings.

METROPOLITAN OPERA, leading US and world opera company. The old Metropolitan Opera House was built in New York City in 1883, but in 1966 the company moved to a new house in New York's Lincoln Center. "The Met" has been as famous for its directors, such as Gatti-Casazza and Rudolf BING, as for its operas and singers, or for conductors like MAHLER and TOSCANINI.

METTERNICH, Clemens Wenzel Nepomuk Lothar von, Prince (1773–1859), Austrian statesman. After a diplomatic career in Saxony, Prussia and France he became Austrian foreign minister in 1809. He gradually dissociated Austria from France and organized an alliance of Austria, Russia and Prussia against Napoleon. However at the Congress of VIENNA, 1814–15, he reestablished a system of power whereby Russia and Prussia were balanced by the combined power of Austria, France and England. Appointed state chancellor in 1821, his authority declined after 1826 and he was overthrown in 1848 (see REVOLUTIONS OF 1848). The period 1815–48 is often called the "Age of Metternich."

METZ, city in NE France on the Moselle R, a center for iron and coal mining. Of pre-Roman origin, it became a bishopric and capital of the Frankish kingdom of Austrasia. France annexed it in 1552 and

Germany held it 1871–1918. Pop 113,360.

MEUSE RIVER, river in W Europe, rising in the Langres Plateau, France and flowing N for about 580mi across Belgium and the Netherlands, where it is named Maas, into the North Sea. It is an important thoroughfare and line of defense for France and Belgium.

MEXICAN WAR (1846–1848), conflict between the US and Mexico. Its immediate cause was the US annexation of Texas. In 1835 Americans in the Mexican state of Texas rebelled against SANTA ANNA's dictatorship. On his defeat Texas became an independent republic, which the US annexed in 1845. Mexico claimed that the Texas boundary was the Nueces R, and the US that it was the Rio Grande. President POLK sent John Slidell to negotiate this question and to discuss the purchase of California and New Mexico from Mexico. The Mexicans refused to negotiate, and in March 1846 Gen. Zachary TAYLOR was sent with troops to the Rio Grande. A Mexican force met him, and Congress declared war in May. It has been debated whether Polk's motives in promoting hostilities were based on a sincere grievance or on his desire to annex California.

US strategy was to invade N.M. and Cal.; to advance along the Rio Grande; and to invade Mexico from the N. The American forces were successful in all these campaigns and General Taylor defeated Santa Anna in Feb. 1847 at Buena Vista. General Winfield SCOTT landed troops at Veracruz, defeated the Mexicans at Cerro Gordo, Contreras and Churubusco, and after the battle of CHAPULTEPEC captured Mexico City in Sept. 1847.

By the Treaty of GUADALUPE HIDALGO, Feb. 1848, Mexico ceded to the US the territory N of the line formed by the Rio Grande, the Gila R., and across the Colorado R to the Pacific. The US agreed to pay $15 million and settle all claims by US citizens against Mexico. Americans were divided over the war, mainly because the extension of territory involved the problem of extending slavery, and debates on this point brought to the forefront of political conflict issues which led to the Civil War.

MEXICO, the third-largest country in Latin America, lies in southermost North America. Straddling the Central American isthmus, it is bounded on the N by the US, about two-thirds of the border following the Rio Grande (Río Bravo in Mexico). In the S it borders on Guatemala and Belize. On the E lies the Gulf of Mexico and on the W, the Gulf of California, which separates Baja (Lower) California from the rest of Mexico

Official name: United Mexican States
Capital: Mexico City
Area: 756,066sq mi
Population: 81,323,000
Languages: Spanish, Indian languages
Religions: Roman Catholic
Monetary unit(s): 1 Mexican peso = 100 centavos

and the Pacific Ocean.

Land. About 75% of Mexico is occupied by a central plateau with low hills, basins and mountains and bounded by the Sierra Madre Occidental and Sierra Madre Oriental. Its S edge is formed by volcanoes, some still active, including Popocatépetl (17,887ft), Iztaccíhuatl (17,343ft) and Citlaltépetl, or Orizaba (18,700ft, highest peak in Mexico). S of the central plateau is another high and rugged region. On the E and W escarpments drop steeply to the coastal plains, the broader being the Gulf Coast plain extending from the Río Bravo to the Yucatán peninsula and consisting mainly of swamps and lagoons. N Mexico is arid and has few rivers. Three main rivers drain the central plateau: the Santiago-Lerma, the Pánuco-Moctezuma and the upper Balsas R.

There are four climatic zones: *tierra caliente* (hot land) lying between sea level and 2,500ft and embracing the Yucatán, coastal lowlands and part of Baja California; *tierra templada* of the central plateau; and *tierra fría* (cold land, 6,000–12,000ft). Above 12,000ft is *tierra helada* (frozen land). Rainfall, heaviest in the SE, decreases inland and to the N.

People. The population continues to increase rapidly due to the high birthrate. Over 60% live in the towns and cities, the largest being Mexico City, the capital. Guadalajara is the second-largest city. About 60% of Mexicans are mestizos (of mixed Indian and white stock), 30% are pure Indians, and 10% whites. Spanish is the official language, but there are many Indian dialects. Though education has progressed, some 12% of the population are still illiterate.

Economy. The economy has expanded since

WWII, but though industrialization has made great progress, agriculture remains the most important sector, employing 40% of the labor force. Less than 15% of the land surface is cultivable. Most cultivated land is on the central plateau. Since the revolution of 1910, most large estates have been expropriated and the land redistributed among the peasants, organized in landholding communities (*ejidos*). The chief subsistence crops are corn and beans. The main commercial crops are wheat, corn, beans, cotton, coffee, sugarcane and sisal. Tropical crops are grown on the coastal lowlands. Irrigation projects have transformed parts of the arid N. Cattle are reared in the N and in the rugged region S of the central plateau. There are valuable forests (pine, mahogany, cedar) and fisheries (sardines, tuna, shrimps).

Mexico is rich in minerals, especially silver, zinc, lead, copper, coal, natural gas and sulfur. Huge petroleum reserves (possibly second-largest in the world) were discovered in mid-1970s. Abundant reserves of iron ore and uranium await development. Large hydroelectric plants have been constructed on some rivers. Major industries include iron and steel (Monterrey, Monclova and the new, much larger Las Truchas project), and textiles (Mexico City and nearby Puebla and Toluca). Mexico also makes chemicals, electric goods, ceramics, paper, footwear, glass, processed foods and other products. Tourism is a major industry and has stimulated highway improvement and new resort centers.

History. People were living in Mexico by 10,000 BC; early maize cultivation led to a farming culture (c1000 BC). Later advanced Indian civilizations developed (see AZTECS; MAYAS; MIXTECS; TOLTEC; ZAPOTEC). The arrival of Hernán CORTÉS (1519) and his destruction of Aztec power (1521) brought Mexico under Spanish rule, which was challenged in 1810 by Father Miguel HIDALGO Y COSTILLA. Independence was achieved in 1821 under the leadership of Agustín de ITURBIDE. The federal republic was created in 1824. Texas broke free of Mexico in 1836, and in the MEXICAN WAR the republic lost NW territories to the US (1848). During 1864–67 Mexico was ruled by MAXIMILIAN of Austria, a puppet emperor supported by France. He was defeated and executed by Benito JUÁREZ. Then followed the long reformist dictatorship of Porfirio DÍAZ (1876–80, 1884–1911) and the MADERO revolution of 1910. A liberal constitution was introduced by President CARRANZA (1917) and further reforms by later presidents, notably Lázaro CÁRDENAS (1934–40). The National Revolutionary Party, formed from all major political groups in 1929 and later renamed the Institutional Revolutionary Party (PRI), governed the country without serious challenge until the late 1980s.

In the late 1940s, Mexico began to enjoy steady economic growth, which turned into a boom after huge oil reserves were discovered in the mid-1970s. A large urban middle class developed. Successive PRI governments appeased the poor with a variety of subsidies and jobs in the huge state apparatus and in government-owned corporations. But falling oil prices and rising foreign debt changed this picture. During the administration of Miguel de la Madrid Hurtado (1982–88), the economy averaged zero growth while the population rose 2.4% a year. Average purchasing power fell 40%. The government struggled with foreign creditors, reduced subsidies and protectionism, encouraged foreign investment, and promised privatization of many state companies.

Meanwhile, popular criticism of the PRI for authoritarianism and corruption mounted. The party had also become inefficient, controlled by old political bosses and ignored by young, foreign-trained technocrats who ran the bureaucracy. The party was stunned in 1988 when its candidate, Carlos Salinas de Gortari, won the presidency with only 50.4% of the vote, the narrowest margin in the party's history, despite reports of widespread vote fraud. Salinas declared that the era of the one-party state was over. An economist, he promised to orient the economy toward growth.

MEXICO CITY, capital of Mexico. Located at an altitude of 7,347ft and at the S end of Mexico's central plateau, it is surrounded by the mountain ranges of Iztaccíhuatl and Popocatépetl. The climate is cool and dry, but the city, built on land reclaimed from Lake Texcoco, has often been damaged by local floods. Subsidence has caused heavy buildings to sink up to 12in in a year. Mexico City is on the site of the old AZTEC capital of Tenochtitlan founded in 1176. CORTES captured the city in 1521, and for the next 300 years it was the seat of the viceroyalty of New Spain; consequently it possesses some of the finest Spanish colonial architecture. Pop (metro) 17,300,000.

MEYER, Adolf (1866–1950), Swiss-born US psychiatrist best known for his concept of *psychobiology*, the use in psychiatry of both psychological and biological processes together.

MEYERBEER, Giacomo (1791–1864), German composer. His romantic and spectacular operas, with librettos by SCRIBE, set the vogue for French opera. Most famous are his *Robert le Diable* (1831), *Les Huguenots* (1836) and *L'Africaine* (1865.)

MEYERHOLD, Vsevolod Yemilyevich (1874–1942), Russian theatrical director and actor, whose work revolutionized the Russian theater. Rejecting stage illusionist conventions, he adopted abstract "constructivist" settings and advocated "biomechanics"—a system of acting methods and responses.

MIA, abbreviation for "missing in action," term for absent combat personnel who cannot be accounted for as killed, wounded, or captured. It became familiar after the Vietnam War when it was widely believed that many MIAs were alive in prison camps in Vietnam and elsewhere. In the decade after the war, more than 1,000 "sightings" of Americans in such circumstances were reported, but most of these were found baseless. The US government listed 1,758 Americans as unaccounted for in Vietnam, 547 in Laos, 83 in Cambodia, and 6 in China. In 1988 Vietnam agreed to permit US investigators to enter the country and search for information about MIAs.

MIAMI, second-largest city in Fla., the seat of Dade Co., located at the mouth of the Miami R on Biscayne Bay. Its fine climate and beaches have made it a world famous resort center. Miami is also a major manufacturing center with a huge port and international airport. Pop (city) 373,000, (metro) 1,753,000.

MIAMI INDIANS, an Algonquian-speaking North American Indian group, of the Great Lakes region. They hunted buffalo and grew crops. In the 18th century they numbered not more than 1,750. They were allies of the French during the FRENCH AND INDIAN WARS and aided the British during the American Revolution.

MIASKOVSKY, Nikolai Yakovlevich (1881–1950), Russian composer and teacher. A professor at the Moscow Conservatory (from 1921), he was the most prominent teacher of composition in the USSR. His 27 symphonies conformed to the esthetic dictates of the Stalin regime.

MICAH, Book of, the sixth of the Old Testament Minor Prophets, the oracles of the Judean prophet Micah (flourished late 8th century BC). Chapters 4 through 7 are thought to be later. Ethical in tenor, the book prophesies judgment for sin and restoration by the MESSIAH, centered on Zion.

MICHAEL (1596–1645), first ROMANOV czar of Russia, 1613–45. During his rule, peace was made with Sweden and Poland, and some western ideas on army organization and industrial methods were introduced. However the peasants were forced further into serfdom.

MICHELANGELO (1475–1564), one of the world's most famous artists. Italian sculptor, painter, architect and poet, Michelangelo Buonarroti was probably the greatest artistic genius of the Renaissance. As a child he was apprenticed to the Florentine painter GHIRLANDAIO. He went to Rome in 1496 where his beautiful and poignant marble *Pieta* in Saint Peter's (1498–99) established him as the foremost living sculptor. In Florence he sculpted the magnificent *David* (1501–04), the largest marble statue carved in Italy since the end of the Roman empire. In 1505 Michelangelo went to Rome to work on a gigantic tomb for Pope JULIUS II. In Rome he painted the ceiling of the SISTINE CHAPEL, and this work has been one of the most influential in the history of art. After living in Florence (1515–34) and building the New Sacristy and library for the MEDICI family, he moved permanently to Rome. He painted the *Last Judgment* in the Sistine Chapel (1536–41), and his last very great work was rebuilding SAINT PETER'S BASILICA (1546–64). His architectural designs were influential throughout Italy, and in France and England.

MICHELET, Jules (1798–1874), French historian, a professor of history and a director of the national archives (1830–51). Among his voluminous works is the monumental *Histoire de France* (1833–67), with its incomparable description of medieval times.

MICHELOZZO MICHELOZZI (1396–1472), Florentine sculptor and architect of the early Renaissance. His architectural works include the Palazzo Medici-Riccardi in Florence (1444–59) which influenced later palace and town house architecture in Italy.

MICHELS, Robert (1876–1936), German political sociologist. He formulated the "iron law of OLIGARCHY" which postulated that political parties and organizations tend to elitist rule even in a democracy. His most famous work, *Political Parties* (1911), sets forth his ideas.

MICHELSON-MORLEY EXPERIMENT, important experiment whose results, by showing that the ETHER does not exist, substantially contributed to EINSTEIN's formulation of RELATIVITY theory. Its genesis was the development by **Albert Abraham Michelson** (1852–1931) of an INTERFEROMETER (1881) whereby a beam of light could be split into two parts sent at right angles to each other and then brought together again. Because of the earth's motion in space, the "drag" of the stationary ether should produce INTERFERENCE effects when the beams are brought together: his early experiments showed no such effects. With E. W. Morley he improved the sensitivity of his equipment, and by 1887 was able to show that there was no "drag," and therefore no ether. Michelson, awarded the Nobel Prize for Physics in 1908, was the first US Nobel prizewinner.

MICHENER, James Albert (1907–), US author. His Pulitzer prize-winning *Tales of the South Pacific* (1947), based on his US Navy experience in WWII, inspired the famous musical *South Pacific* (1949) by RODGERS and HAMMERSTEIN. He also wrote such ambitious, historically based novels as *Hawaii* (1959), *Centennial* (1974), *Chesapeake* (1978), and *Alaska* (1988).

MICHIGAN, state, N midwest US, bounded to the E by Canada and Lakes Huron and Erie, to the S by Oh. and Ind., to the W by Wis. and Lake Michigan, and to the N by Lake Superior.

Name of state: Michigan
Capital: Lansing
Statehood: Jan. 26, 1837 (26th state)
Familiar name: Wolverine State
Area: 58,216 sq mi
Population: 9,145,000
Elevation: Highest—1,980ft, Mt. Curwood.
Lowest—572ft, Lake Erie
Motto: *Si quaeris peninsulam amoenam, circumspice* ("If you seek a pleasant peninsula, look around you")
State flower: Apple blossom
State bird: Robin
State tree: White pine
State song: "Michigan, My Michigan"

Land. Michigan consists of two separate land areas, the Upper Peninsula and the mitten-shaped Lower Peninsula. The two are connected by the Mackinac Bridge. The W half of the Upper Peninsula is a part of the Superior upland regions, a rugged, forested area which possesses some of the nation's richest iron and copper deposits. It is a popular vacation area. The E half of the Upper Peninsula and the entire Lower Peninsula lie in the Great Lakes plain region. While winters in the Upper Peninsula may be extremely severe, the Lower Peninsula has a damp, milder climate, with hot summers and snowy winters. The Lower Peninsula contains most of the state's industry and fertile farmland.

People. About three-fourths of the population live in urban area, and about 90% live in the Lower Peninsula. Famous as the "automobile capital of the world," Detroit remains the state's largest city, although its population dropped almost 30% from 1970 to 1987.

Economy. Michigan's economy is highly industrialized. The state's automobile industry produces about two-fifths of the total US output of motor vehicles and parts. Other leading products are processed foods, machine tools, chemicals and metal and plastic goods. The rich soil of the Lower Peninsula supports livestock and dairy farming. Corn, wheat, hay, dry beans and fruit are also important. Michigan provides about 15% of the nation's iron ore. Tourism and mining are also important to the state's economy, both in winter and summer.

History. The first settlement in what is now Michigan was established by the French in 1668. In 1763 the area came under British control. After the War of 1812 the Michigan area came permanently under the control of the US, and pioneers began to settle the Lower Peninsula in greater numbers. Michigan was admitted to the Union in 1837. The REPUBLICAN PARTY was organized at Jackson (1854). At the end of the 19th century Michigan's population was about 2.4 million, but the state was still primarily rural. This was changed by Henry Ford and others who set up factories in the early 1900s for the mass production of automobiles. By 1920 the population had increased to almost 3.7 million. Apart from very bad years in the 1930s depression, Michigan (still dominated by the automobile industry) prospered into the 1970s. Then the decline of the domestic auto industry brought the state to the brink of another true depression. Auto sales and the state's economy revived in the mid-1980s. In presidential elections 1968–88, Michigan voted Republican 1972–88.

MICHIGAN, Lake, third largest of the

GREAT LAKES, in North America. It is the largest freshwater lake wholly within the US, with an area of 22,178sq mi. In the N, Lake Michigan empties into Lake Huron by the Straits of Mackinac. It is part of the navigable Great Lakes-SAINT LAWRENCE SEAWAY, and there is also a series of connections linking it to the Mississippi R and the Gulf of Mexico. Important ports on the lake include Milwaukee, Wis., Chicago, Ill. and Gary, Ind.

MICKIEWICZ, Adam (1798–1855), Polish poet and patriot. His masterpiece is *Pan Tadeusz* (1834), an epic description of the life of the Polish gentry.

MICMAC INDIANS, Canadian Indians of New France (Nova Scotia, New Brunswick, Prince Edward Island and coastal Quebec), of the Algonquian language group. They lived by hunting and fishing, using canoes for transportation, and numbered about 3,000 in the 17th and 18th centuries. They survive today as a tribal group engaged in guiding and farming.

MICROBIOLOGY, the study of microorganisms, including BACTERIA, VIRUSES, FUNGI and ALGAE. Departments of microbiology include the traditional divisions of ANATOMY, PHYSIOLOGY, GENETICS, TAXONOMY and ECOLOGY, together with various branches of MEDICINE, VETERINARY MEDICINE and PLANT DISEASES, since many microorganisms are pathogenic by nature. Microbiologists also play an important role in the food industry, particularly in baking and brewing. In the pharmaceutical industry, they supervise the production of ANTIBIOTICS.

MICROCHEMISTRY, branch of CHEMISTRY in which very small amounts (1μg to 1mg) are studied. Special techniques and apparatus have been developed for weighing and handling such minute quantities. Tracer methods, especially labeling with radioactive ISOTOPES, are useful, as are instrumental methods of ANALYSIS. Microanalysis is the chief part of microchemistry; another important aspect is the study of rare substances such as the TRANSURANIUM ELEMENTS.

MICROECONOMICS, the study in economics of the basic constituent elements of an economy, the individual consumers (households) and producers (firms). By analyzing their behavior and interaction, microeconomics seeks to explain the relative prices of goods and the amount produced and demanded. (See also MACROECONOMICS.)

MICRONESIA, a NW subdivision of the Pacific islands of OCEANIA. N of MELANESIA and divided from POLYNESIA by the international date line. The 2,250 small islands and atolls have a total land area of less than 1,500sq mi, and include the Caroline, Marshall, Marianas and Gilbert islands, Wake Island, Marcus Island and Nauru.

MICRONESIA, Federated States of, self-governing islands consisting of four constituent states—Yap, Truk, Ponape and Kosrae, each state made up of small islands, many uninhabited—located in the W Pacific just N of the equator.

Official name: Federated States of Micronesia
Capital: Kolonia
Area: 273sq mi
Population: 97,400
Languages: English, indigenous dialects
Religions: Christian
Monetary unit(s): 1 US dollar = 100 cents
Land. The states, part of the Caroline Island group, extend for a length of about 2,000mi. They are composed of both low-lying coral islands and higher volcanic ones that reach a peak elevation of 1,234ft on Truk. Ponape—the largest island—and Kosrae, the most fertile, are wooded and well watered. The climate is hot with little temperature variation. Rainfall reaches 118in per year, and severe storms and typhoons may occur.
People. The indigenous people are Micronesian, although some speak Malayan languages, and Polynesians live on two isolated atolls in Ponape state. On Yap traditional culture survives more strongly than elsewhere.
Economy. Taro, sweet potatoes, bananas, copra and breadfruit are grown on small subsistence holdings, supplemented by fishing. Coconuts and fish constitute virtually the only exports. There is little industry, and the people rely heavily on US aid.
History. The islands, some of which have been inhabited for over 2,000 years, were largely ignored by Europeans until the end of the 18th century. Spain claimed the islands but sold them to Germany in 1898,

and in 1914 they were occupied by Japan. In 1945 the US assumed control and they were incorporated into the US Trust Territory of the Pacific Islands in 1947. The Federated States became internally self-governing in 1979; in 1986 they became a sovereign state in free association with the US, which remained responsible for their defense.

MICROPHONE, device for converting sound waves into electrical impulses. The **carbon microphone** used in TELEPHONE mouthpieces has a thin diaphragm behind which are packed tiny carbon granules. SOUND waves vibrate the diaphragm, exerting a variable pressure on the granules. This varies their resistance, producing fluctuations in a DC current (see ELECTRICITY) passing through them. The **crystal microphone** incorporates a piezoelectric crystal in which pressure changes from the diaphragm produce an alternating voltage. In the **electrostatic microphone** the diaphragm acts as one plate of a CAPACITOR. with vibration producing changes in capacitance. In the **moving-coil microphone** the diaphragm is attached to a coil located between the poles of a permanent magnet: movement induces a varying current in the coil (see INDUCTION). The **ribbon microphone** has, rather than a diaphragm, a metal ribbon held in a magnetic field; vibration of the ribbon induces an electric current in it.

MICROPROCESSOR, an integrated circuit that performs the functions of a COMPUTER on a tiny "chip" of silicon. Unlike a computer, which can be programmed to solve many different problems, a microprocessor is designed for a specific task. Microprocessors are used in a great variety of "smart" devices, including home appliances that remember instructions and the popular electronic games.

MICROSCOPE, an instrument for producing enlarged images of small objects. The simple microscope or magnifying glass, comprising a single converging LENS. was known in ancient times, but the first compound microscope is thought to have been invented by the Dutch spectacle-maker Zacharias Janssen around 1590. However, because of the ABERRATION unavoidable in early lens systems, the simple microscope held its own for many years, Anton van LEEUWENHOEK constructing many fine examples using tiny near-spherical lenses. Compound microscopes incorporating achromatic lenses became available from the mid 1840s.

In the compound microscope a magnified, inverted image of an object resting on the "stage" is produced by the objective lens (system). This image is viewed through the eyepiece (or ocular) lens (system), which acts as a simple microscope, giving a greatly magnified virtual image. In most biological microscopy the object is viewed by transmitted light, illumination being controlled by mirror, diaphragm and "substage condenser" lenses. The near-transparent objects are often stained to make them visible. As this usually proves fatal to the specimen, phase-contrast microscopy, in which a "phase plate" is used to produce a DIFFRACTION effect, can alternatively be employed. Objects which are just too small to be seen directly can be made visible in darkfield illumination. In this an opaque disk prevents direct illumination and the object is viewed in the light diffracted from the remaining oblique illumination. In mineralogical use objects are frequently viewed by reflected light.

Although there is no limit to the theoretical magnifying power of the optical microscope, magnifications greater than about 2000 × can offer no improvement in resolving power (see TELESCOPE) for light of visible wavelengths. The shorter wavelength of ultraviolet light allows better resolution and hence higher useful magnification. For yet finer resolution physicists turn to electron beams and electromagnetic focusing (see ELECTRON MICROSCOPE). The FIELD-ION MICROSCOPE. which offers the greatest magnifications, is a quite dissimilar instrument.

MICROWAVES, ELECTROMAGNETIC RADIATIONS of wavelength between 1mm and 30cm; used in RADAR. telecommunications, SPECTROSCOPY and for cooking (microwave ovens). Their dimensions are such that it is easy to build ANTENNAS of great directional sensitivity and high-efficiency waveguides for them.

MIDDLE AGES, the period in W European history between the fall of the Roman Empire and the dawn of the RENAISSANCE—roughly the 5th to the 15th centuries AD. The centuries preceding the 11th century are often called the DARK AGES. In the 5th century the W half of the Roman Empire broke up. Trade declined, cities shrank in size, law and order broke down. By the 10th century Europe was fragmented into numerous small kingdoms in which economic life for the masses of people was reduced to subsistence level.

Church, feudalism and society. The single unifying institution throughout the Middle Ages was the Christian Church. It provided some care for the poor and sick and its monasteries preserved the writings of the Greeks and Romans. But while the Church provided the spiritual foundations of the Middle Ages, society was ordered according to FEUDALISM. Its most important feature was the idea of service in return for land, protection and justice. At the top of the feudal pyramid was the Holy Roman Emperor (see HOLY ROMAN EMPIRE); then kings and princes, then warrior knights; at the bottom were the peasants. Each had a duty to pay homage to those above him and to provide military service when required to do so. In return each vassal was allowed by his suzerain or overlord to exercise control over his own domain and provided protection and justice for those below him.

Breakup of the old order. Around the 11th century the long phase of European decline was reversed. Population began to grow again, trade revived and cities expanded (see GUILDS). During the 13th and 14th centuries the cities became powerful, allying themselves with the emerging centralized monarchies against the Church and the feudal barons. New centers of learning, the universities, emerged. By the end of the 16th century LUTHER had set Europe aflame with his criticisms of the Catholic Church, GUTENBERG had invented the printing press and COLUMBUS had discovered a New World.

MIDDLE EAST, a large region, mostly in SW Asia but extending into SE Europe and NE Africa. Today the term usually includes the following countries: Bahrain, Cyprus, Egypt, Lebanon, Libya, Syria, Iran, Iraq, Israel, Jordan, Kuwait, Turkey, Sudan, Saudi Arabia and the other countries of the Arabian peninsula. Politically, other countries of predominantly Islamic culture like Algeria, Morocco and Tunisia are sometimes included. The Middle East was the cradle of early civilization. (See EGYPT, ANCIENT; BABYLONIA AND ASSYRIA; MESOPOTAMIA). It was also the birthplace of JUDAISM, CHRISTIANITY and ISLAM. It has been the seat of many great empires, including the OTTOMAN EMPIRE which survived into the present century. Today the Middle East has assumed tremendous geopolitical importance as the world's primary oil-producing region. It is also the focus of international tensions and strife—see, for example, ARAB-ISRAELI WARS; IRAN-IRAQ WAR.

MIDDLE ENGLISH. See ENGLISH.

MIDDLETON, Thomas (c1580–1627), English dramatist. He wrote lively, natural comedies, the Lord Mayor of London's pageants and various masques, and two outstanding tragedies concerning human corruption: *The Changeling* (1653) and *Women Beware Women* (1657). *A Game at Chess* (1624) was his satire on political marriages with Spain, suppressed under James I.

MIDNIGHT SUN, phenomenon observed N of the Arctic Circle and S of the Antarctic Circle. Each summer the sun remains above the horizon for at least one 24-hour period (a corresponding period of darkness occurs in winter), owing to the tilt of the EARTH's equator to the ecliptic.

MIDWAY, Battle of, an air-sea battle of WWII, fought in early June, 1942. It began with an American attack on a hostile Japanese force approaching the American base on Midway Island in the Pacific. The battle was a decisive US naval victory, and marked the passing of the initiative in the Pacific to the Allies.

MIES VAN DER ROHE, Ludwig (1886–1969), German-American architect, famous for his functional but elegant buildings in the INTERNATIONAL STYLE, constructed of brick, steel and glass. His work includes the Illinois Institute of Technology campus in Chicago, and the Seagram Building (with Philip JOHNSON) in New York. Although he had no formal training, he was a director of the BAUHAUS and one of the 20th century's leading architects.

MIFFLIN, Thomas (1744–1800), American soldier and political leader. A member of the First Continental Congress, during the Revolutionary War he rose to the rank of quartermaster general. He was later a delegate to the Constitutional Convention (1787), and the first governor of Pa. (1790–99).

MIGRANT LABOR, workers who move from place to place, usually in search of seasonal agricultural employment. Although found elsewhere, migrant labor is primarily a US phenomenon, particularly in the W and SW. The workers, without fixed homes and unprotected by trade unions or governments, often live in sub-standard conditions. Since 1970, however, California migrant workers organized by Cesar CHAVEZ have secured improvement in their status and working conditions.

MIGRATION, long-distance mass movements made by animals of many different groups, both vertebrate and invertebrate, often at regular intervals. Generally animals move from a breeding area to a feeding place, returning as the breeding season approaches the following year. This is the pattern of annual movements of migratory birds and fishes. Migrations of this nature may be over great distances, up to 7,000mi in some birds. Navigation is extremely accurate: birds may return to the same nest site year after year; migratory fish return to the exact rivulet of their birth to spawn. In other cases, migrations may follow cycles of food abundance: WILDEBEEST in E Africa follow in the wake of the rains grazing on the new grass; CARIBOU in Canada show similar movements. Certain carnivore species may follow these migrations, others capitalize on a temporary abundance as the herds move through their ranges.

MIGRATIONS, mass movements of people which modify world population and culture patterns. Prehistoric hunter-gatherer tribes migrated in search of food following climatic changes as in the ICE AGES. Other migrations include those of the ancestral North American INDIANS from Asia, c25,000 years ago; of the CELTS across Europe in the 2nd millennium BC; of the Aryans into India c1500 BC; of the Germanic GOTHS driven by migrating HUNS into the ROMAN EMPIRE; of the ARAB peoples in the 7th century AD; of the Mongols in the 13th century (see MONGOL EMPIRE); of the TURKS into Anatolia in the 14th century. Since the 16th century colonial expansion, war, political and religious oppression, and poverty at home combined with the opportunity for exploitation abroad have led to massive migrations from Europe. More than 15 million have migrated to India, Africa and Oceania and some 65 million to North and South America. Pogroms in 19th-century Tsarist Russia drove thousands of Jews to W Europe and America, while millions of Jews and others were displaced and annihilated by German Nazis in the 1930s. Major migrations may also occur within a country. In the US, in the 19th century, migrants moved west in search of land, and more recently, blacks in the S have moved N in search of greater opportunities. The 1970s saw an accelerated movement of new settlers to the "sunbelt" states in the W and S. (See also NORMANS; VIKINGS; SAXONS; IMMIGRATION; REFUGEES.)

MIHAJLOVIC, Draza (1893–1946), Yugoslav partisan leader in WWII. A royalist and a Serbian nationalist, he sometimes collaborated with the Germans against TITO and the communists, who after the war accused him of treason and shot him.

MIKOYAN, Anastas Ivanovich (1895–1978), Soviet public official, deputy premier under KHRUSHCHEV 1955–57, 1958–64, and chairman of the Presidium of the Supreme Soviet (i.e., head of state) 1964–65. From 1926 his career was largely in departments of trade. In 1956 he took a lead in denouncing STALIN's regime. He

retired from public life in 1974.

MILAN, city in N Italy. An important European trade and transportation hub, it is Italy's major industrial and commercial center, producing automobiles, airplanes, textiles, chemicals, electrical equipment, machinery and books. Milan was a major late Roman city, and the principal city state of LOMBARDY under the Visconti (1277–1447) and Sforza families. Spanish from 1535, it fell to Austria in 1713, and became a center of the 19th-century RISORGIMENTO. Artistic treasures include the cathedral, LEONARDO DA VINCI's *Last Supper*, the Brera palace and art gallery and La Scala opera house. Pop (city) 1,548,580; (metro) 7,200,000.

MILDEW, general name for the superficial growth of many types of fungi often found on plants and material derived from plants. Powdery mildews are caused by fungi belonging to the Ascomycetes order Erysiphales, the powdery effect being due to the masses of spores. These fungi commonly infest roses, apples, phlox, melons etc. Downy mildews are caused by Phycomycetes. They commonly infest many vegetable crops. Both types of disease can be controlled by use of FUNGICIDES.

MILE, name of many units of length in different parts of the world. The statute mile (st mi) is 1,760 yards (exactly 1,609.344m); the international (US) nautical mile is 1.150,78st mi; the UK nautical mile, 1.151,51st mi. The name derives from the Roman (Latin) *milia passuum*, a thousand paces.

MILES, Nelson Appleton (1839–1925), US soldier, army commander in chief 1895–1903. A Union general in the CIVIL WAR, in the INDIAN WARS he campaigned against the Sioux and also accepted the surrenders of Chiefs JOSEPH (1877) and GERONIMO (1886). He also commanded in Puerto Rico (1898).

MILHAUD, Darius (1892–1974), French composer, one of Les SIX, noted for his polytonality (the simultaneous use of different keys). His vast output includes the jazz-influenced ballet, *Creation of the World* (1923), *Saudades do Brasil* (1921) for piano, symphonies, chamber music and operas, among them *Christophe Colombe* (1930).

MILITARY ACADEMY, US. See WEST POINT.

MILIUKOV, Pavel Nikolayevich (1859–1943), Russian historian and politician. A member of the liberal Constitutional Democratic Party, he was briefly foreign minister after the Feb. 1917 revolution. He emigrated to Paris, where he was active in antibolshevik émigré politics.

MILK, a white liquid containing water, PROTEIN, FAT, SUGAR, VITAMINS and inorganic salts which is secreted by the mammary glands of female mammals. The secretion of milk (LACTATION) is initiated immediately after birth by the hormone prolactin. The milks produced by different mammals all have the same basic constituents, but the proportion of each ingredient differs from species to species and within species. In any species the milk produced is a complete food for the young until weaning. Milk is of high nutritional value, and man has used the milk of other animals as a food for at least 5,000 years. Milk for use by man is produced in the largest volume by cows and water buffalo (especially in India); goat milk is also produced in some areas, particularly the Middle East. Milk is an extremely perishable liquid which must be cooled to $10°C$ within two hours of milking and maintained at that temperature until delivery. The storage life of milk is greatly improved by PASTEURIZATION. Because of the perishable nature of milk large quantities are processed to give a variety of products including BUTTER; CHEESE; cream; evaporated, condensed and dried milk; yogurt; milk protein (casein) and lactose.

MILKY WAY, our GALAXY. It is a disk-shaped spiral galaxy containing some 100 billion stars, and has a radius of about 50,000 light-years. Our SOLAR SYSTEM is in one of the spiral arms and is just over 30,000 light-years from the galactic center, which lies in the direction of Sagittarius. The galaxy slowly rotates about a roughly spherical nucleus, though not at uniform speed; the sun circles the galactic center about every 230 million years. The galaxy is surrounded by a spheroidal halo some 165,000 light-years in diameter composed of gas, dust, occasional stars and GLOBULAR CLUSTERS. The Milky Way derives its name from our view of it as a hazy milk-like band of stars encircling the night sky. Irregular dark patches are caused by intervening clouds of gas and dust.

MILL, James (1773–1836) and **John Stuart** (1806–1873), distinguished British economists and philosophers. James Mill rose from humble origins to a senior position in the East India Company. He was an able apologist for the UTILITARIANISM of his friend Jeremy BENTHAM. A famous account of the education James imposed on his son John Stuart can be found in the latter's *Autobiography* (1873). The younger Mill is noted for his strictly empiricist *A System of Logic* (1843), his *Principles of Political Economy* (1848), and for his essays *On Liberty* (1854) and *Utilitarianism* (1861). J. S. Mill's circle included F. D. Maurice, Thomas CARLYLE and, later, Herbert SPENCER.

MILLAIS, Sir John Everett (1829–1896), English painter, a founder of the PRE-RAPHAELITE "brotherhood" (1848). His *Christ in the Carpenter's Shop* (1850) caused a scandal by its realism; later works such as *The Blind Girl* (1856) and *Bubbles* (1886) became more sentimental.

MILLAY, Edna St. Vincent (1892–1950), US poet of bohemian rebellion. Her reputation was established with *A Few Figs from Thistles* (1920), and *The Harp Weaver* (1922) won a Pulitzer Prize. Other works include *Wine from these Grapes* (1934) and the verse drama *Aria da Capo* (1921).

MILLENNIUM, in Christian ESCHATOLOGY, a 1000-year period in which Jesus Christ will reign gloriously. The doctrine, occurring in Revelation 20, ties in with Old Testament prophecies of the MESSIAH's reign. Millenarianism takes two forms: postmillennialists believe in a golden age of righteousness preceding Christ's SECOND COMING; premillennialists believe in a literal reign of Christ on earth after the Second Coming. Many in the early Church were millenarians (or chiliasts), but the idea was spiritualized by St. AUGUSTINE and recurred mainly in enthusiast Protestant sects, FUNDAMENTALISM and among ADVENTISTS.

MILLER, Arthur (1915–   ), US playwright. A committed liberal, he explores individual and social morality in such plays as *Death of a Salesman* (1949; Pulitzer Prize), *The Crucible* (1953) on the witch trials in Salem, Mass., *A View from the Bridge* (1955; Pulitzer Prize), the partly autobiographical *After the Fall* (1964) and the screenplay *The Misfits* (1961), for his second wife Marilyn MONROE. *Timebends* (1987) is his autobiography.

MILLER, Glenn (1904–1944), US trombonist and band leader in the big band "swing" era of the late 1930s and early 1940s. His blend of instrumental colors, the "Glenn Miller sound," had immense success. Among his most popular recordings were *In the Mood, Moonlight Serenade,* and *Chattanooga Choo–Choo.* He died in a plane crash while touring troop bases in Europe in WWII, but his popularity continues.

MILLER, Henry (1891–1980), US writer, noted for his candid treatment of sex and his espousal of the "natural man." *Tropic of Cancer* (1934) and *Tropic of Capricorn* (1939) were banned as obscene in America until 1961. Other books include the trilogy *The Rosy Crucifixion* (1949–60). He was a major influence on the BEAT GENERATION of writers.

MILLER, Perry Gilbert (1905–1963), US historian and professor at Harvard (1931–63), whose extensive writings on colonial New England history led to a resurgence of interest in Puritan life and thought. His best known works were *The New England Mind* (2 vols., 1939–53), and intellectual biographies of Jonathan Edwards (2 vols., 1948–49) and Roger Williams (1953).

MILLER, William (1782–1849), US religious leader who prophesied the second coming of Christ for 1843. His followers, called **Millerites** or Adventists, laid the foundations of modern ADVENTIST sects.

MILLET, Jean François (1814–1875), French painter. His famous peasant subjects like *The Gleaners* (1857) and *The Angelus* (1859) are naturalistic in style if somewhat romanticized.

MILLIGAN, Ex parte (1866), a US Supreme Court ruling defining the limits of military courts. The civilian Milligan had been condemned to death by a military tribunal in 1864 for pro-South COPPERHEAD agitation. The court ruled that a civilian cannot be tried by military courts, even in wartime, if the civil courts are functioning. Milligan was freed.

MILLS, C(harles) Wright (1916–1962), US sociologist and penetrating critic of US capitalism and militarism whose work was influential with radical social scientists of the 1970s. His books include *White Collar* (1951), *The Power Elite* (1956), *The Causes of World War Three* (1958) and *The Sociological Imagination* (1959), which argues that sociologists should not be passive observers but active agents of social change.

MILLS, Robert (1781–1855), US architect and engineer. From 1836 official architect of public buildings in Washington, D.C., who aimed at an American neo-classical style. He designed the Washington Monument, the Treasury and the old Post Office building.

MILL SPRINGS, Battle of, Jan. 19, 1862, a Confederate defeat in the US CIVIL WAR. The Union forces' victory near the village of Mill Springs, S Ky., opened E Tenn. to them.

MILNE, A(lan) A(lexander) (1882–1956), English writer and dramatist, famous for the children's stories and poems he wrote for his son Christopher Robin. They were *Winnie-the-Pooh* (1926), *The House at Pooh Corner* (1928), *When We Were Very Young* (1924) and *Now We are Six* (1927).

MILNER, Alfred Milner, 1st Viscount (1854–1925), British statesman and colonial administrator. As high commissioner in South Africa (1897–1905) he supported non-Afrikaner whites against the dominant Boers, adding to the tensions that brought on the BOER WAR. After the war he worked to assimilate the Boers into a federal Union of South Africa (established 1910). During WWI he served in the war cabinet, and in 1920 he headed a commission that recommended Egyptian independence.

MILNES, Sherrill (1935–   ), US baritone, with New York's Metropolitan Opera from 1964.

MILOSZ, Czeslaw (1911–   ), Polish poet, critic, translator, and diplomat. A leading leftist poet in the 1930s, he left Poland for the West in 1951 and taught at U of California at Berkeley 1960–78. His *The Captive Mind* (Eng. ed., 1953) condemns the spiritually repressive nature of Communism. In 1980 he won the Nobel Prize for Literature.

MILSTEIN, Nathan (1904–   ), Russian-born US violinist who studied under Leopold Auer in St. Petersburg and left the USSR in 1925. Known for his dazzling technique and intense virtuosity, he performed publicly for more than 50 years and made numerous recordings.

MILTIADES (d. ?489 BC), Greek general who defeated the Persians at MARATHON (490 BC). Before this, he had served the Persian king DARIUS I against the Scythians.

MILTON, John (1608–1674), English poet whose blank-verse epic *Paradise Lost* (1667), detailing Lucifer's revolt against God and the fall of Adam and Eve in the Garden of Eden, is one of the masterpieces of English literature. His major early works are the ode *On The Morning of Christ's Nativity* (1629), *L'Allegro* and *Il Penseroso* (c1631), *Comus*, (c1632) and *Lycidas* (1638). A Puritan supporter during the English Civil War, he wrote many political pamphlets and the famous prose piece in defense of freedom of the press, *Areopagitica* (1644). In retirement after the Restoration (1660), and now totally blind, he dictated his final great works: *Paradise Lost, Paradise Regained* (1671) and *Samson Agonistes* (1671).

MILVIAN BRIDGE, Battle of (312 AD), battle near Rome before which CONSTANTINE I is supposed to have seen a flaming cross in the sky inscribed "In this sign conquer." His victory over Maxentius made him emperor in the West. The next year the Edict of Milan granted toleration to Christianity in the Roman Empire.

MIME, the dramatic art of gesture and facial expression, also any silent acting. Mime was popular in classical times, often featuring topical or obscene subjects. It played an important part in the improvised Italian COMMEDIA DELL' ARTE of the 16th century and in the silent movie era, which produced such subtle masters of the art as CHAPLIN and KEATON. A theater of the mime has an especially strong tradition in France, where BARRAULT and MARCEAU are major contemporary mimes.

MIMICRY, the close resemblance of one organism to another which, because it is unpalatable and conspicuous, is avoided by certain predators. The mimic will thus gain a degree of protection on the strength of the predator's avoidance of the mimicked. Mimicry is well developed among insects. (See also BATES, HENRY W.)

MINDSZENTY, József (1892–1975), Hungarian Roman Catholic cardinal who was sentenced (1949) to life imprisonment for his opposition to communism. Released in the uprising of 1956, he took refuge in the US Legation in Budapest. He refused to leave until the charges against him were withdrawn. This condition was met in 1971 by arrangement between the Vatican and the Hungarian government, and Mindszenty left for Rome.

MINERALS, naturally-occurring substances obtainable by MINING. including COAL, PETROLEUM and NATURAL GAS: more specifically in geology, substances of natural inorganic origin, of more or less definite chemical COMPOSITION, CRYSTAL structure and properties, of which the ROCKS of the earth's crust are composed. (See also GEMS; ORE.) Of the 3,000 minerals known, fewer than 100 are common. They may be identified by their color (though this often varies because of impurities), hardness, luster, specific gravity, crystal forms and cleavage; or by chemical analysis and X-ray diffraction. Minerals are generally classified by their anions—in order of increasing complexity: elements, sulfides, oxides, halides, carbonates, nitrates, sulfates, phosphates and silicates. Others are classed with those which they resemble chemically and structurally, e.g. arsenates with phosphates. A newer system classifies minerals by their topological structure (see TOPOLOGY).

MING, Chinese dynasty 1368–1644, founded with the expulsion of the Mongol YUAN dynasty and terminated with the establishment of the Manchu CH'ING dynasty. Under the Ming, China extended from Burma to Korea and culture flourished. Europeans established settlements at Macao and Canton, and Christian missionaries penetrated the country.

MINIMALISM, an art movement initiated in the 1960s that stresses pure color and geometry. In both painting and sculpture—generally executed with great precision—it rejects emotionalism, striving for an "exclusive, negative, absolute and timeless" quality. Minimalism comprises, among styles and techniques, COLOR-FIELD PAINTING, HARD-EDGE PAINTING, OP ART, the shaped canvas, serial imagery and primary structures.

MINIMUM WAGE, a basic wage which employers are obliged by law to pay employees. They may pay more than this bottom limit, but not less. It is designed to protect the lowest paid workers, who may not have powerful unions to act on their behalf. Critics argue that it contributes to the unemployment of unskilled youths who might be hired at lower wages.

MINING, the means for extracting economically important MINERALS and ORES from the earth. Where the desired minerals lie near the surface, the most economic form of mine is the *open pit*. This usually consists of a series of terraces, which are worked back in parallel so that the mineral is always within convenient reach of the excavating machines. *Strip mining* refers to stripping off a layer of overburden to reach a usually thin mineral seam (often COAL). The excavating machines used in open-pit mining are frequently vast. Soft minerals such as kaolin can be recovered hydraulically—by directing heavy water jets at the pit face and pumping out the resulting slurry. Where a mineral is found in alluvial (river bed) deposits, bucket or suction dredgers may be used. But where minerals lie far below the surface, various deep mining techniques must be used. Sulfur is mined by pumping superheated water down boreholes into the mineral bed. This melts the sulfur, which is then pumped to the surface. Watersoluble minerals such as SALT are often mined in a similar way (*solution mining*). But most often, deep minerals and ores must be won from underground mines. Access to the mineral-bearing strata is obtained via a vertical *shaft* or sloping *incline* driven from the surface, or via a horizontal *adit* driven into the side of a mountain. The geometry of the actual mining area is determined by the type of mineral and the strength of the surrounding material. All underground mines require adequate ventilation and lighting, facilities for pumping out any groundwater or toxic gases seeping into the workings, and means (railroad or conveyor) for removing the ore and waste to the surface. As in open-pit mining, the rock is broken mechanically or with explosives. However, particular care must be exercised when using explosives underground. Several serious occupational diseases (e.g., PNEUMOCONIOSIS) are associated with mining and extraction metallurgy, particularly where high dust levels and toxic substances are involved. (See also SEA-BED MINING.)

MINISTRY, in the Christian Church, those ordained (see ORDINATION) to functions of leadership, preaching, administering the SACRAMENTS. pastoral care, etc. The Anglican churches recognize a "threefold ministry" of BISHOPS. PRIESTS (or presbyters) and DEACONS. The Roman Catholic and Eastern churches have recognized also subdeacons, and the "Minor Orders" of acolytes, readers, exorcists and porters; subdeacons and porters no longer exist in the Roman Catholic Church, and only subdeacons, readers and cantors are retained in the Eastern churches. Other churches usually recognize only pastors (or ministers), elders (or presbyters) and deacons.

MINK, semiaquatic carnivores of the WEASEL family, extensively farmed for their prized fur. There are two species, one (*Mustela lutreola*) of European distribution, the other (*M. vison*) originating in North America but now widely distributed throughout Europe where it has escaped from fur farms. Feeding on small fish, eggs, fledgling birds and small mammals, they are fearless hunters, and often kill more than they can eat—creating havoc when they raid domestic chicken farms.

MINNESINGER, minstrel-poet of medieval Germany who composed and sang songs of courtly love (*minne*). The Minnesingers, heirs to the Provençal TROUBADOURS. flourished from c1150 to c1350. They included WALTHER VON DER VOGELWEIDE and Tannhaüser.

MINNESOTA, state, N midwest US, bounded to the E by Lake Superior and Wis., to the S by Ia., to the W by S.D. and N.D., and to the N by Canada. It is one of the most scenic regions of the nation, with about 15,000 lakes and extensive forests. Its vast wheat fields, flour mills and dairy products have given it the nickname "Bread and Butter State."

Land. The state lies within two major geographical regions: its NE part belongs to the Superior Upland (the S tip of the Canadian Shield); the remainder belongs to the Central Lowland Region of North

Name of state: Minnesota
Capital: St. Paul
Statehood: May 11, 1858 (32nd state)
Familiar name: Gopher State
Area: 84,068sq mi
Population: 4,214,000
Elevation: Highest—2,301ft Eagle Mountain. Lowest—602ft, Lake Superior
Motto: *L'Etoile du Nord* ("The star of the north")
State flower: Pink and white lady's-slipper
State bird: Common loon
State tree: Norway pine
State song: "Hail! Minnesota"

America, mostly a treeless, gently rolling plain, where glaciers have deposited fertile topsoil. Three great river systems rise in Minnesota: the Mississippi, flowing SE from Lake Itasca and joined by the Minnesota R in St. Paul-Minneapolis; the Red R system, flowing N into Hudson Bay; and the St. Louis R (source of the St. Lawrence R), flowing into Lake Superior.

People. Two thirds of the population live in urban areas. Major cities include Minneapolis, St. Paul, Duluth and Rochester. Extensive Scandinavian immigration in the late 19th century made a strong cultural impact on the state. Among Minnesota's approximately 65 institutions of higher education is the University of Minnesota, one of the largest US universities.

Economy. The manufacture of nonelectrical machinery is the largest single industry in the state. Other leading industries include food processing, printing and publishing, and the manufacture of pulp and paper products, chemicals and electrical and electronic equipment. Livestock and dairy products are prominent, and major crops are corn, hay, spring wheat, alfalfa, soybeans, sugar beet, sunflowers and barley. Rich in natural resources, Minnesota contains deposits of iron ore, copper and nickel.

History. First settled by French missionaries and trader-explorers in the 17th century, for over 100 years Minnesota was noted chiefly as a rich fur-trading area. Immigrant settlement began in the early

1800s and accelerated rapidly throughout the century as land was taken from the Indians. The state's prosperity rested on agriculture and timber until manufacturing expanded in the 20th century. The present economy, which is stable and diversified, has stood up well. However, the state was hard hit by the drop in farm prices in the mid-1980s and the great drought of 1988. Politically, the state is known for producing liberals, including Hubert Humphrey, Eugene McCarthy and Walter Mondale. In presidential elections 1968–88, Minnesota voted Democratic in 1968 and 1976–88.

MINOAN LINEAR SCRIPTS, two written languages, samples of which, inscribed on clay tablets, were found in Crete by Sir Arthur EVANS (1900), and named Linear A and B. Linear B was deciphered (1952) by Michael Ventris (1922–1956) and shown to be very early Greek (from c1400 BC). Linear A is yet to be deciphered, though some symbols have been assigned phonetic values. (See also AEGEAN CIVILIZATION.)

MINSTRELS, loose term for often-itinerant medieval entertainers, including the lower-class JONGLEURS and the aristocratic TROUBADOURS and MINNESINGERS.

MINSTREL SHOW, form of entertainment native to the US, in which white performers blacked their faces in imitation of Negroes and alternated jokes with Negro songs, many of which thus became well-known American folksongs. The entertainers, led by a "Mister Interlocutor," sat in a semicircle with the "end men" at each end.

MINT, US Bureau of the, a bureau of the Department of the Treasury responsible for the manufacture of domestic coins and for the handling of gold and silver bullion. The first US Mint was established at Philadelphia in 1792, and the present bureau in 1873.

MINTO, Gilbert John Elliot-Murray-Kynynmound, 4th earl of (1845–1915), British colonial administrator, governor general of Canada (1898–1904) and viceroy of India (1905–10). With secretary of state for India John MORLEY he authored (1909) the Morley-Minto reforms, which increased Indian representation in the viceroy's advisory councils.

MINUET, a French dance in three-quarter time with delicate mincing steps. It became very popular first at the court of Louis XIV and then throughout Europe in the 17th and 18th centuries. It also became a form of lively musical composition, particularly in the works of HAYDN and MOZART.

MINUIT, Peter (1580–1638), colonial administrator in North America. He was the first director-general of NEW NETHERLAND for the Dutch West India Company, and is remembered for buying Manhattan Island from the Indians for about $24 in trinkets in 1626. He founded New Amsterdam, now New York City, and later established NEW SWEDEN on the Delaware R for the Swedes.

MINUTEMEN, volunteer militia in the American REVOLUTIONARY WAR, who were ready to take up arms "at a minute's notice." Mass. minutemen fought at the battles of LEXINGTON and CONCORD (1775). Md., N. H. and Conn. also adopted the system.

MIOCENE, the penultimate epoch of the TERTIARY, which lasted from 25 to 10 million years ago. (See GEOLOGY.)

MIQUELON. See SAINT PIERRE AND MIQUELON.

MIRABEAU, Honoré Gabriel Victor Riqueti, Comte de (1749–1791), French Revolutionary leader. A powerful orator, he became an early moderate leader of the JACOBINS and represented the third estate (the commoners) in the STATES-GENERAL (the French parliament). He worked secretly to establish a constitutional monarchy, but was mistrusted by both revolutionaries and royalists. He was elected president of the National Assembly in 1791, but died a few months later.

MIRACLE, a wonderful event, transcending the known laws of nature, due to supernatural intervention. Belief in miracles is found in all religions; they are important not so much for their own sake as for their religious significance in revealing a god and his character or authenticating his agents. In theistic religions (see THEISM), only God has intrinsic power to work miracles (though he may delegate it). Miracles are immediate acts of God: normal events are ordered by God mediately through natural law. In the Bible, miracles occur in cycles associated with redemption, culminating in those wrought by Jesus Christ, and, above all, in his RESURRECTION. Roman Catholicism claims that miracles have continued in the Church, associated with saints, martyrs, their relics, and images; at least two authenticated posthumous miracles are required for CANONIZATION. Rationalist denial of miracles became important from the 18th century in PANTHEISM, DEISM and the skepticism of David HUME and others. Modern liberal Protestantism explains miracles as myths expressing a religious world-view.

MIRACLE PLAY. See MYSTERY PLAY.

MIRAGE, optical illusion arising from the REFRACTION of light as it passes through air layers of different densities. In *inferior mirages* distant objects appear to be reflected in water at their bases: this is because light rays traveling initially toward the ground have been bent upward by layers of hot air close to the surface. In *superior mirages* objects seem to float in the air: this commonly occurs over cold surfaces such as ice or a cold sea where warmer air overlies cooler, bending rays downward.

MIRANDA, Carmen (Maria do Carmo da Cunha; 1913–1955), Portuguese-born Brazilian entertainer, in the US from 1941 where she made more than a dozen musical films.

MIRANDA, Francisco de (1750–1816), Venezuelan patriot who fought for the forces of freedom on three continents. While an officer in the army of Spain he served in the American Revolution, receiving the British surrender at Pensacola, Fla. He later joined the French revolutionary forces, fighting in several major battles. When in 1810 patriots in Venezuela formed a provisional government, he returned home, where he and Simón Bolívar proclaimed the first South American republic, in Caracas on July 5, 1811. Captured by royalists, he died in prison in Spain.

MIRANDA v. ARIZONA, case establishing the rights of a criminal suspect whom the police or other officials seek to interrogate, as defined by the US Supreme Court in 1963. In its 5-4 ruling the Court specified that prior to any sort of questioning a suspect must be told that he has the right to remain silent, that anything he says can be used against him, and that he has the right to have a lawyer present. Thereafter, if the suspect waives these rights, questioning may proceed.

MIRÓ, Joan (1893–1983), Spanish abstract painter. A pioneer of SURREALISM, his imaginative works are freely drawn and are characterized by bright colors and clusters of symbolic forms. His work includes murals and large ceramic decorations for UNESCO in Paris.

MIRROR, a smooth reflecting surface in which sharp optical images can be formed. Ancient mirrors were usually made of polished bronze, but glass mirrors backed with tin amalgam became the rule in the 17th century. Silvered-glass mirrors were first manufactured in 1840, five years after LIEBIG discovered that a silver mirror was formed on a glass surface when an ammoniacal solution of silver nitrate was reduced by an aldehyde (now usually formaldehyde).

Undistorted but laterally reversed virtual images can be seen in plane (flat) mirrors. (Such images are "virtual" and not "real" because no light actually passes through the apparent position of the image.) Concave spherical mirrors form real inverted images of objects farther away than half the radius of curvature of the mirror and virtual images of closer objects. Concave mirrors (usually with an unglazed metallic surface) are used in astronomical TELESCOPES because of their freedom from many LENS defects. Parabolic concave mirrors, which focus a parallel beam of light in a single point, also find use as reflectors for solar furnaces and searchlights. Convex spherical mirrors always form distorted virtual images but offer a wider field of view than plane mirrors. Half-silvered glass mirrors are used in many optical instruments and can be used to give a one-way mirror effect between a well-lit and a dimly illuminated room. (See also LIGHT; REFLECTION.)

MISES, Ludwig Edler von (1881–1973), Austrian-born US economist, a leader of the Austrian school of free-market economics. He emigrated (1940) to the US, where he taught (1945–69) at New York U.

MISHIMA, Yukio (1925–1970), Japanese author, born Kimitake Hiraoka into a SAMURAI family. His writing is obsessed with the conflict between traditional and post-WWII Japan. He formed a private army devoted to ancient martial arts and committed HARA-KIRI. His work includes the novels *The Temple of the Golden Pavilion* (1956), *Sun and Steel* (1970), *Sea of Fertility* (4 vols., 1970) and *Patriotism* (1966), on ritual suicide, and modern Kabuki and Noh plays.

MISHNAH. See TALMUD.

MISSILE, anything that can be thrown or projected. In modern usage the word most often describes the self-propelled weapons developed during and since WWII, properly called guided missiles.

The first rocket missiles were used by the Chinese in the 13th century, but the ancestors of the modern missile were the German V-1 and V-2 rockets used to bombard London in WWII. There was no defense against the V-2, which could reach 3,500mph. Captured V-2s gave Russia and the US the starting point for further development culminating in intercontinental missiles capable of delivering nuclear warheads to any spot on the globe—and also of launching mankind in space.

Missiles can be classified according to

their range, by the way they approach their target (unguided, guided or ballistic), by their use (surface-to-surface [SSM], surface-to-air [SAM], etc.) or by their target (as with antitank missiles). The *Minuteman III*, for example, is an intercontinental ballistic missile (ICBM), with a range of more than 8,000 miles and a ballistic arc trajectory, after burnout of its last stage, like a shell fired from a gun. The newer guided missiles fall into the category of "smart" or precision-guided weapons, non-nuclear munitions that can be remotely guided to their target after launch. The first of these, the wire-guided, manually controlled French SS10 antitank missile was used in the Arab-Israeli war of 1956.

Missiles are normally propelled by solid-fueled rockets equipped with an oxidant that allows the fuel to burn outside the atmosphere. Liquid propellants are more volatile and not generally used. Larger missiles, such as the *Minuteman*, comprise several stages, each with its own motor. This gives the missile increased speed, range and lifting capacity. The same system is generally used in spacecraft-launching missiles such as *Atlas* or *Saturn*. A few missiles, such as the *Hound Dog* air-to-surface missile carried by the B-52 and the cruise missiles are powered by jets. Britain's *Bloodhound* is driven by a ramjet (see JET PROPULSION).

Guidance systems vary from wire guidance for short-range missiles to elaborate homing systems which eliminate almost all possibility of escape. Wire guidance allows the operator to control the course of the missile through two fine wires paid out behind it. More complex guidance systems rely on radio beams, television, infrared sensors, radar and laser "designator" beams. Computers fed by laser or radar track missiles and correct their courses. Homing systems involve devices which detect waves emitted by or reflected from the target. Some home in on heat in the form of infrared rays; others use radar. To prevent jamming, systems are being provided with Electronic Counter Counter Measures circuitry allowing them to operate on alternating frequencies. Some systems are pre-set with a complete flight plan to guide the missile to a selected target, and to correct any deviation from course. Most long-range missiles have an inertial guidance system to detect changes in course and velocity. Inertial guidance systems do not rely on information obtained outside the missile. They contain elements that sense the magnitude and direction of the acceleration vector and from that compute velocity, then distance covered and direction.

The emergence of the multiple independently targeted reentry vehicle (MIRV) in the 1960s greatly increased missile lethality. MIRV'd missiles contain multiple warheads in their first stage or "bus." Each reentry vehicle can be directed to a different target.

Missile launchers range from the simple tube of the bazooka to the fully tracked mobile carrier used for *Lance*. Larger missiles such as ICBMs require so much elaborate support equipment that they must be stored in heavily defended underground silos. Nuclear-powered missile submarines are more difficult to detect and destroy. The US has over 40 such vessels carrying Polaris, Poseidon and Trident missiles. Surface vessels may also use missiles, gyro-stabilized to allow for the movement of the ship. Aircraft-launched missiles usually have a guidance system enabling the aircraft itself to remain a considerable distance from the target. Planes taking off from aircraft carriers more than 1,000mi from target should be able to launch sea-launched cruise missiles (SLCM) at a distance of 700mi from their objective. The SALT and START talks between the US and Russia resulted from the crippling expense and high risks involved in the uncontrolled development of nuclear missiles and antimissile systems.

MISSIONS, organizations for propagating a religious faith. Found from time to time in most religions, they are most characteristic of Christianity. The basis of Christian mission lies in the saving action of God to all men, found in Hebrew prophetic writings and especially in the New Testament, and in Jesus' commission to his APOSTLES to "make disciples of all nations." Vigorous missionary activity, pioneered by St. PAUL, spread Christianity through the Roman Empire and beyond. From the 5th to the 10th centuries the rest of Europe was converted (sometimes by force), though N Africa was lost to ISLAM. There was then little missionary activity until after the Council of TRENT, when the Roman Catholic Church sent missionaries, especially JESUITS, to the Far East and the empires of Spain, Portugal and France; such work has been administered since 1622 by the Congregation for the Propagation of the Faith. Protestant missionary work began in the 17th century among the American Indians but became a major enterprise only after the evangelical revival, when numerous missionary societies, denominational and voluntary, were formed, starting with the

Baptist Missionary Society (1792). Today, missions operate in most countries of the world, aiming to help native churches and to do medical and educational work.

MISSISSIPPI, state, S US, bounded to the E by Ala., to the W by La. and Ark. across the Mississippi R., and to the N by Tenn. On the S it borders on the Gulf of Mexico and includes a chain of small islands separated from the mainland by the Mississippi Sound.

Name of state: Mississippi
Capital: Jackson
Statehood: Dec. 10, 1817 (20th state)
Familiar name: Magnolia State
Area: 47,716sq mi
Population: 2,625,000
Elevation: Highest—806ft, Woodall Mountain. Lowest—sea level, Gulf of Mexico
Motto: *Virtute et armis* ("By valor and arms")
State flower: Magnolia
State bird: Mockingbird
State tree: Magnolia
State song: "Go, Mississippi"
Land. The W edge of the state is in the fertile Mississippi alluvial plain known as the Delta, which has numerous streams, rivers and lakes. The rest of the state lies in the Gulf coastal plain. Pine forests cover much of the S area (about 55% of the state is commercial woodland), and the NE is hilly agricultural land. The general climate is subtropical with some 200 to 300 days of growing season and average rainfall of 50in per year.
People. The present population is about 50% rural. The white population is more than 98% native-born with primarily British, Irish and N European ancestors, while the black population (about 35% of the total) is also almost wholly native-born, partly descended from the former slave population.
Economy. In the 1960s for the first time Mississippi's income from agriculture came second to that from industry. Although cotton is no longer "king" in what was virtually a one-crop economy until the 1860s, it is still produced in large quantities.

Other important produce includes soybeans, pecans, sweet potatoes, rice, sugarcane, poultry, livestock and fish. Petroleum and natural gas are the main natural resources besides timber. Major manufacturing is concerned with clothing and textiles, paper and wood products, food processing, chemicals and electrical and transportation equipment.
History. Mississippi was discovered by Hernando DE SOTO in 1540. Part of the area was claimed by Britain and was ceded by the French to the British in 1763. Spanish claims in the S were not relinquished until 1798. Mississippi became a slave-based agricultural economy and was the second state to secede from the Union (Jan. 1861) before the CIVIL WAR. The state suffered severely from the war and RECONSTRUCTION. After WWII agriculture in the state was boosted with federal funds and farm programs. During the 1960s Mississippi experienced a period of intense change which brought increasing industrial employment and also bitter strife over black civil rights. By the 1970s the state's economy was more prosperous than it had ever been and its racial problems were generally being confronted in a balanced atmosphere. In 1988 Mississippi had more black elected officials than any other state. In presidential elections 1968–88, Mississippi voted Republican in 1972 and 1980–88.

MISSISSIPPIAN, the antepenultimate period of the PALEOZOIC, lasting from about 345 to 315 million years ago. (See also CARBONIFEROUS; GEOLOGY.)

MISSISSIPPI RIVER, the chief river of the North American continent and one of the world's great rivers. It divides the US from N to S between Lake Itasca in NW Minn. and the Gulf of Mexico below New Orleans, La. Known as the "father of waters," it drains an area of approximately 1,247,000sq mi. With the MISSOURI and OHIO rivers (its chief tributaries) and the Jefferson-Beaverhead-Red Rock system it forms the world's third longest river system (some 3,710mi). Its main course is some 2,348mi. It receives more than 250 tributaries. The Mississippi is noted for sudden changes of course; its length varies by 40–50mi per year. The river's average discharge is 1,640,000cu ft per sec, but in high water season this soars to some 2,300,000cu ft per sec. Flooding is a serious problem, but dikes and levees have been built to contain its periodic massive overflows. The river is a major transportation artery of the US and was of fundamental importance in the development of the American continent.

MISSOURI, a W central US state, bounded by Ia. to the N, Ark. to the S, Kan., Neb. and Okla. to the W; on the E it is separated from Ill., Ky. and Tenn. by the Mississippi R. Its largest cities are St. Louis; Kansas City; Springfield; and Independence, the home of former President Harry TRUMAN.

Name of state: Missouri
Capital: Jefferson City
Statehood: Aug. 10, 1821 (24th state)
Familiar name: Show Me State
Area: 69,686sq mi
Population: 5,066,000
Elevation: Highest—1,772ft, Taum Sauk Mountain. Lowest—230ft, St. Francis River in Dunklin County
Motto: *Salus populi suprema lex esto* ("Let the welfare of the people be the supreme law")
State flower: Hawthorn
State bird: Bluebird
State tree: Flowering dogwood
State song: "Missouri Waltz"
Land. The state's development has been shaped by its two principal rivers. The Missouri was an early pioneering route to the West, while the Mississippi linked the state to the South. The N third of the state above the Missouri lies in the Midwest "corn belt," while the SE corner lies in the fertile Mississippi alluvial plain. In the central and S portion of the state is the forested Ozark plateau, which has poor, stony soil but great scenic beauty and is a popular tourist region.
People. About 65% of the people now live in urban areas, and the population continues to move from rural areas. In 1986 blacks were almost 11% of the state's total population.
Economy. Agriculture has always been an important factor in the state's economy. Livestock raising is a prime source of income as is the production of soybeans, corn, wheat and cotton. Manufacturing is heavily concentrated around the St. Louis and Kansas City areas, which are major mid-continental transportation crossroads

and industrial centers. Production of transportation equipment (automobile assembly, railroad cars, airplanes, rocket engines, space capsules and other aerospace technology) ranks first; the second-largest industry is food processing. Electrical and electronic equipment and chemicals are also produced. Missouri is a leading lead producer. Banking (with Federal Reserve banks in St. Louis and Kansas City) and tourism are also important to the state's economic base.
History. Missouri was explored by the Spanish in the mid-16th century, but claimed for France by LA SALLE in 1682 and was subsequently developed by French fur traders. It was acquired by the US in the LOUISIANA PURCHASE (1803). Under the MISSOURI COMPROMISE, the state entered the Union as a slave state in 1821. Historically, the state was a central point of departure for traders, explorers and pioneers moving westward. It was also a border state between N and S, conservative in politics but generally northern in sympathies. During the Civil War many battles were fought on its territory. Industry expanded with the arrival of German, Irish, Polish and Jewish immigrants.

In 1839, the U. of Mo. was the first state university to be founded W of the Mississippi. Its world-famous School of Journalism (established 1908) was the first in the world. Since WWII technological industrialization has displaced agriculture in the economy and many new industries have created new jobs.

A boundary dispute with Ill., settled in 1970, resulted in Mo. receiving Cottonwoods and Roth Islands. In the 1980s, population growth was a modest 5%. A ten-year court battle over desegregation of the Kansas City schools was settled in 1987 with the busing of white students from the suburbs. In presidential elections 1968–88, Missouri voted Republican in 1968–72 and 1980–88.

MISSOURI COMPROMISE, a measure adopted by the US Congress in 1820, to resolve the issue of Missouri's admission to the Union as a slave state. At the time of Missouri's first petition (1819), there were 11 free and 11 slave states in the Union. The addition of Missouri would have changed the balance of power in the US Senate and reopened the bitterly contested issue between N and S as to whether slavery should be permitted and allowed to spread in the US. Action on Missouri's petition was delayed until Maine (formerly a part of Massachusetts) requested admission as a free state. A series of maneuvers led by

Henry CLAY resulted in Missouri being admitted as a state in which slavery was legal, while Maine was admitted as a state in which it was not, with the added proviso that slavery would not be permitted in the rest of the territory of the LOUISIANA PURCHASE (of which Missouri had been part) N of 36° 30'. The compromise was later repealed in 1854 by the KANSAS-NEBRASKA ACT, which introduced the doctrine of popular sovereignty.

MISSOURI RIVER, longest river in the US (about 2,466mi) and the chief tributary of the MISSISSIPPI, with which it forms the major waterway of the US. Formed in SE Mont. by the Jefferson, Madison and Gallatin rivers in the Rocky Mts, it flows N and then E through Mont. and then enters N Dak., continuing generally SE to empty into the Mississippi R N of St. Louis. Its main tributaries along the way include the Cheyenne, Kansas, Osage, Platte, Yellowstone, James and Milk rivers. The Missouri was explored by JOLIET and MARQUETTE in 1673 and the LEWIS AND CLARK EXPEDITION in 1804–05. Like the Mississippi, it has been subject to disastrous flooding, which has been brought under control in the past three decades.

MISTI, El, a volcano, rising 19,031ft high in the Andes Mts, S Peru, near Arequipa. Its last eruption was in 1600. El Misti has been the source of many legends and played a part in the religion of the INCAS.

MISTLETOE, many species of evergreen plant parasites with small inconspicuous flowers, belonging to the family Loranthaceae. In Europe, the common mistletoe (*Viscum album*) commonly grows on apples, poplar, willow, linden and hawthorns, while the common mistletoes of the US (*Phoradendron spp* and *Arceuthobium spp*) occur on most deciduous trees and some conifers. Mistletoes derive some of their nutrients from the host plants, but being green produce some by PHOTOSYNTHESIS. Seed dispersal is achieved by fruit-eating birds that deposit the seeds on the bark of trees.

MISTRAL, Frédéric (1830–1914), French poet. He won the 1905 Nobel Prize for Literature and for his work as leader of a movement to restore the former glories of the Provençal language and culture. Among his works are the epic poems *Mireio* (1859), *Calendau* (1867), *Nerto* (1884) and *Lou Pouémo dúo Rose* (1897).

MISTRAL, Gabriela (1889–1957), pen name of Chilean poet, educator and diplomat, Lucila Godoy Alcayaga, awarded the Nobel Prize for Literature in 1945. Her simple, lyrical poems express a deep

sympathy with nature and mankind. Her work includes *Desolation* (1922) and *Tenderness* (1924).

MISTRAL, cold wind blowing S from the Central Plateau of France to the NW Mediterranean. It occurs mainly in winter, and speeds up to about 90mph have been recorded. It is a hazard to air and surface transport, crops and buildings.

MITCHELL, John (1870–1919), US labor leader; president of the UNITED MINE WORKERS (1898–1908) and vice-president of the AFL (1899–1914). He was a conservative whose advocacy of harmonious relations between labor and capital alienated him from many union members.

MITCHELL, John Newton (1913–1988), US lawyer and public official, attorney general (1967–72) in the administration of Richard NIXON. Tough on crime and dissent, he was convicted (1975) of conspiracy, obstruction of justice, and perjury for his part in covering up the WATERGATE affair and served 19 months (1977–79) in prison.

MITCHELL, Margaret (1900–1949), US writer. Her best selling and only novel *Gone With the Wind* (1936) won the 1937 Pulitzer Prize and was made into a phenomenally successful film (1939).

MITCHELL, Maria (1818–1889), US astronomer, who discovered a comet in 1847. She was the first woman to be elected to the American Academy of Arts and Sciences (1848) and was professor of astronomy at Vassar College (1865–88).

MITCHELL, Wesley Clair (1874–1948), US economist and educator. He helped organize the National Bureau of Economic Research (1920) and was its research director, 1920–45. He served on many government boards and was a leading authority on business cycles.

MITCHELL, William Lendrum "Billy" (1879–1936), US army officer and aviator. After leading US air services in WWI, he became an active champion for a strong air force independent of army or naval control. Court-martialed for insubordination, and suspended from duty for five years in 1925, he resigned from the army in 1926.

MITFORD, Jessica (1917–   ), English-born US writer known as the "Queen of the Muckrakers." In addition to her exposé of the funeral industry in *The American Way of Death* (1963), she has excoriated the Famous Writers School, "fat farms" for wealthy women, and the US prison system. A sister of Nancy Mitford, she has chronicled her eccentric family in *Daughters and Rebels* (1960) and *A Fine Old Conflict* (1977).

MITFORD, Nancy (1904–1973), English author known for her witty, sophisticated portrayals of the English upper classes in such novels as *Love in a Cold Climate* (1949) and *Don't Tell Alfred* (1960). She also wrote biographies: *Madame de Pompadour* (1954, 1968), *Voltaire in Love* (1957) and *Frederick the Great* (1970).

MITHRA or **MITHRAS**, Indo-Iranian sun-god, one of the ethical lords or gods in ZOROASTRIANISM. By 400 BC, he was the chief Persian deity. His cult spread over most of Asia Minor and, according to Plutarch, reached Rome in 68 BC. Mithraism was especially popular among the Roman legions. Roman Mithraism, which amounted to a virtual parody of Christianity, declined after 200 AD and was officially suppressed in the 4th century.

MITHRADATES VI (c132–63 BC), king of Pontus, on the Black Sea, who fought three wars against the Roman state. In the first (88–84 BC), he overran Asia Minor and massacred its Roman citizens, but was subsequently forced to make peace. He won the second war (83–81 BC) but lost the third (74–63 BC) and fled to the Crimea, where he ordered a mercenary to kill him.

MITOCHONDRIA. See CELL.

MITOSIS, the normal process by which a CELL divides into two. Initially the CHROMOSOMES become visible in the nucleus before longitudinally dividing into a pair of parallel *chromatids*. The chromosomes shorten and thicken and arrange themselves on a spindle across the equator of the cell. The cell then divides so that each daughter contains a full complement of chromosomes.

MITTERRAND, François (1916–), writer, political leader and president of France (1981–). A cabinet minister in 11 governments during the Fourth Republic, he opposed De Gaulle's establishment of the Fifth Republic in 1958. Candidate of the non-Communist left he first ran for the presidency in 1965 and was defeated by De Gaulle. He became head of the Socialist Party in 1971 and again ran unsuccessfully for the presidency in 1974. He finally won in 1981 and was reelected in 1988.

MIX, Tom (1880–1940), US film actor and director whose popular westerns featured spectacular photography and daring horsemanship. He starred in such silent films as *Desert Love* (1920) and *Riders of the Purple Sage* (1925) and in numerous films of the 1930s.

MIXTECS or **Mixtecas,** Indian people occupying Guerrero, Puebla and Oaxaca states, in SW Mexico. They were one of the most important and culturally advanced pre–Columbian peoples in Mesoamerica. They eclipsed the ZAPOTEC INDIANS by the 14th century, but were themselves overshadowed by the AZTECS prior to the arrival of the Spanish, who defeated the last Mixtec kingdom c1550. The Mixtec language is today spoken by some 300,000 Mexican people.

MOBILE, a moving, three-dimensional abstract sculpture. The form was invented by Alexander CALDER c1930 and named by Marcel DUCHAMP. A mobile consists of a group of shapes connected together by rods or wires, and suspended to move freely in the air, changing the spatial relationships among the pieces as they turn.

MOBILE BAY, Battle of, Civil War conflict on Aug. 5, 1864, in which Union admiral FARRAGUT's command broke through the Confederate defensive forts and torpedo lines and destroyed key units of the South's fleet. The battle formed part of the North's wider strategy to encircle the Confederacy.

MÖBIUS STRIP, a topological space (see TOPOLOGY) formed by joining the two ends of a strip of paper or other material after having turned one of the ends through an ANGLE of 180°. It is of interest in that it has only one side: if a line is drawn from a point A on the surface parallel to the edges of the strip it will eventually pass through a point A′ directly through the paper from A. This circle is known as a nonbounding cycle since it does not bound an area of the surface.

MOBUTU SESE SEKO (1930–), born Joseph Désiré Mobutu, president of the Republic of Zaire (formerly the Belgian Congo) from 1965. He ousted President KASAVUBU. He was credited for instilling a national consciousness in a country made up of 200 tribes, in part by suppressing or coopting all opposition and establishing a personality cult. But his government became notorious for its incompetence and corruption. Mobutu himself was alleged to have amassed $5 billion.

MOCKINGBIRDS, a family, Mimidae, of songbirds of the Americas; or, certain species within that family. They are long-tailed birds with short, rounded wings and well-developed legs, which skulk in low scrub feeding on insects and fruit. Certain species may flick their wings when searching for food, perhaps to disturb insects that would otherwise remain undetected.

MODE, in music, the method of tone selection as a basis for melody and harmony. Starting on any "home" note to designate key, each mode follows a fixed progression of tones and semitones to form a

SCALE. By about 1600 Western music retained only the major and minor modes of 14 that grew from the eight plainsong modes of Medieval church music. The eight Greek modes, ancestors of these, were conceived from the top note down.

MODEL PARLIAMENT, an English parliament set up in 1295 by Edward I. The Model Parliament's wide representation of clergy, earls, barons, two knights from each county and two burgesses from each borough indicated Parliament's developing representational role, although these principles of membership were by no means strictly observed through much of the 14th century.

MODERNISM, in Christian theology, a movement in the late 19th and early 20th centuries that aimed to reinterpret traditional doctrine to align it with modern trends in philosophy, history and the sciences. It espoused the liberal, critical view of the Bible, was skeptical about the historicity of Christian origins, and downgraded traditional credal dogma. Modernism became dominant in Protestantism (though opposed by FUNDAMENTALISM). The similar movement in Roman Catholicism was formally condemned by Pius X (1907) and largely disappeared.

MODERNISMO, a movement in Latin American and Spanish poetry in the late 19th and early 20th centuries, influenced by SYMBOLISM and the PARNASSIANS. The exoticism of the Nicaraguan poet Rubén Darío provided the impetus for the movement.

MODIGLIANI, Amedeo (1884–1920), Italian painter and sculptor. He is best known for studies of nudes and for portraits, works characterized by elongated forms and elegant draftsmanship. He was influenced by African sculpture and by BRANCUSI.

MODIGLIANI, Franco (1918–   ), Italian-born US economist, winner of the 1985 Nobel Prize for Economics for analyzing the behavior of household savers and the functioning of financial markets.

MODOC INDIANS, North American Indian tribe who occupied parts of what is now Cal. and Ore. They are closely related to the KLAMATH INDIANS, with whom, in 1864, they agreed to move to an Ore. reservation. In 1870 a Modoc group, led by Chief Kintpuash ("Captain Jack"), fled back to N Cal. The group was attacked by a US army unit, bringing about the Modoc War (1872–73). Gen. Edward Canby was killed during the peace negotiations, and the tribe subsequently returned to Ore.

MOGUL EMPIRE, 16th- and 17th-century empire in India, founded by Babur, who invaded India from Afghanistan in 1526. His son Humayun was defeated by the Afghan Sher Shah Sur, but Mogul power was restored by AKBAR (1556–1605). He established firm, centralized government throughout Afghanistan and N and central India. The Mogul "golden age" was in the reign of SHAH JEHAN (1628–58). During this time, the TAJ MAHAL, the Pearl Mosque of Agra and many of Delhi's finest buildings were erected. In the 1700s, the rising power of the Hindu Mahrattas weakened the empire. In 1803 the British occupied Delhi and in 1857 they deposed the last puppet Mogul emperor, Bahadur Shah II.

MOHACS, Battles of, name of two Turkish battles. In 1526 the Ottoman Sultan Suleiman I defeated the Hungarians, killing Louis II of Hungary and about 25,000 of his army. In 1687 the Turks were routed by forces under Charles V of Lorraine.

MOHAMMED, or **Muhammad** or **Mahomet** (c570–632), "the Praised One," founder of ISLAM, the Muslim faith. He was born in Mecca and was a member of its ruling tribe. He became a merchant and his trade from Mecca brought him into contact with Judaism and Christianity. At the age of 40, he had a vision of the archangel Gabriel which bade him go forth and preach. This, and subsequent visions, were recorded in the KORAN, the Muslim sacred book. Mohammed proclaimed himself God's messenger and called on the Meccans to accept Allah as the only god. At first, he made few converts. Among the earliest were his wife Khadija, his daughter Fatima, her husband and his cousin, Ali, and his friend ABU BAKR. As Mohammed's influence increased, the Meccans began to fear he might gain political control of the city. They persecuted his followers and plotted to murder him. In 622, he fled to Yathrib, which he subsequently renamed MEDINA, "City of the Prophet," with Abu Bakr and some followers. This event is known as the Hegira (departure). Muslim calendars are dated from the Hegira. In Medina, Mohammed formed an Islamic community based upon religious faith rather than tribal or family loyalties. He rapidly extended his territory by conquest and conversion. In 630, after a long period of warfare with Mecca and winning the battles of Badr (624) and Uhud (625), he captured Mecca with little bloodshed, making it both the political and religious capital of Islam. He proclaimed the KAABA a mosque and laid down the ceremonies of the *Hadj* (pilgrimage) to Mecca.

MOHAMMED II (1429–1481), Ottoman sultan (1451–81) who captured Constantinople in 1453, putting an end to the BYZANTINE EMPIRE, then enlarged and consolidated the OTTOMAN EMPIRE in Asia Minor and the Balkan peninsula.

MOHAMMED REZA SHAH PAHLAVI (1919–1980), shah of Iran (1941–79). He succeeded to the throne when his father, REZA SHAH PAHLAVI, was forced into exile by British and Soviet occupation forces. He was himself forced (1953) into a brief exile by the nationalist prime minister Mohammed MOSSADEGH, but the US engineered a coup expelling Mossadegh and restoring the shah to power. The shah used Iran's oil revenues to modernize the country as rapidly as possible, and with US aid he built a large military force. His policies provoked opposition on all sides, particularly among anti-Western Islamic fundamentalists. Dying of cancer, the shah left Iran in Jan. 1979 in the midst of strikes and violent demonstrations. Later that year an Islamic republic was declared by Ayatollah Ruhollah KHOMEINI.

MOHAWK INDIANS, North American tribe of Indians, members of the IROQUOIS League. They aided the British in their victories at Lake George, 1755, and Fort Niagara, 1759, and during the Revolutionary War.

MOHICAN INDIANS, name of two related North American Indian tribes: the Mahican Indians of the upper Hudson R, and the Mohegan Indians of SW Conn. After the coming of the Dutch, the Mahicans dispersed westward. The Mohegans and the PEQUOT INDIANS were at this time living as one tribe. They enjoyed great power under Sassacus and Uncas. Today only a few Mohegans survive.

MOHOLY-NAGY, László (1895–1946), Hungarian painter, designer and member of the German Constructivist school. He was professor at the BAUHAUS 1923–28. He founded the Chicago Institute of Design in 1939 and was an important influence on US industrial design.

MOHOROVICIC DISCONTINUITY, a seismic boundary of the earth originally regarded as separating the crust and mantle (see EARTH), evidenced by rapid increase in the velocity of seismic waves (see EARTHQUAKE). The US project Mohole, designed to drill through the "Moho," was abandoned in 1966. More important are the discontinuities between the core and the mantle (Gutenberg or Oldham Discontinuity), with a radius of about 3,500km; and between the inner and outer cores, with a radius of about 1,200km to 1,650km.

MOJAVE or MOHAVE DESERT, an area of barren mountains and desert valleys in S

Cal. It is swept by strong winds; average annual rainfall is 5in. It includes DEATH VALLEY in the N, and the Joshua Tree National Monument in the S. It is a rich source of minerals.

MOLASSES ACT, prohibitive duties introduced by England in 1733 in an attempt to force the American colonies to import molasses, sugar, rum and other spirits exclusively from the British West Indies. Rendered ineffective through smuggling, it was replaced by the Sugar Act (1764).

MOLD, general name for a number of filamentous FUNGI that produce powdery or fluffy growths on fabrics, foods and decaying plant or animal remains. Best known is the blue bread mold caused by *Penicillium*, from which the ANTIBIOTIC, PENICILLIN, was first discovered.

MOLDAU RIVER. See VLTAVA.

MOLE, pigmented spot or nevus in the SKIN, consisting of a localized group of special cells containing MELANIN. Change in a mole, such as increase in size, change of color and bleeding should lead to suspicion of melanoma.

MOLECULAR BIOLOGY, the study of the structure and function of the MOLECULES which make up living organisms. This includes the study of PROTEINS, ENZYMES, CARBOHYDRATES, FATS and NUCLEIC ACIDS. (See also BIOCHEMISTRY; BIOLOGY; BIOPHYSICS.)

MOLECULAR WEIGHT, the sum of the ATOMIC WEIGHTS of all the atoms in a MOLECULE. It is an integral multiple of the empirical FORMULA weight found by chemical ANALYSIS, and of the equivalent weight. Molecular weights may be found directly by MASS SPECTROSCOPY, or deduced from related physical properties including gas DENSITY; effusion; osmotic pressure (see OSMOSIS), and effects on solvents; lowering of vapor pressure and freezing point, and raising of boiling point; for large molecules the ultracentrifuge is used.

MOLECULE, entity composed of ATOMS linked by chemical BONDS and acting as a unit; the smallest particle of a chemical compound which retains the COMPOSITION and chemical properties of the compound. The composition of a molecule is represented by its molecular FORMULA. Elements may exist as molecules, e.g. oxygen O_2, phosphorus P_4. Free radicals and IONS are merely types of molecules. Molecules range in size from single atoms to **macromolecules**—chiefly PROTEINS and POLYMERS—with MOLECULAR WEIGHTS of 10,000 or more. The chief properties of molecules are their structure (bond lengths and angles)—determined by electron diffraction, X-ray diffraction and SPECTROSCOPY—spectra, and dipole moments.

MOLES, small insectivores adapted to an underground digging existence, family Talpidae. The family includes a number of species of European and American distribution. All have large spade-shaped hands projecting sideways from the body and long, mobile muzzles. The eyes are small, and there is no external ear. They are solitary animals and live in a complicated system of burrows, feeding on soil invertebrates, largely earthworms. Parallel evolution has produced identical adaptations in marsupial moles and golden moles.

MOLIÈRE, stage name of Jean-Baptiste Poquelin (1622–1673), France's greatest comic dramatist, renowned for his satire on hypocrisy and his characters personifying particular vices and types. After touring the provinces as actor-manager and playwright for many years, he eventually became established in Paris with the success of *Les Précieuses ridicules* in 1659. Among his best-known works are *Tartuffe* (1664), *Le Misanthrope* (1666), *Le Bourgeois gentilhomme* (1670) and *Le Malade imaginaire* (1673).

MOLLUSKS, soft-bodied invertebrates, typically having a calcareous shell into which the body can withdraw. They include slugs and SNAILS, limpets, winkles, CLAMS, mussels and OYSTERS, as well as the apparently dissimilar OCTOPUSES and SQUIDS. Mollusks have adapted to an incredible variety of niches in the sea, in fresh water and on land. This has resulted in equal diversity of structure and habit. Major groups of mollusks include BIVALVES, CEPHALOPODA, chitons and gastropoda.

MOLLY MAGUIRES, Irish-American secret society in the Pa. anthracite mining area c1862–79, whose name was borrowed from an Irish anti-landlord organization. In a time of harsh conditions and labor unrest, its members were alleged to have been responsible for intimidation, sabotage and even murder against police and mining officials. They were exposed on the testimony of PINKERTON agent James McParlan, who infiltrated the organization.

MOLLY PITCHER. See PITCHER, MOLLY.

MOLNÁR, Ferenc (1878–1952), Hungarian author and playwright, who lived in the US from 1940. His play *Liliom* (1909) was adapted as the musical *Carousel* (1945). He also wrote novels and short stories.

MOLOCH, the Canaanite god of fire, to whom children were sacrificed, identified in the Old Testament as a god of the Ammonites. His worship, introduced by King Ahaz, was condemned by the prophets, and his sanctuary at Tophet near Jerusalem later became known as Gehenna.

MOLOTOV, Vyacheslav Mikhailovich (1890–1986), born Vyacheslav Mikhailovich Skriabin, Russian diplomat. He became a Bolshevik in 1906, and after the RUSSIAN REVOLUTION quickly rose to power in the Communist Party. He was Soviet premier 1930–41 under Stalin. As foreign minister 1939–49 and 1953–56, he negotiated the 1939 nonaggression pact with Germany and played an important role in the USSR's wartime and postwar relations with the West. Under Khrushchev, he lost power and held only minor posts, and in 1964 it was revealed that he had been expelled from the Communist Party.

MOLTING, the shedding of the skin, fur or feathers by an animal. It may be a seasonal occurrence, as a periodic renewal of fur or plumage in mammals and birds, or it may be associated with GROWTH, as in insects or crustaceans. In birds and mammals the molt is primarily to renew worn fur or feathers so that plumage or pelage is kept in good condition for waterproofing, insulation or flight. In addition it may serve to shed breeding plumage in birds, or to change between summer and winter coats. In invertebrates the rigid external skeleton must be shed and replaced to allow growth within. In larval insects the final molts are involved in the METAMORPHOSIS to adult form.

MOLTKE, Helmuth Johannes Ludwig, Graf von (1848–1916), German chief of staff 1906–14, nephew of Helmuth Karl MOLTKE. Responsible for German strategy at the start of WWI, he was dismissed after losing the first battle of the MARNE.

MOLTKE, Helmuth Karl Bernhard, Graf von (1800–1891), Prussian and, later, German chief of staff 1858–88. A strategist of genius, he won victories against Denmark (1864), Austria (1866), and France (1870–71), greatly furthering German unification (1871).

MOLUCCAS, or Spice Islands, a group of fertile, volcanic islands in E Indonesia, between Celebes and New Guinea. Once the center of the world trade in nutmeg and cloves, the islands now export copra and forest products, as well as spices.

MOLYBDENUM (Mo), silvery-gray metal in Group VIB of the PERIODIC TABLE: a transition element. It is obtained commercially by roasting molybdenite in air and reducing the oxide formed with carbon in an electric furnace or by the thermite process to give ferromolybdenum. Because of its high melting point, it is used to support the filament in electric lamps and for furnace heating elements. It also finds use in corrosion-resistant, high-temperature STEELS and ALLOYS. Molybdenum is unreactive, but forms various covalent compounds. Some are used as industrial catalysts. Molybdenum is a vital trace element in plants and a catalyst in bacterial nitrogen fixation. AW 95.9, mp 2610°C, bp 5560°C, sg 10.2 (20°C).

MOMENTUM, the product of the MASS and linear velocity of a body. Momentum is thus a vector quantity. The linear momentum of a system of interacting particles is the sum of the momenta of its particles, and is constant if no external forces act. The rate of change of momentum with time in the direction of an applied force equals the force (Newton's second law of motion—see MECHANICS). In rotational motion, the analogous concept is **angular momentum,** the product of the moment of inertia and the angular velocity of a body relative to a given rotation axis. If no external forces act on a rotating system, the direction and magnitude of its angular momentum remain constant.

MOMMSEN, Theodor (1817–1903), German liberal classical scholar and historian, winner of the 1902 Nobel Prize for Literature. He was an authority on Roman law, and wrote a famous *History of Rome* (3 vols; 1854–56).

MONACO, independent principality on the Mediterranean near the French-Italian border, about 370 acres in area. It is a tourist center with a yachting harbor and a world-famous casino. Since 1960 land reclamation has increased Monaco's size by 20%.

Official name: Principality of Monaco
Capital: Monaco
Area: 0.7sq mi
Population: 29,000
Languages: French
Religions: Roman Catholic
Monetary unit(s): 1 French franc = 100 centimes.

Monaco's towns are MONTE CARLO, Monaco-Ville (capital), La Condamine (commercial center) and Fontvieille (small industrial area).

The reigning constitutional monarch, Prince Rainier III, succeeded to the throne in 1949 and married the US film actress Grace Kelly in 1956. In 1962, after a crisis with France over Monaco's tax free status, he proclaimed a new constitution, guaranteeing fundamental rights, giving the vote to women and abolishing the death penalty. The government consists of three councillors, headed by a minister of state who must be French. There is an 18-member National Council elected for five-year terms by universal suffrage, which shares legislative powers with the Prince. Foreign relations are controlled by France. In recent years light industry and banking have grown, but the vitally important tourism declined after the death of Princess Grace in 1982.

MONARCH BUTTERFLY, *Danaus plexippus,* an American BUTTERFLY remarkable not only for its size and coloration, but because it is one of those species of butterfly that undertake long MIGRATIONS. In spring they fly north to Canada, returning along exactly the same route in the fall. As an antipredator device, monarchs have an unpleasant taste; the coloration is mimicked for protection by other less distasteful species.

MONARCHY, form of government in which sovereignty is vested in one person, usually for life. The office may be elective but is usually hereditary. A monarch who has unlimited power is an *absolute monarch*; one whose power is limited by custom or constitution is a *constitutional monarch*. In modern parliamentary democracies a monarch is usually a non-party political figure and a symbol of national unity.

MONASTICISM, way of life, usually communal and celibate, always ascetic, conducted according to a religious rule. It is found in all major religions. Christian monasticism aims at holiness by fulfilling vows of poverty, chastity and obedience. It was founded in Egypt by St. ANTONY OF THEBES, and spread rapidly. Most early monks were hermits or lived in small groups; later, CENOBITES predominated, engaging in prayer, manual work, and sometimes in teaching and scholarship. In W Christianity, under the pervasive rule of St. BENEDICT OF NURSIA, communities were contemplative and "enclosed" (see BENEDICTINE ORDERS), as e.g. CISTERCIANS are today; but AUGUSTINIAN, DOMINICAN and FRANCISCAN friars abandoned enclosure in the 13th century. Important monastic centers included Mount ATHOS, CLUNY and MONTE CASSINO. Monasticism was abolished where the REFORMATION succeeded, but has revived and spread since the mid-19th century.

MONCK, Charles Stanley, 1st Baron (1819–1894), Irish peer and British Liberal member of Parliament. As governor general of British North America (1861–67), he promoted confederation of the Canadian provinces and became the first governor general of the Dominion of Canada (1867–68).

MONCK or MONK, George, 1st Duke of Albermarle (1608–1670), English general and naval commander. At first supporting CHARLES I in the English CIVIL WAR, he became CROMWELL's commander-in-chief in Scotland (1650–52; 1654–60). After Cromwell's death he was the architect of the RESTORATION of Charles II. He was a successful commander of the fleet in the DUTCH WARS (1652–54; 1666).

MONDALE, Walter Frederick "Fritz" (1928–   ), 41st US vice-president (1977–81), under James CARTER. His early career was furthered by Hubert HUMPHREY. As a Democratic senator from Minn. (1964–77) he was known as a liberal and populist reformer. Carter and Mondale ran again in 1980 but lost to Ronald REAGAN and George BUSH. He was the unsuccessful Democratic candidate for president in 1984.

MONDRIAN, Piet (1872–1944), Dutch painter and theorist, a founder of the DE STIJL movement. At first a symbolist, he was influenced by CUBISM, and evolved a distinctive abstract style relating primary colors and black and white in grid-like arrangements.

MONET, Claude (1840–1926), French painter, leading exponent of IMPRESSIONISM, a term coined after his picture *Impression, Sunrise* (1872). He worked in and around Paris, in poverty in his early years. Always fascinated by varying light effects, around 1889 he began painting series of pictures of a subject at different times of day, such as those of *Rouen Cathedral* (1892–94). His last pictures of *Water Lilies* are virtually abstract.

MONETARISM, theoretical position in economics, chiefly associated with the work of Milton FRIEDMAN of the University of Chicago. This contemporary theory is based on the 19th-century "quantity-of-money" theory, which directly related changes in price levels to changes in the amount of money in circulation. Monetarism, which stands generally in opposition to Keynesian-

ism, advocates curing inflation and depression not by fiscal measures but rather by control of the nation's money supply—for instance, by varying the interest rate charged by the FEDERAL RESERVE SYSTEM and expanding or limiting the sale of Treasury bills.

MONEY, in any economic system, is a medium of exchange, of labor and products, or for payment of debts. In primitive societies, barter, direct physical exchange, was commonly used. The precise origin of money is unknown. It evolved gradually out of the needs of commerce and trade. A wide variety of objects have at one time or other been used as money: shells, nuts, beads, stones etc. Gradually, metal was adopted because of its easy handling, durability, divisibility, and—especially with gold or silver—for its own value. The oldest coinage dates back to about 700 BC, when COINS of gold and silver alloys were made in Lydia (Asia Minor). Paper money was known in China as early as the 9th century, but it did not develop in Europe until the 17th century. The banknote and the modern BANKING system evolved when goldsmiths began, for safekeeping, to store gold and coins for others. Money thus deposited or invested could be re-used by the borrower, who therefore paid INTEREST as a fee for its availability. The realization that available money could make more money overthrew the medieval Church's view that money was barren and usury wrong. An over-reaction led to MERCANTILISM, in which money was preferred to all other forms of wealth.

The stability and value of paper currency is usually guaranteed by governments or banks (those invested with legal authority to issue currency) with some bullion holdings. However, it is tempting for governments to over-issue money as an easy way to pay their debts. This can lead to INFLATION and devaluation of the currency. (See also FEDERAL RESERVE SYSTEM.)

In the last 20 or 30 years, there has emerged a school of economists who argue that monetary policies (controlling the volume of money in circulation) should be utilized to achieve MACROECONOMIC objectives, such as growth rates, employment levels and curbing inflation.

The monetary system of the US during most of the 19th century was based on bimetalism, with the dollar defined as 371.25 grains of fine silver or 24.75 grains of fine gold. From 1900, the dollar was defined in terms of gold, with the passing of the GOLD STANDARD Act of 1900 and the Gold Reserve Act of 1934. However, in 1970 the dollar's dependency on gold was ended when the requirement set by the Treasury of 25% gold backing for all Federal Reserve notes was dropped.

MONGOL EMPIRE, founded in the 1200s by GENGHIS KHAN, who united the Mongol tribes of central Asia. Already superb horsemen and archers, the Mongols were united by Genghis Khan into a huge, well-disciplined, swiftly-moving army, which had conquered N China by 1215 and then swept W to engulf Bukhara, Samarkand, Gurgan and S Russia in a wave of terror and destruction. After his death, the bloody Mongol invasions were continued under his son Ogotai. During 1237–40, the Mongol general BATU KHAN, a grandson of Genghis Khan, crossed the Volga, crushed the Bulgars and Kumans, devastated central Russia and invaded Poland and Hungary. Further conquest was halted only by the death of Ogotai in 1241.

By about 1260 the Empire was organized into four Khanates: the Il Khanate (Persia); the Kipchak Khanate, founded by the GOLDEN HORDE (Russia); the Jagatai (Turkestan); and the Great Khanate (China). During KUBLAI KHAN'S rule (1260–94) the Great Khanate became the Yüan Dynasty of China. The Empire stretched from the China Seas to the Danube R. After his death, it disintegrated. But the Mongol tradition of conquest was revived by TAMERLANE in the 1300s and BABUR in the 1500s.

MONGOLIAN PEOPLE'S REPUBLIC, previously known as Outer Mongolia, republic in Central Asia between China and the USSR, set up in 1921.

Official name: Mongolian People's Republic
Capital: Ulan Bator
Area: 604,000sq mi
Population: 1,989,000
Languages: Mongolian
Religions: Lamaism
Monetary unit(s): 1 togrog = 100 mongo
Land. The country is a steppe plateau fringed on the N and W by mountains. Much of the SE is part of the Gobi desert. The climate is dry, with harsh extremes of temperature, and the country is very thinly populated. There are forests in the mountainous north.

People. Over 50% of the population live on state collective farms, and almost 25% in the capital, Ulan Bator. Many people continue to practice Tibetan Buddhism (Lamaism), with monasteries allowed to function.

Economy. The economy is based on livestock farming, principally of sheep and goats, but also of horses, cattle, yaks and (in the desert) camels. There is some agriculture and hunting of sable and other wild animals for fur. Coal, iron ore, gold and other minerals are mined. Industry is developing at Choybalsan, Darkhan and Ulan Bator, but is limited to felts, furniture and other consumer goods. Chief exports are of livestock, wool, hides, meat and ores. The Trans-Mongolian railroad links the country with the USSR (its chief trading partner) and China; roads and communications are poor.

History. Formerly the heartland of the MONGOL EMPIRE and a Chinese province since 1691, Mongolia declared itself independent in 1911, but was reoccupied by China in 1919. With Soviet support the country declared its independence again in 1921, and in 1924 adopted its present name and became the world's second communist state. Its communist government has since maintained close links with the USSR.

MONGOLOID, one of the three major divisions of the human RACE. Mongoloids generally have straight black hair, little facial hair, yellow to brown skin and the distinctive epicanthic fold, a fold of skin over the eyes which gives them a slanting appearance. The Amerinds, Eskimos, Polynesians and Patagonians are Mongoloid peoples, as are the Chinese, Japanese, Koreans, Indochinese and many other Asian peoples.

MONGOOSES, small carnivores of the Viverridae, with a reputation for killing snakes and stealing eggs. There are about 48 species occupying a variety of habitats around the Mediterranean, in Africa and southern Asia. Most of them are diurnal, feeding on lizards, snakes, eggs and small mammals. They are usually solitary, although a few species form colonies, often in burrows in termite mounds. All mongooses have great immunity to snake venom. One of the best known species is the common or Egyptian mongoose sometimes known as the ichneumon.

MONISM, any philosophical system asserting the essential unity of things—that all things are matter (see MATERIALISM), or mind (see IDEALISM), or of some other essence. Monism is contrasted with various kinds of DUALISM or pluralism.

MONITOR AND MERRIMACK, two pioneer ironclad warships famous for the first battle fought by iron armored vessels during the US CIVIL WAR at Hampton Roads, Va., on March 9, 1862. The *U.S.S. Merrimack* was a scuttled Union steam frigate, salvaged by the Confederates, renamed the *C.S.S. Virginia* and reinforced with iron plate. The *U.S.S. Monitor* was designed by John Ericsson and equipped with a revolving gun turret. In.1973 the *Monitor* was located on the ocean floor off Cape Hatteras, N.C., and in 1983 its 1,300-pound anchor was recovered.

MONK, Thelonius Sphere (1917?–1982), US jazz pianist and composer who pioneered cool jazz in the 1940s and 1950s.

MONKEY, a term used to describe any higher PRIMATE, suborder *Anthropoidea*, that is not an ape or a man. It includes both New World and Old World forms. There is thus little uniformity in the group; monkeys have adapted to a variety of modes of life. All have flattened faces, the Old and New World groups being distinguished by nose shape. New World, platyrrhine monkeys, family Cebidae, have broad, flat noses with the nostrils widely separated. Old World catarrhines, family Cercopithecidae, have the nostrils separated by only a thin septum. Monkeys are normally restricted to tropical or subtropical areas of the world. Old World forms include langurs, colubuses, macaques, guenons, mangabeys and BABOONS. Monkeys of the New World include sakis, uakaris,, howlers, douroucoulis, squirrel monkeys and capuchins. (See also ANTHROPOID APES.)

MON-KHMER LANGUAGES, a linguistic subfamily and geographical language group of the so-called Austro-Asiatic or Southeast Asian language family, spoken by some 35 million to 45 million people. Khmer is spoken in Kampuchea and Mon in Burma; related dialects are used in S Vietnam, the Malay peninsula, the Nicobar islands and India. (See also MALAYO-POLYNESIAN LANGUAGES.)

MONMOUTH, Battle of, engagement in the REVOLUTIONARY WAR, June 28, 1778, near Monmouth Courthouse (now Freehold, N.J.). Gen. Charles LEE's treacherous orders to retreat led to Sir Henry CLINTON's march on New York City. Molly PITCHER was the legendary American heroine of the battle.

MONNET, Jean (1888–1979), French economist and statesman; known as the architect of a united W Europe. He created the Monnet Plan (1947) to help France's economic recovery from WWII, planned and served as first president of the EUROPEAN COAL AND STEEL COMMUNITY (ECSC) and helped plan the COMMON MARKET.

MONONUCLEOSIS, Infectious, or **glandular fever,** common VIRUS infection of adolescence causing a variety of symptoms including severe sore throat, HEADACHF FEVER, malaise and enlargement of LYMPH nodes and SPLEEN. Skin rashes, hepatitis (see LIVER) with JAUNDICE, pericarditis and involvement of the NERVOUS SYSTEM may also be prominent. Atypical lymphocytes in the BLOOD and specific agglutination reactions (see ANTIBODIES AND ANTIGENS) are diagnostic. Severe cases may require STEROIDS, and convalescence may be lengthy. It can be transmitted in SALIVA and has thus been nicknamed the "kissing disease."

MONOPHYSITE CHURCHES, branches of the EASTERN CHURCH formed in the 6th century by the schismatic adherents of MONOPHYSITISM: the ARMENIAN, COPTIC and JACOBITE CHURCHES. Their doctrine is now essentially orthodox.

MONOPHYSITISM (from Greek *monos*, one, and *physis*, nature), heretical doctrine that in the Person of Christ there is but one (divine) nature. It arose in opposition to the orthodox Council of Chalcedon (451). A confused controversy resulted, and despite reconciliation attempts the schism hardened. (See also INCARNATION.)

MONOPOLY, an economic term describing significant control or ownership of a product or service (and thereby its price) because of command of the product's supply, legal privilege or concerted action. There are different kinds of monopoly. PATENTS and COPYRIGHTS are legal monopolies granted by a government to individuals or companies. A nationalized industry or service such as the US Post Office has a monopoly. A franchise granted by government to a public company to run a public utility (such as an electrical company) creates a monopoly. Trading and industrial monopolies have the power to decide upon supply and price of goods. Sometimes labor unions act as monopolies in the supply of workers' services. In the case of national monopolies, it is considered that they can provide mass-produced goods or services at a lower price, or more efficiently, than could be provided in a competitive situation; in practice this is not always true. Business or manufacturing monopolies may often discourage competitors from entering the field of competition.

There is legislation designed to control monopolies that conspire to restrain price or trade (see SHERMAN ANTITRUST ACT; CLAYTON ANTITRUST ACT; FEDERAL TRADE COMMISSION).

MONOTHEISM, belief in one God, contrasted with POLYTHEISM, PANTHEISM or atheism. Classical monotheism is held by Judaism, Christianity and Islam; some other religions, such as early Zoroastrianism and later Greek religion, are monotheistic to a lesser degree. In the theories of E. B. TYLOR, religions have evolved from animism through polytheism and henotheism (the worship of one god, ignoring others in practice) to monotheism. There is, however, evidence for residual monotheism (the "High God") in primitive religions.

MONROE, James (1758–1831), fifth president of the US, 1817–25. He promulgated the MONROE DOCTRINE, one of the most fundamental statements of foreign policy in the history of American diplomacy.

Monroe was born in Westmoreland Co., Va. He fought in the Revolution, was wounded at Trenton, commended for gallantry and became a lieutenant colonel. In 1780 he began to study law under Thomas JEFFERSON, and with his sponsorship was elected to the Virginia House of Delegates (1782), beginning a career of public service which would last over 40 years. He served in the Congress of the Confederation (1783–86) and began his law practice in 1788. Elected by Va. to the US Senate, he joined Jefferson and James MADISON in forming the Democratic-Republican Party.

Monroe's first diplomatic foray as minister to France (1794) went badly when he criticized the JAY TREATY and was recalled. He withdrew into Virginia politics, becoming governor from 1799 to 1802. During Jefferson's presidency, he was envoy extraordinary to France (1803), where he and Robert LIVINGSTON arranged the terms of the LOUISIANA PURCHASE, but was less successful in Madrid, with the Spaniards, who refused to consider American claims to W Fla. As minister to Great Britain (1806), he was unsatisfactory; his attempt to secure the presidential candidacy from Madison in 1808 was a failure. In 1811 he was once again elected governor of Va., and in the same year he became Madison's secretary of state. After the British burned Washington, D.C., in the WAR OF 1812, he added the duties of secretary of war to those of secretary of state (1814). In 1816 he easily defeated his Federalist opponent for the presidency and was reelected unopposed four years later.

Monroe's administration years were called the "era of good feeling." The country prospered after the war and expanded westward. Monroe was a moderate man who believed in a decentralized federal government. During his presidency, Fla. was purchased from Spain (1819), Mo. was admitted to the Union (1821) under the MISSOURI COMPROMISE, the Rush-Bagot agreement (1817) was concluded with Great Britain, the 49th parallel was established as the US-Canadian boundary, the MONROE DOCTRINE guaranteed that European interference would not be tolerated in the Americas and the Santa Fe Trail to the SW was opened. Monroe retired after his presidency, but served as regent of the U. of Virginia and in 1829 presided over Va.'s constitutional convention.

MONROE, Marilyn (Norma Jean Baker; 1926–1962), US movie star who became world-famous as a blonde sex-symbol. A comic actress of considerable talent, her films include *Gentlemen Prefer Blondes* (1953), *The Seven-Year Itch* (1955), *Bus Stop* (1956) and *Some Like It Hot* (1959).

MONROE DOCTRINE, a declaration of American policy toward the newly independent states of Latin America, issued by President James MONROE before the US Congress on Dec. 2, 1823. It stated in effect that any attempt by European powers to interfere with their old colonies in the western hemisphere would not be tolerated by the US and that the Americas were "henceforth not to be considered as subjects for further colonization by any European powers." The declaration relied for its force on British reluctance, backed by her naval supremacy, to see her own New World position threatened by other European states. President Theodore Roosevelt's corollary to the doctrine (1904) asserted that the US had the power and the right to control any interference in the affairs of the hemisphere by outside governments, and to ensure that acceptable governments were maintained there (this became known as the "big stick" policy; it was repudiated in 1928 by the Clark memorandum). Although the doctrine was mostly ignored until the last decade of the 19th century, it has remained a fundamental policy of the US.

MONSOON, wind system where the prevailing WIND direction reverses in the course of the seasons, occurring where large temperature (hence pressure) differences arise between oceans and large landmasses. Best known is that of SE Asia. In summer, moist winds, with associated HURRICANES, blow from the Indian Ocean into the low-pressure region of NW India that is caused by intense heating of the land. In winter, cold dry winds sweep S from the high-pressure region of S Siberia.

MONTAGE, an art technique in which pictures or picture fragments, usually chosen for their subject matter or message, are mounted together. It is used in advertising, notably with photographs (photomontage), and also in motion-picture editing where contrasting film sequences are spliced together—a technique pioneered by EISENSTEIN in *The Battleship Potemkin* (1925).

MONTAGNA, Bartolomeo (c1450–1523), Italian early Renaissance painter. His stark, somber works were influenced by MANTEGNA and BELLINI and he founded a school of painting at Vicenza. His works include a *Madonna and Child* at the Venice Academy and an *Ecce Homo* in the Louvre, Paris.

MONTAGU, Lady Mary Wortley (1689–1762), English writer. She is noted for her so-called Embassy Letters, written from Turkey, and her society verse. Alexander POPE satirizes her under the name Sappho. She is also remembered as a pioneer in the use of smallpox inoculation, to which she submitted her children.

MONTAIGNE, Michel Eyquem, Seigneur de (1533–1592), French writer, generally regarded as the originator of the personal essay. The first two books of his *Essays*, published in 1580, were written in an informal style and display an insatiable intellectual curiosity tempered by skepticism—his motto was always *Que sais-je?* (What do I know?). A third book of essays appeared in 1588, and the posthumous edition of 1595 includes his last reflections. He studied law, held various provincial political offices in Bordeaux and engaged in diplomacy during the French religious civil wars.

MONTALE, Eugenio (1896–1981), Italian poet who received the 1975 Nobel Prize for Literature.

MONTANA, state, NW US, in the Rocky Mts, bounded on the N by Canada along the 49th parallel, on the E by N.D. and S.D., on the S by Wyo. and on the SW and W by Ida.

Land. The fourth largest state, it can be divided into two physiographic regions: the mountains to the W, rising to Granite Peak (12,799ft), which cover two-fifths of the state and the Great Plains to the E. The state's major rivers include the Missouri (its headwaters are in SW Mont.) the

Name of state: Montana
Capital: Helena
Statehood: Nov. 8, 1889 (41st state)
Familiar name: Treasure State
Area: 147,138sq mi
Population: 819,000
Elevation: Highest—12,799ft, Granite Peak. Lowest—1,800ft Kootenai River in Lincoln County
Motto: *Oro y plata* ("Gold and silver")
State flower: Bitterroot
State bird: Western meadowlark
State tree: Ponderosa pine
State song: "Montana"

Yellowstone, and the Clark Fork, Flathead and Kootenai in the W; there are many other rivers and lakes. About half the state is grassland, and about one-quarter is forest lands (22,400,000 acres). Climatic differences between E and W are marked, but the yearly average temperature ranges are 14°–70°F in the E and 20°–64°F in the W. Annual rainfall averages 15½in, while snow varies from 15in to 300in. The state has an abundance of wildlife and protected herds of buffalo.

People. About 75% of the population lives in rural areas. The largest urban centers are Billings, Great Falls and Missoula. The state contains over 37,250 American Indians (about 5% of the state's total population).

Economy. The economy is dominated by agriculture; livestock brings in about half of the agriculture income, while the other half comes from crops, notably durum wheat, barley, hay, sugar beets, rye, oats and potatoes. Montana is rich in mineral resources including coal, petroleum, copper, gold, lead, zinc and silver. Numerous other minerals are also mined. Lumbering, food processing and the smelting and refining of nonferrous metals are major industries. Natural power resources are supplemented by large-scale hydroelectric power schemes. Tourism is also important throughout the state. Principal attractions include Glacier National Park, Flathead Lake, and the Custer Battlefield National Monument.

History. Under the LOUISIANA PURCHASE, E

Mont. became a US territory (1803). The first recorded exploration was undertaken by the LEWIS AND CLARK EXPEDITION in 1805–06, but except for fur traders and missionaries to the Indians, settlement did not begin until the discovery of gold at Grasshopper Creek (1852). The resulting lawlessness led to the creation of the Montana Territory (1864). Escalating conflict between the settlers and the Indians culminated in the massacre of Gen. CUSTER and his troops by the Sioux at the Battle of the Little Bighorn (1876), but the Sioux surrendered by 1881. The NEZ PERCÉ INDIANS made a dramatic march to freedom across Mont., but surrendered before reaching Canada. In 1889 the territory became a state. At the end of the century there were feuds between mine-owners for control of the copper industry and of state politics. Agriculture prospered until the 1930s. After the depression, industry began to expand, and natural resources were further developed with construction of large dams and many federal reclamation projects. In the 1980s, the state faced difficult policy decisions in the conflict between mining and industrial interests and concern for the environment. Montanans in 1986 outlawed property-tax increases, making it difficult for local governments to maintain services in a declining energy-based economy. In presidential elections 1968–88, Montana voted consistently Republican.

MONTANUS (flourished 2nd century AD), Phrygian founder of the heretical Christian sect of Montanism. Claiming direct inspiration by the Holy Spirit, he prophesied the fulfillment of PENTECOST and the MILLENNIUM. The sect had a strict ascetic discipline and was puritan and anti-intellectual. Its members had ecstatic religious experiences, including GLOSSOLALIA. Montanism separated from the Church and was denounced, but spread widely; TERTULLIAN was a member. Montanism largely died out in the 5th century.

MONT BLANC. See BLANC, MONT.

MONTCALM, Louis Joseph de (1712–1759), French general; military commander in Canada from 1756 during the FRENCH AND INDIAN WARS. He captured Fort Ontario (1756) and Fort William Henry (1757) and repulsed the British at Ticonderoga (1758). He was defeated and killed on the Plains of Abraham (Sept. 13, 1759) while defending Quebec against the British General James WOLFE, who was also killed.

MONTE CARLO, town in the independent principality of MONACO, on the Mediterran-

ean coast known as the French Riviera. It is an international resort with a gambling casino, a yacht harbor and an annual automobile rally and the Monaco Grand Prix car race. It is the home (and tax haven) of many international firms. Pop 10,000.

MONTE CASSINO, an Italian monastery founded by St. BENEDICT OF NURSIA c529 AD, which was the ruling house of the BENEDICTINE ORDERS and an influential cultural and religious center for centuries. Its buildings were destroyed for the fourth time in their history in WWII by bombardment but have since been rebuilt; the abbey is now a national monument.

MONTENEGRO, the smallest of Yugoslavia's six constituent republics, at the S end of the Dinaric Alps on the Adriatic Sea. Its capital is Titograd. Its former capital, Cetinje, was absorbed into Serbia after WWI. The area is mountainous with heavy forests. Mining and the raising of livestock are its chief occupations.

MONTESQUIEU, Charles Louis de Secondat, Baron de la Brède et de (1689–1755), French political philosopher who profoundly influenced 19th and 20th century political and social philosophy. His theory that governmental powers should be separated into legislative, executive and judicial bodies to safeguard personal liberty was developed in his most important work *The Spirit of the Laws* (1748), which influenced the US Constitution and others. Montesquieu's *Persian Letters* (1721) satirized contemporary French sociopolitical institutions.

MONTESSORI, Maria (1870–1952), Italian psychiatrist and educator. The first woman to gain a medical degree in Italy (1894), she developed a system of preschool teaching, the Montessori Method, in which children of 3 to 6 are given a wide range of materials and equipment which enable them to learn by themselves. There are about 600 schools in the US using this method which encourages individual initiative.

MONTEVERDI, Claudio (1567–1643), Italian composer. His innovative operas were the predecessors of modern opera, in which aria, recitative and orchestral accompaniment all enhance dramatic characterization. *Orfeo* (1607) is considered the first modern opera. His other compositions include the ornate *Vespers* (1610) and much other sacred music, the operas *The Return of Ulysses to His Country* (1641) and *The Coronation of Poppea* (1642), and many madrigals.

MONTEVIDEO, capital and largest city of Uruguay and of Montevideo department, located in the S on the Río de la Plata. It is the industrial, cultural and transportation center for the country, as well as a seaport and popular resort. Founded 1724. Pop 1,247,920.

MONTEZ, Lola (c1818–1861), stage name of Marie Dolores Eliza Rosanna Gilbert, a notorious Irish adventuress who became famous in Europe, the US and Australia as a "Spanish" dancer. The mistress of Franz Liszt, Alexander Dumas *père* and then Ludwig I of Bavaria, she gained powerful enemies because of her influence over the king and was forced to leave the country when revolution broke out in 1848.

MONTEZUMA, name of two Aztec rulers of Mexico before its conquest. **Montezuma I** (c1390–1469), was a successful conqueror who ruled from 1440. His descendant **Montezuma II** (1466–1520), was the last Aztec emperor (1502–20). When the Spanish conquistadors arrived, Montezuma failed to resist them because he believed CORTES to be the white god QUETZALCOATL, and he became a hostage. The Aztecs rebelled and Montezuma II was killed in the struggle.

MONTFORT, Simon de, Earl of Leicester (c1208–1265), Anglo-French leader who mounted a revolt to limit Henry III's power by law. The BARONS' WAR followed which ended in the capture of the king (1264). The famous parliament of 1265, summoned by Montfort, was a landmark in English history with representatives from every shire, town and borough. In fighting that followed Montfort was killed at the Battle of Evesham.

MONTGOLFIER, Joseph Michel (1740–1810) and **Jacques Étienne** (1745–1799), French brothers noted for their invention of the first manned aircraft, the first practical (hot-air) BALLOON, which they flew in 1783. Later that same year Jacques assisted Jacques CHARLES in the launching of the first gas (hydrogen) balloon.

MONTGOMERY, Bernard Law, 1st Viscount Montgomery of Alamein (1887–1976), British army leader known as the commander who never lost a battle. He defeated ROMMEL at El Alamein (1942) driving the Germans out of N Africa. Promoted to field marshal, he commanded the British forces in the invasion of Normandy (1944) and later became deputy supreme commander of NATO, 1951–58.

MONTH, name of several periods of time, mostly defined in terms of the motion of the MOON. The synodic month (lunar month or lunation) is the time between successive full moons; it is 29.531 DAYS. The sidereal month, the time taken by the moon to

complete one revolution about the earth relative to the fixed stars, is 27.322 days. The anomalistic month, 27.555 days, is the time between successive passages of the moon through perigee (see ORBIT). The solar month, 30.439 days, is one twelfth of the solar YEAR. Civil or calendar months vary in length throughout the year, lasting from 28 to 31 days (see CALENDAR). In popular usage, the (lunar) month refers to 28 days.

MONTHERLANT, Henri-Marie Joseph Millon de (1896–1972), French novelist and playwright. His work stressed masculine as opposed to feminine virtues and his characters are heroic idealists. His many works include the novels *The Girls* (1936–39) and *Chaos and Night* (1963) and the plays *Malatesta* (1946) and *La Guerre Civile* (1965).

MONTICELLO, a 640-acre estate planned by Thomas JEFFERSON in Va., 3mi from Charlottesville. Construction of the neoclassical mansion atop a small mountain began in 1770; Jefferson moved in before it was completed and lived there for 56 years. His tomb is nearby and the house became a national shrine in 1926, and is open to the public.

MONTREAL, city in S Quebec, Canada, located on the island of Montreal at the confluence of the St. Lawrence and Ottawa rivers. It is a huge inland port, despite its distance of 1000mi from the sea, Canada's largest city and the second-largest French-speaking city in the world. A French mission was built on the site in 1642 and then became an important fur trading center. Ceded to Britain in 1763, the city retained much of its French character. In the 19th century Montreal grew into an important transportation and industrial center aided by its many natural resources and abundance of hydroelectric power. It is the site of McGill U., the U. of Montreal and Sir George Williams U. Pop (city) 980,354; (metro) 2,906,600.

MONTREUX CONVENTION, an international agreement, which gave Turkey military control of the DARDANELLES, signed in 1936. Ratified by Turkey, Great Britain, France, USSR, Germany, Greece, Bulgaria and Yugoslavia (and Japan, with reservations), it closed the straits to warships if Turkey was at war and allowed passage of merchant ships in peace and war (if the countries were neutral to Turkey). The convention still stands.

MOODY, Dwight Lyman (1837–1899), US evangelist, who toured the US and Britain on missions with the hymn writer Ira D. Sankey. He founded several schools and set up a Bible Institute in Chicago (1889) to promote religious learning.

MOODY, Helen Newington Wills. See WILLS, Helen Newington.

MOON, Sun Myung (1920–), Korean evangelist. Excommunicated by the Presbyterian church in Korea, he established the UNIFICATION CHURCH based on doctrines allegedly received in conversations with Jesus, Buddha, and Moses. He brought the church to the US in 1973, where it attracted many youthful followers ("Moonies") and developed extensive business interests. Moon was convicted (1982) of income-tax evasion and served (1984–85) 12 months in prison.

MOON, a SATELLITE, in particular, the earth's largest natural satellite. The moon is so large relative to the earth (it has a diameter two thirds that of MERCURY) that earth and moon are commonly regarded as a double planet. The moon has a diameter of 2,160mi and a mass 0.0123 that of the earth; its escape velocity is around 1.5mi/sec. The orbit of the moon defines the several kinds of MONTH. The distance of the moon from the earth varies between 225,000mi and 252,000mi (perigee and apogee) with a mean of about 240,000mi. The moon rotates on its axis every 27.322 days, hence keeping the same face constantly toward the earth; however, in accordance with KEPLER'S second law, the moon's orbital velocity is not constant and hence there is exhibited the phenomenon known as *libration*: to a particular observer on the earth, marginally different parts of the moon's disk are visible at different times. There is also a very small physical libration due to slight irregularities in its rotational velocity.

The moon is covered with craters, whose sizes range up to 125mi diameter. These sometimes are seen in chains up to 625mi in length. Other features include rilles, trenches a few mi wide and a few hundred mi long; the *maria* (Latin: seas) or great plains; the bright rays which emerge from the large craters, and the lunar mountains. There are also lunar hot spots, generally associated with those larger craters showing bright rays: these remain cooler than their surroundings during lunar daytime, warmer during the lunar night. It has been shown, both by the samples brought back by the Apollo 11 (1969) and subsequent lunar expeditions (see SPACE EXPLORATION) and measurements of crater circularities carried out in 1968, that the smaller lunar craters are in general of meteoritic (see METEOR) origin, the larger of volcanic origin. It is believed that the earth and the moon formed simultaneously, the greater mass of the earth accounting for its higher proportion of metallic iron; the heat of the young earth's atmosphere, which evaporated silicates, accounting for their higher proportion on the moon.

MOONEY, Thomas J. (1883–1942), US labor activist. A key figure in labor's struggle for recognition on the West Coast, he was sentenced to death for his part in a bomb outrage in San Francisco, Cal., in 1916. He was widely believed to be innocent, and his sentence was commuted in 1918. He was pardoned in 1939.

MOONIES. See UNIFICATION CHURCH.

MOORE, Brian (1921–), Irish-born Canadian novelist. In such works as *The Lonely Passion of Judith Hearne* (1955) and *The Luck of Ginger Coffey* (1960), Moore focused on "insignificant" characters who suffer because of their inability to change their lives.

MOORE, Clement Clarke (1779–1863), US educator and poet. He wrote the popular Christmas poem *A Visit from St. Nicholas*, which begins "Twas the night before Christmas" (1823), and was a professor of Oriental and Greek literature at New York City's General Theological Seminary for 29 years.

MOORE, Douglas Stuart (1893–1969), US composer and teacher, at Columbia U 1926–62. Besides symphonies and chamber music, Moore composed operas, including *The Devil and Daniel Webster* (1939) and the Pulitzer Prize-winning *Giants in the Earth* (1951).

MOORE, George Augustus (1852–1933), Irish writer. He spent his youth in Paris and came under the influence of BALZAC and ZOLA, returning to England to stir literary society with realistic novels such as *Esther Waters* (1894) and his masterpiece *Héloise and Abélard* (1921). He contributed much to the Irish literary revival and the ABBEY THEATRE'S success.

MOORE, George Edward (1873–1958), English philosopher who led the 20th-century reaction against IDEALISM and is known for his "ordinary language" approach to philosophy. In his main work, *Principia Ethica* (1903) he held that "good" was not an aspect of the natural world as investigated by science but a simple, indefinable concept.

MOORE, Henry (1898–1986), English sculptor and artist, one of the outstanding sculptors of the 20th century. His inspiration came from natural forms such as stones, roots and bones and often expresses itself in curving abstract shapes perforated with large holes. His work, with repeated themes such as mother and child, is monumental and full of humanity and includes *Family Group* (1949) and *Reclining Figure* (1965).

MOORE, John Bassett (1860–1947), US jurist, author of standard works on international law. A professor at Columbia U (1891–1924), he was on the panel of the HAGUE TRIBUNAL (1912–32) and was the first US judge on the World Court (1921–28).

MOORE, Marianne Craig (1887–1972), US poet, winner of the 1952 Pulitzer Prize for her *Collected Poems*. She edited the *Dial* magazine (1925–29) and translated La Fontaine's *Fables* (1954). Her subjects and themes are often taken from nature.

MOORE, Thomas (1779–1852), Irish poet. He is remembered for his *Irish Melodies* (1808–34), including "The Last Rose of Summer" and other lyrics. Extremely popular in his own day, he also wrote an oriental romance *Lalla Rookh* (1817) and lives of Sheridan (1825) and of Byron (1830).

MOORS, N African people of mixed Berber and Arabic stock who in the 8th century conquered much of Spain and Portugal, basing their rule in Córdoba and Granada. Philosophy and the sciences flourished under their patronage, as did architecture. After losing ground throughout the 13th century, they were finally driven from the peninsula in 1492.

MOOSE, *Alces alces*, a large long-legged DEER of cold climates, known as the ELK in N Europe and Asia and moose in North America. It is characterized by its large size, long legs and overshot muzzle. The males have large, palmate antlers, as much as 7ft across. Often living near water, the moose feeds on aquatic plants as well as browsing from bushes and mature trees.

MORALITY PLAY, form of drama popular in the Middle Ages from about the 14th to the 16th centuries. It was intended to instruct its audience on the eternal struggle between good and evil for human souls. The characters were personifications of virtues and vices. The most noted English example is *Everyman* (from the 1500s) which is still sometimes performed. Morality plays grew out of earlier religious pageants and were an important step in the secularization of drama. (See also MYSTERY PLAY.)

MORAL MAJORITY, strictly, the US religious-political organization headed by the Rev. Jerry Falwell; loosely, the entire religious constituency of the NEW RIGHT. In this second sense, the Moral Majority is the same as the New Christian (or Religious) Right; led chiefly by TV evangelists, it represents fundamentalist Christian beliefs, and proved a potent force in the 1980 presidential and congressional campaigns, especially in the Sun Belt and West.

MORAN, Thomas (1837–1926), English-born US landscape painter. He accompanied (1871, 1873) exploring expeditions on the Yellowstone and Colorado rivers. His large paintings *The Grand Canyon of the Yellowstone* and *Chasm of the Colorado* hang in the Capitol in Washington, D.C.

MORAVIA, Alberto (1907–), Italian novelist, born Alberto Pincherle, whose detached and colloquial style lends realism to his theme of disaffection and aridity in modern life. His novels include *The Woman of Rome* (1947) and *Two Women* (1957).

MORAVIA, central region of Czechoslovakia, bounded on the W by the Bohemian highlands and on the E by the CARPATHIANS. Historically the homeland of the Moravian Empire, from 1029 Moravia was a province of Bohemia. In 1526 it passed under Hapsburg rule, and was part of Austria-Hungary until 1918. Moravia is a fertile and now highly industrialized region. Brno, the largest city, is notable for its manufacture of textiles.

MORAVIAN CHURCH, Protestant church also known as the Church of the Brethren or *Unitas Fratrum*, formed (1457) by Bohemian followers of Jan HUS, believers in simple worship and strict Christian living, with the Bible as their rule of faith. They broke with Rome in 1467. During the THIRTY YEARS' WAR (1618–48), they were persecuted almost to extinction, but revived in Silesia and in 1732 began the missionary work for which they are still known. The first American settlements were in Pa. (1740) and N.C. (1753). The Moravian Church has about 50,000 members in the US, but its influence, especially in shaping modern Protestantism, has been far greater than its numbers suggest. (See also ZINZENDORF.)

MORE, Paul Elmer (1864–1937), US scholar and literary critic, an exponent (with Irving BABBITT) of the New Humanism. His works include *Shelburne Essays* (1904–21) and *The Greek Tradition* (1921–31).

MORE, Sir Thomas (1478–1535), English statesman, writer and saint who was executed for his refusal to take the oath of supremacy recognizing Henry VIII as head of the English Church. A man of brilliance, subtlety and wit, he was much favored by the king. When Cardinal WOLSEY fell in 1529 More was made lord chancellor. Probably because of Henry's determination to divorce Catherine of Aragon in defiance of the pope, More resigned only three years later. Considered dangerously influential even in silence and retirement, More was condemned for high treason. More's best-known work is *Utopia*, a description of an ideal society based on reason. Long recognized as a martyr by the Catholic Church, More was canonized in 1935.

MOREAU, Gustave (1826–1898), French painter noted for his highly dramatic studies of mythological and supernatural scenes, such as *Oedipus and The Sphinx* (1864). As a teacher he greatly influenced MATISSE and ROUAULT.

MORGAN, US banking family famous for its immense financial power and its philanthropic activities. The banking house of J. S. Morgan and Co. was founded by **Junius Spencer Morgan** (1813–1890), and developed into a vast financial and industrial empire (J. P. Morgan & Co.) under his son, **John Pierpont Morgan** (1837–1913). Many of J. P. Morgan's commercial activities aroused controversy, and in 1904 his Northern Securities Company was dissolved as a violation of the SHERMAN ANTITRUST ACT. Notable philanthropic legacies include part of his art collection to the Metropolitan Museum of Art, and the Pierpont Morgan Library, which was endowed by his son. **John Pierpont Morgan, Jr.** (1867–1943) was American agent for the Allies during WWI, when he raised huge funds and organized contracts for military supplies. Most of the large postwar international loans were floated by the house of Morgan.

MORGAN, Sir Henry (c1635–1688), notorious English adventurer and leader of the West Indies buccaneers. The destruction (1671) of Panama City, his most daring exploit, took place after the signing of a treaty between England and Spain. Recalled under arrest, he was subsequently pardoned, knighted (1673) and made lieutenant governor of Jamaica.

MORGAN, John Hunt (1825–1864), Confederate general in the American Civil War, famous for his skilled and daring raids behind Union lines. His great raid (1863) through Kentucky, Indiana and Ohio ended in his capture, but he escaped to resume fighting until killed at Greenville, Tenn.

MORGAN, Lewis Henry (1818–1881), US ethnologist best known for his studies of kinship systems and for his attempts to prove that the Amerinds had migrated into North America, and to discover their place of origin. His techniques and apparently successful results have earned him regard as a father of the science of cultural ANTHROPOLOGY.

MORGAN, Thomas Hunt (1866–1945), US biologist who, through his experiments with the fruit fly *Drosophila*, established the relation between GENES and CHROMOSOMES and thus the mechanism of HEREDITY. For his work he received the 1933 Nobel Prize for Physiology or Medicine.

MORGENTHAU, Hans (1904–1980), German-born US political scientist. He advocated a realistic approach to foreign policy and gained international attention for his opposition to US involvement in Vietnam during the 1960s and 1970s. Among his books are *Politics Among Nations* (1948) and *A New Foreign Policy for the United States* (1969).

MORGENTHAU, Henry Jr. (1891–1967), US secretary of the treasury (1934–45) in the administration of Franklin Roosevelt. He was an early advocate of collective action against German aggression and for aid to Britain and France. He resigned in 1945 when President Harry Truman rejected the "Morgenthau Plan," which called for the partition and deindustrialization of postwar Germany. His father, **Henry Morgenthau** (1856–1946), was a banker and diplomat. A supporter of Woodrow Wilson, he served (1913–16) as US ambassador to Turkey.

MÖRIKE, Eduard (1804–1875), major German lyric poet. His poetry, first collected in the volume *Gedichte* (1838), is small in quantity but richly varied in theme and technique. He also wrote a novel and some short stories.

MORISCOS, Spanish Moors who after 1492 accepted conversion to Christianity rather than banishment. Many continued to practice Islam secretly. Despite persecution by the Inquisition and legal disabilities, the Moriscos prospered until Philip III expelled them in 1609. (See also MARRANOS.)

MORISON, Samuel Eliot (1887–1976), US historian and Harvard professor who wrote the official 15-volume history (1947–62) of the US Navy during WWII. He won Pulitzer Prizes for his *Admiral of the Ocean Sea* (1942), a life of Christopher Columbus, and *John Paul Jones* (1959).

MORLEY, John, Viscount Morley of Blackburn (1838–1923), English statesman and author. Editor (1867–82) of the liberal *Fortnightly Review*, he entered (1883) Parliament as a supporter of William E. GLADSTONE. He worked for home rule in Ireland, opposed the Boer War, and, as secretary of state for India, coauthored (1909) the Morley-Minto reforms, which advanced self-government in India. He was also a noted literary critic and biographer of Voltaire, Rousseau, Burke, Cromwell, and

Gladstone.

MORLEY, Thomas (c1557–?1603), English composer noted especially for his madrigals. A pupil of William BYRD and organist of St. Paul's Cathedral, he also wrote *A Plaine and Easie Introduction to Practicall Musicke* (1597), an invaluable source of information on Elizabethan musical practice.

MORMONS, members of the Church of Jesus Christ of Latter-Day Saints founded (1830) by Joseph SMITH. Mormons accept Smith as having miraculously found and translated a divinely-inspired record of the early history and religion of America, the *Book of Mormon*. With Smith's own writings and the Bible, this forms the Mormon scriptures. Smith's teachings quickly gained a following, but the Mormons' attempts to settle met with recurrent persecution, culminating in the murder of Smith in 1844. It was Brigham YOUNG who led the Mormons in 1847 beyond the frontier to what is now Salt Lake City (still the location of their chief temple). In 1850 Congress granted them the Territory of Utah with Young as Governor. Hostility to the flourishing agricultural community which then developed focused on the Mormon sanction of polygamy and came to a climax with the "Utah War" (1857–58). In 1890 the Mormons abolished polygamy, and Utah was admitted to the Union in 1896. The Mormons have no professional priesthood, but a president and counselors. They stress repentance and believe in the afterlife and the Last Judgment. The Mormons are notably temperate and law-abiding; their religion is an integral part of their lives. They have a membership of about 3 million.

MORO, Aldo (1916–1978), Italian political leader. First elected as a Christian Democrat to the Chamber of Deputies in 1948, he headed five Italian governments as prime minister during the 1960s and 1970s. He was generally expected to be elected Italy's president in 1978 but was kidnapped by the terrorist Red Brigades only weeks before the election. He was found murdered in a car in Rome.

MOROCCO, country in NW Africa, on the Mediterranean and the Atlantic, bordering Algeria (S and E) and Western Sahara (S). **Land.** Topography varies from the fertile coastal region (which includes the Rif Mts along the Mediterranean) to barren desert, with the great ATLAS mountain chain enclosing extensive plains W to E across the center. N Morocco has a Mediterranean climate.

People. Most Moroccans are of Arab

Official name: Kingdom of Morocco
Capital: Rabat
Area: 177,117sq mi
Population: 23,119,000
Languages: Arabic. French, Spanish also spoken
Religion: Muslim
Monetary unit: 1 dirham = 100 centimes

descent, but about one third are BERBERS, and there are Jewish, French and Spanish communities. Less than half of the people are town dwellers. The largest cities are Casablanca, Marrakesh and Rabat (the capital).
Economy. Agriculture employs nearly half of the labor force but provides only a sixth of the gross national product. Wheat, barley, corn, beans, dates, citrus and other fruits are grown. Timber, livestock and fishing are also sources of income, and tourism is increasingly important. The chief mineral is phosphate. Coal, manganese, iron ore, lead, cobalt, zinc, silver and some oil are also produced. There are leather, textile and cement industries. Traditional Moroccan handicrafts are world-famous.
History. The Arabs swept into N Africa from the east (c683 AD), converting the native Berbers to Islam and enlisting their aid in the 8th-century conquest of Spain, but lengthy Arab-Berber strife followed under a succession of dynasties. European (chiefly Portuguese) penetration of Morocco, beginning in 1415, was checked in 1660, but resumed in the 19th and 20th centuries by France, Spain and Germany. Independent since 1956, Morocco is now ruled by King Hassan II, who celebrated his 25th year on the throne in 1986. A UN peace plan to end Morocco's long fight with Polisario Front guerrillas for control of Western Sahara was accepted in principle by both parties in 1988.
MOROS, a group of Muslim people of the S Philippines and Borneo, largely of Malayan origin. Until the 19th century they waged constant war against the Christian Filipinos. An agricultural people noted also for their metal work, they now represent about 5% of Filipinos.

MORPHINE, OPIUM derivative used as a narcotic ANALGESIC and also commonly in DRUG ADDICTION. It depresses RESPIRATION and the COUGH reflex, induces sleep and may cause vomiting and CONSTIPATION. It is valuable in HEART failure and as a premedication for anesthetics; its properties are particularly valuable in terminal malignant DISEASE (see also HEROIN). Addiction and withdrawal syndromes are common.

MORRIS, Gouverneur (1752–1816), American statesman responsible for planning the US decimal coinage system. He was a member of the New York provincial congress (1775–77). At the Constitutional Convention of 1787 he argued for a strong, property-based federal government, and was responsible, as a literary adviser, for much of the wording of the US Constitution. He was minister to France (1792–94) and later played a leading part in promoting the Erie Canal.

MORRIS, Robert (1734–1806), American financier who funded the American Revolution and was a signatory of the Declaration of Independence. As superintendant of finance (1781–84) he saved the nation from bankruptcy by raising money (chiefly from the French) to establish the Bank of North America.

MORRIS, William (1834–1896), English artist, poet and designer. One of the PRE-RAPHAELITES, he sought to counteract the effects of industrialization by a return to the aesthetic standards and craftsmanship of the Middle Ages. In 1861 he set up Morris and Co. to design and make wallpaper, furniture, carpets and other home furnishings. Influenced by RUSKIN, he formed the Socialist League (1884). His founding (1890) of the Kelmscott Press had a primary impact on typographical and book design.

MORRIS DANCE, English folk dance associated with ancient ritual festivals such as May Day. Literary references to the Morris Dance occur from the 1400s, and it still survives today. The dancers performed in groups, often centered around a man symbolically disguised as an animal.

MORROW, Dwight Whitney (1873–1931), US banker and diplomat. A partner in the banking house of J. P. Morgan & Co., he served (1927–30) as US ambassador to Mexico, where he resolved disputes between Mexico and the US over oil rights and between the Mexican government and the Catholic church. His daughter was Anne Morrow LINDBERGH.

MORSE, Samuel Finley Breese (1791–1872), US inventor of an electric TELEGRAPH. His first crude model was designed in 1832, and by 1835 he could demonstrate a working model. With the considerable help of Joseph HENRY (which later he refused to acknowledge) he developed by 1837 electromagnetic relays to extend the range and capabilities of his system. WHEATSTONE'S invention had preceded Morse's, so that he was unable to obtain an English patent, and in the US official support did not come until 1843. His famous message, "What hath God wrought!", was the first sent on his Washington-Baltimore line on May 24, 1844. For this he used MORSE CODE, devised in 1838. In early life, Morse was a noted portrait painter.

MORSE, Wayne Lyman (1900–1974), US senator from Oregon (1945–69). Elected in 1944 as a Republican, he declared himself an independent in 1952 and a Democrat in 1956. He was defeated for reelection in 1968 because of his opposition to the Vietnam War.

MORSE CODE, signal system devised (1838) by Samuel MORSE for use in the wire TELEGRAPH, now used in radiotelegraphy and elsewhere. Letters, numbers and punctuation are represented by combinations of dots (brief taps of the transmitting key) and dashes (three times the length of dots).

MORTGAGE, loan given on the security of the borrower's property. A mortgage is sometimes taken out on property already owned, but is more often used to help finance the purchase of property. If the loan is not repaid on time the mortgage may be foreclosed: that is, the person who loaned the money may obtain a court order to sell the property, and take what he is owed from the proceedings. Mortgages taken out for the purchase of a home usually run for 20 years or more. In the US, most mortgages are granted by banks or savings and loan societies. Mortgages are also issued for the purchase of machinery (especially farm machinery), when property other than real estate is often used as security.

MORTON, Jelly Roll (Ferdinand Joseph LaMenthe Morton; 1885–1941), US jazz pianist whose compositions included "King Porter Stomp" and "Jelly Roll Blues."

MORTON, Thomas (c1590–c1647), English adventurer and colorful leader (from 1626) of the Merry Mount settlement (now Quincy, Mass.). His erection of a maypole, general merriment and commercial rivalry outraged his Puritan neighbors in Plymouth and Boston, who imprisoned and expelled Morton several times. Morton satirized Puritan New England in his book *New*

English Canaan (1637).

MORTON, William Thomas Green (1819–1868), US dentist who pioneered the use of diethyl ETHER as an anesthetic (1844–46). In later years he engaged in bitter litigation over his refusal to recognize the contributions of former colleagues and especially C. W. LONG'S prior use of ether in this way.

MOSAIC, ancient mode of decorating surfaces (mainly floors and walls) by inlaying small pieces of colored stone, marble, or glass, fitted together to form a design. Greek pebble mosaics survive from about 400 BC. There are fine Roman mosaics at Pompeii near Naples and outstanding Byzantine examples may be seen in Ravenna, Italy. American Indian stone mosaics have been found at Chichén Itza in Mexico.

MOSBY, John Singleton (1833–1916), Confederate Civil War hero who led Mosby's Partisan Rangers, a cavalry troop known for their daring raids behind enemy lines in Md. and Union-occupied Va. After the war he became a Republican and entered government service.

MOSCA, Gaetano (1858–1941), Italian politician and jurist who held that all governments are run by entrenched elitist groups and that majority rule is therefore a myth. His ideas, set out in *The Ruling Class* (1896) and other writings, were distorted to suit apologists of FASCISM.

MOSCOW (Moskva), capital of the Soviet Union (USSR) and of the Russian Soviet Federated Socialist Republic, administrative center of Moscow region, on both banks of the Moskva R. It is the USSR's largest city, and its political, cultural, commercial, industrial and communications center. Some leading industries are chemicals, textiles, wood products and a wide range of heavy machinery including aircraft and automobiles. Moscow became the capital of all Russia under IVAN IV in the 16th century. Superseded by St. Petersburg (now LENINGRAD) in 1713, it regained its former status in 1918, following the Russian Revolution. At the city's heart is the KREMLIN, location of the headquarters of government and containing notable architectural relics of tsarist Russia. Immediately east of the Kremlin, from which wide boulevards radiate in all directions, lies Red Square, the site of parades and celebrations, overlooked by the Lenin Mausoleum and St. Basil's Cathedral. Among outstanding cultural and educational institutions are the BOLSHOI THEATER, the Moscow Art Theater, the Maly Theater, Moscow University, the Academy of Sciences, the Tchaikovsky Conservatory and the Lenin State Library. Pop 8,642,000.

MOSCOW ART THEATER, influential Russian repertory theater famed for its ensemble acting and its introduction of new techniques in stage realism. Founded in 1897 by Konstantin STANISLAVSKI and Vladimir NEMIROVICH-DANCHENKO, it introduced plays by such authors as CHEKHOV and GORKI.

MOSES (c13th century BC), Hebrew lawgiver and prophet who led the Israelites out of Egypt. According to the Bible, the infant Moses, hidden to save him from being killed, was found and raised by the pharaoh's daughter. After killing a tyrannical Egyptian, he fled to the desert. From a burning bush, God ordered him to return and demand the Israelites' freedom under threat of the PLAGUES. On PASSOVER night Moses led them out of Egypt (the "exodus"); the Red Sea was parted to let them cross. On Mt. Sinai he received the TEN COMMANDMENTS. After years of ruling the wandering Israelites in the wilderness, Moses died within sight of the promised land. Traditionally he was the author of the PENTATEUCH.

MOSES, Grandma (Anna Mary Robertson Moses; 1860–1961), US artist of the so-called primitive style. Self-taught, she began painting at age 76 and won wide popularity with her lively, unpretentious pictures of rural life in the upstate N.Y. of her youth.

MOSES, Robert (1888–1981), US public official who, though never elected to public office, exerted enormous political influence in New York State as chairman of the state Park Commission (1924–63) and other public authorities. He built the parks, beaches, highways, bridges, and other public works that transformed the New York City area.

MOSLEMS or MUSLIMS (Arabic: ones who submit), adherents of the religion of ISLAM.

MOSLEY, Sir Oswald Ernald (1896–1980), British politician who formed (1932) the British Union of Fascists, popularly called the Blackshirts. He was interned during WWII. In 1948 he founded the extreme right-wing British Union Movement.

MOSQUE, Muslim place of worship. The name derives from the Arabic *masjid*, meaning "a place for prostration" (in prayer). Mosques are typically built with one or more minarets (towers); a courtyard with fountains or wells for ceremonial washing; an area where the faithful assemble for prayers led by the *imam* (priest); a *mihrah* (niche) indicating the direction (*qiblah*) of MECCA; a *mimbar* (pulpit) and sometimes, facing it, a *maqsurah* (enclosed area for important persons). Some mosques include a *madrash* (religious school). (See also ISLAM.)

MOSQUITOES, two-winged flies of the family Culicidae, with penetrating, sucking mouthparts. The females of many species feed on vertebrate blood, using their needle-like stylets to puncture a blood capillary, but usually only when about to lay eggs. The males, and the females at other times, feed on sugary liquids such as nectar. Both the larvae and pupae are entirely aquatic, breathing through spiracles at the tip of the abdomen. In all but the anopheline mosquitoes, the spiracles are at the tip of a tubular siphon, and the larva's body is suspended from this below the surface film. Mosquitoes are involved in the transmission of many diseases in man, including YELLOW FEVER, filariasis, and MALARIA.

MOSSADEGH, Mohammed (c1880–1967), Iranian prime minister (1951–53) who nationalized Iran's British-controlled oil industry. A subsequent boycott by foreign consumers brought Iran near to economic disaster, and Mossadegh was forced out of office and imprisoned (1953–56).

MÖSSBAUER, Rudolf Ludwig (1929–   ), German physicist who shared the 1961 Nobel Prize for Physics for his discovery of the "Mössbauer effect" concerning the emission and absorption of gamma rays by atomic nuclei.

MOSSES, large group of plants belonging to the class Musci, of the division Bryophyta. Each moss plant consists of an erect "stem" to which primitive "leaves" are attached. The plants are anchored by root-like rhizoids. Mosses have worldwide distribution and are usually found in woods and other damp habitats. They are often early colonizers of bare soil and play an important role in preventing soil erosion. Sphagnum debris is an important constituent of PEAT.

MOTET, polyphonic vocal music, usually unaccompanied, which has occupied a place in sacred services, largely Roman Catholic, analogous to that of the Protestant anthem. Like the madrigal, its secular counterpart, the motet reached its zenith in the 16th and 17th centuries. Notable composers of motets include PALESTRINA and BACH.

MOTHER GOOSE, fictitious character to whose authorship many collections of fairy tales and nursery rhymes have been ascribed. The name seems to have been first associated with Charles PERRAULT's *Tales of Mother Goose* (1697).

MOTHER-OF-PEARL, or **nacre,** the iridescent substance of which PEARLS and the inner coating of bivalved mollusk shells are made. It consists of alternate thin layers of aragonite (CALCIUM carbonate) and conchiolin, a horny substance. Valued for its beauty, it is used in thin sheets for ornament, jewelry and for buttons.

MOTHER'S DAY, holiday observed in the US on the second Sunday in May to honor motherhood. It was officially recognized by Congress in 1914. Similar days of remembrance are observed in various other countries.

MOTHER TERESA (Agnes Gonxha Bojaxhiu; 1910–   ), Albanian-born Roman Catholic nun who served the destitute and dying in Calcutta, India, from 1948. She founded the Order of the Missionaries of Charity, which grew into a worldwide movement. She received the 1979 Nobel Peace Prize.

MOTHERWELL, Robert (1915–   ), US painter and theoretician, a leading exponent of ABSTRACT EXPRESSIONISM. His work is characterized by restrained colors and large indefinite shapes.

MOTHS, insects which, together with the BUTTERFLIES, constitute the order LEPIDOPTERA. The differences between moths and butterflies are not clearly defined. Butterflies usually fly by day and rest with the wings raised over the back. Moths are mostly nocturnal and rest with the wings outspread. The antennae of butterflies are usually simple and end in a knob; this is rare in moths, where the antennae, at least in the males, are often feathery. This confers powerful long-range scent perception. In many species females produce "pheromones"—chemical sexual attractants. The males can detect even a single molecule of this, sensing females as far as 1mi away. In many species, melanistic (blacker) forms have developed or increased in numbers in industrial areas. Darker coloration provides a better camouflage against birds on the blackened trees of these regions, an example of evolution in progress.

MOTION PICTURES, a succession of photographs projected rapidly onto a screen to create the illusion of continuous movement. Modern "movies" project 24 frames per second. Film may be 8mm, 16mm, 35mm or 70mm wide and may have a sound track (see SOUND RECORDING).

Research into persistence of vision, using drawings, in the 19th century, and the development of photography, culminated in Thomas EDISON's Kinetoscope (1894), a peep show version of the movies. Projection of motion pictures, using Edison's Vitascope (1896), was a success in vaudeville. Static camera work soon gave way to the creative use of both camera and film-editing processes, and in 1903 Edwin S. Porter exploited these in the one-reel narrative film, *The Great Train Robbery*. The success of this movie helped establish NICKELODEONS in the US, and this led in turn to the building of movie palaces. By 1913 the American film industry was established, aimed at satisfying a mass popular craving. Independent producers moved to Cal. to escape the power of distribution trusts. Cecil B. DE MILLE's *The Squaw Man* (1914) and Mack Sennett's comedies helped finance the establishment of the Hollywood studios. D. W. GRIFFITH was the creative genius of the era. From 1908, he explored the possibilities of film and created "stars" to increase the appeal of his work. He made the first feature length films (1913), and his epics *The Birth of a Nation* (1915) and *Intolerance* (1917) are considered landmarks of cinema history. WWI had stopped film production in Europe, but afterwards German cinema attained influence with films such as *The Cabinet of Dr. Caligari* (1919) and the work of G. W. PABST and Fritz Lang. Russia's Sergei EISENSTEIN and the Scandinavians Carl Dreyer and Victor Sjorström were among those directors who achieved major reputations in a medium which, despite the employment of many technicians, writers and actors, is ultimately controlled artistically by the director and film editor—except in the case of a few extraordinarily creative producers such as David O. Selznick and Irving Thalberg.

The use of motion pictures for other than narrative purposes was established early. Newsreels were produced by Charles Pathé in Paris by 1909; Robert FLAHERTY's *Nanook of the North* (1922) consolidated the appeal of documentary films; cartoons became popular features of cinema programs, especially after Walt DISNEY created Mickey Mouse in the late 1920s.

The coming of sound in *The Jazz Singer*, 1927, briefly set film back as an art: the camera was immobilized, but regained its fluidity when sound techniques were improved and it was realized that sound was merely a useful adjunct. Color techniques were finally established with such films as *The Wizard of Oz* (1939) and the epic *Gone With the Wind* (1939), among the first in which color was an integral part of the effect and not a mere novelty. After WWII the industry experimented with Cinerama, Cinemascope, Vista Vision and even 3-D, but cinema still achieved its most powerful results with techniques of editing and photography used since the silent era.

The great age of Hollywood (1930–1950) occurred partly because of its ability to provide cheap entertainment during the Depression and because of the dominance of totalitarian censorship, which crippled filmmaking in much of Europe (Lang and Joseph von Sternberg were among those who fled to America). The Western and the musical were recognized as uniquely successful North American film genres. The British film industry produced notable successes under Alexander KORDA's production and Alfred HITCHCOCK's direction, while French directors René CLAIR and Jean RENOIR were among the most acclaimed of the era.

Since WWII the split has grown between "art" and popular film. Movies no longer dominate mass entertainment. Television has drastically reduced audiences for theater-shown films, and producers have tried to win them back with wide-screen spectaculars or films exploiting sex and violence. The motion-picture audience today is a youthful one. Yet, film distribution has become more truly international. Directors such as FELLINI, DE SICA, Satyajit RAY, KUROSAWA, Roberto Rosselini, BUÑUEL, TRUFFAUT and Ingmar BERGMAN have made exciting contributions to cinematic art. Hollywood's dominance has been superseded by many independent productions worldwide, and the vigor and popularity of film, both as art and as entertainment, continues unabated, despite competition from television.

MOTION SICKNESS, nausea and vomiting caused by rhythmic movements of the body, particularly the head, set up in automobile, train, ship or airplane travel. In susceptible people, neither stimulation of the EAR labyrinths nor their action on the vomiting centers in the BRAIN stem are adequately suppressed. Hyoscine and phenothiazines can prevent it if taken before travel.

MOTLEY, John Lothrop (1814–1877), US historian known for his books on Dutch history, *The Rise of the Dutch Republic* (1856) and *History of the United Netherlands* (1860–67). He was also sent as a diplomat to Russia, Austria and England.

MOTOR, Electric, a device converting electrical into mechanical energy. Traditional forms are based on the FORCE experienced by a current-carrying wire in a magnetic field (see ELECTROMAGNETISM). Motors can be, and sometimes are, run in reverse as GENERATORS.

Simple direct-current (see ELECTRICITY)

motors consist of a magnet or ELECTROMAGNET (the *stator*) and a coil (the *rotor*) which turns when a current is passed through it because of the force between the current and the stator field. So that the force keeps the same sense as the rotor turns, the current to the rotor is supplied via a *commutator*—a slip ring broken into two semicircular parts, to each of which one end of the coil is connected, so that the current direction is reversed twice each revolution.

For use with alternating-current supplies, small DC motors are often still suitable, but **induction motors** are preferred for heavier duty. In the simplest of these, there is no electrical contact with the rotor, which consists of a cylindrical array of copper bars welded to end rings. The stator field, generated by more than one set of coils, is made to rotate at the supply frequency, including (see INDUCTION, ELECTROMAGNETIC) currents in the rotor when (under load) it rotates more slowly, these in turn producing a force accelerating the rotor. Greater control of the motor speed and torque can be obtained in "wound rotor" types in which the currents induced in coils wound on the rotor are controlled by external resistances connected via slip-ring contacts.

In applications such as electric clocks, **synchronous motors**, which rotate exactly in step with the supply frequency, are used. In these the rotor is usually a permanent magnet dragged round by the rotating stator field, the induction-motor principle being used to start the motor.

The above designs can all be opened out to form **linear motors** producing a lateral rather than rotational drive. The induction type is the most suitable, a plate analogous to the rotor being driven with respect to a stator generating a laterally moving field. Such motors have a wide range of possible applications, from operating sliding doors to driving trains, being much more robust than rotational drive systems, and offering no resistance to manual operation in the event of power cuts. A form of DC linear motor can be used to pump conducting liquids such as molten metals, the force being generated between a current passed through the liquid and a static magnetic field around it.

MOTORCYCLE, a motorized bicycle, first developed in 1885 by Gottlieb DAIMLER. The engine of a motorcycle may be either two-stroke or four-stroke and is usually air cooled. Chain drive is almost universal. In lightweight machines, ignition is often achieved by means of a magneto inside the flywheel. Motorcycles were first widely used by dispatch riders in WWI. Between the wars, the motorcycle industry was dominated by simple, heavy British designs. After WWII, Italy also developed the motor scooter, designed for convenience and economy, with 150cc two-stroke engines. In the 1960s the Japanese introduced a series of highly sophisticated, lightweight machines, which are now seen all over the world. (See INTERNAL COMBUSTION ENGINE.)

MOTT, Lucretia Coffin (1793–1880), US reformer who was one of the first pioneers of women's rights. A Quaker by religion, she founded the Philadelphia Female Anti-Slavery Society (1833), and with Elizabeth STANTON organized the first women's rights convention at Seneca Falls, N.Y., in 1848.

MOUNDS, artificial constructions of earth or, on occasion, piled stones built according to a predetermined plan, found in many areas of the eastern US. The largest known mound is one of the CAHOKIA MOUNDS; the oldest dates from c500AD. Some mounds were built in historic times. Dome-shaped burial mounds served the same purpose as barrows, while mounds in the form of truncated pyramids were used as bases for temples and other buildings. KITCHEN MIDDENS are sometimes erroneously termed mounds. Less common types of mounds are hilltop forts and mounds in effigy form.

MOUNTAIN, a landmass elevated substantially above its surroundings. The difference between a mountain and a hill is essentially one of size: the exact borderline is not clearly defined. Plateaus, or table-mountains, unlike most other mountains, have a large summit area as compared with that of their base. Most mountains occur in groups, ranges or chains. The processes involved in mountain building are termed orogenesis. Periods of orogenesis can largely be explained in terms of the theory of PLATE TECTONICS. Thus the Andes have formed where the Nazca oceanic plate is being subducted beneath (forced under) the South American continental plate, and the Himalayas have arisen at the meeting of two continental plates.

Mountains are traditionally classified as volcanic, block or folded. **Volcanic mountains** occur where LAVA and other debris (e.g., pyroclastic rocks) build up a dome around the vent of a VOLCANO. They are found in certain well-defined belts around the world, marking plate margins. **Block mountains** occur where land has been uplifted between FAULTS in a way akin to that leading to the formation of RIFT VALLEYS. **Folded mountains** occur through deformations of the EARTH'S crust (see FOLD), especially in geosynclinal areas, where vast quantities of sediments whose weight causes deformation accumulate (see also SEDIMENTATION). EROSION eventually reduces all mountains to plains. But it may also play a part in the creation of mountains, as where most of an elevated stretch of land has been eroded away, leaving a few resistant outcrops of rock.

MOUNTAIN LION. See PUMA.

MOUNTAIN MEN, pioneer fur trappers and traders in the Rockies in the 1820s and 1830s. Early mountain men included John Colter, who stayed in the area after the LEWIS AND CLARK EXPEDITION of 1804–06, Thomas Fitzpatrick, Jedediah SMITH and W. S. Williams. Many mountain men, including James BRIDGER, took part in William Ashley's expedition up the Missouri R in 1822. The mountain men were the first to begin opening up the Rockies and make the area's potential known. They were quickly followed by the big fur companies such as the Rocky Mountain Fur Company and the American Fur Company.

MOUNTBATTEN, Louis Francis Albert Victor Nicholas, 1st Earl Mountbatten of Burma (1900–1979), British admiral and statesman. In WWII he was supreme allied commander in SE Asia and liberated Burma from the Japanese. After WWII he was the last British viceroy of India, and led the negotiations for India's and Pakistan's independence. He later served as first sea lord, admiral of the fleet and chief of the defense staff. He was killed by Irish Republican Army terrorists.

MOUNT SAINT HELENS, active volcano in the Cascade Range of SW Wash. Long considered dormant, the volcano became seismically active in Mar. 1980 and erupted for the first time in 120 years on May 18, 1980. The eruption was preceded by two magnitude 5 earthquakes (see RICHTER SCALE) and was the first in the 48 coterminous states since Mt Lassen erupted in 1915. More than 60 people were killed, and there were widespread floods and mudslides. Surrounding forests were scorched or devastated, and much of Wash., Ore., Ida. and Mont. were blanketed with volcanic ash. Subsequent eruptions (particularly in Apr. 1982) were much less destructive.

MOUNT VERNON, the restored Georgian home (1747–99) of George WASHINGTON on the Potomac R in Va., S of Washington. The tomb of Washington and his wife Martha is nearby.

MOUSE, a term applied loosely to almost any small RODENT. The majority however fall into two groups: Old World mice, family Muridae, and New World mice of the family Cricetidae. Very active animals, often nocturnal, they are characteristically shortlived. Feeding on berries and grain, they are, in terms of biomass, extremely important herbivores, and in turn important as prey for many birds and mammals.

MOVIES: See MOTION PICTURES.

MOYNIHAN, Daniel Patrick (1927–   ), US social scientist, diplomat, and Democratic politician. A student of poverty, welfare, ethnicity, and urban affairs, he served in the New York State and federal governments and taught at Harvard U before becoming US ambassador to India (1973–75) and to the United Nations (1975–76). He was US senator from New York from 1977.

MOZAMBIQUE, republic in SE Africa on the Indian Ocean between Tanzania and South Africa.

Official name: People's Republic of Mozambique
Capital: Maputo
Area: 308,642sq mi
Population: 14,516,000
Languages: Portuguese, Bantu languages
Religions: Animist, Christian, Muslim
Monetary unit(s): 1 metical = 100 centavos
Land. A hot and humid coastal plain and low plateaus cover about two-thirds of the country, rising to mountainous regions in the N and W. Most of the coastal plain is infertile except in the Zambezi, Save, Limpopo and small river areas.

People. The population comprises over 60 Bantu tribes and a small group with African-Portuguese ancestry. There are some Europeans and Asians, though their numbers have sharply decreased since independence.

Economy. Mozambique is a poor country, almost completely dependent on agriculture, including forestry, fishing and hunting. Main exports are cashews, seafood and cotton. The government has encouraged collective farming; in the late 1970s drought created acute food shortages. The economy also suffered at that time as a result of Mozambique's support for

Zimbabwe nationalists during the Rhodesian war. Good relations with Zimbabwe and the expansion of port facilities are expected to increase Mozambique's trade and transport opportunities. Although Mozambique is ideologically opposed to its neighbor, South Africa, the countries have strong economic and commercial ties.

History. The first European to reach Mozambique was Vasco da GAMA (1498). During the 1500s and 1600s the Portuguese set up small trading settlements. From the mid-18th until the early-19th century their great source of wealth was the black slave trade. Mozambique became a Portuguese colony in 1910, and Portugal placed controls on its economic growth and the Africans' social advancement. In 1962 the Mozambique nationalists formed the Mozambique Liberation Front (Frelimo), which engaged in fierce guerrilla warfare with Portuguese troops in 1964–74. After the 1974 coup in Portugal negotiations led to the formation in June 1975 of an independent socialist republic in Mozambique. Since independence, Mozambique has been plagued by famine and civil war. The Mozambique National Resistance, or Renamo, supported by right-wing sources in South Africa and the US, waged a campaign of mindless destruction and violence to undermine the leftist government. Other bandits added to the anarchy in the countryside that uprooted more than 1 million people and halted food production by perhaps 2 million farmers.

MOZART, Wolfgang Amadeus (1756–1791), Austrian composer whose brief career produced some of the world's greatest music. He was a child prodigy of the harpsichord, violin and organ at the age of four and toured the European courts. He soon became a prodigious composer. Between 1771–81 he was concertmaster to the archbishop of Salzburg. Much of Mozart's early music is in a pure and elegant classical style, which is also extremely lively and spontaneous. In 1781 he moved to Vienna, where he became Court Composer to Joseph II in 1787. He became a close friend of HAYDN and set Lorenzo Da Ponte's opera librettos *The Marriage of Figaro* (1786) and *Don Giovanni* (1787) to music. In a three-month period during 1788 he wrote three of his greatest symphonies, numbers 39–41. Mozart wrote over 600 works, including 50 symphonies, over 20 operas, nearly 30 piano concertos, 27 string quartets, about 40 violin sonatas and many other instrumental pieces. In all these genres his work shows great expressive beauty and technical mastery, and he advanced the styles and musical forms of each.

MUBARAK, Hosni (1928–   ), president of Egypt from 1981. A graduate of Egypt's military academy, he was trained as a bomber pilot and rose in rank to air force chief of staff (1969) and air force commander (1972). He launched the surprise air attack in the 1973 war with Israel. Chosen by President Sadat to be Egypt's vice president in 1975, Mubarak thereafter concentrated his attention on domestic and international affairs. He became president, by public referendum, after Sadat was assassinated. Domestically, he worked to contain Islamic fundamentalists who opposed efforts at modernization. Internationally, he adopted a cool stance toward Israel after Israel's invasion of Lebanon in 1982. In 1988, however, he undertook an active role as a regional peacemaker by seeking to arrange a rapprochement between PLO leader Yasir Arafat and King Hussein of Jordan in the hope of reviving the stalled peace process with Israel.

MUCKRAKERS, term coined in 1906 by President Theodore Roosevelt to condemn journalists specializing in sensational exposés of corrupt businesses and political procedures. The name was adopted by a group of contemporary reformist writers and journalists. The "Muckrakers" included Lincoln STEFFENS who wrote about political corruption, Ida TARBELL who exposed the exploitative practices of an enormous oil company, and Upton SINCLAIR who uncovered deplorable conditions in the Chicago meat-packing industry.

MUGABE, Robert Gabriel (1924–   ), prime minister of Zimbabwe (1980–   ). A Marxist, he and Joshua Nkomo shared leadership of a guerrilla movement against the white leaders of Rhodesia. When Rhodesia achieved legal independence (as Zimbabwe) and black majority ru.e in 1980, Mugabe became prime minister in a government of national unity. In 1982, however, he expelled Nkomo from his cabinet.

MUGWUMPS, term for independent voters, or sometimes political fence straddlers. It was particularly used for Republicans who voted for Democrat Grover CLEVELAND in 1884.

MUHAMMAD, Elijah (1897–1975), US Black Muslim leader. In 1931 he met Wali "Prophet" Farad, founder of the first Temple of Islam in Detroit, Mich. Elijah became a prominent disciple and on Farad's disappearance (1934) became leader of the movement. He advocated black separatism.

MUHAMMAD ALI. See ALI, MUHAMMAD.

MUIR, John (1838–1914), Scottish-American naturalist and writer, an advocate of US forest conservation. He described his walking journeys in the NW US and Alaska in many influential articles and books. Yosemite and Sequoia national parks and Muir Woods National Monument were established as a result of his efforts.

MULE, a term now commonly used to describe infertile hybrids between various species. The name is properly restricted to the offspring of a male DONKEY and a mare. Mules have the shape and size of a HORSE, and the long ears and small hooves of a donkey. They are favored for their endurance and surefootedness as draft or pack animals.

MULLER, Hermann Joseph (1890–1967), US geneticist awarded the 1946 Nobel Prize for Physiology or Medicine for his work showing that X-RAYS greatly accelerate MUTATION processes.

MÜLLER, Paul Hermann (1899–1965), Swiss chemist who received the 1948 Nobel Prize for Chemistry for developing the insecticide known as DDT.

MULRONEY, M. Brian (1939–), Canadian politician, leader of the Progressive Conservative Party (from 1983) and prime minister (from 1984). A lawyer and business executive, he had never held elective office before being chosen party leader. As prime minister he tried to improve Canadian economic relations with the US.

MULTIPLE SCLEROSIS, or disseminated sclerosis, a relatively common disease of the BRAIN and SPINAL CORD in which myelin is destroyed in plaques of INFLAMMATION. Its cause is unknown although slow VIRUSES, abnormal ALLERGY to viruses and abnormalities of FATS are suspected. It may affect any age group, but particularly young adults. Symptoms and signs indicating disease in widely separate parts of the NERVOUS SYSTEM are typical. They occur episodically, often with intervening recovery or improvement. Blurring of VISION, sometimes with EYE pain; double vision; vertigo; abnormal sensations in the limbs; paralysis; ATAXIA, and BLADDER disturbance are often seen, although individually these can occur in other brain diseases. STEROIDS, certain dietary foods, and DRUGS acting on spasticity in muscles and the bladder are valuable in some cases. The course of the disease is extremely variable, some subjects having but a few mild attacks, while others progress rapidly to permanent disability and dependency.

MUMFORD, Lewis (1895–), US social critic and historian, concerned with the relationship between man and his environment, especially in urban planning. His books include *The Brown Decades* (1931), *The Culture of Cities* (1934), *The City in History* (1961) and *The Pentagon of Power* (1971).

MUMMY, a corpse embalmed, particularly in ancient Egypt, in order to ensure its preservation for a protracted period after death. The earliest known attempts artificially to preserve bodies were about 2600 BC, though many bodies from earlier times were naturally preserved through the desiccating effect of the sand in which they were buried.

MUMPS, common VIRUS infection causing swelling of the parotid salivary GLAND, and occasionally INFLAMMATION of the PANCREAS, an OVARY or a testis. Mild FEVER, HEADACHE and malaise may precede the gland swelling. Rarely a viral MENINGITIS and less often ENCEPHALITIS complicate mumps. Very rarely a bilateral and severe testicular inflammation can cause sterility.

MUNCH, Charles (1891–1968), French orchestra conductor. He conducted the Paris Conservatory orchestra (1936–46), the Boston (Mass.) Symphony orchestra (1949–62), and was director of its Berkshire Music Center (1951–62).

MUNCH, Edvard (1863–1944), Norwegian painter and printmaker. His work foreshadowed EXPRESSIONISM and was influential in the development of modern art. His powerful, often anguished pictures show his obsession with the themes of love, death and loneliness.

MÜNCHHAUSEN, Karl Friedrich Hieronymus, Freiherr (Baron) von (1720–1797), German soldier and country gentleman. His exaggerated adventure tales were the basis of fantastic "tall tales" compiled by R. E. Raspe, published in London (1785). These stories became widely popular. The English *Adventures of Baron Munchhausen* (1793) is the standard edition.

MUNICH, capital of Bavaria, West Germany, on the Isar R about 30mi N of the Alps. A cultural center with a cathedral and palace, it is also heavily industrialized (beer, textiles, publishing), and is Germany's third largest city. Founded in 1158 by Duke Henry the Lion, it was ruled 1255–1918 by the Wittelsbach family (dukes and kings of Bavaria). Munich was the birthplace and headquarters of NAZISM and the scene of Hitler's attempted "beer hall putsch" of 1923. Munich hosted the 1972 OLYMPIC GAMES. Pop 1,266,549.

MUNICH AGREEMENT, a pact, signed

Sept. 30, 1938, prior to WWII, which forced Czechoslovakia to surrender its SUDETENLAND to Nazi Germany. The Sudetenland in W Czechoslovakia contained much of the nation's industry, about 700,000 Czechs as well as 3 million German-speaking citizens, the pretext for Hitler's demands for occupation. The agreement, which allowed an immediate German takeover, was signed by Adolph HITLER, Neville CHAMBERLAIN (Britain), Edouard DALADIER (France) and Benito MUSSOLINI (Italy). Neither the Czechs nor their Russian allies were consulted. The Allies hoped this would be Hitler's "last territorial claim," and that the pact would avert war, but in March 1939 he occupied the rest of Czechoslovakia.

MUNN v. ILLINOIS. See GRANGER CASES.

MUÑOZ MARÍN, Luis (1898–1980), Puerto Rican political leader, the first elected governor of the island (1948–64), founder of the Popular Democratic Party (1938). Elected to the legislature in 1932, he favored social reforms and ties with the US. He led the campaign for Puerto Rican self-government status, achieved in 1952.

MUNRO, Hector Hugh (pseudonym, Saki; 1870–1916), British writer, known for his inventive, satirical and often fantastic short stories. Among his published works are stories collected in *Reginald* (1904) and *Beasts and Super-Beasts* (1914) and a novel, *The Unbearable Bassington* (1912).

MÜNZER, Thomas (c1490–1525), radical German Protestant reformer. Originally a follower of LUTHER, he preached revolution and the establishment of a godly communistic state. He was executed as a leader of the PEASANTS' WAR (1524–25).

MURAL PAINTING, any kind of painting executed on a wall. The earliest are the cave paintings of reindeer and bison at ALTAMIRA, Spain, and LASCAUX, France, which were probably a form of magic to Paleolithic man. Early Roman FRESCO murals were found in POMPEII. Wall paintings of sacred subjects were the chief form of religious instruction in the Byzantine Empire, medieval Europe and India. The fresco technique was adopted by Italian artists like GIOTTO at Padua and Assisi, MICHELANGELO for the ceiling of the SISTINE CHAPEL and TIEPOLO in N Italian palaces, and also by the 20th-century Mexican artist OROZCO.

MURASAKI, Shikibu (c978–1026?), Japanese court lady and author of *Genji Monogatari*, or the *Tale of Genji*, the greatest Japanese classic and probably the world's first novel.

MURAT, Joachim (1767–1815), French marshal under Napoleon Bonaparte and king of Naples 1808–15. Murat gained his reputation as a brilliant cavalry leader in the Italian and Egyptian campaigns (1796–99), and contributed to French successes in the NAPOLEONIC WARS. He married Napoleon's sister Caroline. As king of Naples he fostered the beginnings of Italian nationalism. Although he joined the Allies in 1814, he supported Napoleon during the Hundred Days, and was executed after an attempt to recapture Naples.

MURDOCH, (Jean) Iris (1919–), Irish-born British novelist. Her novels such as *A Fairly Honourable Defeat* (1970), *The Sea, the Sea* (1978) and *The Good Apprentice* (1985) display wit and a gift for analyzing human relations.

MURDOCH, (Keith) Rupert (1931–), Australian-born US newspaper publisher. After creating a sizable communications organization in Australia, he moved aggressively to buy properties in the UK and US, including the London *Times* and the Chicago *Sun-Times*. He also acquired magazines, television stations, and a motion picture company. He became a US citizen in 1985.

MURFREESBORO, or Stones River, Battle of, bitter but indecisive battle (Dec. 31, 1862–Jan. 2, 1863) in the American CIVIL WAR, fought near Murfreesboro, Tenn. The battle site is now the Stones River National Battlefield.

MURILLO, Bartolomé Estéban (1618–1682), Spanish BAROQUE painter, known as the "Raphael of Seville." The most famous painter of his time in Spain, Murillo produced religious narrative scenes expressing deep piety and gentleness, works of realism and fine portraits. Among his many famous paintings are the *Visions of St. Anthony*, the *Two Trinities* (known as the *Holy Family*) and *Beggar Boy.*

MURPHY, Frank (1890–1949), US public official and jurist. A New Deal Democrat, he served as governor general (1933–35) and high commissioner (1935–36) of the Philippines. As governor of Michigan (1936–38) he won national attention for settling the 1937 automobile strike in Flint. Briefly US attorney general (1939–40), he was appointed (1940) to the US Supreme Court.

MURRAY, Gilbert (1866–1957), British classical scholar, best known for his translations of ancient Greek playwrights. He actively promoted the LEAGUE OF NATIONS.

MURRAY, Philip (1886–1952), Scottish-born US labor leader. He was president of the Congress of Industrial Organizations

(CIO) from 1940; prominent leader of the UNITED MINE WORKERS, 1912–42, and organizer and head of the UNITED STEELWORKERS from 1942. In 1949–50 he helped rid the CIO of communist unions.

MURRAY RIVER, chief river of Australia; an important source of irrigation. It rises in the mountains of New South Wales and flows for 1,609mi, passing through Hume reservoir and Lake Victoria, on to Encounter Bay on the Indian Ocean.

MURROW, Edward R. (Edward Egbert Roscoe Murrow; 1908–1965), US broadcaster. He was head of Columbia Broadcasting System's European bureau during WWII; from 1947–60 he produced many acclaimed radio and TV programs, including an exposé of Senator Joseph MCCARTHY (1954). He directed the US Information Agency 1961–63.

MUSCAT AND OMAN. See OMAN.

MUSCLE, the tissue whose contraction produces body movement. In man and other vertebrates there are three types of muscle. **Skeletal or striated muscle** is the type normally associated with the movement of the body. Its action can either be initiated voluntarily, through the central NERVOUS SYSTEM, or it can respond to REFLEX mechanisms. Under the microscope this muscle is seen to be striped or striated. It consists of cylinders of tissue 0.01mm in diameter, showing great variation in length (1–150mm) and containing many nuclei. Each cylinder consists of thousands of filaments, each bathed in cytoplasm (known as sarcoplasm), which is their source of nutrition. Energy for contraction is derived by the oxidation of glucose brought by the BLOOD and stored as granules of glycogen in the sarcoplasm. The oxidation and breakdown of the glucose takes place in the mitochondria (see CELL), the net result being the formation of adenosine triphosphate (ATP). This molecule provides a "high-energy" bond which enables actin and myosin, two proteins in the muscle filament, to slide into each other, an action which, repeated many times throughout the muscle, results in its contraction. The behavior of a particular fiber is governed by an "all-or-none" law, in that it will either contract completely or not at all. Therefore the extent to which a muscle contracts is dependent solely on the number of individual fibers contracting. If a muscle is starved of oxygen, a process termed glycolysis provides the energy. However, glycolysis involves lactic acid production with the consequent risk of CRAMP. Skeletal muscle functions by being attached via TENDONS to two parts of the SKELETON which move relative to each other. The larger attachment is known as the muscle's origin. Contraction of the muscle attempts to draw together the two parts of the skeleton. Muscles are arranged in antagonistic groups so that all movements involve the contraction of some muscles at the same time as their antagonists relax. **Smooth or involuntary muscle** is under the control of the autonomic nervous system, and we are rarely aware of its action. Smooth muscle fibers are constructed in sheets of cells, each with a single nucleus. They are situated in hollow structures such as the gut, bronchi, uterus and BLOOD vessels. Smooth muscle uses the property of "tone" (continual slight tension) to regulate the diameter of tubes such as blood vessels. Being responsive to HORMONES, notably ADRENALINE, it can thus decrease blood supply to nonessential organs during periods of stress. In the gut, the muscle also propels the contents along by contracting along its length in waves (PERISTALSIS). **Cardiac muscle**, found only in the HEART, has the property of never resting throughout life. It combines features of both skeletal and smooth muscle, for it is striped but yet involuntary. The fibers are not discrete but branching and interlinked, thus enabling cardiac muscle to act quickly and in unison when stimulated.

MUSCULAR DYSTROPHY, a group of inherited DISEASES in which MUSCLE fibers are abnormal and undergo atrophy. Most develop in early life or adolescence. *Duchenne dystrophy* occurs in males although the genes for it are carried by females. It starts in early life, when some swelling (pseudohypertrophy) of calf and other muscles may be seen. A similar disease can affect females. Other types, described by muscles mainly affected, include *limb-girdle* and *facio-scapulo-humeral* dystrophies. There are many diverse variants, largely due to structural or biochemical abnormalities in muscle fibers. *Myotonic dystrophy* occurs in older men, causing BALDNESS, CATARACTS, testis atrophy and a characteristic myotonus, in which contraction is involuntarily sustained. Muscular dystrophies usually cause weakness and wasting of muscles, particularly of those close to and in the trunk; a waddling gait and exaggerated curvature of the lower spine are typical. The muscles of RESPIRATION may be affected, with resulting PNEUMONIA and respiratory failure; HEART muscle, too, can also be affected. These two factors in particular may lead to early death in severe cases. Mechanical aids, including, if necessary, ARTIFICIAL RESPIRATION, may greatly improve well-being, mobility and life-span.

MUSES, in Greek mythology, nine patron goddesses of the arts, worshiped especially near Mt Helicon. Daughters of ZEUS and the goddess of memory (Mnemosyne), they were attendants of APOLLO, god of poetry. The chief muse was Calliope (epic poetry); the others were Clio (history), Euterpe (lyric poetry), Thalia (comedy, pastoral poetry), Melpomene (tragedy), Terpsichore (choral dancing), Erato (love poetry), Polyhymnia (sacred song) and Urania (astronomy).

MUSEUM, institution that collects, preserves and exhibits objects—natural or manmade—for cultural and educational purposes. A museum was originally a place sacred to the MUSES; the most famous ancient museum, at Alexandria, Egypt (founded c280 BC), was a center for Greek scholars. Public museums did not exist in the ancient world or in medieval Europe; they developed from private Renaissance collections. The royal collections of works of art at the LOUVRE in Paris were made public in 1793, and the English physician and naturalist Sir Hans Sloane's widely varied collections were bought by the British government which then opened the BRITISH MUSEUM (1759). In the late 19th and 20th centuries numerous public museums were established, tending to specialize in particular subjects or time periods. Museums and their collections are of several kinds: general, art and picture galleries, historical, scientific, natural history, outdoors, specialized (industrial, commercial or professional) and regional or local.

MUSHROOM, popular name given to many gill fungi or agarics. In general, mushrooms are considered to be edible, while poisonous or inedible agarics are called toadstools. The common field mushroom (*Agaricus campestris*) is the most frequent wild species eaten, while *Agaricus bisporus* is the cultivated mushroom. Some mushrooms are serious parasites of wood, plantation trees and garden plants. Although mainly eaten for their flavor, mushrooms are of some food value, containing 5% protein. (See also FUNGI.)

MUSIAL, Stan (Stanley Frank Musial; 1920–   ), US baseball player, outfielder and first baseman for the St. Louis Cardinals (1941–63). He was elected the National League's most valuable player in 1943, 1946, and 1948 and was a member of 24 consecutive All-Star teams.

MUSIC, the art of arranging sound. Music cannot be defined merely as the art of

arranging pleasing sounds; discords have long been used, and many modern composers experiment with almost any kind of sound.

One of the most important elements of western music is HARMONY, the interaction of tones. An elaborate theory and technique of harmony has been evolved and can be used to great effect by a skilled composer. Eastern music, however, has largely developed without harmony and tends to rely more on complex melodic or rhythmic structures, as in the Indian *raga* or *tala*. Here the performer's ability to improvise within the traditional musical framework is important. Chinese musical theory depends on a single note, the *huang chung*, from which arises a series of 12 notes (*lue*), each of which is the basis of a pentatonic SCALE. RHYTHM is the one element common to music of all cultures. Music probably grew up as a rhythmical accompaniment to man's natural urge to dance.

Music has existed in every culture, and often seems to have developed in conjunction with religion. Music was used in Sumerian temple ceremonies c4000 BC. The ancient Greeks used music for religious and dramatic purposes. The Romans made much use of music for ceremonial occasions. The early history of western music is largely that of church music, with secular music taking a significant but secondary place until the Renaissance. Modern NOTATION was developed by the Benedictine monk GUIDO D'ARREZO in the 11th century, allowing a complex musical tradition to evolve. The current repertoire consists largely of music written after 1600, divided roughly into RENAISSANCE, BAROQUE, CLASSICAL, ROMANTIC and modern styles. Recently this has been extended to cover much earlier music, music of other cultures and less traditionally "serious" forms such as JAZZ and BLUES, POP MUSIC and FOLK MUSIC. The last has grown up as a separate tradition from formal music (though interacting with it) in almost all cultures, and has been transmitted orally from generation to generation.

Many people have tried to evolve a philosophy of music, but none has ever satisfactorily explained its power to heighten feeling and to communicate on a deeper level than language. What is certain is that a liking for music in one form or another is one of mankind's most natural and universal instincts. (See also ATONALITY; COUNTERPOINT; POLYPHONY; SOUND; TONALITY.)

MUSICAL NOTATION. See NOTATION.

MUSIL, Robert (1880–1942), Austrian

writer. He is known for *The Man Without Qualities* (3 vols., 1930–43), an encyclopedic novel about the ills of pre-war Austria.

MUSK, a strongly-scented substance used in the manufacture of perfume. The term is strictly applied to that obtained from the musk glands of the male musk deer, but also covers other similar secretions, e.g., civet musk, badger musk.

MUSKIE, Edmund Sixtus (1914–   ), US Democratic politician, senator from Maine (1965–77). In 1968 he was the Democratic candidate for vice president on the ticket headed by Hubert Humphrey. He sought the Democratic presidential nomination in 1972 but did poorly in the primaries. During the WATERGATE investigations it was revealed that his campaign had been sabotaged by "dirty tricksters" working for the reelection of President Nixon.

MUSKOGEAN, one of the nine language families of the major North American Indian language group called Macro-Algonkian. Muskogean has four languages. Today about 20,000 people speak the Choctaw, Chickasaw, Creek and Seminole dialects of Muskogean.

MUSK-OX, *Ovibos moschatus*, a heavily-built bovid from the Arctic of North America, not a true ox but related to sheep and goats. Musk-oxen have thick, shaggy coats and a pronounced hump over the shoulders. They are highly aggressive animals living in herds of up to 100. When threatened, herds form a circle of adults around the calves, with horns facing outward. Musk-oxen have always been hunted for their fur, but now they are also farmed commercially.

MUSKRAT, or **musquash,** *Ondatra zibethica*, of North America, the largest of the voles, measuring up to 2ft. It is an aquatic animal living in fresh water or salt marshes, feeding mainly on water plants. The feet are broad, the hindfeet being webbed, and the fur is thick and waterproof. Muskrats are frequently hunted for their fur.

MUSLIMS (Arabic: ones who submit), adherents of the religion of ISLAM.

MUSSET, (Louis Charles) Alfred de (1810–1857), French Romantic poet and playwright (see ROMANTICISM). After an affair with George SAND, he wrote "Les Nuits" (1835–37), some of the finest love poetry in French, and the autobiographical *Confession d'un Enfant du Siècle* (1836). His witty plays are often produced today.

MUSSOLINI, Benito (1883–1945) Italian founder of FASCISM, dictator of ITALY, 1924–43. Editor of the socialist party paper 1912–14, Mussolini split with the socialists when he advocated Italy's joining the Allies in WWI. In 1919 he formed a Fascist group in Milan which, in that time of political unrest, attracted many Italians with its blend of nationalism and socialism. The Fascist Party was nationally organized 1921; in 1922 the Fascist militia conducted the march on Rome which led the king to make Mussolini premier. He consolidated his position, eliminated opponents, signed the LATERAN TREATY and began an aggressive foreign policy. He brutally conquered Ethiopia 1935–36 (see ITALO-ETHIOPIAN WAR), and annexed Albania 1939. He joined Hitler (see AXIS POWERS) and in 1940 declared war on the ALLIES. Italy suffered defeats in Greece, Africa and at home. Mussolini was captured by the Allies (1943). When rescued by the Germans he headed the Fascist puppet regime in German-occupied N Italy; on its collapse he was shot by Italian PARTISANS.

MUSSORGSKY or **MOUSSORSKY, Modest Petrovich,** (1839–1881), major Russian composer. His *Boris Godunov* (1874) is one of the finest Russian operas. He developed a highly original style around characteristically Russian idioms, as in the song cycle *Songs and Dances of Death* (1875–77) and the piano suite *Pictures from an Exhibition* (1874).

MUSTANG, small feral HORSE of the W US, descended from horses of N African stock brought over by the Spaniards. Well adapted to plains conditions, they were popular as cow ponies. A **bronco** is an untamed mustang.

MUSTARD, herbs of the genus *Sinapis*, which is part of the CABBAGE family, Cruciferae. White mustard (*Sinapis alba*) and black mustard (*S. nigra*), native to the Mediterranean region, are now widely cultivated for their seeds which are used as a condiment.

MUTATION, a sudden and relatively permanent change in a GENE or CHROMOSOME set, the raw material for evolutionary change. Chemical or physical agents which cause mutations are known as *mutagens*. Mutations can occur in any type of CELL at any stage in the life of an organism, but only changes present in the GAMETES are passed on to the offspring. A mutation may be dominant or recessive, viable or lethal. The majority are changes in individual genes (gene mutations), but in some cases changes in the structure or numbers of chromosomes may be seen. The formation of structural chromosome changes is used to test drugs for mutagenic activity. Mutation normally occurs very rarely, though certain mutagens—X-RAYS, gamma rays, NEUTRONS and mustard gas—greatly accelerate mutation.

MUTE. See DUMBNESS.

MUTSUHITO (1852–1912), emperor of Japan from 1867, with regnal name Meiji. The long isolation of Japan under the SHOGUNS ended 1868 with the restoration of imperial power. Mutsuhito guided the transformation of Japan from a feudal empire into a modern nation. He established industries, promoted education, gave farmers titles to their land, and modernized the armed forces.

MUTUAL FUNDS, investment companies which pool their shareholders' funds and invest them in a broad range of stocks and shares. This spreads the risks for a small investor, who receives dividends for his shares in the fund (rather than for individual company shares) and who can always sell his fund shares back to the company at net asset value (see also STOCKS AND STOCK MARKET).

MUYBRIDGE, Eadweard (Edward James Muggeridge; 1830–1904), English-born US photographer. He pioneered studies of human and animal movement using a series of cameras with special shutters, and invented a precursor of the cinema projector to display his results, published in his *Animal Locomotion* portfolio (1887).

MYASTHENIA GRAVIS, a DISEASE of the junctions between the peripheral NERVOUS SYSTEM and the MUSCLES, probably due to abnormal IMMUNITY, and characterized by the fatigability of muscles. It commonly affects EYE muscles, leading to drooping lids and double VISION, but it may involve limb muscles. Weakness of the muscles of RESPIRATION, swallowing and coughing may lead to respiratory failure and aspiration or bacterial PNEUMONIA. Speech is nasal, regurgitation into the nose may occur and the face is weak, lending a characteristic snarl to the mouth. It is associated with disorders of the THYMUS and THYROID glands. Treatment is with cholinesterase inhibitors; STEROIDS and thymus removal may control the causative immune mechanism.

MYCENAE, city of ancient Greece and a late Bronze Age site, 7mi N of Argos in the NE Peloponnesus. The city of HOMER's King Agamemnon, it was destroyed by the Dorian invasion of 1100 BC. Historically the city is important as the center of Mycenaean civilization (see AEGEAN CIVILIZATION). The remains of the city include the Treasury of Atreus and royal beehive and shaft tombs and the Lion Gate of the citadel wall. Heinrich SCHLIEMANN

excavated the site (1876–78) and uncovered weapons, jewels, ornaments, gold and silverware.

MYCOLOGY, the scientific study of FUNGI.

MYOCARDITIS, a rare INFLAMMATION of the HEART muscle caused by VIRUSES, BACTERIA, some metal poisons and drugs. It is a serious complication of acute RHEUMATIC FEVER. Treatment involves bed rest, but the heart may be permanently damaged.

MYOPIA, or near- or shortsightedness, a defect of VISION in which light entering the EYE from distant objects is brought to a focus in front of the retina. The condition may be corrected by use of a diverging spectacle LENS.

MYRDAL, Gunnar (1898–1987), Swedish economist who wrote a classic work on race relations, *An American Dilemma* (1944), and an influential study of Third World economic development, *Asian Drama* (1968). He won the 1974 Nobel Prize in Economic Science.

MYRON (5th century BC), Greek sculptor best-known for his *Discobulus* (The Discus Thrower), a marble reconstruction of which is housed in Rome's National Museum. His work, almost exclusively in bronze, marks the apogee of early classical art. It is predominantly concerned with the human figure at critical moments of poise and balance in the course of generally strenuous, often athletic actions.

MYRRH, the fragrant resin obtained from small thorny trees of the genus *Commiphora* from the family Burseraceae. Myrrh has been used for embalming, in medicines and as incense and is now an important constituent of some PERFUMES.

MYSTERIES, secret religious rites of ancient Greece and Rome. Revealed only to initiated persons, they were called mysteries from the Greek word *mystes*, meaning an initiate. Disclosure of the secrets of the rites was punishable by death, hence the fragmentary nature of our knowledge of them. Of the Classical mysteries the most famous were the ELEUSINIAN MYSTERIES held at Eleusis and later in Athens. These involved purification rites, dance, drama and the display of sacred objects such as an ear of corn. The Orphic mysteries were said to have been founded by ORPHEUS. Other mysteries were connected with nature deities and those of eastern cults such as Cybele, Attis, ISIS, Osiris and MITHRA.

MYSTERY PLAY, medieval religious drama based on biblical themes, chiefly those concerning the Nativity, the Passion and the Resurrection. The form is closely related to that of the miracle play, which is generally based on non-biblical material, such as, for example, the saints' lives. The distinction between the two forms is not clearcut and some authorities refer to both as miracle plays. Mystery plays, which are liturgical in origin, can be extraordinarily ambitious in scale, treating the whole of man's spiritual history from the Creation to Judgment Day in vast cycles which required communal cooperation to perform. Important examples are the English York and Wakefield cycles, the French cycle *Miracle of Notre Dame* and the famous OBERAMMERGAU Passion, of Bavaria. (See also MORALITY PLAY.)

MYSTICISM, belief that man can experience a transcendental union with the divine in this life through meditation and other disciplines. It is at the core of most eastern religions, though it may be only loosely linked with them. The path to this union is usually seen as three stages: cleansing away of physical desires, purification of will and enlightenment of mind. Mysticism is important in most forms of Christianity. The goal is union and communion with God in love and by intuitive knowledge in prayer; mystical experience can be expressed only in metaphors, especially of love and marriage.

MYTHOLOGY, the traditional stories of a people which collectively constitute their folk history and that of their gods and heroes, embody their beliefs and ideas, and represent an affirmation of their culture. Most major mythologies originated in pre-literate societies and were passed on orally. The stories within a mythology fall into three main types: myths proper, which take place in a timeless past and are serious attempts to rationalize the mysterious and unknowable—i.e., the creation of the world, the origin of the gods, death and afterlife, the seasonal renewal of the earth; folk tales, narratives set in historical time and more social than religious in their concerns; and legends and sagas, which recount the embellished exploits of racial heroes.

Comparative studies have revealed fundamental similarities of theme and action among many widely separated mythologies. These similarities are thought by some to be the result of cultural interchanges. For others they constitute evidence of universal archetypes, the embodiments of the unconscious racial memories common to all humanity (see Carl G. JUNG). Sir James FRAZER'S *The Golden Bough* (1890) is the most famous work of comparative mythology.

The mythologies that have had the most profound influence on western thought and literature are those of the ancient Near East (Mesopotamia, Egyptian and Canaanite); classical, or Greco-Roman; Norse, including the Icelandic and Scandinavian sagas (see EDDA) and the Germanic NIBELUNGENLIED; and Celtic, especially Irish mythology.

14th letter of the English alphabet, corresponding with the 14th Semitic letter nūn and the Greek nū. N is the abbreviation for name, noun, neuter and north, among others. (See ALPHABET.)

NAACP. See NATIONAL ASSOCIATION FOR THE ADVANCEMENT OF COLORED PEOPLE.

NABATAEANS, ancient Arabs whose kingdom between the Euphrates R and the Red Sea prospered from the 4th century BC until Roman annexation (106 AD). Petra, S of the Dead Sea, was the center of the Nabataean settlements, which owed their wealth to control of caravan routes from Arabia to the Mediterranean coast.

NABOKOV, Vladimir (1899–1977), Russian-US novelist and critic. Born in St. Petersburg (now Leningrad), he became a US citizen in 1945. Noted for his originality and satiric wit, he published poetry, essays, short stories and novels in Russian and in English. His first English novel was *The Real Life of Sebastian Knight* (1938); he became famous for *Lolita* (1958), the story of a middle-aged man's passion for a young girl. His works include *Pnin* (1957), *Pale Fire* (1962), *Ada* (1969) and an English translation of *Eugene Onegin* (1964).

NABOPOLASSAR, first Chaldean king of Babylonia (626–605 BC); father of NEBUCHADNEZZAR II. With the Medes as allies he captured NINEVEH (612 BC), resulting in the destruction of the Assyrian Empire and the rise of the Neo-Babylonian Empire.

NADELMAN, Elie (1882–1946), Polish-born US sculptor. He interpreted the human form through the eyes of 18th century folk-artists and doll-makers, but was also influenced by "classic" sculptors such as RODIN. Among his more amusing sculptures was *Man in the Open Air.*

NADER, Ralph (1934–   ), US consumer crusader and lawyer. The controversy which greeted his book *Unsafe at Any Speed* (1965), a criticism of safety standards in the auto industry, enabled him to gain widespread support for investigations into other areas of public interest, including chemical food additives, X-ray leakage and government agencies. His work has resulted in Congressional hearings and remedial legislation.

NADIR SHAH (1688–1747), shah of Iran (1736–47), often called the "Napoleon of Iran." He created an Iranian empire reaching from the Indus R to the Caucasus Mts by ruthless military conquest, including the capture of Delhi (and its famous Koh-i-noor diamond and peacock throne).

NAGASAKI, capital of Nagasaki prefecture, a major port, on W Kyushu Island, Japan, and a foreign trading center since 1571. In WWII about 40,000 residents were killed when the US dropped the second atomic bomb (Aug. 9, 1945). Today shipbuilding is the city's major industry. Pop 449,382.

NAGY, Imre (1896–1958), Hungarian communist leader and premier (1953–55). His criticism of Soviet influence led to his removal from office; but during the Oct. 1956 revolution he became premier again briefly. After Soviet troops crushed the uprising, the Russians tried and executed Nagy in secret.

NAHUM, Book of, the seventh of the Old Testament Minor Prophets, the oracles of the prophet Nahum. It graphically relates the fall of Nineveh (612 BC) and is dated shortly before or after this.

NAIL, metal shaft, pointed at one end and usually with a head at the other, that can be hammered into pieces of wood or other materials to fasten them together. In the making of common nails, steel wire is fed discontinuously between a pair of gripper dies, which hold it while a hammer forms the head. The grippers part and the wire moves forward; nippers then shear the shaft, and pliers form the point. Other forms are masonry nails, stamped from a plate, and U-shaped staples.

NAIPAUL, V(idiadhar) S(urajprasad) (1932–), cosmopolitan Indian writer, born in Trinidad. A brilliant critic and essayist, Naipaul has been especially praised for his novels of life in the Third World, including *A House for Mr. Biswas* (1961) and *A Bend in the River* (1979).

NAISMITH, James (1861–1939), US teacher of physical education, at the U of Kansas 1898–1937. In 1891, while a student at the YMCA Training School in Springfield, Mass., he responded to an assignment to invent a game that could occupy students between the football and baseball seasons by inventing BASKETBALL.

NAMATH, Joe (Joseph William Namath; 1943–), US football player. A star quarterback at the U of Alabama (1962–64), he played professionally for the New York Jets (1965–72) and the Los Angeles Rams (1977–78). In 1969 he led the Jets to an upset Superbowl victory over the Baltimore Colts. His playing career was cut short by injuries.

NAMIBIA, or **South West Africa,** a territory under the control of the Republic of South Africa, is bordered by the S Atlantic Ocean, Angola, Zambia, Botswana and South Africa.

Official name: Namibia (South West Africa)
Capital: Windhoek
Area: 318,259sq mi
Population: 1,075,000
Languages: Afrikaans, English, Bantu
Religions: Christian, Animist
Monetary unit(s): 1 South African rand=100 cents
Land. The land rises from the Namib Desert, which stretches N to S on the Atlantic coast, to a plateau averaging 3,500ft above sea level covered by rough grass and scrub. The Kalahari, a desert region, lies to the E. The climate is hot and dry, and there are only two important rivers.
People. The population is overwhelmingly Bantu. Ovambos, the single largest ethnic group, Bushmen and Kavango live in Ovamboland, to the N. The Hereros, Nama and Damara live in the S plateau, chiefly around Windhoek, the capital, which is home to most of the country's Europeans, about 12% of the population. The Rehoboths, or coloureds, of African and European ancestry, are also an important group. All these groups—except the Bushmen—farm, raise cattle or work in mines.
Economy. The mineral sector accounts for most exports, diamonds and uranium being

the leading commodities. Livestock dominates the agricultural sector. Fishing is also an important economic activity. Meat processing and fish canning are the main industries.
History. The territory was annexed by Germany in 1884, and mandated to South Africa after WWI by the League of Nations in 1920. After WWII South Africa refused to place it under UN trusteeship; the UN in 1966 declared the original mandate terminated and tried to bring South West Africa under its control, later renaming it Namibia. In 1971 the International Court of Justice reversed its earlier rulings in favor of South Africa, stating that South Africa's practice of *apartheid* (separation of the races) violated its mandate. South Africa rejected the court's ruling and continued its occupation, which was opposed by the Marxist-leaning South-West Africa People's Organization (SWAPO), founded (1959) and led by Sam Nujoma. In 1988 a US-brokered agreement involving Cuba, Angola, and South Africa provided for the withdrawal of Cuban troops from Angola and the end of South Africa's occupation of Namibia. Because Namibia would remain locked in to the South African economy, however, its independence promised to be more symbolic than real.

NANSEN, Fridtjof (1861–1930), Norwegian explorer, scientist and humanitarian, awarded the 1922 Nobel Peace Prize, best known for his explorations of the Arctic. His most successful attempt at reaching the NORTH POLE was in 1895, when he achieved latitude 86° 14', the farthest north then reached. He also designed the **Nansen bottle,** a device for obtaining water samples at depth.

NANTES, Edict of, proclamation of religious toleration for French Protestants (HUGUENOTS) issued in the city of Nantes by Henry IV in 1598. Protestants were granted civil rights and freedom of private and public worship in many parts of France (but not in Paris). In 1685 Catholic pressure brought Louis XIV to revoke the edict.

NANTUCKET ISLAND, popular summer resort, 25mi S of Cape Cod, Mass., across Nantucket Sound. The 15mi-long island has a mild climate and 88mi of beaches. It was a world famous 18th-century whaling center. Pop 3,774.

NAOROJI, Dadabhai (1825–1917), Indian nationalist leader. He lived in England from 1855, lecturing and writing about British policies in India. He was a founder (1885) of the Indian National Congress and the first Indian elected to the British

Parliament (1892).

NAPALM, a SOAP consisting of the aluminum salt of a mixture of carboxylic acids, with aluminum hydroxide in excess. When about 10% is added to GASOLINE it forms a gel, also called napalm, used in flame throwers and incendiary bombs; it burns hotly and relatively slowly, and sticks to its target. Developed in WWII, it was used in the Vietnam War and caused great havoc. (See also CHEMICAL AND BIOLOGICAL WARFARE.)

NAPIER, John (1550–1617), Scottish mathematician credited with the invention of LOGARITHMS (before 1614). Natural logarithms (to the base e) are often called **Napierian logarithms** for him. He also developed the modern notation for the DECIMAL SYSTEM.

NAPLES, third-largest city in Italy, capital of Naples province and of the Campania region, on N shore of the Bay of Naples, 120mi SE of Rome. Founded by the Greeks (c600 BC), it was the capital of the Kingdom of NAPLES and later the TWO SICILIES. The historic city has a 13th-century cathedral and university (1224), and medieval castles and palaces. Nearby are the ruins of POMPEII. Naples is the financial and intellectual center of S Italy. A major seaport, its industries vary from heavy engineering and textiles to wine and glass manufacture. Pop (city) 1,207,750; (metro) 4,100,000.

NAPLES, Kingdom of. It comprised all of Italy S of the Papal States, including Sicily. It emerged after the conquests of the Norman Robert Guiscard in the 1000s; his nephew Roger II took the title King of Sicily and Apulia (1130). Naples was ruled in turn by the Hohenstaufens, the ANGEVINS, the Aragonese (see ARAGON) and the Spanish Crown. The Austrians conquered the kingdom in 1707, but it was taken by the Spanish BOURBON kings in 1734. NAPOLEON I annexed the kingdom to his empire and made his brother Joseph king (1806) followed by his brother-in-law MURAT. In 1815, after Napoleon's defeat, the Bourbon Ferdinand IV was restored; he reunited Naples and Sicily as the Kingdom of the TWO SICILIES. Bourbon rule collapsed before the advance of the revolutionary forces of GARIBALDI (1860). When Victor Emmanuel was confirmed by the Italian parliament as king of all Italy (Feb. 1861), Naples became a part of the new Italian state, ending 700 years as an independent kingdom.

NAPOLEON I (1769–1821), general and emperor of the French (1804–14). Napoleon Bonaparte was born in Corsica, went to military schools in France and became a lieutenant in the artillery (1785). He associated with JACOBINS on the outbreak of the FRENCH REVOLUTION, drove the British from Toulon (1793), and dispersed a royalist rebellion in Paris (Oct. 1795). Soon after his marriage to JOSÉPHINE de Beauharnais, he defeated the Austro–Sardinian armies in Italy (1796–7) and signed the treaty of Campo Formio extending French territory. He returned to Paris a national hero. He then campaigned in Egypt and the Middle East, threatening Great Britain's position in India. Although he won land battles, the French fleet was destroyed in the Battle of the Nile (Aboukir) Aug. 1798. Napoleon later returned to Paris and helped to engineer the coup d'etat of Nov. 9, 1799, which established a Consulate with himself as first consul and virtual dictator. He reorganized the government, established the Bank of France and the CODE NAPOLÉON, which is still the basis of French law.

Continuing hostilities with Austria and Great Britain resulted in the Treaty of Lunéville, which recognized French dominance on the Continent. The Treaty of Amiens with Britain (March 1802) meant that Europe was at peace for the first time in ten years. Napoleon became first consul for life (1802) and crowned himself emperor (1804). In the NAPOLEONIC WARS he then won a series of great victories over the European alliance at Austerlitz (1805), Jena (1806) and Friedland (1807), dissolving the HOLY ROMAN EMPIRE (1806) and becoming ruler of almost the whole continent. After Jena he inaugurated the Continental System whereby he hoped to keep European ports closed to British trade, but the battle of TRAFALGAR (1805) established the dominance of Britain at sea.

In 1809 Napoleon divorced Joséphine and married Marie Louise, who bore him an heir, NAPOLEON II. The PENINSULAR WAR revealed growing French weakness, and in 1812 Napoleon began his disastrous campaign against Russia. A new alliance of European nations defeated the French at Leipzig (1813); in 1814, after France was invaded, Napoleon abdicated and was exiled to the island of Elba. In March 1815 he escaped, returned to France and ruled for the Hundred Days, which ended in French defeat at WATERLOO (1815). Napoleon was then exiled to SAINT HELENA, where he died in 1821. His remains were brought to Paris in 1840 and buried under the dome of Les Invalides.

NAPOLEON II (1811–1832), son of Napoleon and Marie Louise, proclaimed king of Rome at birth. After his father's abdication (1814), he lived in Austria as Duke of Reichstadt. He died of tuberculosis.

NAPOLEON III (Louis Napoleon Bonaparte; 1808–1873), emperor of the French (1852–70); son of Louis Bonaparte, king of Holland, nephew of Napoleon I. He attempted several coups against King LOUIS PHILIPPE, was jailed but escaped to England (1846). After the 1848 revolution, he was elected president of France; he dissolved the legislature and made himself emperor (1852). His regime promoted domestic prosperity, but by the 1860s opposition to his repressive, corrupt government had grown. He joined in the CRIMEAN WAR (1854–56) but failed to maintain MAXIMILIAN as emperor of Mexico. In 1870 his ill-judged war with Prussia ended in defeat, capture and the collapse of his empire; he died in exile in England.

NAPOLEONIC CODE. See CODE NAPOLÉON.

NAPOLEONIC WARS (1804–15), fought by France after NAPOLEON I became emperor. After the Treaty of Amiens (1802), which had ended the FRENCH REVOLUTIONARY WARS (1792–1802), Britain declared war on France in May, 1803, maintaining that Napoleon was not keeping to the treaty. Napoleon planned to invade Britain, but the British fleet proved too strong for him, especially after TRAFALGAR. The British, Austrians and Russians formed an alliance in July 1805; Napoleon defeated the Austrians and Russians at Austerlitz (Dec. 1805), the Prussians at Jena (1806) and the Russians at Friedland (1807); the Peace of Tilsit (1807) left him nearly master of Europe. Meanwhile Britain had secured supremacy of the seas at the Battle of Trafalgar (1805). The Continental System begun after Jena was Napoleon's attempt to blockade British trade; on the pretext of enforcing it he invaded Portugal (1807) and Spain (1808). During the defeat of his armies by the British in the PENINSULAR WAR (1808–14), he signed the Peace of Schönbrunn (1809) with the defeated Austrians. In 1812 Napoleon invaded Russia with a grand army some 500,000 strong. He barely won the Battle of Borodino (1812) and marched unchallenged to Moscow, but his troops suffered from lack of supplies and the cold weather. Their retreat from Moscow and Russia was horrifying; only about 30,000 of Napoleon's soldiers returned. The French, by now drained of manpower and supplies, were decisively beaten at Leipzig (1813). Paris fell, and on April 6, 1814, Napoleon abdicated. The victorious allies signed the Treaty of Paris with the Bourbons. After Napoleon's escape from Elba and return (the Hundred Days) and his defeat at Waterloo (1815), the second Treaty of Paris was signed in 1815 (see PARIS, TREATIES OF).

NARAYAN, R(asipuram) K(rishnaswamy) (1906–   ), Indian novelist writing in English who created the fictitious South Indian town of Malgudi in a series of novels which dealt with the ironies of daily life in contemporary India. These include *The Bachelor of Arts* (1937), *The Financial Expert* (1952) and *Talkative Man* (1986).

NARCOLEPSY, a disease marked by uncontrollable sleepiness. It is a chronic disease which usually begins during puberty and occurs predominantly in males. It is characterized by two elements: (1) the occurrence, usually several times a day, of attacks of irresistible sleep, lasting on the average 5 to 10 minutes; (2) the fact that under the influence of certain emotions, the muscles of the body relax acutely, so that the person falls down and is unable to move for a while. His consciousness remains completely clear throughout and he soon recovers completely.

NARCOTICS, DRUGS that induce sleep; specifically, the OPIUM-derived ANALGESICS. These affect the higher BRAIN centers causing mild euphoria and sleep (narcosis). They may act as HALLUCINOGENIC DRUGS and are abused in DRUG ADDICTION.

NARODNIKI (Russian: populists), members of a socialist movement in 19th-century Russia. They ineffectually spread political propaganda among the peasants; failure and police repression turned them to terrorism, culminating in Tsar Alexander II's assassination (1881). They were succeeded by the Socialist Revolutionary Party (1901).

NARRAGANSETT BAY, inlet of the Atlantic Ocean, extending about 30 mi into Rhode Island. Three large islands, Conanicut, Aquidneck and Prudence, are so situated in the bay that they divide its mouth into three channels. All five counties of Rhode Island have a shoreline on the bay, and several famous resorts are located there, including Newport on Aquidneck Island.

NARRAGANSETT INDIANS, North American tribe of the Algonquian linguistic family (numbering perhaps 5,000 before 1675) who inhabited most of Rhode Island. They were friendly to the colonists until KING PHILIP'S WAR (1675–76) resulted in their virtual annihilation.

NARVÁEZ, Pánfilo de (c1470–1528), Spanish conquistador. Under VELÁZQUEZ, he played a major role in subjecting Cuba to Spain. In 1520 Velázquez sent him on a punitive expedition against Hernán CORTES in Mexico which failed. He also led an unsuccessful expedition, on which he himself died, to subjugate and exploit Florida.

NARWHAL, *Monodon monoceros*, a "toothed whale" of the Arctic. The teeth are completely absent in both sexes except for a single spiral tusk in the male on the left-hand side of the jaw. This tusk may be up to 2.5m (8.2ft) long; its function is unknown. It is believed that narwhal tusks were once thought to be the horns of unicorns.

NASA. See NATIONAL AERONAUTICS AND SPACE ADMINISTRATION.

NASH, John (1752–1835), British architect, famous for his development of Regent's Park and Regent St, London, begun 1811. He built the Royal Pavilion, Brighton, Sussex; redesigned St. James's Park, London; and began alterations to Buckingham Palace (1821).

NASH, Ogden (1902–1971), US humorous poet with a witty, sometimes satirical style, punctuated by puns, asides, unconventional rhymes and unexpectedly long lines. He published 20 volumes of verse and wrote lyrics for musicals.

NASHVILLE, capital city of Tenn., seat of Davidson Co., on the Cumberland R in N central Tenn. The last major battle of the Civil War was fought nearby (Dec. 1864). Nashville is a commercial, industrial and agricultural city; the center of the country music recording industry; and a religious, educational and publishing center. Pop (city) 462,000, (metro) 910,000.

NASSAU, capital city of the Bahama Islands, a port on NE New Providence Island. Long a pirate haunt, it is now a world-famous tourist resort. Pop (metro) 135,437.

NASSER, Gamal Abdel (1918–1970), Egyptian president and Arab leader. He led the military coup d'etat which overthrew King FAROUK (1952), then ousted General Naguib and named himself prime minister (1954). He ended British military presence in Egypt (1954) and seized the SUEZ CANAL (1956). He was elected president of Egypt unopposed (1956), and was president of the UNITED ARAB REPUBLIC 1958–61. His "Arab socialism" policy brought new land ownership laws and agricultural policies, more schools, increased social services and widespread nationalization. He fought a brief war with Israel in 1956; after the disastrous 1967 ARAB-ISRAELI WAR with Israel, he resigned but resumed office by popular demand.

NAST, Thomas (1840–1902), German-born US cartoonist, creator of the symbols for the Democratic Party (donkey) and the Republican Party (elephant). His attacks on the TAMMANY HALL political machine, symbolized as a tiger, contributed to its disintegration. Nast's drawings of SANTA CLAUS set a US popular image.

NATAL, province of South Africa, on the Indian Ocean, 33,578sq mi in area, with capital Pietermaritzburg. It produces sugar, fruit, cereals and coal and manufactures fertilizers and textiles, mainly near Durban, the chief city. Natal was a British colony 1856–1910.

NATCHEZ   INDIANS, MUSKOGEAN-speaking tribe of SW Miss.; numbering about 6,000 in 1682. Primarily an agricultural people, they worshiped the sun and also maintained a rigid social caste system. They were driven from their villages near today's Natchez, Miss., after three wars with French settlers (1716, 1723, 1729), and mostly joined other tribes.

NATCHEZ TRACE, old road from Natchez, Miss., to Nashville, Tenn.; developed from Indian trails, it was of great importance c1780–1830. The **Natchez Trace National Parkway**, about 450mi long, follows the old route.

NATHAN, George Jean (1882–1958), US editor and drama critic, with H. L. Mencken coeditor (1914–23) of *Smart Set* magazine and cofounder (1924) of the *American Mercury*. As a reviewer, he championed the plays of O'Neill, Pirandello, O'Casey, Molnar, Saroyan, and Giraudoux.

NATION, Carry Amelia (1846–1911), US temperance agitator. She began her campaign against liquor bars in the "dry" state of Kan. Formidable in size and appearance, from 1901 she smashed several saloons with a hatchet. Arrested on about 30 occasions, she paid fines by selling souvenir hatchets and lecturing. She was not supported by the national PROHIBITION movement.

NATIONAL ACADEMY OF DESIGN, US fine arts association, founded 1825. Its 425 members are painters, sculptors, graphic artists, architects, and watercolorists. It has a School of Fine Arts in New York City.

NATIONAL ACADEMY OF SCIENCES, private US organization of scientists and engineers, founded 1863. It officially advises the government on scientific questions, and coordinates major programs. Its 1500 members are elected for distinguished research achievements.

NATIONAL   AERONAUTICS   AND

SPACE ADMINISTRATION (NASA), US government agency responsible for nonmilitary SPACE EXPLORATION and related research. Founded by President Eisenhower (1958) as successor to the National Advisory Committee for Aeronautics (NACA), it has numerous research stations, laboratories and space flight launching centers, including Cape CANAVERAL and the Houston control center. Its headquarters are in Washington, D.C.

NATIONAL AEROSPACE PLANE. See AEROSPACE PLANE, NATIONAL.

NATIONAL ASSOCIATION FOR THE ADVANCEMENT OF COLORED PEOPLE (NAACP), US voluntary interracial organization, founded in New York City (1909) to oppose RACISM and racial segregation and discrimination, and to ensure CIVIL RIGHTS for black Americans. It works for the enactment and enforcement of civil rights laws, supports education programs and engages in direct action. An early success was the ending of LYNCHING. NAACP's membership is about 400,000.

NATIONAL BANK, See BANK OF THE UNITED STATES.

NATIONAL BUREAU OF STANDARDS (NBS), bureau of the US Department of Commerce, established 1901. It determines national WEIGHTS AND MEASURES, tests products and materials, and carries on research in science and technology. It also advises government agencies and industries on safety codes and technical specifications.

NATIONAL COLLEGIATE ATHLETIC ASSOCIATION (NCAA), US advisory body founded 1906. It establishes eligibility and competition rules for intercollegiate athletics. The NCAA compiles statistics on college sports and publishes rule books and guides. It has over 1,000 member institutions.

NATIONAL CONFERENCE OF CHRISTIANS AND JEWS, US organization founded 1928 to fight prejudice, intolerance and bigotry and to promote interfaith harmony. The conference sponsors Brotherhood/Sisterhood Week.

NATIONAL COUNCIL OF THE CHURCHES OF CHRIST IN THE USA, organization of 32 Protestant and Eastern Orthodox churches (with combined membership of 40 million), founded 1950 to promote interdenominational cooperation and understanding. It has educational, evangelistic, ecumenical, political and relief programs, and has allied itself with many other church bodies and missionary societies.

NATIONAL DEBT, the amount of money owed by a government, borrowed to pay expenses not covered by taxation revenue. The US national debt totaled almost $2.8 trillion by 1988. National debts are incurred to pay for wars, public construction programs, etc. To obtain money, governments sell bonds or short-term certificates to banks, other organizations and individuals. Some governments in crisis have defaulted or devalued the currency. The public debt includes not only the national debt but also debts of individual states, cities, etc.

NATIONAL FOREST SYSTEM, administered by the Forest Service in the US Department of Agriculture, comprises 156 national forests, 19 national grasslands, and 17 land utilization projects totaling 191 million acres. The system is managed for timber production, recreation and natural beauty, wildlife habitat, livestock forage, and water supplies. Some 32 million acres are set aside as wilderness and 175,000 acres as primitive areas.

NATIONAL GALLERY OF ART, US museum of nationally-owned works of art, opened 1941, in Washington, D.C. It is part of the SMITHSONIAN INSTITUTION. The initial collection was donated by Andrew MELLON (1937). The gallery possesses Jan van Eyck's *The Annunciation* and Raphael's *The Alba Madonna*; it has many works by Italian, French and American artists.

NATIONAL GEOGRAPHIC SOCIETY, nonprofit scientific and educational organization, established in Washington, D.C. (1888) "for the increase and diffusion of geographic knowledge." It publishes *National Geographic* magazine, books, maps and school bulletins, and sponsors expedition and research projects.

NATIONAL GUARD, volunteer reserve groups of the US Army and Air Force, with a combined authorized strength of about 500,000, originating in the volunteer militia organized in 1792. Each state, territory, and the District of Columbia has its National Guard units. Army units are directed by the National Guard Bureau of the Department of the Army and air units by the Department of the Air Force. The National Defense Acts of 1920 and 1933 empower the president to call up units in time of national crisis. Governors may call up state units during strikes, riots, disasters and other emergencies—in recent years National Guard units have checked civil disturbances, often amid controversy. A guardsman takes a dual oath—to the federal government and to his state. In peacetime he attends 48 drill sessions and a two-week training camp annually.

NATIONAL INSTITUTES OF HEALTH

(NIH), research agency of the US Public Health Service, Department of Health and Human Services. NIH conducts and supports biomedical research into the causes, prevention, and cure of diseases; supports research training and the development of research resources; and makes use of modern methods to communicate biomedical information. Its major components include the National Cancer Institute; the National Heart, Lung, and Blood Institute; the National Institute of Diabetes and Digestive and Kidney Diseases; the National Institute of Allergy and Infectious Diseases; the National Institute of Child Health and Human Development; the National Institute of Dental Research; the National Institute of Environmental Health Sciences; the National Institute of General Medical Sciences; the National Institute of Neurological and Communicative Disorders and Stroke; the National Eye Institute; the National Institute on Aging; and the National Institute of Arthritis and Musculoskeletal and Skin Diseases.

NATIONALISM, political and social attitude of groups of people who share a common culture, language and territory as well as common aims and purposes, and thus feel a deep-seated loyalty to the group to which they belong, as opposed to other groups. Nationalism in the modern sense dates from the FRENCH REVOLUTON, but had its roots in the rise of strong centralized monarchies, in the economic doctrine of MERCANTILISM and the growth of a substantial middle class. Nationalism today is also associated with any drive for national unification or independence. It can represent a destructive force in multinational states.

NATIONALITY, in law, recognized citizenship of a particular country. Nations themselves determine who their nationals are. Two basic principles for deciding nationality are acknowledged by most countries: *jus sanguinis*, the right of blood, based on the nationality of a parent; and *jus soli*, the right of place of birth. (See also CITIZENSHIP; NATURALIZATION.)

NATIONAL LABOR RELATIONS BOARD (NLRB), independent US government agency designed to prevent or correct unfair labor practices. Originally set up to administer the National Labor Relations Act of 1935 and protect fledgling unions from illegal interference, the board has since been granted power to police both illegal union and management practices. Its actions are subject, however, to approval by the federal courts.

NATIONAL MEDIATION BOARD, independent US federal agency which mediates and arbitrates in labor disputes threatening to disrupt interstate (airline and railroad) commerce. Its arbitration decisions are legally binding.

NATIONAL MERIT SCHOLARSHIP CORPORATION, nonprofit, independent corporation, started with a $20 million investment by the FORD FOUNDATION in 1955. The Carnegie Corporation was a leading initial contributor and many philanthropies, businesses, and educational institutions now also are donors. The corporation runs two nationwide scholarship programs; one provides a range of college scholarship grants to some 3,800 high school graduates annually; the other provides similar scholarships for outstanding black students. Awards are based on scores in tests run by the corporation, on extracurricular achievements, school standing and so on.

NATIONAL OCEANIC AND AT-MOSPHERIC ADMINISTRATION (NOAA), US government agency set up in 1970 to coordinate scientific research into atmosphere and oceans. Its specific aims are the monitoring and control of POLLUTION and the investigation of potential resources and weather-control techniques. The NOAA is responsible for the work of several formerly independent agencies, including the Coast and Geodetic Survey (founded in 1807) and the Weather Bureau (founded in 1870).

NATIONAL ORGANIZATION FOR WOMEN (NOW), founded 1966 to promote full equality between men and women in all walks of life. With some 260,000 members, NOW has focused its efforts since 1978 on passage of the EQUAL RIGHTS AMENDMENT. Its first president was Betty FRIEDAN.

NATIONAL PARK SYSTEM, system administered by the US National Park Service, a bureau of the Department of the Interior, whereby land of outstanding scenic or historical interest is protected "for the benefit and enjoyment of the people". The national park idea originated in the US; descriptions in 1870–71 of the wild country at the headwaters of the Yellowstone R in Wyo. led in 1872 to an Act of Congress creating Yellowstone National Park (2,221,733 acres). In Cal., Sequoia and Yosemite were declared parks in 1890, but few other sites were brought under protection until 1916, when President Woodrow Wilson instituted the Park Service. Today it administers more than 46,000sq mi of parkland, comprising about 300 protected areas—and the number is still growing. Of this land, 48 outstanding scenic areas are known simply as national parks. About 80 others, combining scenery with precolonial history, natural or man-made objects, or geological, zoological or botanical phenomena, are called national monuments. The other areas include battlefields (such as Gettysburg), forts and trading posts, pioneer trails, cemeteries, recreation areas, scenic lake shores and waterways, important birthplaces (Washington's, Lincoln's), the National Scientific Reserve, the Statue of Liberty, memorials such as the Washington Monument and Mt Rushmore, and the White House. The service also protects shorelines in danger of erosion.

NATIONAL RECOVERY ADMINIS-TRATION (NRA), principal government agency set up under the NEW DEAL by the National Industrial Recovery Act of 1933 to administer codes of fair practice for businesses and industries. Promise of higher prices and wages stimulated a minor boom which soon collapsed. By early 1934 the laboriously negotiated codes had become intolerably cumbersome; and in May 1935 the Supreme Court ruled it unconstitutional. It was later abolished by the president.

NATIONAL REPUBLICAN PARTY, American political party formed when the Democratic–Republican Party split up in the 1828 presidential election. The party's candidate in 1832, Henry CLAY, was routed and during JACKSON's presidency, in 1836, the party merged with other political groups to form the WHIG party.

NATIONAL RIFLE ASSOCIATION OF AMERICA (NRA), US organization composed of people interested in firearms, founded 1871. It promotes the use of firearms for sport and self-defense, safety and wildlife conservation, and maintains all national records of shooting competitions. The organization is a major lobbying group opposed to gun-control legislation. It has 3 million members.

NATIONAL ROAD, famous old paved road for settlers emigrating to the West. It ran from Cumberland, Md., through Vandalia, Ill., to St. Louis, Mo. The first section, as far as Wheeling, W Va. (the Cumberland Road) was opened in 1818. Today's US Highway 40 closely follows the original route.

NATIONAL SCIENCE FOUNDATON (NSF), US federal agency set up in 1950. It promotes research, education and international exchange in the sciences and funds fellowships, projects such as the International Decade of Ocean Exploration, and several permanent observatories.

NATIONAL SECURITY AGENCY (NSA), agency within the US Department of Defense established by presidential directive in 1952. Its director also heads the Central Security Service (CSS), established by presidential memorandum in 1972 to provide a more unified cryptologic organization within the Defense Department. The NSA/CSS has three primary missions: communications security, computer security, and foreign-intelligence gathering.

NATIONAL SECURITY COUNCIL (NSC), created by Congress in 1947 as part of the executive office of the president, to advise him on a wide range of matters relating to national security and defense policies. Chaired by the president, its permanent members include the vice-president and the secretaries of state and defense. The chairman of the Joint Chiefs of Staff and the director of the Central Intelligence Agency are advisers. The NSC staff is headed by the president's national security adviser.

NATIONAL SERVICE, alternative to a military DRAFT often proposed by critics of the ALL-VOLUNTEER FORCE (AVF). Under national service, all young people — perhaps including women — after the completion of high school would be required to serve the nation either in the armed forces or in such civilian areas as hospitals, jails, schools, poverty neighborhoods, and conservation projects. Proponents argue that this would meet many urgent national needs while providing youths of all classes with experiences of great value in their personal development and citizenship training. Critics point out that coercive national service, employing 4 million youths each year, would require a massive and costly administrative structure and that much of the employment would necessarily be trivial and profitless. In any case, coercive national service would probably be politically unacceptable, particularly if women were exempted. Voluntary national service, already familiar in the PEACE CORPS and ACTION programs, has attracted relatively few youths.

NATIONAL SOCIALISM. See NAZISM.

NATIONAL URBAN LEAGUE, US civil rights organization, founded 1910, with headquarters in New York City. In 1988 it had 50,000 members.

NATIONAL WAR COLLEGE, in Washington, D.C., provides education in national security policy to selected military officers and career civil servants from federal departments and agencies concerned with national security. Its academic program lasts 10 months.

NATIVISM, turning in of a country or society towards its own culture through movements rejecting foreign influences, ideas or immigrants; largely an anthropological term. Nativism is brought on by social stress or disintegration, as with primitive peoples faced by Western civilization. For notable examples of nativist movements in American history see KNOW-NOTHING PARTY; KU KLUX KLAN. (See also CHAUVINISM.)

NATO. See NORTH ATLANTIC TREATY ORGANIZATION (NATO).

NAT TURNER'S REBELLION, or the **Southampton Insurrection,** the largest slave uprising in US history, leading to harsher slave laws in the South and the eclipse of emancipation societies. On Aug. 21, 1831, Nat Turner, a Negro slave and Baptist preacher, believing himself called to free his fellow slaves, murdered his master, John Travis of Southampton Co., Va., and led a brief campaign in which 55 whites were killed. He was captured on Oct. 22, tried and hanged. Thirteen slaves and three free Negroes were also hanged.

NATURAL GAS, mixture of gaseous HYDROCARBONS occurring in reservoirs of porous rock (commonly sand or sandstone) capped by impervious strata. It is often associated with PETROLEUM, with which it has a common origin in the decomposition of organic matter in sedimentary deposits. Natural gas consists largely of METHANE and ethane, with also propane and butane (separated for bottled gas), some higher alkanes (used for GASOLINE), nitrogen, oxygen, carbon dioxide, hydrogen sulfide, and sometimes valuable HELIUM. It is used as an industrial and domestic FUEL, and also to make carbonblack and in chemical synthesis. Natural gas is transported by large pipelines or (as a liquid) in refrigerated tankers.

NATURALISM, attempt to apply the scientific view of the natural world to philosophy and the arts. There is nothing real beyond nature; man is thus a prisoner of his environment and heredity. This aesthetic movement, inspired by Émile ZOLA's argument for a scientific approach to literature in *The Experimental Novel* (1880), had a profound affect on the fine arts, literature and drama. Zola's ideas influenced many writers—Guy de MAUPASSANT, as well as Stephen CRANE and Theodore DREISER in the US; dramatists from Scandinavia's Henrik IBSEN and August STRINDBERG to Russia's Maxim GORKI and the modern American playwrights Arthur MILLER and Tennessee

WILLIAMS; and painters such as the Frenchman Gustave COURBET.

NATURALIZATION, process whereby a resident alien obtains citizenship of a country. In the US, under the Immigration and Nationality Act of 1952, an alien is eligible for naturalization if he is over 18, entered the country legally and has resided there for at least five years, is of "good moral character," names two referees who can vouch for his qualifications, can demonstrate familiarity with written and spoken English and American history and government, and is prepared to renounce all foreign allegiances and take an oath of loyalty and service to his new country. Citizenship may be granted on the recommendation of the immigration service after a court hearing. Alien wives of Americans may normally apply for naturalization after three years' residence. Naturalization of resident aliens in Canada proceeds on much the same lines as in the US, except that the minimum age is 21, and two court hearings are required before the citizenship oath is taken.

NATURAL LAW, the body of law supposed to be innate, discoverable by natural human reason, and common to all mankind. Under this philosophy, man–made or *positive* law, though changeable and culturally dependent, must—if truly just—be derived from the principles of natural law. The concept was rooted in Greek philosophy (see STOICISM) and Roman law, and particularly in the Christian philosophy of Thomas AQUINAS, where natural law—the sense of right and wrong implanted in men by God—is contrasted with revealed law. It lay behind GROTIUS' ideas on international law (17th century). It was used as a basis for ethics, morality, and even for protests against tyranny by SPINOZA, LEIBNIZ, LOCKE, ROUSSEAU and many others, but with the development of scientific philosophies in the 19th century, natural law largely lost its influence.

NATURAL RIGHTS, political philosophy based on a belief that man as a natural being has certain basic rights that cannot be denied by government or society. John LOCKE'S "life, liberty and property" and the American Declaration of Independence's "life, liberty and the pursuit of happiness" are two of the most famous formulations of natural rights. These rights, however derived, form an important basis for the social contract theory of government, for revolutions like the American and the French and, most importantly, for statements like the English Bill of Rights (1689), the US Bill of Rights (1791) and the UN's Universal Declaration of Human Rights (1948). (See also HUMAN RIGHTS.)

NATURAL SELECTION, mechanism for the process of EVOLUTION discovered by Charles DARWIN in the late 1830s, but not made public until 1858. According to Darwin, evolution occurs when an organism is confronted by a changing environment. A degree of variety is always present in the members of an interbreeding population. Normally, the possession of a variant character by an individual confers no particular advantage on it, and the proportion of individuals in the population with a given variation remains constant. But if it ever arises in a changed environment that a given variation increases the chances of an individual's survival, then individuals possessing that character will be more liable to survive—and breed. The frequency with which the variant character occurs in future generations of the organism will thus increase, and, over a large number of generations, the general form of the population will change. The name "natural selection" derives from the analogy Darwin saw between this selection on the part of "nature" and the "artificial selection" practiced by animal breeders.

NAURU, independent island republic in the W Pacific Ocean, 40mi S of the equator. The Polynesian population's revenue comes from phosphate rock which covers the central plateau and is the chief resource and export.

Official name: Republic of Nauru
Capital: Yaren district
Area: 8.2sq mi
Population: 8,100
Languages: Nauruan, English
Monetary unit: 1 Australian dollar =100 cents
History. The island was discovered in 1798 and annexed by Germany in 1888. Australia captured it in WWI and administered it as a trust territory until independence was achieved in 1968. The government, which then took control of the phosphate industry, has invested much of its revenue abroad to provide a source of

income after the phosphate deposits are exhausted in the late 1990s.

NAUTILUS, first nuclear-powered submarine, launched Jan. 1955. Capable of submerged speed of over 20 knots, she made the first transpolar voyage beneath the North Pole on Aug. 3, 1958. She measured 323 ft. in length and had a crew of over 100. The *Nautilus* was decommissioned in 1980.

NAVAHO or **NAVAJO INDIANS**, migrants from the N who settled around 1000 AD in Ariz. and N.M.; cousins to the APACHE Indians. They learned agriculture, weaving and sand painting from the PUEBLO Indians. After the Spanish introduced sheep in the 1600s, they became pastoralists. Inveterate raiders of Spanish and American settlements in the SW, they were finally subdued (1864) by Kit CARSON and held at Fort Sumner, N.M., until their resettlement on a reservation in 1868. Today there are about 100,000 Navahos. The Navaho culture has an elaborate mythology and religion; their folk art includes painting, silver-working and the weaving of rugs and blankets.

NAVAL ACADEMY, US, at Annapolis, Md., founded in 1845 to train officers for the US Navy and Marine Corps, coeducational since 1976. Enrollment in 1988 was 4,500. Graduates are commissioned ensigns in the Navy or 2nd lieutenants in the Marine Corps.

NAVAL OBSERVATORY, US, source of official standard time in the US. Founded in Washington, D.C., in 1833, the observatory has moved several times to obtain better observing conditions. Since 1955 its main station has been in Flagstaff, Ariz.

NAVARINO, Battle of, naval action in the Greek War of Independence (Oct. 1827). It resulted in the destruction of an Egyptian fleet by a combined English-French-Russian fleet intervening on the side of Greece. This was the last major conflict between wooden sailing ships.

NAVARRE, BASQUE province in N Spain. Formerly an independent Basque kingdom, it was important in international politics as a buffer state between Spain and France because it controlled a principal mountain pass (Roncesvalles) into Spain. Most of Navarre was conquered in 1512 by Ferdinand of Aragon; it sank to provincial status in 1841. The northern part of Navarre (also called Lower Navarre) remained independent until 1589, when its king Henry IV became ruler of France as well as of Navarre. Today the area is part of the French department of Basses-Pyrénées.

NAVIGATION, the art and science of directing a vessel from one place to another.

Originally navigation applied only to marine vessels, but now air navigation and, increasingly, space navigation are also important. Although the techniques and applications of navigation have radically changed through time, the basic problems, and hence the principles, have remained much the same.

Marine Navigation. Primitive sailors could not venture out of sight of land without the risk of getting lost. But soon they learned to use sunset and sunrise, the prevailing winds, the North Star and other natural phenomena as aids to direction. Early on, the first fathometer, a weighted rope used to measure depth, was developed. Before the 10th century AD the magnetic COMPASS had appeared. But it was not until the 1730s that the inventions of the SEXTANT and CHRONOMETER heralded the dawn of accurate sea navigation. Both LATITUDE AND LONGITUDE could now be determined within reasonable tolerances. (See also ASTROLABE; GREENWICH OBSERVATORY.) Modern navigation uses electronic aids such as LORAN and the radiocompass; celestial navigation, the determination of position by sightings of celestial bodies; and dead reckoning where, by knowing one's position at a particular past time, the time that has elapsed since, one's direction and speed, one can tell one's present position. (See also MAP; SONAR; SUBMARINE.)

Air navigation uses many of the principles of marine navigation. In addition, the pilot must work in a third dimension, must know his altitude (see ALTIMETER), and in bad visibility must use aids like the instrument landing system. RADAR is also used.

Space navigation is a science in its infancy. Like air navigation, it works in three dimensions, but the problems are exacerbated by the motions both of one's source (the earth) and one's destination, as well as by the distances involved. But, prior to developments in new areas, it seems that SPACE EXPLORATION has inaugurated a new era in navigation by the stars. (See also CELESTIAL SPHERE; GYRO-COMPASS; GYROPILOT.)

NAVIGATION ACTS, laws regulating navigation at sea or in port, or restricting commercial shipping in the national interest. More specifically, regulations promulgated (from 1650) by the British during the American colonial period to try to insure that benefits of commerce would accrue to England (and to a lesser extent, the colonies) rather than to England's enemies. After 1763, strict enforcement of the acts caused friction between England and the American colonies and was a major factor leading to the outbreak of the REVOLUTIONARY WAR.

NAVRATILOVA, Martina (1956–   ), Czech-born US tennis player, eight-time Wimbledon singles champion (1978–79, 1982–87) and four-time US Open winner (1983–84, 1986–87).

NAVY, a seaborne armed force maintained for national defense or attack. In ancient times, armed men often put to sea to explore or raid distant territories. Assyria, Egypt and Phoenicia each deployed merchant fleets on military tasks. Among the first to create a permanent naval force were the Athenians. Their armed *triremes* (galleys with three tiers of oars) defeated the Persians at SALAMIS (480 BC) and were adopted by Carthage and later Rome, which, after the naval battle at ACTIUM in 31 BC, ruled the Mediterranean for 400 years. In Scandinavia, the VIKINGS created marauding fleets which ravaged the coasts of Europe from c800 AD for over 200 years. Only ALFRED THE GREAT withstood their raids by creating an English naval task force. Byzantium, Genoa, Venice and other Italian republics, the Arabs and Turks developed powerful navies in the Mediterranean. By the late 16th century most western European nations had acquired naval forces. Spain emerged as the leading naval power, but after her ARMADA was defeated by the English in 1588, England had mastery of the seas. Her naval supremacy was challenged by Holland (see DUTCH WARS) and France, but the Battle of TRAFALGAR in 1805 restored it for another 100 years. A powerful navy ensured that a country could maintain an overseas empire and world influence. Large armored BATTLESHIPS were built from before WWI, until they were outmoded in WWII, although some are presently being reinstated. The submarine and the aircraft carrier then took over. In the postwar period, Britain was overshadowed as a leading naval power by the US and the USSR. The strike power of modern navies, capable of nuclear warfare, assures them a prominent place in the superpowers' armed forces in the future. (See also NAVY, US.)

NAVY, US, is headed by the chief of naval operations, who is responsible to the civilian secretary of the navy in the US Department of Defense. He is also the Navy member of the JOINT CHIEFS OF STAFF. Major Navy operating commands include the Pacific Fleet; the Atlantic Fleet; Naval Forces, Europe; and the Sealift Command. In 1986, 581,000 men and women served in the US Navy.

NAZARETH, historic town in N Israel, lower Galilee, where Jesus Christ lived as a youth. A place of Christian pilgrimage, the town has many shrines and churches. It also has some light industry and is an agricultural market center. Pop 40,400.

NAZISM, or **National Socialism,** the creed of the National Socialist German Workers' Party (Nazi Party) led by Adolf HITLER from 1921 to 1945. The Nazi movement began (1918–19) when Germany was humiliated and impoverished by defeat in WWI and by the severe terms of the Treaty of VERSAILLES. There was growing economic, political and social chaos, and fear of increasing communist influence. The Nazi Party emerged as a political force during the worldwide GREAT DEPRESSION. From a membership of around 100,000 in 1928, the party increased in strength to 920,000 in 1932. Using Hitler's powerful talent for public oratory and propaganda, the Nazis set forth a program designed to appeal to the grievances of as wide a range of German society as possible. The ideas behind the program were rooted in nationalism, racism (especially ANTI-SEMITISM), authoritarianism and militarism. They were expressed by Hitler in *Mein Kampf* (*My Struggle*, 1923). Recovery of the German nation was to be accomplished by rearmament, territorial expansion to acquire *lebensraum* (living space) for the Teutonic *herrenrasse* (master race) and the restoration of self-respect under a unified military regime—*Ein Reich, Ein Volk, Ein Führer* (one state, one nation, one leader). The movement continued to grow, aided by publicity techniques, military pageantry and intimidation and terrorization of opponents by the party's brownshirted militia, the *Sturm-Abteilung* (S.A.). In 1932 the Nazi party won more than one-third of the seats in the German parliament (*Reichstag*), and in Jan. 1933 politicians who hoped to be able to manipulate Hitler and use his political power base made him chancellor. In 1933–34 he reversed the situation by establishing a Nazi dictatorship. With the aid of the secret police (GESTAPO) and the S.A., Hitler began systematically to intern Jews, other non-Aryans and any opposing groups including labor unions and political parties in CONCENTRATION CAMPS. In the 1940s many of these were used for the systematic extermination of millions of Jews. Hitler's Nazi program of expansionism temporarily improved the German economic position, but led to WORLD WAR II, which resulted in the defeat of Germany and its allies and the end of the Nazi Party. (See also GERMANY; FASCISM.)

NCAA. See NATIONAL COLLEGIATE ATHLETIC ASSOCIATION.

NEANDERTHAL MAN. See PREHISTORIC MAN.

NEARCHUS (d. c312 BC), Cretan-born general under ALEXANDER THE GREAT. On Alexander's return from India, Nearchus commanded the fleet which sailed down the Indus R and up the Persian coast.

NEARSIGHTEDNESS. See MYOPIA.

NEAR v. MINNESOTA, the first case (1931) in which the US Supreme Court applied the 1st Amendment freedom of the press to a state through the "due process" clause of the 14th Amendment. When a Minneapolis newspaper criticized local officials for not acting against a gangster, the state prosecutor, acting under a "newspaper gag law," got an injunction closing down the newspaper. The court held the gag law unconstitutional. It said a state may pass criminal libel laws providing for punishment *after* publication of defamatory material, but it cannot close a newspaper, "even a vicious scandal sheet," to keep it from publishing in the first instance.

NEBRASKA, W central state of the US, bounded on the E by Ia. and Mo. across the Missouri R, on the S by Kan. and Col., to the W by Wyo. and on the N by S.D.

Name of state: Nebraska
Capital: Lincoln
Statehood: March 1, 1867 (37th state)
Familiar name: Cornhusker State
Area: 77,227sq mi
Population: 1,598,000
Elevation: Highest—5,424ft, Kimball County; Lowest—840ft, Richardson County
Motto: "Equality before the law"
State flower: Goldenrod
State bird: Western meadowlark
State tree: Cottonwood
State song: "Beautiful Nebraska"
Land. Nebraska is an undulating plain which slopes gradually from NW to SE. Over half of the state's area is covered with fertile soil. Most of W Nebraska consists of semiarid high plains, often broken by rugged hills called buttes. In the NW corner

of the state lie about 1,000sq mi of badlands, used mostly for grazing. The state is crossed by many rivers (notably the Platte) and contains over 2,000 lakes. The climate is marked by extremes of very cold winters and very hot summers.

People. Although Nebraska is primarily an agricultural state, just over half its people live in urban areas. About 97% of the population is native born. About one-third have German ancestors; other large groups which settled the state were the English and the Irish.

Economy. The states chief field crop is corn, followed by wheat, hay, grain and sorghum. The state contains one of the world's largest cattle markets and is a principal producer of beef cattle. Food processing is the most important industry; other major manufactures include electrical machinery, chemicals, metal products, printed material and electronic and transportation equipment.

History. During the 17th and 18th centuries the French established fur-trading centers there. Nebraska became part of the US with the LOUISIANA PURCHASE (1803), was set up as a territory under the KANSAS–NEBRASKA ACT (1854) and joined the Union in 1867. When the railroad crossed the state in that year, hordes of settlers began to move in. In the next two decades the pioneer farmers were active in the GRANGE and POPULIST movements. The state's prosperity depended upon agricultural productivity, and natural disasters and the Great Depression in the 1930s brought much hardship. In 1937 Nebraska adopted a unicameral (one-house) legislative system. After WWII increasing farm mechanization and new industries benefited the state's economy. Nebraska was hard hit by the agricultural depression of the 1980s, but its economy turned up in 1988 despite the worst drought since 1955. In presidential elections 1968–88, Nebraska voted consistently Republican.

NEBUCHADNEZZAR, name of three kings of Babylonia. **Nebuchadnezzar I** (ruled c1124–1103 BC) conquered Elam and extended Babylonian rule over most of ancient Mesopotamia. **Nebuchadnezzar II** (c630–562 BC) waged many military campaigns to consolidate the Neo-Babylonian or Chaldean Empire (see BABYLONIA AND ASSYRIA). He crushed the kingdom of Judah, destroyed Jerusalem (586), and took many captive Jews to Babylon. **Nebuchadnezzar III** (6th century BC) usurped the throne from DARIUS I for ten weeks before he was killed.

NEBULA, an interstellar cloud of gas or

dust. The term is Latin, meaning "cloud," and was initially used to denote any fuzzy celestial object, including COMETS and external GALAXIES: this practice has now largely been abandoned. There are two main types of nebula. **Diffuse nebulae** are large, formless clouds of gas and dust and may be either bright or dark. *Bright nebulae*, such as the Orion Nebula, appear to shine due to the proximity or more usually presence within them of bright stars, whose light they either reflect (reflection nebula) or absorb and re-emit (emission nebula). *Dark nebulae*, such as the Horsehead Nebula, are not close to, or do not contain, any bright stars, and hence appear as dark patches in the sky obscuring the light from stars beyond them. Study of diffuse nebulae is particularly important since it is generally accepted that they are in the process of condensing to form new STARS. **Planetary nebulae** are very much smaller, and are always connected with a star that has gone NOVA some time in the past. They are, in fact, the material that has been cast off by the star. They are usually symmetrical, forming an expanding shell around the central star, which is often still visible within. The Ring Nebula is an outstanding example.

NEBULAR HYPOTHESIS, theory accounting for the origin of the solar system put forward by LAPLACE. It suggested that a rotating NEBULA had formed gaseous rings which condensed into the planets and moons, the nebula's nucleus forming the sun.

NECKER, Jacques (1732–1804), French banker; finance minister under LOUIS XVI. In 1777 he tried to raise money to support French involvement in the American Revolution. Later, before the STATES GENERAL, he proposed wide-sweeping public reforms, but opposition forced his resignation in 1790.

NEEDLEWORK, work using a needle either for plain sewing like mending, darning, sewing seams or hemming, or for decorative embroidery such as smocking, needlepoint or canvas work (needlework on canvas backing), and drawn-thread work. Quilting involves sewing together two layers of material with padding between; appliqué is attaching small pieces of material to a backing material. LACE may be made with a needle and thread, being then called needlepoint lace; tatting employs shuttles, crochet employs a hook and knitting employs needles: all four are usually termed needlework. Samplers are traditional forms of recording various embroidery stitches and designs; one of the earliest, Jane

Bostocke's (1598), includes satin, chain, ladder, buttonhole, arrowhead and cross stitches in metal thread and silk.

NEFERTITI or **Nefretete** (14th century BC), queen of ancient Egypt, and subject of a famous painted limestone portrait bust now in the Berlin Museum. She was the wife of Pharaoh AKHENATON (reigned c1379–62 BC).

NEGEV, or **Negeb,** a triangular region of hills, plateaus and desert in S Israel, extending S from Beersheba to Elath on the Gulf of Aqaba. It covers an area of around 5,000sq mi, or more than half of Israel. Although it is mainly an arid region, irrigation has made many areas fertile. It is rich in mineral and natural gas resources.

NEGLIGENCE, in law, inadvertent failure to act with the degree of care a situation demands. The degree may be determined by a contractual obligation or what the law defines as the standard of conduct of a "reasonable man." Conduct of an accident victim which contributed to his accident is contributory negligence, and may prevent his receiving compensation, or reduce the amount. Negligence is usually a civil offense, but may lead to a criminal charge such as manslaughter.

NEGRI, Pola (1899?–1987), Polish-born US film vamp of the 1920s, famous for her off-screen romances with Charlie Chaplin, Rudolph Valentino, and others.

NEGRITOS, a Spanish term applied to Negroid peoples of pygmy size living in various parts of the South Pacific. Negritos average less than 5ft in height and include the Eta peoples of the Philippines, the Semang of the Malay Peninsula, and the inhabitants of the Andaman Islands.

NEGROID, one of the racial divisions of man. The RACE is characterized by woolly hair and yellow, dark brown or black skin. Most Negroid peoples originated in Africa, but Melanesians and Negritos are also Negroid.

NEHEMIAH (flourished 5th century BC), Jewish leader of the return from the BABYLONIAN CAPTIVITY. As described in the OLD TESTAMENT Book of Nehemiah (written with the Book of EZRA by the author of CHRONICLES), he rebuilt Jerusalem's walls and enforced moral and religious reforms.

NEHRU, Jawaharlal (1889–1964), first prime minister of independent India. An English-educated lawyer, he embraced the cause of India's freedom after the British massacre of Indian nationalists at Amritsar (1919). In 1929 he became president of the Indian National Congress. He spent most of 1930–36 in prison for his part in civil disobedience campaigns. By 1939 his

Marxist outlook had brought conflict to his long association with GANDHI, but during WWII the two leaders united in their opposition to aiding Britain unless India was freed. Released in 1945 after three years' imprisonment, Nehru began negotiations with Britain which culminated, in 1947, in the establishment of independent India. He was prime minister until his death, successfully guiding his country through the difficult early years of freedom. Although the eventual compromise of his neutralist and non-aggressive policies evoked some criticism, he never lost the profound devotion of his countrymen.

NELSON, Horatio, Viscount Nelson (1758–1805), great British naval hero who defeated the French and Spanish fleets at the Battle of TRAFALGAR. He entered the navy at age 12, was rapidly promoted, and given his first command in the French Revolutionary Wars. He was instrumental in defeating the Spanish fleet off Cape St. Vincent (1797). His destruction of the French fleet off Aboukir (1798) brought him fame and honors. Official disapproval caused by the scandal of his liaison with Emma, Lady HAMILTON, was dispelled by his defeat of the Danes at Copenhagen (1801). His pursuit of the French fleet on the renewal of the war in 1803 culminated in the Battle of Trafalgar, the occasion of his now-famous flag signal, "England expects that every man will do his duty." The victory cost Nelson his life, but ensured British naval supremacy for 100 years.

NEMEROV, Howard (1920–   ), US poet, novelist and critic noted for his satiric power. His *Collected Poems* (1977) won the National Book Award and Pulitzer Prize in 1978. Among his novels are *The Melodramatists* (1949) and *The Homecoming Game* (1957).

NEMIROVICH-DANCHENKO, Vladimir Ivanovich (1858–1943), Russian novelist, playwright and producer, cofounder, with STANISLAVSKI, of the Moscow Art Theater. As a producer, Nemirovich-Danchenko was a great patron of the works of Ibsen and Chekhov.

NEOCLASSICISM, in the visual arts and architecture, a movement, c1750–1850, to return to the style and spirit of classical times. A reaction against the BAROQUE, its ideals of simplicity and proportion were particularly successful in architecture. Leading figures included Thomas JEFFERSON in America, and Inigo JONES and Christopher WREN in England. In music, it was a movement from c1920 looking back to 18th- and 19th-century "classical" composers.

NEOCONSERVATISM, political philosophy of an influential group of former liberals, who in the late 1960s began to oppose many of the policies and principles associated with President Lyndon Johnson's Great Society programs. In particular, the neoconservatives (or new conservatives) objected to affirmative-action programs based on racial quotas, and they deplored a perceived trend toward lower standards and loss of individual initiative. The movement, often characterized as elitist, was first publicized in *Public Interest*, a quarterly edited by Irving Kristol and Daniel Bell. Norman Podhoretz, editor of *Commentary*, took the lead in calling for a strong anti-Soviet foreign policy.

NEOKANTIANISM, movement in late-19th-century European philosophy inspired by the rigorous critical method of Immanuel KANT (1724–1804) and directed against irrationalism and speculative naturalism. The Marburg School, founded by Herman Cohen (1842–1918), sought the application of Kantian methods to the physical sciences; the Heidelberg School, headed by Wilhelm Windelband (1848–1915) and Heinrich Rickert (1863–1936), sought their application to history and the social sciences.

NEOLITHIC AGE. See PRIMITIVE MAN; STONE AGE.

NEOPLATONISM, a school of philosophy based on the work of Plato and dominant from the 3rd to the 6th centuries AD. It was developed by PLOTINUS and formulated in his *Enneads*. Neoplatonic philosophy set forth a systematized order which contained all levels and states of existence. From God, or the One, emanates the Divine Mind, from which the World Soul proceeds, and which in turn comprehends the visible world. Man's ideal is to rise upward toward union with the One. Neoplatonic philosophy greatly influenced early Christian theology through St. Augustine and others.

NEPAL, independent kingdom of S Asia.
Land. It is a land of strongly contrasting climate and terrain, with the Himalayas in the N, the temperate Valley of Nepal in the center, and the low-lying swamplands and forests of the Terai region in the S. Its major rivers rise in Tibet.
People. The population of Nepal is of mixed Mongolian and Indo-Aryan origin. Its main ethnic groups are the Newars, the Bhotias (who include the Sherpas) and the GURKHAS. Hinduism, numerically the dominant religion, has long coexisted with Buddhism. Tribal and caste distinctions retain considerable importance. In spite of rapid educational expansion since 1951, the

Official name: Kingdom of Nepal
Capital: Kathmandu
Area: 56,827sq mi
Population: 17,567,000
Languages: Nepali, Hindu, Tibeto-Burman dialects
Religions: Hindu, Buddhist
Monetary unit(s): 1 Nepali rupee = 100 pice
illiteracy rate is still about 85%.
Economy. Nepal's economy is predominantly agricultural. Crops include rice, wheat, corn, oilseeds, potatoes, jute, tobacco, opium and cotton. Livestock is important. The forests of the Terai provide wood, and medicinal herbs are exported from the slopes of the Himalayas. Nepal's few industries, employing only about 1% of the labor force, rely chiefly on the processing of agricultural products, but include wood and metal handicrafts. Means of transportation, though still severely limited in the remoter areas, now include roads linking the Valley of Nepal with both Tibet and India, and several airports. Infrastructure in the eastern part of the country was damaged by a major earthquake in 1988.
History. Nepal comprised numerous principalities until it was conquered by the Gurkhas in 1768. Political power was in the hands of the Rana family from 1846 to 1951, when it returned to the monarchy. The first democratically-elected government came to power in 1959, but a conflict in 1962 resulted in King Mahendra's banning all political parties. The present king, Birendra, came to the throne in 1972 and continued his father's policies. In 1980 a referendum resulted in the continuance of the partyless government, Panchayat, and the constitution was revised to permit direct parliamentary elections, which were held in 1981 and 1986.

NEPHRITIS, INFLAMMATION affecting the KIDNEYS. The term **glomerulonephritis** covers a variety of diseases, often involving-disordered IMMUNITY, in which renal glomeruli are damaged by immune complex deposition (e.g., BRIGHT'S DISEASE); by direct autoimmune attack (Goodpasture's syndrome), or sometimes as a part of systemic disease (e.g., lupus, endocarditis, DIABETES or hypertension). Acute or chronic renal failure or nephrotic syndrome may result. The treatment is immunosuppressive or with STEROIDS. Acute **pyelonephritis** is bacterial infection of the kidney and renal pelvis, following SEPTICEMIA or lower urinary tract infection. Typically, this involves FEVER, loin pain and painful, frequent urination. The treatment requires ANTIBIOTICS. Chronic pyelonephritis includes recurrent kidney infection with permanent scarring and functional impairment.

NEPHROSIS, or nephrotic syndrome, EDEMA associated with kidney disease (see NEPHRITIS).

NEPTUNE, the fourth-largest planet in the SOLAR SYSTEM and the eighth in position from the sun, with a mean solar distance of 30.07AU. Neptune was first discovered in 1846 by J. G. Galle using computations by U. J. J. Leverrier based on the perturbations of URANUS' orbit. The calculation had been performed independently by John Couch ADAMS in England, but vacillations on the part of the then Astronomer Royal had precluded a rigorous search for the planet. Neptune has two moons, Triton and Nereid, the former having a circular, retrograde orbit, the latter having the most eccentric orbit of any moon in the solar system. Neptune's "year" is 164.8 times that of the earth, its day being 15.8h. Its diameter is about 31,000mi and its mass 17.45 times that of the earth. Its structure and constitution are believed to resemble those of JUPITER.

NERNST, Walther Hermann (1864–1941), German physical chemist awarded the 1920 Nobel Prize for Chemistry for his discovery of the Third Law of THERMODYNAMICS.

NERO (37–68 AD), infamous Roman emperor. Born Lucius Domitius Ahenobarbus, he was adopted by his stepfather, emperor Claudius, whom he succeeded in 54 AD. Nero had Claudius' son Britannicus murdered in 55. In 59 he killed his mother Agrippina, and in 62 his wife Octavia, Claudius' daughter. The wise rule of SENECA and Burrus, to whom Nero had left affairs of state, ended in 62. Nero rebuilt Rome after the fire in 64 AD. Not himself responsible, he attributed the fire to the Christians, and the first Roman persecution followed. His cruelty, instability, and imposition of heavy taxes led to a revolt. Deserted by the PRAETORIAN GUARD, Nero committed suicide.

NERUDA, Pablo (1904–1973), born Neftalí Ricardo Reyes Basualto, influential

Chilean poet, diplomat and communist leader. He won the 1971 Nobel Prize for Literature. His verse collections, written in the surrealist vein, include *Twenty Love Poems and a Song of Despair* (1924) and the highly-regarded *Canto General* (1950).

NERVAL, Gérard de (1808–1855), born Gérard Labrunie, French romantic writer who anticipated the symbolist and surrealist movements in French literature. His works include a collection of sonnets, *Les Chimères* (1854); some short stories, *Les Filles du Feu* (1854); and his autobiography, *Aurélia* (1853–54).

NERVI, Pier Luigi (1891–1979), Italian civil engineer and architect. In the 1940s he invented *ferrocemento*, a new form of reinforced concrete. Notable among his bold and imaginative designs are the Turin exposition hall, the railway station in Naples, the Olympic buildings in Rome, and (in collaboration) the UNESCO headquarters in Paris.

NERVOUS SYSTEM, the system of tissues which coordinates an animal's various activities with each other and with external events by means of nervous impulses conducted rapidly from part to part via nerves. Its responses are generally rapid, whereas those of the endocrine system with which it shares its coordinating and integrating function are generally slow (see GLANDS; HORMONES).

The nervous system can be divided into two parts. The **central nervous system** (CNS), consisting of BRAIN and SPINAL CORD, stores and processes information and sends messages to muscles and glands. The **peripheral nervous system,** consisting of 12 pairs of cranial nerves arising in and near the medulla oblongata of the brain and 31 pairs of spinal nerves arising at intervals from the spinal cord, carries messages to and from the central nervous system.

A third system, the **autonomic nervous system,** normally considered part of the peripheral nervous system, controls involuntary actions such as heartbeat and digestion. It is divisible into two complementary parts: the *sympathetic system* prepares the body for "fight or flight," and the *parasympathetic system* controls the body's vegetative functions. Most internal organs are innervated by both parts.

The nervous system's basic anatomical and functional unit is the highly specialized nerve cell or NEURON, the shape of which varies greatly in different regions. It possesses two kinds of processes: *dendrites*, which together with the cell body receive impulses from other neurons, and an *axon*, which conducts impulses to other neurons. Axons vary greatly in length (up to a few yards) and speed of conduction (up to about 300ft/sec).

Sensory or *afferent neurons* carry information to the central nervous system from sensory receptors (such as skin receptors and muscle stretch receptors), whereas *efferent neurons* carry information away from it. Efferent neurons passing to muscle are called *motor neurons*.

Nerves are formed from many axons, both afferent and efferent, surrounded by their associated sheaths which insulate them from each other. Axons surrounded by a fat and protein sheath, called a myelin sheath, conduct fastest. Just prior to entering the spinal cord each spinal nerve divides into a *dorsal root* containing afferent axons only and a *ventral root* containing efferent axons only.

Adjacent neurons communicate through specialized contact points or *synapses* which are either excitatory or inhibitory. The elaborate neural circuitry arising from synaptic contact in the central nervous system is responsible for much of behavior, from simple reflex action to complex thought-communication patterns.

The nerve impulse, or action potential, is an electrical signal conducted at speeds far slower than ELECTRICITY. An electrical potential difference of about 70mV, called the resting potential, exists between the inside and outside of the neuron due to the ionic concentration imbalance between inside and outside, and a metabolic pump moving IONS across the cell membrane. If the resting potential is reduced below a certain threshold level, as may occur when impulses are received from other neurons, an impulse is initiated. Impulses are all the same strength ("all-or-none" law), and travel to the end of the axon to the synapse, where a chemical transmitter substance is released which initiates a new electrical signal in the next neuron. (See also NEURITIS.)

NESS, Loch, lake in Inverness Co., N central Scotland, about 23mi long, 1mi wide and 750ft deep. As yet there has been no conclusive evidence of the existence of the famous Loch Ness "monster."

NESSELRODE, Karl Robert, Count (1780–1862), Russian statesman, foreign minister 1816–56. A pillar of the conservative HOLY ALLIANCE, he sent Russian troops to help Austria suppress the Hungarian revolution of 1849. His expansionist policy in the E Mediterranean brought on the CRIMEAN WAR.

NEST, a structure prepared by many

animals for the protection of their eggs and young, or for sleeping purposes. In social insects, the nest provides the home of the whole colony, and may have special structures for temperature control and ventilation. The sleeping nests of, for example, the great apes, are commonly no more than crudely woven hammocks of twigs and branches. The sleeping nests of other mammals (which may be used for hibernation) are as complex and woven as any breeding nest. Both these and the nests used by birds and mammals for breeding, must protect the animals within from both weather and predators. Nests can be built of mud, leaves, twigs, down, paper and various human garbage.

NESTORIANS, members of the heretical Christian sect named for Nestorius (Patriarch of Constantinople 428–431), who was condemned by the Council of Ephesus (431) for rejecting the title "Mother of God" for the Virgin MARY, and teaching the existence of two persons—divine and human—in Jesus Christ. The Nestorians expanded vigorously for 800 years, but were persecuted by the Mongols and—in recent times—by the Turks. The modern Nestorian (Assyrian) Church has about 100,000 members, mainly in Iraq, Iran, and Syria.

NETHERLANDS, The, kingdom in W Europe, commonly known as Holland. The land is mostly flat, about 38% is below sea-level. It is protected from the sea by a narrow belt of dunes bordering the North Sea coast and a vast complex of dikes forming POLDERS. The major cities of the Netherlands are located in the polders region, which, with its rich clay soil, contains the finest agricultural land. The higher inland region has natural drainage but relatively poor, sandy soil, except where it is traversed by the Lower Rhine, Waal and Maas (Meuse) rivers. The climate of the Netherlands is mild and damp.

People. The Netherlands is one of the world's most densely populated countries. Nearly half the population lives close to the three largest cities—Amsterdam (the capital), The Hague (the seat of government) and Rotterdam (the chief port). Schooling is compulsory between ages 7 and 15; the literacy rate is one of the highest in the world. There are 11 universities, including the famous public universities at Leiden, Utrecht, Groningen and Amsterdam. There is no official religion.

Economy. Industry now provides 40% of the Netherlands' GNP and employs over a million people. There are reserves of oil,

Official name: Kingdom of the Netherlands
Capital: Amsterdam
Seat of government: The Hague
Area: 16,133sq mi
Population: 14,615,000
Language: Dutch
Religions: Protestant, Roman Catholic
Monetary unit(s): 1 guilder = 100 cents

natural gas and coal, but most raw materials must be imported. Major industries include oil-refining, iron and steel, textiles, machinery, electrical equipment and plastics. Dairy produce, the basis of Holland's intensive agriculture, sustains a large food-processing industry. Financial and transportation services contribute significantly. Tourism is also important. A highly advanced transportation system includes about 4,000mi of natural and artificial waterways. The Netherlands is a member of the EUROPEAN ECONOMIC COMMUNITY and BENELUX. Foreign trade accounts for two-thirds of the nation's GNP.

History. The Low Countries' seven northern provinces (now the Netherlands) broke away from Spanish rule under William the Silent, Prince of Orange, to form the Union of Utrecht in 1579. Independence was declared in 1581 but not recognized by Spain until the Treaty of Westphalia (1648), which ended the THIRTY YEARS' WAR. The 17th century saw the golden age of the Netherlands: made prosperous by overseas trading and colonizing, it was also famed for its religious tolerance and cultural life (see REMBRANDT; VERMEER; SPINOZA). In the 18th century Holland was outrivalled by England and France. Popular sympathy with the French Revolution led (1795) to the establishment of the French-ruled Batavian Republic. After the defeat of Napoleon (1814), the United Kingdom of the Netherlands was formed, joining Holland with present-day Belgium. The latter broke away in 1830. Holland's subsequent history, under its constitutional monarchy, has been marked by a steady growth of prosperity and liberalism. Neutral in WWI, the Dutch recovered rapidly after the devastating German occupation in WWII. Since the war, they have taken a leading part in European integration. The government has been run by a series of coalitions, generally dominated by the Catholic People's Party. Queen Beatrix replaced her mother, Juliana, on the throne in 1980.

NETHERLANDS ANTILLES or the **Dutch West Indies**, two groups of islands in the Caribbean Sea. They are an autonomous part of the Netherlands. The S group comprises Curaçao (location of the capital, Willemstad), Aruba, and Bonaire, about 50mi off Venezuela. The N group, 500mi to the NE, comprises Saba, St. Eustacius, and St. Maarten. The processing of petroleum from Venezuela once accounted for more than 90% of exports; the main refinery on Aruba was shut down in 1985 and the government took control of the leading refinery on Curaçao to avoid a similar closing. There is also some tourism. The S group came under Dutch control in 1634, the N group in 1815. They became self-governing in 1954.

NEUMANN, Johann Balthasar (1687–1753), leading German architect of the late BAROQUE style. He designed palaces, churches, houses, bridges and water systems. Especially notable are the church in Vierzehnheiligen and the Residenz at Würzburg.

NEURALGIA, pain originating in a nerve and characterized by sudden, sharp, often electric-shock-like pain or exacerbations of pain. Nerves commonly affected include the digital nerves of toes and intercostal nerves. Neuralgia may be due to INFLAMMATION or trauma.

NEURATH, Otto (1882–1945), Austrian sociologist and philosopher. A polymath, he played a prominent role in the Vienna Circle of logical positivists during the 1920s, invented an international picture language to overcome barriers separating linguistic groups, and planned and edited the *International Encyclopedia of Unified Science* (1938).

NEURITIS, or **peripheral neuropathy,** any disorder of the peripheral NERVOUS SYSTEM which interferes with sensation, the nerve control of MUSCLE, or both. Its causes include DRUGS and heavy metals (e.g., gold); infection or allergic reaction to it (as with LEPROSY or DIPHTHERIA); inflammatory disease (rheumatoid ARTHRITIS); infiltration, systemic and metabolic disease (e.g., DIABETES or PORPHYRIA); VITAMIN deficiency (BERIBERI); organ failure (e.g., of the LIVER or KIDNEY); genetic disorders, and the nonmetastatic effects of distant CANCER.

Numbness, tingling, weakness and PARALYSIS result, at first affecting the extremities. Diagnosis involves electrical studies of the nerves and as well as the procedure of nerve BIOPSY.

NEUROLOGY, branch of MEDICINE concerned with diseases of the BRAIN, SPINAL CORD, and peripheral NERVOUS SYSTEM. These include MULTIPLE SCLEROSIS, EPILEPSY, migraine (HEADACHE), STROKE, PARKINSON'S DISEASE, NEURITIS, ENCEPHALITIS, MENINGITIS, brain TUMORS, MUSCULAR DYSTROPHY and MYASTHENIA GRAVIS.

NEURON, or **nerve cell,** the basic unit of the NERVOUS SYSTEM (including the BRAIN and SPINAL CORD). Each has a long axon, specialized for transmitting electrical impulses and releasing chemical transmitters that act on MUSCLE or effector cells or other neurons. Branched processes called dendrites integrate the input to neurons.

NEUROSIS, originally any NERVOUS SYSTEM activity; later, any disorder of the nervous system; though in PSYCHOANALYSIS, those mental disorders (e.g., HYSTERIA) unconnected with the nervous system. It is usually seen as based in UNCONSCIOUS conflict, with an unconscious attempt to conform to reality (not escape from it, as in PSYCHOSIS).

NEUTRA, Richard Joseph (1892–1970), Austrian-born US architect who brought the INTERNATIONAL STYLE of architecture to the US. The Tremaine House (1947) in Santa Barbara, Calif., demonstrates his skill in relating a building to its setting.

NEUTRALITY, the status of a country which elects not to participate in a war between other countries. Under international law, a neutral state has the right to have its boundaries and territorial waters respected, and the obligation to remain impartial towards belligerents in its actions. The two World Wars, however, brought many violations of neutrality, e.g. Germany's invasion of Belgium in WWI. Before the US entered WWII, her neutrality was effectively nullified by her support of the Allies. With the need for would-be neutral countries to defend their status (as America in WWI), the viability of neutrality became questionable. Membership in the United Nations is not compatible with neutrality, since members may be called upon to act against aggressors.

NEUTRALITY ACTS, of 1935, 1936 and 1937, US legislation banning arms sales and loans to belligerent states. The acts were aimed at keeping America out of war. They were modified in 1939 and effectively replaced by the LEND LEASE Act of 1941, the purpose of which was to assist the Allies without direct participation in the war.

NEUTRINO. See SUBATOMIC PARTICLES.

NEUTRON (n), uncharged SUBATOMIC PARTICLE with rest mass 1.6748×10^{-27}hg (slightly greater than that of the PROTON) and spin ½. A free neutron is slightly unstable, decaying to a proton, an ELECTRON and an antineutrino with HALF-LIFE 680s:

$$n \rightarrow p^+ + e^- + \bar{v}$$

But neutrons bound within the nucleus of an ATOM are stable. All nuclei save hydrogen contain neutrons, which contribute to the nuclear cohesive forces and separate the mutually repulsive protons. Free neutrons are produced in many nuclear reactions, including nuclear FISSION, and hence nuclear reactors and particle ACCELERATORS are used as sources. The neutron was discovered in 1932 by Sir James CHADWICK, who bombarded beryllium with alpha particles emitted by a radioisotope. Neutrons are highly penetrating but are moderated (slowed down) by colliding with the nuclei of light atoms. They induce certain heavy atoms to undergo fission. Shielding requires thick concrete walls. Neutrons are detected by counting the ionizing particles or gamma rays produced when they react with nuclei. Neutrons have wave properties, and their DIFFRACTION is used to study crystal structures and magnetic properties.

NEUTRON BOMB, hypothetical "clean" variant of the HYDROGEN BOMB that would produce intense lethal neutron radiation but not much structural damage or radioactive fallout.

NEVADA, US western state, situated between the Rocky Mts and the Sierra Nevada, bounded to the E by Ut. and Ariz., to the S and W by Cal., and to the N by Ore. and Ida.

Land. Most of the state lies in the Great Basin, an arid plateau at about 5,000ft above sea level which is broken by many short mountain ranges running from N to S. Nevada's longest river is the Humboldt, and the major lakes are Mead (formed by the Hoover Dam), Tahoe, Pyramid and Walker. The state has the lowest average annual rainfall in the US, and because of its altitude, temperatures drop considerably at night. There are extremes of heat in summer and cold in winter. Much of the state is arid desert.

People. Most of the population of Nevada, which ranks 47th in state populations, is concentrated in Las Vegas and Reno. Over 90% of the population is white, the rest are black or Indian; there are a number of Indian reservations. Carson City is the

Name of state: Nevada
Capital: Carson City
Statehood: Oct. 31, 1864 (36th state)
Familiar name: Silver State, Sagebrush State
Area: 110,540sq mi
Population: 963,000
Elevation: Highest—13,140ft, Boundary Peak; Lowest—470ft, Colorado River in Clark County
Motto: "All for our country"
State flower: Sagebrush
State bird: Mountain bluebird
State tree: Single-leaf piñon
State song: "Home Means Nevada"
smallest state capital in the US.

Economy. The Nevada economy depends heavily on tourism, which its liberal gambling and divorce laws support. Mining, especially of copper and iron ore, is also important. The manufacturing sector is gradually expanding. Principal products include gaming devices, electronic equipment, chemicals and wood and glass items.

History. Nevada was first explored by the Spanish in the 1770s. In 1827 Jedediah Smith crossed Nevada toward Cal., and in the 1840s John FRÉMONT explored it extensively. It first became a US possession by the treaty of GUADELOUPE-HIDALGO after the MEXICAN WAR. In 1859, the discovery of the COMSTOCK LODE, a very rich silver deposit, attracted thousands of prospectors to the area. In 1864 Nevada was made the 36th state, largely to secure its precious metal resources for the Union in the Civil War. In the late 19th century prosperity declined when the gold and silver mines were depleted. But copper mining, high-tech manufacturing, and tourism brought new wealth to the state beginning in the 1970s, along with increased population. In 1987 the state legislature created a new county, Bullfrog, population 0, as the site for the first high-level nuclear waste dump in the US, at Yucca Mountain. In presidential elections 1968–88, Nevada voted consistently Republican.

NEVELSON, Louise (1900–1988), Russian-born US sculptor. She is famous for her intricate wood constructions, both free-standing and wall-hung, which suggest vast ranges of box-like shelves with found objects on them.

NEVINS, Allan (1890–1971), US historian, whose best-known work is the Civil War series, *The Ordeal of the Union* (1947–60). Nevins received Pulitzer Prizes for his biographies, *Grover Cleveland* (1932) and *Hamilton Fish* (1936). His many other works include the biography *John D. Rockefeller* (1953).

NEW AGE MOVEMENT, 1980s intellectual fad drawing upon Eastern mysticism and Western occultism and based on the belief that adherents can partake directly of the inexhaustible cosmic energy that animates the universe through nonrational, intuitive processes. Crystals, Tarot cards, pyramids, and other occult merchandise can help. Related preoccupations are trance channeling (communicating with the dead), reincarnation, altered states of consciousness, UFO abductions, and out-of-body experiences. The most prominent exponent of the New Age is the actress Shirley MacLaine.

NEW BRUNSWICK, second largest of the Canadian Atlantic provinces, one of the Maritime Provinces. Its coast runs some 750mi along the Chaleur Bay, the Gulf of St. Lawrence, Northumberland Strait and the Bay of Fundy.

Name of province: New Brunswick
Joined Confederation: July 1, 1867
Capital: Fredericton
Area: 28,354sq mi
Population: 703,474

Land and People. About 88% of the province is forested. The center is high, and there is a coastal plain in the NE. The province is well-drained by many swift-flowing rivers and streams. The fertile valley of the St. John R provides an excellent farming region. The climate is continental, but ocean breezes moderate extremes along the coast. About half the population live in cities, the largest being Saint John, Moncton and the capital Fredericton. Over 50% of the population is of British origin, and 33% of French. French is the language of instruction in public schools. New Brunswick had been losing population to central Canada, notably Ontario, but in recent years population has grown at a rate of about 1%.

Economy. The economy is largely based on forest industries, pulp and paper manufacturing, food processing, fishing and tourism. Copper, lead, silver and particularly zinc mining are being developed in the NE. Since WWII hydroelectric power has been exploited on an increasing scale. During the past 10 years, the work force has expanded by more than 60,000 people and the manufacturing sector has diversified. Manufactures include fabricated metals, machinery, plastics and electrical products. An important renewable energy resource of potential value is the tidal power of the Bay of Fundy.

History. Jacques CARTIER explored the region in 1534. Samuel de CHAMPLAIN established a settlement in 1604 in what became known as French ACADIA. Britain gained control of the region in 1713, but it was not until the arrival of Loyalists from the US after the Revolution that New Brunswick became a separate province (1784). The boundary with Maine was settled after the Aroostook War by the WEBSTER-ASHBURTON TREATY of 1842. New Brunswick was one of the four original provinces to join the Dominion of Canada in 1867. The province developed slowly; inhabitants emigrated, and it was an under-privileged area. However, the discovery of mineral deposits, the growing importance of the port of Saint John and large federal financial support have helped in economic expansion. Conservatives dominated the provincial government from 1970 to 1987, when they were displaced in a Liberal landslide.

NEWCOMB, Simon (1835–1909), US astronomer. He computed new planetary tables whose data were so accurate that they remained in use for over half a century. Head of the *American Nautical Almanac*, he taught at Johns Hopkins 1884–94.

NEWCOMEN, Thomas (1663–1729), British inventor of the first functional STEAM ENGINE (before 1712). His device, employed mainly to pump water from mines, used steam pressure to raise the piston and, after condensation of the steam, atmospheric pressure to force it down again: it was thus called an "atmospheric" steam engine.

NEW DEAL, program adopted by President Franklin D. ROOSEVELT to alleviate the effects of the GREAT DEPRESSION. On his election in 1933, Roosevelt initiated a dramatic program of relief and reform, known as "the first hundred days." He called an immediate bank holiday and restored confidence in those banks which were allowed to reopen by the Emergency Banking Act. Bank funds and practices were overseen by the FEDERAL DEPOSIT INSURANCE CORPORATION and the FEDERAL RESERVE board. Measures were taken to control the Stock Exchange (see SECURITIES AND EXCHANGE COMMISSION).

Farm recovery was helped by the creation

of credit facilities, subsidies, rural electrification programs and the resettlement of some farmers in more productive areas. The National Recovery Administration (NRA) and the Civilian Conservation Corps (CCC) were set up to boost business and ensure jobs, though many of the NRA's functions were later declared unconstitutional by the Supreme Court. Unions were protected by the Labor Relations Act (1935), and the Fair Labor Standards Act (1938) set a national MINIMUM WAGE. Measures were taken to relieve poverty and unemployment. The SOCIAL SECURITY system was established in 1935, and jobs were created by the Work Projects Administration (WPA), including the massive TENNESSEE VALLEY AUTHORITY (TVA) project. The Home Loan Corporation and the Federal Housing Administration (FHA) helped home owners and aided recovery in the construction industry.

After its initial popularity, the New Deal met increasing opposition in Congress and the Supreme Court. It ended in 1939 as the economy expanded to meet the demands of WWII. The question of its success remains controversial; many believe that only WWII finally ended the Great Depression. Its influence, however, was permanent; it changed the direction of social legislation, centralized control of the economy and altered the US public's attitude to the role of the federal government.

NEW DELHI, capital of India, on the Jumna R, in the N central part of the country. It was built by the British in 1912–29 to the S of Delhi, when the capital was transferred from Calcutta. New Delhi, a spacious city, was designed by the architect Sir Edwin Lutyens. Since independence in 1947 new official buildings, shops and industrial quarters have been added to the city. Pop 273,036.

NEW ECONOMIC POLICY (NEP), economic policy adopted by Soviet Russia during 1921–28 to deal with the effects of the previous war years. The NEP made concessions to private enterprise in industry, trade and agriculture, and allowed the peasants to sell produce profitably. The NEP was very successful and by 1927 had restored the pre-war national income level.

NEW ENGLAND, region of NE US comprising six states—CONNECTICUT, RHODE ISLAND, MASSACHUSETTS, NEW HAMPSHIRE, VERMONT, and MAINE.

NEW ENGLAND CONFEDERATION, colonial alliance organized in 1643 by representatives from Massachusetts Bay, Plymouth, Connecticut and New Haven colonies. They formed "the United Colonies of New England" to settle boundary disputes and arrange defense. Inter-colonial rivalry hindered agreement, and the confederation was dissolved in 1684.

NEWFOUNDLAND, largest Canadian Atlantic province, comprising Newfoundland Island and Labrador and their adjacent islands.
Name of province: Newfoundland
Capital: St. John's
Joined confederation: March 31, 1949
Area: 156,185sq mi
Population: 564,360
Land. Newfoundland Island has a long (6,000mi) indented coastline, with many islands, which is most rugged on the S and E coast; the land rises from the E lowlands to a plateau and mountains, the highest being the Lewis Hills (2,672ft). The central plateau has many lakes and bogs. Avalon peninsula, the most densely populated part of the province, is the location of the capital, St. John's. Labrador is a rugged, forested plateau (mountain peaks reaching 5,160ft) with a rocky coast and many fjords. Its climate is harsher than that of Newfoundland island; winters are severe throughout the whole province. More than 56% of Newfoundland province is forested.
People. The province is sparsely populated, and most of the people live close to the sea. Only 3% live in Labrador, and 10% of these are of Indian or Eskimo descent.
Economy. The economy is based on mining, forestry, fishing and manufacturing. There are very large iron-ore mines in Labrador; copper, gold, lead, silver and zinc are also mined. In the 1970s more than half of Canada's output of iron was produced in western Labrador. The province still contains large reserves of mineral wealth. Exploration of the continental shelf began in 1965, and in 1979 high-quality crude oil was discovered on the southeastern Grand Banks. Fishing is Newfoundland's best-known industry. Fishermen from Europe and Japan are attracted to the famous GRAND BANKS, which abound in cod, haddock and other fish. Fishstocks were seriously depleted in the 1970s but are being restored. Manufacturing accounts for almost half of the economy; industries include paper, steel, textiles and clothing manufacture and food processing. Electricity is mostly provided by hydroelectric plants, the most recent being the gigantic Churchill Falls project; completed in 1974, it is one of the largest generating plants in the world, but all of its power is exported to Quebec. The province's strategic position has made it important in transatlantic air travel; there are large air terminals at

Gander and Goose Bay.

History. Remains of 10th-century Viking settlements have been found on Newfoundland Island. John CABOT rediscovered the island in 1497, and Sir Humphrey GILBERT claimed it for England in 1583. It was not until 1763, after the SEVEN YEARS' WAR, that England gained firm control, although France retained the "French shore" on the W coast until 1904. Newfoundland gained fully responsible government in 1855, but Britain took control again in 1934 when the island's economy was hit by the Great Depression. Newfoundland chose to join the Dominion of Canada in 1949 and became Canada's 10th province. For the next 23 years the provincial government was dominated by the Liberal Party. Conservatives have controlled it since 1972 despite high unemployment and a lagging economy.

NEW FRANCE, North American territories held by France from the 16th century to 1763 which extended W beyond the St. Lawrence to the Great Lakes and NE areas. France lost these territories in a series of colonial wars with Britain.

NEW FREEDOM, program adopted by President WILSON in 1913 which aimed to establish more political and economic opportunities in the US and to free the US economy from tariffs and other restrictions. He obtained the Underwood Tariff Act, the Federal Reserve Act (see FEDERAL RESERVE SYSTEM) and the Antitrust Act in 1913–17.

NEW FRONTIER, collective name for the policies of the administration of President John F. Kennedy, derived from Kennedy's acceptance speech after winning the Democratic nomination in 1960 when he said that the nation stood on "the edge of a new frontier." Characteristic New Frontier programs aimed at space exploration, improved science education, extension of civil-rights protections, and better medical care for the elderly.

NEW GRANADA, Spanish colony in NW South America which included present-day Colombia, Panama, Ecuador and Venezuela, established in the first half of the 16th century. It was named by Gonzalo JIMENEZ DE QUESADA in 1537 and attached to the vice-royalty of Peru until 1717, when it became a vice-royalty itself until independence in 1819.

NEW GUINEA, world's second largest island. It lies in the SW Pacific just S of the equator and is separated from N Australia by the Torres Strait and the Arafura and Coral Seas. The island covers an area of 319,713sq mi, and comprises a series of high central mountain ranges and densely-forested tropical lowlands. Djaja Peak is the highest mountain at 16,535ft. Politically, New Guinea is divided into two parts: Irian Jaya, a province of Indonesia, and PAPUA NEW GUINEA, self-governing since 1973.

Melanesians and Papuans are the two largest population groups in New Guinea. In remote mountain areas there are primitive Negrito groups and Papuans some of whom are head-hunting tribes. Some animals such as the opossum are related to Australian species. There are more than 70 species of snakes, many species of butterflies and birds of paradise.

New Guinea was discovered by the Portuguese in the 16th century and named for Guinea, West Africa. It was colonized by the Dutch, Germans and British; after WWI, Australia gained the German sector. The island was bitterly contested by the Japanese and the Allies during WWII.

NEW HAMPSHIRE, state, NE US, one of the New England states and one of the 13 original states, bounded to the E by Me. and the Atlantic Ocean, to the S by Mass., to the W by Vt. across the Connecticut R and to the N by Canada. Forests cover four-fifths of New Hampshire's surface, and it contains mountains, lakes and streams. Despite its rural appearance and fame as a tourist center it is also one of the most intensively industrialized states of the union.

Name of state: New Hampshire
Capital: Concord
Statehood: June 21, 1788 (9th state)
Familiar name: Granite State
Area: 9,304sq mi
Population: 1,027,000
Elevation: Highest—6,288ft, Mount Washington; Lowest—sea level, Atlantic Ocean
Motto: "Live free or die"
State flower: Purple lilac
State bird: Purple finch
State tree: White birch
State songs: "New Hampshire, My New Hampshire," "Old New Hampshire"
Land. New Hampshire can be divided into three main areas: the White Mountains in the N third of the state; the coastal lowlands

in the extreme SE corner; and the New England Upland, a rolling plateau that covers the central and S portions of the state. The 86-peak Presidential Range includes the highest point in New England, Mount Washington (6,288ft); and the Franconia Range includes Profile Mountain and the steep chasm of the Flume. The Merrimack R drains southward from the White Mountains, and most of the state's major cities, industries and farms are located along its hilly, uneven valley.

People. Most of New Hampshire's people and industries are concentrated in the S, but the scenic beauty of the White Mountains attracts thousands of skiers, hikers, campers and sightseers. About 40% of the population are urban. Cities include Manchester, Nashua and Concord.

Economy. The original importance of agriculture, textiles and leather goods has declined, but under the farsighted planning of the New Business Development Corporation, the development of new and varied industries more than outweighs these losses. Principal manufactures include leather, wood and paper goods, electrical equipment, machinery and metal products. Part of the population commutes to jobs in neighboring Mass.

History. The first settlements were established along the coast in the 1620s, and in 1629 Capt. John Mason was granted the land between the Merrimack and Piscataqua rivers, which he named New Hampshire. Inland settlement was slow and began on a large scale only after the FRENCH AND INDIAN WARS. New Hampshire was the first colony to declare itself independent of British rule and to adopt a new constitution, 1776. Republicans have dominated the state's politics since the Civil War, despite Democratic strength in the industrial cities of Nashua and Manchester. The state has the lowest per-capita taxes in the US. In 1987 the state's booming economy was rocked when Public Service of New Hampshire filed for bankruptcy after failing to put into operation its Seabrook nuclear power plant. PSNH was the first major public utility to file for bankruptcy since the Depression. New Hampshire is a bellwether in national presidential politics by virtue of holding the first primaries after the Iowa caucuses. In presidential elections 1968–88, New Hampshire voted consistently Republican.

NEW HARMONY, town in SW Ind., the site of two cooperative communities in the early 1800s. "Harmonie" was settled in 1814 by George Rapp, leader of the HARMONY SOCIETY. In 1824 the colony was sold to Robert OWEN, and renamed New Harmony. The community, based on socialism and Owen's theories of human freedom, was a noted scientific and cultural center but broke up in 1828. Pop 945.

NEW HAVEN, third-largest city in Conn., its chief port, and famous as the seat of YALE UNIVERSITY. It is a noted cultural center and important for its varied industrial products. It was founded in 1638 by Puritans from Boston led by John DAVENPORT and Theophilus EATON. It was a flourishing port at the end of the 18th century, and only revived as such when a deep water channel was dredged in 1927. Pop (city) 124,000, (metro) 510,000.

NEW JERSEY, state, E US, bounded on the E by N.Y. and the Atlantic Ocean and on the W by Del. and Pa. across the Delaware R, the nation's most highly urbanized and most densely populated state, and one of the 13 original states.

Name of state: New Jersey
Capital: Trenton
Statehood: Dec. 18, 1787 (3rd state)
Familiar name: Garden State
Area: 7,836sq mi
Population: 7,619,000
Elevation: Highest—1,803ft, High Point; Lowest—sea level, Atlantic Ocean
Motto: "Liberty and prosperity"
State flower: Purple violet
State bird: Eastern goldfinch
State tree: Red oak
State song: None

Land. New Jersey can be divided into four natural regions: the Appalachian Valley in the NW; the Appalachian Highlands running NE-SW; the low-lying Piedmont Plateau; and the Atlantic coastal plain. The state's major rivers are the Delaware, Hudson, Passaic and Raritan.

People. More than 90% of New Jersey's population live in urban areas, the largest cities being Newark, Trenton, Jersey City, Paterson, and Elizabeth. Blacks constitute 12.5% of the total population.

Economy. One of the leading industrial states, New Jersey contains a number of small but highly efficient farms. Strategically located amid many rich markets, it has exceptional transport facilities and the most concentrated rail and road network in the nation. After WWII a large number of industrial research centers were established, and these plants play an important role in the state's industrial importance. The leading branch of manufacturing is the chemical industry, followed by the production of electrical machinery, processed food, metal goods, transportation equipment and clothing. Tourism is also a major industry, bolstered in the late 1970s by the legalization of gambling in Atlantic City.

History. On a voyage for the Dutch East India Company, Henry HUDSON sailed up the Hudson R in 1609, and Dutch trading posts were soon established, but the first permanent settlement in present-day New Jersey was not founded until the 2nd half of the 17th century. In 1664 the Dutch possessions in North America were captured by the English (see NEW NETHERLAND), and New Jersey was divided and subdivided among various owners until 1702, when it became a single crown colony. After the British captured New York in 1776, New Jersey became the "cockpit of the Revolution," as armies crossed and recrossed the state, fighting nearly 100 engagements.

Today, New Jersey is a state profoundly divided, two-thirds being farm land and woods, while the highly-industrialized NE corner of the state is more densely populated than Japan. This area is also plagued by air pollution, urban blight, toxic wastes and water management problems. Long-term neglect of the environment was brought forcefully to public attention in 1988 when New Jersey beaches had to be closed because of ocean pollution. In presidential elections 1968–88, New Jersey voted consistently Republican.

NEW JERUSALEM, Church of the. See SWEDENBORG, EMANUEL.

NEWLANDS, Francis Griffith (1848–1917), US politician and lawyer. He represented Nev. in Congress, 1893–1903, and was a Democratic senator 1903–1917. He wrote the Newlands Act (1913), which provided for mediation and conciliation in labor disputes, and was involved in federal trade and transportation affairs.

NEWMAN, Barnett (1905–1970), US painter. A member of the NEW YORK SCHOOL of abstract expressionists, he pioneered COLOR-FIELD PAINTING.

NEWMAN, John Henry (1801–1890), English clergyman and a founder of the OXFORD MOVEMENT in 1833. A Church of England vicar and tutor at Oxford University, he was converted to Roman Catholicism in 1845, becoming a cardinal in 1879. Much of his thought was controversial, opposed by Cardinal Henry MANNING and Charles KINGSLEY. He was a master stylist. His writings include *Apologia pro vita sua* (1864), a religious autobiography that remains his monument.

NEW MEXICO, state, SW US, bounded to the E by Tex., to the S by Tex. and Mexico, to the W by Ariz., and to the N by Col. It is a mixture of three distinct cultures— Anglo-American, Spanish and Indian. Side by side with reminders of the old Indian and Spanish cultures are modern industries and research stations for atomic energy and space travel. The world's first atomic bomb, developed during WWII at the Los Alamos Laboratories north of Santa Fe, was exploded near Alamogordo in July 1945.

Name of state: New Mexico
Capital: Santa Fe
Statehood: Jan. 6, 1912 (47th state)
Familiar name: Land of Enchantment
Area: 122,666sq mi
Population: 1,479,000
Elevation: Highest—13,160ft, Wheeler Peak; Lowest—2,817ft, Red Bluff Reservoir
Motto: *Crescit eundo* ("It grows as it goes")
State flower: Yucca
State bird: Roadrunner
State tree: Piñon, or nut pine
State song: "O, Fair New Mexico"
Land. New Mexico's varied topography and geological history make the area of great interest to geologists. Innumerable fossils have been found in the various geological strata, including many extinct species of plants and animals. The state has an average elevation of about 5,700ft. New Mexico includes parts of four main regions: the Colorado Plateaus in the NW, the Rocky Mountain System in the N central area, the Great Plains in the E and the Basin and Range Region in the central and SW area of the state. The state is generally arid with limited water resources, but it has two

important rivers, the Rio Grande and the Pecos, both of which help to provide irrigation.

People. In 1980 there were more than 104,000 Indians in New Mexico, many of whom lived on reservations. Spanish-Americans account for over 30% of the population, and Spanish influence is evident in architecture and place names as well as in the wide use of the Spanish language. Some 70% of New Mexico's population is concentrated in urban areas, the largest being Albuquerque and Santa Fe.

Economy. New Mexico is basically a mining state with rich deposits of many minerals, particularly uranium. Other important mineral resources are oil, natural gas and potash. Atomic and space research is heavily funded by the federal government and is of great importance to the state's economy. Ranching is the state's most important agricultural activity. Crops include hay, sorghum, grain, onions, cotton and corn. Tourism is also important. In 1987 the Santa Fe Trail was declared a National Historic Trail.

History. Indians have inhabited what is now New Mexico for perhaps 20,000 years. In the 16th century the Spaniards conquered the Indians and colonized the area. In 1821 Mexico won its independence from Spain and took control over New Mexico, only to lose it to the US after the MEXICAN WAR (1846–48). Settlement continued, and in 1859 the GADSDEN PURCHASE was made. In 1980 the state's per capita income was relatively low and unemployment was high. These factors put added strain on the state's meager tax base and contributed to tensions among the Anglo, Spanish and Indian communities. The conviction of some Hispanics that the original Spanish land grants in New Mexico are still valid has sometimes provoked armed conflict. Although still small in comparison to most states, New Mexico's population grew rapidly during the 1970s and 1980s. In presidential elections 1968–88, New Mexico voted consistently Republican.

NEW NATIONALISM, Theodore ROOSEVELT's political philosophy (about 1910) proclaimed in opposition to Woodrow WILSON's Democratic manifesto, the NEW FREEDOM. His ideas included increased federal intervention to regulate the economy and promote social justice, honest government and conservation of natural resources.

NEW NETHERLAND, Dutch colonial territory extending roughly from Albany, N.Y., to Manhattan Island, and including parts of New Jersey, Connecticut and Delaware. It was granted in 1621 by the government of Holland to a group of merchants known as the DUTCH WEST INDIA COMPANY. In 1626 the company purchased Manhattan Island from the Indians and called it New Amsterdam. In 1664, under the British, New Amsterdam became New York City.

NEW ORLEANS, historic city in La., seat of Orleans parish, on the banks of the Mississippi R 107mi from the river's mouth. Excellent transport facilities serve the port, which is also the main gateway for trade with Latin America. New Orleans is surrounded by oil and natural gas deposits. It is a center of aerospace, shipbuilding, oil and chemical industries, and has many manufacturing and processing plants. In the 1980s the city was beset by problems caused by inner-city decay, low oil prices, and a decline in shipping. The city is famed for its picturesque French Quarter (*Vieux Carré*) and Mardi Gras Carnival, and as the birthplace of JAZZ. Its varied population includes French-speaking Creoles who are descended from early French and Spanish settlers (see LOUISIANA PURCHASE). The Creole cookery of New Orleans is famous. Pop (city) 559,000, (metro) 1,324,000.

NEW ORLEANS, Battle of, engagement fought Jan. 8, 1815 in the WAR OF 1812 to prevent the British from occupying New Orleans. US Gen. Andrew JACKSON'S victory made him a national hero, though it did not affect the Treat of GHENT signed Dec. 24, 1814.

NEWPORT, historic resort city in SE R.I., seat of Newport Co., and an important naval base. Founded in 1639, it became a refuge from religious persecution for Quakers and Jews. It was a wealthy resort in the 19th century, and its jazz festivals in the 1950s were famous. Pop 29,259.

NEW REALISM, modern art movement which, in rejecting various painterly schools and the principles of ABSTRACT ART, advocated works that incorporated real materials and artifacts. Based on a manifesto entitled *The New Realism* (Milan, 1960) and related to DADA, it has also been dubbed "junk art."

NEWSPAPER, daily or weekly publication of current domestic and foreign news. In addition newspapers often contain information, humor and advice on a great variety of subjects. In 59 BC Julius Caesar ordered the daily publication of a newssheet, the *Acta Diurna,* which was posted in public places. The first Chinese newspaper was published in the 8th century. Johann GUTENBERG'S invention of movable type in the mid-15th century was an important step in the development of newspapers, and newspaper sheets appeared in Venice and Cologne in the 16th century. In 1620 fact-sheets printed in Amsterdam were sold in England. The *London Gazette* (1665) was the first paper issued regularly in a newspaper format. The first English daily, the *London Daily Courant*, appeared in England in 1702. The first regularly printed American paper was the *Boston Newsletter* (1704). Early newspapers were too expensive for the ordinary reader, but the gap was later filled by James Gordon BENNETT and Horace GREELEY publishing daily penny papers, such as *The New York Sun* (1833), the *New York Herald* (1835) and the *New York Tribune* (1841).

An era of fiercely competitive journalism began with the end of the Civil War, when newspaper initiative took the form of stunts, crusades, scandal and increasing sensationalism. In the late 19th and early 20th centuries Joseph PULITZER, a pioneer of YELLOW JOURNALISM, William Randolph HEARST, Colonel Robert MCCORMICK and Joseph Medill Patterson, and Lords BEAVERBROOK and NORTHCLIFFE in England, were the czars of vast newspaper empires and important forces in national life and international politics. Newspapers in general have since toned down, although the traditions of yellow journalism continue to be followed by some major publishers, notably Australia's Rupert Murdoch.

Radio, and later television, together with rising production costs and shifts in population, have forced many newspapers out of business in recent years, with urban afternoon dailies in the US being especially hard-hit.

NEW SWEDEN, Swedish colony on the Delaware R extending from the site of Trenton, N.J., to the mouth of the Delaware R. In 1633 the New Sweden Company was organized, and in 1638 two Swedish vessels arrived and Peter MINUIT founded Fort Christina (later Wilmington, Del.). The Dutch, led by Peter STUYVESANT, annexed the colony in 1655.

NEW TESTAMENT, the part of the Bible which is distinctively Christian. In it are recorded the life and teachings of JESUS CHRIST and the beginnings of CHRISTIANITY. It comprises the four GOSPELS, the ACTS OF THE APOSTLES, the Epistles and the Book of REVELATION, numbering 27 books in all (for list see BIBLE). The Gospels (lives of Christ) are named for their traditional authors: Saints MATTHEW, MARK, LUKE and JOHN. The Epistles are early evangelical letters, written to local churches or individuals. Thirteen are ascribed to St. PAUL; the others (except the anonymous HEBREWS), are named for their traditional authors. The New Testament is written in everyday 1st-century Greek. The earliest copy fragments date from the early 2nd century. (See also CANON, BIBLICAL.)

NEWTON, Sir Isaac (1642–1726), the most prestigious natural philosopher and mathematician of modern times, the discoverer of the CALCULUS and author of the theory of universal GRAVITATION. Newton went up to Trinity College, Cambridge, in 1661, retiring to Woolsthorp, Lincolnshire, during the Plague of 1665–66, but becoming a fellow in 1667 and succeeding Isaac Barrow in the Lucasian Chair of Mathematics in 1669. He was elected Fellow of the ROYAL SOCIETY in 1672, on the strength of his optical discoveries. In Cambridge, Newton spent much time in alchemical experiments, though, toward the end of the century, he tired of the academic life and accepted a position at the Royal Mint, becoming Master of the Mint in 1699. He resigned his chair and entered Parliament in 1701 and two years later began his presidency of the Royal Society, which he retained until his death. His whole life was one of ceaseless energy—investigating mathematics, optics, chronology, chemistry, theology, mechanics, dynamics and the occult—broken only by a period of mental illness about 1693. His achievements were legion: the method of fluxions and fluents (calculus); the theory of universal gravitation and his derivation of KEPLER'S LAWS; his formulation of the concept of FORCE as expressed in his three laws of motion (see MECHANICS); the corpuscular theory of LIGHT; and the BINOMIAL THEOREM, among many others. These were summed up in his two greatest works: *Philosophiae Naturalis Principia Mathematica* (1687)—the "Principia," which established the mathematical representation of nature as the paradigm of what counted as "science"—and the *Opticks* (1704). Newton's often bitter controversies with his fellow scientists (notably HOOKE and LEIBNIZ) are famous, but his influence is undoubted, even if, in the cases of optical theory and the Newtonian calculus notation, it retarded rather than accelerated the advance of British science.

NEW WAVE, in MOTION PICTURES, denotes a film style of the late 1950s and early '60s identified with such French directors as François TRUFFAUT and Jean Luc Godard, who exercised an unusual degree of control over all phases of the filmmaking process and whose films, such as Truffaut's semiautobiographical *The 400 Blows*

(1959), represented strongly personal statements.

NEW YORK, state, E US, one of the 13 original states, location of the nation's largest metropolis, NEW YORK CITY. It is bounded on the N by Canada and Lake Ontario, E by Vt., Mass. and Conn., S by Pa., N.J. and the Atlantic Ocean, and W by Pa., Lake Erie and Canada.

Name of state: New York
Capital: Albany
Statehood: July 26, 1788 (11th state)
Familiar name: Empire State
Area: 49,576sq mi
Population: 17,772,000
Elevation: Highest—5,344ft, Mt. Marcy; Lowest—sea level, Atlantic Ocean
Motto: *Excelsior* ("Ever upward")
State flower: Rose
State bird: Bluebird
State tree: Sugar maple
State song: "I Love New York"

Land. The topography of N.Y. is rich in variety and scenic beauty. The Appalachian Plateau, its largest land region, slopes upward (NW to SE) from Niagara Falls to the Catskill Mts. In the NE is the Adirondack Upland. There are 1,637sq mi of inland waters in addition to those of the Great Lakes. The Hudson R with its tributary the Mohawk, the St. Lawrence R and the Delaware R all form important transport routes.

People. Almost 90% of the population is urban. New York has traditionally been the immigration center of the nation. The numerically dominant immigrant groups are from Italy, Germany, the Soviet Union, Poland, Ireland and the Caribbean. New York has the largest black population of any state in the US and a growing number of immigrants from the Middle East and Asia.

Economy. New York is one of the nation's leading manufacturing and trading states. Major industries include printing and publishing, clothing, electronic equipment, finance, and food products. New York's intensive agriculture produces milk, grain, potatoes, apples and grapes. The state's varied natural resources are far from sufficient to supply manufacturing needs, but hydroelectricity is provided by the St. Lawrence and Niagara power plants. Tourism, communications, and government operations are also important to New York's economic base.

History. Home of the IROQUOIS and ALGONQUIN INDIANS, New York began (1624) as the Dutch colony of NEW NETHERLAND. In 1664 Peter STUYVESANT, under whose administration the colony had flourished, was forced to surrender to British claims, when the colony together with its capital New Amsterdam was renamed for the Duke of York (later James II of England). New York was a major battlefield during the FRENCH AND INDIAN WARS (1689–1763), and during the REVOLUTIONARY WAR was the scene of the decisive Battle of SARATOGA. The state contributed significantly to Union success during the CIVIL WAR.

The late 19th and early 20th centuries saw increased industrialization and immigration, making New York for many years the leading manufacturing state as well as the most populous. Although no longer growing significantly in population, the state remains the 2nd largest after California, while New York City continues as the nation's largest metropolis. In presidential elections 1968–88, New York voted Democratic in 1968, 1976, and 1988.

NEW YORK CITY, city in SE N.Y., the largest in the US. It is divided into five boroughs: Manhattan, the Bronx, Brooklyn, Queens and Richmond. The long, narrow island of Manhattan, upon which New York's complex network of bridges and tunnels all converge, is the city's economic and cultural heart. New York is the nation's richest port, and a world leader in trade and finance. It is also a manufacturing (notably garments), communications (broadcasting, advertising and publishing) and performing arts center.

In 1626, Dutch settlers of NEW NETHERLAND purchased Manhattan from the resident Indians, reputedly for $24 worth of goods, and it became the site of their major city, New Amsterdam. The city, which had flourished under the firm administration of its last Dutch governor, Peter STUYVESANT, was surrendered to the British in 1664, and renamed New York. Over the next hundred years it developed rapidly as a prosperous trade center. In the late Colonial period New Yorkers were among the most outspoken opponents of British rule, but after the defeat (1776) of George Washington at the Battle of Long Island the city remained in the hands of

English troops until the end of the REVOLUTIONARY WAR, after which it served briefly (1789–90) as the nation's capital. As early as the first census of 1790, New York was the largest city in the US, and by 1860 its population was almost a million. The city's population was doubled in the great wave of immigration between 1880 and 1900. Housing and transport problems caused by this influx were partly eased by the construction of the first elevated railway in 1867, Brooklyn Bridge in 1883, and the first subway system in 1904. Scarcity of land and subsequent high land prices produced a new architectural form—the skyscraper, which was to be for long the very symbol of modernity.

Around the turn of the century bitter conflicts between labor and management resulted in highly progressive labor laws. New York's political leadership, at times notoriously corrupt, has included such notable reformers as Theodore ROOSEVELT and Fiorello LA GUARDIA.

Because of its size, the city tends to experience urban problems sooner—and on a larger scale—than other municipalities. Thus its near-bankruptcy in 1975 presaged the troubles of other cities, as did the stringent cure of layoffs of government workers and cutbacks in a host of social and economic programs. In the 1980s the AIDS epidemic, crack use, and homelessness strained the city's agencies. The continuing problems posed by the loss of jobs in manufacturing and resultant structural unemployment were mitigated in the 1980s by booms in financial services and construction. New York City continues to occupy a central position in the nation's—and the world's—cultural and business affairs.

New York has over 100 parks, some of them achieving a striking atmosphere of serenity within the often hectic bustle of activity which surrounds them. The city's cultural and entertainment facilities offer an enormous range of interest and opportunity. Pop (city) 7,165,000, (metro) 8,466,000.

NEW YORK MARATHON, annual ROAD RACING event inaugurated in 1970. Run at the marathon distance (26 miles, 385 yards), it follows a course that takes the runners into each of New York City's five boroughs.

NEW YORK SCHOOL, a diverse group of painters active in New York City from the early 1940s through the late 1950s. Its initial members included Arshile GORKY, Hans HOFMANN, Willem DE KOONING, Robert MOTHERWELL, Jackson POLLOCK, Mark ROTHKO, and Clyfford Still. All abstractionists, they can be subdivided into "action painters" and painters of the "color field."

NEW YORK STATE BARGE CANAL, inland waterway system which connects the Hudson R with the Great Lakes. It was completed in 1918. Its 524mi length includes the ERIE CANAL.

NEW YORK STOCK EXCHANGE, largest securities market in the US, located at Broad and Wall streets in the financial district of New York City. This world-famous trading market has about 1,350 members and handles over 2,000 issues. It was founded in 1792 and received its present name in 1863.

NEW ZEALAND, sovereign state within the British Commonwealth, 1,200mi SE of Australia, in the S Pacific Ocean. The country comprises the North Island, the South Island (the two principal islands), Stewart Island and the Chatham Islands, with other small outlying islands.

Official name: New Zealand
Capital: Wellington
Area: 103,288sq mi
Population: 3,341,000
Languages: English; Maori also spoken
Religions: Protestant, Roman Catholic
Monetary unit(s): 1 New Zealand dollar = 100 cents
Land. Both major islands are mountainous, with fertile coastal plains. North Island has some volcanic ranges, a region of hot springs surrounding Lake Taupo in the center, and the country's major river, the Waikato. South Island includes large areas of forest and many glaciers and lakes. Plants include subtropical species. There are hardly any native mammals but many rare birds, such as the KIWI. The climate is temperate.
People. About 10% of New Zealand's population are MAORIS, and about 90% are descended from settlers who came from Britain. Over 40% of the population live in urban areas—notably Auckland, Christchurch and the capital, Wellington.
Economy. Sheep and cattle are the main sources of income. Principal exports are

frozen meat (mainly lamb), wool and dairy products. The country's varied light industry is dominated by food-processing. Some minerals are produced. New Zealand's beauty and diversity, and its famous fishing and winter sports attract growing numbers of tourists.

History. The chief Maori migrations (1200–1400) led to the eclipse of the earlier Moriori tribes in New Zealand. The islands were sighted by the Dutch seaman Abel TASMAN in 1642, and named for the Netherlands province of Zeeland. In the 1770s Captain James COOK visited New Zealand and claimed it for England. Missionaries became active in the early 19th century, and systematic colonization was begun in 1840 by the New Zealand Company. Maori chiefs acknowledged British sovereignty in exchange for recognition of their territorial rights at the Treaty of Waitangi (1840), but over the next 30 years the treaty was contravened by white settlers who fought Maoris for their land. It achieved self-government in 1852, became a dominion under the British crown in 1907, and was made completely independent in 1931. A pioneer in social reform, New Zealand was the first country to give women the vote (1893) and inaugurated a progressive social security system in 1898. WESTERN SAMOA gained independence in 1962, and internal self-government was granted to the Cook Islands (1965) and Niue (1974). In 1986, following a decision by Prime Minister David Lange to bar nuclear-armed ships from New Zealand ports, the US suspended its defense agreement with New Zealand under the 1950 ANZUS PACT.

NEY, Michel (1769–1815), French Napoleonic marshal and military hero. His rear-guard defense during NAPOLEON I's retreat from Moscow (1812) was the most notable achievement of a brilliant career. Though he helped persuade Napoleon to abdicate, Ney's allegiance to the Bourbon Louis XVIII did not outlive Napoleon's return from exile. Ney fought with Napoleon at WATERLOO, and afterward was condemned to death for treason by the British.

NEZ PERCÉ INDIANS (French: pierced nose), American Indian tribe of present-day central Idaho. Noted horse-breeders, they ceded (1855) much of their territory to the US. Fraudulently-enforced cession of a further 75% of their land (1863) and many land disputes led to the Nez Percé War of 1877, in which 300 Indians held out for five months against 5,000 US troops before surrendering.

NIACIN. See VITAMINS.

NIAGARA FALLS, cataract in the Niagara R, between W N.Y. and S Ontario, Canada, world-famous spectacle and an important source of hydroelectric power. The river is divided into the American Falls (1,060ft wide and 167ft high) and the Canadian, or Horseshoe Falls (2,600ft wide and 158ft high), by Goat Island before plunging into the deep gorge with its Whirlpool Rapids. Some 212,000cu ft of water per second pass over the Falls, which are gradually moving upstream as they erode the rock.

NIBELUNGENLIED ("Song of the Nibelungs"), German epic written c1200 AD, partly based on Scandinavian myths. It tells how SIEGFRIED, who had gained the treasure of the Nibelungen dwarfs, is given Kriemhild in marriage as a reward for helping Gunther win Brunhild by trickery. Brunhild in revenge has Siegfried killed by Hagen, who hides the treasure in the Rhine. Kriemhild's subsequent vow to avenge Siegfried ends in a holocaust. The story inspired WAGNER'S operatic tetralogy *The Ring of the Nibelungs*.

NICAEA, Councils of, the first and seventh Ecumenical Councils. The first Nicaean Council, called in 325 AD by the Emperor CONSTANTINE, condemned ARIANISM and drew up the NICENE CREED. The second Nicaean Council in 787 ruled in favor of the restoration of images in churches.

NICARAGUA, largest of the Central American republics, bounded on the N by Honduras, E by the Caribbean Sea, S by Costa Rica, and W by the Pacific Ocean.

Official name: Republic of Nicaragua
Capital: Managua
Area: 49,363sq mi
Population: 3,502,000
Language: Spanish
Religion: Roman Catholic
Monetary unit(s): 1 córdoba = 100 centavos
Land. Nicaragua is a country of volcanoes, lakes and forested plains. A prominent physical feature is the long, eastern lowland belt running diagonally across the country, which embraces two large lakes: Nicaragua and Managua. This lowland belt contains

all the large towns and 90% of Nicaragua's relatively sparse population. Earthquakes, such as the one which devastated the capital Managua in 1972, are not uncommon.

People. The people are predominantly (70%) of mixed Spanish-Indian descent, but include pure Spanish, pure Negroes and pure Indians. About half of the population is illiterate.

Economy. Only 10% of land is cultivated, but agriculture is the mainstay of the economy. Forestry and mining also play an important part. The main exports are raw cotton, meat, coffee, gold, timber and rice.

History. Before the arrival of the Spanish conquistador Gil González de Ávila (1522) the country was inhabited by various Indian communities. Another Spanish expedition founded León and Granada in 1524. From 1570 the country was ruled as part of Guatemala. Nicaragua won independence from Spain in 1821 and was then annexed to Mexico, after which it became (1825) part of the Central American Federation. Independent from 1838, the country became convulsed by power struggles. In 1912 the US was asked for aid, and US Marines occupied the country almost continuously until 1933. Ostensibly a democracy, Nicaragua was ruled by members of the powerful Somoza family from 1937 until 1979, when Sandinist guerrillas forced Anastasio Somoza Debayle to resign and leave the country. A junta of Sandinista leaders took power; in 1984, one of them, Daniel ORTEGA, was elected president. With aid from the Soviet Union, the Sandinistas tried to establish a Marxist regime, but they had to devote many of their resources to fighting US-supported contras operating from Honduras. A democratic constitution adopted in 1987 was nullified by the continuing state of emergency under which the government operated. Meanwhile, rampant inflation, shortages of all kinds, and the military draft increased popular discontent. In 1987, the Sandinistas appeared to recognize the necessity of ending the contra war, but a settlement proved elusive and democratic reforms promised by Ortega in a treaty with other Central American presidents were not fulfilled.

NICENE CREED, either of two early CREEDS. The first was issued by the first Council of Nicaea (325) to state orthodoxy against ARIANISM. The second was perhaps issued by the Council of Constantinople (381); much longer, it is used at Holy COMMUNION in both Eastern and Western Churches.

NICHOLAS, Saint, 4th-century patron saint of children, scholars, merchants and sailors and probably bishop of Myra in Lycia, Asia Minor. In many European countries he traditionally visits children and gives them gifts on his feast day (Dec. 6). The custom was brought to America by the Dutch, whose Sinter Klaas became the SANTA CLAUS of Christmas.

NICHOLAS, name of two Russian tsars: **Nicholas I** (1796–1855), emperor and tsar 1825–55, notorious for his despotic rule. His succession was challenged by a liberal revolt (see DECEMBRIST REVOLT) which was quickly crushed. A determined absolutist, he opposed all liberal reform or independence. He expanded Russian territory at the expense of Turkey and was only checked by the CRIMEAN WAR. **Nicholas II** (1868–1918), tsar 1894–1917, whose inflexibility and misgovernment helped bring about the RUSSIAN REVOLUTION and the overthrow of his dynasty. His wife, the empress Alexandra, filled the court with irresponsible favorites of whom the monk RASPUTIN was the most influential. Russian defeats in the RUSSO-JAPANESE WAR (1904–05) led to a popular uprising, and Nicholas granted limited civil rights and called the first representative DUMA (1905). The military defeats of WWI led to his abdication and eventual execution.

NICHOLAS OF CUSA (1401–1464), German cardinal best known for his advanced cosmological views: he held that the earth rotates on its axis, that space is infinite, and that the sun is a star like other stars (see also ASTRONOMY). He also suggested the use of concave lenses for the shortsighted (see GLASSES; LENS).

NICHOLSON, Ben (1894–1982), British abstract sculptor and painter of landscapes and still-lifes. His reliefs, like *White Relief*, 1939, are composed in an elegant pure linear style.

NICKEL (Ni), hard, gray-white, ferromagnetic (see MAGNETISM) metal in Group VIII of the PERIODIC TABLE; a transition element. About half the total world output comes from deposits of pyrrhotite and pentlandite at Sudbury, Ontario; garnierite in New Caledonia is also important. Roasting the ore gives crude nickel oxide, refined by electrolysis or by the Mond process. Nickel is widely used in ALLOYS, including monel metal, invar and German silver. In many countries "silver" coins are made from cupronickel (an alloy of copper and nickel). Nickel-chromium alloys ("nichrome"), resistant to oxidation at high temperatures, are used as heating elements in electric heaters, etc. Nickel is used for nickel plating and as a catalyst for hydrogenation. Chemically nickel resembles IRON and COBALT, being moderately reactive, and forming compounds in the +2 oxidation state; the +4 state is known in ligand complexes. AW 58.7, mp 1453°C, bp 2732°C, sg 8.902 (25°C).

NICKELODEON, early motion-picture theater. The first one opened in 1905 in McKeesport, Pa., and offered for five cents a screen program with piano accompaniment. It was so popular that there were 5,000 nickelodeons in the US by 1907. The name was subsequently applied to coin-operated, automatic phonographs.

NICOLAI, Otto (1810–1849), German composer. Of his many operas, the most famous is *The Merry Wives of Windsor*. He founded the Vienna Philharmonic in 1842.

NICOLAY, John George (1832–1901), German-born US biographer. He was Abraham Lincoln's private secretary from 1860–65. From 1875–90 he wrote (with John HAY) Lincoln's biography. He also edited the *Complete Works of Abraham Lincoln* (1905).

NICOLET, Jean (c1598–1642), French explorer who was probably the first European to visit the Lake Michigan area. In 1634 he set out by canoe through Lake Huron, entered Lake Michigan and explored Green Bay and the Fox River, making friendly contact with the Winnebago Indians.

NICOLLS, Richard (1624–1672), the first British governor of New York. As governor he made the transition from Dutch to English government (1664–68) as gradual as possible, treating the Dutch with "humanity and gentleness."

NICOLSON, Sir Harold (1886–1968), British writer and diplomat. After 20 years' diplomatic service (1909–29), he became a member of Parliament (1935–45). He wrote biographies of Verlaine, Byron, Tennyson, Swinburne and King George V, and many reviews.

NICOTINE, colorless oily liquid, an ALKALOID occurring in tobacco leaves and extracted from tobacco refuse. It is used as an insecticide and to make nicotinic acid (see VITAMINS). Nicotine is one of the most toxic substances known; even the small dose ingested by SMOKING causes blood-vessel constriction, raised blood pressure, nausea, headache and impaired digestion.

NIEBUHR, Reinhold (1892–1971), American Protestant theologian. An active socialist in the early 1930s, he turned back after WWII to traditional Protestant values, relating them to modern society in his "conservative realism." His *Nature and Destiny of Man* (1941–43) greatly influenced American theology.

NIELSEN, Carl August (1865–1931), Danish composer. His six symphonies are most notable for their original harmonic structure. He also wrote operas, concertos for flute, clarinet and violin and chamber music.

NIEMEYER, Oscar (Oscar Niemeyer Soares Filho; 1907–   ), Brazilian architect whose outstanding work in Brazil culminated in that country's capital city, BRASILIA, 1956–60. His most characteristic style is the curved, sculptural use of reinforced concrete.

NIEMÖLLER, Martin (1892–1984), German Lutheran pastor who opposed the Nazis and Adolf Hitler. He was confined in concentration camps (1937–1945). In 1945 he organized the "Declaration of Guilt" in which German Churches admitted their failure to resist the Nazis.

NIEPCE, Joseph Nicéphore (1765–1833), French inventor who in 1826 made the first successful permanent photograph. The image, recorded in asphalt on a pewter plate, required an 8hr exposure in a camera obscura. The method used derived from heliography, Niepce's photoengraving process. In 1829 Niepce went into partnership with Louis Daguerre (see DAGUERROTYPE).

NIETZSCHE, Friedrich (1844–1900), German philosopher, classical scholar and critic of Christianity. In *Thus Spake Zarathustra* (1833–92) he introduced the concept of the "superman," a great-souled hero who transcends the slavish morality of Christianity and whose motivating force is the supreme passion of "will to power," which is directed towards creativity. This passion distinguishes him from inferior human beings. Nietzsche's ideas have been much misrepresented, particularly by the Nazis who misappropriated the concept of the "superman" to justify their own concepts of Aryan racial superiority.

NIGER, the largest state in W Africa, is surrounded by seven countries, with Algeria and Libya to the N, Nigeria and Benin to the S, Chad to the E, and Mali and Burkina to the W.

Land. Despite its vast area, the country is thinly populated. Most of the land is desert: the N is typically Saharan, and the NE is virtually uninhabitable. Moderate rainfall in the S and SW permit cultivation. The Niger R flows through the SW corner, and farmers plant crops there when the river floods. The Air Mts are in N central Niger.

People. The people are divided into several different groups: the Hausa, who form over

Official name: Republic of Niger
Capital: Niamey
Area: 458,074sq mi
Population: 6,947,000
Languages: French, Hausa, Fulani
Religions: Muslim, Animist, Christian
Monetary unit(s): 1 CFA franc=100 centimes

half the population; Djerma-Songhai and Beriberi-Manga in the S are mainly farmers; the Fulani, Tuareg and others in the N are nomadic pastoralists.
Economy. Niger is presently one of the world's poorest countries; however, it is rich in mineral potential. Principal exports are uranium, livestock and vegetables. Chief food crops are millet, cassava, sorghum, vegetables, rice and peanuts.
History. Areas of what is now Niger were part of the Mali and Songhai empires. In 1922 Niger became a French colony; in 1960 it gained independence. In 1974 widespread unrest caused by drought-related food shortages brought about the overthrow of the government by the military. In a 1987 referendum, voters approved a new national charter designed to restore the government to civilian control under military supervision.

NIGERIA, federal republic in West Africa, the most populous country on the African continent. Nigeria is one of Africa's most powerful nations and plays a major role in international affairs.
Land. Bordering on the Gulf of Guinea, it lies between Cameroon on the E and Benin on the W. Behind the coastal strip are lowlands which rise to the Jos Plateau and fall away to sandy high plains in the N. In the S Nigeria has a 475mi coastline of sandbars, mangroves and lagoons, with the great delta of the Niger R as the most prominent natural feature. The N is hot and dry; the S is humid, with the rainfall averaging more than 150in per year.
People. The country has over 200 tribes and languages. There are three major tribal groups: the Yorubas in the W, the Ibos in the E and the Hausa-Fulani in the N; the minority tribes are more or less equal in

Official name: Federal Republic of Nigeria
Capital: Lagos
Area: 356,669sq mi
Population: 100,596,000
Languages: English, Hausa, Ibo, Yoruba
Religions: Muslim, Christian, Animist
Monetary unit(s): 1 naira = 100 kobo

number to these three groups. The population is concentrated mainly in the Muslim N, although the S is also heavily populated. Most Nigerians are farmers, herders or fishermen. Despite widespread illiteracy, Nigeria has a relatively large number of university graduates, many of whom have studied abroad. The government has introduced free primary education. Nigeria is one of the most urbanized countries in Africa; the largest cities are Ibaden, Lagos, Ogbomosho, Kano and Oshogbo. There is a large community of expatriates, most of whom are employed by foreign companies, including oil companies.
Economy. Nigeria is the second largest supplier of oil to the US, after Saudi Arabia. Agricultural products include peanuts, cotton and soybeans in the N, along with livestock, palm oil, cacao, rubber and timber in the S. Manufacturing includes vehicle assembly, food processing, textiles, building materials and furniture.
History. The Nok culture of black settlers on the Jos Plateau, c800 BC–200 AD, is the earliest known in Nigeria. Small trading city-states arose c1000 AD, especially in the N, and by the 1300s became powerful empires such as the Kanem, Mali and the BENIN in the S. The Portuguese reached Nigeria in 1483. Britain annexed areas of Nigeria, establishing it in 1914 as a colony and protectorate. Nigeria became independent, in 1960 and, in 1963, a republic. Political parties had long developed on regional lines, and after disputes over the 1964 election the collapse of law and order led to a series of military regimes until 1966, when General GOWON set up a military government. Gowon reorganized Nigeria into 12 states, but the Ibos seceded to form the independent republic of BIAFRA. Civil war between Biafra and the rest of Nigeria

broke out in 1967 and continued until Biafra surrendered in 1970. In 1975 Gowon was deposed and exiled in a military coup. Civilian government, from 1979 to 1983, was notable for profligacy and corruption. Gen. Ibrahim B. Babangida, president from 1985, faced severe economic problems due to declining oil prices that reduced Nigeria's per capita income by half. Western oriented, he sought to restore a free-market economy, instituting government austerity measures favored by the World Bank and the International Monetary Fund. He established a five-year schedule for restoring civilian government in 1992.

NIGER RIVER, the third longest river in Africa, 2,600mi long. With its eastern branch, the Benue, it drains an area of more than 1 million sq mi. Rising in SW Guinea, it curves NE, E then SE into Nigeria and finally S towards the Gulf of Guinea, where it forms a 14,000sq mi delta.

NIGHT BLINDNESS, or **nyctalopia,** inability to accommodate in or adapt to darkness. It may be a hereditary defect or an early symptom of VITAMIN A deficiency in adults. It is due to a defect in rod VISION.

NIGHTINGALE, Florence (1820–1910), English founder of modern nursing, known as the "Lady with the Lamp" because she worked night and day during the Crimean War. She determined to make a career out of nursing the sick and traveled in Europe in the 1840s studying methods of nursing. In 1854 the British government asked her to tend the wounded of the CRIMEAN WAR. She sailed with 38 nurses to Scutari and established sanitary methods and discipline in the two huge army hospitals. In 1860 she set up a nurses' training school in London.

NIGHTINGALE, *Luscinia megarhynchos,* bird of the thrush subfamily Turdinae, renowned for its beautiful song. A small brown bird, feeding on insects and other invertebrates, it lives in deciduous woodlands throughout most of Europe.

NIHILISM, a doctrine that denies all values, questions all authority, and advocates the destruction of all social and economic institutions. The movement arose in 19th-century Russia in reaction against all authority, especially that of the tsar. It is romantic in origin and anarchist in outlook; its most noted exponent was KROPOTKIN.

NIJINSKY, Vaslav (1890–1950), famous Russian dancer whose outstanding technique and magnetic stage presence contributed greatly to the impact of Russian ballet on the West, when Sergei DIAGHILEV brought a company to Paris in 1909. With Diaghilev's encouragement, Nijinsky devised original choreography, based on Greek vase paintings, for DEBUSSY'S *Afternoon of a Faun.* Mental illness ended his career in 1919.

NIKLAUS, Jack (1940–   ), US golfer who won six Masters, five PGA, and four US Open titles.

NILE RIVER, the longest river in the world, flowing generally N about 4,145mi from central Africa to the Mediterranean. Its remotest headstream is the Luvironza R in Burundi above Victoria Nyanza (Lake Victoria), from which flows the White Nile. The Blue Nile rises above Lake Tana in NW Ethiopia and joins the White Nile at Khartoum, Sudan, to form the Nile proper. N of Cairo it fans out into a 115mi-wide delta with principal outlets at Rosetta near Alexandria and Damietta near Port Said. Silt deposited by the Nile's annual overflow brought agricultural prosperity throughout Egypt's history. The river has been harnessed, notably at the ASWAN HIGH DAM, to supply hydroelectricity as well as constant irrigation. The Nile is navigable the year round from its mouth to Aswan, and in full spate is generally navigable as far south as Uganda.

NIMITZ, Chester William (1885–1966), US admiral who commanded naval operations in the Pacific after America entered WORLD WAR II in 1941. Credited with originating the strategy of "island hopping," he had an outstandingly successful command. On Sept. 2, 1945, the Japanese surrender was signed aboard his flagship, U.S.S. *Missouri.*

NIN, Anaïs (1903–1977), French-born US author whose novels and stories depict the inner worlds of women in surrealistic and psychoanalytic fashion. Her novels include *The House of Incest* (1936) and *Collages* (1964). She is best known, however, for *The Diaries of Anaïs Nin* (7 vols., 1966–80), which span the years 1931–74 and include portraits of such contemporaries as Lawrence Durrell, Henry Miller, William Carlos Williams, and Marguerite Young.

NINEVEH, capital of Assyria in the 7th century BC, on the Tigris R, opposite modern Mosul, Iraq. Invaluable remains survive from its period of greatness under Sennacherib and ASHURBANIPAL. Its destruction by invaders in 612 BC ended the Assyrian Empire. (See also BABYLONIA AND ASSYRIA.)

NINO, El, massive body of warm water whose periodic appearance in the Pacific Ocean off the W coast of South America is responsible for worldwide weather abnormalities. Storms, heavy precipitation, and droughts in the US in 1982–83 were attributed to the effects of an El Niño whose temperatures averaged 12° F above normal Pacific temperatures.

NIPPUR, ancient Mesopotamian city which lay 100mi SE of BABYLON, a religious center sacred to the god En-Lil. Large numbers of SUMERIAN archives have been found there.

NIRVANA, Sanskrit term used in Buddhism, Jainism and Hinduism to denote the highest state of existence, reached when all bodily desires have been quelled and the self is free to dissolve into the ocean of peace or God. It means literally "extinguished," denoting freedom from ego. Nirvana is the final escape from the cycle of rebirth (see TRANSMIGRATION OF SOULS).

NISEI (Japanese: second generation), those born of immigrant Japanese parents in the US. After the Japanese attack on PEARL HARBOR (1941), some 110,000 Americans of Japanese ancestry were forcibly evacuated from their homes on the West Coast and placed in detention centers, in most cases until WWII had ended. Acknowledging the injustice, the US government in 1988 made a compensatory payment of $20,000 to every surviving internee.

NITROGEN (N), nonmetal in Group VA of the PERIODIC TABLE; a colorless, odorless gas (N_2) comprising 78% of the ATMOSPHERE, prepared by fractional distillation of liquid air. Combined nitrogen occurs mainly as nitrates. As a constituent of AMINO ACIDS, it is vital. Molecular nitrogen is inert because of the strong triple bond between the two atoms, but it will react with some elements, especially the alkaline-earth metals, to give nitrides; with oxygen; and with hydrogen. Activated nitrogen, formed in an electric discharge, consists of nitrogen atoms and is much more reactive. Nitrogen is used in nitrogen fixation and to provide an inert atmosphere; liquid nitrogen is a CRYOGENIC refrigerant. AW 14.0, mp $-210°C$, bp $-196°C$.

Nitrogen forms mainly trivalent and pentavalent compounds. **Nitric oxide** (NO), is a colorless gas formed in the electric-arc process; it is readily oxidized further to nitrogen dioxide, mp-164°C, bp-152°C. **Nitrites** are salts (or esters) of **nitrous acid** (HNO_2) and are mild reducing agents. **Nitrous oxide** (N_2O), or laughing gas, is a colorless gas with a sweet odor, prepared by heating ammonium nitrate, and used as a weak anesthetic, sometimes producing mild hysteria, and also as an aerosol propellant. mp $-91°C$, bp$-88°C$. **Nitrogen dioxide** (NO_2), a red-brown toxic gas in equilibrium with its colorless dimer (N_2O_4), is a constituent of automobile exhaust and smog. A powerful oxidizing agent, it is used in the manufacture of sulfuric acid and in rocket fuels. It is also an intermediate in the manufacture of nitric acid. mp $-11°C$, bp 21°C. (See also AMMONIA.)

NITROGLYCERIN ($C_3H_5(ONO_2)_3$), properly called glyceryl trinitrate, the nitrate ester of glycerol, made by its nitration. Since it causes vasodilation, it is used to relieve ANGINA PECTORIS. Its major use, however, is as a very powerful high EXPLOSIVE, though its sensitivity to shock renders it unsafe unless used in the form of DYNAMITE or blasting gelatin. It is a colorless, oily liquid. AW 227.1, mp 13°C.

NIXON, Richard Milhous (1913–   ), 37th president of the US (1969–74). Nixon was born into a Quaker family in Yorba Linda, Cal., and trained and practiced (1937–42) as a lawyer. An aviation ground officer in the navy in WWII, he began his political career with election to congress in 1946. As a Republican congressman he became a prominent member of the House's anti-communist UN-AMERICAN ACTIVITIES COMMITTEE. In 1950 he was elected to the Senate, where his continued and aggressive anti-communist stance probably influenced Dwight D. EISENHOWER's choice of Nixon as running-mate in 1952. As Eisenhower's vice-president (1953–61) Nixon was given an unusually prominent role both at home and abroad. In 1960 he was chosen as the Republican presidential nominee, but was narrowly defeated by John KENNEDY. After running unsuccessfully for the governorship of California in 1962, he announced his retirement to pursue his career in law. Reentering political life in 1964, however, Nixon gradually won wide backing and, with Spiro AGNEW as his running-mate, won the presidency in 1968. He was reelected in 1972 with a large majority.

Nixon had pledged withdrawal from the VIETNAM WAR, which had plagued the presidencies of his two predecessors. Although his actions did not always seem consistent with his electoral promise (notably his ordering of the invasions of Cambodia and Laos and of saturation bombing in North Vietnam), he began pulling US troops out of Vietnam almost at once. Eventually, with Secretary of State Henry KISSINGER as Nixon's chief negotiator, a cease-fire agreement was reached (1973). In the meantime COLD WAR tensions were eased by arms-limitation talks with the USSR in 1969, and again when Nixon visited Moscow (he was the first US president to do so) in 1972. This followed his historic state visit to the People's Republic of China, which reopened contact with the mainland Chinese for the first time in more than 20 years. In domestic affairs, Nixon introduced the "New Federalism," which in principle sought a more balanced relationship between the federal and state governments. A major element of this concept was revenue-sharing, the return to the states of some federal tax money for use as the states saw fit. Nixon also imposed wage and price controls to help offset the nation's severe economic problems of recession and inflation.

Nixon's second term of office was aborted by the scandal of the WATERGATE affair, which led to revelations of widespread corruption, misinformation and the public and an unprecedented increase in the power of the White House at the expense of Congress and the judiciary. Several of Nixon's top aides were tried and imprisoned, and the House Judiciary Committee recommended that Nixon be impeached. On August 9, 1974, Nixon resigned office, the first US president ever to do so.

A month later, Nixon was given a pardon by his successor, Gerald Ford, for any illegal acts he may have committed while president. Barred from practicing law, Nixon wrote his memoirs and other books.

NKRUMAH, Kwame (1901–1972), Ghanian who led his country to independence, and a champion of pan-Africanism. After the electoral victory (1951) of his Convention People's party, he became first prime minister of the then Gold Coast, in which role he established (1957) the independent Republic of Ghana. As president from 1960, his gradual assumption of dictatorial powers won him enemies, and his government was overthrown by a military coup in 1966.

NOBEL, Alfred Bernhard (1833–1896), Swedish-born inventor of dynamite and other explosives. About 1863 he set up a factory to manufacture liquid NITROGLYCERIN, but when in 1864 this blew up, killing his younger brother, Nobel set out to find safe handling methods for the substance, so discovering DYNAMITE, patented 1867 (UK) and 1868 (US). Later he invented gelignite (patented 1876) and ballistite (1888). A lifelong pacifist, he wished his explosives to be used solely for peaceful purposes, and was much embittered by their military use. He left most of his fortune for the establishment of the Nobel Foundation and this fund has been used to award Nobel Prizes since 1901.

NOBEL PRIZES, annual awards given to individuals or institutions judged to confer "the greatest benefit on mankind" in any one of six fields: physics, chemistry, physiology or medicine, literature, peace and economics. Except for the prize in economics, instituted in 1969, the prizes have been awarded since 1901. The award of the peace prize, sometimes controversial, is made by a committee of five elected by the Norwegian parliament; the other prizes are awarded by the appropriate learned bodies in Sweden: the Royal Academy of Science, the Caroline Institute, and the Swedish Academy of Literature. The prize money comes from the foundation set up by Alfred NOBEL.

NOBILE, Umberto (1885–1978), Italian aeronautical engineer and Arctic explorer. He designed the airships *Norge, Roma* and *Italia*, and in 1926 flew over the NORTH POLE in *Norge* with Roald AMUNDSEN and Lincoln ELLSWORTH.

NOBLE GASES, the elements in Group 0 of the PERIODIC TABLE, comprising HELIUM, neon, ARGON, krypton, xenon and radon. They are colorless, odorless gases, prepared by fractional distillation of liquid air (see ATMOSPHERE), except helium and radon. Owing to their stable filled-shell electron configurations, the noble gases are chemically unreactive: only krypton, xenon and radon form isolable compounds. They glow brightly when an electric discharge is passed through them, and so are used in advertising signs: neon tubes glow red, xenon blue, and krypton bluish-white; argon tubes glow pale red at low pressures, blue at high pressures.

NOBLE METALS, the corrosion–resistant precious metals comprising the platinum group, SILVER and GOLD, and sometimes including rhenium.

NOGUCHI, Hideyo (1876–1928), Japanese bacteriologist, at the Rockefeller Institute in New York from 1904, best known for isolating the spirochete that causes syphilis and for developing the skin test for the disease.

NOGUCHI, Isamu (1904–   ), US abstract sculptor whose works, especially those created for specific architectural settings such as the UNESCO building in Paris, have won international recognition. He was a student of BRANCUSI.

NOH or No, the classical drama of Japan, developed under court patronage in the 14th century. Typically, a Noh play dramatizes the spiritual life of its central character, employing speech, singing, instrumental music, dancing and mime. The play is short, but it moves slowly in a highly ritualized style. The performers are all male, and traditional wooden masks are used. Noh gave rise to the more popular KABUKI theater.

NOISE, in electronics, any unwanted or interfering current or voltage in an electrical device or system. Its presence in the amplifying circuits of RADIOS, TELEVISION receivers, etc., may mask or distort signals. Unpredictable random noise exists in any component with resistance because of the thermal motion of the current-carrying ELECTRONS, and in electron tubes due to random cathode emission. Thermal radiations and variations in the atmosphere also cause random noise. Nonrandom noise arises from spurious oscillations and unintended couplings between components.

NOISE, unwanted SOUND. As far as man is concerned this is a subjective definition: people vary in their sensitivity to noise; many sounds are agreeable to some and noisy to others. Blasts or explosions can cause sudden damage to the ear, and prolonged exposure to impulsive sounds such as those created by a pneumatic drill may cause gradual hearing impairment. In general, any sound that is annoying, interferes with speech, damages the hearing or reduces concentration or work efficiency may be considered as noise. From the physical viewpoint, sound waves (either in air or vibrations in solid bodies) that mask required signals or cause fatigue and breakdown of equipment or structures are noise and should be minimized. In air, sound is radiated spherically from its source as a compressional wave, being partly reflected, absorbed or transmitted on hitting an obstacle. Noise is usually a nonperiodic sound wave, as opposed to a periodic pure musical tone or a sine-wave combination. It is characterized by its intensity (measured in decibels or nepers), frequency and spatial variation; a sound-level meter and frequency analyzer measure these properties. Noise may be controlled at its source (e.g., by a muffler), between it and the listener (e.g., by sound-absorbing material) or at the listener (e.g., by wearing ear plugs).

NOLAND, Kenneth (1924–), US painter whose work featured bands of color. With Morris Louis, he developed a technique of employing thinned paints for staining and became one of the best-known color field painters.

NOLDE, Emil (1867–1956), born Emil Hansen, German expressionist, engraver and painter, notably of landscapes and figures, whose bold, visionary and highly emotional style is typified in his *Marsh Landscape* (1916). (See also EXPRESSIONISM.)

NOMAD, member of a tribe or community which moves from one place to another for subsistence. The nomadic way of life, though fast declining, is still to be found among some herdsmen, such as the BEDOUIN Arabs, and hunters such as some groups of Australian ABORIGINES. There are also semi-nomadic peoples, such as the LAPPS, who move from summer to winter pastures.

NOMINALISM, in philosophy, usually as opposed to REALISM, the view that the names of abstract ideas (e.g., beauty) used in describing things (as in, a *beautiful* table) are merely conventions or conveniences, and should not be taken to imply the actual existence of universals corresponding to those names.

NONALIGNED MOVEMENT, or **nonaligned nations,** a group of about 100 countries whose professed aim is close relations with all nations regardless of ideology. These nations are diverse, though mostly THIRD WORLD, and not all (e.g., Cuba) are strictly "nonaligned" with regard to the two superpowers, the US and USSR. The movement's formal beginnings date from a 1961 conference in Belgrade with representatives from 25 countries.

NONCONFORMISTS, or dissenters, those who will not conform to the doctrine or practice of an established church; especially the Protestant dissenters from the Church of England (mainly PURITANS) expelled by the Act of Uniformity (1662). They now include Baptists, Brethren, Congregationalists, Methodists, Presbyterians and Quakers.

NON-EUCLIDEAN GEOMETRY, those branches of GEOMETRY that challenge EUCLIDEAN GEOMETRY'S tenet that through any point A not on a line L there passes one and only one line parallel to L, but which accept in general all other Euclidean axioms with at most minor changes. The geometry based on the hypothesis that no lines pass through A parallel to L is Riemannian geometry; (see RIEMANN); that based on the hypothesis that there is more than one such line is LOBACHEVSKIAN GEOMETRY. The first mathematician to open the doors for non-Euclidean geometry was GAUSS in the 19th century. He did not publish his work, however, and the fathers of non-Euclidean geometry are usually considered to be János Bolyai (1802–60) and LOBACHEVSKY.

NONO, Luigi (1924–), Italian composer of serial or TWELVE-TONE MUSIC. His choral and instrumental works, often political in content, include *Epitaffo per Federico García Lorca* (1952), *Il canto sospeso* (1956) and *Intolleranza* (1961), an antifascist opera. Word sounds and electronic tape and equipment are important elements in much of his music.

NONPARTISAN LEAGUE, political association of farmers and farmworkers founded (1915) and centered in the Dakotas. Formed in response to the power of banking, grain and railroad bosses, the league campaigned for state-run elevators, mills, banks and insurance. Dominating N.D. government 1916–21, it realized most of its demands.

NOOTKA INDIANS, of Wakashan linguistic stock, lived on the W coast of Vancouver Island and in NW Wash. They hunted whales in 60ft seagoing canoes of cedar and lived in long wooden houses, several families to each house. The Nootka used *Dentalia* (tooth) shells for money and carved puppets and masks with moving parts.

NORDENSKJÖLD, Nils Adolf Eric, Baron (1832–1901), Finnish-born Swedish geologist, cartographer and explorer of Spitzbergen (reaching 81° 42'N in 1868) and of Greenland, where he studied inland ice. He was the first to navigate the NORTHEAST PASSAGE (1878–79).

NORMAN CONQUEST, conquest of England by William, Duke of Normandy, following the Battle of HASTINGS (Oct. 14, 1066) when William defeated and killed England's Saxon king, HAROLD. Although illegitimate, William claimed the English throne as EDWARD THE CONFESSOR'S cousin and named successor. Crowned in London, he quickly crushed revolts, building castles as he advanced. The land of the English nobles was distributed to NORMANS in return for their agreement to supply the king with mounted soldiers. The great DOMESDAY BOOK (1086) listed landholdings. The conquerors also brought to England the influence of their French language and innovations in architecture and methods of warfare.

NORMANDY, region of NW France facing the English Channel, noted for dairy products, fruit, brandy, wheat and flax. Le Havre, Dieppe and Cherbourg are the main ports; Rouen and Caen are historic cathedral and university cities. Shipbuilding, steel, iron and textiles are the main industries. Home of the NORMANS, it was later much contested with England before finally going to France in 1450. In WWII it was chosen for the Allied landing, June 6, 1944.

NORMANS, inhabitants of NORMANDY, the former province of NW France. In 911 Rollo, leader of the VIKING raider-settlers, was recognized as duke of the area. Strong, warlike and excellent administrators, the Normans ("Northmen") became Christians in the 10th century and completed the NORMAN CONQUEST of England in the 11th. They were active in the CRUSADES, in the reconquest of Spain, in S Italy and Sicily.

NORRIS, Frank (Benjamin Franklin Norris; 1870–1902), US novelist and newspaperman. His best-known novels are his first, the naturalistic *McTeague* (1899), about life in San Francisco slums and his uncompleted trilogy *The Epic of Wheat* (*The Octopus*, 1901 and *The Pit*, 1903), in which he foreshadowed the MUCKRAKERS.

NORRIS, George William (1861–1944), noted US congressman (1903–43) and reformer. Elected to the House as a Republican from Neb., he led the fight which ousted Speaker Joseph CANNON. In 1913 he moved to the Senate. There his progressive, nonpartisan crusades embraced election reform, setting up the TENNESSEE VALLEY AUTHORITY, labor disputes (the Norris–La Guardia Act), farm relief, the 20th or Lame Duck Amendment which he authored, and POLL TAX abolition.

NORSEMEN. See VIKINGS.

NORTH, Frederick, Baron North (later Earl of Guilford; 1732–1792), British Tory prime minister. His policies precipitated the break with the American colonies. A tool of George III, North answered the BOSTON TEA PARTY with the INTOLERABLE ACTS (1774), including the QUEBEC ACT, which kept Canada loyal to Britain. He resigned in 1782 and the next year formed a brief coalition with Charles James FOX.

NORTH AMERICA, third-largest continent, bounded in the N by the Arctic Ocean, in the S by South America, in the W by the Pacific and Bering Sea, and in the E by the Atlantic. It includes the US, Canada, Mexico, Central America, the Caribbean Islands and Greenland—one-sixth of the earth's land surface (9,361,791sq mi), with over 95,000mi of coastline.

Land. Its regions differ immensely: in the W coastal ranges from Alaska to the Gulf of California run parallel to the Rocky Mts, the continent's backbone. Between lies the Intermountain Region, with the Great Basin and Mexican Plateau. E of the Rockies is the vast Interior Plain which includes the Great Plains, the Canadian Prairies, the US Midwest and the Great Lakes and in the NE the ancient rocks of the Canadian (Laurentian) Shield. In the SE lie the Piedmont and Atlantic Coastal Plain and Appalachian Mts. The CONTINENTAL DIVIDE, created by the Rockies, directs the main rivers: the Colorado, Columbia, Fraser and Yukon flow generally westward; the Mackenzie, St. Lawrence, Rio Grande, Missouri and Mississippi flow in other directions. The climate ranges from polar to tropical. Most of the interior has cold winters and hot summers; rainfall can reach 140in a year on the NW Pacific coast and in S Central America. Vegetation varies widely, with northern tundra in Greenland, Alaska and N Canada, desert in SW US and Mexico, and jungle in Central America. Wildlife is rich and diverse. North America has enormous mineral wealth, and a large proportion of the land has a hospitable climate and fertile soils.

People. The continent ranks third in population, which is densest in the E US, SE Canada, the W coast of both, and in Mexico. The people are mainly Caucasians of European descent, speaking English and French in the N and Spanish in Mexico and Central America. Their ancestors emigrated following the first permanent European contacts made in the 1490s by Columbus in the Caribbean and the Cabots in Newfoundland. The settlers found Indians, descendants of the Mongoloid peoples who are thought to have moved E from Asia across the Bering Strait some 25,000 years ago (see ESKIMO; INDIANS, American). Negroes were brought in from Africa as slaves, and are now concentrated in the Caribbean and the US, where every European nation is represented and 10% of the population are NEGROES or mulattoes. Of Mexicans 60% are mestizos. Varied backgrounds have brought wide differences in culture, religion and standards of living. (See also CANADA; MEXICO; UNITED STATES and other countries.)

NORTH ATLANTIC DRIFT, eastward-flowing ocean current, continuation of the GULF STREAM, notable for its warming effect on the climates of W Europe.

NORTH ATLANTIC TREATY ORGANIZATION (NATO), defense organization of nations adhering to the North Atlantic Treaty. An extension of the 1948 Brussels Treaty for military cooperation among five European nations, the treaty is directed at the threat of armed communist attack in Europe or the N Atlantic or Mediterranean area. The new treaty was signed in April 1949 by Belgium, Canada, Denmark, France, Great Britain, Iceland, Italy, Luxembourg, the Netherlands, Norway, Portugal and the US, by Greece and Turkey in 1951, by West Germany in 1955 and by Spain in 1982. Article 5 states that an armed attack on any one or two members will be taken as an attack on all; other clauses cover military, political and economic cooperation. The supreme body is the North Atlantic Council, backed up by committees. It coordinates with its executive branch, the Military Committee, in Brussels. The presidency of the Military Committee annually rotates among member nations. NATO has three commands: Europe, the Atlantic, and the English Channel and North Sea. The Canada–United States Regional Planning Group coordinates North American defense with NATO. France expelled NATO forces in 1966, and the US, which resents its disproportionate share of cost, is accused of acting unilaterally in political matters, but the alliance holds through mutual self-interest among the members. Its corresponding alliance system is the Soviet-dominated WARSAW PACT.

NORTH CAROLINA, state, E US, bounded to the E by the Atlantic Ocean, to the S by S.C. and Ga., to the W by Tenn. and to the N by Va.; one of the 13 original states.

Name of state: North Carolina
Capital: Raleigh
Statehood: Nov. 21, 1789 (12th state)
Familiar name: Tar Heel State
Area: 52,586sq mi
Population: 6,333,000
Elevation: Highest—6,684ft, Mt Mitchell; Lowest—sea level, Atlantic Ocean
Motto: *Esse quam videri* ("To be, rather than to seem")
State flower: Dogwood
State bird: Cardinal
State tree: Pine
State song: "The Old North State"
Land. The Atlantic coastal plain of swamps and rich farmland, shielded in the E by a long chain of barrier islands, gives way on the W to the rolling hills of the Piedmont, where industry has centered at Raleigh, the capital, the urban complex of Greensboro/Winston-Salem and Charlotte, the biggest city. Farther W lie the BLUE RIDGE and GREAT SMOKY MOUNTAINS areas; Mt Mitchell is the highest peak E of the Mississippi R. The many rivers provide for hydroelectric power. Forests cover over half of the state. The mild climate has a mean annual temperature of 59°F and rainfall of about 50in.

People. Almost all the citizens of North Carolina are US-born. Approximately 23% of the population are black, and almost 45% live in urban communities. Baptists are the largest religious group, followed by Methodists and Presbyterians.

Economy. Industry, intensified after WWII, now accounts for a major proportion of North Carolina's income. The state continues to be one of the leading US manufacturers of textiles, cigarettes and furniture. Chemicals, electrical machinery, processed foods and pulp and paper products are also important to North Carolina's economic base. In agriculture, tobacco leads, followed by soybeans, corn, peanuts and cotton. Tourism, supported by the scenic beauty in the W, five national forests and many historical sites, was the fastest growing industry in the 1980s. Mining centers on construction materials, but North Carolina is also the main source of felspar, lithium and mica in the US.

History. Sir Walter Raleigh failed twice in the 1580s to settle the area, inhabited by Catawba, CHEROKEE and Tuscarora Indians (see LOST COLONY). Grants from Charles I (hence *Carolina*) and II were followed in 1677 of Culpeper's Rebellion by settlers against the governor. North Carolina became a separate colony in 1712 and a royal colony in 1729. It was the first to instruct its delegates to vote for independence and in 1789 became the 12th state of the US. It seceded in 1861 when it failed in efforts to preserve the Union. Development was spurred in the 1900s by a major expansion in education and after WWII by industrial diversification and provision of hydroelectric power. North Carolina is now a pioneer in social legislation and a major industrial force in the South. The state has a healthy mix of manufacturing and agricultural resources, though its farmers still depend heavily on tobacco production. In recent years, the state's textile industry has been hurt by imports, and some mills have closed. Nonetheless, the population increased 24.5% from 1970 to 1986, and urban expansion is rapidly changing the face of the state. In presidential elections 1968–88, North Carolina voted Republican in 1968–72 and 1980–88.

NORTHCLIFFE, Alfred Charles William Harmsworth, Viscount (1865–1922), creator of modern British journalism. On a basis of popular journals starting with *Answers* (1888), he built the world's biggest newspaper empire. He founded or bought the *London Evening News, Daily Mail, Sunday Dispatch, Daily Mirror, Observer* and the *Times*.

NORTH DAKOTA, N central US state, bounded to the E by Minn., to the S by S.D., to the W by Mont. and to the N by Canada. The state lies at the center of the North American land mass.

Name of state: North Dakota
Capital: Bismarck
Statehood: Nov. 2, 1889 (39th state)
Familiar names: Flickertail State, Sioux State
Area: 70,665sq mi
Population: 679,000
Elevation: Highest—3,506ft, White Butte; Lowest—750ft, Red River in Pembina County
Motto: "Liberty and union, now and forever; one and inseparable"
State flower: Wild prairie rose
State bird: Western meadowlark
State tree: American elm
State song: "North Dakota Hymn"

Land. The most populous part is the flat, fertile Red R valley in the E. The Red R of the North forms the E border with Minn. It drains E N.D. and flows N to Lake Winnipeg. The Drift Plains, with fertile glacial deposits and many lakes, roll W some 70mi in the S and 200mi in the N to the Missouri escarpment. The Missouri Plateau, part of the Great Plains, covers the SW of the state. The Missouri R enters N.D. from Montana in the W and flows SE via the huge Garrison hydroelectric dam and reservoir to S.D. Near the W border lie the spectacularly eroded badlands. The continental climate has temperatures averaging 70°F in the summer and 10°F in winter. The rain (only 20in in the E and 14in in the W), falls mostly in the growing season. Only 1% of the land is forested.

People. The people are nearly all native-born, of European descent. Less than 25% of the total population live in urban areas. The largest cities are Fargo, Grand Forks, Bismarck and Minot. Lutherans and Roman Catholics are the largest religious groups.

Economy. A major part of North Dakota's economy is based on agriculture. Wheat, grown in all 53 counties, is by far the most important crop, followed by flax, barley, rye, potatoes and oats. Earnings from livestock products of the W are second to those from wheat. Oil (discovered 1951 in the NW) and lignite (the US's largest deposits, in the SW) are the chief minerals exploited. Natural gas and uranium are also mined. Tourism and manufacturing (food processing and oil refining) roughly equal mineral exploitation in value.

History. The state was part of the 1803 LOUISIANA PURCHASE. Even after the LEWIS AND CLARK expedition, few homesteaders settled there until the arrival of railroads in the 1870s and the 1881 defeat of the SIOUX chief SITTING BULL. Friction between farmers and grain monopolies led to the forming of the NONPARTISAN LEAGUE in 1915. WWII brought recovery from the drought, dust storms and depression of the 1930s. The manufacturing sector remains modest, while agriculture has gradually consolidated, with farms now averaging more than 1,000 acres. The enlargement of farms, and the accompanying mechanization of farm work, has reduced the already sparse population of North Dakota's rural areas—a trend that is expected to continue. The local economy benefited from the building in the 1960s and 1970s of air bases and missile sites in the state. In 1988 the state's already fragile farm economy was badly hurt by the worst drought since 1955; more than 3.5 million acres of farmland were damaged by wind erosion. In presidential elections 1968–88, North Dakota voted consistently Republican.

NORTHEAST PASSAGE, sea passage linking the Atlantic and Pacific oceans. It passes N of the Eurasian mainland along the Arctic coast of Norway and the USSR. Adolf Nordenskjöld, the Swedish explorer, was first to sail its length, 1878–79, although its exploration dates from the 15th century. Explorers of the area have included Willem Barents, Henry Hudson, James Cook and Vitus Bering.

NORTHERN IRELAND. See IRELAND, NORTHERN.

NORTHERN LIGHTS. See AURORA.

NORTHERN MARIANA ISLANDS, a commonwealth of the US, comprises 16 islands in the W Pacific.

Land. Although GUAM is geographically part of the Marianas, it has long been administered separately and is not considered part of the group. Of these volcanic and coral islands, only six are inhabited, with more than 85% of the population living on Saipan, the largest island and administrative center, which is followed in size by Tinian and Rota. The total area is 298sq mi.

People. About 75% of the people are descended from the Chamorro, the indigenous Micronesian group of the Marianas; most of the others are Caroline Islanders. Roman Catholicism predominates. The population numbers 16,758. Saipan is the capital.

Economy. The US government is the largest employer, as Saipan continues to serve as the administrative center of the Trust Territory of the Pacific Islands despite the Northern Marianas' separate status. The leading crops include coconuts, sugar, coffee, taro, breadfruit and yams; cattle raising is of growing importance. Tourism is also a leading source of income.

History. After Spain assumed control of the Marianas in 1565 all the Chamorros were moved to Guam; the other islands remained uninhabited until some resettlement began during the late 17th century. In 1898 control of Guam passed to the US. The other Marianas were sold to Germany, then occupied in 1914 by Japan, which developed commercial sugar plantations. US forces captured the islands in 1944 after heavy fighting, and they subsequently became part of the US Trust Territory of the Pacific Islands. Northern Mariana voters approved separate status as a commonwealth in 1975. The islands ceased to be part of the Trust Territory in 1986 and its residents became US citizens.

NORTHERN RHODESIA. See ZAMBIA.

NORTH PACIFIC CURRENT, ocean current fed by the JAPAN CURRENT, heading E from the region of Japan to the US west coast, where it becomes the Alaska Current and California Current. (See also OCEAN CURRENTS.)

NORTH POLE, the point on the earth's surface some 750km N of Greenland through which passes the earth's axis of rotation. It does not coincide with the earth's N Magnetic Pole, which is over 1,000km away (see EARTH). The Pole lies roughly at the center of the Arctic Ocean, which is permanently ice-covered, and experiences days and nights each of six months. It was first reached by Robert E. Peary (April 6, 1909). (See also CELESTIAL SPHERE; MAGNETISM; SOUTH POLE.)

NORTH SEA, arm of the Atlantic Ocean lying between Britain, Scandinavia and NW Europe, rich in fish, gas and oil. Almost 600mi long, it covers 222,125sq mi with an average depth of 300ft, falling to 2,400ft off Norway. Long a rich commercial fishing ground for flatfish and herring, the North Sea since the early 1960s has been prospected by more than 20 international companies for oil and gas. The first productive gas field was found in 1965, 42mi E of Britain's Humber estuary. Since then, major gas and oil deposits have been found off the Dutch, Norwegian and Scottish coasts.

NORTH STAR. See POLARIS.

NORTHUMBRIA, English Anglo-Saxon kingdom of the 6th–9th centuries, extending from the Mersey and Humber rivers on the S to the Firth of Forth in the N. It became the cultural center of England due to the civilizing work of monks (see BEDE, SAINT). The kingdom was overrun by the Danes, the N remnant becoming subject to Wessex.

NORTHWEST ORDINANCE, ordinance adopted by Congress in 1787, which established the government of the NORTHWEST TERRITORY and provided a form for future territories to follow. It stated that Congress should appoint a territorial governor, a secretary and three judges. Once the territory had a voting population of 5,000 it could elect a legislature and send a non-voting representative to Congress. When the population reached 60,000, the territory could seek full admission to the Union. It barred slavery, guaranteed basic rights and encouraged education.

NORTHWEST PASSAGE, inland water route from the E coast of North America to the Pacific, and thus to the Orient. This was unsuccessfully sought for centuries. John CABOT explored the coast around Newfoundland in 1497 thinking it was China; Henry HUDSON sailed as far as Hudson Bay and beyond (1609–11); William Baffin and Robert Bylot found a way between Baffin Island and Greenland. Explorations opened up important new lands, but not until Robert McClure's expedition of 1850–54 was the existence of a passage weaving among the Arctic islands proved. The first complete journey was made when Roald AMUNDSEN sailed W from Baffin Bay through Lancaster Sound, 1903–06. The entire Atlantic–Pacific crossing was not accomplished until the US Navy navigated the Northwest Passage by atomic submarine in 1958.

NORTHWEST TERRITORIES, federally administered region of Canada comprising the mainland N of 60°N between Yukon Territory and Hudson Bay, the islands in Hudson, James and Ungava Bays and all islands N of the mainland.

Name of territory: The Northwest Territories (Districts: Mackenzie, Keewatin, Franklin)

Joined Confederation: 1870 (as Rupert's Land, purchased by Canada from the Hudson's Bay Company; present boundaries set in 1912)

Capital: Yellowknife (since 1967; previously Ottawa)

Area: 1,304,903sq mi

Population (including districts): 51,384

Land. It is an immense, low-lying, thinly-populated area: about half the region lies within the Arctic Circle. Two-thirds of the mainland is covered by the Mackenzie R, its tributaries and by lakes such as the Great Bear and Great Slave. The Mackenzie Mts to the W rise to 9,000ft. There is permanent sea ice N of Melville Island, where the winter temperature sinks to −40°F compared with −18°F in the Mackenzie delta.

People. More than 60% of the population are Inuit (Eskimo) and Indians. Most of the Indians and whites are in the Mackenzie District, which is the most developed area and where the largest towns, Yellowknife, the capital, Fort Smith and Inuvik are.

Economy. The principal industries are fishing, mining and trapping. Of these, mining is the most important, the territory producing all of Canada's tungsten, 44% of its lead, 26% of its zinc, 20% of its silver and 13% of its gold. Uranium exploration is continuing. Oil and gas exploration boomed in the 1970s, with the Beaufort Sea project and oil drilling in the Arctic Islands. Farming in the region is still in an experimental stage.

History. Early explorers include Sir Martin FROBISHER, who reached Baffin Island in 1576, and the trader-explorers of the HUDSON'S BAY COMPANY. Sir Alexander MACKENZIE explored in the 1780s. The region was part of a larger area sold to Canada in 1870 by the Hudson's Bay Company. The Territories' boundaries were established in 1912.

NORTHWEST TERRITORY, region between the Ohio and Mississippi rivers, extending N around the Great Lakes. It was the first national territory of the US, eventually forming Ohio (1803), Ind. (1816), Ill. (1818), Mich. (1837), Wis. (1848) and part of Minn. Won by Britain from the French who explored it in the 1600s, it was ceded to the US by the Treaty of Paris 1783, and its future determined by the Ordinance of 1787 (see NORTHWEST ORDINANCE). The first governor, Arthur St. Clair, was appointed, and settlement soon followed. Indians were defeated by General Anthony WAYNE at the battle of Fallen Timbers, and most of their lands taken by the Treaty of Greenville, 1795. Ind., Mich. and Ill. became territories prior to statehood.

NORWAY, European constitutional monarchy in the W Scandinavian peninsula between the Atlantic, on the W, and Sweden. Finland and the USSR are to the NE. Norwegian territory also includes thousands of coastal islands.

Official name: Kingdom of Norway
Capital: Oslo
Area: 125,050sq mi
Population: 4,180,000
Languages: Norwegian; Lappish, Finnish spoken in the North
Religion: Evangelical Lutheran
Monetary unit(s): 1 krone = 100 øre
Land. It is a rugged, mountainous land, famous for its beautiful fjords, with many deep lakes and swift rivers. The mountains, covering over half of Norway, extend nearly its whole length. It has the highest peak in Scandinavia (Galdhøpiggen, 8,098ft) and the largest ice field in mainland Europe, the Jostedalsbreen. Because of its maritime situation and on-shore winds, the climate is mild. Rainfall varies from 100in on the coast to 40in inland. Pine and spruce forests cover about a fourth of Norway.
People. The majority of the population are of the fair Nordic type, but there are some Lapps and Finns in the N. The S is the most heavily populated, the largest towns there being Oslo, the capital, Bergen and Stavanger and in the N, Trondheim. There are two official languages, Nynorsk and Bokmål, (see NORWEGIAN LANGUAGE), although the Lapps in the N have their own UGRO-FINNIC speech.
Economy. Norway's natural resources are sparse: mineral deposits are minimal, and less than 3% of the land is under cultivation. Norway has developed a thriving economy since WWII by restricting imports and promoting industrialization, particularly in aluminum production, chemicals, textiles, machinery, paints and furniture. Agriculture, based on farms of 25 acres or less, gives high yields of oats, hay, barley, potatoes, fruits and vegetables. Livestock is raised in the mountains. Forestry and fishing, particularly of mackerel and cod, are very important industries. The Norwegian

merchant fleet is one of the world's largest. Oil and gas from the North Sea fields are the most important sources of foreign exchange.
History. Norway's separate history began about 800 AD when the VIKINGS began to raid European coastal towns. Until the 14th century there was a long series of civil wars. In 1397 Norway merged with Denmark (becoming a Danish province in 1536) and in 1814 with Sweden. In 1905 it became an independent constitutional monarchy under HAAKON VII. Germany occupied all of Norway 1940–45. Norway is a member of the NORTH ATLANTIC TREATY ORGANIZATION and of the EUROPEAN FREE TRADE ASSOCIATION, but refused in a 1972 referendum to join the EUROPEAN ECONOMIC COMMUNITY. In 1981 Gro Harlem Brundtland became the country's first woman prime minister. Although her party lost an election that same year, she was returned to office in 1986.
NORWEGIAN CURRENT, or Norway Current, a continuation of the GULF STREAM passing NE along the NW Norwegian coast. (See also OCEAN CURRENTS.)
NORWEGIAN LANGUAGE, language of Norway, developed from the Norse and influenced by union with Denmark 1397–1814. There are two official versions: *Nynorsk* or *Landsmål*, based on native dialects, and *Bokmål* or *Riksmål*, a Dano-Norwegian used by writers and the press. Differences between them are diminishing.
NOSE, the midline organ of the face, concerned with the perception of smell and the preparation of the air stream for respiration. It is a cartilage extension of the facial bones with two external openings or nostrils. These pass into the nasal cavities, which are separated by a septum and contain turbinates which increase the mucous membrane surface and direct the air flow. The chemoreceptors for smell lie mainly in the roof of the nasal cavities, but fine nerve fibers throughout the nose contribute both to tactile sensation and smell.
NOSTRADAMUS (1503–1566), French astrologer, famed for his prophecies, published in verse and entitled *Centuries* (1555). His real name was Michel de Nostredame, and he was court physician to Charles IX. His prediction of Henry II's death four years ahead made his name, though his prophecies were generally vague.
NOTATION, method of writing down music formalized between the 10th and 18th centuries into a system of stave

notation, now in general use. It consists of five horizontal lines or staves as the framework on which eight notes are written—A, B, C, D, E, F, G (in ascending order of pitch) and thence to A again an octave higher (see also SCALE). Each note's special place on or between the lines depends on its pitch: in the base clef, if low, the treble clef if higher. A middle or alto clef is sometimes used. The KEY of the music is indicated by sharps and flats on the staves next to the clef sign at the beginning of the score. The length of the notes relative to each other is shown by their form. There are commonly seven forms of note from the longest held to the shortest. The beat of the music is shown by dividing the staves by vertical lines into *bars* and marking at the outset how many beats there are to each bar (see also RHYTHM). Other notations are the *tonic sol-fa* in which notes are related to each other, not to the established pitch of the written stave; and *tablature* in which a diagram indicates where to place the fingers on various instruments to obtain notes. New signs for use in ELECTRONIC MUSIC are being invented.

NOTOCHORD, the primitive longitudinal skeletal element characterizing the class Chordata, the first stage in the development of a flexible internal skeleton. All chordates possess a notochord at some time during life. Though replaced by cartilage or bone in the adult VERTEBRATE and absent in the adults of other chordate groups, e.g., tunicates, it is well developed in the embryos or larvae of all these groups, confirming evolutionary relationships within the class.

NOTRE DAME DE PARIS, cathedral church of Paris, on the Ile de la Cité in the Seine R. Begun in 1163, it was finished in 1313 and is one of the finest examples of early Gothic architecture, especially for the rose window of the west facade and the sculptured portals. Some restoration was necessary after the French Revolution. (See also GOTHIC ART AND ARCHITECTURE.)

NOVA, a star which over a short period (usually a few days) increases in brightness by 100 to 1,000,000 times. This is thought to be due to the star undergoing a partial explosion: that is to say, part of the star erupts, throwing out material at a speed greater than the escape velocity of the star. The initial brightness fades quite rapidly, though it is usually some years before the star returns to its previous luminosity, having lost about 0.0001 of its mass. At that time a rapidly expanding planetary NEBULA may be seen to surround the star. Recurrent novae are stars which go nova at irregular periods of a few decades. Dwarf novae are

subdwarf stars which go nova every few weeks or months. Novae have been observed in other galaxies besides the MILKY WAY. (See also SUPERNOVA.)

NOVALIS, the pen name of Friederich Leopold, Freiherr von Hardenberg (1772–1801), German poet. His works, notably the myth-romance *Heinrich von Ofterdingen* (1802), influenced later European exponents of ROMANTICISM. He attempted to unite poetry, philosophy and science into an allegory of the world.

NOVA SCOTIA, one of the four original provinces of the Dominion of Canada; it includes Cape Breton Island to the NE. It is also one of the Maritime Provinces on the Atlantic seaboard. Linked to the mainland by the narrow Chignecto Isthmus, it is bounded on the N by New Brunswick and is separated from Prince Edward Island on the NW by Northumberland Strait; otherwise it is bounded by the Bay of Fundy and the Atlantic Ocean.

Name of province: Nova Scotia
Joined Confederation: July 1st, 1867
Capital: Halifax
Area: 21,425sq mi
Population: 865,442
Land. Nova Scotia has an area of 21,425sq mi (1,023sq mi of inland water). There are many short rivers, the longest being the Mersey and St. Mary's (both run about 72mi). The Atlantic Upland is a distinctive feature of the landscape and is divided into five areas separated by fertile valleys and lowlands, notably the Annapolis Valley, famous for its apple orchards. The province generally has a cool climate, intensified by the cold Labrador Current; average temperatures are 24°F in Jan. with heavy snowfall and 65°F in July. Rainfall ranges from an average of 55in in the E to 40in in the W. About 84% of the province is forested; wildlife and birdlife are abundant.
People. Most Nova Scotians are of British or French ancestry, but important minority groups are descendants of Irish and German immigrants and of former West Indian slaves, and about 3,000 Micmac Indians live in the province. About 16% of the land is occupied by small farms averaging around 190 acres, and while 6% of the people live on farms, 35% live in nonfarm rural areas. In coastal areas farming is combined with fishing, and inland it is combined with dairying.
Economy. Lumbering is an important industry in the province, which has numerous other natural resources including coal, gypsum, barite and natural gas. There are rich fisheries and farmlands. Apples are the chief fruit crop; hay, oats, barley, wheat

and vegetables are grown in substantial quantities. Manufacturing is diversified and chiefly concentrated around Halifax (which is also the main port), Sydney, Pictou County and on the Strait of Canso. The leading industries are coal mining, petroleum refining, food and beverage processing, transportation–equipment manufacturing and paper production. Coal, lead, zinc, gypsum, salt, sand and gravel are mined. Recent finds suggest the possibility of offshore oil and natural gas deposits. The most important exports are from lumber mills and from fish-processing and agricultural processing plants. The province has turned from imported coal to native coal and is assessing hydroelectric potential. Tidal power may be its key to meeting future energy needs.

History. Leif ERICSON may have visited Nova Scotia as early as 1000 AD, but it is certain that John CABOT discovered Cape Breton Island in 1497. Canada's first permanent settlement was established in 1605 on the site of Annapolis Royal. In the 17th century the area was contested by the British and the French, but after the FRENCH AND INDIAN WARS it was gained by England. Nova Scotia became the first Canadian colony to gain responsible government in 1848, and in 1867 it formed the original Dominion with Quebec, Ontario and New Brunswick. Since then, Nova Scotia has been concerned with establishing its rightful place in the nation, alongside much larger and richer provinces. Much economic and social progress has been achieved, aided by large-scale industrial development around the Sydney area and construction of a deep-water port on the Strait of Canso. The provincial government has been in the hands of the Progressive Conservative Party for most of the 20th century.

NOVAYA ZEMLYA, a group of islands (including two main ones) in NW USSR in the Arctic Ocean between the Barents Sea on the W and the Kara Sea on the E. Used as a Soviet nuclear testing site, the islands have a small native population which fishes and hunts in the S tundra areas.

NOVEL, a work of prose fiction (usually over 60,000 words long) generally portraying in one or more plot lines the interrelationship of a number of characters. Rudimentary forms of novel appear to have existed in ancient Egypt as long ago as 2000 BC; the Greek *Daphnis and Cloë* and the eclectic *The Golden Ass* by the Roman APULEIUS are the earliest known in the West. The Japanese *Tale of Genji* (c1000) by Lady MURASAKI is a sophisticated and startlingly modern love novel. The modern European novel developed out of the Italian Renaissance *novella* form, typified by BOCCACCIO's *Decameron*. RABELAIS' *Gargantua and Pantagruel* (1532–52) and CERVANTES' *Don Quixote* (1605–15) are prototypes of the European novel. In English literature the form was established in the works of DEFOE, and in the mid-18th century with the contrasting work of RICHARDSON and FIELDING. The 19th-century novel was a major form of mass entertainment throughout Europe and the Americas; it was also a forum for the discussion of politics and special problems, and so recorded them for posterity. The novels of GOETHE, Sir Walter SCOTT and others inspired much Romantic drama and music. In France George SAND and Victor HUGO were among the first post-Revolutionary novelists of standing. In the US the novel contributed to the development of a national identity and the defining of a specifically American experience.

Giants of the form in both stature and output emerged in the 19th century such as BALZAC, DICKENS, George ELIOT, TOLSTOY, DOSTOYEVSKY and Herman MELVILLE who exploited the vast possibilities of the form. From the time of FLAUBERT there has been less emphasis on "story-telling"; the novel came to be seen as an intense psychological artifact with aesthetic aspirations akin to poetry. Henry JAMES, Marcel PROUST, James JOYCE, Virginia WOOLF and others have elaborated this emphasis, often at the expense of any easy accessibility. Writers such as Thomas HARDY and D. H. LAWRENCE, and HEMINGWAY and other US writers have, in their different styles, favored a more direct and passionate approach, while writers like ORWELL, KOESTLER and even SOLZHENITSYN emphasized political stance and almost documentary reportage. Despite contrary prophecies the novel's vitality appears to remain undiminished today.

NOVEMBER, the 11th month of the year, the ninth in the original Roman CALENDAR; its name derives from the Latin *novem*, nine. It now has 30 days, and the 4th Thurs. is THANKSGIVING DAY in the US.

NOVENA, in Roman Catholicism, prayers either in private or at public religious services on nine days, in petition for divine favor or intercession for a special event. The novena is often in a particular saint's honor. One famous public novena is that of the Feast of the IMMACULATE CONCEPTION (Nov. 30–Dec. 8). Novenas recall the nine days the apostles spent in prayer awaiting the gift of the Holy Spirit. The practice was probably borrowed from pagan Rome, where a nine-day mourning period was held after an emperor's death.

NOVGOROD, historic city and capital of Novgorod oblast, NW USSR. Located on the Volkhov R, it long formed a trade link between the Baltic and the Orient. The city was important as an ancient Varangian capital, a cultural and a commercial center, and was later a trading center of the HANSEATIC LEAGUE. The kremlin (citadel) includes a number of 15th-century churches and watchtowers. Pop 220,000.

NOVOTNÝ, Antonín (1904–1975), Czechoslovak Communist Party leader, president of Czechoslovakia, 1957–68. As a Stalinist and supporter of Moscow, Novotný fell from power in Jan. 1968 after years of economic stagnation and political unrest. He was succeeded by a liberal regime led by Alexander DUBČEK and others.

NOYES, Alfred (1880–1958), English poet, a traditionalist known for his popular, vigorous rhythmic ballads like *The Highwayman* and patriotic sea poems such as *Drake* (1908). His other works include the blank verse *Torch-Bearers* (1922–30) praising scientific progress, and *Collected Poems* (1947).

NOYES, John Humphrey (1811–1886), US religious reformer, founder of the ONEIDA COMMUNITY, 1848. He preached so-called "perfectionism" in his communities at Putney, Vt. and Oneida, N.Y., but "Bible Communism" and a form of polygamy aroused opposition and he fled to Canada in 1879.

NUBIA, ancient region of NE Africa, now mostly in the republic of Sudan, along both banks of the Nile R from Aswan nearly to Khartoum. Called Cush by the Egyptians, Nubia overran Upper Egypt in 750 BC and Lower Egypt in 721 BC. The Assyrians drove the Cushites out about 667 BC. Around 200 AD the Nobatae, a Negro people, settled in Nubia, and by 600 AD their powerful kingdom was Christianized; eventually it disintegrated under Muslim pressure in the later 14th century.

NUCLEAR ENERGY, energy released from an atomic nucleus during a nuclear reaction in which the atomic number (see ATOM), mass number or RADIOACTIVITY of the nucleus changes. The term atomic energy, also used for this energy, which is produced in large amounts by NUCLEAR REACTORS and nuclear weapons, is not strictly appropriate, since nuclear reactions do not involve the orbital ELECTRONS of the atom. Nuclear energy arises from the special forces (about a million times stronger than chemical bonds) that hold the

PROTONS and NEUTRONS together in the small volume of the atomic nucleus (see NUCLEAR PHYSICS). Lighter nuclei have roughly equal numbers of protons and neutrons, but heavier elements are only stable with a neutron:proton ratio of about 1.5:1. If one could overcome the electrostatic repulsion between protons and assemble them with neutrons to form a stable nucleus, its mass would be less than that of the constituent particles by the *mass defect,* Δm, of the nucleus, and the *binding energy,* BE, given by BE=Δmc^2 (where c is the speed of light), would be released. Because c is large, a vast amount of energy would be released, even for a very small value of the mass defect. The binding energy (equivalent to the work needed to split up the nucleus into separate protons and neutrons) is always positive— nuclei are always more stable than their separate nucleons (protons or neutrons)— but is greatest for nuclei of medium mass, decreasing slightly for lighter and heavier elements. The low binding energy of very light elements means that energy can be released by combining e.g., two deuterium nuclei to form a helium nucleus. This combination of two protons and two neutrons is particularly stable (see FUSION, NUCLEAR). For heavy elements the decrease in binding energy indicates that the more positively charged the nucleus becomes, the less stable it is, even though it contains more neutrons than protons. This sets a limit on the number of elements and also explains why the nuclear-fission process, in which a heavy nucleus splits into two or more medium-mass nuclei with higher total binding energy, releases energy.

The first nuclear reaction was performed experimentally in 1919 by RUTHERFORD, who exposed NITROGEN to alpha particles (helium nuclei) from the radioactive element RADIUM, producing OXYGEN and HYDROGEN. But, because nuclei are positively charged and repel each other, it was found difficult to bring them close enough together to react with each other. The discovery of the neutron in 1932 helped overcome this problem. Being uncharged and heavy (on the atomic scale), the neutron has high energy even when moving slowly and is good for initiating nuclear reactions. By 1939 many nuclear reactions had been studied, but none seemed feasible as an energy source. Although energy might be released in a reaction, more energy was expended in producing particles able to initiate the reaction than could be recovered from it. Moreover, only a small fraction of the reagent particles would react as desired, and any product particles would have little chance of reacting again. A breakthrough came around 1939, when the violent reaction of the heavy element uranium on bombardment with slow neutrons (first observed experimentally by FERMI in 1934) was successfully interpreted. It was realized that this was an example of nuclear fission, the slow neutrons delivering enough energy to the small proportion of U^{235} nuclei in natural uranium to split them into two parts. This split does not always occur in the same way, and many radioactive fission products are formed, but each fission is accompanied by the release of much energy and two or three neutrons (these because the lighter nuclei of the fission products have a lower neutron:proton ratio than uranium). These neutrons were the key to the large-scale production of nuclear energy; they could make the uranium "burn" by setting up a chain reaction. Even allowing for the loss of some neutrons, sufficient are left to produce other fissions, each producing two or more neutrons, and so on, leading to an explosive release of energy. The first controlled chain reaction took place in Chicago in 1942, using pure graphite as a moderator to slow down neutrons and natural uranium as fuel. Rods of neutron-absorbing material kept the reaction under control by limiting the number of neutrons available to cause fissions. The possibilities of nuclear energy as a weapon were exploited at once, and WWII ended shortly after the United States dropped two ATOMIC BOMBS on Japan. Later, more powerful bombs exploiting nuclear fusion were developed. An increasing quantity of man's energy is produced in NUCLEAR REACTORS from nuclear fission, although the earth's known natural supplies of fissionable material are surprisingly limited. Moreover, because the fission products from these reactors are radioactive with long HALF-LIVES, atomic waste disposal is a major environmental problem. At present the waste is stored in concrete vaults lined with stainless steel, though the possibilities of converting waste to an insoluble glass are being explored. Disposal in space, in geologically stable parts of the earth's crust or by chemical conversion to safer materials are ideas for the future. Nuclear fusion seems to offer much better long-term prospects for energy supply, although fusion reactors have not yet progressed beyond the research stage.

NUCLEAR PHYSICS, the study of the physical properties and mathematical treatment of the atomic nucleus and SUBATOMIC PARTICLES. The subject was born when RUTHERFORD postulated the existence of the nucleus in 1911. The nature of the short-range exchange forces which hold together the nucleus, acting between positively charged protons and neutral neutrons is still uncertain. Experimental data from MASS SPECTROSCOPY and scattering experiments have enabled various partially successful theoretical models to be devised. Despite the special techniques required to produce nuclear reactions, the subject has rapidly grown with the technical exploitation of NUCLEAR ENERGY.

NUCLEAR REACTOR, device containing sufficient fissionable material, arranged so that a controlled chain reaction may be started up and maintained in it. Many types of reactor exist; all produce NEUTRONS, gamma rays, radioactive fission products and HEAT, but normally use is made of only one of these. Neutrons may be used in nuclear research or for producing useful RADIOISOTOPES. Gamma rays are dangerous to man and must be shielded against, but have some uses. The fragments produced by fission of a heavy nucleus have a large amount of energy, and the heat they produce may be used for carrying out a variety of high-temperature processes or for heating a working fluid (such as steam) to operate a TURBINE and produce ELECTRICITY. This is the function of most commercial reactors, although a number are used to power ships and submarines, since a small amount of nuclear fuel gives these a very long range. In an electricity-generating reactor, the fuel is normally uranium pellets surrounded by a moderator and the cooling fluid is water or liquid sodium (which in turn heats the turbine fluid). There is much insulation and radiation shielding. The fuel is expensive but produces several thousand times the heat of the same weight of coal. After some time it must be replaced (although only partly consumed) because of the build-up of neutron-absorbing fission products. This replacement, and the reprocessing of the radioactive products, needs costly remote handling equipment. New fast breeder reactors with no moderator avoid this problem, since as well as producing fission of U^{235}, they convert nonfissionable U^{238} to plutonium which also undergoes fission chain reactions. Research is continuing into more efficient reactors as power sources for the future.

Questions relating to nuclear safety and the disposal of nuclear wastes (see WASTE DISPOSAL) are still unresolved, however. The 1979 accident at Pennsylvania's Three Mile Island reactor—involving a partial fuel-core meltdown and the release of radioactive gases into the atmosphere—

brought the issue of nuclear safety into the public arena. Since that year, studies of nuclear plants have revealed that in some, machinery is rusting; in a few, the steel shell that surrounds the fuel core has been made brittle by radiation; and in some cases, welds are not strong enough to withstand thermal shock, the rapid cooling that occurs when fuel cores are replaced.

NUCLEAR REGULATORY COMMISSION (NRC), independent US government agency set up in 1975 to take on all the licensing and regulatory functions formerly assigned to the Atomic Energy Commission. Its purpose is to ensure that the civilian uses of nuclear materials and facilities are conducted in a manner consistent with the public health and safety, environmental quality, national security, and the antitrust laws. The major share of the commission's efforts is focused on regulating the use of nuclear energy to generate electric power.

NUCLEAR WINTER, hypothetical consequence of nuclear war. Some scientists have theorized that hundreds of nuclear explosions would throw so much debris into the atmosphere as to block out sunlight for months, thereby causing lower temperatures, crop destruction, and mass starvation. The theory has been tested in large forest fires, where heavy, persistent smoke has in fact reduced sunlight and lowered temperatures in the affected areas. Other scientists, however, believe that the debris from a nuclear war would be washed out of the atmosphere in a relatively short time.

NUCLEIC ACIDS, the vital chemical constituents of living things; a class of complex threadlike molecules comprising two main types: deoxyribonucleic acid (DNA) and ribonucleic acid (RNA). DNA is found almost exclusively in the nucleus of the living CELL, where it forms the chief material of the CHROMOSOMES. It is the DNA molecule's ability to duplicate itself (replicate) that makes cell reproduction possible; and it is DNA, by directing protein synthesis, that controls HEREDITY in all organisms other than certain VIRUSES which contain only RNA. RNA performs several important tasks connected with protein synthesis; it is found throughout the cell.

In both DNA and RNA the backbone of the molecule is a chain of alternate phosphate and sugar groups. To each sugar group is bonded one or other of four nitrogenous side groups, which are either purines or pyrimidines. Each unit consisting of a side group, a sugar and a phosphate, is called a nucleotide. DNA differs chemically from RNA in that its sugar group has one less oxygen atom (hence the prefix "deoxy-"), and one of its side groups, thymine, is replaced in RNA by uracil. DNA molecules are usually very much longer than RNA and may contain a million or so phosphate-sugar links.

It is the sequence in which the side groups are arranged along the DNA molecule that constitutes stored genetic information and so makes the difference between one inherited characteristic and another. This information, in the form of coded instructions for the synthesis of particular protein molecules, is carried outside the cell nucleus by molecules of "messenger RNA," each incorporating a side-group sequence determined by DNA. Floating freely outside the nucleus are AMINO ACIDS, the "building blocks" of proteins, and molecules of another, smaller kind of RNA, "transfer RNA." Each of these RNA molecules is able to capture an amino acid molecule of a particular type and locate it in its proper place in a sequence dictated by messenger RNA.

The DNA molecule has not one but two sugar-phosphate chains twisted around each other to form a double helix. Linking the chains rather like the rungs of a ladder are the side groups, each interlocking with its appropriate opposite number, for a particular side group can be partnered by a side group of only one other kind. The molecule replicates by splitting down the middle, whereupon the side groups of each half bond with the appropriate side groups of free phosphate-sugar units to form a pair of identical DNA molecules. The elucidation of DNA structure, one of the greatest advances of 20th-century biology, is chiefly associated with the work of the Nobel Prize-winners James WATSON, Francis CRICK and Maurice WILKINS.

NUCLEUS, Atomic. See ATOM; SUBATOMIC PARTICLES.

NULLIFICATION, in US history, an act by which a state suspends a federal law within its borders. An extreme interpretation of STATES' RIGHTS, the tactic was particularly used by southern states to protect their minority status. First raised in the KENTUCKY AND VIRGINIA RESOLUTIONS of 1798, the doctrine was forcibly urged by John C. CALHOUN, who argued that the state of S.C. could nullify the so-called "Tariff of Abominations," passed in 1828. When another protective tariff passed in 1832, S.C. declared it null and void, threatening secession if coerced. President Jackson and Congress were ready to enforce the law by military action, but a compromise tariff was passed before the state's nullification order came into effect. The doctrine died when the South lost the Civil War.

NUMBER, an expression of quantity. In everyday terms, numbers are usually used with units: e.g., "three meters" (or 3m); "6.5893 kilograms" (or 6.5893kg).

NUMBERS, the fourth book of the PENTATEUCH, so called because it records two censuses of the Israelites. It narrates their wanderings in the wilderness until they reached Canaan.

NUMISMATICS, the study of coins, including their origin, history, use, mythology and manufacture. A coin is a medium of exchange, usually made in metal and issued by government authority. In its widest sense, numismatics includes a study of medals, tokens, counters and earliest money forms as well as the coinage of all countries from earliest times to the present.

NUN, a woman member of a religious order who devotes her life to religious service. In Roman Catholic canon law, a nun is one who has taken solemn vows of poverty, chastity and obedience; some orders are devoted to prayer and contemplation. Nuns are called sisters, and the term is specifically used of Roman Catholic nuns under "simple vows" (which allow retention of property).

NUNCIO, a permanent diplomatic representative of the ROMAN CATHOLIC CHURCH to a nation or government who acts as a link between the nation's church and papal headquarters in Rome. The post corresponds to and often has the same status as a secular ambassador.

NUREMBERG, historic city of Bavaria, S West Germany, located on the Pegnitz R, 92mi NNW of Munich. Founded in the 11th century, it became a cultural and trading center in the Middle Ages and was the first city to accept the Reformation. Here Hitler staged annual rallies in the 1930s and proclaimed anti-Jewish laws in 1934. Now a major manufacturing city, it was the scene of war crimes trials after WWII. Pop 465,255.

NUREMBERG TRIALS, a series of WAR CRIMES trials held in Nuremberg, West Germany, 1945–1949, by the victors of WWII—the US, USSR, Great Britain and France. The accused, including von RIBBENTROP, GOERING, HESS and heads of the German armed forces, were tried for three kinds of crime: *Crimes Against Peace* (planning and waging aggressive war); *War Crimes* (murder or mistreatment of civilians or prisoners of war, killing of hostages, plunder of property, wanton destruction of communities, etc.); *Crimes Against Humanity* (extermination or enslavement of any civilian population

before or during a war on political, racial or religious grounds; see GENOCIDE). The trials established new principles in the law of nations, above all that every person is responsible for his own acts.

NUREYEV, Rudolf (1938–   ), Russian virtuoso ballet dancer who sought asylum in the West when touring with the Kirov Ballet in 1961. As guest artist of the Royal Ballet, London, he became famed as a leading classical and modern dancer and for his partnership with Margot FONTEYN. He became director of the Paris Opera Ballet in 1983.

NURMI, Paavo Johannes (1897–1973), Finnish long-distance runner who won a total of nine gold medals in three Olympics (1920, 1924, 1928).

NURSERY SCHOOLS, preschool care and early education for children from about three to five years old. Nursery schools developed from 19th-century infant-care programs for factory women's children, launched by Robert OWEN in Great Britain and copied in Europe as the Industrial Revolution spread. Johann PESTALOZZI (1746–1827), Friedrich FROEBEL (1782–1852) and Maria MONTESSORI (1870–1952) all pioneered preschool methods of nursery education. In the US the first nursery schools opened in the 1850s in large cities like New York and Philadelphia to release mothers for factory work. The first American effort to combine early care and educational projects began in 1915 at the U. of Chicago. Nursery schools today have developed programs in which the young learn by experience and through play to understand others, the world around them and themselves.

NURSING, care of the sick, injured or handicapped. Until the 19th century nursing was considered a charitable activity and was administered by religious bodies such as the Sisters of Charity (founded in 1634). In 1860 Florence NIGHTINGALE opened a school in London where experienced nurses and physicians gave instruction in nursing skills. This helped to establish nursing as a career rather than a religious vocation. In the US, nursing schools opened in New York City, Boston and New Haven, Conn., in the 1870s. Until then all nurses had been volunteers. Dorothea DIX was named by the US government as the first superintendent of nurses during the Civil War, after organizing 2,000 women into the Women's Central Association of Relief. By the 1980s there were about 1,350 schools of professional nursing in the US and an estimated 723,000 trained nurses employed.

A nursing career today requires a high school education followed by a choice of three training programs: (1) a diploma after three years' training in hospitals and independent schools in the theory and practice of nursing and in the sciences; (2) a four-year nursing course and general education from a university, leading to a bachelor's degree (B.S.); or (3) a similar but shorter two-year junior college course. After training, graduates must pass a state licensing examination (each state sets its own standards) to obtain registration. "Practical nursing" after one year of study is becoming increasingly popular and valuable, relieving the registered nurse (R.N.), now in short supply, of routine chores. (See also HOSPITAL; MEDICINE.)

NUTRITION, the process by which living organisms take in and utilize nutrients—the substances or foodstuffs required for GROWTH and the maintenance of LIFE. Vital substances that cannot be synthesized within the CELL and must be present in the food are termed "essential nutrients." Organisms such as green plants can derive ENERGY from sunlight and synthesize their nutritional requirements from simple inorganic chemicals present in the soil and air (see PLANT: PHOTOSYNTHESIS). Animals, on the other hand, depend largely on previously synthesized organic materials obtainable only by eating plants or other animals (see ANIMAL; DIGESTIVE SYSTEM; METABOLISM; ECOLOGY).

Human nutrition involves five main groups of nutrients: PROTEINS, FATS, CARBOHYDRATES, VITAMINS and minerals. Proteins, fats and carbohydrates are the body's sources of energy and are required in relatively large amounts. They yield this energy by oxidation in the body cells, and nutritionists measure it in heat units called food CALORIES (properly called kilocalories, each equaling 1,000 gram calories). Carbohydrates (food STARCHES and SUGARS) normally form the most important energy source, contributing nearly half the calories in a well-balanced diet. Cereal products and potatoes are rich in starch; SUCROSE (table sugar) and lactose (present in milk) are two common sugars. Fats, which provide about 40% of the calorie requirement, include butter, edible oils and shortening, and are present in such foods as eggs, fish, meat and nuts. Fats consist largely of fatty acids (carboxylic acids), which divide into two main classes: saturated and unsaturated. Certain fatty acids are essential nutrients; but if there is too much saturated fatty acid in the diet, an excess of CHOLESTEROL may accumulate in the blood. Proteins supply the remaining energy needs, but their real importance lies in the fact that the body tissues, which are largely composed of protein, need certain essential AMINO ACIDS, found in protein foods, for growth and renewal. Protein-rich foods include meat, fish, eggs, cereals, peas and beans. Too little protein in the diet results in malnutritional diseases such as KWASHIORKOR.

Minerals (inorganic elements) and vitamins (certain complex organic molecules) provide no energy but have numerous indispensable functions. Some minerals are components of body structures. Calcium and phosphorus, for example, are essential to BONES and TEETH. Iron in the BLOOD is vital for the transport of oxygen to the tissues: an iron deficiency results in ANEMIA. Milk and milk products are good sources of calcium and phosphorus; liver, red meat and egg yolk, of iron. Other important minerals, normally well supplied in the Western diet, include chlorine, iodine, magnesium, potassium, sodium and sulfur. Vitamins, which are present in small quantities in most foods, are intimately associated with the action of ENZYMES in the body cells, and particular vitamin deficiencies accordingly impair certain of the body's synthetic or metabolic processes. A chronic lack of vitamin A, for example, leads to a hardening and drying of the skin and can result in irreversible damage to the conjunctiva and cornea of the eye. BERIBERI is caused by a vitamin B_1 deficiency, SCURVY by a vitamin C deficiency; RICKETS by a lack of vitamin D.

Despite the fact that the nutritionists now understand the basic requirements of a healthy diet, the difficulty of applying their knowledge world-wide is immense. About two-thirds of the world's population remain severely undernourished and subject to deficiency diseases. Even in the richer countries malnutrition occurs, generally due to an ill-chosen rather than impoverished diet. In the US, the Food and Nutrition Board of the National Academy of Sciences Research Council publishes a table of recommended daily nutrient allowances.

NYASALAND. See MALAWI.

NYE, Gerald Prentice (1892–1971), Republican US senator from North Dakota 1925–45. He chaired committees that investigated the TEAPOT DOME scandal (1926) and the munitions industry (1934–36). During the 1930s he was a leading Senate isolationist.

NYERERE, Julius Kambarage (1921–), founder and first president of the East African state of Tanzania. He led

Tanganyika to independence (1961) and united it with Zanzibar, forming Tanzania (1964). A supporter of nonalignment, he nonetheless accepted aid from communist China. He espoused belief in a one-party socialist democracy. His military intervention helped overthrow Ugandan dictator Amin.

NYLON, group of POLYMERS containing amide groups recurring in a chain. The commonest nylon is made by condensation of adipic acid and hexamethylene diamine. Nylon is chemically inert, heat-resistant, tough and very strong, and is extruded and drawn to make SYNTHETIC FIBERS, or cast and molded into bearings, gears, zippers etc.

15th letter and fourth vowel of the English ALPHABET. It began as the Semitic *'ayin* (eye), and the Greek *omicron*, and became the 14th letter of the Roman alphabet. It also represents the number zero, and the element oxygen.

OAHU, third-largest island (608sq mi) of Hawaii, containing Honolulu (the state capital), the naval base at Pearl Harbor and 80% of Hawaii's population. A fertile valley growing pineapples and sugarcane is flanked by coastal mountain ranges. Pop 817,000.

OAKLEY, Annie (1860–1926), US entertainer, born Phoebe Anne Oakley Mozee. Known as "Little Sure Shot" (she was only 5ft tall), she was a sharpshooter star of BUFFALO BILL'S Wild West Show, together with her husband Frank Butler.

OAK RIDGE, city in E Tenn., 17mi W of Knoxville. The site was chosen in 1942 as the WWII headquarters of the atomic energy program (the MANHATTAN PROJECT) because of its isolation and easy access to necessary resources. It is still a major research center, and houses the American Museum of Atomic Energy. Pop 27,662.

OAKS, trees and shrubs of the genus *Quercus,* which are native to the N Hemisphere. Oaks have cut or lobed leaves; some are evergreen, and the fruit is the acorn. Oaks produce valuable lumber which has great strength and durability. Important white oak species are *Quercus alba, Q. macrocarpa, Q. robur* and *Q. sessiliflora;* important red oaks are *Q. rubra, Q. velutina* and *Q. palustris.* The cork oak (*Q. suber*) is the source of CORK. Family: Fagaccceae.

OAS. See ORGANIZATION OF AMERICAN STATES.

OATES, Joyce Carol (1938–   ), prolific US novelist, short story writer, poet, playwright and critic whose work often deals with insanity, violence and other nightmarish aspects of society. Among her many books are the novels *A Garden of Earthly Delights* (1967), *Them* (1969, National Book Award 1970), and *You Must Remember This* (1987).

OATES, Titus (1649–1705), English conspirator who in 1678 claimed to have discovered a Roman Catholic plot against Charles II—known as the Popish Plot. No such plot existed, but his story set off a wave of persecution in which some 35 persons were executed. Exposed and imprisoned in 1685, he was freed and pensioned (1689) after the GLORIOUS REVOLUTION.

OATS, cereal plants from the genus *Avena.* Oats are cultivated in cool, damp climates in the N Hemisphere. The grain is rich in starch and protein and is mainly used as a livestock feed, but some is processed for human consumption. Chief producers are the US, USSR and Canada, although production is declining. Family: Graminae.

OBADIAH (or Abdias), Book of, shortest book of the Old Testament, fourth book of the Minor Prophets. Probably written in the 6th century BC, its 21 verses foretell the triumph of Israel over its rival Edom. Nothing is known of Obadiah himself.

OBELISK, four-sided pillar tapering to a pyramidal top. Pairs of these, often as much as 105ft high, were erected in front of ancient Egyptian temples, carved with hieroglyphs for decorative, religious and commemorative purposes. CLEOPATRA'S NEEDLES, in London and New York, dating from around 1500 BC, are notable examples.

OBERAMMERGAU, village in the Bavarian Alps of West Germany, famous for its Passion Play. Every 10 years inhabitants of the village reenact the suffering, death and resurrection of Christ, in fulfillment of a vow made by the villagers in 1633 during a plague. Pop 5,000.

OBESITY, the condition of a subject's having excessive weight for his height, build and age. It is common in Western society, overfeeding in infancy being a possible cause. Excess ADIPOSE TISSUE is found in subcutaneous tissue and the ABDOMEN. Obesity predisposes to or is associated with numerous DISEASES including ARTERIO-SCLEROSIS and high blood pressure; here premature DEATH is usual. Strict diet is essential for cure.

OBOE, soprano WIND INSTRUMENT consisting of a double-reed mouthpiece at the end of a conically-bored tube. It is controlled by keys and finger holes. It was developed in 17th-century France, where it was called the *hautbois* (high wood), whence oboe. An orchestral instrument, it has also had important solo music written for it by composers from Purcell onwards.

OBOTE, Milton (1925–   ), president of Uganda (1980–   ). The first prime minister of independent Uganda (1962), Obote made himself president under a new, centralizing constitution (1966). In 1971 he was overthrown by Gen. Idi Amin. When Amin was in turn overthrown by an invasion of Tanzanian troops and Ugandan exiles in 1979, Obote was reelected president of the destitute country.

OBREGÓN, Álvaro (1880–1928), president of Mexico from 1920 to 1924. A planter, he joined Venustiano Carranza in overthrowing President HUERTA in 1914. He subsequently served in Carranza's government, but led the revolt against him in 1920. As president, Obregón promoted important economic and educational reforms. Four years after leaving office he was elected to another term, but was assassinated by a religious fanatic before taking office.

OBSCENITY. See PORNOGRAPHY AND OBSCENITY LAWS.

OBSERVATORY, in astronomy, a site at which observations of the sky are made. The first observatories were set up by ancient civilizations, long before the invention of the telescope. These observatories consisted of structures that indicated the position of objects in the sky at certain dates and times. The observatories acted as calendars and timekeepers. The ancient English monument called Stonehenge is thought to have been such an observatory. It predicted the occurrence of eclipses, and the times of rising of important objects such as the sun and moon. Observatories in their current meaning came into being only around the 16th century, when the Danish astronomer Tycho Brahe used accurate instruments to measure the precise positions of stars and planets.

Contemporary observatories contain optical or radio telescopes. An optical telescope must be housed in a building to protect the lenses or mirrors from the weather. The building usually has a dome that opens and rotates so that the telescope can always point in the required direction despite the earth's motion. Radio telescopes are like giant dish-shaped radio aerials, and are not usually housed in a building.

Many large countries have national observatories which provide precise time signals. In the United States, this task is performed by the Naval Observatory, Washington, D.C. In England, the Royal Greenwich Observatory provides Greenwich Mean Time—the standard time reference used throughout the world.

OBSTETRICS, the care of women during PREGNANCY, delivery and the puerperium, a branch of MEDICINE and SURGERY usually linked with GYNECOLOGY. Antenatal care and the avoidance or control of risk factors for both mother and baby—ANEMIA, toxemia, high blood pressure, DIABETES, VENEREAL DISEASE, frequent miscarriage, etc.—have greatly contributed to the reduction of maternal and fetal deaths. The monitoring and control of labor and BIRTH, with early recognition of complications; induction of labor and the prevention of post-partum HEMORRHAGE with oxytocin; safe forceps delivery and CESARIAN SECTION, and improved anesthetics are important factors in obstetric safety. Asepsis has made PUERPERAL FEVER a rarity.

O'CASEY, Sean (1880–1964), Irish playwright whose sardonic dramas depict the effects of poverty and war on the Irish. His early plays, such as *Juno and the Paycock* (1924), are the most highly regarded. His later works were written in self-imposed exile due to hostility both from theater managements and from Irish nationalists who objected to his unglamorous portrayal of the independence movement.

OCCAM'S RAZOR. See OCKHAM, WILLIAM OF.

OCCUPATIONAL SAFETY AND HEALTH ADMINISTRATION (OSHA), agency within the US Department of Labor established in 1970 to develop occupational safety and health standards, issue regulations, conduct inspections to determine compliance with those regulations, and issue citations and propose penalties for noncompliance.

OCEAN CURRENTS, large-scale permanent or semipermanent movements of water at or beneath the surface of the OCEANS. Currents may be divided into those caused by winds and those caused by differences in DENSITY of seawater. In the former case, FRICTION between the prevailing wind and the water surface causes horizontal motion, and this motion is both modified by and in part transferred to deeper layers by further friction. Density variations may result from temperature differences, differing salinities, etc. The direction of flow of all currents is affected by the CORIOLIS EFFECT. Best known, perhaps, are the GULF STREAM and HUMBOLDT CURRENT.

OCEANIA, vast section of the Pacific Ocean, stretching roughly from Hawaii to New Zealand and from New Guinea to Easter Island, divided into three broad cultural areas: MELANESIA in the SW, MICRONESIA in the NW and POLYNESIA in the E. The area has islands ranging from large masses of ancient rock to minute coral atolls—many of volcanic origin—and the vegetation varies from lush jungle to scanty palm trees. The Pacific Islands were probably peopled from SE Asia, though HEYERDAHL has shown the possibility of influences from South America. The native islanders live mainly by fishing and farming; their basic diet is vegetable, but some pigs and poultry are kept. First European contact was made by MAGELLAN in 1519, but the earliest comprehensive exploration of the area was that of Captain James COOK in the 18th century. Many of the islands were colonized, first by Britain and France and later by the US and Japan. They brought trade and missionaries, but also new diseases which wiped out thousands. The influence of Western culture upon the fragile island societies was generally destructive. Many of the islands are now independent.

OCEANIC LANGUAGES include some 200 aboriginal languages of Australia, about 500 Papuan languages (spoken mostly in New Guinea), and more than 500 MALAYO-POLYNESIAN LANGUAGES.

OCEANS. The oceans cover some 71% of the earth's surface and comprise about 97% of the water of the planet. They provide man with food, chemicals, minerals and transportation; by acting as a reservoir of solar heat energy, they ameliorate the effects of seasonal and diurnal temperature extremes for much of the world. With the atmosphere, they largely determine the world's CLIMATE (see also HYDROLOGIC CYCLE).

Oceanography is the study of all aspects of, and phenomena associated with, the oceans and seas. Most modern maps of the sea floor are compiled by use of echo sounders (see also SONAR), the vessel's position at sea being accurately determined by RADAR or otherwise. Water sampling, in order to determine, for example, salinity and oxygen content, is also important. Sea-floor sampling, to determine the composition of the sea floor, is carried out by use of dredges, grabs, etc., and especially by use of hollow DRILLS which bring up cores of rock.

OCEAN CURRENTS can be studied by use of buoys, drift bottles, etc., and often simply by accurate determinations of the different positions of a ship allowed to drift. Further information about the sea bottom can be obtained by direct observation (see BATHYSCAPHE) or by study of the deflections of seismic waves (see EARTHQUAKE).

Oceanographers generally regard the world's oceans as a single, large ocean. Geographically, however, it is useful to divide this into smaller units: the Atlantic, Pacific, Indian, Arctic and Antarctic (or Southern) oceans (though the Arctic is often considered as part of the Atlantic, the Antarctic as part of the Atlantic, Pacific and Indian). Of these, the Pacific is by far the largest and, on average, the deepest. However, the Atlantic has by far the longest coastline: its many bays and inlets, ideal for natural harbors, have profoundly affected W civilization's history.

OCEAN WAVES, undulations of the ocean surface, generally the result of the action of wind on the water surface. At sea there is no overall translational movement of the water particles: they move up and forward with the crest, down and backward with the trough, describing a vertical circle. Near the shore, FRICTION with the bottom causes increased wave height, and the wave breaks against the land. Waves can thus cause substantial coastal EROSION. (See also TSUNAMI.)

OCELOT, a small, beautifully marked wildcat of forests from the southwestern US to Paraguay. Although the young are taken as pets and the fur is very valuable, the ocelot is quite abundant. Ocelots feed on small animals, occasionally turning to livestock.

OCHS, Adolph Simon (1858–1935), US newspaper publisher largely responsible for creating the prestige of the *New York Times.* He became the paper's manager in 1896, adopting the slogan "All the news that's fit to print."

OCKHAM or **OCCAM, William of** (c1285–1349), English scholar who formulated the principle now known as **Occam's Razor:** "Entities must not unnecessarily be multiplied." This principle, interpreted roughly as "the simplest theory that fits the facts corresponds most closely to reality," has many applications throughout science.

O'CONNELL, Daniel (1775–1847), Irish statesman, called "the Liberator," who led the fight for Catholic emancipation. He founded the Catholic Association (1823) and after his election (1828) to Parliament refused to take his seat until public opinion precipitated the CATHOLIC EMANCIPATION ACT. He contested the 1801 act uniting Ireland with Britain.

O'CONNOR, Flannery (Mary Flannery O'Connor; 1925–1964), US fiction writer noted for her brilliant style and her grotesque vision of life in the South. Her novels include *Wise Blood* (1952).

O'CONNOR, Frank (1903–1966), Irish short-story writer whose works are admired for their oral quality and portrayals of Irish life. His many collections include *Guests of the Nation* (1931), *Bones of Contention and Other Stories* (1936) and *A Set of Variations* (1969). O'Connor also published poetry, criticism and translations of old Irish literature from the Gaelic.

O'CONNOR, Sandra Day (1930–   ), first woman to serve on the US Supreme Court. A lawyer, she was assistant attorney general of Arizona and a state senator. She then served as a trial judge and on the state court of appeals. In 1981 President Reagan nominated her to the Supreme Court and she was confirmed unanimously by the Senate.

OCTAVE, in music, the interval between two pitches of which one has twice the frequency of the other. In the diatonic scale these are the first and the eighth tones. Because of its unique consonance, the octave gives an aural impression of a single tone duplicated.

OCTOBER, the tenth month of the year. It contains 31 days. Its name comes from the Latin *octo* (eight), since it was the eighth month in the Roman calendar.

OCTOBRISTS, Russian political party formed in 1905 by Alexander Ivanovich Guchkov (1862–1935). It was so called because its members (mainly moderates of the upper middle class) supported the new constitution established by the October Manifesto of that year, promising a wider franchise and a parliament with legislative power.

OCTOPUS, a cephalopod MOLLUSK whose most striking feature is the possession of eight tentacle-like "arms" which surround the mouth. Behind the beaked head is a sac-like body containing the viscera. Octopods can alter body form and outline and also change color, thus have excellent protective camouflage. In addition, a black pigment, sepia, can be ejected into the water from a special sac, forming a smoke screen which foils predators.

ODE, a stately lyric poem usually expressing praise. It is often addressed to the person, object or concept (such as "Joy" or "Autumn") being celebrated. It originated in the ancient Greek choral songs. PINDAR used a tripartite structure in his odes: strophe, antistrophe (both in the same meter) and epode (in a different meter). HORACE's odes were in stanzaic form. Poets of the 19th century, such as KEATS and SHELLEY, wrote odes with irregular structures.

ODER-NEISSE LINE, since 1945, the border between East Germany and Poland, formed by the Oder River and its tributary the Neisse.

ODESSA, city and port in the Ukrainian SSR, USSR, on the Black Sea. It is a major transportation, industrial, commercial and cultural center. It was the scene of an abortive workers' revolt in 1905. Pop 1,126,000.

ODETS, Clifford (1906–1963), US playwright and screenwriter famous for his social-protest dramas about ordinary people caught in the Depression. He was a leading figure in the Group Theater in New York City. His works include *Awake and Sing!* (1935), *Waiting for Lefty* (1935) and *Golden Boy* (1937).

ODIN, in Germanic mythology, the chief of the gods, also known as Wotan or Woden (whose name gave us Wednesday). He was the god of war, poetry, wisdom, learning and magic. He had a single all-seeing eye. He made the world from the body of the giant Ymir, man from an ash tree and woman from an elm.

ODOACER (c435–493), Germanic chief who overthrew the last of the West Roman emperors in 476 and was proclaimed king of Italy. The East Roman Emperor Zeno sent Theodoric the Great to depose him. After a long war, Odoacer was treacherously killed by Theodoric.

ODYSSEUS, or Ulysses, legendary hero of ancient Greece, son and successor of King Laertes of Ithaca and husband of Penelope. He was the crafty counselor of the TROJAN WAR (described in Homer's ILIAD). After 10 years' adventures (subject of Homer's ODYSSEY) he returned home disguised as a beggar and, with his son Telemachus, killed the suitors beleaguering his wife.

ODYSSEY, famous ancient Greek epic poem ascribed to HOMER, one of the masterpieces of world literature. Its 24 books relate the adventures of ODYSSEUS and his Greek friends after the TROJAN WAR. Rescued from the land of the Lotus-Eaters, they encountered the one-eyed cyclops Polyphemus, the cannibal Laestrygonians and the sorceress Circe. They resisted the Sirens and the perils of Scylla and Charybdis, but Odysseus alone survived shipwreck at Trinacria. For seven years he lingered with the nymph Calypso before he finally reached his home, Ithaca, to be reunited after 20 years with his wife, Penelope.

OEDIPUS, in Greek legend, king of Thebes who was fated to kill his father King Laius and marry his mother Jocasta. Laius, warned by an oracle that he would be killed by his son, abandoned him to die. Oedipus survived and was adopted by the king of Corinth. As a young man he learned his fate from the oracle and fled Corinth, home of his supposed parents. On the road he killed Laius, an apparent stranger. Reaching Thebes, he solved the riddle of the SPHINX and was rewarded with the hand of the widowed Jocasta. He later discovered the truth and blinded himself. His story and that of his daughter Antigone inspired tragedies by SOPHOCLES.

OEDIPUS COMPLEX, in Freudian theory, complex typical of infantile sexuality, comprising mainly UNCONSCIOUS desires to exclude the parent of the same SEX and possess the parent of the opposite sex.

OERSTED, Hans Christian (1777–1851), Danish physicist whose discovery that a magnetized needle can be deflected by an electric current passing through a wire (1820) gave birth to the science of ELECTROMAGNETISM.

O'FAOLAIN, Sean (1900–), Irish short-story writer, novelist and biographer whose works often give an unflattering, yet sympathetic view of everyday Irish life. Among his many works are *Midsummer Night Madness and Other Stories* (1932), the novel *A Nest of Simple Folk* (1933), *The Great O'Neill: A Biography of Hugh O'Neill* (1942) and his autobiography *Vive Moi!* (1964).

OFFA (d. 796), king of MERCIA who brought that kingdom to its greatest extent. He built Offa's Dyke to protect Mercia against the Welsh.

OFFENBACH, Jacques (1819–1880), French composer. He wrote over 100 operettas including the immensely popular *Orpheus in the Underworld* (1858), containing the famous can-can, and *La Belle Hélène* (1864). His masterpiece is considered to be the more serious *Tales of Hoffmann*, first produced in 1881.

OFFICE OF MANAGEMENT AND BUDGET (OMB), established in the executive office of the president in 1970, monitors the organizational structure and management procedures of the executive branch and develops mechanisms to implement government activities. One of its chief functions is to help the president prepare his annual budget and to supervise and control the administration of the budget.

OFFICE OF STRATEGIC SERVICES (OSS), US government agency formed in 1942 to collect and analyze strategic information during WWII. It was dissolved in 1945.

O'FLAHERTY, Liam (1896–1984), Irish novelist known for his realistic stories of ordinary people in trouble, such as *The Black Soul* (1924), *The Informer* (1925) and *The Assassins* (1928).

OGLETHORPE, James Edward (1696–1785), English philanthropist, general and member of parliament who obtained (1732) a charter to found the colony of Georgia. He settled the colony as a refuge for jailed debtors and was governor until he returned to England in 1743.

O'HARA, John Henry (1905–1970), US fiction writer known principally for his vigorous accounts of urban and suburban life in America. His novels include *Appointment in Samarra* (1934), *Butterfield 8* (1935) and *A Rage to Live* (1949).

O. HENRY. See HENRY, O.

O'HIGGINS, family famous in South American history. **Ambrosio O'Higgins** (c1720–1801), born in Ireland and educated in Spain, went to South America and rose to be governor of Chile (1789) and viceroy of Peru (1796). **Bernardo O'Higgins** (1778–1842), his natural son, liberated Chile from Spanish rule and became its dictator (1817). His reforms aroused such opposition that he was exiled to Peru in 1823.

OHIO, N central state of the US. It is bounded N by Mich. and Lake Erie, E by Pa. and W.Va., S by W.Va. and Ky., and W by Ind. The Ohio R forms the Ky. and W.Va. borders.

Land. Ohio has four land regions: the highland area of the Appalachian Plateau in the E; the narrow strip of Great Lakes Plains bordering Lake Erie; the Till Plains in the SW, the easternmost section of the great fertile Midwestern Corn Belt; and a small wedge of the Bluegrass region extending from Ky. into S Ohio. Excellent ports on Lake Erie have made the state a major transportation hub of the Midwest. Ohio's climate is humid continental with an average annual precipitation of 37in.

People. About 80% of Ohio's citizens live in urban areas. The state's largest cities are Cleveland, Columbus, Cincinnati and Toledo.

Economy. Ohio is one of the country's major industrial states. Widely varied manufactures include non-electrical machinery, primary metals, transportation equipment

Name of state: Ohio
Capital: Columbus
Statehood: March 1, 1803 (17th state)
Familiar name: Buckeye State
Area: 41,222sq mi
Population: 10,752,000
Elevation: Highest—1,550ft, Campbell Hill in Logan County. Lowest—433ft, Ohio River in Hamilton County
Motto: "With God, all things are possible"
State flower: Scarlet carnation
State bird: Cardinal
State tree: Buckeye
State song: "Beautiful Ohio"

and fabricated metal products. Ohio leads the nation in the production of tires, machine tools, playing cards, business machines, glassware and other products. Rubber, coal and iron ore are important resources. New deposits of oil and gas were discovered in SE Ohio in the 1960s. Major agricultural products are livestock, cereal crops, fruit and dairy foods. Tourism is also important.

History. The Iroquois were the dominant Indian group in the area when La Salle investigated the Ohio valley in 1669. His voyage formed the basis for French claims to the entire Ohio valley, but English fur traders also frequented the region, and Va. and other seaboard colonies had been granted parts of the Ohio country in their royal charters. Anglo-French rivalry culminated in the last of the FRENCH AND INDIAN WARS, as a result of which England was awarded the territory. After the Revolution the region was included by Congress (1787) in the NORTHWEST TERRITORY. The first permanent settlement was Marietta, founded in 1788. Ohio itself became a territory in 1799 and was the 17th state to enter the Union (1803). Rapid expansion in the 19th century was aided (1825) by the opening of the ERIE CANAL. In the period leading up to the Civil War, Ohio had an active UNDERGROUND RAILROAD. Ohio has contributed seven presidents to the nation. The state's cultural and educational facilities are outstanding, but the state has been plagued in recent years with many of

the environmental, economic and social problems common to other highly industrialized states. Strip mining of coal has scarred much of its landscape, and pollution of Lake Erie poses a serious threat to the many cities that rely on it for water supplies. A long slump in the state's economy has been aggravated by the decline in the nation's auto industry, in which many Ohio firms are involved. Its cities, particularly Cleveland, have suffered eroding tax bases, as middle- and upper-income people move to the suburbs. From 1980 to 1986 the state lost population (-0.4%) for the first time. An influx of new factories, including 30 built by Honda and other Japanese firms, was expected to boost the economy in the 1990s. In presidential elections 1968–88, Ohio voted Republican 1968–72 and 1980–88.

OHIO RIVER, the main eastern tributary of the Mississippi River, which it joins at Cairo, Ill. It is formed at Pittsburgh, Pa., by the junction of the Allegheny and Monongahela rivers and flows generally southwest for about 980mi. Together with its main tributaries, it drains over 203,000sq mi and is navigable throughout.

OHM, Georg Simon (1789–1854), Bavarian-born German physicist who formulated OHM'S LAW. He also contributed to ACOUSTICS, recognizing the ability of the human ear to resolve mixed SOUND into its component pure (sinusoidal-wave) tones.

OHM'S LAW, the statement due to G. S. Ohm in 1827 that the electric potential difference across a conductor is proportional to the current flowing through it, the constant of proportionality being known as the resistance of the conductor. It holds well for most materials and objects, including solutions, provided that the passage of the current does not heat the conductor, but electron tubes and SEMICONDUCTOR devices show a much more complicated behavior.

OIL, any substance that is insoluble in water, soluble in ETHER and greasy to the touch. There are three main groups: mineral oils (see PETROLEUM); fixed vegetable and animal oils (see FATS), and volatile vegetable oils. Oils are classified as fixed or volatile according to the ease with which they vaporize when heated. Mineral oils include GASOLINE and many other fuel oils, heating oils and lubricants. Fixed vegetable oils are usually divided into three subgroups depending on the physical change that occurs when they absorb oxygen: oils such as linseed and tung, which form a hard film, are known as "drying oils"; "semidrying oils," such as cottonseed or soybean oil, thicken considerably but do not harden;

"nondrying oils," such as castor and olive oil, thicken only slightly. Fixed animal oils include the "marine oils," such as cod-liver and whale oil. Fixed animal and vegetable fats such as butterfat and palm oil are often also classified as oils. Examples of volatile vegetable oils, which usually have a very distinct odor and flavor, include such oils as bitter almond, peppermint and turpentine. When dissolved in alcohol, they are called "essences."

OIL PAINTS, in art, ground pigments combined with oil (usually linseed), a stabilizer, a plasticizer and often a drier to ensure uniformity of drying time. In applying such paints, the artist may add more oil or a thinner, usually turpentine. Oil paints were developed during the 1400s and 1500s in response to the needs of the radically innovative Renaissance painters. Because they are so predictable, versatile, and durable, these pigments gradually displaced other media. They remain the most popular painter's colors today.

OIL SHALE, a fine-grained, dark-colored sedimentary rock from which oil suitable for refining can be extracted. The rock contains an organic substance called kerogen, which may be distilled to yield OIL (see also DISTILLATION). Important deposits occur in Wyo., Col. and adjacent states. (See also SEDIMENTARY ROCKS; SHALE.)

OISTRAKH, David Feodorovich (1908–1974), Russian violinist. His brilliant technique and strong emotional interpretation (especially of the romantic composers) brought him worldwide acclaim. PROKOFIEV and SHOSTAKOVICH wrote works for him. His son, Igor (1931–   ), is also a violinist and conductor of world renown.

OJIBWA INDIANS, or Chippewa, one of the largest ALGONQUIN-speaking tribes of North America. They lived as small bands of hunter-gatherers, mainly in woodland areas around Lakes Superior and Huron, and to the west. They fought frequently with the SIOUX, but had little contact with early white settlers. LONGFELLOW's *The Song of Hiawatha* was based on a study of Ojibwa mythology. Today some 60,000 Ojibwas live on US and Canadian reservations.

O'KEEFFE, Georgia (1887–1986), US painter, noted for her delicate, abstract designs incorporating symbolic motifs drawn from observations of nature. She is also known for large symbolic flower paintings such as *Black Iris* (1926). Her paintings were first exhibited in 1916 by Alfred STIEGLITZ, whom she married in 1924.

OKEFENOKEE SWAMP, swamp and wildlife refuge in SE Ga. and NE Fla. Covering over 650sq mi, it is drained by the St. Marys and Suwannee rivers and has densely forested areas, grassy bog savannas, hummock islands, sand bars and large swamp areas of dark water overgrown by heavy brush and trees. The abundant wildlife includes alligators, deer, bears, raccoons and many species of birds and fish.

OKEGHEM, Jean d' (c1420–1495), Flemish Renaissance composer, whose work is noted for rich, sonorous vocal harmony and masterful contrapuntal technique. He was chaplain and composer to the French court and the teacher of JOSQUIN DES PRES and Bunois. Among his surviving works are 14 masses, 10 motets and 20 chansons.

OKINAWA, largest (454sq mi) and most important of the Ryukyu Islands in the W Pacific, about 500mi SW of Japan. The island is part of Japan's Okinawa prefecture and Naha is its capital city. The island is mountainous and jungle-covered in the S, and hilly in the N. It is fertile—sugarcane, sweet potatoes and rice are grown, and there are good fisheries. Captured by the US during WWII, Okinawa was formally returned to Japan in 1972.

OKLAHOMA, state, S central US, bounded to the E by Mo. and Ark., to the S by Tex., to the W by Tex. and N.M. and to the N by Col. and Kans. The state is shaped somewhat like a saucepan, with a 34mi wide "panhandle" extending W 167mi.

Name of state: Oklahoma
Capital: Oklahoma City
Statehood: Nov. 16, 1907 (46th state)
Familiar name: Sooner State
Area: 69,919sq mi
Population: 3,305,000
Elevation: Highest—4,973ft., Black Mesa in Cimarron County. Lowest—287ft, Little River in McCurtain County
Motto: *Labor omnia vincit* ("Labor conquers all things")
State flower: Mistletoe
State bird: Scissortailed flycatcher
State tree: Redbud
State song: "Oklahoma!"

Land. The state's 69,919sq mi show a wide variation of terrain. Plains in the W give way to rolling hills in the central region and mountain ranges in the E; scrubby sagebrush country contrasts with rich forestlands. The highest point in the state, Black Mesa (4,973ft), is in the far NW corner of the state. Over 65% of Okla. is in the Arkansas R basin and the rest is in the Red R drainage area. Numerous lakes, most of them man-made, provide sources of irrigation and hydroelectric power. All of the larger rivers drain into the Mississippi R. Rainfall is light in the W and heavy in the E. Extremes of temperature occur: the midsummer average is about 83°F, but the overall state average is about 40°F. Timber is a major natural resource with forest and good stands of varied hard- and softwood trees. Wildlife is abundant.

People. The population is more than 85% white, and 5% American Indian. About 65% are urban dwellers, and many live in one of the state's two major metropolitan areas, Oklahoma City and Tulsa.

Economy. Originally a farming state, Oklahoma now depends chiefly upon mineral production and manufacturing. It ranks third among the oil- and natural gas-producing states and also has large reserves of coal, zinc, lead, granite, salt, gravel, gypsum and helium. Manufactures are based mainly on local agricultural and mineral production, but also include non-electrical machinery, transportation equipment, aircraft and fabricated metal, stone, glass and clay products. A large proportion of agricultural income is based on livestock. Major crops are wheat, cotton, corn, beans, peanuts, oats, hay and barley.

History. Oklahoma was acquired by the US as part of the LOUISIANA PURCHASE, and in 1834 the land was designated Indian Territory and became a federal dumping ground for many Indian tribes. Homesteading runs and "land lotteries" (1889–1910) brought a rush of settlers. The first major oilfield was opened in 1901; and on Nov. 16, 1907, after a constitution had been ratified by popular vote, Okla. was admitted to the Union. The state was hard hit by the great drought of the 1930s, which turned many farms to dust and forced the farmers to migrate, but its economy expanded and diversified during WWII, providing the basis for relatively slow but solid growth after the war. Oklahoma's population grew 29% between 1970 and 1986. The drop in world oil prices in the late 1980s battered the state's economy, leading to many real estate foreclosures and bank failures. In presidential elections 1968–88, Oklahoma voted consistently Republican.

OKUMA, Shigenobu (1838–1922), Japanese statesman. As foreign minister (1888–89, 1896–97) he secured the elimination of the unequal clauses in Japan's treaties with Western powers. He was premier (1914–16) when Japan entered WWI on the Allied side and seized German-held Kiaochow in China.

OLD AGE, strictly, a chronological division of human life; however, the term also suggests the manifestations and diseases associated with aging. The SKIN becomes wrinkled and thins, largely due to the effect of ULTRAVIOLET RADIATION on collagen; HAIR production may be disordered, causing BALDNESS or graying. BONE alters (osteoporosis) with thinning of texture and susceptibility to FRACTURE, while the disks between the vertebrae shrink with resulting loss of height. Wear and tear of the JOINTS frequently leads to osteoarthritis. ARTERIOSCLEROSIS, which starts in early life, becomes established in the elderly, resulting in STROKE, CORONARY THROMBOSIS and limb GANGRENE. Degenerative disease due to cell loss is especially important in the BRAIN. IMMUNITY may be less effective, leading to more frequent and serious infections (PNEUMONIA), and may account for the increased incidence of CANCER with age. VITAMIN deficiency diseases due to inadequate diet are common. Special social and psychiatric problems arise from the social isolation, decreased mobility and poor health associated with old age. (See also GERIATRICS; MEDICARE; SOCIAL SECURITY.)

OLD CATHOLICS, group of churches which have seceded from the ROMAN CATHOLIC CHURCH. The Jansenist Church of Utrecht separated in 1724, followed after 1870 by churches in Germany, Austria and Switzerland, led by Johann von Döllinger, which would not accept the dogmas of papal infallibility and jurisdiction defined by the First VATICAN COUNCIL. Several smaller Slavic churches later separated. Virtually high Anglican in doctrine and practice, Old Catholics have been in full communion with the Church of England since 1932.

OLD CHURCH SLAVONIC, a language of the Slavic subfamily of the Indo-European family of languages, devised in the 9th century by Greek scholars and saints CYRIL AND METHODIUS; presumed to be the first written Slavic language. Its descendant, Church Slavonic, was used as a literary language (from 1100 AD to c1700 AD) and is still the most widely used liturgical language in the Eastern Orthodox churches. (See also SLAVONIC LANGUAGES.)

OLDENBARNEVELDT, Johan van

(1547–1619), Dutch statesman. As advocate of Holland (from 1586), he supported self-government for the burgher towns of the United Provinces, recently liberated from Spain, and encouraged commerce during the early years of the Dutch East India Co. He came into conflict with MAURICE OF NASSAU and the nobles over the role of the STATES-GENERAL and in the Calvinist-Remonstrants controversy. Oldenbarneveldt was arrested on unfounded treason charges and executed.

OLDENBURG, Claes (1929–), Swedish-born US artist best known for "soft" sculptures that satirize America. His hamburgers, ice cream cones, telephones and bathroom fixtures are usually larger than life.

OLD ENGLISH. See ENGLISH.

OLD FAITHFUL, name given to an intermittent hot spring, or geyser, a tourist attraction at YELLOWSTONE NATIONAL PARK, Wyo., which at intervals of 66min, varying at times from 33 to 148min, erupts for about 5min up to heights of 150ft.

OLDS, Ransom Eli (1864–1950), pioneer US automobile engineer and manufacturer. He produced the Oldsmobile and Reo cars, and is generally considered the founder of the US automobile industry. His first powered vehicle was a steam-driven three-wheeler (1886). He established the Olds Motor Vehicle Company in 1899, marketed a 3hp Oldsmobile in 1901—the first commercially successful American car—and established the Reo Motor Car Company in 1904.

OLD TESTAMENT, or the Hebrew Bible, the first part of the Christian Bible (for list of books see BIBLE), describing God's covenant with Israel. The Jewish CANON was fixed by the 1st century AD and is followed by the Protestant churches; the Greek SEPTUAGINT version, containing also the APOCRYPHA, was followed by the VULGATE and hence by the Roman Catholic Church. The standard MASORETIC TEXT of the Hebrew Old Testament is now largely confirmed for most books by the DEAD SEA SCROLLS (almost 1000 years earlier). The Old Testament is traditionally divided into three parts: the Law (see PENTATEUCH), the Prophets—the Former Prophets being the earlier historical books, the Latter being the three Major Prophets and the Minor Prophets—and the Writings, including the later historical books, Daniel and the poetic and "wisdom" books. Christianity regards the Old Testament as an inspired record of God's dealings with His people in preparation for the coming of Christ, containing in embryo much New Testament teaching.

OLDUVAI GORGE, a 300ft-deep canyon in N Tanzania, gouged through lake sediment, volcanic ash and other material deposited over the past few million years. In Bed I, the lowest of five layers into which the walls are divided, the anthropologists Louis and Mary LEAKEY found early fossil remains of PREHISTORIC MAN.

OLIGARCHY, a form of government rule, or control of a state or some other organization by a small elite group. The term often carries an implication that rule by an oligarchy is essentially corrupt and dominated by self-interest.

OLIGOCENE, the third epoch of the TERTIARY, extending from about 40 to 25 million years ago. (See also GEOLOGY.)

OLIVARES, Gaspar de Guzmán, Conde-Duque de (1587–1645), Spanish statesman. A favorite of PHILIP IV, he ruled Spain 1621–43 and attempted to abolish court corruption. He overrode the rights of autonomous regions, provoking revolts of the Portuguese and Catalans in 1640.

OLIVE, *Olea europaea,* an evergreen tree growing in Mediterranean climates and one of the world's oldest cultivated crops. Its unripe fruits are pickled, treated with lye solution to remove the bitter taste and stored in brine. When left to ripen they turn black and are pressed for their oil. Family: Oleaceae.

OLIVES, Mount of, ridge of hills E of Jerusalem. On the W slope is the Garden of GETHSEMANE where Jesus went with his disciples after the Last Supper. It is also the site of Christ's Ascension.

OLIVIER, Laurence Kerr, Baron Olivier of Brighton (1907–1989), English actor, producer and director. Immensely versatile and brilliant in classical as well as modern roles, such as John OSBORNE's *The Entertainer,* he made and acted in such films as *Henry V* (1944) and *Hamlet* (1948), which won an Academy Award. He was the director of Britain's National Theatre 1962–73.

OLLIVIER, Emile (1825–1913), French statesman, proponent of the "Liberal Empire" under NAPOLEON III. Premier Jan.-Aug. 1870, he began to transform the empire into a parliamentary regime, but the outbreak of the Franco-Prussian War ended his work.

OLMEC INDIANS, a people of the SE coastal lowlands of ancient Mexico. Their culture, earliest of the major Mexican cultures, flourished from between 1000 BC and 500 BC until c1100 AD. They were skilled in artistic work with stone and produced huge sculptured basalt heads, beautiful jewelry, fine jade, white ware and mosaics. They knew how to record time and had a hieroglyphic form of writing. Their culture may have influenced the ZAPOTECS and TOLTECS.

OLMSTED or **OLMSTEAD, Frederick Law** (1822–1903), American landscape architect and writer. With Calvert Vaux he planned Central Park, New York, and himself designed other parks in Philadelphia, Brooklyn, Montreal and Chicago. In the 1850s he was well known for his perceptive travel books on the South.

OLNEY, Richard (1835–1917), US attorney general (1893–95) and secretary of state (1895–97) under President Cleveland. He is remembered for calling out troops to deal with workers involved in the PULLMAN STRIKE in 1894. He announced the controversial "Olney Corollary" to the Monroe Doctrine in 1895, declaring US willingness to interfere in the internal affairs of South America.

OLSON, Floyd Bjornstjerne (1891–1936), US politician, Farmer-Labor governor of Minnesota from 1931. He won national attention for his vigorous efforts to combat the Depression, including a moratorium on farm foreclosures, relief for the unemployed, and support for labor in a number of strikes.

OLYMPIC GAMES, the oldest international sporting contest traditionally for amateurs, held every four years. The games probably developed from the ancient Greek athletic contests in honor of a god or dead hero. Events such as boxing, wrestling, long jump, discus, javelin, distance running and chariot racing were added to the original sole event, a 210yd race, held in 776 BC at Olympia in honor of ZEUS. The games at Olympia lasted seven days. They lost popularity, largely through the growth of cheating, and were abolished by Emperor Theodosius I in 394 AD. In 1896 the first modern Olympic Games were held in Athens, organized by Pierre de Coubertin. Since then the games have been held in different cities, once every four years except 1916, 1940 and 1944. In 1924 the Winter Olympics were started at Chamonix, France. The 1972 games in Munich were marred by the terrorist massacre of 11 Israelis. In 1976, 21 African countries withdrew, protesting New Zealand's rugby tour of South Africa. In 1980, 62 of the more than 125 nations invited boycotted the Summer Games in Moscow, protesting the Russian invasion of Afghanistan. The 1984 games were boycotted by the USSR and most Eastern bloc countries. The 1988 games were held in Calgary, Alberta,

Canada (winter) and Seoul, South Korea (summer). The 1992 games will be played at Albertville, France (winter) and Barcelona, Spain (summer).

OLYMPIC NATIONAL PARK, scenic region established in 1938, which includes the Olympic Mts. There are glaciers, lakes, temperate rain forest and wildlife sanctuaries.

OLYMPUS, Mount, highest mountain in Greece, rises 9,570ft at the E end of the 25mi range along the Thessaly-Macedonia border. The summit is snowcapped for most of the year. The ancient Greeks believed it to be the home of Zeus and most other gods (the Olympians).

OM, Sanskrit sacred syllable (see MANTRA) signifying the primordial sound and divine energy; in HINDUISM it often represents the Trimurti, and in Buddhism the Absolute. It is commonly chanted repetitively to purify and concentrate the mind for meditation. LAMAISM often uses the mantra *om mani padme hum* (ah! the jewel is indeed in the lotus!).

OMAHA INDIANS, a Siouan-speaking North American tribe. They originally lived in the Ohio valley area, but moved with the Ponca Indians to the Missouri R region and then to what is now NE Neb. They were an agricultural and hunting tribe and lived mainly in earth lodges. Today 1,000–1,500 live on the Nebraska reservation.

Official name: The Sultanate of Oman
Capital: Muscat
Area: 120,000sq mi
Population: 1,331,000
Languages: Arabic, English
Religions: Muslim
Monetary unit(s): 1 rial Omani = 1,000 baizas

OMAN, formerly **Muscat and Oman,** an independent sultanate along the SE Arabian peninsula on the Arabian Sea. One area of the country, a peninsula separated from the rest of Oman by the United Arab Emirates, juts into the strategic Strait of Hormuz. Much of Oman is barren, with little rainfall, and temperatures reaching 130°F. Dates are grown on the Batinah coastal plain, NW of Muscat (the capital), and the Dhofar Province is noted for sugarcane and cattle. Grains and fruits are grown around Jebel Akhdar. Oil was discovered in 1964, and over 200 million barrels are produced yearly. Oman has a population that is mostly Arab, but includes blacks, Indians and Pakistanis. In 1970 the reformist Sultan Qabus bin Said ousted his father and has become a prominent moderate in Middle Eastern affairs. A 1976 ceasefire largely ended guerrilla warfare in the S. Closely associated with Britain since 1798, Oman signed a defense pact with the US in 1980 and established diplomatic relations with the USSR in 1985.

OMAR KHAYYAM, 11th-century Persian poet, astronomer and mathematician. His epic poem *Rubaiyat*, dealing with nature and love, is known in the West through its translation by Edward FitzGerald.

OMAYYADS, or **Umayyads,** a dynasty of caliphs who ruled the Muslim empire from Damascus, 661–750 AD. They were essentially Arab in character and relied heavily upon the Syrian army. The Omayyad Caliphate is sometimes known as the Arab Kingdom. They were replaced by the ABBASIDS of Baghdad. The last Omayyad fled to Spain and set up the Caliphate of Cordoba in 756.

OMBUDSMAN, official appointed by the legislature to investigate complaints by citizens against government officials or agencies. The office originated in Sweden in 1809 and since 1955 has been adopted by Denmark, New Zealand and Britain. In the US ombudsmen operate in some states as well as on the private level.

ONATE, Juan de (c1549–1628), Spanish explorer of the Southwest. He colonized what is now New Mexico from 1598. He led expeditions to the Wichita area of present-day Kansas (1601) and to the Colorado R and Gulf of California (1605).

ONEIDA COMMUNITY, a religious commune founded by J. H. NOYES in 1848 near Oneida, N.Y. The group shared both possessions and partners and thought of themselves as a "family" of God. They set up successful businesses in silver and steel products. The flourishing community was made a joint stock company in 1881 and social experiments were ended.

ONEIDA INDIANS, smallest of the original five nations of the IROQUOIS confederacy. They lived in present-day central N.Y. In the American Revolution they sided with the colonists. About 3,000 remain.

O'NEILL, Eugene (Gladstone) (1888–1953), arguably the US's greatest playwright, winner of the 1936 Nobel Prize for Literature. Son of a popular actor, after trying the sea, journalism and gold prospecting he started to write plays during a convalescence from tuberculosis and was initially involved in early off-Broadway efforts to introduce European seriousness into American theater. Whether expressionistic (*The Emperor Jones*, 1920), naturalistic (*Anna Christie*, 1921), symbolist (*The Hairy Ape*, 1922) or updated Greek tragedy (*Mourning Becomes Electra*, 1931), his large body of work was ambitious in scope and relentlessly tragic (except for the comedy *Ah, Wilderness!*, 1935), and culminated in masterpieces such as *The Iceman Cometh* (1946) and *Long Day's Journey into Night* (1955).

O'NEILL, Margaret "Peggy" (1796–1879), the daughter of a tavern keeper and wife of John Eaton, President JACKSON's secretary of war. The wives of the other cabinet members snubbed her socially, provoking a cabinet crisis in which VAN BUREN replaced CALHOUN as vice-president.

O'NEILL, Thomas P. ("Tip"), Jr. (1912–   ), US politician. A Massachusetts Democrat, he was in the US House of Representatives 1953–87 and was Speaker 1977–87. He wrote *Man of the House* (1987).

ONONDAGA INDIANS, one of the original five nations of the IROQUOIS Confederacy, living in what is now N.Y. Because of their location they played an important role in the confederacy and provided the chairmen. In the 1700s their loyalties were divided between the French and British. About 1,000 now remain in N.Y.

ONTARIO, the richest and most populous province of Canada.
Name of province: Ontario
Joined Confederation: July 1, 1867
Capital: Toronto
Area: 412,582sq mi
Population: 9,042,433
Land. In the N part of Ontario lies the Hudson Bay Lowland, a poorly drained area covered by low forests, tundra and swamps, stretching 100mi to 200mi inland from the coast of Hudson Bay and James Bay. S of this is the Canadian Shield, covering half of Ontario's surface. Nickel, iron, platinum, copper, gold and uranium are among the valuable ores mined there. The Great Lakes Lowland, lying along Lakes Huron, Erie and Ontario, is the site of rich farmland as well as most of the province's industry. There are many rivers

and 250,000 lakes in Ontario, and Ontario has vast resources of hydroelectric power.

People. Between 1970 and 1980 Ontario's population grew by 10%; the fastest growth rates were in the metropolitan areas. Nearly 90% of Ontarians live in the 10% of the province that lies S of the French River and Lake Nipissing, and 80% of the people live in towns. About three-fifths of the people are of British origin, and the second largest ethnic group is the French Canadian population in eastern and northern Ontario. Since WWII over a million European immigrants, including British, Italians, Dutch, Germans and Poles, have settled in Ontario.

Economy. Ontario is responsible for about half of Canada's manufactured goods, a third of its agricultural wealth and a fourth of its mineral production. Metropolitan Toronto is the most important industrial center. There is car manufacturing in Oakville, Oshawa and Windsor, iron and steelmaking in Hamilton, nickel processing in Port Colborne and a petrochemical industry at Sarnia. The SW area of the Great Lakes Lowland is the main field crop region, where hay, tobacco, soybeans, oats, tomatoes and corn are grown. Because of mechanization and specialization, farms have become very productive. Corn is the leading crop. Rich orchards and vineyards lie in the Niagara fruit belt. Beef and dairy cattle are reared in the NE part of the Great Lakes Lowland. The number of beef cattle has doubled since 1965. About two-thirds of farm income is derived from livestock. Ontario provides about 20% of Canada's commercial lumber. The most important wood product is newsprint.

In the 1960s deposits of zinc and copper were found near Porcupine Lake. The Sudbury basin provides more than a third of the world's nickel, 40% of Canada's copper and a large amount of platinum. The Pickering station, opened in 1971, is the world's largest commercial nuclear power facility.

History. In the early 17th century Ontario was explored by Étienne Brûlé and Samuel de CHAMPLAIN. By 1671 the English Hudson's Bay Company had set up a trading post at Moose Factory, and N Ontario became the scene of Anglo-French rivalry until 1763, at the end of the French and Indian Wars, when French North America was ceded to Britain. In the 1780s many American Loyalists settled in S Ontario. In 1791 Ontario broke from Quebec and became the colony of Upper Canada. After the rebellion of 1837–38, led by W. L. Mackenzie, there were political reforms and in 1840 came reunion with Quebec. The Dominion of CANADA was established in 1867 with Ontario, Quebec, New Brunswick and Nova Scotia as original members. At the end of the 1800s many Ontarians left for richer agricultural lands westward and in the US. The coming of industry and the accessibility of rich mines and lumbering areas in the N led to rapidly increasing prosperity which was accelerated by the opening of the SAINT LAWRENCE SEAWAY in 1959. Long Conservative dominance of the provincial government was ended in 1985 by a Liberal-New Democratic coalition. In 1987 the Liberals won a majority on their own despite favoring bilingualism.

ONTARIO, Lake, the smallest (about 7,600sq mi) and farthest E of the five GREAT LAKES. The lake, bisected by the US-Canadian border, is about 193mi long and up to 53mi wide, with a maximum sounded depth of 802ft. A major link in the GREAT LAKES–SAINT LAWRENCE SEAWAY system, its cargo traffic includes coal, grain, lumber and iron ore. Principal ports are Toronto, Hamilton and Kingston (Ontario), and Oswego and Rochester (N.Y.).

OPAL, cryptocrystalline variety of porous hydrated silica, deposited from aqueous solution in all kinds of rocks, and also formed by replacement of other minerals. Opals are variously colored; the best GEM varieties are translucent, with milky or pearly opalescence and iridescence due to light scattering and interference from internal cracks and cavities. Common opal is used as an abrasive, filler and insulator.

OP ART, abstract art style in which patterns and color values are composed to produce an illusion of movement on the picture-surface. The best-known artists in the style, which developed in the 1960s, are Victor Vasarely and Bridget Riley.

OPEC. See ORGANIZATION OF PETROLEUM EXPORTING COUNTRIES.

OPEN DOOR POLICY, policy of equal commercial rights for all nations involved in an area, usually referring to its enunciation in 1899 and during the BOXER REBELLION by US Secretary of State John Hay in notes to the main powers concerned with China. Its roots lay in the Nanking Treaty after the OPIUM WAR. It was confirmed 1921–22, and ended with the clash with Japan's "New Order" in the 1930s and with WWII.

OPEN SHOP. See RIGHT-TO-WORK LAWS.

OPERA, staged dramatic form in which the text is wholly or partly sung to an instrumental or orchestral accompaniment. It originated in 17th-century Italy, in an attempt to recreate Greek drama; this was combined with the popular semi-musical mystery plays and religious dramas into *dramma per musica* (drama through music), and spread through Europe. Much early opera was a mere excuse for spectacle, but works by MONTEVERDI, LULLY, and PURCELL greatly advanced the art and are again popular today. Dramatic standards had declined by the early 18th century (despite fine works by HANDEL), being caught up in stilted convention. GLUCK sought to avoid this by unifying plot, music and staging into a dramatic whole, while MOZART introduced greater depth of feeling into the music and realism of character on stage. The form was still further enriched by the Romantics, BEETHOVEN and WEBER in Germany and BERLIOZ and BIZET in France. The great Italians BELLINI, DONIZETTI and ROSSINI developed the more stylized bel canto form to which VERDI, in his later operas, gave greater depth and naturalism, a trend carried further in the seminal works and theories of Richard WAGNER. He sought to add a philosophical basis to Gluck's synthesis by creating *Gesamtkunstwerk*, the total work of art, and in his later work made extensive use of leitmotifs, short musical statements representing a character, things or ideas. Much of the music in *Der Ring des Nibelungen* consists of leitmotifs woven together, then developed and varied. Wagner influenced many later composers such as Richard STRAUSS and DEBUSSY. The recent Italian *verismo* (naturalistic) school produced smaller scale, often sensational works: PUCCINI mastered both this and a more epic, fantastic style. Among the greatest 20th-century opera composers are JANÁCEK, BERG and BRITTEN. (See also individual composers, especially BOITO; GOUNOD; MASCAGNI; MEYERBEER; MUSSORGSKY; TCHAIKOVSKY.)

OPHTHALMOLOGY, the branch of MEDICINE and SURGERY concerned with diseases of VISION and the EYE. In infancy, congenital BLINDNESS and STRABISMUS, and in adults, glaucoma, uveitis, CATARACT, retinal detachment and vascular diseases are common, as are ocular manifestations of systemic diseases—hypertension and DIABETES. Disorders of eye movement, lids and TEAR production; impaired color vision; infection, and injury are also seen. Surgery to the lens, cornea (including corneal grafting), eye muscles and lids may be used; and cryosurgery (freezing) or coagulation are also employed in retinal disease.

OPHTHALMOSCOPE, instrument for examining the retina and structures of the inner EYE. A powerful light and lens system,

combined with the cornea and lens of the eye, allows the retina and eye blood vessels to be seen at high magnification. It is a valuable aid to diagnosis in OPHTHALMOLOGY and internal MEDICINE.

OPINION POLL. See POLL, PUBLIC OPINION.

OPIUM, narcotic extract from the immature fruits of the opium poppy, *Papaver somniferum*, which is native to Greece and Asia Minor. The milky juice is refined to a powder which has a sharp, bitter taste. Drugs, some of them drugs of abuse (see DRUG ADDICTION), obtained from opium include the narcotic ANALGESICS, HEROIN, MORPHINE and CODEINE. (Synthetic analogues of these include methadone and pethidine.) Older opium preparations, now rarely used, include laudanum and paregoric. The extraction of opium outside the pharmaceutical industry is strictly controlled in the West.

OPIUM WAR (1839–42), fought in China by the British, the first in a series aimed at opening ports and gaining tariff concessions. The pretext was the burning of 20,000 chests of opium by the Chinese. China had banned the opium trade in 1799, but with the aid of corrupt Chinese officials British merchants still made enormous profits from it. British troops occupied Hong Kong in 1841, and the fall of Chinkiang in 1842 threatened Peking itself. The Treaty of Nanking ceded Hong Kong to Britain and granted British merchants full rights of residence in the ports of Amoy, Canton, Foochow, Ningpo and Shanghai; Britain was to receive over $50 million war indemnity. The US gained trade facilities by the 1844 Treaty of Wanghai. Further hostilities, in which French joined British troops (1856), led to more concessions, notably in the Treaties of Tientsin (1858) to which Britain, France, Russia and the US were parties and which legalized the opium trade, and in 1860, when Kowloon was ceded to Britain and part of Manchuria to Russia.

OPOSSUMS, primitive arboreal MARSUPIALS of the Americas. The name has also been applied to Australian forms but these are now usually distinguished as POSSUMS. Opossums are carnivorous and usually have a prehensile tail. The pouch is developed only in some species, but all have an uneven number of teats, as many as 17 in the Virginian opossum. (The teats of all Australian marsupials are paired.) In size, opossums vary from mouse-like to forms about the size of a domestic cat. Family: Didelphidae.

OPPENHEIMER, Julius Robert

(1904–1967), US physicist whose influence as an educator is still felt today and who headed the MANHATTAN PROJECT, which developed the ATOMIC BOMB. His main aim was the peaceful use of nuclear power (he fought against the construction of the HYDROGEN BOMB but was overruled by Truman in 1949); but, because of his left-wing friendships, was unable to pursue his researches in this direction after being labeled a security risk (1954). He also worked out much of the theory of BLACK HOLES.

OPTICAL FIBER, a fine strand of transparent material, usually high-purity glass coated with protective material, that is able to guide light through it by repeated internal reflection from its surface. The technology of these fibers and their applications is called fiber optics. A bundle of parallel fibers can transmit an image no matter how the bundle is bent, each fiber carrying a dot of light from one end to the corresponding point at the other end. Fiber optics is used in this way in medical instruments to explore the gastrointestinal tract. Optical fibers are coming into use as a substitute for telephone cables, the voice information being converted into pulses of LASER light. Communications are expected to be the major application of fiber optics in the future.

OPTICS, the science of light and vision. Physical optics deal with the nature of LIGHT (see also COLOR; DIFFRACTION; INTERFERENCE; POLARIZED LIGHT; SPECTROSCOPY). Geometrical optics consider the behavior of light in optical instruments (see ABERRATION, OPTICAL; CAMERA; MICROSCOPE; REFLECTION; REFRACTION; SPECTRUM; TELESCOPE). Physiological optics are concerned with vision (see EYE).

OPTOMETRY, measurement of the acuity of VISION and the degree of lens correction required to restore "normal vision" in subjects with refractive errors (MYOPIA, HYPEROPIA, ASTIGMATISM). Its principal instrument is a chart of letters which subtend specific angles to the EYE at a given distance; temporary lenses being used to correct each eye. (See GLASSES.)

ORACLE, in ancient times, the answer by a god or goddess to a human questioner, or the shrine at which the answer was given, usually through a priest or priestess (also called oracles). There were oracles in Egypt and Rome, but the greatest were in Greece: at Delphi, where Apollo spoke through a priestess, the Pythia, and Zeus' oracle at Dodona. Answers, often to important political questions, were obtained direct, or derived from dreams, from signs, such as the rustling of leaves in a sacred tree, and from divination by lot.

ORANGE, citrus fruit obtained from a number of trees and shrubs of the genus *Citrus.* Oranges have been in cultivation since ancient times, but probably originated in tropical regions of Asia. The sweet or China orange (*Citrus sinensis*) and the mandarin orange (*C. reticulata*) are the main species in cultivation; their main uses being as dessert fruit and for making orange drinks. The Seville or sour orange (*C. aurantium*) is mainly used in the preparation of marmalades. Family: Rutaceae.

ORANGE, House of, an important dynasty in the Netherlands since the 16th century. The line has included WILLIAM III of England and, since 1815, the monarchs of the Netherlands, including the present Queen Beatrix.

ORANGEMEN, or Loyal Orange Institution, a Protestant (chiefly Ulster) society, which since the first (1795) lodge has identified with the Protestant ascendancy in Ireland and, more recently, union with Britain. The name is from William of Orange (see also BOYNE, BATTLE OF; WILLIAM III).

ORANGUTAN, *Pongo pygmaeus,* a large, red, anthropoid ape of Sumatra and Borneo. Animals of thick rain forests, they are truly arboreal apes—walking quadrupedally along branches, or bipedally, with the arms holding on above. Occasionally the orangutan brachiates for short distances. They can move along the ground, but rarely descend from the trees. Orangutans are vegetarians, feeding mainly on leaves, buds and fruit.

ORATORIANS, Roman Catholic congregation founded c1575 in Rome by St. Philip Neri. Members, organized in autonomous congregations, are secular priests who take no vows. NEWMAN founded oratories in Birmingham (1848) and London (1849). A separate society was founded in 1611 in Paris by Pierre de Bérulle.

ORATORIO, a musical composition for vocal soloists, chorus and orchestra, usually with a religious subject. The form evolved c1600 from medieval sacred drama. Early oratorio composers include SCARLATTI, J. S. BACH and HANDEL, whose *Messiah* is probably the most famous oratorio. Among later oratorio composers are BEETHOVEN, MENDELSSOHN and ELGAR.

ORBIT, the path followed by one celestial body revolving under the influence of gravity (see GRAVITATION) about another. In the SOLAR SYSTEM, the planets orbit the sun, and the moons the planets, in elliptical paths, although Triton's orbit of NEPTUNE is as far as can be determined perfectly circular. The point in the planetary, asteroidal or cometary orbit closest to the sun is called its *perihelion*; the farthest point is termed *aphelion*. In the case of a moon or artificial satellite orbiting a planet or other moon, the corresponding terms are *perigee* and *apogee*. (See also KEPLER'S LAWS.) Celestial objects of similar masses may orbit each other, particularly DOUBLE STARS.

ORCAGNA or **ARCAGNOLO** (c1308–1368), painter, sculptor and architect of Florence, Italy, leading artist in the Byzantine Gothic style. His work includes the Strozzi chapel altarpiece in S. Maria Novella and the Orsanmichele tabernacle, Florence.

ORCHESTRA, the name given to most instrumental groups of more than a few players. The modern orchestra dates from the birth of OPERA c1600. The first great operatic composer, MONTEVERDI, wrote for orchestra, and for some time opera and orchestral music were closely linked. As the VIOLIN family replaced VIOLS, composers like VIVALDI, J. S. BACH and HANDEL began to write purely orchestral music. The SYMPHONY was developed around the same time (1700) from the operatic overture. In the 18th century HAYDN organized the orchestra into four groups: string, woodwind, brass and percussion—a basic pattern that has not altered. With the great 18th- and 19th-century composers, the orchestra came to dominate the musical scene. New and more numerous instruments were introduced, permanent orchestras established, and the art of conducting developed. The 20th century has seen a movement to return to smaller ensembles.

ORCHIDS, plants of the very large family Orchidaceae (15,000–30,000 species) which produce colorful and elaborate flowers. Some species are native to cold and temperate regions, but most occur in tropical, damp climates. Some grow as EPIPHYTES on forest trees. Orchid flowers are specially adapted to insect POLLINATION, some requiring a particular species of insect. Orchids produce minute seeds that are devoid of stored food and thus require the aid of fungi to supply the nourishment needed for germination. Orchids are of little economic importance except as curious ornamental plants; cultivation has developed into an extensive hobby throughout the world. As house plants they should be grown in sunny windows at average house temperatures; they do well in fluorescent-light gardens. The soil should be drenched and then not watered again until almost dry. Propagation is accomplished by planting divisions.

ORDER. See TAXONOMY.

ORDINANCE OF 1787. See NORTHWEST ORDINANCE.

ORDINATION, in the Christian Church, the ceremonial appointment to one of the orders of MINISTRY. The ordination of BISHOPS is usually called consecration. Regarded by the Roman Catholic Church as a SACRAMENT, ordination is performed in Episcopal churches by a bishop (see also APOSTOLIC SUCCESSION), and in Presbyterian churches by the presbytery. The rite includes prayer and the laying on of hands, traditionally in a eucharistic context.

ORDOVICIAN, the second period of the PALEOZOIC, which lasted from about 500 to 440 million years ago and immediately followed the CAMBRIAN. (See GEOLOGY.)

ORE, aggregate of minerals and rocks from which it is commercially worthwhile to extract minerals (usually metals). An ore has three parts: the country rock in which the deposit is found; the gangue, the unwanted ROCKS and minerals of the deposit; and the desired MINERAL itself. MINING techniques depend greatly on the form and position of the deposit.

OREGON, a US state of the Pacific Northwest, bounded by the N by Wash., across the Columbia R., E by Ida., S by Nev. and Cal., and W by the Pacific Ocean. It is known to its millions of visitors for its lofty mountains, deep gorges and fine coastline.

Land. Oregon is divided in two by the Cascade Range of mountains which stretch N-S across the entire state. Between the Coastal Range and the Cascades lies the Willamette Valley, which contains the state's most fertile land and most of its population and industries. This area has a mild and moist marine climate. Most of the land E of the Cascades is part of the Columbia Plateau, occupying two-thirds of Oregon. This area is drier and experiences a greater range of temperatures. Half of Oregon is forested.

People. Two-thirds of Oregon's population live in or around Portland, Eugene and Salem in the Willamette Valley. Oregon's original constitution of 1859 is still in effect, with the amendments of 1902 providing for the initiative and referendum. These two measures, together with direct primaries and procedures for the recall of elected officials, became known as the "Oregon system" and were adopted by many states before WWI.

Name of state: Oregon
Capital: Salem
Statehood: Feb. 14, 1859 (33rd state)
Familiar name: Beaver State
Area: 96,981sq mi
Population: 2,698,000
Elevation: Highest—11,245ft, Mount Hood. Lowest—sea level, Pacific Ocean
Motto: "The Union"
State flower: Oregon grape
State bird: Western meadowlark
State tree: Douglas fir
State song: "Oregon, My Oregon"
Economy. The most important manufactures are wood-processing and food-processing (especially fish canning). Other leading industries are machinery, transportation equipment, and metal processing, in which cheap hydroelectric power is used. Wheat, grown in E Oregon, is the most important crop. Livestock and turkey farming are also of importance. Commercial deposits of natural gas were tapped in 1979 in NW Oregon, and there is a large geothermal potential. Tourism is also of increasing importance to the state's economy.

History. The first American to visit the area (1792) was Captain Robert GRAY. The LEWIS AND CLARK EXPEDITION of 1805–06 to the mouth of the Columbia R reinforced American claims to the region. Although pioneers settled in Oregon from the 1840s (see OREGON TRAIL), development was slow until the coming of the railroad in the 1880s. The first two decades of this century saw the rapid development of the lumbering industry, and the post-WWII period has seen new developments in the metallurgical and electrochemical industries. Despite the state's efforts to control growth, its population increased almost 30% between 1970 and 1986. Oregon's cities have not suffered the same deterioration as older cities in the East, freeing the state to give more emphasis now to conserving its natural resources and protecting the environment. In presidential elections 1968–88, Oregon voted Republican 1968–84 but Democratic in 1988.

OREGON TRAIL, famous pioneer wagon route of 19th-century America between Independence, Mo., on the Missouri, and the Columbia R region of the Pacific Northwest. The 2,000mi trail was most popular in the 1840s, before the beginning of the Californian GOLD RUSH. In that decade at least 10,000 pioneers made the arduous trek from NE Kansas, along the R Platte in Nebraska, to Fort Laramie, Wyoming. From there they crossed the Rockies at South Pass and passed through Snake River country to Fort Vancouver. The journey was recounted in Francis Parkman's classic, *The Oregon Trail* (1849).

ORELLANA, Francisco de (d. c1546), Spanish soldier and explorer. He left Gonzalo Pizarro's South American expedition (c1540) at the Napo R to explore the course of the Amazon R, reaching the Atlantic Ocean in 1541. The great river's name comes from his tales of Indian AMAZONS.

ORFF, Carl (1895–1982), German composer and music teacher. His works are marked by short melodic motifs and strong rhythms from a large and varied percussion section.

ORGAN, a musical instrument in which air is blown into pipes of different shape and size to produce a range of notes. Organ pipes are of two kinds: flue pipes which work like a flute or recorder, and reed pipes which operate on the same principle as a clarinet or oboe. Although organs go back to ancient times, the main developments in organ building took place between the 14th and the 18th centuries. Composers like J. P. Sweelinck (1562–1621) and BUXTEHUDE paved the way for J. S. BACH, the greatest of all composers for the organ. Bach and HANDEL wrote for the baroque organ, a relatively small instrument. In the 19th century many great organs were built, precursors of the huge electric-powered organs built in the 1920s and 1930s in cinemas and theaters. The modern Hammond organ produces its sound electronically. Small electronic organs are now frequently used by pop groups. (See also HARMONIUM.)

ORGANIC CHEMISTRY, major branch of CHEMISTRY comprising the study of CARBON compounds containing hydrogen (simple carbon compounds such as carbon dioxide being usually deemed inorganic). This apparently specialized field is in fact wide and varied, because of carbon's almost unique ability to form linked chains of atoms to any length and complexity; far more organic compounds are known than inorganic. Organic compounds form the basic stuff of living tissue (see also BIOCHEMISTRY), and until the mid-19th century, when organic syntheses were achieved, a "vital force" was thought necessary to make them. The 19th-century development of quantitative ANALYSIS by J. LIEBIG and J. B. A. DUMAS, and of structural theory by S. Cannizzaro and F. A. KEKULÉ, laid the basis for modern organic chemistry. Organic compounds are classified as aliphatic, alicyclic, aromatic and heterocyclic (see HYDROCARBONS), according to the structure of the skeleton of the molecule, and are further subdivided in terms of the functional groups present.

ORGANIZATION FOR ECONOMIC COOPERATION AND DEVELOPMENT (OECD), a consultative organization set up in 1961 to coordinate economic policies and encourage economic growth and world trade. Its 24 members include 19 European countries, the US, Canada, Australia, New Zealand, and Japan.

ORGANIZATION OF AFRICAN UNITY (OAU), an association of the independent African states (excluding South Africa) which aims to promote unity and eradicate colonialism in Africa. Founded in 1963, the OAU has a permanent secretariat in Addis Ababa, Ethiopia, and has had great influence at the United Nations.

ORGANIZATION OF AMERICAN STATES (OAS), an association of 32 republics of the Americas which aims to settle disputes peacefully, to create a collective security system, and to coordinate the work of other intra-American bodies. The OAS was founded in Bogotá, Colombia, in 1948 and has a permanent secretariat in Washington, D.C. Cuba was excluded from membership in 1962.

ORGANIZATION OF PETROLEUM EXPORTING COUNTRIES (OPEC), an association founded in 1960 by Iran, Iraq, Kuwait, Libya, Saudi Arabia and Venezuela. OPEC's membership expanded to include Qatar, Indonesia, United Arab Emirates, Algeria, Nigeria, Ecuador and Gabon, and its power increased dramatically in the 1970s, when many countries in the world became increasingly dependent on its oil to run their economies. In 1973 OPEC quadrupled world oil prices; it tripled them again between 1974 and 1980. In the 1980s, however, OPEC's power to control oil prices declined because of the inability of its members to agree on production limits, the growing number of non-OPEC producers, and the dramatic success of conservation measures in industrial countries.

ORIGEN (c185–c254 AD), one of the foremost radical theologians of the early Christian Church. Born in Alexandria, Egypt, Origen tried to reconcile Greek philosophy with Christian theology in such works as his *De Principiis* and *Contra Celsum*.

ORIGINAL SIN, in Christian theology, the state of sinfulness in which all mankind is born, and which is the root cause of all actual SINS. According to St. PAUL, when Adam disobeyed God (the Fall), the whole human race fell in solidarity with him and inherited his sin and guilt, losing supernatural GRACE and communion with God, and our FREE WILL was made spiritually inoperative. In Catholic theology, original sin is washed away in BAPTISM.

ORINOCO RIVER, great river of Venezuela, N South America, about 1,700mi long. It rises in the Parima highlands of SE Venezuela and eventually flows into the Atlantic Ocean through a 7,000sq mi delta. It is mostly navigable.

ORISKANY, Battle of, fought on Aug. 6, 1777, in central N.Y. during the REVOLUTIONARY WAR. The British and Indians ambushed the Americans, and there were severe losses on both sides.

ORKNEY ISLANDS, group of about 70 islands north of Scotland, of which they are part. Their total area is 376sq mi but fewer than half are inhabited. The climate is mild and the soil fertile. Farming is the chief activity (grains, sheep, cattle, poultry), with some fishing.

ORLANDO, Vittorio Emanuele (1860–1952), Italian statesman, prime minister 1917–19. He led the Italian delegation at the VERSAILLES Peace Conference of 1919–20. Orlando retired from politics with the advent of fascism, but returned after the fall of Mussolini.

ORLÉANS, family name of two branches of the French royal line. The House of Valois-Orléans was founded by Louis, Duke of Orléans (1372–1407), whose grandson ascended the throne (1498) as LOUIS XII. The House of Bourbon-Orléans was founded by Philippe, Duke of Orléans (1640–1701), a brother of king LOUIS XIV. His son, Philippe (1674–1723), was regent of France 1715–23. LOUIS PHILIPPE was the sole member of the House to become king.

ORMANDY, Eugene (1899–1985), Hungarian-born US conductor, a famous interpreter of Romantic works. Trained as a violinist, he became permanent conductor of the Philadelphia Orchestra in 1938.

ORNITHOLOGY, the scientific study of BIRDS. The observation of birds in their natural environment has a long history and is now so popular as to be the most widespread of zoological hobbies.

OROZCO, José Clemente (1883–1949), major Mexican painter, who exploited the fresco technique in his large-scale murals, which express strong social convictions. His most famous works include the fresco *Prometheus* (1930) and a mural *Epic Culture in the New World* (1932–34).

ORPHEUS, in Greek mythology, famous musician of Thrace. Son of the Muse Calliope, he could tame wild beasts with his lyre-playing. After the death of his wife Eurydice, Orpheus sought her in Hades. He was allowed to lead her back to earth providing he did not look back, but he could not resist the temptation, and Eurydice vanished forever. He is said to have been killed by the women followers of DIONYSUS in Thrace. He was regarded as the founder of the Orphic MYSTERY cult.

ORTEGA SAAVEDRA, Daniel (1945–), Nicaraguan revolutionary and politician. A leader of the Marxist Sandinista National Liberation Front (FSLN) in the guerrilla war that drove President Anastasio SOMOZA Debayle from power in 1979, he was one of five Sandinistas who took control of the government. In 1984 he was elected president. He presided over a deteriorating economy while fighting continuously against US-supported contras.

ORTEGA Y GASSET, José (1883–1955), Spanish philosopher, whose best-known work, *The Revolt of the Masses* (1929), attributes Western decadence to the revolt of "mass man" against an intellectual elite. His philosophy attempts to reconcile reason with individual lives and needs.

ORTHODOX CHURCHES, the family of Christian churches that developed out of the EASTERN CHURCH, remaining orthodox when the NESTORIANS and MONOPHYSITE CHURCHES separated. They finally broke with Rome in the GREAT SCHISM of 1054. Each church is independent, but all are in full communion and acknowledge the honorary primacy of the ecumenical patriarch of Constantinople; some are patriarchates, others are governed by synods. The ancient patriarchates of Constantinople, Alexandria, Antioch and Jerusalem are dwarfed by the more recent churches of Russia, Serbia, Romania, Bulgaria, Georgia, Greece, Cyprus and others. There are now approximately 75 million Orthodox worldwide, including about 5 million in the US. Orthodoxy accepts the first seven ecumenical councils, but often prefers not to define dogma very closely; it is characterized by MONASTICISM, veneration of icons and the importance of the laity. It rejects papal claims, the IMMACULATE CONCEPTION and PURGATORY,

and does not require clerical celibacy.

ORTHOPEDICS, speciality within SURGERY, dealing with BONE and soft-tissue disease, damage and deformity. Its name derives from 17th-century treatments designed to produce "straight children." Until the advent of anesthetics, asepsis and X-RAYS, its methods were restricted to AMPUTATION and manipulation for dislocation, etc. Treatment of congenital deformity; FRACTURES and TUMORS of bone; OSTEOMYELITIS; ARTHRITIS, and joint dislocation are common in modern orthopedics. Methods range from the use of splints, PHYSIOTHERAPY and manipulation, to surgical correction of deformity, fixing of fractures and refashioning or replacement of joints. Suture or transposition of TENDONS, MUSCLES or nerves is performed.

ORWELL, George (1903–1950), pen name of the English novelist Eric Arthur Blair, famous principally for *Animal Farm* (1945), a savage satire on communist revolution, and *Nineteen Eighty-Four* (1949), depicting a dehumanizing totalitarian society. Orwell was also a critic and essayist. Other works include the semi-autobiographical *The Road to Wigan Pier* (1937), and *Homage to Catalonia* (1938), an account of his experiences in the SPANISH CIVIL WAR.

OSAGE INDIANS, Plains Indian tribe of the Siouan language group who lived in what is now W Mo. and Ark. in the late 17th century. In 1872 they were moved to a reservation in Okla., and became one of the richest communities in the world when oil was discovered on their reservation two decades later.

OSBORNE, John (1929–), British dramatist whose *Look Back in Anger* (1956) made him the first ANGRY YOUNG MAN of the 1950s and established a new and vigorous realism in the theater. Later plays include *The Entertainer* (1957), *Luther* (1961) and *Inadmissible Evidence* (1964).

OSCARS. See ACADEMY AWARDS.

OSCEOLA (c1804–1838), Indian leader in the Second Seminole War against the US (1835–42), who used guerrilla tactics to resist a US plan to transport the Seminole Indians from Fla. to Okla. He was taken prisoner in 1837 and died in prison.

OSCILLATOR, a device converting direct to alternating current (see ELECTRICITY), used, for example, in generating RADIO waves. Most types are based on an electronic AMPLIFIER, a small portion of the output being returned via a FEEDBACK circuit to the input, so as to make the oscillation self-sustaining. The feedback signal must have the same phase as the input: by varying the components of the feedback circuit, the frequency for which this occurs can be varied, so that the oscillator is easily "tuned." "Crystal" oscillators incorporate a piezoelectric crystal in the tuning circuit for stability; in "heterodyne" oscillators, the output is the beat frequency between two higher frequencies.

OSCILLOSCOPE, a device using a cathode ray tube to produce line GRAPHS of rapidly varying electrical signals. Since nearly every physical effect can be converted into an electrical signal, the oscilloscope is very widely used. Typically, the signal controls the vertical deflection of the beam while the horizontal deflection increases steadily, producing a graph of the signal as a function of time. For periodic (repeating) signals, synchronization of the horizontal scan with the signal is achieved by allowing the attainment by the signal of some preset value to "trigger" a new scan after one is finished. Most models allow two signals to be displayed as functions of each other; dual-beam instruments can display two as a function of time. Oscilloscopes usually operate from DC to high frequencies, and will display signals as low as a few millivolts.

OSIRIS, ancient Egyptian god, brother and husband of Isis, and father of Horus. He was killed by his evil brother Set, but restored to life by Isis. His cult was important in dynastic Egypt, and later became popular in the Roman Empire. A benefactor of mankind, Osiris was ruler of the underworld and also a life-giving power, symbolizing the creative forces of nature.

OSLO, capital, largest city and chief seaport of Norway. Founded c1050, it was rebuilt after the great fire of 1624. Between 1625 and 1925 it was known as Christiania or Kristiania. Today it is Norway's chief commercial, industrial and cultural center. Oslo has many fine museums, castles and parks. The Viking Ship Museum and the Vigeland Sculpture Park are especially noteworthy. Pop 445,357.

OSMOSIS, the diffusion of a solvent through a semipermeable membrane that separates two solutions of different concentration, the movement being from the more dilute to the more concentrated solution, owing to the thermodynamic tendency to equalize the concentrations. The liquid flow may be opposed by applying pressure to the more concentrated solution: the pressure required to reduce the flow to zero from a pure solvent to a given solution is known as the *osmotic pressure of the solution.* Osmosis was studied by Thomas Graham, who coined the term (1858); in

1886 Van't Hoff showed that, for dilute solutions (obeying Henry's Law), the osmotic pressure varies with temperature and concentration as if the solute were a GAS occupying the volume of the solution. This enables MOLECULAR WEIGHTS to be calculated from osmotic pressure measurements, and degrees of ionic dissociation to be estimated. Osmosis is important in DIALYSIS and in water transport in living tissue.

OSPREY, *Pandion haliaetus,* a large fish-eating bird of prey, found throughout the world, except in South America. Also known as the fish hawk, the osprey occupies both marine and freshwater areas, cruising above the water and plunging to take the fish in its talons. The future of the osprey is in some doubt in both Europe and North America, where it has suffered from increased use of persistent pesticides.

OSSIETZKY, Carl von (1889–1938), German journalist and pacifist, editor of the left-wing weekly *Weltbühne* in which he exposed Germany's secret rearmament. In 1933 the Nazis put him in a concentration camp, where he died of tuberculosis. When he was awarded the 1935 Nobel Peace Prize, the Nazi government forbade German citizens from accepting the prize thereafter.

OSTEND MANIFESTO, agreement drawn up in Oostende (Ostend), Belgium in 1854 by three proslavery US diplomats, James BUCHANAN, John Y. Mason and Pierre Soulé. The manifesto implied that if Spain refused to sell Cuba the US would forcibly seize the island. The diplomats, who probably hoped to make Cuba a Union slave state, were denounced by all the political parties.

OSTEOMYELITIS, BACTERIAL infection of BONE, usually caused by STAPHYLOCOCCUS, STREPTOCOCCUS and SALMONELLA carried to the bone by the BLOOD, or gaining access through open FRACTURES. It commonly affects children, causing FEVER and local pain. If untreated or partially treated, it may become chronic with bone destruction and a discharging SINUS. ANTIBIOTICS and surgical drainage are frequently necessary.

OSTEOPATHY, a system of health care founded by Andrew Taylor Still (1828–1917) based on the theory that the body is capable of making its own remedies against disease and other toxic conditions when it is in normal structural relationship and has favorable environmental conditions and adequate nutrition. It utilizes generally accepted physical, pharmacological, and surgical methods of diagnosis and therapy, but goes beyond general medicine in its distinctive recognition of the function of the musculoskeletal system in health and disease. All 50 states and the District of Columbia provide for the unlimited practice of medicine and surgery by osteopathic physicians.

OSTRICH, *Struthio camelus,* the largest living bird, at one time found throughout Africa and SW Asia, but now common in the wild only in E Africa. They are flightless birds, well adapted to a terrestrial life. They have long powerful legs, with two toes on each foot, an adaptation for running over dry grassland parallel to the reduction of digits in the horse's hoof. Ostriches are polygamous, living in groups of a single male and his harem.

OSTROGOTHS (East Goths), branch of the GOTHS, a Germanic people who originally occupied the lands to the N of the Black Sea. The accession of their king Theodoric the Great in 471 heralded an alliance with Zeno, emperor of the East Roman Empire. On Zeno's orders, Theodoric invaded Italy in 488 and reduced it to Ostrogothic rule in 493, ruling from Ravenna. The Byzantine general Belisarius destroyed Ostrogothic rule in the 530s; a subsequent Ostrogothic revolt was swiftly crushed in 552.

OSTROVSKY, Alexander Nikolayevich (1823–1886), Russian dramatist whose plays, usually about merchants and minor officials, are marked by powerful characterization and strong drama. His masterpiece is *The Storm* (1860), a domestic tragedy.

OSWALD, Lee Harvey (1939–1963), the alleged assassin of President John F. KENNEDY in Dallas, Texas on Nov. 22, 1963, and of a local police officer. A former marine, he had lived in the USSR 1959–62. He was himself shot dead by Dallas nightclub owner Jack Ruby while being transferred from the city to the county jail on Nov. 24. The Warren Report (1964) on the investigation of Kennedy's assassination declared Oswald the sole assassin.

OTIS, Elisha Graves (1811–1861), US inventor of the safety elevator (1852), first installed for passenger use in 1856, New York City.

OTTAWA, capital city of Canada, situated at the junction of Ottawa and Rideau Rivers, in SE Ontario. Ottawa is principally a government center; a major tourist attraction is the group of Parliament buildings, built in Victorian Gothic style. The city was built as a logging community, Bytown, in 1827, during the construction of the Rideau canal which divides the city. It became Ottawa (an anglicization of the local Outawouais Indians' name) in 1854, and capital in 1867. Pop (city) 295,160; (metro) 777,700.

OTTAWA INDIANS, large North American tribe of the Algonquian family originally inhabiting, with the OJIBWA and POTAWATOMI INDIANS, the region N of the Great Lakes. The Ottawa later moved to Manitoulin Island. They were active traders and negotiated with the French.

OTTERS, aquatic or semiaquatic carnivores of the weasel family, subfamily Lutrinae. There are five freshwater genera and one marine genus. The body is lithe and muscular, built for vigorous swimming, and covered with thick fur. The paws are generally webbed. The nostrils and eyes may be shut when swimming underwater. The prey consists of small fish, eels, crayfish and frogs. The sea otter's diet is more specialized: sea otters have powerful rounded molars adapted for crushing sea urchins, abalones and mussels. A tool-using animal, it floats on its back, breaking open the urchin- or mussel-shell on a stone anvil balanced on its chest. Unlike most other wild animals, otters remain playful as adults.

OTTO, name of four Holy Roman Emperors: **Otto I the Great** (912–973) was founder and first emperor of the Holy Roman Empire from 962. King of Saxony from 936, he invaded Italy and declared himself king of the Lombards (951). He subdued the Poles and Bohemians and routed the MAGYARS of Hungary (955). Otto was crowned emperor in Rome (962) for helping Pope John XII against Berengar II. **Otto II** (955–983), succeeded his father Otto I as emperor 973–83. He crushed the rebellion of Henry, duke of Bavaria, defeated the Danes (974), but failed to extend his empire in Italy and was badly defeated by the Saracens in S Italy (982). **Otto III** (980–1002) succeeded his father Otto II as emperor 996–1002, after a regency. He lived in Rome and planned to make it the capital of a vast theocratic empire. **Otto IV** (c1174–1218), emperor 1198–1215, was excommunicated by Pope INNOCENT II for attempting to master parts of Italy in 1210, and later deposed.

OTTOMAN EMPIRE, vast empire of the Ottoman Turks which at its height, during the reign of Sultan SULEIMAN I, stretched from the far shore of the Black Sea and the Persian Gulf in the E to Budapest in the N and Algiers in the W. The Ottoman Turks, led by Osman I, entered Asia Minor in the late 1200s and, expanding rapidly, made Bursa their capital in 1326. They crossed to the Balkan Peninsula (1345) and in 1453 CONSTANTINOPLE fell to Mohammed II. The empire continued to expand in the 16th century under Selim I, the Terrible, 1512–20 and reached its zenith under Suleiman I. However, Suleiman I failed to capture Vienna (1529) and was driven back at Malta (1565). Directly after his death, the Ottoman fleet was annihilated at the naval battle of LEPANTO (1571). During the 1700s and 1800s the decaying empire fought against Russia and Greece won its independence. The reformist Young Turk movement led the empire into WWI on the German side, with disastrous results. Finally, the nationalists, led by ATATURK, deposed and exiled the last Sultan, Mohammed VI, and proclaimed the Turkish republic in 1922.

OUIDA, pen name of Maria Louise de la Ramée (1839–1908), melodramatic English novelist. Among her works are *Under Two Flags* (1867), *A Dog of Flanders* (1872), and *Moths* (1880).

OUTER MONGOLIA. See MONGOLIAN PEOPLE'S REPUBLIC.

OVARY, the female reproductive organ. In plants it contains the ovules (see FLOWER); in humans, the follicles in which the eggs (*ova*) develop (see ESTROGEN; FERTILIZATION; GAMETE; PROGESTERONE; REPRODUCTION).

OVERLAND MAIL COMPANY, US stage coach company. It was established under government contract in 1858 by John Butterfield; it provided a 25-day passenger and mail service between St. Louis and San Francisco. The company was acquired by Wells, Fargo, 1866, and ceased operation with the completion of the transcontinental railroad.

OVERLAND TRAIL, name of westward migration routes in the US, in particular for the S alternative route to the OREGON TRAIL, and for the route to the Cal. goldfields. This latter trail went from Fort Bridger to Sutter's Fort, Cal., and duplicated in part the Mormon Trail.

OVERWEIGHT. See OBESITY.

OVID (Publius Ovidius Naso; 43 BC–18 AD), Latin poet. Popular in his time, he was exiled by the emperor Augustus to the Black Sea in 8 AD and died there; his *Sorrows* and *Letters from Pontus* are pleas for his return. He was a master of erotic poetry, as in his *Amores* and *Art of Love*, but his *Metamorphoses*, a collection of myths linked by their common theme of change, is generally considered to be his finest work.

OVULATION. See MENSTRUATION.

OWEN, two industrialists and social reformers. **Robert Owen** (1771–1858) was a socialist and pioneer of the cooperative movement. He introduced better conditions in his cotton mills in Scotland and was active in the trade union movement in Britain. In the US Owen set up short-lived "villages of cooperation," such as that at NEW HARMONY, Ind. **Robert Dale Owen** (1801–1877), his son, campaigned in the US for birth control, women's property rights, state public schools and slave emancipation. He was a member of Congress from Ind. 1843–47.

OWEN, Wilfred (1893–1918), British poet who wrote movingly of the savagery and human sacrifice in WWI; he was deeply influenced by Siegfried SASSOON. Owen was killed in action a week before the end of WWI. Nine of his poems form the text of BRITTEN's *War Requiem* (1962), a powerful anti-war statement.

OWEN GLENDOWER. See GLENDOWER, OWEN.

OWENS, Jesse (1913–1980), famous US black athlete. In 1935–36 he broke three world records at college athletic meets. By winning the 100- and 200-meter dash, the 400-meter relay and the broad jump at the 1936 Berlin Olympics, he shattered Hitler's attempt to demonstrate "Aryan superiority."

OWLS, soft-plumaged, nocturnal birds of prey. Owls have large eyes, directed forward, and all have pronounced facial disks. Some species develop ear tufts and most have extremely sensitive hearing. Many species hunt primarily on auditory cues. The eyes are also extremely powerful: some 35–100 times more sensitive than our own. All owls are soft-feathered and their flight is completely silent. There are two main families, the Tytonidae, or barn owls, with heart-shaped facial disks, and the Strigidae, which contain the orders Buboninae, to which the majority of species belong, and the Striginae.

OX, term zoologically applied to many members of the Bovidae; also, in common usage, a castrated bull used for draft purposes or for its meat.

OXFORD MOVEMENT, 19th-century religious movement aiming to revitalize the Church of England by reintroducing traditional Catholic practices and doctrines. It started in 1833 in Oxford; its leaders, John Keble, J. H. NEWMAN and, later, Edward Pusey, wrote a series of *Tracts for the Times* to publish their opinions. They became known as the "Tractarians." Despite violent controversy over the Romeward tendency of some—culminating in Newman's conversion to Roman Catholicism (1845)—and over ritualism (from 1850), the movement has had great influence in the Anglican Church.

OXFORD UNIVERSITY, English university in Oxford comprising nearly 50 affiliated but autonomous colleges and halls, a great center of learning since its foundation in the 12th century. The oldest mens' college is University (1249), and the oldest womens' college is Lady Margaret Hall (1879). The major university library is the famous Bodleian.

OXUS. See AMU DARYA.

OXYGEN (O), gaseous nonmetal in Group VIA of the PERIODIC TABLE, comprising 21% by volume of the ATMOSPHERE and about 50% by weight of the earth's crust. It was first prepared by SCHEELE and PRIESTLEY, and named *oxygene* by LAVOISIER. Gaseous oxygen is colorless, odorless and tasteless; liquid oxygen is pale blue. Oxygen has two allotropes (see ALLOTROPY): OZONE (O_3), which is metastable; and normal oxygen (O_2), which shows paramagnetism (see MAGNETISM) because its diatomic molecule has two electrons with unpaired spins. Oxygen is prepared in the laboratory by heating mercuric oxide or potassium chlorate (with manganese dioxide catalyst). It is produced industrially by fractional distillation of liquid air. Oxygen is very reactive, yielding oxides with almost all other elements, and in some cases peroxides. Almost all life depends on chemical reactions with oxygen to produce energy. Animals receive oxygen from the air, as do fish from the water (see RESPIRATION): it is circulated through the body in the bloodstream. The amount of oxygen in the air, however, remains constant because of PHOTOSYNTHESIS in plants and the decomposition of the sun's ultraviolet rays of water vapor in the upper atmosphere.

Oxygen is used in vast quantities in smelting and refining, especially of iron and steel. Oxygen and acetylene are used in oxyacetylene torches for cutting and WELDING metals. Liquid oxygen is used in rocket fuels. Oxygen has many medical applications and is used in mixtures breathed by divers and high-altitude fliers. It is also widely used in chemical synthesis. AW 16.0, mp—218°C, bp—183°C.

OYSTERS, bivalve MOLLUSKS of shallow coastal waters. The edible oysters, as distinct from the pearl oysters (see PEARL), belong to the family Ostreidae. While other bivalves are able to move by means of a muscular "foot," oysters have lost this foot and the animal lives cemented to some hard substrate. Like all bivalves, oysters feed by removing suspended organic particles from a feeding current of water drawn into the shell. Food particles are trapped on highly filamentous gill plates. Oysters are extensively fished and cultivated all over the world.

OZAKI, Yukio (1858–1954), Japanese liberal politician, a member of the diet (1890–1953) and mayor of Tokyo (1903–12). He opposed militarism and fought for universal manhood suffrage (achieved 1925). He was jailed during both world wars. The cherry trees in Washington, D.C., are his gift.

OZAWA, Seiji (1935–   ), Japanese conductor, best known for his fiery interpretations of Romantic and modern French composers. He served as director of the San Francisco Symphony Orchestra (1970–76) and of the Boston Symphony Orchestra and the Berkshire Music Festival from 1973.

OZONE (O_3), triatomic allotrope of OXYGEN (see ALLOTROPY); blue gas with a pungent odor. It is a very powerful oxidizing agent and yields ozonides with olefins. It decomposes rapidly above 100°C. Ozone is made by subjecting oxygen to a high-voltage electric discharge. It is used for killing germs, bleaching, removing unpleasant odors from foods, sterilizing water and in the production of azelaic acid. mp—193°C, bp—112°C. The upper ATMOSPHERE contains a layer of ozone, formed when ULTRAVIOLET RADIATION from the sun acts on oxygen; this layer protects the earth from the sun's ultraviolet rays. In recent decades there has been significant reduction in the amount of atmospheric ozone due to the discharge into the atmosphere of chlorofluorocarbons, industrial chemicals widely used in refrigeration, insulating foam, solvents, and aerosol propellants. These remain in the atmosphere for long periods and combine with and destroy ozone molecules. Scientists predict that as the ozone shield thins and more ultraviolet radiation reaches the earth, there will be major increases in skin cancer and eye disease among humans and damage to marine life, crops, and forests. In 1988, the US, which had already banned the use of chlorofluorocarbons in aerosol propellants, became the first major user and producer of chlorofluorocarbons to ratify an international agreement to reduce their production. Adopted in Montreal in September 1987 by 31 countries, the agreement called for freezing the production and use of chlorofluorocarbons at 1986 levels in 1989 and then rolling back production by as much as 50% by 1999. Scientists warned, however, that these controls, even if effected, would prove inadequate and that destruction of the ozone layer would continue for many decades because of the presence of chlorofluorocarbons already in the atmosphere.

16th letter of the English alphabet. It is descended from the Semitic *pe*, the word for mouth. It then became the Greek *pi*, and was incorporated into Latin and English.

PACIFIC, War of the. See WAR OF THE PACIFIC.

PACIFIC ISLANDS, Trust Territory of the, UN trust territory administered by the US, established 1946. It included 2,141 islands (only 96 inhabited) scattered over 3 million sq mi of the Pacific Ocean within the area known as MICRONESIA. The formerly German islands were mandated to Japan in 1922 and after US occupation in WWII to the US. Among constituent territories, the MARIANAS gained separate status as the NORTHERN MARIANAS and became a US commonwealth in 1986. That same year the Marshall Islands and the Federated states of MICRONESIA (Truk, Yap, Ponape, and Kosrae) became sovereign states in free association with the US, which remained responsible for their defense. In 1988, after repeated referendums in Palau on a similar free association compact had failed to pass due to disputes over the nuclear issue, the UN Trusteeship Council voted to approve the dissolution of the territory and leave it to the US and Palau to resolve their differences independently.

PACIFIC OCEAN, world's largest and deepest ocean. Named by the 16th-century navigator MAGELLAN, it extends from the Arctic to the Antarctic Ocean and from the coasts of the Americas to those of Asia. Its area of 70 million sq mi is one-third of the earth's total surface. The equator divides the ocean into the North Pacific and the South Pacific. The average depth of the Pacific is about 14,000ft, and the deepest point is 36,198ft in the Challenger Deep, Marianas Trench, SW of Guam. Plateaus, ridges, trenches (some over 6mi deep), sea mountains and guyots make for many variations in depth. Japan, the Philippines, New Zealand and the thousands of OCEANIA islands lie on the connected series of ridges running from the Bering Straits to the South China Sea, and SE. Despite its name the ocean is not a calm area. In the tropical and subtropical zones over 130 cyclones occur per year. Many bring much-needed rain, but the winds of at least 150mph, the torrential rain and tempestuous seas of the HURRICANES in the NE, E and S, and the 400mph tidal wave, the TSUNAMI, are highly destructive. The first European to sight the Pacific was BALBOA in 1513, and the first to cross it was Magellan, 1520–21. It was explored by DRAKE, TASMAN, BOUGAINVILLE, COOK, Vitus Bering (1681–1741) and George Vancouver (1757–1798).

PACIFIC SCANDAL, corruption charges against Canadian Premier John MACDONALD in 1872–73. In 1872 he awarded the contract to build the Canadian Pacific Railway to Sir Hugh Allan, who had financed his 1872 election campaign. Macdonald consequently resigned and the contract was canceled.

PACIFISM, belief that violence is never justified, and hence that peaceful means should always be employed to settle disputes. A pacifist may not only refuse to use force himself, but also to abet its use, as by refusing to help produce weapons of war. Pacifists who refuse to serve in the armed forces are called CONSCIENTIOUS OBJECTORS. Supporters of nuclear DISARMAMENT or opponents of a specific war are not necessarily pacifist. Among the most successful pacifist statesmen was Mahatma GANDHI. (See also NEUTRALITY.)

PADEREWSKI, Ignacé Jan (1860–1941), Polish statesman, composer and celebrated concert pianist. He was the first prime minister of the Polish republic (1919) and in 1940–41 led the Polish government in exile.

PADUA, historic city in N Italy, a famous RENAISSANCE center and noted for its architecture. Its art treasures include works by GIOTTO, DONATELLO, MANTEGNA and TITIAN. GALILEO taught at its university. It is now an industrial, agricultural and commercial center. Pop 229,950.

PAEZ, José Antonio (1790–1873), Venezuelan soldier and president. He assisted BOLÍVAR in the Spanish defeats at Carabobo (1821) and Puerto Cabello (1823). He led the successful Venezuelan independence movement in 1829 and ruled Venezuela 1831–46 and 1861–63.

PAGANINI, Niccolo (1782–1840), Italian violinist, one of the great virtuosos. By his use of adventurous techniques, such as diverse tuning of strings and the exploitation of harmonics, he extended the compass of the instrument. His best-known compositions are his 24 *Caprices*.

PAGE, Walter Hines (1855–1918), US journalist and diplomat. He edited the

Atlantic Monthly 1896–99 and founded and edited *The World's Book* 1900–13. As President WILSON's ambassador to Great Britain, 1913–18, he opposed US neutrality in WWI.

PAGNOL, Marcel (1895–1974), French playwright, screen writer, director, producer, and critic. He wrote the screenplays of *Marius* (1930) and *Topaze* (1932), both adapted from his own plays. *Marius* was the first in his Provençal trilogy, which also included *Fanny* and *César*.

PAGODA, multistoried circular or polygonal tower of brick, wood or stone, with projecting roofs that may curve upward. Generally Buddhist shrines, they have been built in India and China since the 5th century, and have spread to Burma and Japan.

PAHLAVI, Mohammed Reza Shah. See MOHAMMED REZA SHAH PAHLAVI.

PAHLAVI, Reza Shah. See REZA SHAH PEHLAVI.

PAIGE, "Satchel" (Leroy Robert Paige; 1906–1982), outstanding US baseball pitcher. Barred as a Negro from the major leagues until 1948, he played with the Cleveland Indians through 1951, and with the St. Louis Browns from 1951 until his retirement in 1953.

PAIN, the detection by the nervous system of harmful stimuli. The function of pain is to warn the individual of imminent danger: even the most minor tissue damage will cause pain, so that avoiding action can be taken at a very early stage. The level at which pain can only just be felt is the *pain threshold.* This threshold level varies slightly among individuals and can be raised by, for example, HYPNOSIS, anesthetics, ANALGESICS and the drinking of alcohol. In some psychological illnesses, especially the NEUROSES, it is lowered. The receptors of pain are unencapsulated nerve endings (see NERVOUS SYSTEM), distributed variably about the body. Deep pain, from the internal organs, may be felt as surface pain or in a different part of the body. This phenomenon, *referred pain,* is probably due to the closeness of the nerve tracts entering the SPINAL CORD.

PAINE, Robert Treat (1731–1814), US lawyer, signatory of the DECLARATION OF INDEPENDENCE. He was a delegate to the first CONTINENTAL CONGRESS (1774–78), Mass. attorney general (1777–90) and state supreme court judge (1790–1804).

PAINE, Thomas (1737–1809), English-born writer and radical, a leading figure of the American Revolution. He emigrated to America in 1774; his highly influential pamphlet, *Common Sense,* 1776, urged the American colonies to declare independence. His patriotic pamphlets, *The Crisis* (1776–83), inspired the CONTINENTAL ARMY. He returned to England and wrote *The Rights of Man,* 1791–92, a defense of the FRENCH REVOLUTION and republicanism. Forced to flee to France, he was elected to the National Convention. His controversially deistic *The Age of Man* (1794–95) alienated his US support; he returned there in 1802, and died in obscurity.

PAINT, a fluid applied to a surface in thin layers, forming a colored, solid coating for decoration, representation (see OIL PAINTS; PAINTING) and protection. Paint consists of a pigment dispersed in a "vehicle" or binder which adheres to the substrate and forms the solid film, and usually a solvent or thinner to control the consistency. Natural binders used, now or formerly, include GLUE, natural RESINS and OILS which dry by oxidation—linseed oil used to be the basis of the paint industry. These have been largely displaced by synthetic resins, latex and oils (to which drying agents are added). The solvents used are hydrocarbons or oils, except for the large class of water-thinned paints in which the binder forms an emulsion or is dissolved in the water. Many specialized paints have been developed, e.g., to resist heat or corrosion. After applying a primer, the paint is brushed, rolled or sprayed on; dip coating and electrostatic attraction are more recent methods.

PAINTED DESERT, brightly colored region (about 150mi long) of mesas and plateaus in N central Ariz., E of the Little Colorado R. Centuries of erosion have exposed red, brown and purple rock surfaces.

PAINTING, the depiction in terms of line and color of a subject, rendered representationally or abstractly, on a two-dimensional surface. (For art preceding that of the RENAISSANCE see ALTAMIRA; LASCAUX CAVE; EGYPT, ANCIENT; GREEK ART AND ARCHITECTURE; ROMANESQUE ART; GOTHIC ART.)

Italian painting, 1300–1600. Giotto's fresco works broke away from Byzantine art by his realistic depiction of people and their emotions. His monumental, sculptural style was generally followed in 14th-century Florence. In Siena, the decorative linear style of Duccio and Simone Martini prevailed. The Florentine discovery of linear perspective was first employed by Masaccio, and the tradition was continued by Fra Angelico, Piero Della Francesca and Botticelli. Western painting reached an apogee in the High Renaissance works of

Leonardo da Vinci, Raphael and Michelangelo. MANNERISM, developed by Giulio Romano and Andrea del Sarto, influenced the arresting style of El Greco. From the mid-15th century a distinct Venetian school emerged, notable particularly for its use of color. The most influential Venetian artists were Titian, Tintoretto and Veronese.

Painting outside Italy, 1400–1600. Flemish art was finely detailed, as in the work of Jan Van Eyck who, with his brother Hubert, is credited with innovative oil painting. A more emotional style was developed by Van der Weyden, while Bosch and Pieter Bruegel developed grotesque fantasy pictures. In the late-15th century, German art became influential with Dürer's woodcuts and engravings, Grünewald's Isenheim altar and Hans Holbein's portraits.

Painting, 1600–1850. The prominent artists of the BAROQUE period were the Italian painter Caravaggio; the brilliant and imaginative Flemish painter Rubens; the Spaniard Velazquez; two classical French painters, Poussin and Claude; and Rembrandt. Dutch painters like Steen and Vermeer specialized in GENRE scenes. The ROCOCO style was characterized by elegant, sensuous, often frivolous works by painters like Watteau and Boucher. English portraiture was developed by Reynolds and Gainsborough, influencing the first important American artists, Copley and Benjamin West. The Spanish Rococo painter, Goya, adapted his style to depict the savagery of the Napoleonic wars. The first half of the 19th century in France was dominated by the CLASSICISM of Ingres and the ROMANTICISM of Delacroix.

Painting since 1850. Courbet promoted the rendering of large-scale pictures of ordinary life and Manet influenced IMPRESSIONISM. Monet and Renoir pioneered painting out of doors and experimented with the effects of light. The POSTIMPRESSIONISTS Gauguin and Van Gogh, through their novel use of paint and simplified forms, greatly influenced EXPRESSIONISM and FAUVISM. Cézanne's work was crucial to the development of CUBISM, which was largely invented by Picasso and Braque. Kandinsky and Malevich developed forms of ABSTRACT ART. SURREALISM used imagery taken from dreams, as in the works of Dali and Ernst. In the 1960s POP ART was developed by Jasper Johns, Robert Rauschenberg and Andy Warhol. Later in the decade, OP ART followed. A resurgence of interest in various aspects of REALISM occurred in the 1970s and 1980s.

PAISLEY, Ian Richard Kyle (1926–   ), Northern Ireland politician, leader of militant Protestants in their conflict with the Roman Catholic minority. He was a member of the British Parliament from 1970.

PAIUTE INDIANS, several North American Indian tribes of the SHOSHONE INDIANS. They can be divided into the North Paiute of N Cal. and Nev. and the South Paiute (or Digger Indians) of Ariz. and S Nev. The Paiute GHOST DANCE religion, which began in 1870, led by Wovoka, led to violent uprisings. Today about 4,000 Paiute live on reservations.

PAKENHAM, Sir Edward Michael (1778–1815), British commander whose forces were disastrously defeated at the Battle of NEW ORLEANS (1815) by Andrew JACKSON. Pakenham himself was killed in the action.

PAKISTAN, republic in the NW Indian subcontinent.

Official name: Islamic Republic of Pakistan
Capital: Islamabad
Area: 307,374sq mi
Population: 106,187,000
Languages: Urdu, Sindhi, Punjabi, Pushtu, English
Religion: Muslim
Monetary unit(s): 1 Pakistani rupee=100 paisa
Land. Pakistan, located on the Arabian Sea, between Afghanistan to the NW and India to the SE, with Jammu and KASHMIR to the NE, comprises four provinces: Punjab, Sind, Baluchistan and the North-West Frontier Province. High mountains dominate the N, and dry high plateaus and mountain ranges the W. The S includes part of the Thar Desert and borders on the barren Rann of Kutch. Most of Pakistan consists of the huge INDUS alluvial plain, which receives the five rivers of the Punjab. One of the largest irrigated regions of the world, it has high agricultural productivity. The climate has extremes of temperature, ranging from below freezing to 120°F. Annual rainfall averages less than 10 in.
People. Most of the population are

relatively light-skinned Punjabis. Other groups include the tall, fairer and often blue-eyed Pathans, possibly of Semitic origin, and the Baluchi, an Aryan people; there are many tribal and linguistic differences. Islam is the state religion. The literacy rate is about 16%. The majority of the population live in small villages. The largest cities are Karachi, Lahore, Lyallpur, Hyderabad and Rawalpindi.

Economy. Pakistan is among the world's poorest countries. It has few natural resources and is dependent on its agriculture. Wheat is the main subsistence crop, and fruit and livestock are important in the N. The diverse mineral resources are still to be developed, but low-grade coal and iron ore, chromite, gypsum and limestone are being mined. Deposits of natural gas and oil are potentially large. Pakistan exports wool and cotton textiles (some from cottage industries) and leather goods.

History. Demands for a Muslim state independent of Hindu India grew strong in the early 1900s. In 1906 the MUSLIM LEAGUE was founded and from 1916 was led by by Mohammed Ali JINNAH. He became first governor-general of the independent dominion of Pakistan, formed in 1947; Liaquat ALI KHAN was the prime minister. The country consisted of two parts, East and West Pakistan, separated by 1,000mi of Indian territory. The new states of India and Pakistan fought bitterly, particularly over Kashmir. In the 1950s tension grew between Bengali East Pakistan and Punjabi West Pakistan which dominated the civil service and army. In 1956 a new constitution was adopted and Pakistan formally became a republic within the British Commonwealth (withdrew 1972). Economic problems, cabinet crises, political corruption, and ethnic strife brought Gen. Mohammed AYUB KHAN to power in 1958. Elected president in 1960 and reelected in 1965, he pursued policies of land reform and economic development, created a federal republic consisting of two provinces (East and West Pakistan) and two official languages (Bengali and Urdu), improved relations with India but also established ties with communist China. Bloody riots drove Ayub from power in 1969. Two years later East Pakistan declared its independence as BANGLADESH and, with the support of India, defeated Pakistan. Power in Pakistan then fell to Prime Minister Zulfikar Ali BHUTTO, who recognized Bangladesh and sought to improve economic conditions in Pakistan but was frustrated by continued political turmoil. Elections in 1977 won by Bhutto's Pakistan People's Party resulted in rioting that was ended only by a military coup led by Gen. Mohammed ZIA UL-HAQ, who imposed martial law, arrested and permitted the execution of Bhutto, and thereafter ruled dictatorially. He maintained ties with China and developed Pakistan's nuclear capability as security against India, and he supported US policy in opposition to the Soviet-sponsored government in Afghanistan. In 1985 Zia lifted martial law and allowed the election of a national assembly whose power was purely advisory. Pakistanis elected local governments in 1987, and Zia promised a national election in Nov. 1988. But in May 1988 he deposed the civilian prime minister, dissolved the national assembly and provincial governments, and declared Islamic law supreme in Pakistan—presumably as a unifying force in an ethnically divided country. In Aug. 1988 he was killed in an airplane crash, leaving no obvious successor. In Nov. 1988 the first democratic election in a decade gave the opposition parties a majority in Pakistan's parliament, with the greatest number of seats going to the Pakistan People's Party led by Benazir Bhutto.

PALATE, structure dividing the mouth from the nose and bounded by the upper gums and teeth; it is made of BONE and covered by mucous membrane. At the back, it is a soft mobile connective-tissue structure which can close off the nasopharynx during swallowing and speech.

PALATINATE, two historic states of Germany: the Lower or Rhine Palatinate on the Rhine R bordering France and the Saar, and the Upper Palatinate in NE Bavaria. The Countship Palatine of the former state was created by the Holy Roman Emperor Frederick I in 1156. The counts became electors of the Holy Roman Empire.

PALAU, formerly **Belau,** self-governing Micronesian island group in the W Pacific.

Land and People. The westernmost of the Caroline Island chain, Palau consists of about 200 volcanic and coral islands extending over an area 125mi long and 25mi wide. Babelthuap, the largest island, covers 156sq mi. On the larger islands the terrain consists of gently rolling, fertile, forested hills reaching 641ft on Babelthuap. Only eight of the islands are inhabited, with most people living on Koror, the administrative center and major port. With the exception of some Americans, the inhabitants are Micronesian.

Economy. Much of the labor force is engaged in small-scale agriculture, raising coconuts, breadfruit, bananas, taro and

Official name: Republic of Palau
Capital: Koror
Area: 178sq mi
Population: 13,873
Languages: Palauan, English
Religions: Christian, traditional
Monetary unit(s): 1 US dollar = 100 cents

yams. There is little industry except for a copra-processing plant. Trochus shell, fish and handicrafts are the leading exports. About 40% of the paid labor force is employed by the government, and much government revenue consists of grants from the US.
History. Palau was a Spanish possessiion from 1710 to 1898, when control passed to Germany. Commercial exploitation of Palau's resources begun under the Germans intensified after Japan captured the islands in 1914. With the Japanese defeat at the end of WWII, Palau, and the rest of the Carolines passed to the US, and in 1947 were included in the US Trust Territory of the Pacific Islands. Palau became internally self-governing in 1981, but repeated referendums on a compact of free association that would give Palau sovereignty while responsiblity for its defense remained with the US foundered on the issue of a nuclear ban. In 1988 the UN Trusteeship Council voted to terminate the trusteeship arrangement and allow Palau and the US to resolve their differences independently.

PALEOCENE, the first epoch of the TERTIARY period, which extended between about 65 and 55 million years ago. (See also GEOLOGY.)

PALEOGEOGRAPHY, the construction from geologic, paleontologic and other evidence of maps of parts or all of the earth's surface at specific times in the earth's past. Paleogeography has proved of considerable importance in CONTINENTAL DRIFT studies.

PALEOGRAPHY, the study of handwritten material from ancient and medieval times, excluding that on metal or stone, for purposes of interpretation and the dating of events, and to trace the evolution of the written ALPHABET.

PALEOLITHIC AGE, See PRIMITIVE MAN; STONE AGE.

PALEOMAGNETISM, the study of past changes in the EARTH's magnetic field by examination of rocks containing certain iron-bearing minerals (e.g., hematite, magnetite). Reversals of the field and movements of the magnetic poles can be charted, and information on CONTINENTAL DRIFT may be obtained. (See also PLATE TECTONICS.)

PALEONTOLOGY, or **paleobiology**, the study of fossils or evidences of ancient life. The two principal branches are *paleobotany* and *paleozoology*, dealing with plants and animals respectively. An important subdivision of paleobotany is palynology, the study of pollen and spores. Paleozoology is divisible into *vertebrate paleontology* and *invertebrate paleontology*. The term *micropaleontology* refers to the study of microscopic fossils or microfossils, which include both plant and animal representatives. Paleontologic studies are essential to STRATIGRAPHY and provide important evidence for EVOLUTION and CONTINENTAL DRIFT theories. (See also FOSSILS; RADIOISOTOPE DATING.)

PALEOZOIC, the earliest era of the PHANEROZOIC EON, comprising two sub-eras: the **Lower Paleozoic**, 570–400 million years ago, containing the CAMBRIAN, ORDOVICIAN and SILURIAN periods; and the **Upper Paleozoic**, 400–225 million years ago, containing the DEVONIAN, MISSISSIPPIAN, PENNSYLVANIAN and PERMIAN periods. (See GEOLOGY.)

PALERMO, capital of Sicily, its largest city and chief seaport, on the NW coast. Shipbuilding, textiles and chemicals are leading industries. Palermo was founded by Phoenicians in the 8th–6th centuries BC. Its notable medieval architecture has Byzantine, Norman and Muslim features. The Sicilian Vespers uprising (1282) there against Naples led to Spanish rule of Sicily. Pop 714,246.

PALESTINE, the biblical Holy Land, named for the PHILISTINES and also called Canaan. Its boundaries, often imprecise, have varied widely. Palestine now usually refers to the region bounded W by the Mediterranean, E by the Jordan R and Dead Sea, N by Mt Hermon on the Syria-Lebanon border and S by the Sinai Peninsula. It thus lies almost entirely within modern Israel, though extending into Jordan. There were Paleolithic and Mesolithic cultures in Palestine, and Neolithic JERICHO emerged by 7000 BC. Semites arrived c3000 BC and built a Bronze-Age civilization (3000–1500 BC).

Soon after 2000 BC, Hebrew tribes under Abraham came from Mesopotamia (see JEWS). In 1479 BC Egyptians invaded, enslaving many Hebrews (or Israelites) in Egypt. Their descendants returned under MOSES c1200 BC. Successful wars against Canaanites and Philistines helped unite Hebrew tribes in one kingdom (c1020 BC), ruled by Saul, then David, then Solomon. After Solomon died the kingdom split into (N) Israel and (S) Judah (later Judaea), hence the term "Jew." Both kingdoms worshiped the One God, Yahweh (JEHOVAH), and Judaism developed under religious leaders called prophets. In 721 BC Assyrians overran Israel and in 587 BC Babylonians conquered Judah, deporting many Jews, who returned only after Babylonia fell to Persia's CYRUS THE GREAT in 539 BC. Palestine was later controlled by Alexander the Great (332–323 BC), the Ptolemies of Egypt (323–198 BC) and the Seleucids of Syria (198–168 BC). Then JUDAS MACCABEUS began a national revolt which established the Jewish HASMONEAN dynasty (143–37 BC) in Judaea. Roman rule (63 BC–395 AD) saw the birth of Christianity, but there was also repression, climaxed by the Roman destruction of Jerusalem (70 AD) and massive Jewish emigration. Control passed to the Byzantines (395–611 and 628–633 AD), Persians (611–628) and Arabs, whose conquest in the 630s began 1,300 years of Muslim rule, briefly disturbed by the CRUSADES. In 1918 the OTTOMAN EMPIRE collapsed, and British rule followed. Jewish immigration, which had begun in the 1850s, increased rapidly after the British government's BALFOUR DECLARATION (1917) promising the Jews a national home in Palestine. Britain had also promised (1915–16) the Arabs an independent state in W Asia. The British claim that Palestine was excluded from this promise has never been accepted by the Arabs. The appalling fate of the Jews in Europe after the rise of NAZISM brought widespread support for the creation of a Jewish state. In 1948 Jews, but not Arabs, accepted a UN recommendation to split Palestine into Jewish and Arab states. Jews proclaimed the state of Israel, and at the same time nearby Arab nations invaded the area. Israel occupied the West Bank, Gaza, and the Old City of Jerusalem in 1967 during the third major Arab-Israeli war, and subsequent negotiations failed to meet the demands of Palestinian Arabs for a Palestinian homeland. In December 1987 they launched an uprising in the occupied territories in an effort to end Israeli occupation. The following year, Jordan formally severed its legal and administrative ties to the West Bank. (See also ISRAEL; JORDAN; ARAB-ISRAELI WARS; PALESTINE LIBERATION ORGANIZATION.)

PALESTINE LIBERATION ORGANIZATION (PLO), coordinating body of Palestinian refugee groups, aiming to establish a Palestinian state on land regained from Israel and recognized by many Arabs as the PALESTINE government. Led by Yasir ARAFAT, it committed many acts of terrorism, though official PLO policy became more moderate in the face of worldwide criticism. First using Jordan as a base of operations until forced out in 1970, the PLO later found a haven in Lebanon, from which it engaged Israel in sporadic conflict. In 1982 Israel invaded Lebanon and forced Arafat and his guerrillas to withdraw to other Arab countries. The group then split into factions supporting and opposing Arafat, and terrorist activities increased. The group's inability to meet Palestinian demands for a homeland contributed to a spontaneous Arab uprising in the Israeli-occupied West Bank and Gaza. In Nov. 1988, almost a year after the uprising began, the PLO declared an independent Arab state in Palestine and accepted UN resolutions recognizing the legitimacy of Israel. But it did not offer to negotiate directly with Israel. The Israelis disregarded the PLO declaration.

PALESTRINA, Giovanni Pierluigi da (c1525–1594), Italian RENAISSANCE composer of unaccompanied choral church music. He wrote over 100 masses and is perhaps best known for his *Missa Papae Marcelli.* He was organist and choirmaster in several Roman churches.

PALEY, William (1743–1805), English theologian and utilitarian philosopher whose *Principles of Moral and Political Philosophy* (1785), *A View of the Evidences of Christianity* (1794), and *Natural Theology* (1802) were influential in early 19th-century liberal education on both shores of the Atlantic.

PALEY, William Samuel (1901–   ), US broadcasting executive, creator of the Columbia Broadcasting System, its president (1928-46) and chairman (1946-83).

PALIMPSEST, parchment or other writing material reused after previous writing has been erased. The high cost of parchments made palimpsests common in Greek and Roman times. Some old, erased texts have been deciphered.

PALLADIO, Andrea (1508–1580), Italian architect, born Andrea di Pietro. He created the immensely influential Palladian style. His designs for villas, palaces and churches stressed harmonic proportions and classical symmetry. Palladio's *The Four Books of Architecture* (1570) helped to spread his style through Europe, notably (via Inigo JONES) to England.

PALM, any of over 3,000 species of trees and shrubs of the family Palmae, mainly native to tropical and subtropical regions. Palms are characterized by having an unbranched stem bearing at the tip a bunch of feather-like (pinnate) or fan-like (palmate) leaves. Flowers are greenish, borne in spikes, and the fruits are either dry or fleshy. Palm products are of great economic importance, both locally and in world trade. The COCONUT PALM and date palm produce staple crops; wax is obtained from the carnauba palm; the oil palm yields oils used in food, soap, toiletries and industrial processes. Several palms make good house plants. Indoors, they grow well at average house temperatures and should be placed in a moderately sunny position. The soil should be kept wet to moist, though palms do not tolerate standing water. The foliage should be misted often. They can be propagated from seeds or by planting divisions.

PALME, (Sven) Olof (Joachim) (1927-1986), Swedish Social Democratic politician, premier (1969-76, 1982-86). He was assassinated by an unknown gunman on a Stockholm street.

PALMER, A(lexander) Mitchell (1872-1936), US attorney general (1919–21) notorious for the "Palmer Raids"—mass arrests of supposed subversives, many of whom were deported as aliens. A Democratic congressman 1909–15, he was US alien property custodian in WWI.

PALMER, Daniel David (1845–1913), Canadian-born US founder of CHIROPRACTIC (1895).

PALMER, Nathaniel Brown (1799–1877), US mariner and explorer, the reputed discoverer of the Antarctic continent. In 1820–21 he sighted Palmer Peninsula (now the Antarctic Peninsula) and discovered the South Orkney Islands.

PALMER, Samuel (1805–1881), English landscape painter and etcher, famous for his visionary, pastoral watercolors of southern England. Prime exemplars of ROMANTICISM, his greatest works, those of the 1820s, were influenced by William BLAKE.

PALMERSTON, Henry John Temple, 3rd Viscount (1784–1865), British statesman remembered for his successful and often aggressive foreign policy. As foreign secretary 1830–34, 1835–41 and 1846–51, he was instrumental in securing Belgian independence (1830–31), in upholding the OTTOMAN EMPIRE (1839–41), and in maintaining peace in Europe during the REVOLUTIONS OF 1848. As prime minister 1855–58 and 1859–65, he led Britain to victory in the CRIMEAN WAR and kept out of the American Civil War, despite the TRENT AFFAIR.

PALMISTRY, study of the characteristics of the hand for the purpose of DIVINATION. The various lines on the palm are held to indicate the individual's character and destiny. Over 4,000 years old, palmistry is still widely popular.

PALM OIL, oil obtained from the fruit and seed kernel of the African oil palm. It is a rich source of VITAMIN A and is used in candles, cosmetics, oleomargarine, lubricants and soaps.

PALM SUNDAY, the Sunday before EASTER and the first day of HOLY WEEK, commemorating Christ's triumphal entry into Jerusalem riding on an ass, when palm leaves were spread in his path. Palm leaves are blessed and carried in procession.

PALMYRA, ancient city in central Syria. Prominent as a trading center, Palmyra prospered under Roman rule and reached its height (3rd century AD) as an independent state under Queen Zenobia. In 273 it was largely destroyed by the Romans under Aurelian. Imposing ruins survive.

PALO ALTO, Battle of, first battle of the MEXICAN WAR. On May 8, 1846, about 2,000 US troops under Gen. Zachary TAYLOR defeated about 6,000 Mexicans under Gen. Mariano Arista 12mi NE of Brownsville, S Tex.

PALOMAR OBSERVATORY. See HALE OBSERVATORIES.

PALSY, paralysis, especially a progressive form of paralysis culminating late in life, characterized by tremors of the limbs, muscular weakness and rigidity, and a peculiar gait and attitude.

PAMIRS, mountainous region of central Asia. It forms a hub from which radiate the Hindu Kush, Karakorum, Kunlun and Tien Shan ranges. Most of it lies in the Tadzhik SSR, but parts are in Afghanistan, China and Kashmir. The highest peaks are Communism Peak (24,590ft) and Lenin Peak (23,508ft), both in the USSR.

PAMPAS, grassy plains of SE South America. They stretch about 300,000sq mi over Argentina and into Uruguay. The humid E Pampa bears some crops. The dry W Pampa supports livestock.

PAMPLONA, city in N Spain, capital of Navarre Province. It makes chemicals, processed foods and consumer goods, and has a university and cathedral. It was the capital of the old kingdom of Navarre. A major event every July is the running of the bulls during the Fiesta de San Fermin. Pop 184,460.

PANAMA, Central American republic occupying the Isthmus of Panama, and cut in half by the PANAMA CANAL.

Official name: Republic of Panama
Capital: Panama
Area: 29,762sq mi
Population: 2,274,000
Language: Spanish
Religion: Roman Catholic
Monetary unit(s): 1 balboa=100 centésimos

Land. Panama is traversed by mountain ranges, flanked by well-watered valleys and plains. The climate is hot and rainy. Much of E Panama is dense tropical forest; the Pacific coast has savanna and forest.

People. The population is more than 70% mestizo, about 14% black and 12% European (mainly Spanish). There are about 60,000 Amerindians, mainly in E Panama and on the San Blas Islands off the Caribbean coast. Nearly one-third of Panamanians live in Panama City or Colón, the largest centers. The literacy rate is about 80%.

Economy. The canal provides 25% of the gross national product, but the economy is basically agricultural. The farms, mostly under 25 acres, produce rice, corn, beans, bananas, cacao and coffee. Only half of all arable land is farmed, and Panama imports most of its food. Industry is chiefly consumer oriented. Major exports by value are bananas, shrimps, coffee, sugar, fishmeal and petroleum products. Food, industrial raw materials and manufactured goods largely account for Panama's huge trading deficit. The chief ports are Cristóbal and Balboa. In 1986 Panama had the world's 2nd largest merchant fleet, foreign shipowners registering in Panama to profit from low fees and easy labor laws. Panama is also a center of international banking.

History. First sighted by Europeans in 1501, claimed by Spain and colonized under BALBOA and Pedrarias Dávila, Panama became a springboard for Spanish conquests in the Americas and a route for transshipping Peruvian gold to Spain. Panama lost importance in the 18th century after buccaneer attacks forced treasure ships from Peru to sail around South America. In 1821 Panama broke free from Spain and became part of Colombia. In1903, Panama gained independence with US support. The completion (1914) of the PANAMA CANAL brought some prosperity, but discontent with US control over the canal led to riots in 1959, 1962 and 1964. Gen. Omar Torrijos Herrera came to power after a military coup in 1968; following 1978 elections Gen. Torrijos resigned and political parties were again allowed. In 1977, US and Panama signed two treaties authorizing gradual takeover by Panama of the canal, to be completed in 1999. The military remained a potent force after Torrijos died in a 1981 plane crash. Since 1983, Gen. Manuel Antonio Noriega has headed the Panama Defense Force. President Eric Arturo Delvalle dismissed Noriega in 1988 after the general had been indicted in the US for drug trafficking, but Noriega refused to leave and Delvalle was forced into hiding. The US then imposed economic sanctions that also failed to force Noriega to step down.

PANAMA CANAL, ship canal which crosses the Isthmus of PANAMA to link the Atlantic and Pacific oceans. It runs 40mi SE from Colón on the Caribbean to Balboa on the Pacific. Ships are lifted to 85ft above sea level and lowered again by means of the Gatún, Pedro Miguel and Miraflores locks. Minimum depth is 41ft. Minimum width is 100ft. A French company led by de LESSEPS bought a Colombian canal-building concession, but after eight years' work in Panama (1881–89), labor problems and disease bankrupted the firm. A second French company bought the franchise in 1894, largely to keep it alive. The US negotiated the Hay-Pauncefote Treaty with Britain (1901) and aimed to build a canal through Nicaragua. The French offered the US the rights to the Panamanian project, but Colombia refused the US terms. In 1903, a US warship and US troops helped Panama successfully revolt against Colombia, and the ensuing Hay-Bunau-Varilla Treaty gave the US rights in perpetuity to a 10mi-wide strip across the isthmus. The US completed the canal in 1914, due mainly to the work of the engineer G. W. GOETHALS and the government health officer Dr. W. C. GORGAS. After WWII there was US-Panamanian friction over canal sovereignty. In 1977 the US and Panama signed a treaty under which full control of the canal would pass to Panama in the year 2000. Another treaty signed at the same time guaranteed the neutrality of the canal after 2000 and assured that the canal would be open to ships of all countries. However, the future of the canal has become uncertain because of the availability of such alternatives as pipelines, airlifts, and "intermodal" sea-to-rail transport. Some shipbuilders are building ships too large for the canal. In the late 1980s, a three-nation commission, consisting of Panama, the US, and Japan, was studying the options of improving the present canal, building a new one, or finding new ways to move goods across the isthmus by land.

PANAMA CANAL ZONE, formerly a strip of land extending 5mi on either side of the PANAMA CANAL. It was controlled by the US and the governor, normally a US army officer, was a presidential appointee. Panama took control over the territory in October 1979, after US and Panama signed and ratified two treaties about gradual takeover of the canal by Panama.

PAN-AMERICAN GAMES, quadrennial amateur sports contest between nations of the Americas. The event is based on the OLYMPIC GAMES and includes many of the same events. It was proposed at the 1940 Pan-American Congress, but postponed by WWII and first held in 1951.

PAN-AMERICAN HIGHWAY, highway system linking Latin American countries with each other and with the Interstate Highway system of the US. The highway was conceived at the Fifth International Conference of American States (1923).

PAN AMERICANISM, movement aimed at creating closer cultural, economic, political and social ties among the republics of the Western Hemisphere. It dates from 1826, when BOLÍVAR called a conference of Latin American states which agreed on a treaty of union and assistance. Further conferences followed. US involvement dates from the First International Conference of American States (1889–90) which founded the International Union of American Republics, reorganized in 1910 as the Pan American Union. Later landmarks in cooperation included the founding of the PAN-AMERICAN HIGHWAY, the PAN-AMERICAN GAMES and the ORGANIZATION OF AMERICAN STATES.

PANCHEN LAMA, second-highest lama in Tibetan BUDDHISM (preceded only by the DALAI LAMA), revered as a reincarnation of Amitabha, the Buddha of Light. The current Panchen Lama, unlike the Dalai Lama, supported Chinese rule in Tibet. Removed from public view during the Cultural Revolution, after 1978 he lived in Peking as China's spokesman on Tibet.

PANCREAS, organ consisting partly of exocrine GLAND tissue, secreting into the duodenum, and partly of ENDOCRINE GLAND tissue (the *islets of Langerhans*), whose principal HORMONES include INSULIN and glucagon. The pancreas lies on the back wall of the upper ABDOMEN, much of it within the duodenal loop. Powerful digestive-system ENZYMES (pepsin, trypsin, lipase, amylase) are secreted into the gut; this secretion is in part controlled by intestinal hormones (secretin) and in part by nerve REFLEXES. nsulin and glucagon have important roles in glucose and fat METABOLISM (see DIABETES); other pancreatic hormones affect GASTROINTESTINAL TRACT secretion and activity. Acute INFLAMMATION of the pancreas due to VIRUS disease, ALCOHOLISM or duct obstruction by gall stones may lead to severe abdominal pain with SHOCK and prostration caused by the release of digestive enzymes into the abdomen. Chronic pancreatitis leads to functional impairment and malabsorption. CANCER of the pancreas may cause JAUNDICE by obstructing the BILE duct.

PANDAS, two species of raccoon-like mammals of uncertain relation found in montane bamboo forests of Yunnan and Szechwan provinces in China. Both have an unusual sixth digit, a modified wristbone which has evolved to thumb-like size and flexibility in the giant panda, *Ailuropoda melanoleuca*, remaining vestigial in the lesser or red panda, *Ailurus fulgens*. Though they have evolved from carnivores, both pandas are vegetarians, their diet largely comprising bamboo shoots. The giant panda has been adopted as the emblem of the World Wildlife Fund.

PANDIT, Vijaya Läkshmi (1900–   ), Indian diplomat and political leader, sister of NEHRU. She was active in the struggle for India's independence and helped implement India's postwar policy of nonalignment. She was ambassador to the US 1949–51 and the first woman president of the UN General Assembly 1953–54.

PANGAEA, primeval supercontinent which, under plate tectonic action, split up to form Laurasia in the N and Gondwanaland in the S hemisphere (see PLATE TECTONICS). In turn these, too, split up to form our modern continents. (See also CONTINENTAL DRIFT.)

PANKHURST, Emmeline (1858–1928), English suffragist. In 1903 she and her daughters **Christabel Pankhurst** (1880–1958) and **Sylvia Pankhurst** (1882–

1960) founded the Woman's Social and Political Union, which soon became militant. She was constantly in prison and on hunger strike 1908–14. She died a month before women gained full voting equality with men. (See WOMEN'S MOVEMENT.)

PANMUNJOM, village in N South Korea in the Korean demilitarized zone where the truce to end the Korean War was negotiated (1951–53) and signed (July 27, 1953).

PANOFSKY, Erwin (1892-1968), German-born US art historian, at the Institute for Advanced Studies, Princeton, N.J. 1935-68. His speciality was medieval, Renaissance, mannerist, and baroque iconography.

PAN-SLAVISM, movement for the cultural and political solidarity of the SLAVS. It began in the 1830s. Pan-Slav Congresses were held in Prague (1848) and Moscow (1867). Pan-Slavism was a factor in the events leading to the Russo-Turkish War (1877–78), the Balkan Wars (1912, 1913) and WWI. Both pre- and post-communist Russia attempted to use Pan-Slavism as a cloak for Russian expansionism.

PANTHEISM, religious or philosophical viewpoint in which God and the universe are identified, stressing God's immanence and denying his transcendence. Religious pantheists see finite beings as merely part of God; others deify the universe, nature being the supreme principle. Pantheism is found in HINDUISM, STOICISM, IDEALISM and notably in SPINOZA's thought; Christian MYSTICISM may tend to it.

PANTHEON, historically, a temple dedicated to the worship of all the gods. In modern times it refers to a structure where a nation's heroes are buried or honored. The most famous pantheon is an ancient circular temple (now a church) in Rome, built c120 AD and having a 142ft-diameter dome.

PANTOMIME, originally a drama performed entirely in MIME. Popular in Roman times, it was developed by the COMMEDIA DELL' ARTE and further adapted to become the traditional British Christmas pantomime (or "panto"), with its dialogue, song, spectacle and comedy loosely based on a well-known fairy story.

PAPACY, the office and institution of the pope. As bishop of Rome in succession to St. PETER, the first bishop of Rome, the pope claims to be Christ's representative, with supremacy over all other bishops. This claim is accepted only by Roman Catholics. The title pope, meaning father, was originally applied to all bishops. The authority of the pope at Rome was established in the West during the first five centuries AD but the refusal of the Eastern

churches to accept it resulted (1054) in the first GREAT SCHISM. The papacy had strengthened its secular power in the West after LEO III crowned Charlemagne Holy Roman Emperor in 800. By 1200 the pope had more feudal vassals than any other power and CANON LAW was enforceable throughout Christian Europe. But growing secular forces weakened papal political authority by the late Middle Ages, and the second Great Schism (1378–1417) gravely divided the papacy. Renaissance popes worked to strengthen the PAPAL STATES and created a culturally brilliant papal court, but Church corruption led to demands for reform which culminated in the Protestant REFORMATION. The papacy reacted by founding the JESUITS (1540), reinforcing the INQUISITION (1542), and calling the reformist Council of TRENT. In the 17th and 18th centuries, the power of the papacy was weakened from within by disputes over JANSENISM and from without by increasing secularism and skepticism. In the 19th century the papacy recovered influence as a bulwark of tradition against revolution, and asserted its renewed confidence in such pronouncements as the doctrine of papal infallibility (1870), which held that the pope was infallible in matters of faith and morals when speaking as the vicar of Christ. The Papal States were lost in 1870 but the LATERAN TREATY of 1929 established VATICAN CITY as an independent papal domain. In recent times popes such as JOHN XXIII and JOHN PAUL II have opposed totalitarian rule, encouraged social justice and backed initiatives to renew the Church while maintaining its historic doctrines. (See also ROMAN CATHOLIC CHURCH; VATICAN COUNCILS.)

PAPAGO INDIANS, North American Indian tribe of S Arizona and NW Sonora, Mexico, related to the Pima Indians. They rebelled unsuccessfully against the Spanish (1695 and 1751) and in the 1860s joined the US government against the Apaches. Crops and cattle raising remain the primary economic activities.

PAPAL BULL, papal letter containing a weighty pronouncement and bearing a leaden seal (bulla). It may grant a favor, issue a reprimand, or proclaim the canonization of a saint. It is considered more important than an encyclical.

PAPAL STATES, lands held by the popes as temporal rulers, 754–1870. The states date from the Frankish king Pepin the Short's donation of conquered Lombard lands to the papacy. Later gifts and conquests meant that by the early 1200s the states stretched from coast to coast across central Italy. Victor Emmanuel II annexed the papal states, including, eventually, Rome itself (1870) during the RISORGIMENTO. The papacy refused to accept its loss of lands until the LATERAN TREATY (1929) created an independent VATICAN CITY.

PAPANDREOU, Andreas (1919–   ), premier of Greece from 1981. Imprisoned and then exiled under the military dictatorship (1967–74), he founded while in exile the socialist party known as Pasik (for Panhellenic Socialist Movement). As premier, he instituted numerous reforms. In 1988 his popularity diminished when he announced plans to divorce his wife and marry his mistress. His father, **George Papandreou** (1888–1968), was premier 1964–65. His removal by King Constantine II led to the military coup of 1967 and to the abolition of the monarchy in 1973.

PAPAYA, *Carica papaya,* small tropical fruit tree, widely cultivated for its large edible fruit. The juice of the stem, leaves and unripe fruit contain the protein-digesting enzyme papain. The papaya is sometimes called a papaw. Family: Caricaceae.

PAPEN, Franz von (1879–1969), German statesman. Lacking support as chancellor (June–Nov. 1932), he resigned and helped engineer the appointment of Hitler, supporting the Nazis as a bulwark against communism. He was Hitler's vice-chancellor 1933–34, and as German minister to Vienna (1934–38), he paved the way for German annexation of Austria.

PAPER, felted or matted sheets of CELLULOSE fibers, formed on a wire screen from a water suspension, and used for writing and printing. Rags and cloth—still used for special high-grade papers—were the raw materials used until generally replaced by wood pulp processes developed in the mid-19th century. Logs are now pulped by three methods. Mechanical pulping normally uses a revolving grind-stone. In full chemical pulping, wood chips are cooked under pressure in a solution that dissolves all but the cellulose: the kraft process uses alkaline sodium sulfide solution; the sulfite process uses various bisulfites with excess sulfur dioxide. Semichemical pulping employs mild chemical softening followed by mechanical grinding. The pulp is bleached, washed and refined—i.e., the fibers are crushed, frayed and cut by mechanical beaters. This increases their surface area and bonding power. At this stage various substances are added: fillers (mainly clay and chalk) to make the paper opaque, sizes (rosin and

alum) for resistance, and dyes and pigments as necessary. A dilute aqueous slurry of the pulp is fed to the paper machine, flowing onto a moving belt or cylindrical drum of fine wire mesh, most of the water being drained off by gravity and suction. The newly-formed continuous sheet is pressed between rollers, dried by evaporation, and subjected to calendering. Some paper is coated to give a special surface.

PAPIER-MACHE, molding material of pulped paper mixed with flour paste, glue or resin. It is usually molded while wet but in some industrial processes is pressure-molded. The technique of making papier-mâché decorative objects began in the Orient, and reached Europe in the 18th century.

PAPINEAU, Louis Joseph (1786–1871), Canadian politician, champion of French-Canadian rights in the English-dominated executive and legislature of Lower Canada (Quebec). He framed the Ninety-two Resolutions—a statement of French-Canadian grievances passed by the assembly in 1834. In 1837, a revolt broke out and Papineau fled to the US to avoid arrest. He settled back in Canada in 1845.

PAPP, Joseph (Joseph Papirofsky; 1921–   ), US theatrical producer, founder (1954) of the New York Shakespeare Festival, which presented free theatrical performances in New York's Central Park, and (1967) of the Public Theater, which provided an off-Broadway forum for new playwrights. Many of Papp's productions were successfully moved to Broadway.

PAP SMEAR TEST, CANCER screening test in which cells scraped from the cervix of the WOMB are examined for abnormality under the microscope using the method of G. N. Papanicolaou (1883–1962).

PAPUA NEW GUINEA, independent nation (since 1975), located just N of Australia. The E half of NEW GUINEA Island comprises five-sixths of its territory, which also includes the islands of Bougainville, Buka and the Bismarck Archipelago to the NE and smaller islands to the SE.

Land and People. It is a mountainous, densely forested region with high tempera-ture and rainfall and a rich variety of plant and animal life. The isolating nature of the environment has resulted in a great variety of racial groups and languages: Melanesian in the E and islands, Papuan and sporadic pygmy Negrito groups on the mainland. Most practice animism or tribal religions. In the interior some Stone Age cultures survive.

Economy. Plantation farming has replaced

Official name: Papua New Guinea
Capital: Port Moresby
Area: 178,704sq mi
Population: 3,500,000
Language: local languages; pidgin and standard English
Religions: Christian; Animist; tribal religions
Monetary unit(s): 1 kina = 100 toea
traditional subsistence agriculture in some areas. Exports include timber and coconut products, rubber, cocoa, tea and coffee. Rich mineral deposits, largely undeveloped, include gold, copper and petroleum. Forestry, with exports mainly to Japan, is important.
History. The N mainland and islands were part of German New Guinea 1884–1914. Seized by Australia in 1914, they later became the Trust Territory of New Guinea. The S area was British New Guinea 1884–1905, then, as the Territory of Papua, under Australian rule. The two areas were merged administratively in 1949 as the Australian-administered Territory of Papua and New Guinea. It was renamed Papua New Guinea in 1971, became self-governing in 1973, and independent in 1975. Michael Somare, a leader of the independence movement, was prime minister from 1972 to 1980 and again from 1982 to 1985; he returned to the cabinet as foreign minister under Rabbie Namaliu, who became prime minister in 1988.

PAPYRUS, *Cyperus papyrus,* a stout, reed-like sedge used in ancient civilization as a writing material. It was also used for making sails, baskets and clothing, and the pith prepared as food. Family: Cyperaceae.

PARACELSUS, Philippus Aureolus (1493–1541), Swiss alchemist and physician who channeled the arts of ALCHEMY toward the preparation of medical remedies. Born Theophrastus Bombast von Hohenheim, he adopted the name Paracelsus, boasting that he was superior to the renowned 1st-century Roman medical writer Celsus.

PARACHUTE, collapsible umbrella-like structure used to retard movement through the air. It was invented in the late-18th century, being used for descent from balloons, and made successively from canvas, silk and nylon. When opened—either manually by pulling a ripcord or by a line attached to the aircraft—the canopy fills with air, trapping a large air mass which, because of the parachute's movement, is at a higher pressure than that outside, producing a large retarding force. The canopy consists of numerous strong panels sewn together. Parachutes are used for safe descent of paratroops and others, for dropping airplanes or missiles, and returning space capsules. Sport parachuting, or skydiving, has become popular.

PARADOX, commonly a literary or rhetorical device whereby a supposedly true statement is couched for effect in apparently contradictory terms: e.g., "The last shall be first." A "theoretical paradox" is the conclusion of an apparently convincing argument that is apparently inconsistent with a generally accepted body of theory.

PARAGUAY, landlocked republic of South America, bordered by Brazil, Argentina and Bolivia. The Paraguay R flows N-S and divides the country into two distinct regions.

Official name: Republic of Paraguay
Capital: Asunción
Area: 157,048sq mi
Population: 3,897,000
Languages: Spanish, Guaraní
Religion: Roman Catholic
Monetary unit(s): 1 guaraní = 100 céntimos
Land. The sparsely populated W region known as the Chaco Boreal (part of the GRAN CHACO) is flat, scrubby country, increasingly arid to the W. The smaller but far richer E region is where most of the people live; it is itself divided into two regions by a clifflike ridge running N from the Alton Paraná R near Encarnación. The sparsely populated and densely forested Paraná Plateau lies to the E. To the W, rolling country, rarely above 2,000ft, falls away to more populous low-lying terrain. The climate is mild and constant, with

abundant rains especially in the E.

People and Economy. The majority of the people are mestizo, with Guaraní Indian stock predominating over Spanish influence. More than 40% of the working population are employed on the land, and about 25% of the gross national product comes from agriculture. Products of ranch, farm (cotton, tobacco, coffee) and forest (timber, tannin, oils) are the chief exports. Industry, which developed rapidly in the late 1970s and 1980s, is represented mainly by agricultural product processing. No commercially valuable minerals have been found, though oil deposits exist in the Chaco. Although over half the country is forested, even this resource is mainly unexploited.

History. The country was originally inhabited by Guaranís, settled Indian farmers. Spanish exploration and settlement began in the early 16th century, and by the 1550s the region had become Spain's power base in SE South America. Jesuit influence 1609–1767 contributed significantly to the merging of Guaraní and Spanish cultures. During 1776–1811, Paraguay was part of the Spanish viceroyalty of La Plata. It gained independence in 1811 after a relatively peaceful revolt. Its third ruler, Francisco Solano López, led the disastrous War of the Triple Alliance against Brazil, Uruguay and Argentina (1865–70). Paraguay was laid waste, and more than half the population died. Clashes with Bolivia over a border dispute led to the CHACO WAR (1932–35). Paraguay gained territory but was ruined economically. President Morínigo's comparatively stable and constructive rule (1940–48) ended in civil war. The incumbent president, Gen. Alfredo STROESSNER, seized power in 1954. His regime, which ruled under a continuous state of seige from 1959 to 1987, was often accused of human rights violations.

PARAKEETS, small or medium-sized PARROTS with long tails. They do not form a natural group, the name being given to species of many different genera. Most parakeets are brightly-colored, gregarious birds, feeding on fruits, buds and flowers in semiarid regions throughout the tropics.

PARALLAX, the difference in observed direction of an object due to a difference in position of the observer. Parallax in nearby objects may be observed by closing each eye in turn so that the more distant object appears to move relative to the closer. The brain normally assembles the two images to produce a stereoscopic effect. Should the length and direction of the line between the two points of observation be known, parallax may be used to calculate the distance of the object. In astronomy, the parallax of a star is defined as half the greatest parallactic displacement when viewed from earth at different times of the year.

PARALYSIS, temporary or permanent loss of MUSCLE power or control. It may consist of inability to move a limb or part of a limb or individual muscles, paralysis of the muscles of breathing, swallowing and VOICE production being especially serious. Paralysis may be due to disease of the BRAIN (e.g., STROKE; TUMOR); SPINAL CORD (POLIOMYELITIS); nerve roots (SLIPPED DISK); peripheral NERVOUS SYSTEM (NEURITIS); neuromuscular junction (MYASTHENIA GRAVIS), or muscle (MUSCULAR DYSTROPHY). Disturbance of blood POTASSIUM levels can also lead to paralysis.

PARANÁ RIVER, formed by the confluence of the Rio Grande and the Paranaíba R in S central Brazil. An important commercial artery, it flows 1,827mi S and SW to join the Paraguay R. One of the world's largest hydroelectric plants is under construction at Itaipó.

PARANOIA, a PSYCHOSIS characterized by delusions of persecution (hence the popular term, **persecution mania**) and grandeur, often accompanied by HALLUCINATIONS. The delusions may form a self-consistent system which replaces reality. (See also MENTAL ILLNESS; SCHIZOPHRENIA.)

PARAPLEGIA, PARALYSIS involving the lower part of the body, particularly the legs. Injury to the SPINAL CORD is often the cause.

PARAPSYCHOLOGY, or **psychic research,** a field of study concerned with scientific evaluation of two distinct types of phenomena: those collectively termed ESP, and those concerned with life after death, reincarnation, etc., particularly including claims to communication with souls of the dead (spiritism or, incorrectly, spiritualism). Tests of the former have generally been inconclusive, of the latter almost exclusively negative. But in both cases many "believers" hold that such phenomena, being beyond the bounds of science, cannot be subjected to laboratory evaluation. In spiritism, the prime site of the alleged communication is the séance, in which one individual (the medium) goes into a trance before communicating with the souls of the dead, often through a spirit guide (a spirit associated particularly with the medium). The astonishing disparity among different accounts of the spirit world has led to the whole field being treated with skepticism.

PARASITE, an organism that is for some part of its life-history physiologically dependent on another, the host, from which it obtains nutrition and which may form its total environment. Nearly all the major groups of animals and plants, from viruses to vertebrates and bacteria and angiosperms, have some parasitic members. The most important parasites, besides the viruses which are a wholly parasitic group, occur in the bacteria, protozoa, flatworms and roundworms. Study of the parasitic worms, the platyhelminths, nematodes and acanthocephalans, is termed helminthology. Bloodsucking arthropods, such as mosquitoes, tsetse flies and ticks, are also important because they transmit parasitic diseases and serve as vectors or transport-hosts for other parasites.

PARASITIC DISEASES, infestation by PARASITES, usually referring to nonbacterial and nonviral agents (i.e., to PROTOZOA and helminths). MALARIA, leishmaniasis, trypanosomiasis, Chagas' disease, filariasis, SCHISTOSOMIASIS, toxoplasmosis, amebiasis and TAPEWORM are common examples. Manifestations may depend on the life cycle of the parasite; animal or insect vectors are usual. CHEMOTHERAPY is often effective in treatment.

PARCHMENT, the skin of sheep, ewes or lambs, cleaned, polished, stretched and dried to make a material which can be written on, and also used to make drums and for bookbinding. Invented in the 2nd century BC as a substitute for PAPYRUS, it was widely used for manuscripts until superseded by paper in the 15th century, except for legal documents. **Vellum** is fine-quality parchment made from lamb, kid or calf skin. Both terms are now applied to high-quality paper. Vegetable parchment is paper immersed briefly in sulfuric acid and so made strong and parchment-like.

PARÉ, Ambroise (c1510–1590), French surgeon whose many achievements (e.g., adopting ligatures or liniments in place of cauterization; introducing the use of artificial limbs and organs) have earned him regard as a father of modern SURGERY.

PARESIS, muscular weakness of a part, usually used in distinction from PARALYSIS, which implies complete loss of muscle power. It may be due to disease of the BRAIN, SPINAL CORD, peripheral NERVOUS SYSTEM or MUSCLES.

PARETO, Vilfredo (1848–1923), Italian economist and sociologist. He followed Walras in applying mathematics to economic theory. (See ECONOMICS.) His theories on elites, developed in *Mind and Society* (1916), influenced Mussolini's fascists.

PARIS, capital and largest city of France. It is in the middle of the fertile ILE-DE-FRANCE region. The Seine R winds through Paris, spanned by 30 bridges, and flows 110mi NW to the English Channel. World-famous for its beauty, historic importance and social and cultural life, Paris is an important port and France's chief manufacturing center. In the city itself tourism, dressmaking and luxury trades predominate. Heavier industry (chiefly autos) is based further out in the metropolitan area. On the Left Bank of the Seine lies the SORBONNE in the Latin Quarter, associated with students and artists. Over 2 million tourists a year come to enjoy the Eiffel Tower, LOUVRE museum, NOTRE DAME cathedral, Montmartre, the cafes, gardens and nightlife.

The Parisii Gauls inhabited the Île de la Cité in the middle of the Seine when the Romans set up a colony at this important crossroads in 52 BC. In the early 6th century King Clovis I of the Franks made Paris his capital, a status confirmed when Hugh Capet became king of France in 987 (see CAPETIANS). Growth increased in Philip II's reign (1180–1223) and was maintained even when Louis XIV moved the court to Versailles (1682). The rebuilding of Paris after the FRENCH REVOLUTION (1789) included Georges Haussmann's great tree-lined boulevards. The work was interrupted 1870–71 by the FRANCO-PRUSSIAN WAR and by the PARIS COMMUNE. Though occupied by the Germans during WWII, Paris was little damaged; it was liberated in Aug. 1944. Postwar expansion was particularly striking beyond the western edge of the city. Pop (city) 2,188,960; (metro) 8,510,000.

PARIS, Treaties of, name given to several treaties concluded at Paris. The **Treaty of Paris, 1763,** ended the SEVEN YEARS' WAR including the FRENCH AND INDIAN WARS in America. France lost her military rights in E India (and thus any chance of ousting the British) and her American possessions. Britain gained Florida and parts of Louisiana, and Spain regained Cuba and the Philippines. Freed from the French threat, American colonists stepped up the struggle for independence, which was finally confirmed by the **Treaty of Paris, 1783,** ending the REVOLUTIONARY WAR. US boundaries were agreed as Canada in the N, the Mississippi in the W and Florida (regained by Spain) in the S, and the US won fishing rights off Newfoundland. The **Treaty of Paris, 1814,** attempted to end the NAPOLEONIC WARS after Napoleon's first abdication. France under the restored Bourbon monarchy was allowed to retain her 1792 boundaries and most of her colonies. The **Treaty of Paris, 1815,** signed after Napoleon's final defeat at WATERLOO, dealt with France more harshly. French boundaries were reduced to those of 1790 and France had to pay reparations and support an army of occupation for up to five years. The **Treaty of Paris, 1856,** ending the CRIMEAN WAR, was signed by Russia, Britain, France, Turkey and Sardinia. Designed largely to protect Turkey from Russia, it guaranteed Turkish independence, declared the Black Sea neutral, opened Danube navigation to all nations, and established Moldavia and Walachia (later Romania) as independent states under Turkish suzerainty. The **Treaty of Paris, 1898,** ended the SPANISH-AMERICAN WAR and effectively ended the Spanish empire. Cuba became independent, and the US gained Puerto Rico, Guam and the Philippines. After WWI the treaties of Neuilly, Saint-Germain, Sèvres, Trianon and VERSAILLES were concluded at the Paris Peace Conference. Treaties were also signed at Paris after WWII.

PARIS, University of, France's greatest, and the world's most venerable, institution of higher learning. Growing out of the medieval cathedral schools of Notre Dame, it has granted master's degrees since 1170. The SORBONNE (founded 1253) became its single most famous college. Reconstituted during the Napoleonic era as a modern university, it was reorganized again in 1970 into 13 autonomous units.

PARIS COMMUNE, insurrection of radical Parisians against the pro-royalist National Assembly, March–May 1871, following the humiliation of the FRANCO-PRUSSIAN WAR. The Communards drove the Assembly out of Paris, and elected their own Commune government, while similar movements broke out elsewhere. The Assembly sent in 130,000 troops who crushed the movement in a week of bloody street fighting. More than 17,000 people were executed in reprisals.

PARK, Mungo (1771–1806), Scottish explorer of W Africa. He made two exploratory journeys along the Gambia, upper Senegal and Niger rivers, 1795–97 and 1805–06, publishing *Travels in the Interior Districts of Africa* in 1799. He was drowned at Bussa during attack by hostile Africans.

PARK, Robert Ezra (1864–1944), US sociologist, at the University of Chicago 1914–33, known for his work in urban sociology.

PARK CHUNG HEE (1917–1979), president of South Korea 1963–1979. He served with the Japanese in WWII, became a general in the Korean army and led the 1961 military coup. Becoming progressively more dictatorial, in 1972 he assumed almost unlimited power. He was a strong ally of the US. He was assassinated by the director of the Korean Central Intelligence Agency.

PARKER, Alton Brooks (1852–1926), US jurist and Democratic presidential candidate. He was chief justice of the N.Y. court of appeals 1897–1904, and after losing to Theodore ROOSEVELT in 1904 returned to private practice.

PARKER, Charlie (Charles Christopher Parker; 1920–1955), US jazz musician, known as "Bird" or "Yardbird." An alto saxophonist and composer, he was a leader in developing the BOP style and was also one of the most innovative improvisers in jazz history.

PARKER, Dorothy (1893–1967), American writer, critic and wit. She wrote short stories, satirical verse and newspaper columns, and was a celebrated conversationalist. Her tone is poignant, ironical and often cruelly witty and cynical.

PARKER, Horatio William (1863–1919), US composer. The first head of Yale University's music department (1894–1919), he composed much religious and chamber music and *Mona*, the first full-length opera by an American ever staged by the Metroplitan Opera (Mar. 14, 1912).

PARKER, Theodore (1810–1860), US liberal preacher and social reformer. A Unitarian pastor in West Roxbury, Mass. (1837–46) and Boston (1846–59), he championed abolition of slavery, prison reform, temperance and education for women.

PARKINSON'S DISEASE, a common disorder in the elderly, causing a characteristic mask-like facial appearance, shuffling gait, slowness to move, muscular rigidity and tremor at rest; mental ability is preserved except in those cases following ENCEPHALITIS lethargica. It is a disorder of the basal ganglia of the BRAIN and may be substantially helped by DRUGS (e.g., L-Dopa) that affect impulse transmission in these sites. A surgical treatment, announced in Mexico in 1987, consisted of transplanting tissue from the patient's own adrenal gland into the brain. Surgeons also experimented with implants of tissue from the brain of a human fetus. Both procedures were intended to spur the brain's production of the chemical dopamine, which is believed to be disrupted in Parkinson's patients. Both proved disappointing.

PARKMAN, Francis (1823–1893), great US historian of the Frontier and of the Anglo-French struggle for North America. His chief work is the seven volumes collectively called *France and England in North America* (1865–92). Other works include his *History of the Conspiracy of Pontiac* (1851) and *The Oregon Trail* (1849), an enormously popular account of a journey made in 1846. He later became an expert horticulturalist.

PARKS, Rosa (1913–   ), US civil-rights activist. A seamstress in 1955, she was arrested for refusing to give up her seat on a Montgomery, Ala., bus to a white passenger, thereby sparking a black boycott of city buses that raised Martin Luther KING, Jr., to national prominence. She became known as the "mother of the civil rights movement."

PARKS, areas of land set aside for public recreation. Urban parks gained importance as towns grew in the 19th century and are a distinctive feature of modern cities. Central Park in New York was laid out in 1857 by F. L. OLMSTED to produce the effect of countryside in the middle of a city. Such parks often imitated landscaped English parklands and featured ornamental lakes and artificial hills. In the 20th century the US NATIONAL PARK SYSTEM developed from the need to preserve large areas of countryside from being built on and to safeguard their wildlife. Since the creation of Yellowstone Park in 1872, enormous areas of the US have been so protected.

PARLIAMENT, body of elected representatives responsible for a country's legislation and finance. The term parliamentary government is used to describe a system (distinct from the presidential system) in which the government's chief ministers, including the PRIME MINISTER, are elected members of parliament. This system operates in Britain, most Commonwealth countries and Scandinavia.

In a parliamentary system the head of state (a monarch or president) exists outside parliament and exercises only limited powers; real power rests with the prime minister, who leads the majority party or a coalition of parties. He rules with the help of a CABINET chosen from other elected members. The government in power has the right to dissolve parliament and call a new election before its term of office ends, but is obliged to resign if it fails to command a majority vote of members. All these features differ from presidential government as practiced in the US. The chief model for modern parliamentary govern-ment is the British Parliament, which began to take on its present form in the Middle Ages. (See also HOUSE OF COMMONS; HOUSE OF LORDS; PRESIDENCY.)

PARMENIDES (flourished c475 BC), Greek philosopher of Elea in southern Italy; foremost of the ELEATICS. His philosophy, anchored on the proposition "What is *is*," denied the reality of multiplicity and change. His uncompromising attempt to deduce the properties of the Real—a single eternal solid, all-embracing yet undifferentiated— marks the beginning of the Western tradition of philosophical reasoning. (See also PRE-SOCRATICS.)

PARNASSIANS, group of 19th-century French poets led by LECONTE DE LISLE. Influenced by GAUTIER's "art for art's sake" theories, they emphasized technical skill, restraint and objectivity.

PARNASSUS, mountain in central Greece, N of DELPHI and the Gulf of Corinth. It was once sacred to Dionysus and Apollo and celebrated as a home of the MUSES. It is 8,061ft high.

PARNELL, Charles Stewart (1846–1891), Irish nationalist, leader of the Irish HOME RULE movement from within the British parliament from 1877. He obstructed parliamentary business and demanded Irish land reform, and his supporters' agitation persuaded GLADSTONE to adopt a home rule policy. His political career ended in 1890 when he was named corespondent in a divorce case.

PAROCHIAL SCHOOLS, in the US, elementary and high schools run by religious bodies. The Roman Catholic Church, the Lutheran system and the Jewish Day Schools between them serve more than 10% of the nation's elementary and high-school pupils. Most parochial schools were set up in the 19th century. They expanded until the 1960s, but were then beset by financial problems, complicated by controversies over whether they should receive state and federal aid.

PAROLE, the system of releasing convicts from prison before the end of their sentences. Generally, parole is granted for good behavior in prison, if the parole board considers a prisoner psychologically and socially ready to readjust to the outside world. A parolee must usually observe certain standards of conduct, stay within certain areas, and report to a parole officer. (See also PRISONS; PROBATION.)

PARR, Catherine (1512–1548), sixth wife of King HENRY VIII of England (1543–47). Twice widowed before she married the king, she outlived him to marry again. She was a kindly influence at court and held some power in the reign of EDWARD VI.

PARRINGTON, Vernon Louis (1871–1929), US literary historian who stressed the influence of social and economic affairs upon American writers. His *Main Currents in American Thought* (1927–30) won a Pulitzer prize.

PARRISH, Maxfield (1870–1966), US painter and illustrator with an elegant, richly decorative style. He is noted for murals, posters and book and magazine illustrations.

PARROTS, a family, Psittacidae, of about 320 species of birds distributed throughout the tropics. Most are brightly-colored birds with heavy, hooked bills, of which both mandibles articulate with the skull. Most are arboreal and diurnal, feeding on fruits, berries and leaves; some can mimic speech. There are four subfamilies: the Strigopinae (with only the kakapo of New Zealand) the Cacatuinae (the cockatoos) and the Lorinae (the lories and lorikeets, pygmy parrots and fig parrots). The fourth subfamily, the Psittacinae, contains some 200 species of "true" parrots, including the 130 species of American parrots.

PARSEES or **Parsis,** religious group centered in Bombay and NW India who practice ZOROASTRIANISM. Their ancestors came from Persia in the 8th century to escape Muslim persecution. They now number about 120,000. The Parsees, many of whom are traders, are among the wealthiest and best educated groups in India. They worship at fire temples.

PARSNIP, *Pastinaca sativa,* a carrot-like plant grown for its edible sweet-fllavored yellowish-white root. They are easy to cultivate, but need a long growing season and are harvested in the fall and winter. Family: Umbelliferae.

PARSONS, Louella O. (Louella Oettinger; 1881?–1972), US newspaper columnist who covered Hollywood gossip for the Hearst newspapers 1925–65.

PARSONS, Talcott (1902–1981), US sociologist, who taught at Harvard 1927–74. An inveterate theorizer, he advocated a "structural-functional" analysis of the units that make up a stable social system. Works include *The Structure of Social Action* (1937), *The Social System* (1951) and *Politics and Social Structure* (1969).

PARSONS, Theophilus (1750–1813), US jurist. A member of the ESSEX JUNTO, he helped draft a new Mass. constitution in 1779, and was chief justice of the Mass. Supreme Court from 1806.

PARTCH, Harry (1901–1974), US composer who devised a special notation for his unique microtonal music, which was based on an octave divided into 43 intervals instead of the traditional 12. His works received scant public attention as they could only be performed on bizarre instruments of his own devising.

PARTHENON, the most famous Greek temple, on the ACROPOLIS at Athens. Sacred to the city's patron goddess, Athena Parthenos, it was built of marble 447–432 BC by Ictinus and Callicrates, with PHIDIAS supervising the sculptures. It featured a roof on Doric columns, an inner room and fine sculptures and friezes, including the ELGIN MARBLES. The Parthenon remained well preserved until 1687, when a Venetian bombardment exploded a Turkish powder magazine inside it. It is now threatened by industrial pollution. (See also GREEK ART AND ARCHITECTURE.)

PARTHIA, ancient country SE of the Caspian Sea, where the Arsacid empire was founded c248 BC in revolt against the SELEUCIDS. It reached its zenith under Mithradates I (171–138 BC) and II (123–88 BC). Parthians conquered Persia and nearby lands, and their mounted archers continually withstood Roman aggression. A revolt established the SASSANIANS in power 224 AD. (See also PERSIA, ANCIENT.)

PARTICLES, Elementary. See SUBATOMIC PARTICLES.

PARTISANS, term usually used to describe the resistance movements in German-occupied territories in WWII. The original partisans were the communist supporters (*partizani*) of TITO in Yugoslavia. (See also GUERRILLA WARFARE.)

PARTNERSHIP, business arrangement between two or more people combining labor, funds or property with a view to sharing profits. In law, partners are assumed to exercise joint control and can be held responsible for the liabilities of the partnership. The arrangement is common in professions such as law and accountancy and in small-scale service businesses. In limited partnerships a partner's liability is limited to his investment in the partnership.

PARTRIDGE, Eric Honeywood (1894–1979), New Zealand-born English lexicographer, best known for *A Dictionary of Slang and Unconventional English* (1937).

PARTRIDGES, several genera of game birds distributed through Europe, Asia and Africa. Best known is the gray or common partridge, *Perdix perdix,* of Europe, with a chestnut horseshoe on the breast.

PASCAL, Blaise (1623–1662), French mathematician, physicist and religious philosopher. Though not the first to study what is now called Pascal's triangle, he was first to use it in PROBABILITY studies, the mathematical treatment of which he and FERMAT evolved together, though in different ways. His studies of the cycloid inspired others to formulate the CALCULUS. His experiments (performed by his brother-in-law) observing the heights of the column of a BAROMETER at different altitudes on the mountain Puy-de-Dôme (1646) confirmed that the atmospheric air had weight. He also pioneered HYDRODYNAMICS and FLUID MECHANICS, in doing so discovering PASCAL'S LAW, the basis of HYDRAULICS. His religious thought, which emphasizes "the reasons of the heart" over those of dry logic and intellect, is expressed in his *Provincial Letters* (1656–57) and his posthumously published *Pensées* (1670 onward).

PASCAL'S LAW, in FLUID MECHANICS, states that the pressure in an enclosed body of fluid arising from forces applied to its boundaries is transmitted equally in all directions with unchanged intensity. This pressure acts at right angles to the surface of the fluid container.

PASQUEFLOWER, common name for spring-flowering ANEMONES that are associated with Easter. The American pasqueflower (*Anemone patens*) is abundant in the prairies and the European pasqueflower (*A. pulsatilla*) grows in chalky pastures. Family: Ranunculaceae.

PASSENGER PIGEON, *Ectopistes migratorius*, extinct member of the PIGEON family Columbidae, extremely common until the 19th century over most of North America. They were highly gregarious and social birds migrating in huge flocks. They fed on invertebrates, fruits and grain, often doing extensive damage to crops. Hunted by man both as a pest and for food, they finally became extinct in 1914.

PASSERIFORMES, a single order of BIRDS which contains all the 5,000 plus species of perching birds and song birds. The order is incredibly diverse and its members have become adapted to an enormous variety of niches. All passerines are land birds with feet adapted for perching and walking. Passerine young are "nidicolous"— confined to a nest by their helplessness and cared for by the parents.

PASSION, musical setting of the Gospel texts describing the crucifixion. From early PLAINSONG developed medieval music-drama and Renaissance MOTET forms. Among the first works to use the name were those of SCHÜTZ, who influenced J. S. BACH, composer of the famous *St. John* and *St.*

Matthew passions for soloists, chorus and orchestra.

PASSION, The, the sufferings of Jesus Christ for mankind including the agony in the garden at GETHSEMANE, his trial and crucifixion. **Passiontide,** in the church year, denotes the last two weeks in LENT, from Passion Sunday until the Saturday of Holy Week.

PASSION PLAY, dramatic presentation of Christ's suffering and death. It was one of the popular medieval MYSTERY PLAYS, performed by amateurs at religious festivals. The most famous passion play still performed is that at OBERAMMERGAU, staged every ten years since 1634.

PASSOVER, ancient major Jewish festival held for eight days from 14th *Nisan* (March/April). It celebrates the Israelites' escape from Egyptian slavery, when each family slew a paschal lamb and sprinkled its blood on the doorposts, and the destroying angel passed over. At the *Seder* feast, on the evening of the first two days, special dishes symbolize the Israelites' hardships, and the story of the Exodus is read from the Haggadah. During Passover unleavened bread (matzoth) is eaten; no leaven at all may be used, a reminder of the hasty departure. (See also LAST SUPPER.)

PASSPORT, document issued by governments to citizens of their country, identifying and authorizing them to travel abroad and be readmitted to their homeland. Some countries also require a visitor to have a visa, issued by the consular authorities in his home country. In wartime passports may have restricted use.

PASTEL, drawing medium resembling a stick of colored chalk, and the pictures formed with it. The color is applied in broad areas and may be rubbed with the finger to form different tones. Usually it covers an entire surface, resembling painting rather than drawing. Masters of the art include J. B. S. CHARDIN and DEGAS.

PASTERNAK, Boris Leonidovich (1890–1960), Russian writer, best known for his only novel *Doctor Zhivago* (1958). He won the 1958 Nobel Prize for Literature but official pressure forced him to decline it. He was also a gifted translator of Shakespeare and Goethe, and the author of poems, short stories and an autobiography.

PASTEUR, Louis (1822–1895), French microbiologist and chemist. In his early pioneering studies in STEREOCHEMISTRY he discovered optical isomerism. His attentions then centered around FERMENTATION, in which he demonstrated the role of microorganisms. He developed PASTEUR-IZATION as a way of stopping wine and beer from souring, and experimentally disproved the theory of SPONTANEOUS GENERATION. His "germ theory" of DISEASE proposed that diseases are spread by living germs (i.e., BACTERIA); and his consequent popularization of the STERILIZATION of medical equipment saved many lives. While studying ANTHRAX in cattle and sheep he developed a form of VACCINATION rather different from that of JENNER: he found inoculation with dead anthrax germs gave future IMMUNITY from the disease. Treating RABIES similarly, he concluded that it was caused by a germ too small to be seen—i.e., a VIRUS. The Pasteur Institute was founded in 1888 to lead the fight against rabies.

PASTEURIZATION, a process for partially sterilizing MILK originally invented by L. PASTEUR for improving the storage qualities of wine and beer. Originally the milk was held at 63°C for 30min in a vat. But today the usual method is a continuous process whereby the milk is held at 72°–85°C for 16s. Disease-producing BACTERIA, particularly those causing TUBERCULOSIS, are thus destroyed with a minimum effect on the flavor of the product. Since the process also destroys a majority of the harmless bacteria which sour milk, its keeping properties are also improved.

PASTORAL LITERATURE idealizes simple shepherd life, free from the corruption of the city. Typical forms are the verse elegy, prose romance and drama. Originating with THEOCRITUS in the 3rd century BC, the form was used by VERGIL, and later in England, after a Renaissance revival, by SHAKESPEARE (in *As You Like It*), Sir Philip SIDNEY (in *Arcadia*) and MILTON (in *Comus*).

PATAGONIA, that part of South America S of the Rio Negro or, more usually, the dry tableland in this region between the Andes and Atlantic, including Tierra del Fuego. Both areas lie mainly in Argentina, partly in Chile. Sheep-raising is the main activity of the few inhabitants, and there are oil, iron ore and coal deposits.

PATCH TEST, test used in investigation of skin and systemic ALLERGY, especially contact DERMATITIS. Patches of known or likely sensitizing substances are placed on the SKIN for a short period. Local erythema or HIVES indicate allergy.

PATEL, Vallabhbhai (1975–1950), Indian political leader. A successful criminal lawyer, from 1917 he devoted himself to the nationalist cause and was often imprisoned for his activities. Upon Indian independence, he became deputy prime minister and successfully integrated hundreds of princely states into the union.

PATENT, a grant of certain specified rights by the government of a particular country, usually to a person whose claim to be the true and first inventor of a new invention (or the discoverer of a new process) is upheld. Criteria of the "novelty" of an invention are defined in law. The term derives from "letters patent"—the "open letters" by which a sovereign traditionally confers a special privilege or right on a subject. An inventor (or his assignee) who files an application for and is granted a patent is exclusively entitled to make, use or sell his invention for a limited period—17 years from the granting date, in the US and Canada. By granting the inventor a temporary monopoly, patent law aims to stimulate inventive activity and the rapid exploitation of new inventions for the public benefit.

PATERSON, William (1745–1806), US statesman. A delegate from N.J., he was author of the "New Jersey plan" at the Constitutional Convention (1787), a US senator 1789–90, governor of N.J. 1791–93, and from 1793 associate justice of the US Supreme Court. Paterson, N.J., is named for him.

PATHOLOGY, study of the ANATOMY of DISEASE. Morbid anatomy, the dissection of bodies after DEATH with a view to discovering the cause of disease and the nature of its manifestaions, is complemented and extended by HISTOLOGY. In addition to autopsy, biopsies and surgical specimens are examined; these provide information that may guide treatment. It has been said that pathology is to MEDICINE what anatomy is to PHYSIOLOGY.

PATIÑO, Simón Ituri (1868–1947), Bolivian tin magnate who dominated the country's economic and political life. His holdings were nationalized after a 1952 revolution.

PATON, Alan Stewart (1903–1988), South African writer. His novel *Cry the Beloved Country* (1948), drawing on his experience as principal of a reform school for Africans, describes APARTHEID. In 1953 he became president of the Liberal Party, banned in 1968.

PATRIARCH, Old Testament title of the head of a family or tribe, especially the Israelite fathers, Abraham, Isaac, Jacob and Jacob's sons (see TWELVE TRIBES OF ISRAEL). The title was adopted by the early Christian bishops of Rome, Alexandria and Antioch, and now extends to certain other sees, especially of the ORTHODOX CHURCHES. It implies jurisdiction over other bishops.

PATRICIAN, in ancient Rome, an aristocrat by birth. In the early Republic the heads (Latin: *patres*) of the chief families dominated the Senate. They gradually lost power 500-250 BC to the PLEBEIANS, or common citizens, until *patrician* became a mere honorary title.

PATRICK, Saint, 5th-century missionary bishop, patron saint of Ireland. Controversy surrounds his identity, dates and works. In the popular and official version he was born in Britain c385, was captured by pagan Irish and was a slave six years. After training in Gaul he returned c432 to convert Ireland, with spectacular success in Ulster and at Tara. He founded his see at Armagh. Author of the autobiographical *Confessions*, he died c461. His feast day, an Irish festival the world over, is March 17.

PATROONS, holders of huge estates in the Dutch colony of NEW NETHERLAND (now N.Y.). From 1629 patroonships, with tax exemptions, monopolies and feudal rights, were granted by the Dutch West India Company to sponsors of 50 or more settlers. The Van Rensselaer patroon excepted, the system did not encourage colonization, but vestiges remained until the Anti-Rent War of 1839-46, in which tenant farmers, claiming their land, refused to pay back rents to hereditary landowners. In 1847 the state granted the farmers the land.

PATTERSON, family of US newspaper publishers and editors. **Joseph Medill Patterson** (1879-1946) was coeditor (from 1910) and copublisher (1914-25) of the *Chicago Tribune* (with Robert McCormick). He was cofounder (1919) and coeditor and publisher of the New York *Daily News*, the largest circulation tabloid in the US. His sister, **Eleanor Medill Patterson** (1884-1948), edited the *Washington Herald* (from 1930), leased it and the *Times* (1937-39) and published the merged Washington *Times-Herald* (1939-48). His daughter, **Alicia Patterson** (1906-1963), founded, published and edited the Long Island, N.Y., newspaper *Newsday* (1940-63), which she developed into one of the largest suburban dailies in the US.

PATTON, George Smith, Jr (1885-1945), US general. His ruthlessness and tactical brilliance as a tank commander won him the nickname "Old Blood and Guts." Born of a military family, he graduated from West Point in 1909 and commanded a tank brigade in WWI. In WWII he was highly successful in N Africa and led the Third Army's rapid drive through France to SW Germany. He was killed in an automobile accident in Dec., 1945.

PAUL, Saint (d. c65 AD), APOSTLE to the Gentiles, major figure in the early Christian Church. His life is recorded in the ACTS OF THE APOSTLES. Son of a Roman citizen, he was a zealous Jew, active in the persecution of the Christians until a vision of Christ on the road to Damascus made him a fervent convert to the new faith. He went on extensive missionary journeys to Cyprus, Asia Minor and Greece. Returning to Jerusalem, he was violently attacked by the Jews and imprisoned for two years. An appeal to the Emperor brought a transfer (c60 AD) to Rome, where, according to tradition, he was executed after two years' house arrest. His epistles, some of which are preserved in the NEW TESTAMENT, have had an incalculable influence on Christian belief and practice.

PAUL, name of six popes. **Paul III** (1468-1549), pope from 1534, encouraged the first major reforms of the COUNTER-REFORMATION, recognized the Jesuit order and convened the Council of TRENT (1545). **Paul IV** (1476-1559), reigned from 1555, increased the powers of the Roman Inquisition, enforced segregation of the Jews in Rome and introduced strict censorship. His fanatical reformism proved self-defeating by creating widespread hostility. **Paul V** (1552-1621), pope from 1605, came into conflict with the Venetian Republic over papal jurisdiction, and, as a member of the Borghese family, was notorious for nepotism. **Paul VI** (1897-1978), elected in 1963, continued the modernizing reforms of his predecessor, JOHN XXIII, confirmed the Roman Catholic Church's ban on contraception and became the first pope to travel widely.

PAUL I (Pavel Petrovich; 1754-1801), emperor of Russia from 1796. His despotism at home and erratic policies abroad caused widespread discontent. He was assassinated by army officers anxious to secure the succession of his son Alexander.

PAUL I (1901-1964), king of Greece from 1947, on the death of his brother George II. During his reign Greece was the recipient of US economic aid, and generally followed anti-communist policies. He was succeeded by his son Constantine (r. 1964-73).

PAULDING, James Kirke (1778-1860), US writer and public official who satirized British colonialism in such works as *John Bull in America* (1825), and did much to encourage the development of distinctively American literature. His five novels include *Westward Ho!* (1832).

PAULI, Wolfgang (1900-1958), Austrian-born physicist awarded the 1945 Nobel Prize for Physics for his discovery of the Pauli EXCLUSION PRINCIPLE, that no two fermions (see SUBATOMIC PARTICLES) in a system may have the same four quantum numbers. In terms of the ATOM, this means that at most two electrons may occupy the same orbital (the two having opposite spin).

PAULING, Linus Carl (1901–), US chemist and pacifist awarded the 1954 Nobel Prize for Chemistry for his work on the chemical BOND and the 1962 Nobel Peace Prize for his support of unilateral nuclear disarmament.

PAULIST FATHERS, officially the Society of Missionary Priests of St. Paul the Apostle, an evangelical order of Roman Catholic priests in the US, founded by Isaac HECKER (1858).

PAUL OF THE CROSS, Saint (1694–1775), Italian mystic who founded the Passionist order of monks in 1720, and an order of the same name for nuns in 1770.

PAULUS, Friedrich (1890–1957), German field marshal. As deputy chief of the German general staff from 1940 he helped plan the 1941 invasion of Russia and led the 6th Army (1942) in the attack on Stalingrad. A Soviet counterattack resulted in the surrender of Paulus and his entire army of 300,000 men (1943).

PAUNCEFOTE, Julian, 1st Baron Pauncefote of Preston (1828–1902), British diplomat, permanent undersecretary of foreign affairs (1882) and ambassador to the US (1893). The most significant contribution of a distinguished career was his negotiation of the HAY-PAUNCEFOTE TREATY (1901), which resolved US-British dispute over control of the projected Panama Canal.

PAVAROTTI, Luciano (1935–), Italian tenor, the best Italian bel canto tenor of his day. He became a Metropolitan Opera star after his debut there in 1968.

PAVESE, Cesare (1908–1950), Italian post-WWII novelist and, with Elio Vittorini, a major translator of American writing into Italian.

PAVLOV, Ivan Petrovich (1849–1936), Russian physiologist best known for his work on the conditioned REFLEX. Regularly, over long periods, he rang a bell just before feeding dogs, and found that eventually they salivated on hearing the bell, even when there was no food forthcoming. He also studied the physiology of the DIGESTIVE SYSTEM, and for this received the 1904 Nobel Prize for Physiology or Medicine.

PAVLOVA, Anna Matveyevna (1882–1931), Russian ballerina, considered the greatest of her time. She formed her own company and was famed for her roles in *Giselle* and *The Dying Swan* choreographed for her by Michel FOKINE.

PAWNBROKING, the business activity of lending on the security of personal possessions, which are left with the pawnbroker in return for a sum of money (usually well below the value of the article). The borrower receives a ticket with which he can redeem his property within a certain time, after which it may be sold.

PAWNEE INDIANS, North American Indians of Caddoan linguistic stock who inhabited river valleys of Nebraska and Kansas in the 16th to the 19th centuries. They had an elaborate religion which for a time involved human sacrifice. They lived by farming and buffalo hunting, but by 1876 had ceded all of their land to the US government. They settled on a reservation in Oklahoma, where they numbered about 1,000 in the 1980s.

PAZ, Octavio (1914–), Mexican poet and critic. He was Mexican ambassador to India, but resigned in 1968 to protest the killing of 300 antigovernment demonstrators and lived thereafter in England.

PAZ ESTENSSORO, Victor (1907–), Bolivian political leader, a founder of the National Revolutionary Movement. Elected president in 1951, he was blocked by the army from taking power, but his supporters revolted and Paz became president in 1952, nationalizing tin mines and executing sweeping land reforms. He stepped down in 1956 but was reelected in 1960 and 1964, when he was overthrown by the army. He was again elected president in 1985.

PEA, herbaceous annual leguminous plants that are mainly cultivated for their edible seeds. They have alternate compound leaves, white or purple flowers and for fruit, a many-seeded pod or legume. The garden pea (*Pisum sativum*) is native to Middle Asia and is now widely cultivated in North America, Europe and Asia. Family: Leguminosae.

PEABODY, Elizabeth Palmer (1804–1894), US educator, author and publisher who started the first US kindergarten and introduced FROEBEL's methods of education to the US. She wrote widely on educational theory, published early works of Nathaniel HAWTHORNE, and was an exponent of TRANSCENDENTALISM.

PEABODY, George (1795–1869), US financier and philanthropist. From 1837 he lived in London, where he set up an immensely prosperous investment banking house. His donations made possible such foundations as the Peabody Institute of Baltimore and the George Peabody College in Nashville, Tenn., as well as museums at Harvard and Yale.

PEACE CORPS, agency of the US government established by President John

F. KENNEDY in 1961 (and in 1971 transferred to ACTION, the agency coordinating federal volunteer programs). The aim of the Peace Corps is to help raise living standards in developing countries and to promote international friendship and understanding. Peace Corps projects, ranging from farm assistance to nursing instruction, are established at the request of the host country. Its volunteers normally serve for two years.

PEACE PIPE, or calumet (French: reed), a tobacco pipe, long-stemmed and elaborately decorated, smoked by most North American Indian peoples on ceremonial occasions such as the signing of peace treaties. The peace pipe was a symbol of its owner's power and honor, and as such was held sacred.

PEACE RIVER, in W Canada, the main branch of the Mackenzie R. Formed by the junction of the Finlay and Parsnip rivers in central British Columbia, it flows 1,065mi E into Alberta to join the Slave R near Lake Athabasca.

PEACH, poopular name for *Prunus persica* and its rough-skinned fruit. Native to China, it is now cultivated in warmer regions throughout the world (notably in Calif.). There are several thousand varieties divided into freestone or clingstone types, according to the ease with which the flesh comes away from the stone. The **nectarine** is a variety of peach and has a smoother skin and a richer flavor. Family: Rosaceae.

PEACOCK, Thomas Love (1785–1866), English novelist and poet, a brilliant satirist of contemporary intellectual trends. He was a close friend of SHELLEY and an able administrator in the East India Company. His best poetry is contained in his novels, which he described as comic romances. They include *Headlong Hall* (1816), *Nightmare Abbey* (1818) and *Crotchet Castle* (1831).

PEACOCKS, properly **peafowl,** large exotic ground birds of two genera, *Pavo* and *Afropavo,* well known as ornamental birds. The male, the peacock, has a train of up to 150 tail feathers, which can be erected in display to form a showy fan.

PEALE, an important family of early US painters. The prolific and versatile **Charles Willson Peale** (1741–1827) is best known for his portraits of Washington and other leading figures of the revolutionary period. He studied with Benjamin WEST in London, and in 1784 founded a museum in Philadelphia, later moved to Independence Hall, which housed a portrait gallery together with natural history and technology exhibits. His younger brother **James**

Peale (1749–1831) was best known for his portrait miniatures. Charles' many sons included **Raphaelle Peale** (1774–1825), a pioneer of US still-life painting, and **Rembrandt Peale** (1778–1860), a portraitist and founder of the Peale Museum, Baltimore. His most famous work is a portrait of Thomas Jefferson (1805).

PEALE, Norman Vincent (1898–   ), US clergyman, pastor of New York's Marble Collegiate Church from 1932. He disseminated his inspirational and politically conservative views by radio, television, and newspaper and magazine columns. He is best known as author of *The Power of Positive Thinking* (1952).

PEANO, Giuseppe (1858–1932), Italian mathematician whose ideas in mathematical LOGIC profoundly influenced those of A. N. WHITEHEAD and B. RUSSELL. He also devised the international language *Interlingua,* still occasionally used.

PEANUT, groundnut or **goober** (*Arachis hypogaea*), a low bushy leguminous plant cultivated in tropical and subtropical regions. The "nut" is a fruit normally containing two seeds, which is produced when the yellow flowers grow down into the ground after pollination. Family: Leguminosae.

PEAR, *Pyrus communis* and related species, common name for these deciduous trees and their oval-shaped soft-fleshed fruit. There are hundreds of varieties of the fruit, the "Bartlett" pear being commonest in the US. Family: Rosaceae.

PEA RIDGE, Battle of, US CIVIL WAR battle of NW Ark. on March 7–8, 1862. Gen. Earl van Dorn led a Confederate attack on the Union army under General Samuel R. Curtis and was decisively defeated.

PEARL HARBOR, natural land-locked harbor on the island of Oahu in Hawaii. Of great strategic importance, it is best known as the scene of the Japanese bombing of the US Pacific fleet on Dec. 7, 1941. Most of the fleet was in the harbor when Japanese carrier-based planes attacked without warning. Nineteen ships were damaged or sunk; on the ground at Wheeler Field 188 planes were destroyed. The raid caused over 2,200 casualties with negligible losses to the Japanese. The attack brought the US into WWII.

PEARLS, white spherical gems produced by bivalve mollusks, particularly by pearl oysters, *Pinctada.* In response to an irritation by foreign matter within the shell, the mantle secretes calcium carbonate in the form of nacre (MOTHER-OF-PEARL) around the irritant body. Over several years, this encrustation forms the pearl.

Cultured pearls may be obtained by "seeding" the oyster with an artificial irritant such as a small bead. Pearls are variable and may be black or pink as well as the usual white. Another bivalve group producing marketable pearls is the freshwater pearl mussel, *Margaritifera margaritifera*.

PEARLY NAUTILUS, a shelled member of the cephalopod mollusks, with six species in the genus *Nautilus*, found in the southwestern Indo-Pacific. The shell is coiled and chambered. The growing animal lives always in the last chamber, the empty ones being gas-filled for flotation.

PEARSE, Patrick Henry (1879–1916), Irish educator, writer and patriot, a major figure in the Gaelic revival. He led the Irish Republican Brotherhood in the EASTER RISING of 1916. When it collapsed he was tried and executed.

PEARSON, Drew (Andrew Russell Pearson; 1897–1969), US journalist who specialized in political muckraking and personal feuds in his syndicated column, "Washington Merry-Go-Round."

PEARSON, Karl (1857–1936), British mathematician best known for his pioneering work on STATISTICS (e.g., devising the chi-squared test) and for his *The Grammar of Science* (1892), an important contribution to the philosophy of mathematics. He was also an early worker in the field of EUGENICS.

PEARSON, Lester Bowles (1897–1972), Canadian diplomat, prime minister (1963–68) and winner of the 1957 Nobel Peace Prize for his mediation in the Suez crisis (1956). In 1928 he joined the Department of External Affairs, becoming first secretary, and in 1945 he was appointed ambassador to the US. As secretary of state (1948–57) he made notable contributions to the UN and NATO. In 1958 he became the Liberal leader. After resigning as prime minister he headed the WORLD BANK commission which produced the Pearson Report on developing countries.

PEARY, Robert Edwin (1856–1920), US Arctic explorer who discovered the North Pole. He entered the US Navy in 1881, and first journeyed to the interior of Greenland in 1886. On leaves of absence from the navy, he led a series of exploratory expeditions to Greenland which culminated in his reaching the North Pole on April 6, 1909. Peary's books, including *The North Pole* (1910) and *Secrets of Polar Travel* (1917), give an account of his journeys and an impression of his extraordinary stamina and courage.

PEASANTS' WAR, popular revolt (1524–26), which began in SW Germany and spread to many parts of Germany and Austria. The social turmoil created by the REFORMATION and the decay of FEUDALISM seem to have been at the root of the discontent. The movement collapsed when LUTHER denounced the uprising and supported its ruthless suppression.

PEAT, partly decayed plant material found in layers, usually in marshy areas. It is composed mainly of the peat mosses sphagnum and hypnum, but also of sedges, trees, etc. Under the right geological conditions, peat forms COAL. It is used as a mulch and burned for domestic heating.

PECCARIES, pig-like mammals of the southwestern US and northern South America, inhabiting bushy thickets or forests. There are two species within the family Tayassuidae, the collared peccary (*Pecari tajacu*) and white-lipped peccary (*Tayassu pecari*). Both are long-legged, with thick bristly hair and an erectile mane along the back.

PECKING ORDER, the term given to a dominance hierarchy in BIRDS. The top bird can peck all others; the second can peck all but the top bird, and so on down to the bottom bird, which is pecked by all but can peck none. Frenzied pecking soon decides the rank of any new bird introduced to the group.

PEDIATRICS, branch of MEDICINE concerned with care of children. This starts with newborn, especially premature, babies for whom intensive care is required to protect the baby from, and adapt it to, the environment outside the WOMB. An important aspect is the recognition and treatment of congenital DISEASES in which structural or functional defects occur due to inherited disease (e.g., DOWN'S SYNDROME) or disease acquired during development of EMBRYO or FETUS (e.g., spina bifida). Otherwise, infectious disease, failure to grow or develop normally, MENTAL RETARDATION, DIABETES, ASTHMA and EPILEPSY form the bulk of pediatric practice.

PEDRO, two emperors of Brazil. **Pedro I** (1798–1834) was the son of John VI of Portugal, who fled with his family to Brazil when Napoleon invaded his homeland in 1807. On his father's return to Portugal in 1821, Pedro remained in Brazil, declared Brazilian independence (1822) and was crowned emperor. His subsequent mismanagement led to his abdication (1831). He was succeeded by his son **Pedro II** (1825–1891), declared of age in 1840, who gave Brazil over half a century of stable government. But his liberal policies, especially his attempt to abolish slavery, alienated the Brazilian landowning classes. They organized a bloodless coup in 1889 and made Brazil a republic.

PEEL, Sir Robert (1788–1850), British statesman. As home secretary in the 1820s, Peel set up the British police force and sponsored the CATHOLIC EMANCIPATION ACT (1829). Though he opposed the REFORM BILL (1832), he became more progressive, and after a brief term (1834–35) as prime minister, he organized the new Conservative Party out of the old Tory Party, aided by young politicians such as DISRAELI and GLADSTONE. His second term in office (1841–46) saw the introduction of an income tax, banking controls and Irish land reforms, and the further removal of discriminatory laws against Roman Catholics. The repeal of the CORN LAWS (1846) led to an era of FREE TRADE but caused a party split which led to his resignation.

PEERCE, Jan (Jacob Pincus Perelmuth; 1904–1984), US concert and opera tenor who moved from Radio City Music Hall to New York's Metropolitan Opera (1941–66).

PEGLER, (James) Westbrook (1894–1969), US newspaper columnist, a caustic conservative critic of President Franklin Roosevelt and members of his administration. He also exposed labor union corruption, for which he won a 1941 Pulitzer Prize.

PÉGUY, Charles Pierre (1873–1914), French poet and essayist known for his spiritual ideals. As editor of *Cahiers de la quinzaine*, he defended Dreyfus. An ardent Catholic and nationalist, Péguy wished France to become a Catholic, socialist state.

PEI, I(eoh) M(ing) (1917–   ), Chinese-born US architect of public buildings and urban complexes, e.g., the Mile High Center in Denver, Place Ville Marie in Montreal, the John Hancock Tower in Boston and the National Gallery's East Wing in Washington, DC. Most are noted for their simplicity and environmental harmony.

PEIRCE, Charles Sanders (1839–1914), US philosopher, best known as a pioneer of PRAGMATISM. He is also known for his work on the logic of relations, theory of signs, and other contributions in logic and the philosophy of science. Although he was a rigorous thinker who dealt with all main branches of philosophy, he wrote no comprehensive work but published numerous articles in philosophical journals.

PEKING, or **Beijing,** capital of the People's Republic of China, lying within Hopeh Province, but administratively independent.

It is the political, commercial, cultural and communications center of the country, and embraces a massive industrial complex. The city's rectangular layout was the work of KUBLAI KHAN in the 13th century, and its splendors were described by Marco POLO. It became the permanent capital of China in 1421. Its occupation by French and British troops from 1860 was a contributing cause of the BOXER REBELLION (1900). In 1928 Peking (renamed Peiping) was superseded by Nanking (Nanjing), but regained its capital status and its name with the communist victory in 1949. Peking has two historic districts: the Inner City, enclosing the Imperial City and the Forbidden City, and the Outer City. Pop (city) 5,531,460; (metro) 9,179,660.

PELAGIANISM, Christian heresy based on the teachings of the British theologian **Pelagius** (c353–c425); an ascetic movement chiefly of aristocratic laity. Pelagius held that men are not naturally sinful and have FREE WILL to take the first steps to salvation by their own efforts. This challenged the basic Christian doctrines relating to GRACE, ORIGINAL SIN and Christ's atonement. Pelagianism was opposed by St. AUGUSTINE and condemned by the Council of Ephesus in 431. A middle position, Semi-Pelagianism, was dominant in Gaul until condemned by the Council of Orange (529).

PELÉE, Mount, active volcano on MARTINIQUE, in the French West Indies; 4,583ft high. Its eruption in 1902 destroyed the town of St. Pierre and killed some 40,000 people.

PELICANS, large aquatic birds of the genus *Pelecanus*. The long bills are provided with an expansible pouch attached to the lower mandible, used, not for storage, but simply as a catching apparatus, a scoop-net. They are social birds, breeding in large colonies. Most species also fish in groups, swimming together, herding the fish in horseshoe formation. All are fine fliers.

PELLAGRA, VITAMIN deficiency DISEASE (due to lack of niacin), often found in maize- or millet-dependent populations. A DERMATITIS, initially resembling sunburn, but followed by thickening, scaling and pigmentation, is characteristic; internal EPITHELIUM is affected (sore tongue, DIARRHEA). Confusion, DELIRIUM, hallucination and ultimately dementia may ensue. Niacin replacement is essential and food enrichment is an important preventitive measure.

PELOPONNESIAN WAR (431–404 BC), war between the rival Greek city-states of ATHENS and SPARTA which ended Athenian dominance and marked the beginning of the end of Greek civilization. The war was fought in two phases. The first (431–421) was inconclusive because Athenian sea power was matched by Spartan land power. A stalemate was acknowledged by the Peace of Nicias, named for the third Athenian leader in the war following PERICLES and Cleon. His leadership was then challenged by ALCIBIADES, who initiated the second and decisive phase of the conflict (418–404). In an attack on Syracuse in 413, the Athenians suffered a major defeat. The Spartans, with Persian aid, built up a powerful fleet under the leadership of Lysander, who blockaded Athens and forced the final surrender. (See also GREECE, ANCIENT.)

PELOPONNESUS, peninsula forming the S part of the Greek mainland, linked with the N by the Isthmus of Corinth. It is mostly mountainous, but its fertile lowlands provide wheat, tobacco and fruit crops. Its largest city and port is Patras. In ancient times it was the center of the Mycenaean civilization and, later, was dominated by SPARTA in the SE.

PELVIS, lowest part of the trunk in animals, bounded by the pelvic BONES and in continuity with the ABDOMEN. The principal contents are the BLADDER and lower GASTROINTESTINAL TRACT (rectum) and reproductive organs, particularly in females—the WOMB, OVARIES, FALLOPIAN TUBES and vagina. The pelvic floor is a powerful muscular layer which supports the pelvic and abdominal contents and is important in urinary and fecal continence. The pelvic bones articulate with the legs at the hip JOINTS.

PEN, an instrument for writing with ink. The earliest pens were the Chinese brush and the Egyptian reed pen for use on PAPYRUS. Quill pens, usually made from goose feathers, were used until the mid-19th century, when steel pens largely replaced them. The modern fountain pen was invented in 1884; its nib is supplied with ink from a reservoir in the barrel by capillary action. The BALLPOINT PEN is now very popular.

PENAL COLONY, overseas settlement in which convicts were isolated from society. The forced labor that was part of their punishment was often used for colonial development. All colonial powers had penal colonies, as had Russia in Siberia. Britain transported large numbers of convicts to the American colonies and to Australia. (See also DEVIL'S ISLAND.)

PENAL LAWS, in England and Ireland, a series of discriminatory laws against Roman Catholics after the REFORMATION. In the 16th and 17th centuries these laws deprived Roman Catholics of virtually all civil rights, and harshly penalized participation in Roman Catholic worship. Although enforcement lapsed, the laws were only gradually repealed in successive Acts of 1791, 1829 (see CATHOLIC EMANCIPATION ACT), 1832 and 1926.

PENANCE, a SACRAMENT of the Roman Catholic Church. A priest, after receiving the CONFESSION of a penitent, may grant absolution, imposing a penance and requiring restitution for harm done to others. The penance— now usually prayers, though formerly a rigorous ascetic discipline—represents the temporal punishment for sin. (See also INDULGENCE.)

PENCIL, instrument for writing or drawing, usually consisting of a wooden rod with a core of mixed powdered graphite and clay. The mixture is extruded as a soft paste and placed in the grooves of two half-pencils, which are glued together and dried. The term "lead pencil" comes from an early view that graphite is a form of lead. Pencils vary in hardness, the hardest (10H) containing the most clay, the softest and blackest (8B), the least. HB and F are intermediate grades.

PENDERECKI, Krzysztof (1933–   ), Polish composer. His innovative works used such unorthodox sounds as sawing and typing, scraping instruments and hissing singers, and include *Threnody for the Victims of Hiroshima* (1960) and *St. Luke's Passion* (1965).

PENDERGAST, Thomas Joseph (1872–1945), US politician. He was the Democratic political boss of Kansas City and Mo. during the 1920s and 1930s. Pendergast was convicted and imprisoned for evading income tax (1939).

PENDLETON, Edmund (1721–1803), American jurist and revolutionary statesman who became the first speaker of the Va. House of Delegates after independence. He helped revise the laws of Va., and in 1788 presided over the Va. convention which ratified the Federal Constitution.

PENDULUM, a rigid body mounted on a fixed horizontal axis that is free to rotate under the influence of gravity. Many types of pendulum exist (e.g., Kater's and the FOUCAULT pendulum), the most common consisting of a large weight (the bob) supported at the end of a light string or bar. An idealized simple pendulum, with a string of negligible weight and length, l, the weight of its bob concentrated at a point and a small swing amplitude, executes simple harmonic motion. The time, T, for a complete swing (to and fro) is given by $T=2\pi\sqrt{l/g}$, depending only on the string length and the local value of the gravitational acceleration, g. Actual physical or compound pendulums approximate this behavior if they have a small angle of swing. They are used for measuring absolute values of g or its variation with geographical position, and as control elements in CLOCKS.

PENGUINS, the most highly-specialized of all aquatic birds, with 17 species in the order Sphenisciformes, restricted to the S hemisphere. Completely flightless, the wings are reduced to flippers for "flying" through the water. Ungainly on land, penguins only leave the water to breed. The nest is usually a skimpy affair; emperor and king penguins brood their single eggs on their feet, covering them with only a flap of skin. Most species nest in colonies. Penguins are long-lived birds: the yellow-eyed penguin may live for 20 years or more.

PENICILLIN, substance produced by a class of FUNGI which interferes with cell wall production by BACTERIA and which was one of the first, and remains among the most useful, ANTIBIOTICS. The property was noted by A. FLEMING in 1928, and production of penicillin for medical use was started by E. B. CHAIN and H. W. FLOREY in 1940. Since then numerous penicillin derivatives have been manufactured, extending the range of activity, overcoming resistance in some organisms and allowing some to be taken by mouth. STAPHYLOCOCCUS, STREPTOCOCCUS and the bacteria causing the VENEREAL DISEASES of gonorrhea and syphilis are among the bacteria sensitive to natural penicillin, while bacilli negative to Gram's stain, which cause urinary-tract infection, SEPTICEMIA, etc., are destroyed by semisynthetic penicillins.

PENINSULAR CAMPAIGN, in the US CIVIL WAR, Union campaign against the Confederate capital of Richmond, Va., April to July 1862, led by George B. McCLELLAN across the peninsula between the James and York rivers. Although the Union troops, 100,000 strong, initially inflicted severe losses on the rebels, they were heavily defeated in the Seven Days' Battles (26 June–2 July) by Confederate forces under Robert E. LEE and Richmond was saved from capture.

PENINSULAR WAR (1808–1814), part of the NAPOLEONIC WARS, in which the French, fighting against the British, Portuguese and Spanish, were driven out of the Iberian Peninsula. Anxious to increase his security in Europe, NAPOLEON sent General Junot to occupy Portugal (1807), and in 1808

dispatched Murat to occupy his ally, Spain. The Spanish and the Portuguese soon rebelled, and, with the aid of the British under Arthur Wellesley (later Duke of WELLINGTON), the French were driven out of Portugal (1809). In the long struggle that followed, the British—aided by Portuguese and Spanish guerrillas—gradually gained the upper hand, despite many reverses. By 1813 the French forces in Spain had been defeated, and Wellesley invaded S France. The war ended on Napoleon's abdication.

PENN, William (1644–1718), English QUAKER, advocate of religious tolerance, and founder of PENNSYLVANIA. He wrote numerous tracts on Quaker beliefs and was several times imprisoned for his nonconformity. In 1675 he became involved in American colonization as a trustee for one of the proprietors of W N.J. (then West Jersey). In 1681, he and 11 others bought the rights to E N.J. (then East Jersey), and he received a vast province on the W bank of the Delaware R in settlement of a debt owed by Charles II to Penn's father. Thousands of European Quakers emigrated there in search of religious and political freedom. In 1682 Penn visited the colony and witnessed the fulfillment of his plans for the city of Philadelphia. He returned in 1699 to revise the constitution.

PENNAMITE WARS (1769–71, 1775–84), two major conflicts amid a series of clashes between Conn. and Pa. over their long-standing rivalry for the Wyoming Valley. Both wars ended with the Conn. settlers in possession of the valley, and the controversy ended only in 1799 when Conn. yielded to the claims of Pa., by then legally recognized. A compromise was reached, and the New England culture of the Conn. settlers became a major influence on the state.

PENNEY, James Cash (1875–1971), US retailer who parlayed a single dry-goods store in Wyoming to a national chain of 1,650 J. C. Penney stores at the time of his death.

PENNSYLVANIA, Middle Atlantic state of the US, one of the original 13 states. It is bounded on the N by Lake Erie and N.Y., E by N.Y. and N.J., S by Del., Md. and W. Va., and W by W. Va. and Ohio.
Land. The state embraces the vast ranges of the APPALACHIAN and ALLEGHENY Mts; its only lowlands are the coastal plains SE and NW. The main rivers are the Delaware and the Susquehanna in the E and the Allegheny and Monongahela in the W. The state is still richly forested, and many of its spectacularly beautiful inland regions retain an air of wilderness. Pa. has a moist

Name of state: Pennsylvania
Capital: Harrisburg
Statehood: Dec 12, 1787 (2nd state)
Familiar name: Keystone State
Area: 45,333sq mi
Population: 11,888,000
Elevation: Highest—3,213ft. Mount Davis. Lowest—sea level, Delaware River
Motto: "Virtue, liberty and independence"
State flower: Mountain laurel
State bird: Ruffed grouse
State tree: Hemlock
State song: None

climate with pronounced seasonal variations.

People. Pennsylvania is the fourth-largest state in population. About 10% are black, and nearly two-thirds of the people are urban, the largest cities being PHILADELPHIA and PITTSBURGH. Religious freedom in colonial times attracted diverse groups of immigrants including QUAKERS and the PENNSYLVANIA DUTCH.

Economy. Manufacturing dominates the state's diversified economy. The pig-iron and steel industry, centered in Pittsburgh, produces one-fifth of the national total. Other major manufactures include electrical and other machinery, processed food, metal products and clothing. Tourism, agriculture (mainly livestock) and coal mining are also of major importance. The outstanding communications and distribution facilities of Pennsylvania include the two great ports of Philadelphia and Erie.

History. When Henry Hudson entered Delaware Bay in 1609, the region was inhabited by ALGONQUIN and IROQUOIS Indians. The first permanent settlement was made by the Swedes in 1643. Swedish rule gave way to control by the Dutch in 1655, and in 1664 the region was captured by the English. It was granted (1681) to William PENN. Under Penn's guidance, the colony became a tolerant, peaceful and prosperous community, initially on good terms with the Indians. The peace was broken by the FRENCH AND INDIAN WARS (1754–63) and again by the REVOLUTIONARY WAR, in which the location and resources of

Pa. were vital. The Declaration of Independence was signed in Philadelphia, the nation's capital from 1790 to 1800 and for long its foremost city. Pennsylvanian Quakers had been outspoken opponents of slavery, and the state entered the Civil War on the Union side. It was the scene of the crucial Battle of GETTYSBURG (1863).

For nearly a century, from the end of the Civil War to the end of WWII, the state's steady growth in prosperity was interrupted only by severe floods in 1889 and the Great Depression of the 1930s. After WWII, however, Pennsylvania's economy was buffeted from various directions: out-of-state (and out-of-country) competitors took business away from the old, relatively inefficient plants of the local iron and steel industry; textile mills moved south in search of cheaper labor; the railroads entered a seemingly irreversible decline; and unemployment became chronic in coal-mining regions as users switched to other fuels.

Pittsburgh was substantially renovated in the 1950s, and its air quality was dramatically improved, changing one of the dirtiest cities into one of the cleanest; but Pennsylvania's other major cities, including Philadelphia, remained in need of renewal. Despite its difficulties, Pennsylvania's economic base is still so large and so strong that it remains by any measure one of the wealthiest and most powerful states in the US. In presidential elections 1968–88, Pennsylvania voted Republican in 1972 and 1980–88.

PENNSYLVANIA DUTCH (from German *Deutsch*, meaning German), descendants of German-speaking immigrants who came to Pa. during the 17th and 18th centuries in search of religious freedom. They were mainly Lutheran and Reformed Protestants, but included such Pietist sects as the AMISH, DUNKERS, MENNONITES and MORAVIANS, who still retain their original culture.

PENNSYLVANIAN, the penultimate period of the PALEOZOIC, stretching between about 315 and 280 million years ago. (See CARBONIFEROUS; GEOLOGY.)

PENOBSCOT RIVER, longest river in Me. (350mi from the head of its longest branch). Rising near the Canadian border it flows E and S to Penobscot Bay on the Atlantic. The Penobscot valley saw a number of battles between the English and French from 1673 to 1759, and between the English and Americans during the Revolution and the War of 1812.

PENOLOGY. See PRISONS; PUNISHMENT.

PENROSE, Boies (1860–1921), US senator from Pennsylvania (1897–1921) and Pennsylvania Republican Party boss (from 1904). In the Senate he led forces that defended corporate interests and opposed legislation popularly viewed as progressive.

PENSION, regular payment made to people after they retire from employment because of age or disability, received from the government under SOCIAL SECURITY programs, or from private employers, or both. In the US, almost all large corporations provide pension plans for their employees, based on salary and length of service, and financed either by the company alone or jointly by company and employee (contributory plans). The most common forms are the trust fund, administered by a bank or trust company; the group annuity in which an insurance company collects payments from the corporation to build up the retirement fund; and profit-sharing plans, in which pension funds are accumulated annually as a percentage of company profits.

PENTAGON, The, five-sided building in Arlington, Va., which houses the US Department of Defense, built in 1941–43. The largest office building in the world, it consists of five concentric pentagons covering a total area of 34 acres.

PENTATEUCH (Greek: five books), the first five books of the OLD TESTAMENT: GENESIS, EXODUS, LEVITICUS, NUMBERS and DEUTERONOMY. They were traditionally assigned to MOSES, but are now regarded as a compilation of four or more documents (J, E, P and D) dating from the 9th to the 5th centuries BC and distinguished by style and theological bias. (See also TORAH.)

PENTECOST (Greek: 50th), distinct Jewish and Christian festivals. The Jewish Pentecost, called SHAVUOT, celebrated on the 50th day after PASSOVER, is a harvest feast. The Christian Pentecost (Whitsunday)—the 50th day inclusively after Easter—commemorates the descent of the HOLY SPIRIT upon the Apostles, marking the birth of the Christian Church.

PENTECOSTAL CHURCHES, Protestant churches, fundamentalist (see FUNDAMENTALISM) and revivalist, that emphasize holiness and spiritual power as initiated by an experience ("baptism in the Spirit") in which the recipient "speaks in tongues" (see GLOSSOLALIA). They base their distinctive doctrines and practice of charismata on New Testament teaching and accounts of the bestowal of the Holy Spirit. Pentecostalism began c1906 and spread rapidly; it is now influential in many major denominations. The largest Pentecostal churches in the US are the Assemblies of God and the United Pentecostal Church.

PENTOTHAL SODIUM, or thiopentone, a BARBITURATE drug injected into a vein to produce brief general ANESTHESIA, also used in PSYCHIATRY as a relaxant to remove inhibitions (a so-called "truth drug").

PENZIAS, Arno (1933–), German-born US physicist who shared the 1978 Nobel Prize in Physics for discovering cosmic MICROWAVE radiation emanating from outside of the GALAXY while doing communications research for the Bell Telephone Laboratories. The discovery provided evidence for the "big bang" theory of the origins of the universe.

PEONAGE, form of coercive servitude by which a laborer (peon) worked off his debts—often inescapable and lifelong—to his creditor-master. In Spanish America, where it was most prevalent, and in the Southern states of the US (in a modified form), peonage did not end until the 20th century.

PEPIN THE SHORT (Pepin III; c714–768), first CAROLINGIAN king of the Franks, who succeeded on the deposition (751) of Childeric, the last of the MEROVINGIAN kings. He was the younger son of CHARLES MARTEL and father of CHARLEMAGNE. In return for papal recognition he helped to establish the temporal power of the papacy.

PEPPER, Claude Denson (1900–), US Democratic politician, senator (1936–51) and representative (from 1963) from Florida, particularly identified with legislation on behalf of the elderly.

PEPPER, name for several unrelated plants from which pungent spices are obtained. Both black and white pepper are the dried ground berries of a woody climbing vine (*Piper nigrum*) which grows in India and SE Asia, while long pepper is obtained from the related *P. longum*. Red, green and chili peppers and the pimiento are the fruits of varieties of *Capsicum annuum*; the condiments paprika and cayenne pepper are produced from the pimento. Melegueta pepper is obtained from *Aframomum melegueta. C. annuum* is also sold as a house plant under the name **Christmas pepper,** its main attraction being the bright red fruits produced. It grows well at average house temperatures and requires a sunny position. The soil should be kept evenly moist and the foliage misted often. Christmas peppers are raised from seed.

PEPPERMINT, *Mentha piperita*, a wild herb whose leaves contain an oil widely used for flavoring. Menthol, a derivative, is used in medicines. Family: Labiatae.

PEPPERRELL, Sir William (1696–1759),

American colonial leader and soldier who, backed by a British fleet, conquered (1745) the reputedly impregnable French fortress of LOUISBOURG on Cape Breton, Canada, during the FRENCH AND INDIAN WARS. He was the first American to be created baronet.

PEPSIN, an ENZYME which breaks down PROTEINS in the DIGESTIVE SYSTEM.

PEPYS, Samuel (1633–1703), English diarist. Although he was a successful reforming naval administrator and president of the Royal Society (1684–85), it is his talent in recording contemporary affairs and his own private life for which he is famed today. His diary, written in cipher 1660–69, was not decoded and published until 1825.

PEQUOT INDIANS, North American Indians of the Algonquian language group, who lived in S New England. Their murder of a colonial trader by whom they had been mistreated led to the **Pequot War** (1637), the first major white massacre of Indians in North America, in which almost the entire tribe was slaughtered or enslaved. The Pequot were resettled (1655) on a Connecticut reservation.

PERCEPTION, the recognition or identification of something. External perception relies on the senses, internal perception, which is introverted, relying on the consciousness. Some psychologists hold that perception need not be conscious: in particular, subliminal perception involves reaction of the UNCONSCIOUS to external stimuli and its subsequent influencing of the conscious (see GESTALT PSYCHOLOGY).

PERCUSSION INSTRUMENTS, musical instruments from which sound is produced by striking. These are divided into two main classes: **idiophones,** such as bells, castanets, cymbals and gongs, whose wood or metal substance vibrates to produce sound, and **membranophones,** chiefly drums and tambourines, in which sound is produced by vibrating a stretched skin. Although the piano, celesta, triangle, xylophone and glockenspiel can be classed as percussion, the term commonly denotes those instruments used chiefly for rhythmic effect.

PERCY, Sir Henry (1366–1403), English nobleman, called Hotspur. He supported Henry of Lancaster (later Henry IV) against Richard II but soon quarreled with Henry over the ransom of a relative. Percy and others plotted to dethrone Henry, but the king defeated them at Shrewsbury. Percy was slain in the battle.

PEREGRINE, *Falco peregrinus,* one of the largest and most widespread of the FALCONS. They are found in mountainous areas or on sea cliffs, feeding on birds up to the size of a duck, caught in the air. Numbers are declining all over Europe and North America with the increased use of pesticides.

PERELMAN, S(idney) J(oseph) (1904–1979), US humorous writer noted for his collaboration as screenwriter on several MARX BROTHERS films, humorous books such as *The Rising Gorge* (1961) and for many articles which appeared in the *New Yorker.* He won an Academy Award in 1956.

PERENNIAL, any plant that continues to grow for more than two years. Trees and shrubs are examples of the perennials that have woody stems that thicken with age. The herbaceous perennials such as the peony and daffodil have stems that die down each winter and regrow in the spring from underground perennating organs, such as TUBERS and BULBS. (See ANNUAL.)

PERES, Shimon (1923–   ), Polish-born Israeli politician. Moving to Palestine in 1934, he was responsible in the 1940s for arms purchasing and manpower mobilization for the underground army Haganah. A protégé of Israel's first prime minister, David BEN-GURION, he helped build Israel's defense industry. He became defense minister in 1974 in the Labor government of Yitzhak RABIN. When Rabin resigned in 1977, Peres became party leader, leading the Labor Party to electoral defeats in 1977 and 1981. After inconclusive elections in 1984, a national unity government was formed in which Peres served as prime minister for the first half of the four-year term and as foreign minister for the second half, alternating with the leader of the conservative Likud bloc, Yitzhak SHAMIR. Peres was receptive to US Middle East peace initiatives.

PÉREZ DE CUÉLLAR, Javier (1920–   ), secretary general of the United Nations (1982–   ), successor to Kurt Waldheim. Formerly a Peruvian diplomat, he had represented Peru as ambassador to the Soviet Union (1969–71) and to the United Nations (1971–75).

PERFUME, a blend of substances made from plant oils and synthetic materials which produce a pleasant odor. Perfumes were used in ancient times as incense in religious rites, in medicines and later for adornment. Today they are utilized in cosmetics, toilet waters, detergents, soaps and polishes. A main source of perfumes is the essential oils extracted from different parts of plants, e.g., the flowers of the ROSE, the leaves of lavender, cinnamon from bark and pine from wood. They are extracted by steam distillation; by using volatile solvents;

by coating petals with fat, or by pressing. Animal products, such as AMBERGRIS from the sperm whale, are used as fixatives to preserve fragrance. The development of synthetic perfumes began in the 19th century. There are now a number of synthetic chemicals with flowerlike fragrances—for example, citronellol for rose and benzyl acetate for jasmine

PERGOLESI, Giovanni Battista (1710–1736), Italian opera composer famed for his comic intermezzo *The Maid as Mistress* (1733). He also composed serious opera and religious music, such as the *Mass in F* (1734) and *Stabat Mater* (1736).

PERI, Jacopo (1561–1633), Italian composer whose *Dafne* (1597) may have been the first opera. Only his opera *Euridice* (1600) and the sensitive madrigals of *Le varie musiche* (1609) survive.

PERICLES (c495–429 BC), Athenian general and statesman. A strong critic of the conservative and aristocratic council, he obtained (461) the ostracism of Cimon and became supreme leader of the Athenian democracy. The years 462–454 BC saw the furthering of that democracy, with salaried state offices and supremacy of the assembly. Pericles' expansionist foreign policy led to a defeat of Persia (449), truce with Sparta (445) and the transformation of the DELIAN LEAGUE into an Athenian empire. The peace of 445–431 saw the height of Athenian culture under his rule. The PARTHENON and Propylaea were both built at Pericles' request. One of the instigators of the PELOPONNESIAN WAR, he was deposed but reelected in 429; his death in a plague soon after may have lost Athens the war.

PERIODIC TABLE, a table of the ELEMENTS in order of atomic number (see ATOM), arranged in rows and columns to illustrate periodic similarities and trends in physical and chemical properties. Such classification of the elements began in the early 19th century, when Johann Wolfgang Döbereiner (1780–1849) discovered certain "triads" of similar elements (e.g. calcium, strontium, barium) whose atomic weights were in arithmetic progression. By the 1860s many more elements were known, and their atomic weights determined, and it was noted by John Alexander Reina Newlands (1837–1898) that similar elements recur at intervals of eight—his "law of octaves"—in a sequence in order of atomic weight. In 1869 MENDELEYEV published the first fairly complete periodic table, based on his discovery that the properties of the elements vary periodically with atomic weight. There were gaps in the table corresponding to elements then unknown, whose properties Mendeleyev predicted with remarkable accuracy. Modern understanding of atomic structure has shown that the numbers and arrangement of the electrons in the atom are responsible for the periodicity of properties; hence the atomic number, rather than the atomic weight, is the basis of ordering. Each row, or period, of the table corresponds to the filling of an electron "shell"; hence the numbers of elements in the periods, 2, 8, 8, 18, 18, 32, 32. (There are n^2 orbitals in the nth shell.) The elements are arranged in vertical columns or groups containing those of similar atomic structure and properties, with regular gradation of properties down each group. The longer groups, with members in the first three (short) periods, are known as the Main Groups, usually numbered IA to VIIA, and 0 for the NOBLE GASES. The remaining groups, the transition elements, are numbered IIIB to VIII (a triple group), IB and IIB. The characteristic valence of each group is equal to its number N, or to $(8 - N)$ for some nonmetals. Two series of 14 elements each, the lanthanides and actinides, form a transition block in which the inner f orbitals are being filled; their members have similar properties, and they are usually counted in Group IIIB. (See also TRANSURANIUM ELEMENTS.)

PERIPATETIC SCHOOL, in philosophy, the name given to the school of philosophy founded by ARISTOTLE and THEOPHRASTUS. The term derives from the covered arcade (*peripatos*) at the Lyceum where Aristotle taught in Athens.

PERISCOPE, optical instrument that permits an observer to view his surroundings along a displaced axis, and hence from a concealed, protected or submerged position. The simplest periscope, used in tanks, has two parallel reflecting surfaces (prisms or mirrors). An auxiliary telescopic gunsight may be added. Submarine periscopes have a series of lenses within the tube to widen the field of view, crosswires and a range-finder, and can rotate and retract.

PERISTALSIS, the coordinated movements of hollow visceral organs, especially the GASTROINTESTINAL TRACT, which cause forward propulsion and mixing of the contents. It is effected by autonomic NERVOUS SYSTEM plexuses acting on visceral MUSCLE layers.

PERITONITIS, INFLAMMATION of the peritoneum, usually caused by bacterial infection or chemical irritation of the peritoneum when internal organs become diseased (as with APPENDICITIS) or when

GASTROINTESTINAL TRACT contents escape (as with a perforated peptic ULCER). Characteristic pain occurs, sometimes with SHOCK, FEVER, and temporary cessation of bowel activity (ileus). Urgent treatment of the cause is required, often with SURGERY; ANTIBIOTICS may also be needed.

PERKIN, Sir William Henry (1838–1907), English chemist who, in 1856, while studying under August Wilhelm von Hofmann, discovered mauve, the first synthetic dye (see DYES AND DYEING). He manufactured this and other dyes until 1874, then devoted his remaining years to research. In 1868 he synthesized coumarin, the first synthetic PERFUME.

PERKINS, Frances (1882–1965), US secretary of labor 1933–45, first US woman cabinet member. From 1910 she was active in N.Y. state factory and labor affairs. Appointed labor secretary by President F. D. ROOSEVELT, she administered NEW DEAL programs.

PERKINS, Maxwell Evarts (1884–1947), US book editor at Charles Scribner's Sons who achieved legendary status for his work with F. Scott Fitzgerald, Ernest Hemingway, Ring Lardner, Thomas Wolfe, Alan Paton, James Jones, and Winston Churchill, to whom he proposed the idea of a history of the English-speaking peoples.

PERLMAN, Itzhak (1945–   ), Israeli-born violinist. A favorite of concert audiences, he performed throughout the world, appeared frequently on TV and made several notable recordings.

PERMAFROST, permanently frozen ground, typical of the treeless plains of Siberia (see TUNDRA), though common throughout polar regions.

PERMIAN, the last period of the PALEOZOIC, stretching between about 280 and 225 million years ago. (See also GEOLOGY.)

PERÓN, Juan Domingo (1895–1974), president of Argentina 1946–55, 1973–74. As head of an army clique, he helped overthrow Castillo in 1943. He won union loyalty as secretary of labor. Elected president (after police intervention), he began with his second wife Eva (1919–1952) a program of industrialization and social reform. Church and army opposition to corruption and repression forced him into exile. Peronist influence survived, however; he returned in 1973 and was reelected president. He served until his death and was succeeded by his third wife, Isabel.

PERPENDICULAR STYLE, name given to the period of English Gothic architecture from the late 14th to the middle 16th century. It is characterized by the vertical tracery on windows and wall panels and by fan vaults. King's College chapel, Cambridge, is a famous example of the style.

PERPETUAL MOTION, an age-old goal of inventors: a machine which would work forever without external interference, or at least with 100% efficiency. No such machine has worked or can work, though many are plausible on paper. Perpetual motion machines of the *first kind* are those whose efficiency exceeds 100%—they do work without energy being supplied. They are disallowed by the First Law of THERMODYNAMICS. Those of the *second kind* are machines that take heat from a reservoir (such as the ocean) and convert it wholly into work. Although energy is conserved, they are disallowed by the Second Law of Thermodynamics. Those of the *third kind* are machines that do no work, but merely continue in motion forever. They are approachable but not actually achievable, because some energy is always dissipated as heat by friction, etc. An example, however, of what is in a sense perpetual motion of the third kind is electric current flowing in a superconducting ring (see SUPERCONDUCTIVITY), which continues undiminished indefinitely.

PERRAULT, name of two eminent French brothers. **Charles Perrault** (1628–1703), poet, fairy-tale writer and man of letters, is best known for his *Contes de ma mère l'Oye* (*Tales of Mother Goose*; 1697) which include "Little Red Riding Hood," "Cinderella" and "Puss in Boots." **Claude Perrault** (1613–1688), architect, scientist and physician, is remembered for his buildings, notably the colonnade of the Louvre (1667–70), the Paris Observatory (1667–72) and for his translation of the works of VITRUVIUS (1673).

PERRET, Auguste (1874–1954), French architect known for his use of reinforced concrete in housing projects (Paris, 1903), in the Théâtre des Champs Élysées (1910), and in the Church of Notre Dame, Le Raincy (1922–23).

PERROT, Nicolas (1644–c1718), French explorer. Through work with the Jesuits, then as a fur trader, he gained influence with the Wisconsin Indians. He fought against the Iroquois and gained the upper Mississippi areas for New France (1689).

PERRY, two US brothers who became distinguished naval officers. **Matthew Calbraith Perry** (1794–1858) was instrumental in opening Japan to the US and world trade. He commanded the first US steam warship, the *Fulton II* (1838) and led US naval forces suppressing the slave trade;

he fought in the MEXICAN WAR. In 1853 Perry took four vessels into Tokyo Bay and remained there until a Japanese envoy agreed to receive President FILLMORE's request for a diplomatic and trade treaty. He returned in Feb. 1854 to conclude the treaty, which was a turning point in US-Japan relations. **Oliver Hazard Perry** (1785–1819), became a hero of the WAR OF 1812. After assembling a fleet of nine ships at Erie, Pa., he defeated six British warships on Sep. 10, 1813 off Put-in-Bay, Ohio, in the battle of Lake ERIE. He announced his victory in the famous message "We have met the enemy and they are ours."

PERSE, St.-John (1887–1975), pen name of Alexis Saint-Léger Léger, French poet and diplomat. He was secretary general of the French foreign office (1933–40). His poetry includes *Anabase* (1924), translated by T. S. ELIOT, and *Amers* (1957). In 1960 he was awarded the Nobel Prize for Literature.

PERSEPOLIS, ancient ceremonial capital of the Achaemenian kings of Persia, lying 30mi NE of Shiraz, SW Iran. It flourished under DARIUS I (d. 486 BC) and his successors but was later destroyed by Alexander the Great in 330. In 1971 the 2,500th anniversary of the Iranian monarchy was celebrated among the ruins of the city.

PERSHING, John Joseph (1860–1948), US general. After distinguished service in the Indian Wars (1886, 1890–91), the Spanish-American War (1898) and in the Philippines (1899–1903), he was promoted to brigadier general (1906). He led a punitive expedition to Mexico against VILLA (1916) and a year later became commander of the WWI American Expeditionary Force in Europe. Pershing insisted on independent authority over US forces. In 1919 he became general of the armies, and was chief of staff from 1921 until his 1924 retirement.

PERSIA. See IRAN.

PERSIA, Ancient, the high plateau of Iran, home of several great civilizations. In the 2nd millennium BC the literate civilization of Elam developed in the SW of the plateau, with its capital at Susa. Its W neighbors, BABYLONIA AND ASSYRIA, had trading and political interests in the state and attempted takeovers. The civilization was ended in 639 BC by the invasion of Ashurbanipal of Assyria. Assyrian downfall followed in 612 after the sacking of NINEVEH by the Babylonians and the MEDES, an Aryan kingdom S of the Caspian Sea. The area of Parsumash to the S of the Medes was ruled by the ACHAEMENIANS. CYRUS THE GREAT

expanded the Achaemenid empire, and at his death (529) he controlled the Middle East from the Mediterranean to the Indus R. Under DARIUS I (522–486) Persepolis succeeded Pasagardae as capital; a road system linked the great empire, a canal linked the Nile and Red Sea. Flourishing trade, commerce and public works continued under XERXES I (586–465). Xerxes' murder by his son was followed by intrigues and rebellions that weakened the Achaemenians. In c330 the empire was conquered by ALEXANDER THE GREAT; at his death most of it became part of the brief empire of the SELEUCIDS, who were conquered by the Parthians from SW of the Caspian. The empire of Parthia (3rd century BC–3rd century AD) had its capital at Ctesiphon and halted the nomads in the NE and the Romans in the W, defeating Crassus in 53 BC and later Mark ANTONY. In 224 AD, a successful revolt by Ardashir, ruler of the Fars (the S Persian homeland), established the vigorous Sassanian empire. Arts, architecture and religion (ZOROASTRIANISM) revived, the wars with Rome continued, and in 260 AD Shapur, the son of Ardashir, captured the Emperor Valerian. Later, after constant struggles with the Byzantines, the Sassanian empire was overwhelmed by the Arabs in 651.

PERSIAN, or Farsi, the principal language of Iran, where the great majority of its speakers live (the others are in Afghanistan). It is an INDO-EUROPEAN LANGUAGE. Modern Persian emerged after the Arab conquest in the 7th century. It has many borrowed Arabic words and a modified Arabic alphabet.

PERSIAN GULF, or Arabian Gulf, an arm of the Arabian Sea between Iran and Arabia. About 550mi long and 120mi wide, the gulf is entered from the Gulf of Oman by the Straits of Hormuz. The bordering regions of Iran, Kuwait, Saudi Arabia, Bahrain, Qatar and the United Arab Emirates contain more than half the world's oil and natural gas resources. The gulf was a theater in the IRAN-IRAQ WAR (1980–88), both combatants attacking neutral shipping in order to impede the other's oil exports. In 1987 the US navy entered the gulf to protect Kuwaiti and other foreign oil tankers sailing under the US flag. The US presence, which was interpreted as supportive of Iraq, resulted in an attack by an Iraqi plane on the USS *Stark* in 1987 and the shooting down of an Iranian civilian airliner by the USS *Vincennes* in 1988.

PERSIAN WARS (500–449 BC), wars between Greek states and the Persian empire. Athenian support of the revolt of Greek states within the empire precipitated Persian offensives in Greece. However, by 449 BC Greek strength had secured Europe from further Persian invasions. (See GREECE, ANCIENT.)

PERSPIRATION, or sweat, watery fluid secreted by the SKIN as a means of reducing body temperature. Sweating is common in hot climates, after EXERCISE and in the resolution of FEVER, where the secretion and subsequent evaporation of sweat allow the skin and thus the body to be cooled. Humid atmospheres and high secretion rates delay the evaporation, leaving perspiration on the surface. Excessive fluid loss in sweat, and of salt in the abnormal sweat of CYSTIC FIBROSIS, may lead to SUNSTROKE. Most sweating is regulated by the HYPOTHALAMUS and autonomic NERVOUS SYSTEM. But there is also a separate system of sweat glands, especially on the palms, which secretes at times of stress. *Hyperidrosis* is a condition of abnormally profuse sweating.

PERU, third-largest nation in South America. It has a mountainous backbone and a 1,400mi coastline bordering the Pacific.

Official name: Republic of Peru
Capital: Lima
Area: 496,225sq mi
Population: 20,727,000
Languages: Spanish, Quechua, Aymara
Religion: Roman Catholic
Monetary unit(s): 1 sol = 100 centavos

Land. Peru is divided into three geographical regions. The coastal zone, averaging 40mi in width, contains a third of the population and most of the large cities. It is mainly arid, but fertile where irrigated by rivers flowing down from the mountains. The mountainous region (the *Sierra*) of the Andes consists of parallel ranges, some with peaks over 20,000ft. Although conditions are harsh, over half the population live in the Sierra. The *Montaña*, consisting of the lower slopes of the E Andes and the E plains, forms part of the tropical forest of the Amazon basin. Rainfall is very low (less than 2in per year) in the coastal zone,

moderate in the Sierra and heavy (100in or more) in the E. An earthquake in 1970 was the hemisphere's worst natural disaster, with about 50,000 dead.

People. Peru's population is composed of about 50% Amerindians, 40% *mestizos* (mixed white and Indian) and 10% whites. Spanish and Quechua are both official languages. There is a great division between the poor, less-educated Indians and *mestizos*, and the wealthier, predominantly white Spanish-speakers. About 30% of the population are illiterate.

Economy. Subsistence agriculture provides the means of livelihood for less than half of the population. Cotton, sugarcane and coffee are the main export crops. Peru is the world's leading fishing country, the main catch being *anchovetas*, which are processed into fishmeal, the country's chief export. Copper, iron, silver, phosphates and other minerals are mined and exported, and manufacturing industry is developing. The high mountains make communications difficult, and transportation problems hinder economic growth.

History. The ancient INCA Empire in Peru was destroyed by the Spanish conquistador PIZARRO (1532). Spanish rule, based at Lima, lasted until the revolutions led by BOLIVAR and SAN MARTÍN (1820–24). After independence power continued to be concentrated in the hands of a small number of wealthy landowners. This century has been characterized by unstable governments and military coups. In 1968 Gen. Juan Velasco Alvarado instituted a program of social reform, suspended the constitution, and seized US-owned companies. He was overthrown in 1975 in a military coup led by the more conservative Gen. Francisco Morales Bermudez. But Morales too was unable to cope with the country's economic problems and he called an election in 1980. After 12 years of military rule, Peru elected as president Fernando Belaúnde Terry, who had been president in 1963–68 and was considered the personification of democracy. He hoped to stimulate the economy by ending protectionism, but the result was to devastate local industry and bring on a prolonged recession. The 1985 election was won by Alan García Pérez, a member of the Popular Revolutionary Alliance (APRA), which had been kept from power by military and civilian conservatives since its founding in 1924. García immediately limited payments on Peru's foreign debt to 10% of export revenues. The result was a boom in consumer spending with an economic growth rate in 1986 and 1987 of 8%. But boom was followed by recession and an inflation approaching 400%. Meanwhile, the democratic government was proving ineffective against the Maoist Shining Path guerrilla movement, begun in 1980. Shining Path terrorism provoked similar responses from the security forces and right-wing terrorists.

PERU CURRENT. See HUMBOLDT CURRENT.

PERUGIA, historic city in Umbria, central Italy. Once an Etruscan city, the walled, hilltop town is renowned for its architecture, paintings and archaeological museum. Its 13th-century municipal palace was decorated with paintings by Perugino, who lived in the city, assisted by his young pupil, Raphael.

PERUGINO (Pietro Vannucci; c1446–1523), Italian Renaissance painter, teacher of RAPHAEL. His frescoes in the Vatican SISTINE CHAPEL, including the *Christ Giving the Keys to St. Peter* (1481), established his fame. He worked much in Florence, and later in his native Umbria.

PERUZZI, Baldassare (1481–1536), Italian High Renaissance architect and painter. In Rome he built the Villa Farnesina, which he decorated with illusionist paintings (1508–11), and the Mannerist Palazzo Massimo (1532–36).

PESCADORES, group of about 64 small islands, about 50sq mi of land area, belonging to Taiwan, in the Formosa strait. The chief occupations are fishing and farming.

PESTALOZZI, Johann Heinrich (1746–1827), famous Swiss educator. At his school at Yverdon he stressed the importance of the individual, and based his methods on the child's direct experience, rather than mechanical learning. His teacher-training methods also became renowned. *How Gertrude Teaches Her Children* (1801) was his most influential work.

PESTICIDE, any substance used to kill plants or animals responsible for economic damage to crops, either growing or under storage, or ornamental plants, or which prejudice the well-being of man and domestic or conserved wild animals. Pesticides are subdivided into INSECTICIDES (which kill insects); miticides (which kill mites); HERBICIDES (which kill plants); FUNGICIDES (which kill fungi), and rodenticides (which kill rats and mice). Substances used in the treatment of infectious BACTERIAL DISEASES are not generally regarded as pesticides. The efficient control of pests is of enormous economic importance for man, particularly as farming becomes more intensive. A

major question with all pesticides is the possibility of unfortunate environmental side effects (see ECOLOGY; POLLUTION).

PÉTAIN, Henri Philippe (1856–1951), French WWI hero who became chief of state in the collaborationist VICHY regime (1940). Famous for his defense of Verdun (1916), he was made chief-of-staff (1917), and subsequently held important military offices. In 1934 he served briefly as war minister. Recalled from his post as ambassador to Spain in June 1940, he became premier and negotiated an armistice with the Nazis. As head of the Vichy government, he aided the Nazis, and in 1945 was tried for treason and sentenced to life imprisonment.

PETER, Saint (Simon Peter; d. c64 AD), leader of the 12 APOSTLES, and regarded by Roman Catholics as the first pope. A Galilean fisherman when Jesus called him to be a disciple, he was a dominating but impulsive figure, and denied Jesus after his arrest. He played a leading role in the early Church, especially in Jerusalem, as related in Acts. By tradition, he died a martyr at Rome.

PETER, name of three tsars of Russia. **Peter I, the Great** (1672–1725) became joint tsar in 1682 and sole tsar in 1696. As a young man he traveled in W Europe (1697–98), learning techniques of war and industry and recruiting experts to bring back to Russia. His war against Turkey was intended to gain access to the Mediterranean, and the long conflict with Sweden (1700–21) led to Russian domination of the Baltic Sea. He established his new capital of St. Petersburg on the Baltic, as a symbol of his policy of westernization. Domestically, he introduced sweeping military, administrative and other reforms. A man of enormous size, strength and demonic energy, Peter was also savage in the exercise of power, and although he modernized, reformed and strengthened Russia, it was at great cost. **Peter II** (1715–1730) ruled from 1727. **Peter III** (1728–1762) ruled in 1762.

PETER I (1844–1921), king of Serbia. A Serbian prince, he spent years in exile, and joined the anti-Turkish Herzegovinian revolt in 1875. He became an honorary senator of Montenegro in 1883, and was elected king of Serbia in 1903.

PETER II (1923–1970), king of Yugoslavia. On the death of his father ALEXANDER I his cousin governed as regent (1934–41). Peter fled to London after the Nazi invasion (1941), and set up an exile government. In 1945 Yugoslavia became a republic, and Peter a pretender.

PETER, Epistles of, two New Testament

letters, traditionally attributed to St. PETER. The first is written to encourage persecuted Christians in Asia Minor; the second closely parallels the Epistle of Jude and refers to the Second Coming. The authorship is doubtful, particularly of the second, which some scholars date c150 AD and which was admitted late to the CANON.

PETER CLAVER, Saint (1581–1654), "Apostle of the Negroes." A Spanish Jesuit, he went in 1610 to Cartagena, Colombia, and against official opposition he visited every slave ship that arrived at the port, nursing the sick and preaching.

PETERSON, Roger Tory (1908–   ), US naturalist. Considered to be the foremost ornithologist of his time in the US, Peterson was associated with the National Audubon Society (from 1934). Among his many books was the best-selling *Guide to the Birds* (1934), *A Field Guide to Western Birds* (1941) and *Penguins* (1979).

PETER THE HERMIT (c1050–1115), French monk who preached the First CRUSADE (1095). He led an army into Asia Minor which was annihilated, and later played an undistinguished part at Antioch and Jerusalem.

PETIPA, Marius (1819–1910), French dancer and choreographer who created the modern classical ballet. An outstanding dancer and mime, he joined the Russian ballet at St. Petersburg in 1847, becoming chief choreographer in 1869. There he created over 60 full-length ballets, including *The Nutcracker*, *Swan Lake* and *The Sleeping Beauty*.

PETIT, Roland (1924–   ), French dancer and choreographer. A founder (1945) and premier danseur of Les Ballets des Champs-Élysées, in 1948 he formed Les Ballets de Paris. He choreographed *Carmen* (1949), *La Croqueuse de Diamants* (1950) and many other ballets for stage and film.

PETITION OF RIGHT, document presented to CHARLES I of England by Parliament (1628) in protest against his arbitrary fiscal methods. It asserted four principles: no taxation without parliamentary consent; no imprisonment of subjects without due legal cause; no billeting of soldiers in private houses without payment; no declaring of MARTIAL LAW in peacetime. Accepted but later disregarded by the king, it represents a landmark in English constitutional history.

PETLYURA, Simon (1879–1926), Ukrainian nationalist leader. In 1919 he became head of an independent Ukrainian republic, but when the Ukraine came under Soviet control in 1921, he went into exile, and was assassinated in Paris.

PETRA, ancient ruined city in SW Jordan.

Famous for its tombs and temples cut into sandstone cliffs, it was the capital of the NABATEANS, prospered under the Romans but lost its trade to Palmyra. Its decline continued under Muslim rule, and its ruins were discovered by BURCKHARDT in 1812.

PETRARCH (Francesco Petrarça; 1304–1374), Italian poet and early HUMANIST. Supported by influential patrons, he spent his life in study, travel and writing. He wrote poetry, epistles and other prose works in Latin, but also much in vernacular Italian, of which he is one of the earliest masters. He himself rated his Latin works highest, but his great fame now rests on the Italian *Canzoniere*, mostly sonnets inspired by his love for the enigmatic Laura, who died of plague in 1348.

PETRELS, seabirds of the tubenosed-bird order, Procellariiformes, particularly the typical petrels and shearwaters of the family Procellariidae. All have webbed feet and hooked bills, with nostrils opening through horny tubes on the upper mandible. They are marine birds which swim and fly expertly, feeding far from the shore on fish, squids and offal. Normally they go ashore only to breed.

PETRIE, Sir William Matthew Flinders (1853–1942), British archaeologist who devised a system of sequence dating. A relative CHRONOLOGY could thus be established between sites and dates attributed to the superimposed layers of a site.

PETRIFIED FOREST NATIONAL PARK, a park of 147sq mi in E Ariz. The fossil remains of a TRIASSIC forest are exposed on the surface, creating the largest display of petrified wood in the world.

PETROCHEMICALS, chemicals made from PETROLEUM and NATURAL GAS, i.e., all organic chemicals, plus the inorganic substances carbon black, sulfur, ammonia and hydrogen peroxide. Many petrochemicals are still made also from other raw materials, but the petrochemical industry has grown rapidly since about 1920. Polymers, detergents, solvents and nitrogen fertilizers are major products.

PETROGRAD. See LENINGRAD.

PETROLEUM, naturally-occurring mixture of HYDROCARBONS, usually liquid "crude oil," but sometimes taken to include NATURAL GAS. Petroleum is believed to be formed from organic debris, chiefly of plankton and simple plants, which has been rapidly buried in fine-grained sediment under marine conditions unfavorable to oxidation. After some biodegradation, increasing temperature and pressure cause cracking, and oil is produced. As the source rock is compacted, oil and water are forced out and slowly migrate to porous reservoir rocks, chiefly sandstone or limestone. Finally, secondary migration occurs within the reservoir as the oil coagulates to form a pool, generally capped by impervious strata, and often associated with natural gas. Some oil seeps to the earth's surface: this was used by the early Mesopotamian civilizations. The first oil well was drilled in W Pa. in 1859. The industry thus begun has grown so fast that it now supplies about half the world's energy, as well as the raw materials for PETROCHEMICALS. Modern technology has made possible oil-well drilling to a depth of 3mi, and deep-sea wells in 500ft of water. Rotary drilling is used, with pressurized mud to carry the rock to the surface and to prevent escape of oil. When the well is completed, the oil rises to the surface, usually under its own pressure, though pumping may be required. The chief world oil-producing regions are the Persian Gulf, the US (mainly Tex., La., Okla. and Cal.), the USSR, N and W Africa and Venezuela. After removing salt and water, the petroleum is refined by fractional DISTILLATION, producing the fractions GASOLINE, KEROSENE, diesel oil, fuel oil, lubricating oil and ASPHALT. Undesirable compounds may be removed by solvent extraction, treatment with sulfuric acid, etc., and less-valuable components converted into more valuable ones by cracking, reforming, alkylation and polymerization. The chemical composition of crude petroleum is chiefly alkanes, saturated alicyclic compounds and aromatic compounds (see HYDROCARBONS), with some sulfur compounds, oxygen compounds (carboxylic acids and phenols), nitrogen and salt. (See also OIL SHALE.)

PETROLOGY, branch of geology concerned with the history, composition, occurrence, properties and classification of rocks. (See GEOLOGY; ROCKS.)

PETRONIUS ARBITER, Gaius (d. 66 AD), Roman satirist. He became NERO's "Arbiter of Taste," but fell from favor and committed suicide. *Trimalchio's Dinner* is the best-known fragment of his *Satyricon*, a sensual, amoral and often obscene romance.

PEVSNER, Antoine (1886–1962), Russian-born sculptor who studied in Paris 1911–13 and settled there from 1922. In 1920 he launched CONSTRUCTIVISM with his brother Naum Gabo in Moscow. Light and space play important roles in his sculptures.

PEWTER, class of ALLOYS consisting chiefly of TIN, now hardened with copper and antimony, and usually containing lead. Roman pewter was high in lead and

darkened with age. Pewter has been used for bowls, drinking vessels and candlesticks.

PEYOTE, *Lophophora williamsii* and related cactus species, native to Texas and Mexico. The cut, dried tops are chewed by Indians to release the hallucinogenic drug MESCALINE. This habit was first described in 1560. Family: Cactaceae.

PHAISTOS, ancient city of the MINOAN CIVILIZATION in S Crete. Many remains have been excavated there, particularly of the great palace (dating from c2200 BC).

PHALANX, ancient Greek infantry formation, consisting of rows of eight men, each heavily armed with an overlapping shield and long pike. PHILIP II of Macedon developed a phalanx 16 men deep, which his son ALEXANDER THE GREAT used in defeating the Persians. Only after defeat by Rome in 168 BC did the phalanx become outmoded.

PHANEROZOIC, the eon of visible life, the period of time represented by rock strata in which skeletonized FOSSILS appear, running from about 570 million years ago through to the present and containing the PALEOZOIC, MESOZOIC and CENOZOIC eras. (See also CRYPTOZOIC; GEOLOGY; PRECAMBRIAN.)

PHARISEES, an ancient Jewish sect devoted to strict observance of the holy law and strongly opposed to pagan practices absorbed by Judaism, and to the SADDUCEES. Their moral fervor and initially progressive nature made them an important political force. Tradition has made them synonymous with hypocrisy and self-righteousness, but Jesus only attacked the debasement of their ideals.

PHARMACOLOGY, the study of DRUGS, their chemistry, mode of action, routes of absorption, excretion METABOLISM, interaction, toxicity and side-effects. New drugs, based on older drugs, traditional remedies, chance observations etc., are tested for safety and efficacy, and manufactured by the pharmaceutical industry. The dispensing of drugs is pharmacy. Drug prescription is the cornerstone of the medical treatment of DISEASE.

PHARMACOPEIA, a text containing all available DRUGS and pharmacological preparations, providing a vital source for accurate prescribing in MEDICINE. It lists drugs; their properties and formulation; routes and doses of administration; mode of action, METABOLISM and excretion; known interaction with other drugs; contraindications and precautions in particular DISEASES; toxicity, and side-effects.

PHARMACY, the preparation or dispensing of DRUGS and pharmacological substances used in MEDICINE; also, the place where this is practiced. Most drugs are now formulated by drug companies and the pharmacist need only measure them out and instruct the patient in their use. In the past, however, the pharmacist mixed numerous basic substances to produce a variety of medicines, tonics, etc.

PHARAOH, Hebrew form of the title of the kings of ancient Egypt. The term (actually *per-'o*: great house) described his palace and, by association, the king. The Egyptians believed the pharaoh to be the personification of the gods HORUS and, later, Amon.

PHAROS, a peninsula near Alexandria, Egypt, whose lighthouse was one of the SEVEN WONDERS OF THE WORLD. The tower of white marble was completed about 280 BC. From pictures it seems to have been about 400ft high with a ramp leading to the top, where a beacon was kept burning day and night. It stood for some 1,600 years, until demolished by an earthquake in 1302.

PHARSALUS, Battle of, the decisive struggle of the Roman civil war fought between POMPEY and Julius CAESAR in Epirus (48 BC). After being defeated by an army half the size of his own, Pompey fled to Egypt, where he was killed.

PHARYNX, the back of the throat where the mouth (oropharynx) and nose (nasopharynx) pass back into the ESOPHAGUS. It contains specialized MUSCLE for swallowing. The food and air channels are kept funtionally separate so that swallowing does not interfere with breathing and speech.

PHEASANTS, game birds of the 16 genera of subfamily Phasianinae. They originated in Asia, but are now found all over the world. They are ground birds which scratch the earth for seeds and insects. When they fly they rise almost vertically on short broad wings. Males are usually brightly-colored, and many species are kept as ornamentals.

PHEIDIPPIDES, Athenian courier who, alter running four times to and from Sparta, ran to announce the victory at MARATHON; he died on arrival.

PHENOMENOLOGY, a school of philosophy based largely on a method developed by Edmund HUSSERL. Unlike the naturalist who describes objects without reference to the subjectivity of the observer, the phenomenologist attempts to describe the "invariant essences" of objects as objects "intended" by consciousness. As a first step toward achieving this, he performs the "phenomenological reduction," which involves as far as possible a suspension of all preconceptions about experience. Phenomenology has become a leading tendency in 20th-century philosophy.

PHENOTYPE, the appearance of, and characteristics actually present in, an organism, as contrasted with its GENOTYPE (its genetic make-up). Heterozygotes and homozygotes with a dominant GENE have the same phenotype but differing genotypes. Organisms may also have an identical genotype but differing phenotype due to environmental influences.

PHENYLKETONURIA (PKU), inherited DISEASE in which phenylalanine METABOLISM is disordered due to lack of an ENZYME. It rapidly causes MENTAL RETARDATION, as well as irritability and vomiting, unless dietary foods low in phenylalanine are given soon after birth and indefinitely. Screening of the newborn by urine tests (with confirmation by blood tests) facilitates prompt treatment.

PHI BETA KAPPA, the most prestigious US honor society for college and university students in the liberal arts and sciences. Members are generally elected in their third or fourth year on the basis of academic achievements. The oldest Greek letter society in the US, the fraternity was founded at William and Mary College, Va. in 1776.

PHIDIAS (c500–c432 BC), perhaps the greatest Greek sculptor, whose work showed the human form idealized and with great nobility. As none of his works survive, his reputation rests on contemporary accounts, on Roman copies and on the PARTHENON statues made under his direction. Under Pericles he had artistic control over the ACROPOLIS.

PHILADELPHIA, historic city in SE Pa., the fifth largest in the US. It is a key shipping port with important metal, machinery, clothing, petroleum, chemical and food industries. It has long been a center for publishing, education and the arts, and was one of the first planned cities. Its founder, William PENN, created his colony in 1682 as a "holy experiment" in which all sects could find freedom. Philadelphia (Greek: brotherly love) attracted immigrants and brought commerce that made it the largest and wealthiest of US cities. In the Old City, near the Delaware R, is the Independence National Historical Park, whose buildings include Independence Hall, where both the Declaration of Independence and the Constitution were adopted. The city was US capital 1790–1800; subsequent corruption in government and growth of slums accompanied a decline. In the 1950s massive urban renewal projects were initiated. Today the city has one of the world's largest freshwater ports, linked with the Atlantic by the Delaware R. In 1983 the city elected its first black mayor, W. Wilson

Goode. Philadelphia is part of an urban complex stretching from Boston to Washington D.C. Pop (city) 1,647,000, (metro) 4,784,000.

PHILBY, Kim (Harold Adrian Russell Philby; 1912–), British intelligence officer, recruited as a Soviet spy along with Guy BURGESS, Donald MACLEAN, and Anthony BLUNT while at Cambridge in the 1930s. Philby joined British intelligence during WWII and, while serving as first secretary at the British embassy in Washington 1945–51, was liaison with the FBI and CIA. He fled to the Soviet Union in 1963.

PHILEMON, Epistle to, New Testament letter written c61 AD by St. PAUL to Philemon, a Colossian Christian, asking him to forgive his runaway slave Onesimus, who had become a Christian and who returned with the letter.

PHILIP, Saint, one of the 12 APOSTLES. Born in Bethsaida, he was according to legend martyred at Hierapolis in Phrygia.

PHILIP, six kings of France. Philip I (1052–1108), reigned from 1059. He enlarged his small territories and prevented union of England and Normandy. His practice of simony and his disputed second marriage led him into conflict with the papacy. **Philip II** (Philip Augustus; 1165–1223), reigned from 1179, established France as a European power. He joined the CRUSADES, only to quarrel with RICHARD the Lion Heart and seize his French territories. By 1204 he had added Normandy, Maine, Anjou, Touraine and Brittany to his domain, in which he set up new towns and a system of royal bailiffs. **Philip III** (the Bold; 1245–85), reigned from 1270, secured Auvergne, Poitou and Toulouse for France. **Philip IV** (the Fair; 1268–1314), reigned from 1285, added Navarre and Champagne to the kingdom, but attempts to overrun Flanders led to his defeat at Courtrai in 1302. He seized Pope Boniface VIII in a quarrel about taxation of clergy, obtained the election of Clement V, a puppet pope residing at Avignon (see BABYLONIAN CAPTIVITY), and seized the land of the crusading order of the KNIGHTS TEMPLAR. **Philip V** (1294–1322), reigned from 1317, invoked the Salic Law of male succession and carried out reforms to strengthen royal power. The succession in 1328 of **Philip VI** (1293–1350) through the Salic Law was disputed and led to the HUNDRED YEARS' WAR against England.

PHILIP II (382-336 BC), king of Macedonia from c359 and father of ALEXANDER THE GREAT. His powerfully reorganized army (see PHALANX) conquered N Greece, acquiring the gold mines of Thrace and advancing S as far as Thermopylae, the key to central Greece. He defeated Athens and Thebes at Chaeronea (338) and became ruler of all Greece. His reign marked the end of the independent and warring city-states.

PHILIP, five kings of Spain. Philip I (1478–1506) was archduke of Austria, duke of Burgundy and inheritor of the Netherlands. He became first Hapsburg king of Castile in 1506, ruling jointly with his wife Joanna. **Philip II** (1527–1598), crowned in 1556, united the Iberian peninsula and ruled an empire which included Milan, Naples, Sicily, the Netherlands and vast tracts of the New World. Though son of the Holy Roman Emperor CHARLES V, he never became emperor. A fanatical Catholic, he married MARY I of England, supported the Inquisition and tried in vain to crush the Protestant Netherlands. He was recognized king (Philip I) of Portugal in 1580, but lost naval supremacy to England after the ARMADA (1588). His son **Philip III** (1578–1621), crowned in 1598, made peace with England and the Netherlands but was frustrated in Italy by the THIRTY YEARS' WAR. **Philip IV** (1605–1655), crowned in 1621, son of Philip III and last Hapsburg king of Spain, was the patron of VELÁZQUEZ. He attempted unsuccessfully to dominate Europe by fighting France, Germany and Holland in the THIRTY YEARS' WAR, but lost Portugal in the process (1640). **Philip V** (1683–1746), crowned in 1700, founder of the BOURBON line, restored influence, but his accession in 1700 led to the war of the SPANISH SUCCESSION. By the Treaty of UTRECHT (1713) his title was recognized, though he ceded possessions in Italy and the Netherlands to Austria.

PHILIP, Prince (1921–), consort of Queen ELIZABETH II of England. The son of Prince Andrew of Greece and Princess Alice of Battenberg, he renounced his Greek title, became a British subject and married the then Princess Elizabeth in 1947. He was created duke of Edinburgh in 1947 and prince in 1957.

PHILIP NERI, Saint (Filippo Neri; 1515–1595), a leading figure of the COUNTER-REFORMATION, and founder of the secular order of the Congregation of the Oratory which was devoted to care of the poor and sick. He was canonized in 1622.

PHILIPPI, ancient city of MACEDONIA, in present-day Greece, named for PHILIP II of Macedon. It was there Brutus and Cassius were defeated (42 BC) by Mark Antony and Octavian, and St. PAUL first preached the gospel in Europe.

PHILIPPIANS, Epistle to the, NEW TESTAMENT letter written by St. PAUL from prison in Rome (c62 AD) to the Christians at Philippi, whom he himself had converted. He encourages them affectionately and quotes an early hymn on Christ's humility.

PHILIPPINES, republic in the SW Pacific Ocean, between the equator and the Tropic of Cancer, comprising more than 7,000 islands.

Official name: Republic of the Philippines
Capital: Manila
Area: 115,800sq mi
Population: 57,357,000
Languages: Filipino/Tagalog; English; Spanish
Religions: Roman Catholic; Muslim; Protestant
Monetary unit(s): 1 Philippine peso=100 centavos

Land. The islands range in size from tiny rocks to Luzon (41,845sq mi), the largest. The other principal islands include Mindanao, Samar, Negros, Panay, Mindoro and Leyte. Only 730 of the islands are inhabited, and 11 of these account for most of the total land area and most of the population. All the larger islands are volcanic and mountainous. The climate in the lowlands is humid, with temperatures averaging 80°F.

People. The population is predominantly of Malay origin, but includes groups of Chinese, Indonesians, Moros, Negritos (descendants of the earliest inhabitants) and people of mixed blood. Filipino, based on Tagalog, was adopted as the national language in 1946; numerous native languages are also spoken. The majority of the population are Roman Catholic.

Economy. About 55% of Filipinos work on the land. The leading crops are rice, coconut, corn and sugar. Abaca (Manila hemp) and lumber are important exports. The islands are rich in mineral resources, the most important of which are lead, nickel, zinc, copper and cobalt. Manila, the largest city, is the main industrial center. Manufactures include wood products, processed foods, textiles, aluminum and tobacco.

History. The islands were first visited by Europeans on MAGELLAN's expedition (1521), and were later named in honor of the future Philip II of Spain. By the 1570s Spanish rule there was secure, lasting until the end of the SPANISH-AMERICAN WAR (1898), when the Philippines were ceded to the US. A revolutionary nationalist movement, under the leadership of Emilio AGUINALDO, helped the US defeat Spain. The issue of independence loomed large in US politics until the establishment (1935) of the internally self-governing Commonwealth of the Philippines, with Manuel QUEZON as president. Occupied by the Japanese during WWII, the country was made an independent republic in 1946, with Manuel ROXAS and later Ramon MAGSAYSAY as presidents. Communist revolutionary movements have been active since 1949. The powers of the presidency were greatly increased (1972) with the introduction of martial law under President Ferdinand MARCOS. Notorious for his corruption, Marcos fled the country in 1986 after massive antigovernment demonstrations and the election as president of Corazon AQUINO, widow of an anti-Marcos politician assassinated in 1984. A new constitution was drawn up and overwhelmingly approved in a 1987 plebiscite. A few months later, candidates supported by Aquino won large majorities in the Philippine senate and house. But Aquino had no political party base; her personal popularity was her only strength. Leftist violence and army mutinies kept the government off balance. Despite dramatic improvement in the economy, Aquino's personal popularity declined because of the postponement of promised land redistribution and her support for relatives in provincial and local elections in 1988.

PHILIPS, Wendell (1811–1884), US orator and social reformer. He gave up law in 1835 to campaign for the abolition of slavery with W. L. GARRISON. After the Civil War he worked for Negroes' civil rights, women's suffrage and other reforms.

PHILISTINES, a non-Semitic people who lived in PALESTINE from the 12th century BC. They were hostile to the Israelites and for a time held considerable power. The term "philistine" may nowadays denote an uncultured person.

PHILLIPS, David Graham (1867–1911), US journalist and novelist, a MUCKRAKER famous for his magazine exposés of political corruption. His many novels include *The Great God Success* (1901).

PHILODENDRON, a genus of South American evergreen plants frequently grown as greenhouse and house plants. Many are vigorous climbers and produce attractive foliage, but rarely flower in cultivation. The most popular climbing species are *Philodendron oxycardium* (heart-leaf philodendron), *P. sodiroi* (silver-leafed) and *P. panduraeforme* (fiddle leaf or horsehead), while *P. bipinnatifidum* and *P. selloum* are self-heading cut-leaved types, closely resembling monstera except for their nonclimbing habit. (The closely related *Monstera deliciosa* is sometimes known as *P. pertusum.*) Philodendrons grow best in a bright north or sunny east window (or similar bright position) but the young plants in particular can tolerate less light. They grow well at average house temperatures, failing to thrive below 16°C (60°F). The soil should be kept evenly moist; the foliage benefits from frequent misting. Propagation is by shoot cuttings or air-layering. Family: Araceae.

PHILO JUDEAS (c20 BC–c50 AD), Alexandrine Jewish philosopher whose attempt to fuse Greek philosophical thought with Jewish Biblical religion had a profound influence on both Christian and Jewish theology.

PHILOLOGY, the study of literature and the language employed in it. The term is used also for those branches of LINGUISTICS concerned with the evolution of languages, especially those dealing with the interrelationships between different languages (comparative philology).

PHILOSOPHES, 18th-century French school of thinkers, scientists and men of letters who believed that the methodology of science should be applied to contemporary social, economic and political problems. Inspired by DESCARTES and the school of SKEPTICISM, they included MONTESQUIEU, VOLTAIRE, DIDEROT and ROUSSEAU.

PHILOSOPHY (from *philosophia*, lover of wisdom), term applied to any body of doctrine or opinion as to the nature and ultimate significance of human experience considered as a whole. It is perhaps more properly applied to the critical evaluation of all claims to knowledge—including its own *and* anything that is presupposed about its own nature and task. In this latter respect, it is widely argued, philosophy differs fundamentally from all other disciplines. What philosophy "is" (what methods the philosopher should employ, what criteria he should appeal to, and what goals he should set himself) is as perennial a question for the philosopher as any other. Traditionally, philosophers have concerned themselves with four main topic areas: LOGIC, the study of the formal structure of valid arguments; METAPHYSICS, usually identified with ontology—the study of the nature of "Being" or ultimate reality; EPISTEMOLOGY, or theory of knowledge, sometimes treated as a branch of metaphysics; and axiology, or theory of value—including AESTHETICS, the philosophy of taste (especially as applied to the arts), ETHICS, or moral philosophy, and political philosophy (see POLITICAL SCIENCE). In modern times, as traditional philosophy has yielded up the subject matters of the natural sciences, of other descriptive studies such as PSYCHOLOGY and SOCIOLOGY, and of such formal studies as logic and mathematics, all once numbered among its legitimate concerns, philosophers have become increasingly conscious of their critical role. Most now tend to interest themselves in special philosophies, e.g., philosophy *of* logic, philosophy *of* science (see SCIENTIFIC METHOD) and philosophy *of* religion. The first attempts to answer distinctively philosophical questions were made from about 600 BC by certain Greeks known collectively as the PRE-SOCRATIC PHILOSOPHERS; their intellectual heirs were SOCRATES, PLATO and ARISTOTLE, the three towering figures in ancient philosophy. Later ancient philosophies include EPICUREANISM, STOICISM and NEOPLATONISM. Foremost among medieval philosophers were St. AUGUSTINE and St. Thomas AQUINAS. (See also SCHOLASTICISM; THOMISM; NOMINALISM; REALISM.) Modern philosophy begins with René DESCARTES and a parallel development of RATIONALISM and EMPIRICISM culminating in the philosophy of Immanuel KANT. The IDEALISM of G. F. W. HEGEL and the POSITIVISM of Auguste COMTE were major forces in 19th-century philosophy. The dialectical materialism of Karl MARX had its roots in both. (See MATERIALISM.) The philosophical orientations of most 20th-century philosophers are developments of MARXISM, Kantianism, LOGICAL POSITIVISM, PRAGMATISM, PHENOMENOLOGY or EXISTENTIALISM.

PHIPS, Sir William (1651–1695), colonial governor (1692–94) of Mass. who led (1690) the troops that captured the French colony of Port Royal in the FRENCH AND INDIAN WARS.

PHLEBITIS, INFLAMMATION of the VEINS, usually causing THROMBOSIS (thrombophlebitis) and obstruction to BLOOD flow. It is common in the superficial veins of the legs, especially VARICOSE VEINS, and visceral veins close to inflamed organs or abscesses. Phlebitis may complicate intravenous injections of DRUGS or indwelling cannulae for intravenous fluids. Pain, swelling and erythema over the vein are typical, the vein becoming a thick tender cord. Occasionally, phlebitis indicates systemic DISEASE (e.g., CANCER).

PHLOGISTON, the elementary principle postulated by G. H. Stahl to be lost from substances when they burn. The phlogiston concept provided 18th-century CHEMISTRY with its unifying principle. The phlogiston theory of COMBUSTION found general acceptance until displaced by its inverse—LAVOISIER'S oxygen theory.

PHNOM PENH, capital and river port of Kampuchea (formerly Cambodia), on the Tônlé Sap R where it joins the Mekong. It is the country's administrative, commercial, communications and cultural center. Founded in the 14th century, it was first made Khmer capital in the 1430s. Phnom Penh was the focus of a massive civil war campaign 1970–75. Est pop 393,995.

PHOBIA, a NEUROSIS characterized by exaggerated ANXIETY on confrontation with a specific object or situation; or the anxiety itself. Phobia is sometimes linked with obsessional neurosis, sometimes with HYSTERIA: in each case the object of phobia is usually merely symbolic. Classic phobias are agoraphobia (fear of open spaces) and claustrophobia (fear of enclosed places).

PHOENICIA, ancient territory corresponding roughly to the coastal region of modern Lebanon, inhabited by the Phoenicians (originally called Canaanites) from c3000 BC. It included the city-states of Sidon and TYRE. Being on the trade route between Asia Minor, Mesopotamia and Egypt, Phoenicia became an important center of commerce. By 1200 BC, with the decline of Egyptian dominance, Phoenicians led the Mediterranean world in trading and seafaring. They colonized many Mediterranean areas which later became independent states, such as CARTHAGE and Utica. From the 9th century BC Phoenicia was intermittently dominated by Assyria, and in 538 came under Persian rule. By the time ALEXANDER THE GREAT conquered Tyre (332) Phoenician civilization had largely been eclipsed. The Greeks were the inheritors of their outstanding cultural legacy—most notably their alphabetic script, from which the modern Western alphabet is descended.

PHONETICS, the systematic examination of the sounds made in speech, concerned not only with the classification of these sounds but also with physical and physiological aspects of their production and transmission, and with their reception and interpretation by the listener. Phonology,

the study of phonetic patterns in languages, is of importance in comparative LINGUISTICS.

PHONOGRAPH, or **record player,** instrument for reproducing sound recorded mechanically as modulations in a spiral groove (see SOUND RECORDING). It was invented by Thomas EDISON (1877), whose first machine had a revolving grooved cylinder covered with tinfoil. Sound waves caused a diaphragm to vibrate, and a stylus on the diaphragm made indentations in the foil. These could then be made to vibrate another stylus attached to a reproducing diaphragm. Wax disks and cylinders soon replaced tinfoil, then, when by etching or electroplating metal master disks could be made, copies were mass-produced in rubber, wax or plastic. The main parts of a phonograph are the turntable, to rotate the disk at constant angular velocity; the stylus, which tracks the groove and vibrates with its modulations; the pickup or transducer, which converts these movements piezoelectrically or electromagnetically into electrical signals; the AMPLIFIER; and the loudspeaker. (For high-quality reproduction, see HIGH-FIDELITY.)

PHOSGENE, or **carbonyl chloride** ($COCl_2$), colorless, reactive gas, hydrolyzed by water, made by catalytic combination of CARBON monoxide and CHLORINE, and used to make RESINS and DYES. Highly toxic, it was a poison gas in WWI.

PHOSPHATES, derivatives of phosphoric acid (see PHOSPHORUS): either phosphate ESTERS, or salts containing the various phosphate ions. Like silicates, these are numerous and complex, the simplest being orthophosphate, PO_4^{3-}. Of many phosphate minerals, the most important is apatite. This is treated with sulfuric acid or phosphoric acid to give calcium dihydrogen-phosphate ($Ca[H_2PO_4]_2$), known as superphosphate—the major phosphate FERTILIZER. The alkaline trisodium phosphate (TSP) (Na_3PO_4) is used as a cleansing agent and water softener. Phosphates are used in making GLASS, SOAPS AND DETERGENTS.

PHOSPHOR, a substance exhibiting LUMINESCENCE, i.e., emitting LIGHT (or other ELECTROMAGNETIC RADIATION) on nonthermal stimulation. Important phosphors include those used in TELEVISION picture tubes (where stimulation is by ELECTRONS) and those coated on the inside wall of fluorescent lamp tubes to convert ULTRAVIOLET RADIATION into visible light.

PHOSPHORUS (P), reactive nonmetal in Group VA of the PERIODIC TABLE, occurring naturally as apatite. This is heated with silica and coke, and elementary phosphorus is produced. Phosphorus has three main allotropes (see ALLOTROPY): white phosphorus, a yellow waxy solid composed of P_4 molecules, spontaneously flammable in air, soluble in carbon disulfide, and very toxic; red phosphorus, a dark-red powder, formed by heating white phosphorus (less reactive and insoluble in carbon disulfide) and black phosphorus (a flaky solid resembling graphite, consisting of corrugated layers of atoms). Phosphorus burns in air to give the trioxide and the pentoxide; it also reacts with the halogens, sulfur and some metals. It is used in making matches, ammunition, pesticides, steels, phosphor bronze, phosphoric acid and phosphate fertilizers. Phosphorus is of great biological importance. AW 31.0 mp (wh) 44°C, bp (wh) 280°C, sg (wh) 1.82, (red) 2.20, (bl) 2.69. Phosphorus forms phosphorus (trivalent) and phosphoric (pentavalent) compounds. **Phosphine** (PH_3) is a colorless, flammable gas, highly toxic, and with an odor of garlic. It is a weak BASE, resembling AMMONIA, and forms phosphonium salts (PH_4^+). **Phosphoric acid** (H_3PO_4) is a colorless crystalline solid, forming a syrupy aqueous solution. It is used to flavor food, in dyeing, to clean metals and to make PHOSPHATES. **Phosphorus pentoxide** (P_4O_{10}) is a white powder made by burning phosphorus in excess air. It is very deliquescent (forming phosphoric acid) and is used as a dehydrating agent.

PHOTOCHEMISTRY, branch of PHYSICAL CHEMISTRY dealing with chemical reactions that produce LIGHT (see COMBUSTION) or that are initiated by light (visible or ultraviolet). Important examples include PHOTOSYNTHESIS, PHOTOGRAPHY and bleaching by sunlight. One PHOTON of light of suitable wavelength may be absorbed by a molecule, raising it to an electronically excited state. Re-emission may occur by fluorescence or phosphorescence (see LUMINESCENCE), the energy may be transferred to another molecule, or a reaction may occur, commonly dissociation to form free radicals. The *quantum yield*, or efficiency, of the reaction is the number of molecules of reactant used (or product formed) per photon absorbed; this may be very large for chain reactions. (See also LASER.)

PHOTOELECTRIC CELL, a device with electrical properties which vary according to the LIGHT falling on it. There are three types: PHOTOVOLTAIC CELLS; photoconductive detectors; and phototubes (see PHOTOELECTRIC EFFECT).

PHOTOELECTRIC EFFECT, properly **photoemissive effect,** the emission of ELECTRONS from a surface when struck by ELECTROMAGNETIC RADIATION such as LIGHT. In 1905 EINSTEIN laid one of the twin foundations of QUANTUM THEORY by explaining photoemission in terms of the action of individual PHOTONS. The effect is used in phototubes (electron tubes having a photoemissive cathode), often employed as "electric eye" switches. Special types are used in image intensifiers and in the Image Orthicon TELEVISION camera. The Einstein photoelectric law is: $E_k = hv - \omega$, where E_k is the maximum kinetic energy of emitted electrons, h is Planck's constant, v is the frequency of the radiation and ω is the surface work function for photoemission.

PHOTOGRAPHY, the use of light-sensitive materials to produce permanent visible images (photographs). The most familiar photographic processes depend on the light-sensitivity of the SILVER halides. A photographic emulsion is a preparation of tiny crystals of these salts suspended in a thin layer of gelatin coated on a glass, film or paper support. On brief exposure to light in a CAMERA or other apparatus, a latent image in activated silver salt is formed wherever light has fallen on the emulsion. This image is made visible in development, when the activated silver halide crystals (but not the unexposed ones) are reduced to metallic silver (black) using a weak organic reducing agent (the developer). The silver image is then made permanent by fixing, in the course of which it becomes possible to examine the image in the light for the first time. Fixing agents (fixers) work by dissolving out the silver halide crystals which were not activated on exposure. The image made in this way is densest in silver where the original subject was brightest and lightest where the original was darkest; it is thus a "negative" image. To produce a positive image, the negative (which is usually made on a film or glass support) is itself made the original in the above process, the result being a positive "print" usually on a paper carrier. An alternative method of producing a positive image is to bleach away the developed image on the original film or plate before fixing, and reexpose the unactivated halide in diffuse light. This forms a second latent image which on development produces a positive image of the original subject (reversal processing).

The history of photography from the earliest work of NIÉPCE, Louis Daguerre (see DAGUERROTYPE) and Fox TALBOT to the present has seen successive refinements in materials, techniques and equipment.

Photography became a popular hobby after EASTMAN first marketed roll film in 1889. The silver halides themselves are sensitive to light only from the blue end of the SPECTRUM so that in the earliest photographs other colors appear dark. The color-sensitivity of emulsions was improved from the 1870s onward as small quantities of sensitizing dyes were incorporated. "Orthochromatic" plates became available after 1884, "panchromatic" from 1906.

New sensitizing dyes also opened up the way to infrared and color photography. Modern "tripack" color films have three layers of emulsion, one each sensitive to blue, green and red light from the subject. Positive color transparencies are made using a reversal processing method in which the superposed, positive, silver images are replaced with yellow, magenta and cyan dyes respectively.

Motion-picture photography dates from 1890, when EDISON built a device to expose Eastman's roll film, and rapidly became an important art form (SEE MOTION PICTURES). Not all modern photographic methods employ the silver-halide process; XEROGRAPHY and the blueprint and ozalid processes work differently. False-color photography and the diffusion process used in the Polaroid Land camera are both developments of the silver-halide process.

The photographers themselves have achieved a great diversity of pictorial results. The great portraitists, from Nadar and Julia Margaret Cameron to Richard AVEDON, have demonstrated an ability to breach the surface and capture the souls of their subjects. Documentary work, much of which has earned recognition as art, has ranged from the 19th-century western views of William Henry JACKSON and Timothy O'Sullivan to the scenes of war captured by witnesses from Matthew BRADY to Gene Smith and Robert CAPA. Those who helped establish photography as art included Alfred STIEGLITZ, Edward STEICHEN and Paul Strand. The natural world has been idealized in the fine prints of Edward WESTON, Ansel ADAMS and Eliot Porter. André Kertesz, Henri CARTIER-BRESSON and Robert Frank discovered art in the everyday movements of common men and women.

PHOTON, the quantum of electromagnetic energy (see QUANTUM THEORY), often thought of as the particle associated with LIGHT or other ELECTROMAGNETIC RADIATION. Its ENERGY is given by hv where h is the Planck constant and v the frequency of the radiation.

PHOTOSPHERE, a 75–120mi-thick layer of gas on the sun, visible to us as the sun's apparent surface, emitting most of the sun's light. Its TEMPERATURE is estimated at 6,000K.

PHOTOSYNTHESIS, the process by which green plants convert the ENERGY of sunlight into chemical energy which is then stored as CARBOHYDRATE. Overall, the process may be written as:

$$6CO_2 + 6H_2O \xrightarrow{light} C_6H_{12}O_6 + 6O_2$$

Although in detail photosynthesis is a complex sequence of reactions, two principal stages can be identified. In the "light reaction," CHLOROPHYLL (the key chemical in the whole process) is activated by absorbing a quantum of LIGHT, initiating a sequence of reactions in which the energy-rich compounds ATP (adenosine triphosphate) and TPNH (the reduced form of triphosphopyridine nucleotide—TPN) are made, water being decomposed to give free oxygen in the process. In the second stage, the "dark reaction," the ATP and TPNH provide the energy for the assimilation of carbon dioxide gas, yielding a variety of SUGARS from which other sugars and carbohydrates, including STARCH, can be built up.

PHOTOVOLTAIC CELL, a device for converting LIGHT radiation into ELECTRICITY, used in light meters and for providing spacecraft power supplies. The photovoltage is usually developed in a layer of SEMICONDUCTOR (e.g., selenium) sandwiched between a transparent electrode and one providing support. (See also SOLAR CELL.)

PHRENOLOGY, study of the shape and detailed contours of the skull as indicators of personality, intelligence and individual characteristics. The method, developed by F. J. Gall (1758–1828) and promoted in the UK and US by George Combe (1788–1858), had many 19th-century followers and may have contributed to the more enlightened treatment of offenders and the mentally ill. Today it has little scientific backing.

PHRYGIA, ancient region and sometime kingdom (8th–6th centuries BC) in present-day central Turkey. Its early kings included Midas and Gordius. Excavation shows the Phrygians to have been highly cultured. The Phrygian worship of Cybele was taken over by the Greeks. (See also GORDIAN KNOT.)

PHYFE, Duncan (c1768–1854), US cabinetmaker, designer of the most distinctive US neoclassical furniture. He came to the US from Scotland in 1784, and based his work on European styles such as the SHERATON and the EMPIRE STYLE.

PHYLACTERY, in Jewish religious practice, a small leather case containing extracts from EXODUS and DEUTERONOMY which is worn by men on the left arm and forehead during morning prayers (except on the Sabbath and festivals).

PHYSICAL CHEMISTRY, major branch of CHEMISTRY, in which the theories and methods of PHYSICS are applied to chemical systems. Physical chemistry underlies all the other branches of chemistry and includes theoretical chemistry. Its main divisions are the study of molecular structure; colloids; CRYSTALS; ELECTROCHEMISTRY; chemical equilibrium; GAS laws; chemical kinetics; MOLECULAR WEIGHT determination; PHOTOCHEMISTRY; SOLUTION; SPECTROSCOPY, and chemical THERMODYNAMICS.

PHYSICAL EDUCATION, instruction designed to further the health, growth and athletic capacity of the body. It may include GYMNASTICS, sports, and Oriental techniques such as YOGA. Culturally important in ancient China and ancient Greece, physical education later had a primarily military application until the 19th century, when it began to be incorporated into school programs in Europe and the US.

PHYSICAL THERAPY. See PHYSIOTHERAPY.

PHYSICS, originally, the knowledge of natural things (=natural science); now, the science dealing with the interaction of MATTER and ENERGY (but usually taken to exclude CHEMISTRY). Until the "scientific revolution" of the Renaissance, physics was a branch of PHILOSOPHY dealing with the natures of things. The physics of the heavens, for instance, was quite separate from (and often conflicted with) the descriptions of mathematical and positional ASTRONOMY. But from the time of GALILEO, and particularly through the efforts of HUYGENS and NEWTON, physics became identified with the mathematical description of nature; occult qualities were banished from physical science. Firm on its Newtonian foundation, classical physics gathered more and more phenomena under its wing until, by the late 19th century, comparatively few phenomena seemed to defy explanation. But the interpretation of these effects (notably BLACKBODY radiation and the PHOTOELECTRIC EFFECT) in terms of new concepts due to PLANCK and EINSTEIN involved the thoroughgoing reformulation of the fundamental principles of physical science (SEE QUANTUM THEORY; RELATIVITY). Physics today is divided into many specialties, themselves subdivided manyfold. The principal of these are ACOUSTICS; ELECTRICITY and MAGNETISM; MECHANICS;

NUCLEAR PHYSICS; OPTICS; QUANTUM MECHANICS; RELATIVITY; and THERMODYNAMICS.

PHYSIOCRATS, 18th-century French school of economists founded by François Quesnay, who held that agriculture, rather than industry or commerce, was the basis of a nation's prosperity, and that land alone should be subject to tax. Their belief in a natural economic law, which merely required non-interference to be successful, is reflected in their famous formula *laissez faire* (let it be). The physiocrats influenced Adam SMITH.

PHYSIOLOGY, the study of function in living organisms. Based on knowledge of ANATOMY, physiology seeks to demonstrate the manner in which organs perform their tasks, and in which the body is organized and maintained in a state of homeostasis. Normal responses to various stresses on the whole or on parts of an organism are studied. Important branches of physiology deal with RESPIRATION, BLOOD CIRCULATION, the NERVOUS SYSTEM, the DIGESTIVE SYSTEM, the KIDNEYS, the fluid and electrolyte balance, the ENDOCRINE GLANDS and METABOLISM. Methods of study include experimentation on anesthetized animals and on human volunteers. Knowledge and understanding of physiology is basic to MEDICINE and provides the physician with a perspective in which to view the body's disordered function in DISEASE.

PHYSIOTHERAPY, system of physical treatment for disease or disability. Active and passive muscle movement; electrical stimulation; balancing exercises; HEAT, ULTRAVIOLET or shortwave RADIATION; and manual vibration of the chest wall with postural drainage are some of the techniques used. Rehabilitation after FRACTURE, SURGERY, STROKE or other neurological disease, and the treatment of LUNG infections (PNEUMONIA, BRONCHITIS), are among the aims.

PI (Greek π), the ratio between the circumference of a circle and its diameter. π is an irrational number whose value to five decimal places is 3.14159. Approximate values of π have been known to several ancient civilizations, such as Babylonia, where the accepted value was 3.0.

PIAF, Edith (1915–1963), French singer of cabaret and music-hall. Born Edith Giovanna Gassion, she began singing for a living at 15 and won international fame with such songs as *Milord* and *Je ne regrette rien*.

PIAGET, Jean (1896–1980), Swiss psychologist whose theories of the mental development of children, though now often criticized, have been of paramount importance. His many books include *The Psychology of the Child* (1969), and *Biology and Knowledge* (1971).

PIANO, keyboard instrument in which depression of the keys causes the strings to be struck with hammers. These hammers rebound immediately after striking, so that the strings go on sounding their notes until the keys are released, when the strings' vibrations are stopped with dampers. Bartolommeo Cristofori made the first piano in 1709, and by 1800 it had overtaken the HARPSICHORD and the CLAVICHORD in popularity. Today the two basic types of piano are the upright piano with vertical strings, and the grand piano with horizontal strings, which has a range of seven octaves. Composers noted for their writing for the piano include C.P.E. BACH, MOZART, BEETHOVEN, CHOPIN, LISZT, and RACHMANINOV. (See also KEYBOARD INSTRUMENTS.)

PIATIGORSKY, Gregor (1903–1976), Russian-born US cellist, an internationally renowned soloist from 1928.

PIAZZI, Giuseppe (1746–1826), Italian astronomer who discovered Ceres, the first ASTEROID (1801). Through illness he lost it again, and it was rediscovered the following year by H. W. M. Olbers.

PICABIA, Francis (1879–1953), French painter, successively a cubist, dadist, and surrealist, best known for his images of intricate but useless machines.

PICARDY, pre-Revolutionary province of N France, on the English Channel, now a geographical region that includes the Somme, Oise and Aisne depts. Its principal city and former captial is Amiens.

PICARESQUE NOVEL, early type of the novel in which the episodic adventures of a roguish, antiheroical character are narrated in the first person. Of 16th-century Spanish origin, the picaresque novel was popular until the mid-1700s, and included notable English examples such as Defoe's *Moll Flanders* (1722).

PICASSO, Pablo (Pablo Ruiz y Picasso; 1881–1973). Spanish-born French painter, sculptor, graphic artist and ceramist, considered by many the greatest artist of the 20th century. An extraordinarily precocious painter, after his melancholy "blue period" and his lyrical "rose period" (1901–06) he was influenced by African and primitive art, as shown in *Les Demoiselles d'Avignon,* 1907. Together he and BRAQUE created CUBISM, 1907–14. His friends at this time included APOLLINAIRE, DIAGHILEV (for whom he made stage designs), and Gertrude STEIN. In 1921 he

painted both the cubist *Three Musicians* and the classical *Three Women at the Fountain.* In the 1930s he adopted the style of SURREALISM, using it to horrify in the large anti-war canvas *Guernica,* 1937 (see GUERNICA). His later work employed cubist and surrealist forms and could be beautiful, tender or grotesque. His output was enormous and near the end of his life he produced a brilliant series of etchings.

PICCARD, Auguste Antoine (1884–1962) and **Jean Felix** (1884–1963), Swiss scientists who were twin brothers. Auguste, a physicist, set a world ballooning altitude record (1931), and an ocean-depth record (1953) in the BATHYSCAPHE that he designed. Jean, a chemist, measured cosmic radiation during a 57,000-foot balloon ascent (1934).

PICCOLO. See FLUTE.

PICKENS, Andrew (1739–1817), American Revolutionary commander who fought at the Battle of COWPENS (1781) and other notable victories. He reached the rank of brigadier general and served (1793–95) in Congress.

PICKERING, name of two US astronomers, **Edward Charles Pickering** (1846–1919) and his brother **William Henry Pickering** (1858–1938). Edward made important contributions to stellar photometry and was the inventor of the meridian photometer. William, in 1898, discovered Phoebe, the ninth moon of the planet SATURN.

PICKERING, Timothy (1745–1829), US statesman. After a distinguished military career in the Revolutionary War, he served as postmaster general (1791–95), secretary of state (1795–1800), senator (1803–11) and representative (1813–17).

PICKETT, George Edward (1825–1875), Confederate general in the US CIVIL WAR who led the disastrous assault (July 3, 1863) on Cemetery Ridge in the Battle of GETTYSBURG. Of the 15,000 Confederate troops who charged the Union line some 6,000 were killed. Pickett later suffered a second major defeat at the Battle of Five Forks (April 1, 1865).

PICKFORD, Mary (1893–1979), US movie actress, born Gladys Smith. Her roles in such films as *Daddy Long Legs,* under the direction of D. W. GRIFFITH, won her the title of "America's sweetheart." In 1919 she and her husband, Douglas FAIRBANKS, helped found United Artists.

PICKLE, food that has been preserved in vinegar or brine to prevent the development of putrefying BACTERIA. Spices are usually added for flavor. Cucumbers, onions, beets, tomatoes and cauliflowers are used to make popular pickles. Pigs' feet and corned beef are also sometimes pickled. (See FOOD PRESERVATION.)

PICO DELLA MIRANDOLA, Count Giovanni (1463–1494), Italian Renaissance philosopher and humanist who attempted to reconcile Christianity with NEOPLATONISM. He was a member of Lorenzo de MEDICI's Platonic Academy in Florence. Shortly before his death he became a follower of SAVONAROLA. (See also HUMANISM.)

PICTS, ancient inhabitants of Scotland whose forebears probably came from the European continent c1000 BC. By the 8th century their kingdom extended from Fife to Caithness. In 843 they united with the kingdom of the SCOTS, and were assimilated into the Scottish nation.

PIDGIN, a language of simplified grammar and vocabulary, most often based on a western European language. Pidgins originate as a means of communication (e.g. for trading purposes) between peoples with different mother tongues. Varieties of pidgin English were developed in China and elsewhere.

PIECE OF EIGHT, Spanish silver coin (*peso*) of the 17th and 18th centuries. It was worth eight *reals* and was stamped with the numeral eight.

PIECK, Wilhelm (1876–1960), East German political leader. A communist member of the Reichstag, he went to the Soviet Union when the Nazis came to power, returning in 1945 with the Russian army. He was the first president (1949–60) of the German Democratic Republic.

PIEDMONT, region of NW Italy in the upper valley of the Po R, bounded N and W by the Swiss and French Alps. During Roman times, the Piedmont was a vital link between Italy and the transalpine provinces. Turin, its capital, is one of Italy's chief industrial centers.

PIERCE, Franklin (1804–1869), 14th president of the US (1853–57). The youngest president the nation had then known, Pierce was the inexperienced compromise candidate of a badly divided Democratic Party, and he was unable to cope with the sectional strife that heralded the Civil War. Born in New Hampshire, Pierce trained and practiced as a lawyer before entering politics. After rapid advancement he spent two terms (1833–37) as a Democratic member of the House of Representatives, and then became a member of the Senate. In 1842 he retired from national politics, but 10 years later, at a time when he was virtually unknown, he won the Democratic nomination after the four leading candidates had brought the Baltimore convention to deadlock. In the 1852 election Pierce easily defeated Winfield Scott, last national candidate of the declining Whig Party. As president, Pierce proved to be fatally pliable and vacillating. His initial concentration on fulfilling the electoral promise of an expansionist foreign policy led to such conspicuous failures as his attempt to procure Hawaii and Alaska for the US, and to annex Cuba from Spain (see OSTEND MANIFESTO). On the domestic scene, apart from the acquisition of the GADSDEN PURCHASE from Mexico, Pierce's administration proved equally inept. Pierce had pledged loyalty to the COMPROMISE OF 1850, but in 1854, yielding to pressure, he backed the KANSAS-NEBRASKA ACT. This repealed the MISSOURI COMPROMISE which had prohibited slavery in the Kansas region. The dormant slavery controversy was reopened, and the Northern part of the Democratic Party split to form the new "Republicans." A wild rush of slavery and anti-slavery supporters poured into Kansas, leading to a local civil war. Pierce's mishandling of the crisis wrecked his administration and his chances of renomination. He left office a discredited figure, retired from public life and died in virtual obscurity.

PIERO DELLA FRANCESCA (c1420–1492), Italian painter, one of the greatest RENAISSANCE artists. His concern for the harmonious relationship of figures to their setting was expressed through simple, elegant forms, clear colors and tones, atmospheric light and perspective as is found in his FRESCO, *Legend of the True Cross*, 1452–59 in Arezzo.

PIERO DI COSIMO (1462–1521), Italian RENAISSANCE painter in Florence, remembered for curious poetic pictures like *Death of Procris; Venus, Cupid and Mars* and *Battle of the Centaurs and Lapiths*, which is based on OVID.

PIETÀ, subject in art representing the Virgin Mary supporting the body of the dead Christ after the Deposition. It originated in N Europe in the 14th century and was popular in the Italian RENAISSANCE and carved three times by MICHELANGELO.

PIETISM, 17th-century evangelical revivalist movement in the German LUTHERAN CHURCH. It attacked the prevalent orthodoxy and stressed individual piety and devotion, but tended to MYSTICISM and anti-intellectualism. It influenced the Moravians, Methodists, and American Lutherans.

PIETRO DA CORTONA (1596–1669), Italian BAROQUE painter whose facade for *Santa Maria della Pace*, Rome, 1656–57, made him a leading architect of the period. Another masterpiece was the ceiling painting, *Divine Providence*, 1633–39, an allegory of the Barberini family's fortunes.

PIEZOELECTRICITY, a reversible relationship between mechanical stress and electrostatic potential exhibited by certain CRYSTALS with no center of symmetry, discovered in 1880 during investigations of *pyroelectric* crystals (these are also asymmetric and get oppositely charged faces when heated). When pressure is applied to a piezoelectric crystal such as QUARTZ, positive and negative electric charges appear on opposite crystal faces. Replacing the pressure by tension changes the sign of the charges. If, instead, an electric potential is applied across the crystal, its length changes; this effect is linear. A piezoelectric crystal placed in an alternating electric circuit will alternately expand and contract. Resonance occurs in the circuit when its frequency matches the natural vibration frequency of the crystal, this effect being applied in frequency controllers. This useful way of coupling electrical and mechanical effects is used in microphones, phonograph pickups and ultrasonic generators.

PIG. See HOGS.

PIGEONS, a family, Columbidae, of some 255 species of birds, with worldwide distribution. They are a diverse group, but the typical pigeon is a pastel gray, pink or brown bird with contrasting patches of brighter colors. The body is compact, the neck short and the head and bill fairly small. Most species are gregarious and many are seen in very large flocks. The food may be stored in a distensible crop.

PIG IRON, crude cast iron produced in a BLAST FURNACE and cast into ingots or "pigs." It is used to make wrought iron and steel. (See also IRON.)

PIGMENTS, Natural, chemical substances imparting colors to animals and plants. In animals the most important examples include MELANIN (black), rhodopsin (purple) and the respiratory pigments, HEMOGLOBIN (red) and hemocyanin (blue). (See also MIMICRY; PROTECTIVE COLORATION.) In plants, the CHLOROPHYLLS (green) are important as the key chemicals in PHOTOSYNTHESIS. Other plant pigments include the carotenes and xanthophylls (red-yellow), the anthocyanins (red-blue) and the anthoxanthins (yellow-orange). In nature, whiteness results from the absence of pigment (see ALBINO) and is comparatively uncommon.

PIKE, James Albert (1913–1969), US theologian, dean of New York's Cathedral of St. John the Divine (1952–58) and Episcopal bishop of California (1958–66). His liberal views strongly influenced Protestant religious and social thought.

PIKE, Zebulon Montgomery (1779–1813), US general and explorer, best known as the man who discovered (1806) the Colorado mountain thereafter called PIKES PEAK.

PIKES PEAK, mountain, 14,110ft, in E central Col., part of the Rocky Mts., near Colorado Springs, one of the most famous in the US. Its solitary position and commanding vistas make it a popular tourist attraction.

PILATE, Pontius, Roman procurator of Judea (26–36 AD) who ordered the crucifixion of Christ, afterwards washing his hands to disclaim responsibility. Hated by the Jews, he was recalled to Rome after his behavior had provoked a riot which had to be put down by troops.

PILE, a heavy beam or column made of wood, steel or concrete, sunk into the ground to support a load. When they rest on bedrock they are known as end-bearing piles; when supported by the friction of the soil, friction piles. Some concrete piles are cast in place, but most are driven in by piledrivers, large hammers worked by gravity or by hydraulic or pneumatic power. Vibratory piledrivers are an efficient recent innovation.

PILGRIMAGE OF GRACE, in English history, Catholic rising in N England (1536–37) to protest HENRY VIII's break with the papacy and his suppression of the monasteries. The movement was severely repressed.

PILGRIM FATHERS, 102 English emigrants on the MAYFLOWER, including 35 PURITAN separatists formerly settled in the Netherlands, who became the first English settlers in New England (1620). Their settlement was named PLYMOUTH COLONY. (See also ALDEN, JOHN; BRADFORD, WILLIAM; BREWSTER, WILLIAM; STANDISH, MILES.)

PILGRIMS, those who journey to a holy place for penance or to seek divine help. Pilgrimages today include those by Roman Catholics to ROME, LOURDES and FÁTIMA; by Hindus to Varanasi; by Muslims to MECCA; and by Buddhists to Kandy.

PILLARS OF HERCULES, the rocky summits on each side of the Strait of Gibraltar, in Greek myth set up by HERCULES, and held to mark the W limits of the seas he had made safe for sailing.

PILSUDSKI, Józef (1867–1935), Polish general and statesman. Imprisoned several times for his nationalism, he led a private army against Russia in WWI and directed the RUSSO-POLISH WAR. From 1918 to 1922 he was president of the new Polish republic. After a coup d'etat in 1926 he became virtual dictator.

PILTDOWN MAN, *Eoanthropus dawsoni,* fraudulent human ancestor whose "remains" were found 1908-15 under Piltdown Common, Sussex, UK. These consisted of a skull with ape-like jaw but large, human cranium and teeth worn down unlike those of any extant ape, surrounded by FOSSIL animals that indicated an early PLEISTOCENE date. Piltdown Man was held by many to be an ancestor of *Homo sapiens* until 1953, when the fraud was exposed: the skull was human but relatively recent; the even more recent jaw was that of an orangutan; the teeth had been filed down by hand; and the fossil animals were not of British origin. The remains had been artificially stained to increase confusion. The hoax has been attributed to Sir Arthur Conan DOYLE among others.

PIMA INDIANS, a North American Indian tribe living with Maricopa Indians on the Gila R and Salt R reservations in S Ariz. A sedentary agricultural group, they are related to the PAPAGO INDIANS and descended from the Hohokam peoples. They were noted for their dome-shaped houses and basketry.

PINCHOT, Gifford (1865-1946), US conservationist who was largely responsible for making CONSERVATION a public issue. He headed the Division of Forestry (US Dept. of Agriculture; 1898-1910) and influenced President Theodore Roosevelt to transfer millions of acres of forest land to public reserves. He was a founder of the PROGRESSIVE PARTY (1912) and served as governor of Pennsylvania (1923-27; 1931-35).

PINCKNEY, a wealthy, influential S.C. family which produced a number of important figures in the early days of the Republic. **Elizabeth Lucas Pinckney** (1722-1793) was a successful planter, notably of indigo, as well as a leading patriot and champion of independence. Her son, **Charles Cotesworth Pinckney** (1746-1825), was a soldier in the Revolutionary War and a member of the Constitutional Convention. He is best known for his part in the XYZ AFFAIR. **Thomas Pinckney** (1750-1828), soldier and statesman, arranged PINCKNEY'S TREATY with Spain in 1795. He served as governor of S.C. and was, like his brother, C. C. Pinckney, an unsuccessful FEDERALIST PARTY candidate for the vice-presidency. Their cousin **Charles Pinckney** (1757-1824) brought the "Pinckney Draft" to the Constitutional Convention of 1787.

Most of its clauses were adopted. Three times governor of S.C., Charles Pinckney became US minister to Spain (1801-05).

PINCKNEY'S TREATY (1795), negotiated with Spain by Thomas PINCKNEY, established commercial relations with Spain, opened the entire Mississippi R to American navigation, granted Americans the right of deposit at New Orleans, and fixed the boundaries of Louisiana and E and W Florida.

PINCUS, Gregory Goodwin (1903-1967), US biologist, director (1944-67) of the Worcester (Mass.) Foundation for Experimental Biology. His work in endocrinology and reproductive biology led to the development of oral contraception ("the pill").

PINDAR (c518-c438 BC), Theban noble and greatest of Greek lyric poets, perfector of the choral *epinicion* ODE celebrating a victory in the national games. His odes combine lofty praise of athlete, patron and gods with extended mythical metaphor. From them was developed the Pindaric ode, consisting of a strophe, antistrophe and epode, chiefly used in 17th- and 18th-century English poetry.

PINE, general name for a large group of coniferous trees that produce needle-like leaves in clusters of two to five. The longleaf pine (*Pinus palustris*) has needles up to 18in long. The sugar pine (*P. lambertiana*) is the tallest pine, growing up to 260ft. The term "pine" is generally confined to about 100 species that belong to the genus *Pinus*. In general, they are able to tolerate dry, harsh conditions and are of importance in providing wood, OILS and RESINS. Family: Pinaceae.

PINEAL BODY, or pineal gland, a gland-like structure situated over the BRAIN stem and which appears to be a vestigial remnant of a functioning ENDOCRINE GLAND in other animals. It has no known function in man, although DESCARTES thought it to be the seat of the soul. It has a role in pigmentation in some species; calcium deposition in the pineal makes it a useful marker of midline in skull X-rays.

PINEL, Philippe (1745-1826), French pioneer of the scientific study of MENTAL ILLNESS and the humane treatment of mental patients, whose remarkably modern ideas have earned him regard as a father of psychiatry.

PINERO, Sir Arthur Wing (1855-1934), English playwright, best known for *The Second Mrs. Tanqueray* (1893).

PINKERTON, Allan (1819-1884), Scottish-born founder of a pioneer detective agency. He organized a Civil War espionage network which became the Federal Secret Service. "Pinkerton Men" became famous; they were used to break the HOMESTEAD STRIKE in 1892.

PINKEYE, common name for CONJUNCTIVITIS.

PINKNEY, William (1764–1822), US lawyer and politician. A specialist in constitutional, maritime and international law, he negotiated maritime claims with England and served as US minister there (1807–11) and to Russia (1816–18). He was US attorney general (1811–14) and a Md. congressman and senator.

PINOCHET UGARTE, Augusto (1915–   ), president of Chile (1974–   ). A right-wing general, he led the bloody coup that overthrew the Marxist president, Salvador Allende, in 1973. His authoritarian regime was affirmed by a plebiscite in 1980, but a 1988 referendum rejected his bid for another term as president. He determined to complete his term of office, which did not expire until 1991.

PINTER, Harold (1930–   ), English dramatist and director. His "comedies of menace" had ambiguous and deceptively casual dialogue, cat-and-mouse situations and a fine balance of humor and tension; notable are *The Caretaker* (1960), *The Homecoming* (1965) and *No Man's Land* (1974). He wrote several successful screenplays.

PINTURICCHIO (Bernardino di Betto; c1454–1513), Italian (Umbrian) RENAISSANCE painter. A pupil of PERUGINO, he helped paint the SISTINE CHAPEL. His most important frescoes are in the Vatican and in the Siena cathedral library.

PINYIN, the official system of the People's Republic of China for transliterating Chinese into the Roman alphabet. In the 1970s the new spellings began to replace those of the earlier Wade-Giles system in English-speaking countries. Pinyin spellings include "Beijing" for the conventional "Peking" and "Mao Zedong" instead of "Mao Tse-tung."

PINZA, Ezio (1892–1957), Italian opera singer, at New York's Metropolitan Opera 1926–48. He found a wider audience on Broadway in *South Pacific* (1949) and *Fanny* (1954).

PINZON, family of three Spanish brothers, navigators who took part with COLUMBUS in discovering America. **Martin Alonso** (c1441–1493) commanded the *Pinta;* he left Columbus after reaching Cuba and unsuccessfully tried to reach Spain first. **Francisco Martín** (c1441–1493?) served under him. **Vicente Yáñez** (c1460–1524?) commanded the *Niña* and stayed with Columbus; he went on to discover Brazil (1500) and to explore the coasts of Central and N South America.

PIPES AND PIPELINES, tubes for conveying fluids—liquids, gases or slurries. Pipes vary in diameter considerably, according to the flow rate required and the pressure gradient: oil pipelines may be up to 4ft in diameter. Materials used include steel, cast iron, other metals, reinforced concrete, fired clay, plastic, bitumenized-fiber cylinders, and wood. They are often coated inside and out with bitumen or concrete to prevent corrosion. Concrete, plastic and steel pipes can now be made and laid in one continuous process, but most pipes still need to be joined by means of welding, screw joints, clamped flange joints, couplings, or bell-and-spigot joints caulked with lead or cement. Pipelines, consisting of long lengths of pipe with valves and pumps at regular intervals (about 60mi for oil pipelines), are used chiefly for transporting water, sewage, chemicals, foodstuffs, crude oil and natural gas.

PIRACY, armed robbery on the high seas. It was rife in the Mediterranean in ancient times until suppressed by POMPEY. In the 16th-19th centuries, Muslim corsairs preyed on Mediterranean and Atlantic shipping; in the 16th and 17th centuries, English buccaneers attacked Spanish ships and bases in the West Indies. Chinese pirates operated until WWII, and Indochinese pirates infest the South China Sea today. (See also BARBARY WARS; BLACKBEARD; DRAKE, SIR FRANCIS; KIDD, WILLIAM; LAFFITE, JEAN; MORGAN, SIR HENRY.)

PIRAEUS, chief port and third largest city of Greece, 6mi SW of Athens, whose ancient history it shares. It handles over half the country's seaborne trade. Its industries include shipbuilding, manufacturing and textile production. Pop 196,389.

PIRANDELLO, Luigi (1867–1936), Italian dramatist and author of novels and short stories. A most influential writer, he won the Nobel Prize for Literature in 1934. He is noted for his grimly humorous treatment of psychological themes and of the reality of art compared with "real" life, as in his best-known play *Six Characters in Search of an Author* (1921).

PIRANESI, Giovanni Battista (1720–1778), Italian etcher, draftsman and architect, known for his prints of old and contemporary Roman buildings, *Views of Rome* (begun 1748), and for a series of fantastic *Imaginary Prisons* (c1745). They are notable for their grandeur and lighting contrasts.

PIRANHAS, or **caribes,** small, extremely ferocious, shoaling freshwater fish from South America. The jaws are short but powerful, armed with sharp cutting teeth. They quickly strip the flesh from other fish and mammals and have even been known to attack humans on river crossings. Family: Characidae.

PIRENNE, Henri (1862–1935), Belgian historian whose *Medieval Cities* (1925) and *Mohammed and Charlemagne* (1937) challenged accepted views of medieval economic history.

PISA, historic city of NW central Italy, on the Arno R in Tuscany. GALILEO was born at Pisa, which is famous for its marble campanile (see LEANING TOWER OF PISA) and rich in architecture and art. Pop 107,312.

PISA, Council of (1409), uncanonical Roman Catholic ECUMENICAL COUNCIL of 500 prelates and delegates from all over Europe, met to try to heal the GREAT SCHISM. It deposed the rival popes of Rome and Avignon, and elected a third pope, Alexander V. This, however, merely created three separate parties.

PISANELLO (Antonio Pisano; c1395–c1455), Italian Renaissance painter and medalist, best known for his portrait medals, frescoes (including *St. George and the Princess*) in Verona, and a complete set of drawings now in the Louvre, Paris.

PISANO, two sculptors, father and son, of Pisa, Italy: **Nicolo Pisano** (c1220–1284?), who revived the art of sculpture in Italy; and **Giovanni Pisano** (c1250– after 1314). They combined classical and Gothic forms in works which include richly decorated pulpits at Pisa, Siena and Pistoia, a fountain at Perugia and the facade of Siena cathedral.

PISCATOR, Erwin (1893–1966), German theatrical director of social and political dramas by Bertolt BRECHT and others in which he employed multimedia effects to achieve EPIC THEATER. In the US (1939–51), he directed the Dramatic Workshop of the New School for Social Research in New York. Back in Germany, he managed and directed the Volksbühne in West Berlin.

PISISTRATUS (c600–527 BC), "tyrant" of Athens, whose benign rule and fostering of commerce and the arts made Athens the foremost city in Greece. In 560 BC he seized power in a popular coup d'etat. Aristocrats, having returned from exile, ousted him in 552, but in 541 he established himself firmly. He enforced SOLON's laws, promoted public works, and was succeeded by his sons.

PISSARRO, Camille (1830–1903), leading French Impressionist painter. Born in the West Indies, he went to Paris in 1855. Influenced by the BARBIZON SCHOOL at first, he was with CÉZANNE, MONET and RENOIR a founder of IMPRESSIONISM. His works, most notably landscapes and street scenes, are famous for their freshness, vividness and luminous color.

PISTOL, small firearm that can be conveniently held and operated in one hand. It developed in parallel with the shoulder weapon from the 14th century, first becoming practical in the early 16th century with the invention of the wheel-lock firing mechanism, soon superseded by the flintlock. Modern rapid-fire pistols are usually either revolvers or automatics. Automatic pistols, such as the Colt .45 automatic, contain a magazine of cartridges in the butt and are automatically reloaded and cocked by the energy of recoil when a round is fired. In a revolver, activation of the trigger mechanism, in addition to firing a bullet, moves a revolving five- or six-chamber cylinder to align a fresh chamber with the breech of the barrel. The first practical revolver design was patented by Samuel Colt in 1856.

PISTON, Walter (1894–1976), US neo-classical composer, professor of music at Harvard from 1944 to 1961. His austere but dynamic music incorporates complex rhythm and harmonics in traditional forms. His *7th Symphony* (1961) won a Pulitzer Prize.

PITCAIRN ISLAND, small British colony (2sq mi) in the Pacific midway between New Zealand and Panama, famous as the uninhabited island settled by BOUNTY mutineers and Tahitian women (1790), from whom the present 90-odd English-speaking islanders are descended.

PITCH, Musical, refers to the frequency of the vibrations constituting a SOUND. The frequency associated with a given pitch name (e.g., Middle C) has varied considerably over the years. The present international standard sets Concert A at 440Hz.

PITCHBLENDE, or **uraninite,** brown, black or greenish radioactive mineral, the most important source of URANIUM, RADIUM and polonium. The composition varies between UO_2 and $UO_{2.6}$; thorium, radium, polonium, lead and helium are also present. Principal deposits are in Zaire, Czechoslovakia, at Great Bear Lake, Canada, and in the US Mountain States.

PITCHER, Molly (1754–1832), popular heroine of the American Revolution. Born Mary Ludwig, she earned her nickname by carrying water for the Continental soldiers during the battle of MONMOUTH. According to legends, she manned her husband's gun when he collapsed.

PITMAN, Sir Isaac (1813–1897), English school teacher who invented a famous SHORTHAND based on phonetic principles, still one of the most widely used systems of stenography in English.

PITT, the name of two British statesmen. **William Pitt, Earl of Chatham** (1708–1778), known as "Pitt the Elder," was an outstanding war minister and empire builder during the SEVEN YEARS' WAR. He was also famous for his defense of the rights of the American colonists. By 1761 he had completely transformed Britain's position in Europe and throughout the world. He strengthened the British navy and extended British control in Canada and India. **William Pitt** (1759–1806), second son of the Earl of Chatham, was known as "Pitt the Younger." At 24 he became Britain's youngest prime minister, at the invitation of GEORGE III, and he dominated British politics until his death. In his 1783–1801 ministry he strengthened national finances, but war with France and agitation at home forced him to shelve parliamentary reform measures. His 1804–06 ministry was marked by defeats on land but victory at sea in the NAPOLEONIC WARS.

PITTSBURGH, steel-producing city in SW Penn., seat of Allegheny Co., and the state's second largest city. It occupies over 55sq mi around its business center, the "Golden Triangle," where the Allegheny and Monongahela rivers meet to form the Ohio. Its economic wealth is based on steel mills, coke from Allegheny coal, pig iron, glass and a variety of manufactured products. Pop (city) 403,000, (metro) 2,143,000.

PITUITARY GLAND, major ENDOCRINE GLAND situated just below the BRAIN, under the control of the adjacent HYPOTHALAMUS and in its turn controlling other endocrine glands. The posterior pituitary is a direct extension of certain cells in the hypothalamus and secretes vasopressin and oxytocin into the BLOOD stream. The anterior pituitary develops separately and consists of several cell types which secrete different HORMONES, including growth hormone, follicle stimulating hormone, luteinizing hormone, prolactin,thyrotrophic hormone (which stimulates thyroid gland) and adrenocorticotrophic hormone (ACTH). Growth hormone is concerned with skeletal growth and development as well as regulation of blood sugar (anti-INSULIN activity). The anterior pituitary hormones are controlled by releasing hormones secreted by the hypothalamus into local blood vessels; the higher centers of the brain

and environmental influences act by this route. FEEDBACK from the organs controlled occurs at both the hypothalamic and pituitary levels. Pituitary TUMORS or loss of blood supply may cause loss of function, while some tumors may be functional and produce syndromes such as GIGANTISM or acromegaly . (due to growth hormone imbalance). Pituitary tumors may also affect VISION by compressing the nearby optic nerves. Sophisticated tests of pituitary function are now available.

PIUS, name of twelve popes. **Saint Pius V** (1504–1572) succeeded in 1566. With some severity he restored a degree of discipline and morality to the papacy in the face of the Protestant challenge, and organized the Spanish-Venetian expedition which defeated the Turks at LEPANTO in 1571. **Pius VI** (1717–1799), elected in 1775, drained the Pontine marshes and completed St. Peter's. The French Revolution led to the occupation of the papal territories and Pius' death in captivity. **Pius VII** (1740–1823) succeeded him in 1800. Under an 1801 CONCORDAT French troops were withdrawn, but the PAPAL STATES were later annexed by Napoleon, whom Pius had consecrated emperor in 1804. **Pius IX** (1792–1878) began the longest papal reign in 1846 with liberal reforms, but became an extreme reactionary in both politics and dogma after the REVOLUTIONS OF 1848. The Immaculate Conception became an article of dogma (1854), and papal infallibility was proclaimed in 1870 by the first VATICAN COUNCIL (see ULTRAMONTANISM). In 1871 the new kingdom of Italy passed The Law of Guaranties defining relations between the state and the papacy, but Pius refused to accept the position. **Saint Pius X** (1835–1914), elected in 1903, condemned modernism in the Church. **Pius XI** (1857–1939), elected in 1922, concluded the LATERAN TREATY (1929) with the Italian state and issued encyclicals condemning communism, fascism and racism. **Pius XII** (1876–1958), who reigned from 1939, was an active diplomat in a difficult period and undertook a considerable amount of humanitarian work during WWII although he was criticized for refusing to condemn Nazi policy toward the Jews. His encyclical *Mediator Dei* led to changes in the Mass.

PIZARRO, Francisco (c1474–1541), Spanish conquistador who destroyed the INCA empire in the course of his conquest of PERU. He was with BALBOA when he discovered the Pacific (1513). In 1524 and 1526–27 Pizarro attempted to conquer Peru with Diego de ALMAGRO and Fernando de Luque. In 1531, with royal assent, he began a new campaign and found Peru in an unsettled state under the Inca emperor ATAHUALPA. At Cajamarca in the Andes Pizarro's small band, at first pretending friendship, kidnapped Atahualpa and massacred his unarmed followers; he forced the emperor to pay a massive ransom, then executed him. A vicious and greedy man, Pizarro cheated Almagro and eventually had him killed; he was himself assassinated by Almagro's followers.

PLACENTA, in PLACENTAL MAMMALS including man, specialized structure derived from the WOMB lining and part of the EMBRYO after implantation; it separates and yet ensures a close extensive contact between the maternal (uterine) and fetal (umbilical) BLOOD CIRCULATIONS. This allows nutrients and OXYGEN to pass from the mother to the FETUS, and waste products to pass in the reverse direction. The placenta thus enables the embryo and fetus to live as a PARASITE, dependent on the maternal organs. Gonadotrophins are produced by the placenta which prepares the maternal body for delivery and the BREASTS for LACTATION. The placenta is delivered after the child at BIRTH (the afterbirth) by separation of the blood vessel layers; placental disorders may cause ante- or post-partum HEMORRHAGE or fetal immaturity.

PLACENTAL MAMMALS, true mammals, distinct from MARSUPIALS and monotremes, in which the FETUS is nourished in the womb attached to a highly organized placenta until a comparatively late stage in its development. By contrast, marsupials give birth to far less well developed young, further development occurring while the young is attached to the mother's teat. Other differences are in the structure of the reproductive system and in the BRAIN. Placental mammals have larger brains and possess a *corpus callosum*: threads of tissue connecting the two halves of the brain.

PLACER MINING, the extraction of minerals such as gold, platinum and diamonds from ore that has accumulated through the processes of weathering or EROSION. The earliest and best known form of placer mining is gold panning.

PLACID, Lake, beautiful small lake (4.37sq mi) in the Adirondack Mts., in NW N.Y., 1,860ft above sea level, It is a year-round tourist attraction.

PLAGUE, a highly infectious disease due to a bacterium carried by rodent fleas. It causes greatly enlarged LYMPH nodes (buboes, hence bubonic plague), SEPTICEMIA with FEVER, prostration and COMA; plague

PNEUMONIA is particularly severe. If untreated, DEATH is common and EPIDEMICS occur in areas of overcrowding and poverty. It still occurs on a small rural scale in the Far East; massive epidemics such as the **Black Death**, which perhaps halved the population of Europe in the mid-14th century, are rare. Rat and flea control, disinfection and ANTIBIOTICS are the mainstay of current prevention and treatment.

PLAGUES OF EGYPT, in the Book of EXODUS, the 10 disasters inflicted on Egypt by God when the pharaoh refused MOSES' demand that the Israelites be freed. They were: the rivers turned to blood, frogs, lice, flies, murrain, boils, hail, locusts, darkness, and finally the death of all firstborn. After the last plague, from which the Israelites were protected by the PASSOVER, they were allowed to leave.

PLAINSONG, or **plainchant,** one of the earliest forms of music in Christian Europe, still used in the ROMAN CATHOLIC CHURCH. It is a sung version of the liturgy in which an unaccompanied line of melody, at its simplest all on one note (psalmodic intonation), follows the rhythm of the words. The "Ambrosian chant" developed in Milan under St. AMBROSE (c340–397). Today's Gregorian chant was developed in Rome and codified in the time of Pope GREGORY I (c540–604), adapting Greek modes. (See MODE; NOTATION; POLYPHONY.)

PLANCK, Max Karl Ernst Ludwig (1858–1947), German physicist whose QUANTUM THEORY, with the theory of RELATIVITY, ushered physics into the modern era. Initially influenced by CLAUSIUS, he made fundamental researches in THERMODYNAMICS before turning to investigate BLACKBODY radiation. To describe the electromagnetic radiation emitted from a blackbody he evolved the **Planck Radiation Formula,** which implied that ENERGY, like MATTER, is not infinitely subdivisible—that it can exist only as quanta. Planck himself was unconvinced of this, even after EINSTEIN had applied the theory to the PHOTOELECTRIC EFFECT and BOHR in his model of the ATOM; but for his achievement he received the 1918 Nobel Prize for Physics.

PLANE, a surface having two dimensions only, length and breadth, any two POINTS of which can be joined by a straight LINE composed entirely of points also in the plane. A plane may be determined by two intersecting or parallel lines, by a line and a point that does not lie on the line, or by three points that do not lie in a straight line. The intersection of two planes is a straight line; the intersection of a plane and a line in a different plane is a point. An infinite number of planes may pass through a single point or line. A plane is parallel to another plane if all perpendiculars drawn between them are of equal length.

PLANET, in the SOLAR SYSTEM, one of the nine major celestial bodies orbiting the sun; by extension, a similar body circling any other star. In 1963 it was discovered that Barnard's Star has at least one companion about 1.5 times the size of Jupiter, and in 1983 scientists detected possible evidence of an evolving planetary system around the star Vega.

PLANETARIUM, an instrument designed to represent the relative positions and motions of celestial objects. Originally a mechanical model of the SOLAR SYSTEM, the planetarium of today is an intricate optical device that projects disks and points of light representing sun, moon, planets and stars on to the interior of a fixed hemispherical dome. The various cyclic motions of these bodies as seen from a given latitude on earth can be simulated. Of great assistance to students of ASTRONOMY and celestial NAVIGATION, planetariums also attract large public audiences. The first modern planetarium, built in 1923 by the firm of Carl ZEISS, is still in use at the Deutsches Museum, Munich, West Germany.

PLANKTON, microscopic animals and plants that live in the sea. They drift under the influence of OCEAN CURRENTS and are vitally important links in the marine food chain (see ECOLOGY). A major part of plankton comprises minute plants (phytoplankton), which are mainly ALGAE and include dinoflagellates and diatoms. Phytoplankton may be so numerous as to color the water and cause it to have a "bloom." They are eaten by animals (zooplankton), which comprise the eggs, larvae and adults of a vast array of animal types, from Protozoa to JELLYFISH. Zooplankton is an important food for large animals such as WHALES and countless fishes such as HERRING. Phytoplankton is confined to the upper layers of the sea where light can reach, but zooplankton has been found at great depths. (See also OCEANS.)

PLANNED PARENTHOOD FEDERATION OF AMERICA, federation, founded in 1916 and headquartered in New York City, of 187 local organizations that provide family-planning information and services.

PLANT, a living organism belonging to the PLANT KINGDOM. Green plants are unique in being able to synthesize their own organic molecules from carbon dioxide and water using light energy by the process known as PHOTOSYNTHESIS. Mineral nutrients are absorbed from the environment. Plants are the primary source of food for all other living organisms (see ECOLOGY). The possession of CHLOROPHYLL, the green photosynthetic pigment, is probably the most important distinction between plants and animals, but there are several other differences. Plants are stationary and have no nervous system, and the cell wall contains large amounts of CELLULOSE. But there are exceptions. Some plants, such as ALGAE and BACTERIA, can move about, and others, including FUNGI, bacteria and some PARASITES, do not contain chlorophyll and cannot synthesize their own organic molecules, but absorb them from their environment. Some INSECTIVOROUS PLANTS obtain their food by trapping insects.

Although the more primitive plants vary considerably in their overall structure, the higher plants (GYMNOSPERMS and ANGIOSPERMS) are much the same in their basic anatomy and morphology. In a typical angiosperm, four main regions can be recognized: root, stem, leaf and flower. Each region has one or more basic functions.

When examined under the microscope, a piece of plant tissue can be seen to consist of thousands of tiny CELLS, generally packed tightly together. The cells are not all alike, and each one is adapted to do a certain job. All are derived, however, from a basic pattern. This basic plant cell tends to be rectangular and has a tough wall of cellulose which gives it its shape, but the living boundary of the cell is the delicate cell membrane just inside the wall. Inside the membrane is the PROTOPLASM, which contains the nucleus, the chloroplasts and many other microscopic structures. In the center of the protoplasm there is a large sap-filled vacuole, which maintains the cell's shape and plays an important part in the working of the whole plant.

Both sexual and asexual REPRODUCTION are widespread throughout the plant kingdom. Many plants are capable of both forms, and in some cases the life cycle of the plant may involve the two different forms. (See also BOTANY; FERTILIZATION; GERMINATION; GROWTH; OSMOSIS; PLANT DISEASES; POLLINATION; TRANSPIRATION.)

PLANTAGENETS, name given to the branch of the ANGEVIN dynasty descended from Geoffrey Plantagenet which ruled England 1154–1485. From HENRY II until the deposition of RICHARD II in 1399 the succession was direct. Thereafter the crown passed to other branches of the family until the defeat of the Yorkist Plantagenet RICHARD III at the hands of Henry Tudor

(HENRY VII), who had remote Plantagenet connections.

PLANT DISEASES cause serious losses to crop production; they may kill plants completely, but more often they simply reduce the yield. Most plant diseases are caused by microorganisms which infect the tissues, the most important being FUNGI, including mildew, rusts and smuts. Control methods are based on FUNGICIDES. VIRUSES are the next most damaging group of plant pathogens. Most of them are carried by aphids and other sap-sucking insects, and control is largely a matter of controlling these insect carriers. BACTERIA are less important, their main role being in secondary infection, causing the tissues to rot. Deficiency diseases are caused by a lack of available minerals in the soil. Insect pests, such as the BOLL WEEVIL on cotton, can also cause serious crop damage.

PLANT KINGDOM, the second great group of living organisms. The plant and ANIMAL KINGDOMS together embrace all living things except VIRUSES, and only overlap in the most primitive organisms. The plant kingdom is extremely diverse (over 400,000 species are now known) and is found in almost every conceivable habitat. Plants range in size from microscopic BACTERIA to 375ft sequoias. The plant kingdom can be arranged into an orderly hierarchical pattern of classification (see TAXONOMY) containing divisions (or phyla), classes, orders, families, genera and species. Indeed, several systems have been evolved to do this. In the classical Eichler system there are four divisions: the Thallophyta, including bacteria, slime molds, algae and fungi; the Bryophyta, including liverworts, hornworts and mosses; the Pteridophyta, including ferns, club mosses and horsetails; and the Spermatophyta, including GYMNOSPERMS and ANGIOSPERMS, the latter being divided into dicotyledons and monocotyledons. However, this system has been replaced recently by a more natural arrangement of 11 divisions: Schizophyta, bacteria and blue-green algae; Euglenophyta, euglenoids; Chlorophyta, green algae; Xanthophyta, yellow-green algae; Chrysophyta, golden algae and diatoms; Phaeophyta, brown algae; Rhodophyta, red algae; Pyrrophyta, dinoflagellates and cryptomonads; Mycota, slime molds and fungi; Bryophyta, liverworts and mosses; and Tracheophyta, the vascular plants, including horsetails, ferns, gymnosperms and angiosperms. Under this system some authorities break the plant kingdom into three kingdoms: the Monera, including the division Schizophyta; the Metaphyta, including the Bryophyta and Tracheophyta; and the Protista, which includes all the other divisions.

PLASMA, almost completely ionized GAS, containing equal numbers of free ELECTRONS and positive IONS. Plasmas such as those forming stellar atmospheres (see STAR) or regions in an electron discharge tube are highly conducting but electrically neutral, and many phenomena occur in them that are not seen in ordinary gases. The TEMPERATURE of a plasma is theoretically high enough to support a controlled nuclear FUSION reaction. Because of this, plasmas are being widely studied particularly in magnetohydrodynamics research. Plasmas are formed by heating low-pressure gases until the ATOMS have sufficient energy to ionize each other. Unless the plasma can be successfully contained by electric or magnetic fields, rapid cooling and recombination occur; indeed, the high temperatures needed for thermonuclear reactions cannot as yet be maintained in the laboratory sufficiently long.

PLASMA, the part of the BLOOD remaining when all CELLS have been removed, and which includes CLOTTING factors. It may be used in resuscitation from SHOCK.

PLASTICS, materials that can be molded (at least in production) into desired shapes. A few natural plastics are known, e.g., bitumen, resins and rubber, but almost all are man-made, mainly from PETROCHEMICALS, and are available with a vast range of useful properties: hardness, elasticity, transparency, toughness, low density, insulating ability, inertness and corrosion resistance, etc. They are invariably high POLYMERS with carbon skeletons, each molecule being made up of thousands or even millions of atoms. Plastics fall into two classes: thermoplastic and thermosetting. **Thermoplastics** soften or melt reversibly on heating; they include celluloid and other cellulose plastics, Lucite, nylon, polyethylene, styrene polymers, vinyl polymers, polyformaldehyde and polycarbonates. **Thermosetting** plastics, although moldable when produced as simple polymers, are converted by heat and pressure, and sometimes by an admixed hardener, to a cross-linked, infusible form. These include Bakelite and other phenol resins, epoxy resins, polyesters, silicones, urea-formaldehyde and melamine-formaldehyde resins, and some polyurethanes. Most plastics are mixed with stabilizers, fillers, dyes or pigments and plasticizers if needed. There are several fabrication processes: making films by calendering (squeezing between rollers), casting or extrusion, and making objects by compression molding, injection molding (melting and forcing into a cooled mold) and casting. (See also LAMINATES; SYNTHETIC FIBERS.)

PLASTIC SURGERY, the branch of SURGERY devoted to reconstruction or repair of deformity, surgical defect or the results of injury. Using bone, cartilage, tendon, and skin from other parts of the body, or artificial substitutes, function and appearance may in many cases be restored. In skin grafting, the most common procedure, a piece of skin is cut, usually from the thigh, and stitched to the damaged area. Bone and cartilage (usually from the ribs or hips), or sometimes plastic, are used in cosmetic remodeling and facial reconstruction after injury. Congenital defects such as HARELIP and CLEFT PALATE can be treated in infancy. "Face lifting," the cosmetic removal of excess fat and tightening of the skin, is a delicate and often unsuccessful operation, carrying the added risk of infection.

PLATA, Río de la. See RÍO DE LA PLATA.

PLATAEA, Battle of (479 BC), in Boeotia, Greece. The Greek land forces under Pausanias decisively repulsed the invading Persian army led by XERXES' General Mardonius (see PERSIAN WARS).

PLATELET. See BLOOD.

PLATE TECTONICS, revolutionary unifying theory of modern GEOLOGY, developed in the 1960s when new information concerning the topography of the ocean floor and paleomagnetic studies become available. The theory is now broadly supported by additional evidence from many branches of geology. Plate tectonics explains the earth's dynamics in terms of a series of moving, rigid, slab-like plates of the LITHOSPHERE that are driven slowly by convection currents in the ASTHENOSPHERE. Plate boundaries, outlined by their seismicity and volcanic activity, are of three types: divergent (constructive) boundaries, usually located along major oceanic ridges where the plates are slowly spreading apart, allowing molten rock (MAGMA) to rise to the surface and solidify to form new oceanic crust; convergent (destructive) boundaries, located at deep oceanic trenches, where the leading edge of one plate plunges beneath the other in a subduction zone and remelts in the upper MANTLE, often rising in a molten state through the upper plate to form an arc of volcanic islands fringing the trench; and transform fault (passive) boundaries, where plates slip past each other along fracture zones. The theory provides for the mechanism (and for the necessity) of CONTINENTAL DRIFT, as continents are carried as integral parts of the conveyor-like plates. It also explains the origin of ocean basins through the location of divergent boundaries under continental land masses; the origin of major continental mountain chains through orogenic folding and faulting of sediments trapped in zones of convergence; and it suggests answers for many questions relating to the migration, extinction and EVOLUTION of life through paleogeographic reconstruction of ancient continental locations and paleoclimates. Plate tectonics also has implications in the search for the earth's mineral resources by suggesting likely places for the localization of oil, gas and metallic ores. (See also PALEOMAGNETISM.)

PLATH, Sylvia (1932–1963), US poet whose taut, melodic, highly imagistic works explore the nature of womanhood and her fixation with death. *Ariel* (1965), which appeared after her suicide, won her international acclaim as a major US "confessional" poet. Her other works include *The Bell Jar* (1963), a semi-autobiographical novel about a young woman's emotional breakdown, and her *Complete Poems* (1981) edited by Ted HUGHES.

PLATINUM (Pt), soft, silvery-white metal in the platinum group. In addition to the general uses of these metals, platinum is used as a catalyst. AW 195.1, mp 1772°C, bp 4010°C, sg 21.45 (20°C).

PLATO, Greek philosopher (c427–347 BC). A pupil of SOCRATES, c385 BC he founded the Academy, where ARISTOTLE studied. His early dialogues present a portrait of Socrates as critical arguer, but in the great middle dialogues he develops his own doctrines—such as the theory of Forms (*Republic*), the immortality of the soul (*Phaedo*), knowledge as recollection of the Forms by the soul (*Meno*), virtue as knowledge (*Protagoras*)—and attacks hedonism and the idea that "might is right" (*Gorgias*). The *Symposium* and *Phaedrus* sublimate love into a beatific vision of the Forms of the Good and the Beautiful. The late dialogues (*Sophist, Theaetetus, Politicus, Philebus, Parmenides*) deal with problems of epistemology, ontology and logic; the *Timaeus* contains cosmological speculation. In the *Republic* Plato posits abstract Forms as the supreme reality. The highest function of the human soul is to achieve the vision of the Form of the Good. Drawing an analogy between the soul and the state, he presents his famous ideal state ruled by philosophers, who correspond to the rational part of the soul. In the late *Laws*

Plato develops in detail his ideas of the state. His idealist philosophy, his insistence on order and harmony, his moral fervor and asceticism and his literary genius have made Plato a dominant figure in Western thought.

PLATT, Thomas Collier (1833–1910), US businessman and New York City political boss, a Republican senator in 1881 and 1897–1909. Hoping to weaken Theodore ROOSEVELT's power by securing his nomination as vice-president, he lost influence when Roosevelt became president.

PLATT AMENDMENT, a provision forced through Congress and into the Cuban constitution by Senator Orville Platt in 1901. Setting out conditions for US intervention, it virtually made Cuba a US protectorate. It was abrogated in 1934.

PLATT NATIONAL PARK, in S Okla. near Sulphur. Established in 1906, it is 912 acres in area. It is known for its mineral and freshwater springs.

PLATTSBURGH, Battle of (1814), the most important US naval victory of the WAR OF 1812. The US navy destroyed all the British ships on Lake Champlain, and without naval support the British land forces occupying Plattsburgh, N.Y., were forced to retreat to Canada.

PLATYPUS, or duck-billed platypus, *Ornithorhynchus anatinus*, an amphibious monotreme (egg-laying mammal) found in Australia and Tasmania. They have webbed feet and thick fur (equipping them for an aquatic life); a short, thick tail, and a flat, toothless, bill-like mouth used for taking insects and crustaceans off the surface of the water. Like echidnas, the other monotreme group, they retain many reptilian characteristics. There is no scrotum; the testes are internal. The mammary glands are diffuse and lack distinct teats. Moreover, in the platypus, the right ovary and oviduct are nonfunctional.

PLAUTUS, Titus Maccius (c254–184 BC), Roman writer of comedies, 21 of which have survived. He based them on Greek New Comedy, especially MENANDER, but adapted them to Roman tastes and situations, and added his own brand of lively, bawdy humor. Popular in his time, he influenced SHAKESPEARE and MOLIÈRE among others.

PLAY, a distinctive type of behavior of both adult and juvenile animals, of unknown function and involving the incomplete, ritualized expression of normal adult behavior patterns. Movements are extravagant and exaggerated. Play occurs particularly in carnivores, primates and certain birds.

PLAYING CARDS, pieces of card with numerical and pictorial sequences marked on them, used in games of skill and chance. Probably originating in the Orient, they were known in Europe by the 14th century. Developed from the TAROT deck, the modern pack has 52 cards in four *suits* (clubs, diamonds, hearts, spades). In most card games players attempt to make winning combinations of cards following a particular set of rules. (See BLACKJACK; BRIDGE; CANASTA.)

PLEA BARGAINING involves an agreement between the accused and the prosecutor under which the accused agrees to plead guilty to a lesser offense in order to receive a lighter sentence from the judge. Plea bargaining has been accepted by judges, prosecutors and lawyers as necessary though undesirable. Necessary, to save time and speed up the work of dangerously overcrowded courts; it also gives guilty parties less time in prison than they would get if they went to trial and were convicted. Undesirable, because it denies the accused a fair trial and does not require the prosecutor to prove the accused's guilt beyond a reasonable doubt.

PLEBEIANS, the non-aristocratic classes in ancient Rome. In their continual rivalries with the ruling PATRICIAN aristocracy, they created their own assemblies and officers, and gained full political and civil rights by about 300 BC. (See TRIBUNE.)

PLEBISCITE, in Roman history, a law enacted by the plebeian *comitia*, or assembly of tribes. In modern times a plebiscite is a direct vote of the whole body of citizens on some specific issue (for instance, acceptance of a new constitution).

PLEDGE OF ALLEGIANCE, patriotic avowal of loyalty to the US, written in 1892 by a Baptist minister, Francis Bellamy, for the magazine *The Youth's Companion* for recitation in schools. It reads: "I pledge allegiance to the flag of the United States of America and to the Republic for which it stands, one nation, under God, indivisible, with liberty and justice for all." The words "the flag of the United States of America" were substituted for the original "my flag" when Congress included the pledge in the official flag code adopted in 1942. The words "under God" were added by Congress in 1954. In 1943 the US Supreme Court ruled that students, such as Jehovah's Witnesses, whose religion prohibited their reciting the pledge could not be compelled to do so.

PLÉIADE, seven French poets of the 16th century, the chief being RONSARD and Joachim Du Bellay. Named for an ancient

Alexandrian school, they aimed to develop French as a literary language, while imitating classical and Italian forms.

PLEISTOCENE, the earlier epoch of the QUATERNARY Period, also known as "The Great Ice Age," stretching from between about 2–3 million through 10,000 years ago. (See also GEOLOGY; HOLOCENE.)

PLEKHANOV, Georgi Valentinovich (1857–1918), Russian Marxist thinker. Always opposed to political terror, he at first supported LENIN, but after 1903 he espoused MENSHEVIK views and, during WWI, supported military defense of Russia.

PLESSY v. FERGUSON, important US Supreme Court ruling on segregation in 1896, which held that the provision of "separate but equal" accommodations for blacks on railroad trains did not violate the "equal protection of the laws" clause of the 14th Amendment. This decision was reversed in 1954 when the Supreme Court unanimously ruled against segregation in the case of BROWN V. BOARD OF EDUCATION.

PLEURISY, INFLAMMATION of the pleura, the two thin connective tissue layers covering the outer LUNG surface and the inner chest wall. It causes a characteristic chest pain, which may be localized and is made worse by deep breathing and coughing. It may be caused by infection (e.g., PNEUMONIA, TUBERCULOSIS) or TUMORS and inflammatory disease.

PLIMSOLL MARK, a line on the side of a seagoing ship indicating the safe loading limit. Samuel Plimsoll (1824–1898) first secured its compulsory marking on British ships in 1876.

PLINY, name of two Roman authors. **Pliny the Elder** (c23–79 AD) is known for his *Natural History,* a vast compendium of ancient sciences, which though of little scientific merit was popular throughout antiquity and the Middle Ages. He died attempting to help the citizens of POMPEII in the eruption of Vesuvius. **Pliny the Younger** (c61–113 AD), a nephew of Pliny the Elder, was a lawyer, statesman and administrator, primarily known for his elegant *Letters,* which throw much light on the political, economic and social life of the Roman Empire.

PLIOCENE, the final period of the TERTIARY, immediately preceding the QUATERNARY. lasting from about 10 to 4 million years ago. (See also GEOLOGY.)

PLOTINUS (205–270 AD), Greco-Roman philosopher, founder of NEOPLATONISM. Probably born in Egypt, he became a teacher in Rome; his work, the *Enneads,* was edited by his pupil Porphyry. His complex philosophical cosmology involves a hierarchy of degrees of being, the highest being the ineffable One or Good which controls the rest, down to the lowest (the physical world), by a process of *emanations.* The human soul reaches its highest state in the mystical contemplation of the One.

PLOVERS, small or medium-sized wading birds of the family Charadriidae. The family contains the lapwings and the true plovers. Fairly leggy birds, most plovers have an olive or brown back, with lighter underparts. Typically, they have a dark band across the belly and a white band on a black head. Plovers feed on insects or crustacea in mud and sand.

PLOW, an implement for tilling the soil, which breaks up the surface crust for sowing and turns under stubble and manure. Essentially it is a horizontal blade (*share*) to cut the furrow, and a projecting *moldboard* to turn the soil over. Plows have been used since the Bronze Age. Roman plows had an iron-shod share with a beam to draw it. Wheels were used in Saxon plows, and developments after 1600 led to the steel plow of the US engineer John DEERE (1837), *disk plows* with revolving concave disks instead of shares and moldboards, and tractor-drawn plows making multiple furrows.

PLUM, trees of the genus *Prunus,* which produce soft-fleshed fruits enclosing a single pit. The European plum (*Prunus domestica*) has been cultivated for 2,000 years. Wild species of North American plum include the American plum and Canada plum. Wild species have been crossed with the European plum to make hardy varieties. **Prunes** are plums that have been preserved by drying. Family: Rosaceae.

PLUNKET, Oliver (1629–1681), Irish churchman, primate of all Ireland from 1669. Falsely accused by Titus OATES of planning a foreign invasion of Ireland, he became the last Roman Catholic martyr in England.

PLUTARCH (c46–c120 AD), Greek philosopher and biographer. A native of Boeotia he visited Rome and lectured there, and was for 30 years a priest at DELPHI. His *Parallel Lives* of famous Greeks and Romans, grouped in pairs for comparison, exemplifies the private virtues or vices of great men and has had great influence on European literature, notably on SHAKESPEARE. His *Moralia* is a vast collection of philosophical essays.

PLUTO, the ninth planet of the SOLAR SYSTEM, orbiting the sun at a mean distance of 39.53AU in 248.4 years. Pluto was discovered in 1930 following observations of perturbations in NEPTUNE's orbit. Because of its great distance from us, little is known of Pluto's composition, atmosphere, mass or diameter. Its orbit is very eccentric: indeed, it is occasionally closer to the sun than is Neptune and may be an escaped satellite of that planet. In 1978 Pluto was discovered to have a satellite, named Charon, large enough to make the two bodies a double planet system, like the earth and its moon. The diameter of Pluto is estimated to be about 2,000mi.

PLUTONISM, the geological theory, often associated with the followers of J. HUTTON, that the rocks of the earth were originally molten in origin. In the early 19th century, plutonism rivaled neptunism (the theory that the rocks originally forming the crust of the earth had been precipitated out of aqueous solution) for acceptance as the fundamental geological principle.

PLUTONIUM (Pu), the most important TRANSURANIUM ELEMENT, used as fuel for NUCLEAR REACTORS and for the ATOMIC BOMB. It is one of the actinides and chemically resembles URANIUM. Pu^{239} is produced in breeder reactors by neutron irradiation of uranium (U^{238}); like U^{235}, it undergoes nuclear FISSION, and was used for the Nagasaki bomb in WWII. mp 640°C, bp 3235°C, sg 19.84 (α; 25°C).

PLYMOUTH, city in Devon county, England, on the Plymouth Sound, from which the MAYFLOWER sailed. It was also the home port of Raleigh's and Drake's expeditions to the New World, and was the launching point of the British fleet in its attack on the Spanish Armada in 1588. It is now an important maritime center and naval base. Pop 253,400.

PLYMOUTH COLONY, first English settlement in what is now New England, and the second permanent English settlement in America, founded by the PILGRIM FATHERS in Dec., 1620. In 1691 it was merged with Massachusetts Bay Colony to form Massachusetts. The colony was founded by a group of Puritan Separatists from the Church of England, who were blown off their course to Virginia and agreed in the famous MAYFLOWER COMPACT to form a "civil body politic." The settlers included John CARVER and William BRADFORD, the first two governors. Half the colony died during a bitter first winter, but the survivors were helped by the friendly Indian chief Massasoit, and by 1624 it was thriving.

PLYMOUTH ROCK, a granite boulder on the shore at Plymouth, Mass., on which, according to tradition, the PILGRIM FATHERS first set foot in America in 1620. There is no documentary evidence confirming the legend.

PLYWOOD, strong, light wood composite made of layers of veneer glued with their grain alternately at right angles. Thick plywood may have a central core of sawn lumber. It is made of an odd number of layers, and is termed 3-ply, 5-ply, etc. Being strong in both directions, and almost free from warping and splitting, it is used for construction of all kinds.

PNEUMOCONIOSIS, restrictive disease of the LUNGS caused by deposition of dusts in the lung substance, inhaled during years of exposure, often in extractive industries. SILICOSIS, anthracosis and asbestosis are the principal kinds, although aluminum, iron, tin and cotton fiber also cause pneumoconiosis. Characteristic X-RAY changes are seen in the lungs.

PNEUMONIA, INFLAMMATION and consolidation of LUNG tissue. It is usually caused by bacteria (pneumococcus, STAPHYLOCOCCUS, GRAM'S STAIN negative bacilli), but rarely results from pure VIRUS infection (INFLUENZA, MEASLES); other varieties occur if food, secretions or chemicals are aspirated or inhaled. The inflammatory response causes lung tissue to be filled with exudate and pus, which may center on the bronchi (bronchopneumonia) or be restricted to a single lobe (lobar pneumonia). Cough with yellow or green sputum (sometimes containing BLOOD), FEVER, malaise, and breathlessness are common. The involvement of the pleural surfaces causes PLEURISY. ANTIBIOTICS and PHYSIOTHERAPY are essential in treatment.

PNEUMOTHORAX, presence of air in the pleural space between the LUNG and the chest wall. This may result from trauma, rupture of lung bullae in EMPHYSEMA or in ASTHMA, TUBERCULOSIS, PNEUMOCONIOSIS, CANCER etc., or, in tall, thin athletic males, it may occur without obvious cause. Drainage of the air through a tube inserted in the chest wall allows lung re-expansion.

PO, the longest river in Italy. Rising in the Cottain Alps near the French border, it winds E for 405mi through N Italy to the Adriatic Sea S of Venice. The Po drains almost all N Italy, and helps to make the plain of Lombardy Italy's richest agricultural region.

POCAHONTAS (c1595–1617), daughter of the North American Indian chief POWHATAN, who befriended the settlers at Jamestown, Virginia. According to Captain John SMITH, leader of the colony, Pocahontas saved his life when he had been captured by her father and was about to be executed. In 1614 she was christened, married John ROLFE and went to England, where she died of smallpox.

PODIATRY, or **chiropody,** care of the feet, concerned with the nails, CORNS AND CALLUSES. bunions and toe deformities. Care of the SKIN of the feet is especially important in the elderly and in diabetics.

POE, Edgar Allan (1809–1849), US short-story writer, poet and critic, famous for his tales of mystery and the macabre, such as *The Murders in the Rue Morgue* (1841) and *The Purloined Letter* (1844), prototypes of the detective story, and *The Fall of the House of Usher* (1839). His poems, including "The Raven" (1845) and "Annabel Lee" (1849), are musical and striking in imagery. Poe discussed beauty and form in art in *The Philosophy of Composition* (1846), which influenced BAUDELAIRE and the French Symbolists.

POET LAUREATE, royal appointment held by a British poet. Traditionally he writes poems for state occasions, but the title is now largely honorific. DRYDEN first had the title in 1668, but the custom started when BEN JONSON received a royal pension in 1616.

POETRY, meaningful arrangement of words into an imaginative or emotional discourse, always with a strong rhythmic pattern. The language, seeking to evoke image and idea, uses imagery and metaphor. RHYME or alliteration may also be important elements. The length of poems may vary from brief lyric poetry to long narrative poems such as COLERIDGE's *Ancient Mariner* or EPIC poetry with the length and scope of a novel, such as BYRON's *Don Juan.* The poet may choose BLANK VERSE, FREE VERSE or any simple or complex rhyme scheme as his medium. Traditional forms also exist; BALLADS are often rhymed in quatrains. The poet has a number of devices available that would be obtrusive or pretentious in prose, such as alliteration or onomatopoeia. The kind of forms and devices used most often or most successfully in poetry depends on the language of the poet. Since the sense of poetry is so intimately tied to its sound it is extremely difficult to translate. The heightening of thought as well as of language, however, and the intensifying and concentration of emotion and observation have meant that the great poets of each country and time have become in some measure accessible to the world as a whole. In most cultures poetry, linked by its rhythmic elements to music and dance, develops before prose literature; the poetic form aids oral transmission. Eventually it is written down; a "higher" form then develops, poetry destined largely for the printed page, although a vital oral tradition may accompany it. Even such written poetry, however, must remain to some extent "musical"; this and its great association with the THEATER still remind one of poetry's origins. (See also articles on individual poets.)

POGROM, term (from the Russian for devastation or riot) for the officially condoned mob attacks on Jewish communities in Russia between 1881 and 1921. More generally, it is used to describe any massacre of a defenseless minority, particularly JEWS, such as those organized by the NAZIS. The pogroms were a major factor in the large-scale emigration of European Jews to the US.

POINCARÉ, Jules Henri (1854–1912), French mathematician, cosmologist and scientific philosopher, best known for his many contributions to pure and applied MATHEMATICS and celestial mechanics.

POINCARÉ, Raymond Nicholas Landry (1860–1934), French statesman, three times premier (1912, 1922–24, 1926–29) and president 1913–20. A strongly nationalist conservative, he ordered the French occupation of the RUHR (1923). His financial policies succeeded in stabilizing the currency (1928).

POINSETT, Joel Roberts (1779–1851), US diplomat and statesman. He was minister to Mexico, 1925–29, introduced the POINSETTIA in the US and was VAN BUREN's secretary of war, 1837–41.

POINSETTIA, *Euphorbia pulcherrima,* a plant native to Mexico and Central America. In the wild they grow up to 10ft high; they are extensively cultivated as smaller plants for use as indoor ornamentals. The flowers are small, but the large red, yellow or white bracts (modified leaves) are very attractive. Poinsettias are popular house plants ideally suited to average house temperatures and sunny positions. The soil should be kept evenly moist. Propagation is by shoot tip cuttings taken in the spring.

POINT, in GEOMETRY, entity defined as having none of the dimensions length, breadth or depth. A point may also be defined as the intersection of two straight lines or of a straight line and a PLANE.

POINT FOUR PROGRAM, technical assistance plan for underdeveloped nations proposed by President Harry TRUMAN in his Inaugural Address of Jan., 1949, so named because it was the fourth point in the speech. Launched in 1950 and later merged with other aid programs, it provided technical, educational and health assistance, and aimed to encourage private investment and increase US influence.

POINTILLISM, painting technique, in which tiny paint dots of color are juxtaposed on the canvas to build up the form. The dots of color are additively mixed by the eye of the observer. This method was developed by the impressionist painters, SEURAT and SIGNAC, to achieve more luminosity and greater control of tone.

POISON GAS. See CHEMICAL AND BIOLOGICAL WARFARE.

POISONING, the taking, via ingestion or other routes, of substances which are liable to produce illness or DEATH. Poisoning may be accidental, homicidal or suicidal. DRUGS and medications are often involved, either taken by children in ignorance of their nature from accessible places, or by adults in suicide or attempted suicide. Easily available drugs such as ASPIRIN, paracetamol and mild SEDATIVES are often taken, though in serious suicidal attempts BARBITURATES and ANTIDEPRESSANTS are more common. Chemicals, such as disinfectants, weedkillers, cosmetics and paints are frequently swallowed by children, while poisonous berries may appear attractive. Poisoning by domestic gas or carbon monoxide has been used for suicide and homicide. Heavy metals (see LEAD POISONING, ARSENIC), INSECTICIDES and CYANIDES are common industrial poisons as well as being a risk in the community. Poisons may act by damaging body structures (e.g., weedkillers); preventing OXYGEN uptake by HEMOGLOBIN (carbon monoxide); acting on the NERVOUS SYSTEM (heavy metals); interfering with essential ENZYMES (cyanides, insecticides), with HEART action (antidepressants) or with the control of RESPIRATION (barbiturates). In some cases, antidotes are available which, if used early, can minimize poisoning, but in most cases treatment consists of supporting life until the poison is eliminated.

POISON IVY, POISON OAK, POISON SUMAC, vines or shrubs of the genus *Rhus* native to North America. They contain a poisonous agent, urushiol, that causes itching or blisters, by contact or indirectly through contaminated clothes. Immediate washing with an alkaline soap may prevent the irritation. Family: Anacardiaceae.

POITIERS, Battle of, famous English victory in the HUNDRED YEARS' WAR, fought in 1356, near Poitiers in W central France. The English, led by EDWARD THE BLACK PRINCE, were outnumbered four to one by their French opponents, but won a brilliant victory over John II and Philip the Bold.

POKER, a card game whose earliest forms date back to c1520 in Europe, developing into such bet-and-bluff games as *brag* in England, *pochen* ("bluff") in Germany and *poque* in France. *Poque* was taken by the French to America c1800, where it was developed and reexported to Europe as poker, c1870. It is now one of the world's top three card games. There are many variations, but basically five or seven cards are dealt and each player tries to make up a winning combination, on which he bets and bluffs in a contest of skill and nerves against the unknown combinations of his opponents.

POLAND, people's republic in central Europe on the Baltic Sea, lying between East Germany and the USSR and N of Czechoslovakia.

Official name: Polish People's Republic
Capital: Warsaw
Area: 120,727sq mi
Population: 37,769,000
Language: Polish
Religion: Roman Catholic
Monetary unit(s): 1 zloty = 100 groszy
Land. Poland is very flat with about 90% of the land under 1,000ft, though in the S are the peaks of the Silesian and Carpathian Mountains, forming a natural barrier between Poland and Czechoslovakia. The main rivers, the Vistula (which flows through Warsaw and Kráków), the Oder, Neisse, Bug and Warta, are important for transportation to the large Baltic ports. The principal cities are Warsaw, Lodz, Kraków, Wroclaw, Poznan and Gdánsk (Danzig). The climate is moderate in summer with temperatures averaging about 60°F. Winters are generally cold (32°F–24°F). About 50% of Poland comprises arable land and 25% forests.

People. Most of the population are of Polish descent. After WWI Poland had sizeable minorities of Ukrainians, Jews and Belorussians, comprising over 30% of its people. By the mid-1960s there were only small minority groups, and an estimated 10 million Poles lived abroad.

Economy. Poland was an agricultural

country until WWII; since then it has been rapidly industrialized. State agricultural collectivization was resisted by the peasants, and there are now very few state farms. The chief products are wheat, rye, barley, oats, potatoes and sugar beet. Industry is largely state-owned. Poland is a big producer of coal, zinc, steel, petroleum and sulfur. Manufactures include machinery, textiles, cement and chemicals. There is a sizeable shipbuilding industry at Gdańsk. The principal exports are coal, textiles, metal products and processed meat.

History. Poland's recorded history dates back to the 10th century, when the local Slavic tribes first united. Later Germans settled in Poland, particularly on the Baltic coast. After Swedish invasions in the 17th century, Poland was divided among Austria, Prussia and Russia in 1772. This lasted until 1918. In 1919 the Treaty of VERSAILLES established a new Poland, formed the POLISH CORRIDOR and made GDÁNSK a free city. In 1939 Germany invaded Poland, occupying the western portion. The USSR occupied the east until 1941, when Germany attacked the USSR and took control of all of Poland. The population was decimated by massacre, starvation and imprisonment in concentration camps like AUSCHWITZ. After the last Germans were expelled early in 1945, a provisional government was set up under Soviet auspices. The communists dominated the 1947 elections, and the Russian ROKOSSOVSKY was made minister of defense (1949). The 1952 constitution was modeled on Russian lines. After STALIN's death, opposition to Soviet control led to widespread rioting in 1956, and GOMULKA became leader of the anti-Soviet revolt. He freed Cardinal WYSZYNSKI, and for several years there was considerable freedom in Poland. But by the early 1960s Gomulka was following Russian policies. In 1970 Edward GIEREK replaced Gomulka and instituted many reforms and controlled inflation. In 1972 Germany and Poland ratified the Oder-Neisse line as Poland's W boundary. In the late 1970s a new wave of unrest swept the country, stimulated by higher food prices. Polish workers formed the independent trade union *Solidarność* (Solidarity) in 1980, headed by Lech WALESA, and demanded a greater measure of workers' control in industry. Gierek fell from power that same year; the new leader, Gen. JARUZELSKI, imposed martial law (1981) and arrested the Solidarity leaders. Although martial law was lifted in 1983 and imprisoned leaders were released, unrest continued as economic conditions showed no improvement. In 1987 the government announced economic reforms involving less central planning and bureaucracy, and wage incentives for increased production. Since the plan also involved higher prices and the prospect of unemployment, it was rejected in an unusual nationwide popular referendum that reflected the general lack of confidence in the government. When new price rises were announced in 1988, there were major strikes at Gdansk and elsewhere. These were ended by a combination of wage concessions, force, and negotiations with Solidarity leader Lech Walesa.

POLAR BEAR, *Thalarctos maritimus,* the most carnivorous of the BEARS. Essentially an aquatic and polar animal, rarely found south of 70°N, it can swim strongly and is also agile on land. It hunts seals, whale calves, fishes, and, on land, arctic foxes and even lemmings. A large bear, up to 750kg (1,650lb), it is well adapted to withstand cold conditions.

POLARIS (Alpha Ursae Minoris), a CEPHEID VARIABLE star in the Little Dipper. Because of its close proximity to the N celestial pole (see CELESTIAL SPHERE), Polaris is also known as the Polestar or North Star, and has been used in navigation for centuries: owing to precession (motion of the earth's axis), Polaris is moving away from the N celestial pole.

POLARIZED LIGHT, LIGHT in which the orientation of the wave vibrations displays a definite pattern. In ordinary unpolarized light the wave vibrations (which occur at right-angles to the direction in which the radiation is propagated) are distributed randomly about the axis of propagation. In *plane-polarized light* (produced in reflection from a dielectric such as glass or by transmission through a nicol prism or polarizing filter), the vibrations all occur in a single plane. Polaroid filters work by subtracting the components of light orientated in a particular plane; two filters in sequence with their transmission planes crossed transmit no light. In *elliptically polarized light* (produced when plane-polarized light is reflected from a polished metallic surface) and *circularly polarized light* (produced on transmission through certain CRYSTALS exhibiting double refraction), the electric vector of the radiation at any point describes an ellipse or a circle. Much of the light around us—that of the blue sky, or reflected from lakes, walls and highways—is partially polarized. Polarizing sunglasses reduce glare by eliminating the light polarized by reflection from horizontal surfaces. Polariscopes employing two polarizing filters have proved to be valuable tools in organic chemistry.

POLAROID LAND CAMERA, See CAMERA.

POLAR REGIONS. See ANTARCTICA; ARCTIC REGIONS.

POLDERS, name given in the Netherlands to areas of agricultural land reclaimed by constructing dikes and canals and draining swamps, lakes or shallows. Much of the land around IJsselmeer consists of polders below sea level.

POLE. See NORTH POLE; SOUTH POLE.

POLESTAR. See POLARIS.

POLICE, civil body charged with maintaining public order and protecting persons and property from unlawful acts. While most civilizations have had some kind of law enforcement agency, most modern forces are descended from the Metropolitan Police established in London by Sir Robert PEEL in 1829; in the US, Boston introduced a similar force in 1838, and New York City soon afterwards. Today in the US the police are organized into around 40,000 separate forces, consisting of local, district, county and state police and the sheriffs and deputies of around 35,000 towns and villages. There are also federal police agencies such as the FBI, the Bureau of Narcotics and Dangerous Drugs, the Border Patrol and the Internal Revenue Service, each responsible to its own civil governing authority. Uniformed police are largely responsible for maintaining public order, regulating traffic, highways and crowds, patrolling the streets and arresting lawbreakers in the course of these duties. In many countries they are also responsible for helping strangers, tracing runaway children and many other duties not involving crime. With the increasing complexity and sophistication of crime, however, most forces have introduced "plainclothes" branches, some specially to deal with homicide, robbery and burglary, vice, and crime involving fraud, narcotics, computer fraud, art thefts, and forgery. There are also specialized services such as forensic science laboratories, information and statistics services. Police powers are in most countries strictly circumscribed by law and constitution. In the US and Great Britain they are obliged to inform an arrested person of his rights.

POLICE POWER, in US law, the inherent power of the state to regulate personal and property rights in the public interest. Although not provided for in the Constitution, the courts have held that it does not violate the 14th Amendment.

POLIOMYELITIS, or **infantile paralysis,** VIRAL DISEASE causing muscle PARALYSIS as a result of direct damage to motor nerve cells in the SPINAL CORD. The virus usually enters by the mouth or GASTROINTESTINAL TRACT and causes a mild feverish illness, after which paresis or paralysis begins, often affecting mainly those muscles that have been most used in preceding days. Treatment is with bed rest and avoidance or treatment of complications: contracture; bed sores; venous THROMBOSIS; secondary infection; MYOCARDITIS; respiratory failure, and swallowing difficulties. Current polio vaccine is a live attenuated strain taken by mouth and which colonizes the gut and induces IMMUNITY. Poliomyelitis VACCINATION, developed by Dr. Jonas Salk in the mid-1950s, has been one of the most successful developments in preventive medicine.

POLISH, one of the W group of the Slavic languages. It is the official and literary language of Poland, where it is spoken by more than 36 million people. In the US it is the language of over 2 million. Modern literary Polish, dating from the 16th century, was originally based on dialects in the vicinity of Poznań.

POLISH CORRIDOR, strip of Polish land about 25mi–65mi wide and 90mi long. Formerly German, it was granted to Poland in 1919 to give her access to the Baltic Sea. The predominantly German port of Danzig (now GDAŃSK) adjoining the Corridor was declared a free city. The separation of East Prussia from the rest of Germany by the Corridor precipitated the German invasion of Poland (1939).

POLISH NATIONAL CATHOLIC CHURCH OF AMERICA, an OLD CATHOLIC church founded by immigrant US Polish Catholics in 1897. Its first synod was held in Scranton, Pa., in 1904, and the first bishop, Father Francis Hodur, was consecrated in 1907. There are now four bishops in the US and some 280,000 members.

POLITBURO, in the USSR, permanent secretariat of top political officials, first formed in 1917, which dominates the Central Committee of the Soviet Communist Party. It is the chief policy-making and governing body of the Communist Party and to a large extent of the USSR. Its size varies; usually it has about 11 voting members and 9 nonvoting members.

POLITIAN. See POLIZIANO, ANGELO.

POLITICAL ACTION COMMITTEES (PACs), organizations established by business corporations, professional and trade associations, labor unions, and ideological and issue organizations to raise and distribute funds in support of the political campaigns of candidates for the House and Senate favorable to their views. PAC contributions are limited by law to $5,000 per candidate per election, but there are no limits on what they can spend independently on behalf of candidates. In 1986, 4,157 PACs made contributions to candidates, chiefly incumbents. Measures have been proposed to curb the influence of PACs.

POLITICAL ECONOMY, a social science, equivalent to modern ECONOMICS, concerned with how a state raises, increases and uses its revenues. The study evolved with the 17th-century rise of MERCANTILISM and was developed by Adam SMITH. David RICARDO and John Stuart MILL, whose *Principles of Political Economy* (1848) is a classic statement. The term had fallen out of use by the 20th century.

POLITICAL PARTY, body or organization which puts forward candidates for public office and contends for power in elections. Parties pose alternative programs and candidates and provide a means by which voters can make their desires and opinions felt. Party connections and party loyalty help to coordinate the separate branches and levels of government necessary in the US system. Primarily, however, political parties institutionalize conflict and the struggle for power. The alternation of parties in office is a peaceful means of replacing those in power, thus ensuring change without revolution.

In some countries a **two-party system** exists while in others there is a multiplicity of parties. The US and many English-speaking powers are dominated by two major parties, and a third party may poll a significant number of votes overall without having a single representative elected. By contrast, in European legislatures, representatives are generally chosen under the system of **proportional representation** which allows the election of candidates from a number of parties in exact proportion to their popular strength. Often in such cases no one party may have a simple overall majority and a coalition will be necessary. Communist states and many newly independent states have a **single-party system,** and the political party is in effect part of the state apparatus. (See also DEMOCRATIC PARTY; REPUBLICAN PARTY; TORY; WHIG.)

POLITICAL SCIENCE, the study of government and political institutions and processes. It was initiated by PLATO's *Republic* and ARISTOTLE's *Politics,* and well-known political theories have included those of MACHIAVELLI, BODIN, HOBBES, LOCKE,

MONTESQUIEU, BENTHAM, Jean Jacques ROUSSEAU and MARX. Traditionally, the study had been primarily concerned with the nature of the state, of SOVEREIGNTY and of government. Today greater emphasis is placed on the human associations, the behavior of interest groups and the decision-making processes. The basis of the study is human power over other humans. This leads to a study of social organization. Pertinent areas of inquiry concern the institutions that dispose of power, the systems through which they operate and the motives of those who run them. These questions are closely connected with the question of the morality of power and general theories of man and society. Past theories cannot provide for the complexity of modern society and a standard view today is to regard society as a set of interacting interdependent systems.

In the US almost all advanced students of political science concentrate on some aspect of one of the following areas: political theory, philosophy and methodology; public administration; international organization, politics and law; foreign governments; government and policies of the US; constitutional and administrative law in the US; and US state and local government.

POLIZIANO, Angelo, or **Politian** (1454–1494), Italian poet, scholar and humanist. Perhaps the greatest RENAISSANCE classical scholar, he also wrote the first Italian play, *Orfeo* (1480), and the famous lyrical love poem *Stanze per la Giostra* (1475–78).

POLK, James Knox (1795–1849), 11th president of the US, 1845–49, elected on a Democratic platform pledged to expand the existing territories of the nation according to the doctrine of MANIFEST DESTINY.

In 1825 Polk was elected to the US House of Representatives, and during Andrew JACKSON's presidency he became the administration's leading spokesman in the House. After Jackson's reelection (1832) Polk became chairman of the Ways and Means Committee in 1833. He was speaker of the House 1835–39, and governor of Tennessee 1839–41. Chosen as a compromise candidate by the Democrats, Polk defeated Henry CLAY and was inaugurated as president on March 4, 1845, having campaigned on five main objectives, each of which he managed to achieve. The first, the annexation of Texas, was in fact achieved before Polk took up office, for the outgoing president, John TYLER, had already accepted the Democratic victory as a mandate and sanctioned (March, 1845) the admission of Texas as a slave state of the Union. The second objective was to extend the boundary in Oregon Territory to a latitude of 54°40'. In the event, he compromised with Great Britain in the Oregon Treaty (1846) which established the boundary between the US and British America at the 49th parallel. The third objective, to acquire California from Mexico, involved the US in the MEXICAN WAR, 1846–48. By the Treaty of GUADALUPE HIDALGO (1848) Mexico ceded all her claims to the territory of California and New Mexico and recognized the border at the Rio Grande. The fourth objective, a promise to the South to lower the tariff, was enacted by the Walker Tariff (1846). Polk's final objective, to reestablish an independent treasury system, was achieved by the Independent Treasury Act (1846) which survived with some modifications until 1913. Broken in health by overwork, he chose not to run for reelection and died shortly afterwards, having achieved impressive successes in fulfilling his aims.

POLK, Leonidas (1806–1864), US clergyman, first bishop of Louisiana, 1841–61, and major-general who abandoned the ministry to fight in the Confederate army during the CIVIL WAR. He served in the Army of Tennessee and fought at Shiloh, Murfreesboro and Chickamauga, before being killed in action at Pine Mountain, Ga.

POLKA, dance with a basic 2/4 rhythm originating as a folk dance in Bohemia. It became fashionable in the 19th century and has been especially popular as a dance and musical form in the US, especially among Polish-Americans.

POLL, Public Opinion, technique for measuring the range of opinions held by the general public or by specifically limited groups of people. It developed during the 1920s. Opinion polls rely on certain statistical laws which show that small carefully chosen samples of any group can accurately represent the range of opinions of the whole group or population. The population in question, known as the "universe," may be a general one (all voters in the US) or a limited one (all car workers in Detroit). Accuracy depends on the care with which the sample is constructed and on the size of the sample. Since 1944 all polls have adopted the method of random selection pioneered by the US Census Bureau in which each member of the "universe" has an equal chance of being questioned. Pioneers in US public-opinion polling included George Gallup, Louis Harris and Elmo Roper.

POLLAIUOLO, Antonio (c1431–1498), Florentine goldsmith and painter. Often collaborating with his brother **Piero**, his works include the *Martyrdom of St Sebastian* (1475), many portraits of women in profile and the tomb of Pope Innocent VIII in St. Peter's, Rome. His pictures are noted for their landscapes and his figures for anatomical detail.

POLLINATION, in plants, the transfer of the male GAMETES (*pollen*) from the anthers of a FLOWER to the stigma of the same or another flower, where subsequent growth of the pollen leads to the fertilization of the female gametes (or EGGS) contained in the ovules and the production of SEEDS and fruit. Wind-pollinated plants, such as grasses, produce inconspicuous flowers with large feathery stamens and stigmas and usually large quantities of pollen. Insect-pollinated flowers have large, conspicuous and colorful flowers, produce nectar and have small stigmas. (See PLANT; REPRODUCTION.)

POLLOCK, (Paul) Jackson (1912–1956), US painter, leader of ABSTRACT EXPRESSIONISM. Influenced by SURREALISM, he developed "action painting"—dripping paint on canvas placed flat on the floor, and forming marks in it with sticks, trowels, knives. His pictures, like *Number 32* (1950) and *Blue Poles* (1953) comprise intricate networks of lines.

POLL TAX, a tax levied equally on each individual in a community. In the US a special poll tax was levied on voters in elections, which effectively disenfranchised the blacks and poor whites. This was banned for federal elections by the 24th amendment to the Constitution (1964), and the ban was extended to local elections in 1966.

POLLUTION, the contamination of one substance by another so that the former is unfit for an intended use; or, more broadly, the addition to any natural environmental resource on which life or the quality of life depends of any substance or form of energy at a rate resulting in abnormal concentrations of what is then termed the "pollutant." Air (see AIR POLLUTION), water (see WATER POLLUTION) and soil (see SOLID WASTE) are the natural resources chiefly affected. Some forms of pollution, such as urban sewage and garbage or inshore petroleum spillage, pose an immediate and obvious environmental threat; other forms, such as those involving potentially toxic substances found in industrial wastes and agricultural PESTICIDES, present a more insidious hazard: they may enter biological food chains and, by affecting the metabolism of organisms, create an ecological imbalance (see ECOLOGY). Populations of organisms thriving abnormally at the expense of other populations may themselves be regarded as pollutants. Forms of energy pollution include: NOISE, e.g., factory, airport and traffic noise; THERMAL POLLUTION, e.g., the excessive heating of lakes and rivers by industrial effluents; light pollution, e.g., the glare of city lights when it interferes with astronomical observations, and radiation from radioactive wastes (see RADIOACTIVITY; FALLOUT). The need to control environmental pollution in all its aspects is now widely recognized. (See also RECYCLING.)

POLO, Marco (c1254–1324), Venetian explorer famous for his overland journey to China, 1271–95. Reaching China in 1275 he served as an envoy of the ruler KUBLAI KHAN. He was appointed governor of Yangchow for three years and assisted in the capture of the city of Sainfu. He returned home to Venice (1295) laden with a treasure in precious stones. He commanded a galley against the Genoese at the battle of Curzola (1298) and was captured. In prison, he wrote an important account of his travels which later inspired explorers such as Christopher COLUMBUS to search for a sea passage to the East.

POLO, game played on horseback with a ball and mallets. It is played between two teams of four on a field 300yds long and 200yds wide, with a goal at each end. The object is to score points by striking the 4½ inch diameter ball into the goal with the mallet. The game originated in Persia and spread through Turkey, Tibet and India, China and Japan. It was revived in 19th-century India and learned by British army officers, and introduced into England in 1869 and the US in 1876.

POLONAISE, slow Polish dance in ¾ time, probably developed from the *promenade.* Polonaises were written by MOZART, BEETHOVEN, CHOPIN and many others.

POL POT (Saloth Sar; 1928–   ), Kampuchean (Cambodian) communist leader, organizer (1963) of the Khmer Rouge guerrilla army that seized power in 1975. As premier (1976–79) he directed the liquidation of the Cambodian middle class, emptying the cities and putting everyone to forced agricultural labor. Some 3-4 million people are estimated to have been killed in the process. Driven from power by a Vietnam invasion in 1979, he remained in command of a guerrilla army that enjoyed Chinese support.

POLTAVA, Battle of, fought in 1709 near Poltava in the Northern War between Russia under TSAR PETER I the Great and the combined forces of Charles XII of Sweden and the Cossack chief Mazeppa. It was a major Russian victory.

POLTERGEIST (German; noisy spirit), malicious spirit causing noisy and destructive phenomena. Such phenomena, whatever their cause, commonly occur around pubescent girls.

POLYBIUS (c200 BC–c120 BC), Greek historian whose universal history, tracing the rise of Rome, is considered one of the greatest historical works of all time.

POLYCLITUS THE ELDER, 5th-century BC Greek sculptor, renowned for his bronze statues of athletes, of which numerous marble copies survive. His most famous works were a colossal statue of Hera, now lost, and the *Doryphoros* (Spear Bearer), which became the models for ideal proportion. **Polyclitus the Younger** was known primarily as an architect but also produced figures of athletes.

POLYGAMY, marriage in which husbands may have several wives at one time (*polygyny*), or wives several husbands (*polyandry*). It is still practiced in parts of Asia and Africa; both the Muslim and Hindu religions permit polygyny. It was once also a custom of US MORMONS but is now forbidden by them.

POLYGON, a closed plane figure bounded by three or more straight lines. Polygons with three sides are called triangles; with four, quadrilaterals; with five, pentagons; with six, hexagons, with seven, heptagons; with eight, octagons; with twelve, dodecagons. Polygons may be either convex or concave (except triangles, which are always convex): convex polygons have interior angles that are all acute or obtuse; in concave polygons one or more of these angles is reflex (see ANGLE). A polygon with equal angles and sides equal in length is called a regular polygon. A *spherical polygon* is a closed figure on the surface of a sphere bounded by arcs of great circles. The sum of the interior angles of a plane polygon is given by: $s = (n \times 180°) - 360°$, where s is the sum in degrees and n the number of sides of the polygon.

POLYGRAPH. See LIE DETECTOR.

POLYHEDRON, a three-dimensional figure bounded by four or more plane sides. There are only five types of convex polyhedron that can be regular (i.e., have faces that are equal regular POLYGONS, each face being at equal angles to those adjacent to it): these are the tetrahedron, the octahedron and the isocahedron, with 4, 8 and 20 faces respectively, each face being an equilateral triangle; the hexahedron, with 6 square faces; and the dodecahedron, with 12 pentagonal faces. Regular polyhedrons may be circumscribed about or inscribed in a sphere.

POLYMER, substance composed of very large MOLECULES (macromolecules) built up by repeated linking of small molecules (monomers). Many natural polymers exist, including PROTEINS, NUCLEIC ACIDS, polysaccharides (see CARBOHYDRATES), RESINS, RUBBER, and many minerals (e.g., quartz). The ability to make synthetic polymers to order lies at the heart of modern technology (see PLASTICS; SYNTHETIC FIBERS). Polymerization, which requires that each monomer have two or more functional groups capable of linkage, takes place by two processes: CONDENSATION, with elimination of small molecules, or simple addition. CATALYSIS is usually required, or the use of an initiator to start a chain reaction of free radicals. If more than one kind of monomer is used, the result is a copolymer with the units arranged at random in the chain. Under special conditions it is possible to form stereoregular polymers, with the groups regularly oriented in space; these have useful properties. Linear polymers may form crystals in which the chains are folded sinuously, or they may form an amorphous tangle. Stretching may orient and extend the chains, giving increased tensile strength useful in synthetic fibers. Some crosslinking between the chains produces elasticity; a high degree of cross-linking yields a hard, infusible product (a thermosetting PLASTIC).

POLYMORPHISM, in zoology the existence of more than two forms or types of individual within the same species of animal. An example is seen in some social insects such as ants and bees in which many different types of worker are structurally adapted for different tasks within the colony.

POLYNESIA, archipelagos and islands in the central Pacific, part of Oceania. They include the Hawaiian, Cook, Phoenix, Ellice, and Easter islands, Samoa, French Polynesia, Tonga, and ethnologically if not geographically New Zealand. They are either of volcanic origin, or are atolls built up by coral reefs.

POLYP, benign TUMOR of EPITHELIUM extending above the surface, usually on a stalk. Polyps may cause nasal obstruction, and some (as in the GASTROINTESTINAL TRACT) may have a tendency to become a CANCER.

POLYPHONY (from Greek: many sounds), music made up of several independent but harmonically linked melodic lines. The name is usually applied to the sacred choral music of the late Renaissance, particularly that of PALESTRINA, LASSUS and William BYRD.

POLYTHEISM, belief in many gods, as opposed to MONOTHEISM or DUALISM;

characteristic of most religions, notably HINDUISM and Greek and Roman religion. It may arise from the personification of forces worshiped at a more primitive level in ANIMISM. One god may dominate the others (e.g. ZEUS); sometimes a supreme being is recognized, transcending the gods. (See also MYTHOLOGY.)

POMERANIA, former Prussian province, now mostly part of Poland. It lay S of the Baltic Sea, mainly between the Oder and Vistula rivers. After a history of Polish, Imperial, Brandenburg and Swedish rule, the region was under Prussian rule from 1815 until 1919, when it was divided among Poland, Germany and Danzig (now GDANSK).

POMO INDIANS, Hozan-speaking Indian tribe living in N Cal., famous for their intricate basket making. They were a wealthly tribe with many natural resources and used shells as currency.

POMPADOUR, Jeanne Antoinette Poisson, Marquise de (1721–1764), famous mistress of King LOUIS XV of France from 1745. She was a patroness of the arts and had much influence on the political and artistic life of France.

POMPEII, ancient Roman city in S Italy, buried by an eruption of Mt VESUVIUS in 79 AD. It was rediscovered in 1748. Excavations have revealed a town preserved much as it was on the day of its destruction, even to several bodies. The site has yielded invaluable information of Roman urban life and beautiful examples of Roman art.

POMPEY (Gnaeus Pompeius Magnus; 106 BC–48 BC), known as the Great, Roman general and statesman. He crushed the rebellion in Spain (76 BC), defeated SPARTACUS (72 BC) and King Mithridates of Pontus (63 BC). In 61 BC he entered the First TRIUMVIRATE, becoming the colleague and later rival of Julius CAESAR. In the civil war following the latter's return from Gaul, Pompey was defeated at Pharsalus in 48 BC and fled to Egypt, where he was assassinated.

POMPIDOU, Georges Jean Raymond (1911–1974), French statesman, president of France 1969–74. He joined the DE GAULLE government in 1944 and again in 1958. In 1961 he prepared the truce negotiation with the FLN, the Algerian nationalist organization. He was prime minister 1962–68, and succeeded de Gaulle as president in 1969. He died in office, of cancer.

POMPONAZZI, Pietro (1462–1525), Italian philosopher, author of *De Immortalitate Animae* (1516) and *De Incantationibus* (1520), which provoked controversy by proposing that, despite physical evidence, revealed truth transcended philosophical truth.

PONCA INDIANS, North American Siouan-speaking Indian tribe. In the 17th century they settled in SW Minn. and the Black Hills of South Dakota, but were forced to move to Okla. in 1865. Finding conditions unacceptable they walked 600mi to Neb. to find shelter with the OMAHA. They were arrested and after a sensational trial were freed to settle in Neb. or Okla. Today about 1,000 remain.

PONCE DE LEON, Juan (c1460–1521), Spanish discoverer of Florida. He sailed with Christopher COLUMBUS in 1493, and in 1508 he conquered Puerto Rico and became its governor. Leading an expedition, possibly to find the mythical Fountain of Youth, he discovered and named Florida in 1513, but when he attempted to colonize it in 1521 he was driven off and mortally wounded by Indians.

PONCHIELLI, Amilcare (1834–1886), Italian opera composer. His best-known works are *I Promessi Sposi* (1856) and *La Gioconda* (1876), with its famous ballet, *Dance of the Hours*.

PONIES, small, sturdy HORSES, usually less than 15 hands (1.5m), hardy and able to live on small amounts of poor food. Races of pony include the Exmoor, Dartmoor, Welsh, Shetland, Iceland and Mongolian. All derive from a Celtic stock of prehistoric British and Scandinavian work horses.

PONS, Lily (Alice Joséphine Pons; 1904–1976), French-born US coloratura soprano, at New York's Metropolitan Opera 1931–56.

PONSELLE, Rosa (1897–1981), US soprano, born Rosa Ponzillo. She sang in vaudeville before her sensational Metropolitan Opera debut in 1918 opposite Enrico CARUSO in Verdi's *La Forza del Destino*. Until retiring in 1936 she was one of the company's leading dramatic sopranos.

PONTCHARTRAIN, Lake, shallow lake in SE La., 630sq mi in area. Discovered by Sieur d'IBERVILLE in 1699, it is now crossed by the world's longest highway built over water, and is connected to the Mississippi R and the Gulf of Mexico.

PONTIAC (c1720–1769), chief of the Ottawa Indians. He opposed the English during the FRENCH AND INDIAN WARS, and was one of the leaders of an unsuccessful war against them, called **Pontiac's Rebellion** (1763–65), in which Pa., Va. and Md. were seriously threatened. He signed a peace treaty in 1766.

PONTIFEX, high priest of ancient Rome, one of the 16 members of the Pontifical College presiding over the state religion. The highest religious authority was the *pontifex maximus* (supreme pontiff); this title was adopted by the emperors and later the popes.

PONTINE MARSHES, low-lying area in S Latium, central Italy. Fertile farmland in the Roman period, the area subsequently became a deserted malarial swamp. It was drained and repopulated in the 1930s.

PONTIUS PILATE. See PILATE, PONTIUS.

PONTUS, ancient kingdom in NE Asia Minor by the Black Sea. Dating from the 4th century BC, it reached its height under MITHRIDATES VI, but was annexed by the Roman Empire in 9 BC after it had challenged Roman power.

PONY EXPRESS, famous relay mail service between St. Joseph, Mo., and Sacramento, Cal., from April 1860 to October 1861. It used horses, not ponies, with riders chosen for their small size. The route covered 1,966mi, with stations at 10–15mi intervals. The goal of 10-day delivery was often met, and only one delivery was ever lost. It was superseded by the transcontinental telegraph.

POOL. See BILLIARDS.

POOR CLARES, Franciscan closed order of nuns, founded by St. CLARE and St. FRANCIS OF ASSISI in 1212. They are a mainly ascetic and contemplative order.

POOR LAWS, laws developed in England from the 16th century enforcing parish assistance to the aged, sick and poor. They were revised in 1834 to provide minimal relief for the able-bodied poor, and after WWI were replaced by a system of public welfare services.

POP ART, modern art movement dating from the mid-1950s, based on images of advertising, commercial illustration and mass-produced objects. Developed in England and the US, it included artists like Richard Hamilton, David HOCKNEY, Andy WARHOL and Robert RAUSCHENBERG.

POPE, Alexander (1688–1744), the greatest English poet and satirist of the AUGUSTAN AGE. Only 4ft 6in tall, he was partly crippled by tuberculosis. He first set out his literary ideals in his *Essay on Criticism* (1711), written in rhymed (heroic) couplets. His best-known works are the mock epic *The Rape of the Lock* (1712), his translations of the *Iliad* (1720) and the *Odyssey* (1726), *The Dunciad* (1728 and 1743), a satirical attack on literary critics, and his essays on moral philosophy, *An Essay on Man* (1733–34) and *Moral Essays* (1731–35).

POPE, John (1822–1892), US Union general in the American CIVIL WAR. Leading the newly-organized army of Va. in 1862, he was defeated at the second battle of BULL RUN and was deprived of the command.

POPE, John Russell (1874–1937), US architect who designed, in neoclassical style, the Jefferson Memorial and the National Gallery in Washington, D.C., both completed after his death.

POPHAM, George (c1550–1608), early English colonist of America. With Raleigh Gilbert he founded Fort St. George (1607), the first New England colonial settlement, at the mouth of the Sagadahoc (now Kennebec) R. When he died there it was abandoned.

POPISH PLOT. See OATES, TITUS.

POP MUSIC, the popular music of the latter half of the 20th century. Much of its vitality derives from the interaction of its diverse styles, all largely affected by commercial pressures. Most have their roots in American FOLK MUSIC, especially in the BLUES and its descendant, rhythm'n'blues. This latter led in the 1950s to rock'n'roll, a form based on electronic amplification and a simple, dominant beat. In the 1960s, British performers such as the BEATLES and the Rolling Stones experimented lyrically and musically with pop and traditional forms; while the US underwent a "folk revival" led by Bob DYLAN who, like Joe HILL and Woody GUTHRIE before him, adapted folk styles in pursuit of contemporary relevance, at first chiefly through quasipolitical protest. With increased lyrical sophistication came folk-rock; and its fusion with the "British" style, by now adopted and adapted in the US, was responsible for much of the pop of the late 1960s and early 1970s. Indian (and later, African) music and JAZZ influenced form and instrumentation; technological advance stimulated closer ties with "serious" music; and a reaction from such complexities resulted in the resurgence of the unsophistication of rock'n'roll. (See also ROCK MUSIC.)

POPOVA, Liubov Serbeevna (1889–1924), Russian painter who, having adopted CUBISM and FUTURISM in Paris, became a member of the avant-garde on her return to Russia in 1913. Before her death, she also took up industrial, textile and theatrical design.

POPPER, Sir Karl Raimund (1902–   ), Austrian-born British philosopher, best known for his theory of falsification in the philosophy of science. Popper contends that scientific theories are never more than provisionally adopted and remain acceptable only as long as scientists are devising new experiments to test (falsify) them. His attacks on the doctrine of historicism are in

The Open Society and Its Enemies (1945) and *The Poverty of Historicism* (1957).

POPPY, annual or herbaceous perennial plants of the genus *Papaver* and related genera. There are about 100 species in *Papaver,* which are mostly native to temperate and subtropical areas of Eurasia and N Africa. The flower bud is enclosed by two thick green sepals which drop off to allow the thin petals to unfold. The seeds are enclosed in a capsule. The unripe capsules of the opium poppy yield OPIUM. Family: Papaveraceae.

POPULAR FRONT, coalition of left-wing and center parties formed in the 1930s to present a united front against FASCISM. Reflecting a change in Soviet policy, the idea was proclaimed at the 1935 meeting of the Communist International, and communists cooperated with socialist and liberal parties in forming anti-fascist governments. A Popular Front government led by BLUM ruled France 1936–37; the Spanish Popular Front, elected in 1936, was eventually overthrown by FRANCO.

POPULATION, the inhabitants of a designated territory. For the world as a whole, population doubled between 1930 and 1975, from 2 to 4 billion, and increased to 5 billion by 1988, with a possible 6 billion forecast for the year 2000. The sharpest increases have been in developing nations least able to provide food, education and jobs for all. Averting world famine depends on the few countries able to export food. Many nations now have population-control programs, but the control of infectious diseases and increases in the food supply because of modern growing techniques have combined to encourage population growth. In some societies, however, fertility rates have declined somewhat, and an increase in abortions, approaching the number of live births in a few countries, has helped defuse the population bomb, though not without great controversy. In the US, a "baby boom" occurred after WWII, but after 1957 the birth rate declined and by the 1980s gave indications of approaching ZERO POPULATION GROWTH.

POPULISM, generally, a "grass roots" political movement which is basically agrarian, but which incorporates a farmer-labor coalition. Specifically, it refers to the doctrines of the US People's Party. This grew from the post-Civil War farm depression which created agrarian reform movements such as the GRANGE and the Farmers' Alliance. In 1891–92 delegates from the Farmers' Alliance and labor organizations set up the People's Party, which fielded J. B. WEAVER as presidential candidate in 1892 on a platform including an eight-hour day, government ownership of railroads, graduated income tax, government postal savings banks, direct election of Senators, increase of the money supply and FREE SILVER. Weaver gained over a million votes, and the party gained support rapidly. In the 1896 presidential elections, however, the Democratic candidate, W. J. BRYAN, captured most of the populist vote by campaigning on the issue of free silver, and thereafter the People's Party declined. It failed because its money-supply and free silver theories did not present a sound economic analysis, and because it did not gain urban support.

The term populism is also sometimes applied to any policies appealing to the "little man," such as those advocated by Huey LONG and George WALLACE.

PORCUPINES, large spiny vegetarian rodents of two quite distinct families: one, Erithizontidae, confined to the Americas, the other, Hystricidae, to the tropics of the Old World. Old World forms include about a dozen species in Africa and S Asia. They are among the largest of rodents and the entire body is covered with spines. The American porcupines have an equal armory of spines, but when relaxed, these are concealed in a thick underfur.

PORNOGRAPHY AND OBSCENITY LAWS, in the US are held to exist for the protection of public morality. Pornography may be defined as material designed by its explicitness to appeal exclusively to a prurient interest in sex. The often explicit contents of genuine works of art and literature and medical texts are thus not pornographic, although in certain circumstances may be deemed obscene. Obscenity, like pornography, is not well defined in law, but may be said to be anything tending to corrupt public morals, generally in a sexual sense. Obscenity laws vary widely from country to country, and in the US from state to state, as does the degree of toleration extended by police and public. US Supreme Court decisions such as *US v. Roth* (1957) tended to relax legal strictures against obscenity by taking as their standard of acceptability that of the "average reasonable adult" and laying down that a work must be judged as a whole. This made the law vaguer and hence hard to administer, with the result that a great deal of "hardcore" pornography became freely available. Supreme Court decisions since then tended to reverse the trend without, however, clarifying the definition.

PORPHYRIA, metabolic disease due to disordered HEMOGLOBIN synthesis. It runs in families and may cause episodic abdominal pain, skin changes, NEURITIS and mental changes. Certain DRUGS can precipitate acute attacks. Porphyria may have been the cause of the "madness" of George III of England.

PORPOISES, small toothed whales, family Phocaenidae. Distinguished from DOLPHINS in being smaller, rather tubby and having a rounded head with no projecting beak-like mouth, they feed mainly on shoaling fishes. The name is now sometimes loosely applied in the US to the various species of dolphin kept in captivity.

PORT, a sweet wine, usually red, fortified with brandy. It comes from grapes grown in the Douro Valley, Portugal, and is shipped from Oporto, whence its name.

PORTAL, Charles (1893–1971), British air marshal. As chief of the air staff he was responsible for British air policy throughout WWII. He had strong faith in bombing for strategic and psychological purposes.

PORT ARTHUR AND DAIREN, now Lü-shun and Ta-lien, two ports forming the joint municipality of Lü-ta at the S end of the Liaotung peninsula, China, first developed under Russian (1898) and Japanese (1905) control. Port Arthur is a strategically important naval base, and Dairen a major commercial port and industrial city. Pop 4,000,000.

PORTER, Cole (1893–1964), US popular song composer. After WWI, he achieved great success as a sophisticated writer of songs and musical comedies, providing both the words and music. His prolific output included *Anything Goes* (1934), *Kiss Me, Kate* (1948), *Can-Can* (1953), the film score for *High Society* (1956) and many classic songs.

PORTER, David Dixon (1813–1891), US naval officer, distinguished in the CIVIL WAR. He served successfully in the New Orleans, Vicksburg, Red River and Fort Fisher campaigns, becoming rear admiral in 1863. In an administrative post 1865–69, he was made admiral in 1870.

PORTER, Katherine Anne (1890–1980), US short-story writer and novelist who won the 1966 Pulitzer Prize for her *Collected Short Stories* (1965). Her first collection of stories was *Flowering Judas* (1930), followed by *Pale Horse, Pale Rider* (1939). *Ship of Fools* (1962) is her only novel.

PORTER, William Sidney. See HENRY, O.

PORTINARI, Candido (1903–1962), Brazilian painter. His early canvases utilized warm earth tones to depict agricultural scenes in his native land. His later work became increasingly abstract.

Two of his murals, *War* and *Peace*, decorate the UN General Assembly Building in NYC.

PORTOLÁ, Gaspar de (c1723–c1784), Spanish colonizer of California. In 1769, as governor of the Californias, he mounted an expedition from Mexico which founded San Diego and Monterey.

PORTSMOUTH, Treaty of, the treaty which ended the 1904–05 Russo-Japanese War. After mediation by President Roosevelt, it was signed Sept. 5, 1905, at Portsmouth Navy Yard, N.H. Russia conceded Japanese supremacy in Korea, and Manchuria was restored to China.

PORTUGAL, republic of the W Iberian Peninsula, between Spain and the Atlantic, and including the Azores and Madeira.

Official name: Republic of Portugal
Capital: Lisbon
Area: 35,672sq mi
Population: 10,312,000
Language: Portuguese
Religion: Roman Catholic
Monetary unit(s): 1 escudo=100 centavos
Land. The N half of Portugal consists of mountains and high plateaus, cut by deep valleys. The S is characterized by lower, rolling countryside and plains. Two large rivers, the Tagus and Douro, cut the country from E to W. The climate is mild and humid in winter and warm and dry in summer.
Economy. Portugal is one of Europe's poorer countries. Agriculture still plays an important part in the economy, with most of the population living in villages and small towns. Most farms are very small and poor, although there are some large estates in the S. Grain, livestock, wine, olives, citrus fruits and almonds are the principal products. There are large forests in the mountainous areas, and Portugal is the world's biggest producer of cork. Fishing is important, the chief catches being sardines and tuna. Industries include food-processing, textiles, metals, mining and hydroelectricity. The principal cities are Lisbon, Oporto, Coimbra and Setúbal. Chief exports are cork, wine, sardines and fruit.
History. Portugal became an independent

kingdom in 1143, under Alfonso I. In 1385, John I founded the Aviz dynasty. His reign started a period of colonial expansion, leading to an empire that by the second half of the 16th century included much of South America, Africa and S and SE Asia. In 1580 King Philip II of Spain seized Portugal, and Spanish kings ruled until the successful revolt of 1640, which established the ruling house of Braganza. Portugal had already lost much of her power, especially in the Far East, and in the ensuing period of increasing absolutism never recovered it. During the NAPOLEONIC WARS she was invaded by the French and Spanish (see PENINSULAR WAR). By 1825 Brazil became an independent empire, and a period of conflict and unrest led to the Portuguese republic being declared in 1910. In 1926 there was a military coup, after which SALAZAR became virtual dictator until he was succeeded by Marcello CAETANO in 1968. In 1974 a military coup brought about a new government, ending 40 years of civilian dictatorship. The new president, Gen. António Spínola, soon resigned and was replaced by Gen. Francisco da Costa Gomes, who presided over the granting of independence to GUINEA-BISSAU (formerly Portuguese Guinea) in 1974 and to ANGOLA, MOZAMBIQUE, SÃO TOMÉ E PRÍNCIPE, and CAPE VERDE in 1975. Under a new constitution adopted in 1976, Gen. António Eanes was elected president. He was succeeded in 1986 by Dr. Mário Soares, a socialist. Portugal joined the EUROPEAN ECONOMIC COMMUNITY that same year. In anticipation of the removal of internal trade barriers within the Community in 1992, the government sought to stimulate the backward economy by diversification and the establishment of market incentives. Foreign capital, chiefly from Britain, Spain, West Germany, and the US, poured into the country and the economy grew rapidly. Nevertheless, Portugal remained at or near the bottom when compared with other members of the European Community. Its per capita income in 1988, $3,500, was the lowest in the Community.

PORTUGUESE, official language of Portugal and Brazil. It is one of the ROMANCE LANGUAGES and developed from the Latin spoken in Roman Iberia. Brazilian Portuguese has absorbed words and phrases from the languages of the Indian and African slave populations.

PORTUGUESE GUINEA. See GUINEA-BISSAU.

PORTUGUESE MAN-O'-WAR, *Physalia physalis*, a colorful jellyfish of the Siphonophora. A colonial cnidarian, it consists of an assemblage of four kinds of polyps: the most obvious of which is a gas-filled bladder about 1ft long, which carries a high crest and is colored blue or purple. Below this float are supported other polyps, including the long, stinging tentacles used for catching prey. The sting can be painful to humans.

POSITIVISM, philosophical theory of knowledge associated with the 19th-century French philosopher Auguste COMTE. It holds that the observable, or "positive," data of sense experience constitute the sole basis for assertions about matters of fact; only the truths of logic and mathematics are additionally admitted. The speculative claims of theology and metaphysics, regarded as the primitive antecedents of "positive" or scientific thought, are discounted. (See also LOGICAL POSITIVISM.)

POSITRON, the antiparticle corresponding to the ELECTRON. (See ANTIMATTER.)

POSSUMS, Australian marsupial mammals, members of the Phalangeridae. The term is also used, wrongly, for the OPOSSUMS of the New World.

POST, Emily (1873–1960), US writer who became an accepted authority on correct social behavior through her book *Etiquette* (1922). She broadcast regularly and her daily column was syndicated to over 200 newspapers.

POSTAL SERVICE, US, an independent establishment of the executive branch created in 1970 to process and deliver mail to individuals and businesses within the US. Its chief executive officer, the postmaster general, is appointed by the nine governors of the Postal Service, who are appointed by the president for overlapping nine-year terms. In 1988 the Postal Service employed 780,000 people in almost 40,000 post offices and stations and handled more than 147 billion pieces of mail.

POSTER, printed placard, posted up to advertise an event, product or service, or for propaganda purposes. The invention of lithography made it possible to produce brightly-colored posters cheaply and quickly. Famous artists who designed posters include Jules Chéret, TOULOUSE-LAUTREC and Aubrey BEARDSLEY.

POSTIMPRESSIONISM, term coined to describe the work of certain painters (c1880–90) whose styles, though dissimilar, flowed from IMPRESSIONISM. CÉZANNE. GAUGUIN. SEURAT. and VAN GOGH are considered the principal Postimpressionists.

POTASSIUM (K), a soft, silvery-white, highly reactive alkali metal. It is the seventh most abundant element, and is extensively found as sylvite, carnallite and other mixed salts; it is isolated by ELECTROLYSIS of fused potassium hydroxide. Potassium is chemically very like sodium, but even more reactive. It has one natural radioactive isotope, K^{40}, which has a half-life of 1.28 billion years. K^{40} decays into Ar^{40}, an isotope of argon; the relative amounts of each are used to date ancient rocks. Potassium salts are essential to plant life (hence their use as fertilizers) and are important in animals for the transmission of impulses through the nervous system. AW 39.1, mp 64°C, bp 774°C, sg 0.862 (20°C).

Potassium carbonate (K_2CO_3), or **potash,** is a hygroscopic colorless crystalline solid, made from potassium hydroxide and carbon dioxide, an ALKALI used for making glass. **Potassium chloride** (KCl) is a colorless crystalline solid, found as sylvite. Used in fertilizers and as the raw material for other potassium compounds. **Potassium nitrate** (KNO_3), or **saltpeter,** is a colorless crystalline solid, soluble in water, which decomposes to give off oxygen when heated to 400°C. It is made from sodium nitrate and potassium chloride by fractional crystallization, and is used in gunpowder, matches, fireworks, some rocket ruels, and as a fertilizer.

POTATO, *Solanum tuberosum,* herbaceous plant with an edible, fleshy tuberous underground stem, originating in the South American Andes. The tubers became a popular European foodstuff in the 18th century, the Irish in particular becoming dependent on the crop. Family: Solanaceae.

POTATO FAMINE, in 19th-century Ireland, famine caused by potato blight. The 1845 and 1846 potato crops failed, and in the subsequent famine nearly a million people died and over a million emigrated, particularly to the US. Ireland's population fell from about 8,500,000 in 1845 to 6,550,000 in 1851.

POTAWATOMI INDIANS, a North American Indian tribe of the Algonquian language family. In the 18th century they lived around the S of Lake Michigan. They allied with the French colonists and joined PONTIAC in his rebellion (1763). They later supported the British in the Revolutionary War and in the War of 1812. Coming under pressure from settlers, they moved W, and in 1846 most of them were forced into a reservation in Kan. The Potawatomi in Kansas have preserved much of the aboriginal culture. Other groups live in Mich., Okla. and Wis.

POTEMKIN, Prince Grigori Aleksandrovich (1739–1791), Russian soldier, statesman and favorite of Catherine the

Great. For the last 20 years of his life, he was the most powerful man in Russia. He enlarged the Russian army and navy, and annexed the Crimea in 1782.

POTLATCH, in many tribal cultures, especially among the Indians of the American NW coast, an elaborate ceremonial feast at which the host distributes or destroys wealth to gain status or office in his tribe. Wealthier guests are expected to match or exceed this in turn. Although banned for a while in Canada the potlatch is still an important tribal institution.

POTOMAC RIVER, US river flowing through Washington, D.C. Formed by the confluence of the 110mi long N Branch and the 140mi long S Branch, it flows 287mi into Chesapeake Bay. Navigation for large ships is prevented above Washington D.C., by the Great Falls. The river is noted for its scenic attraction.

POTSDAM, city in E Germany, near Berlin. In the 18th century it was chosen by FREDERICK II as his principal residence and became a center and symbol of Prussian militarism. Noted for its royal palaces, it is now also an industrial city. It was the site of the 1945 POTSDAM CONFERENCE. Pop 140,198.

POTSDAM CONFERENCE (July–Aug. 1945), a "summit" meeting at Potsdam, Germany, between STALIN, TRUMAN and, in succession, CHURCHILL and Clement ATTLEE. They agreed that a four-power Allied Control Council would rule defeated Germany, disarming it and fostering democratic government; Poland would gain part of E Germany; the German economy would be decentralized; Germans in Hungary, Poland and Czechoslovakia would be repatriated. The conference also discussed reparations payments and issued an ultimatum to Japan. The agreements were almost all breached as the COLD WAR hardened. (See also YALTA CONFERENCE.)

POTTER, Beatrix (1866–1943), British author of children's books. Her works, illustrated by herself, include *Peter Rabbit* (1902), *The Tailor of Gloucester* (1903), *Benjamin Bunny* (1904), *Mrs Tiggy-Winkle* (1905), *Jemima Puddle-Duck* (1908) and *Pigling Bland* (1913). Her books have become children's classics and remain widely popular.

POTTER, Paul (1625–1654), Dutch animal and landscape painter. Among his finest works is *Landscape with Cattle* (1647). He was also an accomplished etcher.

POTTERY AND PORCELAIN, CERAMIC articles, especially vessels, made of clay (generally kaolin) and hardened by firing.

The simplest and oldest type of pottery, **earthenware** (nonvitreous), is soft, porous and opaque, usually glazed and used for common tableware. TERRA COTTA is a primitive unglazed kind. Earthenware is fired to about 1,000°C. Stoneware, the first vitreous ware (of low porosity), was developed in China from the 5th to the 7th centuries AD. Fired to about 1,200°C, it is a hard, strong, nonabsorbent ware, opaque and cream to brown in color. From stoneware evolved porcelain during the Sung dynasty (960–1279). This is a hard, nonporous vitreous ware, white and translucent. Made from flint, kaolin and feldspar, it is fired to about 1,350°C.

In the manufacture of pottery the clay is made plastic by blending with water. The article is then shaped: traditionally by hand, by building up layers of strips (coiled pottery), by "throwing" on the potter's wheel or by molding; industrially by high-pressure molding or by a rotating template. The clay is fired in a kiln, slowly at first, then at higher temperatures to oxidize and consolidate it. The glaze (if desired) is then applied by spraying or dipping, and the article refired. Glazes are mixtures of fusible minerals and pigments, similar to those used for ENAMEL, powdered and mixed with water.

Among the most celebrated potters were the ancient Greeks (see GREEK ART) and the Chinese. Chinese porcelain had a profound influence on the ceramic arts of both Islam and W Europe. From the 9th century the Muslims used tin glaze to imitate Chinese ware, and this was in turn imitated in the European faïence and majolica wares. Porcelain was developed as a luxury ware in Europe in the 18th century, the greatest centers being Dresden (see DRESDEN CHINA) and Sèvres. In England the great ceramics manufacturers were Josiah SPODE and Josiah WEDGWOOD. (See also DELFTWARE.)

POULENC, Francis (1899–1963), French composer, member of the post-WWI group of composers called *Les Six*. His music is light in texture, although serious. His best-known works include *Mouvements perpetuels* for piano (1918), the ballet *Les Biches* (1924) and the operas *Les Mamelles de Tirésias* and *Dialogue des Carmélites* (1957). He was also a notable songwriter.

POULTRY FARMING, the rearing of all types of domesticated farm fowls for eggs and flesh. CHICKENS are by far the most popular bird, followed by TURKEYS, DUCKS, GEESE and other types. Important chicken breeds are the Leghorn and Rhode Island Red for eggs, and the Plymouth Rock and Cornish for meat. Modern scientific breeding programs aim at producing strains which will combine all the desirable qualities of the separate breeds. Before WWII, most flocks were kept on general farms. Today, nearly all economically valuable fowls live in controlled environments, with artificial lighting and heating, and small pens for individuals or groups. Chickens are hatched in incubators, reared in brooders and transferred to laying or fattening quarters. An annual output of 200-250 eggs per bird is essential for good profits. Marketing is organized through farmers' cooperatives and marketing boards.

POUND, Ezra Loomis (1885–1972), major 20th-century US poet, critic and translator. A gifted linguist, he went to Europe in 1908, and soon won recognition. His most important works are *Homage to Sextus Propertius* (1918), *Hugh Selwyn Mauberley* (1920) and the epic *Cantos* (1925–60). He championed the IMAGIST and vorticist movements, and influenced T. S. ELIOT, Robert FROST and W. B. YEATS, among others. He supported MUSSOLINI, and after broadcasting pro-fascist propaganda during WWII he was indicted for treason by the Americans, found unfit to plead, and confined to a mental institution until 1958.

POUND, Roscoe (1870–1964), US botanist, jurist and educator who championed flexibility in the law and efficiency in court administration. He was professor of law at Harvard 1910–37, and advocated a "sociological jurisprudence" that would adapt the law to changing social and economic conditions.

POUSSIN, Nicolas (1594–1665), the greatest 17th-century French BAROQUE painter. He worked mostly in Rome, and based his style on RAPHAEL and antiquities. His classical and religious subjects, such as *Shepherds of Arcadia* (c1629), *The Rape of the Sabine Women* (c1635) and *The Seven Sacraments* (1644–48) are rich in color, austere in handling, dramatic, and evocative in mood. He influenced Jacques DAVID, CÉZANNE and PICASSO.

POVERTY, in the US, is defined by a government-formulated poverty index or poverty level. Originally conceived in 1964 as cash income equal to three times the cost of a minimally adequate family diet, the poverty level varies with family size and composition. It is adjusted each year to reflect changes in the Consumer Price Index. In 1988, the poverty level for a family of four was $11,203, about a third of the median income of all four-person families.

Throughout most of American history, poverty was accepted as an inescapable fact of life. Sometimes it was attributed to personal misfortune, but more often to some moral defect in the poor. Only in recent decades have policymakers taken the view that large-scale poverty is a consequence of public policy. Since the GREAT DEPRESSION of the 1930s, government has pursued policies intended to alleviate and reduce poverty (see NEW DEAL; WAR ON POVERTY). It has been estimated that in the late 1940s a third of the entire US population were poor. Between 1960 and 1980 the poverty rate fell from 22.2% to 13.0%. In 1985, 14.0% of the US population lived below the poverty level — 11.4% of whites, 31.3% of blacks, 29.0% of Hispanics. (See also WELFARE.)

POWDERLY, Terence Vincent (1849–1924), US labor leader. A machinist, he became grand master workman (president) of the KNIGHTS OF LABOR (1879–93). He also served three times as mayor of Scranton, Pa. (1878, 1880, 1882) and held high posts in the Bureau of Immigration.

POWELL, Adam Clayton, Jr. (1908–1972), US politician. A clergyman, he was New York's first black city council member (1941). He founded *The People's Voice* (1942) and, as the flamboyant "Voice of Harlem," was a Democratic Representative 1945–71. Excluded from Congress for alleged misuse of funds (1967), he was reelected twice, but defeated in 1970.

POWELL, Anthony (Dymoke) (1905–), English novelist, best known for his contemporary comedy of manners *A Dance to the Music of Time*, a series of novels which started with *A Question of Upbringing* (1951).

POWELL, John Wesley (1834–1902), US geologist and ethnologist best known for his geological and topographical surveys, and for his anthropological studies of the Amerinds.

POWELL, Lewis Franklin, Jr. (1907–), associate justice of the US Supreme Court (1971–87). A lawyer and former president of the American Bar Association, he was appointed to the court by President Nixon and occupied the center of an often-polarized court, casting deciding votes in many important cases.

POWER, the rate at which work is performed, or ENERGY dissipated. Power is thus measured in units of work (energy) per unit time, the SI UNIT being the watt (=joule/second) and other units including the horsepower (=745.70W) and the *cheval-vapeur* (=735.5W). Frequently in engineering (and particularly in transportation) contexts, what matters is the power that a given machine can deliver or utilize—the rate at which it can handle energy—and not the absolute energies involved. A high-power machine is one which can convert or deliver energy quickly. While mechanical power may be derived as a product of a force and a velocity (linear or angular), the electrical power utilized in a circuit is a product of the potential drop and the current flowing in it (volts × amperes = watts). Where the electrical supply is alternating, the root-mean-square (rms) value of the voltage must be used.

POWER OF ATTORNEY, in US law, a legal document authorizing a person to act on behalf of the signatory, usually in business and financial matters. To be officially recorded, it must usually be certified by a notary public. A *general* power allows the agent to act for the signatory in all circumstances, while a *special* power covers only items listed.

POWERS, Hiram (1805–1873), US sculptor. He worked in Florence from 1837. His work includes the famous neoclassic *Greek Slave* (1843) and busts of eminent Americans.

POWHATAN (c1550–1618), personal name Wahunsonacock, chief of the Powhatan Indians and head of the Powhatan Confederacy of tribes, which he enlarged until it covered most of the Virginia tidewater region and part of Maryland. He befriended the JAMESTOWN settlers under their leader John SMITH (1608). Later hostilities were settled when his daughter POCAHONTAS married John ROLFE (1614).

POWHATAN INDIANS, North American tribe in E Va., of Algonquian linguistic stock. They grew corn, hunted, fished and lived in villages with palisades. Under POWHATAN their confederacy dominated some 30 tribes. After his death (1618) violent clashes with encroaching settlers led to their defeat. Some 3,000 Powhatan live in E Va. today.

POWYS, John Cowper (1872–1963), English writer. His work included novels such as *Wolf Solent* (1929) and *A Glastonbury Romance* (1932), his *Autobiography* (1934), poems, essays and lectures.

PRAETOR, in ancient Rome (from 366 BC), a magistrate elected annually to administer justice, second in rank to the CONSUL. By 197 BC there were six praetors, four of whom were responsible for provincial administration.

PRAETORIAN GUARD, the elite household troops of the Roman emperors, consisting of 9 (later 10) cohorts of 1,000 foot soldiers with higher rank and pay than ordinary troops. Instituted by Augustus in 2 BC, they assumed enough power to overthrow emperors. Constantine disbanded them in 312.

PRAETORIUS, Michael (German name Schultheiss; 1571–1621), prolific German composer of choral church music and dances, and author of *Syntagma musicum* (1614–20), a historically important treatise on theory and instruments.

PRAGMATIC SANCTION, an edict by a ruler pronouncing on an important matter of state, such as the succession. The most famous was issued by the Holy Roman Emperor Charles VI in 1713 (published 1718), declaring that his eldest daughter MARIA THERESA should inherit the Austrian throne in the absence of a male heir. This resulted in the War of the AUSTRIAN SUCCESSION.

PRAGMATISM, a philosophical theory of knowledge whose criterion of truth is relative to events and not, as in traditional philosophy, absolute and independent of human experience. A theory is pragmatically true if it "works"—if it has an intended or predicted effect. All human undertakings are viewed as attempts to solve problems in the world of action; if theories are not trial solutions capable of being tested, they are pointless. The philosophy of pragmatism was developed in reaction to late 19th-century IDEALISM mainly by the US philosophers C. S. PEIRCE, William JAMES and John DEWEY.

PRAGUE (Praha), capital of Czechoslovakia, on the Vltava R. One of Europe's great historic cities, it became prominent under Emperor Charles IV, who founded the university, the first in central Europe (1348). The Hapsburgs ruled Prague for nearly 300 years, until Czechoslovakia's independence after WWI. Prague was invaded by the Nazis in 1939 and by Warsaw Pact countries in 1968. The city has great cultural, commercial and industrial importance and is the center of the country's manufacturing industries. Pop 1,190,576.

PRAIRIE DOGS, ground squirrels of the genus *Cynomys*. Social animals of the open plains of North America, they live in large colonies in burrows. They are short-tailed marmot-like creatures, active by day, feeding, grooming or sunbathing near their burrows. They frequently raise themselves on their hindlegs to watch for danger. A sharp whistle, given as warning, sends the colony dashing into the burrows.

PRAIRIE PROVINCES, the popular name

for the Canadian provinces of Manitoba, Saskatchewan and Alberta.

PRAIRIES, the rolling grasslands that once covered much of interior North America. There are three types: tallgrass, midgrass (or mixed-grass) and shortgrass, which is found in the driest areas. Typical prairie animals are the COYOTES, BADGERS, PRAIRIE DOGS and JACK RABBITS and the now largely vanished BISON and WOLF.

PRAIRIE SCHOONER, the "ship of the plains," the typical canvas covered wagon used in migration to the West. It developed about 1820 from the CONESTOGA WAGON but was lighter and often drawn by oxen.

PRAWNS, zoologically, shrimp-like crustaceans of the suborder Natantia, specifically those groups which possess a pointed rostrum projecting between the eyes. In common language, the term is often used interchangeably with SHRIMP, and applied to any large shrimp.

PRAXITELES (active about 370–330 BC), greatest Greek sculptor of his time. Of his major works, which introduced a new delicacy, grace and sinuosity of line, only a marble statue of Hermes carrying the infant Dionysus survives. There are Roman copies of his *Aphrodite of Cnidus* and *Apollo Sauroctonus.* (See GREEK ART AND ARCHITECTURE.)

PRAYING MANTIS. See MANTISES.

PREBLE, Edward (1761–1807), US naval officer. He commanded the first American warship to go beyond the Cape of Good Hope (1799), and in 1804 led the unsuccessful assault on Tripoli (see BARBARY WARS).

PRECAMBRIAN, the whole of geological time from the formation of the planet earth to the start of the PHANEROZOIC (the eon characterized by the appearance of abundant FOSSILS in rock strata), and thus lasting from about 4,550 to 570 million years ago. It is essentially equivalent to the Cryptozoic eon. (See also GEOLOGY.)

PRECESSION, the gyration of the rotational axis of a spinning body, such as a GYROSCOPE, describing a right circular CONE whose vertex lies at the center of the spinning body. Precession is caused by the action of a torque on the body. **Precession of the equinoxes** occurs because the earth is not spherical, but bulges at the EQUATOR, which is at an angle of 23.5° to the ecliptic. Because of the gravitational attraction of the sun, the earth is subject to a torque which attempts to pull the equatorial bulge into the same plane as the ecliptic, therefore causing the planet's poles, and hence the intersections of the equator and ecliptic (the equinoxes), to precess in a period of about

26,000 years. The moon and planets similarly affect the direction of the earth's rotational axis.

PRECIPITATION, in meteorology, all water particles that fall from CLOUDS to the ground; including RAIN and drizzle, SNOW, sleet and hail. Precipitation is important in the HYDROLOGIC CYCLE.

PRE-COLUMBIAN ART, art of what is now Latin America prior to COLUMBUS' discovery of the Americas in 1492. The two main cultural areas were the central Andes (S Colombia, Ecuador, Peru, Bolivia, NW Argentina and N Chile) and Meso-America (Mexico and Central America). In both areas artistic development took place after c3000 BC. Monochrome-decorated pottery, female figurines and elaborately designed textiles have been discovered in Ecuador and Peru dating from 3000–2500 BC. The great Andean classical period noted for textiles, ceramics, gold and silver work, jewelry and stone masonry took place in 1000 BC–800 AD prior to the INCA kingdom. The great city buildings at Cuzco, MACHU PICCHU and Tiahuanaco are striking achievements. The Meso-Americans excelled in the graphic and plastic arts. From about 1000 AD the illuminated codex writings of the MAYAS, MIXTECS and AZTECS recorded mythological stories. Their temples, as at CHICHEN-ITZA, were decorated with elaborately carved stone sculptures and reliefs, with wall frescoes inside. The OLMECS made small jade carvings and colossal stone heads. In Colombia the CHIBCHA INDIANS were skilled in ceramics, textiles and jewelry.

PREDESTINATION, in theology, the belief that through God's decree certain persons (the elect) are destined to be saved. Premised on God's omniscience and omnipotence and buttressed by the doctrines of God's PROVIDENCE and GRACE, predestination was taught especially by St. Paul and was elaborated by St. AUGUSTINE in opposition to PELAGIANISM. CALVINISM taught additionally the predestination of the nonelect to damnation, unlike Catholicism denying individual FREE WILL and regarding saving grace as irresistible and wholly gratuitious. JANSENISM was a similar Roman Catholic movement. ISLAM likewise teaches absolute predestination.

PREEMPTION ACT, an act passed in 1841 by the US Congress allowing Western settlers to claim up to 160 acres of virgin land after 14 months' residence, and to pay just $1.25 an acre. It was later exploited by speculators and repealed in 1891. (See also HOMESTEADING.)

PREGNANCY, in humans the nine-month

period from the fertilization and implantation of an EGG, the development of EMBRYO and FETUS through the BIRTH of a child. Interruption of MENSTRUATION and change in the structure and shape of the BREASTS are early signs; morning sickness, which may be mild or incapacitating, is a common symptom. Later an increase in abdominal size is seen and other abdominal organs are pushed up by the enlarging WOMB. Ligaments and joints become more flexible in preparation for delivery. Multiple pregnancy, hydatidiform mole, spontaneous ABORTION, antepartum HEMORRHAGE, toxemia and premature labor are common disorders of pregnancy. The time following birth is known as the puerperium.

PREHISTORIC ANIMALS, animals which became extinct before mankind began to produce written records, about 5,000 years ago. Our knowledge of these creatures is therefore derived almost entirely from fossils.

Although life on earth is thought to have begun around 3.1 billion years ago, few fossils have been found that are more than 600 million years old. The first plentiful fossils, dating from 550 million years ago, are all invertebrates (animals without backbones) such as ammonites, creatures that lived in spiral shells. Remains of animals resembling jellyfish, snails, clams and worms have also been found. The most plentiful invertebrate seems to have been the trilobite, a kind of flat shellfish with jointed legs.

Fish. The first fishes appeared about 480 million years ago. These were all covered with heavy bony armor, and are called *ostracoderms.* They had no jaws. Fishes as we know them did not appear until 130 million years later, in the Devonian period. Some of these fishes, like their living descendant the coelacanth, had fleshy fins which only needed a little more strengthening to be useful for moving on land. These were probably the ancestors of the amphibians, which first appeared at the end of the Devonian period (see AMPHIBIA).

Land reptiles. The fossil record becomes spectacular with the arrival of the first land vertebrates, the reptiles, which evolved some 290 million years ago. They grew bigger and more powerful than the amphibians and their shelled eggs were able to hatch on land. Reptiles dominated the earth for about 100 million years. Some walked on two legs, and from these came the dinosaurs, pterodactyls, and eventually birds.

Dinosaurs are the best known of all prehistoric animals. Some grew to enormous size, but they all became extinct, possibly because they could not adapt to climatic changes, though some authorities blame competition from early mammals. Among the dinosaurs was the carnivorous *Tyrannosaurus rex,* the 85-ton *Brachiosaurus,* and the 87-ft-long *Diplodocus.* There were others with fantastic horns, such as Triceratops, and armored vegetarians like the Stegosaurs. Flying reptiles began to appear during the Jurassic period. One of these, the *Archaeopteryx,* had claws on its wings and many teeth—it looked like a reptile covered in feathers. It is from creatures like this that modern birds have evolved.

Mammals. The placental mammals (those whose young are carried within the body) have been on earth for about 65 million years, although shrew-like beasts evolved 190 million years ago, probably from carnivorous reptiles. A well-known early mammal is the *Eohippus,* about the size of a small dog. The horse is thought to be descended from it. Later, when mammals dominated the land, some larger versions of modern mammals existed. *Megatherium* was a 20 ft long sloth, and the mammoth—a contemporary of prehistoric man—was a large hairy elephant. Some mammoths have been preserved by being deep-frozen in soil in Siberia.

PREHISTORIC MAN. *Homo sapiens sapiens,* or modern man, appeared on the earth relatively recently. Though the planet's age is estimated at 4.5 billion years, man in his present form may have existed for only some 100,000 years. By comparison, one-celled life began about 3.2 billion years ago, while mammals have flourished for about 200 million years.

Study of early man is hampered by the difficulty of distinguishing between what was to become *Homo sapiens* and the ancestors of our modern apes. The actual point of separation of the two strains is so long ago, probably before either bore any resemblance to their modern descendants, that it is unlikely ever to be discovered. The earliest known form of man may have been **Ramapithecus,** though there is still debate as to whether he should be classed as of the Hominidae (family of man), of the Pongidae (anthropoid-ape family) or of a third lineage that left no descendants. Only small fragments of Ramapithecus fossil skeletons exist, the earliest of these dating from some 15 million years ago, the latest from some 8 million years ago. The first certain ancestor of modern man is **Australopithecus afarensis,** discovered in

1978. This species flourished in Ethiopia and Tanzania from 3.8 to 2.5 million years ago. Adult individuals walked erect at a height of about 4ft and had a brain of about 400cc. They inhabited grasslands and ate a wide variety of food including some meat. *A. afarensis* is one of several species of the genus *Australopithecus*. Another, *A. africanus*, was slightly taller and lighter boned. Still another, *A. robustus*, was, as its name implies, a taller and more robust species. These two species seem to have established family relationships and relied on meat diets, but both are believed to have been evolutionary dead ends.

The genus **Homo**, or true human being, dates back 2 million years in the form of *H. habilia*, who used primitive tools and had a brain capacity of 500 to 750cc. *H. habilia* hunted in groups. *H. erectus* appeared about 1.5 million years ago and had a brain size of 800cc—about half that of modern man—which gradually increased to 1,300cc over a period of one million years. *H. erectus* spread from Africa into Europe and Asia, and originated the use of fire and the ax. The species gradually evolved into *H. sapiens* and into our own subspecies, *H. sapiens sapiens*. During this gradual change, beginning 400,000 years ago, our ancestors cooked meat, wore clothes, made wooden tools and built huts. Facial features continued to flatten into close resemblance to our own. A variant, **Neanderthal man,** who flourished from about 75,000 to 35,000 years ago, may have become extinct or may have been in man's direct line of descent. Not the brute often depicted, the Neanderthal in fact developed a sense of the spiritual.

There is some evidence that *H. sapiens sapiens* may have appeared in southern Africa 115,000 years ago; but he is not known in Europe until 30,000 years ago. There, he is often designated as **Cro-Magnon man** for the site in France where his remains were first discovered. Cro-Magnon man closely resembled modern man; he used a variety of tools and domesticated animals about 18,000 years ago and plants about 12,000 years ago. The lovely cave paintings of France and Spain, 15–20,000 years old, represent another major stride in the development of modern man.

PRENDERGAST, Maurice Brazil (1859–1924), US painter influenced by POSTIMPRESSIONISM, a member of the ASHCAN SCHOOL. His work includes *Umbrellas in the Rain* (1899) and *Central Park* (1901).

PRE-RAPHAELITES, influential group of English artists who formed a "brotherhood" in 1848 in reaction against the prevailing academic style. An allegorical subject, bright colors and minute naturalistic detail are typical of their work, as in *Christ in the Carpenter Shop* (1850) by MILLAIS or *The Scapegoat* (1854) by W.H. HUNT. A third founder member was D. G. ROSSETTI, while BURNE-JONES and William MORRIS were later followers. Critic John RUSKIN was an advocate of the Pre-Raphaelites.

PRESBYTERIANISM, form of church government by elders. Midway between episcopacy and congregationalism, it was espoused at the Reformation by the REFORMED CHURCHES, who viewed it as a rediscovery of the apostolic practice of government by presbyters. There is a hierarchy of church courts: the *kirk-session*, the minister and elders elected by the local congregation; the *presbytery*, representative ministers and elders from a given area; the *synod*, members chosen from several presbyteries; and the *general assembly*, the supreme body, consisting of ministers and elders from all the presbyteries. (Various names are used for these courts.) Presbyterian doctrine is biblical CALVINISM, usually with the WESTMINSTER CONFESSION as a subordinate standard. Worship is simple and dignified.

PRESCOTT, Samuel (1751–c1777), American patriot who in a famous ride with Paul REVERE escaped to warn his home town Concord, Mass., of the British advance (1775). Later captured, he died in prison.

PRESCOTT, William (1726–1795), American Revolutionary colonel. He commanded the militia in the Battle of BUNKER HILL (1775) and took part in the battles of Long Island (1776) and SARATOGA (1777).

PRESCOTT, William Hickling (1796–1859), US historian. Despite the handicap of near blindness he became an authority on Spain and the Spanish conquest of America. His *History of the Reign of Ferdinand and Isabella the Catholic* (1837), *History of the Conquest of Mexico* (1843) and *History of the Conquest of Peru* (1847) became classics, admired for their narrative skill as well as their historical rigor.

PRESIDENCY, in many countries the office of head of state and often of chief executive; also of the head of many business, educational and other organizations. The US president is both head of state and chief executive. The Founding Fathers intended the presidency to act as a point of unity for the separate states and provide a commander in chief for joint defense. The office has been molded by events and by the elected presidents themselves and has steadily grown in power. President and vice-president are the only elected US federal executives. A candidate for president must be over 35 years of age and be a "natural-born" US citizen who has resided in the US for at least 14 years. By a majority vote the ELECTORAL COLLEGE chooses a president for a four-year term. With the adoption of the 22nd Amendment, a president may serve not more than two terms.

The Constitution empowers the president to appoint, with the advice and consent of the Senate, cabinet secretaries, Supreme Court justices, ambassadors and other high officials. The president similarly appoints heads of boards, agencies and commissions set up by Congress. He has powers under the Constitution and statutes to issue executive orders in times of emergency; the TAFT-HARTLEY ACT gives powers to intervene in labor-management disputes. As commander in chief, the president represents the supremacy of civil authority over the military. He plays a customary role of great importance in foreign policy, owing to his ability to use speed, flexibility and secrecy in negotiations. This role is enhanced by his sole authority in determining the use of nuclear weapons. Although the president cannot declare war, he can create a condition of war by sending troops into combat, as did Kennedy, Johnson and Nixon in Laos, Cambodia and Vietnam. Under the Constitution, the legislature, like the judiciary, is independent of the authority of the president, who is responsible for the execution of laws. But the president's ability to VETO legislation and to initiate it through his party carry great weight in the lawmaking process.

The Executive Office of the President provides the agencies, bureaus and councils vital to the execution of presidential duties. The White House Office Staff includes the president's secretaries, military aides, advisors and his personal physician.

The office's great power of political leadership depends ultimately on the political skills of the president. His control of patronage, his leadership of one of the major political parties and his ability to exert pressure on the legislative and judicial branches of government by appealing directly to the people are powerful weapons for the maintenance of presidential power. (See also CHECKS AND BALANCES; SEPARATION OF POWERS; CONGRESS OF THE UNITED STATES; UNITED STATES CONSTITUTION; WATERGATE.)

PRESIDIUM, in the USSR, the supreme state authority between sessions of the SUPREME SOVIET, responsible for legislation. The Supreme Soviet elects its chairman, who is titular head of state, 15 vice-chairmen (one from each union republic), 20 members and secretary. At different times the POLITBURO has also been termed Presidium.

PRESLEY, Elvis (1935–1977), the first major rock'n'roll star and a present-day cult hero. From 1956 until the mid 1960s, Presley's belted-out versions of rhythm-and-blues songs (*Hound Dog*) and ballads (*Love Me Tender*) were instant hits, as were his 33 films. His Memphis home became a shrine for his many fans.

PRE-SOCRATIC PHILOSOPHY, term applied to the thought of the early Greek philosophers (c600–400 BC) whose work came before the influence of SOCRATES. Their works survive mostly in obscure fragments, but their fame and importance lie in their being the first to attempt rational explanations of the universe. They are grouped into the Ionian school in Asia Minor (THALES, ANAXIMANDER, ANAXIMENES, Xenophanes, HERACLITUS, ANAXAGORAS, and the Atomists, Leucippus and DEMOCRITUS); the Pythagoreans (see PYTHAGORAS); and the ELEATICS (PARMENIDES, ZENO and EMPEDOCLES).

PRESSURE, the FORCE per unit area acting on a surface. The SI UNIT of pressure is the pascal (Pa = newton/meter^2) but several other pressure units, including the atmosphere (101.325kPa), the bar (100kPa) and the millimeter of mercury (mmHg = 133.322Pa), are in common use. In the universe, the pressure varies from roughly zero in interstellar space to an atmospheric pressure of roughly 100kPa at the surface of the earth and much higher pressures within massive bodies and in STARS. According to the KINETIC THEORY of matter, the pressure in a closed container of GAS arises from the bombardment of the container walls by gas molecules: it is proportional to the temperature and inversely proportional to the volume of the gas.

PRESTER JOHN, legendary Christian priest-king. A purported letter from "Presbyter John," probably of Western authorship, reached the papal court in 1165. It described a great Christian utopia in the "three Indies," identified in later legend as Ethiopia.

PRETORIUS, Andries Wilhelmus Jacobus (1799–1835), commandant of the BOERS and GREAT TREK leader. His defeat of the Zulus at Blood R (1838) led to the founding of Natal. He led the 1848 trek into the Transvaal.

PRÉVERT, Jacques (1900–1977), French writer. His popular poems, sometimes satirical, sometimes melancholy, include *Paroles* (1946). Among his screenplays is that for Carné's *Les Enfants du Paradis* (1944).

PREVIN, André (1929–   ), German-US pianist, conductor and arranger. Originally an adapter of stage musicals for the screen, he won Academy Awards for his work on the films *Kiss Me Kate* (1953) and *Gigi* (1958). He later directed symphony orchestras in Houston, London, Pittsburgh, and Los Angeles.

PRÉVOST D'EXILES, Antoine François (Abbé Prévost) (1697–1763), French writer, priest and adventurer. *Manon Lescaut* (1731), a love story, is the masterpiece among his novels. It is the basis of operas by Massenet and Puccini.

PRIBILOF ISLANDS, a group of four small islands of volcanic origin in the Bering Sea. They lie about 300mi SW of Alaska and were acquired by the US in 1867. The two largest are St. Paul and St. George. Every spring, about 80% of the world's fur seals visit the islands to breed. Since 1911 the seal herds have been protected and the US regulates the harvesting of seals.

PRICE, Leontyne (1927–   ), US soprano, at New York's Metropolitan Opera 1976–85. She won international fame in VERDI and PUCCINI operas.

PRICE, the amount of money (or goods in a barter system) for which a commodity or service is exchanged. In theory, prices are set in a free enterprise system by SUPPLY AND DEMAND, while in a planned economy (see SOCIALISM) the state decides prices centrally. (See also MONEY; WAGE AND PRICE CONTROL.)

PRICE CONTROL. See WAGE AND PRICE CONTROL.

PRICKLY HEAT, or **heat rash,** an uncomfortable itching sensation due to excessive sweating, mainly seen in Europeans visiting the tropics.

PRIEST, in most religions, a cultic officer who mediates the sacred to the people; a spiritual leader, expert in ritual and generally the offerer of SACRIFICE. In the Old Testament an initial patriarchal priesthood was later restricted to the descendants of Aaron, assisted by Levites (see also HIGH PRIEST). In the Christian Church presbyters came to be called priests—an order of the threefold MINISTRY—with powers to grant absolution and to offer the sacrifice of the MASS. At the Reformation the priesthood of Christ and through him that of all believers, was emphasized. (See also ORDINATION.)

PRIESTLEY, J(ohn)   B(oynton) (1894–1984), English man of letters. His writings include many plays, but he is best known for such popular novels as *The Good Companions* (1929) and *Angel Pavement* (1930) and for his major critical work *Literature and Western Man* (1960).

PRIESTLEY, Joseph (1733–1804), British theologian and chemist. Encouraged and supported by Benjamin FRANKLIN, he wrote *The History and Present State of Electricity* (1767). His most important discovery was OXYGEN (1774—named later by LAVOISIER), whose properties he investigated. However, he never abandoned the PHLOGISTON theory of COMBUSTION. He later discovered many other gases—AMMONIA, CARBON monoxide, hydrogen sulfide—and found that green plants require sunlight and give off oxygen. He coined the name RUBBER. His association in the 1780s with the Lunar Society brought him into contact with scientists such as James WATT and Erasmus Darwin. His theological writings and activity were important in leading some English Presbyterians into Unitarianism; indeed he is regarded as a principal architect of the Unitarian Church. Hostile opinion over this and his support of the French Revolution led to his emigration to the US (1794).

PRIMATES, the order of MAMMALS containing MAN, the ANTHROPOID APES, MONKEYS, tarsiers, pottos, bushbabies and LEMURS. Compared with most mammal groups, primates are peculiarly un-specialized; the brain, however, is proportionately larger and more developed. The stages in the evolution of primates are mostly represented in extant forms. From tarsier-like forms evolved the lemurs and lorises; from the EOCENE Omomyidae arose the Anthropoidea, Catarrhini, Platyrrhini and Hominoidea.

PRIME MINISTER, or **premier,** head of the executive in a parliamentary system. The prime minister appoints and directs his own CABINET, which is the source of all major legislation. He also has the power to make and dismiss ministers and to call an election before the full term of a government. The office developed in England at the time of Robert WALPOLE. Most parliamentary democracies distinguish between the head of state (a monarch or president) and the prime minister, who is head of the government. (See also PARLIAMENT.)

PRIME NUMBER, a natural number which cannot be expressed as the product of other natural numbers, e.g. 1, 2, 3, 5, 7, 11, 13, 17 and 19.

PRIME RATE, in the US, the rate of INTEREST on short-term loans charged to the major corporations by commercial banks. It largely determines the other interest rates charged by commercial banks.

PRIMITIVE MAN, term for societies whose culture has reached a level little, if any, higher than that of the STONE AGE. Although technologically limited and economically unsophisticated, primitive societies may have extremely complex social structures with extensive rules governing behavior such as MARRIAGE, kinship and religion. Most contemporary primitive societies are Neolithic; that is, they practice agriculture, make pots, weave textiles and work stone to make tools. A few, however, are Paleolithic, such as the AUSTRALIAN ABORIGINES, the Tasady of Mindanao in the Philippines, and the recently extinguished Tasmanians. PREHISTORIC MAN probably first formed primitive societies about 250,000 years ago.

PRIMITIVES, in art history, a term describing several groups of painters: the pre-1500 Netherlandish or Flemish school, including VAN EYCK; all Italian painters between GIOTTO and RAPHAEL; and more recent naive, untrained artists such as Henri ROUSSEAU, and the Americans Edward HICKS and Grandma MOSES.

PRIMO DE RIVERA, Miguel (1870–1930), Spanish general and politician. Supported by King Alfonso XIII, he overthrew the government in 1923 and became dictator. Popular discontent, economic failure and loss of army support forced him to resign in 1930. His son, **José Antonio Primo de Rivera,** founded the Falange (a fascist political party) and was executed by Loyalists (republicans) in 1936.

PRIMOGENITURE, law by which the eldest son inherits family lands. It originated in medieval Europe for the support of the son who gave military service to his king. Never widely established in the US, primogeniture is still customary in England.

PRIMROSE, William (1904–1982), Scottish violist, US resident from 1937. He cofounded the Festival Quartet in 1956. Several composers, including Bartók, wrote works especially for him.

PRINCE EDWARD ISLAND, Canadian maritime province. It is Canada's smallest province, both in area and in population, but the most densely populated.

Name of province: Prince Edward Island
Capital: Charlottetown
Joined confederation: July 1, 1873
Area: 2,184sq mi
Population: 125,379
Land. The island lies in the Gulf of St.

Lawrence and is separated from the mainland by the Northumberland Strait. Its length is about 145mi and greatest width 35mi. There are many tidal inlets, known as "rivers," and no point is more than 10mi from the sea. The surface is gently rolling with small hills in the center and SE; the highest point is 450ft above sea level. The climate is milder than on the mainland and often humid. Precipitation averages 40in and heavy snowfalls are common in winter.

People. For many decades the population remained about 110,000 due to emigration to the mainland. But in the last 15 years it has been rising. Some 80% of the population descends from British and 15% from original inhabitants of ACADIA. There are several hundred Micmac Indians living on reservations.

Economy. Prince Edward Island's economy is based on farming, fishing, tourism and light industry. Now self-sufficient in grain production, it will soon become an exporter of grain; tobacco, strawberry and blueberry crops are already valuable exports. Hog production is profitable. Potatoes have always been important to the economy. Nearly half the crop is processed, mainly into frozen french fries. The processing of lumber is important to the island, as is lobster fishing and the more recent oyster cultivation, or aquaculture, operated by the government. Manufacturing of agricultural and fisheries products is becoming more important.

History. Jacques CARTIER was the first European known to have explored the island and in 1603 CHAMPLAIN claimed it for France. Settled by the French in 1719, it became part of the British colony of Nova Scotia in 1763 and was named Prince Edward Island in 1799 for the duke of Kent, a son of George III. In 1851 the island won control of its own affairs, and it hosted the Confederation Conference of 1864, which led to the foundation of the Dominion of Canada. Prince Edward Island joined the Dominion in 1873 and gained financial support for its depressed economy. It has remained basically rural, but after WWII the central government mounted large construction and aid programs for the islanders. Long dominated by Conservatives, the provincial government passed into the hands of Liberals in 1986.

PRINCETON, Battle of (Jan. 3, 1777), in the American REVOLUTIONARY WAR, battle fought in Princeton, N.J., in which the British under Cornwallis were defeated by George Washington in a surprise attack.

PRINCETON UNIVERSITY, private university in Princeton, N.J. Chartered as the College of New Jersey in 1746, it was renamed in 1896. One of the leading universities in the US, it includes world-famous graduate schools of public and international affairs, architecture and scientific research. It has admitted women since 1969.

PRINCIP, Gavrilo (1895–1918), Serbian nationalist who assassinated Archduke Francis Ferdinand of Austria-Hungary on June 28, 1914 at SARAJEVO. The incident precipitated WWI.

PRINCIPATE, period in Roman history from 27 BC to 284 AD (the beginning of Augustus' reign to the beginning of Diocletian's) when the unofficial title of the emperors was *princeps.* The term came to denote autocracy, and under Diocletian was replaced by the Dominate, from his assumption of the title *dominus.*

PRINTING, the reproduction of words and pictures in ink on paper or other suitable media. Despite the advent of INFORMATION RETRIEVAL systems, the dissemination and storage of knowledge are still based primarily on the printed word. Modern printing begins with the work of Johann GUTENBERG, who probably invented movable type and type metal in the 15th century. Individual characters could be used several times. The process was little changed for 400 years until the invention of machines that could cast type as it was required. Letterpress and lithography are today the two most used printing techniques. **Letterpress** uses raised type that is a mirror image of the printed impression. The type is inked and the paper pressed to it. A number of typeset pages (usually 8, 12, 16, 24 or 32) are tightly locked in a metal form such that, when a sheet of paper has been printed on both sides, it may be folded and trimmed to give a *signature* of up to 64 pages. The arrangement of the pages of type is the *imposition.* In **rotary letterpress,** the forms are not flat but curved backward, so that two may be clamped around a cylinder. Paper is fed between this cylinder and another, the impression cylinder. This technique is especially swift when the paper is fed in as a continuous sheet (a *web*). **Lithography** depends on the mutual repulsion of water and oil or grease. In the fine arts, a design is drawn with a grease crayon on the surface of a flat, porous stone, which is then wetted. The water is repelled by the greasy areas; but ink is repelled by the damp and adheres to the greasy regions. Modern mechanized processes use the same principle. Commonest is **photo-offset,** where the copy to be printed is photographed and the image transferred to a plate such that the part to be printed is oleophilic (oil-loving), the rest hydrophilic (water-loving). The plate is clamped around a cylinder and inked. The impression is made on an intermediate "blanket cylinder," which prints onto the paper. **Gravure** is another major printing technique. The plate is covered with a pattern of recessed cells in which the ink is held, greater depth of cell increasing printed intensity. Gravure is good for color and the plates are long-lasting, but high initial plate-making costs render it suitable only for long runs. Little-used for books, it is much used in packaging as it also prints well on media other than paper. **Illustrations,** in letterpress, are reproduced using line or HALFTONE blocks (see also ETCHING). In photo-offset black and white illustrations are printed much as is text; and gravure is inherently suitable for printing tones. For COLOR, the illustration is photographed for each of the colors magenta, cyan, yellow and black, and separate plates or blocks made: the four images are superimposed in printing to give a full-color effect. (See also INK; PAPER; PHOTOGRAPHY.)

PRINTZ, Johan Björnsson (1592–1663), governor of NEW SWEDEN (1643–53), a Swedish colony on the Delaware R. He resigned because of popular dissatisfaction with his rule and returned to Sweden.

PRISM, in GEOMETRY, a solid figure having two faces (the bases) which are parallel equal polygons and several others (the lateral faces) which are parellelograms. Prismatic pieces of transparent materials are much used in optical instruments. In spectroscopes (see SPECTROSCOPY) and devices for producing monochromatic LIGHT, prisms are used to produce dispersion effects, just as Newton first used a triangular prism to reveal that sunlight could be split up to give a SPECTRUM of colors. In binoculars and single-lens reflex cameras reflecting prisms (employing total internal reflection—see REFRACTION) are used in preference to ordinary mirrors. The Nicol prism is used to produce POLARIZED LIGHT.

PRISONER OF WAR, in wartime, combatant who has been captured by or has surrendered to an enemy state. The Hague Convention of 1907 and the GENEVA CONVENTIONS of 1929 and 1949 established rules in international law for the protection of such prisoners, notably that they should not be maltreated nor required to give any information other than their name, rank, and serial number, and that they should be repatriated upon the cessation of hostilities.

PRISONS, institutions for confining people

accused and/or convicted of breaking a law. There are three types of prisons in the US. Jails and lockups are run by city and county governments mainly for those awaiting trial, but also for some convicts serving short sentences. State prisons are operated by the individual states and contain the majority of those convicted of serious crimes. Federal prisons house those convicted of offenses relating to the drug and liquor laws, income tax or immigration laws, misuse of the mails, threats to national security and crimes carried out across state borders.

By the early 1800s, most of the Western world had adopted imprisonment (rather than corporal punishment, CAPITAL PUNISHMENT, or exile to penal colonies) as the chief method of dealing with criminals. The purpose of prisons is threefold: (1) to punish the wrongdoer; (2) to protect society; and (3) to act as a deterrent. Whether more than the first of these functions is fulfilled by modern prison facilities is often debated. Opportunities to learn a useful trade, the provision of psychiatric care, and the relatively normal living and working conditions afforded by open, or minimum-security, facilities or work-release programs and conjugal visits—along with the parole system developed in the 19th century, which gives convicts a chance to readapt to society toward the end of their sentences—are obviously conducive to rehabilitation. Of these, however, only parole is a realistic possibility for the majority of inmates. Prisoners are more likely to do unskilled work, which is underpaid in prison and will again draw low wages on the outside; to experience hostility or mistreatment at the hands of guards; and to live in an environment characterized by serious overcrowding, racial tension, lack of differentiation between violent and non-violent, hardened or novice criminals, and routine violence including widespread sexual abuse. Poor conditions have caused the courts to close a number of facilities. At the start of 1988, federal and state prisons (exclusive of local jails) held 581,609 inmates.

PRITCHETT, Sir V(ictor) S(awdon) (1900–   ), English novelist, short-story writer and literary critic. Based on his travels, many of his works are about Spain, such as *Marching Spain* (nonfiction, 1928), *The Spanish Temper* (nonfiction, 1954), and *Clare Drummer* (novel, 1929). *A Cab at the Door* (1968) and *Midnight Oil* (1971) are autobiographical.

PRIVACY, customary right of a citizen to maintain his private life without "undue" interference or publicity. In many countries, the right of privacy is written into the constitution. The concept represents a balance of interests between the individual and the state. In general, privacy may only be interfered with by constitutionally-approved means such as powers given to the police or other government bodies. In the US, a major threat to privacy arises from government and commercial organizations having acquired and computerized large bodies of information about individuals.

PRIVATEER, armed vessel which was privately owned, but commissioned by a government to prey upon enemy ships in wartime. Privateers thus often supplemented a nation's navy. The practice of privateering was outlawed (1856) by the Declaration of Paris, but the US refused to sign it, and privateers operated during the American Civil War. The practice has since been abandoned by all nations.

PRIVY COUNCIL, in British history, an advisory council to the monarch, by whom its members were chosen. Powerful in the 15th and 16th centuries, it declined with the ascendancy of Parliament.

PROBABILITY, the statistical ratio between the number n of particular outcomes and the number N of possible outcomes: n/N; where all of N are equally likely. For example, when throwing a die there is one way in which a six can turn up and five ways in which a "not six" can turn up. Thus $n=1$ and $N=5+1=6$, and the ratio $n:N=1/6$. If two dice are thrown there are 6×6 (=36) possible pairs of numbers that can turn up: the chance of throwing two sixes is $1/36$. This does not mean that if a six has just been thrown there is only a $1/36$ chance of throwing another: the two events are independent; the probability of their occurring *together* is $1/36$.

Probability theory is intimately linked with STATISTICS. More advanced probability theory has contributed vital understandings in many fields of physics, as in STATISTICAL MECHANICS and the behavior of particles in a colloid (see BROWNIAN MOTION) and molecules in a GAS.

PROBATE, the legal process of proving that a WILL is valid. Before a will can take effect, it must be shown that it is genuine, that it was the deceased's last will, that he signed it voluntarily and that he was of sound mind. Probate requires all possible heirs of the testator's property to be notified before a special hearing is held in a probate court, where objections can be lodged.

PROBATION, an alternative to prison, whereby convicted offenders are placed under the supervision of a probation officer, on condition that they maintain good behavior. The aim is to encourage reform, particularly for the young, when a spell in prison might simply reinforce criminal tendencies. (See also PUNISHMENT.)

PROCLAMATION OF 1763, proclamation made by the British at the end of the FRENCH AND INDIAN WARS, establishing territorial rights for North American Indians. It aimed both to appease the Indians and to prevent land disputes, but it angered (and was in many respects disregarded by) the colonists.

PROCLUS (c410–485), the last major ancient Greek philosopher. A Neoplatonist, he held that ultimate reality was both ideal and one. He wrote commentaries on Plato and Aristotle, and vigorously defended paganism against Christianity.

PROCONSUL, in ancient Rome, a CONSUL whose year of office was prolonged so that he could continue a military campaign. After the beginning of the Roman Empire in 27 BC it referred simply to the governor of a province.

PRODUCT LIABILITY, legal responsibility of a manufacturer for the safety of its product. Early in the century the doctrine of privity of contract — that there had to be a direct contractual relationship between buyer and seller before an injured buyer of a defective product could sue for damages on grounds of negligence — protected most manufacturers, since few sold their products directly to customers. Gradually, however, the courts recognized that some products — food and drugs, for example — directly affected human life, and the doctrine of privity was relaxed. In New York in 1916, the Buick Motor Co. was held liable for injuries resulting from a defective wheel; thereafter, in a growing number of states, manufacturers of defective products were vulnerable to negligence suits. Since 1963 in most states an injured consumer has had to prove only that a product was defective, not that the manufacturer was negligent, in order to recover damages. This doctrine of "strict liability" has given rise to a flood of product-liability cases.

PROGESTERONE, female sex hormone produced by the corpus luteum under the influence of luteinizing hormone. It prepares the WOMB lining for IMPLANTATION and other body organs for the changes of PREGNANCY. It is used in some oral CONTRACEPTIVES to suppress ovulation or implantation.

PROGRAMMED LEARNING, teaching method whereby matter to be learned is arranged in a coherent sequence of small clear steps (programmed) and presented in such a way that the student is able to instruct, test and, if necessary, correct himself at each step. The learning program is usually embodied in a book or booklet or adapted for use in conjunction with a teaching machine. It enables the student to learn at his own pace, with a minimum of wasted effort. There are two basic kinds of programs. The "linear program," based on the work of the Harvard psychologist B. F. SKINNER, obliges the student to compare his own response at each step with the correct response. The "intrinsic (or branching) program," originally developed for instructing US Air Force technicians, offers a limited choice of responses at each step. The correct response is immediately reinforced; an incorrect response obliges the student to follow a corrective subprogram leading back to the point at which the error occurred.

PROGRAM MUSIC, music with extra-musical meaning. It may describe an event, as in Byrd's *The Battell*, or a place, as in Vaughan Williams' *London Symphony*, or it may express specific feelings, as in Beethoven's *Pastoral Symphony*.

PROGRESSIVE PARTY, the name of three American political organizations which fought in 20th century presidential campaigns. Each was largely characterized by programs of social and economic reform. The Progressive Party of 1912 (better known by its nickname, the Bull Moose Party) chose ex-President Theodore Roosevelt as its nominee. It seceded from the Republican Party after the nomination of TAFT, but was reunited with it during the campaign of 1916.

The Progressive Party of 1924 was formed by farm and labor leaders dissatisfied with the conservatism of the Republican administration. Its position, like that of the Bull Moose Party, was that there should be government control of trusts, and it upheld the right of government intervention in private wealth. Its presidential nominee was Robert LA FOLLETTE. The Progressive Party of 1948 nominated former Democratic Vice-President H. A. WALLACE for the presidency. The party sought better relations with the USSR and an end to the Cold War. It had support from many left-wing groups but was labeled a "Communist front" organization. It polled little more than a million votes out of 48 million.

PROHIBITION, restriction or prevention of the manufacture and sale of alcoholic drinks. It refers in particular to the period from 1919 to 1933 when (by means of the 18th Amendment to the Constitution) there was a Federal prohibition law in the US. In spite of the intensive economic and group pressures which had brought it about, it soon became apparent that the law was too unpopular and too expensive to enforce. A now-notorious time of gangsterism followed, with a vast illegal liquor business (the activities involved were known as bootlegging) in the control of men such as Al CAPONE. Prohibition was repealed (1933) by the 21st Amendment. A few states in the US maintained local prohibition laws as late as 1966. (See also VOLSTEAD ACT; NATION, CARRY; WOMAN'S CHRISTIAN TEMPERANCE UNION.)

PROJECTION, in PSYCHOLOGY and PSYCHIATRY. the attribution to others of characteristics which the individual denies in himself. In PSYCHOANALYSIS. the term describes the interpretation of situations or the actions of others in such a way as to justify one's self-opinion or beliefs, as in PARANOIA and paranoid SCHIZOPHRENIA.

PROJECTION TEST, test whereby an individual's personality may be gauged by his completion of unfinished sentences, his interpretation of "pictures" from inkblots, etc.

PROKOFIEV, Sergei (1891–1953), Russian composer. A student at the St. Petersburg Conservatory with RIMSKY-KORSAKOV. Prokofiev created a fierce, dynamic, unemotive style which later became somewhat softer and more eclectic. His works include the popular *Classical Symphony*, the operas *The Love for Three Oranges* (1921) and *War and Peace* (1943); *Peter and the Wolf* (1936), for narrator and orchestra; *Romeo and Juliet* (1936), a ballet; six symphonies; concertos for piano, violin and cello; film scores and chamber music.

PROLETARIAT, name given to industrial employees as a social and economic class. In Marxist theory, the proletariat is exploited by and inimical to the bourgeois class of employers and property owners.

PROMETHEUS, a demi-god of Greek mythology, one of the Titans and a brother of Atlas. He was sometimes said to have created humankind out of earth and water. In a widespread legend, Prometheus stole fire from the gods for the benefit of mankind. ZEUS punished Prometheus by having him bound to a rock, where his liver was devoured by an eagle.

PRONGHORN, *Antilocapra americana,* the only horned animal that sheds its horn sheath, and the only one with branched HORNS as distinct from antlers. They live in groups in arid grasslands and semi-desert of western North America, feeding on forbs

and browse plants. Conservation efforts have restored numbers from an estimated 30,000 in 1924 to a present 400,000.

PROPAGANDA, selected information, true or false, which is promoted with the aim of persuading people to adopt a particular belief, attitude or course of action. During the 20th century all the major political ideologies have employed propaganda and made use of modern media to reach a mass audience. It has an important role in modern warfare and by WWII separate bureaus and ministries were established to promote morale and subvert the enemy. The Nazi Ministry of Propaganda, headed by GOEBBELS, was one of the most effective. In the West there has been an increase in professional propagandists such as people in public relations and ADVERTISING.

PROPELLER, a mechanical device designed to impart forward motion usually to a SHIP or AIRPLANE, operating on the screw principle. It generally consists of two or more inclined blades radiating from a hub, and the amount of THRUST it produces is proportional to the product of the mass of the fluid it acts on and the rate at which it accelerates the fluid. The inclination, or "pitch," of the propeller blades determines the theoretical distance moved forward with each revolution. A "variable-pitch propeller" can be adjusted while in motion, to maximize its efficiency under different operating conditions; it may also be possible to reverse the propeller's pitch, or to "feather" it—i.e., minimize its resistance when not rotating. John FITCH, in 1796, developed the first marine screw propeller; John ERICSSON perfected the first bladed propeller, in 1837.

PROPERTIUS, Sextus (c50–c16 BC), Roman elegaic poet, whose poems center on his celebrated love-affair with his mistress Cynthia. Though often obscure, he is vivid, imaginative and powerful.

PROPERTY, social concept and legal term indicating the ownership of, or the right to enjoy, something of value; it may also be an interest in something owned by another. Under some systems such as FEUDALISM or COMMUNISM, ownership of some or all kinds of property is vested not in the individual but in the state or its head. The US Constitution establishes the individual's right to property. COMMON LAW distinguishes between *real property,* i.e., land and generally non-transportable goods such as houses and trees, and *personal property,* all other kinds; financial rights such as copyrights or patent holdings are personal. The law treats the two kinds differently in such areas as tax, debt, inheritance and other significant obligations and relationships. (See also MORTGAGE.)

PROPHETS, in the Old Testament, men who by special revelation proclaimed the word of God by oracles and symbolic actions; originally seers and ecstatics. Often a scourge of the establishment, they were religious and social reformers who called for righteousness and faithfulness to God, and pronounced judgment on the ungodly. (See also ESCHATOLOGY; OLD TESTAMENT.) In the early Church prophecy was a recognized CHARISMA, but soon died out except in Montanism, a heretical sect. It was revived among ANABAPTISTS, QUAKERS, MORMONS and PENTECOSTALS. In Islam Mohammed is the last and greatest prophet. Oracular prophets are found in many religions. (See also SHAMANISM.)

PROPORTIONAL REPRESENTATION. See ELECTION.

PROPRIETARY COLONIES, in US colonial history, English colonies granted by royal charter to an individual or small group, mostly in the period 1660–90. Large tracts of land in N.Y., N.J., Pa., N.C. and S.C. were allocated in this way. The proprietors had almost despotic power in theory, but in practice had to yield rights to the colonists, and the system was ended after the REVOLUTIONARY WAR.

PROSPECTING, the hunt for MINERALS economically worth exploiting. The simplest technique is direct observation of local surface features characteristically associated with specific mineral deposits. This is often done by prospectors on the ground, but increasingly aerial photography is employed. Other techniques include examining the seismic waves caused by explosions—these supply information about the structures through which they have passed; testing local magnetic fields to detect magnetic metals or the metallic gangues associated with nonmagnetic minerals; and especially for metallic sulfides, testing electric conductivity.

PROSTATE GLAND, male reproductive GLAND which surrounds the urethra at the base of the BLADDER and which secretes semen. This carries sperm made in the testes to the penis. Benign enlargement of prostate in old age is very common and may cause retention of the urine. CANCER of the prostate is also common in the elderly but responds to HORMONE treatment. Both conditions benefit from surgical removal.

PROSTHETICS, mechanical or electrical devices inserted into or onto the body to replace or supplement the function of defective or diseased organs. **Artificial limbs** designed for persons with AMPUTATIONS were among the first prosthetics; but metal or plastic joint replacements or BONE fixations for subjects with severe ARTHRITIS, FRACTURE or deformity are now also available. Replacement TEETH for those lost by caries or trauma are included in **prosthodontics** (see also DENTISTRY). The valves of the HEART may fail as a result of rheumatic or congenital heart disease or bacterial endocarditis, and may need replacement with mechanical valves (usually of ball-and-wire or flap types) sutured in place of the diseased valves under cardiorespiratory bypass. If the natural **pacemaker** of the heart fails, an electrical substitute can be implanted to stimulate the heart muscle at a set rate.

PROTAGORAS (c490–421 BC), most famous of the Greek SOPHISTS, remembered for the maxim "man is the measure of all things." A respected figure in Athens, where he spent most of his life, he taught RHETORIC and the proper conduct of life ("virtue"), and was appointed lawmaker to the Athenian colony of Thurii in 444 BC. Little is known of his teaching, but he is thought to have been a relativist concerning knowledge and a skeptic about the gods, although he upheld conventional morality.

PROTECTIONISM, in INTERNATIONAL TRADE, a policy by which a country seeks to protect its own industries by controlling the import and export of goods. It generally takes the form of restrictive TARIFFS or quotas on imported goods. The US has had a long tradition of protectionism, and still has a number of restrictive import quotas, in spite of the general world trend towards freer trade (see GENERAL AGREEMENT ON TARIFFS AND TRADE).

PROTECTIVE COLORATION. Many animals have adapted their coloration as a means of defense against predators. Except where selection favors bright coloration for breeding or territorial display, most higher animals are colored in such a way that they blend in with their backgrounds—by pure coloration, by disruption of outline with bold lines or patches, or by a combination of the two. The most highly developed camouflage is found in ground-nesting birds, for example, nightjars, or insects, such as walking sticks or leaf insects. Associated with this coloration must be special behavior patterns enabling the animal to seek out the correct background for its camouflage and to "freeze" against it. Certain animals can change the body texture and coloration to match different backgrounds: OCTOPUSES, CHAMELEONS and some flatfishes. An alternative strategy adopted by some animals, particularly insects, is the use of shock-coloration. When approached by a predator, these insects flick open dowdy wings to expose bright colors, often in the form of staring "eyes," to scare the predator.

PROTECTORATE, a country which is nominally independent, but surrenders part of its SOVEREIGNTY, such as control over foreign policy, in return for protection by a stronger state. The degree of control and dependency may vary. Many states in the European colonial empires were governed as protectorates.

PROTECTORATE, The, period of English history from 1653 to 1659 when the country was ruled by a Lord Protector, a Council of State and Parliament. It was, in effect, a dictatorship. Oliver CROMWELL was the first Lord Protector, succeeded in 1658 by his son Richard, who, unable to control army and Parliament, resigned in 1659, paving the way for the RESTORATION.

PROTEIN, a high-molecular-weight compound which yields AMINO ACIDS on HYDROLYSIS. Although hundreds of different amino acids are possible, only 20 are found in appreciable quantities in proteins, and these are all $\propto$-amino acids. Proteins are found throughout all living organisms. Muscle, the major structural material in animals, is mainly protein; the 20% of blood which is not water is mainly protein. ENZYMES may contain other components, but basically they too are protein. Approximately 700 different proteins are known. Of these 200–300 have been studied and over 150 obtained in crystalline form. Some proteins, such as those found in the hides of cattle which can be converted to leather, are very stable, while others are so delicate that even exposure to air will destroy their capability as enzymes. The most important and strongest bond in a protein is the peptide bond joining the amino acids in a chain. Other bonds hold the different chains together: hydrogen bonding, strong disulfide bonds and secondary peptide links are important here. The three-dimensional structure of proteins helps to determine their properties; X-RAY studies have shown that the amino acid chain is sometimes coiled in a spiral or helix. Although proteins are very large molecules (with molecular weights ranging from 12,000 to over 1 million), many of them are partly ionized and hence are soluble in water. Such differences in size, solubility and electrical charge are exploited in methods of separating and purifying proteins. The separation of proteins in an electrical field (electrophoresis) is widely applied to human serum in the diagnosis of certain diseases.

PROTESTANT EPISCOPAL CHURCH. See EPISCOPAL CHURCH, PROTESTANT.

PROTESTANTISM, the principles of the REFORMATION. The name derives from the *Protestatio* of the minority reforming delegates at the Diet of Speyer (1529). Protestantism is characterized by subordinating TRADITION to the Bible as the basis for doctrine and practice, and stresses JUSTIFICATION BY FAITH, biblical preaching and a high personal morality (see also EVANGELICALISM). In reaction to Roman Catholicism it rejected papal claims, the MASS and the worship of the SAINTS. The main original branches were LUTHERANISM, CALVINISM, ANGLICANISM and Zwinglianism (see ZWINGLI, HULDREICH), with small ANABAPTIST sects on the left wing. Exercise of the right of private judgment in interpreting Scripture led to much fragmentation, a trend reversed in recent decades by the ECUMENICAL MOVEMENT. Protestant churches of later genesis include the CONGREGATIONAL CHURCHES, BAPTISTS, QUAKERS, METHODISTS, the MORAVIAN CHURCH, the SALVATION ARMY and the PENTECOSTAL CHURCHES. Initial rapid expansion (see REFORMATION), followed by consolidation and scholastic doctrinal orthodoxy (17th century), was succeeded by a period of liberalism influenced by romantic subjectivism (see SCHLEIERMACHER) and the ENLIGHTENMENT. From this sprang MODERNISM, opposed in different ways by FUNDAMENTALISM and Neoorthodoxy. In some churches desire for détente with Rome has led to repudiation of the term "protestant."

PROTOCOLS OF THE ELDERS OF ZION, document written by tsarist secret police purporting to record the proceedings of a conference of Jewish leaders in which they plotted to take control of the world. First published in 1905, it was taken up and widely disseminated in the US by Henry FORD in the 1920s. It has been frequently used by anti-Semites despite the fact that its fraudulent character has been well documented.

PROTON, stable elementary particle found in the nucleus of all ATOMS. It has a positive charge, equal in magnitude to that of the ELECTRON, and rest mass of 1.67252×10^{-27} kg (slightly less than the NEUTRON mass but 1,836.1 times the electron mass). As the HYDROGEN ion, the proton is chemically important, particularly in aqueous solutions (see ACID), and is widely used in physics as a projectile for bombarding atoms and nuclei.

PROTOPLASM, the substance including and contained within the plasma membrane of animal CELLS but in plants forming only the cell's contents. It is usually differentiated into the nucleus and the cytoplasm. The latter is usually a transparent viscous fluid containing a number of specialized structures; it is the medium in which the main chemical reactions of the cell take place. The nucleus contains the cell's genetic material.

PROTOZOA, animals consisting of a single CELL, with all life functions carried on within that cell, distinct from the Metazoa, multicelled organisms in which cells are differentiated in function and are united into groups in ORGANS or TISSUES. Nearly 50,000 species of Protozoans have been described. They occur all over the world in every possible kind of habitat. They are divided into four classes: the Mastigophora, or flagellated Protozoa; the Sarcodina, which move using pseudopodia; the Sporozoa, nonmotile and parasitic; and the Ciliata, ciliated forms.

PROUDHON, Pierre Joseph (1809–1865), French social thinker, a founder of modern ANARCHISM. From a poor family, he gained an education through scholarships; he also became a printer. He first gained notoriety with his book *What Is Property?* (1840), to which his famous answer was "Property is theft." However, he was not a socialist, believing in a society in which property would be distributed among free individuals who cooperated spontaneously outside a framework of state authority—a philosophy he called *mutualism*. In 1847 he clashed with MARX, thus starting a struggle between libertarian and authoritarian views on socialism which continued long after his death. Proudhon spent his life propagating his ideas, writing much of his work in prison (1849–1852) and in exile (1858–1862). His influence can be traced in SYNDICALISM and in French radicalism.

PROUST, Joseph Louis (1754–1826), French chemist who established the law of definite proportions, or Proust's Law (see COMPOSITION, CHEMICAL).

PROUST, Marcel (1871–1922), French novelist whose seven-part work *Remembrance of Things Past* is one of the greatest novels of the 20th century. It was written during the period 1907–19, after Proust, who suffered continually from asthma, had retired from Parisian high society and become virtually a recluse. A semi-autobiographical exploration of time, memory and consciousness, with an underlying theme of the transcendency of art over the futility of man's best efforts, it broke new ground in the art of the novel, and was enormously influential.

PROVENÇAL, or **langue d'oc,** a ROMANCE LANGUAGE developed from the Latin spoken in S France, principally Provence. During the Middle Ages, Provençal produced a notable literature which reached its highest point with the courtly love poetry of the TROUBADOURS.

PROVENCE, region and former province of France, embracing the lower Rhone R (including the Camargue) and the French Riviera. The chief cities are Nice, Marseilles, Toulon, Avignon, Arles and Aix-en-Provence (the historic capital). It is a sunny and picturesque region, famous for historical associations and its fruit, vineyards and olives. It was the first transalpine Roman province (hence the name), and later it became an independent kingdom (879–933), finally passing to the French kings in 1486.

PROVERBS, Book of, book of the OLD TESTAMENT; an example of the "wisdom literature" popular in post-exilic Judaism. Its eight sections, attributed in their headings to various authors including SOLOMON, consist of numerous pithy proverbs, mostly unconnected moral maxims, probably dating between the 9th and 2nd centuries BC.

PROVIDENCE, in THEISM, the government by God of the universe. By his almighty power, he infallibly determines and regulates all events—in general providence by means of natural laws: in specific providence by miracles or other direct actions. CALVINISM stresses the providential government of free human actions.

PRUD'HON, Pierre Paul (1758–1823), French painter. His best-known works are the portrait of the Empress Josephine (1805) and *Crime Pursued by Vengeance and Justice* (1808). His painting, influenced by CORREGGIO, is soft and sensual in character.

PRUSSIA, militaristic state of N central Europe that dominated Germany until the rise of NAZISM. At the height of its strength it stretched from W of the Rhine to Poland and Russia. The Baltic territory later known as East Prussia was Germanized by the TEUTONIC KNIGHTS in the 1200s and later became the duchy of Prussia. In 1618 it came under the rule of the Electors of nearby Brandenburg, the Hohenzollerns, and FREDERICK I declared himself king of Prussia in 1701. Under his successors, particularly FREDERICK THE GREAT, the Prussian state expanded to become the strongest military power in N Europe. It received a setback in the NAPOLEONIC WARS, but recovered. In 1862 BISMARCK became premier, and as a result of a planned series of wars and skillful diplomacy conducted under his direction, King WILLIAM I of Prussia was declared Emperor of Germany in 1871. Prussia was the largest and most powerful of the states of the united Germany, and continued so until 1934, when by a decree of HITLER the separate German states ceased to exist as political entities. After WWII former Prussian territory was divided among East Germany, Poland and the USSR.

PRZEWALSKI'S HORSE, or Eastern wild horse, the last remaining race of true wild horses. Of the three subspecies of *Equus przewalskii*, two, the steppe tarpan and forest tarpan, were exterminated by the middle of the 19th century. Only Przewalski's horse remained, undiscovered until 1881. Ancestors of the domestic HORSES, they are about the size of a PONY, yellow or red-brown and with an erect mane. It is probable that they, too, are now extinct in the wild.

PSALMS, Book of, collection of 150 songs in the OLD TESTAMENT, used as the hymn book of Judaism since the return from exile, and prominent in Christian liturgy. Metrical psalms are sung in the REFORMED CHURCHES. Many psalms are traditionally ascribed to DAVID; modern scholars date them between the 10th and 2nd centuries BC. Their fine poetry embodies a rich variety of religious experience, both national and individual. (See also BAY PSALM BOOK.)

PSALTERY, musical instrument related to the dulcimer and consisting of strings stretched over a flat soundbox, and plucked. Of Near Eastern origin, it enjoyed great popularity in the West in the 13th–15th centuries. No medieval examples are extant.

PSEUDEPIGRAPHA (Greek: writings falsely ascribed), uncanonical books excluded from the APOCRYPHA and generally pseudonymous. Such Jewish works, written largely from c150 BC to c100 AD, include the *Book of Enoch*, *Assumption of Moses* and *Apocalypse of Baruch*. Christian pseudepigrapha, also called New Testament apocrypha, include numerous Gospels, Acts of most of the apostles, and spurious epistles; they are mostly fanciful and heretical.

PSITTACOSIS, or parrot fever, LUNG disease with FEVER, cough and breathlessness caused by a bedsonia, an organism intermediate between BACTERIA and VIRUSES. It is carried by parrots, pigeons, domestic fowl and related birds.

TETRACYCLINES provide effective treatment, but any infected birds must be destroyed.

PSORIASIS, common SKIN condition characterized by patches of red, thickened and scaling skin. It often affects the elbows, knees and scalp but may be found anywhere. Several forms are recognized and the manifestations may vary in each individual with time. Coal tar preparations are valuable in treatment but STEROID creams and cytotoxic CHEMOTHERAPY may be needed. There is also an associated ARTHRITIS.

PSYCHEDELIC DRUGS. See HALLU-CINOGENIC DRUGS.

PSYCHIATRY, the branch of medicine concerned with the study and treatment of MENTAL ILLNESS. It has two major branches: one is PSYCHOTHERAPY, the application of psychological techniques to the treatment of mental illnesses where a physiological origin is either unknown or does not exist (see also PSYCHOANALYSIS); the other, medical therapy, where attack is made either on the organic source of the disease or, at least, on its physical or behavioral symptoms. (Psychotherapy and medical therapy are often used in tandem.) As a rule of thumb, the former deals with NEUROSES, the latter with PSYCHOSES. (See also PSYCHOLOGY.) DRUGS are perhaps the most widely used tools of psychiatry. Many emotional and other disturbances can be simply treated by the use of mild SEDATIVES or TRANQUILIZERS. (See also PSYCHO-PHARMACOLOGY.) Another somatic therapy is electroshock (electroconvulsive therapy—ECT). In electroshock treatment, an electric current is passed through the brain, producing convulsions and often unconsciousness: it is used in cases of severe depression. Both techniques are unpredictable in result. LOBOTOMY, a surgical operation which severs certain of the neural pathways, is now rarely used.

PSYCHICAL RESEARCH. See PARA-PSYCHOLOGY.

PSYCHOANALYSIS, a system of psychology having as its base the theories of Sigmund FREUD; also, the psychotherapeutic technique based on that system. The distinct forms of psychoanalysis developed by JUNG and ADLER are respectively more correctly termed analytical psychology and individual psychology. Freud's initial interest was in the origins of the NEUROSES. On developing the technique of free association to replace that of HYPNOSIS in his therapy, he observed that certain patients could in some cases associate freely only with difficulty. He decided that this was due to the memories of certain experiences being held back from the conscious mind and noted that the most sensitive areas were in connection with sexual experiences. He thus developed the concept of the UNCONSCIOUS (later to be called the id), and suggested (for a while) that anxiety was the result of repression of the libido. He also defined "resistance" by the conscious to acceptance of ideas and impulses from the unconscious, and "transference," the idea that relationships with people or objects in the past affect the individual's relationships with people or objects in the present. (See also DREAMS; PROJECTION; SEX.)

PSYCHOHISTORY, history written with special attention to psychodynamic factors. The term gained currency in the 1960s with reference to the historical writing of psychoanalyst Erik H. Erikson, especially his biographies of Luther and Gandhi. The psychohistorical approach has been criticized for substituting speculation for research, but its value depends largely on how carefully and intelligently it is done.

PSYCHOLINGUISTICS. See LINGUISTICS.

PSYCHOLOGICAL TESTS, measures, or sets of tasks, devised to elicit information about the psychological characteristics of individuals. Such characteristics may relate to the INTELLIGENCE, vocation, personality or aptitudes of the individual. Tests must be both consistent and accurate to be of value. (See also IQ; PROJECTION TEST; PSYCHOLOGY; STANFORD-BINET TEST.)

PSYCHOLOGY, originally the branch of philosophy dealing with the mind, then the science of mind, and now, considered in its more general context, the science of behavior, whether human or animal, and of human thought processes. (See also ANIMAL BEHAVIOR.) Clearly, psychology is closely connected with, on the one side, MEDICINE and PSYCHIATRY and, on the other, SOCIOLOGY. There are a number of closely interrelated branches of human psychology. **Experimental psychology** embraces all psychological investigations undertaken by the psychologist. His experiments may center on the individual or GROUP, in which latter case STATISTICS will play a large part in the research. **Social psychologists** use statistical and other methods to investigate the effect of the group on the behavior of the individual. In **applied psychology,** the discoveries and theories of psychology are put to practical use as in industrial psychology. **Comparative psychology** deals with the different behavioral organizations of animals (including man). **Physiological psychology** attempts to understand the neurology and physiology of behavior. **Clinical psychologists** diagnose and treat mental disorders, principally using psychological tests, psychotherapy and behavior therapy. They also do research on psychological factors affecting mental illness. (See also Alfred BINET; Francis GALTON; William JAMES; Wilhelm WUNDT; and BEHAVIORISM; GESTALT PSYCHOLOGY; INTELLIGENCE; PARAPSYCHOLOGY; PSYCHOLOGICAL TESTS; PSYCHOPHARMACOLOGY.)

PSYCHOPATH, a mentally disturbed individual who is unconcerned about others to the point of being completely antisocial. Such individuals are lacking in conscience and are often manipulative and exploitative.

PSYCHOPHARMACOLOGY, the study of the effects of DRUGS on the mind, and particularly the development of drugs for treating MENTAL ILLNESS.

PSYCHOSIS, in contrast with NEUROSIS, any MENTAL ILLNESS, whether of neurological or purely psychological origins, which renders the individual incapable of distinguishing reality from unreality or fantasy. If the loss of mental capacity is progressive, the illness is termed a deteriorative psychosis.

PSYCHOSOMATIC ILLNESS, any illness in which some mental activity, usually anxiety or the inhibition of the EMOTIONS, causes or substantially contributes to physiological malfunction. There is debate as to which disorders are psychosomatic, but among the most likely candidates are gastric ULCERS, ulcerative COLITIS and certain types of ASTHMA.

PSYCHOTHERAPY, the application of the theories and discoveries of PSYCHOLOGY to the treatment of MENTAL ILLNESS. Psychotherapy does not involve physical techniques, such as the use of drugs or surgery (see PSYCHIATRY).

PTERODACTYLS, a name which has come to be used for all pterosaurs or flying reptiles, though originally reserved for a single genus. Pterosaurs were a large and diverse group of reptiles adapted for different kinds of flight. The wings consisted of a naked membrane supported by the fourth finger only. Pterosaurs were almost certainly warm-blooded and had a thick fur. *Pteranodon* was the most specialized, with a wing-span of about 30ft, adapted for soaring and gliding over sea cliffs.

PTOLEMY, name used by all 15 Egyptian kings of the Macedonian dynasty (323–30 BC). **Ptolemy I Soter** (c367–283 BC) was one of Alexander the Great's generals. He secured Egypt for himself after Alexander's death and defended it in a series of wars against the other Diadochi (Alexander's generals). He founded the library of Alexandria, which became a center of Hellenistic culture. Ptolemy II Philadelphus (308–246 BC) succeeded in 285. Under him Alexandria reached its height; he completed the PHAROS and appointed CALLIMACHUS librarian. Ptolemy III Euergetes (c280–221 BC) succeeded in 246. He extended the empire to include most of Asia Minor, the E Mediterranean and Aegean Islands. After 221 the Ptolemaic empire entered a long period of decline, gradually losing its overseas possessions. Ptolemy XV Caesarion ("son of Caesar"; 47–30 BC) ruled from 44 BC jointly with his mother CLEOPATRA VII. On their defeat at the battle of Actium (31 BC), Egypt became a Roman province.

PTOLEMY, or Claudius Ptolemaeus (2nd century AD), Alexandrian astronomer, mathematician and geographer. Most important is his book on ASTRONOMY, now called *Almagest* ("the greatest"), a synthesis of Greek astronomical knowledge, especially that of HIPPARCHUS: his geocentric cosmology dominated Western scientific thought until the Copernican Revolution of the 16th century (see COPERNICUS). His *Geography* confirmed Columbus' belief in the westward route to Asia. In his *Optics* he attempted to solve the astronomical problem of atmospheric refraction.

PTOMAINE POISONING, old name for FOOD POISONING.

PUBERTY, the time during the GROWTH of a person at which sexual development occurs, commonly associated with a growth spurt. Female puberty involves several stages—the acquisition of BREAST buds and of sexual hair, and the onset of MENSTRUATION—which may begin at different times. Male puberty involves sexual-hair development, VOICE change, and growth of the testes and penis. Precocious puberty is the abnormally early development of pubertal features (before 9 years in females). The average age of puberty has fallen in recent years.

PUBLIC DEFENDER, in US law, an official paid to defend in court those unable to pay a lawyer. The defender is employed and compensated by the state, county or city.

PUBLIC DOMAIN, in US law, ownership of a property or resource by the people. In 1980 public domain or public land made up 34% of US land. Processes, plans and creative works not protected by PATENT or COPYRIGHT are said to be in the public domain.

PUBLIC HEALTH, the practice and organization of preventative MEDICINE within a community. Many threats to health are beyond individual control. DISEASE, EPIDEMICS, POLLUTION of the air and purity of WATER can only be effectively regulated by laws and health authorities. Among the strictest controls are those on SEWAGE and WASTE DISPOSAL. Most advanced countries have pure food laws controlling food purity, freshness and additives. In the US, these controls are the responsibility of the FOOD AND DRUG ADMINISTRATION. The work of individual countries in the public health field is coordinated by the WORLD HEALTH ORGANIZATION. Some countries have complete public health services which provide free or low-cost medical treatment of all kinds. (See also HEALTH AND HUMAN SERVICES, US DEPARTMENT OF; WELFARE; MEDICARE; JENNER, EDWARD; PASTEUR, LOUIS.)

PUBLIC HEALTH SERVICE (PHS), the chief US health agency, set up in 1870. In 1953, it became a division of the new Department of Health, Education, and Welfare, now the Department of HEALTH AND HUMAN SERVICES.

PUBLIC OPINION POLL. See POLL, PUBLIC OPINION.

PUBLIC RELATIONS (PR), general term for fostering goodwill for a person, corporation, institution, or product without actually paying for advertisements. Practitioners of PR supply information to the media in the hope that the media will not bother to make any changes in what they want to have said. PR people suggest improvements in behavior, grooming, packaging, etc., to a client or employer. The term "public relations" is thought to have been used first by Ivy L. Lee, who styled himself an "advisor" on "public relations" as early as 1919.

PUBLIC WORKS ADMINISTRATION (PWA), or Federal Emergency Administration of Public Works, a NEW DEAL agency set up in 1933 to stimulate employment and purchasing power. Under H. L. ICKES it made loans and grants, mainly to government bodies, for projects which included the GRAND COULEE and BONNEVILLE dams. The PWA was phased out from 1939.

PUCCINI, Giacomo (1858–1924), Italian opera composer. His first international success, *Manon Lescaut* (1893), was followed by *La Bohème* (1896), *Tosca* (1900), *Madame Butterfly* (1904) and *Turandot* (uncompleted at Puccini's death). A lyric style and strong orchestration are characteristic of his operas, which have great dramatic and emotional power. Puccini's works are among the most popular in the operatic repertoire.

PUCK, in medieval English folklore, a malevolent imp. Later he is merely mischievous, as in Shakespeare's *A Midsummer Night's Dream*. He is identified with Robin Goodfellow and Hobgoblin.

PUEBLO INDIANS, several American Indian tribes living in SW US (Ariz. and N.M.) in permanent villages (*pueblos*). They have the oldest and most developed pre-Columbian civilization N of Mexico. The various tribes, which include the HOPI and ZUÑI, are descended from the basket makers and cliff dwellers. Pueblo Indians are noted for their handiworks; their social system and religious practices remain largely intact today.

PUERPERAL FEVER, disease occurring in puerperal women, usually a few days after the BIRTH of the child and caused by infection of the WOMB, often with STREPTOCOCCUS. It causes FEVER, abdominal pain and discharge of PUS from the womb. The introduction of asepsis in OBSTETRICS by I. P. SEMMELWEISS greatly reduced its incidence. Today, ANTIBIOTICS are required if it develops.

PUERTO RICO, West Indian island, farthest E of the Greater Antilles. It is a self-governing commonwealth freely associated with the US.

Name: Commonwealth of Puerto Rico
Capital: San Juan
Became a Commonwealth: July 25, 1952
Area: 3,435sq mi
Population: 3,274,000
Elevation: Highest—4,389, Cerro de Punta. Lowest—sea level.
Motto: *Joannes est nomen ejus* ("John is his name")
Commonwealth song: "La Borinqueña"
Land and Climate. Roughly rectangular in shape, Puerto Rico extends 133mi E–W and 41mi N–S. The Cordillera Central, which rises to 4,398ft, gives way to foothills, valleys and a fertile coastal plain 1–12mi wide. The mild tropical climate, drier in the S, varies little apart from occasional storms July–Nov.

People. Puerto Ricans are US citizens but pay no federal taxes and may not vote in national elections. The Spanish element is predominant in the people's African and Spanish origins. The island is densely populated; two-thirds of the population is in San Juan, Ponce and Mayagüez. Unemployment led many Puerto Ricans to migrate, mainly to New York.

Economy. Formerly a single-crop economy based on sugar, Puerto Rico now depends largely on manufacturing. From the 1940s "Operation Bootstrap" attracted investment. Today metals, chemicals, oil-refining, textiles and sugar products are the principal exports. The US is the main trading partner. Other products include sugarcane, coffee, tobacco and foods.

History. The island was discovered by Columbus in 1493. In 1508, Juan PONCE DE LEÓN founded a colony. The native ARAWAK INDIANS died out under Spanish rule and, from c1510, Negro slaves were imported to work on sugar plantations. Puerto Rico remained under Spanish rule until 1898 when, as a result of the SPANISH-AMERICAN WAR, the island was ceded to the US. In 1917, Puerto Ricans received US citizenship and the right to elect both houses of their legislature, but nationalism, active since the late 1800s, continued. In 1952, the island became a free commonwealth with its own constitution, a status approved in a 1967 plebiscite.

With Operation Bootstrap, Puerto Rico has experienced vigorous economic development. Continuing through the 1980s it has brought Puerto Rico one of the highest standards of living in the Caribbean region, although unemployment, running around 20%, remains extremely high by US standards. The island's relationship to the US is a perennial political issue, with a minority calling for complete independence and the mainstream parties favoring either statehood or maintenance of commonwealth status.

PUFENDORF, Samuel, Baron von (1632–1694), German jurist, philosopher and historian. In his great Latin work *On the Law of Nature and of Nations* (1672) he stressed NATURAL LAW as opposed to positive (man-made) law in international relations.

PUFFINS, stubby sea birds of the AUK family, Alcidae. Black or black-and-white birds, they are characterized by their large and laterally compressed bills, which, at the beginning of the breeding season, become still further enlarged and brightly patterned. Puffins live in colonies on sea cliffs, nesting in burrows.

PUGACHEV, Emelian Ivanovich (c1742–1775), Cossack leader of the great Urals peasant revolt (1773–74). Claiming to be PETER III, murdered husband of CATHERINE II of Russia, he declared serfdom abolished and led an army of serfs and Cossacks which seized several cities and killed thousands before he was captured and executed.

PUGET SOUND, irregular inlet of the Pacific in NW Wash. It extends S about 100mi to Olympia and is navigable by large ships (US navy yard at Bremerton). Seattle and Tacoma lie on its shores, and the state's fish and lumber industries are centered in the area. It was first explored by George Vancouver in 1792.

PUJO, Arsène Paulin (1861–1939), US Democratic politician, representative from Louisiana (1903–13). As chairman of the House Banking and Currency Committee, he conducted (1912) an investigation of the "money trust" that revealed the power exercised by a few great banks. The disclosures contributed to passage of the Federal Reserve Act (1913) and the Clayton Antitrust Act (1914).

PULASKI, Casimir, Count (1748–1779), Polish soldier, hero of the anti-Russian revolt of 1768 who, exiled from Poland, fought in the American Revolutionary War. He fought at the battles of Brandywine and Germantown. In 1778, he formed his own cavalry unit, the Pulaski Legion. He was mortally wounded at the siege of Savannah.

PULITZER, Joseph (1847–1911), Hungarian-born US publisher who created the PULITZER PRIZES. In 1883, he bought the New York *World* and raised the circulation tenfold in seven years by aggressive reporting (the term YELLOW JOURNALISM was coined to describe its style). In the 1890s Pulitzer was involved in a circulation war with William Randolph HEARST's New York *Journal*. He consistently ran liberal crusades. He also endowed the school of journalism at Columbia U.

PULITZER PRIZES, awards for achievement in US journalism and letters, given every May since 1917 through a foundation created by the estate of Joseph PULITZER and administered by Columbia U. There are eight cash awards for journalism, five for literature and four traveling scholarships. An award for music was added in 1943.

PULLEY, grooved wheel mounted on a block and with a cord or belt passing over it. A pulley is a simple MACHINE applying the equilibrium of torques to obtain a mechanical advantage. Thus, the block and tackle is a combination of ropes and pulleys used for hoisting heavy weights. A belt and pulley combination can transmit motion from one part of a machine to another. Variable speed can be obtained from a single-speed driving shaft by the use of stepped or cone-shaped pulleys with diameters that give the correct speed ratios and belt tensions. To help prevent excessive belt wear and slipping, the rim surface of a pulley is adapted to the material of the belt used.

PULLMAN, George Mortimer (1831–1897), US industrialist and inventor of the first modern railroad sleeping car—the "Pullman." In 1880, he built a model company town—Pullman, Ill. (now part of Chicago), later site of the PULLMAN STRIKE.

PULLMAN STRIKE, May–July 1894, famous boycott of rolling stock of the Pullman Palace Car Co., Pullman, Ill. by E. V. DEBS' American Railway Union to protest the company's wage cuts and victimization of union representatives. After the owners obtained a federal injunction the strike was broken by federal troops, and the US labor movement suffered a major setback.

PULQUE or PULKE, intoxicating Mexican drink made from freshly fermented sap of several species of maguey (agave) plants. The alcoholic content is about 6%.

PULSAR, short for pulsating radio star, a celestial radio source emitting brief, extremely regular pulses of ELECTROMAGNETIC RADIATION (with one exception, entirely radio-frequency). Each pulse lasts a few hundredths of a second, and the period between pulses is of the order of one second or less. The pulse frequency varies from pulsar to pulsar. The first pulsar was discovered in 1967 by Anthony Hewish and S. J. Bell. The fastest pulsar yet observed has a period of 0.033s, emitting pulses of the same frequency in the X-ray and visible regions of the spectrum. It is likely that there are some 10,000 pulsars in the MILKY WAY, though less than 100 have as yet been discovered. It is believed that pulsars are the neutron STAR remnants of SUPERNOVAE, rapidly spinning and radiating through loss of rotational energy.

PULSE, the palpable impulse conducted in the ARTERIES representing the transmitted beat of the HEART. A normal pulse rate is between 68 and 80, but athletes may have slower pulses. FEVER, heart disease, anoxia and anxiety increase the rate. The pulse character may suggest specific conditions, loss of pulse possibly indicating arterial block or cessation of the heart.

PUMA, *Felis concolor,* the **cougar** or **mountain lion,** the most widespread of the big CATS of the Americas, occupying an amazing variety of habitats. Powerful cats, resembling a slender and sinuous lioness with a small head, they lead solitary lives, preying on various species of deer. The lifespan of a puma in the wild is about 18 years. A puma can cover up to 20ft in a bound, and will regularly travel up to 50mi when hunting.

PUMICE, porous, frothy volcanic glass, usually silica-rich; formed by the sudden release of vapors as LAVA cools under low pressures. It is used as an ABRASIVE, an aggregate and a railroad ballast.

PUMP, device for taking in and forcing out a fluid, thus giving it kinetic or potential ENERGY. The HEART is a pump for circulating blood around the body. Pumps are commonly used domestically and industrially to transport fluids, to raise liquids, to compress gases or to evacuate sealed containers. Their chief use is to force fluids along pipelines. The earliest pumps were waterwheels, endless chains of buckets, and the ARCHIMEDES screw. Piston pumps, known in classical times, were developed in the 16th and 17th centuries, the suction types (working by atmospheric pressure) being usual, though unable to raise water more than about 34ft. The STEAM ENGINE was developed to power pumps for pumping out mines. Piston pumps—the simplest of which is the syringe—are reciprocating volume-displacement pumps, as are diaphragm pumps, with a pulsating diaphragm instead of the piston. One-way inlet and outlet valves are fitted in the cylinder. Rotary volume-displacement pumps have rotating gear wheels or wheels with lobes or vanes. Kinetic pumps, or fans, work by imparting momentum to the fluid by means of rotating curved vanes in a housing: centrifugal pumps expel the fluid radially outward, and propeller pumps axially forward. Air compressors use the TURBINE principle (see also JET PROPULSION). Air pumps use compressed air to raise liquids from the bottom of wells, displacing one fluid by another. If the fluid must not come into direct contact with the pump, as in a nuclear reactor, electromagnetic pumps are used: an electric current and a magnetic field at right angles induce the conducting fluid to flow at right angles to both (see MOTOR, ELECTRIC); or the principle of the linear induction motor may be used. To achieve a very high vacuum, the diffusion pump is used, in which atoms of condensing mercury vapor entrain the remaining gas molecules.

PUNCH AND JUDY, leading characters in a children's handpuppet show of the same name. Punch is descended from Pulcinella (Punchinello) of the COMMEDIA DELL'ARTE. He is a hooknosed, hunchbacked, wifebeating rogue who usually ends on the gallows or in a crocodile's mouth. He is accompanied by his shrewish wife Judy (originally called Joan) and their dog, Toby. The Devil, Baby, Hangman, Policeman and Doctor may also appear. (See also PUPPET.)

PUNIC WARS, three wars between ancient ROME and CARTHAGE, each marking a crucial phase in the expansion of the Roman empire in the western Mediterranean, the third culminating in the total destruction of Carthage itself. (The Carthaginians, PHOENICIAN by descent, were known to the Romans as *Poeni*; hence *Punic*.) The First Punic War (264–241 BC) turned on a struggle for the strategically important island of Sicily. The Carthaginians had some success on land, notably under Xanthippus and HAMILCAR BARCA, but were defeated at sea, the decisive battle being fought off the Aegadian Isles in 241. Rome's naval supremacy was thenceforth unchallenged. The Second Punic War (218–201 BC), provoked by Roman moves to check Carthaginian expansion in Spain, began with HANNIBAL's daring invasion of Italy via an overland route which obliged him to cross the Alps in winter. Despite several remarkable victories, including the virtual annihilation of a strong Roman army at Cannae (216), his plan to isolate Rome from her Italian allies was ultimately frustrated. Roman counterattacks in Spain and then in Africa—at Zama (202), under SCIPIO Africanus—forced a Carthaginian surrender on terms which included the forfeiture of her Spanish empire and war fleet. Roman misgivings at the subsequent revival of Carthage as a mercantile power led to the Third Punic War (149–146 BC). After a two-year siege of Carthage, SCIPIO Aemilianus took the city and razed it to the ground. Carthaginian territory became the Roman province of "Africa."

PUNISHMENT, imposition of pain or suffering, deprivation or discomfort, on a person who has infringed the law, rule or custom of the community. The ancient individual exaction of "an eye for an eye" in retaliation or revenge has given way to socially imposed retribution. Supernatural or religious authority may be adduced, though this has yielded to arguments based on the well-being of the community. Today revenge is seen by most people as only one aspect of punishment. Another important aspect is deterrence, and in the 19th and 20th centuries the work of reformers such as John HOWARD and Elizabeth FRY led to reform and rehabilitation being considered important factors. (See CRIMINAL LAW; CAPITAL PUNISHMENT; PRISONS.)

PUNJAB (Sanskrit: five rivers), large wheat-growing region in the NW of the Indian subcontinent, on the upper Indus R plain. Formerly the British Indian province of Punjab, it was divided in 1947 into what became known as **Punjab (Pakistan)** and **Punjab (India)**. In 1966 Punjab (India) was divided into two further provinces, **Punjab** (home of a majority of India's Sikhs) and predominantly Hindu **Haryana**. In the 1980s, Sikh extremists in the Indian state of Punjab resorted to violence in an effort to gain greater Sikh autonomy.

PUPA, an immature stage in the development of those insects which have a larva completely different in structure from the adult, and in which "complete" METAMORPHOSIS occurs. The pupa is a resting stage in which the larval structure is reorganized to form the adult: all but the nervous system changes. Feeding and locomotion are meanwhile suspended.

PUPIN, Michael Idvorsky (1858–1935), Hungarian-born US inventor who made many contributions to TELEPHONE science, including a technique whereby longer-distance communication can be sustained.

PUPPET, figure of a person or animal manipulated in dramatic presentations. There are hand, or glove, and finger puppets; jointed *marionettes* string-controlled from above; and rod puppets, often used in shadow plays. Puppetry, with which VENTRILOQUISM is associated, is an ancient entertainment, popular in many countries. (See also PUNCH AND JUDY.)

PURCELL, Henry (c1659–1695), English composer, the foremost of his time. A master of melody and counterpoint, he wrote in every form and style of the period: odes and anthems for royal occasions, many choral and instrumental works, and music for plays and masques, including his opera *Dido and Aeneas* (1689).

PURE FOOD AND DRUG LAWS. See CONSUMER PROTECTION; FOOD AND DRUG ADMINISTRATION.

PURGATORY, in Roman Catholicism, the place where Christians after death undergo purifying punishment and expiate unforgiven venial sins before admission to HEAVEN. INDULGENCES, MASSES and prayers for the dead are held to lighten their suffering.

PURIM, the Feast of Lots, Jewish festival of the 14th day of Adar (Feb.–March), a joyful celebration of the deliverance from massacre of Persian Jews, through intervention by ESTHER and Mordecai. The story is told in the Book of Esther.

PURITANS, English reforming Protestants who aimed for a simpler form of worship expressly warranted by Scripture, devout personal and family life, and the abolition of clerical hierarchy. They stressed self-discipline, work as a vocation and the Christianizing of all spheres of life. Most were strict Calvinists. The term "Puritan" was first used in the 1560s of those dissatisfied with the compromise of the Elizabethan settlement of the CHURCH OF ENGLAND; under James I, after their unsuccessful pleas for reform at the Hampton Court Conference (1604), some separated from the Church of England. Archbishop Laud set about systematic repression of Puritanism, causing some to emigrate to America (see PILGRIM FATHERS). The English CIVIL WAR—known also as the Puritan Revolution—led to the establishment of PRESBYTERIANISM, but under Oliver CROMWELL Puritan dominance was weakened by internal strife. Most Puritans were forced to leave the Church after the Restoration (1660), becoming NONCONFORMISTS. Many New England settlers were Puritan, and their influence on America was marked, especially their concern for education and church democracy. (See also COVENANTERS; HALF-WAY COVENANT.)

PURKINJE, Johannes Evangelista (1787–1869), Bohemian-born Czech physiologist and pioneer of HISTOLOGY, best known for his observations of nerve cells (see NERVOUS SYSTEM) and discovery of the Purkinje Effect, that at different overall light intensities the eye is more sensitive to different colors (see VISION).

PUS, off-white or yellow liquid consisting of inflammatory exudate, the debris of white BLOOD cells and BACTERIA resulting from localized INFLAMMATION, especially ABSCESSES. Pus contained in cavities is relatively inaccessible to ANTIBIOTICS and may require drainage by SURGERY. Pus suggests but does not prove the presence of bacterial infection.

PUSHKIN, Alexander (1799–1837), poet, widely recognized as the founder of modern Russian literature. A sympathizer of the DECEMBRIST REVOLT, he spent his adult life in exile or under police surveillance. His poetic range included the political, humorous, erotic, lyrical, epic, and verse tales or novels like *Ruslan and Ludmila* (1820), *The Prisoner of the Caucasus* (1822) and his masterpiece *Eugene Onegin* (1833). Other works are the great drama *Boris Godunov* (1831) and such prose works as *The Queen of Spades* (1834) and *The Captain's*

Daughter (1836).

PUTNAM, Israel (1718–1790), American patriot and general in the REVOLUTIONARY WAR. A veteran of the FRENCH AND INDIAN WARS, he was prominent in the Battle of BUNKER HILL, but had less success as commander of Continental forces at the Battle of LONG ISLAND.

PUTNAM, Rufus (1738–1824), American pioneer who served in the FRENCH AND INDIAN WARS and in many of the engagements of the REVOLUTIONARY WAR. He emerged a brigadier general and chief engineer of the army, and in 1786 helped organize the Ohio Company of Associates. In 1788 he led the first settlers into Ohio and founded Marietta.

PUTREFACTION, the natural decomposition of dead organic matter, in particular the anaerobic decomposition of its PROTEIN by BACTERIA and FUNGI. This process produces foul-smelling substances such as AMMONIA, hydrogen sulfide and organic SULFUR compounds. The amino-acid nitrogen of the protein is recycled by incorporation in the bacteria and fungi.

P'U YI, Henry (also known as Hsüan-t'ung; 1906–1967), last Chinese emperor of the Ch'ing (Manchu) dynasty (1908–12) and Japan's puppet emperor of Manchukuo (MANCHURIA), 1934–45. He died in Peking.

PYGMY, term used to denote those peoples whose adult males are on average less than 5ft tall. Some Kalahari Desert Bushmen are of pygmy size, but the most notable pygmys are the Mbuti, or Bambuti, of the Ituri Forest, Zaire, who, through their different blood type, skin color and other characteristics, are regarded as distinct from the surrounding peoples and were probably the original inhabitants of the region. A Stone Age people, they are nomadic hunters, living in groups of 50 to 100. Asian pygmies are generally termed **Negritos**. Peoples rather larger than pygmies are described as pygmoid.

PYLE, Ernie (Ernest Taylor Pyle; 1900–1945), US journalist and war correspondent. He accompanied US troops to all the major fronts in N Africa and Europe, and his popular news column won a Pulitzer Prize in 1944. He was killed by Japanese machine-gun fire during the Okinawa campaign.

PYLE, Howard (1853–1911), US writer and illustrator of children's books such as *The Merry Adventures of Robin Hood* (1883) and *The Story of King Arthur and His Knights* (1903).

PYLOS (modern Greek Pilos, formerly Navarino), ancient port in the SW Peloponnese, Greece, site of a Mycenean palace of the 1200s BC associated with king Nestor. (See also AEGEAN CIVILIZATION; NAVARINO, BATTLE OF.)

PYM, John (c1584–1643), English statesman. A PURITAN, he led parliamentary opposition to CHARLES I and organized the impeachment of the Duke of BUCKINGHAM (1626). Dominating the SHORT and LONG PARLIAMENTS, he narrowly escaped arrest by the king in 1642, and arranged an alliance with the COVENANTERS (1643).

PYNCHON, Thomas (1937–), US novelist whose works, influenced by James JOYCE and Vladimir NABOKOV, are noted for their ingenious wordplay and complexity. His novels include *V* (1963), *The Crying of Lot 49* (1966) and *Gravity's Rainbow* (1973), a National Book Award winner.

P'YONGYANG, capital and largest city of North Korea. It lies on the Taedong R in an important coal-mining area and is a major industrial center producing iron, steel, machinery and textiles. An ancient settlement, it was the capital of the Choson kingdom in the 3rd century BC. The city was severely damaged during the Korean War. Pop 1,283,000.

PYORRHEA, or flow of PUS, generally used to refer to the pus related to poor oral hygiene and exuding from the margins of the gums and TEETH; it causes loosening of the teeth and halitosis.

PYRAMID, a polyhedron whose base is a polygon and whose sides are triangles having a common vertex. A pyramid whose base is triangular is termed a tetrahedron (or triangular pyramid); one whose base is regular polygon is termed regular; one with a square base, square; one with a rectangular base, rectangular.

PYRAMIDS, Battle of the (July 21, 1798), battle fought near Embabeh on the W bank of the Nile R, Egypt, in which NAPOLEON shattered the Mameluke army and gained access to Cairo and Egypt.

PYRENEES, mountain range between France and Spain, stretching 270mi from the Bay of Biscay to the Mediterranean and rising to Pico de Aneto (11,168ft) in the central section. The average height is about 3,500ft and the maximum width about 50mi. There are extensive forests and pasture land. Mineral deposits include iron, zinc, bauxite and talc, and there are sports and health resorts and a growing tourist industry.

PYRENEES, Peace of the (Nov. 7, 1659), by which the Franco-Spanish war (1648–59) ended in French preeminence in Europe. France secured Roussillon, parts of Flanders, and a marriage contract between LOUIS XIV and Marie-Thérèse, daughter of

PHILIP IV of Spain.

PYRITE, or iron pyrites (FeS_2, iron (II) disulfide), a hard, yellow, common sulfide known as **fool's gold** from its resemblance to gold. Of worldwide occurrence, it is an ore of SULFUR. It crystallizes in the isometric system, usually as cubes. It alters to goethite and limonite.

PYRRHO OF ELIS (c360–c270 BC), Greek philosopher, the founder of SKEPTICISM. He taught that, as nothing can be known with certainty, suspension of judgment and imperturbability of mind are the true wisdom and source of happiness.

PYRRHUS (c319–272 BC), king of Epirus, NW Greece. King at 12, he served with Demetrius I of Macedonia in Asia Minor, was helped by PTOLEMY I of Egypt to regain his throne, and later won and lost Macedonia. His costly victory over the Romans at Asculum (279), during an Italian campaign, gave rise to the term "Pyrrhic victory." Further campaigns in Macedonia and Sparta failed. He was killed in Argos.

PYTHAGORAS (c570–c500 BC), Greek philosopher who founded the Pythagorean school. Attributed to the school are: the proof of PYTHAGORAS' THEOREM; the suggestion that the earth travels around the sun, the sun in turn around a central fire; observation of the ratios between the lengths of vibrating strings that sound in mutual harmony, and ascription of such ratios to the distances of the planets, which sounded the "harmony of the spheres"; and the proposition that all phenomena may be reduced to numerical relations. The Pythagoreans were also noted for their concept of the soul, the life of moderation and their interest in medicine. They exerted great influence on Plato and ancient philosophizing generally.

PYTHAGORAS' THEOREM, or **Pythagorean Theorem**, the statement that, for any right-angled TRIANGLE, the square of the hypotenuse is equal to the sum of the squares of the other two sides. The earliest known formal statement of the theorem is in the *Elements* of EUCLID, but it seems that the basis of it was known long before this time and, indeed, long before the time of PYTHAGORAS himself. (See also EUCLIDEAN GEOMETRY.)

PYTHEAS (flourished c300 BC), Greek navigator, the first of his countrymen to explore the Atlantic coast of Europe and visit the British Isles. According to the Greek historian POLYBIUS, he reported the existence of an inhabited island called Thule, six days' sail to the north of Britain—possibly Norway or Iceland.

PYTHIAN GAMES, one of four great festivals of ancient Greece, held at Delphi to celebrate Apollo's slaying of the python at Delphi. Staged every eighth year, then after the Delphic Amphictyony (association) took control c582 BC every four years, they included dramatic, poetic, musical, athletic and equestrian contests and continued until at least 424 AD.

PYTHONS, the Old World equivalent of the New World BOAS, like them SNAKES bearing small spurs as the vestiges of hindlimbs. These two groups are clearly the closest relatives of the ancestral snake type. Like boas, pythons are nonvenomous constrictors. They are found from Africa to Australia in a wide variety of habitats. All have bold color patterns in browns and yellows. The largest species, the reticulate python of Asia, reaches 33ft. Pythons feed on small mammals, birds, reptiles and frogs; the larger African species also take small antelope.

17th letter of the alphabet, traceable to the Semitic letter *koph* and the archaic Greek letter *koppa*. Q is used to designate a hypothetical source of the SYNOPTIC GOSPELS.

QADDAFI, Muammar al- (1942–   ), Libyan leader. One of a group of army officers who deposed King Idris in 1969, he became chairman of the ruling Revolutionary Command Council and commander-in-chief of the armed forces. One of the world's most vehemently anti-Israel and supported several insurgent and terrorist groups around the world. The vast oil resources in Libya increased his influence. In the 1980s he sought to overthrow the governments of CHAD and SUDAN.

QATAR, oil-rich state on a peninsula in the Persian Gulf bordering Saudi Arabia on the west. Mainly desert, it is dominated by the oil industry, centered in the Dukhan oilfield in W Qatar, one of the richest in the Middle East. A British protectorate from 1916, the country became independent in 1971. After the petroleum industry was nationalized in

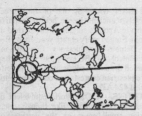

Official name: State of Qatar
Capital: Doha
Area: 4,400sq mi
Population: 414,000
Language: Arabic; English for commercial use
Religion: Muslim
Monetary unit(s): 1 Qatar riyal=100 dirhams
1976, petroleum revenues were used to fund social and economic development. Despite a decline in world petroleum prices in the 1980s, the nation's petroleum exports continued to exceed imports in value.

Q FEVER, or **query fever,** infectious disease due to *Coxiella,* an organism intermediate between BACTERIA and VIRUSES, causing FEVER, HEADACHE and often dry cough and chest pain. It is transmitted by ticks from various farm animals and is common among farm workers and veterinarians. Its course is benign, but TETRACYCLINES may be used.

QUADRANT, a simple astronomical and navigational instrument used in early times to measure the altitudes of the sun and stars. It consisted typically of a pair of sights, a calibrated quadrant (quarter) of a circle, and a plumb line. (See also SEXTANT.)

QUADRAPHONIC SOUND. See HIGH FIDELITY.

QUADRUPLE ALLIANCE, an alliance of four countries. Historically, the most famous are: (1) An alliance between England, France, Austria and the Netherlands formed in 1718 to prevent Spain from changing the terms of the Peace of UTRECHT. Spain later joined the alliance. (2) An alliance between Britain, Austria, Russia and Prussia, signed in 1814 and renewed in 1815. Its purpose was to defeat Napoleon and after his defeat and first abdication to ensure that France abided by the terms of the 1815 Treaty of PARIS.

QUAESTOR or **QUESTOR,** an official in ancient Rome. In the early republic quaestors acted as magistrates in criminal cases. They later took on financial responsibilities. The quaestorship commonly represented the first stage in a senator's political career.

QUAILS, two distinct groups of game birds: Old World and New World quails. Small, rounded ground birds of open country, they feed on insects, grain and shoots. They rarely fly even when disturbed. The tiny painted quail was carried by Chinese mandarins to warm the hands. Family: Phasianidae.

QUAKERS, or **Society of Friends,** a church known for its pacifism, humanitarianism and emphasis on inner quiet. Founded in 17th-century England by George FOX, it was persecuted for its rejection of organized churches and of any dogmatic creed, and many Quakers emigrated to America, where in spite of early persecution they were prominent among the colonizers. In 1681 William PENN established his "Holy Experiment" in Pennsylvania, and from that point the church's main growth took place in America.

The early Quakers adopted a distinctive, simple style of dress and speech, and simplicity of manner is still a characteristic Quaker trait. They have no formal creed and no clergy, putting their trust in the "inward light" of God's guidance. Their meetings for worship, held in "meeting houses," follow a traditional pattern of beginning in silence, with no set service and no single speaker.

The Quakers have exercised a moral influence disproportionate to their numbers through actually practicing what they believe, particularly pacifism. In the US they were prominent abolitionists and have been among the pioneers of social reform. They today number about 126,000 in the US.

QUANTRILL, William Clarke (1837–1865), Confederate guerrilla leader in the American CIVIL WAR. A criminal before the war, Quantrill was made a Confederate captain in 1862. On Aug. 21, 1863, with a force of 450 men he attacked the town of Lawrence, Kan., and slaughtered 150 civilians. He was killed while on a raid in Kentucky.

QUANTUM MECHANICS, fundamental theory of small-scale physical phenomena (such as the motions of ELECTRONS within ATOMS), developed during the 20th century when it became clear that the existing laws of classical mechanics and electromagnetic theory were not successfully applicable to such systems. Because quantum mechanics treats physical events that we cannot directly perceive, it has many concepts unknown in everyday experience. De BROGLIE struck out from the old QUANTUM THEORY when he suggested that particles have a wavelike nature, with a wavelength

h/p (h being the Planck constant and p the particle momentum). This wavelike nature is significant only for particles on the molecular scale or smaller. These ideas were developed by SCHRÖDINGER and others into the branch of quantum mechanics known as WAVE MECHANICS. HEISENBERG worked along parallel lines with a theory incorporating only observable quantities such as ENERGY, using matrix algebra techniques. The UNCERTAINTY PRINCIPLE is fundamental to quantum mechanics, as is Pauli's EXCLUSION PRINCIPLE. DIRAC incorporated relativistic ideas into quantum mechanics.

QUANTUM THEORY, theory developed at the beginning of the 20th century to account for certain phenomena that could not be explained by classical PHYSICS. PLANCK described the previously unexplained distribution of radiation from a BLACKBODY by assuming that ELECTROMAGNETIC RADIATION exists in discrete bundles known as quanta, each with an ENERGY $E=h\nu$ (ν being the radiation frequency and h a universal constant—the Planck constant). EINSTEIN also used the idea of quanta to explain the PHOTOELECTRIC EFFECT, establishing that electromagnetic radiation has a dual nature, behaving both as a WAVE MOTION and as a stream of particle-like quanta. Measurements of other physical quantities, such as the frequencies of lines in atomic spectra and the energy losses of electrons on colliding with atoms, showed that these quantities could not have a continuous range of values, discrete values only being possible. With RUTHERFORD's discovery in 1911 that ATOMS consist of a small positively charged nucleus surrounded by ELECTRONS, attempts were made to understand this atomic structure in the light of quantum ideas, since classically the electrons would radiate energy continuously and collapse into the nucleus. BOHR postulated that an atom only exists in certain stationary (i.e., nonradiating) states with definite energies and that quanta of radiation are emitted or absorbed in transitions between these states; he successfully calculated the stationary states of hydrogen. Some further progress was made along these lines by Bohr and others, but it became clear that the quantum theory was fundamentally weak in being unable to calculate intensities of spectral lines. The new QUANTUM MECHANICS was developed c1925 to take its place.

QUAPAW INDIANS, North American plains Indians of the Siouan language group. By the 17th century they had migrated from the Ohio valley to near the mouth of the Arkansas R. They relinquished most of their lands to the US in 1818. About 750 remain, living on a reserve in Okla.

QUARANTINE, period during which a person or animal must be kept under observation in isolation from the community after having been in contact with an infectious DISEASE. The duration of quarantine depends on the disease(s) concerned and their maximum length of INCUBATION. The term derives from the period of 40 days that ships from the Levant had to wait before their crews could disembark at medieval European ports, from fear of their carrying PLAGUE.

QUARK. See SUBATOMIC PARTICLES.

QUARTZ, rhombohedral form of silica, usually forming hexagonal prisms, colorless when pure ("rock crystal"). A common mineral, it is the chief constituent of SAND, SANDSTONE, quartzite and FLINT, an essential constituent of high-silica igneous rocks such as GRANITE, rhyolite and pegmatite, and also occurs as the GEMS: chalcedony; agate; jasper; and onyx. Quartz is piezoelectric (see PIEZOELECTRICITY) and is used to make oscillators for clocks, radio and radar and to make windows for optical instruments. Crude quartz is used to make glass, glazes and abrasives, and as a flux.

QUASAR, or quasi-stellar object, a telescopically star-like celestial object whose SPECTRUM shows an abnormally large RED SHIFT. Quasars may be extremely distant objects—perhaps the inexplicably bright cores of galaxies near the limits of the known universe—receding from us at high velocities. The spectra of quasars, however, do not seem to be affected by the interpolation of intergalactic gas. Quasars also show variability in light and radio emission (although the first quasars were discovered by RADIO ASTRONOMY, not all are radio sources). These phenomena might indicate that quasars instead are comparatively small objects less than 0.3pc across, and that they are comparatively close to us (larger—and more distant—objects being unlikely to vary in this way). There are about 200 quasars in each square degree of the sky.

QUASIMODO, Salvatore (1901–1968), Italian poet and translator of poetry awarded the 1959 Nobel Prize for Literature. During and after WWII he turned (originally because of his opposition to Fascism) from a complex, introverted hermetic style to social protest and examination of the plight of the individual, as in *Day after Day* (1947).

QUATERNARY, the period of the CENOZOIC whose beginning is marked by the advent of man. It has lasted about 4 million years up to and including the present. (See also TERTIARY; GEOLOGY.)

QUAY, Matthew Stanley (1833–1904), US politician. A lawyer, he fought in the Civil War and later became boss of the Republican Party machine in Pa., making skillful use of patronage. Elected US senator 1887, he was unseated in 1899 after corruption charges, but reelected 1901.

QUAYLE, John Danforth (1947–   ), US politician, vice president of the US (1989–   ). A conservative Indiana Republican, he served in the US House of Representatives (1977–81) and the US Senate (1981–89). In 1988 the Republican presidential nominee, George Bush, selected him as his running mate as representative of the "baby boom" generation.

QUEBEC, the largest province in Canada, stretching from Hudson Bay to S of the St. Lawrence R.

Name of province: Quebec—Québec
Joined Confederation: July 1, 1867
Capital: Quebec
Area: 594,860sq mi
Population: 6,478,190

Land. Over 90% of the province lies within the Canadian Shield, a great rocky plateau, much of it an uninhabited wilderness of forests, lakes and streams. South of the shield are the agricultural St. Lawrence lowlands containing most of the cities of Quebec. The third major region is the Appalachian uplands in the SE. The St. Lawrence R, running through Quebec, has played a key role in its development. The province has severe winters and warm, humid summers.

People. Quebec's population is concentrated in the S. About 85% are urban dwellers. French-Canadians, most of them descendants of 17th- and 18th-century settlers, constitute 80% of the population; there are separate radio and TV stations and newspapers for French and English. French was made the official language of education, business and government by the French Language Charter of 1977. Roman Catholicism dominates the religious life of the province.

Economy. Quebec has vast resources of raw materials and almost limitless hydroelectric power that are still being developed. Industries include paper, aluminum processing, foodstuffs, textiles, chemicals and metal products. Montreal and Quebec City are the leading manufacturing centers with ships, automobiles, aircraft and railway rolling stock the principal manufactures. The chief mineral products are iron ore, asbestos and copper. Dairying is the most important branch of agriculture, and Quebec's forestry accounts for nearly half of Canada's wood and paper products. The development of iron ore mines in the NE has encouraged development of a steel industry. Construction began in 1979 on the La Grande Complex, on the La Grande R, scheduled to be the world's second-largest hydroelectric project.

History. The first permanent settlement in Quebec dates from 1608 when CHAMPLAIN built a trading post at the site of Quebec City. From then until defeat by the British in the FRENCH AND INDIAN WAR (1754–63), the French controlled the province. Since the advent of British rule in 1763, Quebec's history has been dominated by its effort to preserve its French identity, in which the QUEBEC ACT of 1774 played a significant part. In 1837 a revolt under L. J. Papineau flared up. In 1867 Quebec became a founding province of the Dominion of Canada, with considerable autonomy. In the 1960s a French separatist movement emerged, led by the Parti Quebeçois of René Levesque. But the voters rejected independence, and in 1988 the Canadian parliament recognized Quebec as a "distinct society" and granted additional powers to all provincial governments.

QUEBEC, the capital of QUEBEC province, situated on the St. Lawrence R. Founded in 1608 by CHAMPLAIN, it is Canada's oldest city. Quebec has remained essentially French, and more than 90% of its citizens claim French ancestry. Today it is a leading manufacturing center and transatlantic port. Industries include shipbuilding, paper milling, food processing, machinery and textiles. The city is a major tourist attraction. Pop (city) 166,475; (metro) 600,200.

QUEBEC, Battle of, the most important battle of the FRENCH AND INDIAN WAR, whose outcome transferred control of Canada from France to Britain. French troops under MONTCALM were defending Quebec City. On the night of Sept. 12, 1759, British troops under WOLFE silently scaled the cliffs W of the city to the Plains of Abraham. After a short, bloody battle the French fled. Both Wolfe and Montcalm were mortally wounded.

QUEBEC ACT, passed by the British Parliament in 1774, one of the INTOLERABLE ACTS. It guaranteed the use of the French civil code and established religious freedom for the Roman Catholic Church in Quebec, and extended Quebec's boundary to the Ohio and Mississippi rivers.

QUEBEC CONFERENCE, a conference in

the city of Quebec, Oct. 1864, that laid the foundations of the Canadian Confederation. Representatives from the British provinces in N America produced a series of 72 resolutions outlining a centralized federal union. This became the basis of the BRITISH NORTH AMERICA ACT (1867) which created the Dominion of Canada.

QUEBEC CONFERENCES, two important conferences held in the city of Quebec during WWII. In Aug. 1943 ROOSEVELT and CHURCHILL met with the Canadian prime minister and the Chinese foreign minister to make arrangements for operations in the Far East and for the Allied invasion of Europe. In Sept. 1944 Roosevelt and Churchill met again to discuss broad military strategy.

QUECHUA, S American Indians, once part of the INCA empire and now living mostly as peasants in the Andean highlands from Colombia to N Chile. Quechua is also the name of the family to which the official language of the Incas belonged, and some 28 languages of the family are still spoken.

QUEEN, Ellery, pen-name and fictional hero of detective writers Frederic Dannay (1905–1982) and Manfred B. Lee (1905–1972). Their successful *The Roman Hat Mystery* (1929) was followed by over 100 other novels characterized by complexity of plot. *Ellery Queen's Mystery Magazine* was founded in 1941.

QUEEN ANNE'S WAR. See FRENCH AND INDIAN WARS.

QUEENSBERRY RULES, the basic rules of modern BOXING, drawn up in 1865 under the auspices of the 8th Marquess of Queensberry, supplanting the old London prize-ring rules. Innovations included the use of padded gloves instead of bare fists, a 10-second count to determine a knockout, and the division of the bout into rounds with intermissions.

QUEENSTON HEIGHTS, Battle of, battle in the WAR OF 1812, at Queenston Heights, S Ontario, near Niagara Falls (Oct. 13, 1812). Though the British commander, Sir Isaac Brock, was killed, the US invaders, led by Stephen Van Rensselaer, were successfully repulsed.

QUENEAU, Raymond (1903–1976), French novelist and man of letters. His most widely known books are *Exercises de Style* (1947), in which one incident is presented in 99 different literary styles, and the comic *Zazie* (1959).

QUESNAY, François (1694–1774), French economist and a leader of the PHYSIOCRATS. Although trained in medicine—he was physician to Louis XV—his fame rests on his essays in political economy, which first began to appear in 1756 in DIDEROT's *Encyclopédie,* and on his *Economic Table* (1758), which influenced Adam SMITH.

QUETZALCOATL, the plumed serpent, ancient Mexican god identified with the morning and evening star. He is said to have ruled the pre-Aztec TOLTEC empire and to have invented books and the calendar. Whether he was an historical chieftain or merely mythological is not certain. MONTEZUMA II welcomed CORTÉS, believing him to be descended from the god.

QUEVEDO Y VILLEGAS, Francisco Gómez de (1580–1645), great Spanish satirist, poet and prose writer. Master of the *conceptismo* style of terse and arresting intellectual conceits, he is best known for *The Life of a Swindler* (1626), a parody of the PICARESQUE NOVEL, and *Visions* (1627), a bitter, fantastic view of the inhabitants of hell.

QUEZON, Manuel Luis (1878–1944), Filipino statesman who played a leading role in the Philippine independence movement before becoming the first president of the Philippine Commonwealth (1935). His presidency, continued (after Japanese invasion) from 1942 in the US, was marked by efforts to improve conditions for the poor.

QUICHÉ INDIANS, largest Guatemalan Indian group, now numbering about 340,000, found mainly in the W highlands. Of Mayan linguistic stock, they have, since their conquest in 1524 by the Spanish Pedro de Alvarado, colorfully adapted many Western customs and religious traditions to their own.

QUICKSAND, sand saturated with water to form a sand-water suspension possessing the characteristics of a liquid. Quicksands may form at rivermouths or on sandflats, and are dangerous as they appear identical to adjacent SAND. In fact, the DENSITY of the suspension is less than that of the human body so that, if a person does not struggle, he may escape being engulfed.

QUIDDE, Ludwig (1858–1941), German writer and pacifist politician who shared with Ferdinand Buisson the 1927 Nobel Peace Prize.

QUIDS, early US political faction, led by John RANDOLPH, of extreme protagonists of states' rights. Convinced that Thomas JEFFERSON and James MADISON had become virtual nationalists, they attempted to block Madison's Democratic-Republican presidential nomination in 1808.

QUIETISM, mystical religious movement originated in 17th-century Spain by Miguel de Molinos (1640–c1697), which later spread to France as the less extreme

Semiquietism. Molinos advocated a wholly passive mysticism. After papal condemnations, Quietism (1687) and Semiquietism (1699) collapsed.

QUIMBY, Phineas Parkhurst (1802–1866), US pioneer of mental healing, an early user of suggestion as a therapy. A strong influence on Mary Baker EDDY, he is regarded as a father of the New Thought movement.

QUINCY, Josiah (1772–1864), US politician, educator and author. Elected to Congress in 1804, he resigned in 1813 after opposing the WAR of 1812. He later distinguished himself as a reforming mayor of Boston (1823–28) and as president of HARVARD UNIVERSITY (1829–45).

QUINE, Willard Van Orman (1908–), US philosopher and logician, best known for his rejection of such long-standing philosophical claims as that analytic ("self-evident") statements are fundamentally distinguishable from synthetic (observational) statements, and that the concept of synonymy (sameness of meaning) can be exemplified.

QUININE, substance derived from CINCHONA bark from South America, long used in treating a variety of ailments. It was preeminent in early treatment of MALARIA until the 1930s, when atabrine was introduced; after this more suitable quinine derivatives such as chloroquine were synthesized. Quinine is also a mild analgesic and may prevent cramps and suppress heart rhythm disorders. Now rarely used, its side effects include vomiting, deafness, vertigo and vision disturbance.

QUINSY, acute complication of TONSILLITIS in which ABSCESS formation causes spasm of the adjacent jaw muscles, FEVER and severe pain. Incision and drainage of the PUS produce rapid relief, though ANTIBIOTICS are helpful and the TONSILS should be excised later.

QUINTILIAN (Marcus Fabius Quintilianus; c35 AD–c96 AD), Roman rhetoric teacher, whose famous 12-book *Institutio Oratoria*, covering rhetorical techniques, educational theory, literary criticism and morality, deeply influenced Renaissance culture.

QUIRINO, Elpídio (1890–1956), Filipino statesman. Political aide to Manuel QUEZON for many years prior to WWII, he became an underground leader during the Japanese occupation. He was president of the Philippine republic 1948–54.

QUISLING, Vidkun Abraham Lauritz (1887–1945), Norwegian fascist leader who assisted the German invasion of Norway (1940) and was afterward appointed by

HITLER premier of Norway's puppet government (1942–45). He was executed for treason. His name has come to mean "traitor."

QUITO, capital and second largest city of Ecuador and oldest capital in S America, is located just S of the equator at the foot of the Pichincha volcano, at an altitude of 9,350ft. Seized from the INCAS by a Spanish conquistador in 1534, it is famous for its Spanish colonial architecture. It has minor industries. Pop 1,003,875.

QUMRAN, village on the NW shore of the Dead Sea, on the West Bank of Jordan, near the caves where the DEAD SEA SCROLLS were found (1947). Built by ESSENES (c130–c110 BC), it was destroyed by an earthquake (31 BC), rebuilt, and destroyed again by the Romans (68 AD).

18th letter of the alphabet, corresponding to Greek *rho* and Semitic *rēsh* ("head"). Its present capital form comes from classical Latin; the small letter derives from Carolingian script.

RA, sun god of ancient Egypt, one of the most important gods of the pantheon. From the 6th dynasty all pharaohs claimed descent from Ra. He was commonly represented as a falcon or falcon-headed figure with the solar disk on his head.

RABBI (Hebrew: my master, or my teacher), the leader of a Jewish religious congregation with the role of spiritual leader, scholar, teacher and interpreter of Jewish law. The term originated in Palestine, meaning merely religious teacher, after the return from exile and destruction of the hereditary priesthood, the more official role of a rabbi developing from the Middle Ages.

RABBITS, herbivorous members of the Lagomorpha, usually with long ears and a white scut for a tail. Best known is the European rabbit *Oryctolagus cuniculus*. These live in discrete social groups in colonial burrows. Territory is defended by all members of the group and within the group there is distinct dominance ranking. It attains maturity at three months and can breed every month thereafter. In many areas they have reached plague proportions. Numbers have been reduced in Australia and Europe by introducing myxomatosis.

RABELAIS, François (1494?–1553), French monk, doctor and humanist author of *Gargantua and Pantagruel* (four books 1532–52, arguably a fifth 1564). This exuberant mixture of popular anecdote, bawdry and huge erudition with vastly inventive language and broad satire of tyrants and bigots recounts two giants' quest for the secret of life.

RABI, Isidor Isaac (1898–1988), Austrian-born US physicist whose discovery of new ways of measuring the magnetic properties of ATOMS and MOLECULES both paved the way for the development of the maser and the ATOMIC CLOCK and earned him the 1944 Nobel Prize for Physics.

RABIES, or **hydrophobia,** fatal VIRUS disease resulting from the bite of an infected animal, usually a dog. HEADACHE, FEVER, and an overwhelming fear, especially of water, are early symptoms following an INCUBATION period of 3–6 weeks; PARALYSIS, spasm of muscles of swallowing, respiratory paralysis, DELIRIUM, CONVULSIONS and COMA due to an ENCEPHALITIS follow. Wound cleansing, antirabies vaccine and hyperimmune serum must be instituted early in confirmed cases to prevent the onset of these symptoms. Fluid replacement and respiratory support may help, but survival is rare if symptoms appear. Infected animals must be destroyed.

RABIN, Yitzhak (1922–   ), Israeli soldier and Labour Party politician. Chief of staff in the Six-Day War (1967), he was prime minister 1974–77 and defense minister in the national unity government that took office in 1984. He took a hard line against the Palestinian uprising in 1988.

RACCOONS, probably the best known of the American mammals, stout, bear-like animals, 600mm to 1m (2.0–3.3ft) long with a distinctive black mask and five to eight black bands on the bushy tail. They live in trees, alone or in small family groups, descending at night to forage for crayfish, frogs and fish in shallow pools. Family: Procyonidae.

RACE, within a species, a subgroup most of whose members have sufficiently different physical characteristics from those exhibited by most members of another subgroup for it to be considered as a distinct entity. In particular the term is used with respect to the human species, *Homo sapiens*, the three most commonly distinguished races being CAUCASOID, MONGOLOID and NEGROID. However, in practice it is impossible to make unambiguous distinctions between races: a classification by color would yield a quite different result to one by blood-group. According to DARWIN's theories of EVOLUTION, races arise when different groups encounter different environmental situations. Over generations, their physical characteristics evolve until each group as a whole is physically quite different from its parent stock. Should the isolation of the group continue long enough, and the environment be different enough, the divergent race will eventually become a distinct species, unable to mate with the species from which it originally sprang. This has obviously not happened in the case of man, whose races may interbreed successfully and, in many cases, advantageously. It is not known when man became racially differentiated, but certainly it was at a very early stage in his evolution (see PREHISTORIC MAN).

RACHEL (Elisa Félix; 1821–1858), French actress, acclaimed throughout Europe from the 1830s. She died of tuberculosis.

RACHMANINOV, Sergei Vasilyevich (1873–1943), Russian composer and virtuoso pianist. After a successful career in Russia he left in 1917, settling in Switzerland (until 1935) and then the US. His extensive output of piano music, symphonies, songs and choral music includes such popular works as the *Second Piano Concerto* (1901).

RACINE, Jean Baptiste (1639–1699), greatest of French tragic dramatists. After a JANSENIST education at Port Royal schools, he surpassed his rival CORNEILLE with seven tragedies, from *Andromaque* (1667) and *Britannicus* (1669) to *Phèdre* (1677), possibly his masterpiece. His greatness lies in the beauty of his verse, expressing both powerful and subtle emotions, and the creation of tragic suspense in a classically restrained form.

RACING. See AUTOMOBILE RACING; HORSE RACING.

RACISM, the theory that some races are inherently superior to others. The concept of racism in the early 19th century was really an offshoot of NATIONALISM, and emphasis was placed on the development of individual cultures. But at the same time a systematic study of human types was revealing the existence of races distinguished by physical characteristics. Despite the theories of LINNAEUS and BLUMENBACH that environment rather than heredity molded intellectual development, many theorists associated culture with race, and assumed white superiority. Guided by such thinkers as Count de Gobineau (1816–82), a concept of "tribal nationalism" began to appear. It was used to justify IMPERIALISM, the imposition of colonial status on backward peoples, and finally the concept of the "master race" fostered by the NAZIS. The mass exterminations before and during WWII, together with advances in ANTHROPOLOGY, discredited racism as a tenable intellectual doctrine. (See also RACE.)

RACKHAM, Arthur (1867–1939), English artist best known for his fanciful, delicately-colored illustrations for children's books such as *Grimm's Fairy Tales* (1900), *Peter Pan* (1906) and *A Wonder Book* (1922).

RADAR (*radio detection and ranging*), system that detects long-range objects and determines their positions by measuring the time taken for RADIO waves to travel to the objects, be reflected and return. Radar is used for NAVIGATION, air control, fire control, storm detection, in radar astronomy and for catching speeding drivers. It developed out of experiments in the 1920s measuring the distance to the IONOSPHERE by radio pulses. R. A. WATSON-WATT showed that the technique could be applied to detecting aircraft, and from 1935 Britain installed a series of radar stations which were a major factor in winning the Battle of Britain in WWII. From 1940 the UK and the US collaborated to develop radar. There are two main types of radar: **continuous-wave radar**, which transmits continuously, the frequency being varied sinusoidally, and detects the signals received by their instantaneously different frequency; and the more common **pulsed radar**. This latter has a highly directional antenna which scans the area systematically or tracks an object. A cavity magnetron or klystron emits pulses, typically 400 per second, $1\mu s$ across and at a frequency of 3GHz. A duplexer switches the antenna automatically from transmitter to receiver and back as appropriate. The receiver converts the echo pulses to an intermediate frequency of about 30MHz, and they are then amplified, converted to a video signal, and displayed on a CATHODE-RAY TUBE. A synchronizer measures the time-lag between transmission and reception, and this is represented by the position of the pulse on the screen. Electronic processing can reduce noise by adding together successive pulses so that the noise tends to cancel out. Over-the-horizon radar is possible when atmospheric conditions form a "duct" through which the waves travel. Various display modes are used: commonest is the plan-position indicator (PPI),

showing horizontal position in polar coordinates. (See also LORAN.)

RADCLIFFE, Ann (born Ann Ward; 1764–1823), English novelist remembered for her GOTHIC NOVELS, notably *The Mysteries of Udolpho* (1794) and *The Italian* (1797).

RADCLIFFE-BROWN, Alfred Reginald (1881–1955), British anthropologist who wrote important studies of kinship and social organization. His *Andaman Islanders* (1922; rev. 1948) was a pioneering work in structural anthropology.

RADEK, Karl Bernardovich (born Karl Sobelsohn; 1885–1939?), Russian communist politician close to LENIN during the 1917 revolution. Dismissed from the party as a TROTSKY supporter in 1927, readmitted 1930, he fell victim to STALIN'S purges in 1937 and was sent to prison where, it is believed, he died.

RADETZKY, Joseph, Graf Radetzky de Radetz (1766–1858), Austrian field marshal, victorious against CHARLES ALBERT of Sardinia at Custozza (1848) and Novara (1849). Johann Strauss composed the "Radetzky March" in his honor.

RADHAKRISHNAN, Sarvepalli (1888–1975), Indian philosopher and statesman. He taught philosophy at Oxford (1936–52), interpreting the Indian religious and intellectual tradition. He was president of India 1962–67.

RADIATION, the emission and propagation through space of ELECTROMAGNETIC RADIATION or SUBATOMIC PARTICLES. Exposure to X-RAYS and gamma rays is measured in ROENTGEN units; absorbed dose of any high-energy radiation in rads.

RADIATION SICKNESS, malaise, nausea, loss of appetite and vomiting occurring several hours after exposure to ionizing RADIATION in large doses. This occurs as an industrial or war hazard, or more commonly following RADIATION THERAPY for CANCER, LYMPHOMA or LEUKEMIA. Large doses of radiation may cause bone marrow depression with anemia, agranulocytosis and bleeding, or gastrointestinal disturbance with distension and bloody DIARRHEA. Skin erythema and ulceration, lung fibrosis, nephritis and premature arteriosclerosis may follow radiation and there is a risk of malignancy developing.

RADIATION THERAPY, use of ionizing RADIATION, as rays from an outside source or from radium or other radioactive metal implants, in treatment of malignant DISEASE—CANCER, LYMPHOMA and LEUKEMIA. The principle is that rapidly dividing TUMOR cells are more sensitive to the destructive effects of radiation on NUCLEIC

ACIDS and are therefore damaged by doses that are relatively harmless to normal tissues. Certain types of malignancy indeed respond to radiation therapy but RADIATION SICKNESS may also occur.

RADICAL REPUBLICANS, a militant group of the Republican Party active after the US Civil War, putting pressure on LINCOLN and later Andrew JOHNSON to ensure full civil rights for the Southern blacks. Their most important achievement was the RECONSTRUCTION Act (1867).

RADIO, the communication of information between distant points using radio waves, ELECTROMAGNETIC RADIATION of wavelength between 1mm and 100km. Radio waves are also described in terms of their frequency—measured in hertz (Hz) and found by dividing the velocity of the waves (about 300Mm/s) by their wavelength. Radio communications systems link transmitting stations with receiving stations. In a transmitting station a piezoelectric OSCILLATOR is used to generate a steady radio-frequency (RF) "carrier" wave. This is amplified and "modulated" with a signal carrying the information (see INFORMATION THEORY) to be communicated. The simplest method of modulation is to pulse (switch on and off) the carrier with a signal in, say, MORSE CODE, but speech and music, entering the modulator as an audiofrequency (AF) signal from tape or a MICROPHONE, is made to interact with the carrier so that the shape of the audio wave determines either the amplitude of the carrier wave (amplitude modulation—AM) or its frequency within a small band on either side of the original carrier frequency (frequency modulation—FM). The modulated RF signal is then amplified (see AMPLIFIER) to a high power and radiated from an ANTENNA. At the receiving station, another antenna picks up a minute fraction of the energy radiated from the transmitter together with some background NOISE. This RF signal is amplified and the original audio signal is recovered (demodulation or detection). Detection and amplification often involve many stages including FEEDBACK and intermediate frequency (IF) circuits. A radio receiver must of course be able to discriminate between all the different signals acting at any one time on its antenna. This is accomplished with a tuning circuit which allows only the desired frequency to pass to the detector (see also ELECTRONICS). In point-to-point radio communications most stations can both transmit and receive messages but in radio broadcasting a central transmitter broadcasts program sequences to a multitude of individual receivers. Programs are often produced centrally and distributed to a "network" of local broadcasting stations by wire or MICROWAVE link. Because there are potentially so many users of radio communications—aircraft, ships, police and amateur "hams" as well as broadcasting services—the use of the RF portion of the electromagnetic SPECTRUM is strictly controlled to prevent unwanted INTERFERENCE between signals having adjacent carrier frequencies. The International Telecommunication Union (ITU) and national agencies such as the US FEDERAL COMMUNICATIONS COMMISSION (FCC) divide the RF spectrum into bands which they allocate to the various users. Public broadcasting in the US uses MF frequencies between 535kHz and 1605kHz (AM) and VHF bands between 88MHz and 108MHz (FM). VHF reception, though limited to line-of-sight transmissions, offers much higher fidelity of transmission (see HIGH-FIDELITY) and much greater freedom from interference. International broadcasting and local transmissions in other countries frequently use other frequencies in the LF, MF and HF (short wave) bands.

The Development of Radio. The existence of radio waves was first predicted by James Clerk MAXWELL in the 1860s but it was not until 1887 that Heinrich HERTZ succeeded in producing them experimentally. "Wireless" telegraphy was first demonstrated by Sir Oliver LODGE in 1894 and MARCONI made the first trans-Atlantic transmission in 1901. Voice transmission was first achieved in 1900 but transmitter and amplifier powers were restricted before the advent of Lee DE FOREST'S triode electron tube in 1906. Only the development of the TRANSISTOR after 1948 has had as great an impact on radio technology. Commercial broadcasting began in the US in 1920.

RADIO, Amateur, a hobby practiced throughout the world by thousands of enthusiasts, or "hams," who communicate with one another on short-wave radio, by "phone" (voice) or by using International MORSE CODE. Permitted amateur bands include 160, 80, 40, 20, 15 and 10 meters. In the US, the various grades of license may be obtained by passing tests of progressively greater difficulty. CB radio (from "Citizens' Band") is a less structured, more informal kind of "ham" radio which became popular in the US in the late 1970s and resulted in the establishment of a vast network of amateur radio operators.

RADIOACTIVITY, the spontaneous disintegration of certain unstable nuclei, accompanied by the emission of alpha particles (weakly penetrating HELIUM nuclei), beta rays (more penetrating streams of ELECTRONS) or gamma rays (ELECTROMAGNETIC RADIATION capable of penetrating up to 100mm of LEAD). In 1896, BECQUEREL noticed the spontaneous emission of ENERGY from URANIUM compounds (particularly PITCHBLENDE). The intensity of the effect depended on the amount of uranium present, suggesting that it involved individual atoms. The CURIES discovered further radioactive substances such as thorium and RADIUM, and about 40 natural radioactive substances are now known. Their rates of decay are unaffected by chemical changes, pressure, temperature or electromagnetic fields, and each nuclide (nucleus of a particular ISOTOPE) has a characteristic decay constant or HALF-LIFE. RUTHERFORD and Frederick Soddy (1877–1956) suggested in 1902 that a radioactive nuclide decays to a further radioactive nuclide, a series of transformations taking place which ends with the formation of a stable "daughter" nucleus. It is now known that for radioactive elements of high ATOMIC WEIGHT, three decay series (the thorium, actinium and uranium series) exist. As well as the natural radioactive elements, a large number of induced radioactive nuclides have been formed by nuclear reactions taking place in ACCELERATORS or NUCLEAR REACTORS (see also RADIOISOTOPES). Some of these are members of the three natural radioactive series. Various types of radioactivity are known, but beta emission is the most common, normally caused by the decay of a NEUTRON, giving a PROTON, an electron and an antineutrino (see SUBATOMIC PARTICLES). This results in a unit change of atomic number (see ATOM) and no change in mass number. Heavier nuclides often decay to a daughter nucleus with atomic number two less and mass number four less, emitting an alpha particle. If an excited daughter nucleus is formed, gamma-ray emission may accompany both alpha and beta decay. Because the ionizing radiations emitted by radioactive materials are physiologically harmful, special precautions must be taken in handling them.

RADIO ASTRONOMY, the study of the ELECTROMAGNETIC RADIATION emitted or reflected by celestial objects in the approximate wavelength range 1mm–30m, usually by use of a RADIO TELESCOPE. The science was initiated accidentally in 1932 by Karl Jansky, who found an interference in a telephone system he was testing: the source proved to be the MILKY WAY. In 1937 an American, Grote Reber, built a 9.5m radio telescope in his back yard and scanned the sky at a wavelength around 2m. After WWII the science began in earnest. Investigation of the sky revealed that clouds of hydrogen gas in the Milky Way were radio sources, and mapping of these confirmed our galaxy's spiral form (see GALAXY).

The sky is very different for the radio astronomer than for the astronomer. Bright stars are not radio objects (our sun is one solely because it is so close), while many radio objects are optically undetectable. Radio objects include QUASARS, PULSARS, supernova remnants (e.g., the Crab Nebula) and other galaxies. The work of Martin Ryle in the 1960s and 1970s has enabled radio galaxies that are possibly at the farthest extremities of the universe to be mapped. The universe also has an inherent radio "background noise" (see COSMOLOGY).

RADIOCARBON   DATING.   See RADIOISOTOPE DATING.

RADIOCHEMISTRY, the use of RADIOISOTOPES in chemistry, especially in studies involving chemical ANALYSIS, where radioisotopes provide a powerful and sensitive tool. Tracer techniques, in which a particular atom in a molecule is "labeled" by replacement with a radioisotope, are used to study reaction rates and mechanisms.

RADIOISOTOPE, radioactive ISOTOPE of an element. A few elements, such as RADIUM or URANIUM, have naturally occurring radioisotopes, but because of their usefulness in science and industry, a large number of radioisotopes are produced artificially. This is done by irradiation of stable isotopes with PHOTONS, or with particles such as NEUTRONS in an ACCELERATOR or NUCLEAR REACTOR. Radioisotopes with a wide range of HALF-LIVES and activities are available by these means. Because radioisotopes behave chemically and biologically in a very similar way to stable isotopes, and their radiation can easily be monitored even in very small amounts, they are used to "label" particular atoms or groups in studying chemical reaction mechanisms and to "trace" the course of particular components in various physiological processes. The radiation emitted by radioisotopes may also be utilized directly for treating diseased areas of the body (see RADIATION THERAPY), sterilizing foodstuffs or controlling insect pests.

RADIOISOTOPE DATING, means of dating materials from the geological past in terms of the radioisotopes they contain. All radioisotopes are members of various radioactive decay series (see RADIOACTIVITY), whose half-lives (see HALF-LIFE) are known, so that the proportion of the original isotope in the series compared to the percentage of later entrants in the series in a given sample indicates the age of that sample. Several such series are available for investigation by scientists, perhaps the best known of which is the CARBON-14 series used in archaeology and for other relatively recent geological time spans. Because carbon-14 decays fairly rapidly, the method is usually limited to dating the past 50,000 years. Other decay series used for much more ancient times include the potassium-argon method, the rubidium-strontium method, the ionium-thorium method, and various methods involving series that end in the element LEAD.

RADIOLARIANS, single-celled animals possessing an internal skeleton, usually siliceous but sometimes of strontium sulfate. Members of the Sarcodine class of PROTOZOA, all are marine and are abundant in PLANKTON. The skeletons sink after death and build up into thick sediments.

RADIOLOGY, the use of RADIOACTIVITY, gamma rays and X-RAYS in MEDICINE, particularly in diagnosis but also in treatment. (See also RADIATION THERAPY.)

RADIOSONDE, meteorological instrument package attached to a small BALLOON capable of reaching the earth's upper ATMOSPHERE. The instruments measure the TEMPERATURE, PRESSURE and HUMIDITY of the atmosphere at various altitudes, the data being relayed back to earth via a RADIO transmitter. Radiosondes provide a cheap and reliable method of getting information for WEATHER FORECASTING AND CONTROL.

RADIO TELESCOPE, the basic instrument of RADIO ASTRONOMY. The receiving part of the equipment consists of a large parabola, the big dish, which operates on the same principle as the parabolic mirror of a reflecting TELESCOPE. The signals that it receives are then amplified and examined. In practice, it is possible to build radio telescopes effectively far larger than any possible dish by using several connected dishes; this is known as an array.

RADISHCHEV, Aleksandr Nikolayevich (1749–1802), Russian aristocrat who was exiled to Siberia for attacking serfdom in his *Journey from St. Petersburg to Moscow* (1790).

RADISSON, Pierre Esprit (c1636–c1710), French fur trader who worked for both French and British in the exploration of

parts of present-day Minn. and Wis. His reports of the wealth of furs obtainable prompted the creation of the HUDSON'S BAY COMPANY.

RADIUM (Ra), radioactive alkaline-earth METAL similar to BARIUM, isolated from PITCHBLENDE by Marie CURIE in 1898. It has white salts which turn black as the radium decays, and which emit a blue glow due to ionization of the air by radiation. It has four natural ISOTOPES, the commonest being Ra^{226} with HALF-LIFE 1,622 years. Radium is used in industrial and medical radiography. AW 226.0, mp 700°C, bp 1140°C, sg 5.

RADON, odorless radioactive gas produced by the natural decay of radium, which in turn comes from the decay of uranium in soil and rock. The gas normally dissipates harmlessly into the air, but it can accumulate in buildings after seeping in through cracks in the foundation or drain pipes. The amount of radon emission varies with the amount of uranium in the soil. The gas is considered a leading environmental problem. In 1988 the National Academy of Sciences reported that it may be responsible for 13,000 lung-cancer deaths annually in the US.

RAEDER, Erich (1876–1960), German admiral, commander in chief of the German Navy 1928–43. For his aggressive naval strategy, as in the invasions of Denmark and Norway, he was convicted as a war criminal in 1946 (released 1955).

RAFFLES, Sir Thomas Stamford (1781–1826), British colonial administrator who founded Singapore (1819). He persuaded the British government to seize Java, which he governed from 1811 to 1815. His career was marked by his liberalism, especially in his opposition to slavery.

RAGLAN, Fitzroy James Henry Somerset, 1st Baron (1788–1855), commander of British forces in the CRIMEAN WAR. He was widely criticized for the failure of the siege of Sevastopol (1854–55) and for the Earl of CARDIGAN's disastrous charge of the light brigade (1854).

RAGTIME, a style of piano playing in which the left hand provides harmony and a firm beat, while the right hand plays the melody, usually syncopated. Famous exponents of the style, which was the immediate predecessor of JAZZ, are Scott JOPLIN and "Jelly-Roll" Morton.

RAHMAN, Mujibur (called Sheikh Mujib; 1920–1975), first premier (1972–74) and then president (1974–75) of BANGLADESH. He was secretary and president of the Awami League, whose object was autonomy for E Pakistan. He rebuilt Bangladesh following the war of independence (1971), but was assassinated after assuming dictatorial powers.

RAHNER, Karl (1904–1984), German Roman Catholic theologian. His liberal views influenced LIBERATION THEOLOGY.

RAHV, Philip (1908–1973), Russian-born US literary critic and editor. As co-editor of the *Partisan Review* (1934–69), he fostered modernism and promoted the careers of such writers as Saul BELLOW, Robert LOWELL and Karl SHAPIRO. As a critic, Rahv believed that literature must be rooted in history and ideas. His works include *Image and Idea* (1949), *The Myth and the Powerhouse* (1965) and *Essays on Literature and Politics: 1932–1972* (1978).

RAILROAD, land transportation system in which cars with flanged steel wheels run on tracks of two parallel steel rails. From their beginning railroads provided reliable, economical transport for freight and passengers; they promoted the Industrial Revolution and have been vital to continued economic growth ever since, especially in developing countries. Railroads are intrinsically economical in their use of energy because the rolling friction of wheel on rail is very low. However, fixed costs of maintenance are high, so high traffic volume is needed. This, together with rising competition and overmanning, has led to the closure of many minor lines in the US and Europe, though elsewhere many new lines are still being built. Maintenance, signalling and many other functions are now highly automated.

Railroads developed out of the small mining tracks or tramways built in the UK and Europe from the mid-16th century. They used gravity or horse power, and the cars generally ran on flanged rails or plateways. These were hard to switch, however, and the system of flanged wheels on plain rails eventually predominated. The first public freight railroad was the Surrey Iron Railway (1801). The modern era of mechanized traction began with TREVI-THICK's steam locomotive "New Castle" (1804) (see also STEAM ENGINE). Early locomotives ran on toothed racks to prevent slipping, but in 1813 this was found to be unnecessary. The first public railroad to use locomotives and to carry passengers was the Stockton and Darlington Railway (1825). The boom began when the Liverpool and Manchester Railway opened in 1830 using George STEPHENSON's "Rocket," a much superior and more reliable locomotive. Railroads spread rapidly in Britain, Europe and the US. The first US railroad was the Baltimore and Ohio (1830). The rails were laid on wooden (later also concrete) crossties or sleepers, and were joined by fishplates to allow for thermal expansion. Continuous welded rails are now generally used. Track gauges were at first varied, but the "standard gauge" of 4ft 8½in (1.435m) soon predominated. Railroads must be built with shallow curves and gentle gradients, using bridges, embankments, cuttings and tunnels as necessary.

The sharp increases in oil prices, beginning in the early 1970s, appeared to give railroads a new lease on life. However, the popularity of railroads continued to be limited mostly to commuter lines, and the potential for hauling freight was not fully realized. In the US the national AMTRAK system survived with the aid of federal subsidies. (See also SUBWAY.)

RAIMU (Jules Muraire; 1883–1946), French comic actor on stage and screen.

RAIN, water drops falling through the atmosphere; the chief form of precipitation. Raindrops range in size up to 4mm in diameter; if they are smaller than 0.5mm the rain is called drizzle. The quantity of rainfall (independent of the drop size) is measured by a **rain gauge,** an open-top vessel which collects the rain, calibrated in millimeters or inches and so giving a reading independent of the area on which the rain falls. Light rain is less than 0.1in/hr, moderate rain up to 0.3in/hr; and heavy rain more than 0.3in/hr. Rain may result from the melting of snow or hail, as it falls, but is commonly formed by direct condensation. When a parcel of warm air rises, it expands approximately adiabatically, cooling about 1K/325ft. Thus its relative HUMIDITY rises until it reaches saturation, when the water vapor begins to condense as droplets, forming CLOUDS. These droplets may coalesce into raindrops, chiefly through turbulence and nucleation by ice particles or by cloud seeding. Moist air may be lifted by CONVECTION, producing **convective rainfall;** by forced ascent of air as it crosses a mountain range, producing **orographic rainfall;** and by the forces within CYCLONES, producing **cyclonic rainfall.** (See also GROUNDWATER; HYDROLOGIC CYCLE; METEOROLOGY; MONSOON.)

RAINBOW, arch of concentric spectrally colored rings seen in the sky by an observer looking at rain, mist or spray with his back to the sun. The colors are produced by sunlight's being refracted and totally internally reflected (see REFRACTION) by spherical droplets of water. The primary rainbow, with red on the outside and violet inside, results from one total internal reflection. Sometimes a dimmer secondary rainbow with reversed colors is seen, arising from a second total internal reflection.

RAINIER, Mount, extinct volcano in the Cascade Range and highest peak in Wash., 14,410ft high, lying 40mi SE of Tacoma in Mt Rainier National Park. The fine scenery and skiing slopes attract many tourists.

RAIS, or Retz, Gilles de (1404–1440), baron and marshal of France, satanist, noted patron of the arts and soldier, who served with JOAN OF ARC at the relief of Orléans, 1429. He was executed for the abduction and murder of 140 children.

RAISIN RIVER, Battle of, engagement in 1813 during the WAR OF 1812, in which US troops under General James Winchester surrendered to a British and Indian force near Frenchtown (Monroe, Mich.). The US wounded—though protection had been promised by the British—were massacred by the Indians.

RAJA or RAJAH (from Sanskrit *rājan,* king), an Indian or Malay prince (extended to other men of rank during British rule). Higher-ranking princes were styled *maharajas* (or maharajahs). A raja's wife is a *rani.*

RAJPUTS (Sanskrit: kings' sons), military and landowning caste mostly of the Rajasthan (now Rajputana) region, India. Their origins date back nearly 1,500 years, when successive waves of invaders were absorbed into Indian society. Their influence in N and central India has waxed and waned, being at times considerable, and since INDIA's independence (1947) has steadily declined.

RAKOCZY, Francis II (1676–1735), prince of Transylvania who led a Hungarian rising against the Hapsburg Empire. Initially successful, he was elected prince in 1704, but after several crushing defeats he left the country in 1711 and died in exile in Turkey.

RAKOSI, Mátyás (1892–1971), Hungarian politician, secretary general of the Hungarian Communist Party (1945–56) and prime minister (1952–53, 1955–56). A Stalinist, he fled to Russia in the 1956 Hungarian revolution.

RALEIGH or RALEGH, Sir Walter (1554?–1618), English adventurer and poet, a favorite of Queen Elizabeth I. His efforts to organize colonization of the New World resulted in the tragedy of the LOST COLONY. In 1589 he left court and consolidated his friendship with SPENSER, whose *Faerie Queene* was written partly under Raleigh's patronage. Returning he distinguished himself in raids at Cadiz (1596) and the Azores (1597). James I imprisoned him in the Tower of London 1603–16, where he wrote poetry and his uncompleted *History of the World.* After two years' freedom he was executed under the original treason charge.

RAMA, name of seven kings of Thailand (Siam), reigning consecutively since 1782. Their line was founded by the general Chao P'ya Chakri (reigned 1782–1809), who restored order after a Burmese invasion, took the name of the Hindu hero RAMA and established Bangkok as his capital. Following a coup d'état in 1932, the monarchy became constitutional.

RAMA, in N India, the most popular incarnation of the Hindu god VISHNU; he was the son of King Dasaratha of Ayodha, and his legend, narrated in the RAMAYANA, portrays an heroic figure, dedicated more to ridding the earth of evildoers than to conveying spiritual instruction.

RAMADAN, ninth month of the Muslim calendar, during which the revelation of the KORAN to MOHAMMED is commemorated by abstention from food, drink and other bodily pleasures between sunrise and sunset.

RAMAKRISHNA PARAMAHANSA (1836–1886), Indian saint whose teachings, now carried all over the world by the Ramakrishna Mission (founded in Calcutta in 1897), emphasize the unity of all religions and place equal value on social service, worship and meditation. His followers consider him to have been an incarnation of God.

RAMAN, Sir Chandrasekhara Venkata (1888–1970), Indian physicist awarded the 1930 Nobel Prize for Physics for his discovery of the Raman Effect: when molecules are exposed to a beam of INFRARED RADIATION, light scattered by the molecules contains frequencies that differ from that of the beam by amounts characteristic of the molecules. This is the basis for Raman SPECTROSCOPY.

RAMAYANA, major Hindu epic poem, composed in Sanskrit in about the 3rd century BC, concerning the war waged by the legendary hero Rama against Ravān, the demon-king of Lanka, who was terrorizing the earth. Helped by Hanuman, king of the monkeys, Rama eventually rescues his wife, Sita, whom Ravān had abducted, and slays the demon, enabling the righteous once more to live in peace.

RAMEAU, Jean Philippe (1683–1764), French composer and one of the founders of modern harmonic theory. He achieved recognition with his *Treatise on Harmony* (1722), and in Paris became a celebrated teacher and composer of some 30 operas, *Hippolyte et Aricie* (1733) being the first.

RAMPAL, Jean-Pierre (1922–   ),

French flutist. A virtuoso known for his pure luxuriant tone, he revived interest in the flute as a solo instrument.

RAMSAY, Sir William (1852–1916), British chemist awarded the 1904 Nobel Prize for Chemistry for his discovery, prompted by a suggestion from Lord Rayleigh (1892), of all the NOBLE GASES, including (with Frederick Soddy) HELIUM, although it had been earlier detected in the solar spectrum (1868).

RAMSES II (reigned c1304–1237 BC), "Ramses the Great," Egyptian pharaoh who built hundreds of temples and monuments, probably including ABU SIMBEL and the columned hall at Karnak. He campaigned against the HITTITES, and celebrated a battle at Kadesh (1300 BC) on many of his monuments, but was eventually obliged to make peace (c1283 BC). His long reign marked a high point in Egyptian prosperity.

RAMSEY, Arthur Michael (1904–   ), British clergyman, archbishop of Canterbury (1961–74).

RAMUS, Petrus (1515–1572), French humanist and philosopher whose logic was influential among Protestant thinkers, particularly at Cambridge in England where it contributed to the emergence of the scientific spirit.

RANCE, Armand Jean Le Bouthillier de (1626–1700), French monk, abbot of La Trappe, Normandy (1664–95), who founded the TRAPPISTS, a reformed branch of the Roman Catholic Cistercian Order. He was an extreme ascetic, and his rule emphasized silence, prayer, fasting and manual labor.

RAND, Ayn (1905–1982), Russian-born US writer. Her "objectivist" philosophy, individualistic, egoistic and capitalist in inspiration, is at the core of such successful novels as *The Fountainhead* (1943) and *Atlas Shrugged* (1957).

RANDOLPH, name of a well-known Virginia family. **William Randolph** (c1651–1711) was born in England and became a successful planter and colonial administrator. He was attorney general for Virginia 1694–98, a post also held by his son, **Sir John Randolph** (1693–1737), and his grandson, **Peyton Randolph** (1721–1775). **Edmund Jennings Randolph** (1753–1813), a nephew of Peyton, was a lawyer who became attorney general (1776–86) and then governor (1786–88) of Virginia. At the Constitutional Convention (1787) he drafted the "Virginia Plan," calling for representation in Congress to be related to state population. He did not sign the Constitution, but later urged its ratification. He became the first US

attorney general (1789–94) and secretary of state (1794–95). **John Randolph of Roanoke** (1773–1833), great-grandson of William Randolph, entered the US House of Representatives in 1799. A much-feared orator and champion of states' rights, he opposed many popular measures and led Southern opposition to the MISSOURI COMPROMISE in 1820. **George Wythe Randolph** (1818–1867), great-great-great grandson of William Randolph and grandson of Thomas Jefferson, became Confederate secretary of war in 1862.

RANDOLPH, A(sa) Philip (1889–1979), US Negro labor leader. He became an outspoken socialist during WWI and organized the Brotherhood of Sleeping Car Porters in 1925. His campaigning was instrumental in the setting up of the Fair Employment Practices Committee in 1941. In 1963 he directed the March on Washington for Jobs and Freedom.

RANDOLPH, Edward (1632?–1703), British colonial agent whose reports led to the Massachusetts charter being revoked in 1684. He was secretary and register of the Dominion of New England (1685–89), and in 1691 became surveyor general of customs for North America.

RANGOON, capital, largest city and chief port of Burma, on the Rangoon R. It is a commercial and manufacturing center with textile, sawmilling, food-processing and petroleum industries. Its gold-domed Shwe Dagon pagoda is the country's principal Buddhist shrine. Rangoon was founded in 1753 as the Burmese capital. It was occupied by the British 1824–26 and retaken by them in 1852, after which it developed as a modern city. During World War II Rangoon was occupied by the Japanese and suffered heavy damage. Pop 2,458,712.

RANK, Otto (1884–1939), Austrian-born US psychoanalyst best known for his suggestion that the psychological trauma of birth is the basis of later anxiety NEUROSIS; and for applying PSYCHOANALYSIS to artistic creativity.

RANKE, Leopold von (1795–1886), German historian, one of the founders of modern historical research methods. Professor of history at Berlin 1834–71, Ranke insisted on objectivity and the importance of original documents, and wrote a monumental series of works, including the *History of the Popes* (1834–36) and a *History of the Reformation in Germany* (1839–47).

RANKIN, Jeanette (1880–1973), pacifist, feminist, social reformer and first woman elected to the US Congress. She became

Republican Congresswoman at large for Montana 1917–19, and returned to the House in 1941, when she cast the only vote against entering WWII. In the 1960s she reemerged as a leader of the campaign against the war in Vietnam.

RANSOM, John Crowe (1888–1974), US poet and proponent of the New Criticism, which emphasized textual, rather than social or moral, analysis. Professor of poetry at Kenyon College, Ohio, 1937–58, he founded and edited the *Kenyon Review* (1939–59). His poetry includes *Chills and Fever* (1924).

RAOULT, François Marie (1830–1901), French physical chemist best known for his work on the theory of SOLUTIONS. **Raoult's law**, in its most general form, states that the vapor pressure above an ideal solution is given by the sum of the products of the vapor pressure of each component and its mole fraction (the number of moles of the component divided by the total number of moles of all the components).

RAPALLO, Treaty of, name of two separate treaties. One, between Italy and Yugoslavia, signed Nov. 12, 1920, temporarily established Fiume (Rijeka) as a free state. The other, between Germany and the USSR, was signed April 16, 1922. The two countries reestablished diplomatic relations, renounced war debts and claims on one another and agreed on economic cooperation.

RAPHAEL (Raffaello Santi or Sanzio; 1483–1520), Italian High RENAISSANCE painter and architect. Born in Urbino, he was early influenced by PERUGINO, as in *Marriage of the Virgin* (1504). In Florence, 1504–08, he studied the work of MICHELANGELO and LEONARDO DA VINCI, being influenced especially by the latter, and painted his famous Madonnas. From 1508 he decorated the Vatican rooms for JULIUS II: the library frescoes, masterly portrayals of symbolic themes, use Raphael's new knowledge of classical art. His SISTINE CHAPEL tapestries (1515–16) and his sympathetic portraits were much imitated. From 1514 he worked rebuilding SAINT PETER'S BASILICA.

RAPP, George (1757–1847), German-born ascetic who founded the Rappites, a PIETIST sect which emigrated to the US and formed several communes. The sect became known as the HARMONY SOCIETY.

RAPPAHANNOCK RIVER, river flowing 212mi SE from the Blue Ridge Mts, Va., to Chesapeake Bay. It is joined by its main tributary, the Rapidan, above Fredericksburg near the Salem Church Dam.

RARE EARTHS, the elements scandium,

yttrium and the lanthanum series, in Group IIIB of the PERIODIC TABLE, occurring widespread in nature as monazite and other ores. They are separated by CHROMATOGRAPHY and ion-exchange resins. Rare earths are used in ALLOYS, including misch metal; and their compounds (mixed or separately) are used as ABRASIVES, for making glasses and ceramics, as "getters," as catalysts (see CATALYSIS) in the petroleum industry, and to make PHOSPHORS, LASERS and MICROWAVE devices.

RARE GASES, former name for the NOBLE GASES.

RASHI (acronym from Rabbi Shlomo Yitzhaqi; 1040–1105), medieval French commentator on the Bible and TALMUD. His classic commentaries have exercised an enduring influence on Jewish scholarship.

RASMUSSEN, Knud Johan Victor (1879–1933), Danish Arctic explorer and ethnologist. From Thule, Greenland, he undertook many expeditions to study Eskimo culture, including the longest dog-sledge journey known, from Greenland to Alaska (1923–24), described in his *Across Arctic America* (1927).

RASPBERRY, fruit-bearing bushes of the genus *Rubus,* of which some 200 species are known. European cultivated red-fruited varieties are derived from *Rubus idaeus,* while North American varieties, including a number which are black-fruited, are derived from three species. Red raspberries are propagated by suckers and black raspberries by tipping, i.e., by burying a shoot tip in the ground which then roots and produces a new plant. Family: Rosaceae.

RASPE, Rudolph Erich (1737–1794), German scholar and thief best known for *The Adventures of Baron Münchhausen* (1785), a collection of tall stories.

RASPUTIN, Grigori Yefimovich (1872?–1916), Russian mystic, known as the "mad monk," who gained influence over the Tsarina Alexandra Fyodorovna after supposedly curing her son's hemophilia in 1905. The scandal of his debaucheries, as well as his interference in political affairs, contributed to the undermining of the imperial government in WWI. He was assassinated by a group of ultra-conservatives.

RASTRELLI, Bartolomeo Francesco (1700–1771), Italian architect who worked in St. Petersburg (Leningrad). Chief architect to the imperial court from 1736, he did much, through his several baroque and rococo palaces such as the Winter Palace (1754–62), to Europeanize Russian architecture.

RATHENAU, Walther (1867–1922), German industrialist, statesman and political philosopher. Heir to a vast electrical company, during WWI he administered the supply of raw materials. A founder of the German Democratic Party, he became minister of reconstruction in the WEIMAR REPUBLIC (1921), and as foreign minister (1922) concluded the Treaty of RAPALLO. A Jew, he was assassinated by right-wing extremists.

RATIONALISM, the philosophical doctrine that reality has a logical structure accessible to deductive reasoning and proof. Against EMPIRICISM, it holds that reason unsupported by sense experience is a source of knowledge not merely of concepts (as in mathematics and logic) but of the real world. Major rationalists in modern philosophy include DESCARTES, SPINOZA, HEGEL and LEIBNIZ.

RATS, a vast number of species of RODENTS belonging to many different families, largely Muridae and Cricetidae. The name is given to any large mouse-like rodent. The best known rats are perhaps the brown and black rats, *Rattus norvegicus* and *R. rattus*, familiar farmyard and warehouse pests. A strong exploratory urge, with an ability to feed on almost anything, make them persistent pests; in addition, they transmit a number of serious diseases such as TYPHUS and PLAGUE. These rats originated in Asia but are now widespread in Europe and America. The New World has its own, cricetid, rats: the wood rats or pack rats, *Neotoma*; the cotton rats, *Sigmodon*, and the rice rats, *Oryzomys*.

RATTIGAN, Sir Terence Mervyn (1911–1977), popular British playwright. He turned from light comedies such as *French Without Tears* (1936) to the more serious, in *The Winslow Boy* (1946), *Ross* (1960) and *In Praise of Love* (1974).

RATTLESNAKES, two genera, *Crotalus* and *Sistrurus*, of pit vipers of the Americas, named for a rattle on the tip of the tail. This rattle is composed of successive pieces of dead skin sloughed off the tail and is vibrated at great speed. Rattlers have moveable fangs which fold up into the roof of the mouth when not in use and are shed and replaced every three weeks. They are extremely venomous snakes, some quite ready to attack humans.

RATZEL, Friedrich (1844–1904), German geographer. With works such as *Anthropogeography* (1882–91), *Political Geography* (1897), *The History of Mankind* (1896–98) and *Lebensraum* (1901), he strongly influenced later German GEOPOLITICS.

RAUSCHENBERG, Robert (1925–   ),

US artist, an initiator of the POP ART of the 1960s. His "combines" (collages) use brushwork with objects from everyday life such as pop bottles and news photos.

RAUSCHENBUSCH, Walter (1861–1918), US Baptist minister, reformer and theologian. A leader of the SOCIAL GOSPEL movement, he became a national spokesman for social evangelism with his *Christianity and the Social Crisis* (1907).

RAVEL, Maurice Joseph (1875–1937), influential French composer, known for his adventurous harmonic style and the combination of delicacy and power in such orchestral works as *Rhapsodie Espagnole* (1908) and *Bolero* (1928), and the ballets *Daphnis and Chloé* (1912) and *La Valse* (1920). *Gaspard de la Nuit* (1908) is among his many masterpieces for the piano, his favorite instrument.

RAVENNA, city in NE Italy famous for its superb MOSAICS, notably in the 5th-century mausoleum of Galla Placidia and 6th-century churches (notably San Vitale and Sant'Apollinare Nuovo). Emperor Honorius made Ravenna his capital; it was seized by ODOACER in 476 and was later seat of the Byzantine exarch. Modern Ravenna, an agricultural and manufacturing center, has a port and petrochemical plants. Pop 137,011.

RAVENS, large dark CROWS of the genus *Corvus*. They do not form a natural group but are given the name arbitrarily because of their size. There are three species in Africa, one restricted to Australia, one to the Americas. The most cosmopolitan is the common raven *C. corax* of North America and Eurasia.

RAWLINGS, Marjorie Kinnan (1896–1953), US author who left newspaper work to live in backwoods Florida. There she wrote the Pulitzer Prize-winning *The Yearling* (1938) and the autobiographical *Cross Creek* (1942.)

RAWLINSON, Sir Henry Creswicke (1810–1895), British soldier and archaeologist, famous for deciphering the CUNEIFORM inscriptions on the Behistun rock, dating from Persian King DARIUS I.

RAWLS, John (1921–   ), US philosopher, at Harvard U from 1962. His *Theory of Justice* (1971) revived the social contract theory as an alternative to utilitarian political philosophy.

RAY, John (1627–1705), British biologist and natural theologian who, with Francis Willughby (1635–1672), made important contributions to TAXONOMY, especially in *A General History of Plants* (3 vols., 1686–1704).

RAYBURN, Samuel (Sam) Taliaferro

(1882– 1961), longest-serving US House of Representatives speaker (17 years from 1940) and congressman (1913–61). A dedicated Democrat, he helped build NEW DEAL policy and was uniquely esteemed for his political skills and experience.

RAYLEIGH, John William Strutt, 3d Baron (1842–1919), British physicist awarded the 1904 Nobel Prize for Physics for his measurements of the DENSITY of the atmosphere and its component gases, work that led to his isolation of ARGON. He worked in many other fields of physics, and is commemorated in the terms **Rayleigh scattering** (which describes the way that ELECTROMAGNETIC RADIATION is scattered by spherical particles of radius less than 10% of the wavelength of the radiation) and **Rayleigh waves** (see EARTHQUAKES).

RAYMOND, Henry Jarvis (1820–1869), founder-editor of the *New York Times* (1851) who took an active part in forming the REPUBLICAN PARTY. He was in the House of Representatives 1865–67, losing renomination because of his moderate stand on RECONSTRUCTION.

RAYNAUD'S DISEASE, a condition in which the fingers (or toes) suddenly become white and numb, often on exposure to mild cold, and become in turn blue and then red and painful. It is caused by digital artery spasm. Raynaud's disease usually occurs in otherwise fit young women; Raynaud's syndrome is the same symptom as a manifestation of an underlying disease.

RAZIN, Stenka (Stepan Timofeyevich; d. 1671), leader of a great but unsuccessful peasant uprising in 1670–71 in the Volga region against landlords and tsarist absolutism. After his torture and execution he became a Russian folk hero.

REACTOR, Nuclear. See NUCLEAR REACTOR.

READ, Sir Herbert (1893–1968), British poet and critic, champion of art education, free verse and the English 19th-century Romantic writers. His best known works are *The Philosophy of Modern Art* (1952) and *The Tenth Muse* (1959). He edited the *Burlington Magazine* 1933–39.

READING, Rufus Daniel Isaacs, 1st marquess of (1860–1935), British statesman, viceroy of India (1921–26). Appointed viceroy in the troubled aftermath of the Amritsar massacre (1919), he upheld British authority by jailing GANDHI and instituting the salt tax, for which he was greatly criticized at home.

READING, the process of assimilating language in the written form. Initial language development in children is largely as speech (see SPEECH AND SPEECH DISORDERS) and has a primarily auditory or phonetic component; the recognition of letters, words and sentences when written represents a transition from the auditory to the visual mode. The dependence of reading on previous linguistic development with spoken speech is seen in the impaired reading ability of deaf children. Normal reading depends on normal VISION and the ability to recognize the patterns of letter and word order and grammatical variations. In reading, vision is linked with the system controlling EYE movement, so that the page is scanned in an orderly fashion. Reading is represented in essentially the same areas of the brain as are concerned with speech, and disorders of the two often occur together (e.g., APHASIA). In DYSLEXIA, pattern recognition is impaired and a specific defect of reading and language development results. The ability to read and write, and thus to record events, ideas, etc., represented one of the most substantial advances in human civilization after the acquisition of speech itself.

REAGAN, Ronald (1911–   ), 40th president of the US (1981–89). Born in Tampico, Ill., he became a film actor in 1937 and in 1947 was elected president of the Screen Actors Guild. He campaigned for GOLDWATER as a conservative Republican in 1964, and was governor of Cal. 1967–75. Defeated for the Republican presidential nomination in 1976, he won it and the presidency in 1980.

As president, Reagan supported a strong defense budget, but cut federal domestic programs, as he had cut welfare and similar expenditures as governor. His policy of reducing taxes to stimulate the economy resulted in unprecedented budget deficits and high interest rates that clouded the prospects for recovery from the deepest recession and highest unemployment since the 1930s. Other domestic policies alienated advocates of environmental protection, civil rights, civil liberties, and women's issues. In foreign affairs, the president's anti-Soviet policies and rhetoric contributed to a marked worsening of US-Soviet relations. Limited military interventions in Central America and Lebanon raised fears in many Americans of involvement in Vietnam-like quagmires. Nevertheless, Reagan's personal popularity remained high.

Reagan won reelection in 1984 in a 49-state landslide. His second term was marred by the Iran-contra affair, policy failures in Nicaragua and Panama, congressional rejection of a significant Supreme Court nomination, and several unflattering books by former administration insiders. The economy, however, showed dramatic improvement—there was steady economic growth, low inflation, and low unemployment. On the other hand, massive budget and trade deficits continued. In foreign affairs, Reagan moderated his harsh view of the Soviet Union and in 1987 signed a treaty with the USSR reducing intermediage-range nuclear weapons.

Reagan's personal popularity and the sense of national well-being that he communicated contributed to the election of his vice president, George Bush, as president in 1988. Reagan retired to his California ranch.

REALISM, in art and literature, the faithful imitation of real life; more specifically, the artistic movement which started in France c1850 in reaction to the idealized representations of ROMANTICISM and NEOCLASSICISM, with a social dimension derived from scientific progress and the REVOLUTIONS OF 1848. In France the leading painters were COROT, COURBET, DAUMIER and MILLET, and its main literary expression was in the novels of BALZAC, FLAUBERT and ZOLA (see NATURALISM). In the US, EAKINS, Winslow HOMER and the ASHCAN SCHOOL were Realistic painters, and in literature Stephen CRANE, Theodore DREISER, William HOWELLS, Henry JAMES and Frank NORRIS led the movement.

REALISM, in philosophy, is a term with two main technical uses. Philosophers who believe, as PLATO did, that UNIVERSALS exist in their own right, and so independently of perceived objects, are traditionally labeled "realists." Realism in this sense is opposed to NOMINALISM. On the other hand, realism also describes the view that material objects exist independently of our perceptions of them. In this sense it is opposed to certain forms of IDEALISM.

REALPOLITIK, policy based on practicalities and power rather than on doctrine or ethical objectives. Its famous exponent was BISMARCK, who as German chancellor eschewed ideology for national interest.

REAL PRESENCE, term designating those doctrines of Holy COMMUNION that stress the actual presence of Christ's body and blood in the sacrament—whether physically as in TRANSUBSTANTIATION, or in an undefined mode as in moderate ANGLICANISM—as opposed to the more extreme Protestant view that they are present only symbolically.

RÉAUMUR, René Antoine Ferchault de (1683–1757), French scientist whose most important work was in ENTOMOLOGY, but who is best remembered for devising the now little used **Réaumur temperature scale,** in which $0°R = 0°C$ and $80°R = 100°C$.

REBELLION OF 1837–1838, two unsuccessful and parallel uprisings against British colonial rule in Canada, prompted by an economic depression and desire for local self-government. The first, led by Louis PAPINEAU in Lower Canada (roughly Quebec), collapsed swiftly: Papineau fled to the US. While troops were occupied here, colonists in Upper Canada (now Ontario) revolted in Toronto under William Lyon MACKENZIE. After defeat, he too fled to the US (see CAROLINE AFFAIR). Lord DURHAM's subsequent report, accepted in principle by the British government, urged the union of Upper and Lower Canada (which became law with the 1840 Act of Union).

REBER, Grote (1911–   ), US astronomer who built the first RADIO TELESCOPE (1937) and made radio maps of the sky (1940, 1942) which indicated areas of strong radio emissions unrelated to any visible celestial bodies.

RECALL. See INITIATIVE, REFERENDUM AND RECALL.

RÉCAMIER, Juliette (1777–1849), French beauty who presided over a celebrated salon that attracted the leading political and literary figures of the day.

RECLAMATION, US Bureau of, agency of the Department of the Interior, created to administer the Reclamation Act of 1902 for reclaiming arid land by irrigation in the 16 W states. Its responsibilities were later progressively expanded.

RECOMBINANT DNA, DNA from two different organisms. Recombinant DNA, created by splicing a gene from one type of cell into the DNA of a cell of another organism, is the key to the new science of GENETIC ENGINEERING.

RECONSTRUCTION, period (1865–77) when Americans tried to rebuild a stable Union after the Civil War. The deadlock inherited by Andrew JOHNSON on Lincoln's death, over who should control Reconstruction, hardened with increasing congressional hostility toward restoring the South to its old position. Republicans wanted to press home the Union victory by following the 13th Amendment abolishing slavery (1865) with full civil rights for the Negro, including the vote. Instead, while Congress was not in session, Johnson implemented Lincoln's policy of lenience by giving amnesty in return for a loyalty oath. He also condoned BLACK CODES, which practically reintroduced slavery in another guise. Reconvening (1866) with a landslide victory, however, the Radical Republicans took control. Their first Reconstruction Act of

1867 divided ten Southern states into five military areas with a major general for each. Under army scrutiny, black and white voters were registered, and constitutions and governments instituted. In 1868, six Southern states were readmitted to the Union, followed in 1870 by the other four. By ratifying the 14th Amendment (1868) on Negro civil rights, Tenn. escaped the military phase. There were no mass arrests, no indictments for treason and the few Confederate officials jailed were (except for Jefferson DAVIS) soon released. Apart from slaves, the property of the Confederate leaders was untouched, although no help was given to rescue the ruined economy. On readmission, the Southern governments were Republican, supported by enfranchised Negroes, Scalawags (white Republicans) and CARPETBAGGERS (Northern profiteers). Constructive legislation was passed in every state for public schools, welfare taxation and government reform, although the governments were accused of corruption and incompetence. The FREEDMEN'S BUREAU lasted only four years, but it did help to found Atlanta, Howard and Fisk universities for Negroes. Southern conservatives, hostile to the Radical Republican policies, turned to the Democrats; societies like the Ku Klux Klan emerged to crusade against Negroes and radicals. Full citizenship for Negroes, though legally assured by the 14th and 15th (1870) amendments, was denied by intimidation, literacy tests and POLL TAX. The Republican Party, secure again in the North, abandoned the Negro. In 1877, when federal troops withdrew (see HAYES, RUTHERFORD), the last Republican governments collapsed and Reconstruction was over.

RECONSTRUCTION FINANCE CORPORATION (RFC), US government agency set up (1932) under President Hoover to lend money to various enterprises and thus to stimulate the economy. In its 25-year life the RFC loaned some $50 billion.

RECORDER, wind instrument related to the FLUTE but held vertically, with a mouthpiece which channels the airstream, and no keys. Relatively easy to play, soft and sweet in tone, it was most popular about 1600–1700 and is again popular today. There are soprano, alto, and (with some keys) tenor and bass recorders.

RECTIFIER, a device such as an electron tube or SEMICONDUCTOR junction which converts alternating electric current (AC—see ELECTRICITY) to direct current (DC) by allowing more current to flow through it in one direction than another. A halfwave rectifier transmits only one polarity of the alternating current, producing a pulsating direct current; two such devices are combined in full-wave rectification, giving a continuous pulse train which may be smoothed by a filter.

RECYCLING, the recovery and reuse of any waste material. Of obvious economic importance where reusable materials are available more cheaply than fresh supplies of the same materials, the recycling principle is finding ever wider application in the conservation of the world's natural resources and in solving the problems of environmental POLLUTION. The recycling of the wastes of a manufacturing process in the same process—e.g., the resmelting and recasting of metallic turnings and offcuts—is commonplace in industry. So also is the immediate use of wastes or by-products of one industrial process in another—e.g., the manufacture of cattle food from the grain-mash residues found in breweries and distilleries. These are often termed forms of "internal recycling," as opposed to "external recycling": the recovery and reprocessing for reuse of "discarded" materials, such as waste paper, scrap metal and used glass bottles. The burning of garbage to produce electricity and the extraction of pure water from sewage are other common examples of recycling.

RED BRIGADES, an Italian terrorist organization set up in 1970 with the proclaimed aim of being the vanguard of a coming revolution. While its hard-core membership never numbered more than a few hundred, it was organized in small, highly disciplined cells. They attempted to disrupt Italian society by kidnapings, robberies, so-called "people's trials" and murders. Their most celebrated action was the kidnaping and murder of political leader Aldo Moro in 1978. Also reaching headlines was the kidnaping in Verona (Dec. 1981) of US Gen. James Dozier; Italian police rescued him and captured five terrorists a month later.

RED CLOUD (1822–1909), chief of the Oglala Sioux and leader of the Indian struggle against the opening of the Bozeman Trail (see BOZEMAN, JOHN M.). The trail was closed in 1868 following the Fetterman Massacre.

RED CORPUSCLES, or erythrocytes. See BLOOD.

RED CROSS, international agency for the relief of victims of war or disaster. Its two aims are to alleviate suffering and to maintain a rigid neutrality so that it may cross national borders to reach those otherwise unaidable. An international committee founded by J. H. DUNANT and four others from Geneva secured 12 nations' signatures to the first of the GENEVA CONVENTIONS (1864) for the care of the wounded. Aid was given to both sides in the Danish-Prussian War the same year. During WWI and WWII, the Red Cross helped prisoners of war, inspecting camps and sending food and clothing parcels; it investigated about 5 million missing persons and distributed $200 million in relief supplies to civilians. The International Red Cross won the Nobel Peace Prize in 1917 and 1944. It works through the International Committee (1880), made up of 25 Swiss citizens. Over 100 national Red Cross societies (Red Crescent in Muslim countries) carry out peacetime relief and public health work. The US Red Cross (1881) now has some 3,100 chapters.

REDEMPTORISTS (Congregation of the Most Holy Redeemer), a religious order founded 1732 in Naples by St. ALPHONSUS LIGUORI to preach the Gospel to the poor and the abandoned. Now established in five continents, it entered the US in 1832.

REDFIELD, Robert (1897–1958), US cultural anthropologist best known for his comparative studies of primitive and highly civilized cultures, and for his active support of racial integration.

REDGRAVE, family of English actors. **Sir Michael Redgrave** (1908–   ) appeared in many plays and films from 1934. His elder daughter, **Vanessa Redgrave** (1937–   ), scored successes in the films *Morgan!* (1966) and *Isadora* (1968). Her sister, **Lynn Redgrave** (1943–   ), starred in *Georgy Girl* (1966).

REDI, Francesco (1627–1697 or 1698), Italian biological scientist who demonstrated that maggots develop in decaying meat not through SPONTANEOUS GENERATION but from eggs laid there by flies.

RED JACKET (Sagoyewatha; c1758–1830), Seneca Indian chief named for the red coat he wore when an English ally in the Revolution. Later an ally of the US in the War of 1812, he strongly opposed white customs and Christianity for his people in N.Y.

REDMOND, John Edward (1856–1918), Irish nationalist. He succeeded PARNELL as Irish nationalist leader in parliament and secured the passage of the 1914 HOME RULE Bill. After the repression of the 1916 EASTER RISING he lost power to SINN FEIN.

REDON, Odilon (1840–1916), French painter and engraver associated with the Symbolists. His oils, usually of flowers and full of color and light, contrasted with bizarre lithographs such as *The Cyclops,* c1898.

RED RIVER, river in SE Asia, flowing about 500mi SE from Yunnan province, S China (where it is named Yüan Chiang R), across Vietnam (as the Hong R), past Hanoi into the Gulf of Tonkin. Its wide fertile delta E of Hanoi is northern Vietnam's economic center.

RED RIVER, 1,222mi-long river which rises in N Tex. and flows SE to join the Mississippi R between Natchez and Baton Rouge. Named for its red sediment, it drains about 90,000sq mi and forms most of the Okla.-Tex. boundary.

RED RIVER OF THE NORTH, about 540mi long, is formed at Wahpeton, N.D., by the junction of the Bois de Sioux and Otter Trail rivers. It flows N as the N.D.-Minn. boundary and enters Manitoba, Canada, emptying into Lake Winnipeg. It drains some 43,500sq mi of rich wheatlands.

RED RIVER SETTLEMENT, Canadian community founded in 1811 by Lord SELKIRK at the junction of the Red and Assiniboine rivers in present-day S Manitoba, on land granted by the Hudson's Bay Co. Violent hostility from the North West Co. ended with the union of the two fur companies (1821).

RED SEA, sea separating the Arabian Peninsula from NE Africa. It extends some 1,300mi from the Bab al-Mandab strait by the Gulf of Aden in the S to the gulfs of Suez (with the Suez Canal) and Aqaba in the N. It is up to 250mi wide and up to 7,800ft deep.

RED SHIFT, an increase in wavelength of the light from an object, usually caused by its rapid recession (see DOPPLER EFFECT). The spectra of distant GALAXIES show marked red shifts and this is usually, though far from always, interpreted as implying that they are rapidly receding from us. (See also COSMOLOGY.)

REDWOOD NATIONAL PARK, area in N Cal. of 109,207 acres, including 40mi of Pacific Ocean coastline, established in 1968 to preserve groves of ancient redwood trees.

REED, John (1887–1920), US journalist and radical, author of the famous eye-witness *Ten Days That Shook the World* (1919) which recounts the Russian October Revolution.

REED, Sir Carol (1906–1976), British film director of *Odd Man Out* (1946), *The Fallen Idol* (1948), and *The Third Man* (1949).

REED, Stanley Forman (1884–1980), US jurist, associate justice (1938–57) of the US Supreme Court, where his moderate's vote was often decisive. As solicitor general (1935–38) under F. D. Roosevelt he argued important cases arising from NEW DEAL legislation.

REED, Thomas Brackett (1839–1902), US Republican speaker of the House of Representatives 1889–91 and 1895–99, called "Tsar Reed" for his strong control. His "Reed Rules" (1890) are still the basis for procedure in Congress. He supported high tariffs and opposed the Spanish-US war and the annexation of Hawaii.

REED, Walter (1851–1902), US Army pathologist and bacteriologist who, in 1900, demonstrated the role of the mosquito *Aëdes aegypti* as a carrier of YELLOW FEVER, so enabling the disease to be controlled.

REED INSTRUMENTS. See WIND INSTRUMENTS.

REEVE, Tapping (1744–1823), US jurist who started the movement to secure the legal right of married women to dispose of their property. He also founded a famous law school at Litchfield, Conn. (1784).

REFERENDUM. See INITIATIVE, REFERENDUM AND RECALL.

REFLECTION, the bouncing back of energy waves (e.g., LIGHT radiation, SOUND or WATER waves) from a surface. If the surface is smooth, "regular" reflection takes place, the incident and reflected wave paths lying in the same plane as, and at opposed equal angles to, the normal (a line perpendicular to the surface) at the point of reflection. Rough surfaces reflect waves irregularly, so an optically rough surface appears matt or dull while an optically smooth surface looks shiny. Reflected sound waves are known as ECHOES. (See also REFRACTION.)

REFLEX, MUSCLE contraction or secretion resulting from nerve stimulation by a pathway from a stimulus via the NERVOUS SYSTEM to the effector organ without the interference of volition. Basic primitive reflexes are stylized responses to stress of protective value to an infant. Stretch or tendon reflexes (e.g., knee-jerk) are muscle contractions in response to sudden stretching of their TENDONS. **Conditioned reflexes** are more complex responses described by PAVLOV that follow any stimulus which has been repeatedly linked with a stimulus of normal functional significance.

REFORMATION, religious and political upheaval in W Europe in the 16th century. Primarily an attempt to reform the doctrines of the Roman Catholic Church, it led to the establishment of PROTESTANTISM. Anticlericalism spread after the movements led by John WYCLIFFE and the LOLLARDS in

14th-century England and by John HUS in Bohemia in the 15th century. At the same time the PAPACY had lost prestige through its 70-year exile, the BABYLONIAN CAPTIVITY at AVIGNON and the 50-year GREAT SCHISM. RENAISSANCE thought, particularly HUMANISM, stimulated liberal views, spread by the invention of printing. There were many critics, like Martin LUTHER, of the low moral standards of Rome, and of the sale of INDULGENCES, distributed in Germany by TETZEL. Luther also challenged papal authority and the accepted Roman Catholic doctrines, such as TRANSUBSTANTIATION and CELIBACY, and argued strongly for JUSTIFICATION BY FAITH. Luther's ideas spread in Germany after the Diet of WORMS, 1521, and after the PEASANTS' WAR, when Luther won the support of many German princes and of Denmark and Sweden. The protest made by the Lutheran princes at the Diet of Speyer (1529) provided the term "Protestant."

The Swiss divine Huldreich ZWINGLI won a large following in Switzerland and SW Germany. He carried out radical religious reforms in Zürich, abolishing the mass. After his death (1531), John CALVIN led the Swiss reform movement and set up a reformed church in Geneva. Calvin's *Institutes of the Christian Religion* (1536) had great influence, notably in Scotland where CALVINISM was led by John KNOX. In France Calvin's religious followers, the HUGUENOTS, were involved in the complex political struggles leading to the Wars of RELIGION, 1562–98. The Protestant movement in the Low Countries was linked with the national revolt which freed the Dutch from Roman Catholic Spain. The English Reformation was initiated by HENRY VIII, who denied papal authority, dissolved and seized the wealth of the monasteries, and made the CHURCH OF ENGLAND autonomous to increase the royal government's power. Henry VIII remained in doctrine a Catholic but the influence of Reformers such as RIDLEY and LATIMER established Protestantism under EDWARD VI, when Thomas CRANMER issued a new prayer book (1549). There was a Roman Catholic reaction under MARY I but in 1558 ELIZABETH I established moderate Protestantism as the basis of the English Church. The religious position of Europe as a whole, however, was not settled for another century.

REFORMATION, Catholic. See COUNTER-REFORMATION.

REFORM BILLS, three acts of Parliament passed in Britain during the 19th century to extend the franchise. The first (1832) abolished rotten boroughs (boroughs which returned two members to Parliament long after their populations disappeared), and enfranchised industrial cities like Birmingham and Manchester, and the propertied middle class. The second bill (1867) gave the vote to urban dwellers and the third (1884) extended it to agricultural workers.

REFORMED CHURCHES, the Protestant churches arising from the REFORMATION that adhere to CALVINISM doctrinally and to PRESBYTERIANISM in church polity, and thus distinct from the LUTHERAN CHURCHES and the CHURCH OF ENGLAND. They grew up especially in Switzerland, Germany, France (see HUGUENOTS), Holland (see DUTCH REFORMED CHURCH), Scotland (see CHURCH OF SCOTLAND), Hungary and what is now Czechoslovakia. Each had its own simple formal liturgy, and all acknowledged the Reformed Confessions. There are several Reformed Churches in the US, the largest being the Christian Reformed Church.

REFORMED CHURCH IN AMERICA. See DUTCH REFORMED CHURCH.

REFRACTION, the change in direction of energy waves on passing from one medium to another in which they have a different velocity. In the case of LIGHT radiation, refraction is associated with a change in the optical density of the medium. On passing into a denser medium the wave path is bent toward the normal (the line perpendicular to the surface at the point of incidence), the whole wave path and the normal lying in the same plane. The ratio of the sine of the angle of incidence (that between the incident wave path and the normal) to that of the angle of refraction (that between the normal and the refracted wave path) is a constant for a given interface (Snell's law). When measured for light passing from a vacuum into a denser medium, this ratio is known as the refractive index of the medium. Refractive index varies with wavelength. On passing into a less dense medium, light radiation is bent away from the normal but if the angle of incidence is so great that its sine equals or exceeds the index for refraction from the denser to the less dense medium, there is no refraction and total (internal) REFLECTION (applied in the reflecting PRISM) results. Refraction finds its principal application in the design of LENSES.

REFRIGERATION, removal of HEAT from an enclosure in order to lower its TEMPERATURE. It is used for freezing water or food, for FOOD PRESERVATION, for AIR CONDITIONING and for low-temperature chemical processes and CRYOGENICS studies and applications. The ancient Egyptians and Indians used the evaporation of water from porous vessels; and the Chinese, Greeks and Romans used natural ice, a method which became a major industry in the 19th-century US. Modern refrigerators are insulated cabinets containing the cooling elements of a heat pump. The pump may use mechanical compression of refrigerants such as AMMONIA or freon, or may accomplish compression by absorbing the refrigerant in a secondary fluid such as water and pumping the solution through a heat exchanger to a generator where it is heated to drive off the refrigerant at high pressure. Other cycles, similar in principle, using steam or air, are also used.

REFUGEE, person fleeing from his native country to avoid a threat or restriction. In the 15th century MOORS and JEWS were expelled from Spain, and religious refugees fled to the New World in the 17th century. In the 20th century refugees have created a world problem. POGROMS forced Jews to leave Russia; in WWI Greeks and Armenians fled from Turkey and about 1.5 million Russians settled in Europe after the RUSSIAN REVOLUTION. In the 1930s Spaniards and Chinese left their respective homelands. The WWII legacy of about eight million refugees led to the UNITED NATIONS RELIEF AND REHABILITATION ADMINISTRATION, replaced in 1946 by the International Refugee Organization, which in turn was succeeded by the Office of the UNITED NATIONS HIGH COMMISSIONER FOR REFUGEES. They resettled millions of homeless from, for example, the KOREAN WAR. Many thousand Arabs displaced when Israel was created in 1948 still live in Middle Eastern refugee camps and are a serious political problem. The 1971 war between India and Pakistan over BANGLADESH produced nine million refugees, most of whom subsequently settled in Bangladesh. During the 1970s thousands of refugees from SE Asia—the "boat people"—fled to neighboring countries, many later emigrating to the US.

Until WWII, refugees entered the US like other immigrants, subject to the various restrictions and quotas of the immigration laws. The Displaced Persons Act of 1948 admitted 415,000 persons made homeless in WWII, and refugee acts in 1953 and 1960 admitted others. The immigration act of 1965 established a special quota for refugees, whom it defined as people who had fled a communist or communist-dominated country or any country in the Middle East because of persecution on account of race, religion, or political opinion. It also gave the US attorney general authority to admit refugees in special cases at his own discretion. This authority was used to admit Hungarians, Cubans, Ugandans, and Vietnamese. The Refugee Act of 1980 redefined a refugee as anyone from any part of the world—not just communist countries or the Middle East—who has been persecuted or who had a well-founded fear of persecution if he returned to his homeland. It established a ceiling of 50,000 refugees a year, but allowed the president, in consultation with Congress, to admit additional refugees of "grave humanitarian concern" to the US. This latter provision was used to admit Cuban and Haitian BOAT PEOPLE, Soviet Jews, and Soviet Armenians. (See also ASYLUM;SANCTUARY MOVEMENT.)

REGAN, Donald (1918–   ), US financier, chairman of the Wall Street brokerage firm of Merrill Lynch, who served President Ronald Reagan as secretary of the treasury (1981–85) and White House chief of staff (1985–87).

REGENERATION, the regrowing of a lost or damaged part of an organism. In PLANTS this includes the production of, e.g., dormant buds and adventitious organs. All ANIMALS possess some power to regenerate, but its extent varies from that in sponges, in which all the cells in a piece of the body can be almost completely separated and will yet come together again to build up new but smaller sponges, to that in the higher animals, in which regeneration is limited to the healing of wounds.

REGER, Max (1873–1916), German composer and pianist best known for his organ music and orchestral works. His music is characterized by elaborately structured polyphonic forms.

REGGAE, a popular Jamaican musical style that combines American rock and soul music with CALYPSO and other Latin-American rhythms. The 1973 film *The Harder They Come* introduced reggae to the US, where reggae greats like Bob Marley (1945–1981) were to win huge audiences.

REGIOMONTANUS (Johann Müller; 1436–1476), Prussian mathematician and astronomer whose *Five Books on all Types of Triangles* (1533) laid the foundations for modern TRIGONOMETRY.

REGNAULT, Henri Victor (1810–1878), German-born French chemist best known for work on the physical properties of gases (e.g., showing that Boyle's Law works only for ideal gases), and for inventing an air THERMOMETER and a HYGROMETER.

REGULATORS, movement formed in W North Carolina 1764–71 to resist the extortion and oppression of colonial officials. After failing to get reforms against excessive taxes, huge legal fees and multiple office holdings, they rose in revolt, but were defeated at Allemance Creek, 1771, by Governor Tryon, who hanged six leaders for treason.

REGULATORY AGENCIES. See DEREGULATION.

REGULUS, Marcus Atilius (d. c249 BC), Roman general captured in the first PUNIC WAR (255 BC). He was sent to Rome to deliver Carthage's peace terms, under parole to return if they were rejected. He nevertheless urged their rejection, returned and was apparently tortured to death.

REHABILITATION, means of enabling the handicapped to lead lives which are as normal as possible considering their disability. The term can cover social disability (treatment of prisoners) as well as physical or mental difficulty. Physical rehabilitation starts once immediate threat to life is absent and its success calls for the active participation of the patient. When the damage has been assessed, a program is designed to stop degeneration of the unaffected parts, to strengthen the injured area and to encourage the patient to accept his handicap realistically. Also efforts are made to remove external sources of anxiety. With the body so strengthened, the patient is prepared for reentry into daily life, through aids and equipment where appropriate, for example, wheelchairs, artificial limbs. Skills are taught, such as braille, and finally help given by social workers in job-finding. In mental disturbances, treatment tries to break down isolation and prevent self-withdrawal through interaction with others. In hospitals, rehabilitation aims to involve patients in social activities and then gradually to detach them from dependence on the center by trips outside until outpatients' visits only are necessary. The federal agency, the Vocational Rehabilitation Administration, makes grants to states to finance programs and encourage their expansion. It carries out research and advises the state agencies who must direct the actual program. Voluntary bodies, charitable foundations and industrial concerns supplement government provisions.

REHNQUIST, William Hubbs (1924–   ), US jurist. After serving as assistant attorney general, he was appointed (1971) by President Richard Nixon to the US Supreme Court. In 1986 President Ronald Reagan nominated him for chief justice. He was confirmed by a narrow margin after a stormy debate centering on his record on civil rights and his judicial ethics. As chief justice he proved an efficient administrator. In 1988 he surprised some observers with a forceful decision rejecting the administration-supported view that the office of special counsel, created after the Watergate affair to investigate wrong-doing in the executive branch, was unconstitutional.

REICH, Wilhelm (1897–1957), radical Austrian-born US psychoanalyst who broke with FREUD over the function of sexual repression, which Reich saw as the root of individual and collective neurosis. He became known for his controversial theory that there exists a primal life-giving force, *orgone* energy, in living beings and in the atmosphere. His design and sale of orgone boxes for personal therapeutic use led to his imprisonment for violating the Food and Drug Act.

REICHENBACH, Hans (1891–1953), German philosopher of science who was a founder of the Berlin Society for Empirical Philosophy and editor of the *Journal of Unified Science*. He contributed to the theories of probability, relativity and quantum mechanics. He left Germany (1933) and taught at UCLA (1938–53).

REICHSTAG, imperial parliament of the Holy Roman Empire, and from 1871–1945 Germany's lower legislative house, the upper being called the Reichsrat. The ruling body of the WEIMAR REPUBLIC, it was a mere cipher under the NAZI regime. The Reichstag building, burnt down in Jan. 1933, probably as a Nazi propaganda trick, has been restored.

REID, Ogden Mills (1882–1947), US newspaperman who was editor of the New York *Tribune* (from 1913). He acquired the New York *Herald* (1924) and subsequently edited and published the consolidated *Herald Tribune*, one of the most influential newspapers in the US.

REID, Thomas (1710–1796), Scottish philosopher who, through his investigations of and rejection of HUME'S skepticism, is regarded as a founder of the COMMON SENSE SCHOOL of philosophy.

REID, Whitelaw (1837–1912), US journalist, ambassador to Britain 1905–12. Editor of the New York *Tribune* 1872–1912, he was Republican vice-presidential candidate in 1892.

REIGN OF TERROR. See TERROR, THE.

REIMARUS, Hermann Samuel (1694–1768), German philosopher admired by G. LESSING. He held that the truths of a natural religion, the existence of a wise God and the immortality of the soul can be the basis of a universal religion, because they are discoverable by reason. Revealed religion, however, based on miracles and mysteries which can be denied, could not be accepted by all.

REIMS or **Rheims,** city in N France, about 100mi E of Paris on the Besle R. Dating from Roman times, it is famed for its Gothic cathedral built 1211–1430. All but two French kings 1179–1825 were crowned in Reims. Center of champagne and woolen production, it also makes chemicals, machinery and paper. Pop 178,380.

REINCARNATION. See TRANSMIGRATION OF SOULS.

REINDEER, *Rangifer tarandus,* a large ungainly-looking DEER widely distributed in Europe, Asia and North America, where they are referred to as CARIBOU.

REINER, Fritz (1888–1963), Hungarian-born US conductor, director of the orchestras of Cincinnati (1922–28), Pittsburgh (1938–48), Chicago (1953–62), and the Metropolitan Opera (1948–53).

REINHARDT, Adolf (1913–1967), US painter whose symmetrical, geometric abstractions eventually developed into his famous monochrome paintings. His "black" series features only minor contrasts in violet and olive.

REINHARDT, Max (1873–1943), Austrian theatrical director famous for his vast and spectacular productions—especially of *Oedipus Rex* and *Faust*—and for his elaborate and atmospheric use of stage machinery and management of crowds.

RELATIVITY, a frequently referred to but less often understood theory of the nature of space, time and matter. EINSTEIN'S "special theory" of relativity (1905) is based on the premise that different observers moving at a constant speed with respect to each other find the laws of physics to be identical, and, in particular, find the speed of LIGHT waves to be the same (the "principle of relativity"). Among its consequences are: that events occurring simultaneously according to one observer may happen at different times according to an observer moving relative to the first (although the order of two causally related events is never reversed); that a moving object is shortened in the direction of its motion; that time runs more slowly for a moving object; that the velocity of a projectile emitted from a moving body is less than the sum of the relative ejection velocity and the velocity of the body; that a body has a greater MASS when moving than when at rest, and that no massive body can travel as fast as, or faster than, the speed of light (2.998×10^8m/s—at this speed, a body would have zero length and infinite mass, while time would stand still on it).

These effects are too small to be noticed at normal velocities; they have nevertheless found ample experimental verification, and are commonplace considerations in many physical calculations. The relationship between the position and time of a given event according to different observers is known (for H. A. Lorentz) as the Lorentz transformation. In this, time mixes on a similar footing with the three spatial dimensions, and it is in this sense that time has been called the "fourth dimension." The greater mass of a moving body implies a relationship between kinetic ENERGY and mass; Einstein made the bold additional hypothesis that *all* energy was equivalent to mass, according to the famous equation $E = mc^2$. The conversion of mass to energy is now the basis of NUCLEAR REACTORS, and is indeed the source of the energy of the sun itself.

Einstein's "general theory" (1916) is of importance chiefly to cosmologists. It asserts the equivalence of the effects of ACCELERATION and gravitational fields (see GRAVITATION), and that gravitational fields cause space to become "curved," so that light no longer travels in straight lines, while the wavelength of light falls as the light falls through a gravitational field. The direct verification of these last two predictions, among others, has helped deeply to entrench the theory of relativity in the language of physics.

RELIC, in the Roman Catholic Church, an object revered for its association with a holy person, especially a saint—usually all or part of the saint's body, or an article used by him or her.

RELIEF, form of sculpture in which the elements of the design, whether figures or ornament, project from the background. In **high relief** the elements stand out prominently and may even be undercut; in **low relief** they hardly emerge from the plane of the background. Fine examples of low relief are the PARTHENON friezes.

RELIGION, a system of belief to which a social group is committed, in which there is a supernatural object of awe, worship and service. It generally provides a system of ETHICS and a worldview that supply a stable context within which each person can relate himself to others and to the world, and can understand his own significance. Religions are found in all societies, and are generally dominant (modern secularism being an exception). Some form of religion seems to fulfill a basic human need. Some features are common to most religions: the recognition of a sacred realm from which supernatural forces operate; a mediating priesthood; the use of ritual to establish a right relationship with the holy (though ritual used to manipulate the supernatural becomes magic); and a sense of group community. It is uncertain by what stages religion evolved; a linear progression from ANIMISM through POLYTHEISM to MONOTHEISM is not now firmly accepted. (See also DUALISM; MYTHOLOGY; PANTHEISM; DEISM; THEISM.) Some religions have no deity as such, but are natural philosophies: see BUDDHISM; CONFUCIANISM; TAOISM. (See also ANCESTOR WORSHIP; MYTHOLOGY; SACRIFICE; TABOO; THEOLOGY.)

RELIGION, Wars of, French civil wars, 1562–98. They were caused partly by the REFORMATION conflict between the Roman Catholics and the Protestant HUGUENOTS, and partly by the rivalry between the French kings and such great nobles as the dukes of Guise. The worst event was the SAINT BARTHOLOMEW'S DAY MASSACRE (1572). The Edict of NANTES (1598) established religious freedom and concluded the wars.

REMARQUE, Erich Maria (1898–1970), German novelist famous for his powerful anti-war *All Quiet on the Western Front* (1929), describing the horror of the trenches in WWI. In 1932 Remarque emigrated to Switzerland, later becoming a US citizen. Other works include *Arch of Triumph* (1946).

REMBRANDT (Rembrandt Harmenszoon van Rijn; 1606–1669), greatest of Dutch painters. Born and trained in Leiden, he moved to Amsterdam in 1631 and achieved recognition with a group portrait, *The Anatomy Lesson* (1632). Adapting the styles of CARAVAGGIO, HALS and RUBENS, his painting became, during 1632–42, BAROQUE in style, as in *Saskia as Flora* (1634), *Blinding of Samson* (1636) and *Night Watch* (1642). The years 1643–56 were notable for his magnificent drawings and etchings, predominantly of New Testament themes, such as *The Three Crosses* (1653–61). From mid-1650s his painting was more solemn and spiritual in mood and richer in color as shown in portraits (*Jan Six*, 1654, *The Syndics of the Amsterdam Cloth Hall*, 1662), a series of moving self portraits, and religious paintings like *David and Saul* (c1658).

REMINGTON, Frederic (1861–1909), US painter, sculptor and writer chiefly known for his portrayals of the Old West, where he traveled extensively. His paintings, usually of Indians, cowboys and horses, skillfully convey violent action and are notable for authenticity of detail.

REMONSTRANTS, Dutch ARMINIANS who in 1610 published a *Remonstrance* criticizing the doctrine of PREDESTINATION. The Synod of Dort (1618–19) rejected their views and they were persecuted until 1625. They became an independent church in 1795; a small group survives in the Netherlands.

REMOTE SENSING, the observation of the surface of the earth and other planetary bodies through sensors on aircraft and space satellites that detect and record. Aerial photography is the oldest form of remote sensing. Photographic films developed since WWII and sensitive to electromagnetic radiation on the borders of visible light have increased the amount of information that can be captured on photographs. **Near-infrared** photography, utilizing wavelengths slightly longer than visible light, is useful in studies of vegetation, and water pollution, in geological studies, and in mineral exploration. **Far infrared (thermal infrared),** at longer wavelengths, is useful in monitoring areas of high heat flow such as volcanic terrains and can also be used in oceanographic studies where sharp water-temperature contrasts are important. RADAR imagery provides excellent resolution and is unaffected by weather conditions or darkness; geological structures are frequently discerned using this method, which is also useful in monitoring the ocean surface.

REMUS. See ROMULUS AND REMUS.

REMUS, Uncle. See HARRIS, JOEL CHANDLER.

RENAISSANCE (French: rebirth or revival), the transitional period between the MIDDLE AGES and modern times, covering the years c1350–c1650. The term was first applied by the Swiss historian Jakob Burckhardt in 1860. The Renaissance was a period of deeply significant achievement and change. It saw the REFORMATION challenge the unity and supremacy of the Roman Catholic Church, along with the rise of HUMANISM, the growth of large nation-states with powerful kings, far-ranging voyages of exploration and a new emphasis on the importance of the individual. It was a period of extraordinary accomplishment in the arts, in scholarship and the sciences, typified in the universal genius of LEONARDO DA VINCI. The origins of the Renaissance are disputed, but its first flowering occurred in Italy. In the world of learning a new interest in secular Latin literature can be detected in the early 14th century, and by the middle of the century PETRARCH and BOCCACCIO were avidly

searching for old texts and self-consciously cultivating a prose style modeled on CICERO. They inaugurated an age of research and discovery in which the humanists ransacked the monastic libraries of Europe for old manuscripts, and such scholars as FICINO, BESSARION, POLIZIANO and ERASMUS set new standards in learning and critical scholarship. Greek was also studied, particularly after the fall of Constantinople in 1453 drove many Greek scholars to the West. The invention of printing (c1440) and the discovery of the New World (1492) by COLUMBUS gave further impetus to the search for knowledge.

The Renaissance marked the end of FEUDALISM and the rise of national governments, in Spain under FERDINAND II of Aragon, in France under FRANCIS I, in England under HENRY VIII and ELIZABETH I, and in Holland. In Italy, however, independent city states— Ferrara, Florence, Mantua, Milan, Venice, papal Rome—engaged in fierce rivalry, providing MACHIAVELLI with his famous "ideal" of a Renaissance prince. Prosperous trading provided money for the arts, and princes like Cosimo de' MEDICI eagerly patronized artists, musicians and scholars. Renaissance PAINTING and SCULPTURE flourished in Florence and Rome with the works of BOTTICELLI, MICHELANGELO and RAPHAEL. Literary revivals occurred in England, France and Spain; SHAKESPEARE and SPENSER were prominent in Renaissance ENGLISH LITERATURE and some of the finest French writing came from RABELAIS and RONSARD. *Musica Reservata*, composed by JOSQUIN DES PRES and LASSUS, was among the styles of Renaissance music. In science the findings of the astronomers COPERNICUS and GALILEO were the basis of modern astronomy and marked a turning point in scientific and philosophical thought.

RENAN, Joseph Ernest (1823–1892), French historian and orientalist. Agnostic and subtly ironical, he wrote on the origins of Christianity, notably the *Life of Jesus* (1863). Among many other works is the *History of the People of Israel* (1887–93).

RENAULT, Louis (1843–1918), French jurist who was devoted to the advancement and practice of international law. He was professor at the University of Paris and served also on the HAGUE TRIBUNAL. In 1907 he shared the Nobel Peace Prize.

RENAULT, Mary (pseudonym of Mary Challans, 1905–1983), British novelist. Her popular fictional accounts of the lives of ancient Greeks include *The Bull from the Sea* (1962), *The Mask of Apollo* (1966), and *The Persian Boy* (1973).

RENÉ OF ANJOU (1409–1480), duke of Anjou and Provence. He inherited a claim to the kingdom of Naples (1435) but was defeated by Alfonso V of Aragon in 1442. His daughter Margaret of Anjou married HENRY VI of England. René's court at Angers in France was a brilliant cultural center.

RENI, Guido (1575–1642), Italian BAROQUE painter. After studying at the CARRACCI academy he developed an elegant classical style, using light tones, for religious and mythological themes, such as *Aurora* (1613–14) and *Baptism of Christ* (1623).

RENNER, Karl (1870–1950), Austrian socialist statesman. He was the Austrian Republic's first chancellor (1919–20), president of parliament (1931–33) and, after heading the provisional government, president of Austria, 1945–50.

RENOIR, Jean (1894–1979), French film director, son of Pierre Auguste RENOIR. His motion pictures are characterized by a sensitive feeling for atmosphere and a strong pictorial sense. *La Grande Illusion* (1937) and *The Rules of the Game* (1939) are his masterpieces.

RENOIR, Pierre Auguste (1841–1919), French Impressionist painter. He started painting—with MONET, PISSARRO and SISLEY—scenes of Parisian life, such as *La Grenouillère* (1869) and *The Swing* (1876), using vibrant luminous colors. After IMPRESSIONISM he became mostly interested in figure painting, and his later works are usually large female nudes set in rich landscapes.

RENWICK, James (1818–1895), US architect who designed Grace Church (1843–46) and St. Patrick's Cathedral (dedicated 1879), New York, and other notable buildings, including the SMITHSONIAN INSTITUTION (1846) and Vassar College (1860).

REPARATIONS, term applied since WWI to monetary compensation demanded by victorious nations for material losses suffered in war. In 1919 Germany was committed to pay enormous reparations to the Allies (although the US subsequently waived all claim). Again, in 1945, reparations were exacted from Germany, and Japan was also assessed.

REPIN, Ilya Yefimovich (1844–1930), Russian painter. A leading proponent of the realistic style, his paintings often expressed criticism of the Russian social order during the late 19th century. Many of his paintings are on display in the museums of Moscow and Leningrad.

REPRODUCTION, the process by which an organism produces offspring, an ability that is a unique characteristic of ANIMALS and PLANTS. There are two kinds of reproduction: asexual and sexual. In asexual reproduction, parts of an organism split off to form new individuals, a process found in some animals but which is more common in plants: e.g., the FISSION of single-celled plants; the budding of YEASTS; the fragmentation of filamentous ALGAE; SPORE production in BACTERIA, algae and FUNGI, and the production of vegetative organs in flowering plants (bulbs, rhizomes and tubers). In sexual reproduction, special (haploid) CELLS containing half the normal number of CHROMOSOMES, called gametes, are produced: in animals, sperm by males in the testes and ova by females in the OVARY; in plants, pollen by males in the stamens and ovules by females in the ovary. The joining of gametes (FERTILIZATION) produces a (diploid) cell with the normal number of chromosomes, the zygote, which grows to produce an individual with GENES inherited from both parents (see also HEREDITY). Fertilization may take place inside the female (internal fertilization) or outside (external fertilization). Internal fertilization demands that sperm be introduced into the female— insemination by copulation— and is advantageous because the young spend the most vulnerable early stages of their life-histories protected inside the mother.

At the molecular level, the most important aspect of reproduction is the ability of the chromosome to duplicate itself (see NUCLEIC ACIDS). The production of haploid cells is made possible by a process called meiosis and is necessary to prevent doubling of the chromosome number with each generation in sexually reproducing individuals. The advantage of sexual reproduction is that the bringing together of genes derived from two individuals produces variation in each generation enabling populations to change and thus adapt themselves to changing environmental conditions (see also EVOLUTION; NATURAL SELECTION).

REPTILES, once one of the most numerous and diverse groups of animals, today reduced to four groups: the CROCODILES; the LIZARDS and SNAKES; the TORTOISES and TURTLES; and the tuatara. Modern reptiles are characterized by a scaly skin, simple teeth in the jaw, and an undivided heart. They are coldblooded, and sexual reproduction results in the laying of large yolky eggs. However, when fossil groups are considered, the class is not so clearly defined, for the later reptiles merge with their avian and mammalian descendants. Many were fur-covered and warm-blooded and had developed other features of present-day birds and mammals. Some may even have been viviparous.

REPUBLIC (from Latin *res publica*: the state), form of government in which the head of state is not a monarch, and today is usually a president. Popularly, the idea of a republic includes the notion of elected representation and democratic control by the people, but many modern republics do not fulfill this condition. *The Republic* is also the name of the famous dialogue in which PLATO outlined his ideal state.

REPUBLICAN PARTY, one of the two major political parties of the US. It was founded in 1854 by dissidents of the WHIG, DEMOCRATIC and FREE SOIL parties to unify the growing anti-slavery forces. Its first national nominating convention was held in 1856; J. C. FRÉMONT was adopted as presidential candidate. Campaigning for the abolition of slavery and of polygamy in the territories, he captured 11 states. LINCOLN became the first Republican president, and in spite of the unpopularity of the subsequent RECONSTRUCTION policies and the secession of the LIBERAL REPUBLICAN PARTY in 1872, the Republicans remained dominant in US politics, winning 14 out of 18 presidential elections between 1860 and 1932. In an era of scandal, the Republicans consolidated a "pro-business" and "conservative" reputation with the nomination and election of William McKINLEY in 1896. His successor Theodore ROOSEVELT adopted a progressive stance; he defected to the Bull Moose party (see PROGRESSIVE PARTY) in 1912. In 1932 the Democrats swept to power, not to be dislodged until the election of the Republican president EISENHOWER in 1952. His successors KENNEDY and JOHNSON were Democrats. Barry GOLDWATER failed as presidential candidate in 1960, but Richard NIXON's landslide victory in 1972 marked a zenith of party strength. WATERGATE shattered this, contributing to the defeat of Gerald FORD in the 1976 elections. The Republicans rallied again in 1980 to elect Ronald REAGAN; he was reelected in 1984, and his vice president, George BUSH, was elected president in 1988.

REQUIEM, or **requiem mass**, a musical setting of the Roman Catholic MASS for the souls of the dead. The classic settings of the requiem by MOZART and VERDI are generally performed as concert pieces.

REREDOS, an ornamental wall or screen behind the altar in a church. Originally a tapestry, it became a permanent architectural feature, usually of stone or wood and often containing sculpted figures in a richly decorated framework.

RESACA DE LA PALMA, Battle of, second battle of the MEXICAN WAR. On May 9, 1846, after the engagement at PALO ALTO the previous day, US forces under General Zachary TAYLOR pursued and routed the retreating Mexicans.

RESERVE OFFICER TRAINING CORPS (ROTC), US Army recruiting project that holds courses in military leadership in schools and colleges. It grew out of the Land Grant Act of 1862, and began operating full scale under the National Defense Act of 1916. It comprises two to four years of course work and drill plus several weeks of field training. The US Navy and Air Force have similar programs.

RESHEVSKY, Samuel (1911–   ), Polish-born US chess player. Formerly a child prodigy, he was US champion five times between 1936 and 1946, and one of the great modern masters of the game.

RESIN, a high-molecular-weight substance characterized by its gummy or tacky consistency at certain temperatures. Naturally occurring resins include congo copal and bitumen (found as fossils), shellac (from insects) and rosin (from pine trees). Synthetic resins include the wide variety of plastic materials available today and any distinction between PLASTICS and resins is at best arbitrary. The first partially synthetic resins were produced in 1862 using nitrocellulose, vegetable OILS and camphor, and included Xylonite and later, in 1869, CELLULOID. The first totally synthetic resin was Bakelite, which was produced by L. H. BAEKELAND in 1910 from phenol and formaldehyde. The work in the 1920s of H. Staudinger on the polymeric nature of natural RUBBER and styrene resin, which laid the theoretical basis for POLYMER science, was a major factor in stimulating the extremely rapid development of a wide range of synthetic plastics and resins.

RESISTANCE, the ratio of the voltage applied to a conductor to the current flowing through it (see ELECTRICITY; OHM'S LAW), measured in ohms. It is characteristic of the material of which the conductor is made (the resistance presented by a unit cube of a material being called its **resistivity**) and of the physical dimensions of the conductor, increasing as the conductor becomes longer and/or thinner.

RESNAIS, Alain (1922–   ), French film director, important in the "new wave" of the 1950s and 1960s for such films as *Hiroshima Mon Amour* (1959) and *Last Year at Marienbad* (1961).

RESPIGHI, Ottorino (1879–1936), Italian composer, director (1924–26) of the

Accademia di Santa Cecilia in Rome. He is best-known for such tone poems as *The Fountains of Rome* (1917) and *The Pines of Rome* (1924).

RESPIRATION, term applied to several activities and processes occurring in all ANIMALS and PLANTS: e.g., the breathing movements associated with the LUNGS, the uptake of OXYGEN and the release of CARBON dioxide, and the biochemical pathways by which the ENERGY locked in food materials is transferred to energy-rich organic molecules for utilization in the multitude of energy-requiring processes which occur in an organism. Breathing movements, if any, and the exchange of oxygen and carbon dioxide, may be called "external respiration," while the energy-releasing processes which utilize the oxygen and produce carbon dioxide are termed "internal respiration" or "tissue respiration." In man, external respiration is the process whereby air is breathed from the environment into the lungs to provide oxygen for internal respiration. Air, which contains about 20% oxygen, is drawn into the lungs via the nose or mouth, the pharynx, trachea and bronchi. This is achieved by muscular contraction of the intercostal muscles in the chest wall and of the diaphragm; their coordinated movement, controlled by a respiratory center in the brain stem, causes expansion of the chest, and thus of the lung tissue, so that air is drawn in (inspiration). Expiration is usually a passive process of relaxation of the chest wall and diaphragm, allowing the release of the air, which is by now depleted of oxygen and enriched with carbon dioxide. Exchange of gases with the blood circulating in the pulmonary capillaries occurs across the lung alveoli and follows simple diffusion gradients. Disorders of respiration include lung disease (e.g., EMPHYSEMA, PNEUMONIA and PNEUMOCONIOSIS); muscle and nerve disease (e.g., brain-stem STROKE, POLIOMYELITIS, MYASTHENIA GRAVIS and MUSCULAR DYSTROPHY); skeletal deformity; asphyxia, and disorders secondary to metabolic and HEART disease. In man, tissue respiration involves the combination of oxygen with glucose or other nutrients to form high-energy compounds. This reaction also produces carbon dioxide and water.

RESPONSIBLE GOVERNMENT, a government whose executive is responsible to an elected legislature. An example is the British cabinet, which is answerable to the elected House of Commons.

RESTORATION, name given to the return of CHARLES II as king of England in 1660, after the fall of the PROTECTORATE.

Coinciding with a national mood of reaction against the PURITANS, the Restoration was widely popular. The Restoration period (1660 to the fall of JAMES II in 1688) was one of irreverent wit, licentiousness and scientific and literary achievement (see RESTORATION COMEDY). Politically, it was a period of uneasy relations between king and parliament, culminating in the GLORIOUS REVOLUTION.

RESTORATION COMEDY, name given to the witty, bawdy and often satirical comedies written after the reopening of the theaters at the RESTORATION (1660). Masters of the genre include CONGREVE, VANBRUGH and WYCHERLEY.

RESURRECTION, the raising of a dead person to life. The resurrection of JESUS CHRIST on the third day after his death and burial is a basic Christian doctrine attested by earliest New Testament tradition. In recognizable but glorified bodily form he appeared to several groups of disciples; though skeptical, they became convinced that he had overcome death. Christians' eternal life is viewed as participation in Christ's resurrection, culminating in the general bodily resurrection of the dead at the SECOND COMING (see also ESCHATOLOGY; IMMORTALITY).

RETICULO-ENDOTHELIAL SYSTEM, generic name for those CELLS in the body that take up dyes and other foreign material from the BLOOD stream and other body fluids; they are also known as **macrophages.** Blood monocytes are functionally part of the system as are macrophages in the LYMPH nodes, SPLEEN, BONE marrow, LIVER (Kupffer cells) and LUNG alveoli. When foreign material (e.g., BACTERIA) is introduced into the blood stream, macrophages rapidly take it up and destroy it with intracellular ENZYMES. This constitutes a primary defense system and may play a role in establishing IMMUNITY. Similarly, particulate matter in the lungs or liver is cleared by local macrophages.

RETIRED SENIOR VOLUNTEER PROGRAM (RSVP), volunteer program instituted in 1972 and administered by ACTION that provides opportunities for men and women over 60 to serve their communities in such settings as schools, courts, and health care, rehabilitation, day care, youth, and other community centers.

RETIREMENT. The mandatory age for retirement for most workers was raised from 65 to 70 years under a law signed by President Jimmy Carter on Apr. 6, 1978. The law does not apply to businesses with less than 20 employees, nor does it affect people who wish to take voluntary early retirement. The same law also removed the mandatory retirement age of 70 for employees of the federal government.

REUCHLIN, Johann (1455–1522), German Catholic humanist, a famous scholar of Greek and Hebrew. His view that Hebrew books should be preserved and chairs of Hebrew established at German universities set off a quarrel between humanists and church authorities.

REUNION, volcanic island (970sq mi) in the W Indian Ocean, a French possession since 1642 and an overseas department of France since 1946. The islanders, mostly of mixed descent, are nearly all Roman Catholic and speak a Creole patois. Its products include sugar, rum and vanilla. The capital is St. Denis. Pop 535,000.

REUTERS, an international news agency, based in Britain, which distributes information to local agencies, newspapers, television and radio around the world. Founded by P. J. von Reuter (1816–1899) in Germany in 1849, it moved to London 1851, and is today a trust owned mainly by the British press.

REUTHER, Walter Philip (1907–1970), US labor leader, president of the UNITED AUTOMOBILE WORKERS from 1946 until his death in a plane crash. He was president of the Congress of Industrial Organizations 1952–56, and one of the architects of its merger with the AMERICAN FEDERATION OF LABOR, becoming vice president of the combined organization.

REVELATION, the disclosure of truths by God, either directly to PROPHETS or by inspiring Scripture (see BIBLE; KORAN). Whether propositional or embodied in God's "mighty acts," it is the basis of revealed theology as opposed to natural theology. Protestants hold that revelation is sufficiently contained in the Bible; Roman Catholics and Orthodox regard tradition as revelatory.

REVELATION, Book of, or Apocalypse, the last book of the NEW TESTAMENT, traditionally ascribed to St. JOHN the Apostle but probably written by another John, and dated probably c96. After seven letters to the Asia Minor churches, it consists of a series of apocalyptic visions in Old Testament imagery, giving a Christian philosophy of world history.

REVELLE, Roger (1909–   ), US oceanographer, at the U of California's Scripps Institution of Oceanography (1931–64; director, 1950–64). Concerned about ecology, he directed (1964–76) Harvard's Center for Population Studies.

REVELS, Hiram Rhoades (1822–1901), pastor and educator, and first black US

senator. Elected by the Republicans in Miss. for 1870–71, he was subsequently involved in state politics and became president of Alcorn College, Lorman, Miss.

REVERE, Paul (1735–1818), American revolutionary hero, immortalized by LONGFELLOW for his ride from Boston to Lexington (April 18, 1775) to warn the Massachussetts minutemen that "the British are coming." A silversmith and engraver, he joined in the BOSTON TEA PARTY in 1773. During the REVOLUTIONARY WAR, he served the new government, designing and producing the first Continental money, casting official seals and supervising gunpowder and cannon manufacture. After the war he became a prosperous merchant, known for his copper and silver work and his bronze bells.

REVOLUTIONARY WAR, American, in which Britain's 13 North American colonies gained their independence. It was a minor war with immense consequences—the founding of the US and the forging of a new, dynamic democratic ideology in an age of absolutism. Despite elements of civil war and of revolution, the conflict was above all a political, constitutional struggle, and as such began many years before the actual fighting. While the expanding colonies were growing wealthy and independent, Britain adhered to the theory that they were supposed to exist solely for its own profit and were to be tightly ruled by King and Parliament (see MERCANTILISM; NAVIGATION ACTS). Up to 1763, however, control was lax; but after France had been defeated in the New World (see FRENCH AND INDIAN WARS) Britain decided to restore control and tax the colonies to help pay for it. The Navigation Acts were strictly enforced, settlement beyond the Appalachian Mountains was forbidden, a standing army was to be sent to America and quartered at colonial expense, and in 1765 a stamp tax (see STAMP ACT) was imposed. The outraged colonists, near rebellion, drew upon liberal ideas from England and the continent (see ENLIGHTENMENT) to assert the principle of no taxation without representation in the English Parliament. After duties levied by the TOWNSHEND ACTS (1767) resistance centered in Boston, leading to the BOSTON MASSACRE (1770) and the BOSTON TEA PARTY (1773). But after the INTOLERABLE ACTS (1774), aimed at Boston, patriot local assemblies took control in all colonies, and non-importation associations and committees of correspondence flourished, culminating in the First CONTINENTAL CONGRESS (1774). In April-June 1775 fighting flared around disaffected Boston (see battles of

LEXINGTON; CONCORD; BUNKER HILL), and in July George WASHINGTON took command of the Continental Army. In March 1776 the British were forced to evacuate Boston, but an American attempt to conquer Canada (1775–76) failed. Meantime the Second Continental Congress, emboldened by Thomas PAINE's pamphlet *Common Sense*, declared for independence in July 1776.

Washington, with never more than 10–20,000 regulars, plus state militia (see MINUTEMEN), fought a defensive war; the British, with regulars, Tories and mercenaries (see HESSIANS), suffered from confused strategy and extended supply lines across the ocean, and were hindered by the small US Navy and some 2,000 privateers (see JONES, JOHN PAUL). After a brief strike at the South, the British took New York City in September 1776, forcing Washington to retreat into New Jersey. The small victories of TRENTON and PRINCETON heartened the patriots, but Philadelphia fell in September 1777. Meantime General BURGOYNE, sweeping down into New York from Canada, was forced to surrender his troops at SARATOGA in October, an American triumph that brought France in as an ally of the US. But Washington, wintering at VALLEY FORGE, was barely able to keep his troops together.

Turning to the South, the British took Savannah (1778) and Charleston (1780), defeating GATES at Camden, S.C., in August, 1870. But after the defeat of KING'S MOUNTAIN in October, the British gradually withdrew N into Va. In 1781 CORNWALLIS, bottled up in Yorktown, Va. by a French fleet and a Franco-American army under Washington, surrendered on October 19, virtually ending the war, though the Treaty of PARIS was not signed until Sept. 4, 1783. The ideological struggle, which had found its best expression in the Declaration of Independence, came to a noble conclusion with the framing of the Constitution in 1787.

REVOLUTION OF 1688. See GLORIOUS REVOLUTION.

REVOLUTIONS OF 1848, series of unsuccessful revolutionary uprisings in France, Italy, the Austrian Empire and Germany in 1848. They were relatively spontaneous and self-contained, but had a number of common causes: the successful example of the FRENCH REVOLUTION of 1789, economic unrest due to bad harvests and unemployment, and a growing frustration, fired by nationalist fervor, about the repressive policies of conservative statesmen like METTERNICH and GUIZOT. In Feb. 1848, a major uprising in Paris overthrew King LOUIS PHILIPPE and Guizot, but it was

suppressed and the Second Republic proclaimed. In Italy, during the RISORGIMENTO, short-lived republics were proclaimed, and there was agitation to secure independence from Austria, which was itself shaken by revolutions in Vienna, Prague and Hungary. The demand for a representative government led to an all-German Diet in Frankfurt, which failed in its efforts to unite Germany. In England there was working-class agitation (see CHARTISM), and other European countries were also affected.

REXROTH, Kenneth (1905–1982), US poet and critic who also translated Japanese, Chinese, and Greek poetry.

REYES, Rafael (1850–1921), president of Colombia 1904–09. After 10 years exploring the Amazon jungles, he fought in the civil wars 1885–95. Dictatorial as president, he resigned over his treaty with the US recognizing an independent Panama.

REYKJAVÍK, capital of Iceland and its chief port, commercial and industrial center, and home of its cod-fishing fleet. Its name means "smoking bay," from the nearby hot springs which provide the city with central heating. Pop 87,309.

REYNARD THE FOX, leading character in a popular medieval series of FABLES. Appearing first in the area between Flanders and Germany in the 10th century, the tales, with their cunning but sympathetic hero and biting satire, became popular in France, Germany and the Low Countries.

REYNAUD, Paul (1878–1966), conservative French statesman. After holding a number of cabinet posts (from 1930), he became premier in 1940. An opponent of the Nazis, he resigned and spent WWII in prison. Afterwards he returned to politics, held several posts and helped draft the constitution of the Fifth Republic (1958).

REYNOLDS, Sir Joshua (1723–1792), perhaps the most famous English portrait painter. Ambitious and popular, he became first president of the ROYAL ACADEMY OF ARTS in 1768. He held that great art is based on the styles of earlier masters, and espoused the "Grand Style." He painted nearly all his notable contemporaries, including his friend Samuel JOHNSON (1772), and published influential *Discourses* (1769–90).

REZA SHAH PAHLAVI (1877–1944), shah of Iran, 1925–41. An army officer, he led a coup in 1921, becoming prime minister and later (1925) founder of the Pahlavi dynasty. He made important military, administrative and economic reforms, but the Allies forced him to resign in WWII for attempting to keep Iran neutral.

RHAETO-ROMANIC, a group of minor ROMANCE LANGUAGES. They include *Romansh* (spoken in SE Switzerland), *Ladin* (the Italian Tyrol) and *Friulian* (NE Italy), all probably derived from Latin. (See also INDO-EUROPEAN LANGUAGES.)

RHAPSODY, a free musical composition, not written in a set form or style, and often a free or romantic treatment of one or more themes. Well-known examples are LISZT'S *Hungarian Rhapsodies* and GERSHWIN'S *Rhapsody in Blue.*

RHAZES, or **abu Bakr Muhammad ibn Zakariyya al-Razi** (c860–925), Persian physician and practical chemist, the author of numerous medical treatises and possibly the earliest to distinguish MEASLES from SMALLPOX.

RHEE, Syngman (1875–1965), president of South Korea. A leader in the movement to win Korean independence from Japan, he was in exile 1910–45, serving as president of the Korean Provisional Government for 20 years. He returned to Korea after WWII, and became the first president of the Republic of Korea (South Korea) in 1948. He led the nation through the Korean War but was forced from office in 1960 because of corruption and mismanagement by some of his appointees.

RHEIMS. See REIMS.

RHEOSTAT, a variable resistor used to control the current drawn by an electric MOTOR, to dim LIGHTING, etc. It may consist of a resistive wire, wound in a helix, with a sliding contact varying the effective length, or of a series of fixed resistors connected between a row of button contacts. Or, for heavy loads, electrodes dipped in SOLUTIONS can be used, the RESISTANCE being controlled by the immersion depth and separation of the electrodes.

RHESUS MONKEY, *Macaca mulatta,* an omnivorous macaque found in many parts of Asia.

RHETORIC, the art of speaking and writing with the purpose of persuading or influencing others. It was taught by the Greek SOPHISTS in the 5th century BC. The first systematic treatise on it is ARISTOTLE'S *Rhetoric.* CICERO and QUINTILIAN wrote on it, and it was a major course at medieval universities as one of the seven liberal arts.

RHETT, Robert Barnwell (Robert Barnwell Smith; 1800–1876), US "Fire-Eater," representative (1837–49) and senator for S.C. (1850–52). A violent secessionist, he helped draft the Confederate Constitution in 1861.

RHEUMATIC FEVER, feverish illness, following infection with STREPTOCOCCUS and leading to systemic disease. Skin rash, subcutaneous nodules and a migrating ARTHRITIS are commonly seen. Involvement of the HEART may lead to palpitations, chest pain, cardiac failure, MYOCARDITIS and INFLAMMATION of the pericardium; murmurs may be heard and the ELECTROCARDIOGRAPH may show conduction abnormality. Sydenham's CHOREA may also be seen, with awkwardness, clumsiness and involuntary movements. Late effects include chronic valve disease of the heart leading to stenosis or incompetence, particularly of the mitral or aortic valves. Such valve disease may occur in the young and middle aged and may require surgical correction. Treatment of acute rheumatic fever includes bed rest, ASPIRIN and STEROIDS. PENICILLIN treatment of streptococcal disease may prevent recurrence. Patients with valve damage require ANTIBIOTICS during operations, especially dental and urinary tract SURGERY, to prevent bacterial endocarditis.

RHEUMATISM, imprecise term describing various disorders of the joints, including RHEUMATIC FEVER and rheumatoid ARTHRITIS.

Rh FACTOR or **RHESUS FACTOR.** See BLOOD.

RHINE, Joseph Banks (1895–1980), US parapsychologist whose pioneering laboratory studies of ESP demonstrated the possibility of telepathy (see PARAPSYCHOLOGY).

RHINE RIVER (German: *Rhein*), longest river in Western Europe, rising in Switzerland and flowing 820mi through Germany and the Netherlands into the North Sea near Rotterdam. It is of great historical and commercial significance, being navigable by seagoing ships up to Cologne, and by large barges as far as Basel. Canals link it to the Rhône, Marne, Ems, Weser, Elbe, Oder and Danube rivers. Some of its finest scenery is along the gorge between Bingen and Bonn, with terraced vineyards, ruined castles and famous landmarks like the LORELEI rock.

RHINITIS, INFLAMMATION of the mucous membranes of the nose causing runny nasal discharge, and seen in the common COLD, INFLUENZA and HAY FEVER. Irritation in the nose and sneezing are common.

RHINOCEROSES, a family, Rhinocerotidae, of five species of heavy land animals characterized by a long nasal "horn" or "horns." They are bulky animals with thick, hairless skin, often falling in heavy loose folds. They live in transitional habitat between open grassland and high forest, grazing or browsing on the bushes or shrubs. All five species—the square-lipped, or white, rhino; the black rhino; the great Indian; Sumatran, and Javan rhinos—are on the verge of extinction. The horn is not true horn but is formed of a mass of compacted hairs.

RHIZOME, or **rootstock,** the swollen horizontal underground stem of certain PLANTS that acts as an organ of perennation and vegetative propagation. They last for several years and new shoots appear each spring from the axils of scale leaves.

RHODE ISLAND, a New England state in the NE US, the smallest state of the Union. It is bordered on the N and E by Mass., W by Conn., and S by the Atlantic Ocean.

Name of state: Rhode Island (Officially: Rhode Island and Providence Plantations)
Capital: Providence
Statehood: May 29, 1790 (13th state)
Familiar Name: Little Rhody
Area: 1,214sq mi
Population: 975,000
Elevation: Highest—812ft, Jerimoth Hill Lowest—sea level, Atlantic Ocean
Motto: Hope
State Flower: Violet
State Bird: Rhode Island Red
State Tree: Red maple
State Song: "Rhode Island"

Land. Most of Rhode Island lies W of Narrangansett Bay, which extends 28mi inland. There are two major regions: the Seaboard or Coastal Lowlands, including the islands in Narrangansett Bay and the land E of the bay; and the New England Upland to the W. About two-thirds of the state is forested. The climate ranges from about 28°F in winter to about 70°F in summer.

People. The population is heavily urban (87%), and the largest cities are Providence, Warwick, Pawtucket and Cranston. About 97% of the population is white, and over half is Roman Catholic.

Economy. Manufacturing is still of prime importance, with tourism second and agriculture third. The chief farm products are milk, eggs, potatoes and hay. Apples are

the principal fruit crop, and fish and shellfish also contribute to the economy. Principal manufactures include jewelry, electrical machinery, primary and fabricated metals, and plastic and rubber goods.

History. VERRAZANO probably reached Rhode Island in 1524, and in 1636 Roger WILLIAMS established the first settlement at Providence on land purchased from the NARRAGANSETT INDIANS. Charles II of England granted a charter in 1663. Religious and political freedom from the start formed part of the colony's traditions. In the 18th century Rhode Islanders resented British interference in their flourishing trade and Rhode Island was the first colony to declare independence from Britain in 1776 but also the last of the original 13 colonies to ratify the US Constitution. A new liberal state constitution followed after DORR's rebellion in 1842. The fast-expanding textile industry attracted thousands of immigrants while the state became known as the summer home of wealthy industrialists.

Since WWII, varied industries have begun to replace the declining textile industry, but unemployment was a problem until the economic boom that affected all New England in the 1980s. With prosperity came increased concern about the environment, especially ocean pollution. In presidential elections 1968–88, Rhode Island voted Democratic in 1968, 1976–80, and 1988.

RHODES, Cecil John (1853–1902), British statesman and business magnate, who first opened up Rhodesia to European settlement. He founded the De Beers Mining Company in 1880 at Kimberly in South Africa, and in 1889 formed a company to develop the area that is now Zimbabwe. Premier of the Cape Colony from 1890, he was forced to resign through his complicity in the Jameson raid (1896) into the Transvaal. Much of his £6 million fortune went to found the RHODES SCHOLARSHIPS.

RHODES, Greek island (540sq mi) and its capital city off the SW coast of Turkey. Its exports include wine, fruit and olive oil. The city of Rhodes was a prosperous city-state in the 3rd century BC. At its harbor stood the Colossus of Rhodes, a statue that was one of the Seven Wonders of the World.

RHODESIA. See ZIMBABWE.

RHODES SCHOLARSHIPS, instituted at OXFORD UNIVERSITY by the bequest of Cecil RHODES for students from the British Commonwealth, the US and Germany. Elections are based on general grounds as well as on academic ability.

RHODODENDRON, a genus of mostly

evergreen shrubs that are mainly native to the forests of the E Himalayas. They bear leathery dark-green leaves and, in late spring, masses of fragrant blossom. There are many popular horticultural varieties in cultivation. Azaleas are deciduous members of the same genus. Family: Ericaceae.

RHONE RIVER, an important European river, 507mi long, rising in Switzerland and flowing through Lake Geneva and then SW and S through France into the Mediterranean Sea. With its tributaries, particularly the Isère and the Saône, it has a large flow of water, which has been harnessed in major hydroelectric schemes. Navigable in part, it is linked by canal to the Camargue region.

RHUBARB, or pieplant, *Rheum rhaponticum,* was first cultivated in China for its purgative medicinal rootstock. As a vegetable the pink fleshy leaf-stalks, or petioles, are eaten stewed or in pies. The petioles sprout from underground rhizomes and bear large green leaves that can be poisonous. Family: Polygonaceae.

RHUMB LINE, or loxodrome, in NAVIGATION, line of constant compass direction, crossing all lines of longitude at the same angle, and represented by a straight line on the MERCATOR projection. It spirals toward the poles, and is not as short a distance between two points as the great circle route.

RHYME, in poetry, the placing of words with identical or similar sounds in a regular pattern, usually at the ends of lines. Rhymes can be strong (*harp, sharp*), weak (*cotton, rotten*—accent not on last syllable) or imperfect in other ways. Rhyme has characterized much European poetry since the Middle Ages, and certain forms, for example the BALLAD or SONNET, have set rhyme-patterns.

RHYS, Jean (1894–1979), English novelist, born in Dominica, West Indies. The publication of *Wide Sargasso Sea* (1966)—about the early years of Mrs. Rochester, a character in Charlotte Brontë's *Jane Eyre*—led to the "rediscovery" of Rhys's earlier works, which also focused on alienated women in a male-dominated society. These include *Quartet* (1929), *After Leaving Mr. Mackenzie* (1930), *Voyage in the Dark* (1934) and *Good Morning, Midnight* (1939).

RHYTHM, a regular pattern of stressed beats, especially characteristic of MUSIC and POETRY. In Western music the commonest rhythms are 2/4, 3/4, 4/4 and 6/8 (two, three, four and six beats in a bar). A typical 3/4 rhythm is the waltz. Broken rhythms are called SYNCOPATION. In poetry the term

describes the pattern of stressed and unstressed words in a line of verse or a poem.

RHYTHMS, Biological. See BIOLOGICAL CLOCKS.

RIBAUT or **RIBAULT, Jean** (c1520–1565), mariner who colonized Fla. On present-day Parris Island, S.C., he set up a colony in 1562. He fled to England to escape persecution as a HUGUENOT, and in 1563 published *The Whole and True Discouerye of Terra Florida.* In 1565 he was shipwrecked off Fla., and killed by Spanish forces.

RIBBENTROP, Joachim von (1893–1946), German Nazi leader, ambassador to the UK 1936–38 and foreign minister 1938–45. He helped to negotiate the Rome–Berlin Axis in 1936 and the Russo–German non-aggression pact of 1939 and to plan the invasion of Poland, but wielded little influence in WWII. He was hanged for war crimes.

RIBERA, Jusepe de (1591–1652), Spanish painter who lived after 1616 in Naples. His work, influenced by CARAVAGGIO, is noted for its combination of naturalism and mysticism, as in the *Martyrdom of St. Sebastian* (1630) and *The Penitent Magdalen* (c1640).

RIBICOFF, Abraham Alexander (1910–　　), US public official, widely known as a champion of consumer protection. A Democrat, he was a Conn. congressman 1949–53, governor 1955–61 and senator 1963–1981. Under President KENNEDY he was secretary of health, education and welfare 1961–62.

RIBOFLAVIN, or vitamin B₂. See VITAMINS.

RIBONUCLEIC ACID (RNA). See NUCLEIC ACIDS.

RIBOSOMES, tiny granules, of diameter about 10nm, found in CELL cytoplasm. They are composed of PROTEIN and a special form of ribonucleic acid (see NUCLEIC ACIDS) known as ribosomal RNA. The ribosome is the site of protein synthesis.

RICARDO, David (1772–1823), English economist, founder with Adam SMITH of the "classical school." He made a fortune as a stockbroker and then devoted his time to economics and politics, becoming a member of Parliament 1819–23. His main work is *Principles of Political Economy and Taxation* (1817), which pioneered the use of theoretical models in analyzing the distribution of wealth. (See also ECONOMICS; VALUE.)

RICCI, Matteo (1552–1610), Italian Jesuit missionary to China. After teaching in Goa, he entered China in 1583, learned Chinese and eventually won acceptance, reaching Peking in 1601. He introduced Western mathematics, astronomy and geography to the Chinese, and in turn sent the first modern detailed reports of China back to the West.

RICE, Elmer (1892–1967), US dramatist. His plays on social themes include *The Adding Machine* (1923), an expressionist fantasy on mechanization, *Street Scene* (1929), a Pulitzer prize-winning portrait of life in a New York tenement, and the romantic comedy, *Dream Girl* (1945).

RICE, *Oryza sativa*, a grain-yielding annual plant of the GRASS family, Graminae. It is grown chiefly in S and E Asia where it is the staple food of hundreds of millions of people. Rice needs hot moist conditions to grow, which historically made it highly dependent on MONSOON rainfall. But improved irrigation, fertilizers, pesticides and the development of improved varieties have enormously increased the yield. Machinery for planting and harvesting rice is used in the US and parts of South America, but in the Orient rice-farming methods are still primitive, using hand labor. Rice has a reasonable nutrient value, but when "polished" much of its VITAMIN B₁ content is lost, resulting in a high incidence of the deficiency disease, BERIBERI, wherever polished rice is a staple.

RICHARD, name of three kings of England. **Richard I** (1157–1199), called *Coeur de Lion* (the Lion Heart), was the third son of HENRY II, whom he succeeded in 1189. He spent all but six months of his reign out of England, mainly on the Third CRUSADE. After taking Cyprus and Acre in 1191 and recapturing Jaffa in 1192, he was captured returning to England and handed over to the Emperor HENRY VI, who held him for ransom till 1194. After a brief spell in England he spent the rest of his life fighting against PHILIP II in France. **Richard II** (1367–1400), son of EDWARD THE BLACK PRINCE, succeeded his grandfather EDWARD III in 1377. In his minority the country was governed by a group of nobles dominated by his uncle JOHN OF GAUNT. Richard quarreled with them but only began to assert himself after 1397; he executed his uncle the Duke of Gloucester and banished Henry Bolingbroke, Gaunt's son, and confiscated his estates. Bolingbroke returned in 1399 to depose Richard and imprison him in Pontefract castle, where he died. Bolingbroke succeeded as HENRY IV. **Richard III** (1452–1485), third son of Richard Plantagenet, Duke of York, and the younger brother of EDWARD IV, usurped the throne in 1483. The traditional picture of

him as a hunchbacked and cruel ruler who murdered his nephews in the Tower has little historical backing. He instituted many reforms and encouraged trade, but had little hope of defeating his many enemies gathering in France under Henry Tudor (later HENRY VII). They defeated and killed Richard at BOSWORTH FIELD.

RICHARDS, Ivor Armstrong (1893–1979), influential English literary critic and semanticist. He developed with C. K. Ogden the concept of **Basic English**, a primary vocabulary of 850 words. His books include *The Meaning of Meaning* (with Ogden, 1923) and *Principles of Literary Criticism* (1924).

RICHARDSON, Elliot Lee (1920–   ), US lawyer and government official, assistant secretary of health, education and welfare 1957–59, Mass. lieutenant governor (1965–67) and attorney general 1967–69. Secretary of health, education and welfare 1970–73, he was appointed secretary of defense and then attorney general 1973, but resigned over the WATERGATE SCANDAL. He was ambassador to the UK 1975–76 and US secretary of commerce 1976–77.

RICHARDSON, Henry Hobson (1838–1886), influential US architect who pioneered an American Romanesque style. Among his important buildings are the Trinity Church, Boston, and the Marshall Field Wholesale Store in Chicago.

RICHARDSON, Sir Ralph (1902–1983), English actor. A distinguished interpreter of Shakespeare and the classics, he was knighted in 1947. A star on stage, he generally played supporting roles in motion pictures. His films include *Richard III* (1956) and *Long Day's Journey into Night* (1962).

RICHARDSON, Samuel (1689–1761), important English novelist, best known for his novels in epistolary form, especially *Pamela* (1740–41), the story of a servant girl's moral triumph over her lecherous master. *Clarissa* (1747–48), his tragic masterpiece, is also on the theme of seduction. *Sir Charles Grandison* (1753–54) portrays a virtuous hero, in contrast to the amoral hero of FIELDING'S *Tom Jones.*

RICHARDSON, Tony (Cecil Antonio Richardson; 1928–   ), British stage and film director, noted for *Look Back in Anger* (play, 1956; film, 1959), *The Entertainer* (play, 1957; film, 1960), *A Taste of Honey* (play, 1960; film, 1961), and *Loneliness of the Long Distance Runner* (film, 1962).

RICHELIEU, Armand Jean du Plessis, Duc de (1585–1642), French cardinal, statesman and chief minister to LOUIS XIII for 18 years. By a mixture of diplomacy and ruthlessness he helped make France the leading power in Europe with a monarchy secure against internal revolt. He destroyed HUGUENOT power by 1628, foiled an attempt by Maria de MÉDICIS to oust him in 1630, and suppressed the plots of the Duc de Montmorency in 1632 and of Cinq-Mars in 1642, at the same time reducing the power of the nobles. In foreign policy he opposed the HAPSBURGS, intervening against them in the THIRTY YEARS' WAR. Richelieu strengthened the navy, encouraged colonial development and patronized the arts.

RICHMOND, state capital of Va. and from 1861 to 1865 capital of the Confederacy. Located at the navigation head of the James R, it is a port and a financial and distribution center, as well as being an important industrial city, with tobacco and food processing, chemicals, metals and wood products. It has many historic buildings and places of higher education. Pop (city) 219,000, (metro) 801,000.

RICHTER, Conrad (1890–1968), US novelist, author of the frontier trilogy *The Trees* (1940), *The Fields* (1946), and *The Town* (1950).

RICHTER, Hans (1843–1916), Hungarian conductor who presented the first performance of WAGNER'S *Ring* cycle at BAYREUTH in 1876. A BRAHMS specialist also, he conducted in England for many years.

RICHTER, Johann Paul Friedrich (1763–1825), German humorous and sentimental novelist, who wrote as Jean Paul. His early works were satirical; but he achieved popularity with such works as *The Invisible Lodge* (1793), *The Life of Quintus Fixlein* (1796) and the four-volume *Titan* (1800–03).

RICHTER SCALE, scale devised by C. F. Richter (1900–1985), used to measure the magnitudes of EARTHQUAKES in terms of the amplitude and frequency of the surface waves. The largest recorded earthquakes are about 8.5 and a great earthquake of magnitude 8 occurs only once every 5–10 years. Because the scale is logarithmic, an increase of one unit corresponds to a ten-fold increase in the size of an earthquake.

RICHTHOFEN, Manfred, Baron von (1892–1918), German WWI airman, nicknamed the "Red Baron." Known for the daring and chivalry with which he led his squadron, he shot down around 80 opponents and was himself killed in action.

RICKENBACKER, Edward Vernon (1890–1973), US air ace of WWI; he shot down 26 aircraft. After the war he became an automotive and airline executive.

RICKETS, VITAMIN D deficiency disease in children causing disordered BONE growth at the epiphyses, with growth retardation, defective mineralization of bone, epiphyseal irregularity on X-RAY, and pliability and tendency to FRACTURE of bones. It is common among the malnourished, especially in cool climates where vitamin D formation in the SKIN is minimal. Treatment is by vitamin D replacement.

RICKETTSIA, organisms partway between BACTERIA and VIRUSES that are obligatory intracellular organisms but have a more complex structure than viruses. They are responsible for a number of diseases (often borne by TICKS or LICE) including TYPHUS, scrub typhus and ROCKY MOUNTAIN SPOTTED FEVER; related organisms cause Q FEVER and PSITTACOSIS. They are sensitive to TETRACYCLINES and cause characteristic serological reactions cross-specific to proteus bacteria.

RICKEY, Branch Wesley (1881–1965), US baseball executive, nicknamed "The Mahatma." As general manager of the St. Louis Cardinals, he pioneered the minor league "farm system," and as a Brooklyn Dodgers executive in 1947, he signed Jackie ROBINSON, thus breaking baseball's color barrier.

RICKOVER, Hyman George (1900–1986), Russian-born US admiral who brought nuclear power to the US Navy. Head of the Navy's electrical division in WWII, he moved to the Atomic Energy Commission in 1947, and developed the first nuclear-powered submarine, the *Nautilus* (1954). Serving well beyond the usual retirement age, he attained the rank of full admiral at the age of 73.

RIDGWAY, Matthew Bunker (1895–), US military leader. During WWII he led the first full-scale US airborne attack in the invasion of Sicily (1943) and took part in the invasion of France (1944). He became commander of the United Nations forces in Korea (1951), supreme commander of NATO Allied Forces in Europe (1952–53) and US army chief of staff (1953–55).

RIDLEY, Nicholas (c1500–1555), English Protestant martyr. Under CRANMER'S patronage he became a chaplain to HENRY VIII and bishop of Rochester (1547) and London (1550). He helped compile the BOOK OF COMMON PRAYER. On the accession of the Roman Catholic MARY I (1553) he was imprisoned and burnt as a heretic with Hugh Latimer at Oxford.

RIEFENSTAHL, Leni (1902–), German film actress and director whose movie *The Blue Light* (1932) brought her to the attention of Adolf Hitler. She subsequently made two documentaries for the Nazis, *Triumph of the Will* (1935) and *Olympiad* (1938), considered among the most brilliant propaganda films ever produced.

RIEGGER, Wallingford (1885–1961), US composer. In many of his works he used TWELVE-TONE techniques. He wrote ballet scores, symphonies and chamber works.

RIEL, Louis (1844–1885), Canadian *métis* (person of mixed Indian and French descent) and rebel leader. In 1869 he organized the *métis* of Red River, now in Manitoba, to oppose Canada's annexation of these territories. He fled to the US after government troops had moved in (1870). On his return to Canada (1873) he was elected to the House of Commons, but was expelled in 1874 and banished in 1875. In 1884 he led another Indian uprising in Saskatchewan, but was captured in May, 1885. His execution for treason became a cause of friction between English and French Canadians.

RIEMANN, Georg Friedrich Bernhard (1826–1866), German mathematician, whose best known contribution to diverse fields of mathematics is the initiation of studies of NON-EUCLIDEAN GEOMETRY. Elliptic geometry is often named Riemannian geometry for him.

RIEMENSCHNEIDER, Tilman (c1460–1531), German Gothic sculptor in wood and stone. He worked in Würzburg, where many of his works survive, and carved the marble tomb of Emperor Henry II and his wife in Bamberg Cathedral (1499–1513).

RIENZI, Cola di (c1313–1354), Italian popular leader. With papal support, he became "Tribune" of a popular republic in Rome (1347), but his plans for restoring the Roman Empire led to his overthrow by the nobles and exile. He returned triumphantly in 1354 but was killed in a riot.

RIESMAN, David (1909–   ), US sociologist whose best-known work, *The Lonely Crowd* (1950), explores the changing nature of the US social character in a highly industrialized urban society.

RIFLE, strictly any firearm with a "rifled" bore—i.e., with shallow helical grooves cut inside the barrel. These grooves, by causing the bullet to spin, steady it and increase its accuracy, velocity and range. The term "rifle" is more narrowly applied to the long-barreled hand weapon fired from the shoulder. Rifles are generally classified by caliber or decimal fractions or by mode of action. "Single-shot" rifles are manually reloaded after each discharge; "repeaters" are reloaded from a magazine by means of a hand-operated mechanism that ejects the spent cartridge case and drives a fresh cartridge into the breech. In semiautomatic rifles, chambering and ejection operations are powered by gas produced as the weapon is fired. Today, many rifles have an optional fully automatic action, a single squeeze of the trigger emptying the magazine in seconds.

RIFT VALLEY, or graben, a valley formed by the relative downthrow of land between two roughly parallel FAULTS. The best known are the Great Rift Valley of E Africa, and the Rhine Rift Valley between Basel and Bingen.

RIGAUD, Hyacinthe (1659–1743), French portrait painter in the style of VAN DYCK. His subjects included Louis XIV (1701) and Louis XV (1715).

RIGHTS OF MAN, Declaration of the. See DECLARATION OF THE RIGHTS OF MAN AND THE CITIZEN.

RIGHT-TO-DIE LAWS, legislation permitting physicians to withdraw life-sustaining treatment for terminally ill patients under prescribed circumstances. The laws grew out of advances in medicine that permitted doctors to sustain life indefinitely for persons who had no hope for recovery or any ability to function normally. Aside from the expense involved, some patients and their families believed that the right to die with dignity was being denied. In 1976 the N.J. Supreme Court ruled that a hospital respirator being used to sustain the life of Karen Anne Quinlan, 22, long in a comatose state, could be disconnected so that she might "die with grace and dignity"; this was done but she continued to live. That same year Cal. adopted a right-to-die law, and subsequently several more states did the same. The laws required the consent of the patient, if conscious.

RIGHT TO LIFE COMMITTEE, National. See ABORTION CONTROVERSY.

RIGHT-TO-WORK LAWS, laws enforced in 19 US states requiring companies to maintain an "open shop." This means that a person may not be prevented from working because he does not belong to a union, nor may he be forced to take up, or maintain, membership in a union.

RIGOR MORTIS, stiffness of the body MUSCLES occurring some hours after DEATH and caused by biochemical alterations in muscle. The body is set in the position held at the onset of the changes.

RIG VEDA. See VEDA.

RIIS, Jacob August (1849–1914), Danish-born US journalist and social reformer whose book, *How the Other Half Lives* (1890), drew attention to slum conditions in New York City. He worked as a police reporter on the *New York Tribune* (1877–88) and the *New York Evening Sun* (1888–99).

RILEY, James Whitcomb (1849–1916), US poet, known as the "Hoosier poet." *The Old Swimmin' Hole and 'Leven More Poems* (1883) was the first of many popular collections of humorous and sentimental dialect poems.

RILKE, Rainer Maria (1875–1926), German lyric poet. His complex and symbolic poems are preoccupied with spiritual questioning about God and death, as in the *Book of Hours* (1905) and *New Poems* (1907–08). His later *Duino Elegies* (1912–20; published 1923) and the *Sonnets to Orpheus* (1923) are richly mystical. Rilke is one of the great founding figures in modern literature.

RIMBAUD, Arthur (1854–1891), French poet. A precocious youth, he associated with VERLAINE, published *A Season in Hell* in 1873, and thereafter denounced his poetry, becoming an adventurer. His vivid imagery and his "disordering of consciousness," reflected in the fragmented technique of such poems as "The Drunken Boat," have had an enormous influence on modern poetry.

RIMSKY-KORSAKOV, Nikolai Andreyevich (1844–1908), Russian composer. While still a naval officer he started teaching composition at the St. Petersburg Conservatory (1871). He wrote scores for the operas *The Snow Maiden* (1882) and *The Golden Cockerel* (1907) and a colorful symphonic suite, *Scheherazade* (1888).

RINDERPEST, acute VIRUS disease, particularly of cattle, common in N Africa and S Asia. Although there have been outbreaks in other parts of the world, North America has hitherto remained unaffected by this usually fatal disease.

RINEHART, Mary Roberts (1876–1958), American writer of perennially popular detective stories, including *The Circular Staircase* (1908). She also wrote an autobiography, *My Story* (1931).

RINGLING BROTHERS, five US brothers who created the world's largest CIRCUS. Led by **John Ringling** (1866–1936), they started with a one-wagon show and became BARNUM and BAILEY's chief rivals, buying them out in 1907. The combined Ringling Bros., Barnum & Bailey Circus was the world's largest by 1930, and remained in the family's hands until 1967.

RINGWORM, common FUNGUS disease of the SKIN of man and animals which may also affect the HAIR or nails. Ringshaped raised lesions occur, often with central scarring; temporary BALDNESS is seen on hairy skin, together with the disintegration of the nails. ATHLETE'S FOOT is ringworm of the toes, while *tinea cruris* is a variety affecting the groin. Various fungi may be responsible, including *Trichophyton* and *Microspora*. Treatments include topical ointments (e.g., benzyl benzoate) or systemic antifungal ANTIBIOTICS such as Griseofulvin.

RIO DE JANEIRO, second largest city of Brazil, on the Atlantic coast about 200mi W of São Paulo. Located in a picturesque setting, the city is a famous tourist resort. It is also a leading commercial center and port, and also an industrial center, manufacturing clothing, furniture, glassware and foodstuffs. The area was settled by the French (1555–67) and then by the Portuguese. It was the Brazilian capital from 1822 to 1960, when it was supplanted by Brasília. Pop (city) 5,615,149; (metro) 10,400,000.

RIO DE LA PLATA (English: Plate R), an estuary formed by the Paraná R and Uruguay R, separating Argentina to the S and Uruguay to the N. It flows 171mi SE into the Atlantic.

RIO GRANDE, one of the longest rivers in North America, known in Mexico as the Río Bravo del Norte. It rises in the San Juan Mts in SW Col. and flows 1,885mi SE and S to the Gulf of Mexico at Brownsville, Tex., and Matamoros, Mexico. From El Paso, Tex., to its mouth, it forms the US–Mexico border.

RIO TREATY, Inter-American Treaty of Reciprocal Assistance signed in 1947 by all states of the W hemisphere except Canada, Ecuador and Nicaragua. It binds the signatories not to use force on the American continent without the unanimous consent of the others, and regards an attack against one as an attack against all.

RIPARIAN RIGHTS, or water rights, belonging to owners of land on the edge of streams, rivers and lakes. They allow a landowner to use the water for domestic, agricultural or commercial purposes, usually with the provision that such use should not infringe the rights of other riparian owners.

RIPLEY, George (1802–1880), US social reformer and literary critic. Beginning as a Unitarian pastor, he became a TRANSCENDENTALIST, founded and ran the BROOK FARM community, 1841–47. Later he became an influential literary critic with the *New York Tribune*.

RISORGIMENTO (Italian: resurgence), Italian 19th-century period of literary and political nationalism leading to a unified Italy in 1870. After 1815, various states, stirred by revolutionaries like MAZZINI, rose against their Austrian or papal rulers. Unification under VICTOR EMMANUEL II was achieved by CAVOUR, who involved the French in wars against Austria, and by the victories of GARIBALDI.

RITES OF PASSAGE, ceremonies within a community to mark the achievement by an individual of a new stage in his life cycle (e.g., birth, puberty, marriage) and his consequent change of role in the community.

RITTENHOUSE, David (1732–1796), American astronomer and mathematician, who invented the DIFFRACTION grating, built two famous orreries, discovered the atmosphere of VENUS (1768) independently of LOMONOSOV (1761), and built what was probably the first American TELESCOPE.

RITTER, Johann Wilhelm (1776–1810), Silesian-born German physical chemist, a pioneer of ELECTROCHEMISTRY, who first positively identified ULTRAVIOLET RADIATION (1801).

RITTER, Karl (1779–1859), German geographer. Professor at Berlin from 1820, he was one of the founders of modern human and comparative geography. His great work, *Earth Science in Relation to Nature and the History of Man* (1822–59), stresses the influence of environment on man's development.

RIVERA, Diego (1886–1957), Mexican mural painter. He studied in Europe, returning to Mexico in 1921. He painted large murals of social life and political themes throughout Mexico and also in the US, where his Marxist views aroused controversy.

RIVERA, José Eustasio (1889–1928), Colombian novelist. He is famous for his novel *The Vortex* (1924) which tells of the exploitation of rubber gatherers in the dense, hostile rain forest.

RIVER BRETHREN, Christian revivalist sect originating in 1770 among German settlers in Pennsylvania. They were probably called River Brethren because of their ritual of river baptism. Members reject war and worldly pleasures such as alcohol and tobacco, and wear plain dress.

RIVERS, Larry (1923–   ), US painter. He adapted the style of ABSTRACT EXPRESSIONISM to the popular imagery of well-known pictures or commercial advertisements, as in *Dutch Masters Series* (1963).

RIVERS, William Halse Rivers (1864–1922), British anthropologist and psychologist who initiated the study of experimental PSYCHOLOGY at the University of Cambridge (c1893).

RIVERS AND LAKES, bodies of inland water. Rivers flow in natural channels to the sea, lakes or, as tributaries, into other rivers. They are a fundamental component of the HYDROLOGIC CYCLE. Lakes are land-locked stretches of water fed by rivers; though the term may be applied also to temporary widenings of a river's course or to almost-enclosed bays and LAGOONS and to man-made reservoirs. Most lakes have an outflowing stream: where there is great water loss through EVAPORATION there is no such stream and the lake water is extremely saline, as in the Dead Sea. Lakes are comparatively temporary features on the landscape as they are constantly being infilled by silt. In many parts of the world rivers and lakes may exist only during certain seasons, drying up partially or entirely during drought. The main sources of rivers are SPRINGS, lakes and GLACIERS. Near the source a river flows swiftly, the rocks and other abrasive particles that it carries eroding a steep-sided V-shaped valley (see EROSION). Variations in the hardness of the rocks over which it runs may result in waterfalls. In the middle part of its course the gradients become less steep, and lateral (sideways) erosion becomes more important than downcutting. The valley is broader, the flow less swift, and meandering more common. Toward the rivermouth, the flow becomes more sluggish and meandering prominent: the river may form C-shaped oxbow lakes. Sediment may be deposited at the mouth to form a delta (see also HYDROELECTRICITY).

RIVETING, the joining of machine or structural parts, usually plates, by rivets. These are headed bolts, usually steel, which are passed through the plates, a second head then being formed on the plain end by pressure, hammering or an explosive charge. Large rivets are heated for satisfactory closing. Although riveting can be automated, it is slowly being displaced by arc WELDING.

RIVIERA, coastal region of the Mediterranean Sea in SE France and NW Italy. It is a major tourist center, noted for its scenery and pleasant climate. The Riviera's fashionable resorts include Cannes, Nice and St. Tropez in France; Monte Carlo in Monaco; and Bordighera, Portofino, Rapallo and San Remo in Italy.

RIYADH, Saudi Arabia city and seat of the Saudi royal family, about 240mi E of the Persian Gulf. It is an important commercial center and has rapidly expanded because of the oil trade. Pop 666,840.

RIZAL, José (1861–1896), Philippine writer and patriot. His novels, *The Lost Eden* (1886) and *The Subversive* (1891), denounced Spanish rule in the Philippines. His execution by the Spanish on false charges of instigating insurrection led to a full-scale rebellion.

RIZZIO, David (c1533–1566), favorite of MARY QUEEN OF SCOTS. An Italian musician, he became Mary's secretary in 1564. Scottish nobles, including Lord DARNLEY, Mary's husband, assassinated him.

RNA, ribonucleic acid. See NUCLEIC ACIDS.

ROADRUNNERS, two species, genus *Geococcyx,* of large slenderly-built, mainly terrestrial CUCKOOS of arid regions in central America. They fly weakly but have strong legs and run very rapidly, up to 15mph, catching lizards and small rodents. Although they are cuckoos, roadrunners are not nest parasites.

ROANOKE ISLAND, island off the NE coast of N.C., 12mi by 3mi, site of the 16th-century LOST COLONY. Its economy depends on fishing and tourism.

ROBBE-GRILLET, Alain (1922–   ), French novelist, originator of the "new novel." In works such as *The Voyeur* (1955), *Jealousy* (1957) and the screenplay for *Last Year at Marienbad* (1960), structure, objects and events displace character and story.

ROBBIA, della, Italian Florentine family of sculptors who developed the art of glazed TERRA COTTA relief sculptures. **Luca** (c1399–1482) sculpted the famous marble "Singing Gallery" for Florence cathedral (1431–1438) before turning to glazed relief work. The lunette *Madonna and Angels* (c1450) exemplifies the best of his style. His nephew and pupil **Andrea** (1435–1525) made roundels of *Infants in Swaddling Clothes* (1463) for the Hospital of the Innocents in Florence. Andrea's son, **Giovanni** (1469–1529), produced beautiful reliefs for the Church of St. Maria Novella, Florence; another son, **Girolamo** (1488–1566), worked for the French court.

ROBBINS, Jerome (1918–   ), US choreographer and director. He danced major roles with the American Ballet Theatre, 1940–44, where he created his first ballet, *Fancy Free* (1944). With the New York City Ballet he was associate artistic director, 1950–59, a ballet master after 1968 and from 1983 ballet master-in-chief (with Peter Martins). For motion pictures, television and Broadway he choreographed and directed such productions as *West Side Story* (1957) and *Fiddler on the Roof* (1964).

ROBERT GUISCARD (c1015–1085), Norman conqueror of S Italy from Byzantine rule while his brother **Roger Guiscard** (1031–1101) took Sicily from the Arabs.

After Robert's death, Roger ruled the combined Norman possessions. (See NORMANS.)

ROBERTS, Sir Charles George Douglas (1860–1943), Canadian poet and writer. His simple descriptive poems of the Maritime provinces were an important contribution to the emerging Canadian consciousness. Among his best-known works are animal stories such as *Red Fox* (1905).

ROBERTS, Frederick Sleigh, 1st Earl Roberts of Kandahar (1832–1914), British field marshal. Having retired after a distinguished career in India, he was made (1899) commander in chief of British forces in South Africa, where he brought the BOER WAR to a successful conclusion.

ROBERTS, Kenneth Lewis (1885–1957), US writer and *Saturday Evening Post* correspondent. He wrote a series of popular historical novels, including *Arundel* (1930), *Rabble in Arms* (1933) and *Northwest Passage* (1937), receiving a special Pulitzer Prize citation for them in 1957. He also wrote travel books.

ROBERTS, Oral (1918–   ), US Protestant evangelist and faith healer who preached to millions over TV and founded Oral Roberts University in Tulsa, Okla.

ROBERTS, Owen Josephus (1875–1955), associate justice of the US Supreme Court, 1930–45. He was a prosecuting attorney in the TEAPOT DOME scandal 1924 and was involved in economic legislation in the Depression. He led the inquiry into the PEARL HARBOR disaster, 1941.

ROBERTSON, James (1742–1814), American frontier leader who brought settlers from North Carolina to Tennessee in 1771. He explored the Cumberland R area, founded Nashville (1780) and helped draft the Tennessee Constitution (1796).

ROBERT THE BRUCE (1274–1329), King Robert I of Scotland. His family's claim to the throne was disputed by John de Baliol, the English nominee. Bruce was crowned in 1306 in defiance of EDWARD I of England, who favored de Baliol. Pursued as a rebel, he defeated Edward II at BANNOCKBURN (1314). English recognition of Scottish independence was eventually granted in 1328.

ROBESON, Paul (1898–1976), black US singer and stage and film actor. A bass, he made his concert debut in 1925 and became known for his renditions of spirituals. His most famous song was "Ol' Man River" from the musical *Show Boat* (1928). Robeson starred in the play and film of *Emperor Jones* (1925; 1933) and in Shakespeare's *Othello*. Ostracized in the

US for his communist beliefs, he lived and sang in Europe 1958–63.

ROBESPIERRE, Maximilien François Marie Isidore de (1758–94), fanatical idealist leader of the FRENCH REVOLUTION. An Arras lawyer, he was elected as a representative of the third estate to the STATES GENERAL in 1789 and rose to become leader of the radical JACOBINS in the National Convention (1793). He liquidated the rival moderate GIRONDINS and as leader of the Committee of Public Safety he initiated the REIGN OF TERROR. He hoped to establish a "Reign of Virtue" by ridding France of all its internal enemies. However, the National Convention rose against him, alienated by his increasing power, by the mass executions and the threat of further purges, and by the new religious cult of the "Supreme Being." He was arrested, summarily tried and executed.

ROBIN, vernacular name for various unrelated species of small birds with red breasts, referring to different species in different countries. They include the European robin, *Erithacus rubecula,* American robin, *Turdus migratorius,* Pekin robin, *Leiothrix lutea,* and Indian robin, *Saxicoloides fulicata.* Most familiar are the European robin (robin redbreast), an insectivorous thrush of woods and gardens, noted for its beautiful song, and the American robin, a common garden and woodland bird of the US.

ROBIN HOOD, legendary medieval English hero. He is usually depicted as an outlaw, living with his band of "merry men" including Little John, Friar Tuck and Maid Marian in Sherwood Forest in Nottinghamshire and robbing the Norman overlords to give to the poor.

ROBINSON, Edward G. (Emmanuel Goldenberg; 1893–1973), Romanian-born US film actor remembered especially for gangster and other tough-guy roles beginning with *Little Caesar* (1930).

ROBINSON, Edwin Arlington (1869–1935), US poet, known for his series of terse, sometimes bitter verse characterizations of the inhabitants of the fictitious "Tilbury Town." His *Collected Poems* (1921), *The Man Who Died Twice* (1924) and *Tristram* (1927) won Pulitzer prizes.

ROBINSON, Jack Roosevelt "Jackie" (1919–1972), the first black baseball player to be admitted to the major US leagues. He joined the Brooklyn Dodgers in 1947 and maintained a batting average of .311 through 10 seasons.

ROBINSON, James Harvey (1863–1936), US historian. He was one of the founders of the "new history," studying the intellectual,

social and scientific development of man rather than the narrow range of political events.

ROBINSON, John (c1576–1625), English pastor to the PILGRIM FATHERS in Holland. He moved to Leiden with a group of SEPARATISTS in 1609, founded a new church and actively encouraged the voyage of the Pilgrims to America. He wrote several tracts on the Separatist position.

ROBINSON, "Sugar" Ray (born Walter Smith; 1921–), US boxer who won the world welterweight title in 1946 and the middleweight title in 1951. He retired in 1952, but returned in 1955 to regain it, becoming in 1958 the first boxer to win a divisional world championship five times.

ROBINSON CRUSOE. See DEFOE, DANIEL; SELKIRK, ALEXANDER.

ROBOT (from Czech *robota,* work), an automatic machine that simulates and replaces human activity; known as an android if humanoid in form (which most are not). Robots have evolved out of simpler automatic devices, and many are now capable of decision-making, self-programming, and carrying out complex operations. Some have sensory devices. They are increasingly being used in industry and scientific research for tasks such as handling hot or radioactive materials. Science fiction from Čapek to Asimov and beyond has featured robots. (See also MECHANIZATION AND AUTOMATION.)

ROB ROY (1671–1734), nickname of Scottish outlaw Robert MacGregor, romanticized in Sir Walter SCOTT's *Rob Roy.* He was evicted and outlawed for cattle theft in 1712 by the Duke of Montrose, whose tenants he then plundered. Hunted for many years he surrendered in 1722, but was pardoned in 1727.

ROCARD, Michel (1930–), French Socialist Party politician, prime minister from 1988. He was regarded as a market-oriented pragmatist.

ROCHAMBEAU, Jean Baptiste Donatien de Vimeur, Comte de (1725–1807), French general who commanded French troops sent to help WASHINGTON in the American revolution. Involved in the French Revolution, he narrowly escaped execution in the Reign of Terror, and was later pensioned by NAPOLEON.

ROCK, John (1890–1984), US gynecologist and obstetrician who achieved the first test-tube fertilization of a human ovum (with Miriam F. Menkin; 1944). His pioneering experiments with PROGESTERONE in the 1950s led to the development of the birth-control pill by Gregory Pincus and M. C. Chang (1954).

ROCKEFELLER, family of US financiers. **John Davison Rockefeller** (1839–1937) entered the infant oil industry at Cleveland, Ohio, at the age of 24, and ruthlessly unified the oil industry into the Standard Oil Trust. He devoted a large part of his later life to philanthropy, creating the ROCKEFELLER FOUNDATION. **John Davison Rockefeller, Jr.** (1874–1960), only son of John D. Rockefeller, followed his father's business and charitable interests. He donated the land for the UN headquarters and helped found the Rockefeller Center in New York. **Nelson Aldrich Rockefeller** (1908–1979), second son of John, Jr., governor of N.Y. 1959–73, was appointed US vice-president in 1974. He sought presidential nomination in 1960, 1964 and 1968. He expanded transportation, welfare, housing and other social services in N.Y. **Winthrop Rockefeller** (1912–1973), son of John, Jr., was Republican governor of Ark. (1967–1970). **David Rockefeller** (1915–   ), youngest son of John Jr., was president of the Chase Manhattan Bank and chairman of Rockefeller U. **John Davison Rockefeller** (1937–   ), grandson of John D. Rockefeller, Jr., was Democratic governor of W. Va. (1976–84) and US senator (1985–   ).

ROCKEFELLER CENTER, complex of buildings in midtown Manhattan, New York City, including the 70-story RCA Building and Radio City Music Hall.

ROCKEFELLER FOUNDATION, second largest US philanthropic foundation, with assets totaling about $1 billion. Founded in 1913 by John D. ROCKEFELLER, it supports research in three main areas: medical and natural sciences, agricultural sciences, and the humanities and social sciences.

ROCKET, form of JET-PROPULSION engine in which the substances (fuel and oxidizer) needed to produce the propellant gas jet are carried internally. Working by reaction, and being independent of atmospheric oxygen, rockets are used to power interplanetary space vehicles (see SPACE EXPLORATION). In addition to their chief use to power MISSILES, rockets are also used for supersonic and assisted-takeoff airplane propulsion, and sounding rockets are used for scientific investigation of the upper atmosphere. The first rockets—of the firework type, cardboard tubes containing GUNPOWDER—were made in 13th-century China, and the idea quickly spread to the West. Their military use was limited, guns being superior, until they were developed by Sir William Congreve (1772–1828). Later Congreve rockets mounted the guide stick along the central axis; and William Hale eliminated it altogether, placing curved vanes in the exhaust stream, thus stabilizing the rocket's motion by causing it to rotate on its axis. The 20th century saw the introduction of new fuels and oxidants, e.g., a mixture of nitrocellulose and NITROGLYCERIN for solid-fuel rockets, or ETHANOL and liquid oxygen for the more efficient liquid-fuel rockets. The first liquid-fuel rocket was made by R. H. GODDARD, who also invented the multistage rocket. In WWII Germany, and afterward in the US, Wernher VON BRAUN made vast improvements in rocket design. Other propulsion methods, including the use of nuclear furnaces, electrically accelerated PLASMAS and ION PROPULSION, are being developed.

ROCKINGHAM, Charles Watson-Wentworth, 2nd Marquess of (1730–1782), British statesman, prime minister 1765–66. He repealed the Stamp Act, 1765 and tried to conciliate the American colonies. During his second term as premier (1782) he urged peace with the US.

ROCK MUSIC, the dominant pop-music style since the late 1950s. Rock music first emerged in the mid-1950s as "rock'n'roll," a white rendition of the black musical mode called *rhythm-and-blues*—a sophisticated blues style that often used amplified instruments to produce a heavy beat. The first national r'n'r hit, and the one that gave the genre its name, was "Rock Around the Clock," by Bill Haley and his Comets (1955). Rock's first superstar, Elvis PRESLEY, hit on a riveting combination of hard-driving rhythm-and-blues with COUNTRY AND WESTERN MUSIC; his lyrics were simple and earthy, and directly addressed the sexual and emotional concerns of the young.

The impetus for the transformation of r'n'r into rock music came from England, where the BEATLES in 1960, and in 1964 the Rolling Stones, remixed the original ingredients, adding wit, sensuality and new musical textures, forms and rhythms.

The 1960s also saw the emergence of *soul music*, a product of rhythm-and-blues and black gospel styles, which would add its sound to rock; *folk-rock*, as in the later work of Bob DYLAN; *acid rock*, an attempt to reproduce musically the hallucinogenic drug experience, using advanced electronic sound technologies to produce its effects; and *glitter rock*, featuring outrageous costuming and incredible makeup (the pop-rock group Kiss is a later example). In the 1970s acid rock was followed by *hard rock* or *heavy metal*, louder and more repetitive; and by eclectic mixtures of the amplified rock sound with country, jazz, calypso and other styles. Other 1970s innovations were: *punk rock*, an angry, harsh, sometimes violent style that grew out of the postindustrial despair of working-class youth in England; and *disco*, the dance music that uses a rock beat broken into more complex rhythms and with a vocal style directly descended from gospel.

ROCKNE, Knute Kenneth (1888–1931), Norwegian-born US football coach. He played football and was head coach at U of Notre Dame through most of his adult life. He made the small school a national football power, achieving the extraordinary record of 105 victories, five ties and only 12 defeats. He was especially brilliant in devising innovative offensive tactics.

ROCKS, the solid materials making up the earth's LITHOSPHERE. They may be consolidated (e.g., sandstone) or unconsolidated (e.g., sand). The study of rocks is **petrology**. Strictly, the term applies only to those aggregates of one or more minerals, or of organic material, of widespread occurrence at the EARTH'S surface. Unlike MINERALS, rocks are not necessarily homogeneous and have no definite chemical composition. Together, silica and silicates make up about 95% of the crustal rocks. There are three main classes of rocks, igneous, sedimentary and metamorphic. Most IGNEOUS ROCKS form from MAGMA, a molten, subsurface complex of silicates, or from LAVA, a term applied to magma that has reached the earth's surface. They are the primary source of all the earth's rocks. SEDIMENTARY ROCKS are consolidated layered accumulations of inorganic and organic material. They are of three types: detrital (clastic), formed of weathered (see EROSION) particles of other rocks (e.g., SANDSTONE); organic deposits (e.g., COAL, some LIMESTONES); and chemical precipitates (e.g., the evaporites). (See also FOSSILS; STRATIGRAPHY.) METAMORPHIC ROCKS have undergone change within the earth under heat, pressure or chemical action. Sedimentary, igneous and even previously metamorphosed rocks may change in structure or composition in this way. (See also GEOLOGY.)

ROCKWELL, Norman (1894–1978), US illustrator, known for his realistic and humorous scenes of US small town life. His work includes magazine covers for *The Saturday Evening Post* and a series of paintings of the FOUR FREEDOMS.

ROCKY MOUNTAIN NATIONAL PARK, natural wild area in N central Col., in the heart of the Rocky Mts. Founded in 1915, the park is dominated by Longs Peak (14,255ft) and has many glaciers.

ROCKY MOUNTAINS, principal range of W North America. Extending from N Alaska for over 3,000mi to N.M., they form the continental divide; streams rising on the E slopes flow to the Arctic or Atlantic and on the W toward the Pacific. Rivers rising in the Rockies include the Missouri, Rio Grande, Colorado, Columbia and Arkansas. A relatively new system, the Rockies were formed by massive uplifting forces that began about 70 million years ago. The system can be divided into: the Southern Rocky Mts of S Wyo., Col., and N N.M.; the Central Rocky Mts between Mont. and N Ut.; the Northern Rocky Mts of Wash., Mont. and Ida.; the Canadian Rockies of British Columbia, Alberta and Yukon; and continue as the Brooks Range of Alaska. The highest peak is Mt Elbert (14,433ft). National parks in the Rockies include GLACIER, YELLOWSTONE and GRAND TETON. The Rockies are one of the richest mineral deposits in North America, and a major tourist center.

ROCKY MOUNTAIN SPOTTED FEVER, tick-borne rickettsial disease (see RICKETTSIA) seen in much of the US, especially the Rocky Mountain region. It causes FEVER, HEADACHE and a characteristic rash starting on the palms and soles, later spreading elsewhere. TETRACYCLINES are effective, though untreated cases may be fatal.

ROCOCO, 18th century European artistic and architectural style. The term derives from *rocaille* (French: grottowork), whose arabesque and ingenious forms are found in many Rococo works. The style, characterized by lightness and delicacy, emerged c1700 in France, finding expression in the works of BOUCHER, FRAGONARD and others. Some of the greatest achievements of Rococo sculpture and decoration are found in the palaces and pilgrimage churches of Austria and S Germany.

RODCHENKO, Alexander (1891–1956), Russian artist and sculptor, among the most radical of the postrevolutionary avant-garde. He called for an entirely new, wholly abstract art led by artist-engineers, and championed CONSTRUCTIVISM.

RODENTS, the largest order of MAMMALS including some 1,500 species of mice, RATS, PORCUPINES and SQUIRRELS. Rodents are easily identified by the structure and arrangement of the TEETH. There is a single pair of incisors in the upper and lower jaws which continue to grow throughout life. The wearing surface develops a chisel-like edge. Behind the incisors is a gap, or diastema, to allow recirculation of food in chewing.

Furthermore, the cheek skin can be drawn across the diastema in front of the molars and premolars, leaving the incisors free for gnawing. Rodents are predominantly eaters of seeds, grain and other vegetation. Their adaptability in feeding on a variety of vegetable matter allows them to exploit a variety of niches.

RODEO, in the US and Canada, contest and entertainment based on ranching techniques; it derives from late 19th-century cowboy meets when contests were held to celebrate the end of a cattle drive. It usually comprises five main events: *calf-roping*, in which a mounted cowboy must rope a calf, dismount, throw the calf and tie three of its legs together; *steer-wrestling*, in which the cowboy jumps from a galloping horse and wrestles a steer to the ground by its horns; *bareback riding*, on an unbroken horse for 8–10 secs; *saddle-bronc riding*; and *bull-riding*.

RODGERS, Richard Charles (1902–1981), US songwriter and composer. He collaborated with librettist Lorenz HART on *A Connecticut Yankee* (1927), *Pal Joey* (1940) and many other Broadway musicals containing countless popular songs. Later he teamed with Oscar HAMMERSTEIN II on the Pulitzer prize-winning *Oklahoma!* (1943), *South Pacific* (1949) and *The King and I* (1951).

RODIN, Auguste (1840–1917), major French sculptor. He rose to fame c1877, and in 1880 began the never-completed *Gate of Hell*, source of such well known pieces as *The Thinker* (1880) and *The Kiss* (1886). His works, in stone or bronze, were characterized by energy and emotional intensity, as in *The Burghers of Calais* (1884–94).

RODNEY, Caesar (1728–1784), American patriot and statesman who helped to bring Delaware into the Revolutionary War. He was Delaware's delegate to the Continental Congress, 1775–76, signed the Declaration of Independence and was president of Delaware, 1778–81.

RODNEY, George Brydges Rodney, 1st Baron (1719–1792), English admiral. His achievements include capturing Martinique (1762) in the SEVEN YEARS' WAR, relieving Gibraltar from the Spanish in 1780, and defeating the French West Indies fleet in 1782.

ROEBLING, John Augustus (1806–1869), German-born US bridge engineer who pioneered modern suspension bridge design. His most famous works are the Brooklyn Bridge in New York City, and the Niagara Falls Bridge (1885), using wire rope instead of chains. He died before the completion (1883) of the Brooklyn Bridge, finished by his son **Washington Augustus Roebling** (1837–1926).

ROEHM, Ernst (1887–1934), German Nazi leader, organizer of the SA (see STORM TROOPS) and as such a serious rival to HITLER from the 1920s. A dissolute adventurer, he was executed in the June 1934 purge.

ROENTGEN or RÖNTGEN, Wilhelm Conrad (1845–1923), German physicist, recipient in 1901 of the first Nobel Prize for Physics for his discovery of X-RAYS. This discovery was made in 1895 when by chance he (or perhaps his assistant) noticed that a PHOSPHOR screen near a vacuum tube through which he was passing an electric current fluoresced brightly, even when shielded by opaque cardboard.

ROETHKE, Theodore (1908–1963), US poet, influenced by T. S. ELIOT and YEATS, who won a Pulitzer Prize for *The Waking* (1953) and a National Book Award for *Words for the Wind* (1958). Much of his imagery is drawn from nature.

ROE v. WADE. In a 7-2 decision in this 1973 case, the US Supreme Court ruled that states may not prohibit a woman from having a medically initiated abortion in the first trimester of a pregnancy.

ROGERS, Carl Ransom (1902–1987), US psychotherapist who instituted the idea of the patient determining the extent and nature of his course of therapy, the therapist following the patient's lead.

ROGERS, Henry Huttleston (1840–1909), pioneering US oil magnate who developed refining techniques and invented oil pipeline transportation.

ROGERS, James Gamble (1867–1947), US architect who, designed many Yale U. buildings in a mixture of Gothic and Georgian styles. He also designed Butler Library at Columbia U. and the Columbia Presbyterian Medical Center in New York City.

ROGERS, John (1829–1904), US sculptor known for realistic figural groups such as *The Slave Auction*. His extremely popular works were often massproduced.

ROGERS, Robert (1731–1795), American frontiersman who led the famous British–American *Rogers' Rangers*, commandos who adopted Indian tactics, in the FRENCH AND INDIAN WARS. An associate of Jonathan Carver, he was involved in various dubious enterprises and was a Loyalist during the Revolution.

ROGERS, William Penn Adair "Will" (1879–1935), US humorist known for his homespun philosophy and mockery of politics and other subjects previously considered "untouchable." Part Irish and part Cherokee, he became famous in the Ziegfeld Follies of 1916. He also contributed a syndicated column to 350 newspapers.

ROGET, Peter Mark (1779–1869), English scholar and physician, remembered for his definitive *Thesaurus of English Words and Phrases* (1852). He described it as a "dictionary in reverse"; if one has the general idea, the book will provide the precise word to convey it.

RÓHEIM, Géza (1891–1953), Hungarian-born US anthropologist best known for his application of the ideas of PSYCHOANALYSIS to ETHNOLOGY studies. He wrote *Psychoanalysis and Anthropology* (1950).

ROKOSSOVSKY, Konstantin Konstantinovich (1896–1968), Russian army commander who defended Moscow in 1941 and defeated the Germans at Stalingrad in 1943. He was deputy premier of Poland, 1952–56, and Russian deputy defense minister, 1956–58.

ROLAND, one of CHARLEMAGNE's commanders, hero of the CHANSON DE ROLAND. Ambushed by Basques at Roncesvalles in 778, he and his men were massacred because he was too proud to summon help.

ROLAND DE LA PLATIÈRE, Jean Marie (1734–1793), French revolutionary, leader of the GIRONDINS in 1791 and minister of the interior 1792–93. He fled Paris in 1793, after trying to save LOUIS XVI. He committed suicide on hearing of the execution of his wife, Jeanne, whose salon had been an important Girondin intellectual gathering place.

ROLFE, Frederick William (1860–1913), English novelist, also known as Baron Corvo. His works include *Hadrian the Seventh* (1904) and *The Desire and Pursuit of the Whole* (1934).

ROLFE, John (1585–1622), early English settler in Virginia who married the Indian princess POCAHONTAS in 1614. His methods of curing tobacco made it the basis of the colony's later prosperity. He was probably killed in an Indian massacre.

ROLLAND, Romain (1866–1944), French novelist and musicologist who won the 1915 Nobel Prize for Literature. He is best known for his biographies, including *Beethoven* (1909), his WWI pacifist articles *Above the Battle* (1915), and the 10-volume novel-cycle *Jean Christophe* (1904–1912), about the life of a musical genius.

ROLLO, or **Hrolf** (c860–c932), Viking chieftain, first duke of Normandy. Invading NW France, he was granted Normandy in 911 by the French crown when he adopted Christianity.

RØLVAAG, Ole Edvaart (1876–1931), Norwegian-born novelist, who came to the US in 1896 and wrote in Norwegian. His trilogy *Giants in the Earth* (1927–31) is the story of Norwegian settlers in the US.

ROMAGNA, historic region in central Italy. Until the 8th century, it was part of the Byzantine Empire, administered from RAVENNA. It was contested by popes and emperors in the Middle Ages. In the 16th century Pope JULIUS II made it part of the PAPAL STATES.

ROMAINS, Jules, pen name of Louis Farigoule (1885–1972), distinguished French author and exponent of unanimism, or the collective personality. He is known for his plays and his 27-volume cycle *Men of Good Will* (1932–46).

ROMAN ART AND ARCHITECTURE, art of the Roman republic and empire, derived from GREEK ART AND ARCHITECTURE and the art of the ETRUSCANS. In architecture, the Romans combined the arch and column and developed the structural function of vaults and buttresses. Triumphal arches were erected throughout the empire to commemorate important events; the Romans, using concrete instead of stone, excelled in building temples, forums, basilicas, baths, amphitheatres, bridges, aqueducts and sophisticated villas. In art they are known for their realistic portrait busts and carved reliefs on monuments and on triumphal arches. Some of the finest extant Roman painting is at POMPEII, applied to walls as interior decoration. Floor mosaics range from geometric configurations to stylized floral and figure compositions. In the minor arts, the skills of making medallions, coins and cameos, and of carving gems were highly developed.

ROMAN CATHOLIC CHURCH, major branch of the Christian Church, arising out of the Western Church, consisting of those Christians who are in communion with the pope (see PAPACY). It comprises especially the ecclesiastical organization that remained under papal obedience at the REFORMATION, consisting of a hierarchy of bishops and priests (see MINISTRY), with other officers such as CARDINALS. Roman Catholicism stresses the authority of tradition and of the Church (through ecumenical councils and the papacy) to formulate doctrine and regulate the life of the Church. Members participate in GRACE, mediated through the priesthood, by means of the seven SACRAMENTS: the MASS is central to Roman Catholic life and worship. In the Middle Ages the Church influenced all aspects of life in W Europe, and the prelates controlled vast estates. There was a constant struggle with kings and the emperor over the Church's political claims. The challenge of the Reformation was met by the Council of TRENT and by the COUNTER-REFORMATION, many abuses being remedied and large-scale MISSIONS begun. Doctrinally, Roman Catholic theologians since the Reformation have stressed and elaborated the role of the Virgin MARY and the authority and infallibility of the pope. Other distinctive doctrines include clerical celibacy, limbo and PURGATORY. Those held in common with the ORTHODOX CHURCHES (but rejected by Protestants) include the invocation of saints, veneration of images, acceptance of the APOCRYPHA, the entire sacramental system, and MONASTICISM. Especially from the 18th century, anticlericalism weakened the Church's influence, and the loss of the PAPAL STATES was perhaps its political nadir. Since the Second VATICAN COUNCIL there has been a vigorous movement toward accommodation with the modern world, cautious dealings with the ECUMENICAL MOVEMENT and encouragement of lay participation and vernacular liturgy. There are now c600 million Roman Catholics, and the Church's economic and political influence remains moderately strong, especially in S Europe, South America and the Philippines. (See also CHRISTIANITY; MODERNISM; OLD CATHOLICS; UNIATE CHURCHES.)

ROMANCE LANGUAGES, one of the main groups of the INDO-EUROPEAN LANGUAGES. It comprises those languages derived from the vernacular Latin which was spread by Roman soldiers and colonists, and superseded local tongues. The languages include Italian, the Rhaeto-Romanic dialects of Alpine regions, Provençal, French, the Walloon dialect of S Belgium, Spanish, the Catalan dialect around Barcelona, Portuguese and Romanian. Although differentiated by dialects the languages share a similar vocabulary and grammatical development.

ROMAN DE LA ROSE, Le, medieval French poem, an elaborate allegory of love in 22,000 lines, of which 4,058 were written by Guillaume de Lorris c1240. The rest, a meandering dissertation on Christian love, was composed by Jean de Meun, c1280.

ROMAN EMPIRE, See ROME, ANCIENT.

ROMANESQUE ART AND ARCHITECTURE, artistic style prevalent in Western Christian Europe from c950 to c1200. Romanesque preceded GOTHIC ART AND ARCHITECTURE and is so called because its forms are derived from ROMAN ART AND

ARCHITECTURE. The architecture, based on the round Roman arch and improvised systems of vaulting, produced a massive, simple and robust style with great vitality, particularly in the case of Norman architecture. Churches had immense towers; interiors were decorated by FRESCOES of biblical scenes. The sculptural style was very varied, vigorous and expressive, and there were carved, sculptured scenes on column capitals, and larger reliefs and figures on exterior portals and tympanums. The production of metalwork flourished, and many of the pilgrimage churches had elaborate reliquaries and valuable treasuries. There are many fine illuminated manuscripts. The Romanesque style was spread by traveling artists and craftsmen throughout Europe.

ROMANIA or Rumania, republic in SE Europe on the Black Sea, lying between the USSR and Hungary to the N and Bulgaria and Yugoslavia to the S.

Official name: Socialist Republic of Romania
Capital: Bucharest
Area: 91,699sq mi
Population: 22,913,000
Languages: Romanian
Religions: Romanian Orthodox, Roman Catholic
Monetary unit(s): 1 leu=100 bani
Land. In the N is the SE end of the Carpathian Mts, separating Moldavia in the E from Transylvania in the W. The Carpathians join the Transylvanian Alps running from E to W. The principal rivers are the Danube in the S and W and the Prut in the NE. The climate is continental, but with severe winters.
People. Over 60% of the population is rural. About 85% are Romanians, with Hungarian and German minorities. Largest cities are Bucharest, the capital, Brasov, Iasi, Timisoara, Constanta, Cluj and Galati.
Economy. Over 60% of the land area is agricultural, but industry provides two thirds of the national income. More than 90% of farmland is collectivized, grain being the most important crop. About 25%

of Romania is forested, particularly by conifers. With large oil fields in the Prahova R valley, Romania is the second largest producer of petroleum and natural gas in Europe. Copper, lead, coal and iron ore are mined. Principal industries are iron and steel, machinery, textiles and chemicals. The main exports are oil-field equipment, furniture, agricultural machinery and textiles.

History. Most of modern Romania was part of ancient Dacia, thoroughly imbued with Roman language and culture, which survived barbarian conquests. After the 13th century the two principalities of Moldavia and Walachia emerged, Turkish dependencies until 1829 and then Russian protectorates. United in 1861, Romania became independent in 1878. After WWI the Romanian-speaking province of Transylvania was acquired from Austria-Hungary. In the 1930s fascists, especially the Iron Guard, were dominant, and in 1941 dictator Ion ANTONESCU sided with the Axis powers. Overrun by the USSR in 1944, it became a satellite state, and a republic after King Michael's abdication in 1947. In the 1960s and 1970s Romania achieved greater independence under Nicolae CEAUŞESCU, establishing relations with the West. An austerity plan designed to pay off the country's $10 billion foreign debt was adopted in 1981, but the result was an economic slide, popular unrest, and a cabinet shakeup in 1986.

ROMANIAN, official language of ROMANIA. Descended from the Latin of Dacia province, it is a ROMANCE LANGUAGE with Greek, Hungarian, Slavic and Turkish influences. In the 18th century, the script changed from Cyrillic to the Latin alphabet.

ROMAN NUMERALS, letters of the Roman ALPHABET used to represent numbers, the letters I, V, X, L, C, D and M standing for 1, 5, 10, 50, 100, 500 and 1000, respectively. All other numbers are represented by combinations of these letters according to certain rules of addition and subtraction; thus, for example, VIII is 8, XL is 40, MCD is 1400 and MCDXLVIII is 1448.

ROMANOV, ruling dynasty of Russia 1613–1917. The name was adopted by a Russian noble family in the 16th century; the first Romanov tsar was MICHAEL. The last of the direct Romanov line was PETER, but succeeding tsars retained the name of Romanov, down to NICHOLAS II (reigned 1894–1917).

ROMANS, Epistle to the, NEW TESTAMENT book written by St. PAUL to the Christians of Rome c58 AD. It presents his major statement of JUSTIFICATION BY FAITH, and the Christian's consequent freedom from condemnation, sin and the law. It stresses God's sovereignty and grace.

ROMANSH. See RHAETO-ROMANIC.

ROMANTICISM, 19th-century European artistic movement. Its values of emotion, intuition, imagination and individualism were in opposition to the ideals of restraint, reason and harmony of CLASSICISM. The word "Romantic" was first applied to art by Friedrich von SCHLEGEL in 1798, and later to works emphasizing the subjective, spiritual or fantastic, concerned with wild, uncultivated nature, or which seemed fundamentally modern rather than classical. The Middle Ages were thought to express Romantic values. The evocative qualities of nature inspired poets such as WORDSWORTH, COLERIDGE and LAMARTINE, and painters such as TURNER and FRIEDRICH. BLAKE and GOETHE sought to develop new spiritual values; individualism concerned artists as disparate as Walt WHITMAN and GOYA. The lives of BYRON and CHOPIN seemed to act out the Romantic myth. Among the greatest Romantic composers were WEBER, BERLIOZ, MENDELSSOHN, LISZT and WAGNER.

ROMANY, a Dardic Indo-Iranian language, the tongue of GYPSIES, related to SANSKRIT. Gypsies migrated from central to NW India and then to Europe; the three main Romany dialects, Asiatic, Armenian and European, reflect the principal gypsy settlement areas. Romany has acquired much of its vocabulary from the peoples among whom gypsies have traveled.

ROMBERG, Sigmund (1887–1951), Hungarian-born US composer. He settled in the US in 1909, and wrote over 70 operettas and musicals, including *The Student Prince* (1924) and *The Desert Song* (1926). He went on to write many film scores.

ROME (Roma), capital and largest city of Italy, a center of Western civilization for over 2,000 years. "The Eternal City" was capital of the Roman Empire (see ROME, ANCIENT), and is of unique religious significance, with the headquarters of the Roman Catholic Church in VATICAN CITY. Administration (of the Italian government as well as of Roma province and of the region of Latium), religion and tourism are the most important activities of modern Rome, which is also a center for commerce, publishing, movies and fashion. The city is a great transportation hub, but has relatively little industry.

Rome is located on the rolling plain of the Roman Campagna in central Italy, 15mi from the Tyrrhenian Sea, the site of the ancient city being the Seven Hills of Rome. The Tiber R flows through the city from NE to SW. There are many important relics of classical Rome, such as the Forum, the COLOSSEUM, the baths of CARACALLA and the PANTHEON. Rome is famous for its squares, Renaissance palaces, churches, basilicas (see SAINT PETER'S BASILICA), CATACOMBS and fountains, of which the best known is the Trevi fountain. There are also many fine museums, art collections and libraries, the Rome opera house, and the Santa Cecilia music academy, the world's oldest (1584). The university, Italy's largest, was founded in 1303. Pop (city) 2,828,692; (metro) 3,700,000.

ROME, Ancient, initially a tiny city-state in central Italy that, over some six centuries, grew into an empire which at its greatest extent (c117 AD) comprised almost all of the Western world known at the time, including most of Europe, the Middle East, Egypt and N Africa.

According to legend, Rome was founded in 753 BC by ROMULUS AND REMUS, descendants of the Trojan prince AENEAS. Until c500 BC, when the Romans set up an independent republic, the area around the Seven Hills of Rome was controlled by the ETRUSCANS. (See also SABINES.) The Romans were a disciplined, thrifty and industrious people whose genius in organization, administration, building and warfare enabled them not only to create their vast empire, but also to make it one of the most enduring ever.

Throughout the period of the republic (c500–31 BC) warfare was almost continuous. Under government by CONSULS and senate, Rome became master of central and S Italy and defeated CARTHAGE (see PUNIC WARS). Expansion continued: Greece, Asia Minor, Syria, Palestine and Egypt were conquered between 250 and 30 BC; Gaul (58–51 BC) and England (after 43 AD) followed. From about 100 BC, Rome began to move steadily toward dictatorship. Civil wars arose from conflicts between senatorial factions, and between rich and poor, PATRICIAN and PLEBEIAN forces. (See GRACCHUS; MARIUS; SULLA; SPARTACUS.) The army leaders POMPEY and Julius CAESAR emerged to form the first TRIUMVIRATE with Crassus. After Caesar's assassination and the avenging of his death by Mark ANTONY, his nephew Octavian defeated Mark Antony and CLEOPATRA and became the first emperor, AUGUSTUS.

For more than 200 years (27 BC–180 AD) the Roman empire embodied peace and law (the *Pax Romana*) and provided an excellent road and communication system which facilitated the spread of trade and new ideas, particularly Christianity. Its culture sprang from late Hellenism, but Romans surpassed the Greeks in practical achievements such as law (laying the basis for modern CIVIL LAW), civil engineering, a standard coinage and a system of weights and measures In literature, poets such as CATULLUS, VERGIL and HORACE, and dramatists such as PLAUTUS and TERENCE followed Greek models. LIVY and TACITUS were important Roman historians, and CICERO Rome's greatest orator. After Augustus, major emperors were TIBERIUS, CLAUDIUS, NERO, VESPASIAN, DOMITIAN, TRAJAN, HADRIAN and MARCUS AURELIUS. The empire was at its largest under Trajan (emperor 98–117). But from about 200 a decline set in, with internal strife and barbarian raids, particularly by the GOTHS. DIOCLETIAN (joint emperor 284–305) restored order and revived trade. Under his successor CONSTANTINE I (emperor 306–337) the capital was moved to Byzantium (renamed Constantinople after him) and Christianity officially recognized. THEODOSIUS (emperor 379–95) was the last ruler of the united empire; it was then divided into Eastern and Western. From 376, the VISIGOTHS attacked, sacking Rome in 410. The VANDALS followed. The last puppet Western emperor abdicated in 476, but the BYZANTINE EMPIRE lasted until 1453 (see also JUSTINIAN). The HOLY ROMAN EMPIRE was not established until 800.

ROME-BERLIN AXIS. See AXIS POWERS.

RØMER, Ole or **Olaus** (1644–1710), Danish astronomer who first showed that light has a finite velocity. He noticed that JUPITER eclipsed its moons at times differing from those predicted and correctly concluded this was due to the finite nature of light's velocity, which he calculated as 141mi/sec (a modern value is about 186,292mi/sec).

ROMMEL, Erwin (1891–1944), German field marshal, named the "Desert Fox" for his tactical genius as commander of the *Afrika Korps* 1941–43. His E advance ended with the battle of EL ALAMEIN. He commanded Army Group B in N France when the Allies landed in Normandy (he had led an armored division into France, 1940). After being wounded, he was implicated in the July 1944 plot to assassinate Hitler. Given the choice of suicide or trial, he took poison.

ROMNEY, George (1734–1802), English portrait painter, rival of REYNOLDS in late 18th-century London. Influenced by classical sculpture (he spent two years in

Italy), he tended to flatter his sitters, among whom was Lady HAMILTON.

ROMULO, Carlos Peña (1899–1985), Filipino journalist and statesman. His broadcasts during the Japanese occupation of the Philippines were known as "the Voice of Freedom." He won a 1941 Pulitzer Prize, and was ambassador to the US, president of the UN general assembly 1949–50, Filipino education secretary 1966–69, and foreign secretary from 1969.

ROMULUS AND REMUS, mythical founders of Rome (by tradition in 753 BC), twin sons of Rhea Silvia, descendant of AENEAS, by the god Mars. Abandoned as infants, they were suckled by a she-wolf until adopted by a herdsman. After long rivalry, Remus was killed by Romulus, who became the first king of Rome and was later worshiped as the god Quirinus.

ROMULUS AUGUSTULUS ("little Augustus"; b. c461), last Western Roman emperor (475–6), puppet of his father Orestes. The end of the Western Roman empire dates from his overthrow by ODOACER.

RONSARD, Pierre de (1524–1585), 16th-century French "Prince of Poets," leader of the influential PLÉIADE. Best known as a lyric poet, as in *Sonnets for Hélène* (1578), he also wrote lofty *Hymnes* (1556) on more public subjects and an epic, *La Franciade* (1572).

ROON, Count Albrecht Theodor Emil von (1803–1879), Prussian soldier and statesman. His army reorganization, under BISMARCK, made success in the AUSTRO-PRUSSIAN and FRANCO-PRUSSIAN wars possible. War minister 1859–73, he was Prussian premier in 1872.

ROOSEVELT, (Anna) Eleanor (1884–1962), US humanitarian, wife of Franklin Delano Roosevelt and niece of Theodore Roosevelt. Active in politics and social issues (notably for women and minority groups), she was a UN delegate (1945–53, 1961) and coauthored the Universal Declaration of Human Rights. Her many books included *This Is My Story* (1937) and *On My Own* (1958).

ROOSEVELT, Franklin Delano (1882–1945), 32nd and longest-serving US president (1933–45). His twelve years of office included the Great Depression and a global war. Born of Dutch descent in Hyde Park, N.Y., on Jan. 30, 1882, and brought up in "aristocratic" surroundings, he graduated from Harvard and married his distant cousin, Eleanor Roosevelt, in 1905; they had six children. In 1910, after a spell at Columbia U. law school, he worked in a N.Y. law firm until elected as a Democrat

to the N.Y. Senate. He established himself as a leading Democrat and opponent of TAMMANY HALL. In 1913 he became assistant secretary of the navy, and ran unsuccessfully in 1920 as Democratic vice-presidential candidate. He suffered a severe attack of polio in Aug. 1921, and became partially paralyzed. He returned to politics in 1924 and was elected governor of N.Y. in 1928 (reelected 1930) and finally US president in 1932, when he ran against Herbert HOOVER. The GREAT DEPRESSION had begun in 1929, and Roosevelt attempted to combat it with the NEW DEAL, beginning with the "Hundred Days" during which nearly all the initial New Deal legislation was passed. In 1933 he also launched the GOOD NEIGHBOR POLICY in Latin America and recognized the Soviet government. The second phase of the New Deal brought the WAGNER ACT of 1935, the massive relief program of the Works Projects Administration, a tax reform bill, a social security act and a youth administration. Roosevelt was reelected in 1936, but labor violence and his efforts to reform the Supreme Court and purge conservative Congressmen damaged his prestige. Reelected again after WWII had broken out, he tried to keep the US out of war, although aiding Britain (see ATLANTIC CHARTER; FOUR FREEDOMS; LEND-LEASE). But after the PEARL HARBOR attack, he obtained declarations of war against Japan, Germany and Italy. He easily won reelection for a fourth term in 1944, but his health was failing, and he died suddenly on April 12, 1945, of a cerebral hemorrhage.

ROOSEVELT, Nicholas J. (1767–1854), US engineer who, at the request of Robert FULTON and Robert LIVINGSTON, built and operated the *New Orleans,* the first Mississippi paddle-wheel steamer (1811).

ROOSEVELT, Theodore (1858–1919), 26th US president (1901–09), affectionately known as "Teddy" or "T.R.," one of the most popular presidents as well as the youngest, at 42. He was at different times both a progressive and a conservative. His great energy took him outside politics on many hunting and exploring expeditions; he published over 2,000 works on history, politics and his travels. Born in New York City, he graduated from Harvard and in 1880 married Alice Hathaway Lee, who died four years later leaving a daughter. He became a rancher in Dakota Territory. In 1886 he returned to New York City and married Edith Kermit Carow, by whom he had five children. He ran unsuccessfully as Republican candidate for mayor, but established a reputation as an efficient administrator and reformer while a for the Civil Service and the New York City police. As assistant secretary of the navy (1897–98), he advocated the buildup of a strong fleet and when war broke out with Spain, he joined it in Cuba with his famous volunteer cavalry troop, the ROUGH RIDERS. He returned a national hero, and for two years served as governor of N.Y. He was persuaded to run with McKinley for vice-president in 1900 and took over the presidency on Sept. 14, 1901, when McKinley died from an assassin's bullet. He tried to regulate the ever-growing industrial and financial monopolies, using the 1890 SHERMAN ANTITRUST ACT. Despite his "trust-busting," he tried to give both labor and business a "square deal." Reelected in 1904, he secured passage of the Hepburn Act (1906) to prevent abuses in railroad shipping rates, and the Pure Food and Drug Act. He was proudest of his conservation program, which added over 250 million acres to the national forests. His foreign policy was intent on expansion (see PANAMA CANAL), but he won the 1906 Nobel Peace Prize for mediating in the RUSSO-JAPANESE WAR. He also proclaimed the so-called "Roosevelt Corollary" of the MONROE DOCTRINE, reserving the role of international policeman for the US. He did not run for reelection in 1908, choosing W. H. TAFT as his successor; but dissatisfied with Taft, he opposed him in 1912 as the candidate of the PROGRESSIVE PARTY. When Woodrow WILSON was elected as a result of the division among Republicans, Roosevelt retired from politics to lead an expedition into South America. He died of a blood clot in 1919.

ROOSEVELT CAMPOBELLO INTERNATIONAL PARK, jointly administered by the US and Canada, covers 2,722 acres on Campobello Island, SW New Brunswick, Canada, including the home of F. D. ROOSEVELT.

ROOT, Elihu (1845–1937), US statesman. A successful corporation lawyer, he reorganized the command structure of the army as war secretary under President McKinley, and as Theodore Roosevelt's secretary of state developed a pattern of administration for the new possessions won from Spain. A champion of the League of Nations and the World Court, he won the 1912 Nobel Peace Prize for work as an international negotiator. He was also a N.Y. Republican senator 1909–15.

ROOTS, those parts of a PLANT which absorb water and nutrients from the soil and anchor the plant to the ground. Water and nutrients enter a root through minute root hairs sited at the tip of each root. Roots need oxygen to function, and plants growing in swamps have special adaptations to supply it, like the "knees" of bald cypress trees and the aerial roots of mangroves. There are two main types of root systems: the taproot system, where there is a strong main root from which smaller secondary and tertiary roots branch out; and the fibrous root system where a mass of equal-sized roots are produced. In plants such as the SUGAR BEET, the taproot may become swollen with stored food material. Adventitious roots anchor the stems of climbing plants, such as ivy. Epiphytic plants such as ORCHIDS have roots that absorb moisture from the air (see EPIPHYTE). The roots of parasitic plants such as mistletoe and dodder absorb food from other plants.

ROOT-TAKAHIRA AGREEMENT, signed between the US and Japan on Nov. 30, 1908, to maintain the status quo in the Pacific and the OPEN DOOR POLICY in China. War was averted and mutual trade encouraged.

ROPE, or **cordage,** a thick, strong cord made from twisted lengths of natural FIBER. It can be made from manila hemp, henequen, sisal, true hemp, coir (coconut palm fiber), flax, jute and cotton. The last three are generally used for lighter ropes such as cords and twines. SYNTHETIC FIBERS, particularly NYLON and polyesters, are used for lighter and more durable rope. Other ropes are made from wire, for example, for suspension cables in bridge building. Rope-making resembles SPINNING.

ROPER, Elmo Burns, Jr. (1900–1971), US pollster, a pioneer in applying scientific sampling techniques to political polling. His firm, Roper Research Associates (established 1933), gained fame by predicting the results of the 1936–1944 US presidential elections within 1% of the vote.

ROREM, Ned (1923–   ), US composer of melodic art-songs whose texts were drawn from the works of 20th-century American poets. His *Air Music* won the 1976 Pulitzer Prize. He published five volumes of diaries (1966–78).

RORSCHACH, Hermann (1884–1922), Swiss psychoanalyst who devised the **Rorschach Test** (c1920), in which the subject describes what he "sees" in a series of 10 symmetrical inkblots, thereby revealing aspects of his personality.

ROSA, Salvator (1615–1673), Italian artist, poet and musician, famous for his wild landscapes and battle scenes, and regarded in the 19th century as the exemplar of a romantic artist.

ROSARY, closed string of beads used as counters in reciting devotional prayers. The usual Roman Catholic rosary has 5 decades, each of 10 beads and each separated by a larger bead.

ROSAS, Juan Manuel de (1793–1877), Argentine dictatorial governor of Buenos Aires province 1835–52, who built up his own private army of *gauchos* (cowboys). Bribery, force, expansionism and continuous revolt marked his rule, which nevertheless contributed to Argentine unification.

ROSCIUS, Quintus (Quintus Roscius Gallus; d. 62 BC), Roman actor of such renown that "Roscius" was long a compliment for actors.

ROSE, the popular name for various woody shrubs and vines of the genus *Rosa*, with tough thorns and colorful flowers. There are some 100 wild rose species native to the N Hemisphere, but only nine have been involved in the breeding of the hundreds of varieties now available. In many cultivated varieties the stamens become petaloid, producing double flowers. The rose family, Rosaceae, contains many important cultivated plants including the apple, cherry, plum and strawberry.

ROSEBERY, Archibald Philip Primrose, 5th Earl of (1847–1929), British Liberal statesman, foreign secretary (1886, 1892–94) and successor as prime minister to GLADSTONE (1894–95). An opponent of Irish HOME RULE, he resigned because his imperialist views were rejected by his party.

ROSECRANS, William Starke (1819–1898), Union general in the American Civil War. After early successes in W Va. and Miss., he was given command of the Army of the Cumberland in 1862 but was heavily defeated at the Battle of CHICKAMAUGA in Sept., 1863, and relieved of command.

ROSENBERG, Alfred, (1893–1946), Nazi propagandist and newspaper editor, early associate of HITLER. In his *Myth of the 20th Century* (1930) he outlined a theory of Nordic racial superiority used to justify Nazi anti-Semitism and German world conquest. After the NUREMBERG TRIALS he was executed for war crimes.

ROSENBERG, Julius (1918–1953) and **Ethel** (1915–1953), husband and wife, the only US citizens put to death in peacetime for espionage. Convicted (1951) for passing atomic secrets in WWII to the USSR, then a US ally, they were electrocuted on June 19, 1953.

ROSENQUIST, James (1933–   ), US painter who turned his early billboard-painting career into a style of art. His gigantic images of movie stars, such as Kirk Douglas, and objects of cultural impact,

such as *F-111*, put him in the vanguard of POP ART.

ROSENWALD, Julius (1862–1932), US businessman and philanthropist. He worked with Sears Roebuck and Co. for 35 years to make it the largest mail-order firm in the world, and gave some $63 million to charities, including the Julius Rosenwald Fund (1917–48) to provide educational facilities for blacks.

ROSE OF LIMA, Saint (1586–1617), born in Lima, Peru, first canonized saint in the New World and patron saint of South America. She was canonized by Pope Clement X in 1671.

ROSES, Wars of the, intermittent struggle for the English throne between the noble houses of Lancaster (emblem, a red rose) and York (badge, a white rose). Dissatisfied by the weak government of the Lancastrian HENRY VI and the defeats of the English at the end of the HUNDRED YEARS' WAR, the Earl of WARWICK (the "king-maker"), using as figurehead Richard, Duke of York, captured Henry in 1455 and took control of government. Margaret of Anjou, Henry's queen, fought to regain power (1459–64) and killed York but, as Warwick proclaimed York's son king as EDWARD IV, the attempt failed. A second Lancastrian attempt (1471), this time aided by LOUIS XI of France and the disaffected Warwick, also failed. With Warwick and Henry dead and Margaret captured, Edward reigned in peace until his death in 1483. His young son, EDWARD V, was supplanted by his uncle, RICHARD III. The final Lancastrian claim was made by Henry Tudor, who killed Richard at Bosworth (1485) and was crowned HENRY VII in 1485. He linked York and Lancaster by marrying Elizabeth, the daughter of Edward IV.

ROSETTA STONE, an inscribed basalt slab, discovered in 1799, which provided the key to the decipherment of Egyptian HIEROGLYPHICS. About 1.2m long and 0.75m wide, it is inscribed with identical texts in Greek, Egyptian demotic and Egyptian hieroglyphs. Decipherment was begun by Thomas YOUNG (c1818) and completed by Jean-François CHAMPOLLION (c1821–22). Found near Rosetta, Egypt, the stone is now in the British Museum.

ROSE WINDOW, large circular window, often of stained glass, with stone tracery, particularly common in French Gothic cathedrals. The basic design with segments ending in a pointed arch (as at Notre Dame, Paris) developed more intricate curves in the late Gothic flamboyant style.

ROSH HASHANAH (Hebrew: head of the year), the Jewish New Year, observed on the first day of the seventh Jewish month, Tishri (usually in Sept.). It is revered as the Day of Judgment when each person's fate is inscribed in the Book of Life. The *shofar* (ram's horn) calls Jews to ten days of penitence which end on YOM KIPPUR.

ROSICRUCIANS, worldwide group of secret brotherhoods claiming esoteric wisdom, tinged with MYSTICISM, sometimes with MASONRY and the CABALA. The movement's stimulus was *Fama Fraternitatis* (1614), relating the purported travels of, and secrets learned by, Christian Rosenkreuz.

ROSS, Betsy (1752–1836), American seamstress who is said to have made, to George Washington's design, the first US flag (1776).

ROSS, Edward Alsworth (1866–1951), US sociologist and author of *Social Control* (1901), *Social Psychology* (1908) and *The Principles of Sociology* (1920). A political progressive, he taught at the University of Wisconsin (1906–37) and served as chairman of the American Civil Liberties Union (1940–50).

ROSS, Harold Wallace (1892–1951), founder (1925) and lifetime editor of the *New Yorker* magazine. Originally conceived as basically by and for New Yorkers, the magazine won national prestige and has had an enduring effect on American journalism and literature.

ROSS, Sir James Clark (1800–1862), British polar explorer who reached a point farther S (78°10′S) than any explorer until 1900. He made a number of Arctic expeditions, some with his uncle Sir John ROSS, and with William Parry. He located the N Magnetic Pole in 1831. In the historic 1839–43 Antarctic expedition he discovered the Ross Sea and Victoria Island.

ROSS, Sir John (1777–1856), British Arctic explorer whose first, unsuccessful, expedition in search of the NORTHWEST PASSAGE was made in 1818 with James ROSS and William Parry. In a return voyage (1829–33) he discovered and surveyed Boothia Peninsula, the Gulf of Boothia and King William Land.

ROSS, John (1790–1866), of part Cherokee, part Scots parentage, CHEROKEE INDIAN chief and, from 1839, chief of the united Cherokee nations. He led opposition to the US government's attempt to move his people W of the Mississippi R, but in 1838 was forced to lead them to Okla.

ROSS, Nellie (1876–1977), US public official. Elected to succeed her husband, who had died, she was the first woman governor of a state (Wyoming 1935–37). She was director of the US Mint 1933–35.

ROSS, Robert (1766–1814), British soldier in the WAR OF 1812 who commanded a brigade which won the Battle of BLADENSBERG and the same evening burned Washington. Shortly after, he was mortally wounded when attacking Baltimore.

ROSSELINO, two Italian Renaissance sculptor-architects. **Bernardo** (1409–1464) made the tomb of Leonardo Bruni in Santa Croce, Florence. He taught his brother **Antonio** (1427–1479), whose works in Florence and elsewhere include tombs, fine stone reliefs and incisive portraits.

ROSSELLINI, Roberto (1906–1977), Italian film director. His *Open City* (1946), partly made up of footage of the Italian resistance during WWII, established him as a leader of the neorealist movement. He returned to this style in *General della Rovere* (1959), but later turned to educational films.

ROSSETTI, name of two leading English Victorian artists. The poems of **Christina Georgina Rossetti** (1830–1894), a devout Anglican, ranged from fantasy (*Goblin Market*, 1862) to religious poetry. Her brother, **Dante Gabriel Rossetti** (1828–1882), was a founder of the PRE-RAPHAELITES. His paintings, of languid, mystical beauty, have subjects from Dante and medieval romance. As a poet he excelled, notably in his exquisite love sonnets.

ROSSINI, Gioacchino Antonio (1792–1868), Italian composer best known for his comic operas, especially *The Barber of Seville* (1816). The dramatic grand opera *William Tell* (1829), with its famous overture, was his last opera. He was admired by WAGNER and BEETHOVEN, among others.

ROSSO, Il (Giovan Battista di Iacopo di Gasparre; 1495–1540), Italian painter. *The Deposition* (1521) exemplifies the elongated figures, hectic color and emotionalism of his paintings. He decorated the François I gallery at the palace of Fontainebleau and brought MANNERISM to France.

ROSS SEA, Antarctic inlet of the S Pacific Ocean, between Victoria Land and Edward VII Peninsula. Its S limit is the 400mi Ross Ice Shelf, and it contains Ross Island, with the 12,450ft Mt Erebus, the most southerly active volcano known.

ROSTAND, Edmond (1868–1918), French dramatist, famous for his play *Cyrano de Bergerac* (1897), which led a Romantic revival.

ROSTROPOVICH, Mstislav Leopoldovich (1927–), Russian cellist. A celebrated musician, he had works composed for him by PROKOFIEV, SHOSTAKOVICH, and some non-Soviet composers, such as BRITTEN. He made his US debut in 1956, and since the mid-1970s he and his wife, the soprano Galina Vishnevskaya, have lived outside the USSR. He became conductor of the National Symphony Orchestra, Washington, D.C., in 1977.

ROSZAK, Theodore (1907–1981), Polish-born US sculptor. Best known for his sinister, birdlike figures in steel and bronze, he also designed the 45ft spire of the Massachusetts Institute of Technology chapel.

ROTARY INTERNATIONAL, worldwide service organization of business and professional executives, founded 1905, with headquarters in Evanston, Ill. In 1988 it had 1 million members.

ROTH, Philip (1933–   ), leading US novelist and short story writer. His protagonists agonize between a traditional Jewish upbringing and modern urban society. His first novel was *Goodbye Columbus* (1959), and his best-known work is *Portnoy's Complaint* (1969), a hilarious, bitter account of sexual frustration. He also wrote *The Ghost Writer* (1979) and *The Counterlife* (1988).

ROTHKO, Mark (1903–1970), Russian-born US painter, a leader of New York ABSTRACT EXPRESSIONISM. On large canvases he used rich and somber colors to create designs of simple, lightly painted rectangular shapes.

ROTHSCHILD, family of European Jewish bankers who wielded considerable political influence for nearly two centuries. The founder of the house was **Mayer Anselm Rothschild** (1743–1812), who established banks at Frankfurt, Vienna, London, Naples and Paris, with his sons as managers. The financial genius who raised the business to dominance in Europe was his son **Nathan Mayer Rothschild** (1777–1836), who handled Allied loans for the campaign against Napoleon. His son **Baron Lionel de Rothschild,** was the first Jewish member of the British Parliament.

ROTTERDAM, commercial and industrial seaport in South Holland province, second largest city in the Netherlands. Site of the Rotterdam-Europoort industrial and harbor complex, it lies at the center of an extensive canal system connecting with other parts of the Netherlands and the German Rhine ports and RUHR. Major industries include shipyards and oil refineries. Pop (city) 571,226; (metro) 1,023,363.

ROUAULT, Georges (1871–1958), French painter and graphic artist known especially for his intense religious paintings such as *The Three Judges* (1913). Influenced by medieval stained glass work, he developed a distinctive style with the use of thick black outlines.

ROUBILLAC, Louis François (c1702–1762), French sculptor. Influenced by BERNINI, he gained fame in England for his portrait busts and monuments such as *Monument to the Duke of Argyll* (1749).

ROUEN, major port on the Seine R, industrial and commercial city, capital of historic Normandy and today of Seine-Maritime department, NW France. JOAN OF ARC was burned here, and CHAMPLAIN and LA SALLE sailed from here. Pop (city) 101,700; (metro) 380,000.

ROUGET DE LISLE, Claude Joseph (1760–1836), French soldier who composed the MARSEILLAISE (1792).

ROUGH RIDERS (1st Regiment of US Cavalry Volunteers), a unit comprising cowboys and ranchers, organized by Theodore ROOSEVELT and Leonard WOOD at the outbreak of the SPANISH-AMERICAN WAR.

ROULETTE, popular game of chance. The roulette wheel is divided into a series of small compartments, alternatively black and red, numbered 1 to 36 with an additional zero (the US game sometimes has two zeros). A croupier spins the wheel and releases into it a small ivory ball. Players bet on where (usually which number or which color) the ball will settle.

ROUNDHEADS, an originally derogatory name for Puritans in the Parliamentary forces in the English CIVIL WAR. Many wore their hair closely cropped, in sharp contrast to their royalist opponents.

ROUNDWORMS, the nematodes, among the commonest and most widely distributed of invertebrates. Although best known as parasites of man and his domestic animals, the majority are free-living and there are terrestrial, freshwater and marine forms. All roundworms are long and thin, tapering at each end. The outside of the body is covered with a complex cuticle. The sexes are usually separate. The internal organs are suspended within a fluid-filled body cavity or pseudocoel. The free-living and plant-parasitic forms are usually microscopic, but animal-parasitic species may reach a considerable length— the Guinea worm, up to 1m (3.3ft). Nematodes are divided into the Adenophorea, containing the majority of free-living forms, and the Sercenentea, which contains the parasitic orders.

ROUSSEAU, Henri (1844–1910), called *Le Douanier* (the customs inspector, an early occupation), self-taught French "primitive" painter much admired by

GAUGUIN, PICASSO and others. He is known mainly for his portraits, landscapes and jungle paintings, such as *Sleeping Gypsy* (1897) and *Virgin Forest at Sunset* (1907).

ROUSSEAU, Jean Jacques (1712–1778), Swiss-born French writer, philosopher and political theorist. He wrote for DIDEROT'S *Encyclopédie* in Paris from 1745. Made famous by his essay on how arts and sciences corrupt human behavior (1749) he argued in an essay on the *Origin of the Inequality of Man* (1755) that man's golden age was that of primitive communal living. *The Social Contract* (1762), influential in the FRENCH REVOLUTION, claimed that when men form a social contract to live in society they delegate sovereignty to a government; but that sovereignty resides ultimately with the people, who can withdraw it when necessary. His didactic novel *Émile* (1762) suggested that education should build on a child's natural interests and sympathies, gradually developing its potential. *Confessions* (1782) describes Rousseau's romantic feelings of affinity with nature.

ROUSSEAU, Théodore (1812–1867), French landscape painter, a leader of the BARBIZON SCHOOL. His scenes of wooded landscapes at sunset include *Coming out of the Fontainebleau Woods* (c1850).

ROUSSEL, Albert Charles Paul Marie (1869–1937), French composer. Although influenced by DEBUSSY, D'INDY and visits to the East, his music was based on contrapuntal rather than tonal construction, varying in style from *The Feast of the Spider* (1913) to *Padmavati* (1914–18).

ROUX, Pierre Paul Emile (1853–1933), French bacteriologist noted for his work with PASTEUR toward a successful ANTHRAX treatment, with Metchnikov on syphilis, and with Yersin on diphtheria. Using Roux and Yersin's results, von Behring was able to develop the diphtheria antitoxin.

ROWING, propelling a boat by means of oars. In sport there are two types: *sculling*, in which each oarsman uses two oars, and *sweep rowing*, in which each has one. In the US, competitive team rowing is known as *crew*. For speed, the craft (shells) are long, narrow and light. The first recorded race was held on the Thames R, London (1716). The annual Oxford-Cambridge race began in 1829, and the Yale-Harvard race in 1852. The most famous international rowing event is England's annual Henley Royal Regatta (from 1839).

ROWLANDSON, Thomas (1756–1827), English caricaturist, etcher and painter. His work is a valuable though satirical record of contemporary English life. It includes *The English Dance of Death* (1815–16) and illustrations for *The Tour of Dr Syntax in Search of the Picturesque* (3 vols., 1812–21).

ROXAS Y ACUÑA, Manuel (1894–1948), first president of the Philippine republic, 1946–48: earlier he had been a member of the Japanese-sponsored Philippine puppet government in WWII. His administration was marked by corruption.

ROY, Gabrielle (1909–1983), French-Canadian novelist noted for her portrayals of poor urban workers in *The Tin Flute* (1947) and *The Cashier* (1955). Some of her novels, such as *Street of Riches* (1957), are set in the isolated rural landscape of her native Manitoba.

ROYAL ACADEMY OF ARTS, British institution founded 1768 by George III, first president being Joshua REYNOLDS. It has a president, 40 academicians (RA) and 30–35 associates. It maintains an art school and holds an open summer exhibition.

ROYAL CANADIAN MOUNTED POLICE, Canadian federal police force. It was formed 1873, as the North West Mounted Police, to bring law and order to the new Canadian territories. In 1874, the NWMP numbered 300 men and their persistence and determination became legendary: "the Mounties always get their man." In 1904 the force numbered 6,000 and was given the prefix "Royal." In 1920 it absorbed the Dominion Police and received its present name and duties. Its 19,000 members, including 250 women, serve as a provincial police force in the nation's provinces (excluding Ontario and Quebec).

ROYAL GEOGRAPHICAL SOCIETY, British institution founded 1830 as the Geographical Society of London, taking its present name 1859. Its aims are to advance geographical exploration, research and education.

ROYAL INSTITUTION, an English scientific society, founded in 1799 by Benjamin Thompson (see Count RUMFORD) to encourage scientific study and the spread of scientific knowledge. It has associations with many eminent men of science, including Humphry DAVY and Michael FARADAY.

ROYAL SOCIETY OF LONDON FOR THE IMPROVEMENT OF NATURAL KNOWLEDGE, the premier English scientific society. Probably the most famous scientific society in the world, it also has a claim to be the oldest surviving. It had its origins in weekly meetings of scientists in London in the 1640s and was granted a royal charter by Charles II in 1660. Past presidents include Samuel PEPYS, Sir Isaac

NEWTON and Lord RUTHERFORD.

ROYCE, Josiah (1855–1916), US philosopher, a major proponent of IDEALISM. Influenced by HEGEL, and SCHOPENHAUER, he conceived the absolute in terms of will and purpose in *The World and the Individual* (1901–02). Among his other major works was *The Problem of Christianity* (1913), in which he developed his metaphysic of interpretation and community.

RUANDA. See RWANDA.

RUBBER, an elastic substance; that is, one which quickly restores itself to its original size after it has been stretched or compressed. Natural rubber is obtained from many plants, and commercially from *Hevea brasiliensis*, a tree native to South America and cultivated also in SE Asia and W Africa. A slanting cut is made in the bark, and the milky fluid latex, occurring in the inner bark, is tapped off. The latex—an aqueous colloid of rubber and other particles—is coagulated with dilute acid, and the rubber creped or sheeted and smoked. Natural rubber is a chain POLYMER of isoprene, known as caoutchouc when pure; its elasticity is due to the chains being randomly coiled but tending to straighten when the rubber is stretched. Known to have been used by the Aztecs since the 6th century AD, and first known in Europe in the 16th century, it was a mere curiosity until GOODYEAR invented the process of VULCANIZATION. Synthetic rubbers have been produced since WWI, and the industry has developed greatly during and since WWII. They are long-chain polymers, elastomers; the main types are: copolymers of butadiene/styrene, butadiene/nitriles and ethylene/propylene; polymers of chloroprene (neoprene rubber), butadiene, isobutylene and SILICONES; and polyurethanes, polysulfide rubbers and chlorosulfonated polyethylenes. Some latex (natural or synthetic) is used as an adhesive and for making rubber coatings, rubber thread and foam rubber. Most, however, is coagulated, and the rubber is treated by vulcanization and the addition of reinforcing and inert fillers and antioxidants, before being used in tires, shoes, rainwear, belts, hoses, insulation and many other applications.

RUBBER PLANT, or **India rubber fig,** *Ficus elastica,* a popular house plant, native to India and the E Indies. It was once grown for its gum, which was made into india-rubber erasers. Family: Moraceae.

RUBELLA. See GERMAN MEASLES.

RUBENS, Peter Paul (1577–1640), Flemish artist, one of the greatest BAROQUE painters. Influenced by TINTORETTO, TITIAN and VERONESE, he developed an exuberant style depending on a rich handling of color and sensuous effects. His works include portraits and mythological, allegorical and religious subjects such as *Raising of the Cross* (1610), *Descent from the Cross* (1612), *History of Marie de Médicis* (1622–25), *Judgment of Paris* (c1638) and portraits of his wife. His works influenced many artists, including VAN DYCK and RENOIR.

RUBICON, river in N central Italy which formed the boundary between Italy and Cisalpine Gaul during the Roman Republic. In 49 BC, Julius CAESAR led his army across the river into Italy, committing himself to civil war against POMPEY.

RUBINSTEIN, Anton Grigoryevich (1829–1894), Russian piano virtuoso and composer. In 1862 he founded the St. Petersburg Conservatory, where he was director 1862–67 and 1887–91.

RUBINSTEIN, Arthur (1889–1982), Polish-born US pianist who remained at the top of his profession for over 70 years. He was especially famous for his interpretations of CHOPIN.

RUBLEV, Andrei (c1370–c1430), Russian painter famous for his icon of the *Old Testament Trinity,* c1420. As he did not sign his works, it is often difficult to distinguish his style.

RUBY, deep-red GEM stone, a variety of corundum colored by a minute proportion of chromium ions. It is found significantly only in upper Burma, Thailand and Sri Lanka, and is more precious by far than diamonds. The name has been used for other red stones, chiefly varieties of garnet and spinel. Rubies have been synthesized by the Verneuil flame-fusion process (1902). They are used to make ruby LASERS.

RUDE, François (1784–1855), French sculptor. His neoclassical works include the *Neapolitan Fisherboy* (1833), but most of his works, such as *Departure of the Volunteers of 1792* (1835–36), are dramatically realistic.

RUDOLF I (1218–1291), German king, elected in 1273, who established the HAPSBURG dynasty by gaining control of Austria and Styria. The Diet of Augsburg (1282) invested his two sons with these duchies.

RUDOLF II (1552–1612), king of Bohemia and Hungary, succeeded his father Maximilian II as Holy Roman Emperor in 1576. He was a patron of BRAHE and KEPLER, but his religious persecutions and a Hungarian rebellion led to his progressive replacement by his brother Matthias.

RUDOLF (1858–1889), archduke and

crown prince of the Austro–Hungarian Empire. He and 17-year-old Baroness Mary Vetsera were found shot in the royal hunting lodge at Mayerling, apparent victims of a suicide pact. The exact circumstances of the deaths, which caused endless speculation, have never been clarified.

RUDOLPH, Paul Marvin (1918–), US architect connected with Yale U. (1958–65), where his campus buildings include a controversial art and architecture building. He turned away from the International style to experiment with externally visible ducts, a futuristic parking facility and stacking mobile home frames.

RUEF, Abraham (c1865–1936), US political boss who controlled San Francisco in exceptionally corrupt fashion 1901–06 through mayor E. F. Schmitz. He was indicted 1906 and imprisoned 1911–14 for bribery.

RUFFIN, Edmund (1794–1865), US planter, a strong supporter of slavery and secession said to have fired the first shot on Fort Sumter, S.C., at the outbreak of the Civil War. He committed suicide rather than submit to the US government. A noted agriculturalist, he pioneered crop rotation and founded the *Farmers' Register* (1833).

RUGBY, ball game possibly originated at Rugby school, England, during a SOCCER match (1823). Play is on a field 75yd wide by 110yd between goal lines. There are two 40min "halves." In Rugby Union there are 15 players per side, in Rugby League, 13. Each side attempts to ground the oval leather-covered ball beyond the opponents' goal: this, a try, is worth 4 points; place-kicking a goal after a try is 2 further points; and a goal from a free, or penalty kick, or from a drop-kick during play, 3. The game is similar to American FOOTBALL, but little protective equipment is worn and play is almost continuous.

RUGGLES, Carl (1876–1971), controversial US composer. His often dissonant style may be heard in the symphonic poems *Men and Mountains* (1924) and *Sun-Treader* (1927–32). He also achieved recognition as a painter.

RUGS AND CARPETS. Reed mats date from at least 5000 BC, but carpet-weaving with sheep's wool was first highly developed in the Near East. Persian carpets were internationally famous by 600 AD. Their vivid, long-lasting dyes came from natural materials such as bark and roots. Persian designs influenced the 16th- and 17th-century carpets of India's Mogul courts, and the beautiful Chinese carpets produced from the 14th to 17th centuries.

Carpet-weaving spread in the West, particularly in the 17th century, via France, Belgium and England.

Oriental carpets were woven on looms, still the basic technique of carpet-making. Foundation threads (the *warp*) are stretched on the loom; crosswise foundation threads are called the *weft*. The surface material (*pile*) is made by tying small tufts of fiber, usually wool, to the warp. Today, major types of the more expensive loom-made carpets and rugs are: *Axminster, chenille, velvet* and *Wilton*. *Tufted* carpets are made by machines which do the tufting with hundreds of needles onto a prewoven backing, attached to a latex rubber base. Knitted carpets use a combination of loom and tufting processes. (See also TAPESTRY; WEAVING.)

RUHR, great coal-mining and iron-and-steel industrial region in West Germany. It lies mainly E of the Rhine R, between the valleys of the Ruhr and Lippe rivers, and has more than 30 large cities and towns merged into one industrial megalopolis. Chief cities include Düsseldorf, Essen and Dortmund. Materials are transported by the Rhine R, Dortmund-Ems Canal, Rhine-Herne Canal, and road and rail networks.

RUISDAEL, Jacob van (c1629–1682), greatest Dutch landscape painter of the 17th century. He favored a new heroic-romantic style in which small figures are dwarfed by forests, stormy seas and magnificent cloudscapes.

RUIZ CORTINES, Adolfo (1890–1973), Mexican president, 1952–58. During his presidency, corruption was curbed, the "march to the sea" to aid the maritime industry was initiated, agriculture was assisted through widespread irrigation, and women were given the vote.

RUM, alcoholic liquor, usually produced by distilling fermented molasses. It acquires a brown color from the wooden casks in which it is stored and from added caramel or burnt sugar. It is made mainly in the W Indies.

RUMANIA. See ROMANIA.

RUMFORD, Benjamin Thompson, Count (1753–1814), American-born adventurer and scientist best known for his recognition of the relation between work and HEAT (inspired by observation of heat generated by FRICTION during the boring of cannon), which laid the foundations for JOULE's later work. He played a primary role in the founding of the Royal Institution (1799), to which he also introduced Humphry DAVY.

RUMI, or **Jalal-ad-din Rumi** (1207–1273), great Sufi poet and mystic of Persia. His major work was the *Mathnawi*, a poetic exposition of Sufi wisdom in some 27,000 couplets.

RUMINANTS, animals (including goats, sheep, cows) that regurgitate and rechew their food once having swallowed it. They feed by filling one compartment of a three- or four-chambered stomach with unmasticated food, bringing it back up to the mouth again to be fully chewed and finally swallowed. It is an adaptation in many herbivores to increase the time available for the digestion of relatively indigestible vegetable matter.

RUMP PARLIAMENT, 60 remaining members of the British LONG PARLIAMENT after Col. Thomas Pride in "Pride's Purge" had ejected all opposition to Oliver CROMWELL'S army (1648). They created a high court which tried CHARLES I and had him executed (1649), abolished the House of Lords and monarchy, and established a ruling Council of State. The attempt to pass a bill prolonging its life indefinitely led to the Rump's forcible dissolution by Cromwell (1653–59). Purged members returned in 1660, prior to the RESTORATION. (See CIVIL WAR, ENGLISH.)

RUNDSTEDT, Karl Rudolf Gerd von (1875–1953), German field marshal. In WWII he led army groups in Poland, France and Russia, was military ruler of France, and commander, W Europe, on D-DAY and during the BATTLE OF THE BULGE.

RUNES, characters of a pre-Christian writing system used by the Teutonic tribes of N Europe from as early as the 3rd century BC to as late as the 10th century AD, and sometimes after. The three distinct types are Early, Anglo-Saxon and Scandinavian. The Runic alphabet is sometimes known as **Futhork** for its first six characters. (See also WRITING, HISTORY OF.)

RUNNYMEDE, meadow in Surrey, S England, on the bank of the Thames R. Here King John conceded the barons' demands embodied in the MAGNA CARTA (1215). There is a memorial to President John F. Kennedy (unveiled 1965).

RUNYON, Damon (1884–1946), US journalist and writer. His entertaining stories of tough-talking gangsters, Broadway actors and the sporting underworld were written in the colorful vernacular of New York City. *Guys and Dolls* (1932), the first of several collections, was the basis of a successful musical (1950).

RUPERT, Prince (1619–1682), count palatine of the Rhine and duke of Bavaria, brilliant royalist cavalry commander in the English CIVIL WAR. Dismissed by his uncle Charles I after surrendering Bristol to parliamentarians (1645), he commanded a

fleet which harried Commonwealth shipping (1648–50). After the RESTORATION, he was first lord of the admiralty. He introduced mezzotint to Britain and was a founder of the HUDSON'S BAY COMPANY.

RUPERT'S LAND, or **Prince Rupert's Land,** vast, mineral-rich region of NW Canada granted to the HUDSON'S BAY COMPANY in 1670 by Charles II. Named for Prince RUPERT, it comprised the basin of Hudson Bay. In 1818, the US acquired the portion S of the 49th parallel. In 1869, the remainder became part of the NORTHWEST TERRITORIES.

RUPTURE, common name for HERNIA.

RURIK (d. 879), semi-legendary Viking founder of the Russian empire. Based in Novgorod, he ruled from c862. The Rurik dynasty gave way to the house of ROMANOV in the early 17th century.

RUSH, Benjamin (1746–1813), US physician, abolitionist and reformer. His greatest contribution to medical science was his conviction that insanity is a disease (see MENTAL ILLNESS): his *Medical Enquiries and Observations upon the Diseases of the Mind* (1812) was the first US book on PSYCHIATRY.

RUSH, Richard (1780–1859), US statesman, son of Benjamin Rush. Holder of many high US offices, he negotiated with Great Britain the RUSH-BAGOT CONVENTION and the 49th parallel between Canada and the US, prepared the way for the Monroe Doctrine, and helped in founding the SMITHSONIAN INSTITUTION.

RUSH-BAGOT CONVENTION (1817), negotiations after the WAR OF 1812, between US diplomat Richard Rush and British minister to Washington, Sir Charles Bagot, which agreed mutual US-British disarmament on the Great Lakes.

RUSHMORE, Mount, or **Mount Rushmore National Memorial,** rises to 5,600ft in the Black Hills, W S.D. In the granite of the NE face, 60ft portraits of presidents Washington, Jefferson, Lincoln and (Theodore) Roosevelt were carved 1925–41 by Gutzon BORGLUM.

RUSK, (David) Dean (1909–), US secretary of state, 1961–69, in the Kennedy and Johnson administrations. Previously a university professor and WWII army colonel, he worked in the Department of State (1946–52) and was president of the Rockefeller Foundation (1952–60). He became President Johnson's main spokesman on Vietnam. He later taught international law at the University of Georgia.

RUSKIN, John (1819–1900), English art critic, writer and reformer. The first volume of his *Modern Painters* (1843) championed J. M. W. TURNER. A major influence on the arts, he was behind the Victorian GOTHIC REVIVAL. *Unto This Last* (1862), first of his "letters" to workmen, attacked "laissez-faire" philosophy. An autobiography, *Praeterita* (1885–89), was unfinished.

RUSSELL, prominent family in British politics. The first member to gain national fame was **John Russell** (c1486–1555), created 1st earl of Bedford for helping Edward VI to quell a 1549 rebellion. The family fortune, including Woburn Abbey, Bedfordshire, was acquired during this period. **William Russell** (1613–1700), 5th earl, was a parliamentary general in the Civil War. He was created 1st duke of Bedford in 1694, partly because of the fame, as a patriotic martyr, of his son Lord **William Russell** (1639–1683), first notable WHIG in the family. The title of John RUSSELL, 1st Earl Russell, was inherited by his grandson Bertrand RUSSELL.

RUSSELL, Bertrand Arthur William, 3rd Earl Russell (1872–1970), British philosopher, mathematician and man of letters. Initially subscribing to IDEALISM, he broke away in 1898 eventually to become an empiricist (see EMPIRICISM). His most important work was to relate LOGIC and MATHEMATICS. After having written to FREGE pointing out a paradox in Frege's attempt to reduce all mathematics to logical principles, Russell endeavored to perform this task himself. His results appeared in *The Principles of Mathematics* (1903) and, in collaboration with A. N. WHITEHEAD, *Principia Mathematica* (3 vols., 1910–13). Russell was a vehement pacifist for much of his life, his views twice earning him prison sentences (1918, 1961): during the former he wrote his *Introduction to Mathematical Philosophy* (1919). His other works include *Marriage and Morals* (1929), *Education and the Social Order* (1932), *An Inquiry into Meaning and Truth* (1940), *History of Western Philosophy* (1945) and popularizations such as *The ABC of Relativity* (1925), as well as his *Autobiography* (3 vols., 1967–69). He received the 1950 Nobel Prize for Literature and founded the Bertrand Russell Peace Foundation in 1963.

RUSSELL, Charles Marion (1864–1926), US cowboy painter, sculptor and author. His many canvases of frontier life, Indians, horses and cattle camps, usually set in Mont., were enormously popular.

RUSSELL, Charles Taze (1852–1916), US founder of the International Bible Students, forerunner of JEHOVAH'S WITNESSES. He prophesied the return of Jesus and the MILLENNIUM.

RUSSELL, George William (1867–1935), Irish poet, nationalist, mystic and painter, known by the pseudonym "A.E." A theosophist, he was with W. B. YEATS a leader of the CELTIC RENAISSANCE and a cofounder of Dublin's ABBEY THEATRE.

RUSSELL, John, 1st Earl Russell (1792–1878), British Whig statesman and liberal reformer. A leading supporter of the CATHOLIC EMANCIPATION ACT (1830), he also fought for the 1832 REFORM BILL. Twice prime minister (1846–52, 1865–66), he was influential in maintaining British neutrality in the US Civil War.

RUSSELL, Lillian (1861–1922), US singer, actress, flamboyant beauty of the "Gay Nineties." Born Helen Louise Leonard, she became a star in the show *The Great Mogul* (1881). She married four times, but her affair with "Diamond Jim" BRADY spanned 40 years.

RUSSELL, Richard Brevard (1897–1971), influential US Democratic senator from Ga. from 1933. Governor of Ga. 1931–33, he was twice candidate for the presidential nomination.

RUSSELL, Lord William (1639–1683), English Whig statesman who during the Popish Plot led the attempts to bar the duke of York (later JAMES II) from the royal succession. Dubiously implicated in the RYE HOUSE PLOT, he was executed.

RUSSELL SAGE FOUNDATION. See SAGE, RUSSELL.

RUSSIAN, native language of about 140 million Russians, chief official language of the USSR. Most important of the E Slavic INDO-EUROPEAN LANGUAGES (Byelorussian and Ukrainian diverged from c1300), Russian is written in the 33-character Cyrillic alphabet introduced in the 800s by Christian missionaries. A difficult language for English speakers, it has very different word-roots and is heavily inflected in nouns and verbs. By combining colloquialism with the formal Church Slavonic, the poet PUSHKIN did much to shape modern literary Russian, which is based on the Moscow dialect.

RUSSIAN-AMERICAN COMPANY, chartered 1799 by the Russian government, monopoly controller of Russian settlements in North America until 1862. Its first manager, Aleksandr Baranov, virtually governed Alaska and founded New Archangel (1799).

RUSSIAN REVOLUTION, momentous political upheaval which changed the course of world history. It destroyed the autocratic tsarist regime and culminated in the establishment of the world's first communist state, the Soviet Union (1922). Its roots lay in the political and economic backwardness of Russia and the chronic poverty of most of the people, expressed in rising discontent in the middle and lower classes since the late 1800s.

The Revolution of 1905 began on "Bloody Sunday," Jan. 22 (Jan. 9, old Russian calendar), when troops fired on a workers' demonstration in St. Petersburg. Widespread disorders followed, including mutiny on the battleship *Potemkin* and a national general strike organized by the St. Petersburg *soviet* (workers' council). These events, coupled with the disastrous RUSSO-JAPANESE WAR, forced Tsar Nicholas II to grant civil rights and set up an elected *duma* (parliament) in his "October Manifesto." Under premier B. A. STOLYPIN repression continued until late WWI, in which Russia suffered severe reverses.

The February Revolution (1917). Food shortages and strikes provoked riots and mutiny Mar. 8–10 (Feb. 23–25). A provisional government under the progressive Prince Georgi LVOV was set up (later headed by Alexander KERENSKY) and Nicholas II abdicated Mar. 15 (Mar. 2). **The October Revolution (1917).** On Nov. 6 (Oct. 24), the Bolsheviks, led by V. I. LENIN, staged an armed coup. Moscow was seized and the remnants of the provisional government arrested; the constitutional assembly was dispersed by Bolshevik troops and the CHEKA set up. Next day a Council of People's Commissars was set up, headed by Lenin and including Leon TROTSKY and Joseph STALIN. In the civil war (1918–20), the anticommunist "Whites," commanded by A. I. DENIKIN, A. V. KOLCHAK and P. N. WRANGEL were defeated. Russian involvement in WWI ended with the Treaty of BREST-LITOVSK. The tsar and his family were murdered at Ekaterinburg (July, 1918), and the new Soviet constitution made Lenin and the Communist (formerly Bolshevik) Party all-powerful.

RUSSIAN SOVIET FEDERATED SOCIALIST REPUBLIC (RSFSR), largest of the USSR's constituent republics, one of the original four united in the Soviet Union (1922). It holds over 50% of the population, and over 76% of the land area, of the Soviet Union. Its W section is a great plain broken only by the N-S Ural Mts. E of the Yenisey R lie eroded plateaus and ridges, with high, folded mountains in the S. About 83% of the population are Russians and there are some 38 other ethnic groups. The capital and largest city is Moscow, the chief port Leningrad. With 90% of Russia's forests, rich mineral resources and abundant hydroelectric power, the RSFSR provides about 70% of Russia's total industrial and agricultural output. (See UNION OF SOVIET SOCIALIST REPUBLICS.)

RUSSO-FINNISH WARS, two conflicts during WWII. The first, the "Winter War" (1939–40), arose from rejection of Russian demands for military bases in Finland, territorial concessions and the dismantling of the MANNERHEIM line, Finland's defense system across the Karelian isthmus. When the Russians attacked (Nov. 30), the Finns unexpectedly threw them back. But in Feb., 1940 the Mannerheim line was broken and Finland signed the Peace of Moscow (March 12) surrendering about 10% of her territory, including much of Karelia, Petsamo (now Pechenga) and Viipuri (Vyborg). In the "Continuation War" (1941–44), Finland fought alongside Nazi Germany, and was forced to pay $300 million reparations to the USSR and to lease it the Porkkala area (returned in 1956).

RUSSO-GERMAN PACT, nonaggression pact signed by MOLOTOV and RIBBENTROP on Aug. 23, 1939. It cleared the way for Hitler's invasion of Poland (Sept 1.) which precipitated WWII, and for the division of Poland between Nazi Germany and Russia (which invaded Sept. 17 from the E).

RUSSO-JAPANESE WAR, 1904–05, culmination of rivalry in the Far East, where both powers sought expansion at the expense of the decaying Chinese empire. Russia occupied Manchuria during the BOXER REBELLION and coveted Korea. On Feb. 8, 1904 the Japanese attacked the Russian naval base of PORT ARTHUR (now Lü-shun), which they captured in Jan., 1905. The Russians were also defeated at Mukden in Manchuria and their Baltic fleet, sent to retrieve the situation, was destroyed in the battle of TSUSHIMA (May 27, 1905). Mediation by US president Theodore Roosevelt ended the war in the Treaty of PORTSMOUTH (1905). Russia ceded the Liaotung peninsula and S Sakhalin to Japan, recognized Japan's dominance in Korea and returned Manchuria to China. Russia's disastrous defeat was an immediate cause of the 1905 RUSSIAN REVOLUTION and won Japan great power status.

RUSSO-POLISH WAR, 1919–20, started when newly-constituted Poland, under Józef PILSUDSKI, joined with Ukrainian nationalist Simon Petlyura to invade the Ukraine. Driven back by Soviet forces almost to Warsaw, the Poles with French aid forced Russian retreat. By the treaty of Riga (March 18, 1921) the Poles regained parts of Byelorussia and the UKRAINE.

RUSSO-TURKISH WARS, fought intermittently over three centuries, were caused by Russia's determination to absorb the Black Sea coast and Caucasus, dominate the Balkans and control the Bosporus and Dardanelles straits. The first major Russian success was the capture of Azov by Peter I (the Great) in 1696. In two wars against the Turks (1768–74, 1787–91), Catherine the Great, allied with Austria, gained the rest of the Ukraine, the Crimea, and an outlet to the Black Sea and the straits. Russia adopted the role of protecting Christians in the declining OTTOMAN EMPIRE. Russia won Bessarabia in the war of 1806–12 and made further gains in the war of 1828–29. When Russia next pressured the Turks, France and Britain intervened, defeating Russia in the CRIMEAN WAR (1853–56). Russia regained territory in the last war of 1877–78, though the terms of the treaty of San Stefano were modified by the congress of BERLIN (1878). Russia and Turkey were again opponents in WWI, and concluded a separate peace treaty (1921).

RUSSWURM, John Brown (1799–1851), Jamaican-born US abolitionist who led a "back to Africa" movement in the 1820s and eventually settled in Liberia in 1829. He founded (1827) and edited *Freedom's Journal*, the first black-owned US newspaper.

RUST, a large number of FUNGI which cause many PLANT DISEASES. They form red or orange spots, their spore-bearing organs, on the leaves of infected plants. Spores are carried by the wind to infect new plants. Some rusts are heteroecious: they alternate between two different host plants. The most important rust fungus is probably *Puccinia graminis*, which causes black stem rust of wheat.

RUSTIN, Bayard (1910–1987), US civil rights activist and pacifist. He helped found the Southern Christian Leadership Conference and was chief organizer of the 1963 civil rights march on Washington. He became president of the A. Philip Randolph Institute in 1966.

RUTH, Moabite heroine of the Old Testament book bearing her name. Widowed during a famine in the time of the JUDGES, Ruth followed her Judahite mother-in-law, Naomi, to Bethlehem. She survived by gleaning barley from the fields of her husband's next-of-kin, Boaz, who eventually married her. Their great-grandson was DAVID.

RUTH, Babe (George Herman Ruth; 1895–1948), famous US baseball player. An outstanding pitcher and hitter for the Boston Red Sox, he was sold to the New York Yankees in 1920 for the phenomenal sum of $125,000 and was largely responsible for building the team's prestige. In his 22 major league seasons, he hit 714 homeruns and his lifetime batting average was .342. A flamboyant figure, he was elected to the Baseball Hall of Fame in 1936. He established a season record of 60 homeruns in 1927.

RUTHENIA, region SW of the Carpathian Mts. Formerly part of Hungary, then of Czechoslovakia (from 1919), it was ceded to the USSR (1945) and is now Transcarpathian *oblast*, the most westerly in the Ukrainian SSR. Uzhgorod is capital of this mountainous and densely forested region.

RUTHERFORD, Ernest, 1st Baron Rutherford (1871–1937), New Zealand-born British physicist. His early work was with J. J. THOMSON on MAGNETISM and thus on RADIO waves. Following ROENTGEN's discovery of X-RAYS (1895), they studied the conductivity of air bombarded by these rays and the rate at which the IONS produced recombined. This led him to similar studies of the "rays" emitted by URANIUM (see RADIOACTIVITY). He found these were of two types, which he named alpha and beta. As a result of their work on RADIUM, actinium and particularly thorium, he and Frederick Soddy were able in 1903 to put forward their theory of radioactivity. This suggested that the atoms of certain substances spontaneously emit alpha and beta rays, being thereby transformed into atoms of different, but still radioactive, ELEMENTS of lesser ATOMIC WEIGHT. He later showed alpha rays to be positively charged particles, in fact, HELIUM atoms stripped of their two ELECTRONS. He was awarded the 1908 Nobel Prize for Chemistry. In 1911 he proposed his nuclear theory of the ATOM, on which BOHR based his celebrated theory two years later. In 1919 he announced the first artificial disintegration of an atom, NITROGEN being converted into OXYGEN and HYDROGEN by collision with an alpha particle. He was president of the ROYAL SOCIETY from 1925 to 1930. His work was commemorated (1969) by the naming of rutherfordium.

RUTLEDGE, Ann (c1816–1835), daughter of an innkeeper at New Salem, Ill., where Abraham Lincoln lived 1831–37. Her early death deeply grieved Lincoln, but stories of a romance or even engagement are probably apocryphal.

RUTLEDGE, John (1739–1800), US lawyer and statesman, champion of American independence. He was twice delegate to the CONTINENTAL CONGRESS. As a delegate to the 1787 Constitutional Convention, he was largely responsible for concessions to slaveholders. He helped frame S.C.'s constitution (1776) and was governor 1779–82. Washington's nomination of him for Chief Justice (1795) was not confirmed by the Senate. His brother **Edward Rutledge** (1749–1800) was delegate to the Continental Congress 1774–76, a signer of the Declaration of Independence, and S.C. governor, 1798–1800.

RUYSBROECK, Jan van (1293–1381), Dutch mystic. He founded the Augustinian abbey at Groenendaal. His *The Spiritual Espousals* (c1350), a guide for the soul in the quest for God, was influential in Germany, France, Spain and Italy.

RUYSDAEL, Jacob van. See RUISDAEL, JACOB VAN.

RUYTER, Michiel Adriaanszoon de (1607–1676), Dutch admiral who fought the English in the DUTCH WARS. After the first (1652), he became vice-admiral of Holland. In the second, he defeated the English off Dunkirk (1666) and destroyed much of the English fleet in the Medway R (1667). In the third, he prevented an Anglo-French invasion of Holland (1673).

RWANDA, formerly **Ruanda,** small, landlocked independent republic of E central Africa.

Official name: Republic of Rwanda
Capital: Kigali
Area: 10,169sq mi
Population: 6,488,000
Languages: Kinyarwanda, French; Swahili
Religions: Roman Catholic, Animist, Muslim
Monetary unit(s): 1 Rwanda franc=100 centimes
Land. Bordered by Uganda, Tanzania, Burundi and Zaire, Rwanda is largely rugged and mountainous. In the NW, highlands of the GREAT RIFT VALLEY slope in ridges from Mt. Karisimbi (14,784ft); in the E there is a series of plateaus. Average annual temperatures range from 63°F in mountainous areas to 73°F in Rift Valley areas. Average annual rainfall ranges from 30in to 58in.

People. Some 90% of the people are Hutu (Bahutu) Bantu farmers, 9% Tutsi (Watutsi or Watusi) cattle-raisers and 1% pygmy Twa hunters. Many refugees from neighboring Uganda and Burundi live in camps in Rwanda. The population is more than 90% rural, and the illiteracy rate is about 50%.

Economy. Rwanda is among the world's poorest and most overpopulated countries. Soil erosion—due to leaching caused by heavy rains, poor farming techniques and cattle feeding—imperils cultivation, on which the economy depends. Coffee is the principal cash crop. There are deposits of tin and tungsten.

History. In the 1500s, the majority Hutu group were mastered by the taller Tutsi. From 1897, Rwanda was part of German East Africa and, after WWI, part of the Belgian trust territory, Ruanda-Urundi (administered with Belgian Congo 1925–60). In 1959 a bloody Hutu rising destroyed the Tutsi kingdom and ousted the *Mwami* (king), Kigeri V. About 120,000 Tutsi fled to Burundi. The Hutu party (Parmehutu) set up a republican regime. In 1962 Belgium granted full independence. In 1973 a coup established a military government; a 1978 constitution made Rwanda a one-party state whose president is also head of the armed forces. Maj. Gen. Juvenal Habyarimana, the coup leader, was elected president in 1978, 1983, and 1988.

RYAN, Nolan (1947–   ), US baseball pitcher. In 1981 he set a major league record by hurling his fifth no-hitter. He also set records with 19 strikeouts in one game, and 383 in one season. His fastball was once clocked at a record 100.8 mph.

RYDER, Albert Pinkham (1847–1917), major US painter, noted for his darkly poetic landscapes, seascapes and allegorical scenes such as *Toilers of the Sea* (1884), *The Flying Dutchman* (c.1890) and *The Race Track* (1895).

RYDER CUP, golf trophy awarded since 1927 to winners of a biennial Anglo-US professional team match.

RYE, *Secale cereale,* hardiest of all CEREAL CROPS. It can grow in poor, sandy soils in cool and temperate climates. Most rye is used for human consumption, but rye grain and middlings (a byproduct of milling) are also fed to livestock. Rye malt is used to make rye whiskey. Rye is also used for cattle pasture. The leading producer of rye is the USSR. The ERGOT fungus disease of rye produces contaminated grains, which yield a drug that helps control bleeding and relieves migraine.

RYE HOUSE PLOT, radical Whig plot in 1683 to kill Charles II and the Duke of York (later JAMES II) at Rye House, Hertfordshire, and crown the Protestant Duke of Monmouth king. Among Whigs arrested on insubstantial evidence, the Earl of Essex apparently committed suicide, and Lord William Russell and Algernon Sidney were executed.

RYKOV, Alexei Ivanovich (1881–1938), Russian communist leader. Active in the October Revolution (1917), he was Soviet premier 1924–30. An early supporter of STALIN against TROTSKY, he was himself executed after a show trial.

RYLE, Gilbert (1900–1976), English philosopher, a major figure at Oxford in the tradition of "ordinary language" philosophy, which views philosophical problems as conceptual confusions resulting from an unwary use of language. In his best-known work, *The Concept of Mind* (1949), he seeks to expose the legacy of such confusions bequeathed by the DUALISM of DESCARTES.

RYLE, Sir Martin (1918–1984), radio astronomer, corecipient with Anthony Hewish of the 1974 Nobel physics prize. He was the first professor of RADIO ASTRONOMY at Cambridge (1959), knighted in 1966, and became British Astronomer Royal in 1972.

RYSWICK, Treaty of, in 1697, ended the war in which the Great Alliance of the League of Augsburg, England and the Netherlands sought to block expansion of Louis XIV's France (see AUGSBURG, WAR OF THE LEAGUE OF). France gave up most territories won since 1678, but kept all but one of the Hudson's Bay Company forts seized in King William's War (see FRENCH AND INDIAN WARS). France also recognized William of Orange's right to the English throne, taken in the GLORIOUS REVOLUTION. The Dutch gained trade concessions and the right to garrison forts in the Spanish Netherlands.

RYUKYU or RIUKIU ISLANDS, a chain forming a 650mi arc between Japan and Taiwan. Dividing the East China and Philippine seas, the 100-plus islands include the Osumi and Tokara (NE), the Amami and OKINAWA (center) and the Miyako and Yaeyama (SW). Many have coral reefs and some have active volcanoes. There are about 1 million islanders, mostly farmers and fishermen. Disputed with China, the Ryukyus became part of Japan in 1879. After WWII the US gave up the N islands in 1953, and the remainder in 1972. The islands are fully integrated into Japan.

S

19th letter of the English alphabet. It derived from the Semitic language and progressed through Phoenician, Greek and Roman to its present form. It is an abbreviation for *south*, and in some languages (e.g. Italian) for *saint*.

SAADI or SA'DI (c1184–c1292), Persian lyric poet perhaps best known for two ethical works: the *Gulistan* (*The Rose Garden*, 1258), which combines verse and prose, and the more popular poem *Bustan* (*The Orchard*, 1257).

SAADIA BEN JOSEPH (882–942), leading figure in medieval JUDAISM. He was head of the academy at Sura, Babylonia, and orthodox champion against the ascetic Karaites.

SAAR, or Saarland, a West German state bordering France in the S and W. It is a major coal-mining and iron-and-steel region whose control has historically alternated between France and Germany. After WWI, it was administered by France under the League of Nations. It was reunited with Germany after a plebiscite (1935), occupied by France after WWII and became a German state in 1957.

SAARINEN, name of two modern architects, father and son. **Eliel Saarinen** (1873–1950), the leading Finnish architect of his day, designed the influential Helsinki railroad station (1905–14). In 1923, he emigrated to the US, where he designed numerous buildings in the Midwest. **Eero Saarinen** (1910–1961) collaborated with his father 1938–50. His spectacular work includes the General Motors Technical Center (1948–56), the TWA terminal at Kennedy Airport (1962) and Dulles Airport (1962).

SAAVEDRA LAMAS, Carlos (1878–1959), Argentinian lawyer and statesman. As Argentina's foreign minister (1932–38), he presided over the conference that ended the CHACO WAR (1935). He won the 1936 Nobel Peace Prize.

SABAEANS, ancient Semitic people who inhabited SW Arabia, in the area of modern Yemen. They are the Sheba of the Old Testament. The kingdom of Saba lasted from the 8th century BC to the 6th century AD. It was famous for its wealth, in particular its incense, spices, precious stones and gold.

SABBATAI ZEVI (1626–1676), Jewish mystic born in Smyrna, who proclaimed himself the messiah in 1648 and attracted a large following. Arrested in Constantinople, he accepted Islam rather than risk the wrath of Sultan Mohammed IV (1666).

SABBATH, seventh day of the Hebrew week. The Jews observe it as the day of rest laid down in the fourth commandment to commemorate the Creation. It starts at sunset on Friday and ends at sunset on Saturday. Christians adopted Sunday as the Sabbath (Hebrew: rest) to commemorate the Resurrection.

SABBATICAL YEAR. Among ancient Jews every seventh year was a "year of rest" for the land, ordained by the law of Moses. Crops were to be unsown and unreapd, debtors were to be released. Today a professor's sabbatical is for rest or research.

SABER-TOOTHED TIGERS, two genera of extinct CATS of the CENOZOIC: *Smilodon* of North America and *Machairodus* of Europe and Asia. Slightly smaller than lions, but similar in build, saber-toothed tigers had enormous upper canines, up to 230mm (9in) long. They probably preyed on large, thick-skinned animals, using the canines as daggers to pierce the skin.

SABIN, Albert Bruce (1906–   ), US virologist best known for developing an oral POLIOMYELITIS vaccine, made from live viruses (1955).

SABINES, tribe who lived NE of ancient Rome. The legend of the abduction of the Sabine women by the Romans is fictitious, but there were numerous Roman–Sabine wars. Sabines became Roman citizens c268 BC and disappeared as a separate group.

SABLE, *Martes zibellina*, a carnivorous fur-bearing mammal related to the martens. The name is also used for the rich pelt. Sable are ground-living mustelids of coniferous forests, now restricted to parts of N Asia. About 500mm (20in) long, they prey on small rodents.

SACAJAWEA (c1784–1884?), Shoshone Indian guide with the LEWIS AND CLARK EXPEDITION. She was the wife of the interpreter, Toussaint Charbonneau, and joined the expedition in 1805. Although not the expert guide that legend portrays, she was invaluable in the expedition's dealings with Indians.

SACCHARIN, or *o*-sulfobenzoic imide, a sweetening agent, 550 times sweeter than sucrose, normally used as its soluble sodium salt. Not absorbed by the body, it is used by diabetics and in low-calorie dietetic foods.

SACCO-VANZETTI CASE, famous legal battle which polarized opinion between US liberal-radicals and conservatives in the 1920s. In 1921, Nicola Sacco and Bartolomeo Vanzetti were found guilty of murdering a paymaster and factory guard in Braintree, Mass. Opponents of the verdict claimed that there had been insufficient evidence, and that the trial had been unduly influenced by the fact that Sacco and Vanzetti were aliens and anarchists and had also been draft-evaders. The supreme court of Mass. declined to intervene. Eventually, Governor Fuller and an advisory board ruled the trial fair. The two were executed in 1927.

SACHS, Hans (1494–1576), the most popular German poet and dramatist of his time, one of the MEISTERSINGERS, and by trade a shoemaker. His prolific output included *The Nightingale of Wittenberg* (1523), a work in honor of Luther and the Reformation. He was the model for Wagner's *Die Meistersinger.*

SACHS, Julius von (1832–1897), German botanist regarded as the father of experimental plant physiology. Among his many contributions are his discovery of what are now called chloroplasts; the elucidation of the details of the GERMINATION process; and his studies of plant TROPISMS.

SACHS, Nelly (1891–1970), German-Jewish poet who fled to Sweden in 1940. Her poems deal with the sufferings and destiny of the Jewish people. She shared the 1966 Nobel literature prize.

SACKVILLE, Thomas, 1st Earl of Dorset (1536–1608), English statesman and poet. He was co-author of the first English blank-verse tragedy, *Gorboduc* (1561). He is also noted for his poems "Induction" and "Complaint of Buckingham" in the collection *A Mirror for Magistrates* (1563).

SACKVILLE-WEST, Victoria Mary (1892–1962), English poet, novelist and biographer, associated (like her husband Harold Nicolson) with the BLOOMSBURY GROUP. Her works include the poem *The Land* (1926) and the novels *The Edwardians* (1930) and *All Passion Spent* (1931).

SACRAMENT, in Christian theology, a visible sign and pledge of invisible GRACE, ordained by Christ. The traditional seven sacraments (first listed by Peter Lombard) are BAPTISM, Holy COMMUNION, CONFIRMATION, PENANCE, ORDINATION, MARRIAGE and EXTREME UNCTION, of which only the first two are accepted as sacraments by Protestants. In Roman Catholic theology the sacraments, if validly administered, convey grace objectively to the believing recipients; Protestants stress the joining of Word and sacrament, and the necessity of faith.

SACRIFICE, a cultic act found in almost all religions, in which an object is consecrated and offered by a PRIEST in worship to a deity. It often involves the killing of an animal or human being and thus the offering up of its life; sometimes a communion meal follows. Sacrifice may also be seen as the expiation of sin, the sealing of a covenant or a gift to the god which invites blessing in return. Ancient Israel had an elaborate system of sacrifices (chief being that of PASSOVER) which ceased when the Temple was destroyed (70 AD). In Christianity Christ's death is viewed as the one perfect and eternal sacrifice for sin.

SACROILIAC JOINT, the JOINT between the sacrum or lower part of the vertebral column and the iliac bones of the PELVIS. Little movement occurs about the joint but it may be affected by certain types of ARTHRITIS, such as ankylosing spondylitis.

SADAT, Anwar el- (1918–81), president of Egypt from 1970. An army officer, he was active in the coup that overthrew King Faruk in 1952. As vice president, he became president on Nasser's death. He expelled Soviet military advisers. His war with Israel and support of an Arab oil boycott against the West (both 1973) were followed by a policy reversal. Establishing close ties with the US, he took initiatives leading to an Egyptian-Israeli peace treaty (1979). He shared the Nobel Peace Prize for 1978. In 1981, while reviewing a parade, Sadat was assassinated by a fanatical group of army officers.

SADDLE, seat to support a rider on the back of an animal. Most horse saddles are leather and are held in place by a *girth* (strap) passing underneath the horse. Two *stirrup-leathers* (straps) support the *stirrups* in which the rider places his feet. The *English* saddle is light, almost flat, and used by jockeys and horse-show riders. The *Western* saddle is heavier, has a raised frontal horn to which a lariat may be attached, and is used by cowboys and rodeo riders.

SADDUCEES, aristocratic Jewish religious group in Roman Judea, opposed to the PHARISEES. They rejected the Pharisaic Oral Law and based their faith on the TORAH. Their great political influence ended with the destruction of the Temple at Jerusalem (70 AD).

SADE, Donatien Alphonse François, Comte de (1740–1814), usually known as the Marquis de Sade, French soldier and writer who gave his name to sadism. He argued that since sexual deviation and criminal acts exist, they are natural. He spent much of his life in prisons and his last 11 years in Charenton lunatic asylum.

SAFDIE, Moshe (1938–   ), Israeli-born architect who won fame for his prefabricated housing complex, Habitat, at Montreal's Expo 67. He designed housing complexes in Puerto Rico and Israel. He taught at Harvard U from 1978.

SAFETY GLASS, reinforced GLASS used chiefly in automobile windscreens, aircraft, and where bullet resistance is needed. Some safety glass is glass toughened by being heated almost to softening and then cooled; some has wire mesh embedded to guard against shattering; most is a laminate with a thin layer of PLASTIC (polyvinyl butyral) between two glass layers, so that, if broken, the glass fragments adhere to the plastic.

SAFETY LAMP, lamp used to detect explosive "firedamp" (METHANE) in mines, invented in 1815 by the British chemist Sir Humphry DAVY to provide a safe form of lighting underground. A double layer of wire gauze surrounding the flame dissipated its heat, so preventing a methane atmosphere from reaching its ignition temperature, and yet allowed any methane present to cause a noticeable change in the flame's appearance. A safety lamp was also invented independently by George STEPHENSON.

SAFETY VALVE, a VALVE, sealed by a compressed spring or a weight, that opens to allow fluid above a preset pressure to escape. It is then held open until the pressure has fallen by a predetermined amount. They are used on all pressurized vessels (BOILERS, etc.) to prevent explosion.

SAGA, epic narrative, usually in prose, of 11th–14th century Scandinavian and Icelandic literature. Sagas often have historical settings, but their content is mainly fictional; their style is spare and understated, often bleak and grim. Probably the greatest saga author was SNORRI STURLUSON, whose *Heimskringla* (c1230) traced the history of the kings of Norway. Subjects of sagas range from odd incidents to histories of individuals, whole families or, as in *Njal's Saga*, of feuds.

SAGAN, Françoise (1935–   ), pen name of the French novelist Françoise Quoirez, best known for the precocious and highly successful *Bonjour Tristesse* (1954), written when she was 18, and *A Certain Smile* (1956), both of which deal with the disillusionments of gilded youth.

SAGE, Russell (1816–1906), US financier who amassed a fortune from the wholesale grocery, railroad and other businesses. He left $70 million, part of which his widow used to establish the Russell Sage Foundation (1907), which aims to better US social conditions.

SAGEBRUSH, *Artemisia tridentata,* and related species, small aromatic shrubs with purple or yellow flowers, native to plains and mountains of western North America. Sagebrushes are so common in Nev. that it is nicknamed "the sagebrush state." Family: Compositae.

SAHARA DESERT, the world's largest DESERT, covering about 3,500,000sq mi. It stretches across N Africa from the Atlantic to the Red Sea. The terrain includes sand hills, rocky wastes, tracts of gravel and fertile oases. The central plateau, about 1000ft above sea level, has mountain groups rising well above 6,000ft. Rainfall ranges from under 5in to 15in annually and temperatures may soar above 120°F and plunge to under 50°F at night. Since WWII the Sahara has gained economic importance with the discovery of extensive oil, gas and iron-ore deposits.

SAHEL, semi-arid region S of the Sahara desert, with savanna-type grassland and scrub. Rainfall is 4–8in a year, mostly in June–August. Nomadic herders graze livestock in the Sahel during the rainy season and there is some millet and groundnut cultivation. The area suffered severe droughts in 1912–15, 1941–42, 1968–74, and again in the 1980s; rapid desertification is making much of the area uninhabitable.

SAIGON, See HO CHI MINH CITY.

SAINT, term used in the New Testament to refer to all the faithful, and in the early Church to refer to the martyrs: it is now used to denote those who by the exceptional holiness of their lives are recognized by a Church as occupying an exalted position in heaven and being worthy of veneration (see CANONIZATION).

ST. ANDREWS, university city and seaport in Fife, E Scotland. Its university, founded 1410, is the oldest in Scotland. The city is a tourist resort famous for golf, which was played there as early as the 15th century. The Royal and Ancient Club was founded in 1754, and its Old Course is one of the most famous golf links in the world.

SAINT AUGUSTINE, Fla., oldest city (founded 1565) in the US, seat of St. John's Co., on the Atlantic coast 35mi SE of Jacksonville: it did not become part of the US until 1821. It is a tourist center with a fishing industry. Pop 11,985.

SAINT BARTHOLOMEW'S DAY MASSACRE, the killing of French HUGUENOTS which began in Paris on Aug. 24, 1572. Jealous of the influence of the Huguenot COLIGNY on her son King CHARLES IX, Catherine de MÉDICIS plotted to assassinate him. When this failed Catherine, fearing Huguenot reaction, persuaded Charles to order the deaths of all leading Huguenots. On the morning of St. Bartholomew's Day thousands were slaughtered. Despite government orders to stop, the murders continued in the provinces until Oct.

SAINT BERNARD PASSES, two passes over the Alps. The Great St. Bernard (8,100ft) links Martigny in Switzerland with Aosta in Italy. The Little St. Bernard (7,177ft) connects the Isère Valley in France with Aosta.

ST. CHRISTOPHER AND NEVIS, independent nation in the West Indies. Part of the Leeward Islands, St. Kitts–Nevis, when it gained independence in Sept. 1983, became the 12th nation formed in the British Caribbean since 1962.

Official name: Federation of St. Christopher and Nevis
Capital: Basseterre
Area: 103sq mi
Population: 46,500
Language: English
Religion: Christian
Monetary unit(s): 1 East Caribbean dollar = 100 cents
Land. St. Kitts (officially St. Christopher; 65sq mi) and Nevis (36sq mi) are mountainous, volcanic in origin, and separated by a narrow channel. The scenery attracts tourists, as does the climate, which is tropical with a dry season Jul.-Dec.
People and Economy. The population is predominantly of African and British origin. The main town is Basseterre on St. Kitts; Charlestown is the center on Nevis. More than 80,000 tourists visited the country in 1986. In addition to tourism, the economy is based on agriculture, which produces sugar, molasses, cotton and coconuts.
History. Columbus discovered the islands in

1493. The British arrived on St. Kitts in 1623, the French in 1625. Britain definitively gained the islands in 1783. They were part of the Leeward Islands colony 1871–1956 and of the West Indies Federation 1958–62. In 1967 they formed a self-governing state with Anguilla, which subsequently returned to British rule.

ST. CLAIR, Arthur (1736–1818), US soldier and politician. He served in the REVOLUTIONARY WAR, and in 1787 became president of the Continental Congress, then governor of the NORTHWEST TERRITORY. His military career ended with defeat by the Indians in 1791. Unpopular as governor, he was removed from office in 1802.

SAINT CROIX, largest island of the US VIRGIN ISLANDS. A tourist center, it markets sugarcane and rum.

ST. DENIS, Ruth (Ruth Dennis; 1877?–1968), dancer, choreographer and teacher who made a major contribution to US dance. Deeply interested in Hindu philosophy, she staged her first major success, *Radha, the Dance of the Senses,* in 1906. She and her husband, Ted SHAWN, ran the influential Denishawn school of dance, 1914–32.

SAINTE-BEUVE, Charles Augustin (1804–1869), French writer and critic whose biographical approach revolutionized French literary criticism. His works include the collection of critical essays, *Causeries du Lundi* (1851–62).

SAINT ELMO'S FIRE, the glowing electrical discharge seen at the tips of tall, pointed objects—church spires, ship masts, airplane wings, etc.—in stormy weather. The negative electric charge on the storm clouds induces a positive charge on the tall structure. The impressive display is named (corruptly) for St. Erasmus, patron of sailors.

SAINT-EXUPÉRY, Antoine de (1900–1944), French writer and aviator who pioneered air routes over South America and NW Africa. In 1939 he became a military reconnaisance pilot, and was killed in action. His books include *Night Flight* (1932) and the children's classic tale, *The Little Prince* (1943).

SAINT-GAUDENS, Augustus (1848–1907), US sculptor famed for his large public monuments. His works include the Adams Memorial (1891) in Rock Creek Cemetery, Washington D.C., and the Robert G. Shaw monument in Boston (1897).

SAINT GEORGE'S CHANNEL, the strait, about 100mi long and 50–95mi wide, linking the Irish Sea and the Atlantic Ocean.

SAINT-GERMAIN, Treaty of (1919), ended the war between Austria and the Allies in WWI. It reduced Austrian territory, made Austria liable for war reparations, and forbade any alliance with Germany. The treaty was not ratified by the US.

SAINT GOTTHARD PASS, in Switzerland, road and rail route through the Alps from central Europe to Italy. The rail tunnel beneath the pass is over 9mi long and a vehicular tunnel completed in 1980 is the longest in Europe.

SAINT HELENA, British island in the S Atlantic Ocean. Its capital is Jamestown, where NAPOLEON I died in exile in 1821. The climate is temperate, and the island has a growing tourist industry. Pop 6,000.

SAINT JAMES'S PALACE, London, England, situated in Pall Mall and once a royal residence (1698–1837). Royal gatherings are still held here and foreign ambassadors to Britain are received at the Court of St. James.

SAINT-JUST, Louis de (1767–1794), French revolutionary leader. He entered the National Convention 1792 and became president two years later. He supported ROBESPIERRE, helped engineer the downfall of DANTON, and was guillotined when Robespierre fell.

ST. KITTS–NEVIS. See ST. CHRISTOPHER AND NEVIS.

ST. LAURENT, Louis Stephen (1882–1973), Canadian Liberal prime minister 1948–57. He became federal minister of justice and attorney general in 1942, and in 1945 played an important role in the setting up of the UNITED NATIONS. As prime minister he strengthened Canada's position in the COMMONWEALTH OF NATIONS and was instrumental in founding the NORTH ATLANTIC TREATY ORGANIZATION. Domestically, his greatest achievement was the incorporation of Newfoundland as a Canadian province in 1949.

SAINT LAWRENCE RIVER, largest river in Canada, flowing 760mi NE from Lake Ontario to the Gulf of St. Lawrence. It forms 120mi of the US/Canadian border.

SAINT LAWRENCE SEAWAY AND GREAT LAKES WATERWAY, the US/Canadian inland waterway for ocean-going vessels connecting the GREAT LAKES with the Atlantic Ocean, and comprising a 2,342mi-long system of natural waterways, canals, locks, dams and dredged channels (including the WELLAND SHIP CANAL). It was completed in 1959. The waterway, once restricted to small river vessels, has opened the industries and agriculture of the Great Lakes to international trade.

ST. LEGER, Barry (1737–1789), British officer in the American REVOLUTIONARY WAR, and founder of the famous horse race at Doncaster, England, which bears his name.

ST. LOUIS, on the Mississippi R, largest city of Mo. Founded as a fur-trading post by the French in 1763, it was ceded to Spain in 1770, and after reverting briefly to the French became part of the US under the LOUISIANA PURCHASE in 1803. The city expanded rapidly, and became a major inland port, transportation center and market for agricultural products. Pop (city) 429,000, (metro) 2,412,000.

ST. LUCIA, independent island nation of the Windward Island group in the Caribbean, 250mi from the mainland of South America.

Official name: State of St. Lucia
Capital: Castries
Area: 238sq mi
Population: 142,000
Languages: English (official), French patois
Religions: Christian
Monetary unit(s): 1 East Caribbean dollar=100 cents
Land. St. Lucia, 27mi long and 14mi wide. is of volcanic origin with one active volcano. The terrain is hilly, with Morne Gimie reaching 3,145ft. The interior is covered with tropical rain forests. The average annual temperature is 79°F.
People. Most of the inhabitants are of African heritage, descendants of slaves, although a few Carib Indians survive. Roman Catholicism is followed by almost 90% of the population.
Economy. Small-scale agriculture is the principal economic activity, with most farms smaller than 5acres. Bananas, and to a lesser extent cacao, coconuts and citrus fruits are grown for export. Industry, including food processing, electrical components and garments, is being diversified to include an ambitious oil complex. Although tourism is growing, imports exceed exports by 300% and the country is heavily dependent upon foreign aid.

History. The Carib Indians were able to prevent several settlement attempts by the British and French from the early 17th century until 1814 when the island was ceded to Britain. St. Lucia was part of the West Indies Federation from 1958 until it was dissolved in 1962. Full independence from Britain was granted in 1979. The years immediately following independence were marked by political turmoil, but the nation's first prime minister, John Compton, was returned to office in 1982 and reelected in 1987.

SAINT MARK'S CATHEDRAL (San Marco), Venetian 11th-century church, outstanding example of Byzantine architecture, built in the form of a Greek cross surmounted by five large domes. The richly constructed and sculptured west façade has Gothic additions. Its famous four bronze horses were brought from Constantinople in 1204.

SAINT-MIHIEL, town in NE France, famous for its Benedictine abbey founded in 709. Held by the Germans for most of WWI, it was recovered by the Allies in 1918.

SAINT PAUL'S CATHEDRAL, London, baroque church designed by Christopher WREN, built (1675–1710) on the site of earlier churches after the great fire of London (1666). The dome that covers the crossing is one of the world's great domes and a feature of the London skyline. The cathedral was damaged in WWII but rebuilt according to Wren's original plan.

SAINT PETER'S BASILICA, Rome, the world's largest church, built on the supposed tomb of St. PETER between 1506 and 1667 by architects including BRAMANTE, RAPHAEL, SANGALLO, MICHELANGELO, MADERNO and BERNINI. It forms a huge Latin cross capped by a great dome. Gilt, mosaic, bronze and marble embellish the interior and an enormous canopy by Bernini encloses the main altar.

SAINT PETERSBURG. See LENINGRAD.

SAINT PIERRE AND MIQUELON, French islands in the Atlantic Ocean, S of Newfoundland. The capital is Saint Pierre. Chief occupations are codfishing, fox- and mink-farming and tourism. First visited in the 17th century by Breton and Basque fishermen, the islands were long disputed between France and Britain, finally becoming French in 1804, a French Overseas Territory in 1946 and a French overseas department in 1976.

SAINT-SAËNS, Charles Camille (1835–1921), French composer. He composed many large-scale symphonies, piano concertos, symphonic poems and operas, including *Samson and Delilah* (1877), but today it is his lighter music that is best known, especially *Danse Macabre* (1874) and *Carnival of the Animals* (1886).

SAINT-SIMON, Claude Henri de Rouvroy, Comte de (1760–1825), French proto-socialist philosopher who advocated a state organized by scientists and industrialists. Especially concerned by workingclass conditions, his teachings launched the **Saint Simonism** movement, c1830, calling for meritocracy, female emancipation, nation-alization and abolition of inherited wealth.

SAINT-SIMON, Louis de Rouvroy, Duc de (1675–1755), French statesman and writer of *Mémoires* (1739–51), where he brilliantly criticized the court of King LOUIS XIV.

SAINT-SOPHIA. See HAGIA SOPHIA.

SAINT THOMAS, island (32sq mi) of the US VIRGIN ISLANDS. Charlotte Amalie, its capital, is a fine harbor. The economy rests on tourism.

ST. VINCENT, independent island nation, part of the Windward Island group in the Caribbean Sea.

Official name: St. Vincent and the Grenadines
Capital: Kingstown
Area: 150sq mi
Population: 112,000
Languages: English
Religions: Christian
Monetary unit(s): 1 East Caribbean dollar = 100 cents
Land. The principal island, St. Vincent (133sq mi), is of volcanic origin, and a mountainous spine runs down the center of the island reaching 4,000ft at Soufrière, an active volcanic peak that erupted in 1979, causing extensive crop damage. The 5 small main islands of the Grenadines extend to the SW. The climate is tropical, with annual rainfall averaging 60–150in.
People. About 65% of the inhabitants are descendants of slaves brought from Africa; minorities include persons of Portuguese, East Indian and indigenous Carib Indian (2%) descent. Most of the population

belongs to the Anglican church.
Economy. Agriculture employs about 65% of the labor force and provides all exports, principally arrowroot (90% of the world's supply) and bananas, followed by spices and cacao. Staple crops include yams, plantains, maize and peas. The small industrial sector mostly processes food crops.
History. St. Vincent was discovered by Christopher Columbus in 1498. Although both Britain and France subsequently contested control of the island, it was left largely to the Carib Indians until 1797 when, following a war with both the French and Caribs, the British deported most of the Indians. Soon after full independence, achieved in 1979, a secessionist movement in the south was put down with help from Barbados. A tropical storm in 1986 caused considerable damage.

SAINT VINCENT, Cape, SW point of Portugal, thought in ancient times to be the most W tip of Europe. Nearby, HENRY THE NAVIGATOR built his navigation school (c1425).

SAINT VITUS' DANCE, or **Sydenham's chorea.** See CHOREA.

SAIPAN, mountainous and fertile island (c48sq mi) of the MARIANA ISLANDS, capital of the Commonwealth of the Northern Marianas and former (until 1975) headquarters of the Trust Territory of the Pacific Islands. Most of the inhabitants work in government or private service occupations.

SAKE or **saki,** an alcoholic drink made from fermented RICE. It is the national beverage of Japan and contains 14% to 15% by volume of ethanol.

SAKHALIN, long, narrow island in USSR (about 30,000sq mi) off the E Siberian coast. It is mountainous, covered largely with tundra and forest: its resources include oil, coal, timber and fish. Sakhalin, in whole or part, was under Japanese control during various periods. On Sept. 1, 1983, the Soviets shot down a South Korean passenger jet that was off course over Sakhalin; all 269 people aboard were killed, resulting in an international furor.

SAKHAROV, Andrei Dimitrievich (1921–   ), Soviet physicist who played a prominent part in the development of the first Soviet HYDROGEN BOMB. He sub-sequently advocated worldwide nuclear disarmament (being awarded the 1975 Nobel Peace Prize) and became a leading Soviet dissident. His banishment (1981–86) to the city of Gorki provoked international protest.

SAKI. See MUNRO, HECTOR HUGH.

SALADIN (Salah-ad-Din Yusuf ibn-

Ayyub; 1138–1193), Muslim leader who crushed the crusaders in Palestine. Becoming Sultan of Egypt in 1174, he established there his own dynasty. He reclaimed Syria and most of Palestine including Jerusalem (1187) from the crusaders, and forced a stalemate on England's RICHARD I (1192) during the third CRUSADE, leaving the Muslims masters of Palestine. He was famed for his chivalry.

SALAMANDER, general term for all tailed AMPHIBIA, comprising eight families. They are long-bodied and retain the tail throughout their life. Their limbs are usually small and are not used for locomotion to any great extent; most movement is achieved by wriggling, with the belly close to, or touching, the ground—effectively "swimming" on land. Salamanders occupy a variety of aquatic, semiterrestrial and terrestrial habitats throughout the world. Most feed on insects and other invertebrates.

SALAMIS, mountainous and fertile Greek island (35sq mi), about 10mi W of Athens. Salamis, chief town and port, is at the W end. The famous naval battle (480 BC), when THEMISTOCLES destroyed the stronger Persian fleet, was fought in the straits to the E of the island.

SALAZAR, António de Oliveira (1889–1970), dictator of PORTUGAL (1932–68). Although he reorganized public finances and achieved certain modernizations, education and living standards remained almost static and political freedom was restricted.

SALEM, manufacturing city in NE Mass., a seat of Essex Co., NE of Boston. It was founded in 1626, and a number of 17th-century buildings are still standing. It is famous as the site of witchcraft trials (1692) in which 19 were hanged (see SEWALL. SAMUEL), and as the birthplace of Nathaniel HAWTHORNE. Pop 38,220.

SALIC LAW, law code drawn up by the Salian FRANKS. The unconnected **Salic Law of Succession** states that a woman, or one descended through the female line, cannot be heir. It was first cited in France in the early 14th century when PHILIP IV's last son (CHARLES IV) died without direct male heir: EDWARD III of England's consequent exclusion from inheriting France was a cause of the HUNDRED YEARS' WAR.

SALIERI, Antonio (1750–1825), Italian composer who was for nearly 60 years court musician in Vienna. His rivalry with Mozart is celebrated. He taught SCHUBERT, BEETHOVEN and LISZT.

SALINAS GORTARI, Carlos (1948–), Mexican economist and politician, elected president in 1988 by the narrowest margin ever experienced by the ruling Institutional Revolutionary Party (PRI). He advocated free markets and austerity to cope with Mexico's large foreign debt.

SALINGER, J(erome) D(avid) (1919–), US author whose first novel *The Catcher in the Rye* (1951) became one of the most popular postwar books, its adolescent "hero" Holden Caulfield being presented as a spokesman of his generation. Salinger's short stories, many concerning the Glass family, include *For Esmé—With Love and Squalor* (1950).

SALISBURY, Robert Arthur Talbot Gascoyne Cecil, 3rd Marquess of (1830–1903), British statesman, entered parliament 1853. As Conservative prime minister (1885–86, 1886–92, 1895–1902), he opposed parliamentary reform and Irish HOME RULE, and acted as his own foreign minister. He maintained good relations in Europe, and successfully expanded the British Empire in Africa and Asia.

SALISBURY, Robert Cecil, 1st Earl of (1563–1612), English secretary of state under ELIZABETH I from 1596, chief minister from 1598. Before Elizabeth's death he negotiated with JAMES VI that monarch's accession to the English throne, and remained chief minister thereafter.

SALIVA, the watery secretion of the salivary GLANDS which lubricate the mouth and food boluses. It contains mucus, some gamma globulins and ptyalin and is secreted in response to food in the mouth or by conditioned REFLEXES such as the smell or sight of food. Secretion is partly under the control of the parasympathetic autonomic NERVOUS SYSTEM. The various salivary glands—parotid, submandibular and sublingual—secrete slightly different types of saliva, varying in mucus and ENZYME content.

SALK, Jonas Edward (1914–), US virologist best known for developing the first POLIOMYELITIS vaccine, made from killed viruses (1952–54).

SALLUST (Caius Sallustius Crispus; 86–c34 BC), Roman senator, and first Roman historian to interpret the events which he recorded and to describe limited historical periods, though his accounts are flawed by bias and inaccuracy. His major work is *Bellum Catilinarium*, on the CATILINE conspiracy.

SALMON, large, highly palatable fishes of two genera. The Atlantic salmon, *Salmo salar*, lives in the N Atlantic, while in the N Pacific, there are five species in the genus *Onchorhynchus*. All salmon return to freshwater to breed. While the Pacific salmon die on completion of their first spawning, Atlantic salmon return to the sea, and may come back to spawn a second time. Adult salmon return to their natal streams to breed; they spawn in "redds" in the sand or gravel of the stream bed. The young remain in freshwater until they are about 18 months old, then migrate down to the sea. Adults remain in the sea, feeding, for one to two years before returning to breed.

SALMONELLA, bacteria, some species of which cause FOOD POISONING or ENTERITIS; specific types cause TYPHOID and paratyphoid fever.

SALOME (1st century AD), granddaughter of HEROD the Great. Her dancing so pleased her stepfather Herod Antipas that he promised her anything she wanted. Prompted by her mother Herodias, she asked for JOHN THE BAPTIST'S head, which was presented to her on a platter.

SALSA, in popular music, a style that combines Latin and Afro-Cuban rhythms with jazz, soul and rock music. Most popular in the 1950s and 1960s, salsa rhythms are still detectable in many disco compositions.

SALT, common name for **sodium chloride** (NaCl), found in seawater and also as the common mineral rock salt or halite. Pure salt forms white cubic CRYSTALS. Some salt is obtained by solar evaporation from salt pans, shallow depressions periodically flooded with seawater; but most is obtained from underground mines. The most familiar use of salt is to flavor food. (Magnesium carbonate is added to table salt to keep it dry.) It is, however, used in much larger quantities to preserve hides in leathermaking, in soap manufacture, as a food preservative and in keeping highways ice-free in winter. Rock salt is the main industrial source of chlorine and caustic soda. mp $801°C$, bp $1413°C$.

SALT, Chemical, an electrovalent compound (see BOND, CHEMICAL) formed by neutralization of an ACID and a BASE. The vast majority of MINERALS are salts, the best known being common SALT, sodium chloride. Salts are generally ionic solids which are good electrolytes (see ELECTROLYSIS); those of weak acids or bases undergo partial HYDROLYSIS in water. Salts may be classified as normal (fully neutralized), acid (containing some acidic hydrogen, e.g., bicarbonates), or basic (containing hydroxide ions). They may alternatively be classified as simple salts, double salts (two simple salts combined by regular substitution in the crystal lattice) including alums, and complex salts.

SALT I and II. See ARMS CONTROL.

SALTEN, Felix (1869–1945), pen name of Siegmund Salzmann, Austrian novelist and journalist whose books include *Bambi* (1923; filmed by Walt Disney 1942), the anthropomorphized life of a deer.

SALT FLAT, dried-up bed of an enclosed stretch of water that has evaporated, leaving the salts that is held in solution as a crust on the ground. Best known are the Lake Bonneville flats, near Salt Lake City, Ut.

SALT LAKE CITY, 15mi from the Great Salt Lake, capital and largest city in Utah and seat of Salt Lake Co. Founded in 1847 by Brigham YOUNG leading a band of Mormons from persecution, it is the world center of the Church of Jesus Christ of Latter-Day Saints: 65% of its residents are members. It is a commercial and industrial center for minerals, farming, oil refining and chemicals. Pop (city) 165,000, (metro) 1,025,000.

SALTON SEA, large saline lake in SE Cal. Until flooded by the Colorado in 1905, it was a depression, "the Salton Sink," 280ft below sea level. It now covers 370sq mi and is 232ft below sea level.

SALTYKOV-SHCHEDRIN, Mikhail Evgrafovich (1826–1889), one of the finest Russian satirists. His *History of a Town* (1869–70) attacked Russian bureaucrats. His only novel is *The Golovlyov Family* (1876), a story of declining gentry.

SALVAGE, in maritime law, a term given either to the rescue of life and property (a ship and its cargo) from danger on water, or to the reward given by a court to those who effect a rescue (called salvors). Under the law of the sea, it is the duty of a ship's master to go to the aid of an imperiled vessel. If life or property are saved, the owner of the rescue ship, the master and the crew share in the salvage award. These awards are generous in order to encourage seamen and shipowners to risk their lives and property in rescue operations.

SALVATION, a key religious concept: man's deliverance from the evils of life and of death. It is presupposed that man is in bondage to suffering, SIN, disease, death, decay etc., from which he may be rescued and restored to primordial blessedness. In DUALISM salvation is release of the soul from the corrupting prison of the body; in HINDUISM release from the cycle of rebirth (see TRANSMIGRATION OF SOULS). In JUDAISM, CHRISTIANITY and ISLAM it is liberation from evil into communion with God, and hence deliverance from HELL, the RESURRECTION of the body and (in Christian eschatology) the regeneration of the entire universe. In these

W religions salvation is provided by the "mighty acts" of God, who is the savior (see also SACRIFICE); elsewhere salvation may be self-attained by ritual, acquisition of knowledge, asceticism, good deeds or martyrdom. Christianity sees all history as a divine plan of salvation, consequent on Adam's fall (see ORIGINAL SIN), achieved in the INCARNATION, death and resurrection of JESUS CHRIST, and consummated at the LAST JUDGMENT.

SALVATION ARMY, Christian organization founded by William BOOTH (1865). In 1878 the mission became the Army, with Booth as General. Under strict quasimilitary discipline, the members seek to strengthen Christianity and help (also save) the poor and destitute. The Army now operates 8,000 centers in the US alone. Its official journal is *War Cry*.

SALWEEN RIVER, great river of SE Asia. Rising in Tibet it flows 1,750mi SE through China and E Burma into the Gulf of Martaban.

SALZBURG, historic city in central Austria, world famous for its annual music festival (begun 1917). The birthplace of MOZART, it lies on the Salzbach R. Pop 139,426.

SAMARITANS, inhabitants of the ancient district of Samaria. Originally non-Jewish colonists from Assyria, they intermarried with the Israelites and accepted the Jewish TORAH. However, they were not socially accepted—hence the significance of the Good Samaritan in Luke's Gospel.

SAMARKAND, city in Uzbekistan, USSR, in the Zeravshan R valley. One of the world's oldest cities, it was built on the site of Afrosiab (3000 BC or earlier) and was the great conqueror TAMERLANE'S capital. Pop 371,000.

SAMIZDAT, a Russian abbreviation meaning "self-publishing." The term contains an ironic allusion to *Gosizdat*, the standard abbreviation of the State Publishing House in the USSR. It refers to the private reproduction of books, documents, letters, essays, poems, etc. by means of simply typing and retyping them for distribution by hand. *Samizdat* began in the USSR in the 1950s to avoid the state publishing monopoly and the omnipresent censorship. It has spread throughout the countries of the Soviet bloc and is a chief pillar of that clandestine "alternative society" that exists within the official society run by the Communist Party.

SAMMARTINI, Giovanni Battista (1701–1775), Italian composer, influential as an early composer of the concert symphony. His pupils included GLUCK.

SAMNITES, ancient warlike tribes of mountainous S Italy. After three wars with Rome, the Samnites were finally crushed in 290 BC.

SAMOA, chain of 10 islands and several islets in the South Pacific, midway between Honolulu and Sydney. Volcanic and mountainous, their total area is about 1,200sq mi. The people are mostly Polynesians. The soil is fertile, producing cacao, coconuts and bananas, and the climate tropical. Savai'i (the largest), Upolu and the other W islands constitute independent WESTERN SAMOA. **American Samoa** consists of the E islands: Tutuila, the Manua group and the Rose and Swains Islands. Discovered by the Dutch in 1722, Samoa was claimed by Germany, Great Britain and the US in the mid-19th century, but in 1899 the US acquired sole rights to what is now American Samoa.

SAMOTHRACE (modern Samothráki), Greek island (71sq mi) in the NE Aegean Sea, where the WINGED VICTORY OF SAMOTHRACE was found (1863).

SAMPSON, William Thomas (1840–1902), US admiral, commander of the North Atlantic squadron in the SPANISH–AMERICAN WAR.

SAMUEL, two Old Testament books (known to Catholics as 1 and 2 KINGS) which tell of the statesman, general and prophet, Samuel (c11th century BC). He united the tribes under SAUL, and chose DAVID as Saul's successor.

SAMUELSON, Paul Anthony (1915–), US economist, advisor to Presidents KENNEDY and JOHNSON and winner of the 1970 Nobel economics prize. His widely used college textbook, *Economics* (1948; 13th ed. 1989), was translated into 21 languages.

SAMURAI, hereditary military class of Japan. From c1000 AD the Samurai dominated Japan, though after c1600 their activities were less military than cultural. Comprising 5% of Japanese, they exerted influence through BUSHIDO, a code which demanded feudal loyalty and placed honor above life. The class lost its power in the reforms of 1868.

SAN ANDREAS FAULT, break in the earth's crust, running 600mi from Cape Mendocino, NW Cal., to the Colorado desert. It was the sudden movement of land along this FAULT that caused the San Francisco EARTHQUAKE, 1906. The fracture, and the motion responsible for this and other quakes, is a result of the abutment of the eastern Pacific and North American plates (see PLATE TECTONICS).

SAN ANTONIO, city in S Tex., seat of

Bexar Co., on the San Antonio R 150mi N of the Gulf of Mexico. Founded in 1718, it was the site of the ALAMO (1836). It is one of the largest military centers in the US. Pop (city) 843,000, (metro) 1,236,000.

SANCTUARY MOVEMENT, activities of some 400 US churches since 1982 providing help and shelter to undocumented aliens from Central America in defiance of US immigration laws. The churches say their work is based on religious conviction and protected by the 1st Amendment. The US Immigration and Naturalization Service (INS) maintains that the movement is political, inspired by opposition to US policy in Central America. It also argues that the aliens are fleeing economic hardship, not political persecution, and are thus ineligible for asylum. In 1986 eight sanctuary movement activists were convicted on evidence gathered by government informers who infiltrated the movement and used tape recorders and bugging devices within the churches. In 1987 the US Supreme Court found that the standard applied by the INS in granting asylum was too strict.

SAND, George (1804–1876), pseudonym of the French novelist Amandine Aurore Lucie Dupin, Baroness Dudevant. Her novels, at first romantic, later socially oriented, include *Indiana* (1832) and *The Haunted Pool* (1846). Her life-style—coupled with its partial source, her ardent feminism—caused much controversy, her lovers including CHOPIN and notably de MUSSET. Her memoirs, *Histoire de Ma Vie* (1854–55), provide a graceful justification of her views.

SAND, in geology, collection of rock particles with diameters in the range 0.125–2.0mm. It can be graded according to particle size: fine (0.125mm); medium (0.25–0.5mm); coarse 0.5–1.0mm); and very coarse (1–2mm). Sands result from erosion by glaciers, winds, or ocean or other moving water. Their chief constituents are usually quartz and feldspar. (See also DESERT; SANDSTONE.)

SANDALWOOD, a number of trees whose timber exudes a fragrant odor. The wood takes a fine finish. Sandalwood paste, from *Santalum album,* is used for Brahman caste marks in India and in Buddhist funeral rites. Family: Santalaceae.

SANDBURG, Carl (1878–1967), American poet and biographer who won Pulitzer prizes for *Abraham Lincoln: the War Years* in 1940 and *Complete Poems* in 1951. He left school at 13, and at 20 fought in the Spanish-American war. While a journalist in Chicago, he wrote vigorous, earthy, free verse, as in *Chicago Poems* (1916) and

Smoke and Steel (1920). He was also a notable folksong anthologist.

SAND CREEK MASSACRE, unprovoked surprise attack by US soldiers led by Col. John Chivington on CHEYENNE INDIANS in Col. in Nov. 1864. Indians had camped near Fort Lyon to negotiate peace and, although they raised the US and white flags, around 500 were slaughtered and savagely mutilated.

SAN DIEGO, on the Pacific Coast close to the Mexican border, second-largest city of Cal. and seat of San Diego Co. Its natural harbor houses a great Navy base, a large fishing fleet, and lumber and shipbuilding yards. Its heavy industries include aircraft, missiles and electronics factories. Pop (city) 960,000, (metro) 2,133,000.

SANDINISTAS, the Nicaraguan revolutionary movement that overthrew the Somoza family dictatorship in 1979. Named after the Nicaraguan patriot and guerrilla leader of the 1920s César Sandino, it assembled a broad coalition in the country to defeat Anastasio Somoza and his hated Civil Guard. After the revolution the FSLN (Sandinista National Liberation Front) ruled through a five-man junta until the election of Daniel ORTEGA as president in 1984.

SANDINO, Augusto César (1893?–1934), Nicaraguan guerrilla fighter against US marines, 1927–33. After the marines were withdrawn, having established the SOMOZA dictatorship, Sandino was killed by the Somoza national guard. The Sandinista National Liberation Front, which overthrew the Somoza regime in 1979, took its name from him.

SANDOW, Eugene (1867–1925), German world weightlifting champion (1891) who popularized bodybuilding and devised several bodybuilding techniques.

SANDPIPERS, small to medium-sized wading birds forming part of the family Scolopacidae. Most are slim birds, with long straight bills and inconspicuous cryptic plumage. The group includes the stints, knots and "shanks" as well as the true sandpipers, dividing into two major groups, the calidritine and tringine pipers.

SANDSTONE, a SEDIMENTARY ROCK consisting of consolidated sand, cemented postdepositionally by such minerals as quartz, calcite, or hematite, or set in a matrix of clay minerals. The sand grains are chiefly QUARTZ. The chief varieties are quartz-arenite, rich in silica; arkose, feldspar-rich; graywacke, composed of angular grains of quartz and feldspar and/or rock fragments and over 15% matrix; and subgraywacke, with less matrix than graywacke. Sandstone beds may bear NATURAL GAS or PETROLEUM, and are commonly AQUIFERS. Sandstone is quarried for building, and crushed for use as agglomerate.

SANDYS, Sir Edwin (1561–1629), English statesman and a founder of the colony of VIRGINIA. During his management of the LONDON COMPANY, a representative assembly met in Virginia, the first such in the North American colonies (1619).

SAN FRANCISCO, California city and seaport on the Pacific coast, noted for its cosmopolitan charm. Its economy is based on shipping and shipbuilding, with exports of cotton, grain, lumber and petroleum products. It is also the financial, cultural and communications center for the NW Coast. Its many tourist attractions include Chinatown, Fisherman's Wharf and Golden Gate Park. There are several museums and art galleries and the famous opera house. Founded by the Spanish (as Yerba Buena) in 1776, the city passed into US hands in 1846 and was named San Francisco (1847). The GOLD RUSH soon attracted thousands of settlers to the area. Parts of the city were rebuilt after the earthquake of 1906 (see SAN ANDREAS FAULT). A center of the 1960s COUNTERCULTURE, the city was hard hit by the AIDS epidemic in the 1980s. Pop (city) 713,000, (metro) 1,576,000.

SAN FRANCISCO BAY, the world's largest natural harbor, 50mi long and up to 12mi wide, spanned by the GOLDEN GATE and San Francisco–Oakland Bay bridges.

SAN FRANCISCO CONFERENCE, conference, attended by 50 nations, held April–June 1945 to set up the UNITED NATIONS.

SANGALLO, Antonio da (Antonio Cordiani; 1483–1546), Italian architect and military engineer, succeeded RAPHAEL as architect of SAINT PETER'S BASILICA.

SANGER, Frederick (1918–), British biochemist awarded the 1958 Nobel Prize for Chemistry for his work on the PROTEINS, particularly for first determining the complete structure of a protein, that of bovine INSULIN (1955). He shared the 1980 Nobel Prize for Chemistry for his research on NUCLEIC ACIDS, the carriers of genetic traits.

SANGER, Margaret (1883–1966), US pioneer of BIRTH CONTROL and feminism who set up the first birth-control clinic in the US (1916), founded the National Birth Control League (1917), and helped organize the first international birth-control conference (1927).

SANHEDRIN, ruling councils of the Jews in Roman-occupied Palestine. The Great Sanhedrin was made up of 71 SADDUCEES and PHARISEES, presided over by the high priest. It served as a civil and religious court and was thus responsible for the trials of Christ and several of the Apostles. Lesser sanhedrins, made up of 23 members, tried minor offences and criminal cases.

SAN JACINTO, Battle of, decisive engagement (April 21, 1836) in the war for Texan independence. It was won by General HOUSTON whose troops, though outnumbered, surprised and defeated the Mexicans under SANTA ANNA, thereby establishing TEXAS as an independent republic.

SAN JUAN, capital and port of PUERTO RICO on the NE coast of the island. Founded in 1508 by PONCE DE LEON, it is now a trade center producing sugar, rum, metal products, textiles and furniture. Tourism is also important. Pop 434,849.

SAN JUAN HILL, Battle of, victory at Santiago de Cuba won by the ROUGH RIDERS on July 1, 1898, which with the El Caney battle led to CERVERA Y TOPETE's defeat in the SPANISH–AMERICAN WAR.

Official name: Republic of San Marino
Capital: San Marino
Area: 24sq mi
Population: 22,100
Language: Italian
Religion: Roman Catholic
Monetary unit(s): 1 lira = 100 centesimi

SAN MARINO, world's smallest republic and possibly the oldest state in Europe, located in NE Italy. Built on the three peaks of Mt Titano, its townships include San Marino (the capital) and Serravalle. Tradition reports that San Marino was founded as a refuge for persecuted Christians in the 4th century AD. Many historic buildings remain, and the modern state lives mainly by tourism and the sale of postage stamps. The republic is governed by two "captains-regent" assisted by a 60-member council of state. A Communist-led coalition governed the country in 1947–57 and 1978–86.

SAN MARTIN, José de (1778–1850), Argentinian general who, with BOLÍVAR, liberated Chile and much of Peru from Spanish rule. Educated in Spain, he served in the Spanish army before returning to South America in 1812. In 1817 he led the Argentinian army over the Andes to Chile and victory against the Spanish: his friend Bernardo O'HIGGINS became ruler of an independent Chile. In 1821, after a series of military victories, he proclaimed Peru independent and became its protector. In 1822 he retired to France.

SANNAZZARO, Jacopo (c1456–1530), Italian poet whose *Arcadia* (1504), the first lyric pastoral romance, initiated a genre that rapidly spread throughout Western Europe.

SAN SALVADOR ISLAND, name given by COLUMBUS to his first landfall in the New World, now generally accepted to be Watling Island (now called San Salvador: 60sq mi) in the BAHAMAS. Its original Indian name was Guanahani.

SANS-CULOTTES (French: without knee-breeches), in the FRENCH REVOLUTION, the Parisian lower classes, who wore long trousers rather than breeches; the term thus implies extreme radical.

SANSKRIT, classical language of the Hindu peoples of India and the oldest literary language of the Indo-European family of languages. Some early texts date from c1500 BC, including the Vedic texts (see VEDA). Vedic Sanskrit was prevalent roughly 1500–150 BC, Classical Sanskrit roughly 500 BC–900 AD. Sanskrit gave rise to such modern Indian languages as HINDI and URDU, and is distantly related to the CELTIC LANGUAGES, ROMANCE LANGUAGES and SLAVONIC LANGUAGES.

SANSOVINO, Jacopo (Jacopo Tatti; 1486–1570), Italian sculptor and architect, highly influential in Venice where he designed in a classical style the Library of St. Mark's (1536–38) and sculptured *Mars and Neptune* (1554–56).

SANS SOUCI, ROCOCO palace near Potsdam built for FREDERICK II of Prussia in 1745–47, who lived there for 40 years, making it a magnificent cultural center for such notable guests as VOLTAIRE.

SAN STEFANO, Treaty of, peace treaty signed in 1878 between Russia and the Ottoman Empire. Its terms, including the cession of land and payment of a large indemnity, greatly increased Russia's power in SE Europe. The treaty was later revised at the Congress of BERLIN.

SANTA ANNA, Antonio López de (1794–1876), Mexican general and dictator who tried to suppress the Texan revolution and fought US troops in the MEXICAN WAR. He helped establish Mexican independence

in 1821–29 and became president in 1833. When the Texan settlers revolted against his tyranny (1836), he defeated them at the ALAMO but lost the battle of San Jacinto, being himself captured, and had to resign: he was to gain and lose the presidency three further times (1841–44, 1846–47, 1853–55). He spent most of his later years in exile.

SANTA CLAUS, Christmastide bearer of gifts to children. The jolly fat man transported by flying reindeer and dropping presents down chimneys is a comparatively recent (19th-century) legend derived from St. NICHOLAS (introduced as Sinter Klaas to the New World by Dutch settlers), whose feast day (Dec. 6) was a children's holiday. A drawing by cartoonist Thomas NAST is believed to have helped fix the image of a rotund, white-bearded Santa Claus in the popular imagination after such a figure was described in Clement Moore's 1822 poem, *A Visit from St. Nicholas.*

SANTA FE TRAIL, overland trade route between W Mo. and Santa Fe, N.M., in use from its opening-up in 1821 until the coming of the Santa Fe railroad in 1880. Manufactured goods passed W, furs and bullion E.

SANTAYANA, George (1863–1952), Spanish-born US philosopher, writer and critic. He was an influential writer on aesthetics in books such as *The Sense of Beauty* (1896). His philosophy was expressed in *The Life of Reason* (1905–06), where he emphasized the importance of reason in understanding the world but was skeptical of what one can really know. *Skepticism and Animal Faith* (1923) suggests a relationship between faith and knowledge.

SANTIAGO, capital and principal industrial, commercial and cultural city of Chile, on the Mapocho R. Industries include textiles, foodstuffs and iron and steel foundries. It was founded 1541 by VALDIVIA. Numerous earthquakes destroyed most of the colonial buildings and Santiago is now a modern city with parks and wide avenues. Pop 4,099,714.

SANTIAGO DE COMPOSTELA, city in NW Spain, an important Christian pilgrimage center since the discovery in the 9th century of the supposed tomb of the apostle St. JAMES the greater.

SANTO DOMINGO, capital and chief port of the Dominican Republic, at the mouth of the Ozama R. Its official name was Ciudad Trujillo during 1930–61. Founded by COLUMBUS' brother Bartholomew in 1496, it is the oldest continuously inhabited European settlement in the W Hemisphere with a university dating from 1538. Pop (metro) 817,645.

SANTOS-DUMONT, Alberto (1873–1932), Brazilian-born pioneer aviator who experimented with balloons and powered dirigibles before flying his successful box-kite airplane (1906) and "Grasshopper" monoplane with undercarriage (1909).

SÃO PAULO, largest city and industrial center of Brazil. Capital of São Paulo state, it lies 225mi SW of Rio de Janeiro. Founded in 1554, it grew rapidly with the development of the coffee industry in the 1880s, and still sends coffee to the port of Santos. Its other industries are diverse. It is the site of four universities and numerous cultural institutions. Pop (city) 10,099,086; (metro) 15,900,000.

SÃO TOMÉ AND PRÍNCIPE, a republic in the Gulf of Guinea, off the W coast of Africa, comprising two main islands and several islets.

Official name: São Tomé and Príncipe
Capital: São Tomé
Area: 386sq mi
Population: 112,000
Languages: Portuguese, Criolo
Religions: Roman Catholic, Animist
Monetary unit(s): 1 dobra = 100 centavos
Land. São Tomé lies 190mi W of Libreville, Gabon. São Tomé Island (330sq mi) is much larger than Príncipe Island, accounting for almost 90% of the country's area and holding about 90% of its population. The land rises to a 6,640ft peak of volcanic rock, sloping downward to fertile volcanic soil on the E coast. Forests grow near the W shore. Príncipe is similar in land pattern. The islands have a tropical climate.
People and Economy. The country depends heavily on cocoa for its income. Copra, coconuts, palm kernels, bananas and coffee are also important exports. There is a lack of mineral resources and industry is undeveloped. Most of the inhabitants are of mixed African and Portuguese ancestry. African migrant workers and a small group of Europeans are also present.
History. Discovered in the 1400s by the Portuguese, the islands achieved independence in 1975. The withdrawal of skilled Europeans after independence seriously disrupted the former plantation economy. The country is now heavily dependent on foreign aid. Manuel Pinto da Costa, the nation's first president, was reelected in 1980 and 1985.

SAPIR, Edward (1884–1939), US anthropologist, poet and linguist whose most important work was on the relation between language and the culture of which it is a product. He suggested that one's perception of the world is dominated by the language with which one articulates.

SAPPHIRE, all GEM varieties of corundum except those which, being red, are called RUBY; blue sapphires are best-known, but most other colors are found. The best sapphires come from Kashmir, Burma, Thailand, Sri Lanka and Australia. Synthetic stones, made by flame-fusion, are used for jewel bearings, phonograph styluses, etc.

SAPPHO (6th century BC), Greek poet born in Lesbos. Surviving fragments of her work, mainly addressed to young girls, are among the finest classical love lyrics, combining passion with perfect control of many meters. The terms sapphism and lesbianism, meaning female HOMOSEXUALITY, derive from Sappho and Lesbos.

SARACENS, the name given by medieval Christians to the Arab and Turkish Muslims who conquered former Christian territory in SW Asia, N Africa, Spain and Sicily.

SARAJEVO, capital of the republic of Bosnia and Herzegovina in Yugoslavia, on the Bosna R. Here, Austrian Archduke Francis Ferdinand and his wife were assassinated on June 28, 1914, the event which sparked WWI. Pop 319,017.

SARATOGA, Battles of, a key series of engagements in the American Revolution. On Sept. 17, 1777, a British force led by General John BURGOYNE attacked an American encampment around Bemis Heights, N.Y., defended by General Horatio GATES. Burgoyne's force, outnumbered, with heavy losses and without reinforcements was forced to retreat, and after further fighting eventually surrendered at Saratoga on Oct. 17. After this important victory, the French recognized American independence and allied themselves with the rebels. (See also REVOLUTIONARY WAR, AMERICAN.)

SARAWAK, a state of the Malaysia federation. A former British colony, Sarawak comprises 48,000sq mi of mostly mountainous country on the NW coast of

Borneo. Oil, bauxite, rice, pepper, rubber and sago are its principal products. The state capital is Kuching.

SARCOMA, a form of TUMOR derived from connective TISSUE, usually of mesodermal origin in EMBRYOLOGY. It is often distinguished from CANCER as its behavior and natural history may differ, although it is still a malignant tumor. It commonly arises from BONE (osteosarcoma), fibrous tissue (fibrosarcoma) or CARTILAGE (chondrosarcoma). Excision is required, though RADIATION THERAPY may be helpful.

SARDINIA, Italian island in the Mediterranean 120mi to the W of mainland Italy and just S of CORSICA. It is a mountainous area of 9,301sq mi, with some agriculture on the coastal plains and upland valleys. Wheat, olives and vines are grown and sheep and goats raised: fish and cork are also exported. Many different ores are extracted from the ancient mines and tourism is growing in importance. The island is an autonomous region of Italy, with its capital at Caligari.

SARDINIA, Kingdom of, the European state that formed the nucleus of modern, united Italy. In 1720, Sardinia was ceded to Savoy and the duke of Savoy became first ruler of the new kingdom of Sardinia, made up of Savoy, Sardinia and Piedmont, N Italy. In the 19th century Sardinia championed political reform, national unification and independence from Austria. Through the diplomacy of CAVOUR, prime minister of Victor Emmanuel II, and the conquests of GARIBALDI, almost all of Italy was united under the house of Savoy in the period 1859–61, when Victor Emmanuel was proclaimed king of Italy. (See also RISORGIMENTO.)

SARDIS, about 50mi W of modern Izmir, Turkey, the ancient capital of LYDIA and a center of civilization from 650 BC until conquered by the Persians in c546 BC, being finally destroyed by TAMERLANE. Its ruins are Lydian, Roman and Byzantine.

SARGASSO SEA, oval area of the N Atlantic, of special interest as the spawning ground of American EELS, many of whose offspring drift across the Atlantic to form the European eel population. Bounded E by the Canaries Current, S by the N Equatorial Current, W and N by the GULF STREAM, it contains large masses of *Sargassum* weed.

SARGENT, John Singer (1856–1925), US painter famous for his many portraits of high society figures in the US and UK. His most famous picture, *Madame X* (1884), showing the alluring Parisian Madame Gautreau, created a furor that obscured the painting's brilliance.

SARGON, the name of two great rulers in ancient Mesopotamia. **Sargon of Akkad** (reigned c2335–2280 BC) founded the Semite Akkadian dynasty which displaced the SUMERIANS. He built an empire which covered all Mesopotamia and Syria and reached E to Persia, W to the Mediterranean and N to the Black Sea. **Sargon II of Assyria** (ruled 721–705 BC) consolidated the Assyrian empire. He concluded the siege of Samaria in Palestine and conquered Cyprus, Armenia and Babylonia. His method of retaining power was to deport hostile tribes.

SARMATIANS, a central Asian people of Iranian stock who conquered the SCYTHIANS in SE Europe. They held S European Russia 400 BC–400 AD and raided in the Balkans.

SARMIENTO, Domingo Faustino (1811–1888), Argentine educator, writer and statesman, president 1868–74. He helped overthrow the dictator Juan de Rosas (1852), and as president promoted education, commerce, immigration and communications.

SARNOFF, David (1891–1971), Russian-born US radio and television pioneer. Starting his career as a telegraph messenger boy, he became president of RCA, and later founded NBC, the first commercial radio network (1926).

SAROYAN, William (1908–1981), US author. After short stories like *The Daring Young Man on the Flying Trapeze* (1934) came sketches reflecting his Armenian background (*My Name Is Aram*, 1940) and colorful, optimistic accounts of Depression and war years, as in the play *The Time of Your Life* (1939) and the novel *The Human Comedy* (1943), both filmed.

SARRAUTE, Nathalie (1902–   ), Russian-born French writer, creator of the "antinovel." Her technique, in such accounts of bourgeois life and psychology as *Tropisms* (1939) and *Portrait of a Man Unknown* (1947), rejects that of Realist novelists.

SARTON, George Alfred Leon (1884–1956), Belgian-born US historian of science, at Harvard University 1916–51, author of *Introduction to the History of Science* (3 vols., 1927–47). His daughter, **May Sarton** (1912–   ), was a poet and novelist.

SARTRE, Jean Paul (1905–1980), French philosopher, novelist and playwright, famous exponent of EXISTENTIALISM. His works reflect his vision of man as master of his own fate, with his life defined by his actions: "existence precedes essence." Among his novels are *Nausea* (1938) and the trilogy *The Roads to Freedom* (1945–49). His drama includes *The Flies* (1943) and *No Exit* (1944). Sartre founded his review *Les Temps Modernes* in 1945. A close associate of Simone de BEAUVOIR and a communist who spoke eloquently for the left, his influence was international. In 1964 he refused the Nobel Prize for Literature.

SASKATCHEWAN, inland prairie province of W Canada. Fifth largest of Canadian provinces, it is North America's most important wheat-growing region.
Name of province: Saskatchewan
Joined Confederation: Sept. 1, 1905
Capital: Regina
Area: 251,700sq mi
Population: 1,000,227
Land. The N third of the province is made up of the Canadian Shield, the S two-thirds of plains and lowlands. The N contains many forests, lakes, swamps and streams and is rich in mineral deposits including copper, zinc and uranium. The S has the best farming soil, and the majority of the population live there. The climate is continental with cold winters (average 15°F in the S and −20°F in the N) and summer temperatures averaging 57°–67°F.
People. This is the only province that has a variety of ethnic inheritances, without a majority of either British or French. Over 25% of the population lives in the two largest cities, Saskatoon and the capital, Regina.
Economy. The economy is heavily dependent on farming, with 60% of Canada's wheat grown in the area. Other crops are barley, rye and flax. Agriculture is declining in relative importance with the discovery of oil and the growth of service-supply industries. The service sector now accounts for 50% of the total gross domestic product. Food processing and distribution and the manufacture of farm machinery are increasing. Oil refining and steel manufacturing are located in Regina and other northern communities. Heavy-oil pools have been discovered in the Lloydminster area, and the province is second in Canada in crude-oil production. Lignite coal, mined since the 1880s, has been strip-mined since 1956.
History. The paleo-Indians, believed to be the first people there, crossed from Asia 20–30,000 years ago. White traders from the HUDSON'S BAY COMPANY first entered the area in 1690. The area was not properly explored until Sieur de La Vérendrye visited it 40 years later. Farming settlements spread after the purchase in 1870 of the North West Territories by the new Dominion of Canada. Rapid growth

followed after Saskatchewan became a province in 1905. The Depression and war years brought hardship and discontent and led to the rise to power in 1944 of the Cooperative Commonwealth Federation, which remained in office till 1964. Petroleum and petroleum-based industries brought new wealth to the province in the 1970s and 1980s despite the decline of oil prices in the 1980s. Saskatchewan was one of the prime movers behind the Western Accord of 1985, by which Ottawa granted the provinces greater control over their natural resources.

SASSANIANS, or **Sassanids**, the dynasty of rulers of the Persian empire founded by Ardashir I, c224 AD, and based on his capital at Ctesiphon. Named for Sasan, an ancestor of Ardashir, the dynasty included Shapur I and II and Khosru I and II. The empire was overrun by the Arabs in the 7th century. (See also PERSIA, ANCIENT.)

SASSETTA, or **Stefano di Giovanni** (c1400–1450), leading Italian painter of the Sienese school, best known for his narrative altarpieces.

SASSOON, Siegfried (1886–1967), English poet and novelist. Decorated for bravery in WWI, he wrote bitterly satirical poetry such as *The Old Hunstman* (1917) and *Counterattack* (1918), which shocked the public with their graphic portrayal of trench warfare, their attacks on hypocritical patriotism and their pacifist conclusions. His novels include *Memoirs of a Fox-Hunting Man* (1928).

SATELLITE, in astronomy, a celestial object which revolves with or around a larger celestial object. In our SOLAR SYSTEM this includes PLANETS, COMETS, ASTEROIDS, and meteoroids (see METEOR), as well as the moons of the planets; although the term is usually restricted to this last sense. Of the 32 known moons, the largest is Callisto (JUPITER IV), the smallest Phobos (the inner moon of Mars). The MOON is the largest known satellite relative to its parent planet; indeed, the earth-moon system is often considered a double planet.

SATELLITES, Artificial, man-made objects placed in orbit as SATELLITES. First seriously proposed in the 1920s, they were impracticable until large enough ROCKETS were developed. The first artificial satellite, Sputnik 1, was launched by the USSR in Oct. 1957, and was soon followed by a host of others, mainly from the USSR and the US, but also from the UK, France, Canada, West Germany, Italy, Japan and China. They have many scientific, technological and military uses. Astronomical observations (notably X-RAY ASTRONOMY) can be made unobscured by the atmosphere. Studies can be made of the RADIATION and electromagnetic and gravitational fields in which the EARTH is bathed, and of the upper ATMOSPHERE. Experiments have been made on the functioning of animals and plants in space (with zero gravity and increased radiation). Artificial satellites are also used for reconnaissance, surveying, meteorological observation, as navigation aids (position references and signal relays), and in communications for relaying television and radio signals. Manned satellites, especially the historic Soyuz and Mercury series, have paved the way for space stations, which have provided opportunities for diverse research and for developing docking techniques; the USSR Salyut and US Skylab projects are notable. The basic requirements for satellite launching are determined by celestial mechanics. Launching at various velocities between that required for zero altitude and the escape velocity produces an elliptical orbit lying on a conic surface determined by the latitude and time of launch. To reach any other orbit requires considerable extra energy expenditure. Artificial satellites require: a power supply—SOLAR CELLS, BATTERIES, fuel cells or nuclear devices; scientific instruments; a communications system to return encoded data to earth; and instruments and auxiliary rockets to monitor and correct the satellite's position. Most have COMPUTERS for control and data processing, thus reducing remote control to the minimum.

SATIE, Erik (1866–1925), French composer whose witty and highly original music was deliberately opposed to that of classic German composers. The word "surrealism" was first used in Apollinaire's notes to Satie's ballet music *Parade* (1917), scored for such instruments as typewriters and sirens. An influential figure in modern music, he encouraged younger French composers, such as Francis POULENC and Georges AURIC and the US composers Aaron COPLAND and Virgil THOMSON.

SATIRE, in literature or cartoons, on stage or screen, the use of broad humor, parody and irony to ridicule a subject. More serious than BURLESQUE, it contains moral or political criticism. In literature, classical satirists ARTISTOPHANES, HORACE and JUVENAL were followed by such writers as RABELAIS, DEFOE, SWIFT and VOLTAIRE.

SATO, Eisaku (1901–1975), prime minister of Japan 1964–72. A Liberal-Democrat, he presided over the reemergence of Japan as a major economic power and was active in foreign affairs. He won the 1974 Nobel Peace Prize.

SATRAP, governor of a satrapy, a province in the ancient Persian or ACHAEMENIAN empire. Satraps were usually members of the royal family or the nobility and headed the provincial administration and the judiciary.

SATURATION, term applied in many different fields to a state in which further increase in a variable above a critical value produces no increase in a resultant effect. A saturated SOLUTION is one which will dissolve no more solute, an equilibrium having been reached; raising the temperature usually allows more to dissolve: cooling a saturated solution may produce supersaturation, a metastable state, in which sudden crystallization depositing the excess solute occurs if a seed crystal is added. In organic chemistry, a saturated molecule has no double or triple bonds and so does not undergo addition reactions.

SATURN, the second largest planet in the SOLAR SYSTEM and the sixth from the sun. Until the discovery of URANUS (1781), Saturn was the outermost planet known. It orbits the sun in 29.46 years at a mean distance of 9.54AU. Saturn does not rotate uniformly: its period of rotation at the equator is 10.23h, rather longer toward the poles. This rapid rotation causes a noticeable equatorial bulge: the equatorial diameter is 120.9Mm, the polar diameter 108.1Mm. Saturn has the lowest density of any planet in the solar system, less than that of water, and may contain over 60% hydrogen by mass. Its total mass is about 95 times that of the earth. Saturn has 17 known satellites; the largest, Titan, about the same size as MERCURY, has a cold nitrogen atmosphere with traces of methane and other gases. The most striking feature of Saturn is its ring system: composed of countless tiny particles of ice and rock. Three or four major ring divisions are visible from earth, but Voyager space probes revealed the rings to consist of hundreds of narrow ringlets. The rings are about 16km thick and the outermost has an external diameter of about 280Gm.

SATURNALIA, ancient Roman festival in honor of Saturn, god of harvests. Schools and law courts were closed Dec. 17–23, work and commerce ceased, and both slaves and masters indulged in lavish feasting and the exchanging of gifts.

SATYR, in Greek mythology, a male spirit of the forests and mountains, often shown as part man and part goat, with hooves, tail and pointed ears. Companions of DIONYSUS, satyrs played an important part in his orgiastic festivals.

SAUDI ARABIA, kingdom covering most

Official name: Kingdom of Saudi Arabia
Capital: Riyadh
Area: 865,000sq mi
Population: 12,483,000
Language: Arabic
Religion: Muslim
Monetary unit(s): 1 Saudi riyal = 100 halalah
of the Arabian peninsula in SW Asia.

Land and Climate. Along the Red Sea in the W, the Hejaz and Asir mountains rise steeply from the coastal Tahimah plain. In the center is the vast barren plateau of NEJD. The Rub al Khali or Empty Quarter (250,000sq mi) in the SE and the An Nafud (25,000sq mi) in the N are sand deserts. In the E are the oil-rich Hasa lowlands. Coastal areas are very humid. In the interior daytime temperatures sometimes reach 120°F; yearly rainfall is generally less than 5in.

People. The population is almost entirely Arab. RIYADH, the capital, the Red Sea port of Jiddah and the holy cities of MECCA and MEDINA are the main centers. Despite the impact of oil, and the increase in educational and health facilities, many of the people live a traditional life in villages or as nomads. The strictly fundamentalist WAHABI sect of Sunnite Islam is the state religion.

Economy. Saudi Arabia has enormous oil reserves, and the oil and natural gas industry dominates the economy. Profits from exports are being used for industrial development (especially oil refining) and ambitious irrigation projects, and have transformed the country into a world financial power. Other minerals produced include limestone, gypsum, and salt. Chief crops are sorghum, dates, wheat, barley, coffee, citrus fruits and millet. Livestock, raised mainly by nomadic Bedouin, includes camels, cattle, horses, donkeys, sheep and goats.

History. From the 7th century Islam served to unify the Semitic nomad tribes of Saudi Arabia, but rival sheikdoms were later established. In the 1500s Arabia came under control of the OTTOMAN EMPIRE. The WAHABI sect, led by the Saudi rulers of Dariya, conquered most of the Arabian peninsula 1750–1800. Modern Saudi Arabia was founded by IBN SAUD (d. 1953), who conquered Nejd and the Hejaz, joining them with Hasa and Asir, and establishing a hereditary monarchy. Succeeding rulers have been Saud IV (deposed 1964), Faisal (assassinated 1975), Khalid (d. 1982), and Fahd. Saudi Arabia is the world's third largest petroleum producer and plays a major role in the ORGANIZATION OF PETROLEUM EXPORTING COUNTRIES. A decline in world oil prices and a cutback in Saudi production in an effort to stabilize world output led to the curtailment of some development projects in the late 1980s.

SAUK INDIANS, North American tribe of the Algonquian language group. Encountered by the French near Green Bay, Wis. in 1667, they later lived along the Mississippi R, hunting and farming. Many took part in the 1830s BLACK HAWK WAR rather than move W, but they were eventually resettled in Okla. and Ia.

SAUL, first king of Israel, c1000 BC. The son of Kish of the tribe of Benjamin, he was annointed by SAMUEL after the tribes decided to unite under a king. His reign was generally successful, but he killed himself after a defeat by the Philistines. His rival DAVID succeeded him.

SAULT SAINTE MARIE CANALS, three short canals on the St. Marys R, forming part of the SAINT LAWRENCE SEAWAY AND GREAT LAKES WATERWAY between Lake Superior and Lake Huron. Two of the canals (each 1.6mi) are in the US, and one (1.4mi) is in Canada. They are among the busiest in the world.

SAUSSURE, Ferdinand de (1857–1913), Swiss linguist whose contributions to structural linguistics (e.g., the idea that the structure of a language may be studied both as it changes with time and as it is in the present) have had a formative influence on 20th-century studies of GRAMMAR.

SAVAGE, Michael Joseph (1872–1940), New Zealand labor and political leader, prime minister of New Zealand's first Labour government from 1935.

SAVANNA, tropical GRASSLANDS of South America and particularly Africa, lying between equatorial forests and dry deserts.

SAVANNAH, first steamship to cross the Atlantic. A sailing packet on the New York-Le Havre route, she was fitted with engines which were used for 85hrs of the May–June 1819 voyage from Savannah, Ga., to Liverpool. The name Savannah was also given to the world's first (and so far only) nuclear-powered merchant ship, which was launched in 1959 and was in service from 1962 to 1970.

SAVERY, Thomas (c1650–1715), British inventor of an early form of STEAM ENGINE (patented 1698), used for pumping water. His patent covered NEWCOMEN's later invention (c1712), and for this reason the two entered partnership for the development of Newcomen's engine.

SAVIGNY, Friedrich Karl von (1779–1861), German jurist and legal historian, a founder of the historical school of jurisprudence. He believed that law develops gradually from the customs of society: the deliberate effort of the legislator is illusory, since he actually follows custom.

SAVINGS, in economics, that part of current INCOME not spent on consumption and retained after taxes. Today, INTEREST-bearing accounts, and purchase of INSURANCE or a MORTGAGE have replaced the traditional mattress as a way of protecting savings. Savings may be channeled directly into INVESTMENT by buying STOCKS or MUTUAL FUNDS. In MACROECONOMICS, if the total amount invested in a country equals the amount saved, the economy will be in equilibrium. If savings exceed investment, production, income and employment will tend to fall.

SAVONAROLA, Girolamo (1452–1498), Italian reformer. A Dominican friar, he campaigned boldly against the MEDICI in Florence. By 1494 the Medici had left and he had created a democratic republic in Florence. He was excommunicated by his opponent, Pope ALEXANDER VI (1495), but continued to preach until his enemies and the rival Franciscans had him hanged and burnt as a heretic.

SAVOY, former duchy in the W Alps, now comprising the departments of Haute-Savoie and Savoie, SE France. The ruling house, founded in 1026 by Count Humbert, played a leading role in uniting Italy (1859–70) and provided the kings of Italy from 1861 to 1946. The historical capital is Chambéry.

SAW, cutting tool consisting of a flat blade or circular disk, having on its edge a row of sharp teeth of various designs, usually set alternately. Excepting jagged stone knives, the first saws (copper and bronze) were used in Egypt c4000 BC, but only with the use of steel did they become efficient. Hand saws include the crosscut saw for cutting wood to length, the backsaw for joints, the coping saw for shaping, and the hacksaw for cutting metal. Power saws include circular saws, band saws (with a flexible endless steel band running over pulleys) and chain saws.

SAXE, Maurice, Comte de (1696–1750), illegitimate son of elector Frederick Augustus I of Saxony who became a brilliant general and marshal of France. (See AUSTRIAN SUCCESSION, WAR OF THE.) His greatest victory was over the English at Fontenoy (1745), during a successful Netherlands campaign.

SAXO GRAMMATICUS (c1150–c1220), Danish historian who wrote *Gesta Danorum*, the first Danish history, covering the time from the legendary King Dan to the defeat of Pomerania in 1185 by Canute VI.

SAXONS, a Germanic people who with the Angles and the JUTES founded settlements in Britain from c450 AD, supplanting the CELTS (see also ANGLO-SAXONS). From modern Schleswig (N Germany) they also spread along the coast to N France before incorporation in CHARLEMAGNE's empire.

SAXONY (German *Sachsen*, French *Saxe*), region and former duchy, electorate, kingdom and state in E Germany, now part of the German Democratic Republic (districts of Leipzig, Dresden, and Karl-Marx-Stadt, formerly Chemnitz). Rich in minerals, the region has many industries and is noted for its textiles and Dresden china.

SAXOPHONE, a brass instrument, classed as woodwind since its sound is produced by blowing through a reed. Patented by the Belgian Adolphe Sax in 1846, the saxophone exists in soprano, alto, tenor, and baritone forms; the bass is rare. Sometimes used in the symphony orchestra, the saxophone is better known for its important role in JAZZ, where it is a leading solo and ensemble instrument. (See also WIND INSTRUMENTS.)

SAY, Jean-Baptiste (1767–1832), French economist, businessman and author of Say's Law, or the law of markets. This states that supply creates its own demand; hence there can be no overproduction or underproduction. This self-regulating nature of a capitalist economy was widely believed in until the depression of the 1930s.

SAYERS, Dorothy Leigh (1893–1957), English writer of detective stories and creator of the popular, impeccably aristocratic and erudite detective Lord Peter Wimsey. He is the hero of some 16 books, beginning with *Whose Body* (1923). Sayers also wrote religious drama.

SAZONOV, Sergei Dmitreyevich (1861–1927), Russian foreign minister (1910–16) who supported Serbia in resisting the Austro-Hungarian ultimatum of July 23, 1914 and persuaded the tsar on July 30 to order a general rather than a partial mobilization, thereby probably making WWI unavoidable.

SCABIES, infectious SKIN disease caused by a mite which burrows under the skin, often of hands or feet; it causes an intensely itchy skin condition which is partly due to ALLERGY to the mite. Rate of infection has a cyclical pattern. Treatment is with special ointments and should include contacts.

SCALAWAG, in US history, a derisory term for Southern whites who cooperated with military and Republican RECONSTRUCTION governments after the Civil War. Mostly Republican Party members, they ranged from poor whites to rich planters and businessmen.

SCALE, in music, a term used for various sequences or progressions of notes, ascending or descending. The best-known scales are those of the 24 major and minor keys of conventional western harmony, but there are other types (see KEY). The *chromatic scale* progresses through all the notes of a piano keyboard, going up or down by half-tones. The six-note *whole-tone* scale goes up or down by a whole tone, starting from any note. The *pentatonic scale* has five notes, being the black notes on a piano keyboard or any equivalent sequence. The Greek and medieval MODES are another type of scale, and a new type is used in serial or TWELVE-TONE MUSIC.

SCALIA, Antonin (1936–   ), US jurist, on the US Circuit Court of Appeals for the District of Columbia (1982–86), appointed (1986) to the US Supreme Court by President Ronald Reagan.

SCALLOPS, some 300 species of bivalve MOLLUSKS, family Pectinidae, distinguished by a characteristic shell: the valves being rounded, with a series of ribs radiating across the surface in relief. They have especially well developed eyes on the mantle rim. Unique among bivalves, scallops swim extremely well, propelled by jets of water expelled in snapping shut the shell.

SCALPING, removal of an enemy's scalp with hair attached. In North America, the practice, originally limited to the E, spread among Indians and frontiersmen largely as a result of rewards offered by colonial governments.

SCAMOZZI, Vincenzo (1552–1616), Italian architect of the late RENAISSANCE. His work includes, in Venice, several palaces and the Procuratie Nuove and the Villa Pisani at Lonigo. His theoretical *Idea of Universal Architecture* (1615) became a classic.

SCANDINAVIA, region of NW Europe. Geographically it consists of the Scandinavian peninsula (about 300,000sq mi) occupied by Norway, Sweden and NW Finland, but the term normally includes Denmark. Because of close historical development, Iceland and the Faroe Islands are also covered by the term in matters of language, culture, peoples and politics.

SCANDINAVIAN LANGUAGES, a Germanic group of Indo-European languages, comprising Danish, Faroese, Icelandic, Norwegian and Swedish. Icelandic preserves many features of Old Norse, the common tongue of Viking Scandinavia. The Scandinavian colonists who took their language W to N France, Ireland and England, S to Sicily and E to Kiev and Byzantium were later assimilated or died out.

SCAPA FLOW, a large sea basin in the S Orkney Islands off the N coast of Scotland, the principal anchorage of the British navy in WWI and WWII. In 1919 the crews of the interned German fleet scuttled their ships here.

SCAR, area of fibrous tissue which forms a bridge between areas of normal tissue as the end result of wound healing. The fibrous tissue lacks the normal properties of the healed tissue (e.g., it does not tan). The size of a scar depends on the closeness of the wound edges during healing; excess stretching and infection widen scars.

SCARABS, a family of BEETLES which includes the dung beetles, chafers and dor beetles. Most of the 20,000 species are scavengers of decaying organic matter, especially dung, or feed on the foliage and roots of growing plants, as do the chafers, many of which may become agricultural pests.

SCARLATTI, Alessandro (1660–1725), Italian composer. A leading musical scholar and teacher, he composed hundreds of church masses, cantatas and oratorios, and over 100 operas. Few are now performed, but he is important for innovations in harmony, thematic development, and the use of instruments. His son **Domenico Scarlatti** (1685– 1757) also composed operas and church music, but is known for his many brilliant sonatas for harpsichord, which influenced Haydn and Mozart and are still widely played.

SCARLET FEVER, or scarletina, INFECTIOUS DISEASE caused by certain strains of *Streptococcus*. It is common in children and causes sore throat with TONSILLITIS, a characteristic SKIN rash and mild systemic symptoms. PENICILLIN and symptomatic treatment are required. Scarlet fever occurs in EPIDEMICS; some cases are followed by RHEUMATIC FEVER or NEPHRITIS.

SCATTERING, the deflection of moving

1120 SCHACHT

particles and energy waves (such as ELECTRONS, PHOTONS or SOUND waves) through collisions with other particles. RAYLEIGH scattering of sunlight gives rise both to the blue color of the ATMOSPHERE when the sun is high in the sky and to the reds and yellows of the setting sun because the blue light is scattered more strongly than the red.

SCHACHT, Hjalmar Horace Greeley (1877–1970), German financier and banker. He helped halt post-WWI inflation and was finance minister (1934–37) and Reichsbank president (1923–30; 1933–39), but conflict with Goering and Hitler later led to imprisonment. He was acquitted at the NUREMBURG TRIALS.

SCHAPIRO, Meyer (1904–), Lithuanian-born US art historian and critic. One of the most highly regarded and influential art scholars in the US, he taught for many years at Columbia U. Among his books are *Romanesque Art* (1977) and *Modern Art: 19th and 20th Centuries* (1978).

SCHARNHORST, Gerhard Johann David von (1755–1813), Prussian general. After Napoleon's victory (1806) over an army in which he was serving, he reorganized the Prussian army. He laid the foundation of its general staff system and its reliance upon conscripted as opposed to professional men.

SCHECHTER, Solomon (1847–1915), Romanian-born Hebrew scholar. After teaching at Cambridge and London universities, he became president of the Jewish Theological Seminary in New York City (1902). He founded the conservative United Synagogue of America (1913).

SCHECHTER v. US, SUPREME COURT decision (1935) which ruled unconstitutional the 1933 National Industrial Recovery Act. The Schechter Poultry Co. had been convicted of violating a NIRA code regulating interstate commerce. The Court ruled that the NIRA delegated too much legislative power to the US president, thus in effect killing an important part of President Roosevelt's New Deal program.

SCHEELE, Karl (or Carl) Wilhelm (1742–1786), Swedish chemist who discovered OXYGEN (c1773), perhaps a year before Joseph PRIESTLEY's similar discovery. He also discovered CHLORINE (1774).

SCHEER, Reinhard (1863–1928), German naval commander. Famous as a WWI submarine strategist, in 1916 he became commander of the high seas fleet which engaged in the indecisive Battle of JUTLAND.

SCHEIDEMANN, Philipp (1865–1939), German Social Democratic politician who proclaimed the German republic in Nov.

1918 when the kaiser fled. The republic's first chancellor, he resigned (1919) in protest over the Treaty of Versailles. He left Germany in 1933 to escape the Nazis.

SCHEIDT, Samuel (1587–1654), German composer. Famous, like SWEELINCK, for his organ music, he developed counterpoint, adopted Italian staff NOTATION, and also wrote sacred choral works.

SCHELDE RIVER, or Scheldt, important navigable waterway of NW Europe. Rising in Aisne department, NW France, it flows 270mi N and NE to Antwerp, Belgium, then NW, as the East and West Schelde rivers, through Holland to the North Sea. The Delta Plan has sealed off the East outlet. There are canal links to the Rhine and Meuse rivers.

SCHELER, Max (1874–1928), German philosopher whose important work in phenomenology helped spread its influence throughout the world. His best-known works are *Formalism in Ethics and Non-Formal Ethics of Value* (2 vols., 1913–16) and *The Nature of Sympathy* (1928).

SCHELLING, Friedrich Wilhelm Joseph von (1775–1854), German idealist philosopher of the Romantic period, a pioneer of speculative thought after KANT. A student contemporary of HEGEL, Schelling later turned to religious philosophy and mythology. Both EXISTENTIALISM and modern Protestant theology have been influenced by him.

SCHENCK v. US, SUPREME COURT decision (1919) concerning free speech. C. T. Schenck, general secretary of the Socialist Party, was one of over 1,500 prosecuted under laws against espionage and sedition. Applying a test of "clear and present danger" to the nation's security, the Court ruled that Schenck's conviction did not violate the First Amendment right of free speech.

SCHIAPARELLI, Giovanni Virginio (1835–1910), Italian astronomer who discovered the ASTEROID Hesperia (1861) and showed that METEOR showers represent the remnants of COMETS. He is best known for terming the surface markings of MARS *canali* (channels). This was wrongly translated as "canals," implying Martian builders: the resulting controversy lasted for nearly a century.

SCHICK, Béla (1877–1967), Hungarian-born US pediatrician who developed the Schick test to determine immunity to DIPHTHERIA (1913).

SCHIELE, Egon (1890–1918), Austrian expressionist painter. His work, influenced by the linear style of Gustav KLIMT, has great intensity, sometimes expressed in harsh color and brushwork. It includes nudes, portraits and landscapes.

SCHILLER, Johann Christoph Friedrich von (1759–1805), playwright, poet and essayist, a leading figure of German literature second only to his friend GOETHE. Human dignity and spiritual freedom are central to his work, which ranges from the poem "Ode to Joy" to the STURM UND DRANG drama The Robbers (1781) and the popular play Wilhelm Tell (1804). As professor of history at Jena he wrote on the THIRTY YEARS' WAR, later the setting of his great dramatic trilogy Wallenstein (1799).

SCHISM, Great. See GREAT SCHISM; PAPACY.

SCHIST, common group of METAMORPHIC ROCKS which have acquired a high degree of schistosity, i.e., the parallel arrangement of sheety or prismatic minerals resulting from regional metamorphism. Schistosity is similar in nature and origin to slaty cleavage (see SLATE) but is coarser. The major constituents of most schists are either mica, talc, amphiboles or chlorite.

SCHISTOSOMIASIS, or bilharzia, a PARASITIC DISEASE caused by schistosoma species of FLUKES. Infection is usually acquired by bathing in infected water, the different species of parasite causing different manifestations. Infection of the BLADDER causes constriction, calcification and secondary infection, and can predispose to bladder CANCER. Another form leads to GASTROINTESTINAL TRACT disease with LIVER involvement. Antimony compounds are often effective in treatment.

SCHIZOPHRENIA, formerly called dementia praecox, a type of PSYCHOSIS characterized by confusion of identity, HALLUCINATIONS, AUTISM, delusion and illogical thought. The three main types of schizophrenia are catatonia, in which the individual oscillates between excitement and stupor; paranoid schizophrenia, which is similar to PARANOIA except that the intellect deteriorates; and hebephrenia, which is characterized by withdrawal from reality, bizarre or foolish behavior, delusions, hallucinations and self-neglect.

SCHLEGEL, Friedrich von (1772–1829), German philosopher. His stress on the subjective and spiritual in art and his studies of world history and literature greatly influenced ROMANTICISM in Germany.

SCHLEICHER, Kurt von (1882–1934), German soldier and statesman. He held army commands from 1914 to 1931, and became minister of defense in 1932 and later in the same year chancellor. In 1933 he

was succeeded by HITLER. He was murdered by the Nazis during the purge of June 30, 1934.

SCHLEIDEN, Matthias Jakob (1804–1881), German botanist who was among the first to recognize the CELL as the unit of structure and function in living things.

SCHLEIERMACHER, Friedrich Ernst Daniel (1768–1834), German Protestant theologian and philosopher. He became famous with Speeches on Religion (1799), arguing that religion exists independently of morality or science. His great The Christian Faith (1821–22) discussed the essence of religion and Christianity, and the role of doctrine and theology.

SCHLESINGER, name of two famous 20th-century US historians. Arthur Meier Schlesinger (1888–1965) is best known for his The Rise of the City, 1878–1898 (1933) in the series he edited, A History of American Life. He stressed the cultural, social and economic context of history. Arthur Meier Schlesinger, Jr. (1917–   ), his son, won Pulitzer prizes for both The Age of Jackson (1945) and A Thousand Days (1966), the latter written after a period as special assistant to President Kennedy.

SCHLESWIG-HOLSTEIN, state in N West Germany, 6,046sq mi, bordering Denmark. The capital Kiel lies at the E end of Kiel Canal, linking the North and Baltic seas. The main economic activities are dairy farming, fishing, shipbuilding and engineering. Prussia annexed these two Danish duchies in 1866. N Schleswig was reunited with Denmark after WWI.

SCHLEY, Winfield Scott (1839–1911), US naval officer who led an Arctic expedition which rescued A. W. GREELY in 1884. Credit for victory over the Spanish at Santiago de Cuba (1898) was disputed between him and Admiral SAMPSON.

SCHLICK, Moritz (1882–1936), German philosopher regarded as the founder of the Vienna Circle, an influential school of LOGICAL POSITIVISM.

SCHLIEFFEN, Alfred von (1833–1913), German general, later field marshal. He drew up the "Schlieffen Plan" (1905) to combat France and her new ally Russia. The bulk of the German army would rapidly advance through Belgium and Holland to crush the French, before returning E to face the Russians. MOLTKE's modification of this plan failed in WWI.

SCHLIEMANN, Heinrich (1822–1890), German archaeologist, best known for his discoveries of Troy (1871–90) and Mycenae (1876–78). (See AEGEAN CIVILIZATION.)

SCHLÜTER, Andreas (1664–1714), German baroque sculptor who worked in Berlin for the Hohenzollern rulers of Prussia and later for Peter the Great of Russia.

SCHMALKALDIC LEAGUE, the association of German principalities and cities formed 1531, in the early REFORMATION, to defend the Protestant cause against the Holy Roman Emperor CHARLES V and his Catholic allies. Despite the League's defeat in 1547, Lutheranism was legalized by the Peace of AUGSBURG.

SCHMELING, Maximilian (1905–), German boxing champion, hailed by Adolf Hitler as a model Aryan superman. In 1936 he defeated black US boxer Joe LOUIS in a 12th-round knockout, only to be knocked out by Louis in the first round of a 1938 rematch.

SCHMIDT, Bernhard Voldemar (1879–1935), Estonian-born German optician best known for developing the Schmidt TELESCOPE, today one of the most-used tools of astrophotography. Its special advantage is that it avoids LENS coma.

SCHMIDT, Helmut (1918–), chancellor of West Germany 1974–82. A Social Democrat, he was party floor leader in the Bundestag 1962–69, defense minister 1969–72 and finance minister 1972–74. He succeeded Willy Brandt as chancellor when the latter resigned amid a spy scandal. In a continent plagued with economic difficulties, Germany under Schmidt remained stable and prosperous. However, violent radical groups were a problem.

SCHNABEL, Artur (1882–1951), Austrian-US pianist. Best known for his reflective recordings of Beethoven's sonatas (which he edited), he was also a notable interpreter of Mozart and Schubert.

SCHNITZLER, Arthur (1862–1931), Austrian playwright; he wrote about love, lust and the personality basis of racism, particularly anti-Semitism, in the Vienna of Sigmund Freud. His work included *Anatol* (1893), *Playing with Love* (1896) and *Merry-Go-Round* (1897).

SCHOENBERG, Arnold (1874–1951), German composer, theorist and teacher who revolutionized music by introducing TWELVE-TONE MUSIC. His string sextet *Transfigured Night* (1899) with harmonic clashes was followed by the declaimed songs of *Pierrot Lunaire* (1912) and experiments in whole-tone and finally serial or 12-tone music culminating in his unfinished opera *Moses and Aaron* (1930–51). Schoenberg emigrated to the US in 1933. (See also ATONALITY; SCALE.)

SCHOFIELD, John McAllister

(1831–1906), US Union general in the Civil War, from 1864 commander of its Army of the Ohio in the ATLANTA CAMPAIGN. Secretary of war 1868–69, he was commander of the US army 1888–95.

SCHOLASTICISM, the method of medieval Church teachers, or scholastics, who applied philosophic (primarily Aristotelian) ideas to Christian doctrine. They held that though reason was always subordinate to faith, it served to increase the believer's understanding of what he believed. Typical scholastic works are the *commentary* on an authoritative text and the *quaestio*. The latter is a stereotyped form in which the writer sets out opposing authorities and then reconciles them in answering a question. AQUINAS' *Summa Theologica* consists of a systematically constructed series of *quaestiones*. (See also ABELARD; ALBERTUS MAGNUS; BONAVENTURE; DUNS SCOTUS; OCKHAM, WILLIAM OF.)

SCHONGAUER, Martin (1430–1491), German engraver and painter, best known for his engravings of religious subjects.

SCHOOLCRAFT, Henry Rowe (1793–1864), US ethnologist and explorer. Agent for the Lake Superior Indian tribes from 1822, he discovered the source of the Mississippi R in 1832 and published authoritative works on Indian culture and legends.

SCHOPENHAUER, Arthur (1788–1860), German philosopher, noted for his doctrine of the will and systematic pessimism. In *The World as Will and Idea* (1819), his main work, he argued that will is the ultimate reality, but advocated the negation of will to avoid suffering, and the seeking of relief in philosophy and the arts. Schopenhauer's ideas influenced NIETZSCHE and modern EXISTENTIALISM.

SCHOUTEN, Willem Cornelis (1567?–1625), Dutch navigator, discoverer (1616) of CAPE HORN.

SCHRÖDINGER, Erwin (1887–1961), Austrian-born Irish physicist and philosopher of science who shared with Paul Dirac the 1933 Nobel Prize for Physics for his discovery of the **Schrödinger wave equation,** which is of fundamental importance in studies of QUANTUM MECHANICS (1926). It was later shown that his WAVE MECHANICS was equivalent to the matrix mechanics of HEISENBERG.

SCHUBERT, Franz Peter (1797–1828), Viennese composer. He wrote nine symphonies, of which the Fifth (1816), Eighth (1822) and Ninth (1828) are among the world's greatest. He is also famous for his piano pieces and chamber music (especially his string quartets), but above all for his over 600 *lieder* (songs), a form he raised to unprecedented heights of expressiveness and virtuosity. As well as individual lieder such as *The Erl King* and *The Trout*, he wrote song cycles, among them *The Maid of the Mill* and *Winter's Journey*.

SCHULLER, Gunther (1925–   ), US performer, conductor and composer. A horn player with the Metropolitan Opera (1945–59), he became president of the New England Conservatory in 1966. Combining JAZZ and TWELVE-TONE techniques in what he called "third-stream music," he wrote chamber and orchestral works and operas.

SCHULZ, Charles Monroe (1922–   ), US cartoonist, creator (1950) of the comic strip *Peanuts*.

SCHUMAN, Robert (1886–1963), French statesman. Prime minister 1947–48 and foreign minister 1948–52, he launched the "Schuman Plan" which resulted in the EUROPEAN COAL AND STEEL COMMUNITY, precursor of the Common Market.

SCHUMAN, William (1910–   ), US composer. His symphonies, chamber music, ballets and opera are known for their rhythmic vivacity and their debt to jazz. His 1942 cantata, *A Free Song*, won the first Pulitzer Prize for music. He was president of the Juilliard School of Music (1945–62) and of Lincoln Center for the Performing Arts (1962–69).

SCHUMANN, Robert Alexander (1810–1856), major German composer whose compositions and music journal greatly influenced the music of his time. He did much to make known the early music of CHOPIN and BRAHMS. Though he wrote orchestral and chamber music, he best expressed his ardent Romanticism in his piano works and *lieder* (songs), most of the latter composed in 1840, when he married Clara Wieck, a leading pianist.

SCHUMPETER, Joseph Alois (1883–1950), Austrian-born Harvard economist. After studying economic development and business cycles, he concluded that monopoly companies and government intervention would stifle the entrepreneur, the moving force of capitalism, and that socialism would result.

SCHURZ, Carl (1829–1906), German-US statesman. Exiled after the German REVOLUTION OF 1848, he supported Lincoln, who named him minister to Spain (1861). After Civil War service as a brigadier-general he was Republican senator for Mo., and an influential journalist, opposing President Grant's policies. He helped form the LIBERAL REPUBLICAN PARTY and was Hayes' secretary of the interior (1877–81).

SCHUSCHNIGG, Kurt von (1897–1977), Austrian political leader. After Nazis murdered DOLLFUSS in 1934, he succeeded as chancellor, continued the authoritarian Christian Socialist government and tried in vain to preserve independence from Nazi Germany, which occupied Austria and imprisoned him 1938–45. He later taught for 20 years in St. Louis before returning to Austria.

SCHÜTZ, Heinrich (1585–1672), German composer. Apart from madrigals and *Dafne*, Germany's first opera, his works are vocal settings of sacred texts, in German, with or without instruments; his famous Passions influenced Bach.

SCHUYLER, Philip John (1733–1804), American soldier and statesman who served as major-general in the Continental army during the Revolutionary War. He served three terms in the N.Y. senate between 1780 and 1797, and was one of the first two US senators from N.Y. (1789–91 and 1797–98).

SCHWAB, Charles Michael (1862–1939), US industrialist. After helping to build and becoming president of the Carnegie Steel Co. (later J. Pierpont Morgan's US Steel Corp.), he headed and expanded the rival Bethlehem Steel Corp. from 1903.

SCHWANN, Theodor (1810–1882), German biologist who proposed the CELL as the basic unit of animal, as well as of plant, structure (1839), thus laying the foundations of HISTOLOGY. He also discovered the ENZYME pepsin (1836).

SCHWARTZ, Delmore (1913–1966), US poet admired for his rhapsodic yet philosophic style. His works include *In Dreams Begin Responsibilities* (1938), *Summer Knowledge* (1959) and *Last and Lost Poems of Delmore Schwartz* (1979).

SCHWARZKOPF, Elisabeth (1915–   ), German soprano, famous for operatic performances of Mozart, Strauss and Wagner in Vienna and London and later for her expressive singing of German *lieder*.

SCHWARZWALD. See BLACK FOREST.

SCHWEITZER, Albert (1875–1965), German musician, philosopher, theologian, physician and missionary. An authority on Bach, and a noted performer of Bach's organ music, he abandoned an academic career in theology to study medicine and became (1913) a missionary doctor in French Equatorial Africa (now Gabon). He devoted his life to the hospital he founded there. His many writings include *The Quest of the Historical Jesus* (1906). Schweitzer won the 1952 Nobel Peace Prize for his inspiring humanitarian work.

SCHWITTERS, Kurt (1887–1948), German artist and writer associated with DADAISM. He made collages and "*Merzbau*," constructions of discarded objects, and poems of disparate print cuttings. He edited a Dadaist magazine, *Merz*, 1923–32.

SCIATICA, a characteristic pain in the distribution of the sciatic nerve in the leg caused by compression or irritation of the nerve. The pain may resemble an electric shock and be associated with numbness and tingling in the skin area served by the nerve. One of the commonest causes is a SLIPPED DISK in the lower lumbar spine.

SCIENCE FICTION, literary genre which may loosely be defined as fantasy based upon speculation about scientific or social development. Probably the first true science fiction, or sci-fi, work was *Frankenstein* (1818) by Mary SHELLEY; it developed a still popular theme, man's inability to control what his research reveals. Only with the works of Jules VERNE and H. G. WELLS, however, did sci-fi break away from supernatural fantasy. In the US in the 1920s "pulp" magazines popularized the form, but all too often debased it. John W. Campbell's magazine *Astounding* (founded 1937, now called *Analog*) revitalized the genre through its consistently high literary standards; it nurtured writers who today lead the field, among them Isaac ASIMOV, Robert Heinlein, Poul Anderson, Hal Clement, Eric Frank Russell and many others. Many sci-fi writers, such as Asimov, Arthur C. Clarke, Ray BRADBURY, Kurt VONNEGUT and John Wyndham have become household names; others, such as Fritz Leiber, Brian Aldiss, Robert Silverberg, Alfred Bester and Theodore Sturgeon, are less well known outside the field. The critical acclaim they and newer writers such as Larry Niven, Harlan Ellison, Samuel Delany, Stanislav Lem and Ursula K. Le Guin receive indicates that the best science fiction may rank with the best contemporary general fiction.

SCIENTIFIC METHOD. Science (from Latin *scientia*, knowledge) is too diverse an undertaking to be constrained to follow any single method. Yet from the time of Lord BACON, well into the 20th century, the myth has persisted that true science follows a particular method—Bacon's celebrated "inductive method." This allegedly involved collecting a vast number of individual facts about a phenomenon, and then working out what general statements fitted those facts. After the 17th century nobody attempted to follow that program. In the 19th century, philosophers of science came to recognize the possible existence of the "hypothetico-deductive method." According to this model, the scientist studied the phenomena, dreamed up a hypothetical explanation, deduced some additional consequences of his explanation, and then devised experiments to see if these consequences were reflected in nature. If they were, he considered his theory (hypothesis) confirmed. But K. POPPER pointed to the logical fallacy in this last step—the theory had not been confirmed, but merely not falsified; it could, however, be worked with provisionally, so long as new tests did not discredit it. Philosophers of science now recognize that they cannot justly generalize about the psychology of scientific discovery; their role must be confined to the criticism of theories once they have been devised. Historians of science, meanwhile, have pointed to the importance in scientific discovery of "external factors" such as the contemporary intellectual context and the structures of the institutions of science. Once distinct terms— "theory," "model," "hypothesis," "explanation," "description," and "law"— are all now seen to represent different ways of looking at the same thing—the units in what constitutes scientific knowledge at any given time. Indeed there is still no general understanding of how scientists become dissatisfied with a once deeply-entrenched theory and come to replace it with what, for the moment, seems a better version.

SCIENTOLOGY, religio-scientific movement stressing self-redemption which originated in the US in the 1950s and was incorporated as a church in 1965. Based on L. Ron Hubbard's theory of dianetics, a "modern science of mental health," Scientology holds that all aspects of individual human behavior are linked and must be harmonized; it also posits a life energy in the universe at large which affects human behavior.

SCILLY ISLANDS, group of rocky islets, 30mi W of the S tip of Cornwall, SW England. The population of the five inhabited islands (6sq mi) live off tourism and flower growing.

SCIPIO, name of a patrician family of ancient Rome which became famous during the PUNIC WARS. **Publius Cornelius Scipio** (236–184 BC), called Africanus Major, conquered HANNIBAL in the second Punic War. He drove the Carthaginians from Spain, invaded Africa, and forced Hannibal to return from Italy to meet him. The resulting battle of Zama (202 BC) destroyed Carthaginian power. **Publius Cornelius Scipio Aemilianus** (185–129 BC), his adopted grandson, called Africanus Minor, commanded against Carthage in the third Punic War, capturing and destroying the city in 146 BC.

SCOLIOSIS, a curvature of the spine to one side, with twisting. It occurs as a congenital defect or may be secondary to spinal diseases including neurofibromatosis. Severe scoliosis, often associated with kyphosis, causes HUNCHBACK deformity, loss of height, and may restrict cardiac or LUNG function.

SCONE, Stone of, coronation seat of Scottish kings, removed to Westminster Abbey by Edward I in 1296. Scottish nationalists reclaimed it briefly 1950–51. Traditionally, Scone village, E Scotland, was the PICTS' capital.

SCOPES TRIAL, famous 1925 prosecution of a biology teacher for breaking a new Tenn. law forbidding the teaching of EVOLUTION in state-supported schools. Interwar religious fundamentalism secured such laws in several S states. For the defense Clarence DARROW unsuccessfully pitted himself against the orthodoxy of William Jennings BRYAN; the Tenn. supreme court reversed the conviction on a technicality, but the law was repealed only in 1967.

SCOREL, Jan van (1495–1562), Dutch painter. Many of his fine portraits survive. His religious works, largely destroyed by 16th-century Protestant iconoclasts, reflected his wide travels and helped introduce the Italian style to Holland.

SCORPIONS, a homogeneous group of terrestrial arachnids having two formidable palps (claws) held in front of the head and a stinging tail curled forward over the back. All scorpions have a poisonous sting but few are dangerous to man. The sting is usually used in defense, or with the palps in catching prey. Scorpions are restricted to dry, warm regions of the world and feed on grasshoppers, crickets, spiders and other arthropods.

SCOTCH. See WHISKEY.

SCOTCH-IRISH, the people of Scottish descent who emigrated to North America from Northern Ireland after 1713. They were largely descendants of the Scots who had colonized Northern Ireland.

SCOTLAND, former kingdom, now part of the UNITED KINGDOM (see also GREAT BRITAIN). Covering N Britain and the HEBRIDES, ORKNEY and SHETLAND islands, it is 30,414sq mi in area. Over 50% of the population is urban; major cities include Edinburgh, the capital and cultural center, Glasgow, the industrial center, Aberdeen and Dundee. English is spoken everywhere, but some 77,000 Scots in the NW also speak GAELIC. Scotland was one of the first industrialized countries; its economy rests on iron and steel, aluminum, shipbuilding, chemicals, North Sea oil and the immensely lucrative whiskey industry. Agriculture, mainly grain, sheep and cattle, and fishing are also important. Educational standards are among the world's highest, and cultural life flourishes. Scotland's original inhabitants were the PICTS, displaced by the Scots, Britons and Angles. United under Kenneth I MacAlpin, the country maintained an embattled independence from England, ensured by ROBERT THE BRUCE. A brief Renaissance flowering under JAMES IV ended in disaster at FLODDEN FIELD, and in the turmoil of the REFORMATION. James VI (JAMES I of England) united the crowns of Scotland and England, but union of government came only in 1707. It was widely resented, and England fueled this by attacking Scottish autonomy and prosperity; this helped incite the two JACOBITE rebellions (1715 and 1745). A great cultural rebirth followed, but also the hardships of the INDUSTRIAL REVOLUTION and Highland depopulation for sheep farming. Devolution (i.e., greater autonomy) was defeated by referendum vote in 1979.

SCOTLAND, Church of. See CHURCH OF SCOTLAND.

SCOTLAND YARD, headquarters of the Criminal Investigation Department (C.I.D.) of the London Metropolitan Police. Its jurisdiction covers 786sq mi containing more than eight million people. It also coordinates police work throughout Britain and provides national and international criminal records.

SCOTS, English-based dialect of the Scottish Lowlands (not GAELIC, a different language). Its literary form flourished from the 13th to the mid-16th century, in the poetry of William DUNBAR and Gavin Douglas, and was revived by Allan Ramsay and Robert BURNS in the 18th century.

SCOTT, Robert Falcon (1868–1912), British explorer remembered for his fatal attempt to be the first to reach the South Pole. In 1911 he led four men with sleds 950mi from the Ross Ice Shelf to the South Pole. They arrived on Jan. 18, 1912, only to discover that AMUNDSEN had reached the Pole a month before. Scurvy, frostbite, starvation and bitter weather hampered the grueling two-month return journey, and the last three survivors died in a blizzard, only 11mi from the next supply point.

SCOTT, Sir Walter (1771–1832), Scottish poet and the foremost Romantic novelist in the English language. Scott was the inventor of the historical novel, and his vivid recreations of Scotland's past were widely read throughout Europe. He started by writing popular narrative poems, including *The Lay of the Last Minstrel* (1805). After these successes he turned to fiction, and completed 28 novels and many nonfiction works. His novels included *Waverley* (1814), *The Heart of Midlothian* (1818) and *Ivanhoe* (1819).

SCOTT, Winfield (1786–1866), US political and military leader, known as "Old Fuss and Feathers" for his obsession with procedure and detail and for his elaborate uniforms. Scott became a hero for his part in the WAR OF 1812. He was active in the Indian wars and in 1846 was appointed a commander in the MEXICAN WAR, and captured Mexico City. In 1852 he was the unsuccessful Whig presidential candidate. He commanded the Union Army until 1861.

SCOTTSBORO CASES, celebrated US legal cases involving nine uneducated black youths who were accused in 1931 of raping two white women on a freight train in Ala. Indicted and tried in Scottsboro, all the youths were found guilty, and eight were sentenced to death. They had no defense counsel until two lawyers volunteered to aid them on the day of the trial. The first Scottsboro Case, *Powell v. Alabama*, reached the US Supreme Court in 1932. The court reversed the convictions on the ground that failure to provide adequate counsel for the boys violated the "due process" clause of the 14th Amendment. Three years later the second case, *Norris v. Alabama*, reached the US Supreme Court; it reversed the convictions because blacks had been excluded from the grand jury that indicted the youths. Ultimately, all of the youths but one (who escaped) were released from prison.

SCRIABIN, Alexander Nikolayevich (1872 – 1915), Russian composer and brilliant pianist, whose work was based on chords of fourths. He wanted performances of his *Prometheus* (1909–10) to be accompanied by a play of colored lights corresponding to the musical tones.

SCRIBE, Augustin Eugène (1791–1861), French playwright and librettist. Besides his libretto for VERDI's *The Sicilian Vespers* he also wrote librettos for Auber, BELLINI and MEYERBEER.

SCRIBE, professional copier of books by hand before the development of printing, found in royal courts. The name was earlier applied to the ancient Hebrew teachers of the Law, the *Sopherim*, the first of whom was EZRA (c400 BC). Sopherim revised and transmitted the text of the Old Testament, extending the basis of the Oral Law.

SCRIPPS, Edward Wyllis (1854–1926), US newspaper publisher, founder of the first newspaper chain and of the wire service that eventually became United Press International. Beginning in the Midwest and West his chain spread into 15 states, by 1922, when Roy Howard, manager of UPI, became a partner. The Scripps-Howard organization subsequently acquired newspapers in nearly every state in the Union.

SCROFULA, TUBERCULOSIS of the LYMPH nodes of the neck, usually acquired by drinking MILK infected with bovine or atypical mycobacteria, and involving enlargement of the nodes with formation of a cold ABSCESS. The eradication of tuberculosis in cattle has substantially reduced the incidence. Treatment includes antituberculous CHEMOTHERAPY. It used to be called the King's Evil as the royal touch was believed to be curative.

SCRUB TYPHUS, or Tsutsugamushi disease, a disease caused by RICKETTSIA carried by mites, and leading to ulceration at the site of INOCULATION, followed by FEVER, headache, lymph node enlargement and generalized rash. COUGH and chest X-RAY abnormalities are common. ENCEPHALITIS and MYOCARDITIS may occur with fatal outcome. It occurs mainly in the Far East and Australia and is generally seen in people who work on scrubland. TETRACYCLINES eradicate the infection.

SCULPTURE, the artistic creation of three-dimensional forms in materials such as stone, metal, wood, or even canvas or foam rubber. (This article deals mainly with Western sculpture. For some other periods of sculpture see: AEGEAN CIVILIZATION; GREEK ART and ARCHITECTURE; COLUMBIAN ART; ROMAN ART and ARCHITECTURE.)

High cost and durability tended to make ancient sculpture an official and conservative art form. This is evident in the monumental sculpture of Egypt, which changed little in 2,000 years. Greek sculptors, who set enduring standards of taste and technique, aimed to portray beauty of soul as well as body, and idealized the human form. In the Archaic period (about 630–480 BC) Egyptian influence is evident in the frontal, stylized figures, showing little movement or emotion. Greater realism led to the classical perfection of PHIDIAS, and in the 4th century to PRAXITELES, with his more sensuous forms and wider range of expression. The HELLENISTIC AGE favored an exaggerated style, of which the *Laocoön* sculpture and the *Winged Victory of Samothrace* are fine examples. Roman sculpture was deeply indebted to Greek art, but was also under

ETRUSCAN influence, and excelled at realistic portraiture.

The Western tradition revived c1000 AD with the elongated, stylized figures of ROMANESQUE, leading to the more graceful and expressive sculptures of GOTHIC ART. RENAISSANCE sculpture, starting about 1350, was dominated by the Italians. GHIBERTI and DONATELLO treated classical models in a new spirit, and MICHELANGELO gave to works such as his *David* an inner tension quite foreign to classicism. The elegant MANNERISM of Benvenuto CELLINI and the elaborate BAROQUE of BERNINI gave way about 1800 to the neoclassical reaction of HOUDON, CANOVA, and THORVALDSEN. The greatest 19th-century sculptor, RODIN, created a style of partially unworked figures, such as his *Balzac*, influencing EPSTEIN. This century has seen the abstract art of BRANCUSI and ARP, while Henry MOORE and GIACOMETTI showed interest in the human form. Outstanding American sculptors are David SMITH and CALDER, who invented MOBILES.

SCURVY, or VITAMIN C deficiency, involving disease of the SKIN and mucous membranes, poor healing and ANEMIA; in infancy BONE growth is also impaired. It may develop over a few months of low dietary vitamin C, beginning with malaise and weakness. Skin bleeding around HAIR follicles is characteristic, as are swollen, bleeding gums. Treatment and prevention consist of adequate dietary vitamin C.

SCYLLA AND CHARYBDIS, perils faced by ODYSSEUS in the Straits of Messina. Scylla was a six-headed monster who ate all within reach, Charybdis a whirlpool. "Between Scylla and Charybdis" means a straight, narrow course between two dangers.

SCYTHIANS, ancient nomadic people from Central Asia or possibly W Siberia, one of the earliest peoples to learn horsemanship. After the 9th century BC they spread into E Europe and S Russia making raids into the settled Near East. Their power was curbed by the MEDES about 600 BC. The kingdom of the Royal Scyths, 9th–2nd century BC, was defeated by the Sarmatians. The wealth of the Scythians was shown by their gold and silver objects and jewelry.

SEA-BED MINING, the extraction of resources from the ocean floor. Although there are massive mineral deposits in the rocks of the deep-ocean floors, no technology exists at present for extracting them. Current interest is focused mainly on the small (one- to three-inch) round manganese nodules that litter the floors of deep oceans. The nodules contain iron, cobalt, nickel and copper as well as manganese, and represent a potentially rich minerals source awaiting the development of efficient deep-sea mining methods.

SEA BEGGARS, 16th-century Dutch privateers in the struggle for independence from Spain. The epithet "beggars," applied to Dutch petitioners by the Spanish governor, was taken up by the patriots.

SEABURY, Samuel (1729–1796), American clergyman, first bishop of the Protestant EPISCOPAL CHURCH. His consecration, refused by the English bishops, was carried out by the Scottish Episcopal Church (1784) and confirmed by his own church in 1789.

SEA COWS, an order, Sirenia, of aquatic mammals. Probably evolved from a marsh-dwelling ancestor related to the elephants, all the Sirenia are completely aquatic and seal-like, with the forelimbs modified into flippers and the hindlimbs fused into the horizontal flukes of a whale-like tail.

SEA-FLOOR SPREADING, key concept supporting the theory of PLATE TECTONICS. Along midocean ridges (see OCEANS) material emerges from the EARTH's mantle to form new oceanic crust. This material, primarily basalt, spreads out to either side of the ridges at a rate of the order of 10–50mm/yr. Newly formed basalt is able to "fossilize" the prevailing geomagnetism (see PALEOMAGNETISM): the main evidence for sea-floor spreading comes from the symmetric pattern of alternately magnetized strips of basalt on either side of the ridges. Additional evidence comes from the increasing age of rocks as one moves away from the ridges.

SEA HORSES, small, highly-specialized fishes closely related to pipefishes. Unique among fishes in that the head is set at right angles to the body, they swim with the body held vertically. The body is encased in bony rings or plates. There is no tailfin and the hind part of the body is prehensile and may anchor the fish in seaweed. Males brood the eggs in special pouches on the belly.

SEA ISLANDS, chain of more than 100 islands in the Atlantic off the coast of S.C., Ga., and Fla. Settled by the Spanish in the 16th century, the islands were in the early 19th century the first important North American cotton-growing region. Many are now resorts or wildlife sanctuaries.

SEA LIONS, family Otariidae, eared seals, differing from true SEALS in having external ears and an almost hairless body. These are the animals most commonly seen in circuses and zoos. They are large creatures— males may measure between 2–3m (6.6–9.8ft) —and are active marine carnivores, feeding on fishes, squids and other mollusks.

SEALS, members of the mammal order Pinnipedia, which includes both the SEA LIONS, and the true seals of the family Phocidae. True seals have no external ears and have a thick coat of strong guard hairs. Seals are animals of the colder seas of both hemispheres. Northern species (subfamily Phocinae) include the bearded seal, the gray seal and the common or harbor seal. Southern species (subfamily Monachinae) include the monk seals, elephant seals, crabeater and Weddell seals. Most seals are gregarious; all are pelagic and many come ashore only to breed. A single, light-colored pup is born and further mating takes place immediately afterward. Males form harems of females on the breeding grounds. Many species are now uncommon, having been formerly extensively hunted for their skins and meat.

SEARCH WARRANT, in law, a court order issued to give law officers the authority to enter and search private premises for evidence, persons, contraband goods, or illegal equipment such as counterfeiting machinery. "Unreasonable searches and seizures" are forbidden in the Fourth Amendment to the US Constitution, and the scope of such a warrant is severely limited.

SEARS TOWER, tallest inhabited building in the world (1,454ft), built in the mid-1970s, Chicago office building of Sears Roebuck. Prefabricated welded steel frames form a vertical core for the 110 floors.

SEASICKNESS. See MOTION SICKNESS.

SEA SNAKES, a family, Hydrophidae, of poisonous SNAKES that live permanently in the sea and are fully adapted to an aquatic existence, swimming with a sculling action of the paddle-shaped tail. They are fully air-breathing but can submerge for long periods. They feed on small fishes, immobilizing them first with a potent, fast-acting venom.

SEASONS, divisions of the year, characterized by cyclical changes in the predominant weather pattern. In the temperate zones there are four seasons: spring, summer, autumn (fall) and winter. These result from the constant inclination of the earth's polar axis (66½° from the ecliptic) as the earth orbits the sun: during summer in the N Hemisphere the N Pole is tilted toward the sun, in winter—when the solar radiation strikes the hemisphere more obliquely— away from the sun. The summer and winter SOLSTICES (about June 21 and Dec. 22),

popularly known as midsummer and midwinter, strictly speaking mark the beginnings of summer and winter, respectively. Thus spring begins on the day of the vernal EQUINOX (about Mar. 21) and autumn at the autumnal equinox (about Sept. 23).

SEATTLE, largest city in Wash., the financial and commercial center and major port of the Pacific Northwest, seat of King Co. Seattle lies on Elliott Bay (Puget Sound), and its chief industries are aerospace production, steel, shipbuilding, food-processing and chemicals. Settled in 1852, Seattle rapidly expanded after the 1897 Alaska gold rush, and again following the boom created by WWII. Pop (city) 488,000, (metro) 1,724,000.

SEA URCHINS, spiny marine echinoderms with spherical to somewhat flattened form, occurring worldwide. The basic structure is a sphere of 20 columns of calcareous plates. Within this "test," the internal structures, gut, gonads and water-vascular system, are looped around the inside wall. The center of the sphere is empty. The test bears tubercles and short spines, and also the pedicellaria: motile, pincer-like organs which clear the surface of detritus. Tube feet protrude through pores in the test, arranged in double rows down the sides.

SEAWEED, popular name for the ALGAE found around coasts from the shore to fairly deep water. Commonest are the brown algae or wracks. Some, such as bladderwrack, clothe the rocks between tides; others live up to 12m (39.4ft) deep. The large brown algae (kelps) sometimes form thick beds of long, tangled fronds, with tough, well-anchored stems. Gulfweed is another widespread species. Delicate green and red seaweeds live mainly in rock pools. Seaweeds provide food and shelter to sea animals; many are used by man for food, fertilizer, iodine and gelatin.

SEBACEOUS GLANDS, small GLANDS in the SKIN which secrete *sebum*, a fatty substance that acts as a protective and water-repellant layer on skin and allows the epidermis to retain its suppleness. Sebum secretion is fairly constant but varies from individual to individual. Obstructed sebaceous glands become blackheads, which are the basis for ACNE.

SEBASTIAN, Saint (d. c288), early Christian martyr. Legend relates that he was a captain under the Roman Emperor DIOCLETIAN, and was sentenced, as a Christian, to die by archery (a scene recorded in many Italian paintings). He survived but was finally clubbed to death in the Amphitheater.

SEBASTIAN (1554–1578), king of Portugal, successor (1557) to his grandfather John III. A religious fanatic, he refused to marry but led a crusade to Morocco, was defeated and killed in battle at Alcazar-quivir. Rumors that he was alive led to persistent belief in his return to deliver Portugal from her 1580 defeat by Spain.

SEBASTIANO DEL PIOMBO (c1485–1547), Venetian painter. The warm colors of his early portraits and religious works show GIORGIONE's influence. He moved to Rome in his 20s and was associated with MICHELANGELO. His portrait of Christopher Columbus hangs in the Metropolitan Museum.

SEBORRHEA. See DANDRUFF.

SECESSION, in US history, the withdrawal of the Southern states from the Federal Union, 1860–61. A right of secession, arising from a STATES' RIGHTS interpretation of the Constitution, was claimed in the early 1800s by the defeated Federalist Party in New England. The concept died in the US when the CIVIL WAR ended in the Southern states' defeat.

SECOND COMING, or **Parousia** (Greek: arrival), in Christian ESCHATOLOGY, the return of JESUS CHRIST in glory to end the present order, to raise the dead (see RESURRECTION) and to summon all to the LAST JUDGMENT. The Second Coming was prophesied by Christ himself and by St. Paul; the early Church, and many ADVENTIST groups since, regarded it as imminent; some cults such as the JEHOVAH'S WITNESSES have repeatedly forecast its date.

SECRET POLICE, an organization, usually beyond democratic control, which aims its largely covert work at silencing political opposition or "threats to national security." Methods may range from surveillance to torture and murder. Notorious systems have been Fouché's in revolutionary France, the tsarist *Okhrana* and later the CHEKA, KGB and MVD in Russia, the German GESTAPO and the Italian Fascist *Ovra.*

SECRET SERVICE, US, a branch of the US TREASURY Department. Established 1865 to suppress the counterfeiting of currency, it became responsible for protecting the president after the assassination of President William McKINLEY (1901). It now also guards the vice-president, president-elect, and presidential candidates.

SECRET SOCIETIES, groups with secret membership, initiation rituals and recognition signs. Most have specific aims: religious (ROSICRUCIANS; the MYSTERIES of ancient Greece); political (CAMORRA; CARBONARI; KU

KLUX KLAN); social or benevolent (as in MASONRY and college fraternities); or criminal (MAFIA; MOLLY MAGUIRES).

SECULAR HUMANISM, philosophy that rejects the idea of a God who created man and the universe, that locates the values of existence within human life, and that assigns to man the responsibility for making moral distinctions between good and evil, just and unjust. It has been condemned by theists who believe that the authority of religious revelations—however varied and conflicting—is necessary to guide imperfect human nature. In the US in recent decades, fundamentalists have accused the educational system of disseminating secular humanism, resulting in social and political ills of all kinds. (See also HUMANISM.)

SECURITIES AND EXCHANGE COMMISSION (SEC), an independent agency of the US government set up in 1934 to protect investors in securities (stocks and bonds). It requires disclosures of the structure of all public companies and registration of all securities exchanged. SEC hears complaints, initiates investigations, issues brokerage licenses, and has broad powers to penalize fraud. (See STOCKS AND STOCK MARKET.)

SEDAN, manufacturing city in NE France, on the Meuse R, Ardennes department, where, on Sept. 1, 1870 during the FRANCO-PRUSSIAN WAR, Napoleon III with 100,000 men surrendered to the Germans.

SEDATIVES, DRUGS that reduce anxiety and induce relaxation without causing SLEEP; many are also hypnotics, drugs that in adequate doses may induce sleep. BARBITURATES were among the earlier drugs used in sedation, but they have fallen into disfavor because of addiction, side-effects, dangers of overdosage and the availability of safer alternatives. Benzodiazepines (e.g., Valium, Librium) are now the most often used.

SEDIMENTARY ROCKS, one of the three main ROCK classes of the earth's crust. They consist of weathered (see EROSION) detrital fragments of igneous, metamorphic or even sedimentary rock transported, usually by water, and deposited in distinct strata. They may also be of organic origin, as in COAL and some organic limestone, or they may be formed by chemical processes, as in the evaporites. Most common are SHALE, SANDSTONE and LIMESTONE. Sedimentary rocks frequently contain FOSSILS, as well as most of the earth's MINERAL resources.

SEDIMENTATION, in its narrowest sense the process of sediment deposition. In GEOLOGY, the term is often used as a synonym of sedimentology, which refers to the origin, transportation, and deposition of sedimentary materials and may include the postdepositional processes involved in the formation of SEDIMENTARY ROCK. In an even broader sense, sedimentation may also include sedimentary PETROLOGY and sedimentary petrography which encompass the description, classification, and interpretation of sedimentary rocks. STRATIGRAPHY is a closely related field.

SEDITION, advocating the violent overthrow of the government. During WWI, Congress passed sedition and espionage acts that banned communications attacking the US government. In appealing convictions under these acts to the US Supreme Court, defendants claimed a violation of their freedom of speech and press. The Court paid some attention to Justice HOLMES's "clear and present danger" test, but gave more weight to the "evil intent" of the defendants and, without exception, upheld their convictions.

SEECKT, Hans von (1866–1936), German general. After WWI he organized with some secrecy a highly efficient "nucleus" army despite VERSAILLES treaty restrictions, partly with Russian assistance.

SEED, the mature reproductive body of ANGIOSPERMS and GYMNOSPERMS. It also represents a resting stage which enables the PLANTS to survive through unfavorable conditions. The GERMINATION period varies widely from plant to plant. Seeds develop from the fertilized ovule. Each seed is covered with a tough coat called a testa and it contains a young plant or embryo. In most seeds three main regions of embryo can be recognized: a radicle, which gives rise to the root; a plumule, which forms the shoot; and one or two seed leaves or cotyledons which may or may not be taken above ground during germination. Plants that produce one seed leaf are called monocotyledons and those that produce two, dicotyledons. The seed also contains enough stored food (often in the cotyledons) to support embryo growth during and after germination. It is this stored food which is of value to man. Flowering plants produce their seeds inside a FRUIT, but the seeds of conifers lie naked on the scales of the cone. Distribution of seeds is usually by wind, animals or water and the form of seeds is often adapted to a specific means of dispersal. (See also POLLINATION; REPRODUCTION.)

SEEGER, Alan (1888–1916), US poet. He joined the French Foreign Legion at the outbreak of WWI and was killed in France. Among his *Collected Poems* (1916) is the famous "I Have a Rendezvous with Death."

SEEGER, Pete (1919–), US folk singer. A master of the 5-string banjo and 12-string guitar, he led the 1950s revival of interest in folk music with his group the Weavers. Many of his own freedom and pacifist songs have become classics of folk music.

SEEING EYE DOGS, dogs trained to guide the blind. The majority of US guide dogs are German shepherds, and are schooled by The Seeing Eye Inc., founded in 1929 by Dorothy Harrison Eustis.

SEFERIS, George (1900–1971), Greek poet and diplomat. His lyrical, symbolic verse sets tragic modern events against the background of Greece's past. It includes *Turning Point* (1931) and *Poems* (1940). Seferis won the 1963 Nobel Prize for literature.

SEGAL, George (1924–), US sculptor. He is best known for his life-size white figures, resembling plaster casts of his subjects, placed in natural settings, such as a doorway or behind a steering wheel.

SEGHERS, Hercules (c1589–c1638), Dutch etcher and painter famous for his fantastic, forbidding landscapes. To convey light effects he used chiaroscuro and, in his masterly etchings, AQUATINT (the first to do so) and colored paper.

SEGOVIA, Andrés (1893–1987), Spanish guitarist, most celebrated of modern players. He did much to revive serious interest in the guitar, transcribing many pieces for it. FALLA, VILLA-LOBOS and others composed works for him.

SEIFERT, Jaroslav (1901–1986), Czech poet, winner of the 1984 Nobel Prize for Literature.

SEINE RIVER, France's principal waterway. Rising on the Langres Plateau NW of Dijon, it winds 475mi NW to PARIS, where over 30 bridges span it, through Rouen and Normandy, to the English Channel. It is the main artery of a far-reaching river system converging on Paris. Canals link it to the Loire, Rhône, Rhine and Schelde rivers.

SEISMOGRAPH, instrument used to detect and record seismic waves caused by EARTHQUAKES, nuclear explosions, etc.: the record it produces is a **seismogram**. The simplest seismograph has a horizontal bar, pivoted at one end and with a recording pen at the other. The bar, supported by a spring, bears a heavy weight. As the ground moves, the bar remains roughly stationary owing to the INERTIA of the weight, while the rest of the equipment moves. The pen traces the vibrations on a moving belt of paper. Seismographs are used in seismic PROSPECTING.

SEISMOLOGY, a branch of geophysics

concerned with the study of EARTHQUAKES, seismic waves and their propagation through the EARTH's interior.

SELECTIVE SERVICE. See DRAFT.

SELEUCIDS, a Hellenistic dynasty of Syria. It was founded in 312 BC by Seleucus I Nicator (d. 280 BC), a general of Alexander the Great and one of the DIADOCHI, who conquered lands from Thrace to India. Seleucid kings founded many Greek settlements and promoted commerce, but the empire dwindled through secession and revolt, until Syria fell to Rome in 64 BC.

SELJUKS, the Turks who came from central Asia in the 11th century to found dynasties stretching from the borders of India to the Mediterranean Sea. They adopted Arabic culture and championed Islam, but soon fragmented into rival principalities weakened by Crusaders and by the Mongols, to whom they fell in the 13th century. The OTTOMAN EMPIRE rebuilt Turkish power from the 1300s.

SELKIRK, Alexander (1676–1721), Scottish sailor whose life as a castaway inspired Daniel DEFOE's novel *Robinson Crusoe*. In Sept. 1704, after a quarrel with his privateer captain, Selkirk chose to be put ashore on one of the uninhabited Juan Fernández islands. He was rescued in 1709.

SELKIRK, Thomas Douglas, 5th Earl of (1771–1820), Scottish colonizer. He helped refugees from the Scottish highland clearances to settle in Prince Edward Island (1803) and founded the RED RIVER SETTLEMENT in 1811.

SEMANTICS, the study of meaning, concerned both with the relationship of words and symbols to the ideas or objects that they represent, and with tracing the histories of meanings and changes that have taken place in them. Semantics is thus a branch of LINGUISTICS and of LOGIC. **General semantics,** propounded primarily by Alfred KORZYBSKI, holds that habits of thought have lagged behind the language and logic of science: it attacks such Aristotelian logical proposals as that nothing can be both not-x and x, maintaining that these are simplifications no longer valid.

SEMAPHORE, system of visual signaling using movable arms, flags or lights to represent letters and numbers. The first such system was introduced by Claude Chappe (1763–1805): it used towers 8 to 16km apart. Semaphore is still used for signalling between ships and on some railroads.

SEMICONDUCTOR, a material whose electrical conductivity is intermediate between that of an insulator and conductor at room TEMPERATURE and increases with rising temperature and impurity concentration. Typical **intrinsic semiconductors** are single crystals of germanium or SILICON. At low temperatures their valence electron energy levels are filled and NO ELECTRONS are free to conduct ELECTRICITY, but with increasing temperature, some electrons gain enough ENERGY to jump into the empty conduction band, leaving a hole behind in the valence band. Thus there are equal numbers of moving electrons and holes available for carrying electric current. Practical **extrinsic semiconductors** are made by adding a chosen concentration of a particular type of impurity atom to an intrinsic semiconductor (a process known as doping). If the impurity atom has more valence electrons than the semiconductor atom, it is known as a donor and provides spare conduction electrons, creating an **n-type semiconductor.** If the impurity atom has fewer valence electrons, it captures them from the other atoms and is known as an acceptor, leaving behind holes which act as moving positive charge carriers and enhance the conductivity of the **p-type semiconductor** that is formed. An n- and p-type semiconductor junction acts as a rectifier; when it is forward biased, holes cross the junction to the negative end and electrons to the positive end, and current flows through it. If the voltage connections are reversed, the carriers will not cross the junction and no current flows. Semiconductor devices, such as the TRANSISTOR, based on the p-n junction have revolutionized ELECTRONICS since the late 1940s.

SEMINOLE INDIANS, the last Indian tribe to make peace with the US government. They formed in Fla. out of an alliance including refugee CREEK INDIANS (from Ga.), native Apalachee Indians and runaway Negro slaves. They fought Andrew JACKSON's troops in 1817–18 while Fla. was still a Spanish territory. The major Seminole War began in 1835 when the US government ordered their removal to W of the Mississippi. A fierce guerrilla war against overwhelming odds ended in 1842, after which most Seminoles were moved to Okla. However, a small band held out in the Everglades until 1934, when they agreed to a settlement.

SEMIOLOGY, or **semiotics,** the study of signs (including LANGUAGE), their uses, and the way in which they are used. Its branches are pragmatics (dealing with the relation between the signs and those using them), syntactics (the relation between different words and symbols) and SEMANTICS.

SEMIRAMIS, fabled queen of Assyria said to have built Babylon and conquered Persia and Egypt. The historical Semiramis was probably Queen Sammuramat of Assyria (regent c810–805 BC). Semiramis, often identified with the goddess Ishtar, was worshiped for her beauty, valor and wisdom.

SEMITES, in the Old Testament, the "sons of Shem" (who was the son of Noah). The term now generally applies to speakers of SEMITIC LANGUAGES including ancient Akkadians, Babylonians, Assyrians and Phoenicians, modern Arabs and Israelis.

SEMITIC LANGUAGES, important group, found in the Near East and N Africa, of the Hamito-Semitic language family (see HAMITIC LANGUAGES). Most of the group are now extinct, extant members including Hebrew, Arabic and Maltese. A few were written in CUNEIFORM, but most used alphabets. The N Semitic alphabet, the first fully formed alphabetical WRITING system, is of particular importance as it is from this that most of the letters of the Latin ALPHABET have descended.

SEMMELWEISS, Ignaz Philipp (1818–1865), Hungarian obstetrician who, through his discovery that PUERPERAL FEVER was transmitted by failure of obstetricians to thoroughly clean their hands between performing autopsies of mothers who had died of the disease and making examinations of living mothers, first practiced asepsis.

SEMMES, Raphael (1809–1877), American naval officer, commander of the Confederacy's first warship, the *Sumter*, and later the famous *Alabama*, which in two years accounted for some 70 Union ships before it was sunk. (See also ALABAMA CLAIMS.)

SENATE, Roman (Latin *senes*: elders), originally an advisory council to the kings of ancient Rome, in the later Roman republic the chief governing body as PLEBEIANS challenged the PATRICIAN nobility's monopoly of the 300 life appointments to the Senate. Revolts led by the TRIBUNES and by military leaders (see GRACCHI; CINNA; MARIUS) preceded severe curtailment of the powers of the increasingly corrupt Senate, which was thereafter dominated by the emperors.

SENATE, US. See CONGRESS OF THE UNITED STATES.

SENDAK, Maurice Bernard (1928–   ), US illustrator and author of children's books whose inventive renderings of monsters both delight and terrify. His works include the Caldecott Medal winners *Where the Wild Things Are* (1963) and *In the Night Kitchen* (1970). His lively art became known to an even wider public in the 1980s through his stage sets for operas, including *Così fan tutte*.

SENECA, Lucius Annaeus (c4 BC–65 AD), Roman statesman, philosopher and writer. The most important feature of his political life is the role he played in restraining the worst excesses of NERO. Writing in highly rhetorical, epigrammatic style, Seneca advocated STOICISM in his *Moral Letters*, essays, one masterly satire and nine bloody, intense tragedies. After implication in a conspiracy he was commanded to commit suicide.

SENECA FALLS CONVENTION, first women's rights convention in the US, organized by Lucretia MOTT and Elizabeth STANTON and held at Seneca Falls, W central N.Y., 1848. The convention's chief assertion was that women should be entitled to vote.

SENECA INDIANS, of W N.Y. and E Ohio, once the largest nation of the IROQUOIS League. The Seneca Nation, some 4,000 with four reservations, is now a republic.

SENEGAL, a republic located on the bulge of W Africa.

Official name: Republic of Senegal
Capital: Dakar
Area: 75,955sq mi
Population: 6,793,000
Languages: French; Wolof, Fulani, Mende spoken
Religions: Muslim, Christian
Monetary unit(s): 1 CFA franc=100 centimes
Land. Apart from high borderlands in the E and SE, Senegal is a low-lying country of rolling grassland plains. Four rivers—the Senegal and the Gambia among them—cross the country. Tropical rain forests cover the SW. Senegal's climate is varied: cool on the coast and hot inland.
People. Among the major ethnic groups, the most numerous are the Wolof, Foulah, Serere, Toucouleur and Diola. Most of the population is illiterate and about 80% are Muslim. The majority live in rural areas, primarily along the Senegal R, and engage

in agriculture. Dakar, the capital, is a modern port city and site of the national university.

Economy. Senegal is one of the more prosperous and stable countries in Africa, but a recent period of drought sharply reduced national output of peanuts, on which the economy largely depends. Fish and livestock are also important. Industry, mainly in Dakar, centers around food processing. Calcium and phosphates are important mineral exports.

History. Parts of Senegal were within the medieval empires of Ghana, Mali and Songhai. Under French control from 1895, Senegal was part of the Federation of Mali 1959–60, but declared itself independent in 1960. SENGHOR, president for two decades following independence, resigned in 1980. His successor, Abdou Diouf, won presidential elections in 1983 and 1988.

SENGHOR, Léopold-Sédar (1906–   ), Senegalese statesman and poet, Senegal's first president (1960–1980). He became known for his philosophy of *négritude*, a concept of socialism incorporating black African values.

SENNACHERIB (reigned 704–681 BC), one of the last great kings of Assyria. To maintain the great empire established by his father Sargon II, he put down rebellion in Syria and Palestine (but failed to capture Jerusalem) and conquered the Babylonians and Elamites, sacking Babylon as a lesson to his subjects. Finally he rebuilt NINEVEH and made it Assyria's capital.

SENNETT, Mack (1884–1960), Canadian-born US silent movie director-producer, a pioneer of "slapstick humor" on the screen. After working with D. W. GRIFFITH he formed his own Keystone Co. and made over 1,000 "shorts" with his Keystone Kops, Bathing Beauties and stars like CHAPLIN. W. C. FIELDS and Gloria Swanson.

SENSATIONALISM, philosophical theory which in its most extreme forms (see CYRENAICS; CONDILLAC) holds that knowledge is composed wholly of sensations, the mind being regarded as a passive *tabula rasa* (clean slate).

SENSES, the media through which stimuli in the environment of an organism act on it (external senses); also, the internal senses which report on the internal state of the organism (through THIRST AND HUNGER; PAIN, etc.). The organs of sense, the eye, ear, skin etc., all contain specialized cells and nerve endings which communicate with centers in the NERVOUS SYSTEM. Sense organs may be stimulated by pressure (in TOUCH, hearing and balance—see EAR), chemical stimulation (SMELL; TASTE), or electromagnetic radiation (VISION; heat sensors).

SEOUL, capital, largest city and industrial and cultural center of South Korea, on the Han R, 25mi E of Inchon, its seaport. It was founded in 1392 as capital of the Yi dynasty, which it remained until 1910. Seoul changed hands several times in the KOREAN WAR and suffered great damage. Largely rebuilt, it has grown rapidly. It was the site of the 1988 summer Olympics. Pop (metro) 10,300,000.

SEPARATION OF POWERS, political theory developed by MONTESQUIEU from his studies of the British constitution, arguing that the arbitrary exercise of government power should be avoided by dividing it between distinct departments, the executive, legislature and judiciary. This was a basic principle of the Founding Fathers in producing the US Constitution; legislative powers were vested in Congress, judicial powers in the Supreme and subsidiary courts and executive powers in the president and his governmental machinery. Each branch was to have its functions, duties and authority, and in theory no branch could encroach upon another. In practice there has always been a degree of necessary overlap. The legislature can oppose and impeach members of the executive, the president can veto legislation and the Supreme Court can adjudicate the actions of the other branches; its members, in turn, are presidential appointees subject to congressional approval. In US history one branch has always tended to dominate others for long periods, but this "checks and balances" effect has at least ensured that power can and does shift between them.

SEPARATISTS, those English religious congregations who sought independence from the state and established church, beginning in 1580 with the Norwich Brownists (see BROWNE, ROBERT). John ROBINSON led refugee Separatists in Leyden, Holland, who were later prominent among the PILGRIM FATHERS. (See also CONGREGATIONAL CHURCHES.)

SEPHARDIM, Spanish Jews who fled the INQUISITION (1480) for Portugal, N Africa, Italy, Holland (notably Amsterdam), the Balkans (Salonika), Near East and America. Sephardim had their own language, literature and ritual.

SEPOY REBELLION, or Indian Mutiny, a mutiny of Sepoys (Hindi: troops) in the Bengal Army of the EAST INDIA COMPANY. It began at Meerut, near Delhi, in May 1857 and spread over N India. The immediate cause was the issuing of cartridges greased with the fat of cows (sacred to Hindus) and pigs (unclean to Muslims), but years of increasing British domination led to a general revolt which was not suppressed until March 1858. As a result the British government took over the rule of India.

SEPTEMBER, ninth month of the year, derived from Latin *septem,* seven, an indication of its old position in the pre-Julian Roman CALENDAR.

SEPTICEMIA, circulation of infective BACTERIA and the white BLOOD cells responding to them in the blood. Bacteria may transiently enter the blood normally but these are removed by the reticuloen-dothelial system. If this system fails and bacteria continue to circulate, their products and those of the white cells initiate a series of reactions that lead to SHOCK, with warm extremities, FEVER or hypothermia. Septic EMBOLISM may occur causing widespread ABSCESSES. Gran's stain-negative bacteria (usually from urinary or GASTROINTESTINAL TRACT) and STAPHYLOCOCCUS cause severe septicemia. Treatment includes ANTIBIOTICS and resus-citative measures for shock.

SEPTIC TANK, large tank used for SEWAGE disposal from single residences not linked to the public sewer. The liquid part of the sewage drains off to a cesspool or distribution network in sandy soil. The sludge collects at the bottom of the tank and is largely decomposed by bacteria; it is pumped out every few years.

SEPTUAGINT, oldest Greek translation of the Hebrew OLD TESTAMENT, probably from an older source than any now extant. The PENTATEUCH was translated in Alexandria at the behest of PTOLEMY II (c250 BC), according to legend by 70 or 72 scholars (hence the name); completed, including the APOCRYPHA, c130 BC.

SEQUOIA, genus including the two largest trees, the redwood *Sequoia sempervirens* and the giant sequoia (*S. gigantea*), both found only in the Pacific northwest of the US. Furthermore, only the bristlecone pine lives longer. The tallest tree in the world is a redwood in Humboldt Co., Cal. which measures over 360ft high, and the largest living organism in the world is the General Sherman giant sequoia in SEQUOIA NATIONAL PARK, which is over 270ft high with a circumference at the base of over 100ft. Family: Taxodiaceae.

SEQUOIA NATIONAL PARK, 600sq mi park, S central Cal. (administered with the adjacent KINGS CANYON NATIONAL PARK), established 1890 to preserve the groves of giant sequoia. Lying in the S Sierra Nevada, it includes Mt WHITNEY, highest US peak outside Alaska.

SEQUOYA (c1770–1843), Cherokee In-dian silversmith who devised an alphabet whose 85 characters represented every sound in Cherokee language, enabling thousands of Cherokees to read and write. The sequoia tree is named for him.

SERBIA, historic Balkan state, since WWII the easternmost of the six constituent republics of YUGOSLAVIA. The Serbs were SLAVS who settled the Balkans from the 600s onward. Stephen Nemanja (ruled 1168–96) created the first united kingdom, which became a great empire under Stephen Dushan (1331–1355), but after the battle of Kosovo (1389) Serbia remained under Turkish rule until independence was restored in 1878. After WWI occupation by Austria, it became the core of the kingdom of Yugoslavia. Serbia (34,000sq mi) is mountainous and mainly agricultural. Its capital is BELGRADE.

SERBO-CROATIAN, the principal lan-guage of Yugoslavia. One of the SLAVONIC LANGUAGES, it is written in Cyrillic (by the majority Serbs) or Latin (by the Croats) characters.

SERF, a feudal peasant. Under FEUDALISM serfs were bound to the land they worked and had to give some of their labor or produce to an overlord. With the development of CAPITALISM, serfdom died out, although it survived into the 19th century in Russia and parts of E Europe.

SERGIUS, Saint (c1315–1392), Russian religious leader. His monastery at Radon-ezh (modern Zagorsk) near Moscow became a center for the moral and nationalist regeneration of Russia during Tatar oppression.

SERIAL MUSIC. See TWELVE-TONE MUSIC.

SERKIN, Rudolf (1903–   ), Bohemian-born US pianist. He studied with SCHOENBERG in Vienna, made his US debut in 1933 and joined the Curtis Institute of Music, Philadelphia, in 1939. A noted Beethoven interpreter, he has played in concerts all over the world. His son Peter Serkin (1947–   ) is also a prominent pianist.

SERLIO, Sebastiano (1475–1554), Italian architect who worked at Fontainebleau. His *Architecture* (1537–51), first treatise to stress practice rather than theory, diffused MANNERISM and the style of BRAMANTE, RAPHAEL and PERUZZI.

SERMON ON THE MOUNT, Christ's most important discourse, described in Matthew 5–7. Encapsulating most of the principles of Christian ethics, stressing the power of love and God's role as a loving father, it contains also the BEATITUDES and the LORD'S PRAYER.

SERRA, Junípero (1713–1784), Mallorcan Franciscan missionary. A famous preacher and professor, he went to Mexico in 1749 and worked among the Indians of the Sierra Gorda. Franciscans under his leadership established, from 1769 onward, nine missions in present-day Cal., including San Carlos at Monterey.

SERUM, the clear yellowish fluid that separates from BLOOD, LYMPH and other body fluids when they clot. It contains water, PROTEINS, fat, minerals, HORMONES and urea. **Serum therapy** involves injecting (horse or human) serum containing ANTIBODIES (globulins), which can destroy particular pathogens. Occasionally injected serum gives rise to an allergic reaction known as serum sickness; a second injection of the same serum may induce, a severe allergic reaction.

SERVETUS, Michael (1511–1553), Spanish biologist and theologian. In *Christianity Restored* (1553) he mentioned in passing his discovery of the pulmonary circulation (see BLOOD CIRCULATION). For heretical views expressed in this book he was denounced by the Calvinists to the Catholic Inquisition; escaping, he foolishly visited Geneva, where he was seized by the Protestants, tried for heresy and burned alive.

SERVICE, Robert William (1874–1958), British-born Canadian writer. His enormously popular, often humorous ballads, starting with *Songs of a Sourdough* (1907), told of the rugged life and characters of the Yukon and of the KLONDIKE gold rush.

SERVILE WARS, in Roman history, uprisings of agricultural slaves that were severely repressed. The first two (134–132 BC, 104–101 BC) occurred in Sicily, the third (73–71 BC), led by the gladiator SPARTACUS, in S Italy.

SERVOMECHANISM, an automatic control device (see MECHANIZATION AND AUTOMATION) which controls the position, velocity or acceleration of a high-power output device by means of a command signal from a low-power reference device. By FEEDBACK, the error between the actual output state and the state commanded is measured, amplified and made to drive a servomotor which corrects the output. The drive may be electrical, hydraulic or pneumatic.

SESAME, *Sesamum indicum*, a tropical plant, cultivated mainly in China and India for its flat seeds. The seeds yield an oil which is used instead of olive oil as a salad or cooking oil and in margarine, cosmetics and ointments. The residue left after oil extraction is used as a cattle feed and fertilizer. Family: Pedaliaceae.

SESAME STREET, innovative educational television program for young children inaugurated in 1969 by the Public Broadcasting System (PBS).

SESSHU (1420–1506), Japanese master of ink painting. Influenced by Zen Buddhism, and by a visit to China, he painted sensitive but vigorous landscapes in both *shin* and *haboku* styles.

SESSILE ANIMALS, animals that spend part of their lives attached to the ground or sea bed. All have a mobile phase facilitating dispersal.

SESSIONS, Roger Huntington (1896–1985), US composer. He studied with Ernest BLOCH and taught at leading US academic institutions. His orchestral, chamber and choral works are characterized by complexity, POLYPHONY, and rhythmic vitality.

SET or **SETH**, an ancient Egyptian god of evil, represented with an ass's head and a pig's snout. Originally a royal deity, he came to personify evil as killer of OSIRIS, god of goodness. Osiris' son HORUS fought and killed Set.

SET, a collection of objects or quantities, symbolized by a capital letter. Thus
$$S = \{2, 4, 6, 8\}$$
means that S is the set consisting of these four numbers. A member of a set is called an element: symbolically, $2 \in S$ means that 2 is an element of S; $3 \in S$ means that 3 is not an element of S. A set may be infinite, finite or empty: the set of all even numbers is infinite, that of all those less than 10 is finite, and that of all those less than 1 is empty. This empty or **null set** is symbolized $\varnothing$ or O.

If some elements of one set are also elements of another, then those elements are called the intersection of the two sets, symbolized $S_1 \cap S_2$. The set of all elements that are members of at least one of the two sets is their union, written $S_1 \cup S_2$. A set whose members are all members of another set is termed a subset. Thus, if,
$$S_1 = \{a, b, c, d, e\}$$
$$S_2 = \{b, d, f, g\},$$
then
$$S_1 \cap S_2 = \{b, d\}$$
$$S_1 \cup S_2 = \{a, b, c, d, e, f, g\}.$$
Moreover, S_1 and S_2, are subsets of $S_1 \cup S_2$, written $S_1 \subset S_1 \cup S_2$ and $S_2 \subset S_1 \cup S_2$. The set of all elements of all the sets in a particular discussion is the universal set, symbolized by a capital I.

SETI I (ruled c1318–1304 BC), king of Egypt, father of RAMSES II. He restored Egypt's lands and prestige and built the Hypostyle Hall, Karnak, and his own magnificent tomb at THEBES.

SETON, Elizabeth Ann, or **Mother Seton** (née Bayley: 1774–1821), first native-born US saint. A devout Episcopalian, she was widowed at 28 with five children. In 1805, she converted to Catholicism. She opened an elementary school, now regarded as the basis of the US parochial school system, and in 1813 founded the first US religious society, the Sisters of Charity. She was canonized in 1975.

SETTLEMENT HOUSE. See SOCIAL SETTLEMENTS.

SEURAT, Georges (1859–1891), French painter, one of a small group representing Neoimpressionism or POSTIMPRESSIONISM. Interested in color from scientific and artistic points of view, he invented POINTILLISM. Best known of his paintings is probably *A Sunday Afternoon on the Island of La Grande Jatte* (1884–86).

SEUSS, Dr. (1904–), pen name of Theodor Seuss Geisel, US author-illustrator of many children's books. His imaginative verse tales (*Horton Hears a Who*, 1954; *How the Grinch Stole Christmas*, 1957) and humorous pictorial fantasies are tremendously popular with the very young.

SEVASTOPOL, Black Sea port of the CRIMEA peninsula, Ukrainian SSR, USSR. Now a major Soviet naval base, industrial city and railroad terminal, the city suffered long sieges in the CRIMEAN WAR (1854–55) and WWII (1941–42).

SEVEN CITIES OF CIBOLA. See CIBOLA, SEVEN CITIES OF.

SEVEN DAYS BATTLES (June 25–July 2, 1862), series of engagements in the US CIVIL WAR in which Robert E. LEE prevented a Union assault, led by George McCLELLAN, on Richmond, Va., the Confederate capital, so ending the PENINSULAR CAMPAIGN.

SEVEN HILLS OF ROME, on which the ancient city of ROME was built, probably chosen for their strategic position just E of the lowest crossing on the Tiber R. Traditionally, ROMULUS founded the city on the nearest hill, the Palatine, a settlement which soon linked with the neighboring Capitoline to the NW. By 378 BC the Servian Wall enclosed the other hills further out: the Aventine, Caelian, Esquiline, Viminal and Quirinal.

SEVEN SAGES, lawgivers of ancient Greece and Asia Minor (c600 BC), famous for such maxims as "know thyself" and "nothing in excess."

SEVENTH-DAY ADVENTISTS. See ADVENTISTS.

SEVEN WEEKS' WAR. See AUSTRO-PRUSSIAN WAR.

SEVEN WONDERS OF THE WORLD, the seven greatest structures of the ancient world, as listed by Greek scholars. The oldest wonder (and only survivor) are the Pyramids of Egypt: the others were the Hanging Gardens of Babylon; the 30ft statue of Zeus at Olympia; the great temple of Artemis at Ephesus; the Mausoleum at Halicarnassus; the Colossus of Rhodes; and the Pharos of Alexandria.

SEVEN YEARS' WAR (1756–1763), a war between Austria, France, Russia, Saxony, Sweden (from 1757) and (after 1762) Spain on the one side and Britain, Prussia and Hanover on the other. In America the struggle centered on colonial rivalry between Britain and France and formed part of the FRENCH AND INDIAN WARS. In Europe the main dispute was between Austria and Prussia for supremacy in Germany. Austria's MARIA THERESA aimed to recover recently-lost Silesia (see AUSTRIAN SUCCESSION, WAR OF THE). This provoked Prussia to attack Saxony and Bohemia. Although severely pressed, the Prussians avoided complete defeat. By the treaties of Hubertusberg and Paris (1763), Britain emerged as the leading colonial power and Prussia as a major European force.

SEVERN RIVER, Britain's longest river, 220mi long. It rises in E Wales and flows E and S into the Bristol Channel. The Severn bore is famous.

SEVIER, John (1745–1815), US pioneer and first governor of Tenn. He was prominent in the Carolina Campaign of the Revolutionary War and became head of the state of Franklin in 1783. Sevier was made governor of Tenn. in 1796, serving until 1801, and again 1803–09. He was also a congressman (1789–91 and 1811–15).

SEVILLE, city of SW Spain, capital of Seville province and an important industrial center and port on the Guadalquivir R. Seville is famous for its historic buildings and HOLY WEEK processions; it was the birthplace of VELÁZQUEZ and MURILLO. Pop 673,574.

SÈVRES, suburb 6mi SW of Paris, France. It gives its name to the famous Sèvres porcelain, manufactured in the town since 1756. There is a ceramics museum.

SÈVRES, Treaty of (1920), post-WWI treaty between the Allies and Turkey, negotiated at SÈVRES. Never ratified by Turkey, it aimed to abolish the OTTOMAN EMPIRE and protect the independence of surrounding countries. The Turks gained better terms by the Treaty of Lausanne (1923).

SEWAGE, the liquid and semisolid wastes

from dwellings and offices, industrial wastes, and surface and storm waters. Sewage systems collect the sewage, transport and treat it, then discharge it into rivers, lakes or the sea. Vaulted sewers were developed by the Romans but from the Middle Ages and until the mid-19th century sewage flowed through the open gutters of cities, constituting a major health hazard. Then sewage was discharged into storm-water drains which were developed into sewers. But the dumping of large amounts of untreated sewage into rivers led to serious water POLLUTION, and modern treatment methods arose, at least for major cities. An early solution (still sometimes practiced) was sewage farming, raw sewage being used as FERTILIZER. Chemically-aided precipitation was also tried, but neither proved adequate. Noting that natural watercourses can purify a moderate amount of sewage, sanitary engineers imitated natural conditions by allowing atmospheric oxidation of the organic matter, first by passing it intermittently through a shallow tank filled with large stones (the "trickling filter"), and later much more successfully by the **activated-sludge process**, in which compressed air is passed through a sewage tank, the sludge being decomposed by the many microorganisms that it contains. A by-product is sludge gas, chiefly methane, burned as fuel to help power the treatment plant. Sedimentation is carried out before and after decomposition; the filtered solids are buried, incinerated or dried for fertilizer. The sewer system is designed for fast flow (about 1m/s) to carry the solids; the sewers are provided with manholes, drainage inlets, regulators and, finally, outfalls. Dwellings not connected to the sewers have their own SEPTIC TANKS.

SEWALL, Samuel (1652–1730), one of the judges in the Salem witchcraft trials. The trials, as a result of which 19 accused were hanged, were born from malicious rumor and hysteria: Sewall made public apology in 1697 for his support of the sentencings. (See also MATHER, COTTON.) He also wrote the first American antislavery tract.

SEWARD, William Henry (1801–1872), US politician famous for his purchase of ALASKA from Russia in 1867. Seward, a prominent antislavery senator, was appointed secretary of state by President Lincoln in 1861. He did much to keep Britain out of the Civil War (see TRENT AFFAIR). Seward survived an assassination attempt by an accomplice of BOOTH and served as President Johnson's secretary of state.

SEWING MACHINE, machine for sewing cloth, leather or books: a major industrial and domestic labor-saving device. There are two main types: chainstitch machines, using a needle and only one thread, with a hook that pulls each looped stitch through the next; and lock-stitch machines, using two threads, one through the needle eye and the other, which interlocks with the first in the material, from a bobbin/shuttle system (to-and-fro or rotary). Chain-stitch machines—the first to be invented, by Barthélemy Thimmonier (1793–1859)—are now used chiefly for sacks or bags. The lock-stitch machines now in general use are based on that invented by Elias HOWE (1846). Zigzag machines differ from ordinary straight-stitch machines in having variously-shaped cams that move the needle from side to side. Almost all US machines are electrically powered, but foot-treadle machines are common elsewhere.

SEX, the totality of the differences between the male and female partners engaged in sexual REPRODUCTION. Examples of sex are found among all levels of life save the VIRUSES. In the higher orders, fertilization is brought about by the fusion of two GAMETES, the male sperm conveying genetic information to the female EGG, or ovum (see HEREDITY). Many INVERTEBRATES, most PLANTS and some FISHES are HERMAPHRODITE; that is, individuals may possess functioning male *and* female organs. This is not the case with BIRDS and MAMMALS, though these on occasion display **intersexuality**, where an individual may possess a confusion of male and female characteristics. **Sexual behavior** is an important facet of animal behavior: it may also be at the root of AGGRESSION and TERRITORIALITY.

SEX HORMONES. See ANDROGENS; ESTROGENS; GLANDS; HORMONES.

SEXTANT, instrument for NAVIGATION, invented in 1730 and superseding the ASTROLABE. A fixed telescope is pointed at the horizon, and a radial arm is moved against an arc graduated in degrees until a mirror which it bears reflects an image of a known star or the sun down the telescope to coincide with the image of the horizon. The angular elevation of the star, with the exact time (see CHRONOMETER), gives the LATITUDE. The **air sextant** is a similar instrument, usually periscopic, designed for use in aircraft, and has an artificial horizon, generally a bubble level.

SEYCHELLES, independent republic of some 85 islands (largest Mahé) in the Indian Ocean NE of the island of Madagascar. The climate is hot and often humid. About 90% of the population lives on Mahé. Most of the population is of mixed

Official name: Republic of Seychelles
Capital: Victoria, on Mahé
Area: 175sq mi
Population: 66,000
Languages: English, French; Creole patois
Religion: Roman Catholic
Monetary unit(s): 1 rupee = 100 cents
French and African descent. Chief products are coconuts and spices, and fishing and tourism are important. First settled by the French in the mid-1700s the islands were taken by the British in 1794 and made a dependency of Mauritius in 1810. They became a separate colony in 1903 and were granted independence in June 1976. There have been several attempts to overthrow the leftist government headed by Albert René, who came to power in 1977 and won elections in 1979 and 1984 under a new constitution that made Seychelles a one-party state.

SEYMOUR, Horatio (1810–1886), US politician. As Democratic governor of New York (1862–64), he declared the EMANCIPATION PROCLAMATION unconstitutional and opposed national conscription, although encouraging voluntary enlistment. He was defeated by U.S. GRANT in the 1868 presidential election.

SEYMOUR, Jane (c1509–1537), third wife of England's HENRY VIII (from 1536). She died after the birth of her son, EDWARD VI.

SEYSS-INQUART, Arthur (1892–1946), Austrian NAZI leader, governor of Austria (1938–39) and deputy governor of Poland (1939–40). As high commissioner for Holland (1940–45), his cruelty was notorious. He was executed for WAR CRIMES.

SFORZA, Ludovico (c1452–1508), *il Moro* (the Moor), ruler of Milan (1480–99) and patron of BRAMANTE and LEONARDO DA VINCI. Finally deposed by LOUIS XII, he spent his last years in a French prison.

SHACKLETON, Sir Ernest Henry (1874–1922), British Antarctic explorer. He was a member of SCOTT'S 1901–04 expedition, and led his own parties in 1908–09 (when he located the S magnetic pole) and 1914–16. He died during a fourth expedition.

SHAFFER, Peter (Levin) (1926–   ), English playwright whose plays are often concerned with a protagonist's struggle against an incomprehensible God. In *Equus* (1973) a psychiatrist envies the passion that a troubled boy experiences while placating a personal horse-god. Similarly in *Amadeus* (1980) the virtuous and successful but mediocre composer SALIERI blames God for bestowing genius on a conceited, sniggering Mozart.

SHAFTER, William Rufus (1835–1906), US soldier. In the SPANISH-AMERICAN WAR, he led the US expeditionary force which eventually gained the surrender of Santiago, Cuba (1898).

SHAFTESBURY, name of three important English earls. **Anthony Ashley Cooper** (1621–1683), 1st Earl, was a founder of the WHIG party and a staunch Protestant. After supporting both CROMWELL and the RESTORATION, he became lord chancellor in 1672, but was dismissed in 1673 for supporting the TEST ACT. He then built up the Whig opposition to CHARLES II, supporting Monmouth, the pretender, and opposing JAMES II's succession. He was acquitted of treason in 1681, but fled to Holland in 1682. **Anthony Ashley Cooper** (1671–1713), 3rd Earl, was a moral philosopher and pupil of John LOCKE. He aimed to found an ethical system based on an innate moral sense. **Anthony Ashley Cooper** (1801–1885), 7th Earl, was a statesman and leading evangelical Christian who promoted legislation to improve conditions in mines and factories and supported many movements for social improvement.

SHAH, Persian word meaning "king," borne as a title by the rulers of Middle Eastern and some Asian countries. It is used especially to refer to the ruler of Iran (Persia).

SHAH JAHAN (1592–1666), Mogul emperor of India (1628–58), famous for building the TAJ MAHAL. His reign saw the restoration of Islam as state religion, the conquest of S India and the golden age of Mogul art.

SHAHN, Ben (1898–1969), Lithuanian-born US artist. He used a realistic style to draw attention to social and political events. One of his best-known works is a series of paintings on the SACCO-VANZETTI CASE (1931–32).

SHAKERS, originally an abusive term for the United Society of Believers in Christ's Second Appearing, a millenarian sect whose members shook with ecstatic emotion in their worship. Originating among the QUAKERS of England, they were brought by

"Mother" Ann Lee to the US in 1774, where they formed celibate communes which flourished until the mid-19th century.

SHAKESPEARE, William (1564–1616), English poet, playwright and actor-manager, one of the giants of world literature. Little is known with certainty of his early life. Son of a prosperous glover, he was born and educated at Stratford-upon-Avon in Warwickshire. In 1582 he married Ann Hathaway, and they had three children. He moved to London c1589, probably as an actor, and by 1592 had made a name as a playwright. From 1594 he wrote and acted for the Lord Chamberlain's Men, and became a shareholding director of their new Globe Theatre in 1598. The theaters closed during the plague of 1592–94; during this time he wrote the two narrative poems *Venus and Adonis* and *The Rape of Lucrece*, and also the sonnets. The company survived the closure, rivalry and Puritan hostility to become the King's Men on the accession of James I in 1603, and in that year were able to buy the Blackfriars Theatre also. Shakespeare invested his money wisely, and so was able to retire to Stratford c1610, although he probably continued to write until 1613. Immensely successful in his time, Shakespeare stood out even against KYD, MARLOWE and Ben JONSON. He was recognized not only as the most richly endowed dramatist but as a poet of extraordinary sensibility and linguistic gifts.

Because his plays were generally not prepared for publication except to eclipse "pirated" versions, they have come down to us with many corruptions and variant readings. The chronology of the works is uncertain, and even the canon itself is disputed. For example, the *Henry VI* cycle is attributed to him alone, but may well have been a collaboration, as also *Henry VIII*. The first collected edition, known as the First Folio, was published in 1623. He probably revised many plays by others (*Pericles* may be one) and probably had a hand in other works, as in the anonymous plays known as the "Shakespeare Apocrypha." It seems certain, however, that it was Shakespeare and no other who wrote the 37 plays that bear his name, among the most popular of which are *Hamlet, Julius Caesar, Richard III, Macbeth, Othello, Henry IV* (parts I and II), and *A Midsummer Night's Dream.*

SHALE, fine-grained detrital SEDIMENTARY ROCK formed by compaction and dessication of mud (clay and silt). Shales are sometimes rich in FOSSILS; and are laminated (they split readily into layers, or laminae). Their metamorphism (see METAMORPHIC ROCKS) produces SLATE. (See also OIL SHALE.)

SHAMANISM, a primitive religious system centered around a shaman, or **medicine man,** who in trance state is believed to be possessed by spirits that speak and act through him. The shaman (from the language of the Tungus of Siberia) is expected to cure the sick, protect the tribe, foretell the future, etc.

SHAMIR, Yitzhak (1915–   ), Polish-born Israeli politician, prime minister 1986–88. Moving to Palestine in the 1930s, he joind the anti-British underground military organization Irgun Zvai Leumi and, in WWII, was a leader of the "Stern gang," which continued to regard Britain as the principal enemy. In 1955–65 he headed the Paris station of Mossad, the Israeli intelligence service. Elected to the Knesset (parliament) in 1973 as a member of Menachem BEGIN's right-wing Herut Party, he served (1980–83) as foreign minister in Begin's government. Begin retired in 1983, and after an inconclusive national election the conservative Likud bloc (of which Herut was the principal member) formed a coalition government with the Labor Party in which Shamir served as foreign minister for the first 2 years and as prime minister for the second. In both capacities, he rejected US Middle East peace proposals and took a hard line against Palestinian rioters. Another inconclusive election in Nov. 1988 gave Likud 40 seats in parliament and Labor 39. Shamir was asked to form a new government.

SHAMMAI (c50 BC–c30 AD), Jewish scholar and, with HILLEL, the leading sage of his time. He founded the Bet Shammai school of Pharisaic philosophy, which was rigid in its interpretation of Jewish law, in opposition to Hillel's liberalism.

SHAMROCK, popular name in Ireland for several LEGUMINOUS PLANTS, the trifoliate leaves of which were cited by St. Patrick as a symbol of the Christian Trinity. Among the plants called shamrock are the wood sorrel (*Oxalis acetosella*), white clover (*Trifolium repens*) and black medic (*Medicago lupulina*).

SHANG, the first historic Chinese dynasty, traditionally said to have lasted c1766 BC–c1122 BC. The legendary founder was T'ang. The Shang civilization was agriculturally and technically advanced, and is famed for the artistic quality of its bronzes.

SHANGHAI, China's largest city, in SE Kiangsu province. It is a major seaport and a leading commercial and industrial center, producing textiles, iron and steel, ships, petroleum products and a wide range of manufactured goods. In 1842 it was one of the first Chinese ports opened by treaty to foreign trade. Britain (1843), France (1849) and the US (1862) gained concessions to develop the city, and most of it remained under foreign control until after WWII. The British and US concessions were renounced in 1945. Shanghai is now China's film capital and the home of 190 research institutes, colleges and universities. Pop (city) 6,292,960; (metro) 11,785,100.

SHANKAR, Ravi (1920–   ), Indian sitar player. A virtuoso performer, he stimulated interest in Indian classical music throughout the world with his frequent concert appearances and numerous recordings.

SHANKER, Albert (1928–   ), US labor leader. A New York City public school teacher 1952–59, he was active in the teachers' drive for unionization and led strikes over pay and noneconomic issues as president of the United Federation of Teachers 1964–74. He has headed the American Federation of Teachers since 1974.

SHANNON, Claude Elwood (1916–   ), US mathematician who created modern INFORMATION THEORY. He also applied Boolean algebra to the theory of electrical switching circuits.

SHANNON RIVER, chief river in Ireland and longest (240mi) in the British Isles. It rises in N Cavan and flows S and W through several loughs (lakes) into the Atlantic Ocean.

SHAPIRO, Karl (1913–   ), US poet and literary critic. His early poetry, such as *V-Letter and Other Poems* (1944; Pulitzer Prize, 1945), shows the influence of AUDEN and was admired for its verbal conceits. Later work, such as *The Bourgeois Poet* (1964), became more Whitmanesque. His *Collected Poems: 1948–1978* appeared in 1978.

SHAPLEY, Harlow (1885–1972), US astronomer who suggested that CEPHEID VARIABLES are not eclipsing binaries (see DOUBLE STAR) but pulsating stars. He was also the first to deduce the structure and approximate size of the MILKY WAY galaxy, and the position of the sun within it.

SHAPUR, name of two Persian kings of the Sassanian dynasty. **Shapur I** (d. 272 AD), king c241–72, expanded and consolidated his kingdom and decisively defeated the Romans under VALERIAN at Edessa. **Shapur II** (309–379) was proclaimed king at birth. A great general, he brought the Sassanian

empire to the height of its power. Defeating and killing the Roman emperor JULIAN THE APOSTATE in battle, he imposed a humiliating peace on his successor Jovian and annexed Armenia.

SHARAKU TOSHUSAI (18th century), Japanese color-print artist. Himself a professional NOH dancer, in 1794–95 he produced over 136 striking prints of KABUKI theater performers.

SHARANSKY, Natan (Anatoly Borisovich Shcharansky; 1948–   ), Soviet Jewish dissident. A mathematician and computer scientist, he became an active dissident in the 1970s, agitating for human rights and free Jewish emigration. After nine years in prison and labor camps (1977–86) on charges of espionage, he was exchanged for a Soviet spy held in the West. He settled in Isreal.

SHARECROPPING, arrangement whereby a share of a tenant farmer's yearly land yield (usually 50%) went to the landowner in lieu of rent. The tenant provided the labor, while the landowner provided land, equipment and often loans to buy seed. The system was notorious for its abuses.

SHARE-THE-WEALTH MOVEMENTS, inflationary economic programs which arose in the US during the early 1930s, reflecting the anxieties of the Great Depression and hopes of a technological utopia. They sought to redistribute wealth and guarantee minimum incomes without destroying the capitalist system. Notable were the Townsend Plan for old-age pensions, the National Union for Social Justice and Huey LONG's Share-Our-Wealth clubs. They died out after the 1935 Social Security Act was passed.

SHARETT, Moshe (1894–1965), Russian-born Israeli Labor politician, close associate of David BEN-GURION in the creation of Isreal. He served as foreign minister (1948–53) and prime minister (1953–55).

SHARI'A, the Islamic sacred law. Based on divine revelation, it governs all human actions, which it classifies in five grades ranging from absolutely obligatory to absolutely prohibited. It still constitutes the civil law in Saudi Arabia, but other Muslim countries have modified it.

SHARIF, in the Islamic world, an honorific title usually reserved for descendants of Hasan, grandson of Mohammed. Traditionally, the most prominent sharif became ruler of Mecca and Medina.

SHARKS, an order, Pleurotremata, of about 250 species of cartilaginous fishes of marine and fresh waters. Sharks, with the related rays and chimaeras, have a skeleton formed entirely of CARTILAGE. Other distinguishing features are that the GILLS open externally through a series of gill-slits, rather than through a single operculum, and reproduction is by internal fertilization, unlike that of bony fishes. The body is fusiform and the upper lobe of the tail is usually better developed than the lower lobe. Sharks swim by sinuous movements of the whole body; there is no swimbladder and they must swim constantly to avoid sinking. All are extremely fast swimmers and active predators. Despite a universal reputation for unprovoked attack, only 27 out of the 250 known species have been definitely implicated in attacks on man.

SHARON, Ariel (1928–   ), Israeli general and politician. In the 1973 Arab-Israeli war he led Israeli troops across the Suez Canal, cutting off an Egyptian army. As defense minister (1981–82) under Menachem BEGIN he directed the 1982 Israeli invasion of Lebanon. Criticized for his "indirect responsibility" for the massacre of Palestinians in Beirut refugee camps carried out by the Lebanese Christian militia, he resigned the defense portfolio but was soon appointed (1984) minister of industry and commerce.

SHARP, Granville (1735–1813), English abolitionist, philanthropist and biblical scholar. He obtained a ruling (1772) by which slavery was declared illegal in British possessions. A vigorous political and biblical pamphleteer, he founded the Association for the Abolition of Slavery (1787).

SHARPSBURG, Battle of, alternative name for the Battle of ANTIETAM.

SHATT-AL-ARAB, river formed by the confluence of the Tigris R and Euphrates R in SE Iraq. It flows 120mi SE into the Persian Gulf, and forms part of the Iran-Iraq border.

SHAVUOT, Jewish festival celebrated on the sixth and seventh days of the month of Sivan (usually May). Originally an agricultural festival, it commemorates the receiving of the TORAH on Mt Sinai.

SHAW, George Bernard (1856–1950), British dramatist, critic and political propagandist whose witty plays contained serious philosophical and social ideas. Born in Dublin, he went to London (1876) and became a music and theater critic and a leader of the FABIAN SOCIETY. He began writing his brilliantly witty, ironical and polemical comedies in the 1890s. Success came with such plays as *Major Barbara* (1905), *Caesar and Cleopatra* (1906; written 1899), *Androcles and the Lion* (1912) and *Pygmalion* (1913; later adapted as a musical, *My Fair Lady*). He lost popularity for his opposition to WWI, but regained it with *Back to Methuselah* (1921); *St. Joan* (1923), his greatest success, was followed by the 1925 Nobel Prize in Literature. He continued to write up to his death.

SHAW, Irwin (1913–1984), US novelist, short story writer and playwright who lived in Europe after 1951. Concerned with large-scale social and political issues, many of Shaw's works pit "gentle people" against the forces of a morally sick American society. Among his best known novels are *The Young Lions* (1948), *Rich Man, Poor Man* (1970) and *Beggarman, Thief* (1977).

SHAW, Lemuel (1781–1861), US judge. He was chief justice of the Mass. supreme court 1830–60, and many of his decisions influenced succeeding law.

SHAW, Robert Gould (1837–1863), US Union CIVIL WAR hero. Black himself, he led the first regiment of black troops to be raised in a free state. He was killed attacking Fort Wagner, S.C.

SHAWN, Ted (Edwin Meyers Shawn; 1891–1972), US dancer, choreographer and teacher. With his wife, Ruth ST. DENIS, he founded the Denishawn school and company. He led an all-male company of dancers, 1933–40, and in 1941 established an international dance center at Jacob's Pillow in Mass.

SHAWNEE INDIANS, North American tribe of the Algonquian language group. They settled in the Ohio Valley during the 18th century, hunting and cultivating maize. In 1811, the Shawnee chief TECUMSEH attempted to unite the Indian tribes of the region, but his plan failed when the Shawnee were defeated at TIPPECANOE. They were eventually resettled in Okla., where about 2,250 still live.

SHAWNEE PROPHET. See TENSKWATAWA.

SHAYS'S REBELLION, Aug. 1786–Feb. 1787, an armed uprising in Mass., led by Daniel Shays (c1747–1825) to protest high taxes and the severity of legal action against debtors during the postwar depression. The insurgents forced courts to drop actions against debtors, but were defeated attacking a federal arsenal. The uprising led to some reforms.

SHEBA. See SABAEANS.

SHEELER, Charles (1883–1965), US painter and photographer who was fascinated by the abstract geometric shapes he found in industry and architecture.

SHEEN, Fulton John (1895–1979), US Roman Catholic archbishop, widely known in the US for his popular inspirational radio and television talks, and for his strong conservative stance on many issues.

SHEEP, a diverse genus of mammals best known in the various races of the domestic sheep *Ovis aries* bred for both MEAT and WOOL. Wild sheep are a diverse group of mountain-dwelling forms with some 37 races alive today. They divide into two large groups: the Asiatic sheep, which include the mouflons, urials and argalis, and the American sheep, the thinhorns and bighorns. Asiatic sheep are long-legged, lightly-built animals which prefer a gentle rolling terrain. American-type sheep by comparison are heavy-set and barrel-chested, and characteristic of steep slopes and rocky areas, in part filling the role played in Europe and Asia by the IBEX. Sheep are social animals; males usually form bands following a dominant ram and females form separate parties following a mature ewe. The rams use their horns and the specially-thickened bone of their foreheads for combat, not only in the rut but also in dominance struggles.

SHEFFIELD PLATE, articles made from SILVER plated on copper by a method of fusion involving heat and pressure, discovered about 1743 by a Sheffield cutler, Thomas Boulsover. This method was widely used before the advent of electroplating.

SHEIKH, an Arabic title of respect applied to a worthy man over 50 years old, also to chiefs of families, villages and tribes, and to religious leaders.

SHELBY, Isaac (1750–1826), US frontier leader who defeated the British at KING'S MOUNTAIN (1780) and planned the action at COWPENS (1781). He was the first governor of Kentucky, 1792–96. In the WAR OF 1812 he led volunteers who helped defeat the British at the Battle of the Thames in Ontario.

SHELEKHOV, Grigori Ivanovich (1747–1795), Russian merchant who organized an expedition to Alaska (1783) and founded the first Russian colony there (1784). His company later developed into the Russian American Company (1799).

SHELL, any calcareous external covering secreted by an invertebrate, enclosing and protecting the body. The term is used particularly for the shells of MOLLUSKS, but also refers to those of FORAMINIFERANS, and may be used loosely to describe the carapace or chitinous EXOSKELETON of CRUSTACEANS and INSECTS.

SHELLEY, Mary Wollstonecraft (1797–1851), English writer, daughter of William GODWIN and Mary WOLLSTONECRAFT and wife of Percy Bysshe SHELLEY. Her best-known work is the Gothic horror-story *Frankenstein* (1818). She wrote several other novels and edited Shelley's poems.

SHELLEY, Percy Bysshe (1792–1822), English Romantic poet whose work reflects his revolutionary political idealism and his strong faith in the spiritual power of the imagination. It includes long narrative poems such as *Queen Mab* (1813), *The Revolt of Islam* (1818) and *Epipsychidion* (1821), the verse drama *Prometheus Unbound* (1820) and such famous lyrics as the "Ode to the West Wind." He was drowned in a boating accident in Italy, where he had settled with his second wife, Mary.

SHENANDOAH NATIONAL PARK, in the Appalachian Mts, N Va. Covering about 300sq mi along the crest of the Blue Ridge Mts, it is heavily wooded and affords magnificent views along the Skyline Drive, which runs its whole length.

SHENANDOAH VALLEY, between the Allegheny and Blue Ridge Mts in NW Va. About 150mi long and up to 25mi wide, it is a rich farming area famed for its natural beauty. It was the scene of the CIVIL WAR Shenandoah Valley Campaigns (1862–64).

SHEPARD, Alan Bartlett Jr. (1923–   ), first US astronaut (May 5, 1961). He was later grounded by a medical complaint, but overcame this to command the Apollo 14 moon-landing (Jan. 31, 1971).

SHEPARD, Sam (1943–   ), US avant-garde playwright noted for his almost cinematic inventiveness in such plays as *Operation Sidewinder* (1970). His books include *The Unseen Hand, and Other Plays* (1971) and *Mad Dog Blues, and Other Plays* (1972). He won the Pulitzer Prize for *Buried Child* (1979).

SHERATON, Thomas (1751–1806), English furniture designer. His elegant style of furniture was popular around 1800, and his *Cabinet-Maker and Upholsterer's Drawing Book* (1791–94) was very influential.

SHERIDAN, Philip Henry (1831–1888), US general and Union CIVIL WAR hero. After successes in the Chattanooga and Wilderness campaigns, he commanded the army which defeated General Early and devastated the Shenandoah Valley (1864). In 1865 he won the Battle of Five Forks and helped end the war by cutting off Robert E. LEE's line of retreat from Appomattox. He became commander of the US army 1884.

SHERIDAN, Richard Brinsley (1751–1816), Irish-born English dramatist and politician famous for his witty comedies of manners, including *The Rivals* (1775), *The School for Scandal* (1777) and *The Critic* (1779). A Whig member of Parliament (1780–1812), he played a leading part in the impeachment of Warren HASTINGS.

SHERLOCK HOLMES. See DOYLE, SIR ARTHUR CONAN.

SHERMAN, two brothers important in the CIVIL WAR era. **William Tecumseh Sherman** (1820–1891) was a Union commander, second in importance only to General Ulysses S. GRANT. He fought in the battles of BULL RUN (1861), SHILOH (1862) and in the Vicksburg campaign (1862–63). He was given command of the Army of Tennessee and, with Grant, took part in the Chattanooga Campaign (1863). As supreme commander in the West (1864) he invaded Ga., capturing Atlanta and marching on Savannah. He then turned N, pushing General Joseph Johnston's army before him, and accepting its surrender at Durham, N.C., in April, 1865. The destruction he wrought in his attempt to destroy Confederate supplies and communications and break civilian morale made him a hero in the N and a villain in the S. He was US army commander 1869–84. **John Sherman** (1823–1900) was a founding member of the REPUBLICAN PARTY. A senator 1861–77 and 1881–97, and secretary of the treasury 1877–81, he introduced the SHERMAN ANTITRUST ACT and the Sherman Silver Purchase Act.

SHERMAN, James Schoolcraft (1855–1912), US Republican politician, vice-president under W. H. Taft 1909–12. He was a member of the House of Representatives 1887–91, 1893–1909.

SHERMAN, Roger (1721–1793), American patriot who helped draft, and signed, the Declaration of Independence. He was a member of the 1787 Constitutional Convention and, with Oliver ELLSWORTH, introduced the "Connecticut Compromise." (See UNITED STATES CONSTITUTION.) He was US representative (1789–91) and senator (1791–93) for Conn.

SHERMAN ANTITRUST ACT (1890), first major federal action to curb the power of the giant business MONOPOLIES which grew up after the Civil War. Its failure to define key terms, such as *trust, combination* and *restraint of trade*, led to loopholes, and it was strengthened by the CLAYTON ANTITRUST ACT (1914).

SHERMAN SILVER PURCHASE ACT (1890), a compromise measure aiming to placate mineowners and the advocates of FREE SILVER, which required the US government to double its monthly silver purchases. It threatened to undermine gold reserves and was repealed when the panic of 1893 began.

SHERPA, Buddhist people of NE Nepal, famous as Himalayan guides. Of Tibetan origins and speaking a Tibetan language, they number some 85,000 and raise cattle, grow crops and spin wool in the high valleys of the Himalayas.

SHERRINGTON, Sir Charles Scott (1857–1952), British neurophysiologist who shared with E. D. Adrian the 1932 Nobel Prize for Physiology or Medicine for studies of the NERVOUS SYSTEM which form the basis of our modern understanding of its action.

SHERRY, an alcoholic beverage named for Jérez de la Frontera, Spain, where it originated. It is an aperitif wine, matured in wooden casks and fortified with brandy to bring the alcohol level to about 20% by volume.

SHERWOOD, Robert Emmet (1896–1955), US playwright who won four Pulitzer prizes: for *Idiot's Delight* (1936), *Abe Lincoln in Illinois* (1938), *There Shall Be No Night* (1940) and his biography *Roosevelt and Hopkins: An Intimate History* (1948).

SHETLAND ISLANDS, archipelago of some 100 islands off N Scotland, constituting its northernmost county. Less than a quarter are inhabited; Lerwick is the chief town and port. The main occupations are fishing and cattle and sheep raising. The Shetlands are famous for their knitted woolen goods and the SHETLAND PONY.

SHETLAND PONY, tiny and shaggy-haired, the smallest of the PONIES, probably a relict of prehistoric British and Scandinavian HORSES. Once restricted to the Shetland Islands, it has now been widely bred as a riding pony for children.

SHEVARDNADZE, Eduard Amvrosiyevich (1928–   ), Soviet foreign minister from 1985, succeeding Andrei Gromyko. He was named first secretary of the Georgian Communist Party (1972), a member of the Central Committee of the national Communist Party (1976), and a full member of the Politburo (1985).

SHIH-HUANG-TI (259 BC–210 BC), "First Sovereign Emperor," title assumed in 221 BC by King Cheng of Ch'in (NW China) when he had created a unified Chinese empire and founded the CH'IN dynasty. He created the centralized government that was the model for all succeeding dynasties, and built the GREAT WALL OF CHINA.

SHI'ITES, members of an Islamic sect opposed to the orthodox SUNNITES. The Shi'ites reject the first three caliphs and recognize Ali (Mohammed's son-in-law) and his descendants as rightful successors to Mohammed. They number some 40,000,000, concentrated principally in Iran and Iraq.

SHIKOKU, smallest of the four principal islands (7,245sq mi in area) of Japan situated S of Honshu and E of Kyushu. With a subtropical climate, it produces tea, camphor, rice, fruit and tobacco.

SHILOH, Battle of, major conflict of the US CIVIL WAR, fought at Pittsburgh Landing, Tenn. (April 6–7, 1862). The Union army under General Ulysses S. GRANT was forced back by a surprise onslaught of the 40,000-strong Confederate army under General A. S. Johnston. The reinforced Union army routed the Confederates in a counterattack the next day. Casualties were over 10,000 on each side.

SHIMONOSEKI, Treaty of, April 1895, treaty which ended the first SINO-JAPANESE WAR, 1894–95. China's defeat led to Korea's independence and Japan's acquisition of Taiwan and the Pescadores Islands.

SHINGLES, or **herpes zoster,** a VIRUS disorder characterized by development of pain, a vesicular rash and later scarring, often with persistent pain, over the SKIN of part of the face or trunk. The virus seems to settle in or near nerve cells following CHICKENPOX, which is caused by the same virus, and then becomes activated, perhaps years later and sometimes by disease. It then leads to the acute skin eruption which follows the path of the nerve involved.

SHINN, Everett (1876–1953), US painter, member of the ASHCAN SCHOOL. He is best known for his pictures of the theater and music hall world, such as *Revue* (1908).

SHINTO (way of the gods), indigenous religion of Japan originally based on the belief that the royal family was descended from the sun-goddess Amaterasu Omikami. It later absorbed much Buddhist thought and practice. At its core is the idea that *kami* (divine power) is manifest at every moment in every thing; hence attention paid to each moment, however trivial, will lead to the realization of truth. Shinto shrines are plain wooden buildings in which priest and people perform simple rites; the imperial shrine is at Ise. Worship of the emperor and the ZEN influence on martial arts resulted in a close connection between Shinto and Japanese militarism. State Shinto ended after WWII.

SHIP MONEY, in English history, originally an emergency tax for naval defense in wartime. CHARLES I's attempt (1634–39) to establish it as a general and permanent tax was a cause of the English CIVIL WAR.

SHIPS AND SHIPPING, large seagoing vessels and their uses for transport and warfare. The first ships were probably developed from river craft by the Mesopotamians and Egyptians as early as the 4th millennium BC, and the Mediterranean became the home of the first sea-based civilizations. Early ships had a single sail on a fixed yard-arm, a stern oar for a rudder, and one or more banks of oars, a classic example being the Greek trireme. There is evidence that the Phoenicians ventured in such ships as far as Britain and around Africa before 600 BC. Under the Roman Empire the whole Mediterranean was controlled by a navy, and grain-carrying galleys up to 180ft long were built.

In medieval Europe the VIKING longships developed into square-rigged galleons, with fixed stern rudders. These were capable of long sea voyages, and the 15th and 16th centuries saw the great world explorations of Christopher COLUMBUS, Vasco da GAMA and Ferdinand MAGELLAN. In the age of colonial expansion, world trade and naval rivalry which followed, large navies and shipping fleets developed rapidly, and the great "men o' war" and the grain CLIPPER SHIPS represented the culmination of the age of sail.

A steamship first crossed the Atlantic in 1819, and the screw-driven *Great Eastern* (1858) was the first large iron ship. By the early 20th century steel construction and steam turbines dominated, and passenger liners, warships and cargo ships increased spectacularly in size and power. Modern developments include SUBMARINES, AIRCRAFT CARRIERS, nuclear-powered vessels and supertankers of up to 500,000 tons. (See also BATTLESHIP; NAVIGATION; NAVY; YACHTS AND YACHTING.)

SHIPWORM, despite its name, a bivalve MOLLUSK, *Teredo navalis,* notorious for burrowing into the timbers of piers and wooden ships. The body is long and wormlike, with the shell reduced to a tiny pair of abrasive plates at the head end. These are used for rasping into wood—at a rate sometimes exceeding 300mm (1ft) per month.

SHIRER, William Lawrence (1904–   ), US newspaper and radio correspondent in pre-WWII Europe, author of the best-sellers *Berlin Diary* (1941) and *Rise and Fall of the Third Reich* (1960).

SHIVA, important deity of HINDUISM, representing that aspect of the Godhead connected with the destruction necessary for renewal of life. He is sometimes depicted as an ascetic youth. In the role of recreator he is called the happy one. His phallic emblem is worshipped.

SHIVERING, fine contractions of MUSCLES, causing slight repetitive movements, employed for increasing heat production by the body, thus raising body temperature in conditions of cold or when DISEASE induces FEVER. Uncontrollable shivering with gross movements of the whole body is a rigor seen only in some fevers.

SHOCK specifically refers to the development of low blood pressure, inadequate to sustain BLOOD CIRCULATION, usually causing cold, clammy, gray SKIN and extremities, faintness and mental confusion and decreased urine production. It is caused by acute blood loss; burns with PLASMA loss; acute HEART failure; massive pulmonary EMBOLISM, and SEPTICEMIA. If untreated, death ensues. Early replacement of plasma or BLOOD and administration of DRUGS to improve blood circulation are necessary to prevent permanent BRAIN damage and acute KIDNEY failure.

SHOCK THERAPY, or electroconvulsive therapy (ECT), is a form of treatment used in MENTAL ILLNESS, particularly DEPRESSION, in which carefully regulated electric shocks are given to the BRAINS of anesthetized patients. (Muscle relaxants are used to prevent injury through forceful MUSCLE contractions.) The mode of action is unknown but rapid resolution of severe depression may be achieved.

SHOE, protective covering for the foot. The various types include the boot, whose upper extends above the ankle; the clog, a simple wooden-soled shoe; the moccasin, a hunting shoe whose sole extends around and over the foot; the sandal, an open shoe whose sole is secured to the foot by straps, and the slipper, a soft indoor shoe. Shoes have been made from earliest times, the type depending mainly on the climate; clogs, sandals and moccasins predominated until the early Middle Ages, since when boots and typical shoes in widely varying styles have been most popular. LEATHER has always been the main material used, shaped on a *last* of wood or metal, and hand-sewn, the sole being nailed to the upper. In the mid-19th century the SEWING MACHINE was adapted for sewing shoes, and nailing and gluing were also mechanized, allowing mass-production. Other materials have to some extent displaced leather—natural and synthetic RUBBER for the sole and heel, and various PLASTICS and synthetic fibers for the upper.

SHOGUN, title of the hereditary military commanders of Japan who usurped the power of the emperor in the 12th century and ruled the country for about 700 years. In 1867 the last TOKUGAWA shogun was forced to resign and restore sovereignty to the emperor.

SHOLEM ALEICHEM (1859–1916), pseudonym of Solomon Rabinovitch, Russian-born YIDDISH humorous writer. He was an immensely prolific and popular author, and his novels, short stories and plays tell of the serious and absurd aspects of Jewish life in E Europe. His works include *The Old Country* and *Tevye's Daughters.*

SHOLES, Christopher Latham (1819–1890), US inventor (with some help from others) of the TYPEWRITER (patented 1868). He sold his patent rights to the Remington Arms Company in 1873.

SHOLOKHOV, Mikhail Alexandrovich (1905–1984), Russian novelist awarded the Nobel Prize in Literature (1965). He is best known for his stories about the Don Cossacks of S Russia. His greatest work is *And Quiet Flows the Don* (1928–40).

SHORTHAND, or stenography, any writing system permitting the rapid transcription of speech. The three most used today are Isaac Pitman Shorthand, the first to be commercially developed (c1837), and Gregg Shorthand, developed c1888 by John Robert Gregg, both of which are phonetic, using symbols to represent recurring sounds; and Speedwriting, which uses abbreviations. Shorthand is much used by secretaries, journalists, court reporters, etc. (See also STENOTYPE.)

SHORT PARLIAMENT, convened by the English king CHARLES I in April 1640 to finance the Scottish war. The House of Commons wanted first to settle major grievances, so the king dissolved Parliament in May. (See English CIVIL WAR.)

SHORTSIGHTEDNESS. See MYOPIA.

SHORT STORY, form of prose fiction, usually limited in character and situation, and between 500 and 20,000 words long. CHAUCER'S *Canterbury Tales* and BOCCACCIO'S *Decameron* are prototypes of short stories. The art form was revived in the 19th century, and prominent short story writers have been POE, MAUPASSANT, CHEKHOV, O. HENRY, JAMES, MANSFIELD, HEMINGWAY and O'HARA.

SHOSHONE INDIANS, group of North American Indians originally inhabiting the territory between SE Cal. and W Wyo. The Shoshone of E Utah and Wyo. were typical buffalo-hunting tribesmen of the plains. In the 18th century the COMANCHE Indians split off and moved S to modern Tex. There are about 8,000 Shoshone on reservation lands today.

SHOSTAKOVICH, Dmitri (1906–1975), Russian composer. Some of his music is notably patriotic. His works include the opera *Lady Macbeth of Mzensk* (1934) and

15 symphonies of which the most famous are the Fifth (1937), the Seventh, "the Leningrad," written during the siege of Leningrad (1941), and the Tenth (1953). His important works of chamber music include the *Piano Quintet* (1940).

SHOT PUT. See TRACK AND FIELD.

SHREWS, small mouse-like insectivorous mammals with short legs and long pointed noses. They have narrow skulls and sharp, rather unspecialized teeth for feeding on insects, earthworms and small mammal carrion. They are highly active creatures. The somewhat indigestible nature of their food, combined with the high energy consumption of their constant activity, means that they may eat two to three times their own weight of food in a day. Having a pulse rate sometimes approaching 1,000 beats a minute, few shrews live longer than one year. Family: Soricidae.

SHRIKES, aggressive and predatory passerine birds of the family Laniidae, which kill insects, birds or small mammals with their hooked bill. Because they store their victims impaled on thorns like the carcasses hung in a butcher's shop, they are often called butcherbirds. They have a worldwide distribution, living on the edges of woods and forests.

SHRIMP, decapod CRUSTACEANS (suborder Natantia) which use their abdominal limbs to swim instead of crawling like LOBSTERS or CRABS. The body, more or less cylindrical and translucent, bears five pairs of walking legs and two pairs of very long antennae. The eyes are stalked. Shrimp are mostly scavengers or predators and may be found in the open ocean, inshore, in estuaries and even in freshwater. They are fished for food worldwide.

SHROVE TUESDAY, the last day before Lent begins (see ASH WEDNESDAY). It is a traditional day for MARDI GRAS carnivals such as those in New Orleans and Rio de Janeiro.

SHUBERT, family of Russian-born US theater owners and producers. **Lee Shubert** (1873?–1953) and **Jacob Shubert** (1880?–1963) produced vaudeville, operettas, and plays, and at one time controlled 75% of all US theaters.

SHUBUN (flourished early 15th century), Japanese ink painter. His masterly works, many of them landscapes, led to the development of the distinctively Japanese style.

SHULTZ, George Pratt (1920–   ), US secretary of state (1982–89). A former dean of the Graduate School of Business at the University of Chicago, in the Nixon administration he was secretary of labor (1969–70), director of the Office of Management and Budget (1970–72), and secretary of the treasury (1972–74). He was president of the Bechtel Corporation when President Ronald Reagan appointed him to succeed Alexander HAIG as secretary of state.

SIAM. See THAILAND.

SIAMESE TWINS, twins that are physically joined at some part of their anatomy due to a defect in early separation. A variable depth of fusion is seen, most commonly at the head or trunk. SURGERY may be used to separate the twins if no vital organs are shared.

SIAN or **Xian,** city in NE central China, ancient capital of China for 11 dynasties. Today it is a major transportation and industrial center. The scene of CHIANG KAI-SHEK's kidnapping in 1936, it is famous for fabulous archeological finds of life-size terra-cotta warriors and horses at the tomb of Emperor Qin Shi Huang. There are large steel, chemical and textile industries. Pop (metro) 2,285,040.

SIBELIUS, Jean (1865–1957), Finnish composer. His most famous work is *Finlandia* (1900), which expressed his country's growing nationalist feeling. He composed a number of tone poems such as *En Saga* (1892), which evokes the physical beauty and ancient legends of Finland. His works include many pieces for violin and for piano and seven symphonies.

SIBERIA, vast indefinite area of land (about 4,000,000sq mi) in N Asian USSR between the Ural Mts in the W and the Pacific Ocean in the E, forming most of the Russian SFSR. The landscape varies from the Arctic tundra to the great forest zone in the S and the steppes of the W. Summers are mild in most parts, winters extremely severe (as low as −90°F in some parts). Most of the people are Russian; Yakuts, Buryats and Tuvans form autonomous republics. The largest cities are Novosibirsk, Omsk, Krasnoyarsk, Irkutsk and Vladivostok. Siberia has rich natural resources—farmland, forests, fisheries and such minerals as coal, iron ore, tungsten, gold and natural gas. Industrial centers have developed in the regions of Krasnoyarsk and Lake Baikal (the world's deepest lake) and one of the world's largest hydroelectric plants is near Bratsk. Siberia was inhabited in prehistoric times. Russians conquered much of Siberia by 1598. Political prisoners were first sent to Siberia in 1710 and forced-labor camps still exist. The TRANS-SIBERIAN RAILROAD (1905) led to large-scale colonization and economic development.

SICILIAN VESPERS, Sicilian revolt in 1282 against the Angevin French king of Naples and Sicily, Charles I. It led to his overthrow and Aragonese control of Sicily. After killing French soldiers at Vespers on Easter Monday in Palermo, Sicilians massacred 2,000 French inhabitants of the town.

SICILY, largest Mediterranean island (9,925sq mi); part of Italy, but with its own parliament at the capital, Palermo. Its most notable feature is the active volcano, Mt Etna (height varies around 10,900ft). Much of the island is mountainous, but there are lowlands along the coasts. About half the population live in the coastal towns Palermo, Catania, Messina and Syracuse. Agriculture is the mainstay of the economy, though hampered by the low rainfall and feudal land-tenure system. Wheat is the staple crop; grapes, citrus fruits and olives are also grown. Main exports, from Ragusa, are petroleum products. Sicily was the site of Greek, Phoenician and Roman colonies before conquest by the Arabs, who in turn were ousted by Robert Guiscard, the Norman conqueror. The SICILIAN VESPERS (1282) led to Spanish rule, ended by GARIBALDI (1860). In WWII, Sicily was conquered by the Allies (1943) and used as a base for attack on Italy.

SICKERT, Walter Richard (1860–1942), British painter. Trained by WHISTLER and DEGAS, he was from 1905 the main link between English and French art. His scenes of music halls and low-class life are executed in a rich and direct style.

SICKLE CELL ANEMIA, one of many hereditary blood diseases caused by abnormal hemoglobin in the red blood cells. Rather than the normal disk shape, the red cells of persons with this disease have distorted sickle or crescent shapes when their oxygen supply is low. It is from this unusual appearance of the red blood corpuscles that the disease and its abnormal hemoglobin derive their names, the hemoglobin being known as the sickle hemoglobin or hemoglobin S.

The disease was first described by J.B. Herrick in 1910, but it was not until 1949 that Linus Pauling and his associates demonstrated the basic defect to be in the hemoglobin molecule of the red blood cells. Since the discovery of the sickle hemoglobin, more than 100 other abnormal hemoglobins have been described.

Persons who are carriers of sickle cell anemia but do not have the disease are said to have the sickle cell trait, or sicklemia. If a person has both the sickle hemoglobin and other abnormal hemoglobin in his red blood cells, he has a sickle cell variant. The term sickle cell disease is often used to refer to all these states—sickle cell anemia, sickle cell trait and sickle cell variants.

SIDDHARTHA GAUTAMA. See BUDDHA.

SIDDONS, Sarah (*née* Kemble; 1755–1831), English actress who first appeared in London (without success) at the request of GARRICK (1775). She returned at the request of SHERIDAN (1782), and became the leading tragic actress of her day.

SIDEREAL TIME, time referred to the rotation of the earth with respect to the fixed stars. The sidereal DAY is about four minutes shorter than the solar day since the earth moves each day about 1/365 of its orbit about the sun. Sidereal time is used in astronomy when determining the locations of celestial bodies.

SIDEWINDERS, several species of snake, especially of the RATTLESNAKES, which exhibit a peculiar sideways looping motion when moving rapidly. The name is particularly applied to the horned rattlesnake, *Crotalus cerastis*, of the southwestern US.

SIDNEY, Algernon (1622–1683), English politician executed for his alleged part in the RYE HOUSE PLOT to overthrow CHARLES II. His *Discourses Concerning Government* (1698) contributed to the ideology of the American Revolution.

SIDNEY, Sir Philip (1554–1586), Elizabethan poet and courtier, a favorite with the queen and a model of RENAISSANCE chivalry. He had great influence on English poetry, both through his poems, of which the best known are *Arcadia* (c1580) and the love sonnets *Astrophel and Stella* (1591), and through his critical work, *The Defence of Poesie* (1595).

SIDON, great commercial city of ancient PHOENICIA, on the Lebanese coast. Founded in the 3rd millennium BC, it is mentioned in the Bible and in HOMER. It was famed for its purple dyes and glassware.

SIEGFRIED, legendary figure of outstanding strength and courage. He appears in both the Icelandic EDDA and the 13th-century German NIBELUNGENLIED epic, and is the hero of WAGNER's operas *Siegfried* and *Die Götterdämmerung*.

SIEGFRIED LINE, defensive line built on the German W frontier in the 1930s which delayed the US advance in 1944–45.

SIEGMEISTER, Elie (1909–   ), US composer. An authority on American folk music, he wrote for chamber groups and orchestra such works as *Ozark Set* (1943) and a concerto for clarinet (1956) and composed the score for the Broadway production *Sing Out, Sweet Land* (1944).

SIEMENS, German family of technologists and industrialists. **Ernst Werner von Siemens** (1816–1892) invented, among other things, an electroplating process (patented 1842), a differential governor (c1844), and a regenerative STEAM ENGINE, the principle of which was developed by his brothers **Friedrich** (1826–1904) and then **Karl Wilhelm** (1823–1883), later **Sir (Charles) William Siemens**, to form the basis of the open-hearth process. Ernst and Sir William both made many important contributions to TELEGRAPH science, culminating in the laying from the *Faraday*, a ship designed by William, of the ATLANTIC CABLE of 1874 by the company he owned.

SIENA, city in Tuscany, Italy, famous for its GOTHIC ARCHITECTURE and the RENAISSANCE art of DONATELLO, LORENZETTI and PISANO. Its main square is the scene of the historic and colorful *Palio* horse races every summer. Pop 65,700.

SIENKIEWICZ, Henryk (1846–1916), Polish novelist awarded the 1905 Nobel Prize in Literature. His greatest works are a trilogy about 17th-century Poland—*With Fire and Sword* (1884), *The Deluge* (1886) and *Pan Michael* (1888)—and the internationally famous *Quo Vadis?* (1896).

SIERRA LEONE, republic in W Africa on the Atlantic Ocean, sharing a common border with Guinea on the NW, N and NE, and with Liberia on the SE.

Official name: Republic of Sierre Leone
Capital: Freetown
Area: 27,699sq mi
Population: 3,803,000
Languages: English; Krio, Mende, Temne
Religions: Animist, Muslim, Christian
Monetary unit(s): 1 leone = 100 cents
Land. It consists of a swampy coastal area, wooded inland plains crossed by several rivers and rising grassland in the N. The climate is tropical, with an average temperature of 79°F and annual rainfall of 90–150in.
People. The indigenous population includes over 18 tribes, the Mende of the S and the Temne of the N predominating. The Limba

and the Kono are also important ethnic groups. The Creoles, descendants of freed slaves, mainly from the Americas, live around Freetown, the capital and chief port. Bo, Kenema and Port Loko are other urban centers.
Economy. The economy is heavily dependent on diamond mining and production of cocoa and coffee. Rice is the chief food crop. Cattle are raised in the N, pigs and poultry in the W.
History. Named by the Portuguese in 1460, the coastal area became the haunt of slavers: in 1787 the English abolitionist Granville Sharp settled freed slaves there. In 1808 it became a British colony. Independent from 1961, Sierra Leone was declared a republic in 1971 under the presidency of Siaka Stevens, who remained president until his retirement in 1985.

SIERRA MADRE, great mountain system of Mexico. The E range (*Sierra Madre Oriental*) stretches 1,000mi S from the Rio Grande, forming the E edge of the central plateau and reaching 18,700ft in Orizaba (Citlaltépetl). The *Sierra Madre Occidental*, running SW from Ariz. and N.M., borders the plateau on the W, rising to over 10,000ft. The *Sierra Madre de Sur* parallels the SW coast.

SIERRA NEVADA, mountain range, 420mi long, in E Cal., including Mt Whitney (14,494ft), the highest mountain in the US outside Alaska. The spectacular scenery of the three national parks, Yosemite, Kings Canyon and Sequoia, makes the Sierra Nevada a popular vacation area.

SIEYÈS, Emmanuel Joseph (1748–1836), theorist of the FRENCH REVOLUTION and author of *Qu'est-ce que le Tiers État?* (1789). He advocated national sovereignty and organized the National Assembly. Joining the Directory in 1799 he took part in the coup of 18 Brumaire that brought NAPOLEON I to power.

SIGISMUND (1368–1437), Holy Roman Emperor from 1433 and king of Hungary from 1387, of Germany from 1410 and of Bohemia from 1419. He was involved in continual wars to maintain his power against other claimants, HUS's followers and the Turks.

SIGNAC, Paul (1863–1935), French painter, leading theorist of neo-impressionism. A friend of Georges SEURAT, he developed POINTILLISM, painting many views of ports, like *Port of St. Tropez* (1894).

SIGN LANGUAGE, any system of communication using gesture (usually of the hand and arm) rather than speech. The most comprehensive sign language in modern use is that employed by the deaf and dumb, but sophisticated sign languages are also used by many primitive peoples to communicate with other tribes.

SIGNORELLI, Luca (c1440–1523), Italian RENAISSANCE painter. His greatest work, the FRESCO cycle at Orvieto cathedral (1499–1502), reveals, as in *Resurrection of the Dead* and the *Last Judgment*, a masterly depiction of the nude, surpassed at the period only by MICHELANGELO.

SIHANOUK, Norodom (1922–), chief of state of Cambodia (KAMPUCHEA) 1960–70 and 1975–76. King from 1941, he abdicated in 1955 to become premier. Deposed by a coup in 1970, he returned from exile in 1975 as figurehead of the communist victors. He resigned six months later. In 1982 he became the leader of the Government of Democratic Kampuchea and fought against the Vietnamese-supported regime in Phnom Penh.

SIKHS (from Hindi *sikh*, disciple), religious community of about nine million mostly in the PUNJAB, N India. Their religion, based on the sacred book Ādi Granth, combines elements of HINDUISM and BUDDHISM and was founded by the mystic Nānak, their first guru, in the 16th century. There is no professional priesthood and officially no CASTE SYSTEM. In the 19th century, under Ranjit Singh, the Sikhs developed a powerful military state that was subdued (1845–49) by the British. Thereafter Sikhs were prominent in the British army in India. When the partition of India and Pakistan in 1947 divided the Sikhs, many moved from Pakistan to what became the Indian state of Punjab. Since 1982 Sikh extremists have waged a war of terrorism against Hindus and the Indian government to achieve an autonomous Punjab.

SI-KIANG, or **Hsi Chiang,** the longest river of S China. It flows E for 1,250mi from the highlands of Yunnan to the Canton River delta on the South China Sea. Much of it is navigable.

SIKKIM, Indian state (since 1975) in the E Himalayas, formerly a constitutional monarchy and protectorate of India. It lies between Tibet, Nepal, Bhutan and India, and covers 2,851sq mi, ranging from Kanchenjunga (28,146ft) to lush tropical forests barely 700ft above sea level. The economy rests on agriculture (rice, corn, millet, and fruits); and cardamom is the chief cash crop. Hydroelectricity and new roads are being developed.

SIKORSKI, Władysław (1881–1943), Polish prime minister (1922–23), war minister (1923–25) and general. After the German invasion in 1939, he became leader of the Polish forces and government in exile.

SIKORSKY, Igor Ivanovich (1889–1972), Russian-born US aircraft designer best known for his invention of the first successful HELICOPTER (flown in 1939). He also designed several AIRPLANES, including the first to have more than one engine (1913).

SILAGE, winter cattle fodder made from grass, corn, legumes etc., by limited fermentation. The material is harvested when green, chopped and then stored in either a pit or a tower where air access can be carefully controlled. Lactic acid is formed from the CARBOHYDRATES while the loss of other nutrients is minimal.

SILENT FILMS. See MOTION PICTURES.

SILESIA, region of E central Europe, extending from the Sudeten Mts and W Carpathians in the S up the Oder River valley. Mostly in Poland, it covers about 20,000sq mi and has fertile farmlands and forests and great mineral wealth. Upper Silesia is Poland's most important industrial region.

SILICON (Si), nonmetal in Group IVA of the PERIODIC TABLE; the second most abundant element (after oxygen), occurring as silica and silicates. It is made by reducing silica with coke at high temperatures. Silicon forms an amorphous brown powder, or gray semiconducting crystals, metallic in appearance. It oxidizes on heating, and reacts with the halogens, hydrogen fluoride, and alkalis. It is used in alloys, and to make TRANSISTORS and SEMICONDUCTORS. AW 28.1, mp 1410°C, bp 2355°C, sg 2.42 (20°C). Silicon is tetravalent in almost all its compounds, which resemble those of CARBON, except that it does not form multiple bonds, and that chains of silicon atoms are relatively unstable. **Silanes** are series of volatile silicon hydrides, analogous to paraffins, spontaneously flammable in air and hydrolyzed by water. **Silicon tetrachloride** is a colorless fuming liquid, made by reacting chlorine with a mixture of silica and carbon, the starting material for preparing organo-silicon compounds, including SILICONES. mp 70°C, bp 58°C.

SILICONES, POLYMERS with alternate atoms of silicon and oxygen, and organic groups attached to the silicon. They are resistant to water and oxidation, and are stable to heat. Liquid silicones are used for waterproofing, as polishes and anti-foam agents. Silicone greases are high- and low-temperature lubricants, and resins are used as electrical insulators. Silicone rubbers remain flexible at low temperatures.

SILICOSIS, a form of PNEUMOCONIOSIS, or fibrotic LUNG disease, in which long-standing inhalation of fine silica dusts in mining causes a progressive reduction in the functional capacity of the lungs. The normally thin-walled alveoli and small bronchioles become thickened with fibrous tissue and the lungs lose their elasticity. Characteristic X-RAY appearances and changes in lung function occur.

SILK, natural FIBER produced by certain insects and spiders to make cocoons and webs, a glandular secretion extruded from the spinneret and hardened into a filament on exposure to air. Commercial textile silk comes from the various SILKWORMS. The cocooned pupae are killed by steam or hot air, and the cocoons are placed in hot water to soften the gum (sericin) that binds the silk. The filaments from several cocoons are then unwound together to form a single strand of "raw silk," which is reeled. Several strands are twisted together, or "thrown," to form yarn. At this stage, or after weaving, the sericin is washed away. The thickness of the yarn is measured in denier. About 70% of all raw silk is now produced in Japan.

SILK-SCREEN PRINTING, method of PRINTING derived from the stencil process. A stencil is attached to a silk screen or fine wire mesh, or formed on it by a photographic process or by drawing the design in tusche (a greasy ink), sealing the screen with glue and washing out the tusche and its covering glue with an organic solvent. The framed screen is placed on the surface to be printed, and viscous ink is pressed through by a rubber squeegee. Each color requires a different screen. The process, which may be mechanized, is used for printing labels, posters, fabrics, and on bottles and other curved surfaces. Since 1938 it has been used by painters, who call it serigraphy.

SILKWORM, the caterpillar of a moth, *Bombyx mori*, which, like many other caterpillars, spins itself a cocoon of silk in which it pupates. The cocoon of *B. mori* is, however, especially thick and may be composed of a single thread commonly 900m (2,950ft) long. This is unraveled to provide commercial SILK. Originally a native of China, *B. mori* has been introduced to many countries. The caterpillar, which takes about a month to develop, feeds on the leaves of the mulberry tree.

SILLANPAA, Frans Eemil (1888–1964), Finnish novelist awarded the 1939 Nobel Prize in Literature. His best known work is *The Maid Silja* (1931).

SILLIMAN, Benjamin (1779–1864), US chemist and geologist who founded *The American Journal of Science* (1819). The mineral **sillimanite** (a form of aluminum SILICATE, Al_2SiO_5) is named for him.

SILLITOE, Alan (1928–   ), English novelist, short-story writer and poet. Many of his works, such as *Saturday Night and Sunday Morning* (1958) and *The Loneliness of the Long-Distance Runner* (1959), focus on working-class heroes rebelling against an oppressive society.

SILLS, Beverly (1929–   ), US coloratura soprano, born Belle Silverman. She made her debut at the NY City Opera in 1955 and later became internationally known, acclaimed both as an actress and as a singer. She was general director of the NY City Opera 1979–88.

SILONE, Ignazio (1900–1978), pseudonym of Secondo Tranquilli, Italian writer and social reformer. Opposed to fascism, he spent 1931–44 in exile in Switzerland. His novels include *Bread and Wine* (1937).

SILURIAN, the third period of the PALEOZOIC, which lasted between about 440 and 400 million years ago. (See also GEOLOGY.)

SILVER (Ag), soft, white NOBLE METAL in Group IB of the PERIODIC TABLE, a transition element. Silver has been known and valued from earliest times and used for jewelry, ornaments and coinage since the 4th millennium BC. It occurs as the metal, notably in Norway; in COPPER, LEAD and ZINC sulfide ores; and in argentite and other silver ores. It is concentrated by various processes including cupellation and extraction with CYANIDE (see also GOLD), and is refined by electrolysis. Silver has the highest thermal and electrical conductivity of all metals, and is used for printed circuits and electrical contacts. Other modern uses include dental ALLOYS and amalgam, high-output storage batteries, and for monetary reserves. Although the most reactive of the noble metals, silver is not oxidized in air, nor dissolved by alkalis or nonoxidizing acids; it dissolves in nitric and concentrated sulfuric acid. Silver tarnishes by reaction with sulfur or hydrogen sulfide to form a dark silver-sulfide layer. Silver salts are normally monovalent. Ag^+ is readily reduced by mild reducing agents, depositing a silver mirror from solution. AW 107.9, mp 960.8°C, bp 2212°C, sg 10.5 (20°C). **Silver halides** (AgX) are crystalline salts used in PHOTOGRAPHY. The chloride is white, the bromide pale yellow and the iodide yellow. On exposure to light, a crystal of silver halide becomes activated, and is preferentially reduced to silver by a mild reducing agent (the developer). **Silver nitrate** ($AgNO_3$) is a transparent crystalline solid, used as an ANTISEPTIC and astringent, especially for removing WARTS.

SIMENON, Georges Joseph Christian (1903–), Belgian-born French author of over 200 novels and thousands of short stories. He is best known for his detective novels about Inspector Maigret, outstanding works of tightly plotted suspense and psychological insight.

SIMEON STYLITES, Saint (c390–c459) (from Greek *stylos*, pillar), Syrian ascetic and mystic who spent his last 40 years or so on top of a high column. His feast day is Jan. 5.

SIMMS, William Gilmore (1806–1870), US author whose writings on the US South include historical novels, short stories, biographies and poetry. His most important work was *The Yemassee* (1835).

SIMON, Saint, one of the disciples of Christ. His names of "the Canaanite" or "Zelotes" may suggest association with the ZEALOTS. His feast day is Oct. 28.

SIMON, John Allsebrook Simon, 1st Viscount (1873–1954), British statesman, a leading proponent of appeasement of Nazi Germany while foreign secretary (1931–35), home secretary (1935–37), and chancellor of the exchequer (1937–40).

SIMON, Jules (1814–1896), French statesman. A republican opponent of Napoleon III, he served in the government of national defense after the emperor's abdication in the Franco-Prussian War. In the Third Republic, he was a reforming education minister (1870–73) and premier (1876–77). His replacement by the monarchist president, MacMahon, led to the establishment of the principle that the premier was responsible to the legislature rather than to the president.

SIMON (Marvin) Neil (1927–), US playwright, a comedy writer for television before writing an unprecedented succession of hit stage comedies beginning with *Come Blow Your Horn* (1966).

SIMONIDES OF CEOS (c556–469 BC), Greek lyric poet, famous for his epitaphs on the Greeks who fell at MARATHON and THERMOPYLAE. He was also well known for his elegies, odes and epigrams. Very little of his verse has survived.

SIMONS, Menno (c1496–1561), Frisian religious reformer and leader of the peaceful ANABAPTISTS in Holland and Germany. He was a Roman Catholic priest who converted to Anabaptism in 1536. The MENNONITES are named for him.

SIMONY, the buying and selling of sacred privileges. It is named for Simon Magus, a Samarian magician who tried to buy from St. Peter the power of transmitting the Holy Spirit.

SIMPLON PASS, 29mi long and 6,590ft high, between Brig in Switzerland and Isella in Italy. NAPOLEON I built a road along it in 1800–06. In 1906 the Simplon Tunnel, 12.5mi long, Europe's longest and the world's second-longest railroad tunnel, was opened to traffic.

SIMPSON, George Gaylord (1902–1984), US paleontologist, at Columbia U 1945–59 and Harvard U 1959–70, known to the general public for his *Meaning of Evolution* (1949).

SIMPSON, Sir James Young (1811–1870), Scottish obstetrician who pioneered the use of CHLOROFORM as an anesthetic, especially for mothers during childbirth.

SIN, or transgression, an unethical act (see ETHICS) considered as disobedience to the revealed will of God. Sin may be viewed legally as crime—breaking God's commandments—and so deserving punishment (see HELL; PURGATORY), or as an offense that grieves God the loving Father, breaking communion with Him. According to the Bible, sin entered the world in Adam's fall and all mankind became innately sinful (see ORIGINAL SIN). Both for this and for actual sins committed, man becomes guilty and in need of SALVATION. Since sin is rooted in character and will, each sinner bears personal responsibility; hence the need for repentance, CONFESSION and absolution (see also PENANCE). Views as to what constitutes sin vary, being partly determined by church authority, social standards and one's own conscience. The traditional "seven deadly sins" are pride, covetousness, lust, envy, gluttony, anger and sloth. The Roman Catholic Church defines a mortal sin as a serious sin committed willingly and with clear knowledge of its wrongness; a venial sin is less grave, does not wholly deprive the perpetrator of grace, and need not be individually confessed. (See also IMMACULATE CONCEPTION.)

SINAI PENINSULA, mountainous peninsula between the Gulf of Suez and the Gulf of Aqaba, the N arms of the Red Sea. It is thought that Mt Sinai, where MOSES received the TEN COMMANDMENTS, is one of the S peaks (Jebel Serbal or Jebel Musa).

SINATRA, Frank (Francis Albert Sinatra; 1917–), US singer and film star. He achieved fame as a band singer with Tommy Dorsey before becoming a teenagers' idol as a solo performer during

WWII. After making several musical films, he became a dramatic actor of note in *From Here to Eternity* (1953).

SINCLAIR, Upton Beall (1878–1968), novelist and social reformer. He is best known for *The Jungle* (1906), a novel exposing the horrors of the Chicago meat-packing industries, and for the 11 *World's End* novels centered on Lanny Budd, one of which, *Dragon's Teeth* (1942), brought him the 1943 Pulitzer Prize.

SINGAPORE, republic in SE Asia, at the S end of the Malay Peninsula, consisting of Singapore Island and 60 adjacent islets. It is one of the smallest states in the world.

Official name: Republic of Singapore
Capital: Singapore
Area: 240sq mi
Population: 2,616,000
Languages: Malay, Chinese (Mandarin), English, Tamil
Religions: Confucianist, Buddhist, Taoist, Muslim
Monetary unit(s): 1 Singapore dollar = 100 cents

Singapore Island is largely low-lying and fringed by mango swamps, its climate tropical: rainfall averages about 95in yearly. The population is predominantly Chinese, with large Malay and Indian minorities. The capital, Singapore city, has a fine natural harbor and is SE Asia's foremost commercial and shipping center, conducting a flourishing international trade as a free port. It trades in textiles, rubber, petroleum, timber and tin, and produces electrical goods, petroleum products and textiles. Shipbuilding and repair is an important new industry. Singapore was founded as a trading post by Sir Thomas RAFFLES in 1819 and became part of the Straits Settlements in 1826. Self-governing from 1959, it joined MALAYSIA as a constituent state in 1963 but withdrew from the federation in 1965. Lee Kwan Yew, who became prime minister in 1965, oversaw a period of tremendous economic growth and remained firmly in control despite opposition gains in the 1985 and 1988 parliamentary elections.

SINGER, Isaac Bashevis (1904–   ), Polish-born US YIDDISH novelist and short story writer, known for his portrayal of European Jewish life. His work includes *The Family Moskat* (1950), *The Magician of Lublin* (1960) and *The Estate* (1969). He was awarded the 1978 Nobel Prize.

SINGER, Isaac Merrit (1811–1875), US inventor of the first viable domestic SEWING MACHINE (patented 1851). Despite a legal battle with the earlier inventor Elias Howe, the Singer sewing machine soon became the most popular in the world.

SINGER, Israel Joshua (1893–1944), Polish-born US Yiddish novelist, playwright and journalist, best known for his epic novel, *The Brothers Ashkenazi* (1936). He was the older brother of novelist Isaac Bashevis SINGER.

SINGLE TAX, proposed reform that tax on land value should be a government's sole revenue, stated by Henry GEORGE in *Progress and Poverty* (1879). He argued that economic rent of land results from the growth of an economy, not from an individual's effort; therefore, governments are justified in appropriating all economic rents, thus eliminating the need for other taxes. The proposal was never enacted in the US.

SINHALESE, an INDO-ARYAN LANGUAGE, derived from SANSKRIT, spoken by two-thirds of the people of SRI LANKA. Most other Sinhalese speak TAMIL.

SINKIANG, or **Xinjiang,** Uyger Autonomous Region, region in NW China between Mongolia and USSR. A predominantly agricultural and pastoral area covering 16% of China's land area, it has very rich mineral resources and vast oil fields. Because of scant rainfall, Sinkiang has extensive irrigation systems. It is a strategic region for the defense of China and the home of 13 minority ethnic groups, most of whom practice Islam.

SINN FEIN (Irish Gaelic: we, ourselves), Irish nationalist movement which achieved independence for the Irish Free State in 1922. Formed by Arthur GRIFFITH in 1905, it was first widely supported in 1916 when most of the leaders of the EASTER RISING were martyred. Led by DE VALERA, it set up an Irish Parliament, the Dáil Eireann, by 1919. (See also IRELAND; IRISH REPUBLICAN ARMY).

SINO-JAPANESE WARS, two bitter conflicts between China and Japan. The first (1894–95) was precipitated by the rivalry of the two nations over Korea. China's navy was totally destroyed and its army routed by the Japanese. The Treaty of Shimonoseki led to Japan becoming a great power. The second (1937–45) was the result of renewed Japanese expansionism in the Far East. Japan conquered Manchuria in 1931 and gradually penetrated into China. In 1937 Japan seized nearly all the coastal cities and industrial areas. The Chinese Nationalists and the communists united to fight the Japanese. After PEARL HARBOR the fighting became part of WWII.

SINUS, large air space connected with the nose which may become infected and obstructed after upper respiratory infection and cause facial pain and fever (sinusitis). There are four major nasal sinuses: the maxillary, frontal, ethmoid and sphenoid. *Also*, a blind-ended channel which may discharge PUS or other material onto the skin or other surface. These may be embryological remnants or arise from a foreign body or deep chronic infection (e.g., OSTEOMYELITIS). *Also*, a large venous channel, as in the LIVER and in the large vessels draining BLOOD from the BRAIN.

SIOUX INDIANS, the largest North American tribe of the Siouan language group. Also known as the *Dakota* ("allies"), they were originally a federation of seven tribes, the most numerous being the Teton. After repeated revolts against white misrule and treachery, they were finally defeated at WOUNDED KNEE (1890). Today about 35,000 live on reservations.

SIPHON, device, usually consisting of a bent tube with two legs of unequal length, which utilizes atmospheric pressure to transfer liquid over the edge of one container into another at a lower level. The flowing action depends on the difference in the pressures acting on the two liquid surfaces and stops when these coincide.

SIQUEIROS, David Alfaro (1896–1974), Mexican mural painter, best known for his murals in Mexico City on social subjects.

SIRIUS, Alpha Canis Majoris, the Dog Star, the brightest star in the night sky. 2.7pc distant, it is 20 times more luminous than the sun and has absolute magnitude +1.4. A DOUBLE STAR, its major component is twice the size of the sun; its minor component (the Pup), the first white dwarf star to be discovered, has a diameter only 50% greater than that of the earth, but is extremely dense, its mass being just less than that of the sun.

SIROCCO, in S Europe, warm, humid WIND from the S or SE, originating as a dry wind over the Sahara Desert and gaining humidity from passage over the Mediterranean.

SISLEY, Alfred (1839–1899), Anglo-French painter, a founder of IMPRESSIONISM. His fine landscapes and

snow scenes, painted in the 1870s, often show Paris, London and their neighborhoods. His work achieved wide recognition only after his death.

SISTINE CHAPEL, the papal chapel in the Vatican palace, Rome, renowned for its magnificent frescoes by MICHELANGELO and other Renaissance artists like PERUGINO, BOTTICELLI and PINTURICCHIO. It is named for Pope Sixtus IV, who began its construction in 1473, and is used by the College of Cardinals when it meets to elect a new pope.

SITAR, Indian stringed instrument with a long neck and smallish rounded soundbox. There are usually seven strings—five melody and two drone: these are plucked by a player seated on cushions or the floor. In 1957 the Indian sitar virtuoso Ravi SHANKAR made the first of several concert tours of the US, spreading the popularity of the instrument, which has since been used by ROCK MUSIC groups.

SITTER, Willem de (1872–1934), Dutch astronomer who helped to get EINSTEIN'S theory of RELATIVITY widely known and who proposed a modification to it allowing for a gradual expansion of the universe.

SITTING BULL (c1831–1890), chief of the Teton SIOUX INDIANS who led the last major Indian resistance in the US. Born in S.D., he became head of the Sioux nation and inspired the 1876 campaign that resulted in the massacre at Little Bighorn. After the Sioux surrender (1881) he retired to Standing Rock reservation, N.D. During the GHOST DANCE Indian police killed him while attempting his arrest.

SITUATION ETHICS, ethical theory denying the binding force of objective moral laws. It holds that the morality of an act is determined by the conditions of a given situation and the intentions of the actor rather than by the objective nature of the behavior. *Situation Ethics: The New Morality* (1966), by Episcopalian theologian Joseph Fletcher, outlines the theory.

SITWELL, name of three distinguished English writers, children of Sir George Keresley Sitwell. **Dame Edith Sitwell** (1887–1964), leading poet and critic, helped launch *Wheels* (1916), a magazine of experimental poetry, wrote the satirical *Facade* (1922; music by William WALTON), and was a master technician of sound, rhythm and symbol. **Sir Osbert Sitwell** (1892–1969), satirist, novelist and short-story writer, is best known for his fantastic novel *The Man Who Lost Himself* (1929) and his five-volume autobiography. **Sir Sacheverell Sitwell** (1897–1988) was a poet, art critic and traveler whose work includes *Southern Baroque Art* (1924), *All Summer in a Day* (1926) and *Mozart* (1932).

SI UNITS, the internationally adopted abbreviation for the *Système International d'Unités* (International System of Units), a modification of the system known as rationalized MKSA units (Giorgi system) adopted by the 11th General Conference of Weights and Measures (CGPM) in 1960 and subsequently amended. It is the modern version of the METRIC SYSTEM. SI Units are the legal standard in many countries and find almost universal use among scientists.

SIX, Les, term coined in 1920 to group six French composers (Darius MILHAUD, Francis POULENC, Arthur HONEGGER, Georges AURIC, Louis Durey and Germaine Tailleferre) inspired by the work of Erik SATIE and Jean COCTEAU.

SIX-DAY WAR. See ARAB-ISRAELI WARS.

SIX NATIONS, the enlarged IROQUOIS League formed by the joining of the Tuscarora (1722).

SIXTUS, name of five popes. **Sixtus IV** (1414–1484; elected 1471) built the SISTINE CHAPEL. His reign was characterized by nepotism and SIMONY. **Sixtus V** (1521–90; elected 1585) brought the PAPAL STATES to order and made the pope one of Europe's richest princes. His reforms of church administration were part of the COUNTER-REFORMATION.

SKAGERRAK, arm of the North Sea some 140mi long and 80mi wide dividing Norway from Denmark and linking the North Sea with the Baltic Sea through the Kattegat.

SKALDIC POETRY, in Old Norse literature, the poetry of the SAGA, recited by Scandinavian court poets (*skalds*) from about 800 onwards. It is noted for its syllabic metrical structure and elaborate metaphors (*kennings*).

SKANDERBEG (George Kastrioti; c1405–1468), Albanian national hero. He organized the Albanian clans into a guerrilla force that for 25 years repelled the newly arrived Turkish invaders.

SKELETON, in VERTEBRATES, the framework of BONES that supports and protects the soft TISSUES and organs of the body. It acts as an attachment for the MUSCLES, especially those producing movement, and protects vital organs such as the BRAIN, HEART and LUNGS. It is also a store of calcium, magnesium, sodium, phosphorus and PROTEINS, while its bone marrow is the site of red BLOOD-corpuscle formation. In the adult human body, there are about 206 bones, to which more than 600 muscles are attached. The skeleton consists of two parts: the axial skeleton (the skull,

backbone and rib-cage), and the appendicular skeleton (the limbs). The function of the **axial skeleton** is mainly protective. The skull consists of 29 bones, 8 being fused together to form the cranium, protecting the brain. The *vertebral column,* or backbone, consists of 33 small bones (or VERTEBRAE): the upper 25 are joined by ligaments and thick cartilaginous disks and the lower 9 are fused together. It supports the upper body and protects the SPINAL CORD which runs through it. The *rib-cage* consists of 12 pairs of ribs forming a protective cage around the heart and lungs and assists in breathing (see RESPIRATION). The **appendicular skeleton** is primarily concerned with locomotion and consists of the arms and pectoral girdle, and the legs and pelvic girdle. The limbs articulate with their girdles in ball and socket joints which permit the shoulder and hip great freedom of movement but are prone to dislocation. In contrast the elbows and knees are hinge joints permitting movement in one plane only, but which are very strong.

SKELTON, John (c1460–1529), English court poet and satirist, influential tutor to Henry VIII. His works include burlesques (*Philip Sparrow*, 1508), a morality play (*Magnificence*, 1515), and satires directed against Cardinal WOLSEY (*Colin Clout*, 1522).

SKEPTICISM, philosophical attitude of doubting all claims to knowledge, chiefly on the ground that the adequacy of any proposed criterion is itself questionable. Examples of thoroughgoing skeptics, wary of dogmatism in whatever guise, were PYRRHO OF ELIS ("Pyrrhonism" and "skepticism" are virtual synonyms) and HUME. Other thinkers, among them AUGUSTINE, ERASMUS, MONTAIGNE, PASCAL, BAYLE and KIERKEGAARD, sought to defend faith and religion by directing skeptical arguments against the epistemological claims of RATIONALISM and EMPIRICISM. PRAGMATISM and KANT'S critical philosophy represent two influential attempts to resolve skeptical dilemmas. (See also AGNOSTICISM.)

SKIDMORE, Louis (1897–1962), US architect and cofounder of the firm of Skidmore, Owings and Merrill (1936), which designed government and corporate projects such as Oak Ridge, Tenn. (1943–45), the US Air Force Academy in Colorado Springs (1954–62), and the Sears Tower in Chicago (1971–73).

SKIING, the sport of gliding over snow on long, thin runners called skis. It began some 5,000 years ago in N Europe as a form of transport and became a sport in the 1800s. In 1924, the Fédération Internationale de

Ski was formed and the first Winter Olympics held. Today, skiing is ever-increasing in popularity, as either Alpine downhill slalom or giant slalom obstacle courses, Nordic crosscountry skiing, or ski-jumping. Skis are generally made of laminated wood, fiberglass, plastic, metal or a combination of these. They have safety bindings attaching the boot firmly to the ski; ski poles are used for balance.

SKIN, the TISSUE which forms a sensitive, elastic, protective and waterproof covering of the human body, together with its specializations (e.g., nails, HAIR). In the adult human, it weighs 2.75kg, covers an area of $1.7m^2$ and varies in thickness from 1mm (in the eyelids) to 3mm (in the palms and soles). It consists of two layers: the outer, epidermis, and the inner, dermis, or true skin. The outermost part of the **epidermis,** the *stratum corneum,* contains a tough protein called keratin. Consequently it provides protection against mechanical trauma, a barrier against microorganisms, and waterproofing. The epidermis also contains cells which produce the MELANIN responsible for skin pigmentation and which provides protection against the sun's ultraviolet rays. The unique pattern of skin folding on the soles and palms provides a gripping surface, and is the basis of identification by FINGERPRINTS. The **dermis** is usually thicker than the epidermis and contains BLOOD vessels, nerves and sensory receptors, sweat glands, sebaceous glands, hair follicles, fat cells and fibers. Temperature regulation of the body is aided by the evaporative cooling of sweat (see PERSPIRATION); regulation of the skin blood flow, and the erection of hairs which trap an insulating layer of air next to the skin. The rich nerve supply of the dermis is responsible for the reception of touch, pressure, pain and temperature stimuli. Leading into the hair follicles are sebaceous glands which produce the antibacterial sebum, a fluid which keeps the hairs oiled and the skin moist. The action of sunlight on the skin initiates the formation of VITAMIN D which helps prevent RICKETS.

SKINDIVING, underwater SWIMMING AND DIVING with or without self-contained underwater breathing apparatus (SCUBA). The simplest apparatus is the snorkel, generally used with goggles or mask, and flippers. An aqualung consists of compressed air cylinders with an automatic demand regulator, which supplies air at the correct pressure according to the diver's depth. "Closed-circuit" SCUBA contains a chemical which absorbs carbon dioxide from exhaled air.

SKINNER, B(urrhus) F(rederic) (1904–), US psychologist and author whose staunch advocacy of BEHAVIORISM did much to gain it acceptance in 20th-century PSYCHOLOGY. His best known books were *Science and Human Behavior* (1953); *Walden Two* (1961), a Utopian novel based on behaviorism; and *Beyond Freedom and Dignity* (1971).

SKULL, the bony structure of the head and face situated at the top of the vertebral column. It forms a thick bony protection for the BRAIN with small apertures for blood vessels, nerves, the SPINAL CORD etc., and the thinner framework of facial structure.

SKUNKS, carnivorous mammals of the WEASEL family, Mustelidae, renowned for the foul stink they produce when threatened. There are ten species distributed throughout the Americas. All are boldly-patterned in black and white. Most are nocturnal and feed on insects, mice and eggs. In defense a skunk can expel fine jets of foul-smelling liquid from scent glands under the tail. This can be shot out to a distance of 3m (10ft) with a remarkably accurate aim.

SKYSCRAPER, a very tall building. From the mid-19th century the price of land in big cities made it worthwhile to build upward rather than outward, and this became practicable with the development of safe electric elevators. The first skyscraper was the 40m (130ft)-high Equitable Life Assurance Society Building, New York (1870). A major design breakthrough was the use of a load-bearing skeletal iron frame, first used in the 10-story Home Insurance Company Building, Chicago (1885).

SLATE, a fine-grained low grade metamorphic rock formed by the regional metamorphism of shale. The parallel orientation of platy minerals in the rock causes the rock to split evenly (slaty cleavage) in a plane that is perpendicular to the direction of the compressive metamorphic stress. (See also METAMORPHIC ROCKS.)

SLATER, Samuel (1768–1835), British-born founder of the US cotton textile industry. As an apprentice in England he memorized the principles of ARKWRIGHT'S machinery. He set up his spinning mill (now a museum) in Pawtucket, R.I., in 1793.

SLAUGHTERHOUSE CASES, controversy following the granting (1869) by the La. legislature of a New Orleans monopoly in landing and slaughtering cattle to the Crescent City Live Stock Landing and Slaughterhouse Co. In 1873, the US Supreme Court found, against other New Orleans butchers, that there was no infringement of the 14th Amendment.

SLAVERY, a practice found at different times in most parts of the world, now condemned in the Universal Declaration of Human Rights.

Slavery generally means enforced servitude, along with society's recognition that the master has ownership rights over the slave and his labor. Some elements of slavery can be found in serfdom, as practiced during the Middle Ages and in Russia up to 1861; in debt bondage and PEONAGE, both forms of enforced labor for the payment of debts; and in forced labor itself, exacted for punishment or for political or military reasons (examples being the "slave" labor used by the Nazis in WWII and the Soviet labor camps). In some places a form of slavery or bondage is still practiced today under the guise of exacting a bride price, or the "adoption" of poor children by wealthier families for labor purposes. While peonage is still rampant in South America, actual slavery is reputed to exist in Africa, the Arabian Peninsula, Tibet and elsewhere. Slavery in Saudi Arabia was officially abolished only in 1962.

Warfare was the main source of slaves in ancient times, along with enslavement for debt or as punishment, and the selling of children. But there was not necessarily a distinction in race or color between master and slave. Manumission (the granting of freedom) was commonplace, and in Greece and Rome many slaves or freedmen rose to influential posts: a slave dynasty, the Mamelukes, ruled Egypt from 1250 to 1517. In the West the Germans enslaved many Slavic people (hence "slave") in the Dark Ages. By the 13th century feudal serfdom was widespread in Europe. Slavery increased again when the Portuguese, exploring the coast of Africa, began to import black slaves in 1433 to fill a manpower shortage at home. With the discovery of America and the development of plantations, the need for cheap, abundant labor encouraged the slave trade. The British abolished the slave trade in 1807 and slavery in 1833. By constitutional provision, the US slave trade ended in 1808 and the Emancipation Proclamation (1863), issued by President Lincoln, took full effect with the end of the Civil War (1865). See BLACKS, AMERICAN; ABOLITIONISM; MISSOURI COMPROMISE; COMPROMISE OF 1850; KANSAS-NEBRASKA ACT; DRED SCOTT CASE; EMANCIPATION PROCLAMATION; CIVIL WAR, AMERICAN; REPUBLICAN PARTY; RECONSTRUCTION; CIVIL LIBERTIES; and CIVIL RIGHTS.

SLAVONIC LANGUAGES, a group of INDO-EUROPEAN LANGUAGES spoken by some 225 million people in central and E Europe and Siberia. There are three groups: W Slavonic (Polish, Czech and Slovak), S Slavonic (Slovene, Serbo-Croatian, Macedonian and Bulgarian), and E Slavonic (Russian, Ukrainian and Belorussian). Byzantine missionaries in the 9th century first developed written Slavonic, using a modified Greek alphabet known as Cyrillic. Today, SLAVS converted by the Orthodox Church use Cyrillic characters and Slavs converted by the Roman Church use the Latin alphabet.

SLAVOPHILES AND WESTERNIZERS, two groups of 19th-century Russian intellectuals. The Slavophiles opposed the westernization of what they felt was a superior Russian or Slavic way of life. The Westernizers advocated the introduction of Western capitalism, technology and liberalism.

SLAVS, largest European ethnic and language group, living today in central and E Europe and speak SLAVONIC LANGUAGES. About 4,000 years ago they migrated to land N of the Black Sea and later split into three groups: the E Slavs, (Russians, Belorussians and Ukrainians), the W Slavs (Czechs, Slovaks and Poles) and the S Slavs (Serbs, Croats, Slovenes, Macedonians, Montenegrins and Bulgarians). Slavonic nations were formed from the 9th century but almost all were overwhelmed by Turkish or Mongol invaders. In the 15th century Russia gained national independence but it was not until WWI that the other Slav nations regained their national identities.

SLEEP, a state of relative unconsciousness and inactivity. The need for sleep recurs periodically in all animals. If deprived of sleep humans initially experience HALLUCINATIONS, acute anxiety, and become highly suggestible and eventually COMA and sometimes DEATH result. During sleep, the body is relaxed and most bodily activity is reduced. Cortical, or higher, brain activity, as measured by the ELECTROENCEPHALOGRAPH; blood pressure; body TEMPERATURE; rate of heartbeat and breathing are decreased. However, certain activities, such as gastric and alimentary activity, are increased. Sleep tends to occur in daily cycles which exhibit up to 5 or 6 periods of orthodox sleep—characterized by its deepness—alternating with periods of paradoxical, or rapid-eye-movement (REM), sleep—characterized by its restlessness and jerky movements of the eyes. Paradoxical sleep occurs only when we are dreaming and occupies about 20% of total sleeping time. Sleepwalking (SOMNAMBULISM) occurs only during orthodox sleep when we are not dreaming. Sleeptalking occurs mostly in orthodox sleep. Many theories have been proposed to explain sleep but none is completely satisfactory. Separate sleeping and waking centers in the HYPOTHALAMUS cooperate with other parts of the BRAIN in controlling sleep. Sleep as a whole, and particularly paradoxical sleep when dreaming occurs, is essential to health and life. Consequently, the key to why animals sleep may reside in a need to DREAM. **Sleep learning** experiments have so far proved ineffective. A rested brain and concentration are probably the most effective basis for LEARNING.

SLEEPING SICKNESS, INFECTIOUS DISEASE caused by trypanosomes occurring in Africa and carried by TSETSE FLIES. It initially causes FEVER, headache, often a sense of oppression and a rash; later the characteristic somnolence follows and the disease enters a chronic, often fatal stage. Treatment is most effective if started before the late stage of BRAIN involvement and uses arsenical compounds.

SLEEPWALKING. See SOMNAMBULISM.

SLIDELL, John (1793–1871), US political leader. Senator from Louisiana (1853–61), he was appointed Confederate commissioner to France. On the way there he was involved in the TRENT AFFAIR. In France, he failed to get official recognition or aid for the Confederacy from Napoleon III.

SLIDE RULE, an instrument based on LOGARITHMS and used for rapid, though approximate, calculation. Two scales are calibrated identically so that, on each, the distance from the "1" point to any point on the scale is proportional to the logarithm of the number represented by that point. Since $\log (a.b) = \log a + \log b$, the multiplication $a.b$ can be performed by setting the "1" point on scale (1) against a on scale (2), then reading off the number of scale (2) opposite b on scale (1). Division is performed by reversing the procedure. In practice, slide rules have several different scales for different kinds of calculation, and a runner (cursor) to permit more accurate readings.

SLIM, William Joseph (1891–1970), British field marshal. He served in India between the world wars. As commander in Burma in 1942 he had to retreat before superior Japanese forces but saved India. His reconquest of Burma, one of the most difficult campaigns in modern warfare, was the greatest land defeat ever suffered by the Japanese. In 1945 he was supreme allied commander of ground forces in SE Asia. He was chief of the imperial general staff 1948–52 and governor general of Australia 1953–60, when he was created a viscount.

SLIPPED DISK, a common condition in which the intervertebral disks of the spinal column degenerate with extrusion of the central soft portion through the outer fibrous ring. The protruding material may cause back pain, or may press upon the spinal cord or on nerves as they leave the SPINAL CORD (causing SCIATICA). Prolonged bed rest is an effective treatment in many cases, but traction, manipulation or surgery may also be required particularly if there is PARALYSIS or nerve involvement.

SLOAN, Alfred Pritchard (1875–1966), US industrialist, president of General Motors from 1923 and chairman of the board 1937–56. His Sloan Foundation (1934) finances social and medical research, particularly into cancer through the Sloan-Kettering Institute in NYC.

SLOAN, John (1871–1951), US painter, a member of the ASHCAN SCHOOL and influential in the development of US modern art. He is famous for his paintings of nudes and of urban scenes, such as *McSorley's Bar* (1912) and *Wake of the Ferry* (1907).

SLOANE, Sir Hans (1660–1753), British physician and natural historian who served as president of the ROYAL SOCIETY (1727–41) after NEWTON. His collection of books and specimens, left to the nation (for a fee of £20,000 to be paid to his family), formed the basis of the British Museum (founded 1759).

SLOTHS, slow, tree-dwelling edentate mammals. There are two genera of modern tree sloths, the two-toed sloths (*Choloepus*) and three-toed sloths or ai (*Bradypus*), descending from the giant ground sloths, *Megatherium* of the PLEISTOCENE. The arms and legs are long, the digits are bound together by tissue and terminate in long, strong claws. With these the sloth can suspend the body from branches. All sloths are South American in origin and vegetarian, feeding on fruits, shoots and leaves.

SLOVAK, the official language of Slovakia. A W SLAVONIC LANGUAGE, it resembles Czech in dialect and is written in the Roman alphabet.

SLOVAKIA, E part of Czechoslovakia, 18,922sq mi in area. It is mostly mountainous, but the mountains slope down to plains and the Danube R in the S and SW. Slovakia has rich farmlands and mineral deposits; shipbuilding and metal processing are also leading industries. The old capital, Bratislava, is an important port on the Danube. Slovakia was mainly under Hungarian rule from the early 900s to 1918. It was then part of Czechoslovakia until it became a German protectorate in 1939. After WWII it was reincorporated into Czechoslovakia.

SLOVENE, the language of Slovenia. It is a S SLAVONIC LANGUAGE, closely related to Serbo-Croatian, and has 46 individual dialects.

SLOVENIA, NW part of YUGOSLAVIA. It became independent of Austria in 1918 and a constituent republic of Yugoslavia in 1945. Its economy is based chiefly on agriculture and on iron, steel, and aluminum industries. The capital is Ljubljana.

SLUTER, Claus (c1350–1406), Dutch sculptor famous for the portal, the tomb of PHILIP III of France, and a large crucifixion group, the *Well of Moses*, at Chartreuse de Champmol, Dijon.

SMALL BUSINESS ADMINISTRA-TION, independent agency of the US government which furnishes small businesses with practical advice and low-cost loans. The agency also helps small businesses obtain government contracts and aids minority-owned firms.

SMALLPOX, INFECTIOUS DISEASE, now restricted to a few areas, causing FEVER, headache and general malaise, followed by a rash. The rash characteristically affects face and limbs more than trunk and lesions start simultaneously. From a maculopapular appearance, the rash passes into a pustular or vesicular stage and ends with scab formation; the lesions are deep and cause scarring. Major and minor forms of smallpox exist, with high fatality rate in major, often with extensive skin HEMORRHAGE. Transmission is from infected cases by secretions and the SKIN lesions; these are infectious for the duration of the rash. Immunization against smallpox was the earliest form practiced, initially through inoculation with the minor form. Later JENNER introduced VACCINATION with the related cowpox VIRUS (vaccinia is now used). QUARANTINE regulations and contact tracing are important in control of isolated outbreaks. It is important to confirm that apparent cases of CHICKENPOX are not indeed of smallpox.

SMART, Christopher (1722–1771), English poet. His masterpiece, *A Song to David* (1763), was written while he was confined in BEDLAM.

SMELL, sense for detecting and recognizing substances at a distance and for assessing the quality of food. One of the earliest senses to develop in EVOLUTION, it may have been based on the chemotaxis of lower forms. Recognition of environmental odors is of vital importance in recognizing edible substances, detecting other animals or objects of danger, and in sexual behavior and attraction. In recent years, particular odors called **pheromones** that have specific physiological functions in insect and mammal behavior have been recognized. Smell reception in insects is localized to the antennae and detection is by specialist (pheromone) receptors and generalist (other odor) receptors. In man and mammals, the nose is the organ of smell. Respiratory air is drawn into the nostrils and passes across a specialized receptor surface—the olfactory epithelium. Receptor cells detect the tiny concentrations of odors in the air stream and stimulate nerve impulses that pass to olfactory centers in the BRAIN for coding and perception. It is not possible to classify odors in the same way as the primary colors in VISION and it is probable that pattern recognition is more important. Certain animals depend mainly on the sense of smell, while man is predominantly a visual animal. But with training, he can achieve sensitive detection and discrimination of odors.

SMELTING, in METALLURGY, process of extracting a metal from its ORE by heating the ore in a BLAST FURNACE or reverberatory furnace (one in which a shallow hearth is heated by radiation from a low roof heated by flames from the burning fuel). A reducing agent, usually COKE, is used, and a flux is added to remove impurities. Sulfide ores are generally roasted to convert them to oxides before smelting.

SMETANA, Bedřich (1824–1884), Czech composer. Many of his compositions reflect Smetana's ardent Bohemian nationalism; most famous are the comic opera *The Bartered Bride* (1866) and the symphonic poem *Ma Vlast* ("My Country"; 1874–79).

SMIBERT, John (1688–1751), Scottish-born painter in New England. He painted portraits of many notable colonial figures.

SMILES, Samuel (1812–1904), Scottish writer and moralist. He wrote several didactic works based on the work ethic—*Self-Help* (1859), *Character* (1871), *Thrift* (1875), and *Duty* (1880).

SMITH, Adam (1723–1790), Scottish economist and philosopher. The free-market system he advocated in *The Wealth of Nations* (1776) came to be regarded as the classic system of economics. Smith drew on the ideas of TURGOT, Quesnay, MONTESQUIEU and his friend David HUME and argued that if market forces were allowed to operate without state intervention "an invisible hand" would guide self-interest for the well-being of all. His concept of the division of labor and the belief that value derives from productive labor were major insights. An earlier work, *Theory of Moral Sentiments* (1759) contrasts with *The Wealth of Nations* in its emphasis upon sympathy rather than self-interest as a basic force in human nature.

SMITH, Alfred Emanuel (1873–1944), US politician elected governor of New York four times (1918, 1922, 1924, 1926), a TAMMANY HALL politician and a leading figure among the Democrats. Supported by F. D. ROOSEVELT in his bids for the presidency, he failed to gain nomination in 1924 and was beaten by HOOVER in 1928: when Roosevelt became president, Smith opposed the NEW DEAL.

SMITH, Bessie (c1898–1937), US jazz singer, perhaps the greatest BLUES singer. "The Empress of the Blues" came from a poor Tenn. home and first recorded in 1923; later she performed with many leading musicians, including Louis ARMSTRONG and Benny GOODMAN.

SMITH, David (1906–1965), influential US sculptor, famous for his constructions of wrought iron and cut steel. His late works, like *Cubi XVIII* (1964), comprised burnished or painted cubic forms dramatically welded together.

SMITH, Gerald Lyman Kenneth (1898–1976), US radical agitator. A religious fundamentalist, he inveighed against black, Jews, Catholics, communists, and labor unions. He was an organizer of the Union Party (1936), America First Party (1944), and the Christian National Crusade (1947).

SMITH, Gerrit (1797–1874), US reformer. He financed many reforms with his large fortune and was a prominent abolitionist. He organized the LIBERTY PARTY and was a congressman 1853–54. He ran twice for the governorship of N.Y., in 1840 and 1858.

SMITH, Ian Douglas (1919–   ), Rhodesian prime minister 1965–80. As leader of a white minority government he declared unilateral independence from Britain in 1965, and made Rhodesia a republic in 1970. A decade of civil strife ended (1980) with the formation of a black regime in Rhodesia, renamed Zimbabwe.

SMITH, Jedediah Strong (1799–1831), US frontiersman and MOUNTAIN MAN who led fur-trapping expeditions to the Missouri R and to Wind R, and in 1824 discovered the South Pass route to the West. Smith was the first white man to cross the Sierra Nevada and to explore the Cal.-Ore. coast by land.

SMITH, John (c1580–1631), English explorer, soldier and writer who established the first permanent English colony in North America. He sailed to Virginia in 1607 and founded a settlement at JAMESTOWN. Smith claimed to have been captured by Chief POWHATAN in 1607 and saved from death by the chief's daughter POCAHONTAS. Smith charted the coast of New England in 1614, publishing his findings in *A Description of New England* (1616).

SMITH, Joseph (1805–1844), founder of the Church of Jesus Christ of the Latter-Day Saints, based on the Bible and the Book of Mormon, which Smith claimed to have found (in the form of hieroglyphs on gold plates) and translated with the help of the angel Moroni. In 1844 he was accused of conspiracy and, while in prison, was murdered by a mob. (See MORMONS.)

SMITH, Margaret Chase (1897–   ), US Republican politician, a US representative (1940–49) and senator (1949–73) from Maine. In 1964, she became the first woman to have her name placed in nomination as a presidential candidate at a major party convention.

SMITH, Sydney (1771–1845), English preacher, reformer and wit. In his sermons, his *Letters to Peter Plymley* (1807–08) and pieces in the *Edinburgh Review* (which he cofounded in 1802), he combined powerful arguments with biting satire of Protestant bigotry to press for Catholic emancipation.

SMITH, Walter Bedell (1895–1961), WWII US army chief of staff in Europe. He negotiated the surrenders of Italy (1943) and Germany (1945), was ambassador to the USSR 1946–49, CIA director 1950–53 and undersecretary of state 1953–54.

SMITH, William (1769–1839), the "father of stratigraphy." He established that similar sedimentary rock strata in different places may be dated by identifying the fossils each level contains, and made the first geological map of England and Wales (1815).

SMITH ACT (1940), a federal US law making it a criminal offense to advocate the violent overthrow of the government or to belong to any group advocating this. Used to convict Communist Party leaders, the act also required registration and fingerprinting of aliens.

SMITHSON, James (1765–1829), earlier known as James Lewis and Louis Macie, British chemist and mineralogist who left £100,000 (then about $500,000) for the foundation of the SMITHSONIAN INSTITUTION.

SMITHSONIAN INSTITUTION, US

institution of scientific and artistic culture, located in Washington, D.C., and sponsored by the US Government. Founded with money left by James Smithson, it was established by Congress in 1846. It is governed by a board of regents comprising the US Vice-President and Chief Justice, three Senators, three Representatives and nine private citizens appointed by Congress. Although it undertakes considerable scientific research, it is best known as the largest US collection of museums, the "nation's attic:" these include the National Air and Space Museum, the National Gallery of Art, the Freer Gallery of Art, the National Portrait Gallery and the National Museum of American Art.

SMOG. See FOG.

SMOKING, the habit of inhaling or taking into the mouth the smoke of dried tobacco or other leaves from a pipe or wrapped cylinder; it has been practiced for many years in various communities, often using leaves of plants with hallucinogenic or other euphoriant properties. The modern habit of tobacco smoking derived from America and spread to Europe in the 16th century. Mass production of cigarettes began in the 19th century. Since the rise in cigarette consumption, epidemiology has demonstrated an unequivocal association with lung CANCER, chronic BRONCHITIS and EMPHYSEMA and with ARTERIOSCLEROSIS, leading to CORONARY THROMBOSIS and STROKE. Smoking appears to play a part in other forms of cancer and in other diseases such as peptic ULCER. It is not yet clear what part of smoke is responsible for disease. It is now known that nonsmokers may be affected by environmental smoke. A minor degree of physical and a large degree of psychological addiction occur.

SMOKY MOUNTAINS. See GREAT SMOKY MOUNTAINS.

SMOLLETT, Tobias George (1721–1771), British writer who developed the PICARESQUE NOVEL in his satires of 18th-century English society. They include *Roderick Random* (1748), *Peregrine Pickle* (1751) and his masterpiece, *Humphry Clinker* (1771), which is written in letter form.

SMOOT-HAWLEY TARIFF, enacted by Congress in 1930, brought the US tariff to a very high level. It aggravated world depression: foreign countries replied with retaliatory measures and there was a steep decline in US foreign trade.

SMUTS, Jan Christiaan (1870–1950), South African lawyer, soldier and statesman. In the BOER WAR he led Boer guerrilla forces in Cape Colony. He worked with BOTHA to create the Union of South Africa (1910) and was in the WWI British war cabinet. He was South African prime minister 1919–24, and minister of justice 1933–39 in the coalition government led by James Hertzog, whom he succeeded as prime minister (1939–48) to bring South Africa into WWII on the British side.

SNAILS, herbivorous gastropod mollusks with, typically, a spirally coiled shell, found on land, in freshwater or in the sea. The shell is secreted by the underlying "mantle" and houses the internal organs. The internal structure is similar in all groups, though many land snails (pulmonates) have their gills replaced with an air-breathing lung. Nonpulmonate snails are mostly unisexual while pulmonates are typically hermaphrodite.

SNAKE BITE. A very small proportion of the world's snakes produce poisonous venom, and most of these live in the tropics. The venom may lead to HEMORRHAGE, PARALYSIS and central NERVOUS SYSTEM disorders as well as local symptoms of pain, EDEMA and ulceration. Treatment aims to minimize venom absorption, neutralize venom with antiserum, counteract the specific effects and support life until venom is eliminated. Antiserum should be used only for definite bites by identified snakes.

SNAKE RIVER, main tributary of the Columbia R, US. Rising in the Rockies of Yellowstone National Park, Wyo., it winds 1,038mi S, W, N and W through Ida. and Ore. to join the Columbia near Pasco, Wash. It is an important source of power and irrigation.

SNAKES, an order, Squamata, of elongate legless reptiles. Snakes have a deeply-forked tongue covered with sense organs, which is flicked in and out of the mouth to test the surroundings. All snakes are carnivorous, feeding on insects, eggs, rodents and other larger mammals, depending on size. While those that feed on insects usually feed fairly regularly, snakes taking larger prey may feed only infrequently. To facilitate swallowing of large prey, upper and lower jaws may be dislocated and moved independently. All snakes swallow their prey whole without mastication. While many species have no accessories to assist them in the capture of prey, others are venomous, or subdue their prey by constriction before swallowing. Snakes may be aquatic, terrestrial or arboreal.

SNEAD, Sam (Samuel Jackson Snead; 1912–   ), US golfer. He won both the US Masters and PGA tourneys three times but never the US Open.

SNEEZE, explosive expiration through the NOSE and MOUTH stimulated by irritation or INFLAMMATION in the nasal EPITHELIUM. It is a REFLEX attempt to remove the source of irritation.

SNIPES, long-billed birds of the family Scolopacidae with flexible bill tips that can be opened below ground to grasp food items. Active mainly at dawn and dusk, snipes are dumpy birds of marshy areas or open moorland having large eyes set well back on the head. Extraordinarily well-camouflaged, if disturbed at close quarters they rise sharply and escape with an erratic zig-zag flight. In courtship many species produce loud whistling or drumming noises by vibration of the primaries or tail coverts in rapid dives.

SNORING, stertorous respiration of certain persons during sleep, the noise being caused by vibration of the soft PALATE. It is predisposed to by the shape of the PHARYNX and by the sleeping position.

SNORRI STURLUSON (1179–1241), Icelandic poet and historian. The major figure in medieval Scandinavian literature, he wrote the still popular *Heimskringla* (*Orb of the World*), a vivid and eventful history of Norway's kings. He compiled the prose EDDA, a handbook of Norse mythology, poetic diction and meter.

SNOW, C(harles) P(ercy) (1905–1980), English author, physicist and government official, many of whose works deal with the widening gap between art and technology. He is best known for his *Strangers and Brothers* series: 11 novels (1940–70) about the English professional classes.

SNOW, Edgar (1905–1972), US journalist and author. The first Westerner to visit the Chinese Communists in their remote headquarters in Yenan (1936), he wrote a sympathetic account of their programs and idealism in *Red Star Over China* (1937). A personal friend of MAO TSE-TUNG and CHOU EN-LAI, he was one of the few Americans to visit China regularly after the 1949 revolution about which he wrote *The Other Side of the River* (1962) and *The Long Revolution* (1972).

SNOW, precipitation consisting of flakes or clumps of ICE crystals. The crystals are plane hexagonal, showing an infinite variety of beautiful branched forms; needles, columns and irregular forms are also found. Snow forms by direct vapor-to-ice condensation from humid air below 0°C. On reaching the ground, snow crystals lose their structure and become granular. Fresh snow is very light (sg about 0.1), and is a good insulator, protecting underlying plants from severe cold. In time, pressure,

sublimation and melting and refreezing lead to compaction into névé.

SNOW BLINDNESS, temporary loss of VISION with severe pain, tears and EDEMA due to excessive ultraviolet light reflected from snow. Permanent damage is rare but protective polaroid glasses should be used.

SNYDERS, Frans (1579–1657), Flemish BAROQUE painter. A student of BRUEGEL the younger and collaborator with RUBENS, Snyders painted scenes of hunting and of fighting beasts, and elaborate still lifes of fruit and game.

SOANE, Sir John (1753–1837), English architect. The severe linear style of his neo-classical Bank of England gave way to more picturesque eccentricity in Dulwich College gallery and his own London home in Lincoln's Inn Fields (now the Soane Museum).

SOAPS AND DETERGENTS, substances which, when dissolved in water, are cleansing agents. Soap has been known since 600 BC; it was used as a medicine until its use for washing was discovered in the 2nd century AD. Until about 1500 it was made by boiling animal fat with wood ashes (which contain the alkali potassium carbonate). Then caustic soda (see SODIUM), a more effective ALKALI, was used; vegetable FATS and oils were also introduced. Saponification, the chemical reaction in soap-making, is an alkaline HYDROLYSIS of the fat (an ESTER) to yield glycerol and the sodium salt of a long-chain carboxylic acid. The potassium salt is used for soft soap. In the modern process, the hydrolysis is effected by superheated water with a zinc catalyst, and the free acid produced is then neutralized. Synthetic detergents, introduced in WWI, generally consist of the sodium salts of various long-chain sulfonic acids, derived from oils and PETROLEUM products. The principle of soaps and detergents is the same: the hydrophobic long-chain hydrocarbon part of the molecule attaches itself to the grease and dirt particles, and the hydrophilic acid group makes the particles soluble in water, so that by agitation they are loosed from the fabric and dispersed. Detergents do not (unlike soaps) form scum in HARD WATER. Their persistence in rivers, however, causes pollution problems, and biodegradable detergents have been developed. Household detergents may contain several additives: bleaches, brighteners, and ENZYMES to digest protein stains (egg, blood, etc.).

SOAPSTONE, or **steatite,** METAMORPHIC ROCK consisting largely of compacted talc with some serpentine and carbonates, formed by alteration of peridotite. Soft and soapy to the touch, soapstone has been used from prehistoric times for carvings and vessels. When fired, it becomes hard and is used for insulators.

SOARES, Mario Alberto Nobre Lopes (1924–   ), Porguese political leader. A socialist opponent of dictators Antonio SALAZAR and Marcello Caetano, he was twice exiled. After the 1974 military coup, he was foreign minister (1974–75), premier (1976–78, 1983–85), and president (1986–   ).

SOCCER, most popular sport in the world, national sport of most European and Latin American countries and fast increasing in popularity in the US. The field measures 115yd by 75yd, the netted goal is 8yd wide and 8ft high and the inflated leather ball 27–28in round. There are two 45min halves, one referee and two linesmen. The aim of each 11-man team is to score by kicking or heading the ball into the opponents' goal. To advance the ball, a player may *dribble* it (repeatedly kick it as he runs with it) or kick it to a teammate. The ball may not be touched with the hand or arm, except by the goalkeeper in the penalty area in front of his goal. Modern professional soccer began in the UK in 1885, in the US in 1967.

SOCIAL CONTRACT, in political philosophy a concept of the formation of society, in which men agree to surrender part of their "natural" freedom to enjoy the security of the organized state. The idea, though of ancient origin, was first fully formulated in the 17th and 18th centuries by Thomas HOBBES (in *Leviathan*, 1651), LOCKE and ROUSSEAU, and was then controversial because it suggested that heads of state ruled only by their subjects' consent.

SOCIAL CREDIT PARTY, Canadian party formed (1935) by William Aberhart. It aimed to implement Clifford Douglas' policy of avoiding economic depression by distributing surplus money as a "social dividend" to increase purchasing power. It failed in this but governed Alberta 1935–71 and British Columbia 1952–72. The party failed to win seats in the 1980 federal parliamentary elections.

SOCIAL DARWINISM, late 19th-century school of thought which held that society evolved on DARWIN'S biological model. Social inequalities were explained (and made to seem natural and inevitable) by the law of "SURVIVAL OF THE FITTEST." Its chief theorist was Herbert SPENCER.

SOCIAL DEMOCRATIC PARTIES, political parties found in many countries that seek socialism through constitutional reform, not revolution. They usually favor government intervention in the economy

and nationalization of powerful industries. The Social Democratic Party of the US joined with the Socialist Labor Party in 1901 to form the SOCIALIST PARTY. In Britain, moderate leaders of the Labour Party broke away to form the Social Democratic Party in 1981.

SOCIAL GOSPEL, a liberal Protestant social-reform movement in the US c1870–1920. It promoted Christian ideas of love and justice in education and social and political service. Among its leaders were Horace Bushnell, Washington Gladden and Walter Rauschenbusch.

SOCIALISM, an economic philosophy and political movement which aims to achieve a just, classless society through public ownership and operation of the means of production and distribution of goods. Within this framework it has many forms, the principal two of which are, in common usage, social democratic ("reformist") and revolutionary.

Modern socialism arose in reaction to the hardships of the INDUSTRIAL REVOLUTION, its prevailing ideology of LAISSEZ-FAIRE liberalism and its economic system of CAPITALISM. The FRENCH REVOLUTION promoted hopes of a radically changed social order in the early 1800s. Early experimental cooperative communities in the US included BROOK FARM, Nauvoo and the ONEIDA COMMUNITY. In Europe, insurrectionary socialism in the tradition of the Frenchmen BABEUF and BLANQUI played an important role in the REVOLUTIONS OF 1848 and the PARIS COMMUNE (1871). The work of MARX and ENGELS helped build socialism into a potent force. Their *Communist Manifesto* (1848) is the best-known socialist document. MARXISM, and its principle of inevitable class conflict leading to the overthrow of capitalism, formed the theoretical basis of the RUSSIAN REVOLUTION of 1917. The offshoots of ANARCHISM and SYNDICALISM developed in the years leading up to WWI; more important was the split between reformist social democrats like the FABIAN SOCIETY seeking gradual reform, and revolutionaries seeking working-class power through extra-legal means. (See LENIN; BOLSHEVISM).

Despite the efforts of such socialists as Eugene V. DEBS and Norman THOMAS, no strong socialist movement has emerged in the US. In West Europe, the SOCIAL DEMOCRATIC PARTIES have formed numerous governments, most recently in France, Greece and Spain. In Third World countries, socialism has often been linked with independence movements.

SOCIALIST PARTY, US, formed in 1901

by Eugene V. DEBS and V. L. BERGER out of the Social Democratic Party and a split from the revolutionary Socialist Labor Party, and led for many years by Norman THOMAS. It reached its peak in 1912 when, with a membership of 118,000, it got 56 socialist mayors and one congressman (Berger) elected while winning 897,000 votes for its presidential candidate (Debs). It opposed US involvement in WWI. In 1919 many radicals left to join the COMMUNIST PARTY. In 1936 right-wing members separated from the Thomas faction to form the Social Democratic Federation, but in 1958 they rejoined and the party was readmitted to the Socialist International. In 1973 a group led by Michael HARRINGTON split off from the Socialist Party to form the Democratic Socialist Organizing Committee, with the aim of working within the Democratic Party.

SOCIALIST REALISM, USSR Communist Party artistic doctrine since the early 1930s, and the dominant philosophy and style in most communist countries. The doctrine holds that, in order to serve the people and the revolution, artistic and literary works should be realistic (representational), yet portray, with "positive" heroes, the workers' progress towards socialism.

SOCIALIST WORKERS PARTY, US political party founded in 1938 in support of Leon TROTSKY's call for a Fourth International. This Marxist, anti-Soviet party favors nationalizing most industry and eliminating the military budget. It has had little success in US electoral politics.

SOCIALIZATION, in psychology and sociology, the process by which individuals are indoctrinated, by parents, teachers and peers, into accepting and following the written and unwritten rules of conduct of a particular society.

SOCIAL PSYCHOLOGY, a branch of psychology concerned with group processes and interactions among individuals. Subjects studied by social psychologists include conformity, altruism, interpersonal attraction and the development of values.

SOCIAL SCIENCES, group of studies concerned with man in relation to his cultural, social and physical environment; one of the three main divisions of human knowledge, the other two being the natural sciences and the HUMANITIES. Although social scientists usually attempt to model their disciplines on the natural sciences, aspiring to achieve a similar level of consensus, their efforts in this direction continue to be frustrated by the crudeness of

their conceptual tools in relation to the complexity of their subject matter and the limited scope afforded for controlled experiments. The social sciences are usually considered to include: ANTHROPOLOGY; ARCHAEOLOGY; DEMOGRAPHY; ECONOMICS; POLITICAL SCIENCE; PSYCHOLOGY; and SOCIOLOGY.

SOCIAL SECURITY, national program of contributory social insurance that provides monthly cash benefits to partially replace wages lost due to retirement, prolonged disability, death, or unemployment and to cover the cost of medical care during old age and disability. The benefits are paid from trust funds established by Social Security taxes paid by employees, employers, and the self-employed. The program is administered by the Social Security Administration in the US Department of Health and Human Services.

To be eligible for benefits, a worker must have had a specified period of employment in which Social Security taxes were paid. A worker becomes eligible for full benefits at age 65, although reduced benefits may be obtained up to three years earlier. Survivor benefits are payable to dependents of deceased insured workers. Disability benefits are payable to an insured worker under 65 with a prolonged disability and to the disabled worker's dependents on the same basis as dependents of retired workers.

The system was established by the Social Security Act of 1935, which instituted a program of old-age insurance to provide adequate incomes to retired workers. Its history since then has been one of improved protection, expanded coverage, and increased benefits. To the original old-age insurance Congress added survivors insurance in 1939, disability insurance in 1956, and health insurance in 1965 (see MEDICARE). To the workers in industrial and commercial occupations covered by the 1935 act, Congress in 1950 added full-time farm and domestic workers, many self-employed persons, and employees of state and local governments; it later extended coverage to members of the armed forces and to self-employed professionals. In 1983, new federal employees were included. (Still outside the Social Security system are other employees of the federal government, of some state and local governments, and of the railroads.) Over the years, Congress raised Social Security benefits as living costs rose; since 1972, increases have been automatic, pegged to the Consumer Price Index.

Largely because of Social Security, the

percentage of elderly Americans living in poverty declined from 65 in 1940, when the first retirement benefits were paid, to 15.7 in 1980. However, the expansion of coverage and benefits, and the growing proportion of aged persons in the population, then threatened the viability of the system. In 1983 Congress enacted a package of reforms recommended by a bipartisan National Commission on Social Security Reform calculated to ensure the system's viability for 75 years. These included acceleration of already scheduled payroll-tax increases, higher taxes on the self-employed, and raising the age of retirement from 65 to 66 by the year 2009 and to 67 by 2027. (See also ENTITLEMENTS; WELFARE.)

SOCIAL SETTLEMENTS, also known as settlement houses, centers of SOCIAL WORK in deprived areas of cities. The first, Toynbee Hall in London, was set up in 1884. In the US, in the late 19th century, many settlements, such as HULL HOUSE, were formed, often to help new immigrants. Their activities today include counselling, adult education, nurseries, sport and recreation.

SOCIAL WAR, 90–88 BC, conflict which arose when Rome's allies in central and S Italy demanded citizenship. It ended when Rome granted the demands, thereby uniting under Rome all Italy S of the Po R. A war between the Athenians and Thebans (357–355 BC) is also called the Social War.

SOCIAL WORK, the activity of trained social workers which has as its aim the alleviation of social problems. Casework, group work and community organization are employed. Casework involves close cooperation with individuals or families who are under mental, physical or social handicaps. Group work developed from work in early SOCIAL SETTLEMENTS, and involves group education and recreational activities. Community organization involves the identification of community problems and the coordination of local welfare services, both public and private, in solving them. A social worker's training may include psychology, sociology, law, medicine and criminology. She or he might specialize in family service, child welfare or medical, psychiatric or correctional social work. (See also WELFARE.)

SOCIETY ISLANDS, a S Pacific group, in W French Polynesia, including the Windward and Leeward archipelagoes. Named for Britain's Royal Society, the 14 islands have been French since 1843. Most of the population lives on the largest, TAHITI. Copra, sugar and tourism are important.

SOCIETY OF FRIENDS. See QUAKERS.

SOCIETY OF JESUS. See JESUITS.

SOCINIANISM, a 16th-century humanistic religious doctrine developed in Poland by the Italians Laelius Socinus and his nephew Faustus. A forerunner of and profound influence on modern UNITARIANISM, it rejected the Trinity and the divinity of Jesus.

SOCIOBIOLOGY, a controversial theory that attempts to prove the influence of natural selection on human and animal behavior. The theory postulates that genes can influence behavior as well as physiology, and that behavior may therefore be as subject to the laws of evolution as is the physical development of the species.

SOCIOLOGY, systematic study that seeks to describe and explain collective human behavior—as manifested in cultures, societies, communities and subgroups—by exploring the institutional relationships that hold between individuals and so sustain this behavior. Sociology shares its subject matter with ANTHROPOLOGY, which traditionally focuses on small, relatively isolated societies, and social PSYCHOLOGY, where the emphasis is on the study of subgroup behavior. The main emphasis in contemporary sociology is on the study of social structures and institutions and on the causes and effects of social change. Some current areas of inquiry are the family, religion, work, politics, urban life and science. Sociologists attempt to model their investigations on those of the physical sciences. Mainly because of the complexity of its subject matter and the political implications of social change, questions as to its proper aims and methods remain far from settled. There can be little doubt, however, that sociological concepts such as "internalization"—the processes by which the values and norms of a particular society are learned by its members (see SOCIALIZATION)—and "institutionalization"—the processes by which norms are incorporated in a culture as binding rules of behavior—do often illuminate important social problems. The two great pioneers of modern sociology were Emile DURKHEIM and Max WEBER. Leading US sociologists include the pioneers William SUMNER and George MEAD, and Talcott PARSONS and Daniel BELL.

SOCIOMETRY usually refers to techniques of measurement employed mainly by psychologists and sociologists in attempting to determine the relative strengths of interpersonal preferences and the relative status of individuals within groups. The term is sometimes applied to any attempt to quantify interpersonal relationships.

SOCRATES (c469–399 BC), Greek philosopher and mentor of PLATO. He wrote nothing, but much of his life and thought is vividly recorded in the dialogues of PLATO. The exact extent of Plato's indebtedness to Socrates is uncertain—e.g., it is still disputed whether the doctrine of the Forms is Socratic or Platonic; but Socrates made at least two fundamental contributions to Western philosophy: by shifting the focus of Greek philosophy from COSMOLOGY to ETHICS; and by developing the "Socratic method" of inquiry. He argued that the good life is the life illuminated by reason and strove to clarify the ideas of his interlocutors by leading them to detect the inconsistencies in their beliefs. His passion for self-consistency was evident even in his death: ultimately condemned for "impiety," he decided to accept the lawful sentence—and so remain true to his principles—rather than make good an easy escape.

SÖDERBLOM, Nathan (1866–1931), Swedish Lutheran archbishop and student of comparative religion. For his work for church unity and world peace he received the 1930 Nobel Peace Prize.

SOD HOUSE, ancient N European type of house made from strips of turf. These were used like bricks, the roof being reinforced with wood. Sod houses were also built by early settlers on the Great Plains of the US and in W Canada.

SODIUM (Na), a soft, reactive, silvery-white alkali metal. It is the sixth most common element, occurring naturally in common salt and many other important minerals such as cryolite and Chile saltpeter. It is very electropositive, and is produced by ELECTROLYSIS of fused sodium chloride (Downs process). Sodium rapidly oxidizes in air and reacts vigorously with water to give off hydrogen, so it is usually stored under kerosene. Most sodium compounds are highly ionic and soluble in water, their properties being mainly those of the anion. Sodium forms some organic compounds such as alkyls. It is used in making sodium cyanide, sodium hydride and the ANTIKNOCK ADDITIVE tetraethyl lead. Its high heat capacity and conductivity make molten sodium a useful coolant in some nuclear reactors. AW 23.0, mp 98°C, bp 883°C, sg 0.971 (20°C). **Sodium bicarbonate** ($NaHCO_3$) is a white crystalline solid, made from sodium carbonate and carbon dioxide. It gives off carbon dioxide when heated to 270°C or when reacted with acids, and is used in baking powder, fire extinguishers and as an

ANTACID. **Sodium borates** are sodium salts of BORIC ACID, differing in their degree of condensation and hydration; borax is the most important. They are white crystalline solids, becoming glassy when heated, and used in the manufacture of detergents, water softeners, fluxes, glass and ceramic glazes. **Sodium carbonate** (Na_2CO_3), or (washing) **soda,** is a white crystalline solid, made by the Solvay process. It is used in making glass, other sodium compounds, soap and paper. The alkaline solution is used in disinfectants and water softeners. mp 851°C. **Sodium hydroxide** (NaOH), or **caustic soda,** is a white deliquescent solid, usually obtained as pellets. It is a strong ALKALI, and absorbs carbon dioxide from the air. It is made by ELECTROLYSIS of sodium chloride solution or by adding calcium hydroxide to sodium carbonate solution. Caustic soda is used in the production of cellulose, plastics, soap, dyestuffs, paper and in oil refining. mp 318°C, bp 1390°C. **Sodium nitrate** ($NaNO_3$), or **soda niter,** is a colorless crystalline solid, occurring naturally in Chile saltpeter. Its properties are similar to those of potassium nitrate (see POTASSIUM), but as it is hygroscopic it is unsuitable for gunpowder. mp 307°C. **Sodium thiosulfate** ($Na_2S_2O_3$), or **hypo,** is a colorless crystalline solid. It is a mild reducing agent, used to estimate iodine, and as a photographic fixer, dissolving the silver halides which have remained unaffected by light. (For sodium chloride, see SALT.)

SODIUM PENTOTHAL. See PENTOTHAL SODIUM.

SODOM AND GOMORRAH, in the Old Testament, two of the cities in the plain of Jordan which were destroyed by God (Genesis 19) for their wickedness. Only Lot and his family were spared. The cities were in the region of the Dead Sea.

SOFIA, capital and largest city of Bulgaria, its commercial and cultural center, between the Balkan Mts of the N and the Vitosha Mts in the S. Its industry, built up since WWII, includes machinery, textiles and electrical equipment. Pop 1,114,759.

SOFTBALL, type of BASEBALL played with a softer, larger ball (12in in circumference) and a thinner bat. The bases are 60ft apart and the pitcher stands 46ft from the home plate. The ball is pitched underhand and a game lasts only seven innings. Softball was developed in Chicago in 1888 by G. W. Hancock as an indoor form of baseball. Many countries, particularly in the Americas, now compete in the annual amateur world championships.

SOFT DRINKS, nonalcoholic beverages

generally containing fruit acids, sweetening agents, and natural or artificial flavorings and colorings. In the early 19th century, carbonated water ("soda water") was developed in imitation of effervescent spa water or mineral water; this was the antecedent of carbonated soft drinks, made by absorption of CARBON dioxide under pressure. The dissolved gas gives a pleasant, slightly acid taste, and acts as a preservative. Still drinks, without carbon dioxide, are frozen or subjected to PASTEURIZATION.

SOFTWARE, term used in the COMPUTER industry to refer to all the non-hardware elements of a computer system, principally the programs.

SOIL, the uppermost surface layer of the earth, in which plants grow and on which, directly or indirectly, all life on earth depends. Soil consists, in the upper layers, of organic material mixed with inorganic matter resultant from weathering (see EROSION). Soil depth, where soil exists, may reach to many meters. Between the soil and the bedrock is a layer called the subsoil. Mature (or zonal) soil may be described in terms of four **soil horizons:** A, the uppermost layer, containing organic matter, though most of the soluble chemicals have been leached (washed out); B, strongly leached and with little or no organic matter (A and B together are often called the topsoil); C, the subsoil, a layer of weathered and shattered rock; and D, the bedrock. Three main types of soil are commonly distinguished: **pedalfers,** associated with temperate, humid climates, have a leached A-horizon but contain IRON and ALUMINUM salts with clay in the B-horizon; **pedocals,** associated with low-rainfall regions, contain CALCIUM carbonate and other salts, and **laterites** or latosols, tropical red or yellow soils, heavily leached and rich in iron and aluminum. Soils may also be classified in terms of texture (see SAND). Loams, with roughly equal proportions of sand, silt and clay, together with humus, are among the richest agricultural soils. (See also PERMAFROST.)

SOIL EROSION, the wearing away of soil, a primary cause of concern in agriculture. There are two types: **Geological erosion** denotes those naturally occurring EROSION processes that constantly affect the earth's surface features; it is usually a fairly slow process and naturally compensated for. **Accelerated erosion** describes erosion hastened by the intervention of man. **Sheet erosion** occurs usually on plowed fields. A fine sheet of rich topsoil (see SOIL) is removed by the action of RAIN water.

Repetition over the years may render the soil unfit for cultivation. In **rill erosion,** heavy rains may run off the land in streamlets: sufficient water moving swiftly enough cuts shallow trenches that may be plowed over and forgotten until, after years, the soil is found poor. In **gully erosion,** deep trenches are cut by repeated or heavy flow of water. WIND erosion is of importance in exposed, arid areas. (See also CONSERVATION.)

SOLAR CELL, device for converting the ENERGY of the sun's radiation into electrical energy. The commonest form is a large array of SEMICONDUCTOR p-n junction devices in series and parallel. By the PHOTOELECTRIC EFFECT each junction produces a small voltage when illuminated. Solar cells are chiefly used to power artificial SATELLITES. Their low efficiency (about 12%) has so far made them uncompetitive on earth except for mobile or isolated devices. In 1988 scientists announced the development of a new type of cell that achieved an efficiency (28%) sufficient to make the cells (when manufactured in quantity) competitive with oil and coal. Among other design features, these "concentrator cells" use magnifying lenses to concentrate the sun's power 500 times.

SOLAR ENERGY, the ENERGY given off by the SUN as ELECTROMAGNETIC RADIATION. In one year the sun emits about 5.4×10^{33}J of energy, of which half of one-billionth $(2.7 \times 10^{24}$J$)$ reaches the earth. Of this, most is reflected away, only 35% being absorbed. The power reaching the ground is at most $1.2 \mathrm{kW/m^2}$, and on average $0.8 \mathrm{kW/m^2}$. Solar energy is naturally converted into WIND power and into the energy of the HYDROLOGIC CYCLE, increasingly exploited as HYDROELECTRICITY. Plants convert solar energy to chemical energy by PHOTOSYNTHESIS, normally at only 0.1% efficiency; the cultivation of ALGAE in ponds can be up to 0.6% efficient, and is being developed to provide food and fuel. Solar heat energy may be used directly in several ways. Solar evaporation is used to convert brine to SALT and distilled water. Flat-plate collectors—matt-black absorbing plates with attached tubes through which a fluid flows to collect the heat—are beginning to be used for domestic water heating, space heating, and to run air-conditioning systems. Focusing collectors, using a parabolic mirror, are used in solar furnaces, which can give high power absorption at high temperatures. They are used for cooking, for high-temperature research, to power heat engines for generating electricity, and to produce electricity more directly by the Seebeck effect. Solar energy may be directly converted to electrical energy by SOLAR CELLS.

SOLAR PLEXUS, the ganglion of nerve cells and fibers situated at the back of the ABDOMEN which subserve autonomic NERVOUS SYSTEM function for much of the GASTROINTESTINAL TRACT. A sharp blow on the abdomen over the plexus causes visceral pain and "winding."

SOLAR SYSTEM, the sun and all the celestial objects that move in ORBITS around it, including the nine known planets (MERCURY; VENUS; EARTH; MARS; JUPITER; SATURN; URANUS; NEPTUNE; PLUTO), their 32 known moons, the ASTEROIDS, COMETS, meteoroids (see METEOR) and a large quantity of gas and dust. The planets all move in their orbits in the same direction, and, with the exceptions of Venus and Uranus, also rotate on their axes in this direction: this is known as direct motion. Most of the moons of the planets have direct orbits, with the exception of four of Jupiter's minor moons, the outermost moon of Saturn and the inner moon of Neptune, whose orbits are retrograde. Most of the planets move in elliptical, near circular orbits, and roughly in the same plane. The origins of the solar system are not known, though various theories have been proposed. It would not appear to be unique among the stars.

SOLAR WIND, the electrically charged material thrown out by the sun at an average speed of 400km/s. The "quiet" component is a continuous stream to which is added an "active" component produced by bursts of activity on the sun's surface. The solar wind affects the magnetic fields of the earth and Jupiter, and causes the tails of COMETS.

SOLDERING, joining metal objects using a low-melting-point ALLOY, **solder**, as the ADHESIVE. Soft solder, commonly used in electronics to join wires and other components, is an alloy of mainly lead and tin. The parts to be joined are cleaned, and heated by applying a hot soldering iron (usually having a copper bit). A flux is used to dissolve oxides, protect the surfaces, and enable the solder to flow freely. The solder melts when applied, solidifying again to form a strong joint when the iron is withdrawn. Solder is often supplied as wire with a core of noncorrosive rosin flux. Soldering at higher temperatures is termed brazing.

SOLER, Antonio (1729–1783), Spanish composer noted for his instrumental church music. Organist at the ESCORIAL monastery

from 1752, he was taught by Domenico SCARLATTI.

SOLERI, Paolo (1919–   ), Italian-born US architect. A visionary planner, he published in *Sketchbooks* (1971) his designs for Mesa City, a solar-powered desert metropolis. He began work on Acrosanti, a scaled-down version, in 1970. His buildings include Domed Desert House (1951) near Cave Creek, Ariz., and the Solimene Ceramics factory in Vietri sul Mare, Italy.

SOLFERINO, Battle of, 1859, a costly victory for French and Sardinian over Austrian forces near Solferino, Lombardy. The subsequent agreement between NEPOLEON III and FRANCIS JOSEPH ceded Lombardy to Sardinia. DUNANT's presence on the battlefield led to the founding of the Red Cross.

SOLID, one of the three physical states of matter, characterized by the property of cohesion: solids retain their shape unless deformed by external forces. True solids have a definite melting point and are crystalline, their molecules being held together in a regular pattern by stronger intermolecular forces than exist in liquids or gases. Amorphous solids are not crystalline, melt over a wide temperature range and are effectively supercooled liquids.

SOLIDARITY, independent Polish labor union spontaneously formed by workers in 1980 and eventually recognized by the Communist government following nation-wide strikes which began in the shipyards of Gdansk to protest a rise in meat prices. The strike's leader and popular hero, Lech WALESA, was elected head of the 10 million-strong Solidarity Union which together with Rural Solidarity (a union of 2.5 million farmers) rivaled the power of the official government. The democratizing process set in motion by Solidarity inaugurated an ongoing period of tension with the USSR. At the end of 1981 the Polish government tightened the reins, suspending the union and imprisoning most of its leaders. The union leaders were released in 1983, but the union itself remained outlawed—although it continued to command the emotional loyalty of millions of Poles. In 1988 Solidarity reemerged as leader in a major wave of strikes and labor unrest, and Walesa negotiated with the government for legalization of the union.

SOLID STATE PHYSICS, branch of physics concerned with the nature and properties of solid materials, many of which arise from the association and regular arrangement of atoms or molecules in crystalline solids. The term is applied particularly to studies of SEMICONDUCTORS and solid-state electronic devices.

SOLID WASTES can be dry (rubbish, scrap) or wet (garbage, sewage, industrial wastes suspended or dissolved in water). They are classified according to their sources as agricultural, mining, industrial, and municipal.

Agriculture and mining produce about 90% of all solid wastes. Agricultural solid wastes consist of crop residues and animal waste. Crop residues are returned to the land as fertilizer; animal wastes, especially those generated in feedlots and slaughterhouses, are often discharged into water or burned. Mining wastes generally accumulate near the extraction site.

Most industrial solid waste is disposed of on the generator's property. Perhaps 10–15% is hazardous — reactive, corrosive, ignitable, infectious, radioactive, or toxic — and requires "cradle to grave" management. The greatest danger from hazardous waste is contamination of water supplies either by leaching into ground water (half the US population gets its drinking water from wells) or by surface runoff into streams. Hazardous waste may contaminate land as well.

Municipal solid wastes — from residential, commercial, and institutional sources — are usually collected and disposed of by local governments either directly or through private contractors. About 75% is disposed of in open dumps, 13% in sanitary landfills, 8% by burning. Open dumps present aesthetic and health problems in addition to the political problems of their location: space is scarce in urban areas, and smaller communities do not welcome dumps for other people's wastes. Sanitary landfills, where each day's deposit of waste is covered with a layer of soil, are more costly than dumps but in some cases may upgrade low-quality sites for recreational and other uses. In recent years, it has been discovered that even sanitary landfills can be the sources of heavy metal leaching into underground water as well as methane gas, which can explode if not drawn off. Organic wastes, which constitute 75% of municipal solid wastes, can be readily burned, either incinerated or, increasingly, used for fuel in specially adapted electric generating plants. (See also POLLUTION.)

SOLOMON, second son of DAVID and Bathsheba who ruled ancient Israel about 970–933 BC at the height of its prosperity and gained a reputation for great wisdom. His success in establishing lucrative foreign trade and his introduction at home of taxation and forced labor enabled him to finance a massive building program which included a temple and royal palaces on an unprecedented scale of opulence. His story is told in 1 Kings 1–11 and 2 Chronicles 1–9 of the OLD TESTAMENT. Biblical writings later attributed to him include PROVERBS, ECCLESIASTES and the SONG OF SOLOMON.

SOLOMON ISLANDS, an independent country, extending across an area of over 232,000sq mi in the SW Pacific.

Official name: Solomon Islands
Capital: Honiara
Area: 10,640sq mi
Population: 292,000
Languages: English (official), pidgin lingua franca
Religions: Christian
Monetary unit(s): 1 Solomon Island dollar = 100 cents

Land. The mountainous Solomon Island archipelago, composed of 21 large islands and many smaller islets, is of volcanic origin; four volcanoes are intermittently active. The highest peak, Mt Makarakombou (8,028ft), is on Guadalcanal, the largest island where Honiara, the capital, is located. The Solomons are well watered and covered with dense tropical rain forests, with grasslands on the N plains of Guadalcanal. The climate is equatorial, and temperatures vary little during the year; yearly rainfall, averaging 120in, is concentrated from Nov. to Apr.

People and Economy. The population is almost 95% Melanesian with Polynesian, Micronesian, European and Chinese minorities. Most follow the traditional life-style, living in small villages, fishing and growing coconuts, taro, yams and cassava. Exports, formerly exclusively copra, now also include fish and timber. Tourism is increasingly important.

History. The Solomons were largely ignored by Europeans until the 19th century, when islanders were forcibly recruited to labor overseas. By 1900 Britain had assumed control. Invaded by the Japanese in 1942, the islands were only recaptured by US forces after heavy fighting in 1943. The islands became internally self-governing in 1976 and gained full independence in 1978. A cyclone in 1986 left 500,000 people homeless and devastated agriculture.

SOLON (c639–559 BC), Athenian law-giver and poet, one of the Seven Sages. Elected *archon* (government leader) of Athens in 594 BC, he repealed the repressive laws of DRACO and freed those enslaved for debt. Dividing citizens into four income classes, he reformed the Greek oligarchy by allowing members of all four classes to sit in the assembly and the law courts. Later he resisted the tyrant Pisistratus.

SOLOW, Robert Merton (1924–   ), US economist, at the Massachusetts Institute of Technology from 1949, who received the 1987 Nobel Prize for Economics for seminal contributions to the theory of economic growth.

SOLSTICES, the two times each year when the sun is on the points of the ecliptic farthest from the equator (see CELESTIAL SPHERE). At the summer solstice in late June the sun is directly overhead at noon on the TROPIC of Cancer; at winter solstice, in late December, it is overhead at noon on the Tropic of Capricorn.

SOLTI, Sir Georg (1912–   ), Hungarian-born British conductor. He is best known for his great recordings of Wagner and Richard Strauss and was musical director of Covent Garden (1961–71), of the Paris Opera and subsequently of the Chicago Symphony.

SOLUTION, a homogeneous molecular mixture of two or more substances, commonly of a solid and a liquid, though solid/solid solutions also exist. The liquid component is usually termed the *solvent*, the other component, which is dissolved in it, the *solute*. The **solubility** of a solute in a given solvent at a particular temperature is usually stated as the mass which will dissolve in 100g of the solvent to give a saturated solution (see SATURATION). Solubility generally increases with temperature. For slightly soluble ionic compounds, the **solubility product**—the product of the individual ionic solubilities—is a constant at a given temperature. Most substances are solvated when dissolved: that is, their molecules become surrounded by solvent molecules acting as ligands. Ionic crystals dissolve to give individual solvated ions, and some good solvents of high dielectric constant (such as water) cause certain covalent compounds to ionize, wholly or partly (see also ACID). Analogous to an ideal gas, the hypothetical **ideal solution** is one which is formed from its components without change in total volume or internal energy: it obeys Raoult's law and its corollaries, so that the addition of solute produces a lowering of the freezing point, elevation of the boiling point and increase is in osmotic pressure (see OSMOSIS), all proportional to the number of MOLES added. (See also ELECTROLYSIS.)

SOLVENT, a liquid capable of dissolving a substance to form a SOLUTION. Generally "like dissolves like"; thus a nonpolar covalent solid such as naphthalene dissolves well in a hydrocarbon solvent. Overall, best solvents are those with polar molecules and high dielectric constant: WATER is the most effective known.

SOLZHENITSYN, Alexander Isayevich (1918–   ), Russian novelist. His own experience of Stalin's labor camps was described in *One Day in the Life of Ivan Denisovich* (1962), acclaimed in the USSR and abroad. But *The First Circle* and *Cancer Ward* (both 1968) were officially condemned. He accepted the 1970 Nobel Prize for literature by letter. His expulsion in 1974 and his warnings on the moral and political fate of the West drew worldwide publicity. Solzhenitsyn's works include *August 1914* (1971) and *The Gulag Archipelago* (1974).

SOMALIA, a republic occupying the E "horn" of Africa, comprises two former colonies, British Somaliland and Italian Somaliland, which gained independence and united on July 1, 1960.

Official name: Somali Democratic Republic
Capital: Mogadishu
Area: 246,000sq mi
Population: 6,160,000
Languages: Somali, Arabic, English, Italian
Religions: Muslim
Monetary unit(s): 1 Somali shilling = 100 centesimi
Land. Although its E coast lies along the Indian Ocean, Somalia is mainly desert. A narrow, barren N coastal plain, hemmed in by high mountains, gives way to high

plateaus, dry savanna plains and to the country's most fertile area, between the Shibeli and Juba rivers in the S. The climate is hot; yearly rainfall varies from about 3in in the N to 20in in the S. Wildlife includes big game and many species of antelope.

People. The population consists mainly of Somalis belonging to northern nomadic or southern farming clans. Somali, the national language, lacks a written form. Arabic (widely spoken), Italian and English are the written languages. The literacy rate is about 15%. Most Somalis move from place to place with their herds and portable woodframe huts; others live in small villages or trade centers built around a well.

Economy. Somalia ranks as one of the world's poorest countries, its development hampered by various factors, among them a lack of natural resources, undeveloped infrastructure, periodic drought and shortages of skilled labor and expertise. Agriculture accounts for the major share of revenues and employment.

History. Europeans colonized Somalia in the late 1800s. Independent Somalia continued its heavy dependence on US and Italian aid. In 1969 President Shermarke was assassinated and a revolutionary council headed by Maj. Gen. Mohammed Siyad Barre took control. The Somali Democratic Republic was declared a socialist state. An armed conflict with Ethiopia erupted in 1963–64 and again in 1977–78 over the disputed territory of the Ogaden. Despite a tacit truce clashes recurred, and hundreds of thousands of refugees streamed into Somalia. Even with assistance by international agencies, Somalia's already meager resources were further strained. Ethiopia and Somalia restored diplomatic relations in 1988. Later that year, a rebel group that had opposed the government since 1982 intensified its attacks, causing hundreds of thousands of Somalis to seek refuge in Ethiopia.

SOMATOTYPES, in anthropometry, descriptions of physique, sometimes supposedly also descriptive of temperament. The individual is classified by three digits representing the extent of his endomorphy (plumpness), mesomorphy (muscularity) and ectomorphy (slenderness), respectively.

SOMERSET, Edward Seymour, 1st Duke of (c1500–1552), protector of England 1547–49 on the death of HENRY VIII and accession of EDWARD VI. He used his great power to repeal heresy and treason laws. Falsely accused of treason by his rivals, he was finally executed.

SOMME RIVER, in N France, rises near Saint-Quentin and flows W and NW some 150mi through Amiens to its English Channel estuary at Saint-Valéry. Scene of the greatest WWI battle of attrition (July–Nov. 1916), it saw over a million casualties of all nations. On July 1 alone there were 57,000 British casualties (19,000 killed).

SOMNAMBULISM, or sleepwalking, state in which the body is able to walk and perform other automatic tasks while consciousness is diminished. Often seen in anxious children, it is said to be unwise to awaken them as intense fear may be felt.

SOMOZA, the name of a Nicaraguan family, three members of which controlled Nicaragua from 1936 to 1979. In 1936 **Anastasio Somoza Garcia** (1896–1956) deposed his uncle, President Sacasa, becoming president himself in 1937. Assassinated after 20 years of nepotistic dictatorship, he was succeeded by his son **Luis Somoza Debayle** (1922–1967), who held formal office until 1963. In 1967 Anastasio's second son **Anastasio Somoza Debayle** (1925–1980) was elected president. Replaced by a puppet triumvirate in 1972, he retained control of the army and was reelected president in 1974. His corrupt rule led to a revolt in 1977 by leftist Sandinist guerrillas, who gradually gained broad support and forced him to flee the country for exile in Paraguay in 1979. A year later Somoza was assassinated in Asuncíon.

SONAR, *sound navigation and ranging,* technique used at sea for detecting and determining the position of underwater objects (e.g. submarines; shoals of fish) and for finding the depth of water under a ship's keel. Sonar works on the principle of echolocation: high-frequency SOUND pulses are beamed from the ship and the direction of and time taken for any returning ECHOES are measured to give the direction and range of the reflecting objects.

SONATA, in music, term used in the 17th and early 18th centuries to describe works for various small groups of instruments, as opposed to the cantata, originally for voices only. Since the late 18th century, it has been restricted to works for piano or other solo instrument (the latter usually with keyboard accompaniment), generally in three movements.

SONG, a musical setting of words, usually a short poem, often with instrumental accompaniment. There are two basic kinds: songs in which each verse repeats the same tune, and songs with a continuous thematic development. The origins of the song are lost in the history of FOLK MUSIC and POETRY (poetry was originally sung); it became a mature art in Western cultures in OPERA arias, the German *lieder*—those of SCHUBERT are supreme examples—and the French *chanson*. The song-forms that have most influenced 20th-century popular music are probably the BALLAD and the BLUES.

SONGHAI, former West African empire, founded in the 8th century by a Berber farming and trading people around the middle Niger R. Converted to Islam in the 11th century, and adopting Gao as its capital, it expanded mainly at the expense of the MALI EMPIRE, and commanded trans-Saharan trade, reaching its greatest extent under Askia I, who rules 1493–1528. Its breakup in the later 1500s was hastened by a Moroccan invasion (1591).

SONG OF ROLAND. See CHANSON DE ROLAND.

SONG OF SOLOMON, or **Song of Songs,** or **Canticles,** OLD TESTAMENT book traditionally ascribed to SOLOMON. A series of exquisite love poems, it has been interpreted by both Jews and Christians as an allegorical description of God's love for his people.

SONIC BOOM, loud noise generated in the form of a shockwave cone when an airplane traveling faster than the speed of sound overtakes the pressure waves it produces. Because of sonic boom damage, supersonic planes are confined to closely defined flight paths.

SONNET, a lyric poem of fourteen lines with traditional rules of structure and rhyme scheme. Devised in 13th-century Italy and perfected by PETRARCH, it entered English literature in the 16th century, and was adopted by such poets as SHAKESPEARE, MILTON, KEATS and WORDSWORTH as a vehicle for concentrated thought and feeling, very often of love.

SONNINO, Sidney, Barone (1847–1922), Italian statesman, premier 1906, 1909–10. As foreign minister (1915–19), he negotiated the secret Treaty of London (1915) under which Italy entered WWI on the side of the Allies. Sonnino represented Italy at the Paris Peace Conference, where US president Woodrow Wilson resisted the territorial promises made to Italy in the treaty.

SONS OF LIBERTY, members of a patriotic society formed in the American colonies in 1765 to oppose the passage of the STAMP ACT. Their campaign of public protest eventually expanded into a general movement for American independence.

SONTAG, Susan (1933–), US novelist, short-story writer, filmmaker and essayist. Her best-known books include *Against Interpretation* (1966), *On Photography* (1977), *Illness as Metaphor* (1978) and *Under the Sign of Saturn* (1980).

SOONERS, name given to the many Okla. homesteaders who entered the Indian Territory in advance of the date of the first official "run"—April 22, 1889. Okla. is familiarly known to this day as the Sooner State.

SOONG, influential Chinese family of **Charles Jones Soong** (1866–1918), an American-educated Methodist minister and businessman in Shanghai. **Soong Ch'ing-ling** (1890–1981) married SUN YAT-SEN and continued to play a leading role in the Chinese revolution after his death, becoming deputy head of state 1949. **Soong Tzu-wen** (T.V. Soong; 1894–1971), a wealthy financier and politician, held important posts in the Nationalist government (1925–47), but retired to the US in 1949. **Soong Mei-ling** (1897–   ) married CHIANG KAI-SHEK and became a well-known publicist for the Nationalist government, especially during WWII.

SOPHISTS, "wise men," name given to certain teachers in Greece in the 5th and 4th centuries BC, the most famous of whom were GORGIAS and PROTAGORAS. They taught RHETORIC and the qualities needed for success in political life. PLATO attacked them for taking fees, teaching skepticism about law, morality and knowledge, and concentrating on how to win arguments regardless of truth—attacks still reflected in the modern word "sophistry."

SOPHOCLES (c495–406 BC), great Athenian dramatist, together with AESCHYLUS and EURIPIDES one of the founders of Greek tragedy. Only seven plays survive, the best-known being *Oedipus Rex, Oedipus at Colonus, Antigone* and *Electra*. They dwell on the tragic ironies of human existence, particularly on the role of fate. Heroic figures, tricked by fate into acts necessitating moral retribution, suffer in the event more harshly than they seem to deserve. The plays are highly dramatic (Sophocles regularly won first prize in the dramatic competitions), and contain much noble poetry.

SORBONNE, a college founded in Paris in 1253 by Robert de Sorbon. It was a famous medieval theological center, rebuilt in the 17th century by RICHELIEU and re-established in 1808 after being closed in the French Revolution. Its name is often used to refer to the University of Paris, into which it was incorporated in the 19th century.

SOREL, Georges (1847–1922), French sociologist, philosopher of revolutionary SYNDICALISM and author of *Reflections on*

Violence (1908). Despising democracy and the bourgeoisie, he believed in the moral regeneration of society through violence. He influenced both FASCISM and the far left.

SORGHUM, widely cultivated CEREAL CROP (*Sorghum vulgare*), the most important grown in Africa. It grows best in warm conditions and is most important as a drought-resistant crop. For human food, the grain is first ground into a meal and then made up into porridge, bread or cakes. The grain is also used as a cattle feed and the whole plants as forage. There are many types in cultivation including durra and kaffir. Family: Graminae.

SOROKIN, Pitirim Alexandrovich (1889–1968), Russian-US sociologist. He distinguished between "sensate" (empirical, scientific) and "ideational" (mystical, authoritarian) societies, and wrote *Social and Cultural Dynamics* (1937–41).

SOULÉ, Pierre (1801–1870), US politician and diplomat. He emigrated in 1825 from France to New Orleans, where he became a prominent Democrat. A US senator (1847; 1849–53) and minister to Spain (1853–54), he resigned after signing the OSTEND MANIFESTO.

SOUL MUSIC, a flamboyant, highly emotional vocal and instrumental music created by blacks out of the rhythms and style of GOSPEL MUSIC. Soul first became known to the US public at large in the late 1950s through such big-name singers as James Brown and Ray Charles, and reached the height of popularity in the 1960s with the recordings of Aretha Franklin and Otis Redding.

SOUND, mechanical disturbance, such as a change of pressure, particle displacement or stress, propagated in an elastic medium (e.g. air or water), that can be detected by an instrument or by an observer who hears the auditory sensation it produces. Sound is a measurable physical phenomenon and an important stimulus to man. It forms a major means of communication in the form of spoken language, and both natural and manmade sounds (of traffic or machinery) contribute largely to our environment. The EAR is very sensitive and will tolerate a large range of sound energies, but enigmas remain as to exactly how it produces the sensation of hearing. The Greeks appreciated that sound was connected with air motion and that the PITCH of a musical sound produced by a vibrating source depended on the vibration FREQUENCY. Attempts to measure the velocity of sound in air date from the 17th century. Sound is carried as a longitudinal compressional wave in an elastic medium: part of the medium next to

a sound source is compressed, but its elasticity makes it expand again, compressing the region next to it and so on. The velocity of such waves depends on the medium and the temperature, but is always much less than that of light. Sound waves are characterized by their wavelength and frequency. Humans cannot hear sounds of frequencies below 16Hz and above 20kHz, such sounds being known as infrasonic and ULTRASONIC respectively. The sound produced by a tuning fork has a definite frequency, but most sounds are a combination of frequencies. The amount of motion in a sound wave determines its loudness or softness and the intensity falls off with the square of distance from the source. Sound waves may be reflected from surfaces (as in an ECHO), refracted or diffracted, the last property enabling us to hear around corners. The intensity of a sound is commonly expressed in decibels above an arbitrary reference level; its loudness is measured in phons.

SOUND BARRIER, term referring to the extra forces acting on an airplane when it goes supersonic.

SOUND RECORDING, the conversion of SOUND waves into a form in which they can be stored, the original sound being reproducible by use of playback equipment. The first sound recording was made by Thomas EDISON in 1877 (see PHONOGRAPH). In modern electronic recording of all kinds, the sound is first converted by one or more MICROPHONES into electrical signals. In the case of **mechanical recordings** (discs, or records), these signals—temporarily recorded on magnetic tape—are made to vibrate a stylus that cuts a spiral groove in a rotating disc covered with lacquer. The master disc is copied by electroforming to produce stamper dies used to press the plastic copies. (See also HIGH-FIDELITY.) In **magnetic recording,** the microphone signals activate an ELECTROMAGNET which imposes a pattern of magnetization on moving magnetic wire, discs or tape with a ferromagnetic coating (see also MAGNETISM; TAPE RECORDER). **Optical recording,** used for many motion-picture sound tracks, converts the microphone signals into a photographic exposure on film using a light beam and a variable shutter. The sound is played back by shining a light beam through the track onto a PHOTOELECTRIC CELL. As with the playback equipment for the other recording methods, this reproduces electrical signals which are amplified and fed to a loudspeaker.

SOUPHANOUVONG, **Prince** (1909?–   ), Laotian political leader. A nationalist and communist, he helped organize (1950) the Pathet Lao, which fought the French and then noncommunist elements in Laos. When communists took control (1975) of S Vietnam and Cambodia, the Pathet Lao seized power in Laos and installed Souphanouvong as head of state.

SOUSA, John Philip (1854–1932), US band master and composer. He wrote many light operas, but is best remembered today for his military marches, including "The Stars and Stripes Forever" and "The Washington Post." Sousa was leader of the Marine Band in Washington before forming a world-touring band of his own.

SOUSAPHONE, a coiled TUBA, or helicon, named for the US bandleader John Philip Sousa, who had suggested the idea for such an instrument. It is equipped with a flexible end, or "bell," that can be moved about to send sound in any direction.

SOUTH AFRICA, independent republic occupying the southern tip of Africa. It is bounded N by Namibia (South West Africa), Botswana, Zimbabwe, Mozambique and Swaziland, and it surrounds the republic of LESOTHO. It comprises four provinces: the Cape, Natal, Transvaal and the Orange Free State.

Official name: Republic of South Africa
Capital: Pretoria
Area: 470,412sq mi
Population: 34,975,000
Languages: Afrikaans, English
Religions: Christian, Bantu
Monetary unit(s): 1 rand = 100 cents

Land. A vast system of grassland plateaus is separated from narrow coastal plains by the ranges of the Great Escarpment, which reaches 11,000ft in the Drakensberg Mts in the E. The westward-flowing Orange R drains most of the interior plateau. The climate is mainly warm temperate. Much of the land in the W is arid or semiarid. Rainfall is greatest in the S and E.

People. The population is about 74% black African (mainly Zulu and Xhosa), 14% white, 9% of mixed descent and 3% Asiatic. About two-thirds of the whites are Afrikaners. About half the people are urban, the largest cities being Johannesburg, Durban, Cape Town, Pretoria and Port Elizabeth. The black Africans speak a variety of Bantu languages; many speak AFRIKAANS or English as well. Most of the population is Christian, belonging to a wide variety of churches.

Economy. South Africa produces most of the world's gem diamonds and gold, has large coal reserves and is also rich in uranium, iron ore, asbestos, copper, manganese, nickel, chrome, titanium and phosphates. Mining contributes the major share of export earnings, but accounts for only 12–13% of the gross domestic product. The largest contributor is manufacturing, which includes food processing, iron, steel and oil-from-coal production, engineering and textiles. Industry and mining are concentrated in the S and E. South Africa is self-sufficient in food production and is a major exporter of food to neighboring countries. The leading crops are corn, sugarcane and a variety of fruits. Wool is a major export. Dairying also flourishes.

History. South Africa was already inhabited by BUSHMEN, HOTTENTOTS, and Bantu peoples from the N when white settlement began in 1652, with the Dutch establishing a colony at Cape Town. The main period of British rule (1806–1910) saw the GREAT TREK (1835–43), the founding of BOER (Dutch farmer) republics inland, and the BOER WAR (1899–1902). In 1910 the Union of South Africa was formed out of the various colonies (now the four provinces), and during WWI South West Africa was wrested from the Germans. Since 1948 South Africa has been ruled by the Afrikaner-led National Party, which has set up an efficient and repressive state apparatus to implement the policies of APARTHEID. In recent years several tribal and racial "homelands" have been designated (see HOMELANDS). Four—the Transkei, Bophuthatswana, Venda and Ciskei—have already been granted "independence" but are not recognized by any country other than South Africa. Other homelands are: Gazankulu, KwaZulu, Lebowa, Qwaqwa, Ndebele and KaNgwane. The homelands encompass only 13% of South Africa's land area. In 1961 the country became a republic and left the Commonwealth largely because of differences over its apartheid policies. Despite the easing of many apartheid restrictions in the late 1970s and 1980s and the granting of Coloureds and Asians a limited role in the national government under a new constitution in 1983, the economy and government remain firmly under white control.

Increasingly violent black protests against apartheid, particularly in the black townships, led to the imposition of a nationwide state of emergency in 1986. While continuing to suppress dissent at home, the government adopted a more conciliatory posture in regional affairs in 1988, including the signing of a preliminary accord designed to end the civil war in neighboring Angola and bring independence to Namibia, which had been ruled illegally by South Africa since WWII.

SOUTH AFRICA WAR. See BOER WAR.

SOUTH AMERICA, the southern half of the two Western Hemisphere continents, linked with the northern by the narrow land bridge of CENTRAL AMERICA. It comprises twelve independent republics: Argentina, Bolivia, Brazil, Chile, Colombia, Ecuador, Guyana, Paraguay, Peru, Suriname, Uruguay and Venezuela, and one European possession, French Guiana.

Land and resources. Roughly triangular in shape, South America is surrounded by the Caribbean Sea on the N, the Atlantic Ocean on the E and the Pacific Ocean on the W. It has a coastline of about 15,000mi. The most prominent feature is the Andean mountain system, with more than 50 peaks exceeding 20,000ft. Mt Aconcagua (22,834ft) in Argentina is the highest mountain in the Western Hemisphere. Other features include three major river basins: the Amazon (the world's most voluminous river), Paraná, and Orinoco; the Brazilian and Guiana highlands in the E and NE; and the pampas grassland and Patagonian plateau of Argentina. The world's largest tropical rain forest is in the Amazon river basin. The climate varies from extreme cold in the high Andes to tropical humid heat in the lowlands near the equator. Native plants include beans, pumpkins, squashes, tomatoes, peanuts, pineapples, red peppers, tapioca, rubber, tobacco, and cocoa. Produce of the tropical forests, which cover about half the area, includes hardwoods, brazil and cashew nuts, quinine and quebracho bark. Sugarcane, coffee and oil palms are important imported crops. Among the native animal species are hummingbids, parrots, and the condor; jaguar, llama and alpaca; anteaters, sloths, tapirs and armadillos; and piranhas, anacondas and boa constrictors. South America is rich in mineral resources, many far from fully developed. The most abundant resources are oil in the N (mainly in Venezuela) and iron ore (in Brazil, Venezuela, and Colombia); other minerals include copper, tin, lead, zinc, manganese, gold, nitrate and bauxite. There is very little coal but considerable hydroelectric potential.

People. There are four main groups: the native Indians; white Europeans, mainly of Spanish or Portuguese descent; Negroes, who originally came as slaves; and people of mixed Indian, Negro, and European ancestry (mestizo usually means of Indian-European and mulatto of Negro-European origin). The total population is almost 277 million. The chief official languages are Spanish and Portuguese (the latter is spoken in Brazil). In Guyana, Suriname and French Guiana, the official languages are English, Dutch and English, and French, respectively. The most widely spoken Indian languages are Guaraní (in Paraguay), Quechua (in Peru, Bolivia and Ecuador) and Aymará (in Bolivia). Two countries, Argentina and Uruguay, have a predominantly European population; three countries, Peru, Bolivia, and Ecuador, have large Indian populations; and the rest are inhabited by people of mixed descent. About 90% of South Americans are nominally Catholic.

SOUTH CAROLINA, state of the SE US bordered to the N by N.C., S and E by the Atlantic Ocean, and S and SW by Georgia. It is one of the original 13 states.

Name of state: South Carolina
Capital: Columbia
Statehood: May 23, 1788 (8th state)
Familiar name: Palmetto State
Area: 31,055sq mi
Population: 3,377,000
Elevation: Highest—3,560ft., Sassafras Mountain; Lowest—sea level, Atlantic Ocean
Motto: *Animis opibusque parati* ("Prepared in mind and resources"); *Dum spiro spero* ("While I breathe, I hope")
State flower: Yellow jessamine
State bird: Carolina wren
State tree: Palmetto
State song: "Carolina"

Land. The three main regions are the Atlantic coastal plain, occupying the SE two-thirds of the state, the Piedmont plateau in the NW, and the Blue Ridge Mts in the extreme NW. Rivers include the Pee Dee, Santee, Edisto and Savannah. Summers are hot (average daily temperature over 70°F) and winters mild. Rainfall averages 47in per year.

People. The population is about 55% rural, and mainly Protestant. Columbia, Charleston and Greenville are the major cities. Blacks make up about 31% of the population.

Economy. Once overwhelmingly agricultural, the economy is now based principally on manufacturing. Textiles and clothing, employing 40% of the manufacturing workforce, are most important, followed by chemicals, and the manufacture of machinery. Agricultural produce includes tobacco, soybeans, cotton and peaches. Livestock farming is increasing, and the state's forests, covering two-thirds of its area, support growing lumber and paper industries.

History. South Carolina was first settled as a PROPRIETARY COLONY in 1670, but dissatisfaction with the proprietors led the colonists to revolt in 1719, and the province became a royal colony in 1729. During the REVOLUTIONARY WAR, victories at KING'S MOUNTAIN and COWPENS offset the fall of Charleston to the British in 1780. In 1786 the capital was moved to Columbia to help unify the two sections of the state, the rich planters of the lowlands and the poorer farmers of the Piedmont. In the NULLIFICATION and STATES' RIGHTS controversies preceding the CIVIL WAR, slave-owning South Carolina took the radical lead, and became the first state to secede from the Union. The first shots of the Civil War were fired at FORT SUMTER, and South Carolina experienced bitter fighting and an equally bitter Reconstruction period, followed by continuing agricultural depression and chronic political corruption. The black majority was effectively disenfranchised, and even in the 1960s, there was resistance to INTEGRATION. Since WWII an industrial and agricultural revival has brought new prosperity; and South Carolina has been growing rapidly, its population rising 30% from 1970 to 1986. In presidential elections 1968–88, South Carolina voted Republican in 1968–72 and 1980–88.

SOUTH CHINA SEA, part of the Pacific Ocean, bounded by mainland Asia and Malaysia to the N and W, Borneo to the S, and the Philippines to the E. It is tropical, and subject to frequent typhoons.

SOUTH DAKOTA, state of the north-central US, bounded on the N by N.D., E by Ia. and Minn., S by Neb., and W by Mont.

Name of State: South Dakota
Capital: Pierre
Statehood: Nov. 2, 1889 (40th state)
Familiar name: Sunshine State, Coyote State
Area: 77,047sq mi
Population: 708,000
Elevation: Highest—7,242ft., Harney Peak; Lowest—962ft., Big Stone Lake
Motto: Under God the people rule
State flower: American pasqueflower
State bird: Ring-necked pheasant
State tree: Black Hills spruce
State song: "Hail, South Dakota" and Wyo.

Land. South Dakota can be divided into the rugged Great Plains in the W and center, the more fertile Central Lowlands to the E, and the semi-arid badlands and Black Hills to the SW. The state is bisected by the Missouri R. Climate is continental, with low humidity and great seasonal temperature changes. Rainfall ranges from about 13in per year in the NW to 25in in the SE.

People. South Dakota has the lowest population density of all the states E of the Rockies. It is also one of the least urbanized, with only about 45% of the population living in urban areas. Sioux Falls and Rapid City are the biggest cities. There are large Indian reservations bordering Lake Oahe (on the Missouri R.). The largest religious denomination is the Lutheran Church.

Economy. Agriculture, particularly livestock and livestock produce, provides 80% of the total value of all goods produced in the state. Leading crops include wheat, corn and oats. Manufacturing is dominated by food processing. Gold is mined in the Black Hills where the Homestake Mine at Lead is the largest in the Western Hemisphere. The Black Hills, Badlands National Park, and other areas are popular with tourists.

History. Home of the Arikara, CHEYENNE and SIOUX Indians, South Dakota became part of the US with the LOUISIANA PURCHASE (1803) and was explored by LEWIS AND CLARK (1804–06). Settlement was first stimulated by the fur trade, but by the 1850s farmers had begun to move in. In

1861 South Dakota was included in the Dakota territory with its capital at Yankton. Increasing conflict with Indian tribes was settled by the Laramie Treaty (1868) which created the Great Sioux Reservation. General CUSTER violated the treaty in a search for gold in the Black Hills (1874), and soon the area was flooded with miners and prospectors; Indian resistance came to an end at WOUNDED KNEE (1890). New railroads brought more farmers, and the population tripled between 1880 and 1890.

The boundary with North Dakota was drawn and both states entered the Union in 1889, but the boom was already almost over and the state suffered from successive droughts and depressions from which it did not recover until after WWII. Since then hydroelectric projects, control of the Missouri R, farm mechanization, industrial expansion and expanded tourism have brought a new prosperity that continued through the farm depression of the mid-1980s and the drought of 1988. In presidential elections 1968–88, South Dakota voted consistently Republican.

SOUTHEAST ASIA TREATY ORGAN-IZATION (SEATO), a defense treaty signed by Australia, France, Great Britain, New Zealand, Pakistan, the Philippines, Thailand and the US after the French had withdrawn from Indochina in 1954. Its aim was to prevent communist expansion. There was a headquarters at Bangkok, Thailand, but no standing forces. The treaty was invoked by the US in the VIETNAM WAR. Pakistan withdrew in 1972. SEATO terminated itself in 1977.

SOUTHERN RHODESIA. See ZIMBABWE.

SOUTHEY, Robert (1774–1843), English Poet Laureate from 1813, a friend of WORDSWORTH and COLERIDGE. His large output includes long narrative poems, journalism, histories, biographies and verse collections. Famous in his day as a poet, he is now more admired as a prose writer, notably for his *Life of Nelson* (1813).

SOUTH POLE, the point in Antarctica through which passes the earth's axis of rotation. It does not coincide with the earth's S Magnetic Pole (see EARTH). It was first reached by Roald Amundsen (Dec. 14, 1911). (See also CELESTIAL SPHERE; MAGNETISM; NORTH POLE.)

SOUTH SEA BUBBLE, popular name for speculation in the South Sea Company, created in England in 1711 to trade with Spanish America. In 1720 the company's proposal to take over the NATIONAL DEBT, aided by fraudulent promotions, pushed shares to fantastic prices. In the subsequent collapse many were ruined.

SOUTHWELL, Robert (c1561–1595), English Jesuit, devotional poet and Roman Catholic martyr. He returned from Rome to England in 1586 as a missionary to the persecuted Catholics. Arrested in 1592, he was tortured and finally executed.

SOUTH WEST AFRICA. See NAMIBIA.

SOUTINE, Chaim (1894–1943), Russian-born French expressionist painter. His style uses vivid primary colors and twisting, rhythmic forms, as in *Pastry Cook* (1922).

SOVEREIGNTY, supreme political power in a state. In political theory debates on sovereignty center on the role of the sovereign and on the nature of supreme power—by what rights, and by whom, it should be wielded. A *sovereign state* is one that is independent of control by other states (but see INTERNATIONAL LAW; UNITED NATIONS).

SOVIET, the basic political unit of socialist Russia (from *sovet*, a council). The soviets, ranging in importance from rural councils to the Supreme Soviet, the major legislative body of the Soviet Union, are elected policy-making and administrative units. The first soviets were the strike committees set up during the 1905 revolution.

SOVIET UNION. See UNION OF SOVIET SOCIALIST REPUBLICS.

SOYBEAN, *Glycine max* or *G. soja*, a leguminous plant native to E Asia providing food, animal feed and industrial raw material. It has been grown as a staple food in China for over 5,000 years. Richer in PROTEIN than most MEAT, it also contains calcium, VITAMINS, minerals, acids and lecithin. Soy flour is used to make artificial meats and is also an important food in times of famine. Soybean oil is used in the manufacture of margarine, paints, soap, linoleum, textiles, paper and agricultural sprays. Over half of the world's soybean crop is now grown in the US.

SOYER, Raphael (1899–1987), Russian-born US artist. Called the "dean of American realism," Soyer is best known for his street scenes and portraits of lonely inhabitants of New York's Lower East Side. His brothers, **Moses** (1899–1974) and **Isaac** (1907–1981), were also realist painters.

SOYINKA, Wole (1934–   ), Nigerian playwright, novelist and poet, recipient of the 1986 Nobel Prize for Literature.

SPAAK, Paul Henri (1899–1972), Belgium's first Socialist premier (1938–39, 1947–49), and deputy premier (1961–65). He was foreign secretary several times between 1936 and 1966, and was president of the UNITED NATIONS General Assembly in 1946. He was influential in setting up the

EUROPEAN ECONOMIC COMMUNITY and was secretary-general of the NORTH ATLANTIC TREATY ORGANIZATION 1957–61.

SPAATZ, Carl Andrew (1891–1974), US general, WWII commander of US bombing forces in Europe (1944) and then in the Pacific (1945). In 1946 he was made commander of the Army Air Forces and in 1947–48 served as first chief of staff of the US Air Force.

SPACE, in MATHEMATICS, a bounded or unbounded extent. In GEOMETRY this extent may be in one, two or three dimensions, its nature being viewed differently in different geometries. According to EUCLIDEAN GEOMETRY space is uniform and infinite, so that we may talk of a line of infinite extent or a polygon of infinite area. In Riemannian geometry, however, all lines are of less than a certain, finite extent; and in LOBACHEVSKIAN GEOMETRY, there is a similar maximum of area. The term is also often used for sets that have some kind of structure imposed on them, as in "topological space" and "vector space." (See TOPOLOGY; ALGEBRA, ABSTRACT.)

SPACE EXPLORATION. The age of space exploration began on Oct. 5, 1957 (Oct. 4 in the US) with the launching by the Soviet Union of the first artificial earth satellite, Sputnik 1, an aluminum sphere 23in in diameter and weighing 184 lb. Both the US and the USSR had planned to launch satellites during the International Geophysical Year (July 1, 1957–Dec. 31, 1958), when scientists around the world were making a coordinated effort to collect data in all the earth sciences. The missile programs of the two superpowers provided the rocket technology that made such launchings possible. On Nov. 3 the Soviets launched Sputnik 2, which weighed 1,121 lb and carried a live dog. The first US satellite, Explorer 1, weighing 30 lb, was launched on Jan. 31, 1958.

The exploration of space is conducted by means of satellites, unmanned space probes, and manned space flights, including space shuttles and space stations.

Satellites. In 1988, eight countries—the US, USSR, France, Japan, China, Great Britain, India, and Israel—had independent space programs involving artificial satellites. Some had provided launch services or equipment to other countries that had orbited satellites. Thirteen European countries participated in the European Space Agency (ESA) to share the costs and benefits of satellite programs. Satellites are of different kinds and have different purposes: communications, weather observation, navigational aids, scientific re-

search, and military intelligence. (See SATELLITES, ARTIFICIAL.)

Unmanned Space Probes. Unmanned probes beyond the immediate vicinity of the earth began with studies of the moon in preparation for manned landings there. A Soviet spacecraft, Luna 1, flew within 4,600mi of the moon in 1959; that same year, Luna 2 impacted on the moon and Luna 3 transmitted the first pictures of the moon's far side. In 1966, Luna 9 landed on the moon and transmitted pictures of the moon's surface. In 1970, Luna 16 landed on the moon and returned to earth with samples of the moon's soil. Two months later Luna 17 put a wheeled vehicle on the moon equipped with television cameras and research instruments controlled from earth.

US moon probes began with the Pioneer and Ranger programs. Designed to hard-land (crash) on the moon, Ranger spacecraft in 1964 transmitted pictures of the moon's surface before impacting. In 1966–68 Surveyor spacecraft made soft landings on the moon and analyzed the soil, and Lunar Orbiters circled the moon to identify landing sites for US astronauts, who first landed on the moon in 1969.

A systematic study of Venus was made by the Soviet Venera program beginning in 1960. Venera 3 impacted on Venus in 1966, and Venera 7 made a successful soft landing in 1970. Landers from Veneras 13 and 14 analyzed surface materials and transmitted color photographs of the planet in 1982. A US Mariner spacecraft passed within 21,600mi of Venus in 1962. Mariner 10 photographed Venus in 1974 on its way to Mercury, where it transmitted photographs of the surface of that planet.

US Mariner spacecraft photographed the surface of Mars in 1965, 1969, and 1971. Viking spacecraft landed on Mars in 1976, took pictures, and performed experiments. Two Soviet probes of Mars were launched in 1988.

US Pioneer spacecraft flew by Jupiter in 1973. Pioneer 10 was propelled by Jupiter's gravity out of the Solar System, which it left in 1983. Pioneer 11 continued on from Jupiter to Saturn, which it reached in 1979. Voyagers 1 and 2 visited Jupiter in 1979 and Saturn in 1980. Voyager 2 continued on to Uranus (1986) and Neptune (1989).

Manned Space Flight. A Soviet cosmonaut, Yuri Gagarin, was the first person in space, making a one-orbit flight in a Vostok spacecraft on Apr. 12, 1961. In their Voshkod and Soyuz programs the Soviets achieved other "firsts"—the first multiperson flight, the first space walk, and the first transfer of crews between docked spacecraft.

US manned space flights also began in 1961 with Project Mercury. Alan Shepard made a suborbital flight on May 5, 1961, and John Glenn made the first US orbital flight on Feb. 20, 1962. The Mercury program was followed by the Gemini and Apollo programs. From Apollo 11, on July 20, 1969, Neil Armstrong and Edwin Aldrin descended to the surface of the moon in a lunar lander while Michael Collins orbited above.

In the 1970s, the US began development of a SPACE SHUTTLE—a winged vehicle carried aloft by external rockets with sufficient power of its own to maneuver in space and then glide back to earth under the control of its crew—to replace the expendable launchers used since the 1950s. The shuttle promised enhanced flexibility for the US space program: among other things, it would be able to visit space stations, launch high-altitude satellites, and retrieve or service other satellites. The first shuttle was launched on Apr. 12, 1981. The explosion shortly after liftoff of the 25th shuttle flight on Jan. 26, 1986 (see CHALLENGER), caused flights to be suspended until Sept. 1988. In Nov. 1988 the first Soviet space shuttle made an unmanned test flight.

The US has begun work on a SPACE STATION planned to travel in a low orbit near the equator. An international effort involving also the European Space Agency, Canada, and Japan, it is scheduled to be assembled in orbit in the late 1990s. Its proponents describe it as an ideal site for certain kinds of scientific and industrial experiments as well as a staging point for missions to other planets. The Soviets have had space stations in orbit since 1971 in their Salyut program. Salyut 7 was replaced in 1986 by a new, modular space station called Mir ("Peace"). Launched unmanned, it has been furnished with crews and supplies by rocket-launched vehicles. In Dec. 1988 two cosmonauts completed a record 366 days in space aboard Mir.

SPACE MEDICINE, the specialized branch of medicine concerned with the special physical and psychological problems arising from space flight. In particular, the effects of prolonged weightlessness and isolation are studied, simulated space flight forming the basis for much of this work.

SPACE SHUTTLE, nickname for Space Transportation System (STS) spacecraft, the first craft designed to orbit the earth and return intact. It is intended mainly to place payloads in orbit more cheaply than can be done by conventional rockets and retrieve

them if necessary, and also to fly astronauts to and from large space stations. It carries an enormous disposable fuel tank for its rocket engine and two solid-fuel boosters that are dropped by parachute and recovered. When the shuttle returns, it lands like a glider. The first shuttle launch was on Apr. 12, 1981. Four vehicles—*Columbia, Challenger, Discovery,* and *Atlantis*—operated from 1981 to 1986. The 25th shuttle flight, the 10th of *Challenger*, ended in the explosion of the vehicle shortly after liftoff on Jan. 28, 1986. Shuttle flights were not resumed until Sept. 1988, when *Discovery* was launched on a successful 5-day mission. At that time the US shuttle program had not fulfilled its promise of cheap, versatile, and reliable access to space.

Meanwhile the USSR had developed a space shuttle similar in design to the US vehicles. In Nov. 1988 the first Soviet space shuttle made an unmanned test flight.

SPACE STATION, project of the NATIONAL AERONAUTICS AND SPACE ADMINISTRATION aiming to develop a permanently manned space station by the late 1990s. The goal is a base initially accommodating a crew of 6-8 people, two unmann platforms, and accommodations for a previously developed Orbital Maneuvering Vehicle and later a larger Orbital Transfer Vehicle. The space station will make the greatest possible use of automation and robotics and will permit evolutionary growth in both size and capability.

The space station will provide facilities for an orbital laboratory for a wide range of science experiments and technology developments; a manufacturing facility to develop and produce new materials and products; a servicing facility to repair and maintain free-flying platforms and other satellites; permanent observatories for viewing Earth below and outward to the solar system and universe; a staging facility for assembling and servicing spacecraft destined for higher orbits or missions to the moon or planets; and an assembly and storage facility to construct large structures.

SPACE-TIME, a way of describing the geometry of the physical universe arising from EINSTEIN's special theory of RELATIVITY. Space and time are considered as a single 4-dimensional continuum rather than as a 3-dimensional space with a separate infinite 1-dimensional time. Time thus becomes the "fourth dimension." Events in space-time are analogous to points in space and invariant space-time intervals to distances in space.

SPAHN, Warren Edward (1921–   ), US baseball player, a left-handed pitcher who won 363 games for the Boston Braves (1942, 1945–65).

SPAIN, a country occupying about four-fifths of the Iberian Peninsula S of the Pyrenees Mts in SW Europe. It includes the BALEARIC ISLANDS and the CANARY ISLANDS. The largely arid plateau of the Meseta forms most of the interior. The Andalusian or Baetic Mts near the Mediterranean coast include the SIERRA NEVADA, rising to Mulacen (11,421ft), the highest peak in mainland Spain. The Guadalquivir R drains the fertile Andalusian plains, and narrow coastal plains lie along the E and SE coasts. The climate is mainly dry with cold winters and hot summers, more extreme on the Meseta. In N Spain the climate is equable, and the S and E coasts enjoy a Mediterranean climate.

Official name: Spanish State
Capital: Madrid
Area: 194,898sq mi
Population: 38,832,000
Languages: Spanish; Catalan, Galician, Basque
Religions: Roman Catholic
Monetary unit(s): 1 peseta = 100 céntimos
People. About 40% of the population is urban. Regional differences are marked and the BASQUE provinces, GALICIA and CATALONIA have preserved their own languages.
Economy. Tourism makes the most important contribution to Spain's income, followed by industry and agriculture. Mineral wealth includes mercury, iron ore, coal, pyrites, potash and salt. Oil was found near Burgos in 1964. Manufacturing industries center on the N provinces, especially Catalonia, and include textiles, shoes, shipbuilding, rubber, chemicals, iron and steel. Agriculture is equally divided between crops and livestock. Oranges, olive oil and wine are exported. Fishing is important.
History. Spain was settled successively by Celts, Phoenicians, Greeks and Carthaginians (3rd century BC). A more enduring

influence was that of the Romans, who conquered Spain during the second of the PUNIC WARS and remained dominant until the VANDALS and VISIGOTHS appeared in the 5th century AD. The last invaders were the MOORS (711 AD). The Christian kingdoms in the N achieved a gradual reconquest completed in the reign (1474–1504) of Ferdinand V (FERDINAND II of Aragon) and his wife ISABELLA of Castile. They introduced the INQUISITION and financed the voyages of COLUMBUS. Soon Spain had won a vast empire in the New World and N Africa, joined with the HAPSBURG lands by the election of Charles I as CHARLES V, Holy Roman Emperor. Under his son PHILIP II a period of outstanding cultural achievement unfolded with such figures as CERVANTES, LOPE DE VEGA, VELÁSQUEZ and El GRECO. At the same time Spain's political power declined. The Netherlands revolted in 1568, and the ARMADA was defeated in 1588. The War of the SPANISH SUCCESSION resulted in heavy losses. The French, invading in 1808, were driven out in the PENINSULAR WAR; but after the revolt of the Latin American colonies and the SPANISH-AMERICAN WAR the Empire was all but dead. After the SPANISH CIVIL WAR General FRANCO became dictator. On his death (1975) JUAN CARLOS succeeded, thus restoring the monarchy while advocating parliamentary democracy. The Socialists won the 1982 elections by a landslide, to lead the first leftist government since the Civil War. Spain joined the NORTH ATLANTIC TREATY ORGANIZATION in 1982 and the EUROPEAN ECONOMIC COMMUNITY in 1986.

SPALDING, Albert (1888–1953), US violinist. An exquisite and restrained stylist, he was the first internationally recognized US-born violin virtuoso. He played with major orchestras in Europe and the US and composed several compositions for the violin.

SPALLANZANI, Lazzaro (1729–1799), Italian biologist who attacked the contemporary belief in the SPONTANEOUS GENERATION of life by demonstrating that organisms which usually appeared in vegetable infusions failed to do so if the infusions were boiled and kept from contact with the air.

SPANISH, a Romance language spoken by perhaps 260 million people in Spain and Latin America. Modern Spanish arose from the Castilian dialect centered on the town of Burgos in N central Spain.

SPANISH-AMERICAN WAR (1898), war fought between the US and Spain, initially over the conduct of Spanish colonial authorities in CUBA. Strong anti-Spanish feeling was fomented in the US by stories of the cruel treatment meted out to Cuban rebels, and the hardships suffered by American business interests. Though President Cleveland took no action, his successor, William McKINLEY, had promised to recognize Cuban independence. He succeeded in obtaining limited self-government for the Cubans, but an explosion aboard the US battleship *Maine* (1898), from which 260 died, was blamed on the Spanish, and McKinley sent an ultimatum, some of whose terms were actually being implemented when Congress declared war on April 25. On May 1 George DEWEY destroyed the Spanish fleet in Manila harbor. What remained was trapped in Santiago harbor by Admiral W. T. Sampson, and destroyed on July 3 by American forces which had already shattered Spanish land forces. Santiago surrendered on July 17. General Nelson A. Miles occupied Puerto Rico, and on Aug. 13 troops occupied Manila. The Treaty of PARIS (Dec. 10, 1898) ended Spanish rule in Cuba. The US gained the islands of GUAM. PUERTO RICO and the PHILIPPINES, thus acquiring an overseas empire with accompanying world military power and responsibilities.

SPANISH CIVIL WAR (1936–39), major conflict between liberal and conservative forces in Spain. After the bloodless overthrow of the monarchy in 1931, the democratic republican government proposed far-reaching reforms which alienated conservatives. On the election (1936) of the POPULAR FRONT, a left-wing coalition, the rightists under General FRANCO resorted to force. Supported by Hitler and Mussolini, Franco was on the verge of shattering the republicans when the Soviet Union began to send them aid. The West remained aloof. Madrid fell to Franco in 1938, Barcelona in 1939. Over 600,000, many of them foreign volunteers, died in the war, and the country suffered massive damage. The Luftwaffe's systematic destruction of GUERNICA, a preview of Hitler's *blitzkrieg*, shocked the world.

SPANISH MAIN, former name of the N coast of the South American mainland, now part of Colombia and Venezuela. It was the hunting ground of the English pirates and buccaneers who attacked the Spanish treasure fleets.

SPANISH MOSS, or **Florida moss**, *Tillandsia usneoides*, an EPIPHYTE that can be found festooning trees such as oaks and cypresses and even telephone poles and wires in the southeastern US. It absorbs water through scaly hairs on the leaves and stem. It is used as a substitute for horsehair stuffing and for insulation.

SPANISH SAHARA. See WESTERN SAHARA.

SPANISH SUCCESSION, War of the (1701–1714), conflict between France on the one hand and a Grand Alliance of England, Holland, Austria and the smaller states of the Holy Roman Empire on the other. The childless Charles II of Spain willed his kingdom and its empire to France on his deathbed. The Grand Alliance sought to prevent France from becoming the dominant European power. Though the decisive battles were fought in Europe, there were also engagements overseas, including North America (see FRENCH AND INDIAN WARS). The Duke of Marlborough and Prince Eugene of Savoy won such remarkable victories as BLENHEIM (1704), Ramillies (1706) and Malplaquet (1709), but LOUIS XIV fought on. The accession of CHARLES VI as the new emperor removed obstacles to the recognition of Philip of Anjou as PHILIP V of Spain. England made a separate peace in 1712 and a general settlement of differences in the Peace of UTRECHT followed in 1713.

SPARK, Muriel Sarah (1918–), Scottish writer best known for her witty, often satirical novels, including *Memento Mori* (1959), *The Prime of Miss Jean Brodie* (1961; later made into a play and a film) and *The Mandelbaum Gate* (1965).

SPARKS, Jared (1789–1866), US historian best known for the 12-volume *Writings of George Washington* (1834–37). He edited the *North American Review* 1824–30, and was president of Harvard U. 1849–53.

SPARROWS, small gregarious seed-eating birds forming the subfamily Passerinae of the weaver-bird family Ploceidae. There are eight genera, five confined to Africa, the other three, the true sparrows, rock sparrows and snow finches, also found in the Palearctic. Of the true sparrows, one species, the house sparrow, *Passer domesticus*, has been successfully introduced to the Americas. Closely associated with human habitation, it is the only bird not known to occur at all in a "natural" habitat, but always with man.

SPARTA, or **Lacedaemon**, city of ancient Greece, the capital of Laconia in the Peloponnesus, on the Eurotas R. Its society was divided into three classes: the helots (serfs bound to the land), the free perioeci, and the Spartiates, whose rigorous military training became a byword. There were two hereditary kings, though real power resided with the five annually elected ephors (magistrates). Founded in the 13th century

BC, Sparta dominated the Peloponnesus by 550 BC. Despite alliance with Athens in the PERSIAN WARS, Sparta fought and won the PELOPONNESIAN WAR against Athens (431–404 BC) but a series of revolts and defeats destroyed Spartan power, and in 146 BC the city became subject to Roman rule.

SPARTACUS (d. 71 BC), leader of the Gladiators' War, a slave revolt against ancient Rome (73–71 BC). With an army of runaway slaves Spartacus heavily defeated forces sent against him and gained control of S Italy, but after his death in battle the revolt was quickly crushed, and 6,000 slaves were crucified along the Appian Way.

SPARTACUS LEAGUE, German revolutionary socialist group active after WWI and named for the slave leader SPARTACUS by its leaders, Karl LIEBKNECHT and Rosa LUXEMBURG. The league became the nucleus of the German Communist Party, but its attempt to seize power in Jan. 1919 was crushed by the government of Friedrich EBERT, and Liebknecht and Luxemburg were murdered while under arrest.

SPASSKY,   Boris   Vasiliyevich (1937–   ), Russian journalist and chess master. He won the Soviet chess championship in 1962 and was world champion 1969–72. He lost the world title to the young American player, Bobby FISCHER, in 1972 in what was probably the most widely publicized series of chess matches in history.

SPASTIC PARALYSIS, form of PARALYSIS due to DISEASE of BRAIN (e.g., STROKE) or SPINAL CORD (e.g., MULTIPLE SCLEROSIS), in which the involved MUSCLES are in a state of constantly increased tone (or resting contraction). Spasticity is a segmental motor phenomenon where muscle contraction occurs without voluntary control.

SPEAKER, Tristram E. (1888–1958), outstanding American League outfielder elected to the Baseball Hall of Fame in 1937. He compiled a lifetime batting average of .344 and set a major league record for doubles (793).

SPEAKER, the officer presiding in the US House of Representatives. Formally elected by the whole House, the speaker is in fact selected from the majority party by its members, and holds powers of recognition, referral of bills to committee and control of debates. Other, wider powers were stripped from the speaker after the term of Joseph CANNON in 1910.

SPECIAL EFFECTS, in cinema, techniques developed to enhance visual illusion, especially important in "disaster movies" and ambitious science fiction films, such as *Star Wars*. Most effects are produced in special studios, and are added to the film after it is shot. A great many techniques are employed, including animation, the use of miniature models, and slow-speed or fast-speed ("slow motion") photography. An important and increasingly sophisticated technique is the creation of a composite picture—using several different images superimposed within a single film frame—often with the aid of electronic memories and timers to match perspectives, light, and camera angles.

SPECIE CIRCULAR, a treasury circular issued at the orders of President Andrew JACKSON in 1836, directing that only gold and silver be received in payment for public lands. It may have contributed considerably to the 1837 money crisis.

SPECIES. See TAXONOMY.

SPECIFIC GRAVITY (sg), or **relative density,** ratio of the density of a substance to that of a reference material at a specified temperature, usually water at $4°C$. If the sg of an inert substance is less than unity (1), it will float in water at $4°C$. The sg of liquids is measured with a hydrometer.

SPECIFIC HEAT, the HEAT required to raise the temperature of 1 kg of a substance through one kelvin; expressed in $J/K.kg$, and measured by calorimetry. The concept was introduced by Joseph BLACK; Dulong and Petit showed that the specific heat of elements is approximately inversely proportional to their ATOMIC WEIGHTS, which could thus be roughly determined.

SPECTROSCOPY, the production, measurement and analysis of spectra (see SPECTRUM), an essential tool of astronomers, chemists and physicists. All spectra arise from transitions between discrete energy states of matter, as a result of which PHOTONS of corresponding energy (and hence characteristic frequency or wavelength) are absorbed or emitted. From the energy levels thus determined, atomic and molecular structure may be studied. Moreover, by using the observed spectra as "fingerprints," spectroscopy may be a sensitive method of chemical ANALYSIS. Most of the different kinds of spectroscopy, corresponding to the various regions of ELECTROMAGNETIC RADIATION, relate to particular kinds of energy-level transitions. **Gamma-ray spectra** arise from nuclear energy-level transitions; **X-ray spectra** from inner-electron transitions in atoms; **ultraviolet** and **visible spectra** from outer (bonding) electron transitions in molecules (or atoms); **infrared spectra** from molecular vibrations; and **microwave spectra** from molecular rotations. There are several more specialized kinds of spectroscopy. **Raman** spectroscopy, based on the effect discovered by C. V. Raman, scans the scattered light from an intense monochromatic beam. Some of the scattered light is at lower (and higher) frequencies than the incident light, corresponding to vibration/rotation transitions. The technique thus supplements infrared spectroscopy. **Mössbauer spectroscopy**, based on the Mössbauer effect, gives information on the electronic or chemical environments of nuclei; as does **nuclear magnetic resonance spectroscopy** (nmr), based on transitions between nuclear spin states in a strong magnetic field. **Electron spin resonance spectroscopy** (esr) is similarly based on electron spin transitions when there is an unpaired electron in an orbital, and so is used to study free radicals. The instrument used is a **spectroscope**, called a *spectrograph* if the spectrum is recorded photographically all at once, or a *spectrometer* if it is scanned by wavelength and calibrated from the instrument.

SPECTRUM, the array of colors produced on passing LIGHT through a prism; also, by extension, the range of a phenomenon displayed in terms of one of its properties. ELECTROMAGNETIC RADIATION arranged according to wavelength thus forms the electromagnetic spectrum, of which that of visible light is only a minute part. Similarly the mass spectrum of a particular collection of ions displays their relative numbers as a function of their masses. (See SPECTROSCOPY; MASS SPECTROSCOPY.)

SPEECH AND SPEECH DISORDERS. Speech may be subdivided into conception, or formulation, and production, or phonation and articulation, of speech (see VOICE). Speech development in children starts with associating sounds with persons and objects, comprehension usually predating vocalization by some months. Nouns are developed first, often with one or two syllables only; later acquisition of verbs, adjectives, etc., allows the construction of phrases and sentences. A phase of babbling speech, where the child toys with sounds resembling speech, is probably essential for development. READING is closely related to speech development, involving the association of auditory and visual symbols. Speech involves coordination of many aspects of BRAIN function (hearing, vision, etc.) but three areas particularly concerned with aspects of speech are located in the dominant hemisphere of right-handed persons and in either hemisphere of left-handed people (see HANDEDNESS). DISEASE of these parts of the brain leads to characteristic forms of dysphasia or APHASIA. alexia. etc. Development DYSLEXIA is a childhood defect of visual pattern recognition. Stammering or stuttering, with repetition and hesitation over certain syllables, is a common disorder, in some cases representing frustrated left-handedness. Dysarthria is disordered voice production and is due to disease of the neuromuscular control of voice. In speech therapy, attempts are made to overcome or circumvent speech difficulties, this being particularly important in children (see also DEAFNESS).

SPEEDOMETER, instrument for indicating the speed of a motor vehicle. The common type works by magnetic INDUCTION. A circular permanent magnet is rotated by a flexible cable geared to the transmission. The rotating magnetic field induces a magnetic field in an aluminum cup, so tending to turn it in the same direction as the magnet. This torque, proportional to the speed of rotation, is opposed by a spiral spring. The angle through which the cup turns against the spring measures the speed. The speedometer is usually coupled with an **odometer**, a counting device geared to the magnet, which registers the distance traveled.

SPEER, Albert (1905–1981), German Nazi leader who was Hitler's architect. For his organization of slave labor for Germany during WWII, the international tribunal at Nuremberg sentenced him to 20 years imprisonment in Spandau. After his release he wrote revealingly of the inner workings of the Nazi regime.

SPEKE, John Hanning (1827–1864), English explorer, the first European to reach Victoria Nyanza (Lake Victoria) in E Africa, a source of the Nile (1858). Speke and James Grant found the Nile exit (Ripon Falls) in 1862.

SPELEOLOGY, the scientific study of CAVES. The world's first speleological society was founded in France in 1895, and interest soon became worldwide. The US National Speleological Society was founded in 1939. Less academic cave exploration is called spelunking.

SPENCER, Herbert (1820–1903), English philosopher, social theorist and early evolutionist. In his multivolume *System of Synthetic Philosophy* (1862–96), he expounded a world view based on a close study of physical, biological and social phenomena, arguing that species evolve by a process of differentiation from the simple to the complex. His political individualism deeply influenced the growth of SOCIAL

DARWINISM, and, in general, US social thinking.

SPENDER, Stephen Harold (1909–   ), English poet and critic, coeditor of the literary magazine *Encounter* 1953–65. His poetry collections include *Poems* (1933), *Ruins and Visions* (1942) and *The Generous Days* (1971).

SPENER, Philipp Jakob (1635–1705), German Lutheran theologian, founder of PIETISM. He was also a founder of the U of Halle, which became a center of Pietism.

SPENGLER, Oswald (1880–1936), German philosopher whose cyclic view of history is expressed in *The Decline of the West* (1918–22), a study of the rise and fall of civilizations. He believed that Western civilization was entering a period of decline, a view much favored between the wars.

SPENSER, Edmund (c1522–1599), English poet, best known for the six books of his unfinished epic poem *The Faerie Queene* (1590–96), an allegorical work celebrating the moral values of Christian chivalry. Steeped in English folklore, the poem displays the monumental scope of a Homer or Vergil. His other works include *The Shepheardes Calender* (1579) and *Epithalamion* (1595).

SPERM WHALES, or **cachalots,** a family of toothed whales, with two species: the cachalot, *Physeter catodon*, and pigmy sperm whale, *Kogia breviceps*. They are among the best known of all WHALES because of the enormous, squared head. The front of the head contains a huge reservoir of **spermaceti** oil, perhaps used as a lens to focus the sounds produced by the whales in echolocation. Spermaceti solidifies in cool air to form a wax once used for candles and cosmetics. Sperm whales are also the source of AMBERGRIS, a secretion in the gut produced in response to irritation by the beaks of SQUIDS, an important prey item. Sperm whales are found in all oceans, migrating from the poles into warmer waters during the breeding season. It is a deep water whale, capable of diving to 500m (1,640ft) or more. Females and young form large schools of up to several hundred animals. Males tend to travel alone or in small groups.

SPERRY, Elmer Ambrose (1860–1930), US inventor of the GYROCOMPASS (first installed in a ship, 1911) and of a high-intensity arc searchlight (1918).

SPEYER, Diet of (1529), an asssembly summoned by Emperor CHARLES V to settle the relationship between Lutheranism and the Roman Catholic Church. Lutherans protested (hence "Protestant") against its decision to continue hampering Lutheranism.

SPHERE, the surface produced by the rotation of a circle through 180° about one of its diameters. The intersection of a sphere and any plane is circular; should the plane pass through the center, the intersection is a great circle. The surface area of a sphere is $4\pi r^2$, where r is the radius; its volume $4\pi r^3/3$. If mutually perpendicular x-, y- and z-axes are constructed such that they intersect at the center, the sphere's equation is $x^2 + y^2 + z^2 = r^2$.

SPHERICAL GEOMETRY, the branch of GEOMETRY dealing with figures drawn on the surface of a SPHERE; sometimes considered as a special case of Riemannian geometry. A circle whose center coincides with that of the sphere is a great circle, other circles on the sphere's surface being small circles: since a great circle may be drawn through any two points on the sphere's surface, one deals primarily with great circles only. The lengths of arcs of great circles are always given in terms of the radius of the sphere and the angle subtended by the arc at the center; i.e., in the form $r\theta$, where r is the radius and θ the angle. It is usually convenient to consider the sphere as of unit radius, thus expressing the length of an arc as an angle. Problems concerning **spherical triangles** are solved using spherical trigonometry.

SPHINX, mythical monster of the ancient Middle East, in Egypt portrayed as a lion with a human head and used as a symbol of the pharaoh. In Greek mythology the sphinx propounded a riddle to travelers on the road to Thebes: when OEDIPUS answered correctly the sphinx threw herself from her rocky perch.

SPICE, a large number of aromatic plant products which have a distinctive flavor or aroma and are used to season food. Most spices are obtained from tropical plants and were once highly valued as a means of making poor quality food more palatable.

SPICE ISLANDS. See MOLUCCAS.

SPIDERS, an order, Araneida, of the Arachnida, with the body divided into two parts, and with four pairs of walking legs. Unlike INSECTS, spiders have no antennae, have simple, not compound, EYES, and no larval or pupal stages. They are an incredibly diverse group of some 26,000 species. The evolution of spiders is closely linked with that of the insects on which they prey: as insects developed abilities of jumping, gliding and later flying, and evolved stings and other defenses, so the spiders developed so as still to be able to capture their changing prey. Thus from primitive running spiders have evolved such groups as the jumping spiders; wolf spiders; trapdoor spiders, and of course, the web-spinners.

SPIN, intrinsic angular momentum of a nucleus or SUBATOMIC PARTICLE arising from its rotation about an axis within itself. Every particle has a definite spin, s, given by $nh/4\pi$, where n is an integer and h is the Planck constant.

SPINACH, *Spinacia oleracea*, a leafy annual widely cultivated as a vegetable. Spinach leaves have a relatively high content of iron and VITAMINS A and C. Family: Chenopodiceae.

SPINAL COLUMN. See VERTEBRAE.

SPINAL CORD, the part of the central NERVOUS SYSTEM outside the skull. It joins the BRAIN at the base of the skull, forming the *medulla oblongata*, and extends downward in a bony canal enclosed in the VERTEBRAE. Between the bone and cord are three sheaths of connective TISSUE called the *meninges*. A section of the cord shows a central core of *gray matter* (containing the cell bodies of nerve fibers running either to the muscles or within the cord itself), completely surrounded by *white matter* (composed solely of nerve fibers). There is a central canal containing CEREBROSPINAL FLUID, which opens into the cavities of the brain.

SPINAL TAP, or **lumbar puncture**, procedure to remove CEREBROSPINAL FLUID (CSF) from the lumbar spinal canal using a fine needle. It is used in diagnosis of MENINGITIS, ENCEPHALITIS, MULTIPLE SCLEROSIS and TUMORS. In neurology, it may be used in treatment, by reducing CSF pressure or allowing insertion of DRUGS.

SPINELLO DI LUCA SPINELLI (c1346–1410), Italian painter of the late Gothic period, also known as Spinello Aretino, whose most important works are two series of frescoes at the Campo Santo, Pisa and the Palazzo Pubblico, Siena.

SPINET, type of small HARPSICHORD which probably originated in 16th-century Italy. Inside the wing-shaped cabinet a single set of strings is set at an oblique angle to the keyboard. The name is also used for a small upright piano.

SPINGARN, Arthur Barnett (1878–1971), US civil rights leader, vice president (1911–40) and president (1940–66) of the NATIONAL ASSOCIATION FOR THE ADVANCEMENT OF COLORED PEOPLE.

SPINNING, the ancient craft of twisting together FIBERS from a mass to form strong, continuous thread suitable for weaving. The earliest method was merely to roll the fibers between hand and thigh. Later two sticks were used: the distaff to hold the bundle of fibers, and a spindle to twist and wind the yarn. Mechanization began with the spinning wheel, invented in India and spreading to Europe by the 14th century. The wheel turned the spindle by means of a belt drive. In the 15th century the flyer was invented: a device on the spindle shaft that winds the yarn automatically on a spool. Improved WEAVING methods in the Industrial Revolution caused increased demand which provoked several inventions. The spinning jenny, invented by James Hargreaves (c1767), spun as many as 16 threads at once, the spindles all being driven by the same wheel. Richard ARKWRIGHT'S "water frame" (1769), so called from being water-powered, had rollers and produced strong thread. Then Samuel Crompton produced a hybrid of the two—his "mule"—which had a movable carriage, and was the forerunner of the modern machine. The other modern spinning machine is the ring-spinning frame (1828) in which the strands, drawn out by rollers, are twisted by a "traveler" that revolves on a ring around the bobbin on which they are wound.

SPINOZA, Baruch or **Benedict de** (1632–1677), Dutch philosopher and rationalist (see RATIONALISM) who held that God is nature, or all that is, an interpretation which brought him expulsion from the Amsterdam Jewish community. Though influenced by DESCARTES, he rejected Descartes' dual substance theory and claimed that matter and mind are attributes of the one substance: God. His most famous work is *Ethics* (1677). Organized "in the geometric style" like EUCLID'S *Elements*, it contains the development of his PANTHEISM, which is both rationalist and mystical.

SPIRITUAL, a form of religious folk song developed by the Negro slaves and their descendants in the southern US states. It usually consists of a number of verses for solo voice, with a rhythmic choral refrain.

SPIRITUALISM, religious movement based on belief in the survival of the human personality after death and its ability to communicate with those left behind, usually through a medium. Spiritualist beliefs have had powerful effects, both for good and for bad, on the advance of psychic research (see PARAPSYCHOLOGY).

SPIROCHETE, spiral BACTERIA, species of which are responsible for relapsing fever, YAWS and syphilis (see VENEREAL DISEASES).

SPITTELER, Carl Friedrich Georg (1845–1924), Swiss poet, winner of the 1919 Nobel Prize for Literature. His heroic epics *Prometheus and Epimetheus* (1881) and *Olympic Spring* (1900–05; 1910) stressed spiritual nobility.

SPITZ, Mark Andrew (1950–), US swimmer, winner of an unprecedented seven gold medals at the 1972 Olympics.

SPLEEN, spongy vascular lymphoid organ (see LYMPH) between the STOMACH and diaphragm on the left side of the ABDOMEN. A center for the reticuloendothelial system, it also eliminates worn-out red BLOOD cells, recycling their iron. Most of its functions are duplicated by other organs. The spleen was classically the source of black bile, or melancholy.

SPOCK, Benjamin McLane (1903–), known worldwide as "Dr. Spock," US pediatrician and pacifist best known for his (*Common Sense Book of*) *Baby and Child Care* (1946), which advocated a more liberal attitude on the part of parents, and *Bringing up Children in a Difficult Time* (1974).

SPODE, British family of pottery makers. **Josiah Spode** (1733–1797) founded the Spode works at Stoke-on-Trent and introduced transfer decoration and oriental motifs. **Josiah Spode** (1754–1827) developed stone china, porcelain and bone china. He popularized the willow pattern and gained royal patronage. (See also POTTERY AND PORCELAIN.)

SPOHR, Ludwig (Louis) (1784–1859), violinist, composer and one of the first orchestral conductors. As a performer he did much to make Beethoven's early string quartets well known. Among his extensive works are 9 symphonies and 11 operas, including *Faust* (1816) and *Jessonda* (1823).

SPOILS SYSTEM, the use of appointments to public offices to reward supporters of a victorious political party. With the growth of a two-party system in the US, political patronage increased. It was President Jackson's friend Senator William L. Marcy who said in 1832 that "to the victor belong the spoils," and the system soon operated on every political level. The PENDLETON ACT OF 1883, introducing competitive entrance examinations for public employees, marked the gradual introduction of a merit system.

SPONGES, primitive animals of both marine and fresh water, phylum Parazoa (Porifera). Sponges are true ANIMALS, although they have only a simple body wall and no specialized organ or tissue systems. They may be solitary or colonial. They are filter-feeders, straining tiny food particles out of water drawn in through pores all over the body surface, and expelled through one or more exhalant vents. The body wall is strengthened by spicules of calcite or silica, or by a meshwork of PROTEIN fibers: spongin. Sponges with spongin skeletons are fished for bath sponges. Sponges can exhibit regeneration to a remarkable degree. A sponge strained through silk to break it up into its component cells can reorganize itself into a functional sponge.

SPONTANEOUS COMBUSTION, COMBUSTION occurring without external ignition, caused by slow oxidation or FERMENTATION which (if heat cannot readily escape) raises the temperature to burning point. It may occur when hay or small coal is stored.

SPONTANEOUS GENERATION, or **abiogenesis,** theory, dating from the writings of ARISTOTLE, that living creatures can arise from nonliving matter. The idea remained current even after it had become clear that higher orders of life could not be created in this way; and it was only with the work of REDI, showing that maggots did not appear in decaying meat to which flies had been denied access, and PASTEUR, who proved that the equivalent was true of microorganisms (i.e., BACTERIA), that the theory was finally discarded.

SPORE, minute single or multicelled body produced during the process of reproduction of many plants, particularly BACTERIA. ALGAE and FUNGI and in some PROTOZOA. The structure of spores varies greatly and depends upon the means of dissemination from the parent. Some, e.g., the zoospores of algae, are motile.

SPOTSWOOD, Alexander (1676–1740), English lieutenant-governor and administrator of VIRGINIA colony, 1710–22. He promoted settlement to the W and fostered tobacco-growing and the iron industry.

SPOTSYLVANIA COURT HOUSE, Battle of (May 8–19, 1864), in the American CIVIL WAR, bloody failure by General GRANT to dislodge Confederates blocking his way to their capital at Richmond, Va.

SPRAGUE, Frank Julian (1857–1934), US inventor of high-speed electric ELEVATORS and electric RAILROAD systems, including that now used in the New York SUBWAY.

SPRING, a naturally occurring flow of water from the ground. This may be, for example, an outflow from an underground stream; but most often a spring occurs where an AQUIFER saturated with GROUNDWATER intersects with the earth's surface. Such an aquifer, if confined above and below by aquicludes, may travel for hundreds of kilometers underground before emerging to the surface, there, perhaps, in desert areas giving rise to oases. Spring water is generally fairly clean, since it has been filtered through the permeable rocks; but all spring water contains some dissolved

MINERALS. (See also GEYSER; WELL.)

SPRING, mechanical device that exhibits ELASTICITY according to HOOKE's Law. Most springs are made of steel, brass or bronze. The commonest type is the **helical spring,** a helical coil of stiff wire, loose-wound if to be compressed, tight-wound if to be extended under tension. They have many uses, including closing valves, spring balances and accelerometers. The **spiral spring** is a wire or strip coiled in one plane, responding to torque applied at its inner end, and used to store energy, notably in CLOCKS AND WATCHES. The **leaf spring,** used in vehicle suspension systems, consists of several steel strips of different lengths clamped on top of each other at one end. When deformed, springs store potential ENERGY, and exert a restoring FORCE. Hydraulic and air springs work by compression of a fluid in a cylinder.

SPRINGSTEEN, Bruce (1949–   ), US singer and songwriter whose rock ballads such as "Born in the U.S.A." (1984) celebrated blue-collar life.

SPRUCE, evergreen coniferous trees of the genus *Picea* with a conical form. There are some 40 species, all of which grow in the cooler regions of the N Hemisphere. Among the species found in the US are the black (*Picea mariana*), blue (*P. pungens*) and white (*P. glauca*) spruces. Spruce wood is used for pulp and general construction work and the whole trees as Christmas decorations. Family: Pinaceae.

SPUTNIK. See SATELLITES, ARTIFICIAL.

SPYRI, Johanna (née Heusser; 1829–1901), Swiss writer of children's books. *Heidi* (1880–81), set in the Swiss Alps, has become a worldwide classic.

SQUANTO (d.1622), Pawtuxet Indian who befriended the newly arrived PILGRIMS, acting as their interpreter in dealings with MASSASOIT, and teaching them how to grow corn.

SQUARE DANCE, popular, lively American folk dance in which four couples formed in a square carry out steps and formations under the direction of a caller. It dates back to the quadrille dances of 15th-century Europe. (See also FOLK DANCING.)

SQUARE DEAL, policy of Theodore ROOSEVELT, when presidential candidate (1912), seeking to reconcile the demands of both workers and industrialists.

SQUASH, a game similar to rackets but played with a softer, less bouncy ball. Singles squash is played on an indoor court 18½ft wide by 32ft long. Doubles squash requires a larger court. The ball may be hit against any of the four walls as long as it bounces on the front wall before striking the

ground. The opponent must strike the ball before it bounces twice.

SQUATTER SOVEREIGNTY, or popular sovereignty, a doctrine intended to end congressional controversy over the expansion of slavery just before the US Civil War. The inhabitants of a territory were to be allowed to decide for themselves whether or not to permit slavery. It was applied to Ut. and N.M. through the COMPROMISE OF 1850, and a popular sovereignty clause was included in the KANSAS-NEBRASKA ACT (1854) which repealed the MISSOURI COMPROMISE.

SQUIDS, shell-less CEPHALOPOD mollusks, order Teuthoidea. Although a few species live in coastal waters the majority are open ocean forms. Squids are streamlined animals with ten arms around the head, facing forward. The mantle at the rear of the body houses the gills and the openings of the excretory, sex and digestive organs. Sudden contraction of the whole mantle cavity sends out a blast of water that can be directed forward or backward by a movable funnel, providing the main means of propulsion. All squids can swim very rapidly and are active predators of fish, shooting out the long arms, provided with suckers and hooks, to grab their prey.

SQUINT. See STRABISMUS.

SQUIRRELS, one of the largest families, Sciuridae, of rodents. Commonly, the name refers only to tree squirrels, which are found in most forested parts of the world. Typically they have long bushy tails and short muzzles. They are diurnal, feeding on seeds, nuts and leaf buds, with some insect or other animal food. A number of temperate species, while not true hibernants, store food for the winter and enter deep torpor.

SRAFFA, Piero (1898–1983), Italian-born theoretical economist, at Cambridge U from 1927, an influential critic of neoclassical economics.

SRI LANKA, formerly Ceylon, independent island republic within the British Commonwealth, separated from SE India by the Gulf of Mannar, Palk Strait and Adam's Bridge, a 30mi chain of shoals.

Land. Sri Lanka is about 270mi N–S and 140mi E–W. The mountainous central S area rises to Pidurutalagala (8,281ft) and Adam's Peak (7,360ft); the major rivers, including the Mahaweli Ganga, rise here. Around the mountains stretches a coastal plain, up to 100mi wide in the N. Climate is tropical, but the island situation gives more equable temperatures than mainland India (around 81°F at Colombo). Rainfall ranges from 40in in the N to 200in in the SW

Official name: Democratic Socialist Republic of Sri Lanka
Capital: Colombo
Area: 25,332sq mi
Population: 16,353,000
Languages: Sinhalese, English, Tamil
Religions: Buddhist, Hindu, Christian, Muslim
Monetary unit(s): 1 Sri Lanka rupee=100 cents

mountains. In many areas the original dense tropical forest has been cleared for agriculture.

People. The few cities include the capital, Colombo on the W coast, Jaffna in the N, Kandy in the S central mountains, Trincomalee on the E coast and Galle in the SW. Buddhist Sinhalese form 75% of the fast-growing population, and SINHALESE is the official language. Others include the Hindu Tamils (people of S Indian origin, who live mainly in the N and E), the forest Veddas (probably the aboriginal inhabitants), the Burghers (Christian descendants of Dutch-Sinhalese ancestors), the Moors and Malay Muslims.

Economy. Sri Lanka produces about one third of the world's tea and over 150,000 tons of rubber a year. Coconuts are commercially grown for their oil, but rice, the main food crop, has to be supplemented in many years by imports. Several irrigation schemes have, however, improved annual rice yields. The country is the world's chief producer of high-grade graphite. Power is mainly hydroelectric. There is a good road and rail system.

History. The island was settled around 550 BC by Sinhalese, a people from the Indian subcontinent who built Anuradhapura and made the island a center of Buddhist thought after the religion was introduced here in the 3rd century BC. From the 12th to the 16th century the Tamils held the N part. Europeans arrived in the 1500s, lured by the spice trade; they called the island Ceylon. Held by the Portuguese (landed 1505), the Dutch (after 1658) and finally the British (from 1796), the island attained independence in 1948 and became a republic in 1956. In 1972 Ceylon adopted a new constitution and the Sinhalese name Sri Lanka. In the late 1970s and 1980s, long-standing differences between the Sinhalese majority and the Tamil minority erupted into violence. In 1987 India and Sri Lanka signed an accord granting greater autonomy to the Tamil areas. Indian peacekeeping forces were sent to enforce the agreement, which was rejected by militants on both sides. As the violence continued, Junius Jayawardene, who had headed the government since 1977, announced that he would not stand for reelection in 1988.

SS (abbreviation of *Schutzstaffel*: defense echelons) or **Blackshirts**, dreaded elite corps of Nazi Germany, commanded by HIMMLER. It comprised the secret police (see GESTAPO), Hitler's personal bodyguard, the guards of the concentration and extermination camps, and some divisions of picked combat troops. (See NAZISM.)

STAËL, Madame de (Anne Louise Germaine Necker; 1766-1817), French-Swiss novelist and critic, celebrated personality and liberal opponent of Napoleon's regime, daughter of the banker Jacques Necker. A noted interpreter of German ROMANTICISM, she maintained brilliant salons in Paris and in exile near Geneva. She had liaisons with TALLEYRAND and the writer Benjamin CONSTANT.

STAFFORD, Jean (1915–1979), US author noted for her sensitive, well-crafted novels and stories. Her *Collected Stories* (1969) won a Pulitzer Prize in 1970.

STAGECOACH, closed coach, usually seating four to eight passengers and drawn by teams of two to six horses, traveling regularly between two stages. It was the principal means of public transportation in 18th- and 19th-century Europe and the US until superseded by railroads.

STAGE DESIGN. See THEATER.

STAGG, Amos Alonzo (1862–1965), US football coach. His career spanned 71 seasons, including 41 (1892–1932) with the University of Chicago. He was in the first All-American team '(1889), developed many football formations and also promoted basketball.

STAHL, Georg Ernst (1660-1734), Bavarian-born German physician and chemist who developed the PHLOGISTON theory to explain combustion.

STAINED GLASS, pieces of colored glass held in place by a framework, usually of grooved lead strips (cames), to form patterns or pictures in a window. The earliest such windows date from the 11th century, but the art reached its highest development in the great period of GOTHIC

ARCHITECTURE, c1150–1500: the series of windows made 1200–1240 for CHARTRES cathedral is perhaps the most famous example. Interest revived with the work of Edward BURNE-JONES and, in the US, the designs of Louis TIFFANY and John LA FARGE. Among recent masters of stained glass are the painters MATISSE, Fernand LÉGER. ROUAULT and CHAGALL. The glass is colored during manufacture, by mixing it with various metallic oxides; then cut according to the artist's full-scale cartoons. Details may be painted on to the glass with colored enamels, which fuse to the glass surface when it is heated.

STAINLESS STEEL, corrosion-resistant STEEL containing more than 10% chromium, little carbon, and often nickel and other metals. Made in the electric furnace, there are four main types: ferritic, martensitic, austenitic and precipitation-hardening. Stainless steel is used for cutlery and many industrial components.

STALACTITES AND STALAGMITES, rocky structures found growing downward from the roof (stalactites) and upward from the floor (stalagmites) of CAVES formed in LIMESTONE. Rainwater percolates through the rocks above the cave and, as it contains atmospheric CARBON dioxide, can dissolve calcium carbonate en route. On reaching the cave, the water drips from the roof to the floor; as a drop hangs, some water evaporates, leaving a little calcium carbonate as calcite on the roof. Repetition forms a stalactite; and evaporation of the fallen water on the floor forms a stalagmite. On occasion, the rising stalagmite and descending stalactite fuse to form a pillar.

STALIN, Joseph (1879–1953), dictatorial ruler of the Soviet Union from 1929 until his death. Born Josif Vissarionovich Dzhugashvili, a Georgian village shoemaker's son intended for the priesthood, he joined the Georgian Social Democratic Party in 1901, becoming its Tiflis organizer in 1905. In 1912 LENIN coopted him onto the Bolshevik central committee, to which he was elected in 1917. After the RUSSIAN REVOLUTION he advanced rapidly. In 1922 he was elected general secretary of the Russian Communist Party. In the struggle for the leadership after Lenin's death (1924) he ousted from the Politburo first Trotsky (1925) then Kamenev and Zinoviev (1926). In 1928 he launched a vast development and industrialization program that involved the forced collectivization of agriculture and massive social redeployment. He also sought to "Russianize" the Soviet Union, attempting to eradicate by force the separate identities of minorities. Dissent

was met with a powerful secret police, informers, mass deportations, executions and show trials. In 1935 Stalin initiated the first of the great "purges" which spared neither his family nor former political associates. Equally ruthless in foreign affairs, he partitioned Poland with Germany, and invaded Finland (1939) and imposed communist rule on the Baltic states (1940). The reversal of German fortunes on the WWII Eastern Front strengthened his hand. In 1945 at YALTA he sealed the postwar fate of East Europe to his satisfaction. Thereafter, he pursued COLD WAR policies abroad and supported rapid industrial recovery at home until his death, from a brain hemorrhage. Almost immediately a process of "destalinization" began, culminating in KHRUSHCHEV'S 1956 attack on the Stalinist terror and personality cult.

STALINGRAD, Battle of, decisive engagement in WWII, fought in the vicinity of Stalingrad (now Volgograd) from Aug. 1942 to Feb. 1943. The 500,000-strong German 6th army under von Paulus surrounded the city on Sept. 14, 1942, but was itself encircled early in 1943 by a Russian army under ZHUKOV and forced to surrender. Not only was the German invasion halted, but the psychological initiative was wrested from the Nazis for the remainder of the war.

STALWARTS, US Republican Party faction that supported the SPOILS SYSTEM and opposed civil service reform by President HAYES and his "Half-breeds." Later "Stalwarts" campaigned for nomination of Ulysses S. GRANT in 1880 for a third presidential term.

STAMFORD BRIDGE, Battle of, victory in Yorkshire on Sept. 25, 1066, of newly crowned HAROLD II, last Anglo-Saxon king of England, over his brother Tostig and Harald Hardraade of Norway. (See HASTINGS, BATTLE OF.)

STAMITZ, Johann Wenzel Anton (1717–1757), Czech-born German composer and musician. As concertmaster of the court orchestra at Mannheim from 1745 and founder of the Mannheim school of symphonists, he had a profound influence on the work of Mozart.

STAMMER. See SPEECH AND SPEECH DISORDERS.

STAMP ACT (1765), the first direct tax imposed by the English Parliament on the 13 American colonies. All legal and commercial documents, pamphlets, playing cards and newspapers were to carry revenue stamps, which would help finance the British army quartered in America. The colonists balked at the idea of "taxation without representation," and delegates from nine colonies met in the Stamp Act Congress held in New York to protest against the law. A boycott of British goods finally led Parliament to repeal the Stamp Act in March 1766.

STAMP COLLECTING, or philately. The first postage stamps, the famous "Penny Blacks" and "Twopenny Blues," were issued in England on May 1, 1840: the first in the US appeared in 1847, and by 1860 most countries had adopted the prepaid postage stamp system. Today stamp catalogs list over 200,000 items. Serious collectors, who generally specialize in particular countries, periods or themes, make a close study of each stamp's paper, ink, printing method, perforations, cancellation (if used), design, information content and historical occasion. Stamps can also be a good investment: sums of up to $380,000 have been paid for rare specimens.

STANDARD OF LIVING, statistical measure which attempts to rate the quality of life in a nation or a group in terms of its level of consumption of food, clothing, and other basic goods and services including transportation, education and medical care. The standard is generally expressed in monetary terms according to latest costs.

STANDISH, Miles (c1584–1656), Lancashire-born military adviser to the PILGRIMS and an important member of the PLYMOUTH COLONY, serving as its assistant governor and treasurer. About 1631 he helped found Duxbury, Mass. Longfellow's poem about him has no factual basis.

STANFORD, Leland (1824–1893), US railroad pioneer and politician. Governor of Cal. (1861–63) and a Cal. Republican senator (1885–93), he also helped found and became president of the Central Pacific and Southern Pacific railroads and he established Stanford University (1885).

STANFORD-BINET TEST, an adaptation of the Binet-Simon test for INTELLIGENCE, introduced by TERMAN (1916, revised 1937), and used primarily to determine the IQs of children. (See also BINET.)

STANHOPE, Lady Hester Lucy (1776–1839), English traveler. She was secretary (1803–06) to her uncle William PITT the Younger. In 1814 she settled in Syria, and was venerated as a prophetess and ruler by the local Arab community.

STANISLAVSKI, Konstantin (1863–1938), Russian actor, director and producer. Born Konstantin Sergeyevich Alekseyev, he originated an influential approach, known as "the method," which involves subordination of personal style to an attempt to analyze, assimilate and live

out the emotional content of the enacted role. In 1898 he founded the Moscow Art Theater.

STANLEY, Sir Henry Morton (1841–1904), British explorer, soldier and journalist. Born John Rowlands, he took the name of a US merchant who adopted him. He fought in the US Civil War and in 1869 was sent to Africa by the *New York Herald* to find the missionary and explorer David LIVINGSTONE. Their famous meeting by Lake Tanganyika occurred in 1871. Stanley continued Livingstone's exploration (1874–77), crossing the continent E–W.

STANLEY CUP, presented annually to the winner of the National Hockey League post-season playoffs. Lord Stanley, Governor General of Canada, first presented the award to the Canadian champion in 1893. Since 1926 it has been identified solely with the NHL.

STANTON, Edwin McMasters (1814–1869), US politician, an able Civil War secretary of war (1862–68) and important ally of the Radical Republicans during RECONSTRUCTION. As US attorney general in the last months of President BUCHANAN's cabinet, he stood against Southern secession. He resigned following President JOHNSON's narrow escape from impeachment (1868).

STANTON, Elizabeth Cady (1815–1902), US abolitionist and campaigner for women's rights. In 1848, with Mrs. Lucretia MOTT, she organized the first women's rights convention in the US, at Seneca Falls, N.Y., and in 1869 founded the Woman Suffrage Association with Susan B. ANTHONY.

STAPHYLOCOCCUS, BACTERIUM responsible for numerous SKIN, soft tissue and BONE infections, less often causing SEPTICEMIA, a cavitating PNEUMONIA, bacterial endocarditis and enterocolitis. Boils, carbuncles, IMPETIGO and OSTEOMYELITIS are commonly due to staphylococci. Treatment usually requires drainage of PUS from ABSCESSES and ANTIBIOTICS.

STAR, a large incandescent ball of gases held together by its own gravity. The SUN is a fairly normal star in its composition, parameters and color. The lifespan of a star depends upon its mass and luminosity: a very luminous star may have a life of only one million years, the sun a life of ten billion years, the faintest main sequence stars a life of ten thousand billion years. Stars are divided into two categories, Populations I and II. The stars in Population I are slower moving, generally to be found in the spiral arms of GALAXIES, and believed to be younger. Population II stars are generally brighter, faster moving and mainly to be found in the spheroidal halo of stars around a galaxy and in the GLOBULAR CLUSTERS. Many stars are DOUBLE STARS. It is believed that stars originate as condensations out of interstellar matter. In certain circumstances a protostar will form, slowly contracting under its own gravity, part of the energy from this contraction being radiated, the remainder heating up the core: this stage may last several million years. At last the core becomes hot enough for thermonuclear reactions (see FUSION, NUCLEAR) to be sustained, and stops contracting. Eventually the star as a whole ceases contracting and radiates entirely by the thermonuclear conversion of hydrogen into helium: it is then said to be on the main sequence. When all the hydrogen in the core has been converted into helium, the now purely helium core begins to contract while the outer layers continue to "burn" hydrogen: this contraction heats up the core and forces the outer layers outward, so that the star as a whole expands for some 100–200 million years until it becomes a red **giant star**. Although the outer layers are comparatively cool, the core has become far hotter than before, and thermonuclear conversions of helium into carbon begin. The star contracts once more (though some expand still further to become **supergiants**) and ends its life as a white **dwarf star**. It is thought that more massive stars become **neutron stars**, whose matter is so dense that its PROTONS and ELECTRONS are packed together to form NEUTRONS; were the sun to become a neutron star, it would have a radius of less than 20km. Finally, when the star can no longer radiate through thermonuclear or gravitational means, it ceases to shine. Some stars may at this stage undergo ultimate gravitational collapse to form BLACK HOLES. (See also CEPHEID VARIABLES; COSMOLOGY; MILKY WAY; NEBULA; NOVA; PULSAR; QUASAR; SOLAR SYSTEM; SUPERNOVA; VARIABLE STAR.)

STARCH, a CARBOHYDRATE consisting of chains of glucose arranged in one of two forms to give the polysaccharides amylose and amylopectin. Amylose consists of an unbranched chain of 200–500 glucose units, whereas amylopectin consists of chains of 20 glucose units joined by cross links to give a highly branched structure. Most natural starches are mixtures of amylose and amylopectin; e.g., potato and cereal starches are 20%–30% amylose and 70%–80% amylopectin. Starch is found in plants, occurring in grains scattered throughout the cytoplasm. The grains from any particular plant have a characteristic microscopic appearance and an expert can

tell the source of a starch by its appearance under the microscope. Starches in the form of rice, potatoes and wheat or other cereal products supply about 70% of the world's food.

STAR CHAMBER, English law court, formally set up in 1487, abolished (1641) by the LONG PARLIAMENT. Operating outside COMMON LAW, with no jury, it was speedy and efficient, but also arbitrary and cruel, particularly under CHARLES I.

STARFISHES, a class, Asteroidea, of star-shaped marine echinoderms, with five-fold symmetry. A starfish consists of a central disk surrounded by five or more radiating arms. There is a dermal skeleton of calcite plates and a water-vascular system gives rise to rows of tube feet on the lower surface by which the animal moves about. The mouth is on the lower surface. Most species are carnivorous or omnivorous scavengers. Starfishes can regenerate lost or damaged parts.

STARK, John (1728–1822), American revolutionary soldier. After distinguishing himself at the battles of BUNKER HILL and Trenton he was made a brigadier general of New Hampshire militia. Stark won an important battle at BENNINGTON, Vt., and was instrumental in forcing the British surrender at SARATOGA. He was made a major general in 1783.

STARLINGS, a family, Sturnidae, of over 100 species of song birds. They have slender bills, an upright stance and smooth glossy plumage. Originally an Old World group, they are now found elsewhere. They feed on insects, other invertebrates and seeds, probing with the bill into turf or among leaves. They flock for feeding and roosting, with communal roosts of up to 500,000 birds.

STARR, Belle (c1848–1889), US outlaw. Her exploits with Jesse JAMES and Cole Younger were made famous in *Belle Starr, the Bandit Queen; or the Female Jesse James* (1889) by Richard K. Fox. Her Okla. home became famous as an outlaw refuge.

STAR-SPANGLED BANNER, The, US national anthem, officially adopted by act of Congress in 1931. Francis Scott KEY wrote the words in 1814, during the War of 1812, and they were later set to the tune of an old English drinking song, "To Anacreon in Heaven."

START. See ARMS CONTROL.

STAR WARS, popular name, derived from a futuristic motion picture, for the **Strategic Defense Initiative (SDI),** a space-based anti-ballistic-missile defense system proposed by President Ronald REAGAN in

1983. The system would employ orbiting space stations equipped with direct energy weapons (lasers or particle beams) intended to destroy hostile missiles soon after their launching. The technology for SDI does not yet exist, and many scientists doubted that it could be developed or, if developed, that it would prove sufficiently effective. Critics pointed out that the system would be vulnerable to attack or that it could be overwhelmed by a large number of missiles. Others argued that SDI, or even the effort to develop it, would violate existing treaties between the US and USSR and would destabilize the nuclear balance. President Reagan persevered in the conviction that an effective defense would end nuclear competition.

STATE, COUNTY AND MUNICIPAL EMPLOYEES, American Federation of (AFSCME), largest US union of public employees (c1,100,000), chartered in 1936. It represents men and women working for the federal government, nonprofit agencies and universities, as well as state, county and municipal government employees.

STATE, US Department of, oldest executive department of the US government. Originally in charge of domestic as well as foreign affairs, it now conducts US foreign policy. It collects and analyzes information from abroad, gives policy advice to the US president and negotiates treaties and agreements. The US Foreign Service maintains some 280 diplomatic and consular offices. The secretary of state, senior member of the president's cabinet, is assisted by undersecretaries, and assistant secretaries who run regional bureaus.

STATES-GENERAL, or **estates-general,** assemblies in European countries in the late Middle Ages which, in Germany, Poland, France and the Netherlands, evolved into modern parliaments. The "estates" were social classes, usually the clergy, the nobility and privileged commoners such as the new bourgeoisie of the towns. Though peasants were not represented, the estates spoke for the whole country, usually when summoned by the ruler to discuss a specific item. Their role was consultative rather than legislative.

STATES' RIGHTS, the rights of individual states in relation to the US federal government. The states' power, enshrined in the ARTICLES OF CONFEDERATION, was curtailed by the Constitution in the interests of federalism. Controversy soon arose over the relation between states' and federal rights: Thomas JEFFERSON opposed the Federalists' advocacy of strong central government and declared with James MADISON, in the KENTUCKY AND VIRGINIA RESOLUTIONS (1798–99), that individual states could decide whether to enforce federal legislation or not. In the HARTFORD CONVENTION (1814–15), Federalist New England expressed defiance of the Madison administration in the War of 1812, and in the 1850s several Northern states refused to implement the FUGITIVE SLAVE ACTS. The most extreme states' rights position was taken by John CALHOUN and set forth in N.C.'s NULLIFICATION ordinance (1832). Calhoun held that the Constitution in no way diminished state sovereignty; this view led logically to the doctrine of SECESSION. The Northern victory in the Civil War demolished the extreme states' rights position of nullification and secession, but states' rights has remained an important rallying cry, notably in the area of federal civil rights law.

STATIC, an accumulation of electric charge (see ELECTRICITY) responsible, e.g., for the attractive and repulsive properties produced in many plastics and fabrics by rubbing. It leaks away gradually through warm damp air, but otherwise may cause small sparks (and consequent RADIO interference) or violent discharges such as LIGHTNING.

STATICS, branch of MECHANICS dealing with systems in equilibrium, i.e., in which all FORCES are balanced and there is no motion.

STATISTICAL MECHANICS, branch of physics that explains the thermodynamic properties of a material system (see THERMODYNAMICS) in terms of the properties of the molecules or other particles of which it is composed. Statistical mechanics can be regarded as a generalization of KINETIC THEORY. Its foundations were laid by L. BOLTZMANN, who postulated that the ENTROPY of a system in a given state is proportional to the LOGARITHM of the PROBABILITY of the system's being in that state. The other thermodynamic quantities, such as TEMPERATURE and PRESSURE, can then be derived.

STATISTICS, the area of mathematics concerned with the manipulation of numerical information. The science has two branches: descriptive statistics, dealing with the classification and presentation of data, and inferential or analytical statistics, which studies ways of collecting data, its analysis and interpretation. Sampling is fundamental to statistics. Since it is usually impractical to treat of every element in a population (the group under consideration), a representative (often random) sample is instead examined, its properties being ascribed to the whole group. The data is analyzed in series of parameters such as the standard deviation and the mean of the data distribution. The distribution may be presented as a histogram, a frequency polygon, or a frequency curve. Ideally, a statistician aims to devise a mathematical model of the distribution, especially if it approximates to normality; there are many tests which he can use to determine whether or not his model "fits." Statistics is used throughout science, wherever there is an element of PROBABILITY involved, and also in industry, politics, market analysis and traffic control. (See also STOCHASTIC PROCESS.)

STATUE OF LIBERTY. See LIBERTY, STATUE OF.

STAUFFENBERG, Klaus von (1907–1944), German army officer. A leader in the conspiracy to kill Hitler, he planted a bomb in a briefcase in Hitler's headquarters at Rastenburg on July 20, 1944, but the explosion resulted only in slight injury to the dictator. Stauffenberg was seized in Berlin and executed.

STEADY STATE THEORY. See COSMOLOGY.

STEALTH AIRCRAFT, military aircraft whose shape and construction out of nonferrous materials are supposed to make them undetectable by enemy radar. The US B-2 bomber, a "flying wing" scheduled for deployment in the early 1990s, is such a plane.

STEAM ENGINE, the first important heat ENGINE, supplying the power that made the Industrial Revolution possible, and the principal power source for industry and transport (notably railroad locomotives and steamships) until largely superseded in the 20th century by steam TURBINES and the various INTERNAL-COMBUSTION ENGINES. The steam engine is an external-combustion engine, the steam being raised in a boiler heated by a furnace; it is also a reciprocating engine. There are two main types: condensing, in which the pressure drop is caused by cooling the steam and so condensing it back to water; and noncondensing, in which the steam is exhausted to the atmosphere. The first major precursor of the steam engine was Thomas Savery's steam pump (1698), worked by the partial vacuum created by condensing steam in closed chambers. It had no moving parts, however, and the first working reciprocating engine was that of Thomas NEWCOMEN (1712): steam was admitted to the cylinder as the piston moved up, and was condensed by a water spray inside the cylinder, whereupon the air

pressure outside forced the piston down again. James WATT radically improved Newcomen's engine (1769) by condensing the steam outside the cylinder (thus no longer having to reheat the cylinder at each stroke) and by using the steam pressure to force the piston up. He later found that, if steam were admitted for only part of the stroke, its expansion would do a good deal of extra work. (The principles involved were later studied by CARNOT and became the basis of THERMODYNAMICS.) Watt also invented the double-action principle—both strokes being powered, by applying the steam alternately to each end of the piston—the flyball governor, and the crank and "sun-and-planet" devices for converting the piston's linear motion to rotary motion. The compound engine (1781) makes more efficient use of the steam by using the exhaust steam from one cylinder to drive the piston of a second cylinder. Later developments included the use of high-pressure steam by Richard TREVITHICK and Oliver Evans.

STEEL, an ALLOY of IRON and up to 1.7% carbon, with small amounts of manganese, phosphorus, sulfur and silicon. These are termed carbon steels; those with other metals are termed alloy steels; low-alloy steels if they have less than 5% of the alloying metal, high-alloy steels if more than 5%. Carbon steels are far stronger than iron, and their properties can be tailored to their uses by adjusting composition and treatment. Alloy steels—including stainless steel—are used for their special properties. Steel was first mass-produced in the mid-19th century, and steel production is now one of the chief world industries, being basic to all industrial economies. The US, the USSR and Japan are the major producers. Steel's innumerable uses include automobile manufacture, shipbuilding, skyscraper frames, reinforced concrete and machinery of all kinds. All steelmaking processes remove the impurities in the raw materials—pig iron, scrap steel and reduced iron ore—by oxidizing them with an air or oxygen blast. Thus most of the carbon, silicon, manganese, phosphorus and sulfur are converted to their oxides and, together with added flux and other waste matter present, form the slag. The main processes are the Bessemer process, the Linz-Donawitz or basic oxygen process and the similar electric-arc process used for highest-quality steel, and the open-hearth process. Most modern processes use a basic slag and a basic refractory furnace lining: acidic processes are incapable of removing phosphorus. When the impurities have been removed, desired elements are added in calculated proportions. The molten steel is cast as ingots which are shaped while still red-hot in rolling mills, or it may be cast as a continuous bar ("strand casting"). The properties of medium-carbon (0.25% to 0.45% C) and high-carbon (up to 1.7% C) steels may be greatly improved by heat treatment: ANNEALING, casehardening and TEMPERING. Steel metallurgy is somewhat complex: unhardened steel may contain combinations of three phases—austenite, ferrite and cementite—differing in structure and carbon content; hardened steel contains martensite, which may be thought of as ferrite supersaturated with carbon.

STEELE, Sir Richard (1672–1729), English author and politician, best remembered for his wide-ranging essays in two periodicals founded with ADDISON, the *Tatler* (1709) and *Spectator* (1711). He was an active Whig member of Parliament, a journalist and a successful playwright, though his sentimental comedies are not now performed.

STEEN, Jan (1626–1679), Dutch genre painter, a master of color and facial expression. His 700 surviving works include jovial scenes of eating, drinking and revelry, portraits, landscapes and classical and biblical scenes.

STEEPLECHASING, horse-racing over a course with such obstacles as fences, hedges and water. It originated in England as a race from one church steeple to another. The world's most famous steeplechase is the English Grand National, first run in 1839. US steeplechases are normally held at racing tracks or hunts. Steeplechases on foot are now an Olympic sport.

STEFANSSON, Vilhjalmur (1879–1962), Canadian arctic explorer and author. He became an authority on Eskimo life and Arctic survival. Stefansson also charted several islands in the W Canadian Arctic. He was a northern studies consultant at Dartmouth College, N.H., from 1947.

STEFFENS, Lincoln (1866–1936), US journalist. One of the MUCKRAKERS, he wrote for *McClure's Magazine* and the *American Magazine* and was famous for his exposés of corruption in politics and business. A selection of his articles was published in *The Shame of the Cities* (1904) and his autobiography (1931) is a classic of the muckraking era.

STEICHEN, Edward (1879–1973), pioneer US photographer. After studying in Paris he worked in fashion, advertising and theater. At New York City's Museum of Modern Art he mounted the 1955 *Family of Man* exhibition.

STEIN, Gertrude (1874–1946), US author and celebrated personality who lived in Paris from 1903. Her first important work was *Three Lives* (1909). Stein is best known for her experimental syntax and her friendships with such figures as PICASSO, HEMINGWAY, MATISSE and GIDE. They are described in *The Autobiography of Alice B. Toklas* (1933).

STEIN, Heinrich Friedrich Karl, Baron vom und zum (1757–1831), Prussian statesman and reformer. As chief minister (1807–08) after Prussia's defeat in the Napoleonic Wars, he abolished serfdom and introduced many administrative and economic reforms, until he was dismissed by order of Napoleon.

STEINBECK, John (1902–1968), US author who came to the fore in the 1930s with his novels about poverty and social injustice. He won a Pulitzer Prize for *The Grapes of Wrath* (1939), about migrant farm workers in Cal., and the 1962 Nobel Prize for Literature. His other works include *Tortilla Flat* (1935), *Of Mice and Men* (1937), *Cannery Row* (1945), *East of Eden* (1952) and *The Winter of Our Discontent* (1961).

STEINBERG, Saul (1914–   ), Romanian-born US painter and cartoonist whose witty drawings often appeared on the cover of the *New Yorker*.

STEINEM, Gloria (1934–   ), US feminist and writer, notably of a lively column in *New York* magazine; a skillful publicist for the women's movement. A co-founder (1971) of the National Women's Political Caucus, she also founded and edited (1971–87) *Ms.* magazine, whose pages have consistently criticized women's traditional place in society.

STEINER, Rudolf (1861–1925), Austrian founder of Anthroposophy, an attempt to recapture spiritual realities ignored by modern man. He founded the Waldorf School movement, and stressed music and drama as aids to self-discovery. Works include *The Philosophy of Spiritual Activity* (1922).

STEINMAN, David Barnard (1886–1960), US engineer whose pioneering aerodynamic studies led to the construction of extremely long yet stable bridges. He designed more than 400 bridges including the Triborough (NYC; 1936) and Mackinac Straits (Michigan; 1957).

STEINMETZ, Charles Proteus (1865–1923), German-born US electrical engineer who is best remembered for working out the theory of alternating current (1893 onward), thereby making it possible for AC to be used rather than DC in most applications.

STEINWAY, German-American family of piano manufacturers. **Henry Engelhard** (1797–1871), who changed his name from Steinweg after migrating in 1851 from Germany to the US, founded the family business in 1853. In 1855 he began building pianos with cast-iron frames. The business was carried on by his sons **Christian Friedrich Theodore** (1825–1889) and **William** (1835–1896).

STELLA, Frank Philip (1936–   ), US painter who moved from minimalist stripes to hot-colored abstractions.

STELLA, Joseph (1877–1946), Italian-born US artist, best known of America's futurist painters. He was fascinated by the world of steel and electricity and filled his canvases with images of bridges, skyscrapers and subways.

STENDHAL (1783–1842), pen name of Marie-Henri Beyle, French pioneer of the psychological novel. *The Red and the Black* (1830) and *The Charterhouse of Parma* (1839) explore the search for happiness through love and political power, with minute analysis of the hero's feelings. His treatment of the figure of the "outsider," his social criticism and brilliant ironic prose style make him one of the greatest and most "modern" of French novelists.

STENGEL, Casey (1890–1975), US baseball manager. A popular and garrulous figure, he led the New York Yankees to seven world championships 1949–58, and managed the New York Mets 1962–65. He was elected to the Baseball Hall of Fame in 1966.

STENO, Nicolaus (1638–1686), or **Niels Stensen**, Danish geologist, anatomist and bishop. In 1669 he published the results of his geological studies: he recognized that many rocks are sedimentary (see SEDIMENTARY ROCKS); that FOSSILS are the remains of once-living creatures and that they can be used for dating purposes, and established many of the tenets of modern crystallography.

STENOTYPE, system of machine SHORTHAND that uses a keyboard machine like a typewriter except that several keys may be depressed at once. Letter groups phonetically represent words. The machine, silent in operation, is capable of 250 words/min.

STEPHEN, Saint (d. c36 AD), first Christian martyr. Accused of blasphemy, he was stoned to death (Acts 6–8). His feast day is Dec. 26.

STEPHEN I, Saint (977–1038), first king of Hungary, often regarded as founder of the state. His formal coronation in 1000 marked Hungary's entry into Christian Europe. He established a strong church, and modeled his administration on German lines.

STEPHEN, name of nine popes. **Stephen I** (reigned 254–57), famous for his disputes with St. CYPRIAN of Carthage, whose rebaptism of heretics he denounced, died during Emperor Valerian's persecutions. **Stephen II** (reigned 752–57) was supported by PEPIN THE SHORT in his defeat of the Lombards. The PAPAL STATES were founded with land gifts from Pepin. Controversy over papal elections dominated the reign of **Stephen III** (768–72). **Stephen IV** (reigned 816–17) crowned LOUIS I emperor (establishing a prerogative of the papacy) and strengthened links with the Franks. **Stephen VI** (reigned 896–97) declared void the reign of his predecessor, Formosus, but was himself imprisoned and strangled. His rule marked the papacy's lowest point. **Stephen IX** (c1000–1058), reigned from 1057, continued the reforms of LEO IX, enforcing priestly celibacy and attacking simony. But he failed to stop the rift between the Eastern and Western churches.

STEPHEN (c1097–1154), king of England 1135–54. A nephew of Henry I, he was briefly supplanted (1141) by Matilda, Henry's daughter. Though a just and generous ruler, he was not strong enough to govern the warring factions of his realm.

STEPHEN, Sir Leslie (1832–1904), English man of letters. He edited (1882–91) *The Dictionary of National Biography*. A freethinker, he wrote major studies of 18th-century English literature and philosophy. Virginia WOOLF was his daughter.

STEPHENS, Alexander Hamilton (1812–1883), vice-president of the Confederate States of America 1861–65. A congressman from Ga. (1843–59), he opposed secession, but stayed loyal to his state in the Civil War. He led the delegation to the Hampton Roads peace conference (1865). Imprisoned for six months after the war, he returned to serve again in Congress (1873–82) and as governor of Ga. (1882–83).

STEPHENSON, British family of inventors and railroad engineers. **George Stephenson** (1781–1848) first worked on stationary STEAM ENGINES, reconstructing and modifying one by NEWCOMEN (c1812). His first LOCOMOTIVE, the *Blucher*, took to the rails in 1814: it traveled at 4mph (about 6.5km/h) hauling coal for the Killingworth colliery, and incorporated an important development, flanged wheels. About this time, independently of DAVY, he invented a safety lamp; this earned him £1,000, which helped finance further locomotive experiments. In 1821 he was appointed to survey and engineer a line from Darlington to Stockton: in 1825 his *Locomotion* carried 450 people along the line at a rate of 15mph (about 25km/h), and the modern RAILROAD was born. This was followed in 1829 by the success of the *Rocket*, which ran the 40mi (65km) of his new Manchester–Liverpool line at speeds up to 30mph (about 48km/h), the first mainline passenger rail journey. His only son **Robert Stephenson** (1803–1859) helped his father on both of these lines, and with the *Rocket*, but is best known as a BRIDGE builder, notably for the tubular bridges over the Menai Straits, North Wales (1850), and the St. Lawrence at Montreal (1859).

STEPINAC, Aloysius (1898–1960), Yugoslav Roman Catholic cardinal. Archbishop of Zagreb (1937), he denounced TITO's communism, was accused of Nazi collaboration, and imprisoned 1946–51. On his elevation to cardinal (1952) Yugoslavia broke off relations with the Vatican.

STEPPES, extensive temperate GRASSLANDS of Europe and Asia (equivalent to the North American prairies and South American pampas). They extend from SW Siberia to the lower reaches of the Danube River.

STEREOCHEMISTRY, the study of the arrangement in space of atoms in molecules, and of the properties which depend on such arrangements. The two chief branches are the study of stereoisomers and stereospecific reactions (which involve only one isomer); and conformational analysis, including the study of steric effects on reaction rates and mechanisms.

STEREOPHONIC SOUND. See HIGH FIDELITY.

STEREOSCOPE, optical instrument that simulates binocular vision by presenting slightly different pictures to the two eyes so that an apparently three-dimensional image is produced. The simplest stereoscope, invented in the 1830s, used a system of mirrors and prisms (later, converging lenses) to view the pictures. In the color separation method the left image is printed or projected in red and seen through a red filter, and likewise for the right image in blue. A similar method uses images projected by POLARIZED LIGHT and viewed through polarizing filters, the polarization axes being at right angles. The pictures are produced by a stereoscopic camera with two lenses a small distance apart. The stereoscope is useful in making relief maps by aerial photographic survey.

STERILIZATION, surgical procedure in which the FALLOPIAN TUBES are cut and tied to prevent eggs reaching the WOMB, thus providing permanent CONTRACEPTION. The procedure is essentially irreversible and should only be performed when a woman has completed her family. It may be done by a small abdominal operation, at CESARIAN SECTION or through an instrument, the laparoscope. In males, sterilization may be achieved by vasectomy, a simple operation in which the *vas deferens* on each side is ligated and cut to prevent sperm from reaching the seminal vesicles. *Also*, the treatment of medical equipment to ensure that it is not contaminated by BACTERIA and other microorganisms. Metal and linen objects are often sterilized by heat (in autoclaves). Chemical disinfection is also used and plastic equipment is exposed to gamma rays.

STERN, Isaac (1920–   ), US violinist. Born in Kremenets, USSR, he studied and made his debut in 1931 in San Francisco.

STERNBERG, Joseph von (1891–1969), Viennese-born US film director. He is most famous for the films he made with Marlene DIETRICH. These include *The Blue Angel* (1930), *Morocco* (1930) and *Shanghai Express* (1932).

STERNE, Laurence (1713–1768), English novelist and clergyman, author of *The Life and Opinions of Tristram Shandy, Gentleman* (1760–67). One of the most widely read novels of its day, this whimsical work proceeds by association of ideas and conversation rather than by plot structure. *A Sentimental Journey* (1768) recounts travels in France and Italy.

STEROIDS, HORMONES produced in the body from CHOLESTEROL, mainly by the ADRENAL GLANDS, and related to ESTROGENS and ANDROGENS. All have chemical structures based on that of the sterols. Cortisol is the main glucocorticoid (steroids that regulate glucose metabolism) and aldosterone the main mineralocorticoid (regulating SALT, POTASSIUM and WATER balance). Increased amounts of cortisol are secreted during times of stress, e.g., SHOCK, SURGERY and severe infection. Steroids, mainly of the glucocorticoid type, are also given in doses above normal hormone levels to obtain other effects, e.g., the suppression of INFLAMMATION, ALLERGY and IMMUNITY. Diseases that respond to this include ASTHMA, MULTIPLE SCLEROSIS, some forms of NEPHRITIS, inflammatory GASTROINTESTINAL TRACT disease and cerebral EDEMA; SKIN and EYE conditions may be treated with local steroids. High-dose systemic steroids may have adverse effects if used for long periods; they may cause ACNE, osteoporosis, hypertension, fluid retention, altered facial appearance and growth retardation in children.

STETHOSCOPE, instrument devised by René T. H. Laënnec (1781–1826) for listening to sounds within the body, especially those from the HEART, LUNGS, ABDOMEN and blood vessels.

STETTINIUS, Edward Reilly, Jr. (1900–1949), US businessman and statesman. Chairman of United States Steel at 37, he administered the LEND-LEASE program 1941–43, was secretary of state 1944–45 and a founder delegate to the UN.

STEUBEN, Friedrich Wilhelm Augustin, Baron von (1730–1794), Prussian soldier who trained the CONTINENTAL ARMY. Arriving in America in 1777 with an introduction from Benjamin Franklin, he was appointed inspector general of the army by Congress in 1778. He organized Washington's troops in Valley Forge into an effective fighting force, seen at the battle of MONMOUTH (1778) and siege of YORKTOWN (1780).

STEVENS, US family of inventors and engineers. **John Stevens** (1749–1838) made many contributions to steamboat development, including the first with a screw propeller (1802) and the first seagoing steamboat (*Phoenix*, 1809). He also built (1825) the first US steam locomotive. His son **Robert Livingston Stevens** (1787–1856) assisted his father, and invented the inverted-T rail still used in modern RAILROADS (1830) as well as the technique of fastening them to wooden sleepers. **Edwin Augustus Stevens** (1795–1868), another son, also made contributions to railroad technology.

STEVENS, John Paul (1920–   ), US jurist, served on the US Court of Appeals and then, by appointment of President Ford (1975), on the US Supreme Court as an associate justice.

STEVENS, Thaddeus (1792–1868), controversial US politician. A staunch opponent of slavery, he wielded great power as a Vt. congressman and chairman of the US Senate Ways and Means Committee during the Civil War. He afterward dominated the joint committee on RECONSTRUCTION, leading the Radical Republicans with Senator SUMNER. He held that the defeated Southern states were "conquered provinces," subject to the will of Congress. He proposed the 14th Amendment, fought for Negro suffrage, and led in the impeachment of President Andrew Johnson.

STEVENS, Wallace (1879–1955), US poet. He worked for a Connecticut insurance company and achieved wide literary recognition only with the 1955 Pulitzer Prize for his *Collected Poems*. Rich in imagery and vocabulary, his often difficult verse explores the use of imagination to ease tragic reality and give meaning to its confusion.

STEVENSON, family of US politicians. **Adlai Ewing Stevenson** (1835–1914), a lawyer and Democratic representative for Ill. (1875–76, 1879–80), was elected US vice-president in Cleveland's second term (1893–97). **Adlai Ewing Stevenson** (1900–1965), his grandson, also a lawyer, was special assistant to the secretary of the navy (1941–44) and a delegate to the UN (1946–47). In 1948 he was elected governor of Ill., where he backed reform. He was chosen as Democratic presidential candidate in 1952 and 1956 but lost to Eisenhower. His policies of halting the arms race and promoting the economies of Africa and Asia were unpopular at home. He lost the 1960 nomination to Kennedy. From 1961 to his death he was US ambassador to the UN. His son, **Adlai Ewing Stevenson III** (1930–   ), served in the US Senate (1970–81) as a Democrat from Illinois and ran unsuccessfully for governor in 1982.

STEVENSON, Robert Louis (1850–1894), Scottish author best known for such adventure stories as *Treasure Island* (1883) and *Kidnapped* (1886). He also wrote *Dr. Jekyll and Mr. Hyde* (1886), a horrific tale of inherent good and evil, and the sensitive verse of *A Child's Garden of Verses* (1885), as well as short stories, essays and travel books. A sufferer from tuberculosis, he sailed with his US wife to the South Pacific (1888) and settled in Samoa, where he continued to write.

STEVINUS, Simon (1548–1620), or **Simon Stevin**, Dutch mathematician and engineer who made many contributions to FLUID MECHANICS; disproved, before GALILEO, ARISTOTLE's theory that heavy bodies fall more swiftly than light ones; introduced the DECIMAL SYSTEM into popular use; and first used the parallelogram of forces in MECHANICS.

STEWARD, Julian Haynes (1902–1972), US anthropologist. A major exponent of cultural evolution, he was among the first anthropologists to emphasize ecology as a determinant of culture. He edited the *Handbook of South American Indians* (7 vol., 1946–59) and wrote *Theory of Culture Change* (1955).

STEWART, Dugald (1753–1828), Scottish philosopher, a major member of the COMMON SENSE SCHOOL and a principal disciple of Thomas REID.

STEWART, James (1908–   ), boyish US film actor whose memorable credits include *Mr. Smith Goes to Washington* (1939), *The Philadelphia Story* (1940), and *It's a Wonderful Life* (1946).

STEWART, Potter (1915–1985), associate justice of the US Supreme Court 1958–1981. Appointed by President Eisenhower, he held a moderate point of view and often cast a "swing" vote.

STIEGEL, Henry William (1729–1785), German-born US iron and glass manufacturer. He emigrated to Philadelphia in 1750, made a fortune manufacturing iron stoves, and in 1760 founded Manheim, Pa., where he established a famous glassfactory. Extravagance led to bankruptcy in 1774.

STIEGLITZ, Alfred (1864–1946), US photographer who helped make photography a recognized art form; and who founded the gallery "291" in New York, where he put on pioneering exhibitions. A founding member of the Photo-Secession, he is known for his city and cloudscapes and many portraits of his artist wife, Georgia O'KEEFFE.

STIFTER, Adalbert (1805–1868), Austrian writer noted for his fine descriptions of nature and his gentle praise of humble virtues. His works include *Colored Stones* (1853: a collection of short stories) and the novel *Indian Summer* (1857).

STIGMATA, apparent wounds on the hands, feet and side, similar to those of the crucified Christ. The earliest of over 300 recorded cases is that of FRANCIS OF ASSISI.

STILICHO, Flavius (c365–408), greatest general of the late Roman Empire. Chief general under THEODOSIUS I and Honorius, he fought major campaigns against barbarian invaders.

STILL, William Grant (1895–1978), US composer whose three ballets, two symphonies and three operas are largely devoted to black themes. Langston HUGHES wrote the libretto for his opera *Troubled Island* (1938).

STILWELL, Joseph Warren (1883–1946), US commander of the Allied forces in the Far East in WWII. Driven back to India in 1942, he rebuilt his forces and counterattacked through Burma to China (1943–44). He was recalled in 1944 after disagreeing with CHIANG KAI-SHEK, under whom he was serving.

STIMSON, Henry Lewis (1867–1950), US lawyer and statesman, author of the "Stimson Doctrine." As secretary of state (1929–33), he declared at the time of Japan's invasion of Manchuria that the US would not recognize any territorial changes or treaties which impaired US treaty rights or were brought about by force. Recalled from retirement to become secretary of war (1940–45), he strongly advocated development and use of the atomic bomb.

STIMULANT, DRUG that stimulates an organ. NERVOUS SYSTEM stimulants range from ALCOHOL (an apparent stimulant only) and HALLUCINOGENIC DRUGS, to drugs liable to induce convulsions. Cardiac stimulants include DIGITALIS and ADRENALINE and are used in cardiac failure and resuscitation respectively. Bowel stimulants have a LAXATIVE effect. WOMB stimulants (oxytocin and ergometrine) are used in OBSTETRICS to induce labor and prevent postpartum HEMORRHAGE.

STINNES, Hugo (1870–1924), German industrialist. Before, during and after WWI he built up a vast industrial empire. A founder of the right-wing National People's party, he served in the Reichstag (parliament) 1920–24.

STIRLING ENGINE, a type of EXTERNAL-COMBUSTION ENGINE invented in Scotland by the Rev. Robert Stirling in 1816. Long in disuse, the Stirling engine has recently become a subject of investigation as a possible substitute for the gasoline engine, but so far has not proved practical. Different versions of the Stirling engine exist, but all involve a gas (usually air) circulating in a closed system of cylinders and pistons and deriving energy from an external source of heat.

STOA, in ancient Greece, a long, open building with a colonnade supporting the roof. Stoas were used as public meeting-places for business or pleasure.

STOCHASTIC PROCESS, any process governed by the laws of PROBABILITY: for example, the BROWNIAN MOTION of the submicroscopic particles in a colloidal solution. The term is usually confined to processes that develop through time, each step taking place according to probabilities that depend on the results of the previous steps.

STOCKHAUSEN, Karlheinz (1928–   ), German composer and theorist, an experimenter with a variety of avant-garde musical techniques, including electronic, twelve-tone and aleatory music.

STOCKHOLM, capital of Sweden, an architecturally fine city on a network of islands on the E coast. It is Sweden's major commercial, industrial, cultural and financial center, and an important port. Chief industries are machinery, paper and print, shipbuilding, chemicals and foodstuffs. Founded in the 13th century, it was long dominated by the HANSEATIC LEAGUE.

Liberated in a national uprising in 1523, it became the capital in 1634. Pop (city) 659,030; (metro) 1,435,474.

STOCKMAN, David (1946–   ), US public official. A Republican member (1977–79) of the US House of Representatives from Michigan, he served (1981–85) as director of the Office of Management and Budget in the first Reagan administration, then joined the investment banking firm of Salomon Bros. His *The Triumph of Politics* (1986) exposed the inner workings of the Reagan White House.

STOCKS AND STOCK MARKET. Stocks represent shares of ownership in a corporation or public body. Issuing stocks provides a means for companies to raise CAPITAL (see INVESTMENT). Individuals buy stocks because they can easily be converted into cash and may gain in value. The initial par value of a stock is determined by the assets of the company, such as its plant, machinery, property. But par value has no bearing on the market value of a stock, which is the price people are willing to pay. If a company is seen to be doing well, the market value can soar above its original par value. This is one way an investor can make capital gains by owning stocks. A stockholder also expects to receive an annual dividend based on the profits of the company. Stocks can be divided into two categories, preferred and common. The preferred stockholder is entitled to a fixed percentage claim on profits prior to the common stockholder, who then gets the rest. Depending on profits, the common stockholder may either get no dividend, or get a much higher return than the preferred stockholder; common stocks are more speculative.

The stock market, or exchange, is the place where people who want to sell and buy stocks can get together. Most transactions are carried out by stockbrokers, who are paid a commission on each transaction. In the US, a customer may also buy stocks on credit, but he must pay an amount, or margin, specified by the Federal Reserve System, toward the transaction, with the balance advanced by the broker. All stock exchanges in the US are registered and regulated by the SECURITIES AND EXCHANGE COMMISSION. (See AMERICAN STOCK EXCHANGE; NEW YORK STOCK EXCHANGE.)

STOCKTON, Robert Field (1795–1866), US naval officer. In the MEXICAN WAR he captured Los Angeles and proclaimed himself governor of Cal. He was a US senator 1851–53, and played a major part in building and running the Delaware and Raritan canal (1828–38, 1853–66).

STOICISM, ancient Greek school of philosophy founded by ZENO OF CITIUM, who taught in a stoa (a long, open, roofed building) in Athens c300 BC. Much influenced by the CYNICS, the Stoics believed that man should live rationally and in harmony with nature, and that virtue is the only good. In performing his duty the virtuous man should be indifferent to pleasure, as well as to pain and misfortune, thus rising above the effects of chance and achieving spiritual freedom and conformity with the divine reason controlling all nature. Stoicism was influential for many centuries; among the most famous of the later Stoics were SENECA, EPICTETUS and MARCUS AURELIUS.

STOKER, Bram (Abraham Stoker; 1847–1912), British writer and theatrical manager best known for his classic novel of horror, *Dracula* (1897). In addition, he was manager to Henry IRVING 1878–1905.

STOKOWSKI, Leopold (1882–1977), brilliant, flamboyant British-born US conductor. He gained his early reputation as musical director of the Philadelphia Orchestra (1912–36), and it was under his baton that they played the music for Disney's *Fantasia* (1940). He was noted especially for his modern repertoire and innovative orchestration.

STOLYPIN, Pyotr Arkadevich (1862–1911), prime minister of imperial Russia 1906–11. Ruthless in suppressing unrest and opposition, he yet instituted land reforms aimed at creating a conservative landowning peasantry, thereby making left-wing enemies. He was assassinated by a revolutionary who was also a police agent.

STOMACH, the large distensible hopper of the DIGESTIVE SYSTEM. It receives food boluses from the ESOPHAGUS and mixes them with hydrochloric acid and the stomach ENZYMES; fats are partially emulsified. After some time, the pyloric sphincter relaxes and food enters the duodenum and the rest of the GASTROINTESTINAL TRACT. Diseases of the stomach include ULCER, CANCER and pyloric stenosis, causing pain, anorexia or vomiting; these often require SURGERY.

STONE, Edward Durell (1902–1978), US architect whose works include the US pavilion for the 1958 Brussels World's Fair, the US embassy in Delhi (1958) and the J. F. Kennedy Center in Washington, D.C. (1971).

STONE, Harlan Fiske (1872–1946), appointed attorney general in 1924 to restore confidence in the scandal-ridden Justice Department, became associate justice (1925–41) and chief justice

(1941–46) of the US Supreme Court. He was noted for his dissenting opinions, many upholding NEW DEAL legislation.

STONE, Lucy (1818–1893), US reformer and campaigner for women's rights. A fervent abolitionist, she helped to found the American Woman Suffrage Association (1869) and edited its magazine *Woman's Journal* (1870–93).

STONE AGE, the stage in man's cultural development preceding the BRONZE AGE and the IRON AGE (see also PRIMITIVE MAN). It is characterized by man's use of exclusively stone tools and weapons, though some made of bone, wood, etc., may occur. It is split up into three periods: the **Paleolithic,** or Old Stone Age, began with the emergence of man-like creatures, the earliest stone tools being some 2.5 million years old and associated with the australopithecines (see PREHISTORIC MAN). Paleolithic tools, if worked at all, are made of chipped stone. The **Mesolithic,** or Middle Stone Age, was confined exclusively to NW Europe. Here, between c10,000 and c3000 BC, various peoples enjoyed a culture showing similarities with both Paleolithic and Neolithic. The **Neolithic,** or New Stone Age, began in SW Asia about 8000 BC and spread throughout Europe between 6000 and 2000 BC; it was signaled by the development of agriculture, with consequent increase in stability of the population and hence elaboration of social structure. The tools of this period are of polished stone. Apart from farming, men also worked mines. The Neolithic merged slowly into the Early Bronze Age.

STONEHENGE, the ruins of a MEGALITHIC MONUMENT, dating from the STONE AGE and early BRONZE AGE, on Salisbury Plain, S England. Its most noticeable features are concentric rings of stones surrounding a horseshoe of upright stones, and a solitary vertical stone, the Heel Stone, some 100m to the NE. Stonehenge was built between c1900 BC and c1400 BC in three distinct phases. It appears to have been both a religious center and an observatory from which predictions of astronomical events could be made.

STONE MOUNTAIN, 650ft-high granite dome near Atlanta, Ga. A portion of the north face has been sculptured as a memorial to the heroes of the Confederacy, begun in 1928 by G. BORGLUM. It is part of the Stone Mountain Memorial Park, established in 1958.

STONEWARE. See POTTERY AND PORCELAIN.

STOPES, Marie Charlotte Carmichael (1880–1958), British pioneer of sex education and family planning. A professional paleobotanist, she wrote *Wise Parenthood* (1918) and set up (1921) the first birth-control clinic.

STOPPARD, Tom (1937–   ), English playwright best known for *Rosencrantz and Guildenstern Are Dead* (1966), an existentialist drama centering on two minor characters from Shakespeare's *Hamlet.* The scintillating dialogue that critics admired in this play is also evident in *Travesties* (1974).

STOREY, David (Malcolm) (1933–   ), English playwright and novelist whose two best-known works, the novel *This Sporting Life* (1960) and the play *The Changing Room* (1971), are based on his years as a professional rugby player.

STORKS, large, heavily-built birds, family Ciconiidae, with long legs and necks, long, stout bills and commonly black and white plumage. The long legs and slightly webbed feet are adaptations for wading in shallow water, where they feed on freshwater animals and large insects. They tend to be gregarious and characteristic greeting ceremonies may be observed at nests and roosts. The family is largely of tropical distribution, the two temperate-breeding species undertaking long migrations to their breeding grounds.

STORM AND STRESS. See STURM UND DRANG.

STORM TROOPERS (*Sturmabteilungen,* or SA), the strongarm gangs set up in Germany in 1921 by Ernst Roehm to destroy resistance to the Nazis. They grew into a private army 2,000,000 strong, but were virtually disbanded after Hitler had Roehm killed in 1934.

STORY, Joseph (1779–1845), associate justice of the US Supreme Court from 1811, author of nine great legal commentaries and professor of law at Harvard from 1829. He participated in many historic decisions shaping federal law under Chief Justice MARSHALL, and exercised a great influence on US jurisprudence and legal education.

STOSS, Veit (c1447–1533), German sculptor of realistic and expressive carvings in wood and stone. Major works include the altar (1477–89) in St. Mary's, Krakow, Poland, and the *Annunciation* (1517–19) in the church of St. Lorenz, Nuremburg.

STOWE, Harriet Elizabeth Beecher (1811–1896), US author famous for the antislavery novel *Uncle Tom's Cabin* (1852). Born into the BEECHER family, she moved to Cincinnati, Ohio, in 1832, and there learned about slavery in nearby Ky. Her other books include the documentary

The Key to Uncle Tom's Cabin (1853), and the novels *Dred: A Tale of the Great Dismal Swamp* (1856) and *The Minister's Wooing* (1859).

STRABISMUS, cross-eye, or **squint,** a disorder of the EYES in which the alignment of the two ocular axes is not parallel, impairing binocular VISION; the eyes may diverge or converge. It is often congenital and may require SURGERY if orthoptics fail. Acquired squints are usually due to nerve or muscle disease and cause double vision.

STRABO (c63 BC–c23 AD), Greek geographer and historian. His *Historical Sketches* in 47 books are almost entirely lost, but the 17 books of his *Geography* have survived and are a principal source for our knowledge of ancient geography.

STRACHEY, (Giles) Lytton (1880–1932), English biographer and critic prominent in the BLOOMSBURY GROUP. His irreverent studies of the famous in *Eminent Victorians* (1918), and *Queen Victoria* (1921) caused a stir but suited the iconoclastic mood which followed WWI. They are still admired for their wit, irony and style. His last major work was *Elizabeth and Essex* (1928).

STRADELLA, Alessandro (c1642–1682), Italian composer of operas, oratorios, over 200 fine chamber cantatas and some notable orchestral music.

STRADIVARI or **STRADIVARIUS, Antonio** (c1644–1737), Italian violin maker, most famous of a group of fine craftsmen who worked in Cremona (see also AMATI). Stradivarius violins, violas and cellos are today highly prized.

STRAFFORD, Thomas Wentworth, 1st Earl of (1593–1641), English statesman. From opposing CHARLES I's policies 1614–28, he changed sides and became a privy councillor 1629–32, lord deputy in Ireland 1633–39 and with LAUD an efficient and just but ruthless promoter of the king's absolutist ideals. He was executed to appease a hostile parliament.

STRASBOURG, commercial and industrial city in NE France, famed for its Gothic cathedral. A major river port linked with the Rhine and Rhône, it has metallurgical, petroleum, heavy machinery and food-processing industries. Seat of the Council of Europe, it was a free imperial city until French seizure in 1681. Strasbourg was under German rule 1871–1919. Pop 248,040.

STRATEGIC AIR COMMAND (SAC), main US nuclear striking force, containing all US land-based ballistic missiles and long-range bombers. SAC is linked to US warning systems and is a specified command under the Defense Department. Its mission is global.

STRATEGIC ARMS LIMITATION TALKS (SALT). See ARMS CONTROL.

STRATEGIC ARMS REDUCTION TALKS (START). See ARMS CONTROL.

STRATEGIC DEFENSE INITIATIVE (SDI). See STAR WARS.

STRATEGIC PETROLEUM RESERVE (SPR), store of imported crude oil authorized by Congress in 1975 to insure against an interruption of the nation's foreign oil supply. The oil is stored in underground salt domes on the Gulf Coast of Texas and Louisiana. Filling of the reserve, intended to hold 1 billion barrels, was delayed by construction and budgetary problems. The SPR had not been filled by the late 1980s.

STRATEGY, the general design behind a war or military campaign. In a wider sense it involves "grand strategy": delineation of broad political objectives. Strategy cannot be reduced to a set of general rules, but it always involves long-term planning; defining military objectives; analyzing one's own and the enemy's strength; understanding the geography of the land and planning moves accordingly; assessing options and preparing contingency plans; organizing transport, supplies and communications; anticipating enemy actions and determining when and where to fight. Strategy and strategic theories are continually modified by technological, social and political changes. Since WWII, nuclear weapons at one extreme and GUERRILLA WARFARE at the other have made obsolete conventional strategy and it has become impossible to separate purely military strategy from wider political and economic objectives.

STRATEMEYER, Edward (1862–1930), US author who, under various pseudonyms and employing a stable of writers, produced hundreds of Tom Swift, Hardy Boys, Bobbsey Twins, and Nancy Drew books.

STRATFORD-UPON-AVON, market town in W central England, home of SHAKESPEARE. A tourist mecca, it contains his birthplace (now a museum), his tomb in Holy Trinity church, and the riverside theater where the Royal Shakespeare Company performs. Anne Hathaway's cottage is nearby. The town also supports some light industry. Pop 19,449.

STRATHCONA AND MOUNT ROYAL, Donald Alexander Smith, 1st Baron (1820–1914), Canadian fur trader, financier, statesman and builder of the Canadian Pacific railroad (1885). Emigrating from Scotland in 1838, he joined the Hudson's Bay Company, eventually becoming governor in 1889. A member of the Canadian

Parliament 1871–80, 1887–96, he was High Commissioner in London 1896–1914.

STRATIGRAPHY, the branch of GEOLOGY concerned with the description, sequence, classification and correlation of bodies of stratified rock, their depositional environments and their vertical and lateral relationships. (See also PALEONTOLOGY; ROCKS; SEDIMENTARY ROCKS.)

STRATOSPHERE, the layer of the ATMOSPHERE extending upward from the tropopause (upper level of the TROPOSPHERE) to about 18mi above the earth's surface. Its upper level is called the *stratopause*. It includes the OZONE layer.

STRAUS, Nathan (1848–1931), German-born US merchant and philanthropist who purchased R. H. Macy and Co. in New York City and developed it into the world's largest department store. He was a leader in the field of child health and established milk distribution centers throughout the US.

STRAUS, Oscar (1870–1954), Austrian composer, famous for *The Chocolate Soldier* (1908) and about 50 other operettas. He left Europe to escape the Nazis but later returned to Austria.

STRAUSS, David Friedrich (1808–1874), German theologian and philosopher whose *Life of Jesus* (1835–36) caused a storm by denying the historicity of supernatural elements in the Gospels and treating their accounts of Jesus as mythological.

STRAUSS, Franz Joseph (1915–1988), West German political leader, head of the conservative Bavarian Christian Social Union. As federal minister of defense (1956–62), he advocated German rearmament. Criticized for the arrest of the editors of the magazine *Der Spiegel*, he lost his post, but returned as finance minister 1966–69. He was prime minister of Bavaria from 1978.

STRAUSS, Johann, name of two famous Viennese composers of WALTZES. **Johann, the Elder** (1804–1849) achieved immense popularity and established the distinctive light style of the Viennese waltz. **Johann, the Younger** (1825–1899), wrote many favorites, including *The Blue Danube* (1866), *Tales from the Vienna Woods* (1868) and the opera *Die Fledermaus* (*The Bat*, 1873).

STRAUSS, Richard (1864–1949), German composer and conductor, the last of the great Romantic composers. He leapt to fame with the tone poem *Don Juan* (1888). Other symphonic poems include *Till Eulenspiegel* (1895), *Thus Spake Zarathustra* (1896), *Don Quixote* (1898) and *A Hero's Life* (1898). After 1900 he concentrated on vocal music, and with von HOFMANNSTHAL as librettist produced brilliantly scored and popular operas, including *Salome* (1905), *Elektra* (1909), *Der Rosenkavalier* (1911) and *Die Frau ohne Schatten* (1919).

STRAVINSKY, Igor Fyodorovich (1882–1971), one of the greatest modern composers, born in Russia. Taught by RIMSKY-KORSAKOV, he caused a sensation with his scores for DIAGHILEV's ballets: *The Firebird* (1910), *Petrouchka* (1911) and *The Rite of Spring* (1913). From 1920 he lived in France, adopting an austere neoclassical style, as in *Symphonies of Wind Instruments* (1920), the opera *Oedipus Rex* (1927) and *Symphony of Psalms* (1930). Emigrating to the US in 1939, he became a US citizen in 1945. Later works include *Symphony in Three Movements* (1942–45) and the opera *The Rake's Progress* (1951). He finally adopted TWELVE-TONE composition in works like *Agon* (1953–57) and *Threni* (1958).

STRAWBERRY, luscious fruit-bearing plants of the genus *Fragaria,* native to the Americas, Europe and Asia. Strawberries have been cultivated locally for many centuries though most modern varieties originated in crosses between New-World species. The fruit is in fact a swollen part of the flower stalk. Family: Rosaceae.

STREAMLINING, the design of the shape of a body so as to minimize drag as it travels through a fluid; essential to the efficiency of aircraft, ships and submarines. At subsonic speeds turbulent flow is minimized by using a shape rounded in front, tapering to a point behind (see AERODYNAMICS; FLUID MECHANICS). At supersonic speeds a different shape is needed, thin and pointed at both ends, to minimize the shock waves.

STREAM OF CONSCIOUSNESS, a literary technique in which a character's thoughts are presented in the jumbled, inconsequential manner of real life, apparently without the author imposing any framework on them. Its best-known exponents are Marcel PROUST, James JOYCE and Virginia WOOLF.

STREICHER, Julius (1885–1946), German Nazi journalist. In 1923 he founded *Der Stürmer,* a fanatical anti-Semitic periodical which he edited until 1945. He was tried at NUREMBERG and hanged.

STREPTOCOCCUS, BACTERIUM responsible for many common infections including sore throat, TONSILLITIS, SCARLET FEVER, IMPETIGO, cellulitis, ERYSIPELAS and PUERPERAL FEVER; a related organism is a common cause of PNEUMONIA and one type may cause endocarditis on damaged HEART valves. PENICILLIN is the ANTIBIOTIC of choice. RHEUMATIC FEVER and BRIGHT'S DISEASE are late immune responses to streptococcus.

STRESEMAN, Gustav (1878–1929), German statesman awarded the 1926 Nobel Peace Prize. He founded (1918) and led the conservative German People's Party, was chancellor in 1923 and foreign minister 1923–29. He followed a program of moderation and reconciliation with Germany's former enemies, and as an author of the LOCARNO TREATIES (1925) took Germany into the League of Nations as an equal of the other powers.

STRICKLAND, William (1787–1854), US architect and engineer, exponent of the classical style. He designed many public buildings in Philadelphia, including the Second Bank of the US (1819–24).

STRINDBERG, Johan August (1849–1912), Swedish playwright and novelist. His biting, pessimistic plays, *Mäster Olof* (1873), *The Father* (1887) and *Miss Julie* (1888) made a deep mark on modern drama; his novel *The Red Room* (1879) about injustice and hypocrisy won acclaim. Later plays such as *The Ghost Sonata* (1907) combine dream sequences with Swedenborgian religious mysticism.

STRINGED INSTRUMENTS, musical instruments whose sound is produced by vibrating strings or wires, the pitch being controlled by their length and tension. In the balalaika, banjo, guitar, harp, lute, mandolin, sitar, ukulele and zither, the vibration is produced by plucking with the fingers or a plectrum. In the KEYBOARD INSTRUMENTS (clavichord, harpsichord, piano, spinet, virginal) the strings are either plucked or struck by hammers operated by depressing the keys. The violin is played with a horsehair bow, which is drawn across the strings.

STRIP MINING, technique used where ore deposits lie close enough to the surface to be uncovered merely by removal of the overlying material; most used for COAL. (See also MINING.)

STROBOSCOPE, instrument that produces regular brief flashes of intense light, used to study periodic motion, to test machinery and in high-speed photography. When the flash frequency exactly equals that of the rotation or vibration, the object is illuminated in the same position during each cycle, and appears stationary. A gas discharge lamp is used, with flash duration about 1 μs and frequency from 2 to 3,000Hz.

STROESSNER, Alfredo (1912–   ), president of Paraguay since 1954. Army commander in 1951, he ousted his predecessor in a coup, and created an efficient and stable totalitarian regime.

STROKE, or **cerebrovascular accident,** the sudden loss of some aspect of BRAIN function due to lack of BLOOD supply to a given area; control of limbs on one side of the body, APHASIA or dysphasia, loss of part of the visual field or disorders of higher function are common. Stroke may result from EMBOLISM, ARTERIOSCLEROSIS and THROMBOSIS, or HEMORRHAGE (then termed apoplexy). Areas with permanent loss of blood supply do not recover but other areas may take over their function.

STRONTIUM (Sr), reactive, silvery-white alkaline-earth metal, occurring as strontianite ($SrCO_3$) and celestite ($SrSO_4$), found mainly in Scotland, Ark. and Ariz. Strontium is made by ELECTROLYSIS of the chloride or reduction of the oxide with aluminum. It resembles calcium physically and chemically. The radioactive isotope Sr^{90} is produced in nuclear FALLOUT, and is used in nuclear electric-power generators. Strontium compounds are used in fireworks (imparting a crimson color), and to refine sugar. AW 87.6, mp 769°C, bp 1384°C, sg 2.54.

STROUD, Robert (1890–1963), US ornithologist, the Bird-Man of Alcatraz. Imprisoned (1909) for murder, he became an authority on diseases of birds.

STRUVE, Otto (1897–1963), Russian-born US astronomer known for work on stellar evolution (see STAR) and primarily for his contributions to astronomical SPECTROSCOPY, especially his discovery of interstellar matter (1938).

STRYCHNINE, poisonous ALKALOID from NUX VOMICA seeds causing excessive SPINAL CORD stimulation. Death results from spinal convulsions and asphyxia.

STUART, Steuart or **Stewart, House of,** ruled Scotland 1371–1714 and Scotland and England 1603–1714. The first Stuart king, **Robert II** (reigned 1371–90) was a hereditary steward of Scotland whose father had married a daughter of ROBERT THE BRUCE. A descendant, **James IV,** married Margaret, daughter of HENRY VII of England. Their grandson, **James VI,** became JAMES I of England in 1603. Between 1603 and 1714, six Stuarts ruled: James I, his son CHARLES I (1625–49), CHARLES II (1660–85), JAMES II (deposed 1688), MARY II (wife of WILLIAM III) and ANNE (1702–14). (For the Stuart pretenders descended from James II, see JACOBITES.)

STUART, Charles Edward (1720–1788), pretender to the throne of England. The grandson of JAMES II, he was known as the Young Pretender and, in Scotland, as

Bonnie Prince Charlie. After the French refused to support his cause, he rallied the Highland clans to invade England, but was defeated at Culloden in 1746.

STUART, Gilbert (1755–1828), US portrait painter, creator of the famous portrait head of George Washington (1796). Praised for his color, technique and psychological insight, he painted nearly 1,000 portraits and created a distinctive US portrait style.

STUART, James Ewell Brown (1833–1864), Confederate cavalry officer. Resigning from the US Army, he won command of a Confederacy brigade after the first Battle of BULL RUN (1861), and began his famous cavalry raids in 1862. Promoted to command all the cavalry in the N Va. Army, he was killed in the Wilderness campaign.

STUBBS, George (1724–1806), English animal painter famous for his pictures of horses, such as *Mares and Foals* (c1760–70), and *Lion Devouring a Horse* (1769). The etchings of his *Anatomy of the Horse* (1766) came from years of anatomical study.

STUDENTS FOR A DEMOCRATIC SOCIETY (SDS), US left-wing student organization founded in 1960. It spread through US universities and spearheaded opposition to the VIETNAM WAR. By 1970 it had split into many irreconcilable factions, including the WEATHERMEN.

STURM UND DRANG (German: storm and stress), name given to a period of literary ferment in Germany c1770–84. Influenced by ROUSSEAU, its leading figures, HERDER, GOETHE and SCHILLER, espoused an antirationalist and rebellious individualism in opposition to the prevailing classicism.

STUTTER. See SPEECH AND SPEECH DISORDERS.

STUYVESANT, Peter (c1610–1672), Dutch governor (1647) of NEW NETHERLAND. Autocratic and unpopular, he lost Dutch territory to Connecticut in 1650, conquered and annexed NEW SWEDEN in 1655, and finally surrendered New Netherland to England in 1664 after his citizens failed to support him against a surprise English attack. He retired to his farm "the Bouwerie," now New York's Bowery.

STYRON, William (1925–   ), US novelist and winner of the 1968 Pulitzer Prize for *The Confessions of Nat Turner* (1967), a controversial first-person account of an 1831 slave rebellion. Other novels are *Lie Down in Darkness* (1951) and *Sophie's Choice* (1979).

SUÁREZ, Francisco (1548–1617), Spanish Jesuit philosopher who represented a late flowering of SCHOLASTICISM. He was an important political and legal theorist, attacking the divine right of kings and arguing that international law was based on custom, not natural law.

SUBATOMIC PARTICLES, or **elementary particles,** small packets of matter-energy which are constituent of ATOMS or are produced in nuclear reactions or in interactions between other subatomic particles. The first such particle to be discovered was the (negative) ELECTRON (e^-), the constituent of cathode rays. Next, the **nucleons** were discovered; first the (positive) PROTON (p^+); then, in 1932, the (neutral) NEUTRON (n°). The same year saw the discovery of the first antiparticle, the positron (or antielectron, $\bar{e}^+$—see ANTIMATTER), and from that time the number of known subatomic particles, found in COSMIC RAYS or detected using particle ACCELERATORS, grew rapidly, until by the early 1980s more than 100 were known or suspected. As yet no attempt to find theoretical order in this multitude of particles, many of which are highly unstable and have very short HALF-LIVES, has proved entirely successful. A first division of the particles classifies them according to whether their spin, S, is a whole number (bosons) or a whole number plus ½ (fermions). Another division groups them into classons, leptons and hadrons. The **classons** are massless bosons which are associated with the fields known to classical physics: the familiar PHOTON associated with ELECTROMAGNETIC RADIATION and the as yet hypothetical graviton, the particle associated with GRAVITATION. The **leptons** are the electrons, the *neutrinos* and the *muons*. These fermions interact with the classical fields and the "weak force" involved in beta-decay. The neutrinos, of rest MASS zero, are products in various decay processes. The **hadrons,** including the mesons, nucleons and hyperons, interact additionally with the "strong force"—the intense force that holds the atomic nucleus together in spite of the mutual electric repulsion of its constituent protons. Boson hadrons are known as *mesons*; these were originally postulated as mediating the "strong force" in a similar way to that in which photons mediate the classical electromagnetic field. The mesons include the *pions* (pi mesons) and the heavier *kaons* (K-mesons). Fermion hadrons are known as *baryons*. These include the nucleons (protons and neutrons) and the heavier *hyperons*. The omega-minus particle (Ω^-) is a quasi-stable hyperon with a half-life of about 0.1ns. A recent attempt to explain the multiplicity of subatomic particles has involved postulating the existence of an order of yet smaller particles, called **quarks**, supposed to be constituent of all the conventional particles.

SUBLETTE, William Lewis (c1799–1845), US fur trader and explorer in the West. Early associated with William ASHLEY and Jedediah SMITH, he made a fortune and became active in Miss. politics.

SUBMARINE, a ship capable of underwater operation. The idea is an old one, but the first working craft was not built until 1620, by Cornelis Drebbel; it was a wooden frame covered with greased leather. The first submarine used in warfae was invented by David Bushnell (1776). Called the Turtle, it was a one-man, hand-powered, screw-driven vessel designed to attach mines to enemy ships. In the Civil War the Confederate States produced several submarines. Propulsion, the major problem, was partly solved by the Rev. G. W. Garrett, who built a steam-powered submarine (1880). In the 1890s John P. Holland and his rival Simon Lake designed vessels powered by gasoline engines on the surface and by electric motors when submerged, the forerunners of modern submarines. They were armed with TORPEDOES and guns. Great advances were made during WWI and WWII, which demonstrated the submarine's military effectiveness. The German U-boats were notably efficient, and introduced snorkels to hinder detection while recharging batteries. But none of these vessels could remain submerged for very long, and a true (long-term) submarine awaited the advent of nuclear power, independent of the oxygen of the air for propulsion. The first nuclear-powered submarine was the U.S.S. *Nautilus* (1955), which in 1958 made the first voyage under the polar ice-cap. The US, USSR, UK and France have nuclear submarine fleets fitted with ballistic missiles. The US has three classes of SSBNs (ballistic missile submarine, nuclear-powered) in deployment: the Polaris, which is being phased out; the Poseidon; and the ultramodern Trident. Submarines when on station at sea are the most survivable of the nuclear strategic systems.

Modern submarines are streamlined vessels, generally with a double hull, the inner being a pressure hull with fuel and ballast tanks between it and the outer hull. The submarine submerges by flooding its ballast tanks to reach neutral buoyancy, i.e., displacing its own weight of water (see ARCHIMEDES), and dives using its hydrofoil diving planes. Submarines are equipped with PERISCOPES and inertial guidance systems. As well as their military uses, submarines are used for oceanographic research and exploration, salvage and rescue.

SUBWAY, an underground railroad system designed for efficient urban and suburban passenger transport. The TUNNELS usually follow the lines of streets, for ease of construction by the cut-and-cover method in which an arched tunnel is built in an open trench, covered with earth and the street restored. Outlying parts of the system usually emerge to the surface. The first subway was built in London (1860–63) by the cut-and-cover method; it used steam trains and was a success despite fumes. A three-mile section of London subway was built (1886–90) using a shield developed by J. H. Greathead: this is a large cylindrical steel tube forced forward through the clay by hydraulic jacks; the clay is removed and the tunnel walls built. Deep tunnels are thus possible, and there is no surface disturbance. This London "tube" was the first to use electrically-powered trains, which soon replaced steam trains everywhere. Elevators were provided for the deep stations, later mostly replaced by escalators. Many cities throughout the world followed London's lead, notably Paris (the Métro, begun 1898) and New York (begun 1900). The New York subway, using the multiple-unit trains developed by Frank SPRAGUE, is now the largest in the world. The Moscow subway (begun 1931) is noted for its palatial marble stations. With increasing road traffic congestion in the 1960s, the value of subways was apparent, and many cities extended, improved and automated their systems; some introduced quieter rubber-tired trains running on concrete guideways.

SUCCOTH. See SUKKOTH.

SUCCULENTS, plants that have swollen leaves or stems and are thus adapted to living in arid regions. CACTI are the most familiar but representatives occur in other families, notably the Crassulaceae (stonecrops and houseleeks) and Aizoaceae (living stones, mesembryanthemum). Many succulents have attractive foliage and colorful, though often short-lived, flowers.

SUCKLING, Sir John (1609–1642), English poet, wit, soldier and courtier, one of the CAVALIER POETS. He is remembered for his graceful love lyrics, collected after his death in *Fragmenta Aurea* (1646).

SUCRE, Antonio José de (1795–1830), South American revolutionary leader, BOLÍVAR's chief aide and first president of Bolivia (1826–28). He liberated Colombia,

Ecuador and Peru from Spanish rule, with a final victory at Ayacucho (1824). He retired to Ecuador 1828, but returned to repel a Peruvian attack 1829. He was assassinated after presiding over a congress aimed at keeping Ecuador, Colombia and Venezuela united.

SUCRE, legal capital of BOLIVIA, some 8,500ft high in the Andes, about 250mi SE of La Paz, the administrative capital. Founded in 1538, it is now a commercial and agricultural center. Pop 86,609.

SUCROSE ($C_{12}H_{22}O_{11}$), or **cane sugar,** disaccharide CARBOHYDRATE, commercially obtained from SUGAR BEET, SUGARCANE and sweet SORGHUM. As table sugar, sucrose is the most important of the SUGARS. It comprises a glucose unit joined to a fructose unit. Sucrose, glucose and fructose all exhibit optical activity and when sucrose is hydrolyzed the rotation changes from right to left. This is called inversion, and an equimolar mixture of glucose and fructose is called invert sugar. The ENZYME which hydrolyzes sucrose to glucose and fructose is called invertase.

SUDAN, the largest country in Africa, lies S of Egypt and W of Ethiopia; its NE coastline is along the Red Sea.

Official name: Democratic Republic of the Sudan
Capital: Khartoum
Area: 996,757sq mi
Population: 25,562,000
Languages: Arabic; English
Religions: Muslim, Animist, Christian
Monetary unit(s): 1 Sudanese pound = 100 piastres
Land. Sudan has swamp and tropical rain forest in the S, savanna grassland in the central region, desert and semidesert in the N and W. There are mountains in the NE, S, center and W. The country is bisected by the N-flowing Nile and its tributaries, along which the bulk of the population and almost all the towns are found. The climate is hot and rainfall ranges from almost nil in the N to almost 60in per year in the S.
People. There are two main groups: the Arab-speaking Muslims of the N, who

make up over 75% of the population, and the black African and Nilotic peoples of the S, mainly animist in belief. There have been continuing disputes between N and S, the latter resisting Muslim domination. About 70% of the people are rural, and the rate of illiteracy is high. There are, however, several universities.
Economy. The Sudan is basically agricultural, and most people live by subsistence farming. The chief cash crops are cotton, gum arabic and peanuts. Domestic crops include millet, sorghum, wheat and sugarcane. Livestock are raised in large numbers. Manufacturing is limited. The only port is Port Sudan on the Red Sea.
History. Called NUBIA in ancient times, N Sudan was colonized by Egypt c2000 BC. By 800 BC it had come under the Cush kingdom, which by 600 AD had given way to independent Coptic Christian states. In the 13th–15th centuries these collapsed under Muslim expansion, and the Muslim Funj state was established, lasting until Egypt invaded the Sudan in 1821. The nationalist MAHDI led a revolt in 1881, after which a series of campaigns resulted in joint Anglo-Egyptian rule in 1899. Since independence in 1956 the country has had alternating military and civilian governments. President Ja'Far Muhammad Numayri (or Nimeiry), who came to power in 1969, ended a 17-year civil war between N and S in 1972, but fighting began again in 1983 after he imposed Islamic law. He was overthrown by the military in 1985 and the country returned to civilian rule in 1986, but the civil war continued. By 1988 war, drought, floods, and a plague of locusts had left about a third of the population in the S homeless and threatened with starvation in a country once considered the potential breadbasket of Africa.

SUDETENLAND, region of W Czechoslovakia. Originally it designated the area of the Sudetes Mts on the Bohemia-Silesia border, but came to apply to all the German-speaking Bohemian and Moravian borderlands incorporated into Czechoslovakia in 1919. The Sudetenland was ceded to Nazi Germany by the MUNICH AGREEMENT in 1938, and restored to Czechoslovakia in 1945.

SUE, Eugène (1804–1857), French novelist, best known for his sensational serialized tales of low-life Paris such as *The Mysteries of Paris* (1842–43) and *The Wandering Jew* (1844–45); they embraced his ideal of social reform.

SUETONIUS (c69–c140 AD), Roman biographer, author of *Lives of the Caesars*, 12 biographies from Julius Caesar to the emperor Domitian. They are full of entertaining scandal and are also valuable for their verbatim use of historical sources.

SUEZ CANAL, ship canal in Egypt linking the Red Sea with the E Mediterranean; 101mi long, it cut over 4,000mi off the route from Britain to India and has been a major commercial waterway since its opening in 1869. Without locks, the canal runs N–S, passing through Lake Timsah and the Bitter Lakes. It has a minimum width of 179ft and a dredged depth of almost 40ft. Work began in 1859 under de LESSEPS, after the Ottoman khedive of Egypt had conceded a 99-year lease to the Suez Canal Company. The controlling interest was French, and in 1875 the khedive sold his 44% shareholding to the British government, which had initially been hostile. An international convention guaranteeing the canal's neutrality was signed in 1888. Egyptian interest increased after 1936 and culminated in 1956 when NASSER nationalized the canal, prompting an invasion by Britain and France. After UN intervention the canal reopened in 1957 under Egyptian control. It was closed again by the ARAB-ISRAELI WAR of 1967, but in 1974 agreement was reached, and after the canal had been cleared of wreckage it was reopened in 1975. The canal was deepened 1976–80 to permit the passage of oil tankers up to 500,000 tons and 53ft draft.

SUFISM, Muslim mystical philosophical and literary movement dating from the 10th and 11th centuries. Stressing personal communion with God, it has spread throughout Islam in a variety of forms.

SUGAR BEET, *Beta vulgaris,* a plant whose swollen root provides almost half the world's sugar. It was first extensively grown in Europe to replace cane sugar from the W Indies, supplies of which were cut off during the Napoleonic Wars. Careful breeding has improved the sugar yield. Sugar beet is grown in all temperate areas where cool summers ensure good sugar formation. Family: Chenopodiaceae.

SUGARCANE, grass of the genus *Saccharum,* from which the world obtains over half its sugar. Originally native to E Asia, it has been grown extensively in the Indies and America since the 18th century and now is cultivated in most warm humid areas. The fibrous material (bagasse) left after juice extraction is made into board. Family: Gramineae.

SUGARS, sweet, soluble CARBOHYDRATES (of general formula $C_x(H_2O)_y$), comprising the monosaccharides and the disaccharides. **Monosaccharides** cannot be further degraded by HYDROLYSIS and contain a single chain of CARBON atoms. They normally have the suffix -ose and a prefix indicating the length of the carbon chain; thus trioses, tetroses, pentoses, hexoses and heptoses contain 3, 4, 5, 6 and 7 carbon atoms respectively. The most abundant natural monosaccharides are the hexoses, $C_6H_{12}O_6$ (including GLUCOSE), and the pentoses, $C_5H_{10}O_5$ (including xylose). Many different isomers of these sugars are possible and often have names reflecting their source, or a property, e.g., fructose is found in fruit, arabinose in gum arabic and the pentose, xylose, in wool. **Disaccharides** contain two monosaccharide units joined by an oxygen bridge. Their chemical and physical properties are similar to those of monosaccharides. The most important disaccharides are SUCROSE (cane sugar), lactose and maltose. (Table sugar consists of sucrose.) The most characteristic property of sugars is their sweetness. If we accord sucrose an arbitrary sweetness of 100, then glucose scores 74, fructose 173, lactose 16, maltose 33, xylose 40 (compare SACCHARIN 55,000). The sweetness of sugars is correlated with their solubility.

SUGER (c1081–1151), French abbot of St.-Denis and counselor of kings LOUIS VI and LOUIS VII. He rebuilt the famous abbey church, and was Louis VII's regent during the Second Crusade (1147–49).

SUGGESTION, process whereby an individual suspends his critical faculties and thus accepts ideas and beliefs that may be contrary to his own. People under HYPNOSIS are particularly suggestible, as are those in a state of exhaustion. **Heterosuggestion** (dependent on an exterior source) is usually verbally derived, but may involve any of the SENSES. **Autosuggestion** implies that the individual himself is the source. **Mass suggestion** is one of the main aims of advertising.

SUHARTO (1921–   ), president of Indonesia from 1968. A veteran general, he opposed the corrupt SUKARNO regime and crushed the communist coup it sponsored in 1965; he has held effective power since, and has restored the country's prosperity.

SUICIDE, the act of voluntarily taking one's own life. In some societies (notably Japan: see HARA-KIRI) suicide is accepted or even expected in the face of disgrace. Judaism, Islam and Christianity, however, consider it a sin. Until 1961 the UK sought to discourage it by making it a crime, and it still is in some US states. Motivation varies enormously where there is no social sanction; a suicide attempt is often thought to be an implicit "plea" for help, and may result from extreme DEPRESSION. Several notable literary figures have died in this manner, among them Ernest Hemingway, Sylvia Plath, and Arthur Koestler.

SUITE, musical form developed in Germany and France in the 17th and 18th centuries, consisting of a set of dance movements in the same or related keys. The regular combination was allemande, courante, sarabande, gigue; additional movements such as the minuet, gavotte or bourée could be added.

SUKARNO (1901–1970), first president of Indonesia 1945–67. A leader of the independence movement from 1927, he collaborated with the Japanese in WWII, and was instrumental in creating the republic in 1945. His flamboyant and corrupt rule became a dictatorship in 1959; he veered toward the communist bloc, while his policies ruined the economy. Implicated in an attempted communist coup (1965), he was gradually ousted by SUHARTO.

SUKKOTH, or **Feast of Tabernacles,** an autumn Jewish festival lasting eight days, during which meals are taken in huts (*sukkot*) roofed with branches and fruits reminiscent of those built in the fields by ancient harvesters.

SULEIMAN I (1494–1566), sultan of the Ottoman Empire 1520–66. He extended its borders W to Budapest and E to Persia and maintained a powerful Mediterranean fleet. Called the Magnificent by Europeans and *Kanuni* (lawgiver) by his subjects, he brought Turkish culture and statecraft to its zenith.

SULFA DRUGS, or **sulfonamides,** synthetic compounds (containing the —SO_2NH_2 group) that inhibit the multiplication of invading BACTERIA, thus allowing the body's cellular defense mechanisms to suppress infection. The first sulfa drug, sulfanilamide (Prontosil), was synthesized in 1908 and used widely as a dye, before, in 1935, Gerhard Domagk reported its effectiveness against STREPTOCOCCI. Since then it has proved effective against several other bacteria including those causing SCARLET FEVER, certain VENEREAL DISEASES and MENINGITIS. This and the many other sulfa drugs are now generally used in conjunction with ANTIBIOTICS.

SULFUR (S), nonmetal in Group VIA of the PERIODIC TABLE. There are large deposits in Tex. and La., and in Japan, Sicily and Mexico; the American sulfur is extracted by the Frasch process. It is also recovered from natural gas and petroleum. Combined sulfur occurs as sulfates and sulfides. There are two main allotropes of sulfur (see ALLOTROPY): the yellow, brittle rhombic form is stable up to 95.6°C, above which monoclinic sulfur (almost colorless) is

stable. Both forms are soluble in carbon disulfide; they consist of eight-membered rings S_8. Plastic sulphur is an amorphous form made by suddenly cooling boiling sulfur. Sulfur is reactive, combining with most other elements. It is used in gunpowder, matches, as a fungicide and insecticide, and to vulcanize rubber. AW 32.1, mp 113°C (rh), 119°C (mono), bp 445°C, sg 2.07 (rh, 20°C). **Sulfur dioxide** (SO_2) is a colorless, acrid gas, formed by combustion of sulfur. It is an oxidizing and reducing agent and is important as an intermediate in the manufacture of sulfur trioxide and sulfuric acid. It is also used in petroleum refining and as a refrigerant, disinfectant, preservative and bleach. It reacts with water to give sulfurous acid (H_2SO_3), which is corrosive. Thus sulfur dioxide in flue gases is a harmful cause of POLLUTION. mp −73°C, bp −10°C. **Sulfites** are salts containing the ion SO_3^{2-}, formed from sulfur dioxide and BASES; readily oxidized to sulfates. Bisulfites are acid sulfites, containing the ion HSO_3^-. **Sulfur trioxide** (SO_3) is a volatile liquid or solid formed by oxidation of sulfur dioxide. It reacts violently with water to give SULFURIC ACID. mp 17°C (α), bp 45°C (α). **Thiosulfates** are salts containing the ion $S_2O_3^{2-}$, usually prepared by dissolving sulfur in an aqueous sulfite solution. They are mild reducing agents, and form ligand complexes; in acid solution they decompose to give sulfur and sulfur dioxide. (For sodium thiosulfate, see SODIUM.)

SULLA, Lucius Cornelius (138–78 BC), Roman general and dictator. Turning against his former commander MARIUS, he became the first Roman to lead an army against Rome (88 BC). He fought MITHRADATES in Asia Minor, 87–83 BC, and returned to defeat the Marians in a civil war. As dictator, 82–79 BC he massacred opponents for their propertuy and restored the Senate's power.

SULLIVAN, Anne (1866–1936), US teacher of Helen KELLER. Partially blind herself, in 1887 she taught Helen to read and communicate through the touch alphabet, and became her lifelong companion.

SULLIVAN, Sir Arthur Seymour (1842–1900), British composer best known for his partnership with W. S. GILBERT on their famous operettas. He also composed oratorios, grand operas and hymn tunes whose popularity has not endured to the same extent.

SULLIVAN, Harry Stack (1892–1949), US psychiatrist who made important contributions to SCHIZOPHRENIA studies and originated the idea that PSYCHIATRY depends on study of interpersonal relations (including that between therapist and patient).

SULLIVAN, John (1740–1795), US soldier and statesman. He distinguished himself in the REVOLUTIONARY WAR, and was N.H. delegate to the Continental Congress (1774–75, 1780–81) and three times president of N.H. (1786–89).

SULLIVAN, John L(awrence) (1858–1918), US boxer, last world heavyweight champion 1882–89 under London Prize Ring (bareknuckle) rules. He lost his first defense of it under QUEENSBURY RULES in 1892 to "Gentleman" Jim Corbett after 21 rounds. The colorful "Boston Strong Boy" was the first nationally famous boxing champion.

SULLIVAN, Louis Henry (1856–1924), US architect famous for his office buildings that pioneered modern design. He was a partner of Dankmar ADLER in Chicago (1881–95). His works include the Auditorium (1889) and the Carson Pirie Scott building (1899–1904) in Chicago, and the Guaranty Building in Buffalo (1894–95). His functionalism was expressed in his famous maxim "form follows function." Frank Lloyd WRIGHT was his pupil.

SULLY, Maximilien de Béthune, Duc de (1560–1641), French statesman. A Protestant protégé of King HENRY IV, he became superintendent of finances in 1598, and by capable management led the successful reorganization of France after the Wars of RELIGION. He retired after Henry's death in 1610.

SULLY, Thomas (1783–1872), English-born US portrait painter. He studied briefly under Gilbert STUART, and became popular and prolific. Queen Victoria (1839) and several US presidents sat for him.

SULLY-PRUDHOMME, René François Armand (1839–1907), French PARNASSIAN poet, winner of the Nobel Prize for Literature, 1901. He began writing melancholy and subjective poetry, but *La Justice* (1878) and *Le Bonheur* (*Happiness*; 1888) are philosophical.

SULU ARCHIPELAGO, group of over 400 volcanic islands and coral islets in the SW Philippines. They are heavily forested. Marine products (fish, turtles, pearls, sea cucumbers) form the economic mainstay of the population of Muslim MOROS.

SUMATRA, second-largest island of Indonesia. On the Equator, with a hot, wet climate, it is heavily forested and rich in oil, bauxite and coal, producing 70% of Indonesia's wealth. Export crops include rubber, coffee, pepper and tobacco. Medan

and Palembang are the chief cities.

SUMER, S part of ancient MESOPOTAMIA in the fertile area at the head of the Persian Gulf in modern Iraq. It was the site of the SUMERIAN civilization.

SUMERIANS, inhabitants of S MESOPOTAMIA from earliest times, with a great civilization dating from c3300 BC. They established agriculture-based city-states such as Erech, Kish, Nippur and UR, built irrigation canals, and achieved remarkable technical and artistic prowess, developing CUNEIFORM writing. Sumer fell to the Akkad kingdom c2400 BC, and after a brief revival c2000 BC was absorbed into BABYLONIA.

SUMMIT MEETINGS, meetings between heads of government, particularly US presidents and Soviet leaders since 1959 to deal with problems arising from superpower rivalry. The dates, locations, and participants of US-Soviet summit meetings are as follows: Sept. 1959, Camp David, Md. (Eisenhower and Khrushchev); May 1960, Paris (Eisenhower and Khrushchev); June 1961, Vienna (Kennedy and Khrushchev); June 1967, Glassboro, N.J. (Johnson and Kosygin); May 1972, Moscow (Nixon and Brezhnev); June 1973, Washington (Nixon and Brezhnev); June-July 1974, Moscow (Nixon and Brezhnev); Nov. 1974, Vladivostok (Ford and Brezhnev); June 1979, Vienna (Carter and Brezhnev); Nov. 1985, Geneva (Reagan and Gorbachev); Oct. 1986, Reykjavik (Reagan and Gorbachev); May-June 1988, Moscow (Reagan and Gorbachev).

SUMNER, Charles (1811–1874), US antislavery politician, senator from Mass. 1851–74. A law graduate (1833), he became an aggressive abolitionist and worked for world peace and prison and educational reform. Chairman of the Senate Foreign Relations Committee (1861–71), he was a prominent radical Republican during RECONSTRUCTION, and active in impeaching President Andrew JOHNSON.

SUMNER, William Graham (1840–1910), US sociologist who expounded social Darwinism. This belief, based on DARWIN'S theory of evolution, stated that social progress depends upon unrestrained competition, economic LAISSEZ-FAIRE and acceptance of inherent inequalities. He wrote *Folkways* (1907), examining the role of custom in society.

SUMO, type of Japanese wrestling in which great importance is put on size and weight, poundages up to 300 being not uncommon. The contests are usually brief.

SUMTER, Thomas (1734–1832), partisan

of the American Revolution who formed a guerrilla band and harassed the British in the Carolina campaign (1780–81). He had notable successes at Hanging Rock, Fishdam Ford and Blackstock. Fort Sumter in Charleston harbor was named for him.

SUN, the star about which the earth and the other planets of the SOLAR SYSTEM revolve. The sun is an incandescent ball of gases, by mass 69.5% hydrogen; 28% helium; 2.5% carbon, nitrogen, oxygen, sulfur, silicon, iron and magnesium altogether, and traces of other elements. It has a diameter of about 1,393Mm, and rotates more rapidly at the equator (24.65 days) than at the poles (about 34 days). Although the sun is entirely gaseous, its distance creates the optical illusion that it has a surface: this visible edge is called the **photosphere**. It is at a temperature of about 6000K, cool compared to the center of the sun (13,000,000K) or the corona (average 2,000,000K); the photospheres of other stars may be at temperatures of less than 2000K or more than 500,000K. Above the photosphere lies the **chromosphere**, an irregular layer of gases between 1.5Mm and 15Mm in depth. It is in the chromosphere that **sunspots, flares** and **prominences** occur: these last are great plumes of gas that surge out into the corona and occasionally off into space. The **corona** is the sparse outer atmosphere of the sun. During solar ECLIPSES it may be seen to extend several thousand megameters and to be as bright as the full moon, though in fact it extends to the orbit of JUPITER. The earth lies within the particles and radiation flowing outward from the sun, termed the SOLAR WIND. The sun is a normal STAR, common in characteristics although slightly smaller than average. It lies in one of the spiral arms of the MILKY WAY.

SUNBELT AND FROSTBELT, popular terms designating, respectively, the southern tier of states stretching from N.C. to Calif. and the states of the Northeast and Midwest. The Frostbelt states, besides their more rigorous climate, are characterized by aging industrial plants and urban infrastructures, unionized labor, high rates of unemployment and poverty, static or declining populations, and the severe fiscal problems these conditions impose on state and local governments. By (often exaggerated) contrast, the Sunbelt states are characterized by burgeoning economic development, expanding cities, rising populations (due to migration from the Frostbelt states), and increasing political importance.

SUNBURN, burning effect on the SKIN

following prolonged exposure to ULTRAVIOLET RADIATION from the sun, common in travelers from temperate zones to hot climates. First-degree BURNS may occur but usually only a delayed erythema is seen with extreme skin sensitivity. Systemic disturbance occurs in severe cases. Fair-skinned persons are most susceptible.

SUNDA ISLANDS, islands of the W Malay archipelago, lying between the S China Sea and the Indian Ocean. They comprise the Greater Sundas (notably Java, Sumatra, Borneo and Sulawesi), and the Lesser Sundas (notably Bali, Lombok, Alor and Timor).

SUN DANCE, religious ceremony observed by a number of Plains tribes of American Indians during the 19th century, involving fasting, self-torture and the seeking of visions.

SUNDAY, Billy (1862–1935), US revivalist preacher noted for his flamboyance and his vivid version of fundamentalist theology. He claimed to have saved over a million souls and is thought to have collected over $1 million in doing so. He was a professional baseball player before his conversion.

SUNDIAL, ancient type of CLOCK, still used (though rarely) in its original form. It consists of a style parallel to the earth's axis that casts a shadow on the calibrated dial plate, which may be horizontal or vertical. It assumes that the sun's apparent motion lies always on the celestial equator (see CELESTIAL SPHERE). Sundials usually show local TIME but may be calibrated to show standard time.

SUNFLOWER, tall plants of the genus *Helianthus*, with large disk-shaped yellow and brown flowers which twist around to face the sun. Most of the 60 species are native to the US. The common sunflower (*Helianthus annuus*) is cultivated in many parts of the world. The seeds yield an oil and the remainder becomes cattle feed. Family: Compositae.

SUNG, one of the strongest Chinese dynasties, founded in 960 AD by Chao K'uang-yin. It was swept away by the Mongols in the 1270s and replaced by the YUAN dynasty. The empire at its zenith reached from the GREAT WALL OF CHINA in the N to Hainan in the S. The period was one of great economic and cultural advance.

SUNNITES, the orthodox majority of the followers of ISLAM, distinct from the SHI'ITES. The term refers to the traditional Way (*sunna*) of the Prophet MOHAMMED.

SUNSPOTS, apparently dark spots visible on the face of the SUN. Vortices of gas associated with strong electromagnetic activity, their dark appearance is merely one of contrast with the surrounding photosphere. Single spots are known, but mostly they form in groups or pairs. They are never seen at the sun's poles or equator. Their cause is not certainly known. Their prevalence reaches a maximum about every 11 years.

SUNSTROKE, or **heatstroke,** rise in body TEMPERATURE and failure of sweating in hot climates, often following exertion. DELIRIUM, COMA and convulsions may develop suddenly and rapid cooling should be effected.

SUN YAT-SEN (1866–1925), Chinese revolutionary, revered as the ideological father of modern China. Influenced by MARX and Henry GEORGE, he founded (1894) a movement against the MANCHUS. Exiled in 1895, he formulated the principles of *democracy, nationalism* and *socialism* underlying the KUOMINTANG, the party he founded and led. In 1911 the Manchus were overthrown and Sun returned to China. First president of the new republic, he soon resigned (1912) to YÜAN SHIH-K'AI, whose rule became increasingly dictatorial. After a second exile (1913–17), in 1921 Sun led a rival "national" government at Canton. In the ensuing struggle against the rulers in Peking, he cooperated with the communists and organized a military academy under CHIANG KAI-SHEK who succeeded him on his death. (See also CHINA.)

SUPERCOLLIDER, a particle accelerator to be built by the US Department of Energy near Dallas, Tex., at a cost of $6 billion. It will consist of a linear accelerator, three progressively larger circular accelerators, and a main ring 53mi in circumference 150ft below ground. Protons will first be boosted to high energy levels in the linear and three circular accelerators before being fed into the main ring, where they will be propelled by superconducting magnets, some in a clockwise direction, some counterclockwise. At certain sites, special magnets will force the protons to collide, producing debris that is expected to provide insights into the fundamental building blocks and forces of nature.

The supercollider, considered essential for the future of high-energy physics, will be the largest and most costly scientific instrument in the world. At present, the Tevatron accelerator at the Fermi National Laboratory at Batavia, Ill., is the world's largest accelerator and the only one using superconducting magnets. It is about 4mi in circumference and can collide particles with a combined energy of about 2 trillion electron volts. The supercollider will use an accelerator the size of the Tevatron to feed particles into its main ring, where they will collide at a combined energy of about 20 trillion electron volts. (See ACCELERATORS, PARTICLE.)

SUPERCONDUCTIVITY, a condition occurring in many metals, alloys, etc., at low temperatures, involving zero electrical RESISTANCE and perfect diamagnetism. In such a material an electric current will persist indefinitely without any driving voltage and applied magnetic fields are exactly canceled out by the magnetization they produce. In **type I superconductors,** both these properties disappear abruptly when the temperature or applied magnetic field exceeds critical values (typically 5K and 10^4A/m), but in **type II superconductors** the diamagnetism decay is spread over a range of field values. Large ELECTROMAGNETS sometimes use superconducting coils which will carry large currents without overheating, and the exclusion of fields by superconducting materials can be exploited to screen or direct magnetic fields.

Superconductivity was discovered in 1911 by the Dutch physicist Heike Kamerlingh Onnes in frozen mercury cooled almost to absolute zero, the temperature at which atomic motion ceases. In the years that followed, other pure metals and then alloys revealed superconductivity at slightly higher temperatures, making some expensive applications possible. Kamerlingh Onnes received the 1913 Nobel Prize for Physics for his discovery. In 1972 the prize was awarded to John Bardeen, Leon N. Cooper, and John Robert Schreiffer for their theory accounting for the phenomenon of superconductivity—namely, that at very low temperatures ELECTRONS in an electric current move in pairs and can pass through a crystal lattice without their motion being disturbed by collisions with the lattice.

In the 1970s progress toward a truly practical superconductor seemed to stop. In 1986, K. Alex Müller and J. Georg Bednorz at the Zurich Research Laboratory of the International Business Machines Corp. discovered that a ceramic of copper, oxygen, lanthanum, and barium registered complete loss of electrical resistance at about 40° C above absolute zero, a temperature equivalent to –400° F. The next year Paul W. C. Chu of the U of Houston produced superconductivity at –300° F. Because that temperature is above the boiling point of liquid nitrogen, Chu's discovery opened the door to a host of devices cooled by nitrogen, which is relatively inexpensive and easy to handle. Müller and Bednorz received the

1987 Nobel Prize for Physics.

SUPERFLUIDITY, the property whereby "superfluids" such as liquid HELIUM below 2.186K exhibit apparently frictionless flow. The effect requires QUANTUM MECHANICS for its explanation.

SUPERIOR, Lake, largest of the North American GREAT LAKES, the world's largest freshwater lake. It is about 350mi long and 160mi wide, covering approximately 31,800sq mi and having a maximum depth of over 1,330ft. It is bounded E and N by Ontario, W by Minn., and S by Wis. and Mich. Some 200 rivers drain into it, the largest being the St. Louis. It is part of the SAINT LAWRENCE SEAWAY AND GREAT LAKES WATERWAY, its principal port, Duluth-Superior, marking the W end of that system.

SUPERNOVA, a NOVA which initially behaves like other novae but, after a few days at maximum brightness, increases to a far higher level of luminosity (a supernova in the Andromeda galaxy, 1885, was one tenth as bright as the entire galaxy). It is thought that supernovae may be caused by the gravitational collapse of a star, or cloud of gas and dust, into a neutron STAR. A supernova in the galaxy called the Large Magellanic Cloud was detected on earth on Feb. 24, 1987, the first relatively close supernova—160,000 light years away—to appear since 1604.

SUPERSONICS, the study of fluid flow at velocities greater than that of SOUND, usually with reference to the supersonic flight of AIRPLANES and MISSILES when the relative velocity of the solid object and the air is greater than the local velocity of sound propagation.

SUPPÉ, Franz von (1819–1895), Austrian composer of light music, especially light opera in the style of OFFENBACH. His works include *Poet and Peasant* (1846).

SUPPLEMENTAL SECURITY INCOME (SSI), federal WELFARE program that provides monthly cash payments to persons with inadequate incomes (including SOCIAL SECURITY benefits) who are 65 or over, blind, or disabled. The program is administered by the Social Security Administration but financed out of general revenue. Some states supplement the basic SSI grant with grants of their own.

SUPPLY AND DEMAND, in economics, central concepts which seek to explain changes in prices, production and consumption of goods and services. Demand for a product depends largely on its price; usually, the higher the price, the less the quantity demanded. This relationship may be plotted as a demand curve. A supply curve may similarly be obtained showing that supply of a product is related to its price. The intersection of the two curves shows the equilibrium between the amount demanded and the amount supplied at a given price. Demand may also be explained by utility, while supply can be explained by the producer's profit motive. The economic theory of SUPPLY-SIDE ECONOMICS emphasizes the supply of goods, whereas KEYNESIAN ECONOMICS places more attention on demand.

SUPPLY-SIDE ECONOMICS, theory of economic management that focuses on stimulating production rather than manipulating demand. In the traditional dichotomy between supply and demand, supply-side economists emphasize the former as opposed to the emphasis of KEYNESIAN ECONOMICS on the latter. The chief measure advocated by supply-siders for the US today is drastic tax reduction, which is intended to inspire increased investment in business, leading to higher employment. The theory also calls for a cutback in government spending to achieve a balanced and much smaller budget, thus eliminating deficit spending which causes inflation and drains funds from the private sector.

SUPREMATISM, art movement c1913–19 originated by the Russian-Polish painter Kasimir MALEVICH, establishing a system of non-representational composition in terms of pure geometric shapes and patterns. The movement's influence on graphic design and typography has been significant.

SUPREME COURT, highest court of the US, with the authority to adjudicate all cases arising under US law, including constitutional matters. The number of member justices is set by statute and so has varied; presently the Court has a Chief Justice and eight Associate Justices. The president appoints the justices as vacancies arise, but nominees must be confirmed by majority vote of the senate. Most nominees are easily confirmed, but the process is not perfunctory; Richard Nixon had two successive nominees rejected by the senate in 1970. Great care is taken in confirmation since justices serve "during good behavior" for life or until retirement. They can, however, be impeached and convicted for high crimes and misdemeanors. Although theoretically above politics, the Court is vitally important to them, since it alone can determine the constitutionality of both state and federal laws. This power of "judicial review" is not explicitly stated in the Constitution, but is rather an operational precedent established by Chief Justice John

MARSHALL in the cases of MARBURY V. MADISON (1803) and *Martin v. Hunters Lessee* (1816). It may also overrule its own previous decisions, a provision that has kept it a living, vital body able to change with the times. A good example of this is the decision in BROWN V. BOARD OF EDUCATION (1954) forbidding racial segregation in education, which overruled PLESSY V. FERGUSON (1896). In 1981, Sandra Day O'CONNOR became the first woman to sit on the High Court.

SUPREME SOVIET, in the USSR, the supreme state and legislative body. Its two chambers—the 767-member Soviet of the Union and the 750-member Soviet of Nationalities—have equal legislative rights, are elected to four-year terms and meet twice a year. Committees continue work between sessions. The Supreme Soviet elects its PRESIDIUM in joint session, appoints the Supreme Court and approves the Council of Ministers, the top executive and administrative body whose chairman heads the government.

SURFACE TENSION, FORCE existing in any boundary surface of a liquid such that the surface tends to assume the minimum possible area. It is defined as the force perpendicular to a line of unit length drawn on the surface. Surface tension arises from the cohesive forces between liquid molecules and makes a liquid surface behave as if it had an elastic membrane stretched over it. Thus, the weight of a needle floated on water makes a depression in the surface. Surface tension governs the wetting properties of liquids, CAPILLARITY and detergent action.

SURFING, the art of riding a wooden or foam plastic surfboard on the fast-moving incline of a wave. It requires exceptional balance, timing and coordination. Surfing originated in Hawaii and has become an international sport, with particular popularity along the coasts of California, Australia, Brazil, Peru and South Africa.

SURGERY, the branch of MEDICINE chiefly concerned with manual operations to remove or repair diseased, damaged or deformed body tissues. With time, surgery has become more complex and has split up into a number of specialities. In 1970 ten surgical speciality boards existed in the US and Canada: general surgery; OPHTHALMOLOGY; otolaryngology; OBSTETRICS and GYNECOLOGY; ORTHOPEDICS; colon and rectal surgery; urology; PLASTIC SURGERY; neurosurgery; and thoracic (chest) surgery. Otolaryngology deals with the EAR, LARYNX (voicebox) and upper respiratory tract: tonsillectomy is one of its most common operations. Colon and rectal surgery deals with the large intestine. Urological surgery deals with the urinary system (KIDNEYS, ureters, BLADDER, urethra) and male reproductive system. Neurosurgery deals with the NERVOUS SYSTEM (BRAIN, SPINAL CORD, nerves); common operations include the removal of TUMORS, the repair of damage caused by severe injury, and the cutting of dorsal roots (rhizotomy) and certain parts of the spinal cord (cordotomy) to relieve unmanageable pain. Thoracic surgery deals with structures within the chest cavity. There are also a number of subspecialities; thus cardiovascular surgery, a subspeciality of thoracic surgery, deals with the heart and major blood vessels.

SURINAME, republic on the NE coast of South America, bounded W by Guyana, S by Brazil and E by French Guiana.

Official name: Republic of Suriname
Capital: Paramaribo
Area: 63,251 sq mi
Population: 415,000
Languages: Dutch, Sranang Tongo, Hindi, Javanese
Religions: Christian, Hindu, Muslim
Monetary unit(s): 1 Suriname guilder = 100 cents
Land. The country, about the size of Georgia, consists of unexplored forested highlands and flat Atlantic coast. The climate is tropical, with heavy rains.
People and Economy. The population consists of about 38% East Indians, 31% Creoles, 15% Javanese, 10% Bush Negroes and 6% Europeans, Chinese and Amerindians. The official language is Dutch, but most people speak the Creole Sranang Tongo. Hindi, Javanese, Chinese, English, French and Spanish are also spoken. The traditional basis of the economy is bauxite, but antigovernment guerrillas shut down the largest bauxite mine and one of the nation's processing plants in 1987. The main crops are rice, sugar, fruits, coffee and bananas.
History. England gave Suriname to the Dutch (1667) in exchange for New Amsterdam (now New York City), and the

country was subsequently known as Dutch Guiana. It became a self-governing part of the Netherlands in 1954 and gained full independence in 1975. The first years of independence were marked by an exodus of some 40,000 Surinamese to the Netherlands and by border disputes with French Guiana and Guyana. A bloodless military coup took place in 1980. A national assembly was installed in 1985, and legislative elections were held in 1987, but the army remains influential.

SURRATT, Mary Eugenia (1820–1865), woman who was hanged for complicity in the assassination of Abraham LINCOLN, a crime of which she was accused because of her contact with the assassin John Wilkes BOOTH. It is now thought that her trial was flagrantly unjust, and she herself innocent.

SURREALISM, movement in literature and art which flourished between WWI and WWII, centered in Paris. Writers such as André BRETON and COCTEAU, and painters such as DALI, MIRO, MAGRITTE, TANGUY and ERNST were surrealists. They owed much to FREUD, emphasizing the world of dream and fantasy and believing that the unconscious mind reveals a truer reality than the natural world. In paintings, everyday objects were often placed in a dream-like setting and apparently unrelated objects were juxtaposed.

SURREY, Henry Howard, Earl of (c1517–1547), English poet who with his friend Thomas WYATT introduced the SONNET from Italy into England. In his translations from Vergil, Surrey was the first to employ BLANK VERSE in English.

SURROGATE MOTHERHOOD, the bearing of a child for another person. During the 1980s a growing number of commercial surrogacy centers brought hundreds of infertile couples together with women willing to bear a child for pay. In 1988, the New Jersey supreme court, in a decision that was expected to prove influential nationally, ruled that surrogacy for pay was a form of child-selling and therefore illegal. Voluntary surrogacy was not affected. State legislatures have the option of legalizing commercial surrogacy, but none have done so. Louisiana in 1987 banned surrogacy.

SURVEYING, the accurate measurement of distances and features on the earth's surface. For making MAPS and charts, the LATITUDE and LONGITUDE of certain primary points are determined from astronomical observations. Geodetic surveying, for large areas, takes the earth's curvature into account (see GEODESY). After a base line of known length is established, the positions of other points are found by triangulation (measuring the angles of the point from each end of the base line) or by trilateration (measuring all the sides of the triangle formed by point and base line). Trigonometry, in particular the sine rule, yields the distances or angles not directly measured. A series of adjacent triangles is thus formed, each having one side in common with the next. Distances are measured by tape or electronically, sending a frequency-modulated light or microwave beam to the farther point and back, and measuring the phase shift. Angles are measured with the theodolite or (vertically) the alidade. Vertical elevations are determined by levels. Much modern surveying is done by photogrammetry, using the STEREOSCOPE to determine contours.

SURVIVAL OF THE FITTEST, term first used by Herbert SPENCER in his *Principles of Biology* (1864) and adopted by Charles Darwin to describe his theory of EVOLUTION by NATURAL SELECTION.

SUSA, city of ancient Persia, the biblical Shushan. It was capital of ELAM and later a principal city of the ACHAEMENIANS. Its remains, including part of the palace of DARIUS I, stand in SW Iran. The famous legal code of HAMMURABI was found here in 1901.

SUSLOV, Mikhail Andreyevich (1902–1982), Soviet party leader. An orthodox Stalinist while Stalin was alive, Suslov rose steadily through the Communist party ranks, saw important service during WWII and helped form the Cominform in 1947. He was editor of Pravda 1949–50. A member of the ruling Politburo from 1955, he became its most rigid ideologue. With an instinct for survival he at first supported Khrushchev and then helped overthrow him in 1964. He opposed any suggestion of relaxing party rule in the USSR.

SUTHERLAND, George (1862–1942), US statesman and lawyer. A Republican congressman (1901–02) and senator (1905–17), Sutherland was appointed associate justice of the Supreme Court in 1922, and retired in 1938. He was strongly conservative.

SUTHERLAND, Graham (1903–1980), English painter. His work includes landscapes and portraits, but he is best known for his post-WWII *Thorns* series, symbolic of Christ's Passion.

SUTHERLAND, Dame Joan (1926–   ), Australian soprano, internationally known as one of the foremost exponents of the art of bel canto.

SUTRAS, precepts, treatises and commentaries in SANSKRIT literature. Principally written about 500–200 BC on religious and philosophical subjects, they are important in HINDUISM and BUDDHISM. They also include the *Kamasutra*, on love.

SUTTEE, Hindu custom compelling a widow to immolate herself on her husband's funeral pyre. The practice was banned in India by the British in 1829.

SUTTER, John Augustus (1803–1880), Swiss-born pioneer of the US who founded a colony on the site of present-day Sacramento, Cal., and established a rich personal empire based on agriculture. His land was overrun and his property destroyed in the GOLD RUSH of 1849. He died bankrupt.

SUTTNER, Bertha, Baroness von (1843–1914), Austrian writer and pacifist whose novel *Lay Down Your Arms* (1892) was widely influential. She was the first woman to win the Nobel Peace Prize (1905).

SUVERO, Mark Di (1933–), US sculptor. His work is distinguished by its monumental size and moveable parts. Usually made from steel, old tires, aged timbers and similar materials, his "constructivist" sculptures sometimes make political statements.

SUVOROV, Aleksandr Vasilyevich (1729–1800), Russian field marshal. Successful against the Turks and the PUGACHEV and Polish rebellions, he commanded Austro-Russian armies that drove the French out of N Italy (1798-99; see FRENCH REVOLUTIONARY WARS). Russia then left the war, and Napoleon Bonaparte shortly restored French power in Italy.

SUWANNEE RIVER, river which rises in SE Ga. and flows 250mi through N Fla. to the Gulf of Mexico. It is famous as the "Swanee River" of Stephen Foster's song.

SUZMAN, Helen (1917–), South African politician, in parliament from 1953. A founder (1959) of the Progressive (later Progressive Federal) Party, she opposed APARTHEID and fought for civil rights.

SUZUKI, Daisetz Teitaro (1870–1966), Japanese Buddhist scholar who taught at major academic institutions in Japan, Europe and the US and was largely responsible for bringing the teachings of ZEN Buddhism to the Western world.

SVEVO, Italo (1861–1928), Italian fiction writer, born Ettore Schmitz. His masterpiece is the witty and perceptive psychological novel *Confessions of Zeno* (1923). He first became widely known through his friend and admirer James JOYCE.

SWAHILI, a Bantu language (influenced by Arabic) which is the lingua franca of much of E Africa, especially near the coast. It also refers to some of the inhabitants of this area.

SWALLOWS, family, Hirundinidae, of some 78 species of birds. All have long sickle-shaped wings and long forked tails. The plumage is generally dark, often with a metallic sheen. Many species have lighter underparts. The legs and feet are small and weak: they can perch on wires or tree branches, but are adapted to spend most of their time on the wing, feeding on insects caught in flight. Many species are migratory.

SWAMMERDAM, Jan (1637–1680), Dutch microscopist whose precision enabled him to make many discoveries, including red BLOOD cells (before 1658).

SWANS, a small group of large long-necked aquatic birds of the family Anatidae. There are eight species, seven within the genus *Cygnus*. Five of these are found in the N Hemisphere; all are white in adult plumage, but have different colored bills. These are the trumpeter swan, Bewick's swan, whooper, whistling and mute swans. The two remaining cygnids are the black swan of Australia and the black-necked swan of South America. Most feed on vegetation.

SWASTIKA (Sanskrit: good fortune), ancient symbol of well-being and prosperity employed by such diverse peoples as Greeks, Celts, Amerindians and the Hindus of India, based on the form. In the 20th century it gained notoriety as the hated symbol of NAZISM.

SWAZILAND, a kingdom in SE Africa, bordered by Mozambique to the E, and the Republic of South Africa on three sides.

Official name: Swaziland
Capital: Mbabane
Area: 6,704sq mi
Population: 716,000
Languages: English, Siswati, Zulu and Afrikaans
Religions: Christian, Traditional beliefs
Monetary unit(s): 1 lilangeni = 100 cents
Land. It has three main regions: the mountainous High Veld in the W, the lower Middle Veld and the Low Veld rising in the E to the narrow Lebombo range. The four

major rivers, running W–E, are being developed for irrigation and could provide abundant hydroelectricity. Temperatures average from 60°F in the W to 72°F in the E.

People and economy. Swazis and a smaller number of Zulus constitute 97% of the population. Coloureds (of mixed ancestry) and Europeans make up the rest. Agriculture, including forestry, is the largest single sector in the economy. Sugar, wood pulp, asbestos, fruits, iron ore and canned meats are the main exports. Swaziland has close communication, economic and trade links with South Africa, its principal trade partner.

History. Settled by the Swazis, a Bantu people, and unified as a kingdom in the 1800s, Swaziland was administered by both Britain and then South Africa. The country became self-governing in 1963 and fully independent in 1968, under King Sobhuza II. The king died in 1982 and one of his sons was crowned King Mswati III in 1986 after a power struggle within the royal family.

SWEATSHOP, place of work with long hours, poor pay and bad conditions. Such places usually exploited those who found difficulty in obtaining employment, such as women, unskilled laborers, newly arrived immigrants and children. Sweatshops were curbed by the growth of organized labor (see UNIONS).

SWEDEN, Scandinavian kingdom of N Europe, bounded W by Norway, NE by Finland, E by the Gulf of Bothnia, SE by the Baltic Sea and SW by the North Sea.

Official name: Kingdom of Sweden
Capital: Stockholm
Area: 173,732sq mi
Population: 8,387,000
Languages: Swedish
Religions: Swedish Lutheran
Monetary unit(s): 1 krona = 100 öre
Land. There are two main regions. Norrland ("the northland") occupies most of the country and slopes down from the Kölen Mts on the Norwegian border to the Gulf of Bothnia. Its northernmost parts lie within the Arctic Circle and include part of

LAPLAND. Sparsely populated, Norrland contains most of the country's vast wealth of timber and its principal iron mines. To the south are the intensively cultivated lowlands where the major cities, including STOCKHOLM and Göteborg, and the manufacturing industries are concentrated. In Feb., the coldest month, temperatures are below 32°F throughout Sweden but average 5°F and lower in the N. Summer temperatures average 60°F in the N and slightly higher in the S.

People. The population is almost entirely Swedish except for a minority of a few thousand Lapps in the N. More than 75% of the people are urban. Sweden enjoys one of the highest living standards in the world and an outstanding range of social services.

Economy. Sweden's forests cover about 55% of the country; it has rich deposits of iron ore, abundant hydroelectricity and enough good farmland to be almost self-sufficient in food. Metals and metal products dominate industry. Main exports are machinery, iron, steel, paper, wood pulp, timber and motor vehicles.

History. The Swedes were first recorded by the historian Tacitus in the 1st century AD. During the period of the VIKINGS they were known as Varangians in Russia where they pioneered a trade route as far as the Black Sea. Throughout the Middle Ages their history was tied to that of NORWAY and DENMARK. The Danes, dominant from the Kalmar Union (1397) of Denmark, Norway and Sweden, were driven out in 1523. In the 17th century Gustavus II (Gustavus Adolphus) made Sweden a leading European power. In 1809 the monarchy became constitutional; a new constitution took effect in 1975. Sweden took no part in WWI and WWII. The Social Democrats have been the predominant political party through much of Sweden's 20th-century history. The country was shocked by the assassination in 1986 of its popular prime minister, Olaf Palme. His Social Democratic Labor Party was returned to office in 1988 despite dissatisfaction with the government's failure to find the assassin.

SWEDENBORG, Emanuel (1688–1772), Swedish scientist, theologian and religious mystic. He had won recognition as a natural scientist when in 1745 he became the recipient of spiritual revelations. In his subsequent teachings he denied the Trinity, saying that Christ alone was God. He later claimed that Christ's second coming occurred in 1757. The Church of the New Jerusalem, founded (1788) after his death, embodies the theology set forth in his numerous works.

SWEDISH, one of the Germanic SCANDINAVIAN LANGUAGES, spoken by about 9 million people in Sweden, Finland, Estonia, the US and Canada. Old Swedish developed from Old Norse c800 AD and gave place to modern Swedish c1500 with the onset of standardization.

SWEELINCK, Jan Pieterszoon (1562–1621), Dutch composer and organist who is known today for his development of organ techniques in his many compositions. He paved the way for J. S. BACH.

SWEETBREADS, the pancreatic tissue (see PANCREAS) or THYMUS glands of various animals sold as MEAT.

SWEET POTATO, *Ipomoea batatas,* a trailing creeper, native to tropical America and producing a tuberous root which is sweet-tasting when cooked. In North America an orange variety is grown, with roots rich in carotene. Family: Leguminosae.

SWIFT, Gustavus Franklin (1839–1903), US butcher and businessman. First (1875) to slaughter cattle in Chicago for shipment E, he introduced refrigerated railroad cars, founded the giant Swift & Co., and pioneered the manufacture of meat byproducts.

SWIFT, Jonathan (1667–1745), Anglo-Irish writer, a journalist, poet and outstanding prose satirist. He was born in Ireland, and ordained in 1694. Two of his satires were published in 1704: *The Battle of the Books* and *The Tale of a Tub.* He became a Tory in 1710, taking over *The Examiner,* the Tory journal. From 1714, he lived in Ireland, as Dean of St. Patrick's, Dublin. He deplored the plight of the Irish poor in the *Drapier's Letters* (1724). His masterpiece is *Gulliver's Travels* (1726), a children's fantasy as well as a political and social satire.

SWIFTS, small, fast-flying insectivorous birds, very like SWALLOWS but placed with the HUMMINGBIRDS in the order Apodiformes. Both swifts and hummingbirds have very small feet and extremely short arm bones, the major flight feathers being attached to the extended hand bones. Entirely aerial, most species feed and even sleep on the wing.

SWIMMING AND DIVING, most popular of water sports. Common swimming styles include the *side stroke,* a simple sidewise propulsion for distance swimming and lifesaving; *breaststroke,* a froglike arm-and-leg thrust which is probably the oldest stroke; *backstroke,* overarm or, for distance endurance, an inverted breaststroke; and *crawl,* the most common freestyle form, using an overarm pull and a flutter kick rather than the thrusting propulsion characteristic of most other strokes. The *butterfly,* a modified breaststroke which thrusts the head and arms up from the water and incorporates a dolphin kick, has become a popular competitive style. Synchronized swimming, or water ballet, is popular among US women. Distance swimming has produced many well-publicized attempts to cross the English Channel and other large bodies of water. Fancy diving dates back to 17th-century Sweden and Germany. Competitions include forward, backward, reverse, inward, twisting and armstand dives in layout (extended), tuck (rolled in a ball), pike (bent at waist, legs straight) and free positions, from a platform or springboard. Several kinds of swimming and diving events have been part of OLYMPIC GAMES competitions.

SWINBURNE, Algernon Charles (1837–1909), English lyric poet and critic. A friend of the PRE-RAPHAELITES, he led a dissolute life, ending in 30 years' seclusion. He won success with *Atalanta in Calydon* (1865), a poetic drama. *Poems and Ballads* (1866, 1878, 1889) dealt with the psychology of sexual passion. They shocked contemporaries but are now widely appreciated for their resonant language and powerful rhythms.

SWING. See JAZZ.

SWISS GUARDS, Swiss mercenary soldiers who served in various European armies, most notably as bodyguards to the French monarchs 1497–1792 and 1814–30. The colorfully uniformed Papal Swiss Guard at the Vatican Palace in Rome dates back to the late 1400s.

SWITHIN or **SWITHUN, Saint** (c800–862), Anglo-Saxon bishop of Winchester and chaplain to King Egbert. Tradition says that St. Swithin's Day (July 15) determines the weather for the next 40 days.

SWITZERLAND, a landlocked central European confederation.

Land. The country borders Germany, Austria, Liechtenstein, Italy and France. In the far NW the Jura Mountains extend into France. The hills and plains of the Swiss Plateau, a SW–NE band in the NW, contain rich farming land, many lakes (lakes Geneva and Lucerne the largest) and 66% of the people (including Geneva, Lausanne, Bern and Zürich). The Swiss ALPS in the S and SE are little populated but attract many tourists. Climate varies greatly: temperature decreases and precipitation increases the higher the altitude. Sheltered S valleys have hot summers and mild winters, but elsewhere winters are

Official name: Swiss Confederation
Capital: Bern
Area: 15,943sq mi
Population: 6,586,000
Languages: German, French, Italian; Romansh
Religions: Roman Catholic, Protestant
Monetary unit(s): 1 Swiss franc = 100 rappen (German) or centimes (French)

cold, with heavy snowfalls.

People. The four official language groups are German (70%), French (19%), Italian (10%) and Romansh (1%). The population is divided almost equally between Protestant and Roman Catholic. There are over 900,000 foreign, mainly S European, workers. The 23 cantons (states) retain much autonomy and choose a 44-member Council of States, which with the directly elected 200-member National Council elects a 7-member executive Federal Council every 4 years. A president and vice-president are similarly elected each year. Women obtained the vote in 1971.

Economy. Highly industrialized, and with plentiful hydroelectric power, Switzerland exports watches, jewelry, precision tools and instruments, textiles and chemicals. Dairy cattle are raised. Cheese and chocolate are important exports, and tourism and international banking major industries.

History. Rome conquered the Helvetii in 58 BC. The area came under the Alemanni, the Burgundians, the FRANKS, and the HOLY ROMAN EMPIRE (962). HAPSBURG oppression led to the Perpetual Covenant between Uri, Schwyz and Unterwald (1291), the traditional beginning of the Swiss Confederation. Wars against Austria resulted in virtual independence in 1499. Religious civil wars divided the country in the REFORMATION (see CALVIN, JOHN; ZWINGLI, HULDREICH) but it stayed neutral in the Thirty Years' War and independence was formally recognized by the 1648 Peace of WESTPHALIA. French revolutionary armies imposed a centralized Helvetic Republic 1798–1803. The 1815 Congress of VIENNA restored the Confederation. After a three-week civil war a federal democracy was set up in 1848. Switzerland maintained an armed neutrality in both world wars and in the cold war. In 1986 voters rejected a proposal to join the UNITED NATIONS.

SWORD, ancient principal form of hand weapon, its metal blade longer than a dagger. Leaf-shaped Bronze Age swords gave way to short flat blades in Rome, and longer laminated iron (in Damascus) and tempered steel (notably in Toledo) weapons. Asian curved cutting blades (the Turkish *scimitar*) inspired the cavalry *saber*. Japanese SAMURAI used a longer two-handed version. The thrust-and-parry *rapier* became the weapon of the duel and FENCING.

SYCAMORE, popular name for a number of deciduous trees. In North America the name is applied to a plane tree (*Platanus occidentalis*), the bark of which flakes off. In Europe, the sycamore is a MAPLE (*Acer pseudoplatanus*). The sycamore of ancient times is a fig (*Ficus occidentalis*) which is now seldom cultivated.

SYDENHAM, Thomas (1624–1689), "the English Hippocrates," who pioneered the use of QUININE for treating MALARIA and of laudanum as an anesthetic, wrote an important treatise on GOUT, and first described Sydenham's CHOREA (St. Vitus' Dance).

SYDNEY, oldest and largest city in Australia, capital of New South Wales. Famous for its natural harbor, Harbor Bridge and opera house, Sydney was founded as a penal colony in 1788. Sydney ships wool, wheat and meat and is a major commercial, industrial, shipping, cultural and recreational center. Pop (metro) 3,332,000.

SYLLOGISM, the logical form of an argument consisting of three statements: two premises and a conclusion. The conclusion of a valid syllogism follows logically from the premises and is true if the premises are true. (See also LOGIC.)

SYMBIOSIS, the relationship between two organisms of different species in which mutual benefit is derived by both participants. The main types of symbiotic relationship are commensalism and mutualism. **Commensalism** implies eating at the same table, e.g., the sea anemone that lives on the shell occupied by the hermit crab: the anemone hides the crab but feeds on food scattered by the crab. **Mutualism** is more intimate, there being close physiological dependence between participants. An example is seen in bacteria that live in the gut of herbivorous mammals. Here the bacteria aid digestion of plant material.

SYMBOLISM, a literary movement begun by a group of French poets in the late 19th century including Laforgue MALLARMÉ, VALÉRY and VERLAINE. Influenced by BAUDELAIRE, SWEDENBORG and WAGNER, the symbolists aimed to create poetic images, or symbols, which would be apprehended by the senses and reach the preconscious world of the spirit. Though shortlived as a movement, symbolism influenced such great writers as JOYCE, PROUST, RILKE and YEATS.

SYMMETRY, regularity of form describable by the geometrical or other operations that leave the form unchanged. The human body has a rough left-right symmetry; its form is left unchanged by *reflection* (interchange of equidistant points on opposite sides) in a vertical plane through its center. The form of an infinitely long picket fence is left unchanged by *translation* (motion without rotation) by certain amounts to the left or right. A circle is unchanged by any *rotation* about its center. There may be more than one kind of symmetry operation: a circle is also unchanged by reflection in any diameter. Two symmetry operations performed in succession give another symmetry operation. All the symmetry operations that can be applied to a given form constitute a mathematical group.

Symmetry plays an important role in PHYSICS. The possible classes of CRYSTALS are defined by their symmetry groups. All physical laws, so far as is known, are left unchanged by simultaneous reflections of space, time and electric charge (interchange of positive and negative), as well as by rotations of space and translations of space and time. The special theory of RELATIVITY is defined by the LORENTZ group. SUBATOMIC PARTICLES show abstract symmetries in which their interactions with other particles are unchanged when different kinds of particles are substituted for one another in certain ways.

SYMPHONIC POEM, or tone poem, a form of orchestral music in one movement, popular about 1850–1900, which describes a story or a scene. LISZT originated the form, but Richard STRAUSS is the most noted composer in the field.

SYMPHONY, the major form of music for ORCHESTRA. Developed from the OVERTURE, by 1800 it had four movements: a fairly quick movement in SONATA form; a slow movement; a MINUET and trio; and a quick rondo. HAYDN and MOZART played a central role in developing the classical symphony. BEETHOVEN introduced the scherzo and a

new range of emotion. Major symphonic composers include in the 1800s SCHUBERT, BERLIOZ, MENDELSSOHN, BRAHMS, BRUCKNER, DVORAK and MAHLER, and in the 1900s STRAVINSKY, PROKOFIEV, SHOSTAKOVITCH, VAUGHAN WILLIAMS, ELGAR, SIBELIUS and NIELSEN.

SYNAGOGUE (Greek: house of assembly), Jewish place of worship. The synagogue became the center of communal and religious life after destruction of the Temple in Jerusalem (70 AD) and dispersal of the Jews. Most synagogues have an ark containing the TORAH, an "eternal light," two candelabra, pews and a platform (*bimah*) for readings and conduct of services. Orthodox synagogues segregate women. (See JUDAISM.)

SYNAPSE, the point of connection between two nerves or between nerve and muscle. An electrical nerve impulse releases a chemical transmitter (often acetylcholine) which crosses a small gap and initiates electrical excitation (or inhibition) of the succeeding nerve or muscle. (See NERVOUS SYSTEM.)

SYNCOPATION, in music, the conscious contradiction of regular rhythm by stressing a normally unstressed beat, or eliminating the expected beat by a rest or tied note. It is a feature of JAZZ and the music of many modern composers.

SYNCOPE. See FAINTING.

SYNDICALISM (French *syndicat*: labor union), a revolutionary labor movement aiming at seizing control of industry through strikes, sabotage, even violence, and, as its ultimate weapon, the general strike. It originated in late 19th-century France, from the theories of PROUDHON and SOREL. Syndicalists agree with Marxist class analysis (see MARXISM) but like anarchists reject any state organization (see ANARCHISM). Syndicalism was strong in France and Italy in the early 1900s and found US expression in the industrial unionism of the INDUSTRIAL WORKERS OF THE WORLD. WWI and the advance of communism overtook the syndicalists; their influence lasted longest in Spain, but was finally destroyed in the civil war 1936–39.

SYNERGISM, the working together of two or more agencies (e.g., synergistic MUSCLES, or a chemical with a mechanical phenomenon, or even a chemist with a physicist) to greater effect than both would have working independently.

SYNFUELS, synthetic fuels, especially oil and gas derived from coal and shale. Interest in the development of synfuels was stimulated by President Jimmy Carter, who in 1980 signed a bill creating the US Synthetic Fuels Corporation, intended to promote the development of a domestic synfuel industry. Declining oil prices put an end to most major synfuels projects.

SYNGE, John Millington (1871–1909), Irish dramatist. Influenced by the CELTIC RENAISSANCE, he studied Irish peasant life and dramatized his view of Irish myth and character in his plays *In the Shadow of the Glen* (1903), *Riders to the Sea* (1904), *The Tinker's Wedding* (1908), and his most famous work, *The Playboy of the Western World* (1907). He was encouraged by W. B. YEATS and with him helped organize the Abbey Theatre in Dublin.

SYNOD, a Christian ecclesiastical assembly, usually of both lay and clerical representatives from a limited area. Synods decide organizational, doctrinal and other questions. They are particularly important in the ORTHODOX, LUTHERAN and REFORMED CHURCHES.

SYNOPTIC GOSPELS, the three GOSPELS (Matthew, Mark and Luke) which—unlike the Gospel of John—have a large degree of subject-matter and phraseology in common. Modern scholars commonly regard Mark as prior and suppose that Matthew and Luke also used Q, a lost source containing the non-Marcan material common to them, and other sources peculiar to each.

SYNOVIAL FLUID, the small amount of fluid which lubricates JOINTS and the synovial sheaths of TENDONS. It contains hyaluronic acid, which contributes to its lubricating properties.

SYNTAX. See GRAMMAR.

SYNTHETIC FIBER, man-made textile FIBER derived from artificial POLYMERS, as opposed to regenerated fibers (such as rayon) made from natural substances, or to natural fibers. Almost all types of long-chain polymer may be used: NYLON, the first to be discovered, is a polyamide; Dacron is a polyester, useful for nonstretch clothing. Other widely-used synthetic fibers include Orlon, polyethylene and FIBERGLASS. Polyurethane fibers are elastomers, used in stretch fabrics. To make the fibers, the polymer is usually converted to a liquid by melting or dissolving it; this is extruded through a spinneret with minute holes, and forms a filament as the solvent evaporates (dry spinning) or as it passes into a suitable chemical bath (wet spinning). The filaments are drawn (stretched) to increase strength by aligning the polymer molecules. They may then be used as such, or cut into short lengths which are twisted together, forming yarn.

SYPHILIS. See VENEREAL DISEASES.

SYRACUSE, city in SE Sicily. Founded by Corinthians c734 BC, it became a brilliant center of Greek culture, notably under Hiero I and Dionysius the Elder. Syracuse was defeated in the PUNIC WARS by Rome (211 BC). Later conquerors were the Arabs (878) and Normans (1085). The modern provincial capital, a port and tourist center, has many ancient monuments. Pop 118,966.

SYRIA, republic in SW Asia bordered by Turkey (N), Iraq (E), Jordan (S), and Israel, Lebanon and the Mediterranean (W).

Official name: The Syrian Arab Republic
Capital: Damascus
Area: 71,498sq mi
Population: 10,969,000
Languages: Arabic; Armenian, Kurdish, Turkish
Religions: Muslim, Christian, Druze
Monetary unit(s): 1 Syrian pound=100 piastres

Land. The Euphrates R flows SE through Syria. To the N lie rolling plains, to the S the Syrian Desert, ending in the SW with the Jebel Druz plateau and fertile Hauran plains. Further W lie the Anti-Lebanon Mts with Mt Hermon (9,232ft) in the S, and the Ansariya range with the cultivated coastal plain beyond it in the N. The warm Mediterranean climate gives way inland to a more extreme temperature range. Annual rainfall (Nov.–March) is heaviest (about 50in) on the W Ansariya slopes, while the desert has less than 5in.

People. After Damascus the largest cities are Aleppo, Homs and Hama (all in fertile zones E of the mountains) and the seaport of Latakia. Over 80% of the people are Arab-speaking Muslims, mostly SUNNITE, but there are nomadic BEDOUIN, and Kurdish, Turkish and Armenian minorities. Christian Orthodox churches claim some 500,000 members. There are about 120,000 DRUZES. Government programs have reduced illiteracy to some 50%. There are universities at Damascus, Aleppo, and Latakia.

Economy. About a third of the labor force is engaged in agriculture. Many large estates were expropriated beginning in 1958 and redistributed, and attempts are being made to increase yields through modern methods and irrigation. Industry includes textiles, iron and steel, and assembly of transportation and electrical equipment. Exports include cotton, fruits and vegetables, and phosphates. Most oil revenues are derived from pipe lines crossing the country, but income from oil drilled in the NE is increasing. The large Euphrates Dam power station opened in 1978.

History. Part of the ancient HITTITE empire, Syria was conquered by Assyrians, Babylonians, Persians and Greeks. Under the SELEUCIDS after the death of ALEXANDER THE GREAT, it was later incorporated into the Roman empire by POMPEY. The Arabs conquered Syria in the 600s. Part of the OTTOMAN EMPIRE from 1516, Syria was mandated to the French after WWI and became fully independent in 1946. It joined with Egypt in the UNITED ARAB REPUBLIC 1958–61. From the late 1950s, emphasis in trade shifted toward the USSR and E European countries. The ruling Baathist Party, which assumed control of the government in 1963, favors socialism and pan-Arab nationalism. Since 1967 Israel has occupied the Golan Heights in the SW; it formally annexed the area in 1981. Syrian forces backed a 1970 Palestinian uprising in Jordan and have intervened in neighboring Lebanon on behalf of various groups since 1976. In the early 1980s the government faced growing unrest, especially from the fundamentalist Muslim Brotherhood; fundamentalist uprisings in Aleppo (1980) and Hama (1982) were brutally repressed. President Hadiz al-Assad, who was elected to a third term in 1985, also supported Iran in the Iran-Iraq war and has backed radical anti-Arafat factions within the Palestine Liberation Organization. Syria, which condemned the Egyptian-Israeli peace treaty and successfully opposed a 1983 Israel-Lebanon peace accord, remains a key factor in the success of any overall Middle East peace settlement.

SYRIAC, an ARAMAIC language of the NW Semitic group. It was used in early Christian writings but was largely superseded by Arabic after the spread of Islam. Closely related to Hebrew, Syriac is still spoken by small groups in the Middle East.

SZELL, Georg (1897–1970), Hungarian-born US conductor. He established his reputation in Germany but emigrated to the US when the Nazis rose to power. Szell's many recordings with the Cleveland Orchestra have gained international acclaim.

SZIGETI, Joseph (1892–1973), US violinist. Born in Hungary, he emigrated to the US in the 1920s. Szigeti is particularly famous for his performances of virtuoso contemporary works.

SZILARD, Leo (1898–1964), Hungarian-born US physicist largely responsible for the US embarking on the development of the atom bomb (see MANHATTAN PROJECT). In 1945 he was a leader of the movement against using it. Later he made contributions in the field of molecular biology.

SZOLD, Henrietta (1860–1945), founder in 1912 of the Women's Zionist Organization of America (Hadassah). Baltimore born, she moved to Palestine in 1920, and directed medical and rehabilitation work, particularly for children.

20th letter of our alphabet. Last letter of the ancient North Semitic alphabet, it became the 19th letter of the Greek (as *tau*) and Roman alphabets. The small t developed in 6th-century Roman script.

TABERNACLE, a portable temple carried by the Israelites during their nomadic period. According to Exodus its design was given to Moses on Mt. Sinai. The inner chamber contained the Ark of the Covenant, which held the Ten Commandments.

TABERNACLES, Feast of. See SUKKOTH.

TABES DORSALIS, form of teriary syphilis (see VENEREAL DISEASES) in which certain tracts in the SPINAL CORD—particularly those concerned with position sense—degenerate, leading to a characteristic high-stepping gait, sensory abnormalities and sometimes disorganization of JOINTS. Attacks of abdominal pain and abnormal pupil reactions are typical.

TABLE TENNIS, or **Ping Pong,** indoor game similar to a small-scale version of TENNIS. It is played by two or four players on a table divided by a 6in-high net into two 5ft × 4½ft courts. The players use wooden rackets to strike a hollow celluloid ball over the net into the opposite court. The game is administered by the International Table Tennis Federation and biennial world tournaments are held.

TABOO or **tabu,** Polynesian word meaning that which is forbidden. Negative taboos arise from fear of possible ill effects (e.g., incest); positive taboos from awe or reverence (e.g., approaching a god). In tribal society the TOTEM of each clan is often subject to taboo.

TABULA RASA (Latin: erased tablet), philosophical term referring to the condition of the mind before it is modified by experience; often used by empiricists (see EMPIRICISM) to emphasize the dependency of knowledge on the senses.

TACHÉ, Sir Étienne Paschal (1795–1865), Canadian politician, premier 1856–57 and 1864–65 of the province of Canada. He presided over the historic Quebec Convention (1865) leading to federation of British North American colonies.

TACITUS, Cornelius (c55–c120 AD), Roman historian. His most famous works are critical studies of the 1st-century empire, the *Histories* and *Annals.* A son-in-law of AGRICOLA, of whom he wrote a biography, he rose to consul (97), and proconsul of Asia (112). His *Germania* is the earliest study of the Germanic tribes.

TACNA-ARICA DISPUTE, between Peru and Chile, fought over two provinces provisionally ceded by Peru to Chile in 1883 after the WAR OF THE PACIFIC. US arbitration settled the dispute in 1929; Tacna went to Peru and Arica to Chile.

TADPOLES, the larvae of FROGS and TOADS. An aquatic larva is characteristic of all the AMPHIBIA but in salamanders and newts it is similar in appearance to the adult. In frogs and toads, the tadpole is globular with a long muscular tail. A full metamorphosis must be undergone to reach adult form.

TAFT, Lorado (1860–1936), US sculptor, author of a pioneering *History of American Sculpture* (1903). Typical of his allegorical monuments (often fountains) is *The Fountain of the Great Lakes* in Chicago. He taught at Chicago Art Institute from 1886.

TAFT, Robert Alphonso (1889–1953), US senator from Ohio, 1938–53. Eldest son of W. H. TAFT, he studied law, served in the Ohio legislature, and became a leading conservative Republican. Taft was a fiscal conservative, an opponent of the NEW DEAL and an isolationist. His most famous congressional achievement was the TAFT-HARTLEY ACT.

TAFT, William Howard (1857–1930), 27th president of the US (1909–13). An enormous, self-effacing man, he had the misfortune to succeed Theodore ROOSEVELT and suffered in comparison. He never wanted to be president and was politically inept; yet the achievements of his administration were substantial.

After a promising legal career, in which he served as state judge, US solicitor general and federal judge, Taft became first civil governor of the Philippines (1901). In 1904 he became Roosevelt's secretary of war and his concerns included the reorganization of the PANAMA CANAL project and the settlement of the RUSSO-JAPANESE WAR. In 1908 Roosevelt named him his successor, and Taft easily defeated William Jennings Bryan.

The new president's policies were based largely on those of Roosevelt. He increased prosecutions under the SHERMAN ANTITRUST ACT and introduced controls on government expenditure. His domestic reforms included a bill requiring disclosure of campaign funds in federal elections. In foreign affairs his efforts at international peace-keeping failed through poor management, and his "dollar diplomacy" poisoned relations with Latin America. Taft's inability to reduce tariffs effectively, his failure to curb the powers of Speaker CANNON, and his dismissal of chief forester Gifford PINCHOT alienated progressive Republicans. With progressive support Roosevelt began to attack Taft and ran against him in the 1912 election on the Bull Moose ticket. The split allowed the Democrat Woodrow WILSON to sweep into power.

Taft's defeat allowed him to return to his legal career and in 1921 he achieved a lifelong ambition when he was appointed chief justice of the Supreme Court, thus becoming the only man to serve as both chief justice and president.

TAFT-HARTLEY ACT, the Labor-Management Relations Act of 1947, sponsored by Sen. Robert A. TAFT and Rep. Fred Hartley. It was passed over the veto of President TRUMAN and amended the WAGNER ACT. The act defined "unfair labor practices," and banned boycotts, sympathy strikes and strikes in interunion disputes. A federal arbitration service was set up and states were empowered to prohibit union shop agreements. A further controversial provision was presidential power to seek an 80-day injunction against a strike in cases of "national emergency."

TAGALOG, a people who comprise over 20% of the population of the Philippines. Their majority in Manila gives them preeminence in business, administration and the arts. Since 1937 Tagalog has been the national language.

TAGORE, Sir Rabindranath (1861–1941), Bengali Indian poet, painter, musician and mystic who founded what is now

Visva-Bharati U. to blend the best in Indian and Western culture. His literary work includes many songs, poems, plays, novels, short stories and essays. He received the 1913 Nobel Prize for Literature.

TAGUS RIVER, longest river in the Iberian peninsula. It flows W 556mi from the Montes Universales in central Spain to the Atlantic coast of Portugal at LISBON.

TAHITI, largest of the Society Islands in the S Pacific, the center of French Polynesia. Its 400sq mi are mountainous and rich in tropical vegetation. The 95,600 people are Polynesians, with some French and Chinese. Papeete is the capital. Tahiti, claimed for France by BOUGAINVILLE in 1768, was visited by James COOK and William BLIGH. Its beauty inspired GAUGUIN.

TAHOE, Lake, a lake in the Sierra Nevada on the Cal./Nev. border about 6,230ft above sea level, 22mi N–S and 12mi E–W. Discovered in 1844 by John C. FRÉMONT, it is now a tourist resort.

TAIGA, Siberian forest region lying between the TUNDRA and the STEPPES. Conifers predominate, though birches are occasionally found. Much of the ground is swampy. The term is applied also to other, similar, N-Hemisphere forests.

TAINE, Hippolyte Adolphe (1828–1893), French critic and historian who devised a "scientific" method of criticism based on study of an author's environment and historical situation. The implications of his determinism greatly influenced the growth of literary NATURALISM. His most famous work is *History of English Literature* (1864).

TAIPEI, capital and largest city of Taiwan, lying to the N on the Tanshui R. A major industrial city, with steel plants, oil refineries and glass factories, Taipei is also the cultural and educational center of Taiwan. Founded in the early 1700s, it became capital of the Nationalist Chinese government in 1949. Pop (metro) 2,500,000.

TAIPING REBELLION (1851–64), great Chinese peasant uprising. Agrarian discontent was channeled into a mass movement by the mystic leader Hung Hsiu-ch'ûan, who claimed to be the brother of Christ. His regime in Kwangsi province survived 10 years but was finally crushed with the help of Charles GORDON and his 3,000 mercenaries. The rebellion seriously weakened the Manchu dynasty.

TAIWAN. See CHINA, REPUBLIC OF.

TAJ MAHAL, a mausoleum built by the Mogul emperor Shah Jahan for his wife Mumtaz-i-Mahal at Agra in N India. Faced in white marble, the central domed tomb stands on a square plinth with a minaret at each corner, surrounded by water gardens, gateways and walks. It took some 20,000 workmen over 20 years to complete (1632–54).

TAKESHITA, Noboru (1924–   ), Japanese politician, president of the ruling Liberal-Democratic Party and prime minister from 1987, succeeding Yasuhiro Nakasone in both posts. He was finance minister 1982-86.

TALBOT, William Henry Fox (1800–1877), English scientist and inventor of the calotype method of PHOTOGRAPHY. In calotype a latent image in silver iodide is developed in gallic acid and fixed in sodium thiosulfate giving a paper "negative." Thus, for the first time, any number of positive prints could be made from a single exposure by contact printing.

TALC, a hydrous magnesium silicate mineral $Mg_3Si_4O_{10}(OH)_2$, occurring in METAMORPHIC ROCKS, chiefly in the US, USSR, France and Japan. It has a layer structure resembling that of MICA, and is extremely soft (see HARDNESS). Talc is used in ceramics, roof insulation, cosmetics, as an insecticide carrier and as a filler in paints, paper and rubber. Impure, massive talc is called SOAPSTONE.

TALLCHIEF, Maria (1925–   ), US ballerina with the New York City Ballet (1947-67), where she danced in ballets choreographed by George BALANCHINE, her husband 1946-51.

TALLEYRAND-PÉRIGORD,   Charles Maurice de (1754–1838), French statesman. He was a member of the National Assembly during the FRENCH REVOLUTION, helped Napoleon found the First Empire (1804), assisted the restoration of the Bourbon kings (1814), then helped oust them in favor of a constitutional monarchy (1830). Talleyrand is best remembered for his brilliant diplomacy at the Congress of Vienna (see VIENNA, CONGRESS OF) and in the negotiations (1830–31) between France and Britain which set up the state of Belgium.

TALLIS, Thomas (c1505–1585), English composer and organist. He was a close associate of William BYRD, with whom he shared a state monopoly in the printing of music. Tallis is famous for his solemn, elaborately constructed choral church music and for his development of COUNTERPOINT.

TALMADGE, Eugene (1884–1946), US Democratic politician, governor of Georgia 1933-37, 1941-43. Appealing to rural white voters, he opposed the NEW DEAL (because it would not let him distribute relief funds) and dismissed educators who advocated racial equality. His son, **Herman Talmadge** (1913–   ), was governor 1947-55 and US senator 1956-81.

TALMUD (Hebrew: teaching), ancient compilation of Jewish oral law and rabbinical teaching, begun 5th century AD. There are two versions: Babylonian and Palestinian. It has two parts: the Mishnah and the Gemara. These contain a wealth of traditional wisdom, legends and stories, comment on the Old Testament and record early legal decisions. The Talmud is second only to the Bible in prestige, and its study has been the core of Jewish education for over 1,000 years.

TAMAYO, Rufino (1899–   ), Mexican painter. He combined the strength and color of native and pre-Columbian art with Expressionist and Surrealist styles. He painted several frescoes but is best known for his small paintings of Indian figures.

TAMBO, Oliver (1917–   ), black South African political leader, president of the outlawed AFRICAN NATIONAL CONGRESS from 1967.

TAMBOURINE, a PERCUSSION INSTRUMENT comprising a skin stretched across a hoop fitted with bells or 'jingles' which rattle as it is tapped or shaken. Originating in the Middle East, it is used in folk music and in some orchestral scores.

TAMERLANE, or **Timur the Lame** (c1336–1405), Mongol conqueror. Claiming descent from GENGHIS KHAN, by 1370 he controlled from his capital SAMARKAND what is now Soviet Turkmenistan. He conquered Persia (1387), the Caucasus (1392), Syria (1400) and the Ottoman Turks (1402) in the W, and invaded India and sacked Delhi (1398). He died planning to invade China. The empire rapidly disintegrated.

TAMIL, a DRAVIDIAN language spoken by some 40 million, principally in SE India and NE Sri Lanka. It is the main language of Tamil Nadu (formerly Madras) state. Tamil has its own script, and a rich ancient literature.

TAMMANY HALL, nickname from the 1800s for the corrupt New York Democratic Party machine, also the name of its Madison Avenue offices. The patriotic society of Tammany (a wise Delaware Indian chief) was founded in 1789, with a ritual based on Indian custom. It became a Democratic machine, dominating the city after c1830, with corruption common under "bosses" like William TWEED. Its influence spread beyond New York, but the reforms of LA GUARDIA (mayor, 1933–45) led to its decline.

TANCRED (c1076–1112), a Sicilian Norman leader of the First CRUSADE (1096–99). He helped take Nicaea (1098) and Jerusalem (1099). Becoming regent of Antioch (1100) and Edessa (1104), he fought Turks and Byzantines and conquered N Syria.

TANEY, Roger Brooke (1777–1864), chief justice of the US (1836–64) whose DRED SCOTT CASE decision helped bring on the Civil War. As President Jackson's secretary of the treasury (1833–35), he crushed the Second BANK OF THE UNITED STATES. As chief justice, he steered a middle course on STATES' RIGHTS, and continued John MARSHALL's liberal interpretation of the Constitution. (See also SUPREME COURT.)

T'ANG, Chinese dynasty (618–906), a "golden age" in Chinese history. Cofounded by the aristocrat Li Yüan and his son T'ai Tsung (ruled 647–49), the dynasty sent armies W to Central Asia and made China a cosmopolitan empire enjoying a cultural renaissance at its peak under Hsüan Tsung (reigned 712–56). There were remarkable advances in science, technology, printing, the arts and literature, with outstanding lyric verse by Li Po and Tu Fu.

TANGANYIKA. See TANZANIA.

TANGANYIKA, Lake, in W Tanzania and E Zaire, in the Great Rift Valley. Africa's second-largest lake, it is 420mi N–S, 30–45mi E–W and up to 4,710ft deep. It has important fisheries.

TANGE, Kenzo (1913–   ), Japanese architect and city planner who combines modern techniques and materials with traditional Japanese design. His design for the Hiroshima Peace Hall (1955–56) was influenced by LE CORBUSIER. He also designed the dramatic National Gymnasium for the 1964 Tokyo Olympic Games.

TANGIER, seaport and residential and commercial city of Morocco, facing the Strait of Gibraltar. Settled about 15th century BC, it was part of an international zone under French, Spanish and British administrators during 1923–56. Pop (metro) 304,000.

TANGLEWOOD, former estate in Stockbridge and Lenox, Mass., site since 1934 of the summer Berkshire Music Festival at which the Boston Symphony Orchestra performs.

TANGUY, Yves (1900–1955), French Surrealist painter, who lived in the US from 1939. Influenced by CHIRICO, he painted a dream-like world of strange inhuman shapes inhabiting a lunar landscape. (See SURREALISM.)

TANIZAKI, Junichiro (1886–1965), Japanese novelist and short-story writer. A leading neoromantic influenced by POE,

BAUDELAIRE and WILDE, he infused his work with sensuality, cruelty and mysterious demonic forces. Among his works is *The Makioka Sisters* (1948; tr. 1957).

TANK, armored combat vehicle, armed with guns or missiles, and self-propelled on caterpillar treads; the chief modern conventional ground assault weapon. Tanks were first built in 1915 by Britain and used from 1916 against Germany in WWI. These early tanks were very slow, and development between the wars greatly improved speed and firepower. The Spanish Civil War and WWII showed the effectiveness of concentrated tank attacks. Amphibious and airborne tanks were developed. Heavy tanks proved cumbersome, and were generally abandoned in favor of the more maneuverable (though more vulnerable) light and medium tanks. Improved models are now used where heavy guns are needed. Light tanks (less than 25 tons) are used mainly for infantry support.

TANKER, ship designed to carry liquid cargo in bulk, notably crude oil, gasoline or natural gas. The first tanker (1886), a 300ft vessel, carried 3,000 tons of oil. Some tankers today hold 100 times as much: a 483,939-ton vessel (the *Globtik London*, 1975) has been built in Japan. Ships this size greatly reduce per-ton transport costs, but cannot enter many ports; some large tankers transfer their cargo to smaller tankers offshore. In gross tonnage tankers account for over a third of all merchant shipping.

TANNENBERG (Polish: Stebark), village in N Poland, 15mi SE of Ostróda, site of two important battles. In 1410, the TEUTONIC KNIGHTS were defeated by the Lithuanians and Poles, and in WWI (August, 1914), the Germans severely defeated the Russians. Up to 1945 Tannenberg was in Germany.

TANNER, Henry Ossawa (1859-1937), black US painter who lived in Paris from 1891, noted for his paintings of biblical subjects.

TANNING, the conversion of animal hide into leather. After cleaning and soaking, a tanning agent is applied that converts the gelatin of the hide into an insoluble material which cements the PROTEIN fibers together and makes them incorruptible. Until the end of the 19th century vegetable extracts containing tannins were used; then the process was greatly shortened by using CHROMIUM salts, and also formaldehyde and formic acid.

TANTRAS, the texts of Tantrism, a system of esoteric Hindu and Buddhist practices. Tantras are often dialogues between the male and female aspects (in Hinduism Shiva and Shakti) of a supreme deity. They instruct in meditation and YOGA (including ritual sex) as a means of reaching ultimate truth through mind and body. They date from c500 AD.

TANZANIA, republic in E Africa, on the Indian Ocean. It was formed (1964) by the union of Tanganyika with the island of ZANZIBAR.

Official name: United Republic of Tanzania
Capital: Dar es Salaam
Area: 364,881sq mi
Population: 23,217,000
Languages: Swahili, English; Bantu dialects
Religions: Animist, Muslim, Christian
Monetary unit(s): 1 Tanzanian shilling=100 cents
Land. Tanzania is a beautiful country, with plateaus, mountain ranges, Africa's highest peak (Mt. Kilimanjaro), Rift Valley lakes and the S part of Lake Victoria. Inland the climate is hot and dry with some rain Dec.–May. Coral reefs and mangrove swamps line the coast. Grasslands and open woods dominate the extensive plains, famous for their wildlife.
People. The vast majority are rural. There are over 100 Bantu tribes, each with distinctive languages and customs. There are Indian, Arab and European minorities. The illiteracy rate is high, but there is a modern university in Dar es Salaam.
Economy. After independence, Tanzania attempted to institute socialism through communal farming villages. Due to various factors, including some resistance to these programs, food production dropped sharply, creating deep problems in the agriculture-based economy. Coffee and cotton are primary exports. Other important exports are cloves (from Zanzibar), pyrethrum, sisal, tobacco and tea. Manufacturing centers around the processing of primary commodities.
History. OLDUVAI GORGE in N Tanzania has the world's earliest known human and pre-human remains. In historical times, the coast and Zanzibar came under Arab

control from the 700s AD. Germany established a mainland protectorate (1891), but after WWI the region passed to Britain by League of Nations mandate. Tanganyika gained independence in 1961, Zanzibar in 1964, and the country was renamed Tanzania in 1965. Under Julius Nyerere, who served as president of Tanzania until 1985 and remained head of the only political party after his retirement, education and health care were greatly expanded. The economy flourished until 1977, when it began to decline due to drought, rapid population growth, mismanagement, the dissolution of the East African Community, and the high cost of Tanzania's 1979 invasion of neighboring Uganda to overthrow dictator Idi Amin Dada. In the mid-1980s, the government also faced a secessionist movement in Zanzibar. Nyerere's successor, Ali Hassan Mwinyi, instituted free-market economic reforms.

TAOISM, ancient Chinese philosophy, in influence second only to CONFUCIANISM, derived chiefly from the book *Tao-te Ching* (3rd century BC) attributed to LAO-TSE. It advocated a contemplative life in accord with nature, unspoiled by intellectual evaluations. Tao ("The Way") was considered impossible to describe save in cryptic imagery. Taoism later became a polytheistic religion.

TAP DANCE, an exhibition dance in which the toes and heels are tapped rapidly against a hard surface. Metal-tipped shoes clarify the complicated rhythms. Tap dancing developed in black communities in the US and on vaudeville stages, reaching a high point in the dancing of Bill Robinson and being carried to more sophisticated level by Fred ASTAIRE.

TAPE RECORDER, instrument for SOUND RECORDING on magnetic tape, and subsequent playback. The tape, consisting of small magnetic particles of iron oxides on a thin plastic film base, is wound from the supply reel to the take-up reel by a rotating capstan which controls the speed. The tape passes in turn: the erase head, which by applying an alternating field reduces the overall magnetization to zero; the recording head; and the playback head. Standard tape speeds are 1⅞, 3¾, 7½, 15 or 30in/s, the higher speeds being used for HIGH-FIDELITY reproduction. Cassettes contain thin tape handily packaged, running at 1⅞in/s. The somewhat larger **cartridges** contain an endless loop of tape on a single reel. Most recorders use two, four or even more tracks side by side on the tape.

TAPESTRY, a fabric woven with colored threads to form a design and used to cover walls and furniture. Warp threads are stretched on a loom, and colored threads, or wefts, are woven over and under them and then compacted (see also WEAVING). Tapestries were known in ancient Egypt, Syria, Persia and China. N Europe's great era of tapestry-making began in the 1300s, notably at Arras in Flanders. It reached a peak in the GOBELIN tapestries of the 1600s. Great painters who have made tapestry designs include Raphael and Rubens. The BAYEUX TAPESTRY is in fact embroidery.

TAPEWORMS, intestinal parasites, so named because they are long and flat, forming the class Cestoda of the flatworm phylum Platyhelminthes. A scolex, or head, only 1.5–2mm (about 0.06in) in diameter is attached to the gut and behind this the body consists of a ribbon of identical flat segments, or proglottids, each containing reproductive organs. These proglottids are budded off from behind the scolex. Mature proglottids containing eggs pass out with the feces where larval stages can infect intermediate hosts.

TAPIRS, a family, Tapiridae, of large brown or black and white ungulates related to RHINOCEROSES. They are plump, thick-skinned vegetarian animals characterized by a short mobile nasal "trunk" and with four toes on the front feet and three on the hind feet. Of four living species, the largest, *Tapirus indicus*, occurs in Malaya, the others being South American.

TAPPAN, Arthur (1786–1865) and **Lewis** (1788–1873), US silk merchants, abolitionists and philanthropists. They cofounded the American Anti-Slavery Society (1833) and formed a rival group in 1840. Arthur helped establish Kenyon and Oberlin colleges. In 1841 Lewis founded the first US commercial credit-rating agency.

TARA, parish in Co. Meath, Ireland, 22 mi NW of Dublin, site of 507ft Tara Hill, a sacred place from c2100 BC. The high kings of Ireland were crowned and had their seat there until c560 AD.

TARANTULA, popular name, originally of the large wolf spider *Lycosa tarantula*, but now used for various unrelated giant SPIDERS throughout the world. All are long and hairy and eat large insects or small vertebrates. Their venom seldom has serious effects on humans.

TARAWA, atoll in the W central Pacific, capital of KIRIBATI. It is the chief port and commercial center. Occupied by Japan in 1942, it was taken by US Marines in 1943.

TARBELL, Ida Minerva (1857–1944), US journalist, a leader of the MUCKRAKERS. Her exposure of malpractice in *The History of* *the Standard Oil Company* (1904) led to successful prosecution of the company in 1911.

TARGUM, an Aramaic translation or paraphrase of the Hebrew scriptures, or Old Testament, usually with a commentary. Some Targums date from c200 BC, when ARAMAIC was replacing Hebrew as an everyday language among many Jews.

TARIFFS, customs duties on exports or, more commonly, imports. The aim is generally to protect home industries from foreign competition, though it may be merely to provide revenue. During the 17th and 18th centuries the European powers created tariff systems that gave their colonies preferential treatment, but Britain's tariffs, by limiting North America's trade, helped provoke the Revolutionary War. In the early 1800s the FREE TRADE movement, bolstered by the economic philosophy of LAISSEZ-FAIRE, helped limit the spread of tariffs. However, US federal tariffs imposed to aid Northern industry damaged the South and contributed to the Civil War. US and European tariffs were moderate in the early 1900s but, after the Great Depression, both the US and UK adopted high tariffs, with a consequent decline in INTERNATIONAL TRADE. In 1947 the US and 22 other nations signed the GENERAL AGREEMENT ON TARIFFS AND TRADE (GATT) aimed at reducing trade discrimination. GATT has only partly achieved this, notably in the "Kennedy Round" (1964–67), involving over 50 nations and a broad range of commodities. By the 1980s, high Common Market tariffs caused food imports and a general trade recession roused fears of revived PROTECTIONISM. (See also ECONOMICS; EUROPEAN FREE TRADE ASSOCIATION.)

TARKINGTON, Newton Booth (1869–1946), US writer famous for his novels reflecting Midwestern life and character, as in his *Penrod* (1914). He worked for *The Saturday Evening Post*, was an Ind. representative (1902–03), and won two Pulitzer prizes (1919, 1922) for *The Magnificent Ambersons* (1918) and *Alice Adams* (1921).

TARLETON, Sir Banastre (1754–1833), English cavalry soldier, commander of the British Legion in the REVOLUTIONARY WAR. Noted for cruelty, he was successful (1799–80) at Charleston, Waxhaws, Camden and Fishing Creek but lost to Gen. Charles MORGAN at COWPENS.

TAROT, pack of 78 PLAYING CARDS used for fortune telling or for the card game *tarok* (tarot or tarocchi). There are four suits each of 14 cards (cups, pentacles, swords and

wands) and a major arcana of 22 cards (also called tarots) which in the card game operate as permanent trumps.

TARQUINIUS, name of the 5th and of the last of Rome's seven semilegendary kings. **Lucius Tarquinius Priscus** (reigned 616–579 BC) built the Temple of Jupiter, Circus Maximus and Cloaca Maxima, crushed Latium and fought the Sabines. He was assassinated. His despotic son or grandson, **Lucius Tarquinius Superbus** (reigned 534–510 BC), murdered his father-in-law Servius Tullius and was expelled by popular revolt after his son's rape of Lucretia (see ROME, ANCIENT).

TARSKI, Alfred (1902–   ), Polish-born US mathematician and logician who was one of the most influential figures in 20th-century philosophy. A professor at the U. of Cal. at Berkeley (1942–68), he made fundamental contributions to the fields of metamathematics, semantics and symbolic logic.

TARTAGLIA, Niccolò (1499–1557), Italian Renaissance mathematician who discovered a method of solving cubic EQUATIONS. He is also known for an encyclopedic work on elementary mathematics and for his contributions to BALLISTICS.

TARTAN, the checkered fabric of Scotland's native dress. Each clan is ascribed a particular tartan, though often in more than one variety—the hunting tartans are usually somber blues and greens, while reds generally predominate in the dress tartans. The authenticity of ascriptions to clans is questioned, and some tartans are of comparatively recent origin.

TARTARS. See TATARS.

TARTINI, Giuseppe (1692–1770), Italian composer and violinist. He founded (1728) a school of violin playing at Padua, improved the violin and playing techniques, and contributed to musical theory. His works include some 200 concertos and 200 violin sonatas, notably *The Devil's Trill*.

TASHKENT, capital of the Uzbek SSR and fourth largest city in USSR, located in Chirchik Valley W of Chatkal Mts. One of the oldest cities in Asia, it was an important trading center for Arab, Muslim and Mongol empires. Major products are textiles and agricultural machinery. Rebuilt after a devastating earthquake in 1966, it is an important cultural center. Pop 2,030,000.

TASMAN, Abel Janszoon (c1603–1659), Dutch sailor and S Pacific explorer. Sailing from Java in Dutch East India Company service (1642–43, 1644), he discovered Tasmania and New Zealand (1642), which he thought were parts of Australia, then Tonga and Fiji (1643).

TASMANIANS, now extinct native population of Tasmania, perhaps once the native race of Australia and physically and culturally quite unlike the AUSTRALIAN ABORIGINES. The pure stock were extinguished 1804–1876, although a few halfbreeds still exist.

TASS (Telegraph Agency of the Soviet Union), the state monopoly news agency of the USSR. Founded in 1925, it is managed by the Propaganda Department of the Communist Party's Central Committee.

TASSO, Torquato (1544–1595), Italy's major late Renaissance poet, a master of lyrical, sensuous, often mournful verse. His works include the pastoral drama *Aminta* (1573) and his masterpiece *Jerusalem Delivered* (completed 1575), an epic based on the First Crusade.

TASTE, special sense concerned with the differentiation of basic modalities of food or other substances in the mouth; receptors are distributed over the surface of the TONGUE and are able to distinguish salt, sweet, sour, bitter and possibly water as primary tastes. Much of what is colloquially termed taste is actually SMELL, perception of odors reaching the olfactory EPITHELIUM via the naso-pharynx. Receptors for sweet are concentrated at the tip of the tongue, for salt and sour along the sides, with bitter mainly at the back. Taste nerve impulses pass via the BRAIN stem to the cortex.

TATARS or **Tartars,** Turkic-speaking people of the USSR, where some 4,500,000 live in the Tatar Autonomous SSR, along the Volga R, in the Ural Mts. and the Uzbek and Kazakh SSRs. Most are Sunnite Muslims. Tatar also describes the E Mongolian tribes, part of the GOLDEN HORDE, which seized much of Russia in the 1200s (see MONGOL EMPIRE).

TATE, Allen (1899–1979), distinguished US writer, critic and teacher. He edited the literary magazine *Fugitive* and advocated the "new criticism," with its stress on a work's intrinsic qualities. His own work includes several collections of poetry and essays, biographies and a novel.

TATI, Jacques (Jacques Tatischeff; 1908-1982), French film director, writer, and actor who followed *Jour de Fête* (1949) with a series of comedies in which he played the innocent M. Hulot.

TATLIN, Vladimir (1885–1956), Russian painter and sculptor, leader of CONSTRUCTIVISM. Influenced by PICASSO's cubist reliefs, he made in 1913 abstract reliefs of tin, wood, glass and plaster and *Corner-reliefs* (1915) suspended on wire. In 1920 he planned a symbolic monument to the Third INTERNATIONAL.

TATTOOING, decorating the body by injecting colored pigment beneath the surface of the skin, a method of personal adornment used throughout history, but especially elaborated among the Maori.

TAURUS MOUNTAINS, a range in S Turkey, parallel with the Mediterranean coast and extending NE as the Anti-Taurus. It has many peaks of 10,000ft to 12,000ft. The range is well wooded and has various mineral deposits.

TAUSSIG, Helen Brooke (1898–), US pediatrician and cardiologist who developed the "blue baby operation" (1945; with surgeon Alfred Blalock) which increased blood circulation to the lungs and stimulated research on the surgical correction of congenital heart defects.

TAVERNER, John (c1495–1545), English composer whose ornate masses and motets are among the finest early Tudor music. After 1530 he turned from music to suppressing monasteries as an agent of Thomas Cromwell.

TAWNEY, Richard Henry (1880–1962), British historian and social theorist. His best known book, *Religion and the Rise of Capitalism* (1926), connects the hard work and individualism of the Protestants of N Europe in the 16th and 17th centuries with the growth of capitalism there.

TAXATION, the raising of revenue to pay for government expenditure. Broadly speaking, a tax can be described as direct or indirect: income tax is paid directly to the government, but sales taxes are collected indirectly through government charges on goods or services. A tax is also progressive or regressive: income tax is usually progressive (its rate rises as the taxable sum increases); sales taxes tend to be regressive (their burden decreases as the taxpayer's income increases).

Modern taxation serves three purposes. It meets government expenditure on public services, administration and defense. In some countries social justice is promoted by the redistribution of income: the rich are taxed at higher rates than the poor, who may receive grants from revenue. Control of the economy is achieved by adjusting direct or indirect taxes to curb consumption or encourage investment. It is often difficult to achieve all three objectives equally effectively.

In the US the Constitution at first required that taxes be levied in proportion to the population, and that indirect taxes must be uniform throughout all states. An INCOME TAX, which does not meet these requirements, was permitted by the 16th Amendment in 1913, and came to replace TARIFFS and excises as a principal source of revenue. During and after WWI, the federal government developed its individual and corporation income taxes, expanded excises, and introduced an estate INHERITANCE TAX and a social security payroll levy. By WWII federal taxes had reached new peaks and become important in regulating the economy, being used to curb inflation and prevent profiteering. The major form of state and local taxation is now the *property tax*; states also tax gasoline, retail sales and automobiles, and many states and cities tax income. A taxpayers' revolt against high property taxes began in Cal. in 1978, when voters approved a state constitutional amendment restricting taxes on real property, and the revolt soon spread to other states. It also took the form of organized opposition to high federal income tax, which culminated in the election of Ronald REAGAN as president in 1980. (See INCOME TAX.)

TAXATION WITHOUT REPRESENTATION, in US history, a cause of the REVOLUTIONARY WAR. In 1765 the British Parliament passed the STAMP ACT, obliging colonists to buy revenue stamps for documents and newspapers. This provoked the slogan "taxation without representation is tyranny," and a colonial congress in New York rejected as unconstitutional taxes imposed without the people's consent.

TAX COURT, US federal tribunal established in 1924 to rule on disputes between taxpayers and the INTERNAL REVENUE SERVICE. Most decisions may be appealed to the US Court of Appeals.

TAXIDERMY, stuffing animal skins to make lifelike replicas. Taxidermy is now practiced mainly in large museums, though it originated in the production of hunting trophies; nowadays, rather than stuffing, the animal's form is duplicated and the skin stretched over.

TAXONOMY, the science of classifying PLANTS and ANIMALS. The theory of EVOLUTION states that organisms come into being as a result of gradual change and that closely related organisms are descended from a relatively recent common ancestor. One of the main aims of taxonomy is to reflect such changes in a classification of groups, or taxa, which are arranged in a hierarchy such that small taxa contain organisms that are closely related and larger taxa contain organisms that are more distantly related. Taxa commonly employed are (in their conventional typography and starting with the largest): Kingdom,

Phylum, Class, Order, Family, *Genus* and *species.*

TAYLOR, A(lan) J(ohn) P(ercivale) (1906–   ), British historian known for his iconoclastic interpretations of the origins of European wars of the 19th and 20th centuries. His books include *The Struggle for Mastery in Europe, 1848–1918* (1954), *The Origins of the Second World War* (1961) and *Revolutions and Revolutionaries* (1980).

TAYLOR, Edward (c1642–1729), American Puritan clergyman, arguably North America's foremost colonial poet. His devotional verse combines homely diction with the striking imagery of the METAPHYSICAL POETS. His works were rediscovered only in 1937 (*Poetical Works,* 1939).

TAYLOR, Frederick Winslow (1856–1915), US mechanical engineer who pioneered the principles of scientific management. He introduced TIME-AND-MOTION STUDY and held that careful analysis of every factory operation by man and machine alike was necessary for operational efficiency. These theories came to be known as **Taylorism**.

TAYLOR, Jeremy (1613–1667), English Anglican bishop whose devotional writings are considered masterpieces of their kind.

TAYLOR, John (1753–1824), US political theorist and agricultural reformer, known as "John Taylor of Caroline." An early exponent of STATES' RIGHTS, he was thrice elected US senator from Va. (1792, 1803, 1822).

TAYLOR, (Joseph) Deems (1885–1966), US composer. During his long career in music he worked as critic, radio commentator, network consultant and president of the American Society of Composers, Authors and Publishers (ASCAP). His works include the operas *The King's Henchman* (1926) and *Peter Ibbetson* (1931).

TAYLOR, Maxwell Davenport (1901–1987), US general who largely organized the army's first airborne units in WWII. He commanded the Eighth Army in Korea 1953–55, headed the US and UN Far East commands 1954–55, was US army chief of staff 1955–59 and ambassador to Vietnam 1964–65.

TAYLOR, Paul (1930–   ), US dancer and choreographer. He danced (1953–61) for Merce CUNNINGHAM and Martha GRAHAM while choreographing avant-garde dances for his own company, formed in 1954.

TAYLOR, Telford (1908–   ), US legal scholar and attorney, who was chief US prosecutor at the Nuremberg war crimes trials. A law professor at Columbia University (1958–76), he wrote several books including *Nuremberg and Vietnam* (1970), *Courts of Terror* (1976) and *Munich: The Price of Peace* (1979).

TAYLOR, Zachary (1784–1850), 12th US president (1849–50). Known as "Old Rough and Ready" to his soldiers, Taylor was a bold and resourceful general in the Mexican War and one of the most popular presidents of his period. Nevertheless, his brief term in the White House—he died after only 16 months in office—has been all but forgotten, though he did take a bold stand against the extension of slavery, the one burning issue of his term. Three things shaped his life: he was 40 years a soldier (doing much to open the West to settlement); his parents belonged to the wealthy planting aristocracy of old Va.; and he himself was brought up in Ky., on the frontiers of an expanding nation. He fought in the WAR OF 1812 and the BLACK HAWK WAR (1832), and subdued the SEMINOLE INDIANS in Fla.; his defeat of General SANTA ANNA's forces in the MEXICAN WAR made him a national hero.

Standing as a Whig, he became president in 1849; his term was marked by the CLAYTON-BULWER TREATY. More important, the acquisition of vast new territories threatened to upset the precarious balance between slave states and free (15 of each) established by the MISSOURI COMPROMISE of 1820. Determined to prevent expansion of slavery even though it might preserve the Union, and undoubtedly influenced by such advisors as William H. SEWARD, Taylor refused to compromise, even if it meant war. His sudden death in 1850 postponed the issue.

TAY-SACHS DISEASE, an inherited fatal disorder found primarily among Jews of or from eastern Europe. Among this group, as many as one out of 30 may be carriers. The disease is caused by a deficiency or defect in the enzyme hexosaminidase A, or sometimes in both hexosaminidase A and B, which allows fatty substances (sphyngolipids) to accumulate in the brain. The condition usually appears at 3 to 6 months of age and is characterized by mental retardation, blindness, muscular weakness, and a cherry-red spot on the retina of each eye. Death commonly occurs between the ages of 3 and 5 years. Individuals capable of transmitting this disease to their children can be detected by medical screening procedures.

TCHAIKOVSKY, Peter Ilich (1840–1893), Russian composer. He studied with Anton RUBINSTEIN, became professor at Moscow Conservatory and gave concerts of his own music in Europe and the US. His gift for melody and brilliant orchestration, plus the drama, excitement and emotional intensity of his music, make him the most popular of all composers. Works such as the 1st Piano Concerto (1875), the Violin Concerto (1878) and *Pathétique* Symphony (No. 6; 1893) are known and loved by millions, and ballet owes much of its popularity to his *Swan Lake* (1876), *Sleeping Beauty* (1889) and *Nutcracker* (1892). His operas include *Eugene Onegin* (1879) and *The Queen of Spades* (1890).

TCHELITCHEW, Pavel (1898–1957), Russian-born US painter. He designed ballets, notably for DIAGHILEV, but is best known for such studies of perspective and metamorphosis as *Hide-and-Seek* (1941).

TEA, the cured and dried young leaves and tips of the tea plant (*Thea sinensis*) which are made into a drink popular throughout the world. Tea has been drunk in China since early times, but it was not until the early 1600s that the Dutch introduced it into Europe. Although expensive, it soon became fashionable. In the UK and the British colonies, the East India Company enjoyed a monopoly of the China tea trade until 1833; it was the attempt of the British government to levy a tax on tea imports into the American colonies that led to the BOSTON TEA PARTY of 1773. Today, the chief producers are India and Sri Lanka (Ceylon). Tea contains the stimulant CAFFEINE. The term tea is also used to describe many other local drinks produced from the leaves of a vast array of plants. Family: Theaceae.

TEAK, a deciduous tree (*Tectona grandis*) whose wood is one of the most valuable in the world. Teaks grow in tropical climates from E India to Malaysia. The hard, oily wood is used for house construction, furniture, railroad ties, etc. Several other trees produce a similar hardwood also called teak. Family: Verbenaceae.

TEAMSTERS (International Brotherhood of Teamsters, Chauffeurs, Warehousemen and Helpers of America), largest US labor union. Formed by an amalgamation in 1903, it has about 2,300,000 members, largely in trucking and warehousing. Daniel TOBIN was president 1907–52. Several recent presidents were jailed for corruption and in 1957 the Teamsters were expelled from the AFL-CIO. In 1988 the US Department of Justice filed a civil racketeering suit seeking to oust the Teamsters' president and the 18-member executive board because of their purported ties to organized crime.

TEAPOT DOME, scandal over government malpractice under President HARDING. The naval oil reserve at Teapot Dome, Wyo., was leased in 1922 by agreement of secretary of the interior Albert Fall to the Mammoth Oil Co. with no competitive bidding. A Senate investigation followed and the lease was canceled. Fall was later convicted of receiving another bribe in a similar transaction.

TEAR GAS, volatile substance that incapacitates for a time by powerfully irritating the eyes, provoking tears. Various halogenated organic compounds are used, including α–chloracetophenome (Mace gas or CN), and the even more potent CS gas. They are packed in grenades and used for riot control. (See also CHEMICAL AND BIOLOGICAL WARFARE.)

TEARS, watery secretions of the lacrymal GLANDS situated over the EYES which provide continuous lubrication and protection of cornea and sclera. A constant flow runs across the surface of the eye to the nasolacrymal duct at the inner corner, where tears drain into the NOSE. Excess tears produced in states of high emotion and conjunctival or corneal irritation overflow over the lower eyelid.

TECHNOCRACY, government by scientists and technologists who recognize only the dictates of technology. Arising from the ideas of Thorstein VEBLEN and engineer Howard Scott, a radical Technocracy movement roused wide discussion in the early 1930s in the US.

TECTONICS, an area of study in geology dealing with the development of the broader structural features of the EARTH and their deformational origins. (See also PLATE TECTONICS.)

TECUMSEH (c1768–1813), great SHAWNEE INDIAN chief, warrior and orator who sought after the Revolution to unite Midwestern tribes against encroachment of their homelands. Despite British and widespread Indian support the effort failed with defeat of his brother TENSKWATAWA at the battle of TIPPECANOE (1811). Tecumseh died fighting for the British at the battle of the Thames in Ontario.

TEDDER, Arthur William Tedder, 1st Baron (1890–1967), British air marshal. He was commander of the Royal Air Force in the Middle East 1940–43, then headed the Mediterranean Air Command and was deputy Supreme Allied Commander under Eisenhower, helping to plan and carry out the invasion of Europe.

TEETH, the specialized hard structures used for biting and chewing food. Their numbers vary in different species and at different ages, but in most cases an immature set of teeth (milk teeth) is replaced during growth by a permanent set. In man the latter consists of 32 teeth comprising 8 incisors, 4 canines, 8 premolars and 12 molars, of which the rearmost are the late-erupting wisdom teeth. ("Dentition" refers to the numbers and arrangement of the teeth in a species.) Each tooth consists of a crown, or part above the gum line, and a root, or insertion into the BONE of the jaw. The outer surface of the crowns is covered by a thin layer of enamel, the hardest animal tissue. This overlies the dentine, a substance similar to bone, and in the center of each tooth is the pulp which contains blood vessels and nerves. The **incisors** are developed for biting off food with a scissor action, while the **canines** are particularly developed in some species for maintaining a hold on an object. The **molars** and **premolars** are adapted for chewing and macerating food, which partly involves side-to-side movement of one jaw over the other. Maldevelopment and caries of teeth are the commonest problems encountered in DENTISTRY.

TEHERAN or Tehran, capital and largest city of Iran, lies S of the Elburz Mts at about 3,800ft. Dating from the 1100s and Mogul destruction of nearby Ray (1220), it became capital in 1788. Modern Teheran is a manufacturing, transportation, and cultural center. The city was the center of the Iranian revolution of the later 1970s and early 1980s. Pop 5,734,000.

TEHERAN CONFERENCE, inter-allied conference of WWII, held in Teheran Nov.–Dec. 1943 and attended by Stalin, Roosevelt and Churchill. Important items were coordination of landings in France with a Soviet offensive against Germany from the E, future Russian entry into the war against Japan, and agreement on Iran's future independence.

TEILHARD DE CHARDIN, Pierre (1881–1955), French Jesuit, philosopher and paleontologist. He was in China 1923–46, where he studied Peking Man (see PREHISTORIC MAN). *The Phenomenon of Man* (1938–40) attempted to reconcile Christianity and science with a theory of man's evolution toward final spiritual unity. His superiors held his views to be unorthodox and warned against them; fame came to him and his ideas only posthumously.

TEKTITES, controversial, nonvolcanic glassy objects, usually of less than 100mm diameter, found only in certain parts of the world. Most are rich in silica: they resemble obsidian, though have less water. Despite suggestions that they are of extraterrestrial, particularly lunar, origin, it seems most likely that they have resulted from meteoritic impacts on terrestrial rock in the remote past.

TEL AVIV-JAFFA, second-largest city in Israel, on the Mediterranean coast NW of Jerusalem. It is a modern city-port and Israel's chief manufacturing center as well as a tourist resort. Tel Aviv was Israel's first capital, from 1948 to 1950 (when Jaffa was incorporated). Pop (city) 322,800; (metro) 1,607,800.

TELEGRAPH, electrical apparatus for sending coded messages. The term was first applied to Claude Chappe's SEMAPHORE. Experiments began on electric telegraphs after the discovery (1819) that a magnetic needle was deflected by a current in a nearby wire. In 1837 W. F. Cooke and Charles WHEATSTONE patented a system using six wires and five pointers which moved in pairs to indicate letters in a diamond-shaped array. It was used on English railroads. In the same year Samuel MORSE, in partnership with Alfred Vail, and helped by Joseph HENRY, patented a telegraph system using MORSE CODE in the US. The first intercity line was inaugurated in 1844. At first the receiver embossed or printed the code symbols but this was soon replaced by a sounding device. In 1858 Wheatstone invented a high-speed automatic Morse telegraph, using punched paper tape in transmission. The telex system, using teletypewriters, is now most popular. In 1872 Jean-Maurice-Émile Baudot invented a multiplexing system for sharing the time on each transmission line between several operators. Telegraph signals are now transmitted not only by wires and land lines but also by submarine cables and radio.

TELEMANN, Georg Philipp (1681–1767), versatile and prolific German composer, a master of all the musical forms of his day. His oratorios and other sacred music, over 40 operas and many instrumental works, are noted for their liveliness of rhythm and tunefulness.

TELEOLOGY (from Greek *telos*, end), the study of an action, event or thing with reference to its purpose or end. PLATO and ARISTOTLE argued that the purpose, perfection and good of a thing, which Aristotle called its "final cause," was the ultimate explanation of the thing. The teleological view of nature has declined since the rise of science. The teleological argument, or argument "from design," argues from the order and perfection of

nature to the existence of a divine Creator.
TELEPATHY. See ESP.
TELEPHONE, apparatus for transmission and reproduction of sound by means of frequency electric waves. Precursors in telecommunication included the megaphone, the speaking tube and the string telephone—all of which transmitted sound as such—and the TELEGRAPH, working by electrical impulses. Although the principles on which it is based had been known 40 years earlier, the telephone was not invented until 1876, when Alexander Graham BELL obtained his patent. Bell's transmitter worked by the voltage induced in a coil by a piece of iron attached to a vibrating diaphragm. The same apparatus, working in reverse, was used as a receiver. Modern receivers use the same principle, but it was soon found that a more sensitive transmitter was needed, and by 1878 the carbon MICROPHONE (invented by Thomas EDISON) was used. A battery-powered DC circuit connected microphone and receiver. In 1878 the first commercial exchange was opened in New Haven, Conn., and local telephone networks spread rapidly in the US and elsewhere. Technical improvements made for longer-distance transmission included the use of hard-drawn copper wire, underground dry-core cable, and two-wire circuits to avoid the cross-talk that occurred when the circuit was completed via ground. Distortion in long circuits was overcome by introducing loading coils at intervals to increase the inductance. The introduction also of repeaters, or AMPLIFIERS, made long-distance telephone calls possible. Today, microwave radio links, and COMMUNICATIONS SATELLITES and OPTICAL FIBERS are used. Telephone subscribers are connected to a local exchange, these in turn being linked by trunk lines connecting a hierarchy of switching centers so that alternative routes may be used. When a call is dialed, each digit is coded as pulses or pairs of tones which work electromechanical or electronic switches.
TELESCOPE, Optical, instrument used to detect or examine distant objects. It consists of a series of lenses and mirrors capable of producing a magnified image and of collecting more light than the unaided eye. The refracting telescope essentially consists of a tube with a LENS system at each end. Light from a distant object first strikes the objective lens which produces an inverted image at its focal point. In the terrestrial telescope the second lens system, the eyepiece, produces a magnified, erect image of the focal image, but in instruments for astronomical use, where the image is

usually recorded photographically, the image is not reinverted, thus reducing light losses. The reflecting telescope uses a concave mirror to gather and focus the incoming light, the focal image being viewed using many different combinations of lenses and mirrors in the various types of instrument, each seeking to reduce different optical ABERRATIONS. The size of a telescope is measured in terms of the diameter of its objective. Up to about 30cm diameter the resolving power (the ability to distinguish finely separated points) increases with size but for larger objectives the only gain is in light gathering. A 500cm telescope can thus detect much fainter sources but resolve no better than a 30cm instrument. Because mirrors can be supported more easily than large lenses, the largest astronomical telescopes are all reflectors.

Currently, the world's largest telescope, completed in 1974, is a 6m (236in) reflector at Zelenchuskaya in the northern Caucasus, USSR. The largest US instrument is the Hale Telescope on Mount Palomar in California. Completed in 1948, it has a 5m (200in) mirror. There are about a dozen telescopes worldwide with mirrors of at least 2.54m (100in) diameter.

The US is now building a telescope with a 10m (394in) mirror atop the Mauna Kea volcano in Hawaii that is scheduled for completion in the 1990s. A consortium of W European countries is planning to build a telescope in northern Chile with four mirrors whose combined light-gathering power will be equal to that of a single mirror 16m (630in) in diameter. (See also RADIO TELESCOPE.)

TELEVISION, the communication of moving pictures between distant points using wire or radio transmissions. In television broadcasting, centrally prepared programs are transmitted to a multitude of individual receivers, though closed-circuit industrial and education applications are of increasing importance. Often, a sound signal is transmitted together with the picture information. In outline, a television CAMERA is used to form an optical image of the scene to be transmitted and convert it into electrical signals. These are amplified and transmitted, either directly by cable (closed-circuit) or as radio waves, to a receiver where the scene is reconstituted as an optical image on the screen of a CATHODE-RAY TUBE. Today most television cameras are of the image orthicon or vidicon types, these having largely replaced the earlier iconoscope and orthicon designs. Since it is impossible to transmit a whole image at once, the image formed by the

optical LENS system of the camera is scanned as a sequence of 525 horizontal lines, the varying light value along each being converted into a fluctuating electrical signal and the whole scan being repeated 30 times a second to allow an impression of motion to be conveyed without noticeable flicker. The viewer sees the image as a whole because of the persistence of VISION effect. In color television, the light entering the camera is analyzed into red, green and blue components—corresponding to the three primary COLORS of light—and electrical information concerning the saturation of each is superimposed on the ordinary luminance (brightness) monochrome signal. In the color receiver this information is recovered and used to control the three electron beams which, projected through a shadow mask (a screen containing some 200,000 minute, precisely positioned holes), excite the mosaic of red, green and blue PHOSPHOR dots which reproduce the color image. All three color television systems in use around the world allow monochrome receivers to work normally from the color transmissions.

Development of television. Early hopes of practical television date back to the early days of the electric TELEGRAPH, but their realization had to await several key developments. First was the discovery of the photoconductive properties of selenium, followed by the development of the cathode-ray tube (1897) and the electron tube (1904). The first practical television system, demonstrated in London in 1926 by J. L. Baird, used a mechanical scanning method devised by Paul Nipkow in 1884. Electronic scanning dates from 1923 when ZWORYKIN filed a patent for his iconoscope camera tube. Television broadcasting began in London in 1936 using a 405-line standard. In the US public broadcasting began in 1941, with regular color broadcasting in 1954. US television broadcasts are made in the VHF (Channels 2–13) and the UHF (Channels 14–83) regions of the RF spectrum (see RADIO). (See also ELECTRONICS.)

TELL, William, legendary 14th-century Swiss hero. Ordered by the Austrian bailiff Gessler to bow to a hat on a pole as a symbol of Austrian supremacy, he refused and was forced to shoot an apple from his son's head with a crossbow: in this almost impossible task he succeeded. Later he killed Gessler.

TELL EL-AMARNA, site of Akhetaton, capital of the Egyptian pharaoh AKHENATON. It lies on the E bank of the Nile R 60mi N of Asyut. Excavation of this short-lived city revealed naturalistic paintings and reliefs and, in 1887, a famous series of about 300 CUNEIFORM tablets.

TELLER, Edward (1908–), Hungarian-born US nuclear physicist who worked with FERMI on nuclear FISSION at the start of the MANHATTAN PROJECT, but who is best known for his fundamental work on, and advocacy of, the HYDROGEN BOMB.

TELSTAR, US artificial SATELLITE, launched July 10, 1962, the first to relay TELEVISION signals across the Atlantic. It weighed 170lb. Broadcasts ended (Feb. 1963) after Van Allen belt radiation damaged some of the 1,000 transistors.

TELUGU, a DRAVIDIAN language of S India. There are some 40 million Andhras (Telugu speakers), mainly in Andhra Pradesh. The extensive literature is written in a script derived from SANSKRIT.

TEMPERA, painting technique in which dry pigments are "tempered" or bound with egg yolks and water. Applied to a panel coated with gesso, in thin, drying layers, it produces a luminous mat surface. Especially popular 1200–1500 in Italy, it has been revived by modern artists.

TEMPERATURE, the degree of hotness or coldness of a body, as measured quantitatively by thermometers. The various practical scales used are arbitrary: the Fahrenheit scale was originally based on the values 0°F for an equal ice-salt mixture, 32°F for the freezing point of water and 96°F for normal human body temperature. Thermometer readings are arbitrary also because they depend on the particular physical properties of the thermometric fluid etc. There are now certain primary calibration points corresponding to the boiling, freezing, or melting points of particular substances, whose values are fixed by convention. The thermodynamic, or absolute, temperature scale, is not arbitrary; starting at ABSOLUTE ZERO and graduated in kelvins, it is defined with respect to an ideal reversible heat engine working on a Carnot cycle between two temperatures, T_1 and T_2. If Q_1 is the heat received at the higher temperature T_1, and Q_2 the heat lost at the lower temperature T_2, then T_1/T_2 is defined equal to Q_1/Q_2. Such absolute temperature is independent of the properties of particular substances, and is a basic THERMODYNAMIC function. It is an intensive property, unlike HEAT, which is an extensive property—that is, the temperature of a body is independent of its mass or nature; it is thus only indirectly related to the heat content (internal energy) of the body. Heat flows always from a higher temperature to a lower. On the molecular scale, temperature may be defined in terms of the statistical distribution of the kinetic energy of the molecules.

TEMPERATURE, Body. Animals fall into two classes: COLD-BLOODED ANIMALS, which have the same temperature as their surroundings, and WARM-BLOODED ANIMALS, which have an approximately constant temperature maintained by a "thermostat" in the brain. The normal temperature for most such animals lies between 95°F (35°C) and 104°F (40°C); it is greatly reduced during HIBERNATION. For man, the normal mouth temperature usually lies between 97°F (36°C) and 99°F (37.2°C), the average being about 98.6°F (37.0°C). It fluctuates daily, and in women monthly. The temperature setting is higher than normal in FEVER. When the body is too hot, the blood vessels near the skin expand to carry more blood and to lose heat by radiation and convection, and the sweat glands produce PERSPIRATION which cools by evaporation. When the body is too cold, the blood vessels near the skin contract, the metabolic rate increases and shivering occurs to produce more heat. Fat under the skin, and body hair (FUR in other animals), help to keep heat in. If these defenses against cold prove inadequate, **hypothermia** results: body temperature falls, functions become sluggish, and death may result. Controlled cooling may be used in surgery to reduce the need for oxygen.

TEMPERING, heat-treatment process in METALLURGY, used to toughen an ALLOY, notably STEEL. The metal is heated slowly to the desired temperature, held there while stresses are relieved and excess solution precipitates out from the supersaturated solid solution, and then cooled, usually by rapid quenching. The temperature determines the properties produced, and may be chosen to retain hardness.

TEMPLE, Shirley Jane (1928–), US child film star and later a politician. She made her movie debut at three and became pheonomenally popular in such films of the 1930s as *Little Miss Marker* and *The Little Colonel.* She retired from films in 1949. After working on television in the 1950s Shirley Temple Black (her married name) took up Republican politics. She became a US delegate to the UN in 1969, ambassador to Ghana in 1975, and US Chief of Protocol 1976. *Child Star* (1988) is her autobiography.

TEMPLE, William (1881–1944), British churchman, archbishop of York (1929–42) and of Canterbury (1942–44). He was active in social and economic matters and worked toward the formation of the World Council of Churches. His father, **Frederick**

Temple (1821–1902), was also archbishop of Canterbury (1896–1902).

TEMPLE, a (usually large) building for religious worship. The Jewish temple, a successor to the tabernacle, was envisaged by King DAVID and built by SOLOMON at Jerusalem, becoming the central shrine where alone SACRIFICE could legally be offered. This First Temple was destroyed by the Babylonian invasion in 586 BC. The Second Temple was built in 520 BC and was used until HEROD the Great built the most splendid and last temple, destroyed by the Romans in 70 AD.

TENANT, a person who has temporary occupation or use of another person's real property (house or apartment) usually under terms spelled out in a lease. A lease may run for a year or more; to avoid mistakes or misunderstandings it should describe the premises being rented. If the premises are in an apartment building having a garage, laundry room and storage areas, the tenant's right to use these facilities should be specified, along with any extra charges for their use. A tenant cannot sublease a house or apartment to another person (a subtenant) unless the owner (landlord) gives written permission, and the tenant remains responsible for the subtenant's obligations to the landlord. A lease may specify certain other restrictions and responsibilities, e.g., regarding pets or noise.

TEN COMMANDMENTS, or the **Decalogue,** the moral laws delivered by God to Moses on Mt. Sinai, as recorded in the Bible (Exodus 20:2–17; Deuteronomy 5:6–21). They provide the foundation for Jewish and Christian teaching.

TENDON, fibrous structure formed at the ends of most MUSCLES, which transmits the force of contraction to the point of action (usually a BONE). They facilitate mechanical advantage and allow bulky power muscles to be situated away from small bones concerned with fine movements, as in the hands.

TENERIFE, largest of the Spanish CANARY ISLANDS off NW Africa. The 500,000 people on its 795sq mi (Pico de Teide, 12,198ft) engage in farming and tourism. Santa Cruz de Tenerife is the capital.

TENG HSIAO-PING (Deng Xiaoping; 1904?–   ), Chinese political leader. A life-long revolutionary who joined the Chinese Communist Party in the 1920s, Teng became the party's secretary general in the 1950s. During the Cultural Revolution of the 1960s he was dismissed from his post, but he again emerged as a top aide to Premier Chou En-lai in the 1970s.

After the death of Mao Tse-tung in 1976 Teng became China's most prominent leader although nominally he was only vice chairman of the party. Rejecting both Soviet and Maoist policies, he embarked upon a program of economic reforms that produced dramatic results in agriculture though not in industry. He also opened China to foreign trade and investment. Teng sought to replace aging party conservatives with younger, reform-minded pragmatists. In 1987 he resigned from the party's Central Committee, by his example compelling other aged members also to step down. However, he retained his chairmanship of the party's military committee, which in effect made him head of the army.

TENIERS, David, the younger (1610–1690), Flemish painter. A master colorist, he studied under his father, David Teniers the elder (1587–1649), and became one of the most famous, sought-after and prolific painters of his time. His over 2,000 surviving works mainly comprise genre scenes of peasant life, still lifes and landscapes.

TENNENT, Gilbert (1703–1764), American Presbyterian clergyman, a leader of the GREAT AWAKENING. He attacked his more conservative colleagues as religious formalists with such vigor and disregard for authority that the Presbyterian Church became divided for 17 years (1741–58).

TENNESSEE, state of the south central US, bordered on the N by Ky. and Va., E by N.C., S by Ga., Ala., and Miss., and W by Ark. and Mo. across the Mississippi R. It is considered one of the border states between North and South.

Land. It forms a narrow parallelogram extending from the Mississippi R in the W to the Blue Ridge region (with the GREAT SMOKY MOUNTAINS and Clingmans Dome, 6,642ft). Other regions include the Appalachian ridge-and-valley farming region, the coal-rich Cumberland Plateau and the fertile central Nashville Basin bounded by a broad Highland Rim. Farther W the N Gulf Coastal Plain slopes down to the alluvial Mississippi Bottoms. Dams on the Tennessee and Cumberland rivers have formed many lakes (including Kentucky Lake, 247sq mi). The climate is humid (average 50in annual precipitation) and temperate.

People. Over 50% of the population now lives in the metropolitan areas of Memphis, NASHVILLE, Chattanooga and Knoxville. Most Tennesseans are native-born. Blacks constitute about 16% of the population.

Economy. Tennessee is now a predominantly industrial state. Its industries produce

Name of state: Tennessee
Capital: Nashville
Statehood: June 1, 1796 (16th state)
Familiar name: Volunteer State, Big Bend State
Area: 42,244sq mi
Population: 4,803,000
Elevation: Highest—6,642ft., Clingmans Dome. Lowest—182ft., Mississippi River
Motto: Agriculture and Commerce
State flower: Iris
State bird: Mockingbird
State tree: Tulip poplar
State song: "Tennessee Waltz"

chemicals, foodstuffs, electronics, textiles, and metal products. Research centers include OAK RIDGE (atomic energy). Much of the state's electricity is derived from the TENNESSEE VALLEY AUTHORITY, which speeded changeover from a primary-products to a manufacturing economy. Mining (stone, zinc, phosphate, coal), livestock (notably cattle and thoroughbred horses), and tobacco, cotton and corn contribute significantly to the economic base.

History. Among Indians encountered by DE SOTO and later white explorers were the CHEROKEE, CHICKASAW and SHAWNEE. The region was ceded to England by the Treaty of PARIS (1763). Settlers drew up North America's first written constitution, the Watauga Association, in 1772 and formed the independent state of Franklin (1784–88). Bitterly divided over slavery, Tenn., the last Southern state to join the Confederates and the first to rejoin the Union, was the site of major Civil War battles. It has provided three US presidents: Andrew JACKSON, James K. POLK and Andrew JOHNSON. During the 1940s and '50s, Tennessee was transformed from an agricultural state to a basically urbanized, manufacturing state; and with its expanding economy, and generally more liberal attitudes than neighboring states, it emerged as a leader of the revitalized "New South." A number of government scandals in the 1970s receded in the political stability and economic growth of the 1980s, when many new businesses, including several automakers, were attracted to the state. In presidential elections 1968–88, Tennessee voted Republican in 1968–72 and 1980–88.

TENNESSEE RIVER, principal tributary of the Ohio R. Formed by the junction of Holston and French Broad rivers near Knoxville, Tenn., it flows SW into Ala., then NW and N back across Tenn. and into Ky. It drains some 40,000sq mi. On its 652mi length are many dams and power facilities under the control of the TENNESSEE VALLEY AUTHORITY.

TENNESSEE VALLEY AUTHORITY (TVA), US federal agency responsible for developing the water and other resources of the Tennessee R Valley, established (1933) as one of the early measures of Roosevelt's NEW DEAL. The Authority has 26 major dams on the Tennessee R and its tributaries. The dams and reservoirs have made it possible to eliminate major flooding. Locks make the Tennessee navigable throughout, and TVA hydroelectric and steam plants provide most of the region's electricity. TVA projects have involved also conservation, agriculture and forestry.

TENNIEL, Sir John (1820–1914), English artist noted for his illustrations for Lewis CARROLL's *Alice's Adventures in Wonderland* and *Through the Looking-Glass,* and for hundreds of political cartoons for the English satirical magazine, *Punch* (1850–1901).

TENNIS, racket game played on a rectangular court by two or four players. The court, divided by painted lines into sections, is bisected by a net 3½ft high; the object is to hit the hollow ball (of cloth-covered rubber, about 2½in in diameter and 2oz in weight) over the net into the opposite court such that the opposing player is unable to return it. The racket has a metal or laminated wood frame with gut or nylon strings forming an oval "head," is about 27in long and weighs 12oz–1lb. Tennis originated in 15th-century France as indoor *court* tennis, and took its present form, *lawn* tennis, in 1870. It was first played in the US 1874. In 1877 England held the first Wimbledon Championship. Dwight Davis donated the Davis Cup in 1900. The International Lawn Tennis Federation regulates rules and play in over 80 countries.

TENNYSON, Alfred, 1st Baron Tennyson (1809–1892), English poet. His *Poems* (1842) established him as a great poet. His well-known philosophic elegy *In Memoriam* (1850) became the favorite of Queen Victoria, who appointed him POET LAUREATE. "Official" work included *The Charge of the Light Brigade* (1855). *Idylls of the King*

(1842–1885) are based on the legends of King Arthur. His mastery of sound and rhythm, both vigorous and delicate, is perhaps best seen in such haunting lyrics as "The Lotus Eaters" and "The Lady of Shalott."

TENOCHTITLÁN, capital of the AZTECS, now in Mexico City. Founded c1325 on an island in Lake Texcoco, connected to the mainland by causeways, it was a rich city of brick houses, palaces, canals, aqueducts and a great square of temple-topped pyramids. It was destroyed by CORTÉS in 1521.

TENSILE STRENGTH, the resistance of a material to tensile stresses (those which tend to lengthen it). The tensile strength of a substance is the tensile force per unit area of cross-section which must be applied to break it.

TENSKWATAWA, or Shawnee Prophet (c1768–1834), Shawnee Indian who aimed with his twin TECUMSEH for a Northwest Indian confederacy. Famous for his "messages from God" and prediction of an eclipse, he urged rejection of the white man. He rashly engaged in the disastrous battle of TIPPECANOE (1811).

TEOTIHUACÁN, pre-TOLTEC metropolis of central America, c400 BC–c700 AD. Lying 30mi NE of Mexico City, it is laid out in grid pattern along the 1½mi Street of the Dead. Monuments include the Temple of Quetzalcoatl, Pyramid of the Moon and the huge Pyramid of the Sun.

TEQUILA, a type of Mexican brandy or mescal that is produced by the fermentation of the stems and leaf bases of a number of agave species, particularly *Agave tecquilana*.

TER BORCH, Gerard (1617–1681), Dutch painter. Much traveled (Italy, France, England, Westphalia, Spain), he painted small, delicate portraits and dignified interior genre scenes. His group portrait *The Peace of Münster* (1648) is of historical note.

TERENCE (Publius Terentius Afer; c185–159 BC), Roman playwright. All his comedies (most based on MENANDER) survive: *The Woman from Andros, The Mother-in-Law, The Self-Tormentor, The Eunuch, Phormio* and *The Brothers*. Their refined realism, humor and language later influenced development of the comdey of manners.

TERESA OF ÁVILA, Saint (1515–1582), Spanish nun and mystic who reformed the CARMELITES; a patron saint of Spain. Canonized in 1622, she was proclaimed a Doctor of the Roman Catholic Church in 1970. Her *Interior Castle* (1588), *Life* (1611) and other writings are classics of spiritual literature.

TERMAN, Lewis Madison (1877–1956), US psychologist best known for developing the STANFORD-BINET TEST.

TERMITES, or white ants, primitive insects closely related to cockroaches, found in all warm regions. They have a complicated social system and live in well-regulated communities with different castes taking distinct roles. They build large nests of soil mixed with saliva, in which the colony of king, queen, workers, soldiers and juveniles live. Soldiers and workers are sterile individuals whose development has been arrested at an early stage. Termites feed on wood and vegetation, digesting the food with the aid of symbiotic PROTOZOA or BACTERIA in the gut.

TERNS, a subfamily, Sterninae, of the GULL family. All have long, pointed wings and deeply-forked tails while most are white with gray back and black head cap in the breeding season. Terns plunge into the sea to catch fish. The Arctic tern, *Sterna paradisaea*, yearly migrates from the Arctic to the Antarctic and back again.

TERRA COTTA (Italian: baked earth), any fired earthenware product, especially one made from coarse, porous clay, red-brown in color and unglazed. Being cheap, hard and durable, it has been used from ancient times for building and roofing, and for molded architectural ornament and statuettes. Its use for sculpture and plaques was revived in the Renaissance and in the 18th century. (See also POTTERY AND PORCELAIN.)

TERRITORIALITY, a behavioral drive causing animals to set up distinct territories defended against other members of the same species (conspecifics) for the purposes of establishing a breeding site, home range or feeding area. It is an important factor in the spacing out of animal populations. Territoriality is shown by animals of all kinds: birds, mammals, fishes and insects, and may involve displays or the scent-marking of boundaries. A territory may be held by individuals, pairs or even family groups.

TERRITORIAL WATERS, in international law, the belt of sea adjacent to a country and under its territorial jurisdiction. Important for control of shipping, seabeds and fisheries, such limits used to extend 3mi, and more recently 12mi, from low-water mark. A 200mi limit has been accepted by some countries.

TERRITORY, in politics, an area under a government's control. Named territories have lower status than the mother country. All but 19 US states were once territories; Alaska and Hawaii were the last incorporated territories (with full Constitutional rights) to gain statehood. US territories include the Virgin Islands and Guam. Federated States of Micronesia, formerly a UN Trust Territory administered by the US, became a self-governing territory in association with the US in 1981.

TERROR, The, 1793–94, period in the FRENCH REVOLUTION when fanatical Jacobin reformers including ROBESPIERRE, DANTON and HÉBERT, seized control from the GIRONDINS. They guillotined over 2,600 "counterrevolutionaries" (including Danton and Hébert, eventually) in Paris and sanctioned "Terrors" elsewhere, notably in Nantes. The Terror ended with the guillotining of Robespierre himself on July 27 (9 Thermidor), 1794. The ensuing period is called the Thermidorian reaction.

TERRORISM, the use of actual or threatened violence for political ends. The phenomenon is worldwide. During the 1980s it was conspicuous in such widely differing countries as Northern Ireland, Italy, Spain, Lebanon, Israel, India, El Salvador, and Colombia.

TERRY, Dame (Alice) Ellen (1847–1928), English actress. In her partnership with Henry IRVING at the London Lyceum (1878–1902) she became famous in roles from Shakespeare, but also acted in modern plays.

TERTIARY, the period of the CENOZOIC before the advent of man, lasting from about 65 to about 2–3 million years ago. (See also GEOLOGY.)

TERTULLIAN (Quintus Septimius Florens Tertullianus; c160–c225), early Christian Latin writer, born Carthage. Converted on return to Carthage from Rome, he wrote apologetics, polemics and ascetic works in which, aided by his law training, he denounced paganism, heresies and licentiousness.

TESLA, Nikola (1856–1943), Croatianborn US electrical engineer whose discovery of the rotating magnetic field permitted his construction of the first AC induction motor (c1888). Since it is easier to transmit AC than DC over long distances, this invention was of great importance.

TEST ACT (1673), an English law making profession of the Church of England faith a condition of holding public office. The test, which affected both Roman Catholics and Nonconformists, ended in 1828–29.

TESTOSTERONE, ANDROGEN STEROID produced by the interstitial cells of the testes, and to a lesser extent by the ADRENAL GLAND cortex, under the control of luteinizing HORMONES. It is responsible for most male sexual characteristics—VOICE change, HAIR distribution and sex-organ development.

TETANUS, or lockjaw, BACTERIAL DISEASE in which a TOXIN produced by anaerobic tetanus bacilli growing in contaminated wounds causes MUSCLE spasm due to nerve toxicity. Minor cuts may be infected with the bacteria which are common in soil. The first symptom may often be painful contraction of jaw and neck muscles; trunk muscles including those of RESPIRATION and muscles close to the site of injury are also frequently involved. Untreated, many cases are fatal, but ARTIFICIAL RESPIRATION, antiserum and PENICILLIN have improved the outlook. Regular VACCINATION and adequate wound cleansing are important in prevention.

TET OFFENSIVE, in the Vietnam War, a coordinated cluster of attacks against cities and bases in South Vietnam by Vietcong and North Vietnamese forces, beginning on Jan. 30, 1968, the first day of the Tet (New Year) holiday. The offensive, which included a brief occupation of part of the US embassy in Saigon, was costly to the enemy; nevertheless, it converted many Americans to the view that the war could not be won.

TETRACYCLINES, broad-spectrum ANTIBIOTICS (including Aureomycin and Terramycin) which may be given by mouth. While useful in BRONCHITIS and other minor infections, they are especially valuable in diseases due to RICKETTSIA and related organisms; they can also be used in ACNE. Staining of TEETH in children and deterioration in KIDNEY failure cases are important side effects.

TETZEL, Johann (1465–1519), German Dominican monk, appointed (1516) to sell indulgences to raise money for SAINT PETER'S BASILICA, Rome. His preaching near Wittenberg (1517) provoked LUTHER'S 95 theses, chiefly against indulgences. (See also REFORMATION.)

TEUTOBURG FOREST, Battle of (9 AD), the successful ambush of three Roman legions under Varus by Arminius, leader of the Cherusci Germans, which prevented Roman domination of Germany.

TEUTONIC KNIGHTS, religious military order established (1198) in Palestine. It successfully invaded, Germanized and Christianized Prussia in the 1200s. It declined after defeat by a Polish-Lithuanian army at TANNENBERG (1410). Its last branch, in central and S Germany, was dissolved by Napoleon (1805).

TEUTONS, originally a German tribe, defeated by the Romans in Gaul (102 BC). "Teutons" became synonymous with JUTES, Angles and SAXONS, then with "North

Germans" in general; "teutonic" came to describe the languages of Scandinavia, Germany, Belgium and Holland.

TEXAS, second-largest US state, bordered by Mexico, N.M., Okla., Ark., La., and the Gulf of Mexico. It is one of three states (with Vermont and Hawaii) to have been an independent republic before attaining statehood.

Name of state: Texas
Capital: Austin
Statehood: Dec. 29, 1845 (28th state)
Familiar name: Lone Star State
Area: 267,339sq mi
Population: 16,685,000
Elevation: Highest—8,751ft., Guadalupe Peak. Lowest—sea level, Gulf of Mexico
Motto: Friendship
State flower: Bluebonnet
State bird: Mockingbird
State tree: Pecan
State song: "Texas, Our Texas"
Land. The West Gulf Coastal Plain extends inland 150–300mi to the Balcones escarpment and contains the state's richest soils. Less fertile are the Texas Great Plains (W half of the Panhandle and along the Pecos R), which reach W to N.M. In the extreme W the Basin and Range (Trans-Pecos) region is crossed by the Rocky Mts. Sam Rayburn Lake, on the Angelina R, is the largest of many man-made lakes. Mean annual temperature ranges from 55°F in the Panhandle to 74°F along the lower Rio Grande in the S. Annual rainfall is 55in in the E but diminishes to only 10in in the W.
People. As of 1980, Texas was the third most populous state, up from fourth place in 1970. More than 80% of the population is urban, the largest urban areas being HOUSTON, Dallas-Fort Worth, San Antonio, Austin, and El Paso. About 20% are of Spanish origin and were born or have parents who were born in neighboring Mexico. Population densities are highest in the West Gulf Plain and lowest in the drier W.
Economy. Texas leads the states in production of oil and natural gas and is also

rich in sulfur and low-grade coal deposits. It is a leading agricultural state and a major producer of cotton, beef cattle, sheep, citrus, rice, wheat, vegetables, and nuts. Large petrochemical industries are concentrated along the Gulf. Food-processing and manufacture of transportation equipment, machinery, metals and textiles are important. NASA's Manned Spacecraft Center was established near Houston in 1964 and has since stimulated the manufacture of scientific and electronic equipment.
History. The subject of French, Spanish and US (1803) claims, Texas became part of independent Mexico 1821. After defeat at the ALAMO, victory for US settlers at SAN JACINTO preceded the independent republic (1836–45) and entrance into the US. The MEXICAN WAR ended Mexican claims (1848). Despite the views of governor Sam HOUSTON, Texas joined the Confederates (1861); it was readmitted to the Union in 1870. Railroads (later 1800s), discovery of oil (1901) and WWII helped economic development.

During the 1970s, Texas began to diversify its economic base and oil and gas production declined despite extensive drilling. So exuberant was its growth in this period that it became a magnet drawing new residents from all over the US. The population jumped 27.1% during the 1970s, including a net immigration of more than 1 million people. But in the 1980s oil prices plunged and the economy was severely hurt. The real estate boom became a bust. Of the 10 largest banks in 1978 only 2 were still in business in 1988. In presidential elections 1968–88, Texas voted Republican in 1972 and 1980–88.
TEXAS RANGERS, a law enforcement body, part of the Texas department of public safety. The first were ten men employed (1823) by S. F. AUSTIN to protect settlers from Indian and Mexican raiders. In 1935 the Rangers were merged with the state highway patrol.
TEXTILES, fabrics made from natural FIBERS OF SYNTHETIC FIBERS, whether knitted, woven, bonded or felted. The fibers are prepared (WOOL preparation being typical) and spun (see SPINNING) into yarn. This is then formed into fabric by WEAVING or other methods. Finishing processes include bleaching, calendering, mercerizing, dyeing (see DYES AND DYEING), brushing, sizing, fulling and tentering. Chemical processes are used to impart crease-resistance, fireproofing, stain-resistance, water-proofing, or nonshrink properties.
TEY, Josephine (1896–1942), pen name of

Elizabeth Mackintosh, Scottish novelist and playwright who also used the name Gordon Daviot. She wrote several highly successful detective stories, beginning with *The Man in the Queue* (1929).

THACKERAY, William Makepeace (1811–1863), English novelist, essayist and illustrator. He did much to shape *Punch*, and was first editor of *The Cornhill Magazine* (1860). His best known (and best) novel is *Vanity Fair* (1848), a gentle satire of the early 19th-century middle classes; its central character is the sly but good-natured Becky Sharp. His other novels include *Barry Lyndon* (1844), *Pendennis* (1850) and *Henry Esmond* (1852).

THAILAND, formerly **Siam,** monarchy in SE Asia. The N part borders Kampuchea (Cambodia), Laos and Burma; the S extends between the Gulf of Thailand and Bay of Bengal down the Malay Peninsula to Malaysia.

Official name: Prathet Thai
Capital: Bangkok
Area: 198,115sq mi
Population: 53,722,000
Languages: Thai; English, Chinese, Malay, tribal languages
Religions: Buddhist; Muslim, Christian, Animist
Monetary unit(s): 1 baht=100 satangs
Land. In the N are densely wooded N–S hill ranges rich in teak. The populous central region comprises the rice-producing alluvial plain of the Chao Phraya R. The drier NE Khorat Plateau drains E to the Mekong R. The narrow S region is mostly mountainous and forested, with some rice plains and many islands off the W coast. Rainfall ranges from an average 80in in the S and W to 40in in the E.
People. The Thais are of Mongol descent; most are Theravada Buddhists. Thai language is of the Sino-Tibetan family and written in script of Sanskrit origin. Chinese form an important urban minority; there are hill peoples in the N and Malays, most of whom are Muslims, in the S. Bangkok, the capital, and adjacent Thon Buri are by

far the largest cities.
Economy. Rice is the chief crop in an agricultural economy, with sugarcane, cotton, corn, coconuts, rubber and tobacco also grown. Draft water buffalos are the principal livestock, though there are timber elephants. Fishing and forestry (teak, oils, resins, bamboo) are important. Textiles (including famous Thai silks) produced in Bangkok and Thon Buri are among the few manufactures. Thailand is one of the world's largest exporters of rice. Other exports include corn, rubber and teak. Trade is mainly with the West.
History. Archaeologists recently unearthed evidence of a Bronze Age culture at Ban Chiang dating back as early as 4000 BC. The Thais migrated from S China about 1000 AD. Their center moved S under the Sukhothai (c1220–1350), Ayuthia (1350–1778) and Chakri (1782–) dynasties. Siam lost territorial influence in the 1800s to the British (in Burma and Malaya) and French (in Laos and Cambodia) but kept its independence. Thailand was invaded by Japan in WWII. In the early 1950s it sent troops to Korea, joined the SOUTHEAST ASIA TREATY ORGANIZATION (headquartered in Bangkok) and later supported the US in Vietnam and has since—often unwillingly—provided first asylum for more than a million Indochinese refugees. Thailand became a constitutional monarchy following a bloodless revolution in 1932, and since that time civilian and military groups have struggled for control of the government. The present constitution, the 12th since 1932, came into effect in 1978 after a 6-year period of martial law. Prem Tinsulanonda, modern Thailand's longest-serving premier, presided over a period of rapid economic expansion. In 1988, after 8½ years in office, he refused to accept another term.

THALAMUS, two nuclei of the upper BRAIN stem involved in transmission of impulses to and from the cerebral cortex, especially in sensory pathways.

THALES (early 6th century BC), ancient Greek PRE-SOCRATIC philosopher, one of the Seven Sages (lawgivers). He is reputed to have invented geometry and to have attempted the first rational account of the universe, claiming that it originated from water.

THALIDOMIDE, mild SEDATIVE introduced in the late 1950s and withdrawn a few years later on finding that it was responsible for congenital deformities in children born to mothers who took the DRUG. This was due to an effect on the EMBRYO in early PREGNANCY, in particular causing defective limb bud formation.

THAMES, Battle of the (1813), victory of the US troops of William H. HARRISON over British and Indian (under TECUMSEH) forces in Ontario in the WAR OF 1812. Following the battle of Lake ERIE, it consolidated US control of the Northwest.

THAMES RIVER, England's chief waterway, winds E 210mi from the Cotswolds to its North Sea estuary. On its banks lie Oxford, Reading, Eton, Windsor Castle, Runnymede, Hampton Court Palace and Greenwich. Canals link it to the West and Midlands. Above LONDON it displays fine, gentle scenery; below London it is of considerable importance for shipping. It is tidal up to Teddington (10mi W of London).

THANKSGIVING DAY, since 1863, an annual US national holiday to give thanks for blessings received during the year. It is celebrated on the fourth Thursday in November with feasting and prayers. The tradition was begun by the colonists of Plymouth, Mass., in 1621, and can be traced back to the English harvest festivals. In Canada, it is celebrated on the second Monday in October.

THANT, U (1909–1974), Burmese diplomat, UNITED NATIONS secretary-general 1961–71. A cautious and unassertive negotiator, he was involved in the Cuban missile crisis (1962), and in peace negotiations in Indonesia (1962), Congo (1963), Cyprus (1964) and the India-Pakistan war (1965).

THARP, Twyla (1942–   ), US dancer and choreographer, a student of Merce CUNNINGHAM and Alwin Nikolais. She made her debut with the Paul Taylor Dance Company in 1965, then formed her own company. In her many innovative dances, she has blended ballroom, jazz and tap dance with traditional ballet forms.

THATCHER, Margaret (1925–   ), British prime minister. She entered Parliament in 1959 and served 1970–74 as secretary of state for education and science. In 1975 she was elected Conservative Party leader, and in 1979, when the Conservatives won a parliamentary majority, Mrs. Thatcher became Britain's first woman prime minister. She was reelected in 1983 and 1987. From the start, Mrs. Thatcher was determined to dismantle the welfare state built after WWII and encourage a free-market, free-enterprise culture. Her policies caused wrenching readjustment, particularly in mining and industrial areas in the north where unemployment soared. She was perceived as uncaring, domineering, abrasive, and confrontational. But in the late 1980s the economy was growing rapidly, unemployment was declining, and the Conservatives held a solid majority in the House of Commons.

THAYER, Sylvanus (1785–1872), US military engineer and educator. Superintendent of West Point 1817–33, he was largely responsible for creating its world-wide reputation, and earned the title "father of the Military Academy."

THEATER, term used to refer to drama as an art form as well as to the building in which it is performed.

According to Aristotle, the drama of ancient Greece, the ancestor of modern European drama, grew out of the dithyramb (choral song). The invention of TRAGEDY is credited to Thespis and the form was refined successively by AESCHYLUS, SOPHOCLES and EURIPIDES. COMEDY was a separate and later development of Greek theater. The plays of ARISTOPHANES are the only remains of Greek Old Comedy (5th century BC), a form that was extremely licentious and still close to its ritual origins. Middle and New Comedy (4th and 3rd centuries BC respectively) became increasingly sentimental; only the New Comedy plays of MENANDER, with their complex, often romantic plots, remain from these periods. Greek drama was performed at religious festivals in outdoor amphitheaters built into hillsides; that at Epidaurus is still used each summer. The Roman plays of PLAUTUS, TERENCE and SENECA show their Greek antecedents, but MIME and PANTOMIME were the popular theatrical forms in the Roman Empire and, through the COMMEDIA DELL'ARTE, provide the only direct link between ancient and medieval European drama.

Medieval drama evolved in the Church from musical elaborations of the service. Eventually these developed into MYSTERY PLAYS and were moved out of doors onto play wagons. Miracle Plays, based on the lives of the saints and on scripture, also developed; whole cycles of plays were performed at religious festivals. MORALITY PLAYS (such as EVERYMAN) and interludes (comic plays) appeared in the 15th century. During the RENAISSANCE the rediscovery of Greek and Roman dramatic texts led directly to the growth of secular drama. Buildings for the performance of plays were erected in Elizabethan times, one of the most famous being the Globe Theatre, associated with SHAKESPEARE. By the end of his career a roofed building inside which the audience ranged around an open stage came into use. The modern form of the stage, with painted scenery and a *proscenium arch* across which a curtain falls between acts, was established by the 17th century.

In England the drama went through distinct phases associated with the Renaissance, the RESTORATION and NEOCLASSICISM before settling into a long period of melodrama and sentimentality. On the Continent, classical and neoclassical drama, represented supremely by CORNEILLE and RACINE in France, gave way to a period of ROMANTICISM during which SCHILLER and GOETHE in Germany, and later HUGO in France and PUSHKIN in Russia, made lasting contributions.

Drama of the modern era began with efforts by IBSEN, STRINDBERG, CHEKHOV, ZOLA and George Bernard SHAW to reintroduce realism, honest character portrayal and serious social and political debate into the theater. Many experiments with dramatic form (EXPRESSIONISM, SURREALISM, NATURALISM) and language characterize this phase in the theater. This century has produced dramatists of considerable merit such as O'NEILL, BRECHT, LORCA, BECKETT, IONESCO, Tennessee WILLLIAMS, Arthur MILLER, Edward ALBEE, and Harold PINTER. In recent times Western audiences have also become interested in Oriental theater, especially Japanese NOH and KABUKI drama. The term theater comprehends also such forms as musical comedy, VAUDEVILLE and OPERA as well as plays.

THEATER OF THE ABSURD, term used to describe plays in which traditional values are shown as unable to fulfill man's emotional and spiritual needs. Human experience is seen as chaotic and without purpose, and man is often depicted as a victim of technology and bourgeois values. BECKETT, IONESCO, GENET, ALBEE and PINTER have been identified with this genre.

THEBES, chief city in Boeotia, ancient Greece, founded by Cadmus. It was rich in legend (see OEDIPUS). Hostile to Athens, Thebes supported Persia in the PERSIAN WARS, and later Sparta in the PELOPONNESIAN WAR. In 394 BC she turned against Sparta, and after early defeats dominated Greece (371–362 BC) under Epaminondas. The city was destroyed by Alexander the Great in 336 BC.

THEBES, ancient Egyptian city, 419mi S of Cairo, famous for its temples to Amon and its tombs of the pharaohs, capital of Egypt from c2100 BC, reaching its peak under the 17th and 18th dynasties (c1600 BC–1306 BC; see LUXOR; TUTANKHAMEN). Already in decline by 1100 BC, it was sacked by the Assyrians in 661 BC and finally destroyed by the Romans in 29 BC.

THEISM, a philosophical system, as distinguished from DEISM and PANTHEISM, that professes the existence of a personal, transcendent God who created, preserves and governs the world. Orthodox Christian philosophy is a developed form of theism. (See also MONOTHEISM; PROVIDENCE.)

THEMISTOCLES (c525 BC–c460 BC), Athenian statesman and naval strategist. During the PERSIAN WARS, he foresaw that the Persians would return, and persuaded the Athenians to build the fleet with which he won the battle of SALAMIS (480 BC). As archon (leader) from 493 BC, he built up the fortifications of Athens. Aristides and other rivals were exiled by ostracism, and in 471 BC he was ostracized himself by his aristocratic enemies, eventually retiring to Persia.

THEOCRACY, probably the oldest form of government in which power and authority are seen as derived directly from God, and rulers are considered either incarnations or representatives of divine power. In ancient times theocracy was widespread, ranging from the Egyptians to the Inca empires, Persia to China and Japan. During the Middle Ages in Europe the pope claimed ultimate authority in governing based on his religious authority, and later kings used the "divine right of kings" to justify their absolutist rule. Early Puritan colonies in New England like Massachusetts Bay and New Haven had leaders who claimed to derive their authority from God. While today secular and religious authority are for the most part separated in the Western democracies, their fusion in such political units as the Iranian Islamic Republic is still strong.

THEOCRITUS (c300–c250 BC), Alexandrian Greek poet of the HELLENISTIC AGE, whose polished, artificial *Idylls* created the genre of the PASTORAL. He was imitated by VERGIL and many later poets.

THEODICY (from Greek *theos*, god; *dikē*, justice), that part of natural THEOLOGY concerned to justify God's goodness and omnipotence in the face of evil and suffering. The term was coined by LEIBNIZ, whose *Theodicy* on this theme appeared in 1710.

THEODORA (c504–548), wife of Byzantine emperor JUSTINIAN I. Formerly an actress and dancer, she became a MONOPHYSITE Christian. Highly intelligent, she exercised enormous political influence, once saving the dynasty by persuading Justinian to remain in Constantinople during the Nika riots (532).

THEODORIC THE GREAT (c454–526 AD), king of the OSTROGOTHS (471) and conqueror of Italy. Alternately opposing and allying with the BYZANTINE EMPIRE, he became consul under the emperor Zeno (484), who sent him to invade Italy (489). Having defeated and murdered ODOACER (493), he set up an Italian kingdom, ruling with justice and toleration.

THEODOSIUS, name of two Roman emperors. **Theodosius I, the Great** (346–395), was a general's son who was chosen by the emperor Gratian to rule the East (379). In 388 he invaded Italy, defeated the usurper Maximus and restored Valentinian II to power, becoming emperor himself in 392. He was an important opponent of ARIANISM. After his death, the Empire was divided between his sons Arcadius (East) and Honorius (West). **Theodosius II** (401–450), Arcadius' son, became emperor in 408, but his sister, his wife and various ministers held effective power. His *Theodosian Code* (438) is the first collection of imperial legislation.

THEOLOGY, the science of religious knowledge; the formal analysis of what is believed by adherents of a religion, making its doctrine coherent, elucidating it logically and relating it to secular disciplines. Its themes, therefore, are universal: GOD, man, the world, the Scriptures, SALVATION, ETHICS, the cultus, and ESCHATOLOGY. However, most religions have no well-developed theology. The concept arose in Greek thought, but its elaboration took place only in Christianity. The early Church Fathers and Doctors formulated doctrine in contemporary philosophical terms, and major advances were made by resolving controversies. In the Middle Ages SCHOLASTICISM developed, partly in reaction to the influence of NEOPLATONISM, and divided theology into natural theology and revealed theology. From the Reformation each branch of PROTESTANTISM began to develop its own distinctive theology. From the Enlightenment rationalist theology became dominant, leading to MODERNISM and the modern critical view of the Bible. Partly in reaction arose neo-orthodoxy, and the existentialist theology of NIEBUHR and TILLICH. The chief divisions of theology are: biblical studies (including linguistic and other auxiliary disciplines), leading to the interpretation of Scripture; biblical theology (the development of ideas in the biblical writings); historical theology; systematic theology; and apologetics.

THEOPHRASTUS (c370–c285 BC), Greek philosopher, pupil of ARISTOTLE and his successor as head of the PERIPATETIC SCHOOL, generally considered the father of modern BOTANY.

THEOSOPHY (literally, divine wisdom), a mystical system of religious philosophy claiming direct insight into the divine nature. The speculations of such philosophers as PLOTINUS, Jakob BÖHME and SWEDENBORG are often called theosophical, as are many Eastern philosophies. The Theosophical Society was founded 1875 by Madame BLAVATSKY.

THÉRÈSE OF LISIEUX, Saint (1873–1897), the "Little Flower of Jesus," a French Carmelite nun who practiced the "little way"—achieving sanctity in performing the humblest tasks. Her spiritual autobiography was published posthumously.

THERMAL POLLUTION, the release of excessive waste heat into the environment, notably by pumping warm water from power plant cooling towers into rivers and lakes. This may kill off some living species, decrease the oxygen supply, and adversely affect reproduction.

THERMIDOR, 11th month of the new calendar adopted in the FRENCH REVOLUTION, in force 1793–1805. It covered the period July–August (the name signifies heat). The coup marking the downfall of ROBESPIERRE (July 27, 1794) is called the coup of 9 Thermidor.

THERMOCOUPLE, an electric circuit involving two junctions between different METALS or SEMICONDUCTORS; if these are at different temperatures, a small ELECTROMOTIVE FORCE is generated in the circuit (Seebeck effect). Measurement of this emf provides a sensitive, if approximate thermometer, typically for the range 70K–1000K, one junction being held at a fixed temperature and the other providing a compact and robust probe. Semiconductor thermocouples in particular can be run in reverse as small refrigerators. A number of thermocouples connected in series with one set of junctions blackened form a **thermopile,** measuring incident radiation through its heating effect on the blackened surface. **Thermoelectricity** embraces the Seebeck and other effects relating heat transfer, thermal gradients, electric fields and currents.

THERMODYNAMICS, division of PHYSICS concerned with the interconversion of HEAT, work and other forms of ENERGY, and with the states of physical systems. Being concerned only with bulk matter and energy, **classical thermodynamics** is independent of theories of their microscopic nature; its axioms are sturdily empirical, and then from them theorems are derived with mathematical rigor. It is basic to engineering, parts of GEOLOGY, METALLURGY and PHYSICAL CHEMISTRY. Building on earlier studies of the thermodynamic functions TEMPERATURE and heat, Sadi CARNOT pioneered the science by his investigations of the cyclic heat ENGINE (1824), and in 1850 CLAUSIUS stated the first two laws. Thermodynamics was further developed by J. W. GIBBS, H. L. F. von HELMHOLTZ, Lord KELVIN and J. C. MAXWELL.

In thermodynamics, a *system* is any defined collection of matter: a *closed system* is one that cannot exchange matter with its surroundings; an *isolated system* can exchange neither matter nor energy. The *state* of a system is specified by determining all its properties such as pressure, volume, etc. A system in stable equilibrium is said to be in an equilibrium state, and has an equation of state (e.g., the general GAS law) relating its properties. A *process* is a change from one state A to another B, the path being specified by all the intermediate states. A *state function* is a property or FUNCTION of properties which depends only on the state and not on the path by which the state was reached; a differential dX of a function X (not necessarily a state function) is termed a *perfect differential* if it can be integrated between two states to give a value

$X_{AB} = {}_A\int^B dX$ which is independent of the

path from A to B. If this holds for all A and B, X must be a state function.

There are four basic laws of thermodynamics, all having many different formulations that can be shown to be equivalent. The **zeroth law** states that, if two systems are each in thermal equilibrium with a third system, then they are in thermal equilibrium with each other. This underlies the concept of temperature. The **first law** states that for any process the difference of the heat Q supplied to the system and the work W done by the system equals the change in the internal energy U: $\Delta U = Q - W$. U is a state function, though neither Q nor W separately is. Corollaries of the first law include the law of conservation of ENERGY, Hess' law, and the impossibility of PERPETUAL MOTION machines of the first kind. The **second law** (in Clausius' formulation) states that heat cannot be transferred from a colder to a hotter body without some other effect, i.e., without work being done. Corollaries include the impossibility of converting heat entirely into work without some other effect, and the impossibility of PERPETUAL MOTION machines of the second kind. It can

be shown that there is a state function ENTROPY, S, defined by $\Delta S = \int dQ/T$, where T is the absolute temperature. The entropy change ΔS in an isolated system is zero for a reversible process and positive for all irreversible processes. Thus entropy tends to a maximum. It also follows that a heat ENGINE is most efficient when it works on a reversible CARNOT cycle between two temperatures T_1 (the heat source) and T_2 (the heat sink), the EFFICIENCY being $(T_1 - T_2)/T_2$. The **third law** states that the entropy of any finite system in an equilibrium state tends to a finite value (defined to be zero) as the temperature of the system tends to absolute zero. The equivalent NERNST heat theorem states that the entropy change for any reversible isothermal process tends to zero as the temperature tends to zero. Hence absolute entropies can be calculated from specific heat data. Other thermodynamic functions, useful for calculating equilibrium conditions under various contraints, are: **enthalpy** (or heat content) $H = U + pV$; the **Helmholtz free energy** $A = U - TS$; and the **Gibbs free energy** $G = H - TS$. The free energy represents the capacity of the system to perform useful work. **Quantum statistical thermodynamics**, based on QUANTUM MECHANICS, has arisen in the 20th century. It treats a system as an assembly of particles in quantum states. The entropy is given by $S = k \ln P$ where k is the BOLTZMANN constant and P the statistical probability of the state of the system. Thus entropy is a measure of the disorder of the system.

THERMOMETER, instrument for measuring the relative degree of hotness of a substance (its TEMPERATURE) on some reproducible scale. Its operation depends upon a regular relationship between temperature and the change in size of a substance (as in the mercury-in-glass thermometer) or in some other physical property (as in the platinum resistance thermometer). The type of instrument used in a given application depends on the temperature range and accuracy required.

THERMONUCLEAR REACTIONS, the reactions used in nuclear FUSION devices such as the HYDROGEN BOMB.

THERMOPYLAE, Battle of (480 BC), famous battle in which a small Greek force under Leonidas held up the invading Persian army for three days (see PERSIAN WARS). Thermopylae, a narrow pass in E central Greece, was on the principal route from the N. The battle has become celebrated as an example of heroic resistance.

THERMOSTAT, device for maintaining a

material or enclosure at a constant temperature by automatically regulating its HEAT supply. This is cut off if the TEMPERATURE rises and reconnected if it falls below that required. A thermostat comprises a sensor whose dimensions or physical properties change with temperature and a relay device which controls a switch or valve accordingly. **Bimetallic strips** are widely used in thermostats; they consist of two metals with widely different linear thermal coefficients fused together. As the temperature rises, the strip bends away from the side with the larger coefficient. This motion may be sufficient to control a heater directly.

THESSALONIANS, Epistles to the, two NEW TESTAMENT books written c51 AD by St. PAUL to the Christians in Salonika, Macedonia. They contain an early expression of Paul's theological ideas, particularly about Christ's second coming.

THESSALY, fertile region of N central Greece famous in legend as home of ACHILLES and Jason. It was rarely united and, despite its fine cavalry, was militarily weak. From the 4th to 2nd centuries BC it was subject to Macedonia, later passing to Rome, the Byzantines and Turkey. It became Greek in 1881.

THIAMINE, or aneurin, alternative name for VITAMIN B_1.

THIBAUD, Jacques (1880–1953), French violinist who was recognized as the leading master of the French school of classical violin playing. He appeared frequently as part of a trio with cellist Pablo CASALS and pianist Alfred Cortot.

THIERS, Louis Adolphe (1797–1877), French statesman, first president (1871–73) of the Third Republic. An influential journalist and popular historian of the French Revolution, he supported LOUIS PHILIPPE (1830) and held ministerial posts under him; opposed NAPOLEON III (1851) and was briefly exiled; negotiated the FRANCO-PRUSSIAN WAR's peace treaty and crushed the PARIS COMMUNE (1871).

THIEU, Nguyen Van (1923–   ), president of South Vietnam, 1967–75. An army officer, he helped overthrow DIEM (1963), becoming premier in 1965 and president in 1967. He was reelected (1971), but after US troops were withdrawn his dictatorial regime gradually collapsed, and he resigned in April, 1975. (See VIETNAM.)

THIRD WORLD, term often applied to the nonaligned (and mostly developing) nations of Africa, Latin America and Asia as opposed to "Western" and communist countries.

THIRST AND HUNGER, complex specific sensations or desires for water and food respectively, which have a role in regulating their intake. Thirst is the end result of a mixture of physical and psychological effects including dry mouth, altered BLOOD mineral content, and the sight and sound of water; hunger, those of STOMACH contractions, low blood sugar levels, habit, and the smell and sight of food. Repleteness with either inhibits the sensation. Food and water intake are regulated by the HYPOTHALAMUS, and are closely related to the control of HORMONE secretion and other vegetative functions, being part of the system preserving the homeostasis (constancy) of the body's internal environment. DRUGS, SMOKING, systemic disease and local BRAIN damage are among the many factors influencing thirst and hunger. Excessive thirst may be a symptom of DIABETES or KIDNEY failure (UREMIA), but organic excessive hunger is rare.

THIRTY-NINE ARTICLES, set of doctrinal statements, issued in 1571, outlining the position of the CHURCH OF ENGLAND on theological and civil matters. Formal assent to the articles was required of all Anglican clergy until 1865, when a less rigorous requirement of general approval was substituted.

THIRTY TYRANTS, a group of extreme oligarchs who set up a reign of terror in Athens (404–403 BC) after her defeat in the PELOPONNESIAN WAR. They were deposed by Thrasybulus.

THIRTY YEARS' WAR, a series of European wars, 1618–1648. Partly a Catholic-Protestant religious conflict, they were also a political and territorial struggle by different European powers, particularly France, against its greatest rivals the HAPSBURGS, rulers of the HOLY ROMAN EMPIRE. War began when BOHEMIAN Protestants revolted. They were defeated by TILLY (1620), who went on to subjugate the Palatinate (1623). In 1625 Denmark, fearing Hapsburg power, invaded N Germany, but was defeated in 1629, when the emperor FERDINAND II issued the Edict of Restitution, restoring lands to the Roman Catholic Church. In 1630 the Swedish king Gustavus Adolphus led the Protestant German princes against Ferdinand. He was killed at Lützen (1632), and by 1635 the Swedes had lost support in Germany, and the German states concluded the Peace of Prague. But now France, under RICHELIEU, intervened. Further wars ensued, with France, Sweden and the German Protestant states fighting in the Low Countries, Scandinavia, France, Germany, Spain and Italy against the Holy Roman Empire,

Spain (another Hapsburg power) and Denmark. Peace negotiations, begun in 1640, were completed with the Peace of WESTPHALIA (1648).

THISTLE, common name for many prickly, herbaceous plants of the family Compositae. They normally have purple or yellow flowers. When the seeds are ripe, they are dispersed as fluffy "thistledown." Thistles normally produce a thick taproot which can be eaten or used as a coffee substitute.

THO, Le Duc (1911–   ), member of the North Vietnamese politburo who, with Henry KISSINGER, was awarded the Nobel Peace Prize in 1975 for negotiating the ceasefire (1973) ending the VIETNAM WAR. He refused the prize on the ground that peace in Vietnam had not in fact been achieved.

THOMAS, Saint, one of the 12 APOSTLES, known as "Doubting Thomas" because he would not believe Christ's resurrection until he put his fingers in Christ's wounds. His subsequent career, and martyrdom at Madras, are recounted in the apocryphal *Acts of Thomas.*

THOMAS, (Charles Louis) Ambroise (1811–1896), French composer remembered chiefly for his operas *Mignon* (1866) and *Hamlet* (1868). He also wrote several cantatas, chamber music and choral works.

THOMAS, Dylan (1914–1953), Welsh poet who first achieved recognition with *Eighteen Poems* (1934). His prose includes the quasiautobiographical *Portrait of the Artist as a Young Dog* (1940) and *Adventures in the Skin Trade* (1955); his poetry *Deaths and Entrances* (1946) and *Collected Poems* (1952). Perhaps his most famous work is *Under Milk Wood* (1954), originally a radio play.

THOMAS, George Henry (1816–1870), US Union general victorious at MILL SPRINGS (1862) and dubbed the "Rock of Chickamauga" for his stand at that battle (1863). His Army of the Cumberland destroyed HOOD's army at Nashville, Tenn. (1864).

THOMAS, Lowell Jackson (1892–1981), US news broadcaster. A traveler and lecturer, he was assigned by President Wilson to make a film record of WWI. His contacts with Col. T. E. LAWRENCE led to his book *With Lawrence in Arabia* (1924). From 1930 to 1976 he conducted a 15-minute evening news program on CBS radio, but continued to travel and film travelogues.

THOMAS, Martha Carey (1857–1935), US educator and feminist. Appointed (1884) professor of English and dean of Bryn Mawr College, she served as president 1894–1922. She worked for greater educational opportunities and higher educational standards for women and was prominent in the fight for women's suffrage.

THOMAS, Norman Mattoon (1884–1968), US socialist leader who ran six times for the presidency as a Socialist Party candidate. He helped found the American Civil Liberties Union (1920) and the League for Industrial Democracy (1922). An ardent pacifist, he tried to keep the US out of WWII. Many of his radical proposals eventually became law.

THOMAS À BECKET, Saint. See BECKET, THOMAS À, SAINT.

THOMAS À KEMPIS (Thomas Hemerken von Kempen; c1380–1471), German religious writer and Augustinian friar at Zwolle in the Netherlands. He is famous as the probable author of *On the Imitation of Christ* which, for its gentle humanity, has had an influence among Roman Catholics second only to the Bible.

THOMAS AQUINAS, Saint. See AQUINAS, SAINT THOMAS.

THOMISM, philosophical system of Thomas AQUINAS and his commentators, a synthesis of the thinking of ARISTOTLE and such early Church Fathers as AUGUSTINE. Long the official philosophical doctrine of the Roman Catholic Church, it has had a revival since the 1800s (as neo-Thomism). A central theme is the distinction between areas in which faith and reason should operate.

THOMPSON, David (1770–1857), British fur-trader, explorer and geographer who headed (1816–26) a commission to survey the Canadian/US boundary. He worked for HUDSON'S BAY COMPANY 1784–97, then with the rival North West Company. He discovered (1798) Turtle Lake, a source of the Mississippi R and was first to travel the entire Columbia R (1811).

THOMPSON, Dorothy (1894–1961), US journalist. A foreign correspondent during the 1920s, she became a syndicated columnist for the New York *Herald Tribune* (1936) and was one of the most influential women in the US. An aggressive anti-fascist during the 1930s, she became a prominent anti-communist during the Cold War era. She was married to Sinclair LEWIS.

THOMPSON, Edward Palmer (1924–   ), British historian. A communist until 1956, he became a leader of the New Left. His interest in "history from below" resulted in the landmark *Making of the English Working Class* (1963). In the

1970s and 1980s he was active in the nuclear disarmament movement.

THOMSEN, Christian Jürgensen (1788–1865), Danish archaeologist who devised a three-part classification of prehistoric technologies (since applied also to contemporary primitive cultures): STONE AGE, BRONZE AGE, and IRON AGE.

THOMSON, Sir George Paget (1892–1975), British physicist awarded with C. J. Davisson the 1937 Nobel Prize for Physics for showing that ELECTRONS can be diffracted, thus demonstrating their wave nature.

THOMSON, James (1700–1748), British poet who wrote *Rule Britannia* (1740). He is otherwise best known for his blank-verse *The Seasons* (1726–30), a celebration of Nature, which foreshadowed the Romantic period.

THOMSON, Sir Joseph John (1856–1940), British physicist generally regarded as the discoverer of the ELECTRON. It had already been shown that cathode rays could be deflected by a magnetic field; in 1897 Thomson showed that they could also be deflected by an electric field, and could thus be regarded as a stream of negatively charged particles. He showed their mass to be much smaller than that of the HYDROGEN atom—this was the first discovery of a SUBATOMIC PARTICLE. His model of the ATOM, though imperfect, provided a good basis for RUTHERFORD's more satisfactory later attempt. Thomson was awarded the 1906 Nobel Prize for Physics.

THOMSON, Roy, Baron Thomson of Fleet (1894–1976), Canadian-born British newspaper publisher whose Thomson Organization was believed to control more newspapers than any other company in the world. His empire included numerous Canadian papers and radio stations as well as *The Scotsman* and *The Times* of London (acquired 1967).

THOMSON, Tom (1877–1917), Canadian artist who painted Canadian northland scenes in vivid tones. *A Northern Lake*, perhaps his best-known canvas, was purchased by the Canadian government and placed in the Ottawa National Gallery.

THOMSON, Virgil (1896–1989), US composer and music critic. Influenced by the SIX in Paris, he became a leading "Americanist." His works include the operas *Four Saints in Three Acts* (1928) and *The Mother of Us All* (1947) in collaboration with Gertrude STEIN, symphonies and instrumental, chamber and film music. He won a 1949 Pulitzer Prize for his *Louisiana Story* score.

THOREAU, Henry David (1817–1862), US writer, philosopher and naturalist. He was taught TRANSCENDENTALISM by Ralph Waldo EMERSON. *Walden* (1854) records his life in harmony with nature at Walden Pond, near Concord, Mass. A fierce opponent of slavery, Thoreau withheld his poll tax in 1845 in protest, and defended the HARPERS FERRY raid in *A Plea for John Brown* (1859). His essay *Civil Disobedience* (1849) influenced GANDHI, TOLSTOY and modern civil rights leaders with its defense of CIVIL DISOBEDIENCE against an unjust state.

THOREZ, Maurice (1900–1964), French communist leader. Rising rapidly in the party he became secretary general in 1930 and was elected to the chamber of Deputies in 1932, where he adhered to the Soviet line. He headed the party until his death.

THORFINN KARLSEFNI (11th century), Icelandic explorer who colonized North America. He sailed to Greenland, then (c1004) followed the route of Leif ERICSON to VINLAND, where he and 160 others attempted for two to three years to set up colonies.

THORNDIKE, Edward Lee (1874–1949), US psychologist whose system of psychology, connectionism, had a profound influence on US school education techniques, especially his discovery that the learning of one skill only slightly assists in the learning of another, even if related.

THORNTON, William (1759–1828), US architect and inventor. Though without formal training, he won (1793) the competition to design the Capitol, Washington, D.C. His revised designs (1795) were used for the exteriors of the N and S wings.

THORPE, James Francis "Jim" (1888–1953), US athlete, first man to win both decathlon and pentathlon at the Olympic Games (1912). He was half American Indian and starred with the Carlisle (Pa.) Indian school football team. After being barred from amateur athletics for having played semi-pro baseball, he became a legendary professional football star.

THORVALDSEN, Bertel (1770–1844), Danish sculptor, an apostle of NEOCLASSICISM, and one of the most successful sculptors of the 19th century. The Thorvaldsen Museum, Copenhagen, houses many of his works.

THOUSAND ISLANDS, group of over 1,500 islands, some Canadian, some US, in St. Lawrence R at the outlet of Lake Ontario. St. Lawrence Islands National Park includes 13 of them. Thousand Islands International Bridge (actually five bridges) is 8½mi long and carries traffic across the river.

THRACE, ancient region in the E Balkan Peninsula, SE Europe, bordering the Black and Aegean seas. It included modern NE Greece, S Bulgaria and European Turkey. The modern Thrace, an administrative region of Greece, comprises the SW parts of the old; while E Thrace constitutes European Turkey.

THREE MILE ISLAND, site in the Susquehanna River, near Middletown, Penn., of a nuclear reactor that on Mar. 28, 1979, began to emit "puffs" of radiation as a result of malfunction of the cooling system, aggravated by problems with the computer monitors and some human error. Initial reports downplayed the crisis, but it developed that a core meltdown was a possibility and that a large, potentially explosive hydrogen bubble had formed in the reactor; also, it was learned that no workable plans existed for evacuating the area. Catastrophe was averted without fatalities or known injury within 12 days. Cleanup continued in 1989.

THROMBOSIS, the formation of clot (thrombus) in the HEART or BLOOD vessels. It commonly occurs in the legs and is associated with VARICOSE VEINS but is more serious if it occurs in the heart or in the brain arteries. Detachments from a thrombus in the legs may be carried to the lungs as an embolus (see EMBOLISM); this may have a fatal outcome if large vessels are occluded. The treatment includes ANTICOAGULANTS.

THRUSHES, slender-billed song-birds of the subfamily Turdinae. The plumage is often gray or red-brown and many species have speckled or striated breasts. The tail is usually rounded or square and is held erect in some species. Birds of worldwide distribution, they feed largely on insects, worms and snails, but many species also take fruit and berries.

THRUST, in aerodynamics, the FORCE that propels an airplane or missile. The chemical energy converted in a rocket or jet engine exhausts a high-velocity gas stream whose momentum, according to Newton's third law of motion, produces the thrust force.

THUCYDIDES (c460–c400 BC), greatest Greek historian and first to probe the relationship between historical cause and effect. An Athenian general exiled for his loss of Amphipolis (424 BC), he spent the rest of his life traveling, interviewing soldiers and writing his *History of the Peloponnesian War*, in which he stressed accuracy, objectivity and analysis of individual motivation.

THUGS, secret society of ritual murderers in India, dating back to the 1600s. Devotees of Kali, Hindu goddess of destruction, they traveled in gangs, strangling and robbing their victims. The last known Thug was hanged by the British in 1882.

THULE, in classical times, the northernmost land, perhaps Iceland. It is now the name of a settlement on Baffin Bay, NW Greenland, with a USAF base; and of a pre-European Eskimo culture.

THUNDER, the acoustic shock wave caused by the sudden expansion of air heated by a LIGHTNING discharge. Thunder may be a sudden clap or a rumble lasting several seconds if the lightning path is long and thus varies in distance from the hearer. It is audible up to about 9mi; the distance in miles can be roughly estimated as one-fifth the time in seconds between the lightning and thunder.

THURBER, James Grover (1894–1961), US humorist and cartoonist. The sophisticated humor of his writing contrasts with the simplicity of his line drawings. Several stories, such as *The Secret Life of Walter Mitty* (1942), were filmed. He contributed to the *New Yorker* from 1927. His collections include *My Life and Hard Times* (1933) and *The Thurber Carnival* (1945).

THURMOND, **(James)** **Strom** (1902–   ), US political leader, senator from South Carolina (1954–   ). A hardline supporter of states' rights, he opposed federal civil rights legislation and federal welfare. He was governor 1947–51 and the 1948 States' Rights Democratic presidential candidate, carrying four states. During his Senate career he shifted to the Republican party.

THURSTONE, Louis Leon (1887–1955), US psychologist whose application of the techniques of STATISTICS to the results of PSYCHOLOGICAL TESTS permitted their more accurate interpretation and demonstrated that a plurality of factors contributed to an individual's score.

THUTMOSE, name of four 18th-dynasty Egyptian pharaohs. **Thutmose I** (ruled c1525–1510 BC) enlarged the empire S into gold-rich Nubia and N to the Euphrates R. His was the first tomb built in the Valley of the Kings. **Thutmose II** (ruled c1510–c1490 BC) crushed a rebellion in Nubia. **Thutmose III** (ruled c1468–c1436 BC) was overshadowed by his father's wife HATSHEPSUT for 22 years until her death. A great soldier, he made Syria secure and extended Egypt's power in Asia. His many monuments (notably at Karnak and Heliopolis) include "Cleopatra's needles" (one now in New York, the other in London). **Thutmose IV** (ruled c1412–c1400 BC) made peace with the Mitanni in Syria and quelled a Nubian revolt. (See also EGYPT, ANCIENT.)

THYMUS, a ductless two-lobed gland lying just behind the breast bone and mainly composed of lymphoid cells (see LYMPH). It plays a part in setting up the body's IMMUNITY system. Autoimmunity is thought to result from its pathological activity. After PUBERTY it declines in size.

THYROID GLAND, a ductless two-lobed gland lying in front of the trachea in the neck. The principal HORMONES secreted by the thyroid are thyroxine and triiodothyroxine; these play a crucial role in regulating the rate at which cells oxidize fuels to release ENERGY, and strongly influence growth. The release of thyroid hormones is controlled by thyroid stimulating hormone (TSH) released by the PITUITARY GLAND when blood thyroid-hormone levels are low. Deficiency of thyroid hormones (hypothyroidism) in adults leads to **myxedema**, with mental dullness and cool, dry and puffy skin. Oversecretion of thyroid hormones (hyperthyroidism or thyrotoxicosis) produces nervousness, weight loss and increased heart rate. GOITER, an enlargement of the gland, may result when the diet is deficient in iodine. (See also CRETINISM.)

TIAHUANACO, prehistoric empire of Peru and Bolivia in the pre-Incan period. Tiahuanaco ruins near the SE end of Lake Titicaca include monolithic statues, stylized carvings and a Temple of the Sun, dating from c1000 AD.

TIBALDI, Pellegrino (1527–1596), Italian baroque painter and architect whose principal works are in Milan. He also worked in Spain on the frescoes of the ESCORIAL palace.

TIBER, river in central Italy, flowing 252mi from the Appenines S through Umbria and Latium and SW through Rome to the Tyrrhenian Sea near Ostia. Ancient ROME was built on its E bank.

TIBERIUS (Tiberius Claudius Nero; 42BC–37AD), second Roman emperor (from 14 AD). A general, he was adopted heir by AUGUSTUS. His reign, although generally peaceful, was often tyrannical, resulting in unrest in Rome.

TIBET (also Xizang), autonomous region of China in central Asia, bordering Burma, India, Nepal, Bhutan and Sikkim. The 471,660sq mi of Tibet ("The Roof of the World") averages 12,000ft in altitude. The Kunlun Mts. in the N are almost as high as the Himalayas, across the great Ch'iang T'ang plateau to the S. The Brahmaputra, Indus, Mekong and Yangtze rivers rise in Tibet.

Tibetans follow Buddhist LAMAISM, headed by the Dalai Lama and the Panchen Lama. Until 1965 there were many monasteries and 20% of the male population were monks. After 1965, the Chinese expropriated large estates and have greatly decreased emphasis on religion. The pastoral, livestock-based economy has been affected by roadbuilding and new cement, chemical, paper, textile and other industries. Tibet has deposits of coal and iron (exploited in the NE) and other minerals.

By the mid-1950s Chinese rule in eastern Tibet caused open dissent and, in 1959, a revolt which was suppressed. The Dalai Lama fled from the capital Lhasa to India. Tibet became an autonomous region in 1965, and there was an influx of ethnic Chinese. Anti-Chinese riots broke out in Lhasa in 1987 and 1988.

TIC, a stereotyped movement, habit spasm or vocalization which occurs irregularly, but often more under stress, and which is outside voluntary control. Its cause is unknown. **Tic douloureux** is a condition in which part of the face is abnormally sensitive, any touch provoking intense PAIN.

TICKS, a group of parasitic arthropods, with the mites members of the order Acarina. Unlike most other arthropods, there is no head and the thorax and ABDOMEN are fused. All ticks are blood-sucking external parasites of vertebrates. They are divided into two main families: the soft ticks, Argasidae, and hard ticks, Ixodidae. Ticks transmit more diseases to man and domestic animals than any other arthropod group except the mosquitoes.

TICONDEROGA, by Lake George, NE N.Y., village and site of Fort Ticonderoga, which commanded the route between Canada and the Hudson R valley. Taken (1759) by the British in the FRENCH AND INDIAN WARS, it fell (1775) in the REVOLUTIONARY WAR to the GREEN MOUNTAIN BOYS led by Ethan ALLEN and Benedict ARNOLD. It was recaptured (1777) by General BURGOYNE. The fort is now a museum.

TIDAL POWER, form of HYDROELECTRICITY produced by harnessing the ebb and flow of the TIDES. Barriers containing reversible TURBINES are built across an estuary or gulf where the tidal range is great. The Rance power plant, the first to be built (1961–67), produces 240MW power, mostly at ebb tide.

TIDAL WAVE, obsolete term for TSUNAMI.

TIDES, the periodic rise and fall of land and water on the earth. Tidal motions are primarily exhibited by water: the motion of the land is barely detectable. As the earth-moon system rotates about its center of gravity, which is within the earth, the earth bulges in the direction of the moon and in the exactly opposite direction, owing to the resultant of the moon's gravitational attraction and the centrifugal forces resulting from the system's revolution. Toward the moon, the lunar attraction is added to a comparatively small centrifugal force; in the opposite direction it is subtracted from a much larger centrifugal force. As the moon orbits the earth in the same direction as the earth rotates, the bulge "travels" round the earth each lunar day (24.83h); hence most points on the earth have a high tide every 12.42h. The sun produces a similar though smaller tidal effect. Exceptionally high high tides occur at full and new moon (spring tides), particularly if the moon is at perigee (see ORBIT); exceptionally low high tides (neap tides) at first and third quarter. The friction of the tides causes the DAY to lengthen 0.001s per century.

TIECK, Ludwig (1773–1853), German romantic writer, fascinated by the Middle Ages and by fairy tales and folk tales.

TIEN SHAN, great mountain system of Soviet central Asia and W China. It curves E from the NE PAMIRS for 1,500mi and covers some 70,000sq mi. Pobeda Peak (24,406ft) is the range's highest.

TIENTSIN, capital of Hopei province, N China, on the Hai R 80mi SE of Peking. It is a great industrial center and sea, river and canal port with major steel, chemical and textile industries. It is the seaport for Peking and is near major coal-producing areas. The city suffered badly during the 1976 earthquake centered in Tangshan, a few miles away. Pop 5,152,180.

TIEPOLO, Giovanni Battista (1696–1770), great Venetian painter. Influenced initially by VERONESE, he developed his own colorful, airy but exuberant style in frescoes and ceilings in N Italy, Würzburg palace (Germany) and the royal palace in Madrid.

TIERRA DEL FUEGO, island group off S South America. Discovered (1520) by MAGELLAN and now divided between Chile and Argentina, its sparsely populated 28,470sq mi comprise one large and many small islands. Sheep and oil are the economic mainstays.

TIFFANY, Charles Lewis (1812–1902), US jeweler and retailer. The stock in his first store, opened in 1839, was limited mainly to ordinary glassware and stationery, but it soon included Bohemian glass, jewelry, silverware and rare porcelain. Tiffany began manufacturing his own jewelry in 1848, and, by 1870, had extended his operations to Paris and London. The firm name, Tiffany & Co., was adopted in 1853.

TIFFANY, Louis Comfort (1848–1933), US artist and designer, a leader of ART NOUVEAU. Son of jeweler Charles Tiffany (1812–1902), he created decorative objects of iridescent "favrile" or Tiffany glass.

TIGER, *Panthera tigris*, the major CAT of Asia, with distinct races in different parts of that continent. Closely related to LIONS, they are the largest of all the cats, with a tawny coat broken with dark, vertical stripes providing excellent camouflage against natural patterns of light and shade. Tigers do not chase after food but prefer to stalk and spring. For the most part they are solitary animals, hunting in the cool of the day and otherwise lying up in the shade to rest.

TIGLATH-PILESER, three kings of Assyria. **Tiglath-Pileser I** (reigned 1116–1078 BC) extended Assyrian territory into Phoenicia, Anatolia and modern Syria and captured Babylon. Little is known of **Tiglath-Pileser II** (956–934 BC). **Tiglath-Pileser III** (reigned 745–727 BC) reversed the decline of Assyrian power by administrative reform and by conquering Israel and the Philistines, Gaza, Damascus and Babylon, where he proclaimed himself King Pulu. (See BABYLONIA AND ASSYRIA.)

TIGRIS RIVER, more eastern of the two great rivers of ancient Mesopotamia. The Tigris-Euphrates valley was the cradle of Middle-East civilizations (see BABYLONIA; NINEVEH). Baghdad, city of the ABBASIDS, now capital of Iraq, stands on its banks. It rises in the Taurus Mts. in Turkey and flows 1,180mi SE through Iraq to the Euphrates at Al Qurnah.

TIKAL, largest Mayan city, in the Petén jungle, NW Guatemala. The ruined plazas, pyramids, palaces and steles indicate its great cultural and ceremonial importance. Tikal flourished about 300 BC–800 AD and was at its greatest in the 7th century.

TILDEN, Samuel Jones (1814–1886), US lawyer and politician. An early leader of the Barnburners faction of the N.Y. Democratic Party and of the FREE SOIL PARTY, he proved corruption among New York City politicians led by William TWEED. Governor of N.Y. 1875–76, he lost the hotly contested 1876 presidential election when an electoral commission awarded disputed votes to Republican Rutherford B. HAYES.

TILDEN, William (Bill) Tatem (1893–1953), US tennis champion. From

1920 to 1930 he was the top-ranked US player, winning US, Wimbledon singles (first American to do so) and Davis Cup titles. He turned professional in 1931.

TILE, thin slab of TERRA COTTA or other kinds of POTTERY AND PORCELAIN, used in building to cover surfaces. Roof tiles are commonly unglazed and functional; they are either flat, hooked over roof battens, or curved (often S-shaped) and cemented. Floor and structural tiles are hard and vitreous. Wall tiles, used from ancient times, are often decorated with bas-relief molding, painting, and glazing. Seventeenth-century Delft tiles are famous. Plain glazed wall tiles are now commonly used in bathrooms etc. By analogy, squares of linoleum, vinyl polymers and cork are also called tiles.

TILLICH, Paul Johannes (1886–1965), German-born theologian and teacher. He attempted to synthesize Christianity and classical and modern existentialist philosophy in such works as *Systematic Theology* (1951–63) and the shorter, more popular *The Shaking of the Foundations* (1948) and *The Courage to Be* (1952). Dismissed from Frankfurt U. by the Nazis, he taught at the Union Theological Seminary and at Harvard and Chicago universities.

TILLMAN, Benjamin Ryan (1847–1918), US politician, spokesman of the white rural South. "Pitchfork Ben" was S.C. governor (1890–94) and senator (1895–1918). He helped agrarians gain control of the Democratic Party (1896) but accomplished little for the Southern farmer.

TILLY, Johann Tserclaes, Count of (1559–1632), Bavarian general, commander (from 1618) of the Catholic League and (from 1630) of Imperial forces in the THIRTY YEARS' WAR. After several victories over the Protestants, he was defeated at Breitenfeld, Saxony (1631).

TIMBUKTU, trading town and ancient city in central Mali, W Africa, near the Niger R. It was a wealthy trading and Muslim cultural center in the Mali Empire (1300s) and under the Songhai (1400–1500s). Pop 12,000.

TIME, a concept dealing with the order and duration of events. If two events occur nonsimultaneously at a point, they occur in a definite order with a time lapse between them. Two intervals of time are equal if a body in equilibrium moves over equal distances in each of them; such a body constitutes a clock. The sun provided man's earliest clock, the natural time interval being that between successive passages of the sun over the local meridian—the solar DAY. For many centuries the rotation of the

earth provided a standard for time measurements, but in 1967 the SI UNIT of time, the second, was redefined in terms of the frequency associated with a cesium energy-level transition. In everyday life, we can still think of time in the way Newton did, ascribing a single universal time-order to events. We can neglect the very short time needed for light signals to reach us, and believe that all events have a unique chronological order. But when velocities close to that of light are involved, relativistic principles become important; simultaneity is no longer universal and the time scale in a moving framework is "dilated" with respect to one at rest— moving clocks appear to run slow (see RELATIVITY).

TIME-AND-MOTION STUDY, analysis of how a worker performs a given task, by study of his movements, methods and equipment. Changes can be made by laying out the job differently or adding labor-saving tools. F. W. TAYLOR was a pioneer in time-and-motion study.

TIMES SQUARE, area in mid-Manhattan, New York City, where Broadway, Seventh Ave., and 42nd St. intersect. It takes its name from the former Times Tower, once the headquarters of the *New York Times*. Famous for its electric advertising signs and for its New Year's Eve celebrations, the square is still the center of New York's theater district but also of tawdry and dangerous streets frequented by drifters, criminals, and prostitutes. In the late 1980s plans were formed for redeveloping the area with office buildings and hotels while preserving the theaters.

TIMOR, largest and easternmost of the Lesser Sunda Islands, 400mi NW of Australia. Since Dec. 1975, when the former Portuguese (eastern) Timor was occupied by Indonesian troops, the whole island has been under Indonesian control.

TIMOTHY, Saint, one of St. PAUL's companions, said to have been bishop of Ephesus after Paul. He was recipient of two of Paul's epistles (1 and 2 Timothy), which emphasize moral discipline and obedience to civil and religious authority.

TIMPANI, kettledrums, first used in orchestral music in the 1600s, having a calfskin head over a hollow brass or copper hemisphere. A set of timpani usually consists of three drums. Pitch is governed by the tension of the head, which can be adjusted. Tone may be varied by the type of stick and by the region of the head struck.

TIN (Sn), silvery-white metal in Group IVA of the PERIODIC TABLE, occurring as cassiterite in SE Asia, Bolivia, Zaire and Nigeria. The ore is reduced by smelting with coal. Tin exhibits ALLOTROPY: white(β) tin, the normal form, changes below 13.2°C to gray (α) tin, a powdery metalloid form resembling germanium, and known as "tin pest." Tin is unreactive, but dissolves in concentrated acids and alkalis, and is attacked by halogens. It is used as a protective coating for steel, and in alloys including solder (see SOLDERING), BRONZE, PEWTER, babbitt metal and type metal. AW 118.7, mp 232°C, bp 2270°C. Tin forms organotin compounds, used as biocides, and also inorganic compounds; tin (II) and tin (IV) salts. **Tin (IV) oxide** (SnO_2), white powder prepared by calcining cassiterite or burning finely divided tin; used in glazes and as an abrasive. subl 1800°C. **Tin (II) chloride** ($SnCl_2$), white crystalline solid, prepared by dissolving tin in hydrochloric acid, used as a reducing agent, in tinplating, and as a mordant for dyes. mp 246°C, bp 652°C.

TINGUELY, Jean (1925–), Swiss sculptor best known for his *metamécaniques*, machine-like forms of KINETIC ART. Some themselves produce paintings.

TINTORETTO (Jacopo Robusti; 1518–1594), Venetian MANNERIST painter. His paintings and FRESCOES are characterized by free brushwork, dramatic viewpoint, movement, monumental figures and rich colors. He sought to express drama through color and light, as in the Scuola di S. Rocco *Life of Christ* (1564–87).

TIPPECANOE, Battle of (Nov. 7, 1811), between TECUMSEH'S Shawnees, led by TENSKWATAWA, and US troops led by William Henry HARRISON, near the Tippecanoe R, Ind. There were heavy casualties on both sides, but the "great victory" helped Harrison to the presidency in 1840.

TIRE, ring-shaped cushion fitted onto a wheel rim as a shock absorber and to provide traction. The pneumatic tire (filled with compressed air) was patented in 1845 by R. W. Thomson, an English engineer, who used a leather tread and a rubber inner tube. Solid rubber tires were more popular, however, until the pneumatic tire was reinvented by John Boyd Dunlop (1888), whose outer tube was of canvas covered by vulcanized rubber. The modern tubeless tire (without inner tube) dates from the 1950s. The basic structure of a tire comprises layers (plies) of rubberized fabric (usually polyester cord). The plies are combined with "beads"—inner circular wire reinforcements—and the outer tread and sidewalls on a tire-building drum. The tire is then shaped and vulcanized (see VULCANIZATION) in a heated mold under pressure, acquiring its tread design. Three types of tire are made: the bias-ply tire has the plies with cords running diagonally, alternately in opposite directions; the bias-belted tire is similar, with fiberglass belts between plies and tread; the radial-ply tire has the cords running parallel to the axle, and steel-mesh belts.

TIROL or **Tyrol**, a state in W Austria. Over half its original area was ceded to Italy in 1919. Austria's highest peak, Grossglockner (12,461ft), is there. Farming, lumber and tourism are its main activities. The capital is Innsbruck.

TIRPITZ, Alfred von (1849–1930), German admiral. As navy secretary (1897–1916) he built up the battle fleet to rival the British navy, precipitating an Anglo-German arms race. In WWI his fleet proved to be relatively useless.

TIRSO DE MOLINA (Gabriel Téllez; c1584–1648), Spanish dramatist and friar. His historical, cloak-and-dagger and religious works are notable for insight into character. His *Rake of Seville* (1630) introduced DON JUAN to the stage.

TISSUES, similar CELLS grouped together in certain areas of the body of multicellular ANIMALS and PLANTS. These cells are usually specialized for a single function; thus MUSCLE cells contract but do not secrete; nerve cells conduct impulses but have little or no powers of contraction. The cells are held together by intercellular material such as collagen. Having become specialized for a single or at most a very narrow range of functions, they are dependent upon other parts of the organism for items such as food or oxygen. Groups of tissues, each with its own functions, make up organs. **Connective tissue** refers to the material in which all the specialized body organs are embedded and supported. It includes ADIPOSE TISSUE and the material of ligaments and TENDONS. (See also HISTOLOGY.)

TITANIC, 46,328-ton British liner which sank in 1912 after hitting an iceberg on her maiden voyage to New York. At least 1,500 of the 2,200 aboard drowned. After the disaster (caused mainly by excessive speed), lifeboat, radio watch and ice patrol provisions were improved. In 1985, a team of American and French researchers located the ship on the ocean bottom S of Newfoundland. The next year the wreck was explored by remote-controlled robot, and in 1987 salvagers began to bring up objects from the ship.

TITANIUM (Ti), silvery gray metal in Group IVB of the PERIODIC TABLE; a transition element. Titanium occurs in rutile and in ilmenite, from which it is extracted by conversion to titanium (IV) chloride and reduction by magnesium. The metal and its alloys are strong, light, and corrosion- and temperature-resistant, and, although expensive, are used for construction in the aerospace industry. Titanium is moderately reactive, forming tetravalent compounds, including titanates (TiO_3^{2-}), and less stable di- and trivalent compounds. **Titanium (IV) oxide** (TiO_2) is used as a white pigment in paints, ceramics, etc. **Titanium (IV) chloride** ($TiCl_4$) finds use as a catalyst. AW 47.9, mp 1660°C, bp 3287°C, sg. 4.54.

TITCHENER, Edward Bradford (1867–1927), British-born US psychologist, a disciple of WUNDT, who played a large part in establishing experimental PSYCHOLOGY in the US, especially through his *Experimental Psychology* (4 vols., 1901–05).

TITHE (Anglo-Saxon: tenth part), a church tax of one tenth of income or annual produce. Tithes, mentioned in the Bible, were adopted by the Western Church from the 6th century as a means of supporting priests, poor and churches.

TITIAN (c1480/90–1576), Venetian painter, leading Renaissance artist. Born Tiziano Vecellio, he worked for BELLINI and GIORGIONE, who influenced his early work. He became Venice's official painter 1516. His perceptive portraits, monumental altarpieces, historical and mythological scenes, are famous for their energetic composition, use of rich color and original technique.

TITICACA, Lake, on the Peru-Bolivia border in the Andes Mts. About 120mi long, it is the largest lake in South America (3,200sq mi) and the world's highest navigable lake (12,500ft). It was the center of the Tiahuanaco civilization.

TITO (Joseph Broz; 1892–1980), president of YUGOSLAVIA (1953–1980), founder of the post-WWII republic. He became a communist while a WWI prisoner of war in Russia and later spent several years in Yugoslav jails. General secretary of the Communist Party from 1937, Tito organized partisan resistance to the Nazis in WWII, eclipsing the CHETNIKS, and after the war established a socialist republic. He served as prime minister (1945–53) before becoming president. Tito broke with STALIN in 1948. He suppressed home opposition, while working for workers' self-management and reconciliation of national minorities. Later years saw a substantial liberalization of his policies. On the international scene, Tito became an organizer and leading spokesman for "third world" or neutralist countries.

TITUS (Titus Flavius Sabinus Vespasianus; 39–81 AD), Roman emperor, successor (79) to his father VESPASIAN. A successful soldier, he captured (70) Jerusalem in the Jewish revolt (66–70). Berenice, sister of HEROD Agrippa II, became his mistress. He was popular for lavish entertaining, and aid to victims of VESUVIUS (79) and of the fire at Rome (80).

TLINGIT INDIANS, largest group of North American INDIANS of the NW coast, now living in SE Alaska and numbering about 7,000. They belong to the Koluschan linguistic family and resemble Haida Indians in their complex social organization. Many still live by fishing, woodcarving, basketry and weaving. (See also ALASKA.)

TNT, or **trinitrotoluene,** pale yellow crystalline solid made by nitration of toluene. It is the most extensively used high EXPLOSIVE, being relatively insensitive to shock, especially when melted by steam heating and cast. MW 227.1, mp 82°C.

TOADS, name strictly referring only to members of the family Bufonidae, but as the terms "frog" and "toad" are the only common names available for all the 2,000 species of tailless amphibians, "frog" is used for those which have smooth skins and live in or near water, and "toad" for all those with warty skins and living in drier areas. Toads are independent of water except for breeding, the larvae—tadpoles—being purely aquatic. Most toads feed nocturnally on small animals.

TOBACCO, dried and cured leaves of varieties of the tobacco plant (*Nicotiana tabacum*), used for smoking, chewing and as snuff. Native to America, tobacco was introduced to Europe by the Spanish in the 16th century and from there spread to Asia and Africa. Today the US remains the world's largest producer, followed by China, India and the USSR. Consumption is increasing despite the health hazards of SMOKING. Tobacco is grown in alluvial or sandy soils and may be harvested in about four months. Cultivation is dependent on hand labor. Family: Solanaceae.

TOBACCO MOSAIC, VIRUS disease of plants, strains of which affect TOBACCO, TOMATOES, beans and many decorative plants. It restricts growth and causes the leaves to develop a mottled or mosaic pattern. Apart from avoiding infection, no cure has been found for this the most studied of all viruses, having been the first virus to be isolated and the first to be purified. (See also PLANT DISEASES.)

TOBEY, Mark (1890–1976), US painter, strongly influenced by Chinese calligraphy and Zen Buddhism. He developed his "white writing" style in the 1930s in small abstracts representing street scenes. His later, delicately colored abstracts have more intricate linear rhythms.

TOBIN, Daniel Joseph (1875–1955), Irish-born US labor leader. As president of the TEAMSTERS UNION (1907–52), he built it into one of the most powerful unions in the US. He was also a vice-president of the AFL (1933–52).

TOBIN, James (1918–   ), US economist; Yale professor who won the 1981 Nobel Memorial Prize in Economic Science for his research in relating the effects of financial markets to consumption, prices, production and investment, as well as his studies of government monetary policies and budgets. He had served as one of President Kennedy's economic advisers.

TOBIT (Tobias), Book of, in the APOCRYPHA, recounts how Tobias, son of the devout but blinded Jew Tobit (or Tobias), successfully undertakes a dangerous journey, helped by the Angel Raphael, to exorcise a demon from, and marry, Sara. He then helps Tobit regain his sight.

TOCH, Ernst (1887–1964), Austrian-US composer. Leaving Germany in 1933, he settled in the US and taught music at the University of California (Los Angeles). His works include six symphonies, chamber compositions and choral pieces. His *3d Symphony* (1955) won a 1956 Pulitzer prize.

TOCQUEVILLE, Alexis (Charles Henri Clérel) de (1805–1859), French historian famous for his analysis of the strengths and drawbacks of democracy. He discussed his observations in the US in *Democracy in America* (1835–40). He was impressed but foresaw a threat to individual liberty in the "tyranny of the majority," a theme developed in *The Old Regime and the French Revolution* (1856). A moderate liberal politician, he was French foreign minister in 1849.

TOGA, outer garment of freeborn citizens of ancient Rome, wrapped twice around the body and falling in folds. The adult male toga was plain white; boys and, later, magistrates wore one with a purple border; the emporor and triumphant generals wore an embroidered purple toga.

TOGLIATTI, Palmiro (1893–1964), Italian Communist Party leader (1926–64). He cofounded the party, now West Europe's largest, in 1921, became Comintern secretary (1935) and returned from exile in Moscow (1944) to serve in several governments.

TOGO, West African republic, a 70mi-wide strip extending 340mi N from the Gulf of Guinea between Ghana and Benin.

Official name: Republic of Togo
Capital: Lomé
Area: 21,925sq mi
Population: 3,158,000
Languages: French; tribal languages
Religions: Animist; Christian; Muslim
Monetary unit(s): 1 CFA franc=100 centimes

Land and People. From the central Togo Mts. a grassy plateau slopes E to the Mono R and S to the sandy coastal plain. The N is savanna country. The climate is hot and humid, averaging 81°F, with yearly rainfall of 40–70in. The economy is agricultural: chief exports are cacao and coffee, but cassava, corn and cotton are also important. Large phosphate deposits are worked NE of the seaport capital Lomé. About 75% of the people live in rural areas, mostly in the S. The population is made up almost entirely of blacks from the Ewe, Ouatchi, Mina, Kabre and other ethnic groups. French is the official language, Ewe the most widely used.

History. Formerly the E part of the German protectorate of Togoland, the area was administered by France after WWI and became independent in 1960. Since a military coup in 1967 it has been ruled by Étienne Eyadema, who suspended the constitution and dissolved the legislative body. The legislature was restored following adoption of a new constitution in 1979. Edayema, who celebrated the 20th anniversary of his rule in 1987, has survived several coup attempts.

TOGO, Heihachiro, Marquis (1847–1934), Japanese admiral and commander in chief of the Japanese navy in the RUSSO-JAPANESE WAR (1904–05). His ships successfully bombarded Port Arthur and destroyed the Russian fleet at TSUSHIMA (1905).

TOJO, Hideki (1884–1948), Japanese general and militarist statesman, prime minister and virtual dictator (1941–44) who ordered the attack on Pearl Harbor. A professional soldier, he was chief of staff of the army in China (1937), and minister of war from 1940. He was forced to resign when the US took Saipan (1944). Convicted of war crimes, he was hanged.

TOKUGAWA, dynasty of SHOGUNS (military governors) of Japan 1603–1867. Tokugawa Ieyasu (1542–1616), first of 15, ruthlessly unified Japan under his rule after the battle of Sekigahara (1600) and established his capital at Edo (Tokyo). The regime was a centralized feudalism with strict control over the barons. It fell in a revolution precipitated partly by the presence of Westerners.

TOKYO, capital of Japan. It lies at the head of Tokyo Bay on the SE coast of Honshu Island, and contains over 10% of Japan's population. Founded in the 12th century as Edo, it became capital of the TOKUGAWA shoguns in 1603; it was renamed and made imperial capital in 1868. Reconstruction after earthquake and fire (1923) and the air raids of WWII transformed much of Tokyo. It is today a center of government, industry, finance and education: the National Diet (parliament) meets here; most of Japan's great corporations have their head offices in Maurunochi district; Tokyo University (founded 1877) is one of hundreds of educational institutions. Tokyo has many parks, museums and temples, the Imperial Palace and the Kabukiza theater (see KABUKI). Industries (with large complexes to the W) include printing, shipbuilding, metal manufactures, automobiles, chemicals and textiles. The harbor and airport are Japan's busiest. Pop (city) 8,386,030; (metro) 11,904,374.

TOLEDO, city in central Spain 40mi SW of Madrid, seat of Toledo province, former Roman and Visigoth capital, famous for sword blades since prosperous Moorish rule (712–1085). Landmarks are the Alcázar (citadel), Gothic cathedral (the archbishop is Spain's primate) and El GRECO's house. Pop 56,000.

TOLKIEN, John Ronald Reuel (1892–1973), British author and scholar, celebrated for his tales *The Hobbit* (1937) and the trilogy *The Lord of the Rings* (1954–55), which present a mythical world of elves and dwarfs, partly based on Anglo-Saxon and Norse folklore. Tolkien was professor of Anglo-Saxon, then of English language and literature, at Oxford University.

TOLSTOY, Aleksei Nikolaevich, (1883–1945), Russian novelist and playwright, best known for his trilogy *The Road to Calvary* (1921–40), the novella *Nikita's Childhood* (1920) and the novel *Peter the First* (1929–34). A nobleman distantly related to Leo Tolstoy, he left Russia in 1917 but returned in 1922 and became a supporter of Stalin's regime.

TOLSTOY, Leo Nikoleyevich, Count (1828–1910), Russian novelist. Educated at Kazan University, he served in the army, married in 1862 and spent the next 15 years on his estate at Yasnaya Polyana near Moscow. In this happy period he produced his masterpieces: *War and Peace* (1865–69), an epic of vast imaginative scope and variety of character, tells the story of five families against the background of the Napoleonic invasion of Russia. *Anna Karenina* (1875–77), the tragic story of an adulterous affair, is remarkable more for its psychological portrayal. In later years Tolstoy experienced a spiritual crisis, recounted in his *Confession* (1882), and embraced an ascetic philosophy of Christian anarchism. His other works include *Childhood* (1852), *The Cossacks* (1863) and *Resurrection* (1899).

TOLTEC, Indian civilization dominant in the central Mexican highlands between the 900s and 1100s. The Toltec god was QUETZALCOATL. The Toltecs, sophisticated builders and craftsmen, erected their capital at Tollán (ruins near modern Tula, 60mi N of Mexico City). The dominant group were Nahuatl speakers. AZTECS and others overran the area and adopted various aspects of Toltec culture.

TOMAHAWK, light hatchet or war club of certain North American Indians. Originally a chip of stone fixed to a stick, it gained an iron ax head through trade with Europeans. Often incorporating a pipe bowl and stem, it had ceremonial value and was usually buried at the end of hostilities.

TOMATO, *Lycopersicon esculentum*, herbaceous plant, native to South America, but introduced to Europe in the 16th century and now cultivated worldwide. Most of the crop is canned or processed to make prepared foods, a relatively small proportion being grown for salad use. In northern latitudes, tomatoes are grown under glass, but the bulk is grown as a field crop. Italy, Spain, Brazil and Japan are among the leading producers. Family: Solanaceae.

TOM THUMB, General (1838–1883), pseudonym for the US midget Charles Sherwood Stratton, who toured Europe and the US with the entertainer P. T. BARNUM. His adult height was only 40in.

TONALITY, the quality of music based on the tonic, or principal note of a particular KEY, as in most classical music; such music is tonal. Tonality compares with polytonality, the simultaneous use of many keys, and ATONALITY, the use of none.

TONE, Wolfe (1763–1798), Irish nationalist. A cofounder (1791) of the Society of United Irishmen, he was forced to leave Ireland in 1794. Leading a French force to support the rebellion in W Ireland (1798), he was captured and condemned to hang, but committed suicide in prison.

TONE POEM. See SYMPHONIC POEM.

TONGA, or **Friendly Islands**, constitutional monarchy in the S Pacific.

Official name: Kingdom of Tonga
Capital: Nukúalofa
Area: 288sq mi
Population: 94,800
Languages: Tongan, English
Religions: Christian
Monetary unit(s): 1 páanga = 100 seniti
Land. The kingdom comprises over 150 islands of which the chief groups are Tongatapu, Háapai, and Vaváu. The climate is tropical. The capital is Nukúalofa on Tongatapu.

People and Economy. The population is mainly Polynesian with about 300 Europeans. The economy is agricultural, with copra, bananas, and vanilla the chief exports. Promising petroleum deposits were located near Tongatapu in 1977.

History. The islands were discovered in 1616 by the Dutch explorer Jakob Lemaire and later visited by Abel Tasman (1643) and James Cook (1773). In 1900, seven years after the death of George Tupuo I, who founded the present dynasty in 1845, Tonga became a British protectorate. It achieved independence under the constitution of 1875 in 1970. In the 1987 elections, two-thirds of the popularly elected seats in the legislature were captured by opponents of the government, although the body was still dominated by traditional authorities.

TONGUE, muscular organ in the floor of the mouth which is concerned with the formation of food boluses and self-cleansing of the mouth, TASTE sensation and VOICE production. Its mobility allows it to move substances around the mouth and to modulate sound production in speech. In certain animals, the tongue is extremely protrusile and is used to draw food into the mouth from a distance.

TONKIN, historic region of SE Asia, now comprising most of northern VIETNAM. It was the European name for the region around the Red R delta, which became a French protectorate in 1883, part of French INDOCHINA.

TÖNNIES, Ferdinand Julius (1855–1936), German sociologist noted for his distinction between rural communities governed by traditions rooted in the family and urban groupings based on rational self-interest and economic and legal interdependence. His theories are expressed in *Community and Society* (1887).

TONSILLITIS, INFLAMMATION of the TONSILS due to VIRUS or BACTERIA infection. It may follow sore throat or other pharyngeal disease or it may be a primary tonsil disease. Sore throat and red swollen tonsils, which may exude PUS or cause swallowing difficulty, are common; LYMPH nodes at the angle of the jaw are usually tender and swollen. QUINSY is a rare complication. ANTIBIOTIC treatment for the bacterial cause usually leads to a resolution but removal of the tonsils is needed in a few cases.

TONSILS, areas of LYMPH tissue aggregated at the sides of the PHARYNX. They provide a basic site of body defense against infection via the mouth or NOSE and are thus particularly susceptible to primary infection (TONSILLITIS). As with the ADENOIDS, they are particularly important in children first encountering infectious microorganisms in the environment.

TONTI, Henri de (c1650–1704), French explorer and founder of Ill. In 1681–83 he built Fort St. Louis on the Illinois R with LA SALLE and brought settlers from Canada. By 1700 the colony was trading actively with the English in Carolina.

TOPAZ, aluminum silicate mineral of composition $Al_2SiO_4(F, OH)_2$, forming prismatic crystals (orthorhombic) which are variable and unstable in color, and valued as GEM stones. The best topazes come from Brazil, Siberia and the US.

TOPOLOGY, branch of mathematics that studies properties of geometrical figures or abstract spaces that are independent of shape or distance. **Point-set topology** deals with ways of defining "nearness" of elements, or points, of a set without necessarily assigning numerical distances to pairs of points. Such a definition is called "a topology on the set" and the set is called a **topological space**. The topology makes it possible to define continuous FUNCTIONS on the space. **Algebraic topology**, or combinatorial topology, uses abstract algebra (see ALGEBRA, ABSTRACT) to treat the ways in which geometrical figures fit together to form figures of higher dimension, disregarding shape. For example a sphere is topologically the same as a cube, but it is distinct from a torus (doughnut) because if the surfaces of the figures are divided into triangles the algebraic relationships between the triangles will be different in the two cases.

TORAH (Hebrew: law, teaching), the PENTATEUCH (first five books of the Bible) kept in the ark of every SYNAGOGUE. In a wider sense it is the whole body of oral and written teaching central to JUDAISM, and includes the rest of the Hebrew Bible, rabbinic codes, the TALMUD and Midrash.

TORDESILLAS, Treaty of, between Spain and Portugal in 1494, specifying where each might make colonial explorations. A papal bull of 1493 had allocated the New World to Spain and Africa and India to Portugal. The treaty shifted the demarcation W, enabling the Portuguese to claim E Brazil.

TORNADO, the most violent kind of storm; an intense whirlwind of small diameter, extending downward from a convective cloud in a severe thunderstorm, and generally funnel-shaped. Air rises rapidly in the outer region of the funnel, but descends in its core, which is at very low pressure. The funnel is visible owing to the formation of cloud droplets by expansional cooling in this low-pressure region. Very high winds spiral in toward the core. There is almost total devastation and often loss of life in the path of a tornado—which itself may move at up to 200m/s. Though generally rare, tornadoes occur worldwide, especially in the US and Australia in spring and early summer.

TORONTO, capital of Ontario province and York Co., second-largest city in Canada (after Montreal), on the NW shore of Lake Ontario. It is a major port as well as a commercial, manufacturing and educational center and the cultural focus of English-speaking Canada. Its products include chemicals, machinery, electrical goods and clothing. The French Fort Rouillé (c1750) was replaced by the English York (1793), which was sacked in the War of 1812, renamed in 1834 and was Canada's capital 1849–51 and 1855–59. Pop (city) 599,220; (metro) 3,274,200.

TORPEDO, self-propelled streamlined missile that travels underwater, its explosive warhead detonating when it nears or strikes its target. The torpedo was invented by Robert Whitehead, a British engineer, in

1866. Modern torpedoes are launched by dropping from airplanes or by firing from ships or submarines. They are electrically driven by propellers and guided by rudders controlled by a GYROPILOT. Many can be set to home in acoustically on their target. Rocket-propelled torpedoes are fired as guided missiles, and convert into torpedoes when they enter the water near their target. Torpedoes are now chiefly antisubmarine weapons.

TORQUEMADA, Tomás de (1420–1498), Spanish Dominican, fanatical inquisitor general appointed by Ferdinand and Isabella in 1483. Using the INQUISITION to enforce religious and political unity, he was responsible for expelling 200,000 Jews from Spain and burning over 2,000 heretics.

TORRICELLI, Evangelista (1608–1647), Italian physicist and mathematician, a one-time assistant of GALILEO, who improved the telescope and microscope and invented the mercury BAROMETER (1643).

TORT (French: wrong), in law, a wrongful act against a person or his property for which that person can claim damages as compensation. It is distinguished from a crime, which the state will prosecute; it is up to the injured party to sue for redress of a tort. The same wrongful act, an assault for example, may be both actionable as a tort and prosecuted as a crime. Torts range from personal injury to slander or LIBEL; they include trespass and damage or injury arising through negligence. Wrongful breach of an agreement, however, is covered by the law of CONTRACT.

TORTOISES, slow-moving, heavily-armored terrestrial reptiles of the tropics, subtropics and warmer temperate regions. The body is enclosed in a box-like shell into which the head and limbs can be withdrawn. The shell is covered with horny plates or scutes. Toothless, the jaws are covered to form a sharp, horny beak. All tortoises move slowly, feeding on vegetable matter. There are many species, ranging from the familiar garden tortoises to the 1.4m (4.6ft) giant tortoises of the Galapagos and Seychelles.

TORY, popular name of the Conservative and Unionist Party, one of Britain's two chief parties. The term (originally describing Irish highwaymen) was applied in 1679 to supporters of the future JAMES II of England. In the main, Tories became staunch church and king men, and "Tory" was applied to loyalist colonists in the American Revolution.

TOSCANINI, Arturo (1867–1957), Italian conductor, perhaps the greatest of his time, famous for dedication to each composer's intentions. He became musical director of La Scala in Milan (1898) and went on to conduct the New York Metropolitan (1908–14) and Philharmonic orchestras (1926–36). The NBC Symphony Orchestra was created for him in 1937.

TOTALITARIANISM, a system of government in which the state exercises wide-ranging control over individuals within its jurisdiction. Usually, a totalitarian state has but one political party, led by a dictator, and an official ideology that is disseminated through the mass media and educational system, with suppression of dissent. Nazi Germany and the Soviet Union are exemplary totalitarian states.

TOTEM, an object, animal or plant toward which a TRIBE, CLAN or other group feels a special affinity, often considering it a mythical ancestor. Killing of the totemic animal or animals by members of the group is TABOO, except, with some peoples, ritually during religious ceremonies. **Totem poles,** on which are carved human and animal shapes representing the particular warrior's heritage, were at one time common among the Amerinds.

TOUCH, the sensory system concerned with surface sensation, found in all external body surfaces including the SKIN and some mucous membranes. Touch sensation is crucial in the detection and recognition of objects at the body surface, including those explored by the limbs, and also in the protection of these surfaces from injury. Functional categories of touch sensation include light touch (including movement of HAIRS), heat, cold, pressure and pain sensation. These are to some degree physiologically distinct. Receptors for all the senses are particularly concentrated and developed over the face and hands. When the various types of skin receptor are stimulated, they activate nerve impulses in cutaneous nerves; these impulses pass via the SPINAL CORD and brain stem to the BRAIN, where coding and perception occur. With painful stimuli, REFLEX withdrawal movements may be induced at the segmental level.

TOULOUSE, chief city of SW France, seat of Haute-Garonne department. A commercial and industrial center, it produces aircraft (including Concorde) and plastics and has an old university (1229). Pop (city) 345,780; (metro) 523,000.

TOULOUSE-LAUTREC, Henri de (1864–1901), French painter and lithographer who portrayed Parisian nightlife. Of an old aristocratic family, he was crippled at 15, studied art in Paris and settled in Montmartre to paint the entertainers who lived there, such as Jane Avril and Aristide Bruant. Influenced by DEGAS and by Japanese prints, his work did much to popularize the lithographic poster.

TOURÉ, Sékou (1922–1984), president of the Republic of Guinea after he led it to independence in 1958. A labor leader in French colonial times, a Marxist and a political writer, Touré was the winner of the 1960 Lenin Peace Prize.

TOURNAMENT, a series of games, originally a combat between armored knights, usually on horseback. Popular in Europe in the Middle Ages, it provided both entertainment and training for war. In the 13th century the dangerous *melée* was replaced by the *joust* contest between only two knights, who tried to unhorse each other with lance, mace and sword.

TOURNEUR, Cyril (c1575–1626), English dramatist, supposed author of *The Revenger's Tragedy* (1607) and *The Atheist's Tragedy* (1611). These two revenge tragedies are powerful, violent and pessimistic.

TOURS, city in W central France, capital of Indre-et-Loire department, on the Loire R. A farm market and transportation center, it has metal, electrical and pharmaceutical industries. The advance of the Moors was halted here in 732 AD. Pop 133,580.

TOUSSAINT L'OUVERTURE, Pierre François Dominique (c1743–1803), Haitian black patriot and general. A freed slave of French St.-Domingue, W Hispaniola (Haiti), he headed the 1791 slave revolt and through military success and diplomacy took all Haiti amid French, Spanish, British and mulatto resistance. Despite his capture (1802) and death in France, Haiti became independent in 1804.

TOWER OF LONDON, ancient fortress on the Thames R in E London. Built 1078–1300, mainly by WILLIAM I the Conqueror and HENRY III, its massive stone buildings are enclosed by high walls and a moat. It has been palace, prison, arsenal and mint. Today it houses the crown jewels and an armor museum. Here Thomas MORE, Anne BOLEYN and Roger CASEMENT were executed. Rudolf HESS was its last prisoner.

TOWN MEETING, a directly democratic form of local government, mainly in New England (Mass., N.H. and Vt.). In colonial days, all enfranchised citizens met to choose officials, decide taxes and discuss affairs. In the 1800s meetings became an annual event called by warrant. Today, many town meetings are attended only by officials and elected representatives; but others are fully attended by the public when significant local issues are discussed.

TOWNSEND, Francis Everett
(1867–1960), US reformer, author of the
Townsend Plan (1933), a
SHARE-THE-WEALTH program by which
citizens over 60 were to receive $200 a
month, the money to be raised by a federal
tax. Claimed supporters of the plan
numbered 5,000,000, but Congress rejected
it.

TOWNSHEND, Charles (1725–1767),
English statesman who in 1767 as
chancellor of the exchequer originated the
politically disastrous TOWNSHEND ACTS. He
joined William PITT's cabinet in 1766, and
exercised great influence, due partly to
Pitt's illness.

TOWNSHEND ACTS (1767), four British
parliament acts, initiated by Charles
TOWNSHEND, which suspended the Massachusetts Assembly and imposed duties on
lead, glass, paint, paper and tea imports to
America. They proved hugely unpopular.
The BOSTON MASSACRE and repeal of all but
the tea tax took place on the same day in
1770. (See also BOSTON TEA PARTY.)

TOXIC SHOCK SYNDROME (TSS), a
rare and sometimes fatal disease associated
with the use of tampons. TSS is
characterized by high fever, vomiting and
diarrhea, followed by a sharp drop in blood
pressure that may bring on fatal shock. At
greatest risk are women under 30 during
their menstrual periods. The incidence is
low, with a frequency of about 3 cases per
100,000 women annually in the US, and the
mortality rate is about 10%.

TOXIN, a poisonous substance produced by
a living organism. Many microorganisms,
animals and plants produce chemical
substances which are poisonous to some
other organism; the toxin may be released
continuously into the immediate environment or released only when danger is
imminent. Examples include FUNGI which
secrete substances which destroy BACTERIA
(as ANTIBIOTICS these are of great value to
man) and poisonous spiders and snakes
which deliver their toxin via fangs. In some
organisms, the function of toxins is obscure,
but in many others they play an important
role in defense and in killing prey. The
symptoms of many INFECTIOUS DISEASES in
man (e.g., CHOLERA; DIPHTHERIA; TETANUS)
are due to the release of toxins by the
bacteria concerned. (See also ANTITOXINS.)

TOYNBEE, Arnold Joseph (1889–1975),
English historian whose principal work, *A
Study of History* (12 vols., 1934–61)
divides the history of the world into 26
civilizations and analyzes their rise and fall
according to a cycle of "challenge and

response."

TOYS, play-objects, principally for children. Some toys, such as balls, marbles,
tops, rattles, whistles, pull-along toys, dolls,
puppets and miniature animals, have been
universally popular throughout the ages.
Mechanical toys, construction kits and
working models of machinery are more
recent innovations, as is the famous "Teddy
Bear," named for Theodore ("Teddy")
Roosevelt, who once refused to shoot a bear
cub while out hunting. Educationalists such
as FROEBEL and MONTESSORI have stressed
the creative role of play in children's
development, and toys and "play materials"
are now an essential part of the modern
educational curriculum.

TRACHEA, the route by which air reaches
the LUNGS from the pharynx. Air is drawn in
through the mouth or NOSE and passes via
the LARYNX into the trachea, which then
divides into the major bronchi. It may be
seen below the Adam's apple. In
tracheostomy, it is incised to bypass any
obstruction to RESPIRATION.

TRACHOMA, INFECTIOUS DISEASE due to an
organism (bedsonia) intermediate in size
between BACTERIA and VIRUSES, the
commonest cause of BLINDNESS in the world.
It causes acute or chronic CONJUNCTIVITIS
and corneal INFLAMMATION with secondary
blood-vessel extension over the cornea
resulting in loss of translucency. Eyelid
deformity with secondary corneal damage is
also common. It is transmitted by direct
contact; early treatment with SULFA DRUGS
or TETRACYCLINE may prevent permanent
corneal damage.

TRACK AND FIELD, athletic sports
including running, walking, hurdling,
jumping for distance or height and throwing
various objects. In modern times organized
athletic contests developed rapidly from the
1860s onwards. The revival of the OLYMPIC
GAMES in 1896 gave international and
national competition an enormous boost,
and in 1913 the International Amateur
Athletics Federation was set up. Track and
field events now constitute a popular sport
throughout the world, and the training of
champions is a serious business, backed up
by government-sponsored programs, particularly in communist countries. The
Olympic Games have developed into a
quadrennial world championship, conducted in an atmosphere of intense rivalry, and
politics has overtaken professionalism as the
major problem confronting the organizers.
Track events. Distances raced vary from the
60-yd dash sprint to the marathon (26mi
385yds). Hurdlers and steeplechasers have
to clear a set number of obstacles. In relay

races a baton is passed from one runner to the next.

Field events. In high jump and pole vault the contestant who clears the greatest height with the least number of attempts wins. A long jump running or triple jump (hop, step and jump) competitor is permitted six jumps. Throwing events also permit six throws. The javelin is a spear thrown by running up to a line and releasing. The shot, a solid iron ball, is "put" from the shoulder. The discus is a circular plate, released with a sweeping sidearm action. The hammer throw consists of throwing an iron ball attached to a handle by a wire. All-around events include the 10-event decathlon and the 5-event pentathlon.

TRACTOR, self-propelled motor vehicle similar in principle to the AUTOMOBILE, but designed for high power and low speed. Used in agriculture, construction etc., tractors may pull other vehicles or implements, and may carry bulldozer and digging attachments. In the early 20th century the tractor, powered by the internal-combustion engine, largely superseded the steam traction engine and stationary farmi-machinery engines. Many tractors have four-wheel drive or endless crawler tracks.

TRACY, Spencer (1900–1967), durable US film star who received Academy Awards for his work in *Captains Courageous* (1937) and *Boys Town* (1938). He was most popular for his nine films with Katharine Hepburn.

TRADEMARK, device used by manufacturers to distinguish their products. It may be a design conjuring up an image of the product, a symbol, a "brand name" or a phrase. Trademarks are registered with the US Patent Office and their use is legally protected.

TRADE UNIONS. See UNIONS.

TRADE WINDS, persistent warm moist WINDS that blow westward from the high-pressure zones at about 30°N and S latitude toward the doldrums (intertropical convergence zone) at the equator. They are thus northeasterlies in the N Hemisphere and southeasterlies in the S Hemisphere. They are stronger and displaced toward the equator in winter.

TRADITION, in the Christian Church, the accumulated teachings and practices of the Church, handed down from one age to the next, by which Scripture and early Christian doctrine are elucidated and developed. It is embodied in the CREEDS, the decisions of ECUMENICAL COUNCILS and the writings of the Church Fathers and Doctors. The Roman Catholic Church recognizes tradition as authoritative because the Church is guided by the Holy Spirit; Protestants subordinate it to REVELATION and reason.

TRAFALGAR, Battle of, decisive naval engagement of the NAPOLEONIC WARS fought on Oct. 21, 1805. The British fleet of 27 warships under NELSON met a combined French and Spanish fleet of 33 ships off Cape Trafalgar (SW Spain). By attacking in an unorthodox formation Nelson surprised the enemy, sinking or capturing 20 vessels without loss, but was himself killed.

TRAGEDY, form of serious drama originating in ancient Greece, in which exceptional characters are led, by fate and by the very qualities that make them great, to suffer calamity and often death. ARISTOTLE, in his famous definition, spoke of purification (*catharsis*) through the rousing of the emotions of pity and fear. The great classical tragedians were AESCHYLUS, SOPHOCLES and EURIPIDES. Supreme in modern times is SHAKESPEARE. Great tragedians include LOPE DE VEGA, CALDERÓN DE LA BARCA, CORNEILLE, RACINE, GOETHE and SCHILLER. In the 19th and 20th centuries, whose drama usually shuns the heroic dimension of tragedy, the greatest exponents are probably IBSEN and O'NEILL. (See also THEATER.)

TRAHERNE, Thomas (c1637–1674), English religious poet and prose writer. His work, often naive and even childlike in expression, conveys his ardent love of God and a mystical sense of God's presence.

TRAJAN (Marius Ulpius Trajanus; c53–117 AD), famous Roman emperor responsible for great extensions of the empire and vast building programs. He conquered Dacia (Romania) and much of Parthia, and rebuilt the Roman Forum. Adopted heir by Nerva in 97 AD, he became emperor in 98. He was known as a capable administrator and a humane and tolerant ruler.

TRAKL, Georg (1887–1914), Austrian EXPRESSIONIST poet. His intense lyrics, with their haunting imagery, reveal a preoccupation with death and decay. An addict, he died of an overdose of cocaine while serving in the army.

TRANQUILIZERS, agents which induce a state of quietude in anxious or disturbed patients. Minor tranquilizers are SEDATIVES (e.g., benzodiazepines) valuable in the anxious. In psychosis (see MENTAL ILLNESS), especially schizophrenia and (hypo) mania, major tranquilizers are required to suppress abnormal mental activity as well as to sedate; phenothiazines (e.g., chlorpromazine) are often used.

TRANSCENDENTALISM, an idealistic philosophical and literary movement which flourished in New England c1835–60. Regarding rationalist UNITARIANISM and utilitarian philosophy as morally bankrupt and shallow, the Transcendentalists took their inspiration from the German idealists, notably KANT. from COLERIDGE and from Eastern mystical philosophies. They believed in the divinity and unity of man and nature and the supremacy of intuition over sense-perception and reason as a source of knowledge. The major figures were Ralph Waldo EMERSON and Margaret FULLER, who edited *The Dial* (1840–44), Henry David THOREAU and Amos Bronson ALCOTT. The movement had considerable influence on US literature (HAWTHORNE, MELVILLE; WHITMAN) and politics (ABOLITIONISM; BROOK FARM).

TRANSFORMER, a device for altering the voltage of an AC supply (see ELECTRICITY), used chiefly for converting the high voltage at which power is transmitted over distribution systems to the normal domestic supply voltage, and for obtaining from the latter voltages suitable for electronic equipment. It is based on INDUCTION: the "primary" voltage applied to a coil wound on a closed loop of a ferromagnetic core creates a strong oscillating magnetic field which in turn induces in a "secondary" coil wound on the same core an AC voltage proportional to the number of turns in the secondary coil. The core is laminated to prevent the flow of "eddy" currents which would otherwise also be induced by the magnetic field and would waste some ENERGY as HEAT.

TRANSFUSION, Blood, a means of BLOOD replacement in ANEMIA. SHOCK or HEMORRHAGE by intravenous infusion of blood from donors. It is the simplest and most important form of transplant, though, while of enormous value, it carries certain risks. Blood group compatibility based on ANTIBODY AND ANTIGEN reactions is of critical importance as incompatible transfusion may lead to life-threatening shock and KIDNEY failure. Infection (e.g., HEPATITIS) may be transmitted by blood, and FEVER or ALLERGY are common.

TRANSISTOR, electronic device made of semiconducting materials used in a circuit as an AMPLIFIER, rectifier, detector or switch. Its functions are similar to those of an electron tube, but it has the advantage of being smaller, more durable and consuming less power. The early and somewhat unsuccessful point-contact transistor has been superseded by the junction transistor, invented in 1948 by J. Bardeen, W. H. Brattain and W. B. Shockley. The junction transistor is a layered device consisting of two p-n junctions (see SEMICONDUCTOR) joined back to back to give either a p-n-p or n-p-n transistor. The three layers are formed by controlled addition of impurities to a semiconductor crystal, usually SILICON or germanium. The thin central region (p-type in an n-p-n transistor and n-type in a p-n-p one) is known as the *base*, and the two outer regions (n-type semiconductor in an n-p-n transistor) are the *emitter* and *collector*, depending on the way an external voltage is connected. To act as an amplifier in a circuit, an n-p-n transistor needs a negative voltage to the collector and base. If the base is sufficiently thin, it attracts ELECTRONS from the emitter which then pass through it to the positively charged collector. By altering the bias applied to the base (which need only be a few volts), large changes in the current from the collector can be obtained and the device amplified. A collector current up to a hundred times the base current can be obtained. This type of transistor is analogous to a triode electron tube, the emitter and collector being equivalent to the cathode and anode respectively and the base to the control grid. The functioning of a p-n-p transistor is similar to the n-p-n type described, but the collector current is mainly holes rather than electrons. Transistors revolutionized the construction of electronic circuits, but are being replaced by integrated circuits in which they and other components are produced in a single silicon wafer.

TRANSMIGRATION OF SOULS, the belief that on death the souls of men and animals pass into new bodies of the same or different species as punishment or reward for previous actions. Central to Buddhist and Hindu thought (see also KARMA), the doctrine is part of much mystical philosophy, and is often found in mystery cults and theosophical speculations (see MYSTERIES; THEOSOPHY).

TRANSMISSION, in engineering, a device for transmitting and adapting power from its source to its point of application. Most act by changing the angular velocity of the power shaft, either by step-variable means—gears, as in automobiles, or chains, as in bicycles—with fixed ratios and no slip, or by stepless means—belt-and-pulley systems or traction drives employing adjustable rolling contact—with continuously variable ratios but liable to slip. In an AUTOMOBILE with manual transmission, the flywheel on the engine crankshaft is connected to the gearbox via the **clutch,** two plates that are normally held tightly together by springs so that through friction they rotate together. When the clutch pedal is depressed, the plates are forced apart so that the engine is disengaged from the rest of the transmission. This is necessary when changing gear: sliding different sets of gears into engagement by means of a manual lever. Modern gearboxes have **synchromesh** in all forward gears: a coned clutch device that synchronizes the rotation of the gears before meshing. The gearbox is coupled to the final drive by a drive shaft with universal joints. A crown wheel and pinion, connected to the half-shafts of each drive wheel via a differential, complete the system. In **automatic transmission** there is no clutch pedal or gear lever; a fluid clutch, combined with sets of epicyclic gears selected by a governor according to the program set by the driver, provides a continuously variable torque ratio for maximum efficiency at all speeds.

TRANSPIRATION, the loss of water by EVAPORATION from the aerial parts of PLANTS. Considerable quantities of water are lost in this way, far more than is needed for the upward movement of solutes and for the internal metabolism of the plant alone. Transpiration is a necessary corollary of PHOTOSYNTHESIS, in that in order to obtain sufficient CARBON dioxide from the air, considerable areas of wet surface, from which high loss of water by evaporation is inevitable, have to be exposed. Plants have many means for reducing water loss, stomata playing an important part. Xerophytes in particular are adapted for minimizing transpiration.

TRANSPLANTS, organs that are removed from one person and surgically implanted in another to replace lost or diseased organs. Autotransplantation is the moving of an organ from one place to another within a person where the original site has been affected by local disease (e.g., skin grafting—see PLASTIC SURGERY). Blood TRANSFUSION was the first practical form of transplant. Here BLOOD cells and other components are transferred from one person to another. The nature of blood allows free transfusion between those with compatible blood groups. The next, most important, and now most successful of organ transplants, was that of the KIDNEY. Here a single kidney is transplanted from a live donor who is a close relative or from a person who has recently suffered sudden DEATH (e.g., by traffic accident or irreversible BRAIN damage), into a person who suffers from chronic renal failure. The kidney is placed beneath the skin of the abdominal wall and plumbed into the major ARTERIES and VEINS in the pelvis and into the BLADDER. High doses of STEROIDS and IMMUNITY suppressants are used to minimize the body's tendency to reject the foreign tissue of the graft. These doses are gradually reduced to lower maintenance levels, but may need to be increased again if rejection threatens. Here, tissue typing methods are used additionally to blood grouping to minimize rejection. HEART transplantation has been much publicized, but is limited to a few centers, many problems remaining. LIVER and LUNG transplants have also been attempted although here too the difficulties are legion. Corneal grafting is a more widespread technique in which the cornea of the EYE of a recently dead person replaces that of a person with irreversible corneal damage leading to BLINDNESS. The lack of blood vessels in the cornea reduces the problem of rejection. Grafts from nonhuman animals are occasionally used (e.g., pig SKIN as temporary cover in extensive BURNS). Both animal and human heart valves are used in cardiac surgery.

TRANSPORTATION, US Department of, responsible for the development and coordination of national transport policies and agencies. Set up in 1966, it reports to Congress on the optimum use of federal transportation funds. It supervises the federal Aviation, Highway, Railroad and Urban Mass Transportation administrations, the US COAST GUARD, the SAINT LAWRENCE SEAWAY Development Corporation and the National Transportation Safety Board.

TRANS-SIBERIAN RAILROAD, in the USSR, longest railroad in the world, stretching 5,787mi from Moscow to Vladivostock on the Sea of Japan, a journey which takes eight days. Its construction (1891–1916) had a dramatic effect on the development of Siberia.

TRANSUBSTANTIATION, Roman Catholic doctrine that in Holy COMMUNION the substance of the bread and wine is changed into that of the body and blood of Christ. It affirms belief in the Real Presence. (See also CONSUBSTANTIATION.)

TRANSURANIUM ELEMENTS, the elements with atomic numbers greater than that of URANIUM (92—see PERIODIC TABLE; ATOM). None occurs naturally: they are prepared by bombardment (usually with NEUTRONS or alpha particles) of suitably-chosen lighter ISOTOPES. All are radioactive (see RADIOACTIVITY), and those of higher atomic number tend to be less stable. Those so far discovered are the actinides from neptunium through lawrencium, rutherfordium and hahnium. Only neptunium and plutonium have been synthesized in large quantity; most of the others have been produced in weighable amounts, but some with very short HALF-LIVES can be studied only by special tracer methods.

TRANSVAAL, second-largest province in the Republic of South Africa, between the Vaal and Limpopo rivers in the NE. It is mainly high VELD 3,000–6,000ft above sea level. The capital is Pretoria and the largest city is Johannesburg. Mineral wealth includes gold, silver, diamonds, coal, iron ore, platinum, asbestos and chrome. Its farmlands are noted for their cattle, corn and tobacco. (See also BOER WAR; SOUTH AFRICA.)

TRANSYLVANIA, historic region of NW and central Romania. It is a plateau separated from the rest of Romania by the Transylvanian Alps to the S and the Carpathian Mts. to the E and N. It has been under Ottoman, Austrian and Hungarian control. There are rich mineral deposits, large areas of forest and fertile plains. The chief center is Cluj.

TRAPPISTS, popular name for Cistercians of the Reformed, or Strict, Observance, a Roman Catholic monastic order founded by Armand de Rancé, abbot of La Trappe in Normandy, France 1664–1700, who instituted a rigorous discipline of silence, prayer and work. There are 12 US abbeys. The abbot general lives in Rome.

TRASIMENO, Lake, shallow lake in central Italy, 10mi W of Perugia. It was the scene of HANNIBAL'S famous victory over the Romans (217 BC).

TRAVIS, William Barret (1809–1836), US lawyer and hero of the ALAMO. As commander of the garrison at the Alamo that was wiped out by the Mexican army, he became a national hero.

TREASON, behavior by a subject or citizen which could harm his sovereign or state. In many countries, including England before the 19th century, treason has been loosely defined and used as a political weapon. The US Constitution, however, states that treason consists only in levying war against the US or in adhering to its enemies, "giving them Aid and Comfort," and evidence of two witnesses or a confession in open court is necessary to secure a conviction.

TREASURY, US Department of, executive department of the US government, established in 1789 and responsible for federal taxes, customs and expenditure. It also plays a major role in national and international financial and monetary policies. Its head, the secretary of the treasury, the second-ranking member of the President's cabinet, is an *ex officio* governor of the INTERNATIONAL MONETARY FUND. The department's other responsibilities include the US SECRET SERVICE, and the bureaus of Customs, MINT. Engraving and Printing, Internal Revenue and Narcotics.

TREATY, an agreement in writing between two or more states. Treaties are bilateral (between two states) or multilateral (between several states), and cover matters such as trade, tariffs, taxation, economic and technical cooperation, diplomatic relations, international boundaries, extradition of criminals, defense and control of arms and aggression—anything on which international agreement is needed. Historically the most famous treaties have been those ending wars, such as the treaties of PARIS, VERSAILLES, WESTPHALIA. Some treaties, for example the NORTH ATLANTIC TREATY ORGANIZATION, are military; others set up international organizations: examples are the UNITED NATIONS; the COMMON MARKET (set up by the Treaty of Rome); the FOOD AND AGRICULTURE ORGANIZATION; the International Telecommunications Union. These have become an important part of modern INTERNATIONAL RELATIONS. (See also INTERNATIONAL LAW.)

TREATY PORTS, ports, notably in China and Japan, opened by treaty to foreign trade and whose foreign residents enjoyed EXTRATERRITORIALITY. In China 69 ports were opened—the first five to the British in 1842 after the OPIUM WAR. The system in Japan lasted 1854–99 but in China continued until WWII.

TREBIZOND, seaport in NE Turkey on the Black Sea. An early Greek city founded c756 BC, it became the capital of a powerful trade-based empire, 1204–1461 AD, ruled by the former Byzantine imperial family. Byzantine churches and much of the medieval city still remain. Pop 80,795.

TREE, woody perennial PLANT with a well defined main stem, or trunk, which either dominates the form throughout the life cycle (giving a pyramidal shape) or is dominant only in the early stages, later forking to form a number of equally important branches (giving a rounded or flattened form to the tree). It is often difficult to distinguish between a small tree and a shrub, but the former has a single trunk rising some distance from the ground before it branches while the latter produces several stems at, or close to, ground level. The trunk of a tree consists almost wholly of thick-walled water-conducting cells (xylem) which are renewed every year (see WOOD), giving rise to the familiar annual rings. The older wood in the center of the tree (the heartwood) is much denser and harder than the younger, outer sapwood. The outer skin, or the bark, insulates and protects the trunk and often shows characteristic cracks, or falls off leaving a smooth skin. Trees belong to the two most advanced groups of plants, the GYMNOSPERMS and the ANGIOSPERMS (the flowering plants). The former include the cone-bearing trees such as the pine, spruce and cedar; they are nearly all evergreens and mostly live in the cooler regions of the world. The angiosperms have broader leaves and much harder wood; in tropical climates they are mostly evergreen, but in temperate regions they are deciduous. (See also FORESTRY.)

TREITSCHKE, Heinrich von (1834–1896), German historian, at the U of Berlin from 1874. His *History of Germany in the Nineteenth Century* reflected his nationalistic, pro-Prussian, and anti-Semitic biases.

TRENT, Council of (1545–1563), the 19th ecumenical council of the Roman Catholic Church, at Trent, N Italy. In response to the REFORMATION. the council, first summoned by Pope PAUL III, formally redefined the Church's doctrines and banned many abuses. The council's reforms and doctrinal canons were the basis of the COUNTER-REFORMATION and became definitive statements of Catholic belief.

TRENT AFFAIR, naval incident in the US CIVIL WAR that nearly brought Britain to military support of the South. In Nov. 1861, Charles WILKES, commanding *San Jacinto*, stopped the British ship *Trent* and seized two Southern agents, J. M. Mason and John Slidell. Britain demanded an apology for this violation of the freedom of the sea and ordered 8,000 troops to Canada. The men were freed in December.

TRENTON, Battle of, American victory in the REVOLUTIONARY WAR. fought on Dec. 26, 1776. To forestall a British attack on Philadelphia, George WASHINGTON crossed the Delaware R at night and surprised a British force of 1,500 HESSIANS at Trenton, N.J. The battle was won in 45 minutes, rallying Washington's army and the American cause.

TREVELYAN, George Macaulay (1876–1962), British historian who rejected the "scientific" approach to history in favor of a more humanistic and literary approach. He taught at Cambridge (1927–51) and was best known for a colorful study of Garibaldi (3 vols., 1907–11), a one-volume *History of England* (1926), *England Under Queen Anne* (3 vols., 1903–34), and *English Social History* (1942).

TREVITHICK, Richard (1771–1833), British mining engineer and inventor primarily remembered for his work improving the STEAM ENGINE and for building the first railroad LOCOMOTIVE (c1804).

TREVOR-ROPER, Hugh Redwald (1914–), British historian. A professor at Oxford (1957–80), he wrote many works ranging from studies of the Elizabethan era to contemporary history. His best known books include *The Last Days of Hitler* (1947) and *The European Witch-Craze of the 16th and 17th Centuries* (1969).

TRIAL, judicial examination and determination of criminal prosecutions and law suits. In the US the right of an accused person to a speedy and public trial by a jury of his peers is guaranteed in the Constitution. Trials in COMMON LAW countries such as the UK and US are "adversary" proceedings, in which the court impartially decides between the evidence of two parties; under CIVIL LAW systems trials tend to be more "inquisitorial," allowing more scope for pretrial investigation and the court itself a greater role in the gathering of evidence. Under both systems the judge ensures that procedure is followed and that rules of evidence are observed, and determines the guilty offender's sentence; in common law systems he decides questions of law. Questions of fact are left to a JURY, if there is one; jury trial is more expensive and time-consuming, and so is reserved for more serious offenses. Although the US trial system today is designed to be as fair as possible, complexity, delay and expense create many serious flaws.

TRIANGLE, a three-sided polygon. There are three main types of plane triangle: scalene, in which no side is equal in length to another; isosceles, in which two of the sides are equal in length; and equilateral, in which all three sides are equal in length. A right (or right-angled) triangle has one interior angle equal to 90°, and may be either scalene or isosceles (see PYTHAGORAS' THEOREM). The "corners" of a triangle are termed vertices (singular, vertex). The sum of the angles of a plane triangle is 180°. A **spherical triangle** is an area of the surface of a sphere bounded by arcs of three great circles, each arc being less than 180°, each side and interior angle being termed an element. The sum of the three sides is never greater than 360°, the sum of the three angles always in the range 180°–540°.

TRIANGLE FIRE, fire on Mar. 25, 1911, at the Triangle Shirtwaist Co. in New York City in which 146 women died. The proprietors were acquitted of negligence.

New York thereafter enacted a stringent new building code and revised its labor laws.

TRIANGULAR TRADE, trading system in the 18th century. Rum and trinkets from New England were traded for West African slaves and ivory; these were taken to the West Indies and traded for tobacco and molasses, which were carried to New England. The Molasses Act (1733) and the Sugar Act (1764) were British attempts to gain revenue from this trade.

TRIANON, Treaty of, WWI peace settlement between the Allies and Hungary, signed in 1920. Hungary ceded two-thirds of her territory and population to neighboring states, became liable for reparations, and had her army limited to 35,000 men.

TRIASSIC, the first period of the MESOZOIC era, which lasted from about 225 to 190 million years ago. (See also GEOLOGY.)

TRIBONIAN (d. 545 AD), Roman jurist and minister of the Byzantine emperor JUSTINIAN I. During 530–32 and 534–45 he was chief compiler of the codification of Roman law into the *Corpus Iuris Civilis.*

TRIBUNE, an official in ancient Rome representing the PLEBEIANS. By 449 BC, 10 tribunes were elected by the people. They could veto the senate's actions and introduce resolutions (*plebiscita*). After 287 BC, *plebiscita* had the force of law, and tribunes became powerful as both initiators and obstructors of legislation. Famous reforming tribunes were the GRACCHI. By 27 BC tribunes had lost their power. There were also military and financial tribunes.

TRICHINOSIS, infestation with the larva of a worm (*Trichinella*), contracted from eating uncooked pork etc., causing a feverish illness. EDEMA around the eyes, MUSCLE pains and DIARRHEA occur early; later the LUNGS, HEART and BRAIN may be involved. It is avoided by the adequate cooking of pork. CHEMOTHERAPY may be helpful in severe cases.

TRIESTE, city-seaport in NE Italy at the head of the Adriatic Sea, with steel, oil and shipbuilding industries. A busy port in Roman times, it was part of Austria, 1382–1919, and then of Italy. Claimed by Yugoslavia in 1945, it was made a Free Territory 1947–54, then restored to Italy. Pop 244,980.

TRIGONOMETRY, the branch of GEOMETRY that deals with the ratios of the sides of right-angled triangles, and the applications of these ratios. The principal ratios, when considering ANGLE A of triangle ABC whose sides opposite the angles A, B and C respectively are a, b and c, where b is

the hypotenuse, are:

name	abbreviation	ratio
tangent	tan A	$\frac{a}{c}$
sine	sin A	$\frac{a}{b}$
cosine	cos A	$\frac{c}{b}$
cotangent	cot A	$\frac{c}{a}$
cosecant	cosec A	$\frac{b}{a}$
secant	sec A	$\frac{b}{c}$

As can be seen, the cotangent is the reciprocal of the tangent, the cosecant that of the sine, and the secant that of the cosine. The basis of trigonometric calculations is PYTHAGORAS' THEOREM, which in trigonometric form reads $\sin^2 A + \cos^2 A = 1$; this is true for any angle A.

From these ratios are derived the **trigonometric functions,** setting y equal to tan x, sin x, etc. These FUNCTIONS are termed transcendental (nonalgebraic). Of particular importance is the sine wave, in terms of which many naturally-occurring WAVE MOTIONS, such as SOUND and LIGHT, are studied.

TRILLING, Lionel (1905–1975), US literary critic and author. *The Liberal Imagination* (1950), and studies of Matthew Arnold (1939), E. M. Forster (1943) and Freud (1962) are informed by psychological, philosophical and sociological insights and methods.

TRINIDAD AND TOBAGO, independent state in the West Indies consisting of the islands Trinidad (1,864sq mi) and Tobago (116sq mi) off the coast of Venezuela.

Official name: Republic of Trinidad and Tobago
Capital: Port-of-Spain
Area: 1,978sq mi
Population: 1,221,000
Language: English
Religions: Roman Catholic, Hindu, Muslim
Monetary unit(s): 1 Trinidad and Tobago dollar=100 cents
Land. Trinidad is very fertile and mainly

flat, rising to about 3,000ft in the N, and Tobago has a mountain ridge 1,800ft high and is densely forested. The climate is tropical, with a rainfall range of 50-100in.

People. The population is mostly black (43%) and East Indian (36%), and there are also whites and Chinese. The literacy rate is over 90%.

Economy. The country, one of the most prosperous in the Caribbean, is rich in oil, natural gas and asphalt—Trinidad is famous for the large pitch lake near La Brea—and produces sugarcane, cocoa and fruit, but has to import many foodstuffs. Tourism is a growing industry.

History. Trinidad was discovered by COLUMBUS in 1498 and settled by the Spaniards, but British rule was establishd in 1802. Trinidad and Tobago joined the West Indies Federation in 1958 but left in 1962 to become independent. It became a republic in 1976. Eric Williams was premier from 1962 until his death in 1981 and his party, the People's National Movement, controlled the government until 1986.

TRINITY, the central doctrine of Christian theology, that there is one GOD who exists in three Persons and one Substance. The definition of the doctrine, implicit in the New Testament, by the early ecumenical councils (notably NICAEA and Constantinople) was the product of violent controversy with such heresies as ARIANISM, MONOPHYSITISM, NESTORIANISM and Monarchianism. It is classically summed up in the ATHANASIAN CREED. The three Persons—the Father, the Son (see INCARNATION; JESUS CHRIST) and the HOLY SPIRIT—are each fully God: coequal, coeternal and consubstantial, yet are distinct. The Son is "eternally begotten" by the Father; the Holy Spirit "proceeds" from the Father and (in Western theology) from the Son. The doctrine is a mystery, being known by revelation and being above reason (though not unreasonable). Hence it has been challenged by rationalists (see DEISM; SOCINIANISM; UNITARIANISM) and by such sects as the JEHOVAH'S WITNESSES and MORMONS.

TRIPLE ALLIANCE, name of several European alliances: between England, Sweden and the Netherlands against France (1668); between England, France and the Netherlands (1717; see also QUADRUPLE ALLIANCE); between Germany, Austria-Hungary and Italy (1882).

TRIPLE ENTENTE, informal diplomatic understanding between Britain, France and Russia which acted as a counterweight to the TRIPLE ALLIANCE of 1882. It lasted 1907-17. After the outbreak of WWI, it

became a military alliance. (See also ENTENTE.)

TRIST, Nicholas Philip (1800–1874), US diplomat, sent (Apr. 1847) by President James K. POLK to negotiate peace with Mexico during the MEXICAN WAR. When Mexican president SANTA ANNA resigned, Polk recalled Trist, intending to impose severe terms on Mexico. Trist disobeyed and negotiated the Treaty of GUADALUPE HIDALGO, which both countries ratified.

TRIUMVIRATE, in ancient Rome, a group of three leaders sharing office or supreme power. The First Triumvirate (60–53 BC) was formed by Julius CAESAR, POMPEY and CRASSUS. The Second Triumvirate (43–36 BC) consisted of Octavian (later the Emperor AUGUSTUS), Marcus Lepidus and Mark ANTHONY.

TROBRIAND ISLANDS, small group of coral islands in the Solomon Sea, SW Pacific Ocean, part of Papua-New Guinea. Losuia is the principal settlement and stands on the largest island, Kiriwina. The islands are famous through the work of the anthropologist Bronislaw MALINOWSKI.

TROELTSCH, Ernst (1865–1923), German Protestant theologian and historian of religion, known for his comprehensive study of Christian social teachings and his research relating religion to other aspects of cultural and social life.

TROJAN WAR, conflict between Greece and Troy, made famous by HOMER's *Iliad*. Paris, son of Priam of Troy, carried off HELEN, wife of Menelaus of Sparta, and took her to Troy. The Greeks, led by AGAMEMNON, Menelaus, ODYSSEUS, ACHILLES and other heroes, swore to take revenge. They besieged Troy for 10 years, then pretended to sail away, leaving a huge wooden horse outside the city, with Greek soldiers concealed in its belly. The Trojans dragged it into the city, and that night the soldiers opened the city gates to the Greek army. Most of the Trojans were killed and the city was burnt. The legend is thought to have been based on an actual conflict of c1250 BC.

TROLLOPE, Anthony (1815–1882), English novelist, famous for his six *Barsetshire* novels about middle-class life in an imaginary cathedral town, including *The Warden* (1855) and *Barchester Towers* (1857). He was a sharp but sympathetic observer of social and political behavior, as revealed in his political *Palliser* novels, such as *Phineas Finn* (1869) and *The Prime Minister* (1876).

TROMBONE, musical instrument, one of the brass WIND INSTRUMENTS. It has a slide mechanism to alter the length of the playing tube and increase the note range. Developed from the sackbut, it was first used in a symphony by BEETHOVEN in 1808.

TROMP, Maarten Harpertszoon (1597–1653), Dutch admiral. He twice crushed the Spanish fleet in 1639 in the English Channel. In the first DUTCH WAR his defeat of the English admiral Robert BLAKE (1652) led to Dutch control of the Channel. After setbacks in 1653 Tromp was killed in battle.

TROPICAL MEDICINE, branch of MEDICINE concerned with the particular diseases encountered in and sometimes imported from the tropics. These largely comprise infectious diseases due to VIRUSES (e.g., YELLOW FEVER, SMALLPOX, lassa fever), BACTERIA (e.g., CHOLERA), protozoa (e.g., MALARIA, trypanosome diseases) and worms (e.g., filariasis) which are generally restricted to tropical zones. The ANTIBIOTIC treatment and CHEMOTHERAPY of bacterial and PARASITIC DISEASES and their prevention with prophylactic DRUGS and by control of insect or other vectors are important aspects of this specialty. The diseases of MALNUTRITION—KWASHIORKOR, marasmus and the VITAMIN deficiency diseases of BERI-BERI, PELLAGRA etc.—often fall in the province of tropical disease as do SUNSTROKE and SNAKE BITES.

TROPICS, the lines of latitude lying 23½°N (**Tropic of Cancer**) and S (**Tropic of Capricorn**) of the equator. They represent the farthest southerly latitudes where the sun is, at one time of the year, directly overhead at noon. This occurs at the time of the summer SOLSTICE in each hemisphere. The term is used also of the area between the two tropics.

TROPISMS, movements of PLANTS in response to external directional stimuli. If a plant is laid on its side, the stem will soon start to bend upward again. This movement (geotropism) is a response to the force of gravity. The stem is said to be negatively geotropic. Roots are generally positively geotropic and grow downward. Phototropisms are bending movements in response to the direction of illumination. Stems are generally positively phototropic (bend toward the light). Most roots are negatively phototropic, although some appear unaffected by light. Some roots exhibit positive hydrotropism: they bend toward moisture. This response is more powerful than the response to gravity; roots can be deflected from their downward course if the plants are watered only on one side. Tropisms are controlled by differences in concentration of growth HORMONES.

TROPOSPHERE, the lowermost zone of the earth's ATMOSPHERE, extending from the earth's surface to 5-6mi over the poles and 8-10mi over the equator. In this zone normal lapse rates prevail, i.e. temperatures decrease with altitude. The top of the troposphere is called the *tropopause.*

TROTSKY, Leon (Lev Davidovich Bronstein; 1879–1940), Russian revolutionary communist, a founder of the USSR. President of the Petrograd (Leningrad) soviet in the 1905 revolution, he escaped from prison to France, Spain and New York. In 1917 he returned, went over to BOLSHEVISM and led the Bolshevik seizure of power in the October RUSSIAN REVOLUTION. As commissar of foreign affairs (1917–18) he resigned over the treaty of BREST-LITOVSK and became commissar of war (1918–25), organizing the Red Army into an effective force. After LENIN's death (1924) he lost power to STALIN and was deported (1929). Bitterly opposed to Stalin's "socialism in one country," he continued to advocate international revolution, founded the Fourth INTERNATIONAL and attacked Stalinism in *The Revolution Betrayed* (1937). He was murdered in Mexico City by a Stalinist agent.

TROUBADOURS, courtly poet-musicians of Provence, S France, c1100–c1300. Their poems, written in PROVENÇAL, mostly on the theme of love, were sung. Troubadours developed the conventions of courtly love, and influenced poetry and music in Germany (see MINNESINGER), Italy, Spain and England.

TROY, city of ancient NW Asia Minor, near the Dardanelles, described in HOMER's *Iliad* and rediscovered by SCHLIEMANN in 1870. The earliest site (Troy I) dates from c3000 BC. Troy II contained an imposing fortress and had wide trade contacts. Its famous treasure of gold, copper and bronze indicates a wealthy community. Troy VI, c2000–1300 BC, had a citadel surrounded by huge limestone walls, and large houses built on terraces. It was destroyed by earthquake. The rebuilt Troy VIIa was probably Homer's Troy. It was looted and destroyed by fire c1250 BC. Troy VIII was a small Greek village. Troy IX was the Greek and Roman city of Ilium.

TROYES, Treaty of, 1420, agreement between CHARLES VI of France and HENRY V of England, recognizing Henry as heir to the French throne. The disinherited dauphin later repudiated the treaty, becoming CHARLES VII of France.

TRUCIAL STATES. See UNITED ARAB EMIRATES.

TRUCK, automotive vehicle used for transporting freight by road. The typical long-distance truck is an articulated vehicle comprising a two- or three-axled "truck tractor" coupled to a two-axled "semi-trailer." A two- or three-axled "full trailer" may in addition be coupled to the semitrailer. Most trucks are powered by a DIESEL ENGINE, have a manual TRANSMISSION with perhaps as many as 16 forward gears, and have air brakes. In the US, trucks carry about 40% of all intercity freight (compared with the railroads' 30%); the industry is organized under a trade association, American Trucking Associations Inc., while the American Association of State Highway Officials regulates truck sizes and weights. Overall supervision of trucking is undertaken by the INTERSTATE COMMERCE COMMISSION.

TRUCK FARMING, large-scale commercial production of fresh vegetables and fruits for local or distant markets. Modern truck farming has been revolutionized by mechanical harvesting and handling and by modern methods of preserving and transporting fresh produce. The principal US farming regions are in Cal., Fla., Tex., the Atlantic Coastal Plain and the Great Lakes area.

TRUDEAU, Garry (Garretson Beekman Trudeau; 1948–   ), US cartoonist, creator (1970) of the comic strip *Doonesbury.*

TRUDEAU, Pierre Elliott (1919–   ), Canadian prime minister (1968–79, 1980–84). A law professor, he entered parliament in 1965, became minister of justice in 1967 and succeeded Lester PEARSON as prime minister and Liberal Party leader (1968). He has sought to promote a dialogue between the provincial and federal governments and to contain the Quebec separatist movement, giving the French language equal status with English. In 1970 he recognized the People's Republic of China. Briefly out of office (1979–80), he returned to cope anew with the constitutional issue that resulted in the CONSTITUTION ACT, 1982.

TRUFFAUT, François (1932–1984), French film director and critic. A leading New Wave director, he attracted attention for his series of semi-autobiographical films, including *The 400 Blows* (1959), *Stolen Kisses* (1968) and *Day for Night* (1973). His other films include *Jules and Jim* (1961), *Small Change* (1976) and *The Last Metro* (1980).

TRUFFLES, underground fungi of the genus *Tuber* that have long been regarded as a delicacy. Pigs and dogs are trained to find them by scent. Some grow up to 1kg (2.2lb) and resemble potatoes; most are much smaller.

TRUJILLO MOLINA, Rafael Leonidas (1891–1961), Dominican dictator 1930–61, and president 1930–38, 1942–52. He introduced much material progress, but savagely suppressed political opposition and feuded with neighboring countries. He was assassinated.

TRUMAN, Harry S (1884–1972), 33rd president of the US (1945–53). Inexperienced and virtually unknown, he became president after F. D. ROOSEVELT's sudden death, and in the difficult post-WWII years attempted to contain communist expansion and to continue the NEW DEAL programs. Truman entered politics in 1919 with help from the Kansas City Democratic political boss T. J. Pendergast, who in 1934 backed his election as a Mo. senator. In 1940 he gained prominence as head of a committee investigating corruption in defense industries, and in 1944 was chosen by Roosevelt as his vice-presidential candidate to replace Henry Wallace. On becoming president Truman accepted the German surrender, was involved in the establishment of the UNITED NATIONS, attended the POTSDAM CONFERENCE and made the controversial decision to use the atom bomb against Japan, thus ending the war. He took a tough line over Russia's attempted annexation of Poland. At home, amid economic difficulties and labor unrest, a hostile Congress blocked most of his FAIR DEAL program, and passed the TAFT-HARTLEY ACT over Truman's veto. As the COLD WAR hardened, he regarded communist expansion as the major threat, and responded with the TRUMAN DOCTRINE and the MARSHALL PLAN, followed by the POINT FOUR PROGRAM and the setting-up of the NORTH ATLANTIC TREATY ORGANIZATION. (See also BERLIN AIRLIFT.) Truman's unpopularity at home made his decision to run again in 1948 seem hopeless, but despite all predictions he won by a narrow margin. During his second term Truman again had his Fair Deal measures blocked by Congress, except for a Housing Act (1949), was embroiled in the anti-communist hysteria generated by MCCARTHY, and had his seizure of the steel industry during a strike declared unconstitutional. He sent troops to fight the KOREAN WAR, and amid controversy over US Far East policy, removed General MACARTHUR for insubordination.

TRUMAN DOCTRINE, US declaration (1947), aimed to combat communist expansion, particularly in Greece and Turkey, stating the US would "support free peoples who are resisting attempted subjugation by armed minorities or by outside pressures."

TRUMBULL, John (1750–1831), US poet and judge. A leader of the HARTFORD WITS, he is best known for *The Progress of Dulness* (1772–73) and *M'Fingal* (1775–82), a mock-epic based on Samuel BUTLER's *Hudibras*, satirizing the British Tories.

TRUMBULL, John (1756–1843), US painter. He studied with Benjamin WEST in London where he started *The Battle of Bunker's Hill* (1786). He made 36 life portrait studies for his best-known work, *The Signing of the Declaration of Independence* (1786–94), one of his four monumental pictures on revolutionary themes for the US Capitol rotunda (1817–24). He is also well known for his portraits of George Washington.

TRUMPET, musical instrument, one of the brass WIND INSTRUMENTS. The modern trumpet comprises a cylindrical tube in a curved oblong form which flares out into a bell. Three piston valves, first introduced c1815, regulate pitch. The standard orchestral trumpet is generally in B Flat. The trumpet is a popular dance and jazz-band instrument.

TRUST, in law, a legal relationship in which property is administered by a **trustee,** who has some of the powers of an owner, for the benefit of a beneficiary; the trustee is obliged to act only in the beneficiary's best interest, and can derive no advantage except an agreed fee. His powers are limited to those specified or implied in the document establishing the trust. The trustee may be an individual, perhaps looking after the property of a child until it comes of age, or a corporate body; banks and trust corporations often act as trustees of larger properties. Trusts are a major feature of EQUITY law. Certain categories of trust, generally those with some charitable or other aim beneficial to the public, may be given tax relief. Under a specialized form, the corporate trust, a group of trustees held the stock and thus controlled the operations of companies that would normally have been competitors; this enabled Standard Oil Co. and others to control whole industries and to fix prices to suit themselves. These monopolistic business combinations continued to be called trusts even after they were replaced by the "holding company." The Sherman Antitrust Act (1890) attacked the trusts, but enforcement was vitiated by US Supreme Court decisions. Enforcement of antitrust legislation in recent years has been complicated by the growth of huge conglomerates, which control many companies in different industries.

TRUST TERRITORY, formerly a dependent territory administered under UNITED NATIONS supervision. A trustee nation was responsible for developing the trust territory and assisting it to independence. The Trusteeship Council helped the General Assembly and Security Council supervise trust territories. Of the 11 trust territories (mostly former MANDATES of the LEAGUE OF NATIONS)—British Cameroons, French Cameroons, Ruanda-Urundi, Italian Somaliland, Tanganyika, British Togoland, French Togoland, Nauru, Pacific Islands, New Guinea and Western Samoa—the US-administered Pacific Islands was the last to be terminated (1981). In 1986 the Northern Mariana Islands became a US commonwealth, and the Federated States of Micronesia and the Marshall Islands gained sovereignty in free association with the US; the UN Trusteeship Council recommended dissolution of the trusteeship in 1988 despite the inability of Palau (the remaining unit) and the US to reach agreement on a compact of free association.

TRUTH, Sojourner (c1797–1883), US abolitionist. A slave until 1827, originally called Isabella, she traveled the North from 1843 preaching Negro emancipation and women's rights. In the mid-1860s in Washington D.C. she worked to resettle ex-slaves.

TRUTH, philosophical concept understood by philosophers according to three main theories. "Correspondence" theories hold that a statement is true if it corresponds to the "facts" of experience. "Coherence" theories contend, however, that facts are themselves statements of a kind whose truth cannot be tested by looking for further correspondences, but only by considering their logical coherence with other statements about supposed reality. "Pragmatic" theories of truth stress that the only usefully testable "truths" are those that enable us to anticipate or control the course of events. (See also EMPIRICISM; RATIONALISM; PRAGMATISM.)

TRUTH-IN-LENDING ACT, a 1968 law (the Consumer Credit Protection Act) requiring the clear disclosure of credit terms, especially the interest rate figured on an annual basis. The law applies to banks, credit-card companies, car dealers, department stores, and others who extend consumer credit.

TRUTH-IN-PACKAGING ACT, a 1966 US law (the Fair Packaging and Labeling Act) requiring food, drug and cosmetic producers to state on the container label the product's ingredients; to specify the quantity being sold; and not to mislead the consumer with large but underfilled containers.

TRUTH SERUM. See PENTOTHAL, SODIUM.

TRYON, William (1729–1788), British governor of N.C. (1765–71). In 1771, after harshly crushing the revolt of the REGULATORS at the battle of Alamance, he was appointed governor of N.Y.

TSAR, or Czar (from Latin, *Ceasar*), title used by Russian emperors. First adopted by IVAN IV, who in 1547 was crowned "tsar of all Russia," the title continued until 1918 when the last tsar, NICHOLAS II, was murdered.

TSETSE FLIES, 20 species of muscoid flies of the genus *Glossina*. They are true winged flies very like houseflies except that the mouthparts are adapted for piercing the skin of mammals and sucking blood. Widespread in tropical Africa, their significance lies in that some species act as vectors of the trypanosomes which cause SLEEPING SICKNESS in humans.

TSHOMBE, Moise Kapenda (1919–1969), president 1960–63 of the Congolese breakaway state of Katanga. Backed by Belgian interests, he opposed LUMUMBA and the UN. He returned from exile to be premier (1964–65) of the Congo (ZAIRE). Dismissed, he was sentenced to death, and died in prison in Algeria.

TSIOLKOVSKY, Konstantin Eduardovich (1857–1935), Russian physicist who pioneered ROCKET science, but who is perhaps most important for his role in educating the Soviet government and people into acceptance of the future potential of SPACE EXPLORATION. He also built one of the first WIND TUNNELS (c1892). A large crater on the far side of the MOON is named for him; and the timing of Sputnik I's launch marked the 100th anniversary of his birth.

TSUNAMI, formerly called **tidal wave,** fast-moving ocean wave caused by submarine EARTHQUAKES, volcanic eruptions, etc., found mainly in the Pacific, and often taking a high toll of lives in affected coastal areas. In midocean, the wave height is usually under 1m, the distance between succeeding crests of the order of 200km, and the velocity about 750km/h. Near the coast, FRICTION with the sea bottom slows the wave, so that the distance between crests decreases, the wave height increasing to about 25m or more.

TSUSHIMA, Battle of, decisive sea battle of May 1905 which effectively ended the RUSSO-JAPANESE WAR. Japanese Admiral Heihachiro TOGO's fleet destroyed or captured almost all the Russian Baltic Fleet under Admiral Rozhdestvenski. The battle

took place near Tsushima Island, between Japan and Korea.

TSVETAYEVA, Marina Ivanova (1892–1941), Russian modernist poet. Her lyrical poetry, such as *King-Maiden* (1922), is noted for its concise style and variety of rhythms. Away from Russia 1922–39, she returned home, later committing suicide.

TUAREGS, a BERBER tribe in the Sahara, about 300,000 in number. Its people are fair-skinned; the social system comprises noble families, a large number of vassal tribes, and Negro slaves. Adult men, but not women, wear a blue veil. Tuareg script is like that of the ancient Libyans.

TUBA, low-pitched brass musical WIND INSTRUMENT with three to five valves. It is held vertically. There are tenor, baritone, euphonium, bass and contrabass tubas—the CC contrabass being popular in orchestras, the BB contrabass in bands.

TUBER, swollen underground stems and roots which are organs of perennation and vegetative propagation and contain stored food material. The potato is a stem tuber. It swells at the tip of a slender underground stem (or stolon) and gives rise to a new plant the following year. Dahlia tubers are swollen roots.

TUBERCULIN, PROTEIN derivative of the mycobacteria responsible for TUBERCULOSIS. This may be used in tests of cell-mediated IMMUNITY to tuberculosis, providing evidence of previous disease (often subclinical) or immunization. The substance was originally isolated by KOCH.

TUBERCULOSIS (TB), a group of INFECTIOUS DISEASES caused by the bacillus *Mycobacterium tuberculosis*, which kills some 3 million people every year throughout the world. TB may invade any organ but most commonly affects the respiratory system where it has been called consumption or phthisis (see also LUPUS VULGARIS and SCROFULA). In 1906 it killed 1 in every 500 persons in the US, but today it leads to only 1 in 30,000 deaths, because of effective drugs and better living conditions. Recent increases in TB cases have been attributed to the spread of AIDS and to the arrival of infected or high-risk people from other countries. The disease is spread in three ways: inoculation via cuts, etc.; inhalation of infected sputum; and ingestion of infected food. In pulmonary TB there are two stages of infection. In primary infection there are usually no significant symptoms: dormant small hard masses called tubercles are formed by the body's defenses. In postprimary infection the dormant BACTERIA are reactivated due to weakening of the body's defenses and clinical symptoms become evident. Symptoms include fatigue, weight loss, persistent cough with green or yellow sputum and possibly blood. Treatment nowadays is mainly by triple drug therapy with streptomycin, para-aminosalicylic acid (PAS) and isoniazid, together with rest. Recovery takes about 2 years.

The TUBERCULIN skin test can show whether a person has some IMMUNITY to the disease, though the detection of the disease in its early stages, when it is readily curable, is difficult. Control of the disease is accomplished by preventive measures such as X-RAY screening, VACCINATION, isolation of infectious people and food sterilization.

TUBMAN, Harriet Ross (c1820–1913), US fugitive slave and abolitionist. She was active in the UNDERGROUND RAILROAD after 1850. Nicknamed "Moses," she helped over 300 slaves to freedom. In the Civil War she was a Union spy and scout.

TUBMAN, William Vacanarat Shadrach (1895–1971), president of Liberia (1944–71). He made extensive economic, social and educational reforms and extended the rights of tribespeople and women.

TUDOR, Antony (1909–1987), English choreographer who introduced dramatic, emotional themes into US ballet. He was a founder (1939) of the American Ballet Theatre, where his *Dark Elegies* (1937) and *Pillar of Fire* (1942) became part of the repertory.

TUDOR, House of, reigning dynasty of England, 1485–1603. Of Welsh descent, Henry Tudor, Earl of Richmond and heir to the House of LANCASTER, ended the Wars of the ROSES by defeating Richard III in 1485 and became HENRY VII, first Tudor king. After him came HENRY VIII (reigned 1509–47), EDWARD VI (1547–53), MARY I (1553–58) and ELIZABETH I (1558–1603). Under the Tudors England became a major power and enjoyed a flowering of the arts.

TU FU (712–770), one of the greatest Chinese poets. His concise and evocative style, typical of the T'ANG period, expresses the tragic conditions of his life and that of the poor.

TUGWELL, Rexford Guy (1891–1979), US economist and public official. He taught (1920–37) at Columbia U, taking time out to serve as a member of President Franklin Roosevelt's "BRAIN TRUST" and in the US Department of Agriculture. As governor of Puerto Rico (1941–46) he developed plans for the economic development of the island known as Operation Bootstrap. He taught at the U of Chicago 1946–57.

TUKHACHEVSKY, Mikhail Nikolayevich (1893–1937), Soviet marshal. A tsarist officer in WWI and an officer in the Red Army from 1918, he fought in the civil war and the Russo-Polish War, becoming chief of staff (1925–28) and deputy military commissar (from 1931). In 1937 he was charged with treason and executed along with other top military leaders. His reputation was restored by Nikita KHRUSHCHEV in 1957.

TULAREMIA, or rabbit fever, INFECTIOUS DISEASE due to BACTERIA, causing FEVER, ulceration, LYMPH node enlargement and sometimes PNEUMONIA. It is carried by wild animals, particularly rabbits, and insects. ANTIBIOTICS are fully effective in treatment.

TULIP, bulbous plants of the genus *Tulipa* native to Europe and Asia. Cultivated tulips were introduced to Europe via Holland in the 16th century and have become popular spring-flowering garden and pot plants. They have deep, cup-shaped flowers and new varieties are continually being bred. Family: Liliaceae.

TULL, Jethro (1674–1741), British agricultural scientist who invented a horse-drawn hoe for cultivating the ground between the rows (after 1715).

TUMBLEWEED, common name for several plants native to North America that grow in clumps on waste land and dry into loose balls. These break from the soil and are blown by the wind, scattering seeds. Examples are the Russian thistle (*Salsola kali*) and *Amaranthus albus*.

TUMOR, strictly, any swelling on or in the body, but more usually used to refer only to an abnormal overgrowth of tissue (or **neoplasm**). These may be benign proliferations such as fibroids of the WOMB, or they may be forms of CANCER, LYMPHOMA or SARCOMA, which are generally malignant. The rate of growth, the tendency to spread locally and to distant sites via the BLOOD vessels and LYMPH system, and systemic effects determine the degree of malignancy of a given tumor. Tumors may present themselves as a lump, by local compression effects (especially with BRAIN tumors), by bleeding (GASTROINTESTINAL TRACT tumors) or by systemic effects including ANEMIA, weight loss, false HORMONE actions, NEURITIS etc. Treatments include surgery, RADIATION THERAPY and CHEMOTHERAPY.

TUNDRA, the treeless plains of the Arctic Circle. For most of the year the temperature is less than 0°C, and even during the short summer it never rises above 10°C. The soil is a thin coating over PERMAFROST. Tundra vegetation includes lichens, mosses and stunted shrubs. Similar regions on high mountains (but generally without permafrost) are **alpine tundra**.

TUNGSTEN (W), or **wolfram**, hard, silvery-gray metal in Group VIB of the PERIODIC TABLE; a transition element. Its chief ores are scheelite and wolframite. The metal is produced by reduction of heated tungsten dioxide with hydrogen. Its main uses are in tungsten steel ALLOYS for high-temperature applications, and for the filaments of incandescent lamps. It is relatively inert, and resembles MOLYB-DENUM. Cemented **tungsten carbide** (WC) is used in cutting tools. AW 183.9, mp 3410°C, bp 5660°C, sg 19.3 (20°C).

TUNGUS, an ALTAIC LANGUAGE people of subarctic E Siberia, related to the MANCHUS. They comprise two groups. The Evenki live E of the Yenisey R to the Pacific and from the Amur R to the Arctic, while the Lamuti live on the Sea of Okhotsk coast.

TUNING FORK, simple two-pronged instrument which, when struck, emits a pure tone of fixed PITCH—usually A above middle C. It is used to tune musical instruments, expecially pianos.

TUNISIA, North African republic on the Mediterranean Sea, with Algeria to the W and Libya to the SE.

Official name: Republic of Tunisia
Capital: Tunis
Area: 59,664sq mi
Population: 7,662,000
Languages: Arabic; French
Religions: Muslim
Monetary unit(s): 1 dinar=1,000 millimes
Land. The 639mi coastline has several good harbors. In the NW the Atlas mountains form a high wooded plateau and rise to 5,000ft in the W. The Medjerda R is the only permanent river; it irrigates a major wheat-producing area. In the S beyond Chott Djerid and other salt lakes lies the Sahara Desert. The summers are hot and dry, the winters mild and wet. Annual rainfall varies from 30in in the N to 4in in the S.

People. Tunisia is the most densely populated of North African countries. Most people live in the fertile N. The population is predominantly BERBER and Arab. There are small French, Italian and Maltese minorities. Tunis, the capital and primary port, Sfax, Sousse, Bizerta and Kairouan are the largest cities; 40% of the population live in towns.

Economy. Crude petroleum is the country's principal export, followed by clothing, olive oil and phosphates. The main crops are wheat, barley and other grains; olives, citrus, dates and wine grapes; and vegetables. Industry has traditionally centered around food processing but is expanding. Tunisia's rich oil deposits, its political stability and educated work force have enhanced development, but inflation and unemployment have kindled unrest in recent years.

History. Formerly a Phoenician colony, Tunisia was conquered in 146 BC by the Romans, in 439 AD by the VANDALS, in 533 by the Byzantines, in 670 by the Arabs, in 1574 by Turkish pirates and in 1881 by the French who made it a protectorate. Habib BOURGUIBA founded the nationalist Neo-Destour Party in 1934 and after Tunisia's independence (1956) became president of the Tunisian republic in 1957. In 1975 he declared himself president for life. Bourguiba earned a reputation as a moderate and pro-Western Arab leader. In 1965 he suggested that the Arabs should recognize Israel, and in 1987 he sternly suppressed Muslim fundamentalists accused of attempting to overthrow the government. In Nov. 1987 Prime Minister Zine el-Abidine Ben Ali deposed Bourguiba on grounds that the president was too ill and senile to govern. Ben Ali assumed the presidency, promising democratic, constitutional government. The next general election was scheduled for 1991.

TUNNEL, underground passageway, usually designed to carry a highway or railroad, to serve as a conduit for water or sewage, or to provide access to an underground working face (see MINING). Although tunnels have been built since prehistoric times, tunneling methods remained primitive and hazardous until the 19th century. Modern softground tunneling was pioneered by Marc BRUNEL, who in 1824 invented the "tunneling shield"—a device subsequently improved (1869–86) by James Greathead. The Greathead shield is basically a large steel cylinder with a sharp cutting edge driven forward by hydraulic rams. Used in conjunction with a compressed-air atmosphere, it protects excavating workmen against cave-ins and water seepage. Tunneling through hard rock is facilitated by an array of pneumatic drills mounted on a "jumbo" carriage running on rails. Explosives are inserted in a pattern of holes drilled in the rock face and then detonated. Increasingly used today, however, are automatic tunneling machines called "moles," with cutting heads consisting of a rotating or oscillating wheel that digs, grinds or chisels away the working face. Another common tunnel-building method—used in constructing the New York SUBWAY—is "cut-and-cover," which involves excavating a trench, building the tunnel-lining and then covering it. The world's longest tunnel is the 33.6mi Seikan Tunnel between the Japanese islands of Honshu and Hokkaido, which opened in Mar. 1988.

TUNNEY, Gene (James Joseph Tunney; 1898–1978), US world heavyweight boxing champion, 1926–28. In 1926 he beat Jack DEMPSEY in the controversial fight of the "long count." He retired undefeated in 1928, having lost only one of his professional bouts.

TUPAMAROS, Uruguayan urban guerrilla movement. Named for Tupac Amaru, an 18th-century Inca who rebelled against the Spaniards, the Tupamaros sought to exploit growing economic difficulties and social unrest in Uruguay in the 1970s. Their objective was creation of a leftist regime.

TUPOLEV, Andrei Nikolayevich (1888–1972), Russian aircraft designer. He was responsible for more than 100 designs, including the Tu-20 Bear turboprop bomber (1955) and the world's first supersonic passenger airliner, the Tu-144 (1969).

TURBINE, machine for directly converting the kinetic and/or thermal ENERGY of a flowing FLUID into useful rotational energy. The working fluid may be air, hot gas, steam or water. This either pushes against a set of blades mounted on the drive shaft (impulse turbines) or turns the shaft by reaction when the fluid is expelled from nozzles (or nozzle-shaped vanes) around its circumference (reaction turbines). Water turbines were the first to be developed. They now include the vast inward-flow reaction turbines used in the generation of HYDROELECTRICITY and the smaller-scale tangential-flow "Pelton wheel" impulse types used when exploiting a very great "head" of water. In the 1880s, Charles Algernon Parsons (1854–1931), a British engineer, designed the first successful steam turbines, having realized that the efficient use of high-pressure steam demanded that its energy be extracted in a multitude of small stages. Steam turbines thus consist of a series of vanes mounted on a rotating drum with stator vanes redirecting the steam in between the moving ones. They are commonly used as marine engines and in thermal and nuclear power plants. Gas turbines are not as yet widely used except in airplanes (see JET PROPULSION) and for peak-load electricity generation.

TURBOJET. See JET PROPULSION.

TURENNE, Henri de la Tour d'Auvergne, Vicomte de (1611–1675), French military commander. During the THIRTY YEARS' WAR, his brilliant campaigns of 1644–47 helped secure the Peace of WESTPHALIA (1648). He supported first CONDÉ then LOUIS XIV in the FRONDE civil war (1648–50), fought against the Spanish (1654–59) and was killed in action in the third DUTCH WAR of 1672–78.

TURGENEV, Ivan Sergeyevich (1818–1883), great Russian writer. A liberal and pro-Western opponent of serfdom, he wrote of peasant and country life, at the same time embracing social and political themes. After criticism of his greatest novel, *Fathers and Sons* (1862), he lived mostly abroad. His plays include *A Month in the Country* (1850). Short stories such as *Torrents of Spring* (1872) are among his finest works.

TURGOT, Jacques (1727–1781), French economist and reformer. One of the PHYSIOCRATS, he favored free trade and a land tax and anticipated the law of diminishing returns. He lost his post (1776) as comptroller general of finances when he pressed for an end to compulsory labor.

TURIN, city in NW Italy. It is a major industrial center, with automobile (Fiat, Lancia), machinery, chemical and electrical industries. It was the capital of the Kingdom of SARDINIA (1720–1861) and the first capital of united Italy (1861–64). Pop 1,059,505.

TURIN, Shroud of, religious relic venerated for centuries by pious Catholics as the shroud in which the body of Jesus was wrapped. It is a piece of linen bearing the ghostly imprint of a bearded man with spike wounds on his wrists and a crown of thorns on his head. The Catholic church never declared the relic authentic, and in 1988 scientists proved conclusively that it dated from the 14th century.

TURING, Alan Mathison (1912–1954), British mathematician who made fundamental contributions to the development of the COMPUTER.

TURKESTAN or **TURKISTAN**, historic region in central Asia, extending from the Caspian Sea to the Mongolian desert. It consists today of the S Kazakh, Kirgiz, Tadzhik, Turkmen and Uzbek SSRs in the USSR, Chinese Turkestan and part of NE Afghanistan. It has been the home of TURKIC-speaking peoples since c500 AD and was important for its great trade routes linking Europe with the Far East. The chief city is SAMARKAND.

TURKEY, a republic in extreme SE Europe and Asia Minor, bounded by the Black Sea, USSR, Iran, Iraq, Syria, the Mediterranean, Greece and Bulgaria.

Official name: Republic of Turkey
Capital: Ankara
Area: 300,948sq mi
Population: 52,845,000
Languages: Turkish; Kurdish
Religions Muslim
Monetary unit(s): 1 Turkish lira (or pound)=100 kurus (or piastres)

Land. Turkey is mountainous, with an extensive semiarid plateau in Asia Minor; the highest peak is Mt. ARARAT (16,945ft). The Euphrates and the Tigris rivers rise in the E; other rivers include the Kizil Irmak, Sakarya and Büyük Menderes. The strategic BOSPORUS and DARDANELLES separate European from Asian Turkey. Earthquakes occur frequently. The climate is Mediterranean around the coastal lowlands, but more extreme and drier inland, with harsh winters toward the NE.

People. The TURKISH-speaking population descends largely from the TATARS, who entered Asia Minor in the 1000s AD. There are small Kurdish and Arab minorities. Some 60% live in rural areas. Illiteracy is about 40%.

Economy. Agriculture is the basis of the economy. The chief crops are grains, cotton, fruits and tobacco. Cattle are raised on the Anatolian plateau. Turkish industry has been developed greatly since WWII and includes steel, iron and textile manufacture, and food processing. There are large deposits of coal, iron and other metals, borax, and some oil.

History. Formerly part of the HITTITE, PERSIAN, ROMAN, BYZANTINE, SELJUK and OTTOMAN empires, Turkey became a republic in 1923 under ATATURK, who initiated a vast program of reform and modernization aiming at establishing Turkey as a modern democratic state on European lines. Neutral for most of WWII,

Turkey afterwards aligned herself with the West, joining the NORTH ATLANTIC TREATY ORGANIZATION and accepting substantial US aid. Democratic rule was shaken by an army coup in 1960, since when military intervention in government has continued, amid economic difficulties, civil unrest and political instability. Voters approved a new constitution in 1982, and the military transferred power to an elected parliament in 1983. Tension with Greece has almost led to war on several occasions. In 1974 Turkey invaded and occupied the northern third of Cyprus.

TURKEYS, two species of large New World game birds in their own family, Meleagrididae. The common turkey, *Meleagris gallopavo*, occurs in open woodland and scrub of North America and is the ancestor of the domestic turkey. The head and neck of both species are naked and with wattles; a fleshy caruncle overhangs the bill. The naked skin in the common turkey is red; in the ocellated turkey, blue.

TURKIC LANGUAGES, a group of ALTAIC LANGUAGES spoken by the TURKS in Turkey, E Europe and central and N Asia. They include Turkish, Azerbaijani, Turkoman, Uzbek, Kirghiz, Tatar, Kazakh and Chuvash. Vowel harmony and wide use of suffixes are characteristic. Latin or Cyrillic has replaced Arabic script since the 1920s–30s.

TURKISH, a TURKIC language, official language of Turkey, also spoken by minorities in E Europe and SW Asia. Evolved during the OTTOMAN EMPIRE, it was written in Arabic script until ATATURK introduced a modified Latin alphabet in 1928.

TURKS, a family of TURKIC speaking, chiefly Muslim peoples extending from Sinkiang (W China) and Siberia to Turkey, Iran and E European USSR. They include the Tatars, Kazakhs, Uzbeks, Kirghiz, Turkmens, Vighurs, Azerbaijanis and many others. The Turks spread through Asia from the 6th century onwards, were converted to Islam in the 10th century. In the W they controlled vast lands under the SELJUKS (1000s–1200s) and OTTOMAN EMPIRE (1300s–1923).

TURNER, Frederick Jackson (1861–1932), US historian. A Harvard professor (1910–24), he propounded an influential thesis about the American frontier and its role in shaping US individualism and democracy. *The Frontier in American History* (1920) reprinted earlier papers. He won a Pulitzer Prize for his study of sectionalism in the US (1932).

TURNER, Joseph Mallord William

(1775–1851), outstanding Romantic landscape painter, perhaps the greatest British painter. His work is famous for its rich treatment of light and atmosphere, in oil, watercolor or engraving. His paintings include *The Fighting Téméraire* (1839) and *Rain, Steam and Speed* (1844). He left some 20,000 works to the nation. (See also ROMANTICISM.)

TURNVEREIN (German: gymnastic club), an athletic, social and patriotic society set up in early 19th-century Prussia by Friedrich Ludwig JAHN. Though discouraged by German governments for their liberalism, the Turnvereins inspired several similar organizations in other countries.

TURTLES, aquatic relatives of TORTOISES, divisible into freshwater and marine groups. Like the tortoises, the body is encased in a horny shell. There are no teeth in the gums and the mouth has become adapted to form a sharp horny bill. Turtles are largely vegetarians. In freshwater forms the limbs normally retain free fingers and toes; in marine turtles they are modified into flat flippers, increasing their swimming ability. The amount of time spent in the water by the various species varies enormously: many of the freshwater species go for more or less extensive walks on land: others, like the marine turtles, leave the water only to lay their eggs. These are laid in scrapes in sand or soil on beaches and are left to incubate themselves. The young turtles make straight for the water on hatching.

TUSCANY, region in W central Italy, extending from the Apennine Mts. to the W coast. It is mostly mountainous, with fertile river valleys and coastal strip. Agricultural products include cereals, olive oil and Chianti wine. Iron and other minerals are mined; the chief manufactures are textiles, chemicals and machinery. Center of the ancient ETRUSCAN civilization, Tuscany has many famous cities such as Florence, Lucca, Pisa and Siena.

TUSCARORA INDIANS, tribe of North American Indians. They were driven from their lands in N.C. by white settlers and joined the IROQUOIS League in 1722. Some hundreds now live in N.Y. and Ontario.

TUSKEGEE INSTITUTE, private college in Tuskegee, Ala. Founded by Booker T. WASHINGTON in 1881, it was one of the first colleges to educate freed slaves. The institute trained black school teachers and supported the work of George W. CARVER. Today it offers a wide range of subjects and has a fine library of American black history.

TUSSAUD, Marie Grosholtz (1760–1850), Swiss wax modeler. Forced to make death masks of guillotined aristocrats in the French Revolution, she left Paris to found (1802) her famous London Wax Museum. Today it contains tableaus and hundreds of models of well-known people.

TUTANKHAMEN (reigned c1350 BC), Egyptian pharaoh. He died at 18 but is famous for his tomb, discovered in THEBES by Howard CARTER in 1922 with its treasures intact. His solid gold coffin, gold portrait mask and other treasures are in the Cairo museum.

TUTU, Desmond Mpilo (1931–   ), South African religious leader, Anglican archbishop of CapeTown from 1986. A black, he advocated nonviolent resistance to APARTHEID and social reconciliation. He received the 1984 Nobel Peace Prize.

TUVALU, formerly **Ellice Islands,** an independent island nation composed of nine small atolls, spread over more than 500,000sq mi in the W Pacific.

Official name: Tuvalu
Capital: Funafuti
Area: 9.3sq mi
Population: 8,200 on Tuvalu, about 2,000 abroad
Languages: English, Tuvaluan
Religions: Christian
Monetary unit(s): 1 Australian dollar = 100 cents

Land. The largest island, Vaitupu, covers only 2sq mi. No spot on these coral atolls rises more than 16ft above sea level. The soil is poor and there are no rivers and little vegetation besides coconut palms. The average annual temperature is 86°F; most of the rainfall occurs between Nov. and Feb.

People and Economy. The inhabitants are Polynesian, with almost 30% living on the island of Funafuti. Although traditional subsistence farming and fishing are important, about 2,000 Tuvaluans have gone abroad for employment, many to Nauru. Copra is the only export although the sale of postage stamps abroad also produces income.

History. The islands were largely ignored

by Europeans until the 19th century, when whaling took place in the area. The population was reduced from 22,000 to 3,000 between 1850 and 1875 because of disease and forcible recruitment for labor abroad. A British protectorate over both the Ellice and Gilbert (now KIRIBATI) islands was established in 1892. In 1974 Ellice Islanders voted for separate status, achieving independence in 1978. To reduce its long-term dependence on foreign aid, the government solicited foreign grants and established the innovative Tuvalu Trust Fund in 1987; income from the fund is used to offset recurrent budgetary shortfalls.

TWAIN, Mark (1835–1910), pen name of Samuel Langhorne Clemens, US author and popular humorist and lecturer. After being a printer's apprentice (1848–53), he led a wandering life, becoming a Mississippi river pilot (1857–61) and then a journalist, establishing a reputation with his humorous sketches. In 1869 he produced his first bestseller, *The Innocents Abroad*, followed by *The Adventures of Tom Sawyer* (1876), *The Prince and the Pauper* (1882), his masterpiece *Huckleberry Finn* (1884) and the satirical *A Connecticut Yankee in King Arthur's Court* (1889). *Huckleberry Finn*, the story of a raft trip down the Mississippi, exemplifies Twain's gift of blending humor with realism. In later life, Twain lost most of his money through speculation and suffered the loss of his wife and daughters. His works became increasingly pessimistic and bitingly satirical, as in *The Tragedy of Pudd'nhead Wilson* (1894) and *The Man Who Corrupted Hadleyburg* (1899).

TWEED, William Marcy (1823–1878), New York City politician. He became boss of TAMMANY HALL in 1868 and with the help of his cronies, known as the Tweed Ring, exercised corrupt control over the Democratic Party machine running New York. Tweed defrauded the city of over 30 million dollars, but was eventually convicted and died in jail.

TWELVE TABLES, Law of the, the earliest Roman code of laws. Written on tablets c450 BC, they were displayed in the Forum. They contained civil, criminal and sacred legal precepts and became revered as a prime source of law. Only fragments survive.

TWELVE-TONE MUSIC, or serial music, a type of music, developed in the 1920s, which rejects TONALITY as the basis for composition. Its most famous exponent, SCHOENBERG, laid down a method of composition which attempted to free music from the 8-note OCTAVE and its associated conventions. Twelve-tone compositions are constructed around a specific series of the twelve notes of the CHROMATIC SCALE. Later 20th-century composers have used the principles of twelve-tone composition with greater freedom. (See ATONALITY.) Composers of twelve-tone music include STRAVINSKY, SESSIONS, PISTON, KRENEK, HENZE, DALLAPICCOLA, SHOSTAKOVICH and Schoenberg's pupils WEBERN and BERG.

TWELVE TRIBES OF ISRAEL, the twelve family groups into which the ancient Hebrews were divided. According to the Bible they were descended from and named for ten sons of JACOB and two sons of JOSEPH. Those descended from Jacob's sons were Asher, Benjamin, Dan, Gad, Issachar, Judah, Naphtali, Reuben, Simeon, Zebulun; the two from Joseph's sons were Ephraim and Manasseh. When the Hebrews finally reached the Promised Land they divided the country among these twelve family groups. A thirteenth tribe, Levi, had no portion of land set aside for it. (See also JEWS.)

TWO SICILIES, Kingdom of the, a kingdom uniting SICILY and S Italy (see NAPLES). Originally founded by Normans in the 1000s, it was reunited by Alfonso V of Aragon in 1442. A branch of the BOURBON family succeeded to the kingdom in 1759 and held it until 1860, when GARIBALDI conquered both Sicily and Naples and made them part of united Italy.

TYLER, John (1790–1862), tenth US president (1841–45). A Va. aristocrat, he studied law and was elected to the Va. legislature (1811–16, 1823–25, 1839), and served in Congress (1817–21). He became governor of Va. (1825–27), and then a US senator (1827–36). A conservative, he believed in STATES' RIGHTS and the restriction of federal power, opposing the MISSOURI COMPROMISE and the bill authorizing President JACKSON to use force against S.C. during the NULLIFICATION crisis. He broke with the Democrats and was chosen by the WHIGS to run for vice-president with William Henry HARRISON, who became president in 1841 but died within a month of his inauguration.

Tyler was the first vice-president to succeed a president in office and he chose to sit out the full term, although the Constitution was not clear on this issue. He alienated the Whigs by vetoing the nationalist program they presented under the leadership of Senator CLAY, and his entire cabinet, except Daniel WEBSTER, resigned. Nevertheless Tyler continued to veto nationalist bills and Congress responded by refusing to vote money for the upkeep of the White House. He was expelled from the Whig party and threatened with impeachment.

In foreign affairs Tyler was more successful; his major achievement was the conclusion of the WEBSTER-ASHBURTON TREATY (1842). Internally he encouraged settlement in the West, backed MORSE'S telegraph system and reorganized the navy. In 1845 he brought Texas and Florida into the Union, despite Democratic opposition. After leaving office (1845), Tyler retired to Va. In 1861 he presided at a peace conference in Washington, hoping to avert civil war. When the southerners' terms were rejected, he voted for Va.'s sucession and was elected to the Confederate House of Representatives, but died before he could take his seat.

TYLER, Wat (d. 1381), leader of the English Peasants' Revolt (1381), England's first popular rebellion, protesting high taxation after the BLACK DEATH. Tyler and his Kentish followers captured Canterbury, then took the TOWER OF LONDON. RICHARD II promised abolition of serfdom and feudal service. At a second meeting with the king, Tyler was stabbed and the revolt was brutally crushed.

TYLOR, Sir Edward Burnett (1832–1917), British anthropologist whose work, culminating in *Primitive Culture* (1871), established him as a father of cultural ANTHROPOLOGY. In 1896 he was appointed the first Professor of Anthropology in the University of Oxford.

TYNDALE, William (c1494–1536), English bible translator, theologian and Protestant martyr. His NEW TESTAMENT. printed in Germany (1526), was suppressed in England. He lived abroad in hiding, translating the PENTATEUCH (1529–30) and Book of Jonah (1531). In 1535 he was captured in Antwerp, tried and burned for heresy. (See also BIBLE.)

TYNDALL, John (1820–1893), British physicist who, through his studies of the scattering of light by colloidal particles or large molecules in suspension (the **Tyndall effect**), showed that the daytime sky is blue because of the Rayleigh scattering of impingent sunlight by dust and other colloidal particles in the air.

TYPESETTING. See PRINTING.

TYPEWRITER, writing machine activated manually or electrically by means of a keyboard. Normally, when a key is depressed, a pivoted bar bearing a type character strikes an inked ribbon against a sheet of paper carried on a cylindrical rubber "platen," and the platen carriage automatically moves a space to the left. In some electric models all the type is carried on a single rotatable sphere that moves from left to right and strikes a fixed platen. The first efficient typewriter was developed in 1868 by C. L. SHOLES.

TYPHOID FEVER, INFECTIOUS DISEASE due to a SALMONELLA species causing FEVER, a characteristic rash, LYMPH node and SPLEEN enlagement, GASTROINTESTINAL TRACT disturbance with bleeding and ulceration, and usually marked malaise or prostration. It is contracted from other cases or from disease carriers, the latter often harboring asymptomatic infection in the GALL BLADDER or urine, with contaminated food and water as major vectors. Carriers must be treated with ANTIBIOTICS (and have their gall bladder removed if this site is the source); they must also stop handling food until they are free of the bacteria. VACCINATION may help protect high risk persons; antibiotics—chloramphenicol or cotrimoxazole—form the treatment of choice.

TYPHOID MARY. See MALLON, MARY.

TYPHUS, INFECTIOUS DISEASE caused by RICKETTSIA and carried by LICE, leading to a feverish illness with a rash. Severe HEADACHE typically precedes the rash, which may be erythematous or may progress to skin HEMORRHAGE; mild respiratory symptoms of cough and breathlessness are common. Death ensues in a high proportion of untreated adults, usually with profound SHOCK and KIDNEY failure. Recurrences may occur in untreated patients who recover from their first attack, often after many years (Brill-Zinsser disease). A similar disease due to a different but related organism is carried by fleas (murine typhus). Chloramphenicol or TETRACYCLINES provide suitable ANTIBIOTIC therapy.

TYPOGRAPHY, the design and layout of printed type. The object of typography is to enhance the legibility of a printed page, or, as in advertising and display, to attract the reader's attention. Early typefaces were derived from medieval Gothic and Renaissance humanistic scripts. A typeface usually consists of a set or *font* of capital and lower-case letters in three styles, roman, *italic* and **bold**, each cut in a range of sizes (measured in *points*). Famous typefaces include those produced by Baskerville, Bodoni, Garamond and Eric Gill. Good typography calls for intelligent positioning of word patterns set in types of appropriate face and size (see PRINTING).

TYRANT, a dictator in ancient Greece. With the growth of democracy in 5th-century BC Athens the word took on its present pejorative sense though in fact many tyrants were able and popular rulers.

Some of the most famous were Dionysius I and II, Hiero I and II and Pisistratus.

TYRE, town, and ancient PHOENICIAN city-port on the coast of Lebanon. After 1400 BC it began to dominate Mediterranean trade, and established colonies in Spain and CARTHAGE. Frequently mentioned in the Bible and famed for its silks and dyes, it was sacked by ALEXANDER THE GREAT (322) but recovered under the ROMAN EMPIRE. It was finally destroyed by the MAMELUKES in 1291. Today the small town of Sur occupies the site.

TYROL. See TIROL.

TYRRHENIAN SEA, part of the Mediterranean Sea bounded by the W coast of Italy, and by Corsica, Sardinia and Sicily. The strait of Messina in the S connects with the Ionian Sea. Its ports include Naples and Palermo.

TYSON, Mike (1966–   ), US boxer. Holder of WBA and WBC heavyweight titles with a win-loss record of 34-0 (33 by knockouts), he won the IBF title as well when he knocked out Michael Spinks (33-0) in the first round of their bout in Atlantic City on June 27, 1988.

TZARA, Tristan (1896–1963), Romanian-born French poet, founder of the DADA movement. In Paris he published the *Seven Dada Manifestos* (1924), working with André BRETON, to destroy conventional values and language. He moved toward SURREALISM, and his mature lyrical poetry is more humanistic.

TZ'U-HSI (1835–1908), Chinese Dowager Empress. She was regent for her son and later her nephew, and finally ruled directly, dominating Chinese affairs for nearly 50 years. Her corrupt rule through a clique of conservative officials contributed to China's defeat in the SINO-JAPANESE WAR (1895) and to the BOXER REBELLION. Three years after her death the Ch'ing dynasty was overthrown.

21st letter of the English alphabet, derived from the Semitic *waw* via the Greek *upsilon*. In the Roman alphabet, *V* (lower case *u*) was both vowel and consonant, and

the modern *u* and *v* date from the 16th century.

UBANGI RIVER, chief N tributary of the Congo R, central Africa. Formed by the junction of the Bomu and Uele rivers, it flows 700mi W and S, forming part of Zaire's NW frontier.

UCAYALI RIVER, N Peru, chief headstream of the Amazon. Formed by the junction of the Urubamba and Apurimac rivers, central Peru, it flows 1000mi N to the Marañón River SW of Iquitos.

UCCELLO, Paolo (1397–1475), Florentine early RENAISSANCE painter, noted for his use of perspective. His best-known works are the *Creation* and *Noah* scenes (c1431–50) in Santa Maria Novella, Florence, and the three richly decorative panels of *The Battle of San Romano* (c1455–60).

UDALL, Nicholas (c1505–1556), English schoolmaster, scholar and playwright. Headmaster of ETON (1534–41) and Westminster (1554–56), he wrote the first known English comedy, *Ralph Roister Doister* (c1553).

UFFIZI, 16th-century palace in Florence, Italy, built to designs by VASARI for Cosimo I de' MEDICI. It houses one of the world's finest art collections, rich in classical, Dutch, Flemish and, notably, Italian Renaissance paintings and sculptures.

UFO. See FLYING SAUCER.

UGANDA, landlocked republic in E central Africa, bordering Kenya, Sudan, Zaire, Rwanda and Tanzania.

Official name: Republic of Uganda
Co-capitals: Kampala, Entebbe
Area: 93,070sq mi
Population: 15,514,000
Languages: English; Bantu languages, Swahili
Religions: Christian, Muslim; tribal religions
Monetary unit(s): 1 Uganda shilling=100 cents

Land. Uganda lies on the equator and has an average elevation of 4,000ft. The fertile plateau is bounded by the GREAT RIFT VALLEY and Ruwenzori Mts to the W and high mountains to the E. The White Nile, whose source is Lake Victoria in the SE, is harnessed for electricity at Owens Falls dam. Except in the arid N and parts of the S, annual rainfall is about 40in, and temperatures rarely exceed 85°F or fall below 60°F.

People. Uganda has over a dozen major tribes, of which Bantu-speaking groups form a majority. The Baganda in the S are the most numerous. The bulk of the population depends on agriculture, but Nilotic-speaking peoples in the N tend to be herdsmen. Illiteracy is high. Kampala's Makerere University was once regarded as one of Africa's most important seats of learning, but declined during the period that Uganda was ruled by Maj. Gen. Idi AMIN DADA, 1971–79.

Economy. The economy is agricultural and most farms are small, growing subsistence crops and raising livestock. Despite severe economic dislocation under Amin's rule and during the civil war of 1981–86, Uganda remained one of the world's major producers of coffee, which accounts for almost all its export earnings. Other export crops include tea, peanuts, and tobacco. Copper is the principal mineral.

History. The Buganda kingdom, which succeeded the Bunyoro kingdom, became a British protectorate in 1894. The protectorate was extended to other kingdoms and by 1914 the present boundaries of Uganda became fixed. Uganda became independent in 1962. In 1971 Maj. Gen. Idi Amin Dada deposed President Milton Obote in a military coup. In 1972 he expelled Uganda's Asian population, attracting world attention. Through the Amin years internal strife prevailed. In 1979 Tanzania invaded Uganda and Amin fled. After a period of political instability, Obote resumed the presidency in 1980. Opponents of Obote, whose army was also accused of widespread human-rights abuses, launched a civil war that continued even after Obote was ousted by a group of army officers in 1985. Opposition leader Yoweri Museveni captured Kampala in Jan. 1986 and gradually extended his control over the rest of the devastated country.

UGARIT, ancient city discovered in 1929 at Ras Shamra, NW Syria. Settled since the 5th millennium BC, it flourished c1400 BC. Numerous CUNEIFORM tablets have revealed much about Semitic culture and language, important for Old Testament studies.

UGRO-FINNIC LANGUAGES, the more important of the branches of the Uralic language family (see URAL-ALTAIC LANGUAGES). The Finnic division includes Finnish and Estonian; the Ugric,

Hungarian.

UKRAINE, constituent Soviet Socialist Republic in the W USSR, third largest in area and second only to the Russian Republic in population and economic importance. Mostly steppes, the Ukraine extends from the Carpathian Mts E to the Donets Ridge and Sea of Azov, and from the Black Sea N to Belorussia. The Dnieper R flows N dividing the Ukraine. In the NW lie the Polesye (Pripyat, Pripet) marshes; in the S, a fertile chernozem region.

The "breadbasket of the Soviet Union" is the second most productive agricultural area of the USSR (wheat and other grains, root crops and flax) and accounts for 25% of the heavy industrial output. It is rich in oil, gas, coal, hydroelectricity, and iron. Major centers are KIEV (the capital), Dnepropetrovsk, Donetsk (and the Donets Basin), Kharkov, and ODESSA. Culturally distinct UKRAINIAN speakers comprise over 75% of the people. The COSSACKS ("outlaws") arose in opposition to Polish and, later, Russian rule. The Ukraine was briefly independent, 1918–20, and nationalism remains.

UKRAINIAN, or Ruthenian, East Slavic SLAVONIC LANGUAGE. Distinguished from RUSSIAN since c1200 and written in a modified cyrillic alphabet, it emerged as a literary language in the 18th century. It is the official language of the Ukraine, with some 41,000,000 speakers.

ULBRICHT, Walter (1893–1973), leader of post-WWII East Germany. A founder member (1918) of the German Communist Party, he became first deputy premier (1949) and head of state (1960–73) of the German Democratic Republic. An uncompromising Stalinist, he headed the Socialist Unity Party from 1950 until replaced (1971) by Erich Honecker. He built the BERLIN WALL (1961), and in 1968 sent troops to Czechoslovakia.

ULCER, pathological defect in SKIN or other EPITHELIUM, caused by INFLAMMATION secondary to infection, loss of BLOOD supply, failure of venous return or CANCER. Various skin lesions can cause ulcers, including infection, arterial disease, VARICOSE VEINS and skin cancer. Aphthous ulcers in the mouth are painful epithelial ulcers of unknown origin. Peptic ulcers include gastric and duodenal ulcers, although the two have different causes; they may cause characteristic pain, acute HEMORRHAGE, or lead to perforation and PERITONITIS. Severe scarring or EDEMA around the pylorus may cause stenosis with VOMITING and STOMACH distension. ANTACIDS, rest, stopping SMOKING, and licorice derivatives may help peptic ulcer but surgery may also be needed.

ULSTER, historic province split since 1920 into the three-county Ulster province of IRELAND and six-county Northern Ireland (see IRELAND, NORTHERN).

ULTIMATUM, written demands made by one country to another before declaring war. It constitutes a warning of hostilities as agreed at the 1907 HAGUE CONFERENCE. Austria's ultimatum to Serbia in July 1914 led to WWI. Hitler delivered ultimatums to Czechoslovakia and Poland. The Japanese attacked Pearl Harbor without warning.

ULTRAMONTANISM, in Roman Catholicism, the movement to strengthen the authority of the pope and Curia. It arose in reaction to Gallicanism (the 16th-to-18th-century movement for autonomy of the French church), JANSENISM and liberal tendencies, and finally triumphed at the First VATICAN COUNCIL (1870), which defined papal infallibility and universal jurisdiction. Some of its opponents seceded as OLD CATHOLICS.

ULTRASONICS, science of SOUND waves with frequencies above those that humans can hear (>720kHz). With modern piezoelectric techniques, ultrasonic waves having frequencies above 24kHz can readily be generated with high efficiency and intensity in solids and liquids, and exhibit the normal wave properties of REFLECTION, REFRACTION and DIFFRACTION. They can thus be used as investigative tools or for concentrating large amounts of mechanical energy. Low-power waves are used in thickness gauging and HOLOGRAPHY, high-power waves in surgery and for industrial homogenization, cleaning and machining.

ULTRAVIOLET RADIATION, ELECTROMAGNETIC RADIATION of wavelength between 0.1nm and 380nm, produced using gas discharge tubes. Although it constitutes 5% of the energy radiated by the sun, most falling on the earth is filtered out by atmospheric OXYGEN and OZONE, thus protecting life on the surface from destruction by the solar ultraviolet light. This also means that air must be excluded from optical apparatus designed for ultraviolet light, similar strong absorption by glass necessitating that lenses and prisms be made of QUARTZ or fluorite. Detection is photographic or by using fluorescent screens. The principal use is in fluorescent tubes (see LIGHTING) but important medical applications include germicidal lamps, the treatment of RICKETS and some skin diseases and the VITAMIN-D enrichment of milk and eggs.

ULYSSES, Latin name for ODYSSEUS.

UMAYYADS. See OMAYYADS.

UMBILICAL CORD, long structure linking the developing EMBRYO or FETUS to the placenta through most of PREGNANCY. It consists of BLOOD vessels taking blood to and from the placenta, and a gelatinous matrix. At BIRTH the cord is clamped to prevent blood loss and is used to assist delivery of the placenta. It undergoes atrophy and becomes the navel.

UMBRIA, ancient region in the Apennine Mts., central Italy. It is chiefly agricultural, with expanding industry based on hydroelectricity, notably at Terni. The capital is Perugia, center of the medieval Umbrian painters.

UNALASKA, second-largest of the ALEUTIAN ISLANDS, SW Alaska, including Unalaska city (pop 180), the US navy base at Dutch Harbor and Makuskin volcano (6,678ft).

UN-AMERICAN ACTIVITIES COMMITTEE. See HOUSE COMMITTEE ON UN-AMERICAN ACTIVITIES (HUAC).

UNAMUNO, Miguel de (1864–1936), leading Spanish philosopher and writer, rector of Salamanca University from 1900. Influenced by KIERKEGAARD, he explored the faith-reason conflict and man's desire for immortality in *The Tragic Sense of Life* (1913), and in essays and novels such as *Mist* (1914). "The Christ of Velázquez" (1920) is his finest poem. Politically outspoken, he was exiled 1924–30.

UNCAS (c1588–c1683), chief of the Mohican Indians of Connecticut, celebrated in J. F. COOPER's *The Last of the Mohicans* (1826). He supported the colonists in the 1637 war against the related PEQUOT INDIANS. The English forced him to be neutral in KING PHILIP'S WAR (1675).

UNCERTAINTY PRINCIPLE, or **indeterminacy principle,** a restriction, first enunciated by W. K. HEISENBERG in 1927, on the accuracy with which the position and MOMENTUM of an object can be established simultaneously: the product of the accuracies attainable in each cannot be less than the Planck constant. Relevant only near the atomic level, the principle arises from the wave nature of matter: the wave function (see WAVE MECHANICS) of a particle consists of a superposition of waves with slightly different momenta producing a localized disturbance of which neither the position nor the momentum is precisely defined.

UNCIALS, compact, cursive capital letters developed from the 200s AD by Greek and Roman calligraphers and used for some 500 years. Half (lowercase) uncials developed later, notably in the British Isles.

UNCLE REMUS. See HARRIS, JOEL CHANDLER.

UNCLE SAM, popular figure officially adopted as a US national symbol in 1961. He is portrayed as a white-haired and bearded, angular gentleman dressed in the Stars and Stripes. The image was developed by 19th-century cartoonists. The name possibly derives from "Uncle Sam" Wilson, a War of 1812 beef supplier to the US army, from Troy, N.Y.

UNCONSCIOUS, that part of the mind in which events take place of which the individual is unaware; i.e., the part of the mind that is not the conscious. Unconscious processes can, however, alter the behavior of the individual (see also DREAMS; INSTINCT). FREUD termed the unconscious the id.

UNDERGROUND RAILROAD, secret network which helped slaves to escape from the US South to the Northern States and Canada before the Civil War. Neither underground nor a railroad, it was named for its necessary secrecy and for the railroad terms used to refer to its operation. Most of the "conductors" were themselves slaves, Harriet TUBMAN being the best known. Abolitionists, notably Quakers such as Levi Coffin, ran "stations" providing food and shelter along the way. Some 40,000–100,000 slaves escaped this way. (See also ABOLITIONISM.)

UNDERWOOD, Oscar Wilder (1862–1929), US Democratic politician, US representative (1895–96, 1897–1915) and senator (1915–22) from Alabama. He sponsored the Underwood Tariff Act (1913), which significantly reduced tariffs.

UNDERWRITING, insuring against risk. Originally, as at Lloyd's of London, underwriters indicated readiness to share risk by signing insurance contracts. In INSURANCE, an underwriter (often an actuary) assesses risk and sets premiums. In finance, underwriting is an agreement to buy STOCKS.

UNDSET, Sigrid (1882–1949), Norwegian novelist. For her epic trilogy set in medieval Norway, *Kristin Lavransdatter* (1920–22), she won the 1928 Nobel literature prize. Her contemporary novels dealt with modern woman and Roman Catholicism.

UNEMPLOYMENT, in the US, is defined and measured by the BUREAU OF LABOR STATISTICS (BLS) in the US Department of Labor. The BLS counts as unemployed only those unemployed who are actively seeking work; those who are not (e.g., discouraged unemployed workers) are not counted. On the other hand, the BLS counts as employed part-time and temporary workers who might actually prefer full-time, permanent jobs. The unemployment rate published by the BLS is the number of unemployed persons as a percentage of the civilian LABOR FORCE. Although the unemployment rate fluctuates with levels of economic activity, its course in recent decades has been generally upward. It averaged 4.5% in the 1950s, 4.8% in the 1960s, and 6.2% in the 1970s. Between 1980 and 1987, it averaged 7.7%.

Economists distinguish four kinds of unemployment: frictional, demand-related or cyclical, structural, and voluntary.

Frictional unemployment occurs when people lose their jobs in a declining firm while other firms in the same industry prosper. These job-losers can expect to find similar jobs at similar pay in other firms. The only obstacle to their immediate reemployment is lack of information about where other jobs are, but help-wanted ads and employment agencies provide that. Some degree of frictional unemployment is inevitable, but is characteristically of short duration.

Demand-related or cyclical unemployment occurs when aggregate demand declines, fewer workers are necessary, and those not being utilized by their employers are laid off. Cyclical unemployment tends to be of longer duration than frictional unemployment, but it is still considered short-term since business activity may be expected to revive after some months.

Structural unemployment is caused by a shift in technology, a change in demand, or the relocation of an industry. Conspicuous among the structurally unemployed are youths with no job experience or marketable skills. Structural unemployment promises to be long-term, perhaps permanent, unless those unemployed can be trained in new skills to match existing employment opportunities or unless new industries replace those that have declined or departed.

Voluntary unemployment is frequent where jobs, while available, are not considered desirable or when the worker has no pressing need to work. In such circumstances, the unemployed worker may delay returning to work, either to enjoy the leisure or to wait for a particularly attractive job.

Since the GREAT DEPRESSION of the 1930s, government has actively pursued policies to reduce unemployment. Its response to cyclical unemployment is "countercyclical" fiscal and monetary policies — for example, tax cuts and lower interest rates — intended to put money into the pockets of consumers and thereby to increase aggregate demand or goods and services. To deal with structural unemployment, government encourages — through tax abatements, grants, loans, and technical assistance — economic development that will bring new industries to depressed areas. When necessary, it provides public-service employment and job training.

UNEMPLOYMENT INSURANCE, a type of social insurance providing income to people involuntarily unemployed. Most modern industrial nations have programs of this kind, financed by the government, employers, employees, or a combination of these.

In the 1800s some labor unions initiated unemployment benefits for out-of-work members. France introduced a voluntary national scheme in 1905, and Britain the first compulsory insurance program in 1911. In the US the first unemployment insurance law was passed in Wis. in 1932; three years later the Social Security Act established a federal–state program, now administered by the Department of LABOR.

UNESCO. See UNITED NATIONS EDUCATIONAL, SCIENTIFIC AND CULTURAL ORGANIZATION.

UNGARETTI, Giuseppe (1888–1970), Italian poet. Influenced by the poets of French SYMBOLISM, his evocative verse, in a condensed, purified language, marked a new direction in Italian poetry.

UNIATE CHURCHES, those Eastern churches which accept the pope's authority and Roman Catholic doctrines, but retain their own languages, rites and canon laws, the administration of both bread and wine in COMMUNION, baptism by immersion and marriage of the clergy. An example is the MARONITE church. (See also JACOBITE CHURCH.)

UNICEF. See UNITED NATIONS CHILDREN'S FUND.

UNICORN, mythical creature with the body of a white horse and one straight horn in its forehead. It has appeared in the art and legends of India, China, Islam, and medieval Europe, where it was associated with virginity, and with Christ.

UNIDENTIFIED FLYING OBJECT (UFO). See FLYING SAUCER.

UNIFICATION CHURCH, religious organization of Korean origin that became highly visible in the US in the late 1960s. Based on the ideas of the Reverend Sun Myung Moon, who represents himself as an elect leader and seer, the organization recruits and regiments young people, who dedicate their lives to it in highly disciplined fashion. Accused of "programming" its adherents by brain-washing techniques, the Unification Church was investigated by Congress in 1977 and has been attacked by both parents and business competitors. See MOONIES.

UNIFIED FIELD THEORY, theory which tries to incorporate electromagnetic together with the strong and weak nuclear forces into the general theory of RELATIVITY. If successful, one set of equations would describe these fundamental force fields, including gravity, in terms of the geometry of space-time. Einstein made the first attempt to produce such a theory; he wanted to represent physical reality entirely in terms of fields, yet, in his general theory of relativity, particles still exist as singularities—regions where field equations break down. (See FORCES, FUNDAMENTAL.)

UNIFORM CODE OF MILITARY JUSTICE, the law governing all members of the US armed forces. It sets out procedures for court-martial and military justice. Enacted in 1950, it unified the codes and laws of the Army, Navy, Air Force and Coast Guard.

UNIFORMITARIANISM, the principle originally opposed to CATASTROPHISM and attributed to J. HUTTON and C. LYELL that the same geologic processes are at work in nature today as have always existed and operated throughout geologic time. Recently, geologists have suggested discarding this concept in favor of *actualism*, the more general concept that the laws of nature have remained invariant through time.

UNIMAK, largest of the ALEUTIAN ISLANDS and nearest to SW Alaska, in the Fox Islanda group. 70mi long, it includes Shishaldin volcano (9,978ft).

UNION OF SOVIET SOCIALIST REPUBLICS (USSR), or **Soviet Union.** The largest country in the world, it encompasses 8,649,490sq mi of the Eurasian land mass. Its maximum W-E extent, E Europe to the Pacific, exceeds 6,500mi. It extends 1,800mi–3,000mi N-S from the Arctic to its frontiers with Turkey, Iran, Afghanistan, China and Mongolia.

This vast country, most of which lies in the high latitudes N of the 50th parallel, has a population of over 270,000,000, exceeded only by China and India. There are more than 170 ethnic groups, the three chief Slav groups—Russians, Ukrainians and Belorussians—making up more than 70% of the population. The Soviet Union comprises 15 federated republics, each of which is inhabited mainly, but not exclusively, by a major ethnic group. The Russian Soviet Federated Socialist Republic (RSFSR) is the largest and its capital, Moscow, is also the capital and largest city of the USSR. Several republics have subdivisions—

Official name: Union of Soviet Socialist Republics
Capital: Moscow
Area: 8,649,500sq mi
Population: 282,811,000
Languages: Russian; numerous regional languages
Religions: Officially atheist; Russian Orthodox
Monetary unit(s): 1 ruble = 100 kopecks

autonomous republics, autonomous oblasts (regions) and national okrugs (districts)—reflecting minority ethnic groups.

The Land. W of the Yenisey R (about 90°E) are the vast W Siberian and E European plains, divided by the N-S Ural Mts (which also divide Asia from Europe). The W Siberian plain, never above 600ft and with large marshy areas, is drained to the N by the Ob and Irtysh rivers and to the S is separated by the Kazakh hills from the largely arid Aral-Caspian lowlands drained by the Amu and Syr rivers. The E European plain is drained N by the Dvina and Pechora rivers, and S by the Dnieper, Don and Volga rivers. E of the Yenisey are the Central Siberian plateau between the Yenisey and Lena rivers, and the Taimyr region along the Arctic, including the N Siberian lowland. Mountain regions include the Caucasus, NE Siberia and the Kamchatka peninsula (with its active volcanoes) and the Altai-Sayan region NW of Mongolia. Russia's highest peaks are in the Pamir ranges of central Asia near the Afghan-Tibetan border. More modest mountain areas are Baikalia, between Lake Baikal and the Amur R in the SE, and the Amur maritime region between that river and the Pacific Ocean.

Climate and Vegetation. Most of the USSR has a continental climate marked by severe winters. The Arctic coast is icebound for most of the year and more than 50% of the country is snow-covered for about six months. But summers are usually warm; the Crimean coast enjoys mild winters and warm summers. The vegetation zones, N-S, comprise tundra, *taiga* (forest zone), the treeless grassland steppes, the semi-desert and desert zone and the subtropical vegetation zone bordering the Black Sea.

People. The population is unevenly distributed: over two-thirds live in the European plain, with heavy concentrations around Moscow, Leningrad and Kiev, the only three cities with more than 2 million inhabitants. Although there has been some intermingling, the 170 or more ethnic groups are mainly territorially distinct. Slav groups (including Russians, who comprise 55% of USSR population) predominate in the European USSR, Siberia and the far E and non-Slav groups in the Caucasus and Soviet Central Asia. More than 100 languages are spoken along with Russian, the official and universal language.

Economy. The USSR has a planned socialist economy in which all resources and means of production belong to the state. An industrial superpower second only to the US, the USSR is self-sufficient in most minerals and energy resources including coal (Donets and Kuznetsk basins, Karaganda and Pechora), oil and natural gas (Volga-Ural oil field, N Caucasus, Baku, W Siberia) and iron ore (Krivoi Rog, Urals, NW Kazakhstan and E Siberia). Industry is concentrated notably in the Urals and E Ukraine (iron, steel, heavy engineering) and manufacturing in cities like Moscow, Leningrad, Kiev, Kharkov, Minsk, Riga and Voronezh. Only about 10% of the land can be used for farming. About 60% of Soviet agricultural output comes from the 20,800 state farms and 26,500 collective farms. In recent years disastrously small grain harvests have necessitated substantial grain imports from the West (US, Canada, Australia).

Government and Politics. The Soviet Union is a federation of 15 constituent republics. Each republic elects delegates to the Supreme Soviet, which, according to the Soviet constitution, is "the highest organ of state power in the USSR." It is the main legislative body and appoints the Supreme Court and the Council of Ministers and elects the Presidium. It consists of two chambers, the Soviet of the Union (with one deputy for every 300,000 of population) and the Soviet of Nationalities, which has representatives from all constituent and autonomous republics, autonomous regions and national areas. The Supreme Soviet has only two sessions a year so that between sessions the highest state authority is its Presidium, consisting of 37 members elected from both houses. Its chairman is the president of the USSR, the nominal head of state, but executive power rests in the Council of Ministers. Its chairman is premier of the USSR and its members, including the 15 premiers of the constituent republics, are chosen by him with the approval of the Supreme Soviet. Similarly, each republic has its own council of ministers and supreme soviet. The Communist Party of the Soviet Union (CPSU) is the only legal political party and provides all candidates for office whom the voter can only approve or reject. The Soviet constitution guarantees freedom of speech, of the press, of assembly and the right to demonstrate freely, but in practice these rights are reserved for the CPSU. The party comprises a relatively small percentage of the total population, with about 15 million members, and remains an elite organization. An All-Union Party Congress should meet once every four years but often meets less frequently. In theory, the party elects a Central Committee of about 350 members who in turn elect the Politburo and the Party Secretariat, whose first secretary (currently Yuri Andropov) is the most powerful man in both the party and the USSR. In practice, power flows downwards from the Party Secretary.

History. The SLAVS probably first entered Russia from the W in the 400s AD. In the 800s Scandinavian conquerors known as "Russes," led by Rurik, settled in Novgorod and Kiev, whose ruler, VLADIMIR, was converted to Christianity c989. After the 12th-century Tatar invasions (see MOGUL EMPIRE), Moscow rose to preeminence. Its Grand Prince IVAN IV (the Terrible) was the first to be crowned tsar (1547). The election of MICHAEL as tsar (1613) established the ROMANOV dynasty which ruled until the Russian Revolution. PETER the Great founded St. Petersburg (now Leningrad) and made it imperial capital (1721). His program of westernization and Russian expansion continued under CATHERINE the Great. Russia survived invasion by Napoleon (1812) but was in decline during the 19th century (nevertheless the greatest period of Russian literature). Reforms, including liberation of the serfs (1861), failed to check internal unrest which culminated in the Russian Revolution. The throne was toppled and power seized from the moderates under KERENSKY by the BOLSHEVIKS led by LENIN. After civil war (1918–20) the USSR was proclaimed (1922). The power struggle following Lenin's death (1924) was won by Joseph STALIN, who led Russia to victory in WWII. After his death (1953), leadership eventually passed to Nikita KHRUSHCHEV, who denounced Stalin's tyrannies and inaugurated "peaceful co-existence" with

the West. China then broke with the USSR; in the 1960s and 1970s the rift increased. Khrushchev was deposed in 1964. Under his successors—Aleksei Kosygin, Leonid Brezhnev, Yuri Andropov, and Konstantin Chernenko—the Soviet economy stagnated. Geared to support a huge military establishment, industry produced few consumer goods and became increasingly backward technologically. State farms were unable to meet domestic food needs. The selection in 1985 of Mikhail Gorbachev as party general secretary signaled a new direction. To revitalize the Soviet economy, Gorbachev inaugurated a controversial policy of *perestroika* (restructuring) accompanied by *glasnost* (openness). *Perestroika* aimed to reduce the role of centralized economic planning and direction and to allow market forces to play a larger role. In industry, accountability was to shift from Moscow bureaucrats to plant managers and workers. Farms managers were to have more independence and the right to sell more goods at market prices. Individual farmers were to be permitted to lease land from state farms and to farm privately. Encouragement was given to cooperatives and individual initiative in the service sector. Gorbachev also called for greater democratization in government and party affairs. The 19th Communist Party Conference, which met in Moscow in 1988, endorsed an overhaul of the political system designed to reduce the role of the Communist Party while expanding the authority of popularly elected legislatures, or soviets. The reforms, which were to go into effect over a period of years, included deep cuts in the party apparatus and the creation of a new national legislature and of a new and powerful post of president. The current presidency—technically, the chairmanship of the presidium of the Supreme Soviet—is largely honorific. Andrei Gromyko retired from this office and Gorbachev was elected to fill it, thereby combining both party and state leadership in himself. When the new post of president is created, Gorbachev is expected to fill it. The sessions of the party conferences were broadcast live on Soviet television in the spirit of *glasnost.*

The new policies were not universally applauded. Blue-collar workers feared the establishment of productivity-related wages, the possibility of unemployment when unprofitable plants were closed, and the end of state subsidies on food and other necessities. Managers and bureaucrats feared loss of status and jobs in the reorganization, as well as the unaccustomed publicity. Consumers saw no immediate increase in consumer goods or food supplies except at high (market) prices. The relaxation of censorship and police control resulted not only in the publication of some long-banned books but also the expression of discontent by many minority groups. Tatars, Armenians, Ukrainians, Latvians, Lithuanians, and Estonians demonstrated for greater cultural autonomy. Conservatives in the party leadership feared that the loosening of controls would lead to unpredictable and possibly disastrous consequences.

UNIONS, workers' organizations formed to improve pay, working conditions and benefits. There were medieval craft GUILDS in Europe, but modern labor unions arose out of the new concentrations of workers in the INDUSTRIAL REVOLUTION. A craft (horizontal) union organizes workers with a particular skill; an industrial (vertical) union includes all workers in an industry. Employer-controlled company unions are unaffiliated to labor groupings.

Unions negotiate contracts with employers by collective bargaining. A CLOSED SHOP or UNION SHOP increases bargaining strength but may be barred by RIGHT-TO-WORK LAWS. A dispute may be referred to ARBITRATION, or members may resort to strikes, slowdowns or featherbedding, picketing, BOYCOTT, and, rarely, sit-downs or work-ins.

In the US, local craft unions existed from the late 1700s. The influence of the socialistic KNIGHTS OF LABOR (1869–1917) gave way to that of the craft unions of the American Federation of Labor (founded 1886). In the early 1900s a revolutionary upsurge was expressed through the INDUSTRIAL WORKERS OF THE WORLD, but the Protocol of Peace ending the 1910 strike by the International Ladies' Garment Workers' Union set a pattern for union-management cooperation that accelerated in WWI. The industrial-union-based Congress of Industrial Organizations was formed in the 1930s, a time of NEW DEAL legislation to improve industrial relations (see WAGNER ACT). The TAFT-HARTLEY ACT (1947) placed restrictions on unions and the Landrum-Griffin Act (1959) curbed union corruption. In recent years, union organizing has lagged as the US economy has become more service-oriented; the percentage of US workers belonging to unions has declined from nearly 30% in 1964 to less than 25% as of 1980.

The AMERICAN FEDERATION OF LABOR AND CONGRESS OF INDUSTRIAL ORGANIZATIONS merger occurred in 1955. Britain has one Trades Union Congress, but many countries have rival Christian and socialist bodies. Internationally, the Christian World Confederation of Labor claims 12 million members, the communist-led World Federation of Trade Unions 160 million, and the International Confederation of Free Trade Unions (the 1949 AFL-CIO-backed breakaway from the WFTU) 56 million.

UNION SHOP, industrial situation where all new employees at a workplace must join a particular union. (See also CLOSED SHOP.)

UNITARIANISM, unorthodox Protestant faith that rejects the TRINITY and Christ's deity and asserts the unipersonality of God. It developed out of SOCINIANISM; and many 18th-century English Presbyterians became Unitarian. Joseph PRIESTLEY gave it a great impetus in the US, where liberal, rationalist Unitarianism preaching toleration and universal salvation was developing in CONGREGATIONAL CHURCHES. The American Unitarian Association, led by William CHANNING, was founded in 1825. Ralph Waldo EMERSON was a notable Unitarian.

UNITARIAN UNIVERSALIST ASSOCIATION, US Protestant church formed (1961) by merger of the Universalist Church of America and the American Unitarian Association. The Association brings together over 170,000 members from two churches with similar histories and views (see UNITARIANISM; UNIVERSALISM).

UNITED ARAB EMIRATES, formerly **Trucial States,** oil-rich federation of emirates in the E Arabian Peninsula, on the Persian Gulf and Gulf of Oman. It comprises Abu Dhabi, Ajman, Dubai, Fujairah, Ras al-Khaimah, Sharjah and Umm al-Qaiwain.

Official name: United Arab Emirates
Capital: Abu Dhabi
Area: 30,000sq mi
Population: 1,856,000
Languages: Arabic; English
Religions: Muslim
Monetary unit(s): 1 UAE dirham=100 fils
Land and People. The country has a 400mi coastline and is mostly desert, with oases. In

the E mountains rise to over 8,000ft, giving way to a fertile littoral strip where dates, grains and tobacco are cultivated. Herding, fishing and pearling are traditional occupations and Dubai has long been a center of Middle East trade. Most of the people are Sunnite Muslim Arabs and are farmers or nomads. The population has recently increased rapidly; there are Iranian, black, Indian, Pakistani and European minorities, who now outnumber the indigenous population. Oil, from Abu Dhabi, Dubai, and Sharjah, has given the country one of the highest per-capita incomes in the world.

History. From 1820 truces linked the emirates with Britain. Oil was discovered in Abu Dhabi, the largest state, in 1958. The independent federation was formed in 1971, neighboring Bahrain and Qatar opting for separate statehood. Ras al-Khaima joined in 1972. The country was a founding member of the Gulf Cooperation Council (1981) and supported Iraq in the long Iran-Iraq war (1981–88).

UNITED ARAB REPUBLIC, union of Egypt and Syria proclaimed in 1958, as a step toward pan-Arab union. Cairo was capital, and NASSER president. The UAR formed with Yemen the nominal United Arab States (1958–61). Resenting Egyptian dominance, Syria seceded in 1961. A 1963 attempt to unite Egypt, Syria and Iraq failed. Egypt was named the UAR until 1971, when a loose Federation of Arab Republics (Egypt, Syria and Libya) was formed.

UNITED AUTOMOBILE WORKERS (United Automobile, Aerospace and Agricultural Implement Workers of America), the second largest US industrial labor union, with local unions in Canada. Founded in 1935, it won recognition at General Motors, Chrysler and Ford (1937–41). Its 1,200,000 members are in automobile, space, aviation and metal industries. The UAW cofounded the CIO, but left the AFL-CIO in 1968. Walter REUTHER was president 1946–70, Leonard WOODCOCK 1970–77, and Douglas Fraser 1977–. UAW headquarters are in Detroit.

UNITED CHURCH OF CANADA, Canadian Protestant church formed 1925 by union of the Methodist and most Presbyterian and Congregationalist churches. Ecumenical, national and missionary, it has a PRESBYTERIAN form of organization, stresses the rights of congregations, and has men and women ministers. It was joined in 1968 by Canada's Evangelical United Brethren Church and has over a million adult communicants.

UNITED CHURCH OF CHRIST, a US Protestant body set up by the 1957 union (with its 1961 constitution) of the Congregational Christian Churches and the Evangelical and Reformed Church. It gives strong local autonomy combined with national services and organization, and has over 1,700,000 members.

UNITED EMPIRE LOYALISTS, people of the original 13 colonies who remained loyal to Britain during the American Revolution and emigrated to Canada. The largest group, some 50,000, left New York City in 1783, and established New Brunswick (1784) and Upper Canada (now Ontario; 1791).

UNITED IRISHMEN, Society of, political group formed by Wolfe TONE and others in 1791 for the emancipation of Irish Catholics, parliamentary reform and, when forced underground (1794), Irish independence. The British arrested its leaders, intercepted French support, and broke the Irish revolt (1798).

UNITED KINGDOM, or the **United Kingdom of Great Britain and Northern Ireland,** a constitutional monarchy of NW Europe occupying the whole of the British Isles except the Republic of Ireland. The United Kingdom (UK) thus comprises the island of Great Britain (England, Scotland, and Wales) and Northern Ireland. The Isle of Man and the Channel Islands are both Crown dependencies and are not strictly part of the UK.

Official name: United Kingdom of Great Britain and Northern Ireland
Capital: London
Area: 94,251sq mi
Population: 56,878,000
Languages: English; Welsh, Gaelic
Religions: Church of England, Roman Catholic, Church of Scotland
Monetary unit(s): 1 pound = 100 pence
Land. England, largest country in the UK, has a hilly backbone—the Pennines—running N from Derbyshire to the Scottish border. This extends from the Solway Firth to Berwick-upon-Tweed. W of the N Pennines (Cross Fell, 2,930ft), is the scenic

Lake District, set amid the Cumbrian Mts, and containing England's highest point (Scafell Pike, 3,210ft) and largest lake (Windermere, 5.69sq mi). Lowlands, sometimes with low hills, stretch across the rest of England. Among them are the fertile Fens bordering on the Wash and, SE of the Chiltern Hills, the London basin with the Thames R.

Scotland has rolling southern uplands, and fertile central lowlands deeply penetrated by the firths (estuaries) of the Clyde R (leading to Glasgow) and the Forth R (leading past Edinburgh, the capital city). The Tay (118mi) is Scotland's longest river. N of the Ochil hills are the rugged Scottish Highlands. Ben Nevis (4,406ft), in the Grampian Mts, is the highest peak in the British Isles. SE of Glen More (the Great Glen) and its chain of lochs, are the Cairngorm Mts (Ben Macdhui, 4,296ft). Scotland's many islands include the Inner and Outer Hebrides to the NW and the Orkney and Shetland groups to the N.

Wales centers on the Cambrian Mts (Snowdon 3,560ft). The many rivers flowing from the Welsh massif include the Severn (220mi), the UK's longest river.

Northern Ireland is often called Ulster because it occupies most of that ancient province. Lough Neagh (153sq mi) is the largest lake in the British Isles. To the SE are the granite Mourne Mts (Slieve Donard, 2,796ft). The Erne R drains the SW.

Climate. Britain enjoys a mainly mild climate with changeable weather. The warm N Atlantic Drift and prevailing westerly winds are major influences. Rainfall, heaviest in the W and mountains, averages 40in yearly. Winter temperatures average 40°F, summer averages ranging from 54°F in the far N, to 61°F in the usually warmer S.

People. With an estimated population of about 56 million, the UK is one of the world's most densely populated countries. More than five sixths of the people live in England. Most British are urban-dwelling, with London, the nation's capital, the largest of some eight major conurbations.

As a result of immigration the UK now has a multiracial society. Immigrants from India, Pakistan, the West Indies and other Commonwealth countries number at least 1,500,000.

Government. MAGNA CARTA and the English CIVIL WAR checked the power of the monarch. Cabinet government and parliamentary democracy developed during the 18th and 19th centuries. Today the supreme legislative body is Parliament, comprising the House of Commons, whose 635 members are elected for a five-year term by all citizens over 18, and the House of Lords with about 1,170 members. The government is conducted by a prime minister and cabinet, normally provided by the majority party in the Commons from among its members of Parliament.

Culture and Beliefs. Education is free and compulsory from 5 to 16. English is the universal language, but Welsh is widely spoken in Wales, and Gaelic survives in parts of Scotland. There are two established churches, the CHURCH OF ENGLAND and CHURCH OF SCOTLAND. The many other religious groups include Roman Catholics, Methodists, Baptists, Unitarians, Congregationalists, Quakers, Jews and Muslims.

Economy. Scene of the world's first industrial revolution in the 18th century, the UK based its economic development on its coal and iron deposits. Recently North Sea oil and natural gas have been exploited. Industrial raw materials and food, however, often have to be imported. (British farms, though efficient, provide only half of the nation's food.) To pay for imports the UK exports manufactured goods and provides services like banking, insurance and shipping. Major industries include iron and steel, engineering, textiles, electronics, chemicals and shipbuilding. Most industries are privately owned, but some of the most important, like coal mining, iron and steel, electric power, railroads and the chief airlines, are wholly or partly owned by the state. After WWII the UK failed to keep pace in economic growth with other W European countries due to the decline of its relative economic strength and the inflexibility of its management and labor practices. Britain joined the EUROPEAN ECONOMIC COMMUNITY in 1973.

History. After the Roman occupation (c100–400 AD) England was invaded by Angles, Saxons, Jutes and Danes. The Norman conquest (1066) introduced the feudal system and the first centralization of power. Wales, conquered in 1282, was legally joined to England in 1536. Scotland was united with England under the monarchy of James VI and I (1603) and then by Act of Union (1707). Northern Ireland remained part of the UK after the S became independent (1922).

Maritime expansion began under Elizabeth I (1558–1603) and reached its height in the 1700s and 1800s, building up the 19th-century British Empire. British power was greatly weakened by both world wars, and with successive grants of independence from 1945, the empire was transformed into the Commonwealth of Nations. Remaining colonies include the Falkland Islands (claimed by Argentina, which unsuccessfully invaded them in 1982), Gibraltar (claimed by Spain) and Hong Kong (until 1997).

After WWII Britain established a welfare state that involved the nationalization of key industries and the vast expansion of social services. One effect was to diminish the country's competitiveness in the world market; problems such as inflation, trade deficits, and unemployment were chronic. When Conservative Party leader Margaret Thatcher became prime minister in 1977 she resolved to dismantle the welfare state, check the power of labor unions, and instill an entrepreneurial spirit in the country. The change was wrenching, marked by persistent high unemployment especially in the northern industrial cities. But by the late 1980s the economy was growing, unemployment was declining, and taxes were being cut. The prime minister was criticized in many quarters for subordinating traditional British values to the drive for commercial success, but her reelection to a third term in 1987 ensured that her policy would be continued.

UNITED METHODIST CHURCH, second largest US Protestant denomination, formed in 1968 by the union of the EVANGELICAL UNITED BRETHREN CHURCH and the Methodist Church (see METHODISTS). The church stresses ecumenism and social action.

UNITED MINEWORKERS OF AMERICA (UMW), US industrial union formed in 1890. Under John L. LEWIS (president 1920–60), it took militant stands on pay, safety, and political questions. A cofounder of the CIO in 1935 (now unaffiliated), it has about 250,000 members.

UNITED NATIONS, international organization of the world's states which aims to promote peace and international cooperation. Successor to the LEAGUE OF NATIONS, it was founded at the 1945 San Francisco Conference prepared by the "Big Three" Allied Powers of WWII; 51 states signed the charter. Membership had grown to 117 in 1955, and to 159 by 1988. The headquarters are in New York.

The UN has six major organs. The *General Assembly,* composed of delegates from all member states, meets once a year and provides a general forum, but has little power of action. The *Security Council* has five permanent members each with a veto (China, France, Great Britain, the US and the USSR) and ten elected members.

Intended to be a permanent peacekeeping body with emergency executive powers, the Security Council has often dispatched peacekeeping forces to trouble spots at the invitation of the combatants. Most recently, observers were sent to monitor the withdrawal of Soviet forces from Afghanistan and the cease-fire in the Iran-Iraq war. In 1988 the UN peacekeeping forces were awarded the Nobel Peace Prize. The *Economic and Social Council,* with 54 elected members, deals with "nonpolitical" matters, coordinating the work of the specialist agencies and operating important commissions of its own, such as those on children, refugees and human rights. The *Trusteeship Council* is responsible for UN TRUST TERRITORIES. The INTERNATIONAL COURT OF JUSTICE is the UN's principal organ for INTERNATIONAL LAW. The *Secretariat* is the administrative body headed by the Secretary General, who is an important figure with considerable executive power and political influence (see LIE, TRYGVE; HAMMARSKJÖLD, DAG; THANT, U; WALDHEIM, KURT; PÉREZ DE CUÉLLAR, JAVIER).

Other organs are the United Nations Conference on Trade and Development, the Office of the UNITED NATIONS HIGH COMMISSIONER FOR REFUGEES, and the UNITED NATIONS CHILDREN'S FUND.

Major specialized agencies affiliated with the UN include the FOOD AND AGRICULTURE ORGANIZATION, GENERAL AGREEMENT ON TARIFFS AND TRADE, INTERNATIONAL ATOMIC ENERGY AGENCY (UN-sponsored), International Civil Aviation Organization, INTERNATIONAL LABOR ORGANIZATION, INTERNATIONAL MONETARY FUND, International Telecommunication Union, UNITED NATIONS EDUCATIONAL, SCIENTIFIC AND CULTURAL ORGANIZATION, UNIVERSAL POSTAL UNION, WORLD BANK, WORLD HEALTH ORGANIZATION, and WORLD METEOROLOGICAL ORGANIZATION.

UNITED NATIONS CHILDREN'S FUND (UNICEF), UN organization formed 1946 as the UN International Children's Emergency Fund to help in countries devastated in WWII. It became a permanent body in 1953, retaining the UNICEF acronym and specializing in child welfare, family planning and nutrition programs in disaster areas and in many poorer countries. It is financed voluntarily. In 1965 UNICEF was awarded the Nobel Peace Prize.

UNITED NATIONS EDUCATIONAL, SCIENTIFIC AND CULTURAL ORGANIZATION (UNESCO), a UN agency established 1946 to promote international collaboration among states in education, the natural and social sciences, communications, and culture. Its policy-making general conference meets biennially at the Paris headquarters. UNESCO has helped develop education in poorer countries and arranges scientific and cultural exchanges. Charging politicization and mismanagement, the US withdrew from UNESCO in 1984, followed by the UK and Singapore in 1985.

UNITED NATIONS HIGH COMMISSIONER FOR REFUGEES, Office of the, UN agency, the 1951 successor to the International Refugee Organization. It has cared for refugees from many countries, and supports their right to be free from arbitrary expulsion, to work and be educated in their new homes. It received in 1954 the Nobel Peace Prize, and again in 1981 it won the award for its humane work in helping displaced people. The separate UN Relief and Works Agency for Palestine Refugees (established 1949) is based in Beirut.

UNITED NATIONS RELIEF AND REHABILITATION ADMINISTRATION (UNRRA), body set up (1943) by WWII Allied Powers to help newly liberated regions. It provided emergency supplies and refugee camps and repatriated 7,000,000 refugees, mainly in China and E and S Europe. Its successors were the International Refugee Organization (1946–52) and the Office of the UNITED NATIONS HIGH COMMISSIONER FOR REFUGEES.

UNITED PRESBYTERIAN CHURCH IN THE USA, created in 1958 through merger of the Presbyterian Church in the USA and the United Presbyterian Church of North America. It is the largest Presbyterian body in the US, representing almost 9,000 churches with about 2,400,000 members. It has many overseas missionaries and is concerned with Christian social action. (See PRESBYTERIANISM; REFORMED CHURCHES.)

UNITED PRESS INTERNATIONAL (UPI), world's largest independent news agency, created by the 1958 merger of United Press (formed by Edward W. SCRIPPS) and William R. HEARST'S International News Service. At its height in the 1950s, it had some 200 bureaus (half in the US) sending news and pictures to over 5,000 clients.

UNITED SERVICE ORGANIZATIONS (USO), independent, nonprofit grouping of organizations formed 1941 to provide recreational, entertainment, religious and social facilities for the US armed forces. It is recognized by the US Department of Defense. Affiliates include the YMCA, YWCA and Salvation Army.

UNITED STATES CONSTITUTION, the supreme law of the nation. Written in Philadelphia in the summer of 1787, the Constitution was approved by the 55 delegates representing the 13 original states and went into effect on March 4, 1789, after ratification by the required nine states. The document was the sum of the young nation's experience to that point. The actions of the virtually autonomous states and the failure of the country's first constitution, the ARTICLES OF CONFEDERATION, convinced the Founding Fathers that a strong executive and a powerful federal government were needed if the US were to survive as a cohesive entity. Many compromises were necessary before final agreement was reached. The conflicting desires of large and small states resulted in a bicameral legislature, one house based on population size, the other house with an equal number of seats for each state (see CONGRESS OF THE UNITED STATES). North and South compromised on including slaves in population totals. Most important, though, was the eventual, if begrudging, recognition by all states that a strong central government would be needed if the US was to be more than just a loose confederation. The states allayed their fears by constructing a SEPARATION OF POWERS to limit governmental power (see STATES' RIGHTS; EXECUTIVE). A BILL OF RIGHTS to guarantee personal freedoms was also added as the first ten amendments to the Constitution. The document has proven adaptable and flexible; its timelessness is indicated by the addition of only 16 amendments since 1791. (See also PRESIDENCY; ELECTORAL COLLEGE; CONSTITUTIONAL LAW.)

UNITED STATES INFORMATION AGENCY (USIA), independent federal agency established in 1948 to conduct the US government's overseas information and cultural programs, including the VOICE OF AMERICA and the FULBRIGHT SCHOLARSHIP PROGRAM.

UNITED STATES OF AMERICA (USA or US), world's fourth-largest country after the USSR, Canada and China. The 48 conterminous states span North America from coast to coast. With Alaska, separated from them by Canada, they form the continental US. The 50th state is Hawaii. The federal capital is Washington, D.C. (District of Columbia). Overseas territories include Puerto Rico, the American Virgin Islands, Guam, American Samoa and Belau, Marshall Islands, Federated States of Micronesia, and Northern Marianas, formerly in the Trust Territory of the Pacific Islands. Other dependencies include

Official name: United States of America
Capital: Washington, D.C.
Area: 3,536,855sq mi
Population: 246,000,000
Languages: English
Monetary unit(s): 1 US dollar=100 cents

Johnson, Midway, Wake and other Pacific islands.

Land. The conterminous US can be divided into six natural regions: the *Atlantic and Gulf Coastal Lowlands* stretching S from Long Island to Florida and then W to Mexico, averaging 200mi wide, with many lagoons and sandbars and, on the Gulf Coast, the Mississippi R delta; the *Appalachians*, running NE-SW from Nova Scotia (Canada), a low mountain system that includes the White Mts of N.H. (Mt Washington, 6,288ft), the Great Smoky Mts (Clingmans Dome, 6,643ft), the Black Mts of N.C. (Mt Mitchell, 6,684ft) and, to the W, the ridge and valley belt and the Allegheny Plateau; the *Central* or *Interior Plains*, stretching W to the Rocky Mts, a region drained chiefly by the Mississippi-Missouri river system and its branches and containing various uplands such as the Black Hills of Dakota, and the Ozarks; the *Rocky Mts*, with peaks exceeding 14,000ft, glacial features and many national parks; the *Western Plateau and Basin* or *Intermontane Region*, separated from the Pacific coastlands by the Cascade and Sierra Nevada ranges and containing such features as the Grand Canyon and the Great Salt Lake; and the *Pacific Coastlands*, extending S from Puget Sound to the long Central Valley of California.

Climate is greatly influenced by the geographic position of the conterminous US between large oceans on the E and W, with a warm and shallow sea to the S and the Canadian landmass to the N. The W winds from the Pacific bring heavy rainfall to the NW coast in winter and the fall, but rainfall decreases rapidly immediately E of the western mountains before increasing again along the Atlantic and Gulf coasts. Winter temperatures vary greatly, being relatively high along the sheltered Pacific coast, but often extremely low in the interior and the E. Snowfall can be heavy in the N. Summer temperatures are mainly high, averaging over 75°F in most areas. The SE becomes subtropical and humid. Tornadoes can occur in spring, especially in the Mississippi valley, and summer thunderstorms and hurricanes are frequent along the S Gulf and Atlantic coasts.

Vegetation. The natural vegetation ranges from the mixed forests of the Appalachians to the grasslands of the Great Plains, and from the conifers of the Rocky Mts and NW states to the splendid redwoods of California, the cacti and mesquite of the SW deserts, and the tropical palms and mangroves of the Gulf.

People. The US is the world's fourth-largest nation by population after China, India and the USSR. Until 1840 immigrants came mostly from England and Scotland, but thereafter increasingly from other, mainly European, lands including Ireland, Germany, Scandinavia and, from the 1860s, Italy and the Slavic countries. Since 1820 more than 46 million immigrants are estimated to have been admitted. After 1921, quotas favored immigrants from W and N Europe; from 1965, large numbers of Latin Americans and Asians have been admitted. The first blacks came as slaves (from 1619). Today there are some 30 million black Americans, of whom the majority still live in the South and in large cities like Washington, D.C., New York and Chicago. Indians, the original inhabitants, are found in all states, with major concentrations in the Great Plains and the West. Other significant national groups include Spanish-Americans (Mexicans and Puerto Ricans), Chinese and Japanese. About 75% of Americans are urban-dwelling and about 16% of the total population live in the highly urbanized Boston to Washington, D.C. stretch of the Atlantic coastal belt which contains the most densely populated states, New Jersey and Rhode Island. During the 1960s California overtook New York to become the most populous state in the Union. The US has many religious groups, the strongest being the Protestants (73,700,000, chiefly Baptists, Methodists, Lutherans and Presbyterians) and Roman Catholics (52,000,000). There is a nationwide system of public education and only 2% of the population is illiterate.

Economy. In 1986 the Gross National Product of the US was $4.2 trillion, nearly twice that of the USSR, its nearest rival as the world's leading economic nation. The American economy is predominantly free-enterprise. The US can grow nearly all temperate and subtropical crops and is self-sufficient in essential foods. About half the land surface is occupied by farms, with dairying important in the N and NE, livestock and feed grains in the Midwest (the Corn Belt), wheat on the plains, livestock on the High Plains and the intermontane areas of the W, and also in the S (along with dairying and various crops). Texas, the rest of the S, and California lead in cotton and there are various specialty crops like fruit, rice, citrus fruits and sugarcane in the S. There are valuable forests and fisheries. The rich mineral resources include coal (Appalachians, Indiana-Illinois, Alabama), iron ore (near Lake Superior), petroleum and natural gas (Texas, Louisiana, the Great Plains and Alaska) and other vital minerals. But reserves of some minerals are declining and the US has increasingly become an importer of ores and oil. Major products include steel (Pittsburgh, Chicago-Gary and elsewhere), automobiles (Detroit), aircraft and aerospace products (the West and on the Great Plains), electric and electronic equipment (New England and increasingly the Sun Belt states), textiles (North and South Carolina, Georgia) and most kinds of consumer goods. Some consumer goods industries, like tobacco and meat-packing, are located near their raw materials; others are widely scattered to meet their markets.

History. For an account of the original inhabitants of America and their dispossession, see INDIANS; INDIAN WARS. The first permanent European settlement was Spanish (St. Augustine, Florida, 1565). Early English settlements were in Virginia (Jamestown, 1607), Massachusetts (Plymouth, 1620), Maryland (1634), Connecticut (1636) and Pennsylvania (1681). There were French, Dutch and Swedish settlements as well. Opposition to Britain's policy toward its 13 North American colonies led to the REVOLUTIONARY WAR (1775–83) and independence as a federal republic with George WASHINGTON as first President (1789). Expansion westward followed. The area of the US was doubled by the LOUISIANA PURCHASE (1803) and later Florida was purchased from Spain (1819). The WAR of 1812 with Britain ended US prospects of conquering Canada. Texas was annexed in 1845 and other territories gained by the Treaty of Guadalupe Hidalgo ending the MEXICAN WAR (1848). The GADSDEN PURCHASE (1853) brought southern New Mexico and southern Arizona into the

Union, and Alaska was purchased from Russia in 1867. Regional differences between North and South culminated in the CIVIL WAR (1861–65). There followed a period of RECONSTRUCTION (1865–77) and rapid development during which the first transcontinental railroad was completed (1869). Hawaii was annexed in 1898, and other overseas territories came under US rule as a result of the SPANISH-AMERICAN WAR. The US entered WORLD WAR I in 1917, but the prosperity which followed the war was ended by the GREAT DEPRESSION of the 1930s. Franklin D. ROOSEVELT'S NEW DEAL was an innovative program to halt this economic decline. The Japanese attack on PEARL HARBOR (1941) brought the US into WORLD WAR II. The nation emerged from that war as leader of the West and a "superpower" engaged in worldwide rivalry with the communist bloc (see COLD WAR), which led to its participation in the KOREAN WAR (1950–53) and the VIETNAM WAR (1961–73). In domestic affairs, the New Deal emphasis on social welfare was renewed in the War on Poverty and other programs of the 1960s, but this impulse was largely spent by the end of the 1970s. Republicans, who had held the presidency 1969–77, returned to power in 1981 under Ronald Reagan, who slashed government spending in all areas except defense and entitlements and lowered taxes. The result, after an initial sharp recession, was a long economic expansion beginning in Nov. 1982 fueled by budget deficits that nearly tripled the national debt—from $1 trillion in 1980 to almost $2.8 trillion in 1988. Reagan's vice president, George Bush, was elected president in 1988 promising to continue the same policies.

UNITED STEELWORKERS OF AMERICA (USW), third largest US union with 1,200,000 members. Superseding the Amalgamated Association of Iron, Steel and Tin Workers, the CIO's Steel Workers' Organizing Committee, recognized by the US Steel Corporation in 1937, took its present name in 1942.

UNITED WAY OF AMERICA (UWA), US organization which raises funds for health, recreation and welfare agencies, founded 1918. Over 200 major national organizations have been helped by the United Way.

UNIVERSAL DECLARATION OF HUMAN RIGHTS, adopted by the General Assembly of the UNITED NATIONS in 1948, enumerates the HUMAN RIGHTS affirmed by the UN Charter. These include freedom of thought, conscience, and religion; freedom of opinion and expression; freedom of assembly and association; equality before the law; protection against arbitrary arrest; the right to a fair trial; the right to own property; the right to work and to choose one's work freely; the right to equal pay for equal work; the right to form and join trade unions; the right to rest and leisure; the right to an adequate standard of living; the right to education. These rights are held up as a standard for the signatory countries to aspire to; they are not legally enforceable obligations.

UNIVERSALISM, heretical Christian doctrine that everyone will ultimately be saved (see SALVATION). HELL is denied. The Universalist Church in the US was formed by Hosea Ballou and other New England nonconformists. Liberal and syncretist, in 1961 it joined the Unitarians to form the UNITARIAN UNIVERSALIST ASSOCIATION.

UNIVERSAL MILITARY TRAINING (UMT), form of military DRAFT often proposed as an alternative to the ALL-VOLUNTEER FORCE (AVF). Under UMT, all persons — presumably males only since the ultimate purpose of the training would be for combat — turning 18 or 19 would be required to undergo a short period of military training. Proponents argue that UMT would be less costly than the AVF, where pay and conditions must be competitive with civilian jobs. Critics argue that UMT would be no less costly and would contribute little to the nation's military effectiveness. It would be necessary to assign — perhaps by lottery — some trainees to further active duty with the career forces, others to the reserves, and the great majority to inactive status since the available trainees would far exceed the needs of both the active-duty and reserve forces. The inherent unfairness of a draft in circumstances of less-than-total mobilization would thus not be avoided by UMT.

UNIVERSAL POSTAL UNION (UPU), a UN agency (since 1947) that determines procedures for the reciprocal flow of foreign mail. Its operations are based on the first (1875) Universal Postal Convention. The Universal Postal Congress meets every five years. Headquarters are in Bern, Switzerland. (See also POSTAL SERVICE.)

UNKNOWN SOLDIER, in the US and some European countries, an unidentified soldier killed in action whose tomb is a national shrine honoring all war dead. Unknown soldiers of WWI, WWII, the Korean War, and the Vietnam War are buried in the Tomb of the Unknown Soldier in ARLINGTON NATIONAL CEMETERY, Arlington, Va.

UPANISHADS, ancient Hindu scriptures (c1000 BC–600 BC) attached to the latter half of each VEDA and containing secret or mystical doctrine. They are of lesser authority than the *Aranyakas* and *Brahmanas* (expository texts), being intended more for the philosophical inquirer.

UPDIKE, John Hoyer (1932–   ), US novelist, short-story writer, poet and critic. With precise craftsmanship, he dissects contemporary life in such novels as *Rabbit, Run* (1960), *The Centaur* (1963), *Couples* (1968), *Bech: A Book* (1970), *Rabbit Redux* (1971), *The Coup* (1978) and *Rabbit Is Rich* (1981) and short-story collections like *The Music School* (1966).

UPJOHN, Richard (1802–1878), British-born US architect, famous for his Gothic Revival churches, such as Trinity Church, New York City (1846). He was president of the American Institute of Architects 1857–76.

UPPER VOLTA. See BURKINA.

UR, or **Ur of the Chaldees,** ancient city of S MESOPOTAMIA. A center of the SUMERIAN civilization from c3000 BC, it was conquered by the Akkadian SARGON c2340 BC. A new dynasty arose c2060 BC under Ur-Nammu, who built the famous ZIGGURAT. After c1950 BC the city came under Elam and BABYLON. Destroyed and rebuilt several times, it was finally revived by Nebuchadnezzar II (c600 BC), but then declined and was abandoned by 300 BC, isolated by the Euphrates R changing its course. Ur was excavated by Leonard WOOLLEY.

URAL-ALTAIC LANGUAGES, collective term for the Uralic language family and the ALTAIC LANGUAGES. The 20 or so languages of the Uralic family (best known being Finnish and Hungarian) are in two branches, the UGRO-FINNIC LANGUAGES and the relatively unimportant Samoyedic languages.

URAL MOUNTAINS, 1,250mi-long mountain system in W USSR. Running N–S from the Kara Sea into Kazakhstan N of the Aral Sea, they are the traditional boundary between Europe and Asia. Mt Narodnaya (6,214ft), in the N section, is the highest peak. The Urals are heavily forested and rich in minerals.

URANIUM (U), soft, silvery-white radioactive metal in the actinide series; the heaviest natural element. Uranium occurs widely as PITCHBLENDE (uranite), carnotite and other ores, which are concentrated and converted to uranium (IV) fluoride, from which uranium is isolated by electrolysis or reduction with calcium or magnesium. The metal is reactive and electropositive, reacting with hot water and dissolving in acids. Its chief oxidation states are $+4$ and $+6$, and the uranyl (UO_2^{2+}) compounds are common. Uranium has three naturally-occurring ISOTOPES: U^{238} (HALF-LIFE 4.5×10^9yr), U^{235} (half-life 7.1×10^8yr) and U^{234} (half-life 2.5×10^5yr). More than 99% of natural uranium is U^{238}. The isotopes may be separated by fractional DIFFUSION of the volatile uranium (VI) fluoride. Neutron capture by U^{235} leads to nuclear FISSION, and a chain reaction can occur which is the basis of NUCLEAR REACTORS and of the ATOMIC BOMB. U^{238} also absorbs neutrons and is converted to an isotope of PLUTONIUM (Pu^{239}) which (like U^{235}) can be used as a nuclear fuel. Uranium is the starting material for the synthesis of the TRANSURANIUM ELEMENTS. Some of its compounds are used to color ceramics. AW 238.0, mp 1132°C, bp 3818°C, sg 19.05 (α).

URANUS, the third largest planet in the SOLAR SYSTEM and the seventh from the sun. Physically very similar to NEPTUNE, but rather larger (53 mm ± 5% equatorial radius), it orbits the sun every 84.02 years at a mean distance of 19.2AU, rotating in 10.75h. The plane of its equator is tilted 98° to the plane of its orbit, such that the rotation of the planet and the revolution of its five known moons, which orbit closely parallel to the equator, are retrograde. In 1977 the planet was discovered to have five rings, like those of SATURN but much fainter.

URBAN, name of eight popes. **Urban II** (reigned 1088–99) continued the reforms and the struggle against the emperor HENRY IV begun by his great predecessor GREGORY VII. At the Council of Clermont (1095) he initiated the CRUSADES. **Urban III** (reigned 1185–87) was absorbed in a struggle with Emperor FREDERICK I Barbarossa and his son HENRY VI. **Urban IV** (reigned 1261–64) continued the struggle against the Hohenstaufen emperors and gave the crown of Naples and Sicily to Charles I. The learned and pious **Saint Urban V** (reigned 1362–70) attempted to return the papacy to Rome from Avignon and to effect a reconciliation with the Eastern Church (1267–70; see PAPACY). **Urban VI** (reigned 1378–89) was involved in disputes with his cardinals which precipitated the GREAT SCHISM. **Urban VIII** (reigned 1623–44) played an ambiguous role in the THIRTY YEARS' WAR through political opposition to the Roman Catholic HAPSBURGS. An energetic administrator, he tried to increase the temporal power of the papacy.

URDU, Indic language of the Indo-European family, a form of HINDUSTANI (see also HINDI). It has borrowed heavily from Arabic and Persian. Spoken by some 20 million people, it is an official language of India and Pakistan.

UREMIA, the syndrome of symptoms and biochemical disorders seen in KIDNEY failure, associated with a rise in blood urea and other nitrogenous waste products of PROTEIN metabolism. Nausea, vomiting, malaise, itching, pigmentation, ANEMIA and acute disorders of fluid and mineral balance are common presentations, but the manifestations depend on the type of disease, rate of waste buildup, etc. Dietary foods may reduce uremic symptoms in chronic renal failure but dialysis or TRANSPLANTATION may be needed.

UREY, Harold Clayton (1893–1981), US chemist awarded the 1935 Nobel Prize for Chemistry for his discovery of deuterium, an isotope of HYDROGEN having one proton and one neutron in its nucleus, and who played a major role in the MANHATTAN PROJECT. He was also important as a cosmologist: his researches into geological dating using oxygen ISOTOPES enabled him to produce a model of the atmosphere of the primordial planet earth; and hence to formulate a theory of the planets having originated as a gaseous disk about the sun (see SOLAR SYSTEM). He was a leading theorist about the nature and origin of the MOON.

URINE, waste product comprising a dilute solution of excess salts and unwanted nitrogenous material, such as urea and deaminated PROTEIN, excreted by many animals. The wastes are filtered from the BLOOD in the KIDNEYS or equivalent structures and stored in the BLADDER till excreted. The passage of urine serves not only to eliminate wastes, but also provides a mechanism for maintaining the water and salt concentrations and pH of the blood. While all MAMMALS excrete their nitrogenous wastes in urine, other groups—birds, insects and fishes—excrete them as AMMONIA or in solid crystals as URIC ACID.

URSULA, Saint, 4th-century Christian martyr. According to legend, she and 11,000 British maidens returning from a pilgrimage to Rome were martyred by HUNS at Cologne. She is no longer officially recognized by the Roman Catholic Church.

URSULINES, Roman Catholic religious order of women, the first to be devoted exclusively to the education of girls. The order was founded in Brescia, Italy, in 1535 by St. Angela Merici, with St. Ursula as patron saint.

URUGUAY, the smallest republic in South

America, bordered by Argentina (W), Brazil (N and E), the Atlantic and the Río de la Plata in the S.

Official name: Oriental Republic of Uruguay
Capital: Montevideo
Area: 68,037sq mi
Population: 3,058,000
Languages: Spanish
Religions: Roman Catholic
Monetary unit(s): 1 new Uruguayan peso=100 centesimos
Land. A narrow coastal strip rises to low ridges (highest point 1,644ft), grassland plains and wooded valleys. The climate is temperate and rainfall (average 35in) is spread throughout the year. The Uruguay and Negro are the chief rivers.
People. The people are mostly of Spanish and Italian descent, and over 80% urban. About two-fifths of the population live in Montevideo. There are some 300,000 mestizos, mainly in the N.
Economy. The economy is based on cattle and sheep; meat, wool and hides provide 80% of the country's exports. Wheat, oats, flax, oilseeds, grapes, fruit and sugarbeet are grown. Meat-packing and tanning are the chief industries, and textiles, chemicals, plastics, electrical and other goods are manufactured. There are important fisheries, but few mineral resources.
History. The region was visited (1516) and settled (1624) by the Spanish, who resisted Portuguese incursions and founded Montevideo in 1726. José Artigas led the independence movement 1810–20, and Uruguay became independent in 1828. In the early 20th century, the government under José Batlle y Ordóñez introduced economic and social reforms and Uruguay subsequently became one of the most developed Latin American countries. Labor unrest and leftist Tupamaro guerrilla activities in the late 1960s led to a military takeover in 1973. Repression in the following years was widespread. A transitional president was installed in 1981 and the country returned to civilian rule in 1985.

USO. See UNITED SERVICE ORGANIZATIONS.
USSACHEVSKY, Vladimir (1911–   ), US composer who pioneered in electronic and computer music.
USSHER, James (1581–1656), Anglican bishop in Ireland, best remembered for having established a biblical chronology that placed the creation in 4004 BC.
UTAH, a state in the W US, bordered on the N by Ida. and Wyo., on the E by Col., S by Ariz., and W by Nev.

Name of state: Utah
Capital: Salt Lake City
Statehood: Jan. 4, 1896 (45th state)
Familiar name: Beehive State
Area: 84,916sq mi
Population: 1,665,000
Elevation: Highest—13,498ft., Kings Peak Lowest—2,000ft, Beaverdam Creek
Motto: Industry
State flower: Sego lily
State bird: Seagull
State tree: Blue spruce
State song: "Utah, We Love Thee"
Land. Utah falls into three regions: the ROCKY MOUNTAINS in the NE, the Colorado Plateau in the S and E and the GREAT BASIN in the W. The NW is dominated by the GREAT SALT LAKE and desert. The Colorado R and its tributary the Green R drain much of the E half. Average temperatures vary from 84°F in July in the SW to 20°F in January in the NE. Much of Utah is semiarid; annual rainfall varies from less than 5in to 50in (in the Wasatch Mts).
People. Over two-thirds of the population are MORMONS, whose headquarters are at Salt Lake City. Roman Catholics constitute the second-largest denomination. The population is almost all white; Indians number about 19,000. Salt Lake City, the state capital, is by far the largest city, followed by Ogden and Provo.
Economy. Since WWII manufacturing and mining have overtaken farming as the mainstays of the state economy. Large industries produce fabricated metals, transportation equipment, missiles and aerospace components, and foodstuffs including dairy products, flour and meat.

Utah possesses large deposits of copper, oil, bituminous coal, uranium, iron and other metals. Extensive irrigation projects have opened up new farm land. The principal crops are hay, wheat, barley and fruits. Livestock-raising is also important. Tourists are attracted to Zion and four other national parks, to four national monuments, and to many other sites of natural beauty. **History.** Visited by Spanish missionaries in 1776 and later explored by fur traders, Utah was first settled by the persecuted Mormons in 1847. It became part of the US in 1848, but did not become a state until 1896, after decades of strife with the federal government and warfare with the Ute Indians (for whom the state is named). The original 1895 constitution has remained in force. Since WWII, Utah has enjoyed a long period of prosperity. Significant reserves of oil, natural gas, and uranium were discovered, starting in 1948, and irrigation for agriculture was improved by the large Central Utah Project, undertaken in 1967. The state's population, which was under 1 million before 1968, grew by almost 70% in the next 20 years, but it remains remarkably homogeneous and virtually all white, with the result that Utah lacks the ethnic tensions common in other states. Much attention has been given in recent years to controlling development of Utah's natural resources. In 1987 a unique flood-control program was undertaken to lower the level of GREAT SALT LAKE. In presidential elections 1968–88, Utah voted consistently Republican.

UTAH WAR (1857–58), in US history, conflict between the US government and Mormons in Utah Territory. In 1857 President James Buchanan appointed a non-Mormon, Alfred Cumming, to replace Brigham YOUNG as territorial governor. Young resisted, and during the winter of 1857–58 there were sporadic encounters between the Mormon militia and the US army. In June 1858 the army entered Salt Lake City and Cumming was installed as governor.

UTAMARO, Kitagawa (1753–1806), Japanese artist famous for his elegant color prints of women. Highly popular in Japan, they were also admired by the French Impressionists.

UTE INDIANS, a North American tribe of the California-Intermountain group which once roamed parts of Ut., Col. and N.M. Originally peaceful hunter-gatherers, they became marauders and buffalo-hunters after obtaining Spanish horses in the 1800s. Some 4,000 now live in Col. and Ut.

UTERUS. See WOMB.

UTILITARIANISM, a theory of ETHICS that the rightness or wrongness of an action is determined by the amount of happiness its consequences produce for the greatest number of people. Although the good action is that which brings about the greatest amount of happiness, it is not dependent on motive: an agent's bad motive may lead to others' happiness. The theory dates from the 18th-century thinker Jeremy BENTHAM who believed that actions were motivated by pleasure and pain and that happiness can be assessed by the quantity of pleasure; but J. S. MILL's *Utilitarianism* (1863) argued that some pleasures should be sought for their intrinsic quality.

UTILITY, in classical economics, defines the psychological satisfaction of consuming a given quantity of a particular good or service. It is an important concept in explaining demand. Goods with high utility may be in greater demand and command a higher PRICE (see SUPPLY AND DEMAND).

UTOPIA, term now used to denote any imaginary ideal state. Based on Greek words meaning "no place," it was coined by Sir Thomas MORE as the title of his *Utopia* (1516), in which he described a just society free of internal strife. Blueprints for such societies have been offered by many other authors, ranging from PLATO to MARX. Utopian thinking in 19th-century America was largely influenced by the theories of FOURIER; utopian experiments included Brook Farm (1841–47); a popular utopian romance was Edward BELLAMY's *Looking Backward* (1888). Aldous HUXLEY's *Brave New World* (1932) and George ORWELL's *1984*, by contrast, are dystopias, or satirical attacks on totalitarian/utopian schemes.

UTRECHT, Peace of (1713–14), a series of treaties between England, France, the Netherlands, Portugal, Prussia, Spain and the Holy Roman Empire which concluded the War of the SPANISH SUCCESSION (see also FRENCH AND INDIAN WARS). It marked the end of a period of French expansion and the beginnings of the British Empire. Britain gained Newfoundland, Acadia (Nova Scotia) and the Hudson Bay territory from France, which retained New France (Quebec), recognized the Protestant succession in England and renounced PHILIP v of Spain's claim to the French throne. From Spain Britain gained Gibraltar and Minorca and a monopoly over the slave trade. Austria gained Milan, Naples, Sardinia and the Catholic Netherlands.

UTRILLO, Maurice (1883–1955), French painter best known for his Paris street scenes. His finest works, painted between about 1908 and 1914, capture the atmosphere of old Montmartre.

UXMAL, ruined city in Yucatán, Mexico. Built by the MAYAS, it flourished c600-900 AD and has some fine examples of the late-classical Puuc style of architecture. It was finally abandoned c1450 AD.

UZBEK SOVIET SOCIALIST REPUBLIC, Soviet republic in central Asia, bordering on Afghanistan to the S. Tashkent, the capital, and Samarkand are the chief cities. Cotton and rice are the principal crops, made possible by extensive irrigation. Industrialization has been rapid since WWII, when many factories were moved there from European Russia for security.

22nd letter of the English alphabet. Its origins are the same as those of the letter U, out of which it developed. In English the use of "v" for the consonantal sound was firmly established by the 17th century. "V" stands for five in Roman numerals.

VAAL, river in South Africa, flowing about 750mi SW from SE Transvaal to the Orange R. It forms the Transvaal-Orange Free State boundary and is used for irrigation and Witwatersrand industry.

VACCINATION, method of inducing IMMUNITY to INFECTIOUS DISEASE due to BACTERIA or VIRUSES. Based on the knowledge that second attacks of diseases such as SMALLPOX were uncommon, early methods of protection consisted of inducing immunity by deliberate inoculation of material from a mild case. Starting from the observation that farm workers who had accidentally acquired cowpox by milking infected cows were resistant to smallpox, JENNER in the 1790s inoculated cowpox material into nonimmune persons who then showed resistance to smallpox. PASTEUR extended this work to experimental chicken CHOLERA, human ANTHRAX and RABIES. The term vaccination became general for all methods of inducing immunity by inoculation of products of the infectious organism. ANTITOXINS were soon developed in which specific immunity to disease TOXINS was induced. Vaccination leads to the formation of antibodies and the ability to produce large quantities rapidly at a later date (see ANTIBODIES AND ANTIGENS); this gives protection equivalent to that induced by an attack of the disease. It is occasionally followed by a reaction resembling a mild form of the disease, but rarely by the serious manifestations. Patients on STEROIDS, with immunity disorders or ECZEMA may suffer severe reactions and should not generally receive vaccinations.

VACUUM, any region of space devoid of ATOMS and MOLECULES. Such a region will neither conduct HEAT nor transmit SOUND waves. Because all materials which surround a space have a definite vapor pressure, a perfect vacuum is an impossibility and the term is usually used to denote merely a space containing air or other gas at very low PRESSURE. Pressures less than 0.1μPa occur naturally about 800km above the earth's surface, though pressures as low as 0.01nPa can be attained in the laboratory. The low pressures required for many physics experiments are obtained using various designs of vacuum PUMP.

VACUUM BOTTLE, double-walled glass container designed by Sir James Dewar in the late 19th century for storing liquified gases at low temperatures, but equally effective for storing hot substances. Heat transfer from the surroundings is minimized by silvering the glass walls to cut down heat RADIATION and evacuating the space between them to reduce the CONDUCTION of heat through them. A protective casing usually surrounds the glass walls.

VAKHTANGOV, Yevgeni (1883–1922), Soviet actor and director at the Moscow Art Theater and then in his own theater. His productions of *Macbeth* (1914), *The Dybbuk* (1922), and *Turandot* (1922) were memorable. He was also the first director (1917) of the Hebrew-language Habima Theater, which moved (1931) to Palestine and became (1953) Israel's national theater.

VALDIVIA, Pedro de (c1498–1554), Spanish conquistador, one of PIZARRO's officers. He conquered Chile (1540–46) from the ARAUCANIAN INDIANS and founded Santiago, Valparaiso and Concepción. He was killed while attempting to suppress an Indian rebellion.

VALENCIA, third-largest Spanish city in E Spain on the Turia R. A Roman settlement (138 BC), it came under the Moors c750–1238. Today it is a commercial and industrial center. Pop 763,949.

VALENS (c328–378 AD), Roman emperor of the East 364–78, brother of VALENTINIAN

I. He defeated the VISIGOTHS (369) and fought against Persia (372–76). The Visigoths, admitted into the Empire in 377, revolted and defeated him at ADRIANOPLE.

VALENTINE, Saint, a Christian priest in Rome who was martyred c270 AD. His traditional association with love probably reflects the near-coincidence of his feast-day (Feb. 14) with the ancient Roman fertility festival of Lupercalia (held Feb. 15). The practice of sending Valentine cards dates from the 19th century.

VALENTINIAN, name of three Roman emperors of the West. **Valentinian I** (321–375) reigned from 364 and made his brother, VALENS, emperor of the East. He successfully secured the Western Empire's borders against barbarian attacks. **Valentinian II** (371–392), his son, was nominally emperor from 375. His brother Gratian held power until 383, when Maximus took control of most of the West. Valentinian fled in 387, but was restored by THEODOSIUS I in 388. He was later murdered. Galla Placidia was regent for her son, **Valentinian III** (419–455), emperor from 425. His reign was disturbed by HUN and VANDAL invasions. In 454 he murdered Aetius (virtual ruler of the empire from 433), whose followers then killed him.

VALENTINO, Rudolph (1895–1926), Italian-born American cinema actor, known as "the great lover." The greatest romantic male star of the silent film era, Valentino's credits included *The Four Horsemen of the Apocalypse* (1921), *The Sheik* (1921) and *Blood and Sand* (1922).

VALERIAN (c190–c260), Roman emperor (253–60). In 257 he campaigned against the Persians in the East but in 260 he was defeated and captured by the Persian emperor, SHAPUR I, and died in captivity.

VALÉRY, Paul (1871–1945), French poet, essayist and critic. His early verse, *Album de Vers Anciens* (1920), was influenced by MALLARMÉ. His best-known works are *La Jeune Parque* (1917) and *Le Cimetière Marin* (1920). He wrote on poetry in *Monsieur Teste* (1896), and on philosophical and critical themes.

VALHALLA, in Norse mythology, the vast splendid "hall of the slain," in ASGARD where warriors killed in battle were entertained by ODIN. On Ragnarok, the day of doom, they were to march out with Odin to battle with the giants.

VALKYRIES (choosers of the slain), ODIN's battle maidens in Norse myth, who transported the souls of the warriors they had chosen in battle to VALHALLA.

VALLA, Lorenzo (1407–1457), Italian humanist and pioneer of critical scholar-ship. He exposed the DONATION OF CONSTANTINE (1440), attacked SCHOLASTICISM and criticized the VULGATE. His influential *Elegantiae* (1435–44) helped establish classical (as opposed to medieval) Latin as a RENAISSANCE ideal.

VALLANDIGHAM, Clement Laird (1820–1871), US Representative from Ohio (1858–63), leader of the pro-South COPPERHEADS during the Civil War, and a KNIGHTS OF THE GOLDEN CIRCLE commander. Court-martialed for "treasonable" sympathies (1863) he was "exiled" to the Confederacy. He returned to Ohio in 1864, but his political influence waned after the Civil War.

VALLEE, Rudy (Hubert Prior Vallee; 1901–1986), US singer and bandleader, host (1929–39) of a popular radio variety show. He also appeared in films and on Broadway.

VALLEY, long narrow depression in the earth's surface, usually formed by GLACIER or river EROSION. Young valleys are narrow, steep-sided and V-shaped; mature valleys, broader, with gentler slopes. Some, RIFT VALLEYS, are the result of collapse between FAULTS. **Hanging valleys,** of glacial origin, are side valleys whose floor is considerably higher than that of the main valley.

VALLEY FORGE, Revolutionary War encampment of Washington's CONTINENTAL ARMY on the Schuylkill R, 22mi NW of Philadelphia, Pa., Dec. 1777–June 1778. The army of 11,000 men was nearly destroyed by a harsh winter and lack of supplies. Hundreds of soldiers died, many deserted, and mutiny was feared. But morale was restored, and the Prussian Baron VON STEUBEN introduced efficient drilling.

VALMY, Battle of, victory of the French Revolutionary army, under Charles Dumouriez, over the invading Austro-Prussian forces at Valmy, NE France, in Sept. 1792. It saved Paris and the FRENCH REVOLUTION.

VALOIS, House of, French royal dynasty, 1328–1589. Starting with PHILIP VI (1328–50) the direct line ended with Charles VIII, who was followed by LOUIS XII (1498–1515) of the ORLÉANS branch. The Angoulême branch succeeded, ending in HENRY III (1574–89).

VALUE, in classical economics, the quality of a good or service that yields utility when consumed. If a good with use-value can be exchanged for other goods or money, it has exchange-value as well. This is the more common sense of the term. Value theory therefore often coincides with PRICE theory. For SMITH, RICARDO and MARX, the basic measure of value was labor.

VALUE-ADDED TAX (VAT), a tax on the value added to goods or services at each stage in their production and distribution. It originated in France in 1954 and was later extended throughout the Common Market; it has been considered at various times in the US. In effect, VAT is a sales tax computed on the difference between what a producer pays for a raw material or semi-finished product and what he sells it for. The cost of the tax is borne ultimately by consumers. It is a regressive tax because it bears most heavily on low-income people who spend more and save less than those with high incomes. For government, VAT has the advantage of being broader than most sales taxes and thus produces large revenues even at low rates. The tax is virtually self-enforcing; producers who make tax payments submit claims for credit for the taxes included in their suppliers' prices, and this tends to discourage non-payment along the line.

VALVE, mechanical device which, by opening and closing, enables the flow of fluid in a pipe or other vessel to be controlled. Common valve types are generally named after the shape or mode of operation of the movable element, e.g., cone, or needle, valve; gate valve; globe valve; poppet valve; and rotary plug cock. In the butterfly valve a disk pivots on one of its diameters. Self-acting valves include: safety valves, usually spring-loaded and designed to open at a predetermined pressure; nonreturn valves, which permit flow in one direction only; and float-operated valves, set to shut off a feeder pipe before a container overflows.

VAMPIRE, in folklore, a spirit of the dead, which left its grave at night to suck the blood of living persons. Victims who died would be decapitated or buried with a stake through their hearts, to prevent them from also becoming vampires. (See DRACULA; STOKER, BRAM.)

VAMPIRE BATS, BATS which feed on the blood of larger mammals and birds; the only parasitic mammals. A slit is cut with the teeth and blood lapped from the wound, anticoagulants in the saliva ensuring a constant flow. They occur in South and Middle America.

VAN ALLEN RADIATION BELTS, the belts of high-energy charged particles, mainly PROTONS and ELECTRONS, surrounding the earth, named for Van Allen, who discovered them in 1958. They extend from a few hundred to about 50,000km above the earth's surface, and radiate intensely enough that astronauts must be specially

protected from them. The mechanisms responsible for their existence are similar to those involved in the production of the AURORA.

VANBRUGH, Sir John (1664–1726), English dramatist and BAROQUE architect. His comedies include *The Relapse* (1696) and *The Provoked Wife* (1697). With HAWKSMOOR he built several grand houses, such as Blenheim Palace and Castle Howard, noted for the interplay of architectural masses.

VAN BUREN, Martin (1782–1862), eighth US president (1837–41), political heir to JACKSON. A consummate politician, he was called "the little magician" for his political maneuvering, use of patronage and power over the press.

Of Dutch descent and born in Kinderhook, N.Y., the son of a farmer and tavern keeper, he studied law locally and was admitted to the bar (1803). He entered politics, was elected to the N.Y. senate (1813–20), became prominent among the Democrats and rivaled De Witt CLINTON for control of N.Y. Elected to the US senate for 1821–28 he maintained his power through TAMMANY HALL and his creation of the political group called the Albany Regency. As a Jeffersonian Van Buren stood for STATES' RIGHTS and opposed internal improvements. After unsuccessfully promoting W. H. CRAWFORD in 1824, he supported General Jackson for president in 1828. Briefly N.Y. governor for 1828–29, he became Jackson's secretary of state. One of the most powerful men in Washington, he developed the SPOILS SYSTEM. His resignation in 1831 assisted Jackson in removing the followers of vice-president CALHOUN from the government. Van Buren was Jackson's vice-president 1832–36, and in 1836 won the presidency for the Democrats. Shortly after his inauguration a financial panic broke out, bringing Van Buren great unpopularity. One crisis remedy was the Independent Treasury System, passed by Congress in 1840. Van Buren also settled the CAROLINE AFFAIR and the Aroostook War (1838–39), a US-Canadian border conflict. Presidential candidate again in 1840 he was defeated by William HARRISON's "log cabin and hard cider" campaign in which Harrison's frontier background was contrasted with Van Buren's alleged luxurious tastes. In 1844 Van Buren failed to receive the Democratic nomination because he opposed the annexation of Texas. He ran in 1848 for the anti-slavery FREE SOIL PARTY, splitting the Democrats and contributing to Zachary TAYLOR's victory. At the outbreak of the Civil War he supported Lincoln.

VANCE, Cyrus (1917–), US public official. A Wall Street lawyer, he was secretary of the army (1962–63) and deputy secretary of defense (1964–67). An experienced diplomatic troubleshooter, he served as President Jimmy Carter's secretary of state (1977–80) before resigning in protest over the abortive attempt to rescue US diplomatic hostages in Iran.

VANCOUVER, George (1757–1798), English explorer. He took part in Captain COOK's voyages (1772–80) and in 1791–94 led an expedition which explored the Pacific and surveyed the American coast from San Luis Obispo, Cal., to British Columbia. He made surveys of Vancouver Island and the Strait of Georgia, visited Cook's Inlet, Alaska, and failed to find a NORTHWEST PASSAGE.

VANCOUVER, largest city in British Columbia, on the Burrard Inlet, Strait of Georgia, and third-largest in Canada. It is an important Pacific port and a major manufacturing center for wood, paper, iron, steel and chemical products. Other industries are shipbuilding, oil refining and fish processing. After becoming the terminus of the trans-Canada railroad (1886) it rapidly expanded. Pop (city) 414,280; (metro) 1,368,100.

VANDALS, ancient Germanic people. They gradually migrated from S of the Baltic to Pannonia and Dacia. In the 5th century they invaded the Roman Empire, ravaging Gaul and Spain. Under Genseric they established a strong Vandal kingdom in North Africa (429) which extended to Sicily, and in 455 they sacked Rome. The Vandals were finally defeated by the Byzantine Belisarius, after which they disappeared as a unified people.

VANDEGRIFF, Alexander Archer (1887–1973), US Marine Corps officer. He led the 1st Marine Division in the invasion (Aug. 1942) and then the defense of Guadalcanal. In Mar. 1943 he became the first Marine to hold four-star rank.

VANDENBERG, Arthur Hendrick (1884–1951), US Republican senator from Mich. (1928–51). A leading isolationist until PEARL HARBOR, he was an important architect of the post-WWII bipartisan foreign policy, supporting the UN, NATO and the MARSHALL PLAN (1949).

VAN DEPOELE, Charles Joseph (1846–1892), Belgian-born US inventor, developer of the electric street car. Trolley systems designed by him were installed in a dozen cities during the 1880s, making possible rapid urban expansion.

VANDERBILT, wealthy American family whose fortune was built on steamship and railroad empires. **Cornelius Vanderbilt** (1794–1877), known as "Commodore," began with a ferry service which grew into an international steamship business. In the 1860s, he purchased a number of small E railroads. His group dominated the NE by the 1870s and controlled the New York-Chicago route. He established Vanderbilt University at Nashville, Tenn. His son, **William Henry Vanderbilt** (1821–1885), was president of the New York Central Railroad and his eldest son, **Cornelius Vanderbilt II** (1843–1899), next controlled the rail empire and amassed another fortune. Another son, **George Washington Vanderbilt** (1862–1914), established the 100,000 acre Biltmore estate near Asheville, N.C. **Harold Sterling Vanderbilt** (1884–1970) won the AMERICA'S CUP three times and invented contract BRIDGE.

VAN DER GOES, Hugo (c1440–1482), Flemish painter. The sophisticated symbolism, naturalist details and oil paint technique of his major work, the Portinari altarpiece *Adoration of the Shepherds* (c1475), greatly influenced Italian RENAISSANCE art.

VANDERLYN, John (1775–1852), US painter of portraits and historical scenes, including the *Landing of Columbus* in the US Capitol. More popular in Europe than in America, he died in poverty.

VANDER MEER, John Samuel (1914–), US baseball player, left-handed pitcher for the Cincinnati Reds who in 1938 threw consecutive no-hitters against the Boston Braves and Brooklyn Dodgers.

VAN DER WEYDEN, Rogier. See WEYDEN, ROGIER VAN DER.

VAN DEVANTER, Willis (1859–1941), US jurist, associate justice of the US Supreme Court (1910–37), an archconservative opponent of the NEW DEAL. His resignation was influential in causing Congress to reject President Franklin ROOSEVELT's plan to enlarge the court as a means of circumventing its conservative members.

VAN DINE, S. S. (Willard Huntington Wright; 1888–1939), US mystery writer, creator of detective Philo Vance, who appeared in twelve novels during the 1920s and 1930s.

VAN DOREN, Carl Clinton (1885–1950), US writer and editor. He wrote criticism, fiction, history, and biography, receiving (1939) a Pulitzer Prize for his life of Benjamin Franklin. His brother, **Mark Van Doren** (1894–1972), a poet and critic, taught (1920–59) at Columbia U, where he was especially noted for his courses on Shakespeare. His *Collected Poems* (1939) received a Pulitzer Prize.

VAN DRUTEN, John William (1901–1957), English dramatist whose plays include *Bell, Book and Candle* (1950) and *I Am a Camera* (1951), based on Christopher ISHERWOOD'S *Goodbye to Berlin* (1939).

VAN DUSEN, Henry Pitney (1897–1975), US Protestant theologian. A prominent liberal, he was an advocate of the SOCIAL GOSPEL and a leader of the ECUMENICAL MOVEMENT. He was president of Union Theological Seminary in New York (1945–63) and a founder of the WORLD COUNCIL OF CHURCHES (1948).

VAN DYCK, Sir Anthony (1599–1641), Flemish BAROQUE portrait and religious painter. He was a pupil of RUBENS and his portrait style, influenced by his study of Venetian art, was one of elegantly posed figures and rich but refined color and handling, particularly of materials. He painted Italian and English nobility and was court painter from 1632 to CHARLES I of England, who knighted him. He had great influence on the development of English art.

VAN EYCK, Jan (c1390–1441), Flemish painter, the leading early Netherlandish artist who collaborated with his older brother **Hubert** (c1370–1426) on his most famous painting, the Ghent altarpiece. Completed in 1432, it comprises more than 250 figures in 20 panels. Van Eyck's other important works include a number of portraits, among which *Giovanni Arnolfini and His Bride* (1434) is especially familiar. All are remarkable for realistic, closely observed details. He was the first painter to develop effects of richness, brilliance and intensity in oil paint.

VAN GOGH, Vincent (1853–1890), Dutch POSTIMPRESSIONIST painter. His early, dark-toned work, done in Holland, focuses on peasant life. Later (1886–88), in Paris, he met GAUGUIN and SEURAT. In 1888 he moved to Arles, in southern France, where—among many other paintings—he produced *Sunflowers* in a direct style and the symbolic *The Night Café* using color suggestively. After a fit of insanity, in which he cut off his left ear (1889), he painted at the asylums of St. Rémy and Auvers. In *Portrait of Dr. Gachet* (1890) he attempted to express ideas and emotion in and through paint. He committed suicide.

VAN MEEGEREN, Hans (1889–1947), Dutch artist, forger of "works" by Vermeer and Pieter de Hooch that were undetected until his confession.

VANUATU, formerly **New Hebrides,** independent republic composed of about 80 small islands, extending for about 500mi in the W Pacific Ocean.

Official name: Republic of Vanuatu
Capital: Vila
Area: 4,707sq mi
Population: 145,000
Languages: Bislama; English, French
Religions: Christian, animist
Monetary unit(s): 1 Australian dollar=100 cents; 1 vatu = 100 centimes
Land. The largest island, Espiritu Santo (1,524sq mi), is followed in size by Efate, site of Vila, the capital. The islands are of volcanic origin, and there are six active volcanoes. The rugged, mountainous interiors, densely covered with tropical rain forests, give way to narrow coastal strips where most of the inhabitants live. SE trade winds prevail; rainfall averages 90in per year.
People and Economy. The inhabitants, 90% Melanesian, speak a variety of different dialects, giving rise to a mutually intelligible pidgin. There are small Chinese, British and French minorities. About 70% of the people live in rural villages, practicing traditional subsistence agriculture, raising coconuts, other fruits, yams, taro and pigs for both food and ceremonial purposes. Industries process copra, fish and beef for export. Manganese has been mined since 1961. Tourism declined after independence, but special tax laws have made Vanuatu a banking center. The economy was devastated by a cyclone in 1987.
History. Settlements existed at least as early as 1300 BC, but it was not until the 18th century that the British and French explored the islands. During the 19th century strife broke out between native inhabitants and British and French settlers. In 1906 a joint British-French condominium was established to rule the islands. In 1980 on the eve of independence, fighting broke out on Espiritu Santo, where guerrillas demanded separate status. Fighting ended after British and French peacekeeping forces arrived, and independence was granted. After independence,

Vanuatu joined the nonaligned movement, established diplomatic relations with Libya and the USSR, and signed (1987) a controversial fishing agreement with the USSR.

VAN VECHTEN, Carl (1880–1964), US music critic, novelist and photographer. He wrote *The Music of Spain* (1918), novels such as *Peter Whiffle* (1922) and *Nigger Heaven* (1926), and an autobiography, *Sacred and Profane Memories* (1932). Subsequently he took up photography and promoted Negro culture at Yale U.

VARANASI, or **Benares**, city in N central India, on the Ganges R. It is very ancient and is the most holy Hindu city (known in this context as Kasi). It has more than 1500 temples. *Ghats* (steps) lead down to the river where pilgrims bathe. Pop 708,647.

VARANGIANS, name given by the Slavs and Byzantine Greeks to the VIKINGS who threatened Constantinople in the 9th and 10th centuries. They were part of the Byzantine imperial guard from the late 10th century until 1453. In 862, the Rus tribe, under Rurik, established itself at Novgorod, founding the Russian state.

VARÈSE, Edgard (1883–1965), French-born US composer. Trained under ROUSSEL and D'INDY, he went to the US in 1915 and became a citizen in 1926. In 1921 he helped organize the International Composers Guild to promote such avant-gardists as Berg, Schoenberg and Webern. He explored new rhythms, harmonies and the effects of dissonance. From the 1950s his compositions used electronic equipment.

VARGAS, Getulio Dornelles (1883–1954), president of Brazil 1930–45 and 1951–54. He set up a "New State" (1937), and a strongly centralized government-promoted industrial, economic and social development. Opposition during his second term led him to commit suicide.

VARGAS LLOSA, Mario (1936–　), Peruvian novelist whose works powerfully depict contemporary Latin American political and social life. He is best known for *Time of the Hero* (1962), *The Green House* (1965) and *Conversation in the Cathedral* (1970).

VARIABLE STARS, stars that vary in brightness. There are two main categories. **Extrinsic variables** are those whose variation in apparent brightness is caused by an external condition, as in the case of eclipsing binaries (see DOUBLE STAR). **Intrinsic variables** vary in absolute brightness owing to physical changes within them. They may vary either regularly or irregularly: NOVAE and SUPERNOVAE are irregular intrinsic variables, though some

novae erupt in an approximate cycle. Pulsating variables, which vary in size, are the most common type of variable star: they include the RR Lyrae stars, with periods from 1.5h to little over a day, W Virginis stars and RV Tauri stars (all three types appearing principally in GLOBULAR CLUSTERS); long period and semiregular variables, which are red giants; and, possibly erroneously, the CEPHEID VARIABLES. Types of variable stars whose periods are known to have a relationship to their absolute brightness are especially important in that they can be used to determine large astronomical distances.

VARIATION, diversity found in all natural populations of organisms. Variation is the result of differing effects of environmental factors and of differences in the genetic constitution of each individual. Genetic diversity is important because it provides variants, some of which may be more suited to prevailing conditions that others, which provide raw material for NATURAL SELECTION. (See also EVOLUTION.)

VARICOSE VEINS, enlarged or tortuous VEINS in the legs resulting from incompetent or damaged valves in the veins, with the pressure of the venous BLOOD causing venous distension and subsequent changes in the vein wall. Although unpleasant in appearance, they are more important for causing venous stagnation, with skin ECZEMA and ULCERS on the inside of the ankle, HEMORRHAGE and EDEMA. Treatment is by stripping or sclerosing injections.

VARNISH, solution of RESIN which dries to form a hard transparent film; widely applied to wood, metal and masonry to improve surface properties without changing appearance. There are two main types: "spirit varnishes," consisting of natural or synthetic resins dissolved in a volatile solvent such as alcohol; and "oleoresinous varnishes"—more resistant to heat and weather—which are mixtures of resins and drying oils dissolved in turpentine or a petroleum oil. Lacquer, the original wood varnish, is the sap of the varnish tree.

VARRO, Marcus Terentius (116–27 BC), greatest scholar of Ancient Rome, a prolific writer on a great variety of subjects. Of his many books only *On Farming* and *On the Latin Language* have substantially survived.

VASARI, Giorgio (1511–1574), Italian MANNERIST painter, architect and writer. His *Lives of the Most Eminent Italian Architects, Painters & Sculptors* (1550), a major source of knowledge of the Italian RENAISSANCE, is about the progress of art in Italy in the 13th–16th centuries.

VASCULAR SYSTEM, the BLOOD CIRCULATION system, comprising BLOOD, ARTERIES, CAPILLARIES, VEINS and the HEART; the LYMPH vessels form a further subdivision. Its function is to deliver nutrients (including OXYGEN) to, and remove wastes from, all organs, and to transport HORMONES and the agents of body defense.

VASSA, Gustavus (born Olaudah Equiano; 1745–1801), African slave in North America. After receiving his freedom he settled in England. His *The Interesting Narrative of the Life of Olaudah Equiano or Gustavus Vassa, The African* (1789) influenced the US antislavery movement.

Official name: Vatican City State
Area: 0.15sq mi
Population: 1,000
Languages: Italian; Latin (administrative and legislative)
Religions: Roman Catholic
Monetary unit(s): 1 lira = 100 centesimi

VATICAN CITY, the world's smallest independent state, in Rome, Italy, ruled by the Pope, and the spiritual and administrative center of the ROMAN CATHOLIC CHURCH. The city is dominated by SAINT PETER'S BASILICA and by the Vatican Palace, the largest residential palace in the world. The city has many art treasures in the SISTINE CHAPEL, the Vatican Museum, and the Vatican Archive and Library which contain many priceless manuscripts. The Vatican has its own currency, postage stamps, broadcasting station, bank, railroad station, newspaper (*L'Osservatore Romano*) and army of SWISS GUARDS. The city does not have income tax and there is no restriction on the import or export of funds. It maintains diplomatic relations with many countries through ambassadors called *nuncios* and sends apostolic delegates to other countries, including the US and Canada, for religious matters. The official independence of the Vatican City from Italy was established in 1929 in the LATERAN TREATY between the PAPACY and the Italian government.

VATICAN COUNCILS, the two most recent Roman Catholic ecumenical councils, held at the Vatican. The **First Vatican Council** (1869–70), summoned by Pius IX, saw ULTRAMONTANISM's triumph. It restated traditional dogma against materialism, rationalism and liberalism. On the papal primacy, it defined the pope's jurisdiction as universal and immediate; it also declared the pope to be infallible when, speaking *ex cathedra*, he defines a doctrine of faith or morals. Some dissenters seceded as OLD CATHOLICS. The **Second Vatican Council** (1962–65), summoned by John XXIII, aimed at renewal of the Church, the updating of its organization and attitude to the modern world, and the ultimate reunion of all Christian churches (see ECUMENICAL MOVEMENT). Protestant and Orthodox observers attended. Along with calling for a reform of the MINISTRY and liturgy, including increased lay participation and use of vernacular languages, the Council decreed that the bishops with the pope form a body ("collegiality") and that the Virgin MARY is "Mother of the Church."

VATTEL, Emerich de (1714–1767), Swiss jurist. His treatise, *The Law of Nations*, based on Christian von Wolff's *Jus Gentium* (1749), claimed that international law should be based on natural law. His theory of liberty had great influence in the American colonies.

VAUBAN, Sébastien Le Prestre, Marquis de (1633–1707), French military engineer, known for his siege tactics and defense fortifications. In 1673 he dug parallel and concentric trenches around Maastricht and in 1688 introduced ricochet gunfire and socket bayonets.

VAUDEVILLE, term for variety shows, deriving from *Vau de Vire*, a French valley and source of 15th-century songs, or from *Voix de Ville*, French street songs. It was applied from the 1880s to US shows with musical, comic, dramatic, acrobatic and juggling acts. Noted artists included Eddie Cantor, Will ROGERS and W. C. FIELDS. Vaudeville declined in the 1930s.

VAUGHAN, Henry (1622–1695), Welsh poet. Some of his best religious and mystical verse, such as "The Retreate," "The Sap" or "I walkt the other day," influenced by the METAPHYSICAL POET George HERBERT, appeared in his *Silex Scintillans* (1651–55).

VAUGHAN WILLIAMS, Ralph (1872–1959), English composer. He was influenced by secular and religious Tudor music and thus acquired methods of expression which differed from traditional classical music. His works, many drawing on English folk music, include *Norfolk Rhapsodies* (1906–07), *Fantasia on a*

Theme of Tallis (1909), nine symphonies and five operas.

VEBLEN, Thorstein Bunde (1857–1929), influential US economist and social theorist. In *Theory of the Leisure Class* (1899) he used the satirical concept of "conspicuous consumption" (that people acquire goods for their status, rather than for their utility or value). *The Theory of Business Enterprise* (1904) attacked the capitalist system, and *The Engineers and the Price System* (1921) foreshadowed technocracy.

VEDA (Sanskrit: knowledge), most ancient of Indian scriptures, believed to have been inspired by God, and basic to HINDUISM. There are four *Samhitas* or collections of MANTRAS—the Rig, Yajur, Sama and Atharva-Veda. The oldest may date from 1500 BC. Vedic literature consists of the Veda itself, the *Brahmanas* and *Aranyakas* (later expository supplements), and the UPANISHADS.

VEDANTA (Sanskrit: end of knowledge), system of Hindu philosophy, based at first on the UPANISHADS (the final part of the VEDA), and later on the *Brahma Sutras*, commentaries on the Upanishads, which date from the 1st century AD. The Vedanta concern the relation of the individual (*atman*) to the Absolute (*Brahman*).

VEGA, Félix Lope de. See LOPE DE VEGA, FÉLIX.

VEINS, thin-walled collapsible vessels which return BLOOD to the HEART from the tissue CAPILLARIES and provide a variable-sized pool of blood. They contain valves which prevent back-flow—especially in the legs. Blood drains from the major veins into the inferior or superior vena cava. Blood in veins is at low pressure and depends for its return to the heart on intermittent muscle compression, combined with valve action.

VELÁZQUEZ, Diego Rodríguez de Silva y (1599–1660), great Spanish painter. In 1623, he became court painter to King Philip IV of Spain. His style was influenced strongly by his Flemish contemporary RUBENS and also by Italian artists of the High RENAISSANCE. His masterpieces include *The Drunkards, Christ on the Cross* and *Maids of Honor*.

VELD, or **veldt,** open grassland of South Africa, divided into three types: High Veld, around 1,500m above sea level, which is similar to the PRAIRIES; Cape Middle Veld, somewhat lower, covered with scrub and occasional low ridges of hills; and Low Veld, under about 750m above sea level.

VELDE, Henri Clemens van de (1863–1957), Belgian ART NOUVEAU architect and designer, interested in the idea of pure form

in architecture. He founded (1906) and taught at the Weimar School of Applied Art which became the BAUHAUS in 1919.

VELIKOVSKY, Immanuel (1895–1979), Russian-born US scientific controversialist. In *Worlds in Collision* (1950) he hypothesized that a comet had collided with the earth about 1500 BC, supporting this view with evidence from history and mythology. This and other books were best-sellers but dismissed by scientists.

VENA CAVA. The *superior vena cava* is a VEIN collecting BLOOD from the head, neck and arms, and delivering it to the right side of the HEART. The *inferior vena cava* performs the same function with blood from the legs and abdomen.

VENDÉE, maritime department of W France, in Poitou, on the Atlantic. It was the scene of the peasants' counterrevolutionary **War of the Vendée** (1793–96), which threatened the new republican state. Savagely crushed at the outset, the peasants continued to resist and eventually achieved their aims of freedom of worship and freedom from conscription.

VENEREAL DISEASES, those INFECTIOUS DISEASES transmitted mainly or exclusively by sexual contact, usually because the organism responsible is unable to survive outside the body and the close contact of genitalia provides the only means for transmitting viable organisms. **Gonorrhea** is an acute BACTERIAL DISEASE which is frequently asymptomatic in females who therefore act as carriers, although they may suffer mild cervicitis or urethritis. In males it causes a painful urethritis with urethral discharge of PUS. ARTHRITIS, SEPTICEMIA and other systemic manifestations may also occur, and urethral stricture follow. Infection of an infant's eyes by mothers carrying the gonococcus causes neonatal ophthalmia, previously a common cause of childhood BLINDNESS. Gonorrhea is best treated with PENICILLIN. **Syphilis,** due to *Treponema pallidum*, a SPIROCHETE, is a disease with three stages. A painless genital ULCER or chancre—a highly infective lesion—develops in the weeks after contact; this is usually associated with LYMPH node enlargement. Secondary syphilis, starting weeks or months after infection, involves systemic disease with FEVER, malaise and a characteristic rash, mucous membrane lesions and occasionally MENINGITIS, HEPATITIS or other organ disease. If the disease is treated with a full course of penicillin in the early stages, its progression is prevented. Tertiary syphilis takes several forms; e.g., gummas—chronic granulomas affecting SKIN, EPITHELIUM, BONE or internal organs—may develop. Largely a disease of blood vessels, tertiary syphilis causes disease of the AORTA with aneurysm and aortic valve disease of the HEART. Syphilis of the NERVOUS SYSTEM may cause tabes dorsalis, primary EYE disease, chronic meningitis, multifocal vascular disease resembling STROKE or general paresis with mental disturbance, personality change, failure of judgment and muscular weakness. Penicillin may only partially reverse late syphilis. Congenital syphilis is a disease transmitted to the FETUS during PREGNANCY and leads to deformity and visceral disease. Other venereal diseases include Reiter's disease with arthritis, CONJUNCTIVITIS and urethritis (in males only); genital trichomonas; thrush; *Herpes simplex* virus, and "nonspecific urethritis." Tropical venereal diseases include chancroid, lymphogranuloma venereum, and granuloma inguinale.

VENEZUELA, republic of N South America, bounded N by the Caribbean Sea, E by Guyana, S by Brazil and W by Colombia.

Official name: Republic of Venezuela
Capital: Caracas
Area: 352,144sq mi
Population: 18,272,000
Languages: Spanish
Religions: Roman Catholic
Monetary unit(s): 1 bolívar=100 céntimos
Land. The country's four main regions are the Venezuelan Highlands (W and N), an extension of the Andes; the oil-producing Maracaibo Lowlands, almost completely enclosed by mountains; the great central grassland plain of the Orinoco (the llanos); and the mineral-rich Guiana Highlands, S of the Orinoco R, very sparsely populated but covering about half the country.
People. The population is mainly mestizo. Of the rest, about 20% are of European stock (mainly Spanish), 10% blacks and 2% Indians. The population is over 85% urban and the literacy rate is 85%.
Economy. In the 1960s, Venezuela was the world's third largest oil producer, but oil production has declined since the 1970s. It

also produces natural gas and iron ore. Chief agricultural products are coffee, rice and cocoa. Oil revenues finance industrial diversification, public works and welfare programs.
History. Venezuela was discovered by COLUMBUS, but may have been named by VESPUCCI. When the first Spanish settlement was founded (at Cumaná, 1521) the country was inhabited by ARAWAKS and CARIBS. Their fierce resistance did not prevent Spanish penetration. Venezuelan independence, unsuccessfully attempted by Francisco de MIRANDA (1806), was proclaimed by a national congress in 1811. Miranda became dictator in 1812, but was imprisoned by the Spanish. Simón BOLÍVAR led the independence struggle and triumphed in 1821. The country became part of Greater Colombia, but broke free as an independent republic in 1830. Dictatorships and revolts followed. General Juan Vicente Gómez (president 1908–35) granted oil concessions to foreign companies. In 1958, the corrupt Marcos Pérez Jiménez dictatorship was overthrown by Rómulo Bétancourt, and democracy was restored. The petroleum industry was nationalized in 1976. In the 1980s, falling world oil prices contributed to an economic decline, forcing the government to introduce austerity measures.
VENEZUELA BOUNDARY DISPUTE, chiefly from 1841, an Anglo-Venezuelan dispute over the location of the British Guiana-Venezuela border. In 1895 US president Grover Cleveland, invoking the MONROE DOCTRINE, demanded arbitration supervised by the US. This initially strained Anglo-US relations almost to the point of war, but Britain submitted to arbitration and a boundary was agreed upon in 1899.
VENICE, city in NE Italy, seaport capital of the Veneto region and Venezia province. It comprises 118 islands in the Lagoon of Venice at the head of the Adriatic Sea. Transport is mainly along the famous canals by motorboat and gondola. Venice is built on piles sunk deep into the mud and is linked by a causeway to the mainland. The first doge (duke or ruler) was elected in 697. Venice rose to control trade between Europe and the East. At its height (15th century), Venice ruled many areas along the coast of the E Mediterranean, the Aegean and parts of the Black Sea. Its power weakened during the long struggle with the Ottoman Empire (c1453–c1718). Venice is now a major tourist resort, boasting unique beauty and a magnificent cultural heritage. Pop 339,272.
VENIZELOS, Eleutherios (1864–1936),

premier of Greece (1910–15; 1916–20; 1928–32; 1933). He promoted the alliance which defeated Turkey in the first of the BALKAN WARS (1912–13) and, after Constantine I's abdication (1917), brought Greece into WWI on the Allied side.

VENTRILOQUISM, way of speaking to make the voice seem to come from a source other than the speaker's mouth. An ancient art, ventriloquism is still practiced, the ventriloquist usually having a dummy with whom he appears to converse. Edgar Bergen, who created the dummies Charlie McCarthy and Mortimer Snerd, was a popular US entertainer of the 1930s and 1940s.

VENTRIS, Michael George Francis (1922–1956), English linguist who deciphered one of the MINOAN LINEAR SCRIPTS (Linear B).

VENTURI, Robert (1925–   ), US architect. A controversial critic of the purely functional and spare designs of orthodox modern architecture, he set forth his "counterrevolutionary" views in *Complexity and Contradiction in Architecture* (1966) and *Learning from Las Vegas* (1972).

VENUS, the planet second from the sun in the SOLAR SYSTEM. Its diameter is 12.1Mm, slightly smaller than that of the earth. Its face is completely obscured by dense clouds containing sulfuric acid, though the USSR's Venera-9 and Venera-10 (Oct. 1975) landings provided photographs of the planet's rocky surface. Venus revolves about the sun at a mean distance of 0.72AU in 225 days, rotating on its axis in a retrograde direction in 243 days. Its atmosphere is 97% carbon dioxide and its surface temperature is about 750K. Venus has no known moons, and could not support life.

VENUS DE MILO, famous armless statue of the Greek goddess APHRODITE. It was carved in marble c150 BC and was discovered 1820 on the island of Melos. It is now in the Louvre in Paris.

VENUS FLYTRAP, an insect-catching plant that lives in the sandy country of the Carolinas and neighboring states. Its leaves form a rosette against the ground and the outer part of each forms a pad hinged in the middle. Around the edge of the pad are stiff teeth and three spines stick up from the middle of the pad. When an insect brushes the spines the pad rapidly folds up so that the insect is caught behind the teeth. Special secretions digest the soft parts of its body. The remarkable thing about the Venus flytrap is the speed with which it acts. It has even been recorded as catching a small frog. (See also INSECTIVOROUS PLANTS).

VERCINGETORIX (d. 46 BC), chieftain of the Arveni tribe of Gaul who rebelled against Roman rule in 52 BC. He repelled Julius Caesar's forces at Gergovia, but was captured after the siege of Alesia and executed in Rome.

VERDI, Giuseppe (1813–1901), Italian opera composer. He rose to fame during the struggle for Italian unification and independence; early operas such as *Nabucco* (1842) express these political ideals. By the time of *Rigoletto* (1851), *Il Trovatore* (1853) and *La Traviata* (1853) he had developed his powerful individual style well beyond the conventions inherited from ROSSINI, DONIZETTI and BELLINI. *Don Carlos* (1867), *Aida* (1871) and the *Requiem* honoring MANZONI (1874) are works of his maturity. The two great Shakespearian operas of Verdi's old age, *Otello* (1887) and *Falstaff* (1893), were written to libretti by BOITO.

VERDUN, Battle of (Feb.–Dec. 1916), major WORLD WAR I engagement. The Germans launched a concentrated offensive against the fortified salient of Verdun. The French dared not abandon this position and the Germans hoped to compel them to exhaust their forces in its defense. Total casualties were well over 700,000. No significant advantage was gained by either side.

VERDUN, Treaty of (843 AD), treaty concluding the civil war between the heirs of LOUIS I, by which CHARLEMAGNE'S empire was divided between his three grandchildren (Louis' sons). Lothair I kept the title emperor and received Italy and a narrow strip of land from Provence to Friesland. Louis the German received the lands between the Rhine and Elbe. Charles the Bald held the area W of the Rhine.

VERGA, Giovanni (1840–1922), Italian novelist and short-story writer whose work had a strong influence on modern Italian neo-realist fiction. His story *Cavalleria Rusticana* (1880) was the basis for his own play and Pietro Mascagni's opera.

VERGENNES, Charles Gravier, Comte de (1717–1787), French statesman. As foreign minister 1774–87, he supported the American colonies in the Revolutionary War and joined them in a military alliance (1778). He negotiated the Treaty of PARIS (1783).

VERGIL or **VIRGIL** (Publius Vergilius Maro; 70–19 BC), Roman poet, one of the greatest writers of epic. Born at Mantua, he studied at Cremona, Milan and finally Rome, where Maecenas became his patron and Octavian (later the emperor AUGUSTUS) his friend. He won recognition with his *Eclogues* or *Bucolics*, PASTORAL poems reflecting the events of his own day. The *Georgics*, a didactic poem on farming, uses the world of the farmer as a model for the world at large. His last ten years were spent on his epic masterpiece, the *Aeneid*, about the wanderings of AENEAS and his struggle to found ROME.

VERISSIMO, Erico (1905–1975), Brazilian historian and novelist, author of *Crossroads* (1935), *Consider the Lilies of the Field* (1938), and the trilogy *Time and the Wind*.

VERLAINE, Paul Marie (1844–1896), French poet, an early and influential exponent of SYMBOLISM. While imprisoned 1873–75 for shooting and wounding his friend and lover Arthur RIMBAUD, he wrote *Romances sans Paroles* (1874), one of his finest volumes. After a period of religious piety he returned to his life of Bohemian dissipation and died in poverty.

VERMEER, Jan (1632–1675), Dutch painter who spent his entire life in Delft. His interior scenes are noted for superb control of light, precise tonality, cool harmonious coloring and classical composition. Of the fewer than 40 works attributed to him his masterpieces include *The Letter* and *Head of a Girl* (both c1665).

VERMONT, state of the NE US, in New England, bounded N by Quebec, W by N.Y., S by Mass. and E by N.H. It is among the ten smallest and least populated states and the only New England state without a coastline.

Name of state: Vermont
Capital: Montpelier
Statehood: March 4, 1791 (14th state)
Familiar name: Green Mountain State
Area: 9,609sq mi
Population: 541,000
Elevation: Highest—4,393ft, Mount Mansfield; Lowest—95ft, Lake Champlain
Motto: Freedom and Unity
State flower: Red clover
State bird: Hermit thrush
State tree: Sugar maple
State song: "Hail, Vermont!"

Land. The Green Mts form the major geographical region, comprising several virtually continuous ranges running N–S through Vt.'s center. Most fertile are the broad Connecticut R Valley in the E and the Champlain Valley in the NW. The climate is cool, with long, cold winters.

People. Vermont remains a predominantly rural state with fewer than one third of the population living in urban areas. Burlington is the largest city. Most of the population is white, with French-speaking Canadian immigrants a significant minority.

Economy. Manufactures include machine tools, furniture, and dairy products. Also important are the state's marble and granite quarries and talc and asbestos production. Dairy farming is the chief agricultural activity, and Vermont is also famed for its maple sugar products. Tourism is important year-round, with hiking and skiing in the Green Mts being a major attraction.

History. Vt. is one of three states (with Hawaii and Texas) that were recognized by the US government as independent republics before they joined the Union. When the French explorer CHAMPLAIN arrived in 1609, the region was inhabited by Iroquois Indians from N.Y., who had driven out the original Algonquins. Champlain aided the Algonquins in their defeat of the Iroquois and claimed the region for France. In 1763, England gained Vt. as a result of the treaty ending the FRENCH AND INDIAN WARS. In 1770, Ethan Allen organized the GREEN MOUNTAIN BOYS to resist N.Y. claims to Vt. lands and to drive out N.Y. settlers. When the Revolutionary War broke out, the Green Mountain Boys joined other patriots to fight the British. The state's 1777 constitution prohibited slavery and was the first to provide for universal male suffrage. Vt. remained an independent republic until 1791, when it became the 14th state.

Vermont has maintained its independent, almost insular spirit into the 20th century. After more than a hundred years of very slow growth, its population is now beginning to increase more quickly, rising 21% from 1970 to 1986. In presidential elections 1968–88, Vermont voted consistently Republican.

VERMOUTH, alcoholic beverage made from fortified (usually white) wine, various herbs and flavorings. The alcohol content is 10–20%. "French" (pale and dry) and "Italian" (sweet and dark) vermouths are now produced in many countries.

VERNE, Jules (1828–1905), popular French novelist and a father of the modern genre of SCIENCE FICTION. He often incorporated genuine scientific principles in his imaginative adventure fantasies, and anticipated the airplane, submarine, television, space travel, etc. His most famous novels include *Journey to the Center of the Earth* (1864), *Twenty Thousand Leagues Under the Sea* (1870) and *Around the World in Eighty Days* (1873).

VERNIER SCALE, an auxiliary scale used in conjunction with the main scale on many instruments (in particular the vernier caliper), allowing greater precision of reading. The vernier scale is graduated such that nine graduations on the vernier scale equal ten on the main scale. By observing which vernier graduation nearest the zero on the vernier scale coincides with a graduation on the main scale, the precision with which a reading can be made is improved by a factor of 10.

VERONESE, Paolo (Paolo Caliari; 1528–1588), Venetian painter of rich, brilliantly colored religious, historical and mythological pictures. Works such as *Triumph of Venice* (post-1577) include crowds of people in splendid costumes and settings.

VERRAZANO, Giovanni da (c1485–c1528), Italian navigator who discovered New York and Narragansett bays while exploring the North American coast in 1524.

VERRAZANO-NARROWS BRIDGE, suspension bridge across the narrows at the entrance to New York Harbor, completed 1964. It has a main span of 4,260ft, the world's longest.

VERROCCHIO, Andrea del (c1435–1488), Italian RENAISSANCE sculptor and painter. In pictures such as *Madonna and Child* (1468–70) he treated figures and landscape sculpturally. His greatest work, finished by Leopardi, the bronze equestrian *Monument to Bartolommeo Colleoni* (1483–96), in Venice, shows his mastery of composition, technique and rich detailing.

VERSAILLES, French city, 12mi SW of Paris. It is world-famous for its magnificent Palace of Versailles, built for King LOUIS XIV in the mid-1600s. The seat of the French court for over 100 years, it was made a national museum in 1837, and the palace and its formal gardens are one of France's greatest tourist attractions. The modern city is principally a residential suburb of Paris. Pop 100,000.

VERSAILLES, Treaty of, agreement ending WORLD WAR I, imposed on Germany by the Allies on June 28, 1919. It also set up the LEAGUE OF NATIONS. Under the treaty, Germany lost all her colonies, Lorraine was given to France, Eupen-Malmédy to Belgium, Posen and West Prussia to Poland, and Memel (Klaipeda) to the Allies. GDANSK became a free city, the Saar (with its coalfields) was to be under international administration for 15 years, the Rhineland was to be demilitarized and occupied by the Allies for 15 years at German cost. Heavy REPARATIONS were imposed, and Germany's armed forces drastically reduced. German resentment of the treaty's harshness was a factor in the rise of NAZISM and the outbreak of WWII.

VERSE, language with a regular rhythm often characteristic of POETRY. Verse may be used as a general term for all such language (as opposed to prose), or to describe a single line of poetry or a quatrain or stanza of a ballad or hymn. Verse generally has RHYME. The pattern of stressed beats in a line of verse is called the *meter*, and the study of the various types of meter and rhyme in poetry is called *prosody*, which employs a technical language to analyze the rhythmic units (called *feet*) making up the different styles of verse. (See also BLANK VERSE; FREE VERSE.)

VERTEBRAE, BONES forming the backbone or spinal column, which is the central pillar of the SKELETON of the group of animals, including man, called VERTEBRATES. Vertebrae exist for each segmental level of the body and are specialized to provide the trunk with both flexibility and strength. In the neck, cervical vertebrae are small and their joints allow free movement to the head. The thoracic vertebrae provide the bases for the ribs. The lumbar spine consists of large vertebrae with long transverse processes that form the back of the . abdomen; the sacral and coccygeal vertebrae, which are fused in man, link the spine with the bony pelvis. Within the vertebrae there is a continuous canal through which passes the SPINAL CORD; between them run the segmental nerves. Around the spinal column are the powerful spinal muscles and ligaments.

VERTEBRATES, subphylum of the CHORDATES, containing all those classes of animals which possess a backbone—a spinal column made up of bony or cartilaginous VERTEBRAE.

VERTIGO, sensation of rotation in space resulting from functional (spinning of head with sudden stop) or organic disorders of the balance system of the EAR or its central mechanisms. It commonly induces nausea or VOMITING and may be suppressed by DRUGS.

VERWOERD, Hendrik Frensch

(1901–1966), Dutch-born South African politician, premier 1958–66. A professor of psychology from 1927, he became editor of the Afrikaans nationalist newspaper *Die Transvaler* (1937). A senator from 1948, he was appointed minister of native affairs (1950), and enforced APARTHEID rigorously, stressing "separate development" and creating the HOMELANDS. He was assassinated.

VESALIUS, Andreas (1514–1564), Flemish biologist regarded as a father of modern ANATOMY. After considerable experience of dissection, he became one of the leading figures in the revolt against GALEN. In his most important work, *On the Structure of the Human Body* (1543), he described several organs for the first time.

VESEY, Denmark (c1767–1822), self-educated US Negro who bought his freedom in 1800, acquired great wealth and influence and organized in Charleston the biggest slave revolt in US history (1822). The plot was discovered and prevented; Vesey and 34 others were hanged.

VESPASIAN (Titus Flavius Vespasianus; 9–79 AD), Roman emperor from 69. The son of a tax collector, he rose in the army under NERO and was sent in 66 to suppress a rebellion in Judaea. His reign began an era of order and prosperity. He began the building of the COLOSSEUM.

VESPERS, the principal evening service of the Western Church. An ancient monastic service, its main elements are the singing of psalms and the Magnificat. The Anglican Evensong is based on Vespers.

VESPUCCI, Amerigo (1454–1512), Italian navigator for whom America was named. In two voyages (1499–1500, 1501–02) he explored the coast of South America, and deduced that the "New World" must be a continent and not part of Asia. The name "America" first appeared on a map published in 1507.

VESTAL VIRGINS, in ancient Rome, priestesses chosen very young, who had to serve the shrine of Vesta, goddess of the domestic hearth, for 30 years. Punishment for breaking their vow of chastity was burial alive. Their chief responsibility was to tend the sacred flame in Vesta's temple.

VESUVIUS, Mount, the only active volcano on mainland Europe, in S Italy near Naples. Its height, c4,000ft, varies with each eruption. Capped by a plume of smoke, it is a famous landmark. Its lower slopes are extremely fertile. In 79 AD it destroyed the cities of POMPEII and HERCULANEUM. Recent eruptions occurred in 1906, 1929 and 1944.

VETERANS AFFAIRS, US Department of, formerly the **Veterans Administration,** a federal agency established in 1930, responsible for administering all laws authorizing benefits for ex-servicemen and their dependents or beneficiaries. These benefits include: compensation payments for disabilities or death related to military service; pensions; education and rehabilitation; home loan guaranty; burial; and a medical care program incorporating nursing homes, clinics, and 172 medical centers. The VA was elevated to cabinet level in 1988, effective Mar. 1989.

VETERANS DAY, a US holiday, celebrated on 11 November, to honor American servicemen, past and present. Originally known as Armistice Day, it was first designated by Woodrow WILSON to commemorate the end of WWI.

VETERANS OF FOREIGN WARS (VFW), US overseas veterans organization, founded 1899, with headquarters in Kansas City, Mo. In 1988 it had 2 million members.

VETERINARY MEDICINE, the medical care of sick animals, sometimes including the delivery of their young. It is practiced separately from human MEDICINE since animal diseases differ largely from those affecting humans. Veterinarians treat domestic, farm, sport and zoo animals.

VETO, in politics, the power of the executive to reject legislation. It is a Latin word meaning "I forbid," pronounced by the Roman TRIBUNES when they exercised their right to block laws passed by the Senate. Under the US Constitution (Article I, Section 7), the President can veto any bill passed by Congress, but this can be overridden by a two-thirds majority in both houses. In the Security Council of the UNITED NATIONS, the five permanent members (China, France, Great Britain, the US and USSR) possess a veto over proceedings.

VIBRATION, periodic motion, such as that of a swinging PENDULUM or a struck TUNING FORK. The simplest and most regular type of vibration is simple harmonic motion. ENERGY from a vibration is propagated as a WAVE MOTION. Excess mechanical vibration, as with noise pollution, can do considerable damage to buildings.

VICENTE, Gil (c1470–c1536), major Portuguese poet and dramatist. Between 1502 and 1536 he produced some 44 plays for the Portuguese court. Full of verve and satire, and with many exquisite songs, they include comedies, farces, morality plays and tragi-comedies.

VICE-PRESIDENT, the second-highest elected official of the US. Constitutionally and politically this office does not carry great power, and its holder must rely on the confidence and discretion of the president for any power he wields. The vice-president was originally intended to perform two roles: that of a neutral presiding officer in the Senate, and that of a constitutional successor on the death or resignation of a president. Eight vice-presidents have succeeded on the death of their predecessors. In the past vice-presidential nominees were often nonentities chosen for party political reasons rather than for ability (though several became excellent presidents), but the increase in presidential duties with WWII has been partly responsible for giving the vice-president a greater share in political and legislative matters, in particular as a member of the National Security Council.

The 25th Amendment (1967) permits the president to fill a vacancy in the office of vice-president, subject to the approval of Congress. The amendment permits the vice-president to act as president when the president is disabled, and even to declare the president disabled if the latter is unable or unwilling to do so.

VICHY, health resort in S central France, famous for its mineral springs. Its chief industry is bottling Vichy water. In WWII it was the seat of the "Vichy government" of Marshal Henri PÉTAIN, which was set up in unoccupied France in 1940 and under LAVAL continued to collaborate with the Nazis after the whole of France was occupied in 1942.

VICKSBURG, city in W Miss., seat of Warren Co. and site of an important campaign in the US CIVIL WAR. A busy Mississippi R port, it produces chemicals, machinery and metal, lumber and food products. Built on the site of a Spanish outpost in 1791, it had a strategic position that made it a key Confederate bastion, until it was taken by Union forces under GRANT in 1863 after a 14-month siege. Pop 25,434.

VICO, Giambattista (1668–1744), Italian philosopher of history whose ideas, embodied in *The New Science* (1725), greatly influenced 19th- and 20th-century social thought. A professor of rhetoric at Naples, he saw history as the study of human institutions and developed a cyclical theory of their rise and fall.

VICTOR EMMANUEL, name of three Italian kings, **Victor Emmanuel I** (1759–1824) was king of SARDINIA 1802–21. He recovered his mainland possessions after NAPOLEON's fall (1814), but his harsh rule provoked a revolt in Piedmont led by the CARBONARI, and he abdicated. **Victor Emmanuel II**

(1820–1878) was king of Sardinia 1849–61 and first king of united Italy 1861–78. With CAVOUR and GARIBALDI he played a major part in Italy's unification. **Victor Emmanuel III** (1869–1947) was king of Italy 1900–46, emperor of Ethiopia 1936–43 and king of Albania 1939–43. He appointed MUSSOLINI premier in 1922, and became a mere figurehead. His unpopular association with Facism ultimately obliged him to abdicate.

VICTORIA (1819–1901), queen of Great Britain and Ireland from 1837 and empress of India from 1876. As a young queen she depended heavily on the counsel of Lord MELBOURNE. Her life was transformed by marriage in 1840 to Prince ALBERT, who became the greatest influence of her life. A devoted wife and mother (she bore nine children), she mourned for the rest of her life after his death in 1861. She had strong opinions and believed in playing an active role in government, and her relations with a succession of ministers colored the political life of her reign. Her dislike of PALMERSTON and GLADSTONE and fondness for DISRAELI, for example, were notorious. In old age she became immensely popular and a symbol of Britain's imperial greatness.

VICTORIA, Tomás Luis de (c1548–1611), Spanish composer. A priest in Rome, he was influenced by PALESTRINA, and composed some of the finest religious choral music of the Renaissance. Returning to Spain in 1594, he wrote his great *Requiem* in 1605.

VICTORIA, Lake, or **Victoria Nyanza,** lies in the GREAT RIFT VALLEY of East Africa, bordered by Tanzania, Uganda and Kenya. It is the second-largest freshwater lake in the world and the largest lake in Africa, c200mi long and c150mi wide.

VICTORIA FALLS, one of Africa's most spectacular sights, on the Zambesi R in S-central Africa between Zimbabwe and Zambia, where the mile-wide river plunges c400ft into a narrow fissure. They were named for Britain's Queen Victoria by LIVINGSTONE in 1855.

VICUÑA, *Lama vicugna,* a member of the CAMEL family living in the western High Andes at up to 5,000m (16,400ft). They are believed to be the original of the domesticated ALPACAS. Vicuñas are graceful animals living in family groups of a stallion and up to 20 mares, occupying a fixed territory.

VIDEOTAPE, magnetic tape used to record TELEVISION programs. In order to record the vast amounts of information necessary to reconstruct a television picture, 2in-wide tape must be run through the tape heads at 15in/s. The tape heads rotate to record the track crosswise on the tape. (See also TAPE

RECORDER; SOUND RECORDING.)

VIENNA, capital of Austria, on the Danube R, one of the world's great cities. Associated with HAYDN, MOZART, BEETHO-VEN and the STRAUSS family, it is a celebrated musical, theatrical and cultural center, and has many famous buildings and museums, including the Hofburg, Schönbrunn and Belvedere palaces, the Cathedral of St. Stephen, the State Opera, the Art History Museum and the City Hall. A Roman town, it became the residence of the HAPSBURGS in 1282. It was besieged by the Turks in 1529 and 1683. A great period of prosperity and building began in the 18th century, and Vienna was capital of the Austro–Hungarian empire until 1918, when the modern republic of Austria was formed. In WWII it was occupied by the Nazis and bombed by the Allies. The modern city is also a commercial and industrial center, producing machinery, metals, textiles, chemicals, furniture, handicrafts and food products. Pop (city) 1,531,346; (metro) 2,044,331.

VIENNA, Congress of, assembly held in Vienna, 1814–15, to reorganize Europe after the NAPOLEONIC WARS. Effective decision-making was carried out by METTERNICH of Austria, Tsar ALEXANDER I of Russia, CASTLEREAGH and WELLINGTON of Britain, von Humboldt of Prussia and TALLEYRAND of France. Among other territorial adjustments, the Congress established the German Confederation and the kingdoms of the Netherlands and Poland (under Russian rule), and restored the PAPAL STATES and the kingdoms of SARDINIA and NAPLES. Austria gained parts of Italy, Prussia gained parts of Austria, and Britain gained overseas territories. The major powers thus distributed territories to achieve a new balance of power, ignoring the nationalist aspirations of the peoples concerned. (See also PARIS, TREATY OF; TRIPLE ALLIANCE; QUADRUPLE ALLIANCE.)

VIETNAM, republic in SE Asia, united in 1976 after nearly 35 years of war.

Land. Narrow and S-shaped, Vietnam is a 1,000mi-long strip bordered by Kampuchea (Cambodia), Laos and China W and N and the Gulf of Tonkin, the South China Sea and the Gulf of Thailand E and S. A heavily forested mountainous backbone and a narrow coastal strip link the Red R delta in the N and the Mekong R delta in the S. Vietnam has a tropical monsoon climate, with high humidity and rainfall.

People. Nearly 90% of the people are Vietnamese, concentrated in the two great deltas. There are urban Chinese minorities, and several highland tribal peoples, such as

Official name: Socialist Republic of Vietnam
Capital: Hanoi
Area: 128,052sq mi
Population: 62,468,000
Language: Vietnamese
Religions: Buddhist, Taoist
Monetary unit(s): 1 dong=100 xu

the Meo (Hmong), who preserve their own cultures. Hanoi (the capital), Ho Chi Minh City (formerly Saigon), Hue, Da Nang and Haiphong are the chief cities.

Economy. Vietnam has an agricultural economy based principally on rice-growing in the Mekong and Red R deltas. Other crops include corn, cotton, hemp, sugar-cane, rubber, coffee and tea. Fishing and forestry are locally important. Minerals, including coal, iron, tin, zinc, lead and phosphates, are found mainly in the N, where most of the country's industry, chiefly the manufacture of iron and steel, chemicals and textiles, is concentrated. There is also some manufacturing industry around Ho Chi Minh City. Offshore oil deposits have been found.

History. Established as a distinct people by the 2nd century BC, the Vietnamese occupy the historic regions of Tonkin (N), Annam (center) and Cochin China (S). Tonkin and Annam were conquered by China in 111 BC. In the 2nd century AD the Champa kingdom emerged in central Vietnam. The Chinese were driven out in 939, and the Annam empire grew, defeating the Champas (1471) and expanding S into Cochin China. European traders and missionaries began to arrive in the 1500s. The French captured Saigon in 1859 and in 1862 annexed Cochin China, which was later merged into French INDOCHINA. After Japanese occupation in WWII, a republic was proclaimed under HO CHI MINH (1945). The French attempt to reassert their authority (1946–54) ended in defeat at DIEN BIEN PHU. At the Geneva Conference (1954) the country was divided, pending nation-wide free elections, into communist North Vietnam, under Ho Chi Minh, and noncommunist South Vietnam. The French withdrew from Vietnam and, with US backing, the regime of Ngo Dinh DIEM declared an independent republic in the South (1955) and refused to hold free elections (1956). The VIETNAM WAR ensued, with South Vietnam being aided by increasing numbers of US troops. A cease-fire agreement was finally signed in 1973 and US troops were withdrawn. Communist forces, however, launched a major offensive and by 1975 had control of all of South Vietnam. The unified Socialist Republic of Vietnam was proclaimed in 1976. Since 1976, Vietnam has strengthened its ties with Laos, installed (1978) a Vietnamese-backed government in Kampuchea, and had sporadic border clashes with China. In 1988, it agreed to withdraw its forces from Kampuchea by the end of 1990. A variety of domestic economic reforms were instituted in the late 1980s.

VIETNAM VETERANS MEMORIAL, in Washington, D.C., a chevron-shaped structure of polished black granite, its two angled walls, each 250ft long, sloping down into the ground from a height of 10ft at their junction. The names of nearly 58,000 US service personnel who died in the Vietnam War are carved in the granite in the order of their deaths from 1959 to 1975. Designed by Maya Ying Lin, a Yale architectural student, the memorial was dedicated in November 1982.

VIETNAM WAR, conflict in South Vietnam between South Vietnamese government forces backed by the US and communist guerrilla insurgents, the Vietcong, backed by North Vietnam. The conflict originated in 1941 when a Vietminh guerrilla force was formed under HO CHI MINH to fight the Japanese. After 1946 it fought the French colonial government, defeating them at DIEN BIEN PHU. The Geneva Conference then temporarily divided Vietnam at the 17th parallel between the Communists (North) and the Nationalists (South). Ngo Dinh DIEM, the South Vietnamese premier, canceled national elections and declared the South independent in 1956. The *Viet Nam Cong San* (Vietnamese Communists), or Vietcong, was then formed to oppose his increasingly corrupt regime. The Vietcong were equipped and trained by North Vietnam, with Chinese backing, and included North Vietnamese troops especially in the later stages of the war. The Vietcong fought a ferocious guerrilla campaign that led Diem to call in US support forces under the US-South Vietnamese military and economic aid treaty of 1961. In 1963 he was overthrown

by his officers; after a period of turmoil Nguyen Van THIEU became president in 1967. In 1965 the US had begun bombing the North in retaliation for the use of Northern troops in the South. Increasing numbers of US combat troops began to arrive in 1965 and totaled nearly 550,000 by 1968. The large-scale US campaign proved unable to do more than hold back the highly motivated Vietcong. Vietnamese civilians suffered terribly at the hands of both sides. Fruitless peace talks began in Paris (1968) and in 1969 President NIXON announced the "Vietnamization" of the war by building up South Vietnamese forces and withdrawing US combat troops. The war had spread to Cambodia and Laos before a ceasefire signed in Jan. 1973 preceded the total withdrawal of US troops a few months later. The South was then overrun by Vietcong and North Vietnamese forces; the war effectively ended with the fall of Saigon in May 1975.

VIGILANTE, member of a self-appointed committee that demands quick and certain punishment for law breakers. During the 18th century such groups in the US took the law into their own hands when officers and courts were nonexistent or corrupt. In the S and W some vigilante groups were little more than lynch mobs, but those in San Francisco in the 1850s and in Montana and Idaho in the 1860s generally executed only those criminals whose guilt had been clearly established in a trial.

VIGNOLA, Giacomo da (1507–1573), Italian architect, painter and sculptor. He designed the Villa Giulia in Rome (1550–55) and the Villa Farnese at Caprarola (1559–73). His designs for the Jesuit church Il Gesù and his *Rules of the Five Orders of Architecture* (1562) helped create the BAROQUE style.

VIGNY, Alfred Victor, Comte de (1797–1863), French Romantic poet, novelist and playwright. His pessimistic works deal with solitude, alienation and spiritual conflict. The posthumous collection *Les Destinées* (1864) contains his most famous poems.

VIKINGS, or **Norsemen,** the Norwegian, Swedish and Danish seafarers who harassed Europe from the 9th to the 11th centuries. Expert shipbuilders and navigators, they were capable of long sea voyages, and their ferocity made them the terror of Europe. The Norwegians raided Scotland, Ireland and France, and colonized the Hebrides, Orkneys, the Faroes, Iceland and Greenland. They may also have discovered America (see VINLAND). The Danes raided England, France, the Netherlands, Spain and Italy. The Swedes went down the E shores of the Baltic, through what is now W Russia, and reached the Bosporus and Byzantium. In addition to being raiders the Vikings also traded and created permanent settlements. They united the Hebrides and the Isle of Man into a kingdom. The Shetlands, the Orkneys and Caithness became an earldom. Kingdoms were also set up in Ireland and Russia (see VARANGIANS). In 878 the Danish founded the DANELAW in NE England. In N France the Viking ROLLO was granted a dukedom in 911, which was the origin of the NORMAN kingdom. Remarkable for their restless energy, the Vikings exerted a considerable influence on European history.

VILLA, Francisco, known as **Pancho Villa** (1877–1923), Mexican bandit, revolutionary leader and popular hero. He helped MADERO to power in 1911. He then supported CARRANZA (1913–14), but fell out with him. Villa and ZAPATA captured Mexico City but were defeated in 1915 by Gen. Álvaro Obregón. In 1916 he raided US territory and evaded capture by a US punitive force for 11 months. An outlaw until 1920, when the Mexican government retired him with full pay as a general, he was assassinated on his ranch.

VILLA-LOBOS, Heitor (1887–1959), Brazilian composer. Director of national musical education from 1932, he created a synthesis of classical and Brazilian folk music in numerous works, including *Chôros* (1920–29) and *Bachianas Brasileiras* (1930–44).

VILLARD, Henry (1835–1900), German-born US journalist and financier. Correspondent for the *New York Herald* and *New York Tribune* in the Civil War, he later (1881) acquired the New York *Evening Post* and *The Nation*. Entering the railroad business in 1873, he created the Oregon Railway and Navigation Co. (1879), and became president of the Northern Pacific (1881–84, 1888–93). In 1890 he formed the Edison General Electric Co. His son, **Oswald Garrison Villard** (1872–1949), a crusading liberal editor of the New York *Evening Post* (1897–1918) and *The Nation* (1918–32).

VILLEHARDOUIN, Geoffroi de (c1150–c1212), French nobleman, historian and crusader. His account of the years 1199–1207, covering the Fourth CRUSADE and its sack of Constantinople (1204), was the first major French prose work. He was given the title Marshal of Romania and a fief in Thrace (1205).

VILLON, François (1431–after 1463), French poet who led a wandering, criminal life. In his coarse and cynical *Lais*

("Legacy") and *Testament*, which contain some celebrated lyrics, he both relishes and regrets his misspent life and expresses his horror of death.

VINCENT DE PAUL, Saint (c1580–1660), Roman Catholic priest who pioneered charities in France. In 1625 he founded the Congregation of the Mission (Lazarists), an order of secular priests devoted to rural missionary work. Later (1633) he founded the Daughters of Charity to help the poor in towns.

VINE, the general name for plants with climbing or trailing stems that cannot grow upright without support. Vines have either *woody* or *herbaceous* (nonwoody) stems. They can be evergreen or deciduous. Some have tendrils (the sweet pea, the grapevine and the cucumber) and others have adhesive disks (the woodbine or Virginia creeper) or small roots (English ivy) to anchor them to their support. Some twine their stem around the support (the convolvulus and hop) and others simply ramble over the surrounding area, with no means of holding themselves up (the blackbery and the rambler rose). By far the most important vine economically is the grapevine, from which the wine grape is harvested, cultivated in temperate regions since ancient times.

VINLAND, a region of E North America discovered c1000 AD by VIKING explorers, probably led by Leif ERICSON, and briefly settled c1004 by THORFINN KARLSEFNI. Some scholars believe it was in New England, others favor Newfoundland (where Viking remains have been found). The Norse sagas describe the discovery of a fertile region where grapes grew, hence "Vin(e)land." (See also KENSINGTON RUNE STONE.)

VINSON, Frederick Moore (1890–1953), Chief Justice of the US 1946–53. A Ky. Democrat, he was a member of the House of Representatives 1923–29, 1931–37 and Secretary of the Treasury 1945–46. While he was chief justice, the Supreme Court made important civil-liberty rulings.

VIOL, the 15th–17th century forerunner of the VIOLIN. Viols have sloping shoulders, frets, a low bridge and a soft, mellow tone. The six strings are tuned in fourths. The treble, alto, tenor and bass (*viola da gamba*) viols are all held upright, as was the double-bass *violone*, which became today's DOUBLE-BASS. Interest in the viol has revived in the 20th century.

VIOLET, low herbaceous plants of the genus *Viola* that produce characteristically shaped flowers on slender stalks. Most species occur in the Andes, but many are found in North America and Europe.

Several species, including the pansy, are cultivated as garden ornamentals. They grow mainly in moist woods. Family: Violaceae.

VIOLIN, smallest, most versatile and leading member of the bowed, four-stringed violin family (violin, viola, cello, double-bass). Violins succeeded the VIOL in the 1600s, differing in their flexibility, range of tone and pitch, arched bridge, squarer shoulders, narrower body and lack of frets. The violin proper, derived from the 16th-century arm viol, is tuned in fifths and ranges over 4½ octaves above G below middle C. Perfected by the craftsmen of Cremona, it became a major solo instrument. The principal violinist leads the ORCHESTRA, violins forming most of the string section. Classical string quartets have two violins.

VIPERS, a family of SNAKES with highly-developed venom apparatus, found in Europe, Africa and Asia. Vipers are short, stoutly-built and typically terrestrial. They lie in wait for their prey—lizards or small mammals—strike, injecting venom from modified salivary glands through the hollow poison fangs, and then wait for a while before tracking down their victim. One of the best known species is the adder.

VIRAL DISEASES, generally infectious diseases due to VIRUSES. The common COLD, INFLUENZA, CHICKENPOX, MEASLES and GERMAN MEASLES are common in childhood, while SMALLPOX and YELLOW FEVER are important tropical virus diseases. Viruses may also cause specific organ disease such as HEPATITIS, MENINGITIS, ENCEPHALITIS, MYOCARDITIS and pericarditis. Most virus diseases are self-limited and mild, but there are few specific drugs effective in cases of severe illness. Prevention by VACCINATION is therefore crucial.

VIRCHOW, Rudolf (1821–1902), Pomeranian-born German pathologist whose most important work was to apply knowledge concerning the CELL to PATHOLOGY, in course of which he was the first to document LEUKEMIA and EMBOLISM. He was also distinguished as an anthropologist and archaeologist.

VIRGIL. See VERGIL.

VIRGINAL, type of small HARPSICHORD, its strings parallel to the single keyboard. There is one wire per note. Encased in a small rectangular box, the virginal was popular c1550–1650.

VIRGIN BIRTH, Christian doctrine that JESUS CHRIST was conceived by the Virgin MARY through the Holy Spirit's power, without a human father. Though stated in the GOSPELS of Matthew and Luke and embodied in the CREEDS, it has been criticized in the past 100 years as a legendary tradition endangering Jesus' full humanity. (See also INCARNATION.)

VIRGINIA, state of the E US, the largest of the original 13 states. It is bounded N by Md., S by N.C. and Tenn., W by Ky., and NW by W. Va.

Name of state: Virginia
Capital: Richmond
Statehood: June 25, 1788 (10th state)
Familiar names: Old Dominion; Mother of Presidents
Area: 40,817sq mi
Population: 5,787,000
Elevation: Highest—5,729ft, Mount Rogers; Lowest—sea level, Atlantic Ocean
Motto: *Sic semper tyrannis* ("Thus always to tyrants")
State flower: Dogwood
State bird: Cardinal
State tree: Dogwood
State song: "Carry Me Back to Old Virginny"

Land. The major regions are: the tidewater coastal plain, extending about 100mi inland; the Piedmont, a rolling plateau rising to 2,000ft where it meets the Blue Ridge Mts., and the broad Appalachian Ridge and Valley Region in the W. There are many rivers, most of which run SE to Chesapeake Bay. The Potomac R forms most of the Va.–Md. boundary. Nearly two-thirds of Va. is forest. The climate is mild.

People. Since 1950 Virginia has been transformed from a predominantly rural to a predominantly urban state. Population is concentrated in the E where Norfolk-Newport News, Richmond-Petersburg, and the Arlington-Alexandria area of suburbs of Washington, D.C., are the largest metropolitan areas. Portsmouth and Richmond are the largest cities; Roanoke is the largest city in the W.

Economy. Va.'s strong economy is based on government and services, manufacturing (notably chemicals, tobacco, textiles, shipbuilding and foodstuffs) and agriculture (primarily tobacco and livestock).

Tourism is a major addition to the economy. There are large coal deposits in the SW.

History. After Sir Walter RALEIGH'S expedition to North America in the late 16th century, the name "Virginia" (for Elizabeth I, the "Virgin Queen") was applied to all of North America not claimed by Spain or France. In May 1607, colonists sent out by one of the VIRGINIA COMPANIES established the first permanent English settlement in the New World at JAMESTOWN.

In 1612 John ROLFE began to raise tobacco, which was to be for long the basis of Va.'s economy. In 1619 the first Africans came to Va., as indentured servants, and by 1715 constituted about 25% of the population. Intermittent conflicts with the POWHATAN INDIANS reached a peak in 1622 when the Indians killed some 350 colonists in a single attack, reducing the colony by a third. In 1619 the first house of burgesses met at Jamestown, and the settlers' participation in their own governmental affairs continued after Va. became a royal colony in 1624. The British government of the RESTORATION attempted strict enforcement of the NAVIGATION ACTS limiting colonial trade to England. This was a contributing cause of BACON'S REBELLION in 1676.

Va. took a leading role in the REVOLUTIONARY WAR and events leading to it. Her distinguished patriots included Patrick HENRY, Thomas JEFFERSON, and George WASHINGTON. In May 1776, the fifth Virginia Convention declared the colony an independent commonwealth and the following month it became the first American colony to adopt a constitution and a declaration of rights. Va.'s Robert E. LEE led the South during the CIVIL WAR. In 1863 the W counties of Va. which had refused to secede formed the new state of WEST VIRGINIA. In the 20th century, Virginia has become increasingly urbanized and industrialized with numerous military facilities contributing to the state's economic sturdiness. It was dominated for many years (1926–66) by Gov. and later US Sen. Harry F. Byrd Sr., under whose leadership the state vigorously resisted desegregation. But accommodations were reached in the 1970s, and in 1986 the state elected a black lieutenant governor. In presidential elections 1968–88, Virginia voted consistently Republican.

VIRGINIA COMPANIES, two companies of merchant-adventurers granted patents by the English crown in 1606 for colonizing America. The London Company, authorized to settle anywhere from present-day S.C. to N.Y., founded JAMESTOWN in 1607 (see also VIRGINIA). The PLYMOUTH COMPANY, granted rights from present-day Va. to Me., fared badly. It was reorganized (1620) into the Council for New England, which made the original grant to the PILGRIM FATHERS and PURITAN settlers.

VIRGIN ISLANDS, westernmost group of the Lesser Antilles in the WEST INDIES, E of Puerto Rico. The W islands belong to the US and the E group to Britain. Discovered and claimed for Spain by Christopher COLUMBUS (1493), the Virgin Islands were settled chiefly by English and Danes in the 1600s. England secured the British Virgin Islands in 1666. The Danish West Indies were acquired by the US for strategic reasons in 1917 and became the US Virgin Islands. The economy of both groups now depends on tourism but farming (food crops, livestock) and fishing are important. **The Virgin Islands of the US,** a US territory covering 133sq mi, comprise St. Thomas, St. John, St. Croix and some 65 islets. Charlotte Amalie, the capital and only city, stands on St. Thomas. Pop 111,000. **The British Virgin Islands** are separated from the American islands by a strait called The Narrows. Covering 59sq mi, the group consists of about 30 mainly uninhabited islands. The largest is Tortola, which has the capital and chief port, Road Town. Pop 12,000.

VIRGIN ISLANDS NATIONAL PARK, authorized 1956 on most of St. John (19sq mi), VIRGIN ISLANDS of the US, comprises 15,000 acres with interesting marine flora, fauna and remnants of the prehistoric Indian civilization.

VIRGINIUS AFFAIR (1873), incident that nearly provoked war between the US and Spain. The *Virginius,* fraudulently registered as a US vessel and running arms to Cuban rebels against Spain, was seized by a Spanish man-of-war. Over 50 crew and passengers, including some Americans, were executed. Secretary of State Hamilton FISH issued an ultimatum, but a compromise was reached.

VIRUS, submicroscopic parasitic microorganism comprising a PROTEIN or protein/lipid sheath containing nucleic acid (DNA or RNA). Viruses are inert outside living cells, but within appropriate cells they can replicate (using raw material parasitized from the cell) and give rise to the manifestations of the associated viral disease in the host organism. Various viruses infect animals, plants and BACTERIA (in which case they are BACTERIOPHAGES). Few drugs act specifically against viruses, although IMMUNITY can be induced in susceptible cells against particular viruses. Various pathogenic organisms formerly regarded as large viruses are now distinguished as *bedsonia*.

VISCONTI, Luchino (1906–1976), Italian film director, noted especially for *The Leopard* (1963) and *Death in Venice* (1971).

VISCOSITY, the property of a FLUID by which it resists shape change or relative motion within itself. All fluids are viscous, the viscosity arising from internal FRICTION between molecules which tends to oppose the development of velocity differences. The viscosity of liquids decreases as they are heated, but that of gases increases.

VISHINSKY, Andrei Yanuarievich (1883–1954), Russian statesman and jurist. Chief state prosecutor in the purge trials of 1936–38, he was deputy commissar (1940–49) and commissar (1949–53) for foreign affairs, and the USSR's chief UN delegate.

VISHNIAC, Roman (1897–   ), Russian-born US biologist and photographer, a pioneer in photomicrography. He also made a photographic record of East European Jews on the eve of their destruction in the Holocaust.

VISHNU, second deity in the Trimurti (see HINDUISM), representing the preserving and protecting aspect of the godhead. The ancient *Vishnu Purana* text describes him as the primal god, as do his followers (Vaishnavas), who also worship his many avatars such as Rama, BUDDHA, and KRISHNA. Vishnu is often represented dark blue in color, holding in his four hands a lotus, mace, discus and conch. His consort is Lakshmi.

VISIGOTHS (West Goths), Germanic people who in the 200s AD invaded Roman Dacia (Romania), under Fritigern defeated the Romans at Adrianople (378) and, led by ALARIC I, invaded Thrace and N Italy and sacked Rome (410). They founded (419) a kingdom in S Gaul and Spain, but ALARIC II lost (507) the N lands to CLOVIS, king of the Franks. Roderick, last Gothic king of Spain, lost his throne to the Moors 711. (See also OSTROGOTHS.)

VISION, the special sense concerned with reception and interpretation of LIGHT stimuli reaching the EYE; the principal sense in man. Light reaches the cornea and then passes through this, the aqueous humor, the lens and the vitreous humor before impinging on the retina. Here there are two basic types of receptor: **rods** concerned with light and dark distinction, and **cones**, with three subtypes corresponding to three primary visual COLORS: red, green and blue.

Much of vision and most of the cones are located in the central area, the macula, of which the fovea is the central portion; gaze directed at objects brings their images into this area. When receptor cells are stimulated, impulses pass through two nerve cell relays in the retina before passing back toward the BRAIN in the optic nerve. Behind the eyes, information derived from left and right visual fields of either eye is collected together and passes back to the opposite cerebral hemisphere, which it reaches after one further relay. In the cortex are several areas concerned with visual perception and related phenomena. The basic receptor information is coded by nerve interconnections at the various relays in such a way that information about spatial interrelationships is derived with increasing specificity as higher levels are reached. Interference with any of the levels of the visual pathway may lead to visual symptoms and potentially to BLINDNESS.

VISTA. See VOLUNTEERS IN SERVICE TO AMERICA (VISTA).

VITALISM, the theory, dating from ARISTOTLE, that there is a distinguishing vital principle ("life force") in living organisms that is absent from nonliving objects. (See BERGSON.)

VITAMINS, specific nutrient compounds which are essential for body growth or METABOLISM and which should be supplied by normal dietary foods. They are denoted by letters and are often divided into fat-soluble (A, D, E and K) and water-soluble (B and C) groups. **Vitamin A**, or **retinol**, is essential for the integrity of EPITHELIUM and its deficiency causes SKIN, EYE and mucous membrane lesions; it is also the precursor for rhodopsin, the retinal pigment. Vitamin-A excess causes an acute encephalopathy or chronic multisystem disease. Important members of the **vitamin B** group include thiamine (B_1), riboflavin (B_2), niacin, pyridoxine (B_6), folic acid and cyanocobalamin (B_{12}). **Thiamine** acts as a coenzyme in CARBOHYDRATE metabolism and its deficiency, seen in rice-eating populations and alcoholics, causes BERIBERI and a characteristic encephalopathy. **Riboflavin** is also a coenzyme, active in oxidation reactions; its deficiency causes epithelial lesions. **Niacin** is a general term for nicotinic acid and nicotinamide, which are coenzymes in carbohydrate metabolism; their deficiency occurs in millet- or maize-dependent populations and leads to PELLAGRA. **Pyridoxine** provides an enzyme important in energy storage and its deficiency may cause nonspecific disease or ANEMIA. **Folic acid** is an essential cofactor in

NUCLEIC ACID metabolism and its deficiency, which is not uncommon in PREGNANCY and with certain DRUGS, causes a characteristic anemia. **Cyanocobalamin** is essential for all cells, but the development of BLOOD cells and GASTROINTESTINAL TRACT epithelium and NERVOUS SYSTEM function are particularly affected by its deficiency, which occurs in pernicious ANEMIA and in extreme vegetarians. Pantothenic acid, biotin, choline, inositol and para-aminobenzoic acid are other members of the B group. **Vitamin C,** or **ascorbic acid,** is involved in many metabolic pathways and has an important role in healing, blood cell formation and bone and tissue growth; SCURVY is its deficiency disease. **Vitamin D,** or **calciferol,** is a crucial factor in CALCIUM metabolism, including the growth and structural maintenance of BONE; lack causes RICKETS, while overdosage also causes disease. **Vitamin E,** or **tocopherol,** appears to play a role in blood cell and nervous system tissues, but its deficiency is uncommon and its beneficial properties have probably been overstated. **Vitamin K** provides essential cofactors for production of certain CLOTTING factors in the LIVER; it is used to treat some clotting disorders, including that seen in premature infants. Vitamin A is derived from both animal and vegetable tissue and most B vitamins are found in green vegetables, though B_{12} is found only in animal food (e.g., liver). Citrus fruit are rich in vitamin C. Vitamin D is found in animal tissues, cod liver oil providing a rich source. Vitamins E and K are found in most biological material.

VITRUVIUS POLLIO, Marcus (1st century BC), Roman architect, military engineer and author of *Architectura,* dedicated to AUGUSTUS. This sole surviving Roman work on the subject had an enormous influence on RENAISSANCE architects.

VITTORINO DA FELTRE (Vittorino Ramboldini; 1378–1446), Italian educator of the early Renaissance. At his boarding school at Mantua, established 1423 on humanist principles, he taught sons of poor as well as of famous rich citizens.

VIVALDI, Antonio (c1680–1741), Venetian composer, notably for the violin. He wrote vocal music, sonatas, some 450 concertos for violin and other instruments (helping establish the three-movement form: see CONCERTO), and *concerti grossi* including the famous *Four Seasons.* His work has a sparkling clarity, strong rhythms, and a wealth of melody.

VIVISECTION, strictly, the dissection of living animals, usually in the course of physiological or pathological research; however, the use of the term is often extended to cover all animal experimentation. Although the practice remains the subject of considerable popular controversy, it is doubtful whether research, particularly medical, can be effectively carried on without a measure of vivisection.

VLADIMIR, Saint, or **Vladimir I** (c956–1015), Russian grand duke of KIEV (c980–1015) who, after successful wars against Bulgars, Byzantines and Lithuanians, became a Christian c988, married Anna, sister of Byzantine Emperor BASIL II, and began the mass conversion of his people to Eastern Orthodox Christianity.

VLADIVOSTOK, capital of Primorski kray, E Russian SFSR, USSR, chief Pacific naval port of the USSR, on Peter the Great Bay near North Korea. Founded in 1860, it has shipbuilding, manufacturing, chemical and fish-canning industries. It is the E terminus of the Trans-Siberian Railway. Pop 600,000.

VLAMINCK, Maurice de (1876–1958), French painter. An admirer of VAN GOGH and a leader of FAUVISM, he evolved an expressionistic style in thickly painted, often somber, but brilliantly lit landscapes.

VLASOV, Andrei Andreyevich (1900–1946), Soviet general captured by the Germans in 1942 and made nominal head of a Russian Liberation Army composed of Russian war prisoners. He surrendered to the Americans in 1945 but was turned over to the Soviets and executed.

VODKA, a colorless and odorless alcoholic beverage made by diluting fermented grain or potatoes. It is a traditional drink in Russia, Poland, and the Baltic.

VOICE, the sound emitted in speech (see SPEECH AND SPEECH DISORDERS), the method of communication exclusive to *Homo sapiens.* It is dependent for its generation upon the passage of air from the LUNGS through the trachea, larynx, pharynx and mouth and its quality in each individual is largely determined by the shape and size of these structures and the resonance of the nose and nasal sinuses. Phonation is the sounding of the elements of speech by the action of several small muscles on the vocal cords of the larynx; these regulate the air passing through and vibrate when tensed against this air stream. Articulation consists in the modulation of these sounds by the use of the tongue, teeth and lips in different combinations. Vowels are produced mainly by phonation while consonants derive their characteristics principally from articulation.

VOICE OF AMERICA, the radio division of the International Communications Agency (formerly the US Information Agency), established 1942 to explain the US role in WWII. Its network now broadcasts, in English and other languages, a favorable view of life in the US to many (chiefly communist) countries.

VOLCANISM, or **vulcanicity**, the processes whereby MAGMA, a complex of molten silicates containing water and other volatiles in solution, rises toward the earth's surface, there forming IGNEOUS ROCKS. These may be extruded on the earth's surface (see LAVA; VOLCANO) or intruded into subsurface rock layers as, for example, dikes, sills and laccoliths.

VOLCANO, fissure or vent in the earth's crust through which MAGMA and associated material may be extruded onto the surface. This may occur with explosive force. The extruded magma, or LAVA, solidifies in various forms soon after exposure to the atmosphere. In particular it does so around the vent, building up the characteristic volcanic cone, at the top of which is a crater containing the main vent. There may be subsidiary vents forming "parasitic cones" in the slopes of the main cone. If the volcano is dormant or extinct the vents may be blocked with a *plug* (or *neck*) of solidified lava. On occasion these are left standing after the original cone has been eroded away. Volcanoes may be classified according to the violence of their eruptions. In order of increasing violence the main types are: Hawaiian, Strombolian, Vulcanian, Vesuvian, Peléan. Volcanoes are generally restricted to belts of seismic activity, particularly active plate margins (see PLATE TECTONICS), but some intraplate volcanic activity is also known as in the case of Hawaii. At mid-ocean ridges magma rises from deep in the mantle and is added to the receding edges of the plates. In MOUNTAIN regions, where plates are in collision, volatile matter ascends from the subducted edge of a plate, perhaps many km below the surface, bursting through the overlying plate in a series of volcanoes. (See also EARTHQUAKES.)

VOLCKER, Paul (1927–   ), US economist, chairman of the Federal Reserve Board (1979–87). He served as under secretary for monetary affairs in the Treasury department 1969–74 and president of the New York Reserve Bank 1975–79 before being appointed 1979 to head the Federal Reserve by President Carter. He was architect of the Board's tight-money policy that kept interest rates on borrowing high in order to contract the money supply and dampen inflation.

VOLGA RIVER, chief river of Russia and the longest in Europe. It rises in the Valdai Hills NW of Moscow and flows 2,293mi through Gorki, Kazan, Kuibyshev, Saratov, Volgograd and Astrakhan to its Caspian Sea delta. Draining an area of some 530,000sq mi, it is the main artery of the world's greatest network of commercial waterways linking the White, Baltic, Caspian, Azov and Black seas.

VOLGOGRAD, or (1925–51) **Stalingrad** or (to 1925) **Tsaritsyn**, important industrial city on the Volga R, S Russian SFSR, USSR. It was the site of heroic resistance to the Germans in WWII (see STALINGRAD, BATTLE OF). It has iron-and-steel, machine manufacturing, chemical, textile and hydroelectric plants. Pop 974,000.

VOLLEYBALL, a popular game for two teams of six, who volley (using any part of the body above the waist) a large inflated ball across a high net, conceding points by failing to return the ball or by hitting it out of court. Invented at the Holyoke (Mass.) YMCA in 1895 by W. G. Morgan, it became an Olympic event at Tokyo (1964).

VOLSTEAD ACT, the United States National Prohibition Act, introduced by Minn. Representative Andrew J. Volstead. Passed in 1919, over the veto of President Wilson, it provided for enforcement of the 18th Amendment prohibiting the sale, manufacture or transportation in the US of intoxicating liquors. It proved unenforceable, and was modified, then repealed, in 1933. (See PROHIBITION.)

VÖLSUNGA SAGA, late-13th-century Icelandic prose heroic saga, based partly on heroic lays in the *Poetic Edda* (see EDDA). Like the Germanic NIBELUNGENLIED, it recounts the exploits of Sigurd (SIEGFRIED) and the Völsungs. This legendary material inspired WAGNER.

VOLTA, Alessandro Giuseppe Antonio Anastasio (1745–1827), French physicist who invented the voltaic pile (the first BATTERY) and thus provided science with its earliest continuous electric-current source. Volta's invention (c1800) demonstrated that "animal electricity" could be produced using solely inanimate materials, thus ending a long dispute with the supporters of GALVANI's view that it was a special property of animal matter.

VOLTAIRE (1694–1778), pen name of François-Marie Arouet, French satirist, polemicist, poet, dramatist, novelist, historian and letter-writer, one of the PHILOSOPHES and a genius of the ENLIGHTENMENT. An enemy of tyrants everywhere, he spent much of his life in exile, including 23 years at his property on the Swiss border. His *Letters Concerning the English Nation* (1733) extolled religious and political toleration and the ideas of NEWTON and LOCKE. The famous tale *Candide* (1759), a rational skeptic's attack on the optimism of LEIBNIZ, shows Voltaire's astringent style at its best. A friend of FREDERICK II of Prussia, Voltaire contributed to DIDEROT'S *Encyclopedia* and wrote his own *Philosophical Dictionary* (1764).

VOLUNTEERS IN SERVICE TO AMERICA (VISTA), volunteer program instituted in 1964 and administered by ACTION that provides opportunities for Americans to work full-time with locally sponsored projects designed to increase the capability of low-income people to improve their own lives. Volunteers serve one year, living and working among the poor in urban or rural areas and on Indian reservations.

VOLUNTEERS OF AMERICA, a voluntary philanthropic society founded in New York City (1896) by Ballington and Maud BOOTH after a split with the Salvation Army. It aims to win converts to Christianity and provides many social services. Though it retains military forms and titles, it is run democratically.

VOMITING, the return of food or other substance (e.g., blood) from the STOMACH. It occurs by reverse PERISTALSIS after closure of the pyloric sphincter and opening of the esophago-gastric junction. It may be induced by DRUGS, MOTION SICKNESS, GASTROENTERITIS or other infection, UREMIA, stomach or pyloric disorders. Morning vomiting may be a feature of early PREGNANCY. Drugs may be needed to control vomiting, and fluid and nutrient replacement may be needed.

VON BRAUN, Wernher (1912–1977), German ROCKET engineer who designed the first self-contained missile, the V-2, which was used against the UK in 1944. In 1945 he went to America, where he led the team that put the first US artificial SATELLITE in ORBIT (1958). He later developed the Saturn rocket used in the Apollo moon-landing program, and he pioneered the concept of the space shuttle.

VONDEL, Joost van den (1587–1679), Dutch national poet. His sonorous verse celebrated the successes of the United Provinces. He translated French, Latin and Greek authors. His dramas, on political, national and religious themes, include *Palamedes* (1625), *Gijsbrecht van Aemstel* (1637) and *Lucifer* (1654).

VONNEGUT, Kurt, Jr. (1922–   ), US novelist noted for his satire and "black humor," with science, religion and war among his targets. His novels, some of which carry overtones rooted in science fiction, include *Player Piano* (1951), *Cat's Cradle* (1963), *God Bless You, Mr. Rosewater* (1965), *Slaughterhouse Five* (1969) and *Deadeye Dick* (1982).

VON NEUMANN, John (1903–1957), Hungarian-born US mathematician who put QUANTUM MECHANICS on a rigorous mathematical foundation. He created GAME THEORY, and made important contributions to the theory of COMPUTERS as well as many branches of abstract mathematics.

VON STERNBERG, Josef (Jo Sternberg; 1894–1969), Austrian-US film director associated with Marlene DIETRICH, with whom he made the German classic *The Blue Angel* (1930) and a number of American films.

VON STROHEIM, Erich (1885–1957), Austrian-born US film actor and director. His notable credits include *Greed* (1923), which he directed, and *Grand Illusion* (1937) and *Sunset Boulevard* (1950).

VOODOO, a folk religion, chiefly of Haiti, with West African and added Roman Catholic and native West Indian elements. It involves worship of the spirits of saints and ancestors who may "possess" participants. Prayers, drumming, dancing and feasts are part of the ritual. A cult group's priest or priestess is believed to act as a medium, work charms, lay curses and recall zombies (the "living dead").

VOROSHILOV, Kliment Yefremovich (1881–1969), Ukrainian Russian army and political leader. An early Bolshevik and associate of STALIN (whom he succeeded as head of state, 1953–60), he played an important role in organizing Soviet military forces as commissar of defense (1925–1940). He held important military commands during WWII.

VORSTER, Balthazar Johannes (John) (1915–1983), prime minister of South Africa 1966–78. On the right of the Nationalist Party, he was in charge of education (1958–61), and as minister of justice (1961–66) responsible for some of the most repressive of the APARTHEID laws. He sought later to improve relations with black Africa. Elected president in 1978, he resigned in 1979 after being accused of false testimony on expenditure of government funds.

VORTICISM, English modern art movement (1914-15) which aimed to produce an energetic and abstract art form. It was led by P. Wyndham LEWIS, editor of *Blast*, and influenced by FUTURISM. Associated were artists GAUDIER-BRZESKA and EPSTEIN and writers Ezra POUND and

T.S. ELIOT.

VOSGES MOUNTAINS, low range in E France, running some 130mi N-S to the W of the Rhine R. The rounded hills are mostly forested, with some vineyards.

VOTING, formal collective expression of approval or rejection of a candidate for office or of a course of action. The ELECTION of officers is a basic feature of DEMOCRACY, but universal adult suffrage is recent: US women obtained the vote only in 1920. Sometimes voting is compulsory, as in Australia and in communist states.

In the US, voting originally followed English parliamentary practice, with the addition of the New England town meeting. Ballot papers first appeared in Mass. in 1634. Most US states now use voting machines to ensure secrecy, speed and accuracy. Voting through INITIATIVE, REFERENDUM AND RECALL is allowed for in many states. (See also POLL, PUBLIC OPINION; PLEBISCITE.)

VOTING RIGHTS ACT OF 1965, US law aimed at eliminating local laws and practices that served to prevent blacks and other minorities from voting. It was strongly backed by President Lyndon B. Johnson, who signed it into law.

VOYAGER, light-weight experimental aircraft flown around the world nonstop and without refueling in December 1986 by Richard Rutan and Jeana Yeager. The flight began from Edwards Air Force Base near Los Angeles on Dec. 14 and ended there on Dec. 23, having covered 25,012mi in 9 days, 3 min, and 44 secs.

VOYAGER PROGRAM, two unmanned US probes of the outer solar system. Voyager 1 made close approaches to JUPITER in March 1979 and SATURN in Nov. 1980. Voyager 2 by-passed Jupiter in July 1979, swung around Saturn in Aug. 1981, and is scheduled to continue to URANUS in 1986 and NEPTUNE in 1989. The probes provided remarkable close-up views of the two giant planets and their satellites, revealing, among other things, the existence of a ring around Jupiter, active volcanoes on Jupiter's moon Io and a completely unexpected complexity in Saturn's ring system.

VOYAGEURS NATIONAL PARK, authorized in 1971, a scenic 219,431-acre park in N Minn., with lakes, forests and interesting glacial features.

VOZNESENSKY, Andrei, (1933–) Russian poet who became popular in the early 1960s. One of the most outspoken and experimental contemporary Soviet poets, he was criticized by the Soviet literary establishment in the 1970s, but continued to write and publish prolifically.

VRIES, Hugo de (1848–1935), Dutch botanist who rediscovered the Mendelian laws of inheritance (see HEREDITY) and applied them to C. DARWIN's theory of EVOLUTION in his *Mutation Theory* (1900–1903).

VUILLARD, Jean Édouard (1868–1940), French painter known particularly for his intimate and richly decorative interior domestic scenes. He was influenced by Japanese art.

VULCANIZATION, the compounding of raw RUBBER with SULFUR so that it retains its shape and strength over a wide range of temperatures.

VULGATE, the Latin version of the BIBLE, so-called because it became the most widespread (Latin, *vulgata*) in use. Largely the work of St. JEROME, who revised earlier Old Latin translations, it was collected together in the 6th century and universally established by 800. In 1546 the Council of TRENT confirmed the Vulgate as the sole official version of the Roman Catholic Church.

VULTURES, two groups of large, soaring, diurnal birds of prey. The New World vultures are a primitive family, Cathartidae; the Old World vultures are a branch of the Accipitridae, being most closely related to certain EAGLES. All vultures are adapted to feed on animal carrion. Their heads and necks are wholly or partially naked; several have specialized tongues to feed rapidly on liquid flesh or bone marrow.

23rd letter of the English alphabet, originally (as the name indicates) a "double U." The form "uu," appearing in the earliest Old English texts, was replaced by the letter *wen* (*p*) in the 700s, but reinstated by French-speaking scribes after the NORMAN CONQUEST (1066).

WADE, Benjamin Franklin (1800–1878), US lawyer and senator from Ohio 1851–69, chairman of the committee on the conduct of the war during the Civil War. An ardent advocate of RECONSTRUCTION, he was co-author of the WADE-DAVIS BILL and Manifesto (1864).

WADE-DAVIS BILL, plan for RECONSTRUCTION produced by the Congressional committee on the conduct of the Civil War in 1864, named for senators B. F. WADE and H. W. DAVIS. President LINCOLN vetoed it.

WADI, or **arroyo,** stream-bed through which water flows only occasionally, found mainly in semiarid areas. Such **ephemeral streams** can swiftly erode quite deep, flat-bottomed gullies (see EROSION).

WAGE AND PRICE CONTROL, in economics, policy of countering INFLATION by government controls on the separate but interdependent movements of PRICES and wages. The policy may contain percentage or flat-rate limits on increases, and is sometimes preceded by a "freeze" or standstill period. The policy may be legally binding, or voluntary with back-up powers of government intervention. It usually entails a system of notification of price or wage increases. Its use has increased in Western countries since the 1960s, although President Nixon's 90-day wage-price freeze in 1971 only temporarily interrupted the steadily increasing US inflation of the 1970s.

WAGNER, Honus (John Peter Wagner; 1874–1955), US baseball player, one of the greatest shortstops. He played for the Pittsburgh Pirates for 21 years and was their coach for another 19. He was one of the first five men elected to the Baseball Hall of Fame in 1936.

WAGNER, Richard (1813–1883), major German opera composer. His adventurous and influential works mark the high point of Romanticism in music. A conductor in provincial opera houses, he achieved his first success with *Rienzi* (1840). *Der Fliegende Holländer (1841), Tannhäuser* (1844) and *Lohengrin* (1848) pioneered his new ideas in music and drama (see OPERA); these were fulfilled in the myth-cycle *Der Ring des Nibelungen: Das Rheingold* (1853–54), *Die Walküre* (1854–56), *Siegfried* (1856–69) and *Die Götterdämmerung* (1874). Involved in the 1848 Dresden revolution, Wagner fled to Switzerland, where he wrote *Tristan und Isolde* (1859) and the comic opera *Die Meistersinger von Nürnberg* (1868). Ludwig II of Bavaria helped him found the BAYREUTH Festival. *Parsifal* (1882) was his last opera. In private life Wagner was often self-centered and bigoted.

WAGNER, Robert Ferdinand (1877–1953), German-born US reforming politician. After serving as a N.Y. senator (1910–18) and justice (1919–26), he became a Democratic US senator (1927–49), and

helped create the NEW DEAL program, particularly in labor, social security and housing (see WAGNER ACT).

WAGNER, Robert Ferdinand, Jr. (1910–), US politician and administrator. Son of R. F. WAGNER, he held posts in New York (1938–41, 1946–53), and served three terms as mayor (1954–65), introducing controversial reforms in housing, education and civil rights. He was US ambassador to Spain 1968–69.

WAGNER ACT, popular name for the National Labor Relations Act, a key part of the NEW DEAL legislation, enacted in July, 1935. Sponsored by R. F. WAGNER, it guaranteed workers the right to organize and bargain collectively, and defined some unfair labor practices. It also set up the NATIONAL LABOR RELATIONS BOARD.

WAGRAM, Battle of, fought near Vienna between the Austrians and the French on July 5–6, 1809, during the NAPOLEONIC WARS. NAPOLEON was victorious and forced Austria to sign an armistice.

WAHABI, a Muslim reform movement begun in 18th-century Arabia. It aimed to restore ISLAM to its primitive simplicity, and its influence spread as far as Africa and Sumatra. In Arabia the movement followed the fortunes of the royal family, becoming firmly established under IBN SAUD.

WAIKIKI BEACH, seaside resort area on Oahu Island, Hawaii. It is lined with luxury hotels and famous for its surfing.

WAILING WALL, part of the western wall of the ancient temple in Jerusalem, destroyed by the Romans in 70 AD. It is held sacred by the Jews, who gather there to pray and mourn the temple's destruction.

WAINWRIGHT, Jonathan Mayhew (1883–1953), US general, veteran of WWI and hero of BATAAN and CORREGIDOR in the defense of the Philippines during WWII. Despite great courage in a hopeless situation, he had to surrender to the Japanese in 1942. A prisoner of war until 1945, he was awarded the Congressional Medal of Honor on his return.

WAITE, Morrison Remick (1816–1888), US lawyer, chief justice of the US Supreme Court 1874–88. He first gained prominence in the ALABAMA CLAIMS dispute (1871–72). His most influential opinions concerned STATES' RIGHTS and the interpretation of the Fourteenth Amendment.

WAKEFIELD, Edward Gibbon (1796–1862), British advocate of colonial development. Concerned about overpopulation and poverty in England, he urged settlement of the colonies by ordinary citizens rather than convicts and the granting of self-government to them. He helped found colonies in Australia and New Zealand and advised Lord DURHAM in the preparation of his report on Canadian government.

WAKE ISLAND, atoll in the central Pacific Ocean, an unincorporated territory of the US. An important commercial and military airbase, it consists of three islets (Wake, Wilkes and Peale), a total of 3sq mi, around a shallow lagoon. It was occupied by Japan 1941–45.

WAKSMAN, Selman Abraham (1888–1973), Russian-born US biochemist, microbiologist and soil scientist. His isolation of streptomycin, the first specific antibiotic (a term he coined) against TUBERCULOSIS, won him the 1952 Nobel Prize for Physiology or Medicine.

WALACHIA or **WALLACHIA,** most prosperous region of Romania, between the Danube and the Transylvanian Alps, with rich agriculture, oilfields and industry centered on Bucharest. Formerly independent, it was united 1861–62 with MOLDAVIA to form modern Romania.

WALD, Lillian D. (1867–1940), US nurse and social worker who pioneered public health nursing. In 1893 she founded the famous Henry Street Settlement in New York, and in 1902 began the city's public school nursing. She also helped establish the Federal Children's Bureau in 1912.

WALDECK-ROUSSEAU, René (1846–1904), French statesman, premier (1899–1902) at the height of the DREYFUS AFFAIR. He secured (1899) a presidential pardon for Dreyfus and oversaw the passage of anticlerical legislation, particularly the Law of Associations (1901) directed against religious orders.

WALDEN POND, small pond near Concord, NE Mass., made famous by Henry THOREAU, who lived on its shore 1845–47.

WALDENSES, a reforming Christian sect founded in Lyons, France, in the 12th century. They preached poverty, rejected the PAPACY and took the Bible as their sole authority, for which they were excommunicated (1184) and persecuted. The survivors united with the Protestants in the REFORMATION. The Waldensian Church still exists, with several offshoots in the US.

WALDHEIM, Kurt (1918–   ), Austrian and international public official. Austrian foreign minister (1968–70), he served (1971–81) two five-year terms as United Nations secretary general. He was elected president of Austria in 1986 in a stormy campaign during which information came to light that he had lied about his WWII record. Waldheim, who had been drafted

into the German army in 1939, was wounded on the Russian front and claimed that his active military service ended in 1943. In fact, he served as an intelligence lieutenant in the Balkans when the Germans massacred Yugoslav partisans and deported Greek Jews to death camps. His army group commander was later executed for war crimes, and Waldheim himself was listed (1948) by the allied War Crimes Commission for prosecution.

WALDSEEMULLER,   **Martin** (c1470–1518), German cartographer who in 1507 published the first map showing the New World as a separate continent. He named it "America" in honor of Amerigo VESPUCCI, on whose discoveries the map was based.

WALES, historic principality of GREAT BRITAIN, politically united with England since 1536. It is a large roughly rectangular peninsula projecting into the Irish Sea W of England. Covering 8,016sq mi, it is dominated by the Cambrian Mts (Snowdon, 3,560ft). Rivers include the Severn, Wye, Usk, Taff and Teifi. The climate is mild and wet. The population (2,774,700) live mainly in the S near the rich coalfields. About 20% speak both WELSH and English. The largest cities are Cardiff, the capital, and Swansea. Major industries, including coalmining, steel, oil-refining, man-made fibers and electronics, are concentrated in the S. Agriculture, mostly cattle and sheep raising, predominates elsewhere. Devolution (i.e. greater local autonomy), long sought by the Welsh nationalist movement (Plaid Cymru) was defeated by referendum vote in 1979.

WALES, Prince of, the title bestowed on the eldest son of the British sovereign. It was first used by EDWARD I (1301), after he had killed the last Welsh prince, for his newborn son. Prince Charles holds the title at present.

WALESA, Lech (1943–   ), Polish labor leader. An electrician in the Gdansk Lenin Shipyard, he had been active in union organizing for several years before becoming head of SOLIDARITY (1980), a national union that wrung many concessions from the government, unprecedented in the Soviet bloc, before it was suspended in 1981. Walesa was awarded the 1983 Nobel Peace Prize for his contribution "to insure the workers' right to establish their own organizations." In the 1988 labor unrest, he negotiated with the government on behalf of Solidarity, agreeing to persuade strikers to return to work in exchange for talks on legalizing the union.

WALKER, James John (1881–1946), New

York politician. A member (1915–20) and minority leader (1921–25) of the state senate, he became Democratic mayor of New York (1926–32), instituting popular reforms. He resigned in a corruption scandal.

WALKER, Joseph Reddeford (1798–1876), US trapper and guide. He explored the Rockies with BONNEVILLE (1832) and guided expeditions to California (1845–46, 1849, 1861–62). Walker Lake and Pass are named for him.

WALKER, Mary Edwards (1832–1919), US surgeon and feminist, the first woman to be commissioned a surgeon in the Union army (1864). Later she practiced in Washington D.C. and campaigned for women's rights.

WALKER, Robert John (1801–1869), US politician. Senator from Miss. 1836–45, he became an able secretary of the treasury (1845–49) and US financial agent in Europe (1863–64). An ardent expansionist, he was governor of Kan. 1857–58.

WALKER, William (1824–1860), US adventurer. He tried to create a republic out of Lower Cal. and Sonora, Mexico (1853–54), then joined a revolution in Nicaragua, becoming president 1856–57. Ousted partly by VANDERBILT interests, but regarded by many as a hero, he was captured by the British and shot in attempting to regain Nicaragua.

WALKER CUP, a golf competition held every other year between men's amateur teams from the US and Great Britain. This match play competition, consisting of both foursome and single matches, is named for former US Golf Association president George H. Walker.

WALKIE-TALKIE, portable two-way RADIO frequently used by policemen, sportsmen and others on the move to communicate over distances up to a few km. In the US, walkie-talkies operate on one or more of 23 channels lying between 26.960 and 27.255MHz.

WALLABIES, a large and diverse assemblage of kangaroo-like MARSUPIALS, generally smaller than true KANGAROOS, but like them in having large strong hindfeet and limbs and a long tail. They are herbivorous animals of Australia, Tasmania and New Guinea. All wallabies produce a single young, suckling it in the marsupium or pouch.

WALLACE, Alfred Russel (1823–1913), British socialist naturalist regarded as the father of ZOOGEOGRAPHY. His most striking work was his formulation, independently of C. DARWIN, of the theory of NATURAL SELECTION as a mechanism for the origin of species (see EVOLUTION). He and Darwin presented their results in a joint paper in 1858 before the Linnean Society.

WALLACE, Dewitt (1889–1981), US publisher who hit on the idea of condensing "articles of lasting interest" and in 1920, with his wife Lila Bell Acheson Wallace, established the *Reader's Digest*. At his death the pocket-sized monthly had a circulation of 30.5 million copies in 16 languages and 163 countries.

WALLACE, George Corley (1919–   ), US political leader, governor of Ala. 1963–67, 1971–79, 1983–87. He achieved notoriety in 1963 with his unsuccessful attempt to prevent racial integration at the University of Alabama. He ran for president as an independent in 1968, receiving 13% of the vote. He was paralyzed in an attempted assassination while campaigning for the Democratic presidential nomination in 1972. His 1976 campaign for the nomination came to little owing to Jimmy CARTER's successes in the South. He won the 1982 gubernatorial election with black support.

WALLACE, Henry Agard (1888–1965), 33rd vice-president of the US (1941–45). A distinguished agricultural economist and plant geneticist, he was appointed secretary of agriculture in 1933. His success with NEW DEAL farm programs led to the vice-presidency. He became secretary of commerce (1945), but was dismissed in 1946 for criticizing TRUMAN. He ran unsuccessfully in 1948 as presidential candidate of the PROGRESSIVE PARTY.

WALLACE, Lew (1827–1905), US author, soldier and diplomat, known for his best-selling novel *Ben Hur* (1880). He served in the Mexican and Civil Wars, became governor of N.M. (1878–81) and minister to Turkey (1881–85).

WALLACE, Sir William (c1272–1305), Scottish national hero who led the rebellion against the English King EDWARD I. Victor at Stirling Bridge (1297), he was defeated at Falkirk (1298) and fled to Europe to rally support for the Scottish cause. Back in Scotland by 1304, he was captured in 1305 and executed for treason.

WALLENBERG, Raoul (1912–1947?), Swedish diplomat. While representing Sweden in Budapest during WWII, he issued passports to 5,000 Jews to keep them out of Nazi hands. Soviet authorities arrested him as a spy in 1945 and claimed he died in prison in 1947. In 1981 an international association said evidence indicated he might be alive and urged the Soviet Union to investigate.

WALLENDA, Karl (1905–1978), German-born circus performer. He created the first high-wire pyramid with his troupe (1925) and led the "Flying Wallendas," the most successful daredevil act in history, to triumphs throughout the world. He fell to his death while trying to walk a wire between two ten-story buildings in San Juan, Puerto Rico.

WALLENSTEIN, Albrecht Wenzel Eusebius von (1583–1634), Bohemian general in the THIRTY YEARS' WAR. He rose to supreme command under FERDINAND II (1625) and achieved spectacular military success until the German princes, jealous of his power and ambition, forced his dismissal in 1630. Reinstated in 1632 but defeated at Lützen, he intrigued secretly and was murdered as a traitor.

WALLER, Edmund (1606–1687), English poet and politician. His polished love poems and his panegyrics on both Cromwell and Charles II helped establish the heroic couplet as a standard poetic form.

WALLER, Thomas "Fats" (1904–1943), US jazz pianist and composer. Original and influential, he made hundreds of popular recordings and wrote such songs as *Ain't Misbehavin'* and *Honeysuckle Rose*. He was also a brilliant performer on the organ.

WALLIS, Hal B. (1899–1986), US film producer, remembered especially for *Little Caesar* (1930), *The Maltese Falcon* (1941), and *Casablanca* (1943).

WALLIS, John (1616–1703), British mathematician and cryptographer whose *Arithmetica infinitorum* (Arithmetic of Infinities, 1655) laid the foundations for much of modern algebra, introducing the concept of the limit and the symbol ∞ for INFINITY. From this work were later developed CALCULUS and the BINOMIAL THEOREM.

WALLOONS, the French-speakers of the S half of BELGIUM. There has long been friction between them and the Flemish-speaking majority, who have resented French political and cultural domination. Separate regional administrations were set up in 1974.

WALL STREET, the financial center of the US, in lower Manhattan, New York, the home of the New York Stock Exchange, many other commodity exchanges and head offices of banks, insurance and brokerage firms. The term also refers to the nation's aggregate financial interests.

WALNUT, trees of the genus *Juglans*, prized for the wood and nuts. In the US, the black walnut (*Juglans nigra*) grows to 150ft, its wood being used for high-class furniture and gun stocks. The English walnut (*J. regia*), providing edible walnuts,

is naturalized throughout the world. Family: Juglandaceae.

WALPOLE, Horace, 4th Earl of Orford (1717–1797), son of Sir Robert, English novelist, letter-writer and connoisseur. His *Castle of Otranto* (1765) was the first GOTHIC NOVEL; and his famous villa, Strawberry Hill, helped stimulate the GOTHIC REVIVAL. Over 3,000 of his letters survive.

WALPOLE, Sir Robert (1676–1745), English statesman often described as Britain's first prime minister. A WHIG, he held ministerial posts 1708–17. Recalled after the SOUTH SEA BUBBLE to be first lord of the treasury and chancellor of the exchequer (1721), he dominated Parliament, creating political and financial stability. Facing opposition and unpopularity as Britain became involved in European wars from 1739, he resigned in 1742, becoming 1st Earl of Orford.

WALPURGIS NIGHT, the night of Apr. 30/May 1 when, according to central European legend, witches assembled on mountaintops to consort with the devil. Of ancient pagan origin, it has been mistakenly associated with 8th-century German St. Walburga.

WALRUSES, two subspecies of seal-like marine mammals, *Odobenus rosmarus*, distinguished by having the upper canines extended into long tusks which in a mature adult may reach 1m (3.3ft). Walruses are found in shallow water around Arctic coasts, often hauling out onto rocks or ice floes to bask. They feed almost exclusively on mollusks.

WALSH, Thomas James (1859–1933), US politician. Democratic senator from Mont., he advocated arms limitation, fought against child labor and exposed the Elk Hills and TEAPOT DOME scandals. He died before taking office as attorney general.

WALSINGHAM, Sir Francis (c1530–1590), English statesman, ELIZABETH I's secretary of state 1573–90. A skillful diplomat, he created an intelligence system which exposed several plots against Elizabeth, secured MARY QUEEN OF SCOTS' downfall and gained advance knowledge of the ARMADA.

WALTER, Bruno (Bruno Walter Schlesinger; 1876–1962), German-born US conductor. He was a protégé of Gustav MAHLER, but his career in Europe was cut short by the Nazis, and he lived in the US from 1939. He was renowned for his interpretations of Mahler, Wagner, Beethoven and Brahms.

WALTER, Thomas Ustick (1804–1887), US architect, known for his pure classical style. He designed Girard College, Philadelphia (1833–47), and as government architect (1851–65) he added the dome and wings to the Capitol in Washington, D.C.

WALTHER VON DER VOGELWEIDE (c1170–c1230), most famous of the German MINNESINGERS. He wandered from court to court, until granted a fief by Emperor FREDERICK II. Apart from love poems, he composed political and religious poetry.

WALTON, Izaak (1593–1683), English writer remembered for *The Compleat Angler* (1653), a series of dialogues on the art of fishing which also praise the peaceful and simple life. He wrote biographies of friends he admired, like John DONNE.

WALTON, Sir William Turner (1902–1983), English composer. He had a brilliant early success with his music for Edith SITWELL'S *Façade* (1923). Other works include the oratorio *Belshazzar's Feast* (1931), film scores, notably for Shakespeare films, and the opera *Troilus and Cressida* (1954).

WALTZ, dance with three beats to the bar, originating from the ländler, a folk dance. Its popularity in the 19th century was due largely to the music of the STRAUSS family.

WAMPANOAG INDIANS, North American Indians of the Algonquian language family who lived E of Narragansett Bay. Their chief, Massasoit, made friends with the Pilgrim Fathers (1620). His son was the leader during KING PHILIP'S WAR (1675), after which the tribe was virtually exterminated.

WAMPUM, strings of shell beads prized by North American Indians, who used them as money in trading. The early white settlers also accepted them as currency, but the production of counterfeit glass beads undermined their value in the early 18th century.

WANAMAKER, John (1838–1922), US businessman whose department stores pioneered advertising techniques and personnel welfare and training. He was postmaster general 1889–93.

WANDERING JEW, according to a legend first recorded in the 13th century, a Jew who taunted Jesus on the way to Calvary and who was doomed to wander the world until Jesus returned.

WANDERING JEW, or **striped inch plant,** several trailing plants that are grown indoors for their flowers and foliage. *Tradescantia fluminensis variegata* has green leaves, irregularly striped with white; *Callisia elegans* has green leaves with white pinstripes, and *Zebrina pendula* has purple, green and silver striped leaves. They grow best in sunny windows, and the growing tips should be pinched out to maintain bushy growth. The soil should be kept evenly moist. They survive temperatures as low as 13°C (55°F). They are extremely easy to propagate by taking cuttings and rooting them in water and wet sand. Family: Commelinaceae.

WANG WEI (699–759), Chinese painter and poet. He is traditionally the originator of the monochrome ink-wash technique and founder of the renowned "Southern" School of landscape painting. His poetry and painting are imbued with a personal feeling for the beauty of nature.

WANKEL ENGINE, INTERNAL COMBUSTION ENGINE that produces rotary motion directly. Invented by the German engineer Felix Wankel (1902–1988), who completed his first design in 1954, it is now used in automobiles and airplanes. A triangular rotor with spring-loaded sealing plates at its apexes rotates eccentrically inside a cylinder, while the three combustion chambers formed between the sides of the rotor and the walls of the cylinder successively draw in, compress and ignite a fuel-and-air mixture. The Wankel engine is simpler in principle, more efficient and more powerful weight for weight, but more difficult to cool, than a conventional reciprocating engine.

WAPITI, the North American subspecies of the red deer, *Cervus elephas*. It differs from the typical European red deer in being larger and in that the terminal points to the antlers are in the same plane as the beam and do not form a "crown." Wapiti, once the most abundant deer in North America, are now severely reduced in numbers and range.

WAR, organized armed conflict between groups of people or states. War is not found elsewhere in the animal kingdom. Since recorded history began, man has been involved in hostility, for different aims: power, territory, wealth, ideological domination, security, independence. Until modern times, most wars were fought with limited means for limited aims, but modern weapons of mass destruction and total warfare can eliminate whole populations and endanger the survival of the human race. (See GENEVA CONVENTIONS; GUERRILLA WARFARE; STRATEGY; WAR CRIMES.)

WARBECK, Perkin (c1474–1499), Flemish-born pretender to the throne of England who, with Yorkist support, claimed to be a son of EDWARD IV (see ROSES, WARS OF THE). After a second attempt to invade England (1497), he was captured and imprisoned in the Tower of London. In

1498 he escaped but was recaptured and hanged.

WARBLERS, small perching birds related to THRUSHES and flycatchers. Almost all have thin, pointed bills and they are mainly insectivorous. While some, tropical, species are brightly-colored, most are olive or brown. The common name refers to the melodious songs produced by many of the species.

WAR CRIMES, in INTERNATIONAL LAW, the violation of the laws and rules of WAR. The first systematic attempt to frame laws for warfare was by GROTIUS (1625). Since 1864 various agreements have laid down principles for the treatment of combatants and civilians, and attempted to outlaw certain weapons (see GENEVA CONVENTIONS; KELLOGG-BRIAND PACT).

Few have been convicted of war crimes. A Confederate officer, Henry Wirz, was executed in 1865. An attempt was made to try the Kaiser after WWI, and some German officers were tried (mostly acquitted) by a German court. The only major war-crimes trial has been the NUREMBERG TRIALS. Here three categories of war crime were defined: crimes against peace (planning and waging aggressive war); "conventional" war crimes (murder of civilians or prisoners of war, plunder etc.); and crimes against humanity (murder, enslavement or deportation of whole populations). The principle of individual responsibility was also established.

WARD, Aaron Montgomery (1843–1913), US businessman. In 1872, with a capital of $2,400, he started up the mail-order firm which became the vast house of Montgomery Ward & Co.

WARD, Artemas (1727–1800), American leader in the REVOLUTIONARY WAR. As governor of Massachusetts (1774–75), he besieged Boston until WASHINGTON arrived, and was second in command of the Continental Army 1775–76. He served in Congress 1791–95.

WARD, Artemus (1834–1867), pen-name of Charles Farrar Browne, US journalist and humorist. The character of Artemus Ward, an irreverent traveling showman, became a household name for his pungent and comically ungrammatical comments. Browne also became a popular lecturer.

WARD, Barbara (1914–1981), British economist and commentator on the relations between the Western powers and developing nations. She stressed the importance of economic aid and international cooperation in such books as *The Rich Nations and the Poor Nations* (1962),

Spaceship Earth (1968) and *Progress for a Small Planet* (1979).

WARD, Lester Frank (1831–1913), US sociologist and paleontologist. A fervent evolutionist, he pioneered US sociology with such works as *Dynamic Sociology* (1883), *The Psychic Factors of Civilization* (1893) and *Glimpses of the Cosmos* (6 vols., 1913–1918).

WAR HAWKS, group of expansionist US Congressmen who in 1810–12 helped precipitate the WAR OF 1812. Mostly Southerners and Westerners, they hoped to remove British hindrance to expansion in the Northwest and gain Florida from Spain, Britain's ally.

WARHOL, Andy (1930?–1987), US artist and filmmaker, famous for his POP ART paintings. His highly innovative, often erotic and often lengthy films include *Chelsea Girls* (1966) and *Lonesome Cowboys* (1969).

WARM-BLOODED ANIMALS, or **homoiotherms,** animals whose body TEMPERATURE is not dependent on external temperature but is maintained at a constant level by internally-generated metabolic heat. This constant temperature enables the chemical processes of the body, many of them temperature-dependent, to be more efficient. Modern animals which have developed this homoiothermy are the MAMMALS and BIRDS, and it is now believed that PTERODACTYLS, therapsids, and many other extinct REPTILES may also have been warm-blooded.

WARM SPRINGS, health resort in W Ga., the site of the Warm Springs Foundation, established by F. D. ROOSEVELT in 1927 for the treatment of poliomyelitis sufferers.

WARNER, Glenn S. "Pop" (1871–1954), US football coach. He coached at Carlisle Indian School 1899–1915, produced three undefeated U. of Pittsburgh teams 1915–24 and led three Stanford elevens to the Rose Bowl 1924–33. During his 46 years as a coach, Warner pioneered both the single and double wing formations.

WARNER, Jack L. (1892–1978), US film producer who, with his three brothers, founded Warner Brothers, one of the largest and most successful Hollywood film studios. Warner Brothers produced the first full-length sound film, *The Jazz Singer* (1927), and was the first studio to produce for television.

WARNER, Seth (1743–1784), a hero of the American REVOLUTIONARY WAR and a leader of the GREEN MOUNTAIN BOYS. He helped capture Fort TICONDEROGA, took Crown Point (1775) and was largely responsible for the American victory at Bennington

(1777).

WARNER, William Lloyd (1898–1970), US social anthropologist at the U of Chicago 1935–60. He brought the methods of cultural anthropology to the study of class in America, particularly in his "Yankee City" series (5 vols., 1941–59).

WAR OF 1812, conflict between the US and Great Britain, 1812–15. It originated in the maritime policies of Britain and France in the NAPOLEONIC WARS. In 1806 Napoleon tried to prevent neutrals from trading with Britain. Britain retaliated with Orders in Council to prevent neutrals from trading with France. US trade slumped, and after the *Chesapeake* incident (when the British impressed four crewmen from a US frigate) she responded with the Embargo Act (1807) and the Noninterference Act (1809), banning trade with the belligerents. However, the chief sufferer from the ban was the US. Macon's Bill No. 2 (1810) lifted the ban, with certain provisions, but after agreement with Napoleon the US reimposed sanctions against Britain. Anti-British feeling, fed by WAR HAWKS and by the conviction that British support of the Indians (see TIPPECANOE, BATTLE OF) was hindering US expansion, led to war being declared on June 18, 1812.

The US was unprepared and in internal conflict over the war, and her attempted invasion of Canada (1812) was a failure. Early naval successes led to a retaliatory British blockade. US successes came in 1813 with the Battles of Lake ERIE and the Thames (in Ontario). In 1814 US troops held their own at Chippaewa and Lundy's Lane, and by a victory at Plattsburgh halted a British advance on the Hudson Valley. In Chesapeake Bay a British force that had sacked Washington was repelled in its attempt to take Baltimore. There was military stalemate, and peace negotiations started in June, 1814. The Peace of GHENT, signed on Dec. 22, 1814, was essentially a return to the status quo before the war. A fortnight later, Andrew JACKSON, unaware of the peace, defeated the British at the Battle of NEW ORLEANS. The war had several far-reaching effects on the US: the military victories promoted national confidence and encouraged expansionism, while the trade embargo encouraged home manufactures.

WAR OF THE PACIFIC (1879–1884) was fought by Chile against Bolivia and Peru over control of the nitrate-rich Atacama Desert in Bolivia (now N Chile's Antofagasta Province), bordering the Pacific. Chile conquered and annexed the desert and parts of Peru.

WAR ON DRUGS, "national crusade" against the "cancer of drugs," in the words of President Ronald REAGAN in a 1986 television address. The Reagan administration assigned a high priority to the war on drugs, but at its close world drug production was rising and drug consumption in the US was near its all-time high.

Drug use rose rapidly in the US in the 1960s. Marijuana and hashish were popular in the 1960s, heroin in the 1970s, cocaine in the 1980s. Particularly pernicious was "crack," a smokable, highly addictive form of cocaine that could be sold in small quantities at low prices. The extent of the damage drugs have wreaked on American society has been debated. The principal damage may be the increase in crime and the pervasive corruption of law-enforcement personnel. Public opinion regards drugs as a major national problem.

The war on drugs has four fronts: eradication of drugs at their sources; interdiction of the international drug traffic; suppression of drug dealing in the US; and reducing the demand for drugs by treating the addicted and educating the young.

The principal sources of opium are Afghanistan, Iran, Pakistan, Burma, Laos, Thailand, and Mexico; of cocaine, Bolivia, Colombia, Peru, and Ecuador; of marijuana, Mexico, Colombia, Jamaica, and Belize; of hashish, Lebanon, Pakistan, Afghanistan, and Morocco. A number of governments have cooperated with the US by prohibiting and trying to eradicate drug crops, but they have been resisted by powerful drug cartels. In some instances, coca, opium poppies, and marijuana are the best cash crops available to the farmers who grow them.

Most drugs enter the US from Latin America and the Caribbean. Drug money is "laundered" in Panama, Hong Kong, Switzerland, and elsewhere. Drug traffic and money laundering often depend on corrupt law-enforcement, military, and political figures in the countries involved. Such people are often beyond the reach of US authorities or are not pursued because they are useful to the US in other policy areas.

The smuggling of illegal drugs into the US through customs or by small boats and planes provides other opportunities to interdict the traffic. Only a small fraction of incoming drugs are intercepted. In recent years, budget cuts have reduced the effectiveness of the Coast Guard in this area. Once in the country, drugs are distributed by organized criminal gangs. The greatest government expenditures are made in law-enforcement efforts against these dealers, but there has been little diminution in the enormous volume of drugs that eventually reaches the streets.

Most authorities agree that as long as there is a demand for drugs, the large profits to be made by supplying them will ensure continued drug traffic. To curb demand, programs have been instituted to help the addicted overcome their dependency, but these are underfunded and waiting lists are long. Antidrug education and advertising are directed at young people but their effect cannot be measured. In 1988, in a major new antidrug act, Congress shifted funds from law enforcement and interdiction to preventive and treatment programs. (See also DRUG ENFORCEMENT ADMINISTRATION (DEA).)

WAR ON POVERTY, the totality of the administrative programs of President Lyndon B. Johnson that were aimed at eliminating poverty in the US and alleviating its effects. Johnson's declaration of "a war on poverty" occurred in his State of the Union speech of 1964; this crusade was essential to his vision of the Great Society.

WARRANT, judicial order (signed usually by a judge or court clerk) authorizing arrest of a suspect or search of premises. Strict procedures govern the issuing of a warrant. There are also tax warrants and warrants of attorney and of attachment.

WARREN, Earl (1891–1974), US Chief Justice 1953–69. Attorney general (1939–43) and governor (1943–53) of Cal., he was Republican vice-presidential candidate in 1948. Appointed to the Supreme Court by Eisenhower, he led it to a number of liberal judgments, notably the one in BROWN V. BOARD OF EDUCATION OF TOPEKA (1954) declaring racial segregation in schools unconstitutional.

WARREN, Joseph (1741–1775), US physician and patriot. He joined in Massachusetts Wig opposition to the STAMP ACT of 1765 and to British reprisals after the BOSTON TEA PARTY. Elected president of the provincial assembly in 1775, he was killed at the battle of BUNKER HILL on June 14.

WARREN, Josiah (1798–1874), US anarchist. He advocated "sovereignty of the individual" in place of Robert OWEN's socialism in *True Civilization* (1863), and founded a utopian colony, Modern Times (Brentwood), N.Y., and "equity stores" for exchange of goods and labor.

WARREN, Leonard (1911–1960), US singer, with the Metropolitan Opera from 1938. Considered the finest baritone of his time, he died on stage after completing an aria in a performance of Verdi's *La Forza del Destino.*

WARREN, Mercy Otis (1728–1814), American writer, author of patriotic plays and a history of the American Revolution valuable for its portraits of contemporary figures.

WARREN, Robert Penn (1905–1989), US novelist, poet, critic, and university teacher. He was one of the poets associated with *The Fugitive* magazine. Most of his poetry and popular novels have a Southern setting and political and moral themes. His three Pulitzer prizes include one for *All the King's Men* (1946).

WARREN REPORT, report of the commission set up by President Lyndon JOHNSON to investigate the assassination of President John KENNEDY. It comprised Earl WARREN, US representatives Hale Boggs and Gerald FORD, US senators Richard RUSSELL and John S. Cooper, Allen DULLES and John J. McCloy, attorney and ex-president of the World Bank. The report, released in Sept. 1964, concluded that neither putative assassin Lee OSWALD nor his killer Jack Ruby was part of a conspiracy. It criticized the FBI and Secret Service and recommended reforms in presidential security.

WARSAW, largest city and capital of Poland and of Warsaw province, on the Vistula R. It is a commercial, industrial, cultural and educational center and transportation hub. Chief products are machinery, precision instruments, motor vehicles, electrical equipment, textiles and chemicals. Warsaw replaced Kraków as capital in 1596 and has frequently fallen into Swedish, Russian, Prussian or German hands. Much of the city was razed in WWII but it has been carefully reconstructed. Pop 1,650,224.

WARSAW PACT, or Warsaw Treaty Organization, mutual defense pact signed 1955 in Warsaw by the USSR and its communist neighbors Albania, Bulgaria, Czechoslovakia, East Germany, Hungary, Poland and Romania, after formation of the NORTH ATLANTIC TREATY ORGANIZATION (NATO). Its unified command has headquarters in Moscow. In 1968 (when Albania formally withdrew), pact forces invaded Czechoslovakia to overthrow an independent-minded regime. In 1980–81 the USSR used pact maneuvers and threats of intervention by pact members to discourage labor unrest in Poland.

WARS OF RELIGION. See RELIGION, WARS OF.

WARS OF THE ROSES. See ROSES, WARS OF THE.

WART, scaly excrescence on the SKIN caused by a VIRUS which may arise without warning and disappear equally suddenly. Numerous remedies have been suggested but local freezing or cauterization are often effective. **Verrucas** are warts pushed into the soles of the feet by the weight of the body.

WARTBURG, castle overlooking Eisenach, SW East Germany; rebuilt, and made a center of music and poetry, by Hermann I of Thuringia (d. 1217)—a setting used in WAGNER's *Tannhäuser.* St. Elizabeth of Hungary lived there and later Martin LUTHER.

WARWICK, Richard Neville, Earl of (1428–1471), "The Kingmaker," most powerful English noble of his time. A Yorkist (see ROSES, WARS OF THE), he drove out HENRY VI and installed Edward of York as EDWARD IV (1461). He virtually ruled England, but lost royal favor, rose against Edward and reinstated Henry (1471). Warwick was defeated by Edward and killed at the battle of Barnet.

WASHINGTON, Booker Taliaferro (1856–1915), black US educator. Born of a Va. slave family, he was chosen 1881 to head a new school for blacks, the TUSKEGEE INSTITUTE, Ala. This he built up from two unequipped buildings to a complex with over 100 buildings and 1,500 students. Washington urged industrial education as the way to economic independence, favoring racial cooperation rather than political action. His extensive writings included an autobiography, *Up From Slavery* (1901).

WASHINGTON, George (1732–1799), first president of the US (1789–97). Born into a wealthy Va. family, he showed an early aptitude for surveying, in 1749 becoming surveyor of Culpeper Co. He first attracted notice with a report (1753) on the French threat in the Ohio Valley, and became commander in chief of the Va. militia (1755–58) after distinguishing himself in the mission of Edward BRADDOCK (see FRENCH AND INDIAN WARS). Returning to MOUNT VERNON, the estate he inherited in 1760, he married (1759) and became a member of the Va. house of burgesses (1759–74) and a justice of the peace (1760–74). His anti-British feelings were exacerbated by British taxes (see STAMP ACT; TOWNSHEND ACTS). He became a delegate to the CONTINENTAL CONGRESS (1774–75) and was appointed commander in chief of the Continental Army in 1775 (see REVOLUTIONARY WAR). From ill-trained and ill-equipped troops, he created a disciplined army, secured the fall of Boston (1776) but narrowly extricated himself

after defeat at Long Island.

After successes at Trenton and Princeton, 1777 marked a low point in the war. Washington survived an attempt to displace him and wintered 1777–78 in VALLEY FORGE. Alliances with France (1778) and Spain (1779) changed the course of the war. Victory was secured by the capture of YORKTOWN (1781), and after peace had been reached (1783). Washington resigned and returned to Mount Vernon.

Dissatisfied with the 1781 ARTICLES OF CONFEDERATION, Washington played a major role in securing the adoption of the UNITED STATES CONSTITUTION, and was unanimously elected president in 1789. Believing in a strong central government, he created a federal judiciary (1789) and a national bank (1791), and put through other far-reaching financial measures. These led to party conflict centering on Thomas JEFFERSON and Alexander HAMILTON. His second term of office was marked by controversy over foreign affairs, as with the JAY TREATY and his efforts to keep the US neutral in Britain's war with France (1793). There were also Indian insurrections and internal dissension (see WHISKEY REBELLION). He refused a third term of office. His integrity, patience and high sense of duty and justice made him a great leader and won him the title of "Father of His Country."

WASHINGTON, Martha Custis (1731–1802), wife of George Washington and first First Lady of the US. At 17 she married a wealthy planter, Daniel Parke Custis, who died in 1757. She married George Washington in 1759 and moved with her two surviving children to Mount Vernon, which she supervised during Washington's absences.

WASHINGTON, a NW Pacific state of the US bordering Ida., Ore., and British Columbia, Canada.

Land. The state is divided by the N–S CASCADE RANGE, which reaches 14,410ft (Mt RAINIER). The W half of the state is largely fertile lowland, deeply penetrated by Puget Sound. The E is mostly semiarid plateau intersected by deep canyons, the largest of which is dammed by the Grand Coulee Dam on the COLUMBIA RIVER. The Columbia and its tributary Pend Oreille and the Snake and Yakima rivers provide irrigation just E of the Cascades, and a large amount of hydroelectricity. The climate is mild and damp (up to 150in rain per year) in the W, drier and more extreme to the E.

People. The population is predominantly urban and concentrated in the NW on the shores of Puget Sound, where Seattle and

Name of state: Washington
Capital: Olympia
Statehood: Nov. 11, 1889 (42nd state)
Familiar name: Evergreen State; Chinook State
Area: 68,192sq mi
Population: 4,462,000
Elevation: Highest—14,410ft, Mount Rainier; Lowest—sea level, Pacific Ocean
Motto: *Alki* ("By and by")
State flower: Coast rhododendron
State bird: Willow goldfinch
State tree: Western hemlock
State song: "Washington, My Home"

Tacoma are the largest cities. The E is more sparsely populated, with Spokane the principal city. Blacks constitute less than 3% of the population, and there are over 60,000 Indians and more than 20 reservations.

Economy. The economy depends primarily on manufactures, notably aircraft, food-processing, forest products, aluminum and chemicals. Agriculture (apples, cherries, wheat, livestock, and dairying), fishing, mining, lumber (half of Wash. is forest) and tourism are also important. The state is an important producer of hydroelectric power.

History. The first recorded landing on the Wash. coast was made by Spaniards in 1775, and James COOK and George Vancouver soon followed. The LEWIS AND CLARK EXPEDITION descended the Columbia R in 1805, and fur traders gradually moved in. In 1846 the 49th-parallel boundary with Canada was fixed. The area was included in the Oregon Territory (1848); Washington Territory, set up in 1853, lost part of W Ida. in 1863, and achieved statehood in 1889. The opening of the railroad in 1883 and the Alaska and Klondike gold rush in the 1890s boosted population, while labor conflicts gave Wash. a certain notoriety. Though WWI brought a stimulus to the economy (especially shipbuilding), a collapse followed, and the situation worsened in the Great Depression. However, industries set up in WWII, postwar hydroelectric schemes, the expanding aerospace industry and diversification have brought increasing prosperity. The eruption of MOUNT SAINT HELENS in 1980 devastated some 44,000 forested acres of the state. In 1982 the Washington Public Power Supply System abandoned two nuclear power plants under construction and defaulted on the bonds that had been issued to pay for them. A late-1980s boom in forest products kept the state's economy vigorous. Between 1970 and 1986, population increased almost 30%. In presidential elections 1968–88, Washington voted Democratic in 1968 and 1988.

WASHINGTON, D.C., capital of the US, coextensive with the federal District of Columbia. It covers 69.2sq mi on the E bank of the Potomac R, but the metropolitan area now includes parts of Md. and Va. The focal point is the domed CAPITOL, home of the CONGRESS OF THE UNITED STATES. To the NW lies the WHITE HOUSE. Other important buildings are the headquarters of numerous government departments and agencies, the SUPREME COURT, PENTAGON (in Va.), FEDERAL BUREAU OF INVESTIGATION and LIBRARY OF CONGRESS. Also a cultural and educational center, Washington is the site of the SMITHSONIAN INSTITUTION, the NATIONAL GALLERY OF ART and the John F. Kennedy Center for the Performing Arts. There are many parks and famous memorials: the WASHINGTON MONUMENT, the LINCOLN MEMORIAL, and the JEFFERSON MEMORIAL. There is little industry, but many large corporations and other organizations have their offices there, including the FEDERAL RESERVE SYSTEM.

History. In 1783, the CONTINENTAL CONGRESS voted for a federal city. President Washington chose the present site in 1790 as a compromise between North and South, and the capitol was built at its center. In 1800 Congress moved from Philadelphia. During the WAR OF 1812, the government buildings were burned down (1814) by British troops, and new and more splendid plans were made. Since then the population has risen steadily. Washington, long a gateway for blacks emigrating N, is a focus for demonstrations as well as government. There is an elected mayor but Congress retains the right to review the city's budget and legislation. The District of Columbia has voted in presidential elections since 1964; it has voted consistently Democratic. In 1987 the House District of Columbia Committee approved a bill to make the district a state. Pop (city) 623,000, (metro) 3,490,000.

WASHINGTON, Treaty of (1871), agreement by the US and Britain, signed in Washington, D.C., to arbitrate the

ALABAMA CLAIMS and boundary and fishing disputes. It was largely brought about by Hamilton Fish, US secretary of state.

WASHINGTON CONFERENCE, post-WWI meetings convened by US President HARDING and held in Washington, D.C., 1921–22. The US, Britain, Japan, France and Italy agreed to limit their capital ships in the ratio 5:5:3:1⅔:1⅔ respectively, to restrictions on submarine warfare and a ban on use of poison gas. France, Japan, Britain and the US agreed to respect each other's Pacific territories. A nine-power treaty with the additional signatures of Belgium, China, the Netherlands and Portugal guaranteed China's territorial integrity.

WASHINGTON MONUMENT, stone obelisk in Washington, D.C., honoring George WASHINGTON. Begun 1848, it was completed in 1884. Faced with white marble, it is 555ft high. Visitors may go to the top by elevator, or by climbing 898 steps.

WASHINGTON'S BIRTHDAY, a legal holiday in most states, celebrated on the third Monday in February in honor of George Washington. He was born Feb. 11, 1732, but the 1752 calendar reform made it Feb. 22. The Monday holiday also honors Abraham Lincoln, who was born on Feb. 12.

WASHITA, Battle of the, 1868, massacre which ended hostilities by the CHEYENNE INDIANS. The 7th Cavalry, under General CUSTER, surprised and destroyed the camp of Chief Black Kettle on the banks of the Washita R, near Cheyenne, W Okla.

WASPS, stinging insects, banded black and yellow, related to BEES and ANTS in the order Hymenoptera. There are a number of families; most are solitary, but members of the Vespoidea are social, forming true colonies with workers, drones and queen(s). Most of the solitary species are hunting wasps. These make nest cells in soil or decaying wood, in which they place one or more paralyzed insects before the egg is laid, to act as a living larder for the larva when it hatches. Social wasps congregate to form a permanent colony with both adults and young. The nest is usually constructed of "wasp paper," a thick pulp of wood fibers and saliva. The adults feed the developing larvae on dead insects which have been killed by biting in the neck; the sting, which in solitary wasps is used to paralyze the prey, is reserved for defense. Adult wasps feed on carbohydrate: nectar, aphid honeydew or jam.

WASSERMAN, AUGUST PAUL VON (1866–1925), German bacteriologist famous for discovering a diagnostic test for syphilis. He also developed an antitoxin treatment for diphtheria and inoculations against typhoid, cholera, and tetanus.

WASSERMAN, Jakob (1873–1934), German writer popular in the 1920s and 1930s for his novels of intense social criticism, powerful characterization, and mystical longing, especially for *The Maurizius Case* (1928). He is sometimes compared with Dostoyevsky.

WASSERMANN TEST, screening test for syphilis (see VENEREAL DISEASES) based on a nonspecific serological reaction which is seen not only in syphilis but also in YAWS and diseases associated with immune disorders. More specific tests are available to discriminate between these.

WASTE DISPOSAL, disposal of such matter as animal excreta and the waste products of agricultural, industrial and domestic processes, where an unacceptable level of environmental POLLUTION would otherwise result. Where an ecological balance exists (see ECOLOGY), wastes are recycled naturally or by technological means (see RECYCLING) before accumulations affect the quality of life or disrupt the ecosystem. The most satisfactory waste-disposal methods are therefore probably those that involve recycling, as in manuring fields with dung, reclaiming metals from scrap or pulping waste paper for remanufacture. Recycling, however, may be inconvenient, uneconomic or not yet technologically feasible. Many popular waste-disposal methods consequently represent either an exchange of one form of environmental pollution for another less troublesome, at least in the short term—e.g., the dumping or burying of non-degradable garbage or toxic wastes—or a reducing of the rate at which pollutants accumulate—e.g., by compacting or incinerating bulk wastes before dumping. Urban wastes are generally disposed of by means of dumping, sanitary landfill, incineration and SEWAGE processing. Agricultural, mining and mineral-processing operations generate most solid wastes—and some of the most intractable waste-disposal problems: e.g., the "factory" farmer's problem of disposing of surplus organic wastes economically without resorting to incineration or dumping in rivers; the problems created by large mine dumps and open-cast excavations; and the culm-dumps that result from the processing of anthracite COAL. Another increasingly pressing waste-disposal problem is presented by radioactive wastes. Those with a "low level" of RADIOACTIVITY can be safely packaged and buried; but "high-level" wastes, produced in the course of reprocessing the fuel elements of NUCLEAR REACTORS, constitute a permanent hazard. Even the practice of encasing these wastes in thick concrete and dumping them on the ocean bottom is considered by many environmentalists to be an inadequate long-term solution (see also NUCLEAR ENERGY).

WATAUGA ASSOCIATION, 1772–75, government set up on land leased from the Cherokee along the Watauga R, present Washington Co., E Tenn. The settlers, from Va. and (after suppression of the REGULATORS) N.C., became part of the State of Franklin in 1788.

WATER (H_2O), pale-blue odorless liquid which, including that trapped as ICE in icecaps and glaciers, covers about 74% of the earth's surface. Water is essential to LIFE, which began in the watery OCEANS: because of its unique chemical properties, it provides the medium for the reactions of the living CELL. Water is also man's most precious natural resource, which he must conserve and protect from POLLUTION. Chemically, water can be viewed variously as a covalent hydride, an oxide, or a hydroxide. It is a good solvent for many substances, especially ionic and polar compounds; it is ionizing and itself ionizes to give a low concentration of hydroxide and hydrogen ions (see pH). It is thus both a weak ACID and a weak BASE, and conducts electricity. It is a good, though labile, ligand, forming hydrates. Water is a polar molecule, and shows anomalies due to hydrogen bonding, including contraction when heated from 0°C to 4°C. Formed when hydrogen or volatile hydrides are burned in oxygen, water oxidizes reactive metals to their ions, and reduces fluorine and chlorine. It converts basic oxides to hydroxides, and acidic oxides to oxy-acids. (See also HARD WATER; HEAVY WATER; HYDROLYSIS.)mp 0°C, bp 100°C, triple point 0.01°C, sg 1.0.

WATERCOLOR, painting technique in which the pigment is mixed with water before application, more particularly the aquarelle technique of thin washes, mastered by such English artists as John Cotman and J. M. W. TURNER around 1800. Infelicities cannot be painted over, but watercolor permits powerful effects of transparency, brilliance and delicacy. Famous US watercolorists include Winslow HOMER and John MARIN. (See also FRESCO; TEMPERA.)

WATERFALL, a vertical fall of water where a river flows from hard rock to one more easily eroded (see EROSION), or where there has been a rise of the land relative to sea level or blockage of a river by a landslide. Highest in the world is Angel Falls, Venezuela (3,212ft).

WATERFORD, seaport capital of Co. Waterford, SE Ireland, on the Suir R. Famous for its cut glass, Waterford ships meat, dairy products and fish, and makes footwear and electrical goods.

WATERGATE, series of scandals which brought down President NIXON'S administration. On June 17, 1972, five men were arrested carrying electronic eavesdropping equipment in the Watergate office building headquarters of the Democratic Party national committee, Washington, D.C. Investigations opened a trail which led to Nixon's inner councils. Nixon easily won reelection in Nov. 1972; but his public support eroded after a televised US Senate investigation, newspaper revelations (notably by Carl Bernstein and Bob Woodward in the *Washington Post*) and testimony of Republican Party and former governmental officials clearly implicated him and his senior aides in massive abuse of power and obstruction of justice involving campaign contributions, the CIA, the FBI, the Internal Revenue Service, and other agencies. The House of Representatives Judiciary Committee voted to impeach Nixon in July 1974, and his ouster from office became inevitable; he resigned on Aug. 9, 1974. One month later he was granted a full pardon by Gerald FORD. Almost three score individuals, including former US attorney general John Mitchell and senior White House staff were convicted of Watergate crimes, about half serving jail sentences.

WATER LILIES, aquatic plants of the genus *Nymphaea* (unrelated to true LILIES). They grow in calm shallow fresh water, with stems rooted in the mud and floating leaves. Many hybrids are used as ornamentals in water gardens. Family: Nymphaeaceae.

WATERLOO, Battle of (June 18, 1815), the final engagement of the NAPOLEONIC WARS. Having escaped from exile on Elba and reinstated himself with a new army, NAPOLEON I faced a coalition of Austria, Britain, Prussia and Russia. He decided to attack, advancing into Belgium to prevent an Anglo-Dutch army under WELLINGTON from uniting with the Prussians. After separate battles with the British and Prussians on June 16, the French army, led by Marshall NEY, attacked Wellington's strongly defended position at Waterloo, S of Brussels. The intervention of a Prussian force under BLÜCHER allowed Wellington to take the offensive. The French were routed, losing some 25,000 men. Napoleon abdicated four days later.

WATER POLLUTION. The discharge of wastes into water bodies has always been a convenient and inexpensive means of disposal. Most organic wastes are readily degradable in water: bacteria convert them into their inorganic components (nitrogen, phosphorous, and carbon), which nourish microscopic algae and thus enter the aquatic food chain. This process consumes the oxygen present in the water, but the water renews its oxygen supply by absorption from the air and by PHOTOSYNTHESIS. When the volume of organic waste is too great, however, the water's oxygen supply is exhausted and the water body eutrophies or "dies." It then turns slimy and stinks.

Certain wastes are not degradable. These include inorganic and synthetic organic chemicals (for example, the pesticide DDT and the industrial chemical PCB) and metals (for example, mercury and lead). Toxic nondegradable wastes may immediately poison aquatic life, or they may enter the aquatic food chain with consequences equally serious though delayed. Water can do little with nondegradable wastes except dilute them and carry them away from the point of discharge. The success of a water body in cleansing itself of nondegradable as of degradable pollutants depends not only on its size but on its character: a flowing stream is the most successful, a tidal stream less so, a lake least of all. Nondegradable wastes may accumulate in stream beds and lake bottoms. The ocean is the ultimate sink of nondegradable wastes.

WATER POWER. See HYDROELECTRICITY; TURBINE.

WATERS, Ethel (1896–1977), US singer and actress. She followed a singing career in nightclubs and on Broadway with notable dramatic roles in the film *Pinky* (1949) and in *Member of the Wedding* (play, 1950; film, 1952).

WATER SNAKES, nearly 80 species of the genus *Natrix*, which also includes the European grass snake. They are non-venomous snakes living on fish and amphibians. The Eurasian water snakes lay eggs, while the two New-World species are viviparous.

WATERSPOUT, effect of a rotating column of air, or TORNADO, as it passes over water. A funnel-like cloud of condensed water vapor extends from a parent cumulonimbus cloud to the water surface, where it is surrounded by a sheath of spray.

WATER SUPPLY, available WATER resources and the means by which sufficient*

water of a suitable quality is supplied for agricultural, industrial, domestic and other purposes. Water precipitated over land (see HYDROLOGIC CYCLE) is available either as "surface water," in the form of rivers and lakes, usually supplemented by reservoirs, or as GROUND WATER, held underground—typically in an AQUIFER underlaid by impermeable rock—and brought to the surface by pumping or else rising as a spring or ARTESIAN WELL. Water may also be extracted from SEWAGE, purified and recycled (see RECYCLING).

WATER TABLE. See GROUNDWATER.

WATLING ISLAND. See SAN SALVADOR ISLAND.

WATSON, James Dewey (1928–   ), US biochemist who shared with F. H. C. Crick and M. H. F. Wilkins the 1962 Nobel Prize for Physiology or Medicine for his work with Crick establishing the "double helix" molecular model of DNA. His personalized account of the research, *The Double Helix* (1968), became a best-seller.

WATSON, John Broadus (1878–1958), US psychologist who founded BEHAVIORISM, a dominant school of US psychology from the 1920s to 1940s, and whose influence is still strong today.

WATSON, Thomas Edward (1856–1922), US author and political leader from Ga. He attacked blacks, socialists, Catholics and Jews. A Farmers' Alliance (1891–93) and Democratic (from 1920) Congressman, and POPULIST vice-presidential and presidential candidate (1896, 1904), he became a champion of the KU KLUX KLAN.

WATSON, Thomas John (1874–1956), US business executive who took over an ailing computing company in 1914, changed its name to International Business Machines Corp., 1924, and built it into one of the world's largest corporations. Under his presidency, 1914–49, and chairmanship, 1949–56, IBM became the leader in electronic data-processing equipment.

WATSON-WATT, Sir Robert Alexander (1892–1973), British physicist largely responsible for the development of RADAR, patenting his first "radiolocator" in 1919. He perfected his equipment and techniques from 1935 through the years of WWII, his radar being largely responsible for the British victory in the BATTLE OF BRITAIN.

WATT, James (1736–1819), Scottish engineer and inventor. His first major invention was a STEAM ENGINE with a separate condenser and thus far greater efficiency. For the manufacture of such engines he entered partnership with John Roebuck and later (1775), more successful-ly, with Matthew Boulton. Between 1775 and 1800 he invented the sun-and-planet gear wheel, the double-acting engine, a throttle valve, a pressure gauge and the centrifugal governor—as well as taking the first steps toward determining the chemical structure of water. He also coined the term horsepower and was a founding member of the Lunar Society.

WATTEAU, Jean-Antoine (1684–1721), French (of Flemish descent) draftsman and painter, strongly influenced by RUBENS. His gay, sensuous paintings have a melancholy quality. They include theater scenes, *fêtes galantes, The Embarkation for Cythera* (1717) and *Gilles* (c1718).

WATTERSON, Henry (1840–1921), US journalist-politician. A US Congressman 1876–77, he backed TILDEN. His Louisville, Ky., *Courier-Journal* editorials (1868–1919) urged Negro rights and Southern home rule. His editorials favoring US war on Germany won him a 1917 Pulitzer Prize.

WATTS, Andre (1946–   ), US pianist. He made his debut at age 16 with the New York Philharmonic over national television. He is best known for his brilliant interpretations of the music of Franz LISZT.

WATTS, George Frederic (1817–1904), English Victorian artist noted for his allegorical paintings, including *Hope* (1886). He married Ellen TERRY.

WATTS, Isaac (1674–1748), English Dissenting theologian, author of numerous fine hymns (many, like "O God, our help in ages past," still sung today) and philosophical writings.

WATUSI (English version of Swahili *Watutsi*), the Tutsi people of BURUNDI and RWANDA in Central Africa (formerly Ruanda-Urundi). In the 1400s and 1500s the invading Watusi imposed a feudal system on the native Hutu, who revolted in 1959 and drove out their rulers. The Tutsi king of Burundi was deposed in 1966. The Watusi differ ethnically from other African peoples. Many attain a height of 7ft.

WAUBESHIEK (c1794–c1841), North American Indian prophet. Also called White Cloud, he advised Chief Black Hawk that victory would be his, and so perhaps prolonged the BLACK HAWK WAR.

WAUGH, name of three English writers, the sons of journalist and publisher Arthur Waugh (1886–1943). **Alexander Raban (Alec) Waugh** (1898–1981) wrote over 40 novels and travel books including *Loom of Youth* (1918) and *Island in the Sun* (1956). **Evelyn Arthur St. John Waugh** (1903–1966) wrote mainly satire, both elegant and biting. His conversion to Roman Catholicism in 1930 had a deep effect on his work. His novels include *Decline and Fall* (1928), *Vile Bodies* (1930), *Scoop* (1938), *Put out More Flags* (1942), *Brideshead Revisited* (1945) and his WWII trilogy *The Sword of Honour* (1952–61). Evelyn's son **Auberon Alexander Waugh** (1939–   ) is a novelist and miscellaneous writer. His novels include *Bed of Flowers* (1972).

WAVELL, Archibald Percival Wavell, 1st Earl (1883–1950), British field marshal. He served in WWI, and was WWII British commander-in-chief, Middle East, defeating the Italians in N Africa 1940. He was viceroy and governor general of India in the years before independence (1943–47).

WAVE MECHANICS, branch of QUANTUM MECHANICS developed by SCHRÖDINGER which considers MATTER rather in terms of its wavelike properties (see WAVE MOTION) than as systems of particles. Thus an orbital ELECTRON is treated as a 3-dimensional system of standing waves represented by a *wave function*. In accordance with the UNCERTAINTY PRINCIPLE, it is not possible to pinpoint both the instantaneous position and velocity of the electron; however, the square of the wave function yields a measure in space-time. The pattern of such probabilities provides a model for the "shape" of the electron orbital involved. Given wave functions can be obtained from the Schrödinger wave equation. Usually, and not unsurprisingly, this can only be solved for particular values of the ENERGY of the system concerned.

WAVE MOTION, a collective motion of a material or extended object, in which each part of the material oscillates about its undisturbed position, but the oscillations at different places are so timed as to create an illusion of crests and troughs running right through the material. Familiar examples are furnished by surface waves on water, or transverse waves on a stretched rope; SOUND is carried through air by a wave motion in which the air molecules oscillate parallel to the direction of propagation, and LIGHT or RADIO waves involve electromagnetic fields oscillating perpendicular to it. The maximum displacement of the material from the undisturbed position is the *amplitude* of the wave, the separation of successive crests, the *wavelength*, and the number of crests passing a given place each second, the *frequency*. The product of the wavelength and the frequency gives the *velocity of propagation*. According to the direction and form of the local oscillations of the medium, different *polarizations* of the wave are distinguished (see POLARIZED LIGHT). *Standing waves* (apparently stationary waves, where the nodes and antinodes—points of zero and maximum amplitude—appear not to move) arise where identical waves traveling in opposite directions superpose. The characteristic properties of waves include propagation in straight lines; REFLECTION at plane surfaces; REFRACTION—a change in direction of a wave transmitted across a plane interface between two media; DIFFRACTION— diffuse scattering by impenetrable objects of a size comparable with the wavelength; and INTERFERENCE—the cancellation of one wave by another wave half a wavelength out of step (or *phase*) so that the crests of one wave fall on the troughs of the other. If the *wave velocity* is the same for all wavelengths, then quite arbitrary forms of disturbance will travel as waves, and not simply regular successions of crests and troughs. When this is not the case, the wave is said to be *dispersive* and localized disturbances move at a speed (the *group velocity*) quite different from that of the individual crests, which can often be seen moving faster or slower within the disturbance "envelope," which becomes progressively broader as it moves. Waves carry ENERGY and MOMENTUM with them just like solid objects; the identity of the apparently irreconcilable wave and particle concepts of matter is a basic tenet of QUANTUM MECHANICS.

WAX, moldable water-repellent solid. There are several entirely different kinds. Animal waxes were the first known: *wool wax* when purified yields lanolin; *beeswax,* from the honeycomb, is used for some candles and as a sculpture medium (by carving or casting); *spermaceti wax,* from the sperm whale, is used in ointments and cosmetics. Vegetable waxes, like animal waxes, are mixtures of ESTERS of longchain ALCOHOLS and carboxylic acids. *Carnauba wax,* from the leaves of a Brazilian palm tree, is hard and lustrous, and is used to make polishes; *candelilla wax,* from a wild Mexican rush, is similar but more resinous; *Japan wax,* the coating of sumac berries, is fatty and soft but tough and kneadable. Mineral waxes include *montan wax,* extracted from lignite (see COAL), bituminous and resinous; *ozokerite,* an absorbent hydrocarbon wax obtained from wax shales, and *paraffin wax* or petroleum wax, the most important wax commercially: it is obtained from the residues of PETROLEUM refining by solvent extraction, and is used to make candles, to coat paper products, in the electrical industry, to waterproof leather and textiles, etc. Various synthetic waxes are made for special uses.

WAYNE, Anthony (1745–1796), American Revolutionary general whose daring tactics earned him the name "Mad Anthony." In 1779 he executed the brilliant victory of Stony Point over the British, and he was with Lafayette at the siege of YORKTOWN (1781). After defeating the Indians at Fallen Timbers in 1794, he negotiated the Treaty of Greenville (1795), in which the Indians ceded most of Ohio.

WAYNE, John (Marion Morrison; 1907–1979), US film actor, a star of westerns beginning with *Stagecoach* (1939) and war films that made him an icon of US patriotism.

WEASEL, *Mustela nivalis,* a small carnivorous mammal very like the stoat but smaller and lacking the black tail tip. A slender lithe red-brown creature, which often kills prey many times its own size, it measures only up to 280mm (11in) in the male, 200mm (7.9in) in the female. The normal diet is mice, voles and fledgling birds, though rabbits may be taken. The many races of weasel are distributed throughout Europe, Africa and North America.

WEATHER, hour-by-hour variations in atmospheric conditions experienced at a given place. (See ATMOSPHERE; METEOROLOGY; WEATHER FORECASTING AND CONTROL.)

WEATHERFORD, William (c1780–1824), North American Indian chief who fought the Americans in the WAR OF 1812. He led the Creek Indians, roused by TECUMSEH, at the battle of HORSESHOE BEND. He was defeated but pardoned by General Andrew JACKSON.

WEATHER FORECASTING AND CONTROL, the practical application of the knowledge gained through the study of METEOROLOGY. **Weather forecasting,** organized nationally by government agencies such as the US National Weather Service, is coordinated internationally by the WORLD METEOROLOGICAL ORGANIZATION (WMO). There are three basic stages: observation; analysis; and forecasting. Observation involves round-the-clock weather watching and the gathering of meteorological data by land stations, weather ships, and by using radiosondes and weather SATELLITES. In analysis, this information is coordinated at national centers, and plotted in terms of isobars, fronts, etc., on synoptic charts (weather maps). Then, in forecasting, predictions of the future weather pattern are made by the "synoptic method" (in which the forecaster applies his experience of the evolution of past weather patterns to the current situation) and by "numerical forecasting" (which treats the ATMOSPHERE as a fluid of variable density and seeks to use hydrodynamic equations to determine its future parameters). These methods yield short- and medium-term forecasts—up to four days ahead. Long-range forecasting, a recent development, depends additionally on the statistical analysis of past weather records in attempting to discern the future weather trends over the next month or season. **Weather control**, or weather modification, is an altogether less reliable technology. Indeed, the natural variability of weather phenomena makes it difficult to assess the success of experimental procedures. To date, the best results have been obtained in the fields of CLOUD seeding and the dispersal of supercooled fogs.

WEATHERMEN, violent faction within the NEW LEFT, formed in 1969 by radical dissenters from the Students for a Democratic Society. The name comes from a line in a Bob Dylan song, "You don't need a weatherman to know which way the wind blows"; it was subsequently changed to "Weather People" and "Weather Underground." Three members of the group were killed in 1970 when an accident in handling bombs blew up a townhouse in New York City. Thereafter the organization operated in secrecy, but by 1980 three who had long been sought by the FBI had turned themselves in: Mark Rudd, Cathlyn Wilkerson, and Bernadine Dohrn. In Oct. 1981, the Weather Underground again made headlines when three self-described members attempted robbery of a Brink's armored car in Nanuet, N.Y., in which two policemen and a guard were killed.

WEATHER SERVICE, National, a part of the Environmental Science Services Administration (ESSA), in the US Department of Commerce. Its head office in Washington, D.C., near the National Meteorological Center, is where data from 300 weather stations in the US and from many other sources including aircraft, satellites, and balloons are coordinated and incorporated into charts for distribution to the 30 forecast centers across the country. Here long- and short-range forecasts are prepared, and warnings of hurricanes, flooding and other weather hazards given. Research to improve forecasting accuracy is also undertaken. (See also METEOROLOGY.)

WEAVER, James Baird (1833–1912), US politician. Elected to the House of Representatives (1879–80, 1885–88) on the GREENBACK PARTY ticket, he was the party's presidential candidate in 1880. He organized the People's Party and as their presidential candidate (1892) won over a

million popular and 22 electoral votes. His career declined with the demise of POPULISM.

WEAVER, Robert Clifton (1907–   ), US economist and secretary of the Department of HOUSING AND URBAN DEVELOPMENT (1966–69), first black member of the US cabinet. He was the administrator of the N.Y. Rent Commission (1955–59) and led the federal Housing and Home Finance Agency (1961–66).

WEAVER, Warren (1894–1978), US scientist and foundation official, developer with Claude E. SHANNON of INFORMATION THEORY. He was long associated with the Rockefeller Foundation and the Alfred P. Sloan Foundation.

WEAVING, making a fabric by interlacing two or more sets of threads. In "plain" weave, one set of threads—the *warp*—extends along the length of the fabric; the other set—the *woof*, or *weft*—is at right angles to the warp and passes alternately over and under it. Other common weaves include "twill," "satin" and "pile." In basic twill, woof threads, stepped one warp thread further on with each line, pass over two warp threads, under one, then over two again, producing diagonal ridges, or wales, as in denim, flannel and gaberdine. In satin weave, a development of twill, long "float" threads passing under four warp threads give the fabric its characteristically smooth appearance. Pile fabrics, such as corduroy and velvet, have extra warp or weft threads woven into a ground weave in a series of loops that are then cut to produce the pile. Weaving is usually accomplished by means of a hand- or power-operated machine called a loom. Warp threads are stretched on a frame and passed through eyelets in vertical wires (heddles) supported on a frame (the harness). A space (the shed) between sets of warp threads is made by moving the heddles up or down, and a shuttle containing the woof thread is passed through the shed. A special comb (the reed) then pushes home the newly woven line. (See also RUGS AND CARPETS.)

WEBB, name of two English social reformers and economists. **Beatrice Webb** (née Potter, 1858–1943) studied working life for her *Life and Labour of the People in London* (1891–1903). Her husband, **Sidney James Webb** (1859–1947), was a Labour Member of Parliament (1922–29) and held several Cabinet posts. The couple were leading intellectuals of the Labour movement and wrote together a *History of Trade Unionism* (1894). They were FABIANS and helped found the London School of

Economics in 1895, and the left-wing journal *The New Statesman* in 1913.

WEBER, Carl Maria Friedrich Ernst von (1786–1826), German composer, pianist and conductor who established Romantic opera and paved the way in Germany for WAGNER, with the operas *Der Freischütz* (*The Marksman*; 1821), *Euryanthe* (1823) and *Oberon* (1826). He wrote a number of orchestral and chamber works, notably for the piano, including the well-known *Invitation to the Dance* (1819).

WEBER, Max (1864–1920), German economist and sociologist. In *The Protestant Ethic and the Spirit of Capitalism* (1904–05) he argued that the Calvinist emphasis on hard work helped develop business enterprise. He believed that many causes such as law, religion and politics combined with economics to determine the course of history. He defined a methodology for sociology.

WEBER, Max (1881–1961), Russian-born US painter who developed his style from primitive art and Jewish folklore. He studied in Europe (1905–09) but was in general outside the mainstream of modern art.

WEBER AND FIELDS, team of US vaudeville comedians. Immensely popular for their dialect jokes and slapstick, **Joe Weber** (1867–1942) and **Lew Fields** (1867–1941) were forerunners of many later comedy pairs.

WEBERN, Anton von (1883–1945), Austrian composer who studied with SCHOENBERG and developed his TWELVE-TONE MUSIC form into a concentrated and individual style. His works include *Five Pieces for Orchestra* (1911–13), two symphonies, three string quartets and a number of songs.

WEBSTER, Daniel (1782–1852), US statesman, lawyer and orator whose advocacy of strong central government earned him the name of "defender of the Constitution." Early in his career, nonetheless, he defended STATES' RIGHTS and championed New England interests as N.H. member of the House of Representatives (1813–17) and Mass. representative (1823–27) and senator (1827–41). As New England interests changed from shipping to industry, Webster became nationalist, and supported protective tariffs despite his earlier castigation of trade restrictions. His battle against NULLIFICATION began in 1830, and continued throughout the crisis of 1832–33; in his efforts to preserve the Union he supported the COMPROMISE OF 1850. He was twice Secretary of State. (See also WEBSTER-ASHBURTON TREATY.)

WEBSTER, John (c1580–c1625), English Jacobean playwright best remembered for his two powerful revenge tragedies, *The White Devil* (c1610) and *The Duchess of Malfi* (c1615). Both are set in Renaissance Italy. Webster sometimes collaborated with other playwrights, notably John FORD and Thomas DEKKER.

WEBSTER, Margaret (1905–1972), US actress and director noted for her Shakespeare productions, including Paul ROBESON's *Othello* (1943).

WEBSTER, Noah (1758–1843), US lexicographer whose works such as *The Elementary Spelling Book*, called the "Blue-Backed Speller" (1829; earlier versions 1783–87), helped standardize American spelling. He compiled a grammar (1784) and a reader (1785). Working on dictionaries from 1803 he published *An American Dictionary of the English Language* (1828), with 70,000 entries and 12,000 new definitions. Today his name is often applied to dictionaries that are in no way based on his work.

WEBSTER-ASHBURTON TREATY (1842), agreement between the US and Great Britain settling the line of the NE border of the US between Me. and New Brunswick. Signed by Daniel WEBSTER for the US and Lord Ashburton for Great Britain, the treaty also agreed on joint suppression of the slave trade.

WEDDELL SEA, arm of the S Atlantic Ocean in Antarctica between Palmer Land and Coats Land. At its S end are the Ronne and Filchner ice shelves.

WEDEKIND, Frank (1864–1918), German playwright who attacked the hypocrisy and sexual mores of his times, notably in *Spring Awakening* (1891). His "Lulu plays," *Earth-Spirit* (1895) and *Pandora's Box* (1903), center on Lulu, a personification of natural sensuality, and inspired an opera by BERG. Many of his techniques foreshadowed EXPRESSIONISM.

WEDGWOOD, Josiah (1730–1795), outstanding English potter, inventor of Wedgwood ware. He patented his cream Queen's Ware in 1765; for the designs on his blue and white Jasper Ware he frequently employed John Flaxman. Wedgwood introduced new materials and machinery; his factory at Etruria, Staffordshire, was the first to acquire steam engines.

WEED, Thurlow (1797–1882), US journalist and Whig political leader. He used his *Albany Evening Journal* to promote the ANTIMASONIC PARTY. He supported the presidential campaigns of William HARRISON and Zachary TAYLOR and the career of his friend, W. H. SEWARD. He joined the Republicans in 1855 and under LINCOLN was a special agent to England.

WEEDKILLERS. See HERBICIDES.

WEEK, an arbitrary division of time, through most of the Christian era, of duration seven days. In most European languages, the days of the week are named for the planets or deities which were considered to preside over them.

WEEMS, Mason Locke (1759–1825), clergyman and (from 1794) traveling book agent who invented the story of George Washington and the cherry tree in the fifth edition of his *The Life and Memorable Actions of George Washington* (1800).

WEEVILS, the largest animal family, Curculionidae, 35,000 species of oval or pear-shaped BEETLES having a greatly drawn out head or snout bearing strong chewing mouthparts. They feed on hard vegetable matter, seeds and wood; the larvae, developing within seeds, are legless. Weevils are important economic pests of cotton and grain crops; also of stored peas, beans and flour.

WEGENER, Alfred Lothar (1880–1930), German meteorologist, explorer and geologist. His *The Origin of Continents and Oceans* (1915) set forth "Wegener's hypothesis," the theory of CONTINENTAL DRIFT, whose developments were in succeeding decades to revolutionize man's view of the planet he lives on (see also PLATE TECTONICS).

WEIDENREICH, Franz (1873–1948), German-born US physical anthropologist and anatomist best known for his work on fossil remains of *Sinanthropus*, *Pithecanthropus* and *Meganthropus* (see PREHISTORIC MAN), and for his chronological arrangement of the various stages in man's evolution.

WEIGHT, the attractive FORCE experienced by an object in the presence of another massive body in accordance with the law of universal GRAVITATION. The weight of a body (measured in newtons) is given by the product of its MASS and the local ACCELERATION due to gravity (g). Weight differs from mass in being a vector quantity.

WEIGHTLIFTING, bodybuilding exercise and competitive sport. As a contest, it has long been popular in Turkey, Egypt, Japan and Europe and has been a regular event in the Olympic Games since 1920. There are three basic lifts: the snatch (from the floor to over the head in a single motion); the clean and jerk (two movements—first to the chest and then over the head); and the military or two-hand press (similar to the clean and jerk, but retaining a "military" stance).

WEIGHTS AND MEASURES, units of weight, length, area and volume commonly used in the home, in commerce and in industry. Although like other early peoples the Hebrews used measures such as the foot, the cubit (the length of the human forearm) and the span, which could easily be realized in practice using parts of the body, in commerce they also used standard containers and weights. Later, weights were based on the quantity of precious metal in coins. During and after the Middle Ages, each region evolved its own system of weights and measures. In the 19th century these were standardized on a national basis, these national standards in turn being superseded by those of the METRIC SYSTEM. In the western world, only the British Empire and the US retained their own systems (the Imperial System and the US Customary System) into the mid-20th century. With the UK's adoption of the International System of Units (SI UNITS), the US has found itself alone in not using metric units, although, as has been the case since 1959, the US customary units are now defined in terms of their metric counterparts and not on the basis of independent standards. In the US the administration of weights and measures is coordinated by the National Bureau of Standards (NBS).

WEIL, Simone (1909–1943), French, philosopher, religious mystic and left-wing intellectual. She was active in the Spanish Civil War and the French Resistance in WWII. She converted from Judaism to Christianity c1940. Her books include *Oppression and Liberty* (1955).

WEILL, Kurt (1900–1950), German-born US composer. His most original music is for the two satirical operas on which he collaborated with BRECHT, *The Threepenny Opera* (1928) and *The Rise and Fall of the City of Mahagonny* (1930). He came to the US in 1935, and became a successful Broadway composer.

WEIMAR, city in SW East Germany, on the Ilm R, manufacturing agricultural machinery, electrical equipment and chemicals. It was capital of the Saxe-Weimar duchy from 1547, and its court became the German cultural and intellectual center in the 18th and 19th centuries, attracting BACH, GOETHE, SCHILLER, HERDER, LISZT and NIETZSCHE. It was the first site of the BAUHAUS. BUCHENWALD concentration camp was nearby. Pop 62,800.

WEIMAR REPUBLIC, German government (1919–33) based on the democratic republican constitution adopted at Weimar in 1919. Its presidents were EBERT and then von HINDENBURG, who made HITLER chancellor in 1933. Hitler suspended the constitution the same year.

WEINBERGER, Caspar (1917–   ), US secretary of Defense (1981–88). A California Republican, he was appointed state director of finance by then Governor Reagan in 1968. He served in the Nixon administration as deputy director 1970–72 and director 1972 of the Office of Management and Budget, and as secretary of Health, Education and Welfare 1973–75.

WEINGARTNER, Felix (1863–1942), Austrian conductor and composer who conducted the Berlin Royal Opera, the Vienna State Opera and the Vienna Philharmonic. He conducted throughout the world, composed six symphonies and eight operas, and wrote several books on conducting and musical interpretation.

WEISMANN, August (1834–1914), German biologist regarded as a father of modern GENETICS for his demolition of the theory that ACQUIRED CHARACTERISTICS could be inherited, and proposal that CHROMOSOMES are the basis of HEREDITY. He coupled this proposal with his belief in NATURAL SELECTION as the mechanism for EVOLUTION.

WEISS, Peter (1916–1982), German playwright, artist and filmmaker, who lived in Sweden, having fled Nazi Germany in 1934. With the appearance of his innovative *Marat/Sade* (1963), essentially about revolutionary idealism versus aristocratic individualism, Weiss was acclaimed the successor of BRECHT as the foremost German dramatist. He is also well known for *The Investigation* (1965), a five-hour docudrama detailing Nazi atrocities.

WEISSMULLER, Johnny (1904–1984), US swimmer and film actor. He set many swimming records and won five gold medals at both the 1924 and 1928 Olympics. Thereafter he played Tarzan in nearly 20 movies (1932–48).

WEIZMANN, Chaim (1874–1952), Polish-born Zionist leader, first president of Israel from 1949. He emigrated to England in 1904 and became an eminent biochemist and director of the British Admiralty laboratories in 1916. He helped secure the BALFOUR DECLARATION (1917), which promised a Jewish state in Palestine. He was head of the World Zionist Organization (1920–29) and of the Jewish Agency (1929–31, 1935–46). (See ZIONISM.)

WELCH, William Henry (1850–1934), US pathologist and bacteriologist whose most significant achievements were in the field of medical education, playing a large part in the founding (1893) and development of the Johns Hopkins Medical School.

WELD, Theodore Dwight (1803–1895), US abolitionist, a founder of the American Antislavery Society (1833–34). He organized 70 agents to campaign in the North, edited the *Emancipator*, lobbied Congress and wrote the influential *American Slavery As It Is* (1839), a basis for H. B. STOWE's *Uncle Tom's Cabin.*

WELDING, bringing two pieces of metal together under conditions of heat or pressure or both, until they coalesce at the joint. The oldest method is forge welding, in which the surfaces to be joined are heated to welding temperature and then hammered together on an anvil. The most widely used method today is metal-arc welding: an electric arc is struck between an electrode and the workpieces to be joined, and molten metal from a "filler rod"—usually the electrode itself—is added. Gas welding, now largely displaced by metal-arc welding, is usually accomplished by means of an oxyacetylene torch, which delivers the necessary heat by burning acetylene in a pure OXYGEN atmosphere. Sources of heat in other forms of welding include the electrical RESISTANCE of the joint (resistance welding), an electric arc at the joint (flash welding), a focused beam of ELECTRONS (electron-beam welding), pressure alone, usually well in excess of 1,400,000kPa (cold welding), and friction (friction welding). Some more recently applied heat sources include hot PLASMAS, LASERS, ULTRASONIC vibrations and explosive impacts.

WELFARE, federal, state, and local programs that provide both cash and noncash (in-kind) benefits to the needy. The principal cash programs are AID TO FAMILIES WITH DEPENDENT CHILDREN (AFDC), SUPPLEMENTAL SECURITY INCOME (SSI), veterans pensions, emergency assistance, and state and local general assistance. The chief in-kind programs are FOOD STAMPS, child nutrition, MEDICAID, and housing assistance.

Until the 1930s, aid to the needy was the concern of private charities and of state and local welfare agencies. The onset of the GREAT DEPRESSION quickly exhausted the resources of those institutions. In 1933, the Roosevelt administration established the Federal Relief Administration (FEA) to funnel federal funds into state welfare channels. At the same time, the US Department of Agriculture began to distribute surplus agricultural commodities to the needy. These emergency measures of public assistance, and others that followed, were intended as temporary expedients until a revived economy reabsorbed the great numbers of unemployed.

The architects of the Social Security Act of 1935 envisioned a future in which comprehensive social insurance would obviate the need for public assistance. That act created a national income-transfer system — that is, a system by which revenues derived from the better-off portions of the population were used to maintain minimal incomes for the needy portions — with both social-insurance and public-assistance components. The social-insurance component consisted of a federal program of old-age insurance, the original element of the SOCIAL SECURITY system, and a federal-state system of UNEMPLOYMENT INSURANCE. Under both programs, payroll taxes paid by workers and their employers were used to provide incomes for workers who lost their jobs or retired. The public-assistance or welfare component consisted of the provision of federal funds to supplement state programs of public assistance to the aged and blind and to dependent children. Benefits under these programs were based only on need, not on previous contributions.

The authors of the Social Security Act were mistaken in their belief that social insurance would eventually end the need for welfare. The steady expansion of social insurance has been accompanied by a remarkable growth in the size of the nation's welfare system. New welfare programs have been established to meet newly perceived needs. Demographic changes have resulted in greater numbers of people eligible for welfare — for example, the elderly and single mothers. And the participation of eligible citizens has grown as a result of informational campaigns conducted by welfare-rights ogranizations, of court decisions removing arbitrarily restrictive regulations, and of outreach programs conducted by welfare departments themselves.

The Welfare Reform Act of 1988 redefined welfare as a temporary and transitional expedient, requiring that welfare recipients take jobs or job training to prepare for independence.

WELL, man-made hole in the ground used to tap water, gas or minerals from the earth. Most modern wells are drilled and fitted with a lining, usually of steel, to forestall collapse. Though wells are sunk for NATURAL GAS and PETROLEUM oil, the commonest type yields water. Such wells may be horizontal or vertical, but all have their innermost end below the water table (see GROUNDWATER). If it should be below the permanent water table (the lowest annual level of the water table) the well will yield water throughout the year. Most wells require to be pumped, but some operate under natural pressure (see ARTESIAN WELL).

WELLAND SHIP CANAL, Canadian waterway running 27.6mi from Port Colborne on Lake Erie to Port Weller on Lake Ontario to form a major link of the SAINT LAWRENCE SEAWAY AND GREAT LAKES WATERWAY. The canal was built 1912–32, modernized in 1972 and has a minimum depth of about 30ft. It has eight locks to overcome the 326ft difference in height between lakes Erie and Ontario.

WELLES, Gideon (1802–1878), US politician who helped organize the Republican party. Made secretary of the navy (1861–69) by Lincoln, during the CIVIL WAR he blockaded the Confederate coast and built up a powerful Union fleet of IRONCLADS.

WELLES, Orson (1915–1985), US actor, director and producer. In 1938 his Mercury Theater's realistic radio production of H. G. WELLS' *War of the Worlds* made thousands of listeners panic. His first motion picture, of which he was director, co-writer, and star, was *Citizen Kane* (1941), loosely modeled on the life of newspaper magnate W. R. HEARST. Innovative camera work and film editing continued to characterize his work in such films as *The Magnificent Ambersons* (1942), *The Lady from Shanghai* (1947), *Macbeth* (1948) and *Touch of Evil* (1958).

WELLES, Sumner (1892–1961), US diplomat, chief architect of President F. D. Roosevelt's "Good Neighbor Policy." He served as assistant secretary (1933; 1934–37) and later under secretary of state (1937–43) for Latin American affairs.

WELLESLEY, Richard Colley Wellesley, Marquess (1760–1842), British statesman in India. As governor general of Bengal and governor of Madras (1797–1805) he greatly extended British authority in India. When lord lieutenant of Ireland (1821–28, 1833–34), he favored CATHOLIC EMANCIPATION.

WELLINGTON, Arthur Wellesley, 1st Duke of (1769–1852), British general and statesman, "the Iron Duke," who defeated NAPOLEON I at the battle of WATERLOO. After distinguished military service in India (1796–1805), he drove the French from Spain and Portugal in the PENINSULAR WAR and entered France in 1813. After being created duke, he led the victorious forces at Waterloo (1815). Serving the Tory government 1819–27, he became prime minister (1828–30), passed the CATHOLIC EMANCIPATION ACT but opposed Parliamentary reform. In 1842 he became commander-in-chief for life.

WELLINGTON, city, capital of New Zealand since 1865, at the S of North Island. Founded in 1840, it is the nation's second largest city and an important port and transportation center. Pop 342,000.

WELLS, Henry (1805–1878), US pioneer expressman. Associated with W. FARGO from 1844, he founded Wells, Fargo and Co. (1852) to supply express mail to Cal. and the West. By acquiring the Overland Mail Company (1866) he owned the greatest US stagecoach network.

WELLS, H(erbert) G(eorge) (1866–1946), British writer and social reformer. A draper's apprentice, he studied science and taught. After such early science-fiction as *The Time Machine* (1895) and *The War of the Worlds* (1898), he wrote novels on the lower middle class, including *Kipps* (1905) and *The History of Mr. Polly* (1910). A founder of the FABIAN SOCIETY, he became a social prophet (*A Modern Utopia*; 1905). After WWI he popularized knowledge in *Outline of History* (1920) and *The Science of Life* (1931).

WELLS, Horace (1815–1848), US dentist and pioneer of surgical ANESTHESIA, using (largely without success) nitrous oxide (see NITROGEN).

WELSBACH, Carl Auer von, Baron (1858–1929), Austrian chemist who invented the incandescent gas mantle (patented 1885) and the ALLOY, Auer metal, used to make lighter flints.

WELSH, one of the Brythonic group of CELTIC LANGUAGES, still widely spoken in Wales. There is a rich literature, particularly of poetry.

WELTY, Eudora (1909–   ), US novelist and short-story writer, known for sensitive tales of Miss. life. She superbly depicted atmosphere and characters in *The Wide Net* (1943), *The Ponder Heart* (1954), *The Optimist's Daughter* (1972; Pulitzer Prize) and others.

WEN, or sebaceous CYST, blocked sebaceous gland, often over the scalp or forehead, which forms a cyst containing old sebum under the SKIN. It may become infected. Its excision is a simple procedure.

WENCESLAUS, Saint (c907–929), duke of Bohemia, famous for his efforts to Christianize his people. The song *Good King Wenceslaus* refers to him.

WENCESLAUS (1361–1419), Holy Roman Emperor, king of Germany (1378–1400) and of Bohemia (1378–1419). Often drunk and indolent, he failed to prevent wars among German princes, cities and nobility. Deposed as German king and emperor, he also lost effective power in Bohemia.

WENDS, or **Sorbs,** Slavic people who by the 5th century settled between the Elbe and Oder rivers, Germany. German conquest of the Wends lasted from the 6th to the 12th century, by which date many Wends were Christianized. Today Wends are found in Lusatia.

WEREWOLF (Old English: man-wolf), in superstition, a man who can supernaturally turn into a wolf and devour humans. The belief dates from Greek legend and was widespread in medieval Europe and in the 19th-century Balkans.

WERFEL, Franz (1890–1945), Austrian novelist, poet and playwright, whose early plays and poetry such as *Der Spiegelmensch* (1920) were important works of German EXPRESSIONISM. His novels include *Embezzled Heaven* (1939) and *The Song of Bernadette* (1941).

WERNER, Abraham Gottlob (1750–1817), Silesian-born mineralogist who taught for over 40 years at the Freiberg Mining Academy, disseminating the doctrines of NEPTUNISM.

WERTHEIMER, Max (1880–1943), German psychologist who founded (with Kurt Koffka and Wolfgang Köhler) the school of GESTALT PSYCHOLOGY. He taught at Frankfurt and Berlin before emigrating to the US (1933), and wrote *Productive Thinking* (1945).

WESKER, Arnold (1932–   ), English playwright, one of the "angry young men" to emerge in England in 1956. His early plays, such as the trilogy *Chicken Soup with Barley* (1958), *Roots* (1959) and *I'm Talking about Jerusalem* (1960), are committed to the ideals of socialism. The later, more introspective *Chips with Everything* (1962) and *The Friends* (1970) explore themes of "private pain."

WESLEY, name of two evangelistic preachers who with George WHITEFIELD founded Methodism (see METHODISTS). **John Wesley** (1703–1791) and his brother **Charles** (1707–1788) formed an Oxford "Holy Club" of scholarly Christians, known as "Methodists" for their "rule and methods." In 1738 the brothers were profoundly influenced by the MORAVIAN CHURCH and John particularly by LUTHER'S *Preface to the Epistle to the Romans.* Aiming to promote "vital, practical religion" the Wesleys took up evangelistic work by field or open-air preaching. Rejected by the church, they were enthusiastically received by the people, and they organized conferences of itinerant lay preachers. Charles composed more than 5,500 hymns.

WESSEX, Anglo-Saxon kingdom in S England, roughly comprising modern Somerset, Dorset, Wiltshire and Hampshire. Probably first settled by the SAXON Cedric in 495, it was at its largest under King Egbert (802–39). ALFRED THE GREAT (871–99) checked the Danish invasions and by 927 Ethelstan had overturned DANELAW and controlled all England. Thomas HARDY revived the name in his novels.

WEST, Benjamin (1738–1820), American-born painter. After studying in Rome he settled in London (1763), becoming official history painter to King George III and a founder of the ROYAL ACADEMY OF ARTS. His best-known works are *The Death of General Wolfe* (1771) and *Penn's Treaty with the Indians* (1776).

WEST, Mae (1892–1980), US stage and screen actress who was the sultry mistress of provocative innuendo and a sex symbol of Hollywood films of the 1930s. Frequently at odds with the censors, she immortalized the phrase "come up 'n' see me sometime" and starred in such movies as *She Done Him Wrong* (1933), *I'm No Angel* (1933) and *My Little Chickadee* (1940).

WEST, Nathanael (1903–1940), pseudonym of Nathan Weinstein, US novelist. His satiric novels, *Miss Lonelyhearts* (1933), the story of an agony columnist, and *The Day of the Locust* (1939) are bitter and disturbing, with sudden flashes of humor.

WEST, Dame Rebecca (Cicily Isabel Fairfield; 1892–1983), British novelist, critic and journalist. *Black Lamb and Grey Falcon: A Journey through Yugoslavia* (1941) is perhaps her finest work. Her novels include *Birds Fall Down* (1966).

WEST BANK, uplands to the west of the Dead Sea and Jordan River, occupied by Jordan 1948–67 and by Israel since 1967. Historically known as Judea and Samaria, the West Bank contains such famous cities as Bethlehem, Jericho, Hebron, and the Old City of Jerusalem. The status of the West Bank, along with that of the Gaza Strip in southwestern Israel, has been at the center of most Arab-Israeli disputes. The Camp David Agreement of 1978 between Egypt and Israel specified that the 1.3 million Palestinian Arabs in the two areas would be given "full autonomy and self-government" for a five-year period during which the ultimate sovereignty of the territories would be determined. The parties, however, failed to agree about the details of self-government. At the same time, Israeli settlements in the West Bank multiplied. West Bank Arabs launched an uprising in Dec. 1987 in an effort to end Israeli occupation. In 1988, as the uprising continued, Jordan severed all legal and administrative ties to the area.

WESTERMARCK, Edward Alexander (1862–1939), Finnish anthropologist and philosopher. He was equally famous for *The History of Human Marriage* (1891), which demonstrated the importance of monogamy, and for *The Origin and Development of Moral Ideas* (1906–08), in which he held that morality was based on social approval, not truth.

WESTERN CHURCH, one of the two great branches of the Christian Church (see EASTERN CHURCH). The Latin-speaking church of the western Roman empire, it was increasingly dominated by Roman usage and by the papacy, whose claims of supremacy grew and were enforced. It thus developed into the ROMAN CATHOLIC CHURCH, though the Protestant churches formed at the Reformation share the common Western tradition. (See also CHRISTIANITY; GREAT SCHISM.)

WESTERN EUROPEAN UNION (WEU), defensive economic, social and cultural alliance (1955) among Belgium, France, Great Britain, Italy, Luxembourg, the Netherlands and West Germany. It supervised German rearmament. The Council of Europe took over its economic and cultural activities (1960).

WESTERN FEDERATION OF MINERS (WFM), radical US miners' union of the W states formed in 1893. In its earlier days it clashed with federal, state and company forces. In 1905 WFM leader W. D. HAYWOOD, falsely charged, was acquitted of a former governor's murder. The WFM cofounded the INDUSTRIAL WORKERS OF THE WORLD (1905), seceded to rejoin (1911) the AMERICAN FEDERATION OF LABOR and became the International Union of Mine, Mill and Smelter Workers (1916).

WESTERN FICTION, an enduring genre in US literature and the performing arts. Its setting is the plains, mountains and canyons of the West between the end of the Civil War and 1900. Familiar characters are the lanky cowboy, the homesteader's sweet young daughter, the hard-bitten pioneer, the taciturn lawman, the sinister gunslinger and the American Indian—sometimes noble, sometimes savage. The simple recurring themes are love, friendship, greed and determination to tame the wild land. In the early dime novels by Ned Buntline, Zane Grey, Luke Short and others, a lone man on horseback prevails over an outlaw, rustler or renegade Indian. Other novelists, including Owen WISTER (*The Virginian*) and A. B. Guthrie (*The Big Sky*), paid more attention to historical detail. Western films have ranged from dusty shoot'-em-ups to serious dramas by directors like John FORD. Gary Cooper and John Wayne were but two of many Western film heroes. Radio and television presented such continuing adventures as *The Lone Ranger*, *Death Valley Days*, *Gunsmoke* and *Bonanza*, and revived the early movies of such cowboy stars as William Boyd (Hopalong Cassidy). Writers such as Louis L'Amour continue to churn out Western fiction for a market that never seems to flag.

WESTERNIZERS, in Russian history. See SLAVOPHILES AND WESTERNIZERS.

WESTERN RESERVE, NE region of Ohio on the S shore of Lake Erie. In 1786, Conn. refused to cede this area to the NORTHWEST TERRITORY. In 1792, 500,000 acres were granted to Conn. citizens whose land was destroyed during the Revolution. The remaining land was sold to a land company which built Cleveland. The region joined the Northwest Territory 1800.

WESTERN SAHARA, former Spanish province in NW Africa, comprising 102,680sq mi of, mainly, desert on the Atlantic coast, rich in phosphate deposits. Despite active independence movements among native Arabs and Berbers, it was formally divided between neighboring Morocco and Mauritania in 1976. Mauritania renounced its claims in 1979, but Morocco continued to battle Polisario Front guerrillas demanding independence and constructed a series of defensive walls that eventually enclosed most of the territory. In 1988, Morocco and the Polisario Front agreed in principle to accept a UN peace plan calling for a cease-fire and a referendum to determine Western Sahara's future.

WESTERN SAMOA, independent state in the SW Pacific Ocean, comprising two large islands, Savai'i and Upolu, and seven smaller islands, only two of which are inhabited.

Land. Most of the islands are mountainous, volcanic, forested and fertile. The climate is rainy and tropical.

People and Economy. The people are Polynesian and the majority live in Upolu, where Apia, the capital and chief port, stands. Samoans speak probably the oldest Polynesian language in use. The economy is agricultural, the main exports being copra, bananas and cacao. Tourism is also important; more than 40,000 tourists visited

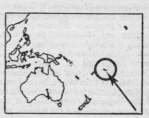

Official name: The Independent State of Western Samoa
Capital: Apia
Area: 1,093sq mi
Population: 161,000
Languages: Samoan; English
Religion: Christian
Monetary unit(s): 1 Western Samoa tala = 100 sene

the country in 1985. The current development program, backed by foreign aid, aims to expand agriculture and encourage modest industrialization (e.g., soap, lumber).

History. The islands were probably discovered by the Dutch explorer Jacob Roggeveen (1722). Germany, Great Britain and the US jointly administered the islands 1889–99 and agreed in 1899 that SAMOA should be divided between the US and Germany. In 1914 New Zealand seized German Samoa, later administering it by League of Nations mandate, and as a UN trust territory. It became independent as Western Samoa in 1962. It joined the UN in 1976.

WEST FLORIDA CONTROVERSIES, two disputes between the US and Spain over a strip of Gulf coast between East Florida (approximately the present state of Fla.) and the Mississippi R. The first dispute, concerning the N boundary of West Florida, was settled in favor of the US in PINCKNEY'S TREATY (1795). The second dispute arose after the LOUISIANA PURCHASE (1803), the US claiming that West Florida was included in the purchase because it had been part of Louisiana when that region had belonged to Spain. American settlers moved into the disputed area and revolted against Spanish rule, and West Florida was incorporated into the US territories of Orleans and Mississippi. Spain finally renounced its claims to West Florida and also ceded East Florida to the US in the ADAMS-ONIS TREATY (1819).

WEST INDIES, chain of islands extending from Fla. to the N coast of South America, separating the Caribbean Sea and the Gulf of Mexico from the Atlantic Ocean. An alternative name (excluding the Bahamas) is the Antilles. The West Indies comprises three main groups: the Bahamas to the NE of Cuba and Hispaniola; the Greater Antilles (Cuba—the largest island in the West Indies, Hispaniola, Jamaica and Puerto Rico); and the Lesser Antilles (Leeward and Windward Islands, Trinidad and Tobago and Barbados); together with the Netherlands Antilles and other islands off the Venezuelan coast. Many of the islands are mountainous and volcanic with lagoons and mangrove swamps on their coastlines. The climate is warm but there are frequent hurricanes. The principal crop is sugarcane. Tourism is an important industry. After COLUMBUS reached the West Indies (1492) they were settled by the Spanish followed by the English, French and Dutch, who exploited the spices and sugar, using African slaves. The political status of the islands varies widely.

WESTINGHOUSE, George (1846–1914), US engineer, inventor and businessman who pioneered the use of high-voltage AC electricity. In 1869 he founded the Westinghouse Air Brake Company to develop the air BRAKES he had invented for RAILROAD use. From 1883 he did pioneering work on the safe transmission of NATURAL GAS. In 1886 he founded the Westinghouse Electric Company, employing notably TESLA, to develop AC induction motors and transmission equipment: this company was largely responsible for the acceptance of AC in preference to DC for most applications—in spite of opposition from the influential EDISON.

WESTMINSTER, Statute of (1931), British parliamentary act abolishing Britain's power to legislate for its dominions. It gave the dominions complete independence in the COMMONWEALTH OF NATIONS although they owed common allegiance to the British crown.

WESTMINSTER ABBEY, great English Gothic church in London, traditional scene of English coronations since that of WILLIAM the Conqueror, and a burial place for English monarchs and famous subjects. The present building, started in 1245, is on the site of a church (1065) built by EDWARD THE CONFESSOR.

WESTMINSTER   CONFESSION, Reformation confession of faith (see CREED) forming the subordinate doctrinal standard of most REFORMED CHURCHES. A detailed statement of CALVINISM, it was produced 1643–46 by the Westminster Assembly, a synod called by the LONG PARLIAMENT to reform the Church of England. The assembly also issued the two Westminster Catechisms. (See also PURITANS.)

WESTMORELAND,   William   Childs (1914–   ), US general, army chief of staff 1968–72. He was superintendent of WEST POINT 1960–63 and the US commander in Vietnam 1964–68.

WESTON, Edward (1886–1958), US photographer, one of the most influential of the 20th century. He aimed for clarity of detail (using large-view cameras and small apertures) and composition, and seldom cropped, enlarged or touched up. His best work is of still lifes, nudes and sand dunes.

WESTPHALIA, Peace of, treaties signed by Sweden, France, Spain, the Holy Roman Empire and the Netherlands concluding the THIRTY YEARS' WAR in 1648. The treaties recognized the sovereignty of the German states of the Holy Roman Empire; declared the Netherlands and Switzerland independent republics; and granted religious freedom to Calvinists and Lutherans in Germany. Sweden acquired W Pomerania and Stettin; France Alsace, Metz, Toul and Verdun; and Brandenburg E Pomerania.

WEST POINT, site of, and common name for, the US Military Academy in SE N.Y., an institute of higher education which trains officers for the regular army. Established by Act of Congress in 1802, its training methods and traditions were set down by Colonel Sylvanus Thayer, superintendent of the academy 1817–33. Candidates for entry (since 1976 of either sex) to the academy must be unmarried US citizens aged 17–22 and must meet minimum academic requirements. Cadets are enlisted in the regular army on entrance. Graduates are awarded a BS and a commission as 2nd lieutenant, and are expected to serve in the army for at least four years.

WEST VIRGINIA, state in E US in the heart of the Appalachians. It is bordered on the N by Ohio, Penn. and Md., on the E by Va.; S by N.C. and Tenn., and W by Ky.

Land. Most of West Virginia lies in the Appalachian Plateau, whose E edge is formed by the hills of Allegheny Front (over 4,500ft), the state's highest area. In the NE the Blue Ridge Mountains region is an area of fertile slopes and river valleys. The state's rugged terrain has the highest average elevation (over 1,500ft) E of the Mississippi. The chief rivers are the Ohio, on the NW border, the Potomac and the Kanawtha. The climate is mild, the annual temperature range 34–70°F, and the annual rainfall about 45 in. Much of the land is forested.

Population. West Virginia is 60% rural. Most urban dwellers live in the industrial centers along the river valleys. Charleston

Name of state: West Virginia
Capital: Charleston
Statehood: June 20, 1863 (35th state)
Familiar name: Mountain State; Panhandle State
Area: 24,181sq mi
Population: 1,918,000
Elevation: Highest—4,863ft, Spruce Knob Lowest—240ft, Potomac River
Motto: *Montani semper liberi* ("Mountaineers are always free")
State flower: Rhododendron
State bird: Cardinal
State tree: Sugar maple
State songs: "The West Virginia Hills," "This is My West Virginia," "West Virginia, My Home Sweet Home"
and Huntington are the largest cities. Over 95% of the people are white.
Economy. The economy is dominated by manufacturing and mining. Its prosperity has long been dependent on its bituminous COAL industry, but today other minerals such as natural gas, petroleum, stone and sand are also exploited. Leading industries produce chemicals, iron and steel. Lumber is a significant resource. Farming is largely confined to the fertile river valleys.
History. West Virginia's history until 1861 is essentially that of VIRGINIA, although West Virginia was distinguished by its isolation from the state capital, the fact that few West Virginians owned slaves, and its economy—small-scale farming and industries based on mineral resources. In 1861 the West Virginians refused to secede from the Union with Va. They declared their independence, adopted a constitution (1862) and became the 35th state to join the Union in 1863.

In the early 20th century, the state's rapid expansion in the coal, gas and steel industries was accompanied by severe labor-management conflicts and by riots, notably in the mines, which were resolved only by the NEW DEAL legislation. Nevertheless, the state remained poor, the land and water resources damaged by coal strip mining, and many people left the state. In 1988 the population was less than it was in

1950. Major efforts have been made to attract new industry, alleviate poverty, and control strip mining. But unemployment is twice the national average, and the state's economic future remains uncertain. In presidential elections 1968–88, West Virginia voted Democratic in 1968, 1976–80, and 1988.

WEYDEN, Rogier Van der (c1400–1464), Flemish painter, the most influential painter of his period. Influenced by VAN EYCK, he is noted for his tragic and emotional depiction of the scenes of the Passion such as *Descent from the Cross* (c1435) and *Calvary Triptych* (c1440–45). His portraits have the same intensity.

WEYL, Hermann (1885–1955), German mathematician and mathematical physicist noted for his contributions to the theories of RELATIVITY and QUANTUM MECHANICS.

WEYLER Y NICOLAU, Valeriano, Marqués de Tenerife (1838–1930), Spanish soldier, governor and military commander of Cuba 1896–97, whose ruthless handling of the Cuban rebellion outraged US public opinion; he was recalled to Spain.

WEYPRECHT, Karl (1838–1881), German Arctic explorer, whose advocacy of internationally coordinated polar exploration led to the first International Polar Year (1882–83). His 1872–74 expedition with Julius von Payer discovered Franz Josef Land.

WHALES, an order, Cetacea, of large wholly-aquatic mammals. All are highly-adapted for life in water, with a torpedo-shaped body, front limbs reduced and modified as steering paddles, and hind limbs absent. They have a tail of two transverse flukes and swim by up-and-down movements of this tail. Most species have a fleshy dorsal fin which acts as a stabilizer. The neck is short, the head flowing directly into the trunk. The body is hairless and the smooth skin lies over a thick layer of blubber which has an insulating function but also acts to smooth out the passage of water over the body in rapid swimming. The nose, or blowhole, is at the top of the head, allowing the animal to breathe as soon as it breaks the surface of the water. Modern whales divide into two suborders, the Mysticeti, or whalebone whales, and the Odontoceti, or toothed whales. Whalebone whales feed on PLANKTON straining the enormous quantities they require from the water with special plates of whalebone, or baleen, developed from the mucus membrane of the upper jaw. Whalebone whales, the right whales, rorqual and gray whales, are usually large and slow-moving. The group includes the blue whale, the largest animal of all time. Toothed whales, equipped with conical teeth, feed on fishes and squids. With the sperm whale and NARWHAL, the group also includes the DOLPHINS and PORPOISES.

WHALING, the hunting of WHALES, originally for oil, meat and baleen, practiced since the 900s if not earlier. The Basques and Dutch hunted from land and pioneered methods of flensing and boiling whale meat. American whaling started in the 1600s, and whaling ports such as Nantucket and New Bedford grew to great size in the 1700s. Whaling became safer after the invention (1856) of harpoons with explosive heads which caused instantaneous death and avoided the dangerous pursuit of a wounded whale. From the 1800s, whalers moved S in pursuit of the sperm whale. Development of factory ships which processed the catch on board facilitated longer expeditions. In the 1900s whaling has centered on Antarctic waters. Reconaissance aircraft and electronic aids are now used. Whale products include oils, AMBERGRIS, spermaceti, meat and bone meal. Despite the (voluntary) restrictions of the International Whaling Convention, whales are still overfished, and many species face extinction.

WHARTON, Edith (1862–1937), US novelist, poet, and short-story writer, a friend of Henry JAMES. She wrote subtle and acerbic accounts of society in New York, New England and Europe, including *The House of Mirth* (1905), *Ethan Frome* (1911) and *The Age of Innocence* (1920, Pulitzer Prize).

WHEAT, *Triticum aestivum*, the world's main CEREAL CROP; about 300 million tons are produced every year, mostly used to make flour for bread and pasta. Wheat has been in cultivation since at least 7000BC and grows best in temperate regions of Europe, America, China and Australia. The USSR is the largest producer, followed by the US and Canada. There are many varieties of wheat and different parts of the grain are used to produce the various types of flour. Grains comprise an outer husk called the bran and a central starchy germ (which is embedded in a PROTEIN known as GLUTEN). Wheat is graded as hard or soft depending on how easily the flour can be separated from the bran. Wheat for bread is hard wheat and contains a lot of gluten. Soft wheat flours containing more STARCH and less protein are used for pastries. There are two main types of wheat; these are sown either in the fall (winter wheat) or in the spring (spring wheat). Harvesting is carried out by combine harvesters which cut and

thresh the crop in one operation. Wheat is vulnerable to several diseases including smut, rust, army worm and Hessian fly. Family: Graminae.

WHEATLEY, Phillis (c1753–1784), black US poet. Born in Africa, she was sold to John Wheatley of Boston, who educated her. Her *Poems on Various Subjects, Religious and Moral* was published in London in 1773.

WHEATSTONE, Sir Charles (1802–1875), British physicist and inventor who popularized the "Wheatstone bridge" for measuring voltages; and invented the electric TELEGRAPH (with the help of Joseph HENRY) before MORSE (1837), the STEREOSCOPE (1838) and the concertina (1829).

WHEATSTONE BRIDGE, an electric circuit used for comparing or measuring resistance. Four resistors, including the unknown one, are connected in a square, with a BATTERY between one pair of diagonally opposite corners and a sensitive galvanometer between the other. When no current flows through the meter, the products of opposite pairs of resistances are equal. Similar bridge circuits are used for impedance measurement.

WHEEL, disk-like mechanical device mediating between rotary and linear motion, widely used to transmit POWER, store ENERGY (the flywheel), and facilitate the movement of heavy objects. Wheels may be solid or spoked, flanged or unflanged, with or without TIRES. Most usefully, they are attached to an axle through the center. Indeed, the wheel and axle is one of the classic simple MACHINES, exemplified in the capstan, the WINCH and transmission gears.

WHEELER, Burton Kendall (1882–1975), US senator from Mont. 1923–47. A Democrat, he ran in 1924 as vice-presidential candidate for the Progressive Party. In WWII he advocated isolationism.

WHEELER, Joseph (1836–1906), US Confederate cavalry general. He fought, often brilliantly, in the Kentucky, Chatanooga and Atlanta Civil War campaigns. He held commands 1898–1900 in the Spanish-American War (in Cuba) and in the Philippines.

WHEELOCK, Eleazar (1711–1779), American educator, Congregationalist preacher and founder of Dartmouth College. He ran a free school for Indians at Lebanon, Conn. (1754–67), and founded Dartmouth College and the town of Hanover, N.H., in 1770.

WHEWELL, William (1794–1866), English philosopher, historian of science, and master of Trinity College, Cambridge

(1841–66). His interests ranged from mineralogy to moral philosophy, but he is chiefly remembered for his *Philosophy of the Inductive Sciences* (1840), which reflected his study of KANT and led to a famous controversy with J. S. MILL.

WHIG, an English and a US political party. In England, the term was applied in 1679 to Protestant opponents of the English Crown led by SHAFTESBURY (see GLORIOUS REVOLUTION). The Whigs enjoyed a period of dominance c1714–60, notably under Robert WALPOLE. Largely out of office under Charles FOX, they were increasingly associated with Nonconformism, mercantile, industrial and reforming interests. After the Whig ministries of 2nd Earl GREY and Lord MELBOURNE, the Whigs helped form the LIBERAL PARTY in the mid 1800s.

The US Whig Party was formed c1836 from diverse opponents, including the NATIONAL REPUBLICANS, of Andrew JACKSON and the Democrats. Its leaders were Henry CLAY and Daniel WEBSTER, and a national economic policy was its principal platform. Whig President W. H. HARRISON died in office and was succeeded 1841 by John TYLER, who was disowned by the Whigs when he vetoed their tariff and banking bills. Clay, the next Whig candidate, lost the 1844 election. During the second Whig presidency (1849–53; Zachary TAYLOR and Millard FILLMORE), the party was already divided by the issues of slavery and national expansion; the COMPROMISE OF 1850 did not last and Winfield SCOTT was heavily defeated in the 1852 election. The party never recovered, and many Whigs joined the new REPUBLICAN PARTY.

WHIP, in US and British politics, party member of a legislative body chosen to enforce party discipline in voting and attendance. The first US whip, Republican congressman James E. Watson, was appointed in 1899.

WHIPPLE, Abraham (1733–1819), American naval officer noted for his successes in the Revolutionary War. In 1779 he captured 11 ships of the British Jamaica fleet. In 1780 he defended Charleston, S.C., but was captured when the city fell.

WHIRLPOOL, a rotary current in water. Permanent whirlpools may arise in the ocean from the interactions of the TIDES (see OCEAN CURRENTS). They occur also in streams or rivers where two currents meet or the shape of the channel dictates. Short-lived whirlpools may be created by wind.

WHIRLWIND, rotating column of air caused by a pocket of low atmospheric pressure formed—unlike a TORNADO—near ground level by surface heating. They are far less violent than tornadoes. Whirlwinds passing over dry dusty country are sometimes called "dust devils."

WHISKEY, strong spirituous distilled liquor, drunk mixed or neat, made from grain. When from Scotland or Canada, whisky is spelt without an "e". The ingredients and preparation vary. In the US corn and rye are commonly used: 51% corn for *bourbon whiskey* and 51% rye for *rye whiskey*. A grain mash is allowed to ferment, then distilled, diluted and left to age. Bourbon and rye whiskey stand in oak barrels for four years. *Canadian whisky* is made from corn, rye and malted (germinated) barley and aged for 4–12 years. *Irish whiskey* uses barley, wheat, oats and rye, and vessels called potstills for the distilling process. *Scotch whisky* is the finest form: the best types are pure barley malt or grain whiskies, but blended varieties are cheaper. The secret of its flavor is supposed to be the peat-flavored water of certain Scottish streams. Whiskey is one of the most popular of alcoholic beverages. In the US an average of 16 bottles per person are drunk every year.

WHISKEY REBELLION, 1794, uprising of W. Pa., mainly Scotch-Irish farmer settlers against the federal excise tax imposed on whiskey by secretary of the treasury HAMILTON in 1791. Federal officers were attacked, some were tarred and feathered and one had his house burnt down. Resistance increased when official measures were taken to obtain the tax. At Hamilton's insistence, President Washington sent in 13,000 militiamen to suppress the insurgents. They met no resistance, and Washington pardoned two ringleaders convicted of treason. Federalists claimed a victory—the federal government had demonstrated the power to enforce its law.

WHISKEY RING, US scandal exposed in 1875. Distillers in St. Louis, Chicago, Milwaukee and elsewhere had evaded tax through payments to Republican Party funds and individuals. The investigations of treasury secretary Bristow led to 237 indictments (including the chief treasury clerk and the president's private secretary) and 110 convictions. President Grant was cleared personally, but his party damaged.

WHIST, four-player card game. A 52-card pack is evenly dealt and the last card exposed to show trumps. Partners (facing players) aim to win tricks. Played in 17th-century England, it became popular and fashionable in the 1800s and 1900s. Solo whist and BRIDGE were 19th-century developments.

WHISTLER, James Abbott McNeill (1834–1903), US painter, etcher, and wit who lived in Paris and London. He advocated "art for art's sake," and stressed simplicity of color and design, as in the famous portrait of his mother, *Arrangement in Gray and Black* (1872), and *Falling Rocket: Nocturne in Black and Gold* (1874). His etchings were among the finest of his day, and his decorated interiors foreshadowed ART NOUVEAU.

WHITBY, Synod of, held 663 or 664 in the kingdom of Northumbria, England, to decide between Celtic and Roman church usage. King Oswy chose Roman practice, thus affecting not only the reckoning of Easter but linking the English church more closely with that of the rest of Europe.

WHITE, Andrew Dickson (1832–1918), US educator and diplomat, first president (1867–85) of Cornell U., founded as a nonsectarian university based on his liberal principles. He was a N.Y. senator 1864–67, US ambassador to Germany 1897–1903 and led the US delegation to the 1899 Hague peace conference.

WHITE, Byron Raymond (1917–   ), US jurist. Once famous as a professional football player, he was appointed by President Kennedy as US deputy attorney general (1961) and associate justice of the Supreme Court (1962–   ).

WHITE, Edward Douglass (1845–1921), US jurist. A judge of the La. supreme court 1879–80, US senator 1890–94 and associate justice of the US Supreme Court from 1894, he was appointed chief justice by Taft in 1910. Generally a conservative, he wrote the "rule of reason" into antitrust law.

WHITE, E(lwyn) B(rooks) (1899–1985), US writer noted for his witty, well-crafted essays in the *New Yorker* (from 1926) and *Harper's* (1938–43). His work includes poems, the satire *Is Sex Necessary?* (1929, with THURBER), and such children's books as *Charlotte's Web* (1952).

WHITE, Gilbert (1720–1793), English naturalist, author of *The Natural History and Antiquities of Selbourne* (1788), a finely written early classic of precise observation of a Hampshire village, in the form of delightful letters to two friends.

WHITE, Minor (1908–1976), US photographer associated with Ansel ADAMS, Alfred STIEGLITZ and Edward WESTON. Known also as a mystical and abstract artist, he co-founded (1952) and edited the journal *Aperture* and taught at several schools, including MIT (1965–74).

WHITE, Patrick (1912–   ), Australian novelist, winner of the 1973 Nobel Prize for Literature. His long novels, set mostly in Australia, include *The Tree of Man* (1955), *Voss* (1957), *Riders in the Chariot* (1961), *The Vivisector* (1970), and *The Eye of the Storm* (1974).

WHITE, Pearl (1889–1939), popular US actress in early silent movies, heroine of such serials as *The Perils of Pauline*, noted for the cliff-hanging ending to each short episode.

WHITE, Peregrine (1620–1704), first New-England-born child of English parentage. Born Nov. 20 abroad the *Mayflower* in Cape Cod Bay, he settled in Marshfield, Mass.

WHITE, Stanford (1853–1906), US architect, noted for interior and decorative work. He cofounded (1879) the famous firm McKim, Mead, and White. Their work developed from domestic Shingle Style to "Beaux Arts" classical-Renaissance, as in the 1890 Madison Square Garden and the Century Club, New York. He was shot dead by the husband of his mistress Evelyn Nesbit Thaw.

WHITE, T(erence) H(anbury) (1906–1964), English novelist, noted for *The Once and Future King* (four books, 1938–58), a retelling of the legends of King Arthur (adapted for the musical *Camelot*) and *The Goshawk* (1951).

WHITE, Walter Francis (1893–1955), US black leader, from 1931 secretary of the National Association for the Advancement of Colored People. His works include his autobiography, *A Man Called White* (1948).

WHITE, William (1748–1836), American clergyman who led the foundation of the Protestant Episcopal Church of the US. Elected bishop of Penn. 1786, and consecrated by English bishops 1787, he drafted the Church's constitution and revised the Book of Common Prayer.

WHITE, William Allen (1868–1944), US journalist and author. A small-town liberal Republican, White became famous for his editorials in his own Emporia (Kan.) *Gazette* (1923 Pulitzer Prize). His posthumous autobiography won a 1946 Pulitzer Prize.

WHITEBOYS, members of small illegal (mainly Roman Catholic) peasant groups in 18th-century Ireland. Protesting against harsh landlords, enclosure of common lands and tithes, they conducted harrassing night raids in white disguise.

WHITEFIELD, George (1714–1770), English evangelist, founder of Calvinist Methodism. He joined the Methodists, led by WESLEY, whom he followed (1738) to Ga., the first of seven missions to America (see GREAT AWAKENING). Adopting Calvinist views on predestination, he led the Calvinist Methodists from 1741.

WHITEHEAD, Alfred North (1861–1947), English mathematician and philosopher. He was co-author with Bertrand RUSSELL of *Principia Mathematica* (1910–13), a major landmark in the philosophy of mathematics; and while teaching at Harvard University (from 1924) he developed a monumental system of metaphysics, most comprehensively expounded in his *Process and Reality* (1929).

WHITE HOUSE, official home of the president of the US, in Washington, D.C. It was designed in the manner of an 18th-century English gentleman's country house by James Hoban (1792). It was severely damaged by the British in 1814, but rebuilt and extended (and painted white) by 1818. In 1824 Hoban added the semicircular south portico. The grounds were landscaped in 1850 by Andrew Downing. Major renovations, including the addition of the executive office building, were carried out in the early 20th century by the architectural firm of McKim, Mead and White. From 1948 onward the building was extensively rebuilt.

WHITEMAN, Paul (1890–1967), US leader of dance and concert orchestras from the 1920s, creator of "symphonic jazz" for popular audiences.

WHITE MOUNTAIN, Battle of the, the first major engagement of the THIRTY YEARS' WAR, Nov. 8, 1620. The Protestants of BOHEMIA, who had revolted, were defeated by TILLY, leading the forces of the German Catholic League and of the emperor FERDINAND II, and Bohemia's independence was destroyed.

WHITE MOUNTAINS, a section of the APPALACHIAN MOUNTAINS covering c1,200sq mi in W Me. and N.H. It includes the Presidential, Sandwich, Carter-Moriah and Franconia ranges. The highest peak, Mt. Washington (6,288ft), is in the Presidential Range. Deep canyons, called "notches," have been carved out by glaciers. The area is noted for scenic beauty.

WHITE NILE, African river flowing 2,300mi north from Lake VICTORIA, joining the BLUE NILE at Khartoum to form the NILE RIVER.

WHITE RUSSIANS, an alternative name for the Belorussians, an East SLAV people who live mostly in the Belorussian Soviet Socialist Republic in W USSR. The name "White Russian" has also been used for the anti-communist groups who fought the BOLSHEVIKS in the RUSSIAN REVOLUTION and Civil War (1917–20).

WHITE SEA, almost landlocked arm of the Arctic Ocean covering 36,000sq mi and extending into NW USSR. It receives the Dvina, Mezen and Onega rivers, and freezes from Nov. to May. Its chief port is ARKHANGELSK.

WHITE SHARK, large aggressive SHARK common on the US Atlantic coast. White on its underside, gray on top, it may reach 20ft in length and weigh over 7,000lb.

WHITE-TAILED DEER, *Odocoileus virginianus,* the most widespread of all the American DEER, named for its longish, white tail, raised erect as a danger signal when the deer is alarmed. It ranges from Canada to northern South America.

WHITEWASH, cheap nondurable paint composed of CHALK, a glue or casein binder, and water; the dry form is called calcimine.

WHITLOCK, Brand (1869–1934), US diplomat and writer. A reform mayor of Toledo (1905–13), he served (1913–22) as US ambassador to Belgium during WWI. He wrote political novels and autobiography.

WHITMAN, Marcus (1802–1847), US physician, pioneer and missionary. He and his wife Narcissa journeyed W in 1836 and helped set up missions to the Indians at Waiilatpu near Walla Walla, Wash., and at Lapwai, Ida. In 1842–43 he made a famous 3,000mi journey E to persuade the Missionary Board not to disband the missions. The Whitmans and 11 others were killed by Indians who blamed them for a measles epidemic.

WHITMAN, Walt (1819–1892), major US poet. Born in Long Island, N.Y., he became a printer and journalist. His *Leaves of Grass* (1855; expanded in successive editions) was praised by EMERSON and THOREAU but did not at first achieve popular recognition. Other works include the Civil War poems, *Drum Taps* (1865); *Democratic Vistas* (1871), studies of American democracy; and the autobiographical *Specimen Days* (1882–83). He rejected regular meter and rhyme in favor of flowing FREE VERSE, and celebrated erotic love, rugged individualism, democracy and equality, and expressed an almost mystical identification with America.

WHITNEY, Eli (1765–1825), US inventor of the COTTON GIN (1793), from which he earned little because of patent infringements, and pioneer of mass production. In 1798 he contracted with the US Government to make 10,000 muskets: he took 8 years to fulfill the 2-year contract, but showed that with unskilled labor muskets could be put together using parts that were precision-made and thus interchangeable, a benefit not only during production but also in later maintenance.

WHITNEY, Gertrude Vanderbilt (1875–1942), US sculptor. She was best known for her monuments commemorating the victims of WWI, and for her fountain sculpture. The Whitney Studio Club, which she established in New York (1918), was a center for American avant-garde art and led to the founding of the Whitney Museum of American Art (1930).

WHITNEY, John Hay (1904–1982), US diplomat and publisher. Born to wealth, he was active in Republican politics and served as ambassador to Great Britain (1957–61). He published the New York *Herald Tribune* (1961–67), served as chairman of the *International Herald Tribune* (from 1967) and published several prominent US magazines.

WHITNEY, Mount, a mountain in the Sierra Nevada range of E central Cal., at 14,494ft the highest in the US outside Alaska. It was named for the geologist Josiah Dwight Whitney (1819–1896), who discovered it in 1864.

WHITNEY MUSEUM OF AMERICAN ART, in New York City, established (1930) by Gertrude Vanderbilt WHITNEY. Its present building on Madison Avenue, opened in 1966, was designed by Marcel BREUER.

WHITTAKER, Charles Evans (1901–1973), US lawyer and judge. A prominent Kansas City lawyer, he became a district and appeals court judge (1954–57) and associate justice of the Supreme Court (1957–61).

WHITTIER, John Greenleaf (1807–1892), US Quaker poet and abolitionist. From 1833 to 1865 he was a campaigning journalist and collected his antislavery poems in *Voices of Freedom* (1846). He later returned to New England themes in his "Yankee pastorals." The autobiographical *Snow-Bound* (1866) and *The Tent on the Beach* (1867) are among his best-known works.

WHITTINGTON, Richard (c1358–1423), English merchant and lord mayor of London, made famous in legend as the poor Dick Whittington with his cat, but in fact the son of a wealthy knight. He was mayor 1397–98, 1407–08 and 1419–20, and bequeathed his considerable fortune to charitable and public purposes.

WHITTLE, Sir Frank (1907–   ), British aeronautical engineer who invented the first aircraft JET PROPULSION unit (patented 1937, first used in flight 1941).

WHOOPING COUGH, or pertussis, BACTERIAL DISEASE of children causing upper respiratory symptoms with a characteristic whoop or inspiratory noise due to IN-FLAMMATION of the LARYNX. It is usually a relatively mild illness, except in the very young, but VACCINATION is widely practiced to prevent it.

WHOOPING CRANE, *Grus americana*, a tall white wading bird with a red cap on the head. Once widespread through North America, they have for several decades been close to extinction and have been preserved only by determined conservation measures.

WHORF, Benjamin Lee (1897–1941), US linguist best known for proposing the theory that a language's structure determines the thought processes of its speakers. (See also LINGUISTICS.)

WIDOR, Charles Marie (1844–1937), French organist and composer, professor at the Paris Conservatoire 1891–1934. As well as 10 organ symphonies he wrote concertos and ballet, opera and chamber music.

WIELAND, Christoph Martin (1733–1813), German poet and novelist. His urbane and satirical works include the verse romance *Oberon* (1780), the psychological novel *Agathon* (1773) and the satire *The Abderites* (1774). He translated much of Shakespeare (1762–66).

WIELAND, Heinrich Otto (1877–1957), German organic chemist noted for his work on STEROIDS, especially his research on BILE acids, which brought him the 1927 Nobel Prize for Chemistry.

WIEN, Wilhelm (1864–1928), Prussian-born German physicist best known for his work on BLACKBODY radiation, work which was later to be a foundation stone for Planck's QUANTUM THEORY.

WIENER, Norbert (1894–1964), US mathematician who created the discipline CYBERNETICS. His major book is *Cybernetics: Or Control and Communication in the Animal and the Machine* (1948).

WIESEL, Elie (1928–   ), Romanian-born US writer. A survivor of the HOLOCAUST, he wrote autobiographical novels and other works meditating upon that experience. He received the 1986 Nobel Peace Prize.

WIESENTHAL, Simon (1908–   ), Polish-born hunter of Nazi war criminals. Having lost a large number of relatives in Nazi concentration camps during WWII, he established the Jewish Documentation Center in Vienna, Austria, through which he located more than 1,000 former Nazis accused of war crimes, including Adolf EICHMANN.

WIG, a covering for the head of real or artificial hair, worn as a cosmetic device, as a mark of rank or office, as a disguise or for theatrical portrayals. Known since ancient times, wigs became fashionable in 17th- and 18th-century Europe, when elaborate headpieces for women and full, curled wigs for men came into wide use. The latter are still worn in British law courts. In the 1960s wigs came back into fashion for women, and the toupee to conceal baldness became acceptable for men.

WIGGIN, Kate Douglas Smith (1856–1923), US author of children's books, including *Rebecca of Sunnybrook Farm* (1903) and *Mother Carey's Chickens* (1911).

WIGGLESWORTH, Michael (1631–1705), English-born American Puritan poet, pastor at Malden, Mass., from 1656. His *Day of Doom* (1662) was extremely popular. He also wrote *Meat Out of the Eater* (1669), on the moral benefits of affliction.

WIGHT, Isle of, diamond-shaped island, 147sq mi, off the S coast of England. Its scenery and mild climate make it a popular resort area. Cowes, the chief port, is a well-known yachting center. Pop 115,300.

WIGNER, Eugene Paul (1902–), Hungarian-born US physicist who shared with J. H. D. Jensen and M. G. Mayer the 1963 Nobel Prize for Physics for his work in the field of nuclear physics. He also worked with FERMI on the MANHATTAN PROJECT, and received the 1960 Atoms for Peace Award.

WIGWAM, Abnaki Indian word for dwelling, especially the oval or round bark-covered homes used by the tribes in E North America. The English used the term to describe any Indian home, including the conical tepee and wickiup.

WILBERFORCE, William (1759–1833), English philanthropist and antislavery campaigner. A member of Parliament (1780–1825), he secured the abolition in the British Empire of the slave trade (1807) and of slavery itself (1833). A leader of the CLAPHAM SECT, he supported missionary work and devoted most of his fortune to evangelical and charitable purposes.

WILBUR, Ray Lyman (1875–1949), US educator and public official, president of Stanford University (1916–43) and US secretary of the interior (1929–33).

WILBUR, Richard (1921–), US poet and critic who won a Pulitzer Prize for *Things of This World* (1956). Using a formal structure and a witty style, he incorporated philosophy and myth into poems about ordinary life.

WILDCAT BANKS, name for numerous unsound state-chartered US banks, c1830–63, which issued paper money (wildcat currency) without having adequate assets. They proliferated after President JACKSON dismantled the BANK OF THE UNITED STATES, and many collapsed in the ·1837 financial panic. By 1863 most were brought under federal control.

WILDCATS, various species of small CATS distributed throughout the world. The name often refers specifically to the European wildcat, *Felis sylvestris*, a heavier version of the domestic cat, living in crevices in rock and preying mainly on mice and voles. It is extremely fierce and intractable.

WILDE, Oscar (1854–1900), Irish wit and playwright. A dandy and aesthete, he achieved celebrity with the novel *The Picture of Dorian Gray* (1891) and witty society comedies such as *Lady Windermere's Fan* (1892), *An Ideal Husband* (1895) and *The Importance of Being Earnest* (1895), and the biblical *Salome* (written in French; 1893). His career was shattered by his imprisonment for homosexuality (1895–97), which prompted his best known poem, *The Ballad of Reading Gaol* (1898).

WILDEBEEST, or **gnu,** ungainly-looking African ANTELOPES of the genus *Connochaetes*. The white-tailed gnu, a southern species, is now rare outside captivity while the brindled gnu (blue wildebeest) still roams the plains of E Africa in vast herds—a major prey of the LION.

WILDER, Billy (1906–), Austrian-born US screenwriter and director. His directing credits include *Lost Weekend* (1945), *Sunset Boulevard* (1950), and *Some Like It Hot* (1959).

WILDER, Laura Ingalls (1867–1957), US children's author whose series of popular autobiographical novels, including *Little House on the Prairie* (1935), depicted pioneer life in the Midwest. Her works provided the basis for a popular TV series (from 1974).

WILDER, Thornton Niven (1897–1975), US novelist and playwright. Novels include *The Bridge of San Luis Rey* (1927; Pulitzer Prize) and *The Ides of March* (1948). Plays such as *Our Town* (1938), *The Skin of Our Teeth* (1942) and *The Matchmaker* (1954) experiment with stylized techniques.

WILDERNESS, Battle of the, the opening engagement, fought on May 5–6, 1864, in central Va. 10mi W of Fredericksburg, of the "Wilderness Campaign" in the US CIVIL WAR. Ulysses GRANT's 118,000-strong Army of the Potomac, advancing to annihilate the Confederate army in open battle, was met and held in heavily wooded country by 60,000 men under Robert E. LEE. Both sides suffered heavy losses. Grant then turned to attack SPOTSYLVANIA COURTHOUSE (May 8–19). Fighting continued in the Wilderness until early June.

WILDERNESS ROAD, an early American pioneer route. It ran from Va. through the Cumberland Gap into the Ohio Valley. Laid out in 1775 by Daniel BOONE, it was the main route W until c1840.

WILDLIFE CONSERVATION. As Americans increased in numbers and advanced westward across the continent, they destroyed many animal habitats and decimated the wildlife population. Several hundred species and subspecies of mammals, birds, insects, fish and other water fauna were entirely destroyed—a rate of extinction vastly greater than that due to natural causes.

The CONSERVATION spirit that arose in the 19th century out of concern for the nation's land, forests, and other resources extended naturally to the nation's wildlife. Hunting was prohibited in national parks after 1894; in 1903 the first national wildlife refuge was established; that same year saw the creation of the Bureau of Fisheries, which later became the Fish and Wildlife Service in the Department of the Interior; the first measure protecting migratory birds was passed in 1916. During the 20th century the US has signed treaties protecting migratory birds, ocean fish, Western Hemisphere wildlife, and endangered fauna and flora worldwide.

Federal and state wildlife management programs, largely financed by hunting taxes, have in some areas been highly successful. Since the early part of this century, the numbers of game animals—notably elk, pronghorn, moose, mule deer, and white-tailed deer—have multiplied to the point of overpopulation. Nongame species have not fared so well. Strenuous efforts are being made to preserve certain conspicuous species, such as the whooping crane, the California condor, and the bald eagle. But in general the extinction of native species proceeds undiminished.

Beginning in 1966, a series of progressively more comprehensive statutes extended federal protection over endangered and threatened species. The acts gave the Fish and Wildlife Service responsibility for maintaining lists of endangered and threatened species of animals and plants and for managing the listed species (e.g., by acquiring their habitats). Taking or trade in the listed species was prohibited. The Endangered Species Act of 1973 prohibited federal agencies from taking any actions that would jeopardize a listed species or its

habitat. In 1978 the US Supreme Court upheld the act against the Tennessee Valley Authority, which was building a dam that threatened the habitat of a small listed fish, the snail darter. The Endangered Species Act was renewed and strengthened in 1988, when the Fish and Wildlife Service's endangered-threatened list contained 1,000 species, about 400 of them in the US.

WILD RICE, *Zizania aquatica,* close relative of cultivated RICE, native to the lakes and streams of North America. The grain has long been eaten by Indians and settlers and is now planted to feed wildfowl. Family: Graminae.

WILEY, Harvey Washington (1844–1930), US chemist whose main achievements were in promoting pure food laws, being largely responsible for instituting the Pure Food and Drugs Act (1906).

WILHELMINA (1880–1962), queen of the Netherlands from 1890 to 1948 (her mother was regent until 1898). She was primarily responsible for Dutch neutrality during WWI. After her golden jubilee in 1948, she abdicated in favor of JULIANA, her daughter.

WILKES, Charles (1798–1877), US naval officer and explorer. Head of the US Navy department of charts and instruments (1833), he explored the Pacific, ANTARCTICA and the NW coast of America (1838–42), and was the first to designate Antarctica a separate continent. In 1861 he precipitated the TRENT AFFAIR.

WILKES, John (1727–1797), English politician and champion of liberty. Expelled from Parliament 1764, reelected and expelled again four times 1768–69, he became a popular champion of electors' rights, individual liberty and freedom of the press. Lord mayor of London (1774), he returned to Parliament (1774–90), where he supported parliamentary reform and opposed the war with America.

WILKINS, Sir George Hubert (1888–1958), Australian polar explorer and pioneer aviator. In 1928 he was the first to fly W to E over the Arctic, from Alaska to Spitsbergen. He managed Lincoln ELLSWORTH'S Antarctic expedition (1933–39) and later advised the US armed services.

WILKINS, Maurice Hugh Frederick (1916–   ), British biophysicist who shared with F. H. Crick and J. D. Watson the 1962 Nobel Prize for Physiology or Medicine for his X-ray diffraction studies of DNA, work that was vital to the determination by Crick and Watson of DNA's molecular structure.

WILKINS, Roy (1901–1981), US CIVIL RIGHTS leader and executive secretary (director) of the NATIONAL ASSOCIATION FOR THE ADVANCEMENT OF COLORED PEOPLE 1955–1970. He was assistant secretary from 1931 and edited the journal, *Crisis* (1934–49). Dedicated to nonviolence, he came under criticism from younger militants in the 1960s and 1970s.

WILKINSON, James (1757–1825), US army officer and adventurer. Involved in the CONWAY CABAL, he resigned as secretary to the Board of War 1778. In 1787 he intrigued with the Spanish to create a pro-Spanish republic in the SW. Governor of La. 1805–06, he was involved with Aaron BURR, but turned chief witness against him. He resumed an unsuccessful army career 1811–15.

WILL, legal document by which a person (the testator) gives instructions concerning the disposal of his or her PROPERTY after death. Under most jurisdictions a will must be attested in order to be legally valid: independent witnesses, who have nothing to gain under the will, must attest that the signature on the will is in fact that of the testator who signed in their presence. Wills may be revoked during the life of the testator or altered by codicils. Wills generally appoint executors to administer the estate of the deceased and carry out his or her instructions. When a person dies intestate (without making a will), the property is normally divided among the next of kin.

WILLAERT, Adrian (c1490–1562), Flemish composer, choirmaster of St. Mark's, Venice (1527–62), and a major influence in developing the MADRIGAL. His works include madrigals, masses, motets, songs and settings of the psalms.

WILLARD, Emma Hart (1787–1870), US campaigner for women's education. In 1821 she founded Troy Female Seminary, later renamed for her, which pioneered collegiate courses for women. She retired in 1838, but continued her educational work.

WILLARD, Frances Elizabeth Caroline (1839–1898), US temperance leader and reformer, president of the WOMAN'S CHRISTIAN TEMPERANCE UNION from 1879. A brilliant speaker and capable organizer, she also worked for women's suffrage and social reforms.

WILLARD, Jess (1883–1968), US heavyweight boxing champion of the world. He won the title by beating Jack JOHNSON in 1915, and lost it in 1919 to Jack DEMPSEY.

WILLIAM (German Wilhelm), name of two German emperors. **William I** (1797–1888), became king of Prussia in 1861. Conservative, autocratic and militaristic, under BISMARCK'S guidance he organized the unification of Germany, largely through the AUSTRO-PRUSSIAN WAR (1866) and the FRANCO-PRUSSIAN WAR (1870–71), from which Prussia emerged as the leading German power. He was proclaimed emperor at Versailles in 1871. **William II** (1859–1941), grandson of William I and also of Queen VICTORIA, succeeded in 1888. Impulsive and with a passion for military affairs, he dismissed Bismarck (1890), reinforced the TRIPLE ALLIANCE and promoted the nationalist imperialism that was a factor leading to WWI. In 1918 he was forced to abdicate, and found asylum in Holland.

WILLIAM, name of four kings of England. **William I, the Conqueror** (1027–1087), duke of Normandy from 1035, became king in 1066 by defeating HAROLD at HASTINGS (see NORMAN CONQUEST), and had suppressed all opposition by 1071. He was a harsh but capable ruler, reorganizing England's military and landholding systems, building many castles and creating a strong feudal government (see FEUDALISM). The DOMESDAY BOOK was compiled by his order. His son, **William II "Rufus"** (the Red; c1056–1100), succeeded in 1087. Autocratic and brutal, he spent much time fighting, in England (against his own barons, 1088), France (1091, 1094, 1097–99), Scotland (1091–92) and Wales (1096–97), and quarreled with St. ANSELM over the independence of the Church. He was killed (probably deliberately) by an arrow while hunting in the New Forest. **William III, Prince of Orange** (1650–1702), was *stadtholder* (ruler) of Holland. His marriage in 1677 to MARY, Protestant daughter of JAMES II, resulted in Parliament inviting him to accept the crown jointly with his wife after the GLORIOUS REVOLUTION (1688). He subdued JACOBITE resistance in Ireland (see BOYNE, BATTLE OF THE) and Scotland, and ruled alone after Mary's death (1694). **William IV** (1765–1837) succeeded his brother GEORGE IV in 1830. He exercised little political influence, and was succeeded by his niece, VICTORIA.

WILLIAM, name of three kings of the Netherlands. **William I** (1772–1843), son of William V, prince of Orange, was proclaimed king of the new kingdom of the Netherlands created at the Congress of VIENNA (1815). Unable to prevent the secession of Belgium (1830–39) and opposed to liberalizing the constitution, he abdicated (1840) in favor of his son, **William II** (1792–1849), who conceded a fully parliamentary constitution in 1848. A soldier, William II had fought with WELLINGTON at WATERLOO. His son, **William**

III (1817–1890), succeeded in 1849 and reigned as a constitutional monarch. He was succeeded by his daughter WILHELMINA.

WILLIAM OF OCKHAM. See OCKHAM. WILLIAM OF.

WILLIAM OF ORANGE. See WILLIAM III (king of England).

WILLIAM RUFUS. See WILLIAM II (king of England).

WILLIAMS, Daniel Hale (1858–1931), US surgeon who carried out the first repair operation on the damaged outer surface of a human heart (1893).

WILLIAMS, Ralph Vaughan. See VAUGHAN WILLIAMS, RALPH.

WILLIAMS, Roger (c1603–1683), British-born clergyman, founder of RHODE ISLAND. A firm believer in religious freedom, he emigrated to Massachusetts Bay Colony in 1631. He became a pastor at Salem, but was banished for criticizing the expropriation of Indian lands and the enforcement of religious principles by civil power. In 1636 he founded Providence in Rhode Island and obtained a charter for the colony (1644). Its constitution exemplified his principles of religious freedom, separation of church and state, democracy and local autonomy, all of which were influential in shaping US traditions.

WILLIAMS, Ted (1918–), US baseball player who achieved a major league batting average of .344 and hit 521 home runs. He joined the Boston Red Sox in 1939 and won six American batting championships before retiring in 1960. A left-hand hitting outfielder, he was the last major leaguer to achieve a .400 season batting average (.406 in 1941).

WILLIAMS, Tennessee (1911–1983), US playwright whose emotionally intense plays deal with the warping effects on sensitive characters of failure, loneliness and futile obsessions. His first success, *The Glass Menagerie* (1945), was followed by *A Streetcar Named Desire* (1947) and *Cat on a Hot Tin Roof* (1955), both of which received Pulitzer Prizes. Other plays include *Sweet Bird of Youth* (1959) and *Night of the Iguana* (1961).

WILLIAMS, William Carlos (1883–1963), US poet. A doctor, he wrote about ordinary life in N.J., especially in the long reflective poem *Paterson* (1946–58). *Pictures from Breughel* (1963) won a Pulitzer Prize. He also wrote plays, fiction and essays, including *In the American Grain* (1925), a study of the American character.

WILLIAMS, William Sherley (1787–1849), US trapper and explorer known as "Old Bill," one of the MOUNTAIN MEN. He ranged over the territories of Cal.,

Col., Ut. and Ore., and was killed on J. C. FRÉMONT's disastrous Rio Grande expedition (1848–49).

WILLIAMSBURG, restored colonial town in SE Va., on the James R. The city (colonial capital of Virginia until 1780) contains over 500 original or reconstructed 18th-century buildings, including the governor's palace and the capitol in which the Virginia assembly met. Much of the restoration work was undertaken by John D. Rockefeller, Jr. Pop 9,870.

WILLIAM THE CONQUEROR. See WILLIAM I (king of England).

WILLIAM THE LION (1143–1214), king of Scotland from 1165. He secured Scotland's ecclesiastical and political independence (1188–89), and began her historic friendship with France (1168).

WILLIAM THE SILENT (1533–1584), founder of Dutch independence. Son of the count of Nassau, he became prince of Orange (1544) and *stadtholder* (ruler) of Holland, Zeeland and Utrecht (1559). Resisting PHILIP II of Spain's oppressive anti-Protestantism, he had his estates confiscated (1567) and fled to Germany. He became a Protestant and led the revolt against Spanish rule, becoming first *stadtholder* of the independent united Northern Provinces in 1579.

WILLKIE, Wendell Lewis (1892–1944), US businessman and political leader. A lawyer and Democrat (1914–33), he became president of a giant utility company and led business opposition to the NEW DEAL. Joining the Republicans, he was presidential candidate in 1940, gaining a large popular vote. *One World* (1943) was a plea for international cooperation.

WILLOW, common name for about 300 species of trees of the genus *Salix*, which occur from the tropics to the Arctic. The leaves are generally sword-like and male and female catkins are borne on separate plants. The willows of the temperate zone are large but the dwarf willow found beyond the tree line of the Arctic grows to only about 150mm (6in). The long, pliable twigs of some species are cut regularly for use in making wicker baskets and furniture. Other species are used for tannins or the light and durable wood. The ornamental weeping willow is a native of China and SW Asia. Family: Salicaceae.

WILL-O'-WISP, or **jack o'lantern,** or **ignis fatuus** (Latin: foolish fire), light seen at night over marshes, caused by SPONTANEOUS COMBUSTION of METHANE produced by putrefying matter. Luring travelers into danger, it was popularly regarded as a wandering damned spirit bearing its own hell-fire.

WILLS, Helen Newington (1906–), US tennis star. Between 1923 and 1938 she won seven US singles titles and eight Wimbledon championships.

WILMOT PROVISO, an attempt by Democratic representative David Wilmot in 1846–47 to outlaw slavery in new US territories. A $5million appropriation for a territorial settlement to the MEXICAN WAR had been proposed in Congress; Wilmot's amendment would have banned slavery in any territory purchased. Twice passed by the House but dropped by the Senate, the Proviso made slavery an explosive issue and led to bitter controversy.

WILSON, Alexander (1766–1813), Scottish-American poet and ornithologist. Author of dialect folk poems, he came to the US (1794), became a teacher, and took up ornithology in 1802, publishing the classic *American Ornithology* (1807–14).

WILSON, Sir Angus (1913–), English novelist and short story writer who satirizes English class attitudes and social life. His novels include *Hemlock and After* (1952), *Anglo-Saxon Attitudes* (1956) and *No Laughing Matter* (1967).

WILSON, Colin (1931–), English writer whose books often explore the dichotomy between reason and vision. His many works include such nonfiction as *The Outsider* (1956), *The Strength to Dream* (1962), *Introduction to the New Existentialism* (1966) and such fiction as *Man without a Shadow* (1963) and *The Space Vampires* (1976).

WILSON, Edmund (1895–1972), US critic and writer who investigated the historical, sociological and psychological background to literature. His prolific imaginative and critical output includes *Axel's Castle* (1931), a study of SYMBOLISM; *To the Finland Station* (1940) on the intellectual sources of the Russian Revolution; *The Wound and the Bow* (1941) on neurosis and literature; the explosive novel *Memoirs of Hecate County* (1949); and *Patriotic Gore* (1962), a study of Civil War literature.

WILSON, Edward Osborne (1929–), US biologist, at Harvard U from 1956. An expert on social insects, he wrote *Sociobiology: The New Synthesis* (1975) in which he argued for the genetic basis of certain patterns of human social behavior.

WILSON, Harold (1916–), British statesman. An Oxford economist, he entered Parliament (1945), became president of the Board of Trade (1947–51), leader of the Labour Party (1963) and prime minister 1964–70 and 1974–76.

Identified initially with the left wing and known for his tactical skill, he preserved party unity during a period of economic crisis and division over the COMMON MARKET He was knighted in 1976.

WILSON, Henry (1812–1875), US anti-slavery politician and vice-president 1873–75. Born Jeremiah Jones Colbath, he was a founder of the FREE SOIL PARTY (1848), senator from Mass. (1855–72) and a leading Radical Republican during RECONSTRUCTION.

WILSON, James (1742–1798), American jurist and signer of the Declaration of Independence, who played an important role in the 1787 Constitutional Convention. He became associate justice of the US Supreme Court from 1789 and first law professor at the University of Pa. from 1790.

WILSON, Woodrow (1856–1924), 28th president of the US, 1913–21. Of Presbyterian stock, Wilson inherited a moral fervor and an impatient idealism which influenced his political life and contributed to the personal tragedy of his last years. After growing up in Ga. and S.C., he studied history and political science at Princeton (BA, 1879) and John Hopkins (PhD, 1886). Teaching followed at Bryn Mawr (1885–88), Wesleyan (1888–90) and Princeton (from 1890), where in 1902 he was elected president. His innovations strengthened the university but his attempt to abolish the aristocratic "eating clubs" aroused bitter controversy. Encouraged by N.J. Democratic political bosses, Wilson in 1910 ran for governor and, on being elected, energetically pushed through ambitious reforms which drew national attention. He captured the 1912 Democratic presidential nomination after 46 ballots and won the ensuing election because of a Republican split. Assuming legislative leadership, and with a Democratic majority in Congress, Wilson achieved much, including the Underwood Tariff (1913), which also provided for graduated income tax; the FEDERAL RESERVE SYSTEM (1913); the FEDERAL TRADE COMMISSION and CLAYTON ANTITRUST ACT (1914); the Federal Child Labor law, the Federal Farm Loans Act and an eight-hour day for railroad employees (1916). The constitutional amendments establishing PROHIBITION, women's votes and direct election of senators were also passed. In foreign affairs Wilson was led to intervene in Haiti, Nicaragua, the Dominican Republic and Mexico. In Europe, he struggled to maintain US neutrality in WWI, before finally declaring war on Germany in 1917. He directed US war moblization and urged a peace of reconciliation based on his famous FOURTEEN POINTS (1918). Wilson headed the US delegation at VERSAILLES (1919). Compromises were forced on him there, but he salvaged the LEAGUE OF NATIONS. In 1919, the Treaty signed, Wilson sought ratification of the League from a Republican-controlled Congress which demanded "reservations" protecting US sovereignty. He refused compromise and went on a countrywide speaking tour to gain support, but collapsed from the strain and suffered a stroke (Oct. 2, 1919). For the remaining 17 months of his term, the government was run informally by the cabinet, aided by his wife. Ratification failed, and although he was awarded the Nobel Peace Prize in 1920, Wilson retired a sick and disappointed man.

WILT, condition where plants droop and wither due to a lack of water in their CELLS. This can be caused by lack of available moisture, physiological disorders, or FUNGI or BACTERIA damaging water-conducting tissues inside roots or stems.

WINCH, device facilitating the hoisting or hauling of loads. It comprises a rotatable drum around which is wound a rope or cable attached to the load. The drum is turned by means of a hand-operated crank or a motor.

WINCKELMANN, Johann Joachim (1717–1768), German archaeologist and art theorist. His *Thoughts on the Imitation of Greek Works in Painting and Sculpture* (1755) and *History of Ancient Art* (1764) created the Greek Revival in art and building.

WIND, body of air moving relative to the earth's surface. The world's major wind systems, are set up to counter the equal heating of the earth's surface and are modified by the rotation of the earth. Surface heating, at its greatest near the equator, creates an equatorial belt of low pressure known as the doldrums and a system of CONVECTION currents transporting heat toward the Poles. The earth's rotation deflects the currents of the N Hemisphere to the right and those of the S Hemisphere to the left of the directions in which they would blow, producing on a nonrotating globe, the NE and SE trade winds, the prevailing westerlies and the polar easterlies. Other factors influencing general wind patterns are the different rates of heating and cooling of land and sea and the seasonal variations in surface heating (see MONSOON). Mixing of air along the boundary between the westerlies and the polar easterlies—the polar front—causes depressions in which winds follow circular paths, counterclockwise in the N Hemis-

phere and clockwise in the S Hemisphere (see CYCLONE). Superimposed on the general wind systems are local winds—winds, such as the chinooks, caused by temperature differentials associated with local topographical features such as mountains and coastal belts, or winds associated with certain CLOUD systems. (See also ATMOSPHERE; HURRICANE; TORNADO.)

WIND CAVE NATIONAL PARK, an area of 28,059 acres in the BLACK HILLS, SW S.D. Established in 1903, it surrounds a cavern with alternating air currents and unusual crystal formations.

WINDERMERE, lake and town in the LAKE DISTRICT, NW England. The lake, 10½mi long and 1 mi wide, is the largest in England and a popular tourist resort.

WINDFALL PROFITS TAX, a special tax often imposed on businesses. When a new law has the effect of increasing the profits of an industry, the tax may be imposed to avoid public criticism. In the US, a windfall profits tax was passed in 1980 to recover from oil companies part of the profits realized from the decontrol of oil prices.

WIND INSTRUMENTS, musical instruments whose sound is produced by blowing air into a tube, causing a vibration within it.

In *woodwind* instruments the vibration is made either by blowing across or into a specially shaped mouthpiece, as with the flute, piccolo, recorder and its relative the flageolet; or by blowing such that a single or double reed vibrates, as in the clarinet, saxophone, oboe, English horn and bassoon. The pitch is altered by opening and closing holes set into the tube.

In *brass* instruments, the vibration is made by the player's lips on the mouthpiece. The bugle and various types of posthorn have a single unbroken tube. The cornet, French horn, trumpet and tuba have valves to vary the effective tube length and increase the range of notes; the trombone has a slide mechanism for the same purpose.

WINDMILL, machine that performs work by harnessing wind power. In the traditional windmill, the power applied to a horizontal shaft by four large radiating sails was transmitted to milling or pumping machinery housed in a sizable supporting structure. The windmill's modern cousin is the wind turbine, often seen in remote rural areas. Here a multibladed turbine wheel mounted on a steel derrick or mast and pointed into the wind by a "fantail" drives a pump or electric generator.

WINDSOR, Duke of, title assumed by Edward VIII of England after his abdication (see EDWARD).

WINDSOR, House of, name of the ruling dynasty of the United Kingdom of Great Britain and Northern Ireland, adopted by King GEORGE V in 1917 to replace Saxe-Coburg-Gotha (from ALBERT, Queen VICTORIA'S husband) when anti-German feeling was high.

WINDSOR CASTLE, principal residence of British sovereigns since the 11th century. Begun by WILLIAM I, it stands about 20mi W of London. The Round Tower, built in 1180, is the castle's center, and St. George's Chapel (1528) is a fine example of English Perpendicular architecture.

WIND TUNNEL, tunnel in which a controlled stream of air is produced in order to observe the effect on scale models or full-size components of airplanes, missiles, automobiles or such structures as bridges and skyscrapers. An important research tool in AERODYNAMICS, the wind tunnel enables a design to be accurately tested without the risks attached to full-scale trials. "Hypersonic" wind tunnels, operating on an impulse principle, can simulate the frictional effects of flight at over five times the speed of sound.

WINDWARD ISLANDS, group of islands in the Lesser Antilles, WEST INDIES, stretching toward Venezuela. They include St. Lucia, St. Vincent, the Grenadines, Grenada, and Martinique. The area is about 950sq mi and the people mainly Negro, producing bananas, cacao, limes, nutmeg and cotton. The tourist industry is growing.

WINDWARD PASSAGE, channel between the E end of Cuba and the NW tip of Hispaniola (Haiti). It links the Caribbean Sea with the Atlantic.

WINE, an alcoholic beverage made from fermented grape juice; wines made from other fruits are always named accordingly. **Table wines** are red, rosé or "white" in color; red wines are made from dark grapes, the skins being left in the fermenting mixture; white wines may be made from dark or pale grapes, the skins being removed. The grapes— normally varieties of *Vitis vinifera*—are allowed to ripen until they attain suitable sugar content—18% or more—and acidity (in cool years or northern areas sugar may have to be added). After crushing, they undergo FERMENTATION in large tanks, a small amount of sulfur dioxide being added to inhibit growth of wild yeasts and bacteria; the wine yeast used, *Saccharomyces cerevisiae*, is resistant to it. When the alcohol and sugar content is right, the wine is cellared, racked off the lees (from which

argol is obtained), clarified by filtration or fining (adding absorbent substances such as bentonite, gelatin and isinglass), aged in the wood and bottled. Sweet wines contain residual sugar; dry wines little or none. The alcohol content of table wines varies from 8% to 14% by volume. **Sparkling wines**—notably champagne—are made by secondary fermentation under pressure, in bottles or in tanks. **Fortified wines,** or dessert wines—including sherry, port and madeira—have brandy added during or after fermentation, and contain about 20% alcohol. Vermouth is a fortified wine flavored with wormwood and other herbs. Major wine-producing areas of the world include France, Germany, Spain and Portugal, Italy, and, in the US, Cal.

WINGATE, Orde Charles (1903–1944), British general whose unorthodox GUERRILLA WARFARE disrupted Japanese operations in WWII. After success in Ethiopia 1940–41 against the Italians, he organized · in Burma WINGATE'S. RAIDERS (1942). Promoted to major general to command the airborne invasion of Burma, he was killed in an airplane crash at the outset of the campaign.

WINGATE'S RAIDERS, or "Chindits," created by Orde WINGATE in 1942, force of British, Gurkha and Burmese guerrillas who operated behind Japanese lines in the Burma jungle, causing serious disruption to the enemy.

WINGED VICTORY OF SAMOTHRACE, statue of the Greek goddess Nike (Victory), carved c200 BC and found in 1863 on Samothrace in the Aegean Sea. It is one of the treasures of the Louvre, Paris.

WINNEBAGO INDIANS, Siouan-speaking tribe of North American Indians from E Wis. Buffalo-hunters and farmers, they were related to the Eastern Woodlands group. Once friendly to the French and English, they joined in the BLACK HAWK WAR (1832) and were removed to reservations in Neb. and Wis. They now number about 2,000.

WINNICOTT, Donald Woods (1896–1971), British pediatrician and child psychiatrist who emphasized the role of transitional objects in human development.

WINNIPEG, captial of Manitoba, Canada, 45mi S of Lake Winnipeg, at the confluence of the Assiniboine and Red rivers. A major transportation and commercial center, it is one of the world's largest grain markets. Industries include food-processing, clothing, railroad stock, agricultural equipment and furniture. Pop (metro) 617,800.

WINSLOW, Edward (1595–1655), a PILGRIM FATHER and founder of PLYMOUTH

COLONY (1621). He became the colony's English agent (1629–1632) and governor (1633–34, 1636–37, 1644–45). After his 1646 voyage to England he stayed to serve CROMWELL.

WINSTANLEY, Gerrard (c1609–c1660), English communistic reformer, founder of the DIGGERS (1649–50). His proposals for complete social and economic equality were set out in *New Law of Righteousness* (1649) and *Law of Freedom* (1652).

WINTERS, Yvor (1900–1968), US poet and critic who argued that a work of art should be "an act of moral judgment" subject to objective evaluation.

WINTHROP, name of three distinguished American colonists. **John Winthrop** (1588–1649) led the English "Great Migration" to Salem in 1630, founded Boston and was 12 times elected governor of the Massachusetts Bay Colony. His journal, *The History of New England*, is an important historical source. His eldest son, **John Winthrop** (1606–1676), went to America in 1631. After founding the colony of Saybrook in 1635, he became governor of Connecticut (1657, 1659–76), receiving in 1662 a charter from Charles II uniting New Haven and Connecticut. His son **John Winthrop** (1638–1707) left Mass. to join CROMWELL'S army in England, returning (1663) to fight the Dutch, the French and the Indians. He was Connecticut's agent in London (1693–97) and from 1698 a popular governor.

WIRE, a length of metal that has been drawn out into a thread. Wire is usually flexible, circular in cross-section and uniform in diameter. Wire diameters generally range from about 0.001 to 0.5in. To manufacture wire, normally a hot-rolled metal rod pointed at one end is coated with a lubricant, threaded through a tungsten-carbide or diamond die and attached to a drum called a draw block. The draw block is rotated and wire of a diameter, or gauge, determined by the diameter of the die is drawn until the entire metal rod is reduced to wire. Steel, iron, aluminum, copper and bronze are the metals most widely used for wire making, although others, including gold, platinum and silver, are used as well. Copper and aluminum are preferred for electrical wiring, since they combine high ductility with low resistance to electric current.

WIRETAPPING, interception of telephone conversations or telegraph messages without the knowledge of those communicating. Wiretapping and the use of other "bugging" devices by private citizens are prohibited by US federal and state laws, but there has always been argument about whether police and other government officials should be able to use wiretapping to detect crimes and collect evidence. In 1968 Congress passed a new law allowing wiretapping to be used in cases involving national security and certain serious crimes, providing that a court order was first obtained. (See also WATERGATE.)

WIRT, William (1772–1834), US lawyer and author of *Letters of a British Spy* (1803) and other collections of sketches. He prosecuted BURR (1807), was US attorney general 1817–29 and presidential candidate 1832 for the ANTI-MASONIC PARTY.

WIRZ, Henry (d. 1865), Confederate army officer in the US CIVIL WAR, director of the ANDERSONVILLE prison camp. After the war he was tried by a military tribunal and hanged.

WISCONSIN, state in the north central US bordered by Lake Michigan (E), Lake Superior and Mich. (N), Minn. and Ia. (W), and Ill. (S).

Name of state: Wisconsin
Capital: Madison
Statehood: May 29, 1848 (30th state)
Familiar name: Badger State
Area: 56,154sq mi
Population: 4,785,000
Elevation: Highest—1,952ft, Timm's Hill Lowest—581ft, Lake Michigan
Motto: Forward
State flower: Wood violet
State bird: Robin
State tree: Sugar maple
State song: "On, Wisconsin!".

Land. Wisconsin consists mostly of gently rolling pasturelands and heavily wooded, hilly upland. There are over 8,000 lakes, formed by glacial action, and much outstandingly beautiful scenery. Some 45% of the surface is forested, the rest rich agricultural land. The largest river, the Wisconsin, drains into the Mississippi. The climate is continental, with hot humid summers and long cold winters.

People. The population is largely of European origin, chiefly German, Polish and Scandinavian. Two-thirds are urban dwellers, of whom half live around

Milwaukee in the more densely populated SE.

Economy. Wisconsin is the leading US producer of milk, cheese and butter, and also produces hay, fruit and vegetables. Food-processing is an important industry, overshadowed, however, by other manufacturing, which produces heavy machinery, transportation equipment, farm and electrical equipment and paper. Tourism is a growing industry. Minerals include sand, gravel, zinc and iron.

History. The area was first visited by the French (1634), who set up fur-trading posts and fought against the Fox Indians (c1690–1740). It became British in 1763 and part of the US in 1783. Intensive settlement began in the 1800s, and resistance by the Fox and Sauk Indians was crushed in the BLACK HAWK WAR (1832). (Other Wis. Indians were the Kickapoo, Menominee, Ojibwa and Winnebago.) Becoming the 30th state in 1848, Wis. acquired a reputation for progressivism under LA FOLLETTE in the early 1900s. Many social welfare laws, including children's aid (1913), were pioneered in the state. In the 1920s, the state became predominantly urban, and it is now an important manufacturing center. In the 1980s service, trade and government were the sources of most new jobs. In 1988 the state's farm economy began to emerge from a 6-year depression. In presidential elections 1968–88, Wisconsin voted Democratic in 1976 and 1988.

WISCONSIN IDEA, name for the progressive reform policies inaugurated by R. M. LA FOLLETTE, governor of Wis. 1901–06. University of Wis. professors were called in to help frame pioneering legislation covering voting procedures, taxes, regulation of railroads and industry, workmen's compensation and minimum wages.

WISDOM OF SOLOMON, a book of the Old Testament APOCRYPHA, traditionally ascribed to Solomon but probably written in the 2nd or 1st century BC. An example of Jewish "wisdom" literature, it praises wisdom and outlines God's care for the Jews.

WISE, Isaac Mayer (1819–1900), Bohemian-born US rabbi, founder of Reform Judaism in the US. He established (1875) the Hebrew Union College in Cincinnati for the training of Reform rabbis.

WISE, John (1652–1725), American Congregationlist clergyman, pastor at Ipswich, Mass., 1680–1725. In two influential pamphlets he defended democracy in church and civil government, and in 1687 led his townsmen in refusing to pay illegal taxes.

WISE, Stephen Samuel (1874–1949), Hungarian-born US rabbi, a leader of American Reform Judaism and Zionism. He founded (1907) the Free Synagogue in New York City, where he worked for many liberal causes.

WISEMAN, Nicholas Patrick Stephen (1802–1865), English Roman Catholic prelate. In 1850, when the Catholic hierarchy was restored in England, Wiseman was appointed bishop of Westminster (the Catholic primate of England) and cardinal (the first English cardinal since the Reformation).

WISSLER, Clark (1870–1947), US anthropologist. In works such as *The American Indian* (1917) and *Man and Culture* (1923) he developed the concept of culture areas, thus making a fundamental contribution to ethnography.

WISTER, Owen (1860–1938), US author, best known for his classic western *The Virginian* (1902) and a biography of his friend Theodore Roosevelt (1930).

WITCHCRAFT, the manipulation of supernatural forces toward usually evil ends. It has existed in most cultures throughout history, and still has its devotees in modern technological society. In the Christian West witchcraft developed from surviving pagan beliefs. Witches were held responsible for disease and misfortune, and to acquire their evil power from the devil, whom they worshiped in obscene rituals (satanism, devil-worship, is not synonymous with witchcraft). From the 14th to the 17th century a witch-hunting epidemic prevailed in Europe, and many thousands of innocent people were tortured and executed in fanatical and hysterical persecutions.

WITCH DOCTOR, popular name for a tribal priest and doctor, or "medicine man," in many primitive cultures. He combines a knowledge of traditional lore and herbal remedies with an authority derived from his alleged magic power, particularly to combat WITCHCRAFT. (See also SHAMANISM.)

WITENAGEMOT (Old English: "meeting of wise men"), the council in Anglo-Saxon England which advised the king. It consisted of nobles and churchmen selected by him, and had no executive powers.

WITHERING, William (1741–1799), British physician, mineralogist and botanist, who first made use of DIGITALIS in the treatment of dropsy (see EDEMA). The mineral **witherite** ($BaCO_3$) is named for him.

WITHERSPOON, John (1723–1794),

Scottish-American clergyman. Emigrating (1768) to become president of the College of New Jersey (now Princeton), he signed the Declaration of Independence and became a leader of the Presbyterian Church in America.

WITT, Jan de. See DE WITT, JAN.

WITTE, Count Sergei Yulyevich (1849–1915), Russian statesman. A capable finance minister (1892–1903), he promoted industry and modernization. Recalled in 1905 to negotiate the Treaty of PORTSMOUTH, he became the first constitutional Russian premier after the 1905 Revolution (1905–06), but conservative pressures forced his dismissal.

WITTELSBACH, German dynasty that ruled BAVARIA as dukes from 1180, electors from 1623, and kings from 1806. The last king was overthrown in the Bavarian revolution of Nov. 1918.

WITTENBERG, city in East Germany on the Elbe R, famous as the center of the REFORMATION, where Martin LUTHER and Philip MELANCHTHON taught. Also the home of Lucas CRANACH, it declined after Dresden became Saxony's capital (1547). It is now a mining and industrial center. Pop 47,000.

WITTGENSTEIN, Ludwig (1889–1951), Austrian philosopher, whose two chief works, *Tractatus Logico-Philosophicus* (1921) and *Philosophical Investigations* (published posthumously in 1953), have profoundly influenced the course of much recent British and US philosophy. The *Tractatus* dwells on the logical nature and limits of language, understood as "picturing" reality. The *Investigations* rejects the assumption in the *Tractatus* that all representations must share a common logical form and instead relates the meanings of sentences to their uses in particular contexts: philosophical problems are attributed to misuses of language. Wittgenstein was professor of philosophy at Cambridge U., England (1929–47).

WITWATERSRAND, or **The Rand,** gold-bearing rocky ridge, 62mi long and 23mi wide, in S Transvaal, NE South Africa. It produces one-third of the world's gold output, and is South Africa's major industrial region, with Johannesburg located in its center.

WITZ, Conrad (c1400–c1445), German painter, active in Basel and Geneva. His *Redemption Altarpiece* (c1435–36) and *Altarpiece of St. Peter* (1444) reveal a striking realism, particularly in their treatment of landscape.

WOBBLIES. See INDUSTRIAL WORKERS OF THE WORLD.

WODEHOUSE, (Sir) P(elham) G(renville) (1881–1975), English humorous novelist and short-story writer. His comic characters include the popular Bertie Wooster and his imperturbable valet, Jeeves. Works include *The Inimitable Jeeves* (1924) and *Much Obliged, Jeeves* (1971). He became a US citizen in 1955.

WOHLER, Friedrich (1800–1882), German chemist who first synthesized an organic compound from inorganic material, urea from ammonium cyanate (1828), and who, with LIEBIG, discovered the benzoyl radical.

WOLCOTT, name of a prominent Connecticut family. **Roger Wolcott** (1679–1767) became chief justice and governor of the colony (1750–54). His *Poetical Meditations* (1725) was the first book of verse published in Conn. His son **Oliver Wolcott** (1726–1797) served in the Continental Congress (1775–78, 1780–84), signed the Declaration of Independence and was governor of Conn. (1796–97). **Oliver Wolcott, Jr.** (1760–1833) was US comptroller (1791–95), secretary of the treasury (1795–1800) and governor of Conn. (1817–27).

WOLF, Hugo (1860–1903), Austrian composer who led an unstable life of poverty and died insane. He is best known for his lieder, published in groups like *The Spanish Song Book* (1889) and *The Italian Song Book* (1891, 1896). He also wrote the opera *Der Corregidor* (1896), a string quartet and the well-known *Italian Serenade* (1894).

WOLF, *Canis lupus,* powerful carnivore ranging throughout the deciduous and coniferous forests and tundra of the N Hemisphere. Broadchested, with small pointed ears and long legs, wolves are pack hunters, preying on the huge northern moose, deer and elk herds. In the summer, with the onset of the breeding season and with small mammal prey more readily available, the packs break up into smaller groups. Wolf packs have distinct territories, and within the pack there is a complex social structure under a top male and female.

WOLFE, James (1727–1759), British general whose capture of Quebec was the decisive victory in the last of the FRENCH AND INDIAN WARS. He fought in the War of the AUSTRIAN SUCCESSION (1742–45) and at Falkirk and CULLODEN MOOR in the JACOBITE rebellion of 1745–46. Second in command under AMHERST (1758), he distinguished himself in the capture of Louisburg, and was chosen to lead the attack on Quebec. By brilliant strategy, aided by good luck, he routed the French but died of his wounds. (See QUEBEC, BATTLE OF.)

WOLFE, Thomas Clayton (1900–1938), US novelist whose works constitute an autobiographical epic. *Look Homeward, Angel* (1929), *Of Time and the River* (1935) and the posthumous *The Web and the Rock* (1939) and *You Can't Go Home Again* (1940) are rich in detail and characterization, and capture the author's vividly felt sense of place.

WOLFE, Tom (Thomas Kennerly Wolfe; 1931–   ), US writer, creator of the "new journalism" combining factual reporting with highly colored subjective reactions. His first novel was *Bonfire of the Vanities* (1987).

WOLFF, Caspar Friedrich (1733–1794), German anatomist regarded as the father of modern EMBRYOLOGY for his demonstration that the organs and other bodily parts form from undifferentiated tissue in the fetus. It had earlier been thought that the fetus was a body in miniature.

WOLFF, Christian (1679–1754), German philosopher and mathematician who developed and popularized the ENLIGHTENMENT in Germany. He championed the ideas of DESCARTES and LEIBNIZ in numerous works published under the general title *Vernünftige Gedanken* ("Rational Ideas").

WOLFRAM VON ESCHENBACH (c1170–1220), medieval German poet and MINNESINGER. His fame rests on a few lyrics and the chivalrous epic *Parzival*, in which the quest for the HOLY GRAIL becomes a spiritual journey.

WOLLASTON, William Hyde (1766–1828), British chemist and physicist who, through the process he devised for isolating platinum in pure and malleable form, founded the technology of powder METALLURGY. He also discovered palladium (1803) and rhodium (1804), was the first to observe the Fraunhofer Lines (1802), and invented the camera lucida (1807) and the reflecting goniometer (1809).

WOLLSTONECRAFT, Mary (1759–1797), English writer and champion of women's rights. Her *Vindication of the Rights of Women* (1792) is an eloquent plea for equality of the sexes in all spheres of life. She married William GODWIN in 1797, and died giving birth to his daughter (later Mary SHELLEY).

WOLSEY, Thomas (c1475–1530), English cardinal and statesman. He became a royal chaplain in 1507, and under HENRY VIII rose to favor, becoming bishop of Lincoln and then archbishop of York in 1514. Made a cardinal and appointed lord chancellor of England in 1515, he amassed great wealth and wielded almost absolute political power until 1529, when he failed to secure the annulment of Henry's marriage and was dismissed. He died journeying to face treason charges.

WOLVERINE, *Gulo gulo,* a large terrestrial carnivore of the weasel family, resembling a heavybodied MARTEN and weighing up to 65lb. They live in tundra regions, males defending a home range of up to 100sq mi. Fierce animals, feeding on insects, fish, small mammals and carrion, they may also attack elk.

WOMAN'S CHRISTIAN TEMPER-ANCE UNION (WCTU), US organization seeking legislation against the consumption of alcohol. Founded 1874, it became a worldwide organization in 1883 through the efforts of Frances WILLARD. It also conducts research into tobacco and narcotics.

WOMB, or **uterus,** female reproductive organ which is specialized for implantation of the egg and development of the EMBRYO and FETUS during PREGNANCY. The regular turnover of its lining under the influence of ESTROGEN and PROGESTERONE is responsible for MENSTRUATION. Disorders of the womb include malformation, abnormal position and disorders of menstruation. Benign tumors or fibroids are a common cause of the latter. CANCER of the womb or its cervix is relatively common and may be detected by the use of regular Papanicolaou tests. Removal of the womb for cancer, fibroids etc., is HYSTERECTOMY.

WOMBATS, heavy, stockily-built, burrowing marsupials of Australia, closely related to KOALAS. They share many anatomical features with placental burrowing rodents. Nocturnal animals, they emerge from their holes to feed on grasses and roots.

WOMEN'S MOVEMENT, movement to achieve political, legal, economic and social equality for women. Following the English common law, the US legal system long assigned women a special and inferior status. Although the Constitution did not use the words "men" and "women" but always "people," "persons," and "citizens," the courts did not interpret these terms to include women. Rather, they classified women with children and imbeciles as incapable of managing their own affairs. Women were denied educations, barred from certain occupations and professions, and excluded from juries and public offices. Married women were virtually the property of their husbands. They were limited in their ability to own property, sign contracts, obtain credit, go into business, control their earnings, write wills. The law regarded home and family as the special province of women, and it did all it could to confine them there in the belief that this was in the best interests of women themselves and of society as a whole.

Early in the 19th century, educated, upper-class women began to enter public life through participation in the many reform movements of the period, especially the abolitionist crusade (see ABOLITIONISM), often in the face of male hostility. The rebuff of women at a World Antislavery Convention in London in 1840 led directly to the organization of a US women's rights movement at Seneca Falls, N.Y. in 1848 (see SENECA FALLS CONVENTION). From the start, a prime objective of the movement was to win for women the right to vote. After the Civil War, the 14th Amendment, in extending the status of citizen to former slaves, introduced the word "male" into the Constitution as a qualification for voting. The 15th Amendment, which enfranchised the former slaves, provided that the right to vote should not be denied or abridged "on account of race, color, or previous condition of servitude" but not on account of sex. When women sought the right to vote on the basis of the 14th Amendment's "privileges and immunities" and "equal protection" clauses, the courts upheld the states' authority to fix voter qualifications.

The states, however, acted to improve the position of women. During the second half of the 19th century, all the states passed Married Women's Property Acts, which largely ended the subordination of women under the common law by dissolving the legal unity of husband and wife. Married women thereby acquired control over their own property and earnings. By 1900 women enjoyed many of the legal advantages of citizenship, the most significant exception being the right to vote. Chivalrous legislators still exempted them from certain responsibilities of citizenship, such as jury duty and poll and property taxes. This benign attitude underlay decisions of the courts early in the 20th century upholding the constitutionality of a number of state and federal laws intended to protect working women (but not men) by regulating their hours, pay, and working conditions.

In 1890 Wyoming entered the union with a state constitution providing for woman suffrage. In the next two decades many states gave women partial voting privileges. Twelve states had given women the unqualified right to vote by 1920 when ratification of the 19th Amendment secured the vote for women nationwide and established the principle of equal political rights for women.

The suffrage did not immediately bring about the removal of gender-based classifications which, in the guise of protecting women, actually confined them to their traditional "separate place." It was, rather, the social changes resulting from two world wars, a major depression, and, more recently, unprecedented national affluence that revolutionized the lives of women and gave new impetus to the feminist movement. Two developments were of particular importance: the development of new and widely accessible birth-control methods liberated women from the necessity of functioning largely as child-bearers and child-rearers; and the rising flood of women into the labor force, mostly into low-paying "women's work," made women of all classes conscious of the disadvantages of their "separate place."

Feminists now perceived all gender-based classifications as discriminatory, including the legislation intended to protect women in the workplace. Not only was that legislation based on the obnoxious "separate place" doctrine but experience showed that it prevented women who wanted to do so from working overtime at premium pay, taking higher-paying jobs that required heavy work, and getting promoted to supervisory positions. A series of federal laws and executive orders has now largely nullified that protective legislation. The Equal Pay Act of 1963 ended discrimination on the basis of sex in the payment of wages. The Civil Rights Act of 1964 ended discrimination in private employment on the basis of sex as well as race, color, religion, and national origin. Executive orders have made it illegal for the federal government and for federal contractors and subcontractors to discriminate on the basis of sex.

But other legal, economic, and social inequities remain. To remove these is the goal of the modern women's movement, whose origin is usually traced to the founding of the NATIONAL ORGANIZATION FOR WOMEN (NOW) in 1966. NOW was soon joined by numerous other women's organizations reflecting a variety of women's interests, including those of black, Hispanic, working, and poor women as well as abortion advocates and lesbians. The presence of these latter groups in the women's rights coalition provided a convenient target for opponents of the movement, who believed it to be the work of an elite of radical and professional women contemptuous of traditional values of home, family, and religion shared by many other women. (See also ABORTION CONTROVERSY;

EQUAL RIGHTS AMENDMENT.)

WOOD, Grant (1891–1942), US painter, exponent of the 1930s style "regionalism." Strongly influenced by Gothic and Early Renaissance painting, he realistically depicted the people and places of Iowa, as in *American Gothic* (1930).

WOOD, Jethro (1774–1834), US inventor of an improved plow (patents 1814, 1819), many of whose features are incorporated in modern plows.

WOOD, Leonard (1860–1927), US general and administrator. He led the Rough Riders' attack (1898) in the SPANISH-AMERICAN WAR. Though an excellent military governor of Cuba (1899–1902), he ruthlessly crushed (1903–08) Philippine opposition to US occupation. He was US chief of staff (1910–14), advocated WWI "preparedness" but had no WWI command. He lost the Republican presidential nomination (1920) and became governor general of the Philippines, reversing the US self-government policy.

WOOD, the hard, dead tissue obtained from the trunks and branches of TREES and SHRUBS. Woody tissue is also found in some herbaceous PLANTS. Botanically, wood consists of *xylem* tissue which is responsible for the conduction of water around the plant. A living tree trunk is composed of (beginning from the center): the *pith* (remains of the primary growth); wood (xylem); cambium (a band of living cells that divide to produce new wood and phloem); phloem (conducting nutrients made in the leaves), and the bark. The wood nearest the cambium is termed *sapwood* because it is capable of conducting water. However, the bulk of the wood is *heartwood* in which the xylem is impregnated with lignin, which gives the cells extra strength but prevents them from conducting water. In temperate regions, a tree's age can be found by counting its annual rings. Commercially, wood is divided into hardwood (from deciduous ANGIOSPERM trees) and softwood (from GYMNOSPERMS). (See also FORESTRY; LUMBER; PAPER.)

WOODBURY, Levi (1789–1851), US jurist and statesman. Senator from N.H. (1825–31, 1841–45), he was secretary of the treasury (1834–41) supporting President JACKSON against the BANK OF THE UNITED STATES. He was US Supreme Court associate justice (1845–51).

WOODCHUCK, or **groundhog,** *Marmota monax,* a familiar ground squirrel of woodlands of North America. A large rodent, up to 600mm (2ft) long, with a short bushy tail, the woodchuck is diurnal,

feeding on greenstuff near the entrance of the communal burrow. The only woodland ground squirrel, it can be a notable pest.

WOODCOCK, Leonard Freel (1911–   ), US labor leader, president of the UNITED AUTOMOBILE WORKERS from 1970 to 1977, when he was named the first US chief of mission to Communist China; he served as ambassador 1979–81.

WOODCUT AND WOOD ENGRAVING, two techniques of producing pictures by incising a design on a block of wood, inking the design and then pressing the inked block onto paper. Those parts of the design which are to be white are cut away and not inked, leaving in relief the areas to be printed. Woodcut is the older method, originating in China and Japan, and used in Europe from the 14th century, particularly for book illustration. The greatest artist in the medium was Albrecht DÜRER. In wood engraving the artist uses a tool called a *burin,* producing a design of white lines on a black background. It became popular in 18th- and 19th-century Europe.

WOODHULL, Victoria Claflin (1838–1927), US social reformer who, with her sister **Tennessee** (1846–1923), advocated woman suffrage, free love and socialism, and published the first English translation of MARX and ENGELS' *Communist Manifesto* in 1872. She was the first woman presidential candidate, for the Equal Rights Party (1872).

WOODPECKERS, a family, Picidae, of birds specialized for obtaining insect food from the trunks and branches of trees. The 210 species occur worldwide except in Australasia. All have wedge-shaped tails which may be pressed against the trunk of a tree as a prop. The bill is strong and straight and the muscles and structure of head and neck are adapted for driving the bill powerfully forward into tree bark and absorbing the shock of the blow. The tongue is long and slender for picking out insects. One group, the sapsuckers, also feed on tree sap. Woodpeckers also use the bill during courtship "drumming" and to hack out nesting holes in tree trunks.

WOODS, Lake of the, on the Canadian-US border, in SE Manitoba, SW Ontario and N Minn. About 70mi long and 1,485sq mi in area, it is fed by the Rainy R and drains into Lake Winnipeg. It is a popular tourist location.

WOODS HOLE OCEANOGRAPHIC IN-STITUTION, research center for oceanography, biology, geology, geophysics and meteorology at Woods Hole, Mass., established in 1930.

WOODSON, Carter Godwin (1875–1950),

US black historian and educator who popularized black studies and founded the Association for the Study of Negro Life and History (1915), which trained black historians, collected historical documentation and issued *The Journal of Negro History*. Woodson's works include *The Negro in Our History* (1922).

WOODSTOCK, rock and folk music festival in 1969 in Bethel, N.Y., near the artists' community of Woodstock, where the festival was originally scheduled. The event came immediately to symbolize the benign aspects of the counterculture spirit of the '60s. Attended by some 400,000 (mostly young) people, the festival was distinguished by disorganization; good humor; good music; marijuana; some nudity; crises with regard to traffic, toilets, and food supplies, and universal opposition to the Vietnam War.

WOODWARD, C(omer) Vann (1908–   ), US historian of the American South. A professor at Johns Hopkins (1946–61) and Yale (1961–77), he wrote several influential works including *Origins of the New South* (1951), *The Strange Career of Jim Crow* (1955), and *The Burden of Southern History* (1960).

WOODWINDS. See WIND INSTRUMENTS.

WOOL, animal FIBER that forms the fleece, or protective coat, of sheep. Coarser than most vegetable or synthetic fibers, wool fibers are wavy (up to 10 waves/cm) and vary in color from the usual white to brown or black. They are composed of the protein keratin, whose molecules are long, coiled chains, giving wool elasticity and resilience. Reactive side groups result in good affinity for DYES, and enable new, desirable properties to be chemically imparted. Wool lasts if well cared for, but is liable to be damaged by some insect larvae (which eat it), by heat, sunlight, alkalis and hot water. It chars and smolders when burned, but is not inflammable. Wool strongly absorbs moisture from the air. It is weakened when wet, and liable to form felt if mechanically agitated in water. Wool has been used from earliest times to make cloth. Sheep are shorn, usually annually, and the fleeces are cleaned—the wool WAX removed is the source of lanolin—and sorted, blended, carded (which disentangles the fibers and removes any foreign bodies) and combed if necessary to remove shorter fibers. A rope of woolen fibers, roving, is thus produced, and is spun (see SPINNING). The woolen yarn is woven into cloth, knitted, or made into carpets or blankets. The main producing countries are Australia, New Zealand, the USSR and India. Because the supply of new (virgin) wool is inadequate, inferior textiles are made of reprocessed wool.

WOOLF, Virginia (1882–1941), English novelist and essayist. The daughter of Sir Leslie STEPHEN, she married the critic **Leonard Sidney Woolf** (1880–1969) and they established the Hogarth Press (1917). Novels using STREAM OF CONSCIOUSNESS, such as *Mrs. Dalloway* (1925), *To the Lighthouse* (1927) and *The Waves* (1931), concern her characters' thoughts and feelings about common experiences. Some of her brilliant criticism was published in *The Common Reader* (1925). Subject to ⁎fits of mental instability, she finally drowned herself.

WOOLLEY, Sir Charles Leonard (1880–1960), English archaeologist, best known for his excavations at UR in Mesopotamia (Iraq) 1922–34, where his most spectacular discoveries were the royal tombs. He also worked in Syria and Turkey.

WOOLMAN, John (1720–1772), American abolitionist and Quaker leader. From 1743 he preached throughout the colonies against slavery. Best remembered for the spiritual autobiography in his *Journal* (1774), he also wrote *Some Considerations on the Keeping of Negroes* (1754–62).

WOOLWORTH, Frank Winfield (1852–1919), US merchant who founded the chain of stores bearing his name. He established his first five-and-ten-cent store in Lancaster, Pa., in 1879. He merged with his competitors in 1912 into the F. W. Woolworth Company, which in 1919 controlled over 1,000 stores.

WORD PROCESSING, the use of electronic equipment to improve the efficiency of office procedures. A **word processor** is basically an electronic typewriter with information-storage devices similar to those of a COMPUTER and a CATHODE-RAY TUBE screen on which text is displayed. This makes it possible to edit or correct the text before it is typed; the processor "remembers" the corrections and prints out the final version. The processor can also make the right-hand margins even and produce documents in any desired format. The automation of offices has gone far beyond this, however, to include word processors, copying machines and computer and data-storage facilities interconnected to provide for input and output wherever needed. In many newspaper offices the word-processing equipment is connected directly to electronic typesetting machines.

WORDSWORTH, William (1770–1850), English poet, one of the greatest poets of ROMANTICISM. He spent much of his life in the Lake District about which he wrote, and his poetry shows his strong affinity with nature. In collaboration with COLERIDGE he composed *Lyrical Ballads* (1798; includes "Tintern Abbey"), written in deliberately ordinary language to suit the simplicity of their themes. In 1805 he wrote *The Prelude* and in 1806 "Ode: Intimations of Immortality," a lament on the loss of the poetic vision of his youth. He was appointed Poet Laureate in 1843.

WORK, alternative name for ENERGY, used particularly in discussing mechanical processes. Work of one joule is done when a FORCE of one newton acts through a distance of one METER.

WORKMEN'S COMPENSATION, the provision by employers of medical, cash and sometimes rehabilitation benefits for workers who are injured in accidents at work. In the US all states have had workmen's compensation laws since 1949, but 20% of all workers are unprotected, notably railroad employees and merchant seamen, who are covered by other legislation. Before the first effective US compensation acts, passed in 1908–11, injured employees were dependent on their employers' financial goodwill or on winning a negligence suit against them. Present laws are based on the principle of "liability without fault," which assumes that accidents are inevitable and that their costs are a legitimate business expense. (See also SOCIAL SECURITY.)

WORK PROJECTS ADMINISTRATION (WPA). See NEW DEAL.

WORLD BANK, officially the International Bank for Reconstruction and Development, a specialized agency of the United Nations, founded 1945. Its headquarters are in Washington, D.C. It lends money to its 150 member states for investments, foreign trade and repayment of debts. The bank is self-sustaining and profit-making.

WORLD COUNCIL OF CHURCHES, international association of about 300 Protestant, Anglican, Eastern Orthodox and Old Catholic churches in some 90 countries. Founded 1948, with headquarters in Geneva, it promotes Christian unity, religious liberty, missionary cooperation, interfaith doctrinal study and service projects such as refugee relief.

WORLD COURT. See INTERNATIONAL COURT OF JUSTICE.

WORLD HEALTH ORGANIZATION (WHO), specialized agency of the United Nations founded 1948 and based in Geneva. Its services are available to all nations and territories. WHO advises countries on how to develop health services, combat epidemics and promote health education

and standards of nutrition and sanitation. It also coordinates the standardization of drugs and health statistics, and researches into mental health and pollution.

WORLD METEOROLOGICAL ORGANIZATION (WMO), specialized agency of the United Nations, in Geneva, established 1951 to promote international meteorological observation and standardization.

WORLD TRADE CENTER, the tallest building in the world when built in the early 1970s in New York City (surpassed by the SEARS TOWER 1973). Built by the N.Y. Port Authority, the twin towers (each 110 stories) rise 1,350ft over the lower west side of Manhattan.

WORLD WAR I, global conflict waged from 1914 to 1918 primarily between two European power blocs: the "Central Powers," Germany and Austria–Hungary; and the "Allies," Britain, France and Russia. Their respective alliance structures, imperial rivalries and mutual distrust escalated a minor conflict into "The Great War." The spark was struck at SARAJEVO on June 28, 1914, when the Austrian Crown Prince FRANZ FERDINAND was assassinated by a Serbian nationalist. Austria, awaiting a pretext for suppressing Slav nationalism, declared war on Serbia (July 28), with Germany's blessing. Russia immediately mobilized, and France rejected a German demand that she declare herself neutral.

The Two Fronts. Germany declared war on Russia (Aug. 1) and on France (Aug. 3) and invaded Belgium, the shortest route to Paris, hoping to win a quick victory in the W before turning to face Russia. Britain entered the war (Aug. 4) in support of Belgium and France. Although initially successful, the German advance was halted by the French at the Marne R (Sept. 1914) and a stalemate developed. Terrible trench warfare along a 300mi front was to drag on for over three years at a cost of several million lives. Meanwhile, the Germans had defeated a Russian invasion force at TANNENBERG in East Prussia (Aug. 1914) and established an eastern front. In Oct., Turkey joined the Central Powers against Russia, and in a vain attempt to aid the Russians the Allies sent a fleet to the Dardanelles and forces to the GALLIPOLI PENINSULA.

Outside Europe. After the Gallipoli disaster, the Allies attacked Turkey through her empire in the Middle East, leaving her ultimately with little more than Anatolia. Farther afield, British, French and South African troops overran Germany's African possessions, while the Japanese (who had entered the war in Sept. 1914) and

Australasian troops captured German possessions in the Far East and the Pacific.

Attrition in the West. Italy was induced to join the Allies in May 1915, and engaged an Austrian army in the Alps. Major features of the stalemate in the W were the German offensive at VERDUN (Feb. 1916) and the Allied counteroffensive at the SOMME (July 1916). Britain maintained a naval blockade of the Continent, while German submarines mauled Allied mercantile shipping. An attempt by the German fleet to lift the blockade at JUTLAND (May 1916) failed. The sinking of three US merchantmen in March 1917 and the ZIMMERMANN TELEGRAM brought the US into the war on April 6. In March 1917 the tsar had been overthrown and Russia's resolve further weakened. In Nov. 1917 the BOLSHEVIKS seized power, and peace terms were concluded between Russia and Germany at BREST-LITOVSK (March 1918). Despite a massive final German offensive in 1918 which drove the Allies back to the Marne, Allied numbers, boosted by US contingents, eventually began to tell. In September the Hindenburg Line was breached. The Central Powers sued for peace, and an armistice came into effect on Nov. 11, 1918. The Treaty of VERSAILLES (June 28, 1919), imposed on Germany, formalized the Allied victory. The dead on both sides totaled 8.4 million.

WORLD WAR II, second global conflict, which lasted from 1939 until 1945, involving civilian populations on an unprecedented scale. The harsh terms of the Treaty of VERSAILLES after WWI had left Germany embittered and unstable. Deep economic depression, the lot of Germany in the 1920s, from 1929 afflicted Japan, Italy, the rest of Europe, and North America. Germany and Italy became FASCIST dictatorships, Japan aggressively militaristic. The Allies were weary of war, but the LEAGUE OF NATIONS, without US membership, proved ineffectual. With the coming to power of HITLER and NAZISM in Germany (1933), the Versailles arrangements began to crumble. Germany rearmed and, on the pretext of defending German ethnic nationals, laid claim to certain neighboring territories. Hitler annexed Austria in March 1938 (see ANSCHLUSS), and by the MUNICH AGREEMENT (Sept. 1939) was given the SUDETENLAND. In March 1939 he occupied the rest of Czechoslovakia, and on Aug. 23 signed a nonaggression pact with the USSR.

Outbreak of War. The German invasion of Poland (Sept. 1, 1939) elicited ultimatums from Britain and France. On Sept. 3 both nations declared war on Germany. The Germans overran Poland; and the USSR, which had invaded Poland from the east, also invaded Finland and the Baltic states. Swift Nazi invasions of Denmark and Norway (April 1940) and of the Low Countries and France (May–June 1940) followed; and within a few weeks of the evacuation of a British expeditionary force from DUNKERQUE, Hitler and his Italian ally MUSSOLINI were unchallenged on the Continent. A concerted German attempt to neutralize Britain's air cover was thwarted by the Royal Air Force in the autumn (see BATTLE OF BRITAIN). Hitler now concentrated on night-bombing and U-boat attacks on British shipping. In June 1941 Germany suddenly invaded the USSR, initially making rapid gains. Late in 1941 Germany and Italy found a new ally in Japan, a nation bent on the conquest of Eastern Asia and the Western Pacific. On Dec. 7, 1941, she surprised and crippled the US fleet at PEARL HARBOR, Hawaii. The US immediately declared war, but at first fared badly in the Pacific.

Turn of the Tide. The first major US victories were recorded in CORAL SEA and MIDWAY (June 1942). In North Africa, Allied supremacy was established at EL ALAMEIN (Oct.–Nov. 1942). On the Russian front, early in 1943, the Germans lost the initiative at STALINGRAD. Sicily fell to Anglo-American forces (July 1943), and Mussolini was driven from power. In September the invasion of Normandy on D-DAY (June 6, 1944) signaled the last phase of the war in Europe. German forces, already expelled from Russia, had by Sept. 1944 been driven from most of France and Belgium. The BATTLE OF THE BULGE (Dec. 1944) proved to be the final German counteroffensive. As Russian forces at last entered Berlin itself, Hitler committed suicide (Apr. 30, 1945) and eight days later all German resistance ceased. The fate of conquered Europe was subsequently settled at the YALTA CONFERENCE and the POTSDAM CONFERENCE. (See also CONCENTRATION CAMPS; NUREMBERG TRIALS.)

Defeat of Japan. Allied forces had begun eroding the Japanese Asian empire from 1943; and by mid-1945 island-hopping assaults by US forces, culminating in IWO JIMA and OKINAWA, had swept Japan from the Western Pacific. The ATOMIC BOMB was dropped on HIROSHIMA and NAGASAKI (Aug. 6 and 9, 1945), and on Aug. 14 Japan accepted terms of unconditional surrender. (See also COLD WAR; UNITED NATIONS.)

WORM, term used for any elongate, cylindrical invertebrate, such as the earthworms, roundworms, hairworms, or acorn worms. The word has no taxonomic validity; animals commonly referred to as worms belong to many unrelated groups—Chordates, Annelids and Platyhelminths. However, the term is sometimes restricted to the phylum Annelida.

WORMS, historic city in SW West Germany, on the Rhine R. It produces the famous Liebfraumilch wine. Important since the 5th century, it was a prominent free city (1156) in the Holy Roman Empire. Pop 77,000.

WORMS, Concordat of, the renunciation in 1122 by the Holy Roman Emperor HENRY V of the right to invest ecclesiastics with the spiritual symbols of their office. This ended the INVESTITURE CONTROVERSY between the emperors and the papacy.

WORMS, Diet of, council of the Holy Roman Empire in 1521 at which Martin LUTHER defended his beliefs. The diet, presided over by Emperor CHARLES V, declared Luther an outlaw.

WORTH, William Jenkins (1794–1849), US general. Victorious against the SEMINOLE Indians (1841–42), he took part in the MEXICAN WAR under SCOTT and successfully stormed Mexico City (1847).

WOUNDED KNEE, Battle of, massacre by US soldiers of more than 200 SIOUX Indian men, women and children at Wounded Knee Creek, SW S.D. on Dec. 29, 1890. The Indians, roused by the GHOST DANCE, had fled from their reservation but had been recaptured and disarmed. A slight Indian scuffle prompted the US attack. In 1973, 200 members of the American Indian Movement occupied the Wounded Knee Reservation for 69 days, demanding a Senate investigation into the conditions of Indians.

WOVOKA (known to whites as Jack Wilson; c1856–1932), American Paiute Indian religious mystic. After a spiritual experience in 1889 he formed the messianic GHOST DANCE religion promising Indians the return of lost lands and warriors. It spread rapidly among W Indians, but Wovoka's popularity waned when his prophecies did not come true.

WRANGEL, Baron Ferdinand Petrovich von (1796–1870), Russian explorer. He led an expedition to the polar regions of NE Siberia 1820–24, was governor of Russian Alaska 1829–35 and director of the Russian-American Company 1840–49. He opposed the sale of Alaska to the US.

WRANGEL, Baron Piotr Nikolayevich (1878–1928), Russian general. Leader 1920–21 of the White Army against the Red Army at the end of the Russian Civil War, he lost the Crimea 1921 but organized an efficient evacuation to Constantinople.

WREN, Sir Christopher (1632–1723), greatest English architect. He had a brilliant early career as a mathematician and professor of astronomy, Oxford (1661–73), and was a founder-member of the ROYAL SOCIETY OF LONDON (president 1681–83). In 1663 he turned to architecture, in which he was largely self-taught. After the Great Fire of London (1666) Wren was appointed principal architect to rebuild London, where he was responsible for 52 churches, all of different design. His greatest building was the new St. Paul's Cathedral, noted for its monumental BAROQUE facade. He also worked at Greenwich (see GREENWICH OBSERVATORY), Oxford and Cambridge.

WRENS, the name of several groups of small birds. The true wrens are the Troglodytidae, a family of 60 species of small perching birds. The name is also used for some 80 species, Malurinae, of warbler of Australia and New Guinea, and the New Zealand wrens, Xenicidae. True wrens are compact little birds with short to long tails cocked upward. They occur in Middle and North America, though one species, *Troglodytes troglodytes*, has spread across Europe. Wrens live in thick cover, feeding on insects picked from foliage with the slender bill.

WRESTLING, in the West, sport in which two persons grapple and try to pin one another's shoulders to the floor by means of various holds. An ancient Greek sport, wrestling became a recognized Olympic sport in 1904. In the US the preferred form is the free-style or catch-as-catch-can. The Greco-Roman form, popular in Europe, forbids holds below the waist or leg holds. Bouts are divided into three periods of 3min each. The match is over when a wrestler pins both his opponent's shoulders for the count of 3 (a fall). Matches can also be won on points awarded by the referee for skilled maneuvers. (See also SUMO.)

WRIGHT, Frances (1795–1852), Scottish–US reformer. After her tour of the US (1818–20) she wrote *Views of Society and Manners in America* (1821) and settled there. She was a radical freethinker, campaigning against slavery and for women's rights and birth control.

WRIGHT, Frank Lloyd (1869–1959), greatest 20th-century US architect. He studied engineering, joined the architect L. SULLIVAN and was influenced by the Arts and Crafts movement. His pioneering "prairie" style (Robie House; 1908–09)—strong, horizontal lines, low-pitched, hipped roofs, open plan and change of internal levels—influenced DE STIJL. He articulated massive forms clearly (Larkin Building, 1904) and, though he liked natural materials and locations, was innovative in his use of reinforced concrete, dramatic cantilevering and screen walls (Falling Water House, 1936–37; Johnson's Wax Building, 1936–49; Guggenheim Museum, 1946–59).

WRIGHT, Joseph (1734–1797), English painter, known as "Wright of Derby," remembered for his realistic portraits, his early treatment of industrial subjects and his candlelight scenes.

WRIGHT, Orville (1871–1948) and **Wilbur** (1867–1912), US aeronautical engineers who built the first successful powered heavier-than-air aircraft, flown first at Kitty Hawk, N.C., on Dec. 17, 1903, over distances of 120–852ft (37–260m). Their early experiments were with gliders, influenced by the work of Otto LILIENTHAL: Wilbur incorporated the aileron (1899), a major step forward in their first man-carrying glider, flown at Kitty Hawk in 1900. In 1901 they built and experimented with a WIND TUNNEL, and their findings were used for their 1902 glider, by far the most advanced of its time. Following their first successful powered flight in 1903, they made further developments and by 1906 they were able to stay aloft for more than an hour. The American Wright Company for manufacturing airplanes was formed in 1909. (See also FLIGHT, HISTORY OF.)

WRIGHT, Quincy (1890–1970), US political scientist, an expert on international law and a supporter of the League of Nations and United Nations. His books include *A Study of War* (2 vols., 1942) and *The Study of International Relations* (1955).

WRIGHT, Richard (1908–1960), black US novelist and social critic. His works include *Uncle Tom's Children* (1938), stories of Southern racial prejudice; *Native Son* (1940) about a victimized black in Chicago; and *Black Boy* (1945) his autobiography.

WRIGHT, Sewall (1889–1988), US geneticist regarded as a founder of population GENETICS, the application of STATISTICS to the study of EVOLUTION.

WRIGHT, Silas (1795–1847), US lawyer and politican. In the 1820s he was a leader of the Albany Regency. He was US senator in 1833–44, known as "Cato of the Union" for his great integrity. As N.Y. governor (1844–46), he suppressed the anti-rent riots by force.

WRIT, a written order of a court of law.

Under English common law, a writ had to be issued before any legal action could be initiated. Most ancient writs have been replaced by summonses and declarations but some, such as writs of certiorari, habeas corpus and mandamus, survive.

WRITING, History of. Human communication has two primary forms: the transient, e.g. speech, sign language; and the permanent or semipermanent, of which the most important is writing. Forerunners of writing are the use of carved sticks or knotted cords to convey information; but the earliest form of writing was the pictography of ancient Sumeria and Egypt. Originally the pictographs depicted objects, but some 5,000 years ago there developed ideograms (representing ideas) and logograms (words). Sumerian CUNEIFORM and Egyptian HIEROGLYPHICS had complex word signs, as does Chinese to this day. The Hittites, Egyptians and Mesopotamians devised symbols for specific sounds; that is, phonetic writing. During the 2nd millennium BC the Semitic ALPHABETS emerged, and from these were derived the Greek and later Roman alphabets and so, in time, our own. (See also LANGUAGE.)

WRITS OF ASSISTANCE, general search warrants issued to customs officers by American colonial courts from 1751. Their use to enforce import duties was imposed by the 1767 TOWNSHEND ACTS and caused a major furor. By 1772 many colonial courts were refusing to issue them. These writs were mentioned by the DECLARATION OF INDEPENDENCE as one of the colonies' grievances against England.

WUNDT, Wilhelm (1832–1920), German psychologist regarded as the father of experimental PSYCHOLOGY. By opening the first psychological institute at Leipzig in 1879, he ushered in the modern era of psychology.

WUORINEN, Charles (1938–   ), US composer who helped found the avant-garde Group for Contemporary Music. His symphonies, vocal music, opera, solo instrumental and chamber works, and electronic music include *Time's Encomium* (1970), which won the first Pulitzer Prize for an all-electronic composition.

WYATT, Sir Thomas (c1503–1542), English poet and courtier who, with the Earl of SURREY, introduced the Italian sonnet form to England. His poems— modeled on PETRARCH'S—were published in *Tottel's Miscellany* (1557). His son, **Sir Thomas the Younger** (c1521–1554), was executed for leading an army from Kent to London against the proposed marriage of Queen MARY to Philip II of Spain (1554).

WYCHERLEY, William (c1640–1716), English playwright of RESTORATION COMEDY. He won success and court favor with *Love in a Wood* (1671). *The Country Wife* (1675) and *The Plain Dealer* (1676) sardonically criticize hedonistic and licentious London society.

WYCLIFFE, John (c1330–1384), English religious reformer, a precursor of the REFORMATION. He attacked the institutional Church and papal authority, and claimed the Bible was the external "exemplar" of the Christian religion and the sole criterion of doctrine. His attack on TRANSUBSTANTIATION forced his retirement in 1382 but he was protected by JOHN OF GAUNT. His followers translated the Latin VULGATE Bible into English. He influenced the LOLLARDS and Jan HUS.

WYETH, Andrew Newell (1917–   ), US painter. His work depicts scenes of strange, lonely rural life in a highly detailed style that seems almost photographic. His best known picture is *Christina's World* (1948).

WYLER, William (1902–1981), US motion-picture director. He won Academy awards for *Mrs Miniver* (1942), *The Best Years of Our Lives* (1946) and *Ben Hur* (1958). His other films include *Wuthering Heights* (1939), *Friendly Persuasion* (1956) and *Funny Girl* (1968).

WYLIE, Elinor Hoyt (1885–1928), US poet and novelist. Her verse included *Nets to Catch the Wind* (1921) and *Black Armour* (1923). Her first novel, *Jennifer Lorn* (1923), is about 18th-century India.

WYLIE, Philip Gordon (1902–1971), US essayist and novelist. His *Generation of Vipers* (1943) is a stinging analysis of US society. He also wrote a number of novels, notably *The Disappearance* (1951).

WYNN, Ed (Isaiah Edwin Leopold; 1886–1966), US entertainer. A vaudeville comedian, he clowned his way through Ziegfield *Follies*, Broadway shows, and a popular 1930s radio program. Late in his career he turned to dramatic roles on television and in films.

WYOMING, a state in the W US, bordered on the N by Montana, E by S.D. and Neb., S by Col. and Utah, and W by Ida. and Utah.

Land. Wyoming has the second highest average elevation of any state (6,700ft) and comprises four major regions: the Great Plains in the E; the Middle Rocky Mts in the W; S Rocky Mts in the S; and the Wyoming Basin in the SW leading to the historic South Pass through the Rockies, whose highest point in the state is Gannett Peak (13,804ft). The Great Plains are 3,100–6,000ft in height. The major rivers

Name of state: Wyoming
Capital: Cheyenne
Statehood: July 10, 1890 (44th state)
Familiar names: Equality State; Cowboy State
Area: 97,914sq mi
Population: 507,000
Elevation: Highest—13,804ft, Gannett Peak
Lowest—3,100ft, Belle Fourche River
Motto: Equal rights
State flower: Indian paintbrush
State bird: Meadow lark
State tree: Cottonwood
State song: "Wyoming"

are the Snake, Green and Yellowstone. The climate is cool and dry; annual rainfall is in the range of 5–40in.

People. Next to Alaska, Wyo. has the smallest population of all the states; its people include about 5,000 Indians and 2,500 blacks. Most of the remaining people trace their ancestry to European countries. About 60% live in towns, the largest cities being Cheyenne and Casper.

Economy. Mining, livestock raising and tourism are the basis of the economy. Coal, oil, and natural gas are the chief mineral products. Cattle provide most of the livestock income, but Wyo. ranks second only to Tex. in sheep and wool production. The important tourist industry is based on the magnificent scenery and the Yellowstone and Grand Teton national parks. Wyo. is one of the least industrialized states, the principal manufactures being processed food and wood and clay products.

History. John Colter made the first records of the region (1807), and expeditions first crossed Wyo. in 1811. Over the next 30 years the fur trade developed and settlers passed through Wyo. on the OREGON TRAIL. Indians resenting encroachment on their lands attacked wagon trains and army forts but peace was restored by 1876. In 1868 Wyoming became a territory and was the first state or territory to enfranchise women (1869). Cattle and oil industries developed in the 1880s. In 1890 Wyoming became a state. The valuable oil resources led to the

TEAPOT DOME scandal (1924). Despite agricultural expansion Wyo. was part of the 1930s DUST BOWL. Since WWII uranium and tourist industries have prospered, and going into the 1980s, the state displayed the signs and scars of rapid, booming success. Between 1970 and 1986 the population grew 52.7%. Strip mining for coal expanded, and many new oil wells came into production in the Overthrust Belt. In the 1980s, however, declining oil prices depressed the state's economy. In 1988 forest fires ravaged 1.2 million acres in and around YELLOWSTONE NATIONAL PARK. In presidential elections 1968–88, Wyoming voted consistently Republican.

WYOMING VALLEY MASSACRE, event in the Revolutionary War. A force of Loyalists, Butler's Rangers and Iroquois Indians led by John Butler defeated a band of 300 Connecticut settlers led by Zebulon Butler in Wyoming Valley (Pa.) in July 1778. A massacre ensued in which the Indians butchered the survivors. The incident horrified both sides; it made the English wary of Indian allies and prompted Washington to attack the Iroquois (1779).

WYSS, Johann David (1743–1818), Swiss author who wrote *The Swiss Family Robinson* (4 vols. 1812–27), edited by his son, **Johann Rudolf** (1781–1830).

WYSZYNSKI, Stefan (1901–1981), Polish Catholic cardinal, archbishop of Warsaw and primate of Poland. Arrested for his attacks on the communist government's persecution of the Church in 1953, he was released after GOMULKA'S rise to power (1956). His funeral was a national event attended by Pope JOHN PAUL II.

WYTHE, George (1726–1806), American judge, friend of Thomas JEFFERSON and first US law professor at the College of William and Mary (1779–90). A member of the Second Continental Congress (1775–76) and a signatory of the Declaration of Independence, he was chancery judge (1778–88) and sole chancellor of Va. (1788–1801).

24th letter of the English alphabet, related to the Greek "chi." "Christ" in Greek begins with chi, so "X" came to be used for Christ, as in Xmas. "X" also stands for ten in Roman numerals.

X AND Y CHROMOSOMES, or sex chromosomes, the CHROMOSOMES which determine the sex of a person (as well as carrying some genetic information not related to sex determination). Sex chromosomes are inherited (see HEREDITY) in the same way as the other 22 human chromosome pairs, normal persons being either XX (female) or XY (male). The Y chromosome carries little genetic information and it is largely the properties of the X chromosome that determine "sex-linked" characteristics in males. Sex-linked characteristics include HEMOPHILIA and COLOR BLINDNESS, which are carried as recessive genes in females.

XANTHIPPE (5th century BC), wife of the Greek philosopher SOCRATES. Her shrewishness and quarrelsome nature became proverbial.

XAVIER, Saint Francis. See FRANCIS XAVIER, SAINT.

XENAKIS, Yannis (1922–   ), Greek avant-garde composer who developed "stochastic" music using computer-programmed sequences based on mathematical probability, as in *Métastasis* (1955) and *Achorripsis* (1958).

XENOPHANES (c570–480 BC), Greek poet and PRE-SOCRATIC philosopher. An IONIAN who emigrated to S Italy, he wrote satires and ridiculed the idea that the gods had human attributes, positing a single, all-embracing diving being. Only some 40 fragments of his works survive.

XENOPHON (431–355 BC), Greek soldier and author. An Athenian and an admirer of SOCRATES, he joined the Greek expedition supporting CYRUS the Younger (401), and after its defeat led the Greeks back in a heroic 1,500mi march recounted in his famous *Anabasis*. He later fought for Sparta, whose conservative militarism he admired. Retiring to the country, he wrote Greek history, memoirs of Socrates, a romanticized account of CYRUS the Great's education, and works on horsemanship and politics.

XEROGRAPHY, an electrostatic copying method. Light reflected from the original is focused onto an electrostatically charged (see ELECTRICITY), selenium-coated drum. Selenium is photoconductive, so where the light strikes the drum, the charge leaks away, leaving a reversed electrostatic image of the original on the drum. This is dusted with "toner," a dry ink powder which sticks only to the charged image. The toner is then transferred to a sheet of ordinary paper and fixed by applying heat. The paper thus carries a positive copy of the original. Each additional copy requires another exposure on the rotating drum. Other electrostatic copying processes form a positive print on paper specially coated with zinc oxide.

XERXES, name of two kings of ancient PERSIA. **Xerxes I** (ruled 486–465 BC) continued the war against Greece started by his father DARIUS I. His vast army crossed the Hellespont in 480 BC, and despite a check at THERMOPYLAE, destroyed Athens. However, his fleet was defeated at SALAMIS, and he returned to Persia leaving the army to be defeated at Plataea (479). He was murdered in a court intrigue. **Xerxes II,** his grandson, was murdered in 424, after ruling for 45 days.

XHOSA, group of related tribes living in Transkei, South Africa. BANTU-speaking, they are mainly agriculturists though some cattle are raised. The Xhosa are organized in patrilineal clans. Many now work as migrant laborers in Johannesburg.

XINJIANG. See SINKIANG.

XOCHIMILCO, Lake, lies 14mi SE of Mexico City, and is famed for its "floating gardens." These were originally soil-covered rafts used by the Indians for growing vegetables and flowers, but they anchored and took root, and are now small islands.

X-RAY ASTRONOMY, the study of the X-RAYS emitted by celestial objects. Since the earth's atmosphere absorbs most X-radiation before it reaches the surface, observations are usually made from high altitude balloons, satellites and rockets. A number of celestial X-ray sources are known, including the sun and the CRAB NEBULA.

X-RAY DIFFRACTION, a technique for determining the structure of CRYSTALS through the way in which they scatter X-RAYS. Because of INTERFERENCE between the waves scattered by different ATOMS, the scattering occurs in directions characteristic of the spatial arrangement of the unit cells of the crystal, while the relative intensity of the different beams reflect the structure of the unit cell itself. Unfortunately, more than one structure can often produce the same DIFFRACTION pattern. The technique is also used to study local ordering in "amorphous" solids and liquids.

X-RAYS, highly energetic, invisible ELECTROMAGNETIC RADIATION of wavelengths ranging between 0.1pm to 1nm. They are usually produced using an evacuated electron tube in which ELECTRONS are accelerated from a heated cathode toward a large tungsten or molybdenum anode by applying a potential difference of perhaps 1MV. The electrons transfer their energy to the anode which then emits X-ray PHOTONS. X-rays are detected using PHOSPHOR screens (as in medical fluoroscopy), with GEIGER and scintillation COUNTERS and on photographic plates. X-rays were discovered by ROENTGEN in 1895, but because of their extremely short wavelength their wave nature was not firmly established until 1911, when von LAUE demonstrated that they could be diffracted from crystal lattices. X-rays find wide use in medicine both for diagnosis and treatment (see RADIOLOGY) and in engineering where radiographs are used to show up minute defects in structural members. X-ray tubes must always be carefully shielded because the radiation causes serious damage to living tissue.

XYLOPHONE, a PERCUSSION INSTRUMENT consisting of a series of tuned wooden blocks set in a frame and struck with special hammers. Of ancient origin, it was widespread in Asia and Africa before being introduced in Europe.

XYZ AFFAIR, diplomatic incident which nearly led to open war between the US and France in 1798. President ADAMS send John MARSHALL and Elbridge Gerry with C. C. PINCKNEY to settle disputes with France following the JAY TREATY. They were met by three unnamed agents, later called X, Y and Z, who demanded US loans and bribes before opening negotiations. When this was announced in Congress, there was uproar, but Adams averted war and reopened negotiations with TALLEYRAND, the French foreign minister.

25th letter of the English alphabet. Like U, V and W it is derived from the Semitic "waw" via the Greek "upsilon," which was transliterated as Y by the Romans. In Old and Middle English Y and I tended to be used interchangeably.

YACHTS AND YACHTING. Now a popular international sport and pastime, yachting developed in the early 19th century as steam began to supplant sail in commercial vessels. It became established on an organized basis with the setting-up of the New York Yacht Club in 1844. In 1851 the first race for the AMERICA'S CUP took place and subsequent races for the cup played a major role in the evolution of yacht design. After WWI the trend moved away from large, expensive yachts, and popular "one-design" classes emerged, with the Bermuda rig predominating. Small-keel yachts and catboats are now raced and sailed for pleasure throughout the world. Ocean racing is also popular and recently single-handed transatlantic and round-the-world races have attracted enormous public attention.

YAEGER, Charles Elwood (1923–   ), US test pilot, the first person to break the sound barrier when, on Oct. 14, 1947, he flew the Bell X-1 research plane on level flight at 670mph. In 1953 he piloted the Air Force's X-1A rocket plane at 1,650mph.

YAK, *Bos mutus,* the shaggy ox of the high plateau of Tibet. Yaks are distinguished by the long fringe of hair on shoulders, flanks, thighs and tail, and the long incurved horns. Wild yaks are large animals, up to 2m (6.6ft) at the shoulder, with black coats. Domestic yaks, kept as beasts of burden and for their milk, are smaller and may be any of a variety of colors.

YAKIMA INDIANS, a North American tribe of Plateau Indians belonging to the Sahaptin-Chinook language family. They lived along the Columbia and Yakima rivers in Wash. In 1859 they were settled in a reservation in Wash. after a three-year war against the white settlers (1855–58). They now number some 7,000.

YALE, Elihu (1649–1721), American-born English merchant who made a fortune in India (1670–99). In 1718 he made a donation to the collegiate school at New Haven which was renamed Yale College (now YALE UNIVERSITY).

YALE, Linus (1821–1868), US inventor of the Yale lock (1861–65) and the dial combination lock (1862). (See LOCKS AND KEYS.)

YALE UNIVERSITY, US university chartered in 1701 as a collegiate school, first at Killingworth, Milford and Saybrook, then (1716) at New Haven, Conn., its present site. Renamed Yale College in 1718 in honor of Elihu Yale (1649–1721), it expanded greatly in the 19th century and was renamed Yale University in 1887.

YALTA, winter and health resort on the Black Sea, in S Crimea, USSR. It was site of the YALTA CONFERENCE. Pop 62,000.

YALTA CONFERENCE, A meeting held near Yalta (Crimea, USSR) Feb. 4-11, 1945, between CHURCHILL, ROOSEVELT and STALIN representing the major Allied powers in WWII. Plans were agreed for the treatment, after the war, of Germany (including its division into occupation zones, elimination of its war industries and prosecution of war criminals). The foundation of a new Polish state was decided upon and the setting-up of the UNITED NATIONS was discussed. The USSR was persuaded to join in the war against Japan.

YALU RIVER, river forming part of the Chinese-North Korean border. It rises in NE China and flows about 500mi into the Bay of Korea.

YAMAGATA, Aritomo (1838–1922), Japanese soldier and statesman, an authoritarian at home and an expansionist abroad. As premier, he ruled that only an active officer could serve as army or navy minister, thus assuring military domination of the cabinet.

YAMAMOTO, Isoroku (1884–1943), commander of the Japanese fleet in WWII. He planned and commanded the attack on PEARL HARBOR (1941) and Midway Island (1941). He was killed in an air ambush.

YAMASAKI, Minoru (1912–1986), US architect. The Lambert-St. Louis air terminal (1951), the McGregor Conference Center at Wayne University (1956) and the US science pavilion at the Seattle Exposition (1962) reveal his mastery of ornamental and sculptural form.

YAMASEE INDIANS, a North American tribe of the MUSKOGEAN language family. Living in S Ga. and N Fla., they were driven into S.C. by the Spanish (1687) and back into Fla. (1715) by the British, who in 1727 destroyed their village near St. Augustine. The survivors eventually assimilated with the Seminole and Creek Indians.

YAMASHITA, Tomoyuki (1885–1946), Japanese army commander in WWII. His forces overran Malaya and captured Singapore (1942). He later commanded Japanese forces in the Philippines, surrendering in 1945. He was hanged by the Allies for the atrocities committed by his troops.

YAMS, herbaceous vines of the genus *Dioscorea,* cultivated for their tubers which weigh up to 100lb. They are an important food in the tropics. For human consumption, they are baked, boiled, or fried. In the US, the SWEET POTATO is incorrectly called a yam. Family: Dioscoreaceae.

YANCEY, William Lowndes (1814–1863), US pro-slavery politician and advocate of SECESSION. A lawyer and US senator (1844–46), he drafted the pro-slavery "Alabama Platform" (1848) in reply to the

WILMOT PROVISO, became a leading "fire-eater," wrote the Ala. ordinance of secession (1860) and served the Confederate government in the Civil War as commissioner to England and France (1861–62).

YANGTZE RIVER, China's longest river. It rises in the Kunlun Mts of Tibet and flows 3,434mi into the E China Sea, draining an area (about 750,000sq mi) which includes China's richest agricultural land along its lower reaches. Its main tributaries are the Min, Wu and Han. It is navigable for oceangoing ships for some 600mi, as far as Wuhan. The $2 billion Gezhouba Dam, China's largest water-control project, is being built on the Yangtze at Yichang.

YANKEE, slang term of uncertain origin, probably Dutch. Outside the US, it refers to anyone from the US; inside the US, it normally refers to a New Englander, especially someone descended from colonists. In the South it refers to Northerners, a tradition dating from the CIVIL WAR.

YANKEE DOODLE, song popular among American troops in the Revolutionary War. It probably originated among the British during the FRENCH AND INDIAN WARS as a song making fun of the Americans, who later adopted it for themselves.

YAP, island group in the W Pacific Ocean, part of the CAROLINE ISLANDS, consisting of four large and ten smaller islands, surrounded by a coral reef. The Micronesian population fish and grow yams, taro, bananas and coconuts.

YAWS, a disease, caused by an organism related to that of syphilis (see VENEREAL DISEASES), common in the tropics. It occurs often in children and consists of a local lesion on the limbs; there is also mild systemic disease. Chronic destructive lesions of SKIN, BONE and CARTILAGE may develop later. The WASSERMANN TEST is positive as in syphilis and PENICILLINS are the treatment of choice.

YAZOO FRAUD, a scandal in which the Ga. state legislature was bribed to sell 35 million acres of land along the Yazoo R to four land companies (1795). In 1796 a new legislature rescinded the act. In a historic decision, the US Supreme Court in 1810 declared the rescinding unconstitutional and awarded compensation to investors who had suffered.

YEAR, name of various units of time, all depending on the revolution of the earth about the sun. The *sidereal year* (365.25636 mean solar DAYS) is the average time the earth takes to complete one revolution measured with respect to a fixed direction in space. The *tropical year* (365.24220 mean solar days), the year measured by the changing seasons, is that in which the mean longitude of the sun moves through 360°. The *anomalistic year* (365.25964 mean solar days) is the average interval between successive terrestrial perihelions (see ORBIT). The *civil year* is a period of variable duration, usually 365 or 366 days (leap year), depending on the type of CALENDAR in use.

YEASTS, single-celled plants classified with the FUNGI. Some cause diseases of the skin and mucous membranes, while others, notably the strains of *Saccharomyces cerevisiae*, baker's yeast, are used in baking, brewing and wine-making. Yeasts employ either or both of two metabolic processes: FERMENTATION involves the anaerobic decomposition of hexose SUGARS to yield alcohol (ETHANOL) and CARBON dioxide; "respiration" involves the exothermic decomposition of various sugars in the presence of oxygen to give carbon dioxide and water. Yeasts are also grown as a source of food rich in B-complex VITAMINS.

YEATS, William Butler (1865–1939), Irish poet and dramatist, leader of the CELTIC RENAISSANCE in Ireland and one of the world's greatest lyric poets. Nationalism is a major element in his early poetry, such as *The Wanderings of Oisin* (1889), which draws on Irish legend. Yeats cofounded (1899) Dublin's Irish Literary Theatre, later the ABBEY THEATRE. His mature poetic works, often symbolic and mystical, treat universal themes. They include *The Wild Swans at Coole* (1917), *The Tower* (1928) and *Last Poems* (1940). Yeats was awarded the Nobel Prize for Literature in 1923.

YELLOW-DOG CONTRACTS, pledges signed by prospective employees promising that they will not join a union. US Supreme Court decisions (1908, 1915) upheld their legality, and they were widely used by anti-union employers in the 1920s. The Norris-La Guardia Act (1932) finally outlawed them.

YELLOW FEVER, INFECTIOUS DISEASE caused by a VIRUS carried by MOSQUITOS of the genus *Aëdes* and occurring in tropical America and Africa. The disease consists of FEVER, headache, backache, prostration and vomiting of sudden onset. PROTEIN loss in the URINE, KIDNEY failure, and LIVER disorder with JAUNDICE are also frequent. HEMORRHAGE from mucous membranes, especially in the GASTROINTESTINAL TRACT, is also common. A moderate number of cases are fatal but a mild form of the disease is also recognized. VACCINATION to induce IMMUNITY is important and effective as no specific therapy is available; mosquito control provides a similarly important preventive measure.

YELLOW JACKETS, a genus, *Vespula*, of HORNETS, social WASPS of the family Vespidae, common in North America. They usually construct an underground nest of paper, frequently in or near human habitation.

YELLOW JOURNALISM, vulgar and sensational newspaper reporting whose sole aim is to attract readers. The term originated with the "Yellow Kid" comic strip in the Sunday supplement of Joseph PULITZER'S New York *World* (1896). This began a "yellow journalism" circulation war in the city with William Randolph HEARST'S *Journal*.

YELLOW RIVER, or **Hwang Ho,** river of N China, flowing 2,903mi from the Kunlun Mts. generally E to the Yellow Sea. It is named for its fertile yellow silt, and often nicknamed "China's Sorrow" because of terrible floods and destructive changes of course. In 1955 a major 50-year flood-control and hydroelectric project was begun.

YELLOW SEA, or **Hwang Hai,** an arm of the Pacific Ocean between Korea and NE China. It opens in the S into the East China Sea. The name arises from the color of its waters, which receive yellow silt from the YELLOW and other rivers.

YELLOWSTONE NATIONAL PARK, oldest and largest US national park, created 1872 and covering 3,472sq mi, mostly in NW Wyo. It contains some of the most spectacular geological wonders in the US, including the OLD FAITHFUL geyser, thousands of hot springs and mud pools, petrified forests, black glass cliffs and the Grand Canyon of the Yellowstone R. Wildlife abounds in the forests covering most of the park. In 1988 the worst forest fires in history ravaged 1 million park acres.

YEMEN, People's Democratic Republic of, also called **Southern Yemen,** independent state in the S of the Arabian peninsula bordering on the Arabian Sea and commanding the entrance to the Red Sea. It includes also the islands of Kamaran, Perim and Socotra. It is bordered by Oman (E), Saudi Arabia (N) and the YEMEN ARAB REPUBLIC (W).

Land. The land rises from the hot, arid coastal plain with its palm oases to a high plateau broken by a ridge of mountains which reach 8,000ft before falling away N to the Rub'al-Khali desert. The Wadi Hadhramaut is a fertile valley running parallel to the coast. Coastal temperatures average 84°F; annual rainfall, 2in on the coast, reaches 20–30in in the highlands

Official name: People's Democratic Republic of Yemen
Capital: Aden
Area: 130,066sq mi
Population: 2,285,000
Languages: Arabic
Religion: Muslim
Monetary units(s): 1 Yemeni dinar=1,000 fils

inland. Dams across the wadis (seasonal rivers) help conserve water for agriculture.

People. Most of the population are SUNNITE Muslim Arabs of various tribes, living in the few fertile areas like the Wadi Hadhramaut, or nomadically in the extreme N. Aden is the largest city and chief port. Other centers are Madinat ash Sha'b and Mukalla.

Economy. Yemen is basically agricultural. Long-staple cotton, coffee, tobacco and dates are exported. Subsistence crops include millet, sesame and sorghum. Fishing along the coast is a major source of food and export revenue. Salt is mined and petroleum deposits were discovered in the mid-1980s but there is little industry, consisting mostly of oil refining. Remittances from Yemenis working abroad are an important source of income. The country is heavily dependent on foreign aid, supplied mostly by the USSR and other Eastern bloc countries.

History. Under British control from the 1830s Southern Yemen became fully independent (1967) under the rule of the Marxist National Liberation Front, after the collapse of the Federation of South Arabia. After a brief war in 1972, unification with the more moderate neighboring Yemen Arab Republic was agreed upon in principle but subsequent border clashes and tense relations between the two governments made unification unlikely. In 1986 there was a bloody power struggle among various factions of the ruling Marxist group, and the president fled the country.

YEMEN ARAB REPUBLIC, independent state on the SW Arabian peninsula bordering on the Red Sea. It is bounded by

Official name: Yemen Arab Republic
Capital: Sana
Area: 75,300sq mi
Population: 8,386,000
Language: Arabic
Religion: Muslim
Monetary unit(s): 1 Yemeni riyal = 100 fils
Saudi Arabia (N and NE) and by the
People's Democratic Republic of YEMEN
(S).
Land. Beyond the Red Sea coast with its
coral reefs and low beaches lies the
Tihamah, a dry coastal plain, and farther
inland a foothill region crossed by wadis
(seasonal rivers). The land then rises E to
lofty mountain crests (some over 12,000ft
high) and a mosaic of plateaus and upland
plains. Fertile valleys leading E eventually
give way to the Rub'al-Khali desert beyond
the basin of the Wadi Abrad. Though the
coastal lowlands are hot, arid and humid (as
are the E desert fringes), the highlands have
the most favored climate in Arabia, with
annual rainfall of 16–32in and sometimes
more.
People. The population is mostly of south
Arabian stock, but with African elements
along the coast and in the S. About half are
SUNNITE Muslims, and the other half
SHI'ITES, a division which creates social and
political problems. Most people live in the
highlands. The largest towns are the port of
Hodeida, Sana (the capital) and Ta'izz.
Economy. The land is the most fertile on the
Arabian peninsula, although agriculture
has been adversely affected by drought and
labor shortages in recent years. Salt was the
only exploited mineral until 1987, when oil
from recently discovered deposits began to
be exported. The small industrial sector
includes textiles, cement, salt processing
and traditional crafts. Many Yemenis work
abroad and their remittances are a major
source of income in a country largely
dependent on foreign aid, coming mostly
from the USSR before 1975 and from the
US, Saudi Arabia and Kuwait since then.
History. Once part of the ancient kingdom
of Saba (the Biblical Sheba), the country
was ruled from the 9th to 20th centuries by
competing local imams, although sometimes under nominal control of foreign
powers including the Ottomans, until 1962
when an army coup led to the proclamation
of a republic. Civil war followed, in which
Saudi Arabia backed the royalist tribes and
Egypt the new republican regime, but was
ended by mediation in 1970, with the
republicans controlling the government.
War with the neighboring Marxist People's
Democratic Republic of Yemen erupted in
1972, and a ceasefire was followed by an
agreement for the two countries to unify,
although brief renewed fighting in 1979 and
1987 made prospects for unification
doubtful. In 1988, the two nations came
close to war over a long-standing territorial
dispute involving a border area believed to
be rich in oil.
YENISEI or **YENISEY,** major river of
central Siberia, USSR. Formed by the
confluence of the Bolshoi and the Maly
Yenisei rivers near the Mongolian border, it
flows 2,566mi N through Siberia into the
Arctic Ocean. It has enormous hydroelectric potential.
YEOMAN, Middle English word denoting
a king's or nobleman's retainer or officer, or
a freehold farmer cultivating his own land,
ranking below the gentry. Yeoman now
refers to a naval petty officer performing
clerical duties.
YEOMAN OF THE GUARD, English royal
bodyguard. They were founded by Henry
VII in 1485 to defend the king's person, and
they still wear Tudor costumes and carry
halberds. Their duties are now largely
ceremonial.
YERKES, Charles Tyson (1837–1905), US
financier. He was highly successful and
controlled Chicago's transportation system.
His financial and political manipulations
caused a public scandal and he was forced to
sell out (1899). He then helped build the
London underground railway system.
YERKES, Robert Mearns (1876–1956),
US pioneer of comparative
(animal/human) PSYCHOLOGY and of intelligence testing. He initiated the first mass
psychological testing program in WWI,
involving nearly 1¾ million US soldiers.
During the 1920s and 1930s he was the
world's foremost authority on PRIMATES.
YERKES OBSERVATORY, the observatory of U. of Chicago. It was set up in 1892
on the shores of Lake Geneva, Wis., by the
astronomer George HALE and financed by
Charles YERKES. The observatory contains
the world's largest refracting telescope
(built 1897), its lens 40in in diameter,
together with several reflecting TELESCOPES.
YERMAK (d. c1584), Russian conqueror of

Siberia. His band of Cossacks, financed by the Stroganovs, a merchant family, conquered the Tartar Khanate of Sibir in 1581 and placed it under the protection of Tsar IVAN IV.

YERSIN, Alexandre Émile John (1863–1943), Swiss bacteriologist who discovered, independently of Kitasato, the PLAGUE bacillus (1894), and developed a SERUM to combat it.

YETI, or abominable snowman, legendary animal—half man, half ape—alleged to inhabit inaccessible regions of the Himalayas.

YEVTUSHENKO, Yevgeny (1933–   ), Russian poet who became a spokesman for "liberal" forces in Soviet literature in the early 1960s. His best-known poems include "Babi Yar" (1961), dealing with Soviet anti-Semitism, and "The Heirs of Stalin" (1963), warning of the persistence of Stalinism.

YIDDISH, a language spoken and written by Jews in many parts of the world, belonging to the Germanic group of INDO-EUROPEAN LANGUAGES. It evolved in Germany in the Middle Ages and was spread by Jewish migrations. It uses the Hebrew alphabet and was standardized in 1934–36 in conferences of the Yiddish Scientific Institute (YIVO).

YIN AND YANG, two principles in Chinese philosophy, representing the passive and the active forces of the universe. Yin stands for earth, female, passive, dark and receiving; Yang for heaven, male, active, light and generative. All things exist through their interaction. The symbol for Yin-Yang is a circle divided into two curved forms, one dark, the other light.

YOGA (Sanskrit: union), forms of spiritual discipline practiced in BUDDHISM and HINDUISM. Through these disciplines the Yogi (one who follows Yoga) strives to free the mind from attachment to the senses and to achieve *Samadhi*, or union with *Brahma*, the deity, and fusion into oneness. There are three varieties of yoga: *karma-yoga*, salvation through action; *jnana-yoga*, salvation through knowledge; and *bhakti-yoga*, salvation through devotion. In each the student passes through eight levels of attainment, supervised by a *guru* or teacher. The practice of *hatha-yoga*, based on physical postures and control, has become increasingly popular in the West.

YOGURT or **YOGHURT,** semisolid cultured MILK food made by inoculating pasteurized milk with a culture of *Streptococcus thermophilus* and *Lactobacillus bulgaricus* and incubating until the desired acidity is achieved. Various

fruits can be added in packaging.

YOKOHAMA, second-largest city in Japan, on the W shore of Tokyo Bay, a leading national seaport and part of Tokyo's industrial belt, S Honshu Island. It is a trading center and supports large shipbuilding, iron, steel, chemical, machinery and oil industries. It also has several universities. Yokohama was a fishing village when visited by Commodore Matthew Perry in 1854. Its growth began in 1859, when it became a foreign-trade port. Pop 3,037,003.

YOM KIPPUR, the Jewish Day of Atonement, the most sacred day in the Jewish religious calendar. It falls on the tenth day after the Jewish New Year and is marked by repentance, prayers and abstention from food, drink, sex and work.

YORITOMO MINAMOTO (1148–1199), Japanese feudal warrior, the first SHOGUN or military dictator of Japan. The victory of his clan in 1185 ended a long period of civil wars and ushered in a century of effective government and flourishing culture.

YORK, Alvin Cullum (1887–1964), US soldier, WWI hero. During the Argonne-Meuse offensive in France in 1918 Sergeant York silenced an entire enemy machine-gun unit, killing at least 25 Germans and taking 132 prisoners. He was awarded the Congressional Medal of Honor and the French Croix de Guerre.

YORK, House of, ruling dynasty of England 1461–1485, a branch of the PLANTAGENET family, whose symbol was the white rose. The three Yorkist kings were EDWARD IV (1461–83), his son EDWARD V (April–June 1483) and RICHARD III (1483–85), who was killed at the Battle of Bosworth Field by Henry Tudor (HENRY VII) who established the House of TUDOR as the ruling family.

YORKTOWN, town in SE Va., seat of York Co., on the York R, site of the last campaign of the REVOLUTIONARY WAR. In Oct. 1781, 16,000 American and French troops, led by Gens. Washington and Rochambeau, laid siege to 7,247 British troops under Lord CORNWALLIS in Yorktown. With naval reinforcements defeated by Adm. de GRASSE and escape impossible, Cornwallis surrendered on Oct. 19th.

YORUBA, African people in SW NIGERIA, characteristically urban dwellers. Yoruba culture exists also in Cuba and Brazil because of large slave importations.

YOSEMITE NATIONAL PARK, park in E Cal., established in 1890, 1,189sq mi of spectacular mountain scenery formed during the last glacial period of the current ice age, on the W slopes of the Sierra Nevada. Its chief attractions are the

Yosemite Valley, its granite walls 2,500–3,500ft high; Yosemite Falls, the highest falls in North America; and the Mariposa Grove of "Big Trees"— 200 giant sequoias.

YOSHIDA, Shigeru (1878–1967), Japanese diplomat and political leader. A career diplomat, he retired in 1938 but became foreign minister in Japan's first postwar government and prime minister 1946–54.

YOUMANS, Vincent (1898–1946), US composer of popular musical comedies of the 1920s, among them *No, No, Nanette* and *Hit the Deck*. His songs included "Tea for Two," "Without a Song" and "I Want To Be Happy."

YOUNG, Arthur (1741–1820), English agriculturalist. He traveled widely to observe agricultural practices and became an influential propagandist for scientific farming.

YOUNG, Brigham (1801–1877), US MORMON leader. He joined the Mormons in 1832 and quickly rose to prominence. After three years as a missionary in England he took over the leadership on the death of Joseph SMITH (1844), and led his people to Salt Lake City, Ut., in 1846. Young established a thriving city on a sound commercial basis and became first governor of Utah in 1850. He may have had as many as 27 wives.

YOUNG, Chic (Murat Young; 1901–1973), US cartoonist, creator (1920) of *Blondie*, which became the world's most widely circulated comic strip.

YOUNG, Coleman Alexander (1918–   ), US Democratic politician. A labor organizer and Michigan State senator, he was elected mayor of Detroit four times (1973, 1977, 1981, 1985).

YOUNG, Denton True (1867–1955), US baseball player, called "Cy", short for cyclone, for his amazingly fast right-hand pitching. He played in major league baseball for 22 seasons, and in 1937 was elected to baseball's Hall of Fame for pitching the most games (906) and winning the most games (511).

YOUNG, Edward (1683–1765), English poet. The melancholy and emotion of his best-known work, *Night Thoughts on Life, Death and Immortality* (1742–45), greatly influenced 18th-century literature and art.

YOUNG, Ella Flagg (1845–1918), US educator. An associate of John Dewey at the U. of Chicago (1899–1904) and a colleague of social reformer Jane Addams, she was a leading figure in American progressive education. She was the first woman to head a major US school system (Chicago, 1909–15) and the first to be president of the National Education Association (1910–11).

YOUNG, Lester Willis (1909–1959), US jazz musician, a tenor saxophonist with Fletcher Henderson and Count Basie and a developer in the 1940s of progressive or cool jazz.

YOUNG, Owen D. (1874–1962), US lawyer, industrial executive and statesman. He had a very successful career in industry, but is chiefly remembered as an international statesman. He presided at the 1929 Paris Reparations Conference and produced the Young Plan for German WWI REPARATIONS, considered a triumph of diplomacy.

YOUNG, Thomas (1773–1829), British linguist, physician and physicist. His most significant achievement was, by demonstrating optical INTERFERENCE, to resurrect the wave theory of LIGHT, which had been occulted by NEWTON's particle theory. He also suggested that the eye responded to mixtures of three primary colors (see VISION), and proposed the modulus of ELASTICITY known as *Young's modulus*. He also helped decipher the ROSETTA STONE.

YOUNG, Whitney Moore, Jr. (1921–1971), US civil rights leader. As director of the National Urban League from 1961 he worked for better job and housing conditions for black Americans and was one of the most influential black leaders of the 1960s.

YOUNGER, Cole (Thomas Coleman Younger; 1844–1916), US outlaw. He was a Confederate guerrilla officer in the Civil War, and with his three brothers joined the Jesse JAMES gang in 1866. In 1876 he was imprisoned for his part in a bank raid but was later pardoned and paroled (1903).

YOUNGHUSBAND, Sir Francis Edward (1863–1942), British explorer in India. He crossed the Mustagh Pass of the Karakoram range in 1887, surveyed the Pamirs in 1889, and opened Tibet to British trade in 1904. He organized early attempts to climb Mount Everest.

YOUNG MEN'S CHRISTIAN ASSOCIATION (YMCA), worldwide organization that seeks, through programs of sport, religious and current affairs study groups and summer camps, to promote a healthy way of life based on Christian ideals. The first US branch was founded in 1851 and there are about 13 million members in 2,000 US associations. The YMCA operates in more than 80 countries.

YOUNG PRETENDER. See STUART, CHARLES EDWARD.

YOUNG WOMEN'S CHRISTIAN ASSOCIATION (YWCA), an international organization which promotes a Christian way of life through educational and recreational activities and social work. The movement, started in the US in 1858, now has 2 million members.

YOURCENAR, Marguerite (1904–1987), pen name of Marguerite de Crayencour, French author who became a US citizen in the 1940s. The first woman elected to the Académie Française (1980), she is best known for the historical novel *Hadrian's Memoirs* (1951) and *Coup de Grâce* (1939).

YPRES, town in W Belgium. It was almost completely destroyed in three terrible WWI battles. There are some 40 military cemeteries nearby. The Ypres textile industry has been famous since the Middle Ages. Pop 20,825.

YUAN, dynasty (1260–1368) of the MONGOL rulers of China. The dynasty was founded by KUBLAI KHAN. The Yuan established extensive postal, road and canal networks and developed trade with the West. The age saw a flowering of Chinese art and culture. Foreign visitors included MARCO POLO.

YÜAN SHIH-K'AI (1859–1916), Chinese soldier and president. His efforts to check Japan in Korea led to the Sino-Japanese war of 1894–95. He supported the Dowager Empress Tz'u Hsi and helped suppress the Boxer movement (1900). Supported by his army during the Revolution of 1911, he emerged as president 1912–16 but was unable to attain his goal of establishing himself emperor.

YUCATÁN, peninsula (55,400sq mi) dividing the Gulf of Mexico from the Caribbean. It contains Belize, part of Guatemala and three Mexican states. The climate is hot and humid, and farming and forestry are the main activities. The N is the leading producer of henequen. The people are of MAYA Indian stock and CHICHÉN ITZÁ, a famed Maya site, is on the peninsula.

YUCCA, genus of plants of the LILY family found in desert regions of the southwestern US and Mexico. The Joshua-tree is a small tree but other yuccas are shrubs or low plants bearing clusters of sword-shaped leaves and white waxy flowers. All depend on the yucca moth for pollination.

YUGOSLAVIA, socialist federal republic, the largest country in the Balkan Peninsula, bordered by Austria, Hungary and Italy to the N, by Romania and Bulgaria to the E, and by Greece to the S.

Land. It is divided into six republics: Serbia, Croatia, Bosnia and Herzegovina, Macedonia, Slovenia and Montenegro. The

Official name: Socialist Federal Republic of Yugoslavia
Capital: Belgrade
Area: 98,766sq mi
Population: 23,433,000
Languages: Serbo-Croatian, Slovenian, Macedonian
Religions: Orthodox, Roman Catholic, Muslim
Monetary unit(s): 1 dinar=100 paras

country comprises four geographical areas: the Alpine NW, the fertile N plains, the rugged mountain region in the S and the beautiful island-studded Dalmatian coast, developed for tourism. Most of Yugoslavia is drained by the Danube R which flows SE from the Hungarian border across the plains. The climate varies from being continental in the N to being warm and mild in the S.

Population. The people include Serbs, Croats, Slovenes, Macedonians, Montenegrins, Albanians, and many minority groups. Both the Roman and Cyrillic alphabets are used. About 41% of the population are urban-dwellers, the largest cities being the federal capital Belgrade, Zagreb, Skopje, Sarajevo and Ljubljana. Industry is widespread, the most important industrial region being the Sava Valley.

Economy. Mining, industry, agriculture and tourism are the basis of the economy. Yugoslavia has rich mineral resources of lignite, iron, lead, copper, bauxite, gas and oil. The chief industrial products are iron, steel, machinery, textiles, metal goods and chemicals. Manufactured goods are the leading exports, traded mainly to West Germany, Italy and the USSR. Crops grown in the Danube R area include corn, wheat, rye, sugar, beets, potatoes and fruit. There are extensive vineyards. Yugoslavia is associated with the COMMON MARKET. All major industries are nationalized.

History. What is now Yugoslavia belonged to the OTTOMAN EMPIRE. By 1914 AUSTRIA-HUNGARY controlled Croatia, Slovenia, and Bosnia and Herzegovina, while Serbia and Montenegro were independent. In 1918 the "Kingdom of the

Serbs, Croats and Slovenes" was created, its name changed to Yugoslavia in 1929. After the German invasion (1941) rival resistance groups were organized by the royalist Draža Mihajlović and the communist TITO. In 1945 Tito proclaimed Yugoslavia a federal republic of six states and established a communist government. Yugoslavia was expelled from the COMINFORM in 1948, and relations with the USSR have since been uneasy, President Tito pursuing an "independent national communism" for Yugoslavia. Internal tensions have been exacerbated by high inflation, chronic unemployment, and problems of intellectual freedom. After the death of Tito in 1980, a collective state presidency was established. Growing ethnic unrest, especially among Croatians and the Albanians in the province of Kosovo, has led the Serbs to demand more authority for the central government.

YUKAWA, Hideki (1907–1981), Japanese physicist who postulated the meson (see SUBATOMIC PARTICLES) as the agent bonding the atomic nucleus together. In fact, the mu-meson discovered shortly afterwards (in 1936) by C. D. Anderson, does not fulfill this role and Yukawa had to wait until C. F. Powell discovered the pi-meson in 1947 for vindication of his theory. He received the 1949 Nobel Prize for Physics.

YUKON RIVER, one of the five longest rivers in North America, flowing from N British Columbia for 1,979mi through Yukon Territory into Alaska, then SW to the Norton Sound on the Bering Sea. It is navigable for about 1,770mi.

YUKON TERRITORY, a subarctic territory in NW Canada lying between the North-West Territories and Alaska.

Name of territory: Yukon
Joined Confederation: June 13, 1898
Capital: Whitehorse
Area: 207,076sq mi
Population: 23,022

The territory consists of high mountain peaks and ranges surrounding a heavily forested central plateau drained by the Yukon R. Winters are long and cold. The original population, Canadian Indians, live as hunters and trappers, and the white population is concentrated in the S and central valleys. The capital is Whitehorse, which contains half the total population. Mining is the chief economic activity with lead, zinc, gold, tungsten and platinum the chief minerals. Some natural gas is produced in the Beaver R field, and the search for petroleum continues. The Klondike gold rush brought prosperity to the area, but gold reserves were running low

by 1911 and the population dropped sharply. It rose again in WWII when the building of the Alaska Highway and airports on the staging route to Alaska brought new settlers. Since then Yukon's economy has expanded gradually.

26th and last letter of the English alphabet. It was taken by the Romans from the Greek "zeta," which in turn came from the ancient Semitic "zayin." Its sound is often represented by "s" in English, as in "busy."

ZADKINE, Ossip (1890–1967), Russian-born French sculptor. He joined the cubists in 1914. His often large works in bronze, wood, and stone include *The Destruction of Rotterdam* (1954).

ZAHARIAS, Mildred "Babe" Didrikson (1914–1956), US athlete. An All-American basketball player (1930), she won (1930–32) national hurdles, javelin, baseball throw, broad- and high-jump titles, set (1932) Olympic 80m hurdles and javelin records, and became top US woman amateur and (after 1947) professional golfer.

ZAHAROFF, Sir Basil (1850–1936), Turkish-born armaments dealer and financier—the "mystery man of Europe"—who sold arms for the Nordenfelt (Swedish) and later Vicker-Armstrong (British) munitions firms. Accused of fomenting world crises and called a "merchant of death," he supplied weapons during the Boer, Russo-Japanese and Balkan wars as well as WWI.

ZAIBATSU, in Japan, large, diversified capitalist combines formed round a single family, with their own banks and controlling large sections of Japanese industry. The four great *zaibatsu* (Mitsubishi, Mitsui, Sumitomo, Yasuda) were supposedly dissolved after WWII by the Allies, but they retain great power.

ZAIRE, a nation in W central Africa and the third-largest country in Africa, formerly known as the Belgian Congo and, after independence, as the Democratic Republic of the Congo. In 1971 it was renamed Zaire.

Official name: Republic of Zaire
Capital: Kinshasa
Area: 905,365sq mi
Population: 31,804,000
Languages: French, Swahili, Tshiluba, Kikongo, Lingala
Religions: Roman Catholic, Protestant, Animist
Monetary unit(s): 1 zaire = 100 makuta = 10,000 sengi

Land. Central Zaire, which straddles the equator, is a large, low plateau covered by rain forest. The plateau rim surrounding the Zaire R basin averages 3,000ft, but highlands in the SE exceed 6,000ft and the Ruwenzori Range (Mts of the Moon) bordering Uganda exceeds 16,000ft. A series of lakes lie on the E border. The CONGO (Zaire) R, one of the largest rivers in Africa, flows W to the Atlantic, where the country narrows to a 25mi-wide coastline. Zaire is a hot, rainy country, with coastal temperatures averaging 79°F. Wild life abounds in the country.

People. The population is divided among numerous groups; about 200 languages are spoken—most of them Bantu. The Kongo people are most numerous. Other important groups are the Mongo, Luba and Zande. Nilotic-speaking peoples live primarily in the N. Pygmies live in the E. About 80% of the population is rural and engaged in agriculture. The rate of literacy is estimated at 35%; there is a national university with three main campuses. The largest cities are Kinshasa, the capital, and Lubumbashi and Kisangani.

Economy. The mainstay of Zaire's economy is its mineral sector. Cobalt is the principal export, followed by copper. Diamonds are also important. Cash crops include coffee, rubber, palm oil, cocoa and tea. Despite its mineral wealth and a diversified industrial sector, Zaire has been beset by severe economic problems, causing it to look to the international banking community for assistance. Hydroelectricity from the newly constructed Inga Dam on the Congo R is expected to play a large role in the nation's future development.

History. In 1885 Belgium's King Leopold II took control of an area he called the Congo Free State; in 1908 it became the Belgian Congo. It gained independence in 1960, with Kasavubu president and Lumumba premier. Unrest erupted shortly afterward, and Tshombe later urged the secession of Katanga (Shaba), a mineral-rich area. The UN sent troops to restore order. In 1965, following continuing unrest, Maj. Gen. Joseph MOBUTU took control. With US support, Mobutu established a one-party regime that pacified the country's 200 tribes and disarmed opposition by a combination of repression and cooptation. His government, however, became notorious for incompetence and corruption. Grandiose but ill-conceived building and development projects, capital flight, deteriorating roads and highways, and declining copper and coffee prices contributed to economic ruin. Self-sufficient agriculturally when it became independent in 1960, Zaire in 1988 imported a quarter of its food. Per capita income in 1988 was only 10% of its 1960 level, the eighth lowest in the world at $180. Corruption was pervasive at every level. Mobutu himself was alleged to have amassed $5 billion.

ZAIRE RIVER. See CONGO RIVER.

ZAMA, ancient site in N central Tunisia, Africa, where the Carthaginian general HANNIBAL was defeated 202 BC by the Romans under SCIPIO Africanus, concluding the second PUNIC WAR.

ZAMBEZI RIVER, SE Africa, fourth-largest river in Africa. Rising in NW Zambia, it flows 1,700mi S, then E along the Zambia-Zimbabwe border, through Mozambique to enter the Mozambique Channel of the Indian Ocean through a 2,500sq mi delta. (See also VICTORIA FALLS.)

ZAMBIA, formerly **Northern Rhodesia,** landlocked republic of S central Africa.

Land. Mostly savanna plateau 3,000-5,000ft above sea level, it rises in the NE to 7,000ft in the Muchinga Mts. Dissecting the plateau are the Kafue and Luangwa rivers, flowing S to join the Zambia R (here marked by the VICTORIA FALLS). In the N are lakes Bangweulu and Mweru and the S end of Lake Tanganyika. Although in the tropics, Zambia has a relatively mild climate because of altitude; however, temperatures can reach 100°F during the hot season (Sept–Nov). Annual rainfall ranges from 20in to 50in.

People. The Zambian people are predominantly Bantu, with over 70 tribes and many languages. About two-thirds live by subsistence agriculture. There are Eur-

Official name: Republic of Zambia
Capital: Lusaka
Area: 290,586sq mi
Population: 7,135,000
Languages: English; Bemba, Nyanja, Tonga
Religions: Christian, Muslim, Hindu
Monetary unit(s): 1 Zambian kwacha=100 ngwee

opean and Asian minorities.

Economy. Zambia is one of the world's top producers of copper, which accounts for the bulk of export earnings. Cobalt is the second-largest export earner; lead, zinc, manganese and sulfur are also exported. Cash crops include tobacco, sugarcane and wheat. Zambia's economy was severely dislocated because of the country's support of Zimbabwe guerrillas during the Rhodesian war. Damage caused by air raids, the disruption of transit routes to the sea and the loss of Rhodesia as a trade partner brought Zambia near economic collapse. In the 1980s Zambia faced severe food shortages due to drought and disease.

History. European traders and missionaries came to Zambia in the 19th century. David LIVINGSTONE came in 1855; in 1888 Cecil RHODES led the way for British commercial interests. As N Rhodesia the area became a British protectorate in 1924. From 1953 to 1963 it formed part of the Federation of Rhodesia and Nyasaland, with S Rhodesia (now Zimbabwe) and Nyasaland (now Malawi). It became independent in 1964, with Kenneth KAUNDA as president. In the late 1980s, Zambia's support of efforts to end apartheid in South Africa led to attacks by South Africa on alleged African National Congress bases in Zambia.

ZAMENHOF, Ludwig Lejzer (Ludovic Lazarus Zamenhof; 1859–1917), Polish doctor, oculist and philologist who devised the international language ESPERANTO (1887).

ZAMYATIN, Yevgeny Ivanovich (1884–1937), Russian writer. His satires include *The Islanders* (1917), about England, and *We* (1922), a forecast of communist society in the 2500s. An early

Bolshevik, he lost favor with Soviet officials (but influenced young writers), and died in Paris.

ZANE, Ebenezer (1747–1812), American pioneer. A Quaker, he cofounded (1769) Zanesburg (now in W Va., renamed Wheeling in 1806) and blazed a trail to Maysville, Ky., known as Zane's Trace.

ZANGWILL, Israel (1864–1926), English writer and Zionist. Born of E European parents, he described Jewish life in *Children of the Ghetto* (1892), *Dreamers of the Ghetto* (1898), and *The Melting Pot* (1903), a play about US Jewish immigrants.

ZANUCK, Darryl F. (1902–1979), US film producer. He co-founded Twentieth Century-Fox (1933), was its production head (1935–52) and its president (1962–71).

ZANZIBAR, island, part of TANZANIA, E. Africa. Center from c1700 of an Omani Arab sultanate with extensive mainland territories, British protectorate (1890–93), independent sultanate (1963), and republic (1964), Zanzibar island united 1964 with nearby Pemba and with Tanganyika to form Tanzania. The chief exports are cloves and copra.

ZAPATA, Emiliano (c1883–1919), Mexican agrarian revolutionary. From 1910 he led his fellow Indian peasants of Morelos state in revolt against DÍAZ and the big landowners. Later he opposed presidents MADERO, HUERTA and CARRANZA for failing to carry out land reforms. He was assassinated by an army officer supporting Carranza.

ZAPOTEC INDIANS, ancient native people of SE Oaxaca, S Mexico, and their descendants. They created a formative pre-Columbian culture about 2,000 years ago. Monte Albán, W of Oaxaca city, contains magnificent ruins of tombs, stelae, temples and plazas.

ZARATHUSTRA. See ZOROASTRIANISM.

ZEALOTS, Jewish religious and political fanatics in Palestine about the time of Christ. Led by Judas of Galilee and Zadok the priest, they resisted Rome and its collaborator HEROD the Great, but later perished 70 AD with the destruction of Jerusalem. St. SIMON the Apostle may have been a Zealot.

ZEBRAS, three species of striped HORSES of Africa. The characteristic black and white striped coat surprisingly makes the animal inconspicuous at long range. The three species—plains zebra, mountain zebra and Grévy's zebra—differ in stripe pattern, habitat and behavior. Plains and mountain zebras live in permanent nonterritorial stallion groups, but mountain zebras are adapted to life in more arid regions. Grévy's zebras, with very narrow stripes, are territorial animals.

ZECHARIAH, 11th of the Minor Prophets of the Old Testament. The book, dated c520 BC, foretells the rebirth of Israel. The more apocalyptic visions in chapters 9–12 are of later, possibly Greek, authorship. With HAGGAI, Zechariah urged the rebuilding of the Temple at Jerusalem.

ZEFFIRELLI, Franco (Gianfranco Corsi; 1923–   ), Italian stage designer and film director. He staged lavish opera productions before becoming a film director with *The Taming of the Shrew* (1967).

ZEISS, Carl (1816–1888), German optical manufacturer who founded a famous workshop at Jena in 1846. Realizing that optical technology had much to gain from scientific research, in the mid-1860s he formed a fruitful association with the physicist, Ernst Abbe.

ZEN (Chinese: *Ch'an*), form of BUDDHISM which developed in China from c500 AD and spread to Japan c1200, exerting great influence on Japanese culture. The word means "meditation." Zen differs markedly from traditional Buddhism, abhorring images and ritual, scriptures and metaphysics. There are some 9,000,000 adherents in two sects in Japan. Rinzai Zen uses *koan* (paradoxical riddles) to shock into sudden enlightenment; Soto Zen stresses contemplation.

ZEND-AVESTA, or **Avesta,** the sacred book of ZOROASTRIANISM, written in Avestan, an Iranian language similar to Vedic Sanskrit. The *Gathas* (songs) derive from Zoroaster himself, but the present Avesta was written down in the Sassanian period (3rd–4th centuries AD). It is the major text of the PARSEES.

ZENGER, John Peter (1697–1746), German-born American printer, whose acquittal (1735) on a charge of seditious libel was an important victory for freedom of the press. Sponsored by opponents of the unpopular New York colonial governor, William Cosby, Zenger had founded the New York *Weekly Journal* in 1733, and proceeded to publish bitter attacks on him. At the trial he was defended by Andrew HAMILTON.

ZENITH, in astronomy, the point on the CELESTIAL SPHERE directly above an observer and exactly 90° from the celestial horizon. It is directly opposite to the nadir.

ZENOBIA, queen of Palmyra, Syria, 267–72, noted for her beauty and ruthlessness. She succeeded her husband Odenathus, conquered much of Asia Minor, N Mesopotamia and Syria, and proclaimed her son emperor before her defeat and capture by Roman emperor Aurelian.

ZENO OF CITIUM (c335–263 BC), ancient Greek philosopher, founder of STOICISM. Influenced by the CYNICS, he developed a complete philosophy, but is most famous for declaring that only virtue is to be desired; a wise man should be indifferent to all else, including pain, pleasure, possessions and wealth.

ZENO OF ELEA (c450 BC), Greek philosopher, member of the ELEATIC school. He is most important for his paradoxes, best known of which is the "Achilles and tortoise" paradox (in a race, the tortoise is given a start: by the time Achilles reaches the point where the tortoise *was*, the tortoise has advanced—therefore Achilles can never overtake the tortoise). Zeno defended the Eleatic concept that being is one and changeless by showing the contradictions entailed in claiming the reality of motion and plurality.

ZEPHANIAH, Old Testament prophet. In the reign of King Josiah of Judah (640–630 BC) he wrote the ninth book of the Minor Prophets, denouncing evil in Judah and predicting the "Day of the Lord." The end of the last (third) chapter, predicting salvation for the remnant, was probably added later.

ZEPPELIN, Count Ferdinand von (1838–1917), German aeronautical engineer who designed and built almost a hundred powered BALLOONS (1900 on), called zeppelins for him.

ZERO, in mathematics, a number smaller than any finite positive number, but larger than any finite negative number. It obeys

$$x \pm 0 = x$$
$$x \times 0 = 0$$
$$0 / x = 0$$
$$x^0 = 1.$$

Division by zero is an undefined operation. Zero may be regarded as the identity element for addition in the field of real numbers.

ZEROMSKI, Stefan (1864–1925), Polish novelist, short-story writer and playwright. He was the first to realistically depict the social injustices of Polish life and has been called "the conscience of Polish literature." He is best known for the novel *Ashes* (3 vols., 1904; tr. 1928).

ZERO POPULATION GROWTH, the close approximation in numbers of births and deaths needed to stabilize a nation's population and prevent annual increases. To stabilize the US population at its present level, the replacement ratio for families (excluding illegitimate births) is 2.54 children per fertile married woman. Zero

Population Growth is also the name of an organization formed in 1968 by Richard Bowers, Paul Ehrlich and Charles Remington to inform the public and legislators of the disadvantages of continued population growth.

ZEUS, supreme god of Greek mythology. His mother Rhea saved him from his jealous father Cronus. Later he led the Olympian gods in overthrowing Cronus and the other Titans. By lot he became god of earth and sky (Poseidon won the sea, Hades the underworld). He ruled from Mt. OLYMPUS, from which his thunderbolt threatened mortals. By his wife Hera, by Metis (Wisdom), Themis (mother of the Seasons and Fates), Eurynome (mother of the Muses), Mnemosyne, and Demeter he sired many gods. Zeus' mortal loves included Leda, Io, and Europa. His offspring included ATHENA and HERCULES. Romans equated him with Jupiter (Jove).

ZEUXIS, Greek painter of the 5th century BC, known for his use of highlights and shading. He is said to have painted grapes so realistically that birds tried to eat them.

ZHAO ZIYANG (1919–   ), general secretary of the Chinese Communist Party from 1987. Purged during the Cultural Revolution, Zhao was later rehabilitated. He was appointed governor of Szechwan (Sichuan) province in 1975 and elected to the Politburo in 1979. He served as premier 1980–87 before replacing Hu Yaobang as party general secretary.

ZHDANOV, Andrei Aleksandrovich (1896–1948), Soviet leader. Chosen (1934) by STALIN to succeed KIROV as Communist Party secretary of LENINGRAD (in whose WWII defense he was active), he became a full member of the POLITBURO (1939) and Supreme Soviet chairman (1946), before organizing the COMINFORM.

ZHUKOV, Georgi Konstantinovich (1896–1974), Soviet general, hero of the defeat of the Germans at STALINGRAD (1943) and entry into Berlin (1945). After the death of STALIN (who had blocked his career), he was defense minister 1955–57, and briefly a full member of the Communist Party presidium (1957).

ZIA UL-HAQ, Mohammad (1924–1988), president of Pakistan from 1977. Army chief of staff, Zia deposed Prime Minister Zulfikar Ali BHUTTO during riots in 1977, imposed martial law, and ruled dictatorially. In 1985 he lifted martial law and permitted political parties to function, but in 1988 he dismissed the civilian prime minister, dissolved the recently elected national assembly and provincial governments, and declared Islamic law supreme.

He died in a plane crash perhaps due to sabotage.

ZIEGFELD, Florenz (1869–1932), US theatrical producer. In 1907 he launched the Ziegfeld Follies, an annual revue famous for its spectacular staging and beautiful girls; it ran for 24 years. Ziegfeld also produced musicals including *Sally* (1920) and *Showboat* (1927).

ZIGGURAT, brick pyramid temple built in many cities of ancient MESOPOTAMIA between about 3,000 and 600 BC. More than 30 are known, with bases up to 320ft square and original heights as much as 150ft. The biblical Tower of Babel may have been a ziggurat.

ZIMBABWE, formerly **Rhodesia,** is a landlocked republic in the heart of southern Africa, bordering Mozambique, South Africa, Botswana and Zambia.

Official name: Republic of Zimbabwe
Capital: Harare (formerly Salisbury)
Area: 150,873sq mi
Population: 8,640,000
Languages: English, Sindebele, Chisona
Religions: Christianity, Animism
Monetary unit(s): 1 Zimbabwe dollar = 100 cents
Land. Zimbabwe lies astride a high plateau between the ZAMBEZI and Limpopo rivers. The High VELD is over 4,000ft and extends SW–NE across the country. The Middle Veld, land between 3,000ft and 4,000ft, is most extensive in the NW. The Low Veld, land below 3,000ft, occupies land near river basins in the N and S. Mt Inyangana in the E highlands rises to 8,503ft. Temperatures are moderated by altitude, ranging between 54°F and 85°F. Rainfall varies from 20in a year in the W to 60in in the E.
People. The African population is primarily Bantu and falls into two broad groups: the Shona and the Ndebele. Other tribes are the Tonga, Sena, Hlengwe, Venda and Sotho. Most live in rural areas, where they depend on subsistence agriculture. Whites (former Rhodesians), Coloureds (of mixed ancestry) and Asians make up about 5% of the population.
Economy. Zimbabwe is a major food

exporter in Southern Africa and is rich in mineral resources. Modern European farms are vital to the economy and produce the main cash crop, tobacco. The black population lives mainly by subsistence farming and by raising cattle, but new government policies have made land available to Africans for commercial agriculture. Gold is the chief export; other important minerals are iron ore, asbestos, chrome, copper and nickel. The industrial sector, which was expanded in response to economic sanctions against Rhodesia in 1965, is diversified and active.

History. Bushmen paintings and tools indicate that Zimbabwe had Stone Age inhabitants. Bantu tribes settled the area c400AD, and during the 1400s the Shona civilization established an empire, calling its capital Zimbabwe. In 1889 the British South Africa Co. of Cecil RHODES (after whom Rhodesia was named) obtained a charter from Britain to colonize and administer the area. In 1953 the country became part of the Federation of Rhodesia and Nyasaland. In 1965, as the wave of independence swept through Africa, Prime Minister Ian SMITH'S government refused to allow black majority rule and illegally declared independence for white-ruled Rhodesia. However, after years of international pressure, local dissension and warfare, and the brief administration of a controversial transitional government, Zimbabwe became legally independent in April 1980 and Robert Mugabe was elected president. In 1987, seats in parliament reserved for whites were abolished and Mugabe, who became executive president, signed a unity agreement with his former rival, Joshua Nkomo, as part of a move to transform the country into a one-party state.

ZIMBABWE, ruined city in the country of Zimbabwe (formerly Rhodesia), 17mi SE of Fort Victoria. Started c1000 AD by the Shona people, the city has a massive oval stone wall surrounding a fortress and a "temple." The site was occupied and developed through several centuries.

ZIMBALIST, Efrem (1890–1985), Russian-born US virtuoso violinist. He directed the Curtis Institute of Music in Philadelphia, 1941–68, and composed several pieces for violin and orchestra.

ZIMMERMANN TELEGRAM, secret message sent by Arthur Zimmermann, the German foreign secretary, in Jan., 1917, proposing a German-Mexican alliance against the US. Sent via the German ambassador in the US to the German minister in Mexico, it was intercepted by the British and shown to President Woodrow WILSON, who made it public. It influenced the US decision to enter WWI.

ZIMMERWALD CONFERENCE, international meeting of socialists held at Zimmerwald, Switzerland, Sept. 4–8, 1915, to discuss their attitude to WWI after the collapse of the Second INTERNATIONAL. LENIN tried to persuade the national socialist parties to convert the "imperialist" war into an international revolutionary war against capitalism, but a much milder resolution was passed.

ZINC (Zn), bluish-white metal in Group IIB of the PERIODIC TABLE, an anomalous transition element. It occurs naturally as sphalerite, smithsonite, hemimorphite and wurtzite, and is extracted by roasting to the oxide and reduction with carbon. It is used for galvanizing; as the cathode of dry cells, and in ALLOYS including BRASS. Zinc is a vital trace element, occurring in red BLOOD cells and in INSULIN. Chemically zinc is reactive, readily forming divalent ionic salts (Zn^{2+}), and zincates (ZnO_2^{2-}) in alkaline solution; it forms many stable ligand complexes. Zinc oxide and sulfide are used as white pigments. Zinc chloride is used as a flux, for fireproofing, in dentistry, and in the manufacture of BATTERIES and FUNGICIDES. AW 65.4, mp 420°C, bp 907°C, sg 7.133 (25°C).

ZINOVIEV, Grigori Evseyevich (1883–1936), Russian communist leader. A close friend of LENIN in exile (1909–17), he became head of the Third INTERNATIONAL (Comintern) 1919–26, and a POLITBURO member 1921–26. After Lenin's death he supported STALIN, who then turned against him; he was finally executed in the 1936 "Great Purge." The "Zinoviev Letter" (1924), containing Zinoviev's purported instructions for a revolution in Britain, was a forgery.

ZINZENDORF, Count Nikolaus Ludwig von (1700–1760), German leader of the MORAVIAN CHURCH. In 1722 he helped some Moravians to form a community called Herrnhut, and became their leader and bishop (1737), founding communities in the Low Countries, England and America. His emphasis on emotion greatly influenced Protestant theology.

ZION, in the Old Testament, the ancient citadel of David, on the SE hill of JERUSALEM. In a wider sense it symbolizes the whole of Jerusalem, and also the Jewish people and their aspirations.

ZIONISM, the movement to establish a Jewish national home in Palestine. Ever since the destruction of their state in 70 AD, the Jews retained their identity and kept alive their dream of an eventual return from exile. The dream turned into a political movement in the 19th century, largely in response to persecution of Jews in Russia and Austria, and Jewish farmers and artisans began to settle in Palestine. The decisive impetus came in 1897, when Theodor HERZL organized the first World Zionist Congress, after which Zionist groups were established all over the world. In 1903 the British government offered the Jews a home in Uganda, but this was rejected. Leadership of the Zionist movement was assumed by Chaim WEIZMANN, who was largely responsible for the BALFOUR DECLARATION (1917). For the setting up of the Jewish state (1947) see JEWS; PALESTINE; ISRAEL.

ZION NATIONAL PARK, established in 1919 and covering 147,035 acres in SW Ut. It is noted for its canyons with multicolored rock formations.

ZIRCON ($ZrSiO_4$), hard silicate mineral, a major ore of zirconium, of widespread occurrence. It forms prismatic crystals in the tetragonal system, which when transparent are used as GEMS. They may be colorless, red, orange, yellow, green or blue, and have a high refractive index. Notable occurrences are in S and SE Asia, Australia and New Zealand.

ZITHER, STRINGED INSTRUMENT related to the DULCIMER and PSALTERY. It is placed across the knees and the strings, which stretch across a shallow sound box, are plucked. The zither is a traditional folk instrument of central Europe.

ZODIAC, the band of the heavens whose outer limits lie 9° on each side of the ecliptic. The 12 main constellations near the ecliptic, corresponding to the 12 signs of the zodiac, are Aries; Taurus; Gemini; Cancer; Leo; Virgo; Libra; Scorpio; Sagittarius; Capricorn; Aquarius; Pisces. The orbits of all the planets except Pluto lie within the zodiac and their positions, as that of the sun, are important in ASTROLOGY. The 12 signs are each equivalent to 30° of arc along the zodiac.

ZOG (1895–1961), king of Albania 1928–39. After serving in the Austrian army he was made premier (1922–24, 1925–28), and proclaimed himself king. He fled when the Italians invaded and spent the rest of his life in exile.

ZOLA, Émile (1840–1902), French novelist and founder of NATURALISM. His works proclaim his "scientific" vision of life determined entirely by heredity and environment. His first success *Thérèse Raquin* (1867) was followed by the *Rougon-Macquart* cycle (20 volumes,

1871–93) depicting, with powerful and often lurid realism, the fortunes of a contemporary family. It includes his celebrated studies of alcoholism (*The Dram-shop,* 1877), prostitution (*Nana,* 1880) and life in a mining community (*Germinal,* 1885). In 1898 Zola threw himself into the DREYFUS AFFAIR with the pamphlet *J'accuse,* attacking the army.

ZOLLVEREIN, German customs union developed after 1818 to provide a free-trade area between Prussia and most of the independent German states. It helped pave the way for German unification (1871), and was then replaced by the Imperial Customs Union.

ZOO, or **zoological garden,** a collection of wild-animal species preserved for public education, scientific research and the breeding of endangered species. The first modern zoo was that of the Royal Zoological Society at Regent's Park, London, established in 1826.

ZOOGEOGRAPHY, the study of the geographical distribution of animal species and populations. Physical barriers, such as wide oceans and mountain ranges, major climatic extremes, intense heat or cold, may prevent the spread of a species into new areas, or may separate two previously like populations, allowing them to develop into distinct species. The presence of these barriers to movement and interbreeding, both now and in the past, are reflected in the distributions and later adaptive radiations of animal species, resulting in the zoogeographical distributions we find today. The major zoogeographic regions of the world are the Ethiopian (sub-Saharan Africa); the Oriental (India and SE Asia); the Australasian (including Australia, New Guinea and New Zealand); the Neotropical (Central and South America), and the Holarctic (the whole northerly region, often divided into the Nearctic—North America—and the Palearctic—most of Eurasia with N Africa).

ZOOLOGY, the scientific study of animal life. Originally concerned with the classification of animal groups (see ANIMAL KINGDOM), comparative ANATOMY and PHYSIOLOGY, the science now embraces studies of EVOLUTION, GENETICS, EMBRYOLOGY, BIOCHEMISTRY, ANIMAL BEHAVIOR and ECOLOGY.

ZOOPLANKTON, the animal elements of the PLANKTON, made up of small marine animals, PROTOZOA, and, principally, the larvae of other marine creatures, mainly MOLLUSKS and CRUSTACEA.

ZORACH, William (1887–1966), Lithuanian-born US sculptor. Abandoning his early painting career, he turned to traditional works of carved wood and stone, noted for their simplicity and monumental character. They include *Spirit of the Dance* (1932).

ZOROASTRIANISM, Persian religion based on the teachings of Zoroaster (Greek form of *Zarathustra*), a sage who lived in the 6th century BC. It was founded on the old Aryan folk-religion, but abolished its polytheism, establishing two predominant spirits: Ahura-Mazda (Ormazd), the spirit of light and good; and Ahriman, the spirit of evil and darkness (see DUALISM). Zoroastrianism includes the belief in eternal reward or punishment after death according to man's deeds. Its scriptures are the ZEND-AVESTA. Almost wiped out in the 7th century by the Muslim conquest of Persia, Zoroastrianism survives among the PARSEES.

ZOSHCHENKO, Mikhail (1895–1958), Russian humorist, born in the Ukraine. His popular short stories of the 1920s satirized everyday Soviet life. Although his works became more conventional in the 1930s, he was attacked by the party and expelled from the Union of Soviet Writers in 1946. He was rehabilitated after Stalin's death.

ZUCKMAYER, Carl (1896–1977), German playwright and novelist, famous for his play *The Captain from Köpenick* (1930), a satire on German militarism. He wrote the screenplay for *The Blue Angel* (1930). Zuckermayer went to the US in 1934 and to Switzerland after WWII.

ZUKERMAN, Pinchas (1948–   ), Israeli-born violinist, violist and conductor who came to New York (1962) as a protégé of Isaac Stern. He performed with orchestras throughout the world and made his conducting debut in 1974.

ZUKOR, Adolph (1873–1976), Hungarian-born US film executive, a founder of Paramount Pictures, of which he was president (1917–35) and later chairman. His interest was in distributing rather than making films.

ZULULAND, the NE region of Natal Province, South Africa. It borders on Mozambique (N), the Indian Ocean (E), Swaziland (W) and the Buffalo and Tugela rivers (S and SW). It produces sugarcane, cotton and maize. Cattle raising is the traditional occupation of the Zulus, a Bantu people who comprise most of the population. Traditionally they live in beehive-shaped huts in fenced compounds called *kraals*. Zululand was annexed by the British in 1887 after prolonged Zulu resistance to white conquest. Many Zulu men now work as MIGRANT LABOR in mines and cities.

ZUÑI INDIANS, North American PUEBLO INDIANS of the Zuñian linguistic stock. They were first discovered by the Spanish in 1539. The Zuñi live mainly by agriculture and produce fine jewelry. They have retained their ancient religion, which they celebrate in magnificent festivals noted for their dancing and costumes. About 4,000 live at Zuñi, W N.M.

ZURBARÁN, Francisco de (1598–1664), Spanish BAROQUE painter. He was influenced by CARAVAGGIO and is known for his realistic and chiaroscuro treatment of religious subjects and still-lifes. Among his masterpieces is *The Apotheosis of St. Thomas Aquinas* (1631).

ZÜRICH, city in N Switzerland, Switzerland's largest city and chief economic, banking and commercial center. It lies on Lake Zürich and the Limmat and Sihl rivers. Zürich manufactures textiles, paper and machine tools. The site was once occupied by Neolithic lake-dwellers, Celtic Helvetii and Romans. Pop (city) 353,033; (metro) 834,538.

ZWEIG, Arnold (1887–1968), German novelist. He wrote an eight-vol. epic that includes his best-known novel, *The Case of Sergeant Grischa* (1927) which powerfully indicted militarism in its description of WWI and its effects on German society.

ZWEIG, Stefan (1881–1942), Austrian biographer and novelist. He is best known for his psychological studies of historical figures and writers such as Erasmus, Mary Queen of Scots and Balzac. He wrote of European culture in *The Tide of Fortune* (1928).

ZWINGLI, Huldreich or **Ulrich** (1484–1531), influential Swiss leader of the REFORMATION. In 1523 the city of Zürich accepted his 67 Articles demanding such reforms as the removal of religious images, simplification of the Mass and the introduction of Bible readings. Zwingli was killed in the war between the Catholic and Protestant cantons.

ZWORYKIN, Vladimir Kosma (1889–1982), Russian-born US electronic engineer regarded as the father of modern TELEVISION: his kinescope (patented 1924), little adapted, is our modern picture tube; and his iconoscope, though now obsolete, represents the basis of the first practical television camera. He also made important contributions to the ELECTRON MICROSCOPE.

ZYGOTE, CELL produced by the fusion of two GAMETES and which contains the diploid chromosome number. The offspring is then produced by mitotic division (see MITOSIS) of the zygote to give 2, 4, 8, 16, 32 ... 2^n cells.